D1159525

LIVING FAITH BIBLE

living faith™

BIBLE

Tyndale House Publishers, Inc.
Wheaton, Illinois

Visit Tyndale's exciting Web site at www.tyndale.com, where you'll find additional information about the *Living Faith Bible* and related products.

Living Faith Bible copyright © 2000 by Tyndale House Publishers, Inc. Wheaton, Illinois, 60189.

Living Faith Bible notes copyright © 2000 by David and Renée Sanford. All rights reserved.

The Bible text used in this edition of the *Living Faith Bible* is the *Holy Bible*, New Living Translation, copyright © 1996 by Tyndale Charitable Trust. All rights reserved.

The text of the *Holy Bible*, New Living Translation, may be quoted in any form (written, visual, electronic, or audio) up to and inclusive of two hundred and fifty (250) verses without express written permission of the publisher, provided that the verses quoted do not account for more than 20 percent of the work in which they are quoted, and provided that a complete book of the Bible is not quoted.

When the *Holy Bible*, New Living Translation, is quoted, one of the following credit lines must appear on the copyright page or title page of the work:

> Scripture quotations marked NLT are taken from the *Holy Bible*, New Living Translation, copyright © 1996. Used by permission of Tyndale House Publishers, Inc., Wheaton, Illinois 60189. All rights reserved.

> Scripture quotations are taken from the *Holy Bible*, New Living Translation, copyright © 1996. Used by permission of Tyndale House Publishers, Inc., Wheaton, Illinois 60189. All rights reserved.

> Unless otherwise indicated, all Scripture quotations are taken from the *Holy Bible*, New Living Translation, copyright © 1996. Used by permission of Tyndale House Publishers, Inc., Wheaton, Illinois 60189. All rights reserved.

When quotations from the NLT text are used in nonsalable media, such as church bulletins, orders of service, newsletters, transparencies, or similar media, a complete copyright notice is not required, but the initials (NLT) must appear at the end of each quotation.

Quotations in excess of two hundred and fifty (250) verses or 20 percent of the work, or other permission requests, must be directed to and approved in writing by Tyndale House Publishers, Inc., P.O. Box 80, Wheaton, Illinois 60189.

New Living and the New Living Translation logo are registered trademarks of Tyndale House Publishers, Inc.

Living Faith is a trademark of Tyndale House Publishers, Inc.

Published in association with the literary agency of Alive Communications, Inc., 7680 Goddard Street, Suite 200, Colorado Springs, CO 80920.

ISBN 0-8423-7359-4 Burgundy Bonded Leather Edition

ISBN 0-8423-7358-6 Hardcover Edition

ISBN 0-8423-7357-8 Softcover Edition

Printed in the United States of America

06 05 04 03 02 01 00
10 9 8 7 6 5 4 3 2 1

Contents

Books of the Bible

Alphabetical Listing of Books

Contributors

Living Faith Notes
David and Renée Sanford

Editorial Review Committee
Barry Andrews
Geoff and Kelly Bard
Linda Blosser
Brian Boys
Steve Burg
Leticia Calçada
Russell Chandler
David Clausen
Wes and Beth Emmert
Damon and Elise Evans
Adrienne Fajen
Jerry Fidler
Earle Fries
Paul and Jean Goodrich
Paul Govert
Mike Hamel
Brian Hansen
Greg Hartman
Kristina Haws
Deborah Hedstrom
Scott Hord
Greg Johnson
Peter and Marie Kenote
Peter Lowe
Greg Matthews
Angela McCollum
Kathy Collard Miller
Paul and Annette Schroth
Floyd and Christine Schneider
Poppy Smith
Sandra Stone
Marty and Linda Trammell
Mike Umlandt
Scott and Leslie Walt
Timothy Walton
W. Terry Whalin
Kevin Williamson

Tyndale House Editors
David P. Barrett
Jill Swanson

Cover and Interior Design
Julie Chen

Typesetter
Judy Stafford

Print Buyer
Kristen Mapstone

Welcome to the *Living Faith Bible*

Every man, woman, and young person faces a profound choice: "Today, am I going to affirm the Bible's truths, obey the Lord's commands, and heed the examples of those who have gone before me? Or am I going to close this book, forget what God has said, and go my own stubborn way?"

What strikingly different ways to live—and what startlingly different outcomes. Scripture says: "Today I have given you the choice between life and death, between blessings and curses. I call on heaven and earth to witness the choice you make. Oh, that you would choose life, that you and your descendants might live! Choose to love the LORD your God and to obey him and commit yourself to him, for he is your life" (Deuteronomy 30:19-20).

The *Living Faith Bible* urges you to choose life! It takes seriously God's promises in Joshua 1, Psalm 1, Psalm 119, 2 Peter 1, and other Scriptures, which teach that God prospers those who delight in his Word, take it to heart, and apply it in every area of life.

What's the goal of presenting the Holy Bible this way?

- ○ To profoundly change the way you think about God and his Word.
- ○ To actively encourage you to open the Bible more often.
- ○ To diligently urge you to reflect on each Scripture longer.
- ○ To continually prompt you to live differently as a result—until you know God's blessings in each area of your life!

AFFIRMING EACH TRUTH IN GOD'S WORD

Remarkably, you and I can read page after page of the Bible without ever stopping to say, "Do I really believe this? And this? And that?" Yet, if we don't wholeheartedly affirm the Bible's truths, we can easily lose our way in this crazy, confusing, mixed-up world of half-truths, misconceptions, and outright lies.

That's why we've published thousands of personal affirmations of belief in this devotional Bible. To encourage you to read God's Word and say "yes!" to its rich and trustworthy declarations about God, Creation, the Fall, the ancient world, God's chosen people, and God's love for the whole world. About Jesus' life, ministry, teaching, miracles, betrayal, death, burial, and resurrection. About the Church's miraculous birth, expansion, teachings, and blessed hope.

As you read these affirmations, remember:

- ○ Many affirmations present profound biblical truths.
- ○ Others affirm basic historical facts from Bible times.
- ○ Still others repeat affirmations written alongside other passages.
- ○ You're free to revise or delete affirmations, if you wish.
- ○ You're also invited to write additional affirmations.

OBEYING EACH COMMAND IN GOD'S WORD

Incredibly, you and I can listen to Scripture, nod our heads, walk out the door, and never once stop to wonder, "What would Jesus have me do in this situation?" Yet if we don't whole-heartedly obey the Lord's commands, we'll quickly go astray, risk our lives in mad pursuit of the tempting and trivial, get terribly hurt in the process, and then have the audacity to point the finger at others—even God.

That's why we've published hundreds of personal affirmations of obedience in this devotional application Bible. To encourage you, as the apostle Paul said, "to turn from godless living and sinful pleasures" and instead "live in this evil world with self-control, right conduct, and devotion to God, while we look forward to that wonderful event when the glory of our great God and Savior, Jesus Christ, will be revealed" (Titus 2:12-13).

As you read these affirmations, remember:
   O There's no one "right" way to write affirmations.
   O Many affirmations simply echo the words of Scripture itself.
   O Other affirmations interpret and apply biblical truths for today.
   O Still others convey a New Testament understanding of Old Testament verses.
   O Some may not apply to you due to gender, marital status, or family size.

HEEDING EACH EXAMPLE IN GOD'S WORD

It's not enough to know the great Sunday school stories about Noah and Sarah, Joshua and Deborah, Ruth and Absalom, Elijah and Esther, Daniel and Mary, Nicodemus and Cornelius, John Mark and Timothy. True, the biblical narratives are intriguing. But what lessons can we learn from each character's faith and failings, victories and vices?

That's why we've published scores of personal profiles showing what life-changing affirmations we can import from the lives of biblical scoundrels (1 Corinthians 10:1-13) and heroes of the faith (Hebrews 11:4-40). After all, experience is the best teacher—especially the experiences of others who have gone before us.

As you read these profiles, remember:
   O Many more affirmations could be drawn from what Scripture says.
   O Most profiles focus on one particular affirmation from a person's life.
   O Almost all the profiles present affirmations applicable to you and me.
   O Many profiles include cross references to other Scripture passages.
   O An index of all 122 profiles appears on pages 1459-1462.

HOW TO USE THE *LIVING FAITH BIBLE*

This is your devotional application Bible.

1. Become familiar with it.
   After reading these introductory notes, be sure to take a few minutes to check out the various features in this Bible. Don't miss the bonus features on pages 1455-1506.

2. Open it often.
   Make a commitment to read from God's Word daily. Three recommended daily reading plans follow on the next page. Choose one and follow it during the next few months.

3. Pray before you read.
   Ask the Lord to speak to you. After all, it's his Word! Like the psalmist, ask God to open your eyes (Psalm 119:18). Ask him to cleanse your heart (Psalm 51:10). Pray that the Holy Spirit will guide you into all truth (John 16:13). Thank him for making you "totally committed to doing what is right" (Titus 2:14).

4. Write in the margins as you read.

Always keep a pen handy to record your thoughts in the margins of this Bible. Feel free to add your own personal affirmation statements. And be sure to sprinkle its pages with exclamation points and an occasional "Yes!"

5. Pray again after you read.

Like Hannah, David, Daniel, Jeremiah, Nehemiah, Mary, and other great men and women of God, keep a prayer journal. This is where most life change begins! In response to each faith affirmation, tell the Lord what you believe—or find hard to believe. Tell him what you obey—or find easy to disobey. Tell him whose example you want to imitate—and whose failures you don't want to repeat.

6. Remember what you read.

Start each day reviewing the previous day's faith affirmations. Echo yesterday's prayers from the heart. Recommit yourself to following the Lord your God with all your soul, strength, and mind—and to loving your neighbor as yourself.

7. Share what you read.

If something in this Bible helps you experience a closer walk with God, why not share it with others? You may give away photocopies of a specific chapter or article. Just be sure to let your friends know it's from the *Living Faith Bible.*

SELECTING YOUR OWN READING PLAN

1. Survey Plan

Here's your opportunity to affirm key truths, commands, and examples from every book of the Bible. Use the table of Contents on page A5 as your guide. Each day, read the introduction to one book of the Bible. Then, using the list at the end of that introduction as a guide, read the most famous passages from that book. You can go from Genesis to Revelation in only 66 days.

2. Biographical Plan

Here's your opportunity to affirm the life-changing examples of the most important people in the Bible. Use the index of Examples to Heed on pages 1459–1462 as your guide. Each day, read one profile and the accompanying Scriptures. You can go from Adam (Genesis 1:26) to John (Revelation 1:9) in only 122 days.

3. One-Year Plan

Here's your opportunity to affirm each truth, command, and example in the Bible. Each day, read four pages of Scripture and the accompanying notes. You can go from Genesis 1–3 to Revelation 20–22 in slightly less than 365 days.

A Note to Readers

With 40 million copies in print, *The Living Bible* has been meeting a great need in people's hearts for more than thirty years. But even good things can be improved, so ninety evangelical scholars from various theological backgrounds and denominations were commissioned in 1989 to begin revising *The Living Bible*. The end result of this seven-year process is the *Holy Bible*, New Living Translation—a general-purpose translation that is accurate, easy to read, and excellent for study.

The goal of any Bible translation is to convey the meaning of the ancient Hebrew and Greek texts as accurately as possible to the modern reader. The New Living Translation is based on the most recent scholarship in the theory of translation. The challenge for the translators was to create a text that would make the same impact in the life of modern readers that the original text had for the original readers. In the New Living Translation, this is accomplished by translating entire thoughts (rather than just words) into natural, everyday English. The end result is a translation that is easy to read and understand and that accurately communicates the meaning of the original text.

We believe that this new translation, which combines the latest in scholarship with the best in translation style, will speak to your heart. We present the New Living Translation with the prayer that God will use it to speak his timeless truth to the church and to the world in a fresh, new way.

The Publishers
July 1996

Introduction to the New Living Translation

TRANSLATION PHILOSOPHY AND METHODOLOGY

There are two general theories or methods of Bible translation. The first has been called "formal equivalence." According to this theory, the translator attempts to render each word of the original language into the receptor language and seeks to preserve the original word order and sentence structure as much as possible. The second has been called "dynamic equivalence" or "functional equivalence." The goal of this translation theory is to produce in the receptor language the closest natural equivalent of the message expressed by the original-language text—both in meaning and in style. Such a translation attempts to have the same impact on modern readers as the original had on its own audience.

A dynamic-equivalence translation can also be called a thought-for-thought translation, as contrasted with a formal-equivalence or word-for-word translation. Of course, to translate the thought of the original language requires that the text be interpreted accurately and then be rendered in understandable idiom. So the goal of any thought-for-thought translation is to be both reliable and eminently readable. Thus, as a thought-for-thought translation, the New Living Translation seeks to be both exegetically accurate and idiomatically powerful.

In making a thought-for-thought translation, the translators must do their best to enter into the thought patterns of the ancient authors and to present the same ideas, connotations, and effects in the receptor language. In order to guard against personal biases and to ensure the accuracy of the message, a thought-for-thought translation should be created by a group of scholars who employ the best exegetical tools and who also understand the receptor language very well. With these concerns in mind, the Bible Translation Committee assigned each book of the Bible to three different scholars. Each scholar made a thorough review of the assigned book and submitted suggested revisions to the appropriate general reviewer. The general reviewer reviewed and summarized these suggestions and then proposed a first-draft revision of the text. This draft served as the basis for several additional phases of exegetical and stylistic committee review. Then the Bible Translation Committee jointly reviewed and approved every verse in the final translation.

A thought-for-thought translation prepared by a group of capable scholars has the potential to represent the intended meaning of the original text even more accurately than a word-for-word translation. This is illustrated by the various renderings of the Hebrew word *hesed*. This term cannot be adequately translated by any single English word because it can connote love, mercy, grace, kindness, faithfulness, and loyalty. The context—not the lexicon—must determine which English term is selected for translation.

The value of a thought-for-thought translation can be illustrated by comparing 1 Kings 2:10 in the King James Version, the New International Version, and the New Living Translation.

"So David slept with his fathers, and was buried in the city of David" (KJV). "Then David rested with his fathers and was buried in the City of David" (NIV). "Then David died and was buried in the City of David" (NLT). Only the New Living Translation clearly translates the real meaning of the Hebrew idiom "slept with his fathers" into contemporary English.

WRITTEN TO BE READ ALOUD

It is evident in Scripture that the biblical documents were written to be read aloud, often in public worship (see Nehemiah 8; Luke 4:16-20; 1 Timothy 4:13; Revelation 1:3). It is still the case today that more people will hear the Bible read aloud in church than are likely to read it for themselves. Therefore, a new translation must communicate with clarity and power when it is read aloud. For this reason, the New Living Translation is recommended as a Bible to be used for public reading. Its living language is not only easy to understand, but it also has an emotive quality that will make an impact on the listener.

THE TEXTS BEHIND THE NEW LIVING TRANSLATION

The translators of the Old Testament used the Masoretic Text of the Hebrew Bible as their standard text. They used the edition known as *Biblia Hebraica Stuttgartensia* (1977) with its up-to-date textual apparatus, a revision of Rudolf Kittel's *Biblia Hebraica* (Stuttgart, 1937). The translators also compared the Dead Sea Scrolls, the Septuagint and other Greek manuscripts, the Samaritan Pentateuch, the Syriac Peshitta, the Latin Vulgate, and any other versions or manuscripts that shed light on textual problems.

The translators of the New Testament used the two standard editions of the Greek New Testament: the *Greek New Testament*, published by the United Bible Societies (fourth revised edition, 1993), and *Novum Testamentum Graece*, edited by Nestle and Aland (twenty-seventh edition, 1993). These two editions, which have the same text but differ in punctuation and textual notes, represent the best in modern textual scholarship.

TRANSLATION ISSUES

The translators have made a conscious effort to provide a text that can be easily understood by the average reader of modern English. To this end, we have used the vocabulary and language structures commonly used by the average person. The result is a translation of the Scriptures written generally at the reading level of a junior high school student. We have avoided using language that is likely to become quickly dated or that reflects a narrow subdialect of English, with the goal of making the New Living Translation as broadly useful as possible.

But our concern for readability goes beyond the concerns of vocabulary and sentence structure. We are also concerned about historical and cultural barriers to understanding the Bible, and we have sought to translate terms shrouded in history or culture in ways that can be immediately understood by the contemporary reader. Thus, our goal of easy readability expresses itself in a number of other ways:

○ Rather than translating ancient weights and measures literally, which communicates little to the modern reader, we have expressed them by means of recognizable contemporary equivalents. We have converted ancient weights and measures to modern English (American) equivalents, and we have rendered the literal Hebrew or Greek measures, along with metric equivalents, in textual footnotes.

○ Instead of translating ancient currency values literally, we have generally expressed them in terms of weights in precious metals. In some cases we have used other common terms to communicate the message effectively. For example, "three shekels of silver" might become "three silver coins" or "three pieces of silver" to convey the intended message. Again, a rendering of the literal Hebrew or Greek is given in textual footnotes.

○ Since the Hebrew lunar calendar fluctuates from year to year in relation to the solar calendar used today, we have translated Hebrew dates in a way that communicates with our modern readership. It was clear that we could not use the names of the Hebrew months, such as *Abib*, which are meaningless to the modern reader. Nor could we use a simple designation such as "first month," because the months of the Hebrew lunar calendar do not correspond with the months of our calendar. Thus, we have often used seasonal references to communicate the time of year when something happened. For example, "the first month" (which occurs in March and April) might be translated "early spring." Where it is possible to define a specific ancient date in terms of our modern calendar, we use modern dates in the text. Textual footnotes then give the literal Hebrew date and state the rationale for our rendering. For example, Ezra 7:9 pinpoints the date when Ezra arrived in Jerusalem: "the first day of the fifth month." This was during the seventh year of King Artaxerxes' reign (Ezra 7:7). We translate that lunar date as August 4, with a footnote giving the Hebrew and identifying the year as 458 B.C.

○ Since ancient references to the time of day differ from our modern methods of denoting time, we used renderings that are instantly understandable to the modern reader. Accordingly, we have rendered specific times of day by using approximate equivalents in terms of our common "o'clock" system. On occasion, translations such as "at dawn the next morning" or "as the sun began to set" have been used when the biblical reference is general.

○ Many words in the original texts made sense to the original audience but communicate something quite different to the modern reader. In such cases, some liberty must be allowed in translation to communicate what was intended. Places identified by the term normally translated "city," for example, are often better identified as "towns" or "villages." Similarly, the term normally translated "mountain" is often better rendered "hill."

○ Many words and phrases carry a great deal of cultural meaning that was obvious to the original readers but needs explanation in our own culture. For example, the phrase "they beat their breasts" (Luke 23:48) in ancient times meant that people were very upset. In our translation we chose to translate this phrase dynamically: "They went home *in deep sorrow.*" In some cases, however, we have simply illuminated the existing expression to make it immediately understandable. For example, we might have expanded the literal phrase to read "they beat their breasts *in sorrow.*"

○ Metaphorical language is often difficult for contemporary readers to understand, so at times we have chosen to translate or illuminate the metaphor. For example, the ancient poet writes, "Your eyes are doves" (Song of Songs 1:15). To help the modern reader, who might be confused or distracted by a literal visualization of this image, we converted the metaphor to a simile to make the meaning immediately clear: "Your eyes are soft *like* doves." Here we also added the modifier "soft" to help the modern reader catch the significance of the metaphoric expression. A few chapters later, the poet writes, "Your neck is like the tower of David" (Song of Songs 4:4). We rendered it "Your neck is *as stately as* the tower of David" to clarify the intended positive meaning of the metaphor.

○ We did not feel obligated to display all Hebrew poetry in English poetic form. Only the book of Psalms is set entirely in poetic lines. Other books, though poetic in nature, are set in prose for the sake of easier reading. Nonetheless, these prose renderings reflect the poetic language of the original Hebrew. Where a portion of text is explicitly said to be a poem or song, however, it has usually been set as such.

○ One challenge we faced was in determining how to translate accurately the ancient biblical text that was originally written in a context where male-oriented terms were used to refer to humanity generally. We needed to respect the nature of the ancient context while also trying to make the translation clear to a modern audience that tends to read male-oriented language as applying only to males. Often the original text, though using masculine nouns and pronouns, clearly intends that the message be applied to both men and women. One example is found in the New Testament epistles, where the believers are called "brothers" (adelphoi). Yet it is clear that these epistles were addressed to all the believers—male and female. Thus, we have usually translated this Greek word "brothers and sisters" in order to represent the historical situation more accurately.

We have also been sensitive to passages where the text applies generally to human beings or to the human condition. In many instances we have used plural pronouns (they, them) in place of the masculine singular (he, him). For example, a traditional rendering of Proverbs 22:6 is: "Train up a child in the way he should go, and when he is old he will not turn from it." We have rendered it: "Teach your children to choose the right path, and when they are older, they will remain upon it." At times, we have also replaced third person pronouns with the second person to ensure clarity. A traditional rendering of Proverbs 26:27 is: "He who digs a pit will fall into it, and he who rolls a stone, it will come back on him." We have rendered it: "If you set a trap for others, you will get caught in it yourself. If you roll a boulder down on others, it will roll back and crush you." All such decisions were driven by the concern to reflect accurately the intended meaning of the original texts of Scripture.

We should emphasize, however, that all masculine nouns and pronouns used to represent God (for example, "Father") have been maintained without exception. We believe that essential traits of God's revealed character can only be conveyed through the masculine language expressed in the original texts of Scripture.

LEXICAL CONSISTENCY IN TERMINOLOGY

For the sake of clarity, we have maintained lexical consistency in areas such as divine names, synoptic passages, rhetorical structures, and nontheological technical terms (i.e., liturgical, cultic, zoological, botanical, cultural, and legal terms). For theological terms, we have allowed a greater semantic range of acceptable English words or phrases for a single Hebrew or Greek word. We avoided weighty theological terms that do not readily communicate to many modern readers. For example, we avoided using words such as "justification," "sanctification," and "regeneration." In place of these words (which are carryovers from Latin), we provided renderings such as "we are made right with God," "we are made holy," and "we are born anew."

THE SPELLING OF PROPER NAMES

Many individuals in the Bible, especially the Old Testament, are known by more than one name or by a number of variant names (e.g., Uzziah/Azariah). For the sake of clarity, we have tried to use a single spelling for any one individual, footnoting the literal spelling whenever we differ from it. This is especially helpful in delineating the kings of Israel and Judah. King Joash/Jehoash of Israel has been consistently called Jehoash, while King Joash/Jehoash of Judah is called Joash. A similar distinction has been used to distinguish between Joram/Jehoram of Israel and Joram/Jehoram of Judah. All such decisions were made with the goal of clarifying the text for the reader. When the ancient biblical writers clearly had a theological purpose in their choice of a variant name (e.g., Eshbaal/Ishbosheth), the different names have been maintained with an explanatory footnote.

THE RENDERING OF DIVINE NAMES

All appearances of *'el, 'elohim,* or *'eloah* have been translated "God," except where the context demands the translation "god(s)." We have rendered the tetragrammaton *(YHWH)* consistently as "the LORD," utilizing a form with small capitals that is common among English translations. This will distinguish it from the name *'adonai,* which we render "Lord." When *'adonai* and *YHWH* appear in conjunction, we have rendered it "Sovereign LORD." This also distinguishes *'adonai YHWH* from cases where *YHWH* appears with *'elohim,* which is rendered "LORD God." When *YH* (the short form of *YHWH*) and *YHWH* appear together, we have rendered it "LORD GOD." The Hebrew word *'adon* is rendered "lord," or "master," or sometimes "sir."

In the New Testament, the Greek word *christos* has been translated as "Messiah" when the context assumes a Jewish audience. When a Gentile audience can be assumed, *christos* has been translated as "Christ." The Greek word *kurios* is consistently translated "Lord," except in four quotations of Psalm 110:1, where it is translated "LORD."

TEXTUAL FOOTNOTES

The New Living Translation provides several kinds of textual footnotes:

○ All Old Testament passages that are clearly quoted in the New Testament are identified in a textual footnote in the New Testament.
○ Some textual footnotes provide cultural and historical information on places, things, and people in the Bible that are probably obscure to modern readers. Such notes should aid the reader in understanding the message of the text. For example, in Acts 12:1, "King Herod" is named in this translation as "King Herod Agrippa" and is identified in a footnote as being "the nephew of Herod Antipas and a grandson of Herod the Great."
○ When various ancient manuscripts contain different readings, these differences are often documented in footnotes. For instance, textual variants are footnoted when the variant reading is very familiar (usually through the King James Version). We have used footnotes when we have selected variant readings that differ from the Hebrew and Greek editions normally followed.
○ When the meaning of a proper name (or a wordplay inherent in a proper name) is relevant to the meaning of the text, it is illuminated with a textual footnote. For example, the footnote at Genesis 3:20 reads: *"Eve* sounds like a Hebrew term that means 'to give life.' " This wordplay in the Hebrew illuminates the meaning of the text, which goes on to say that Eve "would be the mother of all people everywhere." If the meaning of the name is more certain, it is stated more simply. For example, the footnote at Genesis 16:11 reads: *"Ishmael* means 'God hears.' " In this case, Hagar named her son Ishmael after realizing that God had heard her cry for help.
○ When we translate the meaning of a place-name that is often simply transliterated from the Hebrew or Greek, we provide a textual footnote showing the transliteration that appears in many English translations. For example, the name usually transliterated "Havvoth-jair" in Judges 10:4 has been translated "the Towns of Jair," with a footnote that gives the traditional transliteration: "Hebrew *Havvoth-jair.*"

○ Textual footnotes are also used to show alternative renderings. These are prefaced with the word "Or." On occasion, we also provide notes on words or phrases that represent a translation that departs from long-standing tradition. These notes are prefaced with the words "traditionally rendered." For example, a footnote to the translation "contagious skin disease" at Leviticus 13:2 says, "Traditionally rendered *leprosy.*"

AS WE SUBMIT this translation of the Bible for publication, we recognize that any translation of the Scriptures is subject to limitations and imperfections. Anyone who has attempted to communicate the richness of God's Word into another language will realize it is impossible to make a perfect translation. Recognizing these limitations, we sought God's guidance and wisdom throughout this project. Now we pray that he will accept our efforts and use this translation for the benefit of the church and of all people.

We pray that the New Living Translation will overcome some of the barriers of history, culture, and language that have kept people from reading and understanding God's Word. We hope that readers unfamiliar with the Bible will find the words clear and easy to understand and that readers well versed in the Scriptures will gain a fresh perspective. We pray that readers will gain insight and wisdom for living but most of all that they will meet the God of the Bible and be forever changed by knowing him.

The Bible Translation Committee
July 1996

Bible Translation Team

PENTATEUCH

Daniel I. Block, General Reviewer
The Southern Baptist Theological Seminary

GENESIS
Allan Ross, *Trinity Episcopal Seminary*
John Sailhamer, *Northwestern College*
Gordon Wenham, *The Cheltenham and Gloucester College of Higher Education*

EXODUS
Robert Bergen, *Hannibal-LaGrange College*
Daniel I. Block, *The Southern Baptist Theological Seminary*
Eugene Carpenter, *Bethel College, Mishawaka, Indiana*

LEVITICUS
David Baker, *Ashland Theological Seminary*
Victor Hamilton, *Asbury College*
Kenneth Mathews, *Beeson Divinity School, Samford University*

NUMBERS
Dale A. Brueggemann, *Assemblies of God Division of Foreign Missions*
Roland K. Harrison (deceased), *Wycliffe College*
Gerald L. Mattingly, *Johnson Bible College*

DEUTERONOMY
J. Gordon McConville, *The Cheltenham and Gloucester College of Higher Education*
Eugene H. Merrill, *Dallas Theological Seminary*
John A. Thompson, *University of Melbourne*

HISTORICAL BOOKS

Barry J. Beitzel, General Reviewer
Trinity Evangelical Divinity School

JOSHUA/JUDGES
Carl E. Armerding, *Schloss Mittersill Study Centre*
Barry J. Beitzel, *Trinity Evangelical Divinity School*
Lawson Stone, *Asbury Theological Seminary*

1 & 2 SAMUEL
Barry J. Beitzel, *Trinity Evangelical Divinity School*
V. Philips Long, *Covenant Theological Seminary*
J. Robert Vannoy, *Biblical Theological Seminary*

1 & 2 KINGS
Bill T. Arnold, *Asbury Theological Seminary*
William H. Barnes, *Southeastern College of the Assemblies of God*
Frederic W. Bush, *Fuller Theological Seminary*

1 & 2 CHRONICLES
Raymond B. Dillard (deceased), *Westminster Theological Seminary*
David A. Dorsey, *Evangelical School of Theology*
Terry Eves, *Calvin College*

EZRA/NEHEMIAH/ESTHER/RUTH
William C. Williams, *Southern California College*
Hugh G. M. Williamson, *Oxford University*

POETRY

Tremper Longman III, General Reviewer
Westminster Theological Seminary

JOB
August Konkel, *Providence Theological Seminary*
Tremper Longman III, *Westminster Theological Seminary*
Al Wolters, *Redeemer College*

PSALMS 1–75
Mark D. Futato, *Westminster Theological Seminary in California*
Douglas Green, *Westminster Theological Seminary*
Richard Pratt, *Reformed Theological Seminary*

PSALMS 76–150
David M. Howard Jr., *Trinity Evangelical Divinity School*
Raymond C. Ortlund Jr., *Trinity Evangelical Divinity School*
Willem VanGemeren, *Trinity Evangelical Divinity School*

PROVERBS
Ted Hildebrandt, *Grace College*
Richard Schultz, *Wheaton College*
Raymond C. Van Leeuwen, *Eastern College*

ECCLESIASTES/SONG OF SONGS
Daniel C. Fredericks, *Belhaven College*
David Hubbard (deceased), *Fuller Theological Seminary*
Tremper Longman III, *Westminster Theological Seminary*

PROPHETS

John N. Oswalt, General Reviewer
Asbury Theological Seminary

ISAIAH
John N. Oswalt, *Asbury Theological Seminary*
Gary Smith, *Bethel Theological Seminary*
John Walton, *Moody Bible Institute*

JEREMIAH/LAMENTATIONS
G. Herbert Livingston, *Asbury Theological Seminary*
Elmer A. Martens, *Mennonite Brethren Biblical Seminary*

EZEKIEL
Daniel I. Block, *The Southern Baptist Theological Seminary*
David H. Engelhard, *Calvin Theological Seminary*
David Thompson, *Asbury Theological Seminary*

DANIEL/HAGGAI/ZECHARIAH/MALACHI
Joyce Baldwin Caine (deceased), *Trinity College, Bristol*
Douglas Gropp, *Catholic University of America*
Roy Hayden, *Oral Roberts School of Theology*

HOSEA–ZEPHANIAH
Joseph Coleson, *Nazarene Theological Seminary*
Andrew Hill, *Wheaton College*
Richard Patterson, *Professor Emeritus, Liberty University*

GOSPELS AND ACTS
Grant R. Osborne, General Reviewer
Trinity Evangelical Divinity School

MATTHEW
Craig Blomberg, *Denver Conservative Baptist Seminary*
Donald A. Hagner, *Fuller Theological Seminary*
David Turner, *Grand Rapids Baptist Seminary*

MARK
Robert Guelich (deceased), *Fuller Theological Seminary*
Grant R. Osborne, *Trinity Evangelical Divinity School*

LUKE
Darrell Bock, *Dallas Theological Seminary*
Scot McKnight, *North Park College*
Robert Stein, *Bethel Theological Seminary*

JOHN
Gary M. Burge, *Wheaton College*
Philip W. Comfort, *Wheaton College*
Marianne Meye Thompson, *Fuller Theological Seminary*

ACTS
D. A. Carson, *Trinity Evangelical Divinity School*

William J. Larkin, *Columbia Biblical Seminary*
Roger Mohrlang, *Whitworth College*

LETTERS AND REVELATION
Norman R. Ericson, *General Reviewer*
Wheaton College

ROMANS/GALATIANS
Gerald Borchert, *The Southern Baptist Theological Seminary*
Douglas J. Moo, *Trinity Evangelical Divinity School*
Thomas R. Schreiner, *Bethel Theological Seminary*

1 & 2 CORINTHIANS
Joseph Alexanian, *Trinity International University*
Linda Belleville, *North Park Theological Seminary*
Douglas A. Oss, *Central Bible College*
Robert Sloan, *Baylor University*

EPHESIANS–PHILEMON
Harold W. Hoehner, *Dallas Theological Seminary*
Moises Silva, *Gordon-Conwell Theological Seminary*
Klyne Snodgrass, *North Park Theological Seminary*

HEBREWS/JAMES/1 & 2 PETER/JUDE
Peter Davids, *Canadian Theological Seminary*
Norman R. Ericson, *Wheaton College*
William Lane (deceased), *Seattle Pacific University*
J. Ramsey Michaels, *S.W. Missouri State University*

1–3 JOHN/REVELATION
Greg Beale, *Gordon-Conwell Theological Seminary*
Robert Mounce, *Whitworth College*
M. Robert Mulholland Jr., *Asbury Theological Seminary*

SPECIAL REVIEWERS
F. F. Bruce (deceased), *University of Manchester*
Kenneth N. Taylor, *Tyndale House Publishers*

COORDINATING TEAM
Mark R. Norton, *Managing Editor and O.T. Coordinating Editor*
Philip W. Comfort, *N.T. Coordinating Editor*
Ronald A. Beers, *Executive Director and Stylist*
Mark D. Taylor, *Director and Chief Stylist*
Daniel W. Taylor, *Consultant*

OLD testament

GENESIS

THIS FIRST BOOK of the Old Testament shows how deeply God longs to bless those who know and love him.

Right from the start, we see God at work—forming man from the dust of the earth and then walking daily with Adam and Eve in the marvelous Garden of Eden (1:1–2:25). And almost right from the start, we see humanity walking away from God—eating the forbidden fruit, being exiled from Eden, growing increasingly wicked (3:1–6:7).

Sadly, God eventually must judge the ancient world, so he sends a massive flood and commissions Noah's family to make a new start (6:8–9:29).

From one branch of Noah's family (10:1–11:26) we see God choosing a specific family to which he will demonstrate his love and concern for the world (11:27–22:19). That family, far from perfect, becomes a small clan (22:20–47:26) from which the nation of Israel will emerge (47:27–50:26) four centuries later.

As the first great prophet of Israel, Moses wrote this book to remind God's people who they are and where they have come from.

Famous passages in Genesis abound, including

- The creation of Adam (1:26-28)
- The creation of Eve (2:21-25)
- Adam and Eve's fall (3:6-7)
- The prophecy of a coming Savior (3:15)
- God's covenant with Noah (8:21–9:17)
- God calls Abraham (12:1-3)
- Abraham is declared righteous because of his faith (15:6)
- Sodom and Gomorrah are destroyed (19:24-25)
- Abraham's great test of faith (22:1-18)
- Jacob wrestles with God (32:22-32)
- Joseph resists Potiphar's wife's sexual advances (39:6-20)
- Joseph's great affirmation of faith (45:3-13)

CHAPTER 1

The Account of Creation

In the beginning God created* the heavens and the earth. ²The earth was empty, a formless mass cloaked in darkness. And the Spirit of God was hovering over its surface. ³Then God said, "Let there be light," and there was light. ⁴And God saw that it was good. Then he separated the light from the darkness. ⁵God called the light "day" and the darkness "night." Together these made up one day.

⁶And God said, "Let there be space between the waters, to separate water from water." ⁷And so it was. God made this space to separate the waters

I WORSHIP God, the Creator of heaven and earth. (1:1)

1:1 Or *In the beginning when God created,* or *When God began to create.*

above from the waters below. ⁸And God called the space "sky." This happened on the second day.

⁹And God said, "Let the waters beneath the sky be gathered into one place so dry ground may appear." And so it was. ¹⁰God named the dry ground "land" and the water "seas." And God saw that it was good. ¹¹Then God said, "Let the land burst forth with every sort of grass and seed-bearing plant. And let there be trees that grow seed-bearing fruit. The seeds will then produce the kinds of plants and trees from which they came." And so it was. ¹²The land was filled with seed-bearing plants and trees, and their seeds produced plants and trees of like kind. And God saw that it was good. ¹³This all happened on the third day.

¹⁴And God said, "Let bright lights appear in the sky to separate the day from the night. They will be signs to mark off the seasons, the days, and the years. ¹⁵Let their light shine down upon the earth." And so it was. ¹⁶For God made two great lights, the sun and the moon, to shine down upon the earth. The greater one, the sun, presides during the day; the lesser one, the moon, presides through the night. He also made the stars. ¹⁷God set these lights in the heavens to light the earth, ¹⁸to govern the day and the night, and to separate the light from the darkness. And God saw that it was good. ¹⁹This all happened on the fourth day.

²⁰And God said, "Let the waters swarm with fish and other life. Let the skies be filled with birds of every kind." ²¹So God created great sea creatures and every sort of fish and every kind of bird. And God saw that it was good. ²²Then God blessed them, saying, "Let the fish multiply and fill the oceans. Let the birds increase and fill the earth." ²³This all happened on the fifth day.

²⁴And God said, "Let the earth bring forth every kind of animal—livestock, small animals, and wildlife." And so it was. ²⁵God made all sorts of wild animals, livestock, and small animals, each able to reproduce more of its own kind. And God saw that it was good.

²⁶Then God said, "Let us make people* in our image, to be like ourselves. They will be masters over all life—the fish in the sea, the birds in the sky, and all the livestock, wild animals,* and small animals."

²⁷ So God created people in his own image;
God patterned them after himself;
male and female he created them.

²⁸God blessed them and told them, "Multiply and fill the earth and subdue it. Be masters over the fish and birds and all the animals." ²⁹And God said, "Look! I have given you the seed-bearing plants throughout the earth and all the fruit trees for your food. ³⁰And I have given all the grasses and other green plants to the animals and birds for their food." And so it was. ³¹Then God looked over all he had made, and he saw that it was excellent in every way. This all happened on the sixth day.

CHAPTER 2

So the creation of the heavens and the earth and everything in them was completed. ²On the seventh day, having finished his task, God rested from all his work. ³And God blessed the seventh day and declared it holy, because it was the day when he rested from his work of creation.

⁴This is the account of the creation of the heavens and the earth.

The Man and Woman in Eden

When the LORD God made the heavens and the earth, ⁵there were no plants or grain growing on the earth, for the LORD God had not sent any rain. And

I BELIEVE God wants the world to be inhabited by his creatures. (1:22)

Today what truth(s) are you choosing to believe?

I BELIEVE every person is made in the image of God. (1:27)

I BELIEVE God wants people to fill the world, care for it, and serve as masters over all he has created. (1:28)

I GLADLY ACCEPT God's good gifts and provisions, which meet my needs. (1:29)

I SEE AND REJOICE in the good things God has made. (1:31)

1:26a Hebrew *man;* also in 1:27.   1:26b As in Syriac version; Hebrew reads *all the earth.*

no one was there to cultivate the soil. ⁶But water came up out of the ground and watered all the land. ⁷And the LORD God formed a man's body from the dust of the ground and breathed into it the breath of life. And the man became a living person.

⁸Then the LORD God planted a garden in Eden, in the east, and there he placed the man he had created. ⁹And the LORD God planted all sorts of trees in the garden—beautiful trees that produced delicious fruit. At the center of the garden he placed the tree of life and the tree of the knowledge of good and evil.

¹⁰A river flowed from the land of Eden, watering the garden and then dividing into four branches. ¹¹One of these branches is the Pishon, which flows around the entire land of Havilah, where gold is found. ¹²The gold of that land is exceptionally pure; aromatic resin and onyx stone are also found there. ¹³The second branch is the Gihon, which flows around the entire land of Cush. ¹⁴The third branch is the Tigris, which flows to the east of Asshur. The fourth branch is the Euphrates.

¹⁵The LORD God placed the man in the Garden of Eden to tend and care for it. ¹⁶But the LORD God gave him this warning: "You may freely eat any fruit in the garden ¹⁷except fruit from the tree of the knowledge of good and evil. If you eat of its fruit, you will surely die."

I BELIEVE God created the first human with great dignity and worth and endowed him with his very own life-breath. (2:7)

I KNOW God delights to give beautiful things to his creatures. (2:8)

I BELIEVE God intends for work to be a good and purposeful endeavor. (2:15)

I LISTEN to any warnings that come with God's gifts. (2:16)

LIKE ADAM

Genesis 1:26

I am created by God and endowed with eternal dignity and value.

Who doesn't enjoy wandering through the woods, looking out over the desert, walking along an ocean shore, or standing on a prominent hill just before sunset? Everywhere that you and I see the beauty of nature, we see God's handiwork. What we see now, however, is dulled and damaged by the ravages of thousands of years of sin.

Imagine what Adam must have experienced when he first viewed creation fresh from the Creator's hand. Every tree Adam climbed, every lion cub he stroked, every rock he skipped on the Tigris river must have radiated something of God's glory. But no plant, animal, or jewel compared with the wonder of Adam caring for the garden, conversing with the Lord, and listening to his wife's first songs.

Everything in creation was made by God, but only Adam and Eve (and their descendants) were made *like* God. God dreamed up fantastic, intricate designs for each kind of palm tree and polar bear. God patterned humans, however, after himself.

The wonders of nature have immense worth because God created them. But the human race holds an incredible place of honor within the universe (Psalm 8). Why? Because you and I are made in the image of God.

Of course, sin has ravaged more than nature. Scripture makes it clear that through Adam's sin the entire human race has been infected with this fatal disease (Hosea 6:7; Romans 5:12; 1 Corinthians 15:21-22).

Thankfully, through Jesus Christ we can receive forgiveness of sins and the sure hope of new, eternal life (Romans 5:13-21; 1 Corinthians 15:45-49).

○ *Today's Scripture reading is Genesis 1:26–2:17.*

---

¹⁸And the LORD God said, "It is not good for the man to be alone. I will make a companion who will help him." ¹⁹So the LORD God formed from the soil every kind of animal and bird. He brought them to Adam* to see what he would call them, and Adam chose a name for each one. ²⁰He gave names to all the livestock, birds, and wild animals. But still there was no companion suitable for him. ²¹So the LORD God caused Adam to fall into a deep sleep. He

2:19 Hebrew *the man,* and so throughout this chapter.

took one of Adam's ribs* and closed up the place from which he had taken it. ²²Then the LORD God made a woman from the rib and brought her to Adam.

²³"At last!" Adam exclaimed. "She is part of my own flesh and bone! She will be called 'woman,' because she was taken out of a man." ²⁴This explains why a man leaves his father and mother and is joined to his wife, and the two are united into one. ²⁵Now, although Adam and his wife were both naked, neither of them felt any shame.

CHAPTER 3
The Man and Woman Sin

Now the serpent was the shrewdest of all the creatures the LORD God had made. "Really?" he asked the woman. "Did God really say you must not eat any of the fruit in the garden?"

²"Of course we may eat it," the woman told him. ³"It's only the fruit from the tree at the center of the garden that we are not allowed to eat. God says we must not eat it or even touch it, or we will die."

⁴"You won't die!" the serpent hissed. ⁵"God knows that your eyes will be opened when you eat it. You will become just like God, knowing everything, both good and evil."

⁶The woman was convinced. The fruit looked so fresh and delicious, and it would make her so wise! So she ate some of the fruit. She also gave some to her husband, who was with her. Then he ate it, too. ⁷At that moment, their eyes were opened, and they suddenly felt shame at their nakedness. So they strung fig leaves together around their hips to cover themselves.

⁸Toward evening they heard the LORD God walking about in the garden, so they hid themselves among the trees. ⁹The LORD God called to Adam,* "Where are you?"

¹⁰He replied, "I heard you, so I hid. I was afraid because I was naked."

¹¹"Who told you that you were naked?" the LORD God asked. "Have you eaten the fruit I commanded you not to eat?"

¹²"Yes," Adam admitted, "but it was the woman you gave me who brought me the fruit, and I ate it."

¹³Then the LORD God asked the woman, "How could you do such a thing?"

"The serpent tricked me," she replied. "That's why I ate it."

¹⁴So the LORD God said to the serpent, "Because you have done this, you will be punished. You are singled out from all the domestic and wild animals of the whole earth to be cursed. You will grovel in the dust as long as you live, crawling along on your belly. ¹⁵From now on, you and the woman will be enemies, and your offspring and her offspring will be enemies. He will crush your head, and you will strike his heel."

¹⁶Then he said to the woman, "You will bear children with intense pain and suffering. And though your desire will be for your husband,* he will be your master."

¹⁷And to Adam he said, "Because you listened to your wife and ate the fruit I told you not to eat, I have placed a curse on the ground. All your life you will struggle to scratch a living from it. ¹⁸It will grow thorns and thistles for you, though you will eat of its grains. ¹⁹All your life you will sweat to produce food, until your dying day. Then you will return to the ground from which you came. For you were made from dust, and to the dust you will return."

²⁰Then Adam named his wife Eve,* because she would be the mother of all people everywhere. ²¹And the LORD God made clothing from animal skins for Adam and his wife.

²²Then the LORD God said, "The people have become as we are, knowing everything, both good and evil. What if they eat the fruit of the tree of life?

I THANK God for the spouse he gives me. (2:23)

I DO NOT TAKE shortcuts to try to gain wisdom or godliness. (3:6)

I KNOW that disobeying God can produce feelings of guilt or shame. (3:7)

I TAKE responsibility for my own sin instead of blaming others. (3:12)

I BELIEVE that from the very beginning God promised to provide future victory over Satan and sin. (3:15)

I ACCEPT God's covering for the shame of my sin. (3:21)

2:21 Or took a part of Adam's side. 3:9 Hebrew the man, and so throughout this chapter. 3:16 Or And though you may desire to control your husband. 3:20 Eve sounds like a Hebrew term that means "to give life."

Then they will live forever!" ²³So the LORD God banished Adam and his wife from the Garden of Eden, and he sent Adam out to cultivate the ground from which he had been made. ²⁴After banishing them from the garden, the LORD God stationed mighty angelic beings* to the east of Eden. And a flaming sword flashed back and forth, guarding the way to the tree of life.

CHAPTER 4

Cain, Abel, and Seth

Now Adam* slept with his wife, Eve, and she became pregnant. When the time came, she gave birth to Cain,* and she said, "With the LORD's help, I have brought forth* a man!" ²Later she gave birth to a second son and named him Abel.

I ACKNOWLEDGE the Lord's help in conceiving and bearing children. (4:1)

When they grew up, Abel became a shepherd, while Cain was a farmer. ³At harvesttime Cain brought to the LORD a gift of his farm produce, ⁴while Abel brought several choice lambs from the best of his flock. The LORD accepted Abel and his offering, ⁵but he did not accept Cain and his offering. This made Cain very angry and dejected.

I BRING my best as a gift to God. (4:4)

⁶"Why are you so angry?" the LORD asked him. "Why do you look so dejected? ⁷You will be accepted if you respond in the right way. But if you refuse to respond correctly, then watch out! Sin is waiting to attack and destroy you, and you must subdue it."

I LISTEN to God's rebuke, then repent and obey him. (4:7)

LIKE EVE

Genesis 3:21

I know for certain that God forgives even the worst of sins.

Meet the woman who gets blamed for everything.

"If only Eve hadn't eaten the forbidden fruit. . . ." Not that Adam helped matters any! Who knows what life would have been like without that first act of disobedience? But we do know what life is like afterward. And, like Eve, we know that God will not forsake us when we sin.

What worse sin could Eve have committed? There was only one rule, and she broke it. Instead of embracing all that God gave her, she reached for the one thing he kept back (2 Corinthians 11:3). As soon as Adam and Eve ate the fruit, they experienced the bitter aftertaste of sin—exposure, shame, and physically painful consequences.

Quickly, God also gave them the taste of forgiveness. Later, after a sobering discussion, God would give them coverings for their physical nakedness. First, however, he gave them hope for their souls. His forgiveness did not undo the damage, but he promised that one day the serpent and sin would be defeated (Genesis 3:15). This was accomplished in Jesus Christ. In the meantime, despite the presence of sin and death, humanity would continue, with Eve becoming the mother of all people.

Our sin brings pain to ourselves and others. But like Eve, you and I can be confident that God will forgive us. In fact, the Lord promises one day to remove the curse from the ground (Romans 8:20-23) and live with his people once again in the garden of eternity (Revelation 22:1-2).

○ *Today's Scripture reading is Genesis 2:18–3:24.*

⁸Later Cain suggested to his brother, Abel, "Let's go out into the fields."* And while they were there, Cain attacked and killed his brother.

⁹Afterward the LORD asked Cain, "Where is your brother? Where is Abel?"

"I don't know!" Cain retorted. "Am I supposed to keep track of him wherever he goes?"

I DEAL with negative emotions before they erupt into hurtful actions. (4:8)

¹⁰But the LORD said, "What have you done? Listen—your brother's blood cries out to me from the ground! ¹¹You are hereby banished from the ground

3:24 Hebrew *cherubim.* 4:1a Hebrew *the man.* 4:1b *Cain* sounds like a Hebrew term that can mean "bring forth" or "acquire." 4:1c Or *I have acquired.* 4:8 As in Samaritan Pentateuch, Greek and Syriac versions, Latin Vulgate; Masoretic Text lacks *"Let's go out into the fields."*

you have defiled with your brother's blood. ¹²No longer will it yield abundant crops for you, no matter how hard you work! From now on you will be a homeless fugitive on the earth, constantly wandering from place to place."

¹³Cain replied to the LORD, "My punishment* is too great for me to bear! ¹⁴You have banished me from my land and from your presence; you have made me a wandering fugitive. All who see me will try to kill me!"

¹⁵The LORD replied, "They will not kill you, for I will give seven times your punishment to anyone who does." Then the LORD put a mark on Cain to warn anyone who might try to kill him. ¹⁶So Cain left the LORD's presence and settled in the land of Nod,* east of Eden.

¹⁷Then Cain's wife became pregnant and gave birth to a son, and they named him Enoch. When Cain founded a city, he named it Enoch after his son.

¹⁸ Enoch was the father of* Irad.

Irad was the father of Mehujael.

Mehujael was the father of Methushael.

Methushael was the father of Lamech.

¹⁹Lamech married two women—Adah and Zillah. ²⁰Adah gave birth to a baby named Jabal. He became the first of the herdsmen who live in tents. ²¹His brother's name was Jubal, the first musician—the inventor of the harp and flute. ²²To Lamech's other wife, Zillah, was born Tubal-cain. He was the first to work with metal, forging instruments of bronze and iron. Tubal-cain had a sister named Naamah.

²³One day Lamech said to Adah and Zillah, "Listen to me, my wives. I have killed a youth who attacked and wounded me. ²⁴If anyone who kills Cain is to be punished seven times, anyone who takes revenge against me will be punished seventy-seven times!"

²⁵Adam slept with his wife again, and she gave birth to another son. She named him Seth,* for she said, "God has granted me another son in place of Abel, the one Cain killed." ²⁶When Seth grew up, he had a son and named him Enosh. It was during his lifetime that people first began to worship the LORD.

CHAPTER 5
From Adam to Noah

This is the history of the descendants of Adam. When God created people,* he made them in the likeness of God. ²He created them male and female, and he blessed them and called them "human."*

³When Adam was 130 years old, his son Seth was born,* and Seth was the very image of his father.* ⁴After the birth of Seth,* Adam lived another 800 years, and he had other sons and daughters. ⁵He died at the age of 930.

⁶When Seth was 105 years old, his son Enosh was born. ⁷After the birth of Enosh, Seth lived another 807 years, and he had other sons and daughters. ⁸He died at the age of 912.

⁹When Enosh was 90 years old, his son Kenan was born. ¹⁰After the birth of Kenan, Enosh lived another 815 years, and he had other sons and daughters. ¹¹He died at the age of 905.

¹²When Kenan was 70 years old, his son Mahalalel was born. ¹³After the birth of Mahalalel, Kenan lived another 840 years, and he had other sons and daughters. ¹⁴He died at the age of 910.

I THANK God for his mercy. (4:15)

I ACCEPT the consequences of my sin. (4:16)

I BELIEVE God created people in his own likeness. (5:1)

Make a commitment to read from God's Word daily.

4:13 Or *My sin.* 4:16 *Nod* means "wandering." 4:18 Or *the ancestor of,* and so throughout the verse. 4:25 *Seth* probably means "granted"; the name may also mean "appointed." 5:1 Hebrew *man.* 5:2 Hebrew *man.* 5:3a Or *his son, the ancestor of Seth, was born;* similarly in 5:6, 9, 12, 15, 18, 21, 25. 5:3b Hebrew *was in his own likeness, after his image.* 5:4 Or *After the birth of this ancestor of Seth;* similarly in 5:7, 10, 13, 16, 19, 22, 26.

15When Mahalalel was 65 years old, his son Jared was born. 16After the birth of Jared, Mahalalel lived 830 years, and he had other sons and daughters. 17He died at the age of 895.

18When Jared was 162 years old, his son Enoch was born. 19After the birth of Enoch, Jared lived another 800 years, and he had other sons and daughters. 20He died at the age of 962.

21When Enoch was 65 years old, his son Methuselah was born. 22After the birth of Methuselah, Enoch lived another 300 years in close fellowship with God, and he had other sons and daughters. 23Enoch lived 365 years in all. 24He enjoyed a close relationship with God throughout his life. Then suddenly, he disappeared because God took him.

25When Methuselah was 187 years old, his son Lamech was born. 26After the birth of Lamech, Methuselah lived another 782 years, and he had other sons and daughters. 27He died at the age of 969.

28When Lamech was 182 years old, his son Noah was born. 29Lamech named his son Noah,* for he said, "He will bring us relief from the painful labor of farming this ground that the LORD has cursed." 30After the birth of Noah, Lamech lived 595 years, and he had other sons and daughters. 31He died at the age of 777.

32By the time Noah was 500 years old, he had three sons: Shem, Ham, and Japheth.

I LIVE in close fellowship with God. (5:22)

Today what command(s) are you choosing to obey?

I GROW closer and closer to God throughout my entire life. (5:24)

I RECOGNIZE the potential for God's work in my child's life. (5:29)

LIKE ABEL   *I am righteous in God's eyes by faith alone.*

Genesis 4:4

What went wrong?

Why was Cain's offering not accepted? According to Genesis, it does not seem that God had given specific laws for sacrifices yet. It does say that Abel brought the choicest lambs from his flock. Who knows if there were bigger cucumbers growing in Cain's garden?

The reason the Lord didn't accept Cain's offering went deeper than a preference for meat over veggies. Faith is what made Abel's offering acceptable. Faith is what showed him to be a godly, righteous man (Hebrews 11:4).

If faith is what made Abel's offering acceptable, then faith must have been what Cain lacked. When Cain became angry and dejected by God's warnings, he revealed a heart that neither loved nor trusted God. God pleaded with Abel's brother to watch out for sin's onslaughts. Cain refused, further rebelled, and ended up striking down his brother. His sinful actions only proved his lack of faith. But Abel's blood still speaks to us. Why? Because it testifies of his faith (Hebrews 11:4). Like Abel, you and I come to God, not on the merit of what we bring him, but by faith in who he is.

○ *Today's Scripture reading is Genesis 4:1-18.*

CHAPTER 6

Noah and the Flood

When the human population began to grow rapidly on the earth, 2the sons of God saw the beautiful women of the human race and took any they wanted as their wives. 3Then the LORD said, "My Spirit will not put up with humans for such a long time, for they are only mortal flesh. In the future, they will live no more than 120 years."

4In those days, and even afterward, giants* lived on the earth, for whenever the sons of God had intercourse with human women, they gave birth to children who became the heroes mentioned in legends of old.

5Now the LORD observed the extent of the people's wickedness, and he saw that all their thoughts were consistently and totally evil. 6So the LORD was

I AM HEARTBROKEN by the evil of people around me. (6:6)

5:29 *Noah* sounds like a Hebrew term that can mean "relief" or "comfort."   6:4 Hebrew *Nephilim*.

sorry he had ever made them. It broke his heart. [7]And the LORD said, "I will completely wipe out this human race that I have created. Yes, and I will destroy all the animals and birds, too. I am sorry I ever made them." [8]But Noah found favor with the LORD.

[9]This is the history of Noah and his family. Noah was a righteous man, the only blameless man living on earth at the time. He consistently followed God's will and enjoyed a close relationship with him. [10]Noah had three sons: Shem, Ham, and Japheth.

[11]Now the earth had become corrupt in God's sight, and it was filled with violence. [12]God observed all this corruption in the world, and he saw violence and depravity everywhere. [13]So God said to Noah, "I have decided to destroy all living creatures, for the earth is filled with violence because of them. Yes, I will wipe them all from the face of the earth!

[14]"Make a boat* from resinous wood and seal it with tar, inside and out. Then construct decks and stalls throughout its interior. [15]Make it 450 feet long, 75 feet wide, and 45 feet high.* [16]Construct an opening all the way around the boat, 18 inches* below the roof. Then put three decks inside the boat—bottom, middle, and upper—and put a door in the side.

[17]"Look! I am about to cover the earth with a flood that will destroy every living thing. Everything on earth will die! [18]But I solemnly swear to keep you safe in the boat, with your wife and your sons and their wives. [19]Bring a pair of every kind of animal—a male and a female—into the boat with you to keep them alive during the flood. [20]Pairs of each kind of bird and each kind of animal, large and small alike, will come to you to be kept alive. [21]And remember, take enough food for your family and for all the animals."

[22]So Noah did everything exactly as God had commanded him.

CHAPTER 7

The Flood Covers the Earth

Finally, the day came when the LORD said to Noah, "Go into the boat with all your family, for among all the people of the earth, I consider you alone to be righteous. [2]Take along seven pairs of each animal that I have approved for eating and for sacrifice, and take one pair of each of the others. [3]Then select seven pairs of every kind of bird. There must be a male and a female in each pair to ensure that every kind of living creature will survive the flood. [4]One week from today I will begin forty days and forty nights of rain. And I will wipe from the earth all the living things I have created."

[5]So Noah did exactly as the LORD had commanded him. [6]He was 600 years old when the flood came, [7]and he went aboard the boat to escape—he and his wife and his sons and their wives. [8]With them were all the various kinds of animals—those approved for eating and sacrifice and those that were not—along with all the birds and other small animals. [9]They came into the boat in pairs, male and female, just as God had commanded Noah. [10]One week later, the flood came and covered the earth.

[11]When Noah was 600 years old, on the seventeenth day of the second month, the underground waters burst forth on the earth, and the rain fell in mighty torrents from the sky. [12]The rain continued to fall for forty days and forty nights. [13]But Noah had gone into the boat that very day with his wife and his sons—Shem, Ham, and Japheth—and their wives. [14]With them in the boat were pairs of every kind of breathing animal—domestic and wild, large and small—along with birds and flying insects of every kind. [15]Two by two they came into the boat, [16]male and female, just as God had commanded. Then the LORD shut them in.

[17]For forty days the floods prevailed, covering the ground and lifting the

I SEEK to find favor with God in the midst of a wicked society. (6:8)

I LIVE a righteous life, even if I am the only one who does so. (6:9)

I CHOOSE to live a nonviolent life in an often violent world. (6:11)

I BELIEVE God will provide the means to obey his commands. (6:20)

I USE God's way of escape from judgment. (7:7)

I BELIEVE God never idly threatens to bring judgment. (7:11)

I SEEK to bring my family under God's protective hand. (7:13)

6:14 Traditionally rendered *an ark.*   6:15 Hebrew *300 cubits* [135 meters] *long, 50 cubits* [22.5 meters] *wide, and 30 cubits* [13.5 meters] *high.*   6:16 Hebrew *1 cubit* [45 centimeters].

boat high above the earth. [18]As the waters rose higher and higher above the ground, the boat floated safely on the surface. [19]Finally, the water covered even the highest mountains on the earth, [20]standing more than twenty-two feet* above the highest peaks. [21]All the living things on earth died—birds, domestic animals, wild animals, all kinds of small animals, and all the people. [22]Everything died that breathed and lived on dry land. [23]Every living thing on the earth was wiped out—people, animals both large and small, and birds. They were all destroyed, and only Noah was left alive, along with those who were with him in the boat. [24]And the water covered the earth for 150 days.

I BELIEVE God judged the wickedness of the ancient world by sending a massive flood, just as he said he would. (7:23)

CHAPTER 8

The Flood Recedes

But God remembered Noah and all the animals in the boat. He sent a wind to blow across the waters, and the floods began to disappear. [2]The underground water sources ceased their gushing, and the torrential rains stopped. [3]So the flood gradually began to recede. After 150 days, [4]exactly five months from the time the flood began,* the boat came to rest on the mountains of Ararat. [5]Two and a half months later,* as the waters continued to go down, other mountain peaks began to appear.

LIKE ENOCH
Genesis 5:24

I can walk in close fellowship with God my entire life.

Enoch, the father of history's oldest man, Methuselah, lived a relatively short life. But he spent each day of his 365 years right by God's side. Talk about quality versus quantity!

Today, we admire a person who stays true to his or her beliefs and convictions thirty or forty years or more. We toast the couple who remains faithful and as much in love at their fiftieth anniversary as they were at their first.

Enoch beats us all. His fellowship with God stretched over almost four centuries, through the birth of sons and daughters and the rise of civilizations. Enoch never once needed a vacation from his relationship with God. He never let his love grow cold.

Literally, Genesis 5:24 says that Enoch "walked with God," comparing Enoch's close fellowship with God to the deep companionship between two cherished friends accustomed to walking a road together each evening. It seems that Enoch walked so far and so close with God that one day it was as if the two were closer to God's house than to Enoch's. So God just took Enoch home.

True, God may not whisk you or me away while we are reading his Word or praying today. But we can know the same intimacy with God our entire lives—no matter how many years God gives us on earth.

We should long to walk closely with God all of our days, just as Enoch did. To read more about this great man of faith, see Hebrews 11:5-6 and Jude 1:14.

○ *Today's Scripture reading is Genesis 5:18-24.*

---

[6]After another forty days, Noah opened the window he had made in the boat [7]and released a raven that flew back and forth until the earth was dry. [8]Then he sent out a dove to see if it could find dry ground. [9]But the dove found no place to land because the water was still too high. So it returned to the boat, and Noah held out his hand and drew the dove back inside. [10]Seven days later, Noah released the dove again. [11]This time, toward evening, the bird returned to him with a fresh olive leaf in its beak. Noah now knew that the water was almost gone. [12]A week later, he released the dove again, and this time it did not come back.

7:20 Hebrew *15 cubits* [6.8 meters].   8:4 Hebrew *on the seventeenth day of the seventh month;* see 7:11.
8:5 Hebrew *On the first day of the tenth month;* see 7:11 and note on 8:4.

¹³Finally, when Noah was 601 years old, ten and a half months after the flood began,* Noah lifted back the cover to look. The water was drying up. ¹⁴Two more months went by,* and at last the earth was dry! ¹⁵Then God said to Noah, ¹⁶"Leave the boat, all of you. ¹⁷Release all the animals and birds so they can breed and reproduce in great numbers." ¹⁸So Noah, his wife, and his sons and their wives left the boat. ¹⁹And all the various kinds of animals and birds came out, pair by pair.

²⁰Then Noah built an altar to the LORD and sacrificed on it the animals and birds that had been approved for that purpose. ²¹And the LORD was pleased with the sacrifice and said to himself, "I will never again curse the earth, destroying all living things, even though people's thoughts and actions are bent toward evil from childhood. ²²As long as the earth remains, there will be springtime and harvest, cold and heat, winter and summer, day and night."

CHAPTER 9

God's Covenant with Noah

God blessed Noah and his sons and told them, "Multiply and fill the earth. ²All the wild animals, large and small, and all the birds and fish will be afraid of you. I have placed them in your power. ³I have given them to you for food, just as I have given you grain and vegetables. ⁴But you must never eat animals that still have their lifeblood in them. ⁵And murder is forbidden. Animals that kill people must die, and any person who murders must be killed. ⁶Yes, you must execute anyone who murders another person, for to kill a person is to kill a living being made in God's image. ⁷Now you must have many children and repopulate the earth. Yes, multiply and fill the earth!"

⁸Then God told Noah and his sons, ⁹"I am making a covenant with you and your descendants, ¹⁰and with the animals you brought with you—all these birds and livestock and wild animals. ¹¹I solemnly promise never to send another flood to kill all living creatures and destroy the earth." ¹²And God said, "I am giving you a sign as evidence of my eternal covenant with you and all living creatures. ¹³I have placed my rainbow in the clouds. It is the sign of my permanent promise to you and to all the earth. ¹⁴When I send clouds over the earth, the rainbow will be seen in the clouds, ¹⁵and I will remember my covenant with you and with everything that lives. Never again will there be a flood that will destroy all life. ¹⁶When I see the rainbow in the clouds, I will remember the eternal covenant between God and every living creature on earth." ¹⁷Then God said to Noah, "Yes, this is the sign of my covenant with all the creatures of the earth."

Noah's Sons

¹⁸Shem, Ham, and Japheth, the three sons of Noah, survived the Flood with their father. (Ham is the ancestor of the Canaanites.) ¹⁹From these three sons of Noah came all the people now scattered across the earth.

²⁰After the Flood, Noah became a farmer and planted a vineyard. ²¹One day he became drunk on some wine he had made and lay naked in his tent. ²²Ham, the father of Canaan, saw that his father was naked and went outside and told his brothers. ²³Shem and Japheth took a robe, held it over their shoulders, walked backward into the tent, and covered their father's naked body. As they did this, they looked the other way so they wouldn't see him naked. ²⁴When Noah woke up from his drunken stupor, he learned what Ham, his youngest son, had done. ²⁵Then he cursed the descendants of Canaan, the son of Ham:

"A curse on the Canaanites!
May they be the lowest of servants
    to the descendants of Shem and Japheth."

**Sidebar notes (left column):**

I WAIT for God's direction before moving forward into a new situation. (8:15)

I MOVE AHEAD when God tells me. (8:18)

I WORSHIP God for his deliverance. (8:20)

I THANK God for his mercy to humanity, even though we are all sinful from childhood. (8:21)

I ACCEPT God's gifts of meat, fruit, and vegetables for food. (9:3)

I ABHOR murder. (9:5)

I THANK God for his promise to never flood the whole earth again. (9:11)

I THANK God for the rainbow—a sign that he will remember his promise to Noah. (9:16)

I BELIEVE that all people now living are descended from Noah and his sons. (9:19)

I SHOW RESPECT for someone else's modesty, even if that person is willfully immodest. (9:23)

8:13 Hebrew *on the first day of the first month;* see 7:11.   **8:14** Hebrew *The twenty-seventh day of the second month arrived;* see note on 8:13.

²⁶Then Noah said,

"May Shem be blessed by the LORD my God;
and may Canaan be his servant.
²⁷May God enlarge the territory of Japheth,
and may he share the prosperity of Shem;*
and let Canaan be his servant."

²⁸Noah lived another 350 years after the Flood. ²⁹He was 950 years old when he died.

CHAPTER 10

This is the history of the families of Shem, Ham, and Japheth, the three sons of Noah. Many children were born to them after the Flood.

LIKE NOAH
Genesis 6:9

I live a blameless life, even if I am the only one who does so.

Many people today live by the polls. The opinions of others guide their beliefs and votes and choices, as if majority rule could possibly set the standards for right and wrong. If Noah had been interviewed by Gallup on issues of morality and godliness, he would have found himself completely outnumbered. To his credit, that did not stop Noah from living a blameless life.

For the first five hundred years of his life, Noah kept on doing right in a world that was going very wrong. Even after God called him to make a boat that would be his means of rescue from the coming judgment, Noah endured another one hundred years of standing against the tide of growing violence and hatred (Hebrews 11:7). He became a public spectacle, building a ship that no one but his family and the animals would choose to enter, no matter how diligently Noah warned his fellow citizens (2 Peter 2:5). No one listened, and no one cared, and Noah and his family were the only ones left when the Flood swept the inhabited world away (Luke 17:27).

In the end, Noah received the only approval that really mattered: He found favor with God. Because of this, he and his family were spared from otherwise certain destruction.

Like Noah, you and I are never so outnumbered that it is impossible to live by faith, pleasing God.

○ *Today's Scripture reading is Genesis 6:1–9:17.*

Descendants of Japheth
²The descendants of Japheth were Gomer, Magog, Madai, Javan, Tubal, Meshech, and Tiras.
³The descendants of Gomer were Ashkenaz, Riphath, and Togarmah.
⁴The descendants of Javan were Elishah, Tarshish, Kittim, and Rodanim.*
⁵Their descendants became the seafaring peoples in various lands, each tribe with its own language.

Descendants of Ham
⁶The descendants of Ham were Cush, Mizraim,* Put, and Canaan.
⁷The descendants of Cush were Seba, Havilah, Sabtah, Raamah, and Sabteca. The descendants of Raamah were Sheba and Dedan.
⁸One of Cush's descendants was Nimrod, who became a heroic warrior. ⁹He was a mighty hunter in the LORD's sight.* His name became proverbial, and people would speak of someone as being "like Nimrod, a mighty hunter in the LORD's sight." ¹⁰He built the foundation for his empire in the land of Babylonia,* with the cities of Babel, Erech, Akkad, and Calneh. ¹¹From there he extended his reign to Assyria, where he

I WANT to be known for who I am in the Lord's sight. (10:9)

I USE my abilities and authority to accomplish great things for God. (10:10)

9:27 Hebrew *may he live in the tents of Shem.* 10:4 As in some Hebrew manuscripts and Greek version (see also 1 Chr 1:7); most Hebrew manuscripts read *Dodanim.* 10:6 Or *Egypt;* also in 10:13. 10:9 Hebrew *a mighty hunter before the LORD;* also in 10:9b. 10:10 Hebrew *Shinar.*

built Nineveh, Rehoboth-ir, Calah, ¹²and Resen—the main city of the empire, located between Nineveh and Calah.

¹³Mizraim was the ancestor of the Ludites, Anamites, Lehabites, Naphtuhites, ¹⁴Pathrusites, Casluhites, and the Caphtorites, from whom the Philistines came.*

¹⁵Canaan's oldest son was Sidon, the ancestor of the Sidonians. Canaan was also the ancestor of the Hittites, ¹⁶Jebusites, Amorites, Girgashites, ¹⁷Hivites, Arkites, Sinites, ¹⁸Arvadites, Zemarites, and Hamathites. ¹⁹Eventually the territory of Canaan spread from Sidon to Gerar, near Gaza, and to Sodom, Gomorrah, Admah, and Zeboiim, near Lasha.

In response to these affirmations, tell the Lord what you believe—or find hard to believe.

²⁰These were the descendants of Ham, identified according to their tribes, languages, territories, and nations.

Descendants of Shem

²¹Sons were also born to Shem, the older brother of Japheth.* Shem was the ancestor of all the descendants of Eber. ²²The descendants of Shem were Elam, Asshur, Arphaxad, Lud, and Aram.

²³The descendants of Aram were Uz, Hul, Gether, and Mash.

²⁴Arphaxad was the father of Shelah,* and Shelah was the father of Eber. ²⁵Eber had two sons. The first was named Peleg—"division"—for during his lifetime the people of the world were divided into different language groups and dispersed. His brother's name was Joktan.

²⁶Joktan was the ancestor of Almodad, Sheleph, Hazarmaveth, Jerah, ²⁷Hadoram, Uzal, Diklah, ²⁸Obal, Abimael, Sheba, ²⁹Ophir, Havilah, and Jobab. ³⁰The descendants of Joktan lived in the area extending from Mesha toward the eastern hills of Sephar.

³¹These were the descendants of Shem, identified according to their tribes, languages, territories, and nations.

³²These are the families that came from Noah's sons, listed nation by nation according to their lines of descent. The earth was populated with the people of these nations after the Flood.

CHAPTER 11

The Tower of Babel

At one time the whole world spoke a single language and used the same words. ²As the people migrated eastward, they found a plain in the land of Babylonia* and settled there. ³They began to talk about construction projects. "Come," they said, "let's make great piles of burnt brick and collect natural asphalt to use as mortar. ⁴Let's build a great city with a tower that reaches to the skies—a monument to our greatness! This will bring us together and keep us from scattering all over the world."

⁵But the LORD came down to see the city and the tower the people were building. ⁶"Look!" he said. "If they can accomplish this when they have just begun to take advantage of their common language and political unity, just think of what they will do later. Nothing will be impossible for them! ⁷Come, let's go down and give them different languages. Then they won't be able to understand each other."

⁸In that way, the LORD scattered them all over the earth; and that ended the building of the city. ⁹That is why the city was called Babel,* because it was there that the LORD confused the people by giving them many languages, thus scattering them across the earth.

I FOCUS my life and energy on glorifying God. (11:4)

I WORK with others to obey God, not to rebel against him. (11:6)

I BELIEVE the Lord intervenes to keep human rebellion in check. (11:7)

I OBEY God the first time so that he doesn't need to use difficulties to accomplish his purposes in my life. (11:9)

10:14 Hebrew *Casluhites, from whom the Philistines came, Caphtorites.* Compare Jer 47:4; Amos 9:7. 10:21 Or *Shem, whose older brother was Japheth.* 10:24 Greek version reads *Arphaxad was the father of Cainan, Cainan was the father of Shelah.* 11:2 Hebrew *Shinar.* 11:9 *Babel* sounds like a Hebrew term that means "confusion."

From Shem to Abram

¹⁰This is the history of Shem's family.

When Shem was 100 years old, his son Arphaxad was born. This happened two years after the Flood. ¹¹After the birth of Arphaxad, Shem lived another 500 years and had other sons and daughters.
¹²When Arphaxad was 35 years old, his son Shelah was born.* ¹³After the birth of Shelah, Arphaxad lived another 403 years and had other sons and daughters.*
¹⁴When Shelah was 30 years old, his son Eber was born. ¹⁵After the birth of Eber, Shelah lived another 403 years and had other sons and daughters.
¹⁶When Eber was 34 years old, his son Peleg was born. ¹⁷After the birth of Peleg, Eber lived another 430 years and had other sons and daughters.
¹⁸When Peleg was 30 years old, his son Reu was born. ¹⁹After the birth of Reu, Peleg lived another 209 years and had other sons and daughters.
²⁰When Reu was 32 years old, his son Serug was born. ²¹After the birth of Serug, Reu lived another 207 years and had other sons and daughters.
²²When Serug was 30 years old, his son Nahor was born. ²³After the birth of Nahor, Serug lived another 200 years and had other sons and daughters.
²⁴When Nahor was 29 years old, his son Terah was born. ²⁵After the birth of Terah, Nahor lived another 119 years and had other sons and daughters.
²⁶When Terah was 70 years old, he became the father of Abram, Nahor, and Haran.

The Family of Terah

²⁷This is the history of Terah's family. Terah was the father of Abram, Nahor, and Haran; and Haran had a son named Lot. ²⁸But while Haran was still young, he died in Ur of the Chaldeans, the place of his birth. He was survived by Terah, his father. ²⁹Meanwhile, Abram married Sarai, and his brother Nahor married Milcah, the daughter of their brother Haran. (Milcah had a sister named Iscah.) ³⁰Now Sarai was not able to have any children.

³¹Terah took his son Abram, his daughter-in-law Sarai, and his grandson Lot (his son Haran's child) and left Ur of the Chaldeans to go to the land of Canaan. But they stopped instead at the village of Haran and settled there. ³²Terah lived for 205 years* and died while still at Haran.

CHAPTER 12

The Call of Abram

Then the LORD told Abram, "Leave your country, your relatives, and your father's house, and go to the land that I will show you. ²I will cause you to become the father of a great nation. I will bless you and make you famous, and I will make you a blessing to others. ³I will bless those who bless you and curse those who curse you. All the families of the earth will be blessed through you."

⁴So Abram departed as the LORD had instructed him, and Lot went with him. Abram was seventy-five years old when he left Haran. ⁵He took his wife, Sarai, his nephew Lot, and all his wealth—his livestock and all the people who had joined his household at Haran—and finally arrived in Canaan. ⁶Traveling through Canaan, they came to a place near Shechem and set up camp beside the oak at Moreh. At that time, the area was inhabited by Canaanites.

⁷Then the LORD appeared to Abram and said, "I am going to give this land to your offspring.*" And Abram built an altar there to commemorate the

I BELIEVE the Lord has blessed all the families of the earth through Abraham. (12:3)

11:12 Or *his son, the ancestor of Shelah, was born;* similarly in 11:14, 16, 18, 20, 22, 24.   11:12-13 Greek version reads ¹²*When Arphaxad was 135 years old, his son Cainan was born.* ¹³*After the birth of Cainan, Arphaxad lived another 430 years and had other sons and daughters, and then he died. When Cainan was 130 years old, his son Shelah was born. After the birth of Shelah, Cainan lived another 330 years and had other sons and daughters, and then he died.*   11:32 Some ancient versions read *145 years;* compare 11:26; 12:4.   12:7 Hebrew *seed.*

LORD's visit. ⁸After that, Abram traveled southward and set up camp in the hill country between Bethel on the west and Ai on the east. There he built an altar and worshiped the LORD. ⁹Then Abram traveled south by stages toward the Negev.

Abram and Sarai in Egypt

¹⁰At that time there was a severe famine in the land, so Abram went down to Egypt to wait it out. ¹¹As he was approaching the borders of Egypt, Abram said to Sarai, "You are a very beautiful woman. ¹²When the Egyptians see you, they will say, 'This is his wife. Let's kill him; then we can have her!' ¹³But if you say you are my sister, then the Egyptians will treat me well because of their interest in you, and they will spare my life."

¹⁴And sure enough, when they arrived in Egypt, everyone spoke of her beauty. ¹⁵When the palace officials saw her, they sang her praises to their king, the pharaoh, and she was taken into his harem. ¹⁶Then Pharaoh gave Abram many gifts because of her—sheep, cattle, donkeys, male and female servants, and camels.

¹⁷But the LORD sent a terrible plague upon Pharaoh's household because of Sarai, Abram's wife. ¹⁸So Pharaoh called for Abram and accused him sharply. "What is this you have done to me?" he demanded. "Why didn't you tell me she was your wife? ¹⁹Why were you willing to let me marry her, saying she was your sister? Here is your wife! Take her and be gone!" ²⁰Pharaoh then sent them out of the country under armed escort—Abram and his wife, with all their household and belongings.

CHAPTER 13

Abram and Lot Separate

So they left Egypt and traveled north into the Negev—Abram with his wife and Lot and all that they owned, ²for Abram was very rich in livestock, silver, and gold. ³Then they continued traveling by stages toward Bethel, to the place between Bethel and Ai where they had camped before. ⁴This was the place where Abram had built the altar, and there he again worshiped the LORD.

⁵Now Lot, who was traveling with Abram, was also very wealthy with sheep, cattle, and many tents. ⁶But the land could not support both Abram and Lot with all their flocks and herds living so close together. There were too many animals for the available pastureland. ⁷So an argument broke out between the herdsmen of Abram and Lot. At that time Canaanites and Perizzites were also living in the land.

⁸Then Abram talked it over with Lot. "This arguing between our herdsmen has got to stop," he said. "After all, we are close relatives! ⁹I'll tell you what we'll do. Take your choice of any section of the land you want, and we will separate. If you want that area over there, then I'll stay here. If you want to stay in this area, then I'll move on to another place."

¹⁰Lot took a long look at the fertile plains of the Jordan Valley in the direction of Zoar. The whole area was well watered everywhere, like the garden of the LORD or the beautiful land of Egypt. (This was before the LORD had destroyed Sodom and Gomorrah.) ¹¹Lot chose that land for himself—the Jordan Valley to the east of them. He went there with his flocks and servants and parted company with his uncle Abram. ¹²So while Abram stayed in the land of Canaan, Lot moved his tents to a place near Sodom, among the cities of the plain. ¹³The people of this area were unusually wicked and sinned greatly against the LORD.

¹⁴After Lot was gone, the LORD said to Abram, "Look as far as you can see in every direction. ¹⁵I am going to give all this land to you and your offspring* as

13:15 Hebrew *seed.*

I WORSHIP the Lord wherever I go. (12:8)

I DO NOT PLACE my spouse in a morally risky or dangerous situation. (12:15)

I SEEK to live peaceably with my relatives. (13:8)

I AM WILLING to give another person first choice and, when necessary, to use separation as a means to keep peace between others and me. (13:9)

I ACCEPT another person's choice, even if I am left with what looks like the lesser option. (13:12)

a permanent possession. ¹⁶And I am going to give you so many descendants that, like dust, they cannot be counted! ¹⁷Take a walk in every direction and explore the new possessions I am giving you." ¹⁸Then Abram moved his camp to the oak grove owned by Mamre, which is at Hebron. There he built an altar to the LORD.

I AM THANKFUL for all God's promises and gifts to me. (13:17)

CHAPTER 14

Abram Rescues Lot

About this time war broke out in the region. King Amraphel of Babylonia,* King Arioch of Ellasar, King Kedorlaomer of Elam, and King Tidal of Goiim ²fought against King Bera of Sodom, King Birsha of Gomorrah, King Shinab of Admah, King Shemeber of Zeboiim, and the king of Bela (now called Zoar). ³The kings of Sodom, Gomorrah, Admah, Zeboiim, and Bela formed an alliance and mobilized their armies in Siddim Valley (that is, the valley of the Dead Sea*). ⁴For twelve years they had all been subject to King Kedorlaomer, but now in the thirteenth year they rebelled.

⁵One year later, Kedorlaomer and his allies arrived. They conquered the Rephaites in Ashteroth-karnaim, the Zuzites in Ham, the Emites in the plain of Kiriathaim, ⁶and the Horites in Mount Seir, as far as El-paran at the edge of the wilderness. ⁷Then they swung around to En-mishpat (now called Kadesh) and destroyed the Amalekites, and also the Amorites living in Hazazon-tamar.

⁸But now the army of the kings of Sodom, Gomorrah, Admah, Zeboiim, and Bela (now called Zoar) prepared for battle in the valley of the Dead Sea* ⁹against King Kedorlaomer of Elam and the kings of Goiim, Babylonia, and Ellasar—four kings against five. ¹⁰As it happened, the valley was filled with tar pits. And as the army of the kings of Sodom and Gomorrah fled, some slipped into the tar pits, while the rest escaped into the mountains. ¹¹The victorious invaders then plundered Sodom and Gomorrah and began their long journey home, taking all the wealth and food with them. ¹²They also captured Lot—Abram's nephew who lived in Sodom—and took everything he owned. ¹³One of the men who escaped came and told Abram the Hebrew, who was camped at the oak grove belonging to Mamre the Amorite. Mamre and his relatives, Eshcol and Aner, were Abram's allies.

¹⁴When Abram learned that Lot had been captured, he called together the men born into his household, 318 of them in all. He chased after Kedorlaomer's army until he caught up with them in Dan. ¹⁵There he divided his men and attacked during the night from several directions. Kedorlaomer's army fled, but Abram chased them to Hobah, north of Damascus. ¹⁶Abram and his allies recovered everything—the goods that had been taken, Abram's nephew Lot with his possessions, and all the women and other captives.

I COME to the defense of my relatives. (14:14)

Melchizedek Blesses Abram

¹⁷As Abram returned from his victory over Kedorlaomer and his allies, the king of Sodom came out to meet him in the valley of Shaveh (that is, the King's Valley). ¹⁸Then Melchizedek, the king of Salem and a priest of God Most High, brought him bread and wine. ¹⁹Melchizedek blessed Abram with this blessing:

"Blessed be Abram by God Most High,
    Creator of heaven and earth.
²⁰And blessed be God Most High,
    who has helped you conquer your enemies."

Then Abram gave Melchizedek a tenth of all the goods he had recovered.

I BLESS God with gifts, words of praise, and a heart full of thanksgiving. (14:20)

14:1 Hebrew *Shinar*; also in 14:9.   14:3 Hebrew *Salt Sea*.   14:8 Hebrew *in Siddim Valley*; see 14:3.

I KEEP my promises to God, even when it means financial sacrifice. (14:22)

I DO NOT ALLOW others to take the credit for what God has done for me. (14:23)

I AM NOT AFRAID of the future because God protects and rewards me. (15:1)

I BRING my questions to God when I don't understand how his plan will work out. (15:2)

I APPROACH the Sovereign Lord with reverence when I ask for answers to my questions and for confirmations of his promises. (15:8)

I DO what God asks of me when he gives me an answer to my questions. (15:10)

I AM SURE that all God has revealed about the future will happen exactly as he has said. (15:13)

I DO NOT DEVISE my own methods to bring about God's purposes. (16:1)

I DO NOT AGREE to immorality, even if suggested by my spouse. (16:2)

²¹The king of Sodom told him, "Give back my people who were captured. But you may keep for yourself all the goods you have recovered."

²²Abram replied, "I have solemnly promised the LORD, God Most High, Creator of heaven and earth, ²³that I will not take so much as a single thread or sandal thong from you. Otherwise you might say, 'I am the one who made Abram rich!' ²⁴All I'll accept is what these young men of mine have already eaten. But give a share of the goods to my allies—Aner, Eshcol, and Mamre."

CHAPTER 15

The LORD's Covenant with Abram

Afterward the LORD spoke to Abram in a vision and said to him, "Do not be afraid, Abram, for I will protect you, and your reward will be great." ²But Abram replied, "O Sovereign LORD, what good are all your blessings when I don't even have a son? Since I don't have a son, Eliezer of Damascus, a servant in my household, will inherit all my wealth. ³You have given me no children, so one of my servants will have to be my heir."

⁴Then the LORD said to him, "No, your servant will not be your heir, for you will have a son of your own to inherit everything I am giving you." ⁵Then the LORD brought Abram outside beneath the night sky and told him, "Look up into the heavens and count the stars if you can. Your descendants will be like that—too many to count!" ⁶And Abram believed the LORD, and the LORD declared him righteous because of his faith. ⁷Then the LORD told him, "I am the LORD who brought you out of Ur of the Chaldeans to give you this land."

⁸But Abram replied, "O Sovereign LORD, how can I be sure that you will give it to me?"

⁹Then the LORD told him, "Bring me a three-year-old heifer, a three-year-old female goat, a three-year-old ram, a turtledove, and a young pigeon." ¹⁰Abram took all these and killed them. He cut each one down the middle and laid the halves side by side. He did not, however, divide the birds in half. ¹¹Some vultures came down to eat the carcasses, but Abram chased them away. ¹²That evening, as the sun was going down, Abram fell into a deep sleep. He saw a terrifying vision of darkness and horror.

¹³Then the LORD told Abram, "You can be sure that your descendants will be strangers in a foreign land, and they will be oppressed as slaves for four hundred years. ¹⁴But I will punish the nation that enslaves them, and in the end they will come away with great wealth. ¹⁵(But you will die in peace, at a ripe old age.) ¹⁶After four generations your descendants will return here to this land, when the sin of the Amorites has run its course."

¹⁷As the sun went down and it became dark, Abram saw a smoking firepot and a flaming torch pass between the halves of the carcasses. ¹⁸So the LORD made a covenant with Abram that day and said, "I have given this land to your descendants, all the way from the border of Egypt* to the great Euphrates River—¹⁹the land of the Kenites, Kenizzites, Kadmonites, ²⁰Hittites, Perizzites, Rephaites, ²¹Amorites, Canaanites, Girgashites, and Jebusites."

CHAPTER 16

The Birth of Ishmael

But Sarai, Abram's wife, had no children. So Sarai took her servant, an Egyptian woman named Hagar, ²and gave her to Abram so she could bear his children. "The LORD has kept me from having any children," Sarai said to Abram. "Go and sleep with my servant. Perhaps I can have children through her." And Abram agreed. ³So Sarai, Abram's wife, took Hagar the Egyptian servant and gave her to Abram as a wife. (This happened ten years after Abram first arrived in the land of Canaan.)

15:18 Hebrew *the river of Egypt*, referring either to an eastern branch of the Nile River or to the brook of Egypt in the Sinai (see Num 34:5).

⁴So Abram slept with Hagar, and she became pregnant. When Hagar knew she was pregnant, she began to treat her mistress Sarai with contempt. ⁵Then Sarai said to Abram, "It's all your fault! Now this servant of mine is pregnant, and she despises me, though I myself gave her the privilege of sleeping with you. The LORD will make you pay for doing this to me!*"

⁶Abram replied, "Since she is your servant, you may deal with her as you see fit." So Sarai treated her harshly, and Hagar ran away.

⁷The angel of the LORD found Hagar beside a desert spring along the road to Shur. ⁸The angel said to her, "Hagar, Sarai's servant, where have you come from, and where are you going?"

"I am running away from my mistress," she replied.

LIKE ABRAHAM   *I am the recipient of incredible blessings when I believe God.*
Genesis 15:6

At about the age of seventy-five, Abraham (whose was then known as Abram) responded to the call of God on his life. Turning from his pagan past (Joshua 24:2), he repented and put his trust in the one true God. In Genesis 12, we read about the first time the Lord spoke to Abraham.

Here in Genesis 15, Abraham was resting in his large bedouin-style tent when the Lord appeared to him in a second vision. Taking Abraham outside, the Lord said, "Look up into the heavens and count the stars if you can. Your descendants will be like that" (15:5).

Even though he was quite old and didn't have a single child to call his own, Abraham believed that God's promise to make him the father of many peoples would come about—at the right time.

Because Abraham believed, the Lord declared him righteous (15:6). Not that Abraham became perfect overnight. Seven chapters later, however, in Genesis 22, we see Abraham demonstrating complete, unquestioning trust in God.

As a reward for his faith, the Lord blessed Abraham abundantly with many descendants, much land, ongoing protection, a great name, long life, and much more.

Like Abraham, God calls you and me to place our faith in him and continue to trust him to fulfill his promises—no matter how long it takes. To read more about how God rewarded Abraham's faith, see Romans 4:1-25; Hebrews 11:8-19; and James 2:21-24.

○ *Today's Scripture reading is Genesis 15, 17, and 22.*

---

⁹Then the angel of the LORD said, "Return to your mistress and submit to her authority." ¹⁰The angel added, "I will give you more descendants than you can count." ¹¹And the angel also said, "You are now pregnant and will give birth to a son. You are to name him Ishmael,* for the LORD has heard about your misery. ¹²This son of yours will be a wild one—free and untamed as a wild donkey! He will be against everyone, and everyone will be against him. Yes, he will live at odds with the rest of his brothers."

I BELIEVE God will replace present trials with future blessings. (16:10)

¹³Thereafter, Hagar referred to the LORD, who had spoken to her, as "the God who sees me,"* for she said, "I have seen the One who sees me!" ¹⁴Later that well was named Beer-lahairoi,* and it can still be found between Kadesh and Bered.

I BELIEVE God sees and cares about me. (16:13)

¹⁵So Hagar gave Abram a son, and Abram named him Ishmael. ¹⁶Abram was eighty-six years old at that time.

CHAPTER 17

Abram Is Named Abraham

When Abram was ninety-nine years old, the LORD appeared to him and said, "I am God Almighty; serve me faithfully and live a blameless life. ²I will make a covenant with you, by which I will guarantee to make you into

I WILL LIVE a blameless life to the very end of my days. (17:1)

16:5 Hebrew *Let the LORD judge between you and me.*   16:11 *Ishmael* means "God hears."   16:13 Hebrew *El-roi*.
16:14 *Beer-lahairoi* means "well of the Living One who sees me."

a mighty nation." [3]At this, Abram fell face down in the dust. Then God said to him, [4]"This is my covenant with you: I will make you the father of not just one nation, but a multitude of nations! [5]What's more, I am changing your name. It will no longer be Abram; now you will be known as Abraham,* for you will be the father of many nations. [6]I will give you millions of descendants who will represent many nations. Kings will be among them!

[7]"I will continue this everlasting covenant between us, generation after generation. It will continue between me and your offspring* forever. And I will always be your God and the God of your descendants after you. [8]Yes, I will give all this land of Canaan to you and to your offspring forever. And I will be their God.

I RESPOND to God in obedient reverence. (17:3)

I CLAIM God's promises and obey his commands. (17:8)

The Sign of Circumcision

[9]"Your part of the agreement," God told Abraham, "is to obey the terms of the covenant. You and all your descendants have this continual responsibility. [10]This is the covenant that you and your descendants must keep: Each male among you must be circumcised; [11]the flesh of his foreskin must be cut off. This will be a sign that you and they have accepted this covenant. [12]Every male child must be circumcised on the eighth day after his birth. This applies not only to members of your family, but also to the servants born in your household and the foreign-born servants whom you have purchased. [13]All must be circumcised. Your bodies will thus bear the mark of my everlasting covenant. [14]Anyone who refuses to be circumcised will be cut off from the covenant family for violating the covenant."

Sarai Is Named Sarah

[15]Then God added, "Regarding Sarai, your wife—her name will no longer be Sarai; from now on you will call her Sarah.* [16]And I will bless her and give you a son from her! Yes, I will bless her richly, and she will become the mother of many nations. Kings will be among her descendants!"

[17]Then Abraham bowed down to the ground, but he laughed to himself in disbelief. "How could I become a father at the age of one hundred?" he wondered. "Besides, Sarah is ninety; how could she have a baby?" [18]And Abraham said to God, "Yes, may Ishmael enjoy your special blessing!"

I SEEK God's blessing for all my children. (17:18)

I BELIEVE God will keep his promises. (17:19)

[19]But God replied, "Sarah, your wife, will bear you a son. You will name him Isaac,* and I will confirm my everlasting covenant with him and his descendants. [20]As for Ishmael, I will bless him also, just as you have asked. I will cause him to multiply and become a great nation. Twelve princes will be among his descendants. [21]But my covenant is with Isaac, who will be born to you and Sarah about this time next year."

[22]That ended the conversation, and God left Abraham. [23]On that very day Abraham took his son Ishmael and every other male in his household and circumcised them, cutting off their foreskins, exactly as God had told him. [24]Abraham was ninety-nine years old at that time, [25]and Ishmael his son was thirteen. [26]Both were circumcised the same day, [27]along with all the other men and boys of the household, whether they were born there or bought as servants.

CHAPTER 18

A Son Promised to Sarah

The LORD appeared again to Abraham while he was camped near the oak grove belonging to Mamre. One day about noon, as Abraham was sitting at the entrance to his tent, [2]he suddenly noticed three men standing nearby. He got up and ran to meet them, welcoming them by bowing low to the ground.

I OFFER hospitality to strangers. (18:2)

17:5 Abram means "exalted father"; Abraham means "father of many." 17:7 Hebrew seed; also in 17:8. 17:15 Sarah means "princess." 17:19 Isaac means "he laughs."

³"My lord," he said, "if it pleases you, stop here for a while. ⁴Rest in the shade of this tree while my servants get some water to wash your feet. ⁵Let me prepare some food to refresh you. Please stay awhile before continuing on your journey."

"All right," they said. "Do as you have said."

⁶So Abraham ran back to the tent and said to Sarah, "Quick! Get three measures* of your best flour, and bake some bread." ⁷Then Abraham ran out to the herd and chose a fat calf and told a servant to hurry and butcher it. ⁸When the food was ready, he took some cheese curds and milk and the roasted meat, and he served it to the men. As they ate, Abraham waited on them there beneath the trees.

⁹"Where is Sarah, your wife?" they asked him.

"In the tent," Abraham replied.

¹⁰Then one of them said, "About this time next year I will return, and your wife Sarah will have a son."

Now Sarah was listening to this conversation from the tent nearby. ¹¹And since Abraham and Sarah were both very old, and Sarah was long past the age of having children, ¹²she laughed silently to herself. "How could a worn-out woman like me have a baby?" she thought. "And when my master—my husband—is also so old?"

¹³Then the LORD said to Abraham, "Why did Sarah laugh? Why did she say, 'Can an old woman like me have a baby?' ¹⁴Is anything too hard for the LORD? About a year from now, just as I told you, I will return, and Sarah will have a son." ¹⁵Sarah was afraid, so she denied that she had laughed. But he said, "That is not true. You did laugh."

I DO NOT COVER UP my doubts. (18:15)

Abraham Intercedes for Sodom

¹⁶ Then the men got up from their meal and started on toward Sodom. Abraham went with them part of the way.

¹⁷"Should I hide my plan from Abraham?" the LORD asked. ¹⁸"For Abraham will become a great and mighty nation, and all the nations of the earth will be blessed through him. ¹⁹I have singled him out so that he will direct his sons and their families to keep the way of the LORD and do what is right and just. Then I will do for him all that I have promised." ²⁰So the LORD told Abraham, "I have heard that the people of Sodom and Gomorrah are extremely evil, and that everything they do is wicked. ²¹I am going down to see whether or not these reports are true. Then I will know."

I BELIEVE the Lord desires to include his people in his plans. (18:17)

²²The two other men went on toward Sodom, but the LORD remained with Abraham for a while. ²³Abraham approached him and said, "Will you destroy both innocent and guilty alike? ²⁴Suppose you find fifty innocent people there within the city—will you still destroy it, and not spare it for their sakes? ²⁵Surely you wouldn't do such a thing, destroying the innocent with the guilty. Why, you would be treating the innocent and the guilty exactly the same! Surely you wouldn't do that! Should not the Judge of all the earth do what is right?"

I BELIEVE the Lord, the Judge of the earth, will always do what is right. (18:25)

²⁶And the LORD replied, "If I find fifty innocent people in Sodom, I will spare the entire city for their sake."

²⁷Then Abraham spoke again. "Since I have begun, let me go on and speak further to my Lord, even though I am but dust and ashes. ²⁸Suppose there are only forty-five? Will you destroy the city for lack of five?"

And the LORD said, "I will not destroy it if I find forty-five."

I RECOGNIZE my mortality and come to God in humility. (18:27)

²⁹ Then Abraham pressed his request further. "Suppose there are only forty?"

And the LORD replied, "I will not destroy it if there are forty."

18:6 Hebrew 3 seahs, about 15 quarts or 18 liters.

³⁰"Please don't be angry, my Lord," Abraham pleaded. "Let me speak—suppose only thirty are found?"

And the LORD replied, "I will not destroy it if there are thirty."

³¹Then Abraham said, "Since I have dared to speak to the Lord, let me continue—suppose there are only twenty?"

And the LORD said, "Then I will not destroy it for the sake of the twenty."

³²Finally, Abraham said, "Lord, please do not get angry; I will speak but once more! Suppose only ten are found there?"

And the LORD said, "Then, for the sake of the ten, I will not destroy it."

³³The LORD went on his way when he had finished his conversation with Abraham, and Abraham returned to his tent.

CHAPTER 19

Sodom and Gomorrah Destroyed

That evening the two angels came to the entrance of the city of Sodom, and Lot was sitting there as they arrived. When he saw them, he stood up to meet them. Then he welcomed them and bowed low to the ground. ²"My lords," he said, "come to my home to wash your feet, and be my guests for the night. You may then get up in the morning as early as you like and be on your way again."

"Oh no," they said, "we'll just spend the night out here in the city square."

³But Lot insisted, so at last they went home with him. He set a great feast before them, complete with fresh bread made without yeast. After the meal, ⁴as they were preparing to retire for the night, all the men of Sodom, young and old, came from all over the city and surrounded the house. ⁵They shouted to Lot, "Where are the men who came to spend the night with you? Bring them out so we can have sex with them."

⁶Lot stepped outside to talk to them, shutting the door behind him. ⁷"Please, my brothers," he begged, "don't do such a wicked thing. ⁸Look—I have two virgin daughters. Do with them as you wish, but leave these men alone, for they are under my protection."

⁹"Stand back!" they shouted. "Who do you think you are? We let you settle among us, and now you are trying to tell us what to do! We'll treat you far worse than those other men!" And they lunged at Lot and began breaking down the door. ¹⁰But the two angels reached out and pulled Lot in and bolted the door. ¹¹Then they blinded the men of Sodom so they couldn't find the doorway.

¹²"Do you have any other relatives here in the city?" the angels asked. "Get them out of this place—sons-in-law, sons, daughters, or anyone else. ¹³For we will destroy the city completely. The stench of the place has reached the LORD, and he has sent us to destroy it."

¹⁴So Lot rushed out to tell his daughters' fiancés, "Quick, get out of the city! The LORD is going to destroy it." But the young men thought he was only joking.

¹⁵At dawn the next morning the angels became insistent. "Hurry," they said to Lot. "Take your wife and your two daughters who are here. Get out of here right now, or you will be caught in the destruction of the city."

¹⁶When Lot still hesitated, the angels seized his hand and the hands of his wife and two daughters and rushed them to safety outside the city, for the LORD was merciful. ¹⁷"Run for your lives!" the angels warned. "Do not stop anywhere in the valley. And don't look back! Escape to the mountains, or you will die."

¹⁸"Oh no, my lords, please," Lot begged. ¹⁹"You have been so kind to me and saved my life, and you have granted me such mercy. But I cannot go to the mountains. Disaster would catch up to me there, and I would soon die.

I NEVER SACRIFICE the purity and safety of any member of my family. (19:8)

I WARN my loved ones of God's coming judgment. (19:14)

I BELIEVE the Lord is merciful in rescuing me from judgment. (19:16)

²⁰See, there is a small village nearby. Please let me go there instead; don't you see how small it is? Then my life will be saved."

²¹"All right," the angel said, "I will grant your request. I will not destroy that little village. ²²But hurry! For I can do nothing until you are there." From that time on, that village was known as Zoar.*

²³The sun was rising as Lot reached the village. ²⁴Then the LORD rained down fire and burning sulfur from the heavens on Sodom and Gomorrah. ²⁵He utterly destroyed them, along with the other cities and villages of the plain, eliminating all life—people, plants, and animals alike. ²⁶But Lot's wife looked back as she was following along behind him, and she became a pillar of salt.

²⁷The next morning Abraham was up early and hurried out to the place where he had stood in the LORD's presence. ²⁸He looked out across the plain to Sodom and Gomorrah and saw columns of smoke and fumes, as from a furnace, rising from the cities there. ²⁹But God had listened to Abraham's request and kept Lot safe, removing him from the disaster that engulfed the cities on the plain.

Lot and His Daughters

³⁰Afterward Lot left Zoar because he was afraid of the people there, and he went to live in a cave in the mountains with his two daughters. ³¹One day the older daughter said to her sister, "There isn't a man anywhere in this entire area for us to marry. And our father will soon be too old to have children. ³²Come, let's get him drunk with wine, and then we will sleep with him. That way we will preserve our family line through our father." ³³So that night they got him drunk, and the older daughter went in and slept with her father. He was unaware of her lying down or getting up again.

³⁴The next morning the older daughter said to her younger sister, "I slept with our father last night. Let's get him drunk with wine again tonight, and you go in and sleep with him. That way our family line will be preserved." ³⁵So that night they got him drunk again, and the younger daughter went in and slept with him. As before, he was unaware of her lying down or getting up again. ³⁶So both of Lot's daughters became pregnant by their father.

³⁷When the older daughter gave birth to a son, she named him Moab.* He became the ancestor of the nation now known as the Moabites. ³⁸When the younger daughter gave birth to a son, she named him Ben-ammi.* He became the ancestor of the nation now known as the Ammonites.

CHAPTER 20

Abraham Deceives Abimelech

Now Abraham moved south to the Negev and settled for a while between Kadesh and Shur at a place called Gerar. ²Abraham told people there that his wife, Sarah, was his sister. So King Abimelech sent for her and had her brought to him at his palace.

³But one night God came to Abimelech in a dream and told him, "You are a dead man, for that woman you took is married."

⁴But Abimelech had not slept with her yet, so he said, "Lord, will you kill an innocent man? ⁵Abraham told me, 'She is my sister,' and she herself said, 'Yes, he is my brother.' I acted in complete innocence!"

⁶"Yes, I know you are innocent," God replied. "That is why I kept you from sinning against me; I did not let you touch her. ⁷Now return her to her husband, and he will pray for you, for he is a prophet. Then you will live. But if you don't return her to him, you can be sure that you and your entire household will die."

I DO NOT REGRET leaving behind the wickedness of the world. (19:26)

I DO NOT RETREAT from life out of fear of what might happen in the future. (19:30)

I DO NOT USE sexual immorality to conceive children. (19:32)

I BELIEVE God can keep an innocent person from sinning. (20:6)

19:22 Zoar means "little."   19:37 Moab sounds like a Hebrew term that means "from father."   19:38 Ben-ammi means "son of my people."

[8]Abimelech got up early the next morning and hastily called a meeting of all his servants. When he told them what had happened, great fear swept through the crowd. [9]Then Abimelech called for Abraham. "What is this you have done to us?" he demanded. "What have I done to you that deserves treatment like this, making me and my kingdom guilty of this great sin? This kind of thing should not be done! [10]Why have you done this to us?"

[11]"Well," Abraham said, "I figured this to be a godless place. I thought, 'They will want my wife and will kill me to get her.' [12]Besides, she is my sister—we both have the same father, though different mothers—and I married her. [13]When God sent me to travel far from my father's home, I told her, 'Wherever we go, have the kindness to say that you are my sister.' "

[14] Then Abimelech took sheep and oxen and servants—both men and women—and gave them to Abraham, and he returned his wife, Sarah, to him. [15]"Look over my kingdom, and choose a place where you would like to live," Abimelech told him. [16]Then he turned to Sarah. "Look," he said, "I am giving your 'brother' a thousand pieces of silver* to compensate for any embarrassment I may have caused you. This will settle any claim against me in this matter."

[17]Then Abraham prayed to God, and God healed Abimelech, his wife, and the other women of the household, so they could have children. [18]For the LORD had stricken all the women with infertility as a warning to Abimelech for having taken Abraham's wife.

CHAPTER 21

The Birth of Isaac

Then the LORD did exactly what he had promised. [2]Sarah became pregnant, and she gave a son to Abraham in his old age. It all happened at the time God had said it would. [3]And Abraham named his son Isaac.* [4]Eight days after Isaac was born, Abraham circumcised him as God had commanded. [5]Abraham was one hundred years old at the time.

[6]And Sarah declared, "God has brought me laughter! All who hear about this will laugh with me. [7]For who would have dreamed that I would ever have a baby? Yet I have given Abraham a son in his old age!"

Hagar and Ishmael Sent Away

[8]As time went by and Isaac grew and was weaned, Abraham gave a big party to celebrate the happy occasion. [9]But Sarah saw Ishmael—the son of Abraham and her Egyptian servant Hagar—making fun of Isaac. [10]So she turned to Abraham and demanded, "Get rid of that servant and her son. He is not going to share the family inheritance with my son, Isaac. I won't have it!"

[11]This upset Abraham very much because Ishmael was his son. [12]But God told Abraham, "Do not be upset over the boy and your servant wife. Do just as Sarah says, for Isaac is the son through whom your descendants will be counted. [13]But I will make a nation of the descendants of Hagar's son because he also is your son."

[14]So Abraham got up early the next morning, prepared food for the journey, and strapped a container of water to Hagar's shoulders. He sent her away with their son, and she walked out into the wilderness of Beersheba, wandering aimlessly. [15]When the water was gone, she left the boy in the shade of a bush. [16]Then she went and sat down by herself about a hundred yards* away. "I don't want to watch the boy die," she said, as she burst into tears.

[17] Then God heard the boy's cries, and the angel of God called to Hagar from the sky, "Hagar, what's wrong? Do not be afraid! God has heard the

I DO NOT RELY on half-truths to protect myself. (20:12)

I TRUST God to protect my reputation. (20:16)

I BELIEVE God will not allow anything, including the sin of his people, to thwart his plan. (21:1)

I BELIEVE God does all that he says he will do exactly when he says he will do it. (21:2)

I REJOICE in God's gift of children. (21:6)

I RELEASE my children at the right time and entrust them to God's care and his promises. (21:12)

I BELIEVE God hears the prayers of my children and will care for them. (21:17)

20:16 Hebrew *1,000 shekels of silver*, about 25 pounds or 11.4 kilograms in weight.   21:3 *Isaac* means "he laughs."   21:16 Hebrew *a bowshot*.

boy's cries from the place where you laid him. [18]Go to him and comfort him, for I will make a great nation from his descendants."

[19]Then God opened Hagar's eyes, and she saw a well. She immediately filled her water container and gave the boy a drink. [20]And God was with the boy as he grew up in the wilderness of Paran. He became an expert archer, [21]and his mother arranged a marriage for him with a young woman from Egypt.

A Treaty with Abimelech

[22]About this time, Abimelech came with Phicol, his army commander, to visit Abraham. "It is clear that God helps you in everything you do," Abimelech said. [23]"Swear to me in God's name that you won't deceive me, my children, or my grandchildren. I have been loyal to you, so now swear that you will be loyal to me and to this country in which you are living."

[24]Abraham replied, "All right, I swear to it!" [25]Then Abraham complained to Abimelech about a well that Abimelech's servants had taken violently from Abraham's servants.

[26]"This is the first I've heard of it," Abimelech said. "And I have no idea who is responsible. Why didn't you say something about this before?" [27]Then Abraham gave sheep and oxen to Abimelech, and they made a treaty. [28]But when Abraham took seven additional ewe lambs and set them off by themselves, [29]Abimelech asked, "Why are you doing that?"

I BELIEVE God will enable me to provide for my children. (21:19)

I KEEP my promises to other people. (21:24)

LIKE SARAH   *I know that God will always keep his promises.*

Genesis 21:1

It isn't always easy to believe the fantastic promises of God.

For years Sarah (who was then known as Sarai) had heard about the promised blessings to Abraham and his descendants. Tired of waiting, Sarah had even tried to hurry along the process herself by using a surrogate mother. But all she got for her trouble was more sorrow, distress, and pain.

As each year passed, perhaps Sarah felt less and less a part of God's plan. Finally, God stepped through the curtain to reaffirm his promise to Abraham and to remind Sarah that she herself would be the mother of this blessed people. Even Abraham, who had taken a knife to his own flesh to show that he accepted God's covenant, laughed to think that Sarah could mother a child. No wonder Sarah laughed, too, when she heard the angels predict her coming pregnancy.

As the baby grew within Sarah, God gave her plenty of time for her faith to grow as well. "How could it be?" became "Come, laugh and rejoice with me!" Part of Sarah still couldn't grasp what a marvelous thing God had done. A baby born from her own body. The promised son of Abraham (Romans 9:7-9)!

Laughter of disbelief became laughter of delight. Sarah had learned that God will always keep his promises (Isaiah 51:1-3). It's a lesson well worth learning! To read more about this great woman of faith, see Hebrews 11:11 and 1 Peter 3:6.

○ *Today's Scripture reading is Genesis 16:1-15; 18:1-15; and 21:1-7.*

---

[30]Abraham replied, "They are my gift to you as a public confirmation that I dug this well." [31]So ever since, that place has been known as Beersheba—"well of the oath"—because that was where they had sworn an oath. [32]After making their covenant, Abimelech left with Phicol, the commander of his army, and they returned home to the land of the Philistines. [33]Then Abraham planted a tamarisk tree at Beersheba, and he worshiped the LORD, the Eternal God, at that place. [34]And Abraham lived in Philistine country for a long time.

I WORSHIP God wherever I go. (21:33)

CHAPTER 22

Abraham's Obedience Tested

Later on God tested Abraham's faith and obedience. "Abraham!" God called.

"Yes," he replied. "Here I am."

²"Take your son, your only son—yes, Isaac, whom you love so much—and go to the land of Moriah. Sacrifice him there as a burnt offering on one of the mountains, which I will point out to you."

I OBEY God
immediately. (22:3)

³The next morning Abraham got up early. He saddled his donkey and took two of his servants with him, along with his son Isaac. Then he chopped wood to build a fire for a burnt offering and set out for the place where God had told him to go. ⁴On the third day of the journey, Abraham saw the place in the distance. ⁵"Stay here with the donkey," Abraham told the young men. "The boy and I will travel a little farther. We will worship there, and then we will come right back."

⁶Abraham placed the wood for the burnt offering on Isaac's shoulders, while he himself carried the knife and the fire. As the two of them went on together, ⁷Isaac said, "Father?"

"Yes, my son," Abraham replied.

"We have the wood and the fire," said the boy, "but where is the lamb for the sacrifice?"

I TRUST God to provide the strength and means for me to obey him, no matter how difficult his commands. (22:8)

⁸"God will provide a lamb, my son," Abraham answered. And they both went on together.

⁹When they arrived at the place where God had told Abraham to go, he built an altar and placed the wood on it. Then he tied Isaac up and laid him on the altar over the wood. ¹⁰And Abraham took the knife and lifted it up to kill his son as a sacrifice to the LORD. ¹¹At that moment the angel of the LORD shouted to him from heaven, "Abraham! Abraham!"

I WITHHOLD nothing from God, not even what he has given me as a result of his promises. (22:10)

"Yes," he answered. "I'm listening."

¹²"Lay down the knife," the angel said. "Do not hurt the boy in any way, for now I know that you truly fear God. You have not withheld even your beloved son from me."

¹³Then Abraham looked up and saw a ram caught by its horns in a bush. So he took the ram and sacrificed it as a burnt offering on the altar in place of his son. ¹⁴Abraham named the place "The LORD Will Provide."* This name has now become a proverb: "On the mountain of the LORD it will be provided."

¹⁵Then the angel of the LORD called again to Abraham from heaven, ¹⁶"This is what the LORD says: Because you have obeyed me and have not withheld even your beloved son, I swear by my own self that ¹⁷I will bless you richly. I will multiply your descendants into countless millions, like the stars of the sky and the sand on the seashore. They will conquer their enemies, ¹⁸and through your descendants,* all the nations of the earth will be blessed—all because you have obeyed me." ¹⁹Then they returned to Abraham's young men and traveled home again to Beersheba, where Abraham lived for quite some time.

²⁰Soon after this, Abraham heard that Milcah, his brother Nahor's wife, had borne Nahor eight sons. ²¹The oldest was named Uz, the next oldest was Buz, followed by Kemuel (the father of Aram), ²²Kesed, Hazo, Pildash, Jidlaph, and Bethuel. ²³Bethuel became the father of Rebekah. ²⁴In addition to his eight sons from Milcah, Nahor had four other children from his concubine Reumah. Their names were Tebah, Gaham, Tahash, and Maacah.

CHAPTER 23
The Burial of Sarah

I EXPRESS grief when a loved one dies. (23:2)

When Sarah was 127 years old, ²she died at Kiriath-arba (now called Hebron) in the land of Canaan. There Abraham mourned and wept for her. ³Then, leaving her body, he went to the Hittite elders and said, ⁴"Here I am, a stranger in a foreign land, with no place to bury my wife. Please let me have a piece of land for a burial plot."

22:14 Hebrew *Yahweh Yir'eh*.   22:18 Hebrew *seed*.

[5] The Hittites replied to Abraham, [6]"Certainly, for you are an honored prince among us. It will be a privilege to have you choose the finest of our tombs so you can bury her there."

[7]Then Abraham bowed low before them and said, [8]"Since this is how you feel, be so kind as to ask Ephron son of Zohar [9]to let me have the cave of Machpelah, down at the end of his field. I want to pay the full price, of course, whatever is publicly agreed upon, so I may have a permanent burial place for my family."

[10]Ephron was sitting there among the others, and he answered Abraham as the others listened, speaking publicly before all the elders of the town. [11]"No, sir," he said to Abraham, "please listen to me. I will give you the cave and the field. Here in the presence of my people, I give it to you. Go and bury your dead."

[12]Abraham bowed again to the people of the land, [13]and he replied to Ephron as everyone listened. "No, listen to me," he insisted. "I will buy it from you. Let me pay the full price for the field so I can bury my dead there."

I PAY fair price for something that is valuable to me. (23:13)

[14]"Well," Ephron answered, [15]"the land is worth four hundred pieces* of silver, but what is that between friends? Go ahead and bury your dead."

[16]So Abraham paid Ephron the amount he had suggested, four hundred pieces of silver, as was publicly agreed. [17]He bought the plot of land belonging to Ephron at Machpelah, near Mamre. This included the field, the cave that was in it, and all the trees nearby. [18]They became Abraham's permanent possession by the agreement made in the presence of the Hittite elders at the city gate. [19]So Abraham buried Sarah there in Canaan, in the cave of Machpelah, near Mamre, which is at Hebron. [20]The field and the cave were sold to Abraham by the Hittites as a permanent burial place.

I ABIDE by publicly witnessed agreements. (23:16)

CHAPTER 24

Isaac Marries Rebekah

Abraham was now a very old man, and the LORD had blessed him in every way. [2]One day Abraham said to the man in charge of his household, who was his oldest servant, [3]"Swear* by the LORD, the God of heaven and earth, that you will not let my son marry one of these local Canaanite women. [4]Go instead to my homeland, to my relatives, and find a wife there for my son Isaac."

[5] The servant asked, "But suppose I can't find a young woman who will travel so far from home? May I then take Isaac there to live among your relatives?"

I WILL SPARE no expense to help my children find godly spouses. (24:4)

[6]"No!" Abraham warned. "Be careful never to take my son there. [7]For the LORD, the God of heaven, who took me from my father's house and my native land, solemnly promised to give this land to my offspring.* He will send his angel ahead of you, and he will see to it that you find a young woman there to be my son's wife. [8]If she is unwilling to come back with you, then you are free from this oath. But under no circumstances are you to take my son there."

I WILL NOT SPEND a dime to put my children in a godless situation. (24:6)

I HOLD realistic expectations of what others can accomplish for me. (24:8)

[9]So the servant took a solemn oath* that he would follow Abraham's instructions. [10]He loaded ten of Abraham's camels with gifts and set out, taking with him the best of everything his master owned. He traveled to Aram-naharaim* and went to the village where Abraham's brother Nahor had settled. [11]There the servant made the camels kneel down beside a well just outside the village. It was evening, and the women were coming out to draw water.

I CAREFULLY FOLLOW my employer's instructions. (24:9)

23:15 Hebrew *400 shekels*, about 10 pounds or 4.6 kilograms in weight; also in 23:16.   24:3 Hebrew *Put your hand under my thigh, and I will make you swear.*   24:7 Hebrew *seed.*   24:9 Hebrew *put his hand under the thigh of Abraham his master and swore an oath.*   24:10 *Aram-naharaim* means "Aram of the two rivers," thought to have been located between the Euphrates and Balih Rivers in northwestern Mesopotamia.

I PRAY for God's help
to accomplish my task.
(24:12)

¹²"O L ORD , God of my master," he prayed. "Give me success and show kindness to my master, Abraham. Help me to accomplish the purpose of my journey. ¹³See, here I am, standing beside this spring, and the young women of the village are coming out to draw water. ¹⁴This is my request. I will ask one of them for a drink. If she says, 'Yes, certainly, and I will water your camels, too!'—let her be the one you have appointed as Isaac's wife. By this I will know that you have shown kindness to my master."

¹⁵As he was still praying, a young woman named Rebekah arrived with a water jug on her shoulder. Her father was Bethuel, who was the son of Abraham's brother Nahor and his wife, Milcah. ¹⁶Now Rebekah was very beautiful, and she was a virgin; no man had ever slept with her. She went down to the spring, filled her jug, and came up again. ¹⁷Running over to her, the servant asked, "Please give me a drink."

¹⁸"Certainly, sir," she said, and she quickly lowered the jug for him to drink. ¹⁹When he had finished, she said, "I'll draw water for your camels, too, until they have had enough!" ²⁰So she quickly emptied the jug into the watering trough and ran down to the well again. She kept carrying water to the camels until they had finished drinking. ²¹The servant watched her in silence, wondering whether or not she was the one the L ORD intended him to meet. ²²Then at last, when the camels had finished drinking, he gave her a gold ring for her nose and two large gold bracelets* for her wrists.

²³"Whose daughter are you?" he asked. "Would your father have any room to put us up for the night?"

²⁴"My father is Bethuel," she replied. "My grandparents are Nahor and Milcah. ²⁵Yes, we have plenty of straw and food for the camels, and we have a room for guests."

I PRAISE God for
leading me in specific
situations. (24:27)

²⁶The man fell down to the ground and worshiped the L ORD . ²⁷"Praise be to the L ORD , the God of my master, Abraham," he said. "The L ORD has been so kind and faithful to Abraham, for he has led me straight to my master's relatives."

²⁸The young woman ran home to tell her family about all that had happened. ²⁹Now Rebekah had a brother named Laban. ³⁰When he saw the nose-ring and the bracelets on his sister's wrists, and when he heard her story, he rushed out to the spring, where the man was still standing beside his camels. Laban said to him, ³¹"Come and stay with us, you who are blessed by the L ORD . Why do you stand here outside the village when we have a room all ready for you and a place prepared for the camels!"

³²So the man went home with Laban, and Laban unloaded the camels, gave him straw to bed them down, fed them, and provided water for the camel drivers to wash their feet. ³³Then supper was served. But Abraham's servant said, "I don't want to eat until I have told you why I have come."

"All right," Laban said, "tell us your mission."

I TELL the story of
God's answer to my
prayer. (24:34)

³⁴"I am Abraham's servant," he explained. ³⁵"And the L ORD has blessed my master richly; he has become a great man. The L ORD has given him flocks of sheep and herds of cattle, a fortune in silver and gold, and many servants and camels and donkeys. ³⁶When Sarah, my master's wife, was very old, she gave birth to my master's son, and my master has given him everything he owns. ³⁷And my master made me swear that I would not let Isaac marry one of the local Canaanite women. ³⁸Instead, I was to come to his relatives here in this far-off land, to his father's home. I was told to bring back a young woman from here to marry his son.

³⁹" 'But suppose I can't find a young woman willing to come back with me?' I asked him. ⁴⁰'You will,' he told me, 'for the L ORD , in whose presence I have walked, will send his angel with you and will make your mission

24:22 Hebrew *a gold nose-ring weighing a half shekel* [0.2 ounces or 6 grams] *and two gold bracelets weighing 10 shekels* [4 ounces or 114 grams].

successful. Yes, you must get a wife for my son from among my relatives, from my father's family. [41]But if you go to my relatives and they refuse to let her come, you will be free from your oath.'

[42]"So this afternoon when I came to the spring I prayed this prayer: 'O LORD, the God of my master, Abraham, if you are planning to make my mission a success, please guide me in a special way. [43]Here I am, standing beside this spring. I will say to some young woman who comes to draw water, "Please give me a drink of water!" [44]And she will reply, "Certainly! And I'll water your camels, too!" LORD, let her be the one you have selected to be the wife of my master's son.'

[45]"Before I had finished praying these words, I saw Rebekah coming along with her water jug on her shoulder. She went down to the spring and drew water and filled the jug. So I said to her, 'Please give me a drink.' [46]She quickly lowered the jug from her shoulder so I could drink, and she said, 'Certainly, sir, and I will water your camels, too!' And she did. [47]When I asked her whose daughter she was, she told me, 'My father is Bethuel, the son of Nahor and his wife, Milcah.' So I gave her the ring and the bracelets.

[48]"Then I bowed my head and worshiped the LORD. I praised the LORD, the God of my master, Abraham, because he had led me along the right path to find a wife from the family of my master's relatives. [49]So tell me—will you or won't you show true kindness to my master? When you tell me, then I'll know what my next step should be, whether to move this way or that."

[50]Then Laban and Bethuel replied, "The LORD has obviously brought you here, so what can we say? [51]Here is Rebekah; take her and go. Yes, let her be the wife of your master's son, as the LORD has directed."

[52]At this reply, Abraham's servant bowed to the ground and worshiped the LORD. [53]Then he brought out silver and gold jewelry and lovely clothing for Rebekah. He also gave valuable presents to her mother and brother. [54]Then they had supper, and the servant and the men with him stayed there overnight. But early the next morning, he said, "Send me back to my master."

[55]"But we want Rebekah to stay at least ten days," her brother and mother said. "Then she can go."

[56]But he said, "Don't hinder my return. The LORD has made my mission successful, and I want to report back to my master."

[57]"Well," they said, "we'll call Rebekah and ask her what she thinks." [58]So they called Rebekah. "Are you willing to go with this man?" they asked her.

And she replied, "Yes, I will go."

[59]So they said good-bye to Rebekah and sent her away with Abraham's servant and his men. The woman who had been Rebekah's childhood nurse went along with her. [60]They blessed her with this blessing as she parted:

"Our sister, may you become
   the mother of many millions!
May your descendants overcome
   all their enemies."

[61]Then Rebekah and her servants mounted the camels and left with Abraham's servant.

[62]Meanwhile, Isaac, whose home was in the Negev, had returned from Beer-lahairoi. [63]One evening as he was taking a walk out in the fields, meditating, he looked up and saw the camels coming. [64]When Rebekah looked up and saw Isaac, she quickly dismounted. [65]"Who is that man walking through the fields to meet us?" she asked the servant.

And he replied, "It is my master." So Rebekah covered her face with her veil. [66]Then the servant told Isaac the whole story.

[67]And Isaac brought Rebekah into his mother's tent, and she became his

I ALLOW my children to participate in important decisions that affect their lives. (24:57)

I BLESS my loved ones when they leave and move far away. (24:60)

I LOVE my spouse and take comfort in our relationship after the death of another family member. (24:67)

wife. He loved her very much, and she was a special comfort to him after the death of his mother.

CHAPTER 25

The Death of Abraham

Now Abraham married again. Keturah was his new wife, [2]and she bore him Zimran, Jokshan, Medan, Midian, Ishbak, and Shuah. [3]Jokshan's two sons were Sheba and Dedan. Dedan's descendants were the Asshurites, Letushites, and Leummites. [4]Midian's sons were Ephah, Epher, Hanoch, Abida, and Eldaah. These were all descendants of Abraham through Keturah.

[5]Abraham left everything he owned to his son Isaac. [6]But before he died, he gave gifts to the sons of his concubines and sent them off to the east, away from Isaac.

[7]Abraham lived for 175 years, [8]and he died at a ripe old age, joining his ancestors in death. [9]His sons Isaac and Ishmael buried him in the cave of Machpelah, near Mamre, in the field of Ephron son of Zohar the Hittite. [10]This was the field Abraham had purchased from the Hittites, where he had buried his wife Sarah. [11]After Abraham's death, God poured out rich blessings on Isaac, who settled near Beer-lahairoi in the Negev.

Ishmael's Descendants

[12] This is the history of the descendants of Ishmael, the son of Abraham through Hagar, Sarah's Egyptian servant. [13]Here is a list, by their names and clans, of Ishmael's descendants: The oldest was Nebaioth, followed by Kedar, Abdeel, Mibsam, [14]Mishma, Dumah, Massa, [15]Hadad, Tema, Jetur, Naphish, and Kedemah. [16]These twelve sons of Ishmael became the founders of twelve tribes that bore their names, listed according to the places they settled and camped. [17]Ishmael finally died at the age of 137 and joined his ancestors in death. [18]Ishmael's descendants were scattered across the country from Havilah to Shur, which is east of Egypt in the direction of Asshur. The clans descended from Ishmael camped close to one another.*

The Births of Jacob and Esau

[19]This is the history of the family of Isaac, the son of Abraham. [20]When Isaac was forty years old, he married Rebekah, the daughter of Bethuel the Aramean from Paddan-aram and the sister of Laban. [21]Isaac pleaded with the LORD to give Rebekah a child because she was childless. So the LORD answered Isaac's prayer, and his wife became pregnant with twins. [22]But the two children struggled with each other in her womb. So she went to ask the LORD about it. "Why is this happening to me?" she asked.

[23]And the LORD told her, "The sons in your womb will become two rival nations. One nation will be stronger than the other; the descendants of your older son will serve the descendants of your younger son."

[24]And when the time came, the twins were born. [25]The first was very red at birth. He was covered with so much hair that one would think he was wearing a piece of clothing. So they called him Esau.* [26]Then the other twin was born with his hand grasping Esau's heel. So they called him Jacob.* Isaac was sixty years old when the twins were born.

Esau Sells His Birthright

[27]As the boys grew up, Esau became a skillful hunter, a man of the open fields, while Jacob was the kind of person who liked to stay at home. [28]Isaac loved Esau in particular because of the wild game he brought home, but Rebekah favored Jacob.

[29]One day when Jacob was cooking some stew, Esau arrived home ex-

---

I SEEK to give a rich inheritance to my children who obey the Lord and walk in his ways (Galatians 3:28). (25:5)

I JOIN my siblings in honoring my parents when they die. (25:9)

Start each day reviewing the previous day's affirmations.

I BRING my needs and the needs of my loved ones to God in prayer. (25:21)

I INQUIRE of the Lord when I don't understand what is happening to me. (25:22)

I WAIT patiently for answers to prayer, remembering Isaac and Rebekah waited twenty years before the birth of their children. (25:26)

I LOVE each of my children deeply. (25:28)

25:18 The meaning of the Hebrew is uncertain.   25:25 *Esau* sounds like a Hebrew term that means "hair."
25:26 *Jacob* means "he grasps the heel"; this can also figuratively mean "he deceives."

hausted and hungry from a hunt. ³⁰Esau said to Jacob, "I'm starved! Give me some of that red stew you've made." (This was how Esau got his other name, Edom—"Red.")

³¹Jacob replied, "All right, but trade me your birthright for it."

³²"Look, I'm dying of starvation!" said Esau. "What good is my birthright to me now?"

³³So Jacob insisted, "Well then, swear to me right now that it is mine." So Esau swore an oath, thereby selling all his rights as the firstborn to his younger brother. ³⁴Then Jacob gave Esau some bread and lentil stew. Esau ate and drank and went on about his business, indifferent to the fact that he had given up his birthright.

I PLACE a higher priority on my spiritual needs than on my immediate physical needs. (25:32)

I CHERISH my spiritual inheritance from the Lord. (25:34)

CHAPTER 26

Isaac Deceives Abimelech

Now a severe famine struck the land, as had happened before in Abraham's time. So Isaac moved to Gerar, where Abimelech, king of the Philistines, lived.

LIKE ISAAC

Genesis 25:19

I am blessing my family for generations to come by passing on a spiritual heritage to my children.

The young couple beamed as they stood in front of the small congregation, their precious new son in their arms.

On each side of them, their parents looked on with equal pleasure as the minister prayed for their new grandson and dedicated him and his family to the Lord. The baby squirmed and cooed, not realizing the tremendous heritage his father and mother were giving him—his family had served the Lord for four generations, her family for five.

Isaac's heritage went back only one generation, but it would stretch physically and spiritually for scores of generations to come (Romans 9:7). Isaac passed on to his sons not just a hope and a prayer, but a real spiritual blessing. He actually prophesied about Jacob's and Esau's futures (Hebrews 11:20). The Lord had a plan that focused particularly on the younger son. Yet Jacob and Esau each had a choice to make. Would the Lord become their God, too?

Centuries afterward Moses, and later Jesus, spoke of "the God of Abraham, Isaac, and Jacob." And that faith passes not just through physical families but through spiritual birth to the entire family of God. Many a single woman or man or childless couple, although without physical descendants, has gained spiritual children by passing on their faith to others.

Today, all who believe in God are described in Scripture as "children of Abraham," the man of faith. Isaac started passing along the blessing. You and I can do so as well.

○ *Today's Scripture reading is Genesis 24 and 26.*

---

²The LORD appeared to him there and said, "Do not go to Egypt. ³Do as I say, and stay here in this land. If you do, I will be with you and bless you. I will give all this land to you and your descendants, just as I solemnly promised Abraham, your father. ⁴I will cause your descendants to become as numerous as the stars, and I will give them all these lands. And through your descendants* all the nations of the earth will be blessed. ⁵I will do this because Abraham listened to me and obeyed all my requirements, commands, regulations, and laws."

⁶So Isaac stayed in Gerar. ⁷And when the men there asked him about Rebekah, he said, "She is my sister." He was afraid to admit that she was his wife. He thought they would kill him to get her, because she was very beautiful. ⁸But some time later, Abimelech, king of the Philistines, looked out a window and saw Isaac fondling Rebekah.

I DO NOT REPEAT the sins of my parents. (26:7)

26:4 Hebrew *seed.*

I DO NOT USE deceit to protect myself. (26:9)

I DO NOT PUT others in the position of sinning or being sinned against (particularly in a sexual manner), even if it means risking my own life. (26:10)

I AM WILLING to give in during an argument, even if I am not in the wrong. (26:20)

I THANK God when he gives me rest from others who oppose me. (26:22)

I WORSHIP God for renewing his promises to me. (26:25)

⁹Abimelech called for Isaac and exclaimed, "She is obviously your wife! Why did you say she was your sister?"

"Because I was afraid someone would kill me to get her from me," Isaac replied.

¹⁰"How could you treat us this way!" Abimelech exclaimed. "Someone might have taken your wife and slept with her, and you would have made us guilty of great sin." ¹¹Then Abimelech made a public proclamation: "Anyone who harms this man or his wife will die!"

Conflict over Water Rights

¹²That year Isaac's crops were tremendous! He harvested a hundred times more grain than he planted, for the LORD blessed him. ¹³He became a rich man, and his wealth only continued to grow. ¹⁴He acquired large flocks of sheep and goats, great herds of cattle, and many servants. Soon the Philistines became jealous of him, ¹⁵and they filled up all of Isaac's wells with earth. These were the wells that had been dug by the servants of his father, Abraham.

¹⁶And Abimelech asked Isaac to leave the country. "Go somewhere else," he said, "for you have become too rich and powerful for us."

¹⁷So Isaac moved to the Gerar Valley and lived there instead. ¹⁸He reopened the wells his father had dug, which the Philistines had filled in after Abraham's death. Isaac renamed them, using the names Abraham had given them. ¹⁹His shepherds also dug in the Gerar Valley and found a gushing spring.

²⁰But then the local shepherds came and claimed the spring. "This is our water," they said, and they argued over it with Isaac's herdsmen. So Isaac named the well "Argument,"* because they had argued about it with him. ²¹Isaac's men then dug another well, but again there was a fight over it. So Isaac named it "Opposition."* ²²Abandoning that one, he dug another well, and the local people finally left him alone. So Isaac called it "Room Enough,"* for he said, "At last the LORD has made room for us, and we will be able to thrive."

²³From there Isaac moved to Beersheba, ²⁴where the LORD appeared to him on the night of his arrival. "I am the God of your father, Abraham," he said. "Do not be afraid, for I am with you and will bless you. I will give you many descendants, and they will become a great nation. I will do this because of my promise to Abraham, my servant." ²⁵Then Isaac built an altar there and worshiped the LORD. He set up his camp at that place, and his servants dug a well.

A Treaty with Abimelech

²⁶One day Isaac had visitors from Gerar. King Abimelech arrived with his adviser, Ahuzzath, and also Phicol, his army commander. ²⁷"Why have you come?" Isaac asked them. "This is obviously no friendly visit, since you sent me from your land in a most unfriendly way."

²⁸They replied, "We can plainly see that the LORD is with you. So we decided we should have a treaty, a covenant between us. ²⁹Swear that you will not harm us, just as we did not harm you. We have always treated you well, and we sent you away from us in peace. And now look how the LORD has blessed you!"

³⁰So Isaac prepared a great feast for them, and they ate and drank in preparation for the treaty ceremony. ³¹Early the next morning, they each took a solemn oath of nonaggression. Then Isaac sent them home again in peace. ³²That very day Isaac's servants came and told him about a well they had dug. "We've found water!" they said. ³³So Isaac named the well "Oath,"* and

26:20 Hebrew *Esek.* 26:21 Hebrew *Sitnah.* 26:22 Hebrew *Rehoboth.* 26:33 Hebrew *Shibah,* which can mean "oath" or "seven."

from that time to this, the town that grew up there has been called Beersheba—"well of the oath."

³⁴At the age of forty, Esau married a young woman named Judith, the daughter of Beeri the Hittite. He also married Basemath, the daughter of Elon the Hittite. ³⁵But Esau's wives made life miserable for Isaac and Rebekah.

CHAPTER 27

Jacob Steals Esau's Blessing

When Isaac was old and almost blind, he called for Esau, his older son, and said, "My son?"

"Yes, Father?" Esau replied.

²"I am an old man now," Isaac said, "and I expect every day to be my last. ³Take your bow and a quiver full of arrows out into the open country, and hunt some wild game for me. ⁴Prepare it just the way I like it so it's savory and good, and bring it here for me to eat. Then I will pronounce the blessing that belongs to you, my firstborn son, before I die."

I PLEDGE to give my children spiritual blessings before I die. (27:4)

UNLIKE ESAU
Genesis 25:34

I value my relationship with God and the spiritual blessings he offers me.

One rather famous advertising slogan begins, "When you care enough . . ."

Esau's problem was that he just didn't care. Worse than not caring about the needs and wants of others, Esau didn't care about knowing and serving the living Lord God Almighty (Hebrews 12:16).

Esau could count Abraham as his grandfather and Isaac, the son of promise, as his father. The knowledge of God had been specially revealed to his family. Among all the people on earth, the beam of the Lord's spiritual blessings was particularly focused on them. Yet, somehow, this meant little to Esau.

When Jacob and Esau still wrestled in Rebekah's womb, the Lord had told her that the younger son would be the conduit through whom the covenant would flow to create and bless a people of his own. God was not unfair to make this choice. Even if Esau was not the chosen son, he had no reason not to enjoy a personal relationship with the God of his fathers.

Known by his nickname, "Red," Esau was fiery and impatient. His birthright evidently meant nothing to him one day when his physical needs shouted their demands. Indifferent to all he could experience as the blessed of the Lord, he exchanged his inheritance—and all the physical and spiritual wealth it promised—for a bowl of stew!

Unlike Esau, you and I can place great value on our relationship with God and on the spiritual blessings he offers us (Ephesians 1:3-4).

Let's not trade knowing God for anything the world has to offer.

○ *Today's Scripture reading is Genesis 25:27-34.*

⁵But Rebekah overheard the conversation. So when Esau left to hunt for the wild game, ⁶she said to her son Jacob, "I overheard your father asking Esau ⁷to prepare him a delicious meal of wild game. He wants to bless Esau in the LORD's presence before he dies. ⁸Now, my son, do exactly as I tell you. ⁹Go out to the flocks and bring me two fine young goats. I'll prepare your father's favorite dish from them. ¹⁰Take the food to your father; then he can eat it and bless you instead of Esau before he dies."

¹¹"But Mother!" Jacob replied. "He won't be fooled that easily. Think how hairy Esau is and how smooth my skin is! ¹²What if my father touches me? He'll see that I'm trying to trick him, and then he'll curse me instead of blessing me."

¹³"Let the curse fall on me, dear son," said Rebekah. "Just do what I tell you. Go out and get the goats."

¹⁴So Jacob followed his mother's instructions, bringing her the two goats.

I REMAIN calm when circumstances seem likely to thwart the fulfillment of God's will or promises to me. (27:6)

I DO NOT MANIPULATE or deceive others to try to accomplish God's will. (27:10)

I DO NOT GO ALONG with my parent's plan if it is not right in God's eyes. (27:14)

She took them and cooked a delicious meat dish, just the way Isaac liked it. ¹⁵ Then she took Esau's best clothes, which were there in the house, and dressed Jacob with them. ¹⁶She made him a pair of gloves from the hairy skin of the young goats, and she fastened a strip of the goat's skin around his neck. ¹⁷ Then she gave him the meat dish, with its rich aroma, and some freshly baked bread. ¹⁸Jacob carried the platter of food to his father and said, "My father?"

"Yes, my son," he answered. "Who is it—Esau or Jacob?"

¹⁹Jacob replied, "It's Esau, your older son. I've done as you told me. Here is the wild game, cooked the way you like it. Sit up and eat it so you can give me your blessing."

²⁰Isaac asked, "How were you able to find it so quickly, my son?"

"Because the LORD your God put it in my path!" Jacob replied.

²¹Then Isaac said to Jacob, "Come over here. I want to touch you to make sure you really are Esau." ²²So Jacob went over to his father, and Isaac touched him. "The voice is Jacob's, but the hands are Esau's," Isaac said to himself. ²³But he did not recognize Jacob because Jacob's hands felt hairy just like Esau's. So Isaac pronounced his blessing on Jacob. ²⁴"Are you really my son Esau?" he asked.

"Yes, of course," Jacob replied.

²⁵Then Isaac said, "Now, my son, bring me the meat. I will eat it, and then I will give you my blessing." So Jacob took the food over to his father, and Isaac ate it. He also drank the wine that Jacob served him. Then Isaac said, ²⁶"Come here and kiss me, my son."

²⁷So Jacob went over and kissed him. And when Isaac caught the smell of his clothes, he was finally convinced, and he blessed his son. He said, "The smell of my son is the good smell of the open fields that the LORD has blessed. ²⁸May God always give you plenty of dew for healthy crops and good harvests of grain and wine. ²⁹May many nations become your servants. May you be the master of your brothers. May all your mother's sons bow low before you. All who curse you are cursed, and all who bless you are blessed."

³⁰As soon as Isaac had blessed Jacob, and almost before Jacob had left his father, Esau returned from his hunting trip. ³¹Esau prepared his father's favorite meat dish and brought it to him. Then he said, "I'm back, Father, and I have the wild game. Sit up and eat it so you can give me your blessing."

³²But Isaac asked him, "Who are you?"

"Why, it's me, of course!" he replied. "It's Esau, your older son."

³³Isaac began to tremble uncontrollably and said, "Then who was it that just served me wild game? I have already eaten it, and I blessed him with an irrevocable blessing before you came."

³⁴When Esau understood, he let out a loud and bitter cry. "O my father, bless me, too!" he begged.

I DO NOT DECEIVE others to get what I want, even if I deserve it. (27:35)

³⁵But Isaac said, "Your brother was here, and he tricked me. He has carried away your blessing."

³⁶Esau said bitterly, "No wonder his name is Jacob,* for he has deceived me twice, first taking my birthright and now stealing my blessing. Oh, haven't you saved even one blessing for me?"

³⁷Isaac said to Esau, "I have made Jacob your master and have declared that all his brothers will be his servants. I have guaranteed him an abundance of grain and wine—what is there left to give?"

³⁸Esau pleaded, "Not one blessing left for me? O my father, bless me, too!" Then Esau broke down and wept.

³⁹His father, Isaac, said to him, "You will live off the land and what it yields, ⁴⁰and you will live by your sword. You will serve your brother for a time, but then you will shake loose from him and be free."

27:36 *Jacob* means "he grasps the heel"; this can also figuratively mean "he deceives."

Jacob Flees to Paddan-Aram

⁴¹Esau hated Jacob because he had stolen his blessing, and he said to himself, "My father will soon be dead and gone. Then I will kill Jacob."

⁴²But someone got wind of what Esau was planning and reported it to Rebekah. She sent for Jacob and told him, "Esau is threatening to kill you. ⁴³This is what you should do. Flee to your uncle Laban in Haran. ⁴⁴Stay there with him until your brother's fury is spent. ⁴⁵When he forgets what you have done, I will send for you. Why should I lose both of you in one day?"

⁴⁶ Then Rebekah said to Isaac, "I'm sick and tired of these local Hittite women. I'd rather die than see Jacob marry one of them."

CHAPTER 28

So Isaac called for Jacob, blessed him, and said, "Do not marry any of these Canaanite women. ²Instead, go at once to Paddan-aram, to the house of your grandfather Bethuel, and marry one of your uncle Laban's daughters. ³May God Almighty bless you and give you many children. And may your descendants become a great assembly of nations! ⁴May God pass on to you and your descendants the blessings he promised to Abraham. May you own this land where we now are foreigners, for God gave it to Abraham."

I ACCEPT the consequences of my sins and bad decisions instead of blaming and trying to punish others. (27:41)

I GIVE people space after I have wronged them instead of further antagonizing them. (27:45)

I PASS ON to my children the spiritual blessings my parents gave to me. (28:4)

UNLIKE REBEKAH   *I do not attempt to obtain God's blessings*
Genesis 27:10   *through my own schemes.*

Sometimes it almost seems as if God purposely sets up obstacles to fulfilling his promises so that he can then overcome them and build his people's faith.

Like Abraham and Sarah, Isaac and Rebekah were childless—and that's a problem when you're supposed to be the parents of "many nations." Isaac prayed about their difficulty, however, and God allowed Rebekah to conceive (25:21).

Just as God gave Sarah a promise—that she would have a son—so he gave a promise to Rebekah—that her youngest (and favored) son would not only father a nation but also rule over his brother (Romans 9:10-12). When it came to seeing that promise fulfilled, however, Rebekah became desperate and fell into the same trap that Sarah had fallen into.

The day for Isaac to bless his sons approached. These blessings were not "good luck" wishes but real predictions for the destinies of the two sons. The critical moment in which God must act arrived, or so it seemed to Rebekah. To ensure the right outcome, she manipulated the circumstances and used deceit to gain what God had promised.

Rebekah believed God—but not enough to wait for him to overcome what looked impossible. In contrast, you and I don't need to become desperate when his methods and timing don't meet our expectations. We can rest assured that God's promises will come true.

○ *Today's Scripture reading is Genesis 27.*

---

⁵So Isaac sent Jacob away, and he went to Paddan-aram to stay with his uncle Laban, his mother's brother, the son of Bethuel the Aramean.

⁶Esau heard that his father had blessed Jacob and sent him to Paddan-aram to find a wife, and that he had warned Jacob not to marry a Canaanite woman. ⁷He also knew that Jacob had obeyed his parents and gone to Paddan-aram. ⁸It was now very clear to Esau that his father despised the local Canaanite women. ⁹So he visited his uncle Ishmael's family and married one of Ishmael's daughters, in addition to the wives he already had. His new wife's name was Mahalath. She was the sister of Nebaioth and the daughter of Ishmael, Abraham's son.

I LISTEN to my parents' advice about whom to marry—someone who is a godly believer. (28:6)

Jacob's Dream at Bethel

¹⁰Meanwhile, Jacob left Beersheba and traveled toward Haran. ¹¹At sundown he arrived at a good place to set up camp and stopped there for the night.

Jacob found a stone for a pillow and lay down to sleep. ¹²As he slept, he dreamed of a stairway that reached from earth to heaven. And he saw the angels of God going up and down on it.

I BELIEVE God reveals himself and renews his promises to each new generation. (28:13)

¹³At the top of the stairway stood the LORD, and he said, "I am the LORD, the God of your grandfather Abraham and the God of your father, Isaac. The ground you are lying on belongs to you. I will give it to you and your descendants. ¹⁴Your descendants will be as numerous as the dust of the earth! They will cover the land from east to west and from north to south. All the families of the earth will be blessed through you and your descendants.* ¹⁵What's more, I will be with you, and I will protect you wherever you go. I will someday bring you safely back to this land. I will be with you constantly until I have finished giving you everything I have promised."

¹⁶Then Jacob woke up and said, "Surely the LORD is in this place, and I wasn't even aware of it." ¹⁷He was afraid and said, "What an awesome place this is! It is none other than the house of God—the gateway to heaven!" ¹⁸The next morning he got up very early. He took the stone he had used as a pillow and set it upright as a memorial pillar. Then he poured olive oil over it. ¹⁹He named the place Bethel—"house of God"—though the name of the nearby village was Luz.

I TAKE God up on his promises to protect and bless me. (28:20)

²⁰Then Jacob made this vow: "If God will be with me and protect me on this journey and give me food and clothing, ²¹and if he will bring me back safely to my father, then I will make the LORD my God. ²²This memorial pillar will become a place for worshiping God, and I will give God a tenth of everything he gives me."

CHAPTER 29

Jacob Arrives at Paddan-Aram

Jacob hurried on, finally arriving in the land of the east. ²He saw in the distance three flocks of sheep lying in an open field beside a well, waiting to be watered. But a heavy stone covered the mouth of the well. ³It was the custom there to wait for all the flocks to arrive before removing the stone. After watering them, the stone would be rolled back over the mouth of the well. ⁴Jacob went over to the shepherds and asked them, "Where do you live?"

"At Haran," they said.

⁵"Do you know a man there named Laban, the grandson of Nahor?"

"Yes, we do," they replied.

⁶"How is he?" Jacob asked.

"He's well and prosperous. Look, here comes his daughter Rachel with the sheep."

⁷"Why don't you water the flocks so they can get back to grazing?" Jacob asked. "They'll be hungry if you stop so early in the day."

⁸"We don't roll away the stone and begin the watering until all the flocks and shepherds are here," they replied.

I HELP my relatives. (29:10)

⁹As this conversation was going on, Rachel arrived with her father's sheep, for she was a shepherd. ¹⁰And because she was his cousin, the daughter of his mother's brother, and because the sheep were his uncle's, Jacob went over to the well and rolled away the stone and watered his uncle's flock. ¹¹Then Jacob kissed Rachel, and tears came to his eyes. ¹²He explained that he was her cousin on her father's side, her aunt Rebekah's son. So Rachel quickly ran and told her father, Laban.

I WELCOME my relatives when they come to visit. (29:13)

¹³As soon as Laban heard about Jacob's arrival, he rushed out to meet him and greeted him warmly. Laban then brought him home, and Jacob told him his story. ¹⁴"Just think, my very own flesh and blood!" Laban exclaimed.

28:14 Hebrew *seed.*

Jacob Marries Leah and Rachel

After Jacob had been there about a month, ¹⁵Laban said to him, "You shouldn't work for me without pay just because we are relatives. How much do you want?"

¹⁶Now Laban had two daughters: Leah, who was the oldest, and her younger sister, Rachel. ¹⁷Leah had pretty eyes,* but Rachel was beautiful in every way, with a lovely face and shapely figure. ¹⁸Since Jacob was in love with Rachel, he told her father, "I'll work for you seven years if you'll give me Rachel, your younger daughter, as my wife."

¹⁹"Agreed!" Laban replied. "I'd rather give her to you than to someone outside the family."

²⁰So Jacob spent the next seven years working to pay for Rachel. But his love for her was so strong that it seemed to him but a few days. ²¹Finally, the time came for him to marry her. "I have fulfilled my contract," Jacob said to Laban. "Now give me my wife so we can be married."

²²So Laban invited everyone in the neighborhood to celebrate with Jacob at a wedding feast. ²³That night, when it was dark, Laban took Leah to Jacob, and he slept with her. ²⁴And Laban gave Leah a servant, Zilpah, to be her maid.

²⁵But when Jacob woke up in the morning—it was Leah! "What sort of trick is this?" Jacob raged at Laban. "I worked seven years for Rachel. What do you mean by this trickery?"

²⁶"It's not our custom to marry off a younger daughter ahead of the first-born," Laban replied. ²⁷"Wait until the bridal week is over, and you can have Rachel, too—that is, if you promise to work another seven years for me."

²⁸So Jacob agreed to work seven more years. A week after Jacob had married Leah, Laban gave him Rachel, too. ²⁹And Laban gave Rachel a servant, Bilhah, to be her maid. ³⁰So Jacob slept with Rachel, too, and he loved her more than Leah. He then stayed and worked the additional seven years.

Jacob's Many Children

³¹But because Leah was unloved, the LORD let her have a child, while Rachel was childless. ³²So Leah became pregnant and had a son. She named him Reuben,* for she said, "The LORD has noticed my misery, and now my husband will love me." ³³She soon became pregnant again and had another son. She named him Simeon,* for she said, "The LORD heard that I was unloved and has given me another son." ³⁴Again she became pregnant and had a son. She named him Levi,* for she said, "Surely now my husband will feel affection for me, since I have given him three sons!" ³⁵Once again she became pregnant and had a son. She named him Judah,* for she said, "Now I will praise the LORD!" And then she stopped having children.

CHAPTER 30

When Rachel saw that she wasn't having any children, she became jealous of her sister. "Give me children, or I'll die!" she exclaimed to Jacob.

²Jacob flew into a rage. "Am I God?" he asked. "He is the only one able to give you children!"

³Then Rachel told him, "Sleep with my servant, Bilhah, and she will bear children for me." ⁴So Rachel gave him Bilhah to be his wife, and Jacob slept with her. ⁵Bilhah became pregnant and presented him with a son. ⁶Rachel named him Dan,* for she said, "God has vindicated me! He has heard my request and given me a son." ⁷Then Bilhah became pregnant again and gave

I WORK hard to prepare for marriage. (29:18)

I ABIDE by and fulfill the contracts I make. (29:21)

I DO NOT PLAY games with the lives of my children. (29:26)

I THANK God for noticing my misery and providing for me. (29:32)

I COME to the point of praising God when my plans don't work out. (29:35)

I DO NOT BECOME jealous when God blesses someone else in a way he has not blessed me. (30:1)

I DO NOT VIOLATE my marriage vows in order to have a child. (30:3)

29:17 Or *dull eyes.* The meaning of the Hebrew is uncertain.   29:32 *Reuben* means "Look, a son!" It also sounds like the Hebrew for "He has seen my misery."   29:33 *Simeon* probably means "one who hears."   29:34 *Levi* sounds like a Hebrew term that means "being attached" or "feeling affection for."   29:35 *Judah* sounds like the Hebrew term for "praise."   30:6 *Dan* is a play on the Hebrew term meaning "to vindicate" or "to judge."

Jacob a second son. ⁸Rachel named him Naphtali,* for she said, "I have had an intense struggle with my sister, and I am winning!"

⁹Meanwhile, Leah realized that she wasn't getting pregnant anymore, so she gave her servant, Zilpah, to Jacob to be his wife. ¹⁰Soon Zilpah presented him with another son. ¹¹Leah named him Gad,* for she said, "How fortunate I am!" ¹²Then Zilpah produced a second son, ¹³and Leah named him Asher,* for she said, "What joy is mine! The other women will consider me happy indeed!"

¹⁴One day during the wheat harvest, Reuben found some mandrakes growing in a field and brought the roots to his mother, Leah. Rachel begged Leah to give some of them to her. ¹⁵But Leah angrily replied, "Wasn't it enough that you stole my husband? Now will you steal my son's mandrake roots, too?"

Rachel said, "I will let him sleep with you tonight in exchange for the mandrake roots."

¹⁶So that evening, as Jacob was coming home from the fields, Leah went out to meet him. "You must sleep with me tonight!" she said. "I have paid for you with some mandrake roots my son has found." So Jacob slept with her. ¹⁷And God answered her prayers. She became pregnant again and gave birth to her fifth son. ¹⁸She named him Issachar,* for she said, "God has rewarded me for giving my servant to my husband as a wife." ¹⁹Then she became pregnant again and had a sixth son. ²⁰She named him Zebulun,* for she said, "God has given me good gifts for my husband. Now he will honor me, for I have given him six sons." ²¹Later she gave birth to a daughter and named her Dinah.

²²Then God remembered Rachel's plight and answered her prayers by giving her a child. ²³She became pregnant and gave birth to a son. "God has removed my shame," she said. ²⁴And she named him Joseph,* for she said, "May the LORD give me yet another son."

Jacob's Wealth Increases

²⁵Soon after Joseph was born to Rachel, Jacob said to Laban, "I want to go back home. ²⁶Let me take my wives and children, for I have earned them from you, and let me be on my way. You know I have fully paid for them with my service to you."

²⁷"Please don't leave me," Laban replied, "for I have learned by divination that the LORD has blessed me because you are here. ²⁸How much do I owe you? Whatever it is, I'll pay it."

²⁹Jacob replied, "You know how faithfully I've served you through these many years, and how your flocks and herds have grown. ³⁰You had little indeed before I came, and your wealth has increased enormously. The LORD has blessed you from everything I do! But now, what about me? When should I provide for my own family?"

³¹"What wages do you want?" Laban asked again.

Jacob replied, "Don't give me anything at all. Just do one thing, and I'll go back to work for you. ³²Let me go out among your flocks today and remove all the sheep and goats that are speckled or spotted, along with all the dark-colored sheep. Give them to me as my wages. ³³This will make it easy for you to see whether or not I have been honest. If you find in my flock any white sheep or goats that are not speckled, you will know that I have stolen them from you."

³⁴"All right," Laban replied. "It will be as you have said." ³⁵But that very day Laban went out and removed all the male goats that were speckled and

I DO NOT DEPEND solely on my spouse for my feelings of esteem and honor. (30:20)

I PRAY to God if I am childless. (30:22)

I WORK hard and productively for my employer. (30:29)

I REQUEST fair compensation from my employer. (30:31)

I DO NOT THWART my employees or withhold fair benefits from them. (30:34)

30:8 Naphtali means "my struggle." 30:11 Gad means "good fortune." 30:13 Asher means "happy." 30:18 Issachar sounds like a Hebrew term that means "reward." 30:20 Zebulun probably means "honor." 30:24 Joseph means "may he add."

spotted, the females that were speckled and spotted with any white patches, and all the dark-colored sheep. He placed them in the care of his sons, ³⁶and they took them three days' distance from where Jacob was. Meanwhile, Jacob stayed and cared for Laban's flock.

³⁷Now Jacob took fresh shoots from poplar, almond, and plane trees and peeled off strips of the bark to make white streaks on them. ³⁸Then he set up these peeled branches beside the watering troughs so Laban's flocks would see them as they came to drink, for that was when they mated. ³⁹So when the flocks mated in front of the white-streaked branches, all of their offspring were streaked, speckled, and spotted. ⁴⁰Jacob added them to his own flock, thus separating the lambs from Laban's flock. Then at mating time, he turned the flocks toward the streaked and dark-colored rams in Laban's flock. This is how he built his flock from Laban's. ⁴¹Whenever the stronger females were ready to mate, Jacob set up the peeled branches in front of them. ⁴²But he didn't do this with the weaker ones, so the weaker lambs belonged to Laban, and the stronger ones were Jacob's. ⁴³As a result, Jacob's flocks increased rapidly, and he became very wealthy, with many servants, camels, and donkeys.

CHAPTER 31

Jacob Flees from Laban

But Jacob soon learned that Laban's sons were beginning to grumble. "Jacob has robbed our father!" they said. "All his wealth has been gained at our father's expense." ²And Jacob began to notice a considerable cooling in Laban's attitude toward him.

³Then the LORD said to Jacob, "Return to the land of your father and grandfather and to your relatives there, and I will be with you."

⁴Jacob called Rachel and Leah out to the field where he was watching the flocks, ⁵so he could talk things over with them. "Your father has turned against me and is not treating me like he used to," he told them. "But the God of my father has been with me. ⁶You know how hard I have worked for your father, ⁷but he has tricked me, breaking his wage agreement with me again and again. But God has not allowed him to do me any harm. ⁸For if he said the speckled animals were mine, the whole flock began to produce speckled lambs. And when he changed his mind and said I could have the streaked ones, then all the lambs were born streaked. ⁹In this way, God has made me wealthy at your father's expense. ¹⁰During the mating season, I had a dream and saw that the male goats mating with the flock were streaked, speckled, and spotted. ¹¹Then in my dream, the angel of God said to me, 'Jacob!' And I replied, 'Yes, I'm listening!' ¹²The angel said, 'Look, and you will see that only the streaked, speckled, and spotted males are mating with the females of your flock. For I have seen all that Laban has done to you. ¹³I am the God you met at Bethel, the place where you anointed the pillar of stone and made a vow to serve me. Now leave this country and return to the land you came from.' "

¹⁴Rachel and Leah said, "That's fine with us! There's nothing for us here—none of our father's wealth will come to us anyway. ¹⁵He has reduced our rights to those of foreign women. He sold us, and what he received for us has disappeared. ¹⁶The riches God has given you from our father are legally ours and our children's to begin with. So go ahead and do whatever God has told you."

¹⁷So Jacob put his wives and children on camels. ¹⁸He drove the flocks in front of him—all the livestock he had acquired at Paddan-aram—and set out on his journey to the land of Canaan, where his father, Isaac, lived. ¹⁹At the time they left, Laban was some distance away, shearing his sheep. Rachel stole her father's household gods and took them with her. ²⁰They set out secretly and never told Laban they were leaving. ²¹Jacob took all his

I GO where God directs me. (31:3)

I CONSULT with my spouse before I make major life changes. (31:4)

I CREDIT God for taking care of me when others are trying to take advantage of me. (31:5)

I RECOGNIZE when I am being mistreated and when God is working out his plan for my benefit. (31:14)

I DO NOT STEAL from my parents, even if they have not given me my fair share. (31:19)

possessions with him and crossed the Euphrates River, heading for the territory of Gilead.

Laban Pursues Jacob

[22]Laban didn't learn of their flight for three days. [23]But when he did, he gathered a group of his relatives and set out in hot pursuit. He caught up with them seven days later in the hill country of Gilead. [24]But the previous night God had appeared to Laban in a dream. "Be careful about what you say to Jacob!" he was told.

[25]So when Laban caught up with Jacob as he was camped in the hill country of Gilead, he set up his camp not far from Jacob's. [26]"What do you mean by sneaking off like this?" Laban demanded. "Are my daughters prisoners, the plunder of war, that you have stolen them away like this? [27]Why did you slip away secretly? I would have given you a farewell party, with joyful singing accompanied by tambourines and harps. [28]Why didn't you let me kiss my daughters and grandchildren and tell them good-bye? You have acted very foolishly! [29]I could destroy you, but the God of your father appeared to me last night and told me, 'Be careful about what you say to Jacob!' [30]I know you feel you must go, and you long intensely for your childhood home, but why have you stolen my household gods?"

[31]"I rushed away because I was afraid," Jacob answered. "I said to myself, 'He'll take his daughters from me by force.' [32]But as for your household gods, let the person who has taken them die! If you find anything that belongs to you, I swear before all these relatives of ours, I will give it back without question." But Jacob didn't know that Rachel had taken them.

[33]Laban went first into Jacob's tent to search there, then into Leah's, and then he searched the tents of the two concubines, but he didn't find the gods. Finally, he went into Rachel's tent. [34]Rachel had taken the household gods and had stuffed them into her camel saddle, and now she was sitting on them. So although Laban searched all the tents, he couldn't find them. [35]"Forgive my not getting up, Father," Rachel explained. "I'm having my monthly period." So despite his thorough search, Laban didn't find them.

[36]Then Jacob became very angry. "What did you find?" he demanded of Laban. "What is my crime? You have chased me as though I were a criminal. [37]You have searched through everything I own. Now show me what you have found that belongs to you! Set it out here in front of us, before our relatives, for all to see. Let them decide who is the real owner!

[38]"Twenty years I have been with you, and all that time I cared for your sheep and goats so they produced healthy offspring. In all those years I never touched a single ram of yours for food. [39]If any were attacked and killed by wild animals, did I show them to you and ask you to reduce the count of your flock? No, I took the loss! You made me pay for every animal stolen from the flocks, whether the loss was my fault or not. [40]I worked for you through the scorching heat of the day and through cold and sleepless nights. [41]Yes, twenty years—fourteen of them earning your two daughters, and six years to get the flock. And you have reduced my wages ten times! [42]In fact, except for the grace of God—the God of my grandfather Abraham, the awe-inspiring God of my father, Isaac—you would have sent me off without a penny to my name. But God has seen your cruelty and my hard work. That is why he appeared to you last night and vindicated me."

Jacob's Treaty with Laban

[43]Then Laban replied to Jacob, "These women are my daughters, and these children are my grandchildren, and these flocks and all that you have—all are mine. But what can I do now to my own daughters and grandchildren?

I RECOGNIZE that God can keep others from destroying me. (31:29)

I BELIEVE God sees my situation and will vindicate me when I am treated poorly and accused falsely. (31:42)

⁴⁴"Come now, and we will make a peace treaty, you and I, and we will live by its terms."

⁴⁵So Jacob took a stone and set it up as a monument. ⁴⁶He also told his men to gather stones and pile them up in a heap. Jacob and Laban then sat down beside the pile of stones to share a meal. ⁴⁷They named it "Witness Pile," which is Jegar-sahadutha in Laban's language and Galeed* in Jacob's.

⁴⁸"This pile of stones will stand as a witness to remind us of our agreement," Laban said. ⁴⁹This place was also called Mizpah,* for Laban said, "May the LORD keep watch between us to make sure that we keep this treaty when we are out of each other's sight. ⁵⁰I won't know about it if you are harsh to my daughters or if you take other wives, but God will see it. ⁵¹This heap of stones and this pillar ⁵²stand between us as a witness of our vows. I will not cross this line to harm you, and you will not cross it to harm me. ⁵³I call on the God of our ancestors—the God of your grandfather Abraham and the God of my grandfather Nahor—to punish either one of us who harms the other."

So Jacob took an oath before the awesome God of his father, Isaac, to respect the boundary line. ⁵⁴Then Jacob presented a sacrifice to God and invited everyone to a feast. Afterward they spent the night there in the hills. ⁵⁵Laban got up early the next morning, and he kissed his daughters and grandchildren and blessed them. Then he returned home.

CHAPTER 32

Jacob Sends Gifts to Esau

As Jacob and his household started on their way again, angels of God came to meet him. ²When Jacob saw them, he exclaimed, "This is God's camp!" So he named the place Mahanaim.*

³Jacob now sent messengers to his brother, Esau, in Edom, the land of Seir. ⁴He told them, "Give this message to my master Esau: 'Humble greetings from your servant Jacob! I have been living with Uncle Laban until recently, ⁵and now I own oxen, donkeys, sheep, goats, and many servants, both men and women. I have sent these messengers to inform you of my coming, hoping that you will be friendly to us.' "

⁶The messengers returned with the news that Esau was on his way to meet Jacob—with an army of four hundred men! ⁷Jacob was terrified at the news. He divided his household, along with the flocks and herds and camels, into two camps. ⁸He thought, "If Esau attacks one group, perhaps the other can escape."

⁹Then Jacob prayed, "O God of my grandfather Abraham and my father, Isaac—O LORD, you told me to return to my land and to my relatives, and you promised to treat me kindly. ¹⁰I am not worthy of all the faithfulness and unfailing love you have shown to me, your servant. When I left home, I owned nothing except a walking stick, and now my household fills two camps! ¹¹O LORD, please rescue me from my brother, Esau. I am afraid that he is coming to kill me, along with my wives and children. ¹²But you promised to treat me kindly and to multiply my descendants until they become as numerous as the sands along the seashore—too many to count."

¹³Jacob stayed where he was for the night and prepared a present for Esau: ¹⁴two hundred female goats, twenty male goats, two hundred ewes, twenty rams, ¹⁵thirty female camels with their young, forty cows, ten bulls, twenty female donkeys, and ten male donkeys. ¹⁶He told his servants to lead them on ahead, each group of animals by itself, separated by a distance in between.

¹⁷He gave these instructions to the men leading the first group: "When you meet Esau, he will ask, 'Where are you going? Whose servants are you? Whose

I LIVE by the terms of agreements I make. (31:44)

I RELY on God to make sure that an agreement is kept when I am not around. (31:49)

I APPROACH people humbly after I have wronged them. (32:4)

I PLAN for my family's safety. (32:7)

I RELY on God's promises. (32:12)

31:47 *Jegar-sahadutha* means "witness pile" in Aramaic; *Galeed* means "witness pile" in Hebrew. 31:49 *Mizpah* means "watchtower." 32:2 *Mahanaim* means "two camps."

animals are these?' ¹⁸You should reply, 'These belong to your servant Jacob. They are a present for his master Esau! He is coming right behind us.' " ¹⁹Jacob gave the same instructions to each of the herdsmen and told them, "You are all to say the same thing to Esau when you see him. ²⁰And be sure to say, 'Your servant Jacob is right behind us.' " Jacob's plan was to appease Esau with the presents before meeting him face to face. "Perhaps," Jacob hoped, "he will be friendly to us." ²¹So the presents were sent on ahead, and Jacob spent that night in the camp.

Jacob Wrestles with God

²²But during the night Jacob got up and sent his two wives, two concubines, and eleven sons across the Jabbok River. ²³After they were on the other side, he sent over all his possessions. ²⁴This left Jacob all alone in the camp, and a man came and wrestled with him until dawn. ²⁵When the man saw that he couldn't win the match, he struck Jacob's hip and knocked it out of joint at the socket. ²⁶Then the man said, "Let me go, for it is dawn."

But Jacob panted, "I will not let you go unless you bless me."

²⁷"What is your name?" the man asked.

He replied, "Jacob."

²⁸"Your name will no longer be Jacob," the man told him. "It is now Israel,* because you have struggled with both God and men and have won."

²⁹"What is your name?" Jacob asked him.

"Why do you ask?" the man replied. Then he blessed Jacob there.

³⁰Jacob named the place Peniel—"face of God"—for he said, "I have seen God face to face, yet my life has been spared." ³¹The sun rose as he left Peniel,* and he was limping because of his hip. ³²That is why even today the people of Israel don't eat meat from near the hip, in memory of what happened that night.

CHAPTER 33

Jacob and Esau Make Peace

Then, in the distance, Jacob saw Esau coming with his four hundred men. ²Jacob now arranged his family into a column, with his two concubines and their children at the front, Leah and her children next, and Rachel and Joseph last. ³Then Jacob went on ahead. As he approached his brother, he bowed low seven times before him. ⁴Then Esau ran to meet him and embraced him affectionately and kissed him. Both of them were in tears.

⁵Then Esau looked at the women and children and asked, "Who are these people with you?"

"These are the children God has graciously given to me," Jacob replied. ⁶Then the concubines came forward with their children and bowed low before him. ⁷Next Leah came with her children, and they bowed down. Finally, Rachel and Joseph came and made their bows.

⁸"And what were all the flocks and herds I met as I came?" Esau asked.

Jacob replied, "They are gifts, my lord, to ensure your goodwill."

⁹"Brother, I have plenty," Esau answered. "Keep what you have."

¹⁰"No, please accept them," Jacob said, "for what a relief it is to see your friendly smile. It is like seeing the smile of God! ¹¹Please take my gifts, for God has been very generous to me. I have more than enough." Jacob continued to insist, so Esau finally accepted them.

¹²"Well, let's be going," Esau said. "I will stay with you and lead the way."

¹³But Jacob replied, "You can see, my lord, that some of the children are very young, and the flocks and herds have their young, too. If they are driven

Margin notes

I PERSIST in seeking God's blessing. (32:26)

I BELIEVE God met Jacob directly at his point of need, yet spared his life. (32:30)

I APPROACH people humbly after I have wronged them. (33:3)

I RECOGNIZE that my children are gifts from God. (33:5)

I ACTIVELY SEEK to be reconciled with my enemies. (33:10)

I AM CONSIDERATE of the needs of my family and any animals under my care. (33:13)

32:28 *Israel* means "God struggles" or "one who struggles with God." 32:31 Hebrew *Penuel*, a variant name for Peniel.

too hard, they may die. ¹⁴So go on ahead of us. We will follow at our own pace and meet you at Seir."

¹⁵"Well," Esau said, "at least let me leave some of my men to guide and protect you."

"There is no reason for you to be so kind to me," Jacob insisted.

LIKE JACOB

Genesis 32:9

I always recognize God's hand on my life as I pursue his blessings.

Maybe Jacob was originally from Missouri, the "Show Me" state. Raised to be the recipient of God's promises to Abraham and Isaac, Jacob (who was later renamed "Israel") wanted to see for himself that the Lord was at work in his life.

As a young man, he slept on a pillow of stone and dreamed of a stairway to heaven. When he awoke, he realized God's presence with him. Jacob responded by declaring that he would follow the Lord if God would show himself faithful and bring him back safely from a foreign land.

The Lord did bless Jacob and brought him back with tents bursting with children and large flocks and herds grazing under the care of many servants (Hebrews 11:9). Jacob knew that God had more than proven himself, and he was prepared to worship the Lord alone.

On his way home from that foreign land, Jacob found himself wrestling with a mysterious man. Somehow, Jacob knew his opponent was a heavenly messenger. As they wrestled in the dark, Jacob's all-consuming desire to know more of God's blessing compelled him to hold on until he received that blessing. As always, the Lord gave his blessing and more. The man changed Jacob's name from Jacob (which means "he deceives") to Israel ("one who struggles with God"). Jacob knew then that this man was no mere angel. God himself had come to test Jacob's true desires.

God is pleased when the desire of our heart is to know him and enjoy all his good gifts. "Keep on asking, and you will be given what you ask for" (Matthew 7:7). Why? Because our heavenly Father delights to give good gifts to his children (Matthew 7:8-11).

Like Jacob, you and I can cling to the Lord, knowing that in him alone we will find life and blessing. To read more about Jacob's faith even in his old age, see Genesis 48–49 and Hebrews 11:21.

○ *Today's Scripture reading is Genesis 31–32.*

¹⁶So Esau started back to Seir that same day. ¹⁷Meanwhile, Jacob and his household traveled on to Succoth. There he built himself a house and made shelters for his flocks and herds. That is why the place was named Succoth.* ¹⁸Then they arrived safely at Shechem, in Canaan, and they set up camp just outside the town. ¹⁹Jacob bought the land he camped on from the family of Hamor, Shechem's father, for a hundred pieces of silver.* ²⁰And there he built an altar and called it El-Elohe-Israel.*

I WORSHIP God everywhere I go. (33:20)

CHAPTER 34

Revenge against Shechem

One day Dinah, Leah's daughter, went to visit some of the young women who lived in the area. ²But when the local prince, Shechem son of Hamor the Hivite, saw her, he took her and raped her. ³But Shechem's love for Dinah was strong, and he tried to win her affection. ⁴He even spoke to his father about it. "Get this girl for me," he demanded. "I want to marry her."

I ABHOR rape. (34:2)

⁵Word soon reached Jacob that his daughter had been defiled, but his sons were out in the fields herding cattle so he did nothing until they returned. ⁶Meanwhile, Hamor, Shechem's father, came out to discuss the matter with Jacob. ⁷He arrived just as Jacob's sons were coming in from the fields. They were shocked and furious that their sister had been raped. Shechem had done a disgraceful thing against Jacob's family,* a thing that should never have been done.

I TAKE prompt action when my child has been abused. (34:5)

33:17 *Succoth* means "shelters." 33:19 Hebrew *100 kesitahs;* the value or weight of the kesitah is no longer known. 33:20 *El-Elohe-Israel* means "God, the God of Israel." 34:7 Hebrew *in Israel.*

⁸Hamor told Jacob and his sons, "My son Shechem is truly in love with your daughter, and he longs for her to be his wife. Please let him marry her. ⁹We invite you to let your daughters marry our sons, and we will give our daughters as wives for your young men. ¹⁰And you may live among us; the land is open to you! Settle here and trade with us. You are free to acquire property among us."

¹¹Then Shechem addressed Dinah's father and brothers. "Please be kind to me, and let me have her as my wife," he begged. "I will give whatever you require. ¹²No matter what dowry or gift you demand, I will pay it—only give me the girl as my wife."

¹³But Dinah's brothers deceived Shechem and Hamor because of what Shechem had done to their sister. ¹⁴They said to them, "We couldn't possibly allow this, because you aren't circumcised. It would be a disgrace for her to marry a man like you! ¹⁵But here is a solution. If every man among you will be circumcised like we are, ¹⁶we will intermarry with you and live here and unite with you to become one people. ¹⁷Otherwise we will take her and be on our way."

¹⁸Hamor and Shechem gladly agreed, ¹⁹and Shechem lost no time in acting on this request, for he wanted Dinah desperately. Shechem was a highly respected member of his family, ²⁰and he appeared with his father before the town leaders to present this proposal. ²¹"Those men are our friends," they said. "Let's invite them to live here among us and ply their trade. For the land is large enough to hold them, and we can intermarry with them. ²²But they will consider staying here only on one condition. Every one of us men must be circumcised, just as they are. ²³But if we do this, all their flocks and possessions will become ours. Come, let's agree to this so they will settle here among us."

²⁴So all the men agreed and were circumcised. ²⁵But three days later, when their wounds were still sore, two of Dinah's brothers, Simeon and Levi, took their swords, entered the town without opposition, and slaughtered every man there, ²⁶including Hamor and Shechem. They rescued Dinah from Shechem's house and returned to their camp. ²⁷Then all of Jacob's sons plundered the town because their sister had been defiled there. ²⁸They seized all the flocks and herds and donkeys—everything they could lay their hands on, both inside the town and outside in the fields. ²⁹They also took all the women and children and wealth of every kind.

³⁰Afterward Jacob said to Levi and Simeon, "You have made me stink among all the people of this land—among all the Canaanites and Perizzites. We are so few that they will come and crush us. We will all be killed!"

³¹"Should he treat our sister like a prostitute?" they retorted angrily.

CHAPTER 35

Jacob's Return to Bethel

God said to Jacob, "Now move on to Bethel and settle there. Build an altar there to worship me—the God who appeared to you when you fled from your brother, Esau."

²So Jacob told everyone in his household, "Destroy your idols, wash yourselves, and put on clean clothing. ³We are now going to Bethel, where I will build an altar to the God who answered my prayers when I was in distress. He has stayed with me wherever I have gone."

⁴So they gave Jacob all their idols and their earrings, and he buried them beneath the tree near Shechem. ⁵When they set out again, terror from God came over the people in all the towns of that area, and no one attacked them. ⁶Finally, they arrived at Luz (now called Bethel) in Canaan. ⁷Jacob built an altar there and named it El-bethel,* because God had appeared to him there at Bethel when he was fleeing from Esau.

35:7 *El-bethel* means "the God of Bethel."

I DO NOT USE deceit to take revenge. (34:13)

I DO NOT USE violence to take revenge. (34:25)

I PROTECT my loved ones from sexual abuse. (34:26)

I TAKE sexual abuse very seriously. (34:31)

I CLEANSE my life as I prepare to meet with God. (35:4)

I WORSHIP God for fulfilling his promise to care for me. (35:7)

⁸Soon after this, Rebekah's old nurse, Deborah, died. She was buried beneath the oak tree in the valley below Bethel. Ever since, the tree has been called the "Oak of Weeping."*

⁹God appeared to Jacob once again when he arrived at Bethel after traveling from Paddan-aram. God blessed him ¹⁰and said, "Your name is no longer Jacob; you will now be called Israel."* ¹¹Then God said, "I am God Almighty. Multiply and fill the earth! Become a great nation, even many nations. Kings will be among your descendants! ¹²And I will pass on to you the land I gave to Abraham and Isaac. Yes, I will give it to you and your descendants." ¹³Then God went up from the place where he had spoken to Jacob.

¹⁴Jacob set up a stone pillar to mark the place where God had spoken to him. He then poured wine over it as an offering to God and anointed the pillar with olive oil. ¹⁵Jacob called the place Bethel—"house of God"—because God had spoken to him there.

The Deaths of Rachel and Isaac

¹⁶Leaving Bethel, they traveled on toward Ephrath (that is, Bethlehem). But Rachel's pains of childbirth began while they were still some distance away. ¹⁷After a very hard delivery, the midwife finally exclaimed, "Don't be afraid—you have another son!" ¹⁸Rachel was about to die, but with her last breath she named him Ben-oni; the baby's father, however, called him Benjamin.* ¹⁹So Rachel died and was buried on the way to Ephrath (that is, Bethlehem). ²⁰Jacob set up a stone monument over her grave, and it can be seen there to this day.

²¹Jacob* then traveled on and camped beyond the tower of Eder. ²²While he was there, Reuben slept with Bilhah, his father's concubine, and someone told Jacob about it.

These are the names of the twelve sons of Jacob:

²³The sons of Leah were Reuben (Jacob's oldest son), Simeon, Levi, Judah, Issachar, and Zebulun.
²⁴The sons of Rachel were Joseph and Benjamin.
²⁵The sons of Bilhah, Rachel's servant, were Dan and Naphtali.
²⁶The sons of Zilpah, Leah's servant, were Gad and Asher.

These were the sons born to Jacob at Paddan-aram.

²⁷So Jacob came home to his father Isaac in Mamre, which is near Kiriath-arba (now called Hebron), where Abraham had also lived. ²⁸Isaac lived for 180 years, ²⁹and he died at a ripe old age, joining his ancestors in death. Then his sons, Esau and Jacob, buried him.

CHAPTER 36

Descendants of Esau

This is the history of the descendants of Esau (also known as Edom). ²Esau married two young women from Canaan: Adah, the daughter of Elon the Hittite; and Oholibamah, the daughter of Anah and granddaughter of Zibeon the Hivite. ³He also married his cousin Basemath, who was the daughter of Ishmael and the sister of Nebaioth. ⁴Esau and Adah had a son named Eliphaz. Esau and Basemath had a son named Reuel. ⁵Esau and Oholibamah had sons named Jeush, Jalam, and Korah. All these sons were born to Esau in the land of Canaan.

⁶ Then Esau took his wives, children, household servants, cattle, and flocks—all the wealth he had gained in the land of Canaan—and moved away from his brother, Jacob. ⁷There was not enough land to support them

I ACCEPT the new identity God gives me. (35:10)

I BELIEVE God keeps his promises through each generation. (35:12)

I MAKE tangible reminders of God's dealings in my life. (35:14)

I ABHOR incest. (35:22)

I HELP my siblings care for the burial of a parent. (35:29)

I AM WILLING to go somewhere else if it means staying at peace with others. (36:6)

35:8 Hebrew *Allon-bacuth.* 35:10 *Jacob* means "he grasps the heel"; this can also figuratively mean "he deceives"; *Israel* means "God struggles" or "one who struggles with God." 35:18 *Ben-oni* means "son of my sorrow"; *Benjamin* means "son of my right hand." 35:21 Hebrew *Israel;* also in 35:22a.

both because of all their cattle and livestock. ⁸So Esau (also known as Edom) settled in the hill country of Seir.

⁹This is a list of Esau's descendants, the Edomites, who lived in the hill country of Seir.

¹⁰Among Esau's sons were Eliphaz, the son of Esau's wife Adah; and Reuel, the son of Esau's wife Basemath. ¹¹The sons of Eliphaz were Teman, Omar, Zepho, Gatam, and Kenaz. ¹²Eliphaz had another son named Amalek, born to Timna, his concubine. These were all grandchildren of Esau's wife Adah. ¹³The sons of Reuel were Nahath, Zerah, Shammah, and Mizzah. These were all grandchildren of Esau's wife Basemath. ¹⁴Esau also had sons through Oholibamah, the daughter of Anah and granddaughter of Zibeon. Their names were Jeush, Jalam, and Korah.

I BELIEVE God blessed all of the children of his servant Abraham, just as he had promised. (36:15)

¹⁵Esau's children and grandchildren became the leaders of different clans.

The sons of Esau's oldest son, Eliphaz, became the leaders of the clans of Teman, Omar, Zepho, Kenaz, ¹⁶Korah, Gatam, and Amalek. These clans in the land of Edom were descended from Eliphaz, the son of Esau and Adah.

¹⁷The sons of Esau's son Reuel became the leaders of the clans of Nahath, Zerah, Shammah, and Mizzah. These clans in the land of Edom were descended from Reuel, the son of Esau and Basemath.

¹⁸The sons of Esau and his wife Oholibamah became the leaders of the clans of Jeush, Jalam, and Korah. These are the clans descended from Esau's wife Oholibamah, the daughter of Anah.

¹⁹These are all the clans descended from Esau (also known as Edom).

Original Peoples of Edom

²⁰These are the names of the tribes that descended from Seir the Horite, one of the families native to the land of Seir: Lotan, Shobal, Zibeon, Anah, ²¹Dishon, Ezer, and Dishan. These were the Horite clans, the descendants of Seir, who lived in the land of Edom.

²²The sons of Lotan were Hori and Heman. Lotan's sister was named Timna.

²³The sons of Shobal were Alvan, Manahath, Ebal, Shepho, and Onam.

²⁴The sons of Zibeon were Aiah and Anah. This is the Anah who discovered the hot springs in the wilderness while he was grazing his father's donkeys.

²⁵The son of Anah was Dishon, and Oholibamah was his daughter.

²⁶The sons of Dishon* were Hemdan, Eshban, Ithran, and Keran.

²⁷The sons of Ezer were Bilhan, Zaavan, and Akan.

²⁸The sons of Dishan were Uz and Aran.

Ask God to make you "totally committed to doing what is right" (Titus 2:14).

²⁹So the leaders of the Horite clans were Lotan, Shobal, Zibeon, Anah, ³⁰Dishon, Ezer, and Dishan. The Horite clans are named after their clan leaders, who lived in the land of Seir.

Rulers of Edom

³¹These are the kings who ruled in Edom before there were kings in Israel*:

³²Bela son of Beor, who ruled from his city of Dinhabah.

³³When Bela died, Jobab son of Zerah from Bozrah became king.

³⁴When Jobab died, Husham from the land of the Temanites became king.

³⁵When Husham died, Hadad son of Bedad became king and ruled from

36:26 Hebrew *Dishan*, a variant name for Dishon; compare 36:21, 28.　36:31 Or *before an Israelite king ruled over them.*

the city of Avith. He was the one who destroyed the Midianite army in the land of Moab.

[36]When Hadad died, Samlah from the city of Masrekah became king. [37]When Samlah died, Shaul from the city of Rehoboth on the Euphrates River* became king. [38]When Shaul died, Baal-hanan son of Acbor became king. [39]When Baal-hanan died, Hadad* became king and ruled from the city of Pau. Hadad's wife was Mehetabel, the daughter of Matred and granddaughter of Me-zahab.

[40]These are the leaders of the clans of Esau, who lived in the places named for them: Timna, Alvah, Jetheth, [41]Oholibamah, Elah, Pinon, [42]Kenaz, Teman, Mibzar, [43]Magdiel, and Iram. These are the names of the clans of Esau, the ancestor of the Edomites, each clan giving its name to the area it occupied.

I BELIEVE God's blessings continue throughout the generations. (36:43)

CHAPTER 37

Joseph's Dreams

So Jacob settled again in the land of Canaan, where his father had lived.

[2]This is the history of Jacob's family. When Joseph was seventeen years old, he often tended his father's flocks with his half brothers, the sons of his father's wives Bilhah and Zilpah. But Joseph reported to his father some of the bad things his brothers were doing. [3]Now Jacob* loved Joseph more than any of his other children because Joseph had been born to him in his old age. So one day he gave Joseph a special gift—a beautiful robe.* [4]But his brothers hated Joseph because of their father's partiality. They couldn't say a kind word to him.

I DO NOT CREATE jealousy in my children by loving one of them more than the others. (37:3)

[5]One night Joseph had a dream and promptly reported the details to his brothers, causing them to hate him even more. [6]"Listen to this dream," he announced. [7]"We were out in the field tying up bundles of grain. My bundle stood up, and then your bundles all gathered around and bowed low before it!"

I SPEAK carefully to those who hate me. (37:5)

[8]"So you are going to be our king, are you?" his brothers taunted. And they hated him all the more for his dream and what he had said.

[9]Then Joseph had another dream and told his brothers about it. "Listen to this dream," he said. "The sun, moon, and eleven stars bowed low before me!"

[10]This time he told his father as well as his brothers, and his father rebuked him. "What do you mean?" his father asked. "Will your mother, your brothers, and I actually come and bow before you?" [11]But while his brothers were jealous of Joseph, his father gave it some thought and wondered what it all meant.

[12]Soon after this, Joseph's brothers went to pasture their father's flocks at Shechem. [13]When they had been gone for some time, Jacob said to Joseph, "Your brothers are over at Shechem with the flocks. I'm going to send you to them."

"I'm ready to go," Joseph replied.

[14]"Go and see how your brothers and the flocks are getting along," Jacob said. "Then come back and bring me word." So Jacob sent him on his way, and Joseph traveled to Shechem from his home in the valley of Hebron.

[15]When he arrived there, a man noticed him wandering around the countryside. "What are you looking for?" he asked.

36:37 Hebrew *the river.*   36:39 As in some Hebrew manuscripts, Samaritan Pentateuch, and Syriac version (see also 1 Chr 1:50); most Hebrew manuscripts read *Hadar.*   37:3a Hebrew *Israel*; also in 37:13.
37:3b Traditionally rendered *a coat of many colors.* The exact meaning of the Hebrew is uncertain.

¹⁶"For my brothers and their flocks," Joseph replied. "Have you seen them?"

¹⁷"Yes," the man told him, "but they are no longer here. I heard your brothers say they were going to Dothan." So Joseph followed his brothers to Dothan and found them there.

Joseph Sold into Slavery

¹⁸When Joseph's brothers saw him coming, they recognized him in the distance and made plans to kill him. ¹⁹"Here comes that dreamer!" they exclaimed. ²⁰"Come on, let's kill him and throw him into a deep pit. We can tell our father that a wild animal has eaten him. Then we'll see what becomes of all his dreams!"

²¹But Reuben came to Joseph's rescue. "Let's not kill him," he said. ²²"Why should we shed his blood? Let's just throw him alive into this pit here. That way he will die without our having to touch him." Reuben was secretly planning to help Joseph escape, and then he would bring him back to his father.

²³So when Joseph arrived, they pulled off his beautiful robe ²⁴and threw him into the pit. This pit was normally used to store water, but it was empty at the time. ²⁵Then, just as they were sitting down to eat, they noticed a caravan of camels in the distance coming toward them. It was a group of Ishmaelite traders taking spices, balm, and myrrh from Gilead to Egypt.

²⁶Judah said to the others, "What can we gain by killing our brother? That would just give us a guilty conscience. ²⁷Let's sell Joseph to those Ishmaelite traders. Let's not be responsible for his death; after all, he is our brother!" And his brothers agreed. ²⁸So when the traders* came by, his brothers pulled Joseph out of the pit and sold him for twenty pieces* of silver, and the Ishmaelite traders took him along to Egypt.

²⁹Some time later, Reuben returned to get Joseph out of the pit. When he discovered that Joseph was missing, he tore his clothes in anguish and frustration. ³⁰Then he went back to his brothers and lamented, "The boy is gone! What can I do now?"

³¹Then Joseph's brothers killed a goat and dipped the robe in its blood. ³²They took the beautiful robe to their father and asked him to identify it. "We found this in the field," they told him. "It's Joseph's robe, isn't it?"

³³Their father recognized it at once. "Yes," he said, "it is my son's robe. A wild animal has attacked and eaten him. Surely Joseph has been torn in pieces!" ³⁴Then Jacob tore his clothes and put on sackcloth. He mourned deeply for his son for many days. ³⁵His family all tried to comfort him, but it was no use. "I will die in mourning for my son," he would say, and then begin to weep.

³⁶Meanwhile, in Egypt, the traders sold Joseph to Potiphar, an officer of Pharaoh, the king of Egypt. Potiphar was captain of the palace guard.

CHAPTER 38

Judah and Tamar

About this time, Judah left home and moved to Adullam, where he visited a man named Hirah. ²There he met a Canaanite woman, the daughter of Shua, and he married her. ³She became pregnant and had a son, and Judah named the boy Er. ⁴Then Judah's wife had another son, and she named him Onan. ⁵And when she had a third son, she named him Shelah. At the time of Shelah's birth, they were living at Kezib.

⁶When his oldest son, Er, grew up, Judah arranged his marriage to a young woman named Tamar. ⁷But Er was a wicked man in the LORD's sight, so the LORD took his life. ⁸Then Judah said to Er's brother Onan, "You must marry Tamar, as our law requires of the brother of a man who has died. Her first son from you will be your brother's heir."

I NEVER PLOT violence against others. (37:18)

I RESCUE people, including those I dislike, from the violence planned by others. (37:21)

I AM LOYAL to my siblings. (37:26)

I DO NOT COVER UP my sin with deceit. (37:31)

I DO NOT CAUSE grief to my parents by hurting one of my siblings. (37:34)

I RECOGNIZE God may end the life of a wicked person. (38:7)

37:28a Hebrew *Midianites*; also in 37:36.   37:28b Hebrew *20 shekels*, about 8 ounces or 228 grams in weight.

⁹But Onan was not willing to have a child who would not be his own heir. So whenever he had intercourse with Tamar, he spilled the semen on the ground to keep her from having a baby who would belong to his brother. ¹⁰But the LORD considered it a wicked thing for Onan to deny a child to his dead brother. So the LORD took Onan's life, too.

¹¹Then Judah told Tamar, his daughter-in-law, not to marry again at that time but to return to her parents' home. She was to remain a widow until his youngest son, Shelah, was old enough to marry her. (But Judah didn't really intend to do this because he was afraid Shelah would also die, like his two brothers.) So Tamar went home to her parents.

¹²In the course of time Judah's wife died. After the time of mourning was over, Judah and his friend Hirah the Adullamite went to Timnah to supervise the shearing of his sheep. ¹³Someone told Tamar that her father-in-law had left for the sheep-shearing at Timnah. ¹⁴Tamar was aware that Shelah had grown up, but they had not called her to come and marry him. So she changed out of her widow's clothing and covered herself with a veil to disguise herself. Then she sat beside the road at the entrance to the village of Enaim, which is on the way to Timnah. ¹⁵Judah noticed her as he went by and thought she was a prostitute, since her face was veiled. ¹⁶So he stopped and propositioned her to sleep with him, not realizing that she was his own daughter-in-law.

"How much will you pay me?" Tamar asked.

¹⁷"I'll send you a young goat from my flock," Judah promised.

"What pledge will you give me so I can be sure you will send it?" she asked.

¹⁸"Well, what do you want?" he inquired.

She replied, "I want your identification seal, your cord, and the walking stick you are carrying." So Judah gave these items to her. She then let him sleep with her, and she became pregnant. ¹⁹Afterward she went home, took off her veil, and put on her widow's clothing as usual.

²⁰Judah asked his friend Hirah the Adullamite to take the young goat back to her and to pick up the pledges he had given her, but Hirah couldn't find her. ²¹So he asked the men who lived there, "Where can I find the prostitute* who was sitting beside the road at the entrance to the village?"

"We've never had a prostitute here," they replied. ²²So Hirah returned to Judah and told him that he couldn't find her anywhere and that the men of the village had claimed they didn't have a prostitute there.

²³"Then let her keep the pledges!" Judah exclaimed. "We tried our best to send her the goat. We'd be the laughingstock of the village if we went back again."

²⁴About three months later, word reached Judah that Tamar, his daughter-in-law, was pregnant as a result of prostitution. "Bring her out and burn her!" Judah shouted.

²⁵But as they were taking her out to kill her, she sent this message to her father-in-law: "The man who owns this identification seal and walking stick is the father of my child. Do you recognize them?"

²⁶Judah admitted that they were his and said, "She is more in the right than I am, because I didn't keep my promise to let her marry my son Shelah." But Judah never slept with Tamar again.

²⁷In due season the time of Tamar's delivery arrived, and she had twin sons. ²⁸As they were being born, one of them reached out his hand, and the midwife tied a scarlet thread around the wrist of the child who appeared first, saying, "This one came out first." ²⁹But then he drew back his hand, and the other baby was actually the first to be born. "What!" the midwife exclaimed. "How did you break out first?" And ever after, he was called Perez.* ³⁰Then the baby with the scarlet thread on his wrist was born, and he was named Zerah.*

I DO NOT USE deceit to get what I deserve. (38:14)

I ABHOR the thought of using prostitution to meet my sexual needs. (38:16)

I DO NOT USE sexual immorality to conceive children. (38:18)

I ADMIT when I am wrong. (38:26)

38:21 Hebrew *shrine prostitute;* also in 38:21b, 22.   38:29 *Perez* means "breaking out."   38:30 *Zerah* means "scarlet" or "brightness."

CHAPTER 39

Joseph in Potiphar's House

Now when Joseph arrived in Egypt with the Ishmaelite traders, he was purchased by Potiphar, a member of the personal staff of Pharaoh, the king of Egypt. Potiphar was the captain of the palace guard. ²The LORD was with Joseph and blessed him greatly as he served in the home of his Egyptian master. ³Potiphar noticed this and realized that the LORD was with Joseph, giving him success in everything he did. ⁴So Joseph naturally became quite a favorite with him. Potiphar soon put Joseph in charge of his entire household and entrusted him with all his business dealings. ⁵From the day Joseph was put in charge, the LORD began to bless Potiphar for Joseph's sake. All his household affairs began to run smoothly, and his crops and livestock flourished. ⁶So Potiphar gave Joseph complete administrative responsibility over everything he owned. With Joseph there, he didn't have a worry in the world, except to decide what he wanted to eat!

Now Joseph was a very handsome and well-built young man. ⁷And about this time, Potiphar's wife began to desire him and invited him to sleep with her. ⁸But Joseph refused. "Look," he told her, "my master trusts me with everything in his entire household. ⁹No one here has more authority than I do! He has held back nothing from me except you, because you are his wife. How could I ever do such a wicked thing? It would be a great sin against God."

¹⁰She kept putting pressure on him day after day, but he refused to sleep with her, and he kept out of her way as much as possible. ¹¹One day, however, no one else was around when he was doing his work inside the house. ¹²She came and grabbed him by his shirt, demanding, "Sleep with me!" Joseph tore himself away, but as he did, his shirt came off. She was left holding it as he ran from the house.

¹³When she saw that she had his shirt and that he had fled, ¹⁴she began screaming. Soon all the men around the place came running. "My husband has brought this Hebrew slave here to insult us!" she sobbed. "He tried to rape me, but I screamed. ¹⁵When he heard my loud cries, he ran and left his shirt behind with me."

¹⁶She kept the shirt with her, and when her husband came home that night, ¹⁷she told him her story. "That Hebrew slave you've had around here tried to make a fool of me," she said. ¹⁸"I was saved only by my screams. He ran out, leaving his shirt behind!"

Joseph Put in Prison

¹⁹After hearing his wife's story, Potiphar was furious! ²⁰He took Joseph and threw him into the prison where the king's prisoners were held. ²¹But the LORD was with Joseph there, too, and he granted Joseph favor with the chief jailer. ²²Before long, the jailer put Joseph in charge of all the other prisoners and over everything that happened in the prison. ²³The chief jailer had no more worries after that, because Joseph took care of everything. The LORD was with him, making everything run smoothly and successfully.

CHAPTER 40

Joseph Interprets Two Dreams

Some time later, Pharaoh's chief cup-bearer and chief baker offended him. ²Pharaoh became very angry with these officials, ³and he put them in the prison where Joseph was, in the palace of Potiphar, the captain of the guard. ⁴They remained in prison for quite some time, and Potiphar assigned Joseph to take care of them.

⁵One night the cup-bearer and the baker each had a dream, and each

---

I AM BLESSED by the Lord because he is with me. (39:2)

I AM TRUSTWORTHY in all my work. (39:6)

I AVOID anyone who pressures me to sin sexually. (39:10)

I DO everything I can to flee from sexual temptation. (39:12)

I BELIEVE the Lord is with me and will bless me, even in the most difficult situations. (39:21)

I CAN BE TRUSTED no matter what situation I am in. (39:23)

dream had its own meaning. [6]The next morning Joseph noticed the dejected look on their faces. [7]"Why do you look so worried today?" he asked.

[8]And they replied, "We both had dreams last night, but there is no one here to tell us what they mean."

"Interpreting dreams is God's business," Joseph replied. "Tell me what you saw."

[9]The cup-bearer told his dream first. "In my dream," he said, "I saw a vine in front of me. [10]It had three branches that began to bud and blossom, and soon there were clusters of ripe grapes. [11]I was holding Pharaoh's wine cup in my hand, so I took the grapes and squeezed the juice into it. Then I placed the cup in Pharaoh's hand."

[12]"I know what the dream means," Joseph said. "The three branches mean three days. [13]Within three days Pharaoh will take you out of prison and return you to your position as his chief cup-bearer. [14]And please have some pity on me when you are back in his favor. Mention me to Pharaoh, and ask him to let me out of here. [15]For I was kidnapped from my homeland, the land of the Hebrews, and now I'm here in jail, but I did nothing to deserve it."

I DO NOT HIDE the meaning of God's message. (40:12)

I ASK for help when I am in trouble. (40:14)

[16]When the chief baker saw that the first dream had such a good meaning, he told his dream to Joseph, too. "In my dream," he said, "there were three baskets of pastries on my head. [17]In the top basket were all kinds of bakery goods for Pharaoh, but the birds came and ate them."

LIKE JOSEPH

Genesis 39:2

I trust the Lord to use difficulties in my life to bring about good.

Rejected, kidnapped, falsely accused. Sentenced to prison and left to rot. The outline of the script for Joseph's life sounds depressing, an almost sure formula for developing a bitter spirit toward God and others.

Instead, Joseph emerges above his circumstances, confident in God's purposes and able to forgive those who had hurt him most. Amazingly, even in the worst of times, he never gives up on life. He never forgets God's promises. He never stops trusting God.

What hurts and betrayals have you suffered? How have other people hurt you deeply? Joseph's life demonstrates the fact that nothing can separate us from God's love (Romans 8:38-39). Through the triumph of Jesus Christ our Lord, we, like Joseph (Genesis 37:5-11), have a vision of present spiritual blessings and future triumph (Romans 8:18; Colossians 3:1-4).

Like Joseph, we can remain steadfastly confident that whatever evil Satan or someone else may plot against us (Genesis 50:19-20), God will turn it around to bring good into our life and the lives of others (Romans 8:28).

You and I may have to wait out extremely difficult circumstances, but, like Joseph, we can always trust the Lord our God. To read more about Joseph's steadfast faith in God, see Psalm 105:17-22; Acts 7:9-14; and Hebrews 11:22.

○ *Today's Scripture reading is Genesis 39, 41, 43, and 45.*

---

[18]"I'll tell you what it means," Joseph told him. "The three baskets mean three days. [19]Three days from now Pharaoh will cut off your head and impale your body on a pole. Then birds will come and peck away at your flesh."

[20]Pharaoh's birthday came three days later, and he gave a banquet for all his officials and household staff. He sent for his chief cup-bearer and chief baker, and they were brought to him from the prison. [21]He then restored the chief cup-bearer to his former position, [22]but he sentenced the chief baker to be impaled on a pole, just as Joseph had predicted. [23]Pharaoh's cup-bearer, however, promptly forgot all about Joseph, never giving him another thought.

I DECLARE God's message honestly, even when it is unpleasant. (40:18)

I REMEMBER to help those who have helped me. (40:23)

CHAPTER **41**

Pharaoh's Dreams

Two years later, Pharaoh dreamed that he was standing on the bank of the Nile River. ²In his dream, seven fat, healthy-looking cows suddenly came up out of the river and began grazing along its bank. ³Then seven other cows came up from the river, but these were very ugly and gaunt. These cows went over and stood beside the fat cows. ⁴Then the thin, ugly cows ate the fat ones! At this point in the dream, Pharaoh woke up.

⁵Soon he fell asleep again and had a second dream. This time he saw seven heads of grain on one stalk, with every kernel well formed and plump. ⁶Then suddenly, seven more heads appeared on the stalk, but these were shriveled and withered by the east wind. ⁷And these thin heads swallowed up the seven plump, well-formed heads! Then Pharaoh woke up again and realized it was a dream.

⁸The next morning, as he thought about it, Pharaoh became very concerned as to what the dreams might mean. So he called for all the magicians and wise men of Egypt and told them about his dreams, but not one of them could suggest what they meant. ⁹Then the king's cup-bearer spoke up. "Today I have been reminded of my failure," he said. ¹⁰"Some time ago, you were angry with the chief baker and me, and you imprisoned us in the palace of the captain of the guard. ¹¹One night the chief baker and I each had a dream, and each dream had a meaning. ¹²We told the dreams to a young Hebrew man who was a servant of the captain of the guard. He told us what each of our dreams meant, ¹³and everything happened just as he said it would. I was restored to my position as cup-bearer, and the chief baker was executed and impaled on a pole."

¹⁴Pharaoh sent for Joseph at once, and he was brought hastily from the dungeon. After a quick shave and change of clothes, he went in and stood in Pharaoh's presence. ¹⁵"I had a dream last night," Pharaoh told him, "and none of these men can tell me what it means. But I have heard that you can interpret dreams, and that is why I have called for you."

¹⁶"It is beyond my power to do this," Joseph replied. "But God will tell you what it means and will set you at ease."

¹⁷So Pharaoh told him the dream. "I was standing on the bank of the Nile River," he said. ¹⁸"Suddenly, seven fat, healthy-looking cows came up out of the river and began grazing along its bank. ¹⁹But then seven other cows came up from the river. They were very thin and gaunt—in fact, I've never seen such ugly animals in all the land of Egypt. ²⁰These thin, ugly cows ate up the seven fat ones that had come out of the river first, ²¹but afterward they were still as ugly and gaunt as before! Then I woke up.

²²"A little later I had another dream. This time there were seven heads of grain on one stalk, and all seven heads were plump and full. ²³Then out of the same stalk came seven withered heads, shriveled by the east wind. ²⁴And the withered heads swallowed up the plump ones! I told these dreams to my magicians, but not one of them could tell me what they mean."

²⁵"Both dreams mean the same thing," Joseph told Pharaoh. "God was telling you what he is about to do. ²⁶The seven fat cows and the seven plump heads of grain both represent seven years of prosperity. ²⁷The seven thin, ugly cows and the seven withered heads of grain represent seven years of famine. ²⁸This will happen just as I have described it, for God has shown you what he is about to do. ²⁹The next seven years will be a period of great prosperity throughout the land of Egypt. ³⁰But afterward there will be seven years of famine so great that all the prosperity will be forgotten and wiped out. Famine will destroy the land. ³¹This famine will be so terrible that even the memory of the good years will be erased. ³²As for having the dream twice, it means

I SEEK the counsel of others when I am confused or concerned. (41:8)

I ADMIT my shortcomings. (41:9)

that the matter has been decreed by God and that he will make these events happen soon.

[33]"My suggestion is that you find the wisest man in Egypt and put him in charge of a nationwide program. [34]Let Pharaoh appoint officials over the land, and let them collect one-fifth of all the crops during the seven good years. [35]Have them gather all the food and grain of these good years into the royal storehouses, and store it away so there will be food in the cities. [36]That way there will be enough to eat when the seven years of famine come. Otherwise disaster will surely strike the land, and all the people will die."

Joseph Made Ruler of Egypt

[37]Joseph's suggestions were well received by Pharaoh and his advisers. [38]As they discussed who should be appointed for the job, Pharaoh said, "Who could do it better than Joseph? For he is a man who is obviously filled with the spirit of God." [39]Turning to Joseph, Pharaoh said, "Since God has revealed the meaning of the dreams to you, you are the wisest man in the land! [40]I hereby appoint you to direct this project. You will manage my household and organize all my people. Only I will have a rank higher than yours."

[41]And Pharaoh said to Joseph, "I hereby put you in charge of the entire land of Egypt." [42]Then Pharaoh placed his own signet ring on Joseph's finger as a symbol of his authority. He dressed him in beautiful clothing and placed the royal gold chain about his neck. [43]Pharaoh also gave Joseph the chariot of his second-in-command, and wherever he went the command was shouted, "Kneel down!" So Joseph was put in charge of all Egypt. [44]And Pharaoh said to Joseph, "I am the king, but no one will move a hand or a foot in the entire land of Egypt without your approval."

[45]Pharaoh renamed him Zaphenath-paneah* and gave him a wife—a young woman named Asenath, the daughter of Potiphera, priest of Heliopolis.* So Joseph took charge of the entire land of Egypt. [46]He was thirty years old when he entered the service of Pharaoh, the king of Egypt. And when Joseph left Pharaoh's presence, he made a tour of inspection throughout the land.

[47]And sure enough, for the next seven years there were bumper crops everywhere. [48]During those years, Joseph took a portion of all the crops grown in Egypt and stored them for the government in nearby cities. [49]After seven years, the granaries were filled to overflowing. There was so much grain, like sand on the seashore, that the people could not keep track of the amount.

[50]During this time, before the arrival of the first of the famine years, two sons were born to Joseph and his wife, Asenath, the daughter of Potiphera, priest of Heliopolis. [51]Joseph named his older son Manasseh,* for he said, "God has made me forget all my troubles and the family of my father." [52]Joseph named his second son Ephraim,* for he said, "God has made me fruitful in this land of my suffering."

[53]At last the seven years of plenty came to an end. [54]Then the seven years of famine began, just as Joseph had predicted. There were crop failures in all the surrounding countries, too, but in Egypt there was plenty of grain in the storehouses. [55]Throughout the land of Egypt the people began to starve. They pleaded with Pharaoh for food, and he told them, "Go to Joseph and do whatever he tells you." [56]So with severe famine everywhere in the land, Joseph opened up the storehouses and sold grain to the Egyptians. [57]And people from surrounding lands also came to Egypt to buy grain from Joseph because the famine was severe throughout the world.

I PREPARE for the future. (41:33)

I CHOOSE wise people for positions of responsibility. (41:38)

I BELIEVE God fulfilled the dreams he gave Joseph of becoming a ruler. (41:41)

I PREPARE for the future so that I can better care for others. (41:47)

I TAKE comfort in the birth of my children. (41:50)

I CARE for others during times of disaster. (41:56)

41:45a *Zaphenath-paneah* probably means "God speaks and lives."   41:45b Hebrew *of On;* also in 41:50. 41:51 *Manasseh* sounds like a Hebrew term that means "causing to forget."   41:52 *Ephraim* sounds like a Hebrew term that means "fruitful."

CHAPTER 42

Joseph's Brothers Go to Egypt

When Jacob heard that there was grain available in Egypt, he said to his sons, "Why are you standing around looking at one another? ²I have heard there is grain in Egypt. Go down and buy some for us before we all starve to death." ³So Joseph's ten older brothers went down to Egypt to buy grain. ⁴Jacob wouldn't let Joseph's younger brother, Benjamin, go with them, however, for fear some harm might come to him. ⁵So Jacob's* sons arrived in Egypt along with others to buy food, for the famine had reached Canaan as well.

⁶Since Joseph was governor of all Egypt and in charge of the sale of the grain, it was to him that his brothers came. They bowed low before him, with their faces to the ground. ⁷Joseph recognized them instantly, but he pretended to be a stranger. "Where are you from?" he demanded roughly.

"From the land of Canaan," they replied. "We have come to buy grain."

⁸Joseph's brothers didn't recognize him, but Joseph recognized them. ⁹And he remembered the dreams he had had many years before. He said to them, "You are spies! You have come to see how vulnerable our land has become."

¹⁰"No, my lord!" they exclaimed. "We have come to buy food. ¹¹We are all brothers and honest men, sir! We are not spies!"

¹²"Yes, you are!" he insisted. "You have come to discover how vulnerable the famine has made us."

¹³"Sir," they said, "there are twelve of us brothers, and our father is in the land of Canaan. Our youngest brother is there with our father, and one of our brothers is no longer with us."

¹⁴But Joseph insisted, "As I said, you are spies! ¹⁵This is how I will test your story. I swear by the life of Pharaoh that you will not leave Egypt unless your youngest brother comes here. ¹⁶One of you go and get your brother! I'll keep the rest of you here, bound in prison. Then we'll find out whether or not your story is true. If it turns out that you don't have a younger brother, then I'll know you are spies."

¹⁷So he put them all in prison for three days. ¹⁸On the third day Joseph said to them, "I am a God-fearing man. If you do as I say, you will live. ¹⁹We'll see how honorable you really are. Only one of you will remain in the prison. The rest of you may go on home with grain for your families. ²⁰But bring your youngest brother back to me. In this way, I will know whether or not you are telling me the truth. If you are, I will spare you." To this they agreed.

²¹Speaking among themselves, they said, "This has all happened because of what we did to Joseph long ago. We saw his terror and anguish and heard his pleadings, but we wouldn't listen. That's why this trouble has come upon us."

²²"Didn't I tell you not to do it?" Reuben asked. "But you wouldn't listen. And now we are going to die because we murdered him."

²³Of course, they didn't know that Joseph understood them as he was standing there, for he had been speaking to them through an interpreter. ²⁴Now he left the room and found a place where he could weep. Returning, he talked some more with them. He then chose Simeon from among them and had him tied up right before their eyes.

²⁵Joseph then ordered his servants to fill the men's sacks with grain, but he also gave secret instructions to return each brother's payment at the top of his sack. He also gave them provisions for their journey. ²⁶So they loaded up their donkeys with the grain and started for home.

²⁷But when they stopped for the night and one of them opened his sack to get some grain to feed the donkeys, he found his money in the sack.

I BELIEVE God fulfilled the dreams he gave Joseph about ruling over his brothers. (42:6)

I WAIT to see a change in someone's life before I assume they are repentant. (42:8)

I RECOGNIZE when my difficulties are a consequence of my sin. (42:21)

I CARE deeply about others, even when I am in a position to discipline them. (42:24)

42:5 Hebrew *Israel's.*

²⁸"Look!" he exclaimed to his brothers. "My money is here in my sack!" They were filled with terror and said to each other, "What has God done to us?" ²⁹So they came to their father, Jacob, in the land of Canaan and told him all that had happened.

³⁰"The man who is ruler over the land spoke very roughly to us," they told him. "He took us for spies. ³¹But we said, 'We are honest men, not spies. ³²We are twelve brothers, sons of one father; one brother has disappeared, and the youngest is with our father in the land of Canaan.' ³³Then the man, the ruler of the land, told us, 'This is the way I will find out if you are honest men. Leave one of your brothers here with me, and take grain for your families and go on home. ³⁴But bring your youngest brother back to me. Then I will know that you are honest men and not spies. If you prove to be what you say, then I will give you back your brother, and you may come as often as you like to buy grain.' "

³⁵As they emptied out the sacks, there at the top of each one was the bag of money paid for the grain. Terror gripped them, as it did their father. ³⁶Jacob exclaimed, "You have deprived me of my children! Joseph has disappeared, Simeon is gone, and now you want to take Benjamin, too. Everything is going against me!"

³⁷Then Reuben said to his father, "You may kill my two sons if I don't bring Benjamin back to you. I'll be responsible for him."

³⁸But Jacob replied, "My son will not go down with you, for his brother Joseph is dead, and he alone is left of his mother's children. If anything should happen to him, you would bring my gray head down to the grave in deep sorrow."

CHAPTER 43

The Brothers Return to Egypt

But there was no relief from the terrible famine throughout the land. ²When the grain they had brought from Egypt was almost gone, Jacob said to his sons, "Go again and buy us a little food."

³But Judah said, "The man wasn't joking when he warned that we couldn't see him again unless Benjamin came along. ⁴If you let him come with us, we will go down and buy some food. ⁵But if you don't let Benjamin go, we may as well stay at home. Remember that the man said, 'You won't be allowed to come and see me unless your brother is with you.' "

⁶"Why did you ever tell him you had another brother?" Jacob* moaned. "Why did you have to treat me with such cruelty?"

⁷"But the man specifically asked us about our family," they replied. "He wanted to know whether our father was still living, and he asked us if we had another brother so we told him. How could we have known he would say, 'Bring me your brother'?"

⁸Judah said to his father, "Send the boy with me, and we will be on our way. Otherwise we will all die of starvation—and not only we, but you and our little ones. ⁹I personally guarantee his safety. If I don't bring him back to you, then let me bear the blame forever. ¹⁰For we could have gone and returned twice by this time if you had let him come without delay."

¹¹So their father, Jacob, finally said to them, "If it can't be avoided, then at least do this. Fill your bags with the best products of the land. Take them to the man as gifts—balm, honey, spices, myrrh, pistachio nuts, and almonds. ¹²Take double the money that you found in your sacks, as it was probably someone's mistake. ¹³Then take your brother and go back to the man. ¹⁴May God Almighty give you mercy as you go before the man, that he might release

I TAKE the necessary risks to provide for my family. (43:4)

I TAKE responsibility for the welfare of my family. (43:8)

I RETURN money that I rightfully owe. (43:12)

I LOOK to God for mercy from people in authority. (43:14)

43:6 Hebrew *Israel;* also in 43:11.

Simeon and return Benjamin. And if I must bear the anguish of their deaths, then so be it."

¹⁵So they took Benjamin and the gifts and double the money and hurried to Egypt, where they presented themselves to Joseph. ¹⁶When Joseph saw that Benjamin was with them, he said to the manager of his household, "These men will eat with me this noon. Take them inside and prepare a big feast." ¹⁷So the man did as he was told and took them to Joseph's palace.

¹⁸They were badly frightened when they saw where they were being taken. "It's because of the money returned to us in our sacks," they said. "He plans to pretend that we stole it. Then he will seize us as slaves and take our donkeys."

A Feast at Joseph's Palace

I DIRECTLY ADDRESS a situation where I appear to have done something wrong. (43:20)

¹⁹As the brothers arrived at the entrance to the palace, they went over to the man in charge of Joseph's household. ²⁰They said to him, "Sir, after our first trip to Egypt to buy food, ²¹as we were returning home, we stopped for the night and opened our sacks. The money we had used to pay for the grain was there in our sacks. Here it is; we have brought it back again. ²²We also have additional money to buy more grain. We have no idea how the money got into our sacks."

²³"Relax. Don't worry about it," the household manager told them. "Your God, the God of your ancestors, must have put it there. We collected your money all right." Then he released Simeon and brought him out to them.

²⁴The brothers were then led into the palace and given water to wash their feet and food for their donkeys. ²⁵They were told they would be eating there, so they prepared their gifts for Joseph's arrival at noon.

²⁶When Joseph came, they gave him their gifts and bowed low before him. ²⁷He asked them how they had been getting along, and then he said, "How is your father—the old man you spoke about? Is he still alive?"

²⁸"Yes," they replied. "He is alive and well." Then they bowed again before him.

²⁹Looking at his brother Benjamin, Joseph asked, "Is this your youngest brother, the one you told me about? May God be gracious to you, my son."

I AM NOT AFRAID of my emotions. (43:30)

³⁰Then Joseph made a hasty exit because he was overcome with emotion for his brother and wanted to cry. Going into his private room, he wept there. ³¹Then he washed his face and came out, keeping himself under control. "Bring on the food!" he ordered.

³²Joseph ate by himself, and his brothers were served at a separate table. The Egyptians sat at their own table because Egyptians despise Hebrews and refuse to eat with them. ³³Joseph told each of his brothers where to sit, and to their amazement, he seated them in the order of their ages, from oldest to youngest. ³⁴Their food was served to them from Joseph's own table. He gave the largest serving to Benjamin—five times as much as to any of the others. So they all feasted and drank freely with him.

CHAPTER 44

Joseph's Silver Cup

When his brothers were ready to leave, Joseph gave these instructions to the man in charge of his household: "Fill each of their sacks with as much grain as they can carry, and put each man's money back into his sack. ²Then put my personal silver cup at the top of the youngest brother's sack, along with his grain money." So the household manager did as he was told.

³The brothers were up at dawn and set out on their journey with their loaded donkeys. ⁴But when they were barely out of the city, Joseph said to his household manager, "Chase after them and stop them. Ask them, 'Why have you repaid an act of kindness with such evil? ⁵What do you mean by stealing

my master's personal silver drinking cup, which he uses to predict the future? What a wicked thing you have done!' "

⁶So the man caught up with them and spoke to them in the way he had been instructed. ⁷"What are you talking about?" the brothers responded. "What kind of people do you think we are, that you accuse us of such a terrible thing? ⁸Didn't we bring back the money we found in our sacks? Why would we steal silver or gold from your master's house? ⁹If you find his cup with any one of us, let that one die. And all the rest of us will be your master's slaves forever."

I DO NOT MAKE rash vows. (44:9)

¹⁰"Fair enough," the man replied, "except that only the one who stole it will be a slave. The rest of you may go free."

¹¹They quickly took their sacks from the backs of their donkeys and opened them. ¹²Joseph's servant began searching the oldest brother's sack, going on down the line to the youngest. The cup was found in Benjamin's sack! ¹³At this, they tore their clothing in despair, loaded the donkeys again, and returned to the city. ¹⁴Joseph was still at home when Judah and his brothers arrived, and they fell to the ground before him.

¹⁵"What were you trying to do?" Joseph demanded. "Didn't you know that a man such as I would know who stole it?"

¹⁶And Judah said, "Oh, my lord, what can we say to you? How can we plead? How can we prove our innocence? God is punishing us for our sins. My lord, we have all returned to be your slaves—we and our brother who had your cup in his sack."

¹⁷"No," Joseph said. "Only the man who stole the cup will be my slave. The rest of you may go home to your father."

Judah Speaks for His Brothers

¹⁸Then Judah stepped forward and said, "My lord, let me say just this one word to you. Be patient with me for a moment, for I know you could have me killed in an instant, as though you were Pharaoh himself.

I BOLDLY SEEK to defend and obtain mercy for my family members. (44:18)

¹⁹"You asked us, my lord, if we had a father or a brother. ²⁰We said, 'Yes, we have a father, an old man, and a child of his old age, his youngest son. His brother is dead, and he alone is left of his mother's children, and his father loves him very much.' ²¹And you said to us, 'Bring him here so I can see him.' ²²But we said to you, 'My lord, the boy cannot leave his father, for his father would die.' ²³But you told us, 'You may not see me again unless your youngest brother is with you.' ²⁴So we returned to our father and told him what you had said. ²⁵And when he said, 'Go back again and buy us a little food,' ²⁶we replied, 'We can't unless you let our youngest brother go with us. We won't be allowed to see the man in charge of the grain unless our youngest brother is with us.' ²⁷Then my father said to us, 'You know that my wife had two sons, ²⁸and that one of them went away and never returned—doubtless torn to pieces by some wild animal. I have never seen him since. ²⁹If you take away his brother from me, too, and any harm comes to him, you would bring my gray head down to the grave in deep sorrow.'

³⁰"And now, my lord, I cannot go back to my father without the boy. Our father's life is bound up in the boy's life. ³¹When he sees that the boy is not with us, our father will die. We will be responsible for bringing his gray head down to the grave in sorrow. ³²My lord, I made a pledge to my father that I would take care of the boy. I told him, 'If I don't bring him back to you, I will bear the blame forever.' ³³Please, my lord, let me stay here as a slave instead of the boy, and let the boy return with his brothers. ³⁴For how can I return to my father if the boy is not with me? I cannot bear to see what this would do to him."

I CARE about the emotional well-being of my elderly parents. (44:31)

I AM WILLING to make personal sacrifices for others. (44:33)

CHAPTER 45

Joseph Reveals His Identity

Joseph could stand it no longer. "Out, all of you!" he cried out to his attendants. He wanted to be alone with his brothers when he told them who he was. ²Then he broke down and wept aloud. His sobs could be heard throughout the palace, and the news was quickly carried to Pharaoh's palace.

³"I am Joseph!" he said to his brothers. "Is my father still alive?" But his brothers were speechless! They were stunned to realize that Joseph was standing there in front of them. ⁴"Come over here," he said. So they came closer. And he said again, "I am Joseph, your brother whom you sold into Egypt. ⁵But don't be angry with yourselves that you did this to me, for God did it. He sent me here ahead of you to preserve your lives. ⁶These two years of famine will grow to seven, during which there will be neither plowing nor harvest. ⁷God has sent me here to keep you and your families alive so that you will become a great nation. ⁸Yes, it was God who sent me here, not you! And he has made me a counselor to Pharaoh—manager of his entire household and ruler over all Egypt.

⁹"Hurry, return to my father and tell him, 'This is what your son Joseph says: God has made me master over all the land of Egypt. Come down to me right away! ¹⁰You will live in the land of Goshen so you can be near me with all your children and grandchildren, your flocks and herds, and all that you have. ¹¹I will take care of you there, for there are still five years of famine ahead of us. Otherwise you and your household will come to utter poverty.' "

¹²Then Joseph said, "You can see for yourselves, and so can my brother Benjamin, that I really am Joseph! ¹³Tell my father how I am honored here in Egypt. Tell him about everything you have seen, and bring him to me quickly." ¹⁴Weeping with joy, he embraced Benjamin, and Benjamin also began to weep. ¹⁵Then Joseph kissed each of his brothers and wept over them, and then they began talking freely with him.

Pharaoh Invites Jacob to Egypt

¹⁶The news soon reached Pharaoh: "Joseph's brothers have come!" Pharaoh was very happy to hear this and so were his officials. ¹⁷Pharaoh said to Joseph, "Tell your brothers to load their pack animals and return quickly to their homes in Canaan. ¹⁸Tell them to bring your father and all of their families, and to come here to Egypt to live. Tell them, 'Pharaoh will assign to you the very best territory in the land of Egypt. You will live off the fat of the land!' ¹⁹And tell your brothers to take wagons from Egypt to carry their wives and little ones and to bring your father here. ²⁰Don't worry about your belongings, for the best of all the land of Egypt is yours."

²¹So the sons of Jacob* did as they were told. Joseph gave them wagons, as Pharaoh had commanded, and he supplied them with provisions for the journey. ²²And he gave each of them new clothes—but to Benjamin he gave five changes of clothes and three hundred pieces* of silver! ²³He sent his father ten donkeys loaded with the good things of Egypt, and ten donkeys loaded with grain and all kinds of other food to be eaten on his journey. ²⁴So he sent his brothers off, and as they left, he called after them, "Don't quarrel along the way!" ²⁵And they left Egypt and returned to their father, Jacob, in the land of Canaan.

²⁶"Joseph is still alive!" they told him. "And he is ruler over all the land of Egypt!" Jacob was stunned at the news—he couldn't believe it. ²⁷But when they had given him Joseph's messages, and when he saw the wagons loaded with the food sent by Joseph, his spirit revived.

²⁸Then Jacob said, "It must be true! My son Joseph is alive! I will go and see him before I die."

45:21 Hebrew *Israel*; also in 45:28.   45:22 Hebrew *300 shekels*, about 7.5 pounds or 3.4 kilograms in weight.

I AM NOT AFRAID to express my emotions to those I love. (45:2)

I RELEASE others from guilt because I trust in God's plan for my life. (45:5)

I BELIEVE God has a purpose for sending me into difficult circumstances. (45:7)

I CARE for my elderly parents and family with the resources God gives me. (45:11)

I EXPRESS my love to my siblings. (45:14)

CHAPTER 46

Jacob's Journey to Egypt

So Jacob* set out for Egypt with all his possessions. And when he came to Beersheba, he offered sacrifices to the God of his father, Isaac. ²During the night God spoke to him in a vision. "Jacob! Jacob!" he called.

"Here I am," Jacob replied.

³"I am God," the voice said, "the God of your father. Do not be afraid to go down to Egypt, for I will see to it that you become a great nation there. ⁴I will go with you down to Egypt, and I will bring your descendants back again. But you will die in Egypt with Joseph at your side."

⁵So Jacob left Beersheba, and his sons brought him to Egypt. They carried their little ones and wives in the wagons Pharaoh had provided for them. ⁶They brought their livestock, too, and all the belongings they had acquired in the land of Canaan. Jacob and his entire family arrived in Egypt—⁷sons and daughters, grandsons and granddaughters—all his descendants.

⁸These are the names of the Israelites, the descendants of Jacob, who went with him to Egypt:

Reuben was Jacob's oldest son. ⁹The sons of Reuben were Hanoch, Pallu, Hezron, and Carmi.
¹⁰The sons of Simeon were Jemuel, Jamin, Ohad, Jakin, Zohar, and Shaul. (Shaul's mother was a Canaanite woman.)
¹¹The sons of Levi were Gershon, Kohath, and Merari.
¹²The sons of Judah were Er, Onan, Shelah, Perez, and Zerah. (But Er and Onan had died in the land of Canaan.) The sons of Perez were Hezron and Hamul.
¹³The sons of Issachar were Tola, Puah,* Jashub,* and Shimron.
¹⁴The sons of Zebulun were Sered, Elon, and Jahleel.

¹⁵These are the sons of Jacob who were born to Leah in Paddan-aram, along with their sister, Dinah. In all, Jacob's descendants through Leah numbered thirty-three.

¹⁶The sons of Gad were Zephon,* Haggi, Shuni, Ezbon, Eri, Arodi, and Areli.
¹⁷The sons of Asher were Imnah, Ishvah, Ishvi, and Beriah. Their sister was named Serah. Beriah's sons were Heber and Malkiel.

¹⁸These sixteen were descendants of Jacob through Zilpah, the servant given to Leah by her father, Laban.

¹⁹The sons of Jacob's wife Rachel were Joseph and Benjamin.
²⁰Joseph's sons, born in the land of Egypt, were Manasseh and Ephraim. Their mother was Asenath, daughter of Potiphera, priest of Heliopolis.*
²¹Benjamin's sons were Bela, Beker, Ashbel, Gera, Naaman, Ehi, Rosh, Muppim, Huppim, and Ard.

²²These fourteen were the descendants of Jacob and his wife Rachel.

²³The son of Dan was Hushim.
²⁴The sons of Naphtali were Jahzeel, Guni, Jezer, and Shillem.

²⁵These seven were the descendants of Jacob through Bilhah, the servant given to Rachel by her father, Laban.

²⁶So the total number of Jacob's direct descendants who went with him to Egypt, not counting his sons' wives, was sixty-six. ²⁷Joseph also had two

I REMEMBER my spiritual heritage as I worship God. (46:1)

I ANSWER God when he calls my name. (46:2)

I AM NOT AFRAID to go anywhere if it is God's plan. (46:3)

I BELIEVE God had a plan for bringing Jacob and his family to Egypt. (46:4)

46:1 Hebrew *Israel*; also in 46:30.   46:13a As in Syriac version and Samaritan Pentateuch (see also 1 Chr 7:1); Hebrew reads *Puvah*.   46:13b As in some Greek manuscripts and Samaritan Pentateuch (see also Num 26:24; 1 Chr 7:1); Hebrew reads *Iob*.   46:16 As in Greek version and Samaritan Pentateuch (see also Num 26:15); Hebrew reads *Ziphion*.   46:20 Hebrew *of On*.

sons* who had been born in Egypt. So altogether, there were seventy* members of Jacob's family in the land of Egypt.

Jacob's Family Arrives in Goshen

²⁸Jacob sent Judah on ahead to meet Joseph and get directions to the land of Goshen. And when they all arrived there, ²⁹Joseph prepared his chariot and traveled to Goshen to meet his father. As soon as Joseph arrived, he embraced his father and wept on his shoulder for a long time. ³⁰Then Jacob said to Joseph, "Now let me die, for I have seen you with my own eyes and know you are still alive."

³¹And Joseph said to his brothers and to all their households, "I'll go and tell Pharaoh that you have all come from the land of Canaan to join me. ³²And I will tell him, 'These men are shepherds and livestock breeders. They have brought with them their flocks and herds and everything they own.' ³³So when Pharaoh calls for you and asks you about your occupation, ³⁴tell him, 'We have been livestock breeders from our youth, as our ancestors have been for many generations.' When you tell him this, he will let you live here in the land of Goshen, for shepherds are despised in the land of Egypt."

CHAPTER 47

Jacob Blesses Pharaoh

So Joseph went to see Pharaoh and said, "My father and my brothers are here from Canaan. They came with all their flocks and herds and possessions, and they are now in the land of Goshen."

²Joseph took five of his brothers with him and presented them to Pharaoh. ³Pharaoh asked them, "What is your occupation?"

And they replied, "We are shepherds like our ancestors. ⁴We have come to live here in Egypt, for there is no pasture for our flocks in Canaan. The famine is very severe there. We request permission to live in the land of Goshen."

⁵And Pharaoh said to Joseph, "Now that your family has joined you here, ⁶choose any place you like for them to live. Give them the best land of Egypt—the land of Goshen will be fine. And if any of them have special skills, put them in charge of my livestock, too."

⁷Then Joseph brought his father, Jacob, and presented him to Pharaoh, and Jacob blessed Pharaoh. ⁸"How old are you?" Pharaoh asked him.

⁹Jacob replied, "I have lived for 130 hard years, but I am still not nearly as old as many of my ancestors." ¹⁰Then Jacob blessed Pharaoh again before he left.

¹¹So Joseph assigned the best land of Egypt—the land of Rameses—to his father and brothers, just as Pharaoh had commanded. ¹²And Joseph furnished food to his father and brothers in amounts appropriate to the number of their dependents.

Joseph's Leadership in the Famine

¹³Meanwhile, the famine became worse and worse, and the crops continued to fail throughout Egypt and Canaan. ¹⁴Joseph collected all the money in Egypt and Canaan in exchange for grain, and he brought the money to Pharaoh's treasure-house. ¹⁵When the people of Egypt and Canaan ran out of money, they came to Joseph crying again for food. "Our money is gone," they said, "but give us bread. Why should we die?"

¹⁶"Well, then," Joseph replied, "since your money is gone, give me your livestock. I will give you food in exchange." ¹⁷So they gave their livestock to Joseph in exchange for food. Soon all the horses, flocks, herds, and donkeys of Egypt were in Pharaoh's possession. But at least they were able to purchase food for that year.

I EXPRESS my love to my parents. (46:29)

I SPEAK UP on behalf of others. (46:31)

I ACCEPT the generosity of others. (47:5)

I BLESS those who have been kind and generous to me. (47:10)

I CONDUCT business transactions wisely and fairly. (47:14)

46:27a Greek version reads *nine sons*, probably including Joseph's grandsons through Ephraim and Manasseh (see 1 Chr 7:14-20). 46:27b Greek version reads *seventy-five*; see note on Exod 1:5.

¹⁸ The next year they came again and said, "Our money is gone, and our livestock are yours. We have nothing left but our bodies and land. ¹⁹Why should we die before your very eyes? Buy us and our land in exchange for food; we will then become servants to Pharaoh. Just give us grain so that our lives may be saved and so the land will not become empty and desolate."

²⁰So Joseph bought all the land of Egypt for Pharaoh. All the Egyptians sold him their fields because the famine was so severe, and their land then belonged to Pharaoh. ²¹Thus, all the people of Egypt became servants to Pharaoh.* ²²The only land he didn't buy was that belonging to the priests, for they were assigned food from Pharaoh and didn't need to sell their land.

²³Then Joseph said to the people, "See, I have bought you and your land for Pharaoh. I will provide you with seed, so you can plant the fields. ²⁴Then when you harvest it, a fifth of your crop will belong to Pharaoh. Keep four-fifths for yourselves, and use it to plant the next year's crop and to feed yourselves, your households, and your little ones."

²⁵"You have saved our lives!" they exclaimed. "May it please you, sir, to let us be Pharaoh's servants." ²⁶Joseph then made it a law throughout the land of Egypt—and it is still the law—that Pharaoh should receive one-fifth of all the crops grown on his land. But since Pharaoh had not taken over the priests' land, they were exempt from this payment.

²⁷So the people of Israel settled in the land of Goshen in Egypt. And before long, they began to prosper there, and their population grew rapidly. ²⁸Jacob lived for seventeen years after his arrival in Egypt, so he was 147 years old when he died. ²⁹As the time of his death drew near, he called for his son Joseph and said to him, "If you are pleased with me, swear most solemnly that you will honor this, my last request: Do not bury me in Egypt. ³⁰When I am dead, take me out of Egypt and bury me beside my ancestors." So Joseph promised that he would. ³¹"Swear that you will do it," Jacob insisted. So Joseph gave his oath, and Jacob* bowed in worship as he leaned on his staff.*

I HONOR my parents' request for burial. (47:30)

I WILL WORSHIP God to the very end of my life. (47:31)

CHAPTER 48

Jacob Blesses Manasseh and Ephraim
One day not long after this, word came to Joseph that his father was failing rapidly. So Joseph went to visit him, and he took with him his two sons, Manasseh and Ephraim. ²When Jacob heard that Joseph had arrived, he gathered his strength and sat up in bed to greet him.

³Jacob said to Joseph, "God Almighty appeared to me at Luz in the land of Canaan and blessed me. ⁴He said to me, 'I will make you a multitude of nations, and I will give this land of Canaan to you and your descendants as an everlasting possession.' ⁵Now I am adopting as my own sons these two boys of yours, Ephraim and Manasseh, who were born here in the land of Egypt before I arrived. They will inherit from me just as Reuben and Simeon will. ⁶But the children born to you in the future will be your own. The land they inherit will be within the territories of Ephraim and Manasseh. ⁷As I was returning from Paddan, Rachel died in the land of Canaan. We were still on the way, just a short distance from Ephrath (that is, Bethlehem). So with great sorrow I buried her there beside the road to Ephrath."

⁸Then Jacob* looked over at the two boys. "Are these your sons?" he asked.

⁹"Yes," Joseph told him, "these are the sons God has given me here in Egypt."

And Jacob said, "Bring them over to me, and I will bless them."

¹⁰Now Jacob was half blind because of his age and could hardly see. So Joseph brought the boys close to him, and Jacob kissed and embraced them.

I SPEAK to my children of God's promises. (48:3)

I PASS ON spiritual blessings to my grandchildren. (48:5)

47:21 As in Greek version and Samaritan Pentateuch; Hebrew reads *He moved the people into the towns throughout the land of Egypt.* 47:31a Hebrew *Israel.* 47:31b As in Greek version; Hebrew reads *bowed in worship at the head of his bed.* 48:8 Hebrew *Israel;* also in 48:10, 11, 13, 14, 21.

[11]Then Jacob said to Joseph, "I never thought I would see you again, but now God has let me see your children, too."

[12]Joseph took the boys from their grandfather's knees, and he bowed low to him. [13]Then he positioned the boys so Ephraim was at Jacob's left hand and Manasseh was at his right hand. [14]But Jacob crossed his arms as he reached out to lay his hands on the boys' heads. So his right hand was on the head of Ephraim, the younger boy, and his left hand was on the head of Manasseh, the older.

I PRAISE God for shepherding my life. (48:15)

[15]Then he blessed Joseph and said, "May God, the God before whom my grandfather Abraham and my father, Isaac, walked, the God who has been my shepherd all my life, [16]and the angel who has kept me from all harm—may he bless these boys. May they preserve my name and the names of my grandfather Abraham and my father, Isaac. And may they become a mighty nation."

[17]But Joseph was upset when he saw that his father had laid his right hand on Ephraim's head. So he lifted it to place it on Manasseh's head instead. [18]"No, Father," he said, "this one over here is older. Put your right hand on his head."

I ACCEPT God's will for my children and grandchildren. (48:19)

[19]But his father refused. "I know what I'm doing, my son," he said. "Manasseh, too, will become a great people, but his younger brother will become even greater. His descendants will become a multitude of nations!" [20]So Jacob blessed the boys that day with this blessing: "The people of Israel will use your names to bless each other. They will say, 'May God make you as prosperous as Ephraim and Manasseh.' " In this way, Jacob put Ephraim ahead of Manasseh.

I TRUST God to fulfill his plans for and promises to my family. (48:21)

[21]Then Jacob said to Joseph, "I am about to die, but God will be with you and will bring you again to Canaan, the land of your ancestors. [22]And I give you an extra portion* beyond what I have given your brothers—the portion that I took from the Amorites with my sword and bow."

CHAPTER 49

Jacob Blesses His Sons

Then Jacob called together all his sons and said, "Gather around me, and I will tell you what is going to happen to you in the days to come.

I BELIEVE God gave Jacob insight to prophesy about the future of his descendants. (49:1)

[2]"Come and listen, O sons of Jacob;
    listen to Israel, your father.

[3]"Reuben, you are my oldest son,
    the child of my vigorous youth.
You are first on the list in rank and honor.
[4]But you are as unruly as the waves of the sea,
    and you will be first no longer.
For you slept with one of my wives;
    you dishonored me in my own bed.

I FORFEIT a position of privilege or honor when I sin. (49:4)

[5]"Simeon and Levi are two of a kind—
    men of violence.
[6]O my soul, stay away from them.
    May I never be a party to their wicked plans.
For in their anger they murdered men,
    and they crippled oxen just for sport.
[7]Cursed be their anger, for it is fierce;
    cursed be their wrath, for it is cruel.
Therefore, I will scatter their descendants
    throughout the nation of Israel.

I DO NOT CONDONE violence or cruelty. (49:6)

48:22 Or *give you the ridge of land.* The meaning of the Hebrew is uncertain.

⁸ "Judah, your brothers will praise you.
  You will defeat your enemies.
  All your relatives will bow before you.
⁹ Judah is a young lion
    that has finished eating its prey.
  Like a lion he crouches and lies down;
    like a lioness—who will dare to rouse him?
¹⁰ The scepter will not depart from Judah,
    nor the ruler's staff from his descendants,
  until the coming of the one to whom it belongs,*
    the one whom all nations will obey.
¹¹ He ties his foal to a grapevine,
    the colt of his donkey to a choice vine.
  He washes his clothes in wine
    because his harvest is so plentiful.
¹² His eyes are darker than wine,
    and his teeth are whiter than milk.

¹³ "Zebulun will settle on the shores of the sea
    and will be a harbor for ships;
    his borders will extend to Sidon.

¹⁴ "Issachar is a strong beast of burden,
    resting among the sheepfolds.*
¹⁵ When he sees how good the countryside is,
    how pleasant the land,
  he will bend his shoulder to the task
    and submit to forced labor.

¹⁶ "Dan will govern his people
    like any other tribe in Israel.
¹⁷ He will be a snake beside the road,
    a poisonous viper along the path,
  that bites the horse's heels
    so the rider is thrown off.
¹⁸ I trust in you for salvation, O LORD!

¹⁹ "Gad will be plundered by marauding bands,
    but he will turn and plunder them.

²⁰ "Asher will produce rich foods,
    food fit for kings.

²¹ "Naphtali is a deer let loose,
    producing magnificent fawns.

²² "Joseph is a fruitful tree,
    a fruitful tree beside a fountain.
  His branches reach over the wall.
²³ He has been attacked by archers,
    who shot at him and harassed him.
²⁴ But his bow remained strong,
    and his arms were strengthened
  by the Mighty One of Jacob,
    the Shepherd, the Rock of Israel.
²⁵ May the God of your ancestors help you;
    may the Almighty bless you

I BELIEVE God fulfilled his promise to bring forth a ruler— ultimately Jesus—from the tribe of Judah. (49:10)

I TRUST in God's salvation. (49:18)

I WILL BLESS my children before I die. (49:25)

49:10 Or until tribute is brought to him and the peoples obey; traditionally rendered until Shiloh comes.   49:14 Or saddlebags, or hearths.

with the blessings of the heavens above,
    blessings of the earth beneath,
    and blessings of the breasts and womb.
[26] May the blessings of your ancestors
    be greater than the blessings of the eternal mountains,
    reaching to the utmost bounds of the everlasting hills.
These blessings will fall on the head of Joseph,
    who is a prince among his brothers.

[27] "Benjamin is a wolf that prowls.
    He devours his enemies in the morning,
    and in the evening he divides the plunder."

[28] These are the twelve tribes of Israel, and these are the blessings with which Jacob* blessed his twelve sons. Each received a blessing that was appropriate to him.

Jacob's Death and Burial

[29] Then Jacob told them, "Soon I will die. Bury me with my father and grandfather in the cave in Ephron's field. [30] This is the cave in the field of Machpelah, near Mamre in Canaan, which Abraham bought from Ephron the Hittite for a permanent burial place. [31] There Abraham and his wife Sarah are buried. There Isaac and his wife, Rebekah, are buried. And there I buried Leah. [32] It is the cave that my grandfather Abraham bought from the Hittites." [33] Then when Jacob had finished this charge to his sons, he lay back in the bed, breathed his last, and died.

CHAPTER 50

Joseph threw himself on his father and wept over him and kissed him. [2] Then Joseph told his morticians to embalm the body. [3] The embalming process took forty days, and there was a period of national mourning for seventy days. [4] When the period of mourning was over, Joseph approached Pharaoh's advisers and asked them to speak to Pharaoh on his behalf. [5] He told them, "Tell Pharaoh that my father made me swear an oath. He said to me, 'I am about to die; take my body back to the land of Canaan, and bury me in our family's burial cave.' Now I need to go and bury my father. After his burial is complete, I will return without delay."

[6] Pharaoh agreed to Joseph's request. "Go and bury your father, as you promised," he said. [7] So Joseph went, with a great number of Pharaoh's counselors and advisers—all the senior officers of Egypt. [8] Joseph also took his brothers and the entire household of Jacob. But they left their little children and flocks and herds in the land of Goshen. [9] So a great number of chariots, cavalry, and people accompanied Joseph.

[10] When they arrived at the threshing floor of Atad, near the Jordan River, they held a very great and solemn funeral, with a seven-day period of mourning for Joseph's father. [11] The local residents, the Canaanites, renamed the place Abel-mizraim,* for they said, "This is a place of very deep mourning for these Egyptians." [12] So Jacob's sons did as he had commanded them. [13] They carried his body to the land of Canaan and buried it there in the cave of Machpelah. This is the cave that Abraham had bought for a permanent burial place in the field of Ephron the Hittite, near Mamre.

Joseph Reassures His Brothers

[14] Then Joseph returned to Egypt with his brothers and all who had accompanied him to his father's funeral. [15] But now that their father was dead, Joseph's brothers became afraid. "Now Joseph will pay us back for all

49:28 Hebrew *Israel.*   50:11 *Abel-mizraim* means "mourning of the Egyptians."

the evil we did to him," they said. [16]So they sent this message to Joseph: "Before your father died, he instructed us [17]to say to you: 'Forgive your brothers for the great evil they did to you.' So we, the servants of the God of your father, beg you to forgive us." When Joseph received the message, he broke down and wept. [18]Then his brothers came and bowed low before him. "We are your slaves," they said.

[19]But Joseph told them, "Don't be afraid of me. Am I God, to judge and punish you? [20]As far as I am concerned, God turned into good what you meant for evil. He brought me to the high position I have today so I could save the lives of many people. [21]No, don't be afraid. Indeed, I myself will take care of you and your families." And he spoke very kindly to them, reassuring them.

The Death of Joseph
[22]So Joseph and his brothers and their families continued to live in Egypt. Joseph was 110 years old when he died. [23]He lived to see three generations of descendants of his son Ephraim and the children of Manasseh's son Makir, who were treated as if they were his own.

[24]"Soon I will die," Joseph told his brothers, "but God will surely come for you, to lead you out of this land of Egypt. He will bring you back to the land he vowed to give to the descendants of Abraham, Isaac, and Jacob."

[25]Then Joseph made the sons of Israel swear an oath, and he said, "When God comes to lead us back to Canaan, you must take my body back with you." [26]So Joseph died at the age of 110. They embalmed him, and his body was placed in a coffin in Egypt.

I ACCEPT forgiveness when it is offered. (50:17)

I TRUST God to turn into good what others meant for evil (Romans 8:28). (50:20)

I REASSURE others of my forgiveness. (50:21)

I BELIEVE God eventually brought the family of Israel back to Canaan, as he promised. (50:24)

EXODUS

THIS SECOND BOOK of the Bible reveals the amazing lengths to which God will go to save his less-than-perfect people.

The great prophet Moses describes how the emerging nation of Israel was enslaved by the Egyptians (1:1-22). He then dramatically details how God called him to deliver the Israelites (2:1-6:30), how the Lord sent a series of terrible plagues upon the Egyptians (7:1-12:30), and how the Israelites escaped from bondage (12:31-15:21).

Moses also records how the Israelites began complaining against the Lord (15:22-17:7) and how Joshua and others helped lead the people (17:8-18:27). Moses then describes how he received the Ten Commandments and other laws of the Lord (19:1-31:18), how the people quickly began to rebel (32:1-33:23), how God renewed his covenant with his chosen people (34:1-35), and then how the Israelites willingly constructed the Tabernacle according to the Lord's specific instructions (35:1-40:38).

Famous passages in Exodus include

- ◯ The Israelites' enslavement by the Egyptians (1:1-22)
- ◯ The birth of Moses (2:1-25)
- ◯ Moses and the burning bush (3:2-10)
- ◯ God reveals his covenant name (3:14-15)
- ◯ Moses and Aaron first confront Pharaoh (5:1-5)
- ◯ First Passover is observed (12:1-28)
- ◯ The Israelites flee from Egypt (12:37-38)
- ◯ God leads them by fire and cloud (13:21-22)
- ◯ God splits the Red Sea (14:15-22)
- ◯ Ten Commandments (20:1-17)
- ◯ The Israelites worship an idol and repent (32:1-33:6)
- ◯ God reveals his glory to Moses (33:17-34:8)
- ◯ God's glory fills the Tabernacle (40:34-35)

CHAPTER 1

The Israelites in Egypt

These are the sons of Jacob* who went with their father to Egypt, each with his family: ²Reuben, Simeon, Levi, Judah, ³Issachar, Zebulun, Benjamin, ⁴Dan, Naphtali, Gad, and Asher. ⁵Joseph was already down in Egypt. In all, Jacob had seventy* direct descendants.

⁶In time, Joseph and each of his brothers died, ending that generation. ⁷But their descendants had many children and grandchildren. In fact, they multiplied so quickly that they soon filled the land. ⁸Then a new king came to the throne of Egypt who knew nothing about Joseph or what he had done. ⁹He told his people, "These Israelites are becoming a threat to us because there

See Jacob's profile (page 43) at Genesis 32:9.

I BELIEVE children are a blessing from God. (1:7)

1:1 Hebrew *Israel*.   1:5 Dead Sea Scrolls and Greek version read *seventy-five;* see notes on Gen 46:27.

are so many of them. [10]We must find a way to put an end to this. If we don't and if war breaks out, they will join our enemies and fight against us. Then they will escape from the country."

[11]So the Egyptians made the Israelites their slaves and put brutal slave drivers over them, hoping to wear them down under heavy burdens. They forced them to build the cities of Pithom and Rameses as supply centers for the king. [12]But the more the Egyptians oppressed them, the more quickly the Israelites multiplied! The Egyptians soon became alarmed [13]and decided to make their slavery more bitter still. [14]They were ruthless with the Israelites, forcing them to make bricks and mortar and to work long hours in the fields.

[15]Then Pharaoh, the king of Egypt, gave this order to the Hebrew midwives, Shiphrah and Puah: [16]"When you help the Hebrew women give birth, kill all the boys as soon as they are born. Allow only the baby girls to live." [17]But because the midwives feared God, they refused to obey the king and allowed the boys to live, too.

[18]Then the king called for the midwives. "Why have you done this?" he demanded. "Why have you allowed the boys to live?"

[19]"Sir," they told him, "the Hebrew women are very strong. They have their babies so quickly that we cannot get there in time! They are not slow in giving birth like Egyptian women."

[20]So God blessed the midwives, and the Israelites continued to multiply, growing more and more powerful. [21]And because the midwives feared God, he gave them families of their own.

[22]Then Pharaoh gave this order to all his people: "Throw all the newborn Israelite boys into the Nile River. But you may spare the baby girls."

CHAPTER 2

The Birth of Moses

During this time, a man and woman from the tribe of Levi got married. [2]The woman became pregnant and gave birth to a son. She saw what a beautiful baby he was and kept him hidden for three months. [3]But when she could no longer hide him, she got a little basket made of papyrus reeds and waterproofed it with tar and pitch. She put the baby in the basket and laid it among the reeds along the edge of the Nile River. [4]The baby's sister then stood at a distance, watching to see what would happen to him.

[5]Soon after this, one of Pharaoh's daughters came down to bathe in the river, and her servant girls walked along the riverbank. When the princess saw the little basket among the reeds, she told one of her servant girls to get it for her. [6]As the princess opened it, she found the baby boy. His helpless cries touched her heart. "He must be one of the Hebrew children," she said.

[7]Then the baby's sister approached the princess. "Should I go and find one of the Hebrew women to nurse the baby for you?" she asked.

[8]"Yes, do!" the princess replied. So the girl rushed home and called the baby's mother.

[9]"Take this child home and nurse him for me," the princess told her. "I will pay you for your help." So the baby's mother took her baby home and nursed him.

[10]Later, when he was older, the child's mother brought him back to the princess, who adopted him as her son. The princess named him Moses,* for she said, "I drew him out of the water."

Moses Escapes to Midian

[11]Many years later, when Moses had grown up, he went out to visit his people, the Israelites, and he saw how hard they were forced to work. During his visit, he saw an Egyptian beating one of the Hebrew slaves. [12]After looking

I BELIEVE God often allows believers to prosper under persecution. (1:12)

I FEAR God more than any government official. (1:17)

I FIND a way to obey God, no matter what obstacles or risks. (1:19)

I OBEY God even at the risk of my reputation or career. (1:20)

I WILL DO anything to protect my children. (2:3)

I AM BOLD in seeking the welfare of the children in my care. (2:7)

I DO NOT TAKE justice into my own hands. (2:12)

2:10 *Moses* sounds like a Hebrew term that means "to draw out."

around to make sure no one was watching, Moses killed the Egyptian and buried him in the sand. ¹³The next day, as Moses was out visiting his people again, he saw two Hebrew men fighting. "What are you doing, hitting your neighbor like that?" Moses said to the one in the wrong.

¹⁴"Who do you think you are?" the man replied. "Who appointed you to be our prince and judge? Do you plan to kill me as you killed that Egyptian yesterday?"

Moses was badly frightened because he realized that everyone knew what he had done. ¹⁵And sure enough, when Pharaoh heard about it, he gave orders to have Moses arrested and killed. But Moses fled from Pharaoh and escaped to the land of Midian.

LIKE MOSES' PARENTS *I do what is right for my family in*
Exodus 2:3 *obedience to God.*

Some people today wonder if perhaps this world is too full of suffering and danger to bring more children into it.

Jochebed and Amram knew what it meant to bring a child into a life of danger. Living in slavery, they were commanded to destroy their own child. Yet instead of giving in to fear, these parents responded with the strength and determination that comes from faith.

They recognized how special their child was (isn't every child?!) and stopped at nothing to protect him (Hebrews 11:23). For three months they hid him and then watched as God himself placed him in the care of the princess whose father had ordered his death (Acts 7:20-21). All this was done by faith—not fear. Jochebed planned well, worked hard, took risks, and trusted God.

But doing what was right for their baby was no simple matter. Jochebed and Amram knew they could endanger the rest of their family for the sake of one baby. They were willing to disobey the king and suffer dire consequences. They were also willing to make hard choices that didn't feel good. Jochebed did what was right in God's eyes for her child, not just what she wanted for herself as a mother.

Jochebed hung on to that baby when she was commanded to throw him away, but she was willing to let him go when that was the only way to protect his life. Just as God returns what we give to him, he returned Moses to her, in this case for a few more precious years—long enough for her to imprint him with faith for a lifetime. In fact, all of her children were used by God to lead the children of Israel into a new land and a new relationship of worship (Micah 6:4).

Like Jochebed and Amram, you and I are called by God to do what is best for the children in our care, no matter what the potential risks or conflicts with our personal desires.

○ *Today's Scripture reading is Exodus 1:1–2:10.*

When Moses arrived in Midian, he sat down beside a well. ¹⁶Now it happened that the priest of Midian had seven daughters who came regularly to this well to draw water and fill the water troughs for their father's flocks. ¹⁷But other shepherds would often come and chase the girls and their flocks away. This time, however, Moses came to their aid, rescuing the girls from the shepherds. Then he helped them draw water for their flocks.

¹⁸When the girls returned to Reuel, their father, he asked, "How did you get the flocks watered so quickly today?"

¹⁹"An Egyptian rescued us from the shepherds," they told him. "And then he drew water for us and watered our flocks."

²⁰"Well, where is he then?" their father asked. "Did you just leave him there? Go and invite him home for a meal!"

²¹Moses was happy to accept the invitation, and he settled down to live with them. In time, Reuel gave Moses one of his daughters, Zipporah, to be

I HELP those who are being mistreated. (2:17)

I BELIEVE God hears my cries for help and remembers his promises. (2:24)

I BELIEVE God feels deep concern for my welfare. (2:25)

his wife. ²²Later they had a baby boy, and Moses named him Gershom,* for he said, "I have been a stranger in a foreign land."

²³Years passed, and the king of Egypt died. But the Israelites still groaned beneath their burden of slavery. They cried out for help, and their pleas for deliverance rose up to God. ²⁴God heard their cries and remembered his covenant promise to Abraham, Isaac, and Jacob. ²⁵He looked down on the Israelites and felt deep concern for their welfare.

CHAPTER 3

Moses and the Burning Bush

One day Moses was tending the flock of his father-in-law, Jethro,* the priest of Midian, and he went deep into the wilderness near Sinai,* the mountain of God. ²Suddenly, the angel of the LORD appeared to him as a blazing fire in a bush. Moses was amazed because the bush was engulfed in flames, but it didn't burn up. ³"Amazing!" Moses said to himself. "Why isn't that bush burning up? I must go over to see this."

⁴When the LORD saw that he had caught Moses' attention, God called to him from the bush, "Moses! Moses!"

"Here I am!" Moses replied.

I SHOW great reverence for God. (3:5)

⁵"Do not come any closer," God told him. "Take off your sandals, for you are standing on holy ground." ⁶Then he said, "I am the God of your ancestors—the God of Abraham, the God of Isaac, and the God of Jacob." When Moses heard this, he hid his face in his hands because he was afraid to look at God.

I AM CONFIDENT that God sees the misery of his people and is aware of their suffering. (3:7)

⁷Then the LORD told him, "You can be sure I have seen the misery of my people in Egypt. I have heard their cries for deliverance from their harsh slave drivers. Yes, I am aware of their suffering. ⁸So I have come to rescue them from the Egyptians and lead them out of Egypt into their own good and spacious land. It is a land flowing with milk and honey—the land where the Canaanites, Hittites, Amorites, Perizzites, Hivites, and Jebusites live. ⁹The cries of the people of Israel have reached me, and I have seen how the Egyptians have oppressed them with heavy tasks. ¹⁰Now go, for I am sending you to Pharaoh. You will lead my people, the Israelites, out of Egypt."

¹¹"But who am I to appear before Pharaoh?" Moses asked God. "How can you expect me to lead the Israelites out of Egypt?"

¹²Then God told him, "I will be with you. And this will serve as proof that I have sent you: When you have brought the Israelites out of Egypt, you will return here to worship God at this very mountain."

I DO NOT MAKE excuses when God gives me a difficult task. (3:13)

¹³But Moses protested, "If I go to the people of Israel and tell them, 'The God of your ancestors has sent me to you,' they won't believe me. They will ask, 'Which god are you talking about? What is his name?' Then what should I tell them?"

¹⁴God replied, "I AM THE ONE WHO ALWAYS IS.* Just tell them, 'I AM has sent me to you.'" ¹⁵God also said, "Tell them, 'The LORD,* the God of your ancestors—the God of Abraham, the God of Isaac, and the God of Jacob—has sent me to you.' This will be my name forever; it has always been my name, and it will be used throughout all generations.

See the profiles for Abraham (page 19), Isaac (page 31), and Jacob (page 43) at Genesis 15:6, Genesis 25:19, and Genesis 32:9.

¹⁶"Now go and call together all the leaders of Israel. Tell them, 'The LORD, the God of your ancestors—the God of Abraham, Isaac, and Jacob—appeared to me in a burning bush. He said, "You can be sure that I am watching over you and have seen what is happening to you in Egypt. ¹⁷I promise to rescue you from the oppression of the Egyptians. I will lead you to the land now

2:22 *Gershom* sounds like a Hebrew term that means "a stranger there." 3:1a Moses' father-in-law went by two names, Jethro and Reuel. 3:1b Hebrew *Horeb*, another name for Sinai. 3:14 Or *I AM WHO I AM*, or *I WILL BE WHAT I WILL BE.* 3:15 Hebrew *Yahweh*; traditionally rendered *Jehovah*.

occupied by the Canaanites, Hittites, Amorites, Perizzites, Hivites, and Jebusites—a land flowing with milk and honey." '

¹⁸"The leaders of the people of Israel will accept your message. Then all of you must go straight to the king of Egypt and tell him, 'The LORD, the God of the Hebrews, has met with us. Let us go on a three-day journey into the wilderness to offer sacrifices to the LORD our God.'

¹⁹"But I know that the king of Egypt will not let you go except under heavy pressure. ²⁰So I will reach out and strike at the heart of Egypt with all kinds of miracles. Then at last he will let you go. ²¹And I will see to it that the Egyptians treat you well. They will load you down with gifts so you will not leave empty-handed. ²²The Israelite women will ask for silver and gold jewelry and fine clothing from their Egyptian neighbors and their neighbors' guests. With this clothing, you will dress your sons and daughters. In this way, you will plunder the Egyptians!"

CHAPTER 4

Signs of the LORD's Power

But Moses protested again, "Look, they won't believe me! They won't do what I tell them. They'll just say, 'The LORD never appeared to you.' "

²Then the LORD asked him, "What do you have there in your hand?"

"A shepherd's staff," Moses replied.

³"Throw it down on the ground," the LORD told him. So Moses threw it down, and it became a snake! Moses was terrified, so he turned and ran away.

⁴Then the LORD told him, "Take hold of its tail." So Moses reached out and grabbed it, and it became a shepherd's staff again.

⁵"Perform this sign, and they will believe you," the LORD told him. "Then they will realize that the LORD, the God of their ancestors—the God of Abraham, the God of Isaac, and the God of Jacob—really has appeared to you."

⁶Then the LORD said to Moses, "Put your hand inside your robe." Moses did so, and when he took it out again, his hand was white as snow with leprosy.* ⁷"Now put your hand back into your robe again," the LORD said. Moses did, and when he took it out this time, it was as healthy as the rest of his body.

⁸"If they do not believe the first miraculous sign, they will believe the second," the LORD said. ⁹"And if they do not believe you even after these two signs, then take some water from the Nile River and pour it out on the dry ground. When you do, it will turn into blood."

¹⁰But Moses pleaded with the LORD, "O Lord, I'm just not a good speaker. I never have been, and I'm not now, even after you have spoken to me. I'm clumsy with words."

¹¹"Who makes mouths?" the LORD asked him. "Who makes people so they can speak or not speak, hear or not hear, see or not see? Is it not I, the LORD? ¹²Now go, and do as I have told you. I will help you speak well, and I will tell you what to say."

¹³But Moses again pleaded, "Lord, please! Send someone else."

¹⁴Then the LORD became angry with Moses. "All right," he said. "What about your brother, Aaron the Levite? He is a good speaker. And look! He is on his way to meet you now. And when he sees you, he will be very glad. ¹⁵You will talk to him, giving him the words to say. I will help both of you to speak clearly, and I will tell you what to do. ¹⁶Aaron will be your spokesman to the people, and you will be as God to him, telling him what to say. ¹⁷And be sure to take your shepherd's staff along so you can perform the miraculous signs I have shown you."

4:6 Or *with a contagious skin disease.* The Hebrew word used here can describe various skin diseases.

I BELIEVE God is in control of the obstacles I encounter when I serve him. (3:19)

I DO NOT CONTRADICT the promises God gives with his commands. (4:1)

See the profiles for Abraham (page 19), Isaac (page 31), and Jacob (page 43) at Genesis 15:6, Genesis 25:19, and Genesis 32:9.

I DO NOT USE my inadequacies as excuses for not obeying God. (4:10)

I DO NOT RESIST God's call on my life. (4:13)

I BELIEVE God often uses others to help me. (4:14)

Moses Returns to Egypt

I SEEK the counsel of godly relatives. (4:18)

18 Then Moses went back home and talked it over with Jethro, his father-in-law. "With your permission," Moses said, "I would like to go back to Egypt to visit my family. I don't even know whether they are still alive."

"Go with my blessing," Jethro replied.

19 Before Moses left Midian, the LORD said to him, "Do not be afraid to return to Egypt, for all those who wanted to kill you are dead."

20 So Moses took his wife and sons, put them on a donkey, and headed back to the land of Egypt. In his hand he carried the staff of God.

21 Then the LORD reminded him, "When you arrive back in Egypt, go to Pharaoh and perform the miracles I have empowered you to do. But I will make him stubborn so he will not let the people go. 22 Then you will tell him, 'This is what the LORD says: Israel is my firstborn son. 23 I commanded you to let him go, so he could worship me. But since you have refused, be warned! I will kill your firstborn son!' "

24 On the journey, when Moses and his family had stopped for the night, the LORD confronted Moses* and was about to kill him. 25 But Zipporah, his wife, took a flint knife and circumcised her son. She threw the foreskin at Moses' feet and said, "What a blood-smeared bridegroom you are to me!" 26(When she called Moses a "blood-smeared bridegroom," she was referring to the circumcision.) After that, the LORD left him alone.

I AM WILLING to partner with others to accomplish God's purposes. (4:27)

27 Now the LORD had said to Aaron, "Go out into the wilderness to meet Moses." So Aaron traveled to the mountain of God, where he found Moses and greeted him warmly. 28 Moses then told Aaron everything the LORD had commanded them to do and say. And he told him about the miraculous signs they were to perform.

I WORSHIP God when I remember that he cares about my suffering. (4:31)

29 So Moses and Aaron returned to Egypt and called the leaders of Israel to a meeting. 30 Aaron told them everything the LORD had told Moses, and Moses performed the miraculous signs as they watched. 31 The leaders were soon convinced that the LORD had sent Moses and Aaron. And when they realized that the LORD had seen their misery and was deeply concerned for them, they all bowed their heads and worshiped.

CHAPTER 5

Moses and Aaron Speak to Pharaoh

After this presentation to Israel's leaders, Moses and Aaron went to see Pharaoh. They told him, "This is what the LORD, the God of Israel, says: 'Let my people go, for they must go out into the wilderness to hold a religious festival in my honor.' "

I DO NOT QUESTION God's right to tell me what to do. (5:2)

I PERSIST in making a way to do God's will. (5:3)

2 "Is that so?" retorted Pharaoh. "And who is the LORD that I should listen to him and let Israel go? I don't know the LORD, and I will not let Israel go."

3 But Aaron and Moses persisted. "The God of the Hebrews has met with us," they declared. "Let us take a three-day trip into the wilderness so we can offer sacrifices to the LORD our God. If we don't, we will surely die by disease or the sword."

4 "Who do you think you are," Pharaoh shouted, "distracting the people from their tasks? Get back to work! 5 Look, there are many people here in Egypt, and you are stopping them from doing their work."

Making Bricks without Straw

I DO NOT HOLD unfair expectations of my workers. (5:7)

6 That same day Pharaoh sent this order to the slave drivers and foremen he had set over the people of Israel: 7 "Do not supply the people with any more straw for making bricks. Let them get it themselves! 8 But don't reduce their production quotas by a single brick. They obviously don't have enough to do. If they did, they wouldn't be talking about going into the wilderness to

4:24 Or *confronted Moses' son;* Hebrew reads *confronted him.*

offer sacrifices to their God. [9]Load them down with more work. Make them sweat! That will teach them to listen to these liars!"

[10]So the slave drivers and foremen informed the people: "Pharaoh has ordered us not to provide straw for you. [11]Go and get it yourselves. Find it wherever you can. But you must produce just as many bricks as before!" [12]So the people scattered throughout the land in search of straw.

[13]The slave drivers were brutal. "Meet your daily quota of bricks, just as you did before!" they demanded. [14]Then they whipped the Israelite foremen in charge of the work crews. "Why haven't you met your quotas either yesterday or today?" they demanded.

[15]So the Israelite foremen went to Pharaoh and pleaded with him. "Please don't treat us like this," they begged. [16]"We are given no straw, but we are still told to make as many bricks as before. We are beaten for something that isn't our fault! It is the fault of your slave drivers for making such unreasonable demands."

LIKE MOSES

I value my relationship to God more than any earthly possessions or fame.

Exodus 5:1

What did it feel like for Moses to reenter the palaces of Egypt after having been away for forty years? These halls had once been his home. He practically owned them. But now he approached the new pharaoh as a stranger with a wild demand: "Release the Israelites to go and worship their God."

As a brash young prince of Egypt, Moses once attempted to use his own strength and position to identify with his people and bring them justice (see 2:11-13). But as a seasoned old man, he first argued with the Lord and then gave himself completely to him. From that point on, he was known as the friend of God (33:17). None of the splendors of Egypt could ever capture his heart again (Hebrews 3:5).

Like Moses, we live in a country and an era of spectacular culture and extravagant resources. Worldly possessions and praise may seek our attention and affection. But all our attention and affection belong to the Lord God. As we openly identify with him, like Moses, we will find that no cost will be too great to gain friendship with God (see James 4:4). To read more about Moses' remarkable faith in God, see Psalm 90; Acts 7:20-38; and Hebrews 11:24-28.

○ Today's Scripture reading is Exodus 5:1–6:13 and 14:5-31.

---

[17]But Pharaoh replied, "You're just lazy! You obviously don't have enough to do. If you did, you wouldn't be saying, 'Let us go, so we can offer sacrifices to the LORD.' [18]Now, get back to work! No straw will be given to you, but you must still deliver the regular quota of bricks."

[19]Since Pharaoh would not let up on his demands, the Israelite foremen could see that they were in serious trouble. [20]As they left Pharaoh's court, they met Moses and Aaron, who were waiting outside for them. [21]The foremen said to them, "May the LORD judge you for getting us into this terrible situation with Pharaoh* and his officials. You have given them an excuse to kill us!"

[22]So Moses went back to the LORD and protested, "Why have you mistreated your own people like this, Lord? Why did you send me? [23]Since I gave Pharaoh your message, he has been even more brutal to your people. You have not even begun to rescue them!"

I GO to the Lord when I am accused by the very people I am trying to help. (5:22)

CHAPTER 6

Promises of Deliverance

"Now you will see what I will do to Pharaoh," the LORD told Moses. "When he feels my powerful hand upon him, he will let the people go. In fact, he will be so anxious to get rid of them that he will force them to leave his land!"

5:21 Hebrew *for making us a stench in the nostrils of Pharaoh.*

See the profiles for Abraham (page 19), Isaac (page 31), and Jacob (page 43) at Genesis 15:6, Genesis 25:19, and Genesis 32:9.

I BELIEVE God cares about the sufferings of his people and remembers his promises to them. (6:5)

I BELIEVE the Lord uses his own name to declare that his promises are true. (6:8)

I DO NOT BECOME so discouraged by my hardships that I cannot hear God's message and promises. (6:9)

I DO NOT GIVE UP speaking God's message, even though some won't listen to me. (6:12)

Keep a prayer journal. This is where life changes often begin!

See Phinehas's profile (page 717) at Psalm 106:30.

²And God continued, "I am the LORD. ³I appeared to Abraham, to Isaac, and to Jacob as God Almighty,* though I did not reveal my name, the LORD,* to them. ⁴And I entered into a solemn covenant with them. Under its terms, I swore to give them the land of Canaan, where they were living. ⁵You can be sure that I have heard the groans of the people of Israel, who are now slaves to the Egyptians. I have remembered my covenant with them.

⁶"Therefore, say to the Israelites: 'I am the LORD, and I will free you from your slavery in Egypt. I will redeem you with mighty power and great acts of judgment. ⁷I will make you my own special people, and I will be your God. And you will know that I am the LORD your God who has rescued you from your slavery in Egypt. ⁸I will bring you into the land I swore to give to Abraham, Isaac, and Jacob. It will be your very own property. I am the LORD!' "

⁹So Moses told the people what the LORD had said, but they wouldn't listen anymore. They had become too discouraged by the increasing burden of their slavery.

¹⁰Then the LORD said to Moses, ¹¹"Go back to Pharaoh, and tell him to let the people of Israel leave Egypt."

¹²"But LORD!" Moses objected. "My own people won't listen to me anymore. How can I expect Pharaoh to listen? I'm no orator!"

¹³But the LORD ordered Moses and Aaron to return to Pharaoh, king of Egypt, and to demand that he let the people of Israel leave Egypt.

The Ancestors of Moses and Aaron
¹⁴These are the ancestors of clans from some of Israel's tribes:

The descendants of Reuben, Israel's oldest son, included Hanoch, Pallu, Hezron, and Carmi. Their descendants became the clans of Reuben.
¹⁵The descendants of Simeon included Jemuel, Jamin, Ohad, Jakin, Zohar, and Shaul (whose mother was a Canaanite). Their descendants became the clans of Simeon.
¹⁶These are the descendants of Levi, listed according to their family groups. In the first generation were Gershon, Kohath, and Merari. (Levi, their father, lived to be 137 years old.)
¹⁷ The descendants of Gershon included Libni and Shimei, each of whom is the ancestor of a clan.
¹⁸ The descendants of Kohath included Amram, Izhar, Hebron, and Uzziel. (Kohath lived to be 133 years old.)
¹⁹ The descendants of Merari included Mahli and Mushi.

These are the clans of the Levites, listed according to their genealogies.

²⁰Amram married his father's sister Jochebed, and she bore him Aaron and Moses. (Amram lived to be 137 years old.)
²¹The descendants of Izhar included Korah, Nepheg, and Zicri.
²²The descendants of Uzziel included Mishael, Elzaphan, and Sithri.
²³Aaron married Elisheba, the daughter of Amminadab and sister of Nahshon, and she bore him Nadab, Abihu, Eleazar, and Ithamar.
²⁴The descendants of Korah included Assir, Elkanah, and Abiasaph. Their descendants became the clans of Korah.
²⁵Eleazar son of Aaron married one of the daughters of Putiel, and she bore him Phinehas.

These are the ancestors of the Levite clans, listed according to their family groups.

²⁶The Aaron and Moses named in this list are the same Aaron and Moses to whom the LORD said, "Lead all the people of Israel out of the land of Egypt,

6:3a Hebrew *El Shaddai.*   6:3b Hebrew *Yahweh;* traditionally rendered *Jehovah.*

division by division." ²⁷They are the ones who went to Pharaoh to ask permission to lead the people from the land of Egypt.

²⁸At that time, the LORD had said to them, ²⁹"I am the LORD! Give Pharaoh the message I have given you." ³⁰This is the same Moses who had argued with the LORD, saying, "I can't do it! I'm no orator. Why should Pharaoh listen to me?"

CHAPTER 7

Moses' Staff Becomes a Snake

Then the LORD said to Moses, "Pay close attention to this. I will make you seem like God to Pharaoh. Your brother, Aaron, will be your prophet; he will speak for you. ²Tell Aaron everything I say to you and have him announce it to Pharaoh. He will demand that the people of Israel be allowed to leave Egypt. ³But I will cause Pharaoh to be stubborn so I can multiply my miraculous signs and wonders in the land of Egypt. ⁴Even then Pharaoh will refuse to listen to you. So I will crush Egypt with a series of disasters, after which I will lead the forces of Israel out with great acts of judgment. ⁵When I show the Egyptians my power and force them to let the Israelites go, they will realize that I am the LORD."

⁶So Moses and Aaron did just as the LORD had commanded them. ⁷Moses was eighty years old, and Aaron was eighty-three at the time they made their demands to Pharaoh.

⁸Then the LORD said to Moses and Aaron, ⁹"Pharaoh will demand that you show him a miracle to prove that God has sent you. When he makes this demand, say to Aaron, 'Throw down your shepherd's staff,' and it will become a snake."

¹⁰So Moses and Aaron went to see Pharaoh, and they performed the miracle just as the LORD had told them. Aaron threw down his staff before Pharaoh and his court, and it became a snake. ¹¹Then Pharaoh called in his wise men and magicians, and they did the same thing with their secret arts. ¹²Their staffs became snakes, too! But then Aaron's snake swallowed up their snakes. ¹³Pharaoh's heart, however, remained hard and stubborn. He still refused to listen, just as the LORD had predicted.

A Plague of Blood

¹⁴Then the LORD said to Moses, "Pharaoh is very stubborn, and he continues to refuse to let the people go. ¹⁵So go to Pharaoh in the morning as he goes down to the river. Stand on the riverbank and meet him there. Be sure to take along the shepherd's staff that turned into a snake. ¹⁶Say to him, 'The LORD, the God of the Hebrews, has sent me to say, "Let my people go, so they can worship me in the wilderness." Until now, you have refused to listen to him. ¹⁷Now the LORD says, "You are going to find out that I am the LORD." Look! I will hit the water of the Nile with this staff, and the river will turn to blood. ¹⁸The fish in it will die, and the river will stink. The Egyptians will not be able to drink any water from the Nile.' "

¹⁹Then the LORD said to Moses: "Tell Aaron to point his staff toward the waters of Egypt—all its rivers, canals, marshes, and reservoirs. Everywhere in Egypt the water will turn into blood, even the water stored in wooden bowls and stone pots in the people's homes."

²⁰So Moses and Aaron did just as the LORD had commanded them. As Pharaoh and all of his officials watched, Moses raised his staff and hit the water of the Nile. Suddenly, the whole river turned to blood! ²¹The fish in the river died, and the water became so foul that the Egyptians couldn't drink it. There was blood everywhere throughout the land of Egypt. ²²But again the magicians of Egypt used their secret arts, and they, too, turned water into blood. So Pharaoh's heart remained hard and stubborn. He refused to listen to

I BELIEVE God can even use people who argue with him. (6:30)

I PAY close attention to God's instructions. (7:1)

I BELIEVE God used his power to cause the Egyptians to realize that he is indeed the Lord. (7:5)

I AM never too old to obey God's commands and serve him. (7:7)

I BELIEVE God's power is far greater than even the most powerful black magic. (7:12)

I DO NOT HARDEN my heart to God's Word. (7:13)

I DO just what God commands me to do. (7:20)

I DO NOT HARDEN my heart to God's Word and to his miracles. (7:22)

Moses and Aaron, just as the LORD had predicted. ²³Pharaoh returned to his palace and put the whole thing out of his mind. ²⁴Then the Egyptians dug wells along the riverbank to get drinking water, for they couldn't drink from the river. ²⁵An entire week passed from the time the LORD turned the water of the Nile to blood.

CHAPTER 8

A Plague of Frogs

Then the LORD said to Moses, "Go to Pharaoh once again and tell him, 'This is what the LORD says: Let my people go, so they can worship me. ²If you refuse, then listen carefully to this: I will send vast hordes of frogs across your entire land from one border to the other. ³The Nile River will swarm with them. They will come up out of the river and into your houses, even into your bedrooms and onto your beds! Every home in Egypt will be filled with them. They will fill even your ovens and your kneading bowls. ⁴You and your people will be overwhelmed by frogs!' "

⁵Then the LORD said to Moses, "Tell Aaron to point his shepherd's staff toward all the rivers, canals, and marshes of Egypt so there will be frogs in every corner of the land." ⁶Aaron did so, and frogs covered the whole land of Egypt! ⁷But the magicians were able to do the same thing with their secret arts. They, too, caused frogs to come up on the land.

⁸Then Pharaoh summoned Moses and Aaron and begged, "Plead with the LORD to take the frogs away from me and my people. I will let the people go, so they can offer sacrifices to the LORD."

⁹"You set the time!" Moses replied. "Tell me when you want me to pray for you, your officials, and your people. I will pray that you and your houses will be rid of the frogs. Then only the frogs in the Nile River will remain alive."

¹⁰"Do it tomorrow," Pharaoh said.

"All right," Moses replied, "it will be as you have said. Then you will know that no one is as powerful as the LORD our God. ¹¹All the frogs will be destroyed, except those in the river."

¹²So Moses and Aaron left Pharaoh, and Moses pleaded with the LORD about the frogs he had sent. ¹³And the LORD did as Moses had promised. The frogs in the houses, the courtyards, and the fields all died. ¹⁴They were piled into great heaps, and a terrible stench filled the land. ¹⁵But when Pharaoh saw that the frogs were gone, he hardened his heart. He refused to listen to Moses and Aaron, just as the LORD had predicted.

A Plague of Gnats

¹⁶So the LORD said to Moses, "Tell Aaron to strike the dust with his staff. The dust will turn into swarms of gnats throughout the land of Egypt." ¹⁷So Moses and Aaron did just as the LORD had commanded them. Suddenly, gnats infested the entire land, covering the Egyptians and their animals. All the dust in the land of Egypt turned into gnats. ¹⁸Pharaoh's magicians tried to do the same thing with their secret arts, but this time they failed. And the gnats covered all the people and animals.

¹⁹"This is the finger of God!" the magicians exclaimed to Pharaoh. But Pharaoh's heart remained hard and stubborn. He wouldn't listen to them, just as the LORD had predicted.

A Plague of Flies

²⁰Next the LORD told Moses, "Get up early in the morning and meet Pharaoh as he goes down to the river. Say to him, 'This is what the LORD says: Let my people go, so they can worship me. ²¹If you refuse, I will send swarms of flies throughout Egypt. Your homes will be filled with them, and the ground will be covered with them. ²²But it will be very different in the land of Goshen, where the Israelites live. No flies will be found there. Then you will know that

---

I DO whatever the Lord commands. (8:6)

I BELIEVE black magic only causes problems rather than fixes them. (8:7)

I PRAY for people who want to be delivered from God's judgment. (8:9)

I DO NOT HARDEN my heart to God's Word. (8:15)

I BELIEVE God's power is far greater than black magic or any other occult powers. (8:18)

I DO NOT HARDEN my heart to God's miracles. (8:19)

I BELIEVE God can spare his people from judgment to show that he is the Lord Almighty. (8:22)

I am the LORD and that I have power even in the heart of your land. ²³I will make a clear distinction between your people and my people. This miraculous sign will happen tomorrow.' "

²⁴And the LORD did just as he had said. There were terrible swarms of flies in Pharaoh's palace and in every home in Egypt. The whole country was thrown into chaos by the flies.

²⁵Pharaoh hastily called for Moses and Aaron. "All right! Go ahead and offer sacrifices to your God," he said. "But do it here in this land. Don't go out into the wilderness."

²⁶But Moses replied, "That won't do! The Egyptians would detest the sacrifices that we offer to the LORD our God. If we offer them here where they can see us, they will be sure to stone us. ²⁷We must take a three-day trip into the wilderness to offer sacrifices to the LORD our God, just as he has commanded us."

²⁸"All right, go ahead," Pharaoh replied. "I will let you go to offer sacrifices to the LORD your God in the wilderness. But don't go too far away. Now hurry, and pray for me."

²⁹"As soon as I go," Moses said, "I will ask the LORD to cause the swarms of flies to disappear from you and all your people. But I am warning you, don't change your mind again and refuse to let the people go to sacrifice to the LORD."

³⁰So Moses left Pharaoh and asked the LORD to remove all the flies. ³¹And the LORD did as Moses asked and caused the swarms to disappear. Not a single fly remained in the land! ³²But Pharaoh hardened his heart again and refused to let the people go.

CHAPTER 9

A Plague against Livestock

"Go back to Pharaoh," the LORD commanded Moses. "Tell him, 'This is what the LORD, the God of the Hebrews, says: Let my people go, so they can worship me. ²If you continue to oppress them and refuse to let them go, ³the LORD will send a deadly plague to destroy your horses, donkeys, camels, cattle, and sheep. ⁴But the LORD will again make a distinction between the property of the Israelites and that of the Egyptians. Not a single one of Israel's livestock will die!' "

⁵The LORD announced that he would send the plague the very next day, ⁶and he did it, just as he had said. The next morning all the livestock of the Egyptians began to die, but the Israelites didn't lose a single animal from their flocks and herds. ⁷Pharaoh sent officials to see whether it was true that none of the Israelites' animals were dead. But even after he found it to be true, his heart remained stubborn. He still refused to let the people go.

A Plague of Boils

⁸Then the LORD said to Moses and Aaron, "Take soot from a furnace, and have Moses toss it into the sky while Pharaoh watches. ⁹It will spread like fine dust over the whole land of Egypt, causing boils to break out on people and animals alike."

¹⁰So they gathered soot from a furnace and went to see Pharaoh. As Pharaoh watched, Moses tossed the soot into the air, and terrible boils broke out on the people and animals throughout Egypt. ¹¹Even the magicians were unable to stand before Moses, because the boils had broken out on them, too. ¹²But the LORD made Pharaoh even more stubborn, and he refused to listen, just as the LORD had predicted.

A Plague of Hail

¹³Then the LORD said to Moses, "Get up early in the morning. Go to Pharaoh and tell him, 'The LORD, the God of the Hebrews, says: Let my people go, so

I DO NOT TRY to obey God on my terms. (8:25)

I DO NOT HARDEN my heart to God's Word and to his miracles. (8:32)

I REPEAT God's message as often as he commands. (9:1)

I DO NOT HARDEN my heart against God. (9:7)

I BELIEVE there is no
other God like the
Lord in all the earth.
(9:14)

they can worship me. ¹⁴If you don't, I will send a plague that will really speak to you and your officials and all the Egyptian people. I will prove to you that there is no other God like me in all the earth. ¹⁵I could have killed you all by now. I could have attacked you with a plague that would have wiped you from the face of the earth. ¹⁶But I have let you live for this reason—that you might see my power and that my fame might spread throughout the earth. ¹⁷But you are still lording it over my people, and you refuse to let them go. ¹⁸So tomorrow at this time I will send a hailstorm worse than any in all of Egypt's history. ¹⁹Quick! Order your livestock and servants to come in from the fields. Every person or animal left outside will die beneath the hail.' "

I BELIEVE and have
great respect for God's
Word. (9:20)

²⁰Some of Pharaoh's officials believed what the LORD said. They immediately brought their livestock and servants in from the fields. ²¹But those who had no respect for the word of the LORD left them out in the open.

²²Then the LORD said to Moses, "Lift your hand toward the sky, and cause the hail to fall throughout Egypt, on the people, the animals, and the crops."

²³So Moses lifted his staff toward the sky, and the LORD sent thunder and hail, and lightning struck the earth. The LORD sent a tremendous hailstorm against all the land of Egypt. ²⁴Never in all the history of Egypt had there been a storm like that, with such severe hail and continuous lightning. ²⁵It left all of Egypt in ruins. Everything left in the fields was destroyed—people, animals, and crops alike. Even all the trees were destroyed. ²⁶The only spot in all Egypt without hail that day was the land of Goshen, where the people of Israel lived.

I BELIEVE that God can
spare his people from
judgment to show the
greatness of his
power. (9:26)

²⁷Then Pharaoh urgently sent for Moses and Aaron. "I finally admit my fault," he confessed. "The LORD is right, and my people and I are wrong. ²⁸Please beg the LORD to end this terrifying thunder and hail. I will let you go at once."

²⁹"All right," Moses replied. "As soon as I leave the city, I will lift my hands and pray to the LORD. Then the thunder and hail will stop. This will prove to you that the earth belongs to the LORD. ³⁰But as for you and your officials, I know that you still do not fear the LORD God as you should."

I FEAR the Lord as I
should. (9:30)

³¹All the flax and barley were destroyed because the barley was ripe and the flax was in bloom. ³²But the wheat and the spelt were not destroyed because they had not yet sprouted from the ground.

³³So Moses left Pharaoh and went out of the city. As he lifted his hands to the LORD, all at once the thunder and hail stopped, and the downpour ceased. ³⁴When Pharaoh saw this, he and his officials sinned yet again by stubbornly refusing to do as they had promised. ³⁵Pharaoh refused to let the people leave, just as the LORD had predicted.

I DO NOT GO BACK on
my promise to God to
repent and change.
(9:34)

CHAPTER 10

A Plague of Locusts

I BELIEVE the Lord used
the plagues to display
his power to the
Egyptians and to show
the Israelites that he is
indeed the Lord. (10:1)

Then the LORD said to Moses, "Return to Pharaoh and again make your demands. I have made him and his officials stubborn so I can continue to display my power by performing miraculous signs among them. ²You will be able to tell wonderful stories to your children and grandchildren about the marvelous things I am doing among the Egyptians to prove that I am the LORD."

³So Moses and Aaron went to Pharaoh and said, "This is what the LORD, the God of the Hebrews, says: How long will you refuse to submit to me? Let my people go, so they can worship me. ⁴If you refuse, watch out! For tomorrow I will cover the whole country with locusts. ⁵There will be so many that you won't be able to see the ground. They will devour everything that escaped the hailstorm, including all the trees in the fields. ⁶They will overrun your palaces and the homes of your officials and all the houses of Egypt. Never in the history of Egypt has there been a plague like this one!" And with that, Moses turned and walked out.

⁷The court officials now came to Pharaoh and appealed to him. "How long will you let these disasters go on? Please let the Israelites go to serve the LORD their God! Don't you realize that Egypt lies in ruins?"

⁸So Moses and Aaron were brought back to Pharaoh. "All right, go and serve the LORD your God," he said. "But tell me, just whom do you want to take along?"

⁹"Young and old, all of us will go," Moses replied. "We will take our sons and daughters and our flocks and herds. We must all join together in a festival to the LORD."

I INVITE my whole family to worship God with me. (10:9)

¹⁰Pharaoh retorted, "The LORD will certainly need to be with you if you try to take your little ones along! I can see through your wicked intentions. ¹¹Never! Only the men may go and serve the LORD, for that is what you requested." And Pharaoh threw them out of the palace.

¹²Then the LORD said to Moses, "Raise your hand over the land of Egypt to bring on the locusts. Let them cover the land and eat all the crops still left after the hailstorm."

¹³So Moses raised his staff, and the LORD caused an east wind to blow all that day and through the night. When morning arrived, the east wind had brought the locusts. ¹⁴And the locusts swarmed over the land of Egypt from border to border. It was the worst locust plague in Egyptian history, and there has never again been one like it. ¹⁵For the locusts covered the surface of the whole country, making the ground look black. They ate all the plants and all the fruit on the trees that had survived the hailstorm. Not one green thing remained, neither tree nor plant, throughout the land of Egypt.

¹⁶Pharaoh quickly sent for Moses and Aaron. "I confess my sin against the LORD your God and against you," he said to them. ¹⁷"Forgive my sin only this once, and plead with the LORD your God to take away this terrible plague."

¹⁸So Moses left Pharaoh and pleaded with the LORD. ¹⁹The LORD responded by sending a strong west wind that blew the locusts out into the Red Sea.* Not a single locust remained in all the land of Egypt. ²⁰But the LORD made Pharaoh stubborn once again, and he did not let the people go.

I PRAY for people who want to be delivered from God's judgment. (10:18)

A Plague of Darkness

²¹Then the LORD said to Moses, "Lift your hand toward heaven, and a deep and terrifying darkness will descend on the land of Egypt." ²²So Moses lifted his hand toward heaven, and there was deep darkness over the entire land for three days. ²³During all that time the people scarcely moved, for they could not see. But there was light as usual where the people of Israel lived.

I BELIEVE the Lord sent a deep darkness on the land of Egypt. (10:21)

²⁴Then Pharaoh called for Moses. "Go and worship the LORD," he said. "But let your flocks and herds stay here. You can even take your children with you."

²⁵"No," Moses said, "we must take our flocks and herds for sacrifices and burnt offerings to the LORD our God. ²⁶All our property must go with us; not a hoof can be left behind. We will have to choose our sacrifices for the LORD our God from among these animals. And we won't know which sacrifices he will require until we get there."

I OBEY God completely. (10:25)

²⁷So the LORD hardened Pharaoh's heart once more, and he would not let them go. ²⁸"Get out of here!" Pharaoh shouted at Moses. "Don't ever let me see you again! The day you do, you will die!"

²⁹"Very well," Moses replied. "I will never see you again."

CHAPTER 11

Death for Egypt's Firstborn

Then the LORD said to Moses, "I will send just one more disaster on Pharaoh and the land of Egypt. After that, Pharaoh will let you go. In fact, he will be so

10:19 Hebrew *sea of reeds.*

I MAKE bold requests when God tells me to do so. (11:2)

I BELIEVE God can cause even my enemies to respect me. (11:3)

anxious to get rid of you that he will practically force you to leave the country. ²Tell all the Israelite men and women to ask their Egyptian neighbors for articles of silver and gold."

³(Now the LORD had caused the Egyptians to look favorably on the people of Israel, and Moses was considered a very great man in the land of Egypt. He was respected by Pharaoh's officials and the Egyptian people alike.)

⁴So Moses announced to Pharaoh, "This is what the LORD says: About midnight I will pass through Egypt. ⁵All the firstborn sons will die in every family in Egypt, from the oldest son of Pharaoh, who sits on the throne, to the oldest son of his lowliest slave. Even the firstborn of the animals will die. ⁶Then a loud wail will be heard throughout the land of Egypt; there has never been such wailing before, and there never will be again. ⁷But among the Israelites it will be so peaceful that not even a dog will bark. Then you will know that the LORD makes a distinction between the Egyptians and the Israelites. ⁸All the officials of Egypt will come running to me, bowing low. 'Please leave!' they will beg. 'Hurry! And take all your followers with you.' Only then will I go!" Then, burning with anger, Moses left Pharaoh's presence.

⁹Now the LORD had told Moses, "Pharaoh will not listen to you. But this will give me the opportunity to do even more mighty miracles in the land of Egypt." ¹⁰Although Moses and Aaron did these miracles in Pharaoh's presence, the LORD hardened his heart so he wouldn't let the Israelites leave the country.

CHAPTER 12

The First Passover

Now the LORD gave the following instructions to Moses and Aaron while they were still in the land of Egypt: ²"From now on, this month will be the first month of the year for you. ³Announce to the whole community that on the tenth day of this month each family must choose a lamb or a young goat for a sacrifice. ⁴If a family is too small to eat an entire lamb, let them share the lamb with another family in the neighborhood. Whether or not they share in this way depends on the size of each family and how much they can eat. ⁵This animal must be a one-year-old male, either a sheep or a goat, with no physical defects.

I BELIEVE God required the Passover lamb or goat to be perfect, with no defects—a picture of the Lord Jesus Christ. (12:5)

I BELIEVE God required the Israelites to smear the lamb's blood on the top and sides of the doorframe of their home—a picture of the cross on which Jesus shed his blood. (12:7)

I BELIEVE the Lord executed judgment on all the gods of Egypt. (12:12)

⁶"Take special care of these lambs until the evening of the fourteenth day of this first month. Then each family in the community must slaughter its lamb. ⁷They are to take some of the lamb's blood and smear it on the top and sides of the doorframe of the house where the lamb will be eaten. ⁸That evening everyone must eat roast lamb with bitter herbs and bread made without yeast. ⁹The meat must never be eaten raw or boiled; roast it all, including the head, legs, and internal organs. ¹⁰Do not leave any of it until the next day. Whatever is not eaten that night must be burned before morning.

¹¹"Wear your traveling clothes as you eat this meal, as though prepared for a long journey. Wear your sandals, and carry your walking sticks in your hands. Eat the food quickly, for this is the LORD's Passover. ¹²On that night I will pass through the land of Egypt and kill all the firstborn sons and firstborn male animals in the land of Egypt. I will execute judgment against all the gods of Egypt, for I am the LORD! ¹³The blood you have smeared on your doorposts will serve as a sign. When I see the blood, I will pass over you. This plague of death will not touch you when I strike the land of Egypt.

¹⁴"You must remember this day forever. Each year you will celebrate it as a special festival to the LORD. ¹⁵For seven days, you may eat only bread made without yeast. On the very first day you must remove every trace of yeast from your homes. Anyone who eats bread made with yeast at any time during the seven days of the festival will be cut off from the community of Israel. ¹⁶On the first day of the festival, and again on the seventh day, all the people must

gather for a time of special worship. No work of any kind may be done on these days except in the preparation of food.

¹⁷"Celebrate this Festival of Unleavened Bread, for it will remind you that I brought your forces out of the land of Egypt on this very day. This festival will be a permanent regulation for you, to be kept from generation to generation. ¹⁸Only bread without yeast may be eaten from the evening of the fourteenth day of the month until the evening of the twenty-first day of the month. ¹⁹During those seven days, there must be no trace of yeast in your homes. Anyone who eats anything made with yeast during this week will be cut off from the community of Israel. These same regulations apply to the foreigners living with you, as if they had been born among you. ²⁰I repeat, during those days you must not eat anything made with yeast. Wherever you live, eat only bread that has no yeast in it."

²¹Then Moses called for the leaders of Israel and said, "Tell each of your families to slaughter the lamb they have set apart for the Passover. ²²Drain each lamb's blood into a basin. Then take a cluster of hyssop branches and dip it into the lamb's blood. Strike the hyssop against the top and sides of the doorframe, staining it with the blood. And remember, no one is allowed to leave the house until morning. ²³For the LORD will pass through the land and strike down the Egyptians. But when he sees the blood on the top and sides of the doorframe, the LORD will pass over your home. He will not permit the Destroyer to enter and strike down your firstborn.

²⁴"Remember, these instructions are permanent and must be observed by you and your descendants forever. ²⁵When you arrive in the land the LORD has promised to give you, you will continue to celebrate this festival. ²⁶Then your children will ask, 'What does all this mean? What is this ceremony about?' ²⁷And you will reply, 'It is the celebration of the LORD's Passover, for he passed over the homes of the Israelites in Egypt. And though he killed the Egyptians, he spared our families and did not destroy us.' " Then all the people bowed their heads and worshiped.

²⁸So the people of Israel did just as the LORD had commanded through Moses and Aaron. ²⁹And at midnight the LORD killed all the firstborn sons in the land of Egypt, from the firstborn son of Pharaoh, who sat on the throne, to the firstborn son of the captive in the dungeon. Even the firstborn of their livestock were killed. ³⁰Pharaoh and his officials and all the people of Egypt woke up during the night, and loud wailing was heard throughout the land of Egypt. There was not a single house where someone had not died.

Israel's Exodus from Egypt

³¹Pharaoh sent for Moses and Aaron during the night. "Leave us!" he cried. "Go away, all of you! Go and serve the LORD as you have requested. ³²Take your flocks and herds, and be gone. Go, but give me a blessing as you leave." ³³All the Egyptians urged the people of Israel to get out of the land as quickly as possible, for they thought, "We will all die!"

³⁴The Israelites took with them their bread dough made without yeast. They wrapped their kneading bowls in their spare clothing and carried them on their shoulders. ³⁵And the people of Israel did as Moses had instructed and asked the Egyptians for clothing and articles of silver and gold. ³⁶The LORD caused the Egyptians to look favorably on the Israelites, and they gave the Israelites whatever they asked for. So, like a victorious army, they plundered the Egyptians!

³⁷That night the people of Israel left Rameses and started for Succoth. There were about 600,000 men, plus all the women and children. And they were all traveling on foot. ³⁸Many people who were not Israelites went with them, along with the many flocks and herds. ³⁹Whenever they stopped to eat, they baked bread from the yeastless dough they had brought from Egypt. It

I BELIEVE the Passover and Festival of Unleavened Bread were to be kept permanently by the Israelites to remind them of how God brought them out of Egypt. (12:17)

I BELIEVE the Israelites had to put the blood on the doorframe with hyssop and stay in the house all night—a picture of our security of salvation in Jesus Christ. (12:22)

I DO just what God commands. (12:28)

was made without yeast because the people were rushed out of Egypt and had no time to wait for bread to rise.

I TRUST in God's perfect timing for my deliverance. (12:42)

40The people of Israel had lived in Egypt for 430 years. 41In fact, it was on the last day of the 430th year that all the LORD's forces left the land. 42This night had been reserved by the LORD to bring his people out from the land of Egypt, so this same night now belongs to him. It must be celebrated every year, from generation to generation, to remember the LORD's deliverance.

Instructions for the Passover

43Then the LORD said to Moses and Aaron, "These are the regulations for the festival of Passover. No foreigners are allowed to eat the Passover lamb. 44But any slave who has been purchased may eat it if he has been circumcised. 45Hired servants and visiting foreigners may not eat it. 46All who eat the lamb must eat it together in one house. You must not carry any of its meat outside, and you may not break any of its bones. 47The whole community of Israel must celebrate this festival at the same time.

I BELIEVE God made a way for foreigners to eat the Passover lamb if they became part of the Israelite nation. (12:48)

I FOLLOW all of God's instructions. (12:50)

48"If there are foreigners living among you who want to celebrate the LORD's Passover, let all the males be circumcised. Then they may come and celebrate the Passover with you. They will be treated just as if they had been born among you. But an uncircumcised male may never eat of the Passover lamb. 49This law applies to everyone, whether a native-born Israelite or a foreigner who has settled among you."

50So the people of Israel followed all the LORD's instructions to Moses and Aaron. 51And that very day the LORD began to lead the people of Israel out of Egypt, division by division.

CHAPTER 13

Dedication of the Firstborn

Then the LORD said to Moses, 2"Dedicate to me all the firstborn sons of Israel and every firstborn male animal. They are mine."

3So Moses said to the people, "This is a day to remember forever—the day you left Egypt, the place of your slavery. For the LORD has brought you out by his mighty power. (Remember, you are not to use any yeast.) 4This day in early spring* will be the anniversary of your exodus. 5You must celebrate this day when the LORD brings you into the land of the Canaanites, Hittites, Amorites, Hivites, and Jebusites. This is the land he swore to give your ancestors—a land flowing with milk and honey. 6For seven days you will eat only bread without yeast. Then on the seventh day, you will celebrate a great feast to the LORD. 7Eat only bread without yeast during those seven days. In fact, there must be no yeast in your homes or anywhere within the borders of your land during this time.

I TELL my children how God has delivered me. (13:8)

8"During these festival days each year, you must explain to your children why you are celebrating. Say to them, 'This is a celebration of what the LORD did for us when we left Egypt.' 9This annual festival will be a visible reminder to you, like a mark branded on your hands or your forehead. Let it remind you always to keep the LORD's instructions in your minds and on your lips. After all, it was the LORD who rescued you from Egypt with great power.

10"So celebrate this festival at the appointed time each year. 11And remember these instructions when the LORD brings you into the land he swore to give your ancestors long ago, the land where the Canaanites are now living. 12All firstborn sons and firstborn male animals must be presented to the LORD. 13A firstborn male donkey may be redeemed from the LORD by presenting a lamb in its place. But if you decide not to make the exchange, the donkey must be killed by breaking its neck. However, you must redeem every firstborn son.

13:4 Hebrew *in the month of Abib.* This month of the Hebrew lunar calendar usually occurs in March and April.

[14] "And in the future, your children will ask you, 'What does all this mean?' Then you will tell them, 'With mighty power the LORD brought us out of Egypt from our slavery. [15]Pharaoh refused to let us go, so the LORD killed all the firstborn males throughout the land of Egypt, both people and animals. That is why we now offer all the firstborn males to the LORD—except that the firstborn sons are always redeemed.' [16]Again I say, this ceremony will be like a mark branded on your hands or your forehead. It is a visible reminder that it was the LORD who brought you out of Egypt with great power."

Israel's Wilderness Detour

[17]When Pharaoh finally let the people go, God did not lead them on the road that runs through Philistine territory, even though that was the shortest way from Egypt to the Promised Land. God said, "If the people are faced with a battle, they might change their minds and return to Egypt." [18]So God led them along a route through the wilderness toward the Red Sea,* and the Israelites left Egypt like a marching army.

[19]Moses took the bones of Joseph with him, for Joseph had made the sons of Israel swear that they would take his bones with them when God led them out of Egypt—as he was sure God would.

[20]Leaving Succoth, they camped at Etham on the edge of the wilderness. [21]The LORD guided them by a pillar of cloud during the day and a pillar of fire at night. That way they could travel whether it was day or night. [22]And the LORD did not remove the pillar of cloud or pillar of fire from their sight.

CHAPTER 14

Then the LORD gave these instructions to Moses: [2]"Tell the people to march toward Pi-hahiroth between Migdol and the sea. Camp there along the shore, opposite Baal-zephon. [3]Then Pharaoh will think, 'Those Israelites are confused. They are trapped between the wilderness and the sea!' [4]And once again I will harden Pharaoh's heart, and he will chase after you. I have planned this so I will receive great glory at the expense of Pharaoh and his armies. After this, the Egyptians will know that I am the LORD!" So the Israelites camped there as they were told.

The Egyptians Pursue Israel

[5]When word reached the king of Egypt that the Israelites were not planning to return to Egypt after three days, Pharaoh and his officials changed their minds. "What have we done, letting all these slaves get away?" they asked. [6]So Pharaoh called out his troops and led the chase in his chariot. [7]He took with him six hundred of Egypt's best chariots, along with the rest of the chariots of Egypt, each with a commander. [8]The LORD continued to strengthen Pharaoh's resolve, and he chased after the people of Israel who had escaped so defiantly. [9]All the forces in Pharaoh's army—all his horses, chariots, and charioteers—were used in the chase. The Egyptians caught up with the people of Israel as they were camped beside the shore near Pi-hahiroth, across from Baal-zephon.

[10]As Pharaoh and his army approached, the people of Israel could see them in the distance, marching toward them. The people began to panic, and they cried out to the LORD for help.

[11]Then they turned against Moses and complained, "Why did you bring us out here to die in the wilderness? Weren't there enough graves for us in Egypt? Why did you make us leave? [12]Didn't we tell you to leave us alone while we were still in Egypt? Our Egyptian slavery was far better than dying out here in the wilderness!"

[13]But Moses told the people, "Don't be afraid. Just stand where you are and

13:18 Hebrew *sea of reeds.*

I TELL my children about the Lord's mighty power, which delivers his people. (13:14)

I KEEP visible reminders of the Lord's power and deliverance. (13:16)

I BELIEVE God will always do as he has promised. (13:19)

I BELIEVE the Lord guided the Israelites with a pillar of cloud by day and fire by night. (13:21)

I DO NOT CHANGE my mind after I have repented. (14:5)

I CRY OUT to the Lord for help when someone tries to attack me. (14:10)

I WATCH for the Lord to rescue me, and I do not fear. (14:13)

watch the LORD rescue you. The Egyptians that you see today will never be seen again. [14]The LORD himself will fight for you. You won't have to lift a finger in your defense!"

Escape through the Red Sea
[15]Then the LORD said to Moses, "Why are you crying out to me? Tell the people to get moving! [16]Use your shepherd's staff—hold it out over the water, and a path will open up before you through the sea. Then all the people of Israel will walk through on dry ground. [17]Yet I will harden the hearts of the Egyptians, and they will follow the Israelites into the sea. Then I will receive great glory at the expense of Pharaoh and his armies, chariots, and charioteers. [18]When I am finished with Pharaoh and his army, all Egypt will know that I am the LORD!"

[19] Then the angel of God, who had been leading the people of Israel, moved to a position behind them, and the pillar of cloud also moved around behind them. [20]The cloud settled between the Israelite and Egyptian camps. As night came, the pillar of cloud turned into a pillar of fire, lighting the Israelite camp. But the cloud became darkness to the Egyptians, and they couldn't find the Israelites.

[21]Then Moses raised his hand over the sea, and the LORD opened up a path through the water with a strong east wind. The wind blew all that night, turning the seabed into dry land. [22]So the people of Israel walked through the sea on dry ground, with walls of water on each side! [23]Then the Egyptians—all of Pharaoh's horses, chariots, and charioteers—followed them across the bottom of the sea. [24]But early in the morning, the LORD looked down on the Egyptian army from the pillar of fire and cloud, and he threw them into confusion. [25]Their chariot wheels began to come off, making their chariots impossible to drive. "Let's get out of here!" the Egyptians shouted. "The LORD is fighting for Israel against us!"

[26]When all the Israelites were on the other side, the LORD said to Moses, "Raise your hand over the sea again. Then the waters will rush back over the Egyptian chariots and charioteers." [27]So as the sun began to rise, Moses raised his hand over the sea. The water roared back into its usual place, and the LORD swept the terrified Egyptians into the surging currents. [28]The waters covered all the chariots and charioteers—the entire army of Pharaoh. Of all the Egyptians who had chased the Israelites into the sea, not a single one survived.

[29] The people of Israel had walked through the middle of the sea on dry land, as the water stood up like a wall on both sides. [30]This was how the LORD rescued Israel from the Egyptians that day. And the Israelites could see the bodies of the Egyptians washed up on the shore. [31]When the people of Israel saw the mighty power that the LORD had displayed against the Egyptians, they feared the LORD and put their faith in him and his servant Moses.

CHAPTER 15

A Song of Deliverance
Then Moses and the people of Israel sang this song to the LORD:

"I will sing to the LORD, for he has triumphed gloriously;
    he has thrown both horse and rider into the sea.
[2]The LORD is my strength and my song;
    he has become my victory.
He is my God, and I will praise him;
    he is my father's God, and I will exalt him!
[3]The LORD is a warrior;
    yes, the LORD is his name!
[4]Pharaoh's chariots and armies,
    he has thrown into the sea.

I BELIEVE the Lord fights for me. (14:14)

I TAKE the path of deliverance that God opens for me. (14:22)

I FEAR the Lord, who is mighty in power. (14:31)

I PRAISE the Lord because he is my strength and song. (15:2)

The very best of Pharaoh's officers
    have been drowned in the Red Sea.*
⁵The deep waters have covered them;
    they sank to the bottom like a stone.

⁶"Your right hand, O LORD,
    is glorious in power.
Your right hand, O LORD,
    dashes the enemy to pieces.
⁷In the greatness of your majesty,
    you overthrew those who rose against you.
Your anger flashed forth;
    it consumed them as fire burns straw.
⁸At the blast of your breath, the waters piled up!
    The surging waters stood straight like a wall;
    in the middle of the sea the waters became hard.

⁹"The enemy said, 'I will chase them,
    catch up with them, and destroy them.
I will divide the plunder,
    avenging myself against them.
I will unsheath my sword;
    my power will destroy them.'
¹⁰But with a blast of your breath,
    the sea covered them.
They sank like lead
    in the mighty waters.

I BELIEVE the threats of my enemies are powerless before God's might. (15:9)

¹¹"Who else among the gods is like you, O LORD?
    Who is glorious in holiness like you—
so awesome in splendor,
    performing such wonders?
¹²You raised up your hand,
    and the earth swallowed our enemies.

¹³"With unfailing love you will lead
    this people whom you have ransomed.
You will guide them in your strength
    to the place where your holiness dwells.
¹⁴The nations will hear and tremble;
    anguish will grip the people of Philistia.
¹⁵The leaders of Edom will be terrified;
    the nobles of Moab will tremble.
All the people of Canaan will melt with fear;
¹⁶   terror and dread will overcome them.
Because of your great power,
    they will be silent like a stone,
until your people pass by, O LORD,
until the people whom you purchased pass by.
¹⁷You will bring them in and plant them on your own mountain—
    the place you have made as your home, O LORD,
    the sanctuary, O Lord, that your hands have made.
¹⁸The LORD will reign forever and ever!"

I PRAISE the Lord, who reigns forever! (15:18)

¹⁹When Pharaoh's horses, chariots, and charioteers rushed into the sea, the LORD brought the water crashing down on them. But the people of Israel had walked through on dry land!

15:4 Hebrew *sea of reeds*; also in 15:22.

I LEAD God's people in expressive worship for his mighty deeds. (15:20)

I TURN to God in times of trouble instead of attacking his leaders. (15:24)

I LISTEN carefully to God's commands and obey them, doing what is right. (15:26)

I DO NOT SPEAK bitterly against God's appointed leaders. (16:2)

I DO NOT COMPLAIN against the Lord. (16:7)

I BELIEVE God hears the complaints of his people. (16:9)

²⁰Then Miriam the prophet, Aaron's sister, took a tambourine and led all the women in rhythm and dance. ²¹And Miriam sang this song:

"I will sing to the LORD, for he has triumphed gloriously;
  he has thrown both horse and rider into the sea."

Bitter Water at Marah

²²Then Moses led the people of Israel away from the Red Sea, and they moved out into the Shur Desert. They traveled in this desert for three days without water. ²³When they came to Marah, they finally found water. But the people couldn't drink it because it was bitter. (That is why the place was called Marah, which means "bitter.")

²⁴Then the people turned against Moses. "What are we going to drink?" they demanded.

²⁵So Moses cried out to the LORD for help, and the LORD showed him a branch. Moses took the branch and threw it into the water. This made the water good to drink.

It was there at Marah that the LORD laid before them the following conditions to test their faithfulness to him: ²⁶"If you will listen carefully to the voice of the LORD your God and do what is right in his sight, obeying his commands and laws, then I will not make you suffer the diseases I sent on the Egyptians; for I am the LORD who heals you."

²⁷After leaving Marah, they came to Elim, where there were twelve springs and seventy palm trees. They camped there beside the springs.

CHAPTER 16

Manna and Quail from Heaven

Then they left Elim and journeyed into the Sin* Desert, between Elim and Mount Sinai. They arrived there a month after leaving Egypt.* ²There, too, the whole community of Israel spoke bitterly against Moses and Aaron.

³"Oh, that we were back in Egypt," they moaned. "It would have been better if the LORD had killed us there! At least there we had plenty to eat. But now you have brought us into this desert to starve us to death."

⁴Then the LORD said to Moses, "Look, I'm going to rain down food from heaven for you. The people can go out each day and pick up as much food as they need for that day. I will test them in this to see whether they will follow my instructions. ⁵Tell them to pick up twice as much as usual on the sixth day of each week."

⁶Then Moses and Aaron called a meeting of all the people of Israel and told them, "In the evening you will realize that it was the LORD who brought you out of the land of Egypt. ⁷In the morning you will see the glorious presence of the LORD. He has heard your complaints, which are against the LORD and not against us. ⁸The LORD will give you meat to eat in the evening and bread in the morning, for he has heard all your complaints against him. Yes, your complaints are against the LORD, not against us."

⁹Then Moses said to Aaron, "Say this to the entire community of Israel: 'Come into the LORD's presence, and hear his reply to your complaints.'"

¹⁰And as Aaron spoke to the people, they looked out toward the desert. Within the guiding cloud, they could see the awesome glory of the LORD.

¹¹And the LORD said to Moses, ¹²"I have heard the people's complaints. Now tell them, 'In the evening you will have meat to eat, and in the morning you will be filled with bread. Then you will know that I am the LORD your God.'"

¹³That evening vast numbers of quail arrived and covered the camp. The next morning the desert all around the camp was wet with dew. ¹⁴When the

16:1a Not to be confused with the English word *sin.* 16:1b Hebrew *on the fifteenth day of the second month.* The Exodus had occurred on the fourteenth day of the first month (see 12:6).

dew disappeared later in the morning, thin flakes, white like frost, covered the ground. ¹⁵The Israelites were puzzled when they saw it. "What is it?" they asked.

And Moses told them, "It is the food the LORD has given you. ¹⁶The LORD says that each household should gather as much as it needs. Pick up two quarts* for each person."

¹⁷So the people of Israel went out and gathered this food—some getting more, and some getting less. ¹⁸By gathering two quarts for each person, everyone had just enough. Those who gathered a lot had nothing left over, and those who gathered only a little had enough. Each family had just what it needed.

¹⁹Then Moses told them, "Do not keep any of it overnight." ²⁰But, of course, some of them didn't listen and kept some of it until morning. By then it was full of maggots and had a terrible smell. And Moses was very angry with them.

I BELIEVE the Lord provides for my needs. (16:16)

LIKE MIRIAM   *I lead others in praise to God for his goodness.*
Exodus 15:20

Miriam had seen the mighty God at work. The first time was when she was a young girl and her parents had placed her baby brother in a basket in the Nile to save him from certain death. As she watched over her brother, the Lord brought a princess to rescue him. Miriam then saw her parents' faith rewarded as the princess returned baby Moses to his parents for a few more precious years. Years later Miriam also watched as God struck the Egyptians with plagues to show his glorious power and free his people.

Now past her ninetieth birthday, Miriam experienced the Lord's complete deliverance as she and the rest of the Israelites marched through the Red Sea and turned around to see Pharaoh and his army swept away in the crashing waters.

Miriam was called a prophet, and neither age nor gender would keep her from leading in the festival of worship that day. She did more than shout a hearty "Amen!" Tambourine in hand, she led other women in a celebration of rhythm and dance to express with mind, soul, and body their joy at God's wondrous deeds. Their refrain echoed the new nation's heartfelt song of praise.

Miriam would later make the mistake of seeking her own glory and influencing her brother Aaron to do the same (Numbers 12:1). But on this glorious day she gave all the glory to God and helped others do the same

Without seeking our own glory, you and I can help lead people to give glory to God. Opportunities abound, whether helping lead worship in the midst of a large congregation or simply drawing a circle of small children around us.

Together, let's give glory to God and help others to praise him, too!

○ *Today's Scripture reading is Exodus 15:1-21.*

²¹The people gathered the food morning by morning, each family according to its need. And as the sun became hot, the food they had not picked up melted and disappeared. ²²On the sixth day, there was twice as much as usual on the ground—four quarts* for each person instead of two. The leaders of the people came and asked Moses why this had happened. ²³He replied, "The LORD has appointed tomorrow as a day of rest, a holy Sabbath to the LORD. On this day we will rest from our normal daily tasks. So bake or boil as much as you want today, and set aside what is left for tomorrow."

²⁴The next morning the leftover food was wholesome and good, without maggots or odor. ²⁵Moses said, "This is your food for today, for today is a Sabbath to the LORD. There will be no food on the ground today. ²⁶Gather the

16:16 Hebrew *1 omer* [2 liters]; also in 16:18, 32, 33.   16:22 Hebrew *2 omers* [4 liters].

food for six days, but the seventh day is a Sabbath. There will be no food on the ground for you on that day."

I DO NOT LOOK for God to give me something when he has already said no. (16:27)

²⁷Some of the people went out anyway to gather food, even though it was the Sabbath day. But there was none to be found. ²⁸"How long will these people refuse to obey my commands and instructions?" the LORD asked Moses. ²⁹"Do they not realize that I have given them the seventh day, the Sabbath, as a day of rest? That is why I give you twice as much food on the sixth day, so there will be enough for two days. On the Sabbath day you must stay in your places. Do not pick up food from the ground on that day." ³⁰So the people rested on the seventh day.

³¹In time, the food became known as manna.* It was white like coriander seed, and it tasted like honey cakes.

I KEEP mementos to remind my family of God's gracious provision. (16:32)

³²Then Moses gave them this command from the LORD: "Take two quarts of manna and keep it forever as a treasured memorial of the LORD's provision. By doing this, later generations will be able to see the bread that the LORD provided in the wilderness when he brought you out of Egypt."

³³Moses said to Aaron, "Get a container and put two quarts of manna into it. Then store it in a sacred place* as a reminder for all future generations." ³⁴Aaron did this, just as the LORD had commanded Moses. He eventually placed it for safekeeping in the Ark of the Covenant.* ³⁵So the people of Israel ate manna for forty years until they arrived in the land of Canaan, where there were crops to eat.

³⁶(The container used to measure the manna was an omer, which held about two quarts.)*

CHAPTER 17

Water from the Rock

At the LORD's command, the people of Israel left the Sin* Desert and moved from place to place. Eventually they came to Rephidim, but there was no water to be found there. ²So once more the people grumbled and complained to Moses. "Give us water to drink!" they demanded.

I CRY OUT to the Lord instead of complaining when I am in need. (17:2)

"Quiet!" Moses replied. "Why are you arguing with me? And why are you testing the LORD?"

³But tormented by thirst, they continued to complain, "Why did you ever take us out of Egypt? Why did you bring us here? We, our children, and our livestock will all die!"

I CRY OUT to the Lord when people complain about my leadership. (17:4)

⁴Then Moses pleaded with the LORD, "What should I do with these people? They are about to stone me!"

⁵The LORD said to Moses, "Take your shepherd's staff, the one you used when you struck the water of the Nile. Then call some of the leaders of Israel and walk on ahead of the people. ⁶I will meet you by the rock at Mount Sinai.* Strike the rock, and water will come pouring out. Then the people will be able to drink." Moses did just as he was told; and as the leaders looked on, water gushed out.

⁷Moses named the place Massah—"the place of testing"—and Meribah—"the place of arguing"—because the people of Israel argued with Moses and tested the LORD by saying, "Is the LORD going to take care of us or not?"

Israel Defeats the Amalekites

⁸While the people of Israel were still at Rephidim, the warriors of Amalek came to fight against them. ⁹Moses commanded Joshua, "Call the Israelites

16:31 *Manna* means "What is it?" See 16:15.   16:33 Hebrew *before the LORD*.   16:34 Hebrew *in front of the Testimony*.   16:36 Hebrew *An omer is one tenth of an ephah*.   17:1 Not to be confused with the English word *sin*.   17:6 Hebrew *Horeb*, another name for Sinai.

to arms, and fight the army of Amalek. Tomorrow, I will stand at the top of the hill with the staff of God in my hand."

¹⁰So Joshua did what Moses had commanded. He led his men out to fight the army of Amalek. Meanwhile Moses, Aaron, and Hur went to the top of a nearby hill. ¹¹As long as Moses held up the staff with his hands, the Israelites had the advantage. But whenever he lowered his hands, the Amalekites gained the upper hand. ¹²Moses' arms finally became too tired to hold up the staff any longer. So Aaron and Hur found a stone for him to sit on. Then they stood on each side, holding up his hands until sunset. ¹³As a result, Joshua and his troops were able to crush the army of Amalek.

¹⁴Then the LORD instructed Moses, "Write this down as a permanent record, and announce it to Joshua: I will blot out every trace of Amalek from under heaven." ¹⁵Moses built an altar there and called it "The LORD Is My Banner."* ¹⁶He said, "They have dared to raise their fist against the LORD's throne, so now* the LORD will be at war with Amalek generation after generation."

I ENCOURAGE others to rely on God. (17:12)

CHAPTER 18
Jethro's Visit to Moses
Word soon reached Jethro, the priest of Midian and Moses' father-in-law, about all the wonderful things God had done for Moses and his people, the Israelites. He had heard about how the LORD had brought them safely out of Egypt.

²Some time before this, Moses had sent his wife, Zipporah, and his two sons to live with Jethro, his father-in-law. ³The name of Moses' first son was Gershom,* for Moses had said when the boy was born, "I have been a stranger in a foreign land." ⁴The name of his second son was Eliezer,* for Moses had said at his birth, "The God of my fathers was my helper; he delivered me from the sword of Pharaoh." ⁵Jethro now came to visit Moses, and he brought Moses' wife and two sons with him. They arrived while Moses and the people were camped near the mountain of God. ⁶Moses was told, "Jethro, your father-in-law, has come to visit you. Your wife and your two sons are with him."

⁷So Moses went out to meet his father-in-law. He bowed to him respectfully and greeted him warmly. They asked about each other's health and then went to Moses' tent to talk further. ⁸Moses told his father-in-law about everything the LORD had done to rescue Israel from Pharaoh and the Egyptians. He also told him about the problems they had faced along the way and how the LORD had delivered his people from all their troubles. ⁹Jethro was delighted when he heard about all that the LORD had done for Israel as he brought them out of Egypt.

I WILLINGLY SHARE with others the problems I have faced and how God has delivered me. (18:8)

¹⁰"Praise be to the LORD," Jethro said, "for he has saved you from the Egyptians and from Pharaoh. He has rescued Israel from the power of Egypt! ¹¹I know now that the LORD is greater than all other gods, because his people have escaped from the proud and cruel Egyptians."

I PRAISE the Lord for his deliverance. (18:10)

¹²Then Jethro presented a burnt offering and gave sacrifices to God. As Jethro was doing this, Aaron and the leaders of Israel came out to meet him. They all joined him in a sacrificial meal in God's presence.

Jethro's Wise Advice
¹³The next day, Moses sat as usual to hear the people's complaints against each other. They were lined up in front of him from morning till evening.

¹⁴When Moses' father-in-law saw all that Moses was doing for the people, he said, "Why are you trying to do all this alone? The people have been standing here all day to get your help."

17:15 Hebrew *Yahweh Nissi.* 17:16 Or *Hands have been lifted up to the LORD's throne, and now.* 18:3 *Gershom* sounds like a Hebrew term that means "a stranger there." 18:4 *Eliezer* means "God is my helper."

¹⁵Moses replied, "Well, the people come to me to seek God's guidance. ¹⁶When an argument arises, I am the one who settles the case. I inform the people of God's decisions and teach them his laws and instructions."

¹⁷"This is not good!" his father-in-law exclaimed. ¹⁸"You're going to wear yourself out—and the people, too. This job is too heavy a burden for you to handle all by yourself. ¹⁹Now let me give you a word of advice, and may God be with you. You should continue to be the people's representative before God, bringing him their questions to be decided. ²⁰You should tell them God's decisions, teach them God's laws and instructions, and show them how to conduct their lives. ²¹But find some capable, honest men who fear God and hate bribes. Appoint them as judges over groups of one thousand, one hundred, fifty, and ten. ²²These men can serve the people, resolving all the ordinary cases. Anything that is too important or too complicated can be brought to you. But they can take care of the smaller matters themselves. They will help you carry the load, making the task easier for you. ²³If you follow this advice, and if God directs you to do so, then you will be able to endure the pressures, and all these people will go home in peace."

²⁴Moses listened to his father-in-law's advice and followed his suggestions. ²⁵He chose capable men from all over Israel and made them judges over the people. They were put in charge of groups of one thousand, one hundred, fifty, and ten. ²⁶These men were constantly available to administer justice. They brought the hard cases to Moses, but they judged the smaller matters themselves.

²⁷Soon after this, Moses said good-bye to his father-in-law, who returned to his own land.

CHAPTER 19

The LORD Reveals Himself at Sinai

The Israelites arrived in the wilderness of Sinai exactly two months after they left Egypt.* ²After breaking camp at Rephidim, they came to the base of Mount Sinai and set up camp there.

³ Then Moses climbed the mountain to appear before God. The LORD called out to him from the mountain and said, "Give these instructions to the descendants of Jacob, the people of Israel: ⁴'You have seen what I did to the Egyptians. You know how I brought you to myself and carried you on eagle's wings. ⁵Now if you will obey me and keep my covenant, you will be my own special treasure from among all the nations of the earth; for all the earth belongs to me. ⁶And you will be to me a kingdom of priests, my holy nation.' Give this message to the Israelites."

⁷Moses returned from the mountain and called together the leaders of the people and told them what the LORD had said. ⁸They all responded together, "We will certainly do everything the LORD asks of us." So Moses brought the people's answer back to the LORD.

⁹Then the LORD said to Moses, "I am going to come to you in a thick cloud so the people themselves can hear me as I speak to you. Then they will always have confidence in you."

Moses told the LORD what the people had said. ¹⁰Then the LORD told Moses, "Go down and prepare the people for my visit. Purify them today and tomorrow, and have them wash their clothing. ¹¹Be sure they are ready on the third day, for I will come down upon Mount Sinai as all the people watch. ¹²Set boundary lines that the people may not pass. Warn them, 'Be careful! Do not go up on the mountain or even touch its boundaries. Those who do will certainly die!' ¹³Any people or animals that cross the boundary must be stoned to death or shot with arrows. They must not be touched by human hands.' The

I ENLIST capable people to help me. (18:21)

I ALLOW others to help me carry the load of caring for other people. (18:22)

I DELEGATE responsibility to others but willingly take responsibility for major concerns. (18:26)

See Jacob's profile (page 43) at Genesis 32:9.

I COMMIT myself to obey everything the Lord asks of me. (19:8)

I BELIEVE the Lord required his people to be prepared and purified before they heard him speak. (19:10)

19:1 Hebrew *in the third month . . . on the very day*, i.e., two lunar months to the day after leaving Egypt. This day of the Hebrew lunar calendar occurs in late May or early June; compare note on 13:4.

people must stay away from the mountain until they hear one long blast from the ram's horn. Then they must gather at the foot of the mountain."

¹⁴So Moses went down to the people. He purified them for worship and had them wash their clothing. ¹⁵He told them, "Get ready for an important event two days from now. And until then, abstain from having sexual intercourse."

¹⁶On the morning of the third day, there was a powerful thunder and lightning storm, and a dense cloud came down upon the mountain. There was a long, loud blast from a ram's horn, and all the people trembled. ¹⁷Moses led them out from the camp to meet with God, and they stood at the foot of the mountain. ¹⁸All Mount Sinai was covered with smoke because the LORD had descended on it in the form of fire. The smoke billowed into the sky like smoke from a furnace, and the whole mountain shook with a violent earthquake. ¹⁹As the horn blast grew louder and louder, Moses spoke, and God thundered his reply for all to hear. ²⁰The LORD came down on the top of Mount Sinai and called Moses to the top of the mountain. So Moses climbed the mountain.

²¹Then the LORD told Moses, "Go back down and warn the people not to cross the boundaries. They must not come up here to see the LORD, for those who do will die. ²²Even the priests who regularly come near to the LORD must purify themselves, or I will destroy them."

²³"But LORD, the people cannot come up on the mountain!" Moses protested. "You already told them not to. You told me to set boundaries around the mountain and to declare it off limits."

²⁴But the LORD said, "Go down anyway and bring Aaron back with you. In the meantime, do not let the priests or the people cross the boundaries to come up here. If they do, I will punish them."

²⁵So Moses went down to the people and told them what the LORD had said.

CHAPTER 20

The Ten Commandments

Then God instructed the people as follows:

²"I am the LORD your God, who rescued you from slavery in Egypt.

³"Do not worship any other gods besides me.

⁴"Do not make idols of any kind, whether in the shape of birds or animals or fish. ⁵You must never worship or bow down to them, for I, the LORD your God, am a jealous God who will not share your affection with any other god! I do not leave unpunished the sins of those who hate me, but I punish the children for the sins of their parents to the third and fourth generations. ⁶But I lavish my love on those who love me and obey my commands, even for a thousand generations.

⁷"Do not misuse the name of the LORD your God. The LORD will not let you go unpunished if you misuse his name.

⁸"Remember to observe the Sabbath day by keeping it holy. ⁹Six days a week are set apart for your daily duties and regular work, ¹⁰but the seventh day is a day of rest dedicated to the LORD your God. On that day no one in your household may do any kind of work. This includes you, your sons and daughters, your male and female servants, your livestock, and any foreigners living among you. ¹¹For in six days the LORD made the heavens, the earth, the sea, and everything in them; then he rested on the seventh day. That is why the LORD blessed the Sabbath day and set it apart as holy.

¹²"Honor your father and mother. Then you will live a long, full life in the land the LORD your God will give you.

¹³"Do not murder.

¹⁴"Do not commit adultery.

¹⁵"Do not steal.

I BELIEVE the Lord descended on Mount Sinai in the form of great fire in the presence of the entire nation of Israel. (19:18)

I BELIEVE all Israel heard the voice of God from Mount Sinai. (19:19)

I BELIEVE the Israelites could not come close to the Lord's actual presence without fatal consequences. (19:21)

I WORSHIP the Lord my God exclusively (1 Corinthians 10:14). (20:3)

I BELIEVE the Lord never stops lavishing his love on those who love him and obey his commands. (20:6)

I HONOR my father and mother (Matthew 19:19; Ephesians 6:1–3). (20:12)

¹⁶"Do not testify falsely against your neighbor.

¹⁷"Do not covet your neighbor's house. Do not covet your neighbor's wife, male or female servant, ox or donkey, or anything else your neighbor owns."

¹⁸When the people heard the thunder and the loud blast of the horn, and when they saw the lightning and the smoke billowing from the mountain, they stood at a distance, trembling with fear.

¹⁹And they said to Moses, "You tell us what God says, and we will listen. But don't let God speak directly to us. If he does, we will die!"

²⁰"Don't be afraid," Moses said, "for God has come in this way to show you his awesome power. From now on, let your fear of him keep you from sinning!"

²¹As the people stood in the distance, Moses entered into the deep darkness where God was.

Proper Use of Altars

²²And the LORD said to Moses, "Say this to the people of Israel: You are witnesses that I have spoken to you from heaven. ²³Remember, you must not make or worship idols of silver or gold.

²⁴"The altars you make for me must be simple altars of earth. Offer on such altars your sacrifices to me—your burnt offerings and peace offerings, your sheep and goats and your cattle. Build altars in the places where I remind you who I am, and I will come and bless you there. ²⁵If you build altars from stone, use only uncut stones. Do not chip or shape the stones with a tool, for that would make them unfit for holy use. ²⁶And you may not approach my altar by steps. If you do, someone might look up under the skirts of your clothing and see your nakedness.

CHAPTER 21

Fair Treatment of Slaves

"Here are some other instructions you must present to Israel:

²"If you buy a Hebrew slave, he is to serve for only six years. Set him free in the seventh year, and he will owe you nothing for his freedom. ³If he was single when he became your slave and then married afterward, only he will go free in the seventh year. But if he was married before he became a slave, then his wife will be freed with him.

⁴"If his master gave him a wife while he was a slave, and they had sons or daughters, then the man will be free in the seventh year, but his wife and children will still belong to his master. ⁵But the slave may plainly declare, 'I love my master, my wife, and my children. I would rather not go free.' ⁶If he does this, his master must present him before God.* Then his master must take him to the door and publicly pierce his ear with an awl. After that, the slave will belong to his master forever.

⁷"When a man sells his daughter as a slave, she will not be freed at the end of six years as the men are. ⁸If she does not please the man who bought her, he may allow her to be bought back again. But he is not allowed to sell her to foreigners, since he is the one who broke the contract with her. ⁹And if the slave girl's owner arranges for her to marry his son, he may no longer treat her as a slave girl, but he must treat her as his daughter. ¹⁰If he himself marries her and then takes another wife, he may not reduce her food or clothing or fail to sleep with her as his wife. ¹¹If he fails in any of these three ways, she may leave as a free woman without making any payment.

Cases of Personal Injury

¹²"Anyone who hits a person hard enough to cause death must be put to death. ¹³But if it is an accident and God allows it to happen, I will appoint a

21:6 Or *before the judges.*

I DO NOT COVET (Romans 7:6-8). (20:17)

I MAKE tangible reminders of instances when God has shown me who he is. (20:24)

I BELIEVE God gave instructions to the Israelites for the fair treatment of slaves. (21:2)

I BELIEVE God gave instructions to the Israelites for the protection and fair treatment of slave women. (21:7)

I BELIEVE God provided the Israelites with a place of safety for the person who killed someone accidentally. (21:13) place where the slayer can run for safety. ¹⁴However, if someone deliberately attacks and kills another person, then the slayer must be dragged even from my altar and put to death.

¹⁵"Anyone who strikes father or mother must be put to death.

¹⁶"Kidnappers must be killed, whether they are caught in possession of their victims or have already sold them as slaves.

¹⁷"Anyone who curses father or mother must be put to death.

¹⁸"Now suppose two people quarrel, and one hits the other with a stone or fist, causing injury but not death. ¹⁹If the injured person is later able to walk again, even with a crutch, the assailant will be innocent. Nonetheless, the assailant must pay for time lost because of the injury and must pay for the medical expenses.

²⁰"If a male or female slave is beaten and dies, the owner must be punished. ²¹If the slave recovers after a couple of days, however, then the owner should not be punished, since the slave is the owner's property.

²²"Now suppose two people are fighting, and in the process, they hurt a pregnant woman so her child is born prematurely. If no further harm results, then the person responsible must pay damages in the amount the woman's husband demands and the judges approve. ²³But if any harm results, then the offender must be punished according to the injury. If the result is death, the offender must be executed. ²⁴If an eye is injured, injure the eye of the person who did it. If a tooth gets knocked out, knock out the tooth of the person who did it. Similarly, the payment must be hand for hand, foot for foot, ²⁵burn for burn, wound for wound, bruise for bruise.

²⁶"If an owner hits a male or female slave in the eye and the eye is blinded, then the slave may go free because of the eye. ²⁷And if an owner knocks out the tooth of a male or female slave, the slave should be released in payment for the tooth.

²⁸"If a bull gores a man or woman to death, the bull must be stoned, and its flesh may not be eaten. In such a case, however, the owner will not be held liable. ²⁹Suppose, on the other hand, that the owner knew the bull had gored people in the past, yet the bull was not kept under control. If this is true and if the bull kills someone, it must be stoned, and the owner must also be killed. ³⁰However, the dead person's relatives may accept payment from the owner of the bull to compensate for the loss of life. The owner will have to pay whatever is demanded.

³¹"The same principle applies if the bull gores a boy or a girl. ³²But if the bull gores a slave, either male or female, the slave's owner is to be given thirty silver coins* in payment, and the bull must be stoned.

³³"Suppose someone digs or uncovers a well and fails to cover it, and then an ox or a donkey falls into it. ³⁴The owner of the well must pay in full for the dead animal but then gets to keep it.

³⁵"If someone's bull injures a neighbor's bull and the injured bull dies, then the two owners must sell the live bull and divide the money between them. Each will also own half of the dead bull. ³⁶But if the bull was known from past experience to gore, yet its owner failed to keep it under control, the money will not be divided. The owner of the living bull must pay in full for the dead bull but then gets to keep it.

CHAPTER 22

Protection of Property

"A fine must be paid by anyone who steals an ox or sheep and then kills or sells it. For oxen the fine is five oxen for each one stolen. For sheep the fine is four sheep for each one stolen.

21:32 Hebrew *30 shekels of silver*, about 12 ounces or 342 grams in weight.

I BELIEVE God required an assailant to provide restitution to the injured person. (21:18)

I BELIEVE God required that the punishment fit the crime. (21:23)

Ask God to open your eyes as you read his Word (Psalm 119:18).

I BELIEVE God required the Israelites to pay restitution plus a fine when they stole something. (22:1)

²"If a thief is caught in the act of breaking into a house and is killed in the process, the person who killed the thief is not guilty. ³But if it happens in daylight, the one who killed the thief is guilty of murder.

"A thief who is caught must pay in full for everything that was stolen. If payment is not made, the thief must be sold as a slave to pay the debt. ⁴If someone steals an ox or a donkey or a sheep and it is recovered alive, then the thief must pay double the value.

⁵"If an animal is grazing in a field or vineyard and the owner lets it stray into someone else's field to graze, then the animal's owner must pay damages in the form of high-quality grain or grapes.

⁶"If a fire gets out of control and goes into another person's field, destroying the sheaves or the standing grain, then the one who started the fire must pay for the lost crops.

⁷"Suppose someone entrusts money or goods to a neighbor, and they are stolen from the neighbor's house. If the thief is found, the fine is double the value of what was stolen. ⁸But if the thief is not found, God* will determine whether or not it was the neighbor who stole the property.

⁹"Suppose there is a dispute between two people as to who owns a particular ox, donkey, sheep, article of clothing, or anything else. Both parties must come before God* for a decision, and the person whom God declares* guilty must pay double to the other.

¹⁰"Now suppose someone asks a neighbor to care for a donkey, ox, sheep, or any other animal, but it dies or is injured or gets away, and there is no eyewitness to report just what happened. ¹¹The neighbor must then take an oath of innocence in the presence of the LORD. The owner must accept the neighbor's word, and no payment will be required. ¹²But if the animal or property was stolen, payment must be made to the owner. ¹³If it was attacked by a wild animal, the carcass must be shown as evidence, and no payment will be required.

¹⁴"If someone borrows an animal from a neighbor and it is injured or killed, and if the owner was not there at the time, the person who borrowed it must pay for it. ¹⁵But if the owner is there, no payment is required. And no payment is required if the animal was rented because this loss was covered by the rental fee.

Social Responsibility

¹⁶"If a man seduces a virgin who is not engaged to anyone and sleeps with her, he must pay the customary dowry and accept her as his wife. ¹⁷But if her father refuses to let her marry him, the man must still pay the money for her dowry.

¹⁸"A sorceress must not be allowed to live.

¹⁹"Anyone who has sexual relations with an animal must be executed.

²⁰"Anyone who sacrifices to any god other than the LORD must be destroyed.

²¹"Do not oppress foreigners in any way. Remember, you yourselves were once foreigners in the land of Egypt.

²²"Do not exploit widows or orphans. ²³If you do and they cry out to me, then I will surely help them. ²⁴My anger will blaze forth against you, and I will kill you with the sword. Your wives will become widows, and your children will become fatherless.

²⁵"If you lend money to a fellow Hebrew in need, do not be like a money lender, charging interest. ²⁶If you take your neighbor's cloak as a pledge of repayment, you must return it by nightfall. ²⁷Your neighbor will need it to stay warm during the night. If you do not return it and your neighbor cries out to me for help, then I will hear, for I am very merciful.

22:8 Or *the judges.*   22:9a Or *before the judges.*   22:9b Or *whom the judges declare.*

I PAY damages for harm that comes to someone else's property because of my carelessness. (22:5)

I BELIEVE God requires a man to be fully responsible for every sexual action. (22:16)

I CARE about foreigners because God cares about them. (22:21)

I SHOW kindness to widows and orphans. (22:22)

28 "Do not blaspheme God* or curse anyone who rules over you.

29 "Do not hold anything back when you give me the tithe of your crops and your wine.

"You must make the necessary payment for redemption of your firstborn sons.

30 "You must also give me the firstborn of your cattle and sheep. Leave the newborn animal with its mother for seven days; then give it to me on the eighth day.

31 "You are my own holy people. Therefore, do not eat any animal that has been attacked and killed by a wild animal. Throw its carcass out for the dogs to eat.

I DO NOT HOLD anything back when I give tithes to God. (22:29)

CHAPTER 23

A Call for Justice

"Do not pass along false reports. Do not cooperate with evil people by telling lies on the witness stand.

2 "Do not join a crowd that intends to do evil. When you are on the witness stand, do not be swayed in your testimony by the opinion of the majority. 3 And do not slant your testimony in favor of a person just because that person is poor.

4 "If you come upon your enemy's ox or donkey that has strayed away, take it back to its owner. 5 If you see the donkey of someone who hates you struggling beneath a heavy load, do not walk by. Instead, stop and offer to help.

6 "Do not twist justice against people simply because they are poor.

7 "Keep far away from falsely charging anyone with evil. Never put an innocent or honest person to death. I will not allow anyone guilty of this to go free.

8 "Take no bribes, for a bribe makes you ignore something that you clearly see. A bribe always hurts the cause of the person who is in the right.

9 "Do not oppress the foreigners living among you. You know what it is like to be a foreigner. Remember your own experience in the land of Egypt.

I GIVE a completely accurate witness, favoring neither poor nor rich. (23:2)

I AVOID all false charges because God takes very seriously the unjust sentencing of an innocent person. (23:7)

I DO NOT OPPRESS foreigners. (23:9)

10 "Plant and harvest your crops for six years, 11 but let the land rest and lie fallow during the seventh year. Then let the poor among you harvest any volunteer crop that may come up. Leave the rest for the animals to eat. The same applies to your vineyards and olive groves.

12 "Work for six days, and rest on the seventh. This will give your ox and your donkey a chance to rest. It will also allow the people of your household, including your slaves and visitors, to be refreshed.

13 "Be sure to obey all my instructions. And remember, never pray to or swear by any other gods. Do not even mention their names.

Three Annual Festivals

14 "Each year you must celebrate three festivals in my honor. 15 The first is the Festival of Unleavened Bread. For seven days you are to eat bread made without yeast, just as I commanded you before. This festival will be an annual event at the appointed time in early spring,* for that is the anniversary of your exodus from Egypt. Everyone must bring me a sacrifice at that time. 16 You must also celebrate the Festival of Harvest,* when you bring me the first crops of your harvest. Finally, you are to celebrate the Festival of the Final Harvest* at the end of the harvest season. 17 At these three times each year, every man in Israel must appear before the Sovereign LORD.

18 "Sacrificial blood must never be offered together with bread that has yeast in it. And no sacrificial fat may be left unoffered until the next morning.

I BELIEVE I can come before God any day of the year. (23:17)

22:28 Or Do not revile your judges. 23:15 Hebrew in the month of Abib. This month of the Hebrew lunar calendar usually occurs in March and April. 23:16a Or Festival of Weeks. 23:16b This was later called the Festival of Shelters; see Lev 23:33-36.

¹⁹"As you harvest each of your crops, bring me a choice sample of the first day's harvest. It must be offered to the LORD your God.

"You must not cook a young goat in its mother's milk.

A Promise of the LORD's Presence

²⁰"See, I am sending my angel before you to lead you safely to the land I have prepared for you. ²¹Pay attention to him, and obey all of his instructions. Do not rebel against him, for he will not forgive your sins. He is my representative—he bears my name. ²²But if you are careful to obey him, following all my instructions, then I will be an enemy to your enemies, and I will oppose those who oppose you. ²³For my angel will go before you and bring you into the land of the Amorites, Hittites, Perizzites, Canaanites, Hivites, and Jebusites, so you may live there. And I will destroy them. ²⁴Do not worship the gods of these other nations or serve them in any way, and never follow their evil example. Instead, you must utterly conquer them and break down their shameful idols.

²⁵"You must serve only the LORD your God. If you do, I will bless you with food and water, and I will keep you healthy. ²⁶There will be no miscarriages or infertility among your people, and I will give you long, full lives.

²⁷"I will send my terror upon all the people whose lands you invade, and they will panic before you. ²⁸I will send hornets ahead of you to drive out the Hivites, Canaanites, and Hittites. ²⁹But I will not do this all in one year because the land would become a wilderness, and the wild animals would become too many to control. ³⁰I will drive them out a little at a time until your population has increased enough to fill the land. ³¹And I will fix your boundaries from the Red Sea to the Mediterranean Sea,* and from the southern deserts to the Euphrates River.* I will help you defeat the people now living in the land, and you will drive them out ahead of you.

³²"Make no treaties with them and have nothing to do with their gods. ³³Do not even let them live among you! If you do, they will infect you with their sin of idol worship, and that would be disastrous for you."

CHAPTER 24

Israel Accepts the LORD's Covenant

Then the LORD instructed Moses: "Come up here to me, and bring along Aaron, Nadab, Abihu, and seventy of Israel's leaders. All of them must worship at a distance. ²You alone, Moses, are allowed to come near to the LORD. The others must not come too close. And remember, none of the other people are allowed to climb on the mountain at all."

³When Moses had announced to the people all the teachings and regulations the LORD had given him, they answered in unison, "We will do everything the LORD has told us to do."

⁴Then Moses carefully wrote down all the LORD's instructions. Early the next morning he built an altar at the foot of the mountain. He also set up twelve pillars around the altar, one for each of the twelve tribes of Israel. ⁵Then he sent some of the young men to sacrifice young bulls as burnt offerings and peace offerings to the LORD. ⁶Moses took half the blood from these animals and drew it off into basins. The other half he splashed against the altar.

⁷Then he took the Book of the Covenant and read it to the people. They all responded again, "We will do everything the LORD has commanded. We will obey."

⁸Then Moses sprinkled the blood from the basins over the people and said, "This blood confirms the covenant the LORD has made with you in giving you these laws."

23:31a Hebrew *from the sea of reeds to the sea of the Philistines.*   23:31b Hebrew *the river.*

I BELIEVE God is with me, leading me where he wants me to go. (23:20)

I BELIEVE God required the Israelites to conquer certain nations and destroy their false gods. (23:24)

I OBEY all of the Lord's commands. (24:3)

I DO NOT IGNORE any of the Lord's commands. (24:4)

⁹Then Moses, Aaron, Nadab, Abihu, and seventy of the leaders of Israel went up the mountain. ¹⁰There they saw the God of Israel. Under his feet there seemed to be a pavement of brilliant sapphire, as clear as the heavens. ¹¹And though Israel's leaders saw God, he did not destroy them. In fact, they shared a meal together in God's presence!

¹²And the LORD said to Moses, "Come up to me on the mountain. Stay there while I give you the tablets of stone that I have inscribed with my instructions and commands. Then you will teach the people from them." ¹³So Moses and his assistant Joshua climbed up the mountain of God.

¹⁴Moses told the other leaders, "Stay here and wait for us until we come back. If there are any problems while I am gone, consult with Aaron and Hur, who are here with you."

¹⁵Then Moses went up the mountain, and the cloud covered it. ¹⁶And the glorious presence of the LORD rested upon Mount Sinai, and the cloud covered it for six days. On the seventh day the LORD called to Moses from the cloud. ¹⁷The Israelites at the foot of the mountain saw an awesome sight. The awesome glory of the LORD on the mountaintop looked like a devouring fire. ¹⁸Then Moses disappeared into the cloud as he climbed higher up the mountain. He stayed on the mountain forty days and forty nights.

CHAPTER 25

Offerings for the Tabernacle
The LORD said to Moses, ²"Tell the people of Israel that everyone who wants to may bring me an offering. ³Here is a list of items you may accept on my behalf: gold, silver, and bronze; ⁴blue, purple, and scarlet yarn; fine linen; goat hair for cloth; ⁵tanned ram skins and fine goatskin leather; acacia wood; ⁶olive oil for the lamps; spices for the anointing oil and the fragrant incense; ⁷onyx stones, and other stones to be set in the ephod and the chestpiece.

⁸"I want the people of Israel to build me a sacred residence where I can live among them. ⁹You must make this Tabernacle and its furnishings exactly according to the plans I will show you.

Plans for the Ark
¹⁰"Make an Ark of acacia wood—a sacred chest 3³/₄ feet long, 2¹/₄ feet wide, and 2¹/₄ feet high.* ¹¹Overlay it inside and outside with pure gold, and put a molding of gold all around it. ¹²Cast four rings of gold for it, and attach them to its four feet, two rings on each side. ¹³Make poles from acacia wood, and overlay them with gold. ¹⁴Fit the poles into the rings at the sides of the Ark to carry it. ¹⁵These carrying poles must never be taken from the rings; they are to be left there permanently. ¹⁶When the Ark is finished, place inside it the stone tablets inscribed with the terms of the covenant,* which I will give to you.

¹⁷"Then make the Ark's cover—the place of atonement—out of pure gold. It must be 3³/₄ feet long and 2¹/₄ feet wide. ¹⁸Then use hammered gold to make two cherubim, and place them at the two ends of the atonement cover. ¹⁹Attach the cherubim to each end of the atonement cover, making it all one piece. ²⁰The cherubim will face each other, looking down on the atonement cover with their wings spread out above it. ²¹Place inside the Ark the stone tablets inscribed with the terms of the covenant, which I will give to you. Then put the atonement cover on top of the Ark. ²²I will meet with you there and talk to you from above the atonement cover between the gold cherubim that hover over the Ark of the Covenant.* From there I will give you my commands for the people of Israel.

I BELIEVE Moses received the law directly from God's own hand. (24:12)

I BELIEVE the Lord spoke to Moses regarding the offerings and plans for the Tabernacle. (25:1)

I BRING offerings to the Lord willingly. (25:2)

I BELIEVE God asked the Israelites to build a residence for him to live among them (1 Peter 2:5). (25:8)

I FOLLOW God's instructions exactly as he gives them. (25:9)

I BELIEVE the Lord gave exact instructions for making the Ark of the Covenant. (25:10)

I BELIEVE the Lord met with Moses from above the atonement cover of the Ark of the Covenant. (25:22)

25:10 Hebrew 2¹/₂ cubits [1.1 meters] long, 1¹/₂ cubits [0.7 meters] wide, and 1¹/₂ cubits high. In this chapter, the distance measures are calculated from the Hebrew cubit at a ratio of 18 inches or 45 centimeters per cubit. 25:16 Hebrew place inside it the Testimony; also in 25:21. 25:22 Or Ark of the Testimony.

Plans for the Table

I BELIEVE the Lord gave exact instructions for making the table for the Bread of the Presence and the utensils on it. (25:23)

²³"Then make a table of acacia wood, 3 feet long, 1¹/₂ feet wide, and 2¹/₄ feet high. ²⁴Overlay it with pure gold and run a molding of gold around it. ²⁵Put a rim about three inches* wide around the top edge, and put a gold molding all around the rim. ²⁶Make four gold rings, and put the rings at the four corners by the four legs, ²⁷close to the rim around the top. These rings will support the poles used to carry the table. ²⁸Make these poles from acacia wood and overlay them with gold. ²⁹And make gold plates and dishes, as well as pitchers and bowls to be used in pouring out drink offerings. ³⁰You must always keep the special Bread of the Presence on the table before me.

Plans for the Lampstand

I BELIEVE the Lord gave exact instructions for making the lampstand. (25:31)

³¹"Make a lampstand of pure, hammered gold. The entire lampstand and its decorations will be one piece—the base, center stem, lamp cups, buds, and blossoms. ³²It will have six branches, three branches going out from each side of the center stem. ³³Each of the six branches will hold a cup shaped like an almond blossom, complete with buds and petals. ³⁴The center stem of the lampstand will be decorated with four almond blossoms, complete with buds and petals. ³⁵One blossom will be set beneath each pair of branches where they extend from the center stem. ³⁶The decorations and branches must all be one piece with the stem, and they must be hammered from pure gold. ³⁷Then make the seven lamps for the lampstand, and set them so they reflect their light forward. ³⁸The lamp snuffers and trays must also be made of pure gold. ³⁹You will need seventy-five pounds* of pure gold for the lampstand and its accessories.

I FOLLOW God's instructions exactly as he gives them. (25:40)

⁴⁰"Be sure that you make everything according to the pattern I have shown you here on the mountain.

CHAPTER 26

Plans for the Tabernacle

I BELIEVE the Lord gave exact instructions for constructing the Tabernacle. (26:1)

"Make the Tabernacle from ten sheets of fine linen. These sheets are to be decorated with blue, purple, and scarlet yarn, with figures of cherubim skillfully embroidered into them. ²Each sheet must be forty-two feet long and six feet wide.* All ten sheets must be exactly the same size. ³Join five of these sheets together into one set; then join the other five sheets into a second set. ⁴Put loops of blue yarn along the edge of the last sheet in each set. ⁵The fifty loops along the edge of one set are to match the fifty loops along the edge of the other. ⁶Then make fifty gold clasps to fasten the loops of the two sets of sheets together, making the Tabernacle a single unit.

⁷"Make heavy sheets of cloth from goat hair to cover the Tabernacle. There must be eleven of these sheets, ⁸each forty-five feet long and six feet wide. All eleven of these sheets must be exactly the same size. ⁹Join five of these together into one set, and join the other six into a second set. The sixth sheet of the second set is to be doubled over at the entrance of the sacred tent. ¹⁰Put fifty loops along the edge of the last sheet in each set, ¹¹and fasten them together with fifty bronze clasps. In this way, the two sets will become a single unit. ¹²An extra half sheet of this roof covering will be left to hang over the back of the Tabernacle, ¹³and the covering will hang down an extra eighteen inches on each side. ¹⁴On top of these coverings place a layer of tanned ram skins, and over them put a layer of fine goatskin leather. This will complete the roof covering.

¹⁵"The framework of the Tabernacle will consist of frames made of acacia wood. ¹⁶Each frame must be 15 feet high and 2¹/₄ feet wide. ¹⁷There will be two pegs on each frame so they can be joined to the next frame. All the frames

25:25 Hebrew *a handbreadth* [8 centimeters]. 25:39 Hebrew *1 talent* [34 kilograms]. 26:2 Hebrew *28 cubits* [12.6 meters] *long and 4 cubits* [1.8 meters] *wide.* In this chapter, the distance measures are calculated from the Hebrew cubit at a ratio of 18 inches or 45 centimeters per cubit.

must be made this way. ¹⁸Twenty of these frames will support the south side of the Tabernacle. ¹⁹They will fit into forty silver bases—two bases under each frame. ²⁰On the north side there will also be twenty of these frames, ²¹with their forty silver bases, two bases for each frame. ²²On the west side there will be six frames, ²³along with an extra frame at each corner. ²⁴These corner frames will be connected at the bottom and firmly attached at the top with a single ring, forming a single unit. Both of these corner frames will be made the same way. ²⁵So there will be eight frames on that end of the Tabernacle, supported by sixteen silver bases—two bases under each frame.

²⁶"Make crossbars of acacia wood to run across the frames, five crossbars for the north side of the Tabernacle ²⁷and five for the south side. Also make five crossbars for the rear of the Tabernacle, which will face westward. ²⁸The middle crossbar, halfway up the frames, will run all the way from one end of the Tabernacle to the other. ²⁹Overlay the frames with gold and make gold rings to support the crossbars. Overlay the crossbars with gold as well.

³⁰"Set up this Tabernacle according to the design you were shown on the mountain.

³¹"Across the inside of the Tabernacle hang a special curtain made of fine linen, with cherubim skillfully embroidered into the cloth using blue, purple, and scarlet yarn. ³²Hang this inner curtain on gold hooks set into four posts made from acacia wood and overlaid with gold. The posts will fit into silver bases. ³³When the inner curtain is in place, put the Ark of the Covenant* behind it. This curtain will separate the Holy Place from the Most Holy Place.

³⁴"Then put the Ark's cover—the place of atonement—on top of the Ark of the Covenant inside the Most Holy Place. ³⁵Place the table and lampstand across the room from each other outside the inner curtain. The lampstand must be placed on the south side, and the table must be set toward the north.

³⁶"Make another curtain from fine linen for the entrance of the sacred tent, and embroider exquisite designs into it, using blue, purple, and scarlet yarn. ³⁷Hang this curtain on gold hooks set into five posts made from acacia wood and overlaid with gold. The posts will fit into five bronze bases.

CHAPTER 27

Plans for the Altar of Burnt Offering

"Using acacia wood, make a square altar 7¹⁄₂ feet wide, 7¹⁄₂ feet long, and 4¹⁄₂ feet high.* ²Make a horn at each of the four corners of the altar so the horns and altar are all one piece. Overlay the altar and its horns with bronze. ³The ash buckets, shovels, basins, meat hooks, and firepans will all be made of bronze. ⁴Make a bronze grating, with a metal ring at each corner. ⁵Fit the grating halfway down into the firebox, resting it on the ledge built there. ⁶For moving the altar, make poles from acacia wood, and overlay them with bronze. ⁷To carry it, put the poles into the rings at two sides of the altar. ⁸The altar must be hollow, made from planks. Be careful to build it just as you were shown on the mountain.

Plans for the Courtyard

⁹"Then make a courtyard for the Tabernacle, enclosed with curtains made from fine linen. On the south side the curtains will stretch for 150 feet. ¹⁰They will be held up by twenty bronze posts that fit into twenty bronze bases. The curtains will be held up with silver hooks attached to the silver rods that are attached to the posts. ¹¹It will be the same on the north side of the courtyard—150 feet of curtains held up by twenty posts fitted into bronze bases,

I BELIEVE the Lord gave Moses the design for the Tabernacle. (26:30)

I BELIEVE the Lord is most holy, just as the careful placement of the Ark of the Covenant demonstrated. (26:33)

I BELIEVE the Lord gave exact instructions for the arrangement of the Tabernacle. (26:34)

I BELIEVE the Lord gave exact instructions for the building of the altar. (27:1)

I BELIEVE the Lord gave exact instructions for building the courtyard to the Tabernacle. (27:9)

26:33 Or Ark of the Testimony; also in 26:34.　27:1 Hebrew 5 cubits [2.3 meters] wide, 5 cubits long, and 3 cubits [1.4 meters] high. In this chapter, the distance measures are calculated from the Hebrew cubit at a ratio of 18 inches or 45 centimeters per cubit.

with silver hooks and rods. ¹²The curtains on the west end of the courtyard will be 75 feet long, supported by ten posts set into ten bases. ¹³The east end will also be 75 feet long. ¹⁴The courtyard entrance will be on the east end, flanked by two curtains. The curtain on the right side will be 22¹/₂ feet long, supported by three posts set into three bases. ¹⁵The curtain on the left side will also be 22¹/₂ feet long, supported by three posts set into three bases.

¹⁶"For the entrance to the courtyard, make a curtain that is 30 feet long. Fashion it from fine linen, and decorate it with beautiful embroidery in blue, purple, and scarlet yarn. It will be attached to four posts that fit into four bases. ¹⁷All the posts around the courtyard must be connected by silver rods, using silver hooks. The posts are to be set in solid bronze bases. ¹⁸So the entire courtyard will be 150 feet long and 75 feet wide, with curtain walls 7¹/₂ feet high, made from fine linen. The bases supporting its walls will be made of bronze.

¹⁹"All the articles used in the work of the Tabernacle, including all the tent pegs used to support the Tabernacle and the courtyard curtains, must be made of bronze.

²⁰"Tell the people of Israel to bring you pure olive oil for the lampstand, so it can be kept burning continually. ²¹The lampstand will be placed outside the inner curtain of the Most Holy Place in the Tabernacle.* Aaron and his sons will keep the lamps burning in the LORD's presence day and night. This is a permanent law for the people of Israel, and it must be kept by all future generations.

CHAPTER 28

Clothing for the Priests

"Your brother, Aaron, and his sons, Nadab, Abihu, Eleazar, and Ithamar, will be set apart from the common people. They will be my priests and will minister to me. ²Make special clothing for Aaron to show his separation to God—beautiful garments that will lend dignity to his work. ³Instruct all those who have special skills as tailors to make the garments that will set Aaron apart from everyone else, so he may serve me as a priest. ⁴They are to make a chestpiece, an ephod, a robe, an embroidered tunic, a turban, and a sash. They will also make special garments for Aaron's sons to wear when they serve as priests before me. ⁵These items must be made of fine linen cloth and embroidered with gold thread and blue, purple, and scarlet yarn.

Design of the Ephod

⁶"The ephod must be made of fine linen cloth and skillfully embroidered with gold thread and blue, purple, and scarlet yarn. ⁷It will consist of two pieces, front and back, joined at the shoulders with two shoulder-pieces. ⁸And the sash will be made of the same materials: fine linen cloth embroidered with gold thread and blue, purple, and scarlet yarn. ⁹Take two onyx stones and engrave on them the names of the tribes of Israel. ¹⁰Six names will be on each stone, naming all the tribes in the order of their ancestors' births. ¹¹Engrave these names in the same way a gemcutter engraves a seal. Mount the stones in gold settings. ¹²Fasten the two stones on the shoulder-pieces of the ephod as memorial stones for the people of Israel. Aaron will carry these names before the LORD as a constant reminder. ¹³The settings are to be made of gold filigree, ¹⁴and two cords made of pure gold will be attached to the settings on the shoulders of the ephod.

Design of the Chestpiece

¹⁵"Then, with the most careful workmanship, make a chestpiece that will be used to determine God's will. Use the same materials as you did for the ephod: fine linen cloth embroidered with gold thread and blue, purple, and scarlet yarn. ¹⁶This chestpiece will be made of two folds of cloth, forming a

I BELIEVE the Lord gave exact instructions for using bronze for all the articles used for work in the Tabernacle. (27:19)

I BELIEVE the Israelites were to burn the lamps continually in the Lord's presence. (27:21)

I BELIEVE the Lord gave instructions for special clothing to be made for the priests to lend dignity to their work. (28:2)

I BELIEVE the Lord gave exact instructions for the ephod the high priest was to wear. (28:6)

I BELIEVE the high priest carried the names of the tribes of Israel as a reminder before the Lord. (28:12)

I BELIEVE the Lord gave exact instructions for the chestpiece. (28:15)

27:21 Hebrew *in the Tent of Meeting, outside of the inner curtain, in front of the Testimony.*

pouch nine inches* square. [17]Four rows of gemstones* will be attached to it. The first row will contain a red carnelian, a chrysolite, and an emerald. [18]The second row will contain a turquoise, a sapphire, and a white moonstone. [19]The third row will contain a jacinth, an agate, and an amethyst. [20]The fourth row will contain a beryl, an onyx, and a jasper. All these stones will be set in gold. [21]Each stone will represent one of the tribes of Israel, and the name of that tribe will be engraved on it as though it were a seal.

[22]"To attach the chestpiece to the ephod, make braided cords of pure gold. [23] Then make two gold rings and attach them to the top corners of the chestpiece. [24]The two gold cords will go through the rings on the chestpiece, [25]and the ends of the cords will be tied to the gold settings on the shoulder-pieces of the ephod. [26]Then make two more gold rings, and attach them to the two lower inside corners of the chestpiece next to the ephod. [27]And make two more gold rings and attach them to the ephod near the sash. [28]Then attach the bottom rings of the chestpiece to the rings on the ephod with blue cords. This will hold the chestpiece securely to the ephod above the beautiful sash. [29]In this way, Aaron will carry the names of the tribes of Israel on the chestpiece over his heart when he goes into the presence of the LORD in the Holy Place. Thus, the LORD will be reminded of his people continually. [30]Insert into the pocket of the chestpiece the Urim and Thummim, to be carried over Aaron's heart when he goes into the LORD's presence. Thus, Aaron will always carry the objects used to determine the LORD's will for his people whenever he goes in before the LORD.

I BELIEVE the Lord gave exact instructions for attaching the chestpiece to the ephod. (28:22)

I BELIEVE the Lord gave the priest the Urim and Thummim to determine the Lord's will in certain situations. (28:30)

Additional Clothing for the Priests

[31]"Make the robe of the ephod entirely of blue cloth, [32]with an opening for Aaron's head in the middle of it. The opening will be reinforced by a woven collar* so it will not tear. [33]Make pomegranates out of blue, purple, and scarlet yarn, and attach them to the hem of the robe, with gold bells between them. [34]The gold bells and pomegranates are to alternate all the way around the hem. [35]Aaron will wear this robe whenever he enters the Holy Place to minister to the LORD, and the bells will tinkle as he goes in and out of the LORD's presence. If he wears it, he will not die.

[36]"Next make a medallion of pure gold. Using the techniques of an engraver, inscribe it with these words: SET APART AS HOLY TO THE LORD. [37]This medallion will be attached to the front of Aaron's turban by means of a blue cord. [38]Aaron will wear it on his forehead, thus bearing the guilt connected with any errors regarding the sacred offerings of the people of Israel. He must always wear it so the LORD will accept the people.

[39]"Weave Aaron's patterned tunic from fine linen cloth. Fashion the turban out of this linen as well. Also make him an embroidered sash.

[40]"Then for Aaron's sons, make tunics, sashes, and headdresses to give them dignity and respect. [41]Clothe Aaron and his sons with these garments, and then anoint and ordain them. Set them apart as holy so they can serve as my priests. [42]Also make linen underclothes for them, to be worn next to their bodies, reaching from waist to thigh. [43]These must be worn whenever Aaron and his sons enter the Tabernacle* or approach the altar in the Holy Place to perform their duties. Thus they will not incur guilt and die. This law is permanent for Aaron and his descendants.

I BELIEVE the Lord instructed the high priest to wear a medallion so the Lord would accept the Israelites. (28:38)

I BELIEVE the Lord gave exact instructions for the clothing of the other priests. (28:40)

CHAPTER 29

Dedication of the Priests

"This is the ceremony for the dedication of Aaron and his sons as priests: Take a young bull and two rams with no physical defects. [2]Then using fine

I BELIEVE the Lord gave exact instructions for the dedication of Aaron and his sons as priests before God. (29:1)

28:16 Hebrew 1 *span* [23 centimeters].   28:17 The identification of some of these gemstones is uncertain.
28:32 The meaning of the Hebrew is uncertain.   28:43 Hebrew *Tent of Meeting*.

wheat flour and no yeast, make loaves of bread, thin cakes mixed with olive oil, and wafers with oil poured over them. ³Place these various kinds of bread in a single basket, and present them at the entrance of the Tabernacle, along with the young bull and the two rams.

⁴"Present Aaron and his sons at the entrance of the Tabernacle,* and wash them with water. ⁵Then put Aaron's tunic on him, along with the embroidered robe of the ephod, the ephod itself, the chestpiece, and the sash. ⁶And place on his head the turban with the gold medallion. ⁷Then take the anointing oil and pour it over his head. ⁸Next present his sons, and dress them in their tunics ⁹with their woven sashes and their headdresses. They will then be priests forever. In this way, you will ordain Aaron and his sons.

¹⁰"Then bring the young bull to the entrance of the Tabernacle, and Aaron and his sons will lay their hands on its head. ¹¹You will then slaughter it in the LORD's presence at the entrance of the Tabernacle. ¹²Smear some of its blood on the horns of the altar with your finger, and pour out the rest at the base of the altar. ¹³Take all the fat that covers the internal organs, also the long lobe of the liver and the two kidneys with their fat, and burn them on the altar. ¹⁴Then take the carcass (including the skin and the dung) outside the camp, and burn it as a sin offering.

¹⁵"Next Aaron and his sons must lay their hands on the head of one of the rams ¹⁶as it is slaughtered. Its blood will be collected and sprinkled on the sides of the altar. ¹⁷Cut up the ram and wash off the internal organs and the legs. Set them alongside the head and the other pieces of the body, ¹⁸and burn them all on the altar. This is a burnt offering to the LORD, which is very pleasing to him.

¹⁹"Now take the other ram and have Aaron and his sons lay their hands on its head ²⁰as it is slaughtered. Collect the blood and place some of it on the tip of the right earlobes of Aaron and his sons. Also put it on their right thumbs and the big toes of their right feet. Sprinkle the rest of the blood on the sides of the altar. ²¹Then take some of the blood from the altar and mix it with some of the anointing oil. Sprinkle it on Aaron and his sons and on their clothes. In this way, they and their clothing will be set apart as holy to the LORD.

²²"Since this is the ram for the ordination of Aaron and his sons, take the fat of the ram, including the fat tail and the fat that covers the internal organs. Also, take the long lobe of the liver, the two kidneys with their fat, and the right thigh. ²³Then take one loaf of bread, one cake mixed with olive oil, and one wafer from the basket of yeastless bread that was placed before the LORD. ²⁴Put all these in the hands of Aaron and his sons to be lifted up as a special gift to the LORD. ²⁵Afterward take the bread from their hands, and burn it on the altar as a burnt offering that will be pleasing to the LORD. ²⁶Then take the breast of Aaron's ordination ram, and lift it up in the LORD's presence as a special gift to him. Afterward keep it for yourself.

²⁷"Set aside as holy the parts of the ordination ram that belong to Aaron and his sons. This includes the breast and the thigh that were lifted up before the LORD in the ordination ceremony. ²⁸In the future, whenever the people of Israel offer up peace offerings or thanksgiving offerings to the LORD, these parts will be the regular share of Aaron and his descendants.

²⁹"Aaron's sacred garments must be preserved for his descendants who will succeed him, so they can be anointed and ordained in them. ³⁰Whoever is the next high priest after Aaron will wear these clothes for seven days before beginning to minister in the Tabernacle and the Holy Place.

³¹"Take the ram used in the ordination ceremony, and boil its meat in a sacred place. ³²Aaron and his sons are to eat this meat, along with the bread in

I BELIEVE the Lord gave exact instructions for the sacrifices to be given to dedicate Aaron and his sons as priests before God. (29:10)

I BELIEVE Aaron and his sons presented special gifts to the Lord. (29:24)

I BELIEVE the Lord gave parts of the offerings to the priests as their share. (29:28)

I BELIEVE God instructed the special clothing to be used for every succeeding high priest. (29:29)

I BELIEVE the Lord gave exact instructions for the person who should eat the ordination meal and how. (29:31)

29:4 Hebrew *Tent of Meeting*; also in 29:10, 11, 30, 32, 42, 44.

the basket, at the Tabernacle entrance. [33] They alone may eat the meat and bread used for their atonement in the ordination ceremony. The ordinary people may not eat them, for these things are set apart and holy. [34]If any of the ordination meat or bread remains until the morning, it must be burned. It may not be eaten, for it is holy.

[35]"This is how you will ordain Aaron and his sons to their offices. The ordination ceremony will go on for seven days. [36]Each day you must sacrifice a young bull as an offering for the atonement of sin. Afterward make an offering to cleanse the altar. Purify the altar by making atonement for it; make it holy by anointing it with oil. [37]Make atonement for the altar every day for seven days. After that, the altar will be exceedingly holy, and whatever touches it will become holy.

[38]"This is what you are to offer on the altar. Offer two one-year-old lambs each day, [39]one in the morning and the other in the evening. [40]With one of them, offer two quarts of fine flour mixed with one quart of olive oil; also, offer one quart of wine* as a drink offering. [41]Offer the other lamb in the evening, along with the same offerings of flour and wine as in the morning. It will be a fragrant offering to the LORD, an offering made by fire.

[42]"This is to be a daily burnt offering given from generation to generation. Offer it in the LORD's presence at the Tabernacle entrance, where I will meet you and speak with you. [43]I will meet the people of Israel there, and the Tabernacle will be sanctified by my glorious presence. [44]Yes, I will make the Tabernacle and the altar most holy, and I will set apart Aaron and his sons as holy, that they may be my priests. [45]I will live among the people of Israel and be their God, [46]and they will know that I am the LORD their God. I am the one who brought them out of Egypt so that I could live among them. I am the LORD their God.

CHAPTER 30

Plans for the Incense Altar

"Then make a small altar out of acacia wood for burning incense. [2]It must be eighteen inches square and three feet high,* with horns at the corners carved from the same piece of wood as the altar. [3]Overlay the top, sides, and horns of the altar with pure gold, and run a gold molding around the entire altar. [4]Beneath the molding, on opposite sides of the altar, attach two gold rings to support the carrying poles. [5]The poles are to be made of acacia wood and overlaid with gold. [6]Place the incense altar just outside the inner curtain, opposite the Ark's cover—the place of atonement—that rests on the Ark of the Covenant.* I will meet with you there.

[7]"Every morning when Aaron trims the lamps, he must burn fragrant incense on the altar. [8]And each evening when he tends to the lamps, he must again burn incense in the LORD's presence. This must be done from generation to generation. [9]Do not offer any unholy incense on this altar, or any burnt offerings, grain offerings, or drink offerings.

[10]"Once a year Aaron must purify the altar by placing on its horns the blood from the offering made for the atonement of sin. This will be a regular, annual event from generation to generation, for this is the LORD's supremely holy altar."

Money for the Tabernacle

[11]And the LORD said to Moses, [12]"Whenever you take a census of the people of Israel, each man who is counted must pay a ransom for himself to the LORD. Then there will be no plagues among the people as you count them. [13]His

I BELIEVE the Lord gave exact instructions for making the altar holy for the ordination of the priests. (29:35)

I BELIEVE the Lord's glorious presence sanctified the Tabernacle. (29:43)

I REJOICE that the Lord is my God. (29:46)

I BELIEVE the Lord gave exact instructions for the incense altar. (30:1)

I OFFER God what he asks of me. (30:9)

I BELIEVE the priests were to purify the altar each year. (30:10)

29:40 Hebrew 1/10 of an ephah [2 liters] of fine flour . . . 1/4 of a hin [1 liter] of olive oil . . . 1/4 of a hin of wine.
30:2 Hebrew 1 cubit [45 centimeters] square and 2 cubits [90 centimeters] high.   30:6 Or Ark of the Testimony; also in 30:26, 36.

payment to the LORD will be one-fifth of an ounce* of silver. [14]All who have reached their twentieth birthday must give this offering to the LORD. [15]When this offering is given to the LORD to make atonement for yourselves, the rich must not give more, and the poor must not give less. [16]Use this money for the care of the Tabernacle.* It will bring you, the Israelites, to the LORD's attention, and it will make atonement for your lives."

I BELIEVE the Lord required each Israelite man to pay an equal ransom for the care of the Tabernacle. (30:15)

I BELIEVE the Lord gave exact instructions for the bronze washbasin used by the priests. (30:17)

I BELIEVE the priests were to be cleansed when they appeared before God. (30:19)

I BELIEVE God's commands for the Israelite priests did not change from year to year. (30:21)

I BELIEVE the Lord gave exact instructions for the blending of the anointing oil. (30:22)

Plans for the Washbasin

[17]And the LORD said to Moses, [18]"Make a large bronze washbasin with a bronze pedestal. Put it between the Tabernacle and the altar, and fill it with water. [19]Aaron and his sons will wash their hands and feet there [20]before they go into the Tabernacle to appear before the LORD and before they approach the altar to burn offerings to the LORD. They must always wash before ministering in these ways, or they will die. [21]This is a permanent law for Aaron and his descendants, to be kept from generation to generation."

The Anointing Oil

[22]Then the LORD said to Moses, [23]"Collect choice spices—12½ pounds of pure myrrh, 6¼ pounds* each of cinnamon and of sweet cane, [24]12½ pounds of cassia, and one gallon* of olive oil. [25]Blend these ingredients into a holy anointing oil. [26]Use this scented oil to anoint the Tabernacle, the Ark of the Covenant, [27]the table and all its utensils, the lampstand and all its accessories, the incense altar, [28]the altar of burnt offering with all its utensils, and the large washbasin with its pedestal. [29]Sanctify them to make them entirely holy. After this, whatever touches them will become holy. [30]Use this oil also to anoint Aaron and his sons, sanctifying them so they can minister before me as priests. [31]And say to the people of Israel, 'This will always be my holy anointing oil. [32]It must never be poured on the body of an ordinary person, and you must never make any of it for yourselves. It is holy, and you must treat it as holy. [33]Anyone who blends scented oil like it or puts any of it on someone who is not a priest will be cut off from the community.' "

I BELIEVE the Lord gave exact instructions for the blending of the incense. (30:34)

The Incense

[34]These were the LORD's instructions to Moses concerning the incense: "Gather sweet spices—resin droplets, mollusk scent, galbanum, and pure frankincense—weighing out the same amounts of each. [35]Using the usual techniques of the incense maker, refine it to produce a pure and holy incense. [36]Beat some of it very fine and put some of it in front of the Ark of the Covenant, where I will meet with you in the Tabernacle. This incense is most holy. [37]Never make this incense for yourselves. It is reserved for the LORD, and you must treat it as holy. [38]Those who make it for their own enjoyment will be cut off from the community."

CHAPTER 31

Craftsmen: Bezalel and Oholiab

The LORD also said to Moses, [2]"Look, I have chosen Bezalel son of Uri, grandson of Hur, of the tribe of Judah. [3]I have filled him with the Spirit of God, giving him great wisdom, intelligence, and skill in all kinds of crafts. [4]He is able to create beautiful objects from gold, silver, and bronze. [5]He is skilled in cutting and setting gemstones and in carving wood. Yes, he is a master at every craft!

I BELIEVE the Lord gave Bezalel and Oholiab special abilities and wisdom to create objects for the Tabernacle. (31:3)

I USE my skills for God's service and glory. (31:6)

[6]"And I have appointed Oholiab son of Ahisamach, of the tribe of Dan, to be his assistant. Moreover, I have given special skill to all the naturally talented craftsmen so they can make all the things I have instructed you to

30:13 Hebrew *half a shekel* [6 grams], *according to the sanctuary shekel, 20 gerahs to each shekel.* **30:16** Hebrew *Tent of Meeting;* also in 30:18, 20, 26, 36. **30:23** Hebrew *500 shekels* [5.7 kilograms] *of pure myrrh, 250 shekels* [2.9 kilograms]. **30:24** Hebrew *500 shekels* [5.7 kilograms] *of cassia, according to the sanctuary shekel, and 1 hin* [3.8 liters].

make: [7]the Tabernacle itself; the Ark of the Covenant;* the Ark's cover—the place of atonement; all the furnishings of the Tabernacle; [8]the table and all its utensils; the gold lampstand with all its accessories; the incense altar; [9]the altar of burnt offering with all its utensils; the washbasin and its pedestal; [10]the beautifully stitched, holy garments for Aaron the priest, and the garments for his sons to wear as they minister as priests; [11]the anointing oil; and the special incense for the Holy Place. They must follow exactly all the instructions I have given you."

Instructions for the Sabbath

[12]The LORD then gave these further instructions to Moses: [13]"Tell the people of Israel to keep my Sabbath day, for the Sabbath is a sign of the covenant between me and you forever. It helps you to remember that I am the LORD, who makes you holy. [14]Yes, keep the Sabbath day, for it is holy. Anyone who desecrates it must die; anyone who works on that day will be cut off from the community. [15]Work six days only, but the seventh day must be a day of total rest. I repeat: Because the LORD considers it a holy day, anyone who works on the Sabbath must be put to death. [16]The people of Israel must keep the Sabbath day forever. [17]It is a permanent sign of my covenant with them. For in six days the LORD made heaven and earth, but he rested on the seventh day and was refreshed."

[18]Then as the LORD finished speaking with Moses on Mount Sinai, he gave him the two stone tablets inscribed with the terms of the covenant,* written by the finger of God.

CHAPTER 32

The Calf of Gold

When Moses failed to come back down the mountain right away, the people went to Aaron. "Look," they said, "make us some gods who can lead us. This man Moses, who brought us here from Egypt, has disappeared. We don't know what has happened to him."

[2]So Aaron said, "Tell your wives and sons and daughters to take off their gold earrings, and then bring them to me."

[3]All the people obeyed Aaron and brought him their gold earrings. [4]Then Aaron took the gold, melted it down, and molded and tooled it into the shape of a calf. The people exclaimed, "O Israel, these are the gods who brought you out of Egypt!"

[5]When Aaron saw how excited the people were about it, he built an altar in front of the calf and announced, "Tomorrow there will be a festival to the LORD!"

[6]So the people got up early the next morning to sacrifice burnt offerings and peace offerings. After this, they celebrated with feasting and drinking, and indulged themselves in pagan revelry.

[7]Then the LORD told Moses, "Quick! Go down the mountain! The people you brought from Egypt have defiled themselves. [8]They have already turned from the way I commanded them to live. They have made an idol shaped like a calf, and they have worshiped and sacrificed to it. They are saying, 'These are your gods, O Israel, who brought you out of Egypt.'"

[9]Then the LORD said, "I have seen how stubborn and rebellious these people are. [10]Now leave me alone so my anger can blaze against them and destroy them all. Then I will make you, Moses, into a great nation instead of them."

[11]But Moses pleaded with the LORD his God not to do it. "O LORD!" he exclaimed. "Why are you so angry with your own people whom you brought from the land of Egypt with such great power and mighty acts? [12]The Egyptians

---

I FOLLOW God's instructions exactly as he gives them. (31:11)

I REMEMBER the Lord, the one who makes me holy. (31:13)

I BELIEVE the Lord spoke to Moses and gave him the law written by God's own finger. (31:18)

I DO NOT LOOK for answers from pagan sources when I am forced to wait for God. (32:1)

I DO NOT OFFER people an easier, alternate belief system just because they have difficulty trusting the Lord God. (32:4)

I APPEAL to God's own character when I pray. (32:12)

31:7 Hebrew *the Tent of Meeting; the Ark of the Testimony.* 31:18 Hebrew *the Testimony.*

will say, 'God tricked them into coming to the mountains so he could kill them and wipe them from the face of the earth.' Turn away from your fierce anger. Change your mind about this terrible disaster you are planning against your people! ¹³Remember your covenant with your servants—Abraham, Isaac, and Jacob.* You swore by your own self, 'I will make your descendants as numerous as the stars of heaven. Yes, I will give them all of this land that I have promised to your descendants, and they will possess it forever.'"

¹⁴So the LORD withdrew his threat and didn't bring against his people the disaster he had threatened.

¹⁵Then Moses turned and went down the mountain. He held in his hands the two stone tablets inscribed with the terms of the covenant.* They were inscribed on both sides, front and back. ¹⁶These stone tablets were God's work; the words on them were written by God himself.

¹⁷When Joshua heard the noise of the people shouting below them, he exclaimed to Moses, "It sounds as if there is a war in the camp!"

¹⁸But Moses replied, "No, it's neither a cry of victory nor a cry of defeat. It is the sound of a celebration."

¹⁹When they came near the camp, Moses saw the calf and the dancing. In terrible anger, he threw the stone tablets to the ground, smashing them at the foot of the mountain. ²⁰He took the calf they had made and melted it in the fire. And when the metal had cooled, he ground it into powder and mixed it with water. Then he made the people drink it.

²¹After that, he turned to Aaron. "What did the people do to you?" he demanded. "How did they ever make you bring such terrible sin upon them?"

²²"Don't get upset, sir," Aaron replied. "You yourself know these people and what a wicked bunch they are. ²³They said to me, 'Make us some gods to lead us, for something has happened to this man Moses, who led us out of Egypt.' ²⁴So I told them, 'Bring me your gold earrings.' When they brought them to me, I threw them into the fire—and out came this calf!"

²⁵When Moses saw that Aaron had let the people get completely out of control—and much to the amusement of their enemies—²⁶he stood at the entrance to the camp and shouted, "All of you who are on the LORD's side, come over here and join me." And all the Levites came.

²⁷He told them, "This is what the LORD, the God of Israel, says: Strap on your swords! Go back and forth from one end of the camp to the other, killing even your brothers, friends, and neighbors." ²⁸The Levites obeyed Moses, and about three thousand people died that day.

²⁹Then Moses told the Levites, "Today you have been ordained for the service of the LORD, for you obeyed him even though it meant killing your own sons and brothers. Because of this, he will now give you a great blessing."

Moses Intercedes for Israel

³⁰The next day Moses said to the people, "You have committed a terrible sin, but I will return to the LORD on the mountain. Perhaps I will be able to obtain forgiveness for you."

³¹So Moses returned to the LORD and said, "Alas, these people have committed a terrible sin. They have made gods of gold for themselves. ³²But now, please forgive their sin—and if not, then blot me out of the record you are keeping."

³³The LORD replied to Moses, "I will blot out whoever has sinned against me. ³⁴Now go, lead the people to the place I told you about. Look! My angel will lead the way before you! But when I call the people to account, I will certainly punish them for their sins."

32:13 Hebrew *Israel.* 32:15 Hebrew *the Testimony.*

I APPEAL to God's promises when I pray. (32:13)

See the profiles for Abraham (page 19), Isaac (page 31, and Jacob (page 43) at Genesis 15:6 , Genesis 25:19, and Genesis 32:9.

I DO NOT MAKE excuses for my failure to stand up for what is right. (32:22)

I CHOOSE to be on the Lord's side. (32:26)

I OBEY the Lord, even if my family and friends don't obey. (32:29)

I BELIEVE the Lord requires personal repentance from each individual. (32:33)

[35]And the LORD sent a great plague upon the people because they had worshiped the calf Aaron had made.

CHAPTER 33

The LORD said to Moses, "Now that you have brought these people out of Egypt, lead them to the land I solemnly promised Abraham, Isaac, and Jacob. I told them long ago that I would give this land to their descendants. [2]And I will send an angel before you to drive out the Canaanites, Amorites, Hittites, Perizzites, Hivites, and Jebusites. [3]Theirs is a land flowing with milk and honey. But I will not travel along with you, for you are a stubborn, unruly people. If I did, I would be tempted to destroy you along the way."

[4]When the people heard these stern words, they went into mourning and refused to wear their jewelry and ornaments. [5]For the LORD had told Moses to tell them, "You are an unruly, stubborn people. If I were there among you for even a moment, I would destroy you. Remove your jewelry and ornaments until I decide what to do with you." [6]So from the time they left Mount Sinai,* the Israelites wore no more jewelry.

See the profiles for Abraham (page 19), Isaac (page 31), and Jacob (page 43) at Genesis 15:6, Genesis 25:19, and Genesis 32:9.

I MOURN when I have sinned against God. (33:4)

UNLIKE AARON   *I do not give in to the pressure of others to redefine God.*
Exodus 32:2

Peer pressure. Do we ever really outgrow it?

Aaron experienced such great pressure to please other people that even a recent meal in the bright presence of God (see 24:9-11) didn't deter him from giving in soon after.

It probably wasn't that Aaron lost his faith in the Lord God. In the past he had seen God's miracles and great glory. In the future God would set him and his family apart as high priests—the only Israelites allowed in the Most Holy Place (Leviticus 8:2-3, 12). So what went wrong with Aaron?

Left in charge of the Israelites for a mere forty days, Aaron couldn't hold on to what he knew was true against what the people wanted. The Israelites wanted a god they could see, not one who was cloaked in dark clouds and lightning (Exodus 19:16-18). They wanted a religion of wild parties, not one where they must wait to hear from God. And who knew what happened to that guy Moses, anyway? Their needs just weren't being met and they demanded a change (Acts 7:39-41). Giving their gold to Aaron, they begged him for a god they could see to worship. Out of the fire came a calf—a poor imitation of the Sovereign Lord (Exodus 32:22-24).

Aaron didn't lose the priesthood for his part in the Israelites' idolatry, but he did lose an opportunity to lead the people closer to their one true God.

Many people today clamor for a god they can fashion after their own image and a religion that meets what they think are their real needs. When they can't see or understand God's mysterious ways, they redefine him to fit their own understanding. As a result, they create futile idols of their imagination.

You and I can sympathize with others as they wrestle with the unexplained parts of life and God's mysterious ways. But, unlike Aaron, we cannot give in to the pressure to remake God just to make them feel better. Instead, let's hold forth God's Word and wait for him to reveal himself and his ways in his own time.

○ *Today's Scripture reading is Exodus 32.*

[7]It was Moses' custom to set up the tent known as the Tent of Meeting far outside the camp. Everyone who wanted to consult with the LORD would go there.

[8]Whenever Moses went out to the Tent of Meeting, all the people would get up and stand in their tent entrances. They would all watch Moses until he disappeared inside. [9]As he went into the tent, the pillar of cloud would come down and hover at the entrance while the LORD spoke with Moses.

33:6 Hebrew *Horeb*, another name for Sinai.

¹⁰Then all the people would stand and bow low at their tent entrances. ¹¹Inside the Tent of Meeting, the LORD would speak to Moses face to face, as a man speaks to his friend. Afterward Moses would return to the camp, but the young man who assisted him, Joshua son of Nun, stayed behind in the Tent of Meeting.

Moses Sees the LORD's Glory

¹²Moses said to the LORD, "You have been telling me, 'Take these people up to the Promised Land.' But you haven't told me whom you will send with me. You call me by name and tell me I have found favor with you. ¹³Please, if this is really so, show me your intentions so I will understand you more fully and do exactly what you want me to do. Besides, don't forget that this nation is your very own people."

¹⁴And the LORD replied, "I will personally go with you, Moses. I will give you rest—everything will be fine for you."

¹⁵Then Moses said, "If you don't go with us personally, don't let us move a step from this place. ¹⁶If you don't go with us, how will anyone ever know that your people and I have found favor with you? How else will they know we are special and distinct from all other people on the earth?"

¹⁷And the LORD replied to Moses, "I will indeed do what you have asked, for you have found favor with me, and you are my friend."

¹⁸Then Moses had one more request. "Please let me see your glorious presence," he said.

¹⁹The LORD replied, "I will make all my goodness pass before you, and I will call out my name, 'the LORD,' to you. I will show kindness to anyone I choose, and I will show mercy to anyone I choose. ²⁰But you may not look directly at my face, for no one may see me and live." ²¹The LORD continued, "Stand here on this rock beside me. ²²As my glorious presence passes by, I will put you in the cleft of the rock and cover you with my hand until I have passed. ²³Then I will remove my hand, and you will see me from behind. But my face will not be seen."

CHAPTER 34

A New Copy of the Covenant

The LORD told Moses, "Prepare two stone tablets like the first ones. I will write on them the same words that were on the tablets you smashed. ²Be ready in the morning to come up Mount Sinai and present yourself to me there on the top of the mountain. ³No one else may come with you. In fact, no one is allowed anywhere on the mountain. Do not even let the flocks or herds graze near the mountain."

⁴So Moses cut two tablets of stone like the first ones. Early in the morning he climbed Mount Sinai as the LORD had told him, carrying the two stone tablets in his hands.

⁵Then the LORD came down in a pillar of cloud and called out his own name, "the LORD," as Moses stood there in his presence. ⁶He passed in front of Moses and said, "I am the LORD, I am the LORD, the merciful and gracious God. I am slow to anger and rich in unfailing love and faithfulness. ⁷I show this unfailing love to many thousands by forgiving every kind of sin and rebellion. Even so I do not leave sin unpunished, but I punish the children for the sins of their parents to the third and fourth generations."

⁸Moses immediately fell to the ground and worshiped. ⁹And he said, "If it is true that I have found favor in your sight, O Lord, then please go with us. Yes, this is an unruly and stubborn people, but please pardon our iniquity and our sins. Accept us as your own special possession."

¹⁰The LORD replied, "All right. This is the covenant I am going to make with you. I will perform wonders that have never been done before anywhere in

---

I ASK God for understanding to obey him more carefully. (33:12)

I DRAW my self-esteem and sense of worth from knowing that God is with me. (33:16)

I KNOW that when I receive what I ask from God, it is because God, through Jesus Christ, has found favor with me, and I am his friend (John 15:15). (33:17)

I BELIEVE the Lord is merciful, patient, and loving—just as he says he is. (34:6)

I BELIEVE the Lord forgives sin and rebellion, yet he is perfectly just in punishing sin. (34:7)

I WORSHIP God when I consider who he truly is. (34:8)

all the earth or in any nation. And all the people around you will see the power of the LORD—the awesome power I will display through you. ¹¹Your responsibility is to obey all the commands I am giving you today. Then I will surely drive out all those who stand in your way—the Amorites, Canaanites, Hittites, Perizzites, Hivites, and Jebusites.

¹²"Be very careful never to make treaties with the people in the land where you are going. If you do, you soon will be following their evil ways. ¹³Instead, you must break down their pagan altars, smash the sacred pillars they worship, and cut down their carved images. ¹⁴You must worship no other gods, but only the LORD, for he is a God who is passionate about his relationship with you.

¹⁵"Do not make treaties of any kind with the people living in the land. They are spiritual prostitutes, committing adultery against me by sacrificing to their gods. If you make peace with them, they will invite you to go with them to worship their gods, and you are likely to do it. ¹⁶And you will accept their daughters, who worship other gods, as wives for your sons. Then they will cause your sons to commit adultery against me by worshiping other gods. ¹⁷You must make no gods for yourselves at all.

¹⁸"Be sure to celebrate the Festival of Unleavened Bread for seven days, just as I instructed you, at the appointed time each year in early spring,* for that was when you left Egypt.

¹⁹"Every firstborn male belongs to me—of both cattle and sheep. ²⁰A firstborn male donkey may be redeemed from the LORD by presenting a lamb in its place. But if you decide not to make the exchange, you must kill the donkey by breaking its neck. However, you must redeem every firstborn son. No one is allowed to appear before me without a gift.

²¹"Six days are set aside for work, but on the Sabbath day you must rest, even during the seasons of plowing and harvest. ²²And you must remember to celebrate the Festival of Harvest* with the first crop of the wheat harvest, and celebrate the Festival of the Final Harvest* at the end of the harvest season. ²³Three times each year all the men of Israel must appear before the Sovereign LORD, the God of Israel. ²⁴No one will attack and conquer your land when you go to appear before the LORD your God those three times each year. I will drive out the nations that stand in your way and will enlarge your boundaries.

²⁵"You must not offer bread made with yeast as a sacrifice to me. And none of the meat of the Passover lamb may be kept over until the following morning. ²⁶You must bring the best of the first of each year's crop to the house of the LORD your God.

"You must not cook a young goat in its mother's milk."

²⁷And the LORD said to Moses, "Write down all these instructions, for they represent the terms of my covenant with you and with Israel."

²⁸Moses was up on the mountain with the LORD forty days and forty nights. In all that time he neither ate nor drank. At that time he wrote the terms of the covenant—the Ten Commandments—on the stone tablets.

²⁹When Moses came down the mountain carrying the stone tablets inscribed with the terms of the covenant,* he wasn't aware that his face glowed because he had spoken to the LORD face to face. ³⁰And when Aaron and the people of Israel saw the radiance of Moses' face, they were afraid to come near him.

³¹But Moses called to them and asked Aaron and the community leaders to come over and talk with him. ³²Then all the people came, and Moses gave them the instructions the LORD had given him on Mount Sinai. ³³When Moses

I OBEY all the commands God has given me. (34:11)

I ABHOR the worship of other gods, especially knowing that God is passionate about his relationship with me. (34:14)

I BELIEVE the law was given as terms of God's covenant with Israel. (34:27)

I REFLECT the permanent glory that the Spirit of God has brought into my life (2 Corinthians 3:12-13, 18). (34:33)

34:18 Hebrew *in the month of Abib.* This month of the Hebrew lunar calendar usually occurs in March and April. 34:22a Or *Festival of Weeks.* 34:22b This was later called the Festival of Shelters; see Lev 23:33-36. 34:29 Hebrew *the Testimony.*

had finished speaking with them, he put a veil over his face. [34]But whenever he went into the Tent of Meeting to speak with the LORD, he removed the veil until he came out again. Then he would give the people whatever instructions the LORD had given him, [35]and the people would see his face aglow. Afterward he would put the veil on again until he returned to speak with the LORD.

CHAPTER 35

Instructions for the Sabbath

Now Moses called a meeting of all the people and told them, "You must obey these instructions from the LORD. [2]Each week, work for six days only. The seventh day is a day of total rest, a holy day that belongs to the LORD. Anyone who works on that day will die. [3]Do not even light fires in your homes on that day."

Gifts for the Tabernacle

[4]Then Moses said to all the people, "This is what the LORD has commanded. [5]Everyone is invited to bring these offerings to the LORD: gold, silver, and bronze; [6]blue, purple, and scarlet yarn; fine linen; goat hair for cloth; [7]tanned ram skins and fine goatskin leather; acacia wood; [8]olive oil for the lamps; spices for the anointing oil and the fragrant incense; [9]onyx stones, and other stones to be set in the ephod and the chestpiece.

[10]"Come, all of you who are gifted craftsmen. Construct everything that the LORD has commanded: [11]the entire Tabernacle, including the sacred tent and its coverings, the clasps, frames, crossbars, posts, and bases; [12]the Ark and its poles; the Ark's cover—the place of atonement; the inner curtain to enclose the Ark in the Most Holy Place; [13]the table, its carrying poles, and all of its utensils; the Bread of the Presence; [14]the lampstand and its accessories; the lamp cups and the oil for lighting; [15]the incense altar and its carrying poles; the anointing oil and fragrant incense; the curtain for the entrance to the Tabernacle; [16]the altar of burnt offering; the bronze grating of the altar and its carrying poles and utensils; the large washbasin with its pedestal; [17]the curtains for the walls of the courtyard; the posts and their bases; the curtain for the entrance to the courtyard; [18]the tent pegs of the Tabernacle and courtyard and their cords; [19]the beautifully stitched clothing for the priests to wear while ministering in the Holy Place; the sacred garments for Aaron and his sons to wear while officiating as priests."

[20]So all the people left Moses and went to their tents to prepare their gifts. [21]If their hearts were stirred and they desired to do so, they brought to the LORD their offerings of materials for the Tabernacle* and its furnishings and for the holy garments. [22]Both men and women came, all whose hearts were willing. Some brought to the LORD their offerings of gold—medallions, earrings, rings from their fingers, and necklaces. They presented gold objects of every kind to the LORD. [23]Others brought blue, purple, and scarlet yarn, fine linen, or goat hair for cloth. Some gave tanned ram skins or fine goatskin leather. [24]Others brought silver and bronze objects as their offering to the LORD. And those who had acacia wood brought it.

[25]All the women who were skilled in sewing and spinning prepared blue, purple, and scarlet yarn, and fine linen cloth, and they brought them in. [26]All the women who were willing used their skills to spin and weave the goat hair into cloth. [27]The leaders brought onyx stones and the other gemstones to be used for the ephod and the chestpiece. [28]They also brought spices and olive oil for the light, the anointing oil, and the fragrant incense. [29]So the people of Israel—every man and woman who wanted to help in the work the LORD had given them through Moses—brought their offerings to the LORD.

35:21 Hebrew *Tent of Meeting.*

I RESPOND to God's invitation to bring gifts to him. (35:4)

I USE my talents to obey the Lord. (35:10)

In response to these affirmations, tell the Lord what you obey—or find easy to disobey.

I PREPARE my gifts for the Lord. (35:20)

I BRING gifts to the Lord out of a willing heart. (35:21)

I USE my skills to serve the Lord. (35:25)

I SERVE God willingly. (35:29)

[30]And Moses told them, "The LORD has chosen Bezalel son of Uri, grandson of Hur, of the tribe of Judah. [31]The LORD has filled Bezalel with the Spirit of God, giving him great wisdom, intelligence, and skill in all kinds of crafts. [32]He is able to create beautiful objects from gold, silver, and bronze. [33]He is skilled in cutting and setting gemstones and in carving wood. In fact, he has every necessary skill. [34]And the LORD has given both him and Oholiab son of Ahisamach, of the tribe of Dan, the ability to teach their skills to others. [35]The LORD has given them special skills as jewelers, designers, weavers, and embroiderers in blue, purple, and scarlet yarn on fine linen cloth. They excel in all the crafts needed for the work.

CHAPTER 36

"Bezalel, Oholiab, and the other craftsmen whom the LORD has gifted with wisdom, skill, and intelligence will construct and furnish the Tabernacle, just as the LORD has commanded."

[2]So Moses told Bezalel and Oholiab to begin the work, along with all those who were specially gifted by the LORD. [3]Moses gave them the materials donated by the people for the completion of the sanctuary. Additional gifts were brought each morning. [4]But finally the craftsmen left their work to meet with Moses. [5]"We have more than enough materials on hand now to complete the job the LORD has given us to do!" they exclaimed.

[6]So Moses gave the command, and this message was sent throughout the camp: "Bring no more materials! You have already given more than enough." So the people stopped bringing their offerings. [7]Their contributions were more than enough to complete the whole project.

Building the Tabernacle
[8]The skilled weavers first made ten sheets from fine linen. One of the craftsmen then embroidered blue, purple, and scarlet cherubim into them. [9]Each sheet was exactly the same size—forty-two feet long and six feet wide.* [10]Five of these sheets were joined together to make one set, and a second set was made of the other five. [11]Fifty blue loops were placed along the edge of the last sheet in each set. [12]The fifty loops along the edge of the first set of sheets matched the loops along the edge of the second set. [13]Then fifty gold clasps were made to connect the loops on the edge of each set. Thus the Tabernacle was joined together in one piece.

[14]Above the Tabernacle, a roof covering was made from eleven sheets of cloth made from goat hair. [15]Each sheet was exactly the same size—forty-five feet long and six feet wide. [16]The craftsmen joined five of these sheets together to make one set, and the six remaining sheets were joined to make a second set. [17]Then they made fifty loops along the edge of the last sheet in each set. [18]They also made fifty small bronze clasps to couple the loops, so the two sets of sheets were firmly attached to each other. In this way, the roof covering was joined together in one piece. [19]Then they made two more layers for the roof covering. The first was made of tanned ram skins, and the second was made of fine goatskin leather.

[20]For the framework of the Tabernacle, they made frames of acacia wood standing on end. [21]Each frame was 15 feet high and 2¼ feet wide. [22]There were two pegs on each frame so they could be joined to the next frame. All the frames were made this way. [23]They made twenty frames to support the south side, [24]along with forty silver bases, two for each frame. [25]They also made twenty frames for the north side of the Tabernacle, [26]along with forty silver bases, two for each frame. [27]The west side of the Tabernacle, which was its rear, was made from six frames, [28]plus an extra frame at each corner.

I BELIEVE the Lord gave Bezalel and Oholiab special wisdom and skill so that they could construct the Tabernacle. (35:30)

I USE my gifts and skills to serve the Lord. (36:2)

I GIVE until there is more than enough to complete the Lord's work. (36:3)

I BELIEVE the skilled workers of Israel constructed the Tabernacle just as God commanded. (36:8)

36:9 Hebrew *28 cubits* [12.6 meters] *long and 4 cubits* [1.8 meters] *wide.* In this chapter, the distance measures are calculated from the Hebrew cubit at a ratio of 18 inches or 45 centimeters per cubit.

²⁹These corner frames were connected at the bottom and firmly attached at the top with a single ring, forming a single unit from top to bottom. They made two of these, one for each rear corner. ³⁰So for the west side they made a total of eight frames, along with sixteen silver bases, two for each frame.

³¹Then they made five crossbars from acacia wood to tie the frames on the south side together. ³²They made another five for the north side and five for the west side. ³³The middle crossbar of the five was halfway up the frames, along each side, running from one end to the other. ³⁴The frames and crossbars were all overlaid with gold. The rings used to hold the crossbars were made of pure gold.

³⁵The inner curtain was made of fine linen cloth, and cherubim were skillfully embroidered into it with blue, purple, and scarlet yarn. ³⁶This curtain was then attached to four gold hooks set into four posts of acacia wood. The posts were overlaid with gold and set into four silver bases.

³⁷Then they made another curtain for the entrance to the sacred tent. It was made of fine linen cloth and embroidered with blue, purple, and scarlet yarn. ³⁸This curtain was connected by five hooks to five posts. The posts with their decorated tops and bands were overlaid with gold. The five bases were molded from bronze.

CHAPTER 37

Building the Ark

Next Bezalel made the Ark out of acacia wood. It was 3³/₄ feet long, 2¹/₄ feet wide, and 2¹/₄ feet high.* ²It was overlaid with pure gold inside and out, and it had a molding of gold all the way around. ³Four gold rings were fastened to its four feet, two rings at each side. ⁴Then he made poles from acacia wood and overlaid them with gold. ⁵He put the poles into the rings at the sides of the Ark to carry it.

⁶Then, from pure gold, he made the Ark's cover—the place of atonement. It was 3³/₄ feet long and 2¹/₄ feet wide. ⁷He made two figures of cherubim out of hammered gold and placed them at the two ends of the atonement cover. ⁸They were made so they were actually a part of the atonement cover—it was all one piece. ⁹The cherubim faced each other as they looked down on the atonement cover, and their wings were stretched out above the atonement cover to protect it.

Building the Table

¹⁰Then he made a table out of acacia wood, 3 feet long, 1¹/₂ feet wide, and 2¹/₄ feet high. ¹¹It was overlaid with pure gold, with a gold molding all around the edge. ¹²A rim about 3 inches* wide was attached along the edges of the table, and a gold molding ran around the rim. ¹³Then he cast four rings of gold and attached them to the four table legs ¹⁴next to the rim. These were made to hold the carrying poles in place. ¹⁵He made the carrying poles of acacia wood and overlaid them with gold. ¹⁶Next, using pure gold, he made the plates, dishes, bowls, and pitchers to be placed on the table. These utensils were to be used in pouring out drink offerings.

Building the Lampstand

¹⁷Then he made the lampstand, again using pure, hammered gold. Its base, center stem, lamp cups, blossoms, and buds were all of one piece. ¹⁸The lampstand had six branches, three going out from each side of the center stem. ¹⁹Each of the six branches held a cup shaped like an almond blossom, complete with buds and petals. ²⁰The center stem of the lampstand was also decorated with four almond blossoms. ²¹One blossom was set beneath each

I BELIEVE Bezalel constructed the Ark of the Covenant just as God commanded. (37:1)

I BELIEVE Bezalel constructed the table for the Bread of the Presence just as God commanded. (37:10)

I BELIEVE Bezalel constructed the lampstand just as God commanded. (37:17)

37:1 Hebrew 2¹/₂ cubits [1.1 meters] *long,* 1¹/₂ cubits [0.7 meters] *wide, and* 1¹/₂ cubits high. In this chapter, the distance measures are calculated from the Hebrew cubit at a ratio of 18 inches or 45 centimeters per cubit. **37:12** Hebrew *a handbreadth* [8 centimeters].

pair of branches, where they extended from the center stem. ²²The decorations and branches were all one piece with the stem, and they were hammered from pure gold. ²³He also made the seven lamps, the lamp snuffers, and the trays, all of pure gold. ²⁴The entire lampstand, along with its accessories, was made from seventy-five pounds* of pure gold.

Building the Incense Altar
²⁵The incense altar was made of acacia wood. It was eighteen inches square and three feet high, with its corner horns made from the same piece of wood as the altar itself. ²⁶He overlaid the top, sides, and horns of the altar with pure gold and ran a gold molding around the edge. ²⁷Two gold rings were placed on opposite sides, beneath the molding, to hold the carrying poles. ²⁸The carrying poles were made of acacia wood and were overlaid with gold.

²⁹Then he made the sacred oil, for anointing the priests, and the fragrant incense, using the techniques of the most skilled incense maker.

CHAPTER 38
Building the Altar of Burnt Offering
The altar for burning animal sacrifices also was constructed of acacia wood. It was 7¹/₂ feet square at the top and 4¹/₂ feet high.* ²There were four horns, one at each of the four corners, all of one piece with the rest. This altar was overlaid with bronze. ³Then he made all the bronze utensils to be used with the altar—the ash buckets, shovels, basins, meat hooks, and firepans. ⁴Next he made a bronze grating that rested on a ledge about halfway down into the firebox. ⁵Four rings were cast for each side of the grating to support the carrying poles. ⁶The carrying poles themselves were made of acacia wood and were overlaid with bronze. ⁷These poles were inserted into the rings at the side of the altar. The altar was hollow and was made from planks.

Building the Washbasin
⁸The bronze washbasin and its bronze pedestal were cast from bronze mirrors donated by the women who served at the entrance of the Tabernacle.*

Building the Courtyard
⁹Then he constructed the courtyard. The south wall was 150 feet long. It consisted of curtains made of fine linen. ¹⁰There were twenty posts, each with its own bronze base, and there were silver hooks and rods to hold up the curtains. ¹¹The north wall was also 150 feet long, with twenty bronze posts and bases and with silver hooks and rods. ¹²The west end was 75 feet wide. The walls were made from curtains supported by ten posts and bases and with silver hooks and rods. ¹³The east end was also 75 feet wide.

¹⁴The courtyard entrance was on the east side, flanked by two curtains. The curtain on the right side was 22¹/₂ feet long and was supported by three posts set into three bases. ¹⁵The curtain on the left side was also 22¹/₂ feet long and was supported by three posts set into three bases. ¹⁶All the curtains used in the courtyard walls were made of fine linen. ¹⁷Each post had a bronze base, and all the hooks and rods were silver. The tops of the posts were overlaid with silver, and the rods to hold up the curtains were solid silver.

¹⁸The curtain that covered the entrance to the courtyard was made of fine linen cloth and embroidered with blue, purple, and scarlet yarn. It was 30 feet long and 7¹/₂ feet high, just like the curtains of the courtyard walls. ¹⁹It was supported by four posts set into four bronze bases. The tops of the posts were overlaid with silver, and the hooks and rods were also made of silver.

I BELIEVE Bezalel constructed the incense altar just as God commanded. (37:25)

I BELIEVE Bezalel constructed the altar of burnt offering just as God commanded. (38:1)

I GIVE of my personal belongings to serve the Lord. (38:8)

I BELIEVE Bezalel constructed the courtyard just as God commanded. (38:9)

37:24 Hebrew 1 talent [34 kilograms]. 38:1 Hebrew 5 cubits [2.3 meters] square at the top, and 3 cubits [1.4 meters] high. In this chapter, the distance measures are calculated from the Hebrew cubit at a ratio of 18 inches or 45 centimeters per cubit. 38:8 Hebrew Tent of Meeting; also in 38:30.

²⁰All the tent pegs used in the Tabernacle and courtyard were made of bronze.

Inventory of Materials

I KEEP good accounts of offerings entrusted to my use. (38:21)

²¹Here is an inventory of the materials used in building the Tabernacle of the Covenant.* Moses directed the Levites to compile the figures, and Ithamar son of Aaron the priest served as recorder. ²²Bezalel son of Uri, grandson of Hur, of the tribe of Judah, was in charge of the whole project, just as the LORD had commanded Moses. ²³He was assisted by Oholiab son of Ahisamach, of the tribe of Dan, a craftsman expert at engraving, designing, and embroidering blue, purple, and scarlet yarn on fine linen cloth.

²⁴The people brought gifts of gold totaling about 2,200 pounds,* all of which was used throughout the Tabernacle.

²⁵The amount of silver that was given was about 7,545 pounds.* ²⁶It came from the tax of one-fifth of an ounce of silver* collected from each of those registered in the census. This included all the men who were twenty years old or older, 603,550 in all. ²⁷The 100 bases for the frames of the sanctuary walls and for the posts supporting the inner curtain required 7,500 pounds of silver, about 75 pounds for each base.* ²⁸The rest of the silver, about 45 pounds,* was used to make the rods and hooks and to overlay the tops of the posts.

²⁹The people also brought 5,310 pounds* of bronze, ³⁰which was used for casting the bases for the posts at the entrance to the Tabernacle, and for the bronze altar with its bronze grating and altar utensils. ³¹Bronze was also used to make the bases for the posts that supported the curtains around the courtyard, the bases for the curtain at the entrance of the courtyard, and all the tent pegs used to hold the curtains of the courtyard in place.

CHAPTER 39

Clothing for the Priests

I BELIEVE the garments for the priests were made just as God commanded. (39:1)

For the priests, the craftsmen made beautiful garments of blue, purple, and scarlet cloth—clothing to be worn while ministering in the Holy Place. This same cloth was used for Aaron's sacred garments, just as the LORD had commanded Moses.

Making the Ephod

I BELIEVE the ephod for the high priest was made just as God commanded. (39:2)

²The ephod was made from fine linen cloth and embroidered with gold thread and blue, purple, and scarlet yarn. ³A skilled craftsman made gold thread by beating gold into thin sheets and cutting it into fine strips. He then embroidered it into the linen with the blue, purple, and scarlet yarn.

⁴They made two shoulder-pieces for the ephod, which were attached to its corners so it could be tied down. ⁵They also made an elaborate woven sash of the same materials: fine linen cloth; blue, purple, and scarlet yarn; and gold thread, just as the LORD had commanded Moses. ⁶The two onyx stones, attached to the shoulder-pieces of the ephod, were set in gold filigree. The stones were engraved with the names of the tribes of Israel, just as initials are engraved on a seal. ⁷These stones served as reminders to the LORD concerning the people of Israel. All this was done just as the LORD had commanded Moses.

Making the Chestpiece

I BELIEVE the chestpiece was made for the high priest just as God commanded. (39:8)

⁸The chestpiece was made in the same style as the ephod, crafted from fine linen cloth and embroidered with gold thread and blue, purple, and scarlet

38:21 Hebrew *the Tabernacle, the Tabernacle of the Testimony.*   38:24 Hebrew *29 talents* [2,175 pounds or 986 kilograms] *and 730 shekels* [18.3 pounds or 8.3 kilograms], *according to the sanctuary shekel.*   38:25 Hebrew *100 talents* [7,500 pounds or 3,400 kilograms] *and 1,775 shekels* [44.4 pounds or 20.2 kilograms], *according to the sanctuary shekel.*   38:26 Hebrew *1 beka* [6 grams] *per person, that is, half a shekel, according to the sanctuary shekel.*   38:27 Hebrew *100 talents* [3,400 kilograms] *of silver, 1 talent* [34 kilograms] *for each base.*   38:28 Hebrew *1,775 shekels* [20.2 kilograms].   38:29 Hebrew *70 talents* [5,250 pounds or 2,380 kilograms] *and 2,400 shekels* [60 pounds or 27.4 kilograms].

yarn. ⁹It was doubled over to form a pouch, nine inches* square. ¹⁰Four rows of gemstones* were set across it. In the first row were a red carnelian, a chrysolite, and an emerald. ¹¹In the second row were a turquoise, a sapphire, and a white moonstone. ¹²In the third row were a jacinth, an agate, and an amethyst. ¹³In the fourth row were a beryl, an onyx, and a jasper. Each of these gemstones was set in gold. ¹⁴The stones were engraved like a seal, each with the name of one of the twelve tribes of Israel.

¹⁵To attach the chestpiece to the ephod, they made braided cords of pure gold. ¹⁶They also made two gold rings and attached them to the top corners of the chestpiece. ¹⁷The two gold cords were put through the gold rings on the chestpiece, ¹⁸and the ends of the cords were tied to the gold settings on the shoulder-pieces of the ephod. ¹⁹Two more gold rings were attached to the lower inside corners of the chestpiece next to the ephod. ²⁰Then two gold rings were attached to the ephod near the sash. ²¹Blue cords were used to attach the bottom rings of the chestpiece to the rings on the ephod. In this way, the chestpiece was held securely to the ephod above the beautiful sash. All this was done just as the LORD had commanded Moses.

Additional Clothing for the Priests

²²The robe of the ephod was woven entirely of blue yarn, ²³with an opening for Aaron's head in the middle of it. The edge of this opening was reinforced with a woven collar,* so it would not tear. ²⁴Pomegranates were attached to the bottom edge of the robe. These were finely crafted of blue, purple, and scarlet yarn. ²⁵Bells of pure gold were placed between the pomegranates along the hem of the robe, ²⁶with bells and pomegranates alternating all around the hem. This robe was to be worn when Aaron ministered to the LORD, just as the LORD had commanded Moses.

I BELIEVE the robe for the high priest was made just as God commanded. (39:22)

²⁷Tunics were then made for Aaron and his sons from fine linen cloth. ²⁸The turban, the headdresses, and the underclothes were all made of this fine linen. ²⁹The sashes were made of fine linen cloth and embroidered with blue, purple, and scarlet yarn, just as the LORD had commanded Moses. ³⁰Finally, they made the sacred medallion of pure gold to be worn on the front of the turban. Using the techniques of an engraver, they inscribed it with these words: SET APART AS HOLY TO THE LORD. ³¹This medallion was tied to the turban with a blue cord, just as the LORD had commanded Moses.

I BELIEVE the tunics for the priests were made just as God commanded. (39:27)

Moses Inspects the Work

³²And so at last the Tabernacle* was finished. The Israelites had done everything just as the LORD had commanded Moses. ³³And they brought the entire Tabernacle to Moses: the sacred tent with all its furnishings, the clasps, frames, crossbars, posts, and bases; ³⁴the layers of tanned ram skins and fine goatskin leather; the inner curtain that enclosed the Most Holy Place; ³⁵the Ark of the Covenant* and its carrying poles; the Ark's cover—the place of atonement; ³⁶the table and all its utensils; the Bread of the Presence; ³⁷the gold lampstand and its accessories; the lamp cups and the oil for lighting; ³⁸the gold altar; the anointing oil; the fragrant incense; the curtain for the entrance of the sacred tent; ³⁹the bronze altar; the bronze grating; its poles and utensils; the large washbasin and its pedestal; ⁴⁰the curtains for the walls of the courtyard and the posts and bases holding them up; the curtain at the courtyard entrance; the cords and tent pegs; all the articles used in the operation of the Tabernacle; ⁴¹the beautifully crafted garments to be worn while ministering in the Holy Place—the holy garments for Aaron the priest and for his sons to wear while on duty.

I DO everything the Lord commands. (39:32)

⁴²So the people of Israel followed all of the LORD's instructions to Moses.

I FOLLOW all of the Lord's instructions. (39:42)

39:9 Hebrew 1 span [23 centimeters].   39:10 The identification of some of these gemstones is uncertain.
39:23 The meaning of the Hebrew is uncertain.   39:32 Hebrew the Tabernacle, the Tent of Meeting; also in 39:40.
39:35 Or Ark of the Testimony.

⁴³Moses inspected all their work and blessed them because it had been done as the LORD had commanded him.

CHAPTER 40

The Tabernacle Completed

The LORD now said to Moses, ²"Set up the Tabernacle* on the first day of the new year.* ³Place the Ark of the Covenant* inside, and install the inner curtain to enclose the Ark within the Most Holy Place. ⁴Then bring in the table, and arrange the utensils on it. And bring in the lampstand, and set up the lamps.

⁵"Place the incense altar just outside the inner curtain, opposite the Ark of the Covenant. Set up the curtain made for the entrance of the Tabernacle. ⁶Place the altar of burnt offering in front of the Tabernacle entrance. ⁷Set the large washbasin between the Tabernacle* and the altar and fill it with water. ⁸Then set up the courtyard around the outside of the tent, and hang the curtain for the courtyard entrance.

⁹"Take the anointing oil and sprinkle it on the Tabernacle and on all its furnishings to make them holy. ¹⁰Sprinkle the anointing oil on the altar of burnt offering and its utensils, sanctifying them. Then the altar will become most holy. ¹¹Next anoint the large washbasin and its pedestal to make them holy.

¹²"Bring Aaron and his sons to the entrance of the Tabernacle, and wash them with water. ¹³Clothe Aaron with the holy garments and anoint him, setting him apart to serve me as a priest. ¹⁴Then bring his sons and dress them in their tunics. ¹⁵Anoint them as you did their father, so they may serve me as priests. With this anointing, Aaron's descendants are set apart for the priesthood forever, from generation to generation."

¹⁶Moses proceeded to do everything as the LORD had commanded him. ¹⁷So the Tabernacle was set up on the first day of the new year.* ¹⁸Moses put it together by setting its frames into their bases and attaching the crossbars and raising the posts. ¹⁹Then he spread the coverings over the Tabernacle framework and put on the roof layers, just as the LORD had commanded him.

²⁰He placed inside the Ark the stone tablets inscribed with the terms of the covenant,* and then he attached the Ark's carrying poles. He also set the Ark's cover—the place of atonement—on top of it. ²¹Then he brought the Ark of the Covenant into the Tabernacle and set up the inner curtain to shield it from view, just as the LORD had commanded.

²²Next he placed the table in the Tabernacle, along the north side of the Holy Place, just outside the inner curtain. ²³And he arranged the Bread of the Presence on the table that stands before the LORD, just as the LORD had commanded.

²⁴He set the lampstand in the Tabernacle across from the table on the south side of the Holy Place. ²⁵Then he set up the lamps in the LORD's presence, just as the LORD had commanded. ²⁶He also placed the incense altar in the Tabernacle, in the Holy Place in front of the inner curtain. ²⁷On it he burned the fragrant incense made from sweet spices, just as the LORD had commanded.

²⁸He attached the curtain at the entrance of the Tabernacle, ²⁹and he placed the altar of burnt offering near the Tabernacle entrance. On it he offered a burnt offering and a grain offering, just as the LORD had commanded.

³⁰Next he placed the large washbasin between the Tabernacle and the altar. He filled it with water so the priests could use it to wash themselves. ³¹Moses

I RECEIVE God's blessing as I follow his commands. (39:43)

I BELIEVE God spoke to Moses, instructing him where and how to set up the Tabernacle. (40:1)

I BELIEVE God instructed Moses to consecrate Aaron and his sons as priests to serve Israel in each generation. (40:12)

I DO everything the Lord commands. (40:16)

40:2a Hebrew *the Tabernacle, the Tent of Meeting;* also in 40:6, 29.   **40:2b** Hebrew *the first day of the first month.* This day of the Hebrew lunar calendar occurs in March or early April.   **40:3** Or *Ark of the Testimony;* also in 40:5, 21.   **40:7** Hebrew *Tent of Meeting;* also in 40:12, 22, 24, 26, 30, 32, 34, 35.   **40:17** Hebrew *the first day of the first month, in the second year.* See note on 40:2b.   **40:20** Hebrew *the Testimony.*

and Aaron and Aaron's sons washed their hands and feet in the basin. [32]Whenever they walked past the altar to enter the Tabernacle, they were to stop and wash, just as the LORD had commanded Moses.

[33]Then he hung the curtains forming the courtyard around the Tabernacle and the altar. And he set up the curtain at the entrance of the courtyard. So at last Moses finished the work.

The LORD's Glory Fills the Tabernacle

[34]Then the cloud covered the Tabernacle, and the glorious presence of the LORD filled it. [35]Moses was no longer able to enter the Tabernacle because the cloud had settled down over it, and the Tabernacle was filled with the awesome glory of the LORD.

[36]Now whenever the cloud lifted from the Tabernacle and moved, the people of Israel would set out on their journey, following it. [37]But if the cloud stayed, they would stay until it moved again. [38]The cloud of the LORD rested on the Tabernacle during the day, and at night there was fire in the cloud so all the people of Israel could see it. This continued throughout all their journeys.

I BELIEVE God's glory filled the Tabernacle. (40:34)

I FOLLOW God's leading. (40:36)

I DO NOT MOVE ahead of God's leading. (40:37)

I LOOK for God's glory to lead me. (40:38)

LEVITICUS

THIS THIRD BOOK answers the tough question, "Since the Lord is so holy, what must I do to worship him properly?"

Unlike the first two books of Moses, Leviticus contains only a handful of narrative accounts. It's primarily a handbook the Israelites used to know how to worship the Lord properly. In chapters 1–27, we see that sacrifices played a very important role in Old Testament worship as did festivals. In fact, the Lord instructed Israelite families to celebrate at least three festivals each year. These festivals served as tangible reminders of the Lord's covenant with the Israelites.

Many aspects of the Levitical system of worship illustrate our need of God's cleansing and forgiveness. Several key aspects clearly foreshadow the saving work of the promised Savior, Jesus Christ.

Famous passages in Leviticus include
- ◯ Instructions about various sacrifices (1:1–7:38)
- ◯ Moses consecrates Aaron and his sons (8:1–9:24)
- ◯ Two of Aaron's sons sin and are consumed by fire (10:1-5)
- ◯ "Be holy because I am holy" (11:44-45; 19:2; 20:7, 26; 21:8)
- ◯ Instructions about skin diseases (13:1–14:57)
- ◯ Instructions about sexual purity (18:6-23)
- ◯ "Love your neighbor as yourself" (19:18, 34)
- ◯ A man blasphemes and is stoned (24:10-16)
- ◯ Year of Jubilee (25:8-55)

CHAPTER 1

Procedures for the Burnt Offering

The LORD called to Moses from the Tabernacle* and said to him, ²"Give the following instructions to the Israelites: Whenever you present offerings to the LORD, you must bring animals from your flocks and herds.

³"If your sacrifice for a whole burnt offering is from the herd, bring a bull with no physical defects to the entrance of the Tabernacle so it will be accepted by the LORD. ⁴Lay your hand on its head so the LORD will accept it as your substitute, thus making atonement for you. ⁵Then slaughter the animal in the LORD's presence, and Aaron's sons, the priests, will present the blood by sprinkling it against the sides of the altar that stands in front of the Tabernacle. ⁶When the animal has been skinned and cut into pieces, ⁷the sons of Aaron the priest will build a wood fire on the altar. ⁸Aaron's sons will then put the pieces of the animal, including its head and fat, on the wood fire. ⁹But the internal organs and legs must first be washed with water. Then the priests

I ALWAYS BRING the best of my wealth as an offering to the Lord. (1:3)

I BELIEVE the burnt offerings fore-shadowed God's plan to redeem humanity through Jesus, who became the perfect atonement for my sins. (1:4)

1:1 Hebrew *Tent of Meeting;* also in 1:3, 5.

will burn the entire sacrifice on the altar. It is a whole burnt offering made by fire, very pleasing to the LORD.

[10]"If your sacrifice for a whole burnt offering is from the flock, bring a male sheep or goat with no physical defects. [11]Slaughter the animal on the north side of the altar in the LORD's presence. Aaron's sons, the priests, will sprinkle its blood against the sides of the altar. [12]Then you must cut the animal in pieces, and the priests will lay the pieces of the sacrifice, including the head and fat, on top of the wood fire on the altar. [13]The internal organs and legs must first be washed with water. Then the priests will burn the entire sacrifice on the altar. It is a whole burnt offering made by fire, very pleasing to the LORD.

[14]"If you bring a bird as a burnt offering to the LORD, choose either a turtledove or a young pigeon. [15]The priest will take the bird to the altar, twist off its head, and burn the head on the altar. He must then let its blood drain out against the sides of the altar. [16]The priest must remove the crop and the feathers* and throw them to the east side of the altar among the ashes. [17]Then, grasping the bird by its wings, the priest will tear the bird apart, though not completely. Then he will burn it on top of the wood fire on the altar. It is a whole burnt offering made by fire, very pleasing to the LORD.

CHAPTER 2

Procedures for the Grain Offering

"When you bring a grain offering to the LORD, the offering must consist of choice flour. You are to pour olive oil on it and sprinkle it with incense. [2]Bring this offering to one of Aaron's sons, and he will take a handful of the flour mixed with olive oil, together with all the incense, and burn this token portion on the altar fire. It is an offering made by fire, very pleasing to the LORD. [3]The rest of the flour will be given to Aaron and his sons. It will be considered a most holy part of the offerings given to the LORD by fire.

[4]"When you present some kind of baked bread as a grain offering, it must be made of choice flour mixed with olive oil but without any yeast. It may be presented in the form of cakes mixed with olive oil or wafers spread with olive oil. [5]If your grain offering is cooked on a griddle, it must be made of choice flour and olive oil, and it must contain no yeast. [6]Break it into pieces and pour oil on it; it is a kind of grain offering. [7]If your offering is prepared in a pan, it also must be made of choice flour and olive oil.

[8]"No matter how a grain offering has been prepared before being offered to the LORD, bring it to the priests who will present it at the altar. [9]The priests will take a token portion of the grain offering and burn it on the altar as an offering made by fire, and it will be very pleasing to the LORD. [10]The rest of the grain offering will be given to Aaron and his sons as their food. It will be considered a most holy part of the offerings given to the LORD by fire.

[11]"Do not use yeast in any of the grain offerings you present to the LORD, because no yeast or honey may be burned as an offering to the LORD by fire. [12]You may add yeast and honey to the offerings presented at harvesttime, but these must never be burned on the altar as an offering pleasing to the LORD. [13]Season all your grain offerings with salt, to remind you of God's covenant. Never forget to add salt to your grain offerings.

[14]"If you present a grain offering to the LORD from the first portion of your harvest, bring kernels of new grain that have been roasted on a fire. [15]Since it is a grain offering, put olive oil on it and sprinkle it with incense. [16]The priests will take a token portion of the roasted grain mixed with olive oil, together with all the incense, and burn it as an offering given to the LORD by fire.

I CONTINUE TO BRING offerings to the Lord no matter how rich or poor I am. (1:14)

I BRING the best of my wealth to the Lord. (2:1)

I GLADLY HELP support the Lord's servants with my offerings. (2:3)

I BELIEVE that aspects of the Lord's sacrificial requirements served as tangible reminders of his covenant with the Israelites. (2:13)

I GIVE to the Lord first of all that I receive. (2:14)

1:16 Or *the crop and its contents.* The meaning of the Hebrew is uncertain.

CHAPTER 3

Procedures for the Peace Offering

"If you want to present a peace offering from the herd, use either a bull or a cow. The animal you offer to the LORD must have no physical defects. ²Lay your hand on the animal's head, and slaughter it at the entrance of the Tabernacle.* Aaron's sons, the priests, will then sprinkle the animal's blood against the sides of the altar. ³Part of this peace offering must be presented to the LORD as an offering made by fire. This includes the fat around the internal organs, ⁴the two kidneys with the fat around them near the loins, and the lobe of the liver, which is to be removed with the kidneys. ⁵The sons of Aaron will burn these on the altar on top of the burnt offering on the wood fire. It is an offering made by fire, very pleasing to the LORD.

⁶"If you present a peace offering to the LORD from the flock, you may bring either a goat or a sheep. It may be either male or female, and it must have no physical defects. ⁷If you bring a sheep as your gift, present it to the LORD ⁸by laying your hand on its head and slaughtering it at the entrance of the Tabernacle. The sons of Aaron will then sprinkle the sheep's blood against the sides of the altar. ⁹Part of this peace offering must be presented to the LORD as an offering made by fire. This includes the fat of the entire tail cut off near the backbone, the fat around the internal organs, ¹⁰the two kidneys with the fat around them near the loins, and the lobe of the liver, which is to be removed with the kidneys. ¹¹The priest will burn them on the altar as food, an offering given to the LORD by fire.

¹²"If you bring a goat as your offering to the LORD, ¹³lay your hand on its head, and slaughter it at the entrance of the Tabernacle. Then the sons of Aaron will sprinkle the goat's blood against the sides of the altar. ¹⁴Part of this offering must be presented to the LORD as an offering made by fire. This part includes the fat around the internal organs, ¹⁵the two kidneys with the fat around them near the loins, and the lobe of the liver, which is to be removed with the kidneys. ¹⁶The priest will burn them on the altar as food, an offering made by fire; these will be very pleasing to the LORD. Remember, all the fat belongs to the LORD.

¹⁷"You must never eat any fat or blood. This is a permanent law for you and all your descendants, wherever they may live."

CHAPTER 4

Procedures for the Sin Offering

Then the LORD said to Moses, ²"Give the Israelites the following instructions for dealing with those who sin unintentionally by doing anything forbidden by the LORD's commands.

³"If the high priest sins, bringing guilt upon the entire community, he must bring to the LORD a young bull with no physical defects. ⁴He must present the bull to the LORD at the entrance of the Tabernacle,* lay his hand on the bull's head, and slaughter it there in the LORD's presence. ⁵The priest on duty will then take some of the animal's blood into the Tabernacle, ⁶dip his finger into the blood, and sprinkle it seven times before the LORD in front of the inner curtain of the Most Holy Place. ⁷The priest will put some of the blood on the horns of the incense altar that stands in the LORD's presence in the Tabernacle. The rest of the bull's blood must be poured out at the base of the altar of burnt offerings at the entrance of the Tabernacle. ⁸The priest must remove all the fat around the bull's internal organs, ⁹the two kidneys with the fat around them near the loins, and the lobe of the liver. ¹⁰Then he must burn them on the altar of burnt offerings, just as is done with the bull or cow sacrificed as a peace offering. ¹¹But the rest of the bull—its hide, meat, head, legs, internal organs, and dung—¹²must be

I HAVE the freedom to bring different offerings to the Lord from the best of my wealth. (3:6)

I BELIEVE that aspects of the Lord's sacrificial requirements served as tangible reminders of his perpetual covenant with the Israelite people. (3:17)

I BELIEVE a prominent religious leader's sin brings guilt on his entire community of faith. (4:3)

3:2 Hebrew *Tent of Meeting;* also in 3:8, 13.   4:4 Hebrew *Tent of Meeting;* also in 4:5, 7, 14, 16, 18.

carried away to a ceremonially clean place outside the camp, the place where the ashes are thrown. He will burn it all on a wood fire in the ash heap.

[13]"If the entire Israelite community does something forbidden by the LORD and the matter escapes the community's notice, all the people will be guilty. [14]When they discover their sin, the leaders of the community must bring a young bull for a sin offering and present it at the entrance of the Tabernacle. [15]The leaders must then lay their hands on the bull's head and slaughter it there before the LORD. [16]The priest will bring some of its blood into the Tabernacle, [17]dip his finger into the blood, and sprinkle it seven times before the LORD in front of the inner curtain. [18]He will then put some of the blood on the horns of the incense altar that stands in the LORD's presence in the Tabernacle. The rest of the blood must then be poured out at the base of the altar of burnt offerings at the entrance of the Tabernacle. [19]The priest must remove all the animal's fat and burn it on the altar, [20]following the same procedure as with the sin offering for the priest. In this way, the priest will make atonement for the people, and they will be forgiven. [21]The priest must then take what is left of the bull outside the camp and burn it there, just as is done with the sin offering for the high priest. This is a sin offering for the entire community of Israel.

[22]"If one of Israel's leaders does something forbidden by the LORD his God, he will be guilty even if he sinned unintentionally. [23]When he becomes aware of his sin, he must bring as his offering a male goat with no physical defects. [24]He is to lay his hand on the goat's head and slaughter it before the LORD at the place where burnt offerings are slaughtered. This will be his sin offering. [25]Then the priest will dip his finger into the blood of the sin offering, put it on the horns of the altar of burnt offerings, and pour out the rest of the blood at the base of the altar. [26]He must burn all the goat's fat on the altar, just as is done with the peace offering. In this way, the priest will make atonement for the leader's sin, and he will be forgiven.

[27]"If any of the citizens of Israel* do something forbidden by the LORD, they will be guilty even if they sinned unintentionally. [28]When they become aware of their sin, they must bring as their offering a female goat with no physical defects. It will be offered for their sin. [29]They are to lay a hand on the head of the sin offering and slaughter it at the place where burnt offerings are slaughtered. [30]The priest will then dip his finger into the blood, put the blood on the horns of the altar of burnt offerings, and pour out the rest of the blood at the base of the altar. [31]Those who are guilty must remove all the goat's fat, just as is done with the peace offering. Then the priest will burn the fat on the altar, and it will be very pleasing to the LORD. In this way, the priest will make atonement for them, and they will be forgiven.

[32]"If any of the people bring a sheep as their sin offering, it must be a female with no physical defects. [33]They are to lay a hand on the head of the sin offering and slaughter it at the place where the burnt offerings are slaughtered. [34]The priest will then dip his finger into the blood, put it on the horns of the altar of burnt offerings, and pour out the rest of the blood at the base of the altar. [35]Those who are guilty must remove all the sheep's fat, just as is done with a sheep presented as a peace offering. Then the priest will burn the fat on the altar on top of the offerings given to the LORD by fire. In this way, the priest will make atonement for them, and they will be forgiven.

CHAPTER 5
Sins Requiring a Sin Offering

"If any of the people are called to testify about something they have witnessed, but they refuse to testify, they will be held responsible and be subject to punishment.

4:27 Hebrew people of the land.

I BELIEVE the Lord longs to forgive his people, if only they will confess their sins. (4:20)

I BELIEVE a civil leader who sins is guilty, even if he unintentionally violates one of the Lord's commands. (4:22)

I BELIEVE the Lord longs to forgive leaders who confess their sins. (4:26)

I GET RIGHT with God again after I sin. (4:28)

I BELIEVE the Lord was very pleased with sin offerings, which foreshadowed the atonement Jesus made for our sins when he died on the cross. (4:31)

I BELIEVE the Israelites experienced the Lord's forgiveness when they presented a sin offering and a priest made atonement for them. (4:35)

I TESTIFY in court when called to do so. (5:1)

²"Or if they touch something that is ceremonially unclean, such as the dead body of an animal that is ceremonially unclean—whether a wild animal, a domesticated animal, or an animal that scurries along the ground—they will be considered ceremonially unclean and guilty, even if they are unaware of their defilement.

³"Or if they come into contact with any source of human defilement, even if they don't realize they have been defiled, they will be considered guilty as soon as they become aware of it.

⁴"Or if they make a rash vow of any kind, whether its purpose is for good or bad, they will be considered guilty even if they were not fully aware of what they were doing at the time.

⁵"When any of the people become aware of their guilt in any of these ways, they must confess their sin ⁶and bring to the LORD as their penalty a female from the flock, either a sheep or a goat. This will be a sin offering to remove their sin, and the priest will make atonement for them.

⁷"If any of them cannot afford to bring a sheep, they must bring to the LORD two young turtledoves or two young pigeons as the penalty for their sin. One of the birds will be a sin offering, and the other will be a burnt offering. ⁸They must bring them to the priest, who will offer one of the birds as the sin offering. The priest will wring its neck but without severing its head from the body. ⁹Then he will sprinkle some of the blood of the sin offering against the sides of the altar, and the rest will be drained out at the base of the altar. ¹⁰The priest will offer the second bird as a whole burnt offering, following all the procedures that have been prescribed. In this way, the priest will make atonement for those who are guilty, and they will be forgiven.

¹¹"If any of the people cannot afford to bring young turtledoves or pigeons, they must bring two quarts* of choice flour for their sin offering. Since it is a sin offering, they must not mix it with olive oil or put any incense on it. ¹²They must take the flour to the priest, who will scoop out a handful as a token portion. He will burn this flour on the altar just like any other offering given to the LORD by fire. This will be their sin offering. ¹³In this way, the priest will make atonement for those who are guilty, and they will be forgiven. The rest of the flour will belong to the priest, just as with the grain offering."

Procedures for the Guilt Offering

¹⁴Then the LORD said to Moses, ¹⁵"If any of the people sin by unintentionally defiling the LORD's sacred property, they must bring to the LORD a ram from the flock as their guilt offering. The animal must have no physical defects, and it must be of the proper value in silver as measured by the standard sanctuary shekel.* ¹⁶They must then make restitution for whatever holy things they have defiled by paying for the loss, plus an added penalty of 20 percent. When they give their payments to the priest, he will make atonement for them with the ram sacrificed as a guilt offering, and they will be forgiven.

¹⁷"If any of them sin by doing something forbidden by the LORD, even if it is done unintentionally, they will be held responsible. When they become aware of their guilt, ¹⁸they must bring to the priest a ram from the flock as a guilt offering. The animal must have no physical defects, and it must be of the proper value. In this way, the priest will make atonement for those who are guilty, and they will be forgiven. ¹⁹This is a guilt offering, for they have been guilty of an offense against the LORD."

CHAPTER 6

Sins Requiring a Guilt Offering

And the LORD said to Moses, ²"Suppose some of the people sin against the LORD by falsely telling their neighbor that an item entrusted to their

I REFRAIN from making rash vows. (5:4)

I BELIEVE it is important to get right with God whenever I sin. (5:5)

I BELIEVE the Israelites experienced the Lord's forgiveness when they presented a sin offering and a priest made atonement for them. (5:10)

I PAY restitution for any loss I cause. (5:16)

5:11 Hebrew ¹/₁₀ of an ephah [2 liters].   5:15 Each sanctuary shekel was about 0.4 ounces or 11 grams in weight.

safekeeping has been lost or stolen. Or suppose they have been dishonest with regard to a security deposit, or they have taken something by theft or extortion. ³Or suppose they find a lost item and lie about it, or they deny something while under oath, or they commit any other similar sin. ⁴If they have sinned in any of these ways and are guilty, they must give back whatever they have taken by theft or extortion, whether a security deposit, or property entrusted to them, or a lost object that they claimed as their own, ⁵or anything gained by swearing falsely. When they realize their guilt, they must restore the principal amount plus a penalty of 20 percent to the person they have harmed. ⁶They must then bring a guilt offering to the priest, who will present it before the LORD. This offering must be a ram with no physical defects or the animal's equivalent value in silver.* ⁷The priest will then make atonement for them before the LORD, and they will be forgiven."

Further Instructions for the Burnt Offering
⁸Then the LORD said to Moses, ⁹"Give Aaron and his sons the following instructions regarding the whole burnt offering. The burnt offering must be left on the altar until the next morning, and the altar fire must be kept burning all night. ¹⁰The next morning, after dressing in his special linen clothing and undergarments, the priest on duty must clean out the ashes of the burnt offering and put them beside the altar. ¹¹Then he must change back into his normal clothing and carry the ashes outside the camp to a place that is ceremonially clean. ¹²Meanwhile, the fire on the altar must be kept burning; it must never go out. Each morning the priest will add fresh wood to the fire and arrange the daily whole burnt offering on it. He must then burn the fat of the peace offerings on top of this daily whole burnt offering. ¹³Remember, the fire must be kept burning on the altar at all times. It must never go out.

Further Instructions for the Grain Offering
¹⁴"These are the instructions regarding the grain offering. Aaron's sons must present this offering to the LORD in front of the altar. ¹⁵The priest on duty will take a handful of the choice flour that has been mixed with olive oil and sprinkled with incense. He will burn this token portion on the altar, and it will be very pleasing to the LORD. ¹⁶After burning this handful, the rest of the flour will belong to Aaron and his sons for their food. It must, however, be baked without yeast and eaten in a sacred place within the courtyard of the Tabernacle.* ¹⁷Remember, this flour may never be prepared with yeast. I have given it to the priests as their share of the offerings presented to me by fire. Like the sin offering and the guilt offering, it is most holy. ¹⁸Any of Aaron's male descendants, from generation to generation, may eat of the grain offering, because it is their regular share of the offerings given to the LORD by fire. Anyone or anything that touches this food will become holy."

Procedures for the Ordination Offering
¹⁹And the LORD said to Moses, ²⁰"On the day Aaron and his sons are anointed, they must bring to the LORD a grain offering of two quarts* of choice flour, half to be offered in the morning and half to be offered in the evening. ²¹It must be cooked on a griddle with olive oil, and it must be well mixed and broken* into pieces. You must present this grain offering, and it will be very pleasing to the LORD. ²²As the sons of the priests replace their fathers, they will be inducted into office by offering this same sacrifice on the day they are anointed. It is the LORD's regular share, and it must be completely burned up.

6:6 Or *and the animal must be of the proper value;* Hebrew lacks *in silver;* compare 5:15. 6:16 Hebrew *Tent of Meeting;* also in 6:26, 30. 6:20 Hebrew ¹/₁₀ *of an ephah* [2 liters]. 6:21 The meaning of this Hebrew term is uncertain.

I PAY restitution and a penalty for anything I've taken from someone else, and I ask God's forgiveness as well. (6:5)

I BELIEVE the Israelites experienced the Lord's forgiveness when they presented a sin offering and a priest made atonement for them. (6:7)

I BELIEVE that aspects of the Lord's sacrificial requirements served as tangible reminders of his perpetual covenant with the Israelites. (6:13)

I GIVE my offerings to the Lord. (6:14)

I GLADLY HELP support the Lord's servants with my offerings. (6:16)

²³All such grain offerings of the priests must be entirely burned up. None of the flour may be eaten."

Further Instructions for the Sin Offering

²⁴Then the LORD said to Moses, ²⁵"Give Aaron and his sons these further instructions regarding the sin offering. The animal given as a sin offering is most holy and must be slaughtered in the LORD's presence at the place where the burnt offerings are slaughtered. ²⁶The priest who offers the sacrifice may eat his portion in a sacred place within the courtyard of the Tabernacle. ²⁷Anything or anyone who touches the sacrificial meat will become holy, and if the sacrificial blood splatters anyone's clothing, it must be washed off in a sacred place. ²⁸If a clay pot is used to boil the sacrificial meat, it must be broken. If a bronze kettle is used, it must be scoured and rinsed thoroughly with water. ²⁹Only males from a priest's family may eat of this offering, for it is most holy. ³⁰If, however, the blood of a sin offering has been taken into the Tabernacle to make atonement in the Holy Place for the people's sins, none of that animal's meat may be eaten. It must be completely burned up.

CHAPTER 7

Further Instructions for the Guilt Offering

"These are the instructions for the guilt offering, which is most holy. ²The animal sacrificed as a guilt offering must be slaughtered where the burnt offerings are slaughtered, and its blood sprinkled against the sides of the altar. ³The priest will then offer all its fat on the altar, including the fat from the tail, the fat around the internal organs, ⁴the two kidneys with the fat around them near the loins, and the lobe of the liver, which is to be removed with the kidneys. ⁵The priests will burn these parts on the altar as an offering to the LORD made by fire. It is a guilt offering. ⁶All males from a priest's family may eat the meat, and it must be eaten in a sacred place, for it is most holy.

⁷"For both the sin offering and the guilt offering, the meat of the sacrificed animal belongs to the priest in charge of the atonement ceremony. ⁸In the case of the whole burnt offering, the hide of the sacrificed animal also belongs to the priest. ⁹Any grain offering that has been baked in an oven, prepared in a pan, or cooked on a griddle belongs to the priest who presents it. ¹⁰All other grain offerings, whether flour mixed with olive oil or dry flour, are to be shared among all the priests and their sons.

Further Instructions for the Peace Offering

¹¹"These are the instructions regarding the different kinds of peace offerings that may be presented to the LORD. ¹²If you present your peace offering as a thanksgiving offering, the usual animal sacrifice must be accompanied by various kinds of bread—loaves, wafers, and cakes—all made without yeast and soaked with olive oil. ¹³This peace offering of thanksgiving must also be accompanied by loaves of yeast bread. ¹⁴One of each kind of bread must be presented as a gift to the LORD. This bread will then belong to the priest who sprinkles the altar with blood from the sacrificed animal. ¹⁵The animal's meat must be eaten on the same day it is offered. None of it may be saved for the next morning.

¹⁶"However, if you bring an offering to fulfill a vow or as a freewill offering, the meat may be eaten on that same day, and whatever is left over may be eaten on the second day. ¹⁷But anything left over until the third day must be completely burned up. ¹⁸If any of the meat from this peace offering is eaten on the third day, it will not be accepted by the LORD. It will have no value as a sacrifice, and you will receive no credit for bringing it as an offering. By then, the meat will be contaminated; if you eat it, you will have to answer for your sin.

¹⁹"Meat that touches anything ceremonially unclean may not be eaten; it must be completely burned up. And as for meat that may be eaten, it may

I BELIEVE the Lord viewed the body and blood of any Israelite sacrifice as sacred and holy. (6:27)

I BELIEVE sin offerings foreshadowed the atonement Jesus made for our sins when he died on the cross. (6:30)

I HELP support the Lord's servants with my offerings, which are most holy. (7:6)

I HAVE the freedom to give a peace offering to the Lord any time I want. (7:11)

I GIVE generous thanksgiving offerings to the Lord. (7:12)

I BELIEVE the Lord wanted the Israelites to be ceremonially clean, free from any kind of defilement. (7:19) only be eaten by people who are ceremonially clean. [20]Anyone who is ceremonially unclean but eats meat from a peace offering that was presented to the LORD must be cut off from the community. [21]If anyone touches anything that is unclean, whether it is human defilement or an unclean animal, and then eats meat from the LORD's sacrifices, that person must be cut off from the community."

The Forbidden Blood and Fat

[22]Then the LORD said to Moses, [23]"Give the Israelites these instructions: You must never eat fat, whether from oxen or sheep or goats. [24]The fat of an animal found dead or killed by a wild animal may never be eaten, though it may be used for any other purpose. [25]Anyone who eats fat from an offering given to the LORD by fire must be cut off from the community. [26]Even in your homes, you must never eat the blood of any bird or animal. [27]Anyone who eats blood must be cut off from the community."

A Portion for the Priests

[28]Then the LORD said to Moses, [29]"Give these further instructions to the Israelites: When you present a peace offering to the LORD, bring part of it as a special gift to the LORD. [30]Present it to him with your own hands as an offering given to the LORD by fire. Bring the fat of the animal, together with the breast, and present it to the LORD by lifting it up before him. [31]Then the priest will burn the fat on the altar, but the breast will belong to Aaron and his sons. [32]You are to give the right thigh of your peace offering to the priest as a gift. [33]The right thigh must always be given to the priest who sprinkles the blood and offers the fat of the peace offering. [34]For I have designated the breast and the right thigh for the priests. It is their regular share of the peace offerings brought by the Israelites. [35]This is their share. It has been set apart for Aaron and his descendants from the offerings given to the LORD by fire from the time they were appointed to serve the LORD as priests. [36]The LORD commanded that the Israelites were to give these portions to the priests as their regular share from the time of the priests' anointing. This regulation applies throughout the generations to come."

[37]These are the instructions for the whole burnt offering, the grain offering, the sin offering, the guilt offering, the ordination offering, and the peace offering. [38]The LORD gave these instructions to Moses on Mount Sinai when he commanded the Israelites to bring their offerings to the LORD in the wilderness of Sinai.

CHAPTER 8

Ordination of the Priests

The LORD said to Moses, [2]"Now bring Aaron and his sons, along with their special clothing, the anointing oil, the bull for the sin offering, the two rams, and the basket of unleavened bread [3]to the entrance of the Tabernacle.* Then call the entire community of Israel to meet you there."

[4]So Moses followed the LORD's instructions, and all the people assembled at the Tabernacle entrance. [5]Moses announced to them, "The LORD has commanded what I am now going to do!" [6]Then he presented Aaron and his sons and washed them with water. [7]He clothed Aaron with the embroidered tunic and tied the sash around his waist. He dressed him in the robe of the ephod, along with the ephod itself, and attached the ephod with its decorative sash. [8]Then Moses placed the chestpiece on Aaron and put the Urim and the Thummim inside it. [9]He placed on Aaron's head the turban with the gold medallion at its front, just as the LORD had commanded him.

[10]Then Moses took the anointing oil and anointed the Tabernacle and

8:3 Hebrew *Tent of Meeting*; also in 8:4, 31, 33, 35.

I BELIEVE that in Old Testament times the Lord's people were to disown anyone who ate fat or blood, which were strictly forbidden from their diet. (7:25)

I BELIEVE that aspects of the Lord's sacrificial requirements served as tangible reminders of his perpetual covenant with the Israelite people. (7:36)

I BELIEVE the Lord spoke to Moses on Mount Sinai, giving him instructions for the Israelites. (7:38)

I BELIEVE ordination is a public event. (8:3)

I DO what the Lord commands. (8:4)

I ACKNOWLEDGE publicly that I do what the Lord commands. (8:5)

everything in it, thus making them holy. [11]He sprinkled the altar seven times, anointing it and all its utensils and the washbasin and its pedestal, making them holy. [12]Then he poured some of the anointing oil on Aaron's head, thus anointing him and making him holy for his work. [13]Next Moses presented Aaron's sons and clothed them in their embroidered tunics, their sashes, and their turbans, just as the LORD had commanded him.

[14]Then Moses brought in the bull for the sin offering, and Aaron and his sons laid their hands on its head [15]as Moses slaughtered it. Moses took some of the blood, and with his finger he put it on the four horns of the altar to purify it. He poured out the rest of the blood at the base of the altar. In this way, he set the altar apart as holy and made atonement for it.* [16]He took all the fat around the internal organs, the lobe of the liver, and the two kidneys and their fat, and he burned them all on the altar. [17]The rest of the bull, including its hide, meat, and dung, was burned outside the camp, just as the LORD had commanded Moses.

[18]Then Moses presented the ram to the LORD for the whole burnt offering, and Aaron and his sons laid their hands on its head [19]as Moses slaughtered it. Then Moses took the ram's blood and sprinkled it against the sides of the altar. [20]Next he cut the ram into pieces and burned the head, some of its pieces, and the fat on the altar. [21]After washing the internal organs and the legs with water, Moses burned the entire ram on the altar as a whole burnt offering. It was an offering given to the LORD by fire, very pleasing to the LORD. All this was done just as the LORD had commanded Moses.

[22]Next Moses presented the second ram, which was the ram of ordination. Aaron and his sons laid their hands on its head [23]as Moses slaughtered it. Then Moses took some of its blood and put it on the lobe of Aaron's right ear, the thumb of his right hand, and the big toe of his right foot. [24]Next he presented Aaron's sons and put some of the blood on the lobe of their right ears, the thumb of their right hands, and the big toe of their right feet. He then sprinkled the rest of the blood against the sides of the altar.

[25]Next he took the fat, including the fat from the tail, the fat around the internal organs, the lobe of the liver, and the two kidneys with their fat, along with the right thigh. [26]On top of these he placed a loaf of unleavened bread, a cake of unleavened bread soaked with olive oil, and a thin wafer spread with olive oil. All these were taken from the basket of bread made without yeast that was placed in the LORD's presence. [27]He gave all of these to Aaron and his sons, and he presented the portions by lifting them up before the LORD. [28]Moses then took all the offerings back and burned them on the altar on top of the burnt offering as an ordination offering. It was an offering given to the LORD by fire, very pleasing to the LORD. [29]Then Moses took the breast and lifted it up in the LORD's presence. This was Moses' share of the ram of ordination, just as the LORD had commanded him.

[30]Next Moses took some of the anointing oil and some of the blood that was on the altar, and he sprinkled them on Aaron and his clothing and on his sons and their clothing. In this way, he made Aaron and his sons and their clothing holy.

[31]Then Moses said to Aaron and his sons, "Boil the rest of the meat at the Tabernacle entrance, and eat it along with the bread that is in the basket of ordination offerings, just as I commanded you. [32]Any meat or bread that is left over must then be burned up. [33]Do not leave the Tabernacle entrance for seven days, for that is the time it will take to complete the ordination ceremony. [34]What has been done today was commanded by the LORD in order to make atonement for you. [35]Remember, you must stay at the entrance of the Tabernacle day and night for seven days, doing everything the LORD requires.

8:15 Or *that atonement may be made on it.*

Ask God to cleanse your heart as you read his Word (Psalm 51:10).

I GIVE my offerings in obedience to the Lord, who is pleased with them. (8:21)

I BELIEVE the Lord wanted the priests to be ceremonially holy. (8:30)

I DO everything the Lord requires. (8:35)

If you fail in this, you will die. This is what the LORD has said." ³⁶So Aaron and his sons did everything the LORD had commanded through Moses.

CHAPTER 9

The Priests Begin Their Work

After the ordination ceremony, on the eighth day, Moses called together Aaron and his sons and the leaders of Israel. ²He said to Aaron, "Take a young bull for a sin offering and a ram for a whole burnt offering, both with no physical defects, and present them to the LORD. ³Then tell the Israelites to take a male goat for a sin offering for themselves and a year-old calf and a year-old lamb for a whole burnt offering, each with no physical defects. ⁴Also tell them to take a bull* and a ram for a peace offering and flour mixed with olive oil for a grain offering. Tell them to present all these offerings to the LORD because the LORD will appear to them today."

⁵So the people brought all of these things to the entrance of the Tabernacle,* just as Moses had commanded, and the whole community came and stood there in the LORD's presence. ⁶Then Moses told them, "When you have followed these instructions from the LORD, the glorious presence of the LORD will appear to you."

⁷Then Moses said to Aaron, "Approach the altar and present your sin offering and your whole burnt offering to make atonement for yourself. Then present the offerings to make atonement for the people, just as the LORD has commanded."

⁸So Aaron went to the altar and slaughtered the calf as a sin offering for himself. ⁹His sons brought him the blood, and he dipped his finger into it and put it on the horns of the altar. He poured out the rest of the blood at the base of the altar. ¹⁰Then he burned on the altar the fat, the kidneys, and the lobe of the liver from the sin offering, just as the LORD had commanded Moses. ¹¹The meat and the hide, however, he burned outside the camp.

¹²Next Aaron slaughtered the animal for the whole burnt offering. His sons brought him the blood, and he sprinkled it against the sides of the altar. ¹³They handed the animal to him piece by piece, including the head, and he burned each part on the altar. ¹⁴Then he washed the internal organs and the legs and also burned them on the altar as a whole burnt offering.

¹⁵Next Aaron presented the sacrifices for the people. He slaughtered the people's goat and presented it as their sin offering, just as he had done previously for himself. ¹⁶Then he brought the whole burnt offering and presented it in the prescribed way. ¹⁷He also brought the grain offering, burning a handful of the flour on the altar, in addition to the regular morning burnt offering.

¹⁸Then Aaron slaughtered the bull and the ram for the people's peace offering. His sons brought him the blood, and he sprinkled it against the sides of the altar. ¹⁹Then he took the fat of the bull and the ram—the fat from the tail and from around the internal organs—along with the kidneys and the lobe of the liver. ²⁰He placed these fat parts on top of the breasts of these animals and then burned them on the altar. ²¹Aaron then lifted up the breasts and right thighs as an offering to the LORD, just as Moses had commanded.

²²After that, Aaron raised his hands toward the people and blessed them. Then, after presenting the sin offering, the whole burnt offering, and the peace offering, he stepped down from the altar. ²³Next Moses and Aaron went into the Tabernacle, and when they came back out, they blessed the people again, and the glorious presence of the LORD appeared to the whole community. ²⁴Fire blazed forth from the LORD's presence and consumed the burnt offering and the fat on the altar. When the people saw all this, they shouted with joy and fell face down on the ground.

9:4 Or *cow*; also in 9:18, 19.   9:5 Hebrew *Tent of Meeting*; also in 9:23.

I BRING the best of my wealth as an offering to the Lord. (9:2)

I BELIEVE the sin and whole burnt offerings foreshadowed God's plan to redeem humanity through Jesus, who became the perfect atonement for my sins. (9:7)

I BELIEVE the Lord expects religious leaders to acknowledge their sins. (9:8)

I DO what the Lord commands. (9:10)

I REJOICE and humbly worship the Lord for his mighty deeds in the past and his work in my own life today. (9:24)

CHAPTER 10

The Sin of Nadab and Abihu

Aaron's sons Nadab and Abihu put coals of fire in their incense burners and sprinkled incense over it. In this way, they disobeyed the LORD by burning before him a different kind of fire than he had commanded. ²So fire blazed forth from the LORD's presence and burned them up, and they died there before the LORD.

³Then Moses said to Aaron, "This is what the LORD meant when he said,

'I will show myself holy
   among those who are near me.
I will be glorified
   before all the people.' "

And Aaron was silent.

⁴Then Moses called for Mishael and Elzaphan, Aaron's cousins, the sons of Aaron's uncle Uzziel. He said to them, "Come and carry the bodies of your relatives away from the sanctuary to a place outside the camp." ⁵So they came forward and carried them out of the camp by their tunics as Moses had commanded.

⁶Then Moses said to Aaron and his sons Eleazar and Ithamar, "Do not mourn by letting your hair hang loose* or by tearing your clothes. If you do, you will die, and the LORD will be angry with the whole community of Israel. However, the rest of the Israelites, your relatives, may mourn for Nadab and Abihu, whom the LORD has destroyed by fire. ⁷But you are not to leave the entrance of the Tabernacle,* under penalty of death, for the anointing oil of the LORD is upon you." So they did as Moses commanded.

Instructions for Priestly Conduct

⁸Then the LORD said to Aaron, ⁹"You and your descendants must never drink wine or any other alcoholic drink before going into the Tabernacle. If you do, you will die. This is a permanent law for you, and it must be kept by all future generations. ¹⁰You are to distinguish between what is holy and what is ordinary, what is ceremonially unclean and what is clean. ¹¹And you must teach the Israelites all the laws that the LORD has given through Moses."

¹²Then Moses said to Aaron and his remaining sons, Eleazar and Ithamar, "Take what is left of the grain offering after the handful has been presented to the LORD by fire. Make sure there is no yeast in it, and eat it beside the altar, for it is most holy. ¹³It must be eaten in a sacred place, for it has been given to you and your descendants as your regular share of the offerings given to the LORD by fire. These are the commands I have been given. ¹⁴But the breast and thigh that were lifted up may be eaten in any place that is ceremonially clean. These parts have been given to you and to your sons and daughters as your regular share of the peace offerings presented by the people of Israel. ¹⁵The thigh and breast that are lifted up must be lifted up to the LORD along with the fat of the offerings given by fire. Then they will belong to you and your descendants forever, just as the LORD has commanded."

¹⁶When Moses demanded to know what had happened to the goat of the sin offering, he discovered that it had been burned up. As a result, he became very angry with Eleazar and Ithamar, Aaron's remaining sons. ¹⁷"Why didn't you eat the sin offering in the sanctuary area?" he demanded. "It is a holy offering! It was given to you for removing the guilt of the community and for making atonement for the people before the LORD. ¹⁸Since the animal's blood was not taken into the Holy Place, you should have eaten the meat in the sanctuary area as I ordered you."

¹⁹Then Aaron answered Moses on behalf of his sons. "Today my sons

I BELIEVE the Lord is holy—that nothing sinful may enter his glorious presence. (10:3)

I BELIEVE that aspects of the Lord's Levitical requirements served as tangible reminders of his perpetual covenant with Aaron and his descendants. (10:9)

I GLADLY HELP support the Lord's servants with my offerings. (10:13)

10:6 Or *by uncovering your heads.*   10:7 Hebrew *Tent of Meeting;* also in 10:9.

presented both their sin offering and their burnt offering to the LORD," he said. "This kind of thing has also happened to me. Would the LORD have approved if I had eaten the sin offering today?" ²⁰And when Moses heard this, he approved.

CHAPTER 11

Ceremonially Clean and Unclean Animals

Then the LORD said to Moses and Aaron, ²"Give the following instructions to the Israelites: The animals you may use for food ³include those that have completely divided hooves and chew the cud. ⁴You may not, however, eat the animals named here* because they either have split hooves or chew the cud, but not both. The camel may not be eaten, for though it chews the cud, it does not have split hooves. ⁵The same is true of the rock badger* ⁶and the hare, so they also may never be eaten. ⁷And the pig may not be eaten, for though it has split hooves, it does not chew the cud. ⁸You may not eat the meat of these animals or touch their dead bodies. They are ceremonially unclean for you.

⁹"As for marine animals, you may eat whatever has both fins and scales, whether taken from fresh water or salt water. ¹⁰You may not, however, eat marine animals that do not have both fins and scales. You are to detest them, ¹¹and they will always be forbidden to you. You must never eat their meat or even touch their dead bodies. ¹²I repeat, any marine animal that does not have both fins and scales is strictly forbidden to you.

¹³"These are the birds you must never eat because they are detestable for you: the eagle, the vulture, the osprey, ¹⁴the buzzard, kites of all kinds, ¹⁵ravens of all kinds, ¹⁶the ostrich, the nighthawk, the seagull, hawks of all kinds, ¹⁷the little owl, the cormorant, the great owl, ¹⁸the white owl, the pelican, the carrion vulture, ¹⁹the stork, herons of all kinds, the hoopoe, and the bat.

²⁰"You are to consider detestable all swarming insects that walk along the ground. ²¹However, there are some exceptions that you may eat. These include insects that jump with their hind legs: ²²locusts of all varieties, crickets, bald locusts, and grasshoppers. All these may be eaten. ²³But you are to consider detestable all other swarming insects that walk or crawl.

²⁴"The following creatures make you ceremonially unclean. If you touch any of their dead bodies, you will be defiled until evening. ²⁵If you move the dead body of an unclean animal, you must immediately wash your clothes, and you will remain defiled until evening.

²⁶"Any animal that has divided but unsplit hooves or that does not chew the cud is unclean for you. If you touch the dead body of such an animal, you will be defiled until evening. ²⁷Of the animals that walk on all fours, those that have paws are unclean for you. If you touch the dead body of such an animal, you will be defiled until evening. ²⁸If you pick up and move its carcass, you must immediately wash your clothes, and you will remain defiled until evening.

²⁹"Of the small animals that scurry or creep on the ground, these are unclean for you: the mole, the mouse, the great lizard of all varieties, ³⁰the gecko, the monitor lizard, the common lizard, the sand lizard, and the chameleon. ³¹All these small animals are unclean for you. If you touch the dead body of such an animal, you will be defiled until evening. ³²If such an animal dies and falls on something, that object, whatever its use, will be unclean. This is true whether the object is made of wood, cloth, leather, or sackcloth. It must be put into water, and it will remain defiled until evening. After that, it will be ceremonially clean and may be used again.

³³"If such an animal dies and falls into a clay pot, everything in the pot will

I BELIEVE the Lord spoke to Moses and Aaron, giving them instructions for the Israelites regarding clean and unclean animals. (11:1)

I BELIEVE the Lord made a great distinction between the ceremonially clean and unclean foods for the Israelites and now says no foods can make me ceremonially unclean (Mark 7:19). (11:8)

I BELIEVE a dead animal cannot make me ceremonially unclean. (11:24)

11:4 The identification of some of the animals, birds, and insects in this chapter is uncertain. 11:5 Or *coney*, or *hyrax*.

be defiled, and the pot must be smashed. [34]If the water used to cleanse an unclean object touches any food, all of that food will be defiled. And any beverage that is in such an unclean container will be defiled. [35]Any object on which the dead body of such an animal falls will be defiled. If it is a clay oven or cooking pot, it must be smashed to pieces. It has become defiled, and it will remain that way.

[36]"However, if the dead body of such an animal falls into a spring or a cistern, the water will still be clean. But anyone who removes the dead body will be defiled. [37]If the dead body falls on seed grain to be planted in the field, the seed will still be considered clean. [38]But if the seed is wet when the dead body falls on it, the seed will be defiled.

[39]"If an animal that is permitted for eating dies and you touch its carcass, you will be defiled until evening. [40]If you eat any of its meat or carry away its carcass, you must wash your clothes. Then you will remain defiled until evening.

[41]"Consider detestable any animal that scurries along the ground; such animals may never be eaten. [42]This includes all animals that slither along on their bellies, as well as those with four legs and those with many feet. All such animals are to be considered detestable. [43]Never defile yourselves by touching such animals. [44]After all, I, the LORD, am your God. You must be holy because I am holy. So do not defile yourselves by touching any of these animals that scurry along the ground. [45]I, the LORD, am the one who brought you up from the land of Egypt to be your God. You must therefore be holy because I am holy.

[46]"These are the instructions regarding the land animals, the birds, and all the living things that move through the water or swarm over the earth, [47]so you can distinguish between what is unclean and may not be eaten and what is clean and may be eaten."

CHAPTER 12

Purification after Childbirth

The LORD said to Moses, "Give these instructions to the Israelites: [2]When a woman becomes pregnant and gives birth to a son, she will be ceremonially unclean for seven days, just as she is defiled during her menstrual period. [3]On the eighth day, the boy must be circumcised. [4]Then the woman must wait for thirty-three days until the time of her purification from the blood of childbirth is completed. During this time of purification, she must not touch anything that is holy. And she must not go to the sanctuary until her time of purification is over. [5]If a woman gives birth to a daughter, she will be ceremonially defiled for two weeks, just as she is defiled during her menstrual period. She must then wait another sixty-six days to be purified from the blood of childbirth.

[6]"When the time of purification is completed for either a son or a daughter, the woman must bring a year-old lamb for a whole burnt offering and a young pigeon or turtledove for a purification offering. She must take her offerings to the priest at the entrance of the Tabernacle.* [7]The priest will then present them to the LORD and make atonement for her. Then she will be ceremonially clean again after her bleeding at childbirth. These are the instructions to be followed after the birth of a son or a daughter.

[8]"If a woman cannot afford to bring a sheep, she must bring two turtledoves or two young pigeons. One will be for the whole burnt offering and the other for the purification offering. The priest will sacrifice them, thus making atonement for her, and she will be ceremonially clean."

12:6 Hebrew *Tent of Meeting*.

I BELIEVE a creature cannot make me ceremonially unclean. (11:43)

I HONOR the holiness of the Lord by maintaining personal holiness (1 Peter 1:16). (11:44)

I BELIEVE that the Lord wanted the Israelites to be ceremonially clean, free from any kind of defilement, but also that childbirth no longer makes a woman unclean. (12:2)

I BELIEVE the Lord made circumcision a covenantal sign with the Israelites. (12:3)

I BELIEVE the Israelites experienced the Lord's cleansing when they presented the required offerings and a priest made atonement for them. (12:7)

I BELIEVE the Lord is pleased with my offerings, even if I am poor. (12:8)

CHAPTER 13

Contagious Skin Diseases

The LORD said to Moses and Aaron, [2]"If some of the people notice a swelling or a rash or a shiny patch on their skin that develops into a contagious skin disease,* they must be brought to Aaron the priest or to one of his sons. [3]The priest will then examine the affected area of a person's skin. If the hair in the affected area has turned white and appears to be more than skin-deep, then it is a contagious skin disease, and the priest must pronounce the person ceremonially unclean.

[4]"But if the affected area of the skin is white but does not appear to be more than skin-deep, and if the hair in the spot has not turned white, the priest will put the infected person in quarantine for seven days. [5]On the seventh day the priest will make another examination. If the affected area has not changed or spread on the skin, then the priest will put the person in quarantine for seven more days. [6]The priest will examine the skin again on the seventh day. If the affected area has faded and not spread, the priest will pronounce the person ceremonially clean. It was only a temporary rash. So after washing the clothes, the person will be considered free of disease. [7]But if the rash continues to spread after this examination and pronouncement by the priest, the infected person must return to be examined again. [8]If the priest notices that the rash has spread, then he must pronounce this person ceremonially unclean, for it is a contagious skin disease.

[9]"Anyone who develops a contagious skin disease must go to the priest for an examination. [10]If the priest sees that some hair has turned white and an open sore appears in the affected area, [11]it is clearly a contagious skin disease, and the priest must pronounce that person ceremonially unclean. In such cases, the person need not be quarantined for further observation because it is clear that the skin is defiled by the disease.

[12]"Now suppose the priest discovers after his examination that a rash has broken out all over someone's skin, covering the body from head to foot. [13]In such cases, the priest must examine the infected person to see if the disease covers the entire body. If it does, he will pronounce the person ceremonially clean because the skin has turned completely white. [14]But if any open sores appear, the infected person will be pronounced ceremonially unclean. [15]The priest must make this pronouncement as soon as he sees an open sore because open sores indicate the presence of a contagious skin disease. [16]However, if the open sores heal and turn white like the rest of the skin, the person must return to the priest. [17]If, after another examination, the affected areas have indeed turned completely white, then the priest will pronounce the person ceremonially clean.

[18]"If anyone has had a boil on the skin that has started to heal, [19]but a white swelling or a reddish white spot remains in its place, that person must go to the priest to be examined. [20]If the priest finds the disease to be more than skin-deep, and if the hair in the affected area has turned white, then the priest must pronounce that person ceremonially unclean. It is a contagious skin disease that has broken out in the boil. [21]But if the priest sees that there is no white hair in the affected area, and if it doesn't appear to be more than skin-deep and has faded, then the priest is to put the person in quarantine for seven days. [22]If during that time the affected area spreads on the skin, the priest must pronounce the person ceremonially unclean, because it is a contagious skin disease. [23]But if the area grows no larger and does not spread, it is merely the scar from the boil, and the priest will pronounce that person ceremonially clean.

[24]"If anyone has suffered a burn on the skin and the burned area changes

---

I BELIEVE the Lord spoke to Moses and Aaron regarding contagious skin diseases. (13:1)

I BELIEVE the Israelites who might be ceremonially unclean due to a skin disease had to go to a priest. (13:2)

I BELIEVE that the Lord wanted the Israelites to be ceremonially clean, free from any kind of defilement, but also that skin diseases no longer make a person ceremonially unclean. (13:3)

I BELIEVE the Lord had very good reasons spiritually and physically for providing the Israelites with such detailed instructions about skin diseases. (13:4)

13:2 Traditionally rendered *leprosy*. The Hebrew word used throughout this passage is used to describe various skin diseases.

color, becoming either a shiny reddish white or white, [25]then the priest must examine it. If the hair in the affected area turns white and the problem appears to be more than skin-deep, a contagious skin disease has broken out in the burn. The priest must then pronounce that person ceremonially unclean, for it is clearly a contagious skin disease. [26]But if the priest discovers that there is no white hair in the affected area and the problem appears to be no more than skin-deep and has faded, then the priest is to put the infected person in quarantine for seven days. [27]If at the end of that time the affected area has spread on the skin, the priest must pronounce that person ceremonially unclean, for it is clearly a contagious skin disease. [28]But if the affected area has not moved or spread on the skin and has faded, it is simply a scar from the burn. The priest must then pronounce the person ceremonially clean.

[29]"If anyone, whether a man or woman, has an open sore on the head or chin, [30]the priest must examine the infection. If it appears to be more than skin-deep and fine yellow hair is found in the affected area, the priest must pronounce the infected person ceremonially unclean. The infection is a contagious skin disease of the head or chin. [31]However, if the priest's examination reveals that the infection is only skin-deep and there is no black hair in the affected area, then he must put the person in quarantine for seven days. [32]If at the end of that time the affected area has not spread and no yellow hair has appeared, and if the infection does not appear to be more than skin-deep, [33]the infected person must shave off all hair except the hair on the affected area. Then the priest must put the person in quarantine for another seven days, [34]and he will examine the infection again on the seventh day. If it has not spread and appears to be no more than skin-deep, the priest must pronounce that person ceremonially clean. After washing clothes, that person will be clean. [35]But if the infection begins to spread after the person is pronounced clean, [36]the priest must do another examination. If the infection has spread, he must pronounce the infected person ceremonially unclean, even without checking for yellow hair. [37]But if it appears that the infection has stopped spreading and black hair has grown in the affected area, then the infection has healed. The priest will then pronounce the infected person ceremonially clean.

[38]"If anyone, whether a man or woman, has shiny white patches on the skin, [39]the priest must examine the affected area. If the patch is only a pale white, this is a harmless skin rash, and the person is ceremonially clean.

[40]"If a man loses his hair and his head becomes bald, he is still ceremonially clean. [41]And if he loses hair on his forehead, he simply has a bald forehead; he is still clean. [42]However, if a reddish white infection appears on the front or the back of his head, this is a contagious skin disease. [43]The priest must examine him, and if he finds swelling around the reddish white sore, [44]the man is infected with a contagious skin disease and is unclean. The priest must pronounce him ceremonially unclean because of the infection.

[45]"Those who suffer from any contagious skin disease must tear their clothing and allow their hair to hang loose.* Then, as they go from place to place, they must cover their mouth and call out, 'Unclean! Unclean!' [46]As long as the disease lasts, they will be ceremonially unclean and must live in isolation outside the camp.

Treatment of Contaminated Clothing

[47]"Now suppose an infectious mildew* contaminates some woolen or linen clothing, [48]some woolen or linen fabric, the hide of an animal, or anything made of leather. [49]If the affected area in the clothing, the animal hide, the fabric, or the leather has turned bright green or a reddish color, it is contaminated

I BELIEVE the Israelites lamented deeply if they came down with a contagious skin disease, in part because they had to live apart from family, friends, and others in their community. (13:45)

I THANK the Lord that he can heal any disease, no matter how awful or contagious. (13:46)

I BELIEVE that the Lord wanted the Israelites to be ceremonially clean, free from any kind of defilement, but also that mildew no longer makes an article of clothing ceremonially unclean. (13:47)

I BELIEVE the Lord had very good reasons spiritually and physically for providing the Israelites with such detailed instructions about mildew that contaminated clothing. (13:49)

13:45 Or *and uncover their heads.*   13:47 Traditionally rendered *leprosy.* The Hebrew term used throughout this passage is the same term used for the various skin diseases described in 13:1-46.

with an infectious mildew and must be taken to the priest to be examined. [50]After examining the affected spot, the priest will put it away for seven days. [51]On the seventh day the priest must inspect it again. If the affected area has spread, the material is clearly contaminated by an infectious mildew and is unclean. [52]The priest must burn the linen or wool clothing or the piece of leather because it has been contaminated by an infectious mildew. It must be completely destroyed by fire.

[53]"But if the priest examines it again and the affected spot has not spread in the clothing, the fabric, or the leather, [54]the priest will order the contaminated object to be washed and then isolated for seven more days. [55]Then the priest must inspect the object again. If he sees that the affected area has not changed appearance after being washed, even if it did not spread, the object is defiled. It must be completely burned up, whether it is contaminated on the inside or outside. [56]But if the priest sees that the affected area has faded after being washed, he is to cut the spot from the clothing, the fabric, or the leather. [57]If the spot reappears at a later time, however, the mildew is clearly spreading, and the contaminated object must be burned up. [58]But if the spot disappears after the object is washed, it must be washed again; then it will be ceremonially clean.

[59]"These are the instructions for dealing with infectious mildew in woolen or linen clothing or fabric, or in anything made of leather. This is how the priest will determine whether these things are ceremonially clean or unclean."

CHAPTER 14

Cleansing from Skin Diseases

And the LORD said to Moses, [2]"The following instructions must be followed by those seeking purification from a contagious skin disease.* Those who have been healed must be brought to the priest, [3]who will examine them at a place outside the camp. If the priest finds that someone has been healed of the skin disease, [4]he will perform a purification ceremony, using two wild birds of a kind permitted for food, along with some cedarwood, a scarlet cloth, and a hyssop branch. [5]The priest will order one of the birds to be slaughtered over a clay pot that is filled with fresh springwater. [6]He will then dip the living bird, along with the cedarwood, the scarlet cloth, and the hyssop branch, into the blood of the slaughtered bird. [7]The priest will also sprinkle the dead bird's blood seven times over the person being purified, and the priest will pronounce that person to be ceremonially clean. At the end of the ceremony, the priest will set the living bird free so it can fly away into the open fields.

[8]"The people being purified must complete the cleansing ceremony by washing their clothes, shaving off all their hair, and bathing themselves in water. Then they will be ceremonially clean and may return to live inside the camp. However, they must still remain outside their tents for seven days. [9]On the seventh day, they must again shave off all their hair, including the hair of the beard and eyebrows, and wash their clothes and bathe themselves in water. Then they will be pronounced ceremonially clean.

[10]"On the next day, the eighth day, each person cured of the skin disease must bring two male lambs and one female year-old lamb with no physical defects, along with five quarts* of choice flour mixed with olive oil and three-fifths of a pint* of olive oil. [11]Then the officiating priest will present that person for cleansing, along with the offerings, before the LORD at the entrance of the Tabernacle.* [12]The priest will take one of the lambs and the olive oil and offer them as a guilt offering by lifting them up before the LORD.

I BELIEVE the Lord spoke to Moses, giving him instructions regarding individuals seeking purification from skin diseases. (14:1)

I BELIEVE religious leaders must be willing to go to those in need. (14:3)

I BELIEVE the Lord had very good reasons spiritually and physically for providing the Israelites with such detailed instructions about purification from skin diseases. (14:4)

I BRING the best of my wealth as an offering to the Lord. (14:10)

I PRESENT my offerings and myself to the Lord. (14:11)

14:2 Traditionally rendered *leprosy.* See note at 13:2. **14:10a** Hebrew *3/10 of an ephah* [5.4 liters]. **14:10b** Hebrew *1 log* [0.3 liters]; also in 14:21. **14:11** Hebrew *Tent of Meeting;* also in 14:23.

¹³He will then slaughter the lamb there in the sacred area at the place where sin offerings and burnt offerings are slaughtered. As with the sin offering, the guilt offering will be given to the priest. It is a most holy offering. ¹⁴The priest will then take some of the blood from the guilt offering and put it on the tip of the healed person's right ear, on the thumb of the right hand, and on the big toe of the right foot.

¹⁵"Then the priest will pour some of the olive oil into the palm of his own left hand. ¹⁶He will dip his right finger into the oil and sprinkle it seven times before the LORD. ¹⁷The priest will then put some of the oil remaining in his left hand on the tip of the healed person's right ear, on the thumb of the right hand, and on the big toe of the right foot, in addition to the blood of the guilt offering. ¹⁸The oil remaining in the priest's hand will then be poured over the healed person's head. In this way, the priest will make atonement before the LORD for the person being cleansed.

¹⁹"Then the priest must offer the sin offering and again perform the atonement ceremony for the person cured of the skin disease. After that, the priest will slaughter the whole burnt offering ²⁰and offer it on the altar along with the grain offering. In this way, the priest will make atonement for the person being cleansed, and the healed person will be ceremonially clean.

²¹"But anyone who cannot afford two lambs must bring one male lamb for a guilt offering, along with two quarts* of choice flour mixed with olive oil as a grain offering and three-fifths of a pint of olive oil. The guilt offering will be presented by lifting it up, thus making atonement for the person being cleansed. ²²The person being cleansed must also bring two turtledoves or two young pigeons, whichever the person can afford. One of the pair must be used for a sin offering and the other for a whole burnt offering. ²³On the eighth day, the person being cleansed must bring the offerings to the priest for the cleansing ceremony to be performed in the LORD's presence at the Tabernacle entrance. ²⁴The priest will take the lamb for the guilt offering, along with the olive oil, and lift them up before the LORD as an offering to him. ²⁵Then the priest will slaughter the lamb for the guilt offering and put some of its blood on the tip of the person's right ear, on the thumb of the right hand, and on the big toe of the right foot.

²⁶"The priest will also pour some of the olive oil into the palm of his own left hand. ²⁷He will dip his right finger into the oil and sprinkle some of it seven times before the LORD. ²⁸The priest will then put some of the olive oil from his hand on the lobe of the person's right ear, on the thumb of the right hand, and on the big toe of the right foot, in addition to the blood of the guilt offering. ²⁹The oil that is still in the priest's hand will then be poured over the person's head. In this way, the priest will make atonement for the person being cleansed.

³⁰"Then the priest will offer the two turtledoves or the two young pigeons, whichever the person was able to afford. ³¹One of them is for a sin offering and the other for a whole burnt offering, to be presented along with the grain offering. In this way, the priest will make atonement before the LORD for the person being cleansed. ³²These are the instructions for cleansing those who have recovered from a contagious skin disease but who cannot afford to bring the sacrifices normally required for the ceremony of cleansing."

Treatment of Contaminated Houses

³³Then the LORD said to Moses and Aaron, ³⁴"When you arrive in Canaan, the land I am giving you as an inheritance, I may contaminate some of your houses with an infectious mildew.* ³⁵The owner of such a house must then go to the priest and say, 'It looks like my house has some kind of disease.' ³⁶Before the priest examines the house, he must have the house emptied so

I GLADLY HELP support the Lord's servants with my offerings. (14:13)

I BELIEVE the Israelites experienced the Lord's cleansing when they presented the required offerings and a priest made atonement for them. (14:18)

I BELIEVE the Lord is pleased with my offerings, even if I am poor. (14:21)

I BELIEVE the Lord spoke to Moses and Aaron regarding contaminated houses. (14:33)

I BELIEVE that the Lord wanted the Israelites to be ceremonially clean, free from any kind of defilement, but also that mildew no longer makes a house ceremonially unclean. (14:34)

I BELIEVE the Lord had very good reasons spiritually and physically for providing the Israelites with such detailed instructions about mildew that contaminated houses. (14:36)

14:21 Hebrew ¹/₁₀ of an ephah [2 liters].   14:34 Traditionally rendered leprosy. See note at 13:47.

everything inside will not be pronounced unclean. Then the priest will go in and inspect the house. ³⁷If he finds bright green or reddish streaks on the walls of the house and the contamination appears to go deeper than the wall's surface, ³⁸he will leave the house and lock it up for seven days. ³⁹On the seventh day the priest must return for another inspection. If the mildew on the walls of the house has spread, ⁴⁰the priest must order that the stones from those areas be removed. The contaminated material will then be thrown into an area outside the town designated as ceremonially unclean. ⁴¹Next the inside walls of the entire house must be scraped thoroughly and the scrapings dumped in the unclean place outside the town. ⁴²Other stones will be brought in to replace the ones that were removed, and the walls will be replastered.

⁴³"But if the mildew reappears after all these things have been done, ⁴⁴the priest must return and inspect the house again. If he sees that the affected areas have spread, the walls are clearly contaminated with an infectious mildew, and the house is defiled. ⁴⁵It must be torn down, and all its stones, timbers, and plaster must be carried out of town to the place designated as ceremonially unclean. ⁴⁶Anyone who enters the house while it is closed will be considered ceremonially unclean until evening. ⁴⁷All who sleep or eat in the house must wash their clothing.

⁴⁸"But if the priest returns for his inspection and finds that the affected areas have not reappeared after the fresh plastering, then he will pronounce the house clean because the infectious mildew is clearly gone. ⁴⁹To purify the house the priest will need two birds, some cedarwood, a scarlet cloth, and a hyssop branch. ⁵⁰He will slaughter one of the birds over a clay pot that is filled with fresh springwater. ⁵¹Then he will dip the cedarwood, the hyssop branch, the scarlet cloth, and the living bird into the blood of the slaughtered bird, and he will sprinkle the house seven times. ⁵²After he has purified the house in this way, ⁵³he will release the living bird in the open fields outside the town. In this way, the priest will make atonement for the house, and it will be ceremonially clean.

⁵⁴"These are the instructions for dealing with the various kinds of contagious skin disease* and infectious mildew,* ⁵⁵whether in clothing, in a house, ⁵⁶in a swollen area of skin, in a skin rash, or in a shiny patch of skin. ⁵⁷These instructions must be followed when dealing with any contagious skin disease or infectious mildew, to determine when something is ceremonially clean or unclean."

CHAPTER 15

Bodily Discharges

The LORD said to Moses and Aaron, ²"Give these further instructions to the Israelites: Any man who has a genital discharge* is ceremonially unclean because of it. ³This defilement applies whether the discharge continues or is stopped up. In either case the man is unclean. ⁴Any bedding on which he lies and anything on which he sits will be defiled.

⁵"So if you touch the man's bedding, you will be required to wash your clothes and bathe in water, and you will remain ceremonially defiled until evening. ⁶If you sit where the man with the discharge has sat, you will be required to wash your clothes and bathe in water. You will then remain defiled until evening. ⁷The same instructions apply if you touch the man who has the unclean discharge. ⁸And if he spits on you, you must undergo the same procedure. ⁹Any blanket on which the man rides will be defiled. ¹⁰If you touch or carry anything that was under him, you will be required to wash your clothes and bathe in water, and you will remain defiled until evening. ¹¹If the man

I BELIEVE that the Lord wanted the Israelites to be free from any kind of defilement but also that bodily discharges no longer make people ceremonially unclean. (15:2)

14:54 Traditionally rendered *leprosy*. See notes at 13:2 and 13:47. 15:2 Hebrew *a discharge from his flesh;* also in 15:32.

touches you without first rinsing his hands, then you will be required to wash your clothes and bathe in water, and you will remain defiled until evening. [12]Any clay pot touched by the man with the discharge must be broken, and every wooden utensil he touches must be rinsed with water.

[13]"When the man's discharge heals, he must count off a period of seven days. During that time, he must wash his clothes and bathe in fresh springwater. Then he will be ceremonially clean. [14]On the eighth day he must bring two turtledoves or two young pigeons and present himself to the LORD at the entrance of the Tabernacle* and give his offerings to the priest. [15]The priest will present the offerings there, one for a sin offering and the other for a whole burnt offering. In this way, the priest will make atonement for the man before the LORD for his discharge.

[16]"Whenever a man has an emission of semen, he must wash his entire body, and he will remain ceremonially defiled until evening. [17]Any clothing or leather that comes in contact with the semen must be washed, and it will remain defiled until evening. [18]After having sexual intercourse, both the man and the woman must bathe, and they will remain defiled until evening.

I BELIEVE that the Lord wanted the Israelites to be free from any kind of defilement but also that sexual intercourse no longer makes people ceremonially unclean. (15:18)

[19]"Whenever a woman has her menstrual period, she will be ceremonially unclean for seven days. If you touch her during that time, you will be defiled until evening. [20]Anything on which she lies or sits during that time will be defiled. [21]If you touch her bed, you must wash your clothes and bathe in water, and you will remain defiled until evening. [22]The same applies if you touch an object on which she sits, [23]whether it is her bedding or any piece of furniture. [24]If a man has sexual intercourse with her during this time, her menstrual impurity will be transmitted to him. He will remain defiled for seven days, and any bed on which he lies will be defiled.

[25]"If the menstrual flow of blood continues for many days beyond the normal period, or if she discharges blood unrelated to her menstruation, the woman will be ceremonially unclean as long as the discharge continues. [26]Anything on which she lies or sits during that time will be defiled, just as it would be during her normal menstrual period. [27]If you touch her bed or anything on which she sits, you will be defiled. You will be required to wash your clothes and bathe in water, and you will remain defiled until evening.

[28]"When the woman's menstrual discharge stops, she must count off a period of seven days. After that, she will be ceremonially clean. [29]On the eighth day, she must bring two turtledoves or two young pigeons and present them to the priest at the entrance of the Tabernacle. [30]The priest will offer one for a sin offering and the other for a whole burnt offering. In this way, the priest will make atonement for her before the LORD for her menstrual discharge.

[31]"In this way, you will keep the people of Israel separate from things that will defile them, so they will not die as a result of defiling my Tabernacle that is right there among them. [32]These are the instructions for dealing with a man who has been defiled by a genital discharge or an emission of semen; [33]for dealing with a woman during her monthly menstrual period; for dealing with anyone, man or woman, who has had a bodily discharge of any kind; and for dealing with a man who has had intercourse with a woman during her period."

CHAPTER 16

The Day of Atonement

The LORD spoke to Moses after the death of Aaron's two sons, who died when they burned a different kind of fire than the LORD had commanded.* [2]The LORD said to Moses, "Warn your brother Aaron not to enter the Most Holy Place behind the inner curtain whenever he chooses; the penalty for

I BELIEVE the Lord spoke to Moses, giving him instructions regarding the Day of Atonement. (16:1)

I BELIEVE Jesus' death on the cross made full atonement for my sins, granting me access to the Lord's presence to worship him any time, any place (Hebrews 10:19-22). (16:2)

15:14 Hebrew *Tent of Meeting;* also in 15:29.   16:1 Hebrew *when they approached the LORD's presence;* compare 10:1.

intrusion is death. For the Ark's cover—the place of atonement—is there, and I myself am present in the cloud over the atonement cover.

³"When Aaron enters the sanctuary area, he must follow these instructions fully. He must first bring a young bull for a sin offering and a ram for a whole burnt offering. ⁴Then he must wash his entire body and put on his linen tunic and the undergarments worn next to his body. He must tie the linen sash around his waist and put the linen turban on his head. These are his sacred garments. ⁵The people of Israel must then bring him two male goats for a sin offering and a ram for a whole burnt offering.

⁶"Aaron will present the bull as a sin offering, to make atonement for himself and his family. ⁷Then he must bring the two male goats and present them to the LORD at the entrance of the Tabernacle.* ⁸He is to cast sacred lots to determine which goat will be sacrificed to the LORD and which one will be the scapegoat.* ⁹The goat chosen to be sacrificed to the LORD will be presented by Aaron as a sin offering. ¹⁰The goat chosen to be the scapegoat will be presented to the LORD alive. When it is sent away into the wilderness, it will make atonement for the people.

¹¹"Then Aaron will present the young bull as a sin offering for himself and his family. After he has slaughtered this bull for the sin offering, ¹²he will fill an incense burner with burning coals from the altar that stands before the LORD. Then, after filling both his hands with fragrant incense, he will carry the burner and incense behind the inner curtain. ¹³There in the LORD's presence, he will put the incense on the burning coals so that a cloud of incense will rise over the Ark's cover—the place of atonement—that rests on the Ark of the Covenant.* If he follows these instructions, he will not die. ¹⁴Then he must dip his finger into the blood of the bull and sprinkle it on the front of the atonement cover and then seven times against the front of the Ark.

¹⁵"Then Aaron must slaughter the goat as a sin offering for the people and bring its blood behind the inner curtain. There he will sprinkle the blood on the atonement cover and against the front of the Ark, just as he did with the bull's blood. ¹⁶In this way, he will make atonement for the Most Holy Place, and he will do the same for the entire Tabernacle, because of the defiling sin and rebellion of the Israelites. ¹⁷No one else is allowed inside the Tabernacle while Aaron goes in to make atonement for the Most Holy Place. No one may enter until he comes out again after making atonement for himself, his family, and all the Israelites.

¹⁸"Then Aaron will go out to make atonement for the altar that stands before the LORD by smearing some of the blood from the bull and the goat on each of the altar's horns. ¹⁹Then he must dip his finger into the blood and sprinkle it seven times over the altar. In this way, he will cleanse it from Israel's defilement and return it to its former holiness.

²⁰"When Aaron has finished making atonement for the Most Holy Place, the Tabernacle, and the altar, he must bring the living goat forward. ²¹He is to lay both of his hands on the goat's head and confess over it all the sins and rebellion of the Israelites. In this way, he will lay the people's sins on the head of the goat; then he will send it out into the wilderness, led by a man chosen for this task. ²²After the man sets it free in the wilderness, the goat will carry all the people's sins upon itself into a desolate land.

²³"As Aaron enters the Tabernacle, he must take off the linen garments he wore when he entered the Most Holy Place, and he must leave the garments there. ²⁴Then he must bathe his entire body with water in a sacred place, put on his garments, and go out to sacrifice his own whole burnt offering and the whole burnt offering for the people. In this way, he will make atonement for

I BELIEVE the high priest could enter the Lord's presence in the Most Holy Place only on certain occasions after precisely following the Lord's detailed instructions (Hebrews 9:7). (16:3)

I BELIEVE the high priest had to make the required offerings for his own sins and for the sins of the people before entering the Lord's presence in the Most Holy Place. (Hebrews 7:26-27) (16:6)

16:7 Hebrew *Tent of Meeting;* also in 16:16, 17, 20, 23, 33.   16:8 Hebrew *azazel,* which in this context means "the goat of removal"; also in 16:10, 26.   16:13 Hebrew *on the Testimony,* referring to the terms of God's covenant with Israel, which were kept in the Ark.

himself and for the people. ²⁵He must also burn all the fat of the sin offering on the altar.

²⁶"The man chosen to send the goat out into the wilderness as a scapegoat must wash his clothes and bathe in water. Then he may return to the camp.

²⁷"The bull and goat given as sin offerings, whose blood Aaron brought into the Most Holy Place to make atonement for Israel, will be carried outside the camp to be burned. This includes the animals' hides, the internal organs, and the dung. ²⁸The man who does the burning must wash his clothes and bathe himself in water before returning to the camp.

²⁹"On the appointed day in early autumn,* you must spend the day fasting and not do any work. This is a permanent law for you, and it applies to those who are Israelites by birth, as well as to the foreigners living among you. ³⁰On this day, atonement will be made for you, and you will be cleansed from all your sins in the LORD's presence. ³¹It will be a Sabbath day of total rest, and you will spend the day in fasting. This is a permanent law for you. ³²In future generations, the atonement ceremony will be performed by the anointed high priest who serves in place of his ancestor Aaron. He will put on the holy linen garments ³³and make atonement for the Most Holy Place, the Tabernacle, the altar, the priests, and the entire community. ³⁴This is a permanent law for you, to make atonement for the Israelites once each year."

Moses followed all these instructions that the LORD had given to him.

CHAPTER 17

Prohibitions against Eating Blood

Then the LORD said to Moses, ²"Give Aaron and his sons and all the Israelites these commands from the LORD: ³If any Israelite sacrifices a bull* or a lamb or a goat anywhere inside or outside the camp ⁴and does not bring it to the entrance of the Tabernacle* to present it as an offering to the LORD, that person will be guilty of a capital offense.* Such a person has shed blood and must be cut off from the community. ⁵This rule will stop the Israelites from sacrificing animals in the open fields. It will cause them to bring their sacrifices to the priest at the entrance of the Tabernacle, so he can present them to the LORD as peace offerings. ⁶That way the priest will be able to sprinkle the blood and burn the fat on the LORD's altar at the entrance of the Tabernacle, and it will be very pleasing to the LORD. ⁷The people must no longer be unfaithful to the LORD by offering sacrifices to evil spirits* out in the fields. This is a permanent law for them, to be kept generation after generation.

⁸"Give them this command as well, which applies both to Israelites and to the foreigners living among you. If you offer a whole burnt offering or a sacrifice ⁹and do not bring it to the entrance of the Tabernacle to offer it to the LORD, you will be cut off from the community.

¹⁰"And I will turn against anyone, whether an Israelite or a foreigner living among you, who eats or drinks blood in any form. I will cut off such a person from the community, ¹¹for the life of any creature is in its blood. I have given you the blood so you can make atonement for your sins. It is the blood, representing life, that brings you atonement. ¹²That is why I said to the Israelites: 'You and the foreigners who live among you must never eat or drink blood.'

¹³"And this command applies both to Israelites and to the foreigners living among you. If you go hunting and kill an animal or bird that is approved for eating, you must drain out the blood and cover it with earth. ¹⁴The life of every creature is in the blood. That is why I have told the people of Israel never to eat or drink it, for the life of any bird or animal is in the blood. So whoever eats or drinks blood must be cut off.

I BELIEVE the requirement to carry the sin offerings outside the camp pictures Jesus Christ's death and burial outside Jerusalem (Hebrews 13:11). (16:27)

I BELIEVE the Day of Atonement served as a tangible reminder of the Lord's perpetual covenant with the Israelite people. (16:32)

I DO all that the Lord commands. (16:34)

I BELIEVE the Lord spoke to Moses, giving him instructions for the priests and the rest of the people regarding what not to eat. (17:1)

I BELIEVE that the Lord's requirement to sacrifice to him alone served as a tangible reminder of his perpetual covenant with the Israelites. (17:7)

I BELIEVE Jesus, the perfect sacrifice of God, made full atonement for my sins by shedding his blood on the cross (Hebrews 9:22). (17:11)

16:29 Hebrew *On the tenth day of the seventh month.* This day of the Hebrew lunar calendar occurs in September or early October.   17:3 Or *cow.*   17:4a Hebrew *Tent of Meeting;* also in 17:5, 6, 9.   17:4b Hebrew *blood guilt.*   17:7 Or *goat idols.*

I BELIEVE the Lord wanted the Israelites to be free from the defilement of eating from the carcass of an animal that was killed by a wild animal or died of natural causes. (17:15)

I BELIEVE the Lord spoke to Moses, giving him instructions for the Israelites regarding sexual purity (Hebrews 13:4). (18:1)

I DO NOT IMITATE the immoral practices of the world around me. (18:3)

I OBEY all of the Lord's commands, honoring him as my God. (18:4)

I HONOR the Lord and abhor incest. (18:6)

I BELIEVE someone who commits adultery with his neighbor's wife defiles himself and dishonors the Lord (Exodus 20:14). (18:20)

I HONOR the Lord and abhor the thought of doing anything less than protecting my children and nurturing them in the things of God. (18:21)

I ABHOR the immoral, wicked sexual practices of the world around me. (18:24)

¹⁵"And this command also applies both to Israelites and the foreigners living among you. If you eat from the carcass of an animal that died a natural death or was killed by a wild animal, you must wash your clothes and bathe yourselves in water. Then you will remain ceremonially unclean until evening; after that, you will be considered clean. ¹⁶But if you do not wash your clothes and bathe, you will be held responsible."

CHAPTER 18

Forbidden Sexual Practices

Then the LORD said to Moses, ²"Say this to your people, the Israelites: I, the LORD, am your God. ³So do not act like the people in Egypt, where you used to live, or like the people of Canaan, where I am taking you. You must not imitate their way of life. ⁴You must obey all my regulations and be careful to keep my laws, for I, the LORD, am your God. ⁵If you obey my laws and regulations, you will find life through them. I am the LORD.

⁶"You must never have sexual intercourse with a close relative, for I am the LORD. ⁷Do not violate your father by having sexual intercourse with your mother. She is your mother; you must never have intercourse with her. ⁸Do not have sexual intercourse with any of your father's wives, for this would violate your father.

⁹"Do not have sexual intercourse with your sister or half sister, whether she is your father's daughter or your mother's daughter, whether she was brought up in the same family or somewhere else.

¹⁰"Do not have sexual intercourse with your granddaughter, whether your son's daughter or your daughter's daughter; that would violate you. ¹¹Do not have sexual intercourse with the daughter of any of your father's wives; she is your half sister. ¹²Do not have intercourse with your aunt, your father's sister, because she is your father's close relative. ¹³Do not have sexual intercourse with your aunt, your mother's sister, because she is your mother's close relative. ¹⁴And do not violate your uncle, your father's brother, by having sexual intercourse with his wife; she also is your aunt. ¹⁵Do not have sexual intercourse with your daughter-in-law; she is your son's wife. ¹⁶Do not have intercourse with your brother's wife; this would violate your brother.

¹⁷"Do not have sexual intercourse with both a woman and her daughter or marry both a woman and her granddaughter, whether her son's daughter or her daughter's daughter. They are close relatives, and to do this would be a horrible wickedness.

¹⁸"Do not marry a woman and her sister because they will be rivals. But if your wife dies, then it is all right to marry her sister.

¹⁹"Do not violate a woman by having sexual intercourse with her during her period of menstrual impurity.

²⁰"Do not defile yourself by having sexual intercourse with your neighbor's wife.

²¹"Do not give any of your children as a sacrifice to Molech, for you must not profane the name of your God. I am the LORD.

²²"Do not practice homosexuality; it is a detestable sin.

²³"A man must never defile himself by having sexual intercourse with an animal, and a woman must never present herself to a male animal in order to have intercourse with it; this is a terrible perversion.

²⁴"Do not defile yourselves in any of these ways, because this is how the people I am expelling from the Promised Land have defiled themselves. ²⁵As a result, the entire land has become defiled. That is why I am punishing the people who live there, and the land will soon vomit them out. ²⁶You must strictly obey all of my laws and regulations, and you must not do any of these detestable things. This applies both to you who are Israelites by birth and to the foreigners living among you.

²⁷"All these detestable activities are practiced by the people of the land where I am taking you, and the land has become defiled. ²⁸Do not give the land a reason to vomit you out for defiling it, as it will vomit out the people who live there now. ²⁹Whoever does any of these detestable things will be cut off from the community of Israel. ³⁰So be careful to obey my laws, and do not practice any of these detestable activities. Do not defile yourselves by doing any of them, for I, the LORD, am your God."

CHAPTER 19

Holiness in Personal Conduct

The LORD also said to Moses, ²"Say this to the entire community of Israel: You must be holy because I, the LORD your God, am holy. ³Each of you must show respect for your mother and father, and you must always observe my Sabbath days of rest, for I, the LORD, am your God. ⁴Do not put your trust in idols or make gods of metal for yourselves. I, the LORD, am your God.

⁵"When you sacrifice a peace offering to the LORD, offer it properly so it will be accepted on your behalf. ⁶You must eat it on the same day you offer it or on the next day at the latest. Any leftovers that remain until the third day must be burned. ⁷If any of the offering is eaten on the third day, it will be contaminated, and I will not accept it. ⁸If you eat it on the third day, you will answer for the sin of profaning what is holy to the LORD and must be cut off from the community.

⁹"When you harvest your crops, do not harvest the grain along the edges of your fields, and do not pick up what the harvesters drop. ¹⁰It is the same with your grape crop—do not strip every last bunch of grapes from the vines, and do not pick up the grapes that fall to the ground. Leave them for the poor and the foreigners who live among you, for I, the LORD, am your God.

¹¹"Do not steal.

"Do not cheat one another.

"Do not lie.

¹²"Do not use my name to swear a falsehood and so profane the name of your God. I am the LORD.

¹³"Do not cheat or rob anyone.

"Always pay your hired workers promptly.

¹⁴"Show your fear of God by treating the deaf with respect and by not taking advantage of the blind. I am the LORD.

¹⁵"Always judge your neighbors fairly, neither favoring the poor nor showing deference to the rich.

¹⁶"Do not spread slanderous gossip among your people.*

"Do not try to get ahead at the cost of your neighbor's life, for I am the LORD.

¹⁷"Do not nurse hatred in your heart for any of your relatives.

"Confront your neighbors directly so you will not be held guilty for their crimes.

¹⁸"Never seek revenge or bear a grudge against anyone, but love your neighbor as yourself. I am the LORD.

¹⁹"You must obey all my laws.

"Do not breed your cattle with other kinds of animals. Do not plant your field with two kinds of seed. Do not wear clothing woven from two different kinds of fabric.

²⁰"If a man has sexual intercourse with a slave girl who is committed to become someone else's wife, compensation must be paid. But since she had not been freed at the time, the couple will not be put to death. ²¹The man, however, must bring a ram as a guilt offering and present it to the LORD at the entrance of the Tabernacle.* ²²The priest will then make atonement for him

I BELIEVE the Lord spoke to Moses, giving him instructions for the Israelites regarding holiness in personal conduct. (19:1)

I HONOR the holiness of the Lord by maintaining personal holiness (1 Peter 1:16). (19:2)

I HONOR the Lord by sharing with others. (19:9)

I HONOR the Lord by loving my neighbor as myself. (19:18)

19:16 Hebrew *Do not act as a merchant toward your own people.*   19:21 Hebrew *Tent of Meeting.*

before the LORD with the sacrificial ram of the guilt offering, and the man will be forgiven.

²³"When you enter the land and plant fruit trees, leave the fruit unharvested for the first three years and consider it forbidden.* ²⁴In the fourth year the entire crop will be devoted to the LORD as an outburst of praise. ²⁵Finally, in the fifth year you may eat the fruit. In this way, its yield will be increased. I, the LORD, am your God.

²⁶"Never eat meat that has not been drained of its blood.

"Do not practice fortune-telling or witchcraft.

²⁷"Do not trim off the hair on your temples or clip the edges of your beards.

²⁸"Never cut your bodies in mourning for the dead or mark your skin with tattoos, for I am the LORD.

²⁹"Do not defile your daughter by making her a prostitute, or the land will be filled with promiscuity and detestable wickedness.

³⁰"Keep my Sabbath days of rest and show reverence toward my sanctuary, for I am the LORD.

³¹"Do not rely on mediums and psychics, for you will be defiled by them. I, the LORD, am your God.

³²"Show your fear of God by standing up in the presence of elderly people and showing respect for the aged. I am the LORD.

³³"Do not exploit the foreigners who live in your land. ³⁴They should be treated like everyone else, and you must love them as you love yourself. Remember that you were once foreigners in the land of Egypt. I, the LORD, am your God.

³⁵"Do not use dishonest standards when measuring length, weight, or volume. ³⁶Your scales and weights must be accurate. Your containers for measuring dry goods or liquids must be accurate.* I, the LORD, am your God, who brought you out of the land of Egypt. ³⁷You must be careful to obey all of my laws and regulations, for I am the LORD."

CHAPTER 20

Punishments for Disobedience

The LORD said to Moses, ²"Give the Israelites these instructions, which apply to those who are Israelites by birth as well as to the foreigners living among you. If any among them devote their children as burnt offerings to Molech, they must be stoned to death by people of the community. ³I myself will turn against them and cut them off from the community, because they have defiled my sanctuary and profaned my holy name by giving their children to Molech. ⁴And if the people of the community ignore this offering of children to Molech and refuse to execute the guilty parents, ⁵then I myself will turn against them and cut them off from the community, along with all those who commit prostitution by worshiping Molech.

⁶"If any among the people are unfaithful by consulting and following mediums or psychics, I will turn against them and cut them off from the community. ⁷So set yourselves apart to be holy, for I, the LORD, am your God. ⁸Keep all my laws and obey them, for I am the LORD, who makes you holy.

⁹"All who curse their father or mother must be put to death. They are guilty of a capital offense.

¹⁰"If a man commits adultery with another man's wife, both the man and the woman must be put to death. ¹¹If a man has intercourse with his father's wife, both the man and the woman must die, for they are guilty of a capital offense. ¹²If a man has intercourse with his daughter-in-law, both must be

I REFRAIN from any involvement in the occult. (19:26)

I ABHOR prostitution of any kind. (19:29)

I HONOR the Lord by showing respect for the elderly. (19:32)

I HONOR the Lord by showing love to immigrants. (19:33)

I HONOR the Lord by conducting business transactions honestly. (19:36)

I BELIEVE the Lord spoke to Moses, giving him instructions for the Israelites and others in their midst regarding capital offenses. (20:1)

I HONOR the Lord and abhor the thought of doing anything less than protecting my children and nurturing them in the things of God. (20:3)

I HONOR the Lord my God by setting myself apart from the wicked practices of those around me (1 Peter 1:16). (20:7)

I GLADLY AND DILIGENTLY OBEY the Lord, who makes me holy. (20:8)

I DO NOT COMMIT sexual sins of any kind. (20:10)

19:23 Hebrew *consider it uncircumcised.*   19:36 Hebrew *Use an honest ephah* [a dry measure] *and an honest hin* [a liquid measure].

put to death. They have acted contrary to nature and are guilty of a capital offense.

[13] "The penalty for homosexual acts is death to both parties. They have committed a detestable act and are guilty of a capital offense. [14] If a man has intercourse with both a woman and her mother, such an act is terribly wicked. All three of them must be burned to death to wipe out such wickedness from among you.

[15] "If a man has sexual intercourse with an animal, he must be put to death, and the animal must be killed. [16] If a woman approaches a male animal to have intercourse with it, she and the animal must both be put to death. Both must die, for they are guilty of a capital offense.

[17] "If a man has sexual intercourse with his sister, the daughter of either his father or his mother, it is a terrible disgrace. Both of them must be publicly cut off from the community. Since the man has had intercourse with his sister, he will suffer the consequences of his guilt. [18] If a man has intercourse with a woman suffering from a hemorrhage,* both of them must be cut off from the community, because he exposed the source of her flow, and she allowed him to do it.

[19] "If a man has sexual intercourse with his aunt, whether his mother's sister or his father's sister, he has violated a close relative. Both parties are guilty of a capital offense. [20] If a man has intercourse with his uncle's wife, he has violated his uncle. Both the man and woman involved are guilty of a capital offense and will die childless. [21] If a man marries his brother's wife, it is an act of impurity. He has violated his brother, and the guilty couple will remain childless.

[22] "You must carefully obey all my laws and regulations; otherwise the land to which I am bringing you will vomit you out. [23] Do not live by the customs of the people whom I will expel before you. It is because they do these terrible things that I detest them so much. [24] But I have promised that you will inherit their land, a land flowing with milk and honey. I, the LORD, am your God, who has set you apart from all other people.

[25] "You must therefore make a distinction between ceremonially clean and unclean animals, and between clean and unclean birds. You must not defile yourselves by eating any animal or bird or creeping creature that I have forbidden. [26] You must be holy because I, the LORD, am holy. I have set you apart from all other people to be my very own.

[27] "Men and women among you who act as mediums or psychics must be put to death by stoning. They are guilty of a capital offense."

CHAPTER 21

Instructions for the Priests

The LORD said to Moses, "Tell the priests to avoid making themselves ceremonially unclean by touching a dead relative [2] unless it is a close relative—mother or father, son or daughter, brother [3] or virgin sister who was dependent because she had no husband. [4] As a husband among his relatives,* he must not defile himself.

[5] "The priests must never shave their heads, trim the edges of their beards, or cut their bodies. [6] They must be set apart to God as holy and must never dishonor his name. After all, they are the ones who present the offerings to the LORD by fire, providing God with his food, and they must remain holy.

[7] "The priests must not marry women defiled by prostitution or women who have been divorced, for the priests must be set apart to God as holy. [8] You must treat them as holy because they offer up food to your God. You must consider them holy because I, the LORD, am holy, and I make you holy.

Recommit yourself to loving your neighbor as yourself.

I DO NOT COMPROMISE my standards and accept the immoral customs of others. (20:23)

I BELIEVE the Lord spoke to Moses, giving him instructions for the priests regarding personal holiness. (21:1)

I BELIEVE a priest was set apart as holy to the Lord and was always to honor his name. (21:6)

I AM a royal priest set apart to the Lord, who makes me holy (1 Peter 2:9). (21:8)

20:18 Or *a woman who is menstruating.* 21:4 The meaning of the Hebrew is uncertain.

⁹If a priest's daughter becomes a prostitute, defiling her father's holiness as well as herself, she must be burned to death.

¹⁰"The high priest, who has had the anointing oil poured on his head and has been ordained to wear the special priestly garments, must never let his hair hang loose* or tear his clothing. ¹¹He must never defile himself by going near a dead person, even if it is his father or mother. ¹²He must not desecrate the sanctuary of his God by leaving it to attend his parents' funeral, because he has been made holy by the anointing oil of his God. I am the LORD.

¹³"The high priest must marry a virgin. ¹⁴He must not marry a widow, a divorced woman, or a woman defiled by prostitution. She must be a virgin from his own clan, ¹⁵that he may not dishonor his descendants among the members of his clan, because I, the LORD, have made him holy."

¹⁶Then the LORD said to Moses, ¹⁷"Tell Aaron that in all future generations, his descendants who have physical defects will not qualify to offer food to their God. ¹⁸No one who has a defect may come near to me, whether he is blind or lame, stunted or deformed, ¹⁹or has a broken foot or hand, ²⁰or has a humped back or is a dwarf, or has a defective eye, or has oozing sores or scabs on his skin, or has damaged testicles. ²¹Even though he is a descendant of Aaron, his physical defects disqualify him from presenting offerings to the LORD by fire. Since he has a blemish, he may not offer food to his God. ²²However, he may eat from the food offered to God, including the holy offerings and the most holy offerings. ²³Yet because of his physical defect, he must never go behind the inner curtain or come near the altar, for this would desecrate my holy places. I am the LORD who makes them holy."

²⁴So Moses gave these instructions to Aaron and his sons and to all the Israelites.

CHAPTER 22

The LORD said to Moses, ²"Tell Aaron and his sons to treat the sacred gifts that the Israelites set apart for me with great care, so they do not profane my holy name. I am the LORD. ³Remind them that if any of their descendants are ceremonially unclean when they approach the sacred food presented by the Israelites, they must be cut off from my presence. I am the LORD!

⁴"If any of the priests have a contagious skin disease* or any kind of discharge that makes them ceremonially unclean, they may not eat the sacred offerings until they have been pronounced clean. If any of the priests become unclean by touching a corpse, or are defiled by an emission of semen, ⁵or by touching a creeping creature that is unclean, or by touching someone who is ceremonially unclean for any reason, ⁶they will remain defiled until evening. They must not eat any of the sacred offerings until they have purified their bodies with water. ⁷When the sun goes down, they will be clean again and may eat the sacred offerings. After all, this food has been set aside for them. ⁸The priests may never eat an animal that has died a natural death or has been torn apart by wild animals, for this would defile them. I am the LORD. ⁹Warn all the priests to follow these instructions carefully; otherwise they will be subject to punishment and die for violating them. I am the LORD who makes them holy.

¹⁰"No one outside a priest's family may ever eat the sacred offerings, even if the person lives in a priest's home or is one of his hired servants. ¹¹However, if the priest buys slaves with his own money, they may eat of his food. And if his slaves have children, they also may share his food. ¹²If a priest's daughter marries someone outside the priestly family, she may no longer eat the sacred offerings. ¹³But if she becomes a widow or is divorced and has no

I BELIEVE the Lord cares for individuals with physical defects. (21:22)

I BELIEVE the Lord spoke to Moses, giving him instructions for the priests regarding sacred offerings. (22:1)

I BELIEVE only a priest and his immediate family could eat the sacred offerings. (22:10)

21:10 Or *uncover his head.* 22:4 Traditionally rendered *leprosy.* See note at 13:2.

children to support her, and she returns to live in her father's home, she may eat her father's food again. But other than these exceptions, only members of the priests' families are allowed to eat the sacred offerings.

¹⁴"Anyone who eats the sacred offerings without realizing it must pay the priest for the amount eaten, plus an added penalty of 20 percent. ¹⁵No one may defile the sacred offerings brought to the LORD by the Israelites ¹⁶by allowing unauthorized people to eat them. The negligent priest would bring guilt upon the people and require them to pay compensation. I am the LORD, who makes them holy."

Worthy and Unworthy Offerings

¹⁷And the LORD said to Moses, ¹⁸"Give Aaron and his sons and all the Israelites these instructions, which apply to those who are Israelites by birth as well as to the foreigners living among you. If you offer a whole burnt offering to the LORD, whether to fulfill a vow or as a freewill offering, ¹⁹it will be accepted only if it is a male animal with no physical defects. It may be either a bull, a ram, or a male goat. ²⁰Do not bring an animal with physical defects, because it won't be accepted on your behalf.

²¹"If you bring a peace offering to the LORD from the herd or flock, whether to fulfill a vow or as a freewill offering, you must offer an animal that has no physical defects of any kind. ²²An animal that is blind, injured, mutilated, or that has a growth, an open sore, or a scab must never be offered to the LORD by fire on the altar. ²³If the bull* or lamb is deformed or stunted, it may still be offered as a freewill offering, but it may not be offered to fulfill a vow. ²⁴If an animal has damaged testicles or is castrated, it may never be offered to the LORD. ²⁵You must never accept mutilated or defective animals from foreigners to be offered as a sacrifice to your God. Such animals will not be accepted on your behalf because they are defective."

²⁶And the LORD said to Moses, ²⁷"When a bull or a ram or a male goat is born, it must be left with its mother for seven days. From the eighth day on, it will be acceptable as an offering given to the LORD by fire. ²⁸But you must never slaughter a mother animal and her offspring on the same day, whether from the herd or the flock. ²⁹When you bring a thanksgiving offering to the LORD, it must be sacrificed properly so it will be accepted on your behalf. ³⁰Eat the entire sacrificial animal on the day it is presented. Don't leave any of it until the second day. I am the LORD.

³¹"You must faithfully keep all my commands by obeying them, for I am the LORD. ³²Do not treat my holy name as common and ordinary. I must be treated as holy by the people of Israel. It is I, the LORD, who makes you holy. ³³It was I who rescued you from Egypt, that I might be your very own God. I am the LORD."

CHAPTER 23

The Appointed Festivals

The LORD said to Moses, ²"Give the Israelites instructions regarding the LORD's appointed festivals, the days when all of you will be summoned to worship me. ³You may work for six days each week, but on the seventh day all work must come to a complete stop. It is the LORD's Sabbath day of complete rest, a holy day to assemble for worship. It must be observed wherever you live. ⁴In addition to the Sabbath, the LORD has established festivals, the holy occasions to be observed at the proper time each year.

Passover and the Festival of Unleavened Bread

⁵"First comes the LORD's Passover, which begins at twilight on its appointed day in early spring.* ⁶Then the day after the Passover celebration,* the Festival

I BELIEVE the Lord spoke to Moses, giving him instructions for the priests and Israelites and all others regarding worthy and unworthy offerings. (22:17)

I BRING only the best of my wealth as an acceptable offering to the Lord. (22:19)

I HONOR the Lord by faithfully keeping all of his commands. (22:31)

I HONOR the Lord, who is holy and who makes me holy. (22:32)

I HONOR the Lord my God. (22:33)

I HONOR the Lord by setting aside a day of rest and worship. (23:3)

I BELIEVE the Israelites were to set aside a week to celebrate both the Passover, which foreshadowed Jesus Christ's death on the cross, and the Festival of Unleavened Bread, which symbolized cleansing from all sin (Exodus 20:1-20). (23:5)

22:23 Or *cow*; also in 22:27. 23:5 Hebrew *on the fourteenth day of the first month.* This day of the Hebrew lunar calendar occurs in late March or early April. 23:6 Hebrew *On the fifteenth day of the same month.*

of Unleavened Bread begins. This festival to the LORD continues for seven days, and during that time all the bread you eat must be made without yeast. ⁷On the first day of the festival, all the people must stop their regular work and gather for a sacred assembly. ⁸On each of the next seven days, the people must present an offering to the LORD by fire. On the seventh day, the people must again stop all their regular work to hold a sacred assembly."

The Festival of Firstfruits

⁹Then the LORD told Moses ¹⁰to give these instructions to the Israelites: "When you arrive in the land I am giving you and you harvest your first crops, bring the priest some grain from the first portion of your grain harvest. ¹¹On the day after the Sabbath, the priest will lift it up before the LORD so it may be accepted on your behalf. ¹²That same day you must sacrifice a year-old male lamb with no physical defects as a whole burnt offering to the LORD. ¹³A grain offering must accompany it consisting of three quarts* of choice flour mixed with olive oil. It will be an offering given to the LORD by fire, and it will be very pleasing to him. Along with this sacrifice, you must also offer one quart* of wine as a drink offering. ¹⁴Do not eat any bread or roasted grain or fresh kernels on that day until after you have brought this offering to your God. This is a permanent law for you, and it must be observed wherever you live.

The Festival of Harvest

¹⁵"From the day after the Sabbath, the day the bundle of grain was lifted up as an offering, count off seven weeks. ¹⁶Keep counting until the day after the seventh Sabbath, fifty days later, and bring an offering of new grain to the LORD. ¹⁷From wherever you live, bring two loaves of bread to be lifted up before the LORD as an offering. These loaves must be baked from three quarts of choice flour that contains yeast. They will be an offering to the LORD from the first of your crops. ¹⁸Along with this bread, present seven one-year-old lambs with no physical defects, one bull, and two rams as burnt offerings to the LORD. These whole burnt offerings, together with the accompanying grain offerings and drink offerings, will be given to the LORD by fire and will be pleasing to him. ¹⁹Then you must offer one male goat as a sin offering and two one-year-old male lambs as a peace offering.

²⁰"The priest will lift up these offerings before the LORD, together with the loaves representing the first of your later crops. These offerings are holy to the LORD and will belong to the priests. ²¹That same day, you must stop all your regular work and gather for a sacred assembly. This is a permanent law for you, and it must be observed wherever you live.

²²"When you harvest the crops of your land, do not harvest the grain along the edges of your fields, and do not pick up what the harvesters drop. Leave it for the poor and the foreigners living among you. I, the LORD, am your God."

The Festival of Trumpets

²³The LORD told Moses ²⁴to give these instructions to the Israelites: "On the appointed day in early autumn,* you are to celebrate a day of complete rest. All your work must stop on that day. You will call the people to a sacred assembly—the Festival of Trumpets—with loud blasts from a trumpet. ²⁵You must do no regular work on that day. Instead, you are to present offerings to the LORD by fire."

The Day of Atonement

²⁶Then the LORD said to Moses, ²⁷"Remember that the Day of Atonement is to be celebrated on the ninth day after the Festival of Trumpets.* On that day you must humble yourselves, gather for a sacred assembly, and present offer-

---

I PRESENT my offerings to the Lord, thanking him for my salvation. (23:8)

I BELIEVE the Israelites were to set aside one day to celebrate the Festival of Firstfruits, thanking the Lord in advance for that year's harvest. (23:10)

I BELIEVE the Israelites were to set aside one day to celebrate the Festival of Harvest, thanking the Lord in advance for that year's later harvest. (23:15)

I PRESENT my offerings to the Lord, thanking him in advance for his provision. (23:16)

I BELIEVE the Lord's requirements for the festivals served as tangible reminders of his perpetual covenant with the Israelites. (23:21)

I BELIEVE the Israelites were to set aside one day to celebrate the Festival of Trumpets, signaling the beginning of autumn. (23:24)

I BELIEVE the Israelites were to set aside one day to observe the Day of Atonement, fasting and humbling themselves before the Lord. (23:27)

23:13a Hebrew ²/₁₀ of an ephah [3.6 liters]; also in 23:17.   23:13b Hebrew ¹/₄ of a hin [1 liter].   23:24 Hebrew On the first day of the seventh month. This day of the Hebrew lunar calendar occurs in September or early October. 23:27 Hebrew on the tenth day of the seventh month; see 23:24 and the note there.

ings to the LORD by fire. ²⁸Do no work during that entire day because it is the Day of Atonement, when atonement will be made for you before the LORD your God, and payment will be made for your sins. ²⁹Anyone who does not spend that day in humility will be cut off from the community. ³⁰And I will destroy anyone among you who does any kind of work on that day. ³¹You must do no work at all! This is a permanent law for you, and it must be observed wherever you live. ³²This will be a Sabbath day of total rest for you, and on that day you must humble yourselves. This time of rest and fasting will begin the evening before the Day of Atonement* and extend until evening of that day."

The Festival of Shelters

³³And the LORD said to Moses, ³⁴"Tell the Israelites to begin the Festival of Shelters on the fifth day after the Day of Atonement.* This festival to the LORD will last for seven days. ³⁵It will begin with a sacred assembly on the first day, and all your regular work must stop. ³⁶On each of the seven festival days, you must present offerings to the LORD by fire. On the eighth day, you must gather again for a sacred assembly and present another offering to the LORD by fire. This will be a solemn closing assembly, and no regular work may be done that day.

³⁷"These are the LORD's appointed annual festivals. Celebrate them by gathering in sacred assemblies to present all the various offerings to the LORD by fire—whole burnt offerings and grain offerings, sacrificial meals and drink offerings—each on its proper day. ³⁸These festivals must be observed in addition to the LORD's regular Sabbath days. And these offerings must be given in addition to your personal gifts, the offerings you make to accompany your vows, and any freewill offerings that you present to the LORD.

³⁹"Now, on the first day of the Festival of Shelters,* after you have harvested all the produce of the land, you will begin to celebrate this seven-day festival to the LORD. Remember that the first day and closing eighth day of the festival will be days of total rest. ⁴⁰On the first day, gather fruit from citrus trees,* and collect palm fronds and other leafy branches and willows that grow by the streams. Then rejoice before the LORD your God for seven days. ⁴¹You must observe this seven-day festival to the LORD every year. This is a permanent law for you, and it must be kept by all future generations. ⁴²During the seven festival days, all of you who are Israelites by birth must live in shelters. ⁴³This will remind each new generation of Israelites that their ancestors had to live in shelters when I rescued them from the land of Egypt. I, the LORD, am your God."

⁴⁴So Moses gave these instructions regarding the annual festivals of the LORD to the Israelites.

CHAPTER 24

Pure Oil and Holy Bread

The LORD said to Moses, ²"Command the people of Israel to provide you with pure olive oil for the lampstand, so it can be kept burning continually. ³Aaron will set it up outside the inner curtain of the Most Holy Place in the Tabernacle* and must arrange to have the lamps tended continually, from evening until morning, before the LORD. This is a permanent law for you, and it must be kept by all future generations. ⁴The lamps on the pure gold lampstand must be tended continually in the LORD's presence.

⁵"You must bake twelve loaves of bread from choice flour, using three quarts* of flour for each loaf. ⁶Place the bread in the LORD's presence on the

I BELIEVE Jesus' death on the cross made full atonement for my sins, granting me access to the Lord's presence to worship him any time, any place (Hebrews 10:19–22). (23:28)

I BELIEVE the Israelites were to set aside a week to celebrate the Festival of Shelters, remembering how the Lord delivered them. (23:34)

I BELIEVE the Lord spoke to Moses, giving him instructions for the Israelites regarding provisions for the Tabernacle. (24:1)

I BELIEVE the Lord's requirements for the sacred lamps served as a tangible reminder of his perpetual covenant with the Israelites. (24:3)

23:32 Hebrew *the evening of the ninth day of the month;* see 23:24, 27 and the notes there.   23:34 Hebrew *on the fifteenth day of the seventh month;* see 23:24, 27 and the notes there.   23:39 Hebrew *on the fifteenth day of the seventh month;* see 23:24 and the note there.   23:40 Or *fruit from majestic trees.*   24:3 Hebrew *the curtain of the Testimony in the Tent of Meeting.*   24:5 Hebrew ²/₁₀ *of an ephah* [3.6 liters].

pure gold table, and arrange the loaves in two rows, with six in each row. [7]Sprinkle some pure frankincense near each row. It will serve as a token offering, to be burned in place of the bread as an offering given to the LORD by fire. [8]Every Sabbath day this bread must be laid out before the LORD on behalf of the Israelites as a continual part of the covenant. [9]The loaves of bread belong to Aaron and his male descendants, who must eat them in a sacred place, for they represent a most holy portion of the offerings given to the LORD by fire."

An Example of Just Punishment

[10]One day a man who had an Israelite mother and an Egyptian father got into a fight with one of the Israelite men. [11]During the fight, this son of an Israelite woman blasphemed the LORD's name. So the man was brought to Moses for judgment. His mother's name was Shelomith. She was the daughter of Dibri of the tribe of Dan. [12]They put the man in custody until the LORD's will in the matter should become clear.

[13]Then the LORD said to Moses, [14]"Take the blasphemer outside the camp, and tell all those who heard him to lay their hands on his head. Then let the entire community stone him to death. [15]Say to the people of Israel: Those who blaspheme God will suffer the consequences of their guilt and be punished. [16]Anyone who blasphemes the LORD's name must be stoned to death by the whole community of Israel. Any Israelite or foreigner among you who blasphemes the LORD's name will surely die.

[17]"Anyone who takes another person's life must be put to death.

[18]"Anyone who kills another person's animal must pay it back in full—a live animal for the animal that was killed.

[19]"Anyone who injures another person must be dealt with according to the injury inflicted—[20]fracture for fracture, eye for eye, tooth for tooth. Whatever anyone does to hurt another person must be paid back in kind.

[21]"Whoever kills an animal must make full restitution, but whoever kills another person must be put to death.

[22]"These same regulations apply to Israelites by birth and foreigners who live among you. I, the LORD, am your God."

[23]After Moses gave all these instructions to the Israelites, they led the blasphemer outside the camp and stoned him to death, just as the LORD had commanded Moses.

CHAPTER 25

The Sabbath Year

While Moses was on Mount Sinai, the LORD said to him, [2]"Give these instructions to the Israelites: When you have entered the land I am giving you as an inheritance, the land itself must observe a Sabbath to the LORD every seventh year. [3]For six years you may plant your fields and prune your vineyards and harvest your crops, [4]but during the seventh year the land will enjoy a Sabbath year of rest to the LORD. Do not plant your crops or prune your vineyards during that entire year. [5]And don't store away the crops that grow naturally or process the grapes that grow on your unpruned vines. The land is to have a year of total rest. [6]But you, your male and female slaves, your hired servants, and any foreigners who live with you may eat the produce that grows naturally during the Sabbath year. [7]And your livestock and the wild animals will also be allowed to eat of the land's bounty.

The Year of Jubilee

[8]"In addition, you must count off seven Sabbath years, seven years times seven, adding up to forty-nine years in all. [9]Then on the Day of Atonement of the fiftieth year,* blow the trumpets loud and long throughout the land.

I BELIEVE the Lord's requirements for the sacred bread served as a tangible reminder of his perpetual covenant with the Israelites. (24:8)

I DO NOT BLASPHEME the Lord's name. (24:11)

I BELIEVE a criminal should pay full restitution—neither far more nor far less than the cost of the damage caused. (24:19)

I BELIEVE the Lord spoke to Moses, giving him instructions for the Israelites regarding Sabbath years. (25:1)

I BELIEVE the Sabbath years were a demonstration of faith and trust in the Lord's ongoing provision. (25:4)

I BELIEVE the Israelites were to observe an extra Sabbath year—a Year of Jubilee—every fifty years once they entered the Promised Land. (25:8)

25:9 Hebrew *on the tenth day of the seventh month, on the Day of Atonement;* see 23:27 and the note there.

[10]This year will be set apart as holy, a time to proclaim release for all who live there. It will be a jubilee year for you, when each of you returns to the lands that belonged to your ancestors and rejoins your clan. [11]Yes, the fiftieth year will be a jubilee for you. During that year, do not plant any seeds or store away any of the crops that grow naturally, and do not process the grapes that grow on your unpruned vines. [12]It will be a jubilee year for you, and you must observe it as a special and holy time. You may, however, eat the produce that grows naturally in the fields that year. [13]In the Year of Jubilee each of you must return to the lands that belonged to your ancestors.

[14]"When you make an agreement with a neighbor to buy or sell property, you must never take advantage of each other. [15]When you buy land from your neighbor, the price of the land should be based on the number of years since the last jubilee. The seller will charge you only for the crop years left until the next Year of Jubilee. [16]The more the years, the higher the price; the fewer the years, the lower the price. After all, the person selling the land is actually selling you a certain number of harvests. [17]Show your fear of God by not taking advantage of each other. I, the LORD, am your God.

[18]"If you want to live securely in the land, keep my laws and obey my regulations. [19]Then the land will yield bumper crops, and you will eat your fill and live securely in it. [20]But you might ask, 'What will we eat during the seventh year, since we are not allowed to plant or harvest crops that year?' [21]The answer is, 'I will order my blessing for you in the sixth year, so the land will produce a bumper crop, enough to support you for three years. [22]As you plant the seed in the eighth year, you will still be eating the produce of the previous year. In fact, you will eat from the old crop until the new harvest comes in the ninth year.' [23]And remember, the land must never be sold on a permanent basis because it really belongs to me. You are only foreigners and tenants living with me.

Redemption of Property

[24]"With every sale of land there must be a stipulation that the land can be redeemed at any time. [25]If any of your Israelite relatives go bankrupt and are forced to sell some inherited land, then a close relative, a kinsman redeemer, may buy it back for them. [26]If there is no one to redeem the land but the person who sold it manages to get enough money to buy it back, [27]then that person has the right to redeem it from the one who bought it. The price of the land will be based on the number of years until the next Year of Jubilee. After buying it back, the original owner may then return to the land. [28]But if the original owner cannot afford to redeem it, then it will belong to the new owner until the next Year of Jubilee. In the jubilee year, the land will be returned to the original owner.

[29]"Anyone who sells a house inside a walled city has the right to redeem it for a full year after its sale. During that time, the seller retains the right to buy it back. [30]But if it is not redeemed within a year, then the house within the walled city will become the permanent property of the buyer. It will not be returned to the original owner in the Year of Jubilee. [31]But a house in a village—a settlement without fortified walls—will be treated like property in the open fields. Such a house may be redeemed at any time and must be returned to the original owner in the Year of Jubilee.

[32]"The Levites always have the right to redeem any house they have sold within the cities belonging to them. [33]And any property that can be redeemed by the Levites—all houses within the Levitical cities—must be returned in the Year of Jubilee. After all, the cities reserved for the Levites are the only property they own in all Israel. [34]The strip of pastureland around each of the Levitical cities may never be sold. It is their permanent ancestral property.

I DO NOT TAKE advantage of others. (25:17)

I KEEP the Lord's commands and trust him to provide for all of my needs. (25:20)

I BELIEVE the Lord's requirements for the Year of Jubliee served as a tangible reminder of his perpetual covenant with the Israelites. (25:23)

I THANK Jesus Christ for being my kinsman redeemer. (25:25)

I BELIEVE the Lord's requirements for Levitical houses served as a tangible reminder of his perpetual covenant with the Levites. (25:33)

I DO NOT TRY to financially exploit relatives who fall into poverty. (25:35)

Redemption of the Poor and Enslaved

35"If any of your Israelite relatives fall into poverty and cannot support themselves, support them as you would a resident foreigner and allow them to live with you. 36Do not demand an advance or charge interest on the money you lend them. Instead, show your fear of God by letting them live with you as your relatives. 37Remember, do not charge your relatives interest on anything you lend them, whether money or food. 38I, the LORD, am your God, who brought you out of Egypt to give you the land of Canaan and to be your God.

39"If any of your Israelite relatives go bankrupt and sell themselves to you, do not treat them as slaves. 40Treat them instead as hired servants or as resident foreigners who live with you, and they will serve you only until the Year of Jubilee. 41At that time they and their children will no longer be obligated to you, and they will return to their clan and ancestral property. 42The people of Israel are my servants, whom I brought out of the land of Egypt, so they must never be sold as slaves. 43Show your fear of God by treating them well; never exercise your power over them in a ruthless way.

44"However, you may purchase male or female slaves from among the foreigners who live among you. 45You may also purchase the children of such resident foreigners, including those who have been born in your land. You may treat them as your property, 46passing them on to your children as a permanent inheritance. You may treat your slaves like this, but the people of Israel, your relatives, must never be treated this way.

47"If a resident foreigner becomes rich, and if some of your Israelite relatives go bankrupt and sell themselves to such a foreigner, 48they still retain the right of redemption. They may be bought back by a close relative—49an uncle, a nephew, or anyone else who is closely related. They may also redeem themselves if they can get the money. 50The price of their freedom will be based on the number of years left until the next Year of Jubilee—whatever it would cost to hire a servant for that number of years. 51If many years still remain, they will repay most of what they received when they sold themselves. 52If only a few years remain until the Year of Jubilee, then they will repay a relatively small amount for their redemption. 53The foreigner must treat them as servants hired on a yearly basis. You must not allow a resident foreigner to treat any of your Israelite relatives ruthlessly. 54If any Israelites have not been redeemed by the time the Year of Jubilee arrives, then they and their children must be set free at that time. 55For the people of Israel are my servants, whom I brought out of the land of Egypt. I, the LORD, am your God.

I AM a servant of the Lord my God. (25:55)

CHAPTER 26

Blessings for Obedience

"Do not make idols or set up carved images, sacred pillars, or shaped stones to be worshiped in your land. I, the LORD, am your God. 2You must keep my Sabbath days of rest and show reverence for my sanctuary. I am the LORD.

I OBEY the Lord's commands carefully and enjoy his abundant provision and protection as a result. (26:4)

3"If you keep my laws and are careful to obey my commands, 4I will send the seasonal rains. The land will then yield its crops, and the trees will produce their fruit. 5Your threshing season will extend until the grape harvest, and your grape harvest will extend until it is time to plant grain again. You will eat your fill and live securely in your land.

I OBEY the Lord's commands carefully and enjoy his protection as a result. (26:6)

6"I will give you peace in the land, and you will be able to sleep without fear. I will remove the wild animals from your land and protect you from your enemies. 7In fact, you will chase down all your enemies and slaughter them with your swords. 8Five of you will chase a hundred, and a hundred of you will chase ten thousand! All your enemies will fall beneath the blows of your weapons.

I OBEY the Lord's commands carefully and enjoy his abundant provision and presence as a result. (26:9)

9"I will look favorably upon you and multiply your people and fulfill my covenant with you. ¹⁰You will have such a surplus of crops that you will need to get rid of the leftovers from the previous year to make room for each new harvest. ¹¹I will live among you, and I will not despise you. ¹²I will walk among you; I will be your God, and you will be my people. ¹³I, the LORD, am your God, who brought you from the land of Egypt so you would no longer be slaves. I have lifted the yoke of slavery from your neck so you can walk free with your heads held high.

Punishments for Disobedience

¹⁴"However, if you do not listen to me or obey my commands, ¹⁵and if you break my covenant by rejecting my laws and treating my regulations with contempt, ¹⁶I will punish you. You will suffer from sudden terrors, with wasting diseases, and with burning fevers, causing your eyes to fail and your life to ebb away. You will plant your crops in vain because your enemies will eat them. ¹⁷I will turn against you, and you will be defeated by all your enemies. They will rule over you, and you will run even when no one is chasing you!

¹⁸"And if, in spite of this, you still disobey me, I will punish you for your sins seven times over. ¹⁹I will break down your arrogant spirit by making the skies above as unyielding as iron and the earth beneath as hard as bronze. ²⁰All your work will be for nothing, for your land will yield no crops, and your trees will bear no fruit.

²¹"If even then you remain hostile toward me and refuse to obey, I will inflict you with seven more disasters for your sins. ²²I will release wild animals that will kill your children and destroy your cattle, so your numbers will dwindle and your roads will be deserted.

²³"And if you fail to learn a lesson from this and continue your hostility toward me, ²⁴then I myself will be hostile toward you, and I will personally strike you seven times over for your sins. ²⁵I will send armies against you to carry out these covenant threats. If you flee to your cities, I will send a plague to destroy you there, and you will be conquered by your enemies. ²⁶I will completely destroy your food supply, so the bread from one oven will have to be stretched to feed ten families. They will ration your food by weight, and even if you have food to eat, you will not be satisfied.

²⁷"If after this you still refuse to listen and still remain hostile toward me, ²⁸then I will give full vent to my hostility. I will punish you seven times over for your sins. ²⁹You will eat the flesh of your own sons and daughters. ³⁰I will destroy your pagan shrines and cut down your incense altars. I will leave your corpses piled up beside your lifeless idols, and I will despise you. ³¹I will make your cities desolate and destroy your places of worship, and I will take no pleasure in your offerings of incense. ³²Yes, I myself will devastate your land. Your enemies who come to occupy it will be utterly shocked at the destruction they see. ³³I will scatter you among the nations and attack you with my own weapons. Your land will become desolate, and your cities will lie in ruins. ³⁴Then at last the land will make up for its missed Sabbath years as it lies desolate during your years of exile in the land of your enemies. Then the land will finally rest and enjoy its Sabbaths. ³⁵As the land lies in ruins, it will take the rest you never allowed it to take every seventh year while you lived in it.

³⁶"And for those of you who survive, I will demoralize you in the land of your enemies far away. You will live there in such constant fear that the sound of a leaf driven by the wind will send you fleeing. You will run as though chased by a warrior with a sword, and you will fall even when no one is pursuing you. ³⁷Yes, though no one is chasing you, you will stumble over each other in flight, as though fleeing in battle. You will have no power to stand before your enemies. ³⁸You will die among the foreign nations and be

I TRUST the Lord my God, who walks with me day by day. (26:12)

I LISTEN to the Lord and do not show contempt for his commands. (26:14)

I BELIEVE the punishment for rebelling against the Lord's commands is severe. (26:15)

I BELIEVE the punishment for rebellion against the Lord increases in severity the longer someone persists in his or her arrogant hostility against the Lord. (26:21)

I BELIEVE no matter how much people have sinned against the Lord, until their death he longs for them to humble themselves, confess their sins, and turn back to him. (26:40)

I BELIEVE the Lord used exile to prompt the surviving rebellious Israelites to humble themselves, confess their sins, and turn back to him. (26:41)

devoured in the land of your enemies. ³⁹Those still left alive will rot away in enemy lands because of their sins and the sins of their ancestors.

⁴⁰"But at last my people will confess their sins and the sins of their ancestors for betraying me and being hostile toward me. ⁴¹Finally, when I have given full expression to my hostility and have brought them to the land of their enemies, then at last their disobedient hearts will be humbled, and they will pay for their sins. ⁴²Then I will remember my covenant with Jacob, with Isaac, and with Abraham, and I will remember the land. ⁴³And the land will enjoy its years of Sabbath rest as it lies deserted. At last the people will receive the due punishment for their sins, for they rejected my regulations and despised my laws.

⁴⁴"But despite all this, I will not utterly reject or despise them while they are in exile in the land of their enemies. I will not cancel my covenant with them by wiping them out. I, the LORD, am their God. ⁴⁵I will remember my ancient covenant with their ancestors, whom I brought out of Egypt while all the nations watched. I, the LORD, am their God."

⁴⁶These are the laws, regulations, and instructions that the LORD gave to the Israelites through Moses on Mount Sinai.

CHAPTER 27

Redeeming Gifts Offered to the LORD

The LORD said to Moses, ²"Give the following instructions to the Israelites: If you make a special vow to dedicate someone to the LORD by paying the value of that person, ³here is the scale of values to be used. A man between the ages of twenty and sixty is valued at fifty pieces of silver*; ⁴a woman of that age is valued at thirty pieces of silver. ⁵A boy between five and twenty is valued at twenty pieces of silver; a girl of that age is valued at ten pieces of silver. ⁶A boy between the ages of one month and five years is valued at five pieces of silver; a girl of that age is valued at three pieces of silver. ⁷A man older than sixty is valued at fifteen pieces of silver; a woman older than sixty is valued at ten pieces of silver. ⁸If you desire to make such a vow but cannot afford to pay the prescribed amount, go to the priest and he will evaluate your ability to pay. You will then pay the amount decided by the priest.

I BELIEVE the Lord spoke to Moses, giving him instructions for the Israelites regarding redeeming gifts offered to the Lord. (27:1)

I BELIEVE the Israelites were allowed to dedicate themselves or a family member to the Lord and then pay a redemption price. (27:2)

I BELIEVE a priest could lower the redemption price based on someone's ability to pay. (27:8)

I BELIEVE the Israelites were allowed to dedicate a house to the Lord and then pay a redemption price. (27:14)

I BELIEVE the Israelites were allowed to dedicate a piece of property to the Lord and then pay a redemption price based on the time until the next Year of Jubilee. (27:16)

⁹"If your vow involves giving a clean animal—one that is acceptable as an offering to the LORD—then your gift to the LORD will be considered holy. ¹⁰The animal should never be exchanged or substituted for another—neither a good animal for a bad one nor a bad animal for a good one. But if such an exchange is in fact made, then both the original animal and the substitute will be considered holy. ¹¹But if your vow involves an unclean animal—one that is not acceptable as an offering to the LORD—then you must bring the animal to the priest. ¹²He will assess its value, and his assessment will be final. ¹³If you want to redeem the animal, you must pay the value set by the priest, plus 20 percent.

¹⁴"If you dedicate a house to the LORD, the priest must come to assess its value. The priest's assessment will be final. ¹⁵If you wish to redeem the house, you must pay the value set by the priest, plus 20 percent. Then the house will again belong to you.

¹⁶"If you dedicate to the LORD a piece of your ancestral property, its value will be assessed by the amount of seed required to plant it—fifty pieces of silver for an area that produces* five bushels* of barley seed. ¹⁷If the field is dedicated to the LORD in the Year of Jubilee, then the entire assessment will apply. ¹⁸But if the field is dedicated after the Year of Jubilee, the priest must assess the land's value in proportion to the years left until the next Year of

27:3 Hebrew *50 shekels of silver, according to the standard sanctuary shekel*, each about 0.4 ounces or 11 grams in weight. The term *shekels* also appears in 27:4, 5, 6, 7, 16. **27:16a** Or *requires*. **27:16b** Hebrew 1 *homer* [182 liters].

Jubilee. ¹⁹If you decide to redeem the dedicated field, you must pay the land's value as assessed by the priest, plus 20 percent. Then the field will again belong to you. ²⁰But if you decide not to redeem the field, or if the field is sold to someone else by the priests, it can never be redeemed. ²¹When the field is released in the Year of Jubilee, it will be holy, a field specially set apart* for the LORD. It will become the property of the priests.

²²"If you dedicate to the LORD a field that you have purchased but which is not part of your ancestral property, ²³the priest must assess its value based on the years until the next Year of Jubilee. You must then give the assessed value of the land as a sacred donation to the LORD. ²⁴In the Year of Jubilee the field will be released to the original owner from whom you purchased it. ²⁵All the value assessments must be measured in terms of the standard sanctuary shekel.*

²⁶"You may not dedicate to the LORD the firstborn of your cattle or sheep because the firstborn of these animals already belong to him. ²⁷However, if it is the firstborn of a ceremonially unclean animal, you may redeem it by paying the priest's assessment of its worth, plus 20 percent. If you do not redeem it, the priest may sell it to someone else for its assessed value.

²⁸"However, anything specially set apart by the LORD—whether a person, an animal, or an inherited field—must never be sold or redeemed. Anything devoted in this way has been set apart for the LORD as holy. ²⁹A person specially set apart by the LORD for destruction cannot be redeemed. Such a person must be put to death.

³⁰"A tenth of the produce of the land, whether grain or fruit, belongs to the LORD and must be set apart to him as holy. ³¹If you want to redeem the LORD's tenth of the fruit or grain, you must pay its value, plus 20 percent. ³²The LORD also owns every tenth animal counted off from your herds and flocks. They are set apart to him as holy. ³³The tenth animal must not be selected on the basis of whether it is good or bad, and no substitutions will be allowed. If any exchange is in fact made, then both the original animal and the substituted one will be considered holy and cannot be redeemed."

³⁴These are the commands that the LORD gave to the Israelites through Moses on Mount Sinai.

27:21 The Hebrew term used here refers to the complete consecration of things or people to the LORD, either by destroying them or by giving them as an offering; also in 27:28, 29.   27:25 Hebrew *measured according to the sanctuary shekel, 20 gerahs to each shekel.* Each sanctuary shekel was about 0.4 ounces or 11 grams in weight.

I BELIEVE the Israelites were not allowed to redeem anything specially set apart by the Lord for destruction. (27:28)

I THANK the Lord for redeeming me, even though I deserved eternal destruction. (27:29)

I GIVE the Lord a portion of all I receive. (27:30)

NUMBERS

THIS FOURTH BOOK of Moses warns against the tragic consequences of rebelling against the Lord.

A year after the exodus from Egypt, Moses conducts a thorough census of the Israelite nation (chapters 1–4). Then the people rededicate themselves to the Lord (chapters 5–8) and celebrate their second Passover feast (9:1–14). At last, they're prepared to march into the Promised Land and claim it as their own (9:15–10:36)!

Then sin breaks out in the ranks (chapters 11–20), and instead of enjoying God's blessings, the nation ends up wandering until an entire generation lies buried in the wilderness (chapters 21–25). The apostle Paul tells us that "all these events happened to them as examples for us. They were written down to warn us, who live at the time when this age is drawing to a close" (1 Corinthians 10:11).

Only after nearly forty years does a new generation rise up and finally begin to take possession of the Promised Land (chapters 26–36).

Famous passages in Numbers include

- ○ The commissioning of the Levites (3:1–4:49)
- ○ Instructions for taking a Nazirite vow (6:1-21)
- ○ Blessing for the nation of Israel (6:24-26)
- ○ The dedication of the Levites (8:5-22)
- ○ Bitter complaining by the Israelites (11:1-6)
- ○ Complaining by Miriam and Aaron (12:1-15)
- ○ The decision of the Israelites to go back to Egypt (14:1-4)
- ○ The Israelites' loss of God's protection and blessing (14:9, 42-43)
- ○ The rebellion of Korah and others (16:1-50)
- ○ Moses' sin (20:2-13)
- ○ The bronze snake (21:4-9)
- ○ Balaam's blessing over Israel (22:2–24:25; 31:8)

CHAPTER 1

Israel's First Census

One day in midspring,* during the second year after Israel's departure from Egypt, the LORD spoke to Moses in the Tabernacle* in the wilderness of Sinai. He said, ²"Take a census of the whole community of Israel by their clans and families. List the names of all the men ³twenty years old or older who are able to go to war. You and Aaron are to direct the project, ⁴assisted by one family leader from each tribe."

⁵These are the tribes and the names of the leaders chosen for the task:

I BELIEVE the Lord spoke to Moses regarding Israel's first census. (1:1)

I KNOW the people under my authority. (1:2)

1:1a Hebrew *On the first day of the second month.* This day of the Hebrew lunar calendar occurs in April or early May.　1:1b Hebrew *Tent of Meeting.*

Tribe	Leader
Reuben	Elizur son of Shedeur
⁶ Simeon	Shelumiel son of Zurishaddai
⁷ Judah.	Nahshon son of Amminadab
⁸ Issachar	Nethanel son of Zuar
⁹ Zebulun	Eliab son of Helon
¹⁰ Ephraim son of Joseph	Elishama son of Ammihud
Manasseh son of Joseph	Gamaliel son of Pedahzur
¹¹ Benjamin	Abidan son of Gideoni
¹² Dan	Ahiezer son of Ammishaddai
¹³ Asher	Pagiel son of Ocran
¹⁴ Gad	Eliasaph son of Deuel
¹⁵ Naphtali	Ahira son of Enan

¹⁶These tribal leaders, heads of their own families, were chosen from among all the people.

¹⁷Now Moses and Aaron and the chosen leaders ¹⁸called together the whole community of Israel on that very day.* All the people were registered according to their ancestry by their clans and families. The men of Israel twenty years old or older were registered, one by one, ¹⁹just as the LORD had commanded Moses. So Moses counted the people there in the wilderness of Sinai.

²⁰⁻²¹This is the number of men twenty years old or older who were able to go to war, each listed according to his own clan and family*:

Tribe	Number
Reuben (Jacob's* oldest son).	46,500
²²⁻²³ Simeon.	59,300
²⁴⁻²⁵ Gad.	45,650
²⁶⁻²⁷ Judah	74,600
²⁸⁻²⁹ Issachar	54,400
³⁰⁻³¹ Zebulun	57,400
³²⁻³³ Ephraim son of Joseph	40,500
³⁴⁻³⁵ Manasseh son of Joseph	32,200
³⁶⁻³⁷ Benjamin	35,400
³⁸⁻³⁹ Dan	62,700
⁴⁰⁻⁴¹ Asher	41,500
⁴²⁻⁴³ Naphtali.	53,400

⁴⁴These were the men counted by Moses and Aaron and the twelve leaders of Israel, all listed according to their ancestral descent. ⁴⁵They were counted by families—all the men of Israel who were twenty years old or older and able to go to war. ⁴⁶The total number was 603,550.

⁴⁷But this total did not include the Levites. ⁴⁸For the LORD had said to Moses, ⁴⁹"Exempt the tribe of Levi from the census; do not include them when you count the rest of the Israelites. ⁵⁰You must put the Levites in charge of the Tabernacle of the Covenant,* along with its furnishings and equipment. They must carry the Tabernacle and its equipment as you travel, and they must care for it and camp around it. ⁵¹Whenever the Tabernacle is moved, the Levites will take it down and set it up again. Anyone else who goes too near the Tabernacle will be executed. ⁵²Each tribe of Israel will have a designated camping area with its own family banner. ⁵³But the Levites will camp around the Tabernacle of the Covenant to offer the people of Israel protection from

I DO everything just as the Lord commands. (1:19)

I BELIEVE the Levites were called to protect the Tabernacle, not to fight in wars. (1:49)

I FULFILL the tasks God gives me. (1:53)

1:18 Hebrew *on the first day of the second month*; see 1:1.   1:20-21a In the Hebrew text, *number of men . . . family* is repeated in 1:22, 24, 26, 28, 30, 32, 34, 36, 38, 40, 42.   1:20-21b Hebrew *Israel's*.   1:50 Or *Tabernacle of the Testimony*; also in 1:53.

the LORD's fierce anger. The Levites are responsible to stand guard around the Tabernacle."

⁵⁴So the Israelites did everything just as the LORD had commanded Moses.

CHAPTER 2

Organization for Israel's Camp

Then the LORD gave these instructions to Moses and Aaron: ²"Each tribe will be assigned its own area in the camp, and the various groups will camp beneath their family banners. The Tabernacle* will be located at the center of these tribal compounds.

³⁻⁴"The divisions of Judah, Issachar, and Zebulun are to camp toward the sunrise on the east side of the Tabernacle, beneath their family banners. These are the names of the tribes, their leaders, and the number of their available troops:

Tribe	Leader	Number
Judah	Nahshon son of Amminadab	74,600
⁵⁻⁶ Issachar	Nethanel son of Zuar.	54,400
⁷⁻⁸ Zebulun	Eliab son of Helon	57,400

⁹So the total of all the troops on Judah's side of the camp is 186,400. These three tribes are to lead the way whenever the Israelites travel to a new campsite.

¹⁰⁻¹¹"The divisions of Reuben, Simeon, and Gad are to camp on the south side of the Tabernacle, beneath their family banners. These are the names of the tribes, their leaders, and the number of their available troops:

Tribe	Leader	Number
Reuben.	Elizur son of Shedeur	46,500
¹²⁻¹³ Simeon.	Shelumiel son of Zurishaddai.	59,300
¹⁴⁻¹⁵ Gad	Eliasaph son of Deuel*	45,650

¹⁶So the total of all the troops on Reuben's side of the camp is 151,450. These three tribes will be second in line whenever the Israelites travel.

¹⁷"Then the Levites will set out from the middle of the camp with the Tabernacle. All the tribes are to travel in the same order that they camp, each in position under the appropriate family banner.

¹⁸⁻¹⁹"The divisions of Ephraim, Manasseh, and Benjamin are to camp on the west side of the Tabernacle, beneath their family banners. These are the names of the tribes, their leaders, and the number of their available troops:

Tribe	Leader	Number
Ephraim.	Elishama son of Ammihud	40,500
²⁰⁻²¹ Manasseh.	Gamaliel son of Pedahzur.	32,200
²²⁻²³ Benjamin	Abidan son of Gideoni	35,400

²⁴So the total of all the troops on Ephraim's side of the camp is 108,100, and they will follow the Levites in the line of march.

²⁵⁻²⁶"The divisions of Dan, Asher, and Naphtali are to camp on the north side of the Tabernacle, beneath their family banners. These are the names of the tribes, their leaders, and the number of their available troops:

Tribe	Leader	Number
Dan	Ahiezer son of Ammishaddai	62,700
²⁷⁻²⁸ Asher	Pagiel son of Ocran	41,500
²⁹⁻³⁰ Naphtali.	Ahira son of Enan	53,400

I DO everything just as the Lord commands. (1:54)

I BELIEVE the Lord spoke to Moses and Aaron regarding the organization for Israel's camp. (2:1)

I BELIEVE the Lord gave the Israelites instructions for orderly community living. (2:2)

I BELIEVE the Lord gave the Israelites instructions for orderly travel. (2:9)

2:2 Hebrew *Tent of Meeting;* also in 2:17. 2:14-15 As in many Hebrew manuscripts, Samaritan Pentateuch, and Latin Vulgate (see also 1:14); most Hebrew manuscripts read *son of Reuel.*

³¹So the total of all the troops on Dan's side of the camp is 157,600. They are to bring up the rear whenever the Israelites move to a new campsite."

³²In summary, the troops of Israel listed by their families totaled 603,550. ³³The Levites were exempted from this census by the LORD's command to Moses. ³⁴So the people of Israel did everything just as the LORD had commanded Moses. Each clan and family set up camp and marched under their banners exactly as the LORD had instructed them.

CHAPTER 3

Levites Appointed for Service

This is the family line of Aaron and Moses as it was recorded when the LORD spoke to Moses on Mount Sinai: ²Aaron's sons were Nadab (the firstborn), Abihu, Eleazar, and Ithamar. ³They were anointed and set apart to minister as priests. ⁴But Nadab and Abihu died in the LORD's presence in the wilderness of Sinai when they burned before the LORD a different kind of fire than he had commanded. Since they had no sons, this left only Eleazar and Ithamar to serve as priests with their father, Aaron.

⁵Then the LORD said to Moses, ⁶"Call forward the tribe of Levi and present them to Aaron the priest as his assistants. ⁷They will serve Aaron and the whole community, performing their sacred duties in and around the Tabernacle.* ⁸They will also maintain all the furnishings of the sacred tent,* serving in the Tabernacle on behalf of all the Israelites. ⁹Assign the Levites to Aaron and his sons as their assistants. ¹⁰Appoint Aaron and his sons to carry out the duties of the priesthood. Anyone else who comes too near the sanctuary must be executed!"

¹¹And the LORD said to Moses, ¹²"I have chosen the Levites from among the Israelites as substitutes for all the firstborn sons of the people of Israel. The Levites are mine ¹³because all the firstborn sons are mine. From the day I killed all the firstborn sons of the Egyptians, I set apart for myself all the firstborn in Israel of both men and animals. They are mine; I am the LORD."

The Census of the Levites

¹⁴The LORD spoke again to Moses, there in the wilderness of Sinai. He said, ¹⁵"Take a census of the tribe of Levi by its families and clans. Count every male who is one month old or older." ¹⁶So Moses counted them, just as the LORD had commanded.

¹⁷Levi had three sons, who were named Gershon, Kohath, and Merari.
¹⁸The clans descended from Gershon were named for two of his descendants, Libni and Shimei.
¹⁹The clans descended from Kohath were named for four of his descendants, Amram, Izhar, Hebron, and Uzziel.
²⁰The clans descended from Merari were named for two of his descendants, Mahli and Mushi.

These were the Levite clans, listed according to their family groups.

²¹The descendants of Gershon were composed of the clans descended from Libni and Shimei. ²²There were 7,500 males one month old or older among these Gershonite clans. ²³They were assigned the area to the west of the Tabernacle for their camp. ²⁴The leader of the Gershonite clans was Eliasaph son of Lael. ²⁵These two clans were responsible to care for the tent of the Tabernacle with its layers of coverings, its entry curtains, ²⁶the curtains of the courtyard that surrounded the Tabernacle and altar, the curtain at the courtyard entrance, the cords, and all the equipment related to their use.
²⁷The descendants of Kohath were composed of the clans descended from

Marginal notes:

I DO everything just as the Lord commands. (2:34)

I DO NOT TRY to approach God any other way than how he commands. (3:4)

I BELIEVE the Lord spoke to Moses regarding the Levites' service. (3:5)

I AM WILLING to serve the Lord by serving others. (3:7)

I BELIEVE Aaron and his sons were the only Israelites allowed to enter God's inner sanctuary. (3:10)

I BELIEVE the Levites served as substitutes for all the firstborn male Israelites who belonged to the Lord. (3:12)

I BELIEVE the Lord has full rights to whomever he chooses. (3:13)

I PERFORM the tasks given to me as my service to the Lord. (3:25)

3:7 Hebrew *around the Tent of Meeting, doing service at the Tabernacle.*   3:8 Hebrew *Tent of Meeting.*

Amram, Izhar, Hebron, and Uzziel. [28]There were 8,600* males one month old or older among these Kohathite clans. They were responsible for the care of the sanctuary. [29]They were assigned the area south of the Tabernacle for their camp. [30]The leader of the Kohathite clans was Elizaphan son of Uzziel. [31]These four clans were responsible for the care of the Ark, the table, the lampstand, the altars, the various utensils used in the sanctuary, the inner curtain, and all the equipment related to their use. [32]Eleazar the priest, Aaron's son, was the chief administrator over all the Levites, with special responsibility for the oversight of the sanctuary.

[33]The descendants of Merari were composed of the clans descended from Mahli and Mushi. [34]There were 6,200 males one month old or older among these Merarite clans. [35]They were assigned the area north of the Tabernacle for their camp. The leader of the Merarite clans was Zuriel son of Abihail. [36]These two clans were responsible for the care of the frames supporting the Tabernacle, the crossbars, the pillars, the bases, and all the equipment related to their use. [37]They were also responsible for the posts of the courtyard and all their bases, pegs, and cords.

[38]The area in front of the Tabernacle in the east toward the sunrise* was reserved for the tents of Moses and of Aaron and his sons, who had the final responsibility for the sanctuary on behalf of the people of Israel. Anyone other than a priest or Levite who came too near the sanctuary was to be executed.

[39]So among the Levite clans counted by Moses and Aaron at the LORD's command, there were 22,000 males one month old or older.

Redeeming the Firstborn Sons
[40]Then the LORD said to Moses, "Now count all the firstborn sons in Israel who are one month old or older, and register each name. [41]The Levites will be reserved for me as substitutes for the firstborn sons of Israel; I am the LORD. And the Levites' livestock are mine as substitutes for the firstborn livestock of the whole nation of Israel."

[42]So Moses counted the firstborn sons of the people of Israel, just as the LORD had commanded. [43]The total number of firstborn sons who were one month old or older was 22,273.

[44]Now the LORD said to Moses, [45]"Take the Levites in place of the firstborn sons of the people of Israel. And take the livestock of the Levites as substitutes for the firstborn livestock of the people of Israel. The Levites will be mine; I am the LORD. [46]To redeem the 273 firstborn sons of Israel who are in excess of the number of Levites, [47]collect five pieces of silver for each person, each piece weighing the same as the standard sanctuary shekel.* [48]Give the silver to Aaron and his sons as the redemption price for the extra firstborn sons."

[49]So Moses collected redemption money for the firstborn sons of Israel who exceeded the number of Levites. [50]The silver collected on behalf of these firstborn sons of Israel came to about thirty-four pounds in weight.* [51]And Moses gave the redemption money to Aaron and his sons as the LORD had commanded.

CHAPTER 4
Duties of the Kohathite Clan
Then the LORD said to Moses and Aaron, [2]"Take a census of the clans and families of the Kohathite division of the Levite tribe. [3]Count all the men between the ages of thirty and fifty who qualify to work in the Tabernacle.*

[4]"The duties of the Kohathites at the Tabernacle will relate to the most sacred objects. [5]When the camp moves, Aaron and his sons must enter the

I PERFORM the tasks given to me by the Lord. (3:32)

I BELIEVE God always has a plan for redeeming his own. (3:46)

I BELIEVE God gave specific instructions to the Kohathites for the care and moving of the sacred objects. (4:4)

3:28 Some Greek manuscripts read *8,300*; see total in 3:39.   3:38 Hebrew *toward the sunrise, in front of the Tent of Meeting.*   3:47 Hebrew *5 shekels* [2 ounces or 57 grams] *apiece, according to the sanctuary shekel, 20 gerahs to each shekel.*   3:50 Hebrew *1,365 shekels* [15.5 kilograms], *according to the sanctuary shekel.*   4:3 Hebrew *Tent of Meeting;* also in 4:4, 15, 23, 25, 28, 30, 31, 33, 35, 37, 39, 41, 43, 47.

Tabernacle first to take down the inner curtain and cover the Ark of the Covenant* with it. [6] Then they must cover the inner curtain with fine goatskin leather, and the goatskin leather with a dark blue cloth. Finally, they must put the carrying poles of the Ark in place.

[7] "Next they must spread a blue cloth over the table, where the Bread of the Presence is displayed, and place the dishes, spoons, bowls, cups, and the special bread on the cloth. [8] They must spread a scarlet cloth over that, and finally a covering of fine goatskin leather on top of the scarlet cloth. Then they must insert the carrying poles into the table.

[9] "Next they must cover the lampstand with a dark blue cloth, along with its lamps, lamp snuffers, trays, and special jars of olive oil. [10] The lampstand with its utensils must then be covered with fine goatskin leather, and the bundle must be placed on a carrying frame.

[11] "Aaron and his sons must also spread a dark blue cloth over the gold altar and cover this cloth with a covering of fine goatskin leather. Then they are to attach the carrying poles to the altar. [12] All the remaining utensils of the sanctuary must be wrapped in a dark blue cloth, covered with fine goatskin leather, and placed on the carrying frame.

[13] "The ashes must be removed from the altar, and the altar must then be covered with a purple cloth. [14] All the altar utensils—the firepans, hooks, shovels, basins, and all the containers—are to be placed on the cloth, and a covering of fine goatskin leather must be spread over them. Finally, the carrying poles must be put in place. [15] When Aaron and his sons have finished covering the sanctuary and all the sacred utensils, the Kohathites will come and carry these things to the next destination. But they must not touch the sacred objects, or they will die. So these are the objects of the Tabernacle that the Kohathites must carry.

[16] "Eleazar son of Aaron the priest will be responsible for the oil of the lampstand, the fragrant incense, the daily grain offering, and the anointing oil. In fact, the supervision of the entire Tabernacle and everything in it will be Eleazar's responsibility."

[17] Then the LORD said to Moses and Aaron, [18] "Don't let the Kohathite clans be destroyed from among the Levites! [19] This is what you must do so they will live and not die when they approach the most sacred objects. Aaron and his sons must always go in with them and assign a specific duty or load to each person. [20] Otherwise they must not approach the sanctuary and look at the sacred objects for even a moment, or they will die."

Duties of the Gershonite Clan

[21] And the LORD said to Moses, [22] "Take a census of the clans and families of the Gershonite division of the tribe of Levi. [23] Count all the men between the ages of thirty and fifty who are eligible to serve in the Tabernacle.

[24] "The duties of the Gershonites will be in the areas of general service and carrying loads. [25] They must carry the curtains of the Tabernacle, the Tabernacle itself with its coverings, the outer covering of fine goatskin leather, and the curtain for the Tabernacle entrance. [26] They are also to carry the curtains for the courtyard walls that surround the Tabernacle and altar, the curtain across the courtyard entrance, the necessary cords, and all the altar's accessories. The Gershonites are responsible for transporting all these items. [27] Aaron and his sons will direct the Gershonites regarding their duties, whether it involves moving or doing other work. They must assign the Gershonites the loads they are to carry. [28] So these are the duties assigned to the Gershonites at the Tabernacle. They will be directly responsible to Ithamar son of Aaron the priest.

4:5 Or *Ark of the Testimony.*

I BELIEVE touching the sacred objects was a capital offense. (4:15)

I CAREFULLY SUPERVISE the work done by those for whom I am responsible. (4:16)

I BELIEVE the Lord provides a way for people to approach him without dying. (4:19)

I BELIEVE the Lord gave specific instructions to the Gershonites for the tasks of general service and carrying loads—particularly the curtains. (4:24)

I GIVE direction to those working under me. (4:27)

Duties of the Merarite Clan

²⁹"Now take a census of the clans and families of the Merarite division of the Levite tribe. ³⁰Count all the men between the ages of thirty and fifty who are eligible to serve in the Tabernacle.

³¹"Their duties at the Tabernacle will consist of carrying loads. They will be required to carry the frames of the Tabernacle, the crossbars, the pillars with their bases, ³²the posts for the courtyard walls with their bases, pegs, cords, accessories, and everything else related to their use. You must assign the various loads to each man by name. ³³So these are the duties of the Merarites at the Tabernacle. They are directly responsible to Ithamar son of Aaron the priest."

The Census of the Levites

³⁴So Moses, Aaron, and the other leaders of the community counted the Kohathite division by its clans and families. ³⁵The count included all the men between thirty and fifty years of age who were eligible for service in the Tabernacle, ³⁶and the total number came to 2,750. ³⁷So this was the total of all those from the Kohathite clans who were eligible to serve at the Tabernacle. Moses and Aaron counted them, just as the LORD had commanded through Moses.

³⁸The Gershonite division was also counted by its clans and families. ³⁹The count included all the men between thirty and fifty years of age who were eligible for service in the Tabernacle, ⁴⁰and the total number came to 2,630. ⁴¹So this was the total of all those from the Gershonite clans who were eligible to serve at the Tabernacle. Moses and Aaron counted them, just as the LORD had commanded.

⁴²The Merarite division was also counted by its clans and families. ⁴³The count included all the men between thirty and fifty years of age who were eligible for service in the Tabernacle, ⁴⁴and the total number came to 3,200. ⁴⁵So this was the total of all those from the Merarite clans who were eligible for service. Moses and Aaron counted them, just as the LORD had commanded through Moses.

⁴⁶So Moses, Aaron, and the leaders of Israel counted all the Levites by their clans and families. ⁴⁷All the men between thirty and fifty years of age who were eligible for service in the Tabernacle and for its transportation ⁴⁸numbered 8,580. ⁴⁹Each man was assigned his task and told what to carry, just as the LORD had commanded through Moses.

And so the census was completed, just as the LORD had commanded Moses.

CHAPTER 5

Purity in Israel's Camp

The LORD gave these instructions to Moses: ²"Command the people of Israel to remove anyone from the camp who has a contagious skin disease* or a discharge, or who has been defiled by touching a dead person. ³This applies to men and women alike. Remove them so they will not defile the camp, where I live among you." ⁴So the Israelites did just as the LORD had commanded Moses and removed such people from the camp.

⁵Then the LORD said to Moses, ⁶"Give these instructions to the people of Israel: If any of the people—men or women—betray the LORD by doing wrong to another person, they are guilty. ⁷They must confess their sin and make full restitution for what they have done, adding a penalty of 20 percent and returning it to the person who was wronged. ⁸But if the person who was wronged is dead, and there are no near relatives to whom restitution can be made, it belongs to the LORD and must be given to the priest, along with a

5:2 Traditionally rendered *leprosy*. The Hebrew word used here describes various skin diseases.

I BELIEVE the Lord gave specific instructions to the Merarites for carrying loads—particularly the pieces of the Tabernacle. (4:29)

I BELIEVE Moses and Aaron counted the Levite men eligible for service, just as the Lord commanded. (4:37)

I BELIEVE the Lord has a task for each person who serves him. (4:49)

I BELIEVE the Lord gave instructions for health and safety in community living. (5:2)

I BELIEVE the Lord required physical purity in the camp as a sign of the spiritual purity required to live in his presence. (5:3)

I DO whatever the Lord commands to live a pure life. (5:4)

ram for atonement. ⁹All the sacred gifts that the Israelites bring to a priest will belong to him. ¹⁰Each priest may keep the sacred donations that he receives."

Protecting Marital Faithfulness

¹¹And the LORD said to Moses, ¹²"Say to the people of Israel: 'Suppose a man's wife goes astray and is unfaithful to her husband. ¹³Suppose she sleeps with another man, but there is no witness since she was not caught in the act. ¹⁴If her husband becomes jealous and suspicious of his wife, even if she has not defiled herself, ¹⁵the husband must bring his wife to the priest with an offering of two quarts* of barley flour to be presented on her behalf. Do not mix it with olive oil or frankincense, for it is a jealousy offering—an offering of inquiry to find out if she is guilty.

¹⁶" 'The priest must then present her before the LORD. ¹⁷He must take some holy water in a clay jar and mix it with dust from the Tabernacle floor. ¹⁸When he has presented her before the LORD, he must unbind her hair and place the offering of inquiry—the jealousy offering—in her hands to determine whether or not her husband's suspicions are justified. The priest will stand before her, holding the jar of bitter water that brings a curse to those who are guilty. ¹⁹The priest will put the woman under oath and say to her, "If no other man has slept with you, and you have not defiled yourself by being unfaithful, may you be immune from the effects of this bitter water that causes the curse. ²⁰But if you have gone astray while under your husband's authority and defiled yourself by sleeping with another man"—²¹at this point the priest must put the woman under this oath—"then may the people see that the LORD's curse is upon you when he makes you infertile.* ²²Now may this water that brings the curse enter your body and make you infertile.*" And the woman will be required to say, "Yes, let it be so." ²³Then the priest will write these curses on a piece of leather and wash them off into the bitter water. ²⁴He will then make the woman drink the bitter water, so it may bring on the curse and cause bitter suffering in cases of guilt.

²⁵" 'Then the priest will take the jealousy offering from the woman's hand, lift it up before the LORD, and carry it to the altar. ²⁶He will take a handful as a token portion and burn it on the altar. Then he will require the woman to drink the water. ²⁷If she has defiled herself by being unfaithful to her husband, the water that brings the curse will cause bitter suffering. She will become infertile,* and her name will become a curse word among her people. ²⁸But if she has not defiled herself and is pure, she will be unharmed and will still be able to have children.

²⁹" 'This is the ritual law for dealing with jealousy. If a woman defiles herself by being unfaithful to her husband, ³⁰or if a man is overcome with jealousy and suspicion that his wife has been unfaithful, the husband must present his wife before the LORD, and the priest will apply this entire ritual law to her. ³¹The husband will be innocent of any guilt in this matter, but his wife will be held accountable for her sin.' "

CHAPTER 6

Nazirite Laws

Then the LORD said to Moses, "Speak to the people of Israel and give them these instructions: ²If some of the people, either men or women, take the special vow of a Nazirite, setting themselves apart to the LORD in a special way, ³they must give up wine and other alcoholic drinks. They must not use vinegar made from wine, they must not drink other fermented drinks or fresh grape juice, and they must not eat grapes or raisins. ⁴As long as they are

I BELIEVE the Lord spoke to Moses regarding the protection of marital faithfulness. (5:11)

I BELIEVE the Lord provided a way for a woman's guilt or faithfulness to be proven and her husband's jealousy to be resolved. (5:12)

I GO to God with my jealousy. (5:30)

I BELIEVE God gave both men and women an opportunity to serve him as Nazirites. (6:2)

I AM WILLING to voluntarily give up certain things to serve the Lord. (6:3)

5:15 Hebrew ¹/₁₀ of an ephah [2 liters]. 5:21 Hebrew when he causes your thigh to waste away and your abdomen to swell. 5:22 Hebrew enter your body so that your abdomen swells and your thigh wastes away. 5:27 Hebrew Her body will swell and her thigh will waste away.

bound by their Nazirite vow, they are not allowed to eat or drink anything that comes from a grapevine, not even the grape seeds or skins.

[5] "They must never cut their hair throughout the time of their vow, for they are holy and set apart to the LORD. That is why they must let their hair grow long. [6] And they may not go near a dead body during the entire period of their vow to the LORD, [7] even if their own father, mother, brother, or sister has died. They must not defile the hair on their head, because it is the symbol of their separation to God. [8] This applies as long as they are set apart to the LORD.

[9] "If their hair is defiled because someone suddenly falls dead beside them, they must wait for seven days and then shave their heads. Then they will be cleansed from their defilement. [10] On the eighth day they must bring two turtledoves or two young pigeons to the priest at the entrance of the Tabernacle.* [11] The priest will offer one of the birds for a sin offering and the other for a burnt offering. In this way, he will make atonement for the guilt they incurred from the dead body. Then they must renew their vow that day and let their hair begin to grow again. [12] The days of their vow that were completed before their defilement no longer count. They must rededicate themselves to the LORD for the full term of their vow, and each must bring a one-year-old male lamb for a guilt offering.

[13] "This is the ritual law of the Nazirites. At the conclusion of their time of separation as Nazirites, they must each go to the entrance of the Tabernacle [14] and offer these sacrifices to the LORD: a one-year-old male lamb without defect for a burnt offering, a one-year-old female lamb without defect for a sin offering, a ram without defect for a peace offering, [15] a basket of bread made without yeast—cakes of choice flour mixed with olive oil and wafers spread with olive oil—along with their prescribed grain offerings and drink offerings. [16] The priest will present these offerings before the LORD: first the sin offering and the burnt offering; [17] then the ram for a peace offering, along with the basket of bread made without yeast. The priest must also make the prescribed grain offering and drink offering.

[18] "Then the Nazirites will shave their hair at the entrance of the Tabernacle and put it on the fire beneath the peace-offering sacrifice. [19] After each Nazirite's head has been shaved, the priest will take for each of them the boiled shoulder of the ram, one cake made without yeast, and one wafer made without yeast, and put them all into the Nazirite's hands. [20] The priest will then lift the gifts up before the LORD in a gesture of offering. These are holy portions for the priest, along with the breast and thigh pieces that were lifted up before the LORD. After this ceremony the Nazirites may again drink wine.

[21] "This is the ritual law of the Nazirites. If any Nazirites have vowed to give the LORD anything else beyond what is required by their normal Nazirite vow, they must fulfill their special vow exactly as they have promised."

I BELIEVE the Lord gave instructions for the sacrifices to be offered at the completion of the Nazirite's vow. (6:13)

I CHOOSE to give up certain things for a limited time as part of my service to the Lord. (6:20)

I FULFILL my vows to the Lord. (6:21)

The Priestly Blessing

[22] Then the LORD said to Moses, [23] "Instruct Aaron and his sons to bless the people of Israel with this special blessing:

[24] 'May the LORD bless you
   and protect you.
[25] May the LORD smile on you
   and be gracious to you.
[26] May the LORD show you his favor
   and give you his peace.'

[27] This is how Aaron and his sons will designate the Israelites as my people,* and I myself will bless them."

I BLESS other people, just as Aaron and his sons were to bless the people of Israel. (6:23)

6:10 Hebrew *Tent of Meeting;* also in 6:13, 18.   6:27 Hebrew *will put my name on the people of Israel.*

CHAPTER **7**

Offerings of Dedication

On the day Moses set up the Tabernacle, he anointed it and set it apart as holy, along with all its furnishings and the altar with its utensils. ²Then the leaders of Israel—the tribal leaders who had organized the census—came and brought their offerings. ³Together they brought six carts and twelve oxen. There was a cart for every two leaders and an ox for each leader. They presented these to the LORD in front of the Tabernacle.

⁴Then the LORD said to Moses, ⁵"Receive their gifts and use these oxen and carts for the work of the Tabernacle.* Distribute them among the Levites according to the work they have to do." ⁶So Moses presented the carts and oxen to the Levites. ⁷He gave two carts and four oxen to the Gershonite division for their work, ⁸and four carts and eight oxen to the Merarite division for their work. All their work was done under the leadership of Ithamar son of Aaron the priest. ⁹But he gave none of the carts or oxen to the Kohathite division, since they were required to carry the sacred objects of the Tabernacle on their shoulders.

¹⁰The leaders also presented dedication gifts for the altar at the time it was anointed. They each placed their gifts before the altar. ¹¹The LORD said to Moses, "Let each leader bring his gift on a different day for the dedication of the altar."

¹²On the first day Nahshon son of Amminadab, leader of the tribe of Judah, presented his offering.

¹³The offering consisted of a silver platter weighing about 3¼ pounds and a silver basin of about 1¾ pounds.* These were both filled with grain offerings of choice flour mixed with olive oil. ¹⁴He also brought a gold container weighing about four ounces,* which was filled with incense. ¹⁵He brought a young bull, a ram, and a one-year-old male lamb as a burnt offering; ¹⁶a male goat for a sin offering; ¹⁷and two oxen, five rams, five male goats, and five one-year-old male lambs for a peace offering. This was the offering brought by Nahshon son of Amminadab.

¹⁸On the second day Nethanel son of Zuar, leader of the tribe of Issachar, presented his offering.

¹⁹The offering consisted of a silver platter weighing about 3¼ pounds and a silver basin of about 1¾ pounds. These were both filled with grain offerings of choice flour mixed with olive oil. ²⁰He also brought a gold container weighing about four ounces, which was filled with incense. ²¹He brought a young bull, a ram, and a one-year-old male lamb as a burnt offering; ²²a male goat for a sin offering; ²³and two oxen, five rams, five male goats, and five one-year-old male lambs for a peace offering. This was the offering brought by Nethanel son of Zuar.

²⁴On the third day Eliab son of Helon, leader of the tribe of Zebulun, presented his offering.

²⁵The offering consisted of a silver platter weighing about 3¼ pounds and a silver basin of about 1¾ pounds. These were both filled with grain offerings of choice flour mixed with olive oil. ²⁶He also brought a gold container weighing about four ounces, which was filled with incense. ²⁷He brought a young bull, a ram, and a one-year-old male lamb as a burnt offering; ²⁸a male goat for a sin offering; ²⁹and two oxen, five rams, five male goats, and five one-year-old male lambs for a peace offering. This was the offering brought by Eliab son of Helon.

I PRESENT my offerings to the Lord. (7:3)

I SUPPLY God's servants with the tools that they need to do their work. (7:6)

I DO NOT USE shortcuts to accomplish a specific task God has given me. (7:9)

Today what example(s) are you choosing to heed?

7:5 Hebrew *Tent of Meeting*; also in 7:89.   7:13 Hebrew *silver platter weighing 130 shekels* [1.5 kilograms] *and a silver basin weighing 70 shekels* [0.8 kilograms], *according to the sanctuary shekel*; also in 7:19, 25, 31, 37, 43, 49, 55, 61, 67, 73, 79, 85.   7:14 Hebrew *10 shekels* [114 grams]; also in 7:20, 26, 32, 38, 44, 50, 56, 62, 68, 74, 80, 86.

30On the fourth day Elizur son of Shedeur, leader of the tribe of Reuben, presented his offering. 31The offering consisted of a silver platter weighing about 3¼ pounds and a silver basin of about 1¾ pounds. These were both filled with grain offerings of choice flour mixed with olive oil. 32He also brought a gold container weighing about four ounces, which was filled with incense. 33He brought a young bull, a ram, and a one-year-old male lamb as a burnt offering; 34a male goat for a sin offering; 35and two oxen, five rams, five male goats, and five one-year-old male lambs for a peace offering. This was the offering brought by Elizur son of Shedeur.

36On the fifth day Shelumiel son of Zurishaddai, leader of the tribe of Simeon, presented his offering. 37The offering consisted of a silver platter weighing about 3¼ pounds and a silver basin of about 1¾ pounds. These were both filled with grain offerings of choice flour mixed with olive oil. 38He also brought a gold container weighing about four ounces, which was filled with incense. 39He brought a young bull, a ram, and a one-year-old male lamb as a burnt offering; 40a male goat for a sin offering; 41and two oxen, five rams, five male goats, and five one-year-old male lambs for a peace offering. This was the offering brought by Shelumiel son of Zurishaddai.

42On the sixth day Eliasaph son of Deuel, leader of the tribe of Gad, presented his offering. 43The offering consisted of a silver platter weighing about 3¼ pounds and a silver basin of about 1¾ pounds. These were both filled with grain offerings of choice flour mixed with olive oil. 44He also brought a gold container weighing about four ounces, which was filled with incense. 45He brought a young bull, a ram, and a one-year-old male lamb as a burnt offering; 46a male goat for a sin offering; 47and two oxen, five rams, five male goats, and five one-year-old male lambs for a peace offering. This was the offering brought by Eliasaph son of Deuel.

48On the seventh day Elishama son of Ammihud, leader of the tribe of Ephraim, presented his offering. 49The offering consisted of a silver platter weighing about 3¼ pounds and a silver basin of about 1¾ pounds. These were both filled with grain offerings of choice flour mixed with olive oil. 50He also brought a gold container weighing about four ounces, which was filled with incense. 51He brought a young bull, a ram, and a one-year-old male lamb as a burnt offering; 52a male goat for a sin offering; 53and two oxen, five rams, five male goats, and five one-year-old male lambs for a peace offering. This was the offering brought by Elishama son of Ammihud.

54On the eighth day Gamaliel son of Pedahzur, leader of the tribe of Manasseh, presented his offering. 55The offering consisted of a silver platter weighing about 3¼ pounds and a silver basin of about 1¾ pounds. These were both filled with grain offerings of choice flour mixed with olive oil. 56He also brought a gold container weighing about four ounces, which was filled with incense. 57He brought a young bull, a ram, and a one-year-old male lamb as a burnt offering; 58a male goat for a sin offering; 59and two oxen, five rams, five male goats, and five one-year-old male lambs for a peace offering. This was the offering brought by Gamaliel son of Pedahzur.

60On the ninth day Abidan son of Gideoni, leader of the tribe of Benjamin, presented his offering. 61The offering consisted of a silver platter weighing about 3¼ pounds

I BELIEVE the Israelite leaders presented gifts for the altar over twelve days. (7:48)

and a silver basin of about 1³/₄ pounds. These were both filled with grain offerings of choice flour mixed with olive oil. ⁶²He also brought a gold container weighing about four ounces, which was filled with incense. ⁶³He brought a young bull, a ram, and a one-year-old male lamb as a burnt offering; ⁶⁴a male goat for a sin offering; ⁶⁵and two oxen, five rams, five male goats, and five one-year-old male lambs for a peace offering. This was the offering brought by Abidan son of Gideoni.

⁶⁶On the tenth day Ahiezer son of Ammishaddai, leader of the tribe of Dan, presented his offering.
⁶⁷The offering consisted of a silver platter weighing about 3¹/₄ pounds and a silver basin of about 1³/₄ pounds. These were both filled with grain offerings of choice flour mixed with olive oil. ⁶⁸He also brought a gold container weighing about four ounces, which was filled with incense. ⁶⁹He brought a young bull, a ram, and a one-year-old male lamb as a burnt offering; ⁷⁰a male goat for a sin offering; ⁷¹and two oxen, five rams, five male goats, and five one-year-old male lambs for a peace offering. This was the offering brought by Ahiezer son of Ammishaddai.

⁷²On the eleventh day Pagiel son of Ocran, leader of the tribe of Asher, presented his offering.
⁷³The offering consisted of a silver platter weighing about 3¹/₄ pounds and a silver basin of about 1³/₄ pounds. These were both filled with grain offerings of choice flour mixed with olive oil. ⁷⁴He also brought a gold container weighing about four ounces, which was filled with incense. ⁷⁵He brought a young bull, a ram, and a one-year-old male lamb as a burnt offering; ⁷⁶a male goat for a sin offering; ⁷⁷and two oxen, five rams, five male goats, and five one-year-old male lambs for a peace offering. This was the offering brought by Pagiel son of Ocran.

⁷⁸On the twelfth day Ahira son of Enan, leader of the tribe of Naphtali, presented his offering.
⁷⁹The offering consisted of a silver platter weighing about 3¹/₄ pounds and a silver basin of about 1³/₄ pounds. These were both filled with grain offerings of choice flour mixed with olive oil. ⁸⁰He also brought a gold container weighing about four ounces, which was filled with incense. ⁸¹He brought a young bull, a ram, and a one-year-old male lamb as a burnt offering; ⁸²a male goat for a sin offering; ⁸³and two oxen, five rams, five male goats, and five one-year-old male lambs for a peace offering. This was the offering brought by Ahira son of Enan.

I BELIEVE the twelve leaders of the tribes of Israel brought identical gifts for the dedication of the altar. (7:84)

⁸⁴So this was the dedication offering for the altar, brought by the leaders of Israel at the time it was anointed: twelve silver platters, twelve silver basins, and twelve gold incense containers. ⁸⁵In all, the silver objects weighed about 60 pounds,* about 3¹/₄ pounds for each platter and 1³/₄ pounds for each basin. ⁸⁶The weight of the donated gold came to about three pounds,* about four ounces for each of the gold containers that were filled with incense. ⁸⁷Twelve bulls, twelve rams, and twelve one-year-old male lambs were donated for the burnt offerings, along with their prescribed grain offerings. Twelve male goats were brought for the sin offerings. ⁸⁸Twenty-four young bulls, sixty rams, sixty male goats, and sixty one-year-old male lambs were donated for the peace offerings. This was the dedication offering for the altar after it was anointed.

I BELIEVE the Lord spoke with Moses from the place of atonement, between the cherubim above the Ark of the Covenant. (7:89)

⁸⁹Whenever Moses went into the Tabernacle to speak with the LORD, he heard the voice speaking to him from between the two cherubim above the Ark's cover—the place of atonement—that rests on the Ark of the Covenant.* The LORD spoke to him from there.

7:85 Hebrew *2,400 shekels* [27.4 kilograms].   7:86 Hebrew *120 shekels* [1.4 kilograms].   7:89 Or *Ark of the Testimony.*

CHAPTER 8

Preparing the Lamps

The LORD said to Moses, [2]"Tell Aaron that when he sets up the seven lamps in the lampstand, he is to place them so their light shines forward." [3]So Aaron did this. He set up the seven lamps so they reflected their light forward, just as the LORD had commanded Moses. [4]The entire lampstand, from its base to its decorative blossoms, was made of beaten gold. It was built according to the exact design the LORD had shown Moses.

The Levites Dedicated

[5]Then the LORD said to Moses, [6]"Now set the Levites apart from the rest of the people of Israel and make them ceremonially clean. [7]Do this by sprinkling them with the water of purification. And have them shave their entire body and wash their clothing. Then they will be ceremonially clean. [8]Have them bring a young bull and a grain offering of choice flour mixed with olive oil, along with a second young bull for a sin offering. [9]Then assemble the whole community of Israel and present the Levites at the entrance of the Tabernacle.* [10]When you bring the Levites before the LORD, the people of Israel must lay their hands on them. [11]Aaron must present the Levites to the LORD as a special offering from the people of Israel, thus dedicating them to the LORD's service.

[12]"Next the Levites will lay their hands on the heads of the young bulls and present them to the LORD. One will be for a sin offering and the other for a burnt offering, to make atonement for the Levites. [13]Then have the Levites stand in front of Aaron and his sons, and present them as a special offering to the LORD. [14]In this way, you will set the Levites apart from the rest of the people of Israel, and the Levites will belong to me. [15]After this, they may go in and out of the Tabernacle to do their work, because you have purified them and presented them as a special offering.

[16]"Of all the people of Israel, the Levites are reserved for me. I have claimed them for myself in place of all the firstborn sons of the Israelites; I have taken the Levites as their substitutes. [17]For all the firstborn males among the people of Israel are mine, both people and animals. I set them apart for myself on the night I killed all the firstborn sons of the Egyptians. [18]Yes, I claim the Levites in place of all the firstborn sons of Israel. [19]And of all the Israelites, I have assigned the Levites to Aaron and his sons. They will serve in the Tabernacle on behalf of the Israelites and make atonement for them so no plague will strike them when they approach the sanctuary."

[20]So Moses, Aaron, and the whole community of Israel dedicated the Levites, carefully following all the LORD's instructions to Moses. [21]The Levites purified themselves and washed their clothes, and Aaron presented them to the LORD as a special offering. He then performed the rite of atonement over them to purify them. [22]From then on the Levites went into the Tabernacle to perform their duties, helping Aaron and his sons. So they carried out all the commands that the LORD gave Moses concerning the Levites.

[23]The LORD also instructed Moses, [24]"This is the rule the Levites must follow: They must begin serving in the Tabernacle at the age of twenty-five, [25]and they must retire at the age of fifty. [26]After retirement they may assist their fellow Levites by performing guard duty at the Tabernacle, but they may not officiate in the service. This is how you will assign duties to the Levites."

CHAPTER 9

The Second Passover

The LORD gave these instructions to Moses in early spring,* during the second year after Israel's departure from Egypt, while he and the rest of the Israelites

---

I BELIEVE God gave specific instructions for the placement of the lamps. (8:2)

I BELIEVE the Lord required the Levites to be set apart and made ceremonially clean. (8:6)

I IDENTIFY with and support those who serve the Lord in a special way. (8:10)

I BELIEVE the Levites were substitutes for all the firstborn Israelites who belonged to the Lord. (8:16)

I BELIEVE the Lord has full rights to whomever he chooses. (8:17)

I PURIFY myself before the Lord and present myself to him for service. (8:21)

I BELIEVE the Lord gave specific instructions for the Levites' terms of service. (8:24)

8:9 Hebrew *Tent of Meeting;* also in 8:15, 19, 22, 24, 26.   9:1 Hebrew *in the first month.* This month of the Hebrew lunar calendar usually occurs in March and April.

were in the wilderness of Sinai: [2]"Tell the Israelites to celebrate the Passover at the proper time, [3]at twilight on the appointed day in early spring.* Be sure to follow all my laws and regulations concerning this celebration."

[4]So Moses told the people to celebrate the Passover [5]in the wilderness of Sinai as twilight fell on the appointed day.* And they celebrated the festival there, just as the LORD had commanded Moses. [6]But some of the men had been ceremonially defiled by touching a dead person, so they could not offer their Passover lambs that day. So they came to Moses and Aaron that day [7]and said, "We have become ceremonially unclean by touching a dead person. But why should we be excluded from presenting the LORD's offering at the proper time with the rest of the Israelites?"

[8]Moses answered, "Wait here until I have received instructions for you from the LORD."

[9]This was the LORD's reply: [10]"Say to the Israelites: 'If any of the people now or in future generations are ceremonially unclean at Passover time because of touching a dead body, or if they are on a journey and cannot be present at the ceremony, they may still celebrate the LORD's Passover. [11]They must offer the Passover sacrifice one month later,* at twilight on the appointed day. They must eat the lamb at that time with bitter herbs and bread made without yeast. [12]They must not leave any of the lamb until the next morning, and they must not break any of its bones. They must follow all the normal regulations concerning the Passover.

[13]" 'But those who are ceremonially clean and not away on a trip, yet still refuse to celebrate the Passover at the regular time, will be cut off from the community of Israel for failing to present the LORD's offering at the proper time. They will suffer the consequences of their guilt. [14]And if foreigners living among you want to celebrate the Passover to the LORD, they must follow these same laws and regulations. The same laws apply both to you and to the foreigners living among you.' "

The Fiery Cloud

[15]The Tabernacle was set up, and on that day the cloud covered it.* Then from evening until morning the cloud over the Tabernacle appeared to be a pillar of fire. [16]This was the regular pattern—at night the cloud changed to the appearance of fire. [17]When the cloud lifted from over the sacred tent, the people of Israel followed it. And wherever the cloud settled, the people of Israel camped. [18]In this way, they traveled at the LORD's command and stopped wherever he told them to. Then they remained where they were as long as the cloud stayed over the Tabernacle. [19]If the cloud remained over the Tabernacle for a long time, the Israelites stayed for a long time, just as the LORD commanded. [20]Sometimes the cloud would stay over the Tabernacle for only a few days, so the people would stay for only a few days. Then at the LORD's command they would break camp. [21]Sometimes the cloud stayed only overnight and moved on the next morning. But day or night, when the cloud lifted, the people broke camp and followed. [22]Whether the cloud stayed above the Tabernacle for two days, a month, or a year, the people of Israel stayed in camp and did not move on. But as soon as it lifted, they broke camp and moved on. [23]So they camped or traveled at the LORD's command, and they did whatever the LORD told them through Moses.

CHAPTER 10

The Silver Trumpets

Now the LORD said to Moses, [2]"Make two trumpets of beaten silver to be used for summoning the people to assemble and for signaling the breaking of

---

I GIVE God's instructions to the people. (9:4)

I SEEK God's wisdom before answering people's questions. (9:8)

I BELIEVE the Lord provided a way for anyone who wanted to celebrate the Passover. (9:9)

I BELIEVE the consequences of refusing to celebrate the Passover were severe. (9:13)

I BELIEVE the Israelites followed the Lord's leading by cloud and fire. (9:17)

I DO whatever the Lord tells me. (9:23)

I BELIEVE the Lord gave Moses instructions for using the silver trumpets to signal the people of Israel to assemble or move camp. (10:2)

9:3 Hebrew *on the fourteenth day of the first month.* This day of the Hebrew lunar calendar occurs in late March or early April. 9:5 Hebrew *on the fourteenth day of the first month;* see note on 9:3. 9:11 Hebrew *on the fourteenth day of the second month.* This day of the Hebrew lunar calendar occurs in late April or early May. 9:15 Hebrew *covered the Tabernacle, the Tent of the Testimony.*

camp. [3]When both trumpets are blown, the people will know that they are to gather before you at the entrance of the Tabernacle.* [4]But if only one is blown, then only the leaders of the tribes of Israel will come to you.

[5]"When you sound the signal to move on, the tribes on the east side of the Tabernacle will break camp and move forward. [6]When you sound the signal a second time, the tribes on the south will follow. You must sound short blasts to signal moving on. [7]But when you call the people to an assembly, blow the trumpets using a different signal. [8]Only the priests, Aaron's descendants, are allowed to blow the trumpets. This is a permanent law to be followed from generation to generation.

[9]"When you arrive in your own land and go to war against your enemies, you must sound the alarm with these trumpets so the LORD your God will remember you and rescue you from your enemies. [10]Blow the trumpets in times of gladness, too, sounding them at your annual festivals and at the beginning of each month to rejoice over your burnt offerings and peace offerings. The trumpets will remind the LORD your God of his covenant with you. I am the LORD your God."

I BELIEVE the Lord gave Moses instructions for using the silver trumpets to sound a war alarm and demonstrate faith that the Lord would deliver his people. (10:9)

I BELIEVE the Lord gave Moses instructions for using the silver trumpets to sound at times of gladness and sacrifice. (10:10)

The Israelites Leave Sinai

[11]One day in midspring,* during the second year after Israel's departure from Egypt, the cloud lifted from the Tabernacle of the Covenant.* [12]So the Israelites set out from the wilderness of Sinai and traveled on in stages until the cloud stopped in the wilderness of Paran.

[13]When the time to move arrived, the LORD gave the order through Moses. [14]The tribes that camped with Judah headed the march with their banner, under the leadership of Nahshon son of Amminadab. [15]The tribe of Issachar was led by Nethanel son of Zuar. [16]The tribe of Zebulun was led by Eliab son of Helon.

[17]Then the Tabernacle was taken down, and the Gershonite and Merarite divisions of the Levites were next in the line of march, carrying the Tabernacle with them. [18]Then the tribes that camped with Reuben set out with their banner, under the leadership of Elizur son of Shedeur. [19]The tribe of Simeon was led by Shelumiel son of Zurishaddai. [20]The tribe of Gad was led by Eliasaph son of Deuel.

[21]Next came the Kohathite division of the Levites, carrying the sacred objects from the Tabernacle. When they arrived at the next camp, the Tabernacle would already be set up at its new location. [22]Then the tribes that camped with Ephraim set out with their banner, under the leadership of Elishama son of Ammihud. [23]The tribe of Manasseh was led by Gamaliel son of Pedahzur. [24]The tribe of Benjamin was led by Abidan son of Gideoni.

[25]Last of all, the tribes that camped with Dan set out under their banner. They served as the rear guard for all the tribal camps. The tribe of Dan headed this group, under the leadership of Ahiezer son of Ammishaddai. [26]The tribe of Asher was led by Pagiel son of Ocran. [27]The tribe of Naphtali was led by Ahira son of Enan.

[28]This was the order in which the tribes marched, division by division.

[29]One day Moses said to his brother-in-law, Hobab son of Reuel the Midianite, "We are on our way to the Promised Land. Come with us and we will treat you well, for the LORD has given wonderful promises to Israel!"

[30]But Hobab replied, "No, I will not go. I must return to my own land and family."

[31]"Please don't leave us," Moses pleaded. "You know the places in the wilderness where we should camp. [32]Come, be our guide and we will share with you all the good things that the LORD does for us."

I BELIEVE that when God says it's time to move, I should move. (10:12)

I BELIEVE the Israelites traveled by division, in orderly manner, as the Lord commanded. (10:13)

I INVITE others to share in God's blessings with me. (10:29)

I CALL ON others to use their expertise to guide God's people. (10:31)

10:3 Hebrew *Tent of Meeting.*   10:11a Hebrew *On the twentieth day of the second month.* This day of the Hebrew lunar calendar occurs in late April or early May.   10:11b Or *Tabernacle of the Testimony.*

³³They marched for three days after leaving the mountain of the LORD, with the Ark of the LORD's covenant moving ahead of them to show them where to stop and rest. ³⁴As they moved on each day, the cloud of the LORD hovered over them. ³⁵And whenever the Ark set out, Moses would cry, "Arise, O LORD, and let your enemies be scattered! Let them flee before you!" ³⁶And when the Ark was set down, he would say, "Return, O LORD, to the countless thousands of Israel!"

CHAPTER 11

The People Complain to Moses

The people soon began to complain to the LORD about their hardships; and when the LORD heard them, his anger blazed against them. Fire from the LORD raged among them and destroyed the outskirts of the camp. ²The people screamed to Moses for help; and when he prayed to the LORD, the fire stopped. ³After that, the area was known as Taberah—"the place of burning"—because fire from the LORD had burned among them there.

⁴Then the foreign rabble who were traveling with the Israelites began to crave the good things of Egypt, and the people of Israel also began to complain. "Oh, for some meat!" they exclaimed. ⁵"We remember all the fish we used to eat for free in Egypt. And we had all the cucumbers, melons, leeks, onions, and garlic that we wanted. ⁶But now our appetites are gone, and day after day we have nothing to eat but this manna!"

⁷The manna looked like small coriander seeds, pale yellow in color.* ⁸The people gathered it from the ground and made flour by grinding it with hand mills or pounding it in mortars. Then they boiled it in a pot and made it into flat cakes. These cakes tasted like they had been cooked in olive oil. ⁹The manna came down on the camp with the dew during the night.

¹⁰Moses heard all the families standing in front of their tents weeping, and the LORD became extremely angry. Moses was also very aggravated. ¹¹And Moses said to the LORD, "Why are you treating me, your servant, so miserably? What did I do to deserve the burden of a people like this? ¹²Are they my children? Am I their father? Is that why you have told me to carry them in my arms—like a nurse carries a baby—to the land you swore to give their ancestors? ¹³Where am I supposed to get meat for all these people? They keep complaining and saying, 'Give us meat!' ¹⁴I can't carry all these people by myself! The load is far too heavy! ¹⁵I'd rather you killed me than treat me like this. Please spare me this misery!"

Moses Chooses Seventy Leaders

¹⁶Then the LORD said to Moses, "Summon before me seventy of the leaders of Israel. Bring them to the Tabernacle* to stand there with you. ¹⁷I will come down and talk to you there. I will take some of the Spirit that is upon you, and I will put the Spirit upon them also. They will bear the burden of the people along with you, so you will not have to carry it alone.

¹⁸"And tell the people to purify themselves, for tomorrow they will have meat to eat. Tell them, 'The LORD has heard your whining and complaints: "If only we had meat to eat! Surely we were better off in Egypt!" Now the LORD will give you meat, and you will have to eat it. ¹⁹And it won't be for just a day or two, or for five or ten or even twenty. ²⁰You will eat it for a whole month until you gag and are sick of it. For you have rejected the LORD, who is here among you, and you have complained to him, "Why did we ever leave Egypt?" ' "

²¹But Moses said, "There are 600,000 foot soldiers here with me, and yet you promise them meat for a whole month! ²²Even if we butchered all our

11:7 Hebrew *the color of gum resin.*   **11:16** Hebrew *Tent of Meeting.*

I CALL ON the Lord for his presence to be with me and with his people. (10:36)

I PRAY for those who seek help when they are disciplined by God. (11:2)

I DO NOT ANGER the Lord and grieve my leaders by complaining about what I don't have. (11:10)

I GO to the Lord with my frustrations about people under my care. (11:11)

I BELIEVE the Lord will help me when I am overwhelmed with ministry responsibilities. (11:16)

I SEEK Spirit-filled people to help me care for God's people. (11:17)

I BELIEVE God sometimes gives me what I want to teach me that I want the wrong things. (11:18)

I DO NOT QUESTION how God will provide, for he has promised that he will. (11:21)

flocks and herds, would that satisfy them? Even if we caught all the fish in the sea, would that be enough?"

²³Then the LORD said to Moses, "Is there any limit to my power? Now you will see whether or not my word comes true!"

²⁴So Moses went out and reported the LORD's words to the people. Then he gathered the seventy leaders and stationed them around the Tabernacle.* ²⁵And the LORD came down in the cloud and spoke to Moses. He took some of the Spirit that was upon Moses and put it upon the seventy leaders. They prophesied as the Spirit rested upon them, but that was the only time this happened.

²⁶Two men, Eldad and Medad, were still in the camp when the Spirit rested upon them. They were listed among the leaders but had not gone out to the Tabernacle, so they prophesied there in the camp. ²⁷A young man ran and reported to Moses, "Eldad and Medad are prophesying in the camp!" ²⁸Joshua son of Nun, who had been Moses' personal assistant since his youth, protested, "Moses, my master, make them stop!"

²⁹But Moses replied, "Are you jealous for my sake? I wish that all the LORD's people were prophets, and that the LORD would put his Spirit upon them all!" ³⁰Then Moses returned to the camp with the leaders of Israel.

The LORD Sends Quail

³¹Now the LORD sent a wind that brought quail from the sea and let them fall into the camp and all around it! For many miles in every direction from the camp there were quail flying about three feet above the ground.* ³²So the people went out and caught quail all that day and throughout the night and all the next day, too. No one gathered less than fifty bushels*! They spread the quail out all over the camp. ³³But while they were still eating the meat, the anger of the LORD blazed against the people, and he caused a severe plague to break out among them. ³⁴So that place was called Kibroth-hattaavah—"the graves of craving"—because they buried the people there who had craved meat from Egypt. ³⁵From there the Israelites traveled to Hazeroth, where they stayed for some time.

CHAPTER 12

The Complaints of Miriam and Aaron

While they were at Hazeroth, Miriam and Aaron criticized Moses because he had married a Cushite woman. ²They said, "Has the LORD spoken only through Moses? Hasn't he spoken through us, too?" But the LORD heard them.

³Now Moses was more humble than any other person on earth. ⁴So immediately the LORD called to Moses, Aaron, and Miriam and said, "Go out to the Tabernacle,* all three of you!" And the three of them went out. ⁵Then the LORD descended in the pillar of cloud and stood at the entrance of the Tabernacle.* "Aaron and Miriam!" he called, and they stepped forward. ⁶And the LORD said to them, "Now listen to me! Even with prophets, I the LORD communicate by visions and dreams. ⁷But that is not how I communicate with my servant Moses. He is entrusted with my entire house. ⁸I speak to him face to face, directly and not in riddles! He sees the LORD as he is. Should you not be afraid to criticize him?"

⁹The LORD was furious with them, and he departed. ¹⁰As the cloud moved from above the Tabernacle, Miriam suddenly became white as snow with leprosy.* When Aaron saw what had happened, ¹¹he cried out to Moses, "Oh,

I EAGERLY DESIRE that God use other people, not just me. (11:29)

I DO NOT CRAVE the material benefits of this life. (11:34)

I DO NOT CRITICIZE God's servants unjustly, especially over nonissues. (12:1)

See Miriam's profile (page 87) at Exodus 15:20.

I BELIEVE the Lord is the ultimate defender of his servants. (12:6)

11:24 Hebrew *the tent*; also in 11:26.　11:31 Or *there were quail 3 feet* [2 cubits or 90 centimeters] *deep on the ground.*　11:32 Hebrew *10 homers* [1.8 kiloliters].　12:4 Hebrew *Tent of Meeting.*　12:5 Hebrew *the tent*; also in 12:10.　12:10 Or *with a contagious skin disease.* The Hebrew word used here can describe various skin diseases.

my lord! Please don't punish us for this sin we have so foolishly committed. [12]Don't let her be like a stillborn baby, already decayed at birth."

[13]So Moses cried out to the LORD, "Heal her, O God, I beg you!"

I PRAY for those suffering from the consequences of their sins. (12:13)

[14]And the LORD said to Moses, "If her father had spit in her face, wouldn't she have been defiled for seven days? Banish her from the camp for seven days, and after that she may return."

[15]So Miriam was excluded from the camp for seven days, and the people waited until she was brought back before they traveled again. [16]Then they left Hazeroth and camped in the wilderness of Paran.

CHAPTER 13

Twelve Scouts Explore Canaan

The LORD now said to Moses, [2]"Send men to explore the land of Canaan, the land I am giving to Israel. Send one leader from each of the twelve ancestral tribes." [3]So Moses did as the LORD commanded him. He sent out twelve men, all tribal leaders of Israel, from their camp in the wilderness of Paran. [4]These were the tribes and the names of the leaders:

I BELIEVE Moses sent the twelve leaders to explore the land as the Lord commanded. (13:3)

Tribe	Leader
Reuben	Shammua son of Zaccur
[5] Simeon	Shaphat son of Hori
[6] Judah	Caleb son of Jephunneh
[7] Issachar	Igal son of Joseph
[8] Ephraim	Hoshea son of Nun
[9] Benjamin	Palti son of Raphu
[10] Zebulun	Gaddiel son of Sodi
[11] Manasseh son of Joseph	Gaddi son of Susi
[12] Dan	Ammiel son of Gemalli
[13] Asher	Sethur son of Michael
[14] Naphtali	Nahbi son of Vophsi
[15] Gad	Geuel son of Maki

[16]These are the names of the men Moses sent to explore the land. By this time Moses had changed Hoshea's name to Joshua.*

[17]Moses gave the men these instructions as he sent them out to explore the land: "Go northward through the Negev into the hill country. [18]See what the land is like and find out whether the people living there are strong or weak, few or many. [19]What kind of land do they live in? Is it good or bad? Do their towns have walls or are they unprotected? [20]How is the soil? Is it fertile or poor? Are there many trees? Enter the land boldly, and bring back samples of the crops you see." (It happened to be the season for harvesting the first ripe grapes.)

I GLADLY SEEK to learn about all the blessings God promises to give me. (13:20)

[21]So they went up and explored the land from the wilderness of Zin as far as Rehob, near Lebo-hamath. [22]Going northward, they passed first through the Negev and arrived at Hebron, where Ahiman, Sheshai, and Talmai—all descendants of Anak—lived. (The ancient town of Hebron was founded seven years before the Egyptian city of Zoan.) [23]When they came to what is now known as the valley of Eshcol, they cut down a cluster of grapes so large that it took two of them to carry it on a pole between them! They also took samples of the pomegranates and figs. [24]At that time the Israelites renamed the valley Eshcol—"cluster"—because of the cluster of grapes they had cut there.

The Scouting Report

I SHOW others examples of God's blessings. (13:26)

[25]After exploring the land for forty days, the men returned [26]to Moses, Aaron, and the people of Israel at Kadesh in the wilderness of Paran. They reported

13:16 *Hoshea* (see 13:8) means "salvation"; *Joshua* means "The LORD is salvation."

to the whole community what they had seen and showed them the fruit they had taken from the land. ²⁷This was their report to Moses: "We arrived in the land you sent us to see, and it is indeed a magnificent country—a land flowing with milk and honey. Here is some of its fruit as proof. ²⁸But the people living there are powerful, and their cities and towns are fortified and very large. We also saw the descendants of Anak who are living there! ²⁹The Amalekites live in the Negev, and the Hittites, Jebusites, and Amorites live in the hill country. The Canaanites live along the coast of the Mediterranean Sea* and along the Jordan Valley."

³⁰But Caleb tried to encourage the people as they stood before Moses. "Let's go at once to take the land," he said. "We can certainly conquer it!"

³¹But the other men who had explored the land with him answered, "We can't go up against them! They are stronger than we are!" ³²So they spread discouraging reports about the land among the Israelites: "The land we explored will swallow up any who go to live there. All the people we saw were huge. ³³We even saw giants* there, the descendants of Anak. We felt like grasshoppers next to them, and that's what we looked like to them!"

CHAPTER 14

The People Rebel

Then all the people began weeping aloud, and they cried all night. ²Their voices rose in a great chorus of complaint against Moses and Aaron. "We wish we had died in Egypt, or even here in the wilderness!" they wailed. ³"Why is the LORD taking us to this country only to have us die in battle? Our wives and little ones will be carried off as slaves! Let's get out of here and return to Egypt!" ⁴Then they plotted among themselves, "Let's choose a leader and go back to Egypt!"

⁵Then Moses and Aaron fell face down on the ground before the people of Israel. ⁶Two of the men who had explored the land, Joshua son of Nun and Caleb son of Jephunneh, tore their clothing. ⁷They said to the community of Israel, "The land we explored is a wonderful land! ⁸And if the LORD is pleased with us, he will bring us safely into that land and give it to us. It is a rich land flowing with milk and honey, and he will give it to us! ⁹Do not rebel against the LORD, and don't be afraid of the people of the land. They are only helpless prey to us! They have no protection, but the LORD is with us! Don't be afraid of them!"

¹⁰But the whole community began to talk about stoning Joshua and Caleb. Then the glorious presence of the LORD appeared to all the Israelites from above the Tabernacle.* ¹¹And the LORD said to Moses, "How long will these people reject me? Will they never believe me, even after all the miraculous signs I have done among them? ¹²I will disown them and destroy them with a plague. Then I will make you into a nation far greater and mightier than they are!"

Moses Intercedes for the People

¹³"But what will the Egyptians think when they hear about it?" Moses pleaded with the LORD. "They know full well the power you displayed in rescuing these people from Egypt. ¹⁴They will tell this to the inhabitants of this land, who are well aware that you are with this people. They know, LORD, that you have appeared in full view of your people in the pillar of cloud that hovers over them. They know that you go before them in the pillar of cloud by day and the pillar of fire by night. ¹⁵Now if you slaughter all these people, the nations that have heard of your fame will say, ¹⁶'The LORD was not able to bring them into the land he swore to give them, so he killed them in the wilderness.'

I DO NOT LET the challenges of obeying God overshadow the blessings he has promised. (13:28)

I ENCOURAGE others to obey God, confident that we can overcome the challenges by his presence and power. (13:30)

I DO NOT FOCUS on difficulties as an excuse for not obeying God. (13:31)

I DO NOT DISCOURAGE others from obeying God. (13:32)

I DO NOT ASSUME the Lord is seeking to destroy my family when we face difficulties. (14:3)

I CHALLENGE others to obey God and receive his blessing. (14:7)

I ENCOURAGE others not to rebel or be afraid, for the Lord is with us. (14:9)

I AM MORE CONCERNED about the Lord's reputation than my own advancement. (14:13)

13:29 Hebrew *the sea.*   13:33 Hebrew *nephilim.*   14:10 Hebrew *Tent of Meeting.*

I PRAY to God on the basis of his character, not mine. (14:18)

I REMAIN loyal to the Lord and receive his blessings. (14:24)

I BELIEVE the Lord hears everything his people say. (14:27)

I BELIEVE children are affected by the sins of their parents. (14:33)

I BELIEVE it is perilous to dissuade others from trusting the Lord. (14:36)

I KNOW that feeling sorrow for what I've lost isn't the same as repenting of my sin. (14:39)

[17]"Please, Lord, prove that your power is as great as you have claimed it to be. For you said, [18]'The LORD is slow to anger and rich in unfailing love, forgiving every kind of sin and rebellion. Even so he does not leave sin unpunished, but he punishes the children for the sins of their parents to the third and fourth generations.' [19]Please pardon the sins of this people because of your magnificent, unfailing love, just as you have forgiven them ever since they left Egypt."

[20]Then the LORD said, "I will pardon them as you have requested. [21]But as surely as I live, and as surely as the earth is filled with the LORD's glory, [22]not one of these people will ever enter that land. They have seen my glorious presence and the miraculous signs I performed both in Egypt and in the wilderness, but again and again they tested me by refusing to listen. [23]They will never even see the land I swore to give their ancestors. None of those who have treated me with contempt will enter it. [24]But my servant Caleb is different from the others. He has remained loyal to me, and I will bring him into the land he explored. His descendants will receive their full share of that land. [25]Now turn around and don't go on toward the land where the Amalekites and Canaanites live. Tomorrow you must set out for the wilderness in the direction of the Red Sea.*"

The LORD Punishes the Israelites

[26]Then the LORD said to Moses and Aaron, [27]"How long will this wicked nation complain about me? I have heard everything the Israelites have been saying. [28]Now tell them this: 'As surely as I live, I will do to you the very things I heard you say. I, the LORD, have spoken! [29]You will all die here in this wilderness! Because you complained against me, none of you who are twenty years old or older and were counted in the census [30]will enter the land I swore to give you. The only exceptions will be Caleb son of Jephunneh and Joshua son of Nun.

[31]" 'You said your children would be taken captive. Well, I will bring them safely into the land, and they will enjoy what you have despised. [32]But as for you, your dead bodies will fall in this wilderness. [33]And your children will be like shepherds, wandering in the wilderness forty years. In this way, they will pay for your faithlessness, until the last of you lies dead in the wilderness.

[34]" 'Because the men who explored the land were there for forty days, you must wander in the wilderness for forty years—a year for each day, suffering the consequences of your sins. You will discover what it is like to have me for an enemy.' [35]I, the LORD, have spoken! I will do these things to every member of the community who has conspired against me. They will all die here in this wilderness!"

[36]Then the ten scouts who had incited the rebellion against the LORD by spreading discouraging reports about the land [37]were struck dead with a plague before the LORD. [38]Of the twelve who had explored the land, only Joshua and Caleb remained alive.

[39]When Moses reported the LORD's words to the Israelites, there was much sorrow among the people. [40]So they got up early the next morning and set out for the hill country of Canaan. "Let's go," they said. "We realize that we have sinned, but now we are ready to enter the land the LORD has promised us."

[41]But Moses said, "Why are you now disobeying the LORD's orders to return to the wilderness? It won't work. [42]Do not go into the land now. You will only be crushed by your enemies because the LORD is not with you. [43]When you face the Amalekites and Canaanites in battle, you will be slaughtered. The LORD will abandon you because you have abandoned the LORD."

[44]But the people pushed ahead toward the hill country of Canaan, despite the fact that neither Moses nor the Ark of the LORD's covenant left the camp.

14:25 Hebrew *sea of reeds*.

⁴⁵ Then the Amalekites and the Canaanites who lived in those hills came down and attacked them and chased them as far as Hormah.

CHAPTER 15

Laws concerning Offerings

The LORD told Moses to give these instructions to the people of Israel: ²"When you finally settle in the land I am going to give you, ³and you want to please the LORD with a burnt offering or any other offering given by fire, the sacrifice must be an animal from your flocks of sheep and goats or from your herds of cattle. When it is an ordinary burnt offering, a sacrifice to fulfill a vow, a freewill offering, or a special sacrifice at any of the annual festivals, ⁴whoever brings it must also give to the LORD a grain offering of two quarts* of choice flour mixed with one quart* of olive oil. ⁵For each lamb offered as a whole burnt offering, you must also present one quart of wine for a drink offering.

⁶"If the sacrifice is a ram, give three quarts* of choice flour mixed with two and a half pints* of olive oil, ⁷and give two and a half pints of wine for a drink offering. This sacrifice will be very pleasing to the LORD.

⁸"When you present a young bull as a burnt offering or a sacrifice in fulfillment of a special vow or as a peace offering to the LORD, ⁹then the grain offering accompanying it must include five quarts* of choice flour mixed with two quarts* of olive oil, ¹⁰plus two quarts of wine for the drink offering. This will be an offering made by fire, very pleasing to the LORD.

¹¹"These are the instructions for what is to accompany each sacrificial bull, ram, lamb, or young goat. ¹²Each of you must do this with each offering you present. ¹³If you native Israelites want to present an offering by fire that is pleasing to the LORD, you must follow all these instructions. ¹⁴And if any foreigners living among you want to present an offering by fire, pleasing to the LORD, they must follow the same procedures. ¹⁵Native Israelites and foreigners are the same before the LORD and are subject to the same laws. This is a permanent law for you. ¹⁶The same instructions and regulations will apply both to you and to the foreigners living among you."

¹⁷The LORD also said to Moses at this time, ¹⁸"Give the people of Israel the following instructions: When you arrive in the land where I am taking you, ¹⁹you will eat from the crops that grow there. But you must set some aside as a gift to the LORD. ²⁰Present a cake from the first of the flour you grind and set it aside as a gift, as you do with the first grain from the threshing floor. ²¹Throughout the generations to come, you are to present this offering to the LORD each year from the first of your ground flour.

²²"But suppose some of you unintentionally fail to carry out all these commands that the LORD has given you through Moses. ²³And suppose some of your descendants in the future fail to do everything the LORD has commanded through Moses. ²⁴If the mistake was done unintentionally, and the community was unaware of it, the whole community must present a young bull for a burnt offering. It will be pleasing to the LORD, and it must be offered along with the prescribed grain offering and drink offering and with one male goat for a sin offering. ²⁵With it the priest will make atonement for the whole community of Israel, and they will be forgiven. For it was an unintentional sin, and they have corrected it with their offering given to the LORD by fire and by their sin offering. ²⁶The whole community of Israel will be forgiven, including the foreigners living among you, for the entire population was involved in the sin.

²⁷"If the unintentional sin is committed by an individual, the guilty person

I BELIEVE the Israelites pleased the Lord with their sacrifices. (15:7)

I BELIEVE the Lord gave instructions for sacrifices to fulfill a vow or present as a peace offering. (15:8)

I BELIEVE the Israelites were to follow the Lord's instructions precisely in order to please him. (15:13)

I BELIEVE the instructions for sacrifices were the same for Israelites and foreigners. (15:15)

I BELIEVE the Lord gave Moses instructions for presenting the first of the crops of the land as a gift to God. (15:19)

I BELIEVE the Lord provided a way for forgiveness of the community's unintentional failure to carry out all of the Lord's commands. (15:22)

I BELIEVE the Lord provided a way for forgiveness for the unintentional sin of an individual. (15:27)

15:4a Hebrew ¹/₁₀ of an ephah [2 liters]. 15:4b Hebrew ¹/₄ of a hin [1 liter]; also in 15:5. 15:6a Hebrew ²/₁₀ of an ephah [3.6 liters]. 15:6b Hebrew ¹/₃ of a hin [1.3 liters]; also in 15:7. 15:9a Hebrew ³/₁₀ of an ephah [5.4 liters]. 15:9b Hebrew ¹/₂ of a hin [2 liters]; also in 15:10.

must bring a one-year-old female goat for a sin offering. [28] The priest will make atonement for the guilty person before the LORD, and that person will be forgiven. [29] This same law applies both to native Israelites and the foreigners living among you.

[30] "But those who brazenly violate the LORD's will, whether native Israelites or foreigners, blaspheme the LORD, and they must be cut off from the community. [31] Since they have treated the LORD's word with contempt and deliberately disobeyed his commands, they must be completely cut off and suffer the consequences of their guilt."

I BELIEVE there are severe consequences for disobedience and contempt of the Lord's Word. (15:31)

Penalty for Breaking the Sabbath

[32] One day while the people of Israel were in the wilderness, they caught a man gathering wood on the Sabbath day. [33] He was apprehended and taken before Moses, Aaron, and the rest of the community. [34] They held him in custody because they did not know what to do with him. [35] Then the LORD said to Moses, "The man must be put to death! The whole community must stone him outside the camp." [36] So the whole community took the man outside the camp and stoned him to death, just as the LORD had commanded Moses.

Tassels on Clothing

[37] And the LORD said to Moses, [38] "Say to the people of Israel: 'Throughout the generations to come you must make tassels for the hems of your clothing and attach the tassels at each corner with a blue cord. [39] The tassels will remind you of the commands of the LORD, and that you are to obey his commands instead of following your own desires and going your own ways, as you are prone to do. [40] The tassels will help you remember that you must obey all my commands and be holy to your God. [41] I am the LORD your God who brought you out of the land of Egypt that I might be your God. I am the LORD your God!' "

I USE physical reminders to help me obey the Lord. (15:40)

CHAPTER 16

Korah's Rebellion

One day Korah son of Izhar, a descendant of Kohath son of Levi, conspired with Dathan and Abiram, the sons of Eliab, and On son of Peleth, from the tribe of Reuben. [2] They incited a rebellion against Moses, involving 250 other prominent leaders, all members of the assembly. [3] They went to Moses and Aaron and said, "You have gone too far! Everyone in Israel has been set apart by the LORD, and he is with all of us. What right do you have to act as though you are greater than anyone else among all these people of the LORD?"

[4] When Moses heard what they were saying, he threw himself down with his face to the ground. [5] Then he said to Korah and his followers, "Tomorrow morning the LORD will show us who belongs to him and who is holy. The LORD will allow those who are chosen to enter his holy presence. [6] You, Korah, and all your followers must do this: Take incense burners, [7] and burn incense in them tomorrow before the LORD. Then we will see whom the LORD chooses as his holy one. You Levites are the ones who have gone too far!"

I HUMBLE myself before those who criticize and attack me. (16:4)

I ALLOW God to determine my future as a spiritual leader. (16:5)

[8] Then Moses spoke again to Korah: "Now listen, you Levites! [9] Does it seem a small thing to you that the God of Israel has chosen you from among all the people of Israel to be near him as you serve in the LORD's Tabernacle and to stand before the people to minister to them? [10] He has given this special ministry only to you and your fellow Levites, but now you are demanding the priesthood as well! [11] The one you are really revolting against is the LORD! And who is Aaron that you are complaining about him?"

[12] Then Moses summoned Dathan and Abiram, the sons of Eliab, but they replied, "We refuse to come! [13] Isn't it enough that you brought us out of Egypt, a land flowing with milk and honey, to kill us here in this wilderness,

and that you now treat us like your subjects? ¹⁴What's more, you haven't brought us into the land flowing with milk and honey or given us an inheritance of fields and vineyards. Are you trying to fool us? We will not come."

¹⁵ Then Moses became very angry and said to the LORD, "Do not accept their offerings! I have not taken so much as a donkey from them, and I have never hurt a single one of them." ¹⁶And Moses said to Korah, "Come here tomorrow and present yourself before the LORD with all your followers. Aaron will also be here. ¹⁷Be sure that each of your 250 followers brings an incense burner with incense on it, so you can present them before the LORD. Aaron will also bring his incense burner."

¹⁸So these men came with their incense burners, placed burning coals and incense on them, and stood at the entrance of the Tabernacle* with Moses and Aaron. ¹⁹Meanwhile, Korah had stirred up the entire community against Moses and Aaron, and they all assembled at the Tabernacle entrance. Then the glorious presence of the LORD appeared to the whole community, ²⁰and the LORD said to Moses and Aaron, ²¹"Get away from these people so that I may instantly destroy them!"

²²But Moses and Aaron fell face down on the ground. "O God, the God and source of all life," they pleaded. "Must you be angry with all the people when only one man sins?"

²³And the LORD said to Moses, ²⁴"Then tell all the people to get away from the tents of Korah, Dathan, and Abiram."

²⁵So Moses got up and rushed over to the tents of Dathan and Abiram, followed closely by the Israelite leaders. ²⁶"Quick!" he told the people. "Get away from the tents of these wicked men, and don't touch anything that belongs to them. If you do, you will be destroyed for their sins." ²⁷So all the people stood back from the tents of Korah, Dathan, and Abiram. Then Dathan and Abiram came out and stood at the entrances of their tents with their wives and children and little ones.

²⁸And Moses said, "By this you will know that the LORD has sent me to do all these things that I have done—for I have not done them on my own. ²⁹If these men die a natural death, then the LORD has not sent me. ³⁰But if the LORD performs a miracle and the ground opens up and swallows them and all their belongings, and they go down alive into the grave, then you will know that these men have despised the LORD."

³¹He had hardly finished speaking the words when the ground suddenly split open beneath them. ³²The earth opened up and swallowed the men, along with their households and the followers who were standing with them, and everything they owned. ³³So they went down alive into the grave, along with their belongings. The earth closed over them, and they all vanished. ³⁴All of the people of Israel fled as they heard their screams, fearing that the earth would swallow them, too. ³⁵Then fire blazed forth from the LORD and burned up the 250 men who were offering incense.

³⁶And the LORD said to Moses, ³⁷"Tell Eleazar son of Aaron the priest to pull all the incense burners from the fire, for they are holy. Also tell him to scatter the burning incense ³⁸from the burners of these men who have sinned at the cost of their lives. He must then hammer the metal of the incense burners into a sheet as a covering for the altar, for these burners have become holy because they were used in the LORD's presence. The altar covering will then serve as a warning to the people of Israel."

³⁹So Eleazar the priest collected the 250 bronze incense burners that had been used by the men who died in the fire, and they were hammered out into a sheet of metal to cover the altar. ⁴⁰This would warn the Israelites that no unauthorized man—no one who was not a descendant of Aaron—should ever

I GO to God with my anger at my accusers and trust that he knows the true situation. (16:15)

I DO NOT INCITE others against godly leaders. (16:19)

I INTERCEDE for God's mercy on those affected by someone's sin. (16:22)

I TRUST God to prove my call as a spiritual leader. (16:28)

I USE physical items to remind me of God's warnings. (16:39)

16:18 Hebrew *Tent of Meeting*; also in 16:19, 42, 43, 50.

enter the LORD's presence to burn incense. If anyone did, the same thing would happen to him as happened to Korah and his followers. Thus, the LORD's instructions to Moses were carried out. [41]But the very next morning the whole community began muttering again against Moses and Aaron, saying, "You two have killed the LORD's people!" [42]As the people gathered to protest to Moses and Aaron, they turned toward the Tabernacle and saw that the cloud had covered it, and the glorious presence of the LORD appeared.

[43]Moses and Aaron came and stood at the entrance of the Tabernacle, [44]and the LORD said to Moses, [45]"Get away from these people so that I can instantly destroy them!" But Moses and Aaron fell face down on the ground.

[46]And Moses said to Aaron, "Quick, take an incense burner and place burning coals on it from the altar. Lay incense on it and carry it quickly among the people to make atonement for them. The LORD's anger is blazing among them—the plague has already begun."

[47]Aaron did as Moses told him and ran out among the people. The plague indeed had already begun, but Aaron burned the incense and made atonement for them. [48]He stood between the living and the dead until the plague was stopped. [49]But 14,700 people died in that plague, in addition to those who had died in the incident involving Korah. [50]Then because the plague had stopped, Aaron returned to Moses at the entrance of the Tabernacle.

CHAPTER 17

The Budding of Aaron's Staff

Then the LORD said to Moses, [2]"Take twelve wooden staffs, one from each of Israel's ancestral tribes, and inscribe each tribal leader's name on his staff. [3]Inscribe Aaron's name on the staff of the tribe of Levi, for there must be one staff for the leader of each ancestral tribe. [4]Put these staffs in the Tabernacle in front of the Ark of the Covenant,* where I meet with you. [5]Buds will sprout on the staff belonging to the man I choose. Then I will finally put an end to this murmuring and complaining against you."

[6]So Moses gave the instructions to the people of Israel, and each of the twelve tribal leaders, including Aaron, brought Moses a staff. [7]Moses put the staffs in the LORD's presence in the Tabernacle of the Covenant.* [8]When he went into the Tabernacle of the Covenant the next day, he found that Aaron's staff, representing the tribe of Levi, had sprouted, blossomed, and produced almonds!

[9]When Moses brought all the staffs out from the LORD's presence, he showed them to the people. Each man claimed his own staff. [10]And the LORD said to Moses: "Place Aaron's staff permanently before the Ark of the Covenant* as a warning to rebels. This should put an end to their complaints against me and prevent any further deaths." [11]So Moses did as the LORD commanded him.

[12]Then the people of Israel said to Moses, "We are as good as dead! We are ruined! [13]Everyone who even comes close to the Tabernacle of the LORD dies. We are all doomed!"

CHAPTER 18

Duties of Priests and Levites

The LORD now said to Aaron: "You, your sons, and your relatives from the tribe of Levi will be held responsible for any offenses related to the sanctuary. But you and your sons alone will be held liable for violations connected with the priesthood.

[2]"Bring your relatives of the tribe of Levi to assist you and your sons as you

I DO NOT COMPLAIN about God's righteous judgment. (16:41)

I HUMBLY INTERCEDE for those who complain against me and against God. (16:45)

I BELIEVE the Lord warns rebels in order to prevent their deaths. (17:10)

I DO as the Lord commands. (17:11)

17:4 Hebrew *in the Tent of Meeting before the Testimony.*   17:7 Or *Tabernacle of the Testimony;* also in 17:8.   17:10 Hebrew *before the Testimony.*

perform the sacred duties in front of the Tabernacle of the Covenant.* ³But as the Levites go about their duties under your supervision, they must be careful not to touch any of the sacred objects or the altar. If they do, both you and they will die. ⁴The Levites must join with you to fulfill their responsibilities for the care and maintenance of the Tabernacle,* but no one who is not a Levite may officiate with you.

⁵"You yourselves must perform the sacred duties within the sanctuary and at the altar. If you follow these instructions, the LORD's anger will never again blaze against the people of Israel. ⁶I myself have chosen your fellow Levites from among the Israelites to be your special assistants. They are dedicated to the LORD for service in the Tabernacle. ⁷But you and your sons, the priests, must personally handle all the sacred service associated with the altar and everything within the inner curtain. I am giving you the priesthood as your special gift of service. Any other person who comes too near the sanctuary will be put to death."

Support for the Priests and Levites

⁸The LORD gave these further instructions to Aaron: "I have put the priests in charge of all the holy gifts that are brought to me by the people of Israel. I have given these offerings to you and your sons as your regular share. ⁹You are allotted the portion of the most holy offerings that is kept from the fire. From all the most holy offerings—including the grain offerings, sin offerings, and guilt offerings—that portion belongs to you and your sons. ¹⁰You must eat it as a most holy offering. All the males may eat of it, and you must treat it as most holy.

¹¹"All the other offerings presented to me by the Israelites by lifting them up before the altar also belong to you as your regular share. Any member of your family who is ceremonially clean, male and female alike, may eat of these offerings.

¹²"I also give you the harvest gifts brought by the people as offerings to the LORD—the best of the olive oil, wine, and grain. ¹³All the firstfruits of the land that the people present to the LORD belong to you. Any member of your family who is ceremonially clean may eat this food.

¹⁴"Whatever is specially set apart for the LORD* also belongs to you.

¹⁵"The firstborn of every mother, whether human or animal, that is offered to the LORD will be yours. But you must always redeem your firstborn sons and the firstborn males of ritually unclean animals. ¹⁶Redeem them when they are one month old. The redemption price is five pieces of silver, each piece weighing the same as the standard sanctuary shekel.*

¹⁷"However, you may not redeem the firstborn of cattle, sheep, or goats. They are holy and have been set apart for the LORD. Sprinkle their blood on the altar, and burn their fat as an offering given by fire, very pleasing to the LORD. ¹⁸The meat of these animals will be yours, just like the breast and right thigh that are presented by lifting them up before the altar. ¹⁹Yes, I am giving you all these holy offerings that the people of Israel bring to the LORD. They are for you and your sons and daughters, to be eaten as your regular share. This is an unbreakable covenant* between the LORD and you and your descendants."

²⁰And the LORD said to Aaron, "You priests will receive no inheritance of land or share of property among the people of Israel. I am your inheritance and your share. ²¹As for the tribe of Levi, your relatives, I will pay them for their service in the Tabernacle with the tithes from the entire land of Israel.

²²"From now on, Israelites other than the priests and Levites are to stay

I BELIEVE the Lord promised to protect the Israelites from his anger if Aaron and his sons performed the sacred duties given to them. (18:5)

I BELIEVE the Lord gave the priesthood to Aaron and his sons as their form of service to him. (18:7)

I BELIEVE the Lord always required the redemption of firstborn Israelite sons and firstborn unclean animals. (18:15)

I BELIEVE the Lord gave the meat of the firstborn offerings to the priests and their families. (18:18)

I BELIEVE the Lord gave no land inheritance to the priests because he himself was their inheritance. (18:20)

18:2 Or *Tabernacle of the Testimony.* 18:4 Hebrew *Tent of Meeting;* also in 18:6, 21, 22, 23, 31. 18:14 The Hebrew term used here refers to the complete consecration of things or people to the LORD, either by destroying them or by giving them as an offering. 18:16 Hebrew *5 shekels* [about 2 ounces or 57 grams] *of silver, according to the sanctuary shekel, 20 gerahs to each shekel.* 18:19 Hebrew *a covenant of salt.*

away from the Tabernacle. If they come too near, they will be judged guilty and die. ²³The Levites must serve at the Tabernacle, and they will be held responsible for any offenses against it. This is a permanent law among you. But the Levites will receive no inheritance of land among the Israelites, ²⁴because I have given them the Israelites' tithes, which have been set apart as offerings to the LORD. This will be the Levites' share. That is why I said they would receive no inheritance of land among the Israelites."

²⁵The LORD also told Moses, ²⁶"Say this to the Levites: 'When you receive the tithes from the Israelites, give a tenth of the tithes you receive—a tithe of the tithe—to the LORD as a gift. ²⁷The LORD will consider this to be your harvest offering, as though it were the first grain from your own threshing floor or wine from your own winepress. ²⁸You must present one-tenth of the tithe received from the Israelites as a gift to the LORD. From this you must present the LORD's portion to Aaron the priest. ²⁹Be sure to set aside the best portions of the gifts given to you as your gifts to the LORD.'

³⁰"Also say to the Levites: 'When you present the best part, it will be considered as though it came from your own threshing floor or winepress. ³¹You Levites and your families may eat this food anywhere you wish, for it is your compensation for serving in the Tabernacle. ³²You will not be considered guilty for accepting the LORD's tithes if you give the best portion to the priests. But be careful not to treat the holy gifts of the people of Israel as though they were common. If you do, you will die.' "

CHAPTER 19

The Water of Purification

The LORD said to Moses and Aaron, ²"Here is another ritual law required by the LORD: Tell the people of Israel to bring you a red heifer that has no physical defects and has never been yoked to a plow. ³Give it to Eleazar the priest, and it will be taken outside the camp and slaughtered in his presence. ⁴Eleazar will take some of its blood on his finger and sprinkle it seven times toward the front of the Tabernacle.* ⁵As Eleazar watches, the heifer must be burned—its hide, meat, blood, and dung. ⁶Eleazar the priest must then take cedarwood, a hyssop branch, and scarlet thread and throw them into the fire where the heifer is burning.

⁷"Then the priest must wash his clothes and bathe himself in water. Afterward he may return to the camp, though he will remain ceremonially unclean until evening. ⁸The man who burns the animal must also wash his clothes and bathe in water, and he, too, will remain unclean until evening. ⁹Then someone who is ceremonially clean will gather up the ashes of the heifer and place them in a purified place outside the camp. They will be kept there for the people of Israel to use in the water for the purification ceremony. This ceremony is performed for the removal of sin. ¹⁰The man who gathers up the ashes of the heifer must also wash his clothes, and he will remain ceremonially unclean until evening. This is a permanent law for the people of Israel and any foreigners who live among them.

¹¹"All those who touch a dead human body will be ceremonially unclean for seven days. ¹²They must purify themselves on the third and seventh days with the water of purification; then they will be purified. But if they do not do this on the third and seventh days, they will continue to be unclean even after the seventh day. ¹³All those who touch a dead body and do not purify themselves in the proper way defile the LORD's Tabernacle and will be cut off from the community of Israel. Since the water of purification was not sprinkled on them, their defilement continues.

¹⁴"This is the ritual law that applies when someone dies in a tent: Those

I WILLINGLY SHARE what others give to me. (18:27)

I DO NOT TAKE for granted what I receive for serving God. (18:32)

I BELIEVE the Lord required those who prepared the water of purification to cleanse themselves. (19:7)

I BELIEVE the Lord required those who touched a dead body to purify themselves with the water of purification. (19:11)

I BELIEVE the Lord required the individuals and articles in a tent in which someone died to be purified. (19:14)

19:4 Hebrew *Tent of Meeting.*

who enter that tent, and those who were inside when the death occurred, will be ceremonially unclean for seven days. ¹⁵Any container in the tent that was not covered with a lid is also defiled. ¹⁶And if someone outdoors touches the corpse of someone who was killed with a sword or who died a natural death, or if someone touches a human bone or a grave, that person will be unclean for seven days.

¹⁷"To remove the defilement, put some of the ashes from the burnt purification offering in a jar and pour fresh water over them. ¹⁸Then someone who is ceremonially clean must take a hyssop branch and dip it into the water. That person must sprinkle the water on the tent, on all the furnishings in the tent, and on anyone who was in the tent, or anyone who has touched a human bone, or has touched a person who was killed or who died naturally, or has touched a grave. ¹⁹On the third and seventh days the ceremonially clean person must sprinkle the water on those who are unclean. Then on the seventh day the people being cleansed must wash their clothes and bathe themselves, and that evening they will be cleansed of their defilement.

²⁰"But those who become defiled and do not purify themselves will be cut off from the community, for they have defiled the sanctuary of the LORD. Since the water of purification has not been sprinkled on them, they remain defiled. ²¹This is a permanent law. Those who sprinkle the water of purification must afterward wash their clothes, and anyone who touches the water of purification will remain defiled until evening. ²²Anything and anyone that a defiled person touches will be ceremonially defiled until evening."

CHAPTER 20
Moses Strikes the Rock

In early spring* the people of Israel arrived in the wilderness of Zin and camped at Kadesh. While they were there, Miriam died and was buried.

²There was no water for the people to drink at that place, so they rebelled against Moses and Aaron. ³The people blamed Moses and said, "We wish we had died in the LORD's presence with our brothers! ⁴Did you bring the LORD's people into this wilderness to die, along with all our livestock? ⁵Why did you make us leave Egypt and bring us here to this terrible place? This land has no grain, figs, grapes, or pomegranates. And there is no water to drink!"

⁶Moses and Aaron turned away from the people and went to the entrance of the Tabernacle,* where they fell face down on the ground. Then the glorious presence of the LORD appeared to them, ⁷and the LORD said to Moses, ⁸"You and Aaron must take the staff and assemble the entire community. As the people watch, command the rock over there to pour out its water. You will get enough water from the rock to satisfy all the people and their livestock."

⁹So Moses did as he was told. He took the staff from the place where it was kept before the LORD. ¹⁰Then he and Aaron summoned the people to come and gather at the rock. "Listen, you rebels!" he shouted. "Must we bring you water from this rock?" ¹¹Then Moses raised his hand and struck the rock twice with the staff, and water gushed out. So all the people and their livestock drank their fill.

¹²But the LORD said to Moses and Aaron, "Because you did not trust me enough to demonstrate my holiness to the people of Israel, you will not lead them into the land I am giving them!" ¹³This place was known as the waters of Meribah,* because it was where the people of Israel argued with the LORD, and where he demonstrated his holiness among them.

I BELIEVE there were severe consequences for refusing to be cleansed from defilement. (19:20)

See Miriam's profile (page 87) at Exodus 15:20.

I DO NOT REACT to being in need by rebelling against God. (20:2)

I TURN to God when others criticize me. (20:6)

I DO as the Lord tells me. (20:9)

I DO NOT LASH OUT against God or others in my anger. (20:11)

20:1 Hebrew *In the first month.* This month of the Hebrew lunar calendar usually occurs in March and April.
20:6 Hebrew *Tent of Meeting.*   20:13 *Meribah* means "arguing."

Edom Refuses Israel Passage

¹⁴While Moses was at Kadesh, he sent ambassadors to the king of Edom with this message:

"This message is from your relatives, the people of Israel: You know all the hardships we have been through, ¹⁵and that our ancestors went down to Egypt. We lived there a long time and suffered as slaves to the Egyptians. ¹⁶But when we cried out to the LORD, he heard us and sent an angel who brought us out of Egypt. Now we are camped at Kadesh, a town on the border of your land. ¹⁷Please let us pass through your country. We will be careful not to go through your fields and vineyards. We won't even drink water from your wells. We will stay on the king's road and never leave it until we have crossed the opposite border."

¹⁸But the king of Edom said, "Stay out of my land or I will meet you with an army!"

¹⁹The Israelites answered, "We will stay on the main road. If any of our livestock drinks your water, we will pay for it. We only want to pass through your country and nothing else."

²⁰But the king of Edom replied, "Stay out! You may not pass through our land." With that he mobilized his army and marched out to meet them with an imposing force. ²¹Because Edom refused to allow Israel to pass through their country, Israel was forced to turn around.

I ASSIST God's people when they ask me for help. (20:20)

The Death of Aaron

²²The whole community of Israel left Kadesh as a group and arrived at Mount Hor. ²³Then the LORD said to Moses and Aaron at Mount Hor on the border of the land of Edom, ²⁴"The time has come for Aaron to join his ancestors in death. He will not enter the land I am giving the people of Israel, because the two of you rebelled against my instructions concerning the waters of Meribah. ²⁵Now take Aaron and his son Eleazar up Mount Hor. ²⁶There you will remove Aaron's priestly garments and put them on Eleazar, his son. Aaron will die there and join his ancestors."

I BELIEVE the consequences of rebelling against God's instructions are serious. (20:24)

²⁷So Moses did as the LORD commanded. The three of them went up Mount Hor together as the whole community watched. ²⁸At the summit, Moses removed the priestly garments from Aaron and put them on Eleazar, Aaron's son. Then Aaron died there on top of the mountain, and Moses and Eleazar went back down. ²⁹When the people realized that Aaron had died, all Israel mourned for him thirty days.

I ACCEPT God's timing for the end of my life. (20:27)

CHAPTER 21

Victory over the Canaanites

The Canaanite king of Arad, who lived in the Negev, heard that the Israelites were approaching on the road to Atharim. So he attacked the Israelites and took some of them as prisoners. ²Then the people of Israel made this vow to the LORD: "If you will help us conquer these people, we will completely destroy* all their towns." ³The LORD heard their request and gave them victory over the Canaanites. The Israelites completely destroyed them and their towns, and the place has been called Hormah* ever since.

The Bronze Snake

⁴Then the people of Israel set out from Mount Hor, taking the road to the Red Sea* to go around the land of Edom. But the people grew impatient along the way, ⁵and they began to murmur against God and Moses. "Why have you brought us out of Egypt to die here in the wilderness?" they complained.

I DO NOT GET impatient and blame others for the consequences of my own sin. (21:4)

21:2 The Hebrew term used here refers to the complete consecration of things or people to the LORD, either by destroying them or by giving them as an offering; also in 21:3. 21:3 *Hormah* means "destruction." 21:4 Hebrew *sea of reeds.*

"There is nothing to eat here and nothing to drink. And we hate this wretched manna!"

⁶So the LORD sent poisonous snakes among them, and many of them were bitten and died. ⁷Then the people came to Moses and cried out, "We have sinned by speaking against the LORD and against you. Pray that the LORD will take away the snakes." So Moses prayed for the people.

⁸Then the LORD told him, "Make a replica of a poisonous snake and attach it to the top of a pole. Those who are bitten will live if they simply look at it!" ⁹So Moses made a snake out of bronze and attached it to the top of a pole. Whenever those who were bitten looked at the bronze snake, they recovered!

Israel's Journey to Moab

¹⁰The Israelites traveled next to Oboth and camped there. ¹¹Then they went on to Iye-abarim, in the wilderness on the eastern border of Moab. ¹²From there they traveled to the valley of Zered Brook and set up camp. ¹³Then they moved to the far side of the Arnon River, in the wilderness adjacent to the territory of the Amorites. The Arnon is the boundary line between the Moabites and the Amorites. ¹⁴For this reason *The Book of the Wars of the LORD* speaks of "the town of Waheb in the area of Suphah, and the ravines; and the Arnon River ¹⁵and its ravines, which extend as far as the settlement of Ar on the border of Moab."

¹⁶From there the Israelites traveled to Beer,* which is the well where the LORD said to Moses, "Assemble the people, and I will give them water." ¹⁷There the Israelites sang this song:

"Spring up, O well!
    Yes, sing about it!
¹⁸ Sing of this well,
    which princes dug,
which great leaders hollowed out
    with their scepters and staffs."

Then the Israelites left the wilderness and proceeded on through Mattanah, ¹⁹Nahaliel, and Bamoth. ²⁰Then they went to the valley in Moab where Pisgah Peak overlooks the wasteland.*

Victory over Sihon and Og

²¹The Israelites now sent ambassadors to King Sihon of the Amorites with this message:

²²"Let us travel through your land. We will stay on the king's road until we have crossed your territory. We will not trample your fields or touch your vineyards or drink your well water."

²³But King Sihon refused to let them cross his land. Instead, he mobilized his entire army and attacked Israel in the wilderness, engaging them in battle at Jahaz. ²⁴But the Israelites slaughtered them and occupied their land from the Arnon River to the Jabbok River. They went only as far as the Ammonite border because the boundary of the Ammonites was fortified.*

²⁵So Israel captured all the towns of the Amorites and settled in them, including the city of Heshbon and its surrounding villages. ²⁶Heshbon had been the capital of King Sihon of the Amorites. He had conquered a former Moabite king and seized all his land as far as the Arnon River. ²⁷For this reason the ancient poets wrote this about him:

"Come to Heshbon, city of Sihon!
    May it be restored and rebuilt.
²⁸ A fire flamed forth from Heshbon,

I REPENT and ask for prayer when I sin. (21:7)

I BELIEVE that all those who looked at the bronze snake and believed the Lord were saved from death, just as I am saved by looking to Jesus Christ. (21:9)

I SING praise to God for his provision. (21:17)

I AM CAREFUL not to take advantage of other people. (21:22)

I BELIEVE the Lord may give to his people what has been accumulated by his enemies. (21:26)

21:16 *Beer* means "well." 21:20 Or *overlooks Jeshimon.* 21:24 Or *because the terrain of the Ammonite frontier was rugged;* Hebrew *because the boundary of the Ammonites was strong.*

a blaze from the city of Sihon.
It burned the city of Ar in Moab;
    it destroyed the rulers of the Arnon heights.
[29] Your destruction is certain, O people of Moab!
You are finished, O worshipers of Chemosh!
Chemosh has left his sons as refugees,
    and his daughters as captives of Sihon, the Amorite king.
[30] We have utterly destroyed them,
    all the way from Heshbon to Dibon.
We have completely wiped them out
    as far away as Nophah and Medeba.*"

[31] So the people of Israel occupied the territory of the Amorites. [32] After Moses sent men to explore the Jazer area, they captured all the towns in the region and drove out the Amorites who lived there. [33] Then they turned and marched toward Bashan, but King Og of Bashan and all his people attacked them at Edrei. [34] The LORD said to Moses, "Do not be afraid of him, for I have given you victory over Og and his entire army, giving you all his land. You will do the same to him as you did to King Sihon of the Amorites, who ruled in Heshbon." [35] And Israel was victorious and killed King Og, his sons, and his subjects; not a single survivor remained. Then Israel occupied their land.

CHAPTER 22

Balak Sends for Balaam

Then the people of Israel traveled to the plains of Moab and camped east of the Jordan River, across from Jericho. [2] Balak son of Zippor, the Moabite king, knew what the Israelites had done to the Amorites. [3] And when they saw how many Israelites there were, he and his people were terrified. [4] The king of Moab said to the leaders of Midian, "This mob will devour everything in sight, like an ox devours grass!"

So Balak, king of Moab, [5] sent messengers to Balaam son of Beor, who was living in his native land of Pethor* near the Euphrates River.* He sent this message to request that Balaam come to help him:

"A vast horde of people has arrived from Egypt. They cover the face of the earth and are threatening me. [6] Please come and curse them for me because they are so numerous. Then perhaps I will be able to conquer them and drive them from the land. I know that blessings fall on the people you bless. I also know that the people you curse are doomed."

[7] Balak's messengers, officials of both Moab and Midian, set out and took money with them to pay Balaam to curse Israel. They went to Balaam and urgently explained to him what Balak wanted. [8] "Stay here overnight," Balaam said. "In the morning I will tell you whatever the LORD directs me to say." So the officials from Moab stayed there with Balaam.

[9] That night God came to Balaam and asked him, "Who are these men with you?"

[10] So Balaam said to God, "Balak son of Zippor, king of Moab, has sent me this message: [11] 'A vast horde of people has come from Egypt and has spread out over the whole land. Come at once to curse them. Perhaps then I will be able to conquer them and drive them from the land.'"

[12] "Do not go with them," God told Balaam. "You are not to curse these people, for I have blessed them!"

[13] The next morning Balaam got up and told Balak's officials, "Go on home! The LORD will not let me go with you."

I AM NOT AFRAID of those who are preparing to attack me. (21:34)

I BELIEVE that pagans often are afraid of God's people. (22:2)

I RECOGNIZE that unbelievers who hate God will often try anything to hurt God's people. (22:6)

I BELIEVE God can deliver his message through anyone. (22:9)

21:30 Or until fire spread to Medeba. The meaning of the Hebrew is uncertain. 22:5a Or who was at Pethor in the land of the Amavites. 22:5b Hebrew the river.

[14] So the Moabite officials returned to King Balak and reported, "Balaam refused to come with us." [15] Then Balak tried again. This time he sent a larger number of even more distinguished officials than those he had sent the first time. [16] They went to Balaam and gave him this message:

"This is what Balak son of Zippor says: Please don't let anything stop you from coming. [17] I will pay you well and do anything you ask of me. Just come and curse these people for me!"

[18] But Balaam answered them, "Even if Balak were to give me a palace filled with silver and gold, I would be powerless to do anything against the will of the LORD my God. [19] But stay here one more night to see if the LORD has anything else to say to me."

[20] That night God came to Balaam and told him, "Since these men have come for you, get up and go with them. But be sure to do only what I tell you to do."

Balaam and His Donkey

[21] So the next morning Balaam saddled his donkey and started off with the Moabite officials. [22] But God was furious that Balaam was going, so he sent the angel of the LORD to stand in the road to block his way. As Balaam and two servants were riding along, [23] Balaam's donkey suddenly saw the angel of the LORD standing in the road with a drawn sword in his hand. The donkey bolted off the road into a field, but Balaam beat it and turned it back onto the road. [24] Then the angel of the LORD stood at a place where the road narrowed between two vineyard walls. [25] When the donkey saw the angel of the LORD standing there, it tried to squeeze by and crushed Balaam's foot against the wall. So Balaam beat the donkey again. [26] Then the angel of the LORD moved farther down the road and stood in a place so narrow that the donkey could not get by at all. [27] This time when the donkey saw the angel, it lay down under Balaam. In a fit of rage Balaam beat it again with his staff.

[28] Then the LORD caused the donkey to speak. "What have I done to you that deserves your beating me these three times?" it asked Balaam.

[29] "Because you have made me look like a fool!" Balaam shouted. "If I had a sword with me, I would kill you!"

[30] "But I am the same donkey you always ride on," the donkey answered. "Have I ever done anything like this before?"

"No," he admitted.

[31] Then the LORD opened Balaam's eyes, and he saw the angel of the LORD standing in the roadway with a drawn sword in his hand. Balaam fell face down on the ground before him.

[32] "Why did you beat your donkey those three times?" the angel of the LORD demanded. "I have come to block your way because you are stubbornly resisting me. [33] Three times the donkey saw me and shied away; otherwise, I would certainly have killed you by now and spared the donkey."

[34] Then Balaam confessed to the angel of the LORD, "I have sinned. I did not realize you were standing in the road to block my way. I will go back home if you are against my going."

[35] But the angel of the LORD told him, "Go with these men, but you may say only what I tell you to say." So Balaam went on with Balak's officials. [36] When King Balak heard that Balaam was on the way, he went out to meet him at a Moabite town on the Arnon River at the border of his land.

[37] "Did I not send you an urgent invitation? Why didn't you come right away?" Balak asked Balaam. "Didn't you believe me when I said I would reward you richly?"

[38] Balaam replied, "I have come, but I have no power to say just anything. I will speak only the messages that God gives me." [39] Then Balaam accompanied Balak to Kiriath-huzoth, [40] where the king sacrificed cattle and sheep. He

---

I DO NOT ASK God to allow me to do what he has already forbidden. (22:19)

I DO NOT TAKE my anger out on any animal. (22:29)

I CONFESS my sin and willingly go God's way. (22:34)

I DO NOT PUT words in God's mouth. (22:35)

sent portions of the meat to Balaam and the officials who were with him. [41] The next morning Balak took Balaam up to Bamoth-baal. From there he could see the people of Israel spread out below him.

CHAPTER 23

Balaam Blesses Israel

Balaam said to King Balak, "Build me seven altars here, and prepare seven young bulls and seven rams for a sacrifice." [2] Balak followed his instructions, and the two of them sacrificed a young bull and a ram on each altar.

[3] Then Balaam said to Balak, "Stand here by your burnt offerings, and I will go to see if the LORD will respond to me. Then I will tell you whatever he reveals to me." So Balaam went alone to the top of a hill, [4] and God met him there. Balaam said to him, "I have prepared seven altars and have sacrificed a young bull and a ram on each altar."

[5] Then the LORD gave Balaam a message for King Balak and said, "Go back to Balak and tell him what I told you."

[6] When Balaam returned, the king was standing beside his burnt offerings with all the officials of Moab. [7] This was the prophecy Balaam delivered:

I ABHOR the thought of cursing God's people. (23:7)

"Balak summoned me to come from Aram;
   the king of Moab brought me from the eastern hills.
'Come,' he said, 'curse Jacob for me!
   Come and announce Israel's doom.'
[8] But how can I curse
   those whom God has not cursed?
How can I condemn
   those whom the LORD has not condemned?
[9] I see them from the cliff tops;
   I watch them from the hills.
I see a people who live by themselves,
   set apart from other nations.

See Jacob's profile (page 43) at Genesis 32:9.

[10] Who can count Jacob's descendants, as numerous as dust?
   Who can count even a fourth of Israel's people?
Let me die like the righteous;
   let my life end like theirs."

[11] Then King Balak demanded of Balaam, "What have you done to me? I brought you to curse my enemies. Instead, you have blessed them!"

[12] But Balaam replied, "Can I say anything except what the LORD tells me?"

I DO NOT PUT words in God's mouth. (23:12)

I DO NOT SEEK to harm others. (23:13)

Balaam's Second Prophecy

[13] Then King Balak told him, "Come with me to another place. There you will see only a portion of the nation of Israel. Curse at least that many!" [14] So Balak took Balaam to the plateau of Zophim on Pisgah Peak. He built seven altars there and offered a young bull and a ram on each altar.

I SEEK the Lord before speaking his message. (23:15)

[15] Then Balaam said to the king, "Stand here by your burnt offering while I go to meet the LORD."

[16] So the LORD met Balaam and gave him a message. Then he said, "Go back to Balak and give him this message."

[17] So Balaam returned to the place where the king and the officials of Moab were standing beside Balak's burnt offerings. "What did the LORD say?" Balak asked eagerly.

[18] This was the prophecy Balaam delivered:

"Rise up, Balak, and listen!
   Hear me, son of Zippor.
[19] God is not a man, that he should lie.
   He is not a human, that he should change his mind.

Has he ever spoken and failed to act?
    Has he ever promised and not carried it through?
20 I received a command to bless;
    he has blessed, and I cannot reverse it!
21 No misfortune is in sight for Jacob;
    no trouble is in store for Israel.
For the LORD their God is with them;
    he has been proclaimed their king.
22 God has brought them out of Egypt;
    he is like a strong ox for them.
23 No curse can touch Jacob;
    no sorcery has any power against Israel.
For now it will be said of Jacob,
    'What wonders God has done for Israel!'
24 These people rise up like a lioness;
    like a majestic lion they stand.
They refuse to rest
    until they have feasted on prey,
    drinking the blood of the slaughtered!"

25 Then Balak said to Balaam, "If you aren't going to curse them, at least don't bless them!"

26 But Balaam replied, "Didn't I tell you that I must do whatever the LORD tells me?"

Balaam's Third Prophecy

27 Then King Balak said to Balaam, "Come, I will take you to yet another place. Perhaps it will please God to let you curse them from there."

28 So Balak took Balaam to the top of Mount Peor, overlooking the wasteland.* 29 Balaam again told Balak, "Build me seven altars and prepare me seven young bulls and seven rams for a sacrifice." 30 So Balak did as Balaam ordered and offered a young bull and a ram on each altar.

CHAPTER 24

By now Balaam realized that the LORD intended to bless Israel, so he did not resort to divination as he often did. Instead, he turned and looked out toward the wilderness, 2 where he saw the people of Israel camped, tribe by tribe. Then the Spirit of God came upon him, 3 and this is the prophecy he delivered:

"This is the prophecy of Balaam son of Beor,
    the prophecy of the man whose eyes see clearly,
4 who hears the words of God,
    who sees a vision from the Almighty,
    who falls down with eyes wide open:
5 How beautiful are your tents, O Jacob;
    how lovely are your homes, O Israel!
6 They spread before me like groves of palms,
    like fruitful gardens by the riverside.
They are like aloes planted by the LORD,
    like cedars beside the waters.
7 Water will gush out in buckets;
    their offspring are supplied with all they need.
Their king will be greater than Agag;
    their kingdom will be exalted.
8 God brought them up from Egypt,
    drawing them along like a wild ox.

23:28 Or *overlooking Jeshimon.*

I BELIEVE God is the one who brought Israel up from Egypt and destroyed their enemies before them. (24:8)

He devours all the nations that oppose him,
  breaking their bones in pieces,
  shooting them with arrows.
[9] Like a lion, Israel crouches and lies down;
  like a lioness, who dares to arouse her?
Blessed is everyone who blesses you, O Israel,
  and cursed is everyone who curses you."

[10]King Balak flew into a rage against Balaam. He angrily clapped his hands and shouted, "I called you to curse my enemies! Instead, you have blessed them three times. [11]Now get out of here! Go back home! I had planned to reward you richly, but the LORD has kept you from your reward."

[12]Balaam told Balak, "Don't you remember what I told your messengers? I said, [13]'Even if Balak were to give me a palace filled with silver and gold, I am powerless to do anything against the will of the LORD.' I told you that I could say only what the LORD says! [14]Now I am returning to my own people. But first let me tell you what the Israelites will do to your people in the future."

Balaam's Final Prophecies
[15]This is the prophecy Balaam delivered:

"This is the message of Balaam son of Beor,
  the prophecy of the man whose eyes see clearly,
[16]who hears the words of God,
  who has knowledge from the Most High,
  who sees a vision from the Almighty,
  who falls down with eyes wide open:
[17]I see him, but not in the present time.
  I perceive him, but far in the distant future.
A star will rise from Jacob;
  a scepter will emerge from Israel.
It will crush the foreheads of Moab's people,
  cracking the skulls of the people of Sheth.
[18]Edom will be taken over,
  and Seir, its enemy, will be conquered,
  while Israel continues on in triumph.
[19]A ruler will rise in Jacob
  who will destroy the survivors of Ir."

[20]Then Balaam looked over at the people of Amalek and delivered this prophecy:

"Amalek was the greatest of nations,
  but its destiny is destruction!"

[21]Then he looked over at the Kenites and prophesied:

"You are strongly situated;
  your nest is set in the rocks.
[22]But the Kenites will be destroyed
  when Assyria* takes you captive."

[23]Balaam concluded his prophecies by saying:

"Alas, who can survive when God does this?
[24] Ships will come from the coasts of Cyprus*;
they will oppress both Assyria and Eber,
  but they, too, will be utterly destroyed."

[25]Then Balaam and Balak returned to their homes.

24:22 Hebrew *Asshur;* also in 24:24.   24:24 Hebrew *Kittim.*

I WANT no part or profit in cursing God's people. (24:11)

I DO NOT PUT words in God's mouth, even if I can get rich doing so. (24:13)

I BELIEVE God prophesied blessings to Israel through Balaam. (24:15)

I BELIEVE that no one can thwart God's prophecies. (24:23)

CHAPTER 25

Moab Seduces Israel

While the Israelites were camped at Acacia,* some of the men defiled them-selves by sleeping with the local Moabite women. ²These women invited them to attend sacrifices to their gods, and soon the Israelites were feasting with them and worshiping the gods of Moab. ³Before long Israel was joining in the worship of Baal of Peor, causing the LORD's anger to blaze against his people.

⁴The LORD issued the following command to Moses: "Seize all the ring-leaders and execute them before the LORD in broad daylight, so his fierce an-ger will turn away from the people of Israel." ⁵So Moses ordered Israel's judges to execute everyone who had joined in worshiping Baal of Peor.

⁶Just then one of the Israelite men brought a Midianite woman into the camp, right before the eyes of Moses and all the people, as they were weeping at the entrance of the Tabernacle.* ⁷When Phinehas son of Eleazar and grandson of Aaron the priest saw this, he jumped up and left the assembly. Then he took a spear ⁸and rushed after the man into his tent. Phinehas thrust the spear all the way through the man's body and into the woman's stomach. So the plague against the Israelites was stopped, ⁹but not before 24,000 peo-ple had died.

¹⁰Then the LORD said to Moses, ¹¹"Phinehas son of Eleazar and grandson of Aaron the priest has turned my anger away from the Israelites by displaying passionate zeal among them on my behalf. So I have stopped destroying all Israel as I had intended to do in my anger. ¹²So tell him that I am making my special covenant of peace with him. ¹³In this covenant, he and his descen-dants will be priests for all time, because he was zealous for his God and made atonement for the people of Israel."

¹⁴The Israelite man killed with the Midianite woman was named Zimri son of Salu, the leader of a family from the tribe of Simeon. ¹⁵The woman's name was Cozbi; she was the daughter of Zur, the leader of a Midianite clan.

¹⁶Then the LORD said to Moses, ¹⁷"Attack the Midianites and destroy them, ¹⁸because they assaulted you with deceit by tricking you into worshiping Baal of Peor, and because of Cozbi, the daughter of a Midianite leader, who was killed on the day of the plague at Peor."

CHAPTER 26

Israel's Second Census

After the plague had ended, the LORD said to Moses and to Eleazar son of Aaron, the priest, ²"Take a census of all the men of Israel who are twenty years old or older, to find out how many of each family are of military age." ³At that time the entire nation of Israel was camped on the plains of Moab beside the Jordan River, across from Jericho.

So Moses and Eleazar the priest issued these census instructions to the leaders of Israel: ⁴"Count all the men of Israel twenty years old and older, just as the LORD commanded Moses." This is the census record of all the descen-dants of Israel who came out of Egypt.

The Tribe of Reuben

⁵These were the clans descended from Reuben, Jacob's* oldest son:

The Hanochite clan, named after its ancestor Hanoch.

The Palluite clan, named after its ancestor Pallu.

⁶ The Hezronite clan, named after its ancestor Hezron.

The Carmite clan, named after its ancestor Carmi.

⁷The men from all the clans of Reuben numbered 43,730.

I DO NOT BECOME sexually involved with anyone outside of marriage. (25:1)

I DO NOT SPEND TIME in pagan places to pursue a romantic relationship with an unbeliever. (25:2)

I DO NOT PROVOKE God's anger by worshiping other gods. (25:3)

I AM NOT AFRAID to condemn what God has condemned. (25:5)

I DO NOT HOLD ONTO and flaunt my sin, but rather, I weep over my sin and the devastation it brings. (25:6)

I AM ZEALOUS that God's people live godly lives. (25:7)

See Phinehas's profile (page 717) at Psalm 106:30.

I BELIEVE the consequences of sin are far-reaching. (25:9)

I BELIEVE the Lord spoke to Moses, commanding him to take a census of all the men of military age. (26:1)

See Jacob's profile (page 43) at Genesis 32:9.

25:1 Hebrew *Shittim*.   25:6 Hebrew *Tent of Meeting*.   26:5 Hebrew *Israel's*.

⁸Pallu was the ancestor of Eliab, ⁹and Eliab was the father of Nemuel, Dathan, and Abiram. This Dathan and Abiram are the same community leaders who conspired with Korah against Moses and Aaron, defying the LORD. ¹⁰But the earth opened up and swallowed them with Korah, and 250 of their followers were destroyed that day by fire from the LORD. This served as a warning to the entire nation of Israel. ¹¹However, the sons of Korah did not die that day.

The Tribe of Simeon

¹²These were the clans descended from the sons of Simeon:

The Nemuelite clan, named after its ancestor Nemuel.

The Jaminite clan, named after its ancestor Jamin.

The Jakinite clan, named after its ancestor Jakin.

¹³ The Zerahite clan, named after its ancestor Zerah.

The Shaulite clan, named after its ancestor Shaul.

¹⁴The men from all the clans of Simeon numbered 22,200.

The Tribe of Gad

¹⁵These were the clans descended from the sons of Gad:

The Zephonite clan, named after its ancestor Zephon.

The Haggite clan, named after its ancestor Haggi.

The Shunite clan, named after its ancestor Shuni.

¹⁶ The Oznite clan, named after its ancestor Ozni.

The Erite clan, named after its ancestor Eri.

¹⁷ The Arodite clan, named after its ancestor Arodi.*

The Arelite clan, named after its ancestor Areli.

¹⁸The men from all the clans of Gad numbered 40,500.

The Tribe of Judah

¹⁹Judah had two sons, Er and Onan, who had died in the land of Canaan. ²⁰But the following clans descended from Judah's surviving sons:

The Shelanite clan, named after its ancestor Shelah.

The Perezite clan, named after its ancestor Perez.

The Zerahite clan, named after its ancestor Zerah.

²¹These were the subclans descended from the Perezites:

The Hezronites, named after their ancestor Hezron.

The Hamulites, named after their ancestor Hamul.

²²The men from all the clans of Judah numbered 76,500.

The Tribe of Issachar

²³These were the clans descended from the sons of Issachar:

The Tolaite clan, named after its ancestor Tola.

The Puite clan, named after its ancestor Puah.*

²⁴ The Jashubite clan, named after its ancestor Jashub.

The Shimronite clan, named after its ancestor Shimron.

²⁵The men from all the clans of Issachar numbered 64,300.

The Tribe of Zebulun

²⁶These were the clans descended from the sons of Zebulun:

The Seredite clan, named after its ancestor Sered.

The Elonite clan, named after its ancestor Elon.

The Jahleelite clan, named after its ancestor Jahleel.

26:17 As in Samaritan Pentateuch and Syriac version (see also Gen 46:16); Hebrew reads *Arod.*   26:23 As in Samaritan Pentateuch, Greek and Syriac versions, and Latin Vulgate (see also 1 Chr 7:1); Hebrew reads *The Punite clan, named after its ancestor Puvah.*

I TAKE warning when others suffer serious consequences for their sins. (26:10)

I CHOOSE to obey the Lord even if my parents choose to sin against him. (26:11)

²⁷The men from all the clans of Zebulun numbered 60,500.

The Tribe of Manasseh
²⁸Two clans were descended from Joseph through Manasseh and Ephraim.

²⁹These were the clans descended from Manasseh:
The Makirite clan, named after its ancestor Makir.
The Gileadite clan, named after its ancestor Gilead, Makir's son.

³⁰These were the subclans descended from the Gileadites:
The Iezerites, named after their ancestor Iezer.
The Helekites, named after their ancestor Helek.
³¹ The Asrielites, named after their ancestor Asriel.
The Shechemites, named after their ancestor Shechem.
³² The Shemidaites, named after their ancestor Shemida.
The Hepherites, named after their ancestor Hepher.
³³ Hepher's son, Zelophehad, had no sons, but his daughters' names were
Mahlah, Noah, Hoglah, Milcah, and Tirzah.

³⁴The men from all the clans of Manasseh numbered 52,700.

The Tribe of Ephraim
³⁵These were the clans descended from the sons of Ephraim:
The Shuthelahite clan, named after its ancestor Shuthelah.
The Bekerite clan, named after its ancestor Beker.
The Tahanite clan, named after its ancestor Tahan.

³⁶This was the subclan descended from the Shuthelahites:
The Eranites, named after their ancestor Eran.

³⁷The men from all the clans of Ephraim numbered 32,500.

These clans of Manasseh and Ephraim were all descendants of Joseph.

The Tribe of Benjamin
³⁸These were the clans descended from the sons of Benjamin:
The Belaite clan, named after its ancestor Bela.
The Ashbelite clan, named after its ancestor Ashbel.
The Ahiramite clan, named after its ancestor Ahiram.
³⁹ The Shuphamite clan, named after its ancestor Shupham.*
The Huphamite clan, named after its ancestor Hupham.

⁴⁰These were the subclans descended from the Belaites:
The Ardites, named after their ancestor Ard.*
The Naamites, named after their ancestor Naaman.

⁴¹The men from all the clans of Benjamin numbered 45,600.

The Tribe of Dan
⁴²These were the clans descended from the sons of Dan:
The Shuhamite clan, named after its ancestor Shuham.

⁴³All the clans of Dan were Shuhamite clans, and the men from these clans numbered 64,400.

The Tribe of Asher
⁴⁴These were the clans descended from the sons of Asher:
The Imnite clan, named after its ancestor Imnah.
The Ishvite clan, named after its ancestor Ishvi.
The Beriite clan, named after its ancestor Beriah.

Pray that the Holy Spirit will guide you into all truth (John 16:13).

26:39 As in some Hebrew manuscripts, Samaritan Pentateuch, Greek and Syriac versions, and Latin Vulgate; most Hebrew manuscripts read *Shephupham*.   26:40 As in Samaritan Pentateuch, some Greek manuscripts, and Latin Vulgate; Hebrew lacks *named after their ancestor Ard*.

⁴⁵These were the subclans descended from the Beriites:
The Heberites, named after their ancestor Heber.
The Malkielites, named after their ancestor Malkiel.

⁴⁶Asher also had a daughter named Serah.

⁴⁷The men from all the clans of Asher numbered 53,400.

The Tribe of Naphtali
⁴⁸These were the clans descended from the sons of Naphtali:
The Jahzeelite clan, named after its ancestor Jahzeel.
The Gunite clan, named after its ancestor Guni.
⁴⁹ The Jezerite clan, named after its ancestor Jezer.
The Shillemite clan, named after its ancestor Shillem.

⁵⁰The men from all the clans of Naphtali numbered 45,400.

The Census Results
⁵¹So the total number of Israelite men counted in the census numbered 601,730.

⁵²Then the LORD said to Moses, ⁵³"Divide the land among the tribes in proportion to their populations, as indicated by the census. ⁵⁴Give the larger tribes more land and the smaller tribes less land, each group's inheritance reflecting the size of its population. ⁵⁵Make sure you assign the land by lot, and define the inheritance of each ancestral tribe by means of the census listings. ⁵⁶Each inheritance must be assigned by lot among the larger and smaller tribal groups."

The Tribe of Levi
⁵⁷This is the census record for the Levites who were counted according to their clans:
The Gershonite clan, named after its ancestor Gershon.
The Kohathite clan, named after its ancestor Kohath.
The Merarite clan, named after its ancestor Merari.

⁵⁸The Libnites, the Hebronites, the Mahlites, the Mushites, and the Korahites were all subclans of the Levites.

Now Kohath was the ancestor of Amram, ⁵⁹and Amram's wife was named Jochebed. She also was a descendant of Levi, born among the Levites in the land of Egypt. Amram and Jochebed became the parents of Aaron, Moses, and their sister, Miriam. ⁶⁰To Aaron were born Nadab, Abihu, Eleazar, and Ithamar. ⁶¹But Nadab and Abihu died when they burned before the LORD a different kind of fire than he had commanded.

⁶²The men from the Levite clans who were one month old or older numbered 23,000. But the Levites were not included in the total census figure of the people of Israel because they were not given an inheritance of land when it was divided among the Israelites.

⁶³So these are the census figures of the people of Israel as prepared by Moses and Eleazar the priest on the plains of Moab beside the Jordan River, across from Jericho. ⁶⁴Not one person that was counted in this census had been among those counted in the previous census taken by Moses and Aaron in the wilderness of Sinai. ⁶⁵For the LORD had said of them, "They will all die in the wilderness." The only exceptions were Caleb son of Jephunneh and Joshua son of Nun.

CHAPTER 27
The Daughters of Zelophehad
One day a petition was presented by the daughters of Zelophehad—Mahlah, Noah, Hoglah, Milcah, and Tirzah. Their father, Zelophehad, was the son of

---

I BELIEVE God gave the Israelite tribes their lands according to the results of the census. (26:52)

I DISTRIBUTE the Lord's resources fairly, according to need. (26:53)

I DESIRE to help raise children who are used mightily by God. (26:59)

See Miriam's profile (page 87) at Exodus 15:20.

I KNOW that my children must chose for themselves whether to obey God or go their own way. (26:61)

I BELIEVE all who had been counted in the first census died before the second census, just as God had said they would. (26:64)

Hepher, son of Gilead, son of Makir, son of Manasseh, son of Joseph. ²These women went and stood before Moses, Eleazar the priest, the tribal leaders, and the entire community at the entrance of the Tabernacle.* ³"Our father died in the wilderness without leaving any sons," they said. "But he was not among Korah's followers, who rebelled against the LORD. He died because of his own sin. ⁴Why should the name of our father disappear just because he had no sons? Give us property along with the rest of our relatives."

⁵So Moses brought their case before the LORD. ⁶And the LORD replied to Moses, ⁷"The daughters of Zelophehad are right. You must give them an inheritance of land along with their father's relatives. Assign them the property that would have been given to their father. ⁸Moreover announce this to the people of Israel: 'If a man dies and has no sons, then give his inheritance to his daughters. ⁹And if he has no daughters, turn his inheritance over to his brothers. ¹⁰If he has no brothers, give his inheritance to his father's brothers. ¹¹But if his father has no brothers, pass on his inheritance to the nearest relative in his clan. The Israelites must observe this as a general legal requirement, just as the LORD commanded Moses.' "

Joshua Chosen to Lead Israel

¹²One day the LORD said to Moses, "Climb to the top of the mountains east of the river,* and look out over the land I have given the people of Israel. ¹³After you have seen it, you will die as Aaron your brother did, ¹⁴for you both rebelled against my instructions in the wilderness of Zin. When the people of Israel rebelled, you failed to demonstrate my holiness to them at the waters." (These are the waters of Meribah at Kadesh* in the wilderness of Zin.)

¹⁵Then Moses said to the LORD, ¹⁶"O LORD, the God of the spirits of all living things, please appoint a new leader for the community. ¹⁷Give them someone who will lead them into battle, so the people of the LORD will not be like sheep without a shepherd."

¹⁸The LORD replied, "Take Joshua son of Nun, who has the Spirit in him, and lay your hands on him. ¹⁹Present him to Eleazar the priest before the whole community, and publicly commission him with the responsibility of leading the people. ²⁰Transfer your authority to him so the whole community of Israel will obey him. ²¹When direction from the LORD is needed, Joshua will stand before Eleazar the priest, who will determine the LORD's will by means of sacred lots.* This is how Joshua and the rest of the community of Israel will discover what they should do."

²²So Moses did as the LORD commanded and presented Joshua to Eleazar the priest and the whole community. ²³Moses laid his hands on him and commissioned him to his responsibilities, just as the LORD had commanded through Moses.

CHAPTER 28

The Daily Offerings

The LORD said to Moses, ²"Give these instructions to the people of Israel: The offerings you present to me by fire on the altar are my food, and they are very pleasing to me. See to it that they are brought at the appointed times and offered according to my instructions.

³"Say to them: When you present your daily whole burnt offerings to the LORD, you must offer two one-year-old male lambs with no physical defects. ⁴One lamb will be sacrificed in the morning and the other in the evening. ⁵With each lamb you must offer a grain offering of two quarts* of choice flour mixed with one quart* of olive oil. ⁶This is the regular burnt offering

I REQUEST what is fair for my family and me. (27:3)

I PRAY about tough issues. (27:5)

I DEMONSTRATE God's holiness before his people, even when they are rebelling. (27:14)

I CARE about God's people and ask him to provide Spirit-filled leaders for them. (27:17)

I TRANSFER my authority to a successor while I'm still healthy and fit, so people will learn to follow him or her before I must step down. (27:20)

I BELIEVE the Lord spoke to Moses regarding the daily offerings. (28:1)

I PLEASE God by offering to him what is already his. (28:2)

27:2 Hebrew Tent of Meeting.   27:12 Hebrew the mountains of Abarim.   27:14 Hebrew waters of Meribath-kadesh.
27:21 Hebrew of the Urim.   28:5a Hebrew ¹/₁₀ of an ephah [2 liters]; also in 28:13, 21, 29.   28:5b Hebrew ¹/₄ of a hin [1 liter]; also in 28:7.

ordained at Mount Sinai, an offering made by fire, very pleasing to the LORD. [7]Along with it you must present the proper drink offering, consisting of one quart of fermented drink with each lamb, poured out in the Holy Place as an offering to the LORD. [8]Offer the second lamb in the evening with the same grain offering and drink offering. It, too, is an offering made by fire, very pleasing to the LORD.

The Sabbath Offerings

I BELIEVE the Lord gave Moses instructions for the Sabbath offerings. (28:9)

[9]"On the Sabbath day, sacrifice two one-year-old male lambs with no physical defects. They must be accompanied by a grain offering of three quarts* of choice flour mixed with olive oil, and a drink offering. [10]This is the whole burnt offering to be presented each Sabbath day, in addition to the regular daily burnt offering and its accompanying drink offering.

The Monthly Offerings

I BELIEVE the Lord gave Moses instructions for the offerings on the first day of the month. (28:11)

[11]"On the first day of each month, present an extra burnt offering to the LORD of two young bulls, one ram, and seven one-year-old male lambs, all with no physical defects. [12]These will be accompanied by grain offerings of choice flour mixed with olive oil—five quarts* with each bull, three quarts with the ram, [13]and two quarts with each lamb. This burnt offering must be presented by fire, and it will be very pleasing to the LORD. [14]You must also give a drink offering with each sacrifice: two quarts* of wine with each bull, two and a half pints* for the ram, and one quart* for each lamb. Present this monthly burnt offering on the first day of each month throughout the year.

[15]"Also, on the first day of each month you must offer one male goat for a sin offering to the LORD. This is in addition to the regular daily burnt offering and its accompanying drink offering.

Offerings for the Passover

I BELIEVE the Lord gave Moses instructions for the Passover offerings. (28:16)

I COME together with God's people to worship him. (28:18)

[16]"On the appointed day in early spring,* you must celebrate the LORD's Passover. [17]On the following day a joyous, seven-day festival will begin, but no bread made with yeast may be eaten. [18]On the first day of the festival you must call a sacred assembly of the people. None of your regular work may be done on that day. [19]You must present as a burnt offering to the LORD two young bulls, one ram, and seven one-year-old male lambs, all with no physical defects. [20]These will be accompanied by grain offerings of choice flour mixed with olive oil—five quarts with each bull, three quarts with the ram, [21]and two quarts with each of the seven lambs. [22]You must also offer a male goat as a sin offering, to make atonement for yourselves. [23]You will present these offerings in addition to your regular morning sacrifices. [24]On each of the seven days of the festival, this is how you will prepare the food offerings to be presented by fire, very pleasing to the LORD. These will be offered in addition to the regular whole burnt offerings and drink offerings. [25]On the seventh day of the festival you must call another holy assembly of the people. None of your regular work may be done on that day.

Offerings for the Festival of Harvest

I BELIEVE the Lord gave Moses instructions for the Festival of Harvest offerings. (28:26)

[26]"On the first day of the Festival of Harvest,* when you present the first of your new grain to the LORD, you must call a holy assembly of the people. None of your regular work may be done on that day. [27]A special whole burnt offering will be offered that day, very pleasing to the LORD. It will consist of two young bulls, one ram, and seven one-year-old male lambs. [28]These will be accompanied by grain offerings of choice flour mixed with olive oil—five quarts with each bull, three quarts with the ram, [29]and two quarts with each

---

28:9 Hebrew 2/10 of an ephah [3.6 liters]; also in 28:12, 20, 28.   28:12 Hebrew 3/10 of an ephah [5.4 liters]; also in 28:20, 28.   28:14a Hebrew 1/2 of a hin [2 liters].   28:14b Hebrew 1/3 of a hin [1.3 liters].   28:14c Hebrew 1/4 of a hin [1 liter].   28:16 Hebrew On the fourteenth day of the first month. This day of the Hebrew lunar calendar occurs in late March or early April.   28:26 Or Festival of Weeks.

of the seven lambs. ³⁰Also, offer one male goat to make atonement for yourselves. ³¹These special burnt offerings, along with their drink offerings, are in addition to the regular daily burnt offering and its accompanying grain offering. Be sure that all the animals you sacrifice have no physical defects.

CHAPTER 29

Offerings for the Festival of Trumpets

"The Festival of Trumpets will be celebrated on the appointed day in early autumn* each year. You must call a solemn assembly of all the people on that day, and no regular work may be done. ²On that day you must present a burnt offering, very pleasing to the LORD. It will consist of one young bull, one ram, and seven one-year-old male lambs, all with no physical defects. ³These must be accompanied by grain offerings of choice flour mixed with olive oil—five quarts* with the bull, three quarts* with the ram, ⁴and two quarts* with each of the seven lambs. ⁵In addition, you must sacrifice a male goat as a sin offering, to make atonement for yourselves. ⁶These special sacrifices are in addition to your regular monthly and daily burnt offerings, and they must be given with their prescribed grain offerings and drink offerings. These offerings are given to the LORD by fire and are very pleasing to him.

Offerings for the Day of Atonement

⁷"Ten days later,* you must call another holy assembly of all the people. On that day, the Day of Atonement, the people must go without food, and no regular work may be done. ⁸You must present a burnt offering, very pleasing to the LORD. It will consist of one young bull, one ram, and seven one-year-old male lambs, all with no physical defects. ⁹These offerings must be accompanied by the prescribed grain offerings of choice flour mixed with olive oil—five quarts of choice flour with the bull, three quarts of choice flour with the ram, ¹⁰and two quarts of choice flour with each of the seven lambs. ¹¹You must also sacrifice one male goat for a sin offering. This is in addition to the sin offering of atonement and the regular daily burnt offering with its grain offering, and their accompanying drink offerings.

Offerings for the Festival of Shelters

¹²"Five days later,* you must call yet another holy assembly of all the people, and on that day no regular work may be done. It is the beginning of the Festival of Shelters, a seven-day festival to the LORD. ¹³That day you must present a special whole burnt offering by fire, very pleasing to the LORD. It will consist of thirteen young bulls, two rams, and fourteen one-year-old male lambs, all with no physical defects. ¹⁴Each of these offerings must be accompanied by a grain offering of choice flour mixed with olive oil—five quarts for each of the thirteen bulls, three quarts for each of the two rams, ¹⁵and two quarts for each of the fourteen lambs. ¹⁶You must also sacrifice a male goat as a sin offering, in addition to the regular daily burnt offering with its accompanying grain offering and drink offering.

¹⁷"On the second day of this seven-day festival, sacrifice twelve young bulls, two rams, and fourteen one-year-old male lambs, all with no physical defects. ¹⁸Each of these offerings of bulls, rams, and lambs must be accompanied by the prescribed grain offering and drink offering. ¹⁹You must also sacrifice a male goat as a sin offering, in addition to the regular daily burnt offering with its accompanying grain offering and drink offering.

²⁰"On the third day of the festival, sacrifice eleven young bulls, two rams, and fourteen one-year-old male lambs, all with no physical defects. ²¹Each of

I BELIEVE the Lord gave Moses instructions for the Festival of Trumpets offerings. (29:1)

I PLEASE God with my offerings. (29:6)

I CAN WORSHIP God by fasting sometimes. (29:7)

I BELIEVE the Lord gave Moses instructions for the Day of Atonement offerings. (29:8)

I COME together with God's people to worship him. (29:12)

I BELIEVE the Lord gave Moses instructions for the Festival of Shelters offerings. (29:13)

29:1 Hebrew *on the first day of the seventh month*. This day of the Hebrew lunar calendar occurs in September or early October.   29:3a Hebrew ³/₁₀ *of an ephah* [5.4 liters]; also in 29:9, 14.   29:3b Hebrew ²/₁₀ *of an ephah* [3.6 liters]; also in 29:9, 14.   29:4 Hebrew ¹/₁₀ *of an ephah* [2 liters]; also in 29:10, 15.   29:7 Hebrew *On the tenth day of the seventh month*; see 29:1 and the note there.   29:12 Hebrew *On the fifteenth day of the seventh month*; see 29:1, 7 and the notes there.

these offerings of bulls, rams, and lambs must be accompanied by the prescribed grain offering and drink offering. [22]You must also sacrifice a male goat as a sin offering, in addition to the regular daily burnt offering with its accompanying grain offering and drink offering.

[23]"On the fourth day of the festival, sacrifice ten young bulls, two rams, and fourteen one-year-old male lambs, all with no physical defects. [24]Each of these offerings of bulls, rams, and lambs must be accompanied by the prescribed grain offering and drink offering. [25]You must also sacrifice a male goat as a sin offering, in addition to the regular daily burnt offering with its accompanying grain offering and drink offering.

[26]"On the fifth day of the festival, sacrifice nine young bulls, two rams, and fourteen one-year-old male lambs, all with no physical defects. [27]Each of these offerings of bulls, rams, and lambs must be accompanied by the prescribed grain offering and drink offering. [28]You must also sacrifice a male goat as a sin offering, in addition to the regular daily burnt offering with its accompanying grain offering and drink offering.

[29]"On the sixth day of the festival, sacrifice eight young bulls, two rams, and fourteen one-year-old male lambs, all with no physical defects. [30]Each of these offerings of bulls, rams, and lambs must be accompanied by the prescribed grain offering and drink offering. [31]You must also sacrifice a male goat as a sin offering, in addition to the regular daily burnt offering with its accompanying grain offering and drink offering.

[32]"On the seventh day of the festival, sacrifice seven young bulls, two rams, and fourteen one-year-old male lambs, all with no physical defects. [33]Each of these offerings of bulls, rams, and lambs must be accompanied by the prescribed grain offering and drink offering. [34]You must also sacrifice one male goat as a sin offering, in addition to the regular daily burnt offering with its accompanying grain offering and drink offering.

[35]"On the eighth day of the festival, call all the people to another holy assembly. You must do no regular work on that day. [36]You must present a burnt offering, very pleasing to the LORD. It will consist of one young bull, one ram, and seven one-year-old male lambs, all with no physical defects. [37]Each of these offerings must be accompanied by the prescribed grain offering and drink offering. [38]You must also sacrifice one male goat as a sin offering, in addition to the regular daily burnt offering with its accompanying grain offering and drink offering.

[39]"You must present these offerings to the LORD at your annual festivals. These are in addition to the sacrifices and offerings you present in connection with vows, or as freewill offerings, burnt offerings, grain offerings, drink offerings, or peace offerings."

[40]So Moses gave all of these instructions to the people of Israel, just as the LORD had commanded him.

CHAPTER 30

Laws concerning Vows

Now Moses summoned the leaders of the tribes of Israel and told them, "This is what the LORD has commanded: [2]A man who makes a vow to the LORD or makes a pledge under oath must never break it. He must do exactly what he said he would do.

[3]"If a young woman makes a vow to the LORD or a pledge under oath while she is still living at her father's home, [4]and her father hears of the vow or pledge but says nothing, then all her vows and pledges will stand. [5]But if her father refuses to let her fulfill the vow or pledge on the day he hears of it, then all her vows and pledges will become invalid. The LORD will forgive her because her father would not let her fulfill them.

[6]"Now suppose a young woman takes a vow or makes an impulsive pledge

I TELL God's people about his commands in Scripture. (29:40)

I KEEP my vows to the Lord. (30:2)

I BELIEVE God honored the vows of young Israelite women. (30:3)

I BELIEVE God gave Israelite fathers limited authority to revoke their daughters' vows. (30:5)

and later marries. ⁷If her husband learns of her vow or pledge and raises no objections on the day he hears of it, her vows and pledges will stand. ⁸But if her husband refuses to accept her vow or impulsive pledge on the day he hears of it, he nullifies her commitments, and the LORD will forgive her. ⁹If, however, a woman is a widow or is divorced, she must fulfill all her vows and pledges no matter what.

¹⁰"Suppose a woman is married and living in her husband's home when she makes a vow or pledge. ¹¹If her husband hears of it and does nothing to stop her, her vow or pledge will stand. ¹²But if her husband refuses to accept it on the day he hears of it, her vow or pledge will be nullified, and the LORD will forgive her. ¹³So her husband may either confirm or nullify any vows or pledges she makes to deny herself. ¹⁴But if he says nothing on the day he hears of it, then he is agreeing to it. ¹⁵If he waits more than a day and then tries to nullify a vow or pledge, he will suffer the consequences of her guilt."

¹⁶These are the regulations the LORD gave Moses concerning relationships between a man and his wife, and between a father and a young daughter who still lives at home.

CHAPTER 31
Conquest of the Midianites

Then the LORD said to Moses, ²"Take vengeance on the Midianites for leading the Israelites into idolatry. After that, you will die and join your ancestors."

³So Moses said to the people, "Choose some men to fight the LORD's war of vengeance against Midian. ⁴From each tribe of Israel, send one thousand men into battle." ⁵So they chose one thousand men from each tribe of Israel, a total of twelve thousand men armed for battle. ⁶Then Moses sent them out, a thousand men from each tribe, and Phinehas son of Eleazar the priest led them into battle. They carried along the holy objects of the sanctuary and the trumpets for sounding the charge. ⁷They attacked Midian just as the LORD had commanded Moses, and they killed all the men. ⁸All five of the Midianite kings—Evi, Rekem, Zur, Hur, and Reba—died in the battle. They also killed Balaam son of Beor with the sword.

⁹Then the Israelite army captured the Midianite women and children and seized their cattle and flocks and all their wealth as plunder. ¹⁰They burned all the towns and villages where the Midianites had lived. ¹¹After they had gathered the plunder and captives, both people and animals, ¹²they brought them all to Moses and Eleazar the priest, and to the whole community of Israel, which was camped on the plains of Moab beside the Jordan River, across from Jericho. ¹³Moses, Eleazar the priest, and all the leaders of the people went to meet them outside the camp. ¹⁴But Moses was furious with all the military commanders* who had returned from the battle.

¹⁵"Why have you let all the women live?" he demanded. ¹⁶"These are the very ones who followed Balaam's advice and caused the people of Israel to rebel against the LORD at Mount Peor. They are the ones who caused the plague to strike the LORD's people. ¹⁷Now kill all the boys and all the women who have slept with a man. ¹⁸Only the young girls who are virgins may live; you may keep them for yourselves. ¹⁹And all of you who have killed anyone or touched a dead body must stay outside the camp for seven days. You must purify yourselves and your captives on the third and seventh days. ²⁰Also, purify all your clothing and everything made of leather, goat hair, or wood."

²¹Then Eleazar the priest said to the men who were in the battle, "The LORD has given Moses this requirement of the law: ²²Anything made of gold, silver, bronze, iron, tin, or lead—²³that is, metals that do not burn—must be passed through fire in order to be made ceremonially pure. These metal objects must

I BELIEVE God gave Israelite husbands limited authority to revoke their wife's vows. (30:8)

I BELIEVE God held Israelite husbands responsible if they waited more than a day to nullify their wife's vows. (30:15)

See Phinehas's profile (page 717) at Psalm 106:30.

I BECOME ANGRY when the leaders of God's people flagrantly disobey. (31:14)

I OBEY the Lord completely. (31:15)

I BELIEVE the Lord placed great importance on ceremonial cleanliness in Old Testament times. (31:19)

31:14 Hebrew *the commanders of thousands, and the commanders of hundreds;* also in 31:48, 52, 54.

then be further purified with the water of purification. But everything that burns must be purified by the water alone. ²⁴On the seventh day you must wash your clothes and be purified. Then you may return to the camp."

Division of the Spoils

²⁵And the LORD said to Moses, ²⁶"You and Eleazar the priest and the family leaders of each tribe are to make a list of all the plunder taken in the battle, including the people and animals. ²⁷Then divide the plunder into two parts, and give half to the men who fought the battle and half to the rest of the people. ²⁸But first give the LORD his share of the captives, cattle, donkeys, sheep, and goats that belong to the army. Set apart one out of every five hundred as the LORD's share. ²⁹Give this share of their half to Eleazar the priest as an offering to the LORD. ³⁰Also take one of every fifty of the captives, cattle, donkeys, sheep, and goats in the half that belongs to the people of Israel. Give this share to the Levites in charge of maintaining the LORD's Tabernacle." ³¹So Moses and Eleazar the priest did as the LORD commanded Moses.

³²The plunder remaining from the spoils that the fighting men had taken totaled 675,000 sheep, ³³72,000 cattle, ³⁴61,000 donkeys, ³⁵and 32,000 young girls.

³⁶So the half of the plunder given to the fighting men totaled 337,500 sheep, ³⁷of which 675 were the LORD's share; ³⁸36,000 cattle, of which 72 were the LORD's share; ³⁹30,500 donkeys, of which 61 were the LORD's share; ⁴⁰16,000 young girls, of whom 32 were the LORD's share. ⁴¹Moses gave all the LORD's share to Eleazar the priest, just as the LORD had directed him.

⁴²The half of the plunder belonging to the people of Israel, which Moses had separated from the half belonging to the fighting men, ⁴³amounted to 337,500 sheep, ⁴⁴36,000 cattle, ⁴⁵30,500 donkeys, ⁴⁶and 16,000 young girls. ⁴⁷From the half-share given to the people, Moses took one of every fifty prisoners and animals and gave them to the Levites who maintained the LORD's Tabernacle. All this was done just as the LORD had commanded Moses.

⁴⁸Then all the military commanders came to Moses ⁴⁹and said, "Sir, we have accounted for all the men who went out to battle under our command; not one of us is missing! ⁵⁰So we are presenting the items of gold we captured as an offering to the LORD from our share of the plunder—armbands, bracelets, rings, earrings, and necklaces. This will make atonement for our lives before the LORD."

⁵¹So Moses and Eleazar the priest received the gold from all the military commanders, all kinds of jewelry and crafted objects. ⁵²In all, the gold that the commanders presented as a gift to the LORD weighed about 420 pounds.* ⁵³All the fighting men had taken some of the plunder for themselves. ⁵⁴So Moses and Eleazar the priest accepted the gifts from the military commanders and brought the gold to the Tabernacle* as a reminder to the LORD that the people of Israel belong to him.

CHAPTER 32

The Tribes East of the Jordan

Now the tribes of Reuben and Gad owned vast numbers of livestock. So when they saw that the lands of Jazer and Gilead were ideally suited for their flocks and herds, ²they came to Moses, Eleazar the priest, and the other leaders of the people. They said, ³"Ataroth, Dibon, Jazer, Nimrah, Heshbon, Elealeh, Sebam, Nebo, and Beon—⁴the LORD has conquered this whole area for the people of Israel. It is ideally suited for all our flocks and herds. ⁵If we have found favor with you, please let us have this land as our property instead of giving us land across the Jordan River."

31:52 Hebrew *16,750 shekels* [191 kilograms].   31:54 Hebrew *Tent of Meeting.*

I DISPERSE profits justly. (31:27)

I GIVE back to God a portion of what he has given to me. (31:28)

I DO as the Lord commands. (31:31)

I DO all that the Lord commands. (31:47)

I PRAISE God for safety and victory. (31:50)

I REMIND the Lord that I belong to him by giving him gifts and offerings. (31:54)

I RECOGNIZE the good provision of God. (32:1)

⁶"Do you mean you want to stay back here while your brothers go across and do all the fighting?" Moses asked the Reubenites and Gadites. ⁷"Are you trying to discourage the rest of the people of Israel from going across to the land the LORD has given them? ⁸This is what your ancestors did when I sent them from Kadesh-barnea to explore the land. ⁹After they went up to the valley of Eshcol and scouted the land, they discouraged the people of Israel from entering the land the LORD was giving them. ¹⁰Then the LORD was furious with them, and he vowed, ¹¹'Of all those I rescued from Egypt, no one who is twenty years old or older will ever see the land I solemnly promised to Abraham, Isaac, and Jacob, for they have not obeyed me completely. ¹²The only exceptions are Caleb son of Jephunneh the Kenizzite and Joshua son of Nun, for they have wholeheartedly followed the LORD.'

¹³"The LORD was furious with Israel and made them wander in the wilderness for forty years until the whole generation that sinned against him had died. ¹⁴But here you are, a brood of sinners, doing exactly the same thing! You are making the LORD even angrier with Israel. ¹⁵If you turn away from him like this and he abandons them again in the wilderness, you will be responsible for destroying this entire nation!"

¹⁶But they responded to Moses, "We simply want to build sheepfolds for our flocks and fortified cities for our wives and children. ¹⁷Then we will arm ourselves and lead our fellow Israelites into battle until we have brought them safely to their inheritance. Meanwhile, our families will stay in the fortified cities we build here, so they will be safe from any attacks by the local people. ¹⁸We will not return to our homes until all the people of Israel have received their inheritance of land. ¹⁹But we do not want any of the land on the other side of the Jordan. We would rather live here on the east side where we have received our inheritance."

²⁰Then Moses said, "If you keep your word and arm yourselves for the LORD's battles, ²¹and if your troops cross the Jordan until the LORD has driven out his enemies, ²²then you may return when the land is finally subdued before the LORD. You will have discharged your duty to the LORD and to the rest of the people of Israel. And the land on the east side of the Jordan will be your inheritance from the LORD. ²³But if you fail to keep your word, then you will have sinned against the LORD, and you may be sure that your sin will find you out. ²⁴Go ahead and build towns for your families and sheepfolds for your flocks, but do everything you have said."

²⁵Then the people of Gad and Reuben replied, "We are your servants and will follow your instructions exactly. ²⁶Our children, wives, flocks, and cattle will stay here in the towns of Gilead. ²⁷But, sir, all who are able to bear arms will cross over to fight for the LORD, just as you have said."

²⁸So Moses gave orders to Eleazar, Joshua, and the tribal leaders of Israel. ²⁹He said, "If all the men of Gad and Reuben who are able to fight the LORD's battles cross the Jordan with you, then when the land is conquered, you must give them the land of Gilead as their property. ³⁰But if they refuse to cross over and march ahead of you, then they must accept land with the rest of you in the land of Canaan."

³¹The tribes of Gad and Reuben said again, "Sir, we will do as the LORD has commanded! ³²We will cross the Jordan into Canaan fully armed to fight for the LORD, but our inheritance of land will be here on this side of the Jordan."

³³So Moses assigned to the tribes of Gad, Reuben, and half the tribe of Manasseh son of Joseph the territory of King Sihon of the Amorites and the land of King Og of Bashan—the whole land with its towns and surrounding lands.

³⁴The people of Gad built the towns of Dibon, Ataroth, Aroer, ³⁵Atroth-shophan, Jazer, Jogbehah, ³⁶Beth-nimrah, and Beth-haran. These were all fortified cities with sheepfolds for their flocks.

I DO NOT DESERT my family and fellow believers in times of difficulty. (32:6)

See the profiles for Abraham (page 19), Isaac (page 31), and Jacob (page 43) at Genesis 15:6, Genesis 25:19, and Genesis 32:9.

I OBEY the Lord wholeheartedly. (32:12)

I DO NOT REPEAT the sins of my parents. (32:14)

I FULFILL my commitments to others. (32:17)

I DO as the Lord commands. (32:31)

I MAKE good use of what God gives to me. (32:34)

³⁷The people of Reuben built the towns of Heshbon, Elealeh, Kiriathaim, ³⁸Nebo, Baal-meon, and Sibmah. They changed the names of some of the towns they conquered and rebuilt.

³⁹Then the descendants of Makir of the tribe of Manasseh went to Gilead and conquered it, and they drove out the Amorites, who were living there. ⁴⁰So Moses gave Gilead to the Makirites, descendants of Manasseh, and they lived there. ⁴¹The people of Jair, another clan of the tribe of Manasseh, captured many of the towns in Gilead and changed the name of that region to the Towns of Jair.* ⁴²Meanwhile, a man named Nobah captured the town of Kenath and its surrounding villages, and he renamed that area Nobah after himself.

CHAPTER 33

Remembering Israel's Journey

This is the itinerary the Israelites followed as they marched out of Egypt under the leadership of Moses and Aaron. ²At the LORD's direction, Moses kept a written record of their progress. These are the stages of their march, identified by the different places they stopped along the way.

³They set out from the city of Rameses on the morning after the first Passover celebration in early spring.* The people of Israel left defiantly, in full view of all the Egyptians. ⁴Meanwhile, the Egyptians were burying all their firstborn sons, whom the LORD had killed the night before. The LORD had defeated the gods of Egypt that night with great acts of judgment!

⁵After leaving Rameses, the Israelites set up camp at Succoth.

⁶Then they left Succoth and camped at Etham on the edge of the wilderness.

⁷They left Etham and turned back toward Pi-hahiroth, opposite Baal-zephon, and camped near Migdol.

⁸They left Pi-hahiroth and crossed the Red Sea* into the wilderness beyond. Then they traveled for three days into the Etham wilderness and camped at Marah.

⁹They left Marah and camped at Elim, where there are twelve springs of water and seventy palm trees.

¹⁰They left Elim and camped beside the Red Sea.*

¹¹They left the Red Sea and camped in the Sin* Desert.

¹²They left the Sin Desert and camped at Dophkah.

¹³They left Dophkah and camped at Alush.

¹⁴They left Alush and camped at Rephidim, where there was no water for the people to drink.

¹⁵They left Rephidim and camped in the wilderness of Sinai.

¹⁶They left the wilderness of Sinai and camped at Kibroth-hattaavah.

¹⁷They left Kibroth-hattaavah and camped at Hazeroth.

¹⁸They left Hazeroth and camped at Rithmah.

¹⁹They left Rithmah and camped at Rimmon-perez.

²⁰They left Rimmon-perez and camped at Libnah.

²¹They left Libnah and camped at Rissah.

²²They left Rissah and camped at Kehelathah.

²³They left Kehelathah and camped at Mount Shepher.

²⁴They left Mount Shepher and camped at Haradah.

²⁵They left Haradah and camped at Makheloth.

²⁶They left Makheloth and camped at Tahath.

²⁷They left Tahath and camped at Terah.

I KEEP a record of God's direction in my life. (33:2)

I BOLDLY FOLLOW God no matter who opposes me. (33:3)

I FOLLOW the Lord wherever he leads. (33:5)

32:41 Hebrew *Havvoth-jair.* 33:3 Hebrew *on the fifteenth day of the first month.* This day of the Hebrew lunar calendar occurs in late March or early April. 33:8 Hebrew *the sea.* 33:10 Hebrew *sea of reeds;* also in 33:11. 33:11 Not to be confused with the English word *sin.*

²⁸They left Terah and camped at Mithcah.

²⁹They left Mithcah and camped at Hashmonah.

³⁰They left Hashmonah and camped at Moseroth.

³¹They left Moseroth and camped at Bene-jaakan.

³²They left Bene-jaakan and camped at Hor-haggidgad.

³³They left Hor-haggidgad and camped at Jotbathah.

³⁴They left Jotbathah and camped at Abronah.

³⁵They left Abronah and camped at Ezion-geber.

³⁶They left Ezion-geber and camped at Kadesh in the wilderness of Zin.

³⁷They left Kadesh and camped at Mount Hor, at the border of Edom. ³⁸While they were at the foot of Mount Hor, Aaron the priest was directed by the LORD to go up the mountain, and there he died. This happened on a day in midsummer,* during the fortieth year after Israel's departure from Egypt. ³⁹Aaron was 123 years old when he died there on Mount Hor.

⁴⁰It was then that the Canaanite king of Arad, who lived in the Negev in the land of Canaan, heard that the people of Israel were approaching his land.

⁴¹Meanwhile, the Israelites left Mount Hor and camped at Zalmonah.

⁴²Then they left Zalmonah and camped at Punon.

⁴³They left Punon and camped at Oboth.

⁴⁴They left Oboth and camped at Iye-abarim on the border of Moab.

⁴⁵They left Iye-abarim* and camped at Dibon-gad.

⁴⁶They left Dibon-gad and camped at Almon-diblathaim.

⁴⁷They left Almon-diblathaim and camped in the mountains east of the river,* near Mount Nebo.

⁴⁸They left the mountains east of the river and camped on the plains of Moab beside the Jordan River, across from Jericho. ⁴⁹Along the Jordan River they camped from Beth-jeshimoth as far as Abel-shittim on the plains of Moab.

⁵⁰While they were camped near the Jordan River on the plains of Moab opposite Jericho, the LORD said to Moses, ⁵¹"Speak to the Israelites and tell them: 'When you cross the Jordan River into the land of Canaan, ⁵²you must drive out all the people living there. You must destroy all their carved and molten images and demolish all their pagan shrines. ⁵³Take possession of the land and settle in it, because I have given it to you to occupy. ⁵⁴You must distribute the land among the clans by sacred lot and in proportion to their size. A larger inheritance of land will be allotted to each of the larger clans, and a smaller inheritance will be allotted to each of the smaller clans. The decision of the sacred lot is final. In this way, the land will be divided among your ancestral tribes. ⁵⁵But if you fail to drive out the people who live in the land, those who remain will be like splinters in your eyes and thorns in your sides. They will harass you in the land where you live. ⁵⁶And I will do to you what I had planned to do to them.' "

CHAPTER 34

Boundaries of the Land

Then the LORD said to Moses, ²"Give these instructions to the Israelites: When you come into the land of Canaan, which I am giving you as your special possession, these will be the boundaries. ³The southern portion of your country will extend from the wilderness of Zin, along the edge of Edom. The southern boundary will begin on the east at the Dead Sea.* ⁴It will then run south past Scorpion Pass* in the direction of Zin. Its southernmost point will be

I KNOW that God decides how long I will live and when I will die. (33:38)

I BELIEVE the Lord spoke to Moses regarding conquering the Promised Land. (33:50)

I BELIEVE the Lord instructed the Israelites to drive out all the people living in the Promised Land and to destroy their idols. (33:52)

I BELIEVE the Lord allotted the land fairly and according to the needs of each Israelite clan. (33:54)

I DO NOT INFLICT misery on myself by failing to remove all sinful influences from my life. (33:55)

I BELIEVE the Lord instructed the Israelites concerning the boundaries of the Promised Land. (34:2)

33:38 Hebrew *on the first day of the fifth month.* This day of the Hebrew lunar calendar occurs in July or early August.   33:45 As in 33:44; Hebrew reads *Iyim,* another name for Iye-abarim.   33:47 Hebrew *the mountains of Abarim;* also in 33:48.   34:3 Hebrew *Salt Sea;* also in 34:12.   34:4 Hebrew *the ascent of Akrabbim.*

Kadesh-barnea, from which it will go to Hazar-addar, and on to Azmon. ⁵From Azmon the boundary will turn toward the brook of Egypt and end at the Mediterranean Sea.*

⁶"Your western boundary will be the coastline of the Mediterranean Sea.

⁷"Your northern boundary will begin at the Mediterranean Sea and run eastward to Mount Hor, ⁸then to Lebo-hamath, and on through Zedad ⁹and Ziphron to Hazar-enan. This will be your northern boundary.

¹⁰"The eastern boundary will start at Hazar-enan and run south to Shepham, ¹¹then down to Riblah on the east side of Ain. From there the boundary will run down along the eastern edge of the Sea of Galilee,* ¹²and then along the Jordan River to the Dead Sea. These are the boundaries of your land."

¹³Then Moses told the Israelites, "This is the territory you are to divide among yourselves by sacred lot. The LORD commands that the land be divided up among the nine and a half remaining tribes. ¹⁴The families of the tribes of Reuben, Gad, and half the tribe of Manasseh have already received their inheritance of land ¹⁵on the east side of the Jordan River, across from Jericho."

Leaders to Divide the Land

¹⁶And the LORD said to Moses, ¹⁷"These are the men who are to divide the land among the people: Eleazar the priest and Joshua son of Nun. ¹⁸Also enlist one leader from each tribe to help them with the task. ¹⁹These are the tribes and the names of the leaders:

Tribe	Leader
Judah	Caleb son of Jephunneh
²⁰ Simeon	Shemuel son of Ammihud
²¹ Benjamin	Elidad son of Kislon
²² Dan	Bukki son of Jogli
²³ Manasseh son of Joseph	Hanniel son of Ephod
²⁴ Ephraim son of Joseph	Kemuel son of Shiphtan
²⁵ Zebulun	Elizaphan son of Parnach
²⁶ Issachar	Paltiel son of Azzan
²⁷ Asher	Ahihud son of Shelomi
²⁸ Naphtali	Pedahel son of Ammihud

²⁹These are the men the LORD has appointed to oversee the dividing of the land of Canaan among the Israelites."

CHAPTER 35

Towns for the Levites

While Israel was camped beside the Jordan on the plains of Moab, across from Jericho, the LORD said to Moses, ²"Instruct the people of Israel to give to the Levites from their property certain towns to live in, along with the surrounding pasturelands. ³These towns will be their homes, and the surrounding lands will provide pasture for their cattle, flocks, and other livestock. ⁴The pastureland assigned to the Levites around these towns will extend 1,500 feet* from the town walls in every direction. ⁵Measure off 3,000 feet* outside the town walls in every direction—east, south, west, north—with the town at the center. This area will serve as the larger pastureland for the towns.

⁶"You must give the Levites six cities of refuge, where a person who has accidentally killed someone can flee for safety. In addition, give them forty-two other towns. ⁷In all, forty-eight towns with the surrounding pastureland will be given to the Levites. ⁸These towns will come from the property of the

34:5 Hebrew *the sea;* also in 34:6, 7.   34:11 Hebrew *sea of Kinnereth.*   35:4 Hebrew *1,000 cubits* [450 meters].
35:5 Hebrew *2,000 cubits* [900 meters].

I BELIEVE the Lord spoke to Moses regarding leaders to divide the land. (34:16)

I ENLIST good leaders to help with important tasks. (34:18)

I WILLINGLY HELP to provide for God's servants. (35:2)

I BELIEVE the Lord provided six of the Levite towns as cities of refuge for the Israelites. (35:6)

I GIVE in proportion to what I have been given. (35:8)

people of Israel. The larger tribes will give more towns to the Levites, while the smaller tribes will give fewer. Each tribe will give in proportion to its inheritance."

Cities of Refuge

⁹And the LORD said to Moses, ¹⁰"Say this to the people of Israel: 'When you cross the Jordan into the land of Canaan, ¹¹designate cities of refuge for people to flee to if they have killed someone accidentally. ¹²These cities will be places of protection from a dead person's relatives who want to avenge the death. The slayer must not be killed before being tried by the community. ¹³Designate six cities of refuge for yourselves, ¹⁴three on the east side of the Jordan River and three on the west in the land of Canaan. ¹⁵These cities are for the protection of Israelites, resident foreigners, and traveling merchants. Anyone who accidentally kills someone may flee there for safety.

¹⁶" 'But if someone strikes and kills another person with a piece of iron, it must be presumed to be murder, and the murderer must be executed. ¹⁷Or if someone strikes and kills another person with a large stone, it is murder, and the murderer must be executed. ¹⁸The same is true if someone strikes and kills another person with a wooden weapon. It must be presumed to be murder, and the murderer must be executed. ¹⁹The victim's nearest relative is responsible for putting the murderer to death. When they meet, the avenger must execute the murderer. ²⁰So if in premeditated hostility someone pushes another person or throws a dangerous object and the person dies, it is murder. ²¹Or if someone angrily hits another person with a fist and the person dies, it is murder. In such cases, the victim's nearest relative must execute the murderer when they meet.

²²" 'But suppose someone pushes another person without premeditated hostility, or throws something that unintentionally hits another person, ²³or accidentally drops a stone on someone, though they were not enemies, and the person dies. ²⁴If this should happen, the assembly must follow these regulations in making a judgment between the slayer and the avenger, the victim's nearest relative. ²⁵They must protect the slayer from the avenger, and they must send the slayer back to live in a city of refuge until the death of the high priest.

²⁶" 'But if the slayer leaves the city of refuge, ²⁷and the victim's nearest relative finds him outside the city limits and kills him, it will not be considered murder. ²⁸The slayer should have stayed inside the city of refuge until the death of the high priest. But after the death of the high priest, the slayer may return to his own property. ²⁹These are permanent laws for you to observe from generation to generation, wherever you may live.

³⁰" 'All murderers must be executed, but only if there is more than one witness. No one may be put to death on the testimony of only one witness. ³¹Also, you must never accept a ransom payment for the life of someone judged guilty of murder and subject to execution; murderers must always be put to death. ³²And never accept a ransom payment from someone who has fled to a city of refuge, allowing the slayer to return to his property before the death of the high priest. ³³This will ensure that the land where you live will not be polluted, for murder pollutes the land. And no atonement can be made for murder except by the execution of the murderer. ³⁴You must not defile the land where you are going to live, for I live there myself. I am the LORD, who lives among the people of Israel.' "

CHAPTER 36

Women Who Inherit Property

Then the heads of the clan of Gilead—descendants of Makir, son of Manasseh, son of Joseph—came to Moses and the family leaders of Israel

I BELIEVE the Lord instructed the Israelites to provide cities of refuge for anyone who killed another person accidentally. (35:10)

I BELIEVE the Lord gave instructions for determining the difference between accidental killing and murder. (35:16)

I SEEK to protect those who are innocent of premeditated murder. (35:25)

I ACCEPT the merciful terms of my sentence when I have wronged another person. (35:26)

I BELIEVE God required more than one witness to condemn someone to death for murder. (35:30)

I BELIEVE God's presence among the Israelites required their purity. (35:34)

with a petition. [2]They said, "Sir, the LORD instructed you to divide the land by sacred lot among the people of Israel. You were told by the LORD to give the inheritance of our brother Zelophehad to his daughters. [3]But if any of them marries a man from another tribe, their inheritance of land will go with them to the tribe into which they marry. In this way, the total area of our tribal land will be reduced. [4]Then when the Year of Jubilee comes, their inheritance of land will be added to that of the new tribe, causing it to be lost forever to our ancestral tribe."

[5]So Moses gave the Israelites this command from the LORD: "The men of the tribe of Joseph are right. [6]This is what the LORD commands concerning the daughters of Zelophehad: Let them marry anyone they like, as long as it is within their own ancestral tribe. [7]None of the inherited land may pass from tribe to tribe, for the inheritance of every tribe must remain fixed as it was first allotted. [8]The daughters throughout the tribes of Israel who are in line to inherit property must marry within their tribe, so that all the Israelites will keep their ancestral property. [9]No inheritance may pass from one tribe to another; each tribe of Israel must hold on to its allotted inheritance of land."

[10]The daughters of Zelophehad did as the LORD commanded Moses. [11]Mahlah, Tirzah, Hoglah, Milcah, and Noah all married cousins on their father's side. [12]They married into the clans of Manasseh son of Joseph. Thus, their inheritance of land remained within their ancestral tribe.

[13]These are the commands and regulations that the LORD gave to the people of Israel through Moses while they were camped on the plains of Moab beside the Jordan River, across from Jericho.

I ADDRESS the concerns of others from God's Word. (36:5)

I BELIEVE the Lord allowed the daughters of Zelophehad to marry anyone they chose, as long as he was from their tribe. (36:6)

I DO as the Lord commands. (36:10)

DEUTERONOMY

IN THIS FIFTH BOOK of Moses, which contains his last words in the form of a deeply compelling sermon, he reiterates the Lord's covenant with a new generation of Israelites and urges them to claim his blessings diligently. How? By first obeying God's commands faithfully—unlike the previous generation.

In this fast-paced book, Moses reviews the nation's history over the past forty years (chapters 1–3) and challenges them to set a new course (chapters 4–33). What a sermon it is!

Before sunset that same day, Moses climbs Mount Nebo, surveys the Promised Land from a distance, and dies (chapter 34).

Famous passages in Deuteronomy include

- ◯ The warning not to add or subtract from God's commands (4:2)
- ◯ The Ten Commandments repeated (5:6-21)
- ◯ The command to love the Lord wholeheartedly (6:4-9; 10:12-13)
- ◯ A warning against false prophets (13:1-5)
- ◯ The prophecy of the Prophet to come (18:15-19)
- ◯ Blessings and curses (28:1-68)
- ◯ The commissioning of Joshua (31:1-8, 14-23)
- ◯ A song of Moses and Joshua (31:19, 30–32:44)
- ◯ The blessing of Moses on each tribe (33:1-29)

CHAPTER 1

The Command to Leave Sinai

This book records the words that Moses spoke to all the people of Israel while they were in the wilderness east of the Jordan River. They were camped in the Jordan Valley* near Suph, between Paran on one side and Tophel, Laban, Hazeroth, and Di-zahab on the other. ²Normally it takes only eleven days to travel from Mount Sinai* to Kadesh-barnea, going by way of Mount Seir. ³But forty years after the Israelites left Mount Sinai, on a day in midwinter,* Moses gave these speeches to the Israelites, telling them everything the LORD had commanded him to say. ⁴This was after he had defeated King Sihon of the Amorites, who had ruled in Heshbon, and King Og of Bashan, who had ruled in Ashtaroth and Edrei.

⁵So Moses addressed the people of Israel while they were in the land of Moab east of the Jordan River. He began to explain the law as follows: ⁶"When we were at Mount Sinai, the LORD our God said to us, 'You have stayed at this mountain long enough. ⁷It is time to break camp and move on. Go to the hill country of the Amorites and to all the neighboring regions—the Jordan Valley, the hill country, the western foothills,* the Negev,

I GO God's way—avoiding years of disobedience, frustration, heartache, and sorrow. (1:2)

I BELIEVE the Lord spoke to the Israelites, clearly explaining his will and way to realize great blessings. (1:6)

1:1 Hebrew *the Arabah*; also in 1:7. 1:2 Hebrew *Horeb*, another name for Sinai; also in 1:6, 19. 1:3 Hebrew *on the first day of the eleventh month*. This day of the Hebrew lunar calendar occurs in January or early February. 1:7 Hebrew *the Shephelah*.

See the profiles for Abraham (page 19), Isaac (page 31), and Jacob (page 43) at Genesis 15:6, Genesis 25:19, and Genesis 32:9.

I PRAY for the Lord's blessing on others. (1:11)

I AM WILLING to serve God's people, whether that means leading young or old, many or few. (1:15)

I DO NOT SHOW favoritism, regardless of a person's ethnic, financial, or social status. (1:17)

I AM NOT HESITANT to obey the Lord's commands and receive what he has promised. (1:21)

I DO NOT QUIT or demoralize others, no matter how big the obstacles or challenges in life. (1:28)

and the coastal plain. Go to the land of the Canaanites and to Lebanon, and all the way to the great Euphrates River. ⁸I am giving all this land to you! Go in and occupy it, for it is the land the LORD swore to give to your ancestors Abraham, Isaac, and Jacob, and to all their descendants.'

Moses Appoints Leaders from Each Tribe

⁹"At that time I told you, 'You are too great a burden for me to carry all by myself. ¹⁰The LORD your God has made you as numerous as the stars! ¹¹And may the LORD, the God of your ancestors, multiply you a thousand times more and bless you as he promised! ¹²But how can I settle all your quarrels and problems by myself? ¹³Choose some men from each tribe who have wisdom, understanding, and a good reputation, and I will appoint them as your leaders.'

¹⁴"You agreed that my plan was a good one. ¹⁵So I took the wise and respected men you had selected from your tribes and appointed them to serve as judges and officials over you. Some were responsible for a thousand people, some for a hundred, some for fifty, and some for ten. ¹⁶I instructed the judges, 'You must be perfectly fair at all times, not only to fellow Israelites, but also to the foreigners living among you. ¹⁷When you make decisions, never favor those who are rich; be fair to lowly and great alike. Don't be afraid of how they will react, for you are judging in the place of God. Bring me any cases that are too difficult for you, and I will handle them.' ¹⁸And at that time I gave you instructions about everything you were to do.

Scouts Explore the Land

¹⁹"Then, just as the LORD our God directed us, we left Mount Sinai and traveled through the great and terrifying wilderness, which you yourselves saw, and headed toward the hill country of the Amorites. When we arrived at Kadesh-barnea, ²⁰I said to you, 'You have now reached the land that the LORD our God is giving us. ²¹Look! He has placed it in front of you. Go and occupy it as the LORD, the God of your ancestors, has promised you. Don't be afraid! Don't be discouraged!'

²²"But you responded, 'First, let's send out scouts to explore the land for us. They will advise us on the best route to take and decide which towns we should capture.' ²³This seemed like a good idea to me, so I chose twelve scouts, one from each of your tribes. ²⁴They crossed into the hills and came to the valley of Eshcol and explored it. ²⁵They picked some of its fruit and brought it back to us. And they reported that the land the LORD our God had given us was indeed a good land.

Israel Rebels against the LORD

²⁶"But you rebelled against the command of the LORD your God and refused to go in. ²⁷You murmured and complained in your tents and said, 'The LORD must hate us, bringing us here from Egypt to be slaughtered by these Amorites. ²⁸How can we go on? Our scouts have demoralized us with their report. They say that the people of the land are taller and more powerful than we are, and that the walls of their towns rise high into the sky! They have even seen giants there—the descendants of Anak!'

²⁹"But I said to you, 'Don't be afraid! ³⁰The LORD your God is going before you. He will fight for you, just as you saw him do in Egypt. ³¹And you saw how the LORD your God cared for you again and again here in the wilderness, just as a father cares for his child. Now he has brought you to this place.' ³²But even after all he did, you refused to trust the LORD your God, ³³who goes before you looking for the best places to camp, guiding you by a pillar of fire at night and a pillar of cloud by day.

³⁴"When the LORD heard your complaining, he became very angry. So he solemnly swore, ³⁵'Not one of you from this entire wicked generation will

live to see the good land I swore to give your ancestors, [36]except Caleb son of Jephunneh. He will see this land because he has followed the LORD completely. I will give to him and his descendants some of the land he walked over during his scouting mission.'

[37]"And the LORD was also angry with me because of you. He said to me, 'You will never enter the Promised Land! [38]Instead, your assistant, Joshua son of Nun, will lead the people into the land. Encourage him as he prepares to enter it. [39]I will give the land to your innocent children. You were afraid they would be captured, but they will be the ones who occupy it. [40]As for you, turn around now and go on back through the wilderness toward the Red Sea.*'

[41]"Then you confessed, 'We have sinned against the LORD! We will go into the land and fight for it, as the LORD our God has told us.' So your men strapped on their weapons, thinking it would be easy to conquer the hill country.

[42]"But the LORD said to me, 'Tell them not to attack, for I will not go with them. If they do, they will be crushed by their enemies.' [43]This is what I told you, but you would not listen. Instead, you again rebelled against the LORD's command and arrogantly went into the hill country to fight. [44]But the Amorites who lived there came out against you like a swarm of bees. They chased and battered you all the way from Seir to Hormah. [45]Then you returned and wept before the LORD, but he refused to listen. [46]So you stayed there at Kadesh for a long time.

CHAPTER 2

Remembering Israel's Wanderings

"Then we turned around and set out across the wilderness toward the Red Sea,* just as the LORD had instructed me, and we wandered around Mount Seir for a long time. [2]Then at last the LORD said to me, [3]'You have been wandering around in this hill country long enough; turn northward. [4]Give these orders to the people: "You will be passing through the country belonging to your relatives the Edomites, the descendants of Esau, who live in Seir. The Edomites will feel threatened, so be careful. [5]Don't bother them, for I have given them all the hill country around Mount Seir as their property, and I will not give you any of their land. [6]Pay them for whatever food or water you use. [7]The LORD your God has blessed everything you have done and has watched your every step through this great wilderness. During these forty years, the LORD your God has been with you and provided for your every need so that you lacked nothing."' [8]So we went past our relatives, the descendants of Esau, who live in Seir, and avoided the road through the Arabah Valley that comes up from Elath and Ezion-geber.

"Then as we traveled northward along the desert route through Moab, [9]the LORD warned us, 'Do not bother the Moabites, the descendants of Lot, or start a war with them. I have given them Ar as their property, and I will not give you any of their land.' "

[10](A numerous and powerful race of giants called the Emites had once lived in the area of Ar. They were as tall as the Anakites, another race of giants. [11]Both the Emites and the Anakites are often referred to as the Rephaites, but the Moabites called them Emites. [12]In earlier times the Horites had lived at Mount Seir, but they were driven out and displaced by the descendants of Esau. In a similar way the peoples in Canaan were driven from the land that the LORD had assigned to Israel.)

[13]Moses continued, "Then the LORD told us to cross Zered Brook, and we did. [14]So thirty-eight years passed from the time we first arrived at Kadesh-barnea until we finally crossed Zered Brook! For the LORD had vowed

I KNOW that feeling regret for what I've lost isn't the same as repenting for my sin. (1:41)

I KNOW the Lord won't listen to my prayers if I harbor sin in my heart. (1:45)

I KNOW the consequences of sin can last a long time. (2:1)

See Esau's profile (page 33) at Genesis 25:34.

I THANK the Lord for his blessing, care, and provision each step of the way through life, even though I sometimes let him down. (2:7)

I FOLLOW the Lord's directions and obey his commands. (2:13)

1:40 Hebrew *sea of reeds.*   2:1 Hebrew *sea of reeds.*

that this could not happen until all the men old enough to fight in battle had died in the wilderness. [15]The LORD had lifted his hand against them until all of them had finally died.

[16]"When all the men of fighting age had died, [17]the LORD said to me, [18]'Today you will cross the border of Moab at Ar [19]and enter the land of Ammon. But do not bother the Ammonites, the descendants of Lot, or start a war with them. I have given the land of Ammon to them as their property, and I will not give you any of their land.' "

[20](That area, too, was once considered the land of the Rephaites, though the Ammonites referred to them as Zamzummites. [21]They were a numerous and powerful race, as tall as the Anakites. But the LORD destroyed them so the Ammonites could occupy their land. [22]He had similarly helped the descendants of Esau at Mount Seir, for he destroyed the Horites so they could settle there in their place. The descendants of Esau live there to this day. [23]A similar thing happened when the Caphtorites from Crete* invaded and destroyed the Avvites, who had lived in villages in the area of Gaza.)

[24]Moses continued, "Then the LORD said, 'Now cross the Arnon Gorge! Look, I will help you defeat Sihon the Amorite, king of Heshbon, and I will give you his land. Attack him and begin to occupy the land. [25]Beginning today I will make all people throughout the earth terrified of you. When they hear reports about you, they will tremble with dread and fear.'

Victory over Sihon of Heshbon

[26]"Then from the wilderness of Kedemoth I sent ambassadors to King Sihon of Heshbon with this proposal of peace: [27]'Let us pass through your land. We will stay on the main road and won't turn off into the fields on either side. [28]We will pay for every bite of food we eat and all the water we drink. All we want is permission to pass through your land. [29]The descendants of Esau at Mount Seir allowed us to go through their country, and so did the Moabites, who live in Ar. Let us pass through until we cross the Jordan into the land the LORD our God has given us.' [30]But King Sihon refused to allow you to pass through, because the LORD your God made Sihon stubborn and defiant so he could help you defeat them, as he has now done.

[31]"Then the LORD said to me, 'Look, I have begun to hand King Sihon and his land over to you. Begin now to conquer and occupy his land.' [32]Then King Sihon declared war on us and mobilized his forces at Jahaz. [33]But the LORD our God handed him over to us, and we crushed him, his sons, and all his people. [34]We conquered all his towns and completely destroyed* everyone—men, women, and children. Not a single person was spared. [35]We took all the livestock as plunder for ourselves, along with anything of value from the towns we ransacked.

[36]"The LORD our God helped us conquer Aroer on the edge of the Arnon Gorge, the town in the gorge, and the whole area as far as Gilead. No town had walls too strong for us. [37]However, we stayed away from the Ammonites along the Jabbok River and the towns in the hill country—all the places the LORD our God had commanded us to leave alone.

CHAPTER 3

Victory over Og of Bashan

"Next we headed for the land of Bashan, where King Og and his army attacked us at Edrei. [2]But the LORD told me, 'Do not be afraid of him, for I have given you victory over Og and his army, giving you his entire land. Treat him just as you treated King Sihon of the Amorites, who ruled in Heshbon.' [3]So the LORD our God handed King Og and all his people over to us, and we

I BELIEVE the wages of sin is death (see Romans 3:23). (2:15)

I BELIEVE the Israelites under Moses rarely attacked other peoples, and then only if the Lord commanded them to do so. (2:26)

I BELIEVE the Lord spoke to Moses, promising him victory over the pagan king Sihon, who attacked the Israelites. (2:31)

I BELIEVE the Israelites heeded the Lord's warnings not to attack specific peoples. (2:37)

I BELIEVE the Lord spoke to Moses, promising him victory over the pagan king Og, who attacked the Israelites. (3:2)

2:23 Hebrew *from Caphtor.*   2:34 The Hebrew term used here refers to the complete consecration of things or people to the LORD, either by destroying them or by giving them as an offering.

killed them all. [4]We conquered all sixty of his towns, the entire Argob region in his kingdom of Bashan. [5]These were all fortified cities with high walls and barred gates. We also took many unwalled villages at the same time. [6]We completely destroyed* the kingdom of Bashan, just as we had destroyed King Sihon of Heshbon. We destroyed* all the people in every town we conquered—men, women, and children alike. [7]But we kept all the livestock for ourselves and took plunder from all the towns.

[8]"We now possessed all the land of the two Amorite kings east of the Jordan River—from the Arnon Gorge to Mount Hermon. [9](Mount Hermon is called Sirion by the Sidonians; the Amorites call it Senir.) [10]We had now conquered all the cities on the plateau, and all Gilead and Bashan as far as the towns of Salecah and Edrei, which were part of Og's kingdom in Bashan. [11](Incidentally, King Og of Bashan was the last of the giant Rephaites. His iron bed was more than thirteen feet long and six feet wide.* It can still be seen in the Ammonite city of Rabbah.)

Land Division East of the Jordan

[12]"When we took possession of this land, I gave the territory beyond Aroer along the Arnon Gorge, plus half of the hill country of Gilead with its towns, to the tribes of Reuben and Gad. [13]Then I gave the rest of Gilead and all of Bashan—Og's former kingdom—to the half-tribe of Manasseh. (The Argob region of Bashan used to be known as the land of the Rephaites. [14]Jair, a leader from the tribe of Manasseh, acquired the whole Argob region in Bashan all the way to the borders of the Geshurites and Maacathites. Jair renamed this region after himself, calling it the Towns of Jair,* as it is still known today.) [15]I gave Gilead to the clan of Makir. [16]And to the tribes of Reuben and Gad I gave the area extending from Gilead to the middle of the Arnon Gorge, all the way to the Jabbok River on the Ammonite frontier. [17]They also received the Jordan Valley, including the Jordan River and its eastern banks, all the way from the Sea of Galilee down to the Dead Sea,* with the slopes of Pisgah on the east.

I THANK the Lord for what he has given me. (3:12)

[18]"At that time I gave this command to the tribes that will live east of the Jordan: 'Although the LORD your God has given you this land as your property, all your fighting men must cross the Jordan, armed and ready to protect your Israelite relatives. [19]Your wives, children, and numerous livestock, however, may stay behind in the towns I have given you. [20]When the LORD has given security to the rest of the Israelites, as he has to you, and when they occupy the land the LORD your God is giving them across the Jordan River, then you may return here to the land I have given you.'

I DO NOT BECOME complacent when I receive much from the Lord. (3:18)

Moses Forbidden to Enter the Land

[21]"At that time I said to Joshua, 'You have seen all that the LORD your God has done to these two kings. He will do the same to all the kingdoms on the west side of the Jordan. [22]Do not be afraid of the nations there, for the LORD your God will fight for you.'

I ENCOURAGE the next generation of godly leaders. (3:21)

[23]"At that time I pleaded with the LORD and said, [24]'O Sovereign LORD, I am your servant. You have only begun to show me your greatness and power. Is there any god in heaven or on earth who can perform such great deeds as yours? [25]Please let me cross the Jordan to see the wonderful land on the other side, the beautiful hill country and the Lebanon mountains.'

I WORSHIP the Sovereign Lord, who is great and powerful and who does great deeds. (3:24)

[26]"But the LORD was angry with me because of you, and he would not listen to me. 'That's enough!' he ordered. 'Speak of it no more. [27]You can go to Pisgah Peak and view the land in every direction, but you may not cross the Jordan River. [28]But commission Joshua and encourage him, for he will lead

I THANK the Lord for what he has given me. (3:27)

3:6 The Hebrew term used here refers to the complete consecration of things or people to the LORD, either by destroying them or by giving them as an offering.   3:11 Hebrew 9 cubits [4.1 meters] long and 4 cubits [1.8 meters] wide.   3:14 Hebrew Havvoth-jair.   3:17 Hebrew from Kinnereth to the sea of the Arabah, the Salt Sea.

the people across the Jordan. He will give them the land you now see before you.' [29]So we stayed in the valley near Beth-peor.

CHAPTER 4

Moses Urges Israel to Obey

"And now, Israel, listen carefully to these laws and regulations that I am about to teach you. Obey them so that you may live, so you may enter and occupy the land the LORD, the God of your ancestors, is giving you. [2]Do not add to or subtract from these commands I am giving you from the LORD your God. Just obey them. [3]You saw what the LORD did to you at Baal-peor, where the LORD your God destroyed everyone who had worshiped the god Baal of Peor. [4]But all of you who were faithful to the LORD your God are still alive today.

[5]"You must obey these laws and regulations when you arrive in the land you are about to enter and occupy. The LORD my God gave them to me and commanded me to pass them on to you. [6]If you obey them carefully, you will display your wisdom and intelligence to the surrounding nations. When they hear about these laws, they will exclaim, 'What other nation is as wise and prudent as this!' [7]For what great nation has a god as near to them as the LORD our God is near to us whenever we call on him? [8]And what great nation has laws and regulations as fair as this body of laws that I am giving you today?

[9]"But watch out! Be very careful never to forget what you have seen the LORD do for you. Do not let these things escape from your mind as long as you live! And be sure to pass them on to your children and grandchildren. [10]Tell them especially about the day when you stood before the LORD your God at Mount Sinai,* where he told me, 'Summon the people before me, and I will instruct them. That way, they will learn to fear me as long as they live, and they will be able to teach my laws to their children.' [11]You came near and stood at the foot of the mountain, while the mountain was burning with fire. Flames shot into the sky, shrouded in black clouds and deep darkness. [12]And the LORD spoke to you from the fire. You heard his words but didn't see his form; there was only a voice. [13]He proclaimed his covenant, which he commanded you to keep—the Ten Commandments—and wrote them on two stone tablets. [14]It was at that time that the LORD commanded me to issue the laws and regulations you must obey in the land you are about to enter and occupy.

A Warning against Idolatry

[15]"But be careful! You did not see the LORD's form on the day he spoke to you from the fire at Mount Sinai. [16]So do not corrupt yourselves by making a physical image in any form—whether of a man or a woman, [17]an animal or a bird, [18]a creeping creature or a fish. [19]And when you look up into the sky and see the sun, moon, and stars—all the forces of heaven—don't be seduced by them and worship them. The LORD your God designated these heavenly bodies for all the peoples of the earth. [20]Remember that the LORD rescued you from the burning furnace of Egypt to become his own people and special possession; that is what you are today.

[21]"But the LORD was very angry with me because of you. He vowed that I would never cross the Jordan River into the good land the LORD your God is giving you as your special possession. [22]Though you will cross the Jordan to occupy the land, I will die here on this side of the river. [23]So be careful not to break the covenant the LORD your God has made with you. You will break it if you make idols of any shape or form, for the LORD your God has absolutely forbidden this. [24]The LORD your God is a devouring fire, a jealous God.

[25]"In the future, when you have children and grandchildren and have lived

Margin notes

I TEACH others to obey all the Lord's commands so they may enjoy the Lord's presence and blessing in their lives. (4:1)

I REMAIN faithful to the Lord, no matter what others do. (4:4)

I OBEY the Lord's commands carefully, displaying wisdom and intelligence before a watching world. (4:6)

I WILL fear the Lord as long as I live and teach his commands to the next generation. (4:10)

I BELIEVE the Lord is a devouring fire, a jealous God. (4:24)

4:10 Hebrew *Horeb*, another name for Sinai; also in 4:15.

in the land a long time, do not corrupt yourselves by making idols of any kind. This is evil in the sight of the LORD your God and will arouse his anger.

²⁶ "Today I call heaven and earth as witnesses against you. If you disobey me, you will quickly disappear from the land you are crossing the Jordan to occupy. You will live there only a short time; then you will be utterly destroyed. ²⁷ For the LORD will scatter you among the nations, where only a few of you will survive. ²⁸ There, in a foreign land, you will worship idols made from wood and stone, gods that neither see nor hear nor eat nor smell. ²⁹ From there you will search again for the LORD your God. And if you search for him with all your heart and soul, you will find him.

³⁰ "When those bitter days have come upon you far in the future, you will finally return to the LORD your God and listen to what he tells you. ³¹ For the LORD your God is merciful—he will not abandon you or destroy you or forget the solemn covenant he made with your ancestors.

There Is Only One God

³² "Search all of history, from the time God created people on the earth until now. Then search from one end of the heavens to the other. See if anything as great as this has ever happened before. ³³ Has any nation ever heard the voice of God* speaking from fire—as you did—and survived? ³⁴ Has any other god taken one nation for himself by rescuing it from another by means of trials, miraculous signs, wonders, war, awesome power, and terrifying acts? Yet that is what the LORD your God did for you in Egypt, right before your very eyes.

³⁵ "He showed you these things so you would realize that the LORD is God and that there is no other god. ³⁶ He let you hear his voice from heaven so he could instruct you. He let you see his great fire here on earth so he could speak to you from it. ³⁷ Because he loved your ancestors, he chose to bless their descendants and personally brought you out of Egypt with a great display of power. ³⁸ He drove out nations far greater than you, so he could bring you in and give you their land as a special possession, as it is today. ³⁹ So remember this and keep it firmly in mind: The LORD is God both in heaven and on earth, and there is no other god! ⁴⁰ If you obey all the laws and commands that I will give you today, all will be well with you and your children. Then you will enjoy a long life in the land the LORD your God is giving you for all time."

Eastern Cities of Refuge

⁴¹ Then Moses set apart three cities of refuge east of the Jordan River, ⁴² where anyone who had accidentally killed someone without having any previous hostility could flee for safety. ⁴³ These were the cities: Bezer on the wilderness plateau for the tribe of Reuben; Ramoth in Gilead for the tribe of Gad; Golan in Bashan for the tribe of Manasseh.

Introduction to the Law

⁴⁴ This is the law that Moses handed down to the Israelites. ⁴⁵ These are the stipulations, laws, and regulations that Moses gave to the people of Israel when they left Egypt, ⁴⁶ and as they camped in the valley near Beth-peor east of the Jordan River. (This land was formerly occupied by the Amorites under King Sihon of Heshbon. He and his people had been destroyed by Moses and the Israelites as they came up from Egypt. ⁴⁷ Israel conquered his land and that of King Og of Bashan—the two Amorite kings east of the Jordan. ⁴⁸ So Israel conquered all the area from Aroer at the edge of the Arnon Gorge to Mount Sirion,* also called Mount Hermon. ⁴⁹ And they took the eastern bank of the Jordan Valley as far south as the Dead Sea,* below the slopes of Pisgah.)

4:33 Or *voice of a god.* 4:48 As in Syriac version (see also 3:9); Hebrew reads *Mount Sion.* 4:49 Hebrew *took the Arabah on the east side of the Jordan as far as the sea of the Arabah.*

I KNOW I cannot sow disobedience without reaping grave consequences. (4:26)

I BELIEVE the exodus from Egypt and the Ten Commandments at Mount Sinai proved beyond all doubt that the Lord alone is God in heaven and on earth. (4:35)

I BELIEVE the Lord alone is God in heaven and on earth. (4:39)

CHAPTER **5**

The Ten Commandments

Moses called all the people of Israel together and said, "Listen carefully to all the laws and regulations I am giving you today. Learn them and be sure to obey them!

²"While we were at Mount Sinai,* the LORD our God made a covenant with us. ³The LORD did not make this covenant long ago with our ancestors, but with all of us who are alive today. ⁴The LORD spoke to you face to face from the heart of the fire on the mountain. ⁵I stood as an intermediary between you and the LORD, for you were afraid of the fire and did not climb the mountain. He spoke to me, and I passed his words on to you. This is what he said:

⁶"'I am the LORD your God, who rescued you from slavery in Egypt.

⁷"'Do not worship any other gods besides me.

⁸"'Do not make idols of any kind, whether in the shape of birds or animals or fish. ⁹You must never worship or bow down to them, for I, the LORD your God, am a jealous God who will not share your affection with any other god! I do not leave unpunished the sins of those who hate me, but I punish the children for the sins of their parents to the third and fourth generations. ¹⁰But I lavish my love on those who love me and obey my commands, even for a thousand generations.

¹¹"'Do not misuse the name of the LORD your God. The LORD will not let you go unpunished if you misuse his name.

¹²"'Observe the Sabbath day by keeping it holy, as the LORD your God has commanded you. ¹³Six days a week are set apart for your daily duties and regular work, ¹⁴but the seventh day is a day of rest dedicated to the LORD your God. On that day no one in your household may do any kind of work. This includes you, your sons and daughters, your male and female servants, your oxen and donkeys and other livestock, and any foreigners living among you. All your male and female servants must rest as you do. ¹⁵Remember that you were once slaves in Egypt and that the LORD your God brought you out with amazing power and mighty deeds. That is why the LORD your God has commanded you to observe the Sabbath day.

¹⁶"'Honor your father and mother, as the LORD your God commanded you. Then you will live a long, full life in the land the LORD your God will give you.

¹⁷"'Do not murder.

¹⁸"'Do not commit adultery.

¹⁹"'Do not steal.

²⁰"'Do not testify falsely against your neighbor.

²¹"'Do not covet your neighbor's wife. Do not covet your neighbor's house or land, male or female servant, ox or donkey, or anything else your neighbor owns.'

²²"The LORD spoke these words with a loud voice to all of you from the heart of the fire, surrounded by clouds and deep darkness. This was all he said at that time, and he wrote his words on two stone tablets and gave them to me. ²³But when you heard the voice from the darkness, while the mountain was blazing with fire, all your tribal leaders came to me. ²⁴They said, 'The LORD our God has shown us his glory and greatness, and we have heard his voice from the heart of the fire. Today we have seen God speaking to humans, and yet we live! ²⁵But now, why should we die? If the LORD our God speaks to us again, we will certainly die and be consumed by this awesome fire. ²⁶Can any living thing hear the voice of the living God from the heart of the fire and yet survive? ²⁷You go and listen to what the LORD our God says. Then come and tell us everything he tells you, and we will listen and obey.'

5:2 Hebrew *Horeb*, another name for Sinai.

I BELIEVE the Lord spoke to Moses, giving him the Ten Commandments. (5:5)

I BELIEVE the Lord is a jealous God. (5:9)

I BELIEVE the Lord never stops lavishing his love on those who love him and obey his commands. (5:10)

I HONOR my father and mother. (5:16)

I DO NOT COVET. (5:21)

[28]"The LORD heard your request and said to me, 'I have heard what the people have said to you, and they are right. [29]Oh, that they would always have hearts like this, that they might fear me and obey all my commands! If they did, they and their descendants would prosper forever. [30]Go and tell them to return to their tents. [31]But you stay here with me so I can give you all my commands, laws, and regulations. You will teach them to the people so they can obey them in the land I am giving to them as their inheritance.' "

[32]So Moses told the people, "You must obey all the commands of the LORD your God, following his instructions in every detail. [33]Stay on the path that the LORD your God has commanded you to follow. Then you will live long and prosperous lives in the land you are about to enter and occupy.

CHAPTER 6

A Call for Wholehearted Commitment

"These are all the commands, laws, and regulations that the LORD your God told me to teach you so you may obey them in the land you are about to enter and occupy, [2]and so you and your children and grandchildren might fear the LORD your God as long as you live. If you obey all his laws and commands, you will enjoy a long life. [3]Listen closely, Israel, to everything I say. Be careful to obey. Then all will go well with you, and you will have many children in the land flowing with milk and honey, just as the LORD, the God of your ancestors, promised you.

[4]"Hear, O Israel! The LORD is our God, the LORD alone.* [5]And you must love the LORD your God with all your heart, all your soul, and all your strength. [6]And you must commit yourselves wholeheartedly to these commands I am giving you today. [7]Repeat them again and again to your children. Talk about them when you are at home and when you are away on a journey, when you are lying down and when you are getting up again. [8]Tie them to your hands as a reminder, and wear them on your forehead. [9]Write them on the doorposts of your house and on your gates.

[10]"The LORD your God will soon bring you into the land he swore to give your ancestors Abraham, Isaac, and Jacob. It is a land filled with large, prosperous cities that you did not build. [11]The houses will be richly stocked with goods you did not produce. You will draw water from cisterns you did not dig, and you will eat from vineyards and olive trees you did not plant. When you have eaten your fill in this land, [12]be careful not to forget the LORD, who rescued you from slavery in the land of Egypt. [13]You must fear the LORD your God and serve him. When you take an oath, you must use only his name.

[14]"You must not worship any of the gods of neighboring nations, [15]for the LORD your God, who lives among you, is a jealous God. His anger will flare up against you and wipe you from the face of the earth. [16]Do not test the LORD your God as you did when you complained at Massah. [17]You must diligently obey the commands of the LORD your God—all the stipulations and laws he has given you. [18]Do what is right and good in the LORD's sight, so all will go well with you. Then you will enter and occupy the good land that the LORD solemnly promised to give your ancestors. [19]You will drive out all the enemies living in your land, just as the LORD said you would.

[20]"In the future your children will ask you, 'What is the meaning of these stipulations, laws, and regulations that the LORD our God has given us?' [21]Then you must tell them, 'We were Pharaoh's slaves in Egypt, but the LORD brought us out of Egypt with amazing power. [22]Before our eyes the LORD did miraculous signs and wonders, dealing terrifying blows against Egypt and Pharaoh and all his people. [23]He brought us out of Egypt so he could give us this land he had solemnly promised to give our ancestors. [24]And the LORD our

I TEACH the Lord's commands to others so they too can obey them and prosper. (5:31)

I BELIEVE the Lord alone is God in heaven and earth. (6:4)

I LOVE the Lord my God with all my heart, soul, and strength. (6:5)

See the profiles for Abraham (page 19), Isaac (page 31), and Jacob (page 43) at Genesis 15:6, Genesis 25:19, and Genesis 32:9.

I DO NOT BECOME so engrossed in material prosperity that I become spiritually impoverished. (6:12)

I DO NOT TEST the Lord my God by complaining. (6:16)

I BELIEVE the Lord longs for us to do what is right and good in his sight so we can prosper. (6:18)

6:4 Or *The LORD our God is one LORD,* or *The LORD our God, the LORD is one,* or *The LORD is our God, the LORD is one.*

God commanded us to obey all these laws and to fear him for our own prosperity and well-being, as is now the case. ²⁵For we are righteous when we obey all the commands the LORD our God has given us.'

CHAPTER 7

The Privilege of Holiness

"When the LORD your God brings you into the land you are about to enter and occupy, he will clear away many nations ahead of you: the Hittites, Girgashites, Amorites, Canaanites, Perizzites, Hivites, and Jebusites. These seven nations are all more powerful than you. ²When the LORD your God hands these nations over to you and you conquer them, you must completely destroy* them. Make no treaties with them and show them no mercy. ³Do not intermarry with them, and don't let your daughters and sons marry their sons and daughters. ⁴They will lead your young people away from me to worship other gods. Then the anger of the LORD will burn against you, and he will destroy you. ⁵Instead, you must break down their pagan altars and shatter their sacred pillars. Cut down their Asherah poles and burn their idols. ⁶For you are a holy people, who belong to the LORD your God. Of all the people on earth, the LORD your God has chosen you to be his own special treasure.

⁷"The LORD did not choose you and lavish his love on you because you were larger or greater than other nations, for you were the smallest of all nations! ⁸It was simply because the LORD loves you, and because he was keeping the oath he had sworn to your ancestors. That is why the LORD rescued you with such amazing power from your slavery under Pharaoh in Egypt. ⁹Understand, therefore, that the LORD your God is indeed God. He is the faithful God who keeps his covenant for a thousand generations and constantly loves those who love him and obey his commands. ¹⁰But he does not hesitate to punish and destroy those who hate him. ¹¹Therefore, obey all these commands, laws, and regulations I am giving you today.

¹²"If you listen to these regulations and obey them faithfully, the LORD your God will keep his covenant of unfailing love with you, as he solemnly promised your ancestors. ¹³He will love you and bless you and make you into a great nation. He will give you many children and give fertility to your land and your animals. When you arrive in the land he swore to give your ancestors, you will have large crops of grain, grapes, and olives, and great herds of cattle, sheep, and goats. ¹⁴You will be blessed above all the nations of the earth. None of your men or women will be childless, and all your livestock will bear young. ¹⁵And the LORD will protect you from all sickness. He will not let you suffer from the terrible diseases you knew in Egypt, but he will bring them all on your enemies!

¹⁶"You must destroy all the nations the LORD your God hands over to you. Show them no mercy and do not worship their gods. If you do, they will trap you. ¹⁷Perhaps you will think to yourselves, 'How can we ever conquer these nations that are so much more powerful than we are?' ¹⁸But don't be afraid of them! Just remember what the LORD your God did to Pharaoh and to all the land of Egypt. ¹⁹Remember the great terrors the LORD your God sent against them. You saw it all with your own eyes! And remember the miraculous signs and wonders, and the amazing power he used when he brought you out of Egypt. The LORD your God will use this same power against the people you fear. ²⁰And then the LORD your God will send hornets* to drive out the few survivors still hiding from you!

²¹"No, do not be afraid of those nations, for the LORD your God is among you, and he is a great and awesome God. ²²The LORD your God will drive

---

I BELIEVE nations bring destruction upon themselves when they repeatedly sin against the Lord. (7:1)

I BELIEVE it is wrong for a believer to marry an unbeliever. (7:3)

I BELIEVE many people suffer terrible consequences when believers marry unbelievers. (7:4)

I AM PART of a holy people, chosen and treasured by the Lord. (7:6)

I BELIEVE the Lord my God is indeed God— holy, just, faithful and always loving to those who love him and obey his commands. (7:9)

Recommit yourself to loving the Lord with all your heart, soul, strength, and mind.

I THANK the Lord for his mighty presence and power, and I cast off all fear. (7:21)

7:2 The Hebrew term used here refers to the complete consecration of things or people to the LORD, either by destroying them or by giving them as an offering; also in 7:26.   7:20 Or *will spread panic,* or *will send a plague.* The meaning of the Hebrew is uncertain.

those nations out ahead of you little by little. You will not clear them away all at once, for if you did, the wild animals would multiply too quickly for you. ²³But the LORD your God will hand them over to you. He will throw them into complete confusion until they are destroyed. ²⁴He will put their kings in your power, and you will erase their names from the face of the earth. No one will be able to stand against you, and you will destroy them all.

²⁵"You must burn their idols in fire, and do not desire the silver or gold with which they are made. Do not take it or it will become a snare to you, for it is detestable to the LORD your God. ²⁶Do not bring any detestable objects into your home, for then you will be set apart for destruction just like them. You must utterly detest such things, for they are set apart for destruction.

CHAPTER 8

A Call to Remember and Obey

"Be careful to obey all the commands I am giving you today. Then you will live and multiply, and you will enter and occupy the land the LORD swore to give your ancestors. ²Remember how the LORD your God led you through the wilderness for forty years, humbling you and testing you to prove your character, and to find out whether or not you would really obey his commands. ³Yes, he humbled you by letting you go hungry and then feeding you with manna, a food previously unknown to you and your ancestors. He did it to teach you that people need more than bread for their life; real life comes by feeding on every word of the LORD. ⁴For all these forty years your clothes didn't wear out, and your feet didn't blister or swell. ⁵So you should realize that just as a parent disciplines a child, the LORD your God disciplines you to help you.

⁶"So obey the commands of the LORD your God by walking in his ways and fearing him. ⁷For the LORD your God is bringing you into a good land of flowing streams and pools of water, with springs that gush forth in the valleys and hills. ⁸It is a land of wheat and barley, of grapevines, fig trees, pomegranates, olives, and honey. ⁹It is a land where food is plentiful and nothing is lacking. It is a land where iron is as common as stone, and copper is abundant in the hills. ¹⁰When you have eaten your fill, praise the LORD your God for the good land he has given you.

¹¹"But that is the time to be careful! Beware that in your plenty you do not forget the LORD your God and disobey his commands, regulations, and laws. ¹²For when you have become full and prosperous and have built fine homes to live in, ¹³and when your flocks and herds have become very large and your silver and gold have multiplied along with everything else, ¹⁴that is the time to be careful. Do not become proud at that time and forget the LORD your God, who rescued you from slavery in the land of Egypt. ¹⁵Do not forget that he led you through the great and terrifying wilderness with poisonous snakes and scorpions, where it was so hot and dry. He gave you water from the rock! ¹⁶He fed you with manna in the wilderness, a food unknown to your ancestors. He did this to humble you and test you for your own good. ¹⁷He did it so you would never think that it was your own strength and energy that made you wealthy. ¹⁸Always remember that it is the LORD your God who gives you power to become rich, and he does it to fulfill the covenant he made with your ancestors.

¹⁹"But I assure you of this: If you ever forget the LORD your God and follow other gods, worshiping and bowing down to them, you will certainly be destroyed. ²⁰Just as the LORD has destroyed other nations in your path, you also will be destroyed for not obeying the LORD your God.

CHAPTER 9

Victory by God's Grace

"Hear, O Israel! Today you are about to cross the Jordan River to occupy the land belonging to nations much greater and more powerful than you. They

---

I BELIEVE the Lord uses trials to humble and test me, to prove my character, and to show whether I will obey his commands. (8:2)

I BELIEVE the Lord my God disciplines me to help me. (8:5)

I RECOGNIZE that in times of plenty I need to be careful, for I will be tempted to forget the Lord my God and disobey his commands. (8:11)

I BELIEVE the Lord uses trials to humble and test me and to keep me from becoming proud and disobedient during times of prosperity. (8:16)

live in cities with walls that reach to the sky! ²They are strong and tall—descendants of the famous Anakite giants. You've heard the saying, 'Who can stand up to the Anakites?' ³But the LORD your God will cross over ahead of you like a devouring fire to destroy them. He will subdue them so that you will quickly conquer them and drive them out, just as the LORD has promised.

⁴"After the LORD your God has done this for you, don't say to yourselves, 'The LORD has given us this land because we are so righteous!' No, it is because of the wickedness of the other nations that he is doing it. ⁵It is not at all because you are such righteous, upright people that you are about to occupy their land. The LORD your God will drive these nations out ahead of you only because of their wickedness, and to fulfill the oath he had sworn to your ancestors Abraham, Isaac, and Jacob. ⁶I will say it again: The LORD your God is not giving you this good land because you are righteous, for you are not—you are a stubborn people.

Remembering the Gold Calf

⁷"Remember how angry you made the LORD your God out in the wilderness. From the day you left Egypt until now, you have constantly rebelled against him. ⁸Remember how angry you made the LORD at Mount Sinai,* where he was ready to destroy you. ⁹That was when I was on the mountain receiving the tablets of stone inscribed with the covenant that the LORD had made with you. I was there for forty days and forty nights, and all that time I ate nothing and drank no water. ¹⁰The LORD gave me the covenant, the tablets on which God himself had written all the words he had spoken to you from the fire on the mountain.

¹¹"At the end of the forty days and nights, the LORD handed me the two stone tablets with the covenant inscribed on them. ¹²Then the LORD said to me, 'Go down immediately because the people you led out of Egypt have become corrupt. They have already turned from the way I commanded them to live and have cast an idol for themselves from gold.'

¹³"The LORD said to me, 'I have been watching this people, and they are extremely stubborn. ¹⁴Leave me alone so I may destroy them and erase their name from under heaven. Then I will make a mighty nation of your descendants, a nation larger and more powerful than they are.'

¹⁵"So I came down from the fiery mountain, holding in my hands the two stone tablets of the covenant. ¹⁶There below me I could see the gold calf you had made in your terrible sin against the LORD your God. How quickly you had turned from the path the LORD had commanded you to follow! ¹⁷So I raised the stone tablets and dashed them to the ground. I smashed them before your very eyes. ¹⁸Then for forty days and nights I lay prostrate before the LORD, neither eating bread nor drinking water. I did this because you had sinned by doing what the LORD hated, thus making him very angry. ¹⁹How I feared for you, for the LORD was ready to destroy you. But again he listened to me. ²⁰The LORD was so angry with Aaron that he wanted to destroy him. But I prayed for Aaron, and the LORD spared him. ²¹I took your sin—the calf you had made—and I melted it in the fire and ground it into fine dust. I threw the dust into the stream that cascades down the mountain.

²²"You also made the LORD angry at Taberah,* Massah,* and Kibroth-hattaavah.* ²³And at Kadesh-barnea the LORD sent you out with this command: 'Go up and take the land I have given you.' But you rebelled against the command of the LORD your God and refused to trust him or obey

---

I BELIEVE the Lord judged the nations west of the Jordan River because for centuries they had been so wicked. (9:4)

See the profiles for Abraham (page 19), Isaac (page 31), and Jacob (page 43) at Genesis 15:6, Genesis 25:19, and Genesis 32:9.

I BELIEVE the Israelites rebelled against the Lord repeatedly throughout the forty years they wandered in the wilderness. (9:7)

I BELIEVE the Lord would have been right to destroy the Israelites, for they committed gross idolatry almost immediately after he gave them the Ten Commandments. (9:12)

I BELIEVE Moses earnestly interceded with the Lord, who agreed to spare the Israelites. (9:18)

I BELIEVE the Israelites rebelled against the Lord and refused to trust or obey him. (9:23)

9:8 Hebrew *Horeb,* another name for Sinai.   9:22a *Taberah* means "place of burning." See Num 11:1-3.   9:22b *Massah* means "place of testing." See Exod 17:1-7.   9:22c *Kibroth-hattaavah* means "graves of craving." See Num 11:31-34.

him. ²⁴Yes, you have been rebelling against the LORD as long as I have known you. ²⁵"That is why I fell down and lay before the LORD for forty days and nights when he was ready to destroy you. ²⁶I prayed to the LORD and said, 'O Sovereign LORD, do not destroy your own people. They are your special possession, redeemed from Egypt by your mighty power and glorious strength. ²⁷Overlook the stubbornness and sin of these people, but remember instead your servants Abraham, Isaac, and Jacob. ²⁸If you destroy these people, the Egyptians will say, "The LORD destroyed them because he wasn't able to bring them to the land he had sworn to give them." Or they might say, "He destroyed them because he hated them; he brought them into the wilderness to slaughter them." ²⁹But they are your people and your special possession, whom you brought from Egypt by your mighty power and glorious strength.'

See the profiles for Abraham (page 19), Isaac (page 31), and Jacob (page 43) at Genesis 15:6, Genesis 25:19, and Genesis 32:9.

CHAPTER 10

New Tablets of Stone

"At that time the LORD said to me, 'Prepare two stone tablets like the first ones, and make a sacred chest of wood to keep them in. Return to me on the mountain, ²and I will write on the tablets the same words that were on the ones you smashed. Then place the tablets in the sacred chest—the Ark of the Covenant.'

³"So I made a chest of acacia wood and cut two stone tablets like the first two, and I took the tablets up the mountain. ⁴The LORD again wrote the terms of the covenant—the Ten Commandments—on them and gave them to me. They were the same words the LORD had spoken to you from the heart of the fire on the mountain as you were assembled below. ⁵Then I came down and placed the tablets in the Ark of the Covenant, which I had made, just as the LORD commanded me. And the tablets are still there in the Ark.

⁶"The people of Israel set out from the wells of the people of Jaakan* and traveled to Moserah, where Aaron died and was buried. His son Eleazar became the high priest in his place. ⁷Then they journeyed to Gudgodah, and from there to Jotbathah, a land with brooks of water. ⁸At that time the LORD set apart the tribe of Levi to carry the Ark of the LORD's covenant, to minister before the LORD, and to pronounce blessings in his name. These are still their duties. ⁹That is why the Levites have no share or inheritance reserved for them among the other Israelite tribes. The LORD himself is their inheritance, as the LORD your God told them.

¹⁰"As I said before, I stayed on the mountain in the LORD's presence for forty days and nights, as I had done the first time. And once again the LORD yielded to my pleas and didn't destroy you. ¹¹But the LORD said to me, 'Get up and lead the people into the land I swore to give their ancestors, so they may take possession of it.'

A Call to Love and Obedience

¹²"And now, Israel, what does the LORD your God require of you? He requires you to fear him, to live according to his will, to love and worship him with all your heart and soul, ¹³and to obey the LORD's commands and laws that I am giving you today for your own good. ¹⁴The highest heavens and the earth and everything in it all belong to the LORD your God. ¹⁵Yet the LORD chose your ancestors as the objects of his love. And he chose you, their descendants, above every other nation, as is evident today. ¹⁶Therefore, cleanse your sinful hearts and stop being stubborn.

¹⁷"The LORD your God is the God of gods and Lord of lords. He is the great God, mighty and awesome, who shows no partiality and takes no bribes. ¹⁸He gives justice to orphans and widows. He shows love to the foreigners

I BELIEVE the Lord requires me to fear him, to live according to his will, to love and worship him with all my heart and soul, and to obey his commands. (10:12)

I BELIEVE everything in the universe belongs to the Lord my God. (10:14)

I REPENT of my sins and draw near to the Lord. (10:16)

I BELIEVE the Lord my God is the God of gods and Lord of lords, the great God, mighty and awesome, who is holy, just, and compassionate. (10:17)

10:6 Or *set out from Beeroth of Bene-jaakan.*

I AM COMPASSIONATE
to immigrants, whom
the Lord himself loves.
(10:19)

I LOVE the Lord my
God and obey all his
commands. (11:1)

I OBEY all the
commands of the
Lord, who gives me
strength. (11:8)

I BELIEVE the Lord
longed for the
Israelites to worship
him, to love him with
all their heart and
soul, to obey all his
commands carefully,
and to prosper for
many generations in
the Promised Land.
(11:13)

I MEDITATE on the
Lord's commands and
keep them faithfully,
both in my home and
everywhere I go.
(11:18)

I BELIEVE the Lord
would have prospered
the Israelites for all
generations in the
Promised Land if they
would have obeyed his
commands diligently
and persistently.
(11:21)

living among you and gives them food and clothing. ¹⁹You, too, must show love to foreigners, for you yourselves were once foreigners in the land of Egypt. ²⁰You must fear the LORD your God and worship him and cling to him. Your oaths must be in his name alone. ²¹He is your God, the one who is worthy of your praise, the one who has done mighty miracles that you yourselves have seen. ²²When your ancestors went down into Egypt, there were only seventy of them. But now the LORD your God has made you as numerous as the stars in the sky!

CHAPTER 11

"You must love the LORD your God and obey all his requirements, laws, regulations, and commands. ²Listen! I am not talking now to your children, who have never experienced the discipline of the LORD your God or seen his greatness and awesome power. ³They weren't there to see the miraculous signs and wonders he performed in Egypt against Pharaoh and all his land. ⁴They didn't see what the LORD did to the armies of Egypt and to their horses and chariots—how he drowned them in the Red Sea* as they were chasing you, and how he has kept them devastated to this very day! ⁵They didn't see how the LORD cared for you in the wilderness until you arrived here. ⁶They weren't there to see what he did to Dathan and Abiram (the sons of Eliab, a descendant of Reuben) when the earth opened up and swallowed them, along with their households and tents and every living thing that belonged to them. ⁷But you have seen all the LORD's mighty deeds with your own eyes!

The Blessings of Obedience

⁸"Therefore, be careful to obey every command I am giving you today, so you may have strength to go in and occupy the land you are about to enter. ⁹If you obey, you will enjoy a long life in the land the LORD swore to give to your ancestors and to you, their descendants—a land flowing with milk and honey! ¹⁰For the land you are about to enter and occupy is not like the land of Egypt from which you came, where you planted your seed and dug out irrigation ditches with your foot as in a vegetable garden. ¹¹It is a land of hills and valleys with plenty of rain—¹²a land that the LORD your God cares for. He watches over it day after day throughout the year!

¹³"If you carefully obey all the commands I am giving you today, and if you love the LORD your God with all your heart and soul, and if you worship him, ¹⁴then he will send the rains in their proper seasons so you can harvest crops of grain, grapes for wine, and olives for oil. ¹⁵He will give you lush pastureland for your cattle to graze in, and you yourselves will have plenty to eat.

¹⁶"But do not let your heart turn away from the LORD to worship other gods. ¹⁷If you do, the LORD's anger will burn against you. He will shut up the sky and hold back the rain, and your harvests will fail. Then you will quickly die in that good land the LORD is now giving you. ¹⁸So commit yourselves completely to these words of mine. Tie them to your hands as a reminder, and wear them on your forehead. ¹⁹Teach them to your children. Talk about them when you are at home and when you are away on a journey, when you are lying down and when you are getting up again. ²⁰Write them on the doorposts of your house and on your gates, ²¹so that as long as the sky remains above the earth, you and your children may flourish in the land the LORD swore to give your ancestors.

²²"Be careful to obey all the commands I give you; show love to the LORD your God by walking in his ways and clinging to him. ²³Then the LORD will drive out all the nations in your land, though they are much greater and

11:4 Hebrew *sea of reeds.*

stronger than you. [24]Wherever you set your feet, the land will be yours. Your frontiers will stretch from the wilderness in the south to Lebanon in the north, and from the Euphrates River in the east to the Mediterranean Sea in the west.* [25]No one will be able to stand against you, for the LORD your God will send fear and dread ahead of you, as he promised you, wherever you go in the whole land.

[26]"Today I am giving you the choice between a blessing and a curse! [27]You will be blessed if you obey the commands of the LORD your God that I am giving you today. [28]You will receive a curse if you reject the commands of the LORD your God and turn from his way by worshiping foreign gods.

I ENJOY the Lord's blessing on my life by obeying his commands. (11:26)

[29]"When the LORD your God brings you into the land to possess it, you must pronounce a blessing from Mount Gerizim and a curse from Mount Ebal. [30](These two mountains are west of the Jordan River in the land of the Canaanites who live in the Jordan Valley,* near the town of Gilgal. They are located toward the west, not far from the oaks of Moreh.) [31]For you are about to cross the Jordan to occupy the land the LORD your God is giving you. When you are living in that land, [32]you must be careful to obey all the laws and regulations I am giving you today.

CHAPTER 12

The LORD's Chosen Place for Worship

"These are the laws and regulations you must obey as long as you live in the land the LORD, the God of your ancestors, is giving you.

I AM COMMITTED to obeying the Lord's commands as long as I live. (12:1)

[2]"When you drive out the nations that live there, you must destroy all the places where they worship their gods—high on the mountains, up on the hills, and under every green tree. [3]Break down their altars and smash their sacred pillars. Burn their Asherah poles and cut down their carved idols. Erase the names of their gods from those places!

[4]"Do not worship the LORD your God in the way these pagan peoples worship their gods. [5]Rather, you must seek the LORD your God at the place he himself will choose from among all the tribes for his name to be honored. [6]There you will bring to the LORD your burnt offerings, your sacrifices, your tithes, your special gifts, your offerings to fulfill a vow, your freewill offerings, and your offerings of the firstborn animals of your flocks and herds. [7]There you and your families will feast in the presence of the LORD your God, and you will rejoice in all you have accomplished because the LORD your God has blessed you.

I BELIEVE that aspects of the Lord's sacrificial requirements served as tangible reminders of his covenant with the Israelites. (12:6)

[8]"Today you are doing whatever you please, but that is not how it will be [9]when you arrive in the place of rest the LORD your God is giving you. [10]You will soon cross the Jordan River and live in the land the LORD your God is giving you as a special possession. When he gives you rest and security from all your enemies, [11]you must bring everything I command you—your burnt offerings, your sacrifices, your tithes, your special gifts, and your offerings to fulfill a vow—to the place the LORD your God will choose for his name to be honored. [12]You must celebrate there with your sons and daughters and all your servants in the presence of the LORD your God. And remember the Levites who live in your towns, for they will have no inheritance of land as their own. [13]Be careful not to sacrifice your burnt offerings just anywhere. [14]You may do so only at the place the LORD will choose within one of your tribal territories. There you must offer your burnt offerings and do everything I command you.

I BELIEVE the Israelite families were commanded to feast in the presence of the Lord and rejoice because of his evident blessings. (12:7)

I DO everything the Lord commands me to do. (12:14)

[15]"But you may butcher animals for meat in any town, wherever you want, just as you do now with gazelle and deer. You may eat as many animals as the LORD your God gives you. All of you, whether ceremonially clean or unclean,

11:24 Hebrew *to the western sea.*   11:30 Hebrew *the Arabah.*

may eat that meat. [16]The only restriction is that you are not to eat the blood. You must pour it out on the ground like water.

[17]"But your offerings must not be eaten at home—neither the tithe of your grain and new wine and olive oil, nor the firstborn of your flocks and herds, nor an offering to fulfill a vow, nor your freewill offerings, nor your special gifts. [18]You must eat these in the presence of the LORD your God at the place he will choose. Eat them there with your children, your servants, and the Levites who live in your towns, celebrating in the presence of the LORD your God in all you do. [19]Be very careful never to forget the Levites as long as you live in your land.

[20]"When the LORD your God enlarges your territory as he has promised, you may eat meat whenever you want. [21]It might happen that the place the LORD your God chooses for his name to be honored is a long way from your home. If so, you may butcher any of the cattle or sheep the LORD has given you, and you may eat the meat at your home as I have commanded you. [22]Anyone, whether ceremonially clean or unclean, may eat that meat, just as you do now with gazelle and deer. [23]The only restriction is never to eat the blood, for the blood is the life, and you must not eat the life with the meat. [24]Instead, pour out the blood on the ground like water. [25]Do not eat the blood; then all will go well with you and your children, because you will be doing what pleases the LORD. [26]Take your sacred gifts and your offerings given to fulfill a vow to the place the LORD chooses to dwell. [27]You must offer the meat and blood of your burnt offerings on the altar of the LORD your God. The blood of your other sacrifices must be poured out beside the altar of the LORD your God, but you may eat the meat. [28]Be careful to obey all my commands so that all will go well with you and your children, because you will be doing what pleases the LORD your God.

[29]"When the LORD your God destroys the nations and you drive them out and occupy their land, [30]do not be trapped into following their example in worshiping their gods. Do not say, 'How do these nations worship their gods? I want to follow their example.' [31]You must not do this to the LORD your God. These nations have committed many detestable acts that the LORD hates, all in the name of their gods. They have even burned their sons and daughters as sacrifices to their gods. [32]Carefully obey all the commands I give you. Do not add to them or subtract from them.

CHAPTER 13

A Warning against Idolatry

"Suppose there are prophets among you, or those who have dreams about the future, and they promise you signs or miracles, [2]and the predicted signs or miracles take place. If the prophets then say, 'Come, let us worship the gods of foreign nations,' [3]do not listen to them. The LORD your God is testing you to see if you love him with all your heart and soul. [4]Serve only the LORD your God and fear him alone. Obey his commands, listen to his voice, and cling to him. [5]The false prophets or dreamers who try to lead you astray must be put to death, for they encourage rebellion against the LORD your God, who brought you out of slavery in the land of Egypt. Since they try to keep you from following the LORD your God, you must execute them to remove the evil from among you.

[6]"Suppose your brother, son, daughter, beloved wife, or closest friend comes to you secretly and says, 'Let us go worship other gods'—gods that neither you nor your ancestors have known. [7]They might suggest that you worship the gods of peoples who live nearby or who come from the ends of the earth. [8]If they do this, do not give in or listen, and have no pity. Do not spare or protect them. [9]You must put them to death! You must be the one to initiate the execution; then all the people must join in. [10]Stone the guilty ones

I BELIEVE the Israelite households were commanded to offer their sacrifices, celebrate, and feast in the presence of the Lord with the Levites. (12:18)

I BELIEVE the Lord loved the Israelites and instructed them to obey all his commands so that all would go well with them. (12:28)

I REJECT any so-called "prophet" who advocates pagan worship, no matter how persuasive that person may be. (13:2)

I LOVE the Lord my God with all my heart and soul. (13:3)

I SERVE the Lord my God and fear him alone—I obey his commands, and I listen to his voice and cling to him alone. (13:4)

to death because they have tried to draw you away from the LORD your God, who rescued you from the land of Egypt, the place of slavery. ¹¹Then all Israel will hear about it and be afraid, and such wickedness will never again be done among you.

¹²"Suppose you hear in one of the towns the LORD your God is giving you ¹³that some worthless rabble among you have led their fellow citizens astray by encouraging them to worship foreign gods. ¹⁴In such cases, you must examine the facts carefully. If you find it is true and can prove that such a detestable act has occurred among you, ¹⁵you must attack that town and completely destroy* all its inhabitants, as well as all the livestock. ¹⁶Then you must pile all the plunder in the middle of the street and burn it. Put the entire town to the torch as a burnt offering to the LORD your God. That town must remain a ruin forever; it may never be rebuilt. ¹⁷Keep none of the plunder that has been set apart for destruction. Then the LORD will turn from his fierce anger and be merciful to you. He will have compassion on you and make you a great nation, just as he solemnly promised your ancestors.

¹⁸"The LORD your God will be merciful only if you obey him and keep all the commands I am giving you today, doing what is pleasing to him.

CHAPTER 14

Ceremonially Clean and Unclean Animals

"Since you are the people of the LORD your God, never cut yourselves or shave the hair above your foreheads for the sake of the dead. ²You have been set apart as holy to the LORD your God, and he has chosen you to be his own special treasure from all the nations of the earth.

³"You must not eat animals that are ceremonially unclean. ⁴These are the animals* you may eat: the ox, the sheep, the goat, ⁵the deer, the gazelle, the roebuck, the wild goat, the ibex, the antelope, and the mountain sheep.

⁶"Any animal that has split hooves and chews the cud may be eaten, ⁷but if the animal doesn't have both, it may not be eaten. So you may not eat the camel, the hare, or the rock badger.* They chew the cud but do not have split hooves. ⁸And the pig may not be eaten, for though it has split hooves, it does not chew the cud. All these animals are ceremonially unclean for you. You may not eat or even touch the dead bodies of such animals.

⁹"As for marine animals, you may eat whatever has both fins and scales. ¹⁰You may not, however, eat marine animals that do not have both fins and scales. They are ceremonially unclean for you.

¹¹"You may eat any bird that is ceremonially clean. ¹²These are the birds you may not eat: the eagle, the vulture, the osprey, ¹³the buzzard, kites of all kinds, ¹⁴ravens of all kinds, ¹⁵the ostrich, the nighthawk, the seagull, hawks of all kinds, ¹⁶the little owl, the great owl, the white owl, ¹⁷the pelican, the carrion vulture, the cormorant, ¹⁸the stork, herons of all kinds, the hoopoe, and the bat.

¹⁹"All flying insects are ceremonially unclean for you and may not be eaten. ²⁰But you may eat any winged creature that is ceremonially clean.

²¹"Do not eat anything that has died a natural death. You may give it to a foreigner living among you, or you may sell it to a foreigner. But do not eat it yourselves, for you are set apart as holy to the LORD your God.

"Do not boil a young goat in its mother's milk.

The Giving of Tithes

²²"You must set aside a tithe of your crops—one-tenth of all the crops you harvest each year. ²³Bring this tithe to the place the LORD your God chooses

I BELIEVE the Lord promised to be merciful to the Israelites if they obeyed all his commands and did what pleased him. (13:18)

I HONOR the Lord my God by not defacing my body or cutting my hair in pagan ways. (14:1)

I BELIEVE that the Lord made a great distinction between foods that were ceremonially clean and unclean but also that the Lord no longer makes such distinctions. (14:3)

I BELIEVE the Lord wanted the Israelites to be ceremonially clean, free from the defilement of any unclean creatures, but also that touching or eating such creatures no longer makes anyone unclean. (14:6)

I BELIEVE the Israelite families were commanded to fear the Lord and offer a tithe of everything in the presence of the Lord. (14:22)

13:15 The Hebrew term used here refers to the complete consecration of things or people to the LORD, either by destroying them or by giving them as an offering; also in 13:17. 14:4 The identification of some of the animals and birds listed in this chapter is uncertain. 14:7 Or *coney,* or *hyrax.*

for his name to be honored, and eat it there in his presence. This applies to your tithes of grain, new wine, olive oil, and the firstborn males of your flocks and herds. The purpose of tithing is to teach you always to fear the LORD your God. ²⁴Now the place the LORD your God chooses for his name to be honored might be a long way from your home. ²⁵If so, you may sell the tithe portion of your crops and herds and take the money to the place the LORD your God chooses. ²⁶When you arrive, use the money to buy anything you want—an ox, a sheep, some wine, or beer. Then feast there in the presence of the LORD your God and celebrate with your household. ²⁷And do not forget the Levites in your community, for they have no inheritance as you do.

²⁸"At the end of every third year bring the tithe of all your crops and store it in the nearest town. ²⁹Give it to the Levites, who have no inheritance among you, as well as to the foreigners living among you, the orphans, and the widows in your towns, so they can eat and be satisfied. Then the LORD your God will bless you in all your work.

CHAPTER 15

Release for Debtors

"At the end of every seventh year you must cancel your debts. ²This is how it must be done. Creditors must cancel the loans they have made to their fellow Israelites. They must not demand payment from their neighbors or relatives, for the LORD's time of release has arrived. ³This release from debt, however, applies only to your fellow Israelites—not to the foreigners living among you. ⁴There should be no poor among you, for the LORD your God will greatly bless you in the land he is giving you as a special possession. ⁵You will receive this blessing if you carefully obey the commands of the LORD your God that I am giving you today. ⁶The LORD your God will bless you as he has promised. You will lend money to many nations but will never need to borrow! You will rule many nations, but they will not rule over you!

⁷"But if there are any poor people in your towns when you arrive in the land the LORD your God is giving you, do not be hard-hearted or tightfisted toward them. ⁸Instead, be generous and lend them whatever they need. ⁹Do not be mean-spirited and refuse someone a loan because the year of release is close at hand. If you refuse to make the loan and the needy person cries out to the LORD, you will be considered guilty of sin. ¹⁰Give freely without begrudging it, and the LORD your God will bless you in everything you do. ¹¹There will always be some among you who are poor. That is why I am commanding you to share your resources freely with the poor and with other Israelites in need.

Release for Hebrew Slaves

¹²"If an Israelite man or woman voluntarily becomes your servant and serves you for six years, in the seventh year you must set that servant free.

¹³"When you release a male servant, do not send him away empty-handed. ¹⁴Give him a generous farewell gift from your flock, your threshing floor, and your winepress. Share with him some of the bounty with which the LORD your God has blessed you. ¹⁵Remember that you were slaves in the land of Egypt and the LORD your God redeemed you! That is why I am giving you this command. ¹⁶But suppose your servant says, 'I will not leave you,' because he loves you and your family, and he is well off with you. ¹⁷In that case, take an awl and push it through his earlobe into the door. After that, he will be your servant for life.

"You must do the same for your female servants.

¹⁸"Do not consider it a hardship when you release your servants. Remember that for six years they have given you the services worth double

I BELIEVE the Israelite households could sell their tithe, travel to the Lord's appointed city, purchase whatever they wanted, and then feast in the Lord's presence with the Levities. (14:24)

I BELIEVE the Israelites were to give a tithe to the Levites every third year. (14:28)

I BELIEVE the Lord would have greatly prospered the Israelites so that none would have been poor if they would have obeyed his commands carefully. (15:4)

I AM NOT HARD-HEARTED or tightfisted toward the poor in my community. (15:7)

I JOIN hands with other believers to lend to the poor in our community and show generosity. (15:8)

I GIVE cheerfully. (15:10)

I AM GENEROUS to my employees, even when they leave my service. (15:13)

the wages of hired workers, and the LORD your God will bless you in all you do.

Sacrificing Firstborn Male Animals
[19] "You must set aside for the LORD your God all the firstborn males from your flocks and herds. Do not use the firstborn of your herds to work your fields, and do not shear the firstborn of your flocks. [20]Instead, you and your family must eat these animals in the presence of the LORD your God each year at the place he chooses. [21]But if this firstborn animal has any defect, such as being lame or blind, or if anything else is wrong with it, you must not sacrifice it to the LORD your God. [22]Instead, use it for food for your family at home. Anyone may eat it, whether ceremonially clean or unclean, just as anyone may eat a gazelle or deer. [23]But do not eat the blood. You must pour it out on the ground like water.

CHAPTER 16

Passover and the Festival of Unleavened Bread
"In honor of the LORD your God, always celebrate the Passover at the proper time in early spring,* for that was when the LORD your God brought you out of Egypt by night. [2]Your Passover sacrifice may be from either the flock or the herd, and it must be sacrificed to the LORD your God at the place he chooses for his name to be honored. [3]Eat it with bread made without yeast. For seven days eat only bread made without yeast, as you did when you escaped from Egypt in such a hurry. Eat this bread—the bread of suffering—so that you will remember the day you departed from Egypt as long as you live. [4]Let no yeast be found in any house throughout your land for seven days. And do not let any of the meat of the Passover lamb remain until the next morning.

[5]"The Passover must not be eaten in the towns that the LORD your God is giving you. [6]It must be offered at the place the LORD your God will choose for his name to be honored. Sacrifice it there as the sun goes down on the anniversary of your exodus from Egypt. [7]Roast the lamb and eat it in the place the LORD your God chooses. Then go back to your tents the next morning. [8]For the next six days you may not eat bread made with yeast. On the seventh day the people must assemble before the LORD your God, and no work may be done on that day.

The Festival of Harvest
[9]"Count off seven weeks from the beginning of your grain harvest. [10]Then you must celebrate the Festival of Harvest* to honor the LORD your God. Bring him a freewill offering in proportion to the blessings you have received from him. [11]It is a time to celebrate before the LORD your God at the place he chooses for his name to be honored. Celebrate with your whole family, all your servants, the Levites from your towns, and the foreigners, orphans, and widows who live among you. [12]Remember that you were slaves in Egypt, so be careful to obey all these laws.

The Festival of Shelters
[13]"Another celebration, the Festival of Shelters, must be observed for seven days at the end of the harvest season, after the grain has been threshed and the grapes have been pressed. [14]This festival will be a happy time of rejoicing with your family, your servants, and with the Levites, foreigners, orphans, and widows from your towns. [15]For seven days celebrate this festival to honor the LORD your God at the place he chooses, for it is the LORD your God who gives you bountiful harvests and blesses all your work. This festival will be a time of great joy for all.

I CELEBRATE God's provision with my whole family and other believers. (16:11)

I NEVER FORGET what God has delivered me from. (16:12)

I REJOICE in the Lord with my whole family and other believers regarding all that the Lord has given me. (16:14)

16:1 Hebrew *in the month of Abib.* This month of the Hebrew lunar calendar usually occurs in March and April.
16:10 Or *Festival of Weeks;* also in 16:16.

¹⁶"Each year every man in Israel must celebrate these three festivals: the Festival of Unleavened Bread, the Festival of Harvest, and the Festival of Shelters. They must appear before the LORD your God at the place he chooses on each of these occasions, and they must bring a gift to the LORD. ¹⁷All must give as they are able, according to the blessings given to them by the LORD your God.

Justice for the People

¹⁸"Appoint judges and officials for each of your tribes in all the towns the LORD your God is giving you. They will judge the people fairly throughout the land. ¹⁹You must never twist justice or show partiality. Never accept a bribe, for bribes blind the eyes of the wise and corrupt the decisions of the godly. ²⁰Let true justice prevail, so you may live and occupy the land that the LORD your God is giving you.

²¹"You must never set up an Asherah pole beside the altar of the LORD your God. ²²And never set up sacred pillars for worship, for the LORD your God hates them.

CHAPTER 17

"Never sacrifice a sick or defective ox or sheep to the LORD your God, for he detests such gifts.

²"Suppose a man or woman among you, in one of your towns that the LORD your God is giving you, has done evil in the sight of the LORD your God and has violated the covenant ³by serving other gods or by worshiping the sun, the moon, or any of the forces of heaven, which I have strictly forbidden. ⁴When you hear about it, investigate the matter thoroughly. If it is true that this detestable thing has been done in Israel, ⁵then that man or woman must be taken to the gates of the town and stoned to death. ⁶But never put a person to death on the testimony of only one witness. There must always be at least two or three witnesses. ⁷The witnesses must throw the first stones, and then all the people will join in. In this way, you will purge all evil from among you.

⁸"Suppose a case arises in a local court that is too hard for you to decide—for instance, whether someone is guilty of murder or only of manslaughter, or a difficult lawsuit, or a case involving different kinds of assault. Take such cases to the place the LORD your God will choose, ⁹where the Levitical priests and the judge on duty will hear the case and decide what to do. ¹⁰The decision they make at the place the LORD chooses will always stand. You must do exactly what they say. ¹¹After they have interpreted the law and reached a verdict, the sentence they impose must be fully executed; do not modify it in any way. ¹²Anyone arrogant enough to reject the verdict of the judge or of the priest who represents the LORD your God must be put to death. Such evil must be purged from Israel. ¹³Then everyone will hear about it and be afraid to act so arrogantly.

Guidelines for a King

¹⁴"You will soon arrive in the land the LORD your God is giving you, and you will conquer it and settle there. Then you may begin to think, 'We ought to have a king like the other nations around us.' ¹⁵If this happens, be sure that you select as king the man the LORD your God chooses. You must appoint a fellow Israelite, not a foreigner. ¹⁶The king must not build up a large stable of horses for himself, and he must never send his people to Egypt to buy horses there, for the LORD has told you, 'You must never return to Egypt.' ¹⁷The king must not take many wives for himself, because they will lead him away from the LORD. And he must not accumulate vast amounts of wealth in silver and gold for himself.

¹⁸"When he sits on the throne as king, he must copy these laws on a scroll for himself in the presence of the Levitical priests. ¹⁹He must always keep this

---

I GIVE to the Lord as I am able and as he blesses me. (16:17)

I DO NOT ACCEPT a bribe or show partiality in judgment. (16:19)

I DO NOT DEPEND solely on my own judgment for difficult decisions. (17:8)

I BELIEVE the Lord expected the Israelites to follow the judgments of the priests and judges explicitly. (17:12)

I BELIEVE the Lord gave the Israelites guidelines for their king long before they ever crowned one. (17:14)

I READ God's Word daily so that I will obey him completely. (17:19) copy of the law with him and read it daily as long as he lives. That way he will learn to fear the LORD his God by obeying all the terms of this law. ²⁰This regular reading will prevent him from becoming proud and acting as if he is above his fellow citizens. It will also prevent him from turning away from these commands in the smallest way. This will ensure that he and his descendants will reign for many generations in Israel.

CHAPTER 18

Gifts for the Priests and Levites

"Remember that the Levitical priests and the rest of the tribe of Levi will not be given an inheritance of land like the other tribes in Israel. Instead, the priests and Levites will eat from the offerings given to the LORD by fire, for that is their inheritance. ²They will have no inheritance of their own among the Israelites. The LORD himself is their inheritance, just as he promised them.

³"These are the parts the priests may claim as their share from the oxen and sheep that the people bring as offerings: the shoulder, the cheeks, and the stomach. ⁴You must also give to the priests the first share of the grain, the new wine, the olive oil, and the wool at shearing time. ⁵For the LORD your God chose the tribe of Levi out of all your tribes to minister in the LORD's name forever.

⁶"Any Levite who so desires may come from any town in Israel, from wherever he is living, to the place the LORD chooses. ⁷He may minister there in the name of the LORD his God, just like his fellow Levites who are serving the LORD there. ⁸He may eat his share of the sacrifices and offerings, even if he has a private source of income.

A Call to Holy Living

⁹"When you arrive in the land the LORD your God is giving you, be very careful not to imitate the detestable customs of the nations living there. ¹⁰For example, never sacrifice your son or daughter as a burnt offering.* And do not let your people practice fortune-telling or sorcery, or allow them to interpret omens, or engage in witchcraft, ¹¹or cast spells, or function as mediums or psychics, or call forth the spirits of the dead. ¹²Anyone who does these things is an object of horror and disgust to the LORD. It is because the other nations have done these things that the LORD your God will drive them out ahead of you. ¹³You must be blameless before the LORD your God. ¹⁴The people you are about to displace consult with sorcerers and fortune-tellers, but the LORD your God forbids you to do such things.

True and False Prophets

¹⁵"The LORD your God will raise up for you a prophet like me from among your fellow Israelites, and you must listen to that prophet. ¹⁶For this is what you yourselves requested of the LORD your God when you were assembled at Mount Sinai.* You begged that you might never again have to listen to the voice of the LORD your God or see this blazing fire for fear you would die.

¹⁷"Then the LORD said to me, 'Fine, I will do as they have requested. ¹⁸I will raise up a prophet like you from among their fellow Israelites. I will tell that prophet what to say, and he will tell the people everything I command him. ¹⁹I will personally deal with anyone who will not listen to the messages the prophet proclaims on my behalf. ²⁰But any prophet who claims to give a message from another god or who falsely claims to speak for me must die.' ²¹You may wonder, 'How will we know whether the prophecy is from the LORD or not?' ²²If the prophet predicts something in the LORD's name and it does not

I REMEMBER that the Levites received no land inheritance because the Lord was their inheritance. (18:1)

I DO NOT IMITATE the detestable customs of pagan nations. (18:9)

I ABHOR occult practices, such as fortune-telling and witchcraft. (18:10)

I BELIEVE the Lord raised up another Prophet—the Lord Jesus Christ—just as he said he would. (18:15)

I LISTEN to messages that are truly from God. (18:19)

I DO NOT PAY attention to prophets who speak on their own initiative and fail to prophesy correctly. (18:22)

18:10 Or *never make your son or daughter pass through the fire.*   18:16 Hebrew *Horeb,* another name for Sinai.

happen, the LORD did not give the message. That prophet has spoken on his own and need not be feared.

CHAPTER 19

Cities of Refuge

"The LORD your God will soon destroy the nations whose land he is giving you, and you will displace them and settle in their towns and homes. ²Then you must set apart three cities of refuge in the land the LORD your God is giving you to occupy. ³Divide the land the LORD your God is giving you into three districts, with one of these cities in each district. Keep the roads to these cities in good repair so that anyone who has killed someone can flee there for safety.

⁴"If someone accidentally kills a neighbor without harboring any previous hatred, the slayer may flee to any of these cities and be safe. ⁵For example, suppose someone goes into the forest with a neighbor to cut wood. And suppose one of them swings an ax and the ax head flies off the handle, killing the other person. In such cases, the slayer could flee to one of the cities of refuge and be safe. ⁶If the distance to the nearest city of refuge was too far, an enraged avenger might be able to chase down and kill the person who caused the death. The slayer would die, even though there was no death sentence and the first death had been an accident. ⁷That is why I am commanding you to set aside three cities of refuge.

⁸"If the LORD your God enlarges your territory, as he solemnly promised your ancestors, and gives you all the land he promised them, ⁹you must designate three additional cities of refuge. (He will give you this land if you obey all the commands I have given you—if you always love the LORD your God and walk in his ways.) ¹⁰That way you will prevent the death of innocent people in the land the LORD your God is giving you as a special possession, and you will not be held responsible for murder.

¹¹"But suppose someone hates a neighbor and deliberately ambushes and murders that neighbor and then escapes to one of the cities of refuge. ¹²In that case, the leaders of the murderer's hometown must have the murderer brought back from the city of refuge and handed over to the dead person's avenger to be killed. ¹³Do not feel sorry for that murderer! Purge the guilt of murder from Israel so all may go well with you.

Concern for Justice

¹⁴"When you arrive in the land the LORD your God is giving you as a special possession, never steal someone's land by moving the boundary markers your ancestors set up to mark their property.

¹⁵"Never convict anyone of a crime on the testimony of just one witness. The facts of the case must be established by the testimony of two or three witnesses. ¹⁶If a malicious witness comes forward and accuses someone of a crime, ¹⁷then both the accuser and accused must appear before the priests and judges who are on duty before the LORD. ¹⁸They must be closely questioned, and if the accuser is found to be lying, ¹⁹the accuser will receive the punishment intended for the accused. In this way, you will cleanse such evil from among you. ²⁰Those who hear about it will be afraid to do such an evil thing again. ²¹You must never show pity! Your rule should be life for life, eye for eye, tooth for tooth, hand for hand, foot for foot.

CHAPTER 20

Regulations concerning War

"When you go out to fight your enemies and you face horses and chariots and an army greater than your own, do not be afraid. The LORD your God, who brought you safely out of Egypt, is with you! ²Before you go into battle,

I BELIEVE the Lord provided cities of refuge to protect anyone who killed another person accidentally. (19:4)

I BELIEVE the Lord promised to give the Israelites much land if they obeyed all the commands he gave them, always loved him, and walked in his ways. (19:9)

I DO NOT COME to a conclusion about a difficult case without considering the testimony of two or more witnesses. (19:15)

I BELIEVE the Lord requires impartiality and appropriate punishment fitting the crime. (19:21)

I AM NOT AFRAID when I face an enemy, because the Lord is my God who rescues me. (20:1)

the priest will come forward to speak with the troops. ³He will say, 'Listen to me, all you men of Israel! Do not be afraid as you go out to fight today! Do not lose heart or panic. ⁴For the LORD your God is going with you! He will fight for you against your enemies, and he will give you victory!'

⁵"Then the officers of the army will address the troops and say, 'Has anyone just built a new house but not yet dedicated it? If so, go home! You might be killed in the battle, and someone else would dedicate your house! ⁶Has anyone just planted a vineyard but not yet eaten any of its fruit? If so, go home! You might die in battle, and someone else would eat from it! ⁷Has anyone just become engaged? Well, go home and get married! You might die in the battle, and someone else would marry your fiancée.' ⁸Then the officers will also say, 'Is anyone terrified? If you are, go home before you frighten anyone else.' ⁹When the officers have finished saying this to their troops, they will announce the names of the unit commanders.

¹⁰"As you approach a town to attack it, first offer its people terms for peace. ¹¹If they accept your terms and open the gates to you, then all the people inside will serve you in forced labor. ¹²But if they refuse to make peace and prepare to fight, you must attack the town. ¹³When the LORD your God hands it over to you, kill every man in the town. ¹⁴But you may keep for yourselves all the women, children, livestock, and other plunder. You may enjoy the spoils of your enemies that the LORD your God has given you. ¹⁵But these instructions apply only to distant towns, not to the towns of nations nearby.

¹⁶"As for the towns of the nations the LORD your God is giving you as a special possession, destroy every living thing in them. ¹⁷You must completely destroy* the Hittites, Amorites, Canaanites, Perizzites, Hivites, and Jebusites, just as the LORD your God has commanded you. ¹⁸This will keep the people of the land from teaching you their detestable customs in the worship of their gods, which would cause you to sin deeply against the LORD your God.

¹⁹"When you are besieging a town and the war drags on, do not destroy the trees. Eat the fruit, but do not cut down the trees. They are not enemies that need to be attacked! ²⁰But you may cut down trees that you know are not valuable for food. Use them to make the equipment you need to besiege the town until it falls.

CHAPTER 21

Cleansing for Unsolved Murder

"Suppose someone is found murdered in a field in the land the LORD your God is giving you, and you don't know who committed the murder. ²In such cases, your leaders and judges must determine which town is nearest the body. ³Then the leaders of that town must select a young cow that has never been trained or yoked to a plow. ⁴They must lead it to a valley that is neither plowed nor planted with a stream running through it. There they must break the cow's neck. ⁵The Levitical priests must go there also, for the LORD your God has chosen them to minister before him and to pronounce blessings in the LORD's name. And they are to decide all lawsuits and punishments.

⁶"The leaders of the town nearest the body must wash their hands over the young cow whose neck was broken. ⁷Then they must say, 'Our hands did not shed this blood, nor did we see it happen. ⁸O LORD, forgive your people Israel whom you have redeemed. Do not charge your people Israel with the guilt of murdering an innocent person.' Then they will be absolved of the guilt of this person's blood. ⁹By following these instructions and doing what is right in the LORD's sight, you will cleanse the guilt of murder from your community.

I ENCOURAGE others to trust the Lord. (20:3)

I BELIEVE the Lord allowed Israelite men to be excused from battle and go home in certain instances. (20:5)

I BELIEVE the Lord required the Israelites to first offer terms of peace to distant towns. (20:10)

I BELIEVE the Lord required the Israelites to destroy the pagan peoples within the Promised Land because the pagans would teach the Israelites to rebel against God. (20:18)

I BELIEVE the Lord expected the Israelites to be pure. (21:9)

20:17 The Hebrew term used here refers to the complete consecration of things or people to the LORD, either by destroying them or by giving them as an offering.

Marriage to a Captive Woman

[10]"Suppose you go to war against your enemies and the LORD your God hands them over to you and you take captives. [11]And suppose you see among the captives a beautiful woman, and you are attracted to her and want to marry her. [12]If this happens, you may take her to your home, where she must shave her head, cut her fingernails, [13]and change all her clothes. Then she must remain in your home for a full month, mourning for her father and mother. After that you may marry her. [14]But if you marry her and then decide you do not like her, you must let her go free. You may not sell her or treat her as a slave, for you have humiliated her.

Rights of the Firstborn

[15]"Suppose a man has two wives, but he loves one and not the other, and both have given him sons. And suppose the firstborn son is the son of the wife he does not love. [16]When the man divides the inheritance, he may not give the larger inheritance to his younger son, the son of the wife he loves. [17]He must give the customary double portion to his oldest son, who represents the strength of his father's manhood and who owns the rights of the firstborn son, even though he is the son of the wife his father does not love.

Dealing with a Rebellious Son

[18]"Suppose a man has a stubborn, rebellious son who will not obey his father or mother, even though they discipline him. [19]In such cases, the father and mother must take the son before the leaders of the town. [20]They must declare: 'This son of ours is stubborn and rebellious and refuses to obey. He is a worthless drunkard.' [21]Then all the men of the town must stone him to death. In this way, you will cleanse this evil from among you, and all Israel will hear about it and be afraid.

Various Regulations

[22]"If someone has committed a crime worthy of death and is executed and then hanged on a tree, [23]the body must never remain on the tree overnight. You must bury the body that same day, for anyone hanging on a tree is cursed of God. Do not defile the land the LORD your God is giving you as a special possession.

CHAPTER 22

"If you see your neighbor's ox or sheep wandering away, don't pretend not to see it. Take it back to its owner. [2]If it does not belong to someone nearby or you don't know who the owner is, keep it until the owner comes looking for it; then return it. [3]Do the same if you find your neighbor's donkey, clothing, or anything else your neighbor loses. Don't pretend you did not see it.

[4]"If you see your neighbor's ox or donkey lying on the road, do not look the other way. Go and help your neighbor get it to its feet!

[5]"A woman must not wear men's clothing, and a man must not wear women's clothing. The LORD your God detests people who do this.

[6]"If you find a bird's nest on the ground or in a tree and there are young ones or eggs in it with the mother sitting in the nest, do not take the mother with the young. [7]You may take the young, but let the mother go, so you may prosper and enjoy a long life.

[8]"Every new house you build must have a barrier around the edge of its flat rooftop. That way you will not bring the guilt of bloodshed on your household if someone falls from the roof.

[9]"Do not plant any other crop between the rows of your vineyard. If you

I DO NOT REBEL against the discipline from my parents in my youth. (21:18)

I BELIEVE the Lord expected the Israelites to be pure and to learn from the sins and punishments of others. (21:21)

I BELIEVE anyone hanging on a tree was cursed of God. (21:23)

I DO NOT LOOK the other way when I see a need but go and help instead. (22:4)

I TREAT God's creatures carefully and responsibly. (22:6)

I MAKE my home a safe place for others. (22:8)

do, you are forbidden to use either the grapes from the vineyard or the produce of the other crop.

¹⁰"Do not plow with an ox and a donkey harnessed together.

¹¹"Do not wear clothing made of wool and linen woven together.

¹²"You must put tassels on the four corners of your cloaks.

Regulations for Sexual Purity

¹³"Suppose a man marries a woman and, after sleeping with her, changes his mind about her ¹⁴and falsely accuses her of having slept with another man. He might say, 'I discovered she was not a virgin when I married her.' ¹⁵If the man does this, the woman's father and mother must bring the proof of her virginity to the leaders of the town. ¹⁶Her father must tell them, 'I gave my daughter to this man to be his wife, and now he has turned against her. ¹⁷He has accused her of shameful things, claiming that she was not a virgin when he married her. But here is the proof of my daughter's virginity.' Then they must spread the cloth before the judges. ¹⁸The judges must then punish the man. ¹⁹ They will fine him one hundred pieces of silver,* for he falsely accused a virgin of Israel. The payment will be made to the woman's father. The woman will then remain the man's wife, and he may never divorce her.

²⁰"But suppose the man's accusations are true, and her virginity could not be proved. ²¹In such cases, the judges must take the girl to the door of her father's home, and the men of the town will stone her to death. She has committed a disgraceful crime in Israel by being promiscuous while living in her parents' home. Such evil must be cleansed from among you.

²²"If a man is discovered committing adultery, both he and the other man's wife must be killed. In this way, the evil will be cleansed from Israel.

²³"Suppose a man meets a young woman, a virgin who is engaged to be married, and he has sexual intercourse with her. If this happens within a town, ²⁴you must take both of them to the gates of the town and stone them to death. The woman is guilty because she did not scream for help. The man must die because he violated another man's wife. In this way, you will cleanse the land of evil.

²⁵"But if the man meets the engaged woman out in the country, and he rapes her, then only the man should die. ²⁶Do nothing to the young woman; she has committed no crime worthy of death. This case is similar to that of someone who attacks and murders a neighbor. ²⁷Since the man raped her out in the country, it must be assumed that she screamed, but there was no one to rescue her.

²⁸"If a man is caught in the act of raping a young woman who is not engaged, ²⁹he must pay fifty pieces of silver* to her father. Then he must marry the young woman because he violated her, and he will never be allowed to divorce her.

³⁰"A man must not have intercourse with his father's wife, for this would violate his father.

CHAPTER 23

Regulations concerning Worship

"If a man's testicles are crushed or his penis is cut off, he may not be included in the assembly of the LORD.

²"Those of illegitimate birth and their descendants for ten generations may not be included in the assembly of the LORD.

³"No Ammonites or Moabites, or any of their descendants for ten generations, may be included in the assembly of the LORD. ⁴These nations did not welcome you with food and water when you came out of Egypt. Instead, they

---

I MAKE reminders for myself of God's commands. (22:12)

I DO NOT FALSELY ACCUSE my spouse. (22:19)

I CRY OUT for help if I am being attacked or abused. (22:24)

I BELIEVE the Lord gave instructions for dealing gently with a woman raped in a deserted place. (22:26)

I MAKE restitution and take responsibility for my sexual wrongs toward others. (22:28)

I ABHOR incest. (22:30)

22:19 Hebrew *100 shekels of silver*, about 2.5 pounds or 1.1 kilograms in weight.   22:29 Hebrew *50 shekels of silver*, about 1.25 pounds or 570 grams in weight.

I BELIEVE the Lord
turned Balaam's
intended curse into a
blessing because the
Lord loved the
Israelites. (23:5)

tried to hire Balaam son of Beor from Pethor in Aram-naharaim* to curse you. ⁵(But the LORD your God would not listen to Balaam. He turned the intended curse into a blessing because the LORD your God loves you.) ⁶You must never, as long as you live, try to help the Ammonites or the Moabites in any way.

⁷"Do not detest the Edomites or the Egyptians, because the Edomites are your relatives, and you lived as foreigners among the Egyptians. ⁸The third generation of Egyptians who came with you from Egypt may enter the assembly of the LORD.

I BELIEVE the Lord
required the Israelites
to follow his
instructions about
ceremonial cleanness
even during times of
war. (23:9)

I BELIEVE the Lord
required ceremonial
cleanliness throughout
the Israelite army's
camp, for the Lord
was present among
them. (23:14)

I HELP those fleeing
oppression. (23:15)

I ABHOR prostitution.
(23:17)

Miscellaneous Regulations

⁹"When you go to war against your enemies, stay away from everything impure.

¹⁰"Any man who becomes ceremonially defiled because of a nocturnal emission must leave the camp and stay away all day. ¹¹Toward evening he must bathe himself, and at sunset he may return to the camp.

¹²"Mark off an area outside the camp for a latrine. ¹³Each of you must have a spade as part of your equipment. Whenever you relieve yourself, you must dig a hole with the spade and cover the excrement. ¹⁴The camp must be holy, for the LORD your God moves around in your camp to protect you and to defeat your enemies. He must not see any shameful thing among you, or he might turn away from you.

¹⁵"If slaves should escape from their masters and take refuge with you, do not force them to return. ¹⁶Let them live among you in whatever town they choose, and do not oppress them.

¹⁷"No Israelite man or woman may ever become a temple prostitute. ¹⁸Do not bring to the house of the LORD your God any offering from the earnings of a prostitute, whether a man or a woman, for both are detestable to the LORD your God.

¹⁹"Do not charge interest on the loans you make to a fellow Israelite, whether it is money, food, or anything else that may be loaned with interest. ²⁰You may charge interest to foreigners, but not to Israelites, so the LORD your God may bless you in everything you do in the land you are about to enter and occupy.

I FULFILL my vows to
the Lord promptly.
(23:21)

I GIVE careful
consideration before
making a vow to the
Lord and do not rashly
make promises I
cannot keep. (23:22)

I DO NOT TAKE
advantage of my
neighbor's goods.
(23:24)

²¹"When you make a vow to the LORD your God, be prompt in doing whatever you promised him. For the LORD your God demands that you promptly fulfill all your vows. If you don't, you will be guilty of sin. ²²However, it is not a sin to refrain from making a vow. ²³But once you have voluntarily made a vow, be careful to do as you have said, for you have made a vow to the LORD your God.

²⁴"You may eat your fill of grapes from your neighbor's vineyard, but do not take any away in a basket. ²⁵And you may pluck a few heads of your neighbor's grain by hand, but you may not harvest it with a sickle.

CHAPTER 24

"Suppose a man marries a woman but later discovers something about her that is shameful. So he writes her a letter of divorce, gives it to her, and sends her away. ²If she then leaves and marries another man ³and the second husband also divorces her or dies, ⁴the former husband may not marry her again, for she has been defiled. That would be detestable to the LORD. You must not bring guilt upon the land the LORD your God is giving you as a special possession.

⁵"A newly married man must not be drafted into the army or given any

23:4 Aram-naharaim means "Aram of the two rivers," thought to have been located between the Euphrates and Balih Rivers in northwestern Mesopotamia.

other special responsibilities. He must be free to be at home for one year, bringing happiness to the wife he has married.

⁶"It is wrong to take a pair of millstones, or even just the upper millstone, as a pledge, for the owner uses it to make a living.

⁷"If anyone kidnaps a fellow Israelite and treats him as a slave or sells him, the kidnapper must die. You must cleanse the evil from among you.

⁸"Watch all contagious skin diseases* carefully and follow the instructions of the Levitical priests; obey the commands I have given them. ⁹Remember what the LORD your God did to Miriam as you were coming from Egypt.

¹⁰"If you lend anything to your neighbor, do not enter your neighbor's house to claim the security. ¹¹Stand outside and the owner will bring it out to you. ¹²If your neighbor is poor and has only a cloak to give as security, do not keep the cloak overnight. ¹³Return the cloak to its owner by sunset so your neighbor can sleep in it and bless you. And the LORD your God will count it as a righteous act.

¹⁴"Never take advantage of poor laborers, whether fellow Israelites or foreigners living in your towns. ¹⁵Pay them their wages each day before sunset because they are poor and are counting on it. Otherwise they might cry out to the LORD against you, and it would be counted against you as sin.

¹⁶"Parents must not be put to death for the sins of their children, nor the children for the sins of their parents. Those worthy of death must be executed for their own crimes.

¹⁷"True justice must be given to foreigners living among you and to orphans, and you must never accept a widow's garment in pledge of her debt. ¹⁸Always remember that you were slaves in Egypt and that the LORD your God redeemed you. That is why I have given you this command.

¹⁹"When you are harvesting your crops and forget to bring in a bundle of grain from your field, don't go back to get it. Leave it for the foreigners, orphans, and widows. Then the LORD your God will bless you in all you do. ²⁰When you beat the olives from your olive trees, don't go over the boughs twice. Leave some of the olives for the foreigners, orphans, and widows. ²¹This also applies to the grapes in your vineyard. Do not glean the vines after they are picked, but leave any remaining grapes for the foreigners, orphans, and widows. ²²Remember that you were slaves in the land of Egypt. That is why I am giving you this command.

CHAPTER 25

"Suppose two people take a dispute to court, and the judges declare that one is right and the other is wrong. ²If the person in the wrong is sentenced to be flogged, the judge will command him to lie down and be beaten in his presence with the number of lashes appropriate to the crime. ³No more than forty lashes may ever be given; more than forty lashes would publicly humiliate your neighbor.

⁴"Do not keep an ox from eating as it treads out the grain.

⁵"If two brothers are living together on the same property and one of them dies without a son, his widow must not marry outside the family. Instead, her husband's brother must marry her and fulfill the duties of a brother-in-law. ⁶The first son she bears to him will be counted as the son of the dead brother, so that his name will not be forgotten in Israel. ⁷But if the dead man's brother refuses to marry the widow, she must go to the town gate and say to the leaders there, 'My husband's brother refuses to preserve his brother's name in Israel—he refuses to marry me.' ⁸The leaders of the town will then summon him and try to reason with him. If he still insists that he doesn't want to marry her, ⁹the widow must walk over to him in the presence of the leaders,

I DO NOT ASK for collateral that will hinder someone from working. (24:6)

See Miriam's profile (page 87) at Exodus 15:20.

I DO NOT TAKE advantage of poor laborers. (24:14)

I DO NOT PUNISH parents for their children's sins, nor children for their parent's sins. (24:16)

I GIVE true justice to foreigners, widows, and orphans. (24:17)

I OBEY God's command to care for others, remembering my own condition before God redeemed me. (24:22)

I BELIEVE God commanded prompt, fair, and limited punishment for crime. (25:1)

I DO NOT PUBLICLY HUMILIATE my neighbor. (25:3)

24:8 Traditionally rendered *leprosy.* The Hebrew word used here can describe various skin diseases.

pull his sandal from his foot, and spit in his face. She will then say, 'This is what happens to a man who refuses to raise up a son for his brother.' [10]Ever afterward his family will be referred to as 'the family of the man whose sandal was pulled off'!

[11]"If two Israelite men are fighting and the wife of one tries to rescue her husband by grabbing the testicles of the other man, [12]her hand must be cut off without pity.

[13]"You must use accurate scales when you weigh out merchandise, [14]and you must use full and honest measures. [15]Yes, use honest weights and measures, so that you will enjoy a long life in the land the LORD your God is giving you. [16]Those who cheat with dishonest weights and measures are detestable to the LORD your God.

[17]"Never forget what the Amalekites did to you as you came from Egypt. [18]They attacked you when you were exhausted and weary, and they struck down those who were lagging behind. They had no fear of God. [19]Therefore, when the LORD your God has given you rest from all your enemies in the land he is giving you as a special possession, you are to destroy the Amalekites and erase their memory from under heaven. Never forget this!

CHAPTER 26

Harvest Offerings and Tithes

"When you arrive in the land the LORD your God is giving you as a special possession and you have conquered it and settled there, [2]put some of the first produce from each harvest into a basket and bring it to the place the LORD your God chooses for his name to be honored. [3]Go to the priest in charge at that time and say to him, 'With this gift I acknowledge that the LORD your God has brought me into the land he swore to give our ancestors.' [4]The priest will then take the basket from your hand and set it before the altar of the LORD your God. [5]You must then say in the presence of the LORD your God, 'My ancestor Jacob was a wandering Aramean who went to live in Egypt. His family was few in number, but in Egypt they became a mighty and numerous nation. [6]When the Egyptians mistreated and humiliated us by making us their slaves, [7]we cried out to the LORD, the God of our ancestors. He heard us and saw our hardship, toil, and oppression. [8]So the LORD brought us out of Egypt with amazing power, overwhelming terror, and miraculous signs and wonders. [9]He brought us to this place and gave us this land flowing with milk and honey! [10]And now, O LORD, I have brought you a token of the first crops you have given me from the ground.' Then place the produce before the LORD your God and worship him. [11]Afterward go and celebrate because of all the good things the LORD your God has given to you and your household. Remember to include the Levites and the foreigners living among you in the celebration.

[12]"Every third year you must offer a special tithe of your crops. You must give these tithes to the Levites, foreigners, orphans, and widows so that they will have enough to eat in your towns. [13]Then you must declare in the presence of the LORD your God, 'I have taken the sacred gift from my house and have given it to the Levites, foreigners, orphans, and widows, just as you commanded me. I have not violated or forgotten any of your commands. [14]I have not eaten any of it while in mourning; I have not touched it while I was ceremonially unclean; and I have not offered any of it to the dead. I have obeyed the LORD my God and have done everything you commanded me. [15]Look down from your holy dwelling place in heaven and bless your people Israel and the land you have given us—a land flowing with milk and honey—just as you solemnly promised our ancestors.'

I DETEST cheating, as does the Lord. (25:16)

I ACKNOWLEDGE what God has done for me. (26:3)

See Jacob's profile (page 43) at Genesis 32:9.

I CELEBRATE because of all the good things the Lord has given my family and me, and I include needy people in my celebration. (26:11)

I BELIEVE the Israelites were to give a tithe every third year to support Levites, foreigners, and the needy in their community. (26:12)

A Call to Obey the LORD's Commands

[16]"Today the LORD your God has commanded you to obey all these laws and regulations. You must commit yourself to them without reservation. [17]You have declared today that the LORD is your God. You have promised to obey his laws, commands, and regulations by walking in his ways and doing everything he tells you. [18] The LORD has declared today that you are his people, his own special treasure, just as he promised, and that you must obey all his commands. [19]And if you do, he will make you greater than any other nation. Then you will receive praise, honor, and renown. You will be a nation that is holy to the LORD your God, just as he promised."

CHAPTER 27

The Altar on Mount Ebal

Then Moses and the leaders of Israel charged the people as follows: "Keep all these commands that I am giving you today. [2]When you cross the Jordan River and enter the land the LORD your God is giving you, set up some large stones and coat them with plaster. [3] Then write all the terms of this law on them. I repeat, you will soon cross the river to enter the land the LORD your God is giving you, a land flowing with milk and honey, just as the LORD, the God of your ancestors, promised you. [4]When you cross the Jordan, set up these stones at Mount Ebal and coat them with plaster, as I am commanding you today. [5] Then build an altar there to the LORD your God, using natural stones. [6]Do not shape the stones with an iron tool. On the altar you must offer burnt offerings to the LORD your God. [7]Sacrifice peace offerings on it also, and feast there with great joy before the LORD your God. [8]On the stones coated with plaster, you must clearly write all the terms of this law."

[9]Then Moses and the Levitical priests addressed all Israel as follows: "O Israel, be quiet and listen! Today you have become the people of the LORD your God. [10]So obey the LORD your God by keeping all these commands and laws that I am giving you today."

Curses from Mount Ebal

[11]That same day Moses gave this charge to the people: [12]"When you cross the Jordan River, the tribes of Simeon, Levi, Judah, Issachar, Joseph, and Benjamin must stand on Mount Gerizim to proclaim a blessing over the people. [13]And the tribes of Reuben, Gad, Asher, Zebulun, Dan, and Naphtali must stand on Mount Ebal to proclaim a curse. [14]Then the Levites must shout to all the people of Israel:

[15]'Cursed is anyone who carves or casts idols and secretly sets them up. These idols, the work of craftsmen, are detestable to the LORD.'
  And all the people will reply, 'Amen.'

[16]'Cursed is anyone who despises father or mother.'
  And all the people will reply, 'Amen.'

[17]'Cursed is anyone who steals property from a neighbor by moving a boundary marker.'
  And all the people will reply, 'Amen.'

[18]'Cursed is anyone who leads a blind person astray on the road.'
  And all the people will reply, 'Amen.'

[19]'Cursed is anyone who is unjust to foreigners, orphans, and widows.'
  And all the people will reply, 'Amen.'

[20]'Cursed is anyone who has sexual intercourse with his father's wife, for he has violated his father.'
  And all the people will reply, 'Amen.'

I OBEY the Lord without reservation. (26:16)

I BELIEVE Moses and the leaders charged the Israelites to keep all God's commands. (27:1)

I BELIEVE Moses charged all the tribes of Israel to proclaim blessings and curses in a public ceremony on Mount Gerizim and Mount Ebal. (27:11)

I BELIEVE anyone who made and worshiped idols was cursed. (27:15)

I BELIEVE anyone who stole property was cursed. (27:17)

I BELIEVE anyone who was unjust to the needy was cursed. (27:19)

I BELIEVE anyone who committed incest was cursed. (27:20)

²¹'Cursed is anyone who has sexual intercourse with an animal.'
And all the people will reply, 'Amen.'

²²'Cursed is anyone who has sexual intercourse with his sister, whether she is the daughter of his father or his mother.'
And all the people will reply, 'Amen.'

²³'Cursed is anyone who has sexual intercourse with his mother-in-law.'
And all the people will reply, 'Amen.'

²⁴'Cursed is anyone who kills another person in secret.'
And all the people will reply, 'Amen.'

²⁵'Cursed is anyone who accepts payment to kill an innocent person.'
And all the people will reply, 'Amen.'

²⁶'Cursed is anyone who does not affirm the terms of this law by obeying them.'
And all the people will reply, 'Amen.'

CHAPTER 28

Blessings for Obedience

"If you fully obey the LORD your God by keeping all the commands I am giving you today, the LORD your God will exalt you above all the nations of the world. ²You will experience all these blessings if you obey the LORD your God:

³ You will be blessed in your towns and in the country.
⁴ You will be blessed with many children and productive fields.
You will be blessed with fertile herds and flocks.
⁵ You will be blessed with baskets overflowing with fruit, and with kneading bowls filled with bread.
⁶ You will be blessed wherever you go, both in coming and in going.

⁷"The LORD will conquer your enemies when they attack you. They will attack you from one direction, but they will scatter from you in seven! ⁸"The LORD will bless everything you do and will fill your storehouses with grain. The LORD your God will bless you in the land he is giving you. ⁹"If you obey the commands of the LORD your God and walk in his ways, the LORD will establish you as his holy people as he solemnly promised to do. ¹⁰Then all the nations of the world will see that you are a people claimed by the LORD, and they will stand in awe of you. ¹¹"The LORD will give you an abundance of good things in the land he swore to give your ancestors—many children, numerous livestock, and abundant crops. ¹²The LORD will send rain at the proper time from his rich treasury in the heavens to bless all the work you do. You will lend to many nations, but you will never need to borrow from them. ¹³If you listen to these commands of the LORD your God and carefully obey them, the LORD will make you the head and not the tail, and you will always have the upper hand. ¹⁴You must not turn away from any of the commands I am giving you today to follow after other gods and worship them.

Curses for Disobedience

¹⁵"But if you refuse to listen to the LORD your God and do not obey all the commands and laws I am giving you today, all these curses will come and overwhelm you:

¹⁶ You will be cursed in your towns and in the country.
¹⁷ You will be cursed with baskets empty of fruit, and with kneading bowls empty of bread.

I BELIEVE anyone who murdered someone was cursed. (27:24)

I EXPERIENCE blessings as I obey God. (28:2)

I BELIEVE the Israelites would have been blessed in everything if they had obeyed the Lord. (28:8)

I BELIEVE the Lord would have blessed the Israelites with abundance in their families and their farms if they had obeyed him. (28:11)

¹⁸ You will be cursed with few children and barren fields.
  You will be cursed with infertile herds and flocks.
¹⁹ You will be cursed wherever you go, both in coming and in going.

²⁰"The LORD himself will send against you curses, confusion, and disillusionment in everything you do, until at last you are completely destroyed for doing evil and forsaking me. ²¹The LORD will send diseases among you until none of you are left in the land you are about to enter and occupy. ²²The LORD will strike you with wasting disease, fever, and inflammation, with scorching heat and drought, and with blight and mildew. These devastations will pursue you until you die. ²³The skies above will be as unyielding as bronze, and the earth beneath will be as hard as iron. ²⁴The LORD will turn your rain into sand and dust, and it will pour down from the sky until you are destroyed.

²⁵"The LORD will cause you to be defeated by your enemies. You will attack your enemies from one direction, but you will scatter from them in seven! You will be an object of horror to all the kingdoms of the earth. ²⁶Your dead bodies will be food for the birds and wild animals, and no one will be there to chase them away.

²⁷"The LORD will afflict you with the boils of Egypt and with tumors, scurvy, and the itch, from which you cannot be cured. ²⁸The LORD will strike you with madness, blindness, and panic. ²⁹You will grope around in broad daylight, just like a blind person groping in the darkness, and you will not succeed at anything you do. You will be oppressed and robbed continually, and no one will come to save you.

³⁰"You will be engaged to a woman, but another man will ravish her. You will build a house, but someone else will live in it. You will plant a vineyard, but you will never enjoy its fruit. ³¹Your ox will be butchered before your eyes, but you won't get a single bite of the meat. Your donkey will be driven away, never to be returned. Your sheep will be given to your enemies, and no one will be there to help you. ³²You will watch as your sons and daughters are taken away as slaves. Your heart will break as you long for them, but nothing you do will help. ³³A foreign nation you have never heard about will eat the crops you worked so hard to grow. You will suffer under constant oppression and harsh treatment. ³⁴You will go mad because of all the tragedy around you. ³⁵The LORD will cover you from head to foot with incurable boils.

³⁶"The LORD will exile you and the king you crowned to a nation unknown to you and your ancestors. Then in exile you will worship gods of wood and stone! ³⁷You will become an object of horror, a proverb and a mockery among all the nations to which the LORD sends you.

³⁸"You will plant much but harvest little, for locusts will eat your crops. ³⁹You will plant vineyards and care for them, but you will not drink the wine or eat the grapes, for worms will destroy the vines. ⁴⁰You will grow olive trees throughout your land, but you will never use the olive oil, for the trees will drop the fruit before it is ripe. ⁴¹You will have sons and daughters, but you will not keep them, for they will be led away into captivity. ⁴²Swarms of insects will destroy your trees and crops. ⁴³The foreigners living among you will become stronger and stronger, while you become weaker and weaker. ⁴⁴They will lend money to you, not you to them. They will be the head, and you will be the tail!

⁴⁵"If you refuse to listen to the LORD your God and to obey the commands and laws he has given you, all these curses will pursue and overtake you until you are destroyed. ⁴⁶These horrors will serve as a sign and warning among you and your descendants forever. ⁴⁷Because you have not served the LORD your God with joy and enthusiasm for the abundant benefits you have received, ⁴⁸you will serve your enemies whom the LORD will send against you. You will be left hungry, thirsty, naked, and lacking in everything. They will oppress you harshly until you are destroyed.

I BELIEVE the Lord would send disease and drought to destroy the Israelites if they forsook him. (28:21)

I BELIEVE the Lord would cause the Israelites to be defeated by their enemies if they refused to obey him. (28:25)

I BELIEVE the Lord would afflict the Israelites with diseases and madness if they refused to obey him. (28:27)

I BELIEVE the Israelites would lose their families and farms and finally their land if they refused to obey the Lord. (28:30)

I BELIEVE the Lord would exile the Israelites if they refused to obey him. (28:36)

I BELIEVE all the curses would overwhelm and destroy the Israelites if they refused to obey the Lord's commands. (28:45)

I BELIEVE the Israelites would serve their enemies if they refused to serve the Lord with joy. (28:47)

⁴⁹"The LORD will bring a distant nation against you from the end of the earth, and it will swoop down on you like an eagle. It is a nation whose language you do not understand, ⁵⁰a fierce and heartless nation that shows no respect for the old and no pity for the young. ⁵¹Its armies will devour your livestock and crops, and you will starve to death. They will leave you no grain, new wine, olive oil, calves, or lambs, bringing about your destruction. ⁵²They will lay siege to your cities until all the fortified walls in your land—the walls you trusted to protect you—are knocked down. They will attack all the towns in the land the LORD your God has given you. ⁵³The siege will be so severe that you will eat the flesh of your own sons and daughters, whom the LORD your God has given you. ⁵⁴The most tenderhearted man among you will have no compassion for his own brother, his beloved wife, and his surviving children. ⁵⁵He will refuse to give them a share of the flesh he is devouring—the flesh of one of his own children—because he has nothing else to eat during the siege that your enemy will inflict on all your towns. ⁵⁶The most tender and delicate woman among you—so delicate she would not so much as touch her feet to the ground—will be cruel to the husband she loves and to her own son or daughter. ⁵⁷She will hide from them the afterbirth and the new baby she has borne, so that she herself can secretly eat them. She will have nothing else to eat during the siege and terrible distress that your enemy will inflict on all your towns.

⁵⁸"If you refuse to obey all the terms of this law that are written in this book, and if you do not fear the glorious and awesome name of the LORD your God, ⁵⁹then the LORD will overwhelm both you and your children with indescribable plagues. These plagues will be intense and without relief, making you miserable and unbearably sick. ⁶⁰He will bring against you all the diseases of Egypt that you feared so much, and they will claim you. ⁶¹The LORD will bring against you every sickness and plague there is, even those not mentioned in this Book of the Law, until you are destroyed. ⁶²Though you are as numerous as the stars in the sky, few of you will be left because you would not listen to the LORD your God.

⁶³"Just as the LORD has found great pleasure in helping you to prosper and multiply, the LORD will find pleasure in destroying you, until you disappear from the land you are about to enter and occupy. ⁶⁴For the LORD will scatter you among all the nations from one end of the earth to the other. There you will worship foreign gods that neither you nor your ancestors have known, gods made of wood and stone! ⁶⁵There among those nations you will find no place of security and rest. And the LORD will cause your heart to tremble, your eyesight to fail, and your soul to despair. ⁶⁶Your lives will hang in doubt. You will live night and day in fear, with no reason to believe that you will see the morning light. ⁶⁷In the morning you will say, 'If only it were night!' And in the evening you will say, 'If only it were morning!' You will say this because of your terror at the awesome horrors you see around you. ⁶⁸Then the LORD will send you back to Egypt in ships, a journey I promised you would never again make. There you will offer to sell yourselves to your enemies as slaves, but no one will want to buy you."

CHAPTER 29

These are the terms of the covenant the LORD commanded Moses to make with the Israelites while they were in the land of Moab, in addition to the covenant he had made with them at Mount Sinai.*

Moses Reviews the Covenant

²Moses summoned all the Israelites and said to them, "You have seen with your own eyes everything the LORD did in Egypt to Pharaoh and all his servants and his whole country—³all the great tests of strength, the miraculous signs, and the amazing wonders. ⁴But to this day the LORD has not given you minds that understand, nor eyes that see, nor ears that hear!

29:1 Hebrew *Horeb,* another name for Sinai.

I BELIEVE that if the Israelites refused to obey the Lord, foreign enemies would stage a siege of horrifying severity. (28:53)

I BELIEVE the Lord would overwhelm the Israelites with plagues if they refused to obey his law. (28:58)

I BELIEVE the Lord would destroy the nation and scatter the surviving Israelites—who would wander in misery—if they refused to obey him. (28:63)

I BELIEVE God made this covenant, with its conditions for blessings and curses, with the Israelites before they entered the land. (29:1)

I ASK God to help me recognize his great works on my behalf. (29:4)

[5]For forty years I led you through the wilderness, yet your clothes and sandals did not wear out. [6]You had no bread or wine or other strong drink, but he gave you food so you would know that he is the LORD your God. [7]When we came here, King Sihon of Heshbon and King Og of Bashan came out to fight against us, but we defeated them. [8]We took their land and gave it to the tribes of Reuben and Gad and to the half-tribe of Manasseh as their inheritance.

[9]"Therefore, obey the terms of this covenant so that you will prosper in everything you do. [10]All of you—your tribal leaders, your judges, your officers, all the men of Israel—are standing today before the LORD your God. [11]With you are your little ones, your wives, and the foreigners living among you who chop your wood and carry your water. [12]You are standing here today to enter into a covenant with the LORD your God. The LORD is making this covenant with you today, and he has sealed it with an oath. [13]He wants to confirm you today as his people and to confirm that he is your God, just as he promised you, and as he swore to your ancestors Abraham, Isaac, and Jacob. [14]But you are not the only ones with whom the LORD is making this covenant with its obligations. [15]The LORD your God is making this covenant with you who stand in his presence today and also with all future generations of Israel.

[16]"Surely you remember how we lived in the land of Egypt and how we traveled through the lands of enemy nations as we left. [17]You have seen their detestable idols made of wood, stone, silver, and gold. [18]The LORD made this covenant with you so that no man, woman, family, or tribe among you would turn away from the LORD our God to worship these gods of other nations, and so that no root among you would bear bitter and poisonous fruit. [19]Let none of those who hear the warnings of this curse consider themselves immune, thinking, 'I am safe, even though I am walking in my own stubborn way.' This would lead to utter ruin! [20]The LORD will not pardon such people. His anger and jealousy will burn against them. All the curses written in this book will come down on them, and the LORD will erase their names from under heaven. [21]The LORD will separate them from all the tribes of Israel, to pour out on them all the covenant curses recorded in this Book of the Law.

[22]"Then the generations to come, both your own descendants and the foreigners who come from distant lands, will see the devastation of the land and the diseases the LORD will send against it. [23]They will find its soil turned into sulfur and salt, with nothing planted and nothing growing, not even a blade of grass. It will be just like Sodom and Gomorrah, Admah and Zeboiim, which the LORD destroyed in his anger. [24]The surrounding nations will ask, 'Why has the LORD done this to his land? Why was he so angry?'

[25]"And they will be told, 'This happened because the people of the land broke the covenant they made with the LORD, the God of their ancestors, when he brought them out of the land of Egypt. [26]They turned to serve and worship other gods that were foreign to them, gods that the LORD had not designated for them. [27]That is why the LORD's anger burned against this land, bringing down on it all the curses recorded in this book. [28]In great anger and fury the LORD uprooted his people from their land and exiled them to another land, where they still live today!'

[29]"There are secret things that belong to the LORD our God, but the revealed things belong to us and our descendants forever, so that we may obey these words of the law.

CHAPTER 30

A Call to Return to the LORD

"Suppose all these things happen to you—the blessings and the curses I have listed—and you meditate on them as you are living among the nations to which the LORD your God has exiled you. [2]If at that time you return to the LORD your God, and you and your children begin wholeheartedly to obey all

---

See the profiles for Abraham (page 19), Isaac (page 31), and Jacob (page 43) at Genesis 15:6, Genesis 25:19, and Genesis 32:9.

I KNOW I cannot avoid the consequences of disobedience. (29:19)

I BELIEVE the Lord would indeed bring all the curses on the Israelites if they disobeyed. (29:20)

I BELIEVE future generations would wonder at the Lord's anger at Israel for breaking his covenant. (29:22)

I LEAVE secret things to God and obey everything he has revealed. (29:29)

I MEDITATE on how God has kept his word. (30:1)

the commands I have given you today, ³then the LORD your God will restore your fortunes. He will have mercy on you and gather you back from all the nations where he has scattered you. ⁴Though you are at the ends of the earth, the LORD your God will go and find you and bring you back again. ⁵He will return you to the land that belonged to your ancestors, and you will possess that land again. He will make you even more prosperous and numerous than your ancestors!

⁶"The LORD your God will cleanse your heart and the hearts of all your descendants so that you will love him with all your heart and soul, and so you may live! ⁷The LORD your God will inflict all these curses on your enemies and persecutors. ⁸Then you will again obey the LORD and keep all the commands I am giving you today. ⁹The LORD your God will make you successful in everything you do. He will give you many children and numerous livestock, and your fields will produce abundant harvests, for the LORD will delight in being good to you as he was to your ancestors. ¹⁰The LORD your God will delight in you if you obey his voice and keep the commands and laws written in this Book of the Law, and if you turn to the LORD your God with all your heart and soul.

The Choice of Life or Death

¹¹"This command I am giving you today is not too difficult for you to understand or perform. ¹²It is not up in heaven, so distant that you must ask, 'Who will go to heaven and bring it down so we can hear and obey it?' ¹³It is not beyond the sea, so far away that you must ask, 'Who will cross the sea to bring it to us so we can hear and obey it?' ¹⁴The message is very close at hand; it is on your lips and in your heart so that you can obey it.

¹⁵"Now listen! Today I am giving you a choice between prosperity and disaster, between life and death. ¹⁶I have commanded you today to love the LORD your God and to keep his commands, laws, and regulations by walking in his ways. If you do this, you will live and become a great nation, and the LORD your God will bless you and the land you are about to enter and occupy. ¹⁷But if your heart turns away and you refuse to listen, and if you are drawn away to serve and worship other gods, ¹⁸then I warn you now that you will certainly be destroyed. You will not live a long, good life in the land you are crossing the Jordan to occupy.

¹⁹"Today I have given you the choice between life and death, between blessings and curses. I call on heaven and earth to witness the choice you make. Oh, that you would choose life, that you and your descendants might live! ²⁰Choose to love the LORD your God and to obey him and commit yourself to him, for he is your life. Then you will live long in the land the LORD swore to give your ancestors Abraham, Isaac, and Jacob."

CHAPTER 31

Joshua Becomes Israel's Leader

When Moses had finished saying* these things to all the people of Israel, ²he said, "I am now 120 years old and am no longer able to lead you. The LORD has told me that I will not cross the Jordan River. ³But the LORD your God himself will cross over ahead of you. He will destroy the nations living there, and you will take possession of their land. Joshua is your new leader, and he will go with you, just as the LORD promised. ⁴The LORD will destroy the nations living in the land, just as he destroyed Sihon and Og, the kings of the Amorites. ⁵The LORD will hand over to you the people who live there, and you will deal with them as I have commanded you. ⁶Be strong and courageous! Do not be afraid of them! The LORD your God will go ahead of you. He will neither fail you nor forsake you."

*31:1 As in Dead Sea Scrolls and Greek version; Masoretic Text reads *Moses went and spoke.*

I BELIEVE the Lord delights in blessing those who love and obey him. (30:9)

I OBEY God's voice and turn to him with all my heart and soul. (30:10)

Today what command(s) are you willing to obey?

I CHOOSE to love and obey God because he is my life. (30:20)

See the profiles for Abraham (page 19), Isaac (page 31), and Jacob (page 43) at Genesis 15:6, Genesis 25:19, and Genesis 32:9.

I AM STRONG and unafraid because the Lord is with me and will never fail me. (31:6)

[7] Then Moses called for Joshua, and as all Israel watched he said to him, "Be strong and courageous! For you will lead these people into the land that the LORD swore to give their ancestors. You are the one who will deliver it to them as their inheritance. [8] Do not be afraid or discouraged, for the LORD is the one who goes before you. He will be with you; he will neither fail you nor forsake you."

I AM NOT AFRAID or discouraged, because the Lord is with me and will never fail me. (31:8)

Public Reading of the Law

[9] So Moses wrote down this law and gave it to the priests, who carried the Ark of the LORD's covenant, and to the leaders of Israel. [10] Then Moses gave them this command: "At the end of every seventh year, the Year of Release, during the Festival of Shelters, [11] you must read this law to all the people of Israel when they assemble before the LORD your God at the place he chooses. [12] Call them all together—men, women, children, and the foreigners living in your towns—so they may listen and learn to fear the LORD your God and carefully obey all the terms of this law. [13] Do this so that your children who have not known these laws will hear them and will learn to fear the LORD your God. Do this as long as you live in the land you are crossing the Jordan to occupy."

I CALL together others to hear God's Word and obey it. (31:12)

I READ God's Word to my children so they will know how to fear the Lord. (31:13)

Israel's Disobedience Predicted

[14] Then the LORD said to Moses, "The time has come for you to die. Call Joshua and take him with you to the Tabernacle,* and I will commission him there." So Moses and Joshua went and presented themselves at the Tabernacle. [15] And the LORD appeared to them in a pillar of cloud at the entrance to the sacred tent.

[16] The LORD said to Moses, "You are about to die and join your ancestors. After you are gone, these people will begin worshiping foreign gods, the gods of the land where they are going. They will abandon me and break the covenant I have made with them. [17] Then my anger will blaze forth against them. I will abandon them, hiding my face from them, and they will be destroyed. Terrible trouble will come down on them, so that they will say, 'These disasters have come because God is no longer among us!' [18] At that time I will hide my face from them on account of all the sins they have committed by worshiping other gods.

[19] "Now write down the words of this song, and teach it to the people of Israel. Teach them to sing it, so it may serve as a witness against them. [20] For I will bring them into the land I swore to give their ancestors—a land flowing with milk and honey. There they will become prosperous; they will eat all the food they want and become well nourished. Then they will begin to worship other gods; they will despise me and break my covenant. [21] Then great disasters will come down on them, and this song will stand as evidence against them, for it will never be forgotten by their descendants. I know what these people are like, even before they have entered the land I swore to give them." [22] So that very day Moses wrote down the words of the song and taught it to the Israelites.

[23] Then the LORD commissioned Joshua son of Nun with these words: "Be strong and courageous! You must bring the people of Israel into the land I swore to give them. I will be with you."

I BELIEVE God commissioned Joshua to bring the people of Israel into the land. (31:23)

[24] When Moses had finished writing down this entire body of law in a book, [25] he gave these instructions to the Levites who carried the Ark of the LORD's covenant: [26] "Take this Book of the Law and place it beside the Ark of the Covenant of the LORD your God, so it may serve as a witness against the people of Israel. [27] For I know how rebellious and stubborn you are. Even now, while I am still with you, you have rebelled against the LORD. How much more rebellious will you be after my death! [28] Now summon all the

I BELIEVE Moses wrote down the entire Book of the Law and gave it to the Levites. (31:24)

31:14 Hebrew *Tent of Meeting;* also in 31:14b.

leaders and officials of your tribes so that I can speak to them and call heaven and earth to witness against them. [29]I know that after my death you will become utterly corrupt and will turn from the path I have commanded you to follow. In the days to come, disaster will come down on you, for you will make the LORD very angry by doing what is evil in his sight."

The Song of Moses
[30]So Moses recited this entire song to the assembly of Israel:

CHAPTER 32

I CALL others to hear God's Word. (32:1)

[1] "Listen, O heavens, and I will speak!
  Hear, O earth, the words that I say!
[2] My teaching will fall on you like rain;
  my speech will settle like dew.
My words will fall like rain on tender grass,
  like gentle showers on young plants.

I PROCLAIM the perfect works and character of God. (32:3)

[3] I will proclaim the name of the LORD;
  how glorious is our God!
[4] He is the Rock; his work is perfect.
  Everything he does is just and fair.
He is a faithful God who does no wrong;
  how just and upright he is!

[5] "But they have acted corruptly toward him;
  when they act like that, are they really his children?*
  They are a deceitful and twisted generation.

I DO NOT REPAY God's goodness with corrupt living. (32:6)

[6] Is this the way you repay the LORD,
  you foolish and senseless people?
Isn't he your Father who created you?
  Has he not made you and established you?
[7] Remember the days of long ago;
  think about the generations past.
Ask your father and he will inform you.
  Inquire of your elders, and they will tell you.
[8] When the Most High assigned lands to the nations,
  when he divided up the human race,
he established the boundaries of the peoples
  according to the number of angelic beings.*
[9] For the people of Israel belong to the LORD;
  Jacob is his special possession.

[10] "He found them in a desert land,
  in an empty, howling wasteland.
He surrounded them and watched over them;
  he guarded them as his most precious possession.*
[11] Like an eagle that rouses her chicks
  and hovers over her young,
so he spread his wings to take them in
  and carried them aloft on his pinions.
[12] The LORD alone guided them;
  they lived without any foreign gods.
[13] He made them ride over the highlands;
  he let them feast on the crops of the fields.
He nourished them with honey from the cliffs,
  with olive oil from the hard rock.

32:5 The meaning of the Hebrew is uncertain. 32:8 As in Dead Sea Scrolls, which read *of the sons of God,* and Greek version, which reads *of the angels of god;* Masoretic Text reads *of the sons of Israel.* 32:10 Hebrew *as the apple of his eye.*

¹⁴ He fed them curds from the herd and milk from the flock,
　　together with the fat of lambs and goats.
He gave them choice rams and goats from Bashan,
　　together with the choicest wheat.
You drank the finest wine,
　　made from the juice of grapes.
¹⁵ But Israel* soon became fat and unruly;
　　the people grew heavy, plump, and stuffed!
Then they abandoned the God who had made them;
　　they made light of the Rock of their salvation.
¹⁶ They stirred up his jealousy by worshiping foreign gods;
　　they provoked his fury with detestable acts.
¹⁷ They offered sacrifices to demons, non-gods,
　　to gods they had not known before,
　　to gods only recently arrived,
　　to gods their ancestors had never feared.
¹⁸ You neglected the Rock who had fathered you;
　　you forgot the God who had given you birth.

¹⁹ "The LORD saw this and was filled with loathing.
　　He was provoked to anger by his own sons and daughters.
²⁰ He said, 'I will abandon them;
　　I will see to their end!
For they are a twisted generation,
　　children without integrity.
²¹ They have roused my jealousy by worshiping non-gods;
　　they have provoked my fury with useless idols.
Now I will rouse their jealousy by blessing other nations;
　　I will provoke their fury by blessing the foolish Gentiles.
²² For my anger blazes forth like fire
　　and burns to the depths of the grave.*
It devours the earth and all its crops
　　and ignites the foundations of the mountains.
²³ I will heap disasters upon them
　　and shoot them down with my arrows.
²⁴ I will send against them wasting famine,
　　burning fever, and deadly disease.
They will be troubled by the fangs of wild beasts,
　　by poisonous snakes that glide in the dust.
²⁵ Outside, the sword will bring death,
　　and inside, terror will strike
both young men and young women,
　　both infants and the aged.
²⁶ I decided to scatter them,*
　　so even the memory of them would disappear.
²⁷ But I feared the taunt of the enemy,
　　that their adversaries might misunderstand and say,
'Our power has triumphed!
　　It was not the LORD who did this!' '

²⁸ "Israel is a nation that lacks sense;
　　the people are foolish, without understanding.
²⁹ Oh, that they were wise and could understand this!
　　Oh, that they might know their fate!
³⁰ How could one person chase a thousand of them,

I DO NOT NEGLECT God, my Rock, or provoke his jealous anger. (32:18)

I BELIEVE the Lord would make Israel jealous for him by blessing the Gentiles. (32:21)

I BELIEVE the Lord longed for Israel to be wise and understanding. (32:29)

32:15 Hebrew *Jeshurun*, a term of endearment for Israel.　32:22 Hebrew *of Sheol*.　32:26 As in Greek version; the meaning of the Hebrew is uncertain.

and two people put ten thousand to flight,
   unless their Rock had sold them,
   unless the LORD had given them up?
³¹ But the rock of our enemies is not like our Rock,
   as even they recognize.*
³² Their vine grows from the vine of Sodom,
   from the vineyards of Gomorrah.
Their grapes are poison,
   and their clusters are bitter.
³³ Their wine is the venom of snakes,
   the deadly poison of vipers.

³⁴ " 'I am storing up these things,
   sealing them away within my treasury.
³⁵ I will take vengeance; I will repay those who deserve it.
   In due time their feet will slip.
Their day of disaster will arrive,
   and their destiny will overtake them.'

³⁶ "Indeed, the LORD will judge his people,
   and he will change his mind about* his servants,
when he sees their strength is gone
   and no one is left, slave or free.
³⁷ Then he will ask, 'Where are their gods,
   the rocks they fled to for refuge?
³⁸ Where now are those gods,
   who ate the fat of their sacrifices
   and drank the wine of their offerings?
Let those gods arise and help you!
   Let them provide you with shelter!
³⁹ Look now; I myself am he!
   There is no god other than me!
I am the one who kills and gives life;
   I am the one who wounds and heals;
   no one delivers from my power!
⁴⁰ Now I raise my hand to heaven
   and declare, "As surely as I live,
⁴¹ when I sharpen my flashing sword
   and begin to carry out justice,
I will bring vengeance on my enemies
   and repay those who hate me.
⁴² I will make my arrows drunk with blood,
   and my sword will devour flesh—
the blood of the slaughtered and the captives,
   and the heads of the enemy leaders." '

⁴³ "Rejoice with him, O heavens,
   and let all the angels of God worship him,*
   for he will avenge the blood of his servants.
He will take vengeance on his enemies
   and cleanse his land and his people."

⁴⁴ So Moses came with Joshua* son of Nun and recited all the words of this song to the people. ⁴⁵When Moses had finished reciting these words to Israel, ⁴⁶he added: "Take to heart all the words I have given you today. Pass them on

I BELIEVE the Lord holds power over life and death. (32:39)

I TAKE God's commands to heart and pass them on to my children. (32:45)

32:31 The meaning of the Hebrew is uncertain. Greek version reads *our enemies are fools.*   32:36 Or *will take revenge for.*   32:43 As in Dead Sea Scrolls and Greek version; Masoretic Text reads *Rejoice with his people, O nations.*   32:44 Hebrew *Hoshea,* a variant name for Joshua.

as a command to your children so they will obey every word of this law. ⁴⁷These instructions are not mere words—they are your life! By obeying them you will enjoy a long life in the land you are crossing the Jordan River to occupy."

I OBEY God's instructions because I know they are my life! (32:47)

Moses' Death Foretold
⁴⁸That same day the LORD said to Moses, ⁴⁹"Go to Moab, to the mountains east of the river,* and climb Mount Nebo, which is across from Jericho. Look out across the land of Canaan, the land I am giving to the people of Israel as their own possession. ⁵⁰Then you must die there on the mountain and join your ancestors, just as Aaron, your brother, died on Mount Hor and joined his ancestors. ⁵¹For both of you broke faith with me among the Israelites at the waters of Meribah at Kadesh* in the wilderness of Zin. You failed to demonstrate my holiness to the people of Israel there. ⁵²So you will see the land from a distance, but you may not enter the land I am giving to the people of Israel."

I BELIEVE God controls the hour and place of my death. (32:50)

CHAPTER 33

Moses Blesses the People
This is the blessing that Moses, the man of God, gave to the people of Israel before his death:

²"The LORD came from Mount Sinai
and dawned upon us* from Mount Seir;
he shone forth from Mount Paran
and came from Meribah-kadesh
with flaming fire at his right hand.*
³Indeed, you love the people;
all your holy ones are in your hands.
They follow in your steps
and accept your instruction.
⁴Moses charged us with the law,
the special possession of the assembly of Israel.*
⁵The LORD became king in Israel*—
when the leaders of the people assembled,
when the tribes of Israel gathered."

⁶Moses said this about the tribe of Reuben:*

"Let the tribe of Reuben live and not die out,
even though their tribe is small."

⁷Moses said this about the tribe of Judah:

"O LORD, hear the cry of Judah
and bring them again to their people.
Give them strength to defend their cause;
help them against their enemies!"

I CRY OUT to the Lord for strength, and he hears and helps me. (33:7)

⁸Moses said this about the tribe of Levi:

"O LORD, you have given the sacred lots*
to your faithful servants the Levites.
You put them to the test at Massah
and contended with them at the waters of Meribah.
⁹The Levites obeyed your word

32:49 Hebrew *the mountains of Abarim.*   32:51 Hebrew *waters of Meribath-kadesh.*   33:2a As in Greek and Syriac versions; Hebrew reads *upon them.*   33:2b Or *came from myriads of holy ones, from the south, from his mountain slopes.* The meaning of the Hebrew is uncertain.   33:4 Hebrew *of Jacob.*   33:5 Hebrew *in Jeshurun,* a term of endearment for Israel.   33:6 Hebrew lacks *Moses said this about the tribe of Reuben.*   33:8 Hebrew *given your Thummim and Urim.* See Exod 28:30.

and guarded your covenant.
They were more loyal to you
than to their parents, relatives, and children.
¹⁰ Now let them teach your regulations to Jacob;
let them give your instructions to Israel.
They will present incense before you
and offer whole burnt offerings on the altar.
¹¹ Bless the Levites, O LORD,
and accept all their work.
Crush the loins of their enemies;
strike down their foes so they never rise again."

¹² Moses said this about the tribe of Benjamin:

"The people of Benjamin are loved by the LORD
and live in safety beside him.
He surrounds them continuously
and preserves them from every harm."

I AM SURROUNDED by the Lord's love and protection. (33:12)

¹³ Moses said this about the tribes of Joseph:

"May their land be blessed by the LORD
with the choice gift of rain from the heavens,
and water from beneath the earth;
¹⁴ with the riches that grow in the sun,
and the bounty produced each month;
¹⁵ with the finest crops of the ancient mountains,
and the abundance from the everlasting hills;
¹⁶ with the best gifts of the earth and its fullness,
and the favor of the one who appeared in the burning bush.
May these blessings rest on Joseph's head,
crowning the brow of the prince among his brothers.
¹⁷ Joseph has the strength and majesty of a young bull;
his power is like the horns of a wild ox.
He will gore distant nations,
driving them to the ends of the earth.
This is my blessing for the multitudes of Ephraim
and the thousands of Manasseh."

¹⁸ Moses said this about the tribes of Zebulun and Issachar*:

"May the people of Zebulun prosper in their expeditions abroad.
May the people of Issachar prosper at home in their tents.
¹⁹ They summon the people to the mountain
to offer proper sacrifices there.
They benefit from the riches of the sea
and the hidden treasures of the sand."

I AM BLESSED by God wherever I go, at home or abroad. (33:18)

²⁰ Moses said this about the tribe of Gad:

"Blessed is the one who enlarges Gad's territory!
Gad is poised there like a lion
to tear off an arm or a head.
²¹ The people of Gad took the best land for themselves;
a leader's share was assigned to them.
When the leaders of the people were assembled,
they carried out the LORD's justice
and obeyed his regulations for Israel."

I AM BOLD to accomplish the Lord's will. (33:20)

33:18 Hebrew lacks *and Issachar.*

²²Moses said this about the tribe of Dan:

"Dan is a lion's cub,
  leaping out from Bashan."

²³Moses said this about the tribe of Naphtali:

"O Naphtali, you are rich in favor
  and full of the LORD's blessings;
  may you possess the west and the south."

²⁴Moses said this about the tribe of Asher:

"May Asher be blessed above other sons;
  may he be esteemed by his brothers;
  may he bathe his feet in olive oil.
²⁵ May the bolts of your gates be of iron and bronze;
  may your strength match the length of your days!"

²⁶ "There is no one like the God of Israel.*
  He rides across the heavens to help you,
  across the skies in majestic splendor.
²⁷The eternal God is your refuge,
  and his everlasting arms are under you.
He thrusts out the enemy before you;
  it is he who cries, 'Destroy them!'
²⁸ So Israel will live in safety,
  prosperous Jacob in security,
in a land of grain and wine,
  while the heavens drop down dew.
²⁹ How blessed you are, O Israel!
  Who else is like you, a people saved by the LORD?
He is your protecting shield
  and your triumphant sword!
Your enemies will bow low before you,
  and you will trample on their backs!"

I DEPEND on God to help me. (33:26)

I REST in the everlasting arms of the eternal God, my refuge. (33:27)

CHAPTER 34

The Death of Moses

Then Moses went to Mount Nebo from the plains of Moab and climbed Pisgah Peak, which is across from Jericho. And the LORD showed him the whole land, from Gilead as far as Dan; ²all the land of Naphtali; the land of Ephraim and Manasseh; all the land of Judah, extending to the Mediterranean Sea*; ³the Negev; the Jordan Valley with Jericho—the city of palms— as far as Zoar. ⁴Then the LORD said to Moses, "This is the land I promised on oath to Abraham, Isaac, and Jacob, and I told them I would give it to their descendants. I have now allowed you to see it, but you will not enter the land."

⁵So Moses, the servant of the LORD, died there in the land of Moab, just as the LORD had said. ⁶He was buried* in a valley near Beth-peor in Moab, but to this day no one knows the exact place. ⁷Moses was 120 years old when he died, yet his eyesight was clear, and he was as strong as ever. ⁸The people of Israel mourned thirty days for Moses on the plains of Moab, until the customary period of mourning was over.

⁹Now Joshua son of Nun was full of the spirit of wisdom, for Moses had laid his hands on him. So the people of Israel obeyed him and did everything just as the LORD had commanded Moses.

See the profiles for Abraham (page 19), Isaac (page 31), and Jacob (page 43) at Genesis 15:6, Genesis 25:19, and Genesis 32:9.

I BELIEVE Moses died before entering the Promised Land, just as the Lord had said. (34:5)

I MOURN when a godly leader dies. (34:8)

33:26 Hebrew *of Jeshurun,* a term of endearment for Israel.   34:2 Hebrew *the western sea.*   34:6 Hebrew *He buried him,* that is, "The LORD buried him." Samaritan Pentateuch and some Greek manuscripts read *They buried him.*

¹⁰There has never been another prophet like Moses, whom the LORD knew face to face. ¹¹The LORD sent Moses to perform all the miraculous signs and wonders in the land of Egypt against Pharaoh, all his servants, and his entire land. ¹²And it was through Moses that the LORD demonstrated his mighty power and terrifying acts in the sight of all Israel.

JOSHUA

THIS FIRST OF TWELVE Old Testament historical books is filled with *promise*.

Before he died, Moses commissioned Joshua to lead the Israelites into the Promised Land. Now, the Lord himself commissions Joshua with a series of remarkable promises (1:1-9). The people pledge their loyalty to Joshua, as well (1:10-18). Joshua immediately sends out two of his men to spy out the land across the Jordan River (chapter 2).

Joshua then leads the Israelites across the Jordan River (chapters 3-4), renews their covenant with the Lord (chapter 5), and proceeds to overthrow more than thirty corrupt, evil kingdoms that had occupied the Promised Land (chapters 6-12).

After conquering the Promised Land, Joshua begins to divide the land among the Israelite tribes (13:1-15:62). His plans start to go awry, however, when several of the tribes complain they are unable to drive out the remaining hostile inhabitants of the land (15:63-17:18). Joshua sends twenty-one men to survey the remaining land (18:1-10), and then casts lots to assign cities and lands to the Levites and the seven other remaining Israelite tribes (18:11-21:45).

The allegiance of the two and a half tribes living east of the Jordan River is questioned, and civil war is narrowly averted (chapter 22). Before he dies, Joshua delivers a farewell address to the Israelite leaders (chapter 23) and to the people (24:1-28), exhorting them to remain true to the Lord, just as the Lord had remained true to them.

The book ends with an appendix regarding Joshua's death (24:29-33).

Famous passages in Joshua include

- ○ The Lord speaks stirring words to Joshua (1:5-9)
- ○ Rahab assists the two spies (2:1-21)
- ○ The Israelites cross the Jordan River on dry land (3:16-17)
- ○ The Lord's commander appears to Joshua (5:13-15)
- ○ The walls of Jericho come tumbling down (6:20)
- ○ The Gibeonites deceive Joshua (9:3-27)
- ○ The sun stands still during a battle (10:12-14)
- ○ Caleb receives a special inheritance (14:6-15; 15:13-19)
- ○ The Lord keeps all his promises (21:43-45; 23:14)
- ○ The high priest Phinehas helps avert civil war (22:13-34)
- ○ "As for me and my family, we will serve the Lord" (24:15)

CHAPTER 1

The LORD's Charge to Joshua

After the death of Moses the LORD's servant, the LORD spoke to Joshua son of Nun, Moses' assistant. He said, ²"Now that my servant Moses is dead, you must lead my people across the Jordan River into the land I am giving them. ³I promise you what I promised Moses: 'Everywhere you go, you will be on

See Moses' profile (page 73) at Exodus 5:1.

I BELIEVE the Lord commanded Joshua to lead the Israelites into the Promised Land. (1:2)

I BELIEVE the Lord will never fail me or abandon me. (1:5)

I AM STRONG and courageous because the Lord is always with me. (1:6)

I PURSUE success God's way by continually studying the Bible, meditating on it, and obeying all the Lord's commands. (1:8)

I AM NOT AFRAID or discouraged because the Lord is with me wherever I go. (1:9)

land I have given you—⁴from the Negev Desert in the south to the Lebanon mountains in the north, from the Euphrates River on the east to the Mediterranean Sea* on the west, and all the land of the Hittites.' ⁵No one will be able to stand their ground against you as long as you live. For I will be with you as I was with Moses. I will not fail you or abandon you.

⁶"Be strong and courageous, for you will lead my people to possess all the land I swore to give their ancestors. ⁷Be strong and very courageous. Obey all the laws Moses gave you. Do not turn away from them, and you will be successful in everything you do. ⁸Study this Book of the Law continually. Meditate on it day and night so you may be sure to obey all that is written in it. Only then will you succeed. ⁹I command you—be strong and courageous! Do not be afraid or discouraged. For the LORD your God is with you wherever you go."

Joshua's Charge to the Israelites
¹⁰Joshua then commanded the leaders of Israel, ¹¹"Go through the camp and tell the people to get their provisions ready. In three days you will cross the Jordan River and take possession of the land the LORD your God has given you."

¹²Then Joshua called together the tribes of Reuben, Gad, and the half-tribe of Manasseh. He told them, ¹³"Remember what Moses, the servant of the LORD, commanded you: 'The LORD your God is giving you rest and has given you this land.' ¹⁴Your wives, children, and cattle may remain here on the east side of the Jordan River, but your warriors, fully armed, must lead the other tribes across the Jordan to help them conquer their territory. Stay with them ¹⁵until the LORD gives rest to them as he has given rest to you, and until they, too, possess the land the LORD your God is giving them. Only then may you settle here on the east side of the Jordan River in the land that Moses, the servant of the LORD, gave you."

¹⁶They answered Joshua, "We will do whatever you command us, and we will go wherever you send us. ¹⁷We will obey you just as we obeyed Moses. And may the LORD your God be with you as he was with Moses. ¹⁸Anyone who rebels against your word and does not obey your every command will be put to death. So be strong and courageous!"

CHAPTER 2

Rahab Protects the Spies
Then Joshua secretly sent out two spies from the Israelite camp at Acacia.* He instructed them, "Spy out the land on the other side of the Jordan River, especially around Jericho." So the two men set out and came to the house of a prostitute named Rahab and stayed there that night.

Ask the Lord to speak to you. After all, this is his Word!

²But someone told the king of Jericho, "Some Israelites have come here tonight to spy out the land." ³So the king of Jericho sent orders to Rahab: "Bring out the men who have come into your house. They are spies sent here to discover the best way to attack us."

⁴Rahab, who had hidden the two men, replied, "The men were here earlier, but I didn't know where they were from. ⁵They left the city at dusk, as the city gates were about to close, and I don't know where they went. If you hurry, you can probably catch up with them." ⁶(But she had taken them up to the roof and hidden them beneath piles of flax.) ⁷So the king's men went looking for the spies along the road leading to the shallow crossing places of the Jordan River. And as soon as the king's men had left, the city gate was shut.

⁸Before the spies went to sleep that night, Rahab went up on the roof to talk with them. ⁹"I know the LORD has given you this land," she told them.

1:4 Hebrew *the Great Sea.* 2:1 Hebrew *Shittim.*

"We are all afraid of you. Everyone is living in terror. ¹⁰For we have heard how the LORD made a dry path for you through the Red Sea* when you left Egypt. And we know what you did to Sihon and Og, the two Amorite kings east of the Jordan River, whose people you completely destroyed.* ¹¹No wonder our hearts have melted in fear! No one has the courage to fight after hearing such things. For the LORD your God is the supreme God of the heavens above and the earth below. ¹²Now swear to me by the LORD that you will be kind to me and my family since I have helped you. Give me some guarantee that ¹³when Jericho is conquered, you will let me live, along with my father and mother, my brothers and sisters, and all their families."

¹⁴"We offer our own lives as a guarantee for your safety," the men agreed. "If you don't betray us, we will keep our promise when the LORD gives us the land."

¹⁵Then, since Rahab's house was built into the city wall, she let them down by a rope through the window. ¹⁶"Escape to the hill country," she told them. "Hide there for three days until the men who are searching for you have returned; then go on your way."

¹⁷Before they left, the men told her, "We can guarantee your safety ¹⁸only if you leave this scarlet rope hanging from the window. And all your family members—your father, mother, brothers, and all your relatives—must be here inside the house. ¹⁹If they go out into the street, they will be killed, and we cannot be held to our oath. But we swear that no one inside this house will be killed—not a hand will be laid on any of them. ²⁰If you betray us, however, we are not bound by this oath in any way."

²¹"I accept your terms," she replied. And she sent them on their way, leaving the scarlet rope hanging from the window.

²²The spies went up into the hill country and stayed there three days. The men who were chasing them had searched everywhere along the road, but they finally returned to the city without success. ²³Then the two spies came down from the hill country, crossed the Jordan River, and reported to Joshua all that had happened to them. ²⁴"The LORD will certainly give us the whole land," they said, "for all the people in the land are terrified of us."

CHAPTER 3

The Israelites Cross the Jordan

Early the next morning Joshua and all the Israelites left Acacia* and arrived at the banks of the Jordan River, where they camped before crossing. ²Three days later, the Israelite leaders went through the camp ³giving these instructions to the people: "When you see the Levitical priests carrying the Ark of the Covenant of the LORD your God, follow them. ⁴Since you have never traveled this way before, they will guide you. Stay about a half mile* behind them, keeping a clear distance between you and the Ark. Make sure you don't come any closer."

⁵Then Joshua told the people, "Purify yourselves, for tomorrow the LORD will do great wonders among you."

⁶In the morning Joshua said to the priests, "Lift up the Ark of the Covenant and lead the people across the river." And so they started out.

⁷The LORD told Joshua, "Today I will begin to make you great in the eyes of all the Israelites. Now they will know that I am with you, just as I was with Moses. ⁸Give these instructions to the priests who are carrying the Ark of the Covenant: 'When you reach the banks of the Jordan River, take a few steps into the river and stop.'"

⁹So Joshua told the Israelites, "Come and listen to what the LORD your

I BELIEVE the Lord my God is the supreme God of the heavens above and the earth below. (2:11)

I KEEP my promises to others. (2:14)

I BELIEVE what the Lord has said will come to pass. (2:24)

I BELIEVE the Lord did great wonders among the Israelites during the days of Joshua. (3:5)

See Moses' profile (page 73) at Exodus 5:1.

2:10a Hebrew *sea of reeds.*   2:10b The Hebrew term used here refers to the complete consecration of things or people to the LORD, either by destroying them or by giving them as an offering.   3:1 Hebrew *Shittim.*
3:4 Hebrew *about 2,000 cubits* [900 meters].

I BELIEVE the Lord is among his people. (3:10)

I BELIEVE the Israelites crossed the Jordan River on dry ground. (3:17)

I BELIEVE the Lord told Joshua to set up a memorial to commemorate the Jordan crossing. (4:1)

I CREATE lasting reminders of the Lord's miraculous work in my generation. (4:6)

I HURRY to obey the Lord's commands. (4:10)

See Moses' profile (page 73) at Exodus 5:1.

I BELIEVE the Lord told Joshua to bring the Ark of the Covenant out of the Jordan riverbed into the Promised Land. (4:15)

God says. ¹⁰Today you will know that the living God is among you. He will surely drive out the Canaanites, Hittites, Hivites, Perizzites, Girgashites, Amorites, and Jebusites. ¹¹Think of it! The Ark of the Covenant, which belongs to the Lord of the whole earth, will lead you across the Jordan River! ¹²Now choose twelve men, one from each tribe. ¹³The priests will be carrying the Ark of the LORD, the Lord of all the earth. When their feet touch the water, the flow of water will be cut off upstream, and the river will pile up there in one heap."

¹⁴When the people set out to cross the Jordan, the priests who were carrying the Ark of the Covenant went ahead of them. ¹⁵Now it was the harvest season, and the Jordan was overflowing its banks. But as soon as the feet of the priests who were carrying the Ark touched the water at the river's edge, ¹⁶the water began piling up at a town upstream called Adam, which is near Zarethan. And the water below that point flowed on to the Dead Sea* until the riverbed was dry. Then all the people crossed over near the city of Jericho. ¹⁷Meanwhile, the priests who were carrying the Ark of the LORD's covenant stood on dry ground in the middle of the riverbed as the people passed by them. They waited there until everyone had crossed the Jordan on dry ground.

CHAPTER 4

Memorials to the Jordan Crossing

When all the people were safely across the river, the LORD said to Joshua, ²"Now choose twelve men, one from each tribe. ³Tell the men to take twelve stones from where the priests are standing in the middle of the Jordan and pile them up at the place where you camp tonight."

⁴So Joshua called together the twelve men ⁵and told them, "Go into the middle of the Jordan, in front of the Ark of the LORD your God. Each of you must pick up one stone and carry it out on your shoulder—twelve stones in all, one for each of the twelve tribes. ⁶We will use these stones to build a memorial. In the future, your children will ask, 'What do these stones mean to you?' ⁷Then you can tell them, 'They remind us that the Jordan River stopped flowing when the Ark of the LORD's covenant went across.' These stones will stand as a permanent memorial among the people of Israel."

⁸So the men did as Joshua told them. They took twelve stones from the middle of the Jordan River, one for each tribe, just as the LORD had commanded Joshua. They carried them to the place where they camped for the night and constructed the memorial there.

⁹Joshua also built another memorial of twelve stones in the middle of the Jordan, at the place where the priests who carried the Ark of the Covenant were standing. The memorial remains there to this day.

¹⁰The priests who were carrying the Ark stood in the middle of the river until all of the LORD's instructions, which Moses had given to Joshua, were carried out. Meanwhile, the people hurried across the riverbed. ¹¹And when everyone was on the other side, the priests crossed over with the Ark of the LORD. ¹²The armed warriors from the tribes of Reuben, Gad, and the half-tribe of Manasseh led the Israelites across the Jordan, just as Moses had directed. ¹³These warriors—about forty thousand strong—were ready for battle, and they crossed over to the plains of Jericho in the LORD's presence.

¹⁴That day the LORD made Joshua great in the eyes of all the Israelites, and for the rest of his life they revered him as much as they had revered Moses.

¹⁵The LORD had said to Joshua, ¹⁶"Command the priests carrying the Ark of the Covenant* to come up out of the riverbed." ¹⁷So Joshua gave the command. ¹⁸And as soon as the priests carrying the Ark of the LORD's covenant came up out of the riverbed, the Jordan River flooded its banks as before.

3:16 Hebrew *the sea of the Arabah, the Salt Sea.* 4:16 Hebrew *Ark of the Testimony.*

¹⁹The people crossed the Jordan on the tenth day of the first month—the month that marked their exodus from Egypt.* They camped at Gilgal, east of Jericho. ²⁰It was there at Gilgal that Joshua piled up the twelve stones taken from the Jordan River. ²¹Then Joshua said to the Israelites, "In the future, your children will ask, 'What do these stones mean?' ²²Then you can tell them, 'This is where the Israelites crossed the Jordan on dry ground.' ²³For the LORD your God dried up the river right before your eyes, and he kept it dry until you were all across, just as he did at the Red Sea* when he dried it up until we had all crossed over. ²⁴He did this so that all the nations of the earth might know the power of the LORD, and that you might fear the LORD your God forever."

I TELL the next generation about the Lord's miraculous work in my generation. (4:22)

I BELIEVE the Lord's miraculous works show his power to all the nations of the earth so that his chosen ones may fear him forever. (4:24)

LIKE RAHAB
Joshua 2:11

I believe the Lord gladly saves all who turn to him, regardless of their nationality or background.

Rahab had heard all the stories of the mighty God of the wandering Israelites—perhaps since she was a little girl. This God had opened a path for his people through the Red Sea and then defeated the kings Og and Sihon.

Like all the other people of Jericho, Rahab's heart trembled with fear when those same Israelites congregated across the Jordan River. Despite her pagan birth, her low status, and her sinful past, Rahab's heart also held something else: true faith that this God of the Israelites must be the supreme God of the heavens above and the earth below.

God has always had a doorway of faith through which to pass into a relationship with him. Before the coming of Christ, that doorway was through the covenant relationship God had established with Israel. Now, of course, we enter through a personal relationship with Jesus Christ (John 10:9). In both ages, however, God has made the way of faith open to all who want to know him.

Rahab certainly wanted to know God. She believed everything she had heard about God's power. She recognized God's promise to give the Israelites the land. She realized no other "god" compared with him. And she knew she needed to be saved from the coming destruction of her city.

God saw through those thick walls of Jericho into Rahab's heart and brought the two spies to her very door. She immediately seized the opportunity to put her faith into action, first hiding the men and then pleading for her life and the lives of her family members. At the spies' command, Rahab hung the scarlet cord, called her family to her home, and remained behind closed doors until the Israelites came and brought them to safety within their camp.

In rather dramatic fashion, Rahab entered into God's family of faith. By his grace, God also placed this former prostitute and foreigner into the lineage of the coming Messiah (Matthew 1:5).

You and I can give thanks that God gladly saves us if we turn to him, no matter what our nationality, family background, or past sins, for he still rewards the faith of those who diligently seek him (Hebrews 11:6).

To learn more about Rahab's faith, read Hebrews 11:31 and James 2:25.

○ *Today's Scripture reading is Joshua 2 and 6.*

CHAPTER 5

When all the Amorite kings west of the Jordan and all the Canaanite kings who lived along the Mediterranean coast* heard how the LORD had dried up the Jordan River so the people of Israel could cross, they lost heart and were paralyzed with fear.

Israel Reestablishes Covenant Ceremonies

²At that time the LORD told Joshua, "Use knives of flint to make the Israelites a circumcised people again." ³So Joshua made flint knives and circumcised the entire male population of Israel at Gibeath-haaraloth.*

⁴Joshua had to circumcise them because all the men who were old enough

I BELIEVE the Lord told Joshua to reestablish Israel's covenant ceremonies of circumcision and Passover. (5:2)

4:19 Hebrew *the tenth day of the first month.* This day of the Hebrew lunar calendar occurs in late March or early April. 4:23 Hebrew *sea of reeds.* 5:1 Hebrew *along the sea.* 5:3 *Gibeath-haaraloth* means "hill of foreskins."

to bear arms when they left Egypt had died in the wilderness. [5]Those who left Egypt had all been circumcised, but none of those born after the Exodus, during the years in the wilderness, had been circumcised. [6]The Israelites wandered in the wilderness for forty years until all the men who were old enough to bear arms when they left Egypt had died. For they had disobeyed the LORD, and the LORD vowed he would not let them enter the land he had sworn to give us—a land flowing with milk and honey. [7]So Joshua circumcised their sons who had not been circumcised on the way to the Promised Land—those who had grown up to take their fathers' places. [8]After all the males had been circumcised, they rested in the camp until they were healed.

[9]Then the LORD said to Joshua, "Today I have rolled away the shame of your slavery in Egypt." So that place has been called Gilgal* to this day.

[10]While the Israelites were camped at Gilgal on the plains of Jericho, they celebrated Passover on the evening of the fourteenth day of the first month—the month that marked their exodus from Egypt.* [11]The very next day they began to eat unleavened bread and roasted grain harvested from the land. [12]No manna appeared that day, and it was never seen again. So from that time on the Israelites ate from the crops of Canaan.

The LORD's Commander Confronts Joshua

[13]As Joshua approached the city of Jericho, he looked up and saw a man facing him with sword in hand. Joshua went up to him and asked, "Are you friend or foe?"

[14]"Neither one," he replied. "I am commander of the LORD's army."

At this, Joshua fell with his face to the ground in reverence. "I am at your command," Joshua said. "What do you want your servant to do?"

[15]The commander of the LORD's army replied, "Take off your sandals, for this is holy ground." And Joshua did as he was told.

CHAPTER 6

The Fall of Jericho

Now the gates of Jericho were tightly shut because the people were afraid of the Israelites. No one was allowed to go in or out. [2]But the LORD said to Joshua, "I have given you Jericho, its king, and all its mighty warriors. [3]Your entire army is to march around the city once a day for six days. [4]Seven priests will walk ahead of the Ark, each carrying a ram's horn. On the seventh day you are to march around the city seven times, with the priests blowing the horns. [5]When you hear the priests give one long blast on the horns, have all the people give a mighty shout. Then the walls of the city will collapse, and the people can charge straight into the city."

[6]So Joshua called together the priests and said, "Take up the Ark of the Covenant, and assign seven priests to walk in front of it, each carrying a ram's horn." [7]Then he gave orders to the people: "March around the city, and the armed men will lead the way in front of the Ark of the LORD."

[8]After Joshua spoke to the people, the seven priests with the rams' horns started marching in the presence of the LORD, blowing the horns as they marched. And the priests carrying the Ark of the LORD's covenant followed behind them. [9]Armed guards marched both in front of the priests and behind the Ark, with the priests continually blowing the horns. [10]"Do not shout; do not even talk," Joshua commanded. "Not a single word from any of you until I tell you to shout. Then shout!" [11]So the Ark of the LORD was carried around the city once that day, and then everyone returned to spend the night in the camp.

[12]Joshua got up early the next morning, and the priests again carried the Ark of the LORD. [13]The seven priests with the rams' horns marched in front of

---

I BELIEVE the Lord desires to roll away the shame of his people. (5:9)

I THANK the Lord for my daily bread and depend on his provision, no matter what my situation. (5:12)

I BELIEVE the Lord appeared to Joshua just as he appeared to Moses. (5:15)

I DO whatever the Lord commands, confident that he will do exactly what he has promised. (6:7)

5:9 *Gilgal* sounds like the Hebrew word *galal,* meaning "to roll." 5:10 Hebrew *the fourteenth day of the first month.* This day of the Hebrew lunar calendar occurs in late March or early April.

the Ark of the Lord, blowing their horns. Armed guards marched both in front of the priests with the horns and behind the Ark of the Lord. All this time the priests were sounding their horns. [14]On the second day they marched around the city once and returned to the camp. They followed this pattern for six days.

[15]On the seventh day the Israelites got up at dawn and marched around the city as they had done before. But this time they went around the city seven times. [16]The seventh time around, as the priests sounded the long blast on their horns, Joshua commanded the people, "Shout! For the Lord has given you the city! [17]The city and everything in it must be completely destroyed* as an offering to the Lord. Only Rahab the prostitute and the others in her house will be spared, for she protected our spies. [18]Do not take any of the things set apart for destruction, or you yourselves will be completely destroyed, and you will bring trouble on all Israel. [19]Everything made from silver, gold, bronze, or iron is sacred to the Lord and must be brought into his treasury."

[20]When the people heard the sound of the horns, they shouted as loud as they could. Suddenly, the walls of Jericho collapsed, and the Israelites charged straight into the city from every side and captured it. [21]They completely destroyed everything in it—men and women, young and old, cattle, sheep, donkeys—everything.

[22]Then Joshua said to the two spies, "Keep your promise. Go to the prostitute's house and bring her out, along with all her family."

[23]The young men went in and brought out Rahab, her father, mother, brothers, and all the other relatives who were with her. They moved her whole family to a safe place near the camp of Israel.

[24]Then the Israelites burned the city and everything in it. Only the things made from silver, gold, bronze, or iron were kept for the treasury of the Lord's house. [25]So Joshua spared Rahab the prostitute and her relatives who were with her in the house, because she had hidden the spies Joshua sent to Jericho. And she lives among the Israelites to this day.

[26]At that time Joshua invoked this curse:

"May the curse of the Lord fall on anyone
who tries to rebuild the city of Jericho.
At the cost of his firstborn son,
he will lay its foundation.
At the cost of his youngest son,
he will set up its gates."

[27]So the Lord was with Joshua, and his name became famous throughout the land.

CHAPTER 7

Ai Defeats the Israelites

But Israel was unfaithful concerning the things set apart for the Lord.* A man named Achan had stolen some of these things, so the Lord was very angry with the Israelites. Achan was the son of Carmi, of the family of Zimri,* of the clan of Zerah, and of the tribe of Judah.

[2]Joshua sent some of his men from Jericho to spy out the city of Ai, east of Bethel, near Beth-aven. [3]When they returned, they told Joshua, "It's a small town, and it won't take more than two or three thousand of us to destroy it. There's no need for all of us to go there."

I KEEP my promises. (6:17)

I BELIEVE Joshua dedicated everything of value to the Lord from the first city captured inside the Promised Land. (6:19)

I DEDICATE to the Lord whatever he claims as his own. (6:24)

I AM FAITHFUL to the Lord and would never steal from him. (7:1)

I LISTEN to the Lord, not just to the advice of others. (7:3)

6:17 The Hebrew term used here refers to the complete consecration of things or people to the Lord, either by destroying them or by giving them as an offering; also in 6:18, 21. 7:1a The Hebrew term used here refers to the complete consecration of things or people to the Lord, either by destroying them or by giving them as an offering; also in 7:11, 12, 13, 15. 7:1b As in Greek version (see also 1 Chr 2:6); Hebrew reads Zabdi. Also in 7:17, 18.

I BELIEVE others often suffer dire consequences when I sin against the Lord. (7:4)

I DO NOT GIVE UP all hope in dire circumstances. (7:9)

I BELIEVE sin disgraces and ultimately ruins a nation. (7:12)

I BELIEVE the wages of sin is death (see Romans 3:23). (7:15)

I BELIEVE the Lord supernaturally pinpointed the man who had broken his covenant by stealing items set apart for the Lord. (7:18)

⁴So approximately three thousand warriors were sent, but they were soundly defeated. The men of Ai ⁵chased the Israelites from the city gate as far as the quarries,* and they killed about thirty-six who were retreating down the slope. The Israelites were paralyzed with fear at this turn of events, and their courage melted away.

⁶Joshua and the leaders of Israel tore their clothing in dismay, threw dust on their heads, and bowed down facing the Ark of the LORD until evening. ⁷Then Joshua cried out, "Sovereign LORD, why did you bring us across the Jordan River if you are going to let the Amorites kill us? If only we had been content to stay on the other side! ⁸Lord, what am I to say, now that Israel has fled from its enemies? ⁹For when the Canaanites and all the other people living in the land hear about it, they will surround us and wipe us off the face of the earth. And then what will happen to the honor of your great name?"

¹⁰But the LORD said to Joshua, "Get up! Why are you lying on your face like this? ¹¹Israel has sinned and broken my covenant! They have stolen the things that I commanded to be set apart for me. And they have not only stolen them; they have also lied about it and hidden the things among their belongings. ¹² That is why the Israelites are running from their enemies in defeat. For now Israel has been set apart for destruction. I will not remain with you any longer unless you destroy the things among you that were set apart for destruction.

¹³"Get up! Command the people to purify themselves in preparation for tomorrow. For this is what the LORD, the God of Israel, says: Hidden among you, O Israel, are things set apart for the LORD. You will never defeat your enemies until you remove these things. ¹⁴In the morning you must present yourselves by tribes, and the LORD will point out the tribe to which the guilty man belongs. That tribe must come forward with its clans, and the LORD will point out the guilty clan. That clan will then come forward, and the LORD will point out the guilty family. Finally, each member of the guilty family must come one by one. ¹⁵The one who has stolen what was set apart for destruction will himself be burned with fire, along with everything he has, for he has broken the covenant of the LORD and has done a horrible thing in Israel."

Achan's Sin

¹⁶Early the next morning Joshua brought the tribes of Israel before the LORD, and the tribe of Judah was singled out. ¹⁷ Then the clans of Judah came forward, and the clan of Zerah was singled out. Then the families of Zerah came before the LORD, and the family of Zimri was singled out. ¹⁸Every member of Zimri's family was brought forward person by person, and Achan was singled out.

¹⁹Then Joshua said to Achan, "My son, give glory to the LORD, the God of Israel, by telling the truth. Make your confession and tell me what you have done. Don't hide it from me."

²⁰Achan replied, "I have sinned against the LORD, the God of Israel. ²¹For I saw a beautiful robe imported from Babylon,* two hundred silver coins,* and a bar of gold weighing more than a pound.* I wanted them so much that I took them. They are hidden in the ground beneath my tent, with the silver buried deeper than the rest."

²²So Joshua sent some men to make a search. They ran to the tent and found the stolen goods hidden there, just as Achan had said, with the silver buried beneath the rest. ²³ They took the things from the tent and brought them to Joshua and all the Israelites. Then they laid them on the ground in the presence of the LORD.

7:5 Or as far as Shebarim.   7:21a Hebrew Shinar.   7:21b Hebrew 200 shekels of silver, about 5 pounds or 2.3 kilograms in weight.   7:21c Hebrew 50 shekels, about 20 ounces or 570 grams in weight.

²⁴Then Joshua and all the Israelites took Achan, the silver, the robe, the bar of gold, his sons, daughters, cattle, donkeys, sheep, tent, and everything he had, and they brought them to the valley of Achor. ²⁵Then Joshua said to Achan, "Why have you brought trouble on us? The LORD will now bring trouble on you." And all the Israelites stoned Achan and his family and burned their bodies. ²⁶They piled a great heap of stones over Achan, which remains to this day. That is why the place has been called the Valley of Trouble* ever since. So the LORD was no longer angry.

CHAPTER 8

The Israelites Defeat Ai

Then the LORD said to Joshua, "Do not be afraid or discouraged. Take the entire army and attack Ai, for I have given to you the king of Ai, his people, his city, and his land. ²You will destroy them as you destroyed Jericho and its king. But this time you may keep the captured goods and the cattle for yourselves. Set an ambush behind the city."

³So Joshua and the army of Israel set out to attack Ai. Joshua chose thirty thousand fighting men and sent them out at night ⁴with these orders: "Hide in ambush close behind the city and be ready for action. ⁵When our main army attacks, the men of Ai will come out to fight as they did before, and we will run away from them. ⁶We will let them chase us until they have all left the city. For they will say, 'The Israelites are running away from us as they did before.' ⁷Then you will jump up from your ambush and take possession of the city, for the LORD your God will give it to you. ⁸Set the city on fire, as the LORD has commanded. You have your orders."

⁹So they left that night and lay in ambush between Bethel and the west side of Ai. But Joshua remained among the people in the camp that night. ¹⁰Early the next morning Joshua roused his men and started toward Ai, accompanied by the leaders of Israel. ¹¹They camped on the north side of Ai, with a valley between them and the city. ¹²That night Joshua sent five thousand men to lie in ambush between Bethel and Ai, on the west side of the city. ¹³So they stationed the main army north of the city and the ambush west of the city. Joshua himself spent that night in the valley.

¹⁴When the king of Ai saw the Israelites across the valley, he and all his army hurriedly went out early the next morning and attacked the Israelites at a place overlooking the Jordan Valley.* But he didn't realize there was an ambush behind the city. ¹⁵Joshua and the Israelite army fled toward the wilderness as though they were badly beaten, ¹⁶and all the men in the city were called out to chase after them. In this way, they were lured away from the city. ¹⁷There was not a man left in Ai or Bethel* who did not chase after the Israelites, and the city was left wide open.

¹⁸Then the LORD said to Joshua, "Point your spear toward Ai, for I will give you the city." Joshua did as he was commanded. ¹⁹As soon as Joshua gave the signal, the men in ambush jumped up and poured into the city. They quickly captured it and set it on fire.

²⁰When the men of Ai looked behind them, smoke from the city was filling the sky, and they had nowhere to go. For the Israelites who had fled in the direction of the wilderness now turned on their pursuers. ²¹When Joshua and the other Israelites saw that the ambush had succeeded and that smoke was rising from the city, they turned and attacked the men of Ai. ²²Then the Israelites who were inside the city came out and started killing the enemy from the rear. So the men of Ai were caught in a trap, and all of them died. Not a single person survived or escaped. ²³Only the king of Ai was taken alive and brought to Joshua.

I DO NOT BRING suffering on myself and others by purposely disobeying God. (7:25)

I DO whatever the Lord commands, even if I have previously experienced setbacks and defeat. (8:3)

I BELIEVE the Lord can turn attacks by the enemy into victories for the Lord's people. (8:14)

I BELIEVE the Lord told Joshua that he would conquer Ai, and Joshua did what the Lord commanded. (8:18)

7:26 Hebrew *valley of Achor.* 8:14 Hebrew *the Arabah.* 8:17 Some manuscripts lack *or Bethel.*

²⁴When the Israelite army finished killing all the men outside the city, they went back and finished off everyone inside. ²⁵So the entire population of Ai was wiped out that day—twelve thousand in all. ²⁶For Joshua kept holding out his spear until everyone who had lived in Ai was completely destroyed.* ²⁷Only the cattle and the treasures of the city were not destroyed, for the Israelites kept these for themselves, as the LORD had commanded Joshua. ²⁸So Ai* became a permanent mound of ruins, desolate to this very day.

²⁹Joshua hung the king of Ai on a tree and left him there until evening. At sunset the Israelites took down the body and threw it in front of the city gate. They piled a great heap of stones over him that can still be seen today.

The LORD's Covenant Renewed

³⁰Then Joshua built an altar to the LORD, the God of Israel, on Mount Ebal. ³¹He followed the instructions that Moses the LORD's servant had written in the Book of the Law: "Make me an altar from stones that are uncut and have not been shaped with iron tools." Then on the altar they presented burnt offerings and peace offerings to the LORD. ³²And as the Israelites watched, Joshua copied the law of Moses onto the stones of the altar.*

³³Then all the Israelites—foreigners and citizens alike—along with the leaders, officers, and judges, were divided into two groups. One group stood at the foot of Mount Gerizim, the other at the foot of Mount Ebal. Each group faced the other, and between them stood the Levitical priests carrying the Ark of the LORD's covenant. This was all done according to the instructions Moses, the servant of the LORD, had given for blessing the people of Israel.

³⁴Joshua then read to them all the blessings and curses Moses had written in the Book of the Law. ³⁵Every command Moses had ever given was read to the entire assembly, including the women and children and the foreigners who lived among the Israelites.

CHAPTER 9

The Gibeonites Deceive Israel

Now all the kings west of the Jordan heard about what had happened. (These were the kings of the Hittites, Amorites, Canaanites, Perizzites, Hivites, and Jebusites, who lived in the hill country, in the western foothills,* and along the coast of the Mediterranean Sea* as far north as the Lebanon mountains.) ²These kings quickly combined their armies to fight against Joshua and the Israelites.

³But when the people of Gibeon heard what had happened to Jericho and Ai, ⁴they resorted to deception to save themselves. They sent ambassadors to Joshua, loading their donkeys with weathered saddlebags and old patched wineskins. ⁵They put on ragged clothes and worn-out, patched sandals. And they took along dry, moldy bread for provisions. ⁶When they arrived at the camp of Israel at Gilgal, they told Joshua and the men of Israel, "We have come from a distant land to ask you to make a peace treaty with us."

⁷The Israelites replied to these Hivites, "How do we know you don't live nearby? For if you do, we cannot make a treaty with you."

⁸They replied, "We will be your servants."

"But who are you?" Joshua demanded. "Where do you come from?"

⁹They answered, "We are from a very distant country. We have heard of the might of the LORD your God and of all he did in Egypt. ¹⁰We have also heard what he did to the two Amorite kings east of the Jordan River—King Sihon of Heshbon and King Og of Bashan (who lived in Ashtaroth). ¹¹So our leaders

---

I BELIEVE the Lord did not allow the Israelites to spare any pagans set apart for destruction. (8:29)

I FOLLOW the Lord's instructions exactly. (8:31)

See Moses' profile (page 73) at Exodus 5:1.

I BELIEVE the Lord's words are for everyone. (8:35)

I BELIEVE the Lord can turn attacks by the enemy into victories for the Lord's people. (9:2)

I DO NOT RESORT to deception, no matter how desperate my situation. (9:4)

8:26 The Hebrew term used here refers to the complete consecration of things or people to the LORD, either by destroying them or by giving them as an offering. 8:28 *Ai* means "ruin." 8:32 Or *onto stones.* 9:1a Hebrew *the Shephelah.* 9:1b Hebrew *the Great Sea.*

and our people instructed us, 'Prepare for a long journey. Go meet with the people of Israel and declare our people to be their servants, and ask for peace.'

[12] "This bread was hot from the ovens when we left. But now, as you can see, it is dry and moldy. [13] These wineskins were new when we filled them, but now they are old and cracked. And our clothing and sandals are worn out from our long, hard trip."

[14] So the Israelite leaders examined their bread, but they did not consult the LORD. [15] Then Joshua went ahead and signed a peace treaty with them, and the leaders of Israel ratified their agreement with a binding oath.

[16] Three days later, the facts came out—these people of Gibeon lived nearby! [17] The Israelites set out at once to investigate and reached their towns in three days. The names of these towns were Gibeon, Kephirah, Beeroth, and Kiriath-jearim. [18] But the Israelites did not attack the towns, for their leaders had made a vow to the LORD, the God of Israel.

The people of Israel grumbled against their leaders because of the treaty. [19] But the leaders replied, "We have sworn an oath in the presence of the LORD, the God of Israel. We cannot touch them. [20] We must let them live, for God would be angry with us if we broke our oath. [21] Let them live. But we will make them chop the wood and carry the water for the entire community."

So the Israelites kept their promise to the Gibeonites. [22] But Joshua called together the Gibeonite leaders and said, "Why did you lie to us? Why did you say that you live in a distant land when you live right here among us? [23] May you be cursed! From now on you will chop wood and carry water for the house of my God."

[24] They replied, "We did it because we were told that the LORD your God instructed his servant Moses to conquer this entire land and destroy all the people living in it. So we feared for our lives because of you. That is why we have done it. [25] Now we are at your mercy—do whatever you think is right."

[26] Joshua did not allow the people of Israel to kill them. [27] But that day he made the Gibeonites the woodchoppers and water carriers for the people of Israel and for the altar of the LORD—wherever the LORD would choose to build it. That arrangement continues to this day.

CHAPTER 10

Israel Defeats the Southern Kings

Now Adoni-zedek, king of Jerusalem, heard that Joshua had captured and completely destroyed* Ai and killed its king, just as he had destroyed the city of Jericho and killed its king. He also learned that the Gibeonites had made peace with Israel and were now their allies. [2] He and his people became very afraid when they heard all this because Gibeon was a large city—as large as the royal cities and larger than Ai. And the Gibeonite men were mighty warriors. [3] So King Adoni-zedek of Jerusalem sent messengers to several other kings: Hoham of Hebron, Piram of Jarmuth, Japhia of Lachish, and Debir of Eglon. [4] "Come and help me destroy Gibeon," he urged them, "for they have made peace with Joshua and the people of Israel." [5] So these five Amorite kings combined their armies for a united attack. They moved all their troops into place and attacked Gibeon.

[6] The men of Gibeon quickly sent messengers to Joshua at Gilgal, "Don't abandon your servants now!" they pleaded. "Come quickly and save us! For all the Amorite kings who live in the hill country have come out against us with their armies."

[7] So Joshua and the entire Israelite army left Gilgal and set out to rescue Gibeon. [8] "Do not be afraid of them," the LORD said to Joshua, "for I will give

I ASK the Lord for wisdom even in situations where I think I know what to do. (9:14)

I DO NOT MAKE binding agreements quickly before thoroughly examining the facts. (9:15)

I DO NOT BREAK a binding agreement, even if I have made a mistake. (9:19)

I TAKE oaths very seriously, for God does as well. (9:20)

See Moses' profile (page 73) at Exodus 5:1.

I LOOK to God's people to help me when I am in dire straits. (10:6)

I BELIEVE the Lord spoke to Joshua, promising him victory over the pagan kingdoms west and just north of the Dead Sea. (10:8)

10:1 The Hebrew term used here refers to the complete consecration of things or people to the LORD, either by destroying them or by giving them as an offering; also in 10:28, 35, 37, 39, 40.

you victory over them. Not a single one of them will be able to stand up to you."

⁹Joshua traveled all night from Gilgal and took the Amorite armies by surprise. ¹⁰The LORD threw them into a panic, and the Israelites slaughtered them in great numbers at Gibeon. Then the Israelites chased the enemy along the road to Beth-horon and attacked them at Azekah and Makkedah, killing them along the way. ¹¹As the Amorites retreated down the road from Beth-horon, the LORD destroyed them with a terrible hailstorm that continued until they reached Azekah. The hail killed more of the enemy than the Israelites killed with the sword.

¹²On the day the LORD gave the Israelites victory over the Amorites, Joshua prayed to the LORD in front of all the people of Israel. He said,

"Let the sun stand still over Gibeon,
and the moon over the valley of Aijalon."

¹³So the sun and moon stood still until the Israelites had defeated their enemies.

Is this event not recorded in *The Book of Jashar**? The sun stopped in the middle of the sky, and it did not set as on a normal day. ¹⁴The LORD fought for Israel that day. Never before or since has there been a day like that one, when the LORD answered such a request from a human being.

¹⁵Then Joshua and the Israelite army returned to their camp at Gilgal.

Joshua Kills the Five Southern Kings

¹⁶During the battle, the five kings escaped and hid in a cave at Makkedah. ¹⁷When Joshua heard that they had been found, ¹⁸he issued this command: "Cover the opening of the cave with large rocks and place guards at the entrance to keep the kings inside. ¹⁹The rest of you continue chasing the enemy and cut them down from the rear. Don't let them get back to their cities, for the LORD your God has given you victory over them."

²⁰So Joshua and the Israelite army continued the slaughter and wiped out the five armies except for a tiny remnant that managed to reach their fortified cities. ²¹Then the Israelites returned safely to their camp at Makkedah. After that, no one dared to speak a word against Israel.

²²Then Joshua said, "Remove the rocks covering the opening of the cave and bring the five kings to me." ²³So they brought the five kings out of the cave—the kings of Jerusalem, Hebron, Jarmuth, Lachish, and Eglon. ²⁴Joshua told the captains of his army, "Come and put your feet on the kings' necks." And they did as they were told.

²⁵"Don't ever be afraid or discouraged," Joshua told his men. "Be strong and courageous, for the LORD is going to do this to all of your enemies." ²⁶Then Joshua killed each of the five kings and hung them on five trees until evening.

²⁷As the sun was going down, Joshua gave instructions for the bodies of the kings to be taken down from the trees and thrown into the cave where they had been hiding. Then they covered the opening of the cave with a large pile of stones, which remains to this very day.

Israel Destroys the Southern Cities

²⁸That same day Joshua completely destroyed the city of Makkedah, killing everyone in it, including the king. Not one person in the city was left alive. He killed the king of Makkedah as he had killed the king of Jericho. ²⁹Then Joshua and the Israelites went to Libnah and attacked it. ³⁰There, too, the LORD gave them the city and its king. They slaughtered everyone in the city

---

I BELIEVE the Lord fought for Joshua and the Israelites, killing more of the enemy with hail than with the sword. (10:10)

I BELIEVE Joshua prayed publicly, asking the Lord to let the sun and moon stand still, and the Lord answered his prayer. (10:12)

I TRUST the Lord's promises. (10:19)

I ENCOURAGE others to trust in the Lord, even in the midst of adverse circumstances. (10:25)

10:13 Or *The Book of the Upright.*

and left no survivors. Then Joshua killed the king of Libnah just as he had killed the king of Jericho.

³¹From Libnah, Joshua and the Israelites went to Lachish and attacked it. ³²And the LORD gave it to them on the second day. Here, too, the entire population was slaughtered, just as at Libnah. ³³During the attack on Lachish, King Horam of Gezer had arrived with his army to help defend the city. But Joshua's men killed him and destroyed his entire army.

³⁴Then Joshua and the Israelite army went to Eglon and attacked it. ³⁵They captured it in one day, and as at Lachish, they completely destroyed everyone in the city. ³⁶After leaving Eglon, they attacked Hebron, ³⁷capturing it and all of its surrounding towns. And just as they had done at Eglon, they completely destroyed the entire population. Not one person was left alive. ³⁸Then they turned back and attacked Debir. ³⁹They captured the city, its king, and all of its surrounding villages. And they killed everyone in it, leaving no survivors. They completely destroyed Debir just as they had destroyed Libnah and Hebron.

⁴⁰So Joshua conquered the whole region—the kings and people of the hill country, the Negev, the western foothills,* and the mountain slopes. He completely destroyed everyone in the land, leaving no survivors, just as the LORD, the God of Israel, had commanded. ⁴¹Joshua slaughtered them from Kadesh-barnea to Gaza and from Goshen to Gibeon. ⁴²In a single campaign Joshua conquered all these kings and their land, for the LORD, the God of Israel, was fighting for his people. ⁴³Then Joshua and the Israelite army returned to their camp at Gilgal.

> I BELIEVE Joshua and the Israelites conquered the region west and just north of the Dead Sea, just as the Lord had promised. (10:40)

CHAPTER 11

Israel Defeats the Northern Kings

When King Jabin of Hazor heard what had happened, he sent urgent messages to the following kings: King Jobab of Madon; the king of Shimron; the king of Acshaph; ²all the kings of the northern hill country; the kings in the Jordan Valley* south of Galilee*; the kings in the western foothills*; the kings of Naphoth-dor on the west; ³the kings of Canaan, both east and west; the kings of the Amorites; the kings of the Hittites; the kings of the Perizzites; the kings in the Jebusite hill country; and the Hivites in the towns on the slopes of Mount Hermon, in the land of Mizpah.

⁴All these kings responded by mobilizing their warriors and uniting to fight against Israel. Their combined armies, along with a vast array of horses and chariots, covered the landscape like the sand on the seashore. ⁵They established their camp around the water near Merom to fight against Israel.

⁶Then the LORD said to Joshua, "Do not be afraid of them. By this time tomorrow they will all be dead. Cripple their horses and burn their chariots."

⁷So Joshua and his warriors traveled to the water near Merom and attacked suddenly. ⁸And the LORD gave them victory over their enemies. The Israelites chased them as far as Great Sidon and Misrephoth-maim, and eastward into the valley of Mizpah, until not one enemy warrior was left alive. ⁹Then Joshua crippled the horses and burned all the chariots, as the LORD had instructed.

¹⁰Joshua then turned back and captured Hazor and killed its king. (Hazor had at one time been the capital of the federation of all these kingdoms.) ¹¹The Israelites completely destroyed* every living thing in the city. Not a single person was spared. And then Joshua burned the city.

¹²Joshua slaughtered all the other kings and their people, completely

> I BELIEVE the Lord spoke to Joshua, promising him victory over all the pagan kingdoms north and northwest of the Dead Sea. (11:6)

> I OBEY the Lord's commands completely and consistently. (11:12)

10:40 Hebrew *the Shephelah.*   11:2a Hebrew *the Arabah;* also in 11:16.   11:2b Hebrew *of Kinnereth.*
11:2c Hebrew *the Shephelah;* also in 11:16.   11:11 The Hebrew term used here refers to the complete consecration of things or people to the LORD, either by destroying them or by giving them as an offering; also in 11:12, 20, 21.

destroying them, just as Moses, the servant of the LORD, had commanded. [13]However, Joshua did not burn any of the cities built on mounds except Hazor. [14]And the Israelites took all the captured goods and cattle of the ravaged cities for themselves, but they killed all the people. [15]As the LORD had commanded his servant Moses, so Moses commanded Joshua. And Joshua did as he was told, carefully obeying all of the LORD's instructions to Moses.

[16]So Joshua conquered the entire region—the hill country, the Negev, the land of Goshen, the western foothills, the Jordan Valley, and the mountains and lowlands of Israel. [17]The Israelite territory now extended all the way from Mount Halak, which leads up to Seir, to Baal-gad at the foot of Mount Hermon in the valley of Lebanon. Joshua killed all the kings of those territories, [18]waging war for a long time to accomplish this. [19]No one in this region made peace with the Israelites except the Hivites of Gibeon. All the others were defeated. [20]For the LORD hardened their hearts and caused them to fight the Israelites instead of asking for peace. So they were completely and mercilessly destroyed, as the LORD had commanded Moses.

[21]During this period, Joshua destroyed all the descendants of Anak, who lived in the hill country of Hebron, Debir, Anab, and the entire hill country of Judah and Israel. He killed them all and completely destroyed their towns. [22]Not one was left in all the land of Israel, though some still remained in Gaza, Gath, and Ashdod.

[23]So Joshua took control of the entire land, just as the LORD had instructed Moses. He gave it to the people of Israel as their special possession, dividing the land among the tribes. So the land finally had rest from war.

CHAPTER 12

Kings Defeated East of the Jordan

These are the kings east of the Jordan River who had been killed and whose land was taken. Their territory extended from the Arnon Gorge to Mount Hermon and included all the land east of the Jordan Valley.*

[2]King Sihon of the Amorites, who lived in Heshbon, was defeated. His kingdom included Aroer, on the edge of the Arnon Gorge, and extended from the middle of the Arnon Gorge to the Jabbok River, which serves as a boundary for the Ammonites. This territory included half of the present area of Gilead, which lies north of the Jabbok River. [3]Sihon also controlled the Jordan Valley as far north as the western shores of the Sea of Galilee* and as far south as the Dead Sea,* from Beth-jeshimoth to the slopes of Pisgah.

[4]King Og of Bashan, the last of the Rephaites, lived at Ashtaroth and Edrei. [5]He ruled a territory stretching from Mount Hermon to Salecah in the north and to all of Bashan in the east, and westward to the boundaries of the kingdoms of Geshur and Maacah. His kingdom included the northern half of Gilead, the other portion of which was in the territory of King Sihon of Heshbon. [6]Moses, the servant of the LORD, and the Israelites had destroyed the people of King Sihon and King Og. And Moses gave their land to the tribes of Reuben, Gad, and the half-tribe of Manasseh.

Kings Defeated West of the Jordan

[7]The following is a list of the kings Joshua and the Israelite armies defeated on the west side of the Jordan, from Baal-gad in the valley of Lebanon to Mount Halak, which leads up to Seir. (Joshua allotted this land to the tribes of Israel as their inheritance, [8]including the hill country, the western foothills,* the Jordan Valley, the mountain slopes, the Judean wilderness, and the Negev. The people who lived in this region were the Hittites, the

---

I OBEY the Lord's commands completely and teach them to others. (11:15)

See Moses' profile (page 73) at Exodus 5:1.

I BELIEVE Joshua and the Israelites completely destroyed the pagan kingdoms in obedience to the Lord, who had condemned them because of their exceeding wickedness. (11:20)

I BELIEVE the Lord gave the Israelites the Promised Land as their special possession. (11:23)

I BELIEVE Moses and the Israelites completely destroyed two pagan kingdoms east of the Jordan River. (12:6)

See Moses' profile (page 73) at Exodus 5:1.

12:1 Hebrew *the Arabah;* also in 12:3, 8.   12:3a Hebrew *sea of Kinnereth.*   12:3b Hebrew *the sea of the Arabah, the Salt Sea.*   12:8 Hebrew *the Shephelah.*

Amorites, the Canaanites, the Perizzites, the Hivites, and the Jebusites.) These are the kings Israel defeated:

9 The king of Jericho
   The king of Ai, near Bethel
10 The king of Jerusalem
   The king of Hebron
11 The king of Jarmuth
   The king of Lachish
12 The king of Eglon
   The king of Gezer
13 The king of Debir
   The king of Geder
14 The king of Hormah
   The king of Arad
15 The king of Libnah
   The king of Adullam
16 The king of Makkedah
   The king of Bethel
17 The king of Tappuah
   The king of Hepher
18 The king of Aphek
   The king of Lasharon
19 The king of Madon
   The king of Hazor
20 The king of Shimron-meron
   The king of Acshaph
21 The king of Taanach
   The king of Megiddo
22 The king of Kedesh
   The king of Jokneam in Carmel
23 The king of Dor in the city of Naphoth-dor*
   The king of Goyim in Gilgal*
24 The king of Tirzah.

In all, thirty-one kings and their cities were destroyed.

CHAPTER 13

The Land Yet to Be Conquered

When Joshua was an old man, the LORD said to him, "You are growing old, and much land remains to be conquered. 2The people still need to occupy the land of the Philistines and the Geshurites—3territory that belongs to the Canaanites. This land extends from the stream of Shihor, which is on the boundary of Egypt, northward to the boundary of Ekron, 4and includes the five Philistine cities of Gaza, Ashdod, Ashkelon, Gath, and Ekron. The land of the Avvites in the south also remains to be conquered. In the north, this area has not yet been conquered: all the land of the Canaanites, including Mearah (which belongs to the Sidonians), stretching northward to Aphek on the border of the Amorites; 5the land of the Gebalites and all of the Lebanon mountain area to the east, from Baal-gad beneath Mount Hermon to Lebo-hamath; 6and all the hill country from Lebanon to Misrephoth-maim, including all the land of the Sidonians.

"I will drive these people out of the land for the Israelites. So be sure to give this land to Israel as a special possession, just as I have commanded you.

If something in this Bible helps you experience a closer walk with God, why not share it with others?

I BELIEVE Joshua and the Israelites completely destroyed thirty-one pagan kingdoms west of the Jordan River. (12:24)

I BELIEVE the Lord spoke to Joshua, in his old age, about the land yet to be conquered within the Promised Land. (13:1)

I BELIEVE the Lord commanded Joshua to divide the entire Promised Land among the Israelite tribes. (13:6)

12:23a Hebrew *Naphath-dor*, a variant name for Naphoth-dor.   12:23b Greek version reads *Goyim in Galilee*.

I BELIEVE Moses already had assigned inheritances to two and a half Israelite tribes east of the Jordan River. (13:8)

See Moses' profile (page 73) at Exodus 5:1.

I BELIEVE several pagan peoples remained within the borders of the Israelite inheritances east of the Jordan River. (13:13)

I BELIEVE Moses assigned the tribe of Reuben territory east of the Jordan River as an inheritance. (13:15)

I BELIEVE Moses assigned the tribe of Gad territory east of the Jordan River as an inheritance. (13:24)

I BELIEVE Moses assigned the half-tribe of Manasseh territory east of the Jordan River as an inheritance. (13:29)

⁷Include all this territory as Israel's inheritance when you divide the land among the nine tribes and the half-tribe of Manasseh."

The Land Divided East of the Jordan
⁸Half the tribe of Manasseh and the tribes of Reuben and Gad had already received their inheritance on the east side of the Jordan, for Moses, the servant of the LORD, had previously assigned this land to them.

⁹Their territory extended from Aroer on the edge of the Arnon Gorge (including the town in the middle of the gorge) to the plain beyond Medeba, as far as Dibon. ¹⁰It also included all the towns of King Sihon of the Amorites, who reigned in Heshbon, and extended as far as the borders of Ammon. ¹¹It included Gilead, the territory of the kingdoms of Geshur and Maacah, all of Mount Hermon, all of Bashan as far as Salecah, ¹²and all the territory of King Og of Bashan, who had reigned in Ashtaroth and Edrei. King Og was the last of the Rephaites, for Moses had attacked them and driven them out. ¹³But the Israelites failed to drive out the people of Geshur and Maacah, so they continue to live among the Israelites to this day.

An Inheritance for the Tribe of Levi
¹⁴Moses did not assign any land to the tribe of Levi. Instead, as the LORD had promised them, their inheritance came from the offerings burned on the altar to the LORD, the God of Israel.

The Land Given to the Tribe of Reuben
¹⁵Moses had assigned the following area to the families of the tribe of Reuben.

¹⁶Their territory extended from Aroer on the edge of the Arnon Gorge (including the town in the middle of the gorge) to the plain beyond Medeba. ¹⁷It included Heshbon and the other towns on the plain—Dibon, Bamoth-baal, Beth-baal-meon, ¹⁸Jahaz, Kedemoth, Mephaath, ¹⁹Kiriathaim, Sibmah, Zereth-shahar on the hill above the valley, ²⁰Beth-peor, the slopes of Pisgah, and Beth-jeshimoth.
²¹The land of Reuben also included all the towns of the plain and the entire kingdom of Sihon. Sihon was the Amorite king who had reigned in Heshbon and was killed by Moses along with the chiefs of Midian—Evi, Rekem, Zur, Hur, and Reba—princes living in the region who were allied with Sihon. ²²The Israelites also killed Balaam the magician, the son of Beor. ²³The Jordan River marked the western boundary for the tribe of Reuben. The towns and villages in this area were given as an inheritance to the families of the tribe of Reuben.

The Land Given to the Tribe of Gad
²⁴Moses had assigned the following area to the families of the tribe of Gad.

²⁵Their territory included Jazer, all the towns of Gilead, and half of the land of Ammon, as far as the town of Aroer just west of Rabbah. ²⁶It extended from Heshbon to Ramath-mizpeh and Betonim, and from Mahanaim to Lo-debar.* ²⁷In the valley were Beth-haram, Beth-nimrah, Succoth, Zaphon, and the rest of the kingdom of King Sihon of Heshbon. The Jordan River was the western border, extending as far north as the Sea of Galilee.* ²⁸The towns and villages in this area were given as an inheritance to the families of the tribe of Gad.

The Land Given to the Half-Tribe of Manasseh
²⁹Moses had assigned the following area to the families of the half-tribe of Manasseh.

³⁰Their territory extended from Mahanaim, including all of Bashan, all the

13:26 Or *to the territory of Debir.* 13:27 Hebrew *sea of Kinnereth.*

former kingdom of King Og, and the sixty towns of Jair in Bashan. ³¹It also included half of Gilead and King Og's royal cities of Ashtaroth and Edrei. All this was given to the descendants of Makir, who was Manasseh's son.

³² These are the allotments Moses had made while he was on the plains of Moab, across the Jordan River, east of Jericho. ³³But Moses gave no land to the tribe of Levi, for the LORD, the God of Israel, had promised to be their inheritance.

CHAPTER 14

The Land Divided West of the Jordan

The remaining tribes of Israel inherited land in Canaan as allotted by Eleazar the priest, Joshua son of Nun, and the tribal leaders. ²These nine and a half tribes received their inheritance by means of sacred lots, in accordance with the LORD's command through Moses. ³Moses had already given an inheritance of land to the two and a half tribes on the east side of the Jordan River. ⁴The tribe of Joseph had become two separate tribes—Manasseh and Ephraim. And the Levites were given no land at all, only towns to live in and the surrounding pasturelands for their flocks and herds. ⁵So the distribution of the land was in strict accordance with the LORD's instructions to Moses.

Caleb Requests His Land

⁶A delegation from the tribe of Judah, led by Caleb son of Jephunneh the Kenizzite, came to Joshua at Gilgal. Caleb said to Joshua, "Remember what the LORD said to Moses, the man of God, about you and me when we were at Kadesh-barnea. ⁷I was forty years old when Moses, the servant of the LORD, sent me from Kadesh-barnea to explore the land of Canaan. I returned and gave from my heart a good report, ⁸but my brothers who went with me frightened the people and discouraged them from entering the Promised Land. For my part, I followed the LORD my God completely. ⁹So that day Moses promised me, 'The land of Canaan on which you were just walking will be your special possession and that of your descendants forever, because you wholeheartedly followed the LORD my God.'

¹⁰"Now, as you can see, the LORD has kept me alive and well as he promised for all these forty-five years since Moses made this promise—even while Israel wandered in the wilderness. Today I am eighty-five years old. ¹¹I am as strong now as I was when Moses sent me on that journey, and I can still travel and fight as well as I could then. ¹²So I'm asking you to give me the hill country that the LORD promised me. You will remember that as scouts we found the Anakites living there in great, walled cities. But if the LORD is with me, I will drive them out of the land, just as the LORD said."

¹³So Joshua blessed Caleb son of Jephunneh and gave Hebron to him as an inheritance. ¹⁴Hebron still belongs to the descendants of Caleb son of Jephunneh the Kenizzite because he wholeheartedly followed the LORD, the God of Israel. ¹⁵(Previously Hebron had been called Kiriath-arba. It had been named after Arba, a great hero of the Anakites.)

And the land had rest from war.

CHAPTER 15

The Land Given to the Tribe of Judah

The land assigned to the families of the tribe of Judah reached southward to the border of Edom, with the wilderness of Zin being its southernmost point.

²The southern boundary began at the south bay of the Dead Sea,* ³ran south of Scorpion Pass* into the wilderness of Zin and went south of Kadesh-barnea to Hezron. Then it went up to Addar, where it turned toward Karka. ⁴From there it passed to Azmon, until it finally reached the

I BELIEVE Joshua and the other leaders assigned the inheritances by sacred lots, in accordance with the Lord's command through Moses. (14:2)

See Moses' profile (page 73) at Exodus 5:1.

See Joseph's profile (page 51) at Genesis 39:2.

I FOLLOW the Lord my God completely and never discourage others from obeying him. (14:8)

I CLAIM the Lord's promises, confident that he is with me. (14:12)

I BLESS those who claim the Lord's promises. (14:13)

I BELIEVE my descendants will be blessed for years to come if I follow the Lord wholeheartedly. (14:14)

I BELIEVE Joshua assigned a vast inheritance to the tribe of Judah by sacred lot. (15:1)

15:2 Hebrew the Salt Sea; also in 15:5. 15:3 Hebrew Akrabbim.

brook of Egypt, which it followed to the Mediterranean Sea.* This was their* southern boundary.

⁵The eastern boundary extended along the Dead Sea to the mouth of the Jordan River.

The northern boundary began at the bay where the Jordan River empties into the Dead Sea, ⁶crossed to Beth-hoglah, then proceeded north of Beth-arabah to the stone of Bohan. (Bohan was Reuben's son.) ⁷From that point it went through the valley of Achor to Debir, turning north toward Gilgal, which is across from the slopes of Adummim on the south side of the valley. From there the border extended to the springs at En-shemesh and on to En-rogel. ⁸The boundary then passed through the valley of the son of Hinnom, along the southern slopes of the Jebusites, where the city of Jerusalem is located. Then it went west to the top of the mountain above the valley of Hinnom, and on up to the northern end of the valley of Rephaim. ⁹From there the border extended from the top of the mountain to the spring at the waters of Nephtoah,* and from there to the towns on Mount Ephron. Then it turned toward Baalah (that is, Kiriath-jearim). ¹⁰The border circled west of Baalah to Mount Seir, passed along to the town of Kesalon on the northern slope of Mount Jearim, and went down to Beth-shemesh and on to Timnah. ¹¹The boundary line then proceeded to the slope of the hill north of Ekron, where it turned toward Shikkeron and Mount Baalah. It passed Jabneel and ended at the Mediterranean Sea.

¹²The western boundary was the shoreline of the Mediterranean Sea.*

These are the boundaries for the families of the tribe of Judah.

The Land Given to Caleb

I LAY HOLD of what the Lord has promised. (15:13)

¹³The LORD instructed Joshua to assign some of Judah's territory to Caleb son of Jephunneh. So Caleb was given the city of Arba (that is, Hebron), which had been named after Anak's ancestor. ¹⁴Caleb drove out the three Anakites—Sheshai, Ahiman, and Talmai—descendants of Anak.

I KEEP my promises. (15:17)

¹⁵Then he fought against the people living in the town of Debir (formerly called Kiriath-sepher). ¹⁶Caleb said, "I will give my daughter Acsah in marriage to the one who attacks and captures Kiriath-sepher." ¹⁷Othniel, the son of Caleb's brother Kenaz, was the one who conquered it, so Acsah became Othniel's wife.

I DO all I can to see that my children are prosperous when they marry. (15:18)

¹⁸When Acsah married Othniel, she urged him* to ask her father for an additional field. As she got down off her donkey, Caleb asked her, "What is it? What can I do for you?"

¹⁹She said, "Give me a further blessing. You have been kind enough to give me land in the Negev; please give me springs as well." So Caleb gave her the upper and lower springs.

The Towns Judah Inherited

²⁰This was the inheritance given to the families of the tribe of Judah.

²¹The towns of Judah situated along the borders of Edom in the extreme south are Kabzeel, Eder, Jagur, ²²Kinah, Dimonah, Adadah, ²³Kedesh, Hazor, Ithnan, ²⁴Ziph, Telem, Bealoth, ²⁵Hazor-hadattah, Kerioth-hezron (that is, Hazor), ²⁶Amam, Shema, Moladah, ²⁷Hazar-gaddah, Heshmon, Beth-pelet, ²⁸Hazar-shual, Beersheba, Biziothiah, ²⁹Baalah, Iim, Ezem, ³⁰Eltolad, Kesil, Hormah, ³¹Ziklag, Madmannah, Sansannah, ³²Lebaoth, Shilhim, Ain, and Rimmon. In all, there were twenty-nine of these towns with their surrounding villages.

³³The following towns situated in the western foothills* were also

15:4a Hebrew *the sea;* also in 15:11. 15:4b Hebrew *your.* 15:9 Or *the spring at Me-nephtoah.* 15:12 Hebrew *the Great Sea;* also in 15:47. 15:18 Some Greek manuscripts read *Othniel urged her.* 15:33 Hebrew *the Shephelah.*

given to Judah: Eshtaol, Zorah, Ashnah, ³⁴Zanoah, En-gannim, Tappuah, Enam, ³⁵Jarmuth, Adullam, Socoh, Azekah, ³⁶Shaaraim, Adithaim, Gederah, and Gederothaim. In all, there were fourteen towns with their surrounding villages.

³⁷Also included were Zenan, Hadashah, Migdal-gad, ³⁸Dilean, Mizpeh, Joktheel, ³⁹Lachish, Bozkath, Eglon, ⁴⁰Cabbon, Lahmam, Kitlish, ⁴¹Gederoth, Beth-dagon, Naamah, and Makkedah—sixteen towns with their surrounding villages. ⁴²Besides these, there were Libnah, Ether, Ashan, ⁴³Iphtah, Ashnah, Nezib, ⁴⁴Keilah, Aczib, and Mareshah—nine towns with their surrounding villages.

⁴⁵The territory of the tribe of Judah also included all the towns and villages of Ekron. ⁴⁶From Ekron the boundary extended west and included the towns near Ashdod with their surrounding villages. ⁴⁷It also included Ashdod with its towns and villages and Gaza with its towns and villages, as far as the brook of Egypt and along the coast of the Mediterranean Sea.

LIKE CALEB
Joshua 14:12

I never stop taking on challenges to trust and obey God.

In 1962 young adults listened breathlessly to news reports that John Glenn had become the first man to orbit the earth. Thirty-six years later, their grandchildren watched excitedly as the same man, now seventy-seven years old, stepped aboard the space shuttle *Discovery* and once again made history for being the oldest person to orbit the earth.

Like John Glenn, Caleb was a man who seized adventure and challenge just as vigorously in his old age as he had in his youth. More importantly, Caleb renewed his strength and ability by continually trusting and obeying God.

Joshua and Caleb were the only senior citizens left among the Israelites. After spying out the land the first time, they alone believed in God's promises and power to defeat the Canaanites and give them the land. Because of their faith, they alone were spared when everyone else over twenty years of age was sentenced to wander in the wilderness until they died.

More than forty years later after Caleb's first visit to the Promised Land, his faith in the power of God still burned bright. When he saw the great mountains and walled cities a second time, he knew they were still no match for his God. The Lord had promised the Israelites the land, and Moses had promised Caleb those particular mountains. Age didn't matter when it came to trusting God. The Lord was with him, and Caleb knew he could conquer any obstacle.

No Christian need look back wistfully as if the days of trusting and obeying God must be relegated only to one's youthful past. Since the Lord is with us, you and I can take courage—no matter how great the challenge.

○ *Today's Scripture reading is Joshua 14:6–15:19.*

⁴⁸Judah also received the following towns in the hill country: Shamir, Jattir, Socoh, ⁴⁹Dannah, Kiriath-sannah (that is, Debir), ⁵⁰Anab, Eshtemoh, Anim, ⁵¹Goshen, Holon, and Giloh—eleven towns with their surrounding villages.

⁵²Also included were the towns of Arab, Dumah, Eshan, ⁵³Janim, Beth-tappuah, Aphekah, ⁵⁴Humtah, Kiriath-arba (that is, Hebron), and Zior—nine towns with their surrounding villages.

⁵⁵Besides these, there were Maon, Carmel, Ziph, Juttah, ⁵⁶Jezreel, Jokdeam, Zanoah, ⁵⁷Kain, Gibeah, and Timnah—ten towns with their surrounding villages.

⁵⁸In addition, there were Halhul, Beth-zur, Gedor, ⁵⁹Maarath, Beth-anoth, and Eltekon—six towns with their surrounding villages.

⁶⁰There were also Kiriath-baal (that is, Kiriath-jearim) and Rabbah—two towns with their surrounding villages.

⁶¹In the wilderness there were the towns of Beth-arabah, Middin, Secacah, ⁶²Nibshan, the City of Salt, and En-gedi—six towns with their surrounding villages.

⁶³But the tribe of Judah could not drive out the Jebusites, who lived in the city of Jerusalem, so the Jebusites live there among the people of Judah to this day.

CHAPTER 16

The Inheritance of Ephraim and West Manasseh

See Joseph's profile (page 51) at Genesis 39:2.

The allotment to the descendants of Joseph extended from the Jordan River near Jericho, east of the waters of Jericho, through the wilderness and into the hill country of Bethel. ²From Bethel (that is, Luz)* it ran over to Ataroth in the territory of the Arkites. ³Then it descended westward to the territory of the Japhletites as far as Lower Beth-horon, then to Gezer and on over to the Mediterranean Sea.*

The Land Given to Ephraim

⁴The families of Joseph's sons, Manasseh and Ephraim, received their inheritance.

⁵The following territory was given to the families of the tribe of Ephraim as their inheritance.

I BELIEVE Joshua assigned an inheritance to the tribe of Ephraim by sacred lot. (16:5)

The eastern boundary of their inheritance began at Ataroth-addar. From there it ran to Upper Beth-horon, ⁶then on to the Mediterranean Sea. The northern boundary began at the Mediterranean, ran east past Micmethath, then curved eastward past Taanath-shiloh to the east of Janoah. ⁷From Janoah it turned southward to Ataroth and Naarah, touched Jericho, and ended at the Jordan River. ⁸From Tappuah the border extended westward, following the Kanah Ravine to the Mediterranean Sea. This is the inheritance given to the families of the tribe of Ephraim.

I BELIEVE a pagan people remained within the borders of Ephraim's inheritance west of the Jordan River. (16:10)

⁹Ephraim was also given some towns with surrounding villages in the territory of the half-tribe of Manasseh. ¹⁰They did not drive the Canaanites out of Gezer, however, so the people of Gezer live as slaves among the people of Ephraim to this day.

CHAPTER 17

The Land Given to West Manasseh

I BELIEVE Joshua assigned an allotment of land to the half-tribe of Manasseh. (17:1)

See Joseph's profile (page 51) at Genesis 39:2
.

The next allotment of land was given to the half-tribe of Manasseh, the descendants of Joseph's older son. Gilead and Bashan on the east side of the Jordan had already been given to the family of Makir because he was a great warrior. (Makir was Manasseh's oldest son and was the father of Gilead.) ²Land on the west side of the Jordan was allotted to the remaining families within the tribe of Manasseh: Abiezer, Helek, Asriel, Shechem, Hepher, and Shemida.

³However, Zelophehad son of Hepher, who was a descendant of Manasseh, Makir, and Gilead, had no sons. Instead, he had five daughters. Their names were Mahlah, Noah, Hoglah, Milcah, and Tirzah. ⁴These women came to Eleazar the priest, Joshua son of Nun, and the Israelite leaders and said, "The LORD commanded Moses to give us an inheritance along with the men of our tribe."

I KEEP the Lord's command, even when it does not fit with traditional customs. (17:4)

See Moses' profile (page 73) at Exodus 5:1.

So Joshua gave them an inheritance along with their uncles, as the LORD had commanded. ⁵As a result, Manasseh's inheritance came to ten parcels of land, in addition to the land of Gilead and Bashan across the Jordan River,

16:2 As in Greek version (also see 18:13); Hebrew reads *From Bethel to Luz.*   16:3 Hebrew *the sea;* also in 16:6, 8.

⁶because the female descendants of Manasseh received an inheritance along with the male descendants. (The land of Gilead was given to the rest of the male descendants of Manasseh.)

⁷The boundary of the tribe of Manasseh extended from the border of Asher to Micmethath, which is east of Shechem. Then the boundary went south from Micmethath to the people living near the spring of Tappuah. ⁸(The land surrounding Tappuah belonged to Manasseh, but the town of Tappuah, on the border of Manasseh's territory, belonged to the tribe of Ephraim.) ⁹From the spring of Tappuah, the border of Manasseh followed the northern side of the Kanah Ravine to the Mediterranean Sea.* (Several towns in Manasseh's territory belonged to the tribe of Ephraim.) ¹⁰The land south of the ravine belonged to Ephraim, and the land north of the ravine belonged to Manasseh, with the Mediterranean Sea forming Manasseh's western border. North of Manasseh was the territory of Asher, and to the east was the territory of Issachar.

¹¹The following towns within the territory of Issachar and Asher were given to Manasseh: Beth-shan,* Ibleam, Dor (that is, Naphoth-dor),* Endor, Taanach, and Megiddo, with their respective villages. ¹²But the descendants of Manasseh were unable to occupy these towns. They could not drive out the Canaanites who continued to live there. ¹³Later on, however, when the Israelites became strong enough, they forced the Canaanites to work as slaves. But they did not drive them out of the land.

¹⁴The descendants of Joseph came to Joshua and asked, "Why have you given us only one portion of land when the LORD has given us so many people?"

¹⁵Joshua replied, "If the hill country of Ephraim is not large enough for you, clear out land for yourselves in the forest where the Perizzites and Rephaites live."

¹⁶They said, "The hill country is not enough for us, and the Canaanites in the lowlands around Beth-shan and the valley of Jezreel have iron chariots—they are too strong for us."

¹⁷Then Joshua said to the tribes of Ephraim and Manasseh, the descendants of Joseph, "Since you are so large and strong, you will be given more than one portion. ¹⁸The forests of the hill country will be yours as well. Clear as much of the land as you wish and live there. And I am sure you can drive out the Canaanites from the valleys, too, even though they are strong and have iron chariots."

CHAPTER 18

The Allotments of the Remaining Land

Now that the land was under Israelite control, the entire Israelite assembly gathered at Shiloh and set up the Tabernacle.* ²But there remained seven tribes who had not yet been allotted their inheritance.

³Then Joshua asked them, "How long are you going to wait before taking possession of the remaining land the LORD, the God of your ancestors, has given to you? ⁴Select three men from each tribe, and I will send them out to survey the unconquered territory. They will return to me with a written report of their proposed divisions of the inheritance. ⁵The scouts will map the land into seven sections, excluding Judah's territory in the south and Joseph's territory in the north. ⁶Then I will cast sacred lots in the presence of the LORD our God to decide which section will be assigned to each tribe. ⁷However, the Levites will not receive any land. Their role as priests of the LORD is their inheritance. And

I CHALLENGE those with needs to work hard and do their part to provide for themselves. (17:18)

I BELIEVE the Israelites set up the Tabernacle in Shiloh after conquering the Promised Land. (18:1)

I BELIEVE Joshua carefully sought to avoid repeating the mistakes made with the first spies sent out to explore the Promised Land forty-five years earlier. (18:4)

See Joseph's profile (page 51) at Genesis 39:2.

I BELIEVE Joshua used sacred lots to assign inheritances to each Israelite tribe. (18:6)

See Moses' profile (page 73) at Exodus 5:1.

17:9 Hebrew *the sea;* also in 17:10.   17:11a Hebrew *Beth-shean,* a variant name for Beth-shan; also in 17:16. 17:11b The meaning of the Hebrew here is uncertain.   18:1 Hebrew *Tent of Meeting.*

the tribes of Gad, Reuben, and the half-tribe of Manasseh won't receive any more land, for they have already received their inheritance, which Moses, the servant of the LORD, gave them on the east side of the Jordan River."

[8]As the men who were mapping out the land started on their way, Joshua commanded them, "Go and survey the land. Then return to me with your written report, and I will assign the land to the tribes by casting sacred lots in the presence of the LORD here at Shiloh." [9]The men did as they were told and mapped the entire territory into seven sections, listing the towns in each section. Then they returned to Joshua in the camp at Shiloh. [10]There at Shiloh, Joshua cast sacred lots in the presence of the LORD to determine which tribe should have each section.

The Land Given to Benjamin

[11]The first allotment of land went to the families of the tribe of Benjamin. It lay between the territory previously assigned to the tribes of Judah and Joseph.

[12]The northern boundary began at the Jordan River, went north of the slope of Jericho, then west through the hill country and the wilderness of Beth-aven. [13]From there the boundary went south to Luz (that is, Bethel) and proceeded down to Ataroth-addar to the top of the hill south of Lower Beth-horon.

[14]The boundary then ran south along the western edge of the hill facing Beth-horon, ending at the village of Kiriath-baal (that is, Kiriath-jearim), one of the towns belonging to the tribe of Judah. This was the western boundary.

[15]The southern boundary began at the outskirts of Kiriath-jearim. From there it ran westward* to the spring at the waters of Nephtoah,* [16]and down to the base of the mountain beside the valley of the son of Hinnom, at the northern end of the valley of Rephaim. From there it went down the valley of Hinnom, crossing south of the slope where the Jebusites lived, and continued down to En-rogel. [17]From En-rogel the boundary proceeded northeast to En-shemesh and on to Geliloth (which is across from the slopes of Adummim). Then it went down to the stone of Bohan. (Bohan was Reuben's son.) [18]From there it passed along the north side of the slope overlooking the Jordan Valley.* The border then went down into the valley, [19]ran past the north slope of Beth-hoglah, and ended at the north bay of the Dead Sea,* which is the southern end of the Jordan River.

[20]The eastern boundary was the Jordan River.

This was the inheritance for the families of the tribe of Benjamin.

The Towns Given to Benjamin

[21]These were the towns given to the families of the tribe of Benjamin.

Jericho, Beth-hoglah, Emek-keziz, [22]Beth-arabah, Zemaraim, Bethel, [23]Avvim, Parah, Ophrah, [24]Kephar-ammoni, Ophni, and Geba—twelve towns with their villages. [25]Also Gibeon, Ramah, Beeroth, [26]Mizpeh, Kephirah, Mozah, [27]Rekem, Irpeel, Taralah, [28]Zela, Haeleph, Jebus (that is, Jerusalem), Gibeah, and Kiriath-jearim*—fourteen towns with their villages.

This was the inheritance given to the families of the tribe of Benjamin.

CHAPTER 19
The Land Given to Simeon

The second allotment of land went to the families of the tribe of Simeon. Their inheritance was surrounded by Judah's territory.

I BELIEVE Joshua assigned an inheritance to the tribe of Benjamin that was between the territory previously assigned to Ephraim and Manasseh to the north and Judah to the south. (18:11)

18:15a Or it went to Ephron, and. The meaning of the Hebrew is uncertain. 18:15b Or the spring at Me-nephtoah. 18:18 Hebrew the Arabah. 18:19 Hebrew Salt Sea. 18:28 As in Greek version; Hebrew reads Kiriath.

[2]Simeon's inheritance included Beersheba, Sheba, Moladah, [3]Hazar-shual, Balah, Ezem, [4]Eltolad, Bethul, Hormah, [5]Ziklag, Beth-marcaboth, Hazar-susah, [6]Beth-lebaoth, and Sharuhen—thirteen towns with their villages. [7]It also included Ain, Rimmon, Ether, and Ashan—four towns with their villages, [8]including all the villages as far south as Baalath-beer (also known as Ramah of the Negev).

This was the inheritance of the families of the tribe of Simeon. [9]Their inheritance came from part of what had been given to Judah because Judah's territory was too large for them. So the tribe of Simeon received an inheritance within the territory of Judah.

The Land Given to Zebulun
[10]The third allotment of land went to the families of the tribe of Zebulun.

The boundary of Zebulun's inheritance started at Sarid. [11]From there it went west, going past Maralah, touching Dabbesheth, and proceeding to the brook east of Jokneam. [12]In the other direction, the boundary line went east from Sarid to the border of Kisloth-tabor, and from there to Daberath and up to Japhia. [13]Then it continued east to Gath-hepher, Eth-kazin, and Rimmon and turned toward Neah. [14]The northern boundary of Zebulun passed Hannathon and ended at the valley of Iphtah-el. [15]The towns in these areas included Kattath, Nahalal, Shimron, Idalah, and Bethlehem—twelve towns with their surrounding villages.

[16]This was the inheritance of the families of the tribe of Zebulun.

The Land Given to Issachar
[17]The fourth allotment of land went to the families of the tribe of Issachar.

[18]Its boundaries included the following towns: Jezreel, Kesulloth, Shunem, [19]Hapharaim, Shion, Anaharath, [20]Rabbith, Kishion, Ebez, [21]Remeth, En-gannim, En-haddah, and Beth-pazzez. [22]The boundary also touched Tabor, Shahazumah, and Beth-shemesh, ending at the Jordan River—sixteen towns with their surrounding villages.

[23]This was the inheritance of the families of the tribe of Issachar.

The Land Given to Asher
[24]The fifth allotment of land went to the families of the tribe of Asher.

[25]Its boundaries included these towns: Helkath, Hali, Beten, Acshaph, [26]Allammelech, Amad, and Mishal. The boundary on the west went from Carmel to Shihor-libnath, [27]turned east toward Beth-dagon, and ran as far as Zebulun in the valley of Iphtah-el, running north to Beth-emek and Neiel. It then continued north to Cabul, [28]Abdon,* Rehob, Hammon, Kanah, and as far as Greater Sidon. [29]Then the boundary turned toward Ramah and the fortified city of Tyre and came to the Mediterranean Sea* at Hosah. The territory also included Mehebel, Aczib, [30]Ummah, Aphek, and Rehob—twenty-two towns with their surrounding villages.

[31]This was the inheritance of the families of the tribe of Asher.

The Land Given to Naphtali
[32]The sixth allotment of land went to the families of the tribe of Naphtali.

[33]Its boundary ran from Heleph, from the oak at Zaanannim, and extended across to Adami-nekeb, Jabneel, and as far as Lakkum, ending at the Jordan River. [34]The western boundary ran past Aznoth-tabor, then to Hukkok, and touched the boundary of Zebulun in the south, the

I BELIEVE Joshua assigned an inheritance to the tribe of Simeon in the southern region of the Promised Land, within the territory previously assigned to Judah. (19:1)

I BELIEVE Joshua assigned an inheritance to the tribe of Zebulun in the northern regions of the Promised Land. (19:10)

I BELIEVE Joshua assigned an inheritance to the tribe of Issachar in the northern regions of the Promised Land. (19:17)

I BELIEVE Joshua assigned an inheritance to the tribe of Asher in the far northwest corner of the Promised Land. (19:24)

I BELIEVE Joshua assigned an inheritance to the tribe of Naphtali in the far northeast corner of the Promised Land. (19:32)

19:28 As in some Hebrew manuscripts (see also 21:30); most Hebrew manuscripts read *Ebron.*   19:29 Hebrew *the sea.*   19:34 Hebrew *and Judah at the Jordan River.*

boundary of Asher on the west, and the Jordan River* on the east. ³⁵The fortified cities included in this territory were Ziddim, Zer, Hammath, Rakkath, Kinnereth, ³⁶Adamah, Ramah, Hazor, ³⁷Kedesh, Edrei, En-hazor, ³⁸Yiron, Migdal-el, Horem, Beth-anath, and Beth-shemesh—nineteen cities with their surrounding villages.

³⁹This was the inheritance of the families of the tribe of Naphtali.

The Land Given to Dan

⁴⁰The seventh and last allotment of land went to the families of the tribe of Dan.

⁴¹The towns within Dan's inheritance included Zorah, Eshtaol, Ir-shemesh, ⁴²Shaalabbin, Aijalon, Ithlah, ⁴³Elon, Timnah, Ekron, ⁴⁴Eltekeh, Gibbethon, Baalath, ⁴⁵Jehud, Bene-berak, Gath-rimmon, ⁴⁶and Me-jarkon, also Rakkon along with the territory across from Joppa.

⁴⁷But the tribe of Dan had trouble taking possession of their land, so they fought against the town of Laish.* They captured it, slaughtered its people, and settled there. They renamed the city Dan after their ancestor.

⁴⁸This was the inheritance of the families of the tribe of Dan—these towns with their villages.

The Land Given to Joshua

⁴⁹After all the land was divided among the tribes, the Israelites gave a special piece of land to Joshua as his inheritance. ⁵⁰For the LORD had said he could have any town he wanted. He chose Timnath-serah in the hill country of Ephraim. He rebuilt the town and lived there.

⁵¹These are the territories that Eleazar the priest, Joshua son of Nun, and the tribal leaders gave as an inheritance to the tribes of Israel by casting sacred lots in the presence of the LORD at the entrance of the Tabernacle* at Shiloh. So the division of the land was completed.

CHAPTER 20

The Cities of Refuge

The LORD said to Joshua, ²"Now tell the Israelites to designate the cities of refuge, as I instructed Moses. ³Anyone who kills another person unintentionally can run to one of these cities and be protected from the relatives of the one who was killed, for the relatives may seek to avenge the killing.

⁴"Upon reaching one of these cities, the one who caused the accidental death will appear before the leaders at the city gate and explain what happened. They must allow the accused to enter the city and live there among them. ⁵If the relatives of the victim come to avenge the killing, the leaders must not release the accused to them, for the death was accidental. ⁶But the person who caused the death must stay in that city and be tried by the community and found innocent. Then the one declared innocent because the death was accidental must continue to live in that city until the death of the high priest who was in office at the time of the accident. After that, the one found innocent is free to return home."

⁷The following cities were designated as cities of refuge: Kedesh of Galilee, in the hill country of Naphtali; Shechem, in the hill country of Ephraim; and Kiriath-arba (that is, Hebron), in the hill country of Judah. ⁸On the east side of the Jordan River, across from Jericho, the following cities were designated as cities of refuge: Bezer, in the wilderness plain of the tribe of Reuben; Ramoth in Gilead, in the territory of the tribe of Gad; and Golan in Bashan, in the land of the tribe of Manasseh. ⁹These cities were set apart for Israelites as well as the foreigners living among them. Anyone who accidentally killed another person could take refuge in one of these cities. In this way, they could escape being killed in revenge prior to standing trial before the community.

19:47 Hebrew *Leshem*, another name for Laish.   19:51 Hebrew *Tent of Meeting*.

I BELIEVE Joshua assigned an inheritance to the tribe of Dan in the middle of the Promised Land. (19:40)

I BELIEVE the tribe of Dan conquered and added another town to its inheritance. (19:47)

I BELIEVE Joshua received a special inheritance from the nation of Israel. (19:49)

I BELIEVE the Lord told Joshua to designate several cities of refuge. (20:1)

See Moses' profile (page 73) at Exodus 5:1.

I BELIEVE the Lord made provisions to safeguard those who unintentionally killed someone. (20:3)

I BELIEVE Joshua designated cities of refuge both east and west of the Jordan River. (20:7)

CHAPTER 21

The Towns Given to the Levites

Then the leaders of the tribe of Levi came to consult with Eleazar the priest, Joshua son of Nun, and the leaders of the other tribes of Israel. [2]They spoke to them at Shiloh in the land of Canaan, saying, "The LORD instructed Moses to give us towns to live in and pasturelands for our cattle." [3]So by the command of the LORD the Levites were given as their inheritance the following towns with their pasturelands.

[4] The descendants of Aaron, who were members of the Kohathite clan within the tribe of Levi, were given thirteen towns that were originally assigned to the tribes of Judah, Simeon, and Benjamin. [5]The other families of the Kohathite clan were allotted ten towns from the territories of Ephraim, Dan, and the half-tribe of Manasseh.

[6]The clan of Gershon received thirteen towns from the tribes of Issachar, Asher, Naphtali, and the half-tribe of Manasseh in Bashan.

[7]The clan of Merari received twelve cities from the tribes of Reuben, Gad, and Zebulun.

[8]So the Israelites obeyed the LORD's command to Moses and assigned these towns and pasturelands to the Levites by casting sacred lots.

[9]The Israelites gave the following towns from the tribes of Judah and Simeon [10]to the descendants of Aaron, who were members of the Kohathite clan within the tribe of Levi, since the sacred lot fell to them first: [11]Kiriath-arba (that is, Hebron), in the hill country of Judah, along with its surrounding pasturelands. (Arba was an ancestor of Anak.) [12]But the fields beyond the city and the surrounding villages were given to Caleb son of Jephunneh.

[13] The following towns with their pasturelands were given to the descendants of Aaron the priest: Hebron (a city of refuge for those who accidentally killed someone), Libnah, [14]Jattir, Eshtemoa, [15]Holon, Debir, [16]Ain, Juttah, and Beth-shemesh—nine towns from these two tribes.

[17]From the tribe of Benjamin the priests were given the following towns with their surrounding pasturelands: Gibeon, Geba, [18]Anathoth, and Almon—four towns. [19]So thirteen towns were given to the priests, the descendants of Aaron.

[20] The rest of the Kohathite clan from the tribe of Levi was allotted these towns and pasturelands from the tribe of Ephraim: [21]Shechem (a city of refuge for those who accidentally killed someone), Gezer, [22]Kibzaim, and Beth-horon—four towns.

[23] The following towns and pasturelands were allotted to the priests from the tribe of Dan: Eltekeh, Gibbethon, [24]Aijalon, and Gath-rimmon—four towns.

[25] The half-tribe of Manasseh allotted the following towns with their pasturelands to the priests: Taanach and Gath-rimmon—two towns. [26]So ten towns with their pasturelands were given to the rest of the Kohathite clan.

[27] The descendants of Gershon, another clan within the tribe of Levi, received two towns with their pasturelands from the half-tribe of Manasseh: Golan in Bashan (a city of refuge) and Be-eshterah.

[28]From the tribe of Issachar they received Kishion, Daberath, [29]Jarmuth, and En-gannim—four towns with their pasturelands.

[30]From the tribe of Asher they received Mishal, Abdon, [31]Helkath, and Rehob—four towns and their pasturelands.

[32]From the tribe of Naphtali they received Kedesh in Galilee (a city of refuge), Hammoth-dor, and Kartan—three towns with their pasturelands.

[33]So thirteen towns and their pasturelands were allotted to the clan of Gershon.

[34]The rest of the Levites—the Merari clan—were given the following

See Moses' profile (page 73) at Exodus 5:1.

I BELIEVE Joshua gave dozens of towns to the Levites as part of their inheritance. (21:3)

See Aaron's profile (page 107) at Exodus 32:2.

I BELIEVE Joshua gave the rest of the Kohathite clan ten towns originally assigned to three of the central tribes. (21:5)

I BELIEVE Joshua gave the Gershon clan thirteen towns originally assigned to three of the northern tribes and one eastern tribe. (21:6)

I BELIEVE Joshua gave the Merari clan twelve towns from two eastern tribes and one northern tribe. (21:7)

I BELIEVE Joshua assigned forty-eight towns to the Levites in obedience to the Lord's commands. (21:8)

I BELIEVE Joshua assigned two cities of refuge—Hebron and Shechem—to the Kohathite clan. (21:13)

I BELIEVE Joshua assigned two cities of refuge—Golan and Kedesh—to the Gershon clan. (21:27)

towns from the tribe of Zebulun: Jokneam, Kartah, ³⁵Dimnah, and Nahalal—four towns with their pasturelands.

³⁶From the tribe of Reuben they received Bezer, Jahaz,* ³⁷Kedemoth, and Mephaath—four towns with their pasturelands.

³⁸From the tribe of Gad they received Ramoth in Gilead (a city of refuge), Mahanaim, ³⁹Heshbon, and Jazer—four towns with their pasturelands. ⁴⁰So twelve towns were allotted to the clan of Merari.

⁴¹ The total number of towns and pasturelands within Israelite territory given to the Levites came to forty-eight. ⁴²Every one of these towns had pasturelands surrounding it.

⁴³So the LORD gave to Israel all the land he had sworn to give their ancestors, and they conquered it and settled there. ⁴⁴And the LORD gave them rest on every side, just as he had solemnly promised their ancestors. None of their enemies could stand against them, for the LORD helped them conquer all their enemies. ⁴⁵All of the good promises that the LORD had given Israel came true.

CHAPTER 22

The Eastern Tribes Return Home

Then Joshua called together the tribes of Reuben, Gad, and the half-tribe of Manasseh. ²He told them, "You have done as Moses, the servant of the LORD, commanded you, and you have obeyed every order I have given you. ³You have not deserted the other tribes, even though the campaign has lasted for such a long time. You have been careful to obey the commands of the LORD your God up to the present day. ⁴And now the LORD your God has given the other tribes rest, as he promised them. So go home now to the land Moses, the servant of the LORD, gave you on the east side of the Jordan River. ⁵But be very careful to obey all the commands and the law that Moses gave to you. Love the LORD your God, walk in all his ways, obey his commands, be faithful to him, and serve him with all your heart and all your soul."

⁶So Joshua blessed them and sent them home. ⁷Now Moses had given the land of Bashan to the half-tribe of Manasseh east of the Jordan. The other half of the tribe was given land west of the Jordan. As Joshua sent them away, he blessed them ⁸and said, "Share with your relatives back home the great wealth you have taken from your enemies. Share with them your large herds of cattle, your silver and gold, your bronze and iron, and your clothing."

⁹So the men of Reuben, Gad, and the half-tribe of Manasseh left the rest of Israel at Shiloh in the land of Canaan. They started the journey back to their own land of Gilead, the territory that belonged to them according to the LORD's command through Moses.

The Eastern Tribes Build a Memorial

¹⁰But while they were still in Canaan, before they crossed the Jordan River, Reuben, Gad, and the half-tribe of Manasseh built a very large altar near the Jordan River at a place called Geliloth.

¹¹When the rest of Israel heard they had built the altar at Geliloth west of the Jordan River, in the land of Canaan, ¹²the whole assembly gathered at Shiloh and prepared to go to war against their brother tribes. ¹³First, however, they sent a delegation led by Phinehas son of Eleazar, the priest. They crossed the river to talk with the tribes of Reuben, Gad, and the half-tribe of Manasseh. ¹⁴In this delegation were ten high officials of Israel, one from each of the ten tribes, and each a leader within the family divisions of Israel.

¹⁵When they arrived in the land of Gilead, they said to the tribes of Reuben, Gad, and the half-tribe of Manasseh, ¹⁶"The whole community of the LORD demands to know why you are betraying the God of Israel. How could you

---

I BELIEVE Joshua assigned two cities of refuge—Bezer and Ramoth—to the Merari clan. (21:36)

I BELIEVE the Lord gave the Israelites all the land he promised—and peace on every side. (21:43)

I BELIEVE all of the good promises that the Lord had given to Israel came true. (21:45)

See Moses' profile (Page 73) at Exodus 5:1.

I KEEP the commitments that I make to others. (22:3)

I AM VERY CAREFUL to obey all of the Lord's commands, to love the Lord my God, to walk in all of his ways, to be faithful to him, and to serve him with all my heart and soul. (22:5)

I BLESS others and encourage them to bless still others. (22:8)

I INVESTIGATE a matter thoroughly instead of acting rashly. (22:13)

See Phinehas's profile (page 717) at Psalm 106:30.

I ABHOR the thought of ˙raying the Lord ˙˙q against

21:36 Hebrew *Jahzah*, a variant name for Jahaz.

turn away from the LORD and build an altar in rebellion against him? [17]Was our sin at Peor not enough? We are not yet fully cleansed of it, even after the plague that struck the entire assembly of the LORD. [18]And yet today you are turning away from following the LORD. If you rebel against the LORD today, he will be angry with all of us tomorrow. [19]If you need the altar because your land is defiled, then join us on our side of the river, where the LORD lives among us in his Tabernacle, and we will share our land with you. But do not rebel against the LORD or draw us into your rebellion by building another altar for yourselves. There is only one true altar of the LORD our God. [20]Didn't God punish all the people of Israel when Achan, a member of the clan of Zerah, sinned by stealing the things set apart for the LORD*? He was not the only one who died because of that sin."

[21]Then the people of Reuben, Gad, and the half-tribe of Manasseh answered these high officials: [22]"The LORD alone is God! The LORD alone is God! We have not built the altar in rebellion against the LORD. If we have done so, do not spare our lives this day. But the LORD knows, and let all Israel know, too, [23]that we have not built an altar for ourselves to turn away from the LORD. Nor will we use it for our burnt offerings or grain offerings or peace offerings. If we have built it for this purpose, may the LORD himself punish us.

[24]"We have built this altar because we fear that in the future your descendants will say to ours, 'What right do you have to worship the LORD, the God of Israel? [25]The LORD has placed the Jordan River as a barrier between our people and your people. You have no claim to the LORD.' And your descendants may make our descendants stop worshiping the LORD. [26]So we decided to build the altar, not for burnt sacrifices, [27]but as a memorial. It will remind our descendants and your descendants that we, too, have the right to worship the LORD at his sanctuary with our burnt offerings, sacrifices, and peace offerings. Then your descendants will not be able to say to ours, 'You have no claim to the LORD.' [28]If they say this, our descendants can reply, 'Look at this copy of the LORD's altar that our ancestors made. It is not for burnt offerings or sacrifices; it is a reminder of the relationship both of us have with the LORD.' [29]Far be it from us to rebel against the LORD or turn away from him by building our own altar for burnt offerings, grain offerings, or sacrifices. Only the altar of the LORD our God that stands in front of the Tabernacle may be used for that purpose."

[30]When Phinehas the priest and the high officials heard this from the tribes of Reuben, Gad, and the half-tribe of Manasseh, they were satisfied. [31]Phinehas son of Eleazar, the priest, replied to them, "Today we know the LORD is among us because you have not sinned against the LORD as we thought. Instead, you have rescued Israel from being destroyed by the LORD."

[32]Then Phinehas son of Eleazar, the priest, and the ten high officials left the tribes of Reuben and Gad in Gilead and returned to the land of Canaan to tell the Israelites what had happened. [33]And all the Israelites were satisfied and praised God and spoke no more of war against Reuben and Gad. [34]The people of Reuben and Gad named the altar "Witness,"* for they said, "It is a witness between us and them that the LORD is our God, too."

CHAPTER 23

Joshua's Final Words to Israel

The years passed, and the LORD had given the people of Israel rest from all their enemies. Joshua, who was now very old, [2]called together all the elders, leaders, judges, and officers of Israel. He said to them, "I am an old man now. [3]You have seen everything the LORD your God has done for you during my

I AM HAPPY when I see evidences that the Lord is among us. (22:31)

I PRAISE God when I hear a good report. (22:33)

I TAKE time to recall what the Lord has done during my lifetime. (23:3)

22:20 The Hebrew term used here refers to the complete consecration of things or people to the LORD, either by destroying them or by giving them as an offering.   22:34 Hebrew *edh*. Some manuscripts lack this word.

lifetime. The LORD your God has fought for you against your enemies. [4]I have allotted to you as an inheritance all the land of the nations yet unconquered, as well as the land of those we have already conquered—from the Jordan River to the Mediterranean Sea* in the west. [5]This land will be yours, for the LORD your God will drive out all the people living there now. You will live there instead of them, just as the LORD your God promised you.

[6]"So be strong! Be very careful to follow all the instructions written in the Book of the Law of Moses. Do not deviate from them in any way. [7]Make sure you do not associate with the other people still remaining in the land. Do not even mention the names of their gods, much less swear by them or worship them. [8]But be faithful to the LORD your God as you have done until now.

[9]"For the LORD has driven out great and powerful nations for you, and no one has yet been able to defeat you. [10]Each one of you will put to flight a thousand of the enemy, for the LORD your God fights for you, just as he has promised. [11]So be very careful to love the LORD your God.

[12]"But if you turn away from him and intermarry with the survivors of these nations remaining among you, [13]then know for certain that the LORD your God will no longer drive them out from your land. Instead, they will be a snare and a trap to you, a pain in your side and a thorn in your eyes, and you will be wiped out from this good land the LORD your God has given you.

[14]"Soon I will die, going the way of all the earth. Deep in your hearts you know that every promise of the LORD your God has come true. Not a single one has failed! [15]But as surely as the LORD your God has given you the good things he promised, he will also bring disaster on you if you disobey him. He will completely wipe you out from this good land he has given you. [16]If you break the covenant of the LORD your God by worshiping and serving other gods, his anger will burn against you, and you will quickly be wiped out from the good land he has given you."

CHAPTER 24

The LORD's Covenant Renewed

Then Joshua summoned all the people of Israel to Shechem, along with their elders, leaders, judges, and officers. So they came and presented themselves to God.

[2]Joshua said to the people, "This is what the LORD, the God of Israel, says: Your ancestors, including Terah, the father of Abraham and Nahor, lived beyond the Euphrates River,* and they worshiped other gods. [3]But I took your ancestor Abraham from the land beyond the Euphrates and led him into the land of Canaan. I gave him many descendants through his son Isaac. [4]To Isaac I gave Jacob and Esau. To Esau I gave the hill country of Seir, while Jacob and his children went down into Egypt.

[5]"Then I sent Moses and Aaron, and I brought terrible plagues on Egypt; and afterward I brought you out as a free people. [6]But when your ancestors arrived at the Red Sea,* the Egyptians chased after you with chariots and horses. [7]When you cried out to the LORD, I put darkness between you and the Egyptians. I brought the sea crashing down on the Egyptians, drowning them. With your very own eyes you saw what I did. Then you lived in the wilderness for many years.

[8]"Finally, I brought you into the land of the Amorites on the east side of the Jordan. They fought against you, but I gave you victory over them, and you took possession of their land. [9]Then Balak son of Zippor, king of Moab, started a war against Israel. He asked Balaam son of Beor to curse you, [10]but I would not listen to him. Instead, I made Balaam bless you, and so I rescued you from Balak.

**Sidebar (left margin):**

I ENCOURAGE others to be very careful to obey all of the Lord's commands and not deviate from them. (23:6)

See Moses' profile (page 73) at Exodus 5:1.

I BELIEVE the Lord fought for the Israelites, just as he promised. (23:10)

I AM VERY CAREFUL to love the Lord my God. (23:11)

I WOULD NEVER THINK of marrying an unbeliever. (23:12)

I KNOW that every promise of the Lord my God will come true—not a single one will fail! (23:14)

See Abraham's profile (page 19) at Genesis 15:6.

I TAKE the time to review what the Lord has done in the past for his people. (24:3)

See Esau's profile (Page 33) at Genesis 25:34.

See the profiles for Moses (page 73) and Aaron (page 107) at Exodus 5:1 and Exodus 32:2.

23:4 Hebrew *the Great Sea.*   24:2 Hebrew *the river;* also in 24:3, 14, 15.   24:6 Hebrew *sea of reeds.*

[11]"When you crossed the Jordan River and came to Jericho, the men of Jericho fought against you. There were also many others who fought you, including the Amorites, the Perizzites, the Canaanites, the Hittites, the Girgashites, the Hivites, and the Jebusites. But I gave you victory over them. [12]And I sent hornets ahead of you to drive out the two kings of the Amorites. It was not your swords or bows that brought you victory. [13]I gave you land you had not worked for, and I gave you cities you did not build—the cities in which you are now living. I gave you vineyards and olive groves for food, though you did not plant them.

I BELIEVE the Lord fought for the Israelites and gave them victory over many pagan kingdoms. (24:12)

LIKE JOSHUA

Joshua 23:14

I am filled with courage because of God's exceedingly great promises to me.

Even strong men need to take courage.

Joshua was a strong, rugged individual if ever there was one. From his youth as an assistant to Moses to his clandestine exploration of the Promised Land, Joshua had showed himself faithful in service, brave in battle, and mighty in faith.

Yet, as the new leader of Israel after Moses' death, Joshua had many compelling reasons to be afraid. As a good soldier, however, Joshua said yes! to the orders of his Commander: "Be strong. Take courage. Know my Word. Obey my commands. Do not be afraid. And do not forget that I am with you!" (see 1:2-9).

Obeying God's orders, Joshua proceeded to conquer the Promised Land, proving that all God's great promises will come to pass.

Now, at the end of his life, Joshua held out the same challenge to the Israelites: "Be strong. Obey God's Word. And don't forget that the Lord is with you to fight for you!" (see 23:6-11). Joshua had the courage to obey God because he wholeheartedly believed his promises. In turn, he coached his people to take courage. After all, they had seen all God's promises come true, too.

If you and I find ourselves filled with fear, it's because we have forgotten who God is and what he has promised (1 Peter 5:7-11). Like Joshua, we need to continually draw on our abiding source of courage—not our own physical strength or mental abilities but the presence and promises of the Lord God Almighty.

○ *Today's Scripture reading is Joshua 23–24.*

[14]"So honor the LORD and serve him wholeheartedly. Put away forever the idols your ancestors worshiped when they lived beyond the Euphrates River and in Egypt. Serve the LORD alone. [15]But if you are unwilling to serve the LORD, then choose today whom you will serve. Would you prefer the gods your ancestors served beyond the Euphrates? Or will it be the gods of the Amorites in whose land you now live? But as for me and my family, we will serve the LORD."

I HAVE chosen to follow the Lord wholeheartedly. (24:15)

[16] The people replied, "We would never forsake the LORD and worship other gods. [17]For the LORD our God is the one who rescued us and our ancestors from slavery in the land of Egypt. He performed mighty miracles before our very eyes. As we traveled through the wilderness among our enemies, he preserved us. [18]It was the LORD who drove out the Amorites and the other nations living here in the land. So we, too, will serve the LORD, for he alone is our God."

I WILL SERVE the Lord, for he alone is my God. (24:18)

[19]Then Joshua said to the people, "You are not able to serve the LORD, for he is a holy and jealous God. He will not forgive your rebellion and sins. [20]If you forsake the LORD and serve other gods, he will turn against you and destroy you, even though he has been so good to you."

[21]But the people answered Joshua, saying, "No, we are determined to serve the LORD!"

I BELIEVE the Lord is a holy and jealous God who will not ignore national rebellion and sins. (24:19)

²²"You are accountable for this decision," Joshua said. "You have chosen to serve the LORD."

"Yes," they replied, "we are accountable."

²³"All right then," Joshua said, "destroy the idols among you, and turn your hearts to the LORD, the God of Israel."

²⁴The people said to Joshua, "We will serve the LORD our God. We will obey him alone."

I HAVE COMMITTED myself to the Lord permanently. (24:25)

²⁵So Joshua made a covenant with the people that day at Shechem, committing them to a permanent and binding contract between themselves and the LORD. ²⁶Joshua recorded these things in the Book of the Law of God. As a reminder of their agreement, he took a huge stone and rolled it beneath the oak tree beside the Tabernacle of the LORD.

²⁷Joshua said to all the people, "This stone has heard everything the LORD said to us. It will be a witness to testify against you if you go back on your word to God."

²⁸Then Joshua sent the people away, each to his own inheritance.

Leaders Buried in the Promised Land

²⁹Soon after this, Joshua son of Nun, the servant of the LORD, died at the age of 110. ³⁰They buried him in the land he had inherited, at Timnath-serah in the hill country of Ephraim, north of Mount Gaash.

³¹Israel served the LORD throughout the lifetime of Joshua and of the leaders who outlived him—those who had personally experienced all that the LORD had done for Israel.

See Joseph's profile (page 51) at Genesis 39:2.

³²The bones of Joseph, which the Israelites had brought along with them when they left Egypt, were buried at Shechem, in the parcel of ground Jacob had bought from the sons of Hamor for one hundred pieces of silver.* This land was located in the territory allotted to the tribes of Ephraim and Manasseh, the descendants of Joseph.

See Phinehas's profile (page 717) at Psalm 106:30.

³³Eleazar son of Aaron also died. He was buried in the hill country of Ephraim, in the town of Gibeah, which had been given to his son Phinehas.

24:32 Hebrew *100 kesitahs;* the value or weight of the kesitah is no longer known.

JUDGES

THIS SECOND BOOK of Israelite history is filled with *cycles*.

Although Joshua had successfully brought the Israelites into the Promised Land, the tribes were slow to drive out their remaining enemies. The reason the Israelites needed to do this wasn't simply an issue of political survival. It was a question of whether they would obey the Lord.

After Joshua's death, most of the Israelites disregarded the Lord's commands (chapter 1). In fact, many of the people began worshiping foreign gods (2:1-13). As a result, the Lord allowed Israel's enemies to severely oppress them in order to drive them to their knees and back to God (2:14-3:6).

Because Israel was so apt to chase foreign gods—and so slow to repent and truly obey the Lord—for three hundred years the nation repeatedly went from (a) spiritual rebellion to (b) political oppression to (c) national repentance to (d) divine intervention (God raised up judges to deliver them), to another cycle of (a) spiritual rebellion, etc. (3:7-16:31).

This book ends with appendixes describing two of the worst examples of Israel's spiritual rebellion during its first three hundred years in the Promised Land (chapters 17-21).

Famous passages in Judges include

- A summary of the cycles (2:10-19)
- God's plan to test the nation (2:20-3:4)
- Ehud's spectacular victory over King Eglon (3:12-30)
- Deborah and Barak's victory over King Jabin (4:1-24)
- Deborah and Barak's song (5:1-31)
- Gideon's fleece (6:36-40)
- Gideon's army reduced to three hundred (7:1-8)
- Gideon's victory over Kings Zebah and Zalmunna (7:9-8:21)
- Gideon's sacred ephod (8:22-27)
- Gideon's disastrously rebellious son (8:29-9:57)
- The Lord's rejection of Israel's shallow repentance (10:11-14)
- Jephthah's rash and foolish vow (11:29-40)
- Samson's miraculous birth (13:2-25)
- Samson's aborted marriage to a pagan woman (14:1-20)
- Samson's exploits (15:1-20)
- Samson and Delilah (16:4-21)
- Samson's tragic death (16:23-31)
- Appendix A: the idolatry of Micah and the tribe of Dan (17:1-18:31)
- Appendix B: the war against the rebellious tribe of Benjamin (19:1-21:24)
- "The people did whatever seemed right in their own eyes" (17:6; 21:25)

CHAPTER 1

Judah and Simeon Conquer the Land

After Joshua died, the Israelites asked the LORD, "Which tribe should attack the Canaanites first?"

²The LORD answered, "Judah, for I have given them victory over the land."

³The leaders of Judah said to their relatives from the tribe of Simeon, "Join with us to fight against the Canaanites living in the territory allotted to us. Then we will help you conquer your territory." So the men of Simeon went with Judah.

⁴When the men of Judah attacked, the LORD gave them victory over the Canaanites and Perizzites, and they killed ten thousand enemy warriors at the town of Bezek. ⁵While at Bezek they encountered King Adoni-bezek and fought against him, and the Canaanites and Perizzites were defeated. ⁶Adoni-bezek escaped, but the Israelites soon captured him and cut off his thumbs and big toes. ⁷Adoni-bezek said, "I once had seventy kings with thumbs and big toes cut off, eating scraps from under my table. Now God has paid me back for what I did to them." They took him to Jerusalem, and he died there.

⁸The men of Judah attacked Jerusalem and captured it, killing all its people and setting the city on fire. ⁹Then they turned south to fight the Canaanites living in the hill country, the Negev, and the western foothills.* ¹⁰Judah marched against the Canaanites in Hebron (formerly called Kiriath-arba), defeating the forces of Sheshai, Ahiman, and Talmai. ¹¹From there they marched against the people living in the town of Debir (formerly called Kiriath-sepher).

¹²Then Caleb said, "I will give my daughter Acsah in marriage to the one who attacks and captures Kiriath-sepher." ¹³Othniel, the son of Caleb's younger brother Kenaz, was the one who conquered it, so Acsah became Othniel's wife.

¹⁴When Acsah married Othniel, she urged him* to ask her father for an additional field. As she got down off her donkey, Caleb asked her, "What is it? What can I do for you?"

¹⁵She said, "Give me a further blessing. You have been kind enough to give me land in the Negev; please give me springs as well." So Caleb gave her the upper and lower springs.

¹⁶When the tribe of Judah left Jericho,* the Kenites, who were descendants of Moses' father-in-law, traveled with them into the wilderness of Judah. They settled among the people there, near the town of Arad in the Negev.

¹⁷Then Judah joined with Simeon to fight against the Canaanites living in Zephath, and they completely destroyed* the town. So the town was named Hormah.* ¹⁸In addition, Judah captured the cities of Gaza, Ashkelon, and Ekron, along with their surrounding territories.

Israel Fails to Conquer the Land

¹⁹The LORD was with the people of Judah, and they took possession of the hill country. But they failed to drive out the people living in the plains because the people there had iron chariots. ²⁰The city of Hebron was given to Caleb as Moses had promised. And Caleb drove out the people living there, who were descendants of the three sons of Anak. ²¹The tribe of Benjamin, however, failed to drive out the Jebusites, who were living in Jerusalem. So to this day the Jebusites live in Jerusalem among the people of Benjamin.

²²The descendants of Joseph attacked the town of Bethel, and the LORD was with them. ²³They sent spies to Bethel (formerly known as Luz), ²⁴who confronted a man coming out of the city. They said to him, "Show us a way into

I ASK the Lord to direct my steps. (1:1)

See Joshua's profile (page 275) at Joshua 23:14.

I OBEY the Lord's commands. (1:3)

I MAKE promises only if I intend to keep them. (1:12)

See Caleb's profile (page 265) at Joshua 14:12.

I INQUIRE about what my children need and am generous when they marry. (1:14)

See Moses' profile (page 73) at Exodus 5:1.

I BELIEVE the tribes of Judah and Benjamin failed to finish conquering their portions of the Promised Land. (1:19)

See Joseph's profile (page 51) at Genesis 39:2.

1:9 Hebrew the Shephelah.   1:14 Greek version and Latin Vulgate read he urged her.   1:16 Hebrew the city of palms.   1:17a The Hebrew term used here refers to the complete consecration of things or people to the LORD, either by destroying them or by giving them as an offering.   1:17b Hormah means "destruction."

the city, and we will have mercy on you." ²⁵So he showed them a way in, and they killed everyone in the city except for this man and his family. ²⁶Later the man moved to the land of the Hittites, where he built a city. He named the city Luz, and it is known by that name to this day.

²⁷The tribe of Manasseh failed to drive out the people living in Beth-shan,* Taanach, Dor, Ibleam, Megiddo, and their surrounding villages, because the Canaanites were determined to stay in that region. ²⁸When the Israelites grew stronger, they forced the Canaanites to work as slaves, but they never did drive them out of the land.

²⁹The tribe of Ephraim also failed to drive out the Canaanites living in Gezer, and so the Canaanites continued to live there among them.

³⁰The tribe of Zebulun also failed to drive out the Canaanites living in Kitron and Nahalol, who continued to live among them. But they forced them to work as slaves.

³¹The tribe of Asher also failed to drive out the residents of Acco, Sidon, Ahlab, Aczib, Helbah, Aphik, and Rehob. ³²In fact, because they did not drive them out, the Canaanites dominated the land where the people of Asher lived.

³³The tribe of Naphtali also failed to drive out the residents of Beth-shemesh and Beth-anath. Instead, the Canaanites dominated the land where they lived. Nevertheless, the people of Beth-shemesh and Beth-anath were sometimes forced to work as slaves for the people of Naphtali.

³⁴As for the tribe of Dan, the Amorites forced them into the hill country and would not let them come down into the plains. ³⁵The Amorites were determined to stay in Mount Heres, Aijalon, and Shaalbim, but when the descendants of Joseph became stronger, they forced the Amorites to work as slaves. ³⁶The boundary of the Amorites ran from Scorpion Pass* to Sela and continued upward from there.

CHAPTER 2

The LORD's Messenger Comes to Bokim

The angel of the LORD went up from Gilgal to Bokim with a message for the Israelites. He told them, "I brought you out of Egypt into this land that I swore to give your ancestors, and I said I would never break my covenant with you. ²For your part, you were not to make any covenants with the people living in this land; instead, you were to destroy their altars. Why, then, have you disobeyed my command? ³Since you have done this, I will no longer drive out the people living in your land. They will be thorns in your sides, and their gods will be a constant temptation to you." ⁴When the angel of the LORD finished speaking, the Israelites wept loudly. ⁵So they called the place "Weeping,"* and they offered sacrifices to the LORD.

The Death of Joshua

⁶After Joshua sent the people away, each of the tribes left to take possession of the land allotted to them. ⁷And the Israelites served the LORD throughout the lifetime of Joshua and the leaders who outlived him—those who had seen all the great things the LORD had done for Israel.

⁸Then Joshua son of Nun, the servant of the LORD, died at the age of 110. ⁹They buried him in the land he had inherited, at Timnath-serah* in the hill country of Ephraim, north of Mount Gaash.

Israel Disobeys the LORD

¹⁰After that generation died, another generation grew up who did not acknowledge the LORD or remember the mighty things he had done for Israel. ¹¹Then the Israelites did what was evil in the LORD's sight and worshiped the

---

I BELIEVE the tribes of Manasseh and Ephraim failed to finish conquering their portions of the Promised Land. (1:27)

I BELIEVE the tribes of Zebulun, Asher, Naphtali, and Dan failed to finish conquering their portions of the Promised Land. (1:30)

I DO NOT deliberately, obstinately, and persistently disobey the Lord's commands. (2:2)

See Joshua's profile (page 275) at Joshua 23:14.
I WANT to be remembered as a servant of the Lord. (2:8)

I EARNESTLY WANT my children, grandchildren, and great-grandchildren to know the Lord and experience his work in their lives. (2:10)

1:27 Hebrew *Beth-shean,* a variant name for Beth-shan.   1:36 Hebrew *Akrabbim.*   2:5 Hebrew *Bokim.*
2:9 Hebrew *Timnath-heres,* a variant name for Timnath-serah.

images of Baal. [12] They abandoned the LORD, the God of their ancestors, who had brought them out of Egypt. They chased after other gods, worshiping the gods of the people around them. And they angered the LORD. [13] They abandoned the LORD to serve Baal and the images of Ashtoreth. [14] This made the LORD burn with anger against Israel, so he handed them over to marauders who stole their possessions. He sold them to their enemies all around, and they were no longer able to resist them. [15] Every time Israel went out to battle, the LORD fought against them, bringing them defeat, just as he promised. And the people were very distressed.

The LORD Rescues His People

[16] Then the LORD raised up judges to rescue the Israelites from their enemies. [17] Yet Israel did not listen to the judges but prostituted themselves to other gods, bowing down to them. How quickly they turned away from the path of their ancestors, who had walked in obedience to the LORD's commands. [18] Whenever the LORD placed a judge over Israel, he was with that judge and rescued the people from their enemies throughout the judge's lifetime. For the LORD took pity on his people, who were burdened by oppression and suffering. [19] But when the judge died, the people returned to their corrupt ways, behaving worse than those who had lived before them. They followed other gods, worshiping and bowing down to them. And they refused to give up their evil practices and stubborn ways.

[20] So the LORD burned with anger against Israel. He said, "Because these people have violated the covenant I made with their ancestors and have ignored my commands, [21] I will no longer drive out the nations that Joshua left unconquered when he died. [22] I did this to test Israel—to see whether or not they would obey the LORD as their ancestors did." [23] That is why the LORD did not quickly drive the nations out or allow Joshua to conquer them all.

CHAPTER 3

The Nations Left in Canaan

The LORD left certain nations in the land to test those Israelites who had not participated in the wars of Canaan. [2] He did this to teach warfare to generations of Israelites who had no experience in battle. [3] These were the nations: the Philistines (those living under the five Philistine rulers), all the Canaanites, the Sidonians, and the Hivites living in the hill country of Lebanon from Mount Baal-hermon to Lebo-hamath. [4] These people were left to test the Israelites—to see whether they would obey the commands the LORD had given to their ancestors through Moses.

[5] So Israel lived among the Canaanites, Hittites, Amorites, Perizzites, Hivites, and Jebusites, [6] and they intermarried with them. Israelite sons married their daughters, and Israelite daughters were given in marriage to their sons. And the Israelites worshiped their gods.

Othniel Becomes Israel's Judge

[7] The Israelites did what was evil in the LORD's sight. They forgot about the LORD their God, and they worshiped the images of Baal and the Asherah poles. [8] Then the LORD burned with anger against Israel, and he handed them over to King Cushan-rishathaim of Aram-naharaim.* And the Israelites were subject to Cushan-rishathaim for eight years.

[9] But when Israel cried out to the LORD for help, the LORD raised up a man to rescue them. His name was Othniel, the son of Caleb's younger brother, Kenaz. [10] The Spirit of the LORD came upon him, and he became Israel's judge. He went to war against King Cushan-rishathaim of Aram, and the LORD gave

---

I BELIEVE the Lord has every reason to punish those who worship false, demonic gods. (2:14)

I BELIEVE that without true repentance, salvation from one's oppressors is temporal at best. (2:17)

I BELIEVE the Lord allowed some of the pagan peoples to remain in the Promised Land to test the Israelites to see whether they would obey his commands. (3:4)

See Moses' profile (page 73) at Exodus 5:1.

I BELIEVE marriages between believers and unbelievers create countless problems. (3:6)

I TURN BACK to the Lord quickly whenever I sin. (3:8)

See Caleb's profile (page 265) at Joshua 14:12.

3:8 *Aram-naharaim* means "Aram of the two rivers," thought to have been located between the Euphrates and Balih Rivers in northwestern Mesopotamia.

Othniel victory over him. ¹¹So there was peace in the land for forty years. Then Othniel son of Kenaz died.

Ehud Becomes Israel's Judge

¹²Once again the Israelites did what was evil in the LORD's sight, so the LORD gave King Eglon of Moab control over Israel. ¹³Together with the Ammonites and Amalekites, Eglon attacked Israel and took possession of Jericho.* ¹⁴And the Israelites were subject to Eglon of Moab for eighteen years.

¹⁵But when Israel cried out to the LORD for help, the LORD raised up a man to rescue them. His name was Ehud son of Gera, of the tribe of Benjamin, who was left-handed. The Israelites sent Ehud to deliver their tax money to King Eglon of Moab. ¹⁶So Ehud made himself a double-edged dagger that was eighteen inches* long, and he strapped it to his right thigh, keeping it hidden under his clothing. ¹⁷He brought the tax money to Eglon, who was very fat. ¹⁸After delivering the payment, Ehud sent home those who had carried the tax money.

¹⁹But when Ehud reached the stone carvings near Gilgal, he turned back. He came to Eglon and said, "I have a secret message for you." So the king commanded his servants to be silent and sent them all out of the room. ²⁰Ehud walked over to Eglon as he was sitting alone in a cool upstairs room and said, "I have a message for you from God!" As King Eglon rose from his seat, ²¹Ehud reached with his left hand, pulled out the dagger strapped to his right thigh, and plunged it into the king's belly. ²²The dagger went so deep that the handle disappeared beneath the king's fat. So Ehud left the dagger in, and the king's bowels emptied. ²³Then Ehud closed and locked the doors and climbed down the latrine and escaped through the sewage access.

²⁴After Ehud was gone, the king's servants returned and found the doors to the upstairs room locked. They thought he might be using the latrine, ²⁵so they waited. But when the king didn't come out after a long delay, they became concerned and got a key. And when they opened the door, they found their master dead on the floor.

²⁶While the servants were waiting, Ehud escaped, passing the idols on his way to Seirah. ²⁷When he arrived in the hill country of Ephraim, Ehud sounded a call to arms. Then he led a band of Israelites down from the hills. ²⁸"Follow me," he said, "for the LORD has given you victory over Moab your enemy." So they followed him. And the Israelites took control of the shallows of the Jordan River across from Moab, preventing anyone from crossing. ²⁹They attacked the Moabites and killed about ten thousand of their strongest and bravest warriors. Not one of them escaped. ³⁰So Moab was conquered by Israel that day, and the land was at peace for eighty years.

Shamgar Becomes Israel's Judge

³¹After Ehud, Shamgar son of Anath rescued Israel. He killed six hundred Philistines with an ox goad.

CHAPTER 4

Deborah Becomes Israel's Judge

After Ehud's death, the Israelites again did what was evil in the LORD's sight. ²So the LORD handed them over to King Jabin of Hazor, a Canaanite king. The commander of his army was Sisera, who lived in Harosheth-haggoyim. ³Sisera, who had nine hundred iron chariots, ruthlessly oppressed the Israelites for twenty years. Then the Israelites cried out to the LORD for help.

⁴Deborah, the wife of Lappidoth, was a prophet who had become a judge in Israel. ⁵She would hold court under the Palm of Deborah, which stood between Ramah and Bethel in the hill country of Ephraim, and the Israelites

I DO what is right in the Lord's sight. (3:12)

I CRY OUT to the Lord for help in times of distress. (3:15)

I DO what is right in the Lord's sight. (4:1)

I BELIEVE the Lord raised up Deborah as a prophet and judge among the Israelites. (4:4)

3:13 Hebrew *the city of palms.*   3:16 Hebrew *1 cubit* [45 centimeters].

came to her to settle their disputes. ⁶One day she sent for Barak son of Abinoam, who lived in Kedesh in the land of Naphtali. She said to him, "This is what the Lord, the God of Israel, commands you: Assemble ten thousand warriors from the tribes of Naphtali and Zebulun at Mount Tabor. ⁷I will lure Sisera, commander of Jabin's army, along with his chariots and warriors, to the Kishon River. There I will give you victory over him."

⁸Barak told her, "I will go, but only if you go with me!"

⁹"Very well," she replied, "I will go with you. But since you have made this choice, you will receive no honor. For the Lord's victory over Sisera will be at the hands of a woman." So Deborah went with Barak to Kedesh. ¹⁰At Kedesh, Barak called together the tribes of Zebulun and Naphtali, and ten thousand warriors marched up with him. Deborah also marched with them.

¹¹Now Heber the Kenite, a descendant of Moses' brother-in-law* Hobab, had moved away from the other members of his tribe and pitched his tent by the Oak of Zaanannim, near Kedesh.

¹²When Sisera was told that Barak son of Abinoam had gone up to Mount Tabor, ¹³he called for all nine hundred of his iron chariots and all of his warriors, and they marched from Harosheth-haggoyim to the Kishon River.

¹⁴Then Deborah said to Barak, "Get ready! Today the Lord will give you victory over Sisera, for the Lord is marching ahead of you." So Barak led his ten thousand warriors down the slopes of Mount Tabor into battle. ¹⁵When Barak attacked, the Lord threw Sisera and all his charioteers and warriors into a panic. Then Sisera leaped down from his chariot and escaped on foot. ¹⁶Barak chased the enemy and their chariots all the way to Harosheth-haggoyim, killing all of Sisera's warriors. Not a single one was left alive.

¹⁷Meanwhile, Sisera ran to the tent of Jael, the wife of Heber the Kenite, because Heber's family was on friendly terms with King Jabin of Hazor. ¹⁸Jael went out to meet Sisera and said to him, "Come into my tent, sir. Come in. Don't be afraid." So he went into her tent, and she covered him with a blanket.

¹⁹"Please give me some water," he said. "I'm thirsty." So she gave him some milk to drink and covered him again.

²⁰"Stand at the door of the tent," he told her. "If anybody comes and asks you if there is anyone here, say no."

²¹But when Sisera fell asleep from exhaustion, Jael quietly crept up to him with a hammer and tent peg. Then she drove the tent peg through his temple and into the ground, and so he died.

²²When Barak came looking for Sisera, Jael went out to meet him. She said, "Come, and I will show you the man you are looking for." So he followed her into the tent and found Sisera lying there dead, with the tent peg through his temple.

²³So on that day Israel saw God subdue Jabin, the Canaanite king. ²⁴And from that time on Israel became stronger and stronger against King Jabin, until they finally destroyed him.

CHAPTER 5
The Song of Deborah
On that day Deborah and Barak son of Abinoam sang this song:

² "When Israel's leaders take charge,
    and the people gladly follow—
  bless the Lord!

³ "Listen, you kings!
    Pay attention, you mighty rulers!

4:11 Or *father-in-law.*

I ADMIRE the prophet Deborah's bravery. (4:9)

See Moses' profile (page 73) at Exodus 5:1.

I BELIEVE Deborah spoke for the Lord, correctly foretelling the outcome of the battle between Barak and Sisera. (4:14)

I BELIEVE the Lord himself fought for Israel against Sisera and his army. (4:15)

I SING to the Lord and praise his name! (5:3)

For I will sing to the LORD.
I will lift up my song to the LORD, the God of Israel.

[4] "LORD, when you set out from Seir
and marched across the fields of Edom,
the earth trembled
and the cloudy skies poured down rain.
[5] The mountains quaked at the coming of the LORD.
Even Mount Sinai shook in the presence of the LORD, the God of Israel.

LIKE DEBORAH *I bring glory to God by leading others to face difficult battles.*

Judges 4:9

During the time of Israel's judges, Israel had their own Joan of Arc and Rosa Parks in the person of a woman named Deborah.

When strong men shook in fear of their enemies, Deborah gathered people around her and offered God's comfort and counsel. When God's message came to attack the enemy, she did not hesitate to issue his command to the man he had chosen. And when the day of battle dawned, she even helped Barak lead the charge.

Deborah was not a glory seeker. She was ready, however, to step up to any task God gave her. If God called her to settle disputes or proclaim his word or even mobilize soldiers, she would do it. Whether or not that calling fit into her culture or her personal comfort zone, Deborah did whatever God called her to do—for his glory and for the deliverance of his people.

Deborah did not want to be a one-woman show. Her heart was to mother God's people and stir up those who should lead them (5:2; 7-9), while others chased the enemy soldiers down the slopes of Mount Tabor.

Unlike the hesitant Reubenites (5:15), no indecision clouded Deborah's mind. She demonstrated a determination to obey God immediately and face difficulties bravely. Whether listening to disputes, marching into battle, or singing a victory song, she always urged the Israelites to put their trust in God.

Ordinary people living ordinary lives of obedience to God can inspire others to great deeds. You and I can glorify God by being just such examples.

What step is God calling you to take today?

○ *Today's Scripture reading is Judges 4–5.*

---

[6] "In the days of Shamgar son of Anath, and in the days of Jael,
people avoided the main roads,
and travelers stayed on crooked side paths.
[7] There were few people left in the villages of Israel—
until Deborah arose as a mother for Israel.
[8] When Israel chose new gods,
war erupted at the city gates.
Yet not a shield or spear could be seen
among forty thousand warriors in Israel!
[9] My heart goes out to Israel's leaders,
and to those who gladly followed.
Bless the LORD!

[10] "You who ride on fine donkeys
and sit on fancy saddle blankets, listen!
And you who must walk along the road, listen!
[11] Listen to the village musicians* gathered at the watering holes.
They recount the righteous victories of the LORD,

I BELIEVE I will not go unpunished if I choose new gods. (5:8)

5:11 The meaning of the Hebrew is uncertain.

and the victories of his villagers in Israel.
Then the people of the LORD
marched down to the city gates.

¹² "Wake up, Deborah, wake up!
Wake up, wake up, and sing a song!
Arise, Barak!
Lead your captives away, son of Abinoam!

¹³ "Down from Tabor marched the remnant against the mighty.
The people of the LORD marched down against mighty warriors.
¹⁴ They came down from Ephraim—a land that once belonged to the
Amalekites,
and Benjamin also followed you.
From Makir the commanders marched down;
from Zebulun came those who carry the rod of authority.

I DO NOT HESITATE to follow the Lord. (5:15)

¹⁵ The princes of Issachar were with Deborah and Barak.
They followed Barak, rushing into the valley.
But in the tribe of Reuben
there was great indecision.
¹⁶ Why did you sit at home among the sheepfolds—
to hear the shepherds whistle for their flocks?
In the tribe of Reuben
there was great indecision.

I DO NOT IGNORE the Lord's commands. (5:17)

¹⁷ Gilead remained east of the Jordan.
And Dan, why did he stay home?
Asher sat unmoved at the seashore,
remaining in his harbors.
¹⁸ But Zebulun risked his life,
as did Naphtali, on the battlefield.

¹⁹ "The kings of Canaan fought at Taanach near Megiddo's springs,
but they carried off no treasures of battle.
²⁰ The stars fought from heaven.
The stars in their orbits fought against Sisera.

I FOLLOW the Lord with courage. (5:21)

²¹ The Kishon River swept them away—
that ancient river, the Kishon.
March on, my soul, with courage!
²² Then the horses' hooves hammered the ground,
the galloping, galloping of Sisera's mighty steeds.
²³ 'Let the people of Meroz be cursed,' said the angel of the LORD.
'Let them be utterly cursed
because they did not come to help the LORD,
to help the LORD against the mighty warriors.'

²⁴ "Most blessed is Jael,
the wife of Heber the Kenite.
May she be blessed above all women who live in tents.
²⁵ Sisera asked for water,
and Jael gave him milk.
In a bowl fit for kings,
she brought him yogurt.
²⁶ Then with her left hand she reached for a tent peg,
and with her right hand she reached for the workman's hammer.
She hit Sisera, crushing his head.
She pounded the tent peg through his head, piercing his temples.
²⁷ He sank, he fell,
he lay dead at her feet.

²⁸ "From the window Sisera's mother looked out.
   Through the window she watched for his return, saying,
   'Why is his chariot so long in coming?
   Why don't we hear the sound of chariot wheels?'
²⁹ A reply comes from her wise women,
   and she repeats these words to herself:
³⁰ 'They are dividing the captured goods they found—
   a woman or two for every man.
   There are gorgeous robes for Sisera,
   and colorful, beautifully embroidered robes for me.'

³¹ "LORD, may all your enemies die as Sisera did!
   But may those who love you rise like the sun at full strength!"

I LOVE the Lord. (5:31)

Then there was peace in the land for forty years.

CHAPTER 6

Gideon Becomes Israel's Judge

Again the Israelites did what was evil in the LORD's sight. So the LORD handed them over to the Midianites for seven years. ²The Midianites were so cruel that the Israelites fled to the mountains, where they made hiding places for themselves in caves and dens. ³Whenever the Israelites planted their crops, marauders from Midian, Amalek, and the people of the east would attack Israel, ⁴camping in the land and destroying crops as far away as Gaza. They left the Israelites with nothing to eat, taking all the sheep, oxen, and donkeys. ⁵These enemy hordes, coming with their cattle and tents as thick as locusts, arrived on droves of camels too numerous to count. And they stayed until the land was stripped bare. ⁶So Israel was reduced to starvation by the Midianites. Then the Israelites cried out to the LORD for help.

I DO what is right in the Lord's sight. (6:1)

I TURN BACK to the Lord quickly whenever I sin. (6:2)

I CRY OUT to the Lord for help in times of distress. (6:6)

⁷When they cried out to the LORD because of Midian, ⁸the LORD sent a prophet to the Israelites. He said, "This is what the LORD, the God of Israel, says: I brought you up out of slavery in Egypt ⁹and rescued you from the Egyptians and from all who oppressed you. I drove out your enemies and gave you their land. ¹⁰I told you, 'I am the LORD your God. You must not worship the gods of the Amorites, in whose land you now live.' But you have not listened to me."

¹¹Then the angel of the LORD came and sat beneath the oak tree at Ophrah, which belonged to Joash of the clan of Abiezer. Gideon son of Joash had been threshing wheat at the bottom of a winepress to hide the grain from the Midianites. ¹²The angel of the LORD appeared to him and said, "Mighty hero, the LORD is with you!"

I KNOW the Lord is with me. (6:12)

¹³"Sir," Gideon replied, "if the LORD is with us, why has all this happened to us? And where are all the miracles our ancestors told us about? Didn't they say, 'The LORD brought us up out of Egypt'? But now the LORD has abandoned us and handed us over to the Midianites."

I KNOW the Lord is with me even in times of trouble. (6:13)

¹⁴Then the LORD turned to him and said, "Go with the strength you have and rescue Israel from the Midianites. I am sending you!"

I DO NOT QUESTION the Lord's direct commands, no matter how weak I feel. (6:15)

¹⁵"But Lord," Gideon replied, "how can I rescue Israel? My clan is the weakest in the whole tribe of Manasseh, and I am the least in my entire family!"

¹⁶The LORD said to him, "I will be with you. And you will destroy the Midianites as if you were fighting against one man."

I KNOW my greatest strength is the Lord's presence in my life. (6:16)

¹⁷Gideon replied, "If you are truly going to help me, show me a sign to prove that it is really the LORD speaking to me. ¹⁸Don't go away until I come back and bring my offering to you."

The LORD answered, "I will stay here until you return."

¹⁹Gideon hurried home. He cooked a young goat, and with half a bushel*

I DO NOT TEST the Lord by asking for signs. (6:17)

6:19 Hebrew *1 ephah* [18 liters].

of flour he baked some bread without yeast. Then, carrying the meat in a basket and the broth in a pot, he brought them out and presented them to the angel, who was under the oak tree.

²⁰The angel of God said to him, "Place the meat and the unleavened bread on this rock, and pour the broth over it." And Gideon did as he was told. ²¹Then the angel of the LORD touched the meat and bread with the staff in his hand, and fire flamed up from the rock and consumed all he had brought. And the angel of the LORD disappeared.

²²When Gideon realized that it was the angel of the LORD, he cried out, "Sovereign LORD, I have seen the angel of the LORD face to face!"

²³"It is all right," the LORD replied. "Do not be afraid. You will not die." ²⁴And Gideon built an altar to the LORD there and named it "The LORD Is Peace."* The altar remains in Ophrah in the land of the clan of Abiezer to this day.

I WORSHIP the Lord God alone. (6:25)

²⁵That night the LORD said to Gideon, "Take the second best bull from your father's herd, the one that is seven years old. Pull down your father's altar to Baal, and cut down the Asherah pole standing beside it. ²⁶Then build an altar to the LORD your God here on this hill, laying the stones carefully. Sacrifice the bull as a burnt offering on the altar, using as fuel the wood of the Asherah pole you cut down." ²⁷So Gideon took ten of his servants and did as the LORD had commanded. But he did it at night because he was afraid of the other members of his father's household and the people of the town. He knew what would happen if they found out who had done it.

²⁸Early the next morning, as the people of the town began to stir, someone discovered that the altar of Baal had been knocked down and that the Asherah pole beside it was gone. In their place a new altar had been built, and it had the remains of a sacrifice on it. ²⁹The people said to each other, "Who did this?" And after asking around and making a careful search, they learned that it was Gideon, the son of Joash.

³⁰"Bring out your son," they shouted to Joash. "He must die for destroying the altar of Baal and for cutting down the Asherah pole."

³¹But Joash shouted to the mob, "Why are you defending Baal? Will you argue his case? Whoever pleads his case will be put to death by morning! If Baal truly is a god, let him defend himself and destroy the one who knocked down his altar!" ³²From then on Gideon was called Jerubbaal, which means "Let Baal defend himself," because he knocked down Baal's altar.

I AM FILLED with the Spirit of the Lord (Ephesians 5:18). (6:34)

³³Soon afterward the armies of Midian, Amalek, and the people of the east formed an alliance against Israel and crossed the Jordan, camping in the valley of Jezreel. ³⁴Then the Spirit of the LORD took possession of Gideon. He blew a ram's horn as a call to arms, and the men of the clan of Abiezer came to him. ³⁵He also sent messengers throughout Manasseh, Asher, Zebulun, and Naphtali, summoning their warriors, and all of them responded.

³⁶Then Gideon said to God, "If you are truly going to use me to rescue Israel as you promised, ³⁷prove it to me in this way. I will put some wool on the threshing floor tonight. If the fleece is wet with dew in the morning but the ground is dry, then I will know that you are going to help me rescue Israel as you promised." ³⁸And it happened just that way. When Gideon got up the next morning, he squeezed the fleece and wrung out a whole bowlful of water.

³⁹Then Gideon said to God, "Please don't be angry with me, but let me make one more request. This time let the fleece remain dry while the ground around it is wet with dew." ⁴⁰So that night God did as Gideon asked. The fleece was dry in the morning, but the ground was covered with dew.

6:24 Hebrew *Yahweh Shalom*.

CHAPTER 7

Gideon Defeats the Midianites

So Jerubbaal (that is, Gideon) and his army got up early and went as far as the spring of Harod. The armies of Midian were camped north of them in the valley near the hill of Moreh. ²The LORD said to Gideon, "You have too many warriors with you. If I let all of you fight the Midianites, the Israelites will boast to me that they saved themselves by their own strength. ³Therefore, tell the people, 'Whoever is timid or afraid may leave* and go home.' " Twenty-two thousand of them went home, leaving only ten thousand who were willing to fight.

⁴But the LORD told Gideon, "There are still too many! Bring them down to the spring, and I will sort out who will go with you and who will not." ⁵When Gideon took his warriors down to the water, the LORD told him, "Divide the men into two groups. In one group put all those who cup water in their hands and lap it up with their tongues like dogs. In the other group put all those who kneel down and drink with their mouths in the stream." ⁶Only three hundred of the men drank from their hands. All the others got down on their knees and drank with their mouths in the stream. ⁷The LORD told Gideon, "With these three hundred men I will rescue you and give you victory over the Midianites. Send all the others home." ⁸So Gideon collected the provisions and rams' horns of the other warriors and sent them home. But he kept the three hundred men with him.

Now the Midianite camp was in the valley just below Gideon. ⁹During the night, the LORD said, "Get up! Go down into the Midianite camp, for I have given you victory over them! ¹⁰But if you are afraid to attack, go down to the camp with your servant Purah. ¹¹Listen to what the Midianites are saying, and you will be greatly encouraged. Then you will be eager to attack."

So Gideon took Purah and went down to the outposts of the enemy camp. ¹²The armies of Midian, Amalek, and the people of the east had settled in the valley like a swarm of locusts. Their camels were like grains of sand on the seashore—too many to count! ¹³Gideon crept up just as a man was telling his friend about a dream. The man said, "I had this dream, and in my dream a loaf of barley bread came tumbling down into the Midianite camp. It hit a tent, turned it over, and knocked it flat!"

¹⁴His friend said, "Your dream can mean only one thing—God has given Gideon son of Joash, the Israelite, victory over all the armies united with Midian!"

¹⁵When Gideon heard the dream and its interpretation, he thanked God. Then he returned to the Israelite camp and shouted, "Get up! For the LORD has given you victory over the Midianites!" ¹⁶He divided the three hundred men into three groups and gave each man a ram's horn and a clay jar with a torch in it. ¹⁷Then he said to them, "Keep your eyes on me. When I come to the edge of the camp, do just as I do. ¹⁸As soon as my group blows the rams' horns, those of you on the other sides of the camp blow your horns and shout, 'For the LORD and for Gideon!' "

¹⁹It was just after midnight, after the changing of the guard, when Gideon and the one hundred men with him reached the outer edge of the Midianite camp. Suddenly, they blew the horns and broke their clay jars. ²⁰Then all three groups blew their horns and broke their jars. They held the blazing torches in their left hands and the horns in their right hands and shouted, "A sword for the LORD and for Gideon!" ²¹Each man stood at his position around the camp and watched as all the Midianites rushed around in a panic, shouting as they ran. ²²When the three hundred Israelites blew their horns, the LORD caused the warriors in the camp to fight against each other with

7:3 Hebrew *leave Mount Gilead.* The identity of Mount Gilead is uncertain in this context. It is perhaps used here as another name for Mount Gilboa.

I BELIEVE the Lord can use any size group to achieve great results for his glory and honor. (7:2)

I AM NOT TIMID or afraid to do the Lord's will. (7:3)

I OBEY the Lord even when I am afraid. (7:10)

I THANK the Lord for encouraging me when I feel timid or afraid. (7:15)

I BELIEVE the Lord himself fought against the Midianites. (7:22)

their swords. Those who were not killed fled to places as far away as Beth-shittah near Zererah and to the border of Abel-meholah near Tabbath.

²³ Then Gideon sent for the warriors of Naphtali, Asher, and Manasseh, who joined in the chase after the fleeing army of Midian. ²⁴Gideon also sent messengers throughout the hill country of Ephraim, saying, "Come down to attack the Midianites. Cut them off at the shallows of the Jordan River at Beth-barah." And the men of Ephraim did as they were told. ²⁵They captured Oreb and Zeeb, the two Midianite generals, killing Oreb at the rock of Oreb, and Zeeb at the winepress of Zeeb. And they continued to chase the Midianites. Afterward the Israelites brought the heads of Oreb and Zeeb to Gideon, who was by the Jordan.

CHAPTER 8

Gideon Kills Zebah and Zalmunna

Then the people of Ephraim asked Gideon, "Why have you treated us this way? Why didn't you send for us when you first went out to fight the Midianites?" And they argued heatedly with Gideon.

²But Gideon replied, "What have I done compared to you? Aren't the last grapes of Ephraim's harvest better than the entire crop of my little clan of Abiezer? ³God gave you victory over Oreb and Zeeb, the generals of the Midianite army. What have I done compared to that?" When the men of Ephraim heard Gideon's answer, they were no longer angry.

⁴Gideon then crossed the Jordan River with his three hundred men, and though they were exhausted, they continued to chase the enemy. ⁵When they reached Succoth, Gideon asked the leaders of the town, "Will you please give my warriors some food? They are very tired. I am chasing Zebah and Zalmunna, the kings of Midian."

⁶But the leaders of Succoth replied, "You haven't caught Zebah and Zalmunna yet. Catch them first, and then we will feed your warriors."

⁷So Gideon said, "After the LORD gives me victory over Zebah and Zalmunna, I will return and tear your flesh with the thorns and briers of the wilderness."

⁸From there Gideon went up to Peniel* and asked for food, but he got the same answer. ⁹So he said to the people of Peniel, "After I return in victory, I will tear down this tower."

¹⁰By this time Zebah and Zalmunna were in Karkor with a remnant of 15,000 warriors—all that remained of the allied armies of the east—for 120,000 had already been killed. ¹¹Gideon circled around by the caravan route east of Nobah and Jogbehah, taking the Midianite army by surprise. ¹²Zebah and Zalmunna, the two Midianite kings, fled, but Gideon chased them down and captured all their warriors.

¹³After this, Gideon returned by way of Heres Pass. ¹⁴There he captured a young man from Succoth and demanded that he write down the names of all the seventy-seven rulers and leaders in the town. ¹⁵Gideon then returned to Succoth and said to the leaders, "Here are Zebah and Zalmunna. When we were here before, you taunted me, saying, 'You haven't caught Zebah and Zalmunna yet. Catch them first, and then we will feed your exhausted warriors.'" ¹⁶Then Gideon took the leaders of the town and taught them a lesson, punishing them with thorns and briers from the wilderness. ¹⁷He also knocked down the tower of Peniel and killed all the men in the town.

¹⁸Then Gideon asked Zebah and Zalmunna, "The men you killed at Tabor—what were they like?"

"Like you," they replied. "They all had the look of a king's son."

I AM CAREFUL not to become overly angry when I feel slighted. (8:1)

I DO NOT STAY angry over nothing. (8:3)

8:8 Hebrew *Penuel,* a variant name for Peniel; also in 8:9, 17.

[19]"They were my brothers!" Gideon exclaimed. "As surely as the LORD lives, I wouldn't kill you if you hadn't killed them."

[20]Turning to Jether, his oldest son, he said, "Kill them!" But Jether did not draw his sword, for he was only a boy and was afraid.

[21] Then Zebah and Zalmunna said to Gideon, "Don't ask a boy to do a man's job! Do it yourself!" So Gideon killed them both and took the royal ornaments from the necks of their camels.

Gideon's Sacred Ephod

[22] Then the Israelites said to Gideon, "Be our ruler! You and your son and your grandson will be our rulers, for you have rescued us from Midian."

[23]But Gideon replied, "I will not rule over you, nor will my son. The LORD will rule over you! [24]However, I have one request. Each of you can give me an earring out of the treasures you collected from your fallen enemies." (The enemies, being Ishmaelites, all wore gold earrings.)

I AM CAREFUL not to accept undue honor when the Lord accomplishes something great through me. (8:22)

I HONOR the Lord as my God and King. (8:23)

LIKE GIDEON   *I increase my faith by obeying God.*
Judges 7:15

If anyone had tiny mustard-seed faith, it was Gideon.

The Lord had to coax Gideon step-by-step out of hiding to become the mighty hero he wanted him to be.

For some reason, the Lord was patient with each of Gideon's requests for assurance and each of his baby steps of faith. Perhaps the Lord was patient with Gideon because—despite Gideon's need for signs—he was willing to obey the Lord in the midst of extremely difficult circumstances.

Gideon first needed to be sure the Lord himself was speaking to him. When God proved himself, Gideon worshiped him and set about destroying his family's pagan Baal altar and Asherah pole. Soon afterward, the Spirit of the Lord filled Gideon, who summoned armies from the surrounding tribes. After another confirmation from the Lord, he was ready to set forth!

By this point, however, the Lord knew Gideon and his men were all too ready to fight in their own strength. Since God already had proved himself, Gideon readily agreed to whittle down his army as God prescribed.

The Lord, who knows the heart, gave Gideon one final sign he didn't even ask for. A detailed dream recounted by an enemy soldier confirmed to Gideon that he could obey God in full confidence—the battle would be theirs! From cowering in fear to sounding trumpets of triumph, Gideon grew in faith as he obeyed the Lord, who had called him into service.

Sure enough, the Lord's promises came true. With Midianites killing one another in utter confusion, Gideon and the Israelites swooped down and destroyed the fleeing army as if fighting one man. Rescuing Israel in the strength the Lord had given him, Gideon, the mighty hero, came to realize that the Lord was truly with him.

God may or may not give us the assurances we ask for as we seek to follow him and know his will. After all, Gideon had only a few pages, but we have all of God's Word. The question is, Will we obey what God has already told us? Only as we obey will our faith really grow.

To hear other biblical authors recall God's great victory through Gideon, read 1 Samuel 12:10-11; Isaiah 9:4; 10:26; and Hebrews 11:32.

○ *Today's Scripture reading is Judges 6–8.*

---

[25]"Gladly!" they replied. They spread out a cloak, and each one threw in a gold earring he had gathered. [26] The weight of the gold earrings was forty-three pounds,* not including the crescents and pendants, the royal clothing of the kings, or the chains around the necks of their camels. [27]Gideon made a sacred ephod from the gold and put it in Ophrah, his hometown.

I AM CAREFUL not to place too much importance on expensive items. (8:27)

8:26 Hebrew *1,700 shekels* [19.4 kilograms].

But soon all the Israelites prostituted themselves by worshiping it, and it became a trap for Gideon and his family.

²⁸That is the story of how Israel subdued Midian, which never recovered. Throughout the rest of Gideon's lifetime—about forty years—the land was at peace.

²⁹Then Gideon* son of Joash returned home. ³⁰He had seventy sons, for he had many wives. ³¹He also had a concubine in Shechem, who bore him a son named Abimelech. ³²Gideon died when he was very old, and he was buried in the grave of his father, Joash, at Ophrah in the land of the clan of Abiezer.

³³As soon as Gideon was dead, the Israelites prostituted themselves by worshiping the images of Baal, making Baal-berith their god. ³⁴They forgot the LORD their God, who had rescued them from all their enemies surrounding them. ³⁵Nor did they show any loyalty to the family of Jerubbaal (that is, Gideon), despite all the good he had done for Israel.

I BELIEVE the Israelites were prone to forsake the Lord and commit gross idolatry. (8:33)

CHAPTER 9

Abimelech Rules over Shechem

One day Gideon's* son Abimelech went to Shechem to visit his mother's brothers. He said to them and to the rest of his mother's family, ²"Ask the people of Shechem whether they want to be ruled by all seventy of Gideon's sons or by one man. And remember, I am your own flesh and blood!"

³So Abimelech's uncles spoke to all the people of Shechem on his behalf. And after listening to their proposal, they decided in favor of Abimelech because he was their relative. ⁴They gave him seventy silver coins from the temple of Baal-berith, which he used to hire some soldiers who agreed to follow him. ⁵He took the soldiers to his father's home at Ophrah, and there, on one stone, they killed all seventy of his half brothers. But the youngest brother, Jotham, escaped and hid. ⁶Then the people of Shechem and Beth-millo called a meeting under the oak beside the pillar* at Shechem and made Abimelech their king.

Jotham's Parable

I DENOUNCE those who take power by violent means. (9:7)

⁷When Jotham heard about this, he climbed to the top of Mount Gerizim and shouted, "Listen to me, people of Shechem! Listen to me if you want God to listen to you! ⁸Once upon a time the trees decided to elect a king. First they said to the olive tree, 'Be our king!' ⁹But it refused, saying, 'Should I quit producing the olive oil that blesses both God and people, just to wave back and forth over the trees?'

¹⁰"Then they said to the fig tree, 'You be our king!' ¹¹But the fig tree also refused, saying, 'Should I quit producing my sweet fruit just to wave back and forth over the trees?'

¹²"Then they said to the grapevine, 'You be our king!' ¹³But the grapevine replied, 'Should I quit producing the wine that cheers both God and people, just to wave back and forth over the trees?'

¹⁴"Then all the trees finally turned to the thornbush and said, 'Come, you be our king!' ¹⁵And the thornbush replied, 'If you truly want to make me your king, come and take shelter in my shade. If not, let fire come out from me and devour the cedars of Lebanon.'

I BELIEVE those who take power by violent means often continue to act treacherously. (9:15)

¹⁶"Now make sure you have acted honorably and in good faith by making Abimelech your king, and that you have done right by Gideon* and all of his descendants. Have you treated my father with the honor he deserves? ¹⁷For he fought for you and risked his life when he rescued you from the Midianites. ¹⁸But now you have revolted against my father and his descendants, killing his seventy sons on one stone. And you have chosen his slave woman's son,

8:29 Hebrew *Jerubbaal;* see 6:32. 9:1 Hebrew *Jerubbaal's* (see 6:32); also in 9:2, 24. 9:6 The meaning of the Hebrew is uncertain. 9:16 Hebrew *Jerubbaal* (see 6:32); also in 9:19, 28, 57.

Abimelech, to be your king just because he is your relative. ¹⁹If you have acted honorably and in good faith toward Gideon and his descendants, then may you find joy in Abimelech, and may he find joy in you. ²⁰But if you have not acted in good faith, then may fire come out from Abimelech and devour the people of Shechem and Beth-millo; and may fire come out from the people of Shechem and Beth-millo and devour Abimelech!" ²¹Then Jotham escaped and lived in Beer because he was afraid of his brother Abimelech.

Shechem's Revolt against Abimelech

²²After Abimelech had ruled over Israel for three years, ²³God stirred up trouble* between Abimelech and the people of Shechem, and they revolted. ²⁴In the events that followed, God punished Abimelech and the men of Shechem for murdering Gideon's seventy sons. ²⁵The people of Shechem set an ambush for Abimelech on the hilltops and robbed everyone who passed that way. But someone warned Abimelech about their plot.

²⁶At that time Gaal son of Ebed moved to Shechem with his brothers and gained the confidence of the people of Shechem. ²⁷During the annual harvest festival at Shechem, held in the temple of the local god, the wine flowed freely, and everyone began cursing Abimelech. ²⁸"Who is Abimelech?" Gaal shouted. "He's not a true descendant of Shechem!* Why should we be Abimelech's servants? He's merely the son of Gideon, and Zebul is his administrator. Serve the men of Hamor, who are Shechem's true descendants. Why should we serve Abimelech? ²⁹If I were in charge, I would get rid of Abimelech. I would say* to him, 'Get some more soldiers, and come out and fight!' "

³⁰But when Zebul, the leader of the city, heard what Gaal was saying, he was furious. ³¹He sent messengers to Abimelech in Arumah,* telling him, "Gaal son of Ebed and his brothers have come to live in Shechem, and now they are inciting the city to rebel against you. ³²Come by night with an army and hide out in the fields. ³³In the morning, as soon as it is daylight, storm the city. When Gaal and those who are with him come out against you, you can do with them as you wish."

³⁴So Abimelech and his men went by night and split into four groups, stationing themselves around Shechem. ³⁵Gaal was standing at the city gates when Abimelech and his army came out of hiding. ³⁶When Gaal saw them, he said to Zebul, "Look, there are people coming down from the hilltops!"

Zebul replied, "It's just the shadows of the hills that look like men."

³⁷But again Gaal said, "No, people are coming down from the hills.* And another group is coming down the road past the Diviners' Oak.*"

³⁸Then Zebul turned on him triumphantly. "Now where is that big mouth of yours?" he demanded. "Wasn't it you that said, 'Who is Abimelech, and why should we be his servants?' The men you mocked are right outside the city! Go out and fight them!"

³⁹Gaal then led the men of Shechem into battle against Abimelech, ⁴⁰but he was defeated and ran away. Many of Shechem's warriors were killed, and the ground was covered with dead bodies all the way to the city gate. ⁴¹Abimelech stayed in Arumah, and Zebul drove Gaal and his brothers out of Shechem.

⁴²The next day the people of Shechem went out into the fields to battle. When Abimelech heard about it, ⁴³he divided his men into three groups and set an ambush in the fields. When Abimelech saw the people coming out of the city, he and his men jumped up from their hiding places and attacked them. ⁴⁴Abimelech and his group stormed the city gate to keep the men of Shechem from getting back in, while Abimelech's other two groups cut them

I BELIEVE those who take power by the sword often die by the sword. (9:20)

I BELIEVE the Lord doesn't let the violent get away with murder forever. (9:24)

I DO NOT GET DRUNK and make idle boasts. (9:27)

In response to the profiles, tell the Lord whose examples you want to imitate—and whose failures you don't want to repeat.

9:23 Hebrew *sent a disturbing spirit.* 9:28 Hebrew *Who is Shechem?* 9:29 As in Greek version; Hebrew reads *And he said.* 9:31 Hebrew *Tormah;* see 9:41. 9:37a Or *the center of the land.* 9:37b Hebrew *Elon-meonenim.*

down in the fields. ⁴⁵The battle went on all day before Abimelech finally captured the city. He killed the people, leveled the city, and scattered salt all over the ground.

⁴⁶When the people who lived in the tower of Shechem heard what had happened, they took refuge within the walls of the temple of Baal-berith.* ⁴⁷Someone reported to Abimelech that the people were gathered together in the temple, ⁴⁸so he led his forces to Mount Zalmon. He took an ax and chopped some branches from a tree, and he put them on his shoulder. "Quick, do as I have done!" he told his men. ⁴⁹So each of them cut down some branches, following Abimelech's example. They piled the branches against the walls of the temple and set them on fire. So all the people who had lived in the tower of Shechem died, about a thousand men and women.

⁵⁰Then Abimelech attacked the city of Thebez and captured it. ⁵¹But there was a strong tower inside the city, and the entire population fled to it. They barricaded themselves in and climbed up to the roof of the tower. ⁵²Abimelech followed them to attack the tower. But as he prepared to set fire to the entrance, ⁵³a woman on the roof threw down a millstone that landed on Abimelech's head and crushed his skull. ⁵⁴He said to his young armor bearer, "Draw your sword and kill me! Don't let it be said that a woman killed Abimelech!" So the young man stabbed him with his sword, and he died. ⁵⁵When Abimelech's men saw that he was dead, they disbanded and returned to their homes.

⁵⁶Thus, God punished Abimelech for the evil he had done against his father by murdering his seventy brothers. ⁵⁷God also punished the men of Shechem for all their evil. So the curse of Jotham son of Gideon came true.

CHAPTER 10

Tola Becomes Israel's Judge

After Abimelech's death, Tola, the son of Puah and descendant of Dodo, came to rescue Israel. He was from the tribe of Issachar but lived in the town of Shamir in the hill country of Ephraim. ²He was Israel's judge for twenty-three years. When he died, he was buried in Shamir.

Jair Becomes Israel's Judge

³After Tola died, a man from Gilead named Jair judged Israel for twenty-two years. ⁴His thirty sons rode around on thirty donkeys, and they owned thirty towns in the land of Gilead, which are still called the Towns of Jair.* ⁵When Jair died, he was buried in Kamon.

The Ammonites Oppress Israel

⁶Again the Israelites did evil in the LORD's sight. They worshiped images of Baal and Ashtoreth, and the gods of Aram, Sidon, Moab, Ammon, and Philistia. Not only this, but they abandoned the LORD and no longer served him at all. ⁷So the LORD burned with anger against Israel, and he handed them over to the Philistines and the Ammonites, ⁸who began to oppress them that year. For eighteen years they oppressed all the Israelites east of the Jordan River in the land of the Amorites (that is, in Gilead). ⁹The Ammonites also crossed to the west side of the Jordan and attacked Judah, Benjamin, and Ephraim. The Israelites were in great distress. ¹⁰Finally, they cried out to the LORD, saying, "We have sinned against you because we have abandoned you as our God and have served the images of Baal."

¹¹The LORD replied, "Did I not rescue you from the Egyptians, the Amorites, the Ammonites, the Philistines, ¹²the Sidonians, the Amalekites, and the Maonites? When they oppressed you, you cried out to me, and I rescued you. ¹³Yet you have abandoned me and served other gods. So I will not rescue you

---

I ABHOR Abimelech's treachery and murder. (9:50)

I BELIEVE the treacherous often come to a violent end. (9:54)

I BELIEVE the Lord punished Abimelech for his treachery and murder. (9:56)

I BELIEVE the curse of Jotham came true. (9:57)

I BELIEVE the Lord used pagan nations to oppress the Israelites for sinning against him, just as he said he would. (10:7)

9:46 Hebrew El-berith, another name for Baal-berith; compare 9:4.   10:4 Hebrew Havvoth-jair.

anymore. [14]Go and cry out to the gods you have chosen! Let them rescue you in your hour of distress!"

[15]But the Israelites pleaded with the LORD and said, "We have sinned. Punish us as you see fit, only rescue us today from our enemies." [16]Then the Israelites put aside their foreign gods and served the LORD. And he was grieved by their misery.

[17]At that time the armies of Ammon had gathered for war and were camped in Gilead, preparing to attack Israel's army at Mizpah. [18]The leaders of Gilead said to each other, "Whoever attacks the Ammonites first will become ruler over all the people of Gilead."

CHAPTER 11

Jephthah Becomes Israel's Judge

Now Jephthah of Gilead was a great warrior. He was the son of Gilead, but his mother was a prostitute. [2]Gilead's wife also had several sons, and when these half brothers grew up, they chased Jephthah off the land. "You will not get any of our father's inheritance," they said, "for you are the son of a prostitute." [3]So Jephthah fled from his brothers and lived in the land of Tob. Soon he had a large band of rebels following him.

[4]At about this time, the Ammonites began their war against Israel. [5]When the Ammonites attacked, the leaders of Gilead sent for Jephthah in the land of Tob. They said, [6]"Come and be our commander! Help us fight the Ammonites!"

[7]But Jephthah said to them, "Aren't you the ones who hated me and drove me from my father's house? Why do you come to me now when you're in trouble?"

[8]"Because we need you," they replied. "If you will lead us in battle against the Ammonites, we will make you ruler over all the people of Gilead."

[9]Jephthah said, "If I come with you and if the LORD gives me victory over the Ammonites, will you really make me ruler over all the people?"

[10]"The LORD is our witness," the leaders replied. "We promise to do whatever you say."

[11]So Jephthah went with the leaders of Gilead, and he became their ruler and commander of the army. At Mizpah, in the presence of the LORD, Jephthah repeated what he had said to the leaders.

[12]Then Jephthah sent messengers to the king of Ammon, demanding to know why Israel was being attacked. [13]The king of Ammon answered Jephthah's messengers, "When the Israelites came out of Egypt, they stole my land from the Arnon River to the Jabbok River and all the way to the Jordan. Now then, give back the land peaceably."

[14]Jephthah sent this message back to the Ammonite king:

[15]"This is what Jephthah says: Israel did not steal any land from Moab or Ammon. [16]When the people of Israel arrived at Kadesh on their journey from Egypt after crossing the Red Sea,* [17]they sent messengers to the king of Edom asking for permission to pass through his land. But their request was denied. Then they asked the king of Moab for similar permission, but he wouldn't let them pass through either. So the people of Israel stayed in Kadesh.

[18]"Finally, they went around Edom and Moab through the wilderness. They traveled along Moab's eastern border and camped on the other side of the Arnon River. But they never once crossed the Arnon River into Moab.

[19]"Then Israel sent messengers to King Sihon of the Amorites, who ruled from Heshbon, asking for permission to cross through his land to get to their destination. [20]But King Sihon didn't trust Israel to pass

I CONFESS my sins to the Lord in times of great distress and truly repent. (10:15)

I BELIEVE the Lord is grieved by the misery of his people. (10:16)

I ABHOR the idea of taunting someone because of the circumstances surrounding that person's conception and birth. (11:2)

I MAKE vows with the utmost caution and care, knowing that the Lord is my witness whenever I make a promise. (11:10)

I DIRECTLY CONFRONT those who oppose me and seek to understand their reasons for doing so. (11:12)

I PRESENT my case to my opponents by calmly recalling the facts, asking thought-provoking questions, and then presenting a short but strong conclusion. (11:15)

I BELIEVE the Israelites under Moses and Joshua often defeated pagan kingdoms after first being attacked. (11:20)

11:16 Hebrew *sea of reeds.*

through his land. Instead, he mobilized his army at Jahaz and attacked them. [21]But the LORD, the God of Israel, gave his people victory over King Sihon. So Israel took control of all the land of the Amorites, who lived in that region, [22]from the Arnon River to the Jabbok River, and from the wilderness to the Jordan.

[23]"So you see, it was the LORD, the God of Israel, who took away the land from the Amorites and gave it to Israel. Why, then, should we give it to you? [24]You keep whatever your god Chemosh gives you, and we will keep whatever the LORD our God gives us. [25]Are you any better than Balak son of Zippor, king of Moab? Did he try to make a case against Israel for disputed land? Did he go to war? No, of course not. [26]But now after three hundred years you make an issue of this! Israel has been living here all this time, spread across the land from Heshbon to Aroer and in all the towns along the Arnon River. Why have you made no effort to recover it before now? [27]I have not sinned against you. Rather, you have wronged me by attacking me. Let the LORD, who is judge, decide today which of us is right—Israel or Ammon."

[28]But the king of Ammon paid no attention to Jephthah's message.

Jephthah's Vow

[29]At that time the Spirit of the LORD came upon Jephthah, and he went throughout the land of Gilead and Manasseh, including Mizpah in Gilead, and led an army against the Ammonites. [30]And Jephthah made a vow to the LORD. He said, "If you give me victory over the Ammonites, [31]I will give to the LORD the first thing coming out of my house to greet me when I return in triumph. I will sacrifice it as a burnt offering."

[32]So Jephthah led his army against the Ammonites, and the LORD gave him victory. [33]He thoroughly defeated the Ammonites from Aroer to an area near Minnith—twenty towns—and as far away as Abel-keramim. Thus Israel subdued the Ammonites.

[34]When Jephthah returned home to Mizpah, his daughter—his only child—ran out to meet him, playing on a tambourine and dancing for joy. [35]When he saw her, he tore his clothes in anguish. "My daughter!" he cried out. "My heart is breaking! What a tragedy that you came out to greet me. For I have made a vow to the LORD and cannot take it back."

[36]And she said, "Father, you have made a promise to the LORD. You must do to me what you have promised, for the LORD has given you a great victory over your enemies, the Ammonites. [37]But first let me go up and roam in the hills and weep with my friends for two months, because I will die a virgin."

[38]"You may go," Jephthah said. And he let her go away for two months. She and her friends went into the hills and wept because she would never have children. [39]When she returned home, her father kept his vow, and she died a virgin. So it has become a custom in Israel [40]for young Israelite women to go away for four days each year to lament the fate of Jephthah's daughter.

CHAPTER 12

Ephraim Fights with Jephthah

Then the tribe of Ephraim mobilized its army and crossed over to Zaphon. They sent this message to Jephthah: "Why didn't you call for us to help you fight against Ammon? We are going to burn down your house with you in it!"

[2]"I summoned you at the beginning of the dispute, but you refused to come!" Jephthah said. "You failed to help us in our struggle against Ammon. [3]So I risked my life and went to battle without you, and the LORD gave me victory over the Ammonites. So why have you come to fight me?"

I LISTEN to others and do not ignore the facts in a dispute. (11:28)

I AM FILLED with the Holy Spirit (see Ephesians 5:18). (11:29)

I DO NOT MAKE foolish vows as a way to seek the Lord's favor and blessing. (11:30)

I KEEP my vows to the Lord. (11:35)

I DEAL with anger properly and honor God in my responses to others. (12:1)

⁴The leaders of Ephraim responded, "The men of Gilead are nothing more than rejects from Ephraim and Manasseh." So Jephthah called out his army and attacked the men of Ephraim and defeated them.

⁵Jephthah captured the shallows of the Jordan, and whenever a fugitive from Ephraim tried to go back across, the men of Gilead would challenge him. "Are you a member of the tribe of Ephraim?" they would ask. If the man said, "No, I'm not," ⁶they would tell him to say "Shibboleth." If he was from Ephraim, he would say "Sibboleth," because people from Ephraim cannot pronounce the word correctly. Then they would take him and kill him at the shallows of the Jordan River. So forty-two thousand Ephraimites were killed at that time.

I ABHOR "ethnic cleansing." (12:4)

UNLIKE JEPHTHAH   *I do not make a foolish vow to God.*

Judges 11:31

Although soldiers are known to plead with God from foxholes, the Lord is not really interested in bargaining. He is more delighted with a heartfelt prayer than a hasty promise.

Jephthah was a man riding a wave of success that had missed him in the past. He had experienced the sting of social rejection earlier in life as a prostitute's son, but now Jephthah had been called to lead the people of Gilead and face the demands of the pagan Ammonite king.

More important than his obvious talent and calling, Jephthah had the Spirit of the Lord upon him as he gathered the armies together to meet the enemy. God had given him all he needed for victory. Still, Jephthah felt compelled to make a hasty promise to the Lord—a vow that only ensured his own grief, not the battle's outcome.

Whatever Jephthah's motive, his mouth indeed brought him misery. As soon as he heard the shaking tambourine and saw the delighted face of his daughter, his only child, his heart broke. He had given a promise to God to sacrifice the first thing that came out of his house upon his return, and he knew he must keep it. If only he had first stopped to consider what he might have to sacrifice.

Most likely, Jephthah's daughter did not literally lose her life. But she and her father lost something very precious. She was deprived of marriage, children, and the social acceptance they gave in that culture. He lost grandchildren, descendants, posterity.

Years later Solomon would write: "Keep all the promises you make to [God]. It is better to say nothing than to promise something that you don't follow through on" (Ecclesiastes 5:4-5). He also warned: "Don't make rash promises to God" (Ecclesiastes 5:2).

If we promise something (a) that we most likely can't do, (b) that involves others, or (c) that contradicts God's Word, we often bring more hurt on ourselves than glory to God. As Jesus instructed, we should count the cost before we make a commitment (Luke 14:28), make sure our yes means yes (Matthew 5:33-36), and obey God out of love and worship—no strings attached.

You'll find Jephthah listed among the heroes of faith in 1 Samuel 12:11 and Hebrews 11:32.

○ *Today's Scripture reading is Judges 11:1–12:7.*

⁷Jephthah was Israel's judge for six years. When he died, he was buried in one of the towns of Gilead.

Ibzan Becomes Israel's Judge

⁸After Jephthah, Ibzan became Israel's judge. He lived in Bethlehem, ⁹and he had thirty sons and thirty daughters. He married his daughters to men outside his clan and brought in thirty young women from outside his clan to marry his sons. Ibzan judged Israel for seven years. ¹⁰When he died, he was buried at Bethlehem.

Elon Becomes Israel's Judge

¹¹After him, Elon from Zebulun became Israel's judge. He judged Israel for ten years. ¹²When he died, he was buried at Aijalon in Zebulun.

Abdon Becomes Israel's Judge

¹³After Elon died, Abdon son of Hillel, from Pirathon, became Israel's judge. ¹⁴He had forty sons and thirty grandsons, who rode on seventy donkeys. He was Israel's judge for eight years. ¹⁵Then he died and was buried at Pirathon in Ephraim, in the hill country of the Amalekites.

CHAPTER 13

The Birth of Samson

Again the Israelites did what was evil in the LORD's sight, so the LORD handed them over to the Philistines, who kept them in subjection for forty years.

²In those days, a man named Manoah from the tribe of Dan lived in the town of Zorah. His wife was unable to become pregnant, and they had no children. ³The angel of the LORD appeared to Manoah's wife and said, "Even though you have been unable to have children, you will soon become pregnant and give birth to a son. ⁴You must not drink wine or any other alcoholic drink or eat any forbidden food. ⁵You will become pregnant and give birth to a son, and his hair must never be cut. For he will be dedicated to God as a Nazirite from birth. He will rescue Israel from the Philistines."

⁶The woman ran and told her husband, "A man of God appeared to me! He was like one of God's angels, terrifying to look at. I didn't ask where he was from, and he didn't tell me his name. ⁷But he told me, 'You will become pregnant and give birth to a son. You must not drink wine or any other alcoholic drink or eat any forbidden food. For your son will be dedicated to God as a Nazirite from the moment of his birth until the day of his death.' "

⁸Then Manoah prayed to the LORD. He said, "Lord, please let the man of God come back to us again and give us more instructions about this son who is to be born."

⁹God answered his prayer, and the angel of God appeared once again to his wife as she was sitting in the field. But her husband, Manoah, was not with her. ¹⁰So she quickly ran and told her husband, "The man who appeared to me the other day is here again!"

¹¹Manoah ran back with his wife and asked, "Are you the man who talked to my wife the other day?"

"Yes," he replied, "I am."

¹²So Manoah asked him, "When your words come true, what kind of rules should govern the boy's life and work?"

¹³The angel of the LORD replied, "Be sure your wife follows the instructions I gave her. ¹⁴She must not eat grapes or raisins, drink wine or any other alcoholic drink, or eat any forbidden food."

¹⁵Then Manoah said to the angel of the LORD, "Please stay here until we can prepare a young goat for you to eat."

¹⁶"I will stay," the angel of the LORD replied, "but I will not eat anything. However, you may prepare a burnt offering as a sacrifice to the LORD." (Manoah didn't realize it was the angel of the LORD.)

¹⁷Then Manoah asked the angel of the LORD, "What is your name? For when all this comes true, we want to honor you."

¹⁸"Why do you ask my name?" the angel of the LORD replied. "You wouldn't understand if I told you."

¹⁹Then Manoah took a young goat and a grain offering and offered it on a rock as a sacrifice to the LORD. And as Manoah and his wife watched, the LORD did an amazing thing. ²⁰As the flames from the altar shot up toward the sky, the angel of the LORD ascended in the fire. When Manoah and his wife saw this, they fell with their faces to the ground.

²¹The angel did not appear again to Manoah and his wife. Manoah finally realized it was the angel of the LORD, ²²and he said to his wife, "We will die, for we have seen God!"

I AM DEDICATED to God for all my life. (13:7)

I ASK the Lord for wisdom. (13:8)

I BELIEVE what the Lord has said. (13:12)

²³But his wife said, "If the LORD were going to kill us, he wouldn't have accepted our burnt offering and grain offering. He wouldn't have appeared to us and told us this wonderful thing and done these miracles."

²⁴When her son was born, they named him Samson. And the LORD blessed him as he grew up. ²⁵And in Mahaneh-dan, which is located between the towns of Zorah and Eshtaol, the Spirit of the LORD began to take hold of him.

CHAPTER 14

Samson's Riddle

One day when Samson was in Timnah, he noticed a certain Philistine woman. ²When he returned home, he told his father and mother, "I want to marry a young Philistine woman I saw in Timnah."

³His father and mother objected strenuously, "Isn't there one woman in our tribe or among all the Israelites you could marry? Why must you go to the pagan Philistines to find a wife?"

But Samson told his father, "Get her for me. She is the one I want." ⁴His father and mother didn't realize the LORD was at work in this, creating an opportunity to disrupt the Philistines, who ruled over Israel at that time.

⁵As Samson and his parents were going down to Timnah, a young lion attacked Samson near the vineyards of Timnah. ⁶At that moment the Spirit of the LORD powerfully took control of him, and he ripped the lion's jaws apart with his bare hands. He did it as easily as if it were a young goat. But he didn't tell his father or mother about it. ⁷When Samson arrived in Timnah, he talked with the woman and was very pleased with her.

⁸Later, when he returned to Timnah for the wedding, he turned off the path to look at the carcass of the lion. And he found that a swarm of bees had made some honey in the carcass. ⁹He scooped some of the honey into his hands and ate it along the way. He also gave some to his father and mother, and they ate it. But he didn't tell them he had taken the honey from the carcass of the lion.

¹⁰As his father was making final arrangements for the marriage, Samson threw a party at Timnah, as was the custom of the day. ¹¹Thirty young men from the town were invited to be his companions. ¹²Samson said to them, "Let me tell you a riddle. If you solve my riddle during these seven days of the celebration, I will give you thirty plain linen robes and thirty fancy robes. ¹³But if you can't solve it, then you must give me thirty linen robes and thirty fancy robes."

"All right," they agreed, "let's hear your riddle."

¹⁴So he said:

"From the one who eats came something to eat;
  out of the strong came something sweet."

Three days later they were still trying to figure it out. ¹⁵On the fourth* day they said to Samson's wife, "Get the answer to the riddle from your husband, or we will burn down your father's house with you in it. Did you invite us to this party just to make us poor?"

¹⁶So Samson's wife came to him in tears and said, "You don't love me; you hate me! You have given my people a riddle, but you haven't told me the answer."

"I haven't even given the answer to my father or mother," he replied. "Why should I tell you?" ¹⁷So she cried whenever she was with him and kept it up for the rest of the celebration. At last, on the seventh day, he told her the answer because of her persistent nagging. Then she gave the answer to the young men.

14:15 As in Greek version; Hebrew reads *seventh.*

I PRAY that the Lord will bless my children as they grow up. (13:24)

I AM FILLED with the Holy Spirit (see Ephesians 5:18). (13:25)

I AM CAREFUL in making decisions about whom to marry. (14:1)

I ABHOR the idea of marrying an unbeliever. (14:2)

I LISTEN carefully to my parents' counsel about whom to marry. (14:3)

I DO NOT RISK part of my wealth on foolish games. (14:12)

¹⁸So before sunset of the seventh day, the men of the town came to Samson with their answer:

"What is sweeter than honey?
What is stronger than a lion?"

Samson replied, "If you hadn't plowed with my heifer, you wouldn't have found the answer to my riddle!" ¹⁹Then the Spirit of the LORD powerfully took control of him. He went down to the town of Ashkelon, killed thirty men, took their belongings, and gave their clothing to the men who had answered his riddle. But Samson was furious about what had happened, and he went back home to live with his father and mother. ²⁰So his wife was given in marriage to the man who had been Samson's best man at the wedding.

CHAPTER 15

Samson's Vengeance on the Philistines

Later on, during the wheat harvest, Samson took a young goat as a present to his wife. He intended to sleep with her, but her father wouldn't let him in. ²"I really thought you hated her," her father explained, "so I gave her in marriage to your best man. But look, her sister is more beautiful than she is. Marry her instead."

³Samson said, "This time I cannot be blamed for everything I am going to do to you Philistines." ⁴Then he went out and caught three hundred foxes. He tied their tails together in pairs, and he fastened a torch to each pair of tails. ⁵Then he lit the torches and let the foxes run through the fields of the Philistines. He burned all their grain to the ground, including the grain still in piles and all that had been bundled. He also destroyed their grapevines and olive trees.

⁶"Who did this?" the Philistines demanded.

"Samson," was the reply, "because his father-in-law from Timnah gave Samson's wife to be married to his best man." So the Philistines went and got the woman and her father and burned them to death.

⁷"Because you did this," Samson vowed, "I will take my revenge on you, and I won't stop until I'm satisfied!" ⁸So he attacked the Philistines with great fury and killed many of them. Then he went to live in a cave in the rock of Etam.

⁹The Philistines retaliated by setting up camp in Judah and raiding the town of Lehi. ¹⁰The men of Judah asked the Philistines, "Why have you attacked us?"

The Philistines replied, "We've come to capture Samson. We have come to pay him back for what he did to us."

¹¹So three thousand men of Judah went down to get Samson at the cave in the rock of Etam. They said to Samson, "Don't you realize the Philistines rule over us? What are you doing to us?"

But Samson replied, "I only paid them back for what they did to me."

¹²But the men of Judah told him, "We have come to tie you up and hand you over to the Philistines."

"All right," Samson said. "But promise that you won't kill me yourselves."

¹³"We will tie you up and hand you over to the Philistines," they replied. "We won't kill you." So they tied him up with two new ropes and led him away from the rock.

¹⁴As Samson arrived at Lehi, the Philistines came shouting in triumph. But the Spirit of the LORD powerfully took control of Samson, and he snapped the ropes on his arms as if they were burnt strands of flax, and they fell from his wrists. ¹⁵Then he picked up a donkey's jawbone that was lying on the ground and killed a thousand Philistines with it. ¹⁶And Samson said,

I DO NOT CALL OFF my wedding or leave my spouse because I am angry. (14:19)

I DO NOT BELIEVE anyone should be put to death because the community is outraged over a property crime, marital dispute, or some other non-capital offense. (15:6)

I DO NOT TAKE revenge. (15:7)

I AM FILLED with the Holy Spirit (see Ephesians 5:18). (15:14)

"With the jawbone of a donkey,
    I've made heaps on heaps!
With the jawbone of a donkey,
    I've killed a thousand men!"

¹⁷When he finished speaking, he threw away the jawbone; and the place was named Jawbone Hill.*

¹⁸Now Samson was very thirsty, and he cried out to the LORD, "You have accomplished this great victory by the strength of your servant. Must I now die of thirst and fall into the hands of these pagan people?" ¹⁹So God caused water to gush out of a hollow in the ground at Lehi, and Samson was revived as he drank. Then he named that place "The Spring of the One Who Cried Out,"* and it is still in Lehi to this day.

²⁰Samson was Israel's judge for twenty years, while the Philistines ruled the land.

CHAPTER 16

Samson Removes Gaza's Gates

One day Samson went to the Philistine city of Gaza and spent the night with a prostitute. ²Word soon spread that Samson was there, so the men of Gaza gathered together and waited all night at the city gates. They kept quiet during the night, saying to themselves, "When the light of morning comes, we will kill him."

³But Samson stayed in bed only until midnight. Then he got up, took hold of the city gates with its two posts, and lifted them, bar and all, right out of the ground. He put them on his shoulders and carried them all the way to the top of the hill across from Hebron.

Samson and Delilah

⁴Later Samson fell in love with a woman named Delilah, who lived in the valley of Sorek. ⁵The leaders of the Philistines went to her and said, "Find out from Samson what makes him so strong and how he can be overpowered and tied up securely. Then each of us will give you eleven hundred pieces* of silver."

⁶So Delilah said to Samson, "Please tell me what makes you so strong and what it would take to tie you up securely."

⁷Samson replied, "If I am tied up with seven new bowstrings that have not yet been dried, I will be as weak as anyone else."

⁸So the Philistine leaders brought Delilah seven new bowstrings, and she tied Samson up with them. ⁹She had hidden some men in one of the rooms of her house, and she cried out, "Samson! The Philistines have come to capture you!" But Samson snapped the bowstrings as if they were string that had been burned in a fire. So the secret of his strength was not discovered.

¹⁰Afterward Delilah said to him, "You made fun of me and told me a lie! Now please tell me how you can be tied up securely."

¹¹Samson replied, "If I am tied up with brand-new ropes that have never been used, I will be as weak as anyone else."

¹²So Delilah took new ropes and tied him up with them. The men were hiding in the room as before, and again Delilah cried out, "Samson! The Philistines have come to capture you!" But Samson snapped the ropes from his arms as if they were thread.

¹³Then Delilah said, "You have been making fun of me and telling me lies! Won't you please tell me how you can be tied up securely?"

Samson replied, "If you weave the seven braids of my hair into the fabric on your loom and tighten it with the loom shuttle,* I will be as weak as anyone else."

I TRUST the Lord for everything—even for what I eat and drink. (15:18)

I ABHOR sexual immorality, no matter what the world around me says. (16:4)

I PART WAYS immediately if any so-called friend seeks to compromise my commitment to the Lord. (16:6)

I PART WAYS if a so-called friend pressures me to go against my better judgment. (16:10)

I PART WAYS if a so-called friend won't take no for an answer. (16:13)

15:17 Hebrew *Ramath-lehi.*   15:19 Hebrew *En-hakkore.*   16:5 Hebrew *1,100 shekels,* about 28 pounds or 12.5 kilograms in weight.   16:13 As in Greek version; Hebrew lacks *on your loom and tighten it with the loom shuttle.*

So while he slept, Delilah wove the seven braids of his hair into the fabric [14]and tightened it with the loom shuttle. Again she cried out, "Samson! The Philistines have come to capture you!" But Samson woke up, pulled back the loom shuttle, and yanked his hair away from the loom and the fabric.

[15]Then Delilah pouted, "How can you say you love me when you don't confide in me? You've made fun of me three times now, and you still haven't told me what makes you so strong!" [16]So day after day she nagged him until he couldn't stand it any longer.

[17]Finally, Samson told her his secret. "My hair has never been cut," he confessed, "for I was dedicated to God as a Nazirite from birth. If my head were shaved, my strength would leave me, and I would become as weak as anyone else."

[18]Delilah realized he had finally told her the truth, so she sent for the Philistine leaders. "Come back one more time," she said, "for he has told me everything." So the Philistine leaders returned and brought the money with them. [19]Delilah lulled Samson to sleep with his head in her lap, and she called in a man to shave off his hair, making his capture certain. And his strength left him. [20]Then she cried out, "Samson! The Philistines have come to capture you!"

When he woke up, he thought, "I will do as before and shake myself free." But he didn't realize the LORD had left him.

[21]So the Philistines captured him and gouged out his eyes. They took him to Gaza, where he was bound with bronze chains and made to grind grain in the prison. [22]But before long his hair began to grow back.

Samson's Final Victory

[23]The Philistine leaders held a great festival, offering sacrifices and praising their god, Dagon. They said, "Our god has given us victory over our enemy Samson!"

[24]When the people saw him, they praised their god, saying, "Our god has delivered our enemy to us! The one who killed so many of us is now in our power!"

[25]Half drunk by now, the people demanded, "Bring out Samson so he can perform for us!" So he was brought from the prison and made to stand at the center of the temple, between the two pillars supporting the roof. [26]Samson said to the servant who was leading him by the hand, "Place my hands against the two pillars. I want to rest against them." [27]The temple was completely filled with people. All the Philistine leaders were there, and there were about three thousand on the roof who were watching Samson and making fun of him.

[28]Then Samson prayed to the LORD, "Sovereign LORD, remember me again. O God, please strengthen me one more time so that I may pay back the Philistines for the loss of my eyes." [29]Then Samson put his hands on the center pillars of the temple and pushed against them with all his might. [30]"Let me die with the Philistines," he prayed. And the temple crashed down on the Philistine leaders and all the people. So he killed more people when he died than he had during his entire lifetime.

[31]Later his brothers and other relatives went down to get his body. They took him back home and buried him between Zorah and Eshtaol, where his father, Manoah, was buried. Samson had been Israel's judge for twenty years.

CHAPTER 17

Micah's Idols

A man named Micah lived in the hill country of Ephraim. [2]One day he said to his mother, "I heard you curse the thief who stole eleven hundred pieces* of silver from you. Well, here they are. I was the one who took them."

I PART WAYS if a so-called friend pouts and nags until I give in to temptation. (16:15)

I REPENT of my sins immediately, not just in times of great adversity. (16:21)

I ABHOR stealing and believe that those who steal should confess their sin and make restitution. (17:2)

17:2 Hebrew *1,100 shekels*, about 28 pounds or 12.5 kilograms in weight.

"The LORD bless you for admitting it," his mother replied. ³He returned the money to her, and she said, "I now dedicate these silver coins to the LORD. In honor of my son, I will have an image carved and an idol cast." ⁴So his mother took two hundred of the silver coins to a silversmith, who made them into an image and an idol. And these were placed in Micah's house.

> I ABHOR idolatry and the mixing of pagan worship with the worship of the Lord. (17:3)

UNLIKE SAMSON   *I will not let myself be ruined by passions and lusts.*
Judges 16:1

Anyone want to vote for Benedict Arnold as a model of loyalty? or Karl Marx as a champion of free enterprise? or Al Capone as a candidate for sainthood?

What about Samson as a hero of the faith?

Incredibly, Samson rates right up there with "all of the prophets" (Hebrews 11:32) as an Old Testament hero who demonstrated great faith.

Samson?

Yes.

The accounts of Samson's life cover more chapters (four) than anyone else's life in the book of Judges. Those accounts tell of Samson's supernaturally foretold birth, the Lord's blessing on his childhood, his lifelong Nazirite vow, the Spirit's hold on his life, and his incredible strength—as well as his unbridled passions and lusts.

Toward the end of his life, Samson apparently had enough faith to ask for a miracle (15:18-19), only to turn around and sleep with a prostitute (16:1-3), then immediately perform a fantastic feat of strength (16:3), sleep with another woman who betrayed him (16:4-20), lose the Lord's empowerment and suffer at the hands of the Philistines (16:20-27), and then pray to the Lord and perform one last great feat of strength (16:28-30).

The stuff of a hero of the faith?

In the Lord's eyes, yes.

Samson was no saint. He was no prophet or theologian either. Chances are Samson would have had a tough time teaching a first-grade Sunday school class. But through it all, to the very end, he chose to believe the Sovereign Lord could do great things through him.

In many ways, of course, Samson's story is tragically short. One can only imagine how much more he could have done for the Lord if Samson hadn't been ruined by passions and lusts. Perhaps an entire book of the Bible would have been written about him!

Like Samson, you and I have a life story to write. And like Samson, we have important choices to make. Will we run the race of faith to the end? And will we "strip off every weight that slows us down, especially the sin that so easily hinders our progress" (Hebrews 12:1)? Samson did the first but not the second.

Samson made the mistake of thinking he was strong enough to bear up under the growing weight of sin. It's a burden that crushed the strongest man in the world. And Satan would love to see it crush us, too.

Instead of being ruled by passions and lusts, acknowledge the Lord as sovereign over every area of life.

○ *Today's Scripture reading is Judges 13–16.*

⁵Micah set up a shrine, and he made a sacred ephod and some household idols. Then he installed one of his sons as the priest. ⁶In those days Israel had no king, so the people did whatever seemed right in their own eyes.

⁷One day a young Levite from Bethlehem in Judah ⁸arrived in that area of Ephraim, looking for a good place to live. He happened to stop at Micah's house as he was traveling through. ⁹"Where are you from?" Micah asked him.

And he replied, "I am a Levite from Bethlehem in Judah, and I am looking for a place to live."

> I DO what is right in the Lord's eyes, not what merely seems "right" within my culture. (17:6)

¹⁰"Stay here with me," Micah said, "and you can be a father and priest to me. I will give you ten pieces* of silver a year, plus a change of clothes and your food." ¹¹The Levite agreed to this and became like one of Micah's sons. ¹²So Micah ordained the Levite as his personal priest, and he lived in Micah's house. ¹³"I know the LORD will bless me now," Micah said, "because I have a Levite serving as my priest."

CHAPTER 18

Idolatry in the Tribe of Dan

Now in those days Israel had no king. And the tribe of Dan was trying to find a place to settle, for they had not yet driven out the people who lived in the land assigned to them. ²So the men of Dan chose five warriors from among their clans, who lived in the towns of Zorah and Eshtaol, to scout out a land for them to settle in.

When these warriors arrived in the hill country of Ephraim, they came to Micah's home and spent the night there. ³Noticing the young Levite's accent, they took him aside and asked him, "Who brought you here, and what are you doing? Why are you here?" ⁴He told them about his agreement with Micah and that he was Micah's personal priest.

⁵Then they said, "Ask God whether or not our journey will be successful."

⁶"Go in peace," the priest replied. "For the LORD will go ahead of you on your journey."

⁷So the five men went on to the town of Laish, where they noticed the people living carefree lives, like the Sidonians; they were peaceful and secure. The people were also wealthy because their land was very fertile. And they lived a great distance from Sidon and had no allies nearby.

⁸When the men returned to Zorah and Eshtaol, their relatives asked them, "What did you find?"

⁹The men replied, "Let's attack! We have seen the land, and it is very good. You should not hesitate to go and take possession of it. ¹⁰When you get there, you will find the people living carefree lives. God has given us a spacious and fertile land, lacking in nothing!"

¹¹So six hundred warriors from the tribe of Dan set out from Zorah and Eshtaol. ¹²They camped at a place west of Kiriath-jearim in Judah, which is called Mahaneh-dan* to this day. ¹³Then they went up into the hill country of Ephraim and came to the house of Micah.

¹⁴The five men who had scouted out the land around Laish said to the others, "There is a shrine here with a sacred ephod, some household idols, a carved image, and a cast idol. It's obvious what we ought to do." ¹⁵So the five men went over to Micah's house, where the young Levite lived, and greeted him kindly. ¹⁶As the six hundred warriors from the tribe of Dan stood just outside the gate, ¹⁷the five spies entered the shrine and took the carved image, the sacred ephod, the household idols, and the cast idol.

¹⁸When the priest saw the men carrying all the sacred objects out of Micah's shrine, he said, "What are you doing?"

¹⁹"Be quiet and come with us," they said. "Be a father and priest to all of us. Isn't it better to be a priest for an entire tribe of Israel than just for the household of one man?" ²⁰The young priest was quite happy to go with them, so he took along the sacred ephod, the household idols, and the carved image. ²¹They started on their way again, placing their children, livestock, and possessions in front of them.

²²When the people from the tribe of Dan were quite a distance from Micah's home, Micah and some of his neighbors came chasing after them. ²³They were shouting as they caught up with them. The men of Dan turned

I BELIEVE the tribe of Dan failed to finish conquering its portion of the Promised Land. (18:1)

I DO NOT PRESUME or pretend to speak for God. (18:6)

I THINK a group should not presume or pretend to have God's blessing when they go to war, especially if they have consistently and persistently disobeyed God's commands. (18:10)

I ABHOR stealing and plundering. (18:14)

I DO NOT FEIGN friendship. (18:15)

17:10 Hebrew *10 shekels*, about 4 ounces or 114 grams in weight.   **18:12** *Mahaneh-dan* means "the camp of Dan."

around and said, "What do you want? Why have you called these men together and chased after us like this?"

²⁴"What do you mean, What do I want?" Micah replied. "You've taken away all my gods and my priest, and I have nothing left!"

²⁵The men of Dan said, "Watch what you say! Some of us are short-tempered, and they might get angry and kill you and your family." ²⁶So the men of Dan went on their way. When Micah saw that there were too many of them for him to attack, he turned around and went home.

²⁷Then, with Micah's idols and his priest, the men of Dan came to the town of Laish, whose people were peaceful and secure. They attacked and killed all the people and burned the town to the ground. ²⁸There was no one to rescue the residents of the town, for they lived a great distance from Sidon and had no allies nearby. This happened in the valley near Beth-rehob.

Then the people of the tribe of Dan rebuilt the town and lived there. ²⁹They renamed the town Dan after their ancestor, Israel's son, but it had originally been called Laish.

³⁰Then they set up the carved image, and they appointed Jonathan son of Gershom, a descendant of Moses,* as their priest. This family continued as priests for the tribe of Dan until the Exile. ³¹So Micah's carved image was worshiped by the tribe of Dan as long as the Tabernacle of God remained at Shiloh.

CHAPTER 19

The Levite and His Concubine

Now in those days Israel had no king. There was a man from the tribe of Levi living in a remote area of the hill country of Ephraim. One day he brought home a woman from Bethlehem in Judah to be his concubine. ²But she was unfaithful to him and returned to her father's home in Bethlehem. After about four months, ³her husband took a servant and an extra donkey to Bethlehem to persuade her to come back. When he arrived at her father's house, she took him inside, and her father welcomed him. ⁴Her father urged him to stay awhile, so he stayed three days, eating, drinking, and sleeping there.

⁵On the fourth day the man was up early, ready to leave, but the woman's father said, "Have something to eat before you go." ⁶So the two of them sat down together and had something to eat and drink. Then the woman's father said, "Please stay the night and enjoy yourself." ⁷The man got up to leave, but his father-in-law kept urging him to stay, so he finally gave in and stayed the night. ⁸On the morning of the fifth day he was up early again, ready to leave, and again the woman's father said, "Have something to eat; then you can leave some time this afternoon." So they had another day of feasting.

⁹That afternoon, as he and his concubine and servant were preparing to leave, his father-in-law said, "Look, it's getting late. Stay the night and enjoy yourself. Tomorrow you can get up early and be on your way."

¹⁰But this time the man was determined to leave. So he took his two saddled donkeys and his concubine and headed in the direction of Jebus (that is, Jerusalem). ¹¹It was late in the day when they reached Jebus, and the man's servant said to him, "It's getting too late to travel; let's stay in this Jebusite city tonight."

¹²"No," his master said, "we can't stay in this foreign city where there are no Israelites. We will go on to Gibeah. ¹³We will find a place to spend the night in either Gibeah or Ramah." ¹⁴So they went on. The sun was setting as they came to Gibeah, a town in the land of Benjamin, ¹⁵so they stopped there

I ABHOR idolatry and the mixing of pagan worship with the worship of the Lord. (18:30)

See Moses' profile (page 73) at Exodus 5:1.

I BELIEVE in the sanctity of marriage—one man, one woman, committed wholeheartedly for life to God and to each other. (19:1)

I DO NOT PROCRASTINATE if my spouse and I need to be reconciled. (19:3)

I GLADLY OFFER hospitality to close relatives. (19:4)

I DO NOT PUT undue pressure on my relatives. (19:9)

I GLADLY OFFER hospitality to fellow believers visiting my community. (19:15)

18:30 As in an ancient Hebrew tradition, some Greek manuscripts, and Latin Vulgate; Masoretic Text reads *of Manasseh.*

to spend the night. They rested in the town square, but no one took them in for the night.

¹⁶That evening an old man came home from his work in the fields. He was from the hill country of Ephraim, but he was living in Gibeah in the territory of Benjamin. ¹⁷When he saw the travelers sitting in the town square, he asked them where they were from and where they were going.

¹⁸"We have been in Bethlehem in Judah," the man replied. "We are on our way home to a remote area in the hill country of Ephraim, and we're going to the Tabernacle of the LORD. But no one has taken us in for the night, ¹⁹even though we have everything we need. We have straw and fodder for our donkeys and plenty of bread and wine for ourselves."

²⁰"You are welcome to stay with me," the old man said. "I will give you anything you might need. But whatever you do, don't spend the night in the square." ²¹So he took them home with him and fed their donkeys. After they washed their feet, they had supper together.

²²While they were enjoying themselves, some of the wicked men in the town surrounded the house. They began beating at the door and shouting to the old man, "Bring out the man who is staying with you so we can have sex with him."

²³The old man stepped outside to talk to them. "No, my brothers, don't do such an evil thing. For this man is my guest, and such a thing would be shameful. ²⁴Here, take my virgin daughter and this man's concubine. I will bring them out to you, and you can do whatever you like to them. But don't do such a shameful thing to this man."

²⁵But they wouldn't listen to him. Then the Levite took his concubine and pushed her out the door. The men of the town abused her all night, taking turns raping her until morning. Finally, at dawn, they let her go. ²⁶At daybreak the woman returned to the house where her husband was staying. She collapsed at the door of the house and lay there until it was light.

²⁷When her husband opened the door to leave, he found her there. She was lying face down, with her hands on the threshold. ²⁸He said, "Get up! Let's go!" But there was no answer.* So he put her body on his donkey and took her home.

²⁹When he got home, he took a knife and cut his concubine's body into twelve pieces. Then he sent one piece to each tribe of Israel. ³⁰Everyone who saw it said, "Such a horrible crime has not been committed since Israel left Egypt. Shouldn't we speak up and do something about this?"

CHAPTER 20

Israel's War with Benjamin

Then all the Israelites, from Dan to Beersheba and from the land of Gilead, came together in one large assembly and stood in the presence of the LORD at Mizpah. ²The leaders of all the people and all the tribes of Israel—400,000 warriors armed with swords—took their positions in the assembly of the people of God. ³(Word soon reached the land of Benjamin that the other tribes had gone up to Mizpah.) The Israelites then asked how this terrible crime had happened.

⁴The Levite, the husband of the woman who had been murdered, said, "My concubine and I came to Gibeah, a town in the land of Benjamin, to spend the night. ⁵That night some of the leaders of Gibeah surrounded the house, planning to kill me, and they raped my concubine until she was dead. ⁶So I cut her body into twelve pieces and sent the pieces throughout the land of Israel, for these men have committed this terrible and shameful crime.

I UTTERLY ABHOR gang rape and murder. (19:25)

I BELIEVE a careful inquiry should be made, even in the most sensational and public of crimes. (20:3)

I TELL the truth, the whole truth, and nothing but the truth. (20:4)

19:28 Greek version adds *for she was dead.*

[7]Now then, the entire community of Israel must decide what should be done about this!"

[8]And all the people stood up together and replied, "Not one of us will return home. [9]Instead, we will draw lots to decide who will attack Gibeah. [10]One tenth of the men from each tribe will be chosen to supply the warriors with food, and the rest of us will take revenge on Gibeah* for this shameful thing they have done in Israel." [11]So all the Israelites were united, and they gathered together to attack the town.

[12]The Israelites sent messengers to the tribe of Benjamin, saying, "What a terrible thing has been done among you! [13]Give up these evil men from Gibeah so we can execute them and purge Israel of this evil."

But the people of Benjamin would not listen. [14]Instead, they came from their towns and gathered at Gibeah to fight the Israelites. [15]Twenty-six thousand of their warriors armed with swords arrived in Gibeah to join the seven hundred warriors who lived there. [16]Seven hundred of Benjamin's warriors were left-handed, each of whom could sling a rock and hit a target within a hairsbreadth, without missing. [17]Israel had 400,000 warriors armed with swords, not counting Benjamin's warriors.

[18]Before the battle the Israelites went to Bethel and asked God, "Which tribe should lead the attack against the people of Benjamin?"

The LORD answered, "Judah is to go first."

[19]So the Israelites left early the next morning and camped near Gibeah. [20]Then they advanced toward Gibeah to attack the men of Benjamin. [21]But Benjamin's warriors, who were defending the town, came out and killed twenty-two thousand Israelites in the field that day.

[22]But the Israelites took courage and assembled at the same place they had fought the previous day. [23](For they had gone up to Bethel and wept in the presence of the LORD until evening. Then they asked the LORD, "Should we fight against our relatives from Benjamin again?" And the LORD said, "Go out and fight against them.")

[24]So they went out to fight against the warriors of Benjamin, [25]but the men of Benjamin killed another eighteen thousand Israelites, all of whom were experienced with a sword.

[26]Then all the Israelites went up to Bethel and wept in the presence of the LORD and fasted until evening. They also brought burnt offerings and peace offerings to the LORD. [27]And the Israelites went up seeking direction from the LORD. (In those days the Ark of the Covenant of God was in Bethel, [28]and Phinehas son of Eleazar and grandson of Aaron was the priest.) The Israelites asked the LORD, "Should we fight against our relatives from Benjamin again or should we stop?"

The LORD said, "Go! Tomorrow I will give you victory over them."

[29]So the Israelites set an ambush all around Gibeah. [30]They went out on the third day and assembled at the same place as before. [31]When the warriors of Benjamin came out to attack, they were drawn away from the town. And as they had done before, they began to kill the Israelites. About thirty Israelites died in the open fields and along the roads leading to Bethel and Gibeah.

[32]Then the warriors of Benjamin shouted, "We're defeating them as we did in the first battle!" But the Israelites had agreed in advance to run away so that the men of Benjamin would chase them along the roads and be drawn away from the town.

[33]When the main group of Israelite warriors reached Baal-tamar, they turned and prepared to attack. Then the Israelites hiding in ambush west of Gibeah jumped up from where they were [34]and advanced against Benjamin from behind. The fighting was so heavy that Benjamin didn't realize the

I SUPPORT true verdicts and just punishments, even if a friend or relative is found guilty. (20:12)

I WEEP when civil war breaks out. (20:14)

I TAKE courage in the Lord, even after a great tragedy. (20:22)

I CONTINUE to obey God, no matter how many tragedies strike. (20:27)

See the profiles for Aaron (page 107) and Phinehas (page 717) at Exodus 32:2 and Psalm 106:30.

I TRUST in God, not in my own strength, which only leads to disaster. (20:34)

20:10 Hebrew *Geba*, in this case, a variant for Gibeah; also in 20:33.

impending disaster. ³⁵So the LORD helped Israel defeat Benjamin, and that day the Israelites killed 25,100 of Benjamin's warriors, all of whom were experienced with a sword. ³⁶Then the men of Benjamin saw that they were beaten.

The Israelites had retreated from Benjamin's warriors in order to give those hiding in ambush more room to maneuver. ³⁷Then those who were in hiding rushed in from all sides and killed everyone in the town. ³⁸They sent up a large cloud of smoke from the town, ³⁹which was the signal for the Israelites to turn and attack Benjamin's warriors.

By that time Benjamin's warriors had killed about thirty Israelites, and they shouted, "We're defeating them as we did in the first battle!" ⁴⁰But when the warriors of Benjamin looked behind them and saw the smoke rising into the sky from every part of the town, ⁴¹the Israelites turned and attacked. At this point Benjamin's warriors realized disaster was near and became terrified. ⁴²So they ran toward the wilderness, but the Israelites chased after them and killed them. ⁴³The Israelites surrounded the men of Benjamin and were relentless in chasing them down, finally overtaking them east of Gibeah. ⁴⁴Eighteen thousand of Benjamin's greatest warriors died in that day's battle. ⁴⁵The survivors fled into the wilderness toward the rock of Rimmon, but Israel killed five thousand of them along the road. They continued the chase until they had killed another two thousand near Gidom.

⁴⁶So the tribe of Benjamin lost twenty-five thousand brave warriors that day, ⁴⁷leaving only six hundred men who escaped to the rock of Rimmon, where they lived for four months. ⁴⁸Then the Israelites returned and slaughtered every living thing in all the towns—the people, the cattle—everything. They also burned down every town they came to.

CHAPTER 21

Israel Provides Wives for Benjamin
The Israelites had vowed at Mizpah never to give their daughters in marriage to a man from the tribe of Benjamin. ²And the people went to Bethel and sat in the presence of God until evening, raising their voices and weeping bitterly. ³"O LORD, God of Israel," they cried out, "why has this happened? Now one of our tribes is missing!"

⁴Early the next morning the people built an altar and presented their burnt offerings and peace offerings on it. ⁵Then they said, "Was any tribe of Israel not represented when we held our council in the presence of the LORD at Mizpah?" At that time they had taken a solemn oath in the LORD's presence, vowing that anyone who refused to come must die.

⁶The Israelites felt deep sadness for Benjamin and said, "Today we have lost one of the tribes from our family; it is nearly wiped out. ⁷How can we find wives for the few who remain, since we have sworn by the LORD not to give them our daughters in marriage?"

⁸So they asked, "Was anyone absent when we presented ourselves to the LORD at Mizpah?" And they discovered that no one from Jabesh-gilead had attended. ⁹For after they counted all the people, no one from Jabesh-gilead was present. ¹⁰So they sent twelve thousand warriors to Jabesh-gilead with orders to kill everyone there, including women and children. ¹¹"This is what you are to do," they said. "Completely destroy* all the males and every woman who is not a virgin." ¹²Among the residents of Jabesh-gilead they found four hundred young virgins who had never slept with a man, and they brought them to the camp at Shiloh in the land of Canaan.

¹³The Israelite assembly sent a peace delegation to the little remnant of Benjamin who were living at the rock of Rimmon. ¹⁴Then the men of

I DO NOT GIVE IN to fear in the face of impending disaster but immediately turn to God and repent of my sins. (20:41)

I CRY OUT to the Lord after disaster strikes. (21:2)

I ASK the Lord for wisdom instead of doing what merely seems right. (21:7)

21:11 The Hebrew term used here refers to the complete consecration of things or people to the LORD, either by destroying them or by giving them as an offering.

Benjamin returned to their homes, and the four hundred women of Jabesh-gilead who were spared were given to them as wives. But there were not enough women for all of them.

¹⁵The people felt sorry for Benjamin because the LORD had left this gap in the tribes of Israel. ¹⁶So the Israelite leaders asked, "How can we find wives for the few who remain, since all the women of the tribe of Benjamin are dead? ¹⁷There must be heirs for the survivors so that an entire tribe of Israel will not be lost forever. ¹⁸But we cannot give them our own daughters in marriage because we have sworn with a solemn oath that anyone who does this will fall under God's curse."

¹⁹Then they thought of the annual festival of the LORD held in Shiloh, between Lebonah and Bethel, along the east side of the road that goes from Bethel to Shechem. ²⁰They told the men of Benjamin who still needed wives, "Go and hide in the vineyards. ²¹When the women of Shiloh come out for their dances, rush out from the vineyards, and each of you can take one of them home to be your wife! ²²And when their fathers and brothers come to us in protest, we will tell them, 'Please be understanding. Let them have your daughters, for we didn't find enough wives for them when we destroyed Jabesh-gilead. And you are not guilty of breaking the vow since you did not give your daughters in marriage to them.' "

²³So the men of Benjamin did as they were told. They kidnapped the women who took part in the celebration and carried them off to the land of their own inheritance. Then they rebuilt their towns and lived in them. ²⁴So the assembly of Israel departed by tribes and families, and they returned to their own homes.

²⁵In those days Israel had no king, so the people did whatever seemed right in their own eyes.

I ASK the Lord for wisdom instead of relying merely on my own judgment. (21:16)

I ASK the Lord for wisdom instead of doing whatever comes to mind. (21:19)

I DO what is right in the Lord's eyes, not what merely seems "right" within my culture. (21:25)

RUTH

THIS THIRD BOOK of Israelite history is a wonderful story of *redemption*.

The book of Judges ends with two horrific stories associated with the town of Bethlehem. This story, also set in Bethlehem, starts out sad as well. A Jewish family abandons the Promised Land during a severe famine. The matriarch, Naomi, loses her husband and sons in a foreign land (1:1-5). Except for two foreign daughters-in-law, Naomi is utterly destitute and decides to return to Israel. One daughter-in-law, Ruth, refuses to say good-bye, however, and pledges her undying devotion to Naomi (1:6-18). After their return to the Promised Land, Ruth strives to provide for her mother-in-law.

Almost immediately, Ruth meets one of her wealthier relatives. This relative, Boaz, graciously protects and provides for Ruth and Naomi throughout the autumn (1:19–2:23). During a late-night meeting orchestrated by Naomi, Ruth asks Boaz to marry her and legally take on the responsibility of caring for Naomi, as well. Boaz readily accepts her proposal, makes the necessary legal arrangements the next day, and marries Ruth (3:1–4:13).

But the story isn't quite over yet. One of the wonderful results of this unique marriage between a well-respected Israelite and a widowed foreigner was the renowned King David, who was Ruth and Boaz's great-grandson (4:13-22).

Favorite passages in Ruth include
- ◯ Ruth pledges her unfailing loyalty (1:16-17)
- ◯ Naomi tells her sad tale upon returning to Bethlehem (1:20-21)
- ◯ Boaz meets and blesses Ruth (2:11-12)
- ◯ Naomi explains that Boaz is a family redeemer (2:20)
- ◯ Boaz agrees to be Ruth's family redeemer (3:7-13)
- ◯ Boaz secures the legal right to marry Ruth (4:9-10)
- ◯ The leaders and people bless Boaz (4:11-12)
- ◯ Naomi is blessed with a grandson (4:14-17)

CHAPTER 1

Elimelech Moves His Family to Moab

In the days when the judges ruled in Israel, a man from Bethlehem in Judah left the country because of a severe famine. He took his wife and two sons and went to live in the country of Moab. ²The man's name was Elimelech, and his wife was Naomi. Their two sons were Mahlon and Kilion. They were Ephrathites from Bethlehem in the land of Judah. During their stay in Moab, ³Elimelech died and Naomi was left with her two sons. ⁴The two sons married Moabite women. One married a woman named Orpah, and the other a woman named Ruth. But about ten years later, ⁵both Mahlon and Kilion died. This left Naomi alone, without her husband or sons.

Naomi and Ruth Return

⁶Then Naomi heard in Moab that the LORD had blessed his people in Judah by giving them good crops again. So Naomi and her daughters-in-law got

ready to leave Moab to return to her homeland. ⁷With her two daughters-in-law she set out from the place where she had been living, and they took the road that would lead them back to Judah.

⁸But on the way, Naomi said to her two daughters-in-law, "Go back to your mothers' homes instead of coming with me. And may the LORD reward you for your kindness to your husbands and to me. ⁹May the LORD bless you with the security of another marriage." Then she kissed them good-bye, and they all broke down and wept.

¹⁰"No," they said. "We want to go with you to your people."

¹¹But Naomi replied, "Why should you go on with me? Can I still give birth to other sons who could grow up to be your husbands? ¹²No, my daughters, return to your parents' homes, for I am too old to marry again. And even if it were possible, and I were to get married tonight and bear sons, then what? ¹³Would you wait for them to grow up and refuse to marry someone else? No, of course not, my daughters! Things are far more bitter for me than for you, because the LORD himself has caused me to suffer."

¹⁴And again they wept together, and Orpah kissed her mother-in-law good-bye. But Ruth insisted on staying with Naomi. ¹⁵"See," Naomi said to her, "your sister-in-law has gone back to her people and to her gods. You should do the same."

¹⁶But Ruth replied, "Don't ask me to leave you and turn back. I will go wherever you go and live wherever you live. Your people will be my people, and your God will be my God. ¹⁷I will die where you die and will be buried there. May the LORD punish me severely if I allow anything but death to separate us!" ¹⁸So when Naomi saw that Ruth had made up her mind to go with her, she stopped urging her.

¹⁹So the two of them continued on their journey. When they came to Bethlehem, the entire town was stirred by their arrival. "Is it really Naomi?" the women asked.

²⁰"Don't call me Naomi," she told them. "Instead, call me Mara,* for the Almighty has made life very bitter for me. ²¹I went away full, but the LORD has brought me home empty. Why should you call me Naomi when the LORD has caused me to suffer* and the Almighty has sent such tragedy?"

²²So Naomi returned from Moab, accompanied by her daughter-in-law Ruth, the young Moabite woman. They arrived in Bethlehem at the beginning of the barley harvest.

CHAPTER 2

Ruth Works in Boaz's Field

Now there was a wealthy and influential man in Bethlehem named Boaz, who was a relative of Naomi's husband, Elimelech.

²One day Ruth said to Naomi, "Let me go out into the fields to gather leftover grain behind anyone who will let me do it."

And Naomi said, "All right, my daughter, go ahead." ³So Ruth went out to gather grain behind the harvesters. And as it happened, she found herself working in a field that belonged to Boaz, the relative of her father-in-law, Elimelech.

⁴While she was there, Boaz arrived from Bethlehem and greeted the harvesters. "The LORD be with you!" he said.

"The LORD bless you!" the harvesters replied.

⁵Then Boaz asked his foreman, "Who is that girl over there?"

⁶And the foreman replied, "She is the young woman from Moab who came back with Naomi. ⁷She asked me this morning if she could gather grain

---

I SHOW kindness to those in my family. (1:8)

I LOYALLY CARE for those in my family. (1:16)

I CHOOSE God over my culture, my family, my upbringing, and my previous religious background. (1:16)

I DO NOT BECOME bitter toward God when bad things happen to me. (1:20)

I SEEK productive employment to care for the needs of my family. (2:2)

I TRUST God to lead me to safe and profitable employment. (2:3)

I WORK hard for my employer. (2:7)

1:20 *Naomi* means "pleasant"; *Mara* means "bitter." 1:21 Or *has testified against me.*

behind the harvesters. She has been hard at work ever since, except for a few minutes' rest over there in the shelter."

[8]Boaz went over and said to Ruth, "Listen, my daughter. Stay right here with us when you gather grain; don't go to any other fields. Stay right behind the women working in my field. [9]See which part of the field they are harvesting, and then follow them. I have warned the young men not to bother you. And when you are thirsty, help yourself to the water they have drawn from the well."

I NOTICE the good work of my employees and provide for their safety and well-being. (2:9)

[10]Ruth fell at his feet and thanked him warmly. "Why are you being so kind to me?" she asked. "I am only a foreigner."

[11]"Yes, I know," Boaz replied. "But I also know about the love and kindness you have shown your mother-in-law since the death of your husband. I have heard how you left your father and mother and your own land to live here among complete strangers. [12]May the LORD, the God of Israel, under whose wings you have come to take refuge, reward you fully."

I TRUST completely in God's care and provision. (2:12)

LIKE RUTH   *I faithfully care for my loved ones.*

Ruth 1:16

Ruth would not have laughed at even the best comedian's mother-in-law jokes. Even though her widowed mother-in-law, Naomi, was a distraught, despairing old woman, Ruth emphatically declared her commitment to her as they headed back for Naomi's homeland.

Ruth chose to loyally care for Naomi, not just because of family obligation but out of a conscious decision to leave her own pagan culture and embrace the love and community of her Israelite mother-in-law's God.

Ruth first showed her loyalty simply by her presence as they walked the long roads back to Bethlehem. Once they arrived, Ruth immediately began working diligently to provide for Naomi. Ruth's kindness to Naomi did not go unnoticed. God allowed her to work in the fields of Boaz, a relative of Naomi's, who would rescue and redeem them both. Ruth's loyal care for Naomi immediately aroused Boaz's interest and even revived Naomi's own discouraged heart. In turn, Naomi began to care for Ruth, doing her part to bring about a secure marriage and home for her with Boaz.

Ruth chose to care for her mother-in-law and found herself cared for by the God of Israel. Boaz and Naomi were blessed by Ruth's loyal love, and the world itself has been blessed by her descendants—King David and, ultimately, the Lord Jesus Christ.

God calls us to be a blessing as we faithfully care for those in both our physical and spiritual families.

To see Ruth's place in Jesus' lineage, see Matthew 1:5.

○ *Today's Scripture reading is Ruth 1–4.*

[13]"I hope I continue to please you, sir," she replied. "You have comforted me by speaking so kindly to me, even though I am not as worthy as your workers."

[14]At lunchtime Boaz called to her, "Come over here and help yourself to some of our food. You can dip your bread in the wine if you like." So she sat with his harvesters, and Boaz gave her food—more than she could eat.

[15]When Ruth went back to work again, Boaz ordered his young men, "Let her gather grain right among the sheaves without stopping her. [16]And pull out some heads of barley from the bundles and drop them on purpose for her. Let her pick them up, and don't give her a hard time!"

[17]So Ruth gathered barley there all day, and when she beat out the grain that evening, it came to about half a bushel.* [18]She carried it back into town

2:17 Hebrew *about an ephah* [18 liters].

and showed it to her mother-in-law. Ruth also gave her the food that was left over from her lunch.

¹⁹"So much!" Naomi exclaimed. "Where did you gather all this grain today? Where did you work? May the LORD bless the one who helped you!"

So Ruth told her mother-in-law about the man in whose field she had worked. And she said, "The man I worked with today is named Boaz."

²⁰"May the LORD bless him!" Naomi told her daughter-in-law. "He is showing his kindness to us as well as to your dead husband.* That man is one of our closest relatives, one of our family redeemers."

²¹Then Ruth said, "What's more, Boaz even told me to come back and stay with his harvesters until the entire harvest is completed."

²²"This is wonderful!" Naomi exclaimed. "Do as he said. Stay with his workers right through the whole harvest. You will be safe there, unlike in other fields."

²³So Ruth worked alongside the women in Boaz's fields and gathered grain with them until the end of the barley harvest. Then she worked with them through the wheat harvest, too. But all the while she lived with her mother-in-law.

CHAPTER 3
Ruth at the Threshing Floor

One day Naomi said to Ruth, "My daughter, it's time that I found a permanent home for you, so that you will be provided for. ²Boaz is a close relative of ours, and he's been very kind by letting you gather grain with his workers. Tonight he will be winnowing barley at the threshing floor. ³Now do as I tell you—take a bath and put on perfume and dress in your nicest clothes. Then go to the threshing floor, but don't let Boaz see you until he has finished his meal. ⁴Be sure to notice where he lies down; then go and uncover his feet and lie down there. He will tell you what to do."

⁵"I will do everything you say," Ruth replied. ⁶So she went down to the threshing floor that night and followed the instructions of her mother-in-law.

⁷After Boaz had finished his meal and was in good spirits, he lay down beside the heap of grain and went to sleep. Then Ruth came quietly, uncovered his feet, and lay down. ⁸Around midnight, Boaz suddenly woke up and turned over. He was surprised to find a woman lying at his feet! ⁹"Who are you?" he demanded.

"I am your servant Ruth," she replied. "Spread the corner of your covering over me, for you are my family redeemer."

¹⁰"The LORD bless you, my daughter!" Boaz exclaimed. "You are showing more family loyalty now than ever by not running after a younger man, whether rich or poor. ¹¹Now don't worry about a thing, my daughter. I will do what is necessary, for everyone in town knows you are an honorable woman. ¹²But there is one problem. While it is true that I am one of your family redeemers, there is another man who is more closely related to you than I am. ¹³Stay here tonight, and in the morning I will talk to him. If he is willing to redeem you, then let him marry you. But if he is not willing, then as surely as the LORD lives, I will marry you! Now lie down here until morning."

¹⁴So Ruth lay at Boaz's feet until the morning, but she got up before it was light enough for people to recognize each other. For Boaz said, "No one must know that a woman was here at the threshing floor." ¹⁵Boaz also said to her, "Bring your cloak and spread it out." He measured out six scoops* of barley into the cloak and helped her put it on her back. Then Boaz* returned to the town.

2:20 Hebrew *to the living and to the dead.*   3:15a Hebrew *six measures,* an unknown quantity.   3:15b Most Hebrew manuscripts read *he;* many Hebrew manuscripts, Syriac version, and Latin Vulgate read *she.*

I REMEMBER to care for the orphans and widows of my friends and relatives. (2:20)

I LISTEN to the counsel of those who are more experienced than I am. (2:23)

I ENCOURAGE my loved ones toward the joy of a godly marriage. (3:1)

[16]When Ruth went back to her mother-in-law, Naomi asked, "What happened, my daughter?"

Ruth told Naomi everything Boaz had done for her, [17]and she added, "He gave me these six scoops of barley and said, 'Don't go back to your mother-in-law empty-handed.' "

[18]Then Naomi said to her, "Just be patient, my daughter, until we hear what happens. The man won't rest until he has followed through on this. He will settle it today."

I ACT decisively and quickly on behalf of others. (3:18)

CHAPTER 4

Boaz Marries Ruth

So Boaz went to the town gate and took a seat there. When the family redeemer he had mentioned came by, Boaz called out to him, "Come over here, friend. I want to talk to you." So they sat down together. [2]Then Boaz called ten leaders from the town and asked them to sit as witnesses. [3]And Boaz said to the family redeemer, "You know Naomi, who came back from Moab. She is selling the land that belonged to our relative Elimelech. [4]I felt that I should speak to you about it so that you can redeem it if you wish. If you want the land, then buy it here in the presence of these witnesses. But if you don't want it, let me know right away, because I am next in line to redeem it after you."

The man replied, "All right, I'll redeem it."

[5]Then Boaz told him, "Of course, your purchase of the land from Naomi also requires that you marry Ruth, the Moabite widow. That way, she can have children who will carry on her husband's name and keep the land in the family."

I CARE FOR others—especially those within my family—by pursuing all legal and biblical options open to me. (4:1)

[6]"Then I can't redeem it," the family redeemer replied, "because this might endanger my own estate. You redeem the land; I cannot do it."

[7]In those days it was the custom in Israel for anyone transferring a right of purchase to remove his sandal and hand it to the other party. This publicly validated the transaction. [8]So the other family redeemer drew off his sandal as he said to Boaz, "You buy the land."

[9]Then Boaz said to the leaders and to the crowd standing around, "You are witnesses that today I have bought from Naomi all the property of Elimelech, Kilion, and Mahlon. [10]And with the land I have acquired Ruth, the Moabite widow of Mahlon, to be my wife. This way she can have a son to carry on the family name of her dead husband and to inherit the family property here in his hometown. You are all witnesses today."

I HONOR the memory of those who are deceased, particularly if I am marrying a widow or widower. (4:10)

[11]Then the leaders and all the people standing there replied, "We are witnesses! May the LORD make the woman who is now coming into your home like Rachel and Leah, from whom all the nation of Israel descended! May you be great in Ephrathah and famous in Bethlehem. [12]And may the LORD give you descendants by this young woman who will be like those of our ancestor Perez, the son of Tamar and Judah."

I GIVE my blessing to loved ones who marry fellow believers. (4:11)

The Descendants of Boaz

[13]So Boaz married Ruth and took her home to live with him. When he slept with her, the LORD enabled her to become pregnant, and she gave birth to a son. [14]And the women of the town said to Naomi, "Praise the LORD who has given you a family redeemer today! May he be famous in Israel. [15]May this child restore your youth and care for you in your old age. For he is the son of your daughter-in-law who loves you so much and who has been better to you than seven sons!"

I PRAISE God for new life—for the birth of each child. (4:14)

[16]Naomi took care of the baby and cared for him as if he were her own.
[17]The neighbor women said, "Now at last Naomi has a son again!" And they

See David's profile (page 629) at Psalm 3:1.

named him Obed. He became the father of Jesse and the grandfather of David.

[18]This is their family line beginning with their ancestor Perez:

Perez was the father of Hezron.
[19] Hezron was the father of Ram.
Ram was the father of Amminadab.
[20] Amminadab was the father of Nahshon.
Nahshon was the father of Salmon.
[21] Salmon was the father of Boaz.
Boaz was the father of Obed.
[22] Obed was the father of Jesse.
Jesse was the father of David.

1 SAMUEL

THIS FOURTH BOOK of Israelite history is filled with *transitions.*

In a single generation the period of the judges comes to an end, and the first Israelite monarchy begins. Within another generation, the first Israelite dynasty is wiped out and a second dynasty arises.

The story begins with the last and greatest of Israel's judges, Samuel. Samuel's birth comes as a direct answer to his godly mother's prayer (1:1–2:10). In keeping with her vow to the Lord, Hannah dedicates her boy to the Lord's service. The high priest in those days, Eli, brings great dishonor to the Lord's name (2:11–7:2). In contrast, Samuel becomes a godly prophet, priest, and judge. He leads a national revival, judges the nation for many years, and, at the direction of the Lord, establishes a monarchy (7:3–10:25).

The story continues with the rise and fall of Israel's first king, Saul. After his coronation, Saul quietly establishes Israel's first capital. When an eastern Israelite city comes under attack, Saul leads the Israelites in victory over the dreaded Ammonites, and his fame spreads across the land. Samuel reaffirms the monarchy under Saul and formally resigns as Israel's last judge (10:26–12:25).

Almost immediately, however, Saul commits a series of terrible moral blunders. As a result of Saul's growing disobedience, the Lord declares that he has rejected Saul as king and instructs Samuel to secretly anoint David instead. Unaware of David's anointing, Saul asks him to serve in his court (13:1–16:23).

David wins a great battle over the oppressive Philistines, instantly gaining tremendous fame. He also wins the devoted friendship of Saul's son Jonathan. Saul, however, grows jealous of David and for a number of years seeks to take David's life. While David has several opportunities to take Saul's life, he refuses to lay a hand on the king. In the end, Saul and his sons die in a battle against the Philistines (17:1–31:13).

The story of David's dynasty follows in 2 Samuel.

Famous passages in 1 Samuel include

- ○ Hannah prays a psalm of praise (2:1-10)
- ○ The Lord begins to speak to Samuel (3:1-21)
- ○ The Ark is miraculously returned (6:1–7:2)
- ○ Samuel sets up the Ebenezer stone (7:12)
- ○ Samuel warns the people about having a king (8:4-22)
- ○ Saul is anointed and acclaimed as king (10:1-25)
- ○ "I will certainly not sin . . . by ending my prayers for you" (12:23)
- ○ "The LORD has sought out a man after his own heart" (13:14)
- ○ "Obedience is far better than sacrifice . . ." (15:22)
- ○ "People judge by outward appearance . . ." (16:7)
- ○ David defeats the giant Goliath (17:1-51)
- ○ David marries Nabal's widow, Abigail (25:1-42)
- ○ Saul consults the medium at Endor (28:4-25)
- ○ Saul and his sons die in battle (31:1-13)

CHAPTER 1

Elkanah and His Family

There was a man named Elkanah who lived in Ramah* in the hill country of Ephraim. He was the son of Jeroham and grandson of Elihu, from the family of Tohu and the clan of Zuph. ²Elkanah had two wives, Hannah and Peninnah. Peninnah had children, while Hannah did not.

³Each year Elkanah and his family would travel to Shiloh to worship and sacrifice to the LORD Almighty at the Tabernacle. The priests of the LORD at that time were the two sons of Eli—Hophni and Phinehas. ⁴On the day Elkanah presented his sacrifice, he would give portions of the sacrifice to Peninnah and each of her children. ⁵But he gave Hannah a special portion* because he loved her very much, even though the LORD had given her no children. ⁶But Peninnah made fun of Hannah because the LORD had closed her womb. ⁷Year after year it was the same—Peninnah would taunt Hannah as they went to the Tabernacle.* Hannah would finally be reduced to tears and would not even eat.

⁸"What's the matter, Hannah?" Elkanah would ask. "Why aren't you eating? Why be so sad just because you have no children? You have me—isn't that better than having ten sons?"

Hannah's Prayer for a Son

⁹Once when they were at Shiloh, Hannah went over to the Tabernacle* after supper to pray to the LORD. Eli the priest was sitting at his customary place beside the entrance. ¹⁰Hannah was in deep anguish, crying bitterly as she prayed to the LORD. ¹¹And she made this vow: "O LORD Almighty, if you will look down upon my sorrow and answer my prayer and give me a son, then I will give him back to you. He will be yours for his entire lifetime, and as a sign that he has been dedicated to the LORD, his hair will never be cut."*

¹²As she was praying to the LORD, Eli watched her. ¹³Seeing her lips moving but hearing no sound, he thought she had been drinking. ¹⁴"Must you come here drunk?" he demanded. "Throw away your wine!"

¹⁵"Oh no, sir!" she replied, "I'm not drunk! But I am very sad, and I was pouring out my heart to the LORD. ¹⁶Please don't think I am a wicked woman! For I have been praying out of great anguish and sorrow."

¹⁷"In that case," Eli said, "cheer up! May the God of Israel grant the request you have asked of him."

¹⁸"Oh, thank you, sir!" she exclaimed. Then she went back and began to eat again, and she was no longer sad.

Samuel's Birth and Dedication

¹⁹The entire family got up early the next morning and went to worship the LORD once more. Then they returned home to Ramah. When Elkanah slept with Hannah, the LORD remembered her request, ²⁰and in due time she gave birth to a son. She named him Samuel,* for she said, "I asked the LORD for him."

²¹The next year Elkanah, Peninnah, and their children went on their annual trip to offer a sacrifice to the LORD. ²²But Hannah did not go. She told her husband, "Wait until the baby is weaned. Then I will take him to the Tabernacle and leave him there with the LORD permanently."*

²³"Whatever you think is best," Elkanah agreed. "Stay here for now, and may the LORD help you keep your promise." So she stayed home and nursed the baby.

²⁴When the child was weaned, Hannah took him to the Tabernacle in

I DO NOT BELITTLE those who are not blessed by God in the same way I am. (1:6)

I AM WILLING to give back to God whatever he gives me in answer to my prayers. (1:11)

I POUR OUT my heart to God when I am sad or depressed. (1:15)

I PRAY that God will grant the requests of people in sorrow. (1:17)

I WORSHIP God with my family on a regular basis. (1:21)

I HELP my spouse keep his or her promises to God. (1:23)

1:1 Hebrew *Ramathaim-zophim*; compare 1:19.   1:5 Or *a double portion*. The meaning of the Hebrew is uncertain.
1:7 Hebrew *the house of the LORD*; also in 1:24.   1:9 Hebrew *the Temple of the LORD*.   1:11 Some manuscripts add *He will drink neither wine nor intoxicants*.   1:20 *Samuel* sounds like the Hebrew term for "asked of God" or "heard by God."   1:22 Some manuscripts add *I will offer him as a Nazirite for all time*.

Shiloh. They brought along a three-year-old bull* for the sacrifice and half a bushel* of flour and some wine. ²⁵After sacrificing the bull, they took the child to Eli. ²⁶"Sir, do you remember me?" Hannah asked. "I am the woman who stood here several years ago praying to the LORD. ²⁷I asked the LORD to give me this child, and he has given me my request. ²⁸Now I am giving him to the LORD, and he will belong to the LORD his whole life." And they* worshiped the LORD there.

CHAPTER 2

Hannah's Prayer of Praise
Then Hannah prayed:

> "My heart rejoices in the LORD!
> Oh, how the LORD has blessed me!
> Now I have an answer for my enemies,
>   as I delight in your deliverance.
> ²No one is holy like the LORD!
>   There is no one besides you;
>   there is no Rock like our God.
>
> ³"Stop acting so proud and haughty!
>   Don't speak with such arrogance!
> The LORD is a God who knows your deeds;
>   and he will judge you for what you have done.
> ⁴Those who were mighty are mighty no more;
>   and those who were weak are now strong.
> ⁵Those who were well fed are now starving;
>   and those who were starving are now full.
> The barren woman now has seven children;
>   but the woman with many children will have no more.
> ⁶The LORD brings both death and life;
>   he brings some down to the grave but raises others up.
> ⁷The LORD makes one poor and another rich;
>   he brings one down and lifts another up.
> ⁸He lifts the poor from the dust—
>   yes, from a pile of ashes!
> He treats them like princes,
>   placing them in seats of honor.
>
> "For all the earth is the LORD's,
>   and he has set the world in order.
> ⁹He will protect his godly ones,
>   but the wicked will perish in darkness.
> No one will succeed by strength alone.
> ¹⁰ Those who fight against the LORD will be broken.
> He thunders against them from heaven;
>   the LORD judges throughout the earth.
> He gives mighty strength to his king;
>   he increases the might of his anointed one."

¹¹Then Elkanah and Hannah returned home to Ramah without Samuel. And the boy became the LORD's helper, for he assisted Eli the priest.

Eli's Wicked Sons

¹²Now the sons of Eli were scoundrels who had no respect for the LORD ¹³or for their duties as priests. Whenever anyone offered a sacrifice, Eli's sons

I REJOICE in my heart at how the Lord has blessed me! (2:1)

I DO NOT MISUSE offerings to God entrusted to my care. (2:13)

1:24a As in Dead Sea Scrolls, Greek and Syriac versions; Masoretic Text reads *3 bulls.*   1:24b Hebrew *and an ephah* [18 liters].   1:28 Or *he.*

would send over a servant with a three-pronged fork. While the meat of the sacrificed animal was still boiling, ¹⁴the servant would stick the fork into the pot and demand that whatever it brought up be given to Eli's sons. All the Israelites who came to worship at Shiloh were treated this way. ¹⁵Sometimes the servant would come even before the animal's fat had been burned on the altar. He would demand raw meat before it had been boiled so that it could be used for roasting.

¹⁶The man offering the sacrifice might reply, "Take as much as you want, but the fat must first be burned." Then the servant would demand, "No, give it to me now, or I'll take it by force." ¹⁷So the sin of these young men was very serious in the LORD's sight, for they treated the LORD's offerings with contempt.

¹⁸Now Samuel, though only a boy, was the LORD's helper. He wore a linen tunic just like that of a priest.* ¹⁹Each year his mother made a small coat for him and brought it to him when she came with her husband for the sacrifice. ²⁰Before they returned home, Eli would bless Elkanah and his wife and say, "May the LORD give you other children to take the place of this one she gave to the LORD.*" ²¹And the LORD gave Hannah three sons and two daughters. Meanwhile, Samuel grew up in the presence of the LORD.

²²Now Eli was very old, but he was aware of what his sons were doing to the people of Israel. He knew, for instance, that his sons were seducing the young women who assisted at the entrance of the Tabernacle.* ²³Eli said to them, "I have been hearing reports from the people about the wicked things you are doing. Why do you keep sinning? ²⁴You must stop, my sons! The reports I hear among the LORD's people are not good. ²⁵If someone sins against another person, God* can mediate for the guilty party. But if someone sins against the LORD, who can intercede?" But Eli's sons wouldn't listen to their father, for the LORD was already planning to put them to death.

²⁶Meanwhile, as young Samuel grew taller, he also continued to gain favor with the LORD and with the people.

A Warning for Eli's Family

²⁷One day a prophet came to Eli and gave him this message from the LORD: "Didn't I reveal myself to your ancestors when the people of Israel were slaves in Egypt? ²⁸I chose your ancestor Aaron* from among all his relatives to be my priest, to offer sacrifices on my altar, to burn incense, and to wear the priestly garments* as he served me. And I assigned the sacrificial offerings to you priests. ²⁹So why do you scorn my sacrifices and offerings? Why do you honor your sons more than me—for you and they have become fat from the best offerings of my people!

³⁰"Therefore, the LORD, the God of Israel, says: The terrible things you are doing cannot continue! I had promised that your branch of the tribe of Levi* would always be my priests. But I will honor only those who honor me, and I will despise those who despise me. ³¹I will put an end to your family, so it will no longer serve as my priests. All the members of your family will die before their time. None will live to a ripe old age. ³²You will watch with envy as I pour out prosperity on the people of Israel. But no members of your family will ever live out their days. ³³Those who are left alive will live in sadness and grief, and their children will die a violent death.* ³⁴And to prove that what I have said will come true, I will cause your two sons, Hophni and Phinehas, to die on the same day!

³⁵"Then I will raise up a faithful priest who will serve me and do what I tell him to do. I will bless his descendants, and his family will be priests to my

---

*Sidebar notes (left margin):*

I SUPPORT my children in serving the Lord. (2:19)

I BELIEVE God always gives us more than we ever give to him. (2:21)

See Aaron's profile (page 107) at Exodus 32:2.

I HONOR God above my children, putting obedience to him in priority over pleasing my children. (2:29)

I HONOR God and receive his honor. (2:30)

I BELIEVE there are severe consequences for those in leadership who dishonor God. (2:31)

2:18 Hebrew *He wore a linen ephod.* 2:20 As in Greek version; Hebrew reads *this one she requested of the LORD in prayer.* 2:22 Hebrew *Tent of Meeting.* Some manuscripts lack this entire sentence. 2:25 Or *the judges.* 2:28a Hebrew *your father.* 2:28b Hebrew *an ephod.* 2:30 Hebrew *that your house and your father's house.* 2:33 As in Dead Sea Scrolls, which read *die by the sword;* Masoretic Text reads *die like mortals.*

anointed kings forever. ³⁶Then all of your descendants will bow before his descendants, begging for money and food. 'Please,' they will say, 'give us jobs among the priests so we will have enough to eat.' "

CHAPTER 3

The LORD Speaks to Samuel

Meanwhile, the boy Samuel was serving the LORD by assisting Eli. Now in those days messages from the LORD were very rare, and visions were quite uncommon.

I SERVE the Lord by assisting other servants of God. (3:1)

LIKE HANNAH
1 Samuel 2:8

I am confident that God brings joy out of sorrow.

Hannah's story gives us a unique glimpse into an ordinary, God-fearing Israelite family. We meet Hannah as a woman who has so much—especially the devotion of her godly, loving husband, Elkanah—and yet her heart is not full.

In many ways, however, Hannah is not unique in her struggle with infertility. She wasn't unique then, and she wouldn't be today. Sadly, many of God's chosen women who couldn't get pregnant lived in societies where personal esteem and family survival depended on having many children.

Hannah had to bear not only the shame from society but also the verbal scorn from Peninnah, Elkanah's other wife. Even Elkanah's devoted love could not diminish her agony. Her mother's heart longed for a child of her own.

Hannah went to God with her agony of spirit—agony that poured out in soundless words. So deep was her desire that she was willing to give back to God the child she asked for. So deep was her trust that God would bring joy out of sorrow that simply the promise of answered prayer lifted her from her dark despair.

Hannah's prayer reminds the world that things are not always as they appear, and they will not always remain as they now are. The prosperous wicked will be judged, the strong will be defeated, and the weak will be made strong. Those who are full will know hunger, and the hungry will be fed. Women with many children will know what it means to be barren, and the barren woman will have many children to call her own.

Hannah's confidence was in God's ultimate control. After all, the world belongs to the Lord and is ordered by him. In the end, he will set all things right and bring joy out of every sorrow.

Years later, another ordinary Israelite woman received a child from God. Mary, too, praised the Lord for turning the world upside down; for lifting up the lowly and blessing the humble; for bringing joy out of sorrow and victory out of oppression (Luke 1:46-55).

With confidence, we know the Lord will lift us up and turn our sorrow into joy.

○ *Today's Scripture reading is 1 Samuel 1:1–2:21.*

---

²One night Eli, who was almost blind by now, had just gone to bed. ³The lamp of God had not yet gone out, and Samuel was sleeping in the Tabernacle* near the Ark of God. ⁴Suddenly, the LORD called out, "Samuel! Samuel!"

"Yes?" Samuel replied. "What is it?" ⁵He jumped up and ran to Eli. "Here I am. What do you need?"

"I didn't call you," Eli replied. "Go on back to bed." So he did.

⁶Then the LORD called out again, "Samuel!"

Again Samuel jumped up and ran to Eli. "Here I am," he said. "What do you need?"

"I didn't call you, my son," Eli said. "Go on back to bed."

⁷Samuel did not yet know the LORD because he had never had a message from the LORD before. ⁸So now the LORD called a third time, and once more Samuel jumped up and ran to Eli. "Here I am," he said. "What do you need?"

3:3 Hebrew *the Temple of the LORD.*

Then Eli realized it was the LORD who was calling the boy. ⁹So he said to Samuel, "Go and lie down again, and if someone calls again, say, 'Yes, LORD, your servant is listening.' " So Samuel went back to bed.

¹⁰And the LORD came and called as before, "Samuel! Samuel!"

And Samuel replied, "Yes, your servant is listening."

¹¹Then the LORD said to Samuel, "I am about to do a shocking thing in Israel. ¹²I am going to carry out all my threats against Eli and his family. ¹³I have warned him continually that judgment is coming for his family, because his sons are blaspheming God* and he hasn't disciplined them. ¹⁴So I have vowed that the sins of Eli and his sons will never be forgiven by sacrifices or offerings."

Samuel Speaks for the LORD

¹⁵Samuel stayed in bed until morning, then got up and opened the doors of the Tabernacle* as usual. He was afraid to tell Eli what the LORD had said to him. ¹⁶But Eli called out to him, "Samuel, my son."

"Here I am," Samuel replied.

¹⁷"What did the LORD say to you? Tell me everything. And may God punish you if you hide anything from me!" ¹⁸So Samuel told Eli everything; he didn't hold anything back. "It is the LORD's will," Eli replied. "Let him do what he thinks best."

¹⁹As Samuel grew up, the LORD was with him, and everything Samuel said was wise and helpful. ²⁰All the people of Israel from one end of the land to the other knew that Samuel was confirmed as a prophet of the LORD. ²¹The LORD continued to appear at Shiloh and gave messages to Samuel there at the Tabernacle. ¹And Samuel's words went out to all the people of Israel.

CHAPTER 4

The Philistines Capture the Ark

At that time Israel was at war with the Philistines. The Israelite army was camped near Ebenezer, and the Philistines were at Aphek. ²The Philistines attacked and defeated the army of Israel, killing four thousand men. ³After the battle was over, the army of Israel retreated to their camp, and their leaders asked, "Why did the LORD allow us to be defeated by the Philistines?" Then they said, "Let's bring the Ark of the Covenant of the LORD from Shiloh. If we carry it into battle with us, it* will save us from our enemies."

⁴So they sent men to Shiloh to bring back the Ark of the Covenant of the LORD Almighty, who is enthroned between the cherubim. Hophni and Phinehas, the sons of Eli, helped carry the Ark of God to where the battle was being fought. ⁵When the Israelites saw the Ark of the Covenant of the LORD coming into the camp, their shout of joy was so loud that it made the ground shake!

⁶"What's going on?" the Philistines asked. "What's all the shouting about in the Hebrew camp?" When they were told it was because the Ark of the LORD had arrived, ⁷they panicked. "The gods have* come into their camp!" they cried. "This is a disaster! We have never had to face anything like this before! ⁸Who can save us from these mighty gods of Israel? They are the same gods who destroyed the Egyptians with plagues when Israel was in the wilderness. ⁹Fight as you never have before, Philistines! If you don't, we will become the Hebrews' slaves just as they have been ours!"

¹⁰So the Philistines fought desperately, and Israel was defeated again. The slaughter was great; thirty thousand Israelite men died that day. The survivors turned and fled to their tents. ¹¹The Ark of God was captured, and Hophni and Phinehas, the two sons of Eli, were killed.

I ENCOURAGE others to listen and respond to the voice of the Lord. (3:9)

I LISTEN to God. (3:10)

I DISCIPLINE my children if they blaspheme God. (3:13)

I DO NOT HOLD BACK in speaking God's message, even when it seems unpleasant. (3:18)

I DO NOT TRUST in physical things, even spiritual symbols, to save me. (4:3)

I BELIEVE the pagan nations never forgot what God did to save Israel from Egypt. (4:8)

I BELIEVE Hophni and Phinehas died just as God said they would. (4:11)

3:13 As in Greek version; Hebrew reads *his sons have made themselves contemptible.* 3:15 Hebrew *the house of the LORD.* 4:3 Or *he.* 4:7 Or *A god has.*

The Death of Eli

[12]A man from the tribe of Benjamin ran from the battlefront and arrived at Shiloh later that same day. He had torn his clothes and put dust on his head to show his grief. [13]Eli was waiting beside the road to hear the news of the battle, for his heart trembled for the safety of the Ark of God. When the messenger arrived and told what had happened, an outcry resounded throughout the town. [14]"What is all the noise about?" Eli asked.

The messenger rushed over to Eli, [15]who was ninety-eight years old and blind. [16]He said to Eli, "I have just come from the battlefront—I was there this very day."

I AM GRIEVED when God's people are oppressed by unbelievers. (4:12)

UNLIKE ELI   *I do not devalue God in my heart and affections.*

1 Samuel 2:30

Jesus' teaching that each of us must love God more than our own father, mother, spouse, and children (Luke 14:26) seems strange until we see someone who loves family more than God.

Eli was a man who, for all his priestly duties and privileges, had reduced God in his heart. Comfort sat on the throne of his life. His affections were set on the prosperity to be had from the Tabernacle offerings and on the calm to be enjoyed when his sons were not provoked. So he heeded his sons' rebukes more than God's.

Years before, Eli's forefather Phinehas had brandished a sword to protect the nation from gross immorality (Numbers 25:1-13). Eli, however, could barely protest the open immorality and theft committed by his sons within the Tabernacle. The difference between these two men was not some difference in personality. Phinehas acted boldly out of a deep passion for God's holiness. Eli chose not to rouse his behavior beyond mere lip service to the Lord.

Perhaps saddest of all is that even when Eli was confronted with the reality of pending judgment, he didn't seem to comprehend or care. Willing to take the consequences of neglecting God in his heart, he revealed himself as a man who had let God slip to last place in his affections.

Thankfully, as Jesus revealed, loving God "with all your heart, all your soul, all your mind, and all your strength" (Mark 12:30) doesn't preclude loving others as ourselves (Mark 12:31).

On what have you and I set our affections? Whom do we value most? Ourselves? Our loved ones? Or the Lord God?

○ Today's Scripture reading is 1 Samuel 2:27-4:22.

"What happened?" Eli demanded.

[17]"Israel has been defeated," the messenger replied. "Thousands of Israelite troops are dead on the battlefield. Your two sons, Hophni and Phinehas, were killed, too. And the Ark of God has been captured."

[18]When the messenger mentioned what had happened to the Ark, Eli fell backward from his seat beside the gate. He broke his neck and died, for he was old and very fat. He had led Israel for forty years.

[19]Eli's daughter-in-law, the wife of Phinehas, was pregnant and near her time of delivery. When she heard that the Ark of God had been captured and that her husband and father-in-law were dead, her labor pains suddenly began. [20]She died in childbirth, but before she passed away the midwives tried to encourage her. "Don't be afraid," they said. "You have a baby boy!" But she did not answer or respond in any way.

[21]She named the child Ichabod—"Where is the glory?"—murmuring, "Israel's glory is gone." She named him this because the Ark of God had been captured and because her husband and her father-in-law were dead. [22]Then she said, "The glory has departed from Israel, for the Ark of God has been captured."

I AM GRIEVED when God's presence and glory are dishonored by unbelievers. (4:21)

CHAPTER 5

The Ark in Philistia

After the Philistines captured the Ark of God, they took it from the battle-ground at Ebenezer to the city of Ashdod. ²They carried the Ark of God into the temple of Dagon and placed it beside the idol of Dagon. ³But when the citizens of Ashdod went to see it the next morning, Dagon had fallen with his face to the ground in front of the Ark of the LORD! So they set the idol up again. ⁴But the next morning the same thing happened—the idol had fallen face down before the Ark of the LORD again. This time his head and hands had broken off and were lying in the doorway. Only the trunk of his body was left intact. ⁵That is why to this day neither the priests of Dagon nor any-one who enters the temple of Dagon will step on its threshold.

⁶Then the LORD began to afflict the people of Ashdod and the nearby vil-lages with a plague of tumors.* ⁷When the people realized what was happen-ing, they cried out, "We can't keep the Ark of the God of Israel here any longer! He is against us! We will all be destroyed along with our god Dagon." ⁸So they called together the rulers of the five Philistine cities and asked, "What should we do with the Ark of the God of Israel?"

The rulers discussed it and replied, "Move it to the city of Gath." So they moved the Ark of the God of Israel to Gath. ⁹But when the Ark arrived at Gath, the LORD began afflicting its people, young and old, with a plague of tumors, and there was a great panic.

¹⁰So they sent the Ark of God to the city of Ekron, but when the people of Ekron saw it coming they cried out, "They are bringing the Ark of the God of Israel here to kill us, too!" ¹¹So the people summoned the rulers again and begged them, "Please send the Ark of the God of Israel back to its own coun-try, or it* will kill us all." For the plague from God had already begun, and great fear was sweeping across the city. ¹²Those who didn't die were afflicted with tumors; and there was weeping everywhere.

CHAPTER 6

The Philistines Return the Ark

The Ark of the LORD remained in Philistine territory seven months in all. ²Then the Philistines called in their priests and diviners and asked them, "What should we do about the Ark of the LORD? Tell us how to return it to its own land."

³"Send the Ark of the God of Israel back, along with a gift," they were told. "Send a guilt offering so the plague will stop. Then, if the plague doesn't stop, you will know that God didn't send the plague after all."

⁴"What sort of guilt offering should we send?" they asked.

And they were told, "Since the plague has struck both you and your five rulers, make five gold tumors and five gold rats, just like those that have rav-aged your land. ⁵Make these things to show honor to the God of Israel. Per-haps then he will stop afflicting you, your gods, and your land. ⁶Don't be stubborn and rebellious as Pharaoh and the Egyptians were. They wouldn't let Israel go until God had ravaged them with dreadful plagues. ⁷Now build a new cart, and find two cows that have just had calves. Make sure the cows have never been yoked to a cart. Hitch the cows to the cart, but shut their calves away from them in a pen. ⁸Put the Ark of the LORD on the cart, and be-side it place a chest containing the gold rats and gold tumors. Then let the cows go wherever they want. ⁹If they cross the border of our land and go to Beth-shemesh, we will know it was the LORD who brought this great disaster upon us. If they don't, we will know that the plague was simply a coincidence and was not sent by the LORD at all."

5:6 Greek version and Latin Vulgate read *tumors. And rats appeared in their land, and death and destruction were throughout the city.*   5:11 Or *he.*

I BELIEVE false gods are nothing before the Lord. (5:3)

I BELIEVE unbelievers can recognize the work of God. (5:7)

I RECOGNIZE that unbelievers have little understanding of how to truly honor God. (6:5)

I REMEMBER how others have been punished for rebelling against God, and I choose not to make the same mistake. (6:6)

¹⁰So these instructions were carried out. Two cows with newborn calves were hitched to the cart, and their calves were shut up in a pen. ¹¹Then the Ark of the LORD and the chest containing the gold rats and gold tumors were placed on the cart. ¹²And sure enough, the cows went straight along the road toward Beth-shemesh, lowing as they went. The Philistine rulers followed them as far as the border of Beth-shemesh.

LIKE SAMUEL

1 Samuel 3:1

I allow God to use me for his glory no matter what my age.

Four-year-old Cole knew God. And he knew that when his disease took his life, he would be with God. So he told everyone he knew that they needed to know God, too. After his funeral, Cole's uncle and aunt went searching for God and found him in Jesus Christ. All because of four-year-old Cole.

There is no age discrimination with God. He will use anyone who loves and obeys him. He used a four-year-old to bring the message of salvation to his family. He also used the young boy Samuel to bring a message of coming judgment to a sinning priest.

Samuel had been filled with the praise and teachings of God at his mother's knee and had spent his childhood nights and days in the Tabernacle. When God roused him, Samuel was sleeping near the Ark of the Covenant. His heart and life were near to God, ready and available. He did not need to wait for a special age, a special class, or a special experience. Once he knew the voice of God, there was no turning back from obeying him.

That wholehearted, childlike commitment to God never left Samuel. From his youngest days to his old age, he was God's man, always available to be used for God's glory.

From before his birth, Samuel was a promise fulfilled. Even in his death, he came back (so to speak) to declare God's judgment and will (28:11-19).

Just as Paul instructed Timothy, we should not let anyone look down on us if God chooses to use us when we are young (1 Timothy 4:12). Nor should we retire from glorifying and serving God because we are old (Psalm 63:4).

To better understand the role and impact of Samuel's ministry, see Psalm 99:6; Jeremiah 15:1; Acts 3:24; and Hebrews 11:32.

○ *Today's Scripture reading is 1 Samuel 7:3–8:22; 12:1-25.*

---

¹³ The people of Beth-shemesh were harvesting wheat in the valley, and when they saw the Ark, they were overjoyed! ¹⁴The cart came into the field of a man named Joshua and stopped beside a large rock. So the people broke up the wood of the cart for a fire and killed the cows and sacrificed them to the LORD as a burnt offering. ¹⁵Several men of the tribe of Levi lifted the Ark of the LORD and the chest containing the gold rats and gold tumors from the cart and placed them on the large rock. Many burnt offerings and sacrifices were offered to the LORD that day by the people of Beth-shemesh. ¹⁶The five Philistine rulers watched all this and then returned to Ekron that same day.

I GIVE offerings to God in gratitude for his miracles. (6:14)

¹⁷The five gold tumors that were sent by the Philistines as a guilt offering to the LORD were gifts from the rulers of Ashdod, Gaza, Ashkelon, Gath, and Ekron. ¹⁸The five gold rats represented the five Philistine cities and their surrounding villages, which were controlled by the five rulers. The large rock at Beth-shemesh, where they set the Ark of the LORD, still stands in the field of Joshua as a reminder of what happened there.

I RECOGNIZE that unbelievers are watching to see God at work. (6:16)

The Ark Moved to Kiriath-Jearim

¹⁹But the LORD killed seventy men* from Beth-shemesh because they looked into the Ark of the LORD. And the people mourned greatly because of what the LORD had done. ²⁰"Who is able to stand in the presence of the LORD, this

I DO NOT SHOW irreverence toward the things God has declared holy. (6:19)

6:19 As in a few Hebrew manuscripts; most Hebrew manuscripts and Greek version read *50,070 men.* Perhaps the text should be understood to read *the LORD killed 70 men and 50 oxen.*

holy God?" they cried out. "Where can we send the Ark from here?" ²¹So they sent messengers to the people at Kiriath-jearim and told them, "The Philistines have returned the Ark of the LORD. Please come here and get it!"

CHAPTER 7

So the men of Kiriath-jearim came to get the Ark of the LORD. They took it to the hillside home of Abinadab and ordained Eleazar, his son, to be in charge of it. ²The Ark remained in Kiriath-jearim for a long time—twenty years in all. During that time, all Israel mourned because it seemed that the LORD had abandoned them.

Samuel Leads Israel to Victory

³Then Samuel said to all the people of Israel, "If you are really serious about wanting to return to the LORD, get rid of your foreign gods and your images of Ashtoreth. Determine to obey only the LORD; then he will rescue you from the Philistines." ⁴So the Israelites destroyed their images of Baal and Ashtoreth and worshiped only the LORD.

⁵Then Samuel told them, "Come to Mizpah, all of you. I will pray to the LORD for you." ⁶So they gathered there and, in a great ceremony, drew water from a well and poured it out before the LORD. They also went without food all day and confessed that they had sinned against the LORD. So it was at Mizpah that Samuel became Israel's judge.

⁷When the Philistine rulers heard that all Israel had gathered at Mizpah, they mobilized their army and advanced. The Israelites were badly frightened when they learned that the Philistines were approaching. ⁸"Plead with the LORD our God to save us from the Philistines!" they begged Samuel. ⁹So Samuel took a young lamb and offered it to the LORD as a whole burnt offering. He pleaded with the LORD to help Israel, and the LORD answered.

¹⁰Just as Samuel was sacrificing the burnt offering, the Philistines arrived for battle. But the LORD spoke with a mighty voice of thunder from heaven, and the Philistines were thrown into such confusion that the Israelites defeated them. ¹¹The men of Israel chased them from Mizpah to Beth-car, slaughtering them all along the way.

¹²Samuel then took a large stone and placed it between the towns of Mizpah and Jeshanah.* He named it Ebenezer—"the stone of help"—for he said, "Up to this point the LORD has helped us!" ¹³So the Philistines were subdued and didn't invade Israel again for a long time. And throughout Samuel's lifetime, the LORD's powerful hand was raised against the Philistines. ¹⁴The Israelite towns near Ekron and Gath that the Philistines had captured were restored to Israel, along with the rest of the territory that the Philistines had taken. And there was also peace between Israel and the Amorites in those days.

¹⁵Samuel continued as Israel's judge for the rest of his life. ¹⁶Each year he traveled around, setting up his court first at Bethel, then at Gilgal, and then at Mizpah. He judged the people of Israel at each of these places. ¹⁷Then he would return to his home at Ramah, and he would hear cases there, too. And Samuel built an altar to the LORD at Ramah.

CHAPTER 8

Israel Requests a King

As Samuel grew old, he appointed his sons to be judges over Israel. ²Joel and Abijah, his oldest sons, held court in Beersheba. ³But they were not like their father, for they were greedy for money. They accepted bribes and perverted justice.

⁴Finally, the leaders of Israel met at Ramah to discuss the matter with

---

I MOURN when God's people are not experiencing his presence. (7:2)

I DEMONSTRATE that I am serious about returning to God by getting rid of anything that is taking his place in my life. (7:3)

I PRAY for God's people who desire to obey him. (7:5)

I SET UP reminders of God's help in my life. (7:12)

I TRUST in the Lord's powerful hand for protection. (7:13)

I DO NOT PUT my children in positions of responsibility for which they are not qualified. (8:1)

7:12 As in Greek version; Hebrew reads *Shen.*

Samuel. [5]"Look," they told him, "you are now old, and your sons are not like you. Give us a king like all the other nations have."

[6]Samuel was very upset with their request and went to the LORD for advice. [7]"Do as they say," the LORD replied, "for it is me they are rejecting, not you. They don't want me to be their king any longer. [8]Ever since I brought them from Egypt they have continually forsaken me and followed other gods. And now they are giving you the same treatment. [9]Do as they ask, but solemnly warn them about how a king will treat them."

Samuel Warns against a Kingdom

[10]So Samuel passed on the LORD's warning to the people. [11]"This is how a king will treat you," Samuel said. "The king will draft your sons into his army and make them run before his chariots. [12]Some will be commanders of his troops, while others will be slave laborers. Some will be forced to plow in his fields and harvest his crops, while others will make his weapons and chariot equipment. [13]The king will take your daughters from you and force them to cook and bake and make perfumes for him. [14]He will take away the best of your fields and vineyards and olive groves and give them to his own servants. [15]He will take a tenth of your harvest and distribute it among his officers and attendants. [16]He will want your male and female slaves and demand the finest of your cattle* and donkeys for his own use. [17]He will demand a tenth of your flocks, and you will be his slaves. [18]When that day comes, you will beg for relief from this king you are demanding, but the LORD will not help you."

[19]But the people refused to listen to Samuel's warning. "Even so, we still want a king," they said. [20]"We want to be like the nations around us. Our king will govern us and lead us into battle."

[21]So Samuel told the LORD what the people had said, [22]and the LORD replied, "Do as they say, and give them a king." Then Samuel agreed and sent the people home.

CHAPTER 9

Saul Meets Samuel

Kish was a rich, influential man from the tribe of Benjamin. He was the son of Abiel and grandson of Zeror, from the family of Becorath and the clan of Aphiah. [2]His son Saul was the most handsome man in Israel—head and shoulders taller than anyone else in the land.

[3]One day Kish's donkeys strayed away, and he told Saul, "Take a servant with you, and go look for them." [4]So Saul took one of his servants and traveled all through the hill country of Ephraim, the land of Shalishah, the Shaalim area, and the entire land of Benjamin, but they couldn't find the donkeys anywhere. [5]Finally, they entered the region of Zuph, and Saul said to his servant, "Let's go home. By now my father will be more worried about us than about the donkeys!"

[6]But the servant said, "I've just thought of something! There is a man of God who lives here in this town. He is held in high honor by all the people because everything he says comes true. Let's go find him. Perhaps he can tell us which way to go."

[7]"But we don't have anything to offer him," Saul replied. "Even our food is gone, and we don't have a thing to give him."

[8]"Well," the servant said, "I have one small silver piece.* We can at least offer it to him and see what happens!" [9](In those days if people wanted a message from God, they would say, "Let's go and ask the seer," for prophets used to be called seers.)

I LOOK to God alone as my king, not to other people or religions. (8:8)

I WARN people of the probable consequences of their decisions, and then I let them make their own choices. (8:9)

I DO NOT DO things simply because those around me—especially unbelievers—are doing them. (8:20)

I AM CONSIDERATE of others' worries and concerns. (9:5)

I SEEK OUT godly advice for my problems. (9:9)

8:16 As in Greek version; Hebrew reads *young men.* 9:8 Hebrew ¼ *shekel of silver,* about 0.1 ounces or 3 grams in weight.

¹⁰"All right," Saul agreed, "let's try it!" So they started into the town where the man of God was.

¹¹As they were climbing a hill toward the town, they met some young women coming out to draw water. So Saul and his servant asked, "Is the seer here today?"

¹²"Yes," they replied. "Stay right on this road. He is at the town gates. He has just arrived to take part in a public sacrifice up on the hill. ¹³Hurry and catch him before he goes up the hill to eat. The guests won't start until he arrives to bless the food."

¹⁴So they entered the town, and as they passed through the gates, Samuel was coming out toward them to climb the hill. ¹⁵Now the LORD had told Samuel the previous day, ¹⁶"About this time tomorrow I will send you a man from the land of Benjamin. Anoint him to be the leader of my people, Israel. He will rescue them from the Philistines, for I have looked down on my people in mercy and have heard their cry."

¹⁷When Samuel noticed Saul, the LORD said, "That's the man I told you about! He will rule my people."

¹⁸Just then Saul approached Samuel at the gateway and asked, "Can you please tell me where the seer's house is?"

¹⁹"I am the seer!" Samuel replied. "Go on up the hill ahead of me to the place of sacrifice, and we'll eat there together. In the morning I will tell you what you want to know and send you on your way. ²⁰And don't worry about those donkeys that were lost three days ago, for they have been found. And I am here to tell you that you and your family are the focus of all Israel's hopes."

²¹Saul replied, "But I'm only from Benjamin, the smallest tribe in Israel, and my family is the least important of all the families of that tribe! Why are you talking like this to me?"

²²Then Samuel brought Saul and his servant into the great hall and placed them at the head of the table, honoring them above the thirty special guests. ²³Samuel then instructed the cook to bring Saul the finest cut of meat, the piece that had been set aside for the guest of honor. ²⁴So the cook brought it in and placed it before Saul. "Go ahead and eat it," Samuel said. "I was saving it for you even before I invited these others!" So Saul ate with Samuel.

²⁵After the feast, when they had returned to the town, Samuel took Saul up to the roof of the house and prepared a bed for him there.* ²⁶At daybreak the next morning, Samuel called up to Saul, "Get up! It's time you were on your way." So Saul got ready, and he and Samuel left the house together. ²⁷When they reached the edge of town, Samuel told Saul to send his servant on ahead. After the servant was gone, Samuel said, "Stay here, for I have received a special message for you from God."

CHAPTER 10

Samuel Anoints Saul as King

Then Samuel took a flask of olive oil and poured it over Saul's head. He kissed Saul on the cheek and said, "I am doing this because the LORD has appointed you to be the leader of his people Israel.* ²When you leave me today, you will see two men beside Rachel's tomb at Zelzah, on the border of Benjamin. They will tell you that the donkeys have been found and that your father is worried about you and is asking, 'Have you seen my son?'

³"When you get to the oak of Tabor, you will see three men coming toward you who are on their way to worship God at Bethel. One will be bringing three young goats, another will have three loaves of bread, and the third will

---

I BELIEVE God heard Israel's cry and, because of his mercy, sent Saul to rescue them. (9:16)

I GIVE people good news that I know will help them worry less. (9:20)

I GIVE honor to those people God chooses to use. (9:22)

I BELIEVE Samuel spoke for the Lord. (9:27)

I AFFIRM the leaders God appoints. (10:1)

9:25 As in Greek version; Hebrew reads *and talked with him there.*   10:1 Greek version reads *Israel. And you will rule over the LORD's people and save them from their enemies around them. This will be the sign to you that the LORD has appointed you to be leader over his inheritance.*

be carrying a skin of wine. ⁴They will greet you and offer you two of the loaves, which you are to accept.

⁵"When you arrive at Gibeah of God,* where the garrison of the Philistines is located, you will meet a band of prophets coming down from the altar on the hill. They will be playing a harp, a tambourine, a flute, and a lyre, and they will be prophesying. ⁶At that time the Spirit of the LORD will come upon you with power, and you will prophesy with them. You will be changed into a different person. ⁷After these signs take place, do whatever you think is best, for God will be with you. ⁸Then go down to Gilgal ahead of me and wait for me there seven days. I will join you there to sacrifice burnt offerings and peace offerings. When I arrive, I will give you further instructions."

Samuel's Signs Are Fulfilled

⁹As Saul turned and started to leave, God changed his heart, and all Samuel's signs were fulfilled that day. ¹⁰When Saul and his servant arrived at Gibeah, they saw the prophets coming toward them. Then the Spirit of God came upon Saul, and he, too, began to prophesy. ¹¹When his friends heard about it, they exclaimed, "What? Is Saul a prophet? How did the son of Kish become a prophet?" ¹²But one of the neighbors responded, "It doesn't matter who his father is; anyone can become a prophet."* So that is the origin of the saying "Is Saul a prophet?"

¹³When Saul had finished prophesying, he climbed the hill to the altar. ¹⁴"Where in the world have you been?" Saul's uncle asked him.

"We went to look for the donkeys," Saul replied, "but we couldn't find them. So we went to the prophet Samuel to ask him where they were."

¹⁵"Oh? And what did he say?" his uncle asked.

¹⁶"He said the donkeys had been found," Saul replied. But Saul didn't tell his uncle that Samuel had anointed him to be king.

Saul Is Acclaimed King

¹⁷Later Samuel called all the people of Israel to meet before the LORD at Mizpah. ¹⁸And he gave them this message from the LORD, the God of Israel: "I brought you from Egypt and rescued you from the Egyptians and from all of the nations that were oppressing you. ¹⁹But though I have done so much for you, you have rejected me and said, 'We want a king instead!' Now, therefore, present yourselves before the LORD by tribes and clans."

²⁰So Samuel called the tribal leaders together before the LORD, and the tribe of Benjamin was chosen.* ²¹Then he brought each family of the tribe of Benjamin before the LORD, and the family of the Matrites was chosen. And finally Saul son of Kish was chosen from among them. But when they looked for him, he had disappeared! ²²So they asked the LORD, "Where is he?"

And the LORD replied, "He is hiding among the baggage." ²³So they found him and brought him out, and he stood head and shoulders above anyone else.

²⁴Then Samuel said to all the people, "This is the man the LORD has chosen as your king. No one in all Israel is his equal!"

And all the people shouted, "Long live the king!"

²⁵Then Samuel told the people what the rights and duties of a king were. He wrote them down on a scroll and placed it before the LORD. Then Samuel sent the people home again.

²⁶When Saul returned to his home at Gibeah, a band of men whose hearts God had touched became his constant companions. ²⁷But there were some wicked men who complained, "How can this man save us?" And they despised him and refused to bring him gifts. But Saul ignored them.*

Margin notes:
- I AM CHANGED into a different person by the power of the Spirit. (10:6)
- I BELIEVE God can touch the heart of any believer to prophesy and praise him. (10:12)
- I BELIEVE the Israelites were rejecting God's kingship when they asked for a human king. (10:19)
- I BELIEVE the Lord chose Saul to be Israel's king. (10:24)
- I PAY careful attention to the responsibilities my leaders are to fulfill. (10:25)

10:5 Hebrew Gibeath-elohim. 10:12 Hebrew responded, "Who is their father?" 10:20 Hebrew chosen by lot; also in 10:21. 10:27 Dead Sea Scroll 4QSamᵃ continues: Nahash, king of the Ammonites, had been grievously oppressing the Gadites and Reubenites who lived east of the Jordan River. He gouged out the right eye of each of the Israelites living there, and he didn't allow anyone to come and rescue them. In fact, of all the Israelites east of the Jordan, there wasn't a single one whose right eye Nahash had not gouged out. But there were seven thousand men who had escaped from the Ammonites, and they had settled in Jabesh-gilead.

CHAPTER **11**

Saul Defeats the Ammonites

I SEEK a peaceful solution when I am attacked. (11:1)

About a month later,* King Nahash of Ammon led his army against the Israelite city of Jabesh-gilead. But the citizens of Jabesh asked for peace. "Make a treaty with us, and we will be your servants," they pleaded.

²"All right," Nahash said, "but only on one condition. I will gouge out the right eye of every one of you as a disgrace to all Israel!"

I ASK people for help when I am in danger. (11:3)

³"Give us seven days to send messengers throughout Israel!" replied the leaders of Jabesh. "If none of our relatives will come to save us, we will agree to your terms."

⁴When the messengers came to Gibeah, Saul's hometown, and told the people about their plight, everyone broke into tears. ⁵Saul was plowing in the field, and when he returned to town, he asked, "What's the matter? Why is everyone crying?" So they told him about the message from Jabesh.

⁶Then the Spirit of God came mightily upon Saul, and he became very angry. ⁷He took two oxen and cut them into pieces and sent the messengers to carry them throughout Israel with this message: "This is what will happen to the oxen of anyone who refuses to follow Saul and Samuel into battle!" And the LORD made the people afraid of Saul's anger, and all of them came out together as one. ⁸When Saul mobilized them at Bezek, he found that there were 300,000 men of Israel, in addition to 30,000* from Judah.

I MOBILIZE people to rescue those in danger. (11:8)

⁹So Saul sent the messengers back to Jabesh-gilead to say, "We will rescue you by noontime tomorrow!" What joy there was throughout the city when that message arrived!

¹⁰The men of Jabesh then told their enemies, "Tomorrow we will come out to you, and you can do to us as you wish." ¹¹But before dawn the next morning, Saul arrived, having divided his army into three detachments. He launched a surprise attack against the Ammonites and slaughtered them the whole morning. The remnant of their army was so badly scattered that no two of them were left together.

¹²Then the people exclaimed to Samuel, "Now where are those men who said Saul shouldn't rule over us? Bring them here, and we will kill them!"

I FOCUS on God's victory and do not seek revenge when I am shown to be right. (11:13)

¹³But Saul replied, "No one will be executed today, for today the LORD has rescued Israel!"

¹⁴Then Samuel said to the people, "Come, let us all go to Gilgal to reaffirm Saul's kingship." ¹⁵So they went to Gilgal, and in a solemn ceremony before the LORD they crowned him king. Then they offered peace offerings to the LORD, and Saul and all the Israelites were very happy.

CHAPTER **12**

Samuel's Farewell Address

Then Samuel addressed the people again: "I have done as you asked and given you a king. ²I have selected him ahead of my own sons, and I stand here, an old, gray-haired man. I have served as your leader since I was a boy. ³Now tell me as I stand before the LORD and before his anointed one—whose ox or donkey have I stolen? Have I ever cheated any of you? Have I ever oppressed you? Have I ever taken a bribe? Tell me and I will make right whatever I have done wrong."

I SERVE God and his people from my youth to my old age. (12:2)

⁴"No," they replied, "you have never cheated or oppressed us in any way, and you have never taken even a single bribe."

⁵"The LORD and his anointed one are my witnesses," Samuel declared, "that you can never accuse me of robbing you."

"Yes, it is true," they replied.

See the profiles for Moses (page 73) and Aaron (page 107) at Exodus 5:1 and Exodus 32:2.

⁶"It was the LORD who appointed Moses and Aaron," Samuel continued.

11:1 As in Greek version; Hebrew lacks *About a month later*.   11:8 Dead Sea Scrolls and Greek version read 70,000.

"He brought your ancestors out of the land of Egypt. ⁷Now stand here quietly before the LORD as I remind you of all the great things the LORD has done for you and your ancestors.

⁸"When the Israelites were* in Egypt and cried out to the LORD, he sent Moses and Aaron to rescue them from Egypt and to bring them into this land. ⁹But the people soon forgot about the LORD their God, so he let them be conquered by Sisera, the general of Hazor's army, and by the Philistines and the king of Moab.

¹⁰"Then they cried to the LORD again and confessed, 'We have sinned by turning away from the LORD and worshiping the images of Baal and Ashtoreth. But we will worship you and you alone if you will rescue us from our enemies.' ¹¹Then the LORD sent Gideon,* Barak,* Jephthah, and Samuel* to save you, and you lived in safety.

¹²"But when you were afraid of Nahash, the king of Ammon, you came to me and said that you wanted a king to reign over you, even though the LORD your God was already your king. ¹³All right, here is the king you have chosen. Look him over. You asked for him, and the LORD has granted your request.

¹⁴"Now if you will fear and worship the LORD and listen to his voice, and if you do not rebel against the LORD's commands, and if you and your king follow the LORD your God, then all will be well. ¹⁵But if you rebel against the LORD's commands and refuse to listen to him, then his hand will be as heavy upon you as it was upon your ancestors.

¹⁶"Now stand here and see the great thing the LORD is about to do. ¹⁷You know that it does not rain at this time of the year during the wheat harvest. I will ask the LORD to send thunder and rain today. Then you will realize how wicked you have been in asking the LORD for a king!"

¹⁸So Samuel called to the LORD, and the LORD sent thunder and rain. And all the people were terrified of the LORD and of Samuel. ¹⁹"Pray to the LORD your God for us, or we will die!" they cried out to Samuel. "For now we have added to our sins by asking for a king."

²⁰"Don't be afraid," Samuel reassured them. "You have certainly done wrong, but make sure now that you worship the LORD with all your heart and that you don't turn your back on him in any way. ²¹Don't go back to worshiping worthless idols that cannot help or rescue you—they really are useless! ²²The LORD will not abandon his chosen people, for that would dishonor his great name. He made you a special nation for himself.

²³"As for me, I will certainly not sin against the LORD by ending my prayers for you. And I will continue to teach you what is good and right. ²⁴But be sure to fear the LORD and sincerely worship him. Think of all the wonderful things he has done for you. ²⁵But if you continue to sin, you and your king will be destroyed."

CHAPTER 13

Continued War with Philistia

Saul was thirty* years old when he became king, and he reigned for forty-two years.*

²Saul selected three thousand special troops from the army of Israel and sent the rest of the men home. He took two thousand of the chosen men with him to Micmash and the hill country of Bethel. The other thousand went with Saul's son Jonathan to Gibeah in the land of Benjamin.

³Soon after this, Jonathan attacked and defeated the garrison of Philistines at Geba. The news spread quickly among the Philistines that Israel was in

I REMIND God's people of all the great things he has done for them. (12:7)

See the profiles for Gideon (page 289) and Jephthah (page 295) at Judges 7:15 and Judges 11:31.

I OBEY the Lord as my King of kings. (12:12)

I BELIEVE that even when God's people do wrong, the Lord gives them opportunity to worship and obey him. (12:20)

I CONTINUE to pray for people under my spiritual care. (12:23)

I CHOOSE my colaborers carefully. (13:2)

12:8 Hebrew *When Jacob was.*   12:11a Hebrew *Jerubbaal,* another name for Gideon; see Judg 7:1.   12:11b As in Greek and Syriac versions; Hebrew reads *Bedan.*   12:11c Greek and Syriac versions read *Samson.*   13:1a As in a few Greek manuscripts; the number is missing in the Hebrew.   13:1b Hebrew *reigned . . . and two;* the number is incomplete in the Hebrew. Compare Acts 13:21.

revolt, so Saul sounded the call to arms throughout Israel. [4]He announced that the Philistine garrison at Geba had been destroyed, and he warned the people that the Philistines now hated the Israelites more than ever. So the entire Israelite army mobilized again and met Saul at Gilgal.

[5]The Philistines mustered a mighty army of three thousand* chariots, six thousand horsemen, and as many warriors as the grains of sand along the seashore! They camped at Micmash east of Beth-aven. [6]When the men of Israel saw the vast number of enemy troops, they lost their nerve entirely and tried to hide in caves, holes, rocks, tombs, and cisterns. [7]Some of them crossed the Jordan River and escaped into the land of Gad and Gilead.

Saul's Disobedience and Samuel's Rebuke

Meanwhile, Saul stayed at Gilgal, and his men were trembling with fear. [8]Saul waited there seven days for Samuel, as Samuel had instructed him earlier, but Samuel still didn't come. Saul realized that his troops were rapidly slipping away. [9]So he demanded, "Bring me the burnt offering and the peace offerings!" And Saul sacrificed the burnt offering himself. [10]Just as Saul was finishing with the burnt offering, Samuel arrived. Saul went out to meet and welcome him, [11]but Samuel said, "What is this you have done?"

Saul replied, "I saw my men scattering from me, and you didn't arrive when you said you would, and the Philistines are at Micmash ready for battle. [12]So I said, 'The Philistines are ready to march against us, and I haven't even asked for the LORD's help!' So I felt obliged to offer the burnt offering myself before you came."

[13]"How foolish!" Samuel exclaimed. "You have disobeyed the command of the LORD your God. Had you obeyed, the LORD would have established your kingdom over Israel forever. [14]But now your dynasty must end, for the LORD has sought out a man after his own heart. The LORD has already chosen him to be king over his people, for you have not obeyed the LORD's command."

Israel's Military Disadvantage

[15]Samuel then left Gilgal and went on his way, but the rest of the troops went with Saul to meet the army. They went up from Gilgal to Gibeah in the land of Benjamin.* When Saul counted the men who were still with him, he found only six hundred left! [16]Saul and Jonathan and the troops with them were staying at Geba, near Gibeah, in the land of Benjamin. The Philistines set up their camp at Micmash. [17]Three raiding parties soon left the camp of the Philistines. One went north toward Ophrah in the land of Shual, [18]another went west to Beth-horon, and the third moved toward the border above the valley of Zeboim near the wilderness.

[19]There were no blacksmiths in the land of Israel in those days. The Philistines wouldn't allow them for fear they would make swords and spears for the Hebrews. [20]So whenever the Israelites needed to sharpen their plowshares, picks, axes, or sickles,* they had to take them to a Philistine blacksmith. [21](The schedule of charges was as follows: a quarter of an ounce of silver* for sharpening a plowshare or a pick, and an eighth of an ounce* for sharpening an ax, a sickle, or an ox goad.) [22]So none of the people of Israel had a sword or spear, except for Saul and Jonathan.

[23]The pass at Micmash had meanwhile been secured by a contingent of the Philistine army.

CHAPTER 14

Jonathan's Daring Plan

One day Jonathan said to the young man who carried his armor, "Come on, let's go over to where the Philistines have their outpost." But Jonathan did

---

I DO NOT RUN AWAY when I have the Lord on my side. (13:6)

I DO NOT MAKE UP my own solution when God requires me to wait. (13:8)

I BELIEVE Saul's family could have continued to reign over Israel if he had obeyed God's commands. (13:13)

I BELIEVE the Lord sought out and chose a man after his own heart to be king. (13:14)

Always keep a pen handy to record your thoughts in the margins of this Bible.

13:5 As in Greek and Syriac versions; Hebrew reads *30,000*. **13:15** As in Greek version; Hebrew reads *Samuel left Gilgal and went up to Gibeah in the land of Benjamin*. **13:20** As in Greek version; Hebrew reads *or plowshares*. **13:21a** Hebrew *1 pim* [8 grams]. **13:21b** Hebrew *1/3 of a shekel* [4 grams].

not tell his father what he was doing. ²Meanwhile, Saul and his six hundred men were camped on the outskirts of Gibeah, around the pomegranate tree at Migron. ³(Among Saul's men was Ahijah the priest, who was wearing the linen ephod. Ahijah was the son of Ahitub, Ichabod's brother. Ahitub was the son of Phinehas and the grandson of Eli, the priest of the LORD who had served at Shiloh.)

See Eli's profile (page 321) at 1 Samuel 2:30.

No one realized that Jonathan had left the Israelite camp. ⁴To reach the Philistine outpost, Jonathan had to go down between two rocky cliffs that were called Bozez and Seneh. ⁵The cliff on the north was in front of Micmash, and the one on the south was in front of Geba. ⁶"Let's go across to see those pagans," Jonathan said to his armor bearer. "Perhaps the LORD will help us, for nothing can hinder the LORD. He can win a battle whether he has many warriors or only a few!"

I KNOW the Lord can win no matter what the odds. (14:6)

LIKE JONATHAN   *I can overcome any odds by God's power.*
1 Samuel 14:6

David Wilkerson never said it when he lived among the gangs of New York. Amy Carmichael and Mother Teresa never said it while living in the slums of India.

Like these and others who have ventured into dangerous regions or have toiled at difficult tasks, Jonathan never said, "I'm just one person. What can God do through me?"

Bold for God and dependent on him alone, Jonathan attempted difficult tasks for God's glory. He always sought God's will before taking risks, of course. And he didn't go it alone. But neither was his trust in his armor bearer, whom Jonathan instructed to climb up *behind* and not ahead of him.

Down one cliff and up another, Jonathan and his armor bearer were easy targets for the Philistines. But Jonathan was assured that God had a plan to beat the odds. These two men did more than kill twenty soldiers in a skirmish that day. They set in motion a state of panic which, amplified by an earthquake, caused the entire Philistine army to scatter. The Israelite army then pursued and defeated them.

No wonder Jonathan was drawn to David as a committed friend for life. The cliff climber met the giant slayer. The first man went up the side of a mountain on his hands and feet to fight a well-armed contingency. The other man took five small stones and slung one in the face of a giant. Both men knew what it was to trust God's power in the face of overwhelming odds.

Depending on God's power and seeking his glory, you and I can overcome the odds, too.

○ *Today's Scripture reading is 1 Samuel 14 and 20.*

⁷"Do what you think is best," the youth replied. "I'm with you completely, whatever you decide."

I WHOLEHEARTEDLY SUPPORT godly friends who serve the Lord courageously. (14:7)

⁸"All right then," Jonathan told him. "We will cross over and let them see us. ⁹If they say to us, 'Stay where you are or we'll kill you,' then we will stop and not go up to them. ¹⁰But if they say, 'Come on up and fight,' then we will go up. That will be the LORD's sign that he will help us defeat them."

¹¹When the Philistines saw them coming, they shouted, "Look! The Hebrews are crawling out of their holes!" ¹²Then they shouted to Jonathan, "Come on up here, and we'll teach you a lesson!"

I ATTEMPT difficult things for God, since I know he will help me. (14:12)

"Come on, climb right behind me," Jonathan said to his armor bearer, "for the LORD will help us defeat them!" ¹³So they climbed up using both hands and feet, and the Philistines fell back as Jonathan and his armor bearer killed them right and left. ¹⁴They killed about twenty men in all, and their bodies were scattered over about half an acre.* ¹⁵Suddenly, panic broke out in the Philistine army, both in the camp and in the field, including even the

14:14 Hebrew *half a yoke*; a "yoke" was the amount of land plowed by a pair of yoked oxen in one day.

outposts and raiding parties. And just then an earthquake struck, and everyone was terrified.

Israel Defeats the Philistines

16Saul's lookouts in Gibeah saw a strange sight—the vast army of Philistines began to melt away in every direction. 17"Find out who isn't here," Saul ordered. And when they checked, they found that Jonathan and his armor bearer were gone. 18Then Saul shouted to Ahijah, "Bring the ephod here!" For at that time Ahijah was wearing the ephod in front of the Israelites.* 19But while Saul was talking to the priest, the shouting and confusion in the Philistine camp grew louder and louder. So Saul said to Ahijah, "Never mind; let's get going!"*

20Then Saul and his six hundred men rushed out to the battle and found the Philistines killing each other. There was terrible confusion everywhere. 21Even the Hebrews who had gone over to the Philistine army revolted and joined in with Saul, Jonathan, and the rest of the Israelites. 22Likewise, the men who were hiding in the hills joined the chase when they saw the Philistines running away. 23So the LORD saved Israel that day, and the battle continued to rage even out beyond Beth-aven.

Saul's Foolish Oath

24Now the men of Israel were worn out that day, because Saul had made them take an oath, saying, "Let a curse fall on anyone who eats before evening—before I have full revenge on my enemies." So no one ate a thing all day, 25even though they found honeycomb on the ground in the forest. 26They didn't even touch the honey because they all feared the oath they had taken.

27But Jonathan had not heard his father's command, and he dipped a stick into a piece of honeycomb and ate the honey. After he had eaten it, he felt much better. 28But one of the men saw him and said, "Your father made the army take a strict oath that anyone who eats food today will be cursed. That is why everyone is weary and faint."

29"My father has made trouble for us all!" Jonathan exclaimed. "A command like that only hurts us. See how much better I feel now that I have eaten this little bit of honey. 30If the men had been allowed to eat freely from the food they found among our enemies, think how many more we could have killed!"

31But hungry as they were, they chased and killed the Philistines all day from Micmash to Aijalon, growing more and more faint. 32That evening they flew upon the battle plunder and butchered the sheep, cattle, and calves, but they ate them without draining the blood. 33Someone reported to Saul, "Look, the men are sinning against the LORD by eating meat that still has blood in it."

"That is very wrong," Saul said. "Find a large stone and roll it over here. 34Then go out among the troops and tell them, 'Bring the cattle and sheep here to kill them and drain the blood. Do not sin against the LORD by eating meat with the blood still in it.' " So that night all the troops brought their animals and slaughtered them there. 35And Saul built an altar to the LORD, the first one he had ever built.

36Then Saul said, "Let's chase the Philistines all night and destroy every last one of them."

His men replied, "We'll do whatever you think is best."

But the priest said, "Let's ask God first."

37So Saul asked God, "Should we go after the Philistines? Will you help us defeat them?" But God made no reply that day.

14:18 As in some Greek manuscripts; Hebrew reads "Bring the Ark of God." For at that time the Ark of God was with the Israelites. 14:19 Hebrew Withdraw your hand.

³⁸Then Saul said to the leaders, "Something's wrong! I want all my army commanders to come here. We must find out what sin was committed today. ³⁹I vow by the name of the LORD who rescued Israel that the sinner will surely die, even if it is my own son Jonathan!" But no one would tell him what the trouble was. ⁴⁰Then Saul said, "Jonathan and I will stand over here, and all of you stand over there." And the people agreed.

⁴¹Then Saul prayed, "O LORD, God of Israel, please show us who is guilty and who is innocent. Are Jonathan and I guilty, or is the sin among the others?"* And Jonathan and Saul were chosen* as the guilty ones, and the people were declared innocent.

⁴²Then Saul said, "Now choose* between me and Jonathan." And Jonathan was shown to be the guilty one.

⁴³"Tell me what you have done," Saul demanded of Jonathan.

"I tasted a little honey," Jonathan admitted. "It was only a little bit on the end of a stick. Does that deserve death?"

⁴⁴"Yes, Jonathan," Saul said, "you must die! May God strike me dead if you are not executed for this."

⁴⁵But the people broke in and said to Saul, "Should Jonathan, who saved Israel today, die? Far from it! As surely as the LORD lives, not one hair on his head will be touched, for he has been used of God to do a mighty miracle today." So the people rescued Jonathan, and he was not put to death. ⁴⁶Then Saul called back the army from chasing the Philistines, and the Philistines returned home.

Saul's Military Successes

⁴⁷Now when Saul had secured his grasp on Israel's throne, he fought against his enemies in every direction—against Moab, Ammon, Edom, the kings of Zobah, and the Philistines. And wherever he turned, he was victorious. ⁴⁸He did great deeds and conquered the Amalekites, saving Israel from all those who had plundered them.

⁴⁹Saul's sons included Jonathan, Ishbosheth,* and Malkishua. He also had two daughters: Merab, who was older, and Michal. ⁵⁰Saul's wife was Ahinoam, the daughter of Ahimaaz. The commander of Saul's army was his cousin Abner, his uncle Ner's son. ⁵¹Abner's father, Ner, and Saul's father, Kish, were brothers; both were sons of Abiel.

⁵²The Israelites fought constantly with the Philistines throughout Saul's lifetime. So whenever Saul saw a young man who was brave and strong, he drafted him into his army.

CHAPTER 15

Saul Destroys the Amalekites

One day Samuel said to Saul, "I anointed you king of Israel because the LORD told me to. Now listen to this message from the LORD! ²This is what the LORD Almighty says: 'I have decided to settle accounts with the nation of Amalek for opposing Israel when they came from Egypt. ³Now go and completely destroy* the entire Amalekite nation—men, women, children, babies, cattle, sheep, camels, and donkeys.'"

⁴So Saul mobilized his army at Telaim. There were 200,000 troops in addition to 10,000 men from Judah. ⁵Then Saul went to the city of Amalek and lay in wait in the valley. ⁶Saul sent this message to the Kenites: "Move away from where the Amalekites live or else you will die with them. For you were

---

I DO NOT MAKE rash vows before God. (14:39)

I RESCUE those who are unfairly punished. (14:45)

I BELIEVE God settles accounts with his enemies in his perfect timing. (15:2)

I AM CAREFUL to protect innocent people who may be hurt by the punishment of others. (15:6)

14:41a Greek version adds *If the fault is with me or my son Jonathan, respond with Urim; but if the men of Israel are at fault, respond with Thummim.* **14:41b** Hebrew *chosen by lot.* **14:42** Hebrew *draw lots.* **14:49** Hebrew *Ishvi*, a variant name for Ishbosheth; also known as Eshbaal. **15:3** The Hebrew term used here refers to the complete consecration of things or people to the LORD, either by destroying them or by giving them as an offering; also in 15:8, 9, 15, 18, 20, 21.

kind to the people of Israel when they came up from Egypt." So the Kenites packed up and left.

⁷Then Saul slaughtered the Amalekites from Havilah all the way to Shur, east of Egypt. ⁸He captured Agag, the Amalekite king, but completely destroyed everyone else. ⁹Saul and his men spared Agag's life and kept the best of the sheep and cattle, the fat calves and lambs—everything, in fact, that appealed to them. They destroyed only what was worthless or of poor quality.

The LORD Rejects Saul

¹⁰Then the LORD said to Samuel, ¹¹"I am sorry that I ever made Saul king, for he has not been loyal to me and has again refused to obey me." Samuel was so deeply moved when he heard this that he cried out to the LORD all night.

¹²Early the next morning Samuel went to find Saul. Someone told him, "Saul went to Carmel to set up a monument to himself; then he went on to Gilgal."

¹³When Samuel finally found him, Saul greeted him cheerfully. "May the LORD bless you," he said. "I have carried out the LORD's command!"

¹⁴"Then what is all the bleating of sheep and lowing of cattle I hear?" Samuel demanded.

¹⁵"It's true that the army spared the best of the sheep and cattle," Saul admitted. "But they are going to sacrifice them to the LORD your God. We have destroyed everything else."

¹⁶Then Samuel said to Saul, "Stop! Listen to what the LORD told me last night!"

"What was it?" Saul asked.

¹⁷And Samuel told him, "Although you may think little of yourself, are you not the leader of the tribes of Israel? The LORD has anointed you king of Israel. ¹⁸And the LORD sent you on a mission and told you, 'Go and completely destroy the sinners, the Amalekites, until they are all dead.' ¹⁹Why haven't you obeyed the LORD? Why did you rush for the plunder and do exactly what the LORD said not to do?"

²⁰"But I did obey the LORD," Saul insisted. "I carried out the mission he gave me. I brought back King Agag, but I destroyed everyone else. ²¹Then my troops brought in the best of the sheep and cattle and plunder to sacrifice to the LORD your God in Gilgal."

²²But Samuel replied, "What is more pleasing to the LORD: your burnt offerings and sacrifices or your obedience to his voice? Obedience is far better than sacrifice. Listening to him is much better than offering the fat of rams. ²³Rebellion is as bad as the sin of witchcraft, and stubbornness is as bad as worshiping idols. So because you have rejected the word of the LORD, he has rejected you from being king."

Saul Pleads for Forgiveness

²⁴Then Saul finally admitted, "Yes, I have sinned. I have disobeyed your instructions and the LORD's command, for I was afraid of the people and did what they demanded. ²⁵Oh, please, forgive my sin now and go with me to worship the LORD."

²⁶But Samuel replied, "I will not return with you! Since you have rejected the LORD's command, he has rejected you from being the king of Israel."

²⁷As Samuel turned to go, Saul grabbed at him to try to hold him back and tore his robe. ²⁸And Samuel said to him, "See? The LORD has torn the kingdom of Israel from you today and has given it to someone else—one who is better than you. ²⁹And he who is the Glory of Israel will not lie, nor will he change his mind, for he is not human that he should change his mind!"

³⁰Then Saul pleaded again, "I know I have sinned. But please, at least honor me before the leaders and before my people by going with me to

---

I MOURN deeply when leaders grieve God by refusing to obey him. (15:11)

I DO NOT DISOBEY God by making my own interpretations of how to obey his clear commands. (15:20)

I DO NOT LET the demands of others keep me from obeying the Lord completely. (15:24)

I BELIEVE the Lord will not lie or change his mind as humans do. (15:29)

worship the LORD your God." ³¹So Samuel finally agreed and went with him, and Saul worshiped the LORD.

Samuel Executes King Agag

³²Then Samuel said, "Bring King Agag to me." Agag arrived full of smiles, for he thought, "Surely the worst is over, and I have been spared!"* ³³But Samuel said, "As your sword has killed the sons of many mothers, now your mother will be childless." And Samuel cut Agag to pieces before the LORD at Gilgal. ³⁴ Then Samuel went home to Ramah, and Saul returned to his house at Gibeah. ³⁵Samuel never went to meet with Saul again, but he mourned constantly for him. And the LORD was sorry he had ever made Saul king of Israel.

I MOURN deeply when a leader rejects the Lord's will. (15:35)

CHAPTER 16

Samuel Anoints David as King

Finally, the LORD said to Samuel, "You have mourned long enough for Saul. I have rejected him as king of Israel. Now fill your horn with olive oil and go to Bethlehem. Find a man named Jesse who lives there, for I have selected one of his sons to be my new king."

²But Samuel asked, "How can I do that? If Saul hears about it, he will kill me."

"Take a heifer with you," the LORD replied, "and say that you have come to make a sacrifice to the LORD. ³Invite Jesse to the sacrifice, and I will show you which of his sons to anoint for me."

⁴So Samuel did as the LORD instructed him. When he arrived at Bethlehem, the leaders of the town became afraid. "What's wrong?" they asked. "Do you come in peace?"

⁵"Yes," Samuel replied. "I have come to sacrifice to the LORD. Purify yourselves and come with me to the sacrifice." Then Samuel performed the purification rite for Jesse and his sons and invited them, too.

I ACCEPT when it is time to stop grieving over a disobedient person and focus on those who want to follow God. (16:1)

⁶When they arrived, Samuel took one look at Eliab and thought, "Surely this is the LORD's anointed!" ⁷But the LORD said to Samuel, "Don't judge by his appearance or height, for I have rejected him. The LORD doesn't make decisions the way you do! People judge by outward appearance, but the LORD looks at a person's thoughts and intentions."

⁸Then Jesse told his son Abinadab to step forward and walk in front of Samuel. But Samuel said, "This is not the one the LORD has chosen." ⁹Next Jesse summoned Shammah, but Samuel said, "Neither is this the one the LORD has chosen." ¹⁰In the same way all seven of Jesse's sons were presented to Samuel. But Samuel said to Jesse, "The LORD has not chosen any of these." ¹¹Then Samuel asked, "Are these all the sons you have?"

"There is still the youngest," Jesse replied. "But he's out in the fields watching the sheep."

"Send for him at once," Samuel said. "We will not sit down to eat until he arrives."

¹²So Jesse sent for him. He was ruddy and handsome, with pleasant eyes. And the LORD said, "This is the one; anoint him."

¹³So as David stood there among his brothers, Samuel took the olive oil he had brought and poured it on David's head. And the Spirit of the LORD came mightily upon him from that day on. Then Samuel returned to Ramah.

I DO NOT JUDGE people by their outward appearance because I know the Lord sees and judges people by their thoughts and intentions. (16:7)

I FOLLOW God's choice for a spiritual leader. (16:12)

See David's profile (page 629) at Psalm 3:1.

David Serves in Saul's Court

¹⁴Now the Spirit of the LORD had left Saul, and the LORD sent a tormenting spirit that filled him with depression and fear. ¹⁵Some of Saul's servants suggested a remedy. "It is clear that a spirit from God is tormenting you," they said. ¹⁶"Let us find a good musician to play the harp for you whenever

I DISCERN when a person's depression has spiritual causes. (16:15)

15:32 Dead Sea Scrolls and Greek version read *Agag arrived hesitantly, for he thought, "Surely this is the bitterness of death."*

the tormenting spirit is bothering you. The harp music will quiet you, and you will soon be well again."

¹⁷"All right," Saul said. "Find me someone who plays well and bring him here."

¹⁸One of the servants said to Saul, "The son of Jesse is a talented harp player. Not only that; he is brave and strong and has good judgment. He is also a fine-looking young man, and the LORD is with him."

¹⁹So Saul sent messengers to Jesse to say, "Send me your son David, the shepherd." ²⁰Jesse responded by sending David to Saul, along with a young goat and a donkey loaded down with food and wine. ²¹So David went to Saul and served him. Saul liked David very much, and David became one of Saul's armor bearers.

²²Then Saul sent word to Jesse asking, "Please let David join my staff, for I am very pleased with him." ²³And whenever the tormenting spirit from God troubled Saul, David would play the harp. Then Saul would feel better, and the tormenting spirit would go away.

CHAPTER 17

Goliath Challenges the Israelites

The Philistines now mustered their army for battle and camped between Socoh in Judah and Azekah at Ephes-dammim. ²Saul countered by gathering his troops near the valley of Elah. ³So the Philistines and Israelites faced each other on opposite hills, with the valley between them.

⁴Then Goliath, a Philistine champion from Gath, came out of the Philistine ranks to face the forces of Israel. He was a giant of a man, measuring over nine feet* tall! ⁵He wore a bronze helmet and a coat of mail that weighed 125 pounds.* ⁶He also wore bronze leggings, and he slung a bronze javelin over his back. ⁷The shaft of his spear was as heavy and thick as a weaver's beam, tipped with an iron spearhead that weighed fifteen pounds.* An armor bearer walked ahead of him carrying a huge shield.

⁸Goliath stood and shouted across to the Israelites, "Do you need a whole army to settle this? Choose someone to fight for you, and I will represent the Philistines. We will settle this dispute in single combat! ⁹If your man is able to kill me, then we will be your slaves. But if I kill him, you will be our slaves! ¹⁰I defy the armies of Israel! Send me a man who will fight with me!" ¹¹When Saul and the Israelites heard this, they were terrified and deeply shaken.

I AM NOT TERRIFIED by those who defy God and threaten his people. (17:11)

Jesse Sends David to Saul's Camp

¹²Now David was the son of a man named Jesse, an Ephrathite from Bethlehem in the land of Judah. Jesse was an old man at that time, and he had eight sons in all. ¹³Jesse's three oldest sons—Eliab, Abinadab, and Shammah—had already joined Saul's army to fight the Philistines. ¹⁴David was the youngest of Jesse's sons. Since David's three oldest brothers were in the army, they stayed with Saul's forces all the time. ¹⁵But David went back and forth between working for Saul and helping his father with the sheep in Bethlehem.

¹⁶For forty days, twice a day, morning and evening, the Philistine giant strutted in front of the Israelite army.

I CARE ABOUT the welfare of my children who are far away from home. (17:17)

¹⁷One day Jesse said to David, "Take this half-bushel* of roasted grain and these ten loaves of bread to your brothers. ¹⁸And give these ten cuts of cheese to their captain. See how your brothers are getting along, and bring me back a letter from them.*"

¹⁹David's brothers were with Saul and the Israelite army at the valley of Elah, fighting against the Philistines. ²⁰So David left the sheep with another shepherd and set out early the next morning with the gifts. He arrived at the

17:4 Hebrew *6 cubits and 1 span* [which totals about 9.75 feet or 3 meters]; Greek version and Dead Sea Scrolls read *4 cubits and 1 span* [which totals about 6.75 feet or 2 meters].   17:5 Hebrew *5,000 shekels* [57 kilograms].
17:7 Hebrew *600 shekels* [6.8 kilograms].   17:17 Hebrew *ephah* [18 liters].   17:18 Hebrew *and take their pledge.*

outskirts of the camp just as the Israelite army was leaving for the battlefield with shouts and battle cries. ²¹Soon the Israelite and Philistine forces stood facing each other, army against army. ²²David left his things with the keeper of supplies and hurried out to the ranks to greet his brothers. ²³As he was talking with them, he saw Goliath, the champion from Gath, come out from the Philistine ranks, shouting his challenge to the army of Israel.

²⁴As soon as the Israelite army saw him, they began to run away in fright. ²⁵"Have you seen the giant?" the men were asking. "He comes out each day to challenge Israel. And have you heard about the huge reward the king has offered to anyone who kills him? The king will give him one of his daughters for a wife, and his whole family will be exempted from paying taxes!"

²⁶David talked to some others standing there to verify the report. "What will a man get for killing this Philistine and putting an end to his abuse of Israel?" he asked them. "Who is this pagan Philistine anyway, that he is allowed to defy the armies of the living God?" ²⁷And David received the same reply as before: "What you have been hearing is true. That is the reward for killing the giant."

²⁸But when David's oldest brother, Eliab, heard David talking to the men, he was angry. "What are you doing around here anyway?" he demanded. "What about those few sheep you're supposed to be taking care of? I know about your pride and dishonesty. You just want to see the battle!"

²⁹"What have I done now?" David replied. "I was only asking a question!" ³⁰He walked over to some others and asked them the same thing and received the same answer. ³¹Then David's question was reported to King Saul, and the king sent for him.

David Kills Goliath

³²"Don't worry about a thing," David told Saul. "I'll go fight this Philistine!"

³³"Don't be ridiculous!" Saul replied. "There is no way you can go against this Philistine. You are only a boy, and he has been in the army since he was a boy!"

³⁴But David persisted. "I have been taking care of my father's sheep," he said. "When a lion or a bear comes to steal a lamb from the flock, ³⁵I go after it with a club and take the lamb from its mouth. If the animal turns on me, I catch it by the jaw and club it to death. ³⁶I have done this to both lions and bears, and I'll do it to this pagan Philistine, too, for he has defied the armies of the living God! ³⁷The LORD who saved me from the claws of the lion and the bear will save me from this Philistine!"

Saul finally consented. "All right, go ahead," he said. "And may the LORD be with you!"

³⁸Then Saul gave David his own armor—a bronze helmet and a coat of mail. ³⁹David put it on, strapped the sword over it, and took a step or two to see what it was like, for he had never worn such things before. "I can't go in these," he protested. "I'm not used to them." So he took them off again. ⁴⁰He picked up five smooth stones from a stream and put them in his shepherd's bag. Then, armed only with his shepherd's staff and sling, he started across to fight Goliath.

⁴¹Goliath walked out toward David with his shield bearer ahead of him, ⁴²sneering in contempt at this ruddy-faced boy. ⁴³"Am I a dog," he roared at David, "that you come at me with a stick?" And he cursed David by the names of his gods. ⁴⁴"Come over here, and I'll give your flesh to the birds and wild animals!" Goliath yelled.

⁴⁵David shouted in reply, "You come to me with sword, spear, and javelin, but I come to you in the name of the LORD Almighty—the God of the armies of Israel, whom you have defied. ⁴⁶Today the LORD will conquer you, and I will kill you and cut off your head. And then I will give the dead bodies of

I DO NOT RUN AWAY from those who challenge God's people. (17:24)

I CARE passionately about the name of God and his people. (17:26)

I ASK good questions before I commit to a difficult task. (17:30)

I DO NOT UNDERESTIMATE a person's ability because he or she is young. (17:33)

I USE experiences in life to prepare me for greater service for God. (17:34)

I TRUST the Lord to save me from both physical and spiritual enemies. (17:37)

I PREPARE for conflict in the best way I can with the resources God gives me. (17:40)

I TAKE bold action to make God's great power and name known. (17:46)

your men to the birds and wild animals, and the whole world will know that there is a God in Israel! ⁴⁷And everyone will know that the LORD does not need weapons to rescue his people. It is his battle, not ours. The LORD will give you to us!"

⁴⁸As Goliath moved closer to attack, David quickly ran out to meet him. ⁴⁹Reaching into his shepherd's bag and taking out a stone, he hurled it from his sling and hit the Philistine in the forehead. The stone sank in, and Goliath stumbled and fell face downward to the ground. ⁵⁰So David triumphed over the Philistine giant with only a stone and sling. And since he had no sword, ⁵¹he ran over and pulled Goliath's sword from its sheath. David used it to kill the giant and cut off his head.

Israel Routs the Philistines

When the Philistines saw that their champion was dead, they turned and ran. ⁵²Then the Israelites gave a great shout of triumph and rushed after the Philistines, chasing them as far as Gath* and the gates of Ekron. The bodies of the dead and wounded Philistines were strewn all along the road from Shaaraim, as far as Gath and Ekron. ⁵³Then the Israelite army returned and plundered the deserted Philistine camp. ⁵⁴(David took Goliath's head to Jerusalem, but he stored the Philistine's armor in his own tent.)

⁵⁵As Saul watched David go out to fight Goliath, he asked Abner, the general of his army, "Abner, whose son is he?"

"I really don't know," Abner said.

⁵⁶"Well, find out!" the king told him.

⁵⁷After David had killed Goliath, Abner brought him to Saul with the Philistine's head still in his hand. ⁵⁸"Tell me about your father, my boy," Saul said.

And David replied, "His name is Jesse, and we live in Bethlehem."

CHAPTER 18

Saul Becomes Jealous of David

After David had finished talking with Saul, he met Jonathan, the king's son. There was an immediate bond of love between them, and they became the best of friends. ²From that day on Saul kept David with him at the palace and wouldn't let him return home. ³And Jonathan made a special vow to be David's friend, ⁴and he sealed the pact by giving him his robe, tunic, sword, bow, and belt.

⁵Whatever Saul asked David to do, David did it successfully. So Saul made him a commander in his army, an appointment that was applauded by the fighting men and officers alike. ⁶But something happened when the victorious Israelite army was returning home after David had killed Goliath. Women came out from all the towns along the way to celebrate and to cheer for King Saul, and they sang and danced for joy with tambourines and cymbals.* ⁷This was their song:

"Saul has killed his thousands,
and David his ten thousands!"

⁸This made Saul very angry. "What's this?" he said. "They credit David with ten thousands and me with only thousands. Next they'll be making him their king!" ⁹So from that time on Saul kept a jealous eye on David.

¹⁰The very next day, in fact, a tormenting spirit from God overwhelmed Saul, and he began to rave like a madman. David began to play the harp, as he did whenever this happened. But Saul, who had a spear in his hand, ¹¹suddenly hurled it at David, intending to pin him to the wall. But David jumped

I REJOICE in the victory God gives. (17:52)

I MAKE special commitments to my close friends who are believers. (18:3)

I GIVE people positions of responsibility and leadership when they do well. (18:5)

I AM NOT JEALOUS when God uses someone else more than he uses me. (18:8)

17:52 As in some Greek manuscripts; Hebrew reads *a valley*.   18:6 The type of instrument represented by the final word is uncertain.

aside and escaped. This happened another time, too, ¹²for Saul was afraid of him, and he was jealous because the LORD had left him and was now with David. ¹³Finally, Saul banned him from his presence and appointed him commander over only a thousand men, but David faithfully led his troops into battle.

¹⁴David continued to succeed in everything he did, for the LORD was with him. ¹⁵When Saul recognized this, he became even more afraid of him. ¹⁶But all Israel and Judah loved David because he was so successful at leading his troops into battle.

UNLIKE SAUL

I am not jealous when God chooses to honor and use someone else more than me.

1 Samuel 18:9

Saul had it all. Good looks, height, charm, and leadership ability. He was chosen by God, touched by his Spirit, and given the opportunity to be Israel's first and greatest king.

When Saul's own deliberate disobedience against the Lord dashed any opportunity for an enduring dynasty, however, jealous bitterness began to brew in the king's heart.

Saul's own son Jonathan could have felt just as jealous. After all, Jonathan knew full well that he had lost the kingship because of his father's sin—and that David would become king instead. Yet Jonathan was willing to be second to David if that was God's plan. Saul, however, would hear none of it.

Jealousy ate at Saul's tormented mind. Like a man unhinged, he was driven to chase David in the wilderness, bent on destroying the man God had chosen as his replacement. In his jealous rage, Saul eventually viewed his own soldiers as conspirators against his happiness and God's priests as traitors against his life.

Saul's jealousy mushroomed into a terrible cloud of destruction. He murdered hundreds of innocent people but never could catch David. In the end, Saul fell victim to his own sword.

Years later David's son Solomon wrote, "Anger is cruel, and wrath is like a flood, but who can survive the destructiveness of jealousy?" (Proverbs 27:4).

If one of God's most gifted men could not survive jealousy, who are you and I to think we can fare any better by our own strength? Let us continually look to God to help us.

○ *Today's Scripture reading is 1 Samuel 18–19.*

David Marries Saul's Daughter

¹⁷One day Saul said to David, "I am ready to give you my older daughter, Merab, as your wife. But first you must prove yourself to be a real warrior by fighting the LORD's battles." For Saul thought to himself, "I'll send him out against the Philistines and let them kill him rather than doing it myself."

¹⁸"Who am I, and what is my family in Israel that I should be the king's son-in-law?" David exclaimed. "My father's family is nothing!" ¹⁹So* when the time came for the wedding, Saul gave Merab in marriage to Adriel, a man from Meholah.

I DO NOT ASSUME positions of importance for myself. (18:18)

²⁰In the meantime, Saul's daughter Michal had fallen in love with David, and Saul was delighted when he heard about it. ²¹"Here's another chance to see him killed by the Philistines!" Saul said to himself. But to David he said, "I have a way for you to become my son-in-law after all!"

I DO NOT SEEK to cause the downfall or destruction of another person, especially if I am jealous. (18:21)

²²Then Saul told his men to say confidentially to David, "The king really likes you, and so do we. Why don't you accept the king's offer and become his son-in-law?"

²³When Saul's men said these things to David, he replied, "How can a poor man from a humble family afford the bride price for the daughter of a king?"

²⁴When Saul's men reported this back to the king, ²⁵he told them, "Tell

18:19 Or *But.*

David that all I want for the bride price is one hundred Philistine foreskins! Vengeance on my enemies is all I really want." But what Saul had in mind was that David would be killed in the fight.

²⁶David was delighted to accept the offer. So before the time limit expired, ²⁷he and his men went out and killed two hundred Philistines and presented all their foreskins to the king. So Saul gave Michal to David to be his wife.

²⁸When the king realized how much the LORD was with David and how much Michal loved him, ²⁹he became even more afraid of him, and he remained David's enemy for the rest of his life. ³⁰Whenever the Philistine army attacked, David was more successful against them than all the rest of Saul's officers. So David's name became very famous throughout the land.

CHAPTER 19

Saul Tries to Kill David

Saul now urged his servants and his son Jonathan to assassinate David. But Jonathan, because of his close friendship with David, ²told him what his father was planning. "Tomorrow morning," he warned him, "you must find a hiding place out in the fields. ³I'll ask my father to go out there with me, and I'll talk to him about you. Then I'll tell you everything I can find out."

⁴The next morning Jonathan spoke with his father about David, saying many good things about him. "Please don't sin against David," Jonathan pleaded. "He's never done anything to harm you. He has always helped you in any way he could. ⁵Have you forgotten about the time he risked his life to kill the Philistine giant and how the LORD brought a great victory to Israel as a result? You were certainly happy about it then. Why should you murder an innocent man like David? There is no reason for it at all!"

⁶So Saul listened to Jonathan and vowed, "As surely as the LORD lives, David will not be killed." ⁷Afterward Jonathan called David and told him what had happened. Then he took David to see Saul, and everything was as it had been before.

⁸War broke out shortly after that, and David led his troops against the Philistines. He attacked them with such fury that they all ran away.

⁹But one day as Saul was sitting at home, the tormenting spirit from the LORD suddenly came upon him again. As David played his harp for the king, ¹⁰Saul hurled his spear at David in an attempt to kill him. But David dodged out of the way and escaped into the night, leaving the spear stuck in the wall.

Michal Saves David's Life

¹¹Then Saul sent troops to watch David's house. They were told to kill David when he came out the next morning. But Michal, David's wife, warned him, "If you don't get away tonight, you will be dead by morning." ¹²So she helped him climb out through a window, and he escaped. ¹³Then she took an idol* and put it in his bed, covered it with blankets, and put a cushion of goat's hair at its head. ¹⁴When the troops came to arrest David, she told them he was sick and couldn't get out of bed.

¹⁵"Then bring him to me in his bed," Saul ordered, "so I can kill him as he lies there!" And he sent them back to David's house. ¹⁶But when they came to carry David out, they discovered that it was only an idol in the bed with a cushion of goat's hair at its head.

¹⁷"Why have you tricked me and let my enemy escape?" Saul demanded of Michal.

"I had to," Michal replied. "He threatened to kill me if I didn't help him."

¹⁸So David got away and went to Ramah to see Samuel, and he told him all that Saul had done to him. Then Samuel took David with him to live at Naioth. ¹⁹When the report reached Saul that David was at Naioth in Ramah,

19:13 Hebrew teraphim; also in 19:16.

I DO NOT MAKE enemies of godly individuals whom the Lord and others love. (18:29)

I PROTECT my friends from people who would harm them. (19:1)

I SEEK to reconcile people who are estranged from each other. (19:7)

I RECOGNIZE that sometimes there are spiritual reasons behind someone's hatred of me. (19:9)

I WARN those who are in danger and help them escape. (19:11)

I TAKE IN those who are running for their lives. (19:18)

²⁰he sent troops to capture him. But when they arrived and saw Samuel and the other prophets prophesying, the Spirit of God came upon Saul's men, and they also began to prophesy. ²¹When Saul heard what had happened, he sent other troops, but they, too, prophesied! The same thing happened a third time! ²²Finally, Saul himself went to Ramah and arrived at the great well in Secu. "Where are Samuel and David?" he demanded.

"They are at Naioth in Ramah," someone told him. ²³But on the way to Naioth the Spirit of God came upon Saul, and he, too, began to prophesy! ²⁴He tore off his clothes and lay on the ground all day and all night, prophesying in the presence of Samuel. The people who were watching exclaimed, "What? Is Saul a prophet, too?"

CHAPTER 20

Jonathan Helps David

David now fled from Naioth in Ramah and found Jonathan. "What have I done?" he exclaimed. "What is my crime? How have I offended your father that he is so determined to kill me?"

²"That's not true!" Jonathan protested. "I'm sure he's not planning any such thing, for he always tells me everything he's going to do, even the little things. I know he wouldn't hide something like this from me. It just isn't so!"

³Then David took an oath before Jonathan and said, "Your father knows perfectly well about our friendship, so he has said to himself, 'I won't tell Jonathan—why should I hurt him?' But I swear to you that I am only a step away from death! I swear it by the LORD and by your own soul!"

⁴"Tell me what I can do!" Jonathan exclaimed.

⁵David replied, "Tomorrow we celebrate the new moon festival. I've always eaten with your father on this occasion, but tomorrow I'll hide in the field and stay there until the evening of the third day. ⁶If your father asks where I am, tell him I asked permission to go home to Bethlehem for an annual family sacrifice. ⁷If he says, 'Fine!' then you will know all is well. But if he is angry and loses his temper, then you will know he was planning to kill me. ⁸Show me this kindness as my sworn friend—for we made a covenant together before the LORD—or kill me yourself if I have sinned against your father. But please don't betray me to him!"

⁹"Never!" Jonathan exclaimed. "You know that if I had the slightest notion my father was planning to kill you, I would tell you at once."

¹⁰Then David asked, "How will I know whether or not your father is angry?"

¹¹"Come out to the field with me," Jonathan replied. And they went out there together. ¹²Then Jonathan told David, "I promise by the LORD, the God of Israel, that by this time tomorrow, or the next day at the latest, I will talk to my father and let you know at once how he feels about you. If he speaks favorably about you, I will let you know. ¹³But if he is angry and wants you killed, may the LORD kill me if I don't warn you so you can escape and live. May the LORD be with you as he used to be with my father. ¹⁴And may you treat me with the faithful love of the LORD as long as I live. But if I die, ¹⁵treat my family with this faithful love, even when the LORD destroys all your enemies."

¹⁶So Jonathan made a covenant with David,* saying, "May the LORD destroy all your enemies!" ¹⁷And Jonathan made David reaffirm his vow of friendship again, for Jonathan loved David as much as he loved himself.

¹⁸Then Jonathan said, "Tomorrow we celebrate the new moon festival. You will be missed when your place at the table is empty. ¹⁹The day after tomorrow, toward evening, go to the place where you hid before, and wait

20:16 Hebrew *with the house of David.*

I BELIEVE God's Spirit can overcome those who are seeking to hurt his people. (19:20)

I GO to godly, committed friends for help when I am in trouble. (20:1)

I AM EAGER to help my friends when they are in trouble. (20:4)

I DO NOT BETRAY my friends to their enemies. (20:9)

I TREAT my friends' families with the faithful love of the Lord. (20:15)

I REAFFIRM my love and commitment to my friends. (20:17)

I MAKE plans to ensure my friend's safety if he or she is in danger. (20:18) there by the stone pile.* ²⁰I will come out and shoot three arrows to the side of the stone pile as though I were shooting at a target. ²¹Then I will send a boy to bring the arrows back. If you hear me tell him, 'They're on this side,' then you will know, as surely as the LORD lives, that all is well, and there is no trouble. ²²But if I tell him, 'Go farther—the arrows are still ahead of you,' then it will mean that you must leave immediately, for the LORD is sending you away. ²³And may the LORD make us keep our promises to each other, for he has witnessed them."

²⁴So David hid himself in the field, and when the new moon festival began, the king sat down to eat. ²⁵He sat at his usual place against the wall, with Jonathan sitting opposite him* and Abner beside him. But David's place was empty. ²⁶Saul didn't say anything about it that day, for he said to himself, "Something must have made David ceremonially unclean. Yes, that must be why he's not here." ²⁷But when David's place was empty again the next day, Saul asked Jonathan, "Why hasn't the son of Jesse been here for dinner either yesterday or today?"

²⁸Jonathan replied, "David earnestly asked me if he could go to Bethlehem. ²⁹He wanted to take part in a family sacrifice. His brother demanded that he be there, so I told him he could go. That's why he isn't here."

³⁰Saul boiled with rage at Jonathan. "You stupid son of a whore!"* he swore at him. "Do you think I don't know that you want David to be king in your place, shaming yourself and your mother? ³¹As long as that son of Jesse is alive, you'll never be king. Now go and get him so I can kill him!"

³²"But what has he done?" Jonathan demanded. "Why should he be put to death?" ³³Then Saul hurled his spear at Jonathan, intending to kill him. So at last Jonathan realized that his father was really determined to kill David. ³⁴Jonathan left the table in fierce anger and refused to eat all that day, for he was crushed by his father's shameful behavior toward David.

³⁵The next morning, as agreed, Jonathan went out into the field and took a young boy with him to gather his arrows. ³⁶"Start running," he told the boy, "so you can find the arrows as I shoot them." So the boy ran, and Jonathan shot an arrow beyond him. ³⁷When the boy had almost reached the arrow, Jonathan shouted, "The arrow is still ahead of you. ³⁸Hurry, hurry, don't wait." So the boy quickly gathered up the arrows and ran back to his master. ³⁹He, of course, didn't understand what Jonathan meant; only Jonathan and David knew. ⁴⁰Then Jonathan gave his bow and arrows to the boy and told him to take them back to the city.

⁴¹As soon as the boy was gone, David came out from where he had been hiding near the stone pile.* Then David bowed to Jonathan with his face to the ground. Both of them were in tears as they embraced each other and said good-bye, especially David. ⁴²At last Jonathan said to David, "Go in peace, for we have made a pact in the LORD's name. We have entrusted each other and each other's children into the LORD's hands forever." Then David left, and Jonathan returned to the city.

CHAPTER 21

David Runs from Saul

David went to the city of Nob to see Ahimelech the priest. Ahimelech trembled when he saw him. "Why are you alone?" he asked. "Why is no one with you?"

²"The king has sent me on a private matter," David said. "He told me not to tell anyone why I am here. I have told my men where to meet me later.

I TAKE very seriously the commitments that I make to my friends. (20:23)

I FULFILL my promises to my friends. (20:35)

I ENTRUST my friends and their families into the Lord's hands. (20:42)

I GO to God's people for help when I am in trouble. (21:1)

20:19 Hebrew *the stone Ezel*. The meaning of the Hebrew is uncertain.   20:25 As in Greek version; Hebrew reads *with Jonathan standing*.   20:30 Hebrew *You son of a perverse and rebellious woman*.   20:41 As in Greek version; Hebrew reads *near the south edge*.

³Now, what is there to eat? Give me five loaves of bread or anything else you have."

⁴"We don't have any regular bread," the priest replied. "But there is the holy bread, which I guess you can have if your young men have not slept with any women recently."

⁵"Don't worry," David replied. "I never allow my men to be with women when they are on a campaign. And since they stay clean even on ordinary trips, how much more on this one!"

⁶So, since there was no other food available, the priest gave him the holy bread—the Bread of the Presence that was placed before the LORD in the Tabernacle. It had just been replaced that day with fresh bread.

⁷Now Doeg the Edomite, Saul's chief herdsman, was there that day for ceremonial purification.*

⁸David asked Ahimelech, "Do you have a spear or sword? The king's business was so urgent that I didn't even have time to grab a weapon!"

⁹"I only have the sword of Goliath the Philistine, whom you killed in the valley of Elah," the priest replied. "It is wrapped in a cloth behind the ephod. Take that if you want it, for there is nothing else here."

"There is nothing like it!" David replied. "Give it to me!"

¹⁰So David escaped from Saul and went to King Achish of Gath. ¹¹But Achish's officers weren't happy about his being there. "Isn't this David, the king of the land?" they asked. "Isn't he the one the people honor with dances, singing, 'Saul has killed his thousands, and David his ten thousands'?"

¹²David heard these comments and was afraid of what King Achish might do to him. ¹³So he pretended to be insane, scratching on doors and drooling down his beard. ¹⁴Finally, King Achish said to his men, "Must you bring me a madman? ¹⁵We already have enough of them around here! Why should I let someone like this be my guest?"

CHAPTER 22
David at the Cave of Adullam

So David left Gath and escaped to the cave of Adullam. Soon his brothers and other relatives joined him there. ²Then others began coming—men who were in trouble or in debt or who were just discontented—until David was the leader of about four hundred men.

³Later David went to Mizpeh in Moab, where he asked the king, "Would you let my father and mother live here under royal protection until I know what God is going to do for me?" ⁴The king agreed, and David's parents stayed in Moab while David was living in his stronghold.

⁵One day the prophet Gad told David, "Leave the stronghold and return to the land of Judah." So David went to the forest of Hereth. ⁶The news of his arrival in Judah soon reached Saul. At the time, the king was sitting beneath a tamarisk tree on the hill at Gibeah, holding his spear and surrounded by his officers.

⁷"Listen here, you men of Benjamin!" Saul shouted when he heard the news. "Has David promised you fields and vineyards? Has he promised to make you commanders in his army? ⁸Is that why you have conspired against me? For not one of you has ever told me that my own son is on David's side. You're not even sorry for me. Think of it! My own son—encouraging David to try and kill me!"

⁹Then Doeg the Edomite, who was standing there with Saul's men, spoke up. "When I was at Nob," he said, "I saw David talking to Ahimelech the

I PROVIDE God's servants with what they need when they are in trouble. (21:9)

I USE my wits to keep myself safe in a dangerous situation. (21:13)

I ENSURE the welfare of my aged parents. (22:3)

I GO where God directs me, even if it seems dangerous. (22:5)

I DO NOT LET my own anger rile others against an innocent person. (22:7)

21:7 Hebrew *was detained before the LORD.*

priest. ¹⁰Ahimelech consulted the LORD to find out what David should do. Then he gave David food and the sword of Goliath the Philistine."

The Slaughter of the Priests

¹¹King Saul immediately sent for Ahimelech and all his family, who served as priests at Nob. ¹²When they arrived, Saul shouted at him, "Listen to me, you son of Ahitub!"

"What is it, my king?" Ahimelech asked.

¹³"Why have you and David conspired against me?" Saul demanded. "Why did you give him food and a sword? Why have you inquired of God for him? Why did you encourage him to revolt against me and to come here and attack me?"

¹⁴"But sir," Ahimelech replied, "is there anyone among all your servants who is as faithful as David, your son-in-law? Why, he is the captain of your bodyguard and a highly honored member of your household! ¹⁵This was certainly not the first time I had consulted God for him! Please don't accuse me and my family in this matter, for I knew nothing of any plot against you."

¹⁶"You will surely die, Ahimelech, along with your entire family!" the king shouted. ¹⁷And he ordered his bodyguards, "Kill these priests of the LORD, for they are allies and conspirators with David! They knew he was running away from me, but they didn't tell me!" But Saul's men refused to kill the LORD's priests.

¹⁸Then the king said to Doeg, "You do it." So Doeg turned on them and killed them, eighty-five priests in all, all still wearing their priestly tunics. ¹⁹Then he went to Nob, the city of the priests, and killed the priests' families—men and women, children and babies, and all the cattle, donkeys, and sheep.

²⁰Only Abiathar, one of the sons of Ahimelech, escaped and fled to David. ²¹When he told David that Saul had killed the priests of the LORD, ²²David exclaimed, "I knew it! When I saw Doeg there that day, I knew he would tell Saul. Now I have caused the death of all your father's family. ²³Stay here with me, and I will protect you with my own life, for the same person wants to kill us both."

CHAPTER 23

David Protects the Town of Keilah

One day news came to David that the Philistines were at Keilah stealing grain from the threshing floors. ²David asked the LORD, "Should I go and attack them?"

"Yes, go and save Keilah," the LORD told him.

³But David's men said, "We're afraid even here in Judah. We certainly don't want to go to Keilah to fight the whole Philistine army!"

⁴So David asked the LORD again, and again the LORD replied, "Go down to Keilah, for I will help you conquer the Philistines."

⁵So David and his men went to Keilah. They slaughtered the Philistines and took all their livestock and rescued the people of Keilah. ⁶Abiathar the priest went to Keilah with David, taking the ephod with him to get answers for David from the LORD.

⁷Saul soon learned that David was at Keilah. "Good!" he exclaimed. "We've got him now! God has handed him over to me, for he has trapped himself in a walled city!"

⁸So Saul mobilized his entire army to march to Keilah and attack David and his men. ⁹But David learned of Saul's plan and told Abiathar the priest to bring the ephod and ask the LORD what he should do. ¹⁰And David prayed, "O LORD, God of Israel, I have heard that Saul is planning to come and destroy Keilah because I am here. ¹¹Will the men of Keilah surrender me to

---

I REFUSE to hurt innocent people, even if I am commanded to do so. (22:17)

I TAKE responsibility when my actions inadvertently cause harm to other people. (22:22)

I SEEK God's guidance even more earnestly if people I am leading are fearful. (23:4)

I RESCUE those who are being oppressed. (23:5)

him?* And will Saul actually come as I have heard? O LORD, God of Israel, please tell me."

And the LORD said, "He will come."

[12]Again David asked, "Will these men of Keilah really betray me and my men to Saul?"

And the LORD replied, "Yes, they will betray you."

David Hides in the Wilderness

[13]So David and his men—about six hundred of them now—left Keilah and began roaming the countryside. Word soon reached Saul that David had escaped, so he didn't go to Keilah after all. [14]David now stayed in the strongholds of the wilderness and in the hill country of Ziph. Saul hunted him day after day, but God didn't let him be found.

[15]One day near Horesh, David received the news that Saul was on the way to Ziph to search for him and kill him. [16]Jonathan went to find David and encouraged him to stay strong in his faith in God. [17]"Don't be afraid," Jonathan reassured him. "My father will never find you! You are going to be the king of Israel, and I will be next to you, as my father is well aware." [18]So the two of them renewed their covenant of friendship before the LORD. Then Jonathan returned home, while David stayed at Horesh.

[19]But now the men of Ziph went to Saul in Gibeah and betrayed David to him. "We know where David is hiding," they said. "He is in the strongholds of Horesh on the hill of Hakilah, which is in the southern part of Jeshimon. [20]Come down whenever you're ready, O king, and we will catch him and hand him over to you!"

[21]"The LORD bless you," Saul said. "At last someone is concerned about me! [22]Go and check again to be sure of where he is staying and who has seen him there, for I know that he is very crafty. [23]Discover his hiding places, and come back with a more definite report. Then I'll go with you. And if he is in the area at all, I'll track him down, even if I have to search every hiding place in Judah!"

[24]So the men of Ziph returned home ahead of Saul. Meanwhile, David and his men had moved into the wilderness of Maon in the Arabah Valley south of Jeshimon. [25]When David heard that Saul and his men were searching for him, he went even farther into the wilderness to the great rock, and he remained there in the wilderness of Maon. But Saul kept after him. [26]He and David were now on opposite sides of a mountain. Just as Saul and his men began to close in on David and his men, [27]an urgent message reached Saul that the Philistines were raiding Israel again. [28]So Saul quit the chase and returned to fight the Philistines. Ever since that time, the place where David was camped has been called the Rock of Escape.* [29]David then went to live in the strongholds of En-gedi.

CHAPTER **24**

David Spares Saul's Life

After Saul returned from fighting the Philistines, he was told that David had gone into the wilderness of En-gedi. [2]So Saul chose three thousand special troops from throughout Israel and went to search for David and his men near the rocks of the wild goats. [3]At the place where the road passes some sheepfolds, Saul went into a cave to relieve himself. But as it happened, David and his men were hiding in that very cave!

[4]"Now's your opportunity!" David's men whispered to him. "Today is the day the LORD was talking about when he said, 'I will certainly put Saul into your power, to do with as you wish.'" Then David crept forward and cut off a piece of Saul's robe.

I ENCOURAGE my friends to stay strong in their faith. (23:16)

I AM EAGER for my friends to succeed even more than I have, if that is God's will. (23:17)

I RENEW my covenants of friendship. (23:18)

I DO NOT BETRAY innocent people to their enemies. (23:19)

23:11 Some manuscripts lack the first sentence of 23:11.   **23:28** Hebrew *Sela-hammahlekoth.*

I LISTEN to my conscience when I am tempted. (24:5)

⁵But then David's conscience began bothering him because he had cut Saul's robe. ⁶"The LORD knows I shouldn't have done it," he said to his men. "It is a serious thing to attack the LORD's anointed one, for the LORD himself has chosen him." ⁷So David sharply rebuked his men and did not let them kill Saul.

After Saul had left the cave and gone on his way, ⁸David came out and shouted after him, "My lord the king!" And when Saul looked around, David bowed low before him.

⁹Then he shouted to Saul, "Why do you listen to the people who say I am trying to harm you? ¹⁰This very day you can see with your own eyes it isn't true. For the LORD placed you at my mercy back there in the cave, and some of my men told me to kill you, but I spared you. For I said, 'I will never harm him—he is the LORD's anointed one.' ¹¹Look, my father, at what I have in my hand. It is a piece of your robe! I cut it off, but I didn't kill you. This proves that I am not trying to harm you and that I have not sinned against you, even though you have been hunting for me to kill me. ¹²The LORD will decide between us. Perhaps the LORD will punish you for what you are trying to do to me, but I will never harm you. ¹³As that old proverb says, 'From evil people come evil deeds.' So you can be sure I will never harm you. ¹⁴Who is the king of Israel trying to catch anyway? Should he spend his time chasing one who is as worthless as a dead dog or a flea? ¹⁵May the LORD judge which of us is right and punish the guilty one. He is my advocate, and he will rescue me from your power!"

I LEAVE vengeance to God (Romans 12:19). (24:12)

I TRUST the Lord to show who is right and to punish the one who is guilty. (24:15)

I SHOW godly character by repaying good for evil. (24:17)

¹⁶Saul called back, "Is that really you, my son David?" Then he began to cry. ¹⁷And he said to David, "You are a better man than I am, for you have repaid me good for evil. ¹⁸Yes, you have been wonderfully kind to me today, for when the LORD put me in a place where you could have killed me, you didn't do it. ¹⁹Who else would let his enemy get away when he had him in his power? May the LORD reward you well for the kindness you have shown me today. ²⁰And now I realize that you are surely going to be king, and Israel will flourish under your rule. ²¹Now, swear to me by the LORD that when that happens you will not kill my family and destroy my line of descendants!"

²²So David promised, and Saul went home. But David and his men went back to their stronghold.

CHAPTER 25

The Death of Samuel

Now Samuel died, and all Israel gathered for his funeral. They buried him near his home at Ramah.

Nabal Angers David

Then David moved down to the wilderness of Maon.* ²There was a wealthy man from Maon who owned property near the village of Carmel. He had three thousand sheep and a thousand goats, and it was sheep-shearing time. ³This man's name was Nabal, and his wife, Abigail, was a sensible and beautiful woman. But Nabal, a descendant of Caleb, was mean and dishonest in all his dealings.

I CAN BE an honest, good person, even if my spouse is not. (25:3)

See Caleb's profile (page 265) at Joshua 14:12.

⁴When David heard that Nabal was shearing his sheep, ⁵he sent ten of his young men to Carmel. He told them to deliver this message: ⁶"Peace and prosperity to you, your family, and everything you own! ⁷I am told that you are shearing your sheep and goats. While your shepherds stayed among us near Carmel, we never harmed them, and nothing was ever stolen from them. ⁸Ask your own servants, and they will tell you this is true. So would you please be kind to us, since we have come at a time of celebration? Please give

25:1 As in Greek version; Hebrew reads *Paran.*

us any provisions you might have on hand." ⁹David's young men gave this message to Nabal and waited for his reply.

¹⁰"Who is this fellow David?" Nabal sneered. "Who does this son of Jesse think he is? There are lots of servants these days who run away from their masters. ¹¹Should I take my bread and water and the meat I've slaughtered for my shearers and give it to a band of outlaws who come from who knows where?" ¹²So David's messengers returned and told him what Nabal had said.

¹³"Get your swords!" was David's reply as he strapped on his own. Four hundred men started off with David, and two hundred remained behind to guard their equipment.

¹⁴Meanwhile, one of Nabal's servants went to Abigail and told her, "David sent men from the wilderness to talk to our master, and he insulted them. ¹⁵But David's men were very good to us, and we never suffered any harm from them. Nothing was stolen from us the whole time they were with us. ¹⁶In fact, day and night they were like a wall of protection to us and the sheep. ¹⁷You'd better think fast, for there is going to be trouble for our master and his whole family. He's so ill-tempered that no one can even talk to him!"

¹⁸Abigail lost no time. She quickly gathered two hundred loaves of bread, two skins of wine, five dressed sheep, nearly a bushel* of roasted grain, one hundred raisin cakes, and two hundred fig cakes. She packed them on donkeys and said to her servants, ¹⁹"Go on ahead. I will follow you shortly." But she didn't tell her husband what she was doing.

²⁰As she was riding her donkey into a mountain ravine, she saw David and his men coming toward her. ²¹David had just been saying, "A lot of good it did to help this fellow. We protected his flocks in the wilderness, and nothing he owned was lost or stolen. But he has repaid me evil for good. ²²May God deal with me severely if even one man of his household is still alive tomorrow morning!"

Abigail Intercedes for Nabal

²³When Abigail saw David, she quickly got off her donkey and bowed low before him. ²⁴She fell at his feet and said, "I accept all blame in this matter, my lord. Please listen to what I have to say. ²⁵I know Nabal is a wicked and ill-tempered man; please don't pay any attention to him. He is a fool, just as his name suggests.* But I never even saw the messengers you sent.

²⁶"Now, my lord, as surely as the LORD lives and you yourself live, since the LORD has kept you from murdering and taking vengeance into your own hands, let all your enemies be as cursed as Nabal is. ²⁷And here is a present I have brought to you and your young men. ²⁸Please forgive me if I have offended in any way. The LORD will surely reward you with a lasting dynasty, for you are fighting the LORD's battles. And you have not done wrong throughout your entire life.

²⁹"Even when you are chased by those who seek your life, you are safe in the care of the LORD your God, secure in his treasure pouch! But the lives of your enemies will disappear like stones shot from a sling! ³⁰When the LORD has done all he promised and has made you leader of Israel, ³¹don't let this be a blemish on your record. Then you won't have to carry on your conscience the staggering burden of needless bloodshed and vengeance. And when the LORD has done these great things for you, please remember me!"

³²David replied to Abigail, "Praise the LORD, the God of Israel, who has sent you to meet me today! ³³Thank God for your good sense! Bless you for keeping me from murdering the man and carrying out vengeance with my own hands. ³⁴For I swear by the LORD, the God of Israel, who has kept me from hurting you, that if you had not hurried out to meet me, not one of

25:18 Hebrew 5 seahs [30 liters].   25:25 The name Nabal means "fool."

I DO NOT TREAT those who have helped me in a contemptuous, rude way. (25:10)

I DO NOT REACT in instant anger to those who treat me rudely after I have been kind to them. (25:13)

I ACT quickly when people's lives are in danger. (25:18)

I APPROACH people humbly when they are honestly offended and angry. (25:23)

I EXHORT God's servants to keep from sin. (25:31)

I WELCOME the person who exhorts me not to sin against God. (25:32)

I DO NOT KEEP foolish vows that would hurt others. (25:34)

Nabal's men would be alive tomorrow morning." ³⁵Then David accepted her gifts and told her, "Return home in peace. We will not kill your husband."

³⁶When Abigail arrived home, she found that Nabal had thrown a big party and was celebrating like a king. He was very drunk, so she didn't tell him anything about her meeting with David until the next morning. ³⁷The next morning when he was sober, she told him what had happened. As a result he had a stroke,* and he lay on his bed paralyzed. ³⁸About ten days later, the LORD struck him and he died.

David Marries Abigail

³⁹When David heard that Nabal was dead, he said, "Praise the LORD, who has paid back Nabal and kept me from doing it myself. Nabal has received the punishment for his sin." Then David wasted no time in sending messengers to Abigail to ask her to become his wife.

⁴⁰When the messengers arrived at Carmel, they told Abigail, "David has sent us to ask if you will marry him."

⁴¹She bowed low to the ground and responded, "Yes, I am even willing to become a slave to David's servants!" ⁴²Quickly getting ready, she took along five of her servant girls as attendants, mounted her donkey, and went with David's messengers. And so she became his wife. ⁴³David also married Ahinoam from Jezreel, making both of them his wives. ⁴⁴Saul, meanwhile, had given his daughter Michal, David's wife, to a man from Gallim named Palti son of Laish.

CHAPTER 26

David Spares Saul Again

Now some messengers from Ziph came back to Saul at Gibeah to tell him, "David is hiding on the hill of Hakilah, which overlooks Jeshimon." ²So Saul took three thousand of his best troops and went to hunt him down in the wilderness of Ziph. ³Saul camped along the road beside the hill of Hakilah, near Jeshimon, where David was hiding. But David knew of Saul's arrival, ⁴so he sent out spies to watch his movements.

⁵David slipped over to Saul's camp one night to look around. Saul and his general, Abner son of Ner, were sleeping inside a ring formed by the slumbering warriors. ⁶"Will anyone volunteer to go in there with me?" David asked Ahimelech the Hittite and Abishai son of Zeruiah, Joab's brother.

"I'll go with you," Abishai replied. ⁷So David and Abishai went right into Saul's camp and found him asleep, with his spear stuck in the ground beside his head. Abner and the warriors were lying asleep around him. ⁸"God has surely handed your enemy over to you this time!" Abishai whispered to David. "Let me thrust that spear through him. I'll pin him to the ground, and I won't need to strike twice!"

⁹"No!" David said. "Don't kill him. For who can remain innocent after attacking the LORD's anointed one? ¹⁰Surely the LORD will strike Saul down someday, or he will die in battle or of old age. ¹¹But the LORD forbid that I should kill the one he has anointed! But I'll tell you what—we'll take his spear and his jug of water and then get out of here!"

¹²So David took the spear and jug of water that were near Saul's head. Then he and Abishai got away without anyone seeing them or even waking up, because the LORD had put Saul's men into a deep sleep. ¹³David climbed the hill opposite the camp until he was at a safe distance. ¹⁴Then he shouted down to Abner and Saul, "Wake up, Abner!"

"Who is it?" Abner demanded.

¹⁵"Well, Abner, you're a great man, aren't you?" David taunted. "Where in all Israel is there anyone as mighty? So why haven't you guarded your master

---

I AM CAUTIOUS when dealing with those who are ill-tempered or drunk. (25:36)

I DO NOT ATTACK and hurt those who are against me just because I have the opportunity to do so. (26:9)

Today what example(s) are you choosing to heed?

25:37 Hebrew *his heart failed him.*

the king when someone came to kill him? [16]This isn't good at all! I swear by the LORD that you and your men deserve to die, because you failed to protect your master, the LORD's anointed! Look around! Where are the king's spear and the jug of water that were beside his head?"

[17]Saul recognized David's voice and called out, "Is that you, my son David?"

LIKE ABIGAIL
1 Samuel 25:31

I appeal to other believers to resist sinful choices and continue in godliness.

If Abigail held public office today, she probably would be suited best for secretary of state.

Living with an ill-tempered husband, Abigail had plenty of opportunity to sharpen her conflict resolution skills. When Abigail heard that David and his men were on their way to take revenge on her husband, Nabal, and their household for his insolence, it probably wasn't the first time she had to think fast to keep her household safe.

Fortunately, not only was Abigail a quick thinker, she also was a wise communicator. She knew when to speak and when to keep quiet. Most important, she knew how to speak to the heart of a man of God.

Abigail brought gifts and apologies when she met David on the road. But it wasn't the bread or wine, the lamb chops or raisin and fig cakes that diverted him from his course of vengeance on Abigail's husband. Abigail appealed to David by reminding him that he was God's man. After all that the Lord had done to keep him safe, did he want to take vengeance himself? When God repaid David's enemies and made him leader in Israel, did he really want needless bloodshed on his hands and conscience?

David quickly dropped his vow of vengeance when confronted with Abigail's appeal. As a man after God's heart, he recognized that he wanted to be right with God more than he wanted to get even with Nabal. Because of her wise words, he forsook his sinful plan and submitted to God's control.

Where would David have been if Bathsheba had responded as Abigail had? Bathsheba's simple, "Don't do it, David," might have diverted him from another sinful course.

You and I are commanded by God to help other believers make right choices and get back onto the right path when they have sinned (Galatians 6:1). Why? Because, like Abigail, we'll save them from untold grief (James 5:19-20).

○ Today's Scripture reading is 1 Samuel 25.

And David replied, "Yes, my lord the king. [18]Why are you chasing me? What have I done? What is my crime? [19]But now let my lord the king listen to his servant. If the LORD has stirred you up against me, then let him accept my offering. But if this is simply a human scheme, then may those involved be cursed by the LORD. For you have driven me from my home, so I can no longer live among the LORD's people and worship as I should. [20]Must I die on foreign soil, far from the presence of the LORD? Why has the king of Israel come out to search for a single flea? Why does he hunt me down like a partridge on the mountains?"

I MOURN when I am prevented from worshiping God with his people. (26:19)

[21]Then Saul confessed, "I have sinned. Come back home, my son, and I will no longer try to harm you, for you valued my life today. I have been a fool and very, very wrong."

I QUICKLY ADMIT my foolish actions. (26:21)

[22]"Here is your spear, O king," David replied. "Let one of your young men come over and get it. [23]The LORD gives his own reward for doing good and for being loyal, and I refused to kill you even when the LORD placed you in my power, for you are the LORD's anointed one. [24]Now may the LORD value my life, even as I have valued yours today. May he rescue me from all my troubles."

I PROVE by my actions that I have no intent to hurt another person. (26:23)

²⁵And Saul said to David, "Blessings on you, my son David. You will do heroic deeds and be a great conqueror." Then David went away, and Saul returned home.

CHAPTER 27
David among the Philistines

I DO NOT RUN to God's enemies for help when I am in trouble. (27:1)

But David kept thinking to himself, "Someday Saul is going to get me. The best thing for me to do is escape to the Philistines. Then Saul will stop hunting for me, and I will finally be safe."

²So David took his six hundred men and their families and went to live at Gath under the protection of King Achish. ³David brought his two wives along with him—Ahinoam of Jezreel and Abigail of Carmel, Nabal's widow. ⁴Word soon reached Saul that David had fled to Gath, so he stopped hunting for him.

⁵One day David said to Achish, "If it is all right with you, we would rather live in one of the country towns instead of here in the royal city." ⁶So Achish gave him the town of Ziklag (which still belongs to the kings of Judah to this day), ⁷and they lived there among the Philistines for a year and four months.

⁸David and his men spent their time raiding the Geshurites, the Girzites, and the Amalekites—people who had lived near Shur, along the road to Egypt, since ancient times. ⁹David didn't leave one person alive in the villages he attacked. He took the sheep, cattle, donkeys, camels, and clothing before returning home to see King Achish.

¹⁰"Where did you make your raid today?" Achish would ask.

And David would reply, "Against the south of Judah, the Jerahmeelites, and the Kenites."

¹¹No one was left alive to come to Gath and tell where he had really been. This happened again and again while he was living among the Philistines. ¹²Achish believed David and thought to himself, "By now the people of Israel must hate him bitterly. Now he will have to stay here and serve me forever!"

CHAPTER 28
Saul Consults a Medium

About that time the Philistines mustered their armies for another war with Israel. King Achish told David, "You and your men will be expected to join me in battle."

²"Very well!" David agreed. "Now you will see for yourself what we can do."

Then Achish told David, "I will make you my personal bodyguard for life."

I DO NOT USE occult practices to find answers to my questions. (28:3)

³Meanwhile, Samuel had died, and all Israel had mourned for him. He was buried in Ramah, his hometown. And Saul had banned all mediums and psychics from the land of Israel.

I KNOW the Lord may not answer my prayers if I persist in disobedience to him. (28:6)

⁴The Philistines set up their camp at Shunem, and Saul and the armies of Israel camped at Gilboa. ⁵When Saul saw the vast Philistine army, he became frantic with fear. ⁶He asked the LORD what he should do, but the LORD refused to answer him, either by dreams or by sacred lots* or by the prophets. ⁷Saul then said to his advisers, "Find a woman who is a medium, so I can go and ask her what to do."

His advisers replied, "There is a medium at Endor."

⁸So Saul disguised himself by wearing ordinary clothing instead of his royal robes. Then he went to the woman's home at night, accompanied by two of his men.

"I have to talk to a man who has died," he said. "Will you call up his spirit for me?"

28:6 Hebrew *by Urim.*

⁹"Are you trying to get me killed?" the woman demanded. "You know that Saul has expelled all the mediums and psychics from the land. Why are you setting a trap for me?"

¹⁰But Saul took an oath in the name of the LORD and promised, "As surely as the LORD lives, nothing bad will happen to you for doing this."

¹¹Finally, the woman said, "Well, whose spirit do you want me to call up?"

"Call up Samuel," Saul replied.

¹²When the woman saw Samuel, she screamed, "You've deceived me! You are Saul!"

¹³"Don't be afraid!" the king told her. "What do you see?"

"I see a god* coming up out of the earth," she said.

¹⁴"What does he look like?" Saul asked.

"He is an old man wrapped in a robe," she replied. Saul realized that it was Samuel, and he fell to the ground before him.

¹⁵"Why have you disturbed me by calling me back?" Samuel asked.

"Because I am in deep trouble," Saul replied. "The Philistines are at war with us, and God has left me and won't reply by prophets or dreams. So I have called for you to tell me what to do."

¹⁶But Samuel replied, "Why ask me if the LORD has left you and has become your enemy? ¹⁷The LORD has done just as he said he would. He has taken the kingdom from you and given it to your rival, David. ¹⁸The LORD has done this because you did not obey his instructions concerning the Amalekites. ¹⁹What's more, the LORD will hand you and the army of Israel over to the Philistines tomorrow, and you and your sons will be here with me. The LORD will bring the entire army of Israel down in defeat."

²⁰Saul fell full length on the ground, paralyzed with fright because of Samuel's words. He was also faint with hunger, for he had eaten nothing all day and all night. ²¹When the woman saw how distraught he was, she said, "Sir, I obeyed your command at the risk of my life. ²²Now do what I say, and let me give you something to eat so you can regain your strength for the trip back."

²³But Saul refused. The men who were with him also urged him to eat, so he finally yielded and got up from the ground and sat on the couch. ²⁴The woman had been fattening a calf, so she hurried out and killed it. She kneaded dough and baked unleavened bread. ²⁵She brought the meal to Saul and his men, and they ate it. Then they went out into the night.

CHAPTER 29

The Philistines Reject David

The entire Philistine army now mobilized at Aphek, and the Israelites camped at the spring in Jezreel. ²As the Philistine rulers were leading out their troops in groups of one hundred and one thousand, David and his men marched at the rear with King Achish. ³But the Philistine commanders demanded, "What are these Hebrews doing here?"

And Achish told them, "This is David, the man who ran away from King Saul of Israel. He's been with me for years, and I've never found a single fault in him since he defected to me."

⁴But the Philistine commanders were angry. "Send him back!" they demanded. "He can't go into the battle with us. What if he turns against us? Is there any better way for him to reconcile himself with his master than by turning on us in battle? ⁵Isn't this the same David about whom the women of Israel sing in their dances, 'Saul has killed his thousands, and David his ten thousands'?"

⁶So Achish finally summoned David and his men. "I swear by the LORD," he told them, "you are some of the finest men I've ever met. I think you

I DO NOT ATTEMPT to communicate with the dead. (28:15)

I BELIEVE the Lord rejected Saul as king because he disobeyed and refused to destroy the Amalekites as God commanded. (28:18)

I GIVE physical nourishment to those who are traumatized and depressed. (28:22)

I DEMONSTRATE good character even among unbelievers. (29:3)

28:13 Or *gods*.

should go with us, but the other Philistine rulers won't hear of it. ⁷Please don't upset them, but go back quietly."

⁸"What have I done to deserve this treatment?" David demanded. "Why can't I fight the enemies of my lord, the king?"

⁹But Achish insisted, "As far as I'm concerned, you're as perfect as an angel of God. But my commanders are afraid to have you with them in the battle. ¹⁰Now get up early in the morning, and leave with your men as soon as it gets light." ¹¹So David headed back into the land of the Philistines, while the Philistine army went on to Jezreel.

CHAPTER 30

David Destroys the Amalekites

Three days later, when David and his men arrived home at their town of Ziklag, they found that the Amalekites had made a raid into the Negev and had burned Ziklag to the ground. ²They had carried off the women and children, and everyone else but without killing anyone. ³When David and his men saw the ruins and realized what had happened to their families, ⁴they wept until they could weep no more. ⁵David's two wives, Ahinoam of Jezreel and Abigail, the widow of Nabal of Carmel, were among those captured. ⁶David was now in serious trouble because his men were very bitter about losing their wives and children, and they began to talk of stoning him. But David found strength in the LORD his God.

⁷Then he said to Abiathar the priest, "Bring me the ephod!" So Abiathar brought it. ⁸Then David asked the LORD, "Should I chase them? Will I catch them?"

And the LORD told him, "Yes, go after them. You will surely recover everything that was taken from you!" ⁹So David and his six hundred men set out, and they soon came to Besor Brook. ¹⁰But two hundred of the men were too exhausted to cross the brook, so David continued the pursuit with his four hundred remaining troops.

¹¹Some of David's troops found an Egyptian man in a field and brought him to David. They gave him some bread to eat and some water to drink. ¹²They also gave him part of a fig cake and two clusters of raisins because he hadn't had anything to eat or drink for three days and nights. It wasn't long before his strength returned.

¹³"To whom do you belong, and where do you come from?" David asked him.

"I am an Egyptian—the slave of an Amalekite," he replied. "My master left me behind three days ago because I was sick. ¹⁴We were on our way back from raiding the Kerethites in the Negev, the territory of Judah, and the land of Caleb, and we had just burned Ziklag."

¹⁵"Will you lead me to them?" David asked.

The young man replied, "If you swear by God's name that you will not kill me or give me back to my master, then I will guide you to them."

¹⁶So the Egyptian led them to the Amalekite encampment. When David and his men arrived, the Amalekites were spread out across the fields, eating and drinking and dancing with joy because of the vast amount of plunder they had taken from the Philistines and the land of Judah. ¹⁷David and his men rushed in among them and slaughtered them throughout that night and the entire next day until evening. None of the Amalekites escaped except four hundred young men who fled on camels. ¹⁸David got back everything the Amalekites had taken, and he rescued his two wives. ¹⁹Nothing was missing: small or great, son or daughter, nor anything else that had been taken. David brought everything back. ²⁰His troops rounded up all the flocks and herds and drove them on ahead. "These all belong to David as his reward!" they said.

I BELIEVE the Lord will provide a way of escape when it appears that I am about to be forced to sin. (29:10)

I FIND strength in the Lord when people are turning against me. (30:6)

I DO all that I can to rescue my family and others from mistreatment. (30:9)

I GIVE physical nourishment to those who are hungry. (30:11)

See Caleb's profile (page 265) at Joshua 14:12.

[21]When they reached Besor Brook and met the two hundred men who had been too tired to go with them, David greeted them joyfully. [22]But some trouble-makers among David's men said, "They didn't go with us, so they can't have any of the plunder. Give them their wives and children, and tell them to be gone."

[23]But David said, "No, my brothers! Don't be selfish with what the LORD has given us. He has kept us safe and helped us defeat the enemy. [24]Do you think anyone will listen to you when you talk like this? We share and share alike—those who go to battle and those who guard the equipment." [25]From then on David made this a law for all of Israel, and it is still followed.

[26]When he arrived at Ziklag, David sent part of the plunder to the leaders of Judah, who were his friends. "Here is a present for you, taken from the LORD's enemies," he said. [27]The gifts were sent to the leaders of the following towns where David and his men had been: Bethel, Ramoth-negev, Jattir, [28]Aroer, Siphmoth, Eshtemoa, [29]Racal,* the towns of the Jerahmeelites, the towns of the Kenites, [30]Hormah, Bor-ashan, Athach, [31]Hebron, and all the other places they had visited.

CHAPTER 31
The Death of Saul

Now the Philistines attacked Israel, forcing the Israelites to flee. Many were slaughtered on the slopes of Mount Gilboa. [2]The Philistines closed in on Saul and his sons, and they killed three of his sons—Jonathan, Abinadab, and Malkishua. [3]The fighting grew very fierce around Saul, and the Philistine archers caught up with him and wounded him severely. [4]Saul groaned to his armor bearer, "Take your sword and kill me before these pagan Philistines run me through and humiliate me." But his armor bearer was afraid and would not do it. So Saul took his own sword and fell on it. [5]When his armor bearer realized that Saul was dead, he fell on his own sword and died beside the king. [6]So Saul, three of his sons, his armor bearer, and his troops all died together that same day.

[7]When the Israelites on the other side of the Jezreel Valley and beyond the Jordan saw that their army had been routed and that Saul and his sons were dead, they abandoned their towns and fled. So the Philistines moved in and occupied their towns.

[8]The next day, when the Philistines went out to strip the dead, they found the bodies of Saul and his three sons on Mount Gilboa. [9]So they cut off Saul's head and stripped off his armor. Then they proclaimed the news of Saul's death in their pagan temple and to the people throughout the land of Philistia. [10]They placed his armor in the temple of the Ashtoreths, and they fastened his body to the wall of the city of Beth-shan.

[11]But when the people of Jabesh-gilead heard what the Philistines had done to Saul, [12]their warriors traveled all night to Beth-shan and took the bodies of Saul and his sons down from the wall. They brought them to Jabesh, where they burned the bodies. [13]Then they took their remains and buried them beneath the tamarisk tree at Jabesh, and they fasted for seven days.

30:29 Greek version reads *Carmel.*

I AM NOT SELFISH regarding God's provision. (30:22)

I SHARE equally between those who serve the Lord in the front lines and those who serve him behind the scenes. (30:24)

I BELIEVE Saul and his sons died in battle, just as the Lord said they would. (31:2)

I WILL NOT ASSIST a person in taking his or her life. (31:4)

I SHOW reverence for the deceased bodies of those who die in battle. (31:11)

2 SAMUEL

THIS FIFTH BOOK of Israelite history is filled with *contradictions*.

The story of David's reign as Israel's second and most beloved king isn't sugarcoated or air-brushed. Instead, it's quite matter-of-fact about his best and worst days.

This extended account of David's reign begins with a more complete report of Saul's death (1:1-27) and a realistic summary of the nation's political throes before David's coronation in the new capital city of Hebron (2:1-5:5). In the end, David is widely acclaimed as Israel's rightful king.

After David's coronation, he moves Israel's political capital to the city of Jerusalem and moves the religious center there, too (5:6-7:29). During this time David becomes renowned as a man after God's heart.

After this David defeats Israel's enemies on every side (8:1-10:19). One spring, however, David stays in Jerusalem, sending the armies out under the commander of the army, Joab. That same spring, David breaks half of the Ten Commandments while pursuing an adulterous affair. The prophet Nathan rebukes David, who repents (11:1-12:31). Still, David brings great shame and dishonor on himself.

In the aftermath of David's rebellious affair, his children rebel, bringing greater shame on the Davidic dynasty and provoking both revolt and civil war (13:1-20:26). David regains control of the kingdom, but only after suffering great personal losses.

Parallel accounts of David's forty-year reign can be found in 1 Chronicles 10-29, which focus primarily on David's preparations to build a Temple for the Lord in Jerusalem.

This book concludes with several appendixes showing David at his best and worst (21:1-24:25).

The stories of the kings who follow David over the next four hundred years are told in 1 and 2 Kings and in 2 Chronicles.

Famous passages in 2 Samuel include
- David's lament over the death of Saul and Jonathan (1:17-27)
- David's bringing of the Ark of the Covenant to Jerusalem (6:1-19)
- The Lord's great promises to David (7:8-16)
- David's praise of the Lord for his great promises (7:18-29)
- "The LORD gave David victory wherever he went" (8:6, 14)
- David's kindness to Jonathan's son (9:1-13)
- David's adulterous affair with Bathsheba (11:1-27)
- Nathan's rebuke of David (12:1-14)
- David's son Ammon's committing of incest (13:1-19)
- David's son Absalom's murder of Ammon and later revolt (13:20-18:33)
- Absolom's death (18:1-17)
- The Israelites' battles against the Philistine giants (21:15-22)
- David's song of praise (22:1-51)
- David's last words (23:1-7)
- David's mighty men (23:8-39)
- David's census and the plague that followed (24:1-25)

CHAPTER 1

David Learns of Saul's Death

See the profiles for Saul (page 339) and David (page 629) at 1 Samuel 18:9 and Psalm 3:1.

After the death of Saul, David returned from his victory over the Amalekites and spent two days in Ziklag. ²On the third day after David's return, a man arrived from the Israelite battlefront. He had torn his clothes and put dirt on his head to show that he was in mourning. He fell to the ground before David in deep respect.

³"Where have you come from?" David asked.

"I escaped from the Israelite camp," the man replied.

⁴"What happened?" David demanded. "Tell me how the battle went."

The man replied, "Our entire army fled. Many men are dead and wounded on the battlefield, and Saul and his son Jonathan have been killed."

⁵"How do you know that Saul and Jonathan are dead?" David demanded.

⁶The young man answered, "I happened to be on Mount Gilboa. I saw Saul there leaning on his spear with the enemy chariots closing in on him. ⁷When he turned and saw me, he cried out for me to come to him. 'How can I help?' I asked him. ⁸And he said to me, 'Who are you?' I replied, 'I am an Amalekite.' ⁹Then he begged me, 'Come over here and put me out of my misery, for I am in terrible pain and want to die.'

¹⁰"So I killed him," the Amalekite told David, "for I knew he couldn't live. Then I took his crown and one of his bracelets so I could bring them to you, my lord."

¹¹David and his men tore their clothes in sorrow when they heard the news. ¹²They mourned and wept and fasted all day for Saul and his son Jonathan, and for the LORD's army and the nation of Israel, because so many had died that day. ¹³Then David said to the young man who had brought the news, "Where are you from?"

And he replied, "I am a foreigner, an Amalekite, who lives in your land."

¹⁴"Were you not afraid to kill the LORD's anointed one?" David asked. ¹⁵Then David said to one of his men, "Kill him!" So the man thrust his sword into the Amalekite and killed him. ¹⁶"You die self-condemned," David said, "for you yourself confessed that you killed the LORD's anointed one."

David's Song for Saul and Jonathan

¹⁷Then David composed a funeral song for Saul and Jonathan. ¹⁸Later he commanded that it be taught to all the people of Judah. It is known as the Song of the Bow, and it is recorded in *The Book of Jashar*.*

¹⁹Your pride and joy, O Israel, lies dead on the hills!
How the mighty heroes have fallen!
²⁰Don't announce the news in Gath,
or the Philistines will rejoice.
Don't proclaim it in the streets of Ashkelon,
or the pagans will laugh in triumph.

²¹O mountains of Gilboa,
let there be no dew or rain upon you or your slopes.
For there the shield of the mighty was defiled;
the shield of Saul will no longer be anointed with oil.
²²Both Saul and Jonathan killed their strongest foes;
they did not return from battle empty-handed.

²³How beloved and gracious were Saul and Jonathan!
They were together in life and in death.
They were swifter than eagles;
they were stronger than lions.

I DO NOT USE tragic circumstances for my own benefit. (1:7)

I JOIN others in mourning national tragedies. (1:12)

I LEAD others in mourning and in remembering leaders of God's people, whether they were my friends or enemies. (1:17)

I RECOGNIZE and honor the strengths and qualities of others. (1:22)

1:18 Or *The Book of the Upright*.

²⁴O women of Israel, weep for Saul,
for he dressed you in fine clothing and gold ornaments.

²⁵How the mighty heroes have fallen in battle!
Jonathan lies dead upon the hills.
²⁶How I weep for you, my brother Jonathan!
Oh, how much I loved you!
And your love for me was deep,
deeper than the love of women!

²⁷How the mighty heroes have fallen!
Stripped of their weapons, they lie dead.

CHAPTER 2

David Anointed King of Judah

After this, David asked the LORD, "Should I move back to Judah?"
And the LORD replied, "Yes."
Then David asked, "Which town should I go to?"
And the LORD replied, "Hebron."

²David's wives were Ahinoam from Jezreel and Abigail, the widow of Nabal from Carmel. So David and his wives ³and his men and their families all moved to Judah, and they settled near the town of Hebron. ⁴Then Judah's leaders came to David and crowned him king over the tribe of Judah.

When David heard that the men of Jabesh-gilead had buried Saul, ⁵he sent them this message: "May the LORD bless you for being so loyal to your king and giving him a decent burial. ⁶May the LORD be loyal to you in return and reward you with his unfailing love! And I, too, will reward you for what you have done. ⁷And now that Saul is dead, I ask you to be my strong and loyal subjects like the people of Judah, who have anointed me as their new king."

Ishbosheth Crowned King of Israel

⁸But Abner son of Ner, the commander of Saul's army, had already gone to Mahanaim with Saul's son Ishbosheth.* ⁹There he proclaimed Ishbosheth king over Gilead, Jezreel, Ephraim, Benjamin, the land of the Ashurites, and all the rest of Israel. ¹⁰Ishbosheth was forty years old when he became king, and he ruled from Mahanaim for two years. Meanwhile, the tribe of Judah remained loyal to David. ¹¹David made Hebron his capital, and he ruled as king of Judah for seven and a half years.

War between Israel and Judah

¹²One day Abner led some of Ishbosheth's troops from Mahanaim to Gibeon. ¹³About the same time, Joab son of Zeruiah led David's troops from Hebron, and they met Abner at the pool of Gibeon. The two groups sat down there, facing each other from opposite sides of the pool. ¹⁴Then Abner suggested to Joab, "Let's have a few of our warriors put on an exhibition of hand-to-hand combat."

"All right," Joab agreed. ¹⁵So twelve men were chosen from each side to fight against each other. ¹⁶Each one grabbed his opponent by the hair and thrust his sword into the other's side so that all of them died. The place has been known ever since as the Field of Swords.* ¹⁷The two armies then began to fight each other, and by the end of the day Abner and the men of Israel had been defeated by the forces of David.

The Death of Asahel

¹⁸Joab, Abishai, and Asahel, the three sons of Zeruiah, were among David's forces that day. Asahel could run like a deer, ¹⁹and he began chasing Abner.

2:8 Also known as *Eshbaal.*   2:16 Hebrew *Helkath-hazzurim.*

I CREDIT others for the good they have done, even if they have also done harm to me. (1:24)

I PUBLICLY EXPRESS my love for a friend who has died. (1:26)

I SEEK the Lord's direction. (2:1)

See Abigail's profile (page 349) at 1 Samuel 25:31.

I ACCEPT the leadership responsibilities bestowed on me by God. (2:4)

I REWARD those who are loyal and respectful to their deceased leaders. (2:6)

I DO NOT RUSH blindly into danger. (2:19)

He was relentless and single-minded in his pursuit. ²⁰When Abner looked back and saw him coming, he called out, "Is that you, Asahel?"

"Yes, it is," he replied.

²¹"Go fight someone else!" Abner warned. "Take on one of the younger men and strip him of his weapons." But Asahel refused and kept right on chasing Abner.

²²Again Abner shouted to him, "Get away from here! I will never be able to face your brother Joab if I have to kill you!" ²³But Asahel would not give up, so Abner thrust the butt end of his spear through Asahel's stomach, and the spear came out through his back. He stumbled to the ground and died there. And everyone who came by that spot stopped and stood still when they saw Asahel lying there.

²⁴When Joab and Abishai found out what had happened, they set out after Abner. The sun was just going down as they arrived at the hill of Ammah near Giah, along the road to the wilderness of Gibeon. ²⁵Abner's troops from the tribe of Benjamin regrouped there at the top of the hill to take a stand. ²⁶Abner shouted down to Joab, "Must we always solve our differences with swords? Don't you realize the only thing we will gain is bitterness toward each other? When will you call off your men from chasing their Israelite brothers?"

²⁷Then Joab said, "God only knows what would have happened if you hadn't spoken, for we would have chased you all night if necessary." ²⁸So Joab blew his trumpet, and his men stopped chasing the troops of Israel.

²⁹All that night Abner and his men retreated through the Jordan Valley.* They crossed the Jordan River, traveling all through the morning,* and they did not stop until they arrived at Mahanaim.

³⁰Meanwhile, Joab and his men also returned home. When Joab counted his casualties, he discovered that only nineteen men were missing, in addition to Asahel. ³¹But three hundred and sixty of Abner's men, all from the tribe of Benjamin, had been killed. ³²Joab and his men took Asahel's body to Bethlehem and buried him there beside his father. Then they traveled all night and reached Hebron at daybreak.

CHAPTER 3

That was the beginning of a long war between those who had been loyal to Saul and those who were loyal to David. As time passed David became stronger and stronger, while Saul's dynasty became weaker and weaker.

David's Sons Born in Hebron

²These were the sons who were born to David in Hebron:

The oldest was Amnon, whose mother was Ahinoam of Jezreel.
³ The second was Kileab, whose mother was Abigail, the widow of Nabal from Carmel.
The third was Absalom, whose mother was Maacah, the daughter of Talmai, king of Geshur.
⁴ The fourth was Adonijah, whose mother was Haggith.
The fifth was Shephatiah, whose mother was Abital.
⁵ The sixth was Ithream, whose mother was David's wife Eglah.

These sons were all born to David in Hebron.

Abner Joins Forces with David

⁶As the war went on, Abner became a powerful leader among those who were loyal to Saul's dynasty. ⁷One day Ishbosheth,* Saul's son, accused Abner of sleeping with one of his father's concubines, a woman named Rizpah. ⁸Abner became furious. "Am I a Judean dog to be kicked around like this?" he

---

I HEED warnings of imminent danger. (2:23)

I IMPLORE others to solve differences peacefully instead of violently. (2:26)

See Amnon's profile (page 369) at 2 Samuel 13:15.

I FOLLOW God's requirements for the family lives of leaders (see Deuteronomy 17:17). (3:3)

See Abigail's profile (page 349) at 1 Samuel 25:31.

I AM CAREFUL to investigate matters before accusing someone who has proven his or her loyalty to me. (3:7)

I DO NOT USE my power and fury to threaten others for my own advantage. (3:8)

2:29a Hebrew *the Arabah.* 2:29b Or *continued on through the Bithron. The meaning of the Hebrew is uncertain.*
3:7 Also known as *Eshbaal.*

shouted. "After all I have done for you and your father by not betraying you to David, is this my reward—that you find fault with me about this woman? ⁹May God deal harshly with me if I don't help David get all that the LORD has promised him! ¹⁰I should just go ahead and give David the rest of Saul's kingdom. I should set him up as king over Israel as well as Judah, from Dan to Beersheba." ¹¹Ishbosheth didn't dare say another word because he was afraid of what Abner might do.

¹²Then Abner sent messengers to David, saying, "Let's make an agreement, and I will help turn the entire nation of Israel over to you."

¹³"All right," David replied, "but I will not negotiate with you unless you bring back my wife Michal, Saul's daughter, when you come."

¹⁴David then sent this message to Ishbosheth, Saul's son: "Give me back my wife Michal, for I bought her with the lives of one hundred Philistines." ¹⁵So Ishbosheth took Michal away from her husband Palti* son of Laish. ¹⁶Palti followed along behind her as far as Bahurim, weeping as he went. Then Abner told him, "Go back home!" So Palti returned.

¹⁷Meanwhile, Abner had consulted with the leaders of Israel. "For some time now," he told them, "you have wanted to make David your king. ¹⁸Now is the time! For the LORD has said, 'I have chosen David to save my people from the Philistines and from all their other enemies.' " ¹⁹Abner also spoke with the leaders of the tribe of Benjamin. Then he went to Hebron to tell David that all the people of Israel and Benjamin supported him.

> I AM WILLING to use my influence to right any wrongs I have committed. (3:19)

²⁰When Abner came to Hebron with his twenty men, David entertained them with a great feast. ²¹Then Abner said to David, "Let me go and call all the people of Israel to your side. They will make a covenant with you to make you their king. Then you will be able to rule over everything your heart desires." So David sent Abner safely on his way.

Joab Murders Abner

²²But just after Abner left, Joab and some of David's troops returned from a raid, bringing much plunder with them. ²³When Joab was told that Abner had just been there visiting the king and had been sent away in safety, ²⁴he rushed to see the king. "What have you done?" he demanded. "What do you mean by letting Abner get away? ²⁵You know perfectly well that he came to spy on you and to discover everything you are doing!"

²⁶Joab then left David and sent messengers to catch up with Abner. They found him at the pool of Sirah and brought him back with them. But David knew nothing about it. ²⁷When Abner arrived at Hebron, Joab took him aside at the gateway as if to speak with him privately. But then he drew his dagger and killed Abner in revenge for killing his brother Asahel.

> I DO NOT TAKE my own vengeance. (3:27)

²⁸When David heard about it, he declared, "I vow by the LORD that I and my people are innocent of this crime against Abner. ²⁹Joab and his family are the guilty ones. May his family in every generation be cursed with a man who has open sores or leprosy* or who walks on crutches* or who dies by the sword or who begs for food!"

> I PUBLICLY OPPOSE a murder of vengeance. (3:28)

³⁰So Joab and his brother Abishai killed Abner because Abner had killed their brother Asahel at the battle of Gibeon.

David Mourns Abner's Death

³¹Then David said to Joab and all those who were with him, "Tear your clothes and put on sackcloth. Go into deep mourning for Abner." And King David himself walked behind the procession to the grave. ³²They buried Abner in Hebron, and the king and all the people wept at his graveside. ³³Then the king sang this funeral song for Abner:

> I PUBLICLY MOURN the one who was murdered out of vengeance. (3:33)

3:15 As in 1 Sam 25:44; Hebrew reads *Paltiel,* a variant name for Palti.   3:29a Or *or a contagious skin disease.* The Hebrew word used here can describe various skin diseases.   3:29b Or *who is effeminate;* Hebrew reads *who handles a spindle.*

"Should Abner have died as fools die?
³⁴Your hands were not bound;
  your feet were not chained.
No, you were murdered—
  the victim of a wicked plot."

All the people wept again for Abner. ³⁵David had refused to eat anything the day of the funeral, and now everyone begged him to eat. But David had made a vow, saying, "May God kill me if I eat anything before sundown." ³⁶This pleased the people very much. In fact, everything the king did pleased them! ³⁷So everyone in Judah and Israel knew that David was not responsible for Abner's death.

³⁸Then King David said to the people, "Do you not realize that a great leader and a great man has fallen today in Israel? ³⁹And even though I am the anointed king, these two sons of Zeruiah—Joab and Abishai—are too strong for me to control. So may the LORD repay these wicked men for their wicked deeds."

CHAPTER 4

The Murder of Ishbosheth

When Ishbosheth* heard about Abner's death at Hebron, he lost all courage, and his people were paralyzed with fear. ²Now there were two brothers, Baanah and Recab, who were captains of Ishbosheth's raiding parties. They were sons of Rimmon, a member of the tribe of Benjamin who lived in Beeroth. The town of Beeroth is now part of Benjamin's territory ³because the original people of Beeroth fled to Gittaim, where they still live as foreigners.

⁴(Saul's son Jonathan had a son named Mephibosheth,* who was crippled as a child. He was five years old when Saul and Jonathan were killed at the battle of Jezreel. When news of the battle reached the capital, the child's nurse grabbed him and fled. But she fell and dropped him as she was running, and he became crippled as a result.)

⁵One day Recab and Baanah, the sons of Rimmon from Beeroth, went to Ishbosheth's home around noon as he was taking a nap. ⁶The doorkeeper, who had been sifting wheat, became drowsy and fell asleep. So Recab and Baanah slipped past the doorkeeper, went into Ishbosheth's bedroom, and stabbed him in the stomach. Then they escaped. ⁷But before leaving, they cut off his head as he lay there on his bed. Taking his head with them, they fled across the Jordan Valley* through the night. ⁸They arrived at Hebron and presented Ishbosheth's head to David. "Look!" they exclaimed. "Here is the head of Ishbosheth, the son of your enemy Saul who tried to kill you. Today the LORD has given you revenge on Saul and his entire family!"

⁹But David said to Recab and Baanah, "As surely as the LORD lives, the one who saves me from my enemies, I will tell you the truth. ¹⁰Once before, someone told me, 'Saul is dead,' thinking he was bringing me good news. But I seized him and killed him at Ziklag. That's the reward I gave him for his news! ¹¹Now what reward should I give the wicked men who have killed an innocent man in his own house and on his own bed? Should I not also demand your very lives?" ¹²So David ordered his young men to kill them, and they did. They cut off their hands and feet and hung their bodies beside the pool in Hebron. Then they took Ishbosheth's head and buried it in Abner's tomb in Hebron.

CHAPTER 5

David Becomes King of All Israel

Then all the tribes of Israel went to David at Hebron and told him, "We are all members of your family. ²For a long time, even while Saul was our king, you were the one who really led Israel. And the LORD has told you, 'You will be the shepherd of my people Israel. You will be their leader.'" ³So there at

I EXPECT that those who act rashly and violently will suffer the consequences of their actions. (3:39)

I TRY to protect children in my care when they are in danger. (4:4)

I DO NOT DESTROY people to impress and gain favor with their opponents. (4:8)

I MAKE a covenant with those who look to me to lead them. (5:3)

4:1 Also known as *Eshbaal*.   4:4 Also known as *Meribbaal*.   4:7 Hebrew *the Arabah*.

Hebron, David made a covenant with the leaders of Israel before the LORD. And they anointed him king of Israel.

⁴David was thirty years old when he began to reign, and he reigned forty years in all. ⁵He had reigned over Judah from Hebron for seven years and six months, and from Jerusalem he reigned over all Israel and Judah for thirty-three years.

David Captures Jerusalem

⁶David then led his troops to Jerusalem to fight against the Jebusites. "You'll never get in here," the Jebusites taunted. "Even the blind and lame could keep you out!" For the Jebusites thought they were safe. ⁷But David captured the fortress of Zion, now called the City of David.

⁸When the insulting message from the defenders of the city reached David, he told his own troops, "Go up through the water tunnel into the city and destroy those 'lame' and 'blind' Jebusites. How I hate them." That is the origin of the saying, "The blind and the lame may not enter the house."* ⁹So David made the fortress his home, and he called it the City of David. He built additional fortifications around the city, starting at the Millo* and working inward. ¹⁰And David became more and more powerful, because the LORD God Almighty was with him.

¹¹Then King Hiram of Tyre sent messengers to David, along with carpenters and stonemasons to build him a palace. Hiram also sent many cedar logs for lumber. ¹²And David realized that the LORD had made him king over Israel and had made his kingdom great for the sake of his people Israel.

¹³After moving from Hebron to Jerusalem, David married more wives and concubines, and he had many sons and daughters. ¹⁴These are the names of David's sons who were born in Jerusalem: Shimea,* Shobab, Nathan, Solomon, ¹⁵Ibhar, Elishua, Nepheg, Japhia, ¹⁶Elishama, Eliada, and Eliphelet.

David Conquers the Philistines

¹⁷When the Philistines heard that David had been anointed king of Israel, they mobilized all their forces to capture him. But David was told they were coming and went into the stronghold. ¹⁸The Philistines arrived and spread out across the valley of Rephaim. ¹⁹So David asked the LORD, "Should I go out to fight the Philistines? Will you hand them over to me?"

The LORD replied, "Yes, go ahead. I will certainly give you the victory."

²⁰So David went to Baal-perazim and defeated the Philistines there. "The LORD has done it!" David exclaimed. "He burst through my enemies like a raging flood!" So David named that place Baal-perazim (which means "the Lord who bursts through"). ²¹The Philistines had abandoned their idols there, so David and his troops confiscated them.

²²But after a while the Philistines returned and again spread out across the valley of Rephaim. ²³And once again David asked the LORD what to do. "Do not attack them straight on," the LORD replied. "Instead, circle around behind them and attack them near the balsam trees. ²⁴When you hear a sound like marching feet in the tops of the balsam trees, attack! That will be the signal that the LORD is moving ahead of you to strike down the Philistines." ²⁵So David did what the LORD commanded, and he struck down the Philistines all the way from Gibeon* to Gezer.

CHAPTER 6

The Ark Brought to Jerusalem

Then David mobilized thirty thousand special troops. ²He led them to Baalah of Judah* to bring home the Ark of God, which bears the name of the LORD

I RECOGNIZE that my position of leadership is a gift from God to be used for the sake of his people. (5:12)

I FOLLOW God's requirements for the family lives of leaders (see Deuteronomy 17:17). (5:13)

See Solomon's profile (page 753) at Proverbs 2:9.

I CREDIT the Lord for my success and victory. (5:20)

I FOLLOW God's clear guidance in my life. (5:25)

I GIVE priority to publicly honoring the Lord. (6:2)

5:8 The meaning of this saying is uncertain.   5:9 Or *the supporting terraces.* The meaning of the Hebrew is uncertain.   5:14 As in parallel text at 1 Chr 3:5; Hebrew reads *Shammua,* a variant name for Shimea.   5:25 As in Greek version (see also 1 Chr 14:16); Hebrew reads *Geba.*   6:2 *Baalah of Judah* is another name for Kiriath-jearim; compare 1 Chr 13:6.

Almighty, who is enthroned between the cherubim. ³They placed the Ark of God on a new cart and brought it from the hillside home of Abinadab. Uzzah and Ahio, Abinadab's sons, were guiding the cart ⁴with the Ark of God on it, with Ahio walking in front. ⁵David and all the people of Israel were celebrating before the LORD with all their might, singing songs* and playing all kinds of musical instruments—lyres, harps, tambourines, castanets, and cymbals.

⁶But when they arrived at the threshing floor of Nacon, the oxen stumbled, and Uzzah put out his hand to steady the Ark of God. ⁷Then the LORD's anger blazed out against Uzzah for doing this, and God struck him dead beside the Ark of God. ⁸David was angry because the LORD's anger had blazed out against Uzzah. He named that place Perez-uzzah (which means "outbreak against Uzzah"). It is still called that today.

⁹David was now afraid of the LORD and asked, "How can I ever bring the Ark of the LORD back into my care?" ¹⁰So David decided not to move the Ark of the LORD into the City of David. He took it instead to the home of Obed-edom of Gath. ¹¹The Ark of the LORD remained there with the family of Obed-edom for three months, and the LORD blessed him and his entire household.

¹²Then King David was told, "The LORD has blessed Obed-edom's home and everything he has because of the Ark of God." So David went there and brought the Ark to the City of David with a great celebration. ¹³After the men who were carrying it had gone six steps, they stopped and waited so David could sacrifice an ox and a fattened calf. ¹⁴And David danced before the LORD with all his might, wearing a priestly tunic.* ¹⁵So David and all Israel brought up the Ark of the LORD with much shouting and blowing of trumpets.

Michal's Contempt for David

¹⁶But as the Ark of the LORD entered the City of David, Michal, the daughter of Saul, looked down from her window. When she saw King David leaping and dancing before the LORD, she was filled with contempt for him.

¹⁷The Ark of the LORD was placed inside the special tent that David had prepared for it. And David sacrificed burnt offerings and peace offerings to the LORD. ¹⁸When he had finished, David blessed the people in the name of the LORD Almighty. ¹⁹Then he gave a gift of food to every man and woman in Israel: a loaf of bread, a cake of dates,* and a cake of raisins. Then everyone went home.

²⁰When David returned home to bless his family, Michal came out to meet him and said in disgust, "How glorious the king of Israel looked today! He exposed himself to the servant girls like any indecent person might do!"

²¹David retorted to Michal, "I was dancing before the LORD, who chose me above your father and his family! He appointed me as the leader of Israel, the people of the LORD. So I am willing to act like a fool in order to show my joy in the LORD. ²²Yes, and I am willing to look even more foolish than this, but I will be held in honor by the girls of whom you have spoken!" ²³So Michal, the daughter of Saul, remained childless throughout her life.

CHAPTER 7

The LORD's Covenant Promise to David

When the LORD had brought peace to the land and King David was settled in his palace, ²David summoned Nathan the prophet. "Look!" David said. "Here I am living in this beautiful cedar palace, but the Ark of God is out in a tent!"

³Nathan replied, "Go ahead and do what you have in mind, for the LORD is with you."

I DO NOT TREAT the things of the Lord casually. (6:6)

I DO NOT DESPISE those who rejoice before God. (6:16)

I EXPRESS my joy in the Lord by sharing good things with others. (6:19)

I AM WILLING to look foolish in order to show my joy in the Lord. (6:21)

6:5 As in Greek version (see also 1 Chr 13:8); Hebrew reads *cypress trees.* **6:14** Hebrew *a linen ephod.* **6:19** Or *a portion of meat.* The meaning of the Hebrew is uncertain.

[4]But that same night the LORD said to Nathan,

[5]"Go and tell my servant David, 'This is what the LORD says: Are you the one to build me a temple to live in? [6]I have never lived in a temple, from the day I brought the Israelites out of Egypt until now. My home has always been a tent, moving from one place to another. [7]And I have never once complained to Israel's leaders, the shepherds of my people Israel. I have never asked them, "Why haven't you built me a beautiful cedar temple?"'

[8]"Now go and say to my servant David, 'This is what the LORD Almighty says: I chose you to lead my people Israel when you were just a shepherd boy, tending your sheep out in the pasture. [9]I have been with you wherever you have gone, and I have destroyed all your enemies. Now I will make your name famous throughout the earth! [10]And I have provided a permanent homeland for my people Israel, a secure place where they will never be disturbed. It will be their own land where wicked nations won't oppress them as they did in the past, [11]from the time I appointed judges to rule my people. And I will keep you safe from all your enemies.

"'And now the LORD declares that he will build a house for you—a dynasty of kings! [12]For when you die, I will raise up one of your descendants, and I will make his kingdom strong. [13]He is the one who will build a house—a temple—for my name. And I will establish the throne of his kingdom forever. [14]I will be his father, and he will be my son. If he sins, I will use other nations to punish him. [15]But my unfailing love will not be taken from him as I took it from Saul, whom I removed before you. [16]Your dynasty and your kingdom will continue for all time before me, and your throne will be secure forever.'"

[17]So Nathan went back to David and told him everything the LORD had said.

David's Prayer of Thanks

[18]Then King David went in and sat before the LORD and prayed, "Who am I, O Sovereign LORD, and what is my family, that you have brought me this far? [19]And now, Sovereign LORD, in addition to everything else, you speak of giving me a lasting dynasty! Do you deal with everyone this way,* O Sovereign LORD? [20]What more can I say? You know what I am really like, Sovereign LORD. [21]For the sake of your promise and according to your will, you have done all these great things and have shown them to me.

[22]"How great you are, O Sovereign LORD! There is no one like you—there is no other God. We have never even heard of another god like you! [23]What other nation on earth is like Israel? What other nation, O God, have you redeemed from slavery to be your own people? You made a great name for yourself when you rescued your people from Egypt. You performed awesome miracles and drove out the nations and gods that stood in their way. [24]You made Israel your people forever, and you, O LORD, became their God.

[25]"And now, O LORD God, do as you have promised concerning me and my family. Confirm it as a promise that will last forever. [26]And may your name be honored forever so that all the world will say, 'The LORD Almighty is God over Israel!' And may the dynasty of your servant David be established in your presence.

[27]"O LORD Almighty, God of Israel, I have been bold enough to pray this prayer because you have revealed that you will build a house for me—an eternal dynasty! [28]For you are God, O Sovereign LORD. Your words are truth, and you have promised these good things to me, your servant. [29]And now, may it please you to bless me and my family so that our dynasty may continue forever before you. For when you grant a blessing to your servant, O Sovereign LORD, it is an eternal blessing!"

7:19 The meaning of the Hebrew is uncertain.

Today what command(s) are you choosing to obey?

I BELIEVE God promised his unfailing love to David and his family. (7:15)

I BELIEVE God promised that David's dynasty and kingdom would last forever. (7:16)

I COME humbly before God in gratitude for his promises and gifts. (7:18)

I DESIRE that God be glorified as I enjoy the blessings he gives me. (7:26)

I PRAY boldly for the Lord to bless me as he has promised. (7:27)

I BELIEVE God's promised blessings last forever. (7:29)

CHAPTER 8

David's Military Victories

After this, David subdued and humbled the Philistines by conquering Gath, their largest city.* ²David also conquered the land of Moab. He made the people lie down on the ground in a row, and he measured them off in groups with a length of rope. He measured off two groups to be executed for every one group to be spared. The Moabites who were spared became David's servants and brought him tribute money.

³David also destroyed the forces of Hadadezer son of Rehob, king of Zobah, when Hadadezer marched out to strengthen his control along the Euphrates River. ⁴David captured seventeen hundred charioteers* and twenty thousand foot soldiers. Then he crippled all but one hundred of the chariot horses.

⁵When Arameans from Damascus arrived to help Hadadezer, David killed twenty-two thousand of them. ⁶Then he placed several army garrisons in Damascus, the Aramean capital, and the Arameans became David's subjects and brought him tribute money. So the LORD gave David victory wherever he went. ⁷David brought the gold shields of Hadadezer's officers to Jerusalem, ⁸along with a large amount of bronze from Hadadezer's cities of Tebah* and Berothai.

⁹When King Toi of Hamath heard that David had destroyed the army of Hadadezer, ¹⁰he sent his son Joram to congratulate David on his success. Hadadezer and Toi had long been enemies, and there had been many wars between them. Joram presented David with many gifts of silver, gold, and bronze. ¹¹King David dedicated all these gifts to the LORD, along with the silver and gold he had set apart from the other nations he had subdued— ¹²Edom,* Moab, Ammon, Philistia, and Amalek—and from Hadadezer son of Rehob, king of Zobah.

¹³So David became very famous. After his return he destroyed eighteen thousand Edomites* in the Valley of Salt. ¹⁴He placed army garrisons throughout Edom, and all the Edomites became David's subjects. This was another example of how the LORD made David victorious wherever he went.

¹⁵David reigned over all Israel and was fair to everyone. ¹⁶Joab son of Zeruiah was commander of the army. Jehoshaphat son of Ahilud was the royal historian. ¹⁷Zadok son of Ahitub and Ahimelech son of Abiathar were the priests. Seraiah was the court secretary. ¹⁸Benaiah son of Jehoiada was captain of the king's bodyguard.* David's sons served as priestly leaders.*

CHAPTER 9

David's Kindness to Mephibosheth

One day David began wondering if anyone in Saul's family was still alive, for he had promised Jonathan that he would show kindness to them. ²He summoned a man named Ziba, who had been one of Saul's servants. "Are you Ziba?" the king asked.

"Yes sir, I am," Ziba replied.

³The king then asked him, "Is anyone still alive from Saul's family? If so, I want to show God's kindness to them in any way I can."

Ziba replied, "Yes, one of Jonathan's sons is still alive, but he is crippled."

⁴"Where is he?" the king asked.

"In Lo-debar," Ziba told him, "at the home of Makir son of Ammiel." ⁵So

---

I FULFILL the responsibilities God has given me. (8:1)

I GIVE gifts to God when I experience success. (8:7)

I BELIEVE victory comes from the Lord. (8:14)

I AM FAIR to everyone under my leadership. (8:15)

I SEEK to fulfill my promises of kindness. (9:1)

8:1 Hebrew *by conquering Metheg-ammah*, a name which means "the bridle," possibly referring to the size of the city or the tribute money taken from it. Compare 1 Chr 18:1.   **8:4** Greek version reads *1,000 chariots and 7,000 charioteers*; compare 1 Chr 18:4.   **8:8** As in some Greek manuscripts (see also 1 Chr 18:8); Hebrew reads *Betah*. **8:12** As in a few Hebrew manuscripts and Greek and Syriac versions (see also 8:14; 1 Chr 18:11); most Hebrew manuscripts read *Aram*.   **8:13** As in a few Hebrew manuscripts and Greek and Syriac versions (see also 8:14; 1 Chr 18:12); most Hebrew manuscripts read *Arameans*.   **8:18a** Hebrew *of the Kerethites and Pelethites*. **8:18b** Hebrew *David's sons were priests*; compare parallel text at 1 Chr 18:17.

David sent for him and brought him from Makir's home. [6]His name was Mephibosheth*; he was Jonathan's son and Saul's grandson. When he came to David, he bowed low in great fear and said, "I am your servant."

[7]But David said, "Don't be afraid! I've asked you to come so that I can be kind to you because of my vow to your father, Jonathan. I will give you all the land that once belonged to your grandfather Saul, and you may live here with me at the palace!"

[8]Mephibosheth fell to the ground before the king. "Should the king show such kindness to a dead dog like me?" he exclaimed.

[9]Then the king summoned Saul's servant Ziba and said, "I have given your master's grandson everything that belonged to Saul and his family. [10]You and your sons and servants are to farm the land for him to produce food for his family. But Mephibosheth will live here at the palace with me."

Ziba, who had fifteen sons and twenty servants, replied, [11]"Yes, my lord; I will do all that you have commanded." And from that time on, Mephibosheth ate regularly with David, as though he were one of his own sons. [12]Mephibosheth had a young son named Mica. And from then on, all the members of Ziba's household were Mephibosheth's servants. [13]And Mephibosheth, who was crippled in both feet, moved to Jerusalem to live at the palace.

CHAPTER 10

David Defeats the Ammonites

Some time after this, King Nahash of the Ammonites died, and his son Hanun became king. [2]David said, "I am going to show complete loyalty to Hanun because his father, Nahash, was always completely loyal to me." So David sent ambassadors to express sympathy to Hanun about his father's death.

But when David's ambassadors arrived in the land of Ammon, [3]Hanun's advisers said to their master, "Do you really think these men are coming here to honor your father? No! David has sent them to spy out the city so that they can come in and conquer it!" [4]So Hanun seized David's ambassadors and shaved off half of each man's beard, cut off their robes at the buttocks, and sent them back to David in shame. [5]When David heard what had happened, he sent messengers to tell the men to stay at Jericho until their beards grew out, for they were very embarrassed by their appearance.

[6]Now the people of Ammon realized how seriously they had angered David, so they hired twenty thousand Aramean mercenaries from the lands of Beth-rehob and Zobah, one thousand from the king of Maacah, and twelve thousand from the land of Tob. [7]When David heard about this, he sent Joab and the entire Israelite army to fight them. [8]The Ammonite troops drew up their battle lines at the entrance of the city gates, while the Arameans from Zobah and Rehob and the men from Tob and Maacah positioned themselves to fight in the open fields.

[9]When Joab saw that he would have to fight on two fronts, he chose the best troops in his army. He placed them under his personal command and led them out to fight the Arameans in the fields. [10]He left the rest of the army under the command of his brother Abishai, who was to attack the Ammonites. [11]"If the Arameans are too strong for me, then come over and help me," Joab told his brother. "And if the Ammonites are too strong for you, I will come and help you. [12]Be courageous! Let us fight bravely to save our people and the cities of our God. May the LORD's will be done."

[13]When Joab and his troops attacked, the Arameans began to run away. [14]And when the Ammonites saw the Arameans running, they ran from

9:6 Also known as *Meribbaal*.

I SHOW respect to those in leadership. (9:6)

I CARE generously for the children of a deceased friend. (9:7)

I SHOW loyalty to those who have been loyal to me. (10:2)

I ACT peacefully toward those who come in peace. (10:3)

I AM CONSIDERATE of those who have been humiliated. (10:5)

I DO my very best and trust God's will to be done when I face difficult tasks. (10:12)

Abishai and retreated into the city. After the battle was over, Joab returned to Jerusalem.

[15]The Arameans now realized that they were no match for Israel. So when they regrouped, [16]they were joined by additional Aramean troops summoned by Hadadezer from the other side of the Euphrates River.* These troops arrived at Helam under the command of Shobach, the commander of all Hadadezer's forces. [17]When David heard what was happening, he mobilized all Israel, crossed the Jordan River, and led the army to Helam. The Arameans positioned themselves there in battle formation and then attacked David. [18]But again the Arameans fled from the Israelites. This time David's forces killed seven hundred charioteers and forty thousand horsemen,* including Shobach, the commander of their army. [19]When Hadadezer and his Aramean allies realized they had been defeated by Israel, they surrendered to them and became their subjects. After that, the Arameans were afraid to help the Ammonites.

CHAPTER 11

David and Bathsheba

The following spring, the time of year when kings go to war, David sent Joab and the Israelite army to destroy the Ammonites. In the process they laid siege to the city of Rabbah. But David stayed behind in Jerusalem.

[2]Late one afternoon David got out of bed after taking a nap and went for a stroll on the roof of the palace. As he looked out over the city, he noticed a woman of unusual beauty taking a bath. [3]He sent someone to find out who she was, and he was told, "She is Bathsheba, the daughter of Eliam and the wife of Uriah the Hittite." [4]Then David sent for her; and when she came to the palace, he slept with her. (She had just completed the purification rites after having her menstrual period.) Then she returned home. [5]Later, when Bathsheba discovered that she was pregnant, she sent a message to inform David.

[6]So David sent word to Joab: "Send me Uriah the Hittite." [7]When Uriah arrived, David asked him how Joab and the army were getting along and how the war was progressing. [8]Then he told Uriah, "Go on home and relax." David even sent a gift to Uriah after he had left the palace. [9]But Uriah wouldn't go home. He stayed that night at the palace entrance with some of the king's other servants.

[10]When David heard what Uriah had done, he summoned him and asked, "What's the matter with you? Why didn't you go home last night after being away for so long?"

[11]Uriah replied, "The Ark and the armies of Israel and Judah are living in tents,* and Joab and his officers are camping in the open fields. How could I go home to wine and dine and sleep with my wife? I swear that I will never be guilty of acting like that."

[12]"Well, stay here tonight," David told him, "and tomorrow you may return to the army." So Uriah stayed in Jerusalem that day and the next. [13]Then David invited him to dinner and got him drunk. But even then he couldn't get Uriah to go home to his wife. Again he slept at the palace entrance.

David Arranges for Uriah's Death

[14]So the next morning David wrote a letter to Joab and gave it to Uriah to deliver. [15]The letter instructed Joab, "Station Uriah on the front lines where the battle is fiercest. Then pull back so that he will be killed." [16]So Joab assigned Uriah to a spot close to the city wall where he knew the enemy's strongest

---

I DO NOT MAKE arrangements to pursue sin when I am tempted. (11:3)

I DO NOT USE my position or power to secure sexual favors. (11:4)

I DO NOT MANIPULATE others to cover up my sin. (11:13)

I DO NOT PURPOSELY PUT others in positions of mortal danger. (11:15)

I DO NOT COOPERATE with someone's intention to murder. (11:16)

10:16 Hebrew *the river.*   10:18 Some Greek manuscripts read *foot soldiers;* compare parallel text at 1 Chr 19:18. 11:11 Or *at Succoth.*

men were fighting. [17]And Uriah was killed along with several other Israelite soldiers.

[18]Then Joab sent a battle report to David. [19]He told his messenger, "Report all the news of the battle to the king. [20]But he might get angry and ask, 'Why did the troops go so close to the city? Didn't they know there would be shooting from the walls? [21]Wasn't Gideon's son Abimelech killed* at Thebez by a woman who threw a millstone down on him?' Then tell him, 'Uriah the Hittite was killed, too.' "

[22]So the messenger went to Jerusalem and gave a complete report to David. [23]"The enemy came out against us," he said. "And as we chased them back to the city gates, [24]the archers on the wall shot arrows at us. Some of our men were killed, including Uriah the Hittite."

[25]"Well, tell Joab not to be discouraged," David said. "The sword kills one as well as another! Fight harder next time, and conquer the city!"

[26]When Bathsheba heard that her husband was dead, she mourned for him. [27]When the period of mourning was over, David sent for her and brought her to the palace, and she became one of his wives. Then she gave birth to a son. But the LORD was very displeased with what David had done.

See Gideon's profile (page 289) at Judges 7:15.

CHAPTER 12

Nathan Rebukes David

So the LORD sent Nathan the prophet to tell David this story: "There were two men in a certain town. One was rich, and one was poor. [2]The rich man owned many sheep and cattle. [3]The poor man owned nothing but a little lamb he had worked hard to buy. He raised that little lamb, and it grew up with his children. It ate from the man's own plate and drank from his cup. He cuddled it in his arms like a baby daughter. [4]One day a guest arrived at the home of the rich man. But instead of killing a lamb from his own flocks for food, he took the poor man's lamb and killed it and served it to his guest."

[5]David was furious. "As surely as the LORD lives," he vowed, "any man who would do such a thing deserves to die! [6]He must repay four lambs to the poor man for the one he stole and for having no pity."

[7]Then Nathan said to David, "You are that man! The LORD, the God of Israel, says, 'I anointed you king of Israel and saved you from the power of Saul. [8]I gave you his house and his wives and the kingdoms of Israel and Judah. And if that had not been enough, I would have given you much, much more. [9]Why, then, have you despised the word of the LORD and done this horrible deed? For you have murdered Uriah and stolen his wife. [10]From this time on, the sword will be a constant threat to your family, because you have despised me by taking Uriah's wife to be your own.

[11]" 'Because of what you have done, I, the LORD, will cause your own household to rebel against you. I will give your wives to another man, and he will go to bed with them in public view. [12]You did it secretly, but I will do this to you openly in the sight of all Israel.' "

David Confesses His Guilt

[13]Then David confessed to Nathan, "I have sinned against the LORD."

Nathan replied, "Yes, but the LORD has forgiven you, and you won't die for this sin. [14]But you have given the enemies of the LORD great opportunity to despise and blaspheme him, so your child will die."

[15]After Nathan returned to his home, the LORD made Bathsheba's baby deathly ill. [16]David begged God to spare the child. He went without food and lay all night on the bare ground. [17]The leaders of the nation pleaded with him to get up and eat with them, but he refused. [18]Then on the seventh day the baby died. David's advisers were afraid to tell him. "He was so broken up

I CONFRONT God's leaders when they sin against him. (12:7)

I BELIEVE my private sin can have very public consequences. (12:12)

I IMMEDIATELY CONFESS my sin against the Lord when I am confronted. (12:13)

I DO NOT GIVE God's enemies opportunity to despise and blaspheme him. (12:14)

11:21 Hebrew *Was not Abimelech son of Jerubbesheth killed.*

about the baby being sick," they said. "What will he do to himself when we tell him the child is dead?"

¹⁹But when David saw them whispering, he realized what had happened. "Is the baby dead?" he asked.

"Yes," they replied. ²⁰Then David got up from the ground, washed himself, put on lotions, and changed his clothes. Then he went to the Tabernacle and worshiped the LORD. After that, he returned to the palace and ate. ²¹His advisers were amazed. "We don't understand you," they told him. "While the baby was still living, you wept and refused to eat. But now that the baby is dead, you have stopped your mourning and are eating again."

²²David replied, "I fasted and wept while the child was alive, for I said, 'Perhaps the LORD will be gracious to me and let the child live.' ²³But why should I fast when he is dead? Can I bring him back again? I will go to him one day, but he cannot return to me."

²⁴Then David comforted Bathsheba, his wife, and slept with her. She became pregnant and gave birth to a son, and they named him Solomon. The LORD loved the child ²⁵and sent word through Nathan the prophet that his name should be Jedidiah—"beloved of the LORD"—because the LORD loved him.

David Captures Rabbah

²⁶Meanwhile, Joab and the Israelite army were successfully ending their siege of Rabbah, the capital of Ammon. ²⁷Joab sent messengers to tell David, "I have fought against Rabbah and captured its water supply.* ²⁸Now bring the rest of the army and finish the job, so you will get credit for the victory instead of me."

²⁹So David led the rest of his army to Rabbah and captured it. ³⁰David removed the crown from the king's head,* and it was placed on David's own head. The crown was made of gold and set with gems, and it weighed about seventy-five pounds.* David took a vast amount of plunder from the city. ³¹He also made slaves of the people of Rabbah and forced them to labor with saws, picks, and axes, and to work in the brick kilns. That is how he dealt with the people of all the Ammonite cities. Then David and his army returned to Jerusalem.

CHAPTER 13

The Rape of Tamar

David's son Absalom had a beautiful sister named Tamar. And Amnon, her half brother, fell desperately in love with her. ²Amnon became so obsessed with Tamar that he became ill. She was a virgin, and it seemed impossible that he could ever fulfill his love for her.

³Now Amnon had a very crafty friend—his cousin Jonadab. He was the son of David's brother Shimea.* ⁴One day Jonadab said to Amnon, "What's the trouble? Why should the son of a king look so dejected morning after morning?"

So Amnon told him, "I am in love with Tamar, Absalom's sister."

⁵"Well," Jonadab said, "I'll tell you what to do. Go back to bed and pretend you are sick. When your father comes to see you, ask him to let Tamar come and prepare some food for you. Tell him you'll feel better if she feeds you."

⁶So Amnon pretended to be sick. And when the king came to see him, Amnon asked him, "Please let Tamar come to take care of me and cook

---

I WORSHIP God as I accept both his forgiveness and his discipline. (12:20)

I COMFORT my spouse after the death of a loved one. (12:24)

See Solomon's profile (page 753) at Proverbs 2:9.

I DO NOT ALLOW lust to rule my life. (13:2)

I DO NOT LISTEN to schemes to help me get my own way. (13:5)

12:27 Or *captured the city of water.*   **12:30a** Greek version reads *removed the crown of Milcom;* compare 1 Kgs 11:5. Milcom, also called Molech, was the god of the Ammonites.   **12:30b** Hebrew *1 talent* [34 kilograms].
13:3 Hebrew *Shimeah* (also in 13:32), a variant name for Shimea; compare 1 Chr 2:13.

something for me to eat." ⁷So David agreed and sent Tamar to Amnon's house to prepare some food for him.

⁸When Tamar arrived at Amnon's house, she went to the room where he was lying down so he could watch her mix some dough. Then she baked some special bread for him. ⁹But when she set the serving tray before him, he refused to eat. "Everyone get out of here," Amnon told his servants. So they all left. ¹⁰Then he said to Tamar, "Now bring the food into my bedroom and feed it to me here." So Tamar took it to him. ¹¹But as she was feeding him, he grabbed her and demanded, "Come to bed with me, my darling sister."

¹²"No, my brother!" she cried. "Don't be foolish! Don't do this to me! You know what a serious crime it is to do such a thing in Israel. ¹³Where could I go in my shame? And you would be called one of the greatest fools in Israel. Please, just speak to the king about it, and he will let you marry me."

¹⁴But Amnon wouldn't listen to her, and since he was stronger than she was, he raped her. ¹⁵Then suddenly Amnon's love turned to hate, and he hated her even more than he had loved her. "Get out of here!" he snarled at her.

I ABHOR rape. (13:14)

UNLIKE AMNON *I do not allow lust to rule my life.*

2 Samuel 13:15

The men and women in biblical times did not have to deal with the temptations of pornography so readily available today in magazines and movies and on the Internet. But overpowering sexual desire was certainly nothing new to them.

Amnon was a man driven by selfish, uncontrolled desires. As a young man, he desired to have his half sister, Tamar. In that culture, despite their half-sibling relationship, he could have sought her hand in marriage. When he schemed to take her by force, however, his "love" proved to be only lust. He was the first to realize this awful truth as soon as he had used and abused her.

True love gives and pleases. Lust consumes and destroys. Amnon wanted Tamar, but not as a cherished wife. Instead, he wanted her for what he could experience. Having gained the sexual experience he craved, he found the taste bitter and repulsive.

Amnon was not simply a sexual addict. Like any other man, he had a choice to forsake lust and pursue love. Even in the midst of his passion, he still could have chosen the way of love by heeding Tamar's pleas of reason. Instead, he chose the cruel path of lust. As a result, Amnon left Tamar desolate and made himself a target of an enraged brother's revenge.

Pursuing lust always leads to destruction. Broken lives and broken spirits lie strewn in its path. In the end, it never delivers what it promises. You and I can experience true satisfaction only in pursuing relationships of love.

○ *Today's Scripture reading is 2 Samuel 13.*

¹⁶"No, no!" Tamar cried. "To reject me now is a greater wrong than what you have already done to me."

But Amnon wouldn't listen to her. ¹⁷He shouted for his servant and demanded, "Throw this woman out, and lock the door behind her!"

¹⁸So the servant put her out. She was wearing a long, beautiful robe,* as was the custom in those days for the king's virgin daughters. ¹⁹But now Tamar tore her robe and put ashes on her head. And then, with her face in her hands, she went away crying.

²⁰Her brother Absalom saw her and asked, "Is it true that Amnon has been with you? Well, don't be so upset. Since he's your brother anyway, don't worry about it." So Tamar lived as a desolate woman in Absalom's house. ²¹When King David heard what had happened, he was very angry. ²²And

I MOURN if I have been sexually abused. (13:19)

I DO NOT ENCOURAGE anyone to cover up their feelings after they have been sexually abused. (13:20)

I AM ANGERED if I learn that my child has been sexually abused—and I take action. (13:21)

13:18 Or *a robe with sleeves,* or *an ornamented robe.* The meaning of the Hebrew is uncertain.

though Absalom never spoke to Amnon about it, he hated Amnon deeply because of what he had done to his sister.

Absalom's Revenge on Amnon

²³Two years later, when Absalom's sheep were being sheared at Baal-hazor near Ephraim, Absalom invited all the king's sons to come to a feast. ²⁴He went to the king and said, "My sheep-shearers are now at work. Would the king and his servants please come to celebrate the occasion with me?"

²⁵The king replied, "No, my son. If we all came, we would be too much of a burden on you." Absalom pressed him, but the king wouldn't come, though he sent his thanks.

²⁶"Well, then," Absalom said, "if you can't come, how about sending my brother Amnon instead?"

"Why Amnon?" the king asked. ²⁷But Absalom kept on pressing the king until he finally agreed to let all his sons attend, including Amnon.

²⁸Absalom told his men, "Wait until Amnon gets drunk; then at my signal, kill him! Don't be afraid. I'm the one who has given the command. Take courage and do it!" ²⁹So at Absalom's signal they murdered Amnon. Then the other sons of the king jumped on their mules and fled.

³⁰As they were on the way back to Jerusalem, this report reached David: "Absalom has killed all your sons; not one is left alive!" ³¹The king jumped up, tore his robe, and fell prostrate on the ground. His advisers also tore their clothes in horror and sorrow.

³²But just then Jonadab, the son of David's brother Shimea, arrived and said, "No, not all your sons have been killed! It was only Amnon! Absalom has been plotting this ever since Amnon raped his sister Tamar. ³³No, your sons aren't all dead! It was only Amnon." ³⁴Meanwhile Absalom escaped.

Then the watchman on the Jerusalem wall saw a great crowd coming toward the city from the west. He ran to tell the king, "I see a crowd of people coming from the Horonaim road* along the side of the hill."

³⁵"Look!" Jonadab told the king. "There they are now! Your sons are coming, just as I said." ³⁶They soon arrived, weeping and sobbing, and the king and his officials wept bitterly with them. ³⁷And David mourned many days for his son Amnon.

Absalom fled to his grandfather, Talmai son of Ammihud, the king of Geshur. ³⁸He stayed there in Geshur for three years. ³⁹And David, now reconciled to Amnon's death, longed to be reunited with his son Absalom.*

CHAPTER 14

Joab Arranges for Absalom's Return

Joab realized how much the king longed to see Absalom. ²So he sent for a woman from Tekoa who had a reputation for great wisdom. He said to her, "Pretend you are in mourning; wear mourning clothes and don't bathe or wear any perfume. Act like a woman who has been in deep sorrow for a long time. ³Then go to the king and tell him the story I am about to tell you." Then Joab told her what to say.

⁴When the woman approached the king, she fell with her face down to the floor in front of him and cried out, "O king! Help me!"

⁵"What's the trouble?" the king asked.

"I am a widow," she replied. ⁶"My two sons had a fight out in the field. And since no one was there to stop it, one of them was killed. ⁷Now the rest of the family is demanding, 'Let us have your son. We will execute him for murdering his brother. He doesn't deserve to inherit his family's property.' But if I

I DO NOT THWART an estranged family member who wants to be reconciled with me. (13:25)

I DO NOT PLOT my own revenge against someone who has harmed my loved ones. (13:32)

I WORK to reunite family members who are estranged. (14:1)

I SEEK the help of wise individuals. (14:2)

13:34 As in Greek version; Hebrew reads *from the road behind him.* 13:39 Or *no longer felt a need to go out after Absalom.*

do that, I will have no one left, and my husband's name and family will disappear from the face of the earth."

[8]"Leave it to me," the king told her. "Go home, and I'll see to it that no one touches him."

[9]"Oh, thank you, my lord," she replied. "And I'll take the responsibility if you are criticized for helping me like this."

[10]"Don't worry about that!" the king said. "If anyone objects, bring them to me. I can assure you they will never complain again!"

[11]Then she said, "Please swear to me by the LORD your God that you won't let anyone take vengeance against my son. I want no more bloodshed."

"As surely as the LORD lives," he replied, "not a hair on your son's head will be disturbed!"

[12]"Please let me ask one more thing of you!" she said.

"Go ahead," he urged. "Speak!"

[13]She replied, "Why don't you do as much for all the people of God as you have promised to do for me? You have convicted yourself in making this decision, because you have refused to bring home your own banished son. [14]All of us must die eventually. Our lives are like water spilled out on the ground, which cannot be gathered up again. That is why God tries to bring us back when we have been separated from him. He does not sweep away the lives of those he cares about—and neither should you!

[15]"But I have come to plead with you for my son because my life and my son's life have been threatened. I said to myself, 'Perhaps the king will listen to me [16]and rescue us from those who would cut us off from God's people. [17]Yes, the king will give us peace of mind again.' I know that you are like an angel of God and can discern good from evil. May the LORD your God be with you."

[18]"I want to know one thing," the king replied.

"Yes, my lord?" she asked.

[19]"Did Joab send you here?"

And the woman replied, "My lord the king, how can I deny it? Nobody can hide anything from you. Yes, Joab sent me and told me what to say. [20]He did it to place the matter before you in a different light. But you are as wise as an angel of God, and you understand everything that happens among us!"

[21]So the king sent for Joab and told him, "All right, go and bring back the young man Absalom."

[22]Joab fell to the ground before the king and blessed him and said, "At last I know that I have gained your approval, for you have granted me this request!"

[23]Then Joab went to Geshur and brought Absalom back to Jerusalem. [24]But the king gave this order: "Absalom may go to his own house, but he must never come into my presence." So Absalom did not see the king.

Absalom Reconciled to David

[25]Now no one in Israel was as handsome as Absalom. From head to foot, he was the perfect specimen of a man. [26]He cut his hair only once a year, and then only because it was too heavy to carry around. When he weighed it out, it came to five pounds!* [27]He had three sons and one daughter. His daughter's name was Tamar, and she was very beautiful.

[28]Absalom lived in Jerusalem for two years without getting to see the king. [29]Then Absalom sent for Joab to ask him to intercede for him, but Joab refused to come. Absalom sent for him a second time, but again Joab refused to come. [30]So Absalom said to his servants, "Go and set fire to Joab's barley field, the field next to mine." So they set his field on fire, as Absalom had commanded.

I HELP those who are in trouble as I have opportunity. (14:8)

I HELP others see their difficulties and decisions in another light. (14:20)

I PURSUE full, not partial, reconciliation. (14:24)

14:26 Hebrew *200 shekels* [2.3 kilograms] *by the royal standard.*

³¹Then Joab came to Absalom and demanded, "Why did your servants set my field on fire?"

³²And Absalom replied, "Because I wanted you to ask the king why he brought me back from Geshur if he didn't intend to see me. I might as well have stayed there. Let me see the king; if he finds me guilty of anything, then let him execute me."

³³So Joab told the king what Absalom had said. Then at last David summoned his estranged son, and Absalom came and bowed low before the king, and David kissed him.

I PURSUE real reconciliation, not just the appearance of it. (14:33)

CHAPTER 15

Absalom's Rebellion

After this, Absalom bought a chariot and horses, and he hired fifty footmen to run ahead of him. ²He got up early every morning and went out to the gate of the city. When people brought a case to the king for judgment, Absalom would ask where they were from, and they would tell him their tribe. ³Then Absalom would say, "You've really got a strong case here! It's too bad the king doesn't have anyone to hear it. ⁴I wish I were the judge. Then people could bring their problems to me, and I would give them justice!" ⁵And when people tried to bow before him, Absalom wouldn't let them. Instead, he took them by the hand and embraced them. ⁶So in this way, Absalom stole the hearts of all the people of Israel.

⁷After four years,* Absalom said to the king, "Let me go to Hebron to offer a sacrifice to the LORD in fulfillment of a vow I made to him. ⁸For while I was at Geshur, I promised to sacrifice to him in Hebron if he would bring me back to Jerusalem."

⁹"All right," the king told him. "Go and fulfill your vow."

So Absalom went to Hebron. ¹⁰But while he was there, he sent secret messengers to every part of Israel to stir up a rebellion against the king. "As soon as you hear the trumpets," his message read, "you will know that Absalom has been crowned king in Hebron." ¹¹He took two hundred men from Jerusalem with him as guests, but they knew nothing of his intentions. ¹²While he was offering the sacrifices, he sent for Ahithophel, one of David's counselors who lived in Giloh. Soon many others also joined Absalom, and the conspiracy gained momentum.

I DO NOT USE others to gain my own political advantage. (15:11)

I DO NOT JOIN conspiracies against godly leadership. (15:12)

David Escapes from Jerusalem

¹³A messenger soon arrived in Jerusalem to tell King David, "All Israel has joined Absalom in a conspiracy against you!"

¹⁴"Then we must flee at once, or it will be too late!" David urged his men. "Hurry! If we get out of the city before he arrives, both we and the city of Jerusalem will be spared from disaster."

I TAKE action that will preserve the safety of others. (15:14)

¹⁵"We are with you," his advisers replied. "Do what you think is best." ¹⁶So the king and his household set out at once. He left no one behind except ten of his concubines to keep the palace in order. ¹⁷The king and his people set out on foot, and they paused at the edge of the city ¹⁸to let David's troops move past to lead the way. There were six hundred Gittites who had come with David from Gath, along with the king's bodyguard.*

¹⁹Then the king turned to Ittai, the captain of the Gittites, and asked, "Why are you coming with us? Go on back with your men to King Absalom, for you are a guest in Israel, a foreigner in exile. ²⁰You arrived only yesterday, and now should I force you to wander with us? I don't even know where we will go. Go on back and take your troops with you, and may the LORD show you his unfailing love and faithfulness.*"

15:7 As in Greek and Syriac versions; Hebrew reads 40 years.   15:18 Hebrew the Kerethites and Pelethites.
15:20 As in Greek version; Hebrew reads and may unfailing love and faithfulness go with you.

²¹But Ittai said to the king, "I vow by the LORD and by your own life that I will go wherever you go, no matter what happens—whether it means life or death."

²²David replied, "All right, come with us." So Ittai and his six hundred men and their families went along.

²³There was deep sadness throughout the land as the king and his followers passed by. They crossed the Kidron Valley and then went out toward the wilderness.

I AM LOYAL to leaders who are following God. (15:21)

²⁴Abiathar and Zadok and the Levites took the Ark of the Covenant of God and set it down beside the road. Then they offered sacrifices there until everyone had passed by. ²⁵David instructed Zadok to take the Ark of God back into the city. "If the LORD sees fit," David said, "he will bring me back to see the Ark and the Tabernacle again. ²⁶But if he is through with me, then let him do what seems best to him."

I WANT God's will, whether it seems to benefit me or not. (15:26)

UNLIKE ABSALOM   *I do not grab for power.*

2 Samuel 15:6

In many ways Absalom was the perfect politician.

But Absalom pursued what he wanted through all the wrong ways—and for all the wrong reasons. He kept going his way, not God's way, to right the wrongs in his life and to gain the justice and power he thought he deserved.

When Amnon raped Tamar, God's way called for Absalom to seek restitution. Instead, Absalom pursued violent revenge.

Then, when his father, David, verbally pardoned Absalom for murdering his brother, God's way said seek full reconciliation. Instead, Absalom schemed and manipulated to win the public's favor and overthrow his still-grieving father.

In his desire to be king, Absalom looked not to God's will but to his own. He soon decided he wanted to call all the shots, and he plotted to take the Israelite kingdom by cunning and force.

Absalom had what it took to be a national leader—good political sense, excellent counsel, fine leadership. But he grabbed power for himself instead of seeking God's best. And the hand that grabbed for more and more came up empty.

Only when our hands are outstretched and open before God, seeking his glory, can he fill them up with privilege and power and blessing.

Turn to Psalm 3 to read the prayer David wrote during Absalom's revolt.

○ *Today's Scripture reading is 2 Samuel 15, 17, and 18.*

---

²⁷Then the king told Zadok the priest, "Look,* here is my plan. You and Abiathar* should return quietly to the city with your son Ahimaaz and Abiathar's son Jonathan. ²⁸I will stop at the shallows of the Jordan River* and wait there for a message from you. Let me know what happens in Jerusalem before I disappear into the wilderness." ²⁹So Zadok and Abiathar took the Ark of God back to the city and stayed there.

I MAKE wise plans in response to calamity. (15:27)

³⁰David walked up the road that led to the Mount of Olives, weeping as he went. His head was covered and his feet were bare as a sign of mourning. And the people who were with him covered their heads and wept as they climbed the mountain. ³¹When someone told David that his adviser Ahithophel was now backing Absalom, David prayed, "O LORD, let Ahithophel give Absalom foolish advice!"

³²As they reached the spot at the top of the Mount of Olives where people worshiped God, David found Hushai the Arkite waiting for him. Hushai had

15:27a As in Greek version; Hebrew reads *Are you a seer?* or *Do you see?*   **15:27b** Hebrew lacks *and Abiathar;* compare 15:29.   **15:28** Hebrew *at the crossing points of the wilderness.*

torn his clothing and put dirt on his head as a sign of mourning. ³³But David told him, "If you go with me, you will only be a burden. ³⁴Return to Jerusalem and tell Absalom, 'I will now be your adviser, just as I was your father's adviser in the past.' Then you can frustrate and counter Ahithophel's advice. ³⁵Zadok and Abiathar, the priests, are there. Tell them the plans that are being made to capture me, ³⁶and they will send their sons Ahimaaz and Jonathan to find me and tell me what is going on." ³⁷So David's friend Hushai returned to Jerusalem, getting there just as Absalom arrived.

CHAPTER 16

David and Ziba

David was just past the top of the hill when Ziba, the servant of Mephibosheth,* caught up with him. He was leading two donkeys loaded with two hundred loaves of bread, one hundred clusters of raisins, one hundred bunches of summer fruit, and a skin of wine. ²"What are these for?" the king asked Ziba.

And Ziba replied, "The donkeys are for your people to ride on, and the bread and summer fruit are for the young men to eat. The wine is to be taken with you into the wilderness for those who become faint."

³"And where is Mephibosheth?" the king asked him.

"He stayed in Jerusalem," Ziba replied. "He said, 'Today I will get back the kingdom of my grandfather Saul.' "

⁴"In that case," the king told Ziba, "I give you everything Mephibosheth owns."

"Thank you, sir," Ziba replied. "I will always do whatever you want me to do."

Shimei Curses David

⁵As David and his party passed Bahurim, a man came out of the village cursing them. It was Shimei son of Gera, a member of Saul's family. ⁶He threw stones at the king and the king's officers and all the mighty warriors who surrounded them. ⁷"Get out of here, you murderer, you scoundrel!" he shouted at David. ⁸"The LORD is paying you back for murdering Saul and his family. You stole his throne, and now the LORD has given it to your son Absalom. At last you will taste some of your own medicine, you murderer!"

⁹"Why should this dead dog curse my lord the king?" Abishai son of Zeruiah demanded. "Let me go over and cut off his head!"

¹⁰"No!" the king said. "What am I going to do with you sons of Zeruiah! If the LORD has told him to curse me, who am I to stop him?" ¹¹Then David said to Abishai and the other officers, "My own son is trying to kill me. Shouldn't this relative of Saul* have even more reason to do so? Leave him alone and let him curse, for the LORD has told him to do it. ¹²And perhaps the LORD will see that I am being wronged and will bless me because of these curses." ¹³So David and his men continued on, and Shimei kept pace with them on a nearby hillside, cursing as he went and throwing stones at David and tossing dust into the air.

¹⁴The king and all who were with him grew weary along the way, so they rested when they reached the Jordan River.*

Ahithophel Advises Absalom

¹⁵Meanwhile, Absalom and his men arrived at Jerusalem, accompanied by Ahithophel. ¹⁶When David's friend Hushai the Arkite arrived, he went immediately to see Absalom. "Long live the king!" he exclaimed. "Long live the king!"

I HELP those in danger. (16:2)

I DO NOT CURSE God's leaders. (16:5)

I TRUST the Lord to deal with any curses brought against me and to bless me instead. (16:12)

16:1 Also known as *Meribbaal.* 16:11 Hebrew *this Benjaminite.* 16:14 As in Greek version (see also 17:16); Hebrew reads *when they reached their destination.*

¹⁷"Is this the way you treat your friend David?" Absalom asked him. "Why aren't you with him?"

¹⁸"I'm here because I work for the man who is chosen by the LORD and by Israel," Hushai replied. ¹⁹"And anyway, why shouldn't I serve you? I helped your father, and now I will help you!"

²⁰Then Absalom turned to Ahithophel and asked him, "What should I do next?"

²¹Ahithophel told him, "Go and sleep with your father's concubines, for he has left them here to keep the house. Then all Israel will know that you have insulted him beyond hope of reconciliation, and they will give you their support." ²²So they set up a tent on the palace roof where everyone could see it, and Absalom went into the tent to sleep with his father's concubines.

²³Absalom followed Ahithophel's advice, just as David had done. For every word Ahithophel spoke seemed as wise as though it had come directly from the mouth of God.

> I DO NOT BREAK God's law to gain my own political advantage. (16:22)

CHAPTER 17

Now Ahithophel urged Absalom, "Let me choose twelve thousand men to start out after David tonight. ²I will catch up to him while he is weary and discouraged. He and his troops will panic, and everyone will run away. Then I will kill only the king, ³and I will bring all the people back to you as a bride returns to her husband. After all, it is only this man's life that you seek.* Then all the people will remain unharmed and peaceful." ⁴This plan seemed good to Absalom and to all the other leaders of Israel.

Hushai Counters Ahithophel's Advice

⁵But then Absalom said, "Bring in Hushai the Arkite. Let's see what he thinks about this." ⁶When Hushai arrived, Absalom told him what Ahithophel had said. Then he asked, "What is your opinion? Should we follow Ahithophel's advice? If not, speak up."

⁷"Well," Hushai replied, "this time I think Ahithophel has made a mistake. ⁸You know your father and his men; they are mighty warriors. Right now they are probably as enraged as a mother bear who has been robbed of her cubs. And remember that your father is an experienced soldier. He won't be spending the night among the troops. ⁹He has probably already hidden in some pit or cave. And when he comes out and attacks and a few of your men fall, there will be panic among your troops, and everyone will start shouting that your men are being slaughtered. ¹⁰Then even the bravest of them, though they have the heart of a lion, will be paralyzed with fear. For all Israel knows what a mighty man your father is and how courageous his warriors are.

> I GIVE advice that will protect others and accomplish God's will. (17:7)

¹¹"I suggest that you mobilize the entire army of Israel, bringing them from as far away as Dan and Beersheba. That way you will have an army as numerous as the sand on the seashore. And I think that you should personally lead the troops. ¹²When we find David, we can descend on him like the dew that falls to the ground, so that not one of his men is left alive. ¹³And if David has escaped into some city, you will have the entire army of Israel there at your command. Then we can take ropes and drag the walls of the city into the nearest valley until every stone is torn down."

¹⁴Then Absalom and all the leaders of Israel said, "Hushai's advice is better than Ahithophel's." For the LORD had arranged to defeat the counsel of Ahithophel, which really was the better plan, so that he could bring disaster upon Absalom!

> I BELIEVE that God has control over military plans to accomplish his will. (17:14)

Hushai Warns David to Escape

¹⁵Then Hushai reported to Zadok and Abiathar, the priests, what Ahithophel had said and what he himself had suggested instead. ¹⁶"Quick!" he told

17:3 As in Greek version; Hebrew reads *like the return of all is the man whom you seek.*

them. "Find David and urge him not to stay at the shallows of the Jordan River* tonight. He must go across at once into the wilderness beyond. Otherwise he will die and his entire army with him."

[17]Jonathan and Ahimaaz had been staying at En-rogel so as not to be seen entering and leaving the city. Arrangements had been made for a servant girl to bring them the message they were to take to King David. [18]But a boy saw them leaving En-rogel to go to David, and he told Absalom about it. Meanwhile, they escaped to Bahurim, where a man hid them inside a well in his courtyard. [19]The man's wife put a cloth over the top of the well with grain on it to dry in the sun; so no one suspected they were there.

I PROTECT those who are in danger. (17:20)

[20]When Absalom's men arrived, they asked her, "Have you seen Ahimaaz and Jonathan?"

She replied, "They were here, but they crossed the brook." Absalom's men looked for them without success and returned to Jerusalem.

[21]Then the two men crawled out of the well and hurried on to King David. "Quick!" they told him, "cross the Jordan tonight!" And they told him how Ahithophel had advised that he be captured and killed. [22]So David and all the people with him went across the Jordan River during the night, and they were all on the other bank before dawn.

I WOULD NEVER COMMIT suicide to cover up my shame. (17:23)

[23]Meanwhile, Ahithophel was publicly disgraced when Absalom refused his advice. So he saddled his donkey, went to his hometown, set his affairs in order, and hanged himself. He died there and was buried beside his father.

[24]David soon arrived at Mahanaim. By now, Absalom had mobilized the entire army of Israel and was leading his troops across the Jordan River. [25]Absalom had appointed Amasa as commander of his army, replacing Joab, who had been commander under David. (Amasa was Joab's cousin. His father was Jether,* an Ishmaelite.* His mother, Abigail daughter of Nahash, was the sister of Joab's mother, Zeruiah.) [26]Absalom and the Israelite army set up camp in the land of Gilead.

I GIVE nourishment to those who are fleeing from danger. (17:28)

[27]When David arrived at Mahanaim, he was warmly greeted by Shobi son of Nahash of Rabbah, an Ammonite, and by Makir son of Ammiel of Lo-debar, and by Barzillai of Gilead from Rogelim. [28]They brought sleeping mats, cooking pots, serving bowls, wheat and barley flour, roasted grain, beans, lentils, [29]honey, butter, sheep, and cheese for David and those who were with him. For they said, "You must all be very tired and hungry and thirsty after your long march through the wilderness."

CHAPTER **18**

Absalom's Defeat and Death

David now appointed generals and captains to lead his troops. [2]One-third were placed under Joab, one-third under Joab's brother Abishai son of Zeruiah, and one-third under Ittai the Gittite. The king told his troops, "I am going out with you."

I AM WILLING to face danger with others. (18:2)

[3]But his men objected strongly. "You must not go," they urged. "If we have to turn and run—and even if half of us die—it will make no difference to Absalom's troops; they will be looking only for you. You are worth ten thousand of us, and it is better that you stay here in the city and send us help if we need it."

[4]"If you think that's the best plan, I'll do it," the king finally agreed. So he stood at the gate of the city as all the divisions of troops passed by. [5]And the king gave this command to Joab, Abishai, and Ittai: "For my sake, deal gently with young Absalom." And all the troops heard the king give this order to his commanders.

I LISTEN to the wise counsel of people I lead. (18:4)

I AM MERCIFUL. (18:5)

[6]So the battle began in the forest of Ephraim, [7]and the Israelite troops were

17:16 Hebrew *at the crossing points of the wilderness.* 17:25a Hebrew *Ithra,* a variant name for Jether. 17:25b As in some Greek manuscripts (see also 1 Chr 2:17); Hebrew reads *an Israelite.*

beaten back by David's men. There was a great slaughter, and twenty thousand men laid down their lives that day. ⁸The battle raged all across the countryside, and more men died because of the forest than were killed by the sword.

⁹During the battle, Absalom came unexpectedly upon some of David's men. He tried to escape on his mule, but as he rode beneath the thick branches of a great oak, his head got caught. His mule kept going and left him dangling in the air. ¹⁰One of David's men saw what had happened and told Joab, "I saw Absalom dangling in a tree."

¹¹"What?" Joab demanded. "You saw him there and didn't kill him? I would have rewarded you with ten pieces of silver* and a hero's belt!"

> I DO NOT USE violence for my own gain. (18:11)

¹²"I wouldn't do it for a thousand pieces of silver,*" the man replied. "We all heard the king say to you and Abishai and Ittai, 'For my sake, please don't harm young Absalom.' ¹³And if I had betrayed the king by killing his son—and the king would certainly find out who did it—you yourself would be the first to abandon me."

¹⁴"Enough of this nonsense," Joab said. Then he took three daggers and plunged them into Absalom's heart as he dangled from the oak still alive. ¹⁵Ten of Joab's young armor bearers then surrounded Absalom and killed him. ¹⁶Then Joab blew the trumpet, and his men returned from chasing the army of Israel. ¹⁷They threw Absalom's body into a deep pit in the forest and piled a great heap of stones over it. And the army of Israel fled to their homes.

¹⁸During his lifetime, Absalom had built a monument to himself in the King's Valley, for he had said, "I have no son to carry on my name." He named the monument after himself, and it is known as Absalom's Monument to this day.

David Mourns Absalom's Death

¹⁹Then Zadok's son Ahimaaz said, "Let me run to the king with the good news that the LORD has saved him from his enemy Absalom."

²⁰"No," Joab told him, "it wouldn't be good news to the king that his son is dead. You can be my messenger some other time, but not today."

> I CONSIDER how best to communicate bad news. (18:20)

²¹Then Joab said to a man from Cush, "Go tell the king what you have seen." The man bowed and ran off.

²²But Ahimaaz continued to plead with Joab, "Whatever happens, please let me go, too."

"Why should you go, my son?" Joab replied. "There will be no reward for you."

²³"Yes, but let me go anyway," he begged.

Joab finally said, "All right, go ahead." Then Ahimaaz took a shortcut across the plain of the Jordan and got to Mahanaim ahead of the man from Cush.

²⁴While David was sitting at the city gate, the watchman climbed to the roof of the gateway by the wall. As he looked, he saw a lone man running toward them. ²⁵He shouted the news down to David, and the king replied, "If he is alone, he has news."

As the messenger came closer, ²⁶the watchman saw another man running toward them. He shouted down, "Here comes another one!"

The king replied, "He also will have news."

²⁷"The first man runs like Ahimaaz son of Zadok," the watchman said.

"He is a good man and comes with good news," the king replied.

²⁸Then Ahimaaz cried out to the king, "All is well!" He bowed low with his face to the ground and said, "Blessed be the LORD your God, who has handed over the rebels who dared to stand against you."

18:11 Hebrew *10 shekels of silver*, about 4 ounces or 114 grams in weight. 18:12 Hebrew *1,000 shekels*, about 25 pounds or 11.4 kilograms in weight.

²⁹"What about young Absalom?" the king demanded. "Is he all right?"

Ahimaaz replied, "When Joab told me to come, there was a lot of commotion. But I didn't know what was happening."

³⁰"Wait here," the king told him. So Ahimaaz stepped aside.

³¹Then the man from Cush arrived and said, "I have good news for my lord the king. Today the LORD has rescued you from all those who rebelled against you."

³²"What about young Absalom?" the king demanded. "Is he all right?"

And the Cushite replied, "May all of your enemies, both now and in the future, be as that young man is!"

³³The king was overcome with emotion. He went up to his room over the gateway and burst into tears. And as he went, he cried, "O my son Absalom! My son, my son Absalom! If only I could have died instead of you! O Absalom, my son, my son."

CHAPTER 19

Joab Rebukes the King

Word soon reached Joab that the king was weeping and mourning for Absalom. ²As the troops heard of the king's deep grief for his son, the joy of that day's victory was turned into deep sadness. ³They crept back into the city as though they were ashamed and had been beaten in battle. ⁴The king covered his face with his hands and kept on weeping, "O my son Absalom! O Absalom, my son, my son!"

⁵Then Joab went to the king's room and said to him, "We saved your life today and the lives of your sons, your daughters, and your wives and concubines. Yet you act like this, making us feel ashamed, as though we had done something wrong. ⁶You seem to love those who hate you and hate those who love you. You have made it clear today that we mean nothing to you. If Absalom had lived and all of us had died, you would be pleased. ⁷Now go out there and congratulate the troops, for I swear by the LORD that if you don't, not a single one of them will remain here tonight. Then you will be worse off than you have ever been." ⁸So the king went out and sat at the city gate, and as the news spread throughout the city that he was there, everyone went to him.

Meanwhile, the Israelites who supported Absalom had fled to their homes. ⁹And throughout the tribes of Israel there was much discussion and argument going on. The people were saying, "The king saved us from our enemies, the Philistines, but Absalom chased him out of the country. ¹⁰Now Absalom, whom we anointed to rule over us, is dead. Let's ask David to come back and be our king again."

¹¹Then King David sent Zadok and Abiathar, the priests, to say to the leaders of Judah, "Why are you the last ones to reinstate the king? For I have heard that all Israel is ready, and only you are holding out. ¹²Yet you are my relatives, my own tribe, my own flesh and blood! Why are you the last ones to welcome me back?" ¹³And David told them to tell Amasa, "Since you are my nephew, may God strike me dead if I do not appoint you as commander of my army in place of Joab." ¹⁴Then Amasa convinced all the leaders of Judah, and they responded unanimously. They sent word to the king, "Return to us, and bring back all those who are with you."

David's Return to Jerusalem

¹⁵So the king started back to Jerusalem. And when he arrived at the Jordan River, the people of Judah came to Gilgal to meet him and escort him across the river. ¹⁶Then Shimei son of Gera, the man from Bahurim in Benjamin, hurried across with the men of Judah to welcome King David. ¹⁷A thousand men from the tribe of Benjamin were with him, including Ziba, the servant of Saul, and Ziba's fifteen sons and twenty servants. They rushed down to the

---

I MOURN the death of a loved one, even if he or she was estranged from me. (18:33)

I DO NOT MOURN my deceased loved one so much that I hurt or neglect those who are still alive. (19:2)

I CONFRONT those who are hurting and estranging others by their attitudes or actions. (19:5)

I LISTEN to the wise rebuke of my friends and consider their advice. (19:8)

I AM WILLING to be reconciled with those whom I have offended. (19:10)

Jordan to arrive ahead of the king. ¹⁸They all crossed the ford and worked hard ferrying the king's household across the river, helping them in every way they could.

David's Mercy to Shimei

As the king was about to cross the river, Shimei fell down before him. ¹⁹"My lord the king, please forgive me," he pleaded. "Forget the terrible thing I did when you left Jerusalem. ²⁰I know how much I sinned. That is why I have come here today, the very first person in all Israel* to greet you."

²¹Then Abishai son of Zeruiah said, "Shimei should die, for he cursed the LORD's anointed king!"

²²"What am I going to do with you sons of Zeruiah!" David exclaimed. "This is not a day for execution but for celebration! I am once again the king of Israel!" ²³Then, turning to Shimei, David vowed, "Your life will be spared."

David's Kindness to Mephibosheth

²⁴Now Mephibosheth,* Saul's grandson, arrived from Jerusalem to meet the king. He had not washed his feet or clothes nor trimmed his beard since the day the king left Jerusalem. ²⁵"Why didn't you come with me, Mephibosheth?" the king asked him.

²⁶Mephibosheth replied, "My lord the king, my servant Ziba deceived me. I told him, 'Saddle my donkey so that I can go with the king.' For as you know I am crippled. ²⁷Ziba has slandered me by saying that I refused to come. But I know that you are like an angel of God, so do what you think is best. ²⁸All my relatives and I could expect only death from you, my lord, but instead you have honored me among those who eat at your own table! So how can I complain?"

²⁹"All right," David replied. "My decision is that you and Ziba will divide your land equally between you."

³⁰"Give him all of it," Mephibosheth said. "I am content just to have you back again, my lord!"

David's Kindness to Barzillai

³¹Barzillai of Gilead now arrived from Rogelim to conduct the king across the Jordan. ³²He was very old, about eighty, and very wealthy. He was the one who had provided food for the king during his stay in Mahanaim. ³³"Come across with me and live in Jerusalem," the king said to Barzillai. "I will take care of you there."

³⁴"No," he replied, "I am far too old for that. ³⁵I am eighty years old today, and I can no longer enjoy anything. Food and wine are no longer tasty, and I cannot hear the musicians as they play. I would only be a burden to my lord the king. ³⁶Just to go across the river with you is all the honor I need! ³⁷Then let me return again to die in my own town, where my father and mother are buried. But here is my son Kimham. Let him go with you and receive whatever good things you want to give him."

³⁸"Good," the king agreed. "Kimham will go with me, and I will do for him whatever I would have done for you." ³⁹So all the people crossed the Jordan with the king. After David had blessed and embraced him, Barzillai returned to his own home. ⁴⁰The king then went on to Gilgal, taking Kimham with him. All the army of Judah and half the army of Israel escorted him across the river.

An Argument over the King

⁴¹But the men of Israel complained to the king that the men of Judah had gotten to do most of the work in helping him cross the Jordan. ⁴²"Why not?" the

---

I REPENT when I have cursed and hurt another. (19:19)

I AM WILLING to show mercy when my enemy repents. (19:23)

I AM WILLING to listen to an explanation when my friend seems to have deserted me. (19:25)

I VALUE my relationships more than material possessions. (19:30)

I SHOW gratitude to my elderly friends by treating their children kindly. (19:38)

19:20 Hebrew *the house of Joseph.*   19:24 Also known as *Meribbaal.*

men of Judah replied. "The king is one of our own tribe. Why should this make you angry? We have charged him nothing. And he hasn't fed us or even given us gifts!"

⁴³"But there are ten tribes in Israel," the others replied. "So we have ten times as much right to the king as you do. Why did you treat us with such contempt? Remember, we were the first to speak of bringing him back to be our king again." The argument continued back and forth, and the men of Judah were very harsh in their replies.

CHAPTER 20

The Revolt of Sheba

Then a troublemaker named Sheba son of Bicri, a man from the tribe of Benjamin, blew a trumpet and shouted, "We have nothing to do with David. We want no part of this son of Jesse. Come on, you men of Israel, let's all go home!" ²So the men of Israel deserted David and followed Sheba. But the men of Judah stayed with their king and escorted him from the Jordan River to Jerusalem.

³When the king arrived at his palace in Jerusalem, he instructed that the ten concubines he had left to keep house should be placed in seclusion. Their needs were to be cared for, he said, but he would no longer sleep with them. So each of them lived like a widow until she died.

⁴Then the king instructed Amasa to mobilize the army of Judah within three days and to report back at that time. ⁵So Amasa went out to notify the troops, but it took him longer than the three days he had been given. ⁶Then David said to Abishai, "That troublemaker Sheba is going to hurt us more than Absalom did. Quick, take my troops and chase after him before he gets into a fortified city where we can't reach him."

⁷So Abishai and Joab set out after Sheba with an elite guard from Joab's army and the king's own bodyguard.* ⁸As they arrived at the great stone in Gibeon, Amasa met them, coming from the opposite direction. Joab was wearing his uniform with a dagger strapped to his belt. As he stepped forward to greet Amasa, he secretly slipped the dagger from its sheath. ⁹"How are you, my cousin?" Joab said and took him by the beard with his right hand as though to kiss him. ¹⁰Amasa didn't notice the dagger in his left hand, and Joab stabbed him in the stomach with it so that his insides gushed out onto the ground. Joab did not need to strike again, and Amasa soon died. Joab and his brother Abishai left him lying there and continued after Sheba.

¹¹One of Joab's young officers shouted to Amasa's troops, "If you are for Joab and David, come and follow Joab." ¹²But Amasa lay in his blood in the middle of the road, and Joab's officer saw that a crowd was gathering around to stare at him. So he pulled him off the road into a field and threw a cloak over him. ¹³With Amasa's body out of the way, everyone went on with Joab to capture Sheba.

¹⁴Meanwhile, Sheba had traveled across Israel to mobilize his own clan of Bicri at the city of Abel-beth-maacah. ¹⁵When Joab's forces arrived, they attacked Abel-beth-maacah and built a ramp against the city wall and began battering it down. ¹⁶But a wise woman in the city called out to Joab, "Listen to me, Joab. Come over here so I can talk to you." ¹⁷As he approached, the woman asked, "Are you Joab?"

"I am," he replied.

So she said, "Listen carefully to your servant."

"I'm listening," he said.

¹⁸Then she continued, "There used to be a saying, 'If you want to settle an argument, ask advice at the city of Abel.' ¹⁹I am one who is peace loving and

I CARE for the needs of those who have been abused. (20:3)

I DO NOT USE violence to secure my own position. (20:10)

I GIVE wise counsel that will protect innocent people. (20:16)

I SEEK peace for myself and others. (20:19)

20:7 Hebrew *the Kerethites and Pelethites*; also in 20:23.

faithful in Israel. But you are destroying a loyal city. Why do you want to destroy what belongs to the LORD?"

²⁰And Joab replied, "Believe me, I don't want to destroy your city! ²¹All I want is a man named Sheba son of Bicri from the hill country of Ephraim, who has revolted against King David. If you hand him over to me, we will leave the city in peace."

"All right," the woman replied, "we will throw his head over the wall to you." ²²Then the woman went to the people with her wise advice, and they cut off Sheba's head and threw it out to Joab. So he blew the trumpet and called his troops back from the attack, and they all returned to their homes. Joab returned to the king at Jerusalem.

²³Joab once again became the commander of David's army. Benaiah son of Jehoiada was commander of the king's bodyguard. ²⁴Adoniram* was in charge of the labor force. Jehoshaphat son of Ahilud was the royal historian. ²⁵Sheva was the court secretary. Zadok and Abiathar were the priests. ²⁶Ira the Jairite was David's personal priest.

CHAPTER 21

David Avenges the Gibeonites

There was a famine during David's reign that lasted for three years, so David asked the LORD about it. And the LORD said, "The famine has come because Saul and his family are guilty of murdering the Gibeonites."

²So King David summoned the Gibeonites. They were not part of Israel but were all that was left of the nation of the Amorites. Israel had sworn not to kill them, but Saul, in his zeal, had tried to wipe them out. ³David asked them, "What can I do for you to make amends? Tell me so that the LORD will bless his people again."

⁴"Well, money won't do it," the Gibeonites replied. "And we don't want to see the Israelites executed in revenge."

"What can I do then?" David asked. "Just tell me and I will do it for you."

⁵Then they replied, "It was Saul who planned to destroy us, to keep us from having any place at all in Israel. ⁶So let seven of Saul's sons or grandsons be handed over to us, and we will execute them before the LORD at Gibeon, on the mountain of the LORD.*"

"All right," the king said, "I will do it." ⁷David spared Jonathan's son Mephibosheth,* who was Saul's grandson, because of the oath David and Jonathan had sworn before the LORD. ⁸But he gave them Saul's two sons Armoni and Mephibosheth, whose mother was Rizpah daughter of Aiah. He also gave them the five sons of Saul's daughter Merab,* the wife of Adriel son of Barzillai from Meholah. ⁹The men of Gibeon executed them on the mountain before the LORD. So all seven of them died together at the beginning of the barley harvest.

¹⁰Then Rizpah, the mother of two of the men, spread sackcloth on a rock and stayed there the entire harvest season. She prevented vultures from tearing at their bodies during the day and stopped wild animals from eating them at night. ¹¹When David learned what Rizpah, Saul's concubine, had done, ¹²he went to the people of Jabesh-gilead and asked for the bones of Saul and his son Jonathan. (When Saul and Jonathan had died in a battle with the Philistines, it was the people of Jabesh-gilead who had retrieved their bodies from the public square of the Philistine city of Beth-shan.) ¹³So David brought the bones of Saul and Jonathan, as well as the bones of the men the Gibeonites had executed. ¹⁴He buried them all in the tomb of Kish,

I SEEK the Lord regarding causes for suffering. (21:1)

I SEEK to make amends with people who have been sinned against in the past. (21:3)

I DO NOT SEEK money or revenge on innocent people to pay for sins against my family. (21:4)

I ENSURE a proper burial for those who have died. (21:13)

20:24 As in Greek version (see also 1 Kgs 4:6; 5:14); Hebrew reads *Adoram*. 21:6 As in Greek version (see also 21:9); Hebrew reads *at Gibeah of Saul, the chosen of the LORD*. 21:7 Also known as *Meribbaal*. 21:8 As in a few Hebrew and Greek manuscripts and Syriac version (see also 1 Sam 18:19); most Hebrew manuscripts read *Michal*.

Saul's father, at the town of Zela in the land of Benjamin. After that, God ended the famine in the land of Israel.

Battles against Philistine Giants

[15] Once again the Philistines were at war with Israel. And when David and his men were in the thick of battle, David became weak and exhausted. [16] Ishbi-benob was a descendant of the giants*; his bronze spearhead weighed more than seven pounds,* and he was armed with a new sword. He had cornered David and was about to kill him. [17] But Abishai son of Zeruiah came to his rescue and killed the Philistine. After that, David's men declared, "You are not going out to battle again! Why should we risk snuffing out the light of Israel?"

[18] After this, there was another battle against the Philistines at Gob. As they fought, Sibbecai from Hushah killed Saph, another descendant of the giants. [19] In still another battle at Gob, Elhanan son of Jair* from Bethlehem killed the brother of Goliath of Gath.* The handle of his spear was as thick as a weaver's beam! [20] In another battle with the Philistines at Gath, a huge man with six fingers on each hand and six toes on each foot—a descendant of the giants—[21] defied and taunted Israel. But he was killed by Jonathan, the son of David's brother Shimea.* [22] These four Philistines were descended from the giants of Gath, but they were killed by David and his warriors.

I CAN ACCOMPLISH difficult feats with God's help. (21:22)

CHAPTER 22

David's Song of Praise

I PRAISE God for all he has done for me. (22:1)

David sang this song to the LORD after the LORD had rescued him from all his enemies and from Saul. [2] These are the words he sang:

"The LORD is my rock, my fortress, and my savior;
[3]   my God is my rock, in whom I find protection.
He is my shield, the strength of my salvation, and my stronghold,
    my high tower, my savior, the one who saves me from violence.
[4] I will call on the LORD, who is worthy of praise,
    for he saves me from my enemies.

[5] "The waves of death surrounded me;
    the floods of destruction swept over me.
[6] The grave* wrapped its ropes around me;
    death itself stared me in the face.

I CRY OUT to God when I face danger. (22:7)

[7] But in my distress I cried out to the LORD;
    yes, I called to my God for help.
He heard me from his sanctuary;
    my cry reached his ears.

[8] "Then the earth quaked and trembled;
    the foundations of the heavens shook;
    they quaked because of his anger.
[9] Smoke poured from his nostrils;
    fierce flames leaped from his mouth;
    glowing coals flamed forth from him.
[10] He opened the heavens and came down;
    dark storm clouds were beneath his feet.
[11] Mounted on a mighty angel,* he flew,
    soaring* on the wings of the wind.
[12] He shrouded himself in darkness,
    veiling his approach with dense rain clouds.

21:16a As in Greek version; Hebrew reads *a descendant of the Rephaites;* also in 21:18, 20, 22.   21:16b Hebrew *300 shekels* [3.4 kilograms].   21:19a As in parallel text at 1 Chr 20:5; Hebrew reads *son of Jaare-oregim.* 21:19b As in parallel text at 1 Chr 20:5; Hebrew reads *killed Goliath of Gath.*   21:21 As in parallel text at 1 Chr 20:7; Hebrew reads *Shimei,* a variant name for Shimea.   22:6 Hebrew *Sheol.*   22:11a Hebrew *cherub.* 22:11b As in some Hebrew manuscripts (see also Ps 18:10); other Hebrew manuscripts read *appearing.*

¹³ A great brightness shone before him,
    and bolts of lightning blazed forth.
¹⁴ The LORD thundered from heaven;
    the Most High gave a mighty shout.
¹⁵ He shot his arrows and scattered his enemies;
    his lightning flashed, and they were confused.
¹⁶ Then at the command of the LORD,
    at the blast of his breath,
  the bottom of the sea could be seen,
    and the foundations of the earth were laid bare.

¹⁷ "He reached down from heaven and rescued me;
    he drew me out of deep waters.
¹⁸ He delivered me from my powerful enemies,
    from those who hated me and were too strong for me.
¹⁹ They attacked me at a moment when I was weakest,
    but the LORD upheld me.
²⁰ He led me to a place of safety;
    he rescued me because he delights in me.
²¹ The LORD rewarded me for doing right;
    he compensated me because of my innocence.
²² For I have kept the ways of the LORD;
    I have not turned from my God to follow evil.
²³ For all his laws are constantly before me;
    I have never abandoned his principles.
²⁴ I am blameless before God;
    I have kept myself from sin.
²⁵ The LORD rewarded me for doing right,
    because of my innocence in his sight.

²⁶ "To the faithful you show yourself faithful;
    to those with integrity you show integrity.
²⁷ To the pure you show yourself pure,
    but to the wicked you show yourself hostile.
²⁸ You rescue those who are humble,
    but your eyes are on the proud to humiliate them.
²⁹ O LORD, you are my light;
    yes, LORD, you light up my darkness.
³⁰ In your strength I can crush an army;
    with my God I can scale any wall.

³¹ "As for God, his way is perfect.
    All the LORD's promises prove true.
  He is a shield for all who look to him for protection.
³² For who is God except the LORD?
    Who but our God is a solid rock?
³³ God is my strong fortress;
    he has made my way safe.
³⁴ He makes me as surefooted as a deer,
    leading me safely along the mountain heights.
³⁵ He prepares me for battle;
    he strengthens me to draw a bow of bronze.
³⁶ You have given me the shield of your salvation;
    your help* has made me great.
³⁷ You have made a wide path for my feet
    to keep them from slipping.

Make a commitment to read from God's Word daily.

I KEEP God's laws before me constantly. (22:23)

I KEEP myself from sin. (22:24)

I AM RESCUED by the Lord as I humble myself before him. (22:28)

I TRUST in no other God but the Lord. (22:32)

22:36 As in Dead Sea Scrolls; most Hebrew manuscripts read *your answering.*

I EXPERIENCE victory over my enemies because of the Lord. (22:38)

38 "I chased my enemies and destroyed them;
   I did not stop until they were conquered.
39 I consumed them; I struck them down so they could not get up;
   they fell beneath my feet.
40 You have armed me with strength for the battle;
   you have subdued my enemies under my feet.
41 You made them turn and run;
   I have destroyed all who hated me.
42 They called for help, but no one came to rescue them.
   They cried to the LORD, but he refused to answer them.
43 I ground them as fine as the dust of the earth;
   I swept them into the gutter like dirt.

44 "You gave me victory over my accusers.
   You preserved me as the ruler over nations;
   people I don't even know now serve me.
45 Foreigners cringe before me;
   as soon as they hear of me, they submit.
46 They all lose their courage
   and come trembling from their strongholds.

I BLESS AND EXALT the Lord who saves me. (22:47)

47 "The LORD lives! Blessed be my rock!
   May God, the rock of my salvation, be exalted!
48 He is the God who pays back those who harm me;
   he subdues the nations under me
49   and rescues me from my enemies.
   You hold me safe beyond the reach of my enemies;
   you save me from violent opponents.

I PRAISE the Lord's name before all people. (22:50)

50 For this, O LORD, I will praise you among the nations;
   I will sing joyfully to your name.
51 You give great victories to your king;
   you show unfailing love to your anointed,
   to David and all his descendants forever."

CHAPTER 23

David's Last Words

These are the last words of David:

   "David, the son of Jesse, speaks—
   David, the man to whom God gave such wonderful success,
   David, the man anointed by the God of Jacob,
   David, the sweet psalmist of Israel.

See Jacob's profile (page 43) at Genesis 32:9.

2 "The Spirit of the LORD speaks through me;
   his words are upon my tongue.
3 The God of Israel spoke.
   The Rock of Israel said to me:
   'The person who rules righteously,
   who rules in the fear of God,

I BELIEVE the Spirit spoke through David. (23:2)

4 he is like the light of the morning,
   like the sunrise bursting forth in a cloudless sky,
   like the refreshing rains that bring tender grass from the earth.'

I REFRESH others by leading them righteously. (23:4)

5 "It is my family God has chosen!
   Yes, he has made an everlasting covenant with me.
His agreement is eternal, final, sealed.
   He will constantly look after my safety and success.

I TRUST in God's eternal covenant (Hebrews 10:16). (23:5)

⁶ But the godless are like thorns to be thrown away,
   for they tear the hand that touches them.
⁷ One must be armed to chop them down;
   they will be utterly consumed with fire."

David's Mightiest Men

⁸These are the names of David's mightiest men. The first was Jashobeam the Hacmonite,* who was commander of the Three—the three greatest warriors among David's men. He once used his spear to kill eight hundred enemy warriors in a single battle.*

⁹Next in rank among the Three was Eleazar son of Dodai, a descendant of Ahoah. Once Eleazar and David stood together against the Philistines when the entire Israelite army had fled. ¹⁰He killed Philistines until his hand was too tired to lift his sword, and the LORD gave him a great victory that day. The rest of the army did not return until it was time to collect the plunder!

¹¹Next in rank was Shammah son of Agee from Harar. One time the Philistines gathered at Lehi and attacked the Israelites in a field full of lentils. The Israelite army fled, ¹²but Shammah held his ground in the middle of the field and beat back the Philistines. So the LORD brought about a great victory.

¹³Once during harvesttime, when David was at the cave of Adullam, the Philistine army was camped in the valley of Rephaim. The Three (who were among the Thirty—an elite group among David's fighting men) went down to meet him there. ¹⁴David was staying in the stronghold at the time, and a Philistine detachment had occupied the town of Bethlehem. ¹⁵David remarked longingly to his men, "Oh, how I would love some of that good water from the well in Bethlehem, the one by the gate." ¹⁶So the Three broke through the Philistine lines, drew some water from the well, and brought it back to David. But he refused to drink it. Instead, he poured it out before the LORD. ¹⁷"The LORD forbid that I should drink this!" he exclaimed. "This water is as precious as the blood of these men who risked their lives to bring it to me." So David did not drink it. This is an example of the exploits of the Three.

David's Thirty Mighty Men

¹⁸Abishai son of Zeruiah, the brother of Joab, was the leader of the Thirty.* He once used his spear to kill three hundred enemy warriors in a single battle. It was by such feats that he became as famous as the Three. ¹⁹Abishai was the most famous of the Thirty* and was their commander, though he was not one of the Three.

²⁰There was also Benaiah son of Jehoiada, a valiant warrior from Kabzeel. He did many heroic deeds, which included killing two of Moab's mightiest warriors. Another time he chased a lion down into a pit. Then, despite the snow and slippery ground, he caught the lion and killed it. ²¹Another time, armed only with a club, he killed a great Egyptian warrior who was armed with a spear. Benaiah wrenched the spear from the Egyptian's hand and killed him with it. ²²These are some of the deeds that made Benaiah almost as famous as the Three. ²³He was more honored than the other members of the Thirty, though he was not one of the Three. And David made him commander of his bodyguard.

²⁴Other members of the Thirty included:

Asahel, Joab's brother;
Elhanan son of Dodo from Bethlehem;

I HONOR those who have served well. (23:8)

I HOLD my ground and experience victory as a gift from the Lord (Ephesians 6:13–14). (23:12)

I DO NOT TREAT lightly the sacrifices others make for me. (23:17)

I PURSUE my goals zealously and bravely. (23:20)

I HONOR those who serve well. (23:23)

23:8a As in parallel text at 1 Chr 11:11; Hebrew reads *Josheb-basshebeth the Tahkemonite.*   23:8b As in some Greek manuscripts (see also 1 Chr 11:11); the Hebrew is uncertain, though it might be rendered *the Three. It was Adino the Eznite who killed eight hundred men at one time.*   23:18 As in a few Hebrew manuscripts and Syriac version; most Hebrew manuscripts read *the Three.*   23:19 As in Syriac version; Hebrew reads *the Three.*

²⁵ Shammah from Harod;
Elika from Harod;
²⁶ Helez from Pelon*;
Ira son of Ikkesh from Tekoa;
²⁷ Abiezer from Anathoth;
Sibbecai* from Hushah;
²⁸ Zalmon from Ahoah;
Maharai from Netophah;
²⁹ Heled* son of Baanah from Netophah;
Ithai* son of Ribai from Gibeah (from the tribe of Benjamin);
³⁰ Benaiah from Pirathon;
Hurai* from Nahale-gaash*;
³¹ Abi-albon the Arbathite;
Azmaveth from Bahurim;
³² Eliahba from Shaalbon;
the sons of Jashen;
³³ Jonathan son of Shagee* from Harar;
Ahiam son of Sharar from Harar;
³⁴ Eliphelet son of Ahasbai from Maacah;
Eliam son of Ahithophel from Giloh;
³⁵ Hezro from Carmel;
Paarai from Arba;
³⁶ Igal son of Nathan from Zobah;
Bani from Gad;
³⁷ Zelek from Ammon;
Naharai from Beeroth (Joab's armor bearer);
³⁸ Ira from Jattir;
Gareb from Jattir;
³⁹ Uriah the Hittite.

There were thirty-seven in all.

CHAPTER 24

David Takes a Census

Once again the anger of the LORD burned against Israel, and he caused David to harm them by taking a census. "Go and count the people of Israel and Judah," the LORD told him.

²So the king said to Joab, the commander of his army, "Take a census of all the people in the land—from Dan in the north to Beersheba in the south—so that I may know how many people there are."

³But Joab replied to the king, "May the LORD your God let you live until there are a hundred times as many people in your kingdom as there are now! But why do you want to do this?"

I URGE people not to sin against God. (24:3)

⁴But the king insisted that they take the census, so Joab and his officers went out to count the people of Israel. ⁵First they crossed the Jordan and camped at Aroer, south of the town in the valley, in the direction of Gad. Then they went on to Jazer, ⁶then to Gilead in the land of Tahtim-hodshi* and to Dan-jaan and around to Sidon. ⁷Then they came to the stronghold of Tyre, and all the cities of the Hivites and Canaanites. Finally, they went south to Judah as far as Beersheba. ⁸Having gone through the entire land, they completed their task in nine months and twenty days and then returned to

23:26 As in parallel text at 1 Chr 11:27 (see also 1 Chr 27:10); Hebrew reads *from Palti.* 23:27 As in some Greek manuscripts (see also 1 Chr 11:29); Hebrew reads *Mebunnai.* 23:29a As in some Hebrew manuscripts (see also 1 Chr 11:30); most Hebrew manuscripts read *Heleb.* 23:29b As in parallel text at 1 Chr 11:31; Hebrew reads *Ittai.* 23:30a As in some Greek manuscripts (see also 1 Chr 11:32); Hebrew reads *Hiddai.* 23:30b Or *from the ravines of Gaash.* 23:33 As in parallel text at 1 Chr 11:34; Hebrew reads *Jonathan, Shammah*; some Greek manuscripts read *Jonathan son of Shammah.* 24:6 Greek version reads *to Gilead and to Kadesh in the land of the Hittites.*

Jerusalem. ⁹Joab reported the number of people to the king. There were 800,000 men of military age in Israel and 500,000 in Judah.

Judgment for David's Sin

¹⁰But after he had taken the census, David's conscience began to bother him. And he said to the LORD, "I have sinned greatly and shouldn't have taken the census. Please forgive me, LORD, for doing this foolish thing."

¹¹The next morning the word of the LORD came to the prophet Gad, who was David's seer. This was the message: ¹²"Go and say to David, 'This is what the LORD says: I will give you three choices. Choose one of these punishments, and I will do it.' "

¹³So Gad came to David and asked him, "Will you choose three* years of famine throughout the land, three months of fleeing from your enemies, or three days of severe plague throughout your land? Think this over and let me know what answer to give the LORD."

¹⁴"This is a desperate situation!" David replied to Gad. "But let us fall into the hands of the LORD, for his mercy is great. Do not let me fall into human hands."

¹⁵So the LORD sent a plague upon Israel that morning, and it lasted for three days. Seventy thousand people died throughout the nation. ¹⁶But as the death angel was preparing to destroy Jerusalem, the LORD relented and said to the angel, "Stop! That is enough!" At that moment the angel of the LORD was by the threshing floor of Araunah the Jebusite.

¹⁷When David saw the angel, he said to the LORD, "I am the one who has sinned and done wrong! But these people are innocent—what have they done? Let your anger fall against me and my family."

David Builds an Altar

¹⁸That day Gad came to David and said to him, "Go and build an altar to the LORD on the threshing floor of Araunah the Jebusite."

¹⁹So David went to do what the LORD had commanded him. ²⁰When Araunah saw the king and his men coming toward him, he came forward and bowed before the king with his face to the ground. ²¹"Why have you come, my lord?" Araunah asked.

And David replied, "I have come to buy your threshing floor and to build an altar to the LORD there, so that the LORD will stop the plague."

²²"Take it, my lord, and use it as you wish," Araunah said to David. "Here are oxen for the burnt offering, and you can use the threshing tools and ox yokes for wood to build a fire on the altar. ²³I will give it all to you, and may the LORD your God accept your sacrifice."

²⁴But the king replied to Araunah, "No, I insist on buying it, for I cannot present burnt offerings to the LORD my God that have cost me nothing." So David paid him fifty pieces of silver* for the threshing floor and the oxen. ²⁵David built an altar there to the LORD and offered burnt offerings and peace offerings. And the LORD answered his prayer, and the plague was stopped.

24:13 As in Greek version (see also 1 Chr 21:12); Hebrew reads *seven*.   24:24 Hebrew *50 shekels of silver*, about 20 ounces or 570 grams in weight.

I LISTEN to my conscience and repent of my sin. (24:10)

I SEEK God's mercy. (24:14)

I ACCEPT the personal consequences of my sins. (24:17)

I GIVE to God at personal cost to myself, not others. (24:24)

1 KINGS

THIS SIXTH BOOK of Old Testament history is filled with both *greatness* and *tragedy*.

Over the course of the four hundred years of history covered in 1 and 2 Kings, the nation of Israel rises to its greatest glory, only to rebel against the Lord, divide into two kingdoms, grow increasingly pagan, and eventually be destroyed by foreign powers.

The story of 1 Kings begins with a detailed account of King David's last days and of his son Solomon's ascension to the throne (1:1–2:12).

After becoming king, Solomon establishes his rule and becomes renowned for his phenomenal wisdom. His fame spreads to other kingdoms, and the nation of Israel enjoys a season of unparalleled prosperity (2:13–4:34).

During this extraordinary time of blessing, Solomon builds a Temple for the Lord in Jerusalem. Solomon demonstrates his devotion to the Lord by spending vast sums of wealth to build the Temple and dedicate it (5:1–8:5).

After the glory of the Lord fills the Temple, Solomon prays a marvelous prayer of dedication. The Lord rewards Solomon for his devotion but also warns him against ever rebelling against his commands (8:6–9:9).

Solomon continues to gain international fame for his wisdom and wealth. Eventually, however, after marrying many foreign wives, Solomon rebels against the Lord and begins worshiping pagan gods. The Lord warns Solomon, who refuses to repent. As a result, the nation of Israel begins to fall apart (9:10–11:43).

Soon after Solomon's death, the nation splits into two kingdoms. A series of notoriously wicked kings begins to rule the northern kingdom, now called "Israel." A series of alternately wicked and good kings begins to rule the southern kingdom, now called "Judah." In both kingdoms prophets rise up to warn the nation of impending destruction (12:1–22:53).

The story of the final collapse and destruction of both kingdoms is recorded in 2 Kings. Parallel accounts of 1 Kings can be found in 2 Chronicles 1–20.

Famous passages in 1 Kings include

- The Lord's granting of phenomenal wisdom to Solomon (3:5-15)
- Solomon's judgment regarding two prostitutes and a baby (3:16-28)
- Solomon's marvelous prayer of dedication for the Temple (8:15-53)
- The queen of Sheba's visit to Solomon (10:1-13)
- Solomon's many foreign wives, who turn his heart to pagan idols (11:1-8)
- The division of the nation shortly after Solomon's death (12:1-20)
- The northern kingdom's development of its own pagan religion (12:26-33)
- The prophet Ahijah's condemnation of Israel's paganism (14:6-16)
- The southern kingdom's embrace of paganism (14:21-24)
- King Asa's efforts to drive paganism out of Judah (15:9-15)
- The prophet Elijah's efforts to rid Israel of paganism (17:1–19:18)
- Elijah's commissioning of Elisha as his successor (19:19-21)

CHAPTER 1

David in His Old Age

See David's profile (page 629) at Psalm 3:1.

Now King David was very old, and no matter how many blankets covered him, he could not keep warm. [2]So his advisers told him, "We will find a young virgin who will wait on you and be your nurse. She will lie in your arms and keep you warm." [3]So they searched throughout the country for a beautiful girl, and they found Abishag from Shunem and brought her to the king. [4]The girl was very beautiful, and she waited on the king and took care of him. But the king had no sexual relations with her.

Adonijah Claims the Throne

I DO NOT PUSH my way into positions of leadership. (1:5)

[5]About that time David's son Adonijah, whose mother was Haggith, decided to make himself king in place of his aged father. So he provided himself with chariots and horses* and recruited fifty men to run in front of him. [6]Now his father, King David, had never disciplined him at any time, even by asking, "What are you doing?" Adonijah was a very handsome man and had been born next after Absalom. [7]Adonijah took Joab son of Zeruiah and Abiathar the priest into his confidence, and they agreed to help him become king. [8]But among those who remained loyal to David and refused to support Adonijah were Zadok the priest, Benaiah son of Jehoiada, Nathan the prophet, Shimei, Rei, and David's personal bodyguard.

I DISCIPLINE my children as they grow up. (1:6)

See Absalom's profile (page 373) at 2 Samuel 15:6.

I DO NOT ASSIST others in usurping leadership. (1:7)

See Solomon's profile (page 753) at Proverbs 2:9.

[9]Adonijah went to the stone of Zoheleth* near the spring of En-rogel, where he sacrificed sheep, oxen, and fattened calves. He invited all his brothers—the other sons of King David—and all the royal officials of Judah. [10]But he did not invite Nathan the prophet, or Benaiah, or the king's bodyguard, or his brother Solomon.

[11]Then Nathan the prophet went to Bathsheba, Solomon's mother, and asked her, "Did you realize that Haggith's son, Adonijah, has made himself king and that our lord David doesn't even know about it? [12]If you want to save your own life and the life of your son Solomon, follow my counsel. [13]Go at once to King David and say to him, 'My lord, didn't you promise me that my son Solomon would be the next king and would sit upon your throne? Then why has Adonijah become king?' [14]And while you are still talking with him, I will come and confirm everything you have said."

I GIVE counsel that will protect others. (1:12)

[15]So Bathsheba went into the king's bedroom. He was very old now, and Abishag was taking care of him. [16]Bathsheba bowed low before him.

"What can I do for you?" he asked her.

I AM NOT AFRAID to remind people of their promises to me. (1:17)

[17]She replied, "My lord, you vowed to me by the LORD your God that my son Solomon would be the next king and would sit on your throne. [18]But instead, Adonijah has become the new king, and you do not even know about it. [19]He has sacrificed many oxen, fattened calves, and sheep, and he has invited all your sons and Abiathar the priest and Joab, the commander of the army. But he did not invite your servant Solomon. [20]And now, my lord the king, all Israel is waiting for your decision as to who will become king after you. [21]If you do not act, my son Solomon and I will be treated as criminals as soon as you are dead."

[22]While she was still speaking with the king, Nathan the prophet arrived. [23]The king's advisers told him, "Nathan the prophet is here to see you."

Nathan went in and bowed low before the king. [24]He asked, "My lord, have you decided that Adonijah will be the next king and that he will sit on your throne? [25]Today he has sacrificed many oxen, fattened calves, and sheep, and he has invited your sons to attend the celebration. He also invited Joab, the commander of the army,* and Abiathar the priest. They are feasting and drinking with him and shouting, 'Long live King Adonijah!' [26]But I myself,

I GIVE leaders information they need to make wise decisions. (1:24)

1:5 Or *and charioteers.* 1:9 Or *to the Serpent's Stone;* Greek version supports reading *Zoheleth* as a proper name. 1:25 As in Greek version; Hebrew reads *invited the commanders of the army.*

your servant, was not invited; neither were Zadok the priest, Benaiah son of Jehoiada, nor Solomon. ²⁷Has my lord really done this without letting any of his servants know who should be the next king?"

David Makes Solomon King

²⁸"Call Bathsheba," David said. So she came back in and stood before the king. ²⁹And the king vowed, "As surely as the LORD lives, who has rescued me from every danger, ³⁰today I decree that your son Solomon will be the next king and will sit on my throne, just as I swore to you before the LORD, the God of Israel."

³¹Then Bathsheba bowed low before him again and exclaimed, "May my lord King David live forever!"

³²Then King David ordered, "Call Zadok the priest, Nathan the prophet, and Benaiah son of Jehoiada." When they came into the king's presence, ³³the king said to them, "Take Solomon and my officers down to Gihon Spring. Solomon is to ride on my personal mule. ³⁴There Zadok the priest and Nathan the prophet are to anoint him king over Israel. Then blow the trumpets and shout, 'Long live King Solomon!' ³⁵When you bring him back here, he will sit on my throne. He will succeed me as king, for I have appointed him to be ruler over Israel and Judah."

³⁶"Amen!" Benaiah son of Jehoiada replied. "May the LORD, the God of my lord the king, decree it to be so. ³⁷And may the LORD be with Solomon as he has been with you, and may he make Solomon's reign even greater than yours!"

³⁸So Zadok the priest, Nathan the prophet, Benaiah son of Jehoiada, and the king's bodyguard* took Solomon down to Gihon Spring, and Solomon rode on King David's personal mule. ³⁹There Zadok the priest took a flask of olive oil from the sacred tent and poured it on Solomon's head. Then the trumpets were blown, and all the people shouted, "Long live King Solomon!" ⁴⁰And all the people returned with Solomon to Jerusalem, playing flutes and shouting for joy. The celebration was so joyous and noisy that the earth shook with the sound.

⁴¹Adonijah and his guests heard the celebrating and shouting just as they were finishing their banquet. When Joab heard the sound of trumpets, he asked, "What's going on? Why is the city in such an uproar?"

⁴²And while he was still speaking, Jonathan son of Abiathar the priest arrived. "Come in," Adonijah said to him, "for you are a good man. You must have good news."

⁴³"Not at all!" Jonathan replied. "Our lord King David has just declared Solomon king! ⁴⁴The king sent him down to Gihon Spring with Zadok the priest, Nathan the prophet, and Benaiah son of Jehoiada, protected by the king's bodyguard. They had him ride on the king's own mule, ⁴⁵and Zadok and Nathan have anointed him as the new king. They have just returned, and the whole city is celebrating and rejoicing. That's what all the noise is about. ⁴⁶Moreover, Solomon is now sitting on the royal throne as king. ⁴⁷All the royal officials went to King David and congratulated him, saying, 'May your God make Solomon's fame even greater than your own, and may Solomon's kingdom be even greater than yours!' Then the king bowed his head in worship as he lay in his bed, ⁴⁸and he spoke these words: 'Blessed be the LORD, the God of Israel, who today has chosen someone to sit on my throne while I am still alive to see it.' "

⁴⁹Then all of Adonijah's guests jumped up in panic from the banquet table and quickly went their separate ways. ⁵⁰Adonijah himself was afraid of Solomon, so he rushed to the sacred tent and caught hold of the horns of the altar.

I KEEP the promises I make to others. (1:30)

I AM WILLING to pass on my leadership to another person when the right time comes. (1:35)

I CELEBRATE when God provides a good leader for his people. (1:40)

1:38 Hebrew the *Kerethites and Pelethites*; also in 1:44.

[51]Word soon reached Solomon that Adonijah had seized the horns of the altar and that he was pleading, "Let Solomon swear today that he will not kill me!"

[52]Solomon replied, "If he proves himself to be loyal, he will not be harmed.* But if he does not, he will die." [53]So King Solomon summoned Adonijah, and they brought him down from the altar. He came and bowed low before the king, and Solomon dismissed him, saying, "Go on home."

CHAPTER 2

David's Final Instructions to Solomon

As the time of King David's death approached, he gave this charge to his son Solomon: [2]"I am going where everyone on earth must someday go. Take courage and be a man. [3]Observe the requirements of the LORD your God and follow all his ways. Keep each of the laws, commands, regulations, and stipulations written in the law of Moses so that you will be successful in all you do and wherever you go. [4]If you do this, then the LORD will keep the promise he made to me: 'If your descendants live as they should and follow me faithfully with all their heart and soul, one of them will always sit on the throne of Israel.'

[5]"And there is something else. You know that Joab son of Zeruiah murdered my two army commanders, Abner son of Ner and Amasa son of Jether. He pretended that it was an act of war, but it was done in a time of peace,* staining his belt and sandals with the blood of war. [6]Do with him what you think best, but don't let him die in peace.

[7]"Be kind to the sons of Barzillai of Gilead. Make them permanent guests of the king, for they took care of me when I fled from your brother Absalom.

[8]"And remember Shimei son of Gera, the man from Bahurim in Benjamin. He cursed me with a terrible curse as I was fleeing to Mahanaim. When he came down to meet me at the Jordan River, I swore by the LORD that I would not kill him. [9]But that oath does not make him innocent. You are a wise man, and you will know how to arrange a bloody death for him."

[10]Then David died and was buried in the City of David. [11]He had reigned over Israel for forty years, seven of them in Hebron and thirty-three in Jerusalem. [12]Solomon succeeded him as king, replacing his father, David, and he was firmly established on the throne.

Solomon Establishes His Rule

[13]One day Adonijah, whose mother was Haggith, came to see Bathsheba, Solomon's mother. "Have you come to make trouble?" she asked him.

"No," he said, "I come in peace. [14]In fact, I have a favor to ask of you."

"What is it?" she asked.

[15]He replied, "As you know, the kingdom was mine; everyone expected me to be the next king. But the tables were turned, and everything went to my brother instead; for that is the way the LORD wanted it. [16]So now I have just one favor to ask of you. Please don't turn me down."

"What is it?" she asked.

[17]He replied, "Speak to King Solomon on my behalf, for I know he will do anything you request. Ask him to give me Abishag, the girl from Shunem, as my wife."

[18]"All right," Bathsheba replied. "I will speak to the king for you."

[19]So Bathsheba went to King Solomon to speak on Adonijah's behalf. The king rose from his throne to meet her, and he bowed down before her. When he sat down on his throne again, he ordered that a throne be brought for his mother, and she sat at his right hand.

I GIVE people an opportunity to prove their repentance. (1:52)

I CHALLENGE my children to achieve true success that comes only from loving and obeying God. (2:3)

See Moses' profile (page 73) at Exodus 5:1.

I ENSURE that, after I am gone, help continues to be given to those who have helped me. (2:7)

See Absalom's profile (page 373) at 2 Samuel 15:6.

I BELIEVE officials should deal justly with wrongdoers. (2:9)

I DO NOT HARBOR resentment when I am not chosen to be the leader. (2:15)

I DO NOT TRY to use devious methods to regain leadership. (2:17)

1:52 Hebrew *not a hair on his head will be touched.*   2:5 Or *He murdered them during a time of peace as revenge for deaths they had caused in time of war.*

²⁰"I have one small request to make of you," she said. "I hope you won't turn me down."

"What is it, my mother?" he asked. "You know I won't refuse you."

²¹"Then let your brother Adonijah marry Abishag, the girl from Shunem," she replied.

²²"How can you possibly ask me to give Abishag to Adonijah?" Solomon demanded. "You might as well be asking me to give him the kingdom! You know that he is my older brother, and that he has Abiathar the priest and Joab son of Zeruiah on his side." ²³Then King Solomon swore solemnly by the LORD: "May God strike me dead if Adonijah has not sealed his fate with this request. ²⁴The LORD has confirmed me and placed me on the throne of my father, David; he has established my dynasty as he promised. So as surely as the LORD lives, Adonijah will die this very day!" ²⁵So King Solomon ordered Benaiah son of Jehoiada to execute him, and Adonijah was put to death.

²⁶Then the king said to Abiathar the priest, "Go back to your home in Anathoth. You deserve to die, but I will not kill you now, because you carried the Ark of the Sovereign LORD for my father, and you suffered right along with him through all his troubles." ²⁷So Solomon deposed Abiathar from his position as priest of the LORD, thereby fulfilling the decree the LORD had made at Shiloh concerning the descendants of Eli.

²⁸Although he had not followed Absalom earlier, Joab had also joined Adonijah's revolt. When Joab heard about Adonijah's death, he ran to the sacred tent of the LORD and caught hold of the horns of the altar. ²⁹When news of this reached King Solomon, he sent Benaiah son of Jehoiada to execute him.

³⁰Benaiah went into the sacred tent of the LORD and said to Joab, "The king orders you to come out!"

But Joab answered, "No, I will die here."

So Benaiah returned to the king and told him what Joab had said.

³¹"Do as he said," the king replied. "Kill him there beside the altar and bury him. This will remove the guilt of his senseless murders from me and from my father's family. ³²Then the LORD will repay him for the murders of two men who were more righteous and better than he. For my father was no party to the deaths of Abner son of Ner, commander of the army of Israel, and Amasa son of Jether, commander of the army of Judah. ³³May Joab and his descendants be forever guilty of these murders, and may the LORD grant peace to David and his descendants and to his throne forever."

³⁴So Benaiah son of Jehoiada returned to the sacred tent and killed Joab, and Joab was buried at his home in the wilderness. ³⁵Then the king appointed Benaiah to command the army in place of Joab, and he installed Zadok the priest to take the place of Abiathar.

³⁶The king then sent for Shimei and told him, "Build a house here in Jerusalem and live there. But don't step outside the city to go anywhere else. ³⁷On the day you cross the Kidron Valley, you will surely die; your blood will be on your own head."

³⁸Shimei replied, "Your sentence is fair; I will do whatever my lord the king commands." So Shimei lived in Jerusalem for a long time.

³⁹But three years later, two of Shimei's slaves escaped to King Achish of Gath. When Shimei learned where they were, ⁴⁰he saddled his donkey and went to Gath to search for them. When he had found them, he took them back to Jerusalem.

⁴¹Solomon heard that Shimei had left Jerusalem and had gone to Gath and returned. ⁴²So he sent for Shimei and demanded, "Didn't I make you swear by the LORD and warn you not to go anywhere else, or you would surely die? And you replied, 'The sentence is fair; I will do as you say.'

See Eli's profile (page 321) at 1 Samuel 2:30.

I BELIEVE leaders who are not faithful should be removed from office. (2:27)

I BELIEVE justice should be administered when murder has been committed. (2:31)

I GIVE people an opportunity to prove their repentance. (2:36)

I AM TRUE to my word.
(2:43)

⁴³Then why haven't you kept your oath to the Lord and obeyed my command?"

⁴⁴The king also said to Shimei, "You surely remember all the wicked things you did to my father, King David. May the Lord punish you for them. ⁴⁵But may I receive the Lord's rich blessings, and may one of David's descendants always sit on this throne." ⁴⁶Then, at the king's command, Benaiah son of Jehoiada took Shimei outside and killed him.

So the kingdom was now firmly in Solomon's grip.

CHAPTER 3

Solomon Asks for Wisdom

I WILL NOT MARRY an unbeliever for any reason. (3:1)

Solomon made an alliance with Pharaoh, the king of Egypt, and married one of his daughters. He brought her to live in the City of David until he could finish building his palace and the Temple of the Lord and the wall around the city. ²At that time the people of Israel sacrificed their offerings at local altars, for a temple honoring the name of the Lord had not yet been built.

³Solomon loved the Lord and followed all the instructions of his father, David, except that Solomon, too, offered sacrifices and burned incense at the local altars. ⁴The most important of these altars was at Gibeon, so the king went there and sacrificed one thousand burnt offerings. ⁵That night the Lord appeared to Solomon in a dream, and God said, "What do you want? Ask, and I will give it to you!"

⁶Solomon replied, "You were wonderfully kind to my father, David, because he was honest and true and faithful to you. And you have continued this great kindness to him today by giving him a son to succeed him. ⁷O Lord my God, now you have made me king instead of my father, David, but I am like a little child who doesn't know his way around. ⁸And here I am among your own chosen people, a nation so great they are too numerous to count! ⁹Give me an understanding mind so that I can govern your people well and know the difference between right and wrong. For who by himself is able to govern this great nation of yours?"

I RECOGNIZE my need for God's help to carry out all he has called me to do. (3:7)

I ASK God for wisdom to do the job he has called me to do, for the benefit of others and not just myself. (3:9)

¹⁰The Lord was pleased with Solomon's reply and was glad that he had asked for wisdom. ¹¹So God replied, "Because you have asked for wisdom in governing my people and have not asked for a long life or riches for yourself or the death of your enemies—¹²I will give you what you asked for! I will give you a wise and understanding mind such as no one else has ever had or ever will have! ¹³And I will also give you what you did not ask for—riches and honor! No other king in all the world will be compared to you for the rest of your life! ¹⁴And if you follow me and obey my commands as your father, David, did, I will give you a long life."

I GIVE praise and offerings to God when he shows his goodness to me in special ways. (3:15)

¹⁵Then Solomon woke up and realized it had been a dream. He returned to Jerusalem and stood before the Ark of the Lord's covenant, where he sacrificed burnt offerings and peace offerings. Then he invited all his officials to a great banquet.

Solomon Judges Wisely

¹⁶Some time later, two prostitutes came to the king to have an argument settled. ¹⁷"Please, my lord," one of them began, "this woman and I live in the same house. I gave birth to a baby while she was with me in the house. ¹⁸Three days later, she also had a baby. We were alone; there were only two of us in the house. ¹⁹But her baby died during the night when she rolled over on it. ²⁰Then she got up in the night and took my son from beside me while I was asleep. She laid her dead child in my arms and took mine to sleep beside her. ²¹And in the morning when I tried to nurse my son, he was dead! But when I looked more closely in the morning light, I saw that it wasn't my son at all."

²²Then the other woman interrupted, "It certainly was your son, and the living child is mine."

"No," the first woman said, "the dead one is yours, and the living one is mine." And so they argued back and forth before the king.

²³Then the king said, "Let's get the facts straight. Both of you claim the living child is yours, and each says that the dead child belongs to the other. ²⁴All right, bring me a sword." So a sword was brought to the king. ²⁵Then he said, "Cut the living child in two and give half to each of these women!"

²⁶Then the woman who really was the mother of the living child, and who loved him very much, cried out, "Oh no, my lord! Give her the child—please do not kill him!"

But the other woman said, "All right, he will be neither yours nor mine; divide him between us!"

²⁷Then the king said, "Do not kill him, but give the baby to the woman who wants him to live, for she is his mother!"

²⁸Word of the king's decision spread quickly throughout all Israel, and the people were awed as they realized the great wisdom God had given him to render decisions with justice.

I USE wisdom in helping others resolve their conflicts. (3:23)

I CARE more about the welfare of my child than about my own rights. (3:26)

CHAPTER 4

Solomon's Officials and Governors

So Solomon was king over all Israel, ²and these were his high officials:

Azariah son of Zadok was the priest.
³ Elihoreph and Ahijah, the sons of Shisha, were court secretaries.
Jehoshaphat son of Ahilud was the royal historian.
⁴ Benaiah son of Jehoiada was commander of the army.
Zadok and Abiathar were the priests.
⁵ Azariah son of Nathan presided over the district governors.
Zabud son of Nathan, a priest, was a trusted adviser to the king.
⁶ Ahishar was manager of palace affairs.
Adoniram son of Abda was in charge of the labor force.

I APPOINT capable people to positions of leadership. (4:2)

⁷Solomon also had twelve district governors who were over all Israel. They were responsible for providing food from the people for the king's household. Each of them arranged provisions for one month of the year. ⁸These are the names of the twelve governors:

I DIVIDE responsibility wisely. (4:7)

Ben-hur, in the hill country of Ephraim.
⁹ Ben-deker, in Makaz, Shaalbim, Beth-shemesh, and Elon-bethhanan.
¹⁰ Ben-hesed, in Arubboth, including Socoh and all the land of Hepher.
¹¹ Ben-abinadab, in Naphoth-dor.* (He was married to Taphath, one of Solomon's daughters.)
¹² Baana son of Ahilud, in Taanach and Megiddo, all of Beth-shan* near Zarethan below Jezreel, and all the territory from Beth-shan to Abel-meholah and over to Jokmeam.
¹³ Ben-geber, in Ramoth-gilead, including the Towns of Jair (named for Jair son of Manasseh) in Gilead, and in the Argob region of Bashan, including sixty great fortified cities with gates barred with bronze.
¹⁴ Ahinadab son of Iddo, in Mahanaim.
¹⁵ Ahimaaz, in Naphtali. (He was married to Basemath, another of Solomon's daughters.)
¹⁶ Baana son of Hushai, in Asher and in Aloth.
¹⁷ Jehoshaphat son of Paruah, in Issachar.
¹⁸ Shimei son of Ela, in Benjamin.

Ask the Lord to speak to you. After all, this is his Word!

4:11 Hebrew *Naphath-dor*, a variant name for Naphoth-dor.   4:12 Hebrew *Beth-shean*, a variant name for Beth-shan; also in 4:12b.

[19] Geber son of Uri, in the land of Gilead,* including the territories of King Sihon of the Amorites and King Og of Bashan.

And there was one governor over the land of Judah.*

Solomon's Prosperity and Wisdom
[20] The people of Judah and Israel were as numerous as the sand on the seashore. They were very contented, with plenty to eat and drink. [21] King Solomon ruled all the kingdoms from the Euphrates River* to the land of the Philistines, as far south as the border of Egypt. The conquered peoples of those lands sent tribute money to Solomon and continued to serve him throughout his lifetime.

[22] The daily food requirements for Solomon's palace were 150 bushels of choice flour and 300 bushels of meal,* [23] ten oxen from the fattening pens, twenty pasture-fed cattle, one hundred sheep or goats, as well as deer, gazelles, roebucks, and choice fowl.

[24] Solomon's dominion extended over all the kingdoms west of the Euphrates River, from Tiphsah to Gaza. And there was peace throughout the entire land. [25] Throughout the lifetime of Solomon, all of Judah and Israel lived in peace and safety. And from Dan to Beersheba, each family had its own home and garden.

[26] Solomon had four thousand* stalls for his chariot horses and twelve thousand horses.* [27] The district governors faithfully provided food for King Solomon and his court, each during his assigned month. [28] They also brought the necessary barley and straw for the royal horses in the stables.

[29] God gave Solomon great wisdom and understanding, and knowledge too vast to be measured. [30] In fact, his wisdom exceeded that of all the wise men of the East and the wise men of Egypt. [31] He was wiser than anyone else, including Ethan the Ezrahite and Heman, Calcol, and Darda—the sons of Mahol. His fame spread throughout all the surrounding nations. [32] He composed some 3,000 proverbs and wrote 1,005 songs. [33] He could speak with authority about all kinds of plants, from the great cedar of Lebanon to the tiny hyssop that grows from cracks in a wall. He could also speak about animals, birds, reptiles, and fish. [34] And kings from every nation sent their ambassadors to listen to the wisdom of Solomon.

CHAPTER 5

Preparations for Building the Temple
King Hiram of Tyre had always been a loyal friend of David, so when he learned that David's son Solomon was the new king of Israel, Hiram sent ambassadors to congratulate him. [2] Then Solomon sent this message back to Hiram:

[3] "You know that my father, David, was not able to build a Temple to honor the name of the LORD his God because of the many wars he waged with surrounding nations. He could not build until the LORD gave him victory over all his enemies. [4] But now the LORD my God has given me peace on every side, and I have no enemies and all is well. [5] So I am planning to build a Temple to honor the name of the LORD my God, just as he instructed my father that I should do. For the LORD told him, 'Your son, whom I will place on your throne, will build the Temple to honor my name.' [6] Now please command that cedars from Lebanon be cut for me. Let my men work alongside yours, and I will pay your men whatever wages you ask. As you know, there is no one among us who can cut timber like you Sidonians!"

I BELIEVE God blessed the people of Israel during Solomon's reign, just as he had promised David. (4:25)

I OBEY the Lord's commands carefully (see Deuteronomy 17:16). (4:26)

I FULFILL my leadership responsibilities faithfully. (4:27)

I BELIEVE God gave Solomon incredible wisdom, just as he had promised. (4:29)

I SHARE with others the wisdom God gives me. (4:34)

I EXTEND my loyal friendship to the children of any deceased friends. (5:1)

I PAY people good and fair wages for their work. (5:6)

4:19a Greek version reads *of Gad;* compare 4:13.   4:19b As in some Greek manuscripts; Hebrew lacks *of Judah.* The meaning of the Hebrew is uncertain.   4:21 Hebrew *the river;* also in 4:24.   4:22 Hebrew *30 cors* [5.5 kiloliters] *of choice flour and 60 cors* [11 kiloliters] *of meal.*   4:26a As in some Greek manuscripts (see also 2 Chr 9:25); Hebrew reads *40,000.*   4:26b Or *12,000 charioteers.*

⁷When Hiram received Solomon's message, he was very pleased and said, "Praise the LORD for giving David a wise son to be king of the great nation of Israel." ⁸Then he sent this reply to Solomon:

"I have received your message, and I will do as you have asked concerning the timber. I can supply you with both cedar and cypress. ⁹My servants will bring the logs from the Lebanon mountains to the Mediterranean Sea and build them into rafts. We will float them along the coast to whatever place you choose. Then we will break the rafts apart and deliver the timber to you. You can pay me with food for my household."

¹⁰So Hiram produced for Solomon as much cedar and cypress timber as he desired. ¹¹In return Solomon sent him an annual payment of 100,000 bushels* of wheat for his household and 110,000 gallons* of olive oil. ¹²So the LORD gave great wisdom to Solomon just as he had promised. And Hiram and Solomon made a formal alliance of peace.

¹³Then King Solomon enlisted 30,000 laborers from all Israel. ¹⁴He sent them to Lebanon in shifts, 10,000 every month, so that each man would be one month in Lebanon and two months at home. Adoniram was in charge of this labor force. ¹⁵Solomon also enlisted 70,000 common laborers, 80,000 stonecutters in the hill country, ¹⁶and 3,600* foremen to supervise the work. ¹⁷At the king's command, the stonecutters quarried and shaped costly blocks of stone for the foundation of the Temple. ¹⁸Men from the city of Gebal helped Solomon's and Hiram's builders prepare the timber and stone for the Temple.

CHAPTER 6

Solomon Builds the Temple

It was in midspring,* during the fourth year of Solomon's reign, that he began the construction of the Temple of the LORD. This was 480 years after the people of Israel were delivered from their slavery in the land of Egypt. ²The Temple that King Solomon built for the LORD was 90 feet long, 30 feet wide, and 45 feet high.* ³The foyer at the front of the Temple was 30 feet wide, running across the entire width of the Temple. It projected outward 15 feet from the front of the Temple. ⁴Solomon also made narrow, recessed windows throughout the Temple.

⁵A complex of rooms was built against the outer walls of the Temple, all the way around the sides and rear of the building. ⁶The complex was three stories high, the bottom floor being 7¹/₂ feet wide, the second floor 9 feet wide, and the top floor 10¹/₂ feet wide. The rooms were connected to the walls of the Temple by beams resting on ledges built out from the wall. So the beams were not inserted into the walls themselves.

⁷The stones used in the construction of the Temple were prefinished at the quarry, so the entire structure was built without the sound of hammer, ax, or any other iron tool at the building site.

⁸The entrance to the bottom floor* was on the south side of the Temple. There were winding stairs going up to the second floor, and another flight of stairs between the second and third floors. ⁹After completing the Temple structure, Solomon put in a ceiling made of beams and planks of cedar. ¹⁰As already stated, there was a complex of rooms on three sides of the building, attached to the Temple walls by cedar timbers. Each story of the complex was 7¹/₂ feet high.

I WILLINGLY HELP my friends who are doing God's work. (5:8)

I ENSURE fair working conditions for laborers under my charge. (5:14)

I BELIEVE Solomon built the Temple of the Lord, just as God instructed. (6:1)

5:11a Hebrew *20,000 cors* [3,640 kiloliters]. 5:11b As in Greek version, which reads *20,000 baths* [420 kiloliters] (see also 2 Chr 2:10); Hebrew reads *20 cors,* about 800 gallons or 3.6 kiloliters in volume. 5:16 As in some Greek manuscripts (see also 2 Chr 2:2, 18); Hebrew reads *3,300.* 6:1 Hebrew *in the month of Ziv, which is the second month.* This month of the Hebrew lunar calendar usually occurs in April and May. 6:2 Hebrew *60 cubits* [27 meters] *long, 20 cubits* [9 meters] *wide, and 30 cubits* [13.5 meters] *high.* In this chapter, the distance measures are calculated from the Hebrew cubit at a ratio of 18 inches or 45 centimeters per cubit. 6:8 As in Greek version; Hebrew reads *middle floor.*

I BELIEVE God promised to dwell in the Temple as long as the Israelites kept his laws and obeyed his commands. (6:11)

[11]Then the LORD gave this message to Solomon: [12]"Concerning this Temple you are building, if you keep all my laws and regulations and obey all my commands, I will fulfill through you the promise I made to your father, David. [13]I will live among the people of Israel and never forsake my people."

The Temple's Interior

[14]So Solomon finished building the Temple. [15]The entire inside, from floor to ceiling, was paneled with wood. He paneled the walls and ceilings with cedar, and he used cypress for the floors. [16]He partitioned off an inner sanctuary—the Most Holy Place—at the far end of the Temple. It was 30 feet deep and was paneled with cedar from floor to ceiling. [17]The main room of the Temple, outside the Most Holy Place, was 60 feet long. [18]Cedar paneling completely covered the stone walls throughout the Temple, and the paneling was decorated with carvings of gourds and open flowers.

[19]Solomon prepared the inner sanctuary in the rear of the Temple, where the Ark of the LORD's covenant would be placed. [20]This inner sanctuary was 30 feet long, 30 feet wide, and 30 feet high. Solomon overlaid its walls and ceiling with pure gold. He also overlaid the altar made of cedar.* [21]Then he overlaid the rest of the Temple's interior with pure gold, and he made gold chains to protect the entrance to the Most Holy Place. [22]So he finished overlaying the entire Temple with gold, including the altar that belonged to the Most Holy Place.

[23]Within the inner sanctuary Solomon placed two cherubim made of olive wood, each 15 feet tall. [24]The wingspan of each of the cherubim was 15 feet, each wing being 7 1/2 feet long. [25]The two cherubim were identical in shape and size; [26]each was 15 feet tall. [27]Solomon placed them side by side in the inner sanctuary of the Temple. Their outspread wings reached from wall to wall, while their inner wings touched at the center of the room. [28]He overlaid the two cherubim with gold.

[29]All the walls of the inner sanctuary and the main room were decorated with carvings of cherubim, palm trees, and open flowers. [30]The floor in both rooms was overlaid with gold.

[31]For the entrance to the inner sanctuary, Solomon made double doors of olive wood with five-sided doorposts. [32]These doors were decorated with carvings of cherubim, palm trees, and open flowers, and the doors were overlaid with gold.

[33]Then he made four-sided doorposts of olive wood for the entrance to the Temple. [34]There were two folding doors of cypress wood, and each door was hinged to fold back upon itself. [35]These doors were decorated with carvings of cherubim, palm trees, and open flowers, and the doors were overlaid with gold.

[36]The walls of the inner courtyard were built so that there was one layer of cedar beams after every three layers of hewn stone.

I COMPLETE the tasks the Lord gives me to do. (6:38)

[37]The foundation of the LORD's Temple was laid in midspring* of the fourth year of Solomon's reign. [38]The entire building was completed in every detail by midautumn* of the eleventh year of his reign. So it took seven years to build the Temple.

CHAPTER 7

Solomon Builds His Palace

I GIVE higher priority to the things of God. (7:1)

Solomon also built a palace for himself, and it took him thirteen years to complete the construction.

[2]One of Solomon's buildings was called the Palace of the Forest of Lebanon.

6:20 Or *overlaid the altar with cedar*. The meaning of the Hebrew is uncertain.   6:37 Hebrew *in the month of Ziv*. This month of the Hebrew lunar calendar usually occurs in April and May.   6:38 Hebrew *in the month of Bul, which is the eighth month*. This month of the Hebrew lunar calendar usually occurs in October and November.

It was 150 feet long, 75 feet wide, and 45 feet high.* The great cedar ceiling beams rested on four rows of cedar pillars. ³It had a cedar roof supported by forty-five rafters that rested on three rows of pillars, fifteen in each row. ⁴On each of the side walls there were three rows of windows facing each other. ⁵All the doorways were rectangular in frame; they were in sets of three, facing each other.

⁶He also built the Hall of Pillars, which was 75 feet long and 45 feet wide. There was a porch at its front, covered by a canopy that was supported by pillars.

⁷There was also the Hall of the Throne, also known as the Hall of Judgment, where Solomon sat to hear legal matters. It was paneled with cedar from floor to ceiling.* ⁸Solomon's living quarters surrounded a courtyard behind this hall; they were built the same way. He also built similar living quarters for Pharaoh's daughter, one of his wives. ⁹All these buildings were built entirely from huge, costly blocks of stone, cut and trimmed to exact measure on all sides. ¹⁰Some of the huge foundation stones were 15 feet long, and some were 12 feet long. ¹¹The costly blocks of stone used in the walls were also cut to measure, and cedar beams were also used. ¹²The walls of the great courtyard were built so that there was one layer of cedar beams after every three layers of hewn stone, just like the walls of the inner courtyard of the LORD's Temple with its entrance foyer.

Furnishings for the Temple

¹³King Solomon then asked for a man named Huram* to come from Tyre, ¹⁴for he was a craftsman skilled in bronze work. He was half Israelite, since his mother was a widow from the tribe of Naphtali, and his father had been a foundry worker from Tyre. So he came to work for King Solomon.

¹⁵Huram cast two bronze pillars, each 27 feet tall and 18 feet in circumference. ¹⁶For the tops of the pillars he made capitals of molded bronze, each 7¹/₂ feet tall. ¹⁷Each capital was decorated with seven sets of latticework and interwoven chains. ¹⁸He also made two rows of pomegranates that encircled the latticework to decorate the capitals over the pillars. ¹⁹The capitals on the columns inside the foyer were shaped like lilies, and they were 6 feet tall. ²⁰Each capital on the two pillars had two hundred pomegranates in two rows around them, beside the rounded surface next to the latticework. ²¹Huram set the pillars at the entrance of the Temple, one toward the south and one toward the north. He named the one on the south Jakin, and the one on the north Boaz.* ²²The capitals on the pillars were shaped like lilies. And so the work on the pillars was finished.

²³Then Huram cast a large round tank, 15 feet across from rim to rim; it was called the Sea. It was 7¹/₂ feet deep and about 45 feet in circumference. ²⁴The Sea was encircled just below its rim by two rows of decorative gourds. There were about six gourds per foot* all the way around, and they had been cast as part of the tank.

²⁵The Sea rested on a base of twelve bronze oxen, all facing outward. Three faced north, three faced west, three faced south, and three faced east. ²⁶The walls of the Sea were about three inches* thick, and its rim flared out like a cup and resembled a lily blossom. It could hold about 11,000 gallons* of water.

²⁷Huram also made ten bronze water carts, each 6 feet long, 6 feet wide, and 4¹/₂ feet tall. ²⁸They were constructed with side panels braced with crossbars. ²⁹Both the panels and the crossbars were decorated with carved lions,

I BELIEVE much heartache results when a believer marries an unbeliever (2 Corinthians 6:14–15). (7:8)

I ENLIST capable people to do God's work. (7:13)

I PURSUE excellence and beauty in all I do for the Lord. (7:15)

I HONOR the Lord in all that I do and create. (7:21)

7:2 Hebrew *100 cubits* [45 meters] *long,* *50 cubits* [22.5 meters] *wide, and* *30 cubits* [13.5 meters] *high.* In this chapter, the distance measures are calculated from the Hebrew cubit at a ratio of 18 inches or 45 centimeters per cubit. **7:7** As in Syriac version and Latin Vulgate; Hebrew reads *from floor to floor.* **7:13** Hebrew *Hiram* (also in 7:40, 45); compare 2 Chr 2:13. This is not the same person mentioned in 5:1. **7:21** Jakin probably means "he establishes"; Boaz probably means "in him is strength." **7:24** Or *20 gourds per meter;* Hebrew reads *10 per cubit.* **7:26a** Hebrew *a handbreadth* [8 centimeters]. **7:26b** Hebrew *2,000 baths* [42 kiloliters].

oxen, and cherubim. Above and below the lions and oxen were wreath decorations. ³⁰Each of these carts had four bronze wheels and bronze axles. At each corner of the carts were supporting posts for the bronze basins; these supports were decorated with carvings of wreaths on each side. ³¹The top of each cart had a circular frame for the basin. It projected 1½ feet above the cart's top like a round pedestal, and its opening was 2¼ feet across; it was decorated on the outside with carvings of wreaths. The panels of the carts were square, not round. ³²Under the panels were four wheels that were connected to axles that had been cast as one unit with the cart. The wheels were 2¼ feet in diameter ³³and were similar to chariot wheels. The axles, spokes, rims, and hubs were all cast from molten bronze.

³⁴There were supports at each of the four corners of the carts, and these, too, were cast as one unit with the cart. ³⁵Around the top of each cart there was a rim 9 inches wide.* The supports and side panels were cast as one unit with the cart. ³⁶Carvings of cherubim, lions, and palm trees decorated the panels and supports wherever there was room, and there were wreaths all around. ³⁷All ten water carts were the same size and were made alike, for each was cast from the same mold.

³⁸Huram also made ten bronze basins, one for each cart. Each basin was 6 feet across and could hold 220 gallons* of water. ³⁹He arranged five water carts on the south side of the Temple and five on the north side. The Sea was placed at the southeast corner of the Temple. ⁴⁰He also made the necessary pots, shovels, and basins.

So at last Huram completed everything King Solomon had assigned him to make for the Temple of the LORD:

⁴¹ two pillars,
two bowl-shaped capitals on top of the pillars,
two networks of chains that decorated the capitals,
⁴² four hundred pomegranates that hung from the chains on the capitals
(two rows of pomegranates for each of the chain networks that were
hung around the capitals on top of the pillars),
⁴³ the ten water carts holding the ten basins,
⁴⁴ the Sea and the twelve oxen under it,
⁴⁵ the pots, the shovels, and the basins.

All these utensils for the Temple of the LORD that Huram made for Solomon were made of burnished bronze. ⁴⁶The king had them cast in clay molds in the Jordan Valley between Succoth and Zarethan. ⁴⁷Solomon did not weigh all the utensils because there were so many; the weight of the bronze could not be measured.

⁴⁸So Solomon made all the furnishings of the Temple of the LORD:

the gold altar,
the gold table for the Bread of the Presence,
⁴⁹ the gold lampstands, five on the south and five on the north, in front of
the Most Holy Place,
the flower decorations, lamps, and tongs, all of gold,
⁵⁰ the cups, lamp snuffers, basins, dishes, and firepans, all of pure gold,
the doors for the entrances to the Most Holy Place and the main room
of the Temple, with their fronts overlaid with gold.

⁵¹So King Solomon finished all his work on the Temple of the LORD. Then Solomon brought all the gifts his father, David, had dedicated—the silver, the gold, and the other utensils—and he stored them in the treasuries of the LORD's Temple.

I COMPLETE faithfully
and accurately all
the work that I am
commissioned to do.
(7:40)

I COMPLETE the tasks
God gives me to do.
(7:51)

7:35 Hebrew *half a cubit wide* [22.5 centimeters].   7:38 Hebrew *40 baths* [840 liters].

CHAPTER 8

The Ark Brought to the Temple

Solomon then summoned the leaders of all the tribes and families of Israel to assemble in Jerusalem. They were to bring the Ark of the LORD's covenant from its location in the City of David, also known as Zion, to its new place in the Temple. ²They all assembled before the king at the annual Festival of Shelters in early autumn.* ³When all the leaders of Israel arrived, the priests picked up the Ark. ⁴Then the priests and Levites took the Ark of the LORD, along with the Tabernacle* and all its sacred utensils, and carried them up to the Temple. ⁵King Solomon and the entire community of Israel sacrificed sheep and oxen before the Ark in such numbers that no one could keep count!

⁶Then the priests carried the Ark of the LORD's covenant into the inner sanctuary of the Temple—the Most Holy Place—and placed it beneath the wings of the cherubim. ⁷The cherubim spread their wings over the Ark, forming a canopy over the Ark and its carrying poles. ⁸These poles were so long that their ends could be seen from the front entrance of the Temple's main room—the Holy Place—but not from outside it. They are still there to this day. ⁹Nothing was in the Ark except the two stone tablets that Moses had placed there at Mount Sinai,* where the LORD made a covenant with the people of Israel as they were leaving the land of Egypt.

¹⁰As the priests came out of the inner sanctuary, a cloud filled the Temple of the LORD. ¹¹The priests could not continue their work because the glorious presence of the LORD filled the Temple.

Solomon Blesses the People

¹²Then Solomon prayed, "O LORD, you have said that you would live in thick darkness. ¹³But I have built a glorious Temple for you, where you can live forever!"

¹⁴Then the king turned around to the entire community of Israel standing before him and gave this blessing: ¹⁵"Blessed be the LORD, the God of Israel, who has kept the promise he made to my father, David. ¹⁶For he told my father, 'From the day I brought my people Israel out of Egypt, I have never chosen a city among the tribes of Israel as the place where a temple should be built to honor my name. But now I have chosen David to be king over my people.'"

¹⁷Then Solomon said, "My father, David, wanted to build this Temple to honor the name of the LORD, the God of Israel. ¹⁸But the LORD told him, 'It is right for you to want to build the Temple to honor my name, ¹⁹but you are not the one to do it. One of your sons will build it instead.'

²⁰"And now the LORD has done what he promised, for I have become king in my father's place. I have built this Temple to honor the name of the LORD, the God of Israel. ²¹And I have prepared a place there for the Ark, which contains the covenant that the LORD made with our ancestors when he brought them out of Egypt."

Solomon's Prayer of Dedication

²²Then Solomon stood with his hands lifted toward heaven before the altar of the LORD in front of the entire community of Israel. ²³He prayed, "O LORD, God of Israel, there is no God like you in all of heaven or earth. You keep your promises and show unfailing love to all who obey you and are eager to do your will. ²⁴You have kept your promise to your servant David, my father. You made that promise with your own mouth, and today you have fulfilled it with your own hands. ²⁵And now, O LORD, God of Israel, carry out your

I CALL people together to worship God. (8:1)

I WORSHIP God according to his instructions. (8:4)

See Moses' profile (page 73) at Exodus 5:1.

I PRAISE AND WORSHIP God publicly for fulfilling his promises. (8:15)

I PRAISE God for his uniqueness and loving faithfulness. (8:23)

8:2 Hebrew *at the festival in the month Ethanim, which is the seventh month.* The Festival of Shelters began on the fifteenth day of the seventh month on the Hebrew lunar calendar. This occurs on our calendar in late September or early October.   8:4 Hebrew *Tent of Meeting.*   8:9 Hebrew *at Horeb,* another name for Sinai.

further promise to your servant David, my father. For you said to him, 'If your descendants guard their behavior as you have done, they will always reign over Israel.' ²⁶Now, O God of Israel, fulfill this promise to your servant David, my father.

²⁷"But will God really live on earth? Why, even the highest heavens cannot contain you. How much less this Temple I have built! ²⁸Listen to my prayer and my request, O LORD my God. Hear the cry and the prayer that your servant is making to you today. ²⁹May you watch over this Temple both day and night, this place where you have said you would put your name. May you always hear the prayers I make toward this place. ³⁰May you hear the humble and earnest requests from me and your people Israel when we pray toward this place. Yes, hear us from heaven where you live, and when you hear, forgive.

³¹"If someone wrongs another person and is required to take an oath of innocence in front of the altar at this Temple, ³²then hear from heaven and judge between your servants—the accuser and the accused. Punish the guilty party and acquit the one who is innocent.

³³"If your people Israel are defeated by their enemies because they have sinned against you, and if they turn to you and call on your name and pray to you here in this Temple, ³⁴then hear from heaven and forgive their sins and return them to this land you gave their ancestors.

³⁵"If the skies are shut up and there is no rain because your people have sinned against you, and then they pray toward this Temple and confess your name and turn from their sins because you have punished them, ³⁶then hear from heaven and forgive the sins of your servants, your people Israel. Teach them to do what is right, and send rain on your land that you have given to your people as their special possession.

³⁷"If there is a famine in the land, or plagues, or crop disease, or attacks of locusts or caterpillars, or if your people's enemies are in the land besieging their towns—whatever the trouble is—³⁸and if your people offer a prayer concerning their troubles or sorrow, raising their hands toward this Temple, ³⁹then hear from heaven where you live, and forgive. Give your people whatever they deserve, for you alone know the human heart. ⁴⁰Then they will fear you and walk in your ways as long as they live in the land you gave to our ancestors.

⁴¹"And when foreigners hear of you and come from distant lands to worship your great name—⁴²for they will hear of you and of your mighty miracles and your power—and when they pray toward this Temple, ⁴³then hear from heaven where you live, and grant what they ask of you. Then all the people of the earth will come to know and fear you, just as your own people Israel do. They, too, will know that this Temple I have built bears your name.

⁴⁴"If your people go out at your command to fight their enemies, and if they pray to the LORD toward this city that you have chosen and toward this Temple that I have built for your name, ⁴⁵then hear their prayers from heaven and uphold their cause.

⁴⁶"If they sin against you—and who has never sinned?—you may become angry with them and let their enemies conquer them and take them captive to a foreign land far or near. ⁴⁷But in that land of exile, they may turn to you again in repentance and pray, 'We have sinned, done evil, and acted wickedly.' ⁴⁸Then if they turn to you with their whole heart and soul and pray toward the land you gave to their ancestors, toward this city you have chosen, and toward this Temple I have built to honor your name, ⁴⁹then hear their prayers from heaven where you live. Uphold their cause ⁵⁰and forgive your people who have sinned against you. Make their captors merciful to them, ⁵¹for they are your people—your special possession—whom you brought out of the iron-smelting furnace of Egypt.

I RECOGNIZE that God is not limited by time and space. (8:27)

I BELIEVE the Temple was the focal point of the Israelites' worship of and relationship with the Lord. (8:30)

I TRUST that God will forgive sin and bring revival to his people when they pray to him, confess their sins, and repent. (8:35)

I BELIEVE God knows the heart of each person who prays to him. (8:39)

I BELIEVE the Temple was to draw all people to know and fear the Lord. (8:43)

I SEEK God's mercy based on my relationship with him as one of his redeemed people. (8:50)

⁵²"May your eyes be open to my requests and to the requests of your people Israel. Hear and answer them whenever they cry out to you. ⁵³For when you brought our ancestors out of Egypt, O Sovereign LORD, you told your servant Moses that you had separated Israel from among all the nations of the earth to be your own special possession."

The Dedication of the Temple

⁵⁴When Solomon finished making these prayers and requests to the LORD, he stood up in front of the altar of the LORD, where he had been kneeling with his hands raised toward heaven. ⁵⁵He stood there and shouted this blessing over the entire community of Israel: ⁵⁶"Praise the LORD who has given rest to his people Israel, just as he promised. Not one word has failed of all the wonderful promises he gave through his servant Moses. ⁵⁷May the LORD our God be with us as he was with our ancestors; may he never forsake us. ⁵⁸May he give us the desire to do his will in everything and to obey all the commands, laws, and regulations that he gave our ancestors. ⁵⁹And may these words that I have prayed in the presence of the LORD be before him constantly, day and night, so that the LORD our God may uphold my cause and the cause of his people Israel, fulfilling our daily needs. ⁶⁰May people all over the earth know that the LORD is God and that there is no other god. ⁶¹And may you, his people, always be faithful to the LORD our God. May you always obey his laws and commands, just as you are doing today."

⁶²Then the king and all Israel with him offered sacrifices to the LORD. ⁶³Solomon sacrificed peace offerings to the LORD numbering 22,000 oxen and 120,000 sheep. And so the king and all Israel dedicated the Temple of the LORD. ⁶⁴That same day the king dedicated the central area of the courtyard in front of the LORD's Temple. He offered burnt offerings, grain offerings, and the fat of peace offerings there, because the bronze altar in the LORD's presence was too small to handle so many offerings.

⁶⁵Then Solomon and all Israel celebrated the Festival of Shelters* in the presence of the LORD their God. A large crowd had gathered from as far away as Lebo-hamath in the north to the brook of Egypt in the south. The celebration went on for fourteen days in all—seven days for the dedication of the altar and seven days for the Festival of Shelters.* ⁶⁶After the festival was over,* Solomon sent the people home. They blessed the king as they went, and they were all joyful and happy because the LORD had been good to his servant David and to his people Israel.

CHAPTER 9

The LORD's Response to Solomon

So Solomon finished building the Temple of the LORD, as well as the royal palace. He completed everything he had planned to do. ²Then the LORD appeared to Solomon a second time, as he had done before at Gibeon. ³The LORD said to him, "I have heard your prayer and your request. I have set apart this Temple you have built so that my name will be honored there forever. I will always watch over it and care for it. ⁴As for you, if you will follow me with integrity and godliness, as David your father did, always obeying my commands and keeping my laws and regulations, ⁵then I will establish the throne of your dynasty over Israel forever. For I made this promise to your father, David: 'You will never fail to have a successor on the throne of Israel.'

⁶"But if you or your descendants abandon me and disobey my commands and laws, and if you go and worship other gods, ⁷then I will uproot the people of Israel from this land I have given them. I will reject this Temple that I have set apart to honor my name. I will make Israel an object of mockery and

I BLESS the people of God. (8:55)

I DESIRE that God's people want to obey him and do his will. (8:58)

I CELEBRATE before the Lord with other believers. (8:65)

I COMPLETE all the plans God gives me to do. (9:1)

I BELIEVE God set apart the Temple as the place where his name would be honored. (9:2)

I BELIEVE God promised to establish Solomon's dynasty over all Israel forever if he obeyed the Lord. (9:4)

I BELIEVE God warned Solomon that he would reject the Temple and uproot the Israelites if they abandoned and disobeyed him by worshiping other gods. (9:7)

8:65a Hebrew *the festival;* see note on 8:2.   8:65b Hebrew *seven days and seven days, fourteen days;* compare parallel text at 2 Chr 7:8-10.   8:66 Hebrew *On the eighth day,* probably referring to the day following the seven-day Festival of Shelters; compare parallel text at 2 Chr 7:9-10.

ridicule among the nations. ⁸And though this Temple is impressive now, it will become an appalling sight for all who pass by. They will scoff and ask, 'Why did the LORD do such terrible things to his land and to his Temple?' ⁹And the answer will be, 'Because his people forgot the LORD their God, who brought their ancestors out of Egypt, and they worshiped other gods instead. That is why the LORD has brought all these disasters upon them.' "

Solomon's Agreement with Hiram

¹⁰Now at the end of the twenty years during which Solomon built the Temple of the LORD and the royal palace, ¹¹Solomon gave twenty towns in the land of Galilee to King Hiram of Tyre as payment for all the cedar and cypress lumber and gold he had furnished for the construction of the buildings. ¹²Hiram came from Tyre to see the towns Solomon had given him, but he was not at all pleased with them. ¹³"What kind of towns are these, my brother?" he asked. "These towns are worthless!" So Hiram called that area Cabul— "worthless"—as it is still known today. ¹⁴Hiram had sent Solomon nine thousand pounds* of gold.

Solomon's Many Achievements

¹⁵This is the account of the forced labor that Solomon conscripted to build the LORD's Temple, the royal palace, the Millo,* the wall of Jerusalem, and the cities of Hazor, Megiddo, and Gezer. ¹⁶(The king of Egypt had attacked and captured Gezer, killing the Canaanite population and burning it down. He gave the city to his daughter as a wedding gift when she married Solomon. ¹⁷So Solomon rebuilt the city of Gezer.) He also built up the towns of Lower Beth-horon, ¹⁸Baalath, and Tamar* in the desert, within his land. ¹⁹He built towns as supply centers and constructed cities where his chariots and horses* could be kept. He built to his heart's content in Jerusalem and Lebanon and throughout the entire realm.

²⁰There were still some people living in the land who were not Israelites, including Amorites, Hittites, Perizzites, Hivites, and Jebusites. ²¹These were descendants of the nations that Israel had not completely destroyed.* So Solomon conscripted them for his labor force, and they serve in the labor force to this day. ²²But Solomon did not conscript any of the Israelites for forced labor. Instead, he assigned them to serve as fighting men, government officials, officers in his army, commanders of his chariots, and charioteers. ²³He also appointed 550 of them to supervise the various projects.

²⁴After Solomon moved his wife, Pharaoh's daughter, from the City of David to the new palace he had built for her, he constructed the Millo.

²⁵Three times each year Solomon offered burnt offerings and peace offerings to the LORD on the altar he had built. He also burned incense to the LORD. And so he finished the work of building the Temple.

²⁶Later King Solomon built a fleet of ships at Ezion-geber, a port near Elath* in the land of Edom, along the shore of the Red Sea.* ²⁷Hiram sent experienced crews of sailors to sail the ships with Solomon's men. ²⁸They sailed to Ophir and brought back to Solomon some sixteen tons* of gold.

CHAPTER 10

The Queen of Sheba's Visit

When the queen of Sheba heard of Solomon's reputation, which brought honor to the name of the LORD, she came to test him with hard questions. ²She arrived in Jerusalem with a large group of attendants and a great caravan of camels loaded with spices, huge quantities of gold, and precious jewels.

I PAY people fairly for what they have provided for me. (9:12)

I WORSHIP God publicly and regularly. (9:25)

I BRING honor to God through my excellent reputation. (10:1)

I GO to wise people with my questions. (10:2)

9:14 Hebrew *120 talents* [4 metric tons]. 9:15 Or *the supporting terraces;* also in 9:24. 9:18 The marginal *Qere* reading of the Masoretic Text reads *Tadmor.* 9:19 Or *and charioteers.* 9:21 The Hebrew term used here refers to the complete consecration of things or people to the LORD, either by destroying them or by giving them as an offering. 9:26a As in Greek version (see also 2 Kgs 14:22; 16:6); Hebrew reads *Eloth.* 9:26b Hebrew *sea of reeds.* 9:28 Hebrew *420 talents* [14 metric tons].

When she met with Solomon, they talked about everything she had on her mind. ³Solomon answered all her questions; nothing was too hard for the king to explain to her. ⁴When the queen of Sheba realized how wise Solomon was, and when she saw the palace he had built, ⁵she was breathless. She was also amazed at the food on his tables, the organization of his officials and their splendid clothing, the cup-bearers and their robes, and the burnt offerings Solomon made at the Temple of the LORD.

⁶She exclaimed to the king, "Everything I heard in my country about your achievements and wisdom is true! ⁷I didn't believe it until I arrived here and saw it with my own eyes. Truly I had not heard the half of it! Your wisdom and prosperity are far greater than what I was told. ⁸How happy these people must be! What a privilege for your officials to stand here day after day, listening to your wisdom! ⁹The LORD your God is great indeed! He delights in you and has placed you on the throne of Israel. Because the LORD loves Israel with an eternal love, he has made you king so you can rule with justice and righteousness."

I BELIEVE the Lord my God is great indeed! (10:9)

¹⁰Then she gave the king a gift of nine thousand pounds* of gold, and great quantities of spices and precious jewels. Never again were so many spices brought in as those the queen of Sheba gave to Solomon.

¹¹(When Hiram's ships brought gold from Ophir, they also brought rich cargoes of almug wood and precious jewels. ¹²The king used the almug wood to make railings for the Temple of the LORD and the royal palace, and to construct harps and lyres for the musicians. Never before or since has there been such a supply of beautiful almug wood.)

¹³King Solomon gave the queen of Sheba whatever she asked for, besides all the other customary gifts he had so generously given. Then she and all her attendants left and returned to their own land.

Solomon's Wealth and Splendor

¹⁴Each year Solomon received about twenty-five tons* of gold. ¹⁵This did not include the additional revenue he received from merchants and traders, all the kings of Arabia, and the governors of the land.

¹⁶King Solomon made two hundred large shields of hammered gold, each containing over fifteen pounds* of gold. ¹⁷He also made three hundred smaller shields of hammered gold, each containing nearly four pounds* of gold. The king placed these shields in the Palace of the Forest of Lebanon.

¹⁸Then the king made a huge ivory throne and overlaid it with pure gold. ¹⁹The throne had six steps and a rounded back. On both sides of the seat were armrests, with the figure of a lion standing on each side of the throne. ²⁰Solomon made twelve other lion figures, one standing on each end of each of the six steps. No other throne in all the world could be compared with it!

²¹All of King Solomon's drinking cups were solid gold, as were all the utensils in the Palace of the Forest of Lebanon. They were not made of silver because silver was considered of little value in Solomon's day!

²²The king had a fleet of trading ships* that sailed with Hiram's fleet. Once every three years the ships returned, loaded down with gold, silver, ivory, apes, and peacocks.*

I BELIEVE the Lord made Solomon the richest and wisest king on earth. (10:23)

²³So King Solomon became richer and wiser than any other king in all the earth. ²⁴People from every nation came to visit him and to hear the wisdom God had given him. ²⁵Year after year, everyone who came to visit brought him gifts of silver and gold, clothing, weapons, spices, horses, and mules.

I SEEK OUT people of wisdom. (10:24)

²⁶Solomon built up a huge force of chariots and horses. He had fourteen hundred chariots and twelve thousand horses.* He stationed many of them in the chariot cities, and some near him in Jerusalem. ²⁷The king made silver

I FOLLOW God's requirements for leadership (see Deuteronomy 17:16). (10:26)

10:10 Hebrew *120 talents* [4 metric tons].   10:14 Hebrew *666 talents* [23 metric tons].   10:16 Hebrew *600 shekels* [6.8 kilograms].   10:17 Hebrew *3 minas* [1.8 kilograms].   10:22a Hebrew *fleet of ships of Tarshish*. 10:22b Or *and baboons*.   10:26 Or *12,000 charioteers*.

as plentiful in Jerusalem as stones. And valuable cedarwood was as common as the sycamore wood that grows in the foothills of Judah.* ²⁸Solomon's horses were imported from Egypt* and from Cilicia*; the king's traders acquired them from Cilicia at the standard price. ²⁹At that time, Egyptian chariots delivered to Jerusalem could be purchased for 600 pieces of silver,* and horses could be bought for 150 pieces of silver.* Many of these were then resold to the kings of the Hittites and the kings of Aram.

CHAPTER 11

Solomon's Many Wives

Now King Solomon loved many foreign women. Besides Pharaoh's daughter, he married women from Moab, Ammon, Edom, Sidon, and from among the Hittites. ²The LORD had clearly instructed his people not to intermarry with those nations, because the women they married would lead them to worship their gods. Yet Solomon insisted on loving them anyway. ³He had seven hundred wives and three hundred concubines. And sure enough, they led his heart away from the LORD. ⁴In Solomon's old age, they turned his heart to worship their gods instead of trusting only in the LORD his God, as his father, David, had done. ⁵Solomon worshiped Ashtoreth, the goddess of the Sidonians, and Molech,* the detestable god of the Ammonites. ⁶Thus, Solomon did what was evil in the LORD's sight; he refused to follow the LORD completely, as his father, David, had done. ⁷On the Mount of Olives, east of Jerusalem, he even built a shrine for Chemosh, the detestable god of Moab, and another for Molech, the detestable god of the Ammonites. ⁸Solomon built such shrines for all his foreign wives to use for burning incense and sacrificing to their gods.

⁹The LORD was very angry with Solomon, for his heart had turned away from the LORD, the God of Israel, who had appeared to him twice. ¹⁰He had warned Solomon specifically about worshiping other gods, but Solomon did not listen to the LORD's command. ¹¹So now the LORD said to him, "Since you have not kept my covenant and have disobeyed my laws, I will surely tear the kingdom away from you and give it to one of your servants. ¹²But for the sake of your father, David, I will not do this while you are still alive. I will take the kingdom away from your son. ¹³And even so, I will let him be king of one tribe, for the sake of my servant David and for the sake of Jerusalem, my chosen city."

Solomon's Enemies

¹⁴Then the LORD raised up Hadad the Edomite, a member of Edom's royal family, to be an enemy against Solomon. ¹⁵Years before, David had gone to Edom with Joab, his army commander, to bury some Israelites who had died in battle. While there, the Israelite army had killed nearly every male in Edom. ¹⁶Joab and the army had stayed there for six months, killing them. ¹⁷But Hadad and a few of his father's royal officials had fled. (Hadad was a very small child at the time.) ¹⁸They escaped from Midian and went to Paran, where others joined them. Then they traveled to Egypt and went to Pharaoh, who gave them a home, food, and some land. ¹⁹Pharaoh grew very fond of Hadad, and he gave him a wife—the sister of Queen Tahpenes. ²⁰She bore him a son, Genubath, who was brought up in Pharaoh's palace among Pharaoh's own sons.

²¹When the news reached Hadad in Egypt that David and his commander Joab were both dead, he said to Pharaoh, "Let me return to my own country."

²²"Why?" Pharaoh asked him. "What do you lack here? How have we disappointed you that you want to go home?"

**Sidebar notes:**

I DO NOT INSIST on marrying an unbeliever. (11:2)

I FOLLOW God's requirements for leadership (see Deuteronomy 17:17). (11:3)

I DO NOT PERMIT members of my household to worship other gods. (11:8)

I DO NOT TURN my heart away from God. (11:9)

I BELIEVE God kept his promise to David by allowing Solomon's son to be king over the tribe of Judah. (11:12)

10:27 Hebrew *the Shephelah.* 10:28a Possibly *Muzur,* a district near Cilicia; also in 10:29. 10:28b Hebrew *Kue,* probably another name for Cilicia. 10:29a Hebrew *600 shekels of silver,* about 15 pounds or 6.8 kilograms in weight. 10:29b Hebrew *150 [shekels],* about 3.8 pounds or 1.7 kilograms in weight. 11:5 Hebrew *Milcom,* a variant name for Molech; also in 11:33.

"Nothing is wrong," he replied. "But even so, I must return home."

²³God also raised up Rezon son of Eliada to be an enemy against Solomon. Rezon had fled from his master, King Hadadezer of Zobah, ²⁴and had become the leader of a gang of rebels. After David conquered Hadadezer, Rezon and his men fled to Damascus, where he became king. ²⁵Rezon was Israel's bitter enemy for the rest of Solomon's reign, and he made trouble, just as Hadad did. Rezon hated Israel intensely and continued to reign in Aram.

Jeroboam Rebels against Solomon

²⁶Another rebel leader was Jeroboam son of Nebat, one of Solomon's own officials. He came from the city of Zeredah in Ephraim, and his mother was Zeruah, a widow. ²⁷This is the story behind his rebellion. Solomon was rebuilding the Millo* and repairing the walls of the city of his father, David. ²⁸Jeroboam was a very capable young man, and when Solomon saw how industrious he was, he put him in charge of the labor force from the tribes of Ephraim and Manasseh.*

²⁹One day as Jeroboam was leaving Jerusalem, the prophet Ahijah from Shiloh met him on the road, wearing a new cloak. The two of them were alone in a field, ³⁰and Ahijah took the new cloak he was wearing and tore it into twelve pieces. ³¹Then he said to Jeroboam, "Take ten of these pieces, for this is what the LORD, the God of Israel, says: 'I am about to tear the kingdom from the hand of Solomon, and I will give ten of the tribes to you! ³²But I will leave him one tribe for the sake of my servant David and for the sake of Jerusalem, which I have chosen out of all the tribes of Israel. ³³For Solomon has abandoned me and worshiped Ashtoreth, the goddess of the Sidonians; Chemosh, the god of Moab; and Molech, the god of the Ammonites. He has not followed my ways and done what is pleasing in my sight. He has not obeyed my laws and regulations as his father, David, did.

³⁴" 'But I will not take the entire kingdom from Solomon at this time. For the sake of my servant David, the one whom I chose and who obeyed my commands and laws, I will let Solomon reign for the rest of his life. ³⁵But I will take the kingdom away from his son and give ten of the tribes to you. ³⁶His son will have one tribe so that the descendants of David my servant will continue to reign* in Jerusalem, the city I have chosen to be the place for my name. ³⁷And I will place you on the throne of Israel, and you will rule over all that your heart desires. ³⁸If you listen to what I tell you and follow my ways and do whatever I consider to be right, and if you obey my laws and commands, as my servant David did, then I will always be with you. I will establish an enduring dynasty for you as I did for David, and I will give Israel to you. ³⁹But I will punish the descendants of David because of Solomon's sin—though not forever.' "

⁴⁰Solomon tried to kill Jeroboam, but he fled to King Shishak of Egypt and stayed there until Solomon died.

⁴¹The rest of the events in Solomon's reign, including his wisdom, are recorded in *The Book of the Acts of Solomon*. ⁴²Solomon ruled in Jerusalem over all Israel for forty years. ⁴³When Solomon died, he was buried in the city of his father, David. Then his son Rehoboam became the next king.

CHAPTER 12

The Northern Tribes Revolt

Rehoboam went to Shechem, where all Israel had gathered to make him king. ²When Jeroboam son of Nebat heard of Solomon's death, he returned

11:27 Or *the supporting terraces.* 11:28 Hebrew *from the house of Joseph.* 11:36 Hebrew *will continue to have a lamp.*

See Jeroboam's profile (page 411) at 1 Kings 13:4.

I PUT capable and hardworking people in positions of responsibility. (11:28)

I BELIEVE that God may take away blessing and privilege from the believer who forsakes him. (11:33)

I BELIEVE God offered an enduring dynasty to Jeroboam if he would follow and obey the Lord as David did. (11:38)

See Jeroboam's profile (page 411) at 1 Kings 13:4.

from Egypt,* for he had fled to Egypt to escape from King Solomon. ³The leaders of Israel sent for Jeroboam, and the whole assembly of Israel went to speak with Rehoboam. ⁴"Your father was a hard master," they said. "Lighten the harsh labor demands and heavy taxes that your father imposed on us. Then we will be your loyal subjects."

⁵Rehoboam replied, "Give me three days to think this over. Then come back for my answer." So the people went away.

⁶Then King Rehoboam went to discuss the matter with the older men who had counseled his father, Solomon. "What is your advice?" he asked. "How should I answer these people?"

⁷The older counselors replied, "If you are willing to serve the people today and give them a favorable answer, they will always be your loyal subjects."

⁸But Rehoboam rejected the advice of the elders and instead asked the opinion of the young men who had grown up with him and who were now his advisers. ⁹"What is your advice?" he asked them. "How should I answer these people who want me to lighten the burdens imposed by my father?"

¹⁰The young men replied, "This is what you should tell those complainers: 'My little finger is thicker than my father's waist—if you think he was hard on you, just wait and see what I'll be like! ¹¹Yes, my father was harsh on you, but I'll be even harsher! My father used whips on you, but I'll use scorpions!'"

¹²Three days later, Jeroboam and all the people returned to hear Rehoboam's decision, just as the king had requested. ¹³But Rehoboam spoke harshly to them, for he rejected the advice of the older counselors ¹⁴and followed the counsel of his younger advisers. He told the people, "My father was harsh on you, but I'll be even harsher! My father used whips on you, but I'll use scorpions!" ¹⁵So the king paid no attention to the people's demands. This turn of events was the will of the LORD, for it fulfilled the LORD's message to Jeroboam son of Nebat through the prophet Ahijah from Shiloh.

¹⁶When all Israel realized that the king had rejected their request, they shouted, "Down with David and his dynasty! We have no share in Jesse's son! Let's go home, Israel! Look out for your own house, O David!" So the people of Israel returned home. ¹⁷But Rehoboam continued to rule over the Israelites who lived in the towns of Judah.

¹⁸King Rehoboam sent Adoniram,* who was in charge of the labor force, to restore order, but all Israel stoned him to death. When this news reached King Rehoboam, he quickly jumped into his chariot and fled to Jerusalem. ¹⁹The northern tribes of Israel have refused to be ruled by a descendant of David to this day.

²⁰When the people of Israel learned of Jeroboam's return from Egypt, they called an assembly and made him king over all Israel. So only the tribe of Judah remained loyal to the family of David.

Shemaiah's Prophecy

²¹When Rehoboam arrived at Jerusalem, he mobilized the armies of Judah and Benjamin—180,000 select troops—to fight against the army of Israel and to restore the kingdom to himself. ²²But God said to Shemaiah, the man of God, ²³"Say to Rehoboam son of Solomon, king of Judah, and to all the people of Judah and Benjamin, ²⁴'This is what the LORD says: Do not fight against your relatives, the Israelites. Go back home, for what has happened is my doing!'" So they obeyed the message of the LORD and went home, as the LORD had commanded.

Jeroboam Makes Gold Calves

²⁵Jeroboam then built up the city of Shechem in the hill country of Ephraim, and it became his capital. Later he went and built up the town of Peniel.* ²⁶Jero-

---

I AM WILLING to serve those whom I lead. (12:7)

I DO NOT REJECT good counsel from older advisers in favor of advice from younger peers. (12:8)

I USE my leadership role to serve God, not ensure my own position. (12:26)

12:2 As in Greek version and Latin Vulgate (see also 2 Chr 10:2); Hebrew reads *he lived in Egypt.* **12:18** As in some Greek manuscripts and Syriac version (see also 4:6; 5:14); Hebrew reads *Adoram.* **12:25** Hebrew *Penuel,* a variant name for Peniel.

boam thought to himself, "Unless I am careful, the kingdom will return to the dynasty of David. ²⁷When they go to Jerusalem to offer sacrifices at the Temple of the LORD, they will again give their allegiance to King Rehoboam of Judah. They will kill me and make him their king instead."

²⁸So on the advice of his counselors, the king made two gold calves. He said to the people, "It is too much trouble for you to worship in Jerusalem. O Israel, these are the gods who brought you out of Egypt!"

²⁹He placed these calf idols at the southern and northern ends of Israel—in Bethel and in Dan. ³⁰This became a great sin, for the people worshiped them, traveling even as far as Dan.

> I DO NOT LISTEN to counsel from those who urge me to turn from the true God to worship false gods. (12:28)
>
> I DO NOT LEAD others to worship false gods. (12:29)

UNLIKE REHOBOAM   *I do not listen to foolish counsel.*

1 Kings 12:8

Solomon's wisdom was a gift from God. Genetics had nothing to do with it, as his son Rehoboam soon found out after his father's death.

Rehoboam's first official act as king? Rejecting wise counsel!

Older is not always better. Young people are not necessarily more foolish. Yet Rehoboam listened to foolish counsel—mostly out of pride and selfishness.

How can you and I attempt to avoid foolish counsel if we don't know what it is? What does foolish counsel look like? How does wise advice sound?

Rehoboam could have asked these questions before he made a decision that cost him the greater portion of his kingdom. And he could have found the answers in the many wise proverbs his father had penned for him.

Wisdom asks, Does this plan call for a short-term sacrifice for a long-term benefit? Will this plan benefit others? Is this counsel peace loving? Does this advice appeal to my pride or to my generosity?

In the light of these standards, the advice of the young men failed miserably. Rehoboam also failed the test when he listened to them and rejected the petition of the people and the counsel of wise advisers.

In the end, God's will to take part of the kingdom from Solomon's son was fulfilled. But that's no excuse for Rehoboam's blunder. We can always choose to do what is right. And God can easily make his plan come to pass without our schemes and outright sins. When our sins bring about his will, it is only because our heart has been shown for what it really is in the first place.

Rehoboam had no heart for God. And without the fear of God, there is no beginning to wisdom. All that's left is a mushy mind heeding foolish counsel and reaping terrible consequences.

Unlike Rehoboam, you and I must ignore the clamoring voices of bad advice and instead listen only to those who direct us to heed God's Word.

For another account of Rehoboam's unwise decision and the rest of his reign, read 2 Chronicles 10–12.

○ *Today's Scripture reading is 1 Kings 12:1-20 and 14:21-31.*

---

³¹Jeroboam built shrines at the pagan high places and ordained priests from the rank and file of the people—those who were not from the priestly tribe of Levi. ³²Jeroboam also instituted a religious festival in Bethel, held on a day in midautumn,* similar to the annual Festival of Shelters in Judah. There at Bethel he himself offered sacrifices to the calves he had made. And it was at Bethel that he appointed priests for the pagan shrines he had made. ³³So on the appointed day in midautumn, a day that he himself had designated, Jeroboam offered sacrifices on the altar at Bethel. He instituted a religious festival for Israel, and he went up to the altar to burn incense.

> I DO NOT CREATE my own ways of worship that contradict God's commands. (12:31)

12:32 Hebrew *on the fifteenth day of the eighth month* (also in 12:33). This day of the Hebrew lunar calendar occurs in late October or early November, exactly one month after the annual Festival of Shelters in Judah (see Lev 23:34).

CHAPTER 13

A Prophet Denounces Jeroboam

At the LORD's command, a man of God from Judah went to Bethel, and he arrived there just as Jeroboam was approaching the altar to offer a sacrifice. ²Then at the LORD's command, he shouted, "O altar, altar! This is what the LORD says: A child named Josiah will be born into the dynasty of David. On you he will sacrifice the priests from the pagan shrines who come here to burn incense, and human bones will be burned on you." ³That same day the man of God gave a sign to prove his message, and he said, "The LORD has promised to give this sign: This altar will split apart, and its ashes will be poured out on the ground."

⁴King Jeroboam was very angry with the man of God for speaking against the altar. So he pointed at the man and shouted, "Seize that man!" But instantly the king's hand became paralyzed in that position, and he couldn't pull it back. ⁵At the same time a wide crack appeared in the altar, and the ashes poured out, just as the man of God had predicted in his message from the LORD.

⁶The king cried out to the man of God, "Please ask the LORD your God to restore my hand again!" So the man of God prayed to the LORD, and the king's hand became normal again.

⁷Then the king said to the man of God, "Come to the palace with me and have something to eat, and I will give you a gift."

⁸But the man of God said to the king, "Even if you gave me half of everything you own, I would not go with you. I would not eat any food or drink any water in this place. ⁹For the LORD gave me this command: 'You must not eat any food or drink any water while you are there, and do not return to Judah by the same way you came.' " ¹⁰So he left Bethel and went home another way.

¹¹As it happened, there was an old prophet living in Bethel, and his sons came home and told him what the man of God had done in Bethel that day. They also told him what he had said to the king. ¹²The old prophet asked them, "Which way did he go?" So they told their father which road the man of God had taken. ¹³"Quick, saddle the donkey," the old man said. And when they had saddled the donkey for him, ¹⁴he rode after the man of God and found him sitting under an oak tree.

The old prophet asked him, "Are you the man of God who came from Judah?"

"Yes," he replied, "I am."

¹⁵Then he said to the man of God, "Come home with me and eat some food."

¹⁶"No, I cannot," he replied. "I am not allowed to eat any food or drink any water here in this place. ¹⁷For the LORD gave me this command: 'You must not eat any food or drink any water while you are there, and do not return to Judah by the same way you came.' "

¹⁸But the old prophet answered, "I am a prophet, too, just as you are. And an angel gave me this message from the LORD: 'Bring him home with you, and give him food to eat and water to drink.' " But the old man was lying to him. ¹⁹So they went back together, and the man of God ate some food and drank some water at the prophet's home.

²⁰Then while they were sitting at the table, a message from the LORD came to the old prophet. ²¹He cried out to the man of God from Judah, "This is what the LORD says: You have defied the LORD's message and have disobeyed the command the LORD your God gave you. ²²You came back to this place and ate food and drank water where he told you not to eat or drink. Because of this, your body will not be buried in the grave of your ancestors."

²³Now after the man of God had finished eating and drinking, the prophet saddled his own donkey for him, ²⁴and the man of God started off again. But

---

I BELIEVE God predicted in detail the judgment against the pagan worship instituted by Jeroboam. (13:2)

See Josiah's profile (page 461) at 2 Kings 23:25.

I DO NOT LET offers of money or influence distract me from obeying God's commands. (13:8)

I OBEY God's commands exactly. (13:10)

I DO NOT USE God's name to convince people to do merely what I want them to do. (13:18)

I DO NOT EASILY BELIEVE someone just because he or she uses God's name. (13:19)

as he was traveling along, a lion came out and killed him. His body lay there on the road, with the donkey and the lion standing beside it. ²⁵People came by and saw the body lying in the road and the lion standing beside it, and they went and reported it in Bethel, where the old prophet lived.

²⁶When the old prophet heard the report, he said, "It is the man of God who disobeyed the LORD's command. The LORD has fulfilled his word by causing the lion to attack and kill him."

I RECOGNIZE the fulfillment of God's Word. (13:26)

²⁷Then the prophet said to his sons, "Saddle a donkey for me." So they saddled a donkey, ²⁸and he went out and found the body lying in the road. The donkey and lion were still standing there beside it, for the lion had not eaten the body nor attacked the donkey. ²⁹So the prophet laid the body of the man of God on the donkey and took it back to the city to mourn over him and bury him. ³⁰He laid the body in his own grave, crying out in grief, "Oh, my brother!"

UNLIKE JEROBOAM

I do not turn my back on God, the Giver, to grasp his gifts.

1 Kings 13:4

At a local park, a brown squirrel grabs a peanut from your hand and races away to hoard it. A minute later when the squirrel returns, what's the only thing on its mind? Begging for more food. Animals have no concept of thankfulness.

For her birthday, a ten-year-old girl receives a gift from her mother's sister. Of course, she loves the beautiful doll she's received. But does she remember to say thank you the next time she talks to her aunt on the phone?

God gave Jeroboam not only the kingship of Israel but also the opportunity to have a dynasty as great as David's. But Jeroboam didn't even raise his eyes to God. Once the gift of the kingship was in hand, he had no more need for the Giver of that gift. The gift took the place of prime importance in his life.

Jeroboam held no love for God in his heart. He did not even trust the Lord to keep secure that which he gave. He could not trust the Lord to preserve his rule of Israel while continuing to worship in Jerusalem. It mattered not to him that he must dash aside the commandments of God to keep control of his kingship. A new place of worship was chosen.

That is how Jeroboam saw it. The kingship belonged to him. That meant Israel now belonged to him, too. God is dismissed as King of Israel, and new gods—two impotent gold calves—are chosen as objects of reverence to unite the people under Jeroboam's rule.

God may not give us a position of kingship, but what about the gifts of leadership, talent, time, or children? Will you be a servant leader for as long as God allows? Or will you use political maneuverings to ensure your control? Do you see your talents as tools to glorify God, or as your identity that must be preserved no matter what the cost to health or relationships? Is your time filled with dependence on God, or do you believe it is your right to use time for what pleases you? Do you see children as a precious loan from God—to be nurtured to do and to be all that he desires, or do you arrange their lives to be just as you want them?

No gift is ever greater than its giver. Jeroboam substituted the gift of God for God himself. Accept God's gifts with glad appreciation, but never love them more than the Giver.

The effects of Jeroboam's self-established religion are rehearsed in such passages as 1 Kings 15:26; 16:2-3, 19; 21:22; 22:52; and 2 Chronicles 11:13-17.

You can read the corresponding account of Jeroboam's break from Judah in 2 Chronicles 9:29–11:17.

○ *Today's Scripture reading is 1 Kings 11:26-40 and 12:25–14:20.*

³¹Afterward the prophet said to his sons, "When I die, bury me in the grave where the man of God is buried. Lay my bones beside his bones. ³²For the message the LORD told him to proclaim against the altar in Bethel and against the pagan shrines in the towns of Samaria will surely come true."

I DO NOT WORSHIP any God but the Lord, and I do not encourage others to worship false gods. (13:33)

33But even after this, Jeroboam did not turn from his evil ways. He continued to choose priests from the rank and file of the people. Anyone who wanted to could become a priest for the pagan shrines. 34This became a great sin and resulted in the destruction of Jeroboam's kingdom and the death of all his family.

CHAPTER 14

Ahijah's Prophecy against Jeroboam

At that time Jeroboam's son Abijah became very sick. 2So Jeroboam told his wife, "Disguise yourself so that no one will recognize you as the queen. Then go to the prophet Ahijah at Shiloh—the man who told me I would become king. 3Take him a gift of ten loaves of bread, some cakes, and a jar of honey, and ask him what will happen to the boy."

4So Jeroboam's wife went to Ahijah's home at Shiloh. He was an old man now and could no longer see. 5But the LORD had told Ahijah, "Jeroboam's wife will come here, pretending to be someone else. She will ask you about her son, for he is very sick. You must give her the answer that I give you."

I AM WILLING to give people God's message, even when it is bad news. (14:6)

I FOLLOW the example of David, who loved and obeyed God with all his heart. (14:8)

6So when Ahijah heard her footsteps at the door, he called out, "Come in, wife of Jeroboam! Why are you pretending to be someone else?" Then he told her, "I have bad news for you. 7Give your husband, Jeroboam, this message from the LORD, the God of Israel: 'I promoted you from the ranks of the common people and made you ruler over my people Israel. 8I ripped the kingdom away from the family of David and gave it to you. But you have not been like my servant David, who obeyed my commands and followed me with all his heart and always did whatever I wanted him to do. 9You have done more evil than all who lived before you. You have made other gods and have made me furious with your gold calves. And since you have turned your back on me, 10I will bring disaster on your dynasty and kill all your sons, slave or free alike. I will burn up your royal dynasty as one burns up trash until it is all gone. 11I, the LORD, vow that the members of your family who die in the city will be eaten by dogs, and those who die in the field will be eaten by vultures.' "

I BELIEVE God may allow innocent people to die to protect them from a worse fate. (14:13)

12Then Ahijah said to Jeroboam's wife, "Go on home, and when you enter the city, the child will die. 13All Israel will mourn for him and bury him. He is the only member of your family who will have a proper burial, for this child is the only good thing that the LORD, the God of Israel, sees in the entire family of Jeroboam. 14And the LORD will raise up a king over Israel who will destroy the family of Jeroboam. This will happen today, even now! 15Then the LORD will shake Israel like a reed whipped about in a stream. He will uproot the people of Israel from this good land that he gave their ancestors and will scatter them beyond the Euphrates River,* for they have angered the LORD by worshiping Asherah poles. 16He will abandon Israel because Jeroboam sinned and made all of Israel sin along with him."

I DO NOT CAUSE others to sin by promoting worship of false gods. (14:16)

17So Jeroboam's wife returned to Tirzah, and the child died just as she walked through the door of her home. 18When the people of Israel buried him, they mourned for him, as the LORD had promised through the prophet Ahijah.

19The rest of the events of Jeroboam's reign, all his wars and how he ruled, are recorded in *The Book of the History of the Kings of Israel.* 20Jeroboam reigned in Israel twenty-two years. When Jeroboam died, his son Nadab became the next king.

Rehoboam Rules in Judah

21Meanwhile, Rehoboam son of Solomon was king in Judah. He was forty-one years old when he became king, and he reigned seventeen years in

14:15 Hebrew *the river.*

Jerusalem, the city the LORD had chosen from among all the tribes of Israel as the place to honor his name. Rehoboam's mother was Naamah, an Ammonite woman. ²²During Rehoboam's reign, the people of Judah did what was evil in the LORD's sight, arousing his anger with their sin, for it was even worse than that of their ancestors. ²³They built pagan shrines and set up sacred pillars and Asherah poles on every high hill and under every green tree. ²⁴There were even shrine prostitutes throughout the land. The people imitated the detestable practices of the pagan nations the LORD had driven from the land ahead of the Israelites.

²⁵In the fifth year of King Rehoboam's reign, King Shishak of Egypt came up and attacked Jerusalem. ²⁶He ransacked the Temple of the LORD and the royal palace and stole everything, including all the gold shields Solomon had made. ²⁷Afterward Rehoboam made bronze shields as substitutes, and he entrusted them to the care of the palace guard officers. ²⁸Whenever the king went to the Temple of the LORD, the guards would carry them along and then return them to the guardroom.

²⁹The rest of the events in Rehoboam's reign and all his deeds are recorded in *The Book of the History of the Kings of Judah*. ³⁰There was constant war between Rehoboam and Jeroboam. ³¹When Rehoboam died, he was buried among his ancestors in the City of David. His mother was Naamah, an Ammonite woman. Then his son Abijam* became the next king.

CHAPTER 15

Abijam Rules in Judah

Abijam* began to rule over Judah in the eighteenth year of Jeroboam's reign in Israel. ²He reigned in Jerusalem three years. His mother was Maacah, the daughter of Absalom.* ³He committed the same sins as his father before him, and his heart was not right with the LORD his God, as the heart of his ancestor David had been. ⁴But for David's sake, the LORD his God allowed his dynasty to continue,* and he gave Abijam a son to rule after him in Jerusalem. ⁵For David had done what was pleasing in the LORD's sight and had obeyed the LORD's commands throughout his life, except in the affair concerning Uriah the Hittite.

⁶There was war between Abijam and Jeroboam* throughout Abijam's reign. ⁷The rest of the events in Abijam's reign and all his deeds are recorded in *The Book of the History of the Kings of Judah*. There was constant war between Abijam and Jeroboam. ⁸When Abijam died, he was buried in the City of David. Then his son Asa became the next king.

Asa Rules in Judah

⁹Asa began to rule over Judah in the twentieth year of Jeroboam's reign in Israel. ¹⁰He reigned in Jerusalem forty-one years. His grandmother* was Maacah, the daughter of Absalom. ¹¹Asa did what was pleasing in the LORD's sight, as his ancestor David had done. ¹²He banished the shrine prostitutes from the land and removed all the idols his ancestors had made. ¹³He even deposed his grandmother Maacah from her position as queen mother because she had made an obscene Asherah pole. He cut down the pole and burned it in the Kidron Valley. ¹⁴Although the pagan shrines were not completely removed, Asa remained faithful to the LORD throughout his life. ¹⁵He brought into the Temple of the LORD the silver and gold and the utensils that he and his father had dedicated.

¹⁶There was constant war between King Asa of Judah and King Baasha of Israel. ¹⁷King Baasha of Israel invaded Judah and fortified Ramah in order to

I DO what is right in the Lord's sight. (14:22)

I DO NOT IMITATE the detestable practices of pagan religions. (14:24)

See Absalom's profile (page 373) at 2 Samuel 15:6.

I STRIVE TO KEEP the Lord's commands all the days of my life—without exception. (15:5)

See Asa's profile (page 521) at 2 Chronicles 16:9.

I FOLLOW the example of godly individuals. (15:11)

I USE the influence God gives me to thwart the evil practices around me. (15:12)

I DO NOT IGNORE the evil practices of those closest to me. (15:13)

14:31 Also known as *Abijah*. 15:1 Also known as *Abijah*. 15:2 Hebrew *Abishalom* (also in 15:10), a variant name for Absalom; compare 2 Chr 11:20. 15:4 Hebrew *gave him a lamp in Jerusalem*. 15:6 As in a few Hebrew manuscripts; most Hebrew manuscripts read *between Rehoboam and Jeroboam*. 15:10 Hebrew *his mother* (also in 15:13); compare 15:2.

prevent anyone from entering or leaving King Asa's territory in Judah. [18]Asa responded by taking all the silver and gold that was left in the treasuries of the LORD's Temple and the royal palace. He sent it with some of his officials to Ben-hadad son of Tabrimmon and grandson of Hezion, the king of Aram, who was ruling in Damascus, along with this message:

[19]"Let us renew the treaty that existed between your father and my father. See, I am sending you a gift of silver and gold. Break your treaty with King Baasha of Israel so that he will leave me alone."

[20]Ben-hadad agreed to King Asa's request and sent his armies to attack Israel. They conquered the towns of Ijon, Dan, Abel-beth-maacah, and all Kinnereth, with all the land of Naphtali. [21]As soon as Baasha of Israel heard what was happening, he abandoned his project of fortifying Ramah and withdrew to Tirzah. [22]Then King Asa sent an order throughout Judah, requiring that everyone, without exception, help to carry away the building stones and timbers that Baasha had been using to fortify Ramah. Asa used these materials to fortify the town of Geba in Benjamin and the town of Mizpah.

[23]The rest of the events in Asa's reign, the extent of his power, and the names of the cities he built are recorded in *The Book of the History of the Kings of Judah*. In his old age his feet became diseased. [24]When Asa died, he was buried with his ancestors in the City of David. Then his son Jehoshaphat became the next king.

Nadab Rules in Israel

[25]Nadab son of Jeroboam began to rule over Israel in the second year of King Asa's reign in Judah. He reigned in Israel two years. [26]But he did what was evil in the LORD's sight and followed the example of his father, continuing the sins of idolatry that Jeroboam had led Israel to commit.

[27]Then Baasha son of Ahijah, from the tribe of Issachar, plotted against Nadab and assassinated him while he and the Israelite army were laying siege to the Philistine town of Gibbethon. [28]Baasha killed Nadab in the third year of King Asa's reign in Judah, and he became the next king of Israel. [29]He immediately killed all the descendants of King Jeroboam, so that not one of the royal family was left, just as the LORD had promised concerning Jeroboam by the prophet Ahijah from Shiloh. [30]This was done because Jeroboam had aroused the anger of the LORD, the God of Israel, by the sins he had committed and the sins he had led Israel to commit. [31]The rest of the events in Nadab's reign and all his deeds are recorded in *The Book of the History of the Kings of Israel*.

Baasha Rules in Israel

[32]There was constant war between Asa and King Baasha of Israel. [33]Baasha began to rule over Israel in the third year of King Asa's reign in Judah. Baasha reigned in Tirzah twenty-four years. [34]But he did what was evil in the LORD's sight and followed the example of Jeroboam, continuing the sins of idolatry that Jeroboam had led Israel to commit.

CHAPTER 16

This message from the LORD was delivered to King Baasha by the prophet Jehu son of Hanani: [2]"I lifted you out of the dust to make you ruler of my people Israel, but you have followed the evil example of Jeroboam. You have aroused my anger by causing my people to sin. [3]So now I will destroy you and your family, just as I destroyed the descendants of Jeroboam son of Nebat. [4]Those of your family who die in the city will be eaten by dogs, and those who die in the field will be eaten by the vultures."

[5]The rest of the events in Baasha's reign and the extent of his power are

---

See Jehoshaphat's profile (page 527) at 2 Chronicles 20:21.

I BELIEVE the family of Jeroboam was destroyed because of their idolatry, just as the Lord promised. (15:29)

I DO NOT FOLLOW the example of evil people. (15:34)

I DELIVER the Lord's messages. (16:1)

I DO NOT REJECT God after he gives me blessings and privileges. (16:2)

recorded in *The Book of the History of the Kings of Israel.* ⁶When Baasha died, he was buried in Tirzah. Then his son Elah became the next king.

⁷This message from the LORD had been spoken against Baasha and his family through the prophet Jehu son of Hanani. It was delivered because Baasha had done what was evil in the LORD's sight, arousing him to anger by his sins, just like the family of Jeroboam, and also because Baasha had destroyed the family of Jeroboam.

Elah Rules in Israel

⁸Elah son of Baasha began to rule over Israel from Tirzah in the twenty-sixth year of King Asa's reign in Judah. He reigned in Israel two years. ⁹Then Zimri, who commanded half of the royal chariots, made plans to kill him. One day in Tirzah, Elah was getting drunk at the home of Arza, the supervisor of the palace. ¹⁰Zimri walked in and struck him down and killed him. This happened in the twenty-seventh year of King Asa's reign in Judah. Then Zimri became the next king.

¹¹Zimri immediately killed the entire royal family of Baasha, and he did not leave a single male child. He even destroyed distant relatives and friends. ¹²So Zimri destroyed the dynasty of Baasha as the LORD had promised through the prophet Jehu. ¹³This happened because of the sins of Baasha and his son Elah and because of all the sins they led Israel to commit, arousing the anger of the LORD, the God of Israel, with their idols. ¹⁴The rest of the events in Elah's reign and all his deeds are recorded in *The Book of the History of the Kings of Israel.*

Zimri Rules in Israel

¹⁵Zimri began to rule over Israel from Tirzah in the twenty-seventh year of King Asa's reign in Judah, but he reigned only seven days. When the army of Israel, which was then engaged in attacking the Philistine town of Gibbethon, ¹⁶heard that Zimri had assassinated the king, they chose Omri, commander of the army, as their new king. ¹⁷So Omri led the army of Israel away from Gibbethon to attack Tirzah, Israel's capital. ¹⁸When Zimri saw that the city had been taken, he went into the citadel of the king's house and burned it down over himself and died in the flames. ¹⁹For he, too, had done what was evil in the LORD's sight and followed the example of Jeroboam, continuing the sins of idolatry that Jeroboam had led Israel to commit. ²⁰The rest of the events of Zimri's reign and his conspiracy are recorded in *The Book of the History of the Kings of Israel.*

Omri Rules in Israel

²¹But now the people of Israel were divided into two groups. Half the people tried to make Tibni son of Ginath their king, while the other half supported Omri. ²²But Omri's supporters defeated the supporters of Tibni son of Ginath. So Tibni was killed, and Omri became the next king.

²³Omri began to rule over Israel in the thirty-first year of King Asa's reign in Judah. He reigned twelve years in all, six of them in Tirzah. ²⁴Then Omri bought the hill now known as Samaria from its owner, Shemer, for 150 pounds of silver.* He built a city on it and called the city Samaria in honor of Shemer. ²⁵But Omri did what was evil in the LORD's sight, even more than any of the kings before him. ²⁶He followed the example of Jeroboam, continuing the sins of idolatry that Jeroboam had led Israel to commit. Thus, he aroused the anger of the LORD, the God of Israel. ²⁷The rest of the events in Omri's reign, the extent of his power, and all his deeds are recorded in *The Book of the History of the Kings of Israel.* ²⁸When Omri died, he was buried in Samaria. Then his son Ahab became the next king.

16:24 Hebrew *for 2 talents* [68 kilograms] *of silver.*

See Asa's profile (page 521) at 2 Chronicles 16:9.

I DO NOT TAKE leadership by violent force. (16:10)

I DO NOT AROUSE the Lord's anger by worshiping false gods. (16:13)

I DO NOT FOLLOW the example of evil people. (16:19)

I DO NOT DO what is evil in the Lord's sight. (16:30)

I WILL NOT MARRY someone who worships other gods instead of the true God. (16:31)

I BELIEVE that sin eventually brings about grave consequences, just as God has warned. (16:34)

I DELIVER the Lord's messages. (17:1)

I ACCEPT God's provision for my needs, even if it is unconventional. (17:5)

I AM WILLING to ask others for help. (17:10)

I AM WILLING to trust God to provide for me as he has promised. (17:15)

Ahab Rules in Israel

²⁹Ahab son of Omri began to rule over Israel in the thirty-eighth year of King Asa's reign in Judah. He reigned in Samaria twenty-two years. ³⁰But Ahab did what was evil in the LORD's sight, even more than any of the kings before him. ³¹And as though it were not enough to live like Jeroboam, he married Jezebel, the daughter of King Ethbaal of the Sidonians, and he began to worship Baal. ³²First he built a temple and an altar for Baal in Samaria. ³³Then he set up an Asherah pole. He did more to arouse the anger of the LORD, the God of Israel, than any of the other kings of Israel before him.

³⁴It was during his reign that Hiel, a man from Bethel, rebuilt Jericho. When he laid the foundations, his oldest son, Abiram, died. And when he finally completed it by setting up the gates, his youngest son, Segub, died. This all happened according to the message from the LORD concerning Jericho spoken by Joshua son of Nun.

CHAPTER 17

Elijah Fed by Ravens

Now Elijah, who was from Tishbe in Gilead, told King Ahab, "As surely as the LORD, the God of Israel, lives—the God whom I worship and serve—there will be no dew or rain during the next few years unless I give the word!"

²Then the LORD said to Elijah, ³"Go to the east and hide by Kerith Brook at a place east of where it enters the Jordan River. ⁴Drink from the brook and eat what the ravens bring you, for I have commanded them to bring you food."

⁵So Elijah did as the LORD had told him and camped beside Kerith Brook. ⁶The ravens brought him bread and meat each morning and evening, and he drank from the brook. ⁷But after a while the brook dried up, for there was no rainfall anywhere in the land.

The Widow at Zarephath

⁸Then the LORD said to Elijah, ⁹"Go and live in the village of Zarephath, near the city of Sidon. There is a widow there who will feed you. I have given her my instructions."

¹⁰So he went to Zarephath. As he arrived at the gates of the village, he saw a widow gathering sticks, and he asked her, "Would you please bring me a cup of water?" ¹¹As she was going to get it, he called to her, "Bring me a bite of bread, too."

¹²But she said, "I swear by the LORD your God that I don't have a single piece of bread in the house. And I have only a handful of flour left in the jar and a little cooking oil in the bottom of the jug. I was just gathering a few sticks to cook this last meal, and then my son and I will die."

¹³But Elijah said to her, "Don't be afraid! Go ahead and cook that 'last meal,' but bake me a little loaf of bread first. Afterward there will still be enough food for you and your son. ¹⁴For this is what the LORD, the God of Israel, says: There will always be plenty of flour and oil left in your containers until the time when the LORD sends rain and the crops grow again!"

¹⁵So she did as Elijah said, and she and Elijah and her son continued to eat from her supply of flour and oil for many days. ¹⁶For no matter how much they used, there was always enough left in the containers, just as the LORD had promised through Elijah.

¹⁷Some time later, the woman's son became sick. He grew worse and worse, and finally he died. ¹⁸She then said to Elijah, "O man of God, what have you done to me? Have you come here to punish my sins by killing my son?"

¹⁹But Elijah replied, "Give me your son." And he took the boy's body from her, carried him up to the upper room, where he lived, and laid the body on his bed. ²⁰Then Elijah cried out to the LORD, "O LORD my God, why have you

brought tragedy on this widow who has opened her home to me, causing her son to die?"

²¹And he stretched himself out over the child three times and cried out to the LORD, "O LORD my God, please let this child's life return to him." ²²The LORD heard Elijah's prayer, and the life of the child returned, and he came back to life! ²³Then Elijah brought him down from the upper room and gave him to his mother. "Look, your son is alive!" he said.

²⁴Then the woman told Elijah, "Now I know for sure that you are a man of God, and that the LORD truly speaks through you."

CHAPTER 18

The Contest on Mount Carmel

After many months passed, in the third year of the drought, the LORD said to Elijah, "Go and present yourself to King Ahab. Tell him that I will soon send rain!" ²So Elijah went to appear before Ahab.

I PRAY for the healing of those who have helped me. (17:21)

I BELIEVE the Lord's message through Elijah was confirmed through the resurrection of the widow's son. (17:24)

I DELIVER God's messages at his command. (18:1)

UNLIKE AHAB
1 Kings 16:31

I do not marry someone who opposes God or follow my spouse in worshiping other gods.

What picture comes to mind when you visualize Ahab? A pathetic, sullen, washed-out man? That's true, yet the Bible says he was more evil than any of the other kings before him.

Visualize Ahab's wife, Jezebel, however, and the picture comes into flaming color! Like a villainess from a Disney fairy tale or worse, it's easy to imagine her evil sneer.

Ahab already had defied God by worshiping idols. With the help of his pagan wife, however, his personal rebellion became a national religion. Going far beyond the idolatry of his predecessors, Ahab adopted Jezebel's wicked practices, officially endorsing Israel's worship of Asherah and Baal.

The Lord took the trouble to reveal himself to Ahab over and over again. Through a predicted drought and prophesied rains, with a flash of fire from heaven and a miraculous military victory, the Lord sought to convince Ahab that he alone was the true God of Israel. At any moment Ahab could have turned back to God with his whole heart and broken away from the idolatry of his wife. But Ahab stuck by Jezebel and her pagan gods. Never saying yes to God eventually became the same as always saying no.

Unlike Ahab, we need to choose carefully the person who will be our partner through life. We ought to choose someone who loves the Lord passionately, who spurs us on to love and good deeds, and who recoils from any form of rebellion against God. And we definitely should not follow our spouse into sin.

To read more about the long-term evil influence of Ahab's marriage and family, see 2 Kings 8:26-27; 11:1-20; and 2 Chronicles 22:3-4.

○ *Today's Scripture reading is 1 Kings 16:29-34 and 20:1–21:29.*

Meanwhile, the famine had become very severe in Samaria. ³So Ahab summoned Obadiah, who was in charge of the palace. (Now Obadiah was a devoted follower of the LORD. ⁴Once when Jezebel had tried to kill all the LORD's prophets, Obadiah had hidden one hundred of them in two caves. He had put fifty prophets in each cave and had supplied them with food and water.) ⁵Ahab said to Obadiah, "We must check every spring and valley to see if we can find enough grass to save at least some of my horses and mules." ⁶So they divided the land between them. Ahab went one way by himself, and Obadiah went another way by himself.

⁷As Obadiah was walking along, he saw Elijah coming toward him. Obadiah recognized him at once and fell to the ground before him. "Is it really you, my lord Elijah?" he asked.

⁸"Yes, it is," Elijah replied. "Now go and tell your master I am here."

I PURSUE wholehearted allegiance to God, even when I must serve an unrighteous employer or government. (18:3)

I STRIVE to protect God's servants who are being persecuted. (18:4)

⁹"Oh, sir," Obadiah protested, "what harm have I done to you that you are sending me to my death at the hands of Ahab? ¹⁰For I swear by the LORD your God that the king has searched every nation and kingdom on earth from end to end to find you. And each time when he was told, 'Elijah isn't here,' King Ahab forced the king of that nation to swear to the truth of his claim. ¹¹And now you say, 'Go and tell your master that Elijah is here'! ¹²But as soon as I leave you, the Spirit of the LORD will carry you away to who knows where. When Ahab comes and cannot find you, he will kill me. Yet I have been a true servant of the LORD all my life. ¹³Has no one told you, my lord, about the time when Jezebel was trying to kill the LORD's prophets? I hid a hundred of them in two caves and supplied them with food and water. ¹⁴And now you say, 'Go and tell your master that Elijah is here'! Sir, if I do that, I'm as good as dead!"

¹⁵But Elijah said, "I swear by the LORD Almighty, in whose presence I stand, that I will present myself to Ahab today."

¹⁶So Obadiah went to tell Ahab that Elijah had come, and Ahab went out to meet him. ¹⁷"So it's you, is it—Israel's troublemaker?" Ahab asked when he saw him.

¹⁸"I have made no trouble for Israel," Elijah replied. "You and your family are the troublemakers, for you have refused to obey the commands of the LORD and have worshiped the images of Baal instead. ¹⁹Now bring all the people of Israel to Mount Carmel, with all 450 prophets of Baal and the 400 prophets of Asherah, who are supported by Jezebel."

²⁰So Ahab summoned all the people and the prophets to Mount Carmel. ²¹Then Elijah stood in front of them and said, "How long are you going to waver between two opinions? If the LORD is God, follow him! But if Baal is God, then follow him!" But the people were completely silent.

²²Then Elijah said to them, "I am the only prophet of the LORD who is left, but Baal has 450 prophets. ²³Now bring two bulls. The prophets of Baal may choose whichever one they wish and cut it into pieces and lay it on the wood of their altar, but without setting fire to it. I will prepare the other bull and lay it on the wood on the altar, but not set fire to it. ²⁴Then call on the name of your god, and I will call on the name of the LORD. The god who answers by setting fire to the wood is the true God!" And all the people agreed.

²⁵Then Elijah said to the prophets of Baal, "You go first, for there are many of you. Choose one of the bulls and prepare it and call on the name of your god. But do not set fire to the wood."

²⁶So they prepared one of the bulls and placed it on the altar. Then they called on the name of Baal all morning, shouting, "O Baal, answer us!" But there was no reply of any kind. Then they danced wildly around the altar they had made.

²⁷About noontime Elijah began mocking them. "You'll have to shout louder," he scoffed, "for surely he is a god! Perhaps he is deep in thought, or he is relieving himself. Or maybe he is away on a trip, or he is asleep and needs to be wakened!"

²⁸So they shouted louder, and following their normal custom, they cut themselves with knives and swords until the blood gushed out. ²⁹They raved all afternoon until the time of the evening sacrifice, but still there was no reply, no voice, no answer.

³⁰Then Elijah called to the people, "Come over here!" They all crowded around him as he repaired the altar of the LORD that had been torn down. ³¹He took twelve stones, one to represent each of the tribes of Israel,* ³²and he used the stones to rebuild the LORD's altar. Then he dug a trench around the altar large enough to hold about three gallons.* ³³He piled wood on the altar,

---

I DO NOT BLAME the one who brings God's message of judgment for my sin. (18:17)

I CONFRONT those whose sin brings trouble to many others. (18:18)

I AM NOT AFRAID of false gods, for they have no power. (18:27)

I BELIEVE Elijah invited the people to restore their worship of the Lord and to see him prove that he is God. (18:30)

18:31 Hebrew *each of the tribes of the sons of Jacob to whom the LORD had said, "Your name will be Israel."*
18:32 Hebrew *2 seahs* [12 liters] *of seed.*

cut the bull into pieces, and laid the pieces on the wood. Then he said, "Fill four large jars with water, and pour the water over the offering and the wood." After they had done this, ³⁴he said, "Do the same thing again!" And when they were finished, he said, "Now do it a third time!" So they did as he said, ³⁵and the water ran around the altar and even overflowed the trench.

³⁶At the customary time for offering the evening sacrifice, Elijah the prophet walked up to the altar and prayed, "O LORD, God of Abraham, Isaac, and Jacob,* prove today that you are God in Israel and that I am your servant. Prove that I have done all this at your command. ³⁷O LORD, answer me! Answer me so these people will know that you, O LORD, are God and that you have brought them back to yourself."

³⁸Immediately the fire of the LORD flashed down from heaven and burned up the young bull, the wood, the stones, and the dust. It even licked up all the water in the ditch! ³⁹And when the people saw it, they fell on their faces and cried out, "The LORD is God! The LORD is God!"

⁴⁰Then Elijah commanded, "Seize all the prophets of Baal. Don't let a single one escape!" So the people seized them all, and Elijah took them down to the Kishon Valley and killed them there.

Elijah Prays for Rain

⁴¹Then Elijah said to Ahab, "Go and enjoy a good meal! For I hear a mighty rainstorm coming!"

⁴²So Ahab prepared a feast. But Elijah climbed to the top of Mount Carmel and fell to the ground and prayed. ⁴³Then he said to his servant, "Go and look out toward the sea."

The servant went and looked, but he returned to Elijah and said, "I didn't see anything." Seven times Elijah told him to go and look, and seven times he went. ⁴⁴Finally the seventh time, his servant told him, "I saw a little cloud about the size of a hand rising from the sea."

Then Elijah shouted, "Hurry to Ahab and tell him, 'Climb into your chariot and go back home. If you don't hurry, the rain will stop you!' "

⁴⁵And sure enough, the sky was soon black with clouds. A heavy wind brought a terrific rainstorm, and Ahab left quickly for Jezreel. ⁴⁶Now the LORD gave special strength to Elijah. He tucked his cloak into his belt and ran ahead of Ahab's chariot all the way to the entrance of Jezreel.

CHAPTER 19

Elijah Flees to Sinai

When Ahab got home, he told Jezebel what Elijah had done and that he had slaughtered the prophets of Baal. ²So Jezebel sent this message to Elijah: "May the gods also kill me if by this time tomorrow I have failed to take your life like those whom you killed."

³Elijah was afraid and fled for his life. He went to Beersheba, a town in Judah, and he left his servant there. ⁴Then he went on alone into the desert, traveling all day. He sat down under a solitary broom tree and prayed that he might die. "I have had enough, LORD," he said. "Take my life, for I am no better than my ancestors."

⁵Then he lay down and slept under the broom tree. But as he was sleeping, an angel touched him and told him, "Get up and eat!" ⁶He looked around and saw some bread baked on hot stones and a jar of water! So he ate and drank and lay down again.

⁷Then the angel of the LORD came again and touched him and said, "Get up and eat some more, for there is a long journey ahead of you."

⁸So he got up and ate and drank, and the food gave him enough strength to

---

I CALL upon God based upon who he is and what will bring him glory, not upon my pleadings or self-punishment. (18:36)

See the profiles for Abraham (page 19), Isaac (page 31), and Jacob (page 43) at Genesis 15:6, Genesis 25:19, and Genesis 32:9.

I ACKNOWLEDGE the Lord's mighty acts, which prove that he is the true God. (18:39)

I PERSIST in prayer. (18:43)

I PAY ATTENTION to and care for my physical needs when I am struggling emotionally and spiritually. (19:5)

18:36 Hebrew *and Israel.*

travel forty days and forty nights to Mount Sinai,* the mountain of God. ⁹There he came to a cave, where he spent the night.

The LORD Speaks to Elijah

But the LORD said to him, "What are you doing here, Elijah?"

¹⁰Elijah replied, "I have zealously served the LORD God Almighty. But the people of Israel have broken their covenant with you, torn down your altars, and killed every one of your prophets. I alone am left, and now they are trying to kill me, too."

¹¹"Go out and stand before me on the mountain," the LORD told him. And as Elijah stood there, the LORD passed by, and a mighty windstorm hit the mountain. It was such a terrible blast that the rocks were torn loose, but the LORD was not in the wind. After the wind there was an earthquake, but the LORD was not in the earthquake. ¹²And after the earthquake there was a fire, but the LORD was not in the fire. And after the fire there was the sound of a gentle whisper. ¹³When Elijah heard it, he wrapped his face in his cloak and went out and stood at the entrance of the cave.

And a voice said, "What are you doing here, Elijah?"

¹⁴He replied again, "I have zealously served the LORD God Almighty. But the people of Israel have broken their covenant with you, torn down your altars, and killed every one of your prophets. I alone am left, and now they are trying to kill me, too."

¹⁵Then the LORD told him, "Go back the way you came, and travel to the wilderness of Damascus. When you arrive there, anoint Hazael to be king of Aram. ¹⁶Then anoint Jehu son of Nimshi to be king of Israel, and anoint Elisha son of Shaphat from Abel-meholah to replace you as my prophet. ¹⁷Anyone who escapes from Hazael will be killed by Jehu, and those who escape Jehu will be killed by Elisha! ¹⁸Yet I will preserve seven thousand others in Israel who have never bowed to Baal or kissed him!"

The Call of Elisha

¹⁹So Elijah went and found Elisha son of Shaphat plowing a field with a team of oxen. There were eleven teams of oxen ahead of him, and he was plowing with the twelfth team. Elijah went over to him and threw his cloak across his shoulders and walked away again. ²⁰Elisha left the oxen standing there, ran after Elijah, and said to him, "First let me go and kiss my father and mother good-bye, and then I will go with you!"

Elijah replied, "Go on back! But consider what I have done to you."

²¹Elisha then returned to his oxen, killed them, and used the wood from the plow to build a fire to roast their flesh. He passed around the meat to the other plowmen, and they all ate. Then he went with Elijah as his assistant.

CHAPTER 20

Ben-Hadad Attacks Samaria

Now King Ben-hadad of Aram mobilized his army, supported by the chariots and horses of thirty-two allied kings. They went to besiege Samaria, the Israelite capital, and launched attacks against it. ²Ben-hadad sent messengers into the city to relay this message to King Ahab of Israel: "This is what Ben-hadad says: ³'Your silver and gold are mine, and so are the best of your wives and children!'"

⁴"All right, my lord," Ahab replied. "All that I have is yours!"

⁵Soon Ben-hadad's messengers returned again and said, "This is what Ben-hadad says: 'I have already demanded that you give me your silver, gold, wives, and children. ⁶But about this time tomorrow I will send my officials to

I KNOW that simply because a circumstance is impressive doesn't mean it contains a message from God. (19:11)

I CONTINUE to obey the Lord no matter how discouraged I become. (19:15)

See Elisha's profile (page 431) at 2 Kings 2:14.

I REMEMBER that I am never the only believer left—God always has his faithful ones. (19:18)

I WILLINGLY SACRIFICE the comforts of my career and home to follow the call of God. (19:21)

19:8 Hebrew *Horeb*, another name for Sinai.

search your palace and the homes of your people. They will take away everything you consider valuable!' "

⁷Then Ahab summoned all the leaders of the land and said to them, "Look how this man is stirring up trouble! I already agreed when he sent the message demanding that I give him my wives and children and silver and gold."

⁸"Don't give in to any more demands," the leaders and people advised.

⁹So Ahab told the messengers from Ben-hadad, "Say this to my lord the king: 'I will give you everything you asked for the first time, but this last demand of yours I simply cannot meet.' " So the messengers returned to Ben-hadad with the response.

¹⁰Then Ben-hadad sent this message to Ahab: "May the gods bring tragedy on me, and even worse than that, if there remains enough dust from Samaria to provide more than a handful for each of my soldiers."

LIKE ELIJAH
1 Kings 19:18

I know God will meet my needs even in the most desperate of circumstances.

Moses has his place in American cinema with *The Ten Commandments* and *The Prince of Egypt.* It's about time someone commissioned a new epic about one of the Old Testament's other truly great heroes.

The prophet Elijah ranks right up there with Moses as one of the most dramatic prophets of the Lord. At Elijah's word, kings trembled, the rains stopped, a jug of oil never ran dry, a boy was raised from the dead, fire fell from the sky, revival broke out, and hundreds of idolatrous prophets of Baal were executed.

Yet James 5:17 says "Elijah was as human as we are."

After running almost the length of a marathon, this great prophet entered the city of Jezreel just in time to hear wicked Queen Jezebel's murderous threats.

How does Elijah respond? True to life, Scripture says he panicked.

After several days on the run, Elijah collapsed—exhausted, lonely, frightened, and feeling utterly defeated. In his desperation, he foolishly begged the Lord to take his life.

Instead, the Lord renewed Elijah with a double portion of food, drink, and rest. Then he sent him out again with a powerful demonstration of his power, a quiet word to his heart, a new commission, and the assurance that many others were also on his side.

Whether in victory or despair, whether you and I are contending with authority or running for our life, we know God will meet our needs in just the right way. We need to trust the Lord to know exactly what we need for every moment and to provide it abundantly.

To read more about Elijah, see 2 Kings 1:1–2:15; Malachi 4:5-6; Matthew 17:1-13; and James 5:17-18.

○ *Today's Scripture reading is 1 Kings 17:1–19:18.*

---

¹¹The king of Israel sent back this answer: "A warrior still dressing for battle should not boast like a warrior who has already won."

¹²This reply of Ahab's reached Ben-hadad and the other kings as they were drinking in their tents.* "Prepare to attack!" Ben-hadad commanded his officers. So they prepared to attack the city.

Ahab's Victory over Ben-Hadad

¹³Then a prophet came to see King Ahab and told him, "This is what the LORD says: Do you see all these enemy forces? Today I will hand them all over to you. Then you will know that I am the LORD."

¹⁴Ahab asked, "How will he do it?"

And the prophet replied, "This is what the LORD says: The troops of the provincial commanders will do it."

20:12 Or *in Succoth;* also in 20:16.

I BELIEVE the Lord desired to prove to Ahab that he was indeed the true God by conquering his enemies. (20:13)

I LISTEN to God's directions. (20:14)

"Should we attack first?" Ahab asked.

"Yes," the prophet answered.

[15]So Ahab mustered the troops of the 232 provincial commanders. Then he called out the rest of his army of seven thousand men. [16]About noontime, as Ben-hadad and the thirty-two allied kings were still in their tents getting drunk, [17]the troops of the provincial commanders marched out of the city. As they approached, Ben-hadad's scouts reported to him, "Some troops are coming from Samaria."

[18]"Take them alive," Ben-hadad commanded, "whether they have come for peace or for war."

[19]But by now Ahab's provincial commanders had led the army out to fight. [20]Each Israelite soldier killed his Aramean opponent, and suddenly the entire Aramean army panicked and fled. The Israelites chased them, but King Ben-hadad and a few others escaped on horses. [21]However, the other horses and chariots were destroyed, and the Arameans were killed in a great slaughter.

[22]Afterward the prophet said to King Ahab, "Get ready for another attack by the king of Aram next spring."

Ben-Hadad's Second Attack

[23]After their defeat, Ben-hadad's officers said to him, "The Israelite gods are gods of the hills; that is why they won. But we can beat them easily on the plains. [24]Only this time replace the kings with field commanders! [25]Recruit another army like the one you lost. Give us the same number of horses, chariots, and men, and we will fight against them in the plains. There's not a shadow of a doubt that we will beat them." So King Ben-hadad did as they suggested. [26]The following spring he called up the Aramean army and marched out against Israel, this time at Aphek. [27]Israel then mustered its army, set up supply lines, and moved into the battle. But the Israelite army looked like two little flocks of goats in comparison to the vast Aramean forces that filled the countryside!

[28]Then the man of God went to the king of Israel and said, "This is what the LORD says: The Arameans have said that the LORD is a god of the hills and not of the plains. So I will help you defeat this vast army. Then you will know that I am the LORD."

[29]The two armies camped opposite each other for seven days, and on the seventh day the battle began. The Israelites killed 100,000 Aramean foot soldiers in one day. [30]The rest fled behind the walls of Aphek, but the wall fell on them and killed another 27,000. Ben-hadad fled into the city and hid in a secret room. [31]Ben-hadad's officers said to him, "Sir, we have heard that the kings of Israel are very merciful. So let's humble ourselves by wearing sackcloth and putting ropes on our heads. Then perhaps King Ahab will let you live."

[32]So they put on sackcloth and ropes and went to the king of Israel and begged, "Your servant Ben-hadad says, 'Please let me live!' "

The king of Israel responded, "Is he still alive? He is my brother!"

[33]The men were quick to grasp at this straw of hope, and they replied, "Yes, your brother Ben-hadad!"

"Go and get him," the king of Israel told them. And when Ben-hadad arrived, Ahab invited him up into his chariot!

[34]Ben-hadad told him, "I will give back the towns my father took from your father, and you may establish places of trade in Damascus, as my father did in Samaria."

Then Ahab said, "I will let you go under these conditions." So they made a treaty, and Ben-hadad was set free.

Ask God to open your eyes as you read his Word (Psalm 119:18).

I BELIEVE the Lord delivered the Israelites from the Arameans just as he promised. (20:21)

I DO NOT ATTRIBUTE God's work and power to simple coincidence or superstition. (20:23)

I DO NOT PARTNER with those who oppose the Lord's people (2 Corinthians 6:14-15). (20:34)

A Prophet Condemns Ahab

³⁵Meanwhile, the Lord instructed one of the group of prophets to say to another man, "Strike me!" But the man refused to strike the prophet. ³⁶Then the prophet told him, "Because you have not obeyed the voice of the Lord, a lion will kill you as soon as you leave me." And sure enough, when he had gone, a lion attacked and killed him.

³⁷Then the prophet turned to another man and said, "Strike me!" So he struck the prophet and wounded him.

³⁸The prophet waited for the king beside the road, having placed a bandage over his eyes to disguise himself. ³⁹As the king passed by, the prophet called out to him, "Sir, I was in the battle, and a man brought me a prisoner. He said, 'Guard this man; if for any reason he gets away, you will either die or pay a fine of seventy-five pounds* of silver!' ⁴⁰But while I was busy doing something else, the prisoner disappeared!"

"Well, it's your own fault," the king replied. "You have determined your own judgment."

⁴¹Then the prophet pulled the bandage from his eyes, and the king of Israel recognized him as one of the prophets. ⁴²And the prophet told him, "This is what the Lord says: Because you have spared the man I said must be destroyed,* now you must die in his place, and your people will die instead of his people." ⁴³So the king of Israel went home to Samaria angry and sullen.

CHAPTER 21

Naboth's Vineyard

King Ahab had a palace in Jezreel, and near the palace was a vineyard owned by a man named Naboth. ²One day Ahab said to Naboth, "Since your vineyard is so convenient to the palace, I would like to buy it to use as a vegetable garden. I will give you a better vineyard in exchange, or if you prefer, I will pay you for it."

³But Naboth replied, "The Lord forbid that I should give you the inheritance that was passed down by my ancestors." ⁴So Ahab went home angry and sullen because of Naboth's answer. The king went to bed with his face to the wall and refused to eat!

⁵"What in the world is the matter?" his wife, Jezebel, asked him. "What has made you so upset that you are not eating?"

⁶"I asked Naboth to sell me his vineyard or to trade it, and he refused!" Ahab told her.

⁷"Are you the king of Israel or not?" Jezebel asked. "Get up and eat and don't worry about it. I'll get you Naboth's vineyard!"

⁸So she wrote letters in Ahab's name, sealed them with his seal, and sent them to the elders and other leaders of the city where Naboth lived. ⁹In her letters she commanded: "Call the citizens together for fasting and prayer and give Naboth a place of honor. ¹⁰Find two scoundrels* who will accuse him of cursing God and the king. Then take him out and stone him to death."

¹¹So the elders and other leaders followed the instructions Jezebel had written in the letters. ¹²They called for a fast and put Naboth at a prominent place before the people. ¹³Then two scoundrels accused him before all the people of cursing God and the king. So he was dragged outside the city and stoned to death. ¹⁴The city officials then sent word to Jezebel, "Naboth has been stoned to death."

¹⁵When Jezebel heard the news, she said to Ahab, "You know the vineyard Naboth wouldn't sell you? Well, you can have it now! He's dead!" ¹⁶So Ahab immediately went down to the vineyard to claim it.

I AM WILLING to do difficult things to teach and demonstrate God's messages. (20:38)

I DO NOT OBEY God's commands only when I feel like it or make excuses for disobeying. (20:42)

I VALUE my inheritance from the Lord. (21:3)

I DO NOT SULK when I cannot have what I want. (21:4)

I DO NOT USE my position of authority to overrule God's commands. (21:7)

I DO NOT ACCEPT gifts that have been stolen from others. (21:16)

20:39 Hebrew *1 talent* [34 kilograms].   20:42 The Hebrew term used here refers to the complete consecration of things or people to the Lord, either by destroying them or by giving them as an offering.   21:10 Hebrew *two sons of Belial;* also in 21:13.

¹⁷But the LORD said to Elijah, who was from Tishbe, ¹⁸"Go down to meet King Ahab, who rules in Samaria. He will be at Naboth's vineyard in Jezreel, taking possession of it. ¹⁹Give him this message: 'This is what the LORD says: Isn't killing Naboth bad enough? Must you rob him, too? Because you have done this, dogs will lick your blood outside the city just as they licked the blood of Naboth!' "

²⁰"So my enemy has found me!" Ahab exclaimed to Elijah.

"Yes," Elijah answered, "I have come because you have sold yourself to what is evil in the LORD's sight. ²¹The LORD is going to bring disaster to you and sweep you away. He will not let a single one of your male descendants, slave or free alike, survive in Israel! ²²He is going to destroy your family as he did the family of Jeroboam son of Nebat and the family of Baasha son of Ahijah, for you have made him very angry and have led all of Israel into sin. ²³The LORD has also told me that the dogs of Jezreel will eat the body of your wife, Jezebel, at the city wall. ²⁴The members of your family who die in the city will be eaten by dogs, and those who die in the field will be eaten by vultures."

²⁵No one else so completely sold himself to what was evil in the LORD's sight as did Ahab, for his wife, Jezebel, influenced him. ²⁶He was especially guilty because he worshiped idols just as the Amorites had done—the people whom the LORD had driven from the land ahead of the Israelites.

²⁷When Ahab heard this message, he tore his clothing, dressed in sackcloth, and fasted. He even slept in sackcloth and went about in deep mourning.

²⁸Then another message from the LORD came to Elijah, who was from Tishbe: ²⁹"Do you see how Ahab has humbled himself before me? Because he has done this, I will not do what I promised during his lifetime. It will happen to his sons; I will destroy all his descendants."

CHAPTER 22

Jehoshaphat and Ahab

For three years there was no war between Aram and Israel. ²Then during the third year, King Jehoshaphat of Judah went to visit King Ahab of Israel. ³During the visit, Ahab said to his officials, "Do you realize that the Arameans are still occupying our city of Ramoth-gilead? And we haven't done a thing about it!" ⁴Then he turned to Jehoshaphat and asked, "Will you join me in fighting against Ramoth-gilead?"

And Jehoshaphat replied to King Ahab, "Why, of course! You and I are brothers, and my troops are yours to command. Even my horses are at your service." ⁵Then Jehoshaphat added, "But first let's find out what the LORD says."

⁶So King Ahab summoned his prophets, about four hundred of them, and asked them, "Should I go to war against Ramoth-gilead or not?"

They all replied, "Go right ahead! The Lord will give you a glorious victory!"

⁷But Jehoshaphat asked, "Isn't there a prophet of the LORD around, too? I would like to ask him the same question."

⁸King Ahab replied, "There is still one prophet of the LORD, but I hate him. He never prophesies anything but bad news for me! His name is Micaiah son of Imlah."

"You shouldn't talk like that," Jehoshaphat said. "Let's hear what he has to say."

⁹So the king of Israel called one of his officials and said, "Quick! Go and get Micaiah son of Imlah."

I BELIEVE the consequences for murder are severe. (21:19)

See Jeroboam's profile (page 411) at 1 Kings 13:4.

I HUMBLE myself before God when I am confronted with the consequences of my sin. (21:27)

I BELIEVE God extended mercy and delayed judgment because of Ahab's humble response. (21:29)

See Jehoshaphat's profile (page 527) at 2 Chronicles 20:21.

I DO NOT ENTER into partnerships with evil people. (22:4)

I SEEK counsel from God's people, not just secular advisers. (22:7)

I DO NOT RESIST the hard sayings of God's Word. (22:8)

Micaiah Prophesies against Ahab

¹⁰King Ahab of Israel and King Jehoshaphat of Judah, dressed in their royal robes, were sitting on thrones at the threshing floor near the gate of Samaria. All of Ahab's prophets were prophesying there in front of them. ¹¹One of them, Zedekiah son of Kenaanah, made some iron horns and proclaimed, "This is what the LORD says: With these horns you will gore the Arameans to death!"

¹²All the other prophets agreed. "Yes," they said, "go up to Ramoth-gilead and be victorious, for the LORD will give you victory!"

¹³Meanwhile, the messenger who went to get Micaiah said to him, "Look, all the prophets are promising victory for the king. Be sure that you agree with them and promise success."

¹⁴But Micaiah replied, "As surely as the LORD lives, I will say only what the LORD tells me to say."

> I SPEAK the truth of God's Word, no matter what other opinion prevails. (22:14)

¹⁵When Micaiah arrived before the king, Ahab asked him, "Micaiah, should we go to war against Ramoth-gilead or not?"

And Micaiah replied, "Go right ahead! The LORD will give the king a glorious victory!"

¹⁶But the king replied sharply, "How many times must I demand that you speak only the truth when you speak for the LORD?"

¹⁷So Micaiah told him, "In a vision I saw all Israel scattered on the mountains, like sheep without a shepherd. And the LORD said, 'Their master has been killed. Send them home in peace.' "

¹⁸"Didn't I tell you?" the king of Israel said to Jehoshaphat. "He does it every time. He never prophesies anything but bad news for me."

¹⁹Then Micaiah continued, "Listen to what the LORD says! I saw the LORD sitting on his throne with all the armies of heaven around him, on his right and on his left. ²⁰And the LORD said, 'Who can entice Ahab to go into battle against Ramoth-gilead so that he can be killed there?' There were many suggestions, ²¹until finally a spirit approached the LORD and said, 'I can do it!'

²²" 'How will you do this?' the LORD asked.

"And the spirit replied, 'I will go out and inspire all Ahab's prophets to speak lies.'

" 'You will succeed,' said the LORD. 'Go ahead and do it.'

²³"So you see, the LORD has put a lying spirit in the mouths of your prophets. For the LORD has determined disaster for you."

²⁴Then Zedekiah son of Kenaanah walked up to Micaiah and slapped him across the face. "When did the Spirit of the LORD leave me to speak to you?" he demanded.

²⁵And Micaiah replied, "You will find out soon enough when you find yourself hiding in some secret room!"

²⁶King Ahab of Israel then ordered, "Arrest Micaiah and take him back to Amon, the governor of the city, and to my son Joash. ²⁷Give them this order from the king: 'Put this man in prison, and feed him nothing but bread and water until I return safely from the battle!' "

> I DO NOT ATTACK those who confront me with my sin and the truth of God's Word. (22:26)

²⁸But Micaiah replied, "If you return safely, the LORD has not spoken through me!" Then he added to those standing around, "Take note of what I have said."

> I DO NOT DISREGARD the warnings of God's Word. (22:28)

The Death of Ahab

²⁹So the king of Israel and King Jehoshaphat of Judah led their armies against Ramoth-gilead. ³⁰Now King Ahab said to Jehoshaphat, "As we go into battle, I will disguise myself so no one will recognize me, but you wear your royal robes." So Ahab disguised himself, and they went into battle.

³¹Now the king of Aram had issued these orders to his thirty-two charioteers: "Attack only the king of Israel!" ³²So when the Aramean charioteers saw

Jehoshaphat in his royal robes, they went after him. "There is the king of Israel!" they shouted. But when Jehoshaphat cried out, [33]the charioteers realized he was not the king of Israel, and they stopped chasing him.

[34]An Aramean soldier, however, randomly shot an arrow at the Israelite troops, and the arrow hit the king of Israel between the joints of his armor. "Get me out of here!" Ahab groaned to the driver of his chariot. "I have been badly wounded!" [35]The battle raged all that day, and Ahab was propped up in his chariot facing the Arameans. The blood from his wound ran down to the floor of his chariot, and as evening arrived he died. [36]Just as the sun was setting, the cry ran through his troops: "It's all over—return home!" [37]So the king died, and his body was taken to Samaria and buried there. [38]Then his chariot was washed beside the pool of Samaria, where the prostitutes bathed, and dogs came and licked the king's blood, just as the LORD had promised.

I BELIEVE Ahab suffered a violent and humiliating death, just as the Lord said. (22:38)

[39]The rest of the events in Ahab's reign and the story of the ivory palace and the cities he built are recorded in *The Book of the History of the Kings of Israel.* [40]When Ahab died, he was buried among his ancestors. Then his son Ahaziah became the next king.

Jehoshaphat Rules in Judah

See Asa's profile (page 521) at 2 Chronicles 16:9.

I FOLLOW the good example of godly parents. (22:43)

[41]Jehoshaphat son of Asa began to rule over Judah in the fourth year of King Ahab's reign in Israel. [42]He was thirty-five years old when he became king, and he reigned in Jerusalem twenty-five years. His mother was Azubah, the daughter of Shilhi. [43]Jehoshaphat was a good king, following the example of his father, Asa. He did what was pleasing in the LORD's sight. During his reign, however, he failed to remove all the pagan shrines, and the people still offered sacrifices and burned incense there. [44]Jehoshaphat also made peace with the king of Israel.

[45]The rest of the events in Jehoshaphat's reign, the extent of his power, and the wars he waged are recorded in *The Book of the History of the Kings of Judah.* [46]He banished from the land the rest of the shrine prostitutes, who still continued their practices from the days of his father, Asa. [47]There was no king in Edom at that time, only a deputy.

[48]Jehoshaphat also built a fleet of trading ships* to sail to Ophir for gold. But the ships never set sail, for they were wrecked at Ezion-geber. [49]At that time Ahaziah son of Ahab proposed to Jehoshaphat, "Let my men sail an expedition with your men." But Jehoshaphat refused the offer.

[50]When Jehoshaphat died, he was buried with his ancestors in the City of David. Then his son Jehoram became the next king.

Ahaziah Rules in Israel

I DO NOT FOLLOW the bad example of wicked parents. (22:52)

See Jeroboam's profile (page 411) at 1 Kings 13:4.

[51]Ahaziah son of Ahab began to rule over Israel in the seventeenth year of King Jehoshaphat's reign in Judah. He reigned in Samaria two years. [52]But he did what was evil in the LORD's sight, following the example of his father and mother and the example of Jeroboam son of Nebat, who had led Israel into the sin of idolatry. [53]He served Baal and worshiped him, arousing the anger of the LORD, the God of Israel, just as his father had done.

22:48 Hebrew *fleet of ships of Tarshish.*

2 KINGS

THIS SEVENTH BOOK of Old Testament history ends with *destruction*.

In both the northern kingdom of Israel and southern kingdom of Judah, the prophets Elijah, Elisha, Isaiah, and others persistently warn of impending ruin.

Yet for 130 more years, an unbroken string of wicked kings continues to rule the northern kingdom. The worship of the Lord is virtually unknown within its borders. In the end, Assyria destroys the pagan kingdom (1:1–17:41).

And for 265 more years, a series of alternately wicked and good kings continues to rule the southern kingdom. Some revive the worship of the Lord. Others lead the kingdom back to gross paganism. The last few kings of Judah actually serve as puppets of Babylon. For nearly twenty years the Babylonian empire rules over the rebellious kingdom and then crushes it in the end (8:16–25:30).

In Ezra and Nehemiah, we discover that Judah isn't completely erased from world history. After seventy years of captivity, the Lord brings a sizeable remnant back to the Promised Land. That remnant forms a new kingdom committed to worshiping the Lord.

Famous passages in 2 Kings abound

- ○ Elijah calls down fire from heaven (1:9-12)
- ○ Elijah is taken into heaven (2:1-12)
- ○ Elisha takes up Elijah's mantle (2:13-14)
- ○ Elisha performs various miracles (2:19-6:7)
- ○ "There are more on our side than on theirs!" (6:16)
- ○ "This is wonderful news, and we aren't sharing it" (7:9)
- ○ Jehoiada and King Joash lead Judah back to the Lord (11:4-12:16)
- ○ Assyria destroys the kingdom of Israel (17:1-6)
- ○ The sins of Israel leading up to its destruction are reviewed (17:7-23)
- ○ The Lord thwarts Assyria's attempts to crush Judah (18:13-37)
- ○ The Lord predicts that Babylon will crush Judah (20:12-19)
- ○ Judah becomes exceedingly pagan under King Manasseh (21:1-16)
- ○ King Josiah leads Judah back to the Lord, but it's too late (22:1-23:27)
- ○ Babylon conquers and rules over Judah (24:10-17)
- ○ Judah rebels against Babylon, only to be destroyed (24:20-25:21)

CHAPTER 1

Elijah Confronts King Ahaziah

After King Ahab's death, the nation of Moab declared its independence from Israel. ²One day Israel's new king, Ahaziah, fell through the latticework of an upper room at his palace in Samaria, and he was seriously injured. So he sent messengers to the temple of Baal-zebub, the god of Ekron, to ask whether he would recover.

See Ahab's profile (page 417) at 1 Kings 16:31.

I SEEK advice and help from the Lord, not from false gods and religions. (1:3)

See Elijah's profile (page 421) at 1 Kings 19:18.

³But the angel of the LORD told Elijah, who was from Tishbe, "Go and meet the messengers of the king of Samaria and ask them, 'Why are you going to Baal-zebub, the god of Ekron, to ask whether the king will get well? Is there no God in Israel? ⁴Now, therefore, this is what the LORD says: You will never leave the bed on which you are lying, but you will surely die.' " So Elijah went to deliver the message.

⁵When the messengers returned to the king, he asked them, "Why have you returned so soon?"

⁶They replied, "A man came up to us and said, 'Go back to the king and give him this message from the LORD: Why are you sending men to Baal-zebub, the god of Ekron, to ask whether you will get well? Is there no God in Israel? Now, since you have done this, you will never leave the bed on which you are lying, but you will surely die.' "

⁷"Who was this man?" the king demanded. "What did he look like?"

⁸They replied, "He was a hairy man,* and he wore a leather belt around his waist."

I DO NOT ATTACK those who confront me with my sin and the truth of God's Word. (1:9)

"It was Elijah from Tishbe!" the king exclaimed. ⁹Then he sent an army captain with fifty soldiers to arrest him. They found him sitting on top of a hill. The captain said to him, "Man of God, the king has commanded you to come along with us."

¹⁰But Elijah replied to the captain, "If I am a man of God, let fire come down from heaven and destroy you and your fifty men!" Then fire fell from heaven and killed them all.

¹¹So the king sent another captain with fifty men. The captain said to him, "Man of God, the king says that you must come down right away."

¹²Elijah replied, "If I am a man of God, let fire come down from heaven and destroy you and your fifty men!" And again the fire of God fell from heaven and killed them all.

I APPROACH God humbly and ask for mercy for myself and others. (1:13)

¹³Once more the king sent a captain with fifty men. But this time the captain fell to his knees before Elijah. He pleaded with him, "O man of God, please spare my life and the lives of these, your fifty servants. ¹⁴See how the fire from heaven has destroyed the first two groups. But now please spare my life!"

¹⁵Then the angel of the LORD said to Elijah, "Don't be afraid. Go with him." So Elijah got up and went to the king.

¹⁶And Elijah said to the king, "This is what the LORD says: Why did you send messengers to Baal-zebub, the god of Ekron, to ask whether you will get well? Is there no God in Israel? Now, since you have done this, you will never leave the bed on which you are lying, but you will surely die."

See Jehoshaphat's profile (page 527) at 2 Chronicles 20:21.

¹⁷So Ahaziah died, just as the LORD had promised through Elijah. Since Ahaziah did not have a son to succeed him, his brother Joram* became the next king. This took place in the second year of the reign of Jehoram son of Jehoshaphat, king of Judah. ¹⁸The rest of the events in Ahaziah's reign are recorded in *The Book of the History of the Kings of Israel*.

CHAPTER 2

Elijah Taken into Heaven

When the LORD was about to take Elijah up to heaven in a whirlwind, Elijah and Elisha were traveling from Gilgal. ²And Elijah said to Elisha, "Stay here, for the LORD has told me to go to Bethel."

But Elisha replied, "As surely as the LORD lives and you yourself live, I will never leave you!" So they went on together to Bethel.

See Elijah's profile (page 421) at 1 Kings 19:18.

I BELIEVE the Lord revealed his will to the prophets. (2:2)

³The group of prophets from Bethel came to Elisha and asked him, "Did you know that the LORD is going to take your master away from you today?"

1:8 Or *He was wearing clothing made of hair.* 1:17 Hebrew *Jehoram*, a variant name for Joram.

"Quiet!" Elisha answered. "Of course I know it."

⁴Then Elijah said to Elisha, "Stay here, for the LORD has told me to go to Jericho."

But Elisha replied again, "As surely as the LORD lives and you yourself live, I will never leave you." So they went on together to Jericho.

⁵Then the group of prophets from Jericho came to Elisha and asked him, "Did you know that the LORD is going to take your master away from you today?"

"Quiet!" he answered again. "Of course I know it."

⁶Then Elijah said to Elisha, "Stay here, for the LORD has told me to go to the Jordan River."

But again Elisha replied, "As surely as the LORD lives and you yourself live, I will never leave you." So they went on together.

⁷Fifty men from the group of prophets also went and watched from a distance as Elijah and Elisha stopped beside the Jordan River. ⁸Then Elijah folded his cloak together and struck the water with it. The river divided, and the two of them went across on dry ground!

⁹When they came to the other side, Elijah said to Elisha, "What can I do for you before I am taken away?"

And Elisha replied, "Please let me become your rightful successor."*

¹⁰"You have asked a difficult thing," Elijah replied. "If you see me when I am taken from you, then you will get your request. But if not, then you won't."

¹¹As they were walking along and talking, suddenly a chariot of fire appeared, drawn by horses of fire. It drove between them, separating them, and Elijah was carried by a whirlwind into heaven. ¹²Elisha saw it and cried out, "My father! My father! The chariots and charioteers of Israel!" And as they disappeared from sight, Elisha tore his robe in two.

¹³Then Elisha picked up Elijah's cloak and returned to the bank of the Jordan River. ¹⁴He struck the water with the cloak and cried out, "Where is the LORD, the God of Elijah?" Then the river divided, and Elisha went across.

¹⁵When the group of prophets from Jericho saw what happened, they exclaimed, "Elisha has become Elijah's successor!"* And they went to meet him and bowed down before him. ¹⁶"Sir," they said, "just say the word and fifty of our strongest men will search the wilderness for your master. Perhaps the Spirit of the LORD has left him on some mountain or in some valley."

"No," Elisha said, "don't send them." ¹⁷But they kept urging him until he was embarrassed, and he finally said, "All right, send them." So fifty men searched for three days but did not find Elijah. ¹⁸Elisha was still at Jericho when they returned. "Didn't I tell you not to go?" he asked.

Elisha's First Miracles

¹⁹Now the leaders of the town of Jericho visited Elisha. "We have a problem, my lord," they told him. "This town is located in beautiful natural surroundings, as you can see. But the water is bad, and the land is unproductive."

²⁰Elisha said, "Bring me a new bowl with salt in it." So they brought it to him. ²¹Then he went out to the spring that supplied the town with water and threw the salt into it. And he said, "This is what the LORD says: I have made this water wholesome. It will no longer cause death or infertility.*" ²²And sure enough! The water has remained wholesome ever since, just as Elisha said.

²³Elisha left Jericho and went up to Bethel. As he was walking along the road, a group of boys from the town began mocking and making fun of him. "Go away, you baldhead!" they chanted. "Go away, you baldhead!" ²⁴Elisha

Ask God to cleanse your heart as you read his Word (Psalm 51:10).

I SEEK to be used of God as others have been before me. (2:9)

I RESIST pressure to doubt God's miraculous works. (2:17)

I SEEK OUT God's servants when I have a problem. (2:19)

I DO NOT MOCK God's servants. (2:23)

2:9 Hebrew *Let me inherit a double share of your spirit.*   2:15 Hebrew *The spirit of Elijah rests upon Elisha.*
2:21 Or *or make the land unproductive.*

turned around and looked at them, and he cursed them in the name of the LORD. Then two bears came out of the woods and mauled forty-two of them. ²⁵From there Elisha went to Mount Carmel and finally returned to Samaria.

CHAPTER 3

War between Israel and Moab

Ahab's son Joram* began to rule over Israel in the eighteenth year of King Jehoshaphat's reign in Judah. He reigned in Samaria twelve years. ²He did what was evil in the LORD's sight, but he was not as wicked as his father and mother. He at least tore down the sacred pillar of Baal that his father had set up. ³Nevertheless he continued in the sins of idolatry that Jeroboam son of Nebat had led the people of Israel to commit.

⁴King Mesha of Moab and his people were sheep breeders. They used to pay the king of Israel an annual tribute of 100,000 lambs and the wool of 100,000 rams. ⁵But after Ahab's death, the king of Moab rebelled against the king of Israel. ⁶So King Joram mustered the army of Israel and marched from Samaria. ⁷On the way, he sent this message to King Jehoshaphat of Judah: "The king of Moab has rebelled against me. Will you help me fight him?"

And Jehoshaphat replied, "Why, of course! You and I are brothers, and my troops are yours to command. Even my horses are at your service." ⁸Then Jehoshaphat asked, "What route will we take?"

"We will attack from the wilderness of Edom," Joram replied. ⁹The king of Edom and his troops joined them, and all three armies traveled along a roundabout route through the wilderness for seven days. But there was no water for the men or their pack animals.

¹⁰"What should we do?" the king of Israel cried out. "The LORD has brought the three of us here to let the king of Moab defeat us."

¹¹But King Jehoshaphat of Judah asked, "Is there no prophet of the LORD with us? If there is, we can ask the LORD what to do."

One of King Joram's officers replied, "Elisha son of Shaphat is here. He used to be Elijah's personal assistant.*"

¹²Jehoshaphat said, "Then the LORD will speak through him." So the kings of Israel, Judah, and Edom went to consult with Elisha.

¹³"I want no part of you," Elisha said to the king of Israel. "Go to the pagan prophets of your father and mother!"

But King Joram said, "No! For it was the LORD who called us three kings here to be destroyed by the king of Moab!"

¹⁴Elisha replied, "As surely as the LORD Almighty lives, whom I serve, I would not bother with you except for my respect for King Jehoshaphat of Judah. ¹⁵Now bring me someone who can play the harp."

While the harp was being played, the power of the LORD came upon Elisha, ¹⁶and he said, "This is what the LORD says: This dry valley will be filled with pools of water! ¹⁷You will see neither wind nor rain, says the LORD, but this valley will be filled with water. You will have plenty for yourselves and for your cattle and your other animals. ¹⁸But this is only a simple thing for the LORD, for he will make you victorious over the army of Moab! ¹⁹You will conquer the best of their cities, even the fortified ones. You will cut down all their trees, stop up all their springs, and ruin all their good land with stones."

²⁰And sure enough, the next day at about the time when the morning sacrifice was offered, water suddenly appeared! It was flowing from the direction of Edom, and soon there was water everywhere.

²¹Meanwhile, when the people of Moab heard about the three armies marching against them, they mobilized every man who could fight, young and old, and stationed themselves along their border. ²²But when they got up

See Ahab's profile (page 417) at 1 Kings 16:31.

I REMOVE the worship of false gods from my family and my sphere of authority. (3:2)

See Jeroboam's profile (page 411) at 1 Kings 13:4.

I DO NOT PARTNER with wicked individuals. (3:7)

See Jehoshaphat's profile (page 527) at 2 Chronicles 20:21.

I DO NOT BLAME God for mistakes I've made because I wasn't following him. (3:10)

I SEEK God's help with my problems. (3:11)

See Elijah's profile (page 421) at 1 Kings 19:18.

I LISTEN to the words of the Lord, not the words of false prophets. (3:12)

I RESPECT those who love God, even if I disagree with their actions. (3:14)

3:1 Hebrew *Jehoram*, a variant name for Joram; also in 3:6. 3:11 Hebrew *He used to pour water on the hands of Elijah.*

the next morning, the sun was shining across the water, making it look as red as blood. ²³"It's blood!" the Moabites exclaimed. "The three armies have attacked and killed each other! Let's go and collect the plunder!"

²⁴When they arrived at the Israelite camp, the army of Israel rushed out and attacked the Moabites, who turned and ran. The army of Israel chased them into the land of Moab, destroying everything as they went. ²⁵They destroyed the cities, covered their good land with stones, stopped up the springs, and cut down the good trees. Finally, only Kir-hareseth was left, but even that came under attack.*

²⁶When the king of Moab saw that he was losing the battle, he led seven hundred of his warriors in a desperate attempt to break through the enemy lines near the king of Edom, but they failed to escape. ²⁷So he took his oldest son, who would have been the next king, and sacrificed him as a burnt offering on the wall. As a result, the anger against Israel was great, so they withdrew and returned to their own land.

LIKE ELISHA   *I experience the power of God in my own life.*

2 Kings 2:14

God has no grandchildren, and you cannot inherit the personal experience of God's power from a friend.

After Elijah was swept to glory in the fiery chariot, it was time for Elisha to move beyond all he had learned from his teacher and trust himself to the Lord alone.

The big question to be answered: Would Elisha continue dwelling on the past glory days of Elijah, or would he seek to be used and blessed by God daily in a powerful way?

Before he did anything else, Elisha boldly called on the Lord, Elijah's God, to demonstrate his power through him. Elisha continued the ministry of Elijah, declaring to Israel that the Lord was God. Through miraculous signs and miracles, he continued to prove that the Lord was greater than Baal or any other false god around. Yet Elisha's power was not a leftover of Elijah's but Elisha's own experience of God's work through him.

Elisha did more than just succeed Elijah in ministry. Although they preached the same message, God showed his power through these two men in different ways. God poured out even more miracles through Elisha than he did through Elijah. Elisha fulfilled God's purpose for his life as he continued in personal devotion and obedience to the God who called him.

Many have said that there will never be another man quite like Billy Graham. But whether you are Luis Palau preaching in stadiums across the world, or a vacation Bible school teacher bringing the gospel to children at your church, you, too, can experience God's power as he brings others to Christ through you.

"Where is the LORD, the God of Elijah?" He is still near to demonstrate his power to change the life of anyone who trusts him. We may gain the cloak of a good teacher, but the faith must be our own. As we trust God, he will do new and great things in and through us.

Elisha's calling is also recorded in 1 Kings 19:16-21.

○ *Today's Scripture reading is 2 Kings 2, 4, and 6.*

CHAPTER 4

Elisha Helps a Poor Widow

One day the widow of one of Elisha's fellow prophets came to Elisha and cried out to him, "My husband who served you is dead, and you know how he feared the LORD. But now a creditor has come, threatening to take my two sons as slaves."

²"What can I do to help you?" Elisha asked. "Tell me, what do you have in the house?"

I HELP widows and orphans in need. (4:2)

3:25 Hebrew *until only Kir-hareseth was left, with its stones, but the slingers surrounded and attacked it.*

"Nothing at all, except a flask of olive oil," she replied.

³And Elisha said, "Borrow as many empty jars as you can from your friends and neighbors. ⁴Then go into your house with your sons and shut the door behind you. Pour olive oil from your flask into the jars, setting the jars aside as they are filled."

I FOLLOW the counsel of godly individuals. (4:5)

⁵So she did as she was told. Her sons brought many jars to her, and she filled one after another. ⁶Soon every container was full to the brim!

"Bring me another jar," she said to one of her sons.

"There aren't any more!" he told her. And then the olive oil stopped flowing.

⁷When she told the man of God what had happened, he said to her, "Now sell the olive oil and pay your debts, and there will be enough money left over to support you and your sons."

Elisha and the Woman from Shunem

⁸One day Elisha went to the town of Shunem. A wealthy woman lived there, and she invited him to eat some food. From then on, whenever he passed that way, he would stop there to eat.

I PROVIDE opportunities for rest and refreshment for God's servants. (4:10)

See Gehazi's profile (page 435) at 2 Kings 5:22.

I EXPRESS appreciation to those who show hospitality to me. (4:13)

⁹She said to her husband, "I am sure this man who stops in from time to time is a holy man of God. ¹⁰Let's make a little room for him on the roof and furnish it with a bed, a table, a chair, and a lamp. Then he will have a place to stay whenever he comes by."

¹¹One day Elisha returned to Shunem, and he went up to his room to rest. ¹²He said to his servant Gehazi, "Tell the woman I want to speak to her." When she arrived, ¹³Elisha said to Gehazi, "Tell her that we appreciate the kind concern she has shown us. Now ask her what we can do for her. Does she want me to put in a good word for her to the king or to the commander of the army?"

"No," she replied, "my family takes good care of me."

¹⁴Later Elisha asked Gehazi, "What do you think we can do for her?"

He suggested, "She doesn't have a son, and her husband is an old man."

¹⁵"Call her back again," Elisha told him. When the woman returned, Elisha said to her as she stood in the doorway, ¹⁶"Next year at about this time you will be holding a son in your arms!"

"No, my lord!" she protested. "Please don't lie to me like that, O man of God." ¹⁷But sure enough, the woman soon became pregnant. And at that time the following year she had a son, just as Elisha had said.

¹⁸One day when her child was older, he went out to visit his father, who was working with the harvesters. ¹⁹Suddenly he complained, "My head hurts! My head hurts!"

His father said to one of the servants, "Carry him home to his mother."

²⁰So the servant took him home, and his mother held him on her lap. But around noontime he died. ²¹She carried him up to the bed of the man of God, then shut the door and left him there. ²²She sent a message to her husband: "Send one of the servants and a donkey so that I can hurry to the man of God and come right back."

I SEEK OUT the help of God's servants when I am in grief or desperate need. (4:22)

²³"Why today?" he asked. "It is neither a new moon festival nor a Sabbath."

But she said, "It's all right." ²⁴So she saddled the donkey and said to the servant, "Hurry! Don't slow down on my account unless I tell you to."

²⁵As she approached the man of God at Mount Carmel, Elisha saw her in the distance. He said to Gehazi, "Look, the woman from Shunem is coming. ²⁶Run out to meet her and ask her, 'Is everything all right with you, with your husband, and with your child?' "

"Yes," the woman told Gehazi, "everything is fine."

²⁷But when she came to the man of God at the mountain, she fell to the

ground before him and caught hold of his feet. Gehazi began to push her away, but the man of God said, "Leave her alone. Something is troubling her deeply, and the LORD has not told me what it is."

²⁸Then she said, "It was you, my lord, who said I would have a son. And didn't I tell you not to raise my hopes?"

²⁹Then Elisha said to Gehazi, "Get ready to travel; take my staff and go! Don't talk to anyone along the way. Go quickly and lay the staff on the child's face."

³⁰But the boy's mother said, "As surely as the LORD lives and you yourself live, I won't go home unless you go with me." So Elisha returned with her.

³¹Gehazi hurried on ahead and laid the staff on the child's face, but nothing happened. There was no sign of life. He returned to meet Elisha and told him, "The child is still dead."

³²When Elisha arrived, the child was indeed dead, lying there on the prophet's bed. ³³He went in alone and shut the door behind him and prayed to the LORD. ³⁴Then he lay down on the child's body, placing his mouth on the child's mouth, his eyes on the child's eyes, and his hands on the child's hands. And the child's body began to grow warm again! ³⁵Elisha got up and walked back and forth in the room a few times. Then he stretched himself out again on the child. This time the boy sneezed seven times and opened his eyes!

³⁶Then Elisha summoned Gehazi. "Call the child's mother!" he said. And when she came in, Elisha said, "Here, take your son!" ³⁷She fell at his feet, overwhelmed with gratitude. Then she picked up her son and carried him downstairs.

Miracles during a Famine

³⁸Elisha now returned to Gilgal, but there was a famine in the land. One day as the group of prophets was seated before him, he said to his servant, "Put on a large kettle and make some stew for these men."

³⁹One of the young men went out into the field to gather vegetables and came back with a pocketful of wild gourds. He shredded them and put them into the kettle without realizing they were poisonous. ⁴⁰But after the men had eaten a bite or two they cried out, "Man of God, there's poison in this stew!" So they would not eat it.

⁴¹Elisha said, "Bring me some flour." Then he threw it into the kettle and said, "Now it's all right; go ahead and eat." And then it did not harm them!

⁴²One day a man from Baal-shalishah brought the man of God a sack of fresh grain and twenty loaves of barley bread made from the first grain of his harvest. Elisha said, "Give it to the group of prophets* so they can eat."

⁴³"What?" his servant exclaimed. "Feed one hundred people with only this?"

But Elisha repeated, "Give it to the group of prophets so they can eat, for the LORD says there will be plenty for all. There will even be some left over!" ⁴⁴And sure enough, there was plenty for all and some left over, just as the LORD had promised.

CHAPTER 5

The Healing of Naaman

The king of Aram had high admiration for Naaman, the commander of his army, because through him the LORD had given Aram great victories. But though Naaman was a mighty warrior, he suffered from leprosy.*

²Now groups of Aramean raiders had invaded the land of Israel, and among their captives was a young girl who had been given to Naaman's wife

I ACT quickly to help those who are grieving. (4:29)

I PRAY to God for wisdom to help those who are grieving. (4:33)

I BELIEVE God answered Elisha's prayer and raised the Shunemite woman's son from the dead. (4:35)

I BELIEVE God did other miracles through the word of Elisha. (4:41)

I BELIEVE God is in control of the affairs of every nation. (5:1)

4:42 Hebrew *to the people;* also in 4:43. 5:1 Or *from a contagious skin disease.* The Hebrew word used here and throughout this passage can describe various skin diseases.

I SEEK the good of those I serve, even if my circumstances are unfair. (5:3)

I DO NOT BECOME resentful if God doesn't perform a spectacular miracle for me. (5:11)

I AM WILLING to challenge my superiors to rethink a decision if it is for their own good. (5:13)

I AM WILLING to humbly obey what God tells me to do. (5:14)

I DO NOT USE deceit to seek financial gain. (5:22)

as a maid. ³One day the girl said to her mistress, "I wish my master would go to see the prophet in Samaria. He would heal him of his leprosy."

⁴So Naaman told the king what the young girl from Israel had said. ⁵"Go and visit the prophet," the king told him. "I will send a letter of introduction for you to carry to the king of Israel." So Naaman started out, taking as gifts 750 pounds of silver, 150 pounds of gold,* and ten sets of clothing. ⁶The letter to the king of Israel said: "With this letter I present my servant Naaman. I want you to heal him of his leprosy."

⁷When the king of Israel read it, he tore his clothes in dismay and said, "This man sends me a leper to heal! Am I God, that I can kill and give life? He is only trying to find an excuse to invade us again."

⁸But when Elisha, the man of God, heard about the king's reaction, he sent this message to him: "Why are you so upset? Send Naaman to me, and he will learn that there is a true prophet here in Israel."

⁹So Naaman went with his horses and chariots and waited at the door of Elisha's house. ¹⁰But Elisha sent a messenger out to him with this message: "Go and wash yourself seven times in the Jordan River. Then your skin will be restored, and you will be healed of leprosy."

¹¹But Naaman became angry and stalked away. "I thought he would surely come out to meet me!" he said. "I expected him to wave his hand over the leprosy and call on the name of the LORD his God and heal me! ¹²Aren't the Abana River and Pharpar River of Damascus better than all the rivers of Israel put together? Why shouldn't I wash in them and be healed?" So Naaman turned and went away in a rage.

¹³But his officers tried to reason with him and said, "Sir, if the prophet had told you to do some great thing, wouldn't you have done it? So you should certainly obey him when he says simply to go and wash and be cured!" ¹⁴So Naaman went down to the Jordan River and dipped himself seven times, as the man of God had instructed him. And his flesh became as healthy as a young child's, and he was healed!

¹⁵Then Naaman and his entire party went back to find the man of God. They stood before him, and Naaman said, "I know at last that there is no God in all the world except in Israel. Now please accept my gifts."

¹⁶But Elisha replied, "As surely as the LORD lives, whom I serve, I will not accept any gifts." And though Naaman urged him to take the gifts, Elisha refused.

¹⁷Then Naaman said, "All right, but please allow me to load two of my mules with earth from this place, and I will take it back home with me. From now on I will never again offer any burnt offerings or sacrifices to any other god except the LORD. ¹⁸However, may the LORD pardon me in this one thing. When my master the king goes into the temple of the god Rimmon to worship there and leans on my arm, may the LORD pardon me when I bow, too."

¹⁹"Go in peace," Elisha said. So Naaman started home again.

The Greed of Gehazi

²⁰But Gehazi, Elisha's servant, said to himself, "My master should not have let this Aramean get away without accepting his gifts. As surely as the LORD lives, I will chase after him and get something from him." ²¹So Gehazi set off after him.

When Naaman saw him running after him, he climbed down from his chariot and went to meet him. "Is everything all right?" Naaman asked.

²²"Yes," Gehazi said, "but my master has sent me to tell you that two young prophets from the hill country of Ephraim have just arrived. He would like 75 pounds* of silver and two sets of clothing to give to them."

5:5 Hebrew *10 talents* [340 kilograms] *of silver, 6,000 shekels* [68 kilograms] *of gold.* 5:22 Hebrew *1 talent* [34 kilograms].

²³"By all means, take 150 pounds* of silver," Naaman insisted. He gave him two sets of clothing, tied up the money in two bags, and sent two of his servants to carry the gifts for Gehazi. ²⁴But when they arrived at the hill, Gehazi took the gifts from the servants and sent the men back. Then he hid the gifts inside the house.

²⁵When he went in to his master, Elisha asked him, "Where have you been, Gehazi?"

"I haven't been anywhere," he replied.

²⁶But Elisha asked him, "Don't you realize that I was there in spirit when Naaman stepped down from his chariot to meet you? Is this the time to receive money and clothing and olive groves and vineyards and sheep and oxen and servants? ²⁷Because you have done this, you and your children and your children's children will suffer from Naaman's leprosy forever." When Gehazi left the room, he was leprous; his skin was as white as snow.

UNLIKE GEHAZI

2 Kings 5:22

I do not grasp wealth that rightly belongs to God or others.

As Elisha's servant, Gehazi had witnessed the power of God often. Still, when tempted by the chance to fill his own pockets, the glitter of gold shown brighter to Gehazi than did God's glory.

Elisha refused any gift that would distract Naaman from knowing that the Lord alone was God. While God's Word provides for the Lord's servants to receive gifts and support (Deuteronomy 18:1-8 and 1 Timothy 5:17-18), Elisha knew that this was not the time to take money for miracles. Abraham demonstrated this same understanding when he refused payment for rescuing Lot (Genesis 14:22-23). No one but God must get the glory for making Abraham rich or Naaman healthy.

Gehazi had no such insight into God's purposes for bringing the commander of the enemy's army to the prophet of Israel for healing. Even Elisha's words didn't deter Gehazi from going after something for himself. Greed led to deception as he raced after Namaan and asked for the money his master had earlier refused. That greed then led straight to disaster.

Like Achan (Joshua 7:10-26), Gehazi found out that amount is not the issue when we steal from God or others. While Naaman returned home with a healthy body and a committed heart, Gehazi returned home bearing Namaan's leprosy.

God provides abundantly for his children through the gifts of believers and unbelievers alike. But accepting a gift must never detract from God's glory and the free gift of salvation. Otherwise, like Gehazi, we may find that we are robbing both God and others.

○ *Today's Scripture reading is 2 Kings 5.*

CHAPTER 6

The Floating Ax Head

One day the group of prophets came to Elisha and told him, "As you can see, this place where we meet with you is too small. ²Let's go down to the Jordan River, where there are plenty of logs. There we can build a new place for us to meet."

"All right," he told them, "go ahead."

³"Please come with us," someone suggested.

"I will," he said.

⁴When they arrived at the Jordan, they began cutting down trees. ⁵But as one of them was chopping, his ax head fell into the river. "Ah, my lord!" he cried. "It was a borrowed ax!"

⁶"Where did it fall?" the man of God asked. When he showed him the place, Elisha cut a stick and threw it into the water. Then the ax head rose to

I TAKE RESPONSIBILITY for items I borrow from others. (6:5)

5:23 Hebrew *2 talents* [68 kilograms].

the surface and floated. ⁷"Grab it," Elisha said to him. And the man reached out and grabbed it.

Elisha Traps the Arameans

⁸When the king of Aram was at war with Israel, he would confer with his officers and say, "We will mobilize our forces at such and such a place."

⁹But immediately Elisha, the man of God, would warn the king of Israel, "Do not go near that place, for the Arameans are planning to mobilize their troops there." ¹⁰So the king of Israel would send word to the place indicated by the man of God, warning the people there to be on their guard. This happened several times.

¹¹The king of Aram became very upset over this. He called in his officers and demanded, "Which of you is the traitor? Who has been informing the king of Israel of my plans?"

¹²"It's not us, my lord," one of the officers replied. "Elisha, the prophet in Israel, tells the king of Israel even the words you speak in the privacy of your bedroom!"

¹³The king commanded, "Go and find out where Elisha is, and we will send troops to seize him."

And the report came back: "Elisha is at Dothan." ¹⁴So one night the king of Aram sent a great army with many chariots and horses to surround the city. ¹⁵When the servant of the man of God got up early the next morning and went outside, there were troops, horses, and chariots everywhere.

"Ah, my lord, what will we do now?" he cried out to Elisha.

¹⁶"Don't be afraid!" Elisha told him. "For there are more on our side than on theirs!" ¹⁷Then Elisha prayed, "O LORD, open his eyes and let him see!" The LORD opened his servant's eyes, and when he looked up, he saw that the hillside around Elisha was filled with horses and chariots of fire.

¹⁸As the Aramean army advanced toward them, Elisha prayed, "O LORD, please make them blind." And the LORD did as Elisha asked. ¹⁹Then Elisha went out and told them, "You have come the wrong way! This isn't the right city! Follow me, and I will take you to the man you are looking for." And he led them to Samaria. ²⁰As soon as they had entered Samaria, Elisha prayed, "O LORD, now open their eyes and let them see." And the LORD did, and they discovered that they were in Samaria.

²¹When the king of Israel saw them, he shouted to Elisha, "My father, should I kill them?"

²²"Of course not!" Elisha told him. "Do we kill prisoners of war? Give them food and drink and send them home again to their master."

²³So the king made a great feast for them and then sent them home to their king. After that, the Aramean raiders stayed away from the land of Israel.

Ben-Hadad Besieges Samaria

²⁴Some time later, however, King Ben-hadad of Aram mobilized his entire army and besieged Samaria. ²⁵As a result there was a great famine in the city. After a while even a donkey's head sold for two pounds of silver, and a cup of dove's dung cost about two ounces* of silver.

²⁶One day as the king of Israel was walking along the wall of the city, a woman called to him, "Please help me, my lord the king!"

²⁷"If the LORD doesn't help you, what can I do?" he retorted. "I have neither food nor wine to give you." ²⁸But then the king asked, "What is the matter?"

She replied, "This woman proposed that we eat my son one day and her son the next. ²⁹So we cooked my son and ate him. Then the next day I said, 'Kill your son so we can eat him,' but she had hidden him."

I HEED the warnings of God's Word. (6:10)

I SHOW MERCY to prisoners of war. (6:22)

I PUT the welfare of my children before my own welfare in times of disaster. (6:28)

6:25 Hebrew *sold for 80 shekels* [0.9 kilograms] *of silver, and ¼ of a cab* [0.3 liters] *of dove's dung cost 5 shekels* [57 grams]. *Dove's dung may be a variety of wild vegetable.*

³⁰When the king heard this, he tore his clothes in despair. And as the king walked along the wall, the people could see that he was wearing sackcloth underneath next to his skin. ³¹"May God kill me if I don't execute Elisha son of Shaphat this very day," the king vowed.

³²Elisha was sitting in his house at a meeting with the leaders of Israel when the king sent a messenger to summon him. But before the messenger arrived, Elisha said to the leaders, "A murderer has sent a man to kill me. When he arrives, shut the door and keep him out. His master will soon follow him."

³³While Elisha was still saying this, the messenger arrived. And the king* said, "It is the LORD who has brought this trouble on us! Why should I wait any longer for the LORD?"

CHAPTER 7

Elisha replied, "Hear this message from the LORD! This is what the LORD says: By this time tomorrow in the markets of Samaria, five quarts of fine flour will cost only half an ounce of silver,* and ten quarts of barley grain will cost only half an ounce of silver.*"

²The officer assisting the king said to the man of God, "That couldn't happen even if the LORD opened the windows of heaven!"

But Elisha replied, "You will see it happen, but you won't be able to eat any of it!"

Lepers Visit the Enemy Camp

³Now there were four men with leprosy* sitting at the entrance of the city gates. "Why should we sit here waiting to die?" they asked each other. ⁴"We will starve if we stay here, and we will starve if we go back into the city. So we might as well go out and surrender to the Aramean army. If they let us live, so much the better. But if they kill us, we would have died anyway."

⁵So that evening they went out to the camp of the Arameans, but no one was there! ⁶For the Lord had caused the whole army of Aram to hear the clatter of speeding chariots and the galloping of horses and the sounds of a great army approaching. "The king of Israel has hired the Hittites and Egyptians* to attack us!" they cried out. ⁷So they panicked and fled into the night, abandoning their tents, horses, donkeys, and everything else, and they fled for their lives.

⁸When the lepers arrived at the edge of the camp, they went into one tent after another, eating, drinking wine, and carrying out silver and gold and clothing and hiding it. ⁹Finally, they said to each other, "This is not right. This is wonderful news, and we aren't sharing it with anyone! If we wait until morning, some terrible calamity will certainly fall upon us. Come on, let's go back and tell the people at the palace."

¹⁰So they went back to the city and told the gatekeepers what had happened—that they had gone out to the Aramean camp and no one was there! The horses and donkeys were tethered and the tents were all in order, but there was not a single person around. ¹¹Then the gatekeepers shouted the news to the people in the palace.

Israel Plunders the Camp

¹²The king got out of bed in the middle of the night and told his officers, "I know what has happened. The Arameans know we are starving, so they have left their camp and have hidden in the fields. They are expecting us to leave the city, and then they will take us alive and capture the city."

I MOURN the depravity that causes parents to hurt their children. (6:30)

I DO NOT UNFAIRLY BLAME God's people when I am experiencing great difficulties. (6:31)

I DO NOT BLAME God in times of disaster, let alone reject him. (6:33)

I DO NOT DOUBT God's ability to keep his word. (7:2)

I SHARE good news with others. (7:10)

6:33 Hebrew *he.*   7:1a Hebrew *1 seah* [6 liters] *of fine flour will cost 1 shekel* [11 grams]; also in 7:16, 18. 7:1b Hebrew *2 seahs* [12 liters] *of barley grain will cost 1 shekel* [11 grams]; also in 7:16, 18.   7:3 Or *with a contagious skin disease.* The Hebrew word used here and throughout this passage can describe various skin diseases.   7:6 Possibly *and the people of Muzur,* a district near Cilicia.

¹³One of his officers replied, "We had better send out scouts to check into this. Let them take five of the remaining horses. If something happens to them, it won't be a greater loss than if they stay here and die with the rest of us."

¹⁴So two chariots with horses were prepared, and the king sent scouts to see what had happened to the Aramean army. ¹⁵They went all the way to the Jordan River, following a trail of clothing and equipment that the Arameans had thrown away in their mad rush to escape. The scouts returned and told the king about it. ¹⁶Then the people of Samaria rushed out and plundered the Aramean camp. So it was true that five quarts of fine flour were sold that day for half an ounce of silver, and ten quarts of barley grain were sold for half an ounce of silver, just as the LORD had promised. ¹⁷The king appointed his officer to control the traffic at the gate, but he was knocked down and trampled to death as the people rushed out.

So everything happened exactly as the man of God had predicted when the king came to his house. ¹⁸The man of God had said to the king, "By this time tomorrow in the markets of Samaria, five quarts of fine flour will cost half an ounce of silver, and ten quarts of barley grain will cost half an ounce of silver." ¹⁹The king's officer had replied, "That couldn't happen even if the LORD opened the windows of heaven!" And the man of God had said, "You will see it happen, but you won't be able to eat any of it!" ²⁰And so it was, for the people trampled him to death at the gate!

CHAPTER 8

The Woman from Shunem Returns Home

Elisha had told the woman whose son he had brought back to life, "Take your family and move to some other place, for the LORD has called for a famine on Israel that will last for seven years." ²So the woman did as the man of God instructed. She took her family and lived in the land of the Philistines for seven years.

³After the famine ended she returned to the land of Israel, and she went to see the king about getting back her house and land. ⁴As she came in, the king was talking with Gehazi, the servant of the man of God. The king had just said, "Tell me some stories about the great things Elisha has done." ⁵And Gehazi was telling the king about the time Elisha had brought a boy back to life. At that very moment, the mother of the boy walked in to make her appeal to the king.

"Look, my lord!" Gehazi exclaimed. "Here is the woman now, and this is her son—the very one Elisha brought back to life!"

⁶"Is this true?" the king asked her. And she told him that it was. So he directed one of his officials to see to it that everything she had lost was restored to her, including the value of any crops that had been harvested during her absence.

Hazael Murders Ben-Hadad

⁷Now Elisha went to Damascus, the capital of Aram, where King Ben-hadad lay sick. Someone told the king that the man of God had come. ⁸When the king heard the news, he said to Hazael, "Take a gift to the man of God. Then tell him to ask the LORD if I will get well again."

⁹So Hazael loaded down forty camels with the finest products of Damascus as a gift for Elisha. He went in to him and said, "Your servant Ben-hadad, the king of Aram, has sent me to ask you if he will recover."

¹⁰And Elisha replied, "Go and tell him, 'You will recover.' But the LORD has shown me that he will actually die!" ¹¹Elisha stared at Hazael* with a fixed gaze until Hazael became uneasy. Then the man of God started weeping.

8:11 Hebrew *He stared at him.*

I BELIEVE the Lord's warnings and promises always come true. (7:16)

I HEED the warnings of godly individuals. (8:2)

See Gehazi's profile (page 435) at 2 Kings 5:22.

I SEEK help and counsel from godly individuals. (8:8)

I MOURN over the sufferings of others. (8:11)

¹²"What's the matter, my lord?" Hazael asked him.

Elisha replied, "I know the terrible things you will do to the people of Israel. You will burn their fortified cities, kill their young men, dash their children to the ground, and rip open their pregnant women!"

¹³Then Hazael replied, "How could a nobody like me* ever accomplish such a great feat?"

But Elisha answered, "The LORD has shown me that you are going to be the king of Aram."

¹⁴When Hazael went back, the king asked him, "What did Elisha tell you?"

And Hazael replied, "He told me that you will surely recover."

¹⁵But the next day Hazael took a blanket, soaked it in water, and held it over the king's face until he died. Then Hazael became the next king of Aram.

Jehoram Rules in Judah

¹⁶Jehoram son of King Jehoshaphat of Judah began to rule over Judah in the fifth year of King Joram's reign in Israel. Joram was the son of Ahab. ¹⁷Jehoram was thirty-two years old when he became king, and he reigned in Jerusalem eight years. ¹⁸But Jehoram followed the example of the kings of Israel and was as wicked as King Ahab, for he had married one of Ahab's daughters. So Jehoram did what was evil in the LORD's sight. ¹⁹But the LORD was not willing to destroy Judah, for he had made a covenant with David and promised that his descendants would continue to rule forever.*

²⁰During Jehoram's reign, the Edomites revolted against Judah and crowned their own king. ²¹So Jehoram* went with all his chariots to attack the town of Zair.* The Edomites surrounded him and his charioteers, but he escaped at night under cover of darkness. Jehoram's army, however, deserted him and fled. ²²Edom has been independent from Judah to this day. The town of Libnah revolted about that same time.

²³The rest of the events in Jehoram's reign and all his deeds are recorded in *The Book of the History of the Kings of Judah*. ²⁴When Jehoram died, he was buried with his ancestors in the City of David. Then his son Ahaziah became the next king.

Ahaziah Rules in Judah

²⁵Ahaziah son of Jehoram began to rule over Judah in the twelfth year of King Joram's reign in Israel. King Joram was the son of Ahab. ²⁶Ahaziah was twenty-two years old when he became king, and he reigned in Jerusalem one year. His mother was Athaliah, a granddaughter of King Omri of Israel. ²⁷Ahaziah followed the evil example of King Ahab's family, doing what was evil in the LORD's sight, because he was related by marriage to the family of Ahab.

²⁸Ahaziah joined King Joram of Israel in his war against King Hazael of Aram at Ramoth-gilead. When King Joram was wounded in the battle, ²⁹he returned to Jezreel to recover from his wounds. While Joram was there, King Ahaziah of Judah went to visit him.

CHAPTER 9

Jehu Anointed King of Israel

Meanwhile, Elisha the prophet had summoned a member of the group of prophets. "Get ready to go to Ramoth-gilead," he told him. "Take this vial of olive oil with you, ²and find Jehu son of Jehoshaphat and grandson of Nimshi. Call him into a back room away from his friends, ³and pour the oil over his head. Say to him, 'This is what the LORD says: I anoint you to be the king over Israel.' Then open the door and run for your life!"

⁴So the young prophet did as he was told and went to Ramoth-gilead.

See the profiles for Ahab (page 417) and Jehoshaphat (page 527) at 1 Kings 16:31 and 2 Chronicles 20:21.

I BELIEVE God preserved Judah and its king because of his promise to David. (8:19)

See David's profile (page 629) at Psalm 3:1.

I DO NOT FOLLOW the example of wicked individuals, even those in my own family. (8:27)

See Jehoshaphat's profile (page 527) at 2 Chronicles 20:21.

I CARRY OUT my God-given tasks. (9:4)

8:13 Hebrew *a dog.*   8:19 Hebrew *promised to give a lamp to David and his descendants forever.*   8:21a Hebrew *Joram,* a variant name for Jehoram; also in 8:23, 24.   8:21b Greek version reads *Seir.*

⁵When he arrived there, he found Jehu sitting in a meeting with the other army officers. "I have a message for you, Commander," he said.

"For which one of us?" Jehu asked.

"For you, Commander," he replied.

⁶So Jehu left the others and went into the house. Then the young prophet poured the oil over Jehu's head and said, "This is what the LORD, the God of Israel, says: I anoint you king over the LORD's people, Israel. ⁷You are to destroy the family of Ahab, your master. In this way, I will avenge the murder of my prophets and all the LORD's servants who were killed by Jezebel. ⁸The entire family of Ahab must be wiped out—every male, slave and free alike, in Israel. ⁹I will destroy the family of Ahab as I destroyed the families of Jeroboam son of Nebat and of Baasha son of Ahijah. ¹⁰Dogs will eat Ahab's wife, Jezebel, at the plot of land in Jezreel, and no one will bury her." Then the young prophet opened the door and ran.

¹¹Jehu went back to his fellow officers, and one of them asked him, "What did that crazy fellow want? Is everything all right?"

"You know the way such a man babbles on," Jehu replied.

¹²"You're lying," they said. "Tell us." So Jehu told them what the man had said and that at the LORD's command he had been anointed king over Israel.

¹³They quickly spread out their cloaks on the bare steps and blew a trumpet, shouting, "Jehu is king!"

Jehu Kills Joram and Ahaziah

¹⁴So Jehu son of Jehoshaphat and grandson of Nimshi formed a conspiracy against King Joram. (Now Joram had been with the army at Ramoth-gilead, defending Israel against the forces of King Hazael of Aram. ¹⁵But Joram* had been wounded in the fighting and had returned to Jezreel to recover from his wounds.) So Jehu told the men with him, "Since you want me to be king, don't let anyone escape to Jezreel to report what we have done."

¹⁶Then Jehu got into a chariot and rode to Jezreel to find King Joram, who was lying there wounded. King Ahaziah of Judah was there, too, for he had gone to visit him. ¹⁷The watchman on the tower of Jezreel saw Jehu and his company approaching, so he shouted to Joram, "I see a company of troops coming!"

"Send out a rider to find out if they are coming in peace," King Joram shouted back.

¹⁸So a rider went out to meet Jehu and said, "The king wants to know whether you are coming in peace."

Jehu replied, "What do you know about peace? Get behind me!"

The watchman called out to the king, "The rider has met them, but he is not returning."

¹⁹So the king sent out a second rider. He rode up to them and demanded, "The king wants to know whether you come in peace."

Again Jehu answered, "What do you know about peace? Get behind me!"

²⁰The watchman exclaimed, "The rider has met them, but he isn't returning either! It must be Jehu son of Nimshi, for he is driving so recklessly."

²¹"Quick! Get my chariot ready!" King Joram commanded.

Then King Joram of Israel and King Ahaziah of Judah rode out in their chariots to meet Jehu. They met him at the field that had belonged to Naboth of Jezreel. ²²King Joram demanded, "Do you come in peace, Jehu?"

Jehu replied, "How can there be peace as long as the idolatry and witchcraft of your mother, Jezebel, are all around us?"

²³Then King Joram reined the chariot horses around and fled, shouting to King Ahaziah, "Treason, Ahaziah!" ²⁴Then Jehu drew his bow and shot Joram

See Ahab's profile (page 417) at 1 Kings 16:31.

See Jeroboam's profile (page 411) at 1 Kings 13:4.

I DO what the Lord says. (9:10)

I IMMEDIATELY AGREE with what the Lord has said. (9:13)

I LOOK OUT for crazy drivers. (9:20)

9:15 Hebrew *Jehoram*, a variant name for Joram; also in 9:17, 21, 22, 23, 24.

between the shoulders. The arrow pierced his heart, and he sank down dead in his chariot.

²⁵Jehu said to Bidkar, his officer, "Throw him into the field of Naboth of Jezreel. Do you remember when you and I were riding along behind his father, Ahab? The LORD pronounced this message against him: ²⁶'I solemnly swear that I will repay him here on Naboth's property, says the LORD, for the murder of Naboth and his sons that I saw yesterday.' So throw him out on Naboth's field, just as the LORD said."

²⁷When King Ahaziah of Judah saw what was happening, he fled along the road to Beth-haggan. Jehu rode after him, shouting, "Shoot him, too!" So they shot Ahaziah in his chariot at the Ascent of Gur, near Ibleam. He was able to go on as far as Megiddo, but he died there. ²⁸His officials took him by chariot to Jerusalem, where they buried him with his ancestors in the City of David. ²⁹Ahaziah's reign over Judah had begun in the eleventh year of King Joram's reign in Israel.

The Death of Jezebel

³⁰When Jezebel, the queen mother, heard that Jehu had come to Jezreel, she painted her eyelids and fixed her hair and sat at a window. ³¹When Jehu entered the gate of the palace, she shouted at him, "Have you come in peace, you murderer? You are just like Zimri, who murdered his master!"

³²Jehu looked up and saw her at the window and shouted, "Who is on my side?" And two or three eunuchs looked out at him. ³³"Throw her down!" Jehu yelled. So they threw her out the window, and some of her blood spattered against the wall and on the horses. And Jehu trampled her body under his horses' hooves.

³⁴Then Jehu went into the palace and ate and drank. Afterward he said, "Someone go and bury this cursed woman, for she is the daughter of a king." ³⁵But when they went out to bury her, they found only her skull, her feet, and her hands.

³⁶When they returned and told Jehu, he stated, "This fulfills the message from the LORD, which he spoke through his servant Elijah from Tishbe: 'At the plot of land in Jezreel, dogs will eat Jezebel's flesh. ³⁷Her body will be scattered like dung on the field of Jezreel, so that no one will be able to recognize her.' "

CHAPTER 10

Jehu Kills Ahab's Family

Now Ahab had seventy sons living in the city of Samaria. So Jehu wrote a letter and sent copies to Samaria, to the officials of the city,* to the leaders of the people, and to the guardians of King Ahab's sons. The letter said, ²"The king's sons are with you, and you have at your disposal chariots, horses, a fortified city, and weapons. As soon as you receive this letter, ³select the best qualified of King Ahab's sons to be your king, and prepare to fight for Ahab's dynasty."

⁴But they were paralyzed with fear and said, "Two kings couldn't stand against this man! What can we do?" ⁵So the palace and city administrators, together with the other leaders and the guardians of the king's sons, sent this message to Jehu: "We are your servants and will do anything you tell us. We will not make anyone king; do whatever you think is best."

⁶Jehu responded with a second letter: "If you are on my side and are going to obey me, bring the heads of the king's sons to me at Jezreel at about this time tomorrow."

Now the seventy sons of the king were being cared for by the leaders of Samaria, where they had been raised since childhood. ⁷When the letter arrived, the leaders killed all seventy of the king's sons. They placed their heads in

I REMEMBER the prophecies of the Lord. (9:25)

See David's profile (page 629) at Psalm 3:1.

I BELIEVE Jezebel was rebellious to the bitter end. (9:30)

I BELIEVE the Lord's warnings and promises always come true (see 1 Kings 21:23). (9:36)

See Ahab's profile (page 417) at 1 Kings 16:31.

10:1 As in some Greek manuscripts and Latin Vulgate (see also 10:6); Hebrew reads *of Jezreel.*

baskets and presented them to Jehu at Jezreel. [8]A messenger went to Jehu and said, "They have brought the heads of the king's sons."

So Jehu ordered, "Pile them in two heaps at the entrance of the city gate, and leave them there until morning."

[9]In the morning he went out and spoke to the crowd that had gathered around them. "You aren't to blame," he told them. "I am the one who conspired against my master and killed him. But who killed all these? [10]You can be sure that the message of the LORD that was spoken concerning Ahab's family will not fail. The LORD declared through his servant Elijah that this would happen." [11]Then Jehu killed all of Ahab's relatives living in Jezreel and all his important officials, personal friends, and priests. So Ahab was left without a single survivor.

[12]Then Jehu set out for Samaria. Along the way, while he was at Beth-eked of the Shepherds, [13]he met some relatives of King Ahaziah of Judah. "Who are you?" he asked them.

And they replied, "We are relatives of King Ahaziah. We are going to visit the sons of King Ahab and the queen mother."

[14]"Take them alive!" Jehu shouted to his men. And they captured all forty-two of them and killed them at the well of Beth-eked. None of them escaped.

[15]When Jehu left there, he met Jehonadab son of Recab, who was coming to meet him. After they had greeted each other, Jehu said to him, "Are you as loyal to me as I am to you?"

"Yes, I am," Jehonadab replied.

"If you are," Jehu said, "then give me your hand." So Jehonadab put out his hand, and Jehu helped him into the chariot. [16]Then Jehu said, "Now come with me, and see how devoted I am to the LORD." So Jehonadab rode along with him. [17]When Jehu arrived in Samaria, he killed everyone who was left there from Ahab's family, just as the LORD had promised through Elijah.

Jehu Kills the Priests of Baal

[18]Then Jehu called a meeting of all the people of the city and said to them, "Ahab hardly worshiped Baal at all compared to the way I will worship him! [19]Summon all the prophets and worshipers of Baal, and call together all his priests. See to it that every one of them comes, for I am going to offer a great sacrifice to Baal. Any of Baal's worshipers who fail to come will be put to death." But Jehu's plan was to destroy all the worshipers of Baal.

[20]Then Jehu ordered, "Prepare a solemn assembly to worship Baal!" So they did. [21]He sent messengers throughout all Israel summoning those who worshiped Baal. They all came and filled the temple of Baal from one end to the other. [22]And Jehu instructed the keeper of the wardrobe, "Be sure that every worshiper of Baal wears one of these robes." So robes were given to them.

[23]Then Jehu went into the temple of Baal with Jehonadab son of Recab. Jehu said to the worshipers of Baal, "Make sure that only those who worship Baal are here. Don't let anyone in who worships the LORD!" [24]So they were all inside the temple to offer sacrifices and burnt offerings. Now Jehu had surrounded the building with eighty of his men and had warned them, "If you let anyone escape, you will pay for it with your own life."

[25]As soon as Jehu had finished sacrificing the burnt offering, he commanded his guards and officers, "Go in and kill all of them. Don't let a single one escape!" So they killed them all with their swords, and the guards and officers dragged their bodies outside. Then Jehu's men went into the fortress* of the temple of Baal. [26]They dragged out the sacred pillar used in the worship of Baal and destroyed it. [27]They broke down the sacred pillar of Baal and wrecked the temple of Baal, converting it into a public toilet. That is what it is

Margin notes

I BELIEVE the Lord's warnings and promises always come true (see 2 Kings 9:7). (10:10)

See Elijah's profile (page 421) at 1 Kings 19:18.

See Jehonadab's profile (page 893) at Jeremiah 35:19.

I REMOVE false worship from my life and my sphere of authority. (10:19)

10:25 Hebrew *city.*

used for to this day. ²⁸Thus, Jehu destroyed every trace of Baal worship from Israel. ²⁹He did not, however, destroy the gold calves at Bethel and Dan, the great sin that Jeroboam son of Nebat had led Israel to commit.

³⁰Nonetheless the LORD said to Jehu, "You have done well in following my instructions to destroy the family of Ahab. Because of this I will cause your descendants to be the kings of Israel down to the fourth generation." ³¹But Jehu did not obey the law of the LORD, the God of Israel, with all his heart. He refused to turn from the sins of idolatry that Jeroboam had led Israel to commit.

The Death of Jehu

³²At about that time the LORD began to reduce the size of Israel's territory. King Hazael conquered several sections of the country ³³east of the Jordan River, including all of Gilead, Gad, Reuben, and Manasseh. He conquered the area from the town of Aroer by the Arnon Gorge to as far north as Gilead and Bashan.

³⁴The rest of the events in Jehu's reign and all his deeds and achievements are recorded in *The Book of the History of the Kings of Israel*. ³⁵When Jehu died, he was buried with his ancestors in Samaria. Then his son Jehoahaz became the next king. ³⁶In all, Jehu reigned over Israel from Samaria for twenty-eight years.

CHAPTER 11

Athaliah Rules in Judah

When Athaliah, the mother of King Ahaziah of Judah, learned that her son was dead, she set out to destroy the rest of the royal family. ²But Ahaziah's sister Jehosheba, the daughter of King Jehoram,* took Ahaziah's infant son, Joash, and stole him away from among the rest of the king's children, who were about to be killed. Jehosheba put Joash and his nurse in a bedroom to hide him from Athaliah, so the child was not murdered. ³Joash and his nurse remained hidden in the Temple of the LORD for six years while Athaliah ruled over the land.

Revolt against Athaliah

⁴In the seventh year of Athaliah's reign, Jehoiada the priest summoned the commanders, the Carite mercenaries, and the guards to come to the Temple of the LORD. He made a pact with them and made them swear an oath of loyalty there in the LORD's Temple; then he showed them the king's son.

⁵Jehoiada told them, "This is what you must do. A third of you who are on duty on the Sabbath are to guard the royal palace itself. ⁶Another third of you are to stand guard at the Sur Gate. And the final third must stand guard behind the palace guard. These three groups will all guard the palace. ⁷The other two units who are off duty on the Sabbath must stand guard for the king at the LORD's Temple. ⁸Form a bodyguard for the king and keep your weapons in hand. Any unauthorized person who approaches you must be killed. Stay right beside the king at all times."

⁹So the commanders did everything just as Jehoiada the priest ordered. The commanders took charge of the men reporting for duty that Sabbath, as well as those who were going off duty. They brought them all to Jehoiada the priest, ¹⁰and he supplied them with the spears and shields that had once belonged to King David and were stored in the Temple of the LORD. ¹¹The guards stationed themselves around the king, with their weapons ready. They formed a line from the south side of the Temple around to the north side and all around the altar.

¹²Then Jehoiada brought out Joash, the king's son, and placed the crown

11:2 Hebrew *Joram*, a variant name for Jehoram.

I REMOVE anything in my life that competes with true worship of the Lord. (10:29)

See Jeroboam's profile (page 411) at 1 Kings 13:4.

I AM BLESSED by the Lord when I obey his commands. (10:30)

I OBEY the Lord with my whole heart. (10:31)

I PROTECT my family's children when they are in danger of being harmed or abused. (11:2)

I SUPPORT those who are qualified to lead God's people. (11:5)

See David's profile (page 629) at Psalm 3:1.

I BELIEVE that spiritual leaders especially should take God's Word to heart. (11:12)

on his head. He presented Joash with a copy of God's covenant and proclaimed him king. They anointed him, and all the people clapped their hands and shouted, "Long live the king!"

The Death of Athaliah

¹³When Athaliah heard all the noise made by the guards and the people, she hurried to the LORD's Temple to see what was happening. ¹⁴And she saw the newly crowned king standing in his place of authority by the pillar, as was the custom at times of coronation. The officers and trumpeters were surrounding him, and people from all over the land were rejoicing and blowing trumpets. When Athaliah saw all this, she tore her clothes in despair and shouted, "Treason! Treason!"

¹⁵Then Jehoiada the priest ordered the commanders who were in charge of the troops, "Take her out of the Temple, and kill anyone who tries to rescue her. Do not kill her here in the Temple of the LORD." ¹⁶So they seized her and led her out to the gate where horses enter the palace grounds, and she was killed there.

Jehoiada's Religious Reforms

¹⁷Then Jehoiada made a covenant between the LORD and the king and the people that they would be the LORD's people. He also made a covenant between the king and the people. ¹⁸And all the people of the land went over to the temple of Baal and tore it down. They demolished the altars and smashed the idols to pieces, and they killed Mattan the priest of Baal in front of the altars.

Jehoiada the priest stationed guards at the Temple of the LORD. ¹⁹Then the commanders, the Carite mercenaries, the guards, and all the people of the land escorted the king from the Temple of the LORD. They went through the gate of the guards and into the palace, and the king took his seat on the royal throne. ²⁰So all the people of the land rejoiced, and the city was peaceful because Athaliah had been killed at the king's palace.

²¹Joash* was seven years old when he became king.

CHAPTER 12

Joash Repairs the Temple

Joash* began to rule over Judah in the seventh year of King Jehu's reign in Israel. He reigned in Jerusalem forty years. His mother was Zibiah, from Beersheba. ²All his life Joash did what was pleasing in the LORD's sight because Jehoiada the priest instructed him. ³Yet even so, he did not destroy the pagan shrines, and the people still offered sacrifices and burned incense there.

⁴One day King Joash said to the priests, "Collect all the money brought as a sacred offering to the LORD's Temple, whether it is a regular assessment, a payment of vows, or a voluntary gift. ⁵Let the priests take some of that money to pay for whatever repairs are needed at the Temple."

⁶But by the twenty-third year of Joash's reign, the priests still had not repaired the Temple. ⁷So King Joash called for Jehoiada and the other priests and asked them, "Why haven't you repaired the Temple? Don't use any more gifts for your own needs. From now on, it must all be spent on getting the Temple into good condition." ⁸So the priests agreed not to collect any more money from the people, and they also agreed not to undertake the repairs of the Temple themselves.

⁹Then Jehoiada the priest bored a hole in the lid of a large chest and set it on the right-hand side of the altar at the entrance of the Temple of the LORD. The priests guarding the entrance put all of the people's contributions into

I TRAIN young leaders to keep the Lord's commands. (11:17)

I REMOVE false worship from my life and my sphere of authority. (11:18)

I LISTEN to the instruction of godly individuals. (12:2)

I REMOVE anything in my life that competes with true worship of the Lord. (12:3)

I USE the funds given by God's people properly, not for my personal benefit. (12:7)

11:21 Hebrew *Jehoash*, a variant name for Joash. 12:1 Hebrew *Jehoash*, a variant name for Joash; also in 12:2, 4, 6, 7, 18.

the chest. [10]Whenever the chest became full, the court secretary and the high priest counted the money that had been brought to the LORD's Temple and put it into bags. [11]Then they gave the money to the construction supervisors, who used it to pay the people working on the LORD's Temple—the carpenters, the builders, [12]the masons, and the stonecutters. They also used the money to buy timber and cut stone for repairing the LORD's Temple, and they paid any other expenses related to the Temple's restoration.

[13]The money brought to the Temple was not used for making silver cups, lamp snuffers, basins, trumpets, or other articles of gold or silver for the Temple of the LORD. [14]It was paid out to the workmen, who used it for the Temple repairs. [15]No accounting was required from the construction supervisors, because they were honest and faithful workers. [16]However, the money that was contributed for guilt offerings and sin offerings was not brought into the LORD's Temple. It was given to the priests for their own use.

I ENSURE that money donated for the Lord's work is used as intended by the donors. (12:11)

The End of Joash's Reign

[17]About this time King Hazael of Aram went to war against Gath and captured it. Then he turned to attack Jerusalem. [18]King Joash collected all the sacred objects that Jehoshaphat, Jehoram, and Ahaziah, the previous kings of Judah, had dedicated, along with what he himself had dedicated. He sent them all to Hazael, along with all the gold in the treasuries of the LORD's Temple and the royal palace. So Hazael called off his attack on Jerusalem.

See Jehoshaphat's profile (page 527) at 2 Chronicles 20:21.

[19]The rest of the events in Joash's reign and all his deeds are recorded in *The Book of the History of the Kings of Judah.* [20]But his officers plotted against him and assassinated him at Beth-millo on the road to Silla. [21]The assassins were Jozabad son of Shimeath and Jehozabad son of Shomer—both trusted advisers. Joash was buried with his ancestors in the City of David. Then his son Amaziah became the next king.

See David's profile (page 629) at Psalm 3:1.

CHAPTER 13

Jehoahaz Rules in Israel

Jehoahaz son of Jehu began to rule over Israel in the twenty-third year of King Joash's reign in Judah. He reigned in Samaria seventeen years. [2]But he did what was evil in the LORD's sight. He followed the example of Jeroboam son of Nebat, continuing the sins of idolatry that Jeroboam son of Nebat had led Israel to commit. [3]So the LORD was very angry with Israel, and he allowed King Hazael of Aram and his son Ben-hadad to defeat them time after time.

I DO NOT FOLLOW the example of wicked individuals. (13:2)

[4]Then Jehoahaz prayed for the LORD's help, and the LORD heard his prayer. The LORD could see how terribly the king of Aram was oppressing Israel. [5]So the LORD raised up a deliverer to rescue the Israelites from the tyranny of the Arameans. Then Israel lived in safety again as they had in former days. [6]But they continued to sin, following the evil example of Jeroboam. They even set up an Asherah pole in Samaria. [7]Finally, Jehoahaz's army was reduced to fifty mounted troops, ten chariots, and ten thousand foot soldiers. The king of Aram had killed the others like they were dust under his feet.

See Jeroboam's profile (page 411) at 1 Kings 13:4.

I BELIEVE God may allow suffering and defeat in the lives of those who live in rebellion against him. (13:3)

[8]The rest of the events in Jehoahaz's reign and all his deeds, including the extent of his power, are recorded in *The Book of the History of the Kings of Israel.* [9]When Jehoahaz died, he was buried in Samaria with his ancestors. Then his son Jehoash* became the next king.

I PRAY to the Lord for help when I am oppressed. (13:4)

Jehoash Rules in Israel

[10]Jehoash son of Jehoahaz began to rule over Israel in the thirty-seventh year of King Joash's reign in Judah. He reigned in Samaria sixteen years. [11]But he did what was evil in the LORD's sight. He refused to turn from the sins of idolatry that Jeroboam son of Nebat had led Israel to commit. [12]The rest of the

I DO NOT FOLLOW in the footsteps of evil men and women who have gone before me. (13:11)

13:9 Hebrew *Joash,* a variant name for Jehoash; also in 13:10, 12, 13, 14, 25.

events in Jehoash's reign and all his deeds, including the extent of his power and his war with King Amaziah of Judah, are recorded in *The Book of the History of the Kings of Israel.* [13]When Jehoash died, he was buried with his ancestors in Samaria. Then his son Jeroboam II became the next king.

Elisha's Final Prophecy

[14]When Elisha was in his last illness, King Jehoash of Israel visited him and wept over him. "My father! My father! The chariots and charioteers of Israel!" he cried.

[15]Elisha told him, "Get a bow and some arrows." And the king did as he was told.

[16]Then Elisha told the king of Israel to put his hand on the bow, and Elisha laid his own hands on the king's hands. [17]Then he commanded, "Open that eastern window," and he opened it. Then he said, "Shoot!" So he did.

Then Elisha proclaimed, "This is the LORD's arrow, full of victory over Aram, for you will completely conquer the Arameans at Aphek. [18]Now pick up the other arrows and strike them against the ground." So the king picked them up and struck the ground three times. [19]But the man of God was angry with him. "You should have struck the ground five or six times!" he exclaimed. "Then you would have beaten Aram until they were entirely destroyed. Now you will be victorious only three times."

[20]Then Elisha died and was buried.

Groups of Moabite raiders used to invade the land each spring. [21]Once when some Israelites were burying a man, they spied a band of these raiders. So they hastily threw the body they were burying into the tomb of Elisha. But as soon as the body touched Elisha's bones, the dead man revived and jumped to his feet!

[22]King Hazael of Aram had oppressed Israel during the entire reign of King Jehoahaz. [23]But the LORD was gracious to the people of Israel, and they were not totally destroyed. He pitied them because of his covenant with Abraham, Isaac, and Jacob. And to this day he still has not completely destroyed them or banished them from his presence.

[24]King Hazael of Aram died, and his son Ben-hadad became the next king. [25]Then Jehoash son of Jehoahaz recaptured from Ben-hadad son of Hazael the towns that Hazael had taken from Jehoash's father, Jehoahaz. Jehoash defeated Ben-hadad on three occasions, and so recovered the Israelite towns.

CHAPTER 14

Amaziah Rules in Judah

Amaziah son of Joash began to rule over Judah in the second year of the reign of King Jehoash* of Israel. [2]Amaziah was twenty-five years old when he became king, and he reigned in Jerusalem twenty-nine years. His mother was Jehoaddin, from Jerusalem. [3]Amaziah did what was pleasing in the LORD's sight, but not like his ancestor David. Instead, he followed the example of his father, Joash. [4]Amaziah did not destroy the pagan shrines, where the people offered sacrifices and burned incense.

[5]When Amaziah was well established as king, he executed the men who had assassinated his father. [6]However, he did not kill the children of the assassins, for he obeyed the command of the LORD written in the Book of the Law of Moses: "Parents must not be put to death for the sins of their children, nor the children for the sins of their parents. Those worthy of death must be executed for their own crimes."*

[7]It was Amaziah who killed ten thousand Edomites in the Valley of Salt. He also conquered Sela and changed its name to Joktheel, as it is called to this day.

Margin notes (left column)

See Elisha's profile (page 431) at 2 Kings 2:14.

I BELIEVE the Lord graciously protected the Israelites because of his pity and his covenant with Abraham, Isaac, and Jacob. (13:23)

See the profiles for Abraham (page 19), Isaac (page 31), and Jacob (page 43) at Genesis 15:6, Genesis 25:19, and Genesis 32:9.

I PLEASE the Lord by following the examples of godly men and women who have gone before me. (14:3)

See David's profile (page 629) at Psalm 3:1.

I ENSURE that justice is enforced within the sphere of my authority. (14:5)

I DO NOT BELIEVE children should be punished for their parents' sins. (14:6)

14:1 Hebrew *Joash,* a variant name for Jehoash; also in 14:13, 23, 27.   14:6 Deut 24:16.

⁸One day Amaziah sent this challenge to Israel's king Jehoash, the son of Jehoahaz and grandson of Jehu: "Come and meet me in battle!"

⁹But King Jehoash of Israel replied to King Amaziah of Judah with this story: "Out in the Lebanon mountains a thistle sent a message to a mighty cedar tree: 'Give your daughter in marriage to my son.' But just then a wild animal came by and stepped on the thistle, crushing it! ¹⁰You have indeed destroyed Edom and are very proud about it. Be content with your victory and stay at home! Why stir up trouble that will bring disaster on you and the people of Judah?"

¹¹But Amaziah refused to listen, so King Jehoash of Israel mobilized his army against King Amaziah of Judah. The two armies drew up their battle lines at Beth-shemesh in Judah. ¹²Judah was routed by the army of Israel, and its army scattered and fled for home. ¹³King Jehoash of Israel captured King Amaziah of Judah at Beth-shemesh and marched on to Jerusalem. Then Jehoash ordered his army to demolish six hundred feet* of Jerusalem's wall, from the Ephraim Gate to the Corner Gate. ¹⁴He carried off all the gold and silver and all the utensils from the Temple of the LORD, as well as from the palace treasury. He also took hostages and returned to Samaria.

¹⁵The rest of the events in Jehoash's reign, including the extent of his power and his war with King Amaziah of Judah, are recorded in *The Book of the History of the Kings of Israel.* ¹⁶When Jehoash died, he was buried with his ancestors in Samaria. Then his son Jeroboam II became the next king.

¹⁷King Amaziah of Judah lived on for fifteen years after the death of King Jehoash of Israel. ¹⁸The rest of the events in Amaziah's reign are recorded in *The Book of the History of the Kings of Judah.* ¹⁹There was a conspiracy against Amaziah's life in Jerusalem, and he fled to Lachish. But his enemies sent assassins after him, and they killed him there. ²⁰They brought him back to Jerusalem on a horse, and he was buried with his ancestors in the City of David.

²¹The people of Judah then crowned Amaziah's sixteen-year-old son, Uzziah,* as their next king. ²²After his father's death, Uzziah rebuilt the town of Elath and restored it to Judah.

Jeroboam II Rules in Israel

²³Jeroboam II, the son of Jehoash, began to rule over Israel in the fifteenth year of King Amaziah's reign in Judah. Jeroboam reigned in Samaria forty-one years. ²⁴He did what was evil in the LORD's sight. He refused to turn from the sins of idolatry that Jeroboam son of Nebat had led Israel to commit. ²⁵Jeroboam II recovered the territories of Israel between Lebo-hamath and the Dead Sea,* just as the LORD, the God of Israel, had promised through Jonah son of Amittai, the prophet from Gath-hepher. ²⁶For the LORD saw the bitter suffering of everyone in Israel, and how they had absolutely no one to help them. ²⁷And because the LORD had not said he would blot out the name of Israel completely, he used Jeroboam II, the son of Jehoash, to save them.

²⁸The rest of the events in the reign of Jeroboam II and all his deeds, including the extent of his power, his wars, and how he recovered for Israel both Damascus and Hamath, which had belonged to Judah,* are recorded in *The Book of the History of the Kings of Israel.* ²⁹When Jeroboam II died, he was buried with his ancestors, the kings of Israel. Then his son Zechariah became the next king.

CHAPTER 15

Uzziah Rules in Judah

Uzziah* son of Amaziah began to rule over Judah in the twenty-seventh year of the reign of King Jeroboam II of Israel. ²He was sixteen years old when he

See Moses's profile (page 73) at Exodus 5:1.

I RECOGNIZE that any desire on my part to fight can lead to trouble for many others. (14:13)

See Uzziah's profile (page 533) at 2 Chronicles 26:16.

I DO NOT FOLLOW in the footsteps of evil men and women who have gone before me. (14:23)

See Jonah's profile (page 1027) at Jonah 4:2.

I BELIEVE the Lord sees the suffering of his people, even when they have been living in disobedience. (14:26)

See Uzziah's profile (page 533) at 2 Chronicles 26:16.

14:13 Hebrew *400 cubits* [180 meters]. 14:21 Hebrew *Azariah,* a variant name for Uzziah. 14:25 Hebrew *the sea of the Arabah.* 14:28 Or *to Yaudi.* 15:1 Hebrew *Azariah,* a variant name for Uzziah; also in 15:6, 7, 8, 17, 23, 27.

I PLEASE the Lord by following the examples of godly men and women who have gone before me. (15:3)

I REMOVE false worship from my life and my sphere of authority. (15:4)

See David's profile (page 629) at Psalm 3:1.

I DO NOT FOLLOW in the footsteps of evil men and women who have gone before me. (15:9)

See Jeroboam's profile (page 411) at 1 Kings 13:4.

I DO NOT USE violence to further my own agenda. (15:16)

I ABHOR the use of extortion or bribery. (15:20)

became king, and he reigned in Jerusalem fifty-two years. His mother was Jecoliah, from Jerusalem. ³He did what was pleasing in the LORD's sight, just as his father, Amaziah, had done. ⁴But he did not destroy the pagan shrines, where the people offered sacrifices and burned incense. ⁵The LORD struck the king with leprosy,* which lasted until the day of his death; he lived in a house by himself. The king's son Jotham was put in charge of the royal palace, and he governed the people of the land.

⁶The rest of the events in Uzziah's reign and all his deeds are recorded in *The Book of the History of the Kings of Judah.* ⁷When Uzziah died, he was buried near his ancestors in the City of David. Then his son Jotham became the next king.

Zechariah Rules in Israel

⁸Zechariah son of Jeroboam II began to rule over Israel in the thirty-eighth year of King Uzziah's reign in Judah. He reigned in Samaria six months. ⁹Zechariah did what was evil in the LORD's sight, as his ancestors had done. He refused to turn from the sins of idolatry that Jeroboam son of Nebat had led Israel to commit. ¹⁰Then Shallum son of Jabesh conspired against Zechariah, assassinated him in public,* and became the next king. ¹¹The rest of the events in Zechariah's reign are recorded in *The Book of the History of the Kings of Israel.* ¹²So the LORD's message to Jehu came true: "Your descendants will be kings of Israel down to the fourth generation."

Shallum Rules in Israel

¹³Shallum son of Jabesh began to rule over Israel in the thirty-ninth year of King Uzziah's reign in Judah. Shallum reigned in Samaria only one month. ¹⁴Then Menahem son of Gadi went to Samaria from Tirzah and assassinated him, and he became the next king. ¹⁵The rest of the events in Shallum's reign, including his conspiracy, are recorded in *The Book of the History of the Kings of Israel.*

Menahem Rules in Israel

¹⁶At that time Menahem destroyed the town of Tappuah* and all the surrounding countryside as far as Tirzah, because its citizens refused to surrender the town. He killed the entire population and ripped open the pregnant women.

¹⁷Menahem son of Gadi began to rule over Israel in the thirty-ninth year of King Uzziah's reign in Judah. He reigned in Samaria ten years. ¹⁸But Menahem did what was evil in the LORD's sight. During his entire reign, he refused to turn from the sins of idolatry that Jeroboam son of Nebat had led Israel to commit. ¹⁹Then King Tiglath-pileser* of Assyria invaded the land. But Menahem paid him thirty-seven tons* of silver to gain his support in tightening his grip on royal power. ²⁰Menahem extorted the money from the rich of Israel, demanding that each of them pay twenty ounces* of silver in the form of a special tax. So the king of Assyria turned from attacking Israel and did not stay in the land. ²¹The rest of the events in Menahem's reign and all his deeds are recorded in *The Book of the History of the Kings of Israel.* ²²When Menahem died, his son Pekahiah became the next king.

Pekahiah Rules in Israel

²³Pekahiah son of Menahem began to rule over Israel in the fiftieth year of King Uzziah's reign in Judah. He reigned in Samaria two years. ²⁴But Pekahiah did what was evil in the LORD's sight. He refused to turn from the sins of idolatry that Jeroboam son of Nebat had led Israel to commit.

15:5 Or *with a contagious skin disease.* The Hebrew word used here and throughout this passage can describe various skin diseases. 15:10 Or *at Ibleam.* 15:16 As in some Greek manuscripts; Hebrew reads *Tiphsah.* 15:19a Hebrew *Pul,* another name for Tiglath-pileser. 15:19b Hebrew *1,000 talents* [34 metric tons]. 15:20 Hebrew *50 shekels* [570 grams].

²⁵Then Pekah son of Remaliah, the commander of Pekahiah's army, conspired against him. With fifty men from Gilead, Pekah assassinated the king, along with Argob and Arieh, in the citadel of the palace at Samaria. Pekah then became the next king of Israel. ²⁶The rest of the events in Pekahiah's reign and all his deeds are recorded in *The Book of the History of the Kings of Israel.*

Pekah Rules in Israel

²⁷Pekah son of Remaliah began to rule over Israel in the fifty-second year of King Uzziah's reign in Judah. He reigned in Samaria twenty years. ²⁸But Pekah did what was evil in the LORD's sight. He refused to turn from the sins of idolatry that Jeroboam son of Nebat had led Israel to commit. ²⁹During his reign, King Tiglath-pileser of Assyria attacked Israel again, and he captured the towns of Ijon, Abel-beth-maacah, Janoah, Kedesh, and Hazor. He also conquered the regions of Gilead, Galilee, and Naphtali, and he took the people to Assyria as captives. ³⁰Then Hoshea son of Elah conspired against Pekah and assassinated him. He began to rule over Israel in the twentieth year of Jotham son of Uzziah. ³¹The rest of the events in Pekah's reign and all his deeds are recorded in *The Book of the History of the Kings of Israel.*

Jotham Rules in Judah

³²Jotham son of Uzziah began to rule over Judah in the second year of King Pekah's reign in Israel. ³³He was twenty-five years old when he became king, and he reigned in Jerusalem sixteen years. His mother was Jerusha, the daughter of Zadok.

³⁴Jotham did what was pleasing in the LORD's sight, just as his father Uzziah had done. ³⁵But he did not destroy the pagan shrines, where the people offered sacrifices and burned incense. He was the one who rebuilt the upper gate of the Temple of the LORD.

³⁶The rest of the events in Jotham's reign and all his deeds are recorded in *The Book of the History of the Kings of Judah.* ³⁷In those days the LORD began to send King Rezin of Aram and King Pekah of Israel to attack Judah. ³⁸When Jotham died, he was buried with his ancestors in the City of David. Then his son Ahaz became the next king.

CHAPTER 16

Ahaz Rules in Judah

Ahaz son of Jotham began to rule over Judah in the seventeenth year of King Pekah's reign in Israel. ²Ahaz was twenty years old when he became king, and he reigned in Jerusalem sixteen years. He did not do what was pleasing in the sight of the LORD his God, as his ancestor David had done. ³Instead, he followed the example of the kings of Israel, even sacrificing his own son in the fire.* He imitated the detestable practices of the pagan nations the LORD had driven from the land ahead of the Israelites. ⁴He offered sacrifices and burned incense at the pagan shrines and on the hills and under every green tree.

⁵Then King Rezin of Aram and King Pekah of Israel declared war on Ahaz. They besieged Jerusalem but did not conquer it. ⁶At that time the king of Edom* recovered the town of Elath for Edom.* He drove out the people of Judah and sent Edomites* to live there, as they do to this day.

⁷King Ahaz sent messengers to King Tiglath-pileser of Assyria with this message: "I am your servant and your vassal.* Come up and rescue me from the attacking armies of Aram and Israel." ⁸Then Ahaz took the silver and gold from the Temple of the LORD and the palace treasury and sent it as a gift to the Assyrian king. ⁹So the Assyrians attacked the Aramean capital of Damascus

---

I ABHOR political assassinations and other murders. (15:25)

I DO what is pleasing in the Lord's sight. (15:34)

See David's profile (page 629) at Psalm 3:1.

I DO NOT LOOK to the enemies of God for deliverance. (16:7)

16:3 Or *even making his son pass through the fire.*　16:6a As in Latin Vulgate; Hebrew reads *Rezin king of Aram.*　16:6b As in Latin Vulgate; Hebrew reads *Aram.*　16:6c As in marginal *Qere* reading of the Masoretic Text, Greek version, and Latin Vulgate; Hebrew reads *Arameans.*　16:7 Hebrew *your son.*

and led its population away as captives, resettling them in Kir. They also killed King Rezin.

[10]King Ahaz then went to Damascus to meet with King Tiglath-pileser of Assyria. While he was there, he noticed an unusual altar. So he sent a model of the altar to Uriah the priest, along with its design in full detail. [11]Uriah built an altar just like it by following the king's instructions, and it was ready for the king when he returned from Damascus. [12]When the king returned, he inspected the altar and made offerings on it. [13]The king presented a burnt offering and a grain offering, poured a drink offering over it, and sprinkled the blood of peace offerings on it.

[14]Then King Ahaz removed the old bronze altar from the front of the LORD's Temple, which had stood between the entrance and the new altar, and placed it on the north side of the new altar. [15]He said to Uriah the priest, "Use the new altar for the morning sacrifices of burnt offering, the evening grain offering, the king's burnt offering and grain offering, and the offerings of the people, including their drink offerings. The blood from the burnt offerings and sacrifices should be sprinkled over the new altar. The old bronze altar will be only for my personal use." [16]Uriah the priest did just as King Ahaz instructed him.

[17]Then the king removed the side panels and basins from the portable water carts. He also removed the Sea from the backs of the bronze oxen and placed it on the stone pavement. [18]In deference to the king of Assyria, he also removed the canopy that had been constructed inside the palace for use on the Sabbath day,* as well as the king's outer entrance to the Temple of the LORD.

[19]The rest of the events in Ahaz's reign and his deeds are recorded in *The Book of the History of the Kings of Judah.* [20]When Ahaz died, he was buried with his ancestors in the City of David. Then his son Hezekiah became the next king.

CHAPTER 17

Hoshea Rules in Israel

Hoshea son of Elah began to rule over Israel in the twelfth year of King Ahaz's reign in Judah. He reigned in Samaria nine years. [2]He did what was evil in the LORD's sight, but not as much as the kings of Israel who ruled before him.

[3]King Shalmaneser of Assyria attacked and defeated King Hoshea, so Israel was forced to pay heavy annual tribute to Assyria. [4]Then Hoshea conspired against the king of Assyria by asking King So of Egypt* to help him shake free of Assyria's power and by refusing to pay the annual tribute to Assyria. When the king of Assyria discovered this treachery, he arrested him and put him in prison for his rebellion.

[5]Then the king of Assyria invaded the entire land, and for three years he besieged Samaria. [6]Finally, in the ninth year of King Hoshea's reign, Samaria fell, and the people of Israel were exiled to Assyria. They were settled in colonies in Halah, along the banks of the Habor River in Gozan, and among the cities of the Medes.

Samaria Falls to Assyria

[7]This disaster came upon the nation of Israel because the people worshiped other gods, sinning against the LORD their God, who had brought them safely out of their slavery in Egypt. [8]They had imitated the practices of the pagan nations the LORD had driven from the land before them, as well as the practices the kings of Israel had introduced. [9]The people of Israel had also secretly done many things that were not pleasing to the LORD their God. They built pagan shrines for themselves in all their towns, from the smallest outpost to

---

Pray that the Holy Spirit will guide you into all truth (John 16:13).

I DO NOT SUBSTITUTE the worship practices of false religions for the worship God requires. (16:15)

I DO NOT WORSHIP God in a pagan fashion. (16:16)

I DO NOT RESTRICT my worship of God in order to please someone who wields political power. (16:18)

See Hezekiah's profile (page 825) at Isaiah 37:1.

See Elijah's profile (page 421) at 1 Kings 19:18.

I DO NOT TRY to secretly sin against God. (17:9)

16:18 The meaning of the Hebrew is uncertain.   17:4 Or *by asking the king of Egypt at Sais.*

the largest walled city. ¹⁰They set up sacred pillars and Asherah poles at the top of every hill and under every green tree. ¹¹They burned incense at the shrines, just like the nations the LORD had driven from the land ahead of them. So the people of Israel had done many evil things, arousing the LORD's anger. ¹²Yes, they worshiped idols, despite the LORD's specific and repeated warnings. ¹³Again and again the LORD had sent his prophets and seers to warn both Israel and Judah: "Turn from all your evil ways. Obey my commands and laws, which are contained in the whole law that I commanded your ancestors and which I gave you through my servants the prophets."

¹⁴But the Israelites would not listen. They were as stubborn as their ancestors and refused to believe in the LORD their God. ¹⁵They rejected his laws and the covenant he had made with their ancestors, and they despised all his warnings. They worshiped worthless idols and became worthless themselves. They followed the example of the nations around them, disobeying the LORD's command not to imitate them. ¹⁶They defied all the commands of the LORD their God and made two calves from metal. They set up an Asherah pole and worshiped Baal and all the forces of heaven. ¹⁷They even sacrificed their own sons and daughters in the fire.* They consulted fortune-tellers and used sorcery and sold themselves to evil, arousing the LORD's anger.

¹⁸And because the LORD was angry, he swept them from his presence. Only the tribe of Judah remained in the land. ¹⁹But even the people of Judah refused to obey the commands of the LORD their God. They walked down the same evil paths that Israel had established. ²⁰So the LORD rejected all the descendants of Israel. He punished them by handing them over to their attackers until they were destroyed. ²¹For when the LORD tore Israel away from the kingdom of David, they chose Jeroboam son of Nebat as their king. Then Jeroboam drew Israel away from following the LORD and made them commit a great sin. ²²And the people of Israel persisted in all the evil ways of Jeroboam. They did not turn from these sins of idolatry ²³until the LORD finally swept them away, just as all his prophets had warned would happen. So Israel was carried off to the land of Assyria, where they remain to this day.

Foreigners Settle in Israel

²⁴And the king of Assyria transported groups of people from Babylon, Cuthah, Avva, Hamath, and Sepharvaim and resettled them in the towns of Samaria, replacing the people of Israel. So the Assyrians took over Samaria and the other towns of Israel. ²⁵But since these foreign settlers did not worship the LORD when they first arrived, the LORD sent lions among them to kill some of them.

²⁶So a message was sent to the king of Assyria: "The people whom you have resettled in the towns of Israel* do not know how to worship the God of the land. He has sent lions among them to destroy them because they have not worshiped him correctly."

²⁷The king of Assyria then commanded, "Send one of the exiled priests from Samaria back to Israel. Let him teach the new residents the religious customs of the God of the land." ²⁸So one of the priests who had been exiled from Samaria returned to Bethel and taught the new residents how to worship the LORD.

²⁹But these various groups of foreigners also continued to worship their own gods. In town after town where they lived, they placed their idols at the pagan shrines that the people of Israel had built. ³⁰Those from Babylon worshiped idols of their god Succoth-benoth. Those from Cuthah worshiped their god Nergal. And those from Hamath worshiped Ashima. ³¹The Avvites worshiped their gods Nibhaz and Tartak. And the people from Sepharvaim

I DO NOT AROUSE God's anger by copying the pagan worship of evil people. (17:11)

I DO NOT DESPISE the Lord's warnings. (17:12)

I DO NOT REFUSE to obey God's commands. (17:19)

See the profiles for David (page 629) and Jeroboam (page 411) at Psalm 3:1 and 1 Kings 13:4.

I DO NOT PERSIST in the evil ways of those who have gone before me. (17:22)

I FORSAKE any worship practices that are false, pagan, and dishonoring to the Lord. (17:29)

17:17 Or *They even made their sons and daughters pass through the fire.*   17:26 Hebrew *of Samaria;* also in 17:29.

even burned their own children as sacrifices to Adrammelech and Anammelech.

³²These new residents worshiped the LORD, but they appointed from among themselves priests to offer sacrifices at the pagan shrines. ³³And though they worshiped the LORD, they continued to follow the religious customs of the nations from which they came. ³⁴And this is still going on among them today. They follow their former practices instead of truly worshiping the LORD and obeying the laws, regulations, instructions, and commands he gave the descendants of Jacob, whose name he changed to Israel. ³⁵For the LORD had made a covenant with the descendants of Jacob and commanded them: "Do not worship any other gods or bow before them or serve them or offer sacrifices to them. ³⁶Worship only the LORD, who brought you out of Egypt with such mighty miracles and power. You must worship him and bow before him; offer sacrifices to him alone. ³⁷Be careful to obey all the laws, regulations, instructions, and commands that he wrote for you. You must not worship any other gods. ³⁸Do not forget the covenant I made with you, and do not worship other gods. ³⁹You must worship only the LORD your God. He is the one who will rescue you from all your enemies."

⁴⁰But the people would not listen and continued to follow their old ways. ⁴¹So while these new residents worshiped the LORD, they also worshiped their idols. And to this day their descendants do the same.

CHAPTER 18

Hezekiah Rules in Judah

Hezekiah son of Ahaz began to rule over Judah in the third year of King Hoshea's reign in Israel. ²He was twenty-five years old when he became king, and he reigned in Jerusalem twenty-nine years. His mother was Abijah,* the daughter of Zechariah. ³He did what was pleasing in the LORD's sight, just as his ancestor David had done. ⁴He removed the pagan shrines, smashed the sacred pillars, and knocked down the Asherah poles. He broke up the bronze serpent that Moses had made, because the people of Israel had begun to worship it by burning incense to it. The bronze serpent was called Nehushtan.*

⁵Hezekiah trusted in the LORD, the God of Israel. There was never another king like him in the land of Judah, either before or after his time. ⁶He remained faithful to the LORD in everything, and he carefully obeyed all the commands the LORD had given Moses. ⁷So the LORD was with him, and Hezekiah was successful in everything he did. He revolted against the king of Assyria and refused to pay him tribute. ⁸He also conquered the Philistines as far distant as Gaza and its territory, from their smallest outpost to their largest walled city.

⁹During the fourth year of Hezekiah's reign, which was the seventh year of King Hoshea's reign in Israel, King Shalmaneser of Assyria attacked Israel and began a siege on the city of Samaria. ¹⁰Three years later, during the sixth year of King Hezekiah's reign and the ninth year of King Hoshea's reign in Israel, Samaria fell. ¹¹At that time the king of Assyria deported the Israelites to Assyria and put them in colonies in Halah, along the banks of the Habor River in Gozan, and among the cities of the Medes. ¹²For they had refused to listen to the LORD their God. Instead, they had violated his covenant—all the laws the LORD had given through his servant Moses.

Assyria Invades Judah

¹³In the fourteenth year of King Hezekiah's reign, King Sennacherib of Assyria came to attack the fortified cities of Judah and conquered them. ¹⁴King Hezekiah sent this message to the king of Assyria at Lachish: "I have done wrong. I

I OBEY the Lord completely. (17:34)

See Jacob's profile (page 43) at Genesis 32:9.

I AM WILLING to listen and change my old ways. (17:40)

See Elijah's profile (page 421) at 1 Kings 19:18.

See Hezekiah's profile (page 825) at Isaiah 37:1.

I DO what is pleasing in the Lord's sight. (18:3)

See David's profile (page 629) at Psalm 3:1.

See Moses' profile (page 73) at Exodus 5:1.

I AM SUCCESSFUL in the Lord's eyes because I remain faithful to the Lord, carefully obey his commands, and experience his presence in my life. (18:7)

I BELIEVE the Israelites were deported to Assyria because they refused to listen to and obey the Lord. (18:12)

18:2 As in parallel text at 2 Chr 29:1; Hebrew reads *Abi*, a variant name for Abijah. 18:4 *Nehushtan* sounds like the Hebrew terms that mean "snake," "bronze," and "unclean thing."

will pay whatever tribute money you demand if you will only go away." The king of Assyria then demanded a settlement of more than eleven tons of silver and about one ton of gold.* ¹⁵To gather this amount, King Hezekiah used all the silver stored in the Temple of the LORD and in the palace treasury. ¹⁶Hezekiah even stripped the gold from the doors of the LORD's Temple and from the doorposts he had overlaid with gold, and he gave it all to the Assyrian king.

¹⁷Nevertheless the king of Assyria sent his commander in chief, his field commander, and his personal representative from Lachish with a huge army to confront King Hezekiah in Jerusalem. The Assyrians stopped beside the aqueduct that feeds water into the upper pool, near the road leading to the field where cloth is bleached. ¹⁸They summoned King Hezekiah, but the king sent these officials to meet with them: Eliakim son of Hilkiah, the palace administrator, Shebna the court secretary, and Joah son of Asaph, the royal historian.

Sennacherib Threatens Jerusalem

¹⁹Then the Assyrian king's personal representative sent this message to King Hezekiah:

"This is what the great king of Assyria says: What are you trusting in that makes you so confident? ²⁰Do you think that mere words can substitute for military skill and strength? Which of your allies will give you any military backing against Assyria? ²¹Will Egypt? If you lean on Egypt, you will find it to be a stick that breaks beneath your weight and pierces your hand. The pharaoh of Egypt is completely unreliable!

²²"But perhaps you will say, 'We are trusting in the LORD our God!' But isn't he the one who was insulted by King Hezekiah? Didn't Hezekiah tear down his shrines and altars and make everyone in Judah worship only at the altar here in Jerusalem?

²³"I'll tell you what! My master, the king of Assyria, will strike a bargain with you. If you can find two thousand horsemen in your entire army, he will give you two thousand horses for them to ride on! ²⁴With your tiny army, how can you think of challenging even the weakest contingent of my master's troops, even with the help of Egypt's chariots and horsemen*? ²⁵What's more, do you think we have invaded your land without the LORD's direction? The LORD himself told us, 'Go and destroy it!' "

I DO NOT IMMEDIATELY ACCEPT someone's claim that he or she is sent by God. (18:25)

²⁶Then Eliakim son of Hilkiah, Shebna, and Joah said to the king's representative, "Please speak to us in Aramaic, for we understand it well. Don't speak in Hebrew, for the people on the wall will hear."

²⁷But Sennacherib's representative replied, "My master wants everyone in Jerusalem to hear this, not just you. He wants them to know that if you do not surrender, this city will be put under siege. The people will become so hungry and thirsty that they will eat their own dung and drink their own urine."

²⁸Then he stood and shouted in Hebrew to the people on the wall, "Listen to this message from the great king of Assyria! ²⁹This is what the king says: Don't let King Hezekiah deceive you. He will never be able to rescue you from my power. ³⁰Don't let him fool you into trusting in the LORD by saying, 'The LORD will rescue us! This city will never be handed over to the Assyrian king.'

I REJECT the taunts of those who discourage me from trusting the Lord. (18:30)

³¹"Don't listen to Hezekiah! These are the terms the king of Assyria is offering: Make peace with me—open the gates and come out. Then I will allow each of you to continue eating from your own garden and drinking from

I DO NOT COMPROMISE trust in the Lord for immediate and temporary physical benefits. (18:31)

18:14 Hebrew *300 talents* [10 metric tons] *of silver and 30 talents* [1 metric ton] *of gold.*   18:24 Or *and charioteers.*

your own well. ³²Then I will arrange to take you to another land like this one—a country with bountiful harvests of grain and wine, bread and vineyards, olive trees and honey—a land of plenty. Choose life instead of death!

"Don't listen to Hezekiah when he tries to mislead you by saying, 'The LORD will rescue us!' ³³Have the gods of any other nations ever saved their people from the king of Assyria? ³⁴What happened to the gods of Hamath and Arpad? And what about the gods of Sepharvaim, Hena, and Ivvah? Did they rescue Samaria from my power? ³⁵What god of any nation has ever been able to save its people from my power? Name just one! So what makes you think that the LORD can rescue Jerusalem?"

³⁶But the people were silent and did not answer because Hezekiah had told them not to speak. ³⁷Then Eliakim son of Hilkiah, the palace administrator, Shebna the court secretary, and Joah son of Asaph, the royal historian, went back to Hezekiah. They tore their clothes in despair, and they went in to see the king and told him what the Assyrian representative had said.

CHAPTER 19

Hezekiah Seeks the LORD's Help

When King Hezekiah heard their report, he tore his clothes and put on sackcloth and went into the Temple of the LORD to pray. ²And he sent Eliakim the palace administrator, Shebna the court secretary, and the leading priests, all dressed in sackcloth, to the prophet Isaiah son of Amoz. ³They told him, "This is what King Hezekiah says: This is a day of trouble, insult, and disgrace. It is like when a child is ready to be born, but the mother has no strength to deliver it. ⁴But perhaps the LORD your God has heard the Assyrian representative defying the living God and will punish him for his words. Oh, pray for those of us who are left!"

⁵After King Hezekiah's officials delivered the king's message to Isaiah, ⁶the prophet replied, "Say to your master, 'This is what the LORD says: Do not be disturbed by this blasphemous speech against me from the Assyrian king's messengers. ⁷Listen! I myself will move against him, and the king will receive a report from Assyria telling him that he is needed at home. Then I will make him want to return to his land, where I will have him killed with a sword.' "

⁸Meanwhile, the Assyrian representative left Jerusalem and went to consult his king, who had left Lachish and was attacking Libnah. ⁹Soon afterward King Sennacherib received word that King Tirhakah of Ethiopia* was leading an army to fight against him. Before leaving to meet the attack, he sent this message back to Hezekiah in Jerusalem:

¹⁰"This message is for King Hezekiah of Judah. Don't let this God you trust deceive you with promises that Jerusalem will not be captured by the king of Assyria. ¹¹You know perfectly well what the kings of Assyria have done wherever they have gone. They have crushed everyone who stood in their way! Why should you be any different? ¹²Have the gods of other nations rescued them—such nations as Gozan, Haran, Rezeph, and the people of Eden who were in Tel-assar? The former kings of Assyria destroyed them all! ¹³What happened to the king of Hamath and the king of Arpad? What happened to the kings of Sepharvaim, Hena, and Ivvah?"

¹⁴After Hezekiah received the letter and read it, he went up to the LORD's Temple and spread it out before the LORD. ¹⁵And Hezekiah prayed this prayer before the LORD: "O LORD, God of Israel, you are enthroned between the mighty cherubim! You alone are God of all the kingdoms of the earth. You alone created the heavens and the earth. ¹⁶Listen to me, O LORD, and hear! Open your eyes, O LORD, and see! Listen to Sennacherib's words of defiance against the living God.

19:9 Hebrew *of Cush.*

I GRIEVE when God is mocked and his people are in danger of attack. (18:37)

I GO to God in humble mourning when his name is mocked and his people are in danger of attack. (19:1)

See Hezekiah's profile (page 825) at Isaiah 37:1.

See Isaiah's profile (page 801) at Isaiah 6:13.

I TRUST in God and experience peace when unbelievers taunt me and blaspheme his holy name. (19:6)

I REJECT the taunts of those who discourage me from trusting the Lord. (19:10)

I PRAISE the Lord for his greatness as the only true God and Creator. (19:15)

[17]"It is true, LORD, that the kings of Assyria have destroyed all these nations, just as the message says. [18]And they have thrown the gods of these nations into the fire and burned them. But of course the Assyrians could destroy them! They were not gods at all—only idols of wood and stone shaped by human hands. [19]Now, O LORD our God, rescue us from his power; then all the kingdoms of the earth will know that you alone, O LORD, are God."

I RECOGNIZE that all false religions and idols have no power in themselves. (19:18)

Isaiah Predicts Judah's Deliverance

[20]Then Isaiah son of Amoz sent this message to Hezekiah: "This is what the LORD, the God of Israel, says: I have heard your prayer about King Sennacherib of Assyria. [21]This is the message that the LORD has spoken against him:

'The virgin daughter of Zion
  despises you and laughs at you.
The daughter of Jerusalem
  scoffs and shakes her head as you flee.

[22]'Whom do you think you have been insulting and ridiculing?
  Against whom did you raise your voice?
At whom did you look in such proud condescension?
  It was the Holy One of Israel!
[23]By your messengers you have mocked the Lord.
  You have said, "With my many chariots
I have conquered the highest mountains—
  yes, the remotest peaks of Lebanon.
I have cut down its tallest cedars
  and its choicest cypress trees.
I have reached its farthest corners
  and explored its deepest forests.
[24]I have dug wells in many a foreign land
  and refreshed myself with their water.
I even stopped up the rivers of Egypt
  so that my armies could go across!"

I RECOGNIZE that when unbelievers taunt God's people, they are ridiculing God. (19:22)

[25]'But have you not heard?
  It was I, the LORD, who decided this long ago.
Long ago I planned what I am now causing to happen,
  that you should crush fortified cities into heaps of rubble.
[26]That is why their people have so little power
  and are such easy prey for you.
They are as helpless as the grass,
  as easily trampled as tender green shoots.
They are like grass sprouting on a housetop,
  easily scorched by the sun.

[27]'But I know you well—
  your comings and goings and all you do.
  I know the way you have raged against me.
[28]And because of your arrogance against me,
  which I have heard for myself,
I will put my hook in your nose
  and my bridle in your mouth.
I will make you return
  by the road on which you came.' "

I BELIEVE the Lord humbles the arrogant. (19:28)

[29]Then Isaiah said to Hezekiah, "Here is the proof that the LORD will protect this city from Assyria's king. This year you will eat only what grows up by itself, and next year you will eat what springs up from that. But in the third

year you will plant crops and harvest them; you will tend vineyards and eat their fruit. ³⁰And you who are left in Judah, who have escaped the ravages of the siege, will take root again in your own soil, and you will flourish and multiply. ³¹For a remnant of my people will spread out from Jerusalem, a group of survivors from Mount Zion. The passion of the LORD Almighty will make this happen!

³²"And this is what the LORD says about the king of Assyria: His armies will not enter Jerusalem to shoot their arrows. They will not march outside its gates with their shields and build banks of earth against its walls. ³³The king will return to his own country by the road on which he came. He will not enter this city, says the LORD. ³⁴For my own honor and for the sake of my servant David, I will defend it."

See David's profile (page 629) at Psalm 3:1.

³⁵That night the angel of the LORD went out to the Assyrian camp and killed 185,000 Assyrian troops. When the surviving Assyrians* woke up the next morning, they found corpses everywhere. ³⁶Then King Sennacherib of Assyria broke camp and returned to his own land. He went home to his capital of Nineveh and stayed there. ³⁷One day while he was worshiping in the temple of his god Nisroch, his sons Adrammelech and Sharezer killed him with their swords. They then escaped to the land of Ararat, and another son, Esarhaddon, became the next king of Assyria.

CHAPTER 20

Hezekiah's Sickness and Recovery

See the profiles for Hezekiah (page 825) and Isaiah (page 801) at Isaiah 37:1 and Isaiah 6:13.

About that time Hezekiah became deathly ill, and the prophet Isaiah son of Amoz went to visit him. He gave the king this message: "This is what the LORD says: Set your affairs in order, for you are going to die. You will not recover from this illness."

I PRAY to the Lord if I learn I am going to die. (20:2)

²When Hezekiah heard this, he turned his face to the wall and prayed to the LORD, ³"Remember, O LORD, how I have always tried to be faithful to you and do what is pleasing in your sight." Then he broke down and wept bitterly.

I WANT to be faithful to the Lord and please him all my life. (20:3)

See David's profile (page 629) at Psalm 3:1.

⁴But before Isaiah had left the middle courtyard, this message came to him from the LORD: ⁵"Go back to Hezekiah, the leader of my people. Tell him, 'This is what the LORD, the God of your ancestor David, says: I have heard your prayer and seen your tears. I will heal you, and three days from now you will get out of bed and go to the Temple of the LORD. ⁶I will add fifteen years to your life, and I will rescue you and this city from the king of Assyria. I will do this to defend my honor and for the sake of my servant David.' "

⁷Then Isaiah said to Hezekiah's servants, "Make an ointment from figs and spread it over the boil." They did this, and Hezekiah recovered!

⁸Meanwhile, Hezekiah had said to Isaiah, "What sign will the LORD give to prove that he will heal me and that I will go to the Temple of the LORD three days from now?"

⁹Isaiah replied, "This is the sign that the LORD will give you to prove he will do as he promised. Would you like the shadow on the sundial to go forward ten steps or backward ten steps?"

I BELIEVE the Lord can do the miraculous. (20:10)

¹⁰"The shadow always moves forward," Hezekiah replied. "Make it go backward instead." ¹¹So Isaiah asked the LORD to do this, and he caused the shadow to move ten steps backward on the sundial of Ahaz!

Envoys from Babylon

I DO NOT SEEK to impress unbelievers by showing off my wealth. (20:12)

¹²Soon after this, Merodach-baladan son of Baladan, king of Babylon, sent Hezekiah his best wishes and a gift, for he had heard that Hezekiah had been very sick. ¹³Hezekiah welcomed the Babylonian envoys and showed them everything in his treasure-houses—the silver, the gold, the spices, and the

19:35 Hebrew *When they.*

aromatic oils. He also took them to see his armory and showed them all his other treasures—everything! There was nothing in his palace or kingdom that Hezekiah did not show them.

¹⁴Then Isaiah the prophet went to King Hezekiah and asked him, "What did those men want? Where were they from?"

Hezekiah replied, "They came from the distant land of Babylon."

¹⁵"What did they see in your palace?" Isaiah asked.

"They saw everything," Hezekiah replied. "I showed them everything I own—all my treasures."

¹⁶Then Isaiah said to Hezekiah, "Listen to this message from the LORD: ¹⁷The time is coming when everything you have—all the treasures stored up by your ancestors—will be carried off to Babylon. Nothing will be left, says the LORD. ¹⁸Some of your own descendants will be taken away into exile. They will become eunuchs who will serve in the palace of Babylon's king."

¹⁹Then Hezekiah said to Isaiah, "This message you have given me from the LORD is good." But the king was thinking, "At least there will be peace and security during my lifetime."

²⁰The rest of the events in Hezekiah's reign, including the extent of his power and how he built a pool and dug a tunnel to bring water into the city, are recorded in *The Book of the History of the Kings of Judah.* ²¹When Hezekiah died, his son Manasseh became the next king.

CHAPTER 21

Manasseh Rules in Judah

Manasseh was twelve years old when he became king, and he reigned in Jerusalem fifty-five years. His mother was Hephzibah. ²He did what was evil in the LORD's sight, imitating the detestable practices of the pagan nations whom the LORD had driven from the land ahead of the Israelites. ³He rebuilt the pagan shrines his father, Hezekiah, had destroyed. He constructed altars for Baal and set up an Asherah pole, just as King Ahab of Israel had done. He also bowed before all the forces of heaven and worshiped them. ⁴He even built pagan altars in the Temple of the LORD, the place where the LORD had said his name should be honored. ⁵He built these altars for all the forces of heaven in both courtyards of the LORD's Temple. ⁶Manasseh even sacrificed his own son in the fire.* He practiced sorcery and divination, and he consulted with mediums and psychics. He did much that was evil in the LORD's sight, arousing his anger.

⁷Manasseh even took an Asherah pole he had made and set it up in the Temple, the very place where the LORD had told David and his son Solomon: "My name will be honored here forever in this Temple and in Jerusalem—the city I have chosen from among all the other tribes of Israel. ⁸If the Israelites will obey my commands—the whole law that was given through my servant Moses—I will not send them into exile from this land that I gave their ancestors." ⁹But the people refused to listen, and Manasseh led them to do even more evil than the pagan nations whom the LORD had destroyed when the Israelites entered the land.

¹⁰Then the LORD said through his servants the prophets: ¹¹"King Manasseh of Judah has done many detestable things. He is even more wicked than the Amorites, who lived in this land before Israel. He has led the people of Judah into idolatry. ¹²So this is what the LORD, the God of Israel, says: I will bring such disaster on Jerusalem and Judah that the ears of those who hear about it will tingle with horror. ¹³I will judge Jerusalem by the same standard I used for Samaria and by the same measure I used for the family of Ahab. I will wipe away the people of Jerusalem as one wipes a dish and turns it upside

21:6 Or *even made his son pass through the fire.*

See Manasseh's profile (page 543) at 2 Chronicles 33:13.

I DO NOT IMITATE the evil practices of pagan religions. (21:2)

See the profiles for Ahab (page 417) and Hezekiah (page 825) at 1 Kings 16:31 and Isaiah 37:1.

I DO NOT AROUSE the Lord's anger by participating in occult activities. (21:6)

See the profiles for David (page 629) and Solomon (page 753) at Psalm 3:1 and Proverbs 2:9.

See Moses' profile (page 73) at Exodus 5:1.

I DO NOT LEAD God's people into evil practices. (21:9)

down. [14]Then I will reject even those few of my people who are left, and I will hand them over as plunder for their enemies. [15]For they have done great evil in my sight and have angered me ever since their ancestors came out of Egypt."

[16]Manasseh also murdered many innocent people until Jerusalem was filled from one end to the other with innocent blood. This was in addition to the sin that he caused the people of Judah to commit, leading them to do evil in the LORD's sight.

[17]The rest of the events in Manasseh's reign and all his deeds, including the sins he committed, are recorded in *The Book of the History of the Kings of Judah.* [18]When Manasseh died, he was buried in the palace garden, the garden of Uzza. Then his son Amon became the next king.

Amon Rules in Judah

[19]Amon was twenty-two years old when he became king, and he reigned in Jerusalem two years. His mother was Meshullemeth, the daughter of Haruz from Jotbah. [20]He did what was evil in the LORD's sight, just as his father, Manasseh, had done. [21]He followed the example of his father, worshiping the same idols that his father had worshiped. [22]He abandoned the LORD, the God of his ancestors, and he refused to follow the LORD's ways.

[23]Then Amon's own servants plotted against him and assassinated him in his palace. [24]But the people of the land killed all those who had conspired against King Amon, and they made his son Josiah the next king.

[25]The rest of the events in Amon's reign and all his deeds are recorded in *The Book of the History of the Kings of Judah.* [26]He was buried in his tomb in the garden of Uzza. Then his son Josiah became the next king.

CHAPTER 22

Josiah Rules in Judah

Josiah was eight years old when he became king, and he reigned in Jerusalem thirty-one years. His mother was Jedidah, the daughter of Adaiah from Bozkath. [2]He did what was pleasing in the LORD's sight and followed the example of his ancestor David. He did not turn aside from doing what was right.

[3]In the eighteenth year of his reign, King Josiah sent Shaphan son of Azaliah and grandson of Meshullam, the court secretary, to the Temple of the LORD. He told him, [4]"Go up to Hilkiah the high priest and have him count the money the gatekeepers have collected from the people at the LORD's Temple. [5]Entrust this money to the men assigned to supervise the Temple's restoration. Then they can use it to pay workers to repair the Temple of the LORD. [6]They will need to hire carpenters, builders, and masons. Also have them buy the timber and the cut stone needed to repair the Temple. [7]But there will be no need for the construction supervisors to keep account of the money they receive, for they are honest people."

Hilkiah Discovers God's Law

[8]Hilkiah the high priest said to Shaphan the court secretary, "I have found the Book of the Law in the LORD's Temple!" Then Hilkiah gave the scroll to Shaphan, and he read it.

[9]Shaphan returned to the king and reported, "Your officials have given the money collected at the Temple of the LORD to the workers and supervisors at the Temple." [10]Shaphan also said to the king, "Hilkiah the priest has given me a scroll." So Shaphan read it to the king.

[11]When the king heard what was written in the Book of the Law, he tore his clothes in despair. [12]Then he gave these orders to Hilkiah the priest, Ahikam son of Shaphan, Acbor son of Micaiah, Shaphan the court secretary, and Asaiah the king's personal adviser: [13]"Go to the Temple and speak to the

---

I ABHOR the slaughter of innocent people. (21:16)

See Elijah's profile (page 421) at 1 Kings 19:18.

I DO NOT FOLLOW the example of wicked individuals, even if they are members of my own family. (21:20)

See Josiah's profile (page 461) at 2 Kings 23:25.

See David's profile (page 629) at Psalm 3:1.

See Hilkiah's profile (page 545) at 2 Chronicles 34:14.

I ENTRUST qualified individuals with tasks for God's service and glory. (22:5)

I ENTRUST the offerings of God's people to honest individuals. (22:7)

I READ God's Word to others. (22:10)

I MOURN deeply when I read God's Word and am convicted of my sin. (22:11)

LORD for me and for the people and for all Judah. Ask him about the words written in this scroll that has been found. The LORD's anger is burning against us because our ancestors have not obeyed the words in this scroll. We have not been doing what this scroll says we must do."

¹⁴So Hilkiah the priest, Ahikam, Acbor, Shaphan, and Asaiah went to the newer Mishneh section* of Jerusalem to consult with the prophet Huldah. She was the wife of Shallum son of Tikvah and grandson of Harhas, the keeper of the Temple wardrobe. ¹⁵She said to them, "The LORD, the God of Israel, has spoken! Go and tell the man who sent you, ¹⁶'This is what the LORD says: I will destroy this city and its people, just as I stated in the scroll you read. ¹⁷For my people have abandoned me and worshiped pagan gods, and I am very angry with them for everything they have done. My anger is burning against this place, and it will not be quenched.'

¹⁸"But go to the king of Judah who sent you to seek the LORD and tell him: 'This is what the LORD, the God of Israel, says concerning the message you have just heard: ¹⁹You were sorry and humbled yourself before the LORD when you heard what I said against this city and its people, that this land would be cursed and become desolate. You tore your clothing in despair and wept before me in repentance. So I have indeed heard you, says the LORD. ²⁰I will not send the promised disaster against this city until after you have died and been buried in peace. You will not see the disaster I am going to bring on this place.' " So they took her message back to the king.

CHAPTER 23

Josiah's Religious Reforms

Then the king summoned all the leaders of Judah and Jerusalem. ²And the king went up to the Temple of the LORD with all the people of Judah and Jerusalem, and the priests, and the prophets—all the people from the least to the greatest. There the king read to them the entire Book of the Covenant that had been found in the LORD's Temple. ³The king took his place of authority beside the pillar and renewed the covenant in the LORD's presence. He pledged to obey the LORD by keeping all his commands, regulations, and laws with all his heart and soul. In this way, he confirmed all the terms of the covenant that were written in the scroll, and all the people pledged themselves to the covenant.

⁴Then the king instructed Hilkiah the high priest and the leading priests and the Temple gatekeepers to remove from the LORD's Temple all the utensils that were used to worship Baal, Asherah, and all the forces of heaven. The king had all these things burned outside Jerusalem on the terraces of the Kidron Valley, and he carried the ashes away to Bethel. ⁵He did away with the pagan priests, who had been appointed by the previous kings of Judah, for they had burned incense at the pagan shrines throughout Judah and even in the vicinity of Jerusalem. They had also offered incense to Baal, and to the sun, the moon, the constellations, and to all the forces of heaven. ⁶The king removed the Asherah pole from the LORD's Temple and took it outside Jerusalem to the Kidron Valley, where he burned it. Then he ground the pole to dust and threw the dust in the public cemetery. ⁷He also tore down the houses of the shrine prostitutes that were inside the Temple of the LORD, where the women wove coverings for the Asherah pole.

⁸Josiah brought back to Jerusalem all the priests of the LORD, who were living in other towns of Judah. He also defiled all the pagan shrines, where they had burned incense, from Geba to Beersheba. He destroyed the shrines at the entrance to the gate of Joshua, the governor of Jerusalem. This gate was located to the left of the city gate as one enters the city. ⁹The priests who had

I READ AND TEACH God's Word to those under my authority. (23:2)

I COMPLETELY REMOVE all forms and practices of pagan worship from my life and my sphere of authority. (23:4)

See Hilkiah's profile (page 545) at 2 Chronicles 34:14.

I SEEK TO DISMISS those in spiritual authority who seek to lead God's people away from him. (23:5)

I RESTORE faithful individuals to places of spiritual leadership. (23:8)

22:14 Or *the Second Quarter*, a newer section of Jerusalem.

served at the pagan shrines were not allowed to serve at the LORD's altar in Jerusalem, but they were allowed to eat unleavened bread with the other priests.

[10]Then the king defiled the altar of Topheth in the valley of Ben-hinnom, so no one could ever again use it to sacrifice a son or daughter in the fire* as an offering to Molech. [11]He removed from the entrance of the LORD's Temple the horse statues that the former kings of Judah had dedicated to the sun. They were near the quarters of Nathan-melech the eunuch, an officer of the court. The king also burned the chariots dedicated to the sun.

[12]Josiah tore down the altars that the kings of Judah had built on the palace roof above the upper room of Ahaz. The king destroyed the altars that Manasseh had built in the two courtyards of the LORD's Temple. He smashed them to bits and scattered the pieces in the Kidron Valley. [13]The king also desecrated the pagan shrines east of Jerusalem and south of the Mount of Corruption, where King Solomon of Israel had built shrines for Ashtoreth, the detestable goddess of the Sidonians; and for Chemosh, the detestable god of the Moabites; and for Molech,* the detestable god of the Ammonites. [14]He smashed the sacred pillars and cut down the Asherah poles. Then he desecrated these places by scattering human bones over them.

[15]The king also tore down the altar at Bethel, the pagan shrine that Jeroboam son of Nebat had made when he led Israel into sin. Josiah crushed the stones to dust and burned the Asherah pole. [16] Then as Josiah was looking around, he noticed several tombs in the side of the hill. He ordered that the bones be brought out, and he burned them on the altar at Bethel to desecrate it. This happened just as the LORD had promised through the man of God as Jeroboam stood beside the altar at the festival. Then Josiah turned and looked up at the tomb of the man of God* who had predicted these things. [17]"What is that monument over there?" Josiah asked.

And the people of the town told him, "It is the tomb of the man of God who came from Judah and predicted the very things that you have just done to the altar at Bethel!"

[18]Josiah replied, "Leave it alone. Don't disturb his bones." So they did not burn his bones or those of the old prophet from Samaria.

[19]Then Josiah demolished all the buildings at the pagan shrines in the towns of Samaria, just as he had done at Bethel. They had been built by the various kings of Israel and had made the LORD very angry. [20]He executed the priests of the pagan shrines on their own altars, and he burned human bones on the altars to desecrate them. Finally, he returned to Jerusalem.

Josiah Celebrates Passover

[21]King Josiah then issued this order to all the people: "You must celebrate the Passover to the LORD your God, as it is written in the Book of the Covenant." [22]There had not been a Passover celebration like that since the time when the judges ruled in Israel, throughout all the years of the kings of Israel and Judah. [23]This Passover was celebrated to the LORD in Jerusalem during the eighteenth year of King Josiah's reign.

[24]Josiah also exterminated the mediums and psychics, the household gods, and every other kind of idol worship, both in Jerusalem and throughout the land of Judah. He did this in obedience to all the laws written in the scroll that Hilkiah the priest had found in the LORD's Temple. [25]Never before had there been a king like Josiah, who turned to the LORD with all his heart and soul and strength, obeying all the laws of Moses. And there has never been a king like him since.

23:10 Or *to make a son or daughter pass through the fire.*   23:13 Hebrew *Milcom*, a variant name for Molech.
23:16 As in Greek version; Hebrew lacks *as Jeroboam stood beside the altar at the festival. Then Josiah turned and looked up at the tomb of the man of God.*

See Manasseh's profile (page 543) at 2 Chronicles 33:13.

See Solomon's profile (page 753) at Proverbs 2:9.

I REMOVE from my life and my sphere of authority all those things that have caused individuals to sin against God in the past. (23:15)

See Jeroboam's profile (page 411) at 1 Kings 13:4.

I TURN to the Lord with all my heart and soul and strength. (23:25)

See Moses' profile (page 73) at Exodus 5:1.

²⁶Even so, the LORD's anger burned against Judah because of all the great evils of King Manasseh, and he did not hold back his fierce anger from them. ²⁷For the LORD had said, "I will destroy Judah just as I have destroyed Israel. I will banish the people from my presence and reject my chosen city of Jerusalem and the Temple where my name was to be honored."

²⁸The rest of the events in Josiah's reign and all his deeds are recorded in *The Book of the History of the Kings of Judah*.

LIKE JOSIAH
2 Kings 23:25

I lead others by word and example to hear and obey God's Word.

The Gideons place a Bible in every hotel room. For years, Brother Andrew and others have smuggled Bibles into the hands of believers behind the Iron Curtain. Wycliffe missionaries spend years translating Scripture into the language their hearers can truly understand. Like all these people, King Josiah knew the power of the Word of God.

At age twenty-six, Josiah had already been reigning over Israel eighteen years before the scroll of God's law was discovered—hidden and neglected—in the Temple. Even before he heard God's Word, Josiah had chosen to leave the wicked ways of his father and grandfather. He sought after the Lord as David had done. But once he heard the law of the Lord, God's truth bore into Josiah's soul, and he knew the enormity of Judah's sin that angered the Lord. His response turned both the heart of God and the lives of the people.

Even when Josiah was assured that his humble, repentant response had delayed God's judgment, he did not settle back into his palace to enjoy the present peace. As king, he possessed both the power and the authority to give the people what would be their only hope—the very words of God.

Calling all the people to Jerusalem, Josiah took his place of authority and read aloud the Book of the Law. Surely his impassioned voice emphasized the laws that the Israelites had been breaking without qualm, and the blessings and curses that God had promised for obedience or disobedience. Wisely, Josiah used God's words, not his own, to persuade his people to recommit themselves to God's covenant.

Josiah gave the people God's Word and then he gave them the powerful example of his own zeal and obedience. He stormed through both Judah and conquered Israel, destroying idols and desecrating every place of false worship. In place of their abominable pagan practices, he gave the people a Passover celebration such as had never been celebrated before. With the words of the law still ringing in their ears, the people then watched as their king lived out before their eyes the very fulfillment of the law—to love the Lord his God with all his heart and soul and strength.

Josiah knew up front that all his righteous reforms ultimately would not save Israel from punishment. But with a heart motivated by the love and fear of the Lord, he gave his people every chance to live lives that pleased God. Instead of keeping God's Word to himself, he brought it fully to his people and lived it plainly in their sight.

We cannot force another person to love and obey God. But when we give them the Word of God and live it out before them, we are giving them all they need to know and please him.

God had given his people a prophecy about Josiah years before Josiah was even born. To read about this prediction, see 1 Kings 13:2.

○ *Today's Scripture reading is 2 Kings 23.*

---

²⁹While Josiah was king, Pharaoh Neco, king of Egypt, went to the Euphrates River to help the king of Assyria. King Josiah marched out with his army to fight him, but King Neco killed him when they met at Megiddo. ³⁰Josiah's officers took his body back in a chariot from Megiddo to Jerusalem and buried him in his own tomb. Then the people anointed his son Jehoahaz and made him the next king.

Jehoahaz Rules in Judah
³¹Jehoahaz was twenty-three years old when he became king, and he reigned in Jerusalem three months. His mother was Hamutal, the daughter of

I DO NOT FOLLOW the example of wicked individuals. (23:32)

Jeremiah from Libnah. ³²He did what was evil in the LORD's sight, just as his ancestors had done.

³³Pharaoh Neco put Jehoahaz in prison at Riblah in the land of Hamath to prevent him from ruling from Jerusalem. He also demanded that Judah pay 7,500 pounds of silver and 75 pounds of gold* as tribute. ³⁴Pharaoh Neco then installed Eliakim, another of Josiah's sons, to reign in place of his father, and he changed Eliakim's name to Jehoiakim. Jehoahaz was taken to Egypt as a prisoner, where he died.

Jehoiakim Rules in Judah

³⁵In order to get the silver and gold demanded as tribute by Pharaoh Neco, Jehoiakim collected a tax from the people of Judah, requiring them to pay in proportion to their wealth.

³⁶Jehoiakim was twenty-five years old when he became king, and he reigned in Jerusalem eleven years. His mother was Zebidah, the daughter of Pedaiah from Rumah. ³⁷He did what was evil in the LORD's sight, just as his ancestors had done.

CHAPTER 24

See Nebuchadnezzar's profile (page 985) at Daniel 4:37.

I BELIEVE Judah was conquered just as the Lord commanded. (24:3)

I BELIEVE the Lord will not forgive the persistent wickedness of an unrepentant nation. (24:4)

See Manasseh's profile (page 543) at 2 Chronicles 33:13.

During Jehoiakim's reign, King Nebuchadnezzar of Babylon invaded the land of Judah. Jehoiakim surrendered and paid him tribute for three years but then rebelled. ²Then the LORD sent bands of Babylonian,* Aramean, Moabite, and Ammonite raiders against Judah to destroy it, just as the LORD had promised through his prophets. ³These disasters happened to Judah according to the LORD's command. He had decided to remove Judah from his presence because of the many sins of Manasseh. ⁴He had filled Jerusalem with innocent blood, and the LORD would not forgive this.

⁵The rest of the events in Jehoiakim's reign and all his deeds are recorded in *The Book of the History of the Kings of Judah.* ⁶When Jehoiakim died, his son Jehoiachin became the next king. ⁷The king of Egypt never returned after that, for the king of Babylon occupied the entire area formerly claimed by Egypt—from the brook of Egypt to the Euphrates River.

Jehoiachin Rules in Judah

I DO NOT FOLLOW the example of wicked individuals. (24:9)

⁸Jehoiachin was eighteen years old when he became king, and he reigned in Jerusalem three months. His mother was Nehushta, the daughter of Elnathan from Jerusalem. ⁹Jehoiachin did what was evil in the LORD's sight, just as his father had done.

¹⁰During Jehoiachin's reign, the officers of King Nebuchadnezzar of Babylon came up against Jerusalem and besieged it. ¹¹Nebuchadnezzar himself arrived at the city during the siege. ¹²Then King Jehoiachin, along with his advisers, nobles, and officials, and the queen mother, surrendered to the Babylonians.

In the eighth year of Nebuchadnezzar's reign, he took Jehoiachin prisoner. ¹³As the LORD had said beforehand, Nebuchadnezzar carried away all the treasures from the LORD's Temple and the royal palace. They cut apart all the gold vessels that King Solomon of Israel had placed in the Temple. ¹⁴King Nebuchadnezzar took ten thousand captives from Jerusalem, including all the princes and the best of the soldiers, craftsmen, and smiths. So only the poorest people were left in the land.

I BELIEVE Judah was carried into exile just as the Lord had said. (24:13)

See Solomon's profile (page 753) at Proverbs 2:9.

¹⁵Nebuchadnezzar led King Jehoiachin away as a captive to Babylon, along with his wives and officials, the queen mother, and all Jerusalem's elite. ¹⁶He also took seven thousand of the best troops and one thousand craftsmen and smiths, all of whom were strong and fit for war. ¹⁷Then the king of Babylon

23:33 Hebrew *100 talents* [3.4 metric tons] *of silver and 1 talent* [34 kilograms] *of gold.*　24:2 Or *Chaldean.*

installed Mattaniah, Jehoiachin's uncle, as the next king, and he changed Mattaniah's name to Zedekiah.

Zedekiah Rules in Judah

[18]Zedekiah was twenty-one years old when he became king, and he reigned in Jerusalem eleven years. His mother was Hamutal, the daughter of Jeremiah from Libnah. [19]But Zedekiah did what was evil in the LORD's sight, just as Jehoiakim had done. [20]So the LORD, in his anger, finally banished the people of Jerusalem and Judah from his presence and sent them into exile.

The Fall of Jerusalem

Then Zedekiah rebelled against the king of Babylon.

CHAPTER 25

So on January 15,* during the ninth year of Zedekiah's reign, King Nebuchadnezzar of Babylon led his entire army against Jerusalem. They surrounded the city and built siege ramps against its walls. [2]Jerusalem was kept under siege until the eleventh year of King Zedekiah's reign.

[3]By July 18 of Zedekiah's eleventh year,* the famine in the city had become very severe, with the last of the food entirely gone. [4]Then a section of the city wall was broken down, and all the soldiers made plans to escape from the city. But since the city was surrounded by the Babylonians,* they waited for nightfall and fled through the gate between the two walls behind the king's gardens. They made a dash across the fields, in the direction of the Jordan Valley.*

[5]But the Babylonians chased after them and caught the king on the plains of Jericho, for by then his men had all abandoned him. [6]They brought him to the king of Babylon at Riblah, where sentence was passed against him. [7]The king of Babylon made Zedekiah watch as all his sons were killed. Then they gouged out Zedekiah's eyes, bound him in bronze chains, and led him away to Babylon.

The Temple Destroyed

[8]On August 14 of that year,* which was the nineteenth year of Nebuchadnezzar's reign, Nebuzaradan, captain of the guard, an official of the Babylonian king, arrived in Jerusalem. [9]He burned down the Temple of the LORD, the royal palace, and all the houses of Jerusalem. He destroyed all the important buildings in the city. [10]Then the captain of the guard supervised the entire Babylonian* army as they tore down the walls of Jerusalem. [11]Nebuzaradan, captain of the guard, then took as exiles those who remained in the city, along with the rest of the people and the troops who had declared their allegiance to the king of Babylon. [12]But the captain of the guard allowed some of the poorest people to stay behind in Judah to care for the vineyards and fields.

[13]The Babylonians broke up the bronze pillars, the bronze water carts, and the bronze Sea that were at the LORD's Temple, and they carried all the bronze away to Babylon. [14]They also took all the pots, shovels, lamp snuffers, dishes, and all the other bronze utensils used for making sacrifices at the Temple. [15]Nebuzaradan, captain of the guard, also took the firepans and basins, and all the other utensils made of pure gold or silver.

[16]The bronze from the two pillars, the water carts, and the Sea was too great to be weighed. These things had been made for the LORD's Temple in the days

I DO what is right in the Lord's sight. (24:19)

See Nebuchadnezzar's profile (page 985) at Daniel 4:37.

I BELIEVE none of our own efforts can help us escape the Lord's judgment. (25:4)

I BELIEVE the Lord takes no pleasure in places of worship where his name is blasphemed (1 Kings 9:6-9). (25:9)

25:1 Hebrew *on the tenth day of the tenth month,* of the Hebrew calendar. A number of events in 2 Kings can be cross-checked with dates in surviving Babylonian records and related accurately to our modern calendar. This event occurred on January 15, 588 B.C.   25:3 Hebrew *By the ninth day,* that is, "of the fourth month of Zedekiah's eleventh year" (compare Jer 52:6 and the note there). This event of the Hebrew lunar calendar occurred on July 18, 586 B.C.; also see note on 25:1.   25:4a Or *the Chaldeans;* also in 25:5, 13, 25, 26.   25:4b Hebrew *the Arabah.*   25:8 Hebrew *On the seventh day of the fifth month,* of the Hebrew calendar. This day was August 14, 586 B.C.; also see note on 25:1.   25:10 Or *Chaldean;* also in 25:24.

of King Solomon. [17]Each of the pillars was 27 feet* tall. The bronze capital on top of each pillar was 7½ feet* high and was decorated with a network of bronze pomegranates all the way around.

[18]The captain of the guard took with him as prisoners Seraiah the chief priest, his assistant Zephaniah, and the three chief gatekeepers. [19]And of the people still hiding in the city, he took an officer of the Judean army, five of the king's personal advisers, the army commander's chief secretary, who was in charge of recruitment, and sixty other citizens. [20]Nebuzaradan the commander took them all to the king of Babylon at Riblah. [21]And there at Riblah, in the land of Hamath, the king of Babylon had them all put to death. So the people of Judah were sent into exile from their land.

Gedaliah Governs in Judah

[22]Then King Nebuchadnezzar appointed Gedaliah son of Ahikam and grandson of Shaphan as governor over the people left in Judah. [23]When all the army commanders and their men learned that the king of Babylon had appointed Gedaliah as governor, they joined him at Mizpah. These included Ishmael son of Nethaniah, Johanan son of Kareah, Seraiah son of Tanhumeth the Netophathite, and Jaazaniah son of the Maacathite, and all their men.

[24]Gedaliah vowed to them that the Babylonian officials meant them no harm. "Live in the land and serve the king of Babylon, and all will go well for you," he promised. [25]But in midautumn of that year,* Ishmael son of Nethaniah and grandson of Elishama, who was of the royal family, went to Mizpah with ten men and assassinated Gedaliah and everyone with him, both Judeans and Babylonians.

[26]Then all the people of Judah, from the least to the greatest, as well as the army commanders, fled in panic to Egypt, for they were afraid of what the Babylonians would do to them.

Hope for Israel's Royal Line

[27]In the thirty-seventh year of King Jehoiachin's exile in Babylon, Evil-merodach ascended to the Babylonian throne. He was kind to Jehoiachin and released him from prison on April 2 of that year.* [28]He spoke pleasantly to Jehoiachin and gave him preferential treatment over all the other exiled kings in Babylon. [29]He supplied Jehoiachin with new clothes to replace his prison garb and allowed him to dine at the king's table for the rest of his life. [30]The Babylonian king also gave him a regular allowance to cover his living expenses until the day of his death.

I BELIEVE the Lord brings judgment on godless men who mislead his people. (25:19)

See Solomon's profile (page 753) at Proverbs 2:9.

I ABHOR political assassinations and other murders. (25:25)

I FEAR the Lord. (25:26)

25:17a Hebrew *18 cubits* [8.1 meters].   25:17b As in parallel texts at 1 Kgs 7:16, 2 Chr 3:15, and Jer 52:22, all of which read *5 cubits* [2.3 meters]; Hebrew reads *3 cubits*, which is 4.5 feet or 1.4 meters.   25:25 Hebrew *in the seventh month*, of the Hebrew calendar. This month occurred in October and November 586 B.C.   25:27 Hebrew *on the twenty-seventh day of the twelfth month*, of the Hebrew calendar. This day was April 2, 561 B.C.; also see note on 25:1.

1 CHRONICLES

THIS EIGHTH BOOK of Old Testament history begins with an elaborate family tree and ends with a focus on *worship*.

The extensive genealogy spans from Adam to Noah to Abraham to King David and his descendants down to the Babylonian Captivity. It also records the descendants of each Israelite tribe and the names of the families who returned after the Babylonian Captivity. The ungodly are listed right alongside the godly (1:1–9:34).

The next section of this book relates the details of King Saul's family tree and then briefly recounts the story of his death. Nothing is recorded of Saul's great deeds—only of his ungodly end (9:35–10:14).

The rest of this book tells the story of David's reign as Israel's most beloved king. This extended account begins with a description of David's vast military might (11:1–12:40). After David's coronation as king of all Israel, he moves Israel's religious center to the city of Jerusalem (13:1–17:27). David then defeats Israel's enemies on every side (18:1–20:8). Afterward, he builds an altar to stop a violent plague and then decides to build the Temple of God at that location (21:1–22:1). The rest of David's life is devoted to making preparations for his son Solomon to build the Temple (22:2–29:30).

The stories of Solomon and the other kings who come after David over the next four hundred years are told in 2 Chronicles.

Parallel accounts of David's forty-year reign can be found in 2 Samuel, which tells the more personal side of David's greatness, sins, repentance, and family affairs.

Famous passages in 1 Chronicles include
- ○ Uzzah dies when he touches the Ark of God (13:1-14)
- ○ David brings the Ark to Jerusalem and celebrates (15:1-16:43)
- ○ David decides to build a Temple for the Lord (17:1-2)
- ○ The Lord makes a covenant promise to David (17:3-15)
- ○ David gives thanks to the Lord (17:16-27)
- ○ David sins by taking a census (21:1-6)
- ○ David repents before the Lord (21:7-8)
- ○ A plague is sent by the Lord upon Israel (21:9-15)
- ○ David begs the Lord to stop the plague (21:16-30)
- ○ David selects the location for the Temple of God (22:1)
- ○ David instructs Solomon to build the Temple (22:2-19)
- ○ David addresses the nation (28:1-8)
- ○ David commissions the nation to help Solomon build the Temple (28:9-29:25)

CHAPTER 1

From Adam to Noah's Sons

The descendants of Adam were Seth, Enosh, [2]Kenan, Mahalalel, Jared, [3]Enoch, Methuselah, Lamech, [4]and Noah.

The sons of Noah were* Shem, Ham, and Japheth.

Descendants of Japheth

[5]The descendants of Japheth were Gomer, Magog, Madai, Javan, Tubal, Meshech, and Tiras.

[6]The descendants of Gomer were Ashkenaz, Riphath,* and Togarmah.

[7]The descendants of Javan were Elishah, Tarshish, Kittim, and Rodanim.

Descendants of Ham

[8]The descendants of Ham were Cush, Mizraim,* Put, and Canaan.

[9]The descendants of Cush were Seba, Havilah, Sabtah, Raamah, and Sabteca. The descendants of Raamah were Sheba and Dedan. [10]Cush was also the ancestor of Nimrod, who was known across the earth as a heroic warrior.

[11]Mizraim was the ancestor of the Ludites, Anamites, Lehabites, Naphtuhites, [12]Pathrusites, Casluhites, and the Caphtorites, from whom the Philistines came.*

[13]Canaan's oldest son was Sidon, the ancestor of the Sidonians. Canaan was also the ancestor of the Hittites, [14]Jebusites, Amorites, Girgashites, [15]Hivites, Arkites, Sinites, [16]Arvadites, Zemarites, and Hamathites.

Descendants of Shem

[17]The descendants of Shem were Elam, Asshur, Arphaxad, Lud, and Aram.

The descendants of Aram were* Uz, Hul, Gether, and Mash.*

[18]Arphaxad was the father of Shelah. Shelah was the father of Eber. [19]Eber had two sons. The first was named Peleg—"division"—for during his lifetime the people of the world were divided into different language groups and dispersed. His brother's name was Joktan.

[20]Joktan was the ancestor of Almodad, Sheleph, Hazarmaveth, Jerah, [21]Hadoram, Uzal, Diklah, [22]Obal,* Abimael, Sheba, [23]Ophir, Havilah, and Jobab. All these were descendants of Joktan.

[24]So this is the family line descended from Shem: Arphaxad, Shelah,* [25]Eber, Peleg, Reu, [26]Serug, Nahor, Terah, [27]and Abram, later known as Abraham.

Descendants of Abraham

[28]The sons of Abraham were Isaac and Ishmael.

[29]The sons of Ishmael were Nebaioth (the oldest), Kedar, Adbeel, Mibsam, [30]Mishma, Dumah, Massa, Hadad, Tema, [31]Jetur, Naphish, and Kedemah. These were the sons of Ishmael.

[32]The sons of Keturah, Abraham's concubine, were Zimran, Jokshan, Medan, Midian, Ishbak, and Shuah.

The sons of Jokshan were Sheba and Dedan.

[33]The sons of Midian were Ephah, Epher, Hanoch, Abida, and Eldaah.

All these were sons of Abraham by his concubine Keturah.

I BELIEVE everyone is a descendant of Adam. (1:1)

See Adams's profile (page 5) at Genesis 1:26.

See Enoch's profile (page 11) at Genesis 5:24.

I BELIEVE everyone is a descendant of Noah, whom the Lord saved during the Flood. (1:4)

See Noah's profile (page 13) at Genesis 6:9.

I BELIEVE the inhabitants of the world originally spoke one language. (1:19)

See Abraham's profile (page 19) at Genesis 15:6.

1:4 As in Greek version (see also Gen 5:3-32); Hebrew lacks *The sons of Noah were.* **1:6** As in some Hebrew manuscripts and Greek version (see also Gen 10:3); most Hebrew manuscripts read *Diphath.* **1:8** Or *Egypt;* also in 1:11. **1:12** Hebrew *Casluhites, from whom the Philistines came, Caphtorites.* See Jer 47:4; Amos 9:7. **1:17a** As in one Hebrew manuscript and some Greek manuscripts (see also Gen 10:23); most Hebrew manuscripts lack *The descendants of Aram were.* **1:17b** As in parallel text at Gen 10:23; Hebrew reads *and Meshech.* **1:22** As in some Hebrew manuscripts and Syriac version (see also Gen 10:28); most Hebrew manuscripts read *Ebal.* **1:24** Some Greek manuscripts read *Arphaxad, Cainan, Shelah.* See notes on Gen 10:24; 11:12-13.

Descendants of Isaac

³⁴Abraham was the father of Isaac. The sons of Isaac were Esau and Israel.*

Descendants of Esau

³⁵The sons of Esau were Eliphaz, Reuel, Jeush, Jalam, and Korah.
³⁶The sons of Eliphaz were Teman, Omar, Zepho,* Gatam, Kenaz, and Amalek, who was born to Timna.*
³⁷The sons of Reuel were Nahath, Zerah, Shammah, and Mizzah.

Original Peoples of Edom

³⁸The sons of Seir were Lotan, Shobal, Zibeon, Anah, Dishon, Ezer, and Dishan.
³⁹The sons of Lotan were Hori and Heman.* Lotan's sister was named Timna.
⁴⁰The sons of Shobal were Alvan,* Manahath, Ebal, Shepho,* and Onam.
The sons of Zibeon were Aiah and Anah.
⁴¹The son of Anah was Dishon.
The sons of Dishon were Hemdan,* Eshban, Ithran, and Keran.
⁴²The sons of Ezer were Bilhan, Zaavan, and Akan.*
The sons of Dishan* were Uz and Aran.

Rulers of Edom

⁴³These are the kings who ruled in Edom before there were kings in Israel*:

Bela son of Beor, who ruled from his city of Dinhabah.
⁴⁴When Bela died, Jobab son of Zerah from Bozrah became king.
⁴⁵When Jobab died, Husham from the land of the Temanites became king.
⁴⁶When Husham died, Hadad son of Bedad became king and ruled from the city of Avith. He was the one who destroyed the Midianite army in the land of Moab.
⁴⁷When Hadad died, Samlah from the city of Masrekah became king.
⁴⁸When Samlah died, Shaul from the city of Rehoboth on the Euphrates River* became king.
⁴⁹When Shaul died, Baal-hanan son of Acbor became king.
⁵⁰When Baal-hanan died, Hadad became king and ruled from the city of Pau.* His wife was Mehetabel, the daughter of Matred and granddaughter of Me-zahab. ⁵¹Then Hadad died.

The clan leaders of Edom were Timna, Alvah,* Jetheth, ⁵²Oholibamah, Elah, Pinon, ⁵³Kenaz, Teman, Mibzar, ⁵⁴Magdiel, and Iram. These were the clan leaders of Edom.

CHAPTER 2

Descendants of Israel

The sons of Israel* were Reuben, Simeon, Levi, Judah, Issachar, Zebulun, ²Dan, Joseph, Benjamin, Naphtali, Gad, and Asher.

Descendants of Judah

³Judah had three sons through Bathshua, a Canaanite woman. Their names were Er, Onan, and Shelah. But the oldest son, Er, was a wicked man, so

See Isaac's profile (page 31) at Genesis 25:19.

See Esau's profile (page 33) at Genesis 25:34.

See the profiles for Israel (Jacob, page 43) and Joseph (page 51) at Genesis 32:9 and 39:2.

I SEEK to live a godly life in the Lord's sight. (2:3)

1:34 *Israel* is the name that God gave to Jacob.   1:36a As in many Hebrew manuscripts and a few Greek manuscripts (see also Gen 36:11); most Hebrew manuscripts read *Zephi*.   1:36b As in some Greek manuscripts (see also Gen 36:12); Hebrew reads *Kenaz, Timna, and Amalek*.   1:39 As in parallel text at Gen 36:22; Hebrew reads *and Homam*.   1:40a As in many Hebrew manuscripts and a few Greek manuscripts (see also Gen 36:23); most Hebrew manuscripts read *Alian*.   1:40b As in some Hebrew manuscripts (see also Gen 36:23); most Hebrew manuscripts read *Shephi*.   1:41 As in many Hebrew manuscripts and some Greek manuscripts (see also Gen 36:26); most Hebrew manuscripts read *Hamran*.   1:42a As in many Hebrew and Greek manuscripts (see also Gen 36:27); most Hebrew manuscripts read *Jaakan*.   1:42b Hebrew *Dishon;* compare 1:38 and parallel text at Gen 36:28.   1:43 Or *before an Israelite king ruled over them.*   1:48 Hebrew *the river.*   1:50 As in many Hebrew manuscripts, some Greek manuscripts, Syriac version, and Latin Vulgate (see also Gen 36:39); most Hebrew manuscripts read *Pai.*   1:51 As in parallel text at Gen 36:40; Hebrew reads *Aliah.*   2:1 *Israel* is the name that God gave to Jacob.

the LORD killed him. ⁴Later Judah had twin sons through Tamar, his widowed daughter-in-law. Their names were Perez and Zerah. So Judah had five sons in all.

⁵The sons of Perez were Hezron and Hamul.

⁶The sons of Zerah were Zimri, Ethan, Heman, Calcol, and Darda*—five in all.

⁷Achan* son of Carmi, one of Zerah's descendants, brought disaster on Israel by taking plunder that had been set apart for the LORD.*

⁸The son of Ethan was Azariah.

I DO NOT TAKE what rightfully belongs to the Lord. (2:7)

From Judah's Grandson Hezron to David

⁹The sons of Hezron were Jerahmeel, Ram, and Caleb.*

¹⁰ Ram was the father of Amminadab.
Amminadab was the father of Nahshon, a leader of Judah.
¹¹ Nahshon was the father of Salmon.*
Salmon was the father of Boaz.
¹² Boaz was the father of Obed.
Obed was the father of Jesse.

¹³Jesse's first son was Eliab, his second was Abinadab, his third was Shimea, ¹⁴his fourth was Nethanel, his fifth was Raddai, ¹⁵his sixth was Ozem, and his seventh was David.

See David's profile (page 629) at Psalm 3:1.

¹⁶Their sisters were named Zeruiah and Abigail. Zeruiah had three sons named Abishai, Joab, and Asahel. ¹⁷Abigail married a man named Jether, an Ishmaelite, and they had a son named Amasa.

Descendants of Hezron's Son Caleb

¹⁸Hezron's son Caleb had two wives named Azubah and Jerioth. Azubah's sons were named Jesher, Shobab, and Ardon. ¹⁹After Azubah died, Caleb married Ephrathah,* and they had a son named Hur. ²⁰Hur was the father of Uri. Uri was the father of Bezalel.

²¹When Hezron was sixty years old, he married Gilead's sister, the daughter of Makir. They had a son named Segub. ²²Segub was the father of Jair, who ruled twenty-three towns in the land of Gilead. ²³(Later Geshur and Aram captured the Towns of Jair* and also took Kenath and its sixty surrounding villages.) All these were descendants of Makir, the father of Gilead.

²⁴Soon after Hezron died in the town of Caleb-ephrathah, his wife Abijah gave birth to a son named Ashhur (the father of* Tekoa).

Descendants of Hezron's Son Jerahmeel

²⁵The sons of Jerahmeel, the oldest son of Hezron, were Ram (the oldest), Bunah, Oren, Ozem, and Ahijah. ²⁶Jerahmeel had a second wife named Atarah. She was the mother of Onam.

²⁷The sons of Ram, the oldest son of Jerahmeel, were Maaz, Jamin, and Eker.

²⁸The sons of Onam were Shammai and Jada. The sons of Shammai were Nadab and Abishur.

²⁹ The sons of Abishur and his wife Abihail were Ahban and Molid.

³⁰ The sons of Nadab were Seled and Appaim. Seled died without children, ³¹but Appaim had a son named Ishi. The son of Ishi was Sheshan. Sheshan had a descendant named Ahlai.

2:6 As in many Hebrew manuscripts, some Greek manuscripts, and Syriac version (see also 1 Kgs 4:31); Hebrew reads *Dara.* 2:7a Hebrew *Achar;* compare Josh 7:1. *Achar* means "disaster." 2:7b The Hebrew term used here refers to the complete consecration of things or people to the LORD, either by destroying them or by giving them as an offering. 2:9 Hebrew *Kelubai,* a variant name for Caleb; compare 2:18. 2:11 As in Greek version (see also Ruth 4:21); Hebrew reads *Salma.* 2:19 Hebrew *Ephrath,* a variant name for Ephrathah; compare 2:50 and 4:4. 2:23 Or *captured Havvoth-jair.* 2:24 Or *the founder of;* also in 2:42, 45, 49-52 and perhaps other instances where the text reads *the father of.*

[32]Shammai's brother, Jada, had two sons named Jether and Jonathan. Jether died without children, [33]but Jonathan had two sons named Peleth and Zaza. These were all descendants of Jerahmeel.

[34]Sheshan had no sons, though he did have daughters. He also had an Egyptian servant named Jarha. [35]Sheshan gave one of his daughters to be the wife of Jarha, and they had a son named Attai.

[36] Attai was the father of Nathan.
Nathan was the father of Zabad.

[37] Zabad was the father of Ephlal.
Ephlal was the father of Obed.

[38] Obed was the father of Jehu.
Jehu was the father of Azariah.

[39] Azariah was the father of Helez.
Helez was the father of Eleasah.

[40] Eleasah was the father of Sismai.
Sismai was the father of Shallum.

[41] Shallum was the father of Jekamiah.
Jekamiah was the father of Elishama.

Descendants of Hezron's Son Caleb

[42]The oldest son of Caleb, the brother of Jerahmeel, was Mesha, the father of Ziph. Caleb's second son was Mareshah, the father of Hebron.*

[43]The sons of Hebron were Korah, Tappuah, Rekem, and Shema. [44]Shema was the father of Raham. Raham was the father of Jorkeam. Rekem was the father of Shammai. [45]The son of Shammai was Maon. Maon was the father of Beth-zur.

[46]Caleb's concubine Ephah gave birth to Haran, Moza, and Gazez. Haran was the father of Gazez.

[47]The sons of Jahdai were Regem, Jotham, Geshan, Pelet, Ephah, and Shaaph.

[48]Another of Caleb's concubines, Maacah, gave birth to Sheber and Tirhanah. [49]She also gave birth to Shaaph (the father of Madmannah) and Sheva (the father of Macbenah and Gibea). Caleb also had a daughter named Acsah. [50]These were all descendants of Caleb.

Descendants of Caleb's Son Hur

The sons of Hur, the oldest son of Caleb's wife Ephrathah, were Shobal (the father of Kiriath-jearim), [51]Salma (the father of Bethlehem), and Hareph (the father of Beth-gader).

[52]The descendants of Shobal (the father of Kiriath-jearim) were Haroeh, half the Manahathites, [53]and the families of Kiriath-jearim—the Ithrites, Puthites, Shumathites, and Mishraites, from whom came the people of Zorah and Eshtaol.

[54]The descendants of Salma were Bethlehem, the Netophathites, Atroth-beth-joab, the other half of the Manahathites, the Zorites, [55]and the families of scribes living at Jabez—the Tirathites, Shimeathites, and Sucathites. All these were Kenites who descended from Hammath, the father of the family of Recab.*

CHAPTER 3

Descendants of David

These were the sons who were born to David in Hebron:

The oldest was Amnon, whose mother was Ahinoam of Jezreel.
The second was Kileab,* whose mother was Abigail from Carmel.
[2] The third was Absalom, whose mother was Maacah, the daughter of Talmai, king of Geshur.

See the profiles for David (page 629), Amnon (page 369), and Abigail (page 349) at Psalm 3:1, 2 Samuel 13:15, and 1 Samuel 25:31.

See Absalom's profile (page 373) at 2 Samuel 15:6.

2:42 The meaning of the Hebrew is uncertain. 2:55 Or *the founder of Beth-recab*. 3:1 As in parallel text at 2 Sam 3:3; Hebrew reads *Daniel*.

The fourth was Adonijah, whose mother was Haggith. ³ The fifth was Shephatiah, whose mother was Abital. The sixth was Ithream, whose mother was Eglah.

⁴These six sons were born to David in Hebron, where he reigned seven and a half years.

Then David moved the capital to Jerusalem, where he reigned another thirty-three years. ⁵The sons born to David in Jerusalem included Shimea, Shobab, Nathan, and Solomon. Bathsheba,* the daughter of Ammiel, was the mother of these sons. ⁶David also had nine other sons: Ibhar, Elishua,* Elpelet,* ⁷Nogah, Nepheg, Japhia, ⁸Elishama, Eliada, and Eliphelet.

⁹These were the sons of David, not including the sons of his concubines. David also had a daughter named Tamar.

See Solomon's profile (page 753) at Proverbs 2:9.

Descendants of Solomon

¹⁰The descendants of Solomon were Rehoboam, Abijah, Asa, Jehoshaphat, ¹¹Jehoram,* Ahaziah, Joash, ¹²Amaziah, Uzziah,* Jotham, ¹³Ahaz, Hezekiah, Manasseh, ¹⁴Amon, and Josiah.

¹⁵The sons of Josiah were Johanan (the oldest), Jehoiakim (the second), Zedekiah (the third), and Jehoahaz* (the fourth).

¹⁶Jehoiakim was succeeded by his son Jehoiachin; he, in turn, was succeeded by his uncle Zedekiah.*

See the profiles for Solomon (page 753), Rehoboam (page 409), Asa (page 521), and Jehoshaphat (page 527) at Proverbs 2:9, 1 Kings 12:8, 2 Chronicles 16:9, and 2 Chronicles 20:21.

See Uzziah's profile (page 533) at 2 Chronicles 26:16.

Descendants of Jehoiachin

¹⁷The sons of Jehoiachin,* who was taken prisoner by the Babylonians, were Shealtiel, ¹⁸Malkiram, Pedaiah, Shenazzar, Jekamiah, Hoshama, and Nedabiah.

¹⁹The sons of Pedaiah were Zerubbabel and Shimei.

The sons of Zerubbabel were Meshullam and Hananiah. He also had a daughter named Shelomith. ²⁰His five other sons were Hashubah, Ohel, Berekiah, Hasadiah, and Jushab-hesed.

²¹The sons of Hananiah were Pelatiah and Jeshaiah. Jeshaiah's son was Rephaiah. Rephaiah's son was Arnan. Arnan's son was Obadiah. Obadiah's son was Shecaniah.

²²Shecaniah's descendants were Shemaiah and his sons, Hattush, Igal, Bariah, Neariah, and Shaphat—six in all.

²³The sons of Neariah were Elioenai, Hizkiah, and Azrikam—three in all.

²⁴The sons of Elioenai were Hodaviah, Eliashib, Pelaiah, Akkub, Johanan, Delaiah, and Anani—seven in all.

See the profiles for Hezekiah (page 825) and Manasseh (page 543) at Isaiah 37:1 and 2 Chronicles 33:13.

See Josiah's profile (page 461) at 2 Kings 23:25.

CHAPTER 4

Other Descendants of Judah

Some of the descendants of Judah were Perez, Hezron, Carmi, Hur, and Shobal.

²Shobal's son Reaiah was the father of Jahath. Jahath was the father of Ahumai and Lahad. These were the families of the Zorathites.

³The descendants of* Etam were Jezreel, Ishma, Idbash, Hazzelelponi (his daughter), ⁴Penuel (the father of* Gedor), and Ezer (the father of Hushah). These were the descendants of Hur (the firstborn of Ephrathah), the ancestor of Bethlehem.

⁵Ashhur (the father of Tekoa) had two wives, named Helah and Naarah.

3:5 Hebrew *Bathshua,* a variant name for Bathsheba.   3:6a As in some Hebrew and Greek manuscripts (see also 14:5-7 and 2 Sam 5:15); most Hebrew manuscripts read *Elishama.*   3:6b Hebrew *Eliphelet;* compare parallel text at 14:5-7.   3:11 Hebrew *Joram,* a variant name for Jehoram.   3:12 Hebrew *Azariah,* a variant name for Uzziah.   3:15 Hebrew *Shallum,* another name for Jehoahaz.   3:16 Hebrew *The descendants of Jehoiakim were his son Jeconiah* [a variant name for Jehoiachin] *and his son Zedekiah.*   3:17 Hebrew *Jeconiah,* a variant name for Jehoiachin.   4:3 As in Greek version; Hebrew reads *father of.* The meaning of the Hebrew is uncertain.   4:4 Or *the founder of;* also in 4:12, 14, 17-18, and perhaps other instances where the text reads *the father of.*

⁶Naarah gave birth to Ahuzzam, Hepher, Temeni, and Haahashtari. ⁷Helah gave birth to Zereth, Izhar, Ethnan, ⁸and Koz, who became the ancestor of Anub, Zobebah, and all the families of Aharhel son of Harum.

⁹There was a man named Jabez who was more distinguished than any of his brothers. His mother named him Jabez* because his birth had been so painful. ¹⁰He was the one who prayed to the God of Israel, "Oh, that you would bless me and extend my lands! Please be with me in all that I do, and keep me from all trouble and pain!" And God granted him his request.

I ASK the Lord to bless me, prosper me, be with me in all I do, and keep me from further trouble and pain. (4:10)

LIKE JABEZ
1 Chronicles 4:10

I know God wants to prosper me no matter how humble my birth.

Ever feel like life's a pain?

Right in the middle of nine chapters of genealogies, the writer of 1 Chronicles stopped to talk about an obscure descendant of Judah named Jabez.

Who was Jabez?

Well, in a family tree where most individuals were lucky just to get their names mentioned, Jabez landed two verses. But not for being rich, powerful, or famous.

Jabez's life actually got off to a very rough start. So rough that his mother gave him a name that sounded like the Hebrew word for "trouble" or "suffering." Later in life, however, Jabez had the audacity to pray this remarkable prayer to the Lord: "Oh, that you would bless me and extend my lands! Please be with me in all that I do, and keep me from all trouble and pain!" (4:9-10).

How's that for a prayer?

Well, whatever we might think, the Lord liked it! So much so that God said, in essence, "Yes, Jabez, I'll be glad to grant your request!"

Like Jabez, do you long to enjoy more of God's blessing, presence, and protection? If so, why not tell him so right now?

○ *Today's Scripture reading is 1 Chronicles 4:9-10.*

¹¹Kelub (the brother of Shuhah) was the father of Mehir. Mehir was the father of Eshton. ¹²Eshton was the father of Beth-rapha, Paseah, and Tehinnah. Tehinnah was the father of Ir-nahash. These were the descendants of Recah.

¹³The sons of Kenaz were Othniel and Seraiah. Othniel's sons were Hathath and Meonothai.* ¹⁴Meonothai was the father of Ophrah. Seraiah was the father of Joab, the founder of the Valley of Craftsmen,* so called because many craftsmen lived there.

¹⁵The sons of Caleb son of Jephunneh were Iru, Elah, and Naam. The son of Elah was Kenaz.

¹⁶The sons of Jehallelel were Ziph, Ziphah, Tiria, and Asarel.

¹⁷The sons of Ezrah were Jether, Mered, Epher, and Jalon. Mered married an Egyptian woman, who became the mother of Miriam, Shammai, and Ishbah (the father of Eshtemoa). ¹⁸Mered also married a woman of Judah, who became the mother of Jered (the father of Gedor), Heber (the father of Soco), and Jekuthiel (the father of Zanoah). Mered's Egyptian wife was named Bithiah, and she was an Egyptian princess.

¹⁹Hodiah's wife was the sister of Naham. One of her sons was the father of Keilah the Garmite, and another was the father of Eshtemoa the Maacathite.

See Caleb's profile (page 265) at Joshua 14:12.

4:9 *Jabez* sounds like a Hebrew term meaning "distress" or "pain." 4:13 As in some Greek manuscripts and Latin Vulgate; Hebrew lacks *and Meonothai.* 4:14 Or *Joab, the father of Ge-harashim.*

²⁰The sons of Shimon were Amnon, Rinnah, Ben-hanan, and Tilon. The descendants of Ishi were Zoheth and Ben-zoheth.

Descendants of Judah's Son Shelah

²¹Shelah was one of Judah's sons. The descendants of Shelah were Er (the father of Lecah), Laadah (the father of Mareshah), the families of linen workers at Beth-ashbea, ²²Jokim, the people of Cozeba, Joash, and Saraph, who ruled over Moab and Jashubi-lehem. These names all come from ancient records. ²³They were the potters who lived in Netaim and Gederah. They all worked for the king.

Descendants of Simeon

²⁴The sons of Simeon were Nemuel, Jamin, Jarib, Zerah, and Shaul. ²⁵The descendants of Shaul were Shallum, Mibsam, and Mishma. ²⁶The descendants of Mishma were Hammuel, Zaccur, and Shimei. ²⁷Shimei had sixteen sons and six daughters, but none of his brothers had large families. So Simeon's tribe never became as large as the tribe of Judah.

²⁸They lived in Beersheba, Moladah, Hazar-shual, ²⁹Bilhah, Ezem, Tolad, ³⁰Bethuel, Hormah, Ziklag, ³¹Beth-marcaboth, Hazar-susim, Beth-biri, and Shaaraim. These towns were under their control until the time of King David. ³²Their descendants also lived in Etam, Ain, Rimmon, Token, and Ashan—five towns ³³and their surrounding villages as far away as Baalath.* This was their territory, and these names are recorded in their family genealogy.

³⁴Other descendants of Simeon included Meshobab, Jamlech, Joshah son of Amaziah, ³⁵Joel, Jehu son of Joshibiah, son of Seraiah, son of Asiel, ³⁶Elioenai, Jaakobah, Jeshohaiah, Asaiah, Adiel, Jesimiel, Benaiah, ³⁷and Ziza son of Shiphi, son of Allon, son of Jedaiah, son of Shimri, son of Shemaiah.

³⁸These were the names of some of the leaders of Simeon's wealthy clans, ³⁹who traveled to the region of Gedor, in the east part of the valley, seeking pastureland for their flocks. ⁴⁰They found lush pastures there, and the land was quiet and peaceful.

Some of Ham's descendants had been living in the region of Gedor. ⁴¹But during the reign of King Hezekiah of Judah, the leaders of Simeon invaded it and completely destroyed* the homes of the descendants of Ham and of the Meunites. They killed everyone who lived there and took the land for themselves, because they wanted its good pastureland for their flocks. ⁴²Five hundred of these invaders from the tribe of Simeon went to Mount Seir, led by Pelatiah, Neariah, Rephaiah, and Uzziel—all sons of Ishi. ⁴³They destroyed the few Amalekites who had survived, and they have lived there ever since.

CHAPTER 5

Descendants of Reuben

The oldest son of Israel* was Reuben. But since he dishonored his father by sleeping with one of his father's concubines, his birthright was given to the sons of his brother Joseph. For this reason, Reuben is not listed in the genealogy as the firstborn son. ²It was the descendants of Judah that became the most powerful tribe and provided a ruler for the nation,* but the birthright belonged to Joseph.

See David's profile (page 629) at Psalm 3:1.

See Hezekiah's profile (page 825) at Isaiah 37:1.

See Joseph's profile (page 51) at Genesis 39:2.

I HONOR my parents. (5:1)

4:33 As in some Greek manuscripts (see also Josh 19:8); Hebrew reads *Baal.* 4:41 The Hebrew term used here refers to the complete consecration of things or people to the LORD, either by destroying them or by giving them as an offering. 5:1 *Israel* is the name that God gave to Jacob. 5:2 Or *and from Judah came a prince.*

³The sons of Reuben, the oldest son of Israel, were Hanoch, Pallu, Hezron, and Carmi.

⁴The descendants of Joel were Shemaiah, Gog, Shimei, ⁵Micah, Reaiah, Baal, ⁶and Beerah.

Beerah was the leader of the Reubenites when they were taken into captivity by King Tiglath-pileser* of Assyria.

⁷Beerah's relatives are listed in their genealogy by their clans: Jeiel (the leader), Zechariah, ⁸and Bela son of Azaz, son of Shema, son of Joel.

These Reubenites lived in the area that stretches from Aroer to Nebo and Baal-meon. ⁹And since they had so many cattle in the land of Gilead, they spread eastward toward the edge of the desert that stretches to the Euphrates River.

¹⁰During the reign of Saul, the Reubenites defeated the Hagrites in battle. Then they moved into the Hagrite settlements all along the eastern edge of Gilead.

See Saul's profile (page 339) at 1 Samuel 18:9.

Descendants of Gad

¹¹Across from the Reubenites in the land of Bashan lived the descendants of Gad, who were spread as far east as Salecah. ¹²Joel was the leader in the land of Bashan, and Shapham was second-in-command, along with Janai and Shaphat.

¹³Their relatives, the leaders of seven other clans, were Michael, Meshullam, Sheba, Jorai, Jacan, Zia, and Eber. ¹⁴These were all descendants of Abihail son of Huri, son of Jaroah, son of Gilead, son of Michael, son of Jeshishai, son of Jahdo, son of Buz. ¹⁵Ahi son of Abdiel, son of Guni, was the leader of their clans.

¹⁶The Gadites lived in the land of Gilead, in Bashan and its villages, and throughout the Sharon Plain. ¹⁷All of these were listed in the genealogical records during the days of King Jotham of Judah and King Jeroboam of Israel.

See Jeroboam's profile (page 411) at 1 Kings 13:4.

The Tribes East of the Jordan

¹⁸There were 44,760 skilled warriors in the armies of Reuben, Gad, and the half-tribe of Manasseh. They were all skilled in combat and armed with shields, swords, and bows. ¹⁹They waged war against the Hagrites, the Jeturites, the Naphishites, and the Nodabites. ²⁰They cried out to God during the battle, and he answered their prayer because they trusted in him. So the Hagrites and all their allies were defeated. ²¹The plunder taken from the Hagrites included 50,000 camels, 250,000 sheep, 2,000 donkeys, and 100,000 captives. ²²Many of the Hagrites were killed in the battle because God was fighting against them. So they lived in their land until they were taken away into exile.

I TRUST in God, who answers my prayer when I cry out to him. (5:20)

I TRUST in God, who fights for me. (5:22)

²³The half-tribe of Manasseh spread through the land from Bashan to Baal-hermon, Senir, and Mount Hermon. They were very numerous. ²⁴These were the leaders of their clans: Epher, Ishi, Eliel, Azriel, Jeremiah, Hodaviah, and Jahdiel. Each of these men had a great reputation as a warrior and leader. ²⁵But they were unfaithful and violated their covenant with the God of their ancestors. They worshiped the gods of the nations that God had destroyed. ²⁶So the God of Israel caused King Pul of Assyria (also known as Tiglath-pileser) to invade the land and lead away the people of Reuben, Gad, and the half-tribe of Manasseh as captives. The Assyrians exiled them to Halah, Habor, Hara, and the Gozan River, where they remain to this day.

I LIVE a life of faithfulness to God and abhor the worship of false gods. (5:25)

CHAPTER 6

The Priestly Line

The sons of Levi were Gershon, Kohath, and Merari.

²The descendants of Kohath included Amram, Izhar, Hebron, and Uzziel.

5:6 Hebrew *Tilgath-pilneser*, a variant name for Tiglath-pileser; also in 5:26.

See the profiles for Aaron (page 107), Moses (page 73), and Miriam (page 87) at Exodus 32:2, Exodus 5:1, and Exodus 15:20.

³The children of Amram were Aaron, Moses, and Miriam.
The sons of Aaron were Nadab, Abihu, Eleazar, and Ithamar.

⁴ Eleazar was the father of Phinehas.
  Phinehas was the father of Abishua.
⁵ Abishua was the father of Bukki.
  Bukki was the father of Uzzi.
⁶ Uzzi was the father of Zerahiah.
  Zerahiah was the father of Meraioth.
⁷ Meraioth was the father of Amariah.
  Amariah was the father of Ahitub.
⁸ Ahitub was the father of Zadok.
  Zadok was the father of Ahimaaz.
⁹ Ahimaaz was the father of Azariah.
  Azariah was the father of Johanan.

See Solomon's profile (page 753) at Proverbs 2:9.

¹⁰ Johanan was the father of Azariah, the high priest at the Temple built by
  Solomon in Jerusalem.
¹¹ Azariah was the father of Amariah.
  Amariah was the father of Ahitub.
¹² Ahitub was the father of Zadok.
  Zadok was the father of Shallum.

See Hilkiah's profile (page 545) at 2 Chronicles 34:14.

¹³ Shallum was the father of Hilkiah.
  Hilkiah was the father of Azariah.
¹⁴ Azariah was the father of Seraiah.

See Nebuchadnezzar's profile (page 985) at Daniel 4:37.

  Seraiah was the father of Jehozadak, ¹⁵who went into exile when the
  LORD sent the people of Judah and Jerusalem into captivity under
  Nebuchadnezzar.

The Levite Clans
¹⁶The sons of Levi were Gershon,* Kohath, and Merari.
¹⁷The descendants of Gershon included Libni and Shimei.
¹⁸The descendants of Kohath included Amram, Izhar, Hebron, and Uzziel.
¹⁹The descendants of Merari included Mahli and Mushi.

The following were the Levite clans, listed according to their ancestral descent:

²⁰The descendants of Gershon included Libni, Jahath, Zimmah, ²¹Joah,
  Iddo, Zerah, and Jeatherai.
²²The descendants of Kohath included Amminadab, Korah, Assir,
  ²³Elkanah, Abiasaph,* Assir, ²⁴Tahath, Uriel, Uzziah, and Shaul.

See Samuel's profile (page 323) at 1 Samuel 3:1.

²⁵The descendants of Elkanah included Amasai, Ahimoth, ²⁶Elkanah,
  Zophai, Nahath, ²⁷Eliab, Jeroham, Elkanah, and Samuel.*
²⁸The sons of Samuel were Joel* (the older) and Abijah (the second).
²⁹The descendants of Merari included Mahli, Libni, Shimei, Uzzah,
  ³⁰Shimea, Haggiah, and Asaiah.

The Temple Musicians

See David's profile (page 629) at Psalm 3:1.

I MINISTER with music. (6:32)

See Samuel's profile (page 323) at 1 Samuel 3:1.

³¹David assigned the following men to lead the music at the house of the
LORD after he put the Ark there. ³²They ministered with music there at the Tabernacle* until Solomon built the Temple of the LORD in Jerusalem. Then they
carried on their work there, following all the regulations handed down to
them. ³³These are the men who served, along with their sons:

Heman the musician was from the clan of Kohath. His genealogy was
  traced back through Joel, Samuel, ³⁴Elkanah, Jeroham, Eliel, Toah,

6:16 Hebrew *Gershom*, a variant name for Gershon (see 6:1); also in 6:17, 20, 43, 62, 71.   **6:23** Hebrew
Ebiasaph, a variant name for Abiasaph (also in 6:37); compare parallel text at Exod 6:24.   **6:27** As in some Greek
manuscripts (see also 6:33-34); Hebrew lacks *and Samuel*.   **6:28** As in some Greek manuscripts and the Syriac
version (see also 6:33 and 1 Sam 8:2); Hebrew lacks *Joel*.   **6:32** Hebrew *the Tabernacle, the Tent of Meeting.*

[35] Zuph, Elkanah, Mahath, Amasai, [36] Elkanah, Joel, Azariah, Zephaniah, [37] Tahath, Assir, Abiasaph, Korah, [38] Izhar, Kohath, Levi, and Israel.*

[39] Heman's first assistant was Asaph from the clan of Gershon.* Asaph's genealogy was traced back through Berekiah, Shimea, [40] Michael, Baaseiah, Malkijah, [41] Ethni, Zerah, Adaiah, [42] Ethan, Zimmah, Shimei, [43] Jahath, Gershon, and Levi.

[44] Heman's second assistant was Ethan from the clan of Merari. Ethan's genealogy was traced back through Kishi, Abdi, Malluch, [45] Hashabiah, Amaziah, Hilkiah, [46] Amzi, Bani, Shemer, [47] Mahli, Mushi, Merari, and Levi.

[48] Their relatives, also Levites, were appointed to various other tasks in the Tabernacle, the house of God.

Aaron's Descendants

[49] Only Aaron and his descendants served as priests. They presented the offerings on the altar of burnt offering and the altar of incense, and they performed all the other duties related to the Most Holy Place. They made atonement for Israel by following all the commands that Moses, the servant of God, had given them.

[50] The descendants of Aaron were Eleazar, Phinehas, Abishua, [51] Bukki, Uzzi, Zerahiah, [52] Meraioth, Amariah, Ahitub, [53] Zadok, and Ahimaaz.

Territory for the Levites

[54] This is a record of the towns and territory assigned by means of sacred lots to the descendants of Aaron who were from the clan of Kohath. [55] This included Hebron and its surrounding pasturelands in Judah, [56] but the fields and outlying areas were given to Caleb son of Jephunneh. [57] So the descendants of Aaron were given the following towns, each with its surrounding pasturelands: Hebron (a city of refuge), Libnah, Jattir, Eshtemoa, [58] Holon,* Debir, [59] Ain,* Juttah,* and Beth-shemesh. [60] And from the territory of Benjamin they were given Gibeon,* Geba, Alemeth, and Anathoth, each with its pasturelands. So a total of thirteen towns was given to the descendants of Aaron. [61] The remaining descendants of Kohath received ten towns from the territory of the half-tribe of Manasseh by means of sacred lots.

[62] The descendants of Gershon received by sacred lots thirteen towns from the territories of Issachar, Asher, Naphtali, and from the Bashan area of Manasseh, east of the Jordan.

[63] The descendants of Merari received by sacred lots twelve towns from the territories of Reuben, Gad, and Zebulun.

[64] So the people of Israel assigned all these towns and pasturelands to the Levites. [65] The towns in the territories of Judah, Simeon, and Benjamin, mentioned above, were also assigned by means of sacred lots.

[66] The descendants of Kohath received from the territory of Ephraim these towns, each with its surrounding pasturelands: [67] Shechem (a city of refuge in the hill country of Ephraim), Gezer, [68] Jokmeam, Beth-horon, [69] Aijalon, and Gath-rimmon. [70] The remaining descendants of Kohath were assigned these towns from the territory of the half-tribe of Manasseh: Aner and Bileam, each with its pasturelands.

[71] The descendants of Gershon received from the territory of the half-tribe of Manasseh the town of Golan in Bashan with its pasturelands and Ashtaroth with its pasturelands. [72] From the territory of Issachar, they were given Kedesh, Daberath, [73] Ramoth, and Anem, with their pasturelands.

See Israel's (Jacob's) profile (page 43) at Genesis 32:9.

See Asaph's profile (page 687) at Psalm 73:28.

See the profiles for Moses (page 73) and Aaron (page 107) at Exodus 5:1 and Exodus 32:2.

I SERVE the Lord and follow all of his commands. (6:49)

See Phinehas's profile (page 717) at Psalm 106:30.

6:38 *Israel* is the name that God gave to Jacob.   6:39 Hebrew lacks *from the clan of Gershon*; see 6:43.   6:58 As in parallel text at Josh 21:15; Hebrew reads *Hilen*.   6:59a As in parallel text at Josh 21:16; Hebrew reads *Ashan*. 6:59b As in Syriac version (see also Josh 21:16); Hebrew lacks *Juttah*.   6:60 As in parallel text at Josh 21:17; Hebrew lacks *Gibeon*.

74From the territory of Asher, they received Mashal, Abdon, 75Hukok, and Rehob, each with its pasturelands. 76From the territory of Naphtali, they were given Kedesh in Galilee, Hammon, and Kiriathaim, each with its pasturelands.

77The remaining descendants of Merari received from the territory of Zebulun the towns of Jokneam, Kartah,* Rimmono, and Tabor, each with its pasturelands. 78From the territory of Reuben, east of the Jordan River opposite Jericho, they received Bezer (a desert town), Jahaz,* 79Kedemoth, and Mephaath, each with its pasturelands. 80And from the territory of Gad, they received Ramoth in Gilead, Mahanaim, 81Heshbon, and Jazer, each with its pasturelands.

CHAPTER 7

Descendants of Issachar

The four sons of Issachar were Tola, Puah, Jashub, and Shimron. 2The sons of Tola were Uzzi, Rephaiah, Jeriel, Jahmai, Ibsam, and Shemuel. Each of them was the leader of an ancestral clan. At the time of King David, the total number of men available for military service from these families was 22,600. 3The son of Uzzi was Izrahiah. The sons of Izrahiah were Michael, Obadiah, Joel, and Isshiah. These five became the leaders of clans. 4The total number of men available for military service among their descendants was 36,000, for all five of them had many wives and many sons.

5The total number of men available for military service from all the clans of the tribe of Issachar was 87,000. All of them were listed in their tribal genealogy.

Descendants of Benjamin

6Three of Benjamin's sons were Bela, Beker, and Jediael. 7The sons of Bela were Ezbon, Uzzi, Uzziel, Jerimoth, and Iri. These five warriors were the leaders of clans. The total number of men available for military service among their descendants was 22,034. All of them were listed in their family genealogy.

8The sons of Beker were Zemirah, Joash, Eliezer, Elioenai, Omri, Jeremoth, Abijah, Anathoth, and Alemeth. 9According to their family genealogy, there were 20,200 men available for military service among their descendants, in addition to their clan leaders.

10The son of Jediael was Bilhan. The sons of Bilhan were Jeush, Benjamin, Ehud, Kenaanah, Zethan, Tarshish, and Ahishahar. 11They were the leaders of the clans of Jediael, and their descendants included 17,200 men available for military service.

12The sons of Ir were Shuppim and Huppim. Hushim was the son of Aher.

Descendants of Naphtali

13The sons of Naphtali were Jahzeel,* Guni, Jezer, and Shillem.* They were all descendants of Jacob's wife Bilhah.

Descendants of Manasseh

14The sons of Manasseh, born to his Aramean concubine, were Asriel and Makir. Makir was the father of Gilead. 15Makir found wives for Huppim and Shuppim. Makir's sister was named Maacah. One of his descendants was Zelophehad, who had only daughters.

See David's profile (page 629) at Psalm 3:1.

See Jacob's profile (page 43) at Genesis 32:9.

6:77 As in Greek version (see also Josh 21:34); Hebrew lacks Jokneam, Kartah. 6:78 Hebrew Jahzah, a variant name for Jahaz. 7:13a As in parallel text at Gen 46:24; Hebrew reads Jahziel, a variant name for Jahzeel. 7:13b As in some Hebrew and Greek manuscripts (see also Gen 46:24; Num 26:49); most Hebrew manuscripts read Shallum.

[16]Makir's wife, Maacah, gave birth to a son whom she named Peresh. His brother's name was Sheresh. The sons of Peresh were Ulam and Rakem. [17]The son of Ulam was Bedan. All these were considered Gileadites, descendants of Makir son of Manasseh.

[18]Makir's sister Hammoleketh gave birth to Ishhod, Abiezer, and Mahlah. [19]The sons of Shemida were Ahian, Shechem, Likhi, and Aniam.

Descendants of Ephraim

[20]The descendants of Ephraim were Shuthelah, Bered, Tahath, Eleadah, Tahath, [21]Zabad, and Shuthelah.

Ephraim's sons Ezer and Elead were killed trying to steal livestock from the local farmers near Gath. [22]Their father, Ephraim, mourned for them a long time, and his relatives came to comfort him. [23]Afterward Ephraim slept with his wife, and she became pregnant and gave birth to a son. Ephraim named him Beriah* because of the tragedy his family had suffered.

[24]Ephraim had a daughter named Sheerah. She built the towns of Lower and Upper Beth-horon and Uzzen-sheerah.

[25]Ephraim's line of descent was Rephah, Resheph, Telah, Tahan, [26]Ladan, Ammihud, Elishama, [27]Nun, and Joshua.

[28] The descendants of Ephraim lived in the territory that included Bethel and its surrounding towns to the south, Naaran to the east, Gezer and its villages to the west, and Shechem and its surrounding villages to the north as far as Ayyah and its towns. [29]Along the border of Manasseh were the towns of Beth-shan,* Taanach, Megiddo, Dor, and their surrounding villages. The descendants of Joseph son of Israel* lived in these towns.

Descendants of Asher

[30]The sons of Asher were Imnah, Ishvah, Ishvi, and Beriah. They had a sister named Serah.

[31]The sons of Beriah were Heber and Malkiel (the father of Birzaith).

[32]The sons of Heber were Japhlet, Shomer, and Hotham. They had a sister named Shua.

[33]The sons of Japhlet were Pasach, Bimhal, and Ashvath.

[34]The sons of Shomer were Ahi, Rohgah, Hubbah, and Aram.

[35]The sons of his brother Helem* were Zophah, Imna, Shelesh, and Amal.

[36]The sons of Zophah were Suah, Harnepher, Shual, Beri, Imrah, [37]Bezer, Hod, Shamma, Shilshah, Ithran,* and Beera.

[38]The sons of Jether were Jephunneh, Pispah, and Ara.

[39]The sons of Ulla were Arah, Hanniel, and Rizia.

[40]Each of these descendants of Asher was the head of an ancestral clan. They were all skilled warriors and prominent leaders. There were 26,000 men available for military service among the descendants listed in their tribal genealogy.

CHAPTER **8**

Descendants of Benjamin

The sons of Benjamin, in order of age, included Bela (the oldest), Ashbel, Aharah, [2]Nohah, and Rapha.

[3]The sons of Bela were Addar, Gera, Abihud,* [4]Abishua, Naaman, Ahoah, [5]Gera, Shephuphan, and Huram.

[6]The sons of Ehud, leaders of the clans living at Geba, were driven out and moved to Manahath. [7]Ehud's sons were Naaman, Ahijah, and Gera. Gera, the father of Uzza and Ahihud, led them when they moved.

I GO out of my way to comfort relatives who have lost a son or daughter. (7:22)

See Joshua's profile (page 275) at Joshua 23:14.

See the profiles for Joseph (page 51) and Israel (Jacob) (page 43) at Genesis 39:2 and Genesis 32:9.

7:23 *Beriah* sounds like a Hebrew term meaning "tragedy" or "misfortune." **7:29a** Hebrew *Beth-shean*, a variant name for Beth-shan. **7:29b** *Israel* is the name that God gave to Jacob. **7:35** Possibly another name for *Hotham*; compare 7:32. **7:37** Possibly another name for *Jether*; compare 7:38. **8:3** Possibly *Gera the father of Ehud*; compare 8:6.

[8]After Shaharaim divorced his wives Hushim and Baara, he had children in the land of Moab. [9]Hodesh, his new wife, gave birth to Jobab, Zibia, Mesha, Malcam, [10]Jeuz, Sakia, and Mirmah. These sons all became the leaders of clans.

[11]Shaharaim's wife Hushim had already given birth to Abitub and Elpaal. [12]The sons of Elpaal were Eber, Misham, Shemed (who built Ono and Lod and their villages), [13]Beriah, and Shema. They were the leaders of the clans living in Aijalon, and they drove out the inhabitants of Gath.

[14]Ahio, Shashak, Jeremoth, [15]Zebadiah, Arad, Eder, [16]Michael, Ishpah, and Joha were the sons of Beriah.

[17]Zebadiah, Meshullam, Hizki, Heber, [18]Ishmerai, Izliah, and Jobab were the sons of Elpaal.

[19]Jakim, Zicri, Zabdi, [20]Elienai, Zillethai, Eliel, [21]Adaiah, Beraiah, and Shimrath were the sons of Shimei.

[22]Ishpan, Eber, Eliel, [23]Abdon, Zicri, Hanan, [24]Hananiah, Elam, Anthothijah, [25]Iphdeiah, and Penuel were the sons of Shashak.

[26]Shamsherai, Shehariah, Athaliah, [27]Jaareshiah, Elijah, and Zicri were the sons of Jeroham.

[28]These were the leaders of the ancestral clans, and they were listed in their tribal genealogy. They all lived in Jerusalem.

The Family of Saul

[29]Jeiel* (the father of* Gibeon) lived in Gibeon. His wife's name was Maacah, [30]and his oldest son was named Abdon. Jeiel's other sons were Zur, Kish, Baal, Ner,* Nadab, [31]Gedor, Ahio, Zechariah,* [32]and Mikloth, who was the father of Shimeam.* All these families lived near each other in Jerusalem.

[33]Ner was the father of Kish. Kish was the father of Saul. Saul was the father of Jonathan, Malkishua, Abinadab, and Eshbaal.

[34]Jonathan was the father of Meribbaal. Meribbaal was the father of Micah. [35]Micah was the father of Pithon, Melech, Tahrea,* and Ahaz.

[36] Ahaz was the father of Jadah.*
Jadah was the father of Alemeth, Azmaveth, and Zimri.
Zimri was the father of Moza.
[37] Moza was the father of Binea.
Binea was the father of Rephaiah.*
Rephaiah was the father of Eleasah.
Eleasah was the father of Azel.

[38]Azel had six sons: Azrikam, Bokeru, Ishmael, Sheariah, Obadiah, and Hanan. These were the sons of Azel.

[39]Azel's brother Eshek had three sons: Ulam (the oldest), Jeush (the second), and Eliphelet (the third). [40]The sons of Ulam were all skilled warriors and expert archers. They had many sons and grandsons—150 in all.

All these were descendants of Benjamin.

CHAPTER 9

All Israel was listed in the genealogical record in *The Book of the Kings of Israel.*

The Returning Exiles

The people of Judah were exiled to Babylon because they were unfaithful to

See Saul's profile (page 339) at 1 Samuel 18:9.

See Jonathan's profile (page 331) at 1 Samuel 14:6.

I LIVE a life of faithfulness to the Lord. (9:1)

8:29a As in some Greek manuscripts (see also 9:35); Hebrew lacks *Jeiel.*   8:29b Or *the founder of.*   8:30 As in some Greek manuscripts (see also 9:36); Hebrew lacks *Ner.*   8:31 As in parallel text at 9:37; Hebrew reads *Zeker,* a variant name for Zechariah.   8:32 As in parallel text at 9:38; Hebrew reads *Shimeah,* a variant name for Shimeam.   8:35 As in parallel text at 9:41; Hebrew reads *Tarea,* a variant name for Tahrea.   8:36 As in parallel text at 9:42; Hebrew reads *Jehoaddah,* a variant name for Jadah.   8:37 As in parallel text at 9:43; Hebrew reads *Raphah,* a variant name for Rephaiah.

the LORD. ²The first to return to their property in their former towns were common people. With them came some of the priests, Levites, and Temple assistants. ³People from the tribes of Judah, Benjamin, Ephraim, and Manasseh came and settled in Jerusalem.

⁴One family that returned was that of Uthai son of Ammihud, son of Omri, son of Imri, son of Bani, a descendant of Perez son of Judah.
⁵Others returned from the Shilonite clan, including Asaiah (the oldest) and his sons.
⁶From the Zerahite clan, Jeuel returned with his relatives.
In all, 690 families from the tribe of Judah returned.

⁷From the tribe of Benjamin came Sallu son of Meshullam, son of Hodaviah, son of Hassenuah; ⁸Ibneiah son of Jeroham; Elah son of Uzzi, son of Micri; Meshullam son of Shephatiah, son of Reuel, son of Ibnijah.
⁹These men were all leaders of clans, and they were listed in their tribal genealogy. In all, 956 families from the tribe of Benjamin returned.

The Returning Priests

¹⁰Among the priests who returned were Jedaiah, Jehoiarib, Jakin, ¹¹Azariah son of Hilkiah, son of Meshullam, son of Zadok, son of Meraioth, son of Ahitub. Azariah was the chief officer of the house of God.
¹²Other returning priests were Adaiah son of Jeroham, son of Pashhur, son of Malkijah, and Maasai son of Adiel, son of Jahzerah, son of Meshullam, son of Meshillemith, son of Immer.
¹³In all, 1,760 priests returned. They were heads of clans and very able men. They were responsible for ministering at the house of God.

See Hilkiah's profile (page 545) at 2 Chronicles 34:14.

The Returning Levites

¹⁴The Levites who returned were Shemaiah son of Hasshub, son of Azrikam, son of Hashabiah, a descendant of Merari; ¹⁵Bakbakkar; Heresh; Galal; Mattaniah son of Mica, son of Zicri, son of Asaph; ¹⁶Obadiah son of Shemaiah, son of Galal, son of Jeduthun; and Berekiah son of Asa, son of Elkanah, who lived in the area of Netophah.
¹⁷The gatekeepers who returned were Shallum, Akkub, Talmon, Ahiman, and their relatives. Shallum was the chief gatekeeper. ¹⁸Prior to this time, they were responsible for the King's Gate on the east side. These men served as gatekeepers for the camps of the Levites. ¹⁹Shallum was the son of Kore, a descendant of Abiasaph,* from the clan of Korah. He and his relatives, the Korahites, were responsible for guarding the entrance to the sanctuary, just as their ancestors had guarded the Tabernacle in the camp of the LORD.

See Asaph's profile (page 687) at Psalm 73:28.

²⁰Phinehas son of Eleazar had been in charge of the gatekeepers in earlier times, and the LORD had been with him. ²¹And later Zechariah son of Meshelemiah had been responsible for guarding the entrance to the Tabernacle.*

See Phinehas's profile (page 717) at Psalm 106:30.

²²In all, there were 212 gatekeepers in those days, and they were listed by genealogies in their villages. David and Samuel the seer had appointed their ancestors because they were reliable men. ²³These gatekeepers and their descendants, by their divisions, were responsible for guarding the entrance to the house of the LORD, the house that was formerly a tent. ²⁴The gatekeepers were stationed on all four sides—east, west, north, and south. ²⁵From time to time, their relatives in the villages came to share their duties for seven-day periods.
²⁶The four chief gatekeepers, all Levites, were in an office of great trust, for

See the profiles for David (page 629) and Samuel (page 323) at Psalm 3:1 and 1 Samuel 3:1.

9:19 Hebrew *Ebiasaph*, a variant name for Abiasaph; compare Exod 6:24.   **9:21** Hebrew *Tent of Meeting*.

they were responsible for the rooms and treasuries at the house of God. [27]They would spend the night around the house of God, since it was their duty to guard it. It was also their job to open the gates every morning.

[28]Some of the gatekeepers were assigned to care for the various utensils used in worship. They checked them in and out to avoid any loss. [29]Others were responsible for the furnishings, the items in the sanctuary, and the supplies such as choice flour, wine, olive oil, incense, and spices. [30]But it was the priests who prepared the spices and incense. [31]Mattithiah, a Levite and the oldest son of Shallum the Korahite, was entrusted with baking the bread used in the offerings. [32]And some members of the clan of Kohath were in charge of preparing the bread to be set on the table each Sabbath day.

[33]The musicians, all prominent Levites, lived at the Temple. They were exempt from other responsibilities there since they were on duty at all hours. [34]All these men lived in Jerusalem. They were the heads of Levite families and were listed as prominent leaders in their tribal genealogy.

King Saul's Family Tree

[35]Jeiel (the father of* Gibeon) lived in Gibeon. His wife's name was Maacah, [36]and his oldest son was named Abdon. Jeiel's other sons were Zur, Kish, Baal, Ner, Nadab, [37]Gedor, Ahio, Zechariah, and Mikloth. [38]Mikloth was the father of Shimeam. All these families lived near each other in Jerusalem.

[39]Ner was the father of Kish. Kish was the father of Saul. Saul was the father of Jonathan, Malkishua, Abinadab, and Eshbaal. [40]Jonathan was the father of Meribbaal. Meribbaal was the father of Micah. [41]The sons of Micah were Pithon, Melech, Tahrea, and Ahaz.*

[42] Ahaz was the father of Jadah.*
Jadah was the father of Alemeth, Azmaveth, and Zimri.
Zimri was the father of Moza.
[43] Moza was the father of Binea.
Binea's son was Rephaiah.
Rephaiah's son was Eleasah.
Eleasah's son was Azel.

[44]Azel had six sons, and their names were Azrikam, Bokeru, Ishmael, Sheariah, Obadiah, and Hanan. These were the sons of Azel.

See Saul's profile (page 339) at 1 Samuel 18:9.

See Jonathan's profile (page 331) at 1 Samuel 14:6.

CHAPTER 10

The Death of King Saul

See the profiles for Saul (page 339) and Jonathan (page 331) at 1 Samuel 18:9 and 1 Samuel 14:6.

I WILL NOT COMMIT suicide, no matter what trouble I face. (10:4)

Now the Philistines attacked Israel, forcing the Israelites to flee. Many were slaughtered on the slopes of Mount Gilboa. [2]The Philistines closed in on Saul and his sons, and they killed three of his sons—Jonathan, Abinadab, and Malkishua. [3]The fighting grew very fierce around Saul, and the Philistine archers caught up with him and wounded him severely. [4]Saul groaned to his armor bearer, "Take your sword and run me through before these pagan Philistines come and humiliate me." But his armor bearer was afraid and would not do it. So Saul took his own sword and fell on it. [5]When his armor bearer realized that Saul was dead, he fell on his own sword and died. [6]So Saul and his three sons died there together, bringing his dynasty to an end.

[7]When the Israelites in the Jezreel Valley saw that their army had been routed and that Saul and his sons were dead, they abandoned their towns and fled. So the Philistines moved in and occupied their towns.

[8]The next day when the Philistines went out to strip the dead, they found the bodies of Saul and his sons on Mount Gilboa. [9]So they stripped off Saul's armor and cut off his head. Then they proclaimed the news of Saul's death

9:35 Or the founder of. 9:41 As in Syriac version and Latin Vulgate (see also 8:35); Hebrew lacks and Ahaz. 9:42 As in some Hebrew manuscripts and Greek version (see also 8:36); Hebrew reads Jarah.

before their idols and to the people throughout the land of Philistia. ¹⁰They placed his armor in the temple of their gods, and they fastened his head to the wall in the temple of Dagon.

¹¹But when the people of Jabesh-gilead heard what the Philistines had done to Saul, ¹²their warriors went out and brought the bodies of Saul and his three sons back to Jabesh. Then they buried their remains beneath the oak tree at Jabesh, and they fasted for seven days.

¹³So Saul died because he was unfaithful to the LORD. He failed to obey the LORD's command, and he even consulted a medium ¹⁴instead of asking the LORD for guidance. So the LORD killed him and turned his kingdom over to David son of Jesse.

CHAPTER 11

David Becomes King of All Israel

Then all Israel went to David at Hebron and told him, "We are all members of your family. ²For a long time, even while Saul was our king, you were the one who really led Israel. And the LORD your God has told you, 'You will be the shepherd of my people Israel. You will be their leader.' " ³So there at Hebron David made a covenant with the leaders of Israel before the LORD. They anointed him king of Israel, just as the LORD had promised through Samuel.

David Captures Jerusalem

⁴Then David and all Israel went to Jerusalem (or Jebus, as it used to be called), where the Jebusites, original inhabitants of the land, lived. ⁵The people of Jebus said to David, "You will never get in here!" But David captured the fortress of Zion, now called the City of David.

⁶David had said to his troops, "Whoever leads the attack against the Jebusites will become the commander of my armies!" And Joab, the son of David's sister Zeruiah, led the attack, so he became the commander of David's armies.

⁷David made the fortress his home, and that is why it is called the City of David. ⁸He extended the city from the Millo* to the surrounding area, while Joab rebuilt the rest of Jerusalem. ⁹And David became more and more powerful, because the LORD Almighty was with him.

David's Mightiest Men

¹⁰These are the leaders of David's mighty men. Together with all Israel, they determined to make David their king, just as the LORD had promised concerning Israel. ¹¹Here is the record of David's mightiest men:

The first was Jashobeam the Hacmonite, who was commander of the Three—the three greatest warriors among David's men.* He once used his spear to kill three hundred enemy warriors in a single battle.

¹²Next in rank among the Three was Eleazar son of Dodai,* a descendant of Ahoah. ¹³He was with David in the battle against the Philistines at Pas-dammim. The battle took place in a field full of barley, and the Israelite army fled. ¹⁴But Eleazar and David held their ground in the middle of the field and beat back the Philistines. So the LORD saved them by giving them a great victory.

¹⁵Once when David was at the rock near the cave of Adullam, the Philistine army was camped in the valley of Rephaim. The Three (who were among the Thirty—an elite group among David's fighting men) went down to meet him there. ¹⁶David was staying in the stronghold at the time, and a Philistine detachment had occupied the town of Bethlehem. ¹⁷David remarked longingly to his men, "Oh, how I would love some of that good water from the well in

I SHOW RESPECT for my deceased leaders. (10:11)

I FAITHFULLY OBEY the Lord's commands. (10:13)

I BELIEVE Saul died and his dynasty ended because he was unfaithful to the Lord. (10:14)

See David's profile (page 629) at Psalm 3:1.

I FOLLOW godly leaders who are called by God and who lead well. (11:2)

See Saul's profile (page 339) at 1 Samuel 18:9.

See Samuel's profile (page 323) at 1 Samuel 3:1.

I ENTRUST positions of responsibility to capable individuals. (11:6)

I BELIEVE David became powerful because the Lord was with him. (11:9)

I HONOR those who serve well. (11:11)

I STAND my ground and experience victory from the Lord (Ephesians 6:13–14). (11:14)

11:8 Or *the supporting terraces.* The meaning of the Hebrew is uncertain.   11:11 As in some Greek manuscripts (see also 2 Sam 23:8); Hebrew *commander of the Thirty,* or *commander of the captains.*   11:12 As in parallel text at 2 Sam 23:9 (see also 1 Chr 27:4); Hebrew reads *Dodo,* a variant name for Dodai.

Bethlehem, the one by the gate." [18]So the Three broke through the Philistine lines, drew some water from the well, and brought it back to David. But David refused to drink it. Instead, he poured it out before the LORD. [19]"God forbid that I should drink this!" he exclaimed. "This water is as precious as the blood of these men who risked their lives to bring it to me." So David did not drink it. This is an example of the exploits of the Three.

David's Thirty Mighty Men

[20]Abishai, the brother of Joab, was the leader of the Thirty.* He once used his spear to kill three hundred enemy warriors in a single battle. It was by such feats that he became as famous as the Three. [21]Abishai was the most famous of the Thirty and was their commander, though he was not one of the Three.

[22]There was also Benaiah son of Jehoiada, a valiant warrior from Kabzeel. He did many heroic deeds, which included killing two of Moab's mightiest warriors. Another time he chased a lion down into a pit. Then, despite the snow and slippery ground, he caught the lion and killed it. [23]Another time, armed with only a club, he killed an Egyptian warrior who was seven and a half feet* tall and whose spear was as thick as a weaver's beam. Benaiah wrenched the spear from the Egyptian's hand and killed him with it. [24]These are some of the deeds that made Benaiah as famous as the Three. [25]He was more honored than the other members of the Thirty, though he was not one of the Three. And David made him commander of his bodyguard.

[26]These were also included among David's mighty men:

Asahel, Joab's brother;
Elhanan son of Dodo from Bethlehem;
[27] Shammah from Harod;*
Helez from Pelon;
[28] Ira son of Ikkesh from Tekoa;
Abiezer from Anathoth;
[29] Sibbecai from Hushah;
Zalmon* from Ahoah;
[30] Maharai from Netophah;
Heled son of Baanah from Netophah;
[31] Ithai son of Ribai from Gibeah (from the tribe of Benjamin);
Benaiah from Pirathon;
[32] Hurai from near Nahale-gaash*;
Abi-albon* the Arbathite;
[33] Azmaveth from Bahurim*;
Eliahba from Shaalbon;
[34] the sons of Jashen* from Gizon;
Jonathan son of Shagee from Harar;
[35] Ahiam son of Sharar* from Harar;
Eliphal son of Ur;
[36] Hepher from Mekerah;
Ahijah from Pelon;
[37] Hezro from Carmel;
Paarai* son of Ezbai;
[38] Joel, the brother of Nathan;
Mibhar son of Hagri;
[39] Zelek from Ammon;
Naharai from Beeroth (Joab's armor bearer);

I DO NOT TREAT lightly the sacrifices others make for me. (11:19)

I PURSUE the tasks before me with courage. (11:22)

11:20 As in Syriac version; Hebrew reads *the Three*; also in 11:21.   11:23 Hebrew *5 cubits* [2.3 meters].
11:27 As in parallel text at 2 Sam 23:25; Hebrew reads *Shammoth from Haror*.   11:29 As in parallel text at
2 Sam 23:28; Hebrew reads *Ilai*.   11:32a Or *from the ravines of Gaash*.   11:32b As in parallel text at 2 Sam
23:31; Hebrew reads *Abiel*.   11:33 As in parallel text at 2 Sam 23:31; Hebrew reads *Baharum*.   11:34 As in
parallel text at 2 Sam 23:32; Hebrew reads *sons of Hashem*.   11:35 As in parallel text at 2 Sam 23:33; Hebrew
reads *son of Sacar*.   11:37 As in parallel text at 2 Sam 23:35; Hebrew reads *Naarai*.

⁴⁰ Ira from Jattir;
Gareb from Jattir;
⁴¹ Uriah the Hittite;
Zabad son of Ahlai;
⁴² Adina son of Shiza, the Reubenite leader who had thirty men with him;
⁴³ Hanan son of Maacah;
Joshaphat from Mithna;
⁴⁴ Uzzia from Ashtaroth;
Shama and Jeiel, the sons of Hotham, from Aroer;
⁴⁵ Jediael son of Shimri;
Joha, his brother, from Tiz;
⁴⁶ Eliel from Mahavah;
Jeribai and Joshaviah, the sons of Elnaam;
Ithmah from Moab;
⁴⁷ Eliel and Obed;
Jaasiel from Zobah.

CHAPTER **12**

Warriors Join David's Army

The following men joined David at Ziklag while he was hiding from Saul son of Kish. They were among the warriors who fought beside David in battle. ²All of them were expert archers, and they could shoot arrows or sling stones with their left hand as well as their right. They were all relatives of Saul from the tribe of Benjamin. ³Their leader was Ahiezer son of Shemaah from Gibeah; his brother Joash was second-in-command. These were the other warriors:

Jeziel and Pelet, sons of Azmaveth;
Beracah and Jehu from Anathoth;
⁴ Ishmaiah from Gibeon, a famous warrior and leader among the Thirty;
Jeremiah, Jahaziel, Johanan, and Jozabad from Gederah;
⁵ Eluzai, Jerimoth, Bealiah, Shemariah, and Shephatiah from Haruph;
⁶ Elkanah, Isshiah, Azarel, Joezer, and Jashobeam, who were Korahites;
⁷ Joelah and Zebadiah, sons of Jeroham from Gedor.

⁸Some brave and experienced warriors from the tribe of Gad also defected to David while he was at the stronghold in the wilderness. They were expert with both shield and spear, as fierce as lions and as swift as deer on the mountains.

⁹ Ezer was their leader.
Obadiah was second.
Eliab was third.
¹⁰ Mishmannah was fourth.
Jeremiah was fifth.
¹¹ Attai was sixth.
Eliel was seventh.
¹² Johanan was eighth.
Elzabad was ninth.
¹³ Jeremiah was tenth.
Macbannai was eleventh.

¹⁴ These warriors from Gad were army commanders. The weakest among them could take on a hundred regular troops, and the strongest could take on a thousand! ¹⁵They crossed the Jordan River during its seasonal flooding at the beginning of the year and drove out all the people living in the lowlands on both the east and west banks.

¹⁶Others from Benjamin and Judah came to David at the stronghold.

In response to these affirmations, tell the Lord what you believe—or find hard to believe.

See Saul's profile (page 339) at 1 Samuel 18:9.

I FOLLOW godly leaders who are committed to God, not those leaders who turn aside from the Lord. (12:1)

I CHOOSE to follow godly leaders. (12:8)

I ACCEPT the help and partnership of those who come in peace. (12:17)

I AM FILLED with the Holy Spirit (see Ephesians 5:18). (12:18)

[17]David went out to meet them and said, "If you have come in peace to help me, we are friends. But if you have come to betray me to my enemies when I am innocent, then may the God of our ancestors see and judge you."

[18]Then the Spirit came upon Amasai, who later became a leader among the Thirty, and he said,

"We are yours, David!
    We are on your side, son of Jesse.
Peace and prosperity be with you,
    and success to all who help you,
    for your God is the one who helps you."

So David let them join him, and he made them officers over his troops.

[19]Some men from Manasseh defected from the Israelite army and joined David when he went with the Philistines to fight against Saul. But as it turned out, the Philistine leaders refused to let David and his men go with them. After much discussion, they sent them back, for they said, "It will cost us our lives if David switches loyalties to Saul and turns against us."

[20]Here is a list of the men from Manasseh who defected to David as he was returning to Ziklag: Adnah, Jozabad, Jediael, Michael, Jozabad, Elihu, and Zillethai. Each commanded a thousand troops from the tribe of Manasseh.

I SUPPORT AND HELP those who are serving God. (12:21)

I BELIEVE God raised up a mighty army for David. (12:22)

I SUPPORT those who are called by God to lead his people. (12:23)

See Aaron's profile (page 107) at Exodus 32:2.

[21]They helped David chase down bands of raiders, for they were all brave and able warriors who became commanders in his army. [22]Day after day more men joined David until he had a great army, like the army of God.

[23]These are the numbers of armed warriors who joined David at Hebron. They were all eager to see David become king instead of Saul, just as the LORD had promised.

[24]From the tribe of Judah, there were 6,800 warriors armed with shields and spears.
[25]From the tribe of Simeon, there were 7,100 warriors.
[26]From the tribe of Levi, there were 4,600 troops. [27]This included Jehoiada, leader of the family of Aaron, who had 3,700 under his command.
    [28]This also included Zadok, a young warrior, with twenty-two members of his family who were all officers.
[29]From the tribe of Benjamin, Saul's relatives, there were 3,000 warriors. Most of the men from Benjamin had remained loyal to Saul until this time.
[30]From the tribe of Ephraim, there were 20,800 warriors, each famous in his own clan.
[31]From the half-tribe of Manasseh west of the Jordan, 18,000 men were sent for the express purpose of helping David become king.

I USE God-given discernment to counsel others. (12:32)

[32]From the tribe of Issachar, there were 200 leaders of the tribe with their relatives. All these men understood the temper of the times and knew the best course for Israel to take.
[33]From the tribe of Zebulun, there were 50,000 skilled warriors. They were fully armed and prepared for battle and completely loyal to David.
[34]From the tribe of Naphtali, there were 1,000 officers and 37,000 warriors armed with shields and spears.
[35]From the tribe of Dan, there were 28,600 warriors, all prepared for battle.
[36]From the tribe of Asher, there were 40,000 trained warriors, all prepared for battle.
[37]From the east side of the Jordan River—where the tribes of Reuben and Gad and the half-tribe of Manasseh lived—there were 120,000 troops armed with every kind of weapon.

[38]All these men came in battle array to Hebron with the single purpose of making David the king of Israel. In fact, all Israel agreed that David should be

their king. [39] They feasted and drank with David for three days, for preparations had been made by their relatives for their arrival. [40] And people from as far away as Issachar, Zebulun, and Naphtali brought food on donkeys, camels, mules, and oxen. Vast supplies of flour, fig cakes, raisins, wine, olive oil, cattle, and sheep were brought to the celebration. There was great joy throughout the land of Israel.

CHAPTER 13
David Attempts to Move the Ark

David consulted with all his officials, including the generals and captains of his army. [2] Then he addressed the entire assembly of Israel as follows: "If you approve and if it is the will of the LORD our God, let us send messages to all the Israelites throughout the land, including the priests and Levites in their towns and pasturelands. Let us invite them to come and join us. [3] It is time to bring back the Ark of our God, for we neglected it during the reign of Saul."

[4] The whole assembly agreed to this, for the people could see it was the right thing to do. [5] So David summoned all the people of Israel, from one end of the country to the other,* to join in bringing the Ark of God from Kiriath-jearim. [6] Then David and all Israel went to Baalah of Judah (also called Kiriath-jearim) to bring back the Ark of God, which bears the name of the LORD who is enthroned between the cherubim. [7] They transported the Ark of God from the house of Abinadab on a new cart, with Uzzah and Ahio guiding it. [8] David and all Israel were celebrating before God with all their might, singing and playing all kinds of musical instruments—lyres, harps, tambourines, cymbals, and trumpets.

[9] But when they arrived at the threshing floor of Nacon,* the oxen stumbled, and Uzzah put out his hand to steady the Ark. [10] Then the LORD's anger blazed out against Uzzah, and he struck him dead because he had laid his hand on the Ark. So Uzzah died there in the presence of God. [11] David was angry because the LORD's anger had blazed out against Uzzah. He named that place Perez-uzzah (which means "outbreak against Uzzah"). It is still called that today.

[12] David was now afraid of God and asked, "How can I ever bring the Ark of God back into my care?" [13] So David decided not to move the Ark into the City of David. He took it instead to the home of Obed-edom of Gath. [14] The Ark of God remained there with the family of Obed-edom for three months, and the LORD blessed him and his entire household.

CHAPTER 14
David's Palace and Family

Now King Hiram of Tyre sent messengers to David, along with stonemasons and carpenters to build him a palace. Hiram also sent many cedar logs for lumber. [2] And David realized that the LORD had made him king over Israel and had made his kingdom very great for the sake of his people Israel.

[3] Then David married more wives in Jerusalem, and they had many sons and daughters. [4] These are the names of David's sons who were born in Jerusalem: Shimea,* Shobab, Nathan, Solomon, [5] Ibhar, Elishua, Elpelet, [6] Nogah, Nepheg, Japhia, [7] Elishama, Eliada,* and Eliphelet.

David Conquers the Philistines

[8] When the Philistines heard that David had been anointed king over all Israel, they mobilized all their forces to capture him. But David was told they were coming, so he and his men marched out to meet them. [9] The Philistines had arrived in the valley of Rephaim and raided it. [10] So David

---

I CELEBRATE when God provides a godly leader for his people. (12:39)

I SEEK the counsel of others and the will of God before making important decisions. (13:2)

See Saul's profile (page 339) at 1 Samuel 18:9.

I GIVE priority to honoring the name of the Lord publicly. (13:6)

I BELIEVE God blesses those who honor him. (13:14)

See Solomon's profile (page 753) at Proverbs 2:9.

I SEEK the Lord's guidance. (14:10)

13:5 Hebrew *from the Shihor of Egypt to Lebo-hamath.*   13:9 As in parallel text at 2 Sam 6:6; Hebrew reads *Kidon.*
14:4 Hebrew *Shammua,* a variant name for Shimea; compare 3:5.   14:7 Hebrew *Beeliada,* a variant name for Eliada; compare 3:8 and parallel text at 2 Sam 5:16.

asked God, "Should I go out to fight the Philistines? Will you hand them over to me?"

The LORD replied, "Yes, go ahead. I will give you the victory."

¹¹So David and his troops went to Baal-perazim and defeated the Philistines there. "God has done it!" David exclaimed. "He used me to burst through my enemies like a raging flood!" So that place was named Baal-perazim (which means "the Lord who bursts through"). ¹²The Philistines had abandoned their idols* there, so David gave orders to burn them up.

¹³But after a while, the Philistines returned and raided the valley again. ¹⁴And once again David asked God what to do. "Do not attack them straight on," God replied. "Instead, circle around behind them and attack them near the balsam trees. ¹⁵When you hear a sound like marching feet in the tops of the balsam trees, attack! That will be the signal that God is moving ahead of you to strike down the Philistines." ¹⁶So David did what God commanded, and he struck down the Philistine army all the way from Gibeon to Gezer.

¹⁷So David's fame spread everywhere, and the LORD caused all the nations to fear David.

CHAPTER 15

Preparing to Move the Ark

David now built several buildings for himself in the City of David. He also prepared a place for the Ark of God and set up a special tent there to shelter it. ²Then he issued these instructions: "When we transport the Ark of God this time, no one except the Levites may carry it. The LORD has chosen them to carry the Ark of the LORD and to minister before him forever."

³Then David summoned all the Israelites to Jerusalem to bring the Ark of the LORD to the place he had prepared for it. ⁴These are the priests* and Levites who were called together:

⁵There were 120 from the clan of Kohath, with Uriel as their leader.
⁶There were 220 from the clan of Merari, with Asaiah as their leader.
⁷There were 130 from the clan of Gershon,* with Joel as their leader.
⁸There were 200 descendants of Elizaphan, with Shemaiah as their leader.
⁹There were 80 descendants of Hebron, with Eliel as their leader.
¹⁰There were 112 descendants of Uzziel, with Amminadab as their leader.

¹¹Then David summoned the priests, Zadok and Abiathar, and these Levite leaders: Uriel, Asaiah, Joel, Shemaiah, Eliel, and Amminadab. ¹²He said to them, "You are the leaders of the Levite families. You must purify yourselves and all your fellow Levites, so you can bring the Ark of the LORD, the God of Israel, to the place I have prepared for it. ¹³Because you Levites did not carry the Ark the first time, the anger of the LORD our God burst out against us. We failed to ask God how to move it in the proper way." ¹⁴So the priests and the Levites purified themselves in order to bring the Ark of the LORD, the God of Israel, to Jerusalem. ¹⁵Then the Levites carried the Ark of God on their shoulders with its carrying poles, just as the LORD had instructed Moses.

¹⁶David also ordered the Levite leaders to appoint a choir of Levites who were singers and musicians to sing joyful songs to the accompaniment of lyres, harps, and cymbals. ¹⁷So the Levites appointed Heman son of Joel, Asaph son of Berekiah, and Ethan son of Kushaiah from the clan of Merari to direct the musicians. ¹⁸The following men were chosen as their assistants: Zechariah, Jaaziel, Shemiramoth, Jehiel, Unni, Eliab, Benaiah, Maaseiah, Mattithiah, Eliphelehu, Mikneiah, and the gatekeepers, Obed-edom and Jeiel.

¹⁹Heman, Asaph, and Ethan were chosen to sound the bronze cymbals. ²⁰Zechariah, Aziel, Shemiramoth, Jehiel, Unni, Eliab, Maaseiah, and Benaiah

Margin notes: I GIVE glory to God when he gives me victory. (14:11) — I OBEY God's commands. (14:16) — I FOLLOW the Lord's instructions. (15:2) — I LOOK to God's Word for instructions before I begin to serve the Lord. (15:13) — I PURIFY my life in preparation for serving the Lord. (15:14) — See Moses' profile (page 73) at Exodus 5:1. — I GIVE priority to public musical worship. (15:16)

14:12 Hebrew *their gods;* compare parallel text at 2 Sam 5:21.   15:4 Hebrew *descendants of Aaron.*   15:7 Hebrew *Gershom,* a variant name for Gershon.

were chosen to play the lyres.* [21]Mattithiah, Eliphelehu, Mikneiah, Obed-edom, Jeiel, and Azaziah were chosen to play the harps.* [22]Kenaniah, the head Levite, was chosen as the choir leader because of his skill.

[23]Berekiah and Elkanah were chosen to guard the Ark. [24]Shebaniah, Joshaphat, Nethanel, Amasai, Zechariah, Benaiah, and Eliezer—all of whom were priests—were chosen to blow the trumpets as they marched in front of the Ark of God. Obed-edom and Jehiah were chosen to guard the Ark.

Moving the Ark to Jerusalem

[25]Then David and the leaders of Israel and the generals of the army went to the home of Obed-edom to bring the Ark of the LORD's covenant up to Jerusalem with a great celebration. [26]And because God was clearly helping the Levites as they carried the Ark of the LORD's covenant, they sacrificed seven bulls and seven lambs. [27]David was dressed in a robe of fine linen, as were the Levites who carried the Ark, the singers, and Kenaniah the song leader. David was also wearing a priestly tunic.* [28]So all Israel brought up the Ark of the LORD's covenant to Jerusalem with shouts of joy, the blowing of horns and trumpets, the crashing of cymbals, and loud playing on harps and lyres.

[29]But as the Ark of the LORD's covenant entered the City of David, Michal, the daughter of Saul, looked down from her window. When she saw King David dancing and leaping for joy, she was filled with contempt for him.

CHAPTER 16

So they brought the Ark of God into the special tent David had prepared for it, and they sacrificed burnt offerings and peace offerings before God. [2]When he had finished, David blessed the people in the name of the LORD. [3]Then he gave a gift of food to every man and woman in Israel: a loaf of bread, a cake of dates,* and a cake of raisins.

[4]David appointed the following Levites to lead the people in worship before the Ark of the LORD by asking for his blessings and giving thanks and praise to the LORD, the God of Israel. [5]Asaph, the leader of this group, sounded the cymbals. His assistants were Zechariah (the second), then Jeiel, Shemiramoth, Jehiel, Mattithiah, Eliab, Benaiah, Obed-edom, and Jeiel. They played the harps and lyres. [6]The priests, Benaiah and Jahaziel, played the trumpets regularly before the Ark of God's covenant.

David's Song of Praise

[7]That day David gave to Asaph and his fellow Levites this song of thanksgiving to the LORD:

[8]Give thanks to the LORD and proclaim his greatness.
  Let the whole world know what he has done.
[9]Sing to him; yes, sing his praises.
  Tell everyone about his miracles.
[10]Exult in his holy name;
  O worshipers of the LORD, rejoice!
[11]Search for the LORD and for his strength,
  and keep on searching.
[12]Think of the wonderful works he has done,
  the miracles, and the judgments he handed down,
[13]O children of Israel, God's servant,
  O descendants of Jacob, God's chosen one.

[14]He is the LORD our God.
  His rule is seen throughout the land.

I BELIEVE godly, skilled individuals should be appointed to lead public musical worship. (15:22)

I TAKE PART WHOLE-HEARTEDLY in public celebration and worship of the Lord. (15:27)

I DO NOT DESPISE those who worship the Lord enthusiastically. (15:29)

See Saul's profile (page 339) at 1 Samuel 18:9.

I BLESS others in the name of the Lord. (16:2)

I GIVE priority to public worship, thanksgiving, and prayer. (16:4)

I USE my musical gifts to worship God publicly. (16:5)

I REMEMBER all the wonderful things God has done. (16:12)

See Jacob's profile (page 43) at Genesis 32:9.

15:20 Hebrew adds *according to Alamoth*, which is probably a musical term. The meaning of the Hebrew is uncertain.
15:21 Hebrew adds *according to the Sheminith*, which is probably a musical term. The meaning of the Hebrew is uncertain. 15:27 Hebrew *a linen ephod.* 16:3 Or *a portion of meat.* The meaning of the Hebrew is uncertain.

¹⁵ He always stands by his covenant*—
   the commitment he made to a thousand generations.
¹⁶ This is the covenant he made with Abraham
   and the oath he swore to Isaac.
¹⁷ He confirmed it to Jacob as a decree,
   to the people of Israel as a never-ending treaty:
¹⁸ "I will give you the land of Canaan
   as your special possession."

¹⁹ He said this when they were few in number,
   a tiny group of strangers in Canaan.
²⁰ They wandered back and forth between nations,
   from one kingdom to another.
²¹ Yet he did not let anyone oppress them.
   He warned kings on their behalf:
²² "Do not touch these people I have chosen,
   and do not hurt my prophets."

> I SING to the Lord each day and proclaim the good news that he saves. (16:23)
>
> I TELL everyone about the amazing things the Lord does. (16:24)

²³ Let the whole earth sing to the LORD!
   Each day proclaim the good news that he saves.
²⁴ Publish his glorious deeds among the nations.
   Tell everyone about the amazing things he does.
²⁵ Great is the LORD! He is most worthy of praise!
   He is to be revered above all gods.
²⁶ The gods of other nations are merely idols,
   but the LORD made the heavens!
²⁷ Honor and majesty surround him;
   strength and beauty are in his dwelling.

²⁸ O nations of the world, recognize the LORD,
   recognize that the LORD is glorious and strong.
²⁹ Give to the LORD the glory he deserves!
   Bring your offering and come to worship him.
   Worship the LORD in all his holy splendor.
³⁰ Let all the earth tremble before him.
   The world is firmly established and cannot be shaken.

³¹ Let the heavens be glad, and let the earth rejoice!
   Tell all the nations that the LORD is king.
³² Let the sea and everything in it shout his praise!
   Let the fields and their crops burst forth with joy!
³³ Let the trees of the forest rustle with praise before the LORD!
   For he is coming to judge the earth.

> I THANK God for his faithful, enduring love. (16:34)

³⁴ Give thanks to the LORD, for he is good!
   His faithful love endures forever.
³⁵ Cry out, "Save us, O God of our salvation!
   Gather and rescue us from among the nations,
   so we can thank your holy name
   and rejoice and praise you."

³⁶ Blessed be the LORD, the God of Israel,
   from everlasting to everlasting!

And all the people shouted "Amen!" and praised the LORD.

Worship at Jerusalem and Gibeon
³⁷ David arranged for Asaph and his fellow Levites to minister regularly before

---

16:15 As in some Greek manuscripts (see also Ps 105:8); Hebrew reads *Remember his covenant forever.*

the Ark of the LORD's covenant, doing whatever needed to be done each day. [38]This group included Obed-edom (son of Jeduthun), Hosah, and sixty-eight other Levites as gatekeepers.

[39]Meanwhile, David stationed Zadok the priest and his fellow priests at the Tabernacle of the LORD on the hill of Gibeon, where they continued to minister before the LORD. [40]They sacrificed the regular burnt offerings to the LORD each morning and evening on the altar set aside for that purpose, obeying everything written in the law of the LORD, which he had given to Israel. [41]David also appointed Heman, Jeduthun, and the others chosen by name to give thanks to the LORD, "for his faithful love endures forever." [42]They used their trumpets, cymbals, and other instruments to accompany the songs of praise to God. And the sons of Jeduthun were appointed as gatekeepers.

[43]Then all the people returned to their homes, and David returned home to bless his family.

CHAPTER 17

The LORD's Covenant Promise to David

Now when David was settled in his palace, he said to Nathan the prophet, "Here I am living in this beautiful cedar palace, but the Ark of the LORD's covenant is out in a tent!"

[2]Nathan replied, "Go ahead with what you have in mind, for God is with you."

[3]But that same night God said to Nathan,

[4]"Go and tell my servant David, 'This is what the LORD says: You are not the one to build me a temple to live in. [5]I have never lived in a temple, from the day I brought the Israelites out of Egypt until now. My home has always been a tent, moving from one place to another. [6]And I never once complained to Israel's leaders,* the shepherds of my people. I have never asked them, "Why haven't you built me a beautiful cedar temple?"'

[7]"Now go and say to my servant David, 'This is what the LORD Almighty says: I chose you to lead my people Israel when you were just a shepherd boy, tending your sheep out in the pasture. [8]I have been with you wherever you have gone, and I have destroyed all your enemies. Now I will make your name famous throughout the earth! [9]And I have provided a permanent homeland for my people Israel, a secure place where they will never be disturbed. It will be their own land where wicked nations won't oppress them as they did in the past, [10]from the time I appointed judges to rule my people. And I will subdue all your enemies.

" 'And now I declare that the LORD will build a house for you—a dynasty of kings! [11]For when you die, I will raise up one of your sons, and I will make his kingdom strong. [12]He is the one who will build a house—a temple—for me. And I will establish his throne forever. [13]I will be his father, and he will be my son. I will not take my unfailing love from him as I took it from Saul, who ruled before you. [14]I will establish him over my dynasty and my kingdom for all time, and his throne will be secure forever.' "

[15]So Nathan went back to David and told him everything the LORD had said.

David's Prayer of Thanks

[16]Then King David went in and sat before the LORD and prayed, "Who am I, O LORD God, and what is my family, that you have brought me this far? [17]And now, O God, in addition to everything else, you speak of giving me a lasting

---

I OBEY everything the Lord commands. (16:40)

I BLESS my family. (16:43)

I DO NOT INVEST in my own house to the neglect of God's house of worship. (17:1)

See Saul's profile (page 339) at 1 Samuel 18:9.

I HUMBLY WORSHIP the Lord when he blesses me. (17:16)

I AM AWED at the blessings and honor bestowed on me by God. (17:17)

17:6 As in Greek version (see also 2 Sam 7:7); Hebrew reads judges.

dynasty! You speak as though I were someone very great,* O LORD God! ¹⁸What more can I say about the way you have honored me? You know what I am really like. ¹⁹For my sake, O LORD, and according to your will, you have done all these great things and have made them known.

²⁰"O LORD, there is no one like you—there is no other God. We have never even heard of another god like you! ²¹What other nation on earth is like Israel? What other nation, O God, have you redeemed from slavery to be your own people? You made a great name for yourself when you rescued your people from Egypt. You performed awesome miracles and drove out the nations that stood in their way. ²²You chose Israel to be your people forever, and you, O LORD, have become their God.

²³"And now, O LORD, do as you have promised concerning me and my family. May it be a promise that will last forever. ²⁴And may your name be established and honored forever so that all the world will say, 'The LORD Almighty is God over Israel!' And may the dynasty of your servant David be established in your presence.

²⁵"O my God, I have been bold enough to pray this prayer because you have revealed that you will build a house for me—an eternal dynasty! ²⁶For you are God, O LORD. And you have promised these good things to me, your servant. ²⁷And now, it has pleased you to bless me and my family so that our dynasty will continue forever before you. For when you grant a blessing, O LORD, it is an eternal blessing!"

CHAPTER 18

David's Military Victories

After this, David subdued and humbled the Philistines by conquering Gath and its surrounding towns. ²David also conquered the land of Moab, and the Moabites became David's subjects and brought him tribute money.

³Then David destroyed the forces of King Hadadezer of Zobah, as far as Hamath,* when Hadadezer marched out to strengthen his control along the Euphrates River. ⁴David captured one thousand chariots, seven thousand charioteers, and twenty thousand foot soldiers. Then he crippled all but one hundred of the chariot horses.

⁵When Arameans from Damascus arrived to help Hadadezer, David killed twenty-two thousand of them. ⁶Then he placed several army garrisons in Damascus, the Aramean capital, and the Arameans became David's subjects and brought him tribute money. So the LORD gave David victory wherever he went. ⁷David brought the gold shields of Hadadezer's officers to Jerusalem, ⁸along with a large amount of bronze from Hadadezer's cities of Tebah* and Cun. Later Solomon melted the bronze and used it for the Temple. He molded it into the bronze Sea, the pillars, and the various bronze utensils used at the Temple.

⁹When King Toi* of Hamath heard that David had destroyed the army of King Hadadezer of Zobah, ¹⁰he sent his son Joram* to congratulate David on his success. Hadadezer and Toi had long been enemies, and there had been many wars between them. Joram presented David with many gifts of gold, silver, and bronze. ¹¹King David dedicated all these gifts to the LORD, along with the silver and gold he had taken from the other nations he had subdued—Edom, Moab, Ammon, Philistia, and Amalek.

¹²Abishai son of Zeruiah destroyed eighteen thousand Edomites in the Valley of Salt. ¹³He placed army garrisons throughout Edom, and all the

---

I PRAISE the Lord, who alone is God. (17:20)

I PRAY that the name of the Lord will be honored as he fulfills his promises to me. (17:24)

I BELIEVE all of the Lord's promises are true. (17:26)

I BELIEVE the Lord is the one who makes me successful. (18:6)

I GIVE generously to the Lord when he prospers me. (18:8)

I CONGRATULATE those whom God makes successful. (18:10)

17:17 The meaning of the Hebrew is uncertain. 18:3 The meaning of the Hebrew is uncertain. 18:8 Hebrew reads *Tibhath*, a variant name for Tebah; compare parallel text at 2 Sam 8:8. 18:9 As in parallel text at 2 Sam 8:9; Hebrew reads *Tou*; also in 18:10. 18:10 As in parallel text at 2 Sam 8:10; Hebrew reads *Hadoram*, a variant name for Joram.

Edomites became David's subjects. This was another example of how the LORD made David victorious wherever he went.

¹⁴David reigned over all Israel and was fair to everyone. ¹⁵Joab son of Zeruiah was commander of the army. Jehoshaphat son of Ahilud was the royal historian. ¹⁶Zadok son of Ahitub and Ahimelech* son of Abiathar were the priests. Seraiah* was the court secretary. ¹⁷Benaiah son of Jehoiada was captain of the king's bodyguard.* David's sons served as the king's chief assistants.

I TREAT everyone fairly. (18:14)

CHAPTER **19**

David Defeats the Ammonites

Some time after this, King Nahash of the Ammonites died, and his son Hanun* became king. ²David said, "I am going to show complete loyalty to Hanun because his father, Nahash, was always completely loyal to me." So David sent ambassadors to express sympathy to Hanun about his father's death.

But when David's ambassadors arrived in the land of Ammon, ³Hanun's advisers said to him, "Do you really think these men are coming here to honor your father? No! David has sent them to spy out the land so that they can come in and conquer it!" ⁴So Hanun seized David's ambassadors and shaved their beards, cut off their robes at the buttocks, and sent them back to David in shame. ⁵When David heard what had happened, he sent messengers to tell the men to stay at Jericho until their beards grew out, for they were very embarrassed by their appearance.

I SHOW consideration to those who have been unfairly humiliated. (19:5)

⁶Now the people of Ammon realized how seriously they had angered David, so Hanun and the Ammonites sent thirty-eight tons* of silver to hire chariots and troops from Aram-naharaim, Aram-maacah, and Zobah. ⁷They also hired thirty-two thousand chariots and secured the support of the king of Maacah and his army. These forces camped at Medeba, where they were joined by the Ammonite troops that Hanun had recruited from his own towns. ⁸When David heard about this, he sent Joab and all his warriors to fight them. ⁹The Ammonite troops drew up their battle lines at the gate of the city, while the other kings positioned themselves to fight in the open fields.

¹⁰When Joab saw that he would have to fight on two fronts, he chose the best troops in his army. He placed them under his personal command and led them out to fight the Arameans in the fields. ¹¹He left the rest of the army under the command of his brother Abishai, who was to attack the Ammonites. ¹²"If the Arameans are too strong for me, then come over and help me," Joab told his brother. "And if the Ammonites are too strong for you, I will help you. ¹³Be courageous! Let us fight bravely to save our people and the cities of our God. May the LORD's will be done."

I PROCEED wisely in times of crisis. (19:10)

I SERVE the Lord with courage and pray that his will be done. (19:13)

¹⁴When Joab and his troops attacked, the Arameans began to run away. ¹⁵And when the Ammonites saw the Arameans running, they ran from Abishai and retreated into the city. Then Joab returned to Jerusalem.

¹⁶The Arameans now realized that they were no match for Israel, so they summoned additional Aramean troops from the other side of the Euphrates River.* These troops arrived under the command of Shobach,* the commander of all Hadadezer's forces. ¹⁷When David heard what was happening, he mobilized all Israel, crossed the Jordan River, and positioned his troops in battle formation. Then he engaged the enemy troops in battle, and they fought against him. ¹⁸But again the Arameans fled from the Israelites. This

18:16a As in some Hebrew manuscripts, Syriac version, and Latin Vulgate (see also 2 Sam 8:17); most Hebrew manuscripts read *Abimelech.* **18:16b** As in parallel text at 2 Sam 8:17; Hebrew reads *Shavsha.* **18:17** Hebrew *of the Kerethites and Pelethites.* **19:1** Hebrew lacks *Hanun;* compare parallel text at 2 Sam 10:1. **19:6** Hebrew *1,000 talents* [34 metric tons]. **19:16a** Hebrew *the river.* **19:16b** As in parallel text at 2 Sam 10:16; Hebrew reads *Shophach;* also in 19:18.

time David's forces killed seven thousand charioteers and forty thousand foot soldiers, including Shobach, the commander of their army. [19]When the servants of Hadadezer realized they had been defeated by Israel, they surrendered to David and became his subjects. After that, the Arameans were no longer willing to help the Ammonites.

CHAPTER 20

The Capture of Rabbah

The following spring, the time of year when kings go to war, Joab led the Israelite army in successful attacks against the towns and villages of the Ammonites. In the process they laid siege to the city of Rabbah and destroyed it. But David had stayed behind in Jerusalem.

[2]When David arrived at Rabbah, he removed the crown from the king's head,* and it was placed on David's own head. The crown was made of gold and set with gems, and it weighed about seventy-five pounds.* David took a vast amount of plunder from the city. [3]He also made slaves of the people of Rabbah and forced them to labor with saws, picks, and axes.* That is how he dealt with the people of all the Ammonite cities. Then David and his army returned to Jerusalem.

Battles against the Philistines

[4]After this, war broke out with the Philistines at Gezer. As they fought, Sibbecai from Hushah killed Saph,* a descendant of the giants,* and so the Philistines were subdued. [5]During another battle with the Philistines, Elhanan son of Jair killed Lahmi, the brother of Goliath of Gath. The handle of Lahmi's spear was as thick as a weaver's beam! [6]In another battle with the Philistines at Gath, a huge man with six fingers on each hand and six toes on each foot—a descendant of the giants—[7]defied and taunted Israel. But he was killed by Jonathan, the son of David's brother Shimea. [8]These Philistines were descendants of the giants of Gath, but they were killed by David and his warriors.

CHAPTER 21

David Takes a Census

Satan rose up against Israel and caused David to take a census of the Israelites. [2]David gave these orders to Joab and his commanders: "Take a census of all the people in the land—from Beersheba in the south to Dan in the north—and bring me the totals so I may know how many there are."

[3]But Joab replied, "May the LORD increase the number of his people a hundred times over! But why, my lord, do you want to do this? Are they not all your servants? Why must you cause Israel to sin?"

[4]But the king insisted that Joab take the census, so Joab traveled throughout Israel to count the people. Then he returned to Jerusalem [5]and reported the number of people to David. There were 1,100,000 men of military age in Israel, and 470,000 in Judah. [6]But Joab did not include the tribes of Levi and Benjamin in the census because he was so distressed at what the king had made him do.

Judgment for David's Sin

[7]God was very displeased with the census, and he punished Israel for it. [8]Then David said to God, "I have sinned greatly and shouldn't have taken the census. Please forgive me for doing this foolish thing."

[9]Then the LORD spoke to Gad, David's seer. This was the message: [10]"Go

---

I DO NOT SHIRK my leadership responsibilities. (20:1)

I BELIEVE the Lord enabled David and his men to defeat the Philistine giants. (20:8)

I URGE close friends not to sin against the Lord. (21:3)

I BELIEVE God disciplines his people. (21:7)

20:2a Greek version and Latin Vulgate read *removed the crown of Milcom*; compare 1 Kgs 11:5. Milcom, also called Molech, was the god of the Ammonites.   20:2b Hebrew 1 *talent* [34 kilograms].   20:3 As in parallel text at 2 Sam 12:31; Hebrew reads *and saws.*   20:4a As in parallel text at 2 Sam 21:18; Hebrew reads *Sippai.* 20:4b Hebrew *descendant of the Rephaites*; also in 20:6, 8.

and say to David, 'This is what the LORD says: I will give you three choices. Choose one of these punishments, and I will do it.' "

¹¹So Gad came to David and said, "These are the choices the LORD has given you. ¹²You may choose three years of famine, three months of destruction by your enemies, or three days of severe plague as the angel of the LORD brings devastation throughout the land of Israel. Think this over and let me know what answer to give the LORD."

¹³"This is a desperate situation!" David replied to Gad. "But let me fall into the hands of the LORD, for his mercy is very great. Do not let me fall into human hands."

I RELY on God's mercy when I have sinned. (21:13)

¹⁴So the LORD sent a plague upon Israel, and seventy thousand people died as a result. ¹⁵And God sent an angel to destroy Jerusalem. But just as the angel was preparing to destroy it, the LORD relented and said to the death angel, "Stop! That is enough!" At that moment the angel of the LORD was standing by the threshing floor of Araunah* the Jebusite.

¹⁶David looked up and saw the angel of the LORD standing between heaven and earth with his sword drawn, stretched out over Jerusalem. So David and the leaders of Israel put on sackcloth to show their distress and fell down with their faces to the ground. ¹⁷And David said to God, "I am the one who called for the census! I am the one who has sinned and done wrong! But these people are innocent—what have they done? O LORD my God, let your anger fall against me and my family, but do not destroy your people."

I TAKE RESPONSIBILITY for my own sins. (21:17)

David Builds an Altar

¹⁸Then the angel of the LORD told Gad to instruct David to build an altar to the LORD at the threshing floor of Araunah the Jebusite. ¹⁹So David obeyed the instructions the LORD had given him through Gad. ²⁰Araunah, who was busy threshing wheat at the time, turned and saw the angel there. His four sons, who were with him, ran away and hid. ²¹When Araunah saw the king approaching, he left his threshing floor and bowed to the ground before David.

I OBEY the Lord's commands. (21:19)

²²David said to Araunah, "Let me buy this threshing floor from you at its full price. Then I will build an altar to the LORD there, so that he will stop the plague."

²³"Take it, my lord, and use it as you wish," Araunah said to David. "Here are oxen for the burnt offerings, and you can use the threshing tools for wood to build a fire on the altar. And take the wheat for the grain offering. I will give it all to you."

²⁴But the king replied to Araunah, "No, I insist on paying what it is worth. I cannot take what is yours and give it to the LORD. I will not offer a burnt offering that has cost me nothing!" ²⁵So David gave Araunah six hundred pieces of gold* in payment for the threshing floor. ²⁶David built an altar there to the LORD and sacrificed burnt offerings and peace offerings. And when David prayed, the LORD answered him by sending fire from heaven to burn up the offering on the altar. ²⁷Then the LORD spoke to the angel, who put the sword back into its sheath.

I DO NOT GIVE to God what has cost me nothing. (21:24)

²⁸When David saw that the LORD had answered his prayer, he offered sacrifices there at Araunah's threshing floor. ²⁹At that time, the Tabernacle of the LORD and the altar that Moses made in the wilderness were located at the hill of Gibeon. ³⁰But David was not able to go there to inquire of God, because he was terrified by the drawn sword of the angel of the LORD.

See Moses' profile (page 73) at Exodus 5:1.

CHAPTER 22

Then David said, "This will be the location for the Temple of the LORD God and the place of the altar for Israel's burnt offerings!"

21:15 As in parallel text at 2 Sam 24:16; Hebrew reads *Ornan*, another name for Araunah; also in 21:18-28.
21:25 Hebrew *600 shekels of gold*, about 15 pounds or 6.8 kilograms in weight.

Preparations for the Temple

²So David gave orders to call together the foreigners living in Israel, and he assigned them the task of preparing blocks of stone for building the Temple of God. ³David provided large amounts of iron for the nails that would be needed for the doors in the gates and for the clamps, and more bronze than they could ever weigh. ⁴He also provided innumerable cedar logs, for the men of Tyre and Sidon had brought vast amounts of cedar to David. ⁵David said, "My son Solomon is still young and inexperienced, and the Temple of the LORD must be a magnificent structure, famous and glorious throughout the world. So I will begin making preparations for it now." So David collected vast amounts of building materials before his death.

⁶Then David sent for his son Solomon and instructed him to build a Temple for the LORD, the God of Israel. ⁷"I wanted to build a Temple to honor the name of the LORD my God," David told him. ⁸"But the LORD said to me, 'You have killed many men in the great battles you have fought. And since you have shed so much blood before me, you will not be the one to build a Temple to honor my name. ⁹But you will have a son who will experience peace and rest. I will give him peace with his enemies in all the surrounding lands. His name will be Solomon,* and I will give peace and quiet to Israel during his reign. ¹⁰He is the one who will build a Temple to honor my name. He will be my son, and I will be his father. And I will establish the throne of his kingdom over Israel forever.'

¹¹"Now, my son, may the LORD be with you and give you success as you follow his instructions in building the Temple of the LORD your God. ¹²And may the LORD give you wisdom and understanding, that you may obey the law of the LORD your God as you rule over Israel. ¹³For if you carefully obey the laws and regulations that the LORD gave to Israel through Moses, you will be successful. Be strong and courageous; do not be afraid or lose heart!

¹⁴"I have worked hard to provide materials for building the Temple of the LORD—nearly four thousand tons of gold, nearly forty thousand tons of silver,* and so much iron and bronze that it cannot be weighed. I have also gathered lumber and stone for the walls, though you may need to add more. ¹⁵You have many skilled stonemasons and carpenters and craftsmen of every kind available to you. ¹⁶They are expert goldsmiths and silversmiths and workers of bronze and iron. Now begin the work, and may the LORD be with you!"

¹⁷Then David ordered all the leaders of Israel to assist Solomon in this project. ¹⁸"The LORD your God is with you," he declared. "He has given you peace with the surrounding nations. He has handed them over to me, and they are now subject to the LORD and his people. ¹⁹Now seek the LORD your God with all your heart. Build the sanctuary of the LORD God so that you can bring the Ark of the LORD's covenant and the holy vessels of God into the Temple built to honor the LORD's name."

CHAPTER 23

Duties of the Levites

When David was an old man, he appointed his son Solomon to be king over Israel. ²David summoned all the political leaders of Israel, together with the priests and Levites, for the coronation ceremony. ³All the Levites who were thirty years old or older were counted, and the total came to thirty-eight thousand. ⁴Then David said, "Twenty-four thousand of them will supervise the work at the Temple of the LORD. Six thousand are to serve as officials and judges. ⁵Four thousand will work as gatekeepers, and another four thousand will praise the LORD with the musical instruments I have made." ⁶Then David divided the Levites into divisions named after the clans descended from the three sons of Levi—Gershon, Kohath, and Merari.

I GIVE generously to the work of the Lord. (22:3)

I MAKE preparations to assist those who are younger to continue the work of the Lord. (22:5)

See Solomon's profile (page 753) at Proverbs 2:9.

I PRAY that my children will have the wisdom to obey and serve the Lord. (22:12)

See Moses' profile (page 73) at Exodus 5:1.

I ENLIST others to support and aid my children in the work of the Lord. (22:17)

I BELIEVE godly, capable individuals should be appointed to take responsibility for God's work. (23:4)

I BELIEVE godly, skilled individuals should be appointed to lead public musical worship. (23:5)

22:9 Solomon sounds like and is probably derived from the Hebrew word for "peace." 22:14 Hebrew *100,000 talents [3,400 metric tons] of gold, 1,000,000 talents [34,000 metric tons] of silver.*

The Gershonites

[7] The Gershonite family units were defined by their lines of descent from Libni* and Shimei, the sons of Gershon. [8] Three of the descendants of Libni were Jehiel (the family leader), Zetham, and Joel. [9] These were the leaders of the family of Libni.

Three of the descendants of Shimei were Shelomoth, Haziel, and Haran. [10] Four other descendants of Shimei were Jahath, Ziza,* Jeush, and Beriah. [11] Jahath was the family leader, and Ziza was next. Jeush and Beriah were counted as a single family because neither had many sons.

The Kohathites

[12] The descendants of Kohath included Amram, Izhar, Hebron, and Uzziel. [13] The sons of Amram were Aaron and Moses. Aaron and his descendants were set apart to dedicate the most holy things, to offer sacrifices in the LORD's presence, to serve the LORD, and to pronounce blessings in his name forever.

[14] As for Moses, the man of God, his sons were included with the tribe of Levi. [15] The sons of Moses were Gershom and Eliezer. [16] The descendants of Gershom included Shebuel, the family leader. [17] Eliezer had only one son, Rehabiah, the family leader. Rehabiah had numerous descendants. [18] The descendants of Izhar included Shelomith, the family leader. [19] The descendants of Hebron included Jeriah (the family leader), Amariah (the second), Jahaziel (the third), and Jekameam (the fourth). [20] The descendants of Uzziel included Micah (the family leader) and Isshiah (the second).

> I BELIEVE God set apart Aaron's descendants to serve the Lord in his presence. (23:13)
>
> *See the profiles for Aaron (page 107) and Moses (page 73) at Exodus 32:2 and Exodus 5:1.*

The Merarites

[21] The descendants of Merari included Mahli and Mushi.

The sons of Mahli were Eleazar and Kish. [22] Eleazar died with no sons, only daughters. His daughters married their cousins, the sons of Kish. [23] The three sons of Mushi were Mahli, Eder, and Jerimoth.

[24] These were the descendants of Levi by clans, the leaders of their family groups, registered carefully by name. Each had to be twenty years old or older to qualify for service in the house of the LORD. [25] For David said, "The LORD, the God of Israel, has given us peace, and he will always live in Jerusalem. [26] Now the Levites will no longer need to carry the Tabernacle and its utensils from place to place." [27] It was according to David's final instructions that all the Levites twenty years old or older were registered for service.

> I CAREFULLY OVERSEE those who serve the Lord under my direction. (23:24)

[28] The work of the Levites was to assist the priests, the descendants of Aaron, as they served at the house of the LORD. They also took care of the courtyards and side rooms, helped perform the ceremonies of purification, and served in many other ways in the house of God. [29] They were in charge of the sacred bread that was set out on the table, the choice flour for the grain offerings, the wafers made without yeast, the cakes cooked in olive oil, and the other mixed breads. They were also responsible to check all the weights and measures. [30] And each morning and evening they stood before the LORD to sing songs of thanks and praise to him. [31] They assisted with the burnt offerings that were presented to the LORD on Sabbath days, at new moon celebrations, and at all the appointed festivals. The proper number of Levites served in the LORD's presence at all times, following all the procedures they had been given.

> I BELIEVE the Lord made the Levites responsible for serving in his house of worship. (23:28)

[32] And so, under the supervision of the priests, the Levites watched over the Tabernacle and the Temple* and faithfully carried out their duties of service at the house of the LORD.

> I FAITHFULLY CARRY OUT my duties of service to the Lord. (23:32)

23:7 Hebrew *Ladan* (also in 23:8-9), another name for Libni; compare 6:17. 23:10 As in Greek version and Latin Vulgate (see also 23:11); Hebrew reads *Zina*. 23:32 Hebrew *the Tent of Meeting and the sanctuary*.

CHAPTER 24

Duties of the Priests

This is how Aaron's descendants, the priests, were divided into groups for service. The sons of Aaron were Nadab, Abihu, Eleazar, and Ithamar. ²But Nadab and Abihu died before their father did, and they had no sons. So only Eleazar and Ithamar were left to carry on as priests.

³With the help of Zadok, who was a descendant of Eleazar, and of Ahimelech, who was a descendant of Ithamar, David divided Aaron's descendants into groups according to their various duties. ⁴Eleazar's descendants were divided into sixteen groups and Ithamar's into eight, for there were more family leaders among the descendants of Eleazar.

⁵All tasks were assigned to the various groups by means of sacred lots so that no preference would be shown, for there were many qualified officials serving God in the sanctuary from among the descendants of both Eleazar and Ithamar. ⁶Shemaiah son of Nethanel, a Levite, acted as secretary and wrote down the names and assignments in the presence of the king, Zadok the priest, Ahimelech son of Abiathar, and the family leaders of the priests and Levites. The descendants of Eleazar and Ithamar took turns casting lots.

⁷ The first lot fell to Jehoiarib.
   The second lot fell to Jedaiah.
⁸ The third lot fell to Harim.
   The fourth lot fell to Seorim.
⁹ The fifth lot fell to Malkijah.
   The sixth lot fell to Mijamin.
¹⁰ The seventh lot fell to Hakkoz.
    The eighth lot fell to Abijah.
¹¹ The ninth lot fell to Jeshua.
    The tenth lot fell to Shecaniah.
¹² The eleventh lot fell to Eliashib.
    The twelfth lot fell to Jakim.
¹³ The thirteenth lot fell to Huppah.
    The fourteenth lot fell to Jeshebeab.
¹⁴ The fifteenth lot fell to Bilgah.
    The sixteenth lot fell to Immer.
¹⁵ The seventeenth lot fell to Hezir.
    The eighteenth lot fell to Happizzez.
¹⁶ The nineteenth lot fell to Pethahiah.
    The twentieth lot fell to Jehezkel.
¹⁷ The twenty-first lot fell to Jakin.
    The twenty-second lot fell to Gamul.
¹⁸ The twenty-third lot fell to Delaiah.
    The twenty-fourth lot fell to Maaziah.

¹⁹Each group carried out its duties in the house of the LORD according to the procedures established by their ancestor Aaron in obedience to the commands of the LORD, the God of Israel.

Family Leaders among the Levites

²⁰These were the other family leaders descended from Levi:

From the descendants of Amram, the leader was Shebuel.*
From the descendants of Shebuel, the leader was Jehdeiah.
²¹ From the descendants of Rehabiah, the leader was Isshiah.
²² From the descendants of Izhar, the leader was Shelomith.*
From the descendants of Shelomith, the leader was Jahath.

See Aaron's profile (page 107) at Exodus 32:2.

I DEMONSTRATE good organization skills in delegating responsibilities for service to the Lord. (24:3)

I USE fair methods to choose qualified people to serve the Lord. (24:5)

I KEEP good records of those who serve under me and their assignments. (24:6)

I FOLLOW proper procedures in serving the Lord and obeying his commands. (24:19)

24:20 Hebrew *Shubael* (also in 24:20b), a variant name for Shebuel; compare 23:16 and 26:24.   24:22 Hebrew *Shelomoth* (also in 24:22b), a variant name for Shelomith; compare 23:18.

23 From the descendants of Hebron, Jeriah was the leader,* Amariah was second-in-command, Jahaziel was third, and Jekameam was fourth.
24 From the descendants of Uzziel, the leader was Micah.
From the descendants of Micah, the leader was Shamir, 25along with Isshiah, the brother of Micah.
From the descendants of Isshiah, the leader was Zechariah.
26 From the descendants of Merari, the leaders were Mahli and Mushi.
From the descendants of Jaaziah, the leader was Beno.
27 From the descendants of Merari through Jaaziah, the leaders were Beno, Shoham, Zaccur, and Ibri.
28 From the descendants of Mahli, the leader was Eleazar, though he had no sons.
29 From the descendants of Kish, the leader was Jerahmeel.
30 From the descendants of Mushi, the leaders were Mahli, Eder, and Jerimoth.

These were the descendants of Levi in their various families. 31Like the descendants of Aaron, they were assigned to their duties by means of sacred lots, without regard to age or rank. It was done in the presence of King David, Zadok, Ahimelech, and the family leaders of the priests and the Levites.

I BELIEVE qualified individuals should be selected to serve the Lord without regard to age or rank. (24:31)

CHAPTER 25

Duties of the Musicians

David and the army commanders then appointed men from the families of Asaph, Heman, and Jeduthun to proclaim God's messages to the accompaniment of harps, lyres, and cymbals. Here is a list of their names and their work:

I GIVE priority to the public, musical proclamation of God's message. (25:1)

See Asaph's profile (page 687) at Psalm 73:28.

2From the sons of Asaph, there were Zaccur, Joseph, Nethaniah, and Asarelah. They worked under the direction of their father, Asaph, who proclaimed God's messages by the king's orders.
3Jeduthun had six sons: Gedaliah, Zeri, Jeshaiah, Shimei,* Hashabiah, and Mattithiah. They worked under the direction of their father, Jeduthun, who proclaimed God's messages to the accompaniment of the harp, offering thanks and praise to the LORD.
4Heman's sons were Bukkiah, Mattaniah, Uzziel, Shubael,* Jerimoth, Hananiah, Hanani, Eliathah, Geddalti, Romamti-ezer, Joshbekashah, Mallothi, Hothir, and Mahazioth. 5All these were the sons of Heman, the king's seer, for God had honored him with fourteen sons and three daughters.

6All these men were under the direction of their fathers as they made music at the house of the LORD. Their responsibilities included the playing of cymbals, lyres, and harps at the house of God. Asaph, Jeduthun, and Heman reported directly to the king. 7 They and their families were all trained in making music before the LORD, and each of them—288 in all—was an accomplished musician. 8 The musicians were appointed to their particular term of service by means of sacred lots, without regard to whether they were young or old, teacher or student.

I LONG to see my children serve the Lord faithfully. (25:6)

I USE my musical training and talents to make music before the Lord. (25:7)

I BELIEVE qualified individuals should be selected to serve the Lord without regard to age or rank. (25:8)

See Joseph's profile (page 51) at Genesis 39:2.

9 The first lot fell to Joseph of the Asaph clan and twelve of his sons and relatives.*
The second lot fell to Gedaliah and twelve of his sons and relatives.
10 The third lot fell to Zaccur and twelve of his sons and relatives.
11 The fourth lot fell to Zeri* and twelve of his sons and relatives.

24:23 Hebrew *From the descendants of Jeriah;* compare 23:19. 25:3 As in one Hebrew manuscript and some Greek manuscripts (see also 25:17); most Hebrew manuscripts lack *Shimei.* 25:4 Hebrew *Shebuel,* a variant name for Shubael; compare 25:20. 25:9 As in Greek version; Hebrew lacks *and twelve of his sons and relatives.* 25:11 Hebrew *Izri,* a variant name for Zeri; compare 25:3.

¹² The fifth lot fell to Nethaniah and twelve of his sons and relatives.

¹³ The sixth lot fell to Bukkiah and twelve of his sons and relatives.

¹⁴ The seventh lot fell to Asarelah* and twelve of his sons and relatives.

¹⁵ The eighth lot fell to Jeshaiah and twelve of his sons and relatives.

¹⁶ The ninth lot fell to Mattaniah and twelve of his sons and relatives.

¹⁷ The tenth lot fell to Shimei and twelve of his sons and relatives.

¹⁸ The eleventh lot fell to Uzziel* and twelve of his sons and relatives.

¹⁹ The twelfth lot fell to Hashabiah and twelve of his sons and relatives.

²⁰ The thirteenth lot fell to Shubael and twelve of his sons and relatives.

²¹ The fourteenth lot fell to Mattithiah and twelve of his sons and relatives.

²² The fifteenth lot fell to Jerimoth* and twelve of his sons and relatives.

²³ The sixteenth lot fell to Hananiah and twelve of his sons and relatives.

²⁴ The seventeenth lot fell to Joshbekashah* and twelve of his sons and relatives.

²⁵ The eighteenth lot fell to Hanani and twelve of his sons and relatives.

²⁶ The nineteenth lot fell to Mallothi and twelve of his sons and relatives.

²⁷ The twentieth lot fell to Eliathah and twelve of his sons and relatives.

²⁸ The twenty-first lot fell to Hothir and twelve of his sons and relatives.

²⁹ The twenty-second lot fell to Geddalti* and twelve of his sons and relatives.

³⁰ The twenty-third lot fell to Mahazioth and twelve of his sons and relatives.

³¹ The twenty-fourth lot fell to Romamti-ezer and twelve of his sons and relatives.

CHAPTER 26

Duties of the Gatekeepers

These are the divisions of the gatekeepers:

From the Korahites, there was Meshelemiah son of Kore, of the family of Asaph. ²The sons of Meshelemiah were Zechariah (the oldest), Jediael (the second), Zebadiah (the third), Jathniel (the fourth), ³Elam (the fifth), Jehohanan (the sixth), and Eliehoenai (the seventh).

⁴The sons of Obed-edom, also gatekeepers, were Shemaiah (the oldest), Jehozabad (the second), Joah (the third), Sacar (the fourth), Nethanel (the fifth), ⁵Ammiel (the sixth), Issachar (the seventh), and Peullethai (the eighth). God had richly blessed Obed-edom.

⁶Obed-edom's son Shemaiah had sons with great ability who earned positions of great authority in the clan. ⁷Their names were Othni, Rephael, Obed, and Elzabad. Their relatives, Elihu and Semakiah, were also very capable men.

⁸All of these descendants of Obed-edom, including their sons and grandsons—sixty-two of them in all—were very capable men, well qualified for their work.

⁹Meshelemiah's eighteen sons and relatives were also very capable men.

¹⁰Hosah, of the Merari clan, appointed Shimri as the leader among his sons, though he was not the oldest. ¹¹His other sons included Hilkiah (the second), Tebaliah (the third), and Zechariah (the fourth). Hosah's sons and relatives, who served as gatekeepers, numbered thirteen in all.

¹²These divisions of the gatekeepers were named for their family leaders, and like the other Levites, they served at the house of the LORD. ¹³They were assigned

> I LONG to see my children serve the Lord faithfully. (26:6)

> I BELIEVE qualified individuals should be selected to serve the Lord without regard to age or training. (26:13)

25:14 Hebrew *Jesharelah*, a variant name for Asarelah; compare 25:2.   25:18 Hebrew *Azarel*, a variant name for Uzziel; compare 25:4.   25:22 Hebrew *Jeremoth*, a variant name for Jerimoth; compare 25:4.   25:24 Hebrew *Joshbekasha*, a variant name for Joshbekashah; compare 25:4.   25:29 Hebrew *Giddalti*, a variant name for Geddalti; compare 25:4.

by families for guard duty at the various gates, without regard to age or training, for it was all decided by means of sacred lots.

[14] The responsibility for the east gate went to Meshelemiah* and his group. The north gate was assigned to his son Zechariah, a man of unusual wisdom. [15] The south gate went to Obed-edom, and his sons were put in charge of the storehouses. [16] Shuppim and Hosah were assigned the west gate and the gateway leading up to the Temple.* Guard duties were divided evenly. [17] Six Levites were assigned each day to the east gate, four to the north gate, four to the south gate, and two to each of the storehouses. [18] Six were assigned each day to the west gate, four to the gateway leading up to the Temple, and two to the courtyard.*

[19] These were the divisions of the gatekeepers from the clans of Korah and Merari.

I DESIRE to be a wise person. (26:14)

Treasurers and Other Officials

[20] Other Levites, led by Ahijah, were in charge of the treasuries of the house of God and the storerooms. [21] From the family of Libni* in the clan of Gershon, Jehiel* was the leader. [22] The sons of Jehiel, Zetham and his brother Joel, were in charge of the treasuries of the house of the LORD.

[23] These are the leaders that descended from Amram, Izhar, Hebron, and Uzziel:

[24] From the clan of Amram, Shebuel was a descendant of Gershom son of Moses. He was the chief officer of the treasuries. [25] His relatives through Eliezer were Rehabiah, Jeshaiah, Joram, Zicri, and Shelomoth.

See Moses' profile (page 73) at Exodus 5:1.

[26] Shelomoth and his relatives were in charge of the treasuries that held all the things dedicated to the LORD by King David, the family leaders, and the generals and captains and other officers of the army. [27] These men had dedicated some of the plunder they had gained in battle to maintain the house of the LORD. [28] Shelomoth and his relatives also cared for the items dedicated to the LORD by Samuel the seer, Saul son of Kish, Abner son of Ner, and Joab son of Zeruiah. All the other dedicated items were in their care, too.

I TAKE GOOD CARE OF the offerings entrusted to me. (26:28)

[29] From the clan of Izhar came Kenaniah. He and his sons were appointed to serve as public administrators and judges throughout Israel.

[30] From the clan of Hebron came Hashabiah. He and his relatives—seventeen hundred capable men—were put in charge of the Israelite lands west of the Jordan River. They were responsible for all matters related to the things of the LORD and the service of the king in that area.

See the profiles for Samuel (page 323) and Saul (page 339) at 1 Samuel 3:1 and 1 Samuel 18:9.

[31] Also from the clan of Hebron came Jeriah,* who was the leader of the Hebronites according to the genealogical records. (In the fortieth year of David's reign, a search was made in the records, and capable men from the clan of Hebron were found at Jazer in the land of Gilead.) [32] There were twenty-seven hundred capable men among the relatives of Jeriah. King David sent them to the east side of the Jordan River and put them in charge of the tribes of Reuben and Gad and the half-tribe of Manasseh. They were responsible for all matters related to the things of God and the service of the king.

CHAPTER 27

Military Commanders and Divisions

This is the list of Israelite generals and captains, and their officers, who served the king by supervising the army divisions that were on duty each month of

I DIVIDE responsibilities among capable, faithful people. (27:1)

26:14 Hebrew *Shelemiah,* a variant name for Meshelemiah; compare 26:2. **26:16** Or *the gate of Shalleketh on the upper road* (also in 26:18). The meaning of the Hebrew is uncertain. **26:18** Or *the colonnade.* The meaning of the Hebrew is uncertain. **26:21a** Hebrew *Ladan,* another name for Libni; compare 6:17. **26:21b** Hebrew *Jehieli* (also in 26:22), a variant name for Jehiel; compare 23:8. **26:31** Hebrew *Jerijah,* a variant name for Jeriah; compare 23:19.

the year. Each division served for one month and had twenty-four thousand troops.

²Jashobeam son of Zabdiel was commander of the first division, which was on duty during the first month. There were twenty-four thousand troops in his division. ³He was a descendant of Perez and was in charge of all the army officers for the first month.

⁴Dodai, a descendant of Ahoah, was commander of the second division, which was on duty during the second month. There were twenty-four thousand troops in his division, and Mikloth was his chief officer.

⁵Benaiah son of Jehoiada the priest was commander of the third division, which was on duty during the third month. There were twenty-four thousand troops in his division. ⁶This was the Benaiah who commanded David's elite military group known as the Thirty. His son Ammizabad was his chief officer.

⁷Asahel, the brother of Joab, was commander of the fourth division, which was on duty during the fourth month. There were twenty-four thousand troops in his division. Asahel was succeeded by his son Zebadiah.

⁸Shammah* the Izrahite was commander of the fifth division, which was on duty during the fifth month. There were twenty-four thousand troops in his division.

⁹Ira son of Ikkesh from Tekoa was commander of the sixth division, which was on duty during the sixth month. There were twenty-four thousand troops in his division.

¹⁰Helez, a descendant of Ephraim from Pelon, was commander of the seventh division, which was on duty during the seventh month. There were twenty-four thousand troops in his division.

¹¹Sibbecai, a descendant of Zerah from Hushah, was commander of the eighth division, which was on duty during the eighth month. There were twenty-four thousand troops in his division.

¹²Abiezer from Anathoth in the territory of Benjamin was commander of the ninth division, which was on duty during the ninth month. There were twenty-four thousand troops in his division.

¹³Maharai, a descendant of Zerah from Netophah, was commander of the tenth division, which was on duty during the tenth month. There were twenty-four thousand troops in his division.

¹⁴Benaiah from Pirathon in Ephraim was commander of the eleventh division, which was on duty during the eleventh month. There were twenty-four thousand troops in his division.

¹⁵Heled,* a descendant of Othniel from Netophah, was commander of the twelfth division, which was on duty during the twelfth month. There were twenty-four thousand troops in his division.

If something in this Bible helps you experience a closer walk with God, why not share it with others?

Leaders of the Tribes

¹⁶The following were the tribes of Israel and their leaders:

Tribe	Leader
Reuben	Eliezer son of Zicri
Simeon	Shephatiah son of Maacah
¹⁷ Levi	Hashabiah son of Kemuel
Aaron (the priests)	Zadok
¹⁸ Judah	Elihu (a brother of David)
Issachar	Omri son of Michael
¹⁹ Zebulun	Ishmaiah son of Obadiah
Naphtali	Jeremoth son of Azriel

See Aaron's profile (page 107) at Exodus 32:2.

27:8 Hebrew *Shamhuth*, another name for Shammah; compare 11:27 and 2 Sam 23:25. 27:15 Hebrew *Heldai*, a variant name for Heled; compare 11:30 and 2 Sam 23:29.

²⁰ Ephraim . . . . Hoshea son of Azaziah
Manasseh (west). . . . . Joel son of Pedaiah
²¹ Manasseh (east*) . . . . Iddo son of Zechariah
Benjamin . . . . Jaasiel son of Abner
²² Dan . . . . Azarel son of Jeroham

These were the leaders of the tribes of Israel.

²³When David took his census, he did not count those who were younger than twenty years of age, because the LORD had promised to make the Israelites as numerous as the stars in heaven. ²⁴Joab began the census but never finished it because the anger of God broke out against Israel. The final total was never recorded in King David's official records.

Officials of David's Kingdom
²⁵Azmaveth son of Adiel was in charge of the palace treasuries.
Jonathan son of Uzziah was in charge of the regional treasuries throughout the towns, villages, and fortresses of Israel.
²⁶Ezri son of Kelub was in charge of the field workers who farmed the king's lands.
²⁷Shimei from Ramah was in charge of the king's vineyards.
Zabdi from Shepham was responsible for the grapes and the supplies of wine.
²⁸Baal-hanan from Geder was in charge of the king's olive groves and sycamore-fig trees in the foothills of Judah.*
Joash was responsible for the supplies of olive oil.
²⁹Shitrai from Sharon was in charge of the cattle on the Sharon Plain.
Shaphat son of Adlai was responsible for the cattle in the valleys.
³⁰Obil the Ishmaelite was in charge of the camels.
Jehdeiah from Meronoth was in charge of the donkeys.
³¹Jaziz the Hagrite was in charge of the king's sheep.
All these officials were overseers of King David's property.

³²Jonathan, David's uncle, was a wise counselor to the king, a man of great insight, and a scribe. Jehiel the Hacmonite was responsible to teach the king's sons. ³³Ahithophel was the royal adviser. Hushai the Arkite was the king's friend. ³⁴Ahithophel was succeeded by Jehoiada son of Benaiah and by Abiathar. Joab was commander of the Israelite army.

CHAPTER 28

David's Instructions to Solomon
David summoned all his officials to Jerusalem—the leaders of the tribes, the commanders of the twelve army divisions, the other generals and captains, the overseers of the royal property and livestock, the palace officials, the mighty men, and all the other warriors in the kingdom. ²David rose and stood before them and addressed them as follows: "My brothers and my people! It was my desire to build a temple where the Ark of the LORD's covenant, God's footstool, could rest permanently. I made the necessary preparations for building it, ³but God said to me, 'You must not build a temple to honor my name, for you are a warrior and have shed much blood.'

⁴"Yet the LORD, the God of Israel, has chosen me from among all my father's family to be king over Israel forever. For he has chosen the tribe of Judah to rule, and from among the families of Judah, he chose my father's family. And from among my father's sons, the LORD was pleased to make me king over all Israel. ⁵And from among my sons—for the LORD has given me many children—he chose Solomon to succeed me on the throne of his

I BELIEVE the Lord's promises. (27:23)

I GIVE specific responsibilities to the individuals who serve with me. (27:25)

I VALUE wise counsel from godly individuals. (27:32)

I VALUE good friends. (27:33)

I AM WILLING to accept God's will when he does not allow me to serve him in the way I desire. (28:3)

See Solomon's profile (page 753) at Proverbs 2:9.

27:21 Hebrew *in Gilead.*   27:28 Hebrew *the Shephelah.*

kingdom of Israel. [6]He said to me, 'Your son Solomon will build my Temple and its courtyards, for I have chosen him as my son, and I will be his father. [7]And if he continues to obey my commands and regulations as he does now, I will make his kingdom last forever.' [8]So now, with God as our witness, I give you this charge for all Israel, the LORD's assembly: Be careful to obey all the commands of the LORD your God, so that you may possess this good land and leave it to your children as a permanent inheritance.

I URGE others to enjoy the blessings of obeying God's commands. (28:8)

I URGE my children to know God and to worship and serve him wholeheartedly. (28:9)

[9]"And Solomon, my son, get to know the God of your ancestors. Worship and serve him with your whole heart and with a willing mind. For the LORD sees every heart and understands and knows every plan and thought. If you seek him, you will find him. But if you forsake him, he will reject you forever. [10]So take this seriously. The LORD has chosen you to build a Temple as his sanctuary. Be strong, and do the work."

[11]Then David gave Solomon the plans for the Temple and its surroundings, including the treasuries, the upstairs rooms, the inner rooms, and the inner sanctuary where the Ark's cover—the place of atonement—would be kept. [12]David also gave Solomon all the plans he had in mind* for the courtyards of the LORD's Temple, the outside rooms, the treasuries of God's Temple, and the rooms for the dedicated gifts. [13]The king also gave Solomon the instructions concerning the work of the various divisions of priests and Levites in the Temple of the LORD. And he gave specifications for the items in the LORD's Temple which were to be used for worship and sacrifice.

[14]David gave instructions regarding how much gold and silver should be used to make the necessary items. [15]He told Solomon the amount of gold needed for the gold lampstands and lamps, and the amount of silver for the silver lampstands and lamps, depending on how each would be used. [16]He designated the amount of gold for the table on which the Bread of the Presence would be placed and the amount of silver for other tables.

[17]David also designated the amount of gold for the solid gold meat hooks used to handle the sacrificial meat and for the basins, pitchers, and dishes, as well as the amount of silver for every dish. [18]Finally, he designated the amount of refined gold for the altar of incense and for the gold cherubim, whose wings were stretched out over the Ark of the LORD's covenant. [19]"Every part of this plan," David told Solomon, "was given to me in writing from the hand of the LORD.*"

I ENCOURAGE others to trust the Lord and do the work God has given them. (28:20)

[20]Then David continued, "Be strong and courageous, and do the work. Don't be afraid or discouraged by the size of the task, for the LORD God, my God, is with you. He will not fail you or forsake you. He will see to it that all the work related to the Temple of the LORD is finished correctly. [21]The various divisions of priests and Levites will serve in the Temple of God. Others with skills of every kind will volunteer, and the leaders and the entire nation are at your command."

CHAPTER 29

Gifts for Building the Temple

Then King David turned to the entire assembly and said, "My son Solomon, whom God has chosen to be the next king of Israel, is still young and inexperienced. The work ahead of him is enormous, for the Temple he will build is not just another building—it is for the LORD God himself! [2]Using every resource at my command, I have gathered as much as I could for building the Temple of my God. Now there is enough gold, silver, bronze, iron, and wood, as well as great quantities of onyx, other precious stones, costly jewels, and all kinds of fine stone and marble. [3]And now because of my devotion to the Temple of my God, I am giving all of my own private treasures of gold

28:12 Or the plans of the spirit that was with him.   28:19 Or was written under the direction of the LORD.

and silver to help in the construction. This is in addition to the building materials I have already collected for his holy Temple. [4]I am donating more than 112 tons of gold* from Ophir and over 262 tons of refined silver* to be used for overlaying the walls of the buildings [5]and for the other gold and silver work to be done by the craftsmen. Now then, who will follow my example? Who is willing to give offerings to the LORD today?"

[6]Then the family leaders, the leaders of the tribes of Israel, the generals and captains of the army, and the king's administrative officers all gave willingly. [7]For the construction of the Temple of God, they gave almost 188 tons of gold,* 10,000 gold coins,* about 375 tons of silver,* about 675 tons of bronze,* and about 3,750 tons of iron.* [8]They also contributed numerous precious stones, which were deposited in the treasury of the house of the LORD under the care of Jehiel, a descendant of Gershon. [9]The people rejoiced over the offerings, for they had given freely and wholeheartedly to the LORD, and King David was filled with joy.

David's Prayer of Praise
[10]Then David praised the LORD in the presence of the whole assembly: "O LORD, the God of our ancestor Israel,* may you be praised forever and ever! [11]Yours, O LORD, is the greatness, the power, the glory, the victory, and the majesty. Everything in the heavens and on earth is yours, O LORD, and this is your kingdom. We adore you as the one who is over all things. [12]Riches and honor come from you alone, for you rule over everything. Power and might are in your hand, and it is at your discretion that people are made great and given strength.

[13]"O our God, we thank you and praise your glorious name! [14]But who am I, and who are my people, that we could give anything to you? Everything we have has come from you, and we give you only what you have already given us! [15]We are here for only a moment, visitors and strangers in the land as our ancestors were before us. Our days on earth are like a shadow, gone so soon without a trace.

[16]"O LORD our God, even these materials that we have gathered to build a Temple to honor your holy name come from you! It all belongs to you! [17]I know, my God, that you examine our hearts and rejoice when you find integrity there. You know I have done all this with good motives, and I have watched your people offer their gifts willingly and joyously.

[18]"O LORD, the God of our ancestors Abraham, Isaac, and Israel, make your people always want to obey you. See to it that their love for you never changes. [19]Give my son Solomon the wholehearted desire to obey all your commands, decrees, and principles, and to build this Temple, for which I have made all these preparations."

[20]Then David said to the whole assembly, "Give praise to the LORD your God!" And the entire assembly praised the LORD, the God of their ancestors, and they bowed low and knelt before the LORD and the king.

Solomon Named as King
[21]The next day they brought a thousand bulls, a thousand rams, and a thousand male lambs as burnt offerings to the LORD. They also brought drink offerings and many other sacrifices on behalf of Israel. [22]They feasted and drank in the LORD's presence with great joy that day.

And again they crowned David's son Solomon as their new king. They anointed him before the LORD as their leader, and they anointed Zadok as their priest. [23]So Solomon took the throne of the LORD in place of his father,

I CHALLENGE others to join me in giving generously to the work of the Lord (2 Corinthians 9:5-13). (29:5)

I PRAISE God publicly for his greatness, power, glory, and majesty. (29:11)

I BELIEVE the Lord rejoices when his people give with willing, joyful hearts. (29:17)

See the profiles for Abraham (page 19), Isaac (page 31), and Israel (Jacob) (page 43) at Genesis 15:6, Genesis 25:19, and Genesis 32:9.

I PRAY for my children to obey the Lord wholeheartedly. (29:19)

I REJOICE in God's presence when godly people are put in leadership. (29:22)

29:4a Hebrew 3,000 talents [102 metric tons] of gold. 29:4b Hebrew 7,000 talents [238 metric tons] of silver. 29:7a Hebrew 5,000 talents [170 metric tons] of gold. 29:7b Hebrew 10,000 darics [a Persian coin] of gold, about 185 pounds or 84 kilograms in weight. 29:7c Hebrew 10,000 talents [340 metric tons] of silver. 29:7d Hebrew 18,000 talents [612 metric tons] of bronze. 29:7e Hebrew 100,000 talents [3,400 metric tons] of iron. 29:10 Israel is the name that God gave to Jacob.

David, and he prospered greatly, and all Israel obeyed him. ²⁴All the royal officials, the army commanders, and the sons of King David pledged their loyalty to King Solomon. ²⁵And the LORD exalted Solomon so the entire nation of Israel stood in awe of him, and he gave Solomon even greater wealth and honor than his father.

Summary of David's Reign

²⁶So David son of Jesse reigned over all Israel. ²⁷He ruled Israel for forty years in all, seven years from Hebron and thirty-three years from Jerusalem. ²⁸He died at a ripe old age, having enjoyed long life, wealth, and honor. Then his son Solomon ruled in his place. ²⁹All the events of King David's reign, from beginning to end, are written in *The Record of Samuel the Seer*, *The Record of Nathan the Prophet*, and *The Record of Gad the Seer*. ³⁰These accounts include the mighty deeds of his reign and everything that happened to him and to Israel and to all the surrounding kingdoms.

See Samuel's profile (page 323) at 1 Samuel 3:1.

2 CHRONICLES

THIS NINTH BOOK of Old Testament history ends with *destruction*.

Over the course of the four hundred years of history covered in this book, the nation of Israel rises to its greatest glory, only to rebel against the Lord, divide into two kingdoms, grow increasingly pagan, and eventually be destroyed by foreign powers. Unlike 1 and 2 Kings, however, 2 Chronicles focuses almost exclusively on the Davidic dynasty's rise and fall.

After becoming king, Solomon brings about a season of unparalleled prosperity for the nation (1:1-17). Solomon demonstrates his devotion to the Lord by spending vast sums of wealth to build the Temple and dedicate it (2:1-5:14). After the glory of the Lord fills the Temple, Solomon prays a marvelous prayer of dedication. The Lord rewards Solomon, but also warns him against ever rebelling (6:1-7:22). Solomon continues to strengthen the nation and gains international fame for his wisdom and wealth (8:1-9:31).

Soon after Solomon's death, however, the nation splits into two kingdoms. A series of alternately wicked and good kings begin to rule the southern kingdom of Judah.

Some kings actively lead the kingdom into gross paganism. Other kings revive the worship of the Lord, although most forsake the Lord later in life. The last few kings of Judah actually serve as puppets of Babylon. For nearly twenty years the Babylonian empire rules over the rebellious kingdom—and in the end crushes it (10:1-36:19).

Yet Judah isn't completely erased from world history (36:20-23).

Famous passages in 2 Chronicles include
- The glory of the Lord fills the Temple (5:13-6:2; 7:1-3)
- "If my people who are called by my name will humble themselves . . ." (7:14)
- The Queen of Sheba visits Solomon (9:1-12)
- The nation splits shortly after Solomon's death (10:1-19)
- "The LORD" will stay with you as long as you stay with him!" (15:2)
- "The eyes of the LORD search the whole earth" (16:9)
- King Jehoshaphat's faith saves the nation from destruction (20:1-30)
- The Lord thwarts Assyria's attempts to crush Judah (32:1-22)
- King Manasseh refuses to repent until he's defeated (33:1-13)
- King Josiah leads Judah back the Lord, but it's too late (34:1-35:19)
- Egypt attacks and rules over Judah (35:20-36:4)
- Babylon attacks Judah, overthrows the kingdom, and rules over it (36:5-10)
- Judah rebels against Babylon, only to be destroyed (36:11-19)

CHAPTER 1

Solomon Asks for Wisdom

See the profiles for
Solomon (page 753)
and David (page 629) at
Proverbs 2:9 and Psalm
3:1.

See Moses' profile (page
73) at Exodus 5:1.

Solomon, the son of King David, now took firm control of the kingdom, for the LORD his God was with him and made him very powerful. ²He called together all Israel—the generals and captains of the army, the judges, and all the political and clan leaders. ³Then Solomon led the entire assembly to the hill at Gibeon where God's Tabernacle* was located. This was the Tabernacle that Moses, the LORD's servant, had constructed in the wilderness. ⁴David had already moved the Ark of God from Kiriath-jearim to the special tent he had prepared for it in Jerusalem. ⁵But the bronze altar made by Bezalel son of Uri and grandson of Hur was still at Gibeon in front of the Tabernacle of the LORD. So Solomon and the people gathered in front of it to consult the LORD. ⁶There in front of the Tabernacle, Solomon went up to the bronze altar in the LORD's presence and sacrificed a thousand burnt offerings on it.

⁷That night God appeared to Solomon in a dream and said, "What do you want? Ask, and I will give it to you!"

I THANK God for his
faithfulness and
kindness. (1:8)

I ASK God for wisdom
to lead his people
properly. (1:10)

I DESIRE to help God's
people much more
than I want wealth,
honor, or power. (1:11)

⁸Solomon replied to God, "You have been so faithful and kind to my father, David, and now you have made me king in his place. ⁹Now, LORD God, please keep your promise to David my father, for you have made me king over a people as numerous as the dust of the earth! ¹⁰Give me wisdom and knowledge to rule them properly, for who is able to govern this great nation of yours?"

¹¹God said to Solomon, "Because your greatest desire is to help your people, and you did not ask for personal wealth and honor or the death of your enemies or even a long life, but rather you asked for wisdom and knowledge to properly govern my people, ¹²I will certainly give you the wisdom and knowledge you requested. And I will also give you riches, wealth, and honor such as no other king has ever had before you or will ever have again!" ¹³Then Solomon returned to Jerusalem from the Tabernacle at the hill of Gibeon, and he reigned over Israel.

¹⁴Solomon built up a huge military force, which included fourteen hundred chariots and twelve thousand horses.* He stationed many of them in the chariot cities, and some near him in Jerusalem. ¹⁵During Solomon's reign, silver and gold were as plentiful in Jerusalem as stones. And valuable cedarwood was

I OBEY the Lord's
commands carefully
(see Deuteronomy
17:16). (1:16)

as common as the sycamore wood that grows in the foothills of Judah.* ¹⁶Solomon's horses were imported from Egypt* and from Cilicia*; the king's traders acquired them from Cilicia at the standard price. ¹⁷At that time, Egyptian chariots delivered to Jerusalem could be purchased for 600 pieces of silver,* and horses could be bought for 150 pieces of silver.* Many of these were then resold to the kings of the Hittites and the kings of Aram.

CHAPTER 2

Preparations for Building the Temple

Solomon now decided that the time had come to build a Temple for the LORD and a royal palace for himself. ²He enlisted a force of 70,000 common laborers, 80,000 stonecutters in the hill country, and 3,600 foremen. ³Solomon also sent this message to King Hiram* at Tyre:

I FULFILL the
responsibilities given
to me by God and
others. (2:1)

See David's profile
(page 629) at Psalm 3:1.

I PLACE a high priority
on honoring the name
of the Lord. (2:4)

"Send me cedar logs like the ones that were supplied to my father, David, when he was building his palace. ⁴I am about to build a Temple to honor the name of the LORD my God. It will be a place set apart to burn incense and sweet spices before him, to display the special sacrificial bread, and to sacrifice burnt offerings each morning and evening, on the Sabbaths, at

1:3 Hebrew *Tent of Meeting;* also in 1:6, 13.　1:14 Or *12,000 charioteers.*　1:15 Hebrew *the Shephelah.*
1:16a Possibly *Muzur,* a district near Cilicia; also in 1:17.　1:16b Hebrew *Kue,* probably another name for Cilicia.
1:17a Hebrew *600 shekels of silver,* about 15 pounds or 6.8 kilograms in weight.　1:17b Hebrew *150 shekels,*
about 3.8 pounds or 1.7 kilograms in weight.　2:3 Hebrew *Huram,* a variant name for Hiram; also in 2:11, 12.

new moon celebrations, and at the other appointed festivals of the LORD our God. He has commanded Israel to do these things forever.

⁵"This will be a magnificent Temple because our God is an awesome God, greater than any other. ⁶But who can really build him a worthy home? Not even the highest heavens can contain him! So who am I to consider building a Temple for him, except as a place to burn sacrifices to him?

⁷"So send me a master craftsman who can work with gold, silver, bronze, and iron; someone who is expert at dyeing purple, scarlet, and blue cloth; and a skilled engraver who can work with the craftsmen of Judah and Jerusalem who were selected by my father, David. ⁸Also send me cedar, cypress, and almug* logs from Lebanon, for I know that your men are without equal at cutting timber. I will send my men to help them. ⁹An immense amount of timber will be needed, for the Temple I am going to build will be very large and magnificent. ¹⁰I will pay your men 100,000 bushels of crushed wheat, 100,000 bushels of barley,* 110,000 gallons of wine, and 110,000 gallons of olive oil.*"

¹¹King Hiram sent this letter of reply to Solomon:

"It is because the LORD loves his people that he has made you their king! ¹²Blessed be the LORD, the God of Israel, who made the heavens and the earth! He has given David a wise son, gifted with skill and understanding, who will build a Temple for the LORD and a royal palace for himself.

¹³"I am sending you a master craftsman named Huram-abi. He is a brilliant man, ¹⁴the son of a woman from Dan in Israel; his father is from Tyre. He is skillful at making things from gold, silver, bronze, and iron. He also knows all about stonework, carpentry, and weaving. He is an expert in dyeing purple, blue, and scarlet cloth and in working with linen. He is also an engraver and can follow any design given to him. He will work with your craftsmen and those appointed by my lord David, your father.

¹⁵"Send along the wheat, barley, olive oil, and wine that you mentioned. ¹⁶We will cut whatever timber you need from the Lebanon mountains and will float the logs in rafts down the coast of the Mediterranean Sea to Joppa. From there you can transport the logs up to Jerusalem."

¹⁷Solomon took a census of all foreigners in the land of Israel, like the census his father had taken, and he counted 153,600. ¹⁸He enlisted 70,000 of them as common laborers, 80,000 as stonecutters in the hill country, and 3,600 as foremen.

CHAPTER 3
Solomon Builds the Temple
So Solomon began to build the Temple of the LORD in Jerusalem on Mount Moriah, where the LORD had appeared to Solomon's father, King David. The Temple was built on the threshing floor of Araunah* the Jebusite, the site that David had selected. ²The construction began in midspring,* during the fourth year of Solomon's reign.

³The foundation for the Temple of God was ninety feet long and thirty feet wide.* ⁴The foyer at the front of the Temple was thirty feet wide, running across

I BELIEVE the Lord is an awesome God. (2:5)

I PAY a fair amount for the goods I purchase for the Lord's work. (2:10)

I FOLLOW God's instructions regarding how to serve him. (3:1)

See David's profile (page 629) at Psalm 3:1.

2:8 Hebrew *algum,* a variant name for almug; compare 9:10-11 and parallel text at 1 Kgs 10:11-12.
2:10a Hebrew *20,000 cors* [3,640 kiloliters] *of crushed wheat, 20,000 cors of barley.*   2:10b Hebrew *20,000 baths* [420 kiloliters] *of wine, and 20,000 baths of olive oil.*   3:1 Hebrew reads *Ornan,* another name for Araunah; compare 2 Sam 24:16.   3:2 Hebrew *on the second day of the second month.* This day of the Hebrew lunar calendar occurs in April or early May.   3:3 Hebrew *60 cubits* [27 meters] *long and 20 cubits* [9 meters] *wide.* In this chapter, the distance measures are calculated from the Hebrew cubit at a ratio of 18 inches or 45 centimeters per cubit.

the entire width of the Temple. The inner walls of the foyer and the ceiling were overlaid with pure gold. The roof of the foyer was thirty feet* high.

⁵The main room of the Temple was paneled with cypress wood, overlaid with pure gold, and decorated with carvings of palm trees and chains. ⁶The walls of the Temple were decorated with beautiful jewels and with pure gold from the land of Parvaim. ⁷All the walls, beams, doors, and thresholds throughout the Temple were overlaid with gold, and figures of cherubim were carved on the walls.

I PURSUE excellence and beauty in all I do for the Lord. (3:5)

⁸The Most Holy Place was thirty feet wide, corresponding to the width of the Temple, and it was also thirty feet deep. Its interior was overlaid with about twenty-three tons* of pure gold. ⁹They used gold nails that weighed about twenty ounces* each. The walls of the upper rooms were also overlaid with pure gold.

¹⁰Solomon made two figures shaped like cherubim and overlaid them with gold. These were placed in the Most Holy Place. ¹¹The total wingspan of the two cherubim standing side by side was 30 feet. One wing of the first figure was 7¹/₂ feet long, and it touched the Temple wall. The other wing, also 7¹/₂ feet long, touched one of the wings of the second figure. ¹²In the same way, the second figure had one wing 7¹/₂ feet long that touched the opposite wall. The other wing, also 7¹/₂ feet long, touched the wing of the first figure. ¹³So the wingspan of both cherubim together was 30 feet. They both stood and faced out toward the main room of the Temple. ¹⁴Across the entrance of the Most Holy Place, Solomon hung a curtain made of fine linen and blue, purple, and scarlet yarn, with figures of cherubim embroidered on it.

¹⁵For the front of the Temple, Solomon made two pillars that were 27 feet* tall, each topped by a capital extending upward another 7¹/₂ feet. ¹⁶He made a network of interwoven chains and used them to decorate the tops of the pillars. He also made one hundred decorative pomegranates and attached them to the chains. ¹⁷Then he set up the two pillars at the entrance of the Temple, one to the south of the entrance and the other to the north. He named the one on the south Jakin, and the one on the north Boaz.*

I RECOGNIZE God as the one who establishes and strengthens the work of my hands. (3:17)

CHAPTER 4

Furnishings for the Temple

Solomon also made a bronze altar 30 feet long, 30 feet wide, and 15 feet high.* ²Then he cast a large round tank, 15 feet across from rim to rim; it was called the Sea. It was 7¹/₂ feet deep and about 45 feet in circumference. ³The Sea was encircled just below its rim by two rows of figures that resembled oxen. There were about six oxen per foot* all the way around, and they had been cast as part of the tank.

I HELP FURNISH buildings where the Lord is worshiped. (4:1)

⁴The Sea rested on a base of twelve bronze oxen, all facing outward. Three faced north, three faced west, three faced south, and three faced east. ⁵The walls of the Sea were about three inches* thick, and its rim flared out like a cup and resembled a lily blossom. It could hold about 16,500 gallons* of water.

⁶He also made ten basins for water to wash the offerings, five to the south of the Sea and five to the north. The priests used the Sea itself, and not the basins, for their own washing.

⁷Solomon then cast ten gold lampstands according to the specifications that had been given and put them in the Temple. Five were placed against the

I FOLLOW God's instructions. (4:7)

3:4 As in some Greek and Syriac manuscripts, which read *20 cubits* [9 meters]; Hebrew reads *120 cubits*, which is 180 feet or 54 meters. 3:8 Hebrew *600 talents* [20.4 metric tons]. 3:9 Hebrew *50 shekels* [570 grams]. 3:15 As in Syriac version (see also 1 Kgs 7:15; 2 Kgs 25:17; Jer 52:21), which reads *18 cubits* [8.1 meters]; Hebrew reads *35 cubits*, which is 52.5 feet or 15.8 meters. 3:17 Jakin probably means "he establishes"; Boaz probably means "in him is strength." 4:1 Hebrew *20 cubits* [9 meters] *long, 20 cubits wide, and 10 cubits* [4.5 meters] *high*. In this chapter, the distance measures are calculated from the Hebrew cubit at a ratio of 18 inches or 45 centimeters per cubit. 4:3 Or *20 oxen per meter*; Hebrew reads *10 per cubit*. 4:5a Hebrew *a handbreadth* [8 centimeters]. 4:5b Hebrew *3,000 baths* [63 kiloliters].

south wall, and five were placed against the north wall. ⁸He also built ten tables and placed them in the Temple, five along the south wall and five along the north wall. Then he molded one hundred gold basins.

⁹Solomon also built a courtyard for the priests and the large outer courtyard. He made doors for the courtyard entrances and overlaid them with bronze. ¹⁰The Sea was placed near the southeast corner of the Temple.

¹¹Huram-abi also made the necessary pots, shovels, and basins.

So at last Huram-abi completed everything King Solomon had assigned him to make for the Temple of God:

I COMPLETE all the tasks assigned to me for the Lord's service. (4:11)

¹² two pillars,
two bowl-shaped capitals on top of the pillars,
two networks of chains that decorated the capitals,
¹³ four hundred pomegranates that hung from the chains on the capitals
(two rows of pomegranates for each of the chain networks that were hung around the capitals on top of the pillars),
¹⁴ the water carts holding the basins,
¹⁵ the Sea and the twelve oxen under it,
¹⁶ the pots, the shovels, the meat hooks, and all the related utensils.

Huram-abi made all these things out of burnished bronze for the Temple of the LORD, just as King Solomon had requested. ¹⁷The king had them cast in clay molds in the Jordan Valley between Succoth and Zarethan.* ¹⁸Such great quantities of bronze were used that its weight could not be determined.

¹⁹So Solomon made all the furnishings for the Temple of God:

In response to these affirmations, tell the Lord what you obey—or find easy to disobey.

the gold altar;
the tables for the Bread of the Presence;
²⁰ the lampstands and their lamps of pure gold to burn in front of the Most Holy Place as prescribed;
²¹ the flower decorations, lamps, and tongs, all of pure gold;
²² the lamp snuffers, basins, dishes, and firepans, all of pure gold;
the doors for the entrances to the Most Holy Place and the main room of the Temple, overlaid with gold.

CHAPTER 5
The Ark Brought to the Temple
When Solomon had finished all the work related to building the Temple of the LORD, he brought in the gifts dedicated by his father, King David, including all the silver and gold and all the utensils. These were stored in the treasuries of the Temple of God.

See David's profile (page 629) at Psalm 3:1.

²Solomon then summoned the leaders of all the tribes and families of Israel to assemble in Jerusalem. They were to bring the Ark of the LORD's covenant from its location in the City of David, also known as Zion, to its new place in the Temple. ³They all assembled before the king at the annual Festival of Shelters in early autumn.* ⁴When all the leaders of Israel arrived, the Levites moved the Ark, ⁵along with the special tent* and all its sacred utensils. The Levitical priests carried them all up to the Temple. ⁶King Solomon and the entire community of Israel sacrificed sheep and oxen before the Ark in such numbers that no one could keep count!

I WORSHIP God in the congregation of his people. (5:6)

⁷ Then the priests carried the Ark of the LORD's covenant into the inner sanctuary of the Temple—the Most Holy Place—and placed it beneath the wings of the cherubim. ⁸The cherubim spread their wings out over the Ark, forming a canopy over the Ark and its carrying poles. ⁹These poles were so

4:17 As in parallel text at 1 Kgs 7:46; Hebrew reads *Zeredah.* 5:3 Hebrew *at the festival that is in the seventh month.* The Festival of Shelters began on the fifteenth day of the seventh month of the Hebrew lunar calendar. This occurs on our calendar in late September or early October. 5:5 Hebrew *Tent of Meeting.*

long that their ends could be seen from the front entrance of the Temple's main room—the Holy Place—but not from outside it. They are still there to this day. [10]Nothing was in the Ark except the two stone tablets that Moses had placed there at Mount Sinai,* when the LORD made a covenant with the people of Israel after they left Egypt.

[11]Then the priests left the Holy Place. All the priests who were present had purified themselves, whether or not they were on duty that day. [12]And the Levites who were musicians—Asaph, Heman, Jeduthun, and all their sons and brothers—were dressed in fine linen robes and stood at the east side of the altar playing cymbals, harps, and lyres. They were joined by 120 priests who were playing trumpets. [13]The trumpeters and singers performed together in unison to praise and give thanks to the LORD. Accompanied by trumpets, cymbals, and other instruments, they raised their voices and praised the LORD with these words:

> "He is so good!
>   His faithful love endures forever!"

At that moment a cloud filled the Temple of the LORD. [14]The priests could not continue their work because the glorious presence of the LORD filled the Temple of God.

CHAPTER 6

Solomon Blesses the People

Then Solomon prayed, "O LORD, you have said that you would live in thick darkness. [2]But I have built a glorious Temple for you, where you can live forever!"

[3]Then the king turned around to the entire community of Israel standing before him and gave this blessing: [4]"Blessed be the LORD, the God of Israel, who has kept the promise he made to my father, David. For he told my father, [5]'From the day I brought my people out of Egypt, I have never chosen a city among the tribes of Israel as the place where a temple should be built to honor my name. Nor have I chosen a king to lead my people Israel. [6]But now I have chosen Jerusalem as that city, and David as that king.' "

[7]Then Solomon said, "My father, David, wanted to build this Temple to honor the name of the LORD, the God of Israel. [8]But the LORD told him, 'It is right for you to want to build the Temple to honor my name, [9]but you will not be the one to do it. One of your sons will build it instead.'

[10]"And now the LORD has done what he promised, for I have become king in my father's place. I have built this Temple to honor the name of the LORD, the God of Israel. [11]There I have placed the Ark, and in the Ark is the covenant that the LORD made with the people of Israel."

Solomon's Prayer of Dedication

[12]Then Solomon stood with his hands spread out before the altar of the LORD in front of the entire community of Israel. [13]He had made a bronze platform 7½ feet long, 7½ feet wide, and 4½ feet high* and had placed it at the center of the Temple's outer courtyard. He stood on the platform before the entire assembly, and then he knelt down and lifted his hands toward heaven. [14]He prayed, "O LORD, God of Israel, there is no God like you in all of heaven and earth. You keep your promises and show unfailing love to all who obey you and are eager to do your will. [15]You have kept your promise to your servant David, my father. You made that promise with your own mouth, and today you have fulfilled it with your own hands. [16]And now, O LORD, God of Israel, carry out your further promise to your servant David, my father. For you said

---

See Moses' profile (page 73) at Exodus 5:1.

I PURIFY my life before worshiping God, whether I have official duties or not. (5:11)

See Asaph's profile (page 687) at Psalm 73:28.

I GIVE priority to public, musical worship of the Lord. (5:13)

See David's profile (page 629) at Psalm 3:1.

I HONOR the name of the Lord. (6:7)

I WORSHIP the Lord publicly. (6:12)

I BELIEVE there is no other God like the Lord, who keeps his promises and shows his love to those who are eager to do his will. (6:14)

5:10 Hebrew *Horeb,* another name for Sinai.   6:13 Hebrew *5 cubits* [2.3 meters] *long, 5 cubits wide, and 3 cubits* [1.4 meters] *high.*

to him, 'If your descendants guard their behavior and obey my law as you have done, they will always reign over Israel.' [17]Now, O LORD, God of Israel, fulfill this promise to your servant David.

[18]"But will God really live on earth among people? Why, even the highest heavens cannot contain you. How much less this Temple I have built! [19]Listen to my prayer and my request, O LORD my God. Hear the cry and the prayer that your servant is making to you. [20]May you watch over this Temple both day and night, this place where you have said you would put your name. May you always hear the prayers I make toward this place. [21]May you hear the humble and earnest requests from me and your people Israel when we pray toward this place. Yes, hear us from heaven where you live, and when you hear, forgive.

[22]"If someone wrongs another person and is required to take an oath of innocence in front of the altar at this Temple, [23]then hear from heaven and judge between your servants—the accuser and the accused. Punish the guilty party, and acquit the one who is innocent.

I LOOK to God for justice. (6:22)

[24]"If your people Israel are defeated by their enemies because they have sinned against you, and if they turn to you and call on your name and pray to you here in this Temple, [25]then hear from heaven and forgive their sins and return them to this land you gave their ancestors.

I REPENT when I sin and ask the Lord for forgiveness. (6:25)

[26]"If the skies are shut up and there is no rain because your people have sinned against you, and then they pray toward this Temple and confess your name and turn from their sins because you have punished them, [27]then hear from heaven and forgive the sins of your servants, your people Israel. Teach them to do what is right, and send rain on your land that you have given to your people as their special possession.

[28]"If there is a famine in the land, or plagues, or crop disease, or attacks of locusts or caterpillars, or if your people's enemies are in the land besieging their towns—whatever the trouble is—[29]and if your people offer a prayer concerning their troubles or sorrow, raising their hands toward this Temple, [30]then hear from heaven where you live, and forgive. Give your people whatever they deserve, for you alone know the human heart. [31]Then they will fear you and walk in your ways as long as they live in the land you gave to our ancestors.

I LOOK to the Lord in times of trouble and sorrow. (6:28)

I BELIEVE the Lord knows the heart of each person who prays to him. (6:29)

[32]"And when foreigners hear of you and your mighty miracles, and they come from distant lands to worship your great name and to pray toward this Temple, [33]then hear from heaven where you live, and grant what they ask of you. Then all the people of the earth will come to know and fear you, just as your own people Israel do. They, too, will know that this Temple I have built bears your name.

[34]"If your people go out at your command to fight their enemies, and if they pray to you toward this city that you have chosen and toward this Temple that I have built for your name, [35]then hear their prayers from heaven and uphold their cause.

[36]"If they sin against you—and who has never sinned?—you may become angry with them and let their enemies conquer them and take them captive to a foreign land far or near. [37]But in that land of exile, they may turn to you again in repentance and pray, 'We have sinned, done evil, and acted wickedly.' [38]Then if they turn to you with their whole heart and soul and pray toward the land you gave to their ancestors, toward this city you have chosen, and toward this Temple I have built to honor your name, [39]then hear their prayers from heaven where you live. Uphold their cause and forgive your people who have sinned against you.

I BELIEVE there is no one who hasn't sinned against the Lord. (6:36)

[40]"O my God, be attentive to all the prayers made to you in this place. [41]And now, O LORD God, arise and enter this resting place of yours, where your magnificent Ark has been placed. May your priests, O LORD God, be

I REJOICE in God's goodness. (6:41)

clothed with salvation, and may your saints rejoice in your goodness. ⁴²O Lord God, do not reject your anointed one. Remember your unfailing love for your servant David.*"

CHAPTER 7

The Dedication of the Temple

When Solomon finished praying, fire flashed down from heaven and burned up the burnt offerings and sacrifices, and the glorious presence of the Lord filled the Temple. ²The priests could not even enter the Temple of the Lord because the glorious presence of the Lord filled it. ³When all the people of Israel saw the fire coming down and the glorious presence of the Lord filling the Temple, they fell face down on the ground and worshiped and praised the Lord, saying,

> "He is so good!
> His faithful love endures forever!"

⁴Then the king and all the people offered sacrifices to the Lord. ⁵King Solomon offered a sacrifice of 22,000 oxen and 120,000 sheep. And so the king and all the people dedicated the Temple of God. ⁶The priests took their assigned positions, and so did the Levites who were singing, "His faithful love endures forever!" They accompanied the singing with music from the instruments King David had made for praising the Lord. On the other side of the Levites, the priests blew the trumpets, while all Israel stood.

⁷Solomon then dedicated the central area of the courtyard in front of the Lord's Temple so they could present burnt offerings and the fat from peace offerings there. He did this because the bronze altar he had built could not handle all the burnt offerings, grain offerings, and sacrificial fat.

⁸For the next seven days they celebrated the Festival of Shelters* with huge crowds gathered from all the tribes of Israel. They came from as far away as Lebo-hamath in the north, to the brook of Egypt in the south. ⁹On the eighth day they had a closing ceremony, for they had celebrated the dedication of the altar for seven days and the Festival of Shelters for seven days. ¹⁰Then at the end of the celebration,* Solomon sent the people home. They were all joyful and happy because the Lord had been so good to David and Solomon and to his people Israel.

The Lord's Response to Solomon

¹¹So Solomon finished building the Temple of the Lord, as well as the royal palace. He completed everything he had planned to do. ¹²Then one night the Lord appeared to Solomon and said, "I have heard your prayer and have chosen this Temple as the place for making sacrifices. ¹³At times I might shut up the heavens so that no rain falls, or I might command locusts to devour your crops, or I might send plagues among you. ¹⁴Then if my people who are called by my name will humble themselves and pray and seek my face and turn from their wicked ways, I will hear from heaven and will forgive their sins and heal their land. ¹⁵I will listen to every prayer made in this place, ¹⁶for I have chosen this Temple and set it apart to be my home forever. My eyes and my heart will always be here.

¹⁷"As for you, if you follow me as your father, David, did and obey all my commands, laws, and regulations, ¹⁸then I will not let anyone take away your throne. This is the same promise I gave your father, David, when I said, 'You will never fail to have a successor who rules over Israel.'

¹⁹"But if you abandon me and disobey the laws and commands I have

I WORSHIP God for his goodness and faithful love. (7:3)

I GIVE priority to worshiping God with instrumental music and songs of praise. (7:6)

See David's profile (page 629) at Psalm 3:1.

I CELEBRATE God's goodness in the congregation of his people. (7:9)

I BELIEVE the Lord set apart the Temple as the place where his name would be honored. (7:12)

I BELIEVE God promised Solomon to establish his dynasty over Israel forever if he obeyed the Lord. (7:17)

6:42 Or *Remember the faithfulness of your servant David.*   7:8 Hebrew *the festival* (also in 7:9); see note on 5:3.
7:10 Hebrew *Then on the twenty-seventh day of the seventh month.* This day of the Hebrew lunar calendar occurs in late September or early October.

given you, and if you go and worship other gods, [20]then I will uproot the people of Israel from this land of mine that I have given them. I will reject this Temple that I have set apart to honor my name. I will make it a spectacle of contempt among the nations. [21]And though this Temple is impressive now, it will become an appalling sight to all who pass by. They will ask, 'Why has the LORD done such terrible things to his land and to his Temple?' [22]And the answer will be, 'Because his people abandoned the LORD, the God of their ancestors, who brought them out of Egypt, and they worshiped other gods instead. That is why he brought all these disasters upon them.' "

CHAPTER 8

Solomon's Many Achievements

It was now twenty years since Solomon had become king, and the great building projects of the LORD's Temple and his own royal palace were completed. [2]Solomon now turned his attention to rebuilding the towns that King Hiram* had given him, and he settled Israelites in them. [3]It was at this time, too, that Solomon fought against the city of Hamath-zobah and conquered it. [4]He rebuilt Tadmor in the desert and built towns in the region of Hamath as supply centers. [5]He fortified the cities of Upper Beth-horon and Lower Beth-horon, rebuilding their walls and installing barred gates. [6]He also rebuilt Baalath and other supply centers at this time and constructed cities where his chariots and horses* could be kept. He built to his heart's content in Jerusalem and Lebanon and throughout the entire realm.

[7]There were still some people living in the land who were not Israelites, including Hittites, Amorites, Perizzites, Hivites, and Jebusites. [8]These were descendants of the nations that Israel had not completely destroyed. So Solomon conscripted them for his labor force, and they serve in the labor force to this day. [9]But Solomon did not conscript any of the Israelites for forced labor. Instead, he assigned them to serve as fighting men, officers in his army, commanders of his chariots, and charioteers. [10]King Solomon also appointed 250 of them to supervise the various projects.

[11]Solomon moved his wife, Pharaoh's daughter, from the City of David to the new palace he had built for her. He said, "My wife must not live in King David's palace, for the Ark of the LORD has been there, and it is holy ground."

[12]Then Solomon sacrificed burnt offerings to the LORD on the altar he had built in front of the foyer of the Temple. [13]The number of sacrifices varied from day to day according to the commands Moses had given. Extra sacrifices were offered on the Sabbaths, on new moon festivals, and at the three annual festivals—the Passover celebration, the Festival of Harvest,* and the Festival of Shelters. [14]In assigning the priests to their duties, Solomon followed the regulations of his father, David. He also assigned the Levites to lead the people in praise and to assist the priests in their daily duties. And he assigned the gatekeepers to their gates by their divisions, following the commands of David, the man of God. [15]Solomon did not deviate in any way from David's commands concerning the priests and Levites and the treasuries.

[16]So Solomon made sure that all the work related to building the Temple of the LORD was carried out, from the day its foundation was laid to the day of its completion.

[17]Later Solomon went to Ezion-geber and Elath,* ports in the land of Edom, along the shore of the Red Sea.* [18]Hiram sent him ships commanded by his own officers and manned by experienced crews of sailors. These ships sailed to the land of Ophir with Solomon's men and brought back to Solomon almost seventeen tons* of gold.

I SERVE the needs of the people I lead. (8:2)

I TREAT God's people with respect. (8:9)

See David's profile (page 629) at Psalm 3:1.

See Moses' profile (page 73) at Exodus 5:1.

I FAITHFULLY CARRY OUT the work entrusted to me. (8:15)

8:2 Hebrew *Huram,* a variant name for Hiram; also in 8:18.   **8:6** Or *and charioteers.*   **8:13** Or *Festival of Weeks.*
8:17a As in Greek version (see also 2 Kgs 14:22; 16:6); Hebrew reads *Eloth.*   **8:17b** Hebrew *the sea.*
8:18 Hebrew *450 talents* [15.3 metric tons].

CHAPTER 9

The Queen of Sheba's Visit

When the queen of Sheba heard of Solomon's reputation, she came to Jerusalem to test him with hard questions. She arrived with a large group of attendants and a great caravan of camels loaded with spices, huge quantities of gold, and precious jewels. ²When she met with Solomon, they talked about everything she had on her mind. Solomon answered all her questions; nothing was too hard for him to explain to her. ³When the queen of Sheba realized how wise Solomon was, and when she saw the palace he had built, ⁴she was breathless. She was also amazed at the food on his tables, the organization of his officials and their splendid clothing, the cup-bearers and their robes, and the burnt offerings Solomon made at the Temple of the LORD.

⁵She exclaimed to the king, "Everything I heard in my country about your achievements and wisdom is true! ⁶I didn't believe it until I arrived here and saw it with my own eyes. Truly I had not heard the half of it! Your wisdom is far greater than what I was told. ⁷How happy these people must be! What a privilege for your officials to stand here day after day, listening to your wisdom! ⁸The LORD your God is great indeed! He delights in you and has placed you on the throne to rule for him. Because God loves Israel so much and desires this kingdom to last forever, he has made you king so you can rule with justice and righteousness."

⁹Then she gave the king a gift of nine thousand pounds* of gold, and great quantities of spices and precious jewels. Never before had there been spices as fine as those the queen of Sheba gave to Solomon.

¹⁰(When the crews of Hiram and Solomon brought gold from Ophir, they also brought rich cargoes of almug wood* and precious jewels. ¹¹The king used the almug wood to make steps* for the Temple of the LORD and the royal palace, and to construct harps and lyres for the musicians. Never before had there been such beautiful instruments in Judah.)

¹²King Solomon gave the queen of Sheba whatever she asked for—gifts of greater value than the gifts she had given him. Then she and all her attendants left and returned to their own land.

Solomon's Wealth and Splendor

¹³Each year Solomon received about 25 tons* of gold. ¹⁴This did not include the additional revenue he received from merchants and traders. All the kings of Arabia and the governors of the land also brought gold and silver to Solomon.

¹⁵King Solomon made two hundred large shields of hammered gold, each containing over 15 pounds* of gold. ¹⁶He also made three hundred smaller shields of hammered gold, each containing about 7¹/₂ pounds* of gold. The king placed these shields in the Palace of the Forest of Lebanon.

¹⁷Then the king made a huge ivory throne and overlaid it with pure gold. ¹⁸The throne had six steps, and there was a footstool of gold attached to it. On both sides of the seat were armrests, with the figure of a lion standing on each side of the throne. ¹⁹Solomon made twelve other lion figures, one standing on each end of each of the six steps. No other throne in all the world could be compared with it!

²⁰All of King Solomon's drinking cups were solid gold, as were all the utensils in the Palace of the Forest of Lebanon. They were not made of silver because silver was considered of little value in Solomon's day!

²¹The king had a fleet of trading ships* manned by the sailors sent by

---

I PLACE great value on opportunities to meet with godly, wise individuals and ask them my toughest, most pressing questions. (9:2)

I MAKE others happy by leading them wisely and righteously. (9:7)

I PRAISE God because he is the one who appoints wise and righteous rulers. (9:8)

I GIVE priority to worshiping God with musical instruments. (9:11)

9:9 Hebrew *120 talents* [4 metric tons]. 9:10 Hebrew *algum wood* (also in 9:11); compare parallel text at 1 Kgs 10:11-12. 9:11 Or *gateways*. The meaning of the Hebrew is uncertain. 9:13 Hebrew *666 talents* [23 metric tons]. 9:15 Hebrew *600 shekels* [6.8 kilograms]. 9:16 Hebrew *300 shekels* [3.4 kilograms]. 9:21a Hebrew *fleet of ships that could sail to Tarshish.*

Hiram.* Once every three years the ships returned, loaded down with gold, silver, ivory, apes, and peacocks.*

²²So King Solomon became richer and wiser than any other king in all the earth. ²³Kings from every nation came to visit him and to hear the wisdom God had given him. ²⁴Year after year, everyone who came to visit brought him gifts of silver and gold, clothing, weapons, spices, horses, and mules.

²⁵Solomon had four thousand stalls for his chariot horses and twelve thousand horses.* He stationed many of them in the chariot cities, and some near him in Jerusalem. ²⁶He ruled over all the kings from the Euphrates River* to the land of the Philistines and the border of Egypt. ²⁷The king made silver as plentiful in Jerusalem as stones. And valuable cedarwood was as common as the sycamore wood that grows in the foothills of Judah.* ²⁸Solomon's horses were imported from Egypt* and many other countries.

Summary of Solomon's Reign

²⁹The rest of the events of Solomon's reign, from beginning to end, are recorded in *The Record of Nathan the Prophet* and in *The Prophecy of Ahijah from Shiloh,* and also in *The Visions of Iddo the Seer,* concerning Jeroboam son of Nebat. ³⁰Solomon ruled in Jerusalem over all Israel for forty years. ³¹When he died, he was buried in the city of his father, David. Then his son Rehoboam became the next king.

CHAPTER 10

The Northern Tribes Revolt

Rehoboam went to Shechem, where all Israel had gathered to make him king. ²When Jeroboam son of Nebat heard of Solomon's death, he returned from Egypt, for he had fled to Egypt to escape from King Solomon. ³The leaders of Israel sent for Jeroboam, and he and all Israel went together to speak with Rehoboam. ⁴"Your father was a hard master," they said. "Lighten the harsh labor demands and heavy taxes that your father imposed on us. Then we will be your loyal subjects."

⁵Rehoboam replied, "Come back in three days for my answer." So the people went away.

⁶Then King Rehoboam went to discuss the matter with the older men who had counseled his father, Solomon. "What is your advice?" he asked. "How should I answer these people?"

⁷The older counselors replied, "If you are good to the people and show them kindness and do your best to please them, they will always be your loyal subjects."

⁸But Rehoboam rejected the advice of the elders and instead asked the opinion of the young men who had grown up with him and who were now his advisers. ⁹"What is your advice?" he asked them. "How should I answer these people who want me to lighten the burdens imposed by my father?"

¹⁰The young men replied, "This is what you should tell those complainers: 'My little finger is thicker than my father's waist—if you think he was hard on you, just wait and see what I'll be like! ¹¹Yes, my father was harsh on you, but I'll be even harsher! My father used whips on you, but I'll use scorpions!' "

¹²Three days later, Jeroboam and all the people returned to hear Rehoboam's decision, just as the king had requested. ¹³But Rehoboam spoke harshly to them, for he rejected the advice of the older counselors ¹⁴and followed the counsel of his younger advisers. He told the people, "My father was harsh on you, but I'll be even harsher! My father used whips on you, but I'll use scorpions!" ¹⁵So the king paid no attention to the people's demands. This turn of events was the will of God, for it fulfilled the

---

I OBEY the Lord's commands carefully (see Deuteronomy 17:16). (9:25)

I BELIEVE wise public officials ensure that economic prosperity benefits people at all levels of society, not just a select few at the top. (9:27)

See David's profile (page 629) at Psalm 3:1.

See Rehoboam's profile (page 409) at 1 Kings 12:8.

See Jeroboam's profile (page 411) at 1 Kings 13:4.

I LOOK to wise and experienced people for counsel. (10:6)

I WILLINGLY SERVE those I lead. (10:7)

I DO NOT FOOLISHLY reject good counsel. (10:8)

I PAY careful attention to the complaints of those I lead. (10:15)

9:21b Hebrew *Huram,* a variant name for Hiram. 9:21c Or *and baboons.* 9:25 Or *12,000 charioteers.*
9:26 Hebrew *the river.* 9:27 Hebrew *the Shephelah.* 9:28 Possibly *Muzur,* a district near Cilicia.

prophecy of the LORD spoken to Jeroboam son of Nebat by the prophet Ahijah from Shiloh.

See David's profile
(page 629) at Psalm 3:1.

[16]When all Israel realized that the king had rejected their request, they shouted, "Down with David and his dynasty! We have no share in Jesse's son! Let's go home, Israel! Look out for your own house, O David!" So all Israel returned home. [17]But Rehoboam continued to rule over the Israelites who lived in the towns of Judah.

[18]King Rehoboam sent Adoniram,* who was in charge of the labor force, to restore order, but the Israelites stoned him to death. When this news reached King Rehoboam, he quickly jumped into his chariot and fled to Jerusalem. [19]The northern tribes of Israel have refused to be ruled by a descendant of David to this day.

CHAPTER 11

Shemaiah's Prophecy

See Rehoboam's profile
(page 409) at 1 Kings
12:8.

I HEED the Lord's words of warning. (11:4)

See Jeroboam's profile
(page 411) at 1 Kings
13:4.

When Rehoboam arrived at Jerusalem, he mobilized the armies of Judah and Benjamin—180,000 select troops—to fight against the army of Israel and to restore the kingdom to himself. [2]But the LORD said to Shemaiah, the man of God, [3]"Say to Rehoboam son of Solomon, king of Judah, and to all the Israelites in Judah and Benjamin: [4]'This is what the LORD says: Do not fight against your relatives. Go back home, for what has happened is my doing!' " So they obeyed the message of the LORD and did not fight against Jeroboam.

Rehoboam Fortifies Judah

I ENSURE the safety and well-being of the people I lead. (11:11)

[5]Rehoboam remained in Jerusalem and fortified various cities for the defense of Judah. [6]He built up Bethlehem, Etam, Tekoa, [7]Beth-zur, Soco, Adullam, [8]Gath, Mareshah, Ziph, [9]Adoraim, Lachish, Azekah, [10]Zorah, Aijalon, and Hebron. These became the fortified cities of Judah and Benjamin. [11]Rehoboam strengthened their defenses and stationed commanders in them. In each of them, he stored supplies of food, olive oil, and wine. [12]He also put shields and spears in these towns as a further safety measure. So only Judah and Benjamin remained under his control.

[13]But all the priests and Levites living among the northern tribes of Israel sided with Rehoboam. [14]The Levites even abandoned their homes and property and moved to Judah and Jerusalem, because Jeroboam and his sons would not allow them to serve the LORD as priests. [15]Jeroboam appointed his own priests to serve at the pagan shrines, where they worshiped the goat and calf idols he had made. [16]From all over Israel, those who sincerely wanted to worship the LORD, the God of Israel, followed the Levites to Jerusalem, where they could offer sacrifices to the LORD, the God of their ancestors. [17]This strengthened the kingdom of Judah, and for three years they supported Rehoboam son of Solomon and earnestly sought to obey the LORD as they had done during the reigns of David and Solomon.

I SINCERELY WANT to worship the Lord. (11:16)

See David's profile
(page 629) at Psalm 3:1.

Rehoboam's Family

See Absalom's profile
(page 373) at 2 Samuel
15:6.

I OBEY the Lord's commands carefully (see Deuteronomy 17:16). (11:21)

[18]Rehoboam married his cousin Mahalath, the daughter of David's son Jerimoth and of Abihail, the daughter of Eliab. (Eliab was one of David's brothers, a son of Jesse.) [19]Mahalath had three sons—Jeush, Shemariah, and Zaham. [20]Later Rehoboam married another cousin, Maacah, the daughter of Absalom. Maacah gave birth to Abijah, Attai, Ziza, and Shelomith. [21]Rehoboam loved Maacah more than any of his other wives and concubines. In all, he had eighteen wives and sixty concubines, and they gave birth to twenty-eight sons and sixty daughters. [22]Rehoboam made Maacah's son Abijah chief among the princes, making it clear that he would be the next king. [23]Rehoboam also wisely

10:18 Hebrew *Hadoram*, a variant name for Adoniram; compare 1 Kgs 4:6; 5:14; 12:18.

gave responsibilities to his other sons and stationed them in the fortified cities throughout the land of Judah and Benjamin. He provided them with generous provisions and arranged for each of them to have several wives.

CHAPTER 12

Egypt Invades Judah

But when Rehoboam was firmly established and strong, he abandoned the law of the LORD, and all Israel followed him in this sin. [2]Because they were unfaithful to the LORD, King Shishak of Egypt attacked Jerusalem in the fifth year of King Rehoboam's reign. [3]He came with twelve hundred chariots, sixty thousand horsemen, and a countless army of foot soldiers, including Libyans, Sukkites, and Ethiopians.* [4]Shishak conquered Judah's fortified cities and then advanced to attack Jerusalem.

[5]The prophet Shemaiah then met with Rehoboam and Judah's leaders, who had all fled to Jerusalem because of Shishak. Shemaiah told them, "This is what the LORD says: You have abandoned me, so I am abandoning you to Shishak."

[6]The king and the leaders of Israel humbled themselves and said, "The LORD is right in doing this to us!"

[7]When the LORD saw their change of heart, he gave this message to Shemaiah: "Since the people have humbled themselves, I will not completely destroy them and will soon give them some relief. I will not use Shishak to pour out my anger on Jerusalem. [8]But they will become his subjects, so that they can learn how much better it is to serve me than to serve earthly rulers."

[9]So King Shishak of Egypt came to Jerusalem and took away all the treasures of the Temple of the LORD and of the royal palace, including all of Solomon's gold shields. [10]King Rehoboam later replaced them with bronze shields and entrusted them to the care of the captain of his bodyguard. [11]Whenever the king went to the Temple of the LORD, the guards would carry them along and then return them to the guardroom. [12]Because Rehoboam humbled himself, the LORD's anger was turned aside, and he did not destroy him completely. And there was still goodness in the land of Judah.

Summary of Rehoboam's Reign

[13]King Rehoboam firmly established himself in Jerusalem and continued to rule. He was forty-one years old when he became king, and he reigned seventeen years in Jerusalem, the city the LORD had chosen from among all the tribes of Israel as the place to honor his name. Rehoboam's mother was Naamah, a woman from Ammon. [14]But he was an evil king, for he did not seek the LORD with all his heart.

[15]The rest of the events of Rehoboam's reign, from beginning to end, are recorded in *The Record of Shemaiah the Prophet* and in *The Record of Iddo the Seer*, which are part of the genealogical record. Rehoboam and Jeroboam were continually at war with each other. [16]When Rehoboam died, he was buried in the City of David. Then his son Abijah became the next king.

CHAPTER 13

Abijah's War with Jeroboam

Abijah began to rule over Judah in the eighteenth year of Jeroboam's reign in Israel. [2]He reigned in Jerusalem three years. His mother was Maacah,* a daughter of Uriel from Gibeah.

Then war broke out between Abijah and Jeroboam. [3]Judah, led by King Abijah, fielded 400,000 seasoned warriors, while Jeroboam mustered 800,000 courageous men from Israel. [4]When the army of Judah arrived in the

I AM CAREFUL not to disregard God's Word when I become successful and secure. (12:1)

See Rehoboam's profile *(page 409) at 1 Kings 12:8.*

I BELIEVE the Lord shows mercy to those who humble themselves and have a change of heart. (12:7)

I SEEK the Lord with all my heart. (12:14)

See Jeroboam's profile *(page 411) at 1 Kings 13:4.*

See David's profile *(page 629) at Psalm 3:1.*

See Jeroboam's profile *(page 411) at 1 Kings 13:4.*

12:3 Hebrew *and Cushites.* 13:2 As in most Greek manuscripts and Syriac version (see also 2 Chr 11:20-21; 1 Kgs 15:2); Hebrew reads *Micaiah.*

I RECALL God's unbreakable promises and take courage. (13:5)

See David's profile (page 629) at Psalm 3:1.

See Rehoboam's profile (page 409) at 1 Kings 12:8.

hill country of Ephraim, Abijah stood on Mount Zemaraim and shouted to Jeroboam and the Israelite army: "Listen to me! [5]Don't you realize that the LORD, the God of Israel, made an unbreakable covenant* with David, giving him and his descendants the throne of Israel forever? [6]Yet Jeroboam son of Nebat, who was a mere servant of David's son Solomon, became a traitor to his master. [7]Then a whole gang of scoundrels joined him, defying Solomon's son Rehoboam when he was young and inexperienced and could not stand up to them. [8]Do you really think you can stand against the kingdom of the LORD that is led by the descendants of David? Your army is vast indeed, but with you are those gold calves that Jeroboam made as your gods! [9]And you have chased away the priests of the LORD and the Levites and have appointed your own priests, just like the pagan nations. You let anyone become a priest these days! Whoever comes to be dedicated with a young bull and seven rams can become a priest of these so-called gods of yours!

I WILL NOT ABANDON the Lord for any reason. (13:10)

See Aaron's profile (page 107) at Exodus 32:2.

I OBEY the Lord and enjoy his presence in my life. (13:12)

[10]"But as for us, the LORD is our God, and we have not abandoned him. Only the descendants of Aaron serve the LORD as priests, and the Levites alone may help them in their work. [11]They present burnt offerings and fragrant incense to the LORD every morning and evening. They place the Bread of the Presence on the holy table, and they light the gold lampstand every evening. We are following the instructions of the LORD our God, but you have abandoned him. [12]So you see, God is with us. He is our leader. His priests blow their trumpets and lead us into battle against you. O people of Israel, do not fight against the LORD, the God of your ancestors, for you will not succeed!"

I CRY OUT to the Lord for help when I am under attack. (13:14)

[13]Meanwhile, Jeroboam had secretly sent part of his army around behind the men of Judah to ambush them. [14]When Judah realized that they were being attacked from the front and the rear, they cried out to the LORD for help. Then the priests blew the trumpets, [15]and the men of Judah began to shout. At the sound of their battle cry, God defeated Jeroboam and the Israelite army and routed them before Abijah and the army of Judah. [16]The Israelite army fled from Judah, and God handed them over to Judah in defeat. [17]Abijah and his army inflicted heavy losses on them; there were 500,000 casualties among Israel's finest troops that day. [18]So Judah defeated Israel because they trusted in the LORD, the God of their ancestors. [19]Abijah and his army pursued Jeroboam's troops and captured some of his towns, including Bethel, Jeshanah, and Ephron, along with their surrounding villages.

[20]So Jeroboam of Israel never regained his power during Abijah's lifetime, and finally the LORD struck him down and he died. [21]By contrast, Abijah of Judah grew more and more powerful. He married fourteen wives and had twenty-two sons and sixteen daughters. [22]The rest of the events of Abijah's reign, including his words and deeds, are recorded in *The Commentary of Iddo the Prophet.*

CHAPTER **14**
Early Years of Asa's Reign

See the profiles for Asa (page 521) and David (page 629) at 2 Chronicles 16:9 and Psalm 3:1.

I REMOVE false worship from my life and my sphere of authority. (14:3)

When Abijah died, he was buried in the City of David. Then his son Asa became the next king. There was peace in the land for ten years, [2]for Asa did what was pleasing and good in the sight of the LORD his God. [3]He removed the pagan altars and the shrines. He smashed the sacred pillars and cut down the Asherah poles. [4]He commanded the people of Judah to seek the LORD, the God of their ancestors, and to obey his law and his commands. [5]Asa also removed the pagan shrines, as well as the incense altars from every one of Judah's towns. So Asa's kingdom enjoyed a period of peace. [6]During those peaceful years, he was able to build up the fortified cities throughout Judah.

13:5 Hebrew *a covenant of salt.*

No one tried to make war against him at this time, for the LORD was giving him rest from his enemies. [7]Asa told the people of Judah, "Let us build towns and fortify them with walls, towers, gates, and bars. The land is ours because we sought the LORD our God, and he has given us rest from our enemies." So they went ahead with these projects and brought them to completion.

[8]King Asa had an army of 300,000 warriors from the tribe of Judah, armed with large shields and spears. He also had an army of 280,000 warriors from the tribe of Benjamin, armed with small shields and bows. Both armies were composed of courageous fighting men.

[9]Once an Ethiopian* named Zerah attacked Judah with an army of a million men* and three hundred chariots. They advanced to the city of Mareshah, [10]so Asa deployed his armies for battle in the valley north of Mareshah.* [11]Then Asa cried out to the LORD his God, "O LORD, no one but you can help the powerless against the mighty! Help us, O LORD our God, for we trust in you alone. It is in your name that we have come against this vast horde. O LORD, you are our God; do not let mere men prevail against you!"

[12]So the LORD defeated the Ethiopians* in the presence of Asa and the army of Judah, and the enemy fled. [13]Asa and his army pursued them as far as Gerar, and so many Ethiopians fell that they were unable to rally. They were destroyed by the LORD and his army, and the army of Judah carried off vast quantities of plunder. [14]While they were at Gerar, they attacked all the towns in that area, and terror from the LORD came upon the people there. As a result, vast quantities of plunder were taken from these towns, too. [15]They also attacked the camps of herdsmen and captured many sheep and camels before finally returning to Jerusalem.

CHAPTER 15

Asa's Religious Reforms

Then the Spirit of God came upon Azariah son of Oded, [2]and he went out to meet King Asa as he was returning from the battle. "Listen to me, Asa!" he shouted. "Listen, all you people of Judah and Benjamin! The LORD will stay with you as long as you stay with him! Whenever you seek him, you will find him. But if you abandon him, he will abandon you. [3]For a long time, Israel was without the true God, without a priest to teach them, and without God's law. [4]But whenever you were in distress and turned to the LORD, the God of Israel, and sought him out, you found him. [5]During those dark times, it was not safe to travel. Problems troubled the nation on every hand. [6]Nation fought against nation, and city against city, for God was troubling you with every kind of problem. [7]And now, you men of Judah, be strong and courageous, for your work will be rewarded."

[8]When Asa heard this message from Azariah the prophet,* he took courage and removed all the idols in the land of Judah and Benjamin and in the towns he had captured in the hill country of Ephraim. And he repaired the altar of the LORD, which stood in front of the foyer of the LORD's Temple.

[9]Then Asa called together all the people of Judah and Benjamin, along with the people of Ephraim, Manasseh, and Simeon who had settled among them. Many had moved to Judah during Asa's reign when they saw that the LORD his God was with him. [10]The people gathered at Jerusalem in late spring,* during the fifteenth year of Asa's reign. [11]On that day they sacrificed to the LORD some of the animals they had taken as plunder in the battle—seven hundred oxen and seven thousand sheep and goats. [12]Then they entered into a covenant to seek the LORD, the God of their ancestors,

I SEEK the well-being of the people I lead and enjoy that peace and prosperity as a gift from God. (14:7)

I CRY OUT to God, who alone can help when the odds are against me. (14:11)

I CHALLENGE people to continue to seek the Lord. (15:2)

See Asa's profile (page 521) at 2 Chronicles 16:9.

I PLACE more priority on following godly leadership than on following political leadership. (15:9)

14:9a Hebrew *a Cushite.*   14:9b Or *an army of thousands and thousands;* Hebrew reads *an army of a thousand thousands.*   14:10 Or *in the Zephathah Valley near Mareshah.*   14:12 Hebrew *Cushites;* also in 14:13.   15:8 As in Syriac version and Latin Vulgate (see also 15:1); Hebrew reads *from Oded the prophet.*   15:10 Hebrew *in the third month.* This month of the Hebrew lunar calendar usually occurs in May and June.

with all their heart and soul. [13]They agreed that anyone who refused to seek the LORD, the God of Israel, would be put to death—whether young or old, man or woman. [14]They shouted out their oath of loyalty to the LORD with trumpets blaring and horns sounding. [15]All were happy about this covenant, for they had entered into it with all their hearts. Eagerly they sought after God, and they found him. And the LORD gave them rest from their enemies on every side.

[16]King Asa even deposed his grandmother Maacah from her position as queen mother because she had made an obscene Asherah pole. He cut down the pole, broke it up, and burned it in the Kidron Valley. [17]Although the pagan shrines were not completely removed from Israel, Asa remained fully committed to the LORD throughout his life. [18]He brought into the Temple of God the silver and gold and the utensils that he and his father had dedicated. [19]So there was no more war until the thirty-fifth year of Asa's reign.

CHAPTER 16

Final Years of Asa's Reign

In the thirty-sixth year of Asa's reign, King Baasha of Israel invaded Judah and fortified Ramah in order to prevent anyone from entering or leaving King Asa's territory in Judah. [2]Asa responded by taking the silver and gold from the treasuries of the LORD's Temple and from the royal palace. He sent it to King Ben-hadad of Aram, who was ruling in Damascus, along with this message:

[3]"Let us renew the treaty that existed between your father and my father. See, I am sending you a gift of silver and gold. Break your treaty with King Baasha of Israel so that he will leave me alone."

[4]Ben-hadad agreed to King Asa's request and sent his armies to attack Israel. They conquered the towns of Ijon, Dan, Abel-beth-maacah,* and all the store cities in Naphtali. [5]As soon as Baasha of Israel heard what was happening, he abandoned his project of fortifying Ramah. [6]Then King Asa called out all the men of Judah to carry away the building stones and timbers that Baasha had been using to fortify Ramah. Asa used these materials to fortify the towns of Geba and Mizpah.

[7]At that time Hanani the seer came to King Asa and told him, "Because you have put your trust in the king of Aram instead of in the LORD your God, you missed your chance to destroy the army of the king of Aram. [8]Don't you remember what happened to the Ethiopians* and Libyans and their vast army, with all of their chariots and horsemen*? At that time you relied on the LORD, and he handed them all over to you. [9]The eyes of the LORD search the whole earth in order to strengthen those whose hearts are fully committed to him. What a fool you have been! From now on, you will be at war." [10]Asa became so angry with Hanani for saying this that he threw him into prison. At that time, Asa also began to oppress some of his people.

Summary of Asa's Reign

[11]The rest of the events of Asa's reign, from beginning to end, are recorded in *The Book of the Kings of Judah and Israel*. [12]In the thirty-ninth year of his reign, Asa developed a serious foot disease. Even when the disease became life threatening, he did not seek the LORD's help but sought help only from his physicians. [13]So he died in the forty-first year of his reign. [14]He was buried in the tomb he had carved out for himself in the City of David. He was laid on a bed perfumed with sweet spices and ointments, and at his funeral the people built a huge fire in his honor.

16:4 As in parallel text at 1 Kgs 15:20; Hebrew reads *Abel-maim*, another name for Abel-beth-maacah.
16:8a Hebrew *Cushites.* 16:8b Or *and charioteers.*

I FIND happiness in seeking the Lord with all my heart. (15:15)

I WORK to remove from leadership those who promote worship of false gods. (15:16)

I PUT my trust in the Lord, not in my own political maneuverings. (16:2)

I DO NOT ANGRILY ATTACK those who point out my sin and challenge me to trust God. (16:10)

I SEEK the Lord's help when I am sick. (16:12)

See David's profile (page 629) at Psalm 3:1.

CHAPTER 17

Jehoshaphat Rules in Judah

Then Jehoshaphat, Asa's son, became the next king. He strengthened Judah to stand against any attack from Israel. ²He stationed troops in all the fortified cities of Judah, and he assigned additional garrisons to the land of Judah and to the towns of Ephraim that his father, Asa, had conquered.

³The LORD was with Jehoshaphat because he followed the example of his father's early years* and did not worship the images of Baal. ⁴He sought his father's God and obeyed his commands instead of following the practices of the kingdom of Israel. ⁵So the LORD established Jehoshaphat's control over the kingdom of Judah. All the people of Judah brought gifts to Jehoshaphat, so he became very wealthy and highly esteemed. ⁶He was committed to the ways of the LORD. He knocked down the pagan shrines and destroyed the Asherah poles.

I PROTECT the people I lead. (17:1)

See Jehoshaphat's profile (page 527) at 2 Chronicles 20:21.

I FOLLOW the godly example of my parents, as far as they obeyed God. (17:3)

I AM COMMITTED to the ways of God and to removing pagan influences from my life. (17:6)

UNLIKE ASA   *I want to be true to God to the very end.*

2 Chronicles 16:9

Asa was one of those "white sheep" of the family—the godly son of wicked parents. From the beginning of his kingship, Asa determined to reign differently from his father.

Asa set his course to seek the Lord, and God overwhelmingly blessed him for it:

- Asa enjoyed peace instead of war
- The towns of Judah prospered and grew
- God delivered Judah from an army that boasted far more men and greater weapons
- Spiritual revival broke out in Judah and even reached true believers in Israel

Perhaps it is easier in one's youth to take the bold steps of faith Asa took—trusting God in the face of an insurmountable enemy, leading a nation to make a covenant to seek God, and removing his pagan grandmother from her political position.

Unfortunately when Asa was old, seeking and depending on God did not come so easily. His heart was still God's, but his will became his own. He looked only to human resources to rescue him from enemies and then bristled when he was confronted about it.

In pride, Asa kept looking to human help alone, even for his physical well-being. He died without calling to the Lord in his weakness.

Perhaps it is easier to die as a young martyr than to live a long life of dependence on God. The biblical account of Asa's life should prompt each of us to ask, "When I am old, will I still be seeking help from God, or will I have developed my own way of handling life?"

To read more about Asa's reign, see 1 Kings 15:9-24.

○ *Today's Scripture reading is 2 Chronicles 14–16.*

---

⁷In the third year of his reign, Jehoshaphat sent out his officials to teach in all the towns of Judah. These officials included Ben-hail, Obadiah, Zechariah, Nethanel, and Micaiah. ⁸He sent Levites along with them, including Shemaiah, Nethaniah, Zebadiah, Asahel, Shemiramoth, Jehonathan, Adonijah, Tobijah, and Tob-adonijah. He also sent out the priests, Elishama and Jehoram. ⁹They took copies of the Book of the Law of the LORD and traveled around through all the towns of Judah, teaching the people.

I TEACH God's people from his book. (17:9)

¹⁰Then the fear of the LORD fell over all the surrounding kingdoms so that none of them declared war on Jehoshaphat. ¹¹Some of the Philistines brought him gifts and silver as tribute, and the Arabs brought seventy-seven hundred rams and seventy-seven hundred male goats.

¹²So Jehoshaphat became more and more powerful and built fortresses

17:3 Some Hebrew manuscripts read *the example of his father, David.*

and store cities throughout Judah. [13]He stored numerous supplies in Judah's towns and stationed an army of seasoned troops at Jerusalem. [14]His army was enrolled according to ancestral clans.

From Judah, there were 300,000 troops organized in units of one thousand, under the command of Adnah. [15]Next in command was Jehohanan, who commanded 280,000 troops. [16]Next was Amasiah son of Zicri, who volunteered for the LORD's service, with 200,000 troops under his command.

[17]From Benjamin, there were 200,000 troops equipped with bows and shields. They were under the command of Eliada, a veteran soldier. [18]Next in command was Jehozabad, who commanded 180,000 armed men.

[19]These were the troops stationed in Jerusalem to serve the king, besides those Jehoshaphat stationed in the fortified cities throughout Judah.

CHAPTER 18

Jehoshaphat and Ahab

I DO NOT ENCOURAGE my children to marry unbelievers, even if they will gain status and wealth. (18:1)

See the profiles for Ahab (page 417) and Jehoshaphat (page 527) at 1 Kings 16:31 and 2 Chronicles 20:21.

Now Jehoshaphat enjoyed great riches and high esteem, and he arranged for his son to marry the daughter of King Ahab of Israel. [2]A few years later, he went to Samaria to visit Ahab, who prepared a great banquet for him and his officials. They butchered great numbers of sheep and oxen for the feast. Then Ahab enticed Jehoshaphat to join forces with him to attack Ramoth-gilead. [3]"Will you join me in fighting against Ramoth-gilead?" Ahab asked.

And Jehoshaphat replied, "Why, of course! You and I are brothers, and my troops are yours to command. We will certainly join you in battle." [4]Then Jehoshaphat added, "But first let's find out what the LORD says."

I SEEK counsel from God's people, not just secular advisers. (18:6)

I DO NOT RESIST the hard sayings of God's Word. (18:7)

[5]So King Ahab summoned his prophets, four hundred of them, and asked them, "Should we go to war against Ramoth-gilead or not?"

They all replied, "Go ahead, for God will give you a great victory!"

[6]But Jehoshaphat asked, "Isn't there a prophet of the LORD around, too? I would like to ask him the same question."

[7]King Ahab replied, "There is still one prophet of the LORD, but I hate him. He never prophesies anything but bad news for me! His name is Micaiah son of Imlah."

"You shouldn't talk like that," Jehoshaphat said. "Let's hear what he has to say."

[8]So the king of Israel called one of his officials and said, "Quick! Go and get Micaiah son of Imlah."

Micaiah Prophesies against Ahab

I DO NOT TELL people what they want to hear if it is not the truth. (18:10)

[9]King Ahab of Israel and King Jehoshaphat of Judah, dressed in their royal robes, were sitting on thrones at the threshing floor near the gate of Samaria. All of Ahab's prophets were prophesying there in front of them. [10]One of them, Zedekiah son of Kenaanah, made some iron horns and proclaimed, "This is what the LORD says: With these horns you will gore the Arameans to death!"

[11]All the other prophets agreed. "Yes," they said, "go up to Ramoth-gilead and be victorious. The LORD will give you a glorious victory!"

[12]Meanwhile, the messenger who went to get Micaiah said to him, "Look, all the prophets are promising victory for the king. Be sure that you agree with them and promise success."

I SPEAK the truth of God's Word, no matter what other opinion prevails. (18:13)

[13]But Micaiah replied, "As surely as the LORD lives, I will say only what my God tells me to say."

[14]When Micaiah arrived before the king, Ahab asked him, "Micaiah, should we go to war against Ramoth-gilead or not?"

And Micaiah replied, "Go right ahead! It will be a glorious victory!"

¹⁵But the king replied sharply, "How many times must I demand that you speak only the truth when you speak for the LORD?"

¹⁶So Micaiah told him, "In a vision I saw all Israel scattered on the mountains, like sheep without a shepherd. And the LORD said, 'Their master has been killed. Send them home in peace.' "

¹⁷"Didn't I tell you?" the king of Israel said to Jehoshaphat. "He does it every time. He never prophesies anything but bad news for me."

¹⁸Then Micaiah continued, "Listen to what the LORD says! I saw the LORD sitting on his throne with all the armies of heaven on his right and on his left. ¹⁹And the LORD said, 'Who can entice King Ahab of Israel to go into battle against Ramoth-gilead so that he can be killed there?' There were many suggestions, ²⁰until finally a spirit approached the LORD and said, 'I can do it!'

" 'How will you do this?' the LORD asked.

²¹"And the spirit replied, 'I will go out and inspire all Ahab's prophets to speak lies.'

" 'You will succeed,' said the LORD. 'Go ahead and do it.'

²²"So you see, the LORD has put a lying spirit in the mouths of your prophets. For the LORD has determined disaster for you."

²³Then Zedekiah son of Kenaanah walked up to Micaiah and slapped him across the face. "When did the Spirit of the LORD leave me to speak to you?" he demanded.

²⁴And Micaiah replied, "You will find out soon enough, when you find yourself hiding in some secret room!"

²⁵King Ahab of Israel then ordered, "Arrest Micaiah and take him back to Amon, the governor of the city, and to my son Joash. ²⁶Give them this order from the king: 'Put this man in prison, and feed him nothing but bread and water until I return safely from the battle!' "

²⁷But Micaiah replied, "If you return safely, the LORD has not spoken through me!" Then he added to those standing around, "Take note of what I have said."

The Death of Ahab

²⁸So the king of Israel and King Jehoshaphat of Judah led their armies against Ramoth-gilead. ²⁹Now King Ahab said to Jehoshaphat, "As we go into battle, I will disguise myself so no one will recognize me, but you wear your royal robes." So Ahab disguised himself, and they went into battle.

³⁰Now the king of Aram had issued these orders to his charioteers: "Attack only the king of Israel!" ³¹So when the Aramean charioteers saw Jehoshaphat in his royal robes, they went after him. "There is the king of Israel!" they shouted. But Jehoshaphat cried out to the LORD to save him, and God helped him by turning the attack away from him. ³²As soon as the charioteers realized he was not the king of Israel, they stopped chasing him.

³³An Aramean soldier, however, randomly shot an arrow at the Israelite troops, and the arrow hit the king of Israel between the joints of his armor. "Get me out of here!" Ahab groaned to the driver of his chariot. "I have been badly wounded!" ³⁴The battle raged all that day, and Ahab propped himself up in his chariot facing the Arameans until evening. Then, just as the sun was setting, he died.

CHAPTER 19

Jehoshaphat Appoints Judges

When King Jehoshaphat of Judah arrived safely home to Jerusalem, ²Jehu son of Hanani the seer went out to meet him. "Why should you help the wicked and love those who hate the LORD?" he asked the king. "What you have done has brought the LORD's anger against you. ³There is some good in you, however, for

---

I BELIEVE the Lord was in control of even Ahab's prophets to cause them to speak as he wished. (18:18)

I DO NOT ATTACK those who confront me with my sin and the truth of God's Word. (18:25)

I DO NOT DISREGARD the warnings of God's Word or the consequences of disobeying (see verse 22). (18:28)

See Jehoshaphat's profile (page 527) at 2 Chronicles 20:21.

you have removed the Asherah poles throughout the land, and you have committed yourself to seeking God."

I PERSONALLY ENCOURAGE those I lead to return to the Lord. (19:4)

I APPOINT wise leaders for God's people. (19:5)

I CHALLENGE those who make decisions to do so to please God rather than people. (19:6)

⁴So Jehoshaphat lived in Jerusalem, but he went out among the people, traveling from Beersheba to the hill country of Ephraim, encouraging the people to return to the LORD, the God of their ancestors. ⁵He appointed judges throughout the nation in all the fortified cities, ⁶and he gave them these instructions: "Always think carefully before pronouncing judgment. Remember that you do not judge to please people but to please the LORD. He will be with you when you render the verdict in each case that comes before you. ⁷Fear the LORD and judge with care, for the LORD our God does not tolerate perverted justice, partiality, or the taking of bribes."

⁸Jehoshaphat appointed some of the Levites and priests and clan leaders in Israel to serve as judges in Jerusalem for cases concerning both the law of the LORD and civil disputes. ⁹These were his instructions to them: "You must always act in the fear of the LORD, with integrity and with undivided hearts. ¹⁰Whenever a case comes to you from fellow citizens in an outlying town, whether a murder case or some other violation of God's instructions, commands, laws, or regulations, you must warn them not to sin against the LORD, so that his anger will not come against you and them. Do this and you will not be guilty.

¹¹"Amariah the high priest will have final say in all cases concerning the LORD. Zebadiah son of Ishmael, a leader from the tribe of Judah, will have final say in all civil cases. The Levites will assist you in making sure that justice is served. Take courage as you fulfill your duties, and may the LORD be with those who do what is right."

CHAPTER 20

War with Moab, Ammon, and Edom

After this, the armies of the Moabites, Ammonites, and some of the Meunites* declared war on Jehoshaphat. ²Messengers came and told Jehoshaphat, "A vast army from Edom* is marching against you from beyond the Dead Sea.* They are already at Hazazon-tamar." (This was another name for En-gedi.) ³Jehoshaphat was alarmed by this news and sought the LORD for guidance. He also gave orders that everyone throughout Judah should observe a fast. ⁴So people from all the towns of Judah came to Jerusalem to seek the LORD.

I LEAD people in publicly seeking God's guidance. (20:5)

⁵Jehoshaphat stood before the people of Judah and Jerusalem in front of the new courtyard at the Temple of the LORD. ⁶He prayed, "O LORD, God of our ancestors, you alone are the God who is in heaven. You are ruler of all the kingdoms of the earth. You are powerful and mighty; no one can stand against you! ⁷O our God, did you not drive out those who lived in this land when your people arrived? And did you not give this land forever to the descendants of your friend Abraham? ⁸Your people settled here and built this Temple for you. ⁹They said, 'Whenever we are faced with any calamity such as war, disease, or famine, we can come to stand in your presence before this Temple where your name is honored. We can cry out to you to save us, and you will hear us and rescue us.'

I LOOK to God for help, acknowledging that I am powerless and that he is able. (20:12)

¹⁰"And now see what the armies of Ammon, Moab, and Mount Seir are doing. You would not let our ancestors invade those nations when Israel left Egypt, so they went around them and did not destroy them. ¹¹Now see how they reward us! For they have come to throw us out of your land, which you gave us as an inheritance. ¹²O our God, won't you stop them? We are powerless against this mighty army that is about to attack us. We do not know what to do, but we are looking to you for help."

20:1 As in some Greek manuscripts (see also 26:7); Hebrew reads *Ammonites.* 20:2a As in one Hebrew manuscript; most Hebrew manuscripts and ancient versions read *Aram.* 20:2b Hebrew *the sea.*

[13]As all the men of Judah stood before the LORD with their little ones, wives, and children, [14]the Spirit of the LORD came upon one of the men standing there. His name was Jahaziel son of Zechariah, son of Benaiah, son of Jeiel, son of Mattaniah, a Levite who was a descendant of Asaph. [15]He said, "Listen, King Jehoshaphat! Listen, all you people of Judah and Jerusalem! This is what the LORD says: Do not be afraid! Don't be discouraged by this mighty army, for the battle is not yours, but God's. [16]Tomorrow, march out against them. You will find them coming up through the ascent of Ziz at the end of the valley that opens into the wilderness of Jeruel. [17]But you will not even need to fight. Take your positions; then stand still and watch the LORD's victory. He is with you, O people of Judah and Jerusalem. Do not be afraid or discouraged. Go out there tomorrow, for the LORD is with you!"

[18]Then King Jehoshaphat bowed down with his face to the ground. And all the people of Judah and Jerusalem did the same, worshiping the LORD. [19]Then the Levites from the clans of Kohath and Korah stood to praise the LORD, the God of Israel, with a very loud shout.

[20]Early the next morning the army of Judah went out into the wilderness of Tekoa. On the way Jehoshaphat stopped and said, "Listen to me, all you people of Judah and Jerusalem! Believe in the LORD your God, and you will be able to stand firm. Believe in his prophets, and you will succeed." [21]After consulting the leaders of the people, the king appointed singers to walk ahead of the army, singing to the LORD and praising him for his holy splendor. This is what they sang:

"Give thanks to the LORD;
  his faithful love endures forever!"

[22]At the moment they began to sing and give praise, the LORD caused the armies of Ammon, Moab, and Mount Seir to start fighting among themselves. [23]The armies of Moab and Ammon turned against their allies from Mount Seir and killed every one of them. After they had finished off the army of Seir, they turned on each other.

[24]So when the army of Judah arrived at the lookout point in the wilderness, there were dead bodies lying on the ground for as far as they could see. Not a single one of the enemy had escaped. [25]King Jehoshaphat and his men went out to gather the plunder. They found vast amounts of equipment, clothing,* and other valuables—more than they could carry. There was so much plunder that it took them three days just to collect it all! [26]On the fourth day they gathered in the Valley of Blessing,* which got its name that day because the people praised and thanked the LORD there. It is still called the Valley of Blessing today.

[27]Then they returned to Jerusalem, with Jehoshaphat leading them, full of joy that the LORD had given them victory over their enemies. [28]They marched into Jerusalem to the music of harps, lyres, and trumpets and proceeded to the Temple of the LORD. [29]When the surrounding kingdoms heard that the LORD himself had fought against the enemies of Israel, the fear of God came over them. [30]So Jehoshaphat's kingdom was at peace, for his God had given him rest on every side.

Summary of Jehoshaphat's Reign

[31]So Jehoshaphat ruled over the land of Judah. He was thirty-five years old when he became king, and he reigned in Jerusalem twenty-five years. His mother was Azubah, the daughter of Shilhi. [32]Jehoshaphat was a good king, following the ways of his father, Asa. He did what was pleasing in the LORD's

---

I SEEK the Lord's help together with my whole family. (20:13)

See Asaph's profile (page 687) at Psalm 73:28.

I ENTER times of danger and trial with songs of praise to my God (Philippians 4:6-7). (20:21)

I GATHER with God's people to thank the Lord when he has rescued and blessed us. (20:26)

I BELIEVE that unbelievers are often overcome with the fear of the Lord when God's people trust God and are rescued by him. (20:29)

20:25 As in some Hebrew manuscripts and Latin Vulgate; most Hebrew manuscripts read *corpses.* 20:26 Hebrew *valley of Beracah.*

I REMOVE all pagan influence from my sphere of authority. (20:33)

See Asa's profile (page 521) at 2 Chronicles 16:9.

sight. ³³During his reign, however, he failed to remove all the pagan shrines, and the people never fully committed themselves to following the God of their ancestors. ³⁴The rest of the events of Jehoshaphat's reign, from beginning to end, are recorded in *The Record of Jehu Son of Hanani*, which is included in *The Book of the Kings of Israel*.

³⁵But near the end of his life, King Jehoshaphat of Judah made an alliance with King Ahaziah of Israel, who was a very wicked man.* ³⁶Together they built a fleet of trading ships* at the port of Ezion-geber. ³⁷Then Eliezer son of Dodavahu from Mareshah prophesied against Jehoshaphat. He said, "Because you have allied yourself with King Ahaziah, the LORD will destroy your work." So the ships met with disaster and never put out to sea.*

CHAPTER 21

Jehoram Rules in Judah

See David's profile (page 629) at Psalm 3:1.

When Jehoshaphat died, he was buried with his ancestors in the City of David. Then his son Jehoram became the next king. ²Jehoram's brothers—the other sons of Jehoshaphat—were Azariah, Jehiel, Zechariah, Azariahu, Michael, and Shephatiah. ³Their father had given each of them valuable gifts of silver, gold, and costly items, and also the ownership of some of Judah's fortified cities. However, Jehoram became king because he was the oldest. ⁴But when Jehoram had become solidly established as king, he killed all his brothers and some of the other leaders of Israel.

I DO NOT DESTROY my family to gain more power or to get more money. (21:4)

See Ahab's profile (page 417) at 1 Kings 16:31.

I BELIEVE the Lord did not destroy David's dynasty because of his promise to David. (21:7)

⁵Jehoram was thirty-two years old when he became king, and he reigned in Jerusalem eight years. ⁶But Jehoram followed the example of the kings of Israel and was as wicked as King Ahab, for he had married one of Ahab's daughters. So Jehoram did what was evil in the LORD's sight. ⁷But the LORD was not willing to destroy David's dynasty, for he had made a covenant with David and promised that his descendants would continue to rule forever.*

⁸During Jehoram's reign, the Edomites revolted against Judah and crowned their own king. ⁹So Jehoram went to attack Edom with his full army and all his chariots. The Edomites surrounded him and his charioteers, but he escaped at night under cover of darkness. ¹⁰Edom has been independent from Judah to this day. The town of Libnah revolted about that same time, because Jehoram had abandoned the LORD, the God of his ancestors. ¹¹He had built pagan shrines in the hill country of Judah and had led the people of Jerusalem and Judah to give themselves to pagan gods.

¹²Then Elijah the prophet wrote Jehoram this letter:

I FOLLOW the good example of godly family members, not the evil example of wicked family members. (21:12)

See the profiles for Elijah (page 421), David (page 629), Jehoshaphat (page 527), and Asa (page 521) at 1 Kings 19:18, Psalm 3:1, 2 Chronicles 20:21, and 2 Chronicles 16:9.

See Ahab's profile (page 417) at 1 Kings 16:31.

"This is what the LORD, the God of your ancestor David, says: You have not followed the good example of your father, Jehoshaphat, or your grandfather King Asa of Judah. ¹³Instead, you have been as evil as the kings of Israel. You have led the people of Jerusalem and Judah to worship idols, just as King Ahab did in Israel. And you have even killed your own brothers, men who were better than you. ¹⁴So now the LORD is about to strike you, your people, your children, your wives, and all that is yours with a heavy blow. ¹⁵You yourself will be stricken with a severe intestinal disease until it causes your bowels to come out."

¹⁶Then the LORD stirred up the Philistines and the Arabs, who lived near the Ethiopians,* to attack Jehoram. ¹⁷They marched against Judah, broke down its defenses, and carried away everything of value in the royal palace, including his sons and his wives. Only his youngest son, Ahaziah,* was spared.

20:35 Or *who made him do what was wrong.*   20:36 Hebrew *fleet of ships that could go to Tarshish.*   20:37 Hebrew *never set sail for Tarshish.*   21:7 Hebrew *promised to give a lamp to David and his descendants forever.*   21:16 Hebrew *the Cushites.*   21:17 Hebrew *Jehoahaz,* a variant name for Ahaziah; compare 22:1.

[18]It was after this that the LORD struck Jehoram with the severe intestinal disease. [19]In the course of time, at the end of two years, the disease caused his bowels to come out, and he died in agony. His people did not build a great fire to honor him at his funeral as they had done for his ancestors. [20]Jehoram was thirty-two years old when he became king, and he reigned in Jerusalem eight years. No one was sorry when he died. He was buried in the City of David, but not in the royal cemetery.

LIKE JEHOSHAPHAT

I face trials and danger with songs of praise for God's faithful love.

2 Chronicles 20:21

"Thank you, God, for making Mommy all better," a little girl prayed in faith when her mother went to bed early, sick with the flu.

Like that small child, Jehoshaphat led his people to thank the Lord for his promised victory before they ever reached the battlefield. With singers praising God along the way, why wait to celebrate?

Faced with the declaration of war and warned of the approaching army, Jehoshaphat didn't just mouth the words of trust in God and then send off some Temple treasures to appease the enemy. He reacted instead like any good king of Judah. Although he was alarmed in spirit, Jehoshaphat immediately called for the people to seek the Lord in prayer and fasting. Standing before them, Jehoshaphat pleaded with God to remember his power and his promises and to deliver his people. The Lord sent his answer quickly: He would be with them and deliver them. They would not even fight, for it was God's battle and he would win it for them!

What worship followed! Bowing to the ground and shouting aloud, the people expressed their joy.

The next day, Jehoshaphat and the leaders again demonstrated their trust in God's good promises. Calling the people to trust the Lord, they stationed their finest singers in front and marched to the battle accompanied by song. Just as God had promised, they arrived in time to see that the enemy had finished the battle for them. All that was left was to collect the plunder left for the victor.

Though Jehoshaphat had the sure promise of military victory for this battle, the singers praised the Lord for something even more sure: God's faithful love. Circumstances may vary and change. Prayers may seem unanswered. But God's faithful love never changes.

With or without assurances of the outcome, we can march into any situation praising God that his faithful love will be with us to the final, victorious end.

Let us live like Jehoshaphat, entering every circumstance with thanksgiving and praise!

○ *Today's Scripture reading is 2 Chronicles 17–20.*

CHAPTER **22**

Ahaziah Rules in Judah

Then the people of Jerusalem made Ahaziah, Jehoram's youngest son, their next king. The marauding bands of Arabs had killed all the older sons. So Ahaziah son of Jehoram reigned as king of Judah. [2]Ahaziah was twenty-two* years old when he became king, and he reigned in Jerusalem one year. His mother was Athaliah, a granddaughter of King Omri of Israel. [3]Ahaziah also followed the evil example of King Ahab's family, for his mother encouraged him in doing wrong. [4]He did what was evil in the LORD's sight, just as Ahab had done. After the death of his father, members of Ahab's family became his advisers, and they led him to ruin.

[5]Following their evil advice, Ahaziah made an alliance with King Joram,* the son of King Ahab of Israel. They went out to fight King Hazael of Aram at Ramoth-gilead, and the Arameans wounded Joram in the battle. [6]Joram

I DO NOT ENCOURAGE my children to do wrong. (22:3)

See Ahab's profile (page 417) at 1 Kings 16:31.

22:2 As in some Greek manuscripts and Syriac version (see also 2 Kgs 8:26); Hebrew reads *forty-two*.
22:5 Hebrew *Jehoram*, a variant name for Joram; also in 22:6, 7.

returned to Jezreel to recover from his wounds, and King Ahaziah* of Judah went to Jezreel to visit him. ⁷But this turned out to be a fatal mistake, for God had decided to punish Ahaziah. It was during this visit that Ahaziah went out with Joram to meet Jehu son of Nimshi, whom the LORD had appointed to end the dynasty of Ahab.

⁸While Jehu was executing judgment against the family of Ahab, he happened to meet some of Judah's officials and Ahaziah's relatives* who were attending Ahaziah. So Jehu killed them all. ⁹Then Jehu's men searched for Ahaziah, and they found him hiding in the city of Samaria. They brought him to Jehu, who killed him. Ahaziah was given a decent burial because the people said, "He was the grandson of Jehoshaphat—a man who sought the LORD with all his heart." None of the surviving members of Ahaziah's family was capable of ruling the kingdom.

Athaliah Rules in Judah

¹⁰When Athaliah, the mother of King Ahaziah of Judah, learned that her son was dead, she set out to destroy the rest of Judah's royal family. ¹¹But Ahaziah's sister Jehosheba,* the daughter of King Jehoram, took Ahaziah's infant son, Joash, and stole him away from among the rest of the king's children, who were about to be killed. She put Joash and his nurse in a bedroom. In this way, Jehosheba, the wife of Jehoiada the priest, hid the child so that Athaliah could not murder him. ¹²Joash remained hidden in the Temple of God for six years while Athaliah ruled over the land.

CHAPTER 23

Revolt against Athaliah

In the seventh year of Athaliah's reign, Jehoiada the priest decided to act. He got up his courage and made a pact with five army commanders: Azariah son of Jeroham, Ishmael son of Jehohanan, Azariah son of Obed, Maaseiah son of Adaiah, and Elishaphat son of Zicri. ²These men traveled secretly throughout Judah and summoned the Levites and clan leaders in Judah's towns to come to Jerusalem. ³They all gathered at the Temple of God, where they made a covenant with Joash, the young king.

Jehoiada said to them, "The time has come for the king's son to reign! The LORD has promised that a descendant of David will be our king. ⁴This is what you must do. When the priests and Levites come on duty on the Sabbath, a third of them will serve as gatekeepers. ⁵Another third will go over to the royal palace, and the final third will be at the Foundation Gate. Everyone else should stay in the courtyards of the LORD's Temple. ⁶Remember, only the priests and Levites on duty may enter the Temple of the LORD, for they are set apart as holy. The rest of the people must obey the LORD's instructions and stay outside. ⁷You Levites, form a bodyguard for the king and keep your weapons in hand. Any unauthorized person who enters the Temple must be killed. Stay right beside the king at all times."

⁸So the Levites and the people did everything just as Jehoiada the priest ordered. The commanders took charge of the men reporting for duty that Sabbath, as well as those who were going off duty. Jehoiada the priest did not let anyone go home after their shift ended. ⁹Then Jehoiada supplied the commanders with the spears and shields that had once belonged to King David and were stored in the Temple of God. ¹⁰He stationed the guards around the king, with their weapons ready. They formed a line from the south side of the Temple around to the north side and all around the altar.

¹¹Then Jehoiada and his sons brought out Joash, the king's son, and placed

I DO NOT DESTROY my family to gain political power or money. (22:10)

I PROTECT children from family members who would hurt or destroy them. (22:11)

I WORK to ensure that God's will is accomplished within my sphere of authority. (23:3)

See David's profile (page 629) at Psalm 3:1.

I COOPERATE with those who are working to accomplish God's will. (23:8)

22:6 Some Hebrew manuscripts, Greek and Syriac versions, and Latin Vulgate (see also 2 Kgs 8:29); most Hebrew manuscripts read *Azariah*.   22:8 As in Greek version (see also 2 Kgs 10:13); Hebrew reads *and sons of the brothers of Ahaziah*.   22:11 As in parallel text at 2 Kgs 11:2; Hebrew reads *Jehoshabeath*, a variant name for Jehosheba.

the crown on his head. They presented Joash with a copy of God's laws and proclaimed him king. Then they anointed him, and everyone shouted, "Long live the king!"

The Death of Athaliah

¹²When Athaliah heard the noise of the people running and the shouts of praise to the king, she hurried to the LORD's Temple to see what was happening. ¹³And she saw the newly crowned king standing in his place of authority by the pillar at the Temple entrance. The officers and trumpeters were surrounding him, and people from all over the land were rejoicing and blowing trumpets. Singers with musical instruments were leading the people in a great celebration. When Athaliah saw all this, she tore her clothes in despair and shouted, "Treason! Treason!"

¹⁴Then Jehoiada the priest ordered the commanders who were in charge of the troops, "Take her out of the Temple, and kill anyone who tries to rescue her. Do not kill her here in the Temple of the LORD." ¹⁵So they seized her and led her out to the gate where horses enter the palace grounds, and they killed her there.

Jehoiada's Religious Reforms

¹⁶Then Jehoiada made a covenant between himself and the king and the people that they would be the LORD's people. ¹⁷And all the people went over to the temple of Baal and tore it down. They demolished the altars and smashed the idols, and they killed Mattan the priest of Baal in front of the altars.

¹⁸Jehoiada now put the Levitical priests in charge of the Temple of the LORD, following all the instructions given by David. He also commanded them to present burnt offerings to the LORD, as prescribed by the law of Moses, and to sing and rejoice as David had instructed. ¹⁹He stationed gatekeepers at the gates of the LORD's Temple to keep those who were ceremonially unclean from entering.

²⁰Then the commanders, nobles, rulers, and all the people escorted the king from the Temple of the LORD. They went through the Upper Gate and into the palace, and they seated the king on the royal throne. ²¹So all the people of the land rejoiced, and the city was peaceful because Athaliah had been killed.

CHAPTER 24

Joash Repairs the Temple

Joash was seven years old when he became king, and he reigned in Jerusalem forty years. His mother was Zibiah, from Beersheba. ²Joash did what was pleasing in the LORD's sight throughout the lifetime of Jehoiada the priest. ³Jehoiada chose two wives for Joash, and he had sons and daughters.

⁴Some time later, Joash decided to repair and restore the Temple of the LORD. ⁵He summoned the priests and Levites and gave them these instructions: "Go at once to all the towns of Judah and collect the required annual offerings, so that we can repair the Temple of your God. Do not delay!" But the Levites did not act right away.

⁶So the king called for Jehoiada the high priest and asked him, "Why haven't you demanded that the Levites go out and collect the Temple taxes from the towns of Judah and from Jerusalem? Moses, the servant of the LORD, levied this tax on the community of Israel in order to maintain the Tabernacle of the Covenant.*"

⁷Over the years, the followers of wicked Athaliah had broken into the Temple of God, and they had used all the dedicated things from the Temple of the LORD to worship the images of Baal. ⁸So now Joash gave instructions for a

I LEAD God's people in removing idolatry and pagan practices from our midst. (23:17)
See Moses' profile (page 73) at Exodus 5:1.

See Moses' profile (page 73) at Exodus 5:1.

I MAKE provision for the care and support of places of worship to God. (24:8)

24:6 Hebrew *Tent of the Testimony.*

chest to be made and set outside the gate leading to the Temple of the LORD. [9]Then a proclamation was sent throughout Judah and Jerusalem, telling the people to bring to the LORD the tax that Moses, the servant of God, had required of the Israelites in the wilderness. [10]This pleased all the leaders and the people, and they gladly brought their money and filled the chest with it.

[11]Whenever the chest became full, the Levites carried it to the king's officials. Then the court secretary and an officer of the high priest counted the money and took the chest back to the Temple again. This went on day after day, and a large amount of money was collected. [12]The king and Jehoiada gave the money to the construction supervisors, who hired masons and carpenters to restore the Temple of the LORD. They also hired metalworkers, who made articles of iron and bronze for the LORD's Temple.

[13]So the men in charge of the renovation worked hard, and they made steady progress. They restored the Temple of God according to its original design and strengthened it. [14]When all the repairs were finished, they brought the remaining money to the king and Jehoiada. It was used to make utensils for the Temple of the LORD—utensils for worship services and for burnt offerings, including ladles and other vessels made of gold and silver. And the burnt offerings were sacrificed continually in the Temple of the LORD during the lifetime of Jehoiada the priest.

[15]Jehoiada lived to a very old age, finally dying at 130. [16]He was buried among the kings in the City of David, because he had done so much good in Israel for God and his Temple.

Jehoiada's Reforms Reversed

[17]But after Jehoiada's death, the leaders of Judah came and bowed before King Joash and persuaded the king to listen to their advice. [18]They decided to abandon the Temple of the LORD, the God of their ancestors, and they worshiped Asherah poles and idols instead! Then the anger of God burned against Judah and Jerusalem because of their sin. [19]The LORD sent prophets to bring them back to him, but the people would not listen.

[20]Then the Spirit of God came upon Zechariah son of Jehoiada the priest. He stood before the people and said, "This is what God says: Why do you disobey the LORD's commands so that you cannot prosper? You have abandoned the LORD, and now he has abandoned you!"

[21]Then the leaders plotted to kill Zechariah, and by order of King Joash himself, they stoned him to death in the courtyard of the LORD's Temple. [22]That was how King Joash repaid Jehoiada for his love and loyalty—by killing his son. Zechariah's last words as he died were, "May the LORD see what they are doing and hold them accountable!"

The End of Joash's Reign

[23]At the beginning of the year, the Aramean army marched against Joash. They invaded Judah and Jerusalem and killed all the leaders of the nation. Then they sent all the plunder back to their king in Damascus. [24]Although the Arameans attacked with only a small army, the LORD helped them conquer the much larger army of Judah. The people of Judah had abandoned the LORD, the God of their ancestors, so judgment was executed against Joash.

[25]The Arameans withdrew, leaving Joash severely wounded. But his own officials decided to kill him for murdering the son of Jehoiada the priest. They assassinated him as he lay in bed. Then he was buried in the City of David, but not in the royal cemetery. [26]The assassins were Jozabad,* the son of an Ammonite woman named Shimeath, and Jehozabad, the son of a Moabite woman named Shomer.* [27]The complete story about the sons of Joash, the prophecies about him,

I AM HAPPY to give money to support places of worship to God. (24:10)

See David's profile (page 629) at Psalm 3:1.

I DO NOT LISTEN to those who want me to abandon the worship of the Lord. (24:17)

I DO NOT DESTROY those who speak God's truth about my sin and need for repentance. (24:21)

I HONOR the memory of my godly mentors by listening to God's Word instead of resisting it. (24:22)

24:26a As in parallel text at 2 Kgs 12:21; Hebrew reads *Zabad*. 24:26b As in parallel text at 2 Kgs 12:21; Hebrew reads *Shimrith*.

and the record of his restoration of the Temple of God are written in *The Commentary on the Book of the Kings*. When Joash died, his son Amaziah became the next king.

CHAPTER 25

Amaziah Rules in Judah

Amaziah was twenty-five years old when he became king, and he reigned in Jerusalem twenty-nine years. His mother was Jehoaddin,* from Jerusalem. ²Amaziah did what was pleasing in the LORD's sight, but not wholeheartedly.

³When Amaziah was well established as king, he executed the men who had assassinated his father. ⁴However, he did not kill the children of the assassins, for he obeyed the command of the LORD written in the Book of the Law of Moses: "Parents must not be put to death for the sins of their children, nor the children for the sins of their parents. Those worthy of death must be executed for their own crimes."*

⁵Another thing Amaziah did was to organize the army, assigning leaders to each clan from Judah and Benjamin. Then he took a census and found that he had an army of 300,000 men twenty years old and older, all trained in the use of spear and shield. ⁶He also paid about 7,500 pounds* of silver to hire 100,000 experienced fighting men from Israel.

⁷But a man of God came to the king and said, "O king, do not hire troops from Israel, for the LORD is not with Israel. He will not help those people of Ephraim! ⁸If you let them go with your troops into battle, you will be defeated no matter how well you fight. God will overthrow you, for he has the power to help or to frustrate."

⁹Amaziah asked the man of God, "But what should I do about the silver I paid to hire the army of Israel?"

The man of God replied, "The LORD is able to give you much more than this!" ¹⁰So Amaziah discharged the hired troops and sent them back to Ephraim. This made them angry with Judah, and they returned home in a great rage.

¹¹Then Amaziah summoned his courage and led his army to the Valley of Salt, where they killed ten thousand Edomite troops from Seir. ¹²They captured another ten thousand and took them to the top of a cliff and threw them off, dashing them to pieces on the rocks below.

¹³Meanwhile, the hired troops that Amaziah had sent home raided several of the towns of Judah between Samaria and Beth-horon, killing three thousand people and carrying off great quantities of plunder.

¹⁴When King Amaziah returned from defeating the Edomites, he brought with him idols taken from the people of Seir. He set them up as his own gods, bowed down in front of them, and presented sacrifices to them! ¹⁵This made the LORD very angry, and he sent a prophet to ask, "Why have you worshiped gods who could not even save their own people from you?"

¹⁶But the king interrupted him and said, "Since when have I asked your advice? Be quiet now before I have you killed!"

So the prophet left with this warning: "I know that God has determined to destroy you because you have done this and have not accepted my counsel."

¹⁷After consulting with his advisers, King Amaziah of Judah sent this challenge to Israel's king Jehoash,* the son of Jehoahaz and grandson of Jehu: "Come and meet me in battle!"

¹⁸But King Jehoash of Israel replied to King Amaziah of Judah with this story: "Out in the Lebanon mountains, a thistle sent a message to a mighty cedar tree: 'Give your daughter in marriage to my son.' But just then a wild

I WHOLEHEARTEDLY DO what is pleasing to the Lord. (25:2)

See Moses' profile (page 73) at Exodus 5:1.

I AM WILLING to suffer a financial loss in order to trust and obey God. (25:9)

I DO NOT BRING back idols from foreign places. (25:14)

I DO NOT REJECT the warnings God gives through his messengers. (25:16)

25:1 As in parallel text at 2 Kgs 14:2; Hebrew reads *Jehoaddan*, a variant name for Jehoaddin. 25:4 Deut 24:16. 25:6 Hebrew *100 talents* [3.4 metric tons]. 25:17 Hebrew *Joash*, a variant name for Jehoash; also in 25:18, 21, 23, 25.

I WARN others against
provoking a needless
fight. (25:19)

animal came by and stepped on the thistle, crushing it! [19]You may be very proud of your conquest of Edom, but my advice is to stay home. Why stir up trouble that will bring disaster on you and the people of Judah?"

[20]But Amaziah would not listen, for God was arranging to destroy him for worshiping the gods of Edom. [21]So King Jehoash of Israel mobilized his army against King Amaziah of Judah. The two armies drew up their battle lines at Beth-shemesh in Judah. [22]Judah was routed by the army of Israel, and its army scattered and fled for home. [23]King Jehoash of Israel captured King Amaziah of Judah at Beth-shemesh and brought him back to Jerusalem. Then Jehoash ordered his army to demolish six hundred feet* of Jerusalem's wall, from the Ephraim Gate to the Corner Gate. [24]He carried off all the gold and silver and all the utensils from the Temple of God that had been in the care of Obed-edom. He also seized the treasures of the royal palace, along with hostages, and then returned to Samaria.

[25]King Amaziah of Judah lived on for fifteen years after the death of King Jehoash of Israel. [26]The rest of the events of Amaziah's reign, from beginning to end, are recorded in *The Book of the Kings of Judah and Israel.* [27]After Amaziah turned away from the LORD, there was a conspiracy against his life in Jerusalem, and he fled to Lachish. But his enemies sent assassins after him, and they killed him there. [28]They brought him back to Jerusalem on a horse, and he was buried with his ancestors in the City of David.*

CHAPTER 26

Uzziah Rules in Judah

The people of Judah then crowned Amaziah's sixteen-year-old son, Uzziah, as their next king. [2]After his father's death, Uzziah rebuilt the town of Elath* and restored it to Judah. [3]Uzziah was sixteen when he became king, and he reigned in Jerusalem fifty-two years. His mother was Jecoliah, from Jerusalem. [4]He did what was pleasing in the LORD's sight, just as his father, Amaziah, had done.

I SEEK God and learn
from others how to
fear him. (26:5)

[5]Uzziah sought God during the days of Zechariah, who instructed him in the fear of God. And as long as the king sought the LORD, God gave him success.

[6]He declared war on the Philistines and broke down the walls of Gath, Jabneh, and Ashdod. Then he built new towns in the Ashdod area and in other parts of Philistia. [7]God helped him not only with his wars against the Philistines, but also in his battles with the Arabs of Gur* and in his wars with the Meunites. [8]The Meunites* paid annual tribute to him, and his fame spread even to Egypt, for he had become very powerful.

[9]Uzziah built fortified towers in Jerusalem at the Corner Gate, at the Valley Gate, and at the angle in the wall. [10]He also constructed forts in the wilderness and dug many water cisterns, because he kept great herds of livestock in the foothills of Judah* and on the plains. He was also a man who loved the soil. He had many workers who cared for his farms and vineyards, both on the hillsides and in the fertile valleys.

I PROTECT the people
under my authority.
(26:11)

[11]Uzziah had an army of well-trained warriors, ready to march into battle, unit by unit. This great army of fighting men had been mustered and organized by Jeiel, the secretary of the army, and his assistant, Maaseiah. They were under the direction of Hananiah, one of the king's officials. [12]Twenty-six hundred clan leaders commanded these regiments of seasoned warriors. [13]The army consisted of 307,500 men, all elite troops. They were prepared to assist the king against any enemy. [14]Uzziah provided the entire army with shields, spears, helmets, coats of mail, bows, and sling stones.

I PROVIDE my workers
with the tools they
need to do their jobs
well. (26:14)

25:23 Hebrew *400 cubits* [180 meters]. 25:28 As in some Hebrew manuscripts and other ancient versions (see also 2 Kgs 14:20); most Hebrew manuscripts read *the city of Judah.* 26:2 As in Greek version (see also 2 Kgs 14:22; 16:6); Hebrew reads *Eloth.* 26:7 As in Greek version; Hebrew reads *Gur-baal.* 26:8 As in Greek version; Hebrew reads *Ammonites.* Compare 26:7. 26:10 Hebrew *the Shephelah.*

[15]And he produced machines mounted on the walls of Jerusalem, designed by brilliant men to shoot arrows and hurl stones* from the towers and the corners of the wall. His fame spread far and wide, for the LORD helped him wonderfully until he became very powerful.

Uzziah's Sin and Punishment

[16]But when he had become powerful, he also became proud, which led to his downfall. He sinned against the LORD his God by entering the sanctuary of the LORD's Temple and personally burning incense on the altar. [17]Azariah the high priest went in after him with eighty other priests of the LORD, all brave men. [18]They confronted King Uzziah and said, "It is not for you, Uzziah, to burn incense to the LORD. That is the work of the priests alone, the sons of Aaron who are set apart for this work. Get out of the sanctuary, for you have sinned. The LORD God will not honor you for this!"

I DO NOT BECOME proud after I have become powerful. (26:16)

See Aaron's profile (page 107) at Exodus 32:2.

UNLIKE UZZIAH *I humbly keep the Lord as king of*
2 Chronicles 26:16 *my heart and life.*

An old story by the Brothers Grimm tells of a fisherman who found a magic fish who granted him wishes. Unfortunately for the fisherman, he had a wife who wished for bigger and better possessions and power until she had wished herself empress of the world. But when she demanded to be made lord of the sun and moon, she had stretched too far. Both the fisherman and his wife found themselves once again in their miserable hut.

Like the fabled fisherman's wife, King Uzziah enjoyed success and power until his own pride sent him crashing down, and he ended up with less than he began.

Uzziah's fame and power and his productive farms and highly trained and equipped army didn't come from wishes. God himself gave Uzziah wonderful success as long as he sought the Lord. At some point, Uzziah lost sight of God as the true King and put himself on the throne. In pride, Uzziah saw himself as ruler with the power to do whatever he wanted, even if that meant breaking God's law. God commanded that only the priests were to offer incense in the Temple. But Uzziah, as king of the universe (as he saw it), no longer felt that God's rules applied to him.

None of us can usurp God's role as king of our life for very long. As Uzziah learned, pride precedes a very great fall. God struck him with leprosy, and Uzziah lived out the rest of his days excluded from his own palace and the Temple of the Lord.

God will never give his place as King and Lord of our life to another—not even to us. Unlike Uzziah, let us humbly enjoy whatever the Lord gives us and always keep him on the throne of our heart.

To read more about Uzziah's life, see 2 Kings 15:1-7.

○ Today's Scripture reading is 2 Chronicles 26.

[19]Uzziah was furious and refused to set down the incense burner he was holding. But as he was standing there with the priests before the incense altar in the LORD's Temple, leprosy* suddenly broke out on his forehead. [20]When Azariah and the other priests saw the leprosy, they rushed him out. And the king himself was eager to get out because the LORD had struck him. [21]So King Uzziah had leprosy until the day he died. He lived in isolation, excluded from the Temple of the LORD. His son Jotham was put in charge of the royal palace, and he governed the people of the land.

[22]The rest of the events of Uzziah's reign, from beginning to end, are recorded by the prophet Isaiah son of Amoz. [23]So Uzziah died, and since he had leprosy, he was buried nearby in a burial field belonging to the kings. Then his son Jotham became the next king.

I RECOGNIZE when God is disciplining me for sin in my life. (26:20)

I REALIZE that my sin may have consequences that hinder my relationships with others. (26:21)

See Isaiah's profile (page 801) at Isaiah 6:13.

26:15 Or designed by brilliant men to protect those who shot arrows and stones. 26:19 Or a contagious skin disease. The Hebrew word used here and throughout this passage can describe various skin diseases.

CHAPTER 27

Jotham Rules in Judah

Jotham was twenty-five years old when he became king, and he reigned in Jerusalem sixteen years. His mother was Jerusha, the daughter of Zadok. ²He did what was pleasing in the LORD's sight, just as his father, Uzziah, had done. But unlike him, Jotham did not enter the Temple of the LORD. Nevertheless, the people continued in their corrupt ways.

³Jotham rebuilt the Upper Gate to the LORD's Temple and also did extensive rebuilding on the wall at the hill of Ophel. ⁴He built towns in the hill country of Judah and constructed fortresses and towers in the wooded areas. ⁵Jotham waged war against the Ammonites and conquered them. For the next three years, he received from them an annual tribute of 7,500 pounds* of silver, 50,000 bushels of wheat, and 50,000 bushels of barley.*

⁶King Jotham became powerful because he was careful to live in obedience to the LORD his God.

⁷The rest of the events of Jotham's reign, including his wars and other activities, are recorded in *The Book of the Kings of Israel and Judah.* ⁸He was twenty-five years old when he became king, and he reigned in Jerusalem sixteen years. ⁹When he died, he was buried in the City of David, and his son Ahaz became the next king.

CHAPTER 28

Ahaz Rules in Judah

Ahaz was twenty years old when he became king, and he reigned in Jerusalem sixteen years. He did not do what was pleasing in the sight of the LORD, as his ancestor David had done. ²Instead, he followed the example of the kings of Israel and cast images for the worship of Baal. ³He offered sacrifices in the valley of the son of Hinnom, even sacrificing his own sons in the fire.* He imitated the detestable practices of the pagan nations whom the LORD had driven from the land ahead of the Israelites. ⁴He offered sacrifices and burned incense at the pagan shrines and on the hills and under every green tree.

⁵That is why the LORD his God allowed the king of Aram to defeat Ahaz and to exile large numbers of his people to Damascus. The armies of Israel also defeated Ahaz and inflicted many casualties on his army. ⁶In a single day Pekah son of Remaliah, Israel's king, killed 120,000 of Judah's troops because they had abandoned the LORD, the God of their ancestors. ⁷Then Zicri, a warrior from Ephraim, killed Maaseiah, the king's son; Azrikam, the king's palace commander; and Elkanah, the king's second-in-command. ⁸The armies of Israel captured 200,000 women and children from Judah and took tremendous amounts of plunder, which they took back to Samaria.

⁹But a prophet of the LORD named Oded was there in Samaria when the army of Israel returned home. He went out to meet them and said, "The LORD, the God of your ancestors, was angry with Judah and let you defeat them. But you have gone too far, killing them without mercy, and all heaven is disturbed. ¹⁰And now you are planning to make slaves of these people from Judah and Jerusalem. What about your own sins against the LORD your God? ¹¹Listen to me and return these captives you have taken, for they are your own relatives. Watch out, because now the LORD's fierce anger has been turned against you!"

¹²Then some of the leaders of Israel*—Azariah son of Jehohanan, Berekiah son of Meshillemoth, Jehizkiah son of Shallum, and Amasa son of Hadlai—agreed with this and confronted the men returning from battle. ¹³"You must not bring the prisoners here!" they declared. "We cannot afford

---

I FOLLOW the godly example of my parents and avoid their sins and mistakes. (27:2)

I PROVIDE for the care and protection of those under my leadership. (27:3)

See David's profile (page 629) at Psalm 3:1.

I DO what is pleasing to God, just as David did. (28:1)

See David's profile (page 629) at Psalm 3:1.

I PROTEST when victims of war—especially women and children—are treated without mercy. (28:9)

I CONSIDER my own faults and sins carefully so that I treat with mercy those who are being disciplined by God. (28:10)

27:5a Hebrew *100 talents* [3.4 metric tons]. 27:5b Hebrew *10,000 cors* [1,820 kiloliters] *of wheat, and 10,000 cors of barley.* 28:3 Or *even making his sons pass through the fire.* 28:12 Hebrew *Ephraim,* referring to the northern kingdom of Israel.

to add to our sins and guilt. Our guilt is already great, and the LORD's fierce anger is already turned against Israel."

[14]So the warriors released the prisoners and handed over the plunder in the sight of all the leaders and people. [15]Then the four men mentioned by name came forward and distributed clothes from the plunder to the prisoners who were naked. They provided clothing and sandals to wear, gave them enough food and drink, and dressed their wounds with olive oil. They put those who were weak on donkeys and took all the prisoners back to their own land—to Jericho, the city of palms. Then they returned to Samaria.

Ahaz Closes the Temple

[16]About that time King Ahaz of Judah asked the king of Assyria for help against his enemies. [17]The armies of Edom had again invaded Judah and taken captives. [18]And the Philistines had raided towns located in the foothills of Judah* and in the Negev. They had already captured Beth-shemesh, Aijalon, Gederoth, Soco with its villages, Timnah with its villages, and Gimzo with its villages, and the Philistines had occupied these towns. [19]The LORD was humbling Judah because of King Ahaz of Judah,* for he had encouraged his people to sin and had been utterly unfaithful to the LORD. [20]So when King Tiglath-pileser* of Assyria arrived, he oppressed King Ahaz instead of helping him. [21]Ahaz took valuable items from the LORD's Temple, the royal palace, and from the homes of his officials and gave them to the king of Assyria as tribute. But even this did not help him.

[22]And when trouble came to King Ahaz, he became even more unfaithful to the LORD. [23]He offered sacrifices to the gods of Damascus who had defeated him, for he said, "These gods helped the kings of Aram, so they will help me, too, if I sacrifice to them." But instead, they led to his ruin and the ruin of all Israel. [24]The king took the utensils from the Temple of God and broke them into pieces. He shut the doors of the LORD's Temple so that no one could worship there and then set up altars to pagan gods in every corner of Jerusalem. [25]He made pagan shrines in all the towns of Judah for offering sacrifices to other gods. In this way, he aroused the anger of the LORD, the God of his ancestors.

[26]The rest of the events of Ahaz's reign and all his dealings, from beginning to end, are recorded in *The Book of the Kings of Judah and Israel*. [27]When King Ahaz died, he was buried in Jerusalem but not in the royal cemetery. Then his son Hezekiah became the next king.

CHAPTER 29

Hezekiah Rules in Judah

Hezekiah was twenty-five years old when he became the king of Judah, and he reigned in Jerusalem twenty-nine years. His mother was Abijah, the daughter of Zechariah. [2]He did what was pleasing in the LORD's sight, just as his ancestor David had done.

Hezekiah Reopens the Temple

[3]In the very first month of the first year of his reign, Hezekiah reopened the doors of the Temple of the LORD and repaired them. [4]He summoned the priests and Levites to meet him at the courtyard east of the Temple. [5]He said to them, "Listen to me, you Levites! Purify yourselves, and purify the Temple of the LORD, the God of your ancestors. Remove all the defiled things from the sanctuary. [6]Our ancestors were unfaithful and did what was evil in the sight of the LORD our God. They abandoned the LORD and his Temple; they turned their backs on him. [7]They also shut the doors to the Temple's foyer, and they snuffed out the lamps. They stopped burning incense and presenting burnt offerings at

---

I HELP CARE for the needs of prisoners of war. (28:15)

I DO NOT TURN to wicked people instead of the Lord for help. (28:16)

I AM NOT SWAYED to follow other religions, even if they appear to bring others success. (28:23)

See Hezekiah's profile (page 825) at Isaiah 37:1.

See David's profile (page 629) at Psalm 3:1.

I ENCOURAGE the leaders of God's people to purify their lives for worship and service. (29:5)

I OPENLY ADMIT the sins of my family and forefathers. (29:6)

28:18 Hebrew *the Shephelah*.   28:19 Hebrew *of Israel*.   28:20 Hebrew *Tilgath-pilneser*, a variant name for Tiglath-pileser.

the sanctuary of the God of Israel. [8]That is why the LORD's anger has fallen upon Judah and Jerusalem. He has made us an object of dread, horror, and ridicule, as you can so plainly see. [9]Our fathers have been killed in battle, and our sons and daughters and wives are in captivity. [10]But now I will make a covenant with the LORD, the God of Israel, so that his fierce anger will turn away from us. [11]My dear Levites, do not neglect your duties any longer! The LORD has chosen you to stand in his presence, to minister to him, and to lead the people in worship and make offerings to him."

[12]Then these Levites got right to work:

From the clan of Kohath: Mahath son of Amasai and Joel son of Azariah.
From the clan of Merari: Kish son of Abdi and Azariah son of Jehallelel.
From the clan of Gershon: Joah son of Zimmah and Eden son of Joah.
[13] From the family of Elizaphan: Shimri and Jeiel.
From the family of Asaph: Zechariah and Mattaniah.
[14] From the family of Heman: Jehiel and Shimei.
From the family of Jeduthun: Shemaiah and Uzziel.

[15]These men called together their fellow Levites, and they purified themselves. Then they began to purify the Temple of the LORD, just as the king had commanded. They were careful to follow all the LORD's instructions in their work. [16]The priests went into the sanctuary of the Temple of the LORD to cleanse it, and they took out to the Temple courtyard all the defiled things they found. From there the Levites carted it all out to the Kidron Valley. [17]The work began on a day in early spring,* and in eight days they had reached the foyer of the LORD's Temple. Then they purified the Temple of the LORD itself, which took another eight days. So the entire task was completed in sixteen days.

The Temple Rededication

[18]Then the Levites went to King Hezekiah and gave him this report: "We have purified the Temple of the LORD, the altar of burnt offering with all its utensils, and the table of the Bread of the Presence with all its utensils. [19]We have also recovered all the utensils taken by King Ahaz when he was unfaithful and closed the Temple. They are now in front of the altar of the LORD, purified and ready for use."

[20]Early the next morning King Hezekiah gathered the city officials and went to the Temple of the LORD. [21]They brought seven bulls, seven rams, seven lambs, and seven male goats as a sin offering for the kingdom, for the Temple, and for Judah. The king commanded the priests, who were descendants of Aaron, to sacrifice the animals on the altar of the LORD. [22]So they killed the bulls, and the priests took the blood and sprinkled it on the altar. Next they killed the rams and sprinkled their blood on the altar. And finally, they did the same with the lambs. [23]The male goats for the sin offering were then brought before the king and the assembly of people, who laid their hands on them. [24]The priests then killed the goats as a sin offering and sprinkled their blood on the altar to make atonement for the sins of all Israel. The king had specifically commanded that this burnt offering and sin offering should be made for all Israel.

[25]King Hezekiah then stationed the Levites at the Temple of the LORD with cymbals, harps, and lyres. He obeyed all the commands that the LORD had given to King David through Gad, the king's seer, and the prophet Nathan. [26]The Levites then took their positions around the Temple with the instruments of David, and the priests took their positions with the trumpets. [27]Then Hezekiah ordered that the burnt offering be placed on the altar. As the

---

See Aaron's profile (page 107) at Exodus 32:2.

I RESPOND quickly to the call to serve the Lord and lead his people in worship. (29:11)

See Asaph's profile (page 687) at Psalm 73:28.

I COME with other leaders to repent and worship before the Lord. (29:20)

I ASK the Lord to forgive the sins of my nation. (29:24)

29:17 Hebrew *on the first day of the first month.* This day of the Hebrew lunar calendar occurs in March or early April.

burnt offering was presented, songs of praise to the LORD were begun, accompanied by the trumpets and other instruments of David, king of Israel. [28] The entire assembly worshiped the LORD as the singers sang and the trumpets blew, until all the burnt offerings were finished. [29] Then the king and everyone with him bowed down in worship. [30] King Hezekiah and the officials ordered the Levites to praise the LORD with the psalms of David and Asaph the seer. So they offered joyous praise and bowed down in worship.

[31] Then Hezekiah declared, "The dedication ceremony has come to an end. Now bring your sacrifices and thanksgiving offerings to the Temple of the LORD." So the people brought their sacrifices and thanksgiving offerings, and those whose hearts were willing brought burnt offerings, too. [32] The people brought to the LORD seventy bulls, one hundred rams, and two hundred lambs for burnt offerings. [33] They also brought six hundred bulls and three thousand sheep as sacrifices. [34] But there were too few priests to prepare all the burnt offerings, so their relatives the Levites helped them until the work was finished and until more priests had been purified. For the Levites had been more conscientious about purifying themselves than the priests. [35] There was an abundance of burnt offerings, along with the usual drink offerings, and a great deal of fat from the many peace offerings. So the Temple of the LORD was restored to service. [36] And Hezekiah and all the people rejoiced greatly because of what God had done for the people, for everything had been accomplished so quickly.

CHAPTER 30

Preparations for Passover

King Hezekiah now sent word to all Israel and Judah, and he wrote letters of invitation to Ephraim and Manasseh. He asked everyone to come to the Temple of the LORD at Jerusalem to celebrate the Passover of the LORD, the God of Israel. [2] The king, his officials, and all the community of Jerusalem decided to celebrate Passover a month later than usual.* [3] They were unable to celebrate it at the regular time because not enough priests could be purified by then, and the people had not yet assembled at Jerusalem. [4] This plan for keeping the Passover seemed right to the king and all the people. [5] So they sent a proclamation throughout all Israel, from Beersheba in the south to Dan in the north, inviting everyone to come to Jerusalem to celebrate the Passover of the LORD, the God of Israel. The people had not been celebrating it in great numbers as prescribed in the law.

[6] At the king's command, messengers were sent throughout Israel and Judah. They carried letters which said:

"O people of Israel, return to the LORD, the God of Abraham, Isaac, and Israel,* so that he will return to the few of us who have survived the conquest of the Assyrian kings. [7] Do not be like your ancestors and relatives who abandoned the LORD, the God of their ancestors, and became an object of derision, as you yourselves can see. [8] Do not be stubborn, as they were, but submit yourselves to the LORD. Come to his Temple which he has set apart as holy forever. Worship the LORD your God so that his fierce anger will turn away from you. [9] For if you return to the LORD, your relatives and your children will be treated mercifully by their captors, and they will be able to return to this land. For the LORD your God is gracious and merciful. If you return to him, he will not continue to turn his face from you."

Celebration of Passover

[10] The messengers went from town to town throughout Ephraim and Manasseh and as far as the territory of Zebulun. But most of the people just

I GIVE priority to the public worship of the Lord through music. (29:30)

I AM CAREFUL to keep my life pure and available for the Lord's use at any time. (29:34)

I BELIEVE Hezekiah invited everyone from all Judah and Israel to join in the Passover celebration. (30:1)

See Hezekiah's profile (page 825) at Isaiah 37:1.

I AM WILLING to make adjustments if doing so will allow more people to obey and worship the Lord as they should. (30:3)

30:2 Hebrew *in the second month*. This month of the Hebrew lunar calendar usually occurs in April and May.
30:6 *Israel* is the name that God gave to Jacob.

I WILL RETURN to the Lord, even if it means humbling myself before other people. (30:11)

I GATHER with God's people to worship him. (30:13)

See Moses' profile (page 73) at Exodus 5:1.

I BELIEVE the Lord welcomed those Israelites who came to Jerusalem to seek him. (30:18)

I BELIEVE the Lord heard Hezekiah's prayer for the people and healed them. (30:20)

I REJOICE when the Lord is worshiped wholeheartedly. (30:26)

See David's profile (page 629) at Psalm 3:1.

I JOIN with others who are removing pagan influences and idols from their lives. (31:1)

See Hezekiah's profile (page 825) at Isaiah 37:1.

laughed at the messengers and made fun of them. [11]However, some from Asher, Manasseh, and Zebulun humbled themselves and went to Jerusalem. [12]At the same time, God's hand was on the people in the land of Judah, giving them a strong desire to unite in obeying the orders of the king and his officials, who were following the word of the LORD. [13]And so a huge crowd assembled at Jerusalem in midspring* to celebrate Passover and the Festival of Unleavened Bread. [14]They set to work and removed the pagan altars from Jerusalem. They took away all the incense altars and threw them into the Kidron Valley.

[15]On the appointed day in midspring, one month later than usual,* the people slaughtered their Passover lambs. Then the priests and Levites became ashamed, so they purified themselves and brought burnt offerings to the Temple of the LORD. [16]They took their places at the Temple according to the regulations found in the law of Moses, the man of God. The Levites brought the sacrificial blood to the priests, who then sprinkled it on the altar.

[17]Since many of the people there had not purified themselves, the Levites had to slaughter their Passover lambs for them, to set them apart for the LORD. [18]Most of those who came from Ephraim, Manasseh, Issachar, and Zebulun had not purified themselves. But King Hezekiah prayed for them, and they were allowed to eat the Passover meal anyway, even though this was contrary to God's laws. For Hezekiah said, "May the LORD, who is good, pardon those [19]who decide to follow the LORD, the God of their ancestors, even though they are not properly cleansed for the ceremony." [20]And the LORD listened to Hezekiah's prayer and healed the people.

[21]So the people of Israel who were present in Jerusalem celebrated the Festival of Unleavened Bread for seven days with great joy. Each day the Levites and priests sang to the LORD, accompanied by loud instruments.* [22]Hezekiah encouraged the Levites for the skill they displayed as they served the LORD. So for seven days the celebration continued. Peace offerings were sacrificed, and the people confessed their sins to the LORD, the God of their ancestors.

[23]The entire assembly then decided to continue the festival another seven days, so they celebrated joyfully for another week. [24]King Hezekiah gave the people one thousand bulls and seven thousand sheep for offerings, and the officials donated one thousand bulls and ten thousand sheep. Meanwhile, many more priests purified themselves.

[25]The entire assembly of Judah rejoiced, including the priests, the Levites, all who came from the land of Israel, the foreigners who came to the festival, and all those who lived in Judah. [26]There was great joy in the city, for Jerusalem had not seen a celebration like this one since the days of Solomon, King David's son. [27]Then the Levitical priests stood and blessed the people, and God heard them from his holy dwelling in heaven.

CHAPTER 31

Hezekiah's Religious Reforms

Now when the festival ended, the Israelites who attended went to all the towns of Judah, Benjamin, Ephraim, and Manasseh, and they smashed the sacred pillars, cut down the Asherah poles, and removed the pagan shrines and altars. After this, the Israelites returned to their own towns and homes.

[2]Hezekiah then organized the priests and Levites into divisions to offer the burnt offerings and peace offerings, and to worship and give thanks and praise to the LORD at the gates of the Temple. [3]The king also made a personal contribution of animals for the daily morning and evening burnt offerings, as well as for the weekly Sabbath festivals and monthly new moon festivals,

30:13 Hebrew *in the second month.* This month of the Hebrew lunar calendar usually occurs in April and May. 30:15 Hebrew *On the fourteenth day of the second month.* This day of the Hebrew lunar calendar occurs in late April or early May. 30:21 Or *sang to the LORD with all their strength.*

and for the other annual festivals as required in the law of the LORD. [4]In addition, he required the people in Jerusalem to bring the prescribed portion of their income to the priests and Levites, so they could devote themselves fully to the law of the LORD.

[5]The people responded immediately and generously with the first of their crops and grain, new wine, olive oil, honey, and all the produce of their fields. They brought a tithe of all they owned. [6]The people who had moved to Judah from Israel, and the people of Judah themselves, brought in the tithes of their cattle and sheep and a tithe of the things that had been dedicated to the LORD their God, and they piled them up in great heaps. [7]The first of these tithes was brought in late spring,* and the heaps continued to grow until early autumn.* [8]When Hezekiah and his officials came and saw these huge piles, they thanked the LORD and his people Israel!

[9]"Where did all this come from?" Hezekiah asked the priests and Levites.

[10]And Azariah the high priest, from the family of Zadok, replied, "Since the people began bringing their gifts to the LORD's Temple, we have had enough to eat and plenty to spare, for the LORD has blessed his people."

[11]Hezekiah decided to have storerooms prepared in the Temple of the LORD, and this was done. [12]Then all the gifts and tithes were faithfully brought to the Temple. Conaniah the Levite was put in charge, assisted by his brother Shimei. [13]The supervisors under them were Jehiel, Azaziah, Nahath, Asahel, Jerimoth, Jozabad, Eliel, Ismakiah, Mahath, and Benaiah. These appointments were made by King Hezekiah and Azariah, the chief official in the Temple of God.

[14]Kore son of Imnah the Levite, who was the gatekeeper at the East Gate, was put in charge of distributing the freewill offerings of God, the gifts, and the things that had been dedicated to the LORD. [15]His faithful assistants were Eden, Miniamin, Jeshua, Shemaiah, Amariah, and Shecaniah. They distributed the gifts among the families of priests in their towns, by their divisions, dividing the gifts fairly among young and old alike. [16]They also distributed the gifts to all males three years old or older, regardless of their place in the genealogical records, who came daily to the LORD's Temple to perform their official duties, by their divisions. [17]And they distributed gifts to the priests who were listed in the genealogical records by families, and to the Levites twenty years old or older who were listed according to their jobs and their divisions. [18]Food allotments were also given to all the families listed in the genealogical records, including the little babies, the wives, and the sons and daughters. For they had all been faithful in purifying themselves. [19]As for the priests, the descendants of Aaron, who were living in the open villages around the towns, men were appointed to distribute portions to every male among the priests and to all the Levites listed in the genealogical records.

[20]In this way, King Hezekiah handled the distribution throughout all Judah, doing what was pleasing and good in the sight of the LORD his God. [21]In all that he did in the service of the Temple of God and in his efforts to follow the law and the commands, Hezekiah sought his God wholeheartedly. As a result, he was very successful.

CHAPTER 32

Assyria Invades Judah

After Hezekiah had faithfully carried out this work, King Sennacherib of Assyria invaded Judah. He laid siege to the fortified cities, giving orders for his army to break through their walls. [2]When Hezekiah realized that Sennacherib also intended to attack Jerusalem, [3]he consulted with his officials

---

I GIVE from my own personal finances to support the work and worship of the Lord. (31:4)

I PUT faithful people in charge of caring for and distributing offerings given to the Lord. (31:14)

See Aaron's profile (page 107) at Exodus 32:2.

I HANDLE money given to the Lord in a way that pleases him. (31:20)

See Hezekiah's profile (page 825) at Isaiah 37:1.

31:7a Hebrew *in the third month*. This month of the Hebrew lunar calendar usually occurs in May and June.
31:7b Hebrew *in the seventh month*. This month of the Hebrew lunar calendar usually occurs in September and October.

and military advisers, and they decided to stop the flow of the springs outside the city. ⁴They organized a huge work crew to stop the flow of the springs, cutting off the brook that ran through the fields. For they said, "Why should the kings of Assyria come here and find plenty of water?"

⁵Then Hezekiah further strengthened his defenses by repairing the wall wherever it was broken down and by adding to the fortifications and constructing a second wall outside the first. He also reinforced the Millo* in the City of David and manufactured large numbers of weapons and shields. ⁶He appointed military officers over the people and asked them to assemble before him in the square at the city gate. Then Hezekiah encouraged them with this address: ⁷"Be strong and courageous! Don't be afraid of the king of Assyria or his mighty army, for there is a power far greater on our side! ⁸He may have a great army, but they are just men. We have the LORD our God to help us and to fight our battles for us!" These words greatly encouraged the people.

Sennacherib Threatens Jerusalem

⁹Then King Sennacherib of Assyria, while still besieging the town of Lachish, sent officials to Jerusalem with this message for Hezekiah and all the people in the city:

¹⁰"This is what King Sennacherib of Assyria says: What are you trusting in that makes you think you can survive my siege of Jerusalem? ¹¹Hezekiah has said, 'The LORD our God will rescue us from the king of Assyria.' Surely Hezekiah is misleading you, sentencing you to death by famine and thirst! ¹²Surely you must realize that Hezekiah is the very person who destroyed all the LORD's shrines and altars. He commanded Judah and Jerusalem to worship at only the one altar at the Temple and to make sacrifices on it alone.

¹³"Surely you must realize what I and the other kings of Assyria before me have done to all the people of the earth! Were any of the gods of those nations able to rescue their people from my power? ¹⁴Name just one time when any god, anywhere, was able to rescue his people from me! What makes you think your God can do any better? ¹⁵Don't let Hezekiah fool you! Don't let him deceive you like this! I say it again—no god of any nation has ever yet been able to rescue his people from me or my ancestors. How much less will your God rescue you from my power!"

¹⁶And Sennacherib's officials further mocked the LORD God and his servant Hezekiah, heaping insult upon insult. ¹⁷The king also sent letters scorning the LORD, the God of Israel. He wrote, "Just as the gods of all the other nations failed to rescue their people from my power, so the God of Hezekiah will also fail." ¹⁸The Assyrian officials who brought the letters shouted this in the Hebrew language to the people gathered on the walls of the city, trying to terrify them so it would be easier to capture the city. ¹⁹These officials talked about the God of Jerusalem as though he were one of the pagan gods, made by human hands.

²⁰Then King Hezekiah and the prophet Isaiah son of Amoz cried out in prayer to God in heaven. ²¹And the LORD sent an angel who destroyed the Assyrian army with all its commanders and officers. So Sennacherib returned home in disgrace to his own land. And when he entered the temple of his god, some of his own sons killed him there with a sword. ²²That is how the LORD rescued Hezekiah and the people of Jerusalem from King Sennacherib of Assyria and from all the others who threatened them. So there was peace at last throughout the land. ²³From then on King Hezekiah became highly

---

I AM DILIGENT in caring for and protecting the people I lead. (32:5)

See David's profile (page 629) at Psalm 3:1.

I ENCOURAGE God's people by reminding them that the Lord fights our battles for us. (32:8)

I KNOW that my God is stronger and better than all other gods and powers on the earth. (32:14)

I REFUSE to be terrified by unbelievers who mock the Lord. (32:18)

See Isaiah's profile (page 801) at Isaiah 6:13.

32:5 Or *the supporting terraces.*

respected among the surrounding nations, and many gifts for the LORD arrived at Jerusalem, with valuable presents for King Hezekiah, too.

Hezekiah's Sickness and Recovery

²⁴About that time, Hezekiah became deathly ill. He prayed to the LORD, who healed him and gave him a miraculous sign. ²⁵But Hezekiah did not respond appropriately to the kindness shown him, and he became proud. So the LORD's anger came against him and against Judah and Jerusalem. ²⁶Then Hezekiah repented of his pride, and the people of Jerusalem humbled themselves. So the LORD's anger did not come against them during Hezekiah's lifetime.

²⁷Hezekiah was very wealthy and held in high esteem. He had to build special treasury buildings for his silver, gold, precious stones, and spices, and for his shields and other valuable items. ²⁸He also constructed many storehouses for his grain, new wine, and olive oil; and he made many stalls for his cattle and folds for his flocks of sheep and goats. ²⁹He built many towns and acquired vast flocks and herds, for God had given him great wealth. ³⁰He blocked up the upper spring of Gihon and brought the water down through a tunnel to the west side of the City of David. And so he succeeded in everything he did.

³¹However, when ambassadors arrived from Babylon to ask about the remarkable events that had taken place in the land, God withdrew from Hezekiah in order to test him and to see what was really in his heart.

Summary of Hezekiah's Reign

³²The rest of the events of Hezekiah's reign and his acts of devotion are recorded in *The Vision of the Prophet Isaiah Son of Amoz,* which is included in *The Book of the Kings of Judah and Israel.* ³³When Hezekiah died, he was buried in the upper area of the royal cemetery, and all Judah and Jerusalem honored him at his death. Then his son Manasseh became the next king.

CHAPTER 33

Manasseh Rules in Judah

Manasseh was twelve years old when he became king, and he reigned in Jerusalem fifty-five years. ²He did what was evil in the LORD's sight, imitating the detestable practices of the pagan nations whom the LORD had driven from the land ahead of the Israelites. ³He rebuilt the pagan shrines his father Hezekiah had destroyed. He constructed altars for the images of Baal and set up Asherah poles. He also bowed before all the stars of heaven and worshiped them. ⁴He even built pagan altars in the Temple of the LORD, the place where the LORD had said his name should be honored forever. ⁵He put these altars for the stars of heaven in both courtyards of the LORD's Temple. ⁶Manasseh even sacrificed his own sons in the fire* in the valley of the son of Hinnom. He practiced sorcery, divination, and witchcraft, and he consulted with mediums and psychics. He did much that was evil in the LORD's sight, arousing his anger.

⁷Manasseh even took a carved idol he had made and set it up in God's Temple, the very place where God had told David and his son Solomon: "My name will be honored here forever in this Temple and in Jerusalem—the city I have chosen from among all the other tribes of Israel. ⁸If the Israelites will obey my commands—all the instructions, laws, and regulations given through Moses—I will not send them into exile from this land that I gave their ancestors." ⁹But Manasseh led the people of Judah and Jerusalem to do even more evil than the pagan nations whom the LORD had destroyed when the Israelites entered the land.

33:6 Or *even made his sons pass through the fire.*

I WILL PRAY to the Lord for mercy and healing if I become deathly ill. (32:24)

I REPENT when I am confronted with my pride. (32:26)

I BELIEVE the Lord may bring times of testing to show what is really in my heart. (32:31)

I DO NOT IMITATE the evil practices of pagan religions. (33:2)

See Hezekiah's profile (page 825) at Isaiah 37:1.

I DO NOT GIVE other gods, religions, or people the honor and worship that belongs only to the Lord. (33:7)

See David's profile (page 629) at Psalm 3:1.

See Moses' profile (page 73) at Exodus 5:1.

I DO NOT IGNORE God's warnings. (33:10)

I WORK hard to remove the influences of my sin after I have repented. (33:15)

I FOLLOW the example of repentance, not the example of disobeying the Lord. (33:22)

I REALIZE that my children may follow my bad example, even if I have repented and changed. (33:23)

See Josiah's profile (page 461) at 2 Kings 23:25.

See David's profile (page 629) at Psalm 3:1.

I SEEK God while I am still young. (34:3)

[10]The LORD spoke to Manasseh and his people, but they ignored all his warnings. [11]So the LORD sent the Assyrian armies, and they took Manasseh prisoner. They put a ring through his nose, bound him in bronze chains, and led him away to Babylon. [12]But while in deep distress, Manasseh sought the LORD his God and cried out humbly to the God of his ancestors. [13]And when he prayed, the LORD listened to him and was moved by his request for help. So the LORD let Manasseh return to Jerusalem and to his kingdom. Manasseh had finally realized that the LORD alone is God!

[14]It was after this that Manasseh rebuilt the outer wall of the City of David, from west of the Gihon Spring in the Kidron Valley to the Fish Gate, and continuing around the hill of Ophel, where it was built very high. And he stationed his military officers in all of the fortified cities of Judah. [15]Manasseh also removed the foreign gods from the hills and the idol from the LORD's Temple. He tore down all the altars he had built on the hill where the Temple stood and all the altars that were in Jerusalem, and he dumped them outside the city. [16]Then he restored the altar of the LORD and sacrificed peace offerings and thanksgiving offerings on it. He also encouraged the people of Judah to worship the LORD, the God of Israel. [17]However, the people still sacrificed at the pagan shrines, but only to the LORD their God.

[18]The rest of the events of Manasseh's reign, his prayer to God, and the words the seers spoke to him in the name of the LORD, the God of Israel, are recorded in *The Book of the Kings of Israel.* [19]Manasseh's prayer, the account of the way God answered him, and an account of all his sins and unfaithfulness are recorded in *The Record of the Seers.* * It includes a list of the locations where he built pagan shrines and set up Asherah poles and idols before he repented. [20]When Manasseh died, he was buried at his palace. Then his son Amon became the next king.

Amon Rules in Judah
[21]Amon was twenty-two years old when he became king, and he reigned in Jerusalem two years. [22]He did what was evil in the LORD's sight, just as his father Manasseh had done. He worshiped and sacrificed to all the idols his father had made. [23]But unlike his father, he did not humble himself before the LORD. Instead, Amon sinned even more.

[24]At last Amon's own officials plotted against him and assassinated him in his palace. [25]But the people of the land killed all those who had conspired against King Amon, and they made his son Josiah the next king.

CHAPTER 34
Josiah Rules in Judah
Josiah was eight years old when he became king, and he reigned in Jerusalem thirty-one years. [2]He did what was pleasing in the LORD's sight and followed the example of his ancestor David. He did not turn aside from doing what was right.

[3]During the eighth year of his reign, while he was still young, Josiah began to seek the God of his ancestor David. Then in the twelfth year, he began to purify Judah and Jerusalem, destroying all the pagan shrines, the Asherah poles, and the carved idols and cast images. [4]He saw to it that the altars for the images of Baal and their incense altars were torn down. He also made sure that the Asherah poles, the carved idols, and the cast images were smashed and scattered over the graves of those who had sacrificed to them. [5]Then he burned the bones of the pagan priests on their own altars, and so he purified Judah and Jerusalem.

[6]He did the same thing in the towns of Manasseh, Ephraim, and Simeon, even as far as Naphtali. [7]He destroyed the pagan altars and the Asherah poles,

33:19 Or *The Record of Hozai.*

and he crushed the idols into dust. He cut down the incense altars throughout the land of Israel and then returned to Jerusalem.

⁸In the eighteenth year of his reign, after he had purified the land and the Temple, Josiah appointed Shaphan son of Azaliah, Maaseiah the governor of Jerusalem, and Joah son of Joahaz, the royal historian, to repair the Temple of the LORD his God. ⁹They gave Hilkiah the high priest the money that had been collected by the Levites who served as gatekeepers at the Temple of God. The gifts were brought by people from Manasseh, Ephraim, and from all the remnant of Israel, as well as from all Judah, Benjamin, and the people of Jerusalem. ¹⁰He entrusted the money to the men assigned to supervise the restoration of the LORD's Temple. Then they paid the workers who did the repairs and renovation. ¹¹Thus, they hired carpenters and masons and purchased cut stone for the walls and timber for the rafters and beams. They restored what earlier kings of Judah had allowed to fall into ruin.

> **I ENTRUST** money for the Lord's work to people who will use it faithfully and wisely. (34:9)

LIKE MANASSEH
2 Chronicles 33:13

I know it is never too late to turn to God for forgiveness, no matter how horrible my sins.

God visits death row on a regular basis. Prisoners who have committed unspeakable crimes turn to Jesus Christ to find forgiveness and new life. Outside the prison walls, people react in wonder, resentment, or disbelief that God delights to save such wicked individuals.

Manasseh knew God's delight firsthand. From his grimy cell on Babylon's death row, he looked back on years of unspeakable crimes—worshiping the stars and sun in God's own Temple, shedding the blood of innocent people, and sacrificing his own sons to idols. He realized his rebellion had brought him nothing but pain. Then he looked up to the God of his ancestors and cried out for help. Thankfully, the Lord always hears the prayers of the humble and delights to answer their prayers.

Humanly speaking, even God's prophets must have thought Manasseh had gone too far for the Lord to bring him back. After all, his sin had led the people of Judah so deeply into idolatry that God's judgment on the nation could not be canceled. And his despair over his sin could not bring back to life the people he killed and the families he had crushed.

Yet, because of God's grace, Manasseh could come into God's Temple a forgiven man. Freed from Babylon and given another chance to reign, Manasseh took big, bold steps to show his repentance was real—tearing down altars, restoring the Temple, and worshiping the Lord publicly.

May we never choose a life of sin that flouts God's laws and destroys others. We certainly cannot always undo the damage. But we know that the sins of our past are never so great that God's love and mercy cannot forgive us, restore us, and give us a new start.

See 2 Kings 20:21–21:18 for another account of Manasseh's life. Read about the devastating effects of his sin in 2 Kings 21:20; 23:26; 24:3; and Jeremiah 15:4.

○ *Today's Scripture reading is 2 Chronicles 33:1-20.*

¹²The workers served faithfully under the leadership of Jahath and Obadiah, Levites of the Merarite clan, and Zechariah and Meshullam, Levites of the Kohathite clan. Other Levites, all of whom were skilled musicians, ¹³were put in charge of the laborers of the various trades. Still others assisted as secretaries, officials, and gatekeepers.

> **I SERVE** faithfully, whether I supervise or work under the supervision of others to do the Lord's work. (34:12)

Hilkiah Discovers God's Law

¹⁴As Hilkiah the high priest was recording the money collected at the LORD's Temple, he found the Book of the Law of the LORD as it had been given through Moses. ¹⁵Hilkiah said to Shaphan the court secretary, "I have found the Book of the Law in the LORD's Temple!" Then Hilkiah gave the scroll to Shaphan.

¹⁶Shaphan took the scroll to the king and reported, "Your officials are doing everything they were assigned to do. ¹⁷The money that was collected at

> *See Moses' profile (page 73) at Exodus 5:1.*

the Temple of the LORD has been given to the supervisors and workmen." [18]Shaphan also said to the king, "Hilkiah the priest has given me a scroll." So Shaphan read it to the king.

[19]When the king heard what was written in the law, he tore his clothes in despair. [20] Then he gave these orders to Hilkiah, Ahikam son of Shaphan, Acbor son of Micaiah,* Shaphan the court secretary, and Asaiah the king's personal adviser: [21]"Go to the Temple and speak to the LORD for me and for all the remnant of Israel and Judah. Ask him about the words written in this scroll that has been found. The LORD's anger has been poured out against us because our ancestors have not obeyed the word of the LORD. We have not been doing what this scroll says we must do."

[22]So Hilkiah and the other men went to the newer Mishneh section* of Jerusalem to consult with the prophet Huldah. She was the wife of Shallum son of Tikvah and grandson of Harhas,* the keeper of the Temple wardrobe. [23]She said to them, "The LORD, the God of Israel, has spoken! Go and tell the man who sent you, [24]This is what the LORD says: I will certainly destroy this city and its people. All the curses written in the scroll you have read will come true. [25]For the people of Judah have abandoned me and worshiped pagan gods, and I am very angry with them for everything they have done. My anger will be poured out against this place, and nothing will be able to stop it.'

[26]"But go to the king of Judah who sent you to seek the LORD and tell him: 'This is what the LORD, the God of Israel, says concerning the message you have just heard: [27]You were sorry and humbled yourself before God when you heard what I said against this city and its people. You humbled yourself and tore your clothing in despair and wept before me in repentance. So I have indeed heard you, says the LORD. [28]I will not send the promised disaster against this city and its people until after you have died and been buried in peace. You will not see the disaster I am going to bring on this place.' " So they took her message back to the king.

Josiah's Religious Reforms

[29]Then the king summoned all the leaders of Judah and Jerusalem. [30]And the king went up to the Temple of the LORD with all the people of Judah and Jerusalem and the priests and the Levites—all the people from the greatest to the least. There the king read to them the entire Book of the Covenant that had been found in the LORD's Temple. [31]The king took his place of authority beside the pillar and renewed the covenant in the LORD's presence. He pledged to obey the LORD by keeping all his commands, regulations, and laws with all his heart and soul. He promised to obey all the terms of the covenant that were written in the scroll. [32]And he required everyone in Jerusalem and the people of Benjamin to make a similar pledge. As the people of Jerusalem did this, they renewed their covenant with God, the God of their ancestors.

[33]So Josiah removed all detestable idols from the entire land of Israel and required everyone to worship the LORD their God. And throughout the rest of his lifetime, they did not turn away from the LORD, the God of their ancestors.

CHAPTER 35

Josiah Celebrates Passover

Then Josiah announced that the Passover of the LORD would be celebrated in Jerusalem on the appointed day in early spring.* The Passover lambs were slaughtered at twilight of that day. [2]Josiah also assigned the priests to their duties and encouraged them in their work at the Temple of the LORD. [3]He issued

**Sidebar notes (left margin):**

I RESPOND to God's Word when I hear it. (34:19)

I GO to a person who knows and serves the Lord when I need to understand his Word. (34:22)

I KNOW the Lord hears me when his Word reveals my sin and I respond in sorrow and repentance. (34:27)

I MAKE SURE that all people under my spiritual leadership hear and understand God's Word. (34:30)

See Josiah's profile (page 461) at 2 Kings 23:25.

I USE the time the Lord gives me to serve him and his people. (35:3)

34:20 As in parallel text at 2 Kgs 22:12; Hebrew reads *Abdon son of Micah.* **34:22a** Or *the Second Quarter,* a newer section of Jerusalem. **34:22b** As in parallel text at 2 Kgs 22:14; Hebrew reads *son of Tokhath, son of Hasrah.* **35:1** Hebrew *on the fourteenth day of the first month.* This day of the Hebrew lunar calendar occurs in late March or early April.

this order to the Levites, who had been set apart to serve the LORD and were teachers in Israel: "Since the Ark is now in Solomon's Temple and you do not need to carry it back and forth on your shoulders, spend your time serving the LORD your God and his people Israel. ⁴Report for duty according to the family divisions of your ancestors, following the written instructions of King David of Israel and the instructions of his son Solomon. ⁵Then stand in your appointed holy places and help the families assigned to you as they bring their offerings to the Temple. ⁶Slaughter the Passover lambs, purify yourselves, and prepare to help those who come. Follow all the instructions that the LORD gave through Moses."

See David's profile (page 629) at Psalm 3:1.

See Moses' profile (page 73) at Exodus 5:1.

LIKE HILKIAH *I can experience the power of God's Word today.*

2 Chronicles 34:14

Imagine walking slowly through a huge, old, dilapidated building. Your tour guide, a gentle older man named Hilkiah, tells you that because of the wickedness of Manasseh and other terrible kings, the building—the Temple of the Lord—has fallen into ruin. With it, knowledge and worship of the Lord God have fallen into ruin as well.

As high priest, Hilkiah rejoiced to see King Manasseh repent toward the end of his life. Still, the damage was done, national judgment was pending, and copies of the Scriptures were almost nonexistent. To make matters worse, after Manasseh's death, the king's son Amon lived in open rebellion against the Lord and was assassinated only two years into his reign.

In God's providence, however, Manasseh's young grandson, Josiah, became king at age eight. As a teenager, King Josiah trusted the Lord with all his heart and—with the support of Hilkiah—launched a series of zealous religious reforms throughout the land of Judah and beyond.

At age twenty-six, Josiah commissioned several men to repair the Temple and asked the Levites to give all contributions for that work to Hilkiah. One day while recording the money that had been collected at the Lord's Temple, Hilkiah got up to look for something—perhaps an old scroll on which he could write the latest financial figures. While looking about, the high priest found the long lost Book of the Law written by Moses!

Hilkiah immediately brought this discovery to the attention of the king and worked closely with Josiah to enact even greater religious reforms. Those reforms included

- Public reading of Scripture
- Renewal of all aspects of worship in the Temple
- Resumption of the celebration of Passover and the Festival of Unleavened Bread

Toward the end of his life, Hilkiah could only marvel at the changes he had seen! Within a few short years, Babylon would take the kingdom of Judah into captivity as foretold by the prophets Isaiah and Jeremiah. But in God's providence, Hilkiah's discovery ensured the preservation of the earliest books of the Old Testament in Judah's darkest hour.

In addition, Hilkiah's deep love for God's Word later inspired his great grandson, Ezra, who helped lead another national revival after the Exile.

Unlike Hilkiah, you and I don't have to search for God's Word—it's already in our hands to treasure, affirm, and read again and again.

Hilkiah's story also is told in 2 Kings 22:3–23:25.

○ *Today's Scripture reading is 2 Chronicles 34:14-33.*

⁷Then Josiah contributed from his personal property thirty thousand lambs and young goats for the people's Passover offerings, and three thousand bulls. ⁸The king's officials also made willing contributions to the people, priests, and Levites. Hilkiah, Zechariah, and Jehiel, the administrators of God's Temple, gave the priests twenty-six hundred lambs and young goats and three hundred bulls as Passover offerings. ⁹The Levite leaders—

I GIVE willingly to support the work of the Lord. (35:8)

Conaniah and his brothers Shemaiah and Nethanel, and Hashabiah, Jeiel, and Jozabad—gave five thousand lambs and young goats and five hundred bulls to the Levites for their Passover offerings.

¹⁰When everything was ready for the Passover celebration, the priests and the Levites took their places, organized by their divisions, according to the king's orders. ¹¹The Levites then slaughtered the Passover lambs and presented the blood to the priests, who sprinkled the blood on the altar while the Levites prepared the animals. ¹²They divided the burnt offerings among the people by their family groups, so they could offer them to the LORD according to the instructions recorded in the Book of Moses. They did the same with the bulls. ¹³Then they roasted the Passover lambs as prescribed; and they boiled the holy offerings in pots, kettles, and pans, and brought them out quickly so the people could eat them.

¹⁴Afterward the Levites prepared a meal for themselves and for the priests, because the priests had been busy from morning till night offering the burnt offerings and the fat portions. The Levites took responsibility for all these preparations. ¹⁵The musicians, descendants of Asaph, were in their assigned places, following the orders given by David, Asaph, Heman, and Jeduthun, the king's seer. The gatekeepers guarded the gates and did not need to leave their posts of duty, for their meals were brought to them by their fellow Levites.

¹⁶The entire ceremony for the LORD's Passover was completed that day. All the burnt offerings were sacrificed on the altar of the LORD, as King Josiah had ordered. ¹⁷All the Israelites present in Jerusalem celebrated Passover and the Festival of Unleavened Bread for seven days. ¹⁸Never since the time of the prophet Samuel had there been such a Passover. None of the kings of Israel had ever kept a Passover as Josiah did, involving all the priests and Levites, all the people of Jerusalem, and people from all over Judah and Israel. ¹⁹This Passover celebration took place in the eighteenth year of Josiah's reign.

Josiah Dies in Battle

²⁰After Josiah had finished restoring the Temple, King Neco of Egypt led his army up from Egypt to do battle at Carchemish on the Euphrates River, and Josiah and his army marched out to fight him. ²¹But King Neco sent ambassadors to Josiah with this message:

"What do you want with me, king of Judah? I have no quarrel with you today! I only want to fight the nation with which I am at war. And God has told me to hurry! Do not interfere with God, who is with me, or he will destroy you."

²²But Josiah refused to listen to Neco, to whom God had indeed spoken, and he would not turn back. Instead, he led his army into battle on the plain of Megiddo. He laid aside his royal robes so the enemy would not recognize him. ²³But the enemy archers hit King Josiah with their arrows and wounded him. He cried out to his men, "Take me from the battle, for I am badly wounded!"

²⁴So they lifted Josiah out of his chariot and placed him in another chariot. Then they brought him back to Jerusalem, where he died. He was buried there in the royal cemetery. And all Judah and Jerusalem mourned for him. ²⁵The prophet Jeremiah composed funeral songs for Josiah, and to this day choirs still sing these sad songs about his death. These songs of sorrow have become a tradition and are recorded in *The Book of Laments*. ²⁶The rest of the events of Josiah's reign and his acts of devotion done according to the written law of the LORD, ²⁷from beginning to end, are recorded in *The Book of the Kings of Israel and Judah*.

I TAKE responsibility to serve and assist those who are serving the Lord. (35:14)

See Asaph's profile (page 687) at Psalm 73:28.

I LISTEN to those who discourage me from fighting. (35:22)

I MOURN for leaders who die. (35:24)

See Jeremiah's profile (page 855) at Jeremiah 1:19.

See Josiah's profile (page 461) at 2 Kings 23:25.

CHAPTER **36**

Jehoahaz Rules in Judah

Then the people of the land took Josiah's son Jehoahaz and made him the next king in Jerusalem. ²Jehoahaz* was twenty-three years old when he became king, but he reigned only three months. ³Then he was deposed by Neco, the king of Egypt, who demanded a tribute from Judah of 7,500 pounds of silver and 75 pounds of gold.* ⁴The king of Egypt appointed Eliakim, the brother of Jehoahaz, as the next king of Judah and Jerusalem, and he changed Eliakim's name to Jehoiakim. Then Neco took Jehoahaz to Egypt as a prisoner.

Jehoiakim Rules in Judah

⁵Jehoiakim was twenty-five years old when he became king, and he reigned in Jerusalem eleven years. But he did what was evil in the sight of the LORD his God. ⁶Then King Nebuchadnezzar of Babylon came to Jerusalem and captured it, and he bound Jehoiakim in chains and led him away to Babylon. ⁷Nebuchadnezzar also took some of the treasures from the Temple of the LORD, and he placed them in his palace* in Babylon. ⁸The rest of the events of Jehoiakim's reign, including all the evil things he did and everything found against him, are recorded in *The Book of the Kings of Israel and Judah.* Then his son Jehoiachin became the next king.

Jehoiachin Rules in Judah

⁹Jehoiachin was eighteen* years old when he became king, but he reigned in Jerusalem only three months and ten days. Jehoiachin did what was evil in the LORD's sight. ¹⁰In the spring of the following year, Jehoiachin was summoned to Babylon by King Nebuchadnezzar. Many treasures from the Temple of the LORD were taken to Babylon at that time. And Nebuchadnezzar appointed Jehoiachin's uncle,* Zedekiah, to be the next king in Judah and Jerusalem.

Zedekiah Rules in Judah

¹¹Zedekiah was twenty-one years old when he became king, and he reigned in Jerusalem eleven years. ¹²He did what was evil in the sight of the LORD his God, and he refused to humble himself in the presence of the prophet Jeremiah, who spoke for the LORD. ¹³He also rebelled against King Nebuchadnezzar, even though he had taken an oath of loyalty in God's name. Zedekiah was a hard and stubborn man, refusing to turn to the LORD, the God of Israel.

¹⁴All the leaders of the priests and the people became more and more unfaithful. They followed the pagan practices of the surrounding nations, desecrating the Temple of the LORD in Jerusalem.

¹⁵The LORD, the God of their ancestors, repeatedly sent his prophets to warn them, for he had compassion on his people and his Temple. ¹⁶But the people mocked these messengers of God and despised their words. They scoffed at the prophets until the LORD's anger could no longer be restrained and there was no remedy.

The Fall of Jerusalem

¹⁷So the LORD brought the king of Babylon against them. The Babylonians* killed Judah's young men, even chasing after them into the Temple. They had no pity on the people, killing both young and old, men and women, healthy and sick. God handed them all over to Nebuchadnezzar. ¹⁸The king also took home to Babylon all the utensils, large and small, used in the Temple of God,

---

I DO what is right in the sight of the Lord my God. (36:5)

See Nebuchadnezzar's profile (page 985) at Daniel 4:37.

I DO what is right in the sight of the Lord my God and humbly accept all of his words. (36:12)

See Jeremiah's profile (page 855) at Jeremiah 1:19.

I TAKE the Lord's warnings to heart and abhor the thought of scoffing at his words. (36:16)

36:2 Hebrew *Joahaz,* a variant name for Jehoahaz; also in 36:4. **36:3** Hebrew *100 talents* [3.4 metric tons] *of silver and 1 talent* [34 kilograms] *of gold.* **36:7** Or *temple.* **36:9** As in one Hebrew manuscript, some Greek manuscripts, and Syriac version (see also 2 Kgs 24:8); most Hebrew manuscripts read *eight.* **36:10** As in parallel text at 2 Kgs 24:17; Hebrew reads *brother,* or *relative.* **36:17** Or *Chaldeans.*

and the treasures from both the LORD's Temple and the royal palace. He also took with him all the royal princes. [19] Then his army set fire to the Temple of God, broke down the walls of Jerusalem, burned all the palaces, and completely destroyed everything of value.* [20] The few who survived were taken away to Babylon, and they became servants to the king and his sons until the kingdom of Persia came to power. [21] So the message of the LORD spoken through Jeremiah was fulfilled. The land finally enjoyed its Sabbath rest, lying desolate for seventy years, just as the prophet had said.

I BELIEVE the Lord's messages are always fulfilled. (36:21)

Cyrus Allows the Exiles to Return

[22] In the first year of King Cyrus of Persia,* the LORD fulfilled Jeremiah's prophecy by stirring the heart of Cyrus to put this proclamation into writing and to send it throughout his kingdom:

I AM THANKFUL when those in political power acknowledge the Lord's sovereignty. (36:23)

[23] "This is what King Cyrus of Persia says: The LORD, the God of heaven, has given me all the kingdoms of the earth. He has appointed me to build him a Temple at Jerusalem in the land of Judah. All of you who are the LORD's people may return to Israel for this task. May the LORD your God be with you!"

36:19 Or *destroyed all the valuable Temple utensils.*   36:22 The first year of Cyrus's reign was 538 B.C.

EZRA

THIS TENTH BOOK of Israelite history begins the story of *rebuilding*.

Over the course of two centuries, three empires have ruled the regions east of the Mediterranean Sea. The Assyrians destroyed the northern kingdom of Israel. The Babylonians crushed the southern kingdom of Judah. The Persians, however, do the unexpected: They grant permission for the exiled Jews and their descendants to return to the Promised Land and rebuild the Temple (1:1-11).

Nearly fifty thousand Jewish exiles—mostly from the kingdom of Judah—return to the Promised Land (2:1-70). They rebuild the altar of the Lord, then begin rebuilding the Temple, only to face opposition and stop working (3:1-4:5). Such opposition is not unique. Later generations will face even worse opposition (4:6-23). In this situation, however, two prophets of the Lord rise up to spur the people back into action. Almost immediately, enemies challenge the Jews and send an official complaint to King Darius. Surprisingly, Darius commands the enemies to help the Jewish people posthaste! The Temple is finished by late winter, and the Passover is celebrated with great joy a few weeks later (4:24-6:22).

Years later, Ezra the scribe leads another group of Jewish exiles back to the Promised Land. Like the earlier group, these exiles also enjoy official support from the king of Persia (7:1-8:36). After arriving in Jerusalem, however, Ezra learns that many of the Jews have begun intermarrying with pagan neighbors. In front of the Temple, Ezra cries out to the Lord and confesses the nation's sins. His public mourning sparks a national religious revival (9:1-10:44).

The story of rebuilding continues in Nehemiah.

Famous passages in Ezra include
- The Jewish people rebuild the altar and celebrate the Festival of Shelters (3:1-6)
- The Jewish people rebuild the Temple foundation and dedicate it (3:7-13)
- King Darius issues a decree that the Temple must be finished (6:1-12)
- The Jewish people finish the Temple and dedicate it (6:13-18)
- The Jewish people celebrate the Passover with great joy (6:19-22)
- "Ezra had determined to study and obey the law of the LORD" (7:10)
- King Artaxerxes issues a decree supporting the work at the Temple (7:11-26)
- Ezra offers a prayer of thanks to the Lord (7:27-28)
- Ezra and others fast and pray for three days (8:21-23)
- Ezra and others safely journey to Jerusalem (8:31-32)
- Ezra publicly mourns over the sins of the Jewish people (9:3-10:1)
- The people agree to send away their foreign wives and children (10:2-44)

CHAPTER 1

Cyrus Allows the Exiles to Return

In the first year of King Cyrus of Persia,* the LORD fulfilled Jeremiah's prophecy by stirring the heart of Cyrus to put this proclamation into writing and to send it throughout his kingdom:

[2] "This is what King Cyrus of Persia says: The LORD, the God of heaven, has given me all the kingdoms of the earth. He has appointed me to build him a Temple at Jerusalem in the land of Judah. [3] All of you who are his people may return to Jerusalem in Judah to rebuild this Temple of the LORD, the God of Israel, who lives in Jerusalem. And may your God be with you! [4] Those who live in any place where Jewish survivors are found should contribute toward their expenses by supplying them with silver and gold, supplies for the journey, and livestock, as well as a freewill offering for the Temple of God in Jerusalem."

[5] Then God stirred the hearts of the priests and Levites and the leaders of the tribes of Judah and Benjamin to return to Jerusalem to rebuild the Temple of the LORD. [6] And all their neighbors assisted by giving them vessels of silver and gold, supplies for the journey, and livestock. They gave them many choice gifts in addition to all the freewill offerings.

[7] King Cyrus himself brought out the valuable items which King Nebuchadnezzar had taken from the LORD's Temple in Jerusalem and had placed in the temple of his own gods. [8] Cyrus directed Mithredath, the treasurer of Persia, to count these items and present them to Sheshbazzar, the leader of the exiles returning to Judah.* [9] These were the items Cyrus donated:

gold trays	30
silver trays	1,000
silver censers*	29
[10] gold bowls	30
silver bowls	410
other items	1,000

[11] In all, 5,400 gold and silver items were turned over to Sheshbazzar to take back to Jerusalem when the exiles returned there from Babylon.

CHAPTER 2

Exiles Who Returned with Zerubbabel

Here is the list of the Jewish exiles of the provinces who returned from their captivity to Jerusalem and to the other towns of Judah. They had been deported to Babylon by King Nebuchadnezzar. [2] Their leaders were Zerubbabel, Jeshua, Nehemiah, Seraiah, Reelaiah, Mordecai, Bilshan, Mispar, Bigvai, Rehum, and Baanah. This is the number of the men of Israel who returned from exile:

[3]	The family of Parosh	2,172
[4]	The family of Shephatiah	372
[5]	The family of Arah	775
[6]	The family of Pahath-moab (descendants of Jeshua and Joab)	2,812
[7]	The family of Elam	1,254
[8]	The family of Zattu	945
[9]	The family of Zaccai	760
[10]	The family of Bani	642

**Sidebar notes:**

I BELIEVE the Lord always fulfills the words of his prophets, even using pagan emperors to accomplish his purpose and plans. (1:1)

See Jeremiah's profile (page 855) at Jeremiah 1:19.

I BELIEVE the Lord, the God of heaven, is sovereign and places all governments in power—even those who end up rebelling against him. (1:2)

I TAKE ACTION when God stirs my heart to do a good work. (1:5)

See Nebuchadnezzar's profile (page 985) at Daniel 4:37.

See Nebuchadnezzar's profile (page 985) at Daniel 4:37.

I BELIEVE God always preserves a remnant of believers, even when disaster strikes. (2:1)

I RESPECT the leaders God appoints over me. (2:2)

1:1 The first year of Cyrus's reign was 538 B.C. 1:8 Hebrew *Sheshbazzar, the prince of Judah.* 1:9 The meaning of this Hebrew word is uncertain.

¹¹ The family of Bebai 623
¹² The family of Azgad 1,222
¹³ The family of Adonikam 666
¹⁴ The family of Bigvai 2,056
¹⁵ The family of Adin 454
¹⁶ The family of Ater
   (descendants of Hezekiah) 98
¹⁷ The family of Bezai.. 323
¹⁸ The family of Jorah.. 112
¹⁹ The family of Hashum 223
²⁰ The family of Gibbar 95
²¹ The people of Bethlehem...................................... 123
²² The people of Netophah 56
²³ The people of Anathoth....................................... 128
²⁴ The people of Beth-azmaveth* 42
²⁵ The peoples of Kiriath-jearim,*
   Kephirah, and Beeroth...................................... 743
²⁶ The peoples of Ramah and Geba 621
²⁷ The people of Micmash 122
²⁸ The peoples of Bethel and Ai............................... 223
²⁹ The citizens of Nebo... 52
³⁰ The citizens of Magbish 156
³¹ The citizens of Elam 1,254
³² The citizens of Harim.. 320
³³ The citizens of Lod, Hadid,
   and Ono.. 725
³⁴ The citizens of Jericho 345
³⁵ The citizens of Senaah... 3,630

³⁶ These are the priests who returned from exile:
   The family of Jedaiah
   (through the line of Jeshua) 973
³⁷ The family of Immer... 1,052
³⁸ The family of Pashhur... 1,247
³⁹ The family of Harim 1,017

⁴⁰ These are the Levites who returned from exile:
   The families of Jeshua and Kadmiel
   (descendants of Hodaviah)............................... 74
⁴¹ The singers of the family of Asaph 128
⁴² The gatekeepers of the families of
   Shallum, Ater, Talmon, Akkub,
   Hatita, and Shobai.. 139

⁴³ The descendants of the following Temple servants returned from exile:
   Ziha, Hasupha, Tabbaoth,
⁴⁴ Keros, Siaha, Padon,
⁴⁵ Lebanah, Hagabah, Akkub,
⁴⁶ Hagab, Shalmai,* Hanan,
⁴⁷ Giddel, Gahar, Reaiah,
⁴⁸ Rezin, Nekoda, Gazzam,
⁴⁹ Uzza, Paseah, Besai,
⁵⁰ Asnah, Meunim, Nephusim,
⁵¹ Bakbuk, Hakupha, Harhur,

See Hezekiah's profile (page 825) at Isaiah 37:1.

Start each day reviewing the previous day's faith affirmations.

I BELIEVE God preserved a remnant of priests and Levites during the Exile. (2:36)

See Asaph's profile (page 687) at Psalm 73:28.

I BELIEVE God preserved a remnant of Temple servants during the Exile. (2:43)

2:24 As in parallel text at Neh 7:28; Hebrew reads *Azmaveth*.   2:25 As in some Hebrew manuscripts and Greek version (see also Neh 7:29); Hebrew reads *Kiriath-arim*.   2:46 As in the marginal *Qere* reading of the Masoretic Text (see also Neh 7:48); Hebrew text reads *Shamlai*.

⁵² Bazluth, Mehida, Harsha,
⁵³ Barkos, Sisera, Temah,
⁵⁴ Neziah, and Hatipha.

⁵⁵The descendants of these servants of King Solomon returned from exile:
Sotai, Sophereth,* Peruda,
⁵⁶ Jaalah, Darkon, Giddel,
⁵⁷ Shephatiah, Hattil, Pokereth-hazzebaim, and Ami.

⁵⁸In all, the Temple servants and the descendants of Solomon's servants numbered 392.

⁵⁹Another group returned to Jerusalem at this time from the towns of Tel-melah, Tel-harsha, Kerub, Addan, and Immer. However, they could not prove that they or their families were descendants of Israel. ⁶⁰This group consisted of the families of Delaiah, Tobiah, and Nekoda—a total of 652 people.

⁶¹Three families of priests—Hobaiah, Hakkoz, and Barzillai—also returned to Jerusalem. (This Barzillai had married a woman who was a descendant of Barzillai of Gilead, and he had taken her family name.) ⁶²But they had lost their genealogical records, so they were not allowed to serve as priests. ⁶³The governor would not even let them eat the priests' share of food from the sacrifices until there was a priest who could consult the LORD about the matter by means of sacred lots.*

⁶⁴So a total of 42,360 people returned to Judah, ⁶⁵in addition to 7,337 servants and 200 singers, both men and women. ⁶⁶They took with them 736 horses, 245 mules, ⁶⁷435 camels, and 6,720 donkeys.

⁶⁸When they arrived at the Temple of the LORD in Jerusalem, some of the family leaders gave generously toward the rebuilding of God's Temple on its original site, ⁶⁹and each leader gave as much as he could. The total of their gifts came to 61,000 gold coins,* 6,250 pounds* of silver, and 100 robes for the priests.

⁷⁰So the priests, the Levites, the singers, the gatekeepers, the Temple servants, and some of the common people settled in villages near Jerusalem. The rest of the people returned to the other towns of Judah from which they had come.

CHAPTER 3

The Altar Is Rebuilt

Now in early autumn,* when the Israelites had settled in their towns, all the people assembled together as one person in Jerusalem. ²Then Jeshua son of Jehozadak* with his fellow priests and Zerubbabel son of Shealtiel with his family began to rebuild the altar of the God of Israel so they could sacrifice burnt offerings on it, as instructed in the law of Moses, the man of God. ³Even though the people were afraid of the local residents, they rebuilt the altar at its old site. Then they immediately began to sacrifice burnt offerings on the altar to the LORD. They did this each morning and evening.

⁴They celebrated the Festival of Shelters as prescribed in the law of Moses, sacrificing the burnt offerings specified for each day of the festival. ⁵They also offered the regular burnt offerings and the offerings required for the new moon celebrations and the other annual festivals to the LORD. Freewill offerings were also sacrificed to the LORD by the people. ⁶Fifteen days before the Festival of Shelters began,* the priests had begun to sacrifice burnt offerings

---

I BELIEVE God preserved a remnant of palace servants during the Exile. (2:55)

See Solomon's profile (page 753) at Proverbs 2:9.

I RECOGNIZE that a man may take his wife's family name when they marry. (2:61)

I BELIEVE a large contingent returned to Judah after the Exile. (2:64)

I CONTRIBUTE generously toward to the building of new houses in which to worship the Lord. (2:68)

I OBEY the Lord's commands, even if others threaten me. (3:3)

See Moses' profile (page 73) at Exodus 5:1.

2:55 As in parallel text at Neh 7:57; Hebrew reads *Hassophereth.* 2:63 Hebrew *consult the Urim and Thummim about the matter.* 2:69a Hebrew *61,000 darics of gold,* about 1,100 pounds or 500 kilograms in weight. 2:69b Hebrew *5,000 minas* [3 metric tons]. 3:1 Hebrew *in the seventh month.* The year is not specific, so it may have been during Cyrus's first year (538 B.C.) or second year (537 B.C.). The seventh month of the Hebrew lunar calendar occurred in September/October 538 B.C. and October/November 537 B.C. 3:2 Hebrew *Jozadak,* a variant name for Jehozadak; also in 3:8. 3:6 Hebrew *On the first day of the seventh month.* This day of the Hebrew lunar calendar occurs in September or October. The Festival of Shelters began on the fifteenth day of the seventh month.

to the Lord. This was also before they had started to lay the foundation of the Lord's Temple.

The People Rebuild the Temple

⁷Then they hired masons and carpenters and bought cedar logs from the people of Tyre and Sidon, paying them with food, wine, and olive oil. The logs were brought down from the Lebanon mountains and floated along the coast of the Mediterranean Sea to Joppa, for King Cyrus had given permission for this.

⁸The construction of the Temple of God began in midspring,* during the second year after they arrived in Jerusalem. The work force was made up of everyone who had returned from exile, including Zerubbabel son of Shealtiel, Jeshua son of Jehozadak and his fellow priests, and all the Levites. The Levites who were twenty years old or older were put in charge of rebuilding the Lord's Temple. ⁹The workers at the Temple of God were supervised by Jeshua with his sons and relatives, and Kadmiel and his sons, all descendants of Hodaviah.* They were helped in this task by the Levites of the family of Henadad.

¹⁰When the builders completed the foundation of the Lord's Temple, the priests put on their robes and took their places to blow their trumpets. And the Levites, descendants of Asaph, clashed their cymbals to praise the Lord, just as King David had prescribed. ¹¹With praise and thanks, they sang this song to the Lord:

"He is so good!
His faithful love for Israel endures forever!"

Then all the people gave a great shout, praising the Lord because the foundation of the Lord's Temple had been laid.

¹²Many of the older priests, Levites, and other leaders remembered the first Temple, and they wept aloud when they saw the new Temple's foundation. The others, however, were shouting for joy. ¹³The joyful shouting and weeping mingled together in a loud commotion that could be heard far in the distance.

CHAPTER 4

Enemies Oppose the Rebuilding

The enemies of Judah and Benjamin heard that the exiles were rebuilding a Temple to the Lord, the God of Israel. ²So they approached Zerubbabel and the other leaders and said, "Let us build with you, for we worship your God just as you do. We have sacrificed to him ever since King Esarhaddon of Assyria brought us here."

³But Zerubbabel, Jeshua, and the other leaders of Israel replied, "You may have no part in this work, for we have nothing in common. We alone will build the Temple for the Lord, the God of Israel, just as King Cyrus of Persia commanded us."

⁴Then the local residents tried to discourage and frighten the people of Judah to keep them from their work. ⁵They bribed agents to work against them and to frustrate their aims. This went on during the entire reign of King Cyrus of Persia and lasted until King Darius of Persia took the throne.

Later Opposition under King Artaxerxes

⁶Years later when Xerxes* began his reign, the enemies of Judah wrote him a letter of accusation against the people of Judah and Jerusalem. ⁷And even

I JOIN with others in doing the work of the Lord. (3:8)

I HELP DEDICATE new houses in which to worship the Lord with music and great shouts of praise. (3:10)

See the profiles for David (page 629) and Asaph (page 687) at Psalm 3:1 and Psalm 73:28.

I ABHOR AND REJECT combining pagan beliefs and practices with the worship of the Lord. (4:3)

I DO NOT GIVE IN to those who seek to frighten or discourage me from serving the Lord. (4:4)

3:8 Hebrew *in the second month.* This month of the Hebrew lunar calendar occurred in April and May 536 B.C.
3:9 Hebrew *sons of Judah* (i.e., *bene Yehudah*). Bene might also be read here as the proper name Binnui; *Yehudah* is probably another name for Hodaviah. Compare 2:40; Neh 7:43; 1 Esdras 5:58.   4:6 Hebrew *Ahasuerus,* another name for Xerxes. He reigned 486–465 B.C.

later, during the reign of King Artaxerxes of Persia,* the enemies of Judah, led by Bishlam, Mithredath, and Tabeel, sent a letter to Artaxerxes in the Aramaic language, and it was translated for the king. [8]Rehum* the governor and Shimshai the court secretary wrote the letter, telling King Artaxerxes about the situation in Jerusalem. [9]They greeted the king for all their colleagues— the judges and local leaders, the people of Tarpel, the Persians, the Babylonians, and the people of Erech and Susa (that is, Elam). [10]They also sent greetings from the rest of the people whom the great and noble Ashurbanipal* had deported and relocated in Samaria and throughout the neighboring lands of the province west of the Euphrates River. [11]This is a copy of the letter they sent him:

"To Artaxerxes, from your loyal subjects in the province west of the Euphrates River.

[12]"Please be informed that the Jews who came here to Jerusalem from Babylon are rebuilding this rebellious and evil city. They have already laid the foundation for its walls and will soon complete them. [13]But we wish you to know that if this city is rebuilt and its walls are completed, it will be much to your disadvantage, for the Jews will then refuse to pay their tribute, customs, and tolls to you.

I DO NOT FEIGN loyalty. (4:14)

[14]"Since we are loyal to you as your subjects and we do not want to see you dishonored in this way, we have sent you this information. [15]We suggest that you search your ancestors' records, where you will discover what a rebellious city this has been in the past. In fact, it was destroyed because of its long history of sedition against the kings and countries who attempted to control it. [16]We declare that if this city is rebuilt and its walls are completed, the province west of the Euphrates River will be lost to you."

I DO NOT LIBEL others. (4:16)

[17]Then Artaxerxes made this reply:

"To Rehum the governor, Shimshai the court secretary, and their colleagues living in Samaria and throughout the province west of the Euphrates River.

I REVIEW the current situation carefully instead of making an unnecessarily hasty decision based on inaccurate and incomplete information. (4:19)

[18]"Greetings. The letter you sent has been translated and read to me. [19]I have ordered a search to be made of the records and have indeed found that Jerusalem has in times past been a hotbed of insurrection against many kings. In fact, rebellion and sedition are normal there! [20]Powerful kings have ruled over Jerusalem and the entire province west of the Euphrates River and have received vast tribute, customs, and tolls. [21]Therefore, issue orders to have these people stop their work. That city must not be rebuilt except at my express command. [22]Do not delay, for we must not permit the situation to get out of control."

[23]When this letter from King Artaxerxes was read to Rehum, Shimshai, and their colleagues, they hurried to Jerusalem and forced the Jews to stop building.

The Rebuilding Resumes

[24]The work on the Temple of God in Jerusalem had stopped, and it remained at a standstill until the second year of the reign of King Darius of Persia.*

CHAPTER 5

At that time the prophets Haggai and Zechariah son of Iddo prophesied in the name of the God of Israel to the Jews in Judah and Jerusalem. [2]Zerubbabel son

4:7 Artaxerxes reigned 465–424 B.C.   4:8 The original text of 4:8–6:18 is in Aramaic.   4:10 Aramaic *Osnappar*, another name for Ashurbanipal.   4:24 The second year of Darius's reign was 520 B.C.

of Shealtiel and Jeshua son of Jehozadak* responded by beginning the task of rebuilding the Temple of God in Jerusalem. And the prophets of God were with them and helped them.

³But Tattenai, governor of the province west of the Euphrates, and Shethar-bozenai and their colleagues soon arrived in Jerusalem and asked, "Who gave you permission to rebuild this Temple and restore this structure?" ⁴They also asked for a list of the names of all the people who were working on the Temple. ⁵But because their God was watching over them, the leaders of the Jews were not prevented from building until a report was sent to Darius and he returned his decision.

Tattenai's Letter to King Darius
⁶This is the letter that Tattenai the governor, Shethar-bozenai, and the other officials of the province west of the Euphrates River sent to King Darius:

⁷"Greetings to King Darius. ⁸We wish to inform you that we went to the construction site of the Temple of the great God in the province of Judah. It is being rebuilt with specially prepared stones, and timber is being laid in its walls. The work is going forward with great energy and success. ⁹We asked the leaders, 'Who gave you permission to rebuild this Temple and restore this structure?' ¹⁰And we demanded their names so that we could tell you who the leaders were.

¹¹"This was their answer: 'We are the servants of the God of heaven and earth, and we are rebuilding the Temple that was built here many years ago by a great king of Israel. ¹²But because our ancestors angered the God of heaven, he abandoned them to King Nebuchadnezzar of Babylon,* who destroyed this Temple and exiled the people to Babylonia. ¹³However, King Cyrus of Babylon,* during the first year of his reign, issued a decree that the Temple of God should be rebuilt. ¹⁴King Cyrus returned the gold and silver utensils that Nebuchadnezzar had taken from the Temple of God in Jerusalem and had placed in the temple of Babylon. These items were taken from that temple and delivered into the safekeeping of a man named Sheshbazzar, whom King Cyrus appointed as governor of Judah. ¹⁵The king instructed him to return the utensils to their place in Jerusalem and to rebuild the Temple of God there as it had been before. ¹⁶So this Sheshbazzar came and laid the foundations of the Temple of God in Jerusalem. The people have been working on it ever since, though it is not yet completed.'

¹⁷"So now, if it pleases the king, we request that you search in the royal archives of Babylon to discover whether King Cyrus ever issued a decree to rebuild God's Temple in Jerusalem. And then let the king send us his decision in this matter."

CHAPTER 6
Darius Approves the Rebuilding
So King Darius issued orders that a search be made in the Babylonian archives, where treasures were stored. ²But it was at the fortress at Ecbatana in the province of Media that a scroll was found. This is what it said:

³"Memorandum:

"In the first year of King Cyrus's reign, a decree was sent out concerning the Temple of God at Jerusalem. It must be rebuilt on the site where Jews used to offer their sacrifices, retaining the original foundations. Its height will be ninety feet, and its width will be ninety feet.* ⁴Every three

---

I CONTINUE TO DO the Lord's work, even if the law directly goes against God's clear commands. (5:2)

I DO NOT STOP working for the Lord, even if others seek to frighten or discourage me. (5:5)

I BELIEVE that God is indeed great and that his work should go forward with special preparation, great energy, and success. (5:8)

See Nebuchadnezzar's profile (page 985) at Daniel 4:37.

I BELIEVE the Lord uses even pagan emperors to accomplish his purpose and plans. (5:13)

I REVIEW the current situation carefully instead of making an unnecessarily hasty decision based on inaccurate and incomplete information. (6:1)

5:2 Aramaic *Jozadak,* a variant name for Jehozadak.   5:12 Aramaic *Nebuchadnezzar the Chaldean.*   5:13 King Cyrus of Persia is here identified as the king of Babylon because Persia had conquered the Babylonian Empire. 6:3 Aramaic *Its height will be 60 cubits* [27 meters]*, and its width will be 60 cubits.* It is commonly held that this verse should be emended to read: "Its height will be 45 feet, its length will be 90 feet, and its width will be 30 feet"; compare 1 Kgs 6:2. The emendation regarding the width is supported by the Syriac version.

See Nebuchadnezzar's profile (page 985) at Daniel 4:37.

layers of specially prepared stones will be topped by a layer of timber. All expenses will be paid by the royal treasury. [5]And the gold and silver utensils, which were taken to Babylon by Nebuchadnezzar from the Temple of God in Jerusalem, will be taken back to Jerusalem and put into God's Temple as they were before."

[6]So King Darius sent this message:

"To Tattenai, governor of the province west of the Euphrates River, to Shethar-bozenai, and to your colleagues and other officials west of the Euphrates:

"Stay away from there! [7]Do not disturb the construction of the Temple of God. Let it be rebuilt on its former site, and do not hinder the governor of Judah and the leaders of the Jews in their work. [8]Moreover I hereby decree that you are to help these leaders of the Jews as they rebuild this Temple of God. You must pay the full construction costs without delay from my taxes collected in your province so that the work will not be discontinued. [9]Give the priests in Jerusalem whatever is needed in the way of young bulls, rams, and lambs for the burnt offerings presented to the God of heaven. And without fail, provide them with the wheat, salt, wine, and olive oil that they need each day. [10]Then they will be able to offer acceptable sacrifices to the God of heaven and pray for me and my sons.

[11]"Those who violate this decree in any way will have a beam pulled from their house. Then they will be tied to it and flogged, and their house will be reduced to a pile of rubble.* [12]May the God who has chosen the city of Jerusalem as the place to honor his name destroy any king or nation that violates this command and destroys this Temple. I, Darius, have issued this decree. Let it be obeyed with all diligence."

I PRAY for government leaders and for their families. (6:10)

The Temple's Dedication

[13]Tattenai, governor of the province west of the Euphrates River, and Shethar-bozenai and their colleagues complied at once with the command of King Darius. [14]So the Jewish leaders continued their work, and they were greatly encouraged by the preaching of the prophets Haggai and Zechariah son of Iddo. The Temple was finally finished, as had been commanded by the God of Israel and decreed by Cyrus, Darius, and Artaxerxes, the kings of Persia. [15]The Temple was completed on March 12,* during the sixth year of King Darius's reign.

[16]The Temple of God was then dedicated with great joy by the people of Israel, the priests, the Levites, and the rest of the people who had returned from exile. [17]During the dedication ceremony for the Temple of God, one hundred young bulls, two hundred rams, and four hundred lambs were sacrificed. And twelve male goats were presented as a sin offering for the twelve tribes of Israel. [18]Then the priests and Levites were divided into their various divisions to serve at the Temple of God in Jerusalem, following all the instructions recorded in the Book of Moses.

I HELP DEDICATE new houses in which to worship God with great joy, generous offerings, and renewed dedication to assist with the work. (6:16)

See Moses' profile (page 73) at Exodus 5:1.

I HAVE TURNED from the immoral customs of my people to worship the Lord. (6:21)

Celebration of Passover

[19]On April 21* the returned exiles celebrated Passover. [20]The priests and Levites had purified themselves and were ceremonially clean. So they slaughtered the Passover lamb for all the returned exiles, for the other priests, and for themselves. [21]The Passover meal was eaten by the people of Israel who had returned from exile and by the others in the land who had turned

6:11 Aramaic *a dunghill.* 6:15 Aramaic *on the third day of the month Adar,* of the Hebrew calendar. This event occurred on March 12, 515 B.C.; also see note on 3:1. 6:19 Hebrew *On the fourteenth day of the first month,* of the Hebrew calendar. This event occurred on April 21, 515 B.C.; also see note on 3:1.

from their immoral customs to worship the LORD, the God of Israel. [22]They ate the Passover meal and celebrated the Festival of Unleavened Bread for seven days. There was great joy throughout the land because the LORD had changed the attitude of the king of Assyria* toward them, so that he helped them to rebuild the Temple of God, the God of Israel.

CHAPTER 7

Ezra Arrives in Jerusalem

Many years later, during the reign of King Artaxerxes of Persia,* there was a man named Ezra. He was the son* of Seraiah, son of Azariah, son of Hilkiah, [2]son of Shallum, son of Zadok, son of Ahitub, [3]son of Amariah, son of Azariah, son* of Meraioth, [4]son of Zerahiah, son of Uzzi, son of Bukki, [5]son of Abishua, son of Phinehas, son of Eleazar, son of Aaron the high priest. [6]This Ezra was a scribe, well versed in the law of Moses, which the LORD, the God of Israel, had given to the people of Israel. He came up to Jerusalem from Babylon, and the king gave him everything he asked for, because the gracious hand of the LORD his God was on him. [7]Some of the people of Israel, as well as some of the priests, Levites, singers, gatekeepers, and Temple servants, traveled up to Jerusalem with him in the seventh year of King Artaxerxes' reign.

[8]Ezra arrived in Jerusalem in August* of that year. [9]He had left Babylon on April 8* and came to Jerusalem on August 4,* for the gracious hand of his God was on him. [10]This was because Ezra had determined to study and obey the law of the LORD and to teach those laws and regulations to the people of Israel.

Artaxerxes' Letter to Ezra

[11]King Artaxerxes had given a copy of the following letter to Ezra, the priest and scribe who studied and taught the commands and laws of the LORD to Israel:

[12]"Greetings* from Artaxerxes, the king of kings, to Ezra the priest, the teacher of the law of the God of heaven.

[13]"I decree that any of the people of Israel in my kingdom, including the priests and Levites, may volunteer to return to Jerusalem with you. [14]I and my Council of Seven hereby instruct you to conduct an inquiry into the situation in Judah and Jerusalem, based on your God's law, which is in your hand. [15]We also commission you to take with you some silver and gold, which we are freely presenting as an offering to the God of Israel who lives in Jerusalem.

[16]"Moreover you are to take any silver and gold which you may obtain from the province of Babylon, as well as the freewill offerings of the people and the priests that are presented for the Temple of their God in Jerusalem. [17]These donations are to be used specifically for the purchase of bulls, rams, lambs, and the appropriate grain offerings and drink offerings, all of which will be offered on the altar of the Temple of your God in Jerusalem. [18]Any money that is left over may be used in whatever way you and your colleagues feel is the will of your God. [19]But as for the utensils we are entrusting to you for the service of the Temple of your God, deliver them in full to the God of Jerusalem. [20]If you run short of

I REJOICE when the Lord uses even pagan rulers to accomplish his purpose and plans (Proverbs 21:1). (6:22)

See the profiles for Ezra (page 559) and Hilkiah (page 545) at Ezra 8:21 and 2 Chronicles 34:14.

See the profiles for Aaron (page 107) and Phinehas (page 717) at Exodus 32:2 and Psalm 106:30.

See Moses' profile (page 73) at Exodus 5:1.

I MAKE it a priority to study and obey Scripture and to teach God's Word to others (2 Timothy 2:15). (7:10)

I CONSIDER what God's Word says before choosing a course of action. (7:14)

I CONTRIBUTE generously toward the needs of friends and relatives committed to doing God's will in another land. (7:18)

6:22 King Darius of Persia is here identified as the king of Assyria because Persia had conquered the Babylonian Empire, which included the earlier Assyrian Empire. 7:1a Artaxerxes reigned 465–424 B.C. 7:1b Or descendant; see 1 Chr 6:14. 7:3 Or descendant; see 1 Chr 6:6-10. 7:8 Hebrew in the fifth month. This month of the Hebrew lunar calendar occurred in August and September 458 B.C. 7:9a Hebrew on the first day of the first month, of the Hebrew calendar. This event occurred on April 8, 458 B.C.; also see note on 3:1. 7:9b Hebrew on the first day of the fifth month, of the Hebrew calendar. This event occurred on August 4, 458 B.C.; also see note on 3:1. 7:12 The original text of 7:12-26 is in Aramaic.

money for anything necessary for your God's Temple or for any similar needs, you may requisition funds from the royal treasury.

I TEACH God's Word to others. (7:21)

²¹"I, Artaxerxes the king, hereby send this decree to all the treasurers in the province west of the Euphrates River: 'You are to give Ezra whatever he requests of you, for he is a priest and teacher of the law of the God of heaven. ²²You are to give him up to 7,500 pounds* of silver, 500 bushels* of wheat, 550 gallons of wine, 550 gallons of olive oil,* and an unlimited supply of salt. ²³Be careful to provide whatever the God of heaven demands for his Temple, for why should we risk bringing God's anger against the realm of the king and his sons? ²⁴I also decree that no priest, Levite, singer, gatekeeper, Temple servant, or other worker in this Temple of God will be required to pay taxes of any kind.'

²⁵"And you, Ezra, are to use the wisdom God has given you to appoint magistrates and judges who know your God's laws to govern all the people in the province west of the Euphrates River. If the people are not familiar with those laws, you must teach them. ²⁶Anyone who refuses to obey the law of your God and the law of the king will be punished immediately by death, banishment, confiscation of goods, or imprisonment."

I PRAISE the Lord when he uses even pagan rulers to accomplish his purpose and plans (Proverbs 21:1). (7:27)
I PRAISE the Lord when he demonstrates his unfailing love and graciousness toward me. (7:28)

Ezra Praises the LORD

²⁷Praise the LORD, the God of our ancestors, who made the king want to beautify the Temple of the LORD in Jerusalem! ²⁸And praise him for demonstrating such unfailing love to me by honoring me before the king, his council, and all his mighty princes! I felt encouraged because the gracious hand of the LORD my God was on me. And I gathered some of the leaders of Israel to return with me to Jerusalem.

CHAPTER 8

See David's profile (page 629) at Psalm 3:1.
I HUMBLE myself and fast before embarking on a long and dangerous journey. (8:21)

Exiles Who Returned with Ezra

Here is a list of the family leaders and the genealogies of those who came with me from Babylon during the reign of King Artaxerxes:

² From the family of Phinehas: Gershom.
From the family of Ithamar: Daniel.
³ From the family of David: Hattush son of Shecaniah.
From the family of Parosh: Zechariah and 150 other men.
⁴ From the family of Pahath-moab: Eliehoenai son of Zerahiah and 200 other men.
⁵ From the family of Zattu*: Shecaniah son of Jahaziel and 300 other men.
⁶ From the family of Adin: Ebed son of Jonathan and 50 other men.
⁷ From the family of Elam: Jeshaiah son of Athaliah and 70 other men.
⁸ From the family of Shephatiah: Zebadiah son of Michael and 80 other men.
⁹ From the family of Joab: Obadiah son of Jehiel and 218 other men.
¹⁰ From the family of Bani*: Shelomith son of Josiphiah and 160 other men.
¹¹ From the family of Bebai: Zechariah son of Bebai and 28 other men.
¹² From the family of Azgad: Johanan son of Hakkatan and 110 other men.
¹³ From the family of Adonikam, who came later*: Eliphelet, Jeuel, Shemaiah, and 60 other men.
¹⁴ From the family of Bigvai: Uthai, Zaccur, and 70 other men.

7:22a Aramaic *100 talents* [3.4 metric tons]. 7:22b Aramaic *100 cors* [18.2 kiloliters]. 7:22c Aramaic *100 baths* [2.1 kiloliters] *of wine, 100 baths of olive oil.* 8:5 As in some Greek manuscripts (see also 1 Esdras 8:32); Hebrew lacks *Zattu.* 8:10 As in some Greek manuscripts (see also 1 Esdras 8:36); Hebrew lacks *Bani.* 8:13 The meaning of the Hebrew for this phrase is uncertain.

Ezra's Journey to Jerusalem

¹⁵I assembled the exiles at the Ahava Canal, and we camped there for three days while I went over the lists of the people and the priests who had arrived. I found that not one Levite had volunteered to come along. ¹⁶So I sent for Eliezer, Ariel, Shemaiah, Elnathan, Jarib, Elnathan, Nathan, Zechariah, and Meshullam, who were leaders of the people. I also sent for Joiarib and Elnathan, who were very wise men. ¹⁷I sent them to Iddo, the leader of the Levites at Casiphia, to ask him and his relatives and the Temple servants to send us ministers for the Temple of God at Jerusalem. ¹⁸Since the gracious hand of our God was on us, they sent us a man named Sherebiah, along with eighteen of his sons and brothers. He was a very astute man and a descendant of Mahli, who was a descendant of Levi son of Israel.* ¹⁹They also sent Hashabiah, together with Jeshaiah from the descendants of Merari, and twenty of his sons and brothers, ²⁰and 220 Temple servants. The Temple servants were assistants to the Levites—a group of Temple workers first instituted by King David. They were all listed by name.

LIKE EZRA   *I pray to God for safety and protection.*

Ezra 8:21

Many travelers say a hurried prayer for safety as they head down the road. Ezra's prayer for a safe journey, however, was no mere wish for good luck, as are so many of our prayers. Ahead of Ezra and his band of returning refugees lay a desert fraught with danger. Behind them stood the king to whom Ezra desperately wanted to prove the power of God. With prayer and fasting, the entire community asked God to keep them safe on their journey to Jerusalem.

Ezra was no flippant fellow. He knew the trip would be no picnic, and he seriously considered the risks to both limb and luggage. It was not because he was naive or proud that he refused the king's soldiers as escorts. He simply didn't want to be ashamed of proclaiming trust in the Lord while appearing to hide behind the king's protection. Ezra wanted God to be glorified, and in this case it would have been far too easy for the king to take credit for their safety.

Neither did Ezra make assumptions. By setting aside time to fast and ask God to protect them, the people focused their minds on him. They knew from the beginning whom to thank when they got to the end of the road with their children and belongings still safe and sound.

Ezra was not the only leader to make this trip to Jerusalem. To read how Nehemiah accepted the king's guard as God's provision, see Nehemiah 2:7-9. Like Ezra, Nehemiah knew all that was accomplished for Israel was because of the good hand of God upon him. Two different choices for two different journeys—but both men called on God and trusted him for safety (Nehemiah 1:4–2:6).

Whether we go by plane or by train, whether we purchase AAA coverage or not, it is the Lord whom we pray to and depend on for protection every day.

○ *Today's Scripture reading is Ezra 7–9.*

---

²¹And there by the Ahava Canal, I gave orders for all of us to fast and humble ourselves before our God. We prayed that he would give us a safe journey and protect us, our children, and our goods as we traveled. ²²For I was ashamed to ask the king for soldiers and horsemen to accompany us and protect us from enemies along the way. After all, we had told the king, "Our God protects all those who worship him, but his fierce anger rages against those who abandon him." ²³So we fasted and earnestly prayed that our God would take care of us, and he heard our prayer.

²⁴I appointed twelve leaders of the priests—Sherebiah, Hashabiah, and ten other priests—²⁵to be in charge of transporting the silver, the gold, the gold bowls, and the other items that the king, his council, his leaders, and the

I BELIEVE God hears—and answers—prayer. (8:23)

I APPOINT or count on reputable trustees to oversee the wealth of my church, business, and estate. (8:24)

8:18 *Israel* is the name that God gave to Jacob.

I SET UP accurate financial records. (8:26)

people of Israel had presented for the Temple of God. ²⁶I weighed the treasure as I gave it to them and found the totals to be as follows:

24 tons* of silver,
7,500 pounds* of silver utensils,
7,500 pounds* of gold,
²⁷ 20 gold bowls, equal in value to 1,000 gold coins,*
2 fine articles of polished bronze, as precious as gold.

I CAREFULLY GUARD that which has been entrusted to me. (8:29)

I ACCEPT difficult tasks, depending on God to help me fulfill them. (8:30)

²⁸And I said to these priests, "You and these treasures have been set apart as holy to the LORD. This silver and gold is a freewill offering to the LORD, the God of our ancestors. ²⁹Guard these treasures well until you present them, without an ounce lost, to the leading priests, the Levites, and the leaders of Israel at the storerooms of the LORD's Temple in Jerusalem." ³⁰So the priests and the Levites accepted the task of transporting these treasures to the Temple of our God in Jerusalem.

³¹We broke camp at the Ahava Canal on April 19* and started off to Jerusalem. And the gracious hand of our God protected us and saved us from enemies and bandits along the way. ³²So at last we arrived safely in Jerusalem, where we rested for three days.

See Phinehas's profile (page 717) at Psalm 106:30.

³³On the fourth day after our arrival, the silver, gold, and other valuables were weighed at the Temple of our God and entrusted to Meremoth son of Uriah the priest and to Eleazar son of Phinehas, along with Jozabad son of Jeshua and Noadiah son of Binnui—both of whom were Levites. ³⁴Everything was accounted for by number and weight, and the total weight was officially recorded.

³⁵Then the exiles who had returned from captivity sacrificed burnt offerings to the God of Israel. They presented twelve oxen for the people of Israel, as well as ninety-six rams and seventy-seven lambs. They also offered twelve goats as a sin offering. All this was given as a burnt offering to the LORD. ³⁶The king's decrees were delivered to his lieutenants and the governors of the province west of the Euphrates River, who then cooperated by supporting the people and the Temple of God.

CHAPTER 9

Ezra's Prayer concerning Intermarriage

I KEEP myself separate from the detestable practices in my culture that go against God's holy character and Word. (9:1)

I NEVER CONDONE marriages between believers and unbelievers. (9:2)

But then the Jewish leaders came to me and said, "Many of the people of Israel, and even some of the priests and Levites, have not kept themselves separate from the other peoples living in the land. They have taken up the detestable practices of the Canaanites, Hittites, Perizzites, Jebusites, Ammonites, Moabites, Egyptians, and Amorites. ²For the men of Israel have married women from these people and have taken them as wives for their sons. So the holy race has become polluted by these mixed marriages. To make matters worse, the officials and leaders are some of the worst offenders."

³When I heard this, I tore my clothing, pulled hair from my head and beard, and sat down utterly shocked. ⁴Then all who trembled at the words of the God of Israel came and sat with me because of this unfaithfulness of his people. And I sat there utterly appalled until the time of the evening sacrifice.

I PRAY to the Lord as I mourn over the sin rampant among God's people. (9:5)

⁵At the time of the sacrifice, I stood up from where I had sat in mourning with my clothes torn. I fell to my knees, lifted my hands to the LORD my God. ⁶I prayed, "O my God, I am utterly ashamed; I blush to lift up my face to you. For our sins are piled higher than our heads, and our guilt has reached to the

8:26a Hebrew *650 talents* [22 metric tons]. 8:26b Hebrew *100 talents* [3.4 metric tons]. 8:26c Hebrew *100 talents* [3.4 metric tons]. 8:27 Hebrew *1,000 darics,* about 19 pounds or 8.6 kilograms in weight. 8:31 Hebrew *on the twelfth day of the first month,* of the Hebrew calendar. This event occurred on April 19, 458 B.C.; see note on 7:9a.

heavens. [7]Our whole history has been one of great sin. That is why we and our kings and our priests have been at the mercy of the pagan kings of the land. We have been killed, captured, robbed, and disgraced, just as we are today.

[8]"But now we have been given a brief moment of grace, for the LORD our God has allowed a few of us to survive as a remnant. He has given us security in this holy place. Our God has brightened our eyes and granted us some relief from our slavery. [9]For we were slaves, but in his unfailing love our God did not abandon us in our slavery. Instead, he caused the kings of Persia to treat us favorably. He revived us so that we were able to rebuild the Temple of our God and repair its ruins. He has given us a protective wall in Judah and Jerusalem.

[10]"And now, O our God, what can we say after all of this? For once again we have ignored your commands! [11]Your servants the prophets warned us that the land we would possess was totally defiled by the detestable practices of the people living there. From one end to the other, the land is filled with corruption. [12]You told us not to let our daughters marry their sons, and not to let our sons marry their daughters, and not to help those nations in any way. You promised that if we avoided these things, we would become a prosperous nation. You promised that we would enjoy the good produce of the land and leave this prosperity to our children as an inheritance forever.

[13]"Now we are being punished because of our wickedness and our great guilt. But we have actually been punished far less than we deserve, for you, our God, have allowed some of us to survive as a remnant. [14]But now we are again breaking your commands and intermarrying with people who do these detestable things. Surely your anger will destroy us until even this little remnant no longer survives. [15]O LORD, God of Israel, you are just. We stand before you in our guilt as nothing but an escaped remnant, though in such a condition none of us can stand in your presence."

CHAPTER 10

The People Confess Their Sin

While Ezra prayed and made this confession, weeping and throwing himself to the ground in front of the Temple of God, a large crowd of people from Israel—men, women, and children—gathered and wept bitterly with him. [2]Then Shecaniah son of Jehiel, a descendant of Elam, said to Ezra, "We confess that we have been unfaithful to our God, for we have married these pagan women of the land. But there is hope for Israel in spite of this. [3]Let us now make a covenant with our God to divorce our pagan wives and to send them away with their children. We will follow the advice given by you and by the others who respect the commands of our God. We will obey the law of God. [4]Take courage, for it is your duty to tell us how to proceed in setting things straight, and we will cooperate fully."

[5]So Ezra stood up and demanded that the leaders of the priests and the Levites and all the people of Israel swear that they would do as Shecaniah had said. And they all swore a solemn oath. [6]Then Ezra left the front of the Temple of God and went to the room of Jehohanan son of Eliashib. He spent the night* there, but he did not eat any food or drink. He was still in mourning because of the unfaithfulness of the returned exiles. [7]Then a proclamation was made throughout Judah and Jerusalem that all the returned exiles should come to Jerusalem. [8]Those who failed to come within three days would, if the leaders and elders so decided, forfeit all their property and be expelled from the assembly of the exiles.

[9]Within three days, all the people of Judah and Benjamin had gathered in

---

I ACKNOWLEDGE the sins of God's people down through the years. (9:7)

I COME to the Lord in my guilt, confessing that he is just but also that he has allowed his people to survive. (9:15)

I PARTICIPATE in the public confession of the current sins of God's people in my city and nation. (10:1)

I CONFESS my own sins as one of God's people. (10:2)

I COOPERATE in setting things straight after I have sinned. (10:4)

I CONTINUE to mourn over the sin rampant among God's people, even after some confess their unfaithfulness. (10:6)

10:6 As in parallel text at 1 Esdras 9:2; Hebrew reads *He went.*

Jerusalem. This took place on December 19,* and all the people were sitting in the square before the Temple of God. They were trembling both because of the seriousness of the matter and because it was raining. [10] Then Ezra the priest stood and said to them: "You have sinned, for you have married pagan women. Now we are even more deeply under condemnation than we were before. [11]Confess your sin to the LORD, the God of your ancestors, and do what he demands. Separate yourselves from the people of the land and from these pagan women."

I CONFESS the current sins of God's people in my city and nation and then call them to repent. (10:10)

I CONFESS my sins to the Lord my God and do what he commands. (10:11)

[12]Then the whole assembly raised their voices and answered, "Yes, you are right; we must do as you say!" [13]Then they added, "This isn't something that can be done in a day or two, for many of us are involved in this extremely sinful affair. This is the rainy season, so we cannot stay out here much longer. [14]Let our leaders act on behalf of us all. Everyone who has a pagan wife will come at the scheduled time with the leaders and judges of his city, so that the fierce anger of our God may be turned away from us concerning this affair." [15]Only Jonathan son of Asahel and Jahzeiah son of Tikvah opposed this course of action, and Meshullam and Shabbethai the Levite supported them.

I DO NOT OBSTINATELY OPPOSE plans for promoting God's will among his people. (10:15)

[16]So this was the plan that they followed. Ezra selected leaders to represent their families, designating each of the representatives by name. On December 29,* the leaders sat down to investigate the matter. [17]By March 27 of the next year* they had finished dealing with all the men who had married pagan wives.

Those Guilty of Intermarriage
[18]These are the priests who had married pagan wives:

From the family of Jeshua son of Jehozadak* and his brothers: Maaseiah, Eliezer, Jarib, and Gedaliah. [19]They vowed to divorce their wives, and they each acknowledged their guilt by offering a ram as a guilt offering.
[20]From the family of Immer: Hanani and Zebadiah.
[21]From the family of Harim: Maaseiah, Elijah, Shemaiah, Jehiel, and Uzziah.
[22]From the family of Pashhur: Elioenai, Maaseiah, Ishmael, Nethanel, Jozabad, and Elasah.

[23]These are the Levites who were guilty: Jozabad, Shimei, Kelaiah (also called Kelita), Pethahiah, Judah, and Eliezer.

[24]This is the singer who was guilty: Eliashib.

These are the gatekeepers who were guilty: Shallum, Telem, and Uri.

[25]These are the other people of Israel who were guilty:

From the family of Parosh: Ramiah, Izziah, Malkijah, Mijamin, Eleazar, Hashabiah,* and Benaiah.
[26]From the family of Elam: Mattaniah, Zechariah, Jehiel, Abdi, Jeremoth, and Elijah.
[27]From the family of Zattu: Elioenai, Eliashib, Mattaniah, Jeremoth, Zabad, and Aziza.
[28]From the family of Bebai: Jehohanan, Hananiah, Zabbai, and Athlai.
[29]From the family of Bani: Meshullam, Malluch, Adaiah, Jashub, Sheal, and Jeremoth.

10:9 Hebrew *on the twentieth day of the ninth month,* of the Hebrew calendar. This event occurred on December 19, 458 B.C.; also see note on 7:9a.   10:16 Hebrew *On the first day of the tenth month,* of the Hebrew calendar. This event occurred on December 29, 458 B.C.; also see note on 7:9a.   10:17 Hebrew *By the first day of the first month,* of the Hebrew calendar. This event occurred on March 27, 457 B.C.; also see note on 7:9a. 10:18 Hebrew *Jozadak,* a variant name for Jehozadak.   10:25 As in parallel text at 1 Esdras 9:26; Hebrew reads *Malkijah.*

³⁰From the family of Pahath-moab: Adna, Kelal, Benaiah, Maaseiah, Mattaniah, Bezalel, Binnui, and Manasseh.
³¹From the family of Harim: Eliezer, Ishijah, Malkijah, Shemaiah, Shimeon, ³²Benjamin, Malluch, and Shemariah.
³³From the family of Hashum: Mattenai, Mattattah, Zabad, Eliphelet, Jeremai, Manasseh, and Shimei.
³⁴From the family of Bani: Maadai, Amram, Uel, ³⁵Benaiah, Bedeiah, Keluhi, ³⁶Vaniah, Meremoth, Eliashib, ³⁷Mattaniah, Mattenai, and Jaasu.
³⁸From the family of Binnui*: Shimei, ³⁹Shelemiah, Nathan, Adaiah, ⁴⁰Macnadebai, Shashai, Sharai, ⁴¹Azarel, Shelemiah, Shemariah, ⁴²Shallum, Amariah, and Joseph.
⁴³From the family of Nebo: Jeiel, Mattithiah, Zabad, Zebina, Jaddai, Joel, and Benaiah.

⁴⁴Each of these men had a pagan wife, and some even had children by these wives.*

10:37-38 As in Greek version; Hebrew reads *Jaasu,* ³⁸*Bani, Binnui.*   10:44 Or *and they sent them away with their children.* The meaning of the Hebrew is uncertain.

NEHEMIAH

THIS ELEVENTH BOOK of Israelite history finishes the story of *rebuilding*.

Seventy years after the Jewish people finish rebuilding the Temple, the city of Jerusalem still hasn't been rebuilt. The people have been protected by earlier Persian kings. Now they face grave dangers on every side.

One of the most powerful men in King Artaxerxes' court, Nehemiah, mourns deeply for his people. He then puts himself at great risk by bringing a personal petition to the attention of Artaxerxes. Thankfully, the king grants his requests (1:1–2:8).

Shortly after arriving in Jerusalem, Nehemiah urges the Jewish leaders to take up the task of rebuilding the wall (2:9-18). He formulates a plan and divides up the work among various Jewish family groups. When the work begins, the enemies of the Jews fly into a rage, so Nehemiah establishes extra security measures (2:19-4:23).

In the midst of all this, Nehemiah learns that some of the people have been oppressing their fellow Jews. He immediately calls a public meeting to deal with the problem (5:1-19).

In less than two months, the wall is finished. A few days later, Ezra teaches from the law of the Lord and urges the people to once again celebrate the Festival of Shelters (6:1-8:18).

A couple weeks later, all the Jews return to Jerusalem for another extended time of Bible teaching, prayer, and repentance. They vow to obey the Lord's commands and support the Temple. Many agree to move to Jerusalem, as well (9:1-12:26).

Afterward, the priests and Levites dedicate themselves, the people, the gates, and the wall of Jerusalem. Two large choirs walk around the wall and then proceed to the Temple, praising the Lord. At long last, the worship of the Lord is fully restored (12:27-13:3)!

The book ends with an appendix about Nehemiah's other reforms (13:4-31).

Famous passages in Nehemiah include

- ○ Nehemiah's prayer of repentance to the Lord (1:4-11)
- ○ Nehemiah's petition to King Artaxerxes (2:1-8)
- ○ "The God of heaven will help us succeed" (2:20)
- ○ "Our God will fight for us!" (4:20)
- ○ The Water Gate revival (8:1-11)
- ○ The celebration of the Festival of Shelters (8:13-18)
- ○ The prayer of the Levites (9:5-37)

CHAPTER 1

These are the memoirs of Nehemiah son of Hacaliah.

Nehemiah's Concern for Jerusalem

In late autumn of the twentieth year of King Artaxerxes' reign,* I was at the fortress of Susa. ²Hanani, one of my brothers, came to visit me with some other men who had just arrived from Judah. I asked them about the Jews who had survived the captivity and about how things were going in Jerusalem. ³They said to me, "Things are not going well for those who returned to the province of Judah. They are in great trouble and disgrace. The wall of Jerusalem has been torn down, and the gates have been burned."

⁴When I heard this, I sat down and wept. In fact, for days I mourned, fasted, and prayed to the God of heaven. ⁵Then I said, "O LORD, God of heaven, the great and awesome God who keeps his covenant of unfailing love with those who love him and obey his commands, ⁶listen to my prayer! Look down and see me praying night and day for your people Israel. I confess that we have sinned against you. Yes, even my own family and I have sinned! ⁷We have sinned terribly by not obeying the commands, laws, and regulations that you gave us through your servant Moses.

⁸"Please remember what you told your servant Moses: 'If you sin, I will scatter you among the nations. ⁹But if you return to me and obey my commands, even if you are exiled to the ends of the earth, I will bring you back to the place I have chosen for my name to be honored.'

¹⁰"We are your servants, the people you rescued by your great power and might. ¹¹O Lord, please hear my prayer! Listen to the prayers of those of us who delight in honoring you. Please grant me success now as I go to ask the king* for a great favor. Put it into his heart to be kind to me."

In those days I was the king's cup-bearer.

I GRIEVE over the persecution and oppression that fellow believers experience in other lands and pray earnestly for them. (1:4)

I PRAY earnestly to the Lord for fellow believers and for my country, confessing any known sins. (1:6)

See Moses' profile (page 73) at Exodus 5:1.

I ASK the Lord to hear my prayer and grant me success as I seek to help fellow believers. (1:11)

CHAPTER 2

Nehemiah Goes to Jerusalem

Early the following spring,* during the twentieth year of King Artaxerxes' reign, I was serving the king his wine. I had never appeared sad in his presence before this time. ²So the king asked me, "Why are you so sad? You aren't sick, are you? You look like a man with deep troubles."

Then I was badly frightened, ³but I replied, "Long live the king! Why shouldn't I be sad? For the city where my ancestors are buried is in ruins, and the gates have been burned down."

⁴The king asked, "Well, how can I help you?"

With a prayer to the God of heaven, ⁵I replied, "If it please Your Majesty and if you are pleased with me, your servant, send me to Judah to rebuild the city where my ancestors are buried."

⁶The king, with the queen sitting beside him, asked, "How long will you be gone? When will you return?" So the king agreed, and I set a date for my departure.

⁷I also said to the king, "If it please Your Majesty, give me letters to the governors of the province west of the Euphrates River, instructing them to let me travel safely through their territories on my way to Judah. ⁸And please send a letter to Asaph, the manager of the king's forest, instructing him to give me timber. I will need it to make beams for the gates of the Temple fortress, for the city walls, and for a house for myself." And the king granted these requests, because the gracious hand of God was on me.

I ASK God for wisdom, especially when I speak with high government officials. (2:4)

I ASK boldly for assistance in helping fellow believers in other lands. (2:5)

1:1 Hebrew *In the month of Kislev of the twentieth year.* A number of dates in the book of Nehemiah can be cross-checked with dates in surviving Persian records and related accurately to our modern calendar. This month of the Hebrew lunar calendar occurred in November and December 446 B.C. The *twentieth year* probably refers to the reign of King Artaxerxes I; compare 2:1; 5:14. 1:11 Hebrew *stand before this man.* 2:1 Hebrew *In the month of Nisan.* This month of the Hebrew lunar calendar occurred in April and May 445 B.C.

[9]When I came to the governors of the province west of the Euphrates River, I delivered the king's letters to them. The king, I should add, had sent along army officers and horsemen to protect me. [10]But when Sanballat the Horonite and Tobiah the Ammonite official heard of my arrival, they were very angry that someone had come who was interested in helping Israel.

Nehemiah Inspects Jerusalem's Wall

[11]Three days after my arrival at Jerusalem, [12]I slipped out during the night, taking only a few others with me. I had not told anyone about the plans God had put in my heart for Jerusalem. We took no pack animals with us, except the donkey that I myself was riding. [13]I went out through the Valley Gate, past the Jackal's Well,* and over to the Dung Gate to inspect the broken walls and burned gates. [14]Then I went to the Fountain Gate and to the King's Pool, but my donkey couldn't get through the rubble. [15]So I went up the Kidron Valley* instead, inspecting the wall before I turned back and entered again at the Valley Gate.

> I CAREFULLY INVESTIGATE a matter before recommending a costly course of action. (2:12)

LIKE NEHEMIAH *I seek God's very best despite the obstacles in my way.*
Nehemiah 1:11

The first pioneers to travel across the United States to settle the Oregon Territory faced immense obstacles. They left the comforts of home to endure dangerous river crossings, try to avoid deadly prairie fires, traverse the rugged Rocky Mountains, and struggle through largely uncharted forests. Why? All for hopes of a better life in the fertile Willamette Valley of the Pacific Northwest.

Centuries earlier, Nehemiah contemplated making an equally rugged journey to the land of his forefathers. For months after hearing of the dire situation in Jerusalem, Nehemiah poured out his heart before the Lord in prayer. The idea of leaving the comforts of the palace of King Artaxerxes must have been hard, but nothing compared to the thought of asking the king's permission to leave his service!

Still, Nehemiah persisted in prayer and asked the Lord for a miracle when it came time to make his case before the king. Nehemiah risked the king's displeasure and the threat of a swift and almost sure death sentence. Why? In order to seek the welfare of Jerusalem, capital of the reestablished kingdom of Judah.

Once he had the king's ear, Nehemiah then had to ask for financial support and for protection from pagan regional officials who might oppose his efforts to rebuild Jerusalem's walls. Artaxerxes "granted these requests, because the gracious hand of God was on me" (2:8).

Despite letters from the king, Nehemiah still faced fierce opposition from Israel's enemies—and from traitors. At every turn throughout the remainder of this book, Nehemiah rebuked those who opposed the Lord and then prayed earnestly to his God. He worked hard and did his very best to mobilize, lead, provide for, and protect his fellow Israelites.

Even more important, Nehemiah worked closely with Ezra and others to revive the nation's wholehearted worship of the Lord. He refused to tolerate anyone threatening the nation's spiritual and political survival.

Like Nehemiah, you and I face many obstacles that seek to dissuade us from wholeheartedly serving the Lord. But with prayer and hard work, we too can persevere and build a lasting legacy.

○ *Today's Scripture reading is Nehemiah 1–2.*

[16]The city officials did not know I had been out there or what I was doing, for I had not yet said anything to anyone about my plans. I had not yet spoken to the religious and political leaders, the officials, or anyone else in the administration. [17]But now I said to them, "You know full well the tragedy of our city. It lies in ruins, and its gates are burned. Let us rebuild the wall of Jerusalem and rid ourselves of this disgrace!" [18]Then I told them about how the gracious hand of God had been on me, and about my conversation with the king.

> I TELL others about how the gracious hand of God has been on me, encouraging them to actively trust and serve him, as well. (2:18)

2:13 Or *Serpent's Well.* 2:15 Hebrew *the valley.*

They replied at once, "Good! Let's rebuild the wall!" So they began the good work.

[19]But when Sanballat, Tobiah, and Geshem the Arab heard of our plan, they scoffed contemptuously. "What are you doing, rebelling against the king like this?" they asked.

[20]But I replied, "The God of heaven will help us succeed. We his servants will start rebuilding this wall. But you have no stake or claim in Jerusalem."

CHAPTER 3

Rebuilding the Wall of Jerusalem

Then Eliashib the high priest and the other priests started to rebuild at the Sheep Gate. They dedicated it and set up its doors, building the wall as far as the Tower of the Hundred, which they dedicated, and the Tower of Hananel. [2]People from the city of Jericho worked next to them, and beyond them was Zaccur son of Imri.

[3]The Fish Gate was built by the sons of Hassenaah. They did the whole thing—laid the beams, hung the doors, and put the bolts and bars in place. [4]Meremoth son of Uriah and grandson of Hakkoz repaired the next section of wall. Beside him were Meshullam son of Berekiah and grandson of Meshezabel, and then Zadok son of Baana. [5]Next were the people from Tekoa, though their leaders refused to help.

[6]The Old City Gate* was repaired by Joiada son of Paseah and Meshullam son of Besodeiah. They laid the beams, set up the doors, and installed the bolts and bars. [7]Next to them were Melatiah from Gibeon, Jadon from Meronoth, and people from Gibeon and Mizpah, the headquarters of the governor of the province west of the Euphrates River. [8]Next was Uzziel son of Harhaiah, a goldsmith by trade, who also worked on the wall. Beyond him was Hananiah, a manufacturer of perfumes. They left out* a section of Jerusalem as far as the Broad Wall.

[9]Rephaiah son of Hur, the leader of half the district of Jerusalem, was next to them on the wall. [10]Next Jedaiah son of Harumaph repaired the wall beside his own house, and next to him was Hattush son of Hashabneiah. [11]Then came Malkijah son of Harim and Hasshub son of Pahath-moab, who repaired the Tower of the Ovens, in addition to another section of the wall. [12]Shallum son of Hallohesh and his daughters repaired the next section. He was the leader of the other half of the district of Jerusalem.

[13]The people from Zanoah, led by Hanun, rebuilt the Valley Gate, hung its doors, and installed the bolts and bars. They also repaired the fifteen hundred feet* of wall to the Dung Gate.

[14]The Dung Gate was repaired by Malkijah son of Recab, the leader of the Beth-hakkerem district. After rebuilding it, he hung the doors and installed the bolts and bars.

[15]Shallum son of Col-hozeh, the leader of the Mizpah district, repaired the Fountain Gate. He rebuilt it, roofed it, hung its doors, and installed its bolts and bars. Then he repaired the wall of the pool of Siloam* near the king's garden, and he rebuilt the wall as far as the stairs that descend from the City of David. [16]Next to him was Nehemiah son of Azbuk, the leader of half the district of Beth-zur. He rebuilt the wall to a place opposite the royal cemetery as far as the water reservoir and the House of the Warriors.

[17]Next was a group of Levites working under the supervision of Rehum son of Bani. Then came Hashabiah, the leader of half the district of Keilah, who supervised the building of the wall on behalf of his own district. [18]Next down the line were his countrymen led by Binnui* son of Henadad, the leader of the other half of the district of Keilah.

Margin notes (left column)

I DEDICATE my work to the Lord. (3:1)

I PROVIDE practical, hands-on assistance to fellow believers. (3:3)

I DO NOT REFUSE to help others if I am in a position of leadership. (3:5)

I HELP others no matter what my occupation, business, or trade. (3:8)

I ENCOURAGE my daughters and sons to work alongside me to help others. (3:12)

I DO a thorough job when assisting others. (3:15)

See David's profile (page 629) at Psalm 3:1.

3:6 Or *The Mishneh Gate*, or *The Jeshanah Gate*. 3:8 Or *They restored*. 3:13 Hebrew *1,000 cubits* [450 meters].
3:15 Hebrew *pool of Shelah*, another name for the pool of Siloam. 3:18 As in a few Hebrew manuscripts, some Greek manuscripts, and Syriac version (see also 3:24; 10:9); most Hebrew manuscripts read *Bavvai*.

¹⁹Next to them, Ezer son of Jeshua, the leader of Mizpah, repaired another section of wall opposite the armory by the buttress. ²⁰Next to him was Baruch son of Zabbai, who repaired an additional section from the buttress to the door of the home of Eliashib the high priest. ²¹Meremoth son of Uriah and grandson of Hakkoz rebuilt another section of the wall extending from a point opposite the door of Eliashib's house to the side of the house.

²²Then came the priests from the surrounding region. ²³After them, Benjamin, Hasshub, and Azariah son of Maaseiah and grandson of Ananiah repaired the sections next to their own houses. ²⁴Next was Binnui son of Henadad, who rebuilt another section of the wall from Azariah's house to the buttress and the corner. ²⁵Palal son of Uzai carried on the work from a point opposite the buttress and the corner to the upper tower that projects from the king's house beside the court of the guard. Next to him were Pedaiah son of Parosh ²⁶and the Temple servants living on the hill of Ophel, who repaired the wall as far as the Water Gate toward the east and the projecting tower. ²⁷Then came the people of Tekoa, who repaired another section opposite the great projecting tower and over to the wall of Ophel.

²⁸The priests repaired the wall up the hill from the Horse Gate, each one doing the section immediately opposite his own house. ²⁹Next Zadok son of Immer also rebuilt the wall next to his own house, and beyond him was Shemaiah son of Shecaniah, the gatekeeper of the East Gate. ³⁰Next Hananiah son of Shelemiah and Hanun, the sixth son of Zalaph, repaired another section, while Meshullam son of Berekiah rebuilt the wall next to his own house. ³¹Malkijah, one of the goldsmiths, repaired the wall as far as the housing for the Temple servants and merchants, opposite the Inspection Gate. Then he continued as far as the upper room at the corner. ³²The other goldsmiths and merchants repaired the wall from that corner to the Sheep Gate.

CHAPTER 4

Enemies Oppose the Rebuilding

Sanballat was very angry when he learned that we were rebuilding the wall. He flew into a rage and mocked the Jews, ²saying in front of his friends and the Samarian army officers, "What does this bunch of poor, feeble Jews think they are doing? Do they think they can build the wall in a day if they offer enough sacrifices? Look at those charred stones they are pulling out of the rubbish and using again!"

³Tobiah the Ammonite, who was standing beside him, remarked, "That stone wall would collapse if even a fox walked along the top of it!"

⁴Then I prayed, "Hear us, O our God, for we are being mocked. May their scoffing fall back on their own heads, and may they themselves become captives in a foreign land! ⁵Do not ignore their guilt. Do not blot out their sins, for they have provoked you to anger here in the presence of* the builders."

⁶At last the wall was completed to half its original height around the entire city, for the people had worked very hard. ⁷But when Sanballat and Tobiah and the Arabs, Ammonites, and Ashdodites heard that the work was going ahead and that the gaps in the wall were being repaired, they became furious. ⁸They all made plans to come and fight against Jerusalem and to bring about confusion there. ⁹But we prayed to our God and guarded the city day and night to protect ourselves.

¹⁰Then the people of Judah began to complain that the workers were becoming tired. There was so much rubble to be moved that we could never get it done by ourselves. ¹¹Meanwhile, our enemies were saying, "Before they know what's happening, we will swoop down on them and kill them and end their work."

Keep a prayer journal. This is where life changes often begin!

I PRAY to God when slandered or mocked and leave vengeance in his hands. (4:4)

I DO NOT COMPLAIN or despair when I become tired while doing the work of the Lord. (4:10)

4:5 Or *for they have thrown insults in the face of.*

I TAKE physical threats seriously and take the necessary precautions to ensure my safety and the safety of others. (4:13)

I ENCOURAGE others to trust in our great and glorious Lord and not to despair when our physical safety is threatened. (4:14)

¹²The Jews who lived near the enemy came and told us again and again, "They will come from all directions and attack us!"* ¹³So I placed armed guards behind the lowest parts of the wall in the exposed areas. I stationed the people to stand guard by families, armed with swords, spears, and bows.

¹⁴Then as I looked over the situation, I called together the leaders and the people and said to them, "Don't be afraid of the enemy! Remember the Lord, who is great and glorious, and fight for your friends, your families, and your homes!"

¹⁵When our enemies heard that we knew of their plans and that God had frustrated them, we all returned to our work on the wall. ¹⁶But from then on, only half my men worked while the other half stood guard with spears, shields, bows, and coats of mail. The officers stationed themselves behind the people of Judah ¹⁷who were building the wall. The common laborers carried on their work with one hand supporting their load and one hand holding a weapon. ¹⁸All the builders had a sword belted to their side. The trumpeter stayed with me to sound the alarm.

¹⁹Then I explained to the nobles and officials and all the people, "The work is very spread out, and we are widely separated from each other along the wall. ²⁰When you hear the blast of the trumpet, rush to wherever it is sounding. Then our God will fight for us!"

I AM NOT AFRAID of long, hard, exhausting work—especially work done for the Lord. (4:21)

²¹We worked early and late, from sunrise to sunset. And half the men were always on guard. ²²I also told everyone living outside the walls to move into Jerusalem. That way they and their servants could go on guard duty at night as well as work during the day. ²³During this time, none of us—not I, nor my relatives, nor my servants, nor the guards who were with me—ever took off our clothes. We carried our weapons with us at all times, even when we went for water.*

CHAPTER 5

Nehemiah Defends the Oppressed

I PRAY that my family will never be driven into abject poverty. (5:1)

About this time some of the men and their wives raised a cry of protest against their fellow Jews. ²They were saying, "We have such large families. We need more money just so we can buy the food we need to survive." ³Others said, "We have mortgaged our fields, vineyards, and homes to get food during the famine." ⁴And others said, "We have already borrowed to the limit on our fields and vineyards to pay our taxes. ⁵We belong to the same family, and our children are just like theirs. Yet we must sell our children into slavery just to get enough money to live. We have already sold some of our daughters, and we are helpless to do anything about it, for our fields and vineyards are already mortgaged to others."

⁶When I heard their complaints, I was very angry. ⁷After thinking about the situation, I spoke out against these nobles and officials. I told them, "You are oppressing your own relatives by charging them interest when they borrow money!" Then I called a public meeting to deal with the problem.

I PUBLICLY ADDRESS the actions of unscrupulous leaders and privately do all I can to help the poor. (5:8)

⁸At the meeting I said to them, "The rest of us are doing all we can to redeem our Jewish relatives who have had to sell themselves to pagan foreigners, but you are selling them back into slavery again. How often must we redeem them?" And they had nothing to say in their defense.

⁹Then I pressed further, "What you are doing is not right! Should you not walk in the fear of our God in order to avoid being mocked by enemy nations? ¹⁰I myself, as well as my brothers and my workers, have been lending the people money and grain, but now let us stop this business of loans. ¹¹You must restore their fields, vineyards, olive groves, and homes to them this very

4:12 The meaning of the Hebrew is uncertain.   4:23 Hebrew *Each his weapon the water.* The meaning of the Hebrew is uncertain.

day. Repay the interest you charged on their money, grain, wine, and olive oil."

¹²Then they replied, "We will give back everything and demand nothing more from the people. We will do as you say." Then I called the priests and made the nobles and officials formally vow to do what they had promised.

¹³I shook out the fold of my robe and said, "If you fail to keep your promise, may God shake you from your homes and from your property!"

The whole assembly responded, "Amen," and they praised the LORD. And the people did as they had promised.

¹⁴I would like to mention that for the entire twelve years that I was governor of Judah—from the twentieth until the thirty-second year of the reign of King Artaxerxes*—neither I nor my officials drew on our official food allowance. ¹⁵This was quite a contrast to the former governors who had laid heavy burdens on the people, demanding a daily ration of food and wine, besides a pound* of silver. Even their assistants took advantage of the people. But because of my fear of God, I did not act that way. ¹⁶I devoted myself to working on the wall and refused to acquire any land. And I required all my officials to spend time working on the wall. ¹⁷I asked for nothing, even though I regularly fed 150 Jewish officials at my table, besides all the visitors from other lands! ¹⁸The provisions required at my expense for each day were one ox, six fat sheep, and a large number of domestic fowl. And every ten days we needed a large supply of all kinds of wine. Yet I refused to claim the governor's food allowance because the people were already having a difficult time.

¹⁹Remember, O my God, all that I have done for these people, and bless me for it.

CHAPTER 6

Continued Opposition to Rebuilding

When Sanballat, Tobiah, Geshem the Arab, and the rest of our enemies found out that I had finished rebuilding the wall and that no gaps remained—though we had not yet hung the doors in the gates—²Sanballat and Geshem sent me a message asking me to meet them at one of the villages* in the plain of Ono. But I realized they were plotting to harm me, ³so I replied by sending this message to them: "I am doing a great work! I cannot stop to come and meet with you."

⁴Four times they sent the same message, and each time I gave the same reply. ⁵The fifth time, Sanballat's servant came with an open letter in his hand, ⁶and this is what it said:

"Geshem* tells me that everywhere he goes he hears that you and the Jews are planning to rebel and that is why you are building the wall. According to his reports, you plan to be their king. ⁷He also reports that you have appointed prophets to prophesy about you in Jerusalem, saying, 'Look! There is a king in Judah!'

"You can be very sure that this report will get back to the king, so I suggest that you come and talk it over with me."

⁸My reply was, "You know you are lying. There is no truth in any part of your story." ⁹They were just trying to intimidate us, imagining that they could break our resolve and stop the work. So I prayed for strength to continue the work.

¹⁰Later I went to visit Shemaiah son of Delaiah and grandson of Mehetabel, who was confined to his home. He said, "Let us meet together

I CALL unscrupulous leaders to formally vow to do what they have promised to help the poor. (5:12)

I ASK God to remember all that I have done for others and to bless me. (5:19)

I DO NOT BECOME distracted from the Lord's work by petty issues, no matter how hard and often I am pressured. (6:4)

I DENY any libelous charges brought against me publicly, ask the Lord for strength, and continue to serve him wholeheartedly. (6:8)

5:14 That is, from 445 to 433 B.C.   5:15 Hebrew *40 shekels* [456 grams].   6:2 As in Greek version; Hebrew reads at *Kephirim*.   6:6 Hebrew *Gashmu*, another name for Geshem.

This is page 572.

inside the Temple of God and bolt the doors shut. Your enemies are coming to kill you tonight."

[11]But I replied, "Should someone in my position run away from danger? Should someone in my position enter the Temple to save his life? No, I won't do it!" [12]I realized that God had not spoken to him, but that he had uttered this prophecy against me because Tobiah and Sanballat had hired him. [13]They were hoping to intimidate me and make me sin by following his suggestion. Then they would be able to accuse and discredit me.

[14]Remember, O my God, all the evil things that Tobiah and Sanballat have done. And remember Noadiah the prophet and all the prophets like her who have tried to intimidate me.

The Builders Complete the Wall

[15]So on October 2* the wall was finally finished—just fifty-two days after we had begun. [16]When our enemies and the surrounding nations heard about it, they were frightened and humiliated. They realized that this work had been done with the help of our God.

[17]During those fifty-two days, many letters went back and forth between Tobiah and the officials of Judah. [18]For many in Judah had sworn allegiance to him because his father-in-law was Shecaniah son of Arah and because his son Jehohanan was married to the daughter of Meshullam son of Berekiah. [19]They kept telling me what a wonderful man Tobiah was, and then they told him everything I said. And Tobiah sent many threatening letters to intimidate me.

CHAPTER 7

After the wall was finished and I had hung the doors in the gates, the gatekeepers, singers, and Levites were appointed. [2]I gave the responsibility of governing Jerusalem to my brother Hanani, along with Hananiah, the commander of the fortress, for he was a faithful man who feared God more than most. [3]I said to them, "Do not leave the gates open during the hottest part of the day.* And while the gatekeepers are still on duty, have them shut and bar the doors. Appoint the residents of Jerusalem to act as guards, everyone on a regular watch. Some will serve at their regular posts and some in front of their own homes."

Nehemiah Registers the People

[4]At that time the city was large and spacious, but the population was small. And only a few houses were scattered throughout the city. [5]So my God gave me the idea to call together all the leaders of the city, along with the ordinary citizens, for registration. I had found the genealogical record of those who had first returned to Judah. This is what was written there:

[6]"Here is the list of the Jewish exiles of the provinces who returned from their captivity to Jerusalem and to the other towns of Judah. They had been deported to Babylon by King Nebuchadnezzar. [7]Their leaders were Zerubbabel, Jeshua, Nehemiah, Seraiah,* Reelaiah,* Nahamani, Mordecai, Bilshan, Mispar,* Bigvai, Rehum,* and Baanah. This is the number of men of Israel who returned from exile:

8	The family of Parosh	2,172
9	The family of Shephatiah	372
10	The family of Arah	652
11	The family of Pahath-moab (descendants of Jeshua and Joab)	2,818
12	The family of Elam	1,254

**Sidebar notes (left column):**

I REFUSE to act cowardly and disobey the Lord, even if someone "godly" pressures me to sin. (6:11)

I DO God's work despite a flurry of libelous charges and threats. (6:17)

I WORK until the job is finished. (7:1)

I DELEGATE some of my leadership authority and responsibilities to other faithful, God-fearing individuals. (7:2)

I DELEGATE responsibilities and provide clear, concise instructions. (7:3)

I CREDIT God for good ideas. (7:5)

See Nebuchadnezzar's profile (page 985) at Daniel 4:37.

I BELIEVE a large number of Jewish exiles returned to Judah from Babylon. (7:6)

6:15 Hebrew *on the twenty-fifth day of the month Elul,* of the Hebrew calendar. This event occurred on October 2, 445 B.C.; also see note on 1:1. 7:3 Or *Keep the gates of Jerusalem closed until the sun is hot.* 7:7a As in parallel text at Ezra 2:2; Hebrew reads *Azariah.* 7:7b As in parallel text at Ezra 2:2; Hebrew reads *Raamiah.* 7:7c As in parallel text at Ezra 2:2; Hebrew reads *Mispereth.* 7:7d As in parallel text at Ezra 2:2; Hebrew reads *Nehum.*

13 The family of Zattu. 845
14 The family of Zaccai. 760
15 The family of Bani* 648
16 The family of Bebai 628
17 The family of Azgad 2,322
18 The family of Adonikam 667
19 The family of Bigvai 2,067
20 The family of Adin 655
21 The family of Ater (descendants of Hezekiah) 98
22 The family of Hashum 328
23 The family of Bezai. 324
24 The family of Jorah* 112
25 The family of Gibbar* 95
26 The peoples of Bethlehem and Netophah 188
27 The people of Anathoth. 128
28 The people of Beth-azmaveth 42
29 The peoples of Kiriath-jearim, Kephirah, and Beeroth 743
30 The peoples of Ramah and Geba 621
31 The people of Micmash 122
32 The peoples of Bethel and Ai. 123
33 The people of Nebo 52
34 The citizens of Elam 1,254
35 The citizens of Harim. 320
36 The citizens of Jericho 345
37 The citizens of Lod, Hadid, and Ono 721
38 The citizens of Senaah. 3,930

39 "These are the priests who returned from exile:
   The family of Jedaiah (through the line of Jeshua) 973
40 The family of Immer. 1,052
41 The family of Pashhur. 1,247
42 The family of Harim 1,017

43 "These are the Levites who returned from exile:
   The families of Jeshua and Kadmiel (descendants of Hodaviah*) . . . 74
44 The singers of the family of Asaph 148
45 The gatekeepers of the families of Shallum, Ater, Talmon, Akkub,
   Hatita, and Shobai. 138

46 "The descendants of the following Temple servants returned from exile:
   Ziha, Hasupha, Tabbaoth,
47 Keros, Siaha,* Padon,
48 Lebanah, Hagabah, Shalmai,
49 Hanan, Giddel, Gahar,
50 Reaiah, Rezin, Nekoda,
51 Gazzam, Uzza, Paseah,
52 Besai, Meunim, Nephusim,*
53 Bakbuk, Hakupha, Harhur,
54 Bazluth,* Mehida, Harsha,
55 Barkos, Sisera, Temah,
56 Neziah, and Hatipha.

57 "The descendants of these servants of King Solomon returned from exile:
   Sotai, Sophereth, Peruda,*

7:15 As in parallel text at Ezra 2:10; Hebrew reads *Binnui*.   7:24 As in parallel text at Ezra 2:18; Hebrew reads *Hariph*.   7:25 As in parallel text at Ezra 2:20; Hebrew reads *Gibeon*.   7:43 As in parallel text at Ezra 2:40; Hebrew reads *Hodevah*.   7:47 As in parallel text at Ezra 2:44; Hebrew reads *Sia*.   7:52 As in parallel text at Ezra 2:50; Hebrew reads *Nephushesim*.   7:54 As in parallel text at Ezra 2:52; Hebrew reads *Bazlith*.   7:57 As in parallel text at Ezra 2:55; Hebrew reads *Perida*.

See Hezekiah's profile (page 825) at Isaiah 37:1.

I BELIEVE a large number of priests and Levites returned to Judah after the Exile. (7:39)

See Asaph's profile (page 687) at Psalm 73:28.

I BELIEVE a large number of Temple servants and royal servants returned to Judah after the Exile. (7:46)

See Solomon's profile (page 753) at Proverbs 2:9.

⁵⁸ Jaalah,* Darkon, Giddel,
⁵⁹ Shephatiah, Hattil, Pokereth-hazzebaim, and Ami.*

⁶⁰"In all, the Temple servants and the descendants of Solomon's servants numbered 392.

⁶¹"Another group returned to Jerusalem at this time from the towns of Tel-melah, Tel-harsha, Kerub, Addan,* and Immer. However, they could not prove that they or their families were descendants of Israel. ⁶²This group included the families of Delaiah, Tobiah, and Nekoda—a total of 642 people.

⁶³"Three families of priests—Hobaiah, Hakkoz, and Barzillai—also returned to Jerusalem. (This Barzillai had married a woman who was a descendant of Barzillai of Gilead, and he had taken her family name.) ⁶⁴But they had lost their genealogical records, so they were not allowed to serve as priests. ⁶⁵The governor would not even let them eat the priests' share of food from the sacrifices until there was a priest who could consult the LORD about the matter by means of sacred lots.*

⁶⁶"So a total of 42,360 people returned to Judah, ⁶⁷in addition to 7,337 servants and 245 singers, both men and women. ⁶⁸They took with them 736 horses, 245 mules,* ⁶⁹435 camels, and 6,720 donkeys.

⁷⁰"Some of the family leaders gave gifts for the work. The governor gave to the treasury 1,000 gold coins,* 50 gold basins, and 530 robes for the priests. ⁷¹The other leaders gave to the treasury a total of 20,000 gold coins* and some 2,750 pounds* of silver for the work. ⁷²The rest of the people gave 20,000 gold coins, about 2,500 pounds* of silver, and 67 robes for the priests.

⁷³"So the priests, the Levites, the gatekeepers, the singers, the Temple servants, along with some of the people—that is to say, all Israel—settled in their own towns."

Ezra Reads the Law

Now in midautumn,* when the Israelites had settled in their towns, ¹all the people assembled together as one person at the square just inside the Water Gate. They asked Ezra the scribe to bring out the Book of the Law of Moses, which the LORD had given for Israel to obey.

CHAPTER 8

²So on October 8* Ezra the priest brought the scroll of the law before the assembly, which included the men and women and all the children old enough to understand. ³He faced the square just inside the Water Gate from early morning until noon and read aloud to everyone who could understand. All the people paid close attention to the Book of the Law. ⁴Ezra the scribe stood on a high wooden platform that had been made for the occasion. To his right stood Mattithiah, Shema, Anaiah, Uriah, Hilkiah, and Maaseiah. To his left stood Pedaiah, Mishael, Malkijah, Hashum, Hashbaddanah, Zechariah, and Meshullam. ⁵Ezra stood on the platform in full view of all the people. When they saw him open the book, they all rose to their feet.

⁶Then Ezra praised the LORD, the great God, and all the people chanted, "Amen! Amen!" as they lifted their hands toward heaven. Then they bowed down and worshiped the LORD with their faces to the ground.

⁷Now the Levites—Jeshua, Bani, Sherebiah, Jamin, Akkub, Shabbethai,

---

I BELIEVE a large contingent of people returned to Judah after the Exile. (7:66)

I CONTRIBUTE generously toward the building of new houses to worship the Lord. (7:70)

See the profiles for Ezra (page 559) and Moses (page 73) at Ezra 8:21 and Exodus 5:1.

I BELIEVE men, women, and all children old enough to understand should listen regularly to the preaching of God's Word. (8:2)

I PAY CLOSE ATTENTION to the reading of God's Word. (8:3)

I SHOW respect for the public reading of God's Word. (8:5)

7:58 As in parallel text at Ezra 2:56; Hebrew reads *Jaala*. 7:59 As in parallel text at Ezra 2:57; Hebrew reads *Amon*. 7:61 As in parallel text at Ezra 2:59; Hebrew reads *Addon*. 7:65 Hebrew *consult the Urim and Thummim about the matter*. 7:68 As in some Hebrew manuscripts (see also Ezra 2:66); most Hebrew manuscripts lack this verse. 7:70 Hebrew *1,000 darics of gold*, about 19 pounds or 8.6 kilograms in weight. 7:71a Hebrew *20,000 darics of gold*, about 375 pounds or 170 kilograms in weight; also in 7:72. 7:71b Hebrew *2,200 minas* [1.3 metric tons]. 7:72 Hebrew *2,000 minas* [1.2 metric tons]. 7:73 Hebrew *in the seventh month*. This month of the Hebrew lunar calendar occurred in October and November 445 B.C. 8:2 Hebrew *on the first day of the seventh month*, of the Hebrew calendar. This event occurred on October 8, 445 B.C.; also see note on 1:1.

Hodiah, Maaseiah, Kelita, Azariah, Jozabad, Hanan, and Pelaiah—instructed the people who were standing there. ⁸They read from the Book of the Law of God and clearly explained the meaning of what was being read, helping the people understand each passage. ⁹Then Nehemiah the governor, Ezra the priest and scribe, and the Levites who were interpreting for the people said to them, "Don't weep on such a day as this! For today is a sacred day before the LORD your God." All the people had been weeping as they listened to the words of the law.

¹⁰And Nehemiah* continued, "Go and celebrate with a feast of choice foods and sweet drinks, and share gifts of food with people who have nothing prepared. This is a sacred day before our Lord. Don't be dejected and sad, for the joy of the LORD is your strength!"

¹¹And the Levites, too, quieted the people, telling them, "Hush! Don't weep! For this is a sacred day." ¹²So the people went away to eat and drink at a festive meal, to share gifts of food, and to celebrate with great joy because they had heard God's words and understood them.

The Festival of Shelters

¹³On October 9* the family leaders and the priests and Levites met with Ezra to go over the law in greater detail. ¹⁴As they studied the law, they discovered that the LORD had commanded through Moses that the Israelites should live in shelters during the festival to be held that month.* ¹⁵He had said that a proclamation should be made throughout their towns and especially in Jerusalem, telling the people to go to the hills to get branches from olive, wild olive, myrtle, palm, and fig trees. They were to use these branches to make shelters in which they would live during the festival, as it was prescribed in the law.

¹⁶So the people went out and cut branches and used them to build shelters on the roofs of their houses, in their courtyards, in the courtyards of God's Temple, or in the squares just inside the Water Gate and the Ephraim Gate. ¹⁷So everyone who had returned from captivity lived in these shelters for the seven days of the festival, and everyone was filled with great joy! The Israelites had not celebrated this way since the days of Joshua son of Nun. ¹⁸Ezra read from the Book of the Law of God on each of the seven days of the festival. Then on October 15* they held a solemn assembly, as the law of Moses required.

CHAPTER 9

The People Confess Their Sins

On October 31* the people returned for another observance. This time they fasted and dressed in sackcloth and sprinkled dust on their heads. ²Those of Israelite descent separated themselves from all foreigners as they confessed their own sins and the sins of their ancestors. ³The Book of the Law of the LORD their God was read aloud to them for about three hours.* Then for three more hours they took turns confessing their sins and worshiping the LORD their God. ⁴Some of the Levites were standing on the stairs, crying out to the LORD their God. Their names were Jeshua, Bani, Kadmiel, Shebaniah, Bunni, Sherebiah, Bani, and Kenani. ⁵Then the leaders of the Levites—Jeshua, Kadmiel, Bani, Hashabneiah, Sherebiah, Hodiah, Shebaniah, and Pethahiah—called out to the people:

I EXPLAIN God's Word carefully, so that everyone can understand it. (8:8)

I BELIEVE leaders have a greater obligation than others to go over God's Word in detail. (8:13)

I SET ASIDE significant periods of time to receive extensive biblical instruction, confess my sins, and worship the Lord my God. (9:3)

8:10 Hebrew *he.*   8:13 Hebrew *On the second day,* of the seventh month of the Hebrew calendar. This event occurred on October 9, 445 B.C.; also see notes on 1:1 and 8:2.   8:14 Hebrew *in the seventh month.* This month of the Hebrew lunar calendar usually occurs in September and October. See Lev 23:39-43.   8:18 Hebrew *on the eighth day,* of the seventh month of the Hebrew calendar. This event occurred on October 15, 445 B.C.; also see notes on 1:1 and 8:2.   9:1 Hebrew *On the twenty-fourth day of that same month,* the seventh month of the Hebrew calendar. This event occurred on October 31, 445 B.C.; also see note on 1:1.   9:3 Hebrew *for a quarter of a day.*

"Stand up and praise the LORD your God, for he lives from everlasting to everlasting!"

Then they continued, "Praise his glorious name! It is far greater than we can think or say. ⁶You alone are the LORD. You made the skies and the heavens and all the stars. You made the earth and the seas and everything in them. You preserve and give life to everything, and all the angels of heaven worship you.

⁷"You are the LORD God, who chose Abram and brought him from Ur of the Chaldeans and renamed him Abraham. ⁸When he had proved himself faithful, you made a covenant with him to give him and his descendants the land of the Canaanites, Hittites, Amorites, Perizzites, Jebusites, and Girgashites. And you have done what you promised, for you are always true to your word.

⁹"You saw the sufferings and sorrows of our ancestors in Egypt, and you heard their cries from beside the Red Sea.* ¹⁰You displayed miraculous signs and wonders against Pharaoh, his servants, and all his people, for you knew how arrogantly the Egyptians were treating them. You have a glorious reputation that has never been forgotten. ¹¹You divided the sea for your people so they could walk through on dry land! And then you hurled their enemies into the depths of the sea. They sank like stones beneath the mighty waters. ¹²You led our ancestors by a pillar of cloud during the day and a pillar of fire at night so that they could find their way.

¹³"You came down on Mount Sinai and spoke to them from heaven. You gave them regulations and instructions that were just, and laws and commands that were true. ¹⁴You instructed them concerning the laws of your holy Sabbath. And you commanded them, through Moses your servant, to obey all your commands, laws, and instructions.

¹⁵"You gave them bread from heaven when they were hungry and water from the rock when they were thirsty. You commanded them to go and take possession of the land you had sworn to give them. ¹⁶But our ancestors were a proud and stubborn lot, and they refused to obey your commands.

¹⁷"They refused to listen and did not remember the miracles you had done for them. Instead, they rebelled and appointed a leader to take them back to their slavery in Egypt! But you are a God of forgiveness, gracious and merciful, slow to become angry, and full of unfailing love and mercy. You did not abandon them, ¹⁸even though they made an idol shaped like a calf and said, 'This is your god who brought you out of Egypt!' They sinned and committed terrible blasphemies. ¹⁹But in your great mercy you did not abandon them to die in the wilderness. The pillar of cloud still led them forward by day, and the pillar of fire showed them the way through the night. ²⁰You sent your good Spirit to instruct them, and you did not stop giving them bread from heaven or water for their thirst. ²¹For forty years you sustained them in the wilderness. They lacked nothing in all that time. Their clothes did not wear out, and their feet did not swell!

²²"Then you helped our ancestors conquer great kingdoms and many nations, and you placed your people in every corner of the land. They completely took over the land of King Sihon of Heshbon and the land of King Og of Bashan. ²³You made their descendants as numerous as the stars in the sky and brought them into the land you had promised to their ancestors. ²⁴They went in and took possession of the land. You subdued whole nations before them. Even the kings and the Canaanites, who inhabited the land, were powerless! Your people could deal with them as they pleased. ²⁵Our ancestors captured fortified cities and fertile land. They took over houses full of good things, with cisterns already dug and vineyards and olive groves and orchards

See Abram's (Abraham's) profile (page 19) at Genesis 15:6.

I WORSHIP the Lord, who is always true to his Word. (9:8)

I WORSHIP the Lord, who revealed his Word through Moses, other Old Testament prophets, and the apostles. (9:14)

See Moses' profile (page 73) at Exodus 5:1.

I WORSHIP the Lord and abhor idolatry. (9:18)

9:9 Hebrew *sea of reeds.*

in abundance. So they ate until they were full and grew fat and enjoyed themselves in all your blessings.

²⁶"But despite all this, they were disobedient and rebelled against you. They threw away your law, they killed the prophets who encouraged them to return to you, and they committed terrible blasphemies. ²⁷So you handed them over to their enemies. But in their time of trouble they cried to you, and you heard them from heaven. In great mercy, you sent them deliverers who rescued them from their enemies.

²⁸"But when all was going well, your people turned to sin again, and once more you let their enemies conquer them. Yet whenever your people cried to you again for help, you listened once more from heaven. In your wonderful mercy, you rescued them repeatedly! ²⁹You warned them to return to your law, but they became proud and obstinate and disobeyed your commands. They did not follow your regulations, by which people will find life if only they obey. They stubbornly turned their backs on you and refused to listen. ³⁰In your love, you were patient with them for many years. You sent your Spirit, who, through the prophets, warned them about their sins. But still they wouldn't listen! So once again you allowed the pagan inhabitants of the land to conquer them. ³¹But in your great mercy, you did not destroy them completely or abandon them forever. What a gracious and merciful God you are!

³²"And now, our God, the great and mighty and awesome God, who keeps his covenant of unfailing love, do not let all the hardships we have suffered be as nothing to you. Great trouble has come upon us and upon our kings and princes and priests and prophets and ancestors from the days when the kings of Assyria first triumphed over us until now. ³³Every time you punished us you were being just. We have sinned greatly, and you gave us only what we deserved. ³⁴Our kings, princes, priests, and ancestors did not obey your law or listen to your commands and solemn warnings. ³⁵Even while they had their own kingdom, they did not serve you even though you showered your goodness on them. You gave them a large, fertile land, but they refused to turn from their wickedness.

³⁶"So now today we are slaves here in the land of plenty that you gave to our ancestors! We are slaves among all this abundance! ³⁷The lush produce of this land piles up in the hands of the kings whom you have set over us because of our sins. They have power over us and our cattle. We serve them at their pleasure, and we are in great misery.

³⁸"Yet in spite of all this,* we are making a solemn promise and putting it in writing. On this sealed document are the names of our princes and Levites and priests."

CHAPTER 10

The People Agree to Obey

The document was ratified and sealed with the following names:

Nehemiah the governor, the son of Hacaliah.
The priests who signed were Zedekiah, ²Seraiah, Azariah, Jeremiah,
 ³Pashhur, Amariah, Malkijah, ⁴Hattush, Shebaniah, Malluch, ⁵Harim,
 Meremoth, Obadiah, ⁶Daniel, Ginnethon, Baruch, ⁷Meshullam, Abijah,
 Mijamin, ⁸Maaziah, Bilgai, and Shemaiah. These were the priests.
⁹The Levites who signed were Jeshua son of Azaniah, Binnui from the family of Henadad, Kadmiel, ¹⁰and their fellow Levites: Shebaniah, Hodiah,
 Kelita, Pelaiah, Hanan, ¹¹Mica, Rehob, Hashabiah, ¹²Zaccur, Sherebiah,
 Shebaniah, ¹³Hodiah, Bani, and Beninu.
¹⁴The leaders who signed were Parosh, Pahath-moab, Elam, Zattu, Bani,
 ¹⁵Bunni, Azgad, Bebai, ¹⁶Adonijah, Bigvai, Adin, ¹⁷Ater, Hezekiah, Azzur,

9:38 Or *Because of all this.*

I WORSHIP the Lord and do not rebel against him when life is good. (9:26)

I LISTEN to the Lord and find the life he promises to those who obey his commands (Galatians 3:12; Revelation 7:10; 10:5). (9:29)

I WORSHIP the Lord, the great and mighty and awesome God, who keeps his covenant of unfailing love and who does not disregard my suffering. (9:32)

I DO NOT MAKE flippant vows to the Lord. (9:38)

I PROMISE to obey the Lord's commands. (10:1)

I JOIN with other leaders in pledging to obey the Lord's commands. (10:2)

[18]Hodiah, Hashum, Bezai, [19]Hariph, Anathoth, Nebai, [20]Magpiash, Meshullam, Hezir, [21]Meshezabel, Zadok, Jaddua, [22]Pelatiah, Hanan, Anaiah, [23]Hoshea, Hananiah, Hasshub, [24]Hallohesh, Pilha, Shobek, [25]Rehum, Hashabnah, Maaseiah, [26]Ahiah, Hanan, Anan, [27]Malluch, Harim, and Baanah.

[28]The rest of the people—the priests, Levites, gatekeepers, singers, Temple servants, and all who had separated themselves from the pagan people of the land in order to serve God, and who were old enough to understand—[29]now all heartily bound themselves with an oath. They vowed to accept the curse of God if they failed to obey the law of God as issued by his servant Moses. They solemnly promised to carefully follow all the commands, laws, and regulations of the LORD their Lord.

The Vow of the People

[30]"We promise not to let our daughters marry the pagan people of the land, nor to let our sons marry their daughters. [31]We further promise that if the people of the land should bring any merchandise or grain to be sold on the Sabbath or on any other holy day, we will refuse to buy it. And we promise not to do any work every seventh year and to cancel the debts owed to us by other Jews.

[32]"In addition, we promise to obey the command to pay the annual Temple tax of an eighth of an ounce of silver,* so that there will be enough money to care for the Temple of our God. [33]This will provide for the Bread of the Presence; for the regular grain offerings and burnt offerings; for the offerings on the Sabbaths, the new moon celebrations, and the annual festivals; for the holy offerings; and for the sin offerings to make atonement for Israel. It will also provide for the other items necessary for the work of the Temple of our God.

[34]"We have cast sacred lots to determine when—at regular times each year—the families of the priests, Levites, and the common people should bring wood to God's Temple to be burned on the altar of the LORD our God, as required in the law.

[35]"We promise always to bring the first part of every harvest to the LORD's Temple—whether it be a crop from the soil or from our fruit trees. [36]We agree to give to God our oldest sons and the firstborn of all our herds and flocks, just as the law requires. We will present them to the priests who minister in the Temple of our God. [37]We will store the produce in the storerooms of the Temple of our God. We will bring the best of our flour and other grain offerings, the best of our fruit, and the best of our new wine and olive oil. And we promise to bring to the Levites a tenth of everything our land produces, for it is the Levites who collect the tithes in all our rural towns. [38]A priest—a descendant of Aaron—will be with the Levites as they receive these tithes. And a tenth of all that is collected as tithes will be delivered by the Levites to the Temple of our God and placed in the storerooms. [39]The people and the Levites must bring these offerings of grain, new wine, and olive oil to the Temple and place them in the sacred containers near the ministering priests, the gatekeepers, and the singers.

"So we promise together not to neglect the Temple of our God."

CHAPTER 11

The People Occupy Jerusalem

Now the leaders of the people were living in Jerusalem, the holy city, at this time. A tenth of the people from the other towns of Judah and Benjamin were chosen by sacred lots to live there, too, while the rest stayed where they were.

10:32 Hebrew *tax of* ⅓ *of a shekel* [4 grams].

Margin notes

I AM DEDICATED to serving God. (10:28)

I SOLEMNLY PROMISE to obey all the Lord's commands. (10:29)

See Moses' profile (page 73) at Exodus 5:1.

I TRY to dissuade my children from marrying unbelievers. (10:30)

I PLACE a higher priority on worship than on commercial activity during time set aside to worship the Lord. (10:31)

I PROMISE to give to the Lord's work. (10:32)

I PROMISE to give a tithe of all I earn to the Lord. (10:35)

See Aaron's profile (page 107) at Exodus 32:2.

I PROMISE not to neglect my local house of worship or those who serve there. (10:39)

[2]And the people commended everyone who volunteered to resettle in Jerusalem.

[3]Here is a list of the names of the provincial officials who came to Jerusalem. Most of the people, priests, Levites, Temple servants, and descendants of Solomon's servants continued to live in their own homes in the various towns of Judah, [4]but some of the people from Judah and Benjamin resettled in Jerusalem.

From the tribe of Judah: Athaiah son of Uzziah, son of Zechariah, son of Amariah, son of Shephatiah, son of Mahalalel, of the family of Perez; [5]and Maaseiah son of Baruch, son of Col-hozeh, son of Hazaiah, son of Adaiah, son of Joiarib, son of Zechariah, of the family of Shelah.* [6]There were also 468 descendants of Perez who lived in Jerusalem—all outstanding men.

[7]From the tribe of Benjamin: Sallu son of Meshullam, son of Joed, son of Pedaiah, son of Kolaiah, son of Maaseiah, son of Ithiel, son of Jeshaiah; [8]and after him there were Gabbai and Sallai, and a total of 928 relatives. [9]Their chief officer was Joel son of Zicri, who was assisted by Judah son of Hassenuah, second-in-command over the city.

[10]From the priests: Jedaiah son of Joiarib; Jakin; [11]and Seraiah son of Hilkiah, son of Meshullam, son of Zadok, son of Meraioth, son of Ahitub, the supervisor of the Temple of God; [12]together with 822 of their associates, who worked at the Temple. Also, there was Adaiah son of Jeroham, son of Pelaliah, son of Amzi, son of Zechariah, son of Pashhur, son of Malkijah; [13]and 242 of his associates, who were heads of their families. There were also Amashsai son of Azarel, son of Ahzai, son of Meshillemoth, son of Immer; [14]and 128 of his outstanding associates. Their chief officer was Zabdiel son of Haggedolim.

[15]From the Levites: Shemaiah son of Hasshub, son of Azrikam, son of Hashabiah, son of Bunni; [16]Shabbethai and Jozabad, who were in charge of the work outside the Temple of God; [17]Mattaniah son of Mica, son of Zabdi, a descendant of Asaph, who opened the thanksgiving services with prayer; Bakbukiah, who was Mattaniah's assistant; and Abda son of Shammua, son of Galal, son of Jeduthun. [18]In all, there were 284 Levites in the holy city.

[19]From the gatekeepers: Akkub, Talmon, and 172 of their associates, who guarded the gates.

[20]The other priests, Levites, and the rest of the Israelites lived wherever their family inheritance was located in any of the towns of Judah. [21]However, the Temple servants, whose leaders were Ziha and Gishpa, all lived on the hill of Ophel.

[22]The chief officer of the Levites in Jerusalem was Uzzi son of Bani, son of Hashabiah, son of Mattaniah, son of Mica, a descendant of Asaph, whose family served as singers at God's Temple. [23]They were under royal orders, which determined their daily activities.

[24]Pethahiah son of Meshezabel, a descendant of Zerah son of Judah, was the king's agent in all matters of public administration.

[25]Some of the people of Judah lived in Kiriath-arba with its villages, Dibon with its villages, and Jekabzeel with its villages. [26]They also lived in Jeshua, Moladah, Beth-pelet, [27]Hazar-shual, Beersheba with its villages, [28]Ziklag, and Meconah with its villages. [29]They were also in En-rimmon, Zorah, Jarmuth, [30]Zanoah, and Adullam with their villages. They were also in Lachish and its nearby fields and Azekah with its surrounding villages. So the people of Judah were living all the way from Beersheba to the valley of Hinnom.

11:5 Hebrew son of the Shilonite.

I COMMEND those who volunteer to serve the Lord. (11:2)

I BELIEVE hundreds of individuals from the tribe of Judah resettled in Jerusalem. (11:4)

I BELIEVE hundreds of individuals from the tribe of Benjamin resettled in Jerusalem. (11:7)

I AM WILLING to move somewhere else to help accomplish God's work. (11:15)

See Asaph's profile (page 687) at Psalm 73:28.

³¹Some of the people of Benjamin lived at Geba, Micmash, Aija, and Bethel with its surrounding villages. ³²They were also in Anathoth, Nob, Ananiah, ³³Hazor, Ramah, Gittaim, ³⁴Hadid, Zeboim, Neballat, ³⁵Lod, Ono, and the Valley of Craftsmen.* ³⁶Some of the Levites who lived in Judah were sent to live with the tribe of Benjamin.

CHAPTER 12

A History of the Priests and Levites

Here is the list of the priests and Levites who had returned with Zerubbabel son of Shealtiel and Jeshua the high priest:

Seraiah, Jeremiah, Ezra,
² Amariah, Malluch, Hattush,
³ Shecaniah, Harim,* Meremoth,
⁴ Iddo, Ginnethon,* Abijah,
⁵ Miniamin, Moadiah,* Bilgah,
⁶ Shemaiah, Joiarib, Jedaiah,
⁷ Sallu, Amok, Hilkiah, and Jedaiah.

These were the leaders of the priests and their associates in the days of Jeshua.

⁸The Levites who had returned with them were Jeshua, Binnui, Kadmiel, Sherebiah, Judah, and Mattaniah, who with his associates was in charge of the songs of thanksgiving. ⁹Their associates, Bakbukiah and Unni, stood opposite them during the service.

¹⁰ Jeshua the high priest was the father of Joiakim.
Joiakim was the father of Eliashib.
Eliashib was the father of Joiada.
¹¹ Joiada was the father of Johanan.*
Johanan was the father of Jaddua.

¹²Now when Joiakim was high priest, the family leaders of the priests were as follows:

Meraiah was leader of the family of Seraiah.
Hananiah was leader of the family of Jeremiah.
¹³ Meshullam was leader of the family of Ezra.
Jehohanan was leader of the family of Amariah.
¹⁴ Jonathan was leader of the family of Malluch.*
Joseph was leader of the family of Shecaniah.*
¹⁵ Adna was leader of the family of Harim.
Helkai was leader of the family of Meremoth.*
¹⁶ Zechariah was leader of the family of Iddo.
Meshullam was leader of the family of Ginnethon.
¹⁷ Zicri was leader of the family of Abijah.
There was also a* leader of the family of Miniamin.
Piltai was leader of the family of Moadiah.
¹⁸ Shammua was leader of the family of Bilgah.
Jehonathan was leader of the family of Shemaiah.
¹⁹ Mattenai was leader of the family of Joiarib.
Uzzi was leader of the family of Jedaiah.
²⁰ Kallai was leader of the family of Sallu.*
Eber was leader of the family of Amok.

I BELIEVE the records that were kept about the priests and Levites who returned from exile with Zerubbabel and Jeshua. (12:1)

See Ezra's profile (page 559) at Ezra 8:21.

I BELIEVE the records that were kept about the priests who served under Joiakim, Jeshua's son. (12:12)

11:35 Or *and Ge-harashim.* 12:3 Hebrew *Rehum;* compare 7:42; 12:15; Ezra 2:39. 12:4 As in some Hebrew manuscripts and Latin Vulgate (see also 12:16); most Hebrew manuscripts read *Ginnethoi.* 12:5 Hebrew *Mijamin, Maadiah;* compare 12:17. 12:11 Hebrew *Jonathan;* compare 12:22. 12:14a As in Greek version (see also 10:4; 12:2); Hebrew reads *Malluchi.* 12:14b As in many Hebrew manuscripts, some Greek manuscripts, and Syriac version; most Hebrew manuscripts read *Shebaniah.* 12:15 As in some Greek manuscripts (see also 12:3); Hebrew reads *Meraioth.* 12:17 Hebrew lacks the name of this family leader. 12:20 Hebrew *Sallai;* compare 12:7.

21 Hashabiah was leader of the family of Hilkiah.

Nethanel was leader of the family of Jedaiah.

22During the reign of Darius II of Persia,* a list was compiled of the family leaders of the Levites and the priests in the days of the following high priests: Eliashib, Joiada, Johanan, and Jaddua. 23The heads of the Levite families were recorded in *The Book of History* down to the days of Johanan, the grandson* of Eliashib.

24These were the family leaders of the Levites: Hashabiah, Sherebiah, Jeshua, Binnui,* Kadmiel, and other associates, who stood opposite them during the ceremonies of praise and thanksgiving, one section responding to the other, just as commanded by David, the man of God. 25This included Mattaniah, Bakbukiah, and Obadiah.

Meshullam, Talmon, and Akkub were the gatekeepers in charge of the storerooms at the gates. 26These all served in the days of Joiakim son of Jeshua, son of Jehozadak,* and in the days of Nehemiah the governor and of Ezra the priest and scribe.

Dedication of Jerusalem's Wall

27During the dedication of the new wall of Jerusalem, the Levites throughout the land were asked to come to Jerusalem to assist in the ceremonies. They were to take part in the joyous occasion with their songs of thanksgiving and with the music of cymbals, lyres, and harps. 28The singers were brought together from Jerusalem and its surrounding villages and from the villages of the Netophathites. 29They also came from Beth-gilgal and the area of Geba and Azmaveth, for the singers had built their own villages around Jerusalem. 30The priests and Levites first dedicated themselves, then the people, the gates, and the wall.

31I led the leaders of Judah to the top of the wall and organized two large choirs to give thanks. One of the choirs proceeded southward* along the top of the wall to the Dung Gate. 32Hoshaiah and half the leaders of Judah followed them, 33along with Azariah, Ezra, Meshullam, 34Judah, Benjamin, Shemaiah, Jeremiah, 35and some priests who played trumpets. Then came Zechariah son of Jonathan, son of Shemaiah, son of Mattaniah, son of Micaiah, son of Zaccur, a descendant of Asaph. 36And finally came Zechariah's colleagues Shemaiah, Azarel, Milalai, Gilalai, Maai, Nethanel, Judah, and Hanani. They used the musical instruments prescribed by David, the man of God. Ezra the scribe led this procession. 37At the Fountain Gate they went straight up the steps on the ascent of the city wall toward the City of David. They passed the house of David and then proceeded to the Water Gate on the east.

38The second choir went northward* around the other way to meet them. I followed them, with the other half of the people, along the top of the wall past the Tower of the Ovens to the Broad Wall, 39then past the Ephraim Gate to the Old City Gate,* past the Fish Gate and the Tower of Hananel, and went on to the Tower of the Hundred. Then we continued on to the Sheep Gate and stopped at the Guard Gate.

40The two choirs that were giving thanks then proceeded to the Temple of God, where they took their places. So did I, together with the group of leaders who were with me. 41We went together with the trumpet-playing priests— Eliakim, Maaseiah, Miniamin, Micaiah, Elioenai, Zechariah, and Hananiah— 42and the singers—Maaseiah, Shemaiah, Eleazar, Uzzi, Jehohanan, Malkijah,

I BELIEVE the records that were kept about the priests, Levites, and gatekeepers who served under Joiakim in the days of Nehemiah. (12:22)

See David's profile (page 629) at Psalm 3:1.

I JOYFULLY DEDICATE what I have built for the Lord with songs of thanksgiving. (12:27)

I VALUE songs of thanksgiving presented by godly choirs and orchestras. (12:31)

See Asaph's profile (page 687) at Psalm 73:28.

I JOIN other believers in worshiping the Lord with music. (12:42)

12:22 Hebrew *Darius the Persian.*   12:23 Hebrew *son;* compare 12:10-11.   12:24 Hebrew *son of* (i.e., *ben*), which should probably be read here as the proper name Binnui; compare Ezra 3:9 and the note there. 12:26 Hebrew *Jozadak,* a variant name for Jehozadak.   12:31 Hebrew *to the right.*   12:38 Hebrew *to the left.* 12:39 Or *the Mishneh Gate,* or *the Jeshanah Gate.*

Elam, and Ezer. They played and sang loudly and clearly under the direction of Jezrahiah the choir director.

[43]Many sacrifices were offered on that joyous day, for God had given the people cause for great joy. The women and children also participated in the celebration, and the joy of the people of Jerusalem could be heard far away.

Provisions for Temple Worship

[44]On that day men were appointed to be in charge of the storerooms for the gifts, the first part of the harvest, and the tithes. They were responsible to collect these from the fields as required by the law for the priests and Levites, for all the people of Judah valued the priests and Levites and their work. [45]They performed the service of their God and the service of purification, as required by the laws of David and his son Solomon, and so did the singers and the gatekeepers. [46]The custom of having choir directors to lead the choirs in hymns of praise and thanks to God began long ago in the days of David and Asaph. [47]So now, in the days of Zerubbabel and of Nehemiah, the people brought a daily supply of food for the singers, the gatekeepers, and the Levites. The Levites, in turn, gave a portion of what they received to the priests, the descendants of Aaron.

CHAPTER 13

Nehemiah's Various Reforms

On that same day, as the Book of Moses was being read, the people found a statement which said that no Ammonite or Moabite should ever be permitted to enter the assembly of God. [2]For they had not been friendly to the Israelites when they left Egypt. Instead, they hired Balaam to curse them, though our God turned the curse into a blessing. [3]When this law was read, all those of mixed ancestry were immediately expelled from the assembly.

[4]Before this had happened, Eliashib the priest, who had been appointed as supervisor of the storerooms of the Temple of our God and who was also a relative of Tobiah, [5]had converted a large storage room and placed it at Tobiah's disposal. The room had previously been used for storing the grain offerings, frankincense, Temple utensils, and tithes of grain, new wine, olive oil, and the special portion set aside for the priests. Moses had decreed that these offerings belonged to the Levites, the singers, and the gatekeepers.

[6]I was not in Jerusalem at that time, for I had returned to the king in the thirty-second year of the reign of King Artaxerxes of Babylon,* though I later received his permission to return. [7]When I arrived back in Jerusalem and learned the extent of this evil deed of Eliashib—that he had provided Tobiah with a room in the courtyards of the Temple of God—[8]I became very upset and threw all of Tobiah's belongings from the room. [9]Then I demanded that the rooms be purified, and I brought back the utensils for God's Temple, the grain offerings, and the frankincense.

[10]I also discovered that the Levites had not been given what was due them, so they and the singers who were to conduct the worship services had all returned to work their fields. [11]I immediately confronted the leaders and demanded, "Why has the Temple of God been neglected?" Then I called all the Levites back again and restored them to their proper duties. [12]And once more all the people of Judah began bringing their tithes of grain, new wine, and olive oil to the Temple storerooms.

[13]I put Shelemiah the priest, Zadok the scribe, and Pedaiah, one of the Levites, in charge of the storerooms. And I appointed Hanan son of Zaccur and grandson of Mattaniah as their assistant. These men had an excellent reputation, and it was their job to make honest distributions to their fellow Levites.

13:6 The thirty-second year of Artaxerxes was 433 B.C.

I BELIEVE men, women, and children alike should participate in worshiping the Lord. (12:43)

I APPOINT new individuals for the Lord's service if duties have been neglected or if someone has been disqualified. (12:44)

See Solomon's profile (page 753) at Proverbs 2:9.

See Aaron's profile (page 107) at Exodus 32:2.

I BELIEVE the Lord was jealous for the spiritual purity of the Israelites, commanding them not to marry pagans. (13:1)

See Moses' profile (page 73) at Exodus 5:1.

I DO NOT ALLOW unbelievers to misuse what is meant for God's service. (13:4)

I SPEAK UP for God's servants when they are not paid what is due them. (13:10)

I APPOINT godly individuals to positions of authority and responsibility—individuals who have an excellent and honest reputation. (13:13)

[14]Remember this good deed, O my God, and do not forget all that I have faithfully done for the Temple of my God.

[15]One Sabbath day I saw some men of Judah treading their winepresses. They were also bringing in bundles of grain and loading them on their donkeys. And on that day they were bringing their wine, grapes, figs, and all sorts of produce to Jerusalem to sell. So I rebuked them for selling their produce on the Sabbath. [16]There were also some men from Tyre bringing in fish and all kinds of merchandise. They were selling it on the Sabbath to the people of Judah—and in Jerusalem at that!

[17]So I confronted the leaders of Judah, "Why are you profaning the Sabbath in this evil way? [18]Wasn't it enough that your ancestors did this sort of thing, so that our God brought the present troubles upon us and our city? Now you are bringing even more wrath upon the people of Israel by permitting the Sabbath to be desecrated in this way!" [19]So I commanded that from then on the gates of the city should be shut as darkness fell every Friday evening,* not to be opened until the Sabbath ended. I also sent some of my own servants to guard the gates so that no merchandise could be brought in on the Sabbath day. [20]The merchants and tradesmen with a variety of wares camped outside Jerusalem once or twice. [21]But I spoke sharply to them and said, "What are you doing out here, camping around the wall? If you do this again, I will arrest you!" And that was the last time they came on the Sabbath. [22]Then I commanded the Levites to purify themselves and to guard the gates in order to preserve the holiness of the Sabbath.

Remember this good deed also, O my God! Have compassion on me according to your great and unfailing love.

[23]About the same time I realized that some of the men of Judah had married women from Ashdod, Ammon, and Moab. [24]Even worse, half their children spoke in the language of Ashdod or some other people and could not speak the language of Judah at all. [25]So I confronted them and called down curses on them. I beat some of them and pulled out their hair. I made them swear before God that they would not let their children intermarry with the pagan people of the land.

[26]"Wasn't this exactly what led King Solomon of Israel into sin?" I demanded. "There was no king from any nation who could compare to him, and God loved him and made him king over all Israel. But even he was led into sin by his foreign wives. [27]How could you even think of committing this sinful deed and acting unfaithfully toward God by marrying foreign women?"

[28]One of the sons of Joiada* son of Eliashib the high priest had married a daughter of Sanballat the Horonite, so I banished him from my presence.

[29]Remember them, O my God, for they have defiled the priesthood and the promises and vows of the priests and Levites.

[30]So I purged out everything foreign and assigned tasks to the priests and Levites, making certain that each knew his work. [31]I also made sure that the supply of wood for the altar was brought at the proper times and that the first part of the harvest was collected for the priests.

Remember this in my favor, O my God.

13:19 Hebrew *on the day before the Sabbath.*   13:28 Hebrew *Jehoiada,* a variant name for Joiada.

I BELIEVE godly leaders will be held responsible if they allow public sin among God's people to continue unchecked. (13:18)

I DO NOT PROMOTE commercial activity that takes people away from worshiping the Lord. (13:19)

I ABHOR the thought of marrying an unbeliever. (13:26)

See Solomon's profile (page 753) at Proverbs 2:9.

I TRUST God to remember my service for him and reward me someday. (13:31)

ESTHER

THIS LAST BOOK of Israelite history is an intriguing story of *deliverance*.

Two generations have passed since the first large group of exiles returned to the Promised Land. A generation before the next group would return under Ezra, however, the Jewish people throughout the entire Persian Empire are threatened with extermination.

The story begins in the courtyard of King Xerxes. On the seventh day of a great feast, his queen refuses to let him make a public spectacle of her beauty. Enraged, Xerxes deposes her and later selects a new queen, Esther. Unknown to him, Esther is Jewish (1:1–2:20).

Esther's cousin, Mordecai, helps her save the king's life. Later, however, Xerxes promotes Haman, a sworn enemy of the Jewish people. Xerxes approves Haman's wicked decree to destroy the Jews throughout the empire (2:21–3:15).

Mordecai urges Esther to try to save her people by appealing to the king. They fast and pray for three days, and then Esther speaks to Xerxes. Instead of presenting her petition immediately, she invites the king and Haman to a banquet. Later that day, Haman builds an immense gallows and plans to execute Mordecai the next morning. That night, however, Xerxes can't sleep. He orders one of his attendants to read the historical records of his kingdom, only to be reminded how Mordecai had saved his life. The next morning, Haman's plot begins to unravel, and that afternoon Esther exposes his plot. Later that same day, Haman is hung on his own gallows (4:1–7:10).

Esther and Mordecai then receive permission from Xerxes to reverse Haman's wicked decree. Instead of being exterminated, the Jews triumph over their enemies. The annual Festival of Purim commemorates that victory (8:1–9:32).

An appendix notes that for many years Mordecai served as prime minister of Persia (10:1-3).

Famous passages in Esther abound

- King Xerxes plans to display Queen Vashti's beauty (1:11)
- Queen Vashti's disobedience provokes talk of a crisis (1:12-20)
- Esther is brought into King Xerxes' harem (2:8)
- King Xerxes makes Esther his new queen (2:15-18)
- ". . . for just such a time as this?" (4:14)
- "If I must die, I am willing to die" (4:16)
- King Xerxes holds out the golden scepter to Queen Esther (5:2; 8:4)
- "What is your request? I will give it to you" (5:3, 6; 7:2)
- "Do just as you have said for Mordecai the Jew" (6:10)
- "This wicked Haman is our enemy" (7:6)
- The Festival of Purim celebrated (9:17-32)

CHAPTER 1

The King's Banquet

This happened in the days of King Xerxes,* who reigned over 127 provinces stretching from India to Ethiopia.* ²At that time he ruled his empire from his throne at the fortress of Susa. ³In the third year of his reign, he gave a banquet for all his princes and officials. He invited all the military officers of Media and Persia, as well as the noblemen and provincial officials. ⁴The celebration lasted six months*—a tremendous display of the opulent wealth and glory of his empire.

⁵When it was all over, the king gave a special banquet for all the palace servants and officials—from the greatest to the least. It lasted for seven days and was held at Susa in the courtyard of the palace garden. ⁶The courtyard was decorated with beautifully woven white and blue linen hangings, fastened by purple ribbons to silver rings embedded in marble pillars. Gold and silver couches stood on a mosaic pavement of porphyry, marble, mother-of-pearl, and other costly stones. ⁷Drinks were served in gold goblets of many designs, and there was an abundance of royal wine, just as the king had commanded. ⁸The only restriction on the drinking was that no one should be compelled to take more than he wanted. But those who wished could have as much as they pleased, for the king had instructed his staff to let everyone decide this matter for himself.

⁹Queen Vashti gave a banquet for the women of the palace at the same time.

Queen Vashti Deposed

¹⁰On the seventh day of the feast, when King Xerxes was half drunk with wine, he told Mehuman, Biztha, Harbona, Bigtha, Abagtha, Zethar, and Carcas, the seven eunuchs who attended him, ¹¹to bring Queen Vashti to him with the royal crown on her head. He wanted all the men to gaze on her beauty, for she was a very beautiful woman. ¹²But when they conveyed the king's order to Queen Vashti, she refused to come. This made the king furious, and he burned with anger.

¹³He immediately consulted with his advisers, who knew all the Persian laws and customs, for he always asked their advice. ¹⁴The names of these men were Carshena, Shethar, Admatha, Tarshish, Meres, Marsena, and Memucan—seven high officials of Persia and Media. They were his closest associates and held the highest positions in the empire. ¹⁵"What must be done to Queen Vashti?" the king demanded. "What penalty does the law provide for a queen who refuses to obey the king's orders, properly sent through his eunuchs?"

¹⁶Memucan answered the king and his princes, "Queen Vashti has wronged not only the king but also every official and citizen throughout your empire. ¹⁷Women everywhere will begin to despise their husbands when they learn that Queen Vashti has refused to appear before the king. ¹⁸Before this day is out, the wife of every one of us, your officials throughout the empire, will hear what the queen did and will start talking to their husbands the same way. There will be no end to the contempt and anger throughout your realm. ¹⁹So if it please the king, we suggest that you issue a written decree, a law of the Persians and Medes that cannot be revoked. It should order that Queen Vashti be forever banished from your presence and that you choose another queen more worthy than she. ²⁰When this decree is published throughout your vast empire, husbands everywhere, whatever their rank, will receive proper respect from their wives!"

²¹The king and his princes thought this made good sense, so he followed Memucan's counsel. ²²He sent letters to all parts of the empire, to each province in its own script and language, proclaiming that every man should be the ruler of his home.

1:1a Hebrew *Ahasuerus*, another name for Xerxes; also throughout the book of Esther.   1:1b Hebrew *to Cush*.
1:4 Hebrew *180 days*.

I DO NOT MAKE decisions when I am not fully coherent. (1:10)

I DO NOT PURPOSELY PUT my wife in situations where other men will lust after her. (1:11)

I DO NOT TAKE PART in immorality, even if my husband tells me to do so. (1:12)

I DO NOT ENCOURAGE an angry person to make a rash or harsh decision. (1:16)

CHAPTER 2

Esther Becomes Queen

But after Xerxes' anger had cooled, he began thinking about Vashti and what she had done and the decree he had made. ²So his attendants suggested, "Let us search the empire to find beautiful young virgins for the king. ³Let the king appoint agents in each province to bring these beautiful young women into the royal harem at Susa. Hegai, the eunuch in charge, will see that they are all given beauty treatments. ⁴After that, the young woman who pleases you most will be made queen instead of Vashti." This advice was very appealing to the king, so he put the plan into effect immediately.

⁵Now at the fortress of Susa there was a certain Jew named Mordecai son of Jair. He was from the tribe of Benjamin and was a descendant of Kish and Shimei. ⁶His family* had been exiled from Jerusalem to Babylon by King Nebuchadnezzar, along with King Jehoiachin* of Judah and many others. ⁷This man had a beautiful and lovely young cousin, Hadassah, who was also called Esther. When her father and mother had died, Mordecai adopted her into his family and raised her as his own daughter. ⁸As a result of the king's decree, Esther, along with many other young women, was brought to the king's harem at the fortress of Susa and placed in Hegai's care. ⁹Hegai was very impressed with Esther and treated her kindly. He quickly ordered a special menu for her and provided her with beauty treatments. He also assigned her seven maids specially chosen from the king's palace, and he moved her and her maids into the best place in the harem.

¹⁰Esther had not told anyone of her nationality and family background, for Mordecai had told her not to. ¹¹Every day Mordecai would take a walk near the courtyard of the harem to ask about Esther and to find out what was happening to her.

¹²Before each young woman was taken to the king's bed, she was given the prescribed twelve months of beauty treatments—six months with oil of myrrh, followed by six months with special perfumes and ointments. ¹³When the time came for her to go in to the king, she was given her choice of whatever clothing or jewelry she wanted to enhance her beauty. ¹⁴That evening she was taken to the king's private rooms, and the next morning she was brought to the second harem,* where the king's wives lived. There she would be under the care of Shaashgaz, another of the king's eunuchs. She would live there for the rest of her life, never going to the king again unless he had especially enjoyed her and requested her by name.

¹⁵When it was Esther's turn* to go to the king, she accepted the advice of Hegai, the eunuch in charge of the harem. She asked for nothing except what he suggested, and she was admired by everyone who saw her. ¹⁶When Esther was taken to King Xerxes at the royal palace in early winter* of the seventh year of his reign, ¹⁷the king loved her more than any of the other young women. He was so delighted with her that he set the royal crown on her head and declared her queen instead of Vashti. ¹⁸To celebrate the occasion, he gave a banquet in Esther's honor for all his princes and servants, giving generous gifts to everyone and declaring a public festival for the provinces.

¹⁹Even after all the young women had been transferred to the second harem* and Mordecai had become a palace official, ²⁰Esther continued to keep her nationality and family background a secret. She was still following Mordecai's orders, just as she did when she was living in his home.

I DO NOT USE beauty and pleasure as the criteria for choosing a spouse. (2:3)

I BELIEVE God honored David's mercy to Shimei by using Shimei's descendant, Mordecai, to protect Israel. (2:5)

See Nebuchadnezzar's profile (page 985) at Daniel 4:37.

I CARE FOR the orphan children of my relatives. (2:7)

I HEED the wise counsel of my guardians. (2:10)

I CONSIDER the advice of those who are skilled in their field. (2:15)

2:6a Hebrew *He.*   2:6b Hebrew *Jeconiah,* a variant name for Jehoiachin.   2:14 Or *to another part of the harem.*
2:15 Hebrew *the turn of Esther, the daughter of Abihail, who was Mordecai's uncle, who had adopted her.*   2:16 Hebrew *in the tenth month, the month of Tebeth.* A number of dates in the book of Esther can be cross-checked with dates in surviving Persian records and related accurately to our modern calendar. This month of the Hebrew lunar calendar occurred in December 479 B.C. and January 478 B.C.   2:19 The meaning of the Hebrew is uncertain.

Mordecai's Loyalty to the King

²¹One day as Mordecai was on duty at the palace, two of the king's eunuchs, Bigthana* and Teresh—who were guards at the door of the king's private quarters—became angry at King Xerxes and plotted to assassinate him. ²²But Mordecai heard about the plot and passed the information on to Queen Esther. She then told the king about it and gave Mordecai credit for the report. ²³When an investigation was made and Mordecai's story was found to be true, the two men were hanged on a gallows.* This was all duly recorded in *The Book of the History of King Xerxes' Reign.*

> I PASS ON information that will protect the life of another person. (2:22)

CHAPTER 3

Haman's Plot against the Jews

Some time later, King Xerxes promoted Haman son of Hammedatha the Agagite to prime minister, making him the most powerful official in the empire next to the king himself. ²All the king's officials would bow down before Haman to show him respect whenever he passed by, for so the king had commanded. But Mordecai refused to bow down or show him respect.

³Then the palace officials at the king's gate asked Mordecai, "Why are you disobeying the king's command?" ⁴They spoke to him day after day, but still he refused to comply with the order. So they spoke to Haman about this to see if he would tolerate Mordecai's conduct, since Mordecai had told them he was a Jew.

⁵When Haman saw that Mordecai would not bow down or show him respect, he was filled with rage. ⁶So he decided it was not enough to lay hands on Mordecai alone. Since he had learned that Mordecai was a Jew, he decided to destroy all the Jews throughout the entire empire of Xerxes.

> I DO NOT TAKE OUT my anger on a whole group of people to pay back the insult or injury of just one person. (3:6)
>
> I DO NOT TRY to destroy other people just because they are different and they don't treat me as I want. (3:8)

⁷So in the month of April,* during the twelfth year of King Xerxes' reign, lots were cast (the lots were called *purim*) to determine the best day and month to take action. And the day selected was March 7, nearly a year later.*

⁸Then Haman approached King Xerxes and said, "There is a certain race of people scattered through all the provinces of your empire. Their laws are different from those of any other nation, and they refuse to obey the laws of the king. So it is not in the king's interest to let them live. ⁹If it please Your Majesty, issue a decree that they be destroyed, and I will give 375 tons* of silver to the government administrators so they can put it into the royal treasury."

> I DO NOT GIVE people power and permission to hurt others. (3:10)

¹⁰The king agreed, confirming his decision by removing his signet ring from his finger and giving it to Haman son of Hammedatha the Agagite—the enemy of the Jews. ¹¹"Keep the money," the king told Haman, "but go ahead and do as you like with these people."

¹²On April 17* Haman called in the king's secretaries and dictated letters to the princes, the governors of the respective provinces, and the local officials of each province in their own scripts and languages. These letters were signed in the name of King Xerxes, sealed with his ring, ¹³and sent by messengers into all the provinces of the empire. The letters decreed that all Jews—young and old, including women and children—must be killed, slaughtered, and annihilated on a single day. This was scheduled to happen nearly a year later on March 7.* The property of the Jews would be given to those who killed them. ¹⁴A copy of this decree was to be issued in every

---

2:21 Hebrew *Bigthan;* compare 6:2.   2:23 Or *on a pole.*   3:7a Hebrew *in the first month, the month of Nisan.* This month of the Hebrew lunar calendar occurred in April and May 474 B.C.; also see note on 2:16.   3:7b As in Greek version, which reads *the thirteenth day of the twelfth month, the month of Adar* (see also 3:13). Hebrew reads *in the twelfth month,* of the Hebrew calendar. The date selected was March 7, 473 B.C.; also see note on 2:16. 3:9 Hebrew *10,000 talents* [340 metric tons].   3:12 Hebrew *On the thirteenth day of the first month,* of the Hebrew calendar. This event occurred on April 17, 474 B.C.; also see note on 2:16.   3:13 Hebrew *on the thirteenth day of the twelfth month, the month of Adar,* of the Hebrew calendar. The date selected was March 7, 473 B.C.; also see note on 2:16.

province and made known to all the people, so that they would be ready to do their duty on the appointed day. [15]At the king's command, the decree went out by the swiftest messengers, and it was proclaimed in the fortress of Susa. Then the king and Haman sat down to drink, but the city of Susa fell into confusion.

CHAPTER 4

Mordecai Requests Esther's Help

When Mordecai learned what had been done, he tore his clothes, put on sackcloth and ashes, and went out into the city, crying with a loud and bitter wail. [2]He stood outside the gate of the palace, for no one was allowed to enter while wearing clothes of mourning. [3]And as news of the king's decree reached all the provinces, there was great mourning among the Jews. They fasted, wept, and wailed, and many people lay in sackcloth and ashes.

[4]When Queen Esther's maids and eunuchs came and told her about Mordecai, she was deeply distressed. She sent clothing to him to replace the sackcloth, but he refused it. [5]Then Esther sent for Hathach, one of the king's eunuchs who had been appointed as her attendant. She ordered him to go to Mordecai and find out what was troubling him and why he was in mourning. [6]So Hathach went out to Mordecai in the square in front of the palace gate.

[7]Mordecai told him the whole story and told him how much money Haman had promised to pay into the royal treasury for the destruction of the Jews. [8]Mordecai gave Hathach a copy of the decree issued in Susa that called for the death of all Jews, and he asked Hathach to show it to Esther. He also asked Hathach to explain it to her and to urge her to go to the king to beg for mercy and plead for her people. [9]So Hathach returned to Esther with Mordecai's message.

[10]Then Esther told Hathach to go back and relay this message to Mordecai: [11]"The whole world knows that anyone who appears before the king in his inner court without being invited is doomed to die unless the king holds out his gold scepter. And the king has not called for me to come to him in more than a month." [12]So Hathach gave Esther's message to Mordecai.

[13]Mordecai sent back this reply to Esther: "Don't think for a moment that you will escape there in the palace when all other Jews are killed. [14]If you keep quiet at a time like this, deliverance for the Jews will arise from some other place, but you and your relatives will die. What's more, who can say but that you have been elevated to the palace for just such a time as this?"

[15]Then Esther sent this reply to Mordecai: [16]"Go and gather together all the Jews of Susa and fast for me. Do not eat or drink for three days, night or day. My maids and I will do the same. And then, though it is against the law, I will go in to see the king. If I must die, I am willing to die." [17]So Mordecai went away and did as Esther told him.

CHAPTER 5

Esther's Request to the King

Three days later, Esther put on her royal robes and entered the inner court of the palace, just across from the king's hall. The king was sitting on his royal throne, facing the entrance. [2]When he saw Queen Esther standing there in the inner court, he welcomed her, holding out the gold scepter to her. So Esther approached and touched its tip.

[3]Then the king asked her, "What do you want, Queen Esther? What is your request? I will give it to you, even if it is half the kingdom!"

[4]And Esther replied, "If it please Your Majesty, let the king and Haman come today to a banquet I have prepared for the king."

[5]The king turned to his attendants and said, "Tell Haman to come quickly

I DO NOT CAUSE trauma and confusion by issuing rash and harmful orders to those under my authority. (3:15)

I MOURN over the injustices done to God's people. (4:1)

I CARE enough about other people to find out why they are troubled and in mourning. (4:5)

I VIEW my position in life as God's gift and allow him to accomplish his purposes through me. (4:14)

I RELY ON the prayers and support of others when I am making important decisions or taking strategic action. (4:16)

I PREPARE before I make important requests. (5:1)

I TAKE every opportunity given me to approach those who have the authority to help others. (5:2)

to a banquet, as Esther has requested." So the king and Haman went to Esther's banquet.

⁶And while they were drinking wine, the king said to Esther, "Now tell me what you really want. What is your request? I will give it to you, even if it is half the kingdom!"

⁷Esther replied, "This is my request and deepest wish. ⁸If Your Majesty is pleased with me and wants to grant my request, please come with Haman tomorrow to the banquet I will prepare for you. Then tomorrow I will explain what this is all about."

Haman's Plan to Kill Mordecai

⁹What a happy man Haman was as he left the banquet! But when he saw Mordecai sitting at the gate, not standing up or trembling nervously before him, he was furious. ¹⁰However, he restrained himself and went on home. Then he gathered together his friends and Zeresh, his wife, ¹¹and boasted to them about his great wealth and his many children. He bragged about the honors the king had given him and how he had been promoted over all the other officials and leaders.

¹²Then Haman added, "And that's not all! Queen Esther invited only me and the king himself to the banquet she prepared for us. And she has invited me to dine with her and the king again tomorrow!" ¹³Then he added, "But all this is meaningless as long as I see Mordecai the Jew just sitting there at the palace gate."

¹⁴So Haman's wife, Zeresh, and all his friends suggested, "Set up a gallows* that stands seventy-five feet* tall, and in the morning ask the king to hang Mordecai on it. When this is done, you can go on your merry way to the banquet with the king." This pleased Haman immensely, and he ordered the gallows set up.

CHAPTER 6

The King Honors Mordecai

That night the king had trouble sleeping, so he ordered an attendant to bring the historical records of his kingdom so they could be read to him. ²In those records he discovered an account of how Mordecai had exposed the plot of Bigthana and Teresh, two of the eunuchs who guarded the door to the king's private quarters. They had plotted to assassinate the king. ³"What reward or recognition did we ever give Mordecai for this?" the king asked.

His attendants replied, "Nothing has been done."

⁴"Who is that in the outer court?" the king inquired. Now, as it happened, Haman had just arrived in the outer court of the palace to ask the king to hang Mordecai from the gallows* he had prepared.

⁵So the attendants replied to the king, "Haman is out there."

"Bring him in," the king ordered. ⁶So Haman came in, and the king said, "What should I do to honor a man who truly pleases me?"

Haman thought to himself, "Whom would the king wish to honor more than me?" ⁷So he replied, "If the king wishes to honor someone, ⁸he should bring out one of the king's own royal robes, as well as the king's own horse with a royal emblem on its head. ⁹Instruct one of the king's most noble princes to dress the man in the king's robe and to lead him through the city square on the king's own horse. Have the prince shout as they go, 'This is what happens to those the king wishes to honor!' "

¹⁰"Excellent!" the king said to Haman. "Hurry and get the robe and my horse, and do just as you have said for Mordecai the Jew, who sits at the gate of the palace. Do not fail to carry out everything you have suggested."

¹¹So Haman took the robe and put it on Mordecai, placed him on the

I DO NOT LET my anger at one person control my whole life. (5:13)

I DO NOT ENCOURAGE others to act violently. (5:14)

I DO NOT FORGET the good that others have done for me. (6:2)

I SEEK to honor those who have protected and helped me. (6:6)

5:14a Or *a pole.* 5:14b Hebrew *50 cubits* [22.5 meters]. 6:4 Or *from the pole.*

king's own horse, and led him through the city square, shouting, "This is what happens to those the king wishes to honor!" [12]Afterward Mordecai returned to the palace gate, but Haman hurried home dejected and completely humiliated.

[13]When Haman told his wife, Zeresh, and all his friends what had happened, they said, "Since Mordecai—this man who has humiliated you—is a Jew, you will never succeed in your plans against him. It will be fatal to continue to oppose him." [14]While they were still talking, the king's eunuchs arrived to take Haman to the banquet Esther had prepared.

I BELIEVE that the person who is proud will be humbled. (6:12)

LIKE ESTHER
Esther 4:16

I act courageously even when I am afraid because I know that God is in control.

A prominent display at the Holocaust Museum in Washington, D.C., lists the names of thousands of individuals who risked their lives to protect and rescue Jewish people during World War II. How many of these people were inspired by a woman who risked her life to save her people twenty-five hundred years ago?

Esther, also called Hadassah, was separated from her family and friends, only to become the queen of her pagan adopted country. She accepted God's plan for her life, thus fulfilling a purpose she could little fathom beforehand: saving the entire Jewish population from annihilation.

Esther made the choice to act in the difficult place God put her. She even risked her life to plead with the king for her people. As queen, it would seem natural that Esther would have the clout to enter the king's throne room uninvited. But that wasn't the case during the reign of the kings of Persia and Media. Esther very easily could have met the sword. Esther faced her fear with the prayers of others and the conviction that God indeed was in control—no matter what the outcome.

Esther couldn't see God's control clearly. He was at work behind the scenes. The very structure of her story reveals this. Although this story does not contain any obvious references to the Lord's name, readers of Hebrew can spot the letters YHWH—the Lord's covenantal name—repeated in acrostic form four times in the original text.

Because Esther trusted God's sovereignty and acted courageously, God used her to spare the Jewish nation and crush their enemies. As well, Esther's relative Mordecai gained political power to continue serving the good of his people. Esther herself is still remembered each year at Purim—the Jewish holiday celebrating her bravery and God's providence.

The same God is still in control today as he was in Esther's time. Even in times of difficulty and danger, we can act courageously because our God will work all things together for the good of his children (Romans 8:28-37).

○ *Today's Scripture reading is Esther 2:1-23; 4:1–5:8; 7:1–8:8.*

CHAPTER 7
The King Executes Haman

So the king and Haman went to Queen Esther's banquet. [2]And while they were drinking wine that day, the king again asked her, "Tell me what you want, Queen Esther. What is your request? I will give it to you, even if it is half the kingdom!"

[3]And so Queen Esther replied, "If Your Majesty is pleased with me and wants to grant my request, my petition is that my life and the lives of my people will be spared. [4]For my people and I have been sold to those who would kill, slaughter, and annihilate us. If we had only been sold as slaves, I could remain quiet, for that would have been a matter too trivial to warrant disturbing the king."

[5]"Who would do such a thing?" King Xerxes demanded. "Who would dare touch you?"

[6]Esther replied, "This wicked Haman is our enemy." Haman grew pale

I USE my position and opportunities to speak up for the lives of those in danger. (7:3)

I DO NOT FAIL to speak up when people's lives are in danger. (7:4)

I STRIVE to expose those who plan great evil. (7:6)

with fright before the king and queen. ⁷Then the king jumped to his feet in a rage and went out into the palace garden.

But Haman stayed behind to plead for his life with Queen Esther, for he knew that he was doomed. ⁸In despair he fell on the couch where Queen Esther was reclining, just as the king returned from the palace garden. "Will he even assault the queen right here in the palace, before my very eyes?" the king roared. And as soon as the king spoke, his attendants covered Haman's face, signaling his doom.

⁹Then Harbona, one of the king's eunuchs, said, "Haman has set up a gallows* that stands seventy-five feet* tall in his own courtyard. He intended to use it to hang Mordecai, the man who saved the king from assassination."

"Then hang Haman on it!" the king ordered. ¹⁰So they hanged Haman on the gallows he had set up for Mordecai, and the king's anger was pacified.

CHAPTER 8

A Decree to Help the Jews

On that same day King Xerxes gave the estate of Haman, the enemy of the Jews, to Queen Esther. Then Mordecai was brought before the king, for Esther had told the king how they were related. ²The king took off his signet ring—which he had taken back from Haman—and gave it to Mordecai. And Esther appointed Mordecai to be in charge of Haman's property.

³Now once more Esther came before the king, falling down at his feet and begging him with tears to stop Haman's evil plot against the Jews. ⁴Again the king held out the gold scepter to Esther. So she rose and stood before him ⁵and said, "If Your Majesty is pleased with me and if he thinks it is right, send out a decree reversing Haman's orders to destroy the Jews throughout all the provinces of the king. ⁶For how can I endure to see my people and my family slaughtered and destroyed?"

⁷Then King Xerxes said to Queen Esther and Mordecai the Jew, "I have given Esther the estate of Haman, and he has been hanged on the gallows* because he tried to destroy the Jews. ⁸Now go ahead and send a message to the Jews in the king's name, telling them whatever you want, and seal it with the king's signet ring. But remember that whatever is written in the king's name and sealed with his ring can never be revoked."

⁹So on June 25* the king's secretaries were summoned. As Mordecai dictated, they wrote a decree to the Jews and to the princes, governors, and local officials of all the 127 provinces stretching from India to Ethiopia.* The decree was written in the scripts and languages of all the peoples of the empire, including the Jews. ¹⁰Mordecai wrote in the name of King Xerxes and sealed the message with the king's signet ring. He sent the letters by swift messengers, who rode horses especially bred for the king's service.

¹¹The king's decree gave the Jews in every city authority to unite to defend their lives. They were allowed to kill, slaughter, and annihilate anyone of any nationality or province who might attack them or their children and wives, and to take the property of their enemies. ¹²The day chosen for this event throughout all the provinces of King Xerxes was March 7 of the next year.* ¹³A copy of this decree was to be recognized as law in every province and proclaimed to all the people. That way the Jews would be ready on that day to take revenge on their enemies. ¹⁴So urged on by the king's command, the messengers rode out swiftly on horses bred for the king's service. The same decree was also issued at the fortress of Susa.

¹⁵Then Mordecai put on the royal robe of blue and white and the great

---

I PERSIST in seeking to preserve people's lives from destruction. (8:3)

I GIVE the proper authority to those who are trying to protect people. (8:8)

I STRIVE to make lifesaving news known to everyone. (8:9)

7:9a Or *a pole;* also in 7:10. 7:9b Hebrew *50 cubits* [22.5 meters]. 8:7 Or *on the pole.* 8:9a Hebrew *on the twenty-third day of the third month, the month of Sivan,* of the Hebrew calendar. This event occurred on June 25, 474 B.C.; also see note on 2:16. 8:9b Hebrew *to Cush.* 8:12 Hebrew *the thirteenth day of the twelfth month, the month of Adar,* of the Hebrew calendar. The date selected was March 7, 473 B.C.; also see note on 2:16.

crown of gold, and he wore an outer cloak of fine linen and purple. And the people of Susa celebrated the new decree. ¹⁶The Jews were filled with joy and gladness and were honored everywhere. ¹⁷In every city and province, wherever the king's decree arrived, the Jews rejoiced and had a great celebration and declared a public festival and holiday. And many of the people of the land became Jews themselves, for they feared what the Jews might do to them.

I CELEBRATE when the Lord rescues his people from destruction. (8:17)

LIKE MORDECAI *I use every opportunity to work for the good of others.*
Esther 10:3

At pivotal points in history ordinary people have risen to positions of greatness and used their position to serve the greater good of others.

During the time after the Babylonian Captivity, that person was Mordecai. Mordecai, whether humbled or honored, used every opportunity to seek the welfare of those around him.

When Mordecai adopted his young cousin as his own daughter, little did he know he was raising the next queen. For Esther's own benefit, Mordecai nurtured a trust and respect in their relationship that would later give him an audience with the king.

By reporting an assassination plot, Mordecai risked his own life to save the pagan king from death. In God's timing, Mordecai later received special honor for that deed—and gained greater authority to serve even more people.

When the decree to destroy the Jews went out from the palace, Mordecai immediately left the palace to mourn with his people. Yet even from outside the palace gates, Mordecai seized the opportunity to use his influence in the inner courts. Esther was the only one who could reach the king for help. Mordecai appealed without hesitation to her loyalty and destiny—asking her to do what she alone could to save her people from otherwise certain death.

After wicked Haman's plot was exposed, Mordecai received both Haman's estate and his position to preserve the Jewish people. The royal robes of the prime minister hung easily on his shoulders. No longer an ordinary Jewish citizen in a foreign country, Mordecai did not shrink back from a position of honor and authority that gave him incredible power.

With that power, Mordecai sent out decrees, instituted traditions, and preserved lives from Ethiopia to India. All Jews everywhere knew that they had a friend in the royal courts.

Whether as father, servant, or political powerhouse, Mordecai lived to seek the good of others. God gives opportunities in many disguises. Whether humble or honored, you and I can seize each one to serve others and—at some point—perhaps even save their life.

○ *Today's Scripture reading is Esther 3:1-15; 5:9–6:14; 10:1-3.*

CHAPTER 9
The Victory of the Jews

So on March 7* the two decrees of the king were put into effect. On that day, the enemies of the Jews had hoped to destroy them, but quite the opposite happened. ²The Jews gathered in their cities throughout all the king's provinces to defend themselves against anyone who might try to harm them. But no one could make a stand against them, for everyone was afraid of them. ³And all the commanders of the provinces, the princes, the governors, and the royal officials helped the Jews for fear of Mordecai. ⁴For Mordecai had been promoted in the king's palace, and his fame spread throughout all the provinces as he became more and more powerful.

I STAND with others to protect people from harm. (9:2)

⁵But the Jews went ahead on the appointed day and struck down their enemies with the sword. They killed and annihilated their enemies and did as they pleased with those who hated them. ⁶They killed five hundred people in the fortress of Susa. ⁷ They also killed Parshandatha, Dalphon, Aspatha,

9:1 Hebrew *on the thirteenth day of the twelfth month, the month of Adar,* of the Hebrew calendar. This event occurred on March 7, 473 B.C.; also see note on 2:16.

I AM MORE INTERESTED in justice than in money. (9:10)

[8]Poratha, Adalia, Aridatha, [9]Parmashta, Arisai, Aridai, and Vaizatha—[10]the ten sons of Haman son of Hammedatha, the enemy of the Jews. But they did not take any plunder.

[11]That evening, when the king was informed of the number of people killed in the fortress of Susa, [12]he called for Queen Esther and said, "The Jews have killed five hundred people in the fortress of Susa alone and also Haman's ten sons. If they have done that here, what has happened in the rest of the provinces? But now, what more do you want? It will be granted to you; tell me and I will do it."

[13]And Esther said, "If it please Your Majesty, give the Jews in Susa permission to do again tomorrow as they have done today, and have the bodies of Haman's ten sons hung from the gallows.*"

[14]So the king agreed, and the decree was announced in Susa. They also hung the bodies of Haman's ten sons from the gallows. [15]Then the Jews at Susa gathered together on March 8* and killed three hundred more people, though again they took no plunder.

[16]Meanwhile, the other Jews throughout the king's provinces had gathered together to defend their lives. They gained relief from all their enemies, killing seventy-five thousand of those who hated them. But they did not take any plunder. [17]Throughout the provinces this was done on March 7.* Then on the following day* they rested, celebrating their victory with a day of feasting and gladness. [18]But the Jews at Susa continued killing their enemies on the second day also, and then rested on the third day,* making that their day of feasting and gladness. [19]So to this day, rural Jews living in unwalled villages celebrate an annual festival and holiday in late winter,* when they rejoice and send gifts to each other.

I TAKE time each year to celebrate deliverance. (9:19)

The Festival of Purim

[20]Mordecai recorded these events and sent letters to the Jews near and far, throughout all the king's provinces, [21]encouraging them to celebrate an annual festival on these two days. [22]He told them to celebrate these days with feasting and gladness and by giving gifts to each other and to the poor. This would commemorate a time when the Jews gained relief from their enemies, when their sorrow was turned into gladness and their mourning into joy.

I ENCOURAGE others to celebrate and commemorate God's deliverance. (9:22)

[23]So the Jews adopted Mordecai's suggestion and began this annual custom. [24]Haman son of Hammedatha the Agagite, the enemy of the Jews, had plotted to crush and destroy them on the day and month determined by casting lots (the lots were called *purim*). [25]But when Esther came before the king, he issued a decree causing Haman's evil plot to backfire, and Haman and his sons were hanged on the gallows. [26](That is why this celebration is called Purim, because it is the ancient word for casting lots.) So because of Mordecai's letter and because of what they had experienced, [27]the Jews throughout the realm agreed to inaugurate this tradition and to pass it on to their descendants and to all who became Jews. They declared they would never fail to celebrate these two prescribed days at the appointed time each year. [28]These days would be remembered and kept from generation to generation and celebrated by every family throughout the provinces and cities of the empire. These days would never cease to be celebrated among the Jews, nor would the memory of what happened ever die out among their descendants.

I MAINTAIN traditions that pass on to my descendants the memory of God's deliverance. (9:27)

[29]Then Queen Esther, the daughter of Abihail, along with Mordecai the Jew, wrote another letter putting the queen's full authority behind Mordecai's letter

9:13 Or *the pole;* also in 9:14, 25.   9:15 Hebrew *the fourteenth day of the month of Adar,* of the Hebrew calendar. This event occurred on March 8, 473 B.C.; also see note on 2:16.   9:17a Hebrew *on the thirteenth day of the month of Adar,* of the Hebrew calendar. This event occurred on March 7, 473 B.C.; also see note on 2:16. 9:17b Hebrew *on the fourteenth day,* of the Hebrew month of Adar.   9:18 Hebrew *killing their enemies on the thirteenth day and the fourteenth day, and then rested on the fifteenth day,* of the Hebrew month of Adar. 9:19 Hebrew *on the fourteenth day of the month of Adar.* This day of the Hebrew lunar calendar usually occurs in March.

to establish the Festival of Purim. [30]In addition, letters wishing peace and security were sent to the Jews throughout the 127 provinces of the empire of Xerxes. [31] These letters established the Festival of Purim—an annual celebration of these days at the appointed time, decreed by both Mordecai the Jew and Queen Esther. (The people decided to observe this festival, just as they had decided for themselves and their descendants to establish the times of fasting and mourning.) [32]So the command of Esther confirmed the practices of Purim, and it was all written down in the records.

CHAPTER 10

The Greatness of Xerxes and Mordecai

King Xerxes imposed tribute throughout his empire, even to the distant coastlands. [2]His great achievements and the full account of the greatness of Mordecai, whom the king had promoted, are recorded in *The Book of the History of the Kings of Media and Persia.* [3]Mordecai the Jew became the prime minister, with authority next to that of King Xerxes himself. He was very great among the Jews, who held him in high esteem, because he worked for the good of his people and was a friend at the royal court for all of them.

I USE my position and authority to work for the good of God's people. (10:3)

JOB

THIS FIRST BOOK of Hebrew poetry is an *elaborate play.*

This is an intense drama with a purpose. The story is real, the characters are true to life, and the question they debate is timeless. Why in the world does God allow horrible things to happen to really good people?

In chapters 1–2, a wealthy and godly gentleman named Job loses all his livestock and his children in one fell swoop. Of course, Job has no inkling of the heavenly drama that surrounds this sudden, tragic series of events.

In chapters 3–31, Job pours out his complaint to three of his most respected friends, who in turn accuse Job of covering up various terrible sins. Job charges them with slander and maintains he is still righteous. Job also laments God's silence and challenges God to explain what's going on.

In chapters 32–37, another character takes center stage, rebuking Job and his other friends, but this younger friend proves no wiser than the others.

Then in chapters 38–42, the Lord comes down from heaven and challenges Job with a rapid-fire series of questions. Even though the Lord doesn't explain the reasons behind the tumultuous series of events that have transpired, Job repents. The Lord then blesses Job and restores double what he has lost due to Satan's fiery attacks.

Famous verses in Job include
- Job's godly character and integrity (1:1)
- Satan's vicious accusations (1:6-12; 2:1-6)
- "The LORD gave me everything I had, and the LORD has taken it away" (1:21)
- "Those who plant trouble and cultivate evil will harvest the same" (4:8)
- "Can a mortal be just and upright before God?" (4:17)
- "Does the Almighty twist what is right?" (8:3)
- "Can you solve the mysteries of God?" (11:7)
- "If mortals die, can they live again?" (14:14)
- "What miserable comforters you are!" (16:2)
- "But as for me, I know that my Redeemer lives, and that he will stand upon the earth at last" (19:25)
- "After my body has decayed, yet in my body I will see God!" (19:26)
- "The fear of the Lord is true wisdom" (28:28)
- Job's recounting of his past blessings and present anguish (29:1-30:31)
- Job's repentance before the Lord (40:3-5; 42:1-6)
- The Lord's blessing of Job once again (42:10-17)

CHAPTER 1

Prologue

There was a man named Job who lived in the land of Uz. He was blameless, a man of complete integrity. He feared God and stayed away from evil. ²He had seven sons and three daughters. ³He owned seven thousand sheep, three thousand camels, five hundred teams of oxen, and five hundred female donkeys, and he employed many servants. He was, in fact, the richest person in that entire area.

⁴Every year when Job's sons had birthdays, they invited their brothers and sisters to join them for a celebration. On these occasions they would get together to eat and drink. ⁵When these celebrations ended—and sometimes they lasted several days—Job would purify his children. He would get up early in the morning and offer a burnt offering for each of them. For Job said to himself, "Perhaps my children have sinned and have cursed God in their hearts." This was Job's regular practice.

Job's First Test

⁶One day the angels* came to present themselves before the LORD, and Satan the Accuser came with them. ⁷"Where have you come from?" the LORD asked Satan.

And Satan answered the LORD, "I have been going back and forth across the earth, watching everything that's going on."

⁸Then the LORD asked Satan, "Have you noticed my servant Job? He is the finest man in all the earth—a man of complete integrity. He fears God and will have nothing to do with evil."

⁹Satan replied to the LORD, "Yes, Job fears God, but not without good reason! ¹⁰You have always protected him and his home and his property from harm. You have made him prosperous in everything he does. Look how rich he is! ¹¹But take away everything he has, and he will surely curse you to your face!"

¹²"All right, you may test him," the LORD said to Satan. "Do whatever you want with everything he possesses, but don't harm him physically." So Satan left the LORD's presence.

¹³One day when Job's sons and daughters were dining at the oldest brother's house, ¹⁴a messenger arrived at Job's home with this news: "Your oxen were plowing, with the donkeys feeding beside them, ¹⁵when the Sabeans raided us. They stole all the animals and killed all the farmhands. I am the only one who escaped to tell you."

¹⁶While he was still speaking, another messenger arrived with this news: "The fire of God has fallen from heaven and burned up your sheep and all the shepherds. I am the only one who escaped to tell you."

¹⁷While he was still speaking, a third messenger arrived with this news: "Three bands of Chaldean raiders have stolen your camels and killed your servants. I am the only one who escaped to tell you."

¹⁸While he was still speaking, another messenger arrived with this news: "Your sons and daughters were feasting in their oldest brother's home. ¹⁹Suddenly, a powerful wind swept in from the desert and hit the house on all sides. The house collapsed, and all your children are dead. I am the only one who escaped to tell you."

²⁰Job stood up and tore his robe in grief. Then he shaved his head and fell to the ground before God. ²¹He said,

"I came naked from my mother's womb,
  and I will be stripped of everything when I die.
The LORD gave me everything I had,
  and the LORD has taken it away.
Praise the name of the LORD!"

²²In all of this, Job did not sin by blaming God.

1:6 Hebrew *the sons of God.*

I INTERCEDE for my children and long for them to honor God. (1:5)

I FEAR God and have nothing to do with evil. (1:8)

I BELIEVE God controls how much influence Satan can exert in my life. (1:12)

I GRIEVE deeply when a loved one dies. (1:20)

I BELIEVE the Lord has given me everything I have. (1:21)

I DO NOT SIN by blaming God for my troubles. (1:22)

CHAPTER 2

Job's Second Test

One day the angels* came again to present themselves before the LORD, and Satan the Accuser came with them. ²"Where have you come from?" the LORD asked Satan.

And Satan answered the LORD, "I have been going back and forth across the earth, watching everything that's going on."

LIKE JOB   *I cling to God in the midst of my deepest pain.*

Job 1:21

A terrible storm wipes out your entire livelihood. An envious competitor destroys your business. A madman goes on a rampage and your employees are brutally murdered. Your children die suddenly—celebrating a birthday one moment and disappearing the next.

Overnight, your health deteriorates. You suffer incredible, unrelenting physical pain the best medical treatment can't even begin to dull. Your friends pretend to care but question your character. Your spouse grows increasingly bitter in the midst of your shared pain—and finally urges you to curse God and die.

Even one of these situations would be trauma enough for one person in one lifetime. Two of these crises would be considered by many to be enough of an excuse to doubt God and walk away from him completely.

Job experienced all these tragedies—almost simultaneously. In his pain he wrestled with God. He questioned the reasons for his suffering. He cried out for answers and mercy and even death. He despaired—but he never deserted God. When his wife told him to curse the Lord and die, he refused. Job knew he had to accept whatever God had allowed to happen in his life.

Job's strength wore thin, his mind reeled from trying to understand his grief, and his voice grew hoarse from crying out. Still, he knew walking away from God was not an option. Job simply clung harder and cried out louder.

Finally God broke through Job's darkness. Not with answers but in person—convincing Job of the Lord's complete power, control, and right to run the universe. Job did not need to run back to God—the Lord had never left. Instead, Job simply stopped flailing and rested in the everlasting arms that had never let him go.

Job would have agreed with Peter, who told the Lord Jesus, "Lord, to whom would we go? You alone have the words that give eternal life" (John 6:68). As Job discovered, nothing can separate you and me from God's love (Romans 8:35).

When we cling to God in the midst of our pain, we find that he's the one holding on tighter. We can rest assured that he will never leave us or forsake us.

To read the end of the story, see Job 42 and James 5:11.

O *Today's Scripture reading is Job 1–2.*

---

³Then the LORD asked Satan, "Have you noticed my servant Job? He is the finest man in all the earth—a man of complete integrity. He fears God and will have nothing to do with evil. And he has maintained his integrity, even though you persuaded me to harm him without cause."

⁴Satan replied to the LORD, "Skin for skin—he blesses you only because you bless him. A man will give up everything he has to save his life. ⁵But take away his health, and he will surely curse you to your face!"

⁶"All right, do with him as you please," the LORD said to Satan. "But spare his life." ⁷So Satan left the LORD's presence, and he struck Job with a terrible case of boils from head to foot.

⁸Then Job scraped his skin with a piece of broken pottery as he sat among the ashes. ⁹His wife said to him, "Are you still trying to maintain your integrity? Curse God and die."

I MAINTAIN my integrity even in the most difficult circumstances. (2:3)

2:1 Hebrew *the sons of God.*

¹⁰But Job replied, "You talk like a godless woman. Should we accept only good things from the hand of God and never anything bad?" So in all this, Job said nothing wrong.

Job's Three Friends Share His Anguish

¹¹ Three of Job's friends were Eliphaz the Temanite, Bildad the Shuhite, and Zophar the Naamathite. When they heard of the tragedy he had suffered, they got together and traveled from their homes to comfort and console him. ¹²When they saw Job from a distance, they scarcely recognized him. Wailing loudly, they tore their robes and threw dust into the air over their heads to demonstrate their grief. ¹³Then they sat on the ground with him for seven days and nights. And no one said a word, for they saw that his suffering was too great for words.

CHAPTER 3

Job's First Speech

At last Job spoke, and he cursed the day of his birth. ²He said:

³"Cursed be the day of my birth, and cursed be the night when I was conceived. ⁴Let that day be turned to darkness. Let it be lost even to God on high, and let it be shrouded in darkness. ⁵Yes, let the darkness and utter gloom claim it for its own. Let a black cloud overshadow it, and let the darkness terrify it. ⁶Let that night be blotted off the calendar, never again to be counted among the days of the year, never again to appear among the months. ⁷Let that night be barren. Let it have no joy. ⁸Let those who are experts at cursing—those who are ready to rouse the sea monster*—curse that day. ⁹Let its morning stars remain dark. Let it hope for light, but in vain; may it never see the morning light. ¹⁰Curse it for its failure to shut my mother's womb, for letting me be born to all this trouble.

¹¹"Why didn't I die at birth as I came from the womb? ¹²Why did my mother let me live? Why did she nurse me at her breasts? ¹³For if I had died at birth, I would be at peace now, asleep and at rest. ¹⁴I would rest with the world's kings and prime ministers, famous for their great construction projects. ¹⁵I would rest with wealthy princes whose palaces were filled with gold and silver. ¹⁶Why was I not buried like a stillborn child, like a baby who never lives to see the light? ¹⁷For in death the wicked cease from troubling, and the weary are at rest. ¹⁸Even prisoners are at ease in death, with no guards to curse them. ¹⁹Rich and poor are there alike, and the slave is free from his master.

²⁰"Oh, why should light be given to the weary, and life to those in misery? ²¹They long for death, and it won't come. They search for death more eagerly than for hidden treasure. ²²It is a blessed relief when they finally die, when they find the grave. ²³Why is life given to those with no future, those destined by God to live in distress? ²⁴I cannot eat for sighing; my groans pour out like water. ²⁵What I always feared has happened to me. What I dreaded has come to be. ²⁶I have no peace, no quietness. I have no rest; instead, only trouble comes."

CHAPTER 4

Eliphaz's First Response to Job

Then Eliphaz the Temanite replied to Job:

²"Will you be patient and let me say a word? For who could keep from speaking out?

³"In the past you have encouraged many a troubled soul to trust in God; you have supported those who were weak. ⁴Your words have strengthened the fallen; you steadied those who wavered. ⁵But now when trouble strikes, you faint and are broken. ⁶Does your reverence for God give you no confidence? Shouldn't you believe that God will care for those who are upright?

**Sidebar notes (left column):**

I ACCEPT all things from the hand of God. (2:10)

I COMFORT a friend first with my presence—later with words. (2:13)

I MAY CURSE the day of my birth if my suffering is intense, but I will never curse God. (3:1)

Ask the Lord to make you "totally committed to doing what is right" (Titus 2:14).

I DO NOT BELIEVE death is the answer to this life's worst troubles. (3:11)

I MAY LONG for death when my pain is great, but I will never take my life. (3:21)

I BELIEVE I do have a future—thanks to God. (3:23)

I REFRAIN from arguing with someone who is suffering. (4:1)

I ENCOURAGE those who are troubled to trust in God. (4:3)

I DO NOT BELIEVE that only the wicked suffer. (4:7)

3:8 Hebrew *rouse Leviathan.*

[7]"Stop and think! Does the innocent person perish? When has the upright person been destroyed? [8]My experience shows that those who plant trouble and cultivate evil will harvest the same. [9]They perish by a breath from God. They vanish in a blast of his anger. [10]Though they are fierce young lions, they will all be broken and destroyed. [11]The fierce lion will starve, and the cubs of the lioness will be scattered.

[12]"This truth was given me in secret, as though whispered in my ear. [13]It came in a vision at night as others slept. [14]Fear gripped me; I trembled and shook with terror. [15]A spirit* swept past my face. Its wind sent shivers up my spine. [16]It stopped, but I couldn't see its shape. There was a form before my eyes, and a hushed voice said, [17]'Can a mortal be just and upright before God? Can a person be pure before the Creator?'

> I BELIEVE every person has sinned against God (Romans 3:23). (4:17)

UNLIKE ELIPHAZ, BILDAD, AND ZOPHAR

I do not assume God must be punishing those who suffer.

Job 4:7

You're wise, intelligent, brilliant, and internationally respected. So what do you say to a friend who has suddenly lost everything?

If anyone should know, it was

- Eliphaz, an elder from the Edomite city of Teman—famed for the wisdom of its people
- Bildad, an honored descendant of Shuah, who was the father of an Arab tribe and youngest son of Abraham by his second wife, Keturah
- Zophar, an esteemed gentleman from the Arabic city of Naamath and, tradition says, king of the Minaeans

At first, Job's three friends did the smart thing—and said nothing. For an entire week they grieved with him—without saying a word (2:12-13).

Then, when Job began to verbalize his grief, Eliphaz, Bildad, and Zophar all did something rather shocking. Instead of consoling their dear friend, they began to criticize him severely. In essence, they told Job, "You wouldn't have suffered so much from the hand of God if you hadn't been doing wicked things."

These three wrongly believed that God doesn't let horrible things happen to good people. Worse, they compounded their error by slandering Job's reputation, judging his motives, and accusing him of all sorts of evil deeds. As if insisting that Job must be a vile person somehow made God look better!

No wonder Job finally said, "What miserable comforters you are!" (16:2).

In the end, the Lord rebuked Job's three friends, who repented (42:7-9).

Unlike Eliphaz, Bildad, and Zophar, we should not try to "protect" God's character by suggesting that a suffering friend must have sinned against God. Instead, by our presence, we should seek to bring consolation.

○ *Today's Scripture reading is Job 4–7.*

---

[18]"If God cannot trust his own angels and has charged some of them with folly, [19]how much less will he trust those made of clay! Their foundation is dust, and they are crushed as easily as moths. [20]They are alive in the morning, but by evening they are dead, gone forever without a trace. [21]Their tent collapses; they die in ignorance.

CHAPTER 5

Eliphaz's Response Continues

"You may cry for help, but no one listens. You may turn to the angels,* but they give you no help. [2]Surely resentment destroys the fool, and jealousy kills

4:15 Or *wind*.   5:1 Hebrew *the holy ones*.

I DO NOT TURN from God in futile pursuit of worldly success. (5:3)

I BELIEVE God's works are too marvelous to understand. (5:9)

I BELIEVE in the end God makes everything right. (5:16)

I DO NOT DESPISE the chastening of the Almighty when I sin. (5:17)

I LEARN from experience and counsel—and apply what agrees with God's Word. (5:27)

I LISTEN when a friend is suffering. (6:2)

I DO NOT DENY God's truth in the midst of severe pain. (6:10)

I DO NOT GIVE UP all hope when adversity strikes. (6:13)

I DO NOT BELIEVE all suffering is a direct result of someone's own sins. (6:14)

the simple. [3]From my experience, I know that fools who turn from God may be successful for the moment, but then comes sudden disaster. [4]Their children are abandoned far from help, with no one to defend them. [5]Their harvests are stolen, and their wealth satisfies the thirst of many others, not themselves! [6]But evil does not spring from the soil, and trouble does not sprout from the earth. [7]People are born for trouble as predictably as sparks fly upward from a fire.

[8]"My advice to you is this: Go to God and present your case to him. [9]For he does great works too marvelous to understand. He performs miracles without number. [10]He gives rain for the earth. He sends water for the fields. [11]He gives prosperity to the poor and humble, and he takes sufferers to safety. [12]He frustrates the plans of the crafty, so their efforts will not succeed. [13]He catches those who think they are wise in their own cleverness, so that their cunning schemes are thwarted. [14]They grope in the daylight as though they were blind; they see no better in the daytime than at night. [15]He rescues the poor from the cutting words of the strong. He saves them from the clutches of the powerful. [16]And so at last the poor have hope, and the fangs of the wicked are broken.

[17]"But consider the joy of those corrected by God! Do not despise the chastening of the Almighty when you sin. [18]For though he wounds, he also bandages. He strikes, but his hands also heal. [19]He will rescue you again and again so that no evil can touch you. [20]He will save you from death in time of famine, from the power of the sword in time of war. [21]You will be safe from slander and will have no fear of destruction when it comes. [22]You will laugh at destruction and famine; wild animals will not terrify you. [23]You will be at peace with the stones of the field, and its wild animals will be at peace with you. [24]You will know that your home is kept safe. When you visit your pastures, nothing will be missing. [25]Your children will be many; your descendants will be as plentiful as grass! [26]You will live to a good old age. You will not be harvested until the proper time!

[27]"We have found from experience that all this is true. Listen to my counsel, and apply it to yourself."

CHAPTER 6

Job's Second Speech: A Response to Eliphaz

Then Job spoke again:

[2]"If my sadness could be weighed and my troubles be put on the scales, [3]they would be heavier than all the sands of the sea. That is why I spoke so rashly. [4]For the Almighty has struck me down with his arrows. He has sent his poisoned arrows deep within my spirit. All God's terrors are arrayed against me. [5]Don't I have a right to complain? Wild donkeys bray when they find no green grass, and oxen low when they have no food. [6]People complain when there is no salt in their food. And how tasteless is the uncooked white of an egg! [7]My appetite disappears when I look at it; I gag at the thought of eating it!

[8]"Oh, that I might have my request, that God would grant my hope. [9]I wish he would crush me. I wish he would reach out his hand and kill me. [10]At least I can take comfort in this: Despite the pain, I have not denied the words of the Holy One. [11]But I do not have the strength to endure. I do not have a goal that encourages me to carry on. [12]Do I have strength as hard as stone? Is my body made of bronze? [13]No, I am utterly helpless, without any chance of success.

[14]"One should be kind to a fainting friend, but you have accused me without the slightest fear of the Almighty. [15]My brother, you have proved as unreliable as a seasonal brook that overflows its banks in the spring [16]when it is swollen with ice and melting snow. [17]But when the hot weather arrives, the

water disappears. The brook vanishes in the heat. ¹⁸The caravans turn aside to be refreshed, but there is nothing there to drink, and so they perish in the desert. ¹⁹With high hopes, the caravans from Tema and from Sheba stop for water, ²⁰but finding none, their hopes are dashed. ²¹You, too, have proved to be of no help. You have seen my calamity, and you are afraid. ²²But why? Have I ever asked you for a gift? Have I begged you to use any of your wealth on my behalf? ²³Have I ever asked you to rescue me from my enemies? Have I asked you to save me from ruthless people?

²⁴"All I want is a reasonable answer—then I will keep quiet. Tell me, what have I done wrong? ²⁵Honest words are painful, but what do your criticisms amount to? ²⁶Do you think your words are convincing when you disregard my cry of desperation? ²⁷You would even send an orphan into slavery* or sell a friend. ²⁸Look at me! Would I lie to your face? ²⁹Stop assuming my guilt, for I am righteous. Don't be so unjust. ³⁰Do you think I am lying? Don't I know the difference between right and wrong?

I AM NOT QUICK to harshly criticize someone who has falsely accused me. (6:24)

CHAPTER 7

"Is this not the struggle of all humanity? A person's life is long and hard, like that of a hired hand, ²like a worker who longs for the day to end, like a servant waiting to be paid. ³I, too, have been assigned months of futility, long and weary nights of misery. ⁴When I go to bed, I think, 'When will it be morning?' But the night drags on, and I toss till dawn. ⁵My skin is filled with worms and scabs. My flesh breaks open, full of pus.

Job Cries Out to God

⁶"My days are swifter than a weaver's shuttle flying back and forth. They end without hope. ⁷O God, remember that my life is but a breath, and I will never again experience pleasure. ⁸You see me now, but not for long. Your eyes will be on me, but I will be dead. ⁹Just as a cloud dissipates and vanishes, those who die will not come back. ¹⁰They are gone forever from their home—never to be seen again.

I PRAY to God when my suffering is intense. (7:7)

¹¹"I cannot keep from speaking. I must express my anguish. I must complain in my bitterness. ¹²Am I a sea monster that you place a guard on me? ¹³If I think, 'My bed will comfort me, and I will try to forget my misery with sleep,' ¹⁴you shatter me with dreams. You terrify me with visions. ¹⁵I would rather die of strangulation than go on and on like this. ¹⁶I hate my life. I do not want to go on living. Oh, leave me alone for these few remaining days.

I MAY GIVE full expression to my anguish, but I will never curse God. (7:11)

I MAY LONG for death when my pain is great, but I will never take my life. (7:15)

¹⁷"What are mere mortals, that you should make so much of us? ¹⁸For you examine us every morning and test us every moment. ¹⁹Why won't you leave me alone—even for a moment*? ²⁰Have I sinned? What have I done to you, O watcher of all humanity? Why have you made me your target? Am I a burden to you? ²¹Why not just pardon my sin and take away my guilt? For soon I will lie down in the dust and die. When you look for me, I will be gone."

I THANK God that he has pardoned my sin and taken away my guilt. (7:21)

CHAPTER 8

Bildad's First Response to Job

Then Bildad the Shuhite replied to Job:

²"How long will you go on like this? Your words are a blustering wind. ³Does God twist justice? Does the Almighty twist what is right? ⁴Your children obviously sinned against him, so their punishment was well deserved. ⁵But if you pray to God and seek the favor of the Almighty, ⁶if you are pure and live with complete integrity, he will rise up and restore your happy home. ⁷And though you started with little, you will end with much.

⁸"Just ask the former generation. Pay attention to the experience of our ancestors. ⁹For we were born but yesterday and know so little. Our days on earth

I REFRAIN from arguing with someone who is suffering. (8:2)

I LEARN from experience and counsel—and trust most what God himself says in his Word. (8:8)

6:27 Hebrew *even gamble over an orphan.*   7:19 Hebrew *long enough to swallow my spittle.*

are as transient as a shadow. ¹⁰But those who came before us will teach you. They will teach you from the wisdom of former generations.

¹¹"Can papyrus reeds grow where there is no marsh? Can bulrushes flourish where there is no water? ¹²While they are still flowering, not ready to be cut, they begin to wither. ¹³Such is the fate of all who forget God. The hope of the godless comes to nothing. ¹⁴Everything they count on will collapse. They are leaning on a spiderweb. ¹⁵They cling to their home for security, but it won't last. They try to hold it fast, but it will not endure. ¹⁶The godless seem so strong, like a lush plant growing in the sunshine, its branches spreading across the garden. ¹⁷Its roots grow down through a pile of rocks to hold it firm. ¹⁸But when it is uprooted, it isn't even missed! ¹⁹That is the end of its life, and others spring up from the earth to replace it.

²⁰"But look! God will not reject a person of integrity, nor will he make evildoers prosper. ²¹He will yet fill your mouth with laughter and your lips with shouts of joy. ²²Those who hate you will be clothed with shame, and the tent of the wicked will be destroyed."

CHAPTER 9

Job's Third Speech: A Response to Bildad
Then Job spoke again:

²"Yes, I know this is all true in principle. But how can a person be declared innocent in the eyes of God? ³If someone wanted to take God to court,* would it be possible to answer him even once in a thousand times? ⁴For God is so wise and so mighty. Who has ever challenged him successfully?

⁵"Without warning, he moves the mountains, overturning them in his anger. ⁶He shakes the earth from its place, and its foundations tremble. ⁷If he commands it, the sun won't rise and the stars won't shine. ⁸He alone has spread out the heavens and marches on the waves of the sea. ⁹He made all the stars—the Bear, Orion, the Pleiades, and the constellations of the southern sky. ¹⁰His great works are too marvelous to understand. He performs miracles without number.

¹¹"Yet when he comes near, I cannot see him. When he moves on, I do not see him go. ¹²If he sends death to snatch someone away, who can stop him? Who dares to ask him, 'What are you doing?' ¹³And God does not restrain his anger. The mightiest forces against him* are crushed beneath his feet.

¹⁴"And who am I, that I should try to answer God or even reason with him? ¹⁵Even if I were innocent, I would have no defense. I could only plead for mercy. ¹⁶And even if I summoned him and he responded, he would never listen to me. ¹⁷For he attacks me without reason,* and he multiplies my wounds without cause. ¹⁸He will not let me catch my breath, but fills me instead with bitter sorrows. ¹⁹As for strength, he has it. As for justice, who can challenge him? ²⁰Though I am innocent, my own mouth would pronounce me guilty. Though I am blameless, it* would prove me wicked.

²¹"I am innocent, but it makes no difference to me—I despise my life. ²²Innocent or wicked, it is all the same to him. That is why I say, 'He destroys both the blameless and the wicked.' ²³He laughs when a plague suddenly kills the innocent. ²⁴The whole earth is in the hands of the wicked, and God blinds the eyes of the judges and lets them be unfair. If not he, then who?

²⁵"My life passes more swiftly than a runner. It flees away, filled with tragedy. ²⁶It disappears like a swift boat, like an eagle that swoops down on its prey. ²⁷If I decided to forget my complaints, if I decided to end my sadness and be cheerful, ²⁸I would dread all the pain he would send. For I know you will not hold me innocent, O God. ²⁹Whatever happens, I will be found

---

I BELIEVE God offers hope to those who are suffering. (8:21)

I KNOW I cannot be declared innocent before God on my own. (9:2)

I BELIEVE God is infinitely wise and almighty. (9:4)

I BELIEVE God's works are too marvelous to fully understand. (9:10)

I DO NOT BELIEVE God allows pain in my life for no reason. (9:17)

I DO NOT BELIEVE innocence and wickedness are the same to God. (9:22)

I DO NOT BELIEVE God perverts justice throughout the earth. (9:24)

I AM NOT FATALISTIC— convinced that God is somehow out to ruin me. (9:25)

9:3 Or *If God wanted to take a person to court.*   9:13 Hebrew *The helpers of Rahab,* the name of a mythical sea monster that represents chaos in ancient literature.   9:17 As in Syriac version; Hebrew reads *with a storm.*
9:20 Or *he.*

guilty. So what's the use of trying? ³⁰Even if I were to wash myself with soap and cleanse my hands with lye to make them absolutely clean, ³¹you would plunge me into a muddy ditch, and I would be so filthy my own clothing would hate me.

³²"God is not a mortal like me, so I cannot argue with him or take him to trial. ³³If only there were a mediator who could bring us together, but there is none. ³⁴The mediator could make God stop beating me, and I would no longer live in terror of his punishment. ³⁵Then I could speak to him without fear, but I cannot do that in my own strength.

I THANK the Lord Jesus for being my mediator (1 Timothy 2:5). (9:33)

CHAPTER 10

Job Frames His Plea to God

"I am disgusted with my life. Let me complain freely. I will speak in the bitterness of my soul. ²I will say to God, 'Don't simply condemn me—tell me the charge you are bringing against me. ³What do you gain by oppressing me? Why do you reject me, the work of your own hands, while sending joy and prosperity to the wicked? ⁴Are your eyes only those of a human? Do you see things as people see them? ⁵Is your lifetime merely human? Is your life so short ⁶that you are in a hurry to probe for my guilt, to search for my sin? ⁷Although you know I am not guilty, no one can rescue me from your power.

I LONG to know the charge God seems to be bringing against me when I suffer terribly. (10:2)

⁸" 'You formed me with your hands; you made me, and yet you completely destroy me. ⁹Remember that I am made of dust—will you turn me back to dust so soon? ¹⁰You guided my conception and formed me in the womb.* ¹¹You clothed me with skin and flesh, and you knit my bones and sinews together. ¹²You gave me life and showed me your unfailing love. My life was preserved by your care.

I BELIEVE God gave me life from my conception and showed me his unfailing love. (10:12)

¹³" 'Yet your real motive—I know this was your intent—¹⁴was to watch me, and if I sinned, you would not forgive my iniquity. ¹⁵If I am guilty, too bad for me. And even if I'm innocent, I am filled with shame and misery so that I can't hold my head high. ¹⁶And if I hold my head high, you hunt me like a lion and display your awesome power against me. ¹⁷Again and again you witness against me. You pour out an ever-increasing volume of anger upon me and bring fresh armies against me.

I DO NOT JUDGE God or his motives when it seems that I am suffering without cause. (10:13)

¹⁸" 'Why, then, did you bring me out of my mother's womb? Why didn't you let me die at birth? ¹⁹Then I would have been spared this miserable existence. I would have gone directly from the womb to the grave. ²⁰I have only a little time left, so leave me alone—that I may have a little moment of comfort ²¹before I leave for the land of darkness and utter gloom, never to return. ²²It is a land as dark as midnight, a land of utter gloom where confusion reigns and the light is as dark as midnight.' "

I MAY CURSE the day of my birth if my suffering is intense, but I will never curse God. (10:18)

CHAPTER 11

Zophar's First Response to Job

Then Zophar the Naamathite replied to Job:

²"Shouldn't someone answer this torrent of words? Is a person proved innocent just by talking a lot? ³Should I remain silent while you babble on? When you mock God, shouldn't someone make you ashamed? ⁴You claim, 'My teaching is pure,' and 'I am clean in the sight of God.' ⁵If only God would speak; if only he would tell you what he thinks! ⁶If only he would tell you the secrets of wisdom, for true wisdom is not a simple matter. Listen! God is doubtless punishing you far less than you deserve!

I REFRAIN from arguing with or shaming someone who is suffering. (11:2)

⁷"Can you solve the mysteries of God? Can you discover everything there is to know about the Almighty? ⁸Such knowledge is higher than the heavens—but who are you? It is deeper than the underworld*—what can you

I BELIEVE God knows far more than I will ever understand (Romans 11:33). (11:7)

10:10 Hebrew *You poured me out like milk and curdled me like cheese.* 11:8 Hebrew *Sheol.*

know in comparison to him? ⁹It is broader than the earth and wider than the sea. ¹⁰If God comes along and puts a person in prison, or if he calls the court to order, who is going to stop him? ¹¹For he knows those who are false, and he takes note of all their sins. ¹²An empty-headed person won't become wise any more than a wild donkey can bear human offspring*!

¹³"If only you would prepare your heart and lift up your hands to him in prayer! ¹⁴Get rid of your sins and leave all iniquity behind you. ¹⁵Then your face will brighten in innocence. You will be strong and free of fear. ¹⁶You will forget your misery. It will all be gone like water under the bridge. ¹⁷Your life will be brighter than the noonday. Any darkness will be as bright as morning. ¹⁸You will have courage because you will have hope. You will be protected and will rest in safety. ¹⁹You will lie down unafraid, and many will look to you for help. ²⁰But the wicked will lose hope. They have no escape. Their hope becomes despair."

CHAPTER 12

Job's Fourth Speech: A Response to Zophar

Then Job spoke again:

²"You really know everything, don't you? And when you die, wisdom will die with you! ³Well, I know a few things myself—and you're no better than I am. Who doesn't know these things you've been saying? ⁴Yet my friends laugh at me. I am a man who calls on God and receives an answer. I am a just and blameless man, yet they laugh at me. ⁵People who are at ease mock those in trouble. They give a push to people who are stumbling. ⁶But even robbers are left in peace, and those who provoke God—and God has them in his power—live in safety!

⁷"Ask the animals, and they will teach you. Ask the birds of the sky, and they will tell you. ⁸Speak to the earth, and it will instruct you. Let the fish of the sea speak to you. ⁹They all know that the LORD has done this. ¹⁰For the life of every living thing is in his hand, and the breath of all humanity. ¹¹Just as the mouth tastes good food, so the ear tests the words it hears. ¹²Wisdom belongs to the aged, and understanding to those who have lived many years.

¹³"But true wisdom and power are with God; counsel and understanding are his. ¹⁴What he destroys cannot be rebuilt. When he closes in on someone, there is no escape. ¹⁵If he holds back the rain, the earth becomes a desert. If he releases the waters, they flood the earth.

¹⁶"Yes, strength and wisdom are with him; deceivers and deceived are both in his power. ¹⁷He leads counselors away stripped of good judgment; he drives judges to madness. ¹⁸He removes the royal robe of kings. With ropes around their waist, they are led away. ¹⁹He leads priests away stripped of status; he overthrows the mighty. ²⁰He silences the trusted adviser, and he removes the insight of the elders. ²¹He pours disgrace upon princes and confiscates weapons from the strong.

²²"He floods the darkness with light; he brings light to the deepest gloom. ²³He raises up nations, and he destroys them. He makes nations expand, and he abandons them. ²⁴He takes away the understanding of kings, and he leaves them wandering in a wasteland without a path. ²⁵They grope in the darkness without a light. He makes them stagger like drunkards.

CHAPTER 13

Job Wants to Argue His Case with God

"Look, I have seen many instances such as you describe. I understand what you are saying. ²I know as much as you do. You are no better than I am. ³Oh, how I long to speak directly to the Almighty. I want to argue my case with

*Sidebar notes (left margin):*

I BELIEVE God knows who are false and takes note of their sins. (11:11)

I HOPE in God and take courage. (11:18)

I DO NOT BELIEVE God perverts justice. (12:6)

I BELIEVE the life of every living thing is in God's hand. (12:10)

I LEARN from experience and counsel—and trust most what God himself says in his Word. (12:12)

I BELIEVE strength and wisdom are God's to give and to take away. (12:16)

11:12 Or *bear a tame colt.*

God himself. ⁴For you are smearing me with lies. As doctors, you are worth-less quacks. ⁵Please be quiet! That's the smartest thing you could do. ⁶Listen to my charge; pay attention to my arguments.

⁷"Are you defending God by means of lies and dishonest arguments? ⁸You should be impartial witnesses, but will you slant your testimony in his favor? Will you argue God's case for him? ⁹Be careful that he doesn't find out what you are doing! Or do you think you can fool him as easily as you fool people? ¹⁰No, you will be in serious trouble with him if even in your hearts you slant your testimony in his favor. ¹¹Doesn't his majesty strike terror into your heart? Does not your fear of him seize you? ¹²Your statements have about as much value as ashes. Your defense is as fragile as a clay pot.

¹³"Be silent now and leave me alone. Let me speak—and I will face the consequences. ¹⁴Yes, I will take my life in my hands and say what I really think. ¹⁵God might kill me, but I cannot wait. I am going to argue my case with him. ¹⁶But this is what will save me: that I am not godless. If I were, I would be thrown from his presence.

¹⁷"Listen closely to what I am about to say. Hear me out. ¹⁸I have prepared my case; I will be proved innocent. ¹⁹Who can argue with me over this? If you could prove me wrong, I would remain silent until I die.

Job Asks How He Has Sinned

²⁰"O God, there are two things I beg of you, and I will be able to face you. ²¹Remove your hand from me, and don't terrify me with your awesome presence. ²²Now summon me, and I will answer! Or let me speak to you, and you reply. ²³Tell me, what have I done wrong? Show me my rebellion and my sin. ²⁴Why do you turn away from me? Why do you consider me your enemy? ²⁵Would you terrify a leaf that is blown by the wind? Would you chase a dry stalk of grass?

²⁶"You write bitter accusations against me and bring up all the sins of my youth. ²⁷You put my feet in stocks. You watch all my paths. You trace all my footprints. ²⁸I waste away like rotting wood, like a moth-eaten coat.

CHAPTER 14

"How frail is humanity! How short is life, and how full of trouble! ²Like a flower, we blossom for a moment and then wither. Like the shadow of a pass-ing cloud, we quickly disappear. ³Must you keep an eye on such a frail crea-ture and demand an accounting from me? ⁴Who can create purity in one born impure? No one! ⁵You have decided the length of our lives. You know how many months we will live, and we are not given a minute longer. ⁶So give us a little rest, won't you? Turn away your angry stare. We are like hired hands, so let us finish the task you have given us.

⁷"If a tree is cut down, there is hope that it will sprout again and grow new branches. ⁸Though its roots have grown old in the earth and its stump decays, ⁹at the scent of water it may bud and sprout again like a new seedling.

¹⁰"But when people die, they lose all strength. They breathe their last, and then where are they? ¹¹As water evaporates from a lake and as a river disap-pears in drought, ¹²people lie down and do not rise again. Until the heavens are no more, they will not wake up nor be roused from their sleep.

¹³"I wish you would hide me with the dead and forget me there until your anger has passed. But mark your calendar to think of me again! ¹⁴If mortals die, can they live again? This thought would give me hope, and through my struggle I would eagerly wait for release. ¹⁵You would call and I would an-swer, and you would yearn for me, your handiwork. ¹⁶For then you would count my steps, instead of watching for my sins. ¹⁷My sins would be sealed in a pouch, and you would cover over my iniquity.

¹⁸"But as mountains fall and crumble and as rocks fall from a cliff, ¹⁹as water

---

I DO NOT SMEAR others with lies. (13:4)

I DO NOT TRY to defend God by means of lies and dishonest arguments. (13:7)

I AM SAVED by trusting Jesus Christ, who died to take away my sins (Romans 4:24-25). (13:16)

I LONG to know if my sin has caused my suffering. (13:23)

I DO NOT PRESUME that God is accusing me or punishing me for my sin just because I am suffering. (13:26)

I BELIEVE life is frail—so quickly over. (14:1)

I AM MADE PURE in God's eyes because I trust Jesus Christ to take away my sins (Romans 5:8-10). (14:4)

I DO NOT LIVE in dread that God is angry with me (1 Thessalonians 5:9). (14:13)

I HAVE hope because of the promise of resurrection and eternal life in Jesus Christ (Romans 5:20-21). (14:14)

I BELIEVE only the wicked and unbelieving are punished after death (Romans 2:5-8). (14:22)

I REFRAIN from arguing with someone who is suffering. (15:2)

I AM NOT QUICK to suggest that someone is suffering because of personal sin. (15:5)

I AM THANKFUL for God's comfort. (15:11)

I WILL NEVER TURN against God. (15:13)

I AM MADE PURE in God's eyes because I have trusted Jesus Christ to take away my sins. (Romans 6:22-23). (15:14)

I LEARN from experience and counsel—and trust most what God himself says in his Word. (15:17)

I ABHOR the thought of clenching my fists against God. (15:25)

wears away the stones and floods wash away the soil, so you destroy people's hope. [20]You always overpower them, and then they pass from the scene. You disfigure them in death and send them away. [21]They never know if their sons grow up in honor or sink to insignificance. [22]They are absorbed in their own pain and grief."

CHAPTER 15

Eliphaz's Second Response to Job

Then Eliphaz the Temanite replied:

[2]"You are supposed to be a wise man, and yet you give us all this foolish talk. You are nothing but a windbag. [3]It isn't right to speak so foolishly. What good do such words do? [4]Have you no fear of God, no reverence for him? [5]Your sins are telling your mouth what to say. Your words are based on clever deception. [6]But why should I condemn you? Your own mouth does!

[7]"Were you the first person ever born? Were you born before the hills were made? [8]Were you listening at God's secret council? Do you have a monopoly on wisdom? [9]What do you know that we don't? What do you understand that we don't? [10]On our side are aged, gray-haired men much older than your father!

[11]"Is God's comfort too little for you? Is his gentle word not enough? [12]What has captured your reason? What has weakened your vision, [13]that you turn against God and say all these evil things? [14]Can a mortal be pure? Can a human be just? [15]Why, God doesn't even trust the angels*! Even the heavens cannot be absolutely pure in his sight. [16]How much less pure is a corrupt and sinful person with a thirst for wickedness!

[17]"If you will listen, I will answer you from my own experience. [18]And it is confirmed by the experience of wise men who have heard the same thing from their fathers, [19]those to whom the land was given long before any foreigners arrived.

[20]"Wicked people are in pain throughout their lives. [21]They are surrounded by terrors, and even on good days they fear the attack of the destroyer. [22]They dare not go out into the darkness for fear they will be murdered. [23]They wander abroad for bread, saying, 'Where is it?'* They know their ruin is certain. [24]That dark day terrifies them. They live in distress and anguish, like a king preparing for an attack. [25]For they have clenched their fists against God, defying the Almighty. [26]Holding their strong shields, they defiantly charge against him.

[27]"These wicked people are fat and rich, [28]but their cities will be ruined. They will live in abandoned houses that are ready to tumble down. [29]They will not continue to be rich. Their wealth will not endure, and their possessions will no longer spread across the horizon.

[30]"They will not escape the darkness. The flame will burn them up, and the breath of God will destroy everything they have. [31]Let them no longer trust in empty riches. They are only fooling themselves, for emptiness will be their only reward. [32]They will be cut down in the prime of life, and all they counted on will disappear. [33]They will be like a vine whose grapes are harvested before they are ripe, like an olive tree that sheds its blossoms so the fruit cannot form. [34]For the godless are barren. Their homes, enriched through bribery, will be consumed by fire. [35]They conceive trouble and evil, and their hearts give birth only to deceit."

CHAPTER 16

Job's Fifth Speech: A Response to Eliphaz

Then Job spoke again:

[2]"I have heard all this before. What miserable comforters you are! [3]Won't you ever stop your flow of foolish words? What have I said that makes you

Recommit yourself to loving the Lord with all your heart, soul, strength, and mind.

15:15 Hebrew *the holy ones.*   15:23 Greek version reads *He is appointed to be food for a vulture.*

speak so endlessly? ⁴I could say the same things if you were in my place. I could spout off my criticisms against you and shake my head at you. ⁵But that's not what I would do. I would speak in a way that helps you. I would try to take away your grief. ⁶But as it is, my grief remains no matter how I defend myself. And it does not help if I refuse to speak.

⁷"O God, you have ground me down and devastated my family. ⁸You have reduced me to skin and bones—as proof, they say, of my sins. ⁹God hates me and tears angrily at my flesh. He gnashes his teeth at me and pierces me with his eyes. ¹⁰People jeer and laugh at me. They slap my cheek in contempt. A mob gathers against me. ¹¹God has handed me over to sinners. He has tossed me into the hands of the wicked.

¹²"I was living quietly until he broke me apart. He took me by the neck and dashed me to pieces. Then he set me up as his target. ¹³His archers surrounded me, and his arrows pierced me without mercy. The ground is wet with my blood.* ¹⁴Again and again he smashed me, charging at me like a warrior. ¹⁵Here I sit in sackcloth. I have surrendered, and I sit in the dust. ¹⁶My eyes are red with weeping; darkness covers my eyes. ¹⁷Yet I am innocent, and my prayer is pure.

¹⁸"O earth, do not conceal my blood. Let it cry out on my behalf. ¹⁹Even now my witness is in heaven. My advocate is there on high. ²⁰My friends scorn me, but I pour out my tears to God. ²¹Oh, that someone would mediate between God and me, as a person mediates between friends. ²²For soon I must go down that road from which I will never return.

CHAPTER 17

Job Continues to Defend His Innocence

"My spirit is crushed, and I am near death. The grave is ready to receive me. ²I am surrounded by mockers. I watch how bitterly they taunt me.

³"You must defend my innocence, O God, since no one else will stand up for me. ⁴You have closed their minds to understanding, but do not let them triumph. ⁵They denounce their companions for their own advantage, so let their children faint with hunger.

⁶"God has made a mockery of me among the people; they spit in my face. ⁷My eyes are dim with weeping, and I am but a shadow of my former self. ⁸The upright are astonished when they see me. The innocent are aroused against the ungodly. ⁹The righteous will move onward and forward, and those with pure hearts will become stronger and stronger.

¹⁰"As for all of you, come back and try again! But I will not find a wise man among you. ¹¹My days are over. My hopes have disappeared. My heart's desires are broken. ¹²They say that night is day and day is night; how they pervert the truth! ¹³I might go to the grave and make my bed in darkness. ¹⁴And I might call the grave my father, and the worm my mother and my sister. ¹⁵But where then is my hope? Can anyone find it? ¹⁶No, my hope will go down with me to the grave. We will rest together in the dust!"

CHAPTER 18

Bildad's Second Response to Job

Then Bildad the Shuhite replied:

²"How long before you stop talking? Speak sense if you want us to answer! ³Do you think we are cattle? Do you think we have no intelligence? ⁴You may tear your hair out in anger, but will that cause the earth to be abandoned? Will it make rocks fall from a cliff?

⁵"The truth remains that the light of the wicked will be snuffed out. The sparks of their fire will not glow. ⁶The light in their tent will grow dark. The

I REFRAIN from arguing with someone who is suffering. (16:5)

I DO NOT ACCUSE God of hating me or maliciously attacking me. (16:9)

I LOOK to the Lord Jesus to be my advocate before God the Father (1 John 2:1). (16:19)

I KNOW I need the Lord Jesus to be my mediator (1 Timothy 2:5). (16:21)

I LOOK to God to defend my innocence when others accuse me of suffering for my sin. (17:3)

I DO NOT GIVE UP hope in God, no matter how grave my circumstances. (17:16)

I REFRAIN from arguing with someone who is suffering. (18:2)

16:13 Hebrew *my gall.*

I BELIEVE the schemes of the wicked will be their downfall. (18:7)

I BELIEVE the schemes of the wicked will be their downfall. (18:7)

I BELIEVE God's judgment of the wicked will be terrible. (18:15)

I BELIEVE God's judgment is for those who reject him, not for those who follow him. (18:21)

I DO NOT ACCUSE God of wronging me. (19:6)

I DO NOT ACCUSE God of maliciously attacking me. (19:8)

I DO NOT AVOID relatives or friends when calamity strikes them. (19:13)

I KNOW that my Redeemer lives (John 20:1-31). (19:25)

I HAVE great hope because of the resurrection promise that I will see God! (1 Corinthians 15:42-58). (19:26)

lamp hanging above them will be quenched. ⁷The confident stride of the wicked will be shortened. Their own schemes will be their downfall.

⁸"The wicked walk into a net. They fall into a pit that's been dug in the path. ⁹A trap grabs them by the heel. A noose tightens around them. ¹⁰A snare lies hidden in the ground. A rope lies coiled on their path.

¹¹"Terrors surround the wicked and trouble them at every step. ¹²Their vigor is depleted by hunger, and calamity waits for them to stumble. ¹³Disease eats their skin; death devours their limbs. ¹⁴They are torn from the security of their tent, and they are brought down to the king of terrors. ¹⁵The home of the wicked will disappear beneath a fiery barrage of burning sulfur. ¹⁶Their roots will dry up, and their branches will wither. ¹⁷All memory of their existence will perish from the earth. No one will remember them. ¹⁸They will be thrust from light into darkness, driven from the world. ¹⁹They will have neither children nor grandchildren, nor any survivor in their home country. ²⁰People in the west are appalled at their fate; people in the east are horrified. ²¹They will say, 'This was the home of a wicked person, the place of one who rejected God.' "

CHAPTER 19

Job's Sixth Speech: A Response to Bildad

Then Job spoke again:

²"How long will you torture me? How long will you try to break me with your words? ³Ten times now you have meant to insult me. You should be ashamed of dealing with me so harshly. ⁴And even if I have sinned, that is my concern, not yours. ⁵You are trying to overcome me, using my humiliation as evidence of my sin, ⁶but it is God who has wronged me. I cannot defend myself, for I am like a city under siege.

⁷"I cry out for help, but no one hears me. I protest, but there is no justice. ⁸God has blocked my way and plunged my path into darkness. ⁹He has stripped me of my honor and removed the crown from my head. ¹⁰He has demolished me on every side, and I am finished. He has destroyed my hope. ¹¹His fury burns against me; he counts me as an enemy. ¹²His troops advance. They build up roads to attack me. They camp all around my tent.

¹³"My relatives stay far away, and my friends have turned against me. ¹⁴My neighbors and my close friends are all gone. ¹⁵The members of my household have forgotten me. The servant girls consider me a stranger. I am like a foreigner to them. ¹⁶I call my servant, but he doesn't come; I even plead with him! ¹⁷My breath is repulsive to my wife. I am loathsome to my own family. ¹⁸Even young children despise me. When I stand to speak, they turn their backs on me. ¹⁹My close friends abhor me. Those I loved have turned against me. ²⁰I have been reduced to skin and bones and have escaped death by the skin of my teeth.

²¹"Have mercy on me, my friends, have mercy, for the hand of God has struck me. ²²Why must you persecute me as God does? Why aren't you satisfied with my anguish?

²³"Oh, that my words could be written. Oh, that they could be inscribed on a monument, ²⁴carved with an iron chisel and filled with lead, engraved forever in the rock.

²⁵"But as for me, I know that my Redeemer lives, and that he will stand upon the earth at last. ²⁶And after my body has decayed, yet in my body I will see God*! ²⁷I will see him for myself. Yes, I will see him with my own eyes. I am overwhelmed at the thought!

²⁸"How dare you go on persecuting me, saying, 'It's his own fault'? ²⁹I warn you, you yourselves are in danger of punishment for your attitude. Then you will know that there is judgment."

19:26 Or *without my body I will see God.*

CHAPTER 20

Zophar's Second Response to Job

Then Zophar the Naamathite replied:

²"I must reply because I am greatly disturbed. ³I have had to endure your insults, but now my spirit prompts me to reply.

⁴"Don't you realize that ever since people were first placed on the earth, ⁵the triumph of the wicked has been short-lived and the joy of the godless has been only temporary? ⁶Though the godless man's pride reaches to the heavens and though his head touches the clouds, ⁷yet he will perish forever, thrown away like his own dung. Those who knew him will ask, 'Where is he?' ⁸He will fade like a dream and not be found. He will vanish like a vision in the night. ⁹Neither his friends nor his family will ever see him again. ¹⁰His children will beg from the poor, for he must give back his ill-gotten wealth. ¹¹He was just a young man, but his bones will lie in the dust.

¹²"He enjoyed the taste of his wickedness, letting it melt under his tongue. ¹³He savored it, holding it long in his mouth. ¹⁴But suddenly, the food he has eaten turns sour within him, a poisonous venom in his stomach. ¹⁵He will vomit the wealth he swallowed. God won't let him keep it down. ¹⁶He will suck the poison of snakes. The viper will kill him. ¹⁷He will never again enjoy abundant streams of olive oil or rivers of milk and honey. ¹⁸His labors will not be rewarded. His wealth will bring him no joy. ¹⁹For he oppressed the poor and left them destitute. He foreclosed on their homes. ²⁰He was always greedy but never satisfied. Of all the things he dreamed about, nothing remains. ²¹Nothing is left after he finishes gorging himself; therefore, his prosperity will not endure.

²²"In the midst of plenty, he will run into trouble, and disasters will destroy him. ²³May God give him a bellyful of trouble. May God rain down his anger upon him. ²⁴He will try to escape, but God's arrow will pierce him. ²⁵The arrow is pulled from his body, and the arrowhead glistens with blood.* The terrors of death are upon him.

²⁶"His treasures will be lost in deepest darkness. A wildfire will devour his goods, consuming all he has left. ²⁷The heavens will reveal his guilt, and the earth will give testimony against him. ²⁸A flood will sweep away his house. God's anger will descend on him in torrents. ²⁹This is the fate that awaits the wicked. It is the inheritance decreed by God."

CHAPTER 21

Job's Seventh Speech: A Response to Zophar

Then Job spoke again:

²"Listen closely to what I am saying. You can console me by listening to me. ³Bear with me, and let me speak. After I have spoken, you may mock me.

⁴"My complaint is with God, not with people. No wonder I'm so impatient. ⁵Look at me and be stunned. Put your hand over your mouth in shock. ⁶When I think about what I am saying, I shudder. My body trembles.

⁷"The truth is that the wicked live to a good old age. They grow old and wealthy. ⁸They live to see their children grow to maturity, and they enjoy their grandchildren. ⁹Their homes are safe from every fear, and God does not punish them. ¹⁰Their bulls never fail to breed. Their cows bear calves without miscarriage. ¹¹Their children skip about like lambs in a flock of sheep. ¹²They sing with tambourine and harp. They make merry to the sound of the flute. ¹³They spend their days in prosperity; then they go down to the grave in peace. ¹⁴All this, even though they say to God, 'Go away. We want no part of you and your ways.¹⁵Who is the Almighty, and why should we obey him?

I REFRAIN from arguing with someone who is suffering. (20:2)

I BELIEVE the triumph of the wicked is temporary, but that does not mean that everyone who suffers is sinful. (20:5)

I BELIEVE the wicked will perish forever. (20:7)

I BELIEVE the prosperity of the wicked will not last. (20:21)

I BELIEVE the wicked will not escape God's coming judgment. (20:24)

I DO NOT COMPLAIN against God. (21:4)

I RECOGNIZE that the wicked sometimes avoid punishment here on earth. (21:9)

20:25 Hebrew *with gall.*

I WILL HAVE nothing to do with godless thinking that questions obeying God. (21:16)

I DO NOT FAULT God for the apparent prosperity of the wicked. (21:17)

I BELIEVE God is the supreme Judge (Romans 11:34). (21:22)

I RECOGNIZE that evil people sometimes escape the calamity they deserve. (21:28)

I DO NOT MAKE UP explanations when I do not understand another person's suffering. (21:34)

I REFRAIN from arguing with someone who is suffering. (22:2)

I DO NOT FALSELY ACCUSE someone of sin in order to explain suffering. (22:5)

I DO NOT MAKE UP charges against someone else to "prove" he or she is wicked. (22:6)

I BELIEVE God is higher than the heavens. (22:12)

I DO NOT QUARREL with God. (22:21)

I LISTEN to God's commands and store them in my heart. (22:22)

What good will it do us if we pray?' ¹⁶But their prosperity is not of their own doing, so I will have nothing to do with that kind of thinking.

¹⁷"Yet the wicked get away with it time and time again. They rarely have trouble, and God skips them when he distributes sorrows in his anger. ¹⁸Are they driven before the wind like straw? Are they carried away by the storm? Not at all!

¹⁹" 'Well,' you say, 'at least God will punish their children!' But I say that God should punish the ones who sin, not their children! Let them feel their own penalty. ²⁰Let their own eyes see their destruction. Let them drink deeply of the anger of the Almighty. ²¹For when they are dead, they will not care what happens to their family.

²²"But who can teach a lesson to God, the supreme Judge? ²³One person dies in prosperity and security, ²⁴the very picture of good health. ²⁵Another person dies in bitter poverty, never having tasted the good life. ²⁶Both alike are buried in the same dust, both eaten by the same worms.

²⁷"Look, I know your thoughts. I know the schemes you plot against me. ²⁸You will tell me of rich and wicked people who came to disaster because of their sins. ²⁹But I tell you to ask those who have been around, and they can tell you the truth. ³⁰Evil people are spared in times of calamity and are allowed to escape. ³¹No one rebukes them openly. No one repays them for what they have done. ³²When they are carried to the grave, an honor guard keeps watch at their tomb. ³³A great funeral procession goes to the cemetery. Many pay their respects as the body is laid to rest and the earth gives sweet repose.

³⁴"How can you comfort me? All your explanations are wrong!"

CHAPTER 22

Eliphaz's Third Response to Job
Then Eliphaz the Temanite replied:

²"Can a person's actions be of benefit to God? Can even a wise person be helpful to him? ³Is it any pleasure to the Almighty if you are righteous? Would it be any gain to him if you were perfect? ⁴Is it because of your reverence for him that he accuses and judges you? ⁵Not at all! It is because of your wickedness! Your guilt has no limit!

⁶"For example, you must have lent money to your friend and then kept the clothing he gave you as a pledge. Yes, you stripped him to the bone. ⁷You must have refused water for the thirsty and food for the hungry. ⁸After all, you think the land belongs to the powerful and that those who are privileged have a right to it! ⁹You must have sent widows away without helping them and crushed the strength of orphans. ¹⁰That is why you are surrounded by traps and sudden fears. ¹¹That is why you cannot see in the darkness, and waves of water cover you.

¹²"God is so great—higher than the heavens, higher than the farthest stars. ¹³But you reply, 'That's why God can't see what I am doing! How can he judge through the thick darkness? ¹⁴For thick clouds swirl about him, and he cannot see us. He is way up there, walking on the vault of heaven.'

¹⁵"Will you continue on the old paths where evil people have walked? ¹⁶They were snatched away in the prime of life, and the foundations of their lives were washed away forever. ¹⁷For they said to God, 'Leave us alone! What can the Almighty do for us?' ¹⁸But they forgot that he had filled their homes with good things, so I will have nothing to do with that kind of thinking.

¹⁹"Now the righteous will be happy to see the wicked destroyed, and the innocent will laugh them to scorn. ²⁰They will say, 'Surely our enemies have been destroyed. The last of them have been consumed in the fire.'

²¹"Stop quarreling with God! If you agree with him, you will have peace at last, and things will go well for you. ²²Listen to his instructions, and store

them in your heart. ²³If you return to the Almighty and clean up your life, you will be restored. ²⁴Give up your lust for money, and throw your precious gold into the river. ²⁵Then the Almighty himself will be your treasure. He will be your precious silver!

²⁶"Then you will delight yourself in the Almighty and look up to God. ²⁷You will pray to him, and he will hear you, and you will fulfill your vows to him. ²⁸Whatever you decide to do will be accomplished, and light will shine on the road ahead of you. ²⁹If someone is brought low and you say, 'Help him up,' God will save the downcast. ³⁰Then even sinners will be rescued by your pure hands."

CHAPTER 23

Job's Eighth Speech: A Response to Eliphaz
Then Job spoke again:

²"My complaint today is still a bitter one, and I try hard not to groan aloud. ³If only I knew where to find God, I would go to his throne and talk with him there. ⁴I would lay out my case and present my arguments. ⁵Then I would listen to his reply and understand what he says to me. ⁶Would he merely argue with me in his greatness? No, he would give me a fair hearing. ⁷Fair and honest people can reason with him, so I would be acquitted by my Judge.

⁸"I go east, but he is not there. I go west, but I cannot find him. ⁹I do not see him in the north, for he is hidden. I turn to the south, but I cannot find him. ¹⁰But he knows where I am going. And when he has tested me like gold in a fire, he will pronounce me innocent.

¹¹"For I have stayed in God's paths; I have followed his ways and not turned aside. ¹²I have not departed from his commands but have treasured his word in my heart. ¹³Nevertheless, his mind concerning me remains unchanged, and who can turn him from his purposes? Whatever he wants to do, he does. ¹⁴So he will do for me all he has planned. He controls my destiny. ¹⁵No wonder I am so terrified in his presence. When I think of it, terror grips me. ¹⁶God has made my heart faint; the Almighty has terrified me. ¹⁷Darkness is all around me; thick, impenetrable darkness is everywhere.

I BELIEVE God knows exactly where I am going. (23:10)

I TREASURE God's Word in my heart and follow his commands. (23:12)

I BELIEVE God is sovereign—he does whatever he wants. (23:13)

CHAPTER 24

Job Asks Why the Wicked Are Not Punished
"Why doesn't the Almighty open the court and bring judgment? Why must the godly wait for him in vain? ²Evil people steal land by moving the boundary markers. They steal flocks of sheep, ³and they even take donkeys from the poor and fatherless. A poor widow must surrender her valuable ox as collateral for a loan. ⁴The poor are kicked aside; the needy must hide together for safety. ⁵Like the wild donkeys in the desert, the poor must spend all their time just getting enough to keep body and soul together. They go into the desert to search for food for their children. ⁶They harvest a field they do not own, and they glean in the vineyards of the wicked. ⁷All night they lie naked in the cold, without clothing or covering. ⁸They are soaked by mountain showers, and they huddle against the rocks for want of a home.

⁹"The wicked snatch a widow's child from her breast; they take the baby as a pledge for a loan. ¹⁰The poor must go about naked, without any clothing. They are forced to carry food while they themselves are starving. ¹¹They press out olive oil without being allowed to taste it, and they tread in the winepress as they suffer from thirst. ¹²The groans of the dying rise from the city, and the wounded cry for help, yet God does not respond to their moaning.

¹³"Wicked people rebel against the light. They refuse to acknowledge its ways. They will not stay in its paths. ¹⁴The murderer rises in the early dawn to kill the poor and needy; at night he is a thief. ¹⁵The adulterer waits for the twilight, for he says, 'No one will see me then.' He masks his face so no one will

I GRIEVE that so many are cruelly oppressed by the wicked. (24:2)

I KNOW God does not always immediately stop the oppression of the poor. (24:12)

know him. [16]They break into houses at night and sleep in the daytime. They are not acquainted with the light. [17]The black night is their morning. They ally themselves with the terrors of the darkness.

[18]"But they disappear from the earth as quickly as foam is swept down a river. Everything they own is cursed, so that no one enters their vineyard. [19]Death consumes sinners just as drought and heat consume snow. [20]Even the sinner's own mother will forget him. Worms will find him sweet to eat. No one will remember him. Wicked people are broken like a tree in the storm. [21]For they have taken advantage of the childless who have no protecting sons. They refuse to help the needy widows.

[22]"God, in his power, drags away the rich. They may rise high, but they have no assurance in life. [23]They may be allowed to live in security, but God is always watching them. [24]And though they are great now, in a moment they will be gone like all others, withered like heads of grain.

[25]"Can anyone claim otherwise? Who can prove me wrong?"

CHAPTER 25

Bildad's Third Response to Job

Then Bildad the Shuhite replied:

[2]"God is powerful and dreadful. He enforces peace in the heavens. [3]Who is able to count his heavenly army? Does his light not shine on all the earth? [4]How can a mere mortal stand before God and claim to be righteous? Who in all the earth is pure? [5]God is so glorious that even the moon and stars scarcely shine compared to him. [6]How much less are mere people, who are but worms in his sight?"

CHAPTER 26

Job's Ninth Speech: A Response to Bildad

Then Job spoke again:

[2]"How you have helped the powerless! How you have saved a person who has no strength! [3]How you have enlightened my stupidity! What wise things you have said! [4]Where have you gotten all these wise sayings? Whose spirit speaks through you?

[5]"The dead tremble in their place beneath the waters. [6]The underworld* is naked in God's presence. There is no cover for the place of destruction. [7]God stretches the northern sky over empty space and hangs the earth on nothing. [8]He wraps the rain in his thick clouds, and the clouds do not burst with the weight. [9]He shrouds his throne with his clouds. [10]He created the horizon when he separated the waters; he set the boundaries for day and night. [11]The foundations of heaven tremble at his rebuke. [12]By his power the sea grew calm. By his skill he crushed the great sea monster.* [13]His Spirit made the heavens beautiful, and his power pierced the gliding serpent.

[14]"These are some of the minor things he does, merely a whisper of his power. Who can understand the thunder of his power?"

CHAPTER 27

Job's Final Speech

Job continued speaking:

[2]"I make this vow by the living God, who has taken away my rights, by the Almighty who has embittered my soul. [3]As long as I live, while I have breath from God, [4]my lips will speak no evil, and my tongue will speak no lies. [5]I will never concede that you are right; until I die, I will defend my innocence. [6]I will maintain my innocence without wavering. My conscience is clear for as long as I live.

26:6 Hebrew *Sheol*.   26:12 Hebrew *Rahab*, the name of a mythical sea monster that represents chaos in ancient literature.

I BELIEVE the wicked will one day perish suddenly. (24:18)

I BELIEVE God will not forget to judge the wicked (Revelation 11–15). (24:22)

I BELIEVE God is powerful. (25:2)

I BELIEVE God is glorious. (25:5)

I BELIEVE nothing is hidden from God. (26:5)

I KNOW that what I see in heaven and earth is a mere whisper of God's power. (26:14)

I WILL KEEP my words pure and true, no matter how much I suffer. (27:4)

[7] "May my enemy be punished like the wicked, my adversary like evil men. [8] For what hope do the godless have when God cuts them off and takes away their life? [9] Will God listen to their cry when trouble comes upon them? [10] Can they take delight in the Almighty? Can they call to God at any time?

[11] "I will teach you about God's power. I will not conceal anything that concerns the Almighty. [12] But I don't need to, for you yourselves have seen all this; yet you are saying all these useless things to me.

[13] "This is what the wicked will receive from God; this is their inheritance from the Almighty. [14] If they have a multitude of children, their children will die in war or starve to death. [15] Those who survive will be brought down to the grave by a plague, with no one to mourn them, not even their wives.

[16] "Evil people may have all the money in the world, and they may store away mounds of clothing. [17] But the righteous will wear that clothing, and the innocent will divide all that money. [18] The houses built by the wicked are as fragile as a spiderweb, as flimsy as a shelter made of branches.

[19] "The wicked go to bed rich but wake up to find that all their wealth is gone. [20] Terror overwhelms them, and they are blown away in the storms of the night. [21] The east wind carries them away, and they are gone. It sweeps them away. [22] It whirls down on them without mercy. They struggle to flee from its power. [23] But everyone jeers at them and mocks them.

CHAPTER 28

Job Speaks of Wisdom and Understanding

"People know how to mine silver and refine gold. [2] They know how to dig iron from the earth and smelt copper from stone. [3] They know how to put light into darkness and explore the farthest, darkest regions of the earth as they search for ore. [4] They sink a mine shaft into the earth far from where anyone lives. They descend on ropes, swinging back and forth. [5] Bread comes from the earth, but below the surface the earth is melted as by fire.

[6] "People know how to find sapphires and gold dust—[7] treasures that no bird of prey can see, no falcon's eye observe—[8] for they are deep within the mines. No wild animal has ever walked upon those treasures; no lion has set his paw there. [9] People know how to tear apart flinty rocks and overturn the roots of mountains. [10] They cut tunnels in the rocks and uncover precious stones. [11] They dam up the trickling streams and bring to light the hidden treasures.

[12] "But do people know where to find wisdom? Where can they find understanding? [13] No one knows where to find it, for it is not found among the living. [14] 'It is not here,' says the ocean. 'Nor is it here,' says the sea.

[15] "It cannot be bought for gold or silver. [16] Its value is greater than all the gold of Ophir, greater than precious onyx stone or sapphires. [17] Wisdom is far more valuable than gold and crystal. It cannot be purchased with jewels mounted in fine gold. [18] Coral and valuable rock crystal are worthless in trying to get it. The price of wisdom is far above pearls. [19] Topaz from Ethiopia* cannot be exchanged for it. Its value is greater than the purest gold.

[20] "But do people know where to find wisdom? Where can they find understanding? [21] For it is hidden from the eyes of all humanity. Even the sharp-eyed birds in the sky cannot discover it. [22] But Destruction and Death say, 'We have heard a rumor of where wisdom can be found.'

[23] "God surely knows where it can be found, [24] for he looks throughout the whole earth, under all the heavens. [25] He made the winds blow and determined how much rain should fall. [26] He made the laws of the rain and prepared a path for the lightning. [27] Then, when he had done all this, he saw wisdom and measured it. He established it and examined it thoroughly.

28:19 Hebrew *from Cush.*

I PLACE my hope in God. (27:8)

I BELIEVE the wicked will receive great judgment from God. (27:13)

I BELIEVE the wicked have no lasting security. (27:16)

I SEARCH for wisdom with the intensity of one searching for precious jewels. (28:1)

I BELIEVE wisdom cannot be bought with gold or silver—it is far too valuable. (28:15)

I BELIEVE wisdom is hidden from most people. (28:20)

I BELIEVE God established wisdom and has examined it thoroughly. (28:27)

28And this is what he says to all humanity: 'The fear of the Lord is true wisdom; to forsake evil is real understanding.' "

CHAPTER 29

Job Speaks of His Former Blessings

Job continued speaking:

2"I long for the years gone by when God took care of me, 3when he lighted the way before me and I walked safely through the darkness. 4In my early years, the friendship of God was felt in my home. 5The Almighty was still with me, and my children were around me. 6In those days my cows produced milk in abundance, and my olive groves poured out streams of olive oil.

7"Those were the days when I went to the city gate and took my place among the honored leaders. 8The young stepped aside when they saw me, and even the aged rose in respect at my coming. 9The princes stood in silence and put their hands over their mouths. 10The highest officials of the city stood quietly, holding their tongues in respect.

11"All who heard of me praised me. All who saw me spoke well of me. 12For I helped the poor in their need and the orphans who had no one to help them. 13I helped those who had lost hope, and they blessed me. And I caused the widows' hearts to sing for joy. 14All I did was just and honest. Righteousness covered me like a robe, and I wore justice like a turban. 15I served as eyes for the blind and feet for the lame. 16I was a father to the poor and made sure that even strangers received a fair trial. 17I broke the jaws of godless oppressors and made them release their victims.

18"I thought, 'Surely I will die surrounded by my family after a long, good life. 19For I am like a tree whose roots reach the water, whose branches are refreshed with the dew. 20New honors are constantly bestowed on me, and my strength is continually renewed.'

21"Everyone listened to me and valued my advice. They were silent as they waited for me to speak. 22And after I spoke, they had nothing to add, for my counsel satisfied them. 23They longed for me to speak as they longed for rain. They waited eagerly, for my words were as refreshing as the spring rain. 24When they were discouraged, I smiled at them. My look of approval was precious to them. 25I told them what they should do and presided over them as their chief. I lived as a king among his troops and as one who comforts those who mourn.

CHAPTER 30

Job Speaks of His Anguish

"But now I am mocked by those who are younger than I, by young men whose fathers are not worthy to run with my sheepdogs. 2A lot of good they are to me—those worn-out wretches! 3They are gaunt with hunger and flee to the deserts and the wastelands, desolate and gloomy. 4They eat coarse leaves, and they burn the roots of shrubs for heat. 5They are driven from civilization, and people shout after them as if they were thieves. 6So now they live in frightening ravines and in caves and among the rocks. 7They sound like animals as they howl among the bushes; they huddle together for shelter beneath the nettles. 8They are nameless fools, outcasts of civilization.

9"And now their sons mock me with their vulgar song! They taunt me! 10They despise me and won't come near me, except to spit in my face. 11For God has cut the cords of my tent. He has humbled me, so they have thrown off all restraint. 12These outcasts oppose me to my face. They send me sprawling; they lay traps in my path. 13They block my road and do everything they can to hasten my calamity, knowing full well that I have no one to help me. 14They come at me from all directions. They rush upon me when I am down.

I BELIEVE the fear of the Lord is true wisdom—to forsake evil is real understanding (Psalm 110:10; Proverbs 1:7; 9:10). (28:28)

I BELIEVE God takes care of me. (29:2)

I CHERISH my friendship with God and make it a part of my home. (29:4)

I BELIEVE God is with me—even in the most severe trials. (29:5)

I DO what is just and honest, helping the poor and needy. (29:14)

I AM CAUTIOUS not to presume about the future. (29:18)

I REFRESH others with my words. (29:23)

I DO NOT BLAME God for my troubles. (30:11)

¹⁵I live in terror now. They hold me in contempt, and my prosperity has vanished as a cloud before a strong wind.

¹⁶"And now my heart is broken. Depression haunts my days. ¹⁷My weary nights are filled with pain as though something were relentlessly gnawing at my bones. ¹⁸With a strong hand, God grabs my garment. He grips me by the collar of my tunic. ¹⁹He has thrown me into the mud. I have become as dust and ashes.

²⁰"I cry to you, O God, but you don't answer me. I stand before you, and you don't bother to look. ²¹You have become cruel toward me. You persecute me with your great power. ²²You throw me into the whirlwind and destroy me in the storm. ²³And I know that you are sending me to my death—the destination of all who live.

²⁴"Surely no one would turn against the needy when they cry for help. ²⁵Did I not weep for those in trouble? Was I not deeply grieved for the needy? ²⁶So I looked for good, but evil came instead. I waited for the light, but darkness fell. ²⁷My heart is troubled and restless. Days of affliction have come upon me. ²⁸I walk in gloom, without sunlight. I stand in the public square and cry for help. ²⁹But instead, I am considered a brother to jackals and a companion to ostriches. ³⁰My skin has turned dark, and my bones burn with fever. ³¹My harp plays sad music, and my flute accompanies those who weep.

CHAPTER 31

Job's Final Protest of Innocence

"I made a covenant with my eyes not to look with lust upon a young woman. ²What has God above chosen for us? What is our inheritance from the Almighty on high? ³It is calamity for the wicked, misfortune for those who do evil. ⁴He sees everything I do and every step I take.

⁵"Have I lied to anyone or deceived anyone? ⁶Let God judge me on the scales of justice, for he knows my integrity. ⁷If I have strayed from his pathway, or if my heart has lusted for what my eyes have seen, or if I am guilty of any other sin, ⁸then let someone else harvest the crops I have planted, and let all that I have planted be uprooted.

⁹"If my heart has been seduced by a woman, or if I have lusted for my neighbor's wife, ¹⁰then may my wife belong to another man; may other men sleep with her. ¹¹For lust is a shameful sin, a crime that should be punished. ¹²It is a devastating fire that destroys to hell. It would wipe out everything I own.

¹³"If I have been unfair to my male or female servants, if I have refused to hear their complaints, ¹⁴how could I face God? What could I say when he questioned me about it? ¹⁵For God created both me and my servants. He created us both.

¹⁶"Have I refused to help the poor, or crushed the hopes of widows who looked to me for help? ¹⁷Have I been stingy with my food and refused to share it with hungry orphans? ¹⁸No, from childhood I have cared for orphans, and all my life I have cared for widows. ¹⁹Whenever I saw someone who was homeless and without clothes, ²⁰did they not praise me for providing wool clothing to keep them warm? ²¹If my arm has abused an orphan because I thought I could get away with it, ²²then let my shoulder be wrenched out of place! Let my arm be torn from its socket! ²³That would be better than facing the judgment sent by God. For if the majesty of God opposes me, what hope is there?

²⁴"Have I put my trust in money or felt secure because of my gold? ²⁵Does my happiness depend on my wealth and all that I own? ²⁶Have I looked at the sun shining in the skies, or the moon walking down its silver pathway, ²⁷and

I DO NOT ACCUSE God of troubling me. (30:18)

I CRY to the Lord—even if I feel he does not see or answer me. (30:20)

I BEG God to help me in my need as I have helped others who were needy. (30:24)

I HAVE MADE a covenant with my eyes not to look with lust on anyone. (31:1)

I BELIEVE God sees everything I do and every step I take, and he will judge me fairly. (31:4)

I DO NOT LIE or deceive others. (31:5)

I DO NOT LUST after what others have. (31:7)

I DO NOT TREAT unfairly those who work for me, because we are both made by God. (31:13)

I DO NOT NEGLECT the poor and needy but generously care for them. (31:16)

I DO NOT PUT my trust in riches. (31:24)

I AM NOT ENTICED to worship nature, God's creation. (31:26)

been secretly enticed in my heart to worship them? [28]If so, I should be punished by the judges, for it would mean I had denied the God of heaven.

[29]"Have I ever rejoiced when my enemies came to ruin or become excited when harm came their way? [30]No, I have never cursed anyone or asked for revenge. [31]My servants have never let others go hungry. [32]I have never turned away a stranger but have opened my doors to everyone. [33]Have I tried to hide my sins as people normally do, hiding my guilt in a closet? [34]Have I feared the crowd and its contempt, so that I refused to acknowledge my sin and would not go outside?

[35]"If only I had someone who would listen to me and try to see my side! Look, I will sign my name to my defense. Let the Almighty show me that I am wrong. Let my accuser write out the charges against me. [36]I would face the accusation proudly. I would treasure it like a crown. [37]For I would tell him exactly what I have done. I would come before him like a prince.

[38]"If my land accuses me and all its furrows weep together, [39]or if I have stolen its crops or murdered its owners, [40]then let thistles grow on that land instead of wheat and weeds instead of barley."

Job's words are ended.

CHAPTER 32

Elihu Responds to Job's Friends

Job's three friends refused to reply further to him because he kept insisting on his innocence.

Recommit yourself to loving your neighbor as yourself.

[2]Then Elihu son of Barakel the Buzite, of the clan of Ram, became angry. He was angry because Job refused to admit that he had sinned and that God was right in punishing him. [3]He was also angry with Job's three friends because they had condemned God* by their inability to answer Job's arguments. [4]Elihu had waited for the others to speak because they were older than he. [5]But when he saw that they had no further reply, he spoke out angrily.

I DO NOT INSIST that others are suffering because God is punishing them. (32:2)

I DO NOT PRESUME to know more than others about why someone suffers. (32:4)

I BELIEVE God's Spirit gives us wisdom and understanding. (32:8)

[6]Elihu son of Barakel the Buzite said, "I am young and you are old, so I held back and did not dare to tell you what I think. [7]I thought, 'Those who are older should speak, for wisdom comes with age.' [8]Surely it is God's Spirit within people, the breath of the Almighty within them, that makes them intelligent. [9]But sometimes the elders are not wise. Sometimes the aged do not understand justice. [10]So listen to me and let me express my opinion.

[11]"I have waited all this time, listening very carefully to your arguments, listening to you grope for words. [12]I have listened, but not one of you has refuted Job or answered his arguments. [13]And don't tell me, 'He is too wise for us. Only God can convince him.' [14]If Job had been arguing with me, I would not answer with that kind of logic! [15]You sit there baffled, with no further response. [16]Should I continue to wait, now that you are silent? Must I also remain silent? [17]No, I will say my piece. I will speak my mind. I surely will. [18]For I am pent up and full of words, and the spirit within me urges me on. [19]I am like a wine cask without a vent. My words are ready to burst out! [20]I must speak to find relief, so let me give my answers. [21]I won't play favorites or try to flatter anyone. [22]And if I tried, my Creator would soon do away with me.

I DO NOT ALWAYS NEED to speak my mind— especially when I am angry. (32:17)

CHAPTER 33

Elihu Presents His Case against Job

"Listen, Job, to what I have to say. [2]Now that I have begun to speak, let me continue. [3]I speak with all sincerity; I speak the truth. [4]For the Spirit of God

I DO NOT INSIST that my opinion is God's truth. (33:3)

I BELIEVE the Spirit of God has made one and all. (33:4)

32:3 As in ancient Hebrew scribal tradition; the Masoretic Text makes no reference to God.

has made me, and the breath of the Almighty gives me life. ⁵Answer me, if you can; make your case and take your stand.

⁶"Look, you and I are the same before God. I, too, was formed from clay. ⁷So you don't need to be afraid of me. I am not some great person to make you nervous and afraid.

⁸"You have said it in my hearing. I have heard your very words. ⁹You said, 'I am pure; I am innocent; I have not sinned. ¹⁰God is picking a quarrel with me, and he considers me to be his enemy. ¹¹He puts my feet in the stocks and watches every move I make.'

I DO NOT ACCUSE God of attacking me. (33:10)

¹²"In this you are not right, and I will show you why. As you yourself have said, 'God is greater than any person.' ¹³So why are you bringing a charge against him? You say, 'He does not respond to people's complaints.' ¹⁴But God speaks again and again, though people do not recognize it. ¹⁵He speaks in dreams, in visions of the night when deep sleep falls on people as they lie in bed. ¹⁶He whispers in their ear and terrifies them with his warning. ¹⁷He causes them to change their minds; he keeps them from pride. ¹⁸He keeps them from the grave, from crossing over the river of death. ¹⁹Or God disciplines people with sickness and pain, with ceaseless aching in their bones. ²⁰They lose their appetite and do not care for even the most delicious food. ²¹They waste away to skin and bones. ²²They are at death's door; the angels of death wait for them.

I BELIEVE God has spoken, but people do not recognize his words. (33:14)

I BELIEVE God sometimes disciplines people with sickness and pain. (33:19)

UNLIKE ELIHU   *I do not presume to know God's reasons.*

Job 32:10

Who's smarter? The individual who speaks up first? Or the person who gets in the last word?

Like Eliphaz, Bildad, and Zophar, Elihu was an intelligent, well-respected gentleman. And, like Bildad, Elihu was a relative of Abraham, the patriarch of the faith. Unlike Job's other friends, however, Elihu was a younger man. So, following the customs of the time, Elihu waited until the other three men had finished debating Job before he stated his own case.

As his long speech revealed, Elihu was greatly frustrated with all four other men. He was angry that Job's other three friends couldn't refute Job's claims and thus condemned God. And he was upset that Job insisted he was innocent of wrongdoing, accusing him of blasphemy against God.

Like the other men, Elihu asserted many important truths about God. But he also authoritatively presented a number of half-truths and outright errors. Apparently the others were in no mood, however, to argue with Elihu.

Interestingly, the Lord called on the other three men to repent, but not Elihu. No one knows why; maybe he ran away in terror when the Lord first appeared in Job 38:1.

No matter how smart we think we are, let's never assume we know what's on God's mind.

○ *Today's Scripture reading is Job 32–37.*

²³"But if a special messenger from heaven is there to intercede for a person, to declare that he is upright, ²⁴God will be gracious and say, 'Set him free. Do not make him die, for I have found a ransom for his life.' ²⁵Then his body will become as healthy as a child's, firm and youthful again. ²⁶When he prays to God, he will be accepted. And God will receive him with joy and restore him to good standing. ²⁷He will declare to his friends, 'I sinned, but it was not worth it. ²⁸God rescued me from the grave, and now my life is filled with light.'

I BELIEVE God gladly receives those who repent and then restores them. (33:26)

²⁹"Yes, God often does these things for people. ³⁰He rescues them from the grave so they may live in the light of the living. ³¹Mark this well, Job. Listen to me, and let me say more. ³²But if you have anything to say, go ahead. I want to hear it, for I am anxious to see you justified. ³³But if not, then listen to me. Keep silent and I will teach you wisdom!"

CHAPTER 34

Elihu Accuses Job of Arrogance

Then Elihu said:

²"Listen to me, you wise men. Pay attention, you who have knowledge. ³'Just as the mouth tastes good food, the ear tests the words it hears.' ⁴So let us discern for ourselves what is right; let us learn together what is good. ⁵For Job has said, 'I am innocent, but God has taken away my rights. ⁶I am innocent, but they call me a liar. My suffering is incurable, even though I have not sinned.'

⁷"Has there ever been a man as arrogant as Job, with his thirst for irreverent talk? ⁸He seeks the companionship of evil people. He spends his time with wicked men. ⁹He has even said, 'Why waste time trying to please God?'

¹⁰"Listen to me, you who have understanding. Everyone knows that God doesn't sin! The Almighty can do no wrong. ¹¹He repays people according to their deeds. He treats people according to their ways. ¹²There is no truer statement than this: God will not do wrong. The Almighty cannot twist justice. ¹³Who put the world in his care? Who has set the whole world in place? ¹⁴If God were to take back his spirit* and withdraw his breath, ¹⁵all life would cease, and humanity would turn again to dust.

¹⁶"Listen now and try to understand. ¹⁷Could God govern if he hated justice? Are you going to condemn the almighty Judge? ¹⁸For he says to kings and nobles, 'You are wicked and unjust.' ¹⁹He doesn't care how great a person may be, and he doesn't pay any more attention to the rich than to the poor. He made them all. ²⁰In a moment they die. At midnight they all pass away; the mighty are removed without human hand.

²¹"For God carefully watches the way people live; he sees everything they do. ²²No darkness is thick enough to hide the wicked from his eyes. ²³For it is not up to mortals to decide when to come before God in judgment. ²⁴He brings the mighty to ruin without asking anyone, and he sets up others in their places. ²⁵He watches what they do, and in the night he overturns them, destroying them. ²⁶He openly strikes them down for their wickedness. ²⁷For they turned aside from following him. They have no respect for any of his ways. ²⁸So they cause the poor to cry out, catching God's attention. Yes, he hears the cries of the needy. ²⁹When he is quiet, who can make trouble? But when he hides his face, who can find him? ³⁰He prevents the godless from ruling so they cannot be a snare to the people.

³¹"Why don't people say to God, 'I have sinned, but I will sin no more'? ³²Or 'I don't know what evil I have done; tell me, and I will stop at once'?

³³"Must God tailor his justice to your demands? But you have rejected him! The choice is yours, not mine. Go ahead, share your wisdom with us. ³⁴After all, bright people will tell me, and wise people will hear me say, ³⁵'Job speaks without knowledge; his words lack insight.' ³⁶Job, you deserve the maximum penalty for the wicked way you have talked. ³⁷For now you have added rebellion and blasphemy against God to your other sins."

CHAPTER 35

Elihu Reminds Job of God's Justice

Then Elihu said:

²"Do you think it is right for you to claim, 'I am righteous before God'? ³Yet you also ask, 'What's the use of living a righteous life? How will it benefit me?'

⁴"I will answer you and all your friends, too. ⁵Look up into the sky and see the clouds high above you. ⁶If you sin, what do you accomplish against him? Even if you sin again and again, what effect will it have on him? ⁷If you are good, is this some great gift to him? What could you possibly give him? ⁸No,

34:14 Or *his Spirit.*

I DO NOT FALSELY ACCUSE those who are suffering.

I KNOW God never sins. (34:10)

I BELIEVE God cannot and will not twist justice. (34:12)

I BELIEVE God sees everything that people do. (34:21)

I BELIEVE God hears the cries of the needy. (34:28)

I DO NOT SLANDER others or falsely accuse them of sinning against God. (34:37)

I KNOW God is never in my debt. (35:7)

your sins affect only people like yourself, and your good deeds affect only other people.

⁹"The oppressed cry out beneath the wrongs that are done to them. They groan beneath the power of the mighty. ¹⁰Yet they don't ask, 'Where is God my Creator, the one who gives songs in the night? ¹¹Where is the one who makes us wiser than the animals and birds?'

¹²"And if they do cry out and God does not answer, it is because of their pride. ¹³But it is wrong to say God doesn't listen, to say the Almighty isn't concerned. ¹⁴And it is even more false to say he doesn't see what is going on. He will bring about justice if you will only wait. ¹⁵But do you cry out against him because he does not respond in anger? ¹⁶Job, you have protested in vain. You have spoken like a fool."

CHAPTER 36

Elihu continued speaking:

²"Let me go on, and I will show you the truth of what I am saying. For I have not finished defending God! ³I will give you many illustrations of the righteousness of my Creator. ⁴I am telling you the honest truth, for I am a man of well-rounded knowledge.

⁵"God is mighty, yet he does not despise anyone! He is mighty in both power and understanding. ⁶He does not let the wicked live but gives justice to the afflicted. ⁷His eyes never leave the innocent, but he establishes and exalts them with kings forever. ⁸If troubles come upon them and they are enslaved and afflicted, ⁹he takes the trouble to show them the reason. He shows them their sins, for they have behaved proudly. ¹⁰He gets their attention and says they must turn away from evil.

¹¹"If they listen and obey God, then they will be blessed with prosperity throughout their lives. All their years will be pleasant. ¹²But if they refuse to listen to him, they will perish in battle and die from lack of understanding. ¹³For the godless are full of resentment. Even when he punishes them, they refuse to cry out to him for help. ¹⁴They die young after wasting their lives in immoral living. ¹⁵But by means of their suffering, he rescues those who suffer. For he gets their attention through adversity.

¹⁶"God has led you away from danger, giving you freedom. You have prospered in a wide and pleasant valley. ¹⁷But you are too obsessed with judgment on the godless. Don't worry, justice will be upheld. ¹⁸But watch out, or you may be seduced with wealth. Don't let yourself be bribed into sin. ¹⁹Could all your wealth and mighty efforts keep you from distress? ²⁰Do not long for the cover of night, for that is when people will be destroyed. ²¹Be on guard! Turn back from evil, for it was to prevent you from getting into a life of evil that God sent this suffering.

Elihu Reminds Job of God's Power

²²"Look, God is all-powerful. Who is a teacher like him? ²³No one can tell him what to do. No one can say to him, 'You have done wrong.' ²⁴Instead, glorify his mighty works, singing songs of praise. ²⁵Everyone has seen these things, but only from a distance.

²⁶"Look, God is exalted beyond what we can understand. His years are without number. ²⁷He draws up the water vapor and then distills it into rain. ²⁸The rain pours down from the clouds, and everyone benefits from it. ²⁹Can anyone really understand the spreading of the clouds and the thunder that rolls forth from heaven? ³⁰See how he spreads the lightning around him and how it lights up the depths of the sea. ³¹By his mighty acts he governs the people, giving them food in abundance. ³²He fills his hands with lightning bolts. He hurls each at its target. ³³The thunder announces his presence; the storm announces his indignant anger.*

36:33 Or *even the cattle know when a storm is coming.* The meaning of the Hebrew is uncertain.

I BELIEVE God listens to me and is concerned about me. (35:13)

I BELIEVE God sees what is going on and will bring about justice in time. (35:14)

I BELIEVE God is mighty in both power and understanding, yet he despises no one. (36:5)

I LISTEN to God and obey him. (36:11)

I BELIEVE God sometimes gets our attention through adversity. (36:15)

I DO NOT PRESUME to speak for God or know the reasons why others suffer. (36:21)

I GLORIFY God's mighty works, singing songs of praise. (36:24)

I BELIEVE God is exalted beyond what we can understand. (36:26)

CHAPTER 37

"My heart pounds as I think of this. It leaps within me. ²Listen carefully to the thunder of God's voice as it rolls from his mouth. ³It rolls across the heavens, and his lightning flashes out in every direction. ⁴Then comes the roaring of the thunder—the tremendous voice of his majesty. He does not restrain the thunder when he speaks. ⁵God's voice is glorious in the thunder. We cannot comprehend the greatness of his power.

⁶"He directs the snow to fall on the earth and tells the rain to pour down. ⁷Everyone stops working at such a time so they can recognize his power. ⁸The wild animals hide in the rocks or in their dens. ⁹The stormy wind comes from its chamber, and the driving winds bring the cold. ¹⁰God's breath sends the ice, freezing wide expanses of water. ¹¹He loads the clouds with moisture, and they flash with his lightning. ¹²The clouds turn around and around under his direction. They do whatever he commands throughout the earth. ¹³He causes things to happen on earth, either as a punishment or as a sign of his unfailing love.

¹⁴"Listen, Job; stop and consider the wonderful miracles of God! ¹⁵Do you know how God controls the storm and causes the lightning to flash forth from his clouds? ¹⁶Do you understand how he balances the clouds with wonderful perfection and skill? ¹⁷When you are sweltering in your clothes and the south wind dies down and everything is still, ¹⁸he makes the skies reflect the heat like a giant mirror. Can you do that?

¹⁹"You think you know so much, so teach the rest of us what to say to God. We are too ignorant to make our own arguments. ²⁰Should God be told that I want to speak? Can we speak when we are confused? ²¹We cannot look at the sun, for it shines brightly in the sky when the wind clears away the clouds. ²²Golden splendor comes from the mountain of God. He is clothed in dazzling splendor. ²³We cannot imagine the power of the Almighty, yet he is so just and merciful that he does not oppress us. ²⁴No wonder people everywhere fear him. People who are truly wise show him reverence."

CHAPTER 38

The LORD Challenges Job

Then the LORD answered Job from the whirlwind:

²"Who is this that questions my wisdom with such ignorant words? ³Brace yourself, because I have some questions for you, and you must answer them.

⁴"Where were you when I laid the foundations of the earth? Tell me, if you know so much. ⁵Do you know how its dimensions were determined and who did the surveying? ⁶What supports its foundations, and who laid its cornerstone ⁷as the morning stars sang together and all the angels* shouted for joy?

⁸"Who defined the boundaries of the sea as it burst from the womb, ⁹and as I clothed it with clouds and thick darkness? ¹⁰For I locked it behind barred gates, limiting its shores. ¹¹I said, 'Thus far and no farther will you come. Here your proud waves must stop!'

¹²"Have you ever commanded the morning to appear and caused the dawn to rise in the east? ¹³Have you ever told the daylight to spread to the ends of the earth, to bring an end to the night's wickedness? ¹⁴For the features of the earth take shape as the light approaches, and the dawn is robed in red. ¹⁵The light disturbs the haunts of the wicked, and it stops the arm that is raised in violence.

¹⁶"Have you explored the springs from which the seas come? Have you walked about and explored their depths? ¹⁷Do you know where the gates of death are located? Have you seen the gates of utter gloom? ¹⁸Do you realize the extent of the earth? Tell me about it if you know!

38:7 Hebrew *sons of God.*

I CANNOT COMPREHEND the greatness of God's power. (37:5)

I HEED the example of creation and do whatever God commands. (37:12)

I STOP AND CONSIDER the miracles of God in nature. (37:14)

I FEAR the Lord and show him reverence for his power, mercy, and justice. (37:24)

I BELIEVE the Lord spoke to Job from the whirlwind. (38:1)

I DO NOT QUESTION the Lord's wisdom. (38:2)

I BELIEVE the Lord alone laid the foundations of the earth. (38:4)

I BELIEVE the Lord defined the boundaries of the sea. (38:8)

I BELIEVE the Lord alone commands the morning to appear. (38:12)

[19] "Where does the light come from, and where does the darkness go? [20]Can you take it to its home? Do you know how to get there? [21]But of course you know all this! For you were born before it was all created, and you are so very experienced!

[22]"Have you visited the treasuries of the snow? Have you seen where the hail is made and stored? [23]I have reserved it for the time of trouble, for the day of battle and war. [24]Where is the path to the origin of light? Where is the home of the east wind?

[25]"Who created a channel for the torrents of rain? Who laid out the path for the lightning? [26]Who makes the rain fall on barren land, in a desert where no one lives? [27]Who sends the rain that satisfies the parched ground and makes the tender grass spring up?

[28]"Does the rain have a father? Where does dew come from? [29]Who is the mother of the ice? Who gives birth to the frost from the heavens? [30]For the water turns to ice as hard as rock, and the surface of the water freezes.

[31]"Can you hold back the movements of the stars? Are you able to restrain the Pleiades or Orion? [32]Can you ensure the proper sequence of the seasons or guide the constellation of the Bear with her cubs across the heavens? [33]Do you know the laws of the universe and how God rules the earth?

[34]"Can you shout to the clouds and make it rain? [35]Can you make lightning appear and cause it to strike as you direct it? [36]Who gives intuition and instinct? [37]Who is wise enough to count all the clouds? Who can tilt the water jars of heaven, [38]turning the dry dust to clumps of mud?

[39]"Can you stalk prey for a lioness and satisfy the young lions' appetites [40]as they lie in their dens or crouch in the thicket? [41]Who provides food for the ravens when their young cry out to God as they wander about in hunger?

CHAPTER 39

The LORD's Challenge Continues

"Do you know when the mountain goats give birth? Have you watched as the wild deer are born? [2]Do you know how many months they carry their young? Are you aware of the time of their delivery? [3]They crouch down to give birth to their young and deliver their offspring. [4]Their young grow up in the open fields, then leave their parents and never return.

[5]"Who makes the wild donkey wild? [6]I have placed it in the wilderness; its home is the wasteland. [7]It hates the noise of the city, and it has no driver to shout at it. [8]The mountains are its pastureland, where it searches for every blade of grass.

[9]"Will the wild ox consent to being tamed? Will it stay in your stall? [10]Can you hitch a wild ox to a plow? Will it plow a field for you? [11]Since it is so strong, can you trust it? Can you go away and trust the ox to do your work? [12]Can you rely on it to return, bringing your grain to the threshing floor?

[13]"The ostrich flaps her wings grandly, but they are no match for the feathers of the stork. [14]She lays her eggs on top of the earth, letting them be warmed in the dust. [15]She doesn't worry that a foot might crush them or that wild animals might destroy them. [16]She is harsh toward her young, as if they were not her own. She is unconcerned though they die, [17]for God has deprived her of wisdom. He has given her no understanding. [18]But whenever she jumps up to run, she passes the swiftest horse with its rider.

[19]"Have you given the horse its strength or clothed its neck with a flowing mane? [20]Did you give it the ability to leap forward like a locust? Its majestic snorting is something to hear! [21]It paws the earth and rejoices in its strength. When it charges to war, [22]it is unafraid. It does not run from the sword. [23]The arrows rattle against it, and the spear and javelin flash. [24]Fiercely it paws the ground and rushes forward into battle when the trumpet blows. [25]It snorts at

---

I BELIEVE the Lord created light out of nothing. (38:19)

I BELIEVE the Lord orchestrates the movements of the stars. (38:31)

I BELIEVE the Lord established the laws of the universe and rules the earth. (38:33)

I BELIEVE the Lord knows all the secrets of nature. (39:1)

I RECOGNIZE that I cannot give orders to a wild creature, let alone to God. (39:9)

I BELIEVE God has made each creature distinct. (39:13)

I RECOGNIZE that I cannot match a horse's strength, let alone God's. (39:19)

the sound of the bugle. It senses the battle even at a distance. It quivers at the noise of battle and the shout of the captain's commands.

²⁶"Are you the one who makes the hawk soar and spread its wings to the south? ²⁷Is it at your command that the eagle rises to the heights to make its nest? ²⁸It lives on the cliffs, making its home on a distant, rocky crag. ²⁹From there it hunts its prey, keeping watch with piercing eyes. ³⁰Its nestlings gulp down blood, for it feeds on the carcass of the slaughtered."

I RECOGNIZE that I cannot give orders to wild birds, let alone argue with God. (39:26)

CHAPTER 40

Then the LORD said to Job, ²"Do you still want to argue with the Almighty? You are God's critic, but do you have the answers?"

I BELIEVE the Lord spoke to Job. (40:1)

Job Responds to the LORD
³Then Job replied to the LORD, ⁴"I am nothing—how could I ever find the answers? I will put my hand over my mouth in silence. ⁵I have said too much already. I have nothing more to say."

I CLOSE my mouth and confess that I can say nothing to criticize or answer the Lord. (40:3)

The LORD Challenges Job Again
⁶Then the LORD answered Job from the whirlwind:

⁷"Brace yourself, because I have some questions for you, and you must answer them. ⁸Are you going to discredit my justice and condemn me so you can say you are right? ⁹Are you as strong as God, and can you thunder with a voice like his? ¹⁰All right then, put on your robes of state, your majesty and splendor. ¹¹Give vent to your anger. Let it overflow against the proud. ¹²Humiliate the proud with a glance; walk on the wicked where they stand. ¹³Bury them in the dust. Imprison them in the world of the dead. ¹⁴Then even I would praise you, for your own strength would save you.

I DO NOT DISCREDIT the Lord's justice or condemn him. (40:8)

I COULD NEVER BEGIN to match the Lord's strength. (40:9)

I COULD NEVER BEGIN to match the Lord's majesty. (40:10)

¹⁵"Take a look at the mighty hippopotamus.* I made it, just as I made you. It eats grass like an ox. ¹⁶See its powerful loins and the muscles of its belly. ¹⁷Its tail is as straight as a cedar. The sinews of its thighs are tightly knit together. ¹⁸Its bones are tubes of bronze. Its limbs are bars of iron. ¹⁹It is a prime example of God's amazing handiwork. Only its Creator can threaten it. ²⁰The mountains offer it their best food, where all the wild animals play. ²¹It lies down under the lotus plants, hidden by the reeds. ²²The lotus plants give it shade among the willows beside the stream. ²³It is not disturbed by raging rivers, not even when the swelling Jordan rushes down upon it. ²⁴No one can catch it off guard or put a ring in its nose and lead it away.

CHAPTER 41

The LORD's Challenge Continues
"Can you catch a crocodile* with a hook or put a noose around its jaw? ²Can you tie it with a rope through the nose or pierce its jaw with a spike? ³Will it beg you for mercy or implore you for pity? ⁴Will it agree to work for you? Can you make it be your slave for life? ⁵Can you make it a pet like a bird, or give it to your little girls to play with? ⁶Will merchants try to buy it? Will they sell it in their shops? ⁷Will its hide be hurt by darts, or its head by a harpoon? ⁸If you lay a hand on it, you will never forget the battle that follows, and you will never try it again!

I HAVE no power over God's ferocious creatures, much less over God, the Creator. (41:1)

⁹"No, it is useless to try to capture it. The hunter who attempts it will be thrown down. ¹⁰And since no one dares to disturb the crocodile, who would dare to stand up to me? ¹¹Who will confront me and remain safe*? Everything under heaven is mine.

¹²"I want to emphasize the tremendous strength in the crocodile's limbs and throughout its enormous frame. ¹³Who can strip off its hide, and who can penetrate its double layer of armor*? ¹⁴Who could pry open its jaws? For its teeth are terrible! ¹⁵The overlapping scales on its back make a shield.

I KNOW everything under heaven is the Lord's. (41:11)

40:15 Hebrew *at behemoth.* **41:1** Hebrew *Leviathan;* also throughout the following passage. **41:11** As in Greek version; Hebrew reads *confront me that I must pay.* **41:13** As in Greek version; Hebrew reads *its bridle.*

[16]They are close together so no air can get between them. [17]They lock together so nothing can penetrate them.

[18]"When it sneezes, it flashes light! Its eyes are like the red of dawn. [19]Fire and sparks leap from its mouth. [20]Smoke streams from its nostrils like steam from a boiling pot on a fire of dry rushes. [21]Yes, its breath would kindle coals, for flames shoot from its mouth.

[22]"The tremendous strength in its neck strikes terror wherever it goes. [23]Its flesh is hard and firm, not soft and fat. [24]Its heart is as hard as rock, as hard as a millstone. [25]When it rises, the mighty are afraid, gripped by terror. [26]No sword can stop it, nor spear nor dart nor pointed shaft. [27]To the crocodile, iron is nothing but straw, and bronze is rotten wood. [28]Arrows cannot make it flee. Stones shot from a sling are as ineffective as straw. [29]Clubs do no good, and it laughs at the swish of the javelins. [30]Its belly is covered with scales as sharp as glass. They tear up the ground as it drags through the mud.

[31]"The crocodile makes the water boil with its commotion. It churns the depths. [32]The water glistens in its wake. One would think the sea had turned white. [33]There is nothing else so fearless anywhere on earth. [34]Of all the creatures, it is the proudest. It is the king of beasts."

I BELIEVE that no creature, no matter how fierce, could ever begin to match the Lord's overwhelming greatness. (41:33)

CHAPTER 42

Job Responds to the LORD

Then Job replied to the LORD:

[2]"I know that you can do anything, and no one can stop you. [3]You ask, 'Who is this that questions my wisdom with such ignorance?' It is I. And I was talking about things I did not understand, things far too wonderful for me.

I BELIEVE the Lord can do anything (Genesis 18:14; Matthew 19:26). (42:2)

[4]"You said, 'Listen and I will speak! I have some questions for you, and you must answer them.'

[5]"I had heard about you before, but now I have seen you with my own eyes. [6]I take back everything I said, and I sit in dust and ashes to show my repentance."

I DO NOT QUESTION the Lord's wisdom and argue about things I do not understand. (42:3)

I REPENT when the Lord rebukes me (Isaiah 6:5; Luke 5:8). (42:6)

Conclusion: The LORD Blesses Job

[7]After the LORD had finished speaking to Job, he said to Eliphaz the Temanite: "I am angry with you and with your two friends, for you have not been right in what you said about me, as my servant Job was. [8]Now take seven young bulls and seven rams and go to my servant Job and offer a burnt offering for yourselves. My servant Job will pray for you, and I will accept his prayer on your behalf. I will not treat you as you deserve, for you have not been right in what you said about me, as my servant Job was."

I PRAY for my friends, even if they have hurt me deeply. (42:8)

[9]So Eliphaz the Temanite, Bildad the Shuhite, and Zophar the Naamathite did as the LORD commanded them, and the LORD accepted Job's prayer.

[10]When Job prayed for his friends, the LORD restored his fortunes. In fact, the LORD gave him twice as much as before! [11]Then all his brothers, sisters, and former friends came and feasted with him in his home. And they consoled him and comforted him because of all the trials the LORD had brought against him. And each of them brought him a gift of money* and a gold ring.

I BELIEVE the Lord accepted Job's prayer and restored his fortunes—twice as much as before. (42:10)

I COMFORT those who have suffered severe trials. (42:11)

[12]So the LORD blessed Job in the second half of his life even more than in the beginning. For now he had fourteen thousand sheep, six thousand camels, one thousand teams of oxen, and one thousand female donkeys. [13]He also gave Job seven more sons and three more daughters. [14]He named his first daughter Jemimah, the second Keziah, and the third Keren-happuch. [15]In all the land there were no other women as lovely as the daughters of Job. And their father put them into his will along with their brothers.

[16]Job lived 140 years after that, living to see four generations of his children and grandchildren. [17]Then he died, an old man who had lived a long, good life.

42:11 Hebrew *a kesitah*; the value or weight of the kesitah is no longer known.

PSALMS

THIS SECOND BOOK of Hebrew poetry is an extensive collection of *songs*.

David (author of more than seventy psalms), Asaph (a dozen), Solomon (two), and others contributed to this longest of all books in the Bible.

Like any good collection of lyrics, these 150 psalms cover a wide variety of themes. Some of the psalms call the community to praise the Lord for who he is and what he said. Some record a writer's urgent pleas to God and praise for his deliverance. Some present important truths. Some express great heartache and sorrow. Others call on the Lord to judge the wicked and vindicate the righteous. Still others recount and confess the writer's own sins against the Lord.

Most of these psalms were written during David's reign (c. 1000 B.C.), but at least one was written more than four hundred years earlier (Psalm 90, by Moses), and another was penned four hundred years after David's reign (Psalm 137, anonymous). Several of the psalms include distinct prophecies about Jesus Christ. Other psalms foreshadow aspects of Jesus Christ's life, ministry, death, resurrection, glory, and reign over all the earth.

The poetry in these Hebrew psalms "rhymes" ideas—the first line makes a statement, and the next line repeats, expands, or contrasts that idea. This unique parallel poetic structure translates especially well into other languages.

Psalms by Moses, Deborah and Barak, Hannah, David, Hezekiah, Jonah, Mary, Zechariah, Simeon, John, and others appear elsewhere in Scripture.

Famous verses in Psalms abound, including those that describe
- The benefits of meditating on God's Word (Psalms 1, 19, 119)
- The value the Lord places on every individual (Psalms 8, 23, 103, 139)
- The folly of disbelieving and disobeying God (Psalms 14, 53, 58, 64, 82, 83)
- The wisdom of walking uprightly before God (Psalms 15, 26, 101, 112)
- The hope we can have beyond the grave (Psalms 16:8-11; 17:15; 23:6)
- The Lord's greatness (Psalms 29, 45, 84, 93, 95, 96, 100, 110, 111, 113)
- The psalmist's intense desire for the Lord (Psalms 42:1-4; 63:1-8)
- The psalmist's humble confession of sin (Psalms 32, 51)
- The psalmist's trust in the Lord (Psalms 54–56, 73, 77, 115)
- The Lord's great acts in the past (Psalms 104-107, 114, 135, 136)
- Songs for the ascent to Jerusalem (Psalms 120-134)
- Concluding songs of praise to the Lord (Psalms 145-150)

BOOK ONE (Psalms 1–41)

PSALM 1

¹Oh, the joys of those
  who do not follow the advice of the wicked,
  or stand around with sinners,
  or join in with scoffers.

I DO NOT FOLLOW the advice of wicked individuals or join in with them. (1:1)

² But they delight in doing everything the LORD wants;
    day and night they think about his law.
³ They are like trees planted along the riverbank,
    bearing fruit each season without fail.
Their leaves never wither,
    and in all they do, they prosper.

⁴ But this is not true of the wicked.
    They are like worthless chaff, scattered by the wind.
⁵ They will be condemned at the time of judgment.
    Sinners will have no place among the godly.

⁶ For the LORD watches over the path of the godly,
    but the path of the wicked leads to destruction.

PSALM 2

¹ Why do the nations rage?
    Why do the people waste their time with futile plans?
² The kings of the earth prepare for battle;
    the rulers plot together
against the LORD
    and against his anointed one.
³ "Let us break their chains," they cry,
    "and free ourselves from this slavery."

⁴ But the one who rules in heaven laughs.
    The Lord scoffs at them.
⁵ Then in anger he rebukes them,
    terrifying them with his fierce fury.
⁶ For the LORD declares, "I have placed my chosen king on the throne
    in Jerusalem, my holy city.*"

⁷ The king proclaims the LORD's decree:
"The LORD said to me, 'You are my son.*
    Today I have become your Father.*
⁸ Only ask, and I will give you the nations as your inheritance,
    the ends of the earth as your possession.
⁹ You will break them with an iron rod
    and smash them like clay pots.'"

¹⁰ Now then, you kings, act wisely!
    Be warned, you rulers of the earth!
¹¹ Serve the LORD with reverent fear,
    and rejoice with trembling.
¹² Submit to God's royal son, or he will become angry,
    and you will be destroyed in the midst of your pursuits—
    for his anger can flare up in an instant.

But what joy for all who find protection in him!

PSALM 3

A psalm of David, regarding the time David fled from his son Absalom.

¹ O LORD, I have so many enemies;
    so many are against me.
² So many are saying,
    "God will never rescue him!"   *Interlude**

I ENJOY a fruitful life because I delight in the Lord's Word and obey him. (1:3)

I KNOW the Lord scoffs at human attempts to overthrow his kingship. (2:4)

In response to the profiles, tell the Lord whose examples you want to imitate—and whose failures you don't want to repeat.

I SERVE the Lord with fear and rejoicing because he is King of all. (2:11)

I SUBMIT to God's Son and find protection in him (Hebrews 12:28-29). (2:12)

See Absalom's profile (page 373) at 2 Samuel 15:6.

2:6 Hebrew *on Zion, my holy mountain.*   2:7a Or *Son;* also in 2:12.   2:7b Or *Today I reveal you as my son.*
3:2 Hebrew *Selah.* The meaning of this word is uncertain, though it is probably a musical or literary term. It is rendered *Interlude* throughout the Psalms.

³ But you, O LORD, are a shield around me,
   my glory, and the one who lifts my head high.
⁴ I cried out to the LORD,
   and he answered me from his holy mountain.   *Interlude*

I TRUST the Lord to
protect and honor me.
(3:3)

LIKE DAVID
Psalm 3:1

I share my heart with God in any and every circumstance.

Why was David a man after God's own heart? Perhaps because David's every heartbeat pulsed in rhythm with God's own. Few thoughts crossed his mind that did not find their way to David's Lord. His conversation with God was rarely put on hold and never abandoned with disinterest. No matter what happened to David, God was the first to hear about it.

David shared his heart with God in every circumstance of his life:

- He cried out to the Lord when his life was in danger from enemies and no one else held out any hope (Psalm 3:1-2).
- He called out to the Lord for mercy when his reputation was attacked (Psalm 4:1-2).
- He sobbed and pleaded with God for compassion when he was weak in body and sick of heart (Psalm 6:1-3, 6).
- He expressed marvel and amazement as he spent the night under the stars—and told God how he wondered at his exaltation of humanity (Psalm 8:3-4).
- He thanked God with all his heart when he was rescued from danger (Psalm 9:1-2).
- He questioned the Lord when he felt as if God were far away and wicked people were getting away with murder (Psalm 10:1-6).
- He confidently called on God to bring about justice for the oppressed, because he knew God really did care (Psalm 10:12-14).
- He cried out for help when he felt alone in obeying God (Psalm 12:1).
- He blessed God for his constant guidance and presence (Psalm 16:7-8).
- He told the Lord that he loved him (Psalm 18:1).
- He freely admitted that his strength was in God alone (Psalm 21:1).
- He cried out to God when he felt forsaken and deserted and petitioned the Lord to rescue him (Psalm 22:1, 19-21).
- He expressed gratitude for all the Lord provided and reaffirmed his trust in God's care (Psalm 23).
- He confessed his sin and sought forgiveness when he had failed (Psalms 32:3-5; 51:1-2), because more than anything, he wanted to be right with God again (Psalm 51:8, 11).

David's heart lay open before God in anguish, grief, joy, and exaltation—every emotion expressed to God in prayer. David spoke his heartfelt prayers to God, and God gave David's prayers back to us as part of Scripture.

Whether we echo David's words or come up with our own, we need to share our whole heart and life with our Lord.

Be sure to read some of the stories about David in 1 Samuel 17–31; 2 Samuel 1–24; and 1 Chronicles 11–29.

○ *Today's Scripture reading is Psalms 3–8.*

---

⁵ I lay down and slept.
   I woke up in safety,
   for the LORD was watching over me.
⁶ I am not afraid of ten thousand enemies
   who surround me on every side.

I AM NOT AFRAID, even
when I am surrounded
by enemies. (3:6)

⁷ Arise, O LORD!
   Rescue me, my God!
Slap all my enemies in the face!
Shatter the teeth of the wicked!

⁸Victory comes from you, O LORD.
  May your blessings rest on your people. *Interlude*

PSALM 4

For the choir director: A psalm of David, to be accompanied by stringed instruments.

Today what example(s) are you choosing to heed?

¹Answer me when I call,
  O God who declares me innocent.
Take away my distress.
  Have mercy on me and hear my prayer.

²How long will you people ruin my reputation?
  How long will you make these groundless accusations?
  How long will you pursue lies? *Interlude*

³You can be sure of this:
  The LORD has set apart the godly for himself.
  The LORD will answer when I call to him.

I DO NOT LET anger control me when I am attacked. (4:4)

⁴Don't sin by letting anger gain control over you.
  Think about it overnight and remain silent. *Interlude*
⁵Offer proper sacrifices,
  and trust in the LORD.

⁶Many people say, "Who will show us better times?"
  Let the smile of your face shine on us, LORD.

I TAKE greater joy in the Lord than in earthly pleasures. (4:7)

⁷You have given me greater joy
  than those who have abundant harvests of grain and wine.

⁸I will lie down in peace and sleep,
  for you alone, O LORD, will keep me safe.

PSALM 5

For the choir director: A psalm of David, to be accompanied by the flute.

I GROAN in prayer to the Lord my King. (5:1)

¹O LORD, hear me as I pray;
  pay attention to my groaning.
²Listen to my cry for help, my King and my God,
  for I will never pray to anyone but you.
³Listen to my voice in the morning, LORD.
  Each morning I bring my requests to you and wait expectantly.

⁴O God, you take no pleasure in wickedness;
  you cannot tolerate the slightest sin.
⁵Therefore, the proud will not be allowed to stand in your presence,
  for you hate all who do evil.
⁶You will destroy those who tell lies.
  The LORD detests murderers and deceivers.

I CAN COME into God's holy presence because of his unfailing love. (5:7)

⁷Because of your unfailing love, I can enter your house;
  with deepest awe I will worship at your Temple.
⁸Lead me in the right path, O LORD,
  or my enemies will conquer me.
Tell me clearly what to do,
  and show me which way to turn.

⁹My enemies cannot speak one truthful word.
  Their deepest desire is to destroy others.
Their talk is foul, like the stench from an open grave.
  Their speech is filled with flattery.

¹⁰ O God, declare them guilty.
    Let them be caught in their own traps.
    Drive them away because of their many sins,
        for they rebel against you.

¹¹ But let all who take refuge in you rejoice;
    let them sing joyful praises forever.
    Protect them,
        so all who love your name may be filled with joy.
¹² For you bless the godly, O LORD,
        surrounding them with your shield of love.

I BELIEVE I am surrounded by God's shield of love. (5:12)

PSALM 6

For the choir director: A psalm of David, to be accompanied by an eight-stringed instrument. *

¹ O LORD, do not rebuke me in your anger
    or discipline me in your rage.
² Have compassion on me, LORD, for I am weak.
    Heal me, LORD, for my body is in agony.
³ I am sick at heart.
    How long, O LORD, until you restore me?

I SEEK the Lord's mercy and compassion. (6:1)

I SEEK the Lord's restoration and healing. (6:3)

⁴ Return, O LORD, and rescue me.
    Save me because of your unfailing love.
⁵ For in death, who remembers you?
    Who can praise you from the grave?

⁶ I am worn out from sobbing.
    Every night tears drench my bed;
    my pillow is wet from weeping.
⁷ My vision is blurred by grief;
    my eyes are worn out because of all my enemies.

⁸ Go away, all you who do evil,
    for the LORD has heard my crying.
⁹ The LORD has heard my plea;
    the LORD will answer my prayer.
¹⁰ May all my enemies be disgraced and terrified.
    May they suddenly turn back in shame.

I AM CONFIDENT that the Lord has heard my weeping. (6:8)

PSALM 7

A psalm of David, which he sang to the LORD concerning Cush of the tribe of Benjamin.

¹ I come to you for protection, O LORD my God.
    Save me from my persecutors—rescue me!
² If you don't, they will maul me like a lion,
    tearing me to pieces with no one to rescue me.

I LOOK to God for protection from my enemies. (7:1)

³ O LORD my God, if I have done wrong
    or am guilty of injustice,
⁴ if I have betrayed a friend
    or plundered my enemy without cause,
⁵ then let my enemies capture me.
    Let them trample me into the ground.
    Let my honor be left in the dust.   *Interlude*

6:TITLE Hebrew *with stringed instruments; according to the sheminith.*

⁶Arise, O Lᴏʀᴅ, in anger!
　　Stand up against the fury of my enemies!
　　Wake up, my God, and bring justice!
⁷Gather the nations before you.
　　Sit on your throne high above them.
⁸The Lᴏʀᴅ passes judgment on the nations.
　　Declare me righteous, O Lᴏʀᴅ,
　　for I am innocent, O Most High!
⁹End the wickedness of the ungodly,
　　but help all those who obey you.
For you look deep within the mind and heart,
　　O righteous God.

¹⁰God is my shield,
　　saving those whose hearts are true and right.
¹¹God is a judge who is perfectly fair.
　　He is angry with the wicked every day.

¹²If a person does not repent,
　　God* will sharpen his sword;
　　he will bend and string his bow.
¹³He will prepare his deadly weapons
　　and ignite his flaming arrows.

¹⁴The wicked conceive evil;
　　they are pregnant with trouble
　　and give birth to lies.
¹⁵They dig a pit to trap others
　　and then fall into it themselves.
¹⁶They make trouble,
　　but it backfires on them.
They plan violence for others,
　　but it falls on their own heads.

¹⁷I will thank the Lᴏʀᴅ because he is just;
　　I will sing praise to the name of the Lᴏʀᴅ Most High.

PSALM 8

For the choir director: A psalm of David, to be accompanied by a stringed instrument. *

¹O Lᴏʀᴅ, our Lord, the majesty of your name fills the earth!
　　Your glory is higher than the heavens.

²You have taught children and nursing infants
　　to give you praise.*
They silence your enemies
　　who were seeking revenge.

³When I look at the night sky and see the work of your fingers—
　　the moon and the stars you have set in place—
⁴what are mortals that you should think of us,
　　mere humans that you should care for us?*
⁵For you made us only a little lower than God,*
　　and you crowned us with glory and honor.
⁶You put us in charge of everything you made,
　　giving us authority over all things—

I LOOK to God to declare me righteous when I am innocent in a matter. (7:8)

I KNOW that God sees the heart and mind of every person. (7:9)

I THANK God for his justice in a world of violent people. (7:17)

I PRAISE the Lord's majesty. (8:1)

I MARVEL that God has honored humans with glory and authority. (8:5)

7:12 Hebrew *he.*　8:TITLE Hebrew *according to the gittith.*　8:2 As in Greek version; Hebrew reads *to show strength.*　8:4 Hebrew *what is man that you should think of him, the son of man that you should care for him?*　8:5 Or *a little lower than the angels;* Hebrew reads *Elohim.*

⁷ the sheep and the cattle
and all the wild animals,
⁸ the birds in the sky, the fish in the sea,
and everything that swims the ocean currents.

⁹ O Lord, our Lord, the majesty of your name fills the earth!

PSALM 9

For the choir director: A psalm of David, to be sung to the tune "Death of the Son."

¹ I will thank you, Lord, with all my heart;
I will tell of all the marvelous things you have done.
² I will be filled with joy because of you.
I will sing praises to your name, O Most High.

³ My enemies turn away in retreat;
they are overthrown and destroyed before you.
⁴ For you have judged in my favor;
from your throne, you have judged with fairness.

⁵ You have rebuked the nations and destroyed the wicked;
you have wiped out their names forever.
⁶ My enemies have met their doom;
their cities are perpetual ruins.
Even the memory of their uprooted cities is lost.

⁷ But the Lord reigns forever,
executing judgment from his throne.
⁸ He will judge the world with justice
and rule the nations with fairness.

⁹ The Lord is a shelter for the oppressed,
a refuge in times of trouble.
¹⁰ Those who know your name trust in you,
for you, O Lord, have never abandoned anyone who searches
for you.

¹¹ Sing praises to the Lord who reigns in Jerusalem.*
Tell the world about his unforgettable deeds.
¹² For he who avenges murder cares for the helpless.
He does not ignore those who cry to him for help.

¹³ Lord, have mercy on me.
See how I suffer at the hands of those who hate me.
Snatch me back from the jaws of death.
¹⁴ Save me, so I can praise you publicly at Jerusalem's gates,
so I can rejoice that you have rescued me.

¹⁵ The nations have fallen into the pit they dug for others.
They have been caught in their own trap.
¹⁶ The Lord is known for his justice.
The wicked have trapped themselves in their own snares.

*Quiet Interlude**

¹⁷ The wicked will go down to the grave.*
This is the fate of all the nations who ignore God.

> I THANK the Lord publicly for all he has done. (9:1)

> I BELIEVE the Lord reigns forever, judging the whole world with justice. (9:7)

> I SEARCH for the Lord and trust in him, for he will never abandon me (John 5:24). (9:10)

9:11 Hebrew *Zion;* also in 9:14. 9:16 Hebrew *Higgaion Selah.* The meaning of this phrase is uncertain. 9:17 Hebrew *to Sheol.*

¹⁸ For the needy will not be forgotten forever;
    the hopes of the poor will not always be crushed.

I PRAY to God for justice among the nations. (9:19)

¹⁹ Arise, O LORD!
    Do not let mere mortals defy you!
    Let the nations be judged in your presence!
²⁰ Make them tremble in fear, O LORD.
    Let them know they are merely human.   *Interlude*

PSALM 10

I TURN to God, not away from him, when I am in pain and feel that God is far away from me. (10:1)

I CALL UPON God to deal with those who praise the greedy and curse the Lord. (10:3)

¹ O LORD, why do you stand so far away?
    Why do you hide when I need you the most?
² Proud and wicked people viciously oppress the poor.
    Let them be caught in the evil they plan for others.
³ For they brag about their evil desires;
    they praise the greedy and curse the LORD.
⁴ These wicked people are too proud to seek God.
    They seem to think that God is dead.
⁵ Yet they succeed in everything they do.
    They do not see your punishment awaiting them.
    They pour scorn on all their enemies.
⁶ They say to themselves, "Nothing bad will ever happen to us!
    We will be free of trouble forever!"

⁷ Their mouths are full of cursing, lies, and threats.
    Trouble and evil are on the tips of their tongues.
⁸ They lurk in dark alleys,
    murdering the innocent who pass by.

Today what truth(s) are you choosing to believe?

They are always searching
    for some helpless victim.
⁹ Like lions they crouch silently,
    waiting to pounce on the helpless.
Like hunters they capture their victims
    and drag them away in nets.
¹⁰ The helpless are overwhelmed and collapse;
    they fall beneath the strength of the wicked.
¹¹ The wicked say to themselves, "God isn't watching!
    He will never notice!"

¹² Arise, O LORD!
    Punish the wicked, O God!
    Do not forget the helpless!
¹³ Why do the wicked get away with cursing God?
    How can they think, "God will never call us to account"?

I BELIEVE that the Lord sees the wicked and that he will punish them and rescue the helpless. (10:14)

¹⁴ But you do see the trouble and grief they cause.
    You take note of it and punish them.
The helpless put their trust in you.
    You are the defender of orphans.

¹⁵ Break the arms of these wicked, evil people!
    Go after them until the last one is destroyed!
¹⁶ The LORD is king forever and ever!
    Let those who worship other gods be swept from the land.

I KNOW that the Lord knows the hopes of the helpless and comforts them. (10:17)

¹⁷ LORD, you know the hopes of the helpless.
    Surely you will listen to their cries and comfort them.
¹⁸ You will bring justice to the orphans and the oppressed,
    so people can no longer terrify them.

PSALM 11

For the choir director: A psalm of David.

¹ I trust in the LORD for protection.
  So why do you say to me,
"Fly to the mountains for safety!
² The wicked are stringing their bows
  and setting their arrows in the bowstrings.
  They shoot from the shadows at those who do right.
³ The foundations of law and order have collapsed.
  What can the righteous do?"

⁴ But the LORD is in his holy Temple;
  the LORD still rules from heaven.
He watches everything closely,
  examining everyone on earth.
⁵ The LORD examines both the righteous and the wicked.
  He hates everyone who loves violence.
⁶ He rains down blazing coals on the wicked,
  punishing them with burning sulfur and scorching winds.
⁷ For the LORD is righteous, and he loves justice.
  Those who do what is right will see his face.

See David's profile (page 629) at Psalm 3:1.

I RECOGNIZE that I am helpless in my own strength when the foundations of law and order collapse. (11:3)

I TRUST in the Lord, who rules and watches from heaven. (11:4)

PSALM 12

For the choir director: A psalm of David, to be accompanied by an eight-stringed instrument. *

¹ Help, O LORD, for the godly are fast disappearing!
  The faithful have vanished from the earth!
² Neighbors lie to each other,
  speaking with flattering lips and insincere hearts.
³ May the LORD bring their flattery to an end
  and silence their proud tongues.
⁴ They say, "We will lie to our hearts' content.
  Our lips are our own—who can stop us?"

⁵ The LORD replies, "I have seen violence done to the helpless,
  and I have heard the groans of the poor.
Now I will rise up to rescue them,
  as they have longed for me to do."
⁶ The LORD's promises are pure,
  like silver refined in a furnace,
  purified seven times over.

⁷ Therefore, LORD, we know you will protect the oppressed,
  preserving them forever from this lying generation,
⁸ even though the wicked strut about,
  and evil is praised throughout the land.

I CRY OUT to the Lord for help when faithful people are few. (12:1)

I BELIEVE the Lord sees the suffering of the helpless and will rescue them. (12:5)

PSALM 13

For the choir director: A psalm of David.

¹ O LORD, how long will you forget me? Forever?
  How long will you look the other way?
² How long must I struggle with anguish in my soul,
  with sorrow in my heart every day?
  How long will my enemy have the upper hand?

I CRY OUT to the Lord when I feel forgotten. (13:1)

12:TITLE Hebrew *according to the sheminith.*

³Turn and answer me, O LORD my God!
   Restore the light to my eyes, or I will die.
⁴Don't let my enemies gloat, saying, "We have defeated him!"
   Don't let them rejoice at my downfall.

I TRUST in the Lord's love and rejoice in his rescue. (13:5)

⁵But I trust in your unfailing love.
   I will rejoice because you have rescued me.
⁶I will sing to the LORD
   because he has been so good to me.

PSALM 14
For the choir director: A psalm of David.

I BELIEVE in God! (14:1)

¹Only fools say in their hearts,
   "There is no God."
They are corrupt, and their actions are evil;
   no one does good!

²The LORD looks down from heaven
   on the entire human race;
he looks to see if there is even one with real understanding,
   one who seeks for God.
³But no, all have turned away from God;
   all have become corrupt.
No one does good,
   not even one!

⁴Will those who do evil never learn?
   They eat up my people like bread;
   they wouldn't think of praying to the LORD.
⁵Terror will grip them,
   for God is with those who obey him.
⁶The wicked frustrate the plans of the oppressed,
   but the LORD will protect his people.

I LONG for the Lord to rescue, redeem, and restore his people. (14:7)

⁷Oh, that salvation would come from Mount Zion to rescue Israel!
   For when the LORD restores his people,
   Jacob will shout with joy, and Israel will rejoice.

PSALM 15
A psalm of David.

I WANT to live a life that is fitting for those who worship in God's presence. (15:1)

I SPEAK the truth sincerely and kindly. (15:2)

¹Who may worship in your sanctuary, LORD?
   Who may enter your presence on your holy hill?

²Those who lead blameless lives
   and do what is right,
   speaking the truth from sincere hearts.
³Those who refuse to slander others
   or harm their neighbors
   or speak evil of their friends.
⁴Those who despise persistent sinners,
   and honor the faithful followers of the LORD
   and keep their promises even when it hurts.

I LIVE righteously and will never be shaken (2 Peter 1:10). (15:5)

⁵Those who do not charge interest on the money they lend,
   and who refuse to accept bribes to testify against the innocent.

Such people will stand firm forever.

PSALM 16

A psalm of David.

[1] Keep me safe, O God,
for I have come to you for refuge.

[2] I said to the LORD, "You are my Master!
All the good things I have are from you."
[3] The godly people in the land
are my true heroes!
I take pleasure in them!
[4] Those who chase after other gods will be filled with sorrow.
I will not take part in their sacrifices
or even speak the names of their gods.

[5] LORD, you alone are my inheritance, my cup of blessing.
You guard all that is mine.
[6] The land you have given me is a pleasant land.
What a wonderful inheritance!

[7] I will bless the LORD who guides me;
even at night my heart instructs me.
[8] I know the LORD is always with me.
I will not be shaken, for he is right beside me.

[9] No wonder my heart is filled with joy,
and my mouth* shouts his praises!
My body rests in safety.
[10] For you will not leave my soul among the dead*
or allow your godly one* to rot in the grave.
[11] You will show me the way of life,
granting me the joy of your presence
and the pleasures of living with you forever.

I ACKNOWLEDGE the Lord as my Master who gives me all good things. (16:2)

I REST in God's guidance. (16:7)

I TAKE JOY in the life God gives me now and forever in his presence. (16:11)

PSALM 17

A prayer of David.

[1] O LORD, hear my plea for justice.
Listen to my cry for help.
Pay attention to my prayer,
for it comes from an honest heart.
[2] Declare me innocent,
for you know those who do right.

[3] You have tested my thoughts and examined my heart in the night.
You have scrutinized me and found nothing amiss,
for I am determined not to sin in what I say.
[4] I have followed your commands,
which have kept me from going along with cruel and evil people.
[5] My steps have stayed on your path;
I have not wavered from following you.

[6] I am praying to you because I know you will answer, O God.
Bend down and listen as I pray.
[7] Show me your unfailing love in wonderful ways.
You save with your strength
those who seek refuge from their enemies.
[8] Guard me as the apple of your eye.
Hide me in the shadow of your wings.

I CRY OUT to the Lord for justice when I am wronged. (17:1)

I BELIEVE the Lord knows when I am innocent of wrongdoing. (17:3)

I ASK the Lord to guard and protect me from those who would hurt me. (17:8)

16:9 As in Greek version; Hebrew reads *glory.*   16:10a Hebrew *in Sheol.*   16:10b Or *your Holy One.*

⁹Protect me from wicked people who attack me,
   from murderous enemies who surround me.

¹⁰They are without pity.
   Listen to their boasting.
¹¹They track me down, surround me,
   and throw me to the ground.
¹²They are like hungry lions, eager to tear me apart—
   like young lions in hiding, waiting for their chance.

¹³Arise, O LORD!
   Stand against them and bring them to their knees!
   Rescue me from the wicked with your sword!
¹⁴Save me by your mighty hand, O LORD,
   from those whose only concern is earthly gain.
May they have their punishment in full.
   May their children inherit more of the same,
   and may the judgment continue to their children's children.

¹⁵But because I have done what is right, I will see you.
   When I awake, I will be fully satisfied,
   for I will see you face to face.

PSALM 18

For the choir director: A psalm of David, the servant of the LORD. He sang this song to the LORD on the day the LORD rescued him from all his enemies and from Saul.

See Saul's profile (page 339) at 1 Samuel 18:9.

I TELL the Lord how much I love him! (18:1)

I FIND all my strength and protection in the Lord. (18:2)

¹I love you, LORD; you are my strength.
²The LORD is my rock, my fortress, and my savior;
   my God is my rock, in whom I find protection.
He is my shield, the strength of my salvation, and my stronghold.
³I will call on the LORD, who is worthy of praise,
   for he saves me from my enemies.

⁴The ropes of death surrounded me;
   the floods of destruction swept over me.
⁵The grave* wrapped its ropes around me;
   death itself stared me in the face.

I CRY OUT to the Lord because he will hear and answer me. (18:6)

⁶But in my distress I cried out to the LORD;
   yes, I prayed to my God for help.
He heard me from his sanctuary;
   my cry reached his ears.

I BELIEVE the Lord acts mightily in answer to prayer. (18:7)

⁷Then the earth quaked and trembled;
   the foundations of the mountains shook;
   they quaked because of his anger.
⁸Smoke poured from his nostrils;
   fierce flames leaped from his mouth;
   glowing coals flamed forth from him.
⁹He opened the heavens and came down;
   dark storm clouds were beneath his feet.
¹⁰Mounted on a mighty angel,* he flew,
   soaring on the wings of the wind.
¹¹He shrouded himself in darkness,
   veiling his approach with dense rain clouds.
¹²The brilliance of his presence broke through the clouds,
   raining down hail and burning coals.

18:5 Hebrew *Sheol.*   18:10 Hebrew *a cherub.*

¹³ The LORD thundered from heaven;
the Most High gave a mighty shout.*
¹⁴ He shot his arrows and scattered his enemies;
his lightning flashed, and they were greatly confused.
¹⁵ Then at your command, O LORD,
at the blast of your breath,
the bottom of the sea could be seen,
and the foundations of the earth were laid bare.

¹⁶ He reached down from heaven and rescued me;
he drew me out of deep waters.
¹⁷ He delivered me from my powerful enemies,
from those who hated me and were too strong for me.
¹⁸ They attacked me at a moment when I was weakest,
but the LORD upheld me.
¹⁹ He led me to a place of safety;
he rescued me because he delights in me.
²⁰ The LORD rewarded me for doing right;
he compensated me because of my innocence.
²¹ For I have kept the ways of the LORD;
I have not turned from my God to follow evil.
²² For all his laws are constantly before me;
I have never abandoned his principles.
²³ I am blameless before God;
I have kept myself from sin.
²⁴ The LORD rewarded me for doing right,
because of the innocence of my hands in his sight.

I BELIEVE I will one day be rewarded by God if I do what is right. (18:20)

²⁵ To the faithful you show yourself faithful;
to those with integrity you show integrity.
²⁶ To the pure you show yourself pure,
but to the wicked you show yourself hostile.
²⁷ You rescue those who are humble,
but you humiliate the proud.
²⁸ LORD, you have brought light to my life;
my God, you light up my darkness.
²⁹ In your strength I can crush an army;
with my God I can scale any wall.

I SEEK to live a life of faithfulness and integrity (Titus 1:15). (18:25)

³⁰ As for God, his way is perfect.
All the LORD's promises prove true.
He is a shield for all who look to him for protection.
³¹ For who is God except the LORD?
Who but our God is a solid rock?
³² God arms me with strength;
he has made my way safe.
³³ He makes me as surefooted as a deer,
leading me safely along the mountain heights.
³⁴ He prepares me for battle;
he strengthens me to draw a bow of bronze.
³⁵ You have given me the shield of your salvation.
Your right hand supports me;
your gentleness has made me great.
³⁶ You have made a wide path for my feet
to keep them from slipping.

I TRUST in no other God but the Lord. (18:31)

18:13 As in Greek version (see also 2 Sam 22:14); Hebrew adds *raining down hail and burning coals.*

³⁷ I chased my enemies and caught them;
  I did not stop until they were conquered.
³⁸ I struck them down so they could not get up;
  they fell beneath my feet.

I LOOK to the Lord for strength in the midst of life's battles. (18:39)

³⁹ You have armed me with strength for the battle;
  you have subdued my enemies under my feet.
⁴⁰ You made them turn and run;
  I have destroyed all who hated me.
⁴¹ They called for help, but no one came to rescue them.
  They cried to the LORD, but he refused to answer them.
⁴² I ground them as fine as dust carried by the wind.
  I swept them into the gutter like dirt.

⁴³ You gave me victory over my accusers.
  You appointed me as the ruler over nations;
  people I don't even know now serve me.
⁴⁴ As soon as they hear of me, they submit;
  foreigners cringe before me.
⁴⁵ They all lose their courage
  and come trembling from their strongholds.

I EXALT the God of my salvation! (18:46)

⁴⁶ The LORD lives! Blessed be my rock!
  May the God of my salvation be exalted!
⁴⁷ He is the God who pays back those who harm me;
  he subdues the nations under me
⁴⁸ and rescues me from my enemies.
  You hold me safe beyond the reach of my enemies;
  you save me from violent opponents.

I PRAISE the Lord for victory. (18:49)

⁴⁹ For this, O LORD, I will praise you among the nations;
  I will sing joyfully to your name.
⁵⁰ You give great victories to your king;
  you show unfailing love to your anointed,
  to David and all his descendants forever.

PSALM 19

For the choir director: A psalm of David.

I BELIEVE God's creation, the universe, makes his glory known (Romans 1:19-20). (19:1)

¹ The heavens tell of the glory of God.
  The skies display his marvelous craftsmanship.
² Day after day they continue to speak;
  night after night they make him known.
³ They speak without a sound or a word;
  their voice is silent in the skies;*
⁴ yet their message has gone out to all the earth,
  and their words to all the world.

  The sun lives in the heavens
  where God placed it.
⁵ It bursts forth like a radiant bridegroom
  after his wedding.
  It rejoices like a great athlete
  eager to run the race.
⁶ The sun rises at one end of the heavens
  and follows its course to the other end.
  Nothing can hide from its heat.

19:3 Or *There is no speech or language where their voice is not heard.*

⁷The law of the LORD is perfect,
 reviving the soul.
The decrees of the LORD are trustworthy,
 making wise the simple.
⁸The commandments of the LORD are right,
 bringing joy to the heart.
The commands of the LORD are clear,
 giving insight to life.
⁹Reverence for the LORD is pure,
 lasting forever.
The laws of the LORD are true;
 each one is fair.
¹⁰They are more desirable than gold,
 even the finest gold.
They are sweeter than honey,
 even honey dripping from the comb.
¹¹They are a warning to those who hear them;
 there is great reward for those who obey them.

> I GAIN joy and insight from the Lord's commandments. (19:8)

¹²How can I know all the sins lurking in my heart?
 Cleanse me from these hidden faults.
¹³Keep me from deliberate sins!
 Don't let them control me.
Then I will be free of guilt
 and innocent of great sin.

> I ASK God to cleanse me of my hidden faults and keep me from deliberate sin. (19:12)

¹⁴May the words of my mouth and the thoughts of my heart
 be pleasing to you,
O LORD, my rock and my redeemer.

> I DESIRE to please the Lord with my thoughts and words. (19:14)

PSALM 20

For the choir director: A psalm of David.

¹In times of trouble, may the LORD respond to your cry.
 May the God of Israel* keep you safe from all harm.
²May he send you help from his sanctuary
 and strengthen you from Jerusalem.*
³May he remember all your gifts
 and look favorably on your burnt offerings. *Interlude*

⁴May he grant your heart's desire
 and fulfill all your plans.
⁵May we shout for joy when we hear of your victory,
 flying banners to honor our God.
May the LORD answer all your prayers.

> I PRAY that others will see their prayers and heart's desire fulfilled. (20:4)

⁶Now I know that the LORD saves his anointed king.
 He will answer him from his holy heaven
 and rescue him by his great power.
⁷Some nations boast of their armies and weapons,*
 but we boast in the LORD our God.
⁸Those nations will fall down and collapse,
 but we will rise up and stand firm.

> I BELIEVE the Lord saved and answered King David because he boasted and trusted in God alone. (20:6)

⁹Give victory to our king, O LORD!
 Respond to our cry for help.

20:1 Hebrew *of Jacob.*   20:2 Hebrew *Zion.*   20:7 Hebrew *chariots and horses.*

PSALM 21

For the choir director: A psalm of David.

I REJOICE when God
answers my requests
and gives me my
desires. (21:1)

¹How the king rejoices in your strength, O Lord!
  He shouts with joy because of your victory.
²For you have given him his heart's desire;
  you have held back nothing that he requested.   *Interlude*

³You welcomed him back with success and prosperity.
  You placed a crown of finest gold on his head.
⁴He asked you to preserve his life,
  and you have granted his request.
  The days of his life stretch on forever.
⁵Your victory brings him great honor,
  and you have clothed him with splendor and majesty.
⁶You have endowed him with eternal blessings.
  You have given him the joy of being in your presence.

I PRAISE the Lord, as
David did, for the
eternal blessings he
gives. (21:6)

I TRUST in the Lord's
love to keep me from
stumbling. (21:7)

⁷For the king trusts in the Lord.
  The unfailing love of the Most High will keep him from stumbling.

⁸You will capture all your enemies.
  Your strong right hand will seize all those who hate you.
⁹You will destroy them as in a flaming furnace
  when you appear.
  The Lord will consume them in his anger;
  fire will devour them.
¹⁰You will wipe their children from the face of the earth;
  they will never have descendants.
¹¹Although they plot against you,
  their evil schemes will never succeed.
¹²For they will turn and run
  when they see your arrows aimed at them.

¹³We praise you, Lord, for all your glorious power.
  With music and singing we celebrate your mighty acts.

PSALM 22

For the choir director: A psalm of David, to be sung to the tune "Doe of the Dawn."

I CRY OUT to the Lord
when I feel forsaken.
(22:1)

¹My God, my God! Why have you forsaken me?
  Why do you remain so distant?
  Why do you ignore my cries for help?
²Every day I call to you, my God, but you do not answer.
  Every night you hear my voice, but I find no relief.

³Yet you are holy.
  The praises of Israel surround your throne.
⁴Our ancestors trusted in you,
  and you rescued them.
⁵You heard their cries for help and saved them.
  They put their trust in you and were never disappointed.

I GROAN before the
Lord when I am
despised and treated
as if lower than dirt.
(22:6)

⁶But I am a worm and not a man.
  I am scorned and despised by all!
⁷Everyone who sees me mocks me.
  They sneer and shake their heads, saying,
⁸"Is this the one who relies on the Lord?
  Then let the Lord save him!

If the LORD loves him so much,
let the LORD rescue him!"

⁹ Yet you brought me safely from my mother's womb
and led me to trust you when I was a nursing infant.
¹⁰ I was thrust upon you at my birth.
You have been my God from the moment I was born.

¹¹ Do not stay so far from me,
for trouble is near,
and no one else can help me.
¹² My enemies surround me like a herd of bulls;
fierce bulls of Bashan have hemmed me in!
¹³ Like roaring lions attacking their prey,
they come at me with open mouths.
¹⁴ My life is poured out like water,
and all my bones are out of joint.
My heart is like wax,
melting within me.
¹⁵ My strength has dried up like sunbaked clay.
My tongue sticks to the roof of my mouth.
You have laid me in the dust and left me for dead.

¹⁶ My enemies surround me like a pack of dogs;
an evil gang closes in on me.
They have pierced my hands and feet.
¹⁷ I can count every bone in my body.
My enemies stare at me and gloat.
¹⁸ They divide my clothes among themselves
and throw dice* for my garments.

¹⁹ O LORD, do not stay away!
You are my strength; come quickly to my aid!
²⁰ Rescue me from a violent death;
spare my precious life from these dogs.
²¹ Snatch me from the lions' jaws,
and from the horns of these wild oxen.

²² Then I will declare the wonder of your name to my brothers and sisters.
I will praise you among all your people.
²³ Praise the LORD, all you who fear him!
Honor him, all you descendants of Jacob!
Show him reverence, all you descendants of Israel!
²⁴ For he has not ignored the suffering of the needy.
He has not turned and walked away.
He has listened to their cries for help.

²⁵ I will praise you among all the people;
I will fulfill my vows in the presence of those who worship you.
²⁶ The poor will eat and be satisfied.
All who seek the LORD will praise him.
Their hearts will rejoice with everlasting joy.
²⁷ The whole earth will acknowledge the LORD and return to him.
People from every nation will bow down before him.
²⁸ For the LORD is king!
He rules all the nations.

22:18 Hebrew cast lots.

I TRUST in the Lord, who has sustained me since birth. (22:9)

I RECOGNIZE that sometimes God alone can save me from harm. (22:11)

I BELIEVE David foretold the agony of Jesus Christ when he described his own sufferings (Matthew 27:34-46). (22:14)

I DECLARE the praises of God's name to his people when the Lord rescues me. (22:22)

See Jacob's profile (page 43) at Genesis 32:9.

²⁹ Let the rich of the earth feast and worship.
Let all mortals—those born to die—bow down in his presence.
³⁰ Future generations will also serve him.
Our children will hear about the wonders of the Lord.
³¹ His righteous acts will be told to those yet unborn.
They will hear about everything he has done.

PSALM 23

A psalm of David.

¹ The LORD is my shepherd;
  I have everything I need.
² He lets me rest in green meadows;
  he leads me beside peaceful streams.
³ He renews my strength.
He guides me along right paths,
  bringing honor to his name.

⁴ Even when I walk
  through the dark valley of death,*
I will not be afraid,
  for you are close beside me.
Your rod and your staff
  protect and comfort me.

⁵ You prepare a feast for me
  in the presence of my enemies.
You welcome me as a guest,
  anointing my head with oil.
  My cup overflows with blessings.
⁶ Surely your goodness and unfailing love will pursue me
  all the days of my life,
and I will live in the house of the LORD
  forever.

PSALM 24

A psalm of David.

¹ The earth is the LORD's, and everything in it.
  The world and all its people belong to him.
² For he laid the earth's foundation on the seas
  and built it on the ocean depths.

³ Who may climb the mountain of the LORD?
  Who may stand in his holy place?
⁴ Only those whose hands and hearts are pure,
  who do not worship idols
  and never tell lies.
⁵ They will receive the LORD's blessing
  and have right standing with God their savior.
⁶ They alone may enter God's presence
  and worship the God of Israel.*   *Interlude*

⁷ Open up, ancient gates!
  Open up, ancient doors,
  and let the King of glory enter.
⁸ Who is the King of glory?

23:4 Or *the darkest valley.*   **24:6** Hebrew *of Jacob.*

I WILL TELL my children and their children of the wonders of the Lord. (22:30)

I RECEIVE God's renewal of my soul and guidance for my life. (23:2)

I TRUST the Lord and am not afraid in the midst of great difficulty—even the threat of death. (23:4)

I EMBRACE the Lord's unfailing love, which pursues me and promises me a place in his house forever. (23:6)

I BELIEVE the world and all its people belong to the Lord, because he made them. (24:1)

I WANT to live a pure life and receive God's blessing (James 4:8). (24:4)

The LORD, strong and mighty,
the LORD, invincible in battle.
⁹ Open up, ancient gates!
Open up, ancient doors,
and let the King of glory enter.
¹⁰ Who is the King of glory?
The LORD Almighty—
he is the King of glory.

Interlude

Today what command(s) are you choosing to obey?

PSALM 25

A psalm of David.

¹ To you, O LORD, I lift up my soul.
²   I trust in you, my God!
Do not let me be disgraced,
or let my enemies rejoice in my defeat.
³ No one who trusts in you will ever be disgraced,
but disgrace comes to those who try to deceive others.

⁴ Show me the path where I should walk, O LORD;
point out the right road for me to follow.
⁵ Lead me by your truth and teach me,
for you are the God who saves me.
All day long I put my hope in you.

I ASK the Lord to lead me in his truth, and I will follow. (25:5)

⁶ Remember, O LORD, your unfailing love and compassion,
which you have shown from long ages past.
⁷ Forgive the rebellious sins of my youth;
look instead through the eyes of your unfailing love,
for you are merciful, O LORD.

I APPEAL to the Lord's unfailing love and seek his forgiveness for the sins of my youth. (25:7)

⁸ The LORD is good and does what is right;
he shows the proper path to those who go astray.
⁹ He leads the humble in what is right,
teaching them his way.
¹⁰ The LORD leads with unfailing love and faithfulness
all those who keep his covenant and obey his decrees.

¹¹ For the honor of your name, O LORD,
forgive my many, many sins.
¹² Who are those who fear the LORD?
He will show them the path they should choose.
¹³ They will live in prosperity,
and their children will inherit the Promised Land.
¹⁴ Friendship with the LORD is reserved for those who fear him.
With them he shares the secrets of his covenant.
¹⁵ My eyes are always looking to the LORD for help,
for he alone can rescue me from the traps of my enemies.

I FEAR the Lord and enjoy intimate friendship with him. (25:14)

¹⁶ Turn to me and have mercy on me,
for I am alone and in deep distress.
¹⁷ My problems go from bad to worse.
Oh, save me from them all!
¹⁸ Feel my pain and see my trouble.
Forgive all my sins.
¹⁹ See how many enemies I have,
and how viciously they hate me!
²⁰ Protect me! Rescue my life from them!
Do not let me be disgraced, for I trust in you.

I CRY OUT to the Lord and trust him to save me from disgrace and defeat. (25:20)

²¹ May integrity and honesty protect me,
for I put my hope in you.

²² O God, ransom Israel
from all its troubles.

PSALM 26

A psalm of David.

¹ Declare me innocent, O LORD,
for I have acted with integrity;
I have trusted in the LORD without wavering.
² Put me on trial, LORD, and cross-examine me.
Test my motives and affections.
³ For I am constantly aware of your unfailing love,
and I have lived according to your truth.

⁴ I do not spend time with liars
or go along with hypocrites.
⁵ I hate the gatherings of those who do evil,
and I refuse to join in with the wicked.

⁶ I wash my hands to declare my innocence.
I come to your altar, O LORD,
⁷ singing a song of thanksgiving
and telling of all your miracles.
⁸ I love your sanctuary, LORD,
the place where your glory shines.

⁹ Don't let me suffer the fate of sinners.
Don't condemn me along with murderers.
¹⁰ Their hands are dirty with wicked schemes,
and they constantly take bribes.

¹¹ But I am not like that; I do what is right.
So in your mercy, save me.
¹² I have taken a stand,
and I will publicly praise the LORD.

PSALM 27

A psalm of David.

¹ The LORD is my light and my salvation—
so why should I be afraid?
The LORD protects me from danger—
so why should I tremble?

² When evil people come to destroy me,
when my enemies and foes attack me,
they will stumble and fall.
³ Though a mighty army surrounds me,
my heart will know no fear.
Even if they attack me,
I remain confident.

⁴ The one thing I ask of the LORD—
the thing I seek most—
is to live in the house of the LORD all the days of my life,
delighting in the LORD's perfections
and meditating in his Temple.

I ASK the Lord to test my motives and affections. (26:2)

I LIVE according to God's truth because I am aware of his love. (26:3)

I WORSHIP the Lord wholeheartedly and seek to keep myself innocent of wrongdoing. (26:6)

I WILL BE CONFIDENT, though enemies come against me and attack me. (27:3)

⁵ For he will conceal me there when troubles come;
    he will hide me in his sanctuary.
    He will place me out of reach on a high rock.
⁶ Then I will hold my head high,
    above my enemies who surround me.
  At his Tabernacle I will offer sacrifices with shouts of joy,
    singing and praising the LORD with music.

⁷ Listen to my pleading, O LORD.
    Be merciful and answer me!
⁸ My heart has heard you say, "Come and talk with me."
    And my heart responds, "LORD, I am coming."
⁹ Do not hide yourself from me.
    Do not reject your servant in anger.
    You have always been my helper.
  Don't leave me now; don't abandon me,
    O God of my salvation!
¹⁰ Even if my father and mother abandon me,
    the LORD will hold me close.

> I RESPOND to the Lord's invitation to spend time with him. (27:8)

¹¹ Teach me how to live, O LORD.
    Lead me along the path of honesty,
    for my enemies are waiting for me to fall.
¹² Do not let me fall into their hands.
    For they accuse me of things I've never done
    and breathe out violence against me.
¹³ Yet I am confident that I will see the LORD's goodness
    while I am here in the land of the living.

> I TRUST in the Lord to hold on to me, even when everyone else abandons me. (27:10)

¹⁴ Wait patiently for the LORD.
    Be brave and courageous.
    Yes, wait patiently for the LORD.

PSALM 28

A psalm of David.

¹ O LORD, you are my rock of safety.
    Please help me; don't refuse to answer me.
  For if you are silent,
    I might as well give up and die.
² Listen to my prayer for mercy
    as I cry out to you for help,
    as I lift my hands toward your holy sanctuary.

> I BEG God for help and mercy. (28:2)

³ Don't drag me away with the wicked—
    with those who do evil—
  those who speak friendly words to their neighbors
    while planning evil in their hearts.
⁴ Give them the punishment they so richly deserve!
    Measure it out in proportion to their wickedness.
  Pay them back for all their evil deeds!
    Give them a taste of what they have done to others.
⁵ They care nothing for what the LORD has done
    or for what his hands have made.
  So he will tear them down like old buildings,
    and they will never be rebuilt!

> I ASK the Lord to spare me from being punished along with people who plan evil. (28:3)

⁶ Praise the LORD!
    For he has heard my cry for mercy.

⁷The LORD is my strength, my shield from every danger.
    I trust in him with all my heart.
He helps me, and my heart is filled with joy.
    I burst out in songs of thanksgiving.

I PRAISE the Lord for protecting and blessing his people. (28:8)

⁸The LORD protects his people
    and gives victory to his anointed king.
⁹Save your people!
    Bless Israel, your special possession!
Lead them like a shepherd,
    and carry them forever in your arms.

PSALM 29

A psalm of David.

I WORSHIP the Lord and honor his glorious name. (29:2)

¹Give honor to the LORD, you angels;
    give honor to the LORD for his glory and strength.
²Give honor to the LORD for the glory of his name.
    Worship the LORD in the splendor of his holiness.

³The voice of the LORD echoes above the sea.
    The God of glory thunders.
    The LORD thunders over the mighty sea.
⁴The voice of the LORD is powerful;
    the voice of the LORD is full of majesty.
⁵The voice of the LORD splits the mighty cedars;
    the LORD shatters the cedars of Lebanon.
⁶He makes Lebanon's mountains skip like a calf
    and Mount Hermon* to leap like a young bull.
⁷The voice of the LORD strikes with lightning bolts.
⁸The voice of the LORD makes the desert quake;
    the LORD shakes the desert of Kadesh.

I SHOUT, "Glory!" because of the Lord's might and power over all his creation. (29:9)

⁹The voice of the LORD twists mighty oaks*
    and strips the forests bare.
In his Temple everyone shouts, "Glory!"

¹⁰The LORD rules over the floodwaters.
    The LORD reigns as king forever.
¹¹The LORD gives his people strength.
    The LORD blesses them with peace.

PSALM 30

A psalm of David, sung at the dedication of the Temple.

¹I will praise you, LORD, for you have rescued me.
    You refused to let my enemies triumph over me.
²O LORD my God, I cried out to you for help,
    and you restored my health.
³You brought me up from the grave, O LORD.
    You kept me from falling into the pit of death.

I URGE others to sing to the Lord and praise him. (30:4)

I REVEL in God's favor and the joy he brings after discipline and sorrow. (30:5)

⁴Sing to the LORD, all you godly ones!
    Praise his holy name.
⁵His anger lasts for a moment,
    but his favor lasts a lifetime!
Weeping may go on all night,
    but joy comes with the morning.

29:6 Hebrew *Sirion,* another name for Mount Hermon.   29:9 Or *causes the deer to writhe in labor.*

⁶ When I was prosperous I said,
  "Nothing can stop me now!"
⁷ Your favor, O LORD, made me as secure as a mountain.
  Then you turned away from me, and I was shattered.

⁸ I cried out to you, O LORD.
  I begged the Lord for mercy, saying,
⁹ "What will you gain if I die,
  if I sink down into the grave?
  Can my dust praise you from the grave?
  Can it tell the world of your faithfulness?
¹⁰ Hear me, LORD, and have mercy on me.
  Help me, O LORD."

I BEG the Lord to allow me to live so that I can praise him to the world. (30:8)

¹¹ You have turned my mourning into joyful dancing.
  You have taken away my clothes of mourning and clothed me with joy,
¹² that I might sing praises to you and not be silent.
  O LORD my God, I will give you thanks forever!

PSALM 31

For the choir director: A psalm of David.

¹ O LORD, I have come to you for protection;
  don't let me be put to shame.
  Rescue me, for you always do what is right.
² Bend down and listen to me;
  rescue me quickly.
  Be for me a great rock of safety,
  a fortress where my enemies cannot reach me.

³ You are my rock and my fortress.
  For the honor of your name, lead me out of this peril.
⁴ Pull me from the trap my enemies set for me,
  for I find protection in you alone.
⁵ I entrust my spirit into your hand.
  Rescue me, LORD, for you are a faithful God.

I TRUST the Lord to protect me for the honor of his name. (31:3)

⁶ I hate those who worship worthless idols.
  I trust in the LORD.
⁷ I am overcome with joy because of your unfailing love,
  for you have seen my troubles,
  and you care about the anguish of my soul.
⁸ You have not handed me over to my enemy
  but have set me in a safe place.

I FIND joy because God loves me and cares about my troubles (1 Peter 5:7). (31:7)

⁹ Have mercy on me, LORD, for I am in distress.
  My sight is blurred because of my tears.
  My body and soul are withering away.
¹⁰ I am dying from grief;
  my years are shortened by sadness.
  Misery* has drained my strength;
  I am wasting away from within.
¹¹ I am scorned by all my enemies
  and despised by my neighbors—
  even my friends are afraid to come near me.
  When they see me on the street,
  they turn the other way.

I ASK for the Lord's mercy when I am wasting away from grief and misery. (31:9)

31:10 Or *Sin.*

¹²I have been ignored as if I were dead,
    as if I were a broken pot.
¹³I have heard the many rumors about me,
    and I am surrounded by terror.
My enemies conspire against me,
    plotting to take my life.

¹⁴But I am trusting you, O LORD,
    saying, "You are my God!"

I AM TRUSTING in the Lord for my future. (31:15)

¹⁵My future is in your hands.
    Rescue me from those who hunt me down relentlessly.
¹⁶Let your favor shine on your servant.
    In your unfailing love, save me.
¹⁷Don't let me be disgraced, O LORD,
    for I call out to you for help.
Let the wicked be disgraced;
    let them lie silent in the grave.
¹⁸May their lying lips be silenced—
    those proud and arrogant lips that accuse the godly.

I PRAISE the Lord for his goodness and love, which bless his servants before the watching world. (31:19)

¹⁹Your goodness is so great!
    You have stored up great blessings for those who honor you.
You have done so much for those who come to you for protection,
    blessing them before the watching world.
²⁰You hide them in the shelter of your presence,
    safe from those who conspire against them.
You shelter them in your presence,
    far from accusing tongues.

²¹Praise the LORD,
    for he has shown me his unfailing love.
He kept me safe when my city was under attack.
²²In sudden fear I had cried out,
    "I have been cut off from the LORD!"
But you heard my cry for mercy
    and answered my call for help.

I URGE God's people to love him. (31:23)

²³Love the LORD, all you faithful ones!
    For the LORD protects those who are loyal to him,
    but he harshly punishes all who are arrogant.
²⁴So be strong and take courage,
    all you who put your hope in the LORD!

PSALM 32

A psalm of David.

I REJOICE because my sins are forgiven! (32:1)

¹Oh, what joy for those
    whose rebellion is forgiven,
    whose sin is put out of sight!
²Yes, what joy for those
    whose record the LORD has cleared of sin,
    whose lives are lived in complete honesty!

³When I refused to confess my sin,
    I was weak and miserable,
    and I groaned all day long.
⁴Day and night your hand of discipline was heavy on me.
    My strength evaporated like water in the summer heat. *Interlude*

[5] Finally, I confessed all my sins to you
and stopped trying to hide them.
I said to myself, "I will confess my rebellion to the LORD."
And you forgave me! All my guilt is gone.   *Interlude*

[6] Therefore, let all the godly confess their rebellion to you while there is
time,
that they may not drown in the floodwaters of judgment.
[7] For you are my hiding place;
you protect me from trouble.
You surround me with songs of victory.   *Interlude*

[8] The LORD says, "I will guide you along the best pathway for your life.
I will advise you and watch over you.
[9] Do not be like a senseless horse or mule
that needs a bit and bridle to keep it under control."

[10] Many sorrows come to the wicked,
but unfailing love surrounds those who trust the LORD.
[11] So rejoice in the LORD and be glad, all you who obey him!
Shout for joy, all you whose hearts are pure!

PSALM 33

[1] Let the godly sing with joy to the LORD,
for it is fitting to praise him.
[2] Praise the LORD with melodies on the lyre;
make music for him on the ten-stringed harp.
[3] Sing new songs of praise to him;
play skillfully on the harp and sing with joy.

[4] For the word of the LORD holds true,
and everything he does is worthy of our trust.
[5] He loves whatever is just and good,
and his unfailing love fills the earth.

[6] The LORD merely spoke,
and the heavens were created.
He breathed the word,
and all the stars were born.
[7] He gave the sea its boundaries
and locked the oceans in vast reservoirs.

[8] Let everyone in the world fear the LORD,
and let everyone stand in awe of him.
[9] For when he spoke, the world began!
It appeared at his command.

[10] The LORD shatters the plans of the nations
and thwarts all their schemes.
[11] But the LORD's plans stand firm forever;
his intentions can never be shaken.

[12] What joy for the nation whose God is the LORD,
whose people he has chosen for his own.

[13] The LORD looks down from heaven
and sees the whole human race.
[14] From his throne he observes
all who live on the earth.
[15] He made their hearts,
so he understands everything they do.

I CONFESS my sins to God (1 John 1:9). (32:5)

I SHOUT with great joy because the Lord has made my heart pure. (32:11)

I PRAISE the Lord because he is totally trustworthy. (33:4)

I BELIEVE the Lord's plans stand firm, but he shatters the plans of his enemies. (33:10)

I BELIEVE the Lord sees and understands every person on the earth. (33:13)

¹⁶The best-equipped army cannot save a king,
  nor is great strength enough to save a warrior.
¹⁷Don't count on your warhorse to give you victory—
  for all its strength, it cannot save you.

¹⁸But the LORD watches over those who fear him,
  those who rely on his unfailing love.
¹⁹He rescues them from death
  and keeps them alive in times of famine.

²⁰We depend on the LORD alone to save us.
  Only he can help us, protecting us like a shield.
²¹In him our hearts rejoice,
  for we are trusting in his holy name.
²²Let your unfailing love surround us, LORD,
  for our hope is in you alone.

PSALM 34

A psalm of David, regarding the time he pretended to be insane in front of Abimelech, who sent him away.

¹I will praise the LORD at all times.
  I will constantly speak his praises.
²I will boast only in the LORD;
  let all who are discouraged take heart.
³Come, let us tell of the LORD's greatness;
  let us exalt his name together.

⁴I prayed to the LORD, and he answered me,
  freeing me from all my fears.
⁵Those who look to him for help will be radiant with joy;
  no shadow of shame will darken their faces.
⁶I cried out to the LORD in my suffering, and he heard me.
  He set me free from all my fears.
⁷For the angel of the LORD guards all who fear him,
  and he rescues them.

⁸Taste and see that the LORD is good.
  Oh, the joys of those who trust in him!
⁹Let the LORD's people show him reverence,
  for those who honor him will have all they need.
¹⁰Even strong young lions sometimes go hungry,
  but those who trust in the LORD will never lack any good thing.

¹¹Come, my children, and listen to me,
  and I will teach you to fear the LORD.
¹²Do any of you want to live
  a life that is long and good?
¹³Then watch your tongue!
  Keep your lips from telling lies!
¹⁴Turn away from evil and do good.
  Work hard at living in peace with others.

¹⁵The eyes of the LORD watch over those who do right;
  his ears are open to their cries for help.
¹⁶But the LORD turns his face against those who do evil;
  he will erase their memory from the earth.

¹⁷The LORD hears his people when they call to him for help.
  He rescues them from all their troubles.

I DO NOT COUNT on my own strength and resources to save me. (33:17)

I AM SURROUNDED by the Lord's unfailing love, so I hope in him. (33:22)

I URGE others to talk with me about the Lord and his greatness. (34:3)

I CRY OUT to the Lord, who sets me free from fear and shame (see 1 Samuel 21:10-15). (34:6)

I TEACH children how to fear the Lord. (34:11)

[18] The LORD is close to the brokenhearted;
he rescues those who are crushed in spirit.

[19] The righteous face many troubles,
but the LORD rescues them from each and every one.
[20] For the LORD protects them from harm—
not one of their bones* will be broken!

I TRUST in the Lord's protection, even in the midst of troubles. (34:19)

[21] Calamity will surely overtake the wicked,
and those who hate the righteous will be punished.
[22] But the LORD will redeem those who serve him.
Everyone who trusts in him will be freely pardoned.

I ENJOY the Lord's redemption and pardon. (34:22)

PSALM 35

A psalm of David.

[1] O LORD, oppose those who oppose me.
Declare war on those who are attacking me.
[2] Put on your armor, and take up your shield.
Prepare for battle, and come to my aid.
[3] Lift up your spear and javelin
and block the way of my enemies.
Let me hear you say,
"I am your salvation!"

I CALL ON the Lord to fight my enemies for me. (35:1)

[4] Humiliate and disgrace those trying to kill me;
turn them back in confusion.
[5] Blow them away like chaff in the wind—
a wind sent by the angel of the LORD.
[6] Make their path dark and slippery,
with the angel of the LORD pursuing them.
[7] Although I did them no wrong,
they laid a trap for me.
Although I did them no wrong,
they dug a pit for me.
[8] So let sudden ruin overtake them!
Let them be caught in the snare they set for me!
Let them fall to destruction in the pit they dug for me.

[9] Then I will rejoice in the LORD.
I will be glad because he rescues me.
[10] I will praise him from the bottom of my heart:
"LORD, who can compare with you?
Who else rescues the weak and helpless from the strong?
Who else protects the poor and needy from those who want to rob them?"

I PRAISE the Lord, who rescues the weak and needy from the strong and oppressive. (35:10)

[11] Malicious witnesses testify against me.
They accuse me of things I don't even know about.
[12] They repay me with evil for the good I do.
I am sick with despair.
[13] Yet when they were ill,
I grieved for them.
I even fasted and prayed for them,
but my prayers returned unanswered.
[14] I was sad, as though they were my friends or family,
as if I were grieving for my own mother.

34:20 Hebrew *protects him from harm—not one of his bones.*

¹⁵ But they are glad now that I am in trouble;
  they gleefully join together against me.
 I am attacked by people I don't even know;
  they hurl slander at me continually.
¹⁶ They mock me with the worst kind of profanity,
  and they snarl at me.

¹⁷ How long, O Lord, will you look on and do nothing?
  Rescue me from their fierce attacks.
  Protect my life from these lions!
¹⁸ Then I will thank you in front of the entire congregation.
  I will praise you before all the people.

¹⁹ Don't let my treacherous enemies
  rejoice over my defeat.
 Don't let those who hate me without cause
  gloat over my sorrow.
²⁰ They don't talk of peace;
  they plot against innocent people
  who are minding their own business.
²¹ They shout that they have seen me doing wrong.
  "Aha," they say. "Aha!
  With our own eyes we saw him do it!"

²² O LORD, you know all about this.
  Do not stay silent.
  Don't abandon me now, O Lord.
²³ Wake up! Rise to my defense!
  Take up my case, my God and my Lord.
²⁴ Declare me "not guilty," O LORD my God, for you give justice.
  Don't let my enemies laugh about me in my troubles.
²⁵ Don't let them say, "Look! We have what we wanted!
  Now we will eat him alive!"

²⁶ May those who rejoice at my troubles
  be humiliated and disgraced.
 May those who triumph over me
  be covered with shame and dishonor.

²⁷ But give great joy to those
  who have stood with me in my defense.
 Let them continually say, "Great is the LORD,
  who enjoys helping his servant."
²⁸ Then I will tell everyone of your justice and goodness,
  and I will praise you all day long.

PSALM **36**

For the choir director: A psalm of David, the servant of the LORD.

¹ Sin whispers to the wicked, deep within their hearts.
  They have no fear of God to restrain them.
² In their blind conceit,
  they cannot see how wicked they really are.
³ Everything they say is crooked and deceitful.
  They refuse to act wisely or do what is good.
⁴ They lie awake at night, hatching sinful plots.
  Their course of action is never good.
  They make no attempt to turn from evil.

I THANK the Lord publicly when I am rescued from mocking and slander. (35:18)

I PRAY that hurtful people will not know success in their schemes. (35:19)

I LOOK to the Lord to declare me not guilty and to clear me before my enemies. (35:24)

I ASK the Lord to bless those who have helped and defended me. (35:27)

I FEAR the Lord and restrain myself from sin. (36:1)

⁵Your unfailing love, O LORD, is as vast as the heavens;
  your faithfulness reaches beyond the clouds.
⁶Your righteousness is like the mighty mountains,
  your justice like the ocean depths.
You care for people and animals alike, O LORD.
⁷ How precious is your unfailing love, O God!
All humanity finds shelter
  in the shadow of your wings.
⁸You feed them from the abundance of your own house,
  letting them drink from your rivers of delight.
⁹For you are the fountain of life,
  the light by which we see.

¹⁰Pour out your unfailing love on those who love you;
  give justice to those with honest hearts.
¹¹Don't let the proud trample me;
  don't let the wicked push me around.
¹²Look! They have fallen!
  They have been thrown down, never to rise again.

PSALM 37

A psalm of David.

¹Don't worry about the wicked.
  Don't envy those who do wrong.
²For like grass, they soon fade away.
  Like springtime flowers, they soon wither.

³Trust in the LORD and do good.
  Then you will live safely in the land and prosper.
⁴Take delight in the LORD,
  and he will give you your heart's desires.

⁵Commit everything you do to the LORD.
  Trust him, and he will help you.
⁶He will make your innocence as clear as the dawn,
  and the justice of your cause will shine like the noonday sun.

⁷Be still in the presence of the LORD,
  and wait patiently for him to act.
Don't worry about evil people who prosper
  or fret about their wicked schemes.

⁸Stop your anger!
  Turn from your rage!
Do not envy others—
  it only leads to harm.
⁹For the wicked will be destroyed,
  but those who trust in the LORD will possess the land.

¹⁰In a little while, the wicked will disappear.
  Though you look for them, they will be gone.
¹¹Those who are gentle and lowly will possess the land;
  they will live in prosperous security.

¹²The wicked plot against the godly;
  they snarl at them in defiance.
¹³But the Lord just laughs,
  for he sees their day of judgment coming.

I TREASURE the Lord's unfailing and tender care. (36:7)

I LOOK to the Lord as the source of light and life for all humanity. (36:9)

I DO NOT FRET because of evil people or become envious of those who do wrong. (37:1)

I COMMIT my way to the Lord and trust in him to help me. (37:5)

I DO NOT GET ANGRY when evil individuals prosper. (37:8)

If something in this Bible helps you experience a closer walk with God, why not share it with others?

14 The wicked draw their swords
   and string their bows
 to kill the poor and the oppressed,
   to slaughter those who do right.
15 But they will be stabbed through the heart with their own swords,
   and their bows will be broken.

16 It is better to be godly and have little
   than to be evil and possess much.
17 For the strength of the wicked will be shattered,
   but the LORD takes care of the godly.

I BELIEVE that the Lord cares for me and that he will give me a lasting reward. (37:18)

18 Day by day the LORD takes care of the innocent,
   and they will receive a reward that lasts forever.
19 They will survive through hard times;
   even in famine they will have more than enough.

20 But the wicked will perish.
   The LORD's enemies are like flowers in a field—
   they will disappear like smoke.

21 The wicked borrow and never repay,
   but the godly are generous givers.
22 Those blessed by the LORD will inherit the land,
   but those cursed by him will die.

I AM CONFIDENT that the Lord delights in every detail of my life. (37:23)

23 The steps of the godly are directed by the LORD.
   He delights in every detail of their lives.
24 Though they stumble, they will not fall,
   for the LORD holds them by the hand.

25 Once I was young, and now I am old.
   Yet I have never seen the godly forsaken,
   nor seen their children begging for bread.
26 The godly always give generous loans to others,
   and their children are a blessing.

I TURN from evil and do good, knowing I will enjoy God's blessings forever. (37:27)

27 Turn from evil and do good,
   and you will live in the land forever.
28 For the LORD loves justice,
   and he will never abandon the godly.

He will keep them safe forever,
   but the children of the wicked will perish.
29 The godly will inherit the land
   and will live there forever.

30 The godly offer good counsel;
   they know what is right from wrong.
31 They fill their hearts with God's law,
   so they will never slip from his path.

I DO NOT SLIP from God's path, for his Word fills my heart. (37:31)

32 Those who are evil spy on the godly,
   waiting for an excuse to kill them.
33 But the LORD will not let the wicked succeed
   or let the godly be condemned when they are brought before the judge.

I WAIT for the Lord and stay on his path, trusting that he will honor me and give me a rich inheritance. (37:34)

34 Don't be impatient for the LORD to act!
   Travel steadily along his path.
He will honor you, giving you the land.
   You will see the wicked destroyed.

³⁵ I myself have seen it happen—
proud and evil people thriving like mighty trees.
³⁶ But when I looked again, they were gone!
Though I searched for them, I could not find them!

³⁷ Look at those who are honest and good,
for a wonderful future lies before those who love peace.
³⁸ But the wicked will be destroyed;
they have no future.

³⁹ The LORD saves the godly;
he is their fortress in times of trouble.
⁴⁰ The LORD helps them,
rescuing them from the wicked.
He saves them,
and they find shelter in him.

PSALM 38

A psalm of David, to bring us to the LORD's remembrance.

¹ O LORD, don't rebuke me in your anger!
Don't discipline me in your rage!
² Your arrows have struck deep,
and your blows are crushing me.

³ Because of your anger, my whole body is sick;
my health is broken because of my sins.
⁴ My guilt overwhelms me—
it is a burden too heavy to bear.
⁵ My wounds fester and stink
because of my foolish sins.
⁶ I am bent over and racked with pain.
My days are filled with grief.
⁷ A raging fever burns within me,
and my health is broken.
⁸ I am exhausted and completely crushed.
My groans come from an anguished heart.

⁹ You know what I long for, Lord;
you hear my every sigh.
¹⁰ My heart beats wildly, my strength fails,
and I am going blind.
¹¹ My loved ones and friends stay away, fearing my disease.
Even my own family stands at a distance.
¹² Meanwhile, my enemies lay traps for me;
they make plans to ruin me.
They think up treacherous deeds all day long.
¹³ But I am deaf to all their threats.
I am silent before them as one who cannot speak.
¹⁴ I choose to hear nothing,
and I make no reply.

¹⁵ For I am waiting for you, O LORD.
You must answer for me, O Lord my God.
¹⁶ I prayed, "Don't let my enemies gloat over me
or rejoice at my downfall."
¹⁷ I am on the verge of collapse,
facing constant pain.
¹⁸ But I confess my sins;
I am deeply sorry for what I have done.

I KNOW that salvation comes from the Lord and that he alone is my fortress in times of trouble. (37:39)

I ADMIT when my suffering is a result of my foolish sin. (38:5)

I FOCUS completely on the Lord and wait for his answer when I am weak, suffering, or abandoned. (38:15)

I CONFESS my sins and am deeply sorry when I have done wrong. (38:18)

I PRAY to God when people hate me without reason or because I stand for what is right. (38:19)

¹⁹ My enemies are many;
    they hate me though I have done nothing against them.
²⁰ They repay me evil for good
    and oppose me because I stand for the right.

²¹ Do not abandon me, LORD.
    Do not stand at a distance, my God.
²² Come quickly to help me, O Lord my savior.

PSALM 39

For Jeduthun, the choir director: A psalm of David.

I CURB my tongue when I am frustrated with life so that I will not sin by dishonoring the Lord. (39:1)

¹ I said to myself, "I will watch what I do
    and not sin in what I say.
  I will curb my tongue
    when the ungodly are around me."
² But as I stood there in silence—
    not even speaking of good things—
    the turmoil within me grew to the bursting point.
³ My thoughts grew hot within me
    and began to burn,
    igniting a fire of words:
⁴ "LORD, remind me how brief my time on earth will be.
    Remind me that my days are numbered,
    and that my life is fleeing away.
⁵ My life is no longer than the width of my hand.
    An entire lifetime is just a moment to you;
    human existence is but a breath."   *Interlude*

⁶ We are merely moving shadows,
    and all our busy rushing ends in nothing.
    We heap up wealth for someone else to spend.

I PUT my hope in the Lord, not the length or meaningfulness of my life. (39:7)

⁷ And so, Lord, where do I put my hope?
    My only hope is in you.
⁸ Rescue me from my rebellion,
    for even fools mock me when I rebel.
⁹ I am silent before you; I won't say a word.
    For my punishment is from you.
¹⁰ Please, don't punish me anymore!
    I am exhausted by the blows from your hand.
¹¹ When you discipline people for their sins,
    their lives can be crushed like the life of a moth.
    Human existence is as frail as breath.   *Interlude*

I PRAY for God's help as I pass briefly through this life. (39:12)

¹² Hear my prayer, O LORD!
    Listen to my cries for help!
    Don't ignore my tears.
  For I am your guest—
    a traveler passing through,
    as my ancestors were before me.
¹³ Spare me so I can smile again
    before I am gone and exist no more.

PSALM 40

For the choir director: A psalm of David.

¹ I waited patiently for the LORD to help me,
    and he turned to me and heard my cry.

[2] He lifted me out of the pit of despair,
   out of the mud and the mire.
He set my feet on solid ground
   and steadied me as I walked along.
[3] He has given me a new song to sing,
   a hymn of praise to our God.
Many will see what he has done and be astounded.
   They will put their trust in the LORD.

[4] Oh, the joys of those who trust the LORD,
   who have no confidence in the proud,
   or in those who worship idols.
[5] O LORD my God, you have done many miracles for us.
   Your plans for us are too numerous to list.
If I tried to recite all your wonderful deeds,
   I would never come to the end of them.

[6] You take no delight in sacrifices or offerings.
   Now that you have made me listen, I finally understand—
   you don't require burnt offerings or sin offerings.
[7] Then I said, "Look, I have come.
   And this has been written about me in your scroll:
[8] I take joy in doing your will, my God,
   for your law is written on my heart."

[9] I have told all your people about your justice.
   I have not been afraid to speak out,
   as you, O LORD, well know.
[10] I have not kept this good news hidden in my heart;
   I have talked about your faithfulness and saving power.
I have told everyone in the great assembly
   of your unfailing love and faithfulness.

[11] LORD, don't hold back your tender mercies from me.
   My only hope is in your unfailing love and faithfulness.
[12] For troubles surround me—
   too many to count!
They pile up so high
   I can't see my way out.
They are more numerous than the hairs on my head.
   I have lost all my courage.

[13] Please, LORD, rescue me!
   Come quickly, LORD, and help me.
[14] May those who try to destroy me
   be humiliated and put to shame.
May those who take delight in my trouble
   be turned back in disgrace.
[15] Let them be horrified by their shame,
   for they said, "Aha! We've got him now!"

[16] But may all who search for you
   be filled with joy and gladness.
May those who love your salvation
   repeatedly shout, "The LORD is great!"

[17] As for me, I am poor and needy,
   but the Lord is thinking about me right now.
You are my helper and my savior.
   Do not delay, O my God.

I SING my song of God's praise so other people will worship and trust him. (40:3)

I KNOW God values my obedience more than sacrifices and offerings. (40:6)

I BELIEVE the Lord's scroll foretold the coming Lord Jesus' joy in doing God's will and in offering himself as the perfect sacrifice (Hebrews 10:5-7). (40:7)

I TELL everyone around me about God's justice, goodness, power, and love. (40:9)

I BELIEVE the Lord is thinking about me and that he will help and save me. (40:17)

PSALM **41**

For the choir director: A psalm of David.

I SHOW kindness to the poor and enjoy God's protection in times of trouble. (41:1)

¹ Oh, the joys of those who are kind to the poor.
   The LORD rescues them in times of trouble.
² The LORD protects them
   and keeps them alive.
He gives them prosperity
   and rescues them from their enemies.
³ The LORD nurses them when they are sick
   and eases their pain and discomfort.

I PRAY for God's healing when I am suffering because of my sin. (41:4)

I APPEAL to the Lord when others are glad about my suffering. (41:5)

⁴ "O LORD," I prayed, "have mercy on me.
   Heal me, for I have sinned against you."
⁵ But my enemies say nothing but evil about me.
   "How soon will he die and be forgotten?" they ask.
⁶ They visit me as if they are my friends,
   but all the while they gather gossip,
   and when they leave, they spread it everywhere.
⁷ All who hate me whisper about me,
   imagining the worst for me.
⁸ "Whatever he has, it is fatal," they say.
   "He will never get out of that bed!"
⁹ Even my best friend, the one I trusted completely,
   the one who shared my food,
   has turned against me.

¹⁰ LORD, have mercy on me.
   Make me well again, so I can pay them back!
¹¹ I know that you are pleased with me,
   for you have not let my enemy triumph over me.
¹² You have preserved my life because I am innocent;
   you have brought me into your presence forever.

¹³ Bless the LORD, the God of Israel,
   who lives forever from eternal ages past.
   Amen and amen!

BOOK TWO (Psalms 42–72)

PSALM **42**

For the choir director: A psalm of the descendants of Korah.

I THIRST for God and long to meet with him each day. (42:1)

¹ As the deer pants for streams of water,
   so I long for you, O God.
² I thirst for God, the living God.
   When can I come and stand before him?
³ Day and night, I have only tears for food,
   while my enemies continually taunt me, saying,
   "Where is this God of yours?"

⁴ My heart is breaking
   as I remember how it used to be:
I walked among the crowds of worshipers,
   leading a great procession to the house of God,
singing for joy and giving thanks—
   it was the sound of a great celebration!

I REMEMBER God's kindness and put my hope in him when I am discouraged. (42:5)

⁵ Why am I discouraged?
   Why so sad?

I will put my hope in God!
   I will praise him again—
   my Savior and [6]my God!

Now I am deeply discouraged,
   but I will remember your kindness—
from Mount Hermon, the source of the Jordan,
   from the land of Mount Mizar.
[7]I hear the tumult of the raging seas
   as your waves and surging tides sweep over me.

[8]Through each day the LORD pours his unfailing love upon me,
   and through each night I sing his songs,
   praying to God who gives me life.

[9]"O God my rock," I cry,
   "Why have you forsaken me?
Why must I wander in darkness,
   oppressed by my enemies?"
[10]Their taunts pierce me like a fatal wound.
   They scoff, "Where is this God of yours?"

[11]Why am I discouraged?
   Why so sad?
I will put my hope in God!
   I will praise him again—
   my Savior and my God!

PSALM 43

[1]O God, take up my cause!
   Defend me against these ungodly people.
   Rescue me from these unjust liars.
[2]For you are God, my only safe haven.
   Why have you tossed me aside?
Why must I wander around in darkness,
   oppressed by my enemies?

[3]Send out your light and your truth;
   let them guide me.
Let them lead me to your holy mountain,
   to the place where you live.
[4]There I will go to the altar of God,
   to God—the source of all my joy.
I will praise you with my harp,
   O God, my God!

[5]Why am I discouraged?
   Why so sad?
I will put my hope in God!
   I will praise him again—
   my Savior and my God!

PSALM 44

For the choir director: A psalm of the descendants of Korah.

[1]O God, we have heard it with our own ears—
   our ancestors have told us
of all you did in other days,
   in days long ago:

I SING the Lord's songs each night and bask in his love each day. (42:8)

I POUR OUT my questions to God, who understands my struggles. (43:2)

I PUT my hope in God when I am discouraged and sad. (43:5)

I RECOUNT to the Lord all that he has done for his people. (44:2)

2 You drove out the pagan nations
  and gave all the land to our ancestors;
you crushed their enemies,
  setting our ancestors free.
3 They did not conquer the land with their swords;
  it was not their own strength that gave them victory.
It was by your mighty power that they succeeded;
  it was because you favored them and smiled on them.

I CALL upon God as my King. (44:4)

4 You are my King and my God.
  You command victories for your people.*
5 Only by your power can we push back our enemies;
  only in your name can we trample our foes.
6 I do not trust my bow;
  I do not count on my sword to save me.
7 It is you who gives us victory over our enemies;
  it is you who humbles those who hate us.
8 O God, we give glory to you all day long
  and constantly praise your name.   *Interlude*

I CONTINUE TO PRAY to the Lord when I feel deserted by him. (44:9)

9 But now you have tossed us aside in dishonor.
  You no longer lead our armies to battle.
10 You make us retreat from our enemies
  and allow them to plunder our land.
11 You have treated us like sheep waiting to be slaughtered;
  you have scattered us among the nations.
12 You sold us—your precious people—for a pittance.
  You valued us at nothing at all.

13 You have caused all our neighbors to mock us.
  We are an object of scorn and derision to the nations around us.
14 You have made us the butt of their jokes;
  we are scorned by the whole world.
15 We can't escape the constant humiliation;
  shame is written across our faces.
16 All we hear are the taunts of our mockers.
  All we see are our vengeful enemies.

17 All this has happened despite our loyalty to you.
  We have not violated your covenant.
18 Our hearts have not deserted you.
  We have not strayed from your path.
19 Yet you have crushed us in the desert.
  You have covered us with darkness and death.

I BELIEVE the Lord knows if his people worship other gods in their hearts. (44:20)

20 If we had turned away from worshiping our God
  or spread our hands in prayer to foreign gods,
21 God would surely have known it,
  for he knows the secrets of every heart.
22 For your sake we are killed every day;
  we are being slaughtered like sheep.

I CRY OUT to the Lord for help when his people are suffering and oppressed. (44:23)

23 Wake up, O Lord! Why do you sleep?
  Get up! Do not reject us forever.
24 Why do you look the other way?
  Why do you ignore our suffering and oppression?

44:4 Hebrew *for Jacob.*

²⁵ We collapse in the dust,
  lying face down in the dirt.
²⁶ Rise up! Come and help us!
  Save us because of your unfailing love.

PSALM 45

For the choir director: A psalm of the descendants of Korah, to be sung to the tune "Lilies." A love song.

¹ My heart overflows with a beautiful thought!
  I will recite a lovely poem to the king,
    for my tongue is like the pen of a skillful poet.

² You are the most handsome of all.
  Gracious words stream from your lips.
  God himself has blessed you forever.
³ Put on your sword, O mighty warrior!
  You are so glorious, so majestic!
⁴ In your majesty, ride out to victory,
  defending truth, humility, and justice.
  Go forth to perform awe-inspiring deeds!
⁵ Your arrows are sharp,
  piercing your enemies' hearts.
The nations fall before you,
  lying down beneath your feet.

⁶ Your throne, O God,* endures forever and ever.
  Your royal power is expressed in justice.
⁷ You love what is right and hate what is wrong.
  Therefore God, your God, has anointed you,
    pouring out the oil of joy on you more than on anyone else.
⁸ Your robes are perfumed with myrrh, aloes, and cassia.
  In palaces decorated with ivory,
  you are entertained by the music of harps.
⁹ Kings' daughters are among your concubines.
  At your right side stands the queen,
  wearing jewelry of finest gold from Ophir!

¹⁰ Listen to me, O royal daughter; take to heart what I say.
  Forget your people and your homeland far away.
¹¹ For your royal husband delights in your beauty;
  honor him, for he is your lord.
¹² The princes of Tyre* will shower you with gifts.
  People of great wealth will entreat your favor.

¹³ The bride, a princess, waits within her chamber,
  dressed in a gown woven with gold.
¹⁴ In her beautiful robes, she is led to the king,
  accompanied by her bridesmaids.
¹⁵ What a joyful, enthusiastic procession
  as they enter the king's palace!

¹⁶ Your sons will become kings like their father.
  You will make them rulers over many lands.

¹⁷ I will bring honor to your name in every generation.
  Therefore, the nations will praise you forever and ever.

45:6 Or *Your divine throne.* 45:12 Hebrew *The daughter of Tyre.*

I EXALT the Lord, who reigns forever. (45:6)

I LOVE what is right and hate what is wrong. (45:7)

I BELIEVE that people from every nation will praise the Lord forever. (45:17)

PSALM 46

For the choir director: A psalm of the descendants of Korah, to be sung by soprano voices. A song.*

I LOOK to God for help when I am weak and in trouble, knowing he is always there for me. (46:1)

¹God is our refuge and strength,
   always ready to help in times of trouble.
²So we will not fear, even if earthquakes come
   and the mountains crumble into the sea.
³Let the oceans roar and foam.
   Let the mountains tremble as the waters surge!   *Interlude*

⁴A river brings joy to the city of our God,
   the sacred home of the Most High.

I BELIEVE that God will not abandon his people and that his presence provides security and help. (46:5)

⁵God himself lives in that city; it cannot be destroyed.
   God will protect it at the break of day.
⁶The nations are in an uproar,
   and kingdoms crumble!
God thunders,
   and the earth melts!

I AM CONFIDENT that God is in control, even though the world around me is in turmoil. (46:6)

⁷The LORD Almighty is here among us;
   the God of Israel* is our fortress.   *Interlude*

⁸Come, see the glorious works of the LORD:
   See how he brings destruction upon the world
⁹and causes wars to end throughout the earth.
   He breaks the bow and snaps the spear in two;
   he burns the shields with fire.

I AM AT PEACE because I know that God will do what he has promised. (46:10)

¹⁰"Be silent, and know that I am God!
   I will be honored by every nation.
   I will be honored throughout the world."

¹¹The LORD Almighty is here among us;
   the God of Israel is our fortress.   *Interlude*

PSALM 47

For the choir director: A psalm of the descendants of Korah.

I INVITE everyone to praise God with joyful clapping and shouting because he is the King of all the earth! (47:1)

See Jacob's profile (page 43) at Genesis 32:9.

¹Come, everyone, and clap your hands for joy!
   Shout to God with joyful praise!
²For the LORD Most High is awesome.
   He is the great King of all the earth.
³He subdues the nations before us,
   putting our enemies beneath our feet.
⁴He chose the Promised Land as our inheritance,
   the proud possession of Jacob's descendants, whom he loves.   *Interlude*

I PRAISE God, who has ascended in triumph to reign as King. (47:5)

⁵God has ascended with a mighty shout.
   The LORD has ascended with trumpets blaring.
⁶Sing praise to God, sing praises;
   sing praise to our King, sing praises!

⁷For God is the King over all the earth.
   Praise him with a psalm!
⁸God reigns above the nations,
   sitting on his holy throne.

See Abraham's profile (page 19) at Genesis 15:6.

⁹The rulers of the world have gathered together.
   They join us in praising the God of Abraham.

46:TITLE Hebrew *according to alamoth.*   46:7 Hebrew *of Jacob;* also in 46:11.

For all the kings of the earth belong to God.
    He is highly honored everywhere.

PSALM 48

A psalm of the descendants of Korah. A song.

[1] How great is the LORD,
    and how much we should praise him
in the city of our God,
    which is on his holy mountain!
[2] It is magnificent in elevation—
    the whole earth rejoices to see it!
Mount Zion, the holy mountain,*
    is the city of the great King!
[3] God himself is in Jerusalem's towers.
    He reveals himself as her defender.

I REJOICE in how the Lord chose Jerusalem to reveal himself to Israel and the world. (48:2)

[4] The kings of the earth joined forces
    and advanced against the city.
[5] But when they saw it, they were stunned;
    they were terrified and ran away.
[6] They were gripped with terror,
    like a woman writhing in the pain of childbirth
[7] or like the mighty ships of Tarshish
    being shattered by a powerful east wind.

I BELIEVE the pagan nations were terrified when God defended Jerusalem. (48:5)

[8] We had heard of the city's glory,
    but now we have seen it ourselves—
    the city of the LORD Almighty.
It is the city of our God;
    he will make it safe forever.

Interlude

[9] O God, we meditate on your unfailing love
    as we worship in your Temple.
[10] As your name deserves, O God,
    you will be praised to the ends of the earth.
    Your strong right hand is filled with victory.
[11] Let the people on Mount Zion rejoice.
Let the towns of Judah be glad,
    for your judgments are just.

[12] Go, inspect the city of Jerusalem.*
    Walk around and count the many towers.
[13] Take note of the fortified walls,
    and tour all the citadels,
that you may describe them
    to future generations.
[14] For that is what God is like.
    He is our God forever and ever,
    and he will be our guide until we die.

I TELL others what God is like. (48:14)

PSALM 49

For the choir director: A psalm of the descendants of Korah.

[1] Listen to this, all you people!
    Pay attention, everyone in the world!
[2] High and low,
    rich and poor—listen!

48:2 Or *Mount Zion, in the far north*; Hebrew reads *Mount Zion, the heights of Zaphon.*   48:12 Hebrew *Zion.*

³ For my words are wise,
and my thoughts are filled with insight.
⁴ I listen carefully to many proverbs
and solve riddles with inspiration from a harp.

I DO NOT NEED to fear in times of trouble. (49:5)

⁵ There is no need to fear when times of trouble come,
when enemies are surrounding me.
⁶ They trust in their wealth
and boast of great riches.
⁷ Yet they cannot redeem themselves from death*
by paying a ransom to God.

I BELIEVE no one could ever pay enough to live forever. (49:8)

⁸ Redemption does not come so easily,
for no one can ever pay enough
⁹ to live forever
and never see the grave.

¹⁰ Those who are wise must finally die,
just like the foolish and senseless,
leaving all their wealth behind.
¹¹ The grave is their eternal home,
where they will stay forever.
They may name their estates after themselves,
but they leave their wealth to others.
¹² They will not last long despite their riches—
they will die like the animals.
¹³ This is the fate of fools,
though they will be remembered as being so wise.   *Interlude*

¹⁴ Like sheep, they are led to the grave,
where death will be their shepherd.
In the morning the godly will rule over them.
Their bodies will rot in the grave,
far from their grand estates.

I KNOW that God himself will redeem me from death. (49:15)

¹⁵ But as for me, God will redeem my life.
He will snatch me from the power of death.   *Interlude*

¹⁶ So don't be dismayed when the wicked grow rich,
and their homes become ever more splendid.
¹⁷ For when they die, they carry nothing with them.
Their wealth will not follow them into the grave.
¹⁸ In this life they consider themselves fortunate,
and the world loudly applauds their success.
¹⁹ But they will die like all others before them
and never again see the light of day.

I DO NOT BOAST of my wealth, because it can't keep a person from dying. (49:20)

²⁰ People who boast of their wealth don't understand
that they will die like the animals.

PSALM 50

A psalm of Asaph.

See Asaph's profile (page 687) at Psalm 73:28.

¹ The mighty God, the LORD, has spoken;
he has summoned all humanity from east to west!
² From Mount Zion, the perfection of beauty,
God shines in glorious radiance.
³ Our God approaches with the noise of thunder.
Fire devours everything in his way,
and a great storm rages around him.

49:7 Or *no one can redeem the life of another.*

[4] Heaven and earth will be his witnesses
  as he judges his people:
[5] "Bring my faithful people to me—
  those who made a covenant with me by giving sacrifices."
[6] Then let the heavens proclaim his justice,
  for God himself will be the judge.   *Interlude*

[7] "O my people, listen as I speak.
  Here are my charges against you, O Israel:
  I am God, your God!
[8] I have no complaint about your sacrifices
  or the burnt offerings you constantly bring to my altar.
[9] But I want no more bulls from your barns;
  I want no more goats from your pens.
[10] For all the animals of the forest are mine,
  and I own the cattle on a thousand hills.
[11] Every bird of the mountains
  and all the animals of the field belong to me.
[12] If I were hungry, I would not mention it to you,
  for all the world is mine and everything in it.
[13] I don't need the bulls you sacrifice;
  I don't need the blood of goats.
[14] What I want instead is your true thanks to God;
  I want you to fulfill your vows to the Most High.
[15] Trust me in your times of trouble,
  and I will rescue you,
  and you will give me glory."

[16] But God says to the wicked:
  "Recite my laws no longer,
  and don't pretend that you obey me.
[17] For you refuse my discipline
  and treat my laws like trash.
[18] When you see a thief, you help him,
  and you spend your time with adulterers.
[19] Your mouths are filled with wickedness,
  and your tongues are full of lies.
[20] You sit around and slander a brother—
  your own mother's son.
[21] While you did all this, I remained silent,
  and you thought I didn't care.
  But now I will rebuke you,
  listing all my charges against you.
[22] Repent, all of you who ignore me,
  or I will tear you apart,
  and no one will help you.
[23] But giving thanks is a sacrifice that truly honors me.
  If you keep to my path,
  I will reveal to you the salvation of God."

PSALM 51

For the choir director: A psalm of David, regarding the time Nathan the prophet came to him after David had committed adultery with Bathsheba.

[1] Have mercy on me, O God,
  because of your unfailing love.
  Because of your great compassion,
  blot out the stain of my sins.

I BELIEVE God judges his people with justice. (50:4)

I BELIEVE all the creatures of the earth belong to God. (50:10)

I THANK the Lord and fulfill my promises to him. (50:14)

I TRUST the Lord and give him glory when he rescues me. (50:15)

I BELIEVE the Lord calls those who ignore him to repent. (50:22)

See David's profile (page 629) at Psalm 3:1.

I BELIEVE God shows mercy, unfailing love, and great compassion toward me. (51:1)

² Wash me clean from my guilt.
  Purify me from my sin.

³ For I recognize my shameful deeds—
  they haunt me day and night.

Ask God to cleanse your heart as you read his Word.

⁴ Against you, and you alone, have I sinned;
  I have done what is evil in your sight.
  You will be proved right in what you say,
  and your judgment against me is just.

⁵ For I was born a sinner—
  yes, from the moment my mother conceived me.
⁶ But you desire honesty from the heart,
  so you can teach me to be wise in my inmost being.

I DELIGHT in the Lord's cleansing and forgiveness. (51:7)

⁷ Purify me from my sins,* and I will be clean;
  wash me, and I will be whiter than snow.
⁸ Oh, give me back my joy again;
  you have broken me—
  now let me rejoice.
⁹ Don't keep looking at my sins.
  Remove the stain of my guilt.
¹⁰ Create in me a clean heart, O God.
  Renew a right spirit within me.
¹¹ Do not banish me from your presence,
  and don't take your Holy Spirit from me.

I REJOICE in the Holy Spirit's permanent presence in my life (Romans 8:9). (51:11)

¹² Restore to me again the joy of your salvation,
  and make me willing to obey you.
¹³ Then I will teach your ways to sinners,
  and they will return to you.
¹⁴ Forgive me for shedding blood, O God who saves;
  then I will joyfully sing of your forgiveness.
¹⁵ Unseal my lips, O Lord,
  that I may praise you.

¹⁶ You would not be pleased with sacrifices,
  or I would bring them.
  If I brought you a burnt offering,
  you would not accept it.

I AM BROKEN and repentant before God when I sin. (51:17)

¹⁷ The sacrifice you want is a broken spirit.
  A broken and repentant heart, O God,
  you will not despise.

¹⁸ Look with favor on Zion and help her;
  rebuild the walls of Jerusalem.
¹⁹ Then you will be pleased with worthy sacrifices
  and with our whole burnt offerings;
  and bulls will again be sacrificed on your altar.

PSALM 52

See Saul's profile (page 339) at 1 Samuel 18:9.

For the choir director: A psalm of David, regarding the time Doeg the Edomite told Saul that Ahimelech had given refuge to David.

I AM APPALLED at the cruelty of evil individuals (1 Samuel 22:9-19). (52:1)

¹ You call yourself a hero, do you?
  Why boast about this crime of yours,
  you who have disgraced God's people?

51:7 Hebrew Purify me with the hyssop branch.

² All day long you plot destruction.
    Your tongue cuts like a sharp razor;
    you're an expert at telling lies.
³ You love evil more than good
    and lies more than truth.   *Interlude*

⁴ You love to say things that harm others,
    you liar!
⁵ But God will strike you down once and for all.
    He will pull you from your home
    and drag you from the land of the living.   *Interlude*

I BELIEVE God will punish those who destroy others. (52:5)

⁶ The righteous will see it and be amazed.
    They will laugh and say,
⁷ "Look what happens to mighty warriors
    who do not trust in God.
They trust their wealth instead
    and grow more and more bold in their wickedness."

⁸ But I am like an olive tree,
    thriving in the house of God.
I trust in God's unfailing love
    forever and ever.
⁹ I will praise you forever, O God,
    for what you have done.
I will wait for your mercies
    in the presence of your people.

PSALM 53

For the choir director: A meditation of David.

¹ Only fools say in their hearts,
    "There is no God."
They are corrupt, and their actions are evil;
    no one does good!

² God looks down from heaven
    on the entire human race;
he looks to see if there is even one with real understanding,
    one who seeks for God.
³ But no, all have turned away from God;
    all have become corrupt.
No one does good,
    not even one!

I BELIEVE no one is good, not even one (Romans 3:10). (53:3)

⁴ Will those who do evil never learn?
    They eat up my people like bread;
    they wouldn't think of praying to God.
⁵ But then terror will grip them,
    terror like they have never known before.
God will scatter the bones of your enemies.
    You will put them to shame, for God has rejected them.

I BELIEVE God will reject those who refuse to pray to him. (53:4)

⁶ Oh, that salvation would come from Mount Zion to rescue Israel!
    For when God restores his people,
    Jacob will shout with joy, and Israel will rejoice.

PSALM 54

See Saul's profile (page 339) at 1 Samuel 18:9.

For the choir director: A meditation of David, regarding the time the Ziphites came and said to Saul, "We know where David is hiding." To be accompanied by stringed instruments.

I PLEAD with God to defend me from those who hate me (1 Samuel 23:19–29). (54:3)

I THANK God for keeping me alive! (54:4)

[1] Come with great power, O God, and rescue me!
   Defend me with your might.
[2] O God, listen to my prayer.
   Pay attention to my plea.

[3] For strangers are attacking me;
   violent men are trying to kill me.
   They care nothing for God.   *Interlude*

[4] But God is my helper.
   The Lord is the one who keeps me alive!
[5] May my enemies' plans for evil be turned against them.
   Do as you promised and put an end to them.

[6] I will sacrifice a voluntary offering to you;
   I will praise your name, O LORD,
      for it is good.
[7] For you will rescue me from my troubles
   and help me to triumph over my enemies.

PSALM 55

For the choir director: A psalm of David, to be accompanied by stringed instruments.

I BEG God to listen to me when I am overwhelmed. (55:2)

[1] Listen to my prayer, O God.
   Do not ignore my cry for help!
[2] Please listen and answer me,
   for I am overwhelmed by my troubles.
[3] My enemies shout at me,
   making loud and wicked threats.
   They bring trouble on me,
   hunting me down in their anger.

[4] My heart is in anguish.
   The terror of death overpowers me.
[5] Fear and trembling overwhelm me.
   I can't stop shaking.
[6] Oh, how I wish I had wings like a dove;
   then I would fly away and rest!
[7] I would fly far away
   to the quiet of the wilderness.   *Interlude*
[8] How quickly I would escape—
   far away from this wild storm of hatred.

I ASK God to thwart those who stir up hatred and violence. (55:9)

I RECOGNIZE the danger of wickedness within my society. (55:10)

[9] Destroy them, Lord, and confuse their speech,
   for I see violence and strife in the city.
[10] Its walls are patrolled day and night against invaders,
   but the real danger is wickedness within the city.
[11] Murder and robbery are everywhere there;
   threats and cheating are rampant in the streets.

[12] It is not an enemy who taunts me—
   I could bear that.
   It is not my foes who so arrogantly insult me—
   I could have hidden from them.

[13] Instead, it is you—my equal,
   my companion and close friend.
[14] What good fellowship we enjoyed
   as we walked together to the house of God.

[15] Let death seize my enemies by surprise;
   let the grave* swallow them alive,
   for evil makes its home within them.

[16] But I will call on God,
   and the LORD will rescue me.
[17] Morning, noon, and night
   I plead aloud in my distress,
   and the LORD hears my voice.
[18] He rescues me and keeps me safe
   from the battle waged against me,
   even though many still oppose me.
[19] God, who is king forever,
   will hear me and will humble them.
   For my enemies refuse to change their ways;
   they do not fear God.

[20] As for this friend of mine, he betrayed me;
   he broke his promises.
[21] His words are as smooth as cream,
   but in his heart is war.
   His words are as soothing as lotion,
   but underneath are daggers!

[22] Give your burdens to the LORD,
   and he will take care of you.
   He will not permit the godly to slip and fall.

[23] But you, O God, will send the wicked
   down to the pit of destruction.
   Murderers and liars will die young,
   but I am trusting you to save me.

Interlude

I CALL on the Lord because I know he will hear me and rescue me. (55:16)

I GIVE my burdens to the Lord (1 Peter 5:7). (55:22)

PSALM 56

For the choir director: A psalm of David, regarding the time the Philistines seized him in Gath. To be sung to the tune "Dove on Distant Oaks."

[1] O God, have mercy on me.
   The enemy troops press in on me.
   My foes attack me all day long.
[2] My slanderers hound me constantly,
   and many are boldly attacking me.
[3] But when I am afraid,
   I put my trust in you.
[4] O God, I praise your word.
   I trust in God, so why should I be afraid?
   What can mere mortals do to me?

[5] They are always twisting what I say;
   they spend their days plotting ways to harm me.
[6] They come together to spy on me—
   watching my every step, eager to kill me.
[7] Don't let them get away with their wickedness;
   in your anger, O God, throw them to the ground.

I ASK God for mercy when I am slandered and attacked (1 Samuel 21:10-15). (56:1)

55:15 Hebrew *let Sheol.*

I BELIEVE the Lord knows and remembers each of my sorrows. (56:8)

⁸You keep track of all my sorrows.
 You have collected all my tears in your bottle.
 You have recorded each one in your book.

⁹On the very day I call to you for help,
 my enemies will retreat.
 This I know: God is on my side.*
¹⁰O God, I praise your word.
 Yes, LORD, I praise your word.
¹¹I trust in God, so why should I be afraid?
 What can mere mortals do to me?

I THANK God and keep my promises to him when he rescues me. (56:12)

¹²I will fulfill my vows to you, O God,
 and offer a sacrifice of thanks for your help.
¹³For you have rescued me from death;
 you have kept my feet from slipping.
So now I can walk in your presence, O God,
 in your life-giving light.

PSALM 57

See Saul's profile (page 339) at 1 Samuel 18:9.

I LOOK to God for protection (1 Samuel 23:29–24:1-22). (57:1)

For the choir director: A psalm of David, regarding the time he fled from Saul and went into the cave. To be sung to the tune "Do Not Destroy!"

¹Have mercy on me, O God, have mercy!
 I look to you for protection.
I will hide beneath the shadow of your wings
 until this violent storm is past.

²I cry out to God Most High,
 to God who will fulfill his purpose for me.
³He will send help from heaven to save me,
 rescuing me from those who are out to get me. *Interlude*
My God will send forth his unfailing love and faithfulness.

⁴I am surrounded by fierce lions
 who greedily devour human prey—
whose teeth pierce like spears and arrows,
 and whose tongues cut like swords.

I WANT God's glory to be known and exalted throughout the earth. (57:5)

⁵Be exalted, O God, above the highest heavens!
 May your glory shine over all the earth.

⁶My enemies have set a trap for me.
 I am weary from distress.
They have dug a deep pit in my path,
 but they themselves have fallen into it. *Interlude*

⁷My heart is confident in you, O God;
 no wonder I can sing your praises!
⁸Wake up, my soul!
 Wake up, O harp and lyre!
 I will waken the dawn with my song.
⁹I will thank you, Lord, in front of all the people.
 I will sing your praises among the nations.
¹⁰For your unfailing love is as high as the heavens.
 Your faithfulness reaches to the clouds.

¹¹Be exalted, O God, above the highest heavens.
 May your glory shine over all the earth.

56:9 Or *By this I will know that God is on my side.*

PSALM 58

For the choir director: A psalm of David, to be sung to the tune "Do Not Destroy!"

¹ Justice—do you rulers know the meaning of the word?
   Do you judge the people fairly?
² No, all your dealings are crooked;
   you hand out violence instead of justice.
³ These wicked people are born sinners;
   even from birth they have lied and gone their own way.
⁴ They spit poison like deadly snakes;
   they are like cobras that refuse to listen,
⁵ ignoring the tunes of the snake charmers,
   no matter how skillfully they play.

⁶ Break off their fangs, O God!
   Smash the jaws of these lions, O LORD!
⁷ May they disappear like water into thirsty ground.
   Make their weapons useless in their hands.*
⁸ May they be like snails that dissolve into slime,
   like a stillborn child who will never see the sun.
⁹ God will sweep them away, both young and old,
   faster than a pot heats on an open flame.

¹⁰ The godly will rejoice when they see injustice avenged.
   They will wash their feet in the blood of the wicked.
¹¹ Then at last everyone will say,
   "There truly is a reward for those who live for God;
   surely there is a God who judges justly here on earth."

I PLEAD with God to punish leaders who pervert justice. (58:6)

I REJOICE when God avenges injustice. (58:10)

PSALM 59

For the choir director: A psalm of David, regarding the time Saul sent soldiers to watch David's house in order to kill him. To be sung to the tune "Do Not Destroy!"

¹ Rescue me from my enemies, O God.
   Protect me from those who have come to destroy me.
² Rescue me from these criminals;
   save me from these murderers.

³ They have set an ambush for me.
   Fierce enemies are out there waiting,
   though I have done them no wrong, O LORD.
⁴ Despite my innocence, they prepare to kill me.
   Rise up and help me! Look on my plight!
⁵ O LORD God Almighty, the God of Israel,
   rise up to punish hostile nations.
   Show no mercy to wicked traitors.   *Interlude*

⁶ They come at night,
   snarling like vicious dogs
   as they prowl the streets.
⁷ Listen to the filth that comes from their mouths,
   the piercing swords that fly from their lips.
   "Who can hurt us?" they sneer.

⁸ But LORD, you laugh at them.
   You scoff at all the hostile nations.

See Saul's profile (page 339) at 1 Samuel 18:9.

I PRAY for God to rescue me when I am unfairly attacked (1 Samuel 19:11-17). (59:1)

I BELIEVE the Lord scoffs at those who are hostile to him. (59:8)

58:7 Or *Let them be trodden down and wither like grass.* The meaning of the Hebrew is uncertain.

⁹You are my strength; I wait for you to rescue me,
  for you, O God, are my place of safety.
¹⁰In his unfailing love, my God will come and help me.
  He will let me look down in triumph on all my enemies.

¹¹Don't kill them, for my people soon forget such lessons;
  stagger them with your power, and bring them to their knees,
  O Lord our shield.
¹²Because of the sinful things they say,
  because of the evil that is on their lips,
  let them be captured by their pride,
  their curses, and their lies.

I WANT evil to be punished for God's glory, not mine. (59:13)

¹³Destroy them in your anger!
  Wipe them out completely!
Then the whole world will know
  that God reigns in Israel.*   *Interlude*

¹⁴My enemies come out at night,
  snarling like vicious dogs
  as they prowl the streets.
¹⁵They scavenge for food
  but go to sleep unsatisfied.*

I REJOICE in God's love and find safety in him. (59:16)

¹⁶But as for me, I will sing about your power.
  I will shout with joy each morning because of your unfailing love.
For you have been my refuge,
  a place of safety in the day of distress.

¹⁷O my Strength, to you I sing praises,
  for you, O God, are my refuge,
  the God who shows me unfailing love.

PSALM 60

For the choir director: A psalm of David useful for teaching, regarding the time David fought Aram-naharaim and Aram-zobah, and Joab returned and killed twelve thousand Edomites in the Valley of Salt. To be sung to the tune "Lily of the Testimony."

I ASK God to restore his favor after he has disciplined me. (60:1)

¹You have rejected us, O God, and broken our defenses.
  You have been angry with us; now restore us to your favor.
²You have shaken our land and split it open.
  Seal the cracks before it completely collapses.
³You have been very hard on us,
  making us drink wine that sent us reeling.
⁴But you have raised a banner for those who honor you—
  a rallying point in the face of attack.   *Interlude*

I LOOK to the Lord's strong arm to rescue his beloved people. (60:5)

⁵Use your strong right arm to save us,
  and rescue your beloved people.
⁶God has promised this by his holiness*:
  "I will divide up Shechem with joy.
  I will measure out the valley of Succoth.
⁷Gilead is mine,
  and Manasseh is mine.
Ephraim will produce my warriors,
  and Judah will produce my kings.

59:13 Hebrew *in Jacob.*   59:15 Or *and growl if they don't get enough.*   60:6 Or *in his sanctuary.*

⁸ Moab will become my lowly servant,
   and Edom will be my slave.
   I will shout in triumph over the Philistines."

⁹ But who will bring me into the fortified city?
   Who will bring me victory over Edom?
¹⁰ Have you rejected us, O God?
   Will you no longer march with our armies?
¹¹ Oh, please help us against our enemies,
   for all human help is useless.
¹² With God's help we will do mighty things,
   for he will trample down our foes.

I BELIEVE God will help his people do mighty things (2 Samuel 8). (60:12)

PSALM 61

For the choir director: A psalm of David, to be accompanied by stringed instruments.

¹ O God, listen to my cry!
   Hear my prayer!
² From the ends of the earth,
   I will cry to you for help,
   for my heart is overwhelmed.
   Lead me to the towering rock of safety,
³   for you are my safe refuge,
   a fortress where my enemies cannot reach me.
⁴ Let me live forever in your sanctuary,
   safe beneath the shelter of your wings!
⁵ For you have heard my vows, O God.
   You have given me an inheritance reserved for those who fear
      your name.

Interlude

I CRY OUT to the Lord for help when I am overwhelmed. (61:2)

⁶ Add many years to the life of the king!
   May his years span the generations!
⁷ May he reign under God's protection forever.
   Appoint your unfailing love and faithfulness to watch over him.

⁸ Then I will always sing praises to your name
   as I fulfill my vows day after day.

I ASK the Lord to give me the time and strength to fulfill his purposes. (61:6)

PSALM 62

For Jeduthun, the choir director: A psalm of David.

¹ I wait quietly before God,
   for my salvation comes from him.
² He alone is my rock and my salvation,
   my fortress where I will never be shaken.

I FIND security and salvation in God alone. (62:2)

³ So many enemies against one man—
   all of them trying to kill me.
   To them I'm just a broken-down wall
   or a tottering fence.
⁴ They plan to topple me from my high position.
   They delight in telling lies about me.
   They are friendly to my face,
   but they curse me in their hearts.

Interlude

⁵ I wait quietly before God,
   for my hope is in him.

⁶He alone is my rock and my salvation,
   my fortress where I will not be shaken.
⁷My salvation and my honor come from God alone.
   He is my refuge, a rock where no enemy can reach me.

⁸O my people, trust in him at all times.
   Pour out your heart to him,
      for God is our refuge.   *Interlude*

⁹From the greatest to the lowliest—
   all are nothing in his sight.
If you weigh them on the scales,
   they are lighter than a puff of air.
¹⁰Don't try to get rich
   by extortion or robbery.
And if your wealth increases,
   don't make it the center of your life.

¹¹God has spoken plainly,
   and I have heard it many times:
Power, O God, belongs to you;
¹²   unfailing love, O Lord, is yours.
Surely you judge all people
   according to what they have done.

PSALM 63

A psalm of David, regarding a time when David was in the wilderness of Judah.

¹O God, you are my God;
   I earnestly search for you.
My soul thirsts for you;
   my whole body longs for you
in this parched and weary land
   where there is no water.

²I have seen you in your sanctuary
   and gazed upon your power and glory.
³Your unfailing love is better to me than life itself;
   how I praise you!
⁴I will honor you as long as I live,
   lifting up my hands to you in prayer.
⁵You satisfy me more than the richest of foods.
   I will praise you with songs of joy.

⁶I lie awake thinking of you,
   meditating on you through the night.
⁷I think how much you have helped me;
   I sing for joy in the shadow of your protecting wings.
⁸I follow close behind you;
   your strong right hand holds me securely.

⁹But those plotting to destroy me will come to ruin.
   They will go down into the depths of the earth.
¹⁰They will die by the sword
   and become the food of jackals.

¹¹But the king will rejoice in God.
   All who trust in him will praise him,
      while liars will be silenced.

I POUR OUT my heart to God because he alone is my refuge. (62:8)

I KNOW that human power and riches are meaningless before God. (62:9)

I PRAISE AND CHERISH the Lord's unfailing love to me. (63:3)

I TRUST in the Lord and praise him. (63:11)

PSALM 64

For the choir director: A psalm of David.

¹O God, listen to my complaint.
    Do not let my enemies' threats overwhelm me.
²Protect me from the plots of the wicked,
    from the scheming of those who do evil.
³Sharp tongues are the swords they wield;
    bitter words are the arrows they aim.
⁴They shoot from ambush at the innocent,
    attacking suddenly and fearlessly.
⁵They encourage each other to do evil
    and plan how to set their traps.
    "Who will ever notice?" they ask.
⁶As they plot their crimes, they say,
    "We have devised the perfect plan!"
    Yes, the human heart and mind are cunning.

⁷But God himself will shoot them down.
    Suddenly, his arrows will pierce them.
⁸Their own words will be turned against them, destroying them.
    All who see it happening will shake their heads in scorn.
⁹Then everyone will stand in awe,
    proclaiming the mighty acts of God,
    realizing all the amazing things he does.

¹⁰The godly will rejoice in the LORD
    and find shelter in him.
And those who do what is right
    will praise him.

> I ASK God to protect me from those who attack me verbally. (64:2)

> I REJOICE in the Lord and find shelter in him. (64:10)

PSALM 65

For the choir director: A psalm of David. A song.

¹What mighty praise, O God,
    belongs to you in Zion.
We will fulfill our vows to you,
² for you answer our prayers,
    and to you all people will come.
³Though our hearts are filled with sins,
    you forgive them all.
⁴What joy for those you choose to bring near,
    those who live in your holy courts.
What joys await us
    inside your holy Temple.

⁵You faithfully answer our prayers with awesome deeds,
    O God our savior.
You are the hope of everyone on earth,
    even those who sail on distant seas.
⁶You formed the mountains by your power
    and armed yourself with mighty strength.
⁷You quieted the raging oceans
    with their pounding waves
    and silenced the shouting of the nations.
⁸Those who live at the ends of the earth
    stand in awe of your wonders.
From where the sun rises to where it sets,
    you inspire shouts of joy.

> I THANK God for answering my prayers. (65:1)

> I PRAISE the Lord, who inspires me to shout for joy. (65:8)

⁹You take care of the earth and water it,
  making it rich and fertile.
The rivers of God will not run dry;
  they provide a bountiful harvest of grain,
  for you have ordered it so.
¹⁰You drench the plowed ground with rain,
  melting the clods and leveling the ridges.
You soften the earth with showers
  and bless its abundant crops.
¹¹You crown the year with a bountiful harvest;
  even the hard pathways overflow with abundance.
¹²The wilderness becomes a lush pasture,
  and the hillsides blossom with joy.
¹³The meadows are clothed with flocks of sheep,
  and the valleys are carpeted with grain.
They all shout and sing for joy!

PSALM 66

For the choir director: A psalm. A song.

¹Shout joyful praises to God, all the earth!
² Sing about the glory of his name!
  Tell the world how glorious he is.
³Say to God, "How awesome are your deeds!
  Your enemies cringe before your mighty power.
⁴Everything on earth will worship you;
  they will sing your praises,
  shouting your name in glorious songs."   *Interlude*

⁵Come and see what our God has done,
  what awesome miracles he does for his people!
⁶He made a dry path through the Red Sea,*
  and his people went across on foot.
  Come, let us rejoice in who he is.
⁷For by his great power he rules forever.
  He watches every movement of the nations;
  let no rebel rise in defiance.   *Interlude*

⁸Let the whole world bless our God
  and sing aloud his praises.
⁹Our lives are in his hands,
  and he keeps our feet from stumbling.
¹⁰You have tested us, O God;
  you have purified us like silver melted in a crucible.
¹¹You captured us in your net
  and laid the burden of slavery on our backs.
¹²You sent troops to ride across our broken bodies.
  We went through fire and flood.
  But you brought us to a place of great abundance.

¹³Now I come to your Temple with burnt offerings
  to fulfill the vows I made to you—
¹⁴yes, the sacred vows you heard me make
  when I was in deep trouble.
¹⁵That is why I am sacrificing burnt offerings to you—
  the best of my rams as a pleasing aroma.
  And I will sacrifice bulls and goats.   *Interlude*

I TELL others how awesome are God's deeds! (66:3)

I WANT the whole world to praise the Lord. (66:8)

66:6 Hebrew *the sea.*

¹⁶ Come and listen, all you who fear God,
   and I will tell you what he did for me.
¹⁷ For I cried out to him for help,
   praising him as I spoke.
¹⁸ If I had not confessed the sin in my heart,
   my Lord would not have listened.
¹⁹ But God did listen!
   He paid attention to my prayer.

²⁰ Praise God, who did not ignore my prayer
   and did not withdraw his unfailing love from me.

I TELL others what God has done for me. (66:16)

I PRAISE God for hearing my prayers and not withholding his love. (66:20)

PSALM 67

For the choir director: A psalm, to be accompanied by stringed instruments.
A song.

¹ May God be merciful and bless us.
   May his face shine with favor upon us.   *Interlude*
² May your ways be known throughout the earth,
   your saving power among people everywhere.
³ May the nations praise you, O God.
   Yes, may all the nations praise you.

⁴ How glad the nations will be, singing for joy,
   because you govern them with justice
   and direct the actions of the whole world.   *Interlude*
⁵ May the nations praise you, O God.
   Yes, may all the nations praise you.

⁶ Then the earth will yield its harvests,
   and God, our God, will richly bless us.
⁷ Yes, God will bless us,
   and people all over the world will fear him.

I WANT the whole world to know God. (67:2)

I WANT to see all the nations praise God. (67:3)

PSALM 68

For the choir director: A psalm of David. A song.

¹ Arise, O God, and scatter your enemies.
   Let those who hate God run for their lives.
² Drive them off like smoke blown by the wind.
   Melt them like wax in fire.
   Let the wicked perish in the presence of God.
³ But let the godly rejoice.
   Let them be glad in God's presence.
   Let them be filled with joy.

⁴ Sing praises to God and to his name!
   Sing loud praises to him who rides the clouds.
   His name is the LORD—
   rejoice in his presence!

⁵ Father to the fatherless, defender of widows—
   this is God, whose dwelling is holy.
⁶ God places the lonely in families;
   he sets the prisoners free and gives them joy.
   But for rebels, there is only famine and distress.

⁷ O God, when you led your people from Egypt,
   when you marched through the wilderness,   *Interlude*

I REJOICE in God's presence. (68:3)

I BELIEVE God cares for the deserted, the lonely, and the captive. (68:5)

I BELIEVE God cared for his people Israel when he rescued them from Egypt and brought them to the Promised Land. (68:7)

⁸the earth trembled, and the heavens poured rain
  before you, the God of Sinai,
  before God, the God of Israel.
⁹You sent abundant rain, O God,
  to refresh the weary Promised Land.
¹⁰There your people finally settled,
  and with a bountiful harvest, O God,
  you provided for your needy people.

¹¹The Lord announces victory,
  and throngs of women shout the happy news.
¹²Enemy kings and their armies flee,
  while the women of Israel divide the plunder.
¹³Though they lived among the sheepfolds,
  now they are covered with silver and gold,
  as a dove is covered by its wings.
¹⁴The Almighty scattered the enemy kings
  like a blowing snowstorm on Mount Zalmon.

¹⁵The majestic mountains of Bashan
  stretch high into the sky.
¹⁶Why do you look with envy, O rugged mountains,
  at Mount Zion, where God has chosen to live,
  where the LORD himself will live forever?

I BELIEVE the Lord came victoriously into his Tabernacle to dwell with the Israelites. (68:17)

¹⁷Surrounded by unnumbered thousands of chariots,
  the Lord came from Mount Sinai into his sanctuary.
¹⁸When you ascended to the heights,
  you led a crowd of captives.
You received gifts from the people,
  even from those who rebelled against you.
  Now the LORD God will live among us here.

I PRAISE the Lord because he still carries his people in his arms. (68:19)

¹⁹Praise the Lord; praise God our savior!
  For each day he carries us in his arms.   Interlude
²⁰Our God is a God who saves!
  The Sovereign LORD rescues us from death.

²¹But God will smash the heads of his enemies,
  crushing the skulls of those who love their guilty ways.
²²The Lord says, "I will bring my enemies down from Bashan;
  I will bring them up from the depths of the sea.
²³You, my people, will wash your feet in their blood,
  and even your dogs will get their share!"

²⁴Your procession has come into view, O God—
  the procession of my God and King
  as he goes into the sanctuary.
²⁵Singers are in front, musicians are behind;
  with them are young women playing tambourines.
²⁶Praise God, all you people of Israel;
  praise the LORD, the source of Israel's life.
²⁷Look, the little tribe of Benjamin leads the way.
  Then comes a great throng of rulers from Judah
  and all the rulers of Zebulun and Naphtali.

I PRAY that God will once again display his power to the nations. (68:28)

²⁸Summon your might, O God.
  Display your power, O God, as you have in the past.
²⁹The kings of the earth are bringing tribute
  to your Temple in Jerusalem.

³⁰ Rebuke these enemy nations—
    these wild animals lurking in the reeds,
    this herd of bulls among the weaker calves.
  Humble those who demand tribute from us.*
    Scatter the nations that delight in war.
³¹ Let Egypt come with gifts of precious metals;
    let Ethiopia* bow in submission to God.
³² Sing to God, you kingdoms of the earth.
    Sing praises to the Lord.   *Interlude*

³³ Sing to the one who rides across the ancient heavens,
    his mighty voice thundering from the sky.
³⁴ Tell everyone about God's power.
    His majesty shines down on Israel;
    his strength is mighty in the heavens.
³⁵ God is awesome in his sanctuary.
    The God of Israel gives power and strength to his people.

  Praise be to God!

I TELL others about the majesty and power that God demonstrated to Israel. (68:34)

PSALM 69

For the choir director: A psalm of David, to be sung to the tune "Lilies."

¹ Save me, O God,
    for the floodwaters are up to my neck.
² Deeper and deeper I sink into the mire;
    I can't find a foothold to stand on.
  I am in deep water,
    and the floods overwhelm me.
³ I am exhausted from crying for help;
    my throat is parched and dry.
  My eyes are swollen with weeping,
    waiting for my God to help me.

⁴ Those who hate me without cause
    are more numerous than the hairs on my head.
  These enemies who seek to destroy me
    are doing so without cause.
  They attack me with lies,
    demanding that I give back what I didn't steal.

⁵ O God, you know how foolish I am;
    my sins cannot be hidden from you.
⁶ Don't let those who trust in you stumble because of me,
    O Sovereign LORD Almighty.
  Don't let me cause them to be humiliated,
    O God of Israel.
⁷ For I am mocked and shamed for your sake;
    humiliation is written all over my face.
⁸ Even my own brothers pretend they don't know me;
    they treat me like a stranger.

⁹ Passion for your house burns within me,
    so those who insult you are also insulting me.
¹⁰ When I weep and fast before the LORD,
    they scoff at me.
¹¹ When I dress in sackcloth to show sorrow,
    they make fun of me.

I ASK the Lord not to let others stumble when I sin. (69:6)

68:30 Or *Humble them until they submit, bringing pieces of silver as tribute.*   68:31 Hebrew *Cush.*

¹²I am the favorite topic of town gossip,
and all the drunkards sing about me.

I KEEP PRAYING to the Lord even when I am mocked and humiliated. (69:13)

¹³But I keep right on praying to you, LORD,
hoping this is the time you will show me favor.
In your unfailing love, O God,
answer my prayer with your sure salvation.
¹⁴Pull me out of the mud;
don't let me sink any deeper!
Rescue me from those who hate me,
and pull me from these deep waters.
¹⁵Don't let the floods overwhelm me,
or the deep waters swallow me,
or the pit of death devour me.

I ASK God to answer me out of his unfailing love and mercy. (69:16)

¹⁶Answer my prayers, O LORD,
for your unfailing love is wonderful.
Turn and take care of me,
for your mercy is so plentiful.
¹⁷Don't hide from your servant;
answer me quickly, for I am in deep trouble!
¹⁸Come and rescue me;
free me from all my enemies.

I KNOW the Lord sees all I have endured from those who hate me. (69:19)

¹⁹You know the insults I endure—
the humiliation and disgrace.
You have seen all my enemies
and know what they have said.
²⁰Their insults have broken my heart,
and I am in despair.
If only one person would show some pity;
if only one would turn and comfort me.
²¹But instead, they give me poison for food;
they offer me sour wine to satisfy my thirst.

I BELIEVE the Lord Jesus was mocked in the same way the psalmist was, being offered sour wine to quench his thirst (Luke 23:36). (69:21)

²²Let the bountiful table set before them become a snare,
and let their security become a trap.
²³Let their eyes go blind so they cannot see,
and let their bodies grow weaker and weaker.
²⁴Pour out your fury on them;
consume them with your burning anger.
²⁵May their homes become desolate
and their tents be deserted.
²⁶To those you have punished, they add insult to injury;
they scoff at the pain of those you have hurt.
²⁷Pile their sins up high,
and don't let them go free.
²⁸Erase their names from the Book of Life;
don't let them be counted among the righteous.

I BELIEVE the punishment of those who hate God and his people will be certain and severe. (69:27)

²⁹I am suffering and in pain.
Rescue me, O God, by your saving power.

I GIVE God the sacrifice of thanksgiving and praise. (69:30)

³⁰Then I will praise God's name with singing,
and I will honor him with thanksgiving.
³¹For this will please the LORD more than sacrificing an ox
or presenting a bull with its horns and hooves.
³²The humble will see their God at work and be glad.
Let all who seek God's help live in joy.

[33] For the LORD hears the cries of his needy ones;
  he does not despise his people who are oppressed.

[34] Praise him, O heaven and earth,
  the seas and all that move in them.
[35] For God will save Jerusalem*
  and rebuild the towns of Judah.
 His people will live there
  and take possession of the land.
[36] The descendants of those who obey him will inherit the land,
  and those who love him will live there in safety.

I AM CONFIDENT God will restore those who obey him. (69:36)

PSALM 70

For the choir director: A psalm of David, to bring us to the LORD's remembrance.

[1] Please, God, rescue me!
  Come quickly, LORD, and help me.
[2] May those who try to destroy me
  be humiliated and put to shame.
 May those who take delight in my trouble
  be turned back in disgrace.
[3] Let them be horrified by their shame,
  for they said, "Aha! We've got him now!"
[4] But may all who search for you
  be filled with joy and gladness.
 May those who love your salvation
  repeatedly shout, "God is great!"
[5] But I am poor and needy;
  please hurry to my aid, O God.
 You are my helper and my savior;
  O LORD, do not delay!

I BEG God to hurry to my aid and not delay! (70:5)

PSALM 71

[1] O LORD, you are my refuge;
  never let me be disgraced.
[2] Rescue me! Save me from my enemies, for you are just.
  Turn your ear to listen and set me free.
[3] Be to me a protecting rock of safety,
  where I am always welcome.
 Give the order to save me,
  for you are my rock and my fortress.

[4] My God, rescue me from the power of the wicked,
  from the clutches of cruel oppressors.
[5] O Lord, you alone are my hope.
  I've trusted you, O LORD, from childhood.
[6] Yes, you have been with me from birth;
  from my mother's womb you have cared for me.
 No wonder I am always praising you!

I BELIEVE God has cared for me since before my birth. (71:6)

[7] My life is an example to many,
  because you have been my strength and protection.
[8] That is why I can never stop praising you;
  I declare your glory all day long.

[9] And now, in my old age, don't set me aside.
  Don't abandon me when my strength is failing.

69:35 Hebrew *Zion.*

I WANT to prove God's faithfulness to those who think he has abandoned me. (71:10)

¹⁰ For my enemies are whispering against me.
    They are plotting together to kill me.
¹¹ They say, "God has abandoned him.
    Let's go and get him,
    for there is no one to help him now."

¹² O God, don't stay away.
    My God, please hurry to help me.
¹³ Bring disgrace and destruction on those who accuse me.
    May humiliation and shame cover
    those who want to harm me.

¹⁴ But I will keep on hoping for you to help me;
    I will praise you more and more.

I AM continually overwhelmed by all God has done for me. (71:15)

¹⁵ I will tell everyone about your righteousness.
    All day long I will proclaim your saving power,
    for I am overwhelmed by how much you have done for me.
¹⁶ I will praise your mighty deeds, O Sovereign LORD.
    I will tell everyone that you alone are just and good.

¹⁷ O God, you have taught me from my earliest childhood,
    and I have constantly told others about the wonderful things you do.

I WANT to tell the next generation of God's power and miracles. (71:18)

¹⁸ Now that I am old and gray,
    do not abandon me, O God.
    Let me proclaim your power to this new generation,
    your mighty miracles to all who come after me.

¹⁹ Your righteousness, O God, reaches to the highest heavens.
    You have done such wonderful things.
    Who can compare with you, O God?
²⁰ You have allowed me to suffer much hardship,
    but you will restore me to life again
    and lift me up from the depths of the earth.
²¹ You will restore me to even greater honor
    and comfort me once again.

²² Then I will praise you with music on the harp,
    because you are faithful to your promises, O God.
    I will sing for you with a lyre,
    O Holy One of Israel.
²³ I will shout for joy and sing your praises,
    for you have redeemed me.
²⁴ I will tell about your righteous deeds
    all day long,
    for everyone who tried to hurt me
    has been shamed and humiliated.

PSALM 72

See Solomon's profile (page 753) at Proverbs 2:9.

A psalm of Solomon.

¹ Give justice to the king, O God,
    and righteousness to the king's son.
² Help him judge your people in the right way;
    let the poor always be treated fairly.
³ May the mountains yield prosperity for all,
    and may the hills be fruitful,
    because the king does what is right.
⁴ Help him to defend the poor,
    to rescue the children of the needy,
    and to crush their oppressors.

⁵May he live* as long as the sun shines,
   as long as the moon continues in the skies.
   Yes, forever!
⁶May his reign be as refreshing as the springtime rains—
   like the showers that water the earth.
⁷May all the godly flourish during his reign.
   May there be abundant prosperity until the end of time.

⁸May he reign from sea to sea,
   and from the Euphrates River* to the ends of the earth.
⁹Desert nomads will bow before him;
   his enemies will fall before him in the dust.
¹⁰The western kings of Tarshish and the islands
   will bring him tribute.
   The eastern kings of Sheba and Seba
   will bring him gifts.
¹¹All kings will bow before him,
   and all nations will serve him.

¹²He will rescue the poor when they cry to him;
   he will help the oppressed, who have no one to defend them.
¹³He feels pity for the weak and the needy,
   and he will rescue them.
¹⁴He will save them from oppression and from violence,
   for their lives are precious to him.

¹⁵Long live the king!
   May the gold of Sheba be given to him.
   May the people always pray for him
   and bless him all day long.
¹⁶May there be abundant crops throughout the land,
   flourishing even on the mountaintops.
   May the fruit trees flourish as they do in Lebanon,
   sprouting up like grass in a field.
¹⁷May the king's name endure forever;
   may it continue as long as the sun shines.
   May all nations be blessed through him
   and bring him praise.

¹⁸Bless the LORD God, the God of Israel,
   who alone does such wonderful things.
¹⁹Bless his glorious name forever!
   Let the whole earth be filled with his glory.
   Amen and amen!

²⁰(This ends the prayers of David son of Jesse.)

BOOK THREE (Psalms 73–89)

PSALM 73

A psalm of Asaph.

¹Truly God is good to Israel,
   to those whose hearts are pure.

²But as for me, I came so close to the edge of the cliff!
   My feet were slipping, and I was almost gone.
³For I envied the proud
   when I saw them prosper despite their wickedness.

I PRAY that my influence will be a blessing to many people for a long time. (72:5)

I PRAY that my influence will extend far beyond my community. (72:8)

I SAY yes when the poor and oppressed ask for my help. (72:12)

I BLESS the Lord for all the wonderful things he does. (72:18)

I BELIEVE God blesses those whose hearts are pure (Matthew 5:8). (73:1)

I DO NOT ENVY the apparent good fortune of the wicked. (73:3)

72:5 As in Greek version; Hebrew reads *May they fear you.*   72:8 Hebrew *the river.*

⁴They seem to live such a painless life;
  their bodies are so healthy and strong.
⁵They aren't troubled like other people
  or plagued with problems like everyone else.
⁶They wear pride like a jeweled necklace,
  and their clothing is woven of cruelty.
⁷These fat cats have everything
  their hearts could ever wish for!
⁸They scoff and speak only evil;
  in their pride they seek to crush others.
⁹They boast against the very heavens,
  and their words strut throughout the earth.
¹⁰And so the people are dismayed and confused,
  drinking in all their words.
¹¹"Does God realize what is going on?" they ask.
  "Is the Most High even aware of what is happening?"
¹²Look at these arrogant people—
  enjoying a life of ease while their riches multiply.

¹³Was it for nothing that I kept my heart pure
  and kept myself from doing wrong?
¹⁴All I get is trouble all day long;
  every morning brings me pain.

¹⁵If I had really spoken this way,
  I would have been a traitor to your people.
¹⁶So I tried to understand why the wicked prosper.
  But what a difficult task it is!
¹⁷Then one day I went into your sanctuary, O God,
  and I thought about the destiny of the wicked.
¹⁸Truly, you put them on a slippery path
  and send them sliding over the cliff to destruction.
¹⁹In an instant they are destroyed,
  swept away by terrors.
²⁰Their present life is only a dream
  that is gone when they awake.
  When you arise, O Lord,
  you will make them vanish from this life.

²¹Then I realized how bitter I had become,
  how pained I had been by all I had seen.
²²I was so foolish and ignorant—
  I must have seemed like a senseless animal to you.
²³Yet I still belong to you;
  you are holding my right hand.
²⁴You will keep on guiding me with your counsel,
  leading me to a glorious destiny.
²⁵Whom have I in heaven but you?
  I desire you more than anything on earth.
²⁶My health may fail, and my spirit may grow weak,
  but God remains the strength of my heart;
  he is mine forever.

²⁷But those who desert him will perish,
  for you destroy those who abandon you.
²⁸But as for me, how good it is to be near God!
  I have made the Sovereign LORD my shelter,
  and I will tell everyone about the wonderful things you do.

I KNOW the destiny of the wicked will be far different from their current life of ease (Psalm 73:17). (73:12)

I DO NOT CAUSE others to doubt God's righteousness, justice, and truth. (73:15)

I REFRAIN from becoming bitter toward God. (73:21)

I DESIRE God more than anything else in the universe. (73:25)

PSALM 74

A psalm of Asaph.

¹O God, why have you rejected us forever?
  Why is your anger so intense against the sheep of your own pasture?
²Remember that we are the people you chose in ancient times,
  the tribe you redeemed as your own special possession!
And remember Jerusalem,* your home here on earth.

I CRY OUT to God in the midst of a terrible crisis. (74:1)

LIKE ASAPH *I turn to God when my faith is shaken.*

Psalm 73:28

Even the strongest believers can struggle with big questions and serious doubts.

Asaph spent his life serving God. He was a professional. Gifted by God as a "seer," he was appointed by King David to lead the Levites in public worship (1 Chronicles 16:7, 37 and 2 Chronicles 29:30).

But serving nine to five in the Tabernacle didn't shelter Asaph from the harsh realities of life. He heard all the news, talked with government insiders, and saw the hypocrites who worshiped one moment and defied God's law the next.

Slowly, the unfairness of it all—the prosperity of wicked people who lived their lives for themselves and reaped all the benefits—began to wear on Asaph. His faith was shaken.

Why waste my time in obeying and serving God, Asaph wondered, *when others disobey and prosper and live to boast about it?*

Asaph's doubts are not unique, but his response was right on target. He was a man of faith about to go over the edge—but he was still a man of faith. Stopping to look at the world through God's eyes, he finally understood that the prosperity of the wicked was only temporary. And he saw himself—foolish for a moment but loved and guided by God.

So what if I don't get all the perks in this life? Asaph realized. *If I have God, I can know true satisfaction and will enjoy great rewards in the life to come.*

By being completely open before the Lord about his struggles, Asaph also was wide open to receive God's answer. Asaph discovered God's answer was usually a new revelation of himself (Psalms 73:22-26 and 77:10-14)—a new revelation of God's character, promises, and ability to make everything come together in the end.

Afterward, Asaph admitted he was glad he had waited until he and God had wrestled and worked through his doubts before he opened his mouth and said anything publicly (Psalm 73:15). He didn't hide his struggles, but he wanted others to know the end of the story—from God's perspective. He wanted to help people in their faith, not deter them with doubts before he had answers and assurance.

Like Asaph, we need to take our doubts and hurts to God. Ultimately, he alone can answer our questions and bring solace to our heart.

To read more of Asaph's honest prayers to God and his encouragement to other believers, see Psalms 50 and 78–83.

○ *Today's Scripture reading is Psalms 73–77.*

---

³Walk through the awful ruins of the city;
  see how the enemy has destroyed your sanctuary.
⁴There your enemies shouted their victorious battle cries;
  there they set up their battle standards.
⁵They chopped down the entrance
  like woodcutters in a forest.
⁶With axes and picks,
  they smashed the carved paneling.
⁷They set the sanctuary on fire, burning it to the ground.
  They utterly defiled the place that bears your holy name.

74:2 Hebrew *Mount Zion.*

⁸Then they thought, "Let's destroy everything!"
So they burned down all the places where God was worshiped.

I LOOK to God for answers when it seems his help is not coming. (74:9)

⁹We see no miraculous signs
as evidence that you will save us.
All the prophets are gone;
no one can tell us when it will end.
¹⁰How long, O God, will you allow our enemies to mock you?
Will you let them dishonor your name forever?
¹¹Why do you hold back your strong right hand?
Unleash your powerful fist and deliver a deathblow.

I AFFIRM that God is my King. (74:12)

¹²You, O God, are my king from ages past,
bringing salvation to the earth.
¹³You split the sea by your strength
and smashed the sea monster's heads.
¹⁴You crushed the heads of Leviathan
and let the desert animals eat him.
¹⁵You caused the springs and streams to gush forth,
and you dried up rivers that never run dry.
¹⁶Both day and night belong to you;
you made the starlight* and the sun.
¹⁷You set the boundaries of the earth,
and you make both summer and winter.

¹⁸See how these enemies scoff at you, LORD.
A foolish nation has dishonored your name.
¹⁹Don't let these wild beasts destroy your doves.
Don't forget your afflicted people forever.

I REMIND God of his covenant promises. (74:20)

²⁰Remember your covenant promises,
for the land is full of darkness and violence!
²¹Don't let the downtrodden be constantly disgraced!
Instead, let these poor and needy ones give praise to your name.

²²Arise, O God, and defend your cause.
Remember how these fools insult you all day long.
²³Don't overlook these things your enemies have said.
Their uproar of rebellion grows ever louder.

PSALM 75

For the choir director: A psalm of Asaph, to be sung to the tune "Do Not Destroy!" A song.

¹We thank you, O God!
We give thanks because you are near.
People everywhere tell of your mighty miracles.

I BELIEVE God will bring justice on the earth in due time. (75:2)

²God says, "At the time I have planned,
I will bring justice against the wicked.
³When the earth quakes and its people live in turmoil,
I am the one who keeps its foundations firm.   *Interlude*

⁴"I warned the proud, 'Stop your boasting!'
I told the wicked, 'Don't raise your fists!'
⁵Don't lift your fists in defiance at the heavens
or speak with rebellious arrogance.' "

74:16 Or *moon;* Hebrew reads *light.*

⁶ For no one on earth—from east or west,
   or even from the wilderness—
   can raise another person up.
⁷ It is God alone who judges;
   he decides who will rise and who will fall.
⁸ For the Lord holds a cup in his hand;
   it is full of foaming wine mixed with spices.
  He pours the wine out in judgment,
   and all the wicked must drink it,
   draining it to the dregs.

⁹ But as for me, I will always proclaim what God has done;
   I will sing praises to the God of Israel.*

¹⁰ For God says, "I will cut off the strength of the wicked,
   but I will increase the power of the godly."

I BELIEVE God alone has the right and power to bring ultimate judgment upon the wicked. (75:7)

PSALM 76

For the choir director: A psalm of Asaph, to be accompanied by stringed instruments. A song.

¹ God is well known in Judah;
   his name is great in Israel.
² Jerusalem* is where he lives;
   Mount Zion is his home.
³ There he breaks the arrows of the enemy,
   the shields and swords and weapons of his foes.   Interlude

⁴ You are glorious and more majestic
   than the everlasting mountains.*
⁵ The mightiest of our enemies have been plundered.
   They lie before us in the sleep of death.
   No warrior could lift a hand against us.
⁶ When you rebuked them, O God of Jacob,
   their horses and chariots stood still.

I PRAISE God for his glory and majesty. (76:4)

⁷ No wonder you are greatly feared!
   Who can stand before you when your anger explodes?
⁸ From heaven you sentenced your enemies;
   the earth trembled and stood silent before you.
⁹ You stand up to judge those who do evil, O God,
   and to rescue the oppressed of the earth.   Interlude

I KNOW no one can stand against God's righteous anger. (76:7)

¹⁰ Human opposition only enhances your glory,
   for you use it as a sword of judgment.*

¹¹ Make vows to the Lord your God, and fulfill them.
   Let everyone bring tribute to the Awesome One.
¹² For he breaks the spirit of princes
   and is feared by the kings of the earth.

I BELIEVE human opposition only enhances God's glory (Romans 9:17). (76:10)

PSALM 77

For Jeduthun, the choir director: A psalm of Asaph.

¹ I cry out to God without holding back.
   Oh, that God would listen to me!
² When I was in deep trouble,
   I searched for the Lord.

I HOLD nothing back when I cry out to God. (77:1)

75:9 Hebrew *of Jacob.*   76:2 Hebrew *Salem,* another name for Jerusalem.   76:4 As in Greek version; Hebrew reads *than mountains filled with beasts of prey.*   76:10 The meaning of the Hebrew is uncertain.

All night long I pray, with hands lifted toward heaven, pleading.
There can be no joy for me until he acts.
³ I think of God, and I moan,
overwhelmed with longing for his help. *Interlude*

⁴ You don't let me sleep.
I am too distressed even to pray!
⁵ I think of the good old days, long since ended,
⁶ when my nights were filled with joyful songs.
I search my soul and think about the difference now.
⁷ Has the Lord rejected me forever?
Will he never again show me favor?
⁸ Is his unfailing love gone forever?
Have his promises permanently failed?
⁹ Has God forgotten to be kind?
Has he slammed the door on his compassion? *Interlude*

¹⁰ And I said, "This is my fate,
that the blessings of the Most High have changed to hatred."
¹¹ I recall all you have done, O LORD;
I remember your wonderful deeds of long ago.
¹² They are constantly in my thoughts.
I cannot stop thinking about them.

¹³ O God, your ways are holy.
Is there any god as mighty as you?
¹⁴ You are the God of miracles and wonders!
You demonstrate your awesome power among the nations.
¹⁵ You have redeemed your people by your strength,
the descendants of Jacob and of Joseph by your might. *Interlude*

¹⁶ When the Red Sea* saw you, O God,
its waters looked and trembled!
The sea quaked to its very depths.
¹⁷ The clouds poured down their rain;
the thunder rolled and crackled in the sky.
Your arrows of lightning flashed.
¹⁸ Your thunder roared from the whirlwind;
the lightning lit up the world!
The earth trembled and shook.
¹⁹ Your road led through the sea,
your pathway through the mighty waters—
a pathway no one knew was there!
²⁰ You led your people along that road like a flock of sheep,
with Moses and Aaron as their shepherds.

PSALM 78

A psalm of Asaph.

¹ O my people, listen to my teaching.
Open your ears to what I am saying,
² for I will speak to you in a parable.
I will teach you hidden lessons from our past—
³ stories we have heard and know,
stories our ancestors handed down to us.
⁴ We will not hide these truths from our children
but will tell the next generation about the glorious deeds of the LORD.
We will tell of his power and the mighty miracles he did.

77:16 Hebrew *the waters.*

I REMEMBER my times of joy when I go through a time of sorrow. (77:5)

I BRING my questions to God when his love and compassion seem far away. (77:7)

I NEVER STOP thinking about God's wonderful deeds. (77:12)

I REMEMBER how God led and delivered his people. (77:14)

See the profiles for Jacob (page 43) and Joseph (page 51) at Genesis 32:9 and Genesis 39:2.

See the profiles for Moses (page 73) and Aaron (page 107) at Exodus 5:1 and Exodus 32:2.

I REMEMBER God's dealings in the past. (78:2)

I TELL others about God's mighty power and deeds. (78:4)

⁵ For he issued his decree to Jacob;
  he gave his law to Israel.
He commanded our ancestors
  to teach them to their children,
⁶ so the next generation might know them—
  even the children not yet born—
  that they in turn might teach their children.
⁷ So each generation can set its hope anew on God,
  remembering his glorious miracles
  and obeying his commands.
⁸ Then they will not be like their ancestors—
  stubborn, rebellious, and unfaithful,
  refusing to give their hearts to God.

⁹ The warriors of Ephraim, though fully armed,
  turned their backs and fled when the day of battle came.
¹⁰ They did not keep God's covenant,
  and they refused to live by his law.
¹¹ They forgot what he had done—
  the wonderful miracles he had shown them,
¹² the miracles he did for their ancestors in Egypt, on the plain of Zoan.
¹³ For he divided the sea before them and led them through!
  The water stood up like walls beside them!
¹⁴ In the daytime he led them by a cloud,
  and at night by a pillar of fire.
¹⁵ He split open the rocks in the wilderness
  to give them plenty of water, as from a gushing spring.
¹⁶ He made streams pour from the rock,
  making the waters flow down like a river!

I DO NOT FORGET what wonderful miracles God has done in the past. (78:11)

¹⁷ Yet they kept on with their sin,
  rebelling against the Most High in the desert.
¹⁸ They willfully tested God in their hearts,
  demanding the foods they craved.
¹⁹ They even spoke against God himself, saying,
  "God can't give us food in the desert.
²⁰ Yes, he can strike a rock so water gushes out,
  but he can't give his people bread and meat."
²¹ When the LORD heard them, he was angry.
  The fire of his wrath burned against Jacob.
  Yes, his anger rose against Israel,
²² for they did not believe God
  or trust him to care for them.
²³ But he commanded the skies to open—
  he opened the doors of heaven—
²⁴ and rained down manna for them to eat.
  He gave them bread from heaven.
²⁵ They ate the food of angels!
  God gave them all they could hold.
²⁶ He released the east wind in the heavens
  and guided the south wind by his mighty power.
²⁷ He rained down meat as thick as dust—
  birds as plentiful as the sands along the seashore!
²⁸ He caused the birds to fall within their camp
  and all around their tents.
²⁹ The people ate their fill.
  He gave them what they wanted.

I DO NOT KEEP rebelling after God saves me. (78:17)

I DO NOT WILLFULLY TEST God by demanding that he provide what I want. (78:18)

I BELIEVE God demonstrated his ability to provide for the Israelites. (78:23)

I BELIEVE God punished those Israelites who were greedy, ungrateful, and unbelieving (Numbers 11:18-20). (78:31)

I DO NOT KEEP rebelling after God has provided for me and disciplined me. (78:32)

I REJOICE that God is my rock and redeemer. (78:35)

I FOLLOW the Lord with my whole heart. (78:37)

In response to these affirmations, tell the Lord what you believe—or find hard to believe.

I REMEMBER the plagues God poured out on Egypt. (78:49)

30 But before they finished eating this food they had craved,
while the meat was yet in their mouths,
31 the anger of God rose against them,
and he killed their strongest men;
he struck down the finest of Israel's young men.
32 But in spite of this, the people kept on sinning.
They refused to believe in his miracles.
33 So he ended their lives in failure
and gave them years of terror.

34 When God killed some of them, the rest finally sought him.
They repented and turned to God.
35 Then they remembered that God was their rock,
that their redeemer was the Most High.
36 But they followed him only with their words;
they lied to him with their tongues.
37 Their hearts were not loyal to him.
They did not keep his covenant.
38 Yet he was merciful and forgave their sins
and didn't destroy them all.
Many a time he held back his anger
and did not unleash his fury!
39 For he remembered that they were merely mortal,
gone in a moment like a breath of wind, never to return.

40 Oh, how often they rebelled against him in the desert
and grieved his heart in the wilderness.
41 Again and again they tested God's patience
and frustrated the Holy One of Israel.
42 They forgot about his power
and how he rescued them from their enemies.
43 They forgot his miraculous signs in Egypt,
his wonders on the plain of Zoan.
44 For he turned their rivers into blood,
so no one could drink from the streams.
45 He sent vast swarms of flies to consume them
and hordes of frogs to ruin them.
46 He gave their crops to caterpillars;
their harvest was consumed by locusts.
47 He destroyed their grapevines with hail
and shattered their sycamores with sleet.
48 He abandoned their cattle to the hail,
their livestock to bolts of lightning.
49 He loosed on them his fierce anger—
all his fury, rage, and hostility.
He dispatched against them
a band of destroying angels.
50 He turned his anger against them;
he did not spare the Egyptians' lives
but handed them over to the plague.
51 He killed the oldest son in each Egyptian family,
the flower of youth throughout the land of Egypt.*
52 But he led his own people like a flock of sheep,
guiding them safely through the wilderness.
53 He kept them safe so they were not afraid;
but the sea closed in upon their enemies.

78:51 Hebrew *in the tents of Ham.*

54 He brought them to the border of his holy land,
   to this land of hills he had won for them.
55 He drove out the nations before them;
   he gave them their inheritance by lot.
   He settled the tribes of Israel into their homes.

56 Yet though he did all this for them,
   they continued to test his patience.
   They rebelled against the Most High
   and refused to follow his decrees.
57 They turned back and were as faithless as their parents had been.
   They were as useless as a crooked bow.
58 They made God angry by building altars to other gods;
   they made him jealous with their idols.
59 When God heard them, he was very angry,
   and he rejected Israel completely.
60 Then he abandoned his dwelling at Shiloh,
   the Tabernacle where he had lived among the people.
61 He allowed the Ark of his might to be captured;
   he surrendered his glory into enemy hands.
62 He gave his people over to be butchered by the sword,
   because he was so angry with his own people—his special possession.
63 Their young men were killed by fire;
   their young women died before singing their wedding songs.
64 Their priests were slaughtered,
   and their widows could not mourn their deaths.
65 Then the Lord rose up as though waking from sleep,
   like a mighty man aroused from a drunken stupor.
66 He routed his enemies
   and sent them to eternal shame.
67 But he rejected Joseph's descendants;
   he did not choose the tribe of Ephraim.
68 He chose instead the tribe of Judah,
   Mount Zion, which he loved.
69 There he built his towering sanctuary,
   as solid and enduring as the earth itself.
70 He chose his servant David,
   calling him from the sheep pens.
71 He took David from tending the ewes and lambs
   and made him the shepherd of Jacob's descendants—
   God's own people, Israel.
72 He cared for them with a true heart
   and led them with skillful hands.

I DO NOT TEST God's patience to see how much I can rebel before he punishes me. (78:56)

I BELIEVE God rescued his people Israel from their enemies. (78:66)

I BELIEVE God chose Jerusalem (Mount Zion) as his new place to dwell with his people Israel. (78:68)

I BELIEVE God chose David to be his servant and shepherd to the Israelites. (78:70)

See the profiles for David (page 629) and Jacob (page 43) at Psalm 3:1 and Genesis 32:9.

PSALM 79

A psalm of Asaph.

1 O God, pagan nations have conquered your land, your special
      possession.
   They have defiled your holy Temple
   and made Jerusalem a heap of ruins.
2 They have left the bodies of your servants
   as food for the birds of heaven.
   The flesh of your godly ones
   has become food for the wild animals.
3 Blood has flowed like water all around Jerusalem;
   no one is left to bury the dead.

4 We are mocked by our neighbors,
   an object of scorn and derision to those around us.

I TELL God about the suffering of his people and beg for his mercy. (79:5)

5 O LORD, how long will you be angry with us? Forever?
   How long will your jealousy burn like fire?
6 Pour out your wrath on the nations that refuse to recognize you—
   on kingdoms that do not call upon your name.
7 For they have devoured your people Israel,*
   making the land a desolate wilderness.
8 Oh, do not hold us guilty for our former sins!
   Let your tenderhearted mercies quickly meet our needs,
   for we are brought low to the dust.

I ASK for God to forgive his people for the honor of his name. (79:9)

9 Help us, O God of our salvation!
   Help us for the honor of your name.
   Oh, save us and forgive our sins
   for the sake of your name.
10 Why should pagan nations be allowed to scoff,
   asking, "Where is their God?"
   Show us your vengeance against the nations,
   for they have spilled the blood of your servants.
11 Listen to the moaning of the prisoners.
   Demonstrate your great power by saving those condemned to die.

12 O Lord, take sevenfold vengeance on our neighbors
   for the scorn they have hurled at you.
13 Then we your people, the sheep of your pasture,
   will thank you forever and ever,
   praising your greatness from generation to generation.

PSALM 80

For the choir director: A psalm of Asaph, to be sung to the tune "Lilies of the Covenant."

I PRAY that God will listen to his people and rescue them. (80:1)

1 Please listen, O Shepherd of Israel,
   you who lead Israel* like a flock.
   O God, enthroned above the cherubim,
   display your radiant glory
2   to Ephraim, Benjamin, and Manasseh.
   Show us your mighty power.
   Come to rescue us!

3 Turn us again to yourself, O God.
   Make your face shine down upon us.
   Only then will we be saved.

4 O LORD God Almighty,
   how long will you be angry and reject our prayers?
5 You have fed us with sorrow
   and made us drink tears by the bucketful.
6 You have made us the scorn of neighboring nations.
   Our enemies treat us as a joke.

I ASK God to show his loving attention and save his people. (80:7)

7 Turn us again to yourself, O God Almighty.
   Make your face shine down upon us.
   Only then will we be saved.
8 You brought us from Egypt as though we were a tender vine;
   you drove away the pagan nations and transplanted us into your land.

79:7 Hebrew Jacob.   80:1 Hebrew Joseph.

9 You cleared the ground for us,
   and we took root and filled the land.
10 The mountains were covered with our shade;
   the mighty cedars were covered with our branches.
11 We spread our branches west to the Mediterranean Sea,
   our limbs east to the Euphrates River.*
12 But now, why have you broken down our walls
   so that all who pass may steal our fruit?
13 The boar from the forest devours us,
   and the wild animals feed on us.

14 Come back, we beg you, O God Almighty.
   Look down from heaven and see our plight.
   Watch over and care for this vine
15   that you yourself have planted,
   this son you have raised for yourself.
16 For we are chopped up and burned by our enemies.
   May they perish at the sight of your frown.
17 Strengthen the man you love,
   the son of your choice.
18 Then we will never forsake you again.
   Revive us so we can call on your name once more.

19 Turn us again to yourself, O LORD God Almighty.
   Make your face shine down upon us.
   Only then will we be saved.

I BEG God to care for his people in their time of need. (80:14)

I ASK God to strengthen his people so they may call on his name. (80:18)

PSALM 81

For the choir director: A psalm of Asaph, to be accompanied by a stringed instrument. *

1 Sing praises to God, our strength.
   Sing to the God of Israel.*
2 Sing! Beat the tambourine.
   Play the sweet lyre and the harp.
3 Sound the trumpet for a sacred feast
   when the moon is new,
   when the moon is full.
4 For this is required by the laws of Israel;
   it is a law of the God of Jacob.
5 He made it a decree for Israel*
   when he attacked Egypt to set us free.

   I heard an unknown voice that said,
6 "Now I will relieve your shoulder of its burden;
   I will free your hands from their heavy tasks.
7 You cried to me in trouble, and I saved you;
   I answered out of the thundercloud.
   I tested your faith at Meribah,
   when you complained that there was no water.   *Interlude*

8 "Listen to me, O my people, while I give you stern warnings.
   O Israel, if you would only listen!
9 You must never have a foreign god;
   you must not bow down before a false god.

I SING praises to God, my strength. (81:1)

80:11 Hebrew *west to the sea, . . . east to the river.*   81:TITLE Hebrew *according to the gittith.*   81:1 Hebrew of *Jacob.*   81:5 Hebrew *for Joseph.*

I GLADLY ACCEPT the good things the Lord promises to give me. (81:10)

¹⁰ For it was I, the LORD your God,
who rescued you from the land of Egypt.
Open your mouth wide, and I will fill it with good things.

¹¹ "But no, my people wouldn't listen.
Israel did not want me around.
¹² So I let them follow their blind and stubborn way,
living according to their own desires.

I LISTEN to the Lord, follow him, and obey his commands. (81:13)

¹³ But oh, that my people would listen to me!
Oh, that Israel would follow me, walking in my paths!
¹⁴ How quickly I would then subdue their enemies!
How soon my hands would be upon their foes!
¹⁵ Those who hate the LORD would cringe before him;
their desolation would last forever.
¹⁶ But I would feed you with the best of foods.
I would satisfy you with wild honey from the rock."

PSALM 82

A psalm of Asaph.

I BELIEVE God will judge those who judge unjustly. (82:1)

¹ God presides over heaven's court;
he pronounces judgment on the judges:
² "How long will you judges hand down unjust decisions?
How long will you shower special favors on the wicked?   *Interlude*

³ "Give fair judgment to the poor and the orphan;
uphold the rights of the oppressed and the destitute.

I RESCUE the poor, helpless, and oppressed. (82:4)

⁴ Rescue the poor and helpless;
deliver them from the grasp of evil people.
⁵ But these oppressors know nothing;
they are so ignorant!
And because they are in darkness,
the whole world is shaken to the core.
⁶ I say, 'You are gods
and children of the Most High.
⁷ But in death you are mere men.
You will fall as any prince,
for all must die.' "

⁸ Rise up, O God, and judge the earth,
for all the nations belong to you.

PSALM 83

A psalm of Asaph. A song.

¹ O God, don't sit idly by,
silent and inactive!

I ASK God to take note of the violent plans of his enemies. (83:2)

² Don't you hear the tumult of your enemies?
Don't you see what your arrogant enemies are doing?
³ They devise crafty schemes against your people,
laying plans against your precious ones.
⁴ "Come," they say, "let us wipe out Israel as a nation.
We will destroy the very memory of its existence."
⁵ This was their unanimous decision.
They signed a treaty as allies against you—
⁶ these Edomites and Ishmaelites,
Moabites and Hagrites,
⁷ Gebalites, Ammonites, and Amalekites,
and people from Philistia and Tyre.

8 Assyria has joined them, too,
   and is allied with the descendants of Lot. *Interlude*

I LOOK to God to avenge his enemies as he has done in the past. (83:9)

9 Do to them as you did to the Midianites
   or as you did to Sisera and Jabin at the Kishon River.
10 They were destroyed at Endor,
   and their decaying corpses fertilized the soil.
11 Let their mighty nobles die as Oreb and Zeeb did.
   Let all their princes die like Zebah and Zalmunna,
12 for they said, "Let us seize for our own use
   these pasturelands of God!"

13 O my God, blow them away like whirling dust,
   like chaff before the wind!
14 As a fire roars through a forest
   and as a flame sets mountains ablaze,
15 chase them with your fierce storms;
   terrify them with your tempests.
16 Utterly disgrace them
   until they submit to your name, O LORD.
17 Let them be ashamed and terrified forever.
   Make them failures in everything they do,
18 until they learn that you alone are called the LORD,
   that you alone are the Most High, supreme over all the earth.

I PRAY that God's enemies will continue to fail until they see that God alone is the Lord Most High. (83:18)

PSALM 84

For the choir director: A psalm of the descendants of Korah, to be accompanied by a stringed instrument. *

1 How lovely is your dwelling place,
   O LORD Almighty.
2 I long, yes, I faint with longing
   to enter the courts of the LORD.
   With my whole being, body and soul,
   I will shout joyfully to the living God.
3 Even the sparrow finds a home there,
   and the swallow builds her nest
   and raises her young—
   at a place near your altar,
   O LORD Almighty, my King and my God!
4 How happy are those who can live in your house,
   always singing your praises. *Interlude*

I PRAISE God with my whole being. (84:2)

I REJOICE that God lives within me (1 John 4:15-16). (84:4)

5 Happy are those who are strong in the LORD,
   who set their minds on a pilgrimage to Jerusalem.
6 When they walk through the Valley of Weeping, *
   it will become a place of refreshing springs,
   where pools of blessing collect after the rains!
7 They will continue to grow stronger,
   and each of them will appear before God in Jerusalem. *

8 O LORD God Almighty, hear my prayer.
   Listen, O God of Israel. * *Interlude*

9 O God, look with favor upon the king, our protector!
   Have mercy on the one you have anointed.

84:TITLE Hebrew *according to the gittith.*   84:6 Hebrew *valley of Baca.*   84:7 Hebrew *Zion.*   84:8 Hebrew *of Jacob.*

¹⁰A single day in your courts
  is better than a thousand anywhere else!
I would rather be a gatekeeper in the house of my God
  than live the good life in the homes of the wicked.
¹¹For the LORD God is our light and protector.
  He gives us grace and glory.
No good thing will the LORD withhold
  from those who do what is right.
¹²O LORD Almighty,
  happy are those who trust in you.

PSALM 85

For the choir director: A psalm of the descendants of Korah.

¹LORD, you have poured out amazing blessings on your land!
  You have restored the fortunes of Israel.*
²You have forgiven the guilt of your people—
  yes, you have covered all their sins.   *Interlude*

³You have withdrawn your fury.
  You have ended your blazing anger.
⁴Now turn to us again, O God of our salvation.
  Put aside your anger against us.
⁵Will you be angry with us always?
  Will you prolong your wrath to distant generations?
⁶Won't you revive us again,
  so your people can rejoice in you?
⁷Show us your unfailing love, O LORD,
  and grant us your salvation.

⁸I listen carefully to what God the LORD is saying,
  for he speaks peace to his people, his faithful ones.
  But let them not return to their foolish ways.
⁹Surely his salvation is near to those who honor him;
  our land will be filled with his glory.

¹⁰Unfailing love and truth have met together.
  Righteousness and peace have kissed!
¹¹Truth springs up from the earth,
  and righteousness smiles down from heaven.
¹²Yes, the LORD pours down his blessings.
  Our land will yield its bountiful crops.
¹³Righteousness goes as a herald before him,
  preparing the way for his steps.

PSALM 86

A prayer of David.

¹Bend down, O LORD, and hear my prayer;
  answer me, for I need your help.
²Protect me, for I am devoted to you.
  Save me, for I serve you and trust you.
  You are my God.
³Be merciful, O Lord,
  for I am calling on you constantly.
⁴Give me happiness, O Lord,
  for my life depends on you.

85:1 Hebrew *of Jacob.*

I BELIEVE God withholds nothing good from his children. (84:11)

I AM AMAZED at the blessings the Lord pours out on me. (85:1)

I PRAISE the Lord because he forgives my guilt and my sins. (85:2)

I LISTEN carefully to God and follow his ways, not my own. (85:8)

See David's profile (page 629) at Psalm 3:1.

I FIND true happiness in the Lord alone. (86:4)

⁵ O Lord, you are so good, so ready to forgive,
  so full of unfailing love for all who ask your aid.
⁶ Listen closely to my prayer, O LORD;
  hear my urgent cry.
⁷ I will call to you whenever trouble strikes,
  and you will answer me.

⁸ Nowhere among the pagan gods is there a god like you, O Lord.
  There are no other miracles like yours.
⁹ All the nations—and you made each one—
  will come and bow before you, Lord;
  they will praise your great and holy name.
¹⁰ For you are great and perform great miracles.
  You alone are God.

¹¹ Teach me your ways, O LORD,
  that I may live according to your truth!
  Grant me purity of heart,
  that I may honor you.
¹² With all my heart I will praise you, O Lord my God.
  I will give glory to your name forever,
¹³ for your love for me is very great.
  You have rescued me from the depths of death*!

¹⁴ O God, insolent people rise up against me;
  violent people are trying to kill me.
  And you mean nothing to them.
¹⁵ But you, O Lord, are a merciful and gracious God,
  slow to get angry,
  full of unfailing love and truth.
¹⁶ Look down and have mercy on me.
  Give strength to your servant;
  yes, save me, for I am your servant.
¹⁷ Send me a sign of your favor.
  Then those who hate me will be put to shame,
  for you, O LORD, help and comfort me.

I LONG FOR a pure heart that I may honor God. (86:11)

I PRAY for God's strength and protection in my life. (86:16)

PSALM 87

A psalm of the descendants of Korah. A song.

¹ On the holy mountain stands the city founded by the LORD.
²   He loves the city of Jerusalem
  more than any other city in Israel.*
³ O city of God,
  what glorious things are said of you!   *Interlude*

⁴ I will record Egypt* and Babylon among those who know me—
  also Philistia and Tyre, and even distant Ethiopia.*
  They have all become citizens of Jerusalem!
⁵ And it will be said of Jerusalem,*
  "Everyone has become a citizen here."
  And the Most High will personally bless this city.
⁶ When the LORD registers the nations,
  he will say, "This one has become a citizen of Jerusalem."   *Interlude*

⁷ At all the festivals, the people will sing,
  "The source of my life is in Jerusalem!"

I BELIEVE the Lord is calling people from every nation to himself. (87:4)

86:13 Hebrew *of Sheol.*   87:2 Hebrew *He loves the gates of Zion more than all the dwellings of Jacob.*   87:4a Hebrew
Rahab, the name of a mythical sea monster that represents chaos in ancient literature. The name is used here as a
poetic name for Egypt.   87:4b Hebrew *Cush.*   87:5 Hebrew *Zion.*

PSALM **88**

For the choir director: A psalm of the descendants of Korah, to be sung to the tune "The Suffering of Affliction." A psalm of Heman the Ezrahite. A song.

¹O LORD, God of my salvation,
    I have cried out to you day and night.
²Now hear my prayer;
    listen to my cry.
³For my life is full of troubles,
    and death draws near.
⁴I have been dismissed as one who is dead,
    like a strong man with no strength left.
⁵They have abandoned me to death,
    and I am as good as dead.
I am forgotten,
    cut off from your care.
⁶You have thrust me down to the lowest pit,
    into the darkest depths.
⁷Your anger lies heavy on me;
    wave after wave engulfs me.   *Interlude*

⁸You have caused my friends to loathe me;
    you have sent them all away.
I am in a trap with no way of escape.
⁹   My eyes are blinded by my tears.
Each day I beg for your help, O LORD;
    I lift my pleading hands to you for mercy.
¹⁰Of what use to the dead are your miracles?
    Do the dead get up and praise you?   *Interlude*

¹¹Can those in the grave declare your unfailing love?
    In the place of destruction, can they proclaim your faithfulness?
¹²Can the darkness speak of your miracles?
    Can anyone in the land of forgetfulness talk about your righteousness?

¹³O LORD, I cry out to you.
    I will keep on pleading day by day.
¹⁴O LORD, why do you reject me?
    Why do you turn your face away from me?
¹⁵I have been sickly and close to death since my youth.
    I stand helpless and desperate before your terrors.
¹⁶Your fierce anger has overwhelmed me.
    Your terrors have cut me off.
¹⁷They swirl around me like floodwaters all day long.
    They have encircled me completely.
¹⁸You have taken away my companions and loved ones;
    only darkness remains.

PSALM **89**

A psalm of Ethan the Ezrahite.

¹I will sing of the tender mercies of the LORD forever!
    Young and old will hear of your faithfulness.
²Your unfailing love will last forever.
    Your faithfulness is as enduring as the heavens.

³The LORD said, "I have made a solemn agreement with David, my chosen
    servant.

I DO NOT THINK that I am so smart that I don't need to cry out to God in the midst of desperate circumstances (1 Kings 4:31). (88:3)

I KEEP PLEADING with the Lord, even when it seems as if he has rejected me. (88:13)

I DO NOT THINK that I am so smart that I don't need to put my trust in what the Lord says (1 Kings 4:31). (89:3)

I have sworn this oath to him:
⁴ 'I will establish your descendants as kings forever;
    they will sit on your throne from now until eternity.' "   *Interlude*

⁵ All heaven will praise your miracles, LORD;
    myriads of angels will praise you for your faithfulness.
⁶ For who in all of heaven can compare with the LORD?
    What mightiest angel is anything like the LORD?
⁷ The highest angelic powers stand in awe of God.
    He is far more awesome than those who surround his throne.
⁸ O LORD God Almighty!
    Where is there anyone as mighty as you, LORD?
    Faithfulness is your very character.

I BELIEVE no angel can compare with the Lord God Almighty (Hebrews 1:4–2:8). (89:6)

⁹ You are the one who rules the oceans.
    When their waves rise in fearful storms, you subdue them.
¹⁰ You are the one who crushed the great sea monster.*
    You scattered your enemies with your mighty arm.
¹¹ The heavens are yours, and the earth is yours;
    everything in the world is yours—you created it all.
¹² You created north and south.
    Mount Tabor and Mount Hermon praise your name.
¹³ Powerful is your arm!
    Strong is your hand!
    Your right hand is lifted high in glorious strength.

I PRAISE God's powerful and glorious strength. (89:13)

¹⁴ Your throne is founded on two strong pillars—righteousness and justice.
    Unfailing love and truth walk before you as attendants.
¹⁵ Happy are those who hear the joyful call to worship,
    for they will walk in the light of your presence, LORD.
¹⁶ They rejoice all day long in your wonderful reputation.
    They exult in your righteousness.
¹⁷ You are their glorious strength.
    Our power is based on your favor.
¹⁸ Yes, our protection comes from the LORD,
    and he, the Holy One of Israel, has given us our king.

I TRUST in the Lord's protection. (89:18)

¹⁹ You once spoke in a vision to your prophet and said,
    "I have given help to a warrior.
    I have selected him from the common people to be king.
²⁰ I have found my servant David.
    I have anointed him with my holy oil.
²¹ I will steady him,
    and I will make him strong.

I BELIEVE the Lord chose David to be Israel's king. (89:20)

²² His enemies will not get the best of him,
    nor will the wicked overpower him.
²³ I will beat down his adversaries before him
    and destroy those who hate him.
²⁴ My faithfulness and unfailing love will be with him,
    and he will rise to power because of me.
²⁵ I will extend his rule from the Mediterranean Sea in the west
    to the Tigris and Euphrates rivers in the east.*
²⁶ And he will say to me, 'You are my Father,
    my God, and the Rock of my salvation.'
²⁷ I will make him my firstborn son,
    the mightiest king on earth.

89:10 Hebrew *Rahab*, the name of a mythical sea monster that represents chaos in ancient literature.
89:25 Hebrew *I will set his hand on the sea, his right hand on the rivers.*

I BELIEVE the Lord's promises to David will never end. (89:28)

28 I will love him and be kind to him forever;
    my covenant with him will never end.
29 I will preserve an heir for him;
    his throne will be as endless as the days of heaven.
30 But if his sons forsake my law
    and fail to walk in my ways,
31 if they do not obey my decrees
    and fail to keep my commands,
32 then I will punish their sin with the rod,
    and their disobedience with beating.

I BELIEVE the Lord will never let his promises to David fail. (89:33)

33 But I will never stop loving him,
    nor let my promise to him fail.
34 No, I will not break my covenant;
    I will not take back a single word I said.
35 I have sworn an oath to David,
    and in my holiness I cannot lie:
36 His dynasty will go on forever;
    his throne is as secure as the sun,
37   as eternal as the moon,
    my faithful witness in the sky!"   *Interlude*

38 But now you have rejected him.
    Why are you so angry with the one you chose as king?

I KEEP BELIEVING the Lord's promises, even when it seems as if he has renounced them. (89:39)

39 You have renounced your covenant with him,
    for you have thrown his crown in the dust.
40 You have broken down the walls protecting him
    and laid in ruins every fort defending him.
41 Everyone who comes along has robbed him
    while his neighbors mock.
42 You have strengthened his enemies against him
    and made them all rejoice.
43 You have made his sword useless
    and have refused to help him in battle.
44 You have ended his splendor
    and overturned his throne.
45 You have made him old before his time
    and publicly disgraced him.   *Interlude*

I THANK God for his great mercy and abiding presence in my life (Titus 3:5-6). (89:46)

46 O LORD, how long will this go on?
    Will you hide yourself forever?
    How long will your anger burn like fire?
47 Remember how short my life is,
    how empty and futile this human existence!
48 No one can live forever; all will die.
    No one can escape the power of the grave.   *Interlude*

I REMIND God of his promises in the midst of my suffering. (89:49)

49 Lord, where is your unfailing love?
    You promised it to David with a faithful pledge.
50 Consider, Lord, how your servants are disgraced!
    I carry in my heart the insults of so many people.
51 Your enemies have mocked me, O LORD;
    they mock the one you anointed as king.

52 Blessed be the LORD forever!
    Amen and amen!

BOOK FOUR (Psalms 90–106)

PSALM 90

A prayer of Moses, the man of God.

¹ Lord, through all the generations
you have been our home!
² Before the mountains were created,
before you made the earth and the world,
you are God, without beginning or end.

³ You turn people back to dust, saying,
"Return to dust!"
⁴ For you, a thousand years are as yesterday!
They are like a few hours!
⁵ You sweep people away like dreams that disappear
or like grass that springs up in the morning.
⁶ In the morning it blooms and flourishes,
but by evening it is dry and withered.
⁷ We wither beneath your anger;
we are overwhelmed by your fury.
⁸ You spread out our sins before you—
our secret sins—and you see them all.
⁹ We live our lives beneath your wrath.
We end our lives with a groan.

¹⁰ Seventy years are given to us!
Some may even reach eighty.
But even the best of these years are filled with pain and trouble;
soon they disappear, and we are gone.
¹¹ Who can comprehend the power of your anger?
Your wrath is as awesome as the fear you deserve.
¹² Teach us to make the most of our time,
so that we may grow in wisdom.

¹³ O LORD, come back to us!
How long will you delay?
Take pity on your servants!
¹⁴ Satisfy us in the morning with your unfailing love,
so we may sing for joy to the end of our lives.
¹⁵ Give us gladness in proportion to our former misery!
Replace the evil years with good.
¹⁶ Let us see your miracles again;
let our children see your glory at work.
¹⁷ And may the Lord our God show us his approval
and make our efforts successful.
Yes, make our efforts successful!

PSALM 91

¹ Those who live in the shelter of the Most High
will find rest in the shadow of the Almighty.
² This I declare of the LORD:
He alone is my refuge, my place of safety;
he is my God, and I am trusting him.
³ For he will rescue you from every trap
and protect you from the fatal plague.
⁴ He will shield you with his wings.
He will shelter you with his feathers.
His faithful promises are your armor and protection.

See Moses' profile (page 73) at Exodus 5:1.

I BELIEVE the Lord knows how frail and short my life is here on earth. (90:3)

Recommit yourself to following the Lord with all your heart, soul, strength, and mind.

I KNOW all my sins are completely open to God and that I, on my own, deserve his wrath. (90:8)

I PRAY for God's help to use my short time on earth wisely. (90:12)

I PRAY for God's approval and blessings on my efforts in this life. (90:17)

I LET others know that I am putting my trust in the Lord. (91:2)

⁵Do not be afraid of the terrors of the night,
  nor fear the dangers of the day,
⁶nor dread the plague that stalks in darkness,
  nor the disaster that strikes at midday.
⁷Though a thousand fall at your side,
  though ten thousand are dying around you,
  these evils will not touch you.
⁸But you will see it with your eyes;
  you will see how the wicked are punished.

I AM CONFIDENT that evil cannot destroy me, because the Lord is my refuge. (91:9)

⁹If you make the LORD your refuge,
  if you make the Most High your shelter,
¹⁰no evil will conquer you;
  no plague will come near your dwelling.
¹¹For he orders his angels
  to protect you wherever you go.
¹²They will hold you with their hands
  to keep you from striking your foot on a stone.
¹³You will trample down lions and poisonous snakes;
  you will crush fierce lions and serpents under your feet!

I LOVE the Lord and thank him for answering my cries for help. (91:14)

¹⁴The LORD says, "I will rescue those who love me.
  I will protect those who trust in my name.
¹⁵When they call on me, I will answer;
  I will be with them in trouble.
  I will rescue them and honor them.
¹⁶I will satisfy them with a long life
  and give them my salvation."

PSALM 92

A psalm to be sung on the LORD's Day. A song.

¹It is good to give thanks to the LORD,
  to sing praises to the Most High.
²It is good to proclaim your unfailing love in the morning,
  your faithfulness in the evening,
³accompanied by the harp and lute
  and the harmony of the lyre.
⁴You thrill me, LORD, with all you have done for me!
  I sing for joy because of what you have done.

I AM THRILLED by everything the Lord has done for me! (92:4)

⁵O LORD, what great miracles you do!
  And how deep are your thoughts.
⁶Only an ignorant person would not know this!
  Only a fool would not understand it.
⁷Although the wicked flourish like weeds,
  and evildoers blossom with success,
  there is only eternal destruction ahead of them.
⁸But you are exalted in the heavens.
  You, O LORD, continue forever.
⁹Your enemies, LORD, will surely perish;
  all evildoers will be scattered.

I KNOW that, while the wicked may prosper now, they will face eternal destruction if they don't repent (2 Peter 3:9). (92:7)

¹⁰But you have made me as strong as a wild bull.
  How refreshed I am by your power!
¹¹With my own eyes I have seen the downfall of my enemies;
  with my own ears I have heard the defeat of my wicked opponents.

¹² But the godly will flourish like palm trees
and grow strong like the cedars of Lebanon.
¹³ For they are transplanted into the LORD's own house.
They flourish in the courts of our God.
¹⁴ Even in old age they will still produce fruit;
they will remain vital and green.
¹⁵ They will declare, "The LORD is just!
He is my rock!
There is nothing but goodness in him!"

I TELL others about the Lord's goodness to me. (92:15)

PSALM 93

¹ The LORD is king! He is robed in majesty.
Indeed, the LORD is robed in majesty and armed with strength.
The world is firmly established;
it cannot be shaken.

² Your throne, O LORD, has been established from time immemorial.
You yourself are from the everlasting past.
³ The mighty oceans have roared, O LORD.
The mighty oceans roar like thunder;
the mighty oceans roar as they pound the shore.
⁴ But mightier than the violent raging of the seas,
mightier than the breakers on the shore—
the LORD above is mightier than these!
⁵ Your royal decrees cannot be changed.
The nature of your reign, O LORD, is holiness forever.

I PRAISE the Lord for his majestic reign over all the earth. (93:2)

PSALM 94

¹ O LORD, the God to whom vengeance belongs,
O God of vengeance, let your glorious justice be seen!
² Arise, O judge of the earth.
Sentence the proud to the penalties they deserve.
³ How long, O LORD?
How long will the wicked be allowed to gloat?
⁴ Hear their arrogance!
How these evildoers boast!
⁵ They oppress your people, LORD,
hurting those you love.
⁶ They kill widows and foreigners
and murder orphans.
⁷ "The LORD isn't looking," they say,
"and besides, the God of Israel* doesn't care."

I CALL on the Lord to show his justice. (94:1)

I CRY OUT to God when the proud and wicked oppress his people because they think the Lord doesn't care. (94:3)

⁸ Think again, you fools!
When will you finally catch on?
⁹ Is the one who made your ears deaf?
Is the one who formed your eyes blind?
¹⁰ He punishes the nations—won't he also punish you?
He knows everything—doesn't he also know what you are doing?
¹¹ The LORD knows people's thoughts,
that they are worthless!

I BELIEVE that God sees and knows everything people do. (94:10)

¹² Happy are those whom you discipline, LORD,
and those whom you teach from your law.
¹³ You give them relief from troubled times
until a pit is dug for the wicked.

94:7 Hebrew *of Jacob.*

¹⁴The LORD will not reject his people;
    he will not abandon his own special possession.
¹⁵Judgment will come again for the righteous,
    and those who are upright will have a reward.

¹⁶Who will protect me from the wicked?
    Who will stand up for me against evildoers?
¹⁷Unless the LORD had helped me,
    I would soon have died.
¹⁸I cried out, "I'm slipping!"
    and your unfailing love, O LORD, supported me.
¹⁹When doubts filled my mind,
    your comfort gave me renewed hope and cheer.

²⁰Can unjust leaders claim that God is on their side—
    leaders who permit injustice by their laws?
²¹They attack the righteous
    and condemn the innocent to death.
²²But the LORD is my fortress;
    my God is a mighty rock where I can hide.
²³God will make the sins of evil people fall back upon them.
    He will destroy them for their sins.
    The LORD our God will destroy them.

I TRUST that the Lord will one day reward those who trust and obey him. (94:15)

I AM SO GLAD the Lord is my fortress and protector. (94:22)

PSALM 95

¹Come, let us sing to the LORD!
    Let us give a joyous shout to the rock of our salvation!
²Let us come before him with thanksgiving.
    Let us sing him psalms of praise.
³For the LORD is a great God,
    the great King above all gods.
⁴He owns the depths of the earth,
    and even the mightiest mountains are his.
⁵The sea belongs to him, for he made it.
    His hands formed the dry land, too.

⁶Come, let us worship and bow down.
    Let us kneel before the LORD our maker,
⁷ for he is our God.
We are the people he watches over,
    the sheep under his care.

Oh, that you would listen to his voice today!
⁸The LORD says, "Don't harden your hearts as Israel did at Meribah,
    as they did at Massah in the wilderness.
⁹For there your ancestors tried my patience;
    they courted my wrath though they had seen my many miracles.
¹⁰For forty years I was angry with them, and I said,
    'They are a people whose hearts turn away from me.
    They refuse to do what I tell them.'
¹¹So in my anger I made a vow:
    'They will never enter my place of rest.'"

I PRAISE the Lord because he is a great God, the King over all. (95:3)

I DO NOT HARDEN my heart against the Lord. (95:8)

PSALM 96

¹Sing a new song to the LORD!
    Let the whole earth sing to the LORD!
²Sing to the LORD; bless his name.
    Each day proclaim the good news that he saves.

I PROCLAIM the good news of the Lord's salvation each day. (96:2)

³ Publish his glorious deeds among the nations.
    Tell everyone about the amazing things he does.
⁴ Great is the LORD! He is most worthy of praise!
    He is to be revered above all the gods.
⁵ The gods of other nations are merely idols,
    but the LORD made the heavens!
⁶ Honor and majesty surround him;
    strength and beauty are in his sanctuary.

⁷ O nations of the world, recognize the LORD;
    recognize that the LORD is glorious and strong.
⁸ Give to the LORD the glory he deserves!
    Bring your offering and come to worship him.
⁹ Worship the LORD in all his holy splendor.
    Let all the earth tremble before him.
¹⁰ Tell all the nations that the LORD is king.
    The world is firmly established and cannot be shaken.
    He will judge all peoples fairly.

¹¹ Let the heavens be glad, and let the earth rejoice!
    Let the sea and everything in it shout his praise!
¹²   Let the fields and their crops burst forth with joy!
    Let the trees of the forest rustle with praise
¹³   before the LORD!
  For the LORD is coming!
    He is coming to judge the earth.
  He will judge the world with righteousness
    and all the nations with his truth.

PSALM 97

¹ The LORD is king! Let the earth rejoice!
    Let the farthest islands be glad.
² Clouds and darkness surround him.
    Righteousness and justice are the foundation of his throne.
³ Fire goes forth before him
    and burns up all his foes.
⁴ His lightning flashes out across the world.
    The earth sees and trembles.
⁵ The mountains melt like wax before the LORD,
    before the Lord of all the earth.
⁶ The heavens declare his righteousness;
    every nation sees his glory.
⁷ Those who worship idols are disgraced—
    all who brag about their worthless gods—
    for every god must bow to him.
⁸ Jerusalem* has heard and rejoiced,
    and all the cities of Judah are glad
    because of your justice, LORD!
⁹ For you, O LORD, are most high over all the earth;
    you are exalted far above all gods.

¹⁰ You who love the LORD, hate evil!
    He protects the lives of his godly people
    and rescues them from the power of the wicked.
¹¹ Light shines on the godly,
    and joy on those who do right.

97:8 Hebrew *Zion*.

I TALK with others about the amazing deeds of God in my life. (96:3)

I BELIEVE the Lord will judge the world with righteousness and truth. (96:13)

I WORSHIP the Lord for his righteousness and glory. (97:6)

I AM HAPPY in the Lord and do what is right. (97:11)

¹²May all who are godly be happy in the LORD
and praise his holy name!

PSALM 98

A psalm.

¹Sing a new song to the LORD,
for he has done wonderful deeds.
He has won a mighty victory
by his power and holiness.
²The LORD has announced his victory
and has revealed his righteousness to every nation!
³He has remembered his promise to love and be faithful to Israel.
The whole earth has seen the salvation of our God.

⁴Shout to the LORD, all the earth;
break out in praise and sing for joy!
⁵Sing your praise to the LORD with the harp,
with the harp and melodious song,
⁶ with trumpets and the sound of the ram's horn.
Make a joyful symphony before the LORD, the King!

I PRAISE the Lord with song and instruments. (98:5)

⁷Let the sea and everything in it shout his praise!
Let the earth and all living things join in.
⁸ Let the rivers clap their hands in glee!
Let the hills sing out their songs of joy
⁹ before the LORD.
For the LORD is coming to judge the earth.
He will judge the world with justice,
and the nations with fairness.

I PRAISE the Lord because he will judge the world with justice. (98:9)

PSALM 99

¹The LORD is king!
Let the nations tremble!
He sits on his throne between the cherubim.
Let the whole earth quake!
²The LORD sits in majesty in Jerusalem,*
supreme above all the nations.
³Let them praise your great and awesome name.
Your name is holy!
⁴Mighty king, lover of justice,
you have established fairness.
You have acted with justice
and righteousness throughout Israel.*
⁵Exalt the LORD our God!
Bow low before his feet, for he is holy!

I PRAISE God's awesome and holy name. (99:3)

⁶Moses and Aaron were among his priests;
Samuel also called on his name.
They cried to the LORD for help,
and he answered them.
⁷He spoke to them from the pillar of cloud,
and they followed the decrees and principles he gave them.
⁸O LORD our God, you answered them.
You were a forgiving God,
but you punished them when they went wrong.

See the profiles for Moses (page 73), Aaron (page 107), and Samuel (page 323) at Exodus 5:1, Exodus 32:2, and 1 Samuel 3:1.

I THANK the Lord for his righteousness and forgiveness. (99:8)

99:2 Hebrew *Zion.*   99:4 Hebrew *Jacob.*

⁹ Exalt the LORD our God
   and worship at his holy mountain in Jerusalem,
   for the LORD our God is holy!

PSALM 100

A psalm of thanksgiving.

¹ Shout with joy to the LORD, O earth!
² Worship the LORD with gladness.
   Come before him, singing with joy.
³ Acknowledge that the LORD is God!
   He made us, and we are his.
   We are his people, the sheep of his pasture.

⁴ Enter his gates with thanksgiving;
   go into his courts with praise.
   Give thanks to him and bless his name.
⁵ For the LORD is good.
   His unfailing love continues forever,
   and his faithfulness continues to each generation.

I URGE the whole earth to shout with joy to the Lord. (100:1)

I ACKNOWLEDGE that the Lord is God and that we belong to him. (100:3)

PSALM 101

A psalm of David.

¹ I will sing of your love and justice.
   I will praise you, LORD, with songs.
² I will be careful to live a blameless life—
   when will you come to my aid?
   I will lead a life of integrity
   in my own home.
³ I will refuse to look at
   anything vile and vulgar.
   I hate all crooked dealings;
   I will have nothing to do with them.
⁴ I will reject perverse ideas
   and stay away from every evil.
⁵ I will not tolerate people who slander their neighbors.
   I will not endure conceit and pride.

⁶ I will keep a protective eye on the godly,
   so they may dwell with me in safety.
   Only those who are above reproach
   will be allowed to serve me.
⁷ I will not allow deceivers to serve me,
   and liars will not be allowed to enter my presence.
⁸ My daily task will be to ferret out criminals
   and free the city of the LORD from their grip.

See David's profile (page 629) at Psalm 3:1.

I SING praises to the Lord for his love and justice. (101:1)

I DO NOT LOOK AT or have anything to do with vile or illegal things. (101:3)

I RESIST slanderous and proud conversations. (101:5)

PSALM 102

A prayer of one overwhelmed with trouble, pouring out problems before the LORD.

¹ LORD, hear my prayer!
   Listen to my plea!
² Don't turn away from me
   in my time of distress.
   Bend down your ear
   and answer me quickly when I call to you,
³ for my days disappear like smoke,
   and my bones burn like red-hot coals.

I BEG for God to listen to me when I am in distress. (102:2)

⁴ My heart is sick, withered like grass,
  and I have lost my appetite.
⁵ Because of my groaning,
  I am reduced to skin and bones.
⁶ I am like an owl in the desert,
  like a lonely owl in a far-off wilderness.
⁷ I lie awake,
  lonely as a solitary bird on the roof.
⁸ My enemies taunt me day after day.
  They mock and curse me.
⁹ I eat ashes instead of my food.
  My tears run down into my drink
¹⁰ because of your anger and wrath.
  For you have picked me up and thrown me out.
¹¹ My life passes as swiftly as the evening shadows.
  I am withering like grass.

¹² But you, O LORD, will rule forever.
  Your fame will endure to every generation.
¹³ You will arise and have mercy on Jerusalem* —
  and now is the time to pity her,
  now is the time you promised to help.
¹⁴ For your people love every stone in her walls
  and show favor even to the dust in her streets.
¹⁵ And the nations will tremble before the LORD.
  The kings of the earth will tremble before his glory.
¹⁶ For the LORD will rebuild Jerusalem.
  He will appear in his glory.
¹⁷ He will listen to the prayers of the destitute.
  He will not reject their pleas.

¹⁸ Let this be recorded for future generations,
  so that a nation yet to be created will praise the LORD.
¹⁹ Tell them the LORD looked down
  from his heavenly sanctuary.
  He looked to the earth from heaven
²⁰ to hear the groans of the prisoners,
  to release those condemned to die.
²¹ And so the LORD's fame will be celebrated in Zion,
  his praises in Jerusalem,
²² when multitudes gather together
  and kingdoms come to worship the LORD.

²³ He has cut me down in midlife,
  shortening my days.
²⁴ But I cried to him, "My God, who lives forever,
  don't take my life while I am still so young!
²⁵ In ages past you laid the foundation of the earth,
  and the heavens are the work of your hands.
²⁶ Even they will perish, but you remain forever;
  they will wear out like old clothing.
  You will change them like a garment,
  and they will fade away.
²⁷ But you are always the same;
  your years never end.

102:13 Hebrew *Zion;* also in 102:16.

*Sidebar notes:*

Keep a prayer journal. This is where life changes often begin!

I ACKNOWLEDGE that the Lord's rule continues forever. (102:12)

I TRUST the Lord to help his people at just the right time. (102:13)

I BELIEVE the kings and the nations will one day tremble before the Lord. (102:15)

I RECORD God's care and deliverance so future generations will praise the Lord. (102:18)

I WILL ASK God to extend my life if it is threatened at a young age. (102:24)

²⁸The children of your people
 will live in security.
 Their children's children
 will thrive in your presence."

PSALM 103

A psalm of David.

¹Praise the LORD, I tell myself;
 with my whole heart, I will praise his holy name.
²Praise the LORD, I tell myself,
 and never forget the good things he does for me.
³He forgives all my sins
 and heals all my diseases.
⁴He ransoms me from death
 and surrounds me with love and tender mercies.
⁵He fills my life with good things.
 My youth is renewed like the eagle's!
⁶The LORD gives righteousness
 and justice to all who are treated unfairly.
⁷He revealed his character to Moses
 and his deeds to the people of Israel.
⁸The LORD is merciful and gracious;
 he is slow to get angry and full of unfailing love.
⁹He will not constantly accuse us,
 nor remain angry forever.
¹⁰He has not punished us for all our sins,
 nor does he deal with us as we deserve.
¹¹For his unfailing love toward those who fear him
 is as great as the height of the heavens above the earth.
¹²He has removed our rebellious acts
 as far away from us as the east is from the west.
¹³The LORD is like a father to his children,
 tender and compassionate to those who fear him.
¹⁴For he understands how weak we are;
 he knows we are only dust.
¹⁵Our days on earth are like grass;
 like wildflowers, we bloom and die.
¹⁶The wind blows, and we are gone—
 as though we had never been here.
¹⁷But the love of the LORD remains forever
 with those who fear him.
 His salvation extends to the children's children
¹⁸ of those who are faithful to his covenant,
 of those who obey his commandments!

¹⁹The LORD has made the heavens his throne;
 from there he rules over everything.
²⁰Praise the LORD, you angels of his,
 you mighty creatures who carry out his plans,
 listening for each of his commands.
²¹Yes, praise the LORD, you armies of angels
 who serve him and do his will!
²²Praise the LORD, everything he has created,
 everywhere in his kingdom.
 As for me—I, too, will praise the LORD.

I BELIEVE God's children will always know security in his presence. (102:28)

See David's profile (page 629) at Psalm 3:1.

I WILL NEVER FORGET the good things the Lord has done for me. (103:2)

I AM SO THANKFUL that the Lord is merciful, gracious, and slow to anger. (103:8)

I MARVEL at the height and depth of the Lord's unfailing love (Romans 8:38-39). (103:11)

I ACKNOWLEDGE the Lord's sovereign rule over everything. (103:19)

I JOIN with all creation in praising the Lord. (103:22)

PSALM 104

I TELL the Lord how great he is! (104:1)

I SEE God's majesty in the sky—the stars and clouds and wind and rain. (104:2)

I THANK God for his provision and care for all his creatures. (104:10)

I KNOW that even the strongest creatures are dependent on God. (104:21)

¹Praise the LORD, I tell myself;
  O LORD my God, how great you are!
You are robed with honor and with majesty;
² you are dressed in a robe of light.
You stretch out the starry curtain of the heavens;
³ you lay out the rafters of your home in the rain clouds.
You make the clouds your chariots;
  you ride upon the wings of the wind.
⁴The winds are your messengers;
  flames of fire are your servants.

⁵You placed the world on its foundation
  so it would never be moved.
⁶You clothed the earth with floods of water,
  water that covered even the mountains.
⁷At the sound of your rebuke, the water fled;
  at the sound of your thunder, it fled away.
⁸Mountains rose and valleys sank
  to the levels you decreed.
⁹Then you set a firm boundary for the seas,
  so they would never again cover the earth.

¹⁰You make the springs pour water into ravines,
  so streams gush down from the mountains.
¹¹They provide water for all the animals,
  and the wild donkeys quench their thirst.
¹²The birds nest beside the streams
  and sing among the branches of the trees.
¹³You send rain on the mountains from your heavenly home,
  and you fill the earth with the fruit of your labor.
¹⁴You cause grass to grow for the cattle.
  You cause plants to grow for people to use.
  You allow them to produce food from the earth—
¹⁵ wine to make them glad,
  olive oil as lotion for their skin,
  and bread to give them strength.
¹⁶The trees of the LORD are well cared for—
  the cedars of Lebanon that he planted.
¹⁷There the birds make their nests,
  and the storks make their homes in the firs.
¹⁸High in the mountains are pastures for the wild goats,
  and the rocks form a refuge for rock badgers.*
¹⁹You made the moon to mark the seasons
  and the sun that knows when to set.
²⁰You send the darkness, and it becomes night,
  when all the forest animals prowl about.
²¹Then the young lions roar for their food,
  but they are dependent on God.
²²At dawn they slink back
  into their dens to rest.
²³Then people go off to their work;
  they labor until the evening shadows fall again.

²⁴O LORD, what a variety of things you have made!
  In wisdom you have made them all.
  The earth is full of your creatures.

104:18 Or *coneys*, or *hyraxes*.

²⁵ Here is the ocean, vast and wide,
  teeming with life of every kind,
  both great and small.
²⁶ See the ships sailing along,
  and Leviathan, which you made to play in the sea.
²⁷ Every one of these depends on you
  to give them their food as they need it.
²⁸ When you supply it, they gather it.
  You open your hand to feed them, and they are satisfied.
²⁹ But if you turn away from them, they panic.
  When you take away their breath, they die
  and turn again to dust.
³⁰ When you send your Spirit, new life is born
  to replenish all the living of the earth.

³¹ May the glory of the LORD last forever!
  The LORD rejoices in all he has made!
³² The earth trembles at his glance;
  the mountains burst into flame at his touch.
³³ I will sing to the LORD as long as I live.
  I will praise my God to my last breath!
³⁴ May he be pleased by all these thoughts about him,
  for I rejoice in the LORD.
³⁵ Let all sinners vanish from the face of the earth;
  let the wicked disappear forever.
  As for me—I will praise the LORD!

  Praise the LORD!

PSALM 105

¹ Give thanks to the LORD and proclaim his greatness.
  Let the whole world know what he has done.
² Sing to him; yes, sing his praises.
  Tell everyone about his miracles.
³ Exult in his holy name;
  O worshipers of the LORD, rejoice!
⁴ Search for the LORD and for his strength,
  and keep on searching.
⁵ Think of the wonderful works he has done,
  the miracles and the judgments he handed down,
⁶ O children of Abraham, God's servant,
  O descendants of Jacob, God's chosen one.
⁷ He is the LORD our God.
  His rule is seen throughout the land.
⁸ He always stands by his covenant—
  the commitment he made to a thousand generations.
⁹ This is the covenant he made with Abraham
  and the oath he swore to Isaac.
¹⁰ He confirmed it to Jacob as a decree,
  to the people of Israel as a never-ending treaty:
¹¹ "I will give you the land of Canaan
  as your special possession."

¹² He said this when they were few in number,
  a tiny group of strangers in Canaan.
¹³ They wandered back and forth between nations,
  from one kingdom to another.

I BELIEVE the Lord rejoices in all he has made. (104:31)

I WILL SING praises to the Lord to my last breath! (104:33)

I DESIRE to please the Lord by thinking about him and his marvelous works! (104:34)

I TELL the whole world to praise the Lord for his greatness! (105:1)

I URGE others to remember the wonderful works and words of the Lord. (105:5)

See the profiles for Abraham (page 19) and Jacob (page 43) at Genesis 15:6 and Genesis 32:9.

I REMIND God's people of how he kept his promises to Abraham, Isaac, and Jacob. (105:8)

See Isaac's profile (page 31) at Genesis 25:19.

I REMIND God's people of how the Lord cared for Jacob and his children before they became the nation of Israel. (105:14)

I REMIND God's people of how he sent Joseph ahead to Egypt in order to save Jacob's family. (105:17)

See Joseph's profile (page 51) at Genesis 39:2.

I REMIND God's people of how the Lord made Jacob's family into a mighty nation in the land of Egypt. (105:23)

I REMIND God's people of how he sent Moses to perform signs and send plagues to punish the Egyptians. (105:26)

See the profiles for Moses (page 73) and Aaron (page 107) at Exodus 5:1 and Exodus 32:2.

I REMIND God's people of how he led and provided for the Israelites to bring them to the Promised Land. (105:39)

14 Yet he did not let anyone oppress them.
   He warned kings on their behalf:
15 "Do not touch these people I have chosen,
   and do not hurt my prophets."
16 He called for a famine on the land of Canaan,
   cutting off its food supply.
17 Then he sent someone to Egypt ahead of them—
   Joseph, who was sold as a slave.
18 There in prison, they bruised his feet with fetters
   and placed his neck in an iron collar.
19 Until the time came to fulfill his word,
   the LORD tested Joseph's character.
20 Then Pharaoh sent for him and set him free;
   the ruler of the nation opened his prison door.
21 Joseph was put in charge of all the king's household;
   he became ruler over all the king's possessions.
22 He could instruct the king's aides as he pleased
   and teach the king's advisers.

23 Then Israel arrived in Egypt;
   Jacob lived as a foreigner in the land of Ham.
24 And the LORD multiplied the people of Israel
   until they became too mighty for their enemies.
25 Then he turned the Egyptians against the Israelites,
   and they plotted against the LORD's servants.

26 But the LORD sent Moses his servant,
   along with Aaron, whom he had chosen.
27 They performed miraculous signs among the Egyptians,
   and miracles in the land of Ham.
28 The LORD blanketed Egypt in darkness,
   for they had defied his commands to let his people go.
29 He turned the nation's water into blood,
   poisoning all the fish.
30 Then frogs overran the land;
   they were found even in the king's private rooms.
31 When he spoke, flies descended on the Egyptians,
   and gnats swarmed across Egypt.
32 Instead of rain, he sent murderous hail,
   and flashes of lightning overwhelmed the land.
33 He ruined their grapevines and fig trees
   and shattered all the trees.
34 He spoke, and hordes of locusts came—
   locusts beyond number.
35 They ate up everything green in the land,
   destroying all the crops.
36 Then he killed the oldest child in each Egyptian home,
   the pride and joy of each family.

37 But he brought his people safely out of Egypt, loaded with silver and gold;
   there were no sick or feeble people among them.
38 Egypt was glad when they were gone,
   for the dread of them was great.
39 The LORD spread out a cloud above them as a covering
   and gave them a great fire to light the darkness.
40 They asked for meat, and he sent them quail;
   he gave them manna—bread from heaven.

⁴¹ He opened up a rock, and water gushed out
    to form a river through the dry and barren land.
⁴² For he remembered his sacred promise
    to Abraham his servant.
⁴³ So he brought his people out of Egypt with joy,
    his chosen ones with rejoicing.
⁴⁴ He gave his people the lands of pagan nations,
    and they harvested crops that others had planted.
⁴⁵ All this happened so they would follow his principles
    and obey his laws.

Praise the LORD!

I REMIND God's people that he brought the Israelites out of Egypt and gave them the Promised Land so that they would follow and obey him. (105:45)

PSALM 106

¹ Praise the LORD!

Give thanks to the LORD, for he is good!
    His faithful love endures forever.
² Who can list the glorious miracles of the LORD?
    Who can ever praise him half enough?
³ Happy are those who deal justly with others
    and always do what is right.

I CAN NEVER RUN OUT of reasons to praise the Lord. (106:2)

⁴ Remember me, too, LORD, when you show favor to your people;
    come to me with your salvation.
⁵ Let me share in the prosperity of your chosen ones.
    Let me rejoice in the joy of your people;
    let me praise you with those who are your heritage.

I ASK the Lord to make me a part of his people who know his salvation. (106:4)

⁶ Both we and our ancestors have sinned.
    We have done wrong! We have acted wickedly!
⁷ Our ancestors in Egypt
    were not impressed by the LORD's miracles.
They soon forgot his many acts of kindness to them.
    Instead, they rebelled against him at the Red Sea.*
⁸ Even so, he saved them—
    to defend the honor of his name
    and to demonstrate his mighty power.
⁹ He commanded the Red Sea* to divide, and a dry path appeared.
    He led Israel across the sea bottom that was as dry as a desert.
¹⁰ So he rescued them from their enemies
    and redeemed them from their foes.
¹¹ Then the water returned and covered their enemies;
    not one of them survived.
¹² Then at last his people believed his promises.
    Then they finally sang his praise.

I ACKNOWLEDGE my sin and the sin of my ancestors. (106:6)

¹³ Yet how quickly they forgot what he had done!
    They wouldn't wait for his counsel!
¹⁴ In the wilderness, their desires ran wild,
    testing God's patience in that dry land.
¹⁵ So he gave them what they asked for,
    but he sent a plague along with it.
¹⁶ The people in the camp were jealous of Moses
    and envious of Aaron, the LORD's holy priest.
¹⁷ Because of this, the earth opened up;
    it swallowed Dathan
    and buried Abiram and the other rebels.

I REMEMBER how the Lord saved Israel and how he saved me, and I wait for his counsel. (106:13)

I DO NOT LET my desires run wild, testing God's patience. (106:14)

See the profiles for Moses (page 73) and Aaron (page 107) at Exodus 5:1 and Exodus 32:2.

106:7 Hebrew *at the sea, the sea of reeds.*   106:9 Hebrew *sea of reeds;* also in 106:22.

¹⁸Fire fell upon their followers;
a flame consumed the wicked.

¹⁹The people made a calf at Mount Sinai*;
they bowed before an image made of gold.

²⁰They traded their glorious God
for a statue of a grass-eating ox!

²¹They forgot God, their savior,
who had done such great things in Egypt—

²²such wonderful things in that land,
such awesome deeds at the Red Sea.

²³So he declared he would destroy them.
But Moses, his chosen one, stepped between the LORD and the people.
He begged him to turn from his anger and not destroy them.

²⁴The people refused to enter the pleasant land,
for they wouldn't believe his promise to care for them.

²⁵Instead, they grumbled in their tents
and refused to obey the LORD.

²⁶Therefore, he swore
that he would kill them in the wilderness,

²⁷that he would scatter their descendants among the nations,
exiling them to distant lands.

²⁸Then our ancestors joined in the worship of Baal at Peor;
they even ate sacrifices offered to the dead!

²⁹They angered the LORD with all these things,
so a plague broke out among them.

³⁰But Phinehas had the courage to step in,
and the plague was stopped.

³¹So he has been regarded as a righteous man
ever since that time.

³²At Meribah, too, they angered the LORD,
causing Moses serious trouble.

³³They made Moses angry,*
and he spoke foolishly.

³⁴Israel failed to destroy the nations in the land,
as the LORD had told them to.

³⁵Instead, they mingled among the pagans
and adopted their evil customs.

³⁶They worshiped their idols,
and this led to their downfall.

³⁷They even sacrificed their sons
and their daughters to the demons.

³⁸They shed innocent blood,
the blood of their sons and daughters.
By sacrificing them to the idols of Canaan,
they polluted the land with murder.

³⁹They defiled themselves by their evil deeds,
and their love of idols was adultery in the LORD's sight.

⁴⁰That is why the LORD's anger burned against his people,
and he abhorred his own special possession.

⁴¹He handed them over to pagan nations,
and those who hated them ruled over them.

I DO NOT TRADE my glorious God for an imitation god (Romans 1:23). (106:20)

I DO NOT REFUSE to enter into all that God has promised to give me. (106:24)

I STEP IN to put a stop to sin among God's people. (106:30)

I DO NOT ADD anything pagan to my worship of God. (106:35)

I BELIEVE that Israel committed adultery against the Lord by loving idols. (106:39)

106:19 Hebrew at Horeb, another name for Sinai.   106:33 Hebrew They embittered his spirit.

⁴²Their enemies crushed them
  and brought them under their cruel power.
⁴³Again and again he delivered them,
  but they continued to rebel against him,
  and they were finally destroyed by their sin.
⁴⁴Even so, he pitied them in their distress
  and listened to their cries.
⁴⁵He remembered his covenant with them
  and relented because of his unfailing love.
⁴⁶He even caused their captors
  to treat them with kindness.

⁴⁷O LORD our God, save us!
  Gather us back from among the nations,
so we can thank your holy name
  and rejoice and praise you.

⁴⁸Blessed be the LORD, the God of Israel,
  from everlasting to everlasting!
Let all the people say, "Amen!"

Praise the LORD!

I BELIEVE the Lord allowed Israel to be ruled by pagan nations because they rebelled against him. (106:42)

I BELIEVE the Lord pitied and rescued Israel because of his covenant and his unfailing love. (106:45)

LIKE PHINEHAS *I am willing to stand up for what's right.*

Psalm 106:30

George Washington. Abraham Lincoln. Martin Luther King, Jr. Every three to four generations, another giant stands out in American history for valiantly fighting for what's right.

Many centuries earlier, halfway around the world, Phinehas lived in a much different era, when God's people lived in a theocracy—that is, they were directly governed by the Lord himself. Still, Phinehas's courage in the midst of several national crises was nothing short of remarkable.

On one occasion, the nation was in the midst of a moral rebellion. Many flocked to pagan cities to engage in adultery and idolatry in open defiance of the Lord's commands. A terrible plague erupted—stopped only by Phinehas's passionate zeal for God's holiness.

On another occasion, the nation was on the verge of civil war. Again, Phinehas stood up for what was right, investigated matters thoroughly, and brought about a peaceful resolution to the conflict.

Because of his mighty deeds, the Lord commended Phinehas and made a special covenant with him—a promise that his descendants would be the priests of Israel for all time (Numbers 25:11-13).

Like Phinehas, the Lord calls you and me to stand up for what's true and right and just and pure (see Philippians 4:8-9).

To learn more about Phinehas's great courage, see Numbers 25:1-13; 31:1-8; and Joshua 22:10-34.

○ *Today's Scripture reading is Psalms 105-106.*

BOOK FIVE (Psalms 107–150)

PSALM 107

¹Give thanks to the LORD, for he is good!
  His faithful love endures forever.
²Has the LORD redeemed you? Then speak out!
  Tell others he has saved you from your enemies.
³For he has gathered the exiles from many lands,
  from east and west, from north and south.

⁴Some wandered in the desert,
  lost and homeless.

I GIVE THANKS to the Lord because he is good and his love endures forever. (107:1)

⁵ Hungry and thirsty,
 they nearly died.
⁶ "LORD, help!" they cried in their trouble,
 and he rescued them from their distress.
⁷ He led them straight to safety,
 to a city where they could live.
⁸ Let them praise the LORD for his great love
 and for all his wonderful deeds to them.
⁹ For he satisfies the thirsty
 and fills the hungry with good things.

¹⁰ Some sat in darkness and deepest gloom,
 miserable prisoners in chains.
¹¹ They rebelled against the words of God,
 scorning the counsel of the Most High.
¹² That is why he broke them with hard labor;
 they fell, and no one helped them rise again.
¹³ "LORD, help!" they cried in their trouble,
 and he saved them from their distress.
¹⁴ He led them from the darkness and deepest gloom;
 he snapped their chains.
¹⁵ Let them praise the LORD for his great love
 and for all his wonderful deeds to them.
¹⁶ For he broke down their prison gates of bronze;
 he cut apart their bars of iron.

¹⁷ Some were fools in their rebellion;
 they suffered for their sins.
¹⁸ Their appetites were gone,
 and death was near.
¹⁹ "LORD, help!" they cried in their trouble,
 and he saved them from their distress.
²⁰ He spoke, and they were healed—
 snatched from the door of death.
²¹ Let them praise the LORD for his great love
 and for all his wonderful deeds to them.
²² Let them offer sacrifices of thanksgiving
 and sing joyfully about his glorious acts.

²³ Some went off in ships,
 plying the trade routes of the world.
²⁴ They, too, observed the LORD's power in action,
 his impressive works on the deepest seas.
²⁵ He spoke, and the winds rose,
 stirring up the waves.
²⁶ Their ships were tossed to the heavens
 and sank again to the depths;
 the sailors cringed in terror.
²⁷ They reeled and staggered like drunkards
 and were at their wits' end.
²⁸ "LORD, help!" they cried in their trouble,
 and he saved them from their distress.
²⁹ He calmed the storm to a whisper
 and stilled the waves.
³⁰ What a blessing was that stillness
 as he brought them safely into harbor!
³¹ Let them praise the LORD for his great love
 and for all his wonderful deeds to them.

I PRAISE the Lord when he rescues exiles who call out to him. (107:6)

I PRAISE the Lord when he saves prisoners who repent of their sins. (107:13)

I PRAISE the Lord when he saves sinners who cry out to him. (107:19)

I PRAISE the Lord when he saves travelers who cry out to him. (107:28)

[32] Let them exalt him publicly before the congregation
   and before the leaders of the nation.

[33] He changes rivers into deserts,
   and springs of water into dry land.
[34] He turns the fruitful land into salty wastelands,
   because of the wickedness of those who live there.
[35] But he also turns deserts into pools of water,
   the dry land into flowing springs.
[36] He brings the hungry to settle there
   and build their cities.
[37] They sow their fields, plant their vineyards,
   and harvest their bumper crops.
[38] How he blesses them!
   They raise large families there,
   and their herds of cattle increase.

[39] When they decrease in number and become impoverished
   through oppression, trouble, and sorrow,
[40] the LORD pours contempt on their princes,
   causing them to wander in trackless wastelands.
[41] But he rescues the poor from their distress
   and increases their families like vast flocks of sheep.
[42] The godly will see these things and be glad,
   while the wicked are stricken silent.
[43] Those who are wise will take all this to heart;
   they will see in our history the faithful love of the LORD.

PSALM 108

A psalm of David. A song.

[1] My heart is confident in you, O God;
   no wonder I can sing your praises!
 Wake up, my soul!
[2] Wake up, O harp and lyre!
   I will waken the dawn with my song.
[3] I will thank you, LORD, in front of all the people.
   I will sing your praises among the nations.
[4] For your unfailing love is higher than the heavens.
   Your faithfulness reaches to the clouds.
[5] Be exalted, O God, above the highest heavens.
   May your glory shine over all the earth.

[6] Use your strong right arm to save me,
   and rescue your beloved people.
[7] God has promised this by his holiness*:
   "I will divide up Shechem with joy.
   I will measure out the valley of Succoth.
[8] Gilead is mine,
   and Manasseh is mine.
 Ephraim will produce my warriors,
   and Judah will produce my kings.
[9] Moab will become my lowly servant,
   and Edom will be my slave.
   I will shout in triumph over the Philistines."

108:7 Or *in his sanctuary.*

I PRAISE the Lord for
his control over
nature. (107:33)

I PRAISE the Lord for
making a place for
families to thrive.
(107:38)

I PRAISE the Lord for
rescuing and blessing
the poor in the midst
of troubles. (107:41)

I AM GLAD when I see
the Lord faithfully
loving and caring for
his own. (107:42)

See David's profile
(page 629) at Psalm
3:1.

I AM CONFIDENT in
God. (108:1)

I LONG TO SEE God's
glory shine over all
the earth. (108:5)

I CAN FIND no one but God to give me victory. (108:10)

¹⁰ But who will bring me into the fortified city?
Who will bring me victory over Edom?
¹¹ Have you rejected us, O God?
Will you no longer march with our armies?
¹² Oh, please help us against our enemies,
for all human help is useless.
¹³ With God's help we will do mighty things,
for he will trample down our foes.

PSALM 109

For the choir director: A psalm of David.

¹ O God, whom I praise,
don't stand silent and aloof
² while the wicked slander me
and tell lies about me.
³ They are all around me with their hateful words,
and they fight against me for no reason.
⁴ I love them, but they try to destroy me—
even as I am praying for them!
⁵ They return evil for good,
and hatred for my love.

I ASK God for help when people slander and lie about me. (109:2)

⁶ Arrange for an evil person to turn on him.
Send an accuser to bring him to trial.
⁷ When his case is called for judgment,
let him be pronounced guilty.
Count his prayers as sins.
⁸ Let his years be few;
let his position be given to someone else.
⁹ May his children become fatherless,
and may his wife become a widow.
¹⁰ May his children wander as beggars;
may they be evicted from their ruined homes.
¹¹ May creditors seize his entire estate,
and strangers take all he has earned.
¹² Let no one be kind to him;
let no one pity his fatherless children.
¹³ May all his offspring die.
May his family name be blotted out in a single generation.
¹⁴ May the LORD never forget the sins of his ancestors;
may his mother's sins never be erased from the record.
¹⁵ May these sins always remain before the LORD,
but may his name be cut off from human memory.

I LEAVE the punishment of my enemies to God. (109:6)

I GET TRULY ANGRY about the oppression of needy people. (109:16)

¹⁶ For he refused all kindness to others;
he persecuted the poor and needy,
and he hounded the brokenhearted to death.
¹⁷ He loved to curse others;
now you curse him.
He never blessed others;
now don't you bless him.
¹⁸ Cursing is as much a part of him as his clothing,
or as the water he drinks,
or the rich food he eats.
¹⁹ Now may his curses return and cling to him like clothing;
may they be tied around him like a belt.

[20] May those curses become the LORD's punishment for my accusers
 who are plotting against my life.
[21] But deal well with me, O Sovereign LORD,
 for the sake of your own reputation!
Rescue me because you are so faithful and good.
[22] For I am poor and needy,
 and my heart is full of pain.
[23] I am fading like a shadow at dusk;
 I am falling like a grasshopper that is brushed aside.
[24] My knees are weak from fasting,
 and I am skin and bones.
[25] I am an object of mockery to people everywhere;
 when they see me, they shake their heads.

[26] Help me, O LORD my God!
 Save me because of your unfailing love.
[27] Let them see that this is your doing,
 that you yourself have done it, LORD.
[28] Then let them curse me if they like,
 but you will bless me!
When they attack me, they will be disgraced!
But I, your servant, will go right on rejoicing!
[29] Make their humiliation obvious to all;
 clothe my accusers with disgrace.
[30] But I will give repeated thanks to the LORD,
 praising him to everyone.
[31] For he stands beside the needy,
 ready to save them from those who condemn them.

I ASK the Lord to rescue me for the sake of his reputation. (109:21)

I AM NOT AFRAID of curses, because I know the Lord will bless me. (109:28)

I CONTINUALLY REPEAT the Lord's praise to everyone, because he saves the needy and the condemned. (109:30)

PSALM 110

A psalm of David.

[1] The LORD said to my Lord,
 "Sit in honor at my right hand
until I humble your enemies,
 making them a footstool under your feet."

[2] The LORD will extend your powerful dominion from Jerusalem*;
 you will rule over your enemies.
[3] In that day of battle,
 your people will serve you willingly.
Arrayed in holy garments,
 your vigor will be renewed each day like the morning dew.
[4] The LORD has taken an oath and will not break his vow:
 "You are a priest forever in the line of Melchizedek."
[5] The Lord stands at your right hand to protect you.
He will strike down many kings in the day of his anger.
[6] He will punish the nations
 and fill them with their dead;
he will shatter heads
 over the whole earth.
[7] But he himself will be refreshed from brooks along the way.
 He will be victorious.

I BELIEVE God the Father will give the Lord Jesus Christ rule over the nations (Matthew 22:44; Hebrews 1:13). (110:1)

I BELIEVE the Lord foretold and kept his promise to make Jesus an enduring priest before him (Hebrews 5:6; 7:15–22). (110:4)

110:2 Hebrew *Zion.*

PSALM 111

I USE the time with God's people to thank the Lord with my whole heart. (111:1)

¹ Praise the LORD!

I will thank the LORD with all my heart
    as I meet with his godly people.
² How amazing are the deeds of the LORD!
    All who delight in him should ponder them.
³ Everything he does reveals his glory and majesty.
    His righteousness never fails.

I AM REMINDED of the Lord's grace and mercy when I think about the wonders he performs. (111:4)

⁴ Who can forget the wonders he performs?
    How gracious and merciful is our LORD!
⁵ He gives food to those who trust him;
    he always remembers his covenant.
⁶ He has shown his great power to his people
    by giving them the lands of other nations.
⁷ All he does is just and good,
    and all his commandments are trustworthy.

I OBEY God's commands because they are all trustworthy. (111:8)

⁸ They are forever true,
    to be obeyed faithfully and with integrity.
⁹ He has paid a full ransom for his people.
    He has guaranteed his covenant with them forever.
    What a holy, awe-inspiring name he has!
¹⁰ Reverence for the LORD is the foundation of true wisdom.
    The rewards of wisdom come to all who obey him.

Praise his name forever!

PSALM 112

¹ Praise the LORD!

Happy are those who fear the LORD.
    Yes, happy are those who delight in doing what he commands.

I BENEFIT others by the blessings God gives me when I obey him. (112:2)

² Their children will be successful everywhere;
    an entire generation of godly people will be blessed.
³ They themselves will be wealthy,
    and their good deeds will never be forgotten.
⁴ When darkness overtakes the godly, light will come bursting in.
    They are* generous, compassionate, and righteous.
⁵ All goes well for those who are generous,
    who lend freely and conduct their business fairly.
⁶ Such people will not be overcome by evil circumstances.
    Those who are righteous will be long remembered.
⁷ They do not fear bad news;
    they confidently trust the LORD to care for them.
⁸ They are confident and fearless
    and can face their foes triumphantly.
⁹ They give generously to those in need.
    Their good deeds will never be forgotten.
    They will have influence and honor.

I OVERCOME evil people by doing good. (112:10)

¹⁰ The wicked will be infuriated when they see this.
    They will grind their teeth in anger;
    they will slink away, their hopes thwarted.

PSALM 113

¹ Praise the LORD!

Yes, give praise, O servants of the LORD.
    Praise the name of the LORD!

I URGE the Lord's servants to praise the Lord. (113:1)

112:4 Greek version reads *The LORD is.*

² Blessed be the name of the LORD
    forever and ever.
³ Everywhere—from east to west—
    praise the name of the LORD.
⁴ For the LORD is high above the nations;
    his glory is far greater than the heavens.

⁵ Who can be compared with the LORD our God,
    who is enthroned on high?
⁶ Far below him are the heavens and the earth.
    He stoops to look,
⁷ and he lifts the poor from the dirt
    and the needy from the garbage dump.
⁸ He sets them among princes,
    even the princes of his own people!
⁹ He gives the barren woman a home,
    so that she becomes a happy mother.

    Praise the LORD!

> I ACKNOWLEDGE that no one compares to the Lord our God. (113:5)

> I PRAISE the Lord, who stoops from high above the earth to care for the needy. (113:7)

PSALM 114

¹ When the Israelites escaped from Egypt—
    when the family of Jacob left that foreign land—
² the land of Judah became God's sanctuary,
    and Israel became his kingdom.

³ The Red Sea* saw them coming and hurried out of their way!
    The water of the Jordan River turned away.
⁴ The mountains skipped like rams,
    the little hills like lambs!
⁵ What's wrong, Red Sea, that made you hurry out of their way?
    What happened, Jordan River, that you turned away?
⁶ Why, mountains, did you skip like rams?
    Why, little hills, like lambs?

⁷ Tremble, O earth, at the presence of the Lord,
    at the presence of the God of Israel.*
⁸ He turned the rock into pools of water;
    yes, springs of water came from solid rock.

> I BELIEVE God made Israel his kingdom when he brought the Israelites out of Egypt. (114:2)

> I BELIEVE the sea and mountains trembled at the presence of God when he brought the Israelites into their land. (114:6)

PSALM 115

¹ Not to us, O LORD, but to you goes all the glory
    for your unfailing love and faithfulness.
² Why let the nations say,
    "Where is their God?"
³ For our God is in the heavens,
    and he does as he wishes.
⁴ Their idols are merely things of silver and gold,
    shaped by human hands.
⁵ They cannot talk, though they have mouths,
    or see, though they have eyes!
⁶ They cannot hear with their ears,
    or smell with their noses,
⁷   or feel with their hands,
    or walk with their feet,
    or utter sounds with their throats!

> I DO NOT TAKE credit for myself but give all glory to God for his unfailing love and faithfulness. (115:1)

114:3 Hebrew *the sea*; also in 114:5.   114:7 Hebrew *of Jacob.*

I RECOGNIZE that trusting in self-made gods and religions makes a person powerless. (115:8)

See Aaron's profile (page 107) at Exodus 32:2.

⁸ And those who make them are just like them,
  as are all who trust in them.

⁹ O Israel, trust the LORD!
  He is your helper; he is your shield.
¹⁰ O priests of Aaron, trust the LORD!
  He is your helper; he is your shield.
¹¹ All you who fear the LORD, trust the LORD!
  He is your helper; he is your shield.

¹² The LORD remembers us,
  and he will surely bless us.
  He will bless the people of Israel
  and the family of Aaron, the priests.
¹³ He will bless those who fear the LORD,
  both great and small.

I BELIEVE the Lord will remember and bless his people who fear him. (115:13)

¹⁴ May the LORD richly bless
  both you and your children.
¹⁵ May you be blessed by the LORD,
  who made heaven and earth.
¹⁶ The heavens belong to the LORD,
  but he has given the earth to all humanity.

¹⁷ The dead cannot sing praises to the LORD,
  for they have gone into the silence of the grave.
¹⁸ But we can praise the LORD
  both now and forever!

I TAKE every opportunity to praise the Lord. (115:18)

  Praise the LORD!

PSALM 116

¹ I love the LORD because he hears
  and answers my prayers.
² Because he bends down and listens,
  I will pray as long as I have breath!
³ Death had its hands around my throat;
  the terrors of the grave* overtook me.
  I saw only trouble and sorrow.
⁴ Then I called on the name of the LORD:
  "Please, LORD, save me!"
⁵ How kind the LORD is! How good he is!
  So merciful, this God of ours!
⁶ The LORD protects those of childlike faith;
  I was facing death, and then he saved me.
⁷ Now I can rest again,
  for the LORD has been so good to me.
⁸ He has saved me from death,
  my eyes from tears,
  my feet from stumbling.
⁹ And so I walk in the LORD's presence
  as I live here on earth!
¹⁰ I believed in you, so I prayed,
  "I am deeply troubled, LORD."
¹¹ In my anxiety I cried out to you,
  "These people are all liars!"

I LOVE the Lord because he listens to me. (116:1)

I CRY OUT to the Lord when my life is in danger. (116:4)

I PRAISE God when he rescues me from death. (116:6)

116:3 Hebrew *of Sheol.*

¹²What can I offer the LORD
 for all he has done for me?
¹³I will lift up a cup symbolizing his salvation;
 I will praise the LORD's name for saving me.
¹⁴I will keep my promises to the LORD
 in the presence of all his people.

¹⁵The LORD's loved ones are precious to him;
 it grieves him when they die.
¹⁶O LORD, I am your servant;
 yes, I am your servant, the son of your handmaid,
 and you have freed me from my bonds!
¹⁷I will offer you a sacrifice of thanksgiving
 and call on the name of the LORD.
¹⁸I will keep my promises to the LORD
 in the presence of all his people,
¹⁹in the house of the LORD,
 in the heart of Jerusalem.

Praise the LORD!

PSALM 117

¹Praise the LORD, all you nations.
 Praise him, all you people of the earth.
²For he loves us with unfailing love;
 the faithfulness of the LORD endures forever.

Praise the LORD!

PSALM 118

¹Give thanks to the LORD, for he is good!
 His faithful love endures forever.

²Let the congregation of Israel repeat:
 "His faithful love endures forever."
³Let Aaron's descendants, the priests, repeat:
 "His faithful love endures forever."
⁴Let all who fear the LORD repeat:
 "His faithful love endures forever."

⁵In my distress I prayed to the LORD,
 and the LORD answered me and rescued me.
⁶The LORD is for me, so I will not be afraid.
 What can mere mortals do to me?
⁷Yes, the LORD is for me; he will help me.
 I will look in triumph at those who hate me.
⁸It is better to trust the LORD
 than to put confidence in people.
⁹It is better to trust the LORD
 than to put confidence in princes.

¹⁰Though hostile nations surrounded me,
 I destroyed them all in the name of the LORD.
¹¹Yes, they surrounded and attacked me,
 but I destroyed them all in the name of the LORD.
¹²They swarmed around me like bees;
 they blazed against me like a roaring flame.
 But I destroyed them all in the name of the LORD.

I WORSHIP the Lord for all he has done for me. (116:12)

I BELIEVE the Lord is grieved when a loved one dies. (116:15)

I URGE everyone to praise the Lord because his love and faithfulness last forever! (117:1)

I WANT everyone to thank the Lord for his goodness and everlasting love. (118:1)

See Aaron's profile (page 107) at Exodus 32:2.

I URGE all who fear the Lord to keep telling of his faithful love that lasts forever. (118:4)

I AM NOT AFRAID of what others can do to me, because the Lord is for me (Romans 8:31). (118:6)

I PUT my trust in the Lord, not in people. (118:8)

I REMEMBER the victories that God has given me. (118:10)

¹³You did your best to kill me, O my enemy,
   but the LORD helped me.
¹⁴The LORD is my strength and my song;
   he has become my victory.
¹⁵Songs of joy and victory are sung in the camp of the godly.
   The strong right arm of the LORD has done glorious things!
¹⁶The strong right arm of the LORD is raised in triumph.
   The strong right arm of the LORD has done glorious things!
¹⁷I will not die, but I will live
   to tell what the LORD has done.
¹⁸The LORD has punished me severely,
   but he has not handed me over to death.

¹⁹Open for me the gates where the righteous enter,
   and I will go in and thank the LORD.
²⁰Those gates lead to the presence of the LORD,
   and the godly enter there.
²¹I thank you for answering my prayer
   and saving me!

²²The stone rejected by the builders
   has now become the cornerstone.
²³This is the LORD's doing,
   and it is marvelous to see.
²⁴This is the day the LORD has made.
   We will rejoice and be glad in it.
²⁵Please, LORD, please save us.
   Please, LORD, please give us success.
²⁶Bless the one who comes in the name of the LORD.
   We bless you from the house of the LORD.
²⁷The LORD is God, shining upon us.
   Bring forward the sacrifice and put it on the altar.
²⁸You are my God, and I will praise you!
   You are my God, and I will exalt you!

²⁹Give thanks to the LORD, for he is good!
   His faithful love endures forever.

PSALM 119

¹Happy are people of integrity,
   who follow the law of the LORD.
²Happy are those who obey his decrees
   and search for him with all their hearts.
³They do not compromise with evil,
   and they walk only in his paths.
⁴You have charged us
   to keep your commandments carefully.
⁵Oh, that my actions would consistently
   reflect your principles!
⁶Then I will not be disgraced
   when I compare my life with your commands.
⁷When I learn your righteous laws,
   I will thank you by living as I should!
⁸I will obey your principles.
   Please don't give up on me!

I PRAISE the Lord with joyful song for the victories he gives me. (118:14)

I USE every day the Lord gives me breath to tell others about how he has helped me. (118:17)

I GIVE the Lord thanks for answering prayer. (118:21)

I REJOICE because the Lord chose his son Jesus, even though he was rejected by his own people (Acts 4:10-11). (118:22)

I BLESS the Lord Jesus Christ, who came in the name of the Lord (Luke 13:35; 19:38). (118:26)

I PRAISE the Lord, for he is my God! (118:28)

I AM HAPPIEST when I follow the Lord's decrees. (119:1)

I DESIRE to live a life that consistently reflects God's commands. (119:5)

---

119 This psalm is a Hebrew acrostic poem; there are 22 stanzas, one for each letter of the Hebrew alphabet. The 8 verses within each stanza begin with the Hebrew letter of its section.

⁹How can a young person stay pure?
  By obeying your word and following its rules.
¹⁰I have tried my best to find you—
  don't let me wander from your commands.
¹¹I have hidden your word in my heart,
  that I might not sin against you.
¹²Blessed are you, O LORD;
  teach me your principles.
¹³I have recited aloud
  all the laws you have given us.
¹⁴I have rejoiced in your decrees
  as much as in riches.
¹⁵I will study your commandments
  and reflect on your ways.
¹⁶I will delight in your principles
  and not forget your word.

¹⁷Be good to your servant,
  that I may live and obey your word.
¹⁸Open my eyes to see
  the wonderful truths in your law.
¹⁹I am but a foreigner here on earth;
  I need the guidance of your commands.
  Don't hide them from me!
²⁰I am overwhelmed continually
  with a desire for your laws.
²¹You rebuke those cursed proud ones
  who wander from your commands.
²²Don't let them scorn and insult me,
  for I have obeyed your decrees.
²³Even princes sit and speak against me,
  but I will meditate on your principles.
²⁴Your decrees please me;
  they give me wise advice.

²⁵I lie in the dust, completely discouraged;
  revive me by your word.
²⁶I told you my plans, and you answered.
  Now teach me your principles.
²⁷Help me understand the meaning of your commandments,
  and I will meditate on your wonderful miracles.
²⁸I weep with grief;
  encourage me by your word.
²⁹Keep me from lying to myself;
  give me the privilege of knowing your law.
³⁰I have chosen to be faithful;
  I have determined to live by your laws.
³¹I cling to your decrees.
  LORD, don't let me be put to shame!
³²If you will help me,
  I will run to follow your commands.

³³Teach me, O LORD,
  to follow every one of your principles.
³⁴Give me understanding and I will obey your law;
  I will put it into practice with all my heart.
³⁵Make me walk along the path of your commands,
  for that is where my happiness is found.

I KEEP my life pure by obeying God's Word. (119:9)

I HIDE God's Word in my heart so that I might not sin against him. (119:11)

Ask God to open your eyes as you read his Word.

I ASK the Lord to give me understanding to see the truths in his Word. (119:18)

I FIND refreshment and encouragement from God's Word. (119:25)

I ASK the Lord to help me know the truth about myself and the truth about his Word. (119:29)

I FIND my greatest happiness in following the Lord's commands. (119:35)

³⁶Give me an eagerness for your decrees;
do not inflict me with love for money!
³⁷Turn my eyes from worthless things,
and give me life through your word.*
³⁸Reassure me of your promise,
which is for those who honor you.
³⁹Help me abandon my shameful ways;
your laws are all I want in life.
⁴⁰I long to obey your commandments!
Renew my life with your goodness.

⁴¹LORD, give to me your unfailing love,
the salvation that you promised me.
⁴²Then I will have an answer for those who taunt me,
for I trust in your word.
⁴³Do not snatch your word of truth from me,
for my only hope is in your laws.
⁴⁴I will keep on obeying your law
forever and forever.
⁴⁵I will walk in freedom,
for I have devoted myself to your commandments.
⁴⁶I will speak to kings about your decrees,
and I will not be ashamed.
⁴⁷How I delight in your commands!
How I love them!
⁴⁸I honor and love your commands.
I meditate on your principles.

⁴⁹Remember your promise to me,
for it is my only hope.
⁵⁰Your promise revives me;
it comforts me in all my troubles.
⁵¹The proud hold me in utter contempt,
but I do not turn away from your law.
⁵²I meditate on your age-old laws;
O LORD, they comfort me.
⁵³I am furious with the wicked,
those who reject your law.
⁵⁴Your principles have been the music of my life
throughout the years of my pilgrimage.
⁵⁵I reflect at night on who you are, O LORD,
and I obey your law because of this.
⁵⁶This is my happy way of life:
obeying your commandments.

⁵⁷LORD, you are mine!
I promise to obey your words!
⁵⁸With all my heart I want your blessings.
Be merciful just as you promised.
⁵⁹I pondered the direction of my life,
and I turned to follow your statutes.
⁶⁰I will hurry, without lingering,
to obey your commands.
⁶¹Evil people try to drag me into sin,
but I am firmly anchored to your law.

I ASK the Lord to help me leave behind my sin and embrace his commands. (119:39)

I EXPERIENCE freedom when I obey God's commandments. (119:45)

I FIND comfort in God's promises. (119:50)

I FIND happiness in obeying the Lord through every season of my life. (119:56)

I OBEY the Lord's commands without hesitation. (119:60)

119:37 Some manuscripts read *in your ways.*

⁶²At midnight I rise to thank you
  for your just laws.
⁶³Anyone who fears you is my friend—
  anyone who obeys your commandments.
⁶⁴O LORD, the earth is full of your unfailing love;
  teach me your principles.

⁶⁵You have done many good things for me, LORD,
  just as you promised.
⁶⁶I believe in your commands;
  now teach me good judgment and knowledge.
⁶⁷I used to wander off until you disciplined me;
  but now I closely follow your word.
⁶⁸You are good and do only good;
  teach me your principles.
⁶⁹Arrogant people have made up lies about me,
  but in truth I obey your commandments with all my heart.
⁷⁰Their hearts are dull and stupid,
  but I delight in your law.
⁷¹The suffering you sent was good for me,
  for it taught me to pay attention to your principles.
⁷²Your law is more valuable to me
  than millions in gold and silver!

⁷³You made me; you created me.
  Now give me the sense to follow your commands.
⁷⁴May all who fear you find in me a cause for joy,
  for I have put my hope in your word.
⁷⁵I know, O LORD, that your decisions are fair;
  you disciplined me because I needed it.
⁷⁶Now let your unfailing love comfort me,
  just as you promised me, your servant.
⁷⁷Surround me with your tender mercies so I may live,
  for your law is my delight.
⁷⁸Bring disgrace upon the arrogant people who lied about me;
  meanwhile, I will concentrate on your commandments.
⁷⁹Let me be reconciled
  with all who fear you and know your decrees.
⁸⁰May I be blameless in keeping your principles;
  then I will never have to be ashamed.

⁸¹I faint with longing for your salvation;
  but I have put my hope in your word.
⁸²My eyes are straining to see your promises come true.
  When will you comfort me?
⁸³I am shriveled like a wineskin in the smoke, exhausted with waiting.
  But I cling to your principles and obey them.
⁸⁴How long must I wait?
  When will you punish those who persecute me?
⁸⁵These arrogant people who hate your law
  have dug deep pits for me to fall into.
⁸⁶All your commands are trustworthy.
  Protect me from those who hunt me down without cause.
⁸⁷They almost finished me off,
  but I refused to abandon your commandments.
⁸⁸In your unfailing love, spare my life;
  then I can continue to obey your decrees.

I REGARD as my friend anyone who loves and obeys the Lord. (119:63)

I LEARN from difficult circumstances to pay attention to God's Word. (119:71)

I ACKNOWLEDGE that the Lord disciplines me for my good (Hebrews 12:10-11). (119:75)

I ASK the Lord to spare my life so I can keep obeying his Word. (119:88)

I AFFIRM that the Lord's Word stands forever (1 Peter 1:25). (119:89)

⁸⁹ Forever, O LORD,
   your word stands firm in heaven.
⁹⁰ Your faithfulness extends to every generation,
   as enduring as the earth you created.
⁹¹ Your laws remain true today,
   for everything serves your plans.
⁹² If your law hadn't sustained me with joy,
   I would have died in my misery.
⁹³ I will never forget your commandments,
   for you have used them to restore my joy and health.
⁹⁴ I am yours; save me!
   For I have applied myself to obey your commandments.
⁹⁵ Though the wicked hide along the way to kill me,
   I will quietly keep my mind on your decrees.
⁹⁶ Even perfection has its limits,
   but your commands have no limit.

I LOVE pondering the Lord's Word all day long. (119:97)

I GAIN great wisdom from knowing and keeping God's commands. (119:98)

⁹⁷ Oh, how I love your law!
   I think about it all day long.
⁹⁸ Your commands make me wiser than my enemies,
   for your commands are my constant guide.
⁹⁹ Yes, I have more insight than my teachers,
   for I am always thinking of your decrees.
¹⁰⁰ I am even wiser than my elders,
   for I have kept your commandments.
¹⁰¹ I have refused to walk on any path of evil,
   that I may remain obedient to your word.
¹⁰² I haven't turned away from your laws,
   for you have taught me well.

I FIND satisfaction and delight in God's words. (119:103)

¹⁰³ How sweet are your words to my taste;
   they are sweeter than honey.
¹⁰⁴ Your commandments give me understanding;
   no wonder I hate every false way of life.

¹⁰⁵ Your word is a lamp for my feet
   and a light for my path.
¹⁰⁶ I've promised it once, and I'll promise again:
   I will obey your wonderful laws.

I RENEW my promise to obey God's Word. (119:106)

¹⁰⁷ I have suffered much, O LORD;
   restore my life again, just as you promised.
¹⁰⁸ LORD, accept my grateful thanks
   and teach me your laws.
¹⁰⁹ My life constantly hangs in the balance,
   but I will not stop obeying your law.
¹¹⁰ The wicked have set their traps for me along your path,
   but I will not turn from your commandments.
¹¹¹ Your decrees are my treasure;
   they are truly my heart's delight.

I AM DETERMINED to keep God's principles to the very end. (119:112)

I STEER CLEAR of those who try to pull me away from obeying the Lord's commands. (119:115)

¹¹² I am determined to keep your principles,
   even forever, to the very end.

¹¹³ I hate those who are undecided about you,
   but my choice is clear—I love your law.
¹¹⁴ You are my refuge and my shield;
   your word is my only source of hope.
¹¹⁵ Get out of my life, you evil-minded people,
   for I intend to obey the commands of my God.

¹¹⁶ LORD, sustain me as you promised, that I may live!
    Do not let my hope be crushed.
¹¹⁷ Sustain me, and I will be saved;
    then I will meditate on your principles continually.
¹¹⁸ But you have rejected all who stray from your principles.
    They are only fooling themselves.
¹¹⁹ All the wicked of the earth are the scum you skim off;
    no wonder I love to obey your decrees!
¹²⁰ I tremble in fear of you;
    I fear your judgments.

¹²¹ Don't leave me to the mercy of my enemies,
    for I have done what is just and right.
¹²² Please guarantee a blessing for me.
    Don't let those who are arrogant oppress me!
¹²³ My eyes strain to see your deliverance,
    to see the truth of your promise fulfilled.
¹²⁴ I am your servant;
    deal with me in unfailing love,
    and teach me your principles.
¹²⁵ Give discernment to me, your servant;
    then I will understand your decrees.
¹²⁶ LORD, it is time for you to act,
    for these evil people have broken your law.
¹²⁷ Truly, I love your commands
    more than gold, even the finest gold.
¹²⁸ Truly, each of your commandments is right.
    That is why I hate every false way.

¹²⁹ Your decrees are wonderful.
    No wonder I obey them!
¹³⁰ As your words are taught, they give light;
    even the simple can understand them.
¹³¹ I open my mouth, panting expectantly,
    longing for your commands.
¹³² Come and show me your mercy,
    as you do for all who love your name.
¹³³ Guide my steps by your word,
    so I will not be overcome by any evil.
¹³⁴ Rescue me from the oppression of evil people;
    then I can obey your commandments.
¹³⁵ Look down on me with love;
    teach me all your principles.
¹³⁶ Rivers of tears gush from my eyes
    because people disobey your law.

¹³⁷ O LORD, you are righteous,
    and your decisions are fair.
¹³⁸ Your decrees are perfect;
    they are entirely worthy of our trust.
¹³⁹ I am overwhelmed with rage,
    for my enemies have disregarded your words.
¹⁴⁰ Your promises have been thoroughly tested;
    that is why I love them so much.
¹⁴¹ I am insignificant and despised,
    but I don't forget your commandments.
¹⁴² Your justice is eternal,
    and your law is perfectly true.

I AM the Lord's servant, whom he loves. (119:124)

I BELIEVE the Lord's words give light to everyone. (119:130)

I MOURN deeply because so many people disobey God's commands. (119:136)

I FIND joy in God's commands, even when pressure and stress bear down on me. (119:143)

¹⁴³ As pressure and stress bear down on me,
    I find joy in your commands.
¹⁴⁴ Your decrees are always fair;
    help me to understand them, that I may live.

¹⁴⁵ I pray with all my heart; answer me, LORD!
    I will obey your principles.
¹⁴⁶ I cry out to you; save me,
    that I may obey your decrees.

I CRY OUT for God's help and put my hope in his words. (119:147)

¹⁴⁷ I rise early, before the sun is up;
    I cry out for help and put my hope in your words.
¹⁴⁸ I stay awake through the night,
    thinking about your promise.
¹⁴⁹ In your faithful love, O LORD, hear my cry;
    in your justice, save my life.
¹⁵⁰ Those lawless people are coming near to attack me;
    they live far from your law.
¹⁵¹ But you are near, O LORD,
    and all your commands are true.
¹⁵² I have known from my earliest days
    that your decrees never change.

I ASK God to rescue me because I have not forgotten his Word. (119:153)

¹⁵³ Look down upon my sorrows and rescue me,
    for I have not forgotten your law.
¹⁵⁴ Argue my case; take my side!
    Protect my life as you promised.
¹⁵⁵ The wicked are far from salvation,
    for they do not bother with your principles.
¹⁵⁶ LORD, how great is your mercy;
    in your justice, give me back my life.
¹⁵⁷ Many persecute and trouble me,
    yet I have not swerved from your decrees.
¹⁵⁸ I hate these traitors
    because they care nothing for your word.

I LOVE the Lord's commands. (119:159)

¹⁵⁹ See how I love your commandments, LORD.
    Give back my life because of your unfailing love.
¹⁶⁰ All your words are true;
    all your just laws will stand forever.

¹⁶¹ Powerful people harass me without cause,
    but my heart trembles only at your word.
¹⁶² I rejoice in your word
    like one who finds a great treasure.
¹⁶³ I hate and abhor all falsehood,
    but I love your law.

I PRAISE God continually because his laws are just. (119:164)

¹⁶⁴ I will praise you seven times a day
    because all your laws are just.
¹⁶⁵ Those who love your law have great peace
    and do not stumble.
¹⁶⁶ I long for your salvation, LORD,
    so I have obeyed your commands.
¹⁶⁷ I have obeyed your decrees,
    and I love them very much.

I OBEY God's commandments because he knows everything I do. (119:168)

¹⁶⁸ Yes, I obey your commandments and decrees,
    because you know everything I do.

¹⁶⁹ O LORD, listen to my cry;
    give me the discerning mind you promised.

[170] Listen to my prayer;
  rescue me as you promised.
[171] Let my lips burst forth with praise,
  for you have taught me your principles.
[172] Let my tongue sing about your word,
  for all your commands are right.
[173] Stand ready to help me,
  for I have chosen to follow your commandments.
[174] O LORD, I have longed for your salvation,
  and your law is my delight.
[175] Let me live so I can praise you,
  and may your laws sustain me.
[176] I have wandered away like a lost sheep;
  come and find me,
  for I have not forgotten your commands.

I ASK the Lord to find me when I wander (Isaiah 53:6). (119:176)

PSALM 120

A song for the ascent to Jerusalem.

[1] I took my troubles to the LORD;
  I cried out to him, and he answered my prayer.
[2] Rescue me, O LORD, from liars
  and from all deceitful people.
[3] O deceptive tongue, what will God do to you?
  How will he increase your punishment?
[4] You will be pierced with sharp arrows
  and burned with glowing coals.

[5] How I suffer among these scoundrels of Meshech!
  It pains me to live with these people from Kedar!
[6] I am tired of living here
  among people who hate peace.
[7] As for me, I am for peace;
  but when I speak, they are for war!

I ASK God for help, and I am confident that he will answer me when others lie about me. (120:1)

I LONG FOR peace, even when those around me only want war. (120:7)

PSALM 121

A song for the ascent to Jerusalem.

[1] I look up to the mountains—
  does my help come from there?
[2] My help comes from the LORD,
  who made the heavens and the earth!

[3] He will not let you stumble and fall;
  the one who watches over you will not sleep.
[4] Indeed, he who watches over Israel
  never tires and never sleeps.

[5] The LORD himself watches over you!
  The LORD stands beside you as your protective shade.
[6] The sun will not hurt you by day,
  nor the moon at night.
[7] The LORD keeps you from all evil
  and preserves your life.
[8] The LORD keeps watch over you as you come and go,
  both now and forever.

I LOOK UP because I know my help comes from the Lord. (121:1)

I KNOW the Lord watches over me day and night, and I trust him to protect me from harm. (121:5)

PSALM 122

A song for the ascent to Jerusalem. A psalm of David.

See David's profile (page 629) at Psalm 3:1.

I SHARE in the joy of worshiping God with others. (122:1)

¹ I was glad when they said to me,
  "Let us go to the house of the LORD."
² And now we are standing here
  inside your gates, O Jerusalem.
³ Jerusalem is a well-built city,
  knit together as a single unit.
⁴ All the people of Israel—the LORD's people—
  make their pilgrimage here.
  They come to give thanks to the name of the LORD
  as the law requires.
⁵ Here stand the thrones where judgment is given,
  the thrones of the dynasty of David.

⁶ Pray for the peace of Jerusalem.
  May all who love this city prosper.
⁷ O Jerusalem, may there be peace within your walls
  and prosperity in your palaces.
⁸ For the sake of my family and friends, I will say,
  "Peace be with you."
⁹ For the sake of the house of the LORD our God,
  I will seek what is best for you, O Jerusalem.

I PRAY FOR and seek peace for Jerusalem for the sake of God's people and for the sake of the Lord. (122:9)

PSALM 123

A song for the ascent to Jerusalem.

¹ I lift my eyes to you,
  O God, enthroned in heaven.
² We look to the LORD our God for his mercy,
  just as servants keep their eyes on their master,
  as a slave girl watches her mistress for the slightest signal.

³ Have mercy on us, LORD, have mercy,
  for we have had our fill of contempt.
⁴ We have had our fill of the scoffing of the proud
  and the contempt of the arrogant.

I LOOK to God for mercy because he is my master. (123:2)

I KNOW that at times my soul will be burdened with the ridicule of the proud and the arrogant. (123:4)

PSALM 124

A song for the ascent to Jerusalem. A psalm of David.

See David's profile (page 629) at Psalm 3:1.

¹ If the LORD had not been on our side—
  let Israel now say—
² if the LORD had not been on our side
  when people rose up against us,
³ they would have swallowed us alive
  because of their burning anger against us.
⁴ The waters would have engulfed us;
  a torrent would have overwhelmed us.
⁵ Yes, the raging waters of their fury
  would have overwhelmed our very lives.

⁶ Blessed be the LORD,
  who did not let their teeth tear us apart!
⁷ We escaped like a bird from a hunter's trap.
  The trap is broken, and we are free!
⁸ Our help is from the LORD,
  who made the heavens and the earth.

I CREDIT God for protecting Israel—and for protecting me. (124:6)

I AM THANKFUL for the help of my powerful and trustworthy Creator. (124:8)

PSALM **125**

A song for the ascent to Jerusalem.

[1] Those who trust in the LORD are as secure as Mount Zion;
   they will not be defeated but will endure forever.
[2] Just as the mountains surround and protect Jerusalem,
   so the LORD surrounds and protects his people, both now and
      forever.
[3] The wicked will not rule the godly,
   for then the godly might be forced to do wrong.
[4] O LORD, do good to those who are good,
   whose hearts are in tune with you.
[5] But banish those who turn to crooked ways, O LORD.
   Take them away with those who do evil.
   And let Israel have quietness and peace.

I BELIEVE that those who trust in the Lord are as secure as the enduring mountains. (125:1)

I ASK God to do good to those who are good, to those whose hearts are right before him. (125:4)

PSALM **126**

A song for the ascent to Jerusalem.

[1] When the LORD restored his exiles to Jerusalem,*
   it was like a dream!
[2] We were filled with laughter,
   and we sang for joy.
And the other nations said,
   "What amazing things the LORD has done for them."
[3] Yes, the LORD has done amazing things for us!
   What joy!

[4] Restore our fortunes, LORD,
   as streams renew the desert.
[5] Those who plant in tears
   will harvest with shouts of joy.
[6] They weep as they go to plant their seed,
   but they sing as they return with the harvest.

I AM ELATED over all God has done for me. (126:2)

I BELIEVE that even those who seem to spend years planting seeds of sorrow can return to God with a harvest of joy (Galatians 6:9). (126:6)

PSALM **127**

A song for the ascent to Jerusalem. A psalm of Solomon.

[1] Unless the LORD builds a house,
   the work of the builders is useless.
Unless the LORD protects a city,
   guarding it with sentries will do no good.
[2] It is useless for you to work so hard
   from early morning until late at night,
anxiously working for food to eat;
   for God gives rest to his loved ones.

[3] Children are a gift from the LORD;
   they are a reward from him.
[4] Children born to a young man
   are like sharp arrows in a warrior's hands.
[5] How happy is the man whose quiver is full of them!
   He will not be put to shame when he confronts his accusers at the city
      gates.

See Solomon's profile (page 753) at Proverbs 2:9.

I BELIEVE that no plan or project, no matter how worthy, succeeds unless the Lord wills it. (127:1)

I EMBRACE my children as gifts from the Lord. (127:3)

126:1 Hebrew *Zion.*

PSALM 128

A song for the ascent to Jerusalem.

I EXPERIENCE great happiness when I possess a deep respect for God and follow him. (128:1)

¹ How happy are those who fear the LORD—
 all who follow his ways!
² You will enjoy the fruit of your labor.
 How happy you will be! How rich your life!
³ Your wife will be like a fruitful vine,
 flourishing within your home.
 And look at all those children!
 There they sit around your table
 as vigorous and healthy as young olive trees.
⁴ That is the LORD's reward
 for those who fear him.

I BELIEVE that God brings happiness to those who possess a deep respect for him. (128:4)

⁵ May the LORD continually bless you from Zion.
 May you see Jerusalem prosper as long as you live.
⁶ May you live to enjoy your grandchildren.
 And may Israel have quietness and peace.

PSALM 129

A song for the ascent to Jerusalem.

I AM THANKFUL for each time the Lord has rescued me when I remember great sorrows in my past. (129:2)

¹ From my earliest youth my enemies have persecuted me—
 let Israel now say—
² from my earliest youth my enemies have persecuted me,
 but they have never been able to finish me off.
³ My back is covered with cuts,
 as if a farmer had plowed long furrows.
⁴ But the LORD is good;
 he has cut the cords used by the ungodly to bind me.

I KNOW that because the Lord is good, he sets his people free. (129:4)

I ASK God to make his enemies fragile and unproductive, so that they will have no way to spread their evil. (129:6)

⁵ May all who hate Jerusalem*
 be turned back in shameful defeat.
⁶ May they be as useless as grass on a rooftop,
 turning yellow when only half grown,
⁷ ignored by the harvester,
 despised by the binder.
⁸ And may those who pass by refuse to give them this blessing:
 "The LORD's blessings be upon you;
 we bless you in the LORD's name."

PSALM 130

A song for the ascent to Jerusalem.

I AM THANKFUL that the Lord offers forgiveness if I confess my sins (1 John 1:9). (130:4)

¹ From the depths of despair, O LORD,
 I call for your help.
² Hear my cry, O Lord.
 Pay attention to my prayer.

³ LORD, if you kept a record of our sins,
 who, O Lord, could ever survive?
⁴ But you offer forgiveness,
 that we might learn to fear you.

I WAIT for the Lord with my whole being, and I find hope in his Word. (130:5)

⁵ I am counting on the LORD;
 yes, I am counting on him.
 I have put my hope in his word.

129:5 Hebrew *Zion.*

⁶I long for the Lord
  more than sentries long for the dawn,
  yes, more than sentries long for the dawn.

⁷O Israel, hope in the LORD;
  for with the LORD there is unfailing love
  and an overflowing supply of salvation.
⁸He himself will free Israel
  from every kind of sin.

PSALM 131

A song for the ascent to Jerusalem. A psalm of David.

¹LORD, my heart is not proud;
  my eyes are not haughty.
I don't concern myself with matters too great
  or awesome for me.
²But I have stilled and quieted myself,
  just as a small child is quiet with its mother.
  Yes, like a small child is my soul within me.

³O Israel, put your hope in the LORD—
  now and always.

See David's profile (page 629) at Psalm 3:1.

I WILL WAIT quietly in the midst of the unknowns of life, content in the Lord's presence. (131:2)

PSALM 132

A song for the ascent to Jerusalem.

¹LORD, remember David
  and all that he suffered.
²He took an oath before the LORD.
  He vowed to the Mighty One of Israel,*
³"I will not go home;
  I will not let myself rest.
⁴I will not let my eyes sleep
  nor close my eyelids in slumber
⁵   until I find a place to build a house for the LORD,
  a sanctuary for the Mighty One of Israel."
⁶We heard that the Ark was in Ephrathah;
  then we found it in the distant countryside of Jaar.
⁷Let us go to the dwelling place of the LORD;
  let us bow low before him.
⁸Arise, O LORD, and enter your sanctuary,
  along with the Ark, the symbol of your power.
⁹Your priests will be agents of salvation;
  may your loyal servants sing for joy.

¹⁰For the sake of your servant David,
  do not reject the king you chose for your people.
¹¹The LORD swore to David
  a promise he will never take back:
  "I will place one of your descendants on your throne.
¹²If your descendants obey the terms of my covenant
  and follow the decrees that I teach them,
  then your royal line will never end."

¹³For the LORD has chosen Jerusalem*;
  he has desired it as his home.

I STAY FOCUSED on my promise to serve the Lord. (132:4)

I REMIND the Lord of his promises when I pray. (132:11)

I BELIEVE the Lord desired to dwell with and bless his people Israel in Jerusalem. (132:13)

132:2 Hebrew *of Jacob;* also in 132:5.   132:13 Hebrew *Zion.*

¹⁴ "This is my home where I will live forever," he said.
"I will live here, for this is the place I desired.
¹⁵ I will make this city prosperous
and satisfy its poor with food.
¹⁶ I will make its priests the agents of salvation;
its godly people will sing for joy.
¹⁷ Here I will increase the power of David;
my anointed one will be a light for my people.
¹⁸ I will clothe his enemies with shame,
but he will be a glorious king."

PSALM 133

A song for the ascent to Jerusalem. A psalm of David.

¹ How wonderful it is, how pleasant,
when brothers live together in harmony!
² For harmony is as precious as the fragrant anointing oil
that was poured over Aaron's head,
that ran down his beard
and onto the border of his robe.
³ Harmony is as refreshing as the dew from Mount Hermon
that falls on the mountains of Zion.
And the LORD has pronounced his blessing,
even life forevermore.

PSALM 134

A song for the ascent to Jerusalem.

¹ Oh, bless the LORD, all you servants of the LORD,
you who serve as night watchmen in the house of the LORD.
² Lift your hands in holiness,
and bless the LORD.

³ May the LORD, who made heaven and earth,
bless you from Jerusalem.*

PSALM 135

¹ Praise the LORD!

Praise the name of the LORD!
Praise him, you who serve the LORD,
² you who serve in the house of the LORD,
in the courts of the house of our God.
³ Praise the LORD, for the LORD is good;
celebrate his wonderful name with music.
⁴ For the LORD has chosen Jacob for himself,
Israel for his own special treasure.

⁵ I know the greatness of the LORD—
that our Lord is greater than any other god.
⁶ The LORD does whatever pleases him
throughout all heaven and earth,
and on the seas and in their depths.
⁷ He causes the clouds to rise over the earth.
He sends the lightning with the rain
and releases the wind from his storehouses.

See David's profile (page 629) at Psalm 3:1.

I DELIGHT in living in harmony with others!
(133:1)

See Aaron's profile (page 107) at Exodus 32:2.

I ENCOURAGE the Lord's servants to bless the Lord, for he will bless them.
(134:1)

I REMIND myself of the Lord's greatness.
(135:5)

I ACKNOWLEDGE that the Lord has control over all of nature.
(135:6)

134:3 Hebrew *Zion.*

⁸ He destroyed the firstborn in each Egyptian home,
  both people and animals.
⁹ He performed miraculous signs and wonders in Egypt;
  Pharaoh and all his people watched.
¹⁰ He struck down great nations
  and slaughtered mighty kings—
¹¹ Sihon king of the Amorites,
  Og king of Bashan,
  and all the kings of Canaan.
¹² He gave their land as an inheritance,
  a special possession to his people Israel.
¹³ Your name, O Lord, endures forever;
  your fame, O Lord, is known to every generation.
¹⁴ For the Lord will vindicate his people
  and have compassion on his servants.

¹⁵ Their idols are merely things of silver and gold,
  shaped by human hands.
¹⁶ They cannot talk, though they have mouths,
  or see, though they have eyes!
¹⁷ They cannot hear with their ears
  or smell with their noses.
¹⁸ And those who make them are just like them,
  as are all who trust in them.

¹⁹ O Israel, praise the Lord!
  O priests of Aaron, praise the Lord!
²⁰ O Levites, praise the Lord!
  All you who fear the Lord, praise the Lord!
²¹ The Lord be praised from Zion,
  for he lives here in Jerusalem.

  Praise the Lord!

PSALM 136

¹ Give thanks to the Lord, for he is good!
  His faithful love endures forever.
² Give thanks to the God of gods.
  His faithful love endures forever.
³ Give thanks to the Lord of lords.
  His faithful love endures forever.
⁴ Give thanks to him who alone does mighty miracles.
  His faithful love endures forever.
⁵ Give thanks to him who made the heavens so skillfully.
  His faithful love endures forever.
⁶ Give thanks to him who placed the earth on the water.
  His faithful love endures forever.
⁷ Give thanks to him who made the heavenly lights—
  His faithful love endures forever.
⁸ the sun to rule the day,
  His faithful love endures forever.
⁹ and the moon and stars to rule the night.
  His faithful love endures forever.

¹⁰ Give thanks to him who killed the firstborn of Egypt.
  His faithful love endures forever.
¹¹ He brought Israel out of Egypt.
  His faithful love endures forever.

I DECLARE that the Lord showed his greatness and power when he rescued the Israelites from Egypt and gave them the Promised Land. (135:12)

I PRAISE the Lord because his name endures forever. (135:13)

I URGE the Lord's servants to praise the Lord. (135:19)

See Aaron's profile (page 107) at Exodus 32:2.

I GIVE THANKS to the Lord because he is good. (136:1)

I CONTINUALLY REPEAT praise for the Lord's enduring, faithful love. (136:3)

I GIVE THANKS to the Lord for each detail of his creation. (136:5)

Ask the Lord to speak to you. After all, this is his Word!

¹² He acted with a strong hand and powerful arm.
His faithful love endures forever.
¹³ Give thanks to him who parted the Red Sea.*
His faithful love endures forever.
¹⁴ He led Israel safely through,
His faithful love endures forever.
¹⁵ but he hurled Pharaoh and his army into the sea.
His faithful love endures forever.
¹⁶ Give thanks to him who led his people through the wilderness.
His faithful love endures forever.

I THANK the Lord every time he defeats his foes. (136:17)

¹⁷ Give thanks to him who struck down mighty kings.
His faithful love endures forever.
¹⁸ He killed powerful kings—
His faithful love endures forever.
¹⁹ Sihon king of the Amorites,
His faithful love endures forever.
²⁰ and Og king of Bashan.
His faithful love endures forever.
²¹ God gave the land of these kings as an inheritance—
His faithful love endures forever.
²² a special possession to his servant Israel.
His faithful love endures forever.

²³ He remembered our utter weakness.
His faithful love endures forever.
²⁴ He saved us from our enemies.
His faithful love endures forever.

I GIVE THANKS to the Lord for providing for all living things. (136:25)

²⁵ He gives food to every living thing.
His faithful love endures forever.
²⁶ Give thanks to the God of heaven.
His faithful love endures forever.

PSALM 137

¹ Beside the rivers of Babylon, we sat and wept
as we thought of Jerusalem.*
² We put away our lyres,
hanging them on the branches of the willow trees.
³ For there our captors demanded a song of us.
Our tormentors requested a joyful hymn:
"Sing us one of those songs of Jerusalem!"
⁴ But how can we sing the songs of the LORD
while in a foreign land?

I MOURN when I am far from the Lord's presence. (137:4)

⁵ If I forget you, O Jerusalem,
let my right hand forget its skill upon the harp.
⁶ May my tongue stick to the roof of my mouth
if I fail to remember you,
if I don't make Jerusalem my highest joy.

I BRING to God my desire to see him punish the enemies of his people. (137:7)

⁷ O LORD, remember what the Edomites did
on the day the armies of Babylon captured Jerusalem.
"Destroy it!" they yelled.
"Level it to the ground!"
⁸ O Babylon, you will be destroyed.
Happy is the one who pays you back
for what you have done to us.

136:13 Hebrew *sea of reeds;* also in 136:15.   137:1 Hebrew *Zion;* also in 137:3.

⁹Happy is the one who takes your babies
  and smashes them against the rocks!

PSALM 138

A psalm of David.

¹I give you thanks, O LORD, with all my heart;
  I will sing your praises before the gods.
²I bow before your holy Temple as I worship.
  I will give thanks to your name
  for your unfailing love and faithfulness,
  because your promises are backed
  by all the honor of your name.
³When I pray, you answer me;
  you encourage me by giving me the strength I need.

⁴Every king in all the earth will give you thanks, O LORD,
  for all of them will hear your words.
⁵Yes, they will sing about the LORD's ways,
  for the glory of the LORD is very great.
⁶Though the LORD is great, he cares for the humble,
  but he keeps his distance from the proud.

⁷Though I am surrounded by troubles,
  you will preserve me against the anger of my enemies.
  You will clench your fist against my angry enemies!
  Your power will save me.
⁸The LORD will work out his plans for my life—
  for your faithful love, O LORD, endures forever.
  Don't abandon me, for you made me.

PSALM 139

For the choir director: A psalm of David.

¹O LORD, you have examined my heart
  and know everything about me.
²You know when I sit down or stand up.
  You know my every thought when far away.
³You chart the path ahead of me
  and tell me where to stop and rest.
  Every moment you know where I am.
⁴You know what I am going to say
  even before I say it, LORD.
⁵You both precede and follow me.
  You place your hand of blessing on my head.
⁶Such knowledge is too wonderful for me,
  too great for me to know!

⁷I can never escape from your spirit!
  I can never get away from your presence!
⁸If I go up to heaven, you are there;
  if I go down to the place of the dead,* you are there.
⁹If I ride the wings of the morning,
  if I dwell by the farthest oceans,
¹⁰even there your hand will guide me,
  and your strength will support me.

139:8 Hebrew *to Sheol.*

See David's profile (page 629) at Psalm 3:1.

I BOW AND GIVE THANKS for the Lord, whose love never fails and whose promises are true. (138:2)

I TRUST the Lord to work out his plans for my life (Philippians 1:6). (138:8)

I AM AWED by the Lord's knowledge and guidance of my life. (139:6)

I REVEL in God's continual presence with me wherever I go. (139:7)

¹¹ I could ask the darkness to hide me
　and the light around me to become night—
¹² but even in darkness I cannot hide from you.
To you the night shines as bright as day.
　Darkness and light are both alike to you.

¹³ You made all the delicate, inner parts of my body
　and knit me together in my mother's womb.
¹⁴ Thank you for making me so wonderfully complex!
　Your workmanship is marvelous—and how well I know it.
¹⁵ You watched me as I was being formed in utter seclusion,
　as I was woven together in the dark of the womb.
¹⁶ You saw me before I was born.
　Every day of my life was recorded in your book.
Every moment was laid out
　before a single day had passed.

¹⁷ How precious are your thoughts about me,* O God!
　They are innumerable!
¹⁸ I can't even count them;
　they outnumber the grains of sand!
And when I wake up in the morning,
　you are still with me!

I THANK the Lord for making me and planning my life from before my birth. (139:14)

¹⁹ O God, if only you would destroy the wicked!
　Get out of my life, you murderers!
²⁰ They blaspheme you;
　your enemies take your name in vain.
²¹ O LORD, shouldn't I hate those who hate you?
　Shouldn't I despise those who resist you?
²² Yes, I hate them with complete hatred,
　for your enemies are my enemies.

I DO NOT TEAM UP with those who hate God or who are actively sinning against him. (139:19)

²³ Search me, O God, and know my heart;
　test me and know my thoughts.
²⁴ Point out anything in me that offends you,
　and lead me along the path of everlasting life.

I ASK the Lord to show me where I sin and to lead me in his way. (139:24)

PSALM 140

For the choir director: A psalm of David.

¹ O LORD, rescue me from evil people.
　Preserve me from those who are violent,
² those who plot evil in their hearts
　and stir up trouble all day long.
³ Their tongues sting like a snake;
　the poison of a viper drips from their lips. *Interlude*

⁴ O LORD, keep me out of the hands of the wicked.
　Preserve me from those who are violent,
　for they are plotting against me.
⁵ The proud have set a trap to catch me;
　they have stretched out a net;
　they have placed traps all along the way. *Interlude*

⁶ I said to the LORD, "You are my God!"
　Listen, O LORD, to my cries for mercy!
⁷ O Sovereign LORD, my strong savior,
　you protected me on the day of battle.

I ASK the Lord to preserve me from violent people. (140:1)

139:17 Or *How precious to me are your thoughts.*

⁸ LORD, do not give in to their evil desires.
  Do not let their evil schemes succeed, O God.   *Interlude*

⁹ Let my enemies be destroyed
  by the very evil they have planned for me.
¹⁰ Let burning coals fall down on their heads,
  or throw them into the fire,
  or into deep pits from which they can't escape.
¹¹ Don't let liars prosper here in our land.
  Cause disaster to fall with great force on the violent.

I LOOK to God to deal with violent and lying people who cause trouble for the whole land. (140:11)

¹² But I know the LORD will surely help those they persecute;
  he will maintain the rights of the poor.
¹³ Surely the godly are praising your name,
  for they will live in your presence.

I PRAISE the Lord through every circumstance, because I am living in his presence. (140:13)

PSALM 141

A psalm of David.

¹ O LORD, I am calling to you. Please hurry!
  Listen when I cry to you for help!
² Accept my prayer as incense offered to you,
  and my upraised hands as an evening offering.

³ Take control of what I say, O LORD,
  and keep my lips sealed.
⁴ Don't let me lust for evil things;
  don't let me participate in acts of wickedness.
  Don't let me share in the delicacies
  of those who do evil.

I GIVE the control of my lips to the Lord. (141:3)

⁵ Let the godly strike me!
  It will be a kindness!
  If they reprove me, it is soothing medicine.
  Don't let me refuse it.

I ASK the Lord to guide and reprove me through the words of godly people. (141:5)

But I am in constant prayer
  against the wicked and their deeds.
⁶ When their leaders are thrown down from a cliff,
  they will listen to my words and find them pleasing.
⁷ Even as a farmer breaks up the soil and brings up rocks,
  so the bones of the wicked will be scattered without a decent burial.

⁸ I look to you for help, O Sovereign LORD.
  You are my refuge; don't let them kill me.
⁹ Keep me out of the traps they have set for me,
  out of the snares of those who do evil.
¹⁰ Let the wicked fall into their own snares,
  but let me escape.

I ASK the Lord to protect me from the wicked and to deal justly with them. (141:9)

PSALM 142

A psalm of David, regarding his experience in the cave. A prayer.

¹ I cry out to the LORD;
  I plead for the LORD's mercy.
² I pour out my complaints before him
  and tell him all my troubles.
³ For I am overwhelmed,
  and you alone know the way I should turn.

I TELL the Lord all my troubles (see 1 Samuel 23:29–24:22). (142:2)

Wherever I go,
my enemies have set traps for me.
⁴I look for someone to come and help me,
but no one gives me a passing thought!
No one will help me;
no one cares a bit what happens to me.
⁵Then I pray to you, O LORD.
I say, "You are my place of refuge.
You are all I really want in life.
⁶Hear my cry,
for I am very low.
Rescue me from my persecutors,
for they are too strong for me.
⁷Bring me out of prison
so I can thank you.
The godly will crowd around me,
for you treat me kindly."

I ASK the Lord to rescue me so that godly people will thank him with me. (142:7)

PSALM 143

A psalm of David.

I ASK the Lord to hear me because he is faithful and righteous— not because I am deserving. (143:1)

¹Hear my prayer, O LORD;
listen to my plea!
Answer me because you are faithful and righteous.
²Don't bring your servant to trial!
Compared to you, no one is perfect.
³My enemy has chased me.
He has knocked me to the ground.
He forces me to live in darkness like those in the grave.
⁴I am losing all hope;
I am paralyzed with fear.

I REMEMBER God's works in the past when I am paralyzed with fear. (143:5)

⁵I remember the days of old.
I ponder all your great works.
I think about what you have done.
⁶I reach out for you.
I thirst for you as parched land thirsts for rain.   *Interlude*

⁷Come quickly, LORD, and answer me,
for my depression deepens.
Don't turn away from me,
or I will die.
⁸Let me hear of your unfailing love to me in the morning,
for I am trusting you.
Show me where to walk,
for I have come to you in prayer.
⁹Save me from my enemies, LORD;
I run to you to hide me.
¹⁰Teach me to do your will,
for you are my God.
May your gracious Spirit lead me forward
on a firm footing.

I ASK the Lord to guide me by his Spirit into obedience and stability. (143:10)

¹¹For the glory of your name, O LORD, save me.
In your righteousness, bring me out of this distress.
¹²In your unfailing love, cut off all my enemies
and destroy all my foes,
for I am your servant.

PSALM 144

A psalm of David.

¹ Bless the LORD, who is my rock.
  He gives me strength for war
  and skill for battle.
² He is my loving ally and my fortress,
  my tower of safety, my deliverer.
He stands before me as a shield, and I take refuge in him.
He subdues the nations* under me.

³ O LORD, what are mortals that you should notice us,
  mere humans that you should care for us?
⁴ For we are like a breath of air;
  our days are like a passing shadow.

I AM AMAZED at the Lord's notice and care of his human creatures. (144:3)

⁵ Bend down the heavens, LORD, and come down.
  Touch the mountains so they billow smoke.
⁶ Release your lightning bolts and scatter your enemies!
  Release your arrows and confuse them!
⁷ Reach down from heaven and rescue me;
  deliver me from deep waters,
  from the power of my enemies.
⁸ Their mouths are full of lies;
  they swear to tell the truth, but they lie.

⁹ I will sing a new song to you, O God!
  I will sing your praises with a ten-stringed harp.
¹⁰ For you grant victory to kings!
  You are the one who rescued your servant David.
¹¹ Save me from the fatal sword!
  Rescue me from the power of my enemies.
Their mouths are full of lies;
  they swear to tell the truth, but they lie.

I SING a new song of praise to the Lord for rescuing me from those who attack me with lies. (144:9)

¹² May our sons flourish in their youth
  like well-nurtured plants.
May our daughters be like graceful pillars,
  carved to beautify a palace.
¹³ May our farms be filled
  with crops of every kind.
May the flocks in our fields multiply by the thousands,
  even tens of thousands,
¹⁴ and may our oxen be loaded down with produce.
May there be no breached walls, no forced exile,
  no cries of distress in our squares.
¹⁵ Yes, happy are those who have it like this!
  Happy indeed are those whose God is the LORD.

I FIND happiness in the blessings of having the Lord as my God. (144:15)

PSALM 145

A psalm of praise of David.

¹ I will praise you, my God and King,
  and bless your name forever and ever.
² I will bless you every day,
  and I will praise you forever.
³ Great is the LORD! He is most worthy of praise!
  His greatness is beyond discovery!

144:2 Some manuscripts read *my people.*

I TELL the next generation the story of the Lord's mighty acts. (145:4)

⁴ Let each generation tell its children
    of your mighty acts.
⁵ I will meditate* on your majestic, glorious splendor
    and your wonderful miracles.
⁶ Your awe-inspiring deeds will be on every tongue;
    I will proclaim your greatness.
⁷ Everyone will share the story of your wonderful goodness;
    they will sing with joy of your righteousness.

I DECLARE that the Lord is kind, merciful, loving, and good to everyone (Exodus 34:6). (145:8)

⁸ The LORD is kind and merciful,
    slow to get angry, full of unfailing love.
⁹ The LORD is good to everyone.
    He showers compassion on all his creation.
¹⁰ All of your works will thank you, LORD,
    and your faithful followers will bless you.
¹¹ They will talk together about the glory of your kingdom;
    they will celebrate examples of your power.
¹² They will tell about your mighty deeds
    and about the majesty and glory of your reign.
¹³ For your kingdom is an everlasting kingdom.
    You rule generation after generation.

The LORD is faithful in all he says;
    he is gracious in all he does.*
¹⁴ The LORD helps the fallen
    and lifts up those bent beneath their loads.

I PRAISE the Lord for providing for the needs of every living thing. (145:15)

¹⁵ All eyes look to you for help;
    you give them their food as they need it.
¹⁶ When you open your hand,
    you satisfy the hunger and thirst of every living thing.

¹⁷ The LORD is righteous in everything he does;
    he is filled with kindness.

I TAKE comfort and courage because the Lord is close to all who call on him (Ephesians 2:13). (145:18)

¹⁸ The LORD is close to all who call on him,
    yes, to all who call on him sincerely.
¹⁹ He fulfills the desires of those who fear him;
    he hears their cries for help and rescues them.
²⁰ The LORD protects all those who love him,
    but he destroys the wicked.

²¹ I will praise the LORD,
    and everyone on earth will bless his holy name
    forever and forever.

PSALM 146

I CONTINUALLY REMIND myself to praise the Lord. (146:1)

¹ Praise the LORD!

Praise the LORD, I tell myself.
² I will praise the LORD as long as I live.
    I will sing praises to my God even with my dying breath.

³ Don't put your confidence in powerful people;
    there is no help for you there.
⁴ When their breathing stops, they return to the earth,
    and in a moment all their plans come to an end.

I HAPPILY PUT my confidence in the God of Israel as my helper. (146:5)

⁵ But happy are those who have the God of Israel* as their helper,
    whose hope is in the LORD their God.

145:5 Some manuscripts read *They will speak.*   145:13 The last two lines of 145:13 are not found in many of the ancient manuscripts.   146:5 Hebrew *of Jacob.*

6 He is the one who made heaven and earth,
the sea, and everything in them.
He is the one who keeps every promise forever,
7   who gives justice to the oppressed
and food to the hungry.
The LORD frees the prisoners.
8   The LORD opens the eyes of the blind.
The LORD lifts the burdens of those bent beneath their loads.
The LORD loves the righteous.
9 The LORD protects the foreigners among us.
He cares for the orphans and widows,
but he frustrates the plans of the wicked.

10 The LORD will reign forever.
O Jerusalem,* your God is King in every generation!

Praise the LORD!

I BELIEVE the Lord loves the righteous and cares for all the needy. (146:8)

PSALM 147

1 Praise the LORD!

How good it is to sing praises to our God!
How delightful and how right!
2 The LORD is rebuilding Jerusalem
and bringing the exiles back to Israel.
3 He heals the brokenhearted,
binding up their wounds.
4 He counts the stars
and calls them all by name.
5 How great is our Lord! His power is absolute!
His understanding is beyond comprehension!
6 The LORD supports the humble,
but he brings the wicked down into the dust.

7 Sing out your thanks to the LORD;
sing praises to our God, accompanied by harps.
8 He covers the heavens with clouds,
provides rain for the earth,
and makes the green grass grow in mountain pastures.
9 He feeds the wild animals,
and the young ravens cry to him for food.
10 The strength of a horse does not impress him;
how puny in his sight is the strength of a man.
11 Rather, the LORD's delight is in those who honor him,
those who put their hope in his unfailing love.

12 Praise the LORD, O Jerusalem!
Praise your God, O Zion!
13 For he has fortified the bars of your gates
and blessed your children within you.
14 He sends peace across your nation
and satisfies you with plenty of the finest wheat.
15 He sends his orders to the world—
how swiftly his word flies!
16 He sends the snow like white wool;
he scatters frost upon the ground like ashes.

I PRAISE the Lord because it is so good and delightful to do so! (147:1)

I PRAISE our great Lord, who knows each star and cares for each hurting person. (147:5)

I PUT my hope in the Lord's love and know that he delights in me. (147:11)

I PRAISE the Lord for his command over all of nature. (147:15)

146:10 Hebrew *Zion.*

¹⁷ He hurls the hail like stones.
　Who can stand against his freezing cold?
¹⁸ Then, at his command, it all melts.
　He sends his winds, and the ice thaws.

¹⁹ He has revealed his words to Jacob,
　his principles and laws to Israel.
²⁰ He has not done this with any other nation;
　they do not know his laws.

I PRAISE the Lord for giving his Word to his people, Israel. (147:20)

Praise the LORD!

PSALM **148**

¹ Praise the LORD!

Praise the LORD from the heavens!
　Praise him from the skies!
² Praise him, all his angels!
　Praise him, all the armies of heaven!
³ Praise him, sun and moon!
　Praise him, all you twinkling stars!
⁴ Praise him, skies above!
　Praise him, vapors high above the clouds!

I CALL on every created thing to praise the Lord! (148:5)

⁵ Let every created thing give praise to the LORD,
　for he issued his command, and they came into being.
⁶ He established them forever and forever.
　His orders will never be revoked.

⁷ Praise the LORD from the earth,
　you creatures of the ocean depths,
⁸ fire and hail, snow and storm,
　wind and weather that obey him,
⁹ mountains and all hills,
　fruit trees and all cedars,
¹⁰ wild animals and all livestock,
　reptiles and birds,
¹¹ kings of the earth and all people,
　rulers and judges of the earth,
¹² young men and maidens,
　old men and children.

I URGE all people to praise the Lord for his greatness and glory. (148:13)

¹³ Let them all praise the name of the LORD.
　For his name is very great;
　his glory towers over the earth and heaven!
¹⁴ He has made his people strong,
　honoring his godly ones—
　the people of Israel who are close to him.

Praise the LORD!

PSALM **149**

¹ Praise the LORD!

I URGE God's people to rejoice in their Maker and King with singing and dancing. (149:2)

Sing to the LORD a new song.
　Sing his praises in the assembly of the faithful.
² O Israel, rejoice in your Maker.
　O people of Jerusalem,* exult in your King.

149:2 Hebrew *Zion.*

³ Praise his name with dancing,
   accompanied by tambourine and harp.
⁴ For the LORD delights in his people;
   he crowns the humble with salvation.
⁵ Let the faithful rejoice in this honor.
   Let them sing for joy as they lie on their beds.
⁶ Let the praises of God be in their mouths,
   and a sharp sword in their hands—
⁷ to execute vengeance on the nations
   and punishment on the peoples,
⁸ to bind their kings with shackles
   and their leaders with iron chains,
⁹ to execute the judgment written against them.
   This is the glory of his faithful ones.

Praise the LORD!

PSALM 150
¹ Praise the LORD!

Praise God in his heavenly dwelling;
   praise him in his mighty heaven!
² Praise him for his mighty works;
   praise his unequaled greatness!
³ Praise him with a blast of the trumpet;
   praise him with the lyre and harp!
⁴ Praise him with the tambourine and dancing;
   praise him with stringed instruments and flutes!
⁵ Praise him with a clash of cymbals;
   praise him with loud clanging cymbals.
⁶ Let everything that lives sing praises to the LORD!

Praise the LORD!

I CALL on the Lord's faithful people to sing for joy because the Lord gives them his delight and his salvation. (149:5)

I BELIEVE the Lord used his people Israel to praise him and to punish wicked nations. (149:6)

I CALL OUT praises for the Lord's mighty works and greatness! (150:2)

I CALL on every living thing to praise the Lord with music and singing and dancing! (150:6)

PROVERBS

THIS THIRD BOOK of Hebrew poetry is an extensive collection of *wise sayings*.

Solomon (chapters 1–29), Agur (chapter 30), Lemuel (31:1–9), and at least one anonymous writer (31:10–31) contributed to this profoundly practical book.

Some of the most prominent themes in this book include the fear of the Lord, wisdom, righteousness, speech, adultery, purity, justice, wealth, wickedness, and the value of a godly wife. Other significant themes include alcohol, anger, evil, honor, discipline, God's sovereignty, happiness, laziness, politics, prayer, pride, protecting the poor, relationships, self-control, violence, and God's Word.

In 1:1–9:18, Solomon develops some of the book's key themes. In 10:1–22:16, Solomon presents a collection of hundreds of short proverbs or wise sayings. In 22:17–24:22, the writer discusses thirty important topics. In 24:23–34, the writer discusses a few more subjects. In 25:1–29:27, some of Hezekiah's advisers present a collection of nearly 140 more of Solomon's 3,000 proverbs (1 Kings 4:32). In 30:1–31:31 we read the wise sayings of three other writers.

Famous passages in Proverbs abound, including

- The importance of fearing the Lord (1:7; 3:7; 9:10; 15:33; 16:6; 22:4)
- The folly of following wicked people (1:8-19; 2:12-15; 4:10-19)
- The value of acquiring wisdom (1:20-33; 2:1-11; 3:13-26; 4:5-9; 8:1–9:12)
- The folly of committing adultery (2:16-19; 5:1-23; 6:20–7:27; 9:13-18)
- The value of a good wife (5:15-19; 12:4; 18:22; 19:14; 31:10-31)
- "There are six things the LORD hates" (6:16-19)
- "Hope deferred makes the heart sick" (13:12)
- "Whoever walks with the wise will become wise" (13:20)
- "There is a path before each person that seems right, but . . ." (14:12; 16:25)
- The value of a happy heart (14:30; 15:13, 15, 30; 16:24; 17:22)
- "Godliness exalts a nation" (14:34)
- "A gentle answer turns away wrath" (15:1)
- "Teach your children to choose the right path" (22:6)
- "Rescue those who are unjustly sentenced to death" (24:11)
- "Don't brag about tomorrow" (27:1)
- "People who cover over their sins will not prosper" (28:13)
- "There are three other things . . ." (30:15-31)

CHAPTER 1

The Purpose of Proverbs

These are the proverbs of Solomon, David's son, king of Israel.

²The purpose of these proverbs is to teach people wisdom and discipline, and to help them understand wise sayings. ³Through these proverbs, people will receive instruction in discipline, good conduct, and doing what is right,

See the profiles for Solomon (page 753) and David (page 629) at Proverbs 2:9 and Psalm 3:1.

I LEARN wisdom from the proverbs. (1:2)

just, and fair. ⁴These proverbs will make the simpleminded clever. They will give knowledge and purpose to young people.

⁵Let those who are wise listen to these proverbs and become even wiser. And let those who understand receive guidance ⁶by exploring the depth of meaning in these proverbs, parables, wise sayings, and riddles.

⁷Fear of the LORD is the beginning of knowledge. Only fools despise wisdom and discipline.

A Father's Exhortation: Acquire Wisdom

⁸Listen, my child,* to what your father teaches you. Don't neglect your mother's teaching. ⁹What you learn from them will crown you with grace and clothe you with honor.

¹⁰My child, if sinners entice you, turn your back on them! ¹¹They may say, "Come and join us. Let's hide and kill someone! Let's ambush the innocent! ¹²Let's swallow them alive as the grave swallows its victims. Though they are in the prime of life, they will go down into the pit of death. ¹³And the loot we'll get! We'll fill our houses with all kinds of things! ¹⁴Come on, throw in your lot with us; we'll split our loot with you."

¹⁵Don't go along with them, my child! Stay far away from their paths. ¹⁶They rush to commit crimes. They hurry to commit murder. ¹⁷When a bird sees a trap being set, it stays away. ¹⁸But not these people! They set an ambush for themselves; they booby-trap their own lives! ¹⁹Such is the fate of all who are greedy for gain. It ends up robbing them of life.

Wisdom Shouts in the Streets

²⁰Wisdom shouts in the streets. She cries out in the public square. ²¹She calls out to the crowds along the main street, and to those in front of city hall. ²²"You simpletons!" she cries. "How long will you go on being simpleminded? How long will you mockers relish your mocking? How long will you fools fight the facts? ²³Come here and listen to me! I'll pour out the spirit of wisdom upon you and make you wise.

²⁴"I called you so often, but you didn't come. I reached out to you, but you paid no attention. ²⁵You ignored my advice and rejected the correction I offered. ²⁶So I will laugh when you are in trouble! I will mock you when disaster overtakes you—²⁷when calamity overcomes you like a storm, when you are engulfed by trouble, and when anguish and distress overwhelm you.

²⁸"I will not answer when they cry for help. Even though they anxiously search for me, they will not find me. ²⁹For they hated knowledge and chose not to fear the LORD. ³⁰They rejected my advice and paid no attention when I corrected them. ³¹That is why they must eat the bitter fruit of living their own way. They must experience the full terror of the path they have chosen. ³²For they are simpletons who turn away from me—to death. They are fools, and their own complacency will destroy them. ³³But all who listen to me will live in peace and safety, unafraid of harm."

CHAPTER 2

The Benefits of Wisdom

My child,* listen to me and treasure my instructions. ²Tune your ears to wisdom, and concentrate on understanding. ³Cry out for insight and understanding. ⁴Search for them as you would for lost money or hidden treasure. ⁵Then you will understand what it means to fear the LORD, and you will gain knowledge of God. ⁶For the LORD grants wisdom! From his mouth come knowledge and understanding. ⁷He grants a treasure of good sense to the godly. He is their shield, protecting those who walk with integrity. ⁸He guards the paths of justice and protects those who are faithful to him.

I FEAR the Lord and gain knowledge and wisdom. (1:7)

I TURN AWAY from the enticements of evil individuals. (1:10)

I STAY AWAY from violent individuals and resist their plans. (1:15)

I AVOID those who are greedy for gain. (1:19)

I DO NOT IGNORE wise counsel and correction. (1:25)

I LOVE knowledge and choose to fear the Lord. (1:29)

I TREASURE wisdom and seek it diligently. (2:2)

I WALK with integrity before the Lord, who protects me. (2:7)

1:8 Hebrew *my son*; also in 1:10, 15.   2:1 Hebrew *My son*.

⁹Then you will understand what is right, just, and fair, and you will know how to find the right course of action every time. ¹⁰For wisdom will enter your heart, and knowledge will fill you with joy. ¹¹Wise planning will watch over you. Understanding will keep you safe.

UNLIKE SOLOMON

Proverbs 2:9

I apply the wisdom of God's Word to my everyday life.

In his day, Albert Einstein was a genius—but not compared to Solomon.

The Lord tells us no one will ever be as wise as King Solomon (1 Kings 3:12). During Solomon's reign, "He was wiser than anyone else" and "His fame spread throughout all the surrounding nations" (1 Kings 4:31).

Solomon's knowledge encompassed the details of the natural, religious, social, economic, and political worlds of his time. With insight he analyzed the motives and plans of individuals and entire nations. He knew the right course of action to take in every situation.

Early in his forty-year reign as king of Israel, Solomon also led a national revival (1 Kings 8). Unfortunately, just because Solomon always knew the right thing to do doesn't mean he consistently did it.

Over the course of many years, Solomon penned observations about the realities of life. He left some of those writings to his sons—and to us. His writings include two psalms (Psalms 72, 127), hundreds of proverbs (Proverbs 1–29), a poetic essay (Ecclesiastes), and much more. Yet even though wisdom flowed from Solomon's pen, he started growing cynical and, much later, finally put down his pen, turned his back on the Lord, worshiped man-made idols, and finished life as an old fool.

How could the man who had it all figured out in his head end up missing it so badly in real life?

"Above all else," Solomon once observed, "guard your heart, for it affects everything you do" (Proverbs 4:23). These wise words aptly explain Solomon's own foolish downfall. With each foreign wife that Solomon added to his harem, his heart drifted further from the Lord (1 Kings 11:1-10). Yes, Solomon knew the Lord's specific command not to marry foreign women, let alone worship their false gods. And yes, Solomon himself had praised the joys of marriage (Song of Songs). Yet it isn't enough to *know*. Solomon let his guard down, polluted his heart, and in most areas of life blew it—badly.

From Solomon we learn it's not enough to know—if we don't *do*. To become truly wise, God's Word must flow from our head into our heart and out through our life.

Be sure to read some of the stories about Solomon in 1 Kings 1–11 and 2 Chronicles 1–10.

○ *Today's Scripture reading is Proverbs 2–4.*

¹²Wisdom will save you from evil people, from those whose speech is corrupt. ¹³These people turn from right ways to walk down dark and evil paths. ¹⁴They rejoice in doing wrong, and they enjoy evil as it turns things upside down. ¹⁵What they do is crooked, and their ways are wrong.

I DO NOT TURN from right ways to walk down dark and evil paths. (2:13)

¹⁶Wisdom will save you from the immoral woman, from the flattery of the adulterous woman. ¹⁷She has abandoned her husband and ignores the covenant she made before God. ¹⁸Entering her house leads to death; it is the road to hell.* ¹⁹The man who visits her is doomed. He will never reach the paths of life.

I HEED wisdom and avoid anyone who desires to have an adulterous affair with me. (2:16)

²⁰Follow the steps of good men instead, and stay on the paths of the righteous. ²¹For only the upright will live in the land, and those who have integrity will remain in it. ²²But the wicked will be removed from the land, and the treacherous will be destroyed.

CHAPTER 3

Trusting in the LORD

My child,* never forget the things I have taught you. Store my commands in your heart, ²for they will give you a long and satisfying life. ³Never let loyalty

Make a commitment to read from God's Word daily.

2:18 Hebrew *to the spirits of the dead.*   3:1 Hebrew *My son;* also in 3:11, 21.

and kindness get away from you! Wear them like a necklace; write them deep within your heart. [4]Then you will find favor with both God and people, and you will gain a good reputation.

[5]Trust in the LORD with all your heart; do not depend on your own understanding. [6]Seek his will in all you do, and he will direct your paths.

[7]Don't be impressed with your own wisdom. Instead, fear the LORD and turn your back on evil. [8]Then you will gain renewed health and vitality.

[9]Honor the LORD with your wealth and with the best part of everything your land produces. [10]Then he will fill your barns with grain, and your vats will overflow with the finest wine.

[11]My child, don't ignore it when the LORD disciplines you, and don't be discouraged when he corrects you. [12]For the LORD corrects those he loves, just as a father corrects a child* in whom he delights.

[13]Happy is the person who finds wisdom and gains understanding. [14]For the profit of wisdom is better than silver, and her wages are better than gold. [15]Wisdom is more precious than rubies; nothing you desire can compare with her. [16]She offers you life in her right hand, and riches and honor in her left. [17]She will guide you down delightful paths; all her ways are satisfying. [18]Wisdom is a tree of life to those who embrace her; happy are those who hold her tightly.

[19]By wisdom the LORD founded the earth; by understanding he established the heavens. [20]By his knowledge the deep fountains of the earth burst forth, and the clouds poured down rain.

[21]My child, don't lose sight of good planning and insight. Hang on to them, [22]for they fill you with life and bring you honor and respect. [23]They keep you safe on your way and keep your feet from stumbling. [24]You can lie down without fear and enjoy pleasant dreams. [25]You need not be afraid of disaster or the destruction that comes upon the wicked, [26]for the LORD is your security. He will keep your foot from being caught in a trap.

[27]Do not withhold good from those who deserve it when it's in your power to help them. [28]If you can help your neighbor now, don't say, "Come back tomorrow, and then I'll help you."

[29]Do not plot against your neighbors, for they trust you. [30]Don't make accusations against someone who hasn't wronged you.

[31]Do not envy violent people; don't copy their ways. [32]Such wicked people are an abomination to the LORD, but he offers his friendship to the godly.

[33]The curse of the LORD is on the house of the wicked, but his blessing is on the home of the upright.

[34]The LORD mocks at mockers, but he shows favor to the humble.

[35]The wise inherit honor, but fools are put to shame!

CHAPTER 4

A Father's Wise Advice

My children,* listen to me. Listen to your father's instruction. Pay attention and grow wise, [2]for I am giving you good guidance. Don't turn away from my teaching. [3]For I, too, was once my father's son, tenderly loved by my mother as an only child.

[4]My father told me, "Take my words to heart. Follow my instructions and you will live. [5]Learn to be wise, and develop good judgment. Don't forget or turn away from my words. [6]Don't turn your back on wisdom, for she will protect you. Love her, and she will guard you. [7]Getting wisdom is the most important thing you can do! And whatever else you do, get good judgment. [8]If you prize wisdom, she will exalt you. Embrace her and she will honor you.

I DEPEND wholeheartedly on the Lord and seek his will. (3:5)

I HONOR the Lord by always giving him part of my earnings. (3:9)

I VALUE wisdom above silver and gold and rubies. (3:14)

I BELIEVE that by wisdom the Lord created the universe. (3:19)

I LIVE without fear because the Lord gives me good insight. (3:25)

I DO NOT PUT OFF paying what I owe (Romans 13:7). (3:27)

I BRING God's blessing on my home by living an upright life. (3:33)

I TAKE wise words to heart. (4:4)

I MAKE the pursuit of wisdom one of my life's top priorities. (4:7)

3:12 Hebrew *a son.* 4:1 Hebrew *My sons.*

⁹She will place a lovely wreath on your head; she will present you with a beautiful crown."

¹⁰My child,* listen to me and do as I say, and you will have a long, good life. ¹¹I will teach you wisdom's ways and lead you in straight paths. ¹²If you live a life guided by wisdom, you won't limp or stumble as you run. ¹³Carry out my instructions; don't forsake them. Guard them, for they will lead you to a fulfilled life.

¹⁴Do not do as the wicked do or follow the path of evildoers. ¹⁵Avoid their haunts. Turn away and go somewhere else, ¹⁶for evil people cannot sleep until they have done their evil deed for the day. They cannot rest unless they have caused someone to stumble. ¹⁷They eat wickedness and drink violence!

¹⁸The way of the righteous is like the first gleam of dawn, which shines ever brighter until the full light of day. ¹⁹But the way of the wicked is like complete darkness. Those who follow it have no idea what they are stumbling over.

²⁰Pay attention, my child, to what I say. Listen carefully. ²¹Don't lose sight of my words. Let them penetrate deep within your heart, ²²for they bring life and radiant health to anyone who discovers their meaning.

²³Above all else, guard your heart, for it affects everything you do.*

²⁴Avoid all perverse talk; stay far from corrupt speech.

²⁵Look straight ahead, and fix your eyes on what lies before you. ²⁶Mark out a straight path for your feet; then stick to the path and stay safe. ²⁷Don't get sidetracked; keep your feet from following evil.

> I AVOID close association with wicked individuals (1 Corinthians 15:33). (4:15)
>
> I WANT my life to shine with righteousness. (4:18)
>
> I PAY ATTENTION to wise counsel. (4:20)
>
> I GUARD my heart diligently! (4:23)

CHAPTER 5

Avoid Immoral Women

My son, pay attention to my wisdom; listen carefully to my wise counsel. ²Then you will learn to be discreet and will store up knowledge.

³The lips of an immoral woman are as sweet as honey, and her mouth is smoother than oil. ⁴But the result is as bitter as poison, sharp as a double-edged sword. ⁵Her feet go down to death; her steps lead straight to the grave.* ⁶For she does not care about the path to life. She staggers down a crooked trail and doesn't even realize where it leads.

⁷So now, my sons, listen to me. Never stray from what I am about to say: ⁸Run from her! Don't go near the door of her house! ⁹If you do, you will lose your honor and hand over to merciless people everything you have achieved in life. ¹⁰Strangers will obtain your wealth, and someone else will enjoy the fruit of your labor. ¹¹Afterward you will groan in anguish when disease consumes your body, ¹²and you will say, "How I hated discipline! If only I had not demanded my own way! ¹³Oh, why didn't I listen to my teachers? Why didn't I pay attention to those who gave me instruction? ¹⁴I have come to the brink of utter ruin, and now I must face public disgrace."

¹⁵Drink water from your own well—share your love only with your wife.* ¹⁶Why spill the water of your springs in public, having sex with just anyone?* ¹⁷You should reserve it for yourselves. Don't share it with strangers.

¹⁸Let your wife be a fountain of blessing for you. Rejoice in the wife of your youth. ¹⁹She is a loving doe, a graceful deer. Let her breasts satisfy you always. May you always be captivated by her love. ²⁰Why be captivated, my son, with an immoral woman, or embrace the breasts of an adulterous woman?

²¹For the LORD sees clearly what a man does, examining every path he takes. ²²An evil man is held captive by his own sins; they are ropes that catch and hold him. ²³He will die for lack of self-control; he will be lost because of his incredible folly.

> I PAY ATTENTION to wise counsel about avoiding immoral relationships. (5:1)
>
> I UNDERSTAND that immoral individuals don't care that sexual sins inflict untold harm on others. (5:6)
>
> I RUN AWAY from someone who desires an immoral sexual relationship with me. (5:8)
>
> I DO NOT HAVE SEX with someone just because I feel like it. (5:16)
>
> I AM CAPTIVATED BY and sexually involved with my spouse alone. (5:20)

4:10 Hebrew *My son;* also in 4:20.   4:23 Hebrew *for from it flow the springs of life.*   5:5 Hebrew *to Sheol.*
5:15 Hebrew *Drink water from your own cistern, flowing water from your own well.*   5:16 Hebrew *Why spill your springs in public, your streams in the streets?*

CHAPTER 6

Lessons for Daily Life

My child,* if you co-sign a loan for a friend or guarantee the debt of someone you hardly know—²if you have trapped yourself by your agreement and are caught by what you said—³quick, get out of it if you possibly can! You have placed yourself at your friend's mercy. Now swallow your pride; go and beg to have your name erased. ⁴Don't put it off. Do it now! Don't rest until you do. ⁵Save yourself like a deer escaping from a hunter, like a bird fleeing from a net.

⁶Take a lesson from the ants, you lazybones. Learn from their ways and be wise! ⁷Even though they have no prince, governor, or ruler to make them work, ⁸they labor hard all summer, gathering food for the winter. ⁹But you, lazybones, how long will you sleep? When will you wake up? I want you to learn this lesson: ¹⁰A little extra sleep, a little more slumber, a little folding of the hands to rest—¹¹and poverty will pounce on you like a bandit; scarcity will attack you like an armed robber.

¹²Here is a description of worthless and wicked people: They are constant liars, ¹³signaling their true intentions to their friends by making signs with their eyes and feet and fingers. ¹⁴Their perverted hearts plot evil. They stir up trouble constantly. ¹⁵But they will be destroyed suddenly, broken beyond all hope of healing.

¹⁶There are six things the LORD hates—no, seven things he detests:
¹⁷ haughty eyes,
a lying tongue,
hands that kill the innocent,
¹⁸ a heart that plots evil,
feet that race to do wrong,
¹⁹ a false witness who pours out lies,
a person who sows discord among brothers.

²⁰My son, obey your father's commands, and don't neglect your mother's teaching. ²¹Keep their words always in your heart. Tie them around your neck. ²²Wherever you walk, their counsel can lead you. When you sleep, they will protect you. When you wake up in the morning, they will advise you. ²³For these commands and this teaching are a lamp to light the way ahead of you. The correction of discipline is the way to life.

²⁴These commands and this teaching will keep you from the immoral woman, from the smooth tongue of an adulterous woman. ²⁵Don't lust for her beauty. Don't let her coyness seduce you. ²⁶For a prostitute will bring you to poverty, and sleeping with another man's wife may cost you your very life. ²⁷Can a man scoop fire into his lap and not be burned? ²⁸Can he walk on hot coals and not blister his feet? ²⁹So it is with the man who sleeps with another man's wife. He who embraces her will not go unpunished.

³⁰Excuses might be found for a thief who steals because he is starving. ³¹But if he is caught, he will be fined seven times as much as he stole, even if it means selling everything in his house to pay it back. ³²But the man who commits adultery is an utter fool, for he destroys his own soul. ³³Wounds and constant disgrace are his lot. His shame will never be erased. ³⁴For the woman's husband will be furious in his jealousy, and he will have no mercy in his day of vengeance. ³⁵There is no compensation or bribe that will satisfy him.

CHAPTER 7

Another Warning about Immoral Women

Follow my advice, my son; always treasure my commands. ²Obey them and live! Guard my teachings as your most precious possession.* ³Tie them on your fingers as a reminder. Write them deep within your heart.

6:1 Hebrew *My son.*   7:2 Hebrew *as the apple of your eye.*

I ACT quickly to be released from an agreement if I've co-signed a loan. (6:3)

I CHOOSE not to bring poverty on myself by my own laziness. (6:11)

I KEEP my life free from the sins the Lord hates. (6:16)

I BELIEVE the Lord hates a person who sows discord. (6:19)

I TREASURE wise teaching and make it a part of my life. (6:21)

I KNOW the consequences of sexual immorality are painful and severe. (6:26)

I REALIZE that those who commit adultery destroy their own souls. (6:32)

I GREATLY VALUE wise teachings. (7:2)

⁴Love wisdom like a sister; make insight a beloved member of your family. ⁵Let them hold you back from an affair with an immoral woman, from listening to the flattery of an adulterous woman.

⁶I was looking out the window of my house one day ⁷and saw a simple-minded young man who lacked common sense. ⁸He was crossing the street near the house of an immoral woman. He was strolling down the path by her house ⁹at twilight, as the day was fading, as the dark of night set in. ¹⁰The woman approached him, dressed seductively and sly of heart. ¹¹She was the brash, rebellious type who never stays at home. ¹²She is often seen in the streets and markets, soliciting at every corner.

¹³She threw her arms around him and kissed him, and with a brazen look she said, ¹⁴"I've offered my sacrifices and just finished my vows. ¹⁵It's you I was looking for! I came out to find you, and here you are! ¹⁶My bed is spread with colored sheets of finest linen imported from Egypt. ¹⁷I've perfumed my bed with myrrh, aloes, and cinnamon. ¹⁸Come, let's drink our fill of love until morning. Let's enjoy each other's caresses, ¹⁹for my husband is not home. He's away on a long trip. ²⁰He has taken a wallet full of money with him, and he won't return until later in the month."

²¹So she seduced him with her pretty speech. With her flattery she enticed him. ²²He followed her at once, like an ox going to the slaughter or like a trapped stag, ²³awaiting the arrow that would pierce its heart. He was like a bird flying into a snare, little knowing it would cost him his life.

²⁴Listen to me, my sons, and pay attention to my words. ²⁵Don't let your hearts stray away toward her. Don't wander down her wayward path. ²⁶For she has been the ruin of many; numerous men have been her victims. ²⁷Her house is the road to the grave.* Her bedroom is the den of death.

CHAPTER 8

Wisdom Calls for a Hearing

Listen as wisdom calls out! Hear as understanding raises her voice! ²She stands on the hilltop and at the crossroads. ³At the entrance to the city, at the city gates, she cries aloud, ⁴"I call to you, to all of you! I am raising my voice to all people. ⁵How naive you are! Let me give you common sense. O foolish ones, let me give you understanding. ⁶Listen to me! For I have excellent things to tell you. Everything I say is right, ⁷for I speak the truth and hate every kind of deception. ⁸My advice is wholesome and good. There is nothing crooked or twisted in it. ⁹My words are plain to anyone with understanding, clear to those who want to learn.

¹⁰"Choose my instruction rather than silver, and knowledge over pure gold. ¹¹For wisdom is far more valuable than rubies. Nothing you desire can be compared with it.

¹²"I, Wisdom, live together with good judgment. I know where to discover knowledge and discernment. ¹³All who fear the LORD will hate evil. That is why I hate pride, arrogance, corruption, and perverted speech. ¹⁴Good advice and success belong to me. Insight and strength are mine. ¹⁵Because of me, kings reign, and rulers make just laws. ¹⁶Rulers lead with my help, and nobles make righteous judgments.

¹⁷"I love all who love me. Those who search for me will surely find me. ¹⁸Unending riches, honor, wealth, and justice are mine to distribute. ¹⁹My gifts are better than the purest gold, my wages better than sterling silver! ²⁰I walk in righteousness, in paths of justice. ²¹Those who love me inherit wealth, for I fill their treasuries.

²²"The LORD formed me from the beginning, before he created anything else. ²³I was appointed in ages past, at the very first, before the earth began. ²⁴I was

7:27 Hebrew *to Sheol.*

I LET wisdom and insight steer me away from sexual sin. (7:5)

I USE common sense to avoid sin. (7:7)

I AVOID known places of sexual temptation. (7:8)

I DO NOT LISTEN to the flattery of someone who wants to seduce me. (7:13)

I RUN AWAY from the sexual advances of an adulterous person. (7:22)

I BELIEVE wisdom is available to all who will listen and learn. (8:4)

I VALUE wisdom above any material wealth. (8:11)

I FEAR the Lord and hate evil. (8:13)

I REAP rich rewards by seeking godly wisdom. (8:17)

I BELIEVE the Lord formed wisdom before he created anything else. (8:22)

born before the oceans were created, before the springs bubbled forth their waters. [25]Before the mountains and the hills were formed, I was born—[26]before he had made the earth and fields and the first handfuls of soil.

[27]"I was there when he established the heavens, when he drew the horizon on the oceans. [28]I was there when he set the clouds above, when he established the deep fountains of the earth. [29]I was there when he set the limits of the seas, so they would not spread beyond their boundaries. And when he marked off the earth's foundations, [30]I was the architect at his side. I was his constant delight, rejoicing always in his presence. [31]And how happy I was with what he created—his wide world and all the human family!

[32]"And so, my children,* listen to me, for happy are all who follow my ways. [33]Listen to my counsel and be wise. Don't ignore it.

[34]"Happy are those who listen to me, watching for me daily at my gates, waiting for me outside my home! [35]For whoever finds me finds life and wins approval from the LORD. [36]But those who miss me have injured themselves. All who hate me love death."

CHAPTER 9

Wisdom has built her spacious house with seven pillars. [2]She has prepared a great banquet, mixed the wines, and set the table. [3]She has sent her servants to invite everyone to come. She calls out from the heights overlooking the city. [4]"Come home with me," she urges the simple. To those without good judgment, she says, [5]"Come, eat my food, and drink the wine I have mixed. [6]Leave your foolish ways behind, and begin to live; learn how to be wise."

[7]Anyone who rebukes a mocker will get a smart retort. Anyone who rebukes the wicked will get hurt. [8]So don't bother rebuking mockers; they will only hate you. But the wise, when rebuked, will love you all the more. [9]Teach the wise, and they will be wiser. Teach the righteous, and they will learn more.

[10]Fear of the LORD is the beginning of wisdom. Knowledge of the Holy One results in understanding.

[11]Wisdom will multiply your days and add years to your life. [12]If you become wise, you will be the one to benefit. If you scorn wisdom, you will be the one to suffer.

Folly Calls for a Hearing
[13]The woman named Folly is loud and brash. She is ignorant and doesn't even know it. [14]She sits in her doorway on the heights overlooking the city. [15]She calls out to men going by who are minding their own business. [16]"Come home with me," she urges the simple. To those without good judgment, she says, [17]"Stolen water is refreshing; food eaten in secret tastes the best!" [18]But the men don't realize that her former guests are now in the grave.*

CHAPTER 10
The Proverbs of Solomon
The proverbs of Solomon:

A wise child* brings joy to a father; a foolish child brings grief to a mother.
[2]Ill-gotten gain has no lasting value, but right living can save your life.
[3]The LORD will not let the godly starve to death, but he refuses to satisfy the craving of the wicked.
[4]Lazy people are soon poor; hard workers get rich.
[5]A wise youth works hard all summer; a youth who sleeps away the hour of opportunity brings shame.
[6]The godly are showered with blessings; evil people cover up their harmful intentions.

8:32 Hebrew *my sons.* 9:18 Hebrew *in Sheol.* 10:1 Hebrew *son;* also in 10:1b.

I BELIEVE the Lord used wisdom as the architect for all creation. (8:30)

I AM EAGER to gain more wisdom today. (8:34)

I BELIEVE even simple individuals with poor judgment can learn wisdom. (9:4)

I DO NOT WASTE my efforts by trying to instruct those who refuse to listen to sound judgment. (9:8)

I BELIEVE it is impossible to be truly wise without fearing the Lord. (9:10)

I SHUN folly's false, alluring temptations. (9:16)

See Solomon's profile (page 753) at Proverbs 2:9.

I VALUE hard work. (10:4)

⁷We all have happy memories of the godly, but the name of a wicked person rots away.

⁸The wise are glad to be instructed, but babbling fools fall flat on their faces.

⁹People with integrity have firm footing, but those who follow crooked paths will slip and fall.

¹⁰People who wink at wrong cause trouble, but a bold reproof promotes peace.*

¹¹The words of the godly lead to life; evil people cover up their harmful intentions.

¹²Hatred stirs up quarrels, but love covers all offenses.

¹³Wise words come from the lips of people with understanding, but fools will be punished with a rod.

¹⁴Wise people treasure knowledge, but the babbling of a fool invites trouble.

¹⁵The wealth of the rich is their fortress; the poverty of the poor is their calamity.

¹⁶The earnings of the godly enhance their lives, but evil people squander their money on sin.

¹⁷People who accept correction are on the pathway to life, but those who ignore it will lead others astray.

¹⁸To hide hatred is to be a liar; to slander is to be a fool.

¹⁹Don't talk too much, for it fosters sin. Be sensible and turn off the flow!

²⁰The words of the godly are like sterling silver; the heart of a fool is worthless.

²¹The godly give good advice, but fools are destroyed by their lack of common sense.

²²The blessing of the LORD makes a person rich, and he adds no sorrow with it.

²³Doing wrong is fun for a fool, while wise conduct is a pleasure to the wise.

²⁴The fears of the wicked will all come true; so will the hopes of the godly.

²⁵Disaster strikes like a cyclone, whirling the wicked away, but the godly have a lasting foundation.

²⁶Lazy people are a pain to their employer. They are like smoke in the eyes or vinegar that sets the teeth on edge.

²⁷Fear of the LORD lengthens one's life, but the years of the wicked are cut short.

²⁸The hopes of the godly result in happiness, but the expectations of the wicked are all in vain.

²⁹The LORD protects the upright but destroys the wicked.

³⁰The godly will never be disturbed, but the wicked will be removed from the land.

³¹The godly person gives wise advice, but the tongue that deceives will be cut off.

³²The godly speak words that are helpful, but the wicked speak only what is corrupt.

CHAPTER 11

The LORD hates cheating, but he delights in honesty.

²Pride leads to disgrace, but with humility comes wisdom.

³Good people are guided by their honesty; treacherous people are destroyed by their dishonesty.

I ENJOY learning from wise individuals. (10:8)

I OVERLOOK offenses instead of stirring up a fight. (10:12)

I REFRAIN from secretly hating or publicly slandering anyone. (10:18)

I CHOOSE my words carefully so that they promote godliness, not sin. (10:19)

I BELIEVE the godly have a foundation in the Lord in times of trouble. (10:25)

I TRUST in the Lord's protection and know the wicked will receive their due. (10:29)

10:10 As in Greek version; Hebrew reads *but babbling fools fall flat on their faces.*

⁴Riches won't help on the day of judgment, but right living is a safeguard against death.

⁵The godly are directed by their honesty; the wicked fall beneath their load of sin.

⁶The godliness of good people rescues them; the ambition of treacherous people traps them.

⁷When the wicked die, their hopes all perish, for they rely on their own feeble strength.

⁸God rescues the godly from danger, but he lets the wicked fall into trouble.

⁹Evil words destroy one's friends; wise discernment rescues the godly.

¹⁰ The whole city celebrates when the godly succeed; they shout for joy when the godless die.

¹¹Upright citizens bless a city and make it prosper, but the talk of the wicked tears it apart.

¹²It is foolish to belittle a neighbor; a person with good sense remains silent.

¹³A gossip goes around revealing secrets, but those who are trustworthy can keep a confidence.

¹⁴Without wise leadership, a nation falls; with many counselors, there is safety.

¹⁵Guaranteeing a loan for a stranger is dangerous; it is better to refuse than to suffer later.

¹⁶Beautiful women obtain wealth, and violent men get rich.

¹⁷Your own soul is nourished when you are kind, but you destroy yourself when you are cruel.

¹⁸Evil people get rich for the moment, but the reward of the godly will last.

¹⁹Godly people find life; evil people find death.

²⁰The LORD hates people with twisted hearts, but he delights in those who have integrity.

²¹You can be sure that evil people will be punished, but the children of the godly will go free.

²²A woman who is beautiful but lacks discretion is like a gold ring in a pig's snout.

²³ The godly can look forward to happiness, while the wicked can expect only wrath.

²⁴It is possible to give freely and become more wealthy, but those who are stingy will lose everything.

²⁵ The generous prosper and are satisfied; those who refresh others will themselves be refreshed.

²⁶People curse those who hold their grain for higher prices, but they bless the one who sells to them in their time of need.

²⁷If you search for good, you will find favor; but if you search for evil, it will find you!

²⁸Trust in your money and down you go! But the godly flourish like leaves in spring.

²⁹Those who bring trouble on their families inherit only the wind. The fool will be a servant to the wise.

³⁰ The godly are like trees that bear life-giving fruit, and those who save lives are wise.

³¹If the righteous are rewarded here on earth, how much more true that the wicked and the sinner will get what they deserve!

CHAPTER **12**

To learn, you must love discipline; it is stupid to hate correction.

²The LORD approves of those who are good, but he condemns those who plan wickedness.

³Wickedness never brings stability; only the godly have deep roots.

I BELIEVE the godly avoid untold disasters. (11:6)

I CELEBRATE when good people are successful. (11:10)

I DO NOT CRITICIZE other people behind their backs. (11:12)

I BELIEVE leaders should seek input from many sources before making important decisions. (11:14)

I NOURISH my own soul by being kind to others. (11:17)

I FREELY SHARE what I have with others (2 Corinthians 9:6). (11:24)

I TRUST in God, not in money! (11:28)

I WILLINGLY ACCEPT discipline and correction. (12:1)

⁴A worthy wife is her husband's joy and crown; a shameful wife saps his strength.

⁵The plans of the godly are just; the advice of the wicked is treacherous.

⁶The words of the wicked are like a murderous ambush, but the words of the godly save lives.

In response to these affirmations, tell the Lord what you obey—or find easy to disobey.

⁷The wicked perish and are gone, but the children of the godly stand firm.

⁸Everyone admires a person with good sense, but a warped mind is despised.

⁹It is better to be a nobody with a servant than to be self-important but have no food.

¹⁰The godly are concerned for the welfare of their animals, but even the kindness of the wicked is cruel.

¹¹Hard work means prosperity; only fools idle away their time.

I WORK HARD and make good use of my time. (12:11)

¹²Thieves are jealous of each other's loot, while the godly bear their own fruit.

¹³The wicked are trapped by their own words, but godly escape such trouble.

¹⁴People can get many good things by the words they say; the work of their hands also gives them many benefits.

¹⁵Fools think they need no advice, but the wise listen to others.

I LISTEN to the advice of others. (12:15)

¹⁶A fool is quick-tempered, but a wise person stays calm when insulted.

¹⁷An honest witness tells the truth; a false witness tells lies.

¹⁸Some people make cutting remarks, but the words of the wise bring healing.

I USE words that build up others instead of tearing them down. (12:18)

¹⁹Truth stands the test of time; lies are soon exposed.

²⁰Deceit fills hearts that are plotting evil; joy fills hearts that are planning peace!

²¹No real harm befalls the godly, but the wicked have their fill of trouble.

²²The LORD hates those who don't keep their word, but he delights in those who do.

I KEEP my word. (12:22)

²³Wise people don't make a show of their knowledge, but fools broadcast their folly.

²⁴Work hard and become a leader; be lazy and become a slave.

²⁵Worry weighs a person down; an encouraging word cheers a person up.

²⁶The godly give good advice to their friends;* the wicked lead them astray.

I CHEER UP others with encouraging words. (12:25)

²⁷Lazy people don't even cook the game they catch, but the diligent make use of everything they find.

²⁸The way of the godly leads to life; their path does not lead to death.

CHAPTER 13

A wise child* accepts a parent's discipline; a young mocker refuses to listen.

²Good people enjoy the positive results of their words, but those who are treacherous crave violence.

³Those who control their tongue will have a long life; a quick retort can ruin everything.

⁴Lazy people want much but get little, but those who work hard will prosper and be satisfied.

⁵Those who are godly hate lies; the wicked come to shame and disgrace.

I HATE lying. (13:5)

⁶Godliness helps people all through life, while the evil are destroyed by their wickedness.

⁷Some who are poor pretend to be rich; others who are rich pretend to be poor.

⁸The rich can pay a ransom, but the poor won't even get threatened.

12:26 Or *The godly are cautious in friendship,* or *the godly are freed from evil.* The meaning of the Hebrew is uncertain. **13:1** Hebrew *son.*

⁹The life of the godly is full of light and joy, but the sinner's light is snuffed out.

¹⁰Pride leads to arguments; those who take advice are wise.

¹¹Wealth from get-rich-quick schemes quickly disappears; wealth from hard work grows.

¹²Hope deferred makes the heart sick, but when dreams come true, there is life and joy.

¹³People who despise advice will find themselves in trouble; those who respect it will succeed.

¹⁴The advice of the wise is like a life-giving fountain; those who accept it avoid the snares of death.

¹⁵A person with good sense is respected; a treacherous person walks a rocky road.

¹⁶Wise people think before they act; fools don't and even brag about it!

¹⁷An unreliable messenger stumbles into trouble, but a reliable messenger brings healing.

¹⁸If you ignore criticism, you will end in poverty and disgrace; if you accept criticism, you will be honored.

¹⁹It is pleasant to see dreams come true, but fools will not turn from evil to attain them.

²⁰Whoever walks with the wise will become wise; whoever walks with fools will suffer harm.

²¹Trouble chases sinners, while blessings chase the righteous!

²²Good people leave an inheritance to their grandchildren, but the sinner's wealth passes to the godly.

²³A poor person's farm may produce much food, but injustice sweeps it all away.

²⁴If you refuse to discipline your children, it proves you don't love them; if you love your children, you will be prompt to discipline them.

²⁵The godly eat to their hearts' content, but the belly of the wicked goes hungry.

CHAPTER 14

A wise woman builds her house; a foolish woman tears hers down with her own hands.

²Those who follow the right path fear the LORD; those who take the wrong path despise him.

³The talk of fools is a rod for their backs,* but the words of the wise keep them out of trouble.

⁴An empty stable stays clean, but no income comes from an empty stable.

⁵A truthful witness does not lie; a false witness breathes lies.

⁶A mocker seeks wisdom and never finds it, but knowledge comes easily to those with understanding.

⁷Stay away from fools, for you won't find knowledge there.

⁸The wise look ahead to see what is coming, but fools deceive themselves.

⁹Fools make fun of guilt, but the godly acknowledge it and seek reconciliation.

¹⁰Each heart knows its own bitterness, and no one else can fully share its joy.

¹¹The house of the wicked will perish, but the tent of the godly will flourish.

¹²There is a path before each person that seems right, but it ends in death.

¹³Laughter can conceal a heavy heart; when the laughter ends, the grief remains.

14:3 Hebrew *a rod of pride.*

I WORK HARD and shun all get-rich-quick schemes. (13:11)

I LISTEN to criticism and accept it as a path to honor. (13:18)

I SEEK OUT the company of wise, godly individuals. (13:20)

I WANT to leave a good inheritance to those who come after me. (13:22)

I WANT to please the Lord above all else. (14:2)

I SEEK forgiveness and reconciliation when I have wronged someone. (14:9)

[14]Backsliders get what they deserve; good people receive their reward.

[15]Only simpletons believe everything they are told! The prudent carefully consider their steps.

I WEIGH the input I receive and think before acting. (14:15)

[16]The wise are cautious* and avoid danger; fools plunge ahead with great confidence.

[17]Those who are short-tempered do foolish things, and schemers are hated.

[18]The simpleton is clothed with folly, but the wise person is crowned with knowledge.

[19]Evil people will bow before good people; the wicked will bow at the gates of the godly.

[20]The poor are despised even by their neighbors, while the rich have many "friends."

I HONOR AND HELP the poor, no matter what others may think. (14:20)

[21]It is sin to despise one's neighbors; blessed are those who help the poor.

[22]If you plot evil, you will be lost; but if you plan good, you will be granted unfailing love and faithfulness.

[23]Work brings profit, but mere talk leads to poverty!

[24]Wealth is a crown for the wise; the effort of fools yields only folly.

[25]A truthful witness saves lives, but a false witness is a traitor.

[26]Those who fear the LORD are secure; he will be a place of refuge for their children.

[27]Fear of the LORD is a life-giving fountain; it offers escape from the snares of death.

[28]A growing population is a king's glory; a dwindling nation is his doom.

[29]Those who control their anger have great understanding; those with a hasty temper will make mistakes.

I CONTROL my temper and learn to avoid mistakes (James 1:19). (14:29)

[30]A relaxed attitude lengthens life; jealousy rots it away.

[31]Those who oppress the poor insult their Maker, but those who help the poor honor him.

I HONOR the Lord by helping the poor. (14:31)

[32]The wicked are crushed by their sins, but the godly have a refuge when they die.

[33]Wisdom is enshrined in an understanding heart; wisdom is not* found among fools.

[34]Godliness exalts a nation, but sin is a disgrace to any people.

I BELIEVE godliness exalts a nation. (14:34)

[35]A king rejoices in servants who know what they are doing; he is angry with those who cause trouble.

CHAPTER 15

A gentle answer turns away wrath, but harsh words stir up anger.

[2]The wise person makes learning a joy; fools spout only foolishness.

[3]The LORD is watching everywhere, keeping his eye on both the evil and the good.

I SOOTHE angry feelings with gentle words. (15:1)

[4]Gentle words bring life and health; a deceitful tongue crushes the spirit.

[5]Only a fool despises a parent's discipline; whoever learns from correction is wise.

[6]There is treasure in the house of the godly, but the earnings of the wicked bring trouble.

[7]Only the wise can give good advice; fools cannot do so.

[8]The LORD hates the sacrifice of the wicked, but he delights in the prayers of the upright.

I BELIEVE the Lord delights in the prayers of the upright. (15:8)

[9]The LORD despises the way of the wicked, but he loves those who pursue godliness.

[10]Whoever abandons the right path will be severely punished; whoever hates correction will die.

14:16 Hebrew *The wise fear.*   **14:33** As in Greek version; Hebrew lacks *not.*

[11] Even the depths of Death and Destruction* are known by the LORD. How much more does he know the human heart!

[12] Mockers don't love those who rebuke them, so they stay away from the wise.

[13] A glad heart makes a happy face; a broken heart crushes the spirit.

[14] A wise person is hungry for truth, while the fool feeds on trash.

[15] For the poor, every day brings trouble; for the happy heart, life is a continual feast.

[16] It is better to have little with fear for the LORD than to have great treasure with turmoil.

[17] A bowl of soup with someone you love is better than steak with someone you hate.

[18] A hothead starts fights; a cool-tempered person tries to stop them.

[19] A lazy person has trouble all through life; the path of the upright is easy!

[20] Sensible children bring joy to their father; foolish children despise their mother.

[21] Foolishness brings joy to those who have no sense; a sensible person stays on the right path.

[22] Plans go wrong for lack of advice; many counselors bring success.

[23] Everyone enjoys a fitting reply; it is wonderful to say the right thing at the right time!

[24] The path of the wise leads to life above; they leave the grave* behind.

[25] The LORD destroys the house of the proud, but he protects the property of widows.

[26] The LORD despises the thoughts of the wicked, but he delights in pure words.

[27] Dishonest money brings grief to the whole family, but those who hate bribes will live.

[28] The godly think before speaking; the wicked spout evil words.

[29] The LORD is far from the wicked, but he hears the prayers of the righteous.

[30] A cheerful look brings joy to the heart; good news makes for good health.

[31] If you listen to constructive criticism, you will be at home among the wise.

[32] If you reject criticism, you only harm yourself; but if you listen to correction, you grow in understanding.

[33] Fear of the LORD teaches a person to be wise; humility precedes honor.

CHAPTER 16

We can gather our thoughts, but the LORD gives the right answer.

[2] People may be pure in their own eyes, but the LORD examines their motives.

[3] Commit your work to the LORD, and then your plans will succeed.

[4] The LORD has made everything for his own purposes, even the wicked for punishment.

[5] The LORD despises pride; be assured that the proud will be punished.

[6] Unfailing love and faithfulness cover sin; evil is avoided by fear of the LORD.

[7] When the ways of people please the LORD, he makes even their enemies live at peace with them.

[8] It is better to be poor and godly than rich and dishonest.

[9] We can make our plans, but the LORD determines our steps.

[10] The king speaks with divine wisdom; he must never judge unfairly.

[11] The LORD demands fairness in every business deal; he sets the standard.

[12] A king despises wrongdoing, for his rule depends on his justice.

I BELIEVE the Lord knows what's in my heart. (15:11)

I PLACE higher value on pleasing God and living at peace with others than on accumulating wealth. (15:16)

I OBTAIN advice from a variety of sources before making important decisions. (15:22)

I AM CAREFUL about what I say. (15:28)

I LISTEN carefully to constructive criticism. (15:31)

I DO everything for the Lord's glory and seek his approval. (16:3)

I MAKE plans, knowing the Lord guides my life. (16:9)

15:11 Hebrew *Sheol and Abaddon.* 15:24 Hebrew *Sheol.*

¹³The king is pleased with righteous lips; he loves those who speak honestly.

¹⁴The anger of the king is a deadly threat; the wise do what they can to appease it.

I USE DISCRETION when I speak and interact with political leaders. (16:14)

¹⁵When the king smiles, there is life; his favor refreshes like a gentle rain.

¹⁶How much better to get wisdom than gold, and understanding than silver!

¹⁷The path of the upright leads away from evil; whoever follows that path is safe.

¹⁸Pride goes before destruction, and haughtiness before a fall.

¹⁹It is better to live humbly with the poor than to share plunder with the proud.

²⁰Those who listen to instruction will prosper; those who trust the LORD will be happy.

I ENJOY the success and happiness that come from trusting and obeying the Lord. (16:20)

²¹The wise are known for their understanding, and instruction is appreciated if it's well presented.

²²Discretion is a life-giving fountain to those who possess it, but discipline is wasted on fools.

²³From a wise mind comes wise speech; the words of the wise are persuasive.

²⁴Kind words are like honey—sweet to the soul and healthy for the body.

I SPEAK kind words that benefit others. (16:24)

²⁵There is a path before each person that seems right, but it ends in death.

²⁶It is good for workers to have an appetite; an empty stomach drives them on.

²⁷Scoundrels hunt for scandal; their words are a destructive blaze.

I RECOGNIZE how much damage someone can inflict with scandalous words. (16:27)

²⁸A troublemaker plants seeds of strife; gossip separates the best of friends.

²⁹Violent people deceive their companions, leading them down a harmful path.

³⁰With narrowed eyes, they plot evil; without a word, they plan their mischief.

³¹Gray hair is a crown of glory; it is gained by living a godly life.

³²It is better to be patient than powerful; it is better to have self-control than to conquer a city.

I BELIEVE in the Lord, not in dumb luck. (16:33)

³³We may throw the dice, but the LORD determines how they fall.

CHAPTER 17

A dry crust eaten in peace is better than a great feast with strife.

²A wise slave will rule over the master's shameful sons and will share their inheritance.

³Fire tests the purity of silver and gold, but the LORD tests the heart.

⁴Wrongdoers listen to wicked talk; liars pay attention to destructive words.

⁵Those who mock the poor insult their Maker; those who rejoice at the misfortune of others will be punished.

⁶Grandchildren are the crowning glory of the aged; parents are the pride of their children.

I VALUE AND RESPECT the oldest members of my family. (17:6)

⁷Eloquent speech is not fitting for a fool; even less are lies fitting for a ruler.

⁸A bribe seems to work like magic for those who give it; they succeed in all they do.

⁹Disregarding another person's faults preserves love; telling about them separates close friends.

I DO NOT SEEK to find fault with those I love (1 Peter 4:8). (17:9)

¹⁰A single rebuke does more for a person of understanding than a hundred lashes on the back of a fool.

¹¹Evil people seek rebellion, but they will be severely punished.

¹²It is safer to meet a bear robbed of her cubs than to confront a fool caught in folly.

¹³If you repay evil for good, evil will never leave your house.

I NEVER REPAY evil for good. (17:13)

¹⁴Beginning a quarrel is like opening a floodgate, so drop the matter before a dispute breaks out.

¹⁵The LORD despises those who acquit the guilty and condemn the innocent.

¹⁶It is senseless to pay tuition to educate a fool who has no heart for wisdom.

I HELP loved ones in their times of need. (17:17)

¹⁷A friend is always loyal, and a brother is born to help in time of need.

¹⁸It is poor judgment to co-sign a friend's note, to become responsible for a neighbor's debts.

¹⁹Anyone who loves to quarrel loves sin; anyone who speaks boastfully* invites disaster.

²⁰The crooked heart will not prosper; the twisted tongue tumbles into trouble.

²¹It is painful to be the parent of a fool; there is no joy for the father of a rebel.

I NURTURE my health with a cheerful, positive attitude. (17:22)

²²A cheerful heart is good medicine, but a broken spirit saps a person's strength.

²³The wicked accept secret bribes to pervert justice.

²⁴Sensible people keep their eyes glued on wisdom, but a fool's eyes wander to the ends of the earth.

²⁵A foolish child* brings grief to a father and bitterness to a mother.

²⁶It is wrong to fine the godly for being good or to punish nobles for being honest!

I CHOOSE my words carefully. (17:27)

²⁷A truly wise person uses few words; a person with understanding is even-tempered.

²⁸Even fools are thought to be wise when they keep silent; when they keep their mouths shut, they seem intelligent.

CHAPTER 18

A recluse is self-indulgent, snarling at every sound principle of conduct.

²Fools have no interest in understanding; they only want to air their own opinions.

³When the wicked arrive, contempt, shame, and disgrace are sure to follow.

I SPEAK words that refresh others. (18:4)

⁴A person's words can be life-giving water; words of true wisdom are as refreshing as a bubbling brook.

⁵It is wrong for a judge to favor the guilty or condemn the innocent.

⁶Fools get into constant quarrels; they are asking for a beating.

⁷The mouths of fools are their ruin; their lips get them into trouble.

⁸What dainty morsels rumors are—but they sink deep into one's heart.

⁹A lazy person is as bad as someone who destroys things.

I PUT my trust in the strong name of the Lord. (18:10)

¹⁰The name of the LORD is a strong fortress; the godly run to him and are safe.

¹¹The rich think of their wealth as an impregnable defense; they imagine it is a high wall of safety.

¹²Haughtiness goes before destruction; humility precedes honor.

¹³What a shame, what folly, to give advice before listening to the facts!

I LISTEN to all the facts carefully before giving advice to others. (18:13)

¹⁴The human spirit can endure a sick body, but who can bear it if the spirit is crushed?

¹⁵Intelligent people are always open to new ideas. In fact, they look for them.

I AM EAGER to consider and test new ideas. (18:15)

¹⁶Giving a gift works wonders; it may bring you before important people!

¹⁷Any story sounds true until someone sets the record straight.

17:19 Or *who builds up defenses;* Hebrew reads *who makes a high gate.* **17:25** Hebrew *son.*

¹⁸Casting lots can end arguments and settle disputes between powerful opponents.

¹⁹It's harder to make amends with an offended friend than to capture a fortified city. Arguments separate friends like a gate locked with iron bars.

²⁰Words satisfy the soul as food satisfies the stomach; the right words on a person's lips bring satisfaction.

²¹Those who love to talk will experience the consequences, for the tongue can kill or nourish life.

²²The man who finds a wife finds a treasure and receives favor from the LORD.

²³The poor plead for mercy; the rich answer with insults.

²⁴There are "friends" who destroy each other, but a real friend sticks closer than a brother.

I AM LOYAL to my close friends. (18:24)

CHAPTER 19

It is better to be poor and honest than to be a fool and dishonest.

²Zeal without knowledge is not good; a person who moves too quickly may go the wrong way.

³People ruin their lives by their own foolishness and then are angry at the LORD.

⁴Wealth makes many "friends"; poverty drives them away.

⁵A false witness will not go unpunished, nor will a liar escape.

⁶Many beg favors from a prince; everyone is the friend of a person who gives gifts!

⁷If the relatives of the poor despise them, how much more will their friends avoid them. The poor call after them, but they are gone.

⁸To acquire wisdom is to love oneself; people who cherish understanding will prosper.

⁹A false witness will not go unpunished, and a liar will be destroyed.

¹⁰It isn't right for a fool to live in luxury or for a slave to rule over princes!

¹¹People with good sense restrain their anger; they earn esteem by overlooking wrongs.

¹²The king's anger is like a lion's roar, but his favor is like dew on the grass.

¹³A foolish child* is a calamity to a father; a nagging wife annoys like a constant dripping.

¹⁴Parents can provide their sons with an inheritance of houses and wealth, but only the LORD can give an understanding wife.

¹⁵A lazy person sleeps soundly—and goes hungry.

¹⁶Keep the commandments and keep your life; despising them leads to death.

¹⁷If you help the poor, you are lending to the LORD—and he will repay you!

¹⁸Discipline your children while there is hope. If you don't, you will ruin their lives.

¹⁹Short-tempered people must pay their own penalty. If you rescue them once, you will have to do it again.

²⁰Get all the advice and instruction you can, and be wise the rest of your life.

²¹You can make many plans, but the LORD's purpose will prevail.

²²Loyalty makes a person attractive. And it is better to be poor than dishonest.

²³Fear of the LORD gives life, security, and protection from harm.

²⁴Some people are so lazy that they won't even lift a finger to feed themselves.

I DO NOT BLAME the Lord for the consequences of my own foolish mistakes. (19:3)

I GAIN the respect of others by controlling my anger and overlooking wrongs. (19:11)

I BELIEVE helping the poor is the same as lending to the Lord—he is the one who will repay me! (2 Corinthians 9:6-10). (19:17)

I DISCIPLINE my children while I still have the opportunity to make a difference in their lives. (19:18)

I WORK HARD to provide for my own needs. (19:24)

19:13 Hebrew *son*; also in 19:27.

²⁵If you punish a mocker, the simpleminded will learn a lesson; if you reprove the wise, they will be all the wiser.

²⁶Children who mistreat their father or chase away their mother are a public disgrace and an embarrassment.

²⁷If you stop listening to instruction, my child, you have turned your back on knowledge.

²⁸A corrupt witness makes a mockery of justice; the mouth of the wicked gulps down evil.

²⁹Mockers will be punished, and the backs of fools will be beaten.

CHAPTER 20

Wine produces mockers; liquor leads to brawls. Whoever is led astray by drink cannot be wise.

²The king's fury is like a lion's roar; to rouse his anger is to risk your life.

³Avoiding a fight is a mark of honor; only fools insist on quarreling.

⁴If you are too lazy to plow in the right season, you will have no food at the harvest.

⁵Though good advice lies deep within a person's heart, the wise will draw it out.

⁶Many will say they are loyal friends, but who can find one who is really faithful?

⁷The godly walk with integrity; blessed are their children after them.

⁸When a king judges, he carefully weighs all the evidence, distinguishing the bad from the good.

⁹Who can say, "I have cleansed my heart; I am pure and free from sin"?

¹⁰The LORD despises double standards of every kind.

¹¹Even children are known by the way they act, whether their conduct is pure and right.

¹²Ears to hear and eyes to see—both are gifts from the LORD.

¹³If you love sleep, you will end in poverty. Keep your eyes open, and there will be plenty to eat!

¹⁴The buyer haggles over the price, saying, "It's worthless," then brags about getting a bargain!

¹⁵Wise speech is rarer and more valuable than gold and rubies.

¹⁶Be sure to get collateral from anyone who guarantees the debt of a stranger. Get a deposit if someone guarantees the debt of a foreigner.*

¹⁷Stolen bread tastes sweet, but it turns to gravel in the mouth.

¹⁸Plans succeed through good counsel; don't go to war without the advice of others.

¹⁹A gossip tells secrets, so don't hang around with someone who talks too much.

²⁰If you curse your father or mother, the lamp of your life will be snuffed out.

²¹An inheritance obtained early in life is not a blessing in the end.

²²Don't say, "I will get even for this wrong." Wait for the LORD to handle the matter.

²³The LORD despises double standards; he is not pleased by dishonest scales.

²⁴How can we understand the road we travel? It is the LORD who directs our steps.

²⁵It is dangerous to make a rash promise to God before counting the cost.

²⁶A wise king finds the wicked, lays them out like wheat, then runs the crushing wheel over them.

I RESPECT AND CARE FOR my parents. (19:26)

I AM NOT ASHAMED to avoid a fight or quarrel. (20:3)

I AM HONEST about my shortcomings and sins (1 John 1:8). (20:9)

I OBEY the Lord instead of partaking of the fleeting pleasures of sin (Hebrews 11:25). (20:17)

I LET the Lord handle matters when I feel like getting even. (20:22)

I DO NOT MAKE rash promises to God. (20:25)

20:16 An alternate reading in the Hebrew text is *the debt of an adulterous woman;* compare 27:13.

²⁷The LORD's searchlight penetrates the human spirit,* exposing every hidden motive.

²⁸Unfailing love and faithfulness protect the king; his throne is made secure through love.

²⁹The glory of the young is their strength; the gray hair of experience is the splendor of the old.

³⁰Physical punishment cleanses away evil;* such discipline purifies the heart.

I WILL USE my strength for the Lord when I am young and my experience for his glory when I am old. (20:29)

CHAPTER 21

The king's heart is like a stream of water directed by the LORD; he turns it wherever he pleases.

²People may think they are doing what is right, but the LORD examines the heart.

³The LORD is more pleased when we do what is just and right than when we give him sacrifices.

⁴Haughty eyes, a proud heart, and evil actions are all sin.

⁵Good planning and hard work lead to prosperity, but hasty shortcuts lead to poverty.

I SEEK to prosper by planning ahead and working hard. (21:5)

⁶Wealth created by lying is a vanishing mist and a deadly trap.*

⁷Because the wicked refuse to do what is just, their violence boomerangs and destroys them.

⁸The guilty walk a crooked path; the innocent travel a straight road.

⁹It is better to live alone in the corner of an attic than with a contentious wife in a lovely home.

¹⁰Evil people love to harm others; their neighbors get no mercy from them.

¹¹A simpleton can learn only by seeing mockers punished; a wise person learns from instruction.

I DO NOT MAKE my home a miserable place by arguing all the time. (21:9)

¹²The Righteous One* knows what is going on in the homes of the wicked; he will bring the wicked to disaster.

¹³Those who shut their ears to the cries of the poor will be ignored in their own time of need.

¹⁴A secret gift calms anger; a secret bribe pacifies fury.

¹⁵Justice is a joy to the godly, but it causes dismay among evildoers.

¹⁶The person who strays from common sense will end up in the company of the dead.

I REJOICE when justice is carried out. (21:15)

¹⁷Those who love pleasure become poor; wine and luxury are not the way to riches.

¹⁸Sometimes the wicked are punished to save the godly, and the treacherous for the upright.

I AVOID poverty by not overindulging in pleasure, luxuries, or wine. (21:17)

¹⁹It is better to live alone in the desert than with a crabby, complaining wife.

²⁰The wise have wealth and luxury, but fools spend whatever they get.

²¹Whoever pursues godliness and unfailing love will find life, godliness, and honor.

²²The wise conquer the city of the strong and level the fortress in which they trust.

²³If you keep your mouth shut, you will stay out of trouble.

I KNOW when to avoid trouble by keeping my mouth shut. (21:23)

²⁴Mockers are proud and haughty; they act with boundless arrogance.

²⁵The desires of lazy people will be their ruin, for their hands refuse to work. ²⁶They are always greedy for more, while the godly love to give!

²⁷God loathes the sacrifice of an evil person, especially when it is brought with ulterior motives.

I WORK HARD and generously share my wealth with others. (21:25)

20:27 Or *The human spirit is the LORD's searchlight.* 20:30 The meaning of the Hebrew is uncertain. 21:6 As in Greek version; Hebrew reads *mist for those who seek death.* 21:12 Or *The righteous man.*

²⁸A false witness will be cut off, but an attentive witness will be allowed to speak.

²⁹The wicked put up a bold front, but the upright proceed with care.

³⁰Human plans, no matter how wise or well advised, cannot stand against the LORD.

³¹The horses are prepared for battle, but the victory belongs to the LORD.

CHAPTER 22

Choose a good reputation over great riches, for being held in high esteem is better than having silver or gold.

²The rich and the poor have this in common: The LORD made them both.

³A prudent person foresees the danger ahead and takes precautions; the simpleton goes blindly on and suffers the consequences.

⁴True humility and fear of the LORD lead to riches, honor, and long life.

⁵The deceitful walk a thorny, treacherous road; whoever values life will stay away.

⁶Teach your children to choose the right path, and when they are older, they will remain upon it.

⁷Just as the rich rule the poor, so the borrower is servant to the lender.

⁸Those who plant seeds of injustice will harvest disaster, and their reign of terror will end.

⁹Blessed are those who are generous, because they feed the poor.

¹⁰Throw out the mocker, and fighting, quarrels, and insults will disappear.

¹¹Anyone who loves a pure heart and gracious speech is the king's friend.

¹²The LORD preserves knowledge, but he ruins the plans of the deceitful.

¹³The lazy person is full of excuses, saying, "If I go outside, I might meet a lion in the street and be killed!"

¹⁴The mouth of an immoral woman is a deep pit; those living under the LORD's displeasure will fall into it.

¹⁵A youngster's heart is filled with foolishness, but discipline will drive it away.

¹⁶A person who gets ahead by oppressing the poor or by showering gifts on the rich will end in poverty.

Thirty Sayings of the Wise

¹⁷Listen to the words of the wise; apply your heart to my instruction. ¹⁸For it is good to keep these sayings deep within yourself, always ready on your lips. ¹⁹I am teaching you today—yes, you—so you will trust in the LORD. ²⁰I have written thirty sayings for you, filled with advice and knowledge. ²¹In this way, you may know the truth and bring an accurate report to those who sent you.

²²Do not rob the poor because they are poor or exploit the needy in court. ²³For the LORD is their defender. He will injure anyone who injures them.

²⁴Keep away from angry, short-tempered people, ²⁵or you will learn to be like them and endanger your soul.

²⁶Do not co-sign another person's note or put up a guarantee for someone else's loan. ²⁷If you can't pay it, even your bed will be snatched from under you.

²⁸Do not steal your neighbor's property by moving the ancient boundary markers set up by your ancestors.

²⁹Do you see any truly competent workers? They will serve kings rather than ordinary people.

CHAPTER 23

When dining with a ruler, pay attention to what is put before you. ²If you are a big eater, put a knife to your throat, ³and don't desire all the delicacies—deception may be involved.

I TEACH my children to choose the right path. (22:6)

I AM NOT LAZY and full of excuses. (22:13)

I DISCIPLINE my children so they will outgrow their foolishness. (22:15)

I LISTEN to God's Word and apply his instructions to my life. (22:17)

I DO NOT BECOME friends with angry, impatient people. (22:24)

I DO NOT ENDANGER myself by co-signing someone else's loan. (22:26)

[4]Don't weary yourself trying to get rich. Why waste your time? [5]For riches can disappear as though they had the wings of a bird!

[6]Don't eat with people who are stingy; don't desire their delicacies. [7]"Eat and drink," they say, but they don't mean it. They are always thinking about how much it costs. [8]You will vomit up the delicious food they serve, and you will have to take back your words of appreciation for their "kindness."

[9]Don't waste your breath on fools, for they will despise the wisest advice.

[10]Don't steal the land of defenseless orphans by moving the ancient boundary markers, [11]for their Redeemer is strong. He himself will bring their charges against you.

[12]Commit yourself to instruction; attune your ears to hear words of knowledge.

[13]Don't fail to correct your children. They won't die if you spank them. [14]Physical discipline may well save them from death.*

[15]My child,* how I will rejoice if you become wise. [16]Yes, my heart will thrill when you speak what is right and just.

[17]Don't envy sinners, but always continue to fear the LORD. [18]For surely you have a future ahead of you; your hope will not be disappointed.

[19]My child, listen and be wise. Keep your heart on the right course. [20]Do not carouse with drunkards and gluttons, [21]for they are on their way to poverty. Too much sleep clothes a person with rags.

[22]Listen to your father, who gave you life, and don't despise your mother's experience when she is old. [23]Get the truth and don't ever sell it; also get wisdom, discipline, and discernment. [24]The father of godly children has cause for joy. What a pleasure it is to have wise children.* [25]So give your parents joy! May she who gave you birth be happy.

[26]O my son, give me your heart. May your eyes delight in my ways of wisdom. [27]A prostitute is a deep pit; an adulterous woman is treacherous.* [28]She hides and waits like a robber, looking for another victim who will be unfaithful to his wife.

[29]Who has anguish? Who has sorrow? Who is always fighting? Who is always complaining? Who has unnecessary bruises? Who has bloodshot eyes? [30]It is the one who spends long hours in the taverns, trying out new drinks. [31]Don't let the sparkle and smooth taste of wine deceive you. [32]For in the end it bites like a poisonous serpent; it stings like a viper. [33]You will see hallucinations, and you will say crazy things. [34]You will stagger like a sailor tossed at sea, clinging to a swaying mast. [35]And you will say, "They hit me, but I didn't feel it. I didn't even know it when they beat me up. When will I wake up so I can have another drink?"

CHAPTER 24

Don't envy evil people; don't desire their company. [2]For they spend their days plotting violence, and their words are always stirring up trouble.

[3]A house is built by wisdom and becomes strong through good sense. [4]Through knowledge its rooms are filled with all sorts of precious riches and valuables.

[5]A wise man is mightier than a strong man,* and a man of knowledge is more powerful than a strong man. [6]So don't go to war without wise guidance; victory depends on having many counselors.

[7]Wisdom is too much for a fool. When the leaders gather, the fool has nothing to say.

[8]A person who plans evil will get a reputation as a troublemaker. [9]The schemes of a fool are sinful; everyone despises a mocker.

[10]If you fail under pressure, your strength is not very great.

I DO NOT SPEND all my energy trying to get rich. (23:4)

I DO NOT WASTE my breath trying to teach those who refuse to listen. (23:9)

I DISCIPLINE AND CORRECT my children for their good. (23:13)

I LIVE to please the Lord and am not envious of sinful people. (23:17)

I LISTEN to godly teaching and bring joy to my parents. (23:24)

I ABHOR prostitution and adultery. (23:27)

I DO NOT LET alcohol consume my life. (23:29)

I ENRICH my home by growing in wisdom and knowledge. (24:3)

Recommit yourself to loving your neighbor as yourself.

23:14 Hebrew *from Sheol.*   23:15 Hebrew *My son;* also in 23:19.   23:24 Hebrew *a wise son.*   23:27 Hebrew *is a narrow well.*   24:5 As in Greek version; Hebrew reads *A wise man is strength.*

I DO whatever I can to rescue innocent people who are sentenced to death. (24:11)

I DO NOT GLOAT when my enemies get hurt (Matthew 5:44-45). (24:17)

I DO NOT ENVY wicked individuals, for their day of judgment is coming. (24:19)

I FEAR the Lord and respect those in leadership over me (1 Peter 2:17). (24:21)

[11]Rescue those who are unjustly sentenced to death; don't stand back and let them die. [12]Don't try to avoid responsibility by saying you didn't know about it. For God knows all hearts, and he sees you. He keeps watch over your soul, and he knows you knew! And he will judge all people according to what they have done.

[13]My child,* eat honey, for it is good, and the honeycomb is sweet to the taste. [14]In the same way, wisdom is sweet to your soul. If you find it, you will have a bright future, and your hopes will not be cut short.

[15]Do not lie in wait like an outlaw at the home of the godly. And don't raid the house where the godly live. [16]They may trip seven times, but each time they will rise again. But one calamity is enough to lay the wicked low.

[17]Do not rejoice when your enemies fall into trouble. Don't be happy when they stumble. [18]For the LORD will be displeased with you and will turn his anger away from them.

[19]Do not fret because of evildoers; don't envy the wicked. [20]For the evil have no future; their light will be snuffed out.

[21]My child, fear the LORD and the king, and don't associate with rebels. [22]For you will go down with them to sudden disaster. Who knows where the punishment from the LORD and the king will end?

More Sayings of the Wise

[23]Here are some further sayings of the wise:

It is wrong to show favoritism when passing judgment. [24]A judge who says to the wicked, "You are innocent," will be cursed by many people and denounced by the nations. [25]But blessings are showered on those who convict the guilty.

[26]It is an honor to receive an honest reply.

[27]Develop your business first before building your house.

[28]Do not testify spitefully against innocent neighbors; don't lie about them. [29]And don't say, "Now I can pay them back for all their meanness to me! I'll get even!"

[30]I walked by the field of a lazy person, the vineyard of one lacking sense. [31]I saw that it was overgrown with thorns. It was covered with weeds, and its walls were broken down. [32]Then, as I looked and thought about it, I learned this lesson: [33]A little extra sleep, a little more slumber, a little folding of the hands to rest—[34]and poverty will pounce on you like a bandit; scarcity will attack you like an armed robber.

I WORK HARD to make sure I can support my family. (24:27)

I WORK HARD to avoid financial ruin. (24:32)

CHAPTER 25

More Proverbs of Solomon

These are more proverbs of Solomon, collected by the advisers of King Hezekiah of Judah.

[2]It is God's privilege to conceal things and the king's privilege to discover them.

[3]No one can discover the height of heaven, the depth of the earth, or all that goes on in the king's mind!

[4]Remove the dross from silver, and the sterling will be ready for the silversmith. [5]Remove the wicked from the king's court, and his reign will be made secure by justice.

[6]Don't demand an audience with the king or push for a place among the great. [7]It is better to wait for an invitation than to be sent to the end of the line, publicly disgraced!

Just because you see something, [8]don't be in a hurry to go to court. You might go down before your neighbors in shameful defeat. [9]So discuss the

See the profiles for Solomon (page 753) and Hezekiah (page 825) at Proverbs 2:9 and Isaiah 37:1.

I DO NOT PUSH for a place among important people. (25:6)

I SEEK to resolve matters privately instead of rushing into court. (25:8)

24:13 Hebrew My son; also in 24:21.

matter with them privately. Don't tell anyone else, [10]or others may accuse you of gossip. Then you will never regain your good reputation.

[11]Timely advice is as lovely as golden apples in a silver basket.

[12]Valid criticism is as treasured by the one who heeds it as jewelry made from finest gold.

[13]Faithful messengers are as refreshing as snow in the heat of summer. They revive the spirit of their employer.

[14]A person who doesn't give a promised gift is like clouds and wind that don't bring rain.

[15]Patience can persuade a prince, and soft speech can crush strong opposition.

[16]Do you like honey? Don't eat too much of it, or it will make you sick!

[17]Don't visit your neighbors too often, or you will wear out your welcome.

[18]Telling lies about others is as harmful as hitting them with an ax, wounding them with a sword, or shooting them with a sharp arrow.

[19]Putting confidence in an unreliable person is like chewing with a toothache or walking on a broken foot.

[20]Singing cheerful songs to a person whose heart is heavy is as bad as stealing someone's jacket in cold weather or rubbing salt in a wound.

[21]If your enemies are hungry, give them food to eat. If they are thirsty, give them water to drink. [22]You will heap burning coals on their heads, and the LORD will reward you.

[23]As surely as a wind from the north brings rain, so a gossiping tongue causes anger!

[24]It is better to live alone in the corner of an attic than with a contentious wife in a lovely home.

[25]Good news from far away is like cold water to the thirsty.

[26]If the godly compromise with the wicked, it is like polluting a fountain or muddying a spring.

[27]Just as it is not good to eat too much honey, it is not good for people to think about all the honors they deserve.

[28]A person without self-control is as defenseless as a city with broken-down walls.

CHAPTER 26

Honor doesn't go with fools any more than snow with summer or rain with harvest.

[2]Like a fluttering sparrow or a darting swallow, an unfair curse will not land on its intended victim.

[3]Guide a horse with a whip, a donkey with a bridle, and a fool with a rod to his back!

[4]When arguing with fools, don't answer their foolish arguments, or you will become as foolish as they are.

[5]When arguing with fools, be sure to answer their foolish arguments, or they will become wise in their own estimation.

[6]Trusting a fool to convey a message is as foolish as cutting off one's feet or drinking poison!

[7]In the mouth of a fool, a proverb becomes as limp as a paralyzed leg.

[8]Honoring a fool is as foolish as tying a stone to a slingshot.

[9]A proverb in a fool's mouth is as dangerous as a thornbush brandished by a drunkard.

[10]An employer who hires a fool or a bystander is like an archer who shoots recklessly.

[11]As a dog returns to its vomit, so a fool repeats his folly.

[12]There is more hope for fools than for people who think they are wise.

I VALUE the beauty of well-timed advice. (25:11)

I DO NOT TAKE ADVANTAGE of the hospitality of others. (25:17)

I AM GENEROUS and kind to my enemies. (25:21)

I DO NOT FOCUS on the honor and appreciation I think I deserve. (25:27)

I TRY TO AVOID arguing with fools. (26:4)

I DO NOT THINK I am too smart to learn. (26:12)

¹³The lazy person is full of excuses, saying, "I can't go outside because there might be a lion on the road! Yes, I'm sure there's a lion out there!"

¹⁴As a door turns back and forth on its hinges, so the lazy person turns over in bed.

¹⁵Some people are so lazy that they won't lift a finger to feed themselves.

¹⁶Lazy people consider themselves smarter than seven wise counselors.

I DO NOT GET involved in other people's arguments. (26:17)

¹⁷Yanking a dog's ears is as foolish as interfering in someone else's argument.

¹⁸Just as damaging as a mad man shooting a lethal weapon ¹⁹is someone who lies to a friend and then says, "I was only joking."

²⁰Fire goes out for lack of fuel, and quarrels disappear when gossip stops.

²¹A quarrelsome person starts fights as easily as hot embers light charcoal or fire lights wood.

I AVOID gossip and rumors. (26:22)

²²What dainty morsels rumors are—but they sink deep into one's heart.

²³Smooth* words may hide a wicked heart, just as a pretty glaze covers a common clay pot.

²⁴People with hate in their hearts may sound pleasant enough, but don't believe them. ²⁵Though they pretend to be kind, their hearts are full of all kinds of evil. ²⁶While their hatred may be concealed by trickery, it will finally come to light for all to see.

I DO NOT HARM people with lies and flattery. (26:28)

²⁷If you set a trap for others, you will get caught in it yourself. If you roll a boulder down on others, it will roll back and crush you.

²⁸A lying tongue hates its victims, and flattery causes ruin.

CHAPTER **27**

Don't brag about tomorrow, since you don't know what the day will bring.

²Don't praise yourself; let others do it!

I DO NOT MAKE boastful assumptions about the future (James 4:13–16). (27:1)

³A stone is heavy and sand is weighty, but the resentment caused by a fool is heavier than both.

⁴Anger is cruel, and wrath is like a flood, but who can survive the destructiveness of jealousy?

⁵An open rebuke is better than hidden love!

I ACCEPT AND HEED the rebuke of a friend. (27:5)

⁶Wounds from a friend are better than many kisses from an enemy.

⁷Honey seems tasteless to a person who is full, but even bitter food tastes sweet to the hungry.

⁸A person who strays from home is like a bird that strays from its nest.

⁹The heartfelt counsel of a friend is as sweet as perfume and incense.

I VALUE AND GIVE heartfelt counsel. (27:9)

¹⁰Never abandon a friend—either yours or your father's. Then in your time of need, you won't have to ask your relatives for assistance. It is better to go to a neighbor than to a relative who lives far away.

¹¹My child,* how happy I will be if you turn out to be wise! Then I will be able to answer my critics.

¹²A prudent person foresees the danger ahead and takes precautions. The simpleton goes blindly on and suffers the consequences.

I LOOK AHEAD and prepare for the future. (27:12)

¹³Be sure to get collateral from anyone who guarantees the debt of a stranger. Get a deposit if someone guarantees the debt of an adulterous woman.

¹⁴If you shout a pleasant greeting to your neighbor too early in the morning, it will be counted as a curse!

¹⁵A nagging wife is as annoying as the constant dripping on a rainy day. ¹⁶Trying to stop her complaints is like trying to stop the wind or hold something with greased hands.

I DO NOT IRRITATE my family by constantly nagging and complaining. (27:15)

¹⁷As iron sharpens iron, a friend sharpens a friend.

26:23 As in Greek version; Hebrew reads *Burning*.   27:11 Hebrew *My son.*

¹⁸Workers who tend a fig tree are allowed to eat its fruit. In the same way, workers who protect their employer's interests will be rewarded.

¹⁹As a face is reflected in water, so the heart reflects the person.

²⁰Just as Death and Destruction* are never satisfied, so human desire is never satisfied.

²¹Fire tests the purity of silver and gold, but a person is tested by being praised.

²²You cannot separate fools from their foolishness, even though you grind them like grain with mortar and pestle.

²³Know the state of your flocks, and put your heart into caring for your herds, ²⁴for riches don't last forever, and the crown might not be secure for the next generation. ²⁵After the hay is harvested, the new crop appears, and the mountain grasses are gathered in, ²⁶your sheep will provide wool for clothing, and your goats will be sold for the price of a field. ²⁷And you will have enough goats' milk for you, your family, and your servants.

I PAY CLOSE ATTENTION to my business and financial affairs. (27:23)

CHAPTER 28

The wicked run away when no one is chasing them, but the godly are as bold as lions.

²When there is moral rot within a nation, its government topples easily. But with wise and knowledgeable leaders, there is stability.

³A poor person who oppresses the poor is like a pounding rain that destroys the crops.

⁴To reject the law is to praise the wicked; to obey the law is to fight them.

I RESPECT justice and obey the law. (28:4)

⁵Evil people don't understand justice, but those who follow the LORD understand completely.

⁶It is better to be poor and honest than rich and crooked.

⁷Young people who obey the law are wise; those who seek out worthless companions bring shame to their parents.

⁸A person who makes money by charging interest will lose it. It will end up in the hands of someone who is kind to the poor.

I DO NOT MAKE money by taking advantage of people in poverty. (28:8)

⁹The prayers of a person who ignores the law are despised.

¹⁰Those who lead the upright into sin will fall into their own trap, but the honest will inherit good things.

¹¹Rich people picture themselves as wise, but their real poverty is evident to the poor.

¹²When the godly succeed, everyone is glad. When the wicked take charge, people go into hiding.

¹³People who cover over their sins will not prosper. But if they confess and forsake them, they will receive mercy.

I CONFESS my sins and forsake them. (28:13)

¹⁴Blessed are those who have a tender conscience,* but the stubborn are headed for serious trouble.

I MAINTAIN a tender conscience. (28:14)

¹⁵A wicked ruler is as dangerous to the poor as a lion or bear attacking them.

¹⁶Only a stupid prince will oppress his people, but a king will have a long reign if he hates dishonesty and bribes.

¹⁷A murderer's tormented conscience will drive him into the grave. Don't protect him!

¹⁸The honest will be rescued from harm, but those who are crooked will be destroyed.

¹⁹Hard workers have plenty of food; playing around brings poverty.

²⁰The trustworthy will get a rich reward. But the person who wants to get rich quick will only get into trouble.

I WORK HARD and shun all get-rich-quick schemes. (28:20)

27:20 Hebrew *Sheol and Abaddon.* 28:14 Hebrew *those who fear.*

²¹Showing partiality is never good, yet some will do wrong for something as small as a piece of bread.

²²A greedy person tries to get rich quick, but it only leads to poverty.

²³In the end, people appreciate frankness more than flattery.

²⁴Robbing your parents and then saying, "What's wrong with that?" is as serious as committing murder.

²⁵Greed causes fighting; trusting the LORD leads to prosperity.

²⁶Trusting oneself is foolish, but those who walk in wisdom are safe.

²⁷Whoever gives to the poor will lack nothing. But a curse will come upon those who close their eyes to poverty.

²⁸When the wicked take charge, people hide. When the wicked meet disaster, the godly multiply.

CHAPTER 29

Whoever stubbornly refuses to accept criticism will suddenly be broken beyond repair.

²When the godly are in authority, the people rejoice. But when the wicked are in power, they groan.

³The man who loves wisdom brings joy to his father, but if he hangs around with prostitutes, his wealth is wasted.

⁴A just king gives stability to his nation, but one who demands bribes destroys it.

⁵To flatter people is to lay a trap for their feet.

⁶Evil people are trapped by sin, but the righteous escape, shouting for joy.

⁷The godly know the rights of the poor; the wicked don't care to know.

⁸Mockers can get a whole town agitated, but those who are wise will calm anger.

⁹If a wise person takes a fool to court, there will be ranting and ridicule but no satisfaction.

¹⁰The bloodthirsty hate the honest, but the upright seek out the honest.

¹¹A fool gives full vent to anger, but a wise person quietly holds it back.

¹²If a ruler honors liars, all his advisers will be wicked.

¹³The poor and the oppressor have this in common—the LORD gives light to the eyes of both.

¹⁴A king who is fair to the poor will have a long reign.

¹⁵To discipline and reprimand a child produces wisdom, but a mother is disgraced by an undisciplined child.

¹⁶When the wicked are in authority, sin increases. But the godly will live to see the tyrant's downfall.

¹⁷Discipline your children, and they will give you happiness and peace of mind.

¹⁸When people do not accept divine guidance, they run wild. But whoever obeys the law is happy.

¹⁹For a servant, mere words are not enough—discipline is needed. For the words may be understood, but they are not heeded.

²⁰There is more hope for a fool than for someone who speaks without thinking.

²¹A servant who is pampered from childhood will later become a rebel.

²²A hot-tempered person starts fights and gets into all kinds of sin.

²³Pride ends in humiliation, while humility brings honor.

²⁴If you assist a thief, you are only hurting yourself. You will be punished if you report the crime, but you will be cursed if you don't.

²⁵Fearing people is a dangerous trap, but to trust the LORD means safety.

²⁶Many seek the ruler's favor, but justice comes from the LORD.

²⁷The godly despise the wicked; the wicked despise the godly.

I TRUST the wisdom of others, not my own judgment. (28:26)

I ACCEPT criticism and learn from it. (29:1)

I PAY ATTENTION to and respect the rights of the poor. (29:7)

I DO NOT GIVE full vent to my anger. (29:11)

I DISCIPLINE my children and teach them to be wise. (29:15)

I THINK before speaking. (29:20)

I KNOW that justice ultimately comes from the Lord, not from people in leadership. (29:26)

CHAPTER **30**

The Sayings of Agur

The message of Agur son of Jakeh. An oracle.*

I am weary, O God; I am weary and worn out, O God.* ²I am too ignorant to be human, and I lack common sense. ³I have not mastered human wisdom, nor do I know the Holy One.

⁴Who but God goes up to heaven and comes back down? Who holds the wind in his fists? Who wraps up the oceans in his cloak? Who has created the whole wide world? What is his name—and his son's name? Tell me if you know!

⁵Every word of God proves true. He defends all who come to him for protection. ⁶Do not add to his words, or he may rebuke you, and you will be found a liar. ⁷O God, I beg two favors from you before I die. ⁸First, help me never to tell a lie. Second, give me neither poverty nor riches! Give me just enough to satisfy my needs. ⁹For if I grow rich, I may deny you and say, "Who is the LORD?" And if I am too poor, I may steal and thus insult God's holy name.

¹⁰Never slander a person to his employer. If you do, the person will curse you, and you will pay for it.

¹¹Some people curse their father and do not thank their mother. ¹²They feel pure, but they are filthy and unwashed. ¹³They are proud beyond description and disdainful. ¹⁴They devour the poor with teeth as sharp as swords or knives. They destroy the needy from the face of the earth.

¹⁵The leech has two suckers that cry out, "More, more!"* There are three other things—no, four!—that are never satisfied:

¹⁶ the grave,
the barren womb,
the thirsty desert,
the blazing fire.

¹⁷The eye that mocks a father and despises a mother will be plucked out by ravens of the valley and eaten by vultures.

¹⁸There are three things that amaze me—no, four things I do not understand:

¹⁹ how an eagle glides through the sky,
how a snake slithers on a rock,
how a ship navigates the ocean,
how a man loves a woman.

²⁰Equally amazing is how an adulterous woman can satisfy her sexual appetite, shrug her shoulders, and then say, "What's wrong with that?"

²¹There are three things that make the earth tremble—no, four it cannot endure:

²² a slave who becomes a king,
an overbearing fool who prospers,
²³ a bitter woman who finally gets a husband,
a servant girl who supplants her mistress.

²⁴There are four things on earth that are small but unusually wise:

²⁵ Ants—they aren't strong,
but they store up food for the winter.
²⁶ Rock badgers*—they aren't powerful,
but they make their homes among the rocky cliffs.
²⁷ Locusts—they have no king,
but they march like an army in ranks.

I BELIEVE every word of God is true. (30:5)

I DO NOT TRY to add to or change God's Word (Revelation 22:18). (30:6)

I ASK God to spare me from poverty and riches. (30:8)

I EXPRESS appreciation to my parents. (30:11)

I AM INTRIGUED by the wonders of nature and the mysteries of love. (30:18)

I SEE God's wisdom on display in even the most common of creatures. (30:24)

30:1a Or *son of Jakeh from Massa.*   30:1b The Hebrew can also be translated *The man declares this to Ithiel, to Ithiel and to Ucal.*   30:15 Hebrew *two daughters who cry out, "Give, give!"*   30:26 Or *coneys,* or *hyraxes.*

²⁸ Lizards—they are easy to catch,
but they are found even in kings' palaces.

²⁹There are three stately monarchs on the earth—no, four:
³⁰ the lion, king of animals, who won't turn aside for anything,
³¹ the strutting rooster,
the male goat,
a king as he leads his army.

³²If you have been a fool by being proud or plotting evil, don't brag about it—cover your mouth with your hand in shame.
³³As the beating of cream yields butter, and a blow to the nose causes bleeding, so anger causes quarrels.

CHAPTER 31

The Sayings of King Lemuel
These are the sayings of King Lemuel, an oracle* that his mother taught him.
²O my son, O son of my womb, O son of my promises, ³do not spend your strength on women, on those who ruin kings.
⁴And it is not for kings, O Lemuel, to guzzle wine. Rulers should not crave liquor. ⁵For if they drink, they may forget their duties and be unable to give justice to those who are oppressed. ⁶Liquor is for the dying, and wine for those in deep depression. ⁷Let them drink to forget their poverty and remember their troubles no more.
⁸Speak up for those who cannot speak for themselves; ensure justice for those who are perishing. ⁹Yes, speak up for the poor and helpless, and see that they get justice.

A Wife of Noble Character
¹⁰Who can find a virtuous and capable wife? She is worth more than precious rubies. ¹¹Her husband can trust her, and she will greatly enrich his life. ¹²She will not hinder him but help him all her life.
¹³She finds wool and flax and busily spins it. ¹⁴She is like a merchant's ship; she brings her food from afar. ¹⁵She gets up before dawn to prepare breakfast for her household and plan the day's work for her servant girls. ¹⁶She goes out to inspect a field and buys it; with her earnings she plants a vineyard.
¹⁷She is energetic and strong, a hard worker. ¹⁸She watches for bargains; her lights burn late into the night. ¹⁹Her hands are busy spinning thread, her fingers twisting fiber.
²⁰She extends a helping hand to the poor and opens her arms to the needy.
²¹She has no fear of winter for her household because all of them have warm* clothes. ²²She quilts her own bedspreads. She dresses like royalty in gowns of finest cloth.
²³Her husband is well known, for he sits in the council meeting with the other civic leaders.
²⁴She makes belted linen garments and sashes to sell to the merchants.
²⁵She is clothed with strength and dignity, and she laughs with no fear of the future. ²⁶When she speaks, her words are wise, and kindness is the rule when she gives instructions. ²⁷She carefully watches all that goes on in her household and does not have to bear the consequences of laziness.
²⁸Her children stand and bless her. Her husband praises her: ²⁹"There are many virtuous and capable women in the world, but you surpass them all!"
³⁰Charm is deceptive, and beauty does not last; but a woman who fears the LORD will be greatly praised. ³¹Reward her for all she has done. Let her deeds publicly declare her praise.

31:1 Or *of Lemuel, king of Massa.* 31:21 As in Greek version; Hebrew *scarlet.*

I DO NOT BRAG about doing something wrong. (30:32)

I DO NOT WASTE my strength on sexual immorality or drunkenness. (31:3)

I FIGHT for justice for those who cannot speak up for themselves. (31:8)

I WORK HARD to provide for the needs of my family. (31:15)

I MAKE wise financial investments. (31:16)

I REACH OUT to the poor and help them. (31:20)

I USE wise and kind words to speak to my loved ones. (31:26)

I PRAISE my loved ones who fear the Lord. (31:30)

ECCLESIASTES

THIS FOURTH BOOK of Hebrew poetry explores a nagging, age-old question: What is the meaning of life?

This *poetic essay*, probably written by Solomon about halfway through his reign as king of Israel, ponders the apparent meaninglessness of life "under the sun."

The phrase "under the sun" aptly describes Solomon's perspective through most of this book (1:1–12:12). He isn't looking at life as the Lord in heaven sees it but from the perspective of an immensely wise, fabulously wealthy, and politically powerful individual here on earth.

From his famed vantage point, Solomon concludes that everything is meaningless, "utterly meaningless!" (1:2; 12:8).

Nevertheless, throughout Ecclesiastes Solomon alludes to basic beliefs in God's justice, graciousness, sovereignty, omniscience, transcendence, revelation, mystery, creative power, and eternal nature.

Solomon wraps up the book by saying: "Here is my final conclusion: Fear God and obey his commands, for this is the duty of every person. God will judge us for everything we do, including every secret thing, whether good or bad" (12:13-14).

Solomon leaves it to the reader to decide who God is and how he reveals his commands. It's quite likely that Solomon simply assumed his readers were already well versed in the commands the Lord God in heaven had revealed to Moses and other prophets. It's also possible that Solomon may have distributed copies of this book to foreign visitors as a means of provoking their interest in the God of Israel.

Famous passages in Ecclesiastes include
- "Nothing under the sun is truly new" (1:9)
- "There is a time for everything . . ." (3:1-8)
- God "has planted eternity in the human heart" (3:11)
- Everyone should fear God (3:14; 5:7; 12:13)
- God will judge everyone (3:17; 11:9; 12:14)
- Two are better than one (4:9-12)
- Don't make rash promises to God (5:1-6)
- Think about the day of your death (7:1-4)
- God blesses those who fear him (7:18; 8:12-13)
- No one "is always good and never sins" (7:20)
- "Whatever you do, do well" (9:10)
- Wisdom helps you succeed (10:10)
- Don't forget your Creator (12:1)

CHAPTER 1

These are the words of the Teacher,* King David's son, who ruled in Jerusalem.

Everything Is Meaningless

²"Everything is meaningless," says the Teacher, "utterly meaningless!"

³What do people get for all their hard work? ⁴Generations come and go, but nothing really changes. ⁵The sun rises and sets and hurries around to rise again. ⁶The wind blows south and north, here and there, twisting back and forth, getting nowhere. ⁷The rivers run into the sea, but the sea is never full. Then the water returns again to the rivers and flows again to the sea. ⁸Everything is so weary and tiresome! No matter how much we see, we are never satisfied. No matter how much we hear, we are not content.

⁹History merely repeats itself. It has all been done before. Nothing under the sun is truly new. ¹⁰What can you point to that is new? How do you know it didn't already exist long ago? ¹¹We don't remember what happened in those former times. And in future generations, no one will remember what we are doing now.

The Futility of Wisdom

¹²I, the Teacher, was king of Israel, and I lived in Jerusalem. ¹³I devoted myself to search for understanding and to explore by wisdom everything being done in the world. I soon discovered that God has dealt a tragic existence to the human race. ¹⁴Everything under the sun is meaningless, like chasing the wind. ¹⁵What is wrong cannot be righted. What is missing cannot be recovered.

¹⁶I said to myself, "Look, I am wiser than any of the kings who ruled in Jerusalem before me. I have greater wisdom and knowledge than any of them." ¹⁷So I worked hard to distinguish wisdom from foolishness. But now I realize that even this was like chasing the wind. ¹⁸For the greater my wisdom, the greater my grief. To increase knowledge only increases sorrow.

CHAPTER 2

The Futility of Pleasure

I said to myself, "Come now, let's give pleasure a try. Let's look for the 'good things' in life." But I found that this, too, was meaningless. ²"It is silly to be laughing all the time," I said. "What good does it do to seek only pleasure?" ³After much thought, I decided to cheer myself with wine. While still seeking wisdom, I clutched at foolishness. In this way, I hoped to experience the only happiness most people find during their brief life in this world.

⁴I also tried to find meaning by building huge homes for myself and by planting beautiful vineyards. ⁵I made gardens and parks, filling them with all kinds of fruit trees. ⁶I built reservoirs to collect the water to irrigate my many flourishing groves. ⁷I bought slaves, both men and women, and others were born into my household. I also owned great herds and flocks, more than any of the kings who lived in Jerusalem before me. ⁸I collected great sums of silver and gold, the treasure of many kings and provinces. I hired wonderful singers, both men and women, and had many beautiful concubines. I had everything a man could desire!

⁹So I became greater than any of the kings who ruled in Jerusalem before me. And with it all, I remained clear-eyed so that I could evaluate all these things. ¹⁰Anything I wanted, I took. I did not restrain myself from any joy. I even found great pleasure in hard work, an additional reward for all my labors. ¹¹But as I looked at everything I had worked so hard to accomplish, it was all so meaningless. It was like chasing the wind. There was nothing really worthwhile anywhere.

1:1 Hebrew Koheleth; this term is rendered "the Teacher" throughout this book.

I BELIEVE life is utterly meaningless apart from knowing, worshiping, and obeying God (Ecclesiastes 12:13). (1:2)

I RECOGNIZE that nothing on earth will ever truly satisfy me. (1:8)

I DO NOT IGNORE the past; instead, I learn from the experiences of others. (1:9)

See Solomon's profile (page 753) at Proverbs 2:9.

I REALIZE that knowledge cannot eliminate sorrow—it may only increase one's grief. (1:18)

I HAVE DISCOVERED that the pursuit of pleasure is futile. (2:1)

I DO NOT SEEK my significance in life from my home, possessions, or wealth. (2:4)

See Solomon's profile (page 753) at Proverbs 2:9.

The Wise and the Foolish

¹²So I decided to compare wisdom and folly, and anyone else would come to the same conclusions I did. ¹³Wisdom is of more value than foolishness, just as light is better than darkness. ¹⁴For the wise person sees, while the fool is blind. Yet I saw that wise and foolish people share the same fate. ¹⁵Both of them die. Just as the fool will die, so will I. So of what value is all my wisdom? Then I said to myself, "This is all so meaningless!" ¹⁶For the wise person and the fool both die, and in the days to come, both will be forgotten.

> I VALUE wisdom, but I also know it will not shield me from dying one day. (2:14)

The Futility of Work

¹⁷So now I hate life because everything done here under the sun is so irrational. Everything is meaningless, like chasing the wind. ¹⁸I am disgusted that I must leave the fruits of my hard work to others. ¹⁹And who can tell whether my successors will be wise or foolish? And yet they will control everything I have gained by my skill and hard work. How meaningless!

> I REALIZE that life often doesn't make sense from a rational, human perspective. (2:17)

²⁰So I turned in despair from hard work. It was not the answer to my search for satisfaction in this life. ²¹For though I do my work with wisdom, knowledge, and skill, I must leave everything I gain to people who haven't worked to earn it. This is not only foolish but highly unfair. ²²So what do people get for all their hard work? ²³Their days of labor are filled with pain and grief; even at night they cannot rest. It is all utterly meaningless.

> I RECOGNIZE that the profits of hard work aren't lasting. (2:20)

²⁴So I decided there is nothing better than to enjoy food and drink and to find satisfaction in work. Then I realized that this pleasure is from the hand of God. ²⁵For who can eat or enjoy anything apart from him? ²⁶God gives wisdom, knowledge, and joy to those who please him. But if a sinner becomes wealthy, God takes the wealth away and gives it to those who please him. Even this, however, is meaningless, like chasing the wind.

> I THANK the Lord for the daily pleasures of life. (2:24)

CHAPTER 3

A Time for Everything

¹There is a time for everything,
a season for every activity under heaven.
²A time to be born and a time to die.
A time to plant and a time to harvest.
³A time to kill and a time to heal.
A time to tear down and a time to rebuild.
⁴A time to cry and a time to laugh.
A time to grieve and a time to dance.
⁵A time to scatter stones and a time to gather stones.
A time to embrace and a time to turn away.
⁶A time to search and a time to lose.
A time to keep and a time to throw away.
⁷A time to tear and a time to mend.
A time to be quiet and a time to speak up.
⁸A time to love and a time to hate.
A time for war and a time for peace.

> I BELIEVE God has appointed a time for everything. (3:1)
>
> I BELIEVE there is a time to be born and a time to die. (3:2)

⁹What do people really get for all their hard work? ¹⁰I have thought about this in connection with the various kinds of work God has given people to do. ¹¹God has made everything beautiful for its own time. He has planted eternity in the human heart, but even so, people cannot see the whole scope of God's work from beginning to end. ¹²So I concluded that there is nothing better for people than to be happy and to enjoy themselves as long as they can. ¹³And people should eat and drink and enjoy the fruits of their labor, for these are gifts from God.

> I BELIEVE God has planted eternity in the human heart. (3:11)

¹⁴And I know that whatever God does is final. Nothing can be added to it or taken from it. God's purpose in this is that people should fear him.

> I FEAR the Lord and accept his sovereignty over time and eternity. (3:14)

[15]Whatever exists today and whatever will exist in the future has already existed in the past. For God calls each event back in its turn.*

The Injustices of Life

[16]I also noticed that throughout the world there is evil in the courtroom. Yes, even the courts of law are corrupt! [17]I said to myself, "In due season God will judge everyone, both good and bad, for all their deeds."

[18]Then I realized that God allows people to continue in their sinful ways so he can test them. That way, they can see for themselves that they are no better than animals. [19]For humans and animals both breathe the same air,* and both die. So people have no real advantage over the animals. How meaningless! [20]Both go to the same place—the dust from which they came and to which they must return. [21]For who can prove that the human spirit goes upward and the spirit of animals goes downward into the earth? [22]So I saw that there is nothing better for people than to be happy in their work. That is why they are here! No one will bring them back from death to enjoy life in the future.

I BELIEVE that in due time God will judge everyone, both good and bad (2 Corinthians 5:10). (3:17)

CHAPTER 4

Again I observed all the oppression that takes place in our world. I saw the tears of the oppressed, with no one to comfort them. The oppressors have great power, and the victims are helpless. [2]So I concluded that the dead are better off than the living. [3]And most fortunate of all are those who were never born. For they have never seen all the evil that is done in our world.

I DO NOT TURN a blind eye to the oppression and suffering of others. (4:1)

[4]Then I observed that most people are motivated to success by their envy of their neighbors. But this, too, is meaningless, like chasing the wind.

[5]Foolish people refuse to work and almost starve. [6]They feel it is better to be lazy and barely survive than to work hard, especially when in the long run everything is so futile.

The Advantages of Companionship

[7]I observed yet another example of meaninglessness in our world. [8]This is the case of a man who is all alone, without a child or a brother, yet who works hard to gain as much wealth as he can. But then he asks himself, "Who am I working for? Why am I giving up so much pleasure now?" It is all so meaningless and depressing.

I DO NOT POUR my life into the acquisition of wealth. (4:8)

[9]Two people can accomplish more than twice as much as one; they get a better return for their labor. [10]If one person falls, the other can reach out and help. But people who are alone when they fall are in real trouble. [11]And on a cold night, two under the same blanket can gain warmth from each other. But how can one be warm alone? [12]A person standing alone can be attacked and defeated, but two can stand back-to-back and conquer. Three are even better, for a triple-braided cord is not easily broken.

I PLACE great value on teamwork. (4:10)

The Futility of Political Power

[13]It is better to be a poor but wise youth than to be an old and foolish king who refuses all advice. [14]Such a youth could come from prison and succeed. He might even become king, though he was born in poverty. [15]Everyone is eager to help such a youth, even to help him take the throne. [16]He might become the leader of millions and be very popular. But then the next generation grows up and rejects him! So again, it is all meaningless, like chasing the wind.

I WOULD RATHER BE poor, young, and wise than rich, old, and foolish. (4:13)

CHAPTER 5

The Importance of Fearing God

As you enter the house of God, keep your ears open and your mouth shut! Don't be a fool who doesn't realize that mindless offerings to God are evil.

3:15 Hebrew For God calls the past to account.   3:19 Or both have the same spirit.

[2]And don't make rash promises to God, for he is in heaven, and you are only here on earth. So let your words be few.

[3]Just as being too busy gives you nightmares, being a fool makes you a blabbermouth.

[4]So when you make a promise to God, don't delay in following through, for God takes no pleasure in fools. Keep all the promises you make to him. [5]It is better to say nothing than to promise something that you don't follow through on. [6]In such cases, your mouth is making you sin. And don't defend yourself by telling the Temple messenger that the promise you made was a mistake. That would make God angry, and he might wipe out everything you have achieved.

[7]Dreaming all the time instead of working is foolishness. And there is ruin in a flood of empty words. Fear God instead.

The Futility of Wealth

[8]If you see a poor person being oppressed by the powerful and justice being miscarried throughout the land, don't be surprised! For every official is under orders from higher up, and matters of justice only get lost in red tape and bureaucracy. [9]Even the king milks the land for his own profit!*

[10]Those who love money will never have enough. How absurd to think that wealth brings true happiness! [11]The more you have, the more people come to help you spend it. So what is the advantage of wealth—except perhaps to watch it run through your fingers!

[12]People who work hard sleep well, whether they eat little or much. But the rich are always worrying and seldom get a good night's sleep.

[13]There is another serious problem I have seen in the world. Riches are sometimes hoarded to the harm of the saver, [14]or they are put into risky investments that turn sour, and everything is lost. In the end, there is nothing left to pass on to one's children. [15]People who live only for wealth come to the end of their lives as naked and empty-handed as on the day they were born.

[16]And this, too, is a very serious problem. As people come into this world, so they depart. All their hard work is for nothing. They have been working for the wind, and everything will be swept away. [17]Throughout their lives, they live under a cloud—frustrated, discouraged, and angry.

[18]Even so, I have noticed one thing, at least, that is good. It is good for people to eat well, drink a good glass of wine, and enjoy their work—whatever they do under the sun—for however long God lets them live. [19]And it is a good thing to receive wealth from God and the good health to enjoy it. To enjoy your work and accept your lot in life—that is indeed a gift from God. [20]People who do this rarely look with sorrow on the past, for God has given them reasons for joy.

CHAPTER 6

There is another serious tragedy I have seen in our world. [2]God gives great wealth and honor to some people and gives them everything they could ever want, but then he doesn't give them the health to enjoy it. They die, and others get it all! This is meaningless—a sickening tragedy.

[3]A man might have a hundred children and live to be very old. But if he finds no satisfaction in life and in the end does not even get a decent burial, I say he would have been better off born dead. [4]I realize that his birth would have been meaningless and ended in darkness. He wouldn't even have had a name, [5]and he would never have seen the sun or known of its existence. Yet he would have had more peace than he has in growing up to be an unhappy

5:9 The meaning of the Hebrew is uncertain.

I DO NOT MAKE rash promises to God. (5:2)

I AM GRIEVED but not surprised by the injustices that occur in my city or nation. (5:8)

I ENJOY the satisfaction of working hard and not having to worry about having too many possessions. (5:12)

I DO NOT LIVE under a cloud—frustrated, discouraged, and angry. (5:17)

I DO NOT WASTE my life being an unhappy person. (6:5)

man. [6]He might live a thousand years twice over but not find contentment. And since he must die like everyone else—well, what's the use?

[7]All people spend their lives scratching for food, but they never seem to have enough. [8]Considering this, do wise people really have any advantage over fools? Do poor people gain anything by being wise and knowing how to act in front of others?

[9]Enjoy what you have rather than desiring what you don't have. Just dreaming about nice things is meaningless; it is like chasing the wind.

The Future—Determined and Unknown
[10]Everything has already been decided. It was known long ago what each person would be. So there's no use arguing with God about your destiny.

[11]The more words you speak, the less they mean. So why overdo it?

[12]In the few days of our empty lives, who knows how our days can best be spent? And who can tell what will happen in the future after we are gone?

CHAPTER 7
Wisdom for Life
A good reputation is more valuable than the most expensive perfume. In the same way, the day you die is better than the day you are born.

[2]It is better to spend your time at funerals than at festivals. For you are going to die, and you should think about it while there is still time.

[3]Sorrow is better than laughter, for sadness has a refining influence on us.

[4]A wise person thinks much about death, while the fool thinks only about having a good time now.

[5]It is better to be criticized by a wise person than to be praised by a fool! [6]Indeed, a fool's laughter is quickly gone, like thorns crackling in a fire. This also is meaningless.

[7]Extortion turns wise people into fools, and bribes corrupt the heart.

[8]Finishing is better than starting. Patience is better than pride.

[9]Don't be quick-tempered, for anger is the friend of fools.

[10]Don't long for "the good old days," for you don't know whether they were any better than today.

[11]Being wise is as good as being rich; in fact, it is better. [12]Wisdom or money can get you almost anything, but it's important to know that only wisdom can save your life.

[13]Notice the way God does things; then fall into line. Don't fight the ways of God, for who can straighten out what he has made crooked?

[14]Enjoy prosperity while you can. But when hard times strike, realize that both come from God. That way you will realize that nothing is certain in this life.

The Limits of Human Wisdom
[15]In this meaningless life, I have seen everything, including the fact that some good people die young and some wicked people live on and on. [16]So don't be too good or too wise! Why destroy yourself? [17]On the other hand, don't be too wicked either—don't be a fool! Why should you die before your time? [18]So try to walk a middle course—but those who fear God will succeed either way.

[19]A wise person is stronger than the ten leading citizens of a town!

[20]There is not a single person in all the earth who is always good and never sins.

[21]Don't eavesdrop on others—you may hear your servant laughing at you. [22]For you know how often you yourself have laughed at others.

[23]All along I have tried my best to let wisdom guide my thoughts and actions. I said to myself, "I am determined to be wise." But it didn't really work. [24]Wisdom is always distant and very difficult to find. [25]I searched everywhere,

I ENJOY what God gives me instead of wasting my time wishing I had something else. (6:9)

I TAKE time to consider the outcome and end of my life. (7:2)

I VALUE the criticism of a wise person but ignore the flattery of fools. (7:5)

I DO NOT LONG for "the good old days." (7:10)

I RECOGNIZE that life is unpredictable. (7:15)

I KNOW that no one on earth is perfect and without sin (Romans 3:23). (7:20)

determined to find wisdom and to understand the reason for things. I was determined to prove to myself that wickedness is stupid and that foolishness is madness.

²⁶I discovered that a seductive woman is more bitter than death. Her passion is a trap, and her soft hands will bind you. Those who please God will escape from her, but sinners will be caught in her snare.

I FLEE from anyone who is seductive. (7:26)

²⁷"This is my conclusion," says the Teacher. "I came to this result after looking into the matter from every possible angle. ²⁸Just one out of every thousand men I interviewed can be said to be upright, but not one woman! ²⁹I discovered that God created people to be upright, but they have each turned to follow their own downward path."

CHAPTER 8

How wonderful to be wise, to be able to analyze and interpret things. Wisdom lights up a person's face, softening its hardness.

Obedience to the King

²Obey the king because you have vowed before God to do this. ³Don't try to avoid doing your duty, and don't take a stand with those who plot evil. For the king will punish those who disobey him. ⁴The king's command is backed by great power. No one can resist or question it. ⁵Those who obey him will not be punished. Those who are wise will find a time and a way to do what is right. ⁶Yes, there is a time and a way for everything, even as people's troubles lie heavily upon them.

⁷Indeed, how can people avoid what they don't know is going to happen? ⁸None of us can hold back our spirit from departing. None of us has the power to prevent the day of our death. There is no escaping that obligation, that dark battle. And in the face of death, wickedness will certainly not rescue those who practice it.

I KNOW that no one can escape the reality of death. (8:8)

The Wicked and the Righteous

⁹I have thought deeply about all that goes on here in the world, where people have the power to hurt each other. ¹⁰I have seen wicked people buried with honor. How strange that they were the very ones who frequented the Temple and are praised* in the very city where they committed their crimes! ¹¹When a crime is not punished, people feel it is safe to do wrong. ¹²But even though a person sins a hundred times and still lives a long time, I know that those who fear God will be better off. ¹³The wicked will never live long, good lives, for they do not fear God. Their days will never grow long like the evening shadows.

I KNOW some wicked people go their whole lives without getting the punishment they deserve. (8:10)

¹⁴And this is not all that is meaningless in our world. In this life, good people are often treated as though they were wicked, and wicked people are often treated as though they were good. This is so meaningless!

¹⁵So I recommend having fun, because there is nothing better for people to do in this world than to eat, drink, and enjoy life. That way they will experience some happiness along with all the hard work God gives them.

I THANK the Lord for the daily pleasures of life. (8:15)

¹⁶In my search for wisdom, I tried to observe everything that goes on all across the earth. I discovered that there is ceaseless activity, day and night. ¹⁷This reminded me that no one can discover everything God has created in our world, no matter how hard they work at it. Not even the wisest people know everything, even if they say they do.

CHAPTER 9

Death Comes to All

This, too, I carefully explored: Even though the actions of godly and wise people are in God's hands, no one knows whether or not God will show

8:10 As in some Hebrew manuscripts and Greek version; many Hebrew manuscripts read *and are forgotten.*

them favor in this life. ²The same destiny ultimately awaits everyone, whether they are righteous or wicked, good or bad,* ceremonially clean or unclean, religious or irreligious. Good people receive the same treatment as sinners, and people who take oaths are treated like people who don't.

³It seems so tragic that one fate comes to all. That is why people are not more careful to be good. Instead, they choose their own mad course, for they have no hope. There is nothing ahead but death anyway. ⁴There is hope only for the living. For as they say, "It is better to be a live dog than a dead lion!"

⁵The living at least know they will die, but the dead know nothing. They have no further reward, nor are they remembered. ⁶Whatever they did in their lifetime—loving, hating, envying—is all long gone. They no longer have a part in anything here on earth. ⁷So go ahead. Eat your food and drink your wine with a happy heart, for God approves of this! ⁸Wear fine clothes, with a dash of cologne!

⁹Live happily with the woman you love through all the meaningless days of life that God has given you in this world. The wife God gives you is your reward for all your earthly toil. ¹⁰Whatever you do, do well. For when you go to the grave, there will be no work or planning or knowledge or wisdom.

¹¹I have observed something else in this world of ours. The fastest runner doesn't always win the race, and the strongest warrior doesn't always win the battle. The wise are often poor, and the skillful are not necessarily wealthy. And those who are educated don't always lead successful lives. It is all decided by chance, by being at the right place at the right time.

¹²People can never predict when hard times might come. Like fish in a net or birds in a snare, people are often caught by sudden tragedy.

Thoughts on Wisdom and Folly

¹³Here is another bit of wisdom that has impressed me as I have watched the way our world works. ¹⁴There was a small town with only a few people living in it, and a great king came with his army and besieged it. ¹⁵There was a poor, wise man living there who knew how to save the town, and so it was rescued. But afterward no one thought any more about him. ¹⁶Then I realized that though wisdom is better than strength, those who are wise will be despised if they are poor. What they say will not be appreciated for long. ¹⁷But even so, the quiet words of a wise person are better than the shouts of a foolish king. ¹⁸A wise person can overcome weapons of war, but one sinner can destroy much that is good.

CHAPTER 10

Dead flies will cause even a bottle of perfume to stink! Yes, an ounce of foolishness can outweigh a pound of wisdom and honor.

²The hearts of the wise lead them to do right, and the hearts of the foolish lead them to do evil. ³You can identify fools just by the way they walk down the street!

⁴If your boss is angry with you, don't quit! A quiet spirit can overcome even great mistakes.

⁵There is another evil I have seen as I have watched the world go by. Kings and rulers make a grave mistake ⁶if they give foolish people great authority, and if they fail to give people of proven worth their rightful place of dignity. ⁷I have even seen servants riding like princes—and princes walking like servants.

⁸When you dig a well, you may fall in. When you demolish an old wall, you could be bitten by a snake. ⁹When you work in a quarry, stones might fall and crush you! When you chop wood, there is danger with each stroke of your ax! Such are the risks of life.

I PLEASE God when I enjoy every happiness he gives me during the short time I'm alive on this earth. (9:7)

I TAKE advantage of every opportunity God gives me. (9:10)

I DO NOT EXPECT life to be fair. (9:11)

I AM NOT SURPRISED when tragedy strikes. (9:12)

I SEEK to be wise in all things large and small. (10:1)

I DO NOT GIVE UP when I make a big mistake. (10:4)

I RECOGNIZE that every endeavor has inherent risks. (10:8)

9:2 As in Greek and Syriac versions, and Latin Vulgate; Hebrew lacks *or bad*.

¹⁰Since a dull ax requires great strength, sharpen the blade. That's the value of wisdom; it helps you succeed.

¹¹It does no good to charm a snake after it has bitten you.

¹²It is pleasant to listen to wise words, but the speech of fools brings them to ruin.

¹³Since fools base their thoughts on foolish premises, their conclusions will be wicked madness.

¹⁴Foolish people claim to know all about the future and tell everyone the details! But who can really know what is going to happen?

> I DO NOT LISTEN to fools who claim to know all about the future. (10:14)

¹⁵Fools are so exhausted by a little work that they have no strength for even the simplest tasks.

¹⁶Destruction is certain for the land whose king is a child* and whose leaders feast in the morning. ¹⁷Happy is the land whose king is a nobleman and whose leaders feast only to gain strength for their work, not to get drunk.

¹⁸Laziness lets the roof leak, and soon the rafters begin to rot.

¹⁹A party gives laughter, and wine gives happiness, and money gives everything!

²⁰Never make light of the king, even in your thoughts. And don't make fun of a rich man, either. A little bird may tell them what you have said.

CHAPTER 11

Generosity and Diligence

Give generously, for your gifts will return to you later.* ²Divide your gifts among many, for you do not know what risks might lie ahead.

> I SHARE my money generously and invest it broadly. (11:1)

³When the clouds are heavy, the rains come down.

When a tree falls, whether south or north, there it lies.

⁴If you wait for perfect conditions, you will never get anything done.

> I DO NOT PROCRASTINATE, for I realize that conditions never will be perfect. (11:4)

⁵God's ways are as hard to discern as the pathways of the wind, and as mysterious as a tiny baby being formed in a mother's womb.

⁶Be sure to stay busy and plant a variety of crops, for you never know which will grow—perhaps they all will.

Advice for Old and Young

⁷Light is sweet; it's wonderful to see the sun! ⁸When people live to be very old, let them rejoice in every day of life. But let them also remember that the dark days will be many. Everything still to come is meaningless.

⁹Young man, it's wonderful to be young! Enjoy every minute of it. Do everything you want to do; take it all in. But remember that you must give an account to God for everything you do. ¹⁰So banish grief and pain, but remember that youth, with a whole life before it, still faces the threat of meaninglessness.

CHAPTER 12

Don't let the excitement of youth cause you to forget your Creator. Honor him in your youth before you grow old and no longer enjoy living. ²It will be too late then to remember him, when the light of the sun and moon and stars is dim to your old eyes, and there is no silver lining left among the clouds. ³Your limbs will tremble with age, and your strong legs will grow weak. Your teeth will be too few to do their work, and you will be blind, too. ⁴And when your teeth are gone, keep your lips tightly closed when you eat! Even the chirping of birds will wake you up. But you yourself will be deaf and tuneless, with a quavering voice. ⁵You will be afraid of heights and of falling, white-haired and withered, dragging along without any sexual desire. You

> I DO NOT PUT OFF knowing, worshiping, and obeying God. (12:1)

> I RECOGNIZE that as I grow older I have less strength to enjoy life and live for God. (12:3)

10:16 Or *whose king is a servant.* 11:1 Hebrew *Throw your bread on the waters, for after many days you will find it again.*

will be standing at death's door. And as you near your everlasting home, the mourners will walk along the streets.

⁶Yes, remember your Creator now while you are young, before the silver cord of life snaps and the golden bowl is broken. Don't wait until the water jar is smashed at the spring and the pulley is broken at the well. ⁷For then the dust will return to the earth, and the spirit will return to God who gave it.

⁸"All is meaningless," says the Teacher, "utterly meaningless."

Concluding Thoughts

⁹Because the Teacher was wise, he taught the people everything he knew. He collected proverbs and classified them. ¹⁰Indeed, the Teacher taught the plain truth, and he did so in an interesting way.

¹¹A wise teacher's words spur students to action and emphasize important truths. The collected sayings of the wise are like guidance from a shepherd.

¹²But, my child,* be warned: There is no end of opinions ready to be expressed. Studying them can go on forever and become very exhausting!

¹³Here is my final conclusion: Fear God and obey his commands, for this is the duty of every person. ¹⁴God will judge us for everything we do, including every secret thing, whether good or bad.

12:12 Hebrew *my son.*

See Solomon's profile (page 753) at Proverbs 2:9.

I BELIEVE my duty in life is to fear God and obey his commands. (12:13)

SONG OF SONGS

THIS FIFTH BOOK of Hebrew poetry is a *passionate duet.*

As with the book of Ecclesiastes, you won't find much formal theology in the Song of Songs. Instead, from start to finish (chapters 1–8), this poem celebrates the joys of marital love.

Interwoven with the sensuous lyrics of a young man and woman, we also occasionally hear a few lines from a chorus of young women and, toward the end, four brief lines from the young woman's brothers.

Over the millennia, the Jewish people have publicly read this "song of songs" during their first and greatest festival of the year, Passover.

Although this duet isn't an allegory, per se, many believe it pictures something of the Lord's great love for his people.

Famous verses in Song of Songs include

- ○ "How beautiful you are, my beloved" (1:15; 4:1; see 4:7; 7:6)
- ○ "I am the rose of Sharon" (2:1)
- ○ "He brings me to the banquet hall" (2:4)
- ○ "His left hand is under my head" (2:6; see 8:3)
- ○ Don't "awaken love until the time is right" (2:7; 3:5; 8:4)
- ○ "Rise up, my beloved . . . and come away" (2:10; see 2:13)
- ○ "Catch all the little foxes" (2:15)
- ○ "My lover is . . . better than ten thousand others!" (5:10)
- ○ "I am my lover's" (6:3; 7:10)
- ○ "For love is as strong as death" (8:6)
- ○ "Come quickly, my love!" (8:14)

CHAPTER 1

This is Solomon's song of songs, more wonderful than any other.

Young Woman: * ²"Kiss me again and again, for your love is sweeter than wine. ³How fragrant your cologne, and how pleasing your name! No wonder all the young women love you! ⁴Take me with you. Come, let's run! Bring me into your bedroom, O my king.* "

Young Women of Jerusalem: "How happy we are for him! We praise his love even more than wine."

Young Woman: "How right that the young women love you!

⁵"I am dark and beautiful, O women of Jerusalem, tanned as the dark tents of Kedar. Yes, even as the tents of Solomon!

⁶"Don't look down on me, you fair city girls, just because my complexion is so dark. The sun has burned my skin. My brothers were

See Solomon's profile (page 753) at Proverbs 2:9.

I AM NOT DISHEARTENED if my appearance doesn't conform to some of the world's changing standards for beauty. (1:6)

1:1 The headings identifying the speakers are not in the original text, though the Hebrew usually gives clues by means of the gender of the person speaking.   1:4 Or *The king has brought me into his bedroom.*

angry with me and sent me out to tend the vineyards in the hot sun. Now see what it has done to me!*

⁷"Tell me, O my love, where are you leading your flock today? Where will you rest your sheep at noon? For why should I wander like a prostitute* among the flocks of your companions?"

Young Man: ⁸"If you don't know, O most beautiful woman, follow the trail of my flock to the shepherds' tents, and there feed your young goats. ⁹What a lovely filly you are, my beloved one!* ¹⁰How lovely are your cheeks, with your earrings setting them afire! How stately is your neck, accented with a long string of jewels. ¹¹We will make earrings of gold for you and beads of silver."

Young Woman: ¹²"The king is lying on his couch, enchanted by the fragrance of my perfume. ¹³My lover is like a sachet of myrrh lying between my breasts. ¹⁴He is like a bouquet of flowers in the gardens of En-gedi."

Young Man: ¹⁵"How beautiful you are, my beloved, how beautiful! Your eyes are soft like doves."

Young Woman: ¹⁶"What a lovely, pleasant sight you are, my love, as we lie here on the grass, ¹⁷shaded by cedar trees and spreading firs."

CHAPTER 2

Young Woman: "I am the rose of Sharon, the lily of the valley."

Young Man: ²"Yes, compared to other women, my beloved is like a lily among thorns."

Young Woman: ³"And compared to other youths, my lover is like the finest apple tree in the orchard. I am seated in his delightful shade, and his fruit is delicious to eat. ⁴He brings me to the banquet hall, so everyone can see how much he loves me. ⁵Oh, feed me with your love—your 'raisins' and your 'apples'—for I am utterly lovesick! ⁶His left hand is under my head, and his right hand embraces me.

⁷"Promise me, O women of Jerusalem, by the swift gazelles and the deer of the wild, not to awaken love until the time is right.*

⁸"Ah, I hear him—my lover! Here he comes, leaping on the mountains and bounding over the hills. ⁹My lover is like a swift gazelle or a young deer. Look, there he is behind the wall! Now he is looking in through the window, gazing into the room.

¹⁰"My lover said to me, 'Rise up, my beloved, my fair one, and come away. ¹¹For the winter is past, and the rain is over and gone. ¹²The flowers are springing up, and the time of singing birds has come, even the cooing of turtledoves. ¹³The fig trees are budding, and the grapevines are in blossom. How delicious they smell! Yes, spring is here! Arise, my beloved, my fair one, and come away.' "

Young Man: ¹⁴"My dove is hiding behind some rocks, behind an outcrop on the cliff. Let me see you; let me hear your voice. For your voice is pleasant, and you are lovely."

Young Women of Jerusalem: ¹⁵"Quick! Catch all the little foxes before they ruin the vineyard of your love, for the grapevines are all in blossom."

Young Woman: ¹⁶"My lover is mine, and I am his. He feeds among the lilies! ¹⁷Before the dawn comes and the shadows flee away, come back to me, my love. Run like a gazelle or a young stag on the rugged mountains.*"

CHAPTER 3

Young Woman: "One night as I lay in bed, I yearned deeply for my lover, but he did not come. ²So I said to myself, 'I will get up now and roam

---

I TELL my wife how beautiful she is. (1:15)

I TELL my husband how much I enjoy looking at him. (1:16)

I KNOW how valuable I am. (2:1)

I PRIZE my wife over all other women. (2:2)

I PRIZE my husband over all other men. (2:3)

I PROTECT my marriage relationship. (2:15)

I LONG for my husband and dream about him. (3:1)

1:6 Hebrew *My own vineyard I have neglected.* 1:7 Hebrew *like a veiled woman.* 1:9 Hebrew *I compare you, my beloved, to a mare among Pharaoh's chariots.* 2:7 Or *not to awaken love until it is ready.* 2:17 Or *on the hills of Bether.*

the city, searching for him in all its streets and squares.' But my search was in vain. ³The watchmen stopped me as they made their rounds, and I said to them, 'Have you seen him anywhere, this one I love so much?' ⁴A little while later I found him and held him. I didn't let him go until I had brought him to my childhood home, into my mother's bedroom, where I had been conceived.

⁵"Promise me, O women of Jerusalem, by the swift gazelles and the deer of the wild, not to awaken love until the time is right.*"

Young Women of Jerusalem: ⁶"Who is this sweeping in from the deserts like a cloud of smoke along the ground? Who is it that smells of myrrh and frankincense and every other spice? ⁷Look, it is Solomon's carriage, with sixty of Israel's mightiest men surrounding it. ⁸They are all skilled swordsmen and experienced warriors. Each one wears a sword on his thigh, ready to defend the king against an attack during the night.

⁹"King Solomon has built a carriage for himself from wood imported from Lebanon's forests. ¹⁰Its posts are of silver, its canopy is gold, and its seat is upholstered in purple cloth. Its interior was a gift of love from the young women of Jerusalem."

Young Woman: ¹¹"Go out to look upon King Solomon, O young women of Jerusalem.* See the crown with which his mother crowned him on his wedding day, the day of his gladness."

See Solomon's profile (page 753) at Proverbs 2:9.

CHAPTER 4

Young Man: "How beautiful you are, my beloved, how beautiful! Your eyes behind your veil are like doves. Your hair falls in waves, like a flock of goats frisking down the slopes of Gilead. ²Your teeth are as white as sheep, newly shorn and washed. They are perfectly matched; not one is missing. ³Your lips are like a ribbon of scarlet. Oh, how beautiful your mouth! Your cheeks behind your veil are like pomegranate halves—lovely and delicious. ⁴Your neck is as stately as the tower of David, jeweled with the shields of a thousand heroes. ⁵Your breasts are like twin fawns of a gazelle, feeding among the lilies. ⁶Before the dawn comes and the shadows flee away, I will go to the mountain of myrrh and to the hill of frankincense. ⁷You are so beautiful, my beloved, so perfect in every part.

⁸"Come with me from Lebanon, my bride. Come down* from the top of Mount Amana, from Mount Senir and Mount Hermon, where lions have their dens and panthers prowl. ⁹You have ravished my heart, my treasure, my bride. I am overcome by one glance of your eyes, by a single bead of your necklace. ¹⁰How sweet is your love, my treasure, my bride! How much better it is than wine! Your perfume is more fragrant than the richest of spices. ¹¹Your lips, my bride, are as sweet as honey. Yes, honey and cream are under your tongue. The scent of your clothing is like that of the mountains and the cedars of Lebanon.

¹²"You are like a private garden, my treasure, my bride! You are like a spring that no one else can drink from, a fountain of my own. ¹³You are like a lovely orchard bearing precious fruit, with the rarest of perfumes: ¹⁴nard and saffron, calamus and cinnamon, myrrh and aloes, perfume from every incense tree, and every other lovely spice. ¹⁵You are a garden fountain, a well of living water, as refreshing as the streams from the Lebanon mountains."

Young Woman: ¹⁶"Awake, north wind! Come, south wind! Blow on my garden and waft its lovely perfume to my lover. Let him come into his garden and eat its choicest fruits."

I TELL my wife in detail how very beautiful she is. (4:1)

See David's profile (page 629) at Psalm 3:1.

I TREASURE exclusive love with my wife. (4:12)

3:5 Or *not to awaken love until it is ready.*   **3:11** Hebrew *Zion.*   **4:8** Or *Look down.*

CHAPTER 5

Young Man: "I am here in my garden, my treasure, my bride! I gather my myrrh with my spices and eat my honeycomb with my honey. I drink my wine with my milk."

Young Women of Jerusalem: "Oh, lover and beloved, eat and drink! Yes, drink deeply of this love!"

Young Woman: ²"One night as I was sleeping, my heart awakened in a dream. I heard the voice of my lover. He was knocking at my bedroom door. 'Open to me, my darling, my treasure, my lovely dove,' he said, 'for I have been out in the night. My head is soaked with dew, my hair with the wetness of the night.'

³"But I said, 'I have taken off my robe. Should I get dressed again? I have washed my feet. Should I get them soiled?'

⁴"My lover tried to unlatch the door, and my heart thrilled within me. ⁵I jumped up to open it. My hands dripped with perfume, my fingers with lovely myrrh, as I pulled back the bolt. ⁶I opened to my lover, but he was gone. I yearned for even his voice! I searched for him, but I couldn't find him anywhere. I called to him, but there was no reply. ⁷The watchmen found me as they were making their rounds; they struck and wounded me. The watchman on the wall tore off my veil.

⁸"Make this promise to me, O women of Jerusalem! If you find my beloved one, tell him that I am sick with love."

Young Women of Jerusalem: ⁹"O woman of rare beauty, what is it about your loved one that brings you to tell us this?"

Young Woman: ¹⁰"My lover is dark and dazzling, better than ten thousand others! ¹¹His head is the finest gold, and his hair is wavy and black. ¹²His eyes are like doves beside brooks of water; they are set like jewels. ¹³His cheeks are like sweetly scented beds of spices. His lips are like perfumed lilies. His breath is like myrrh. ¹⁴His arms are like round bars of gold, set with chrysolite. His body is like bright ivory, aglow with sapphires. ¹⁵His legs are like pillars of marble set in sockets of the finest gold, strong as the cedars of Lebanon. None can rival him. ¹⁶His mouth is altogether sweet; he is lovely in every way. Such, O women of Jerusalem, is my lover, my friend."

CHAPTER 6

Young Women of Jerusalem: "O rarest of beautiful women, where has your lover gone? We will help you find him."

Young Woman: ²"He has gone down to his garden, to his spice beds, to graze and to gather the lilies. ³I am my lover's, and my lover is mine. He grazes among the lilies!"

Young Man: ⁴"O my beloved, you are as beautiful as the lovely town of Tirzah. Yes, as beautiful as Jerusalem! You are as majestic as an army with banners! ⁵Look away, for your eyes overcome me! Your hair falls in waves, like a flock of goats frisking down the slopes of Gilead. ⁶Your teeth are as white as newly washed sheep. They are perfectly matched; not one is missing. ⁷Your cheeks behind your veil are like pomegranate halves—lovely and delicious. ⁸There may be sixty wives, all queens, and eighty concubines and unnumbered virgins available to me. ⁹But I would still choose my dove, my perfect one, the only beloved daughter of her mother! The young women are delighted when they see her; even queens and concubines sing her praises! ¹⁰'Who is this,' they ask, 'arising like the dawn, as fair as the moon, as bright as the sun, as majestic as an army with banners?'

¹¹"I went down into the grove of nut trees and out to the valley to see the new growth brought on by spring. I wanted to see whether the

Margin notes:

I SEEK to restore our marriage relationship when we are estranged. (5:6)

I AM DEEPLY ATTRACTED to my husband. (5:10)

I ENJOY exclusive love with my spouse. (6:3)

I TELL my wife how beautiful she is. (6:4)

I TELL my wife that I choose her over any other woman. (6:9)

grapevines were budding yet, or whether the pomegranates were blossoming. [12]Before I realized it, I found myself in my princely bed with my beloved one.*"

Young Women of Jerusalem: [13]"Return, return to us, O maid of Shulam. Come back, come back, that we may see you once again."

Young Man: "Why do you gaze so intently at this young woman of Shulam, as she moves so gracefully between two lines of dancers?*"

CHAPTER 7

Young Man: "How beautiful are your sandaled feet, O queenly maiden. Your rounded thighs are like jewels, the work of a skilled craftsman. [2]Your navel is as delicious as a goblet filled with wine. Your belly is lovely, like a heap of wheat set about with lilies. [3]Your breasts are like twin fawns of a gazelle. [4]Your neck is as stately as an ivory tower. Your eyes are like the sparkling pools in Heshbon by the gate of Bath-rabbim. Your nose is as fine as the tower of Lebanon overlooking Damascus. [5]Your head is as majestic as Mount Carmel, and the sheen of your hair radiates royalty. A king is held captive in your queenly tresses.

[6]"Oh, how delightful you are, my beloved; how pleasant for utter delight! [7]You are tall and slim like a palm tree, and your breasts are like its clusters of dates. [8]I said, 'I will climb up into the palm tree and take hold of its branches.' Now may your breasts be like grape clusters, and the scent of your breath like apples. [9]May your kisses be as exciting as the best wine, smooth and sweet, flowing gently over lips and teeth.*"

Young Woman: [10]"I am my lover's, the one he desires. [11]Come, my love, let us go out into the fields and spend the night among the wildflowers.* [12]Let us get up early and go out to the vineyards. Let us see whether the vines have budded, whether the blossoms have opened, and whether the pomegranates are in flower. And there I will give you my love. [13]There the mandrakes give forth their fragrance, and the rarest fruits are at our doors, the new as well as old, for I have stored them up for you, my lover."

CHAPTER 8

Young Woman: "Oh, if only you were my brother, who nursed at my mother's breast. Then I could kiss you no matter who was watching, and no one would criticize me. [2]I would bring you to my childhood home, and there you would teach me. I would give you spiced wine to drink, my sweet pomegranate wine. [3]Your left hand would be under my head and your right hand would embrace me.

[4]"I want you to promise, O women of Jerusalem, not to awaken love until the time is right.*"

Young Women of Jerusalem: [5]"Who is this coming up from the desert, leaning on her lover?"

Young Woman: "I aroused you under the apple tree, where your mother gave you birth, where in great pain she delivered you. [6]Place me like a seal over your heart, or like a seal on your arm. For love is as strong as death, and its jealousy is as enduring as the grave. Love flashes like fire, the brightest kind of flame. [7]Many waters cannot quench love; neither can rivers drown it. If a man tried to buy love with everything he owned, his offer would be utterly despised."

The Young Woman's Brothers: [8]"We have a little sister too young for breasts. What will we do if someone asks to marry her? [9]If she is chaste, we will

I TELL my wife how beautiful her body is to me. (7:1)

I KEEP myself totally faithful and committed to my spouse. (8:6)

I VALUE our relationship as a priceless treasure. (8:7)

6:12 Or *among the royal chariots of my people,* or *among the chariots of Amminadab.* The meaning of the Hebrew is uncertain.   6:13 Or *as you would at the movements of two armies?* or *as you would at the dance of Mahanaim?* The meaning of the Hebrew is uncertain.   7:9 As in Greek and Syriac versions and Latin Vulgate; Hebrew reads *over lips of sleepers.*   7:11 Or *in the villages.*   8:4 Or *not to awaken love until it is ready.*

I AM PURE before
marriage and enjoy
my husband's passion
after we marry. (8:10)

*See Solomon's profile
(page 753) at Proverbs
2:9.*

I ENJOY listening to
my wife's voice. (8:13)

strengthen and encourage her. But if she is promiscuous, we will shut her off from men.*"

Young Woman: [10]"I am chaste, and I am now full breasted. And my lover is content with me.

[11]"Solomon has a vineyard at Baal-hamon, which he rents to some farmers there. Each of them pays one thousand pieces of silver* for its use. [12]But as for my own vineyard, O Solomon, you can take my thousand pieces of silver. And I will give two hundred pieces of silver* to those who care for its vines."

Young Man: [13]"O my beloved, lingering in the gardens, how wonderful that your companions can listen to your voice. Let me hear it, too!"

Young Woman: [14]"Come quickly, my love! Move like a swift gazelle or a young deer on the mountains of spices."

8:9 Hebrew *If she is a wall, we will build battlements of silver on her; but if she is a door, we will surround her with panels of cedar.*   8:11 Hebrew *1,000 shekels of silver,* about 25 pounds or 11.4 kilograms in weight; also in 8:12. 8:12 Hebrew *200 [shekels],* about 5 pounds or 2.3 kilograms in weight.

ISAIAH

THIS FIRST OF seventeen prophetic books in the Old Testament urges readers to humble themselves before "the Holy One of Israel."

The phrase "the Holy One of Israel" appears more than fifteen times both in the first half (chapters 1–39) and in the second half (chapters 40–66) of this book. The title speaks of the Lord's majesty and glory and abhorrence of human wickedness and evil.

Many of the prophecies in the first half of Isaiah warn the kingdoms of Israel and Judah and the surrounding nations of impending judgment and destruction. The most prominent sins of these nations are pride, idolatry, and oppression of the poor and downcast.

In the midst of his warnings, Isaiah offers words of comfort and hope to those who humble themselves before the Lord and survive the coming judgments. This theme becomes especially prevalent in the second half of the book.

In the middle of his prophecies, Isaiah includes a historical interlude (chapters 36–39) that anticipates the kingdom of Judah's upcoming Babylonian captivity.

Isaiah's prophecies speak of days both near at hand and far into the future. In several remarkable passages, Isaiah clearly and compellingly presents the gospel message nearly seven hundred years before Jesus Christ's coming.

So remarkable are Isaiah's predictions that the New Testament makes a special note that "he was given a vision of the Messiah's glory" (John 12:41). Matthew, Mark, Luke, John, Peter, Paul, and Jesus quoted from his prophecies scores of times—far more than all the other prophets put together.

Famous verses in Isaiah abound, including

- "I can make you as white as wool" (1:18)
- "The nations will beat their swords into plowshares" (2:4)
- "Holy, holy, holy, is the LORD Almighty!" (6:3)
- "Lord, I'll go! Send me" (6:8)
- "Look! The virgin will conceive a child!" (7:14)
- "For a child is born to us, a son is given to us" (9:6)
- "You will keep in perfect peace all who trust in you" (26:3)
- "Those who belong to God will live; their bodies will rise again!" (26:19)
- "They honor me with their lips, but their hearts are far away" (29:13)
- "But those who wait on the LORD will find new strength" (40:31)
- "When you go through deep waters . . . I will be with you" (43:2)
- "How beautiful . . . are the feet of those who bring good news" (52:7)
- "All of us have strayed away like sheep" (53:6)
- "So are my ways higher than your ways" (55:9)
- No one came to help except the Lord alone (59:16; 63:5)
- Our righteous deeds are but filthy rags (64:6)
- "I will answer them before they even call to me" (65:24)

CHAPTER 1

These visions concerning Judah and Jerusalem came to Isaiah son of Amoz during the reigns of Uzziah, Jotham, Ahaz, and Hezekiah—all kings of Judah.

A Message for Rebellious Judah

²Hear, O heavens! Listen, O earth! This is what the LORD says: "The children I raised and cared for have turned against me. ³Even the animals—the donkey and the ox—know their owner and appreciate his care, but not my people Israel. No matter what I do for them, they still do not understand."

⁴Oh, what a sinful nation they are! They are loaded down with a burden of guilt. They are evil and corrupt children who have turned away from the LORD. They have despised the Holy One of Israel, cutting themselves off from his help.

⁵Why do you continue to invite punishment? Must you rebel forever? Your head is injured, and your heart is sick. ⁶You are sick from head to foot—covered with bruises, welts, and infected wounds—without any ointments or bandages. ⁷Your country lies in ruins, and your cities are burned. As you watch, foreigners plunder your fields and destroy everything they see. ⁸Jerusalem* stands abandoned like a watchman's shelter in a vineyard or field after the harvest is over. It is as helpless as a city under siege. ⁹If the LORD Almighty had not spared a few of us, we would have been wiped out as completely as Sodom and Gomorrah.

¹⁰Listen to the LORD, you leaders of Israel! Listen to the law of our God, people of Israel. You act just like the rulers and people of Sodom and Gomorrah. ¹¹"I am sick of your sacrifices," says the LORD. "Don't bring me any more burnt offerings! I don't want the fat from your rams or other animals. I don't want to see the blood from your offerings of bulls and rams and goats. ¹²Why do you keep parading through my courts with your worthless sacrifices? ¹³The incense you bring me is a stench in my nostrils! Your celebrations of the new moon and the Sabbath day, and your special days for fasting—even your most pious meetings—are all sinful and false. I want nothing more to do with them. ¹⁴I hate all your festivals and sacrifices. I cannot stand the sight of them! ¹⁵From now on, when you lift up your hands in prayer, I will refuse to look. Even though you offer many prayers, I will not listen. For your hands are covered with the blood of your innocent victims. ¹⁶Wash yourselves and be clean! Let me no longer see your evil deeds. Give up your wicked ways. ¹⁷Learn to do good. Seek justice. Help the oppressed. Defend the orphan. Fight for the rights of widows.

¹⁸"Come now, let us argue this out," says the LORD. "No matter how deep the stain of your sins, I can remove it. I can make you as clean as freshly fallen snow. Even if you are stained as red as crimson, I can make you as white as wool. ¹⁹If you will only obey me and let me help you, then you will have plenty to eat. ²⁰But if you keep turning away and refusing to listen, you will be destroyed by your enemies. I, the LORD, have spoken!"

Unfaithful Jerusalem

²¹See how Jerusalem, once so faithful, has become a prostitute. Once the home of justice and righteousness, she is now filled with murderers. ²²Once like pure silver, you have become like worthless slag. Once so pure, you are now like watered-down wine. ²³Your leaders are rebels, the companions of thieves. All of them take bribes and refuse to defend the orphans and the widows.

²⁴Therefore, the Lord, the LORD Almighty, the Mighty One of Israel, says, "I will pour out my fury on you, my enemies! ²⁵I will turn against you. I will

See the profiles for Uzziah (page 533) and Hezekiah (page 825) at 2 Chronicles 26:16 and Isaiah 37:1.

I DO NOT REBEL against God and invite his punishment. (1:5)

I KNOW the Lord's mercy alone saves sinners from complete destruction. (1:9)

I DO NOT INSULT the Lord by pretending to worship him while living in rebellion. (1:13)

I LISTEN to the Lord and ask him to wash away my sins. (1:18)

I DO NOT TURN away from the righteous way I've lived. (1:22)

1:8 Hebrew *The daughter of Zion.*

melt you down and skim off your slag. I will remove all your impurities. [26]Afterward I will give you good judges and wise counselors like the ones you used to have. Then Jerusalem will again be called the Home of Justice and the Faithful City."

[27]Because the LORD is just and righteous, the repentant people of Jerusalem* will be redeemed. [28]But all sinners will be completely destroyed, for they refuse to come to the LORD.

[29]Shame will cover you when you think of the times you offered sacrifices to idols in your groves of sacred oaks. You will blush when you think of all the sins you committed in your sacred gardens. [30]You will wither away like an oak or garden without water. [31]The strongest among you will disappear like burning straw. Your evil deeds are the spark that will set the straw on fire, and no one will be able to put it out.

CHAPTER 2

The LORD's Future Reign

This is another vision that Isaiah son of Amoz saw concerning Judah and Jerusalem:

[2]In the last days, the Temple of the LORD in Jerusalem will become the most important place on earth. People from all over the world will go there to worship. [3]Many nations will come and say, "Come, let us go up to the mountain of the LORD, to the Temple of the God of Israel.* There he will teach us his ways, so that we may obey him." For in those days the LORD's teaching and his word will go out from Jerusalem.

[4]The LORD will settle international disputes. All the nations will beat their swords into plowshares and their spears into pruning hooks. All wars will stop, and military training will come to an end. [5]Come, people of Israel, let us walk in the light of the LORD!

A Warning of Judgment

[6]The LORD has rejected the people of Israel because they have made alliances with foreigners from the East who practice magic and divination, just like the Philistines. [7]Israel has vast treasures of silver and gold and many horses and chariots. [8]The land is filled with idols. The people bow down and worship these things they have made. [9]So now everyone will be humbled and brought low. The LORD cannot simply ignore their sins!

[10]Crawl into caves in the rocks. Hide from the terror of the LORD and the glory of his majesty. [11]The day is coming when your pride will be brought low and the LORD alone will be exalted. [12]In that day the LORD Almighty will punish the proud, bringing them down to the dust. [13]He will cut down the tall cedars of Lebanon and the mighty oaks of Bashan. [14]He will level the high mountains and hills. [15]He will break down every high tower and wall. [16]He will destroy the great trading ships* and all the small boats in the harbor. [17]The arrogance of all people will be brought low. Their pride will lie in the dust. The LORD alone will be exalted! [18]Idols will be utterly abolished and destroyed.

[19]When the LORD rises to shake the earth, his enemies will crawl with fear into holes in the ground. They will hide in caves in the rocks from the terror of the LORD and the glory of his majesty. [20]They will abandon their gold and silver idols to the moles and bats. [21]They will crawl into caverns and hide among the jagged rocks at the tops of cliffs. In this way, they will try to escape the terror of the LORD and the glory of his majesty as he rises to shake the earth.

[22]Stop putting your trust in mere humans. They are as frail as breath. How can they be of help to anyone?

1:27 Hebrew *Zion.* 2:3 Hebrew *of Jacob;* also in 2:5, 6. 2:16 Hebrew *every ship of Tarshish.*

I BELIEVE the Lord one day will keep his promise to make Jerusalem a place of justice again. (1:26)

I BELIEVE sinners will be destroyed if they continually refuse to come to the Lord. (1:28)

I BELIEVE the Lord will one day bring all the peoples of the world together to worship him. (2:2)

I BELIEVE the Lord one day will bring true peace to the earth. (2:4)

I DO NOT foolishly expect the Lord to ignore my sins. (2:9)

I BELIEVE the Lord one day will punish all arrogance and pride. (2:17)

I DO NOT PUT my trust in frail human strength. (2:22)

CHAPTER 3

Judgment against Judah

The Lord, the LORD Almighty, will cut off the supplies of food and water from Jerusalem and Judah. ²He will destroy all the nation's leaders—the heroes, soldiers, judges, prophets, diviners, elders, ³army officers, honorable citizens, advisers, skilled magicians, and expert enchanters. ⁴Then he will appoint children to rule over them, and anarchy will prevail. ⁵People will take advantage of each other—man against man, neighbor fighting neighbor. Young people will revolt against authority, and nobodies will sneer at honorable people.

⁶In those days a man will say to his brother, "Since you have a cloak, you be our leader! Take charge of this heap of ruins!"

⁷"No!" he will reply. "I can't help. I don't have any extra food or clothes. Don't ask me to get involved!"

⁸Judah and Jerusalem will lie in ruins because they speak out against the LORD and refuse to obey him. They have offended his glorious presence among them. ⁹The very look on their faces gives them away and displays their guilt. They sin openly like the people of Sodom. They are not one bit ashamed. How terrible it will be for them! They have brought about their own destruction.

¹⁰But all will be well for those who are godly. Tell them, "You will receive a wonderful reward!" ¹¹But say to the wicked, "Your destruction is sure. You, too, will get what you deserve. Your well-earned punishment is on the way."

¹²Children oppress my people, and women rule over them. O my people, can't you see what fools your rulers are? They are leading you down a pretty garden path to destruction.

¹³The LORD takes his place in court. He is the great prosecuting attorney, presenting his case against his people! ¹⁴The leaders and the princes will be the first to feel the LORD's judgment. "You have ruined Israel, which is my vineyard. You have taken advantage of the poor, filling your barns with grain extorted from helpless people. ¹⁵How dare you grind my people into the dust like that!" demands the Lord, the LORD Almighty.

A Warning for Jerusalem's Women

¹⁶Next the LORD will judge the women of Jerusalem,* who walk around with their noses in the air, with tinkling ornaments on their ankles. Their eyes rove among the crowds, flirting with the men. ¹⁷The Lord will send a plague of scabs to ornament their heads. Yes, the LORD will make them bald for all to see!

¹⁸The Lord will strip away their artful beauty—their ornaments, headbands, and crescent necklaces; ¹⁹their earrings, bracelets, and veils of shimmering gauze. ²⁰Gone will be their scarves, ankle chains, sashes, perfumes, and charms; ²¹their rings, jewels, ²²party clothes, gowns, capes, and purses; ²³their mirrors, linen garments, head ornaments, and shawls. ²⁴Instead of smelling of sweet perfume, they will stink. They will wear ropes for sashes, and their well-set hair will fall out. They will wear rough sackcloth instead of rich robes. Their beauty will be gone. Only shame will be left to them.

²⁵The men of the city will die in battle. ²⁶The gates of Jerusalem* will weep and mourn. The city will be like a ravaged woman, huddled on the ground.

CHAPTER 4

In that day few men will be left alive. Seven women will fight over each of them and say, "Let us all marry you! We will provide our own food and clothing. Only let us be called by your name so we won't be mocked as old maids."

A Promise of Restoration

²But in the future, Israel—the branch of the LORD—will be lush and beautiful, and the fruit of the land will be the pride of its people. ³All those whose names

Sidenotes:

I BELIEVE the Lord accurately warned Judah of the judgment he would bring upon them for rejecting him. (3:1)

I BELIEVE those who rebel against God bring about their own destruction. (3:9)

I LIVE a godly life and am confident the Lord will one day reward me. (3:10)

I BELIEVE the Lord will one day call to account any leaders who oppress the weak. (3:14)

I AM MORE CONCERNED about inner beauty than outward attractiveness (1 Peter 3:3-4). (3:16)

I BELIEVE the Lord one day will make Israel lush and beautiful again. (4:2)

3:16 Hebrew *the daughters of Zion.*   3:26 Hebrew *Zion.*

are written down, who have survived the destruction of Jerusalem, will be a holy people. [4]The Lord will wash the moral filth from the women of Jerusalem.* He will cleanse Jerusalem of its bloodstains by a spirit of judgment that burns like fire. [5]Then the LORD will provide shade for Jerusalem* and all who assemble there. There will be a canopy of smoke and cloud throughout the day and clouds of fire at night, covering the glorious land. [6]It will be a shelter from daytime heat and a hiding place from storms and rain.

I BELIEVE the Lord will keep his promise to cleanse his people from their sins. (4:4)

CHAPTER 5

A Song about the LORD's Vineyard

Now I will sing a song for the one I love about his vineyard:

My beloved has a vineyard
　on a rich and fertile hill.
[2]He plowed the land, cleared its stones,
　and planted it with choice vines.
In the middle he built a watchtower
　and carved a winepress in the nearby rocks.
Then he waited for a harvest of sweet grapes,
　but the grapes that grew were wild and sour.
[3]"Now, you people of Jerusalem and Judah,
　you have heard the case; you be the judges.
[4]What more could I have done
　to cultivate a rich harvest?
Why did my vineyard give me wild grapes
　when I expected sweet ones?
[5]Now this is what I am going to do to my vineyard:
I will tear down its fences
　and let it be destroyed.
I will break down its walls
　and let the animals trample it.
[6]I will make it a wild place.
　I will not prune the vines or hoe the ground.
　I will let it be overgrown with briers and thorns.
I will command the clouds
　to drop no more rain on it."

Today what truth(s) are you choosing to believe?

[7]This is the story of the LORD's people.
　They are the vineyard of the LORD Almighty.
Israel and Judah are his pleasant garden.
He expected them to yield a crop of justice,
　but instead he found bloodshed.
He expected to find righteousness,
　but instead he heard cries of oppression.

I BELONG to the Lord and live righteously and justly. (5:7)

Judah's Guilt and Judgment

[8]Destruction is certain for you who buy up property so others have no place to live. Your homes are built on great estates so you can be alone in the land. [9]But the LORD Almighty has sealed your awful fate. With my own ears I heard him say, "Many beautiful homes will stand deserted, the owners dead or gone. [10]Ten acres* of vineyard will not produce even six gallons* of wine. Ten measures of seed will yield only one measure* of grain."

[11]Destruction is certain for you who get up early to begin long drinking bouts that last late into the night. [12]You furnish lovely music and wine at your

I DO NOT FOCUS on my own pleasure so much that I fail to see what the Lord is doing. (5:12)

4:4 Hebrew *from the daughters of Zion.*　4:5 Hebrew *Mount Zion.*　5:10a Hebrew *A ten yoke,* that is, the area of land plowed by ten teams of oxen in one day.　5:10b Hebrew *a bath* [21 liters].　5:10c Hebrew *A homer* [5 bushels or 182 liters] *of seed will yield only an ephah* [0.5 bushels or 18.2 liters].

grand parties; the harps, lyres, tambourines, and flutes are superb! But you never think about the LORD or notice what he is doing. [13]So I will send my people into exile far away because they do not know me. The great and honored among them will starve, and the common people will die of thirst.

[14]The grave* is licking its chops in anticipation of Jerusalem, this delicious morsel. Her great and lowly will be swallowed up, with all her drunken crowds. [15]In that day the arrogant will be brought down to the dust; the proud will be humbled. [16]But the LORD Almighty is exalted by his justice. The holiness of God is displayed by his righteousness. [17]In those days flocks will feed among the ruins; lambs and kids* will pasture there.

[18]Destruction is certain for those who drag their sins behind them, tied with cords of falsehood. [19]They even mock the Holy One of Israel and say, "Hurry up and do something! Quick, show us what you can do. We want to see what you have planned."

[20]Destruction is certain for those who say that evil is good and good is evil; that dark is light and light is dark; that bitter is sweet and sweet is bitter.

[21]Destruction is certain for those who think they are wise and consider themselves to be clever.

[22]Destruction is certain for those who are heroes when it comes to drinking, who boast about all the liquor they can hold. [23]They take bribes to pervert justice. They let the wicked go free while punishing the innocent.

[24]Therefore, they will all disappear like burning straw. Their roots will rot and their flowers wither, for they have rejected the law of the LORD Almighty. They have despised the word of the Holy One of Israel. [25]That is why the anger of the LORD burns against his people. That is why he has raised his fist to crush them. The hills tremble, and the rotting bodies of his people are thrown as garbage into the streets. But even then the LORD's anger will not be satisfied. His fist is still poised to strike!

[26]He will send a signal to the nations far away. He will whistle to those at the ends of the earth, and they will come racing toward Jerusalem. [27]They will not get tired or stumble. They will run without stopping for rest or sleep. Not a belt will be loose, not a sandal thong broken. [28]Their arrows will be sharp and their bows ready for battle. Sparks will fly from their horses' hooves as the wheels of their chariots spin like the wind. [29]Roaring like lions, they will pounce on their prey. They will seize my people and carry them off into captivity, and no one will be there to rescue them. [30]The enemy nations will growl over their victims like the roaring of the sea. A cloud of darkness and sorrow will hover over Israel. The clouds will blot out the light.

CHAPTER 6

Isaiah's Cleansing and Call

In the year King Uzziah died, I saw the Lord. He was sitting on a lofty throne, and the train of his robe filled the Temple. [2]Hovering around him were mighty seraphim, each with six wings. With two wings they covered their faces, with two they covered their feet, and with the remaining two they flew. [3]In a great chorus they sang, "Holy, holy, holy is the LORD Almighty! The whole earth is filled with his glory!" [4]The glorious singing shook the Temple to its foundations, and the entire sanctuary was filled with smoke.

[5]Then I said, "My destruction is sealed, for I am a sinful man and a member of a sinful race. Yet I have seen the King, the LORD Almighty!"

[6]Then one of the seraphim flew over to the altar, and he picked up a burning coal with a pair of tongs. [7]He touched my lips with it and said, "See, this coal has touched your lips. Now your guilt is removed, and your sins are forgiven."

5:14 Hebrew *Sheol.* 5:17 As in Greek version; Hebrew reads *strangers.*

I BELIEVE the Lord displays his justice and holiness by punishing the proud and caring for the weak. (5:16)

I DO NOT MOCK God when he delays his judgment. (5:19)

I DO NOT DESPISE or reject the Word of the Lord. (5:24)

I BELIEVE the Lord may use pagan nations to punish those who should know him but turn away. (5:26)

I BELIEVE the Lord allowed the prophet Isaiah to see his glory. (6:1)

See Uzziah's profile (page 533) at 2 Chronicles 26:16.

I ASK the Lord to cleanse me of all sin and guilt. (6:7)

⁸Then I heard the Lord asking, "Whom should I send as a messenger to my people? Who will go for us?"

And I said, "Lord, I'll go! Send me."

⁹And he said, "Yes, go. But tell my people this: 'You will hear my words, but you will not understand. You will see what I do, but you will not perceive its meaning.' ¹⁰Harden the hearts of these people. Close their ears, and shut their eyes. That way, they will not see with their eyes, hear with their ears, understand with their hearts, and turn to me for healing."

¹¹Then I said, "Lord, how long must I do this?"

And he replied, "Until their cities are destroyed, with no one left in them. Until their houses are deserted and the whole country is an utter wasteland. ¹²Do not stop until the LORD has sent everyone away to distant lands and the entire land of Israel lies deserted. ¹³Even if only a tenth—a remnant—survive, it will be invaded again and burned. Israel will remain a stump, like a tree that is cut down, but the stump will be a holy seed that will grow again."

I DO NOT STOP talking about God's Word, even if many ignore what it says. (6:12)

LIKE ISAIAH
Isaiah 6:13

I proclaim the Lord's salvation, knowing that I, too, need the Savior.

Isaiah was no stuck-up prophet looking down his nose at others.

Before Isaiah began to proclaim God's Word, he experienced firsthand the awfulness of his guilt and the astounding miracle of the Lord's cleansing. He knew experientially what it meant to deserve destruction—and to receive forgiveness. And he knew that, of all people, he needed God's deliverance most of all.

Like the apostle Paul—who called himself "the worst" of all sinners (1 Timothy 1:15)—Isaiah saw his own sinfulness in vivid detail. Unlike Paul, however, Isaiah didn't have blood on his hands. He probably was a well-respected gentleman.

After one glimpse of the Holy One, however, Isaiah knew he was a goner—like every other person in the human race.

In this first vision, Isaiah saw the Lord in all his heavenly majesty (John 12:39-41). In a later vision, Isaiah saw the Lord Jesus laboring to carry a blood-stained Roman cross up the hill to Calvary (see John 12:37-38 and Isaiah 52:13–53:12). What an awful picture! Isaiah was equally shocked to realize, "I'm the one who went astray. Yet he is being crushed. I'm the one who sinned. But the Messiah is being put to death."

Throughout history people have asked, "Who killed Jesus?" Fingers point at the Roman guards, at the Jewish leaders, at the fickle crowds. Isaiah knew the real answer: "He died because of me."

When you and I grasp something of the holiness of the Lord and the horrible price he paid to redeem us (1 Peter 1:18-20), like Isaiah we'll be compelled to proclaim his salvation with humility.

○ *Today's Scripture reading is Isaiah 6, 40, and 53.*

CHAPTER 7
A Message for Ahaz

During the reign of Ahaz son of Jotham and grandson of Uzziah, Jerusalem was attacked by King Rezin of Aram and King Pekah of Israel, the son of Remaliah. The city withstood the attack, however, and was not taken.

²The news had come to the royal court: "Aram is allied with Israel* against us!" So the hearts of the king and his people trembled with fear, just as trees shake in a storm.

³Then the LORD said to Isaiah, "Go out to meet King Ahaz, you and your son Shear-jashub.* You will find the king at the end of the aqueduct that feeds water into the upper pool, near the road leading to the field where cloth is bleached. ⁴Tell him to stop worrying. Tell him he doesn't need to fear the

See Uzziah's profile (page 533) at 2 Chronicles 26:16.

I PROCLAIM God's message of deliverance to those who are worried and fearful. (7:4)

7:2 Hebrew *Ephraim*, referring to the northern kingdom of Israel; also in 7:5, 8, 9, 17.   7:3 *Shear-jashub* means "A remnant will return."

fierce anger of those two burned-out embers, King Rezin of Aram and Pekah son of Remaliah.

⁵"Yes, the kings of Aram and Israel are coming against you. They are saying, ⁶'We will invade Judah and throw its people into panic. Then we will fight our way into Jerusalem and install the son of Tabeel as Judah's king.'

⁷"But this is what the Sovereign LORD says: This invasion will never happen, ⁸because Aram is no stronger than its capital, Damascus. And Damascus is no stronger than its king, Rezin. As for Israel, within sixty-five years it will be crushed and completely destroyed. ⁹Israel is no stronger than its capital, Samaria. And Samaria is no stronger than its king, Pekah son of Remaliah. You do not believe me? If you want me to protect you, learn to believe what I say."

The Sign of Immanuel

¹⁰Not long after this, the LORD sent this message to King Ahaz: ¹¹"Ask me for a sign, Ahaz, to prove that I will crush your enemies as I have promised. Ask for anything you like, and make it as difficult as you want."

¹²But the king refused. "No," he said, "I wouldn't test the LORD like that."

¹³Then Isaiah said, "Listen well, you royal family of David! You aren't satisfied to exhaust my patience. You exhaust the patience of God as well! ¹⁴All right then, the Lord himself will choose the sign. Look! The virgin* will conceive a child! She will give birth to a son and will call him Immanuel—'God is with us.' ¹⁵By the time this child is old enough to eat curds and honey, he will know enough to choose what is right and reject what is wrong. ¹⁶But before he knows right from wrong, the two kings you fear so much—the kings of Israel and Aram—will both be dead.

¹⁷"The LORD will bring a terrible curse on you, your nation, and your family. You will soon experience greater terror than has been known in all the years since Solomon's empire was divided into Israel and Judah. The mighty king of Assyria will come with his great army!"

¹⁸In that day the LORD will whistle for the army of Upper Egypt and for the army of Assyria. They will swarm around you like flies. Like bees, they will sting and kill. ¹⁹They will come in vast hordes, spreading across the whole land. They will settle in the fertile areas and also in the desolate valleys, caves, and thorny places. ²⁰In that day the Lord will take this "razor"—these Assyrians you have hired to protect you—and use it to shave off everything: your land, your crops, and your people.*

²¹When they finally stop plundering, a farmer will be fortunate to have a cow and two sheep left. ²²The few people still left in the land will live on curds and wild honey because that is all the land will produce. ²³In that day the lush vineyards, now worth as much as a thousand pieces of silver,* will become patches of briers and thorns. ²⁴The entire land will be one vast brier patch, a hunting ground overrun by wildlife. ²⁵No one will go to the fertile hillsides where the gardens once grew, for briers and thorns will cover them. Cattle, sheep, and goats will graze there.

CHAPTER 8

The Coming Assyrian Invasion

Again the LORD said to me, "Make a large signboard and clearly write this name on it: Maher-shalal-hash-baz.*" ²I asked Uriah the priest and Zechariah son of Jeberekiah, both known as honest men, to testify that I had written it before the child was conceived.

³Then I slept with my wife, and she became pregnant and had a son. And the LORD said, "Call him Maher-shalal-hash-baz. ⁴This name prophesies that

---

*Sidebar notes:*

I BELIEVE in God's Word more than any threat. (7:7)

I BELIEVE everything the Lord says about the future and trust him to protect me. (7:9)

See David's profile (page 629) at Psalm 3:1.

I BELIEVE the Lord himself chose to use a virgin to bear a child as a sign that he would save his people (Matthew 1:23). (7:14)

See Solomon's profile (page 753) at Proverbs 2:9.

I BELIEVE the Lord accurately warned King Ahaz of the coming invasion by the Egyptians and the Assyrians. (7:18)

I BELIEVE the Lord gave Isaiah a son as a sign of the coming judgment and destruction of Damascus and Samaria. (8:4)

7:14 Or *young woman.*   7:20 Hebrew *shave off the head, the hair of the legs, and the beard.*   7:23 Hebrew *1,000 shekels of silver,* about 25 pounds or 11.4 kilograms in weight.   8:1 *Maher-shalal-hash-baz* means "Swift to plunder and quick to spoil."

within a couple of years, before this child is old enough to say 'Papa' or 'Mama,' the king of Assyria will invade both Damascus and Samaria and carry away their riches."

⁵Then the LORD spoke to me again and said, ⁶"The people of Judah have rejected my gentle care* and are rejoicing over what will happen to King Rezin and King Pekah. ⁷Therefore, the Lord will overwhelm them with a mighty flood from the Euphrates River*—the king of Assyria and all his mighty armies. ⁸This flood will overflow all its channels and sweep into Judah. It will submerge Immanuel's land from one end to the other.

⁹"The Assyrians will cry, 'Do your best to defend yourselves, but you will be shattered! Listen all you nations. Prepare for battle—and die! Yes, die! ¹⁰Call your councils of war, develop your strategies, prepare your plans of attack—and then die! For God is with us!*' "

A Call to Trust the LORD

¹¹The LORD has said to me in the strongest terms: "Do not think like everyone else does. ¹²Do not be afraid that some plan conceived behind closed doors will be the end of you. ¹³Do not fear anything except the LORD Almighty. He alone is the Holy One. If you fear him, you need fear nothing else. ¹⁴He will keep you safe. But to Israel and Judah he will be a stone that causes people to stumble and a rock that makes them fall. And for the people of Jerusalem he will be a trap that entangles them. ¹⁵Many of them will stumble and fall, never to rise again. Many will be captured."

¹⁶I will write down all these things as a testimony of what the LORD will do. I will entrust it to my disciples, who will pass it down to future generations. ¹⁷I will wait for the LORD to help us, though he has turned away from the people of Israel.* My only hope is in him. ¹⁸I and the children the LORD has given me have names* that reveal the plans the LORD Almighty has for his people. ¹⁹So why are you trying to find out the future by consulting mediums and psychics? Do not listen to their whisperings and mutterings. Can the living find out the future from the dead? Why not ask your God?

²⁰"Check their predictions against my testimony," says the LORD. "If their predictions are different from mine, it is because there is no light or truth in them. ²¹My people will be led away as captives, weary and hungry. And because they are hungry, they will rage and shake their fists at heaven and curse their king and their God. ²²Wherever they look, there will be trouble and anguish and dark despair. They will be thrown out into the darkness."

CHAPTER 9

Hope in the Messiah

Nevertheless, that time of darkness and despair will not go on forever. The land of Zebulun and Naphtali will soon be humbled, but there will be a time in the future when Galilee of the Gentiles, which lies along the road that runs between the Jordan and the sea, will be filled with glory. ²The people who walk in darkness will see a great light—a light that will shine on all who live in the land where death casts its shadow. ³Israel will again be great, and its people will rejoice as people rejoice at harvesttime. They will shout with joy like warriors dividing the plunder. ⁴For God will break the chains that bind his people and the whip that scourges them, just as he did when he destroyed the army of Midian with Gideon's little band. ⁵In that day of peace, battle gear will no longer be issued. Never again will uniforms be bloodstained by war. All such equipment will be burned.

⁶For a child is born to us, a son is given to us. And the government will rest on his shoulders. These will be his royal titles: Wonderful Counselor,*

I DO NOT REJECT the Lord's gentle care. (8:6)

I DO NOT THINK like those who don't know the Lord. (8:11)

I BELIEVE the Lord Jesus was the one the Israelites had to accept or reject (Luke 2:34; Romans 9:30-33). (8:14)

I PUT my hope in the Lord, even when it seems he has turned away from his people for a time. (8:17)

I BELIEVE the Lord accurately foretold that the coming Messiah, Jesus Christ, would bring light to all peoples (Matthew 4:15-16). (9:1)

I BELIEVE the Lord accurately foretold that Jesus will rule the world with peace and justice (Luke 1:32-33). (9:6)

8:6 Hebrew rejected the gently flowing waters of Shiloah. 8:7 Hebrew the river. 8:10 Hebrew Immanuel! 8:17 Hebrew the house of Jacob. 8:18 Isaiah means "The LORD will save"; Shear-jashub means "A remnant will return"; and Maher-shalal-hash-baz means "Swift to plunder and quick to spoil." 9:6 Or Wonderful, Counselor.

See David's profile (page 629) at Psalm 3:1.

Mighty God, Everlasting Father, Prince of Peace. [7]His ever expanding, peaceful government will never end. He will rule forever with fairness and justice from the throne of his ancestor David. The passionate commitment of the LORD Almighty will guarantee this!

The LORD's Anger against Israel

[8]The Lord has spoken out against that braggart Israel, [9]and the people of Israel* and Samaria will soon discover it. In their pride and arrogance they say, [10]"Our land lies in ruins now, but we will rebuild it better than before. We will replace the broken bricks with cut stone, the fallen sycamore trees with cedars." [11]The LORD will reply to their bragging by bringing Rezin's enemies, the Assyrians, against them—[12]along with Arameans from the east and Philistines from the west. With bared fangs, they will devour Israel. But even then the LORD's anger will not be satisfied. His fist is still poised to strike. [13]For after all this punishment, the people will still not repent and turn to the LORD Almighty.

[14]Therefore, in a single day, the LORD will destroy both the head and the tail, the palm branch and the reed. [15]The leaders of Israel are the head, and the lying prophets are the tail. [16]For the leaders of the people have led them down the path of destruction. [17]That is why the Lord has no joy in the young men and no mercy on even the widows and orphans. For they are all hypocrites, speaking wickedness with lies. But even then the LORD's anger will not be satisfied. His fist is still poised to strike.

[18]This wickedness is like a brushfire. It burns not only briers and thorns but the forests, too. Its burning sends up vast clouds of smoke. [19]The land is blackened by the fury of the LORD Almighty. The people are fuel for the fire, and no one spares anyone else. [20]They fight against their own neighbors to steal food, but they will still be hungry. In the end they will even eat their own children.* [21]Manasseh will feed on Ephraim, Ephraim will feed on Manasseh, and both will devour Judah. But even then the LORD's anger will not be satisfied. His fist is still poised to strike.

I DO NOT arrogantly assume I can fix my own life. (9:10)

I REPENT when the Lord punishes me in order to draw me back to himself. (9:13)

CHAPTER 10

I BELIEVE the Lord will punish those who deny justice to the weak. (10:1)

Destruction is certain for the unjust judges, for those who issue unfair laws. [2]They deprive the poor, the widows, and the orphans of justice. Yes, they rob widows and fatherless children! [3]What will you do when I send desolation upon you from a distant land? To whom will you turn for help? Where will your treasures be safe? [4]I will not help you. You will stumble along as prisoners or lie among the dead. But even then the LORD's anger will not be satisfied. His fist is still poised to strike.

Judgment against Assyria

I BELIEVE the Lord sometimes uses unbelievers to accomplish his purposes. (10:7)

[5]"Destruction is certain for Assyria, the whip of my anger. Its military power is a club in my hand. [6]Assyria will enslave my people, who are a godless nation. It will plunder them, trampling them like dirt beneath its feet. [7]But the king of Assyria will not know that it is I who sent him. He will merely think he is attacking my people as part of his plan to conquer the world. [8]He will say, 'Each of my princes will soon be a king, ruling a conquered land. [9]We will destroy Calno just as we did Carchemish. Hamath will fall before us as Arpad did. And we will destroy Samaria just as we did Damascus. [10]Yes, we have finished off many a kingdom whose gods were far greater than those in Jerusalem and Samaria. [11]So when we have defeated Samaria and her gods, we will destroy Jerusalem with hers.' "

[12]After the Lord has used the king of Assyria to accomplish his purposes in Jerusalem, he will turn against the king of Assyria and punish him—for he is

---

9:9 Hebrew *of Ephraim*, referring to the northern kingdom of Israel.   9:20 Or *eat their own arms.*

proud and arrogant. [13]He boasts, "By my own power and wisdom I have won these wars. By my own strength I have captured many lands, destroyed their kings, and carried off their treasures. [14]By my greatness I have robbed their nests of riches and gathered up kingdoms as a farmer gathers eggs. No one can even flap a wing against me or utter a peep of protest."

[15]Can the ax boast greater power than the person who uses it? Is the saw greater than the person who saws? Can a whip strike unless a hand is moving it? Can a cane walk by itself?

[16]Listen now, king of Assyria! Because of all your evil boasting, the Lord, the LORD Almighty, will send a plague among your proud troops, and a flaming fire will ignite your glory. [17]The LORD, the Light of Israel and the Holy One, will be a flaming fire that will destroy them. In a single night he will burn those thorns and briers, the Assyrians. [18]Assyria's vast army is like a glorious forest, yet it will be destroyed. The LORD will completely destroy Assyria's warriors, and they will waste away like sick people in a plague. [19]Only a few from all that mighty army will survive—so few that a child could count them!

Hope for the LORD's People

[20]Then at last those left in Israel and Judah* will trust the LORD, the Holy One of Israel. They will no longer depend on the Assyrians, who would destroy them. [21]A remnant of them will return* to the Mighty God. [22]But though the people of Israel are as numerous as the sand on the seashore, only a few of them will return at that time. The LORD has rightly decided to destroy his people. [23]Yes, the Lord, the LORD Almighty, has already decided to consume them.

[24]So this is what the Lord, the LORD Almighty, says: "My people in Jerusalem,* do not be afraid of the Assyrians when they oppress you just as the Egyptians did long ago. [25]It will not last very long. In a little while my anger against you will end, and then my anger will rise up to destroy them."

[26]The LORD Almighty will beat them with his whip, as he did when Gideon triumphed over the Midianites at the rock of Oreb, or when the LORD's staff was raised to drown the Egyptian army in the sea. [27]In that day the LORD will end the bondage of his people. He will break the yoke of slavery and lift it from their shoulders.*

[28]Look, the mighty armies of Assyria are coming! They are now at Aiath, now at Migron. They are storing some of their equipment at Micmash. [29]They are crossing the pass and are staying overnight at Geba. Fear strikes the city of Ramah. All the people of Gibeah—the city of Saul—are running for their lives. [30]Well may you scream in terror, you people of Gallim! Shout out a warning to Laishah, for the mighty army comes. Poor Anathoth, what a fate is yours! [31]There go the people of Madmenah, all fleeing. And the citizens of Gebim are preparing to run. [32]But the enemy stops at Nob for the rest of that day. He shakes his fist at Mount Zion in Jerusalem.

[33]But look! The Lord, the LORD Almighty, will chop down the mighty tree! He will destroy all that vast army of Assyria—officers and high officials alike. [34]The Mighty One will cut down the enemy as an ax cuts down the forest trees in Lebanon.

CHAPTER 11

A Branch from David's Line

Out of the stump of David's family* will grow a shoot—yes, a new Branch bearing fruit from the old root. [2]And the Spirit of the LORD will rest on him—the Spirit of wisdom and understanding, the Spirit of counsel and might, the Spirit of knowledge and the fear of the LORD. [3]He will delight in

I DO NOT BOAST when the Lord uses me to accomplish his purposes. (10:14)

I BELIEVE the Lord accurately foretold that the Assyrians would be judged and destroyed for their pride. (10:16)

I BELIEVE the Lord kept his promise to restore the remnant of his people who returned to him. (10:20)

I BELIEVE the Lord kept his promise to rescue the Israelites and punish the Assyrians. (10:25)

I BELIEVE the Lord accurately foretold that the Spirit of the Lord would rest on the coming Messiah, Jesus Christ (John 1:32). (11:2)

10:20 Hebrew *and the house of Jacob.* 10:21 Hebrew *Shear-jashub;* see 7:3; 8:18. 10:24 Hebrew *Zion.* 10:27 As in Greek version; Hebrew reads *The yoke will be broken, for you have grown so fat.* 11:1 Hebrew *the line of Jesse.* Jesse was King David's father.

obeying the LORD. He will never judge by appearance, false evidence, or hearsay. [4]He will defend the poor and the exploited. He will rule against the wicked and destroy them with the breath of his mouth. [5]He will be clothed with fairness and truth.

[6]In that day the wolf and the lamb will live together; the leopard and the goat will be at peace. Calves and yearlings will be safe among lions, and a little child will lead them all. [7]The cattle will graze among bears. Cubs and calves will lie down together. And lions will eat grass as the livestock do. [8]Babies will crawl safely among poisonous snakes. Yes, a little child will put its hand in a nest of deadly snakes and pull it out unharmed. [9]Nothing will hurt or destroy in all my holy mountain. And as the waters fill the sea, so the earth will be filled with people who know the LORD.

[10]In that day the heir to David's throne* will be a banner of salvation to all the world. The nations will rally to him, for the land where he lives will be a glorious place. [11]In that day the Lord will bring back a remnant of his people for the second time, returning them to the land of Israel from Assyria, Lower Egypt, Upper Egypt, Ethiopia,* Elam, Babylonia,* Hamath, and all the distant coastlands.

[12]He will raise a flag among the nations for Israel to rally around. He will gather the scattered people of Judah from the ends of the earth. [13]Then at last the jealousy between Israel* and Judah will end. They will not fight against each other anymore. [14]They will join forces to swoop down on Philistia to the west. Together they will attack and plunder the nations to the east. They will occupy all the lands of Edom, Moab, and Ammon.

[15]The LORD will make a dry path through the Red Sea.* He will wave his hand over the Euphrates River,* sending a mighty wind to divide it into seven streams that can easily be crossed. [16]He will make a highway from Assyria for the remnant there, just as he did for Israel long ago when they returned from Egypt.

CHAPTER 12

Songs of Praise for Salvation
In that day you will sing:

"Praise the LORD!
He was angry with me,
  but now he comforts me.
[2]See, God has come to save me.
  I will trust in him and not be afraid.
The LORD GOD is my strength and my song;
  he has become my salvation."

[3]With joy you will drink deeply from the fountain of salvation! [4]In that wonderful day you will sing:

"Thank the LORD!
  Praise his name!
Tell the world what he has done.
  Oh, how mighty he is!
[5]Sing to the LORD,
  for he has done wonderful things.
  Make known his praise around the world.
[6]Let all the people of Jerusalem* shout his praise with joy!
  For great is the Holy One of Israel who lives among you."

I BELIEVE the Lord accurately foretold that Jesus would look into each person's heart (John 2:24-25). (11:3)

I BELIEVE the Lord promised that Jesus will bring all nations together to worship and serve the Lord. (11:10)

I BELIEVE the Lord promised that the Israelites will one day rejoice and be comforted in his salvation. (12:1)

I PRAISE the Lord for all the wonderful things he has done. (12:5)

11:10 Hebrew *the root of Jesse.*   11:11a Hebrew *Pathros, Cush.*   11:11b Hebrew *Shinar.*   11:13 Hebrew *Ephraim*, referring to the northern kingdom of Israel.   11:15a Hebrew *sea of Egypt.*   11:15b Hebrew *the river.*   12:6 Hebrew *Zion.*

CHAPTER 13

A Message about Babylon

Isaiah son of Amoz received this message concerning the destruction of Babylon:

²"See the flags waving as the enemy attacks. Cheer them on, O Israel! Wave to them as they march against Babylon to destroy the palaces of the high and mighty. ³I, the LORD, have assigned this task to these armies, and they will rejoice when I am exalted. I have called them to satisfy my anger."

⁴Hear the noise on the mountains! Listen, as the armies march! It is the noise and the shout of many nations. The LORD Almighty has brought them here to form an army. ⁵They came from countries far away. They are the LORD's weapons; they carry his anger with them and will destroy the whole land. ⁶Scream in terror, for the LORD's time has arrived—the time for the Almighty to destroy. ⁷Every arm is paralyzed with fear. Even the strongest hearts melt ⁸and are afraid. Fear grips them with terrible pangs, like those of a woman about to give birth. They look helplessly at one another as the flames of the burning city reflect on their faces. ⁹For see, the day of the LORD is coming—the terrible day of his fury and fierce anger. The land will be destroyed and all the sinners with it. ¹⁰The heavens will be black above them. No light will shine from stars or sun or moon.

¹¹"I, the LORD, will punish the world for its evil and the wicked for their sin. I will crush the arrogance of the proud and the haughtiness of the mighty. ¹²Few will be left alive when I have finished my work. People will be as scarce as gold—more rare than the gold of Ophir. ¹³For I will shake the heavens, and the earth will move from its place. I, the LORD Almighty, will show my fury and fierce anger."

¹⁴Everyone will run until exhausted, rushing back to their own lands like hunted deer, wandering like sheep without a shepherd. ¹⁵Anyone who is captured will be run through with a sword. ¹⁶Their little children will be dashed to death right before their eyes. Their homes will be sacked and their wives raped by the attacking hordes. ¹⁷For I will stir up the Medes against Babylon, and no amount of silver or gold will buy them off. ¹⁸The attacking armies will shoot down the young people with arrows. They will have no mercy on helpless babies and will show no compassion for the children.

¹⁹Babylon, the most glorious of kingdoms, the flower of Chaldean culture, will be devastated like Sodom and Gomorrah when God destroyed them. ²⁰Babylon will never rise again. Generation after generation will come and go, but the land will never again be lived in. Nomads will refuse to camp there, and shepherds will not allow their sheep to stay overnight. ²¹Wild animals of the desert will move into the ruined city. The houses will be haunted by howling creatures. Ostriches will live among the ruins, and wild goats will come there to dance. ²²Hyenas will howl in its fortresses, and jackals will make their dens in its palaces. Babylon's days are numbered; its time of destruction will soon arrive.

CHAPTER 14

A Taunt for Babylon's King

But the LORD will have mercy on the descendants of Jacob. Israel will be his special people once again. He will bring them back to settle once again in their own land. And people from many different nations will come and join them there and become a part of the people of Israel.* ²The nations of the world will help the LORD's people to return, and those who come to live in their land will serve them. Those who captured Israel will be captured, and Israel will rule over its enemies.

14:1 Hebrew *the house of Jacob.*

I BELIEVE that—before the Babylonians even invaded Israel—the Lord accurately foretold the destruction of Babylon. (13:2)

I BELIEVE the Lord can use any nation to carry out his purposes. (13:5)

I BELIEVE the day of the Lord's judgment will be a time of terror for those who hate him. (13:9)

I MOURN when I think of those whom the Lord will have to judge if they don't repent of their sins. (13:11)

I BELIEVE the Lord accurately foretold that Babylon would be destroyed completely—never to be inhabited again. (13:20)

See Jacob's profile (page 43) at Genesis 32:9.

I BELIEVE the Lord accurately foretold that the nations would help the Israelites return to their land. (14:2)

Pray that the Holy Spirit will guide you into all truth (John 16:13).

³In that wonderful day when the LORD gives his people rest from sorrow and fear, from slavery and chains, ⁴you will taunt the king of Babylon. You will say, "The mighty man has been destroyed. Yes, your insolence is ended. ⁵For the LORD has crushed your wicked power and broken your evil rule. ⁶You persecuted the people with unceasing blows of rage and held the nations in your angry grip. Your tyranny was unrestrained. ⁷But at last the land is at rest and is quiet. Finally it can sing again! ⁸Even the trees of the forest—the cypress trees and the cedars of Lebanon—sing out this joyous song: 'Your power is broken! No one will come to cut us down now!'

⁹"In the place of the dead* there is excitement over your arrival. World leaders and mighty kings long dead are there to see you. ¹⁰With one voice they all cry out, 'Now you are as weak as we are! ¹¹Your might and power are gone; they were buried with you. All the pleasant music in your palace has ceased. Now maggots are your sheet and worms your blanket.'

I BELIEVE the Lord accurately predicted the end of the power of the king of Babylon. (14:11)

¹²"How you are fallen from heaven, O shining star, son of the morning! You have been thrown down to the earth, you who destroyed the nations of the world. ¹³For you said to yourself, 'I will ascend to heaven and set my throne above God's stars. I will preside on the mountain of the gods far away in the north. ¹⁴I will climb to the highest heavens and be like the Most High.' ¹⁵But instead, you will be brought down to the place of the dead, down to its lowest depths. ¹⁶Everyone there will stare at you and ask, 'Can this be the one who shook the earth and the kingdoms of the world? ¹⁷Is this the one who destroyed the world and made it into a wilderness? Is this the king who demolished the world's greatest cities and had no mercy on his prisoners?'

I BELIEVE anyone who exalts himself above God will be brought down to the place of the dead. (14:15)

¹⁸"The kings of the nations lie in stately glory in their tombs, ¹⁹but you will be thrown out of your grave like a worthless branch. Like a corpse trampled underfoot, you will be dumped into a mass grave with those killed in battle. You will descend to the pit. ²⁰You will not be given a proper burial, for you have destroyed your nation and slaughtered your people. Your son will not succeed you as king. ²¹Kill the children of this sinner! Do not let them rise and conquer the land or rebuild the cities of the world."

²²This is what the LORD Almighty says: "I, myself, have risen against him! I will destroy his children and his children's children, so they will never sit on his throne. ²³I will make Babylon into a desolate land, a place of porcupines, filled with swamps and marshes. I will sweep the land with the broom of destruction. I, the LORD Almighty, have spoken!"

I BELIEVE the Lord kept his promise to punish the Babylonians because of their pride and violence. (14:22)

A Message about Assyria

²⁴The LORD Almighty has sworn this oath: "It will all happen as I have planned. It will come about according to my purposes. ²⁵I will break the Assyrians when they are in Israel; I will trample them on my mountains. My people will no longer be their slaves. ²⁶I have a plan for the whole earth, for my mighty power reaches throughout the world. ²⁷The LORD Almighty has spoken—who can change his plans? When his hand moves, who can stop him?"

I BELIEVE the Lord has a plan for the whole earth and that no one can stop him from carrying it out. (14:26)

A Message about Philistia

²⁸This message came to me the year King Ahaz died:

²⁹Do not rejoice, you Philistines, that the king who attacked you is dead. For even though that whip is broken, his son will be worse than his father ever was. From that snake a poisonous snake will be born, a fiery serpent to destroy you! ³⁰I will feed the poor in my pasture; the needy will lie down in peace. But as for you, I will wipe you out with famine. I will destroy the few who remain.

I BELIEVE the Lord kept his promise to protect his people and punish the Philistines. (14:30)

³¹Weep, you Philistine cities, for you are doomed! Melt in fear, for every-

14:9 Hebrew *Sheol*; also in 14:15.

one will be destroyed. A powerful army is coming out of the north. Each soldier rushes forward ready to fight. [32]What should we tell the enemy messengers? Tell them that the LORD has built Jerusalem,* and that the poor of his people will find refuge in its walls.

CHAPTER 15

A Message about Moab

This message came to me concerning Moab:

In one night your cities of Ar and Kir will be destroyed. [2]Your people in Dibon will mourn at their temples and shrines, weeping for the fate of Nebo and Medeba. They will shave their heads in sorrow and cut off their beards. [3]They will wear sackcloth as they wander the streets. From every home will come the sound of weeping. [4]The cries from the cities of Heshbon and Elealeh will be heard far away, even in Jahaz! The bravest warriors of Moab will cry out in utter terror.

[5]My heart weeps for Moab. Its people flee to Zoar and Eglath-shelishiyah. Weeping, they climb the road to Luhith. Their crying can be heard all along the road to Horonaim. [6]Even the waters of Nimrim are dried up! The grassy banks are scorched, and the tender plants are gone. [7]The desperate refugees take only the possessions they can carry and flee across the Ravine of Willows. [8]The whole land of Moab is a land of weeping from one end to the other—from Eglaim to Beer-elim. [9]The stream near Dibon* runs red with blood, but I am still not finished with Dibon! Lions will hunt down the survivors, both those who try to run and those who remain behind.

CHAPTER 16

Moab's refugees at Sela send lambs to Jerusalem* as a token of alliance with the king of Judah. [2]The women of Moab are left like homeless birds at the shallow crossings of the Arnon River. [3]"Help us," they cry. "Defend us against our enemies. Protect us from their relentless attack. Do not betray us. [4]Let our outcasts stay among you. Hide them from our enemies until the terror is past."

When oppression and destruction have ceased and enemy raiders have disappeared, [5]then David's throne will be established by love. From that throne a faithful king will reign, one who always does what is just and right.

[6]Is this Moab, the proud land we have heard so much about? Its pride and insolence are all gone now! [7]The entire land of Moab weeps. Yes, you people of Moab, mourn for the delicacies of Kir-hareseth. [8]Weep for the abandoned farms of Heshbon and the vineyards at Sibmah. The wine from those vineyards used to make the rulers of the nations drunk. Moab was once like a spreading grapevine. Her tendrils spread out as far as Jazer and trailed out into the desert. Her shoots once reached as far as the Dead Sea.* [9]But now the enemy has completely destroyed that vine. So I wail and lament for Jazer and the vineyards of Sibmah. My tears will flow for Heshbon and Elealeh, for their summer fruits and harvests have all been destroyed.

[10]Gone now is the gladness; gone is the joy of harvest. The happy singing in the vineyards will be heard no more. The treading out of grapes in the winepresses has ceased forever. I have ended all their harvest joys. [11]I will weep for Moab. My sorrow for Kir-hareseth* will be very great. [12]On the hilltops the people of Moab will pray in anguish to their idols, but it will do them no good. They will cry to the gods in their temples, but no one will come to save them.

[13]The LORD has already said this about Moab in the past. [14]But now the

---

I BELIEVE the Lord accurately foretold the destruction of Moab. (15:1)

I MOURN for those who are being destroyed—even if they are getting what they deserve. (15:5)

I RECOGNIZE that pride and insolence eventually produce sorrow and shame. (16:6)

I KNOW those who look to false gods will have no one to save them. (16:12)

I BELIEVE the Lord accurately predicted that Moab would fall. (16:13)

14:32 Hebrew *Zion.* 15:9 As in Dead Sea Scrolls, some Greek manuscripts, and Latin Vulgate; Masoretic Text reads *Dimon;* also in 15:9b. 16:1 Hebrew *to the daughter of Zion.* 16:8 Hebrew *the sea.* 16:11 Hebrew *Kir-heres,* a variant name for Kir-hareseth.

LORD says, "Within three years, without fail, the glory of Moab will be ended, and few of its people will be left alive."

CHAPTER **17**

A Message about Damascus and Israel

This message came to me concerning Damascus:

"Look, Damascus will disappear! It will become a heap of ruins. ²The cities of Aroer will be deserted. Sheep will graze in the streets and lie down unafraid. There will be no one to chase them away. ³The fortified cities of Israel* will also be destroyed, and the power of Damascus will end. The few left in Aram will share the fate of Israel's departed glory," says the LORD Almighty.

⁴"In that day the glory of Israel* will be very dim, for poverty will stalk the land. ⁵Israel will be abandoned like the grainfields in the valley of Rephaim after the harvest. ⁶Only a few of its people will be left, like the stray olives left on the tree after the harvest. Only two or three remain in the highest branches, four or five out on the tips of the limbs. Yes, Israel will be stripped bare of people," says the LORD, the God of Israel.

⁷Then at last the people will think of their Creator and have respect for the Holy One of Israel. ⁸They will no longer ask their idols for help or worship what their own hands have made. They will never again bow down to their Asherah poles or burn incense on the altars they built.

⁹Their largest cities will be as deserted as overgrown thickets. They will become like the cities the Amorites abandoned when the Israelites came here so long ago. ¹⁰Why? Because you have turned from the God who can save you—the Rock who can hide you. You may plant the finest imported grapevines, ¹¹and they may grow so well that they blossom on the very morning you plant them, but you will never pick any grapes from them. Your only harvest will be a load of grief and incurable pain.

¹²Look! The armies rush forward like waves thundering toward the shore. ¹³But though they roar like breakers on a beach, God will silence them. They will flee like chaff scattered by the wind or like dust whirling before a storm. ¹⁴In the evening Israel waits in terror, but by dawn its enemies are dead. This is the just reward of those who plunder and destroy the people of God.

CHAPTER **18**

A Message about Ethiopia

Destruction is certain for the land of Ethiopia,* which lies at the headwaters of the Nile. Its winged sailboats glide along the river, ²and ambassadors are sent in fast boats down the Nile. Go home, swift messengers! Take a message to your land divided by rivers, to your tall, smooth-skinned people, who are feared far and wide for their conquests and destruction.

³When I raise my battle flag on the mountain, let all the world take notice. When I blow the trumpet, listen! ⁴For the LORD has told me this: "I will watch quietly from my dwelling place—as quietly as the heat rises on a summer day, or as the dew forms on an autumn morning during the harvest."

⁵Even before you begin your attack, while your plans are ripening like grapes, the LORD will cut you off as though with pruning shears. He will snip your spreading branches. ⁶Your mighty army will be left dead in the fields for the mountain birds and wild animals to eat. The vultures will tear at corpses all summer. The wild animals will gnaw at bones all winter.

⁷But the time will come when the LORD Almighty will receive gifts from this land divided by rivers, from this tall, smooth-skinned people, who are feared far and wide for their conquests and destruction. They will bring the gifts to the LORD Almighty in Jerusalem,* the place where his name dwells.

Margin notes

I BELIEVE the Lord accurately foretold the destruction of Damascus. (17:1)

I THINK of my Creator and have respect for the Holy One. (17:7)

I DO NOT TURN AWAY from the God who can save me. (17:10)

I BELIEVE the Lord kept his promise to judge Israel's enemies who sought to destroy them. (17:14)

I BELIEVE the Lord accurately foretold the destruction of Ethiopia. (18:1)

I BELIEVE the Lord accurately foretold the day when the Ethiopians would worship him in his presence. (18:7)

17:3 Hebrew *of Ephraim,* referring to the northern kingdom of Israel. 17:4 Hebrew *of Jacob.* 18:1 Hebrew *Cush.* 18:7 Hebrew *on Mount Zion.*

CHAPTER 19

A Message about Egypt

This message came to me concerning Egypt:

Look! The Lord is advancing against Egypt, riding on a swift cloud. The idols of Egypt tremble. The hearts of the Egyptians melt with fear.

²"I will make the Egyptians fight against each other—brother against brother, neighbor against neighbor, city against city, province against province. ³The Egyptians will lose heart, and I will confuse their plans. They will plead with their idols for wisdom. They will call on spirits, mediums, and psychics to show them which way to turn. ⁴I will hand Egypt over to a hard, cruel master, to a fierce king," says the Lord, the Lord Almighty.

⁵The waters of the Nile will fail to rise and flood the fields. The riverbed will be parched and dry. ⁶The canals of the Nile will dry up, and the streams of Egypt will become foul with rotting reeds and rushes. ⁷All the greenery along the riverbank will wither and blow away. All the crops will dry up, and everything will die. ⁸The fishermen will weep for lack of work. Those who fish with hooks and those who use nets will all be unemployed. ⁹The weavers will have no flax or cotton, for the crops will fail. ¹⁰The weavers and all the workers will be sick at heart.

¹¹What fools are the counselors of Zoan! Their best counsel to the king of Egypt is stupid and wrong. Will they still boast of their wisdom? Will they dare tell Pharaoh about their long line of wise ancestors? ¹²What has happened to your wise counselors, Pharaoh? If they are so wise, let them tell you what the Lord Almighty is going to do to Egypt. ¹³The wise men from Zoan are fools, and those from Memphis* are deluded. The leaders of Egypt have ruined the land with their foolish counsel. ¹⁴The Lord has sent a spirit of foolishness on them, so all their suggestions are wrong. They cause the land of Egypt to stagger like a sick drunkard. ¹⁵Nobody in Egypt, whether rich or poor, important or unknown, can offer any help.

¹⁶In that day the Egyptians will be as weak as women. They will cower in fear beneath the upraised fist of the Lord Almighty. ¹⁷Just to speak the name of Israel will strike deep terror in their hearts, for the Lord Almighty has laid out his plans against them.

¹⁸In that day five of Egypt's cities will follow the Lord Almighty. They will even begin to speak the Hebrew language.* One of these will be Heliopolis, the City of the Sun. ¹⁹In that day there will be an altar to the Lord in the heart of Egypt, and there will be a monument to the Lord at its border. ²⁰It will be a sign and a witness to the Lord Almighty in the land of Egypt. When the people cry to the Lord for help against those who oppress them, he will send them a savior who will rescue them.

²¹In that day the Lord will make himself known to the Egyptians. Yes, they will know the Lord and will give their sacrifices and offerings to him. They will make promises to the Lord and keep them. ²²The Lord will strike Egypt in a way that will bring healing. For the Egyptians will turn to the Lord, and he will listen to their pleas and heal them.

²³In that day Egypt and Assyria will be connected by a highway. The Egyptians and Assyrians will move freely between their lands, and they will worship the same God. ²⁴And Israel will be their ally. The three will be together, and Israel will be a blessing to them. ²⁵For the Lord Almighty will say, "Blessed be Egypt, my people. Blessed be Assyria, the land I have made. Blessed be Israel, my special possession!"

CHAPTER 20

A Message about Egypt and Ethiopia

In the year when King Sargon of Assyria captured the Philistine city of Ashdod, ²the Lord told Isaiah son of Amoz, "Take off all your clothes, including your sandals." Isaiah did as he was told and walked around naked and barefoot.

I BELIEVE the Lord accurately foretold the civil war in Egypt. (19:2)

I BELIEVE the Lord accurately foretold the drought and famine in Egypt. (19:5)

I BELIEVE the Lord is in control of the advisers to world leaders. (19:14)

I BELIEVE the Lord kept his promise to make himself known to the Egyptians. (19:21)

I BELIEVE the Lord promised to bless Egypt and Assyria and be their God. (19:25)

19:13 Hebrew *Noph.*   **19:18** Hebrew *the language of Canaan.*

³Then the LORD said, "My servant Isaiah has been walking around naked and barefoot for the last three years. This is a sign—a symbol of the terrible troubles I will bring upon Egypt and Ethiopia.* ⁴For the king of Assyria will take away the Egyptians and Ethiopians* as prisoners. He will make them walk naked and barefoot, both young and old, their buttocks uncovered, to the shame of Egypt. ⁵How dismayed will be the Philistines, who counted on the power of Ethiopia and boasted of their allies in Egypt! ⁶They will say, 'If this can happen to Egypt, what chance do we have? For we counted on Egypt to protect us from the king of Assyria.' "

I DO NOT TRUST in those who are too weak to save themselves. (20:6)

CHAPTER 21

A Message about Babylon

This message came to me concerning the land of Babylonia*:

Disaster is roaring down on you from the desert, like a whirlwind sweeping in from the Negev. ²I see an awesome vision: I see you plundered and destroyed. Go ahead, you Elamites and Medes, take part in the siege. Babylon will fall, and the groaning of all the nations she enslaved will end. ³My stomach aches and burns with pain. Sharp pangs of horror are upon me, like the pangs of a woman giving birth. I grow faint when I hear what God is planning; I am blinded with dismay. ⁴My mind reels; my heart races. The sleep I once enjoyed at night is now a faint memory. I lie awake, trembling.

⁵Look! They are preparing a great feast. They are spreading rugs for people to sit on. Everyone is eating and drinking. Quick! Grab your shields and prepare for battle! You are being attacked!

I WATCH to see when God's Word is fulfilled. (21:6)

⁶Meanwhile, the Lord said to me, "Put a watchman on the city wall to shout out what he sees. ⁷Tell him to sound the alert when he sees chariots drawn by horses and warriors mounted on donkeys and camels."

⁸ Then the watchman* called out, "Day after day I have stood on the watchtower, my lord. Night after night I have remained at my post. ⁹Now at last—look! Here come the chariots and warriors!" Then the watchman said, "Babylon is fallen! All the idols of Babylon lie broken on the ground!"

I TELL God's people everything he says. (21:10)

¹⁰O my people, threshed and winnowed, I have told you everything the LORD Almighty, the God of Israel, has said.

A Message about Edom

¹¹This message came to me concerning Edom*:

Someone from Edom* keeps calling to me, "Watchman, how much longer until morning? When will the night be over?"

¹²The watchman replies, "Morning is coming, but night will soon follow. If you wish to ask again, then come back and ask."

A Message about Arabia

¹³This message came to me concerning Arabia:

O caravans from Dedan, hide in the deserts of Arabia. ¹⁴O people of Tema, bring food and water to these weary refugees. ¹⁵They have fled from drawn swords and sharp arrows and the terrors of war. ¹⁶"But within a year,"* says the Lord, "all the glory of Kedar will come to an end. ¹⁷Only a few of its courageous archers will survive. I, the LORD, the God of Israel, have spoken!"

I BELIEVE what the Lord has spoken. (21:17)

CHAPTER 22

A Message about Jerusalem

This message came to me concerning Jerusalem*:

What is happening? Why is everyone running to the rooftops? ²The whole

20:3 Hebrew *Cush*; also in 20:5. 20:4 Hebrew *Cushites*. 21:1 Hebrew *the desert of the sea*. 21:8 As in Dead Sea Scrolls and Syriac version; Masoretic Text reads *a lion*. 21:11a Hebrew *Dumah*, which means "silence" or "stillness." It is a wordplay on the word *Edom*. 21:11b Hebrew *Seir*, another name for Edom. 21:16 Hebrew *Within a year, like the years of a hired hand*. Some ancient manuscripts read *Within three years*, as in 16:14. 22:1 Hebrew *concerning the Valley of Vision*.

city is in a terrible uproar. What do I see in this reveling city? Bodies are lying everywhere, killed by famine and disease.* ³All your leaders flee. They surrender without resistance. The people try to slip away, but they are captured, too. ⁴Leave me alone to weep; do not try to comfort me. Let me cry for my people as I watch them being destroyed.

⁵Oh, what a day of crushing trouble! What a day of confusion and terror the Lord, the LORD Almighty, has brought upon the Valley of Vision! The walls of Jerusalem have been broken, and cries of death echo from the mountainsides. ⁶Elamites are the archers; Arameans drive the chariots. The men of Kir hold up the shields. ⁷They fill your beautiful valleys and crowd against your gates. ⁸Judah's defenses have been stripped away. You run to the armory for your weapons. ⁹You inspect the walls of Jerusalem* to see what needs to be repaired. You store up water in the lower pool. ¹⁰You check the houses and tear some down to get stone to fix the walls. ¹¹Between the city walls, you build a reservoir for water from the old pool. But all your feverish plans are to no avail because you never ask God for help. He is the one who planned this long ago.

¹²The Lord, the LORD Almighty, called you to weep and mourn. He told you to shave your heads in sorrow for your sins and to wear clothes of sackcloth to show your remorse. ¹³But instead, you dance and play; you slaughter sacrificial animals, feast on meat, and drink wine. "Let's eat, drink, and be merry," you say. "What's the difference, for tomorrow we die." ¹⁴The LORD Almighty has revealed to me that this sin will never be forgiven you until the day you die. That is the judgment of the Lord, the LORD Almighty.

A Message for Shebna

¹⁵Furthermore, the Lord, the LORD Almighty, told me to confront Shebna, the palace administrator, and to give him this message: ¹⁶"Who do you think you are, building a beautiful tomb for yourself in the rock? ¹⁷For the LORD is about to seize you and hurl you away. He is going to send you into captivity, you strong man! ¹⁸He will crumple you up into a ball and toss you away into a distant, barren land. There you will die, and there your glorious chariots will remain, broken and useless. You are a disgrace to your master.

¹⁹"Yes, I will drive you out of office," says the LORD. "I will pull you down from your high position. ²⁰And then I will call my servant Eliakim son of Hilkiah to replace you. ²¹He will have your royal robes, your title, and your authority. And he will be a father to the people of Jerusalem and Judah. ²²I will give him the key to the house of David—the highest position in the royal court. He will open doors, and no one will be able to shut them; he will close doors, and no one will be able to open them. ²³He will bring honor to his family name, for I will drive him firmly in place like a tent stake. ²⁴He will be loaded down with responsibility, and he will bring honor to even the lowliest members of his family."

²⁵The LORD Almighty says: "When that time comes, I will pull out the stake that seemed so firm. It will come out and fall to the ground. Everything it supports will fall with it. I, the LORD, have spoken!"

CHAPTER 23

A Message about Tyre

This message came to me concerning Tyre:

Weep, O ships of Tarshish, returning home from distant lands! Weep for your harbor at Tyre because it is gone! The rumors you heard in Cyprus* are all true. ²Mourn in silence, you people of the coast and you merchants of Sidon. Your traders crossed the sea, ³sailing over deep waters. They brought

I MOURN when I see God's people suffering—even if they are getting what they deserve. (22:4)

I ASK God for help instead of trying to fix my problems myself. (22:11)

I DO NOT COVER UP my sin or ignore its consequences by seeking temporary pleasures. (22:13)

I USE my position of authority and responsibility to care for God's people. (22:21)

See David's profile (page 629) at Psalm 3:1.

I BELIEVE the Lord spoke through Isaiah. (23:1)

22:2 Hebrew killed, but not by sword and not in battle. 22:9 Hebrew the city of David. 23:1 Hebrew Kittim; also in 23:12.

you grain from Egypt* and harvests from along the Nile. You were the merchandise mart of the world.

⁴But now you are put to shame, city of Sidon, fortress on the sea. For the sea says, "Now I am childless; I have no sons or daughters." ⁵When Egypt hears the news about Tyre, there will be great sorrow. ⁶Flee now to Tarshish! Wail, you people who live by the sea! ⁷How can this silent ruin be all that is left of your once joyous city? What a history was yours! Think of all the colonists you sent to distant lands.

I BELIEVE the Lord punished Tyre for its pride. (23:9)

⁸Who has brought this disaster on Tyre, empire builder and chief trader of the world? ⁹The LORD Almighty has done it to destroy your pride and show his contempt for all human greatness. ¹⁰Come, Tarshish, sweep over your mother Tyre like the flooding Nile, for the city is defenseless. ¹¹The LORD holds out his hand over the seas. He shakes the kingdoms of the earth. He has spoken out against Phoenicia* and depleted its strength. ¹²He says, "Never again will you rejoice, O daughter of Sidon. Once you were a lovely city, but you will never again be strong. Even if you flee to Cyprus, you will find no rest."

¹³Look at the land of Babylonia*—the people of that land are gone! The Assyrians have handed Babylon over to the wild beasts. They have built siege ramps against its walls, torn down its palaces, and turned it into a heap of rubble.

¹⁴Wail, O ships of Tarshish, for your home port is destroyed! ¹⁵For seventy years, the length of a king's life, Tyre will be forgotten. But then the city will come back to life and sing sweet songs like a prostitute. ¹⁶Long absent from her lovers, she will take a harp, walk the streets, and sing her songs, so that she will again be remembered. ¹⁷Yes, after seventy years the LORD will revive Tyre. But she will be no different than she was before. She will return again to all her evil ways around the world. ¹⁸But in the end her businesses will give their profits to the LORD. Her wealth will not be hoarded but will be used to provide good food and fine clothing for the LORD's priests.

I BELIEVE the Lord kept his promise to use Tyre's profits to benefit his own people. (23:18)

CHAPTER 24

Destruction of the Earth

Look! The LORD is about to destroy the earth and make it a vast wasteland. See how he is scattering the people over the face of the earth. ²Priests and laypeople, servants and masters, maids and mistresses, buyers and sellers, lenders and borrowers, bankers and debtors—none will be spared. ³The earth will be completely emptied and looted. The LORD has spoken!

I DO NOT TWIST God's instructions or break his covenant. (24:5)

⁴The earth dries up, the crops wither, the skies refuse to rain. ⁵The earth suffers for the sins of its people, for they have twisted the instructions of God, violated his laws, and broken his everlasting covenant. ⁶Therefore, a curse consumes the earth and its people. They are left desolate, destroyed by fire. Few will be left alive.

⁷All the joys of life will be gone. The grape harvest will fail, and there will be no wine. The merrymakers will sigh and mourn. ⁸The clash of tambourines will be stilled; the happy cries of celebration will be heard no more. The melodious chords of the harp will be silent. ⁹Gone are the joys of wine and song; strong drink now turns bitter in the mouth.

¹⁰The city writhes in chaos; every home is locked to keep out looters. ¹¹Mobs gather in the streets, crying out for wine. Joy has reached its lowest ebb. Gladness has been banished from the land. ¹²The city is left in ruins, with its gates battered down. ¹³Throughout the earth the story is the same—like the stray olives left on the tree or the few grapes left on the vine after harvest, only a remnant is left.

23:3 Hebrew *from Shihor,* a branch of the Nile River.   23:11 Hebrew *Canaan.*   23:13 Or *Chaldea.*

[14]But all who are left will shout and sing for joy. Those in the west will praise the LORD's majesty. [15]In eastern lands, give glory to the LORD. In the coastlands of the sea, praise the name of the LORD, the God of Israel. [16]Listen to them as they sing to the LORD from the ends of the earth. Hear them singing praises to the Righteous One!

But my heart is heavy with grief. I am discouraged, for evil still prevails, and treachery is everywhere. [17]Terror and traps and snares will be your lot, you people of the earth. [18]Those who flee in terror will fall into a trap, and those who escape the trap will step into a snare.

Destruction falls on you from the heavens. The world is shaken beneath you. [19]The earth has broken down and has utterly collapsed. Everything is lost, abandoned, and confused. [20]The earth staggers like a drunkard. It trembles like a tent in a storm. It falls and will not rise again, for its sins are very great.

[21]In that day the LORD will punish the fallen angels in the heavens and the proud rulers of the nations on earth. [22]They will be rounded up and put in prison until they are tried and condemned. [23]Then the LORD Almighty will mount his throne on Mount Zion. He will rule gloriously in Jerusalem, in the sight of all the leaders of his people. There will be such glory that the brightness of the sun and moon will seem to fade away.

I BELIEVE the righteous who are left after God's judgment will praise him. (24:14)

I BELIEVE people from the ends of the earth will sing praises to the Lord. (24:16)

I BELIEVE the Lord one day will judge and punish the fallen angels (Jude 1:6). (24:21)

I BELIEVE the Lord one day will rule the earth with his glory. (24:23)

CHAPTER 25

Praise for Judgment and Salvation

O LORD, I will honor and praise your name, for you are my God. You do such wonderful things! You planned them long ago, and now you have accomplished them. [2]You turn mighty cities into heaps of ruins. Cities with strong walls are turned to rubble. Beautiful palaces in distant lands disappear and will never be rebuilt. [3]Therefore, strong nations will declare your glory; ruthless nations will revere you.

[4]But to the poor, O LORD, you are a refuge from the storm. To the needy in distress, you are a shelter from the rain and the heat. For the oppressive acts of ruthless people are like a storm beating against a wall, [5]or like the relentless heat of the desert. But you silence the roar of foreign nations. You cool the land with the shade of a cloud. So the boastful songs of ruthless people are stilled.

[6]In Jerusalem,* the LORD Almighty will spread a wonderful feast for everyone around the world. It will be a delicious feast of good food, with clear, well-aged wine and choice beef. [7]In that day he will remove the cloud of gloom, the shadow of death that hangs over the earth. [8]He will swallow up death forever! The Sovereign LORD will wipe away all tears. He will remove forever all insults and mockery against his land and people. The LORD has spoken!

[9]In that day the people will proclaim, "This is our God. We trusted in him, and he saved us. This is the LORD, in whom we trusted. Let us rejoice in the salvation he brings!" [10]For the LORD's good hand will rest on Jerusalem.

Moab will be crushed like trampled straw and left to rot. [11]God will push down Moab's people as a swimmer pushes down water with his hands. He will end their pride and all their evil works. [12]The high walls of Moab will be demolished and ground to dust.

I PRAISE the Lord for the wonderful things he has planned from long ago. (25:1)

I PRAISE the Lord for being a refuge to the poor and needy. (25:4)

I BELIEVE the Lord one day will wipe away all tears and death (Revelation 21:4). (25:8)

CHAPTER 26

A Song of Praise to the LORD

In that day, everyone in the land of Judah will sing this song:

Our city is now strong!
We are surrounded by the walls of God's salvation.

25:6 Hebrew *On this mountain;* also in 25:10.

² Open the gates to all who are righteous;
  allow the faithful to enter.
³ You will keep in perfect peace all who trust in you,
  whose thoughts are fixed on you!
⁴ Trust in the LORD always,
  for the LORD GOD is the eternal Rock.
⁵ He humbles the proud
  and brings the arrogant city to the dust.
  Its walls come crashing down!
⁶ The poor and oppressed trample it underfoot.

⁷ But for those who are righteous,
  the path is not steep and rough.
  You are a God of justice,
  and you smooth out the road ahead of them.
⁸ LORD, we love to obey your laws;
  our heart's desire is to glorify your name.
⁹ All night long I search for you;
  earnestly I seek for God.
  For only when you come to judge the earth
  will people turn from wickedness and do what is right.
¹⁰ Your kindness to the wicked does not make them do good.
  They keep doing wrong and take no notice of the LORD's majesty.
¹¹ O LORD, they do not listen when you threaten.
  They do not see your upraised fist.
  Show them your eagerness to defend your people.
  Perhaps then they will be ashamed.
  Let your fire consume your enemies.

¹² LORD, you will grant us peace,
  for all we have accomplished is really from you.
¹³ O LORD our God, others have ruled us,
  but we worship you alone.
¹⁴ Those we served before are dead and gone.
  Never again will they return!
  You attacked them and destroyed them,
  and they are long forgotten.
¹⁵ We praise you, LORD!
  You have made our nation great;
  you have extended our borders!

¹⁶ LORD, in distress we searched for you.
  We were bowed beneath the burden of your discipline.
¹⁷ We were like a woman about to give birth,
  writhing and crying out in pain.
  When we are in your presence, LORD,
¹⁸ we, too, writhe in agony,
  but nothing comes of our suffering.
  We have done nothing to rescue the world;
  no one has been born to populate the earth.

¹⁹ Yet we have this assurance:
  Those who belong to God will live;
  their bodies will rise again!
  Those who sleep in the earth
  will rise up and sing for joy!
  For God's light of life will fall like dew
  on his people in the place of the dead!

I FIX my thoughts on the Lord, trust in him, and enjoy perfect peace. (26:3)

I LOVE to obey the Lord's laws and desire to glorify his name. (26:8)

I ACKNOWLEDGE that all I accomplish is from the Lord. (26:12)

I TURN BACK to the Lord when he disciplines me. (26:16)

I AM CONFIDENT that all who belong to God will rise again to new life! (26:19)

Restoration for Israel

²⁰Go home, my people, and lock your doors! Hide until the LORD's anger against your enemies has passed. ²¹Look! The LORD is coming from heaven to punish the people of the earth for their sins. The earth will no longer hide those who have been murdered. They will be brought out for all to see.

Ask the Lord to make you "totally committed to doing what is right" (Titus 2:14).

CHAPTER 27

In that day the LORD will take his terrible, swift sword and punish Leviathan, the swiftly moving serpent, the coiling, writhing serpent, the dragon of the sea.

²"In that day we will sing of the pleasant vineyard. ³I, the LORD, will watch over it and tend its fruitful vines. Each day I will water them; day and night I will watch to keep enemies away. ⁴My anger against Israel will be gone. If I find briers and thorns bothering her, I will burn them up. ⁵These enemies will be spared only if they surrender and beg for peace and protection."

I BELIEVE the Lord one day will restore his vineyard, Israel. (27:3)

⁶The time is coming when my people will take root. Israel will bud and blossom and fill the whole earth with her fruit! ⁷Has the LORD punished Israel in the same way he has punished her enemies? No, for he devastated her enemies, ⁸but he has punished Israel only a little. He has exiled her from her land as though blown away in a storm from the east. ⁹The LORD did this to purge away Israel's* sin. When he has finished, all the pagan altars will be crushed to dust. There won't be an Asherah pole or incense altar left standing. ¹⁰Israel's fortified cities will be silent and empty, the houses abandoned, the streets covered with grass. Cattle will graze there, chewing on twigs and branches.

I BELIEVE the Lord punished his people Israel so that he could cleanse and restore them. (27:7)

¹¹The people are like the dead branches of a tree, broken off and used for kindling beneath the cooking pots. Israel is a foolish and stupid nation, for its people have turned away from God. Therefore, the one who made them will show them no pity or mercy. ¹²Yet the time will come when the LORD will gather them together one by one like handpicked grain. He will bring them to his great threshing floor—from the Euphrates River* in the east to the brook of Egypt in the west. ¹³In that day the great trumpet will sound. Many who were dying in exile in Assyria and Egypt will return to Jerusalem to worship the LORD on his holy mountain.

I BELIEVE the Lord accurately predicted that he would bring his people Israel back to their land. (27:12)

CHAPTER 28

A Message about Samaria

Destruction is certain for the city of Samaria—the pride and joy of the drunkards of Israel*! It sits in a rich valley, but its glorious beauty will suddenly disappear. Destruction is certain for that city—the pride of a people brought low by wine. ²For the Lord will send the mighty Assyrian army against it. Like a mighty hailstorm and a torrential rain, they will burst upon it and dash it to the ground. ³The proud city of Samaria—the pride and joy of the drunkards of Israel—will be trampled beneath its enemies' feet. ⁴It sits in a fertile valley, but its glorious beauty will suddenly disappear. It will be greedily snatched up, as an early fig is hungrily picked and eaten.

I BELIEVE the Lord accurately predicted that Samaria would be destroyed because of its pride. (28:1)

⁵Then at last the LORD Almighty will himself be Israel's crowning glory. He will be the pride and joy of the remnant of his people. ⁶He will give a longing for justice to their judges. He will give great courage to their warriors who stand at the gates.

⁷Now, however, Israel is being led by drunks! The priests and prophets reel and stagger from beer and wine. They make stupid mistakes as they carry out their responsibilities. ⁸Their tables are covered with vomit; filth is everywhere. ⁹They say, "Who does the LORD think we are? Why does he speak to us

I DO NOT MOCK or challenge the Lord's decrees. (28:9)

27:9 Hebrew *Jacob's.*   27:12 Hebrew *the river.*   28:1 Hebrew *of Ephraim,* referring to the northern kingdom of Israel; also in 28:3.

like this? Are we little children, barely old enough to talk? [10]He tells us everything over and over again, a line at a time, in very simple words!*"

[11]Since they refuse to listen, God will speak to them through foreign oppressors who speak an unknown language! [12]God's people could have rest in their own land if they would only obey him, but they will not listen. [13]So the LORD will spell out his message for them again, repeating it over and over, a line at a time, in very simple words. Yet they will stumble over this simple, straightforward message. They will be injured, trapped, and captured.

[14]Therefore, listen to this message from the LORD, you scoffing rulers in Jerusalem. [15]You boast that you have struck a bargain to avoid death and have made a deal to dodge the grave.* You say, "The Assyrians can never touch us, for we have built a strong refuge made of lies and deception." [16]Therefore, this is what the Sovereign LORD says: "Look! I am placing a foundation stone in Jerusalem.* It is firm, a tested and precious cornerstone that is safe to build on. Whoever believes need never run away again.*

[17]"I will take the measuring line of justice and the plumb line of righteousness to check the foundation wall you have built. Your refuge looks strong, but since it is made of lies, a hailstorm will knock it down. Since it is made of deception, the enemy will come like a flood to sweep it away. [18]I will cancel the bargain you made to avoid death, and I will overturn your deal to dodge the grave. When the terrible enemy floods in, you will be trampled into the ground. [19]Again and again that flood will come, morning after morning, day and night, until you are carried away."

This message will bring terror to your people. [20]For you have no place of refuge—the bed you have made is too short to lie on. The blankets are too narrow to cover you. [21]The LORD will come suddenly and in anger, as he did against the Philistines at Mount Perazim and against the Amorites at Gibeon. He will come to do a strange, unusual thing: He will destroy his own people! [22]So scoff no more, or your punishment will be even greater. For the Lord, the LORD Almighty, has plainly told me that he is determined to crush you.

[23]Listen to me; listen as I plead! [24]Does a farmer always plow and never sow? Is he forever cultivating the soil and never planting it? [25]Does he not finally plant his seeds for dill, cumin, wheat, barley, and spelt, each in its own section of his land? [26]The farmer knows just what to do, for God has given him understanding. [27]He doesn't thresh all his crops the same way. A heavy sledge is never used on dill; rather, it is beaten with a light stick. A threshing wheel is never rolled on cumin; instead, it is beaten softly with a flail. [28]Bread grain is easily crushed, so he doesn't keep on pounding it. He threshes it under the wheels of a cart, but he doesn't pulverize it. [29]The LORD Almighty is a wonderful teacher, and he gives the farmer great wisdom.

CHAPTER 29

A Message about Jerusalem

"Destruction is certain for Ariel,* the City of David. Year after year you offer your many sacrifices. [2]Yet I will bring disaster upon you, and there will be much weeping and sorrow. For Jerusalem will become as her name Ariel means—an altar covered with blood. [3]I will be your enemy, surrounding Jerusalem and attacking its walls. I will build siege towers around it and will destroy it. [4]Your voice will whisper like a ghost from the earth where you will lie buried.

[5]"But suddenly, your ruthless enemies will be driven away like chaff before the wind. [6]In an instant, I, the LORD Almighty, will come against them with

---

I OBEY the clear teaching of God's Word. (28:11)

I BUILD my life on the Lord, the only sure foundation. (28:16)

I PLEAD with God's people to listen to his message and respond to his discipline. (28:23)

I BELIEVE the Lord knows how to correctly discipline each person. (28:29)

See David's profile (page 629) at Psalm 3:1.

I BELIEVE the Lord has promised to one day completely deliver Jerusalem from her enemies. (29:5)

28:10 The Hebrew text for this verse may simply be childish sounds that have no meaning, or perhaps a childish mimicking of the prophet's words. Also in 28:13. 28:15 Hebrew *Sheol;* also in 28:18. 28:16a Hebrew in *Zion.* 28:16b Greek version reads *Anyone who believes in him will not be disappointed.* 29:1 *Ariel* sounds like a Hebrew term that means "hearth" or "altar."

thunder and earthquake and great noise, with whirlwind and storm and consuming fire. [7]All the nations fighting against Jerusalem* will vanish like a dream! Those who are attacking her walls will vanish like a vision in the night. [8]A hungry person dreams of eating but is still hungry. A thirsty person dreams of drinking but is still faint from thirst when morning comes. In the same way, your enemies will dream of a victorious conquest over Jerusalem,* but all to no avail."

[9]Are you amazed and incredulous? Do you not believe it? Then go ahead and be blind if you must. You are stupid, but not from wine! You stagger, but not from beer! [10]For the LORD has poured out on you a spirit of deep sleep. He has closed the eyes of your prophets and visionaries. [11]All these future events are a sealed book to them. When you give it to those who can read, they will say, "We can't read it because it is sealed." [12]When you give it to those who cannot read, they will say, "Sorry, we don't know how to read."

[13]And so the Lord says, "These people say they are mine. They honor me with their lips, but their hearts are far away. And their worship of me amounts to nothing more than human laws learned by rote.* [14]Because of this, I will do wonders among these hypocrites. I will show that human wisdom is foolish and even the most brilliant people lack understanding."

[15]Destruction is certain for those who try to hide their plans from the LORD, who try to keep him in the dark concerning what they do! "The LORD can't see us," you say to yourselves. "He doesn't know what is going on!" [16]How stupid can you be? He is the Potter, and he is certainly greater than you. You are only the jars he makes! Should the thing that was created say to the one who made it, "He didn't make us"? Does a jar ever say, "The potter who made me is stupid"?

[17]Soon—and it will not be very long—the wilderness of Lebanon will be a fertile field once again. And the fertile fields will become a lush and fertile forest. [18]In that day deaf people will hear words read from a book, and blind people will see through the gloom and darkness. [19]The humble will be filled with fresh joy from the LORD. Those who are poor will rejoice in the Holy One of Israel. [20]Those who intimidate and harass will be gone, and all those who plot evil will be killed. [21]Those who make the innocent guilty by their false testimony will disappear. And those who use trickery to pervert justice and tell lies to tear down the innocent will be no more.

[22]That is why the LORD, who redeemed Abraham, says to the people of Israel,* "My people will no longer pale with fear or be ashamed. [23]For when they see their many children and material blessings, they will recognize the holiness of the Holy One of Israel. They will stand in awe of the God of Israel. [24]Those in error will then believe the truth, and those who constantly complain will accept instruction.

CHAPTER 30

Judah's Worthless Treaty with Egypt

"Destruction is certain for my rebellious children," says the LORD. "You make plans that are contrary to my will. You weave a web of plans that are not from my Spirit, thus piling up your sins. [2]For without consulting me, you have gone down to Egypt to find help. You have put your trust in Pharaoh for his protection. [3]But in trusting Pharaoh, you will be humiliated and disgraced. [4]For though his power extends to Zoan and Hanes, [5]it will all turn out to your shame. He will not help you even one little bit."

[6]Look at the animals moving slowly across the terrible desert to Egypt—donkeys and camels loaded with treasure to pay for Egypt's aid. On through the wilderness they go, where lions and poisonous snakes live. All

---

I BELIEVE the Lord closed the eyes of the Israelites because of their unbelief (see 2 Corinthians 4:3-4). (29:10)

I WORSHIP the Lord with my whole heart and keep his laws. (29:13)

I AM FILLED with joy when I live humbly before God. (29:19)

See Abraham's profile (page 19) at Genesis 15:6.

I BELIEVE the Israelites one day will recognize the holiness of the Lord and worship and obey him. (29:23)

I DO NOT PUT my trust in worldly powers instead of the Lord. (30:2)

29:7 Hebrew *Ariel.* 29:8 Hebrew *Mount Zion.* 29:13 Greek version reads *Their worship is a farce, for they merely teach human commands and teachings.* 29:22 Hebrew *of Jacob;* also in 29:23.

this, and Egypt will give you nothing in return. ⁷Egypt's promises are worthless! I call her the Harmless Dragon.*

A Warning for Rebellious Judah

⁸Now go and write down these words concerning Egypt. They will then stand until the end of time as a witness to Israel's unbelief. ⁹For these people are stubborn rebels who refuse to pay any attention to the LORD's instructions.

I DO NOT RESIST the Lord's warnings. (30:11)

¹⁰They tell the prophets, "Shut up! We don't want any more of your reports." They say, "Don't tell us the truth. Tell us nice things. Tell us lies. ¹¹Forget all this gloom. We have heard more than enough about your 'Holy One of Israel.' We are tired of listening to what he has to say."

¹²This is the reply of the Holy One of Israel: "Because you despise what I tell you and trust instead in oppression and lies, ¹³calamity will come upon you suddenly. It will be like a bulging wall that bursts and falls. In an instant it will collapse and come crashing down. ¹⁴You will be smashed like a piece of pottery—shattered so completely that there won't be a piece left that is big enough to carry coals from a fireplace or a little water from the well."

I AM SAVED by returning to the Holy One and waiting for him. (30:15)

¹⁵The Sovereign LORD, the Holy One of Israel, says, "Only in returning to me and waiting for me will you be saved. In quietness and confidence is your strength. But you would have none of it. ¹⁶You said, 'No, we will get our help from Egypt. They will give us swift horses for riding into battle.' But the only swiftness you are going to see is the swiftness of your enemies chasing you! ¹⁷One of them will chase a thousand of you. Five of them will make all of you flee. You will be left like a lonely flagpole on a distant mountaintop."

Blessings for the LORD's People

I BELIEVE the Lord still waits for his people Israel and longs to show them his love and compassion. (30:18)

¹⁸But the LORD still waits for you to come to him so he can show you his love and compassion. For the LORD is a faithful God. Blessed are those who wait for him to help them.

I ASK the Lord for help, knowing he will respond to my cries and guide me even in my suffering. (30:19)

¹⁹O people of Zion, who live in Jerusalem, you will weep no more. He will be gracious if you ask for help. He will respond instantly to the sound of your cries. ²⁰Though the Lord gave you adversity for food and affliction for drink, he will still be with you to teach you. You will see your teacher with your own eyes, ²¹and you will hear a voice say, "This is the way; turn around and walk here." ²²Then you will destroy all your silver idols and gold images. You will throw them out like filthy rags. "Ugh!" you will say to them. "Begone!"

²³Then the LORD will bless you with rain at planting time. There will be wonderful harvests and plenty of pastureland for your cattle. ²⁴The oxen and donkeys that till the ground will eat good grain, its chaff having been blown away by the wind. ²⁵In that day, when your enemies are slaughtered, there will be streams of water flowing down every mountain and hill. ²⁶The moon will be as bright as the sun, and the sun will be seven times brighter—like the light of seven days! So it will be when the LORD begins to heal his people and cure the wounds he gave them.

I BELIEVE the Lord promises to punish his proud enemies. (30:28)

²⁷Look! The LORD is coming from far away, burning with anger, surrounded by a thick, rising smoke. His lips are filled with fury; his words consume like fire. ²⁸His anger pours out like a flood on his enemies, sweeping them all away. He will sift out the proud nations. He will bridle them and lead them off to their destruction.

I JOIN others in singing songs of joy to God. (30:29)

²⁹But the people of God will sing a song of joy, like the songs at the holy festivals. You will be filled with joy, as when a flutist leads a group of pilgrims to Jerusalem—the mountain of the LORD—to the Rock of Israel. ³⁰And the LORD will make his majestic voice heard. With angry indignation he will bring down his mighty arm on his enemies. It will descend with devouring flames, with cloudbursts, thunderstorms, and huge hailstones, bringing their

30:7 Hebrew *Rahab who sits still.* Rahab is the name of a mythical sea monster that represents chaos in ancient literature. The name is used here as a poetic name for Egypt.

destruction. ³¹At the LORD's command, the Assyrians will be shattered. He will strike them down with his rod. ³²And as the LORD strikes them, his people will keep time with the music of tambourines and harps. ³³Topheth—the place of burning—has long been ready for the Assyrian king; it has been piled high with wood. The breath of the LORD, like fire from a volcano, will set it ablaze.

CHAPTER 31

The Futility of Relying on Egypt

Destruction is certain for those who look to Egypt for help, trusting their cavalry and chariots instead of looking to the LORD, the Holy One of Israel. ²In his wisdom, the LORD will send great disaster; he will not change his mind. He will rise against those who are wicked, and he will crush their allies, too. ³For these Egyptians are mere humans, not God! Their horses are puny flesh, not mighty spirits! When the LORD clenches his fist against them, they will stumble and fall among those they are trying to help. They will all fall down and die together.

⁴But the LORD has told me this: "When a lion, even a young one, kills a sheep, it pays no attention to the shepherd's shouts and noise. It just goes right on eating. In the same way, the LORD Almighty will come and fight on Mount Zion. He will not be frightened away! ⁵The LORD Almighty will hover over Jerusalem as a bird hovers around its nest. He will defend and save the city; he will pass over it and rescue it."

⁶Therefore, my people, though you are such wicked rebels, come and return to the LORD. ⁷I know the glorious day will come when every one of you will throw away the gold idols and silver images that your sinful hands have made.

⁸"The Assyrians will be destroyed, but not by the swords of men. The sword of God will strike them, and they will panic and flee. The strong young Assyrians will be taken away as captives. ⁹Even their generals will quake with terror and flee when they see the battle flags," says the LORD, whose flame burns brightly in Jerusalem.

CHAPTER 32

Israel's Ultimate Deliverance

Look, a righteous king is coming! And honest princes will rule under him. ²He will shelter Israel from the storm and the wind. He will refresh her as a river in the desert and as the cool shadow of a large rock in a hot and weary land. ³Then everyone who can see will be looking for God, and those who can hear will listen to his voice. ⁴Even the hotheads among them will be full of sense and understanding. Those who stammer in uncertainty will speak out plainly.

⁵In that day ungodly fools will not be heroes. Wealthy cheaters will not be respected as outstanding citizens. ⁶Everyone will recognize ungodly fools for what they are. They spread lies about the LORD; they deprive the hungry of food and give no water to the thirsty. ⁷The smooth tricks of evil people will be exposed, including all the lies they use to oppress the poor in the courts. ⁸But good people will be generous to others and will be blessed for all they do.

⁹Listen, you women who lie around in lazy ease. Listen to me, and I will tell you of your reward. ¹⁰In a short time—in just a little more than a year—you careless ones will suddenly begin to care. For your fruit crop will fail, and the harvest will never take place. ¹¹Tremble, you women of ease; throw off your unconcern. Strip off your pretty clothes, and wear sackcloth in your grief. ¹²Beat your breasts in sorrow for your bountiful farms that will soon be gone, and for those fruitful vines of other years. ¹³For your land will be overgrown with thorns and briers. Your joyful homes and happy cities

I BELIEVE the Lord kept his promise to destroy the Egyptians, on whom the Israelites had foolishly depended for help. (31:2)

I BELIEVE nothing can deter the Lord from accomplishing what he has planned. (31:4)

I BELIEVE the Lord's promise that one day ungodly people will not be acclaimed for their sins. (32:5)

I BELIEVE the Lord's promise that one day good people will be rewarded for all they do. (32:8)

I BELIEVE the Lord kept his promise to pour out his Spirit on his people (Acts 2:4, 17-18). (32:15)

I TRUST God to bless his people even in the midst of troubles. (32:19)

will be gone. [14]The palace and the city will be deserted, and busy towns will be empty. Herds of donkeys and goats will graze on the hills where the watchtowers are, [15]until at last the Spirit is poured down upon us from heaven. Then the wilderness will become a fertile field, and the fertile field will become a lush and fertile forest. [16]Justice will rule in the wilderness and righteousness in the fertile field. [17]And this righteousness will bring peace. Quietness and confidence will fill the land forever.

[18]My people will live in safety, quietly at home. They will be at rest. [19]Even though the forest will be destroyed and the city torn down, [20]God will greatly bless his people. Wherever they plant seed, bountiful crops will spring up. Their flocks and herds will graze in green pastures.

CHAPTER 33

A Message about Assyria

Destruction is certain for you Assyrians,* who have destroyed everything around you but have never felt destruction yourselves. You expect others to respect their promises to you, while you betray your promises to them. Now you, too, will be betrayed and destroyed!

[2]But LORD, be merciful to us, for we have waited for you. Be our strength each day and our salvation in times of trouble. [3]The enemy runs at the sound of your voice. When you stand up, the nations flee! [4]Just as locusts strip the fields and vines, so Jerusalem will strip the fallen army of Assyria!

I BELIEVE the Lord will one day dwell with his people and make Jerusalem his home of righteousness and justice (Revelation 21:1-3). (33:5)

I FEAR the Lord and always seek to please him. (33:6)

[5]Though the LORD is very great and lives in heaven, he will make Jerusalem* his home of justice and righteousness. [6]In that day he will be your sure foundation, providing a rich store of salvation, wisdom, and knowledge. The fear of the LORD is the key to this treasure.

[7]But now your ambassadors weep in bitter disappointment, for Assyria has refused their petition for peace. [8]Your roads are deserted; no one travels them anymore. The Assyrians have broken their peace pact and care nothing for the promises they made before witnesses.* They have no respect for anyone. [9]All the land of Israel is in trouble. Lebanon has been destroyed. The plain of Sharon is now a wilderness. Bashan and Carmel have been plundered.

[10]But the LORD says: "I will stand up and show my power and might. [11]You Assyrians will gain nothing by all your efforts. Your own breath will turn to fire and kill you. [12]Your people will be burned up completely, like thorns cut down and tossed in a fire. [13]Listen to what I have done, you nations far away! And you that are near, acknowledge my might!"

I LIVE in the Lord's presence because I am cleansed from sin and seek to please him (Ephesians 4:17-32). (33:15)

[14]The sinners in Jerusalem* shake with fear. "Which one of us," they cry, "can live here in the presence of this all-consuming fire?" [15]The ones who can live here are those who are honest and fair, who reject making a profit by fraud, who stay far away from bribes, who refuse to listen to those who plot murder, who shut their eyes to all enticement to do wrong. [16]These are the ones who will dwell on high. The rocks of the mountains will be their fortress of safety. Food will be supplied to them, and they will have water in abundance.

[17]Your eyes will see the king in all his splendor, and you will see a land that stretches into the distance. [18]You will think back to this time of terror when the Assyrian officers outside your walls counted your towers and estimated how much plunder they would get from your fallen city. [19]But soon they will all be gone. These fierce, violent people with a strange, unknown language will disappear.

I BELIEVE the Lord's promise one day to make Jerusalem a place of worship and celebration. (33:20)

[20]Instead, you will see Zion as a place of worship and celebration. You will see Jerusalem, a city quiet and secure. [21]The LORD will be our Mighty One. He

33:1 Hebrew *for you, O destroyer . . . O betrayer.* The Hebrew text does not specifically name Assyria as the object of this prophecy. 33:5 Hebrew *Zion.* 33:8 As in Dead Sea Scrolls; Masoretic Text reads *care nothing for the cities.* 33:14 Hebrew *in Zion.*

will be like a wide river of protection that no enemy can cross. ²²For the LORD is our judge, our lawgiver, and our king. He will care for us and save us. ²³The enemies' sails hang loose on broken masts with useless tackle. Their treasure will be divided by the people of God. Even the lame will win their share! ²⁴The people of Israel will no longer say, "We are sick and helpless," for the LORD will forgive their sins.

CHAPTER 34

A Message for the Nations

Come here and listen, O nations of the earth. Let the world and everything in it hear my words. ²For the LORD is enraged against the nations. His fury is against all their armies. He will completely destroy* them, bringing about their slaughter. ³Their dead will be left unburied, and the stench of rotting bodies will fill the land. The mountains will flow with their blood. ⁴The heavens above will melt away and disappear like a rolled-up scroll. The stars will fall from the sky, just as withered leaves and fruit fall from a tree.

⁵And when my sword has finished its work in the heavens, then watch. It will fall upon Edom, the nation I have completely destroyed. ⁶The sword of the LORD is drenched with blood. It is covered with fat as though it had been used for killing lambs and goats and rams for a sacrifice. Yes, the LORD will offer a great sacrifice in the rich city of Bozrah. He will make a mighty slaughter in Edom. ⁷The strongest will die—veterans and young men, too. The land will be soaked with blood and the soil enriched with fat. ⁸For it is the day of the LORD's vengeance, the year when Edom will be paid back for all it did to Israel.* ⁹ The streams of Edom will be filled with burning pitch, and the ground will be covered with fire.

¹⁰This judgment on Edom will never end; the smoke of its burning will rise forever. The land will lie deserted from generation to generation. No one will live there anymore. ¹¹It will be haunted by the horned owl, the hawk, the screech owl, and the raven.* For God will bring chaos and destruction to that land. ¹²It will be called the Land of Nothing, and its princes soon will all be gone. ¹³Thorns will overrun its palaces; nettles will grow in its forts. The ruins will become a haunt for jackals and a home for ostriches. ¹⁴Wild animals of the desert will mingle there with hyenas, their howls filling the night. Wild goats will bleat at one another among the ruins, and night creatures will come there to rest. ¹⁵There the owl will make her nest and lay her eggs. She will hatch her young and cover them with her wings. And the vultures will come, each one with its mate.

¹⁶Search the book of the LORD, and see what he will do. He will not miss a single detail. Not one of these birds and animals will be missing, and none will lack a mate, for the LORD has promised this. His Spirit will make it all come true. ¹⁷He has surveyed and divided the land and deeded it over to those creatures. They will possess it forever, from generation to generation.

CHAPTER 35

Hope for Restoration

Even the wilderness will rejoice in those days. The desert will blossom with flowers. ²Yes, there will be an abundance of flowers and singing and joy! The deserts will become as green as the mountains of Lebanon, as lovely as Mount Carmel's pastures and the plain of Sharon. There the LORD will display his glory, the splendor of our God.

³With this news, strengthen those who have tired hands, and encourage those who have weak knees. ⁴Say to those who are afraid, "Be strong, and do

---

I BELIEVE the Lord is the judge, lawgiver, and king of his people. (33:22)

I BELIEVE the Lord one day will judge all the nations who oppose him. (34:2)

I BELIEVE the Lord accurately predicted the judgment and destruction of Edom. (34:5)

I BELIEVE the Lord's words come true—every detail. (34:16)

34:2 The Hebrew term used here refers to the complete consecration of things or people to the LORD, either by destroying them or by giving them as an offering; also in 34:5. 34:8 Hebrew *to Zion.* 34:11 The identification of some of these birds is uncertain.

I BELIEVE the Lord Jesus brought sight and hearing to his people. (35:5)

I BELIEVE the Lord Jesus brought singing and satisfaction to his people. (35:6)

I BELIEVE the Lord will make a way for all his people to come into his presence to worship him in joy and gladness forever. (35:10)

not fear, for your God is coming to destroy your enemies. He is coming to save you." ⁵And when he comes, he will open the eyes of the blind and unstop the ears of the deaf. ⁶The lame will leap like a deer, and those who cannot speak will shout and sing! Springs will gush forth in the wilderness, and streams will water the desert. ⁷The parched ground will become a pool, and springs of water will satisfy the thirsty land. Marsh grass and reeds and rushes will flourish where desert jackals once lived.

⁸And a main road will go through that once deserted land. It will be named the Highway of Holiness. Evil-hearted people will never travel on it. It will be only for those who walk in God's ways; fools will never walk there. ⁹Lions will not lurk along its course, and there will be no other dangers. Only the redeemed will follow it. ¹⁰Those who have been ransomed by the LORD will return to Jerusalem,* singing songs of everlasting joy. Sorrow and mourning will disappear, and they will be overcome with joy and gladness.

CHAPTER 36

Assyria Invades Judah

In the fourteenth year of King Hezekiah's reign, King Sennacherib of Assyria came to attack the fortified cities of Judah and conquered them. ²Then the king of Assyria sent his personal representative with a huge army from Lachish to confront King Hezekiah in Jerusalem. The Assyrians stopped beside the aqueduct that feeds water into the upper pool, near the road leading to the field where cloth is bleached.

³These are the officials who went out to meet with them: Eliakim son of Hilkiah, the palace administrator, Shebna the court secretary, and Joah son of Asaph, the royal historian. ⁴Then the Assyrian king's personal representative sent this message to King Hezekiah:

"This is what the great king of Assyria says: What are you trusting in that makes you so confident? ⁵Do you think that mere words can substitute for military skill and strength? Which of your allies will give you any military backing against Assyria? ⁶Will Egypt? If you lean on Egypt, you will find it to be a stick that breaks beneath your weight and pierces your hand. The Pharaoh of Egypt is completely unreliable!

⁷"But perhaps you will say, 'We are trusting in the LORD our God!' But isn't he the one who was insulted by King Hezekiah? Didn't Hezekiah tear down his shrines and altars and make everyone in Judah worship only at the altar here in Jerusalem?

⁸"I'll tell you what! My master, the king of Assyria, will strike a bargain with you. If you can find two thousand horsemen in your entire army, he will give you two thousand horses for them to ride on! ⁹With your tiny army, how can you think of challenging even the weakest contingent of my master's troops, even with the help of Egypt's chariots and horsemen*? ¹⁰What's more, do you think we have invaded your land without the LORD's direction? The LORD himself told us, 'Go and destroy it!' "

I CONTINUE to trust in the Lord my God, even when others mock his power. (36:7)

¹¹Then Eliakim, Shebna, and Joah said to the king's representative, "Please speak to us in Aramaic, for we understand it well. Don't speak in Hebrew, for the people on the wall will hear."

I SEEK to protect the people under my care from the threats and mockery of God's enemies. (36:11)

¹²But Sennacherib's representative replied, "My master wants everyone in Jerusalem to hear this, not just you. He wants them to know that if you do not surrender, this city will be put under siege. The people will become so hungry and thirsty that they will eat their own dung and drink their own urine."

¹³Then he stood and shouted in Hebrew to the people on the wall, "Listen to this message from the great king of Assyria! ¹⁴This is what the king says:

35:10 Hebrew *Zion.* 36:9 Or *and charioteers.*

Don't let King Hezekiah deceive you. He will never be able to rescue you. [15]Don't let him fool you into trusting in the LORD by saying, 'The LORD will rescue us! This city will never be handed over to the Assyrian king.'

[16]"Don't listen to Hezekiah! These are the terms the king of Assyria is offering: Make peace with me—open the gates and come out. Then I will allow each of you to continue eating from your own garden and drinking from your own well. [17]Then I will arrange to take you to another land like this one—a country with bountiful harvests of grain and wine, bread and vineyards—a land of plenty.

[18]"Don't let Hezekiah mislead you by saying, 'The LORD will rescue us!' Have the gods of any other nations ever saved their people from the king of Assyria? [19]What happened to the gods of Hamath and Arpad? And what about the gods of Sepharvaim? Did they rescue Samaria from my power? [20]What god of any nation has ever been able to save its people from my power? Name just one! So what makes you think that the LORD can rescue Jerusalem?"

[21]But the people were silent and did not answer because Hezekiah had told them not to speak. [22]Then Eliakim son of Hilkiah, the palace administrator, Shebna the court secretary, and Joah son of Asaph, the royal historian, went back to Hezekiah. They tore their clothes in despair, and they went in to see the king and told him what the Assyrian representative had said.

> I TRUST the Lord, who is greater than any human or spirit power. (36:18)

CHAPTER 37
Hezekiah Seeks the LORD's Help

When King Hezekiah heard their report, he tore his clothes and put on sackcloth and went into the Temple of the LORD to pray. [2]And he sent Eliakim the palace administrator, Shebna the court secretary, and the leading priests, all dressed in sackcloth, to the prophet Isaiah son of Amoz. [3]They told him,

> I SEEK the Lord before I reply to the taunts of his enemies. (37:1)

LIKE HEZEKIAH
Isaiah 37:1

I go to God in prayer when I am attacked and the Lord is blasphemed.

When King Sennacherib's army surrounded Jerusalem, King Hezekiah faced not just a war of weapons but a war of words.

Before a single arrow was shot, the Assyrian king's representative verbally pounded the king and his people in an attempt to destroy their trust in the living God. "Your God is no better than those of any of the other nations we have destroyed," he charged.

Hezekiah did not take the Assyrian threats of siege and famine lightly. The Assyrians had indeed conquered stronger nations than Judah—and they had the corpses and captives to prove it. This was no time for political weakness or wavering.

Thankfully, Hezekiah's first instinct was neither to cower before the enemy nor to present a false bravado before his people. He didn't even bother to set the record straight concerning his zealous obedience to God. Without delay, Hezekiah traded his royal robes for sackcloth and went straight to prayer.

Soon after the Lord's assurance and deliverance came another attack—this time in the form of a blasphemous letter. Once again Hezekiah spread the letter out before the Lord and asked him to save the nation so "all the kingdoms of the earth will know that you alone, O LORD, are God" (37:20).

Today, voices come from every direction—mocking those who trust the Lord, denying his power to save them. "Come with us," they call, "and we will create a new life devoid of your stifling, old-fashioned concepts about 'God.' Why are you leaning on that old crutch anymore?"

Like Hezekiah, you and I can take these taunts directly to the Lord in prayer. We can spread out the blasphemous book or article or editorial and ask the Lord to reveal himself anew to a lost world.

You can read more about Hezekiah's life and faith in 2 Kings 18–20 and 2 Chronicles 29–32.

○ Today's Scripture reading is Isaiah 36–37.

"This is what King Hezekiah says: This is a day of trouble, insult, and disgrace. It is like when a child is ready to be born, but the mother has no strength to deliver it. ⁴But perhaps the LORD your God has heard the Assyrian representative defying the living God and will punish him for his words. Oh, pray for those of us who are left!"

⁵After King Hezekiah's officials delivered the king's message to Isaiah, ⁶the prophet replied, "Say to your master, 'This is what the LORD says: Do not be disturbed by this blasphemous speech against me from the Assyrian king's messengers. ⁷Listen! I myself will make sure that the king will receive a report from Assyria telling him that he is needed at home. Then I will make him want to return to his land, where I will have him killed with a sword.' "

⁸Meanwhile, the Assyrian representative left Jerusalem and went to consult his king, who had left Lachish and was attacking Libnah. ⁹Soon afterward King Sennacherib received word that King Tirhakah of Ethiopia* was leading an army to fight against him. Before leaving to meet the attack, he sent this message back to Hezekiah in Jerusalem:

¹⁰"This message is for King Hezekiah of Judah. Don't let this God you trust deceive you with promises that Jerusalem will not be captured by the king of Assyria. ¹¹You know perfectly well what the kings of Assyria have done wherever they have gone. They have crushed everyone who stood in their way! Why should you be any different? ¹²Have the gods of other nations rescued them—such nations as Gozan, Haran, Rezeph, and the people of Eden who were in Tel-assar? The former kings of Assyria destroyed them all! ¹³What happened to the king of Hamath and the king of Arpad? What happened to the kings of Sepharvaim, Hena, and Ivvah?"

¹⁴After Hezekiah received the letter and read it, he went up to the LORD's Temple and spread it out before the LORD. ¹⁵And Hezekiah prayed this prayer before the LORD: ¹⁶"O LORD Almighty, God of Israel, you are enthroned between the mighty cherubim! You alone are God of all the kingdoms of the earth. You alone created the heavens and the earth. ¹⁷Listen to me, O LORD, and hear! Open your eyes, O LORD, and see! Listen to Sennacherib's words of defiance against the living God.

¹⁸"It is true, LORD, that the kings of Assyria have destroyed all these nations, just as the message says. ¹⁹And they have thrown the gods of these nations into the fire and burned them. But of course the Assyrians could destroy them! They were not gods at all—only idols of wood and stone shaped by human hands. ²⁰Now, O LORD our God, rescue us from his power; then all the kingdoms of the earth will know that you alone, O LORD, are God."

Isaiah Predicts Judah's Deliverance

²¹Then Isaiah son of Amoz sent this message to Hezekiah: "This is what the LORD, the God of Israel, says: This is my answer to your prayer concerning King Sennacherib of Assyria. ²²This is the message that the LORD has spoken against him:

'The virgin daughter of Zion
    despises you and laughs at you.
The daughter of Jerusalem
    scoffs and shakes her head as you flee.

²³ 'Whom do you think you have been insulting and ridiculing?
    Against whom did you raise your voice?
At whom did you look in such proud condescension?
    It was the Holy One of Israel!

37:9 Hebrew *of Cush.*

I SEEK OUT the prayer of godly people when the Lord and his people are mocked and threatened. (37:4)

I BELIEVE the Lord accurately foretold that the Assyrian king would be called away and killed. (37:7)

I GO to the Lord in prayer when others mock the Lord. (37:14)

I AFFIRM the majesty and kingship of the Lord Almighty when others challenge his power and promises. (37:16)

I ASK the Lord to rescue his people and show the world that he alone is God. (37:20)

²⁴ By your messengers you have mocked the Lord.
  You have said, "With my many chariots
I have conquered the highest mountains—
  yes, the remotest peaks of Lebanon.
I have cut down its tallest cedars
  and its choicest cypress trees.
I have reached its farthest corners
  and explored its deepest forests.
²⁵ I have dug wells in many a foreign land
  and refreshed myself with their water.
I even stopped up the rivers of Egypt
  so that my armies could go across!"

²⁶ 'But have you not heard?
  It was I, the LORD, who decided this long ago.
Long ago I planned what I am now causing to happen,
  that you should crush fortified cities into heaps of rubble.
²⁷ That is why their people have so little power
  and are such easy prey for you.
They are as helpless as the grass,
  as easily trampled as tender green shoots.
They are like grass sprouting on a housetop,
  easily scorched by the sun.

²⁸ 'But I know you well—
  your comings and goings and all you do.
I know the way you have raged against me.
²⁹ And because of your arrogance against me,
  which I have heard for myself,
I will put my hook in your nose
  and my bridle in your mouth.
I will make you return
  by the road on which you came.' "

³⁰ Then Isaiah said to Hezekiah, "Here is the proof that the LORD will protect this city from Assyria's king. This year you will eat only what grows up by itself, and next year you will eat what springs up from that. But in the third year you will plant crops and harvest them; you will tend vineyards and eat their fruit. ³¹ And you who are left in Judah, who have escaped the ravages of the siege, will take root again in your own soil, and you will flourish and multiply. ³² For a remnant of my people will spread out from Jerusalem, a group of survivors from Mount Zion. The passion of the LORD Almighty will make this happen!

³³ "And this is what the LORD says about the king of Assyria: His armies will not enter Jerusalem to shoot their arrows. They will not march outside its gates with their shields and build banks of earth against its walls. ³⁴ The king will return to his own country by the road on which he came. He will not enter this city, says the LORD. ³⁵ For my own honor and for the sake of my servant David, I will defend it."

³⁶ That night the angel of the LORD went out to the Assyrian camp and killed 185,000 Assyrian troops. When the surviving Assyrians* woke up the next morning, they found corpses everywhere. ³⁷ Then King Sennacherib of Assyria broke camp and returned to his own land. He went home to his capital of Nineveh and stayed there. ³⁸ One day while he was worshiping in the temple of his god Nisroch, his sons Adrammelech and Sharezer killed him

37:36 Hebrew When they.

I BELIEVE the Lord made his plans for world history long, long ago. (37:26)

I BELIEVE the Lord gave Hezekiah proof that he would save Jerusalem from the Assyrians. (37:30)

See David's profile (page 629) at Psalm 3:1.

I BELIEVE the Lord kept his promise to destroy much of the Assyrian army and caused them to leave. (37:36)

with their swords. They then escaped to the land of Ararat, and another son, Esarhaddon, became the next king of Assyria.

CHAPTER 38

Hezekiah's Sickness and Recovery

About that time Hezekiah became deathly ill, and the prophet Isaiah son of Amoz went to visit him. He gave the king this message: "This is what the LORD says: Set your affairs in order, for you are going to die. You will not recover from this illness."

²When Hezekiah heard this, he turned his face to the wall and prayed to the LORD, ³"Remember, O LORD, how I have always tried to be faithful to you and do what is pleasing in your sight." Then he broke down and wept bitterly.

⁴Then this message came to Isaiah from the LORD: ⁵"Go back to Hezekiah and tell him, 'This is what the LORD, the God of your ancestor David, says: I have heard your prayer and seen your tears. I will add fifteen years to your life, ⁶and I will rescue you and this city from the king of Assyria. Yes, I will defend this city.

⁷" 'And this is the sign that the LORD will give you to prove he will do as he promised: ⁸I will cause the sun's shadow to move ten steps backward on the sundial of Ahaz!' " So the shadow on the sundial moved backward ten steps.

Hezekiah's Poem of Praise

⁹When King Hezekiah was well again, he wrote this poem about his experience:

¹⁰I said, "In the prime of my life,
    must I now enter the place of the dead?
    Am I to be robbed of my normal years?"
¹¹I said, "Never again will I see the LORD GOD
    while still in the land of the living.
Never again will I see my friends
    or laugh with those who live in this world.
¹²My life has been blown away
    like a shepherd's tent in a storm.
It has been cut short,
    as when a weaver cuts cloth from a loom.
    Suddenly, my life was over.
¹³I waited patiently all night,
    but I was torn apart as though by lions.
    Suddenly, my life was over.
¹⁴Delirious, I chattered like a swallow or a crane,
    and then I moaned like a mourning dove.
My eyes grew tired of looking to heaven for help.
    I am in trouble, Lord. Help me!"

¹⁵But what could I say?
    For he himself had sent this sickness.
Now I will walk humbly throughout my years
    because of this anguish I have felt.
¹⁶Lord, your discipline is good,
    for it leads to life and health.
You have restored my health
    and have allowed me to live!
¹⁷Yes, it was good for me to suffer this anguish,
    for you have rescued me from death
    and have forgiven all my sins.

I BELIEVE the Lord heard Hezekiah's prayer and gave him fifteen more years to live. (38:5)

See David's profile (page 629) at Psalm 3:1.

I KEEP a record of God's miraculous workings in my life. (38:9)

I WILL LOOK to the Lord for help when I am mourning the end of my life. (38:14)

I HUMBLY LEARN from the trials and anguish the Lord sends into my life. (38:15)

¹⁸ For the dead cannot praise you;
　　they cannot raise their voices in praise.
　Those who go down to destruction
　　can no longer hope in your faithfulness.
¹⁹ Only the living can praise you as I do today.
　　Each generation can make known your faithfulness to the next.
²⁰ Think of it—the LORD has healed me!
　　I will sing his praises with instruments
　every day of my life
　　in the Temple of the LORD.

²¹Isaiah had said to Hezekiah's servants, "Make an ointment from figs and spread it over the boil, and Hezekiah will recover."

²²And Hezekiah had asked, "What sign will prove that I will go to the Temple of the LORD three days from now?"

CHAPTER 39

Envoys from Babylon

Soon after this, Merodach-baladan son of Baladan, king of Babylon, sent Hezekiah his best wishes and a gift. He had heard that Hezekiah had been very sick and that he had recovered. ²Hezekiah welcomed the Babylonian envoys and showed them everything in his treasure-houses—the silver, the gold, the spices, and the aromatic oils. He also took them to see his armory and showed them all his other treasures—everything! There was nothing in his palace or kingdom that Hezekiah did not show them.

³Then Isaiah the prophet went to King Hezekiah and asked him, "What did those men want? Where were they from?"

Hezekiah replied, "They came from the distant land of Babylon."

⁴"What did they see in your palace?" asked Isaiah.

"They saw everything," Hezekiah replied. "I showed them everything I own—all my treasures."

⁵Then Isaiah said to Hezekiah, "Listen to this message from the LORD Almighty: ⁶The time is coming when everything you have—all the treasures stored up by your ancestors—will be carried off to Babylon. Nothing will be left, says the LORD. ⁷Some of your own descendants will be taken away into exile. They will become eunuchs who will serve in the palace of Babylon's king."

⁸Then Hezekiah said to Isaiah, "This message you have given me from the LORD is good." But the king was thinking, "At least there will be peace and security during my lifetime."

CHAPTER 40

Comfort for God's People

"Comfort, comfort my people," says your God. ²"Speak tenderly to Jerusalem. Tell her that her sad days are gone and that her sins are pardoned. Yes, the LORD has punished her in full for all her sins."

³Listen! I hear the voice of someone shouting, "Make a highway for the LORD through the wilderness. Make a straight, smooth road through the desert for our God. ⁴Fill the valleys and level the hills. Straighten out the curves and smooth off the rough spots. ⁵Then the glory of the LORD will be revealed, and all people will see it together. The LORD has spoken!"

⁶A voice said, "Shout!"

I asked, "What should I shout?"

"Shout that people are like the grass that dies away. Their beauty fades as quickly as the beauty of flowers in a field. ⁷The grass withers, and the flowers

I DO NOT BOAST about and flaunt my possessions and power, especially not to those who oppose God. (39:2)

I BELIEVE the Lord prophesied through Isaiah that Babylon would carry off all the king's treasures and take his people into exile. (39:5)

Start each day by reviewing the previous day's faith affirmations.

I BELIEVE that human life is frail, but God's Word is eternal (1 Peter 1:24–25). (40:8)

I BELIEVE the Lord loves and cares for his people. (40:11)

I BELIEVE the Lord knows everything. (40:13)

I KNOW that nothing on earth can compare to God's greatness. (40:18)

I DO NOT ACCUSE the Lord of not seeing or caring about my troubles. (40:27)

I WAIT on the Lord and find new strength. (40:31)

fade beneath the breath of the LORD. And so it is with people. [8]The grass withers, and the flowers fade, but the word of our God stands forever."

[9]Messenger of good news, shout to Zion from the mountaintops! Shout louder to Jerusalem—do not be afraid. Tell the towns of Judah, "Your God is coming!" [10]Yes, the Sovereign LORD is coming in all his glorious power. He will rule with awesome strength. See, he brings his reward with him as he comes. [11]He will feed his flock like a shepherd. He will carry the lambs in his arms, holding them close to his heart. He will gently lead the mother sheep with their young.

[12]Who else has held the oceans in his hand? Who has measured off the heavens with his fingers? Who else knows the weight of the earth or has weighed out the mountains and the hills? [13]Who is able to advise the Spirit of the LORD? Who knows enough to be his teacher or counselor? [14]Has the LORD ever needed anyone's advice? Does he need instruction about what is good or what is best? [15]No, for all the nations of the world are nothing in comparison with him. They are but a drop in the bucket, dust on the scales. He picks up the islands as though they had no weight at all. [16]All Lebanon's forests do not contain sufficient fuel to consume a sacrifice large enough to honor him. All Lebanon's sacrificial animals would not make an offering worthy of our God. [17]The nations of the world are as nothing to him. In his eyes they are less than nothing—mere emptiness and froth.

[18]To whom, then, can we compare God? What image might we find to resemble him? [19]Can he be compared to an idol formed in a mold, overlaid with gold, and decorated with silver chains? [20]Or is a poor person's wooden idol better? Can God be compared to an idol that must be placed on a stand so it won't fall down?

[21]Have you never heard or understood? Are you deaf to the words of God—the words he gave before the world began? Are you so ignorant? [22]It is God who sits above the circle of the earth. The people below must seem to him like grasshoppers! He is the one who spreads out the heavens like a curtain and makes his tent from them. [23]He judges the great people of the world and brings them all to nothing. [24]They hardly get started, barely taking root, when he blows on them and their work withers. The wind carries them off like straw.

[25]"To whom will you compare me? Who is my equal?" asks the Holy One.

[26]Look up into the heavens. Who created all the stars? He brings them out one after another, calling each by its name. And he counts them to see that none are lost or have strayed away.

[27]O Israel, how can you say the LORD does not see your troubles? How can you say God refuses to hear your case? [28]Have you never heard or understood? Don't you know that the LORD is the everlasting God, the Creator of all the earth? He never grows faint or weary. No one can measure the depths of his understanding. [29]He gives power to those who are tired and worn out; he offers strength to the weak. [30]Even youths will become exhausted, and young men will give up. [31]But those who wait on the LORD will find new strength. They will fly high on wings like eagles. They will run and not grow weary. They will walk and not faint.

CHAPTER 41

God's Help for Israel

"Listen in silence before me, you lands beyond the sea. Bring your strongest arguments. Come now and speak. The court is ready for your case.

[2]"Who has stirred up this king from the east, who meets victory at every step? Who, indeed, but the LORD? He gives him victory over many nations and permits him to trample their kings underfoot. He puts entire armies to the sword. He scatters them in the wind with his bow. [3]He chases them away

and goes on safely, though he is walking over unfamiliar ground. ⁴Who has done such mighty deeds, directing the affairs of the human race as each new generation marches by? It is I, the LORD, the First and the Last. I alone am he."

⁵The lands beyond the sea watch in fear. Remote lands tremble and mobilize for war. ⁶They encourage one another with the words, "Be strong!" ⁷The craftsmen rush to make new idols. The carver hurries the goldsmith, and the molder helps at the anvil. "Good," they say. "It's coming along fine." Carefully they join the parts together, then fasten the thing in place so it won't fall over.

⁸"But as for you, Israel my servant, Jacob my chosen one, descended from my friend Abraham, ⁹I have called you back from the ends of the earth so you can serve me. For I have chosen you and will not throw you away. ¹⁰Don't be afraid, for I am with you. Do not be dismayed, for I am your God. I will strengthen you. I will help you. I will uphold you with my victorious right hand.

¹¹"See, all your angry enemies lie there, confused and ashamed. Anyone who opposes you will die. ¹²You will look for them in vain. They will all be gone! ¹³I am holding you by your right hand—I, the LORD your God. And I say to you, 'Do not be afraid. I am here to help you. ¹⁴Despised though you are, O Israel, don't be afraid, for I will help you. I am the LORD, your Redeemer. I am the Holy One of Israel.' ¹⁵You will be a new threshing instrument with many sharp teeth. You will tear all your enemies apart, making chaff of mountains. ¹⁶You will toss them in the air, and the wind will blow them all away; a whirlwind will scatter them. And the joy of the LORD will fill you to overflowing. You will glory in the Holy One of Israel.

¹⁷"When the poor and needy search for water and there is none, and their tongues are parched from thirst, then I, the LORD, will answer them. I, the God of Israel, will never forsake them. ¹⁸I will open up rivers for them on high plateaus. I will give them fountains of water in the valleys. In the deserts they will find pools of water. Rivers fed by springs will flow across the dry, parched ground. ¹⁹I will plant trees—cedar, acacia, myrtle, olive, cypress, fir, and pine—on barren land. ²⁰Everyone will see this miracle and understand that it is the LORD, the Holy One of Israel, who did it.

²¹"Can your idols make such claims as these? Let them come and show what they can do!" says the LORD, the King of Israel.* ²²"Let them try to tell us what happened long ago or what the future holds. ²³Yes, that's it! If you are gods, tell what will occur in the days ahead. Or perform a mighty miracle that will fill us with amazement and fear. Do something, whether good or bad! ²⁴But no! You are less than nothing and can do nothing at all. Anyone who chooses you becomes filthy, just like you!

²⁵"But I have stirred up a leader from the north and east. He will come against the nations and call on my name, and I will give him victory over kings and princes. He will trample them as a potter treads on clay.

²⁶"Who but I have told you this would happen? Who else predicted this, making you admit that he was right? No one else said a word! ²⁷I was the first to tell Jerusalem, 'Look! Help is on the way!' ²⁸Not one of your idols told you this. Not one gave any answer when I asked. ²⁹See, they are all foolish, worthless things. Your idols are all as empty as the wind.

CHAPTER 42

The LORD's Chosen Servant

"Look at my servant, whom I strengthen. He is my chosen one, and I am pleased with him. I have put my Spirit upon him. He will reveal justice to the nations. ²He will be gentle—he will not shout or raise his voice in public. ³He

41:21 Hebrew *the King of Jacob.*

I BELIEVE the Lord directs the affairs of the human race. (41:4)

See the profiles for Abraham (page 19) and Jacob (page 43) at Genesis 15:6 and Genesis 32:9.

I BELIEVE the Lord chose Israel to be his servant. (41:9)

I AM NOT DISMAYED, for the Lord upholds and strengthens me. (41:10)

I BELIEVE the Lord, the Redeemer, kept his promise to help his people Israel, even though they were despised. (41:14)

I BELIEVE the Lord's promise that he will never forsake those who seek him and that he will quench their thirst. (41:17)

I BELIEVE the Lord proved to Israel that he was indeed their King, more powerful than worthless idols. (41:26)

I BELIEVE Jesus Christ is God's chosen servant (Matthew 3:16-17). (42:1)

will not crush those who are weak or quench the smallest hope. He will bring full justice to all who have been wronged. [4]He will not stop until truth and righteousness prevail throughout the earth. Even distant lands beyond the sea will wait for his instruction."

[5]God, the LORD, created the heavens and stretched them out. He created the earth and everything in it. He gives breath and life to everyone in all the world. And it is he who says, [6]"I, the LORD, have called you to demonstrate my righteousness. I will guard and support you, for I have given you to my people as the personal confirmation of my covenant with them. And you will be a light to guide all nations to me. [7]You will open the eyes of the blind and free the captives from prison. You will release those who sit in dark dungeons.

[8]"I am the LORD; that is my name! I will not give my glory to anyone else. I will not share my praise with carved idols. [9]Everything I prophesied has come true, and now I will prophesy again. I will tell you the future before it happens."

A Song of Praise to the LORD
[10]Sing a new song to the LORD!
    Sing his praises from the ends of the earth!
    Sing, all you who sail the seas,
        all you who live in distant coastlands.
[11]Join in the chorus, you desert towns;
    let the villages of Kedar rejoice!
    Let the people of Sela sing for joy;
        shout praises from the mountaintops!
[12]Let the coastlands glorify the LORD;
    let them sing his praise.
[13]The LORD will march forth like a mighty man;
    he will come out like a warrior, full of fury.
    He will shout his thundering battle cry,
        and he will crush all his enemies.
[14]He will say, "I have long been silent;
    yes, I have restrained myself.
    But now I will give full vent to my fury;
        I will gasp and pant like a woman giving birth.
[15]I will level the mountains and hills
    and bring a blight on all their greenery.
    I will turn the rivers into dry land
        and will dry up all the pools.
[16]I will lead blind Israel down a new path,
    guiding them along an unfamiliar way.
    I will make the darkness bright before them
        and smooth out the road ahead of them.
    Yes, I will indeed do these things;
        I will not forsake them.
[17]But those who trust in idols,
    calling them their gods—
        they will be turned away in shame.

Israel's Failure to See and Listen
[18]"Oh, how deaf and blind you are toward me! Why won't you listen? Why do you refuse to see? [19]Who in all the world is as blind as my own people, my servant? Who is as deaf as my messengers? Who is as blind as my chosen people, the servant of the LORD? [20]You see and understand what is right but refuse to act on it. You hear, but you don't really listen."

[21]The LORD has magnified his law and made it truly glorious. Through it he

I BELIEVE that God's chosen servant, Jesus, will bring truth and righteousness to the earth. (42:4)

I BELIEVE the Lord gave his servant, Jesus, to confirm his covenant with his people Israel and to guide all nations to him (Luke 2:32). (42:6)

I BELIEVE that everything the Lord prophesies comes true. (42:9)

I DO NOT REFUSE to listen to the Lord or act on his words. (42:20)

had planned to show the world that he is righteous. ²²But what a sight his people are, for they have been robbed, enslaved, imprisoned, and trapped. They are fair game for all and have no one to protect them. ²³Will not even one of you apply these lessons from the past and see the ruin that awaits you? ²⁴Who allowed Israel to be robbed and hurt? Was it not the LORD? It was the LORD whom we sinned against, for the people would not go where he sent them, nor would they obey his law. ²⁵That is why he poured out such fury on them and destroyed them in battle. They were set on fire and burned, but they still refused to understand.

CHAPTER 43

The Savior of Israel

But now, O Israel, the LORD who created you says: "Do not be afraid, for I have ransomed you. I have called you by name; you are mine. ²When you go through deep waters and great trouble, I will be with you. When you go through rivers of difficulty, you will not drown! When you walk through the fire of oppression, you will not be burned up; the flames will not consume you. ³For I am the LORD, your God, the Holy One of Israel, your Savior. I gave Egypt, Ethiopia,* and Seba as a ransom for your freedom. ⁴Others died that you might live. I traded their lives for yours because you are precious to me. You are honored, and I love you.

I KNOW the Lord loves me. (43:4)

⁵"Do not be afraid, for I am with you. I will gather you and your children from east and west ⁶and from north and south. I will bring my sons and daughters back to Israel from the distant corners of the earth. ⁷All who claim me as their God will come, for I have made them for my glory. It was I who created them."

⁸Bring out the people who have eyes but are blind, who have ears but are deaf. ⁹Gather the nations together! Which of their idols has ever foretold such things? Can any of them predict something even a single day in advance? Where are the witnesses of such predictions? Who can verify that they spoke the truth?

¹⁰"But you are my witnesses, O Israel!" says the LORD. "And you are my servant. You have been chosen to know me, believe in me, and understand that I alone am God. There is no other God; there never has been and never will be. ¹¹I am the LORD, and there is no other Savior. ¹²First I predicted your deliverance; I declared what I would do, and then I did it—I saved you. No foreign god has ever done this before. You are witnesses that I am the only God," says the LORD. ¹³"From eternity to eternity I am God. No one can oppose what I do. No one can reverse my actions."

I BELIEVE there is no God or Savior but the Lord. (43:11)

I BELIEVE the Lord alone is God from eternity past to eternity future. (43:13)

The LORD's Promise of Victory

¹⁴The LORD your Redeemer, the Holy One of Israel, says: "For your sakes I will send an invading army against Babylon. And the Babylonians* will be forced to flee in those ships they are so proud of. ¹⁵I am the LORD, your Holy One, Israel's Creator and King. ¹⁶I am the LORD, who opened a way through the waters, making a dry path through the sea. ¹⁷I called forth the mighty army of Egypt with all its chariots and horses. I drew them beneath the waves, and they drowned, their lives snuffed out like a smoldering candlewick.

I BELIEVE the Lord is my Creator and King. (43:15)

¹⁸"But forget all that—it is nothing compared to what I am going to do. ¹⁹For I am about to do a brand-new thing. See, I have already begun! Do you not see it? I will make a pathway through the wilderness for my people to come home. I will create rivers for them in the desert! ²⁰The wild animals in the fields will thank me, the jackals and ostriches, too, for giving them water in the wilderness. Yes, I will make springs in the desert, so that my chosen

43:3 Hebrew *Cush.*   **43:14** Or *Chaldeans.*

I BELIEVE the Israelites one day will honor the Lord before the whole world. (43:21)

people can be refreshed. [21]I have made Israel for myself, and they will some-day honor me before the whole world.

[22]"But, my dear people, you refuse to ask for my help. You have grown tired of me! [23]You have not brought me lambs for burnt offerings. You have not honored me with sacrifices, though I have not burdened and wearied you with my requests for grain offerings and incense. [24]You have not brought me fragrant incense or pleased me with the fat from sacrifices. Instead, you have burdened me with your sins and wearied me with your faults.

[25]"I—yes, I alone—am the one who blots out your sins for my own sake and will never think of them again. [26]Let us review the situation together, and you can present your case if you have one. [27]From the very beginning, your ancestors sinned against me—all your leaders broke my laws. [28]That is why I have disgraced your priests and assigned Israel a future of complete destruction* and shame.

CHAPTER 44

I AM NOT AFRAID, because the Lord has chosen me. (44:2)

See Jacob's profile (page 43) at Genesis 32:9.

"But now, listen to me, Jacob my servant, Israel my chosen one. [2]The LORD who made you and helps you says: O Jacob, my servant, do not be afraid. O Israel,* my chosen one, do not fear. [3]For I will give you abundant water to quench your thirst and to moisten your parched fields. And I will pour out my Spirit and my blessings on your children. [4]They will thrive like watered grass, like willows on a riverbank. [5]Some will proudly claim, 'I belong to the LORD.' Others will say, 'I am a descendant of Jacob.' Some will write the LORD's name on their hands and will take the honored name of Israel as their own.

The Foolishness of Idols

I BELIEVE the Lord Almighty, my King and Redeemer, is the only God. (44:6)

I BELIEVE God is the only one who can accurately proclaim his purposes before they occur. (44:8)

[6]"This is what the LORD, Israel's King and Redeemer, the LORD Almighty, says: I am the First and the Last; there is no other God. [7]Who else can tell you what is going to happen in the days ahead? Let them tell you if they can and thus prove their power. Let them do as I have done since ancient times. [8]Do not tremble; do not be afraid. Have I not proclaimed from ages past what my purposes are for you? You are my witnesses—is there any other God? No! There is no other Rock—not one!"

[9]How foolish are those who manufacture idols to be their gods. These highly valued objects are really worthless. They themselves are witnesses that this is so, for their idols neither see nor know. No wonder those who worship them are put to shame. [10]Who but a fool would make his own god—an idol that cannot help him one bit! [11]All who worship idols will stand before the LORD in shame, along with all these craftsmen—mere humans—who claim they can make a god. Together they will stand in terror and shame.

[12]The blacksmith stands at his forge to make a sharp tool, pounding and shaping it with all his might. His work makes him hungry and thirsty, weak and faint. [13]Then the wood-carver measures and marks out a block of wood, takes the tool, and carves the figure of a man. Now he has a wonderful idol that cannot even move from where it is placed! [14]He cuts down cedars; he selects the cypress and the oak; he plants the cedar in the forest to be nourished by the rain. [15]And after his care, he uses part of the wood to make a fire to warm himself and bake his bread. Then—yes, it's true—he takes the rest of it and makes himself a god for people to worship! He makes an idol and bows down and praises it! [16]He burns part of the tree to roast his meat and to keep

I NEVER WOULD CALL anything I've created my "god" or "savior." (44:17)

himself warm. [17]Then he takes what's left and makes his god: a carved idol! He falls down in front of it, worshiping and praying to it. "Rescue me!" he says. "You are my god!"

[18]Such stupidity and ignorance! Their eyes are closed, and they cannot see.

43:28 The Hebrew term used here refers to the complete consecration of things or people to the LORD, either by destroying them or by giving them as an offering. 44:2 Hebrew *Jeshurun,* a term of endearment for Israel.

Their minds are shut, and they cannot think. [19]The person who made the idol never stops to reflect, "Why, it's just a block of wood! I burned half of it for heat and used it to bake my bread and roast my meat. How can the rest of it be a god? Should I bow down to worship a chunk of wood?" [20]The poor, deluded fool feeds on ashes. He is trusting something that can give him no help at all. Yet he cannot bring himself to ask, "Is this thing, this idol that I'm holding in my hand, a lie?"

Restoration for Jerusalem

[21]"Pay attention, O Israel, for you are my servant. I, the LORD, made you, and I will not forget to help you. [22]I have swept away your sins like the morning mists. I have scattered your offenses like the clouds. Oh, return to me, for I have paid the price to set you free."

[23]Sing, O heavens, for the LORD has done this wondrous thing. Shout, O earth! Break forth into song, O mountains and forests and every tree! For the LORD has redeemed Jacob and is glorified in Israel.

[24]The LORD, your Redeemer and Creator, says: "I am the LORD, who made all things. I alone stretched out the heavens. By myself I made the earth and everything in it. [25]I am the one who exposes the false prophets as liars by causing events to happen that are contrary to their predictions. I cause wise people to give bad advice, thus proving them to be fools. [26]But I carry out the predictions of my prophets! When they say Jerusalem will be saved and the towns of Judah will be lived in once again, it will be done! [27]When I speak to the rivers and say, 'Be dry!' they will be dry. [28]When I say of Cyrus, 'He is my shepherd,' he will certainly do as I say. He will command that Jerusalem be rebuilt and that the Temple be restored."

CHAPTER 45

Cyrus, the LORD's Chosen One

This is what the LORD says to Cyrus, his anointed one, whose right hand he will empower. Before him, mighty kings will be paralyzed with fear. Their fortress gates will be opened, never again to shut against him. [2]This is what the LORD says: "I will go before you, Cyrus, and level the mountains.* I will smash down gates of bronze and cut through bars of iron. [3]And I will give you treasures hidden in the darkness—secret riches. I will do this so you may know that I am the LORD, the God of Israel, the one who calls you by name.

[4]"And why have I called you for this work? It is for the sake of Jacob my servant, Israel my chosen one. I called you by name when you did not know me. [5]I am the LORD; there is no other God. I have prepared you, even though you do not know me, [6]so all the world from east to west will know there is no other God. I am the LORD, and there is no other. [7]I am the one who creates the light and makes the darkness. I am the one who sends good times and bad times. I, the LORD, am the one who does these things. [8]Open up, O heavens, and pour out your righteousness. Let the earth open wide so salvation and righteousness can sprout up together. I, the LORD, created them.

[9]"Destruction is certain for those who argue with their Creator. Does a clay pot ever argue with its maker? Does the clay dispute with the one who shapes it, saying, 'Stop, you are doing it wrong!' Does the pot exclaim, 'How clumsy can you be!' [10]How terrible it would be if a newborn baby said to its father and mother, 'Why was I born? Why did you make me this way?' "

[11]This is what the LORD, the Creator and Holy One of Israel, says: "Do you question what I do? Do you give me orders about the work of my hands? [12]I am the one who made the earth and created people to live on it. With my hands I stretched out the heavens. All the millions of stars are at my command. [13]I will raise up Cyrus to fulfill my righteous purpose, and I will guide

45:2 As in Dead Sea Scrolls and Greek version; Masoretic Text reads *the swellings.*

I RETURN to the Lord because he has paid the price to set me free (1 Peter 1:18-19). (44:22)

I BELIEVE the Lord is the Creator of the whole earth and the Redeemer of his people. (44:24)

I BELIEVE the Lord accurately foretold the coming of Cyrus by name and used him for his own purposes. (45:2)

See Jacob's profile (page 43) at Genesis 32:9.

I DO NOT QUESTION my Creator or try to tell him what to do. (45:11)

all his actions. He will restore my city and free my captive people—and not for a reward! I, the LORD Almighty, have spoken!"

Future Conversion of Gentiles

[14]This is what the LORD says: "The Egyptians, Ethiopians,* and Sabeans will be subject to you. They will come to you with all their merchandise, and it will all be yours. They will follow you as prisoners in chains. They will fall to their knees in front of you and say, 'God is with you, and he is the only God.' "

[15]Truly, O God of Israel, our Savior, you work in strange and mysterious ways. [16]All who make idols will be humiliated and disgraced. [17]But the LORD will save the people of Israel with eternal salvation. They will never again be humiliated and disgraced throughout everlasting ages. [18]For the LORD is God, and he created the heavens and earth and put everything in place. He made the world to be lived in, not to be a place of empty chaos.

"I am the LORD," he says, "and there is no other. [19]I publicly proclaim bold promises. I do not whisper obscurities in some dark corner so no one can understand what I mean. And I did not tell the people of Israel* to ask me for something I did not plan to give. I, the LORD, speak only what is true and right.

[20]"Gather together and come, you fugitives from surrounding nations. What fools they are who carry around their wooden idols and pray to gods that cannot save! [21]Consult together, argue your case, and state your proofs that idol worship pays. Who made these things known long ago? What idol ever told you they would happen? Was it not I, the LORD? For there is no other God but me—a just God and a Savior—no, not one! [22]Let all the world look to me for salvation! For I am God; there is no other. [23]I have sworn by my own name, and I will never go back on my word: Every knee will bow to me, and every tongue will confess allegiance to my name."

[24]The people will declare, "The LORD is the source of all my righteousness and strength." And all who were angry with him will come to him and be ashamed. [25]In the LORD all the generations of Israel will be justified, and in him they will boast.

CHAPTER 46

Babylon's False Gods

The idols of Babylon, Bel and Nebo, are being hauled away on ox carts. But look! The beasts are staggering under the weight! [2]Both the idols and the ones carrying them are bowed down. The gods cannot protect the people, and the people cannot protect the gods. They go off into captivity together.

[3]"Listen to me, all you who are left in Israel. I created you and have cared for you since before you were born. [4]I will be your God throughout your lifetime—until your hair is white with age. I made you, and I will care for you. I will carry you along and save you.

[5]"To whom will you compare me? Who is my equal? [6]Some people pour out their silver and gold and hire a craftsman to make a god from it. Then they bow down and worship it! [7]They carry it around on their shoulders, and when they set it down, it stays there. It cannot even move! And when someone prays to it, there is no answer. It has no power to get anyone out of trouble.

[8]"Do not forget this, you guilty ones. [9]And do not forget the things I have done throughout history. For I am God—I alone! I am God, and there is no one else like me. [10]Only I can tell you what is going to happen even before it happens. Everything I plan will come to pass, for I do whatever I wish. [11]I will call a swift bird of prey from the east—a leader from a distant land who will come and do my bidding. I have said I would do it, and I will. [12]Listen to me, you stubborn, evil people! [13]For I am ready to set things right, not in the

45:14 Hebrew *Cushites.* 45:19 Hebrew *of Jacob.*

I BELIEVE the Lord's promise to save the people of Israel (Romans 11:25-26). (45:17)

I BELIEVE the Lord speaks what is right and accomplishes all he says he will do. (45:19)

I BELIEVE one day the whole world will bow before the Lord Jesus, who is the only way of salvation (Acts 4:12; Philippians 2:10). (45:22)

I TRUST in the Lord, who carries his people from before their birth to their old age. (46:4)

I CAN MAKE no comparison to the Lord, for he has no equal. (46:5)

I DO NOT FORGET what God has done throughout history. (46:9)

distant future, but right now! I am ready to save Jerusalem* and give my glory to Israel.

CHAPTER 47

Prediction of Babylon's Fall

"Come, Babylon, unconquered one, sit in the dust. For your days of glory, pomp, and honor have ended. O daughter of Babylonia,* never again will you be the lovely princess, tender and delicate. ²Take heavy millstones and grind the corn. Remove your veil and strip off your robe. Expose yourself to public view. ³You will be naked and burdened with shame. I will take vengeance against you and will not negotiate."

⁴Our Redeemer, whose name is the LORD Almighty, is the Holy One of Israel.

⁵"O daughter of Babylonia, sit now in darkness and silence. Never again will you be known as the queen of kingdoms. ⁶For I was angry with my chosen people and began their punishment by letting them fall into your hands. But you, Babylon, showed them no mercy. You have forced even the elderly to carry heavy burdens. ⁷You thought, 'I will reign forever as queen of the world!' You did not care at all about my people or think about the consequences of your actions.

⁸"You are a pleasure-crazy kingdom, living at ease and feeling secure, bragging as if you were the greatest in the world! You say, 'I'm self-sufficient and not accountable to anyone! I will never be a widow or lose my children.' ⁹Well, those two things will come upon you in a moment: widowhood and the loss of your children. Yes, these calamities will come upon you, despite all your witchcraft and magic.

¹⁰"You felt secure in all your wickedness. 'No one sees me,' you said. Your 'wisdom' and 'knowledge' have caused you to turn away from me and claim, 'I am self-sufficient and not accountable to anyone!' ¹¹So disaster will overtake you suddenly, and you won't be able to charm it away. Calamity will fall upon you, and you won't be able to buy your way out. A catastrophe will arise so fast that you won't know what hit you.

¹²"Call out the demon hordes you have worshiped all these years. Ask them to help you strike terror into the hearts of people once again. ¹³You have more than enough advisers, astrologers, and stargazers. Let them stand up and save you from what the future holds. ¹⁴But they are as useless as dried grass burning in a fire. They cannot even save themselves! You will get no help from them at all. Their hearth is not a place to sit for warmth. ¹⁵And all your friends, those with whom you have done business since childhood, will slip away and disappear, unable to help.

CHAPTER 48

God's Stubborn People

"Listen to me, O family of Jacob, who are called by the name of Israel and born into the family of Judah. Listen, you who take oaths in the name of the LORD and call on the God of Israel. You don't follow through on any of your promises, ²even though you call yourself the holy city and talk about depending on the God of Israel, whose name is the LORD Almighty. ³Time and again I warned you about what was going to happen in the future. Then suddenly I took action, and all my predictions came true.

⁴"I know how stubborn and obstinate you are. Your necks are as unbending as iron. You are as hardheaded as bronze. ⁵That is why I told you ahead of time what I was going to do. That way, you could never say, 'My idols did it. My wooden image and metal god commanded it to happen!' ⁶You have

I SHOW MERCY to those under God's discipline. (47:6)

I BELIEVE the Lord kept his word to bring calamity on Babylon for being prideful and thinking she was self-sufficient. (47:10)

I BELIEVE astrologers and demons can do nothing to save someone from God's judgment. (47:14)

See Jacob's profile (page 43) at Genesis 32:9.

I DO NOT stubbornly resist the Lord. (48:4)

46:13 Hebrew *Zion.*   **47:1** Or *Chaldea;* also in 47:5.

heard my predictions and seen them fulfilled, but you refuse to admit it. Now I will tell you new things I have not mentioned before, secrets you have not yet heard. [7]They are brand new, not things from the past. So you cannot say, 'We knew that all the time!'

[8]"Yes, I will tell you of things that are entirely new, for I know so well what traitors you are. You have been rebels from your earliest childhood, rotten through and through. [9]Yet for my own sake and for the honor of my name, I will hold back my anger and not wipe you out. [10]I have refined you but not in the way silver is refined. Rather, I have refined you in the furnace of suffering. [11]I will rescue you for my sake—yes, for my own sake! That way, the pagan nations will not be able to claim that their gods have conquered me. I will not let them have my glory!

Freedom from Babylon

[12]"Listen to me, O family of Jacob, Israel my chosen one! I alone am God, the First and the Last. [13]It was my hand that laid the foundations of the earth. The palm of my right hand spread out the heavens above. I spoke, and they came into being.

[14]"Have any of your idols ever told you this? Come, all of you, and listen: 'The LORD has chosen Cyrus as his ally. He will use him to put an end to the empire of Babylon, destroying the Babylonian* armies.' [15]I have said it: I am calling Cyrus! I will send him on this errand and will help him succeed. [16]Come closer and listen. I have always told you plainly what would happen so you would have no trouble understanding."

And now the Sovereign LORD and his Spirit have sent me with this message: [17]"The LORD, your Redeemer, the Holy One of Israel, says: I am the LORD your God, who teaches you what is good and leads you along the paths you should follow. [18]Oh, that you had listened to my commands! Then you would have had peace flowing like a gentle river and righteousness rolling like waves. [19]Then you would have become as numerous as the sands along the seashore—too many to count! There would have been no need for your destruction."

[20]Yet even now, be free from your captivity! Leave Babylon and the Babylonians,* singing as you go! Shout to the ends of the earth that the LORD has redeemed his servants, the people of Israel.* [21]They were not thirsty when he led them through the desert. He divided the rock, and water gushed out for them to drink.

[22]"But there is no peace for the wicked," says the LORD.

CHAPTER 49

The LORD's Servant Commissioned

Listen to me, all of you in far-off lands! The LORD called me before my birth; from within the womb he called me by name. [2]He made my words of judgment as sharp as a sword. He has hidden me in the shadow of his hand. I am like a sharp arrow in his quiver.

[3]He said to me, "You are my servant, Israel, and you will bring me glory."

[4]I replied, "But my work all seems so useless! I have spent my strength for nothing and to no purpose at all. Yet I leave it all in the LORD's hand; I will trust God for my reward."

[5]And now the LORD speaks—he who formed me in my mother's womb to be his servant, who commissioned me to bring his people of Israel back to him. The LORD has honored me, and my God has given me strength. [6]He says, "You will do more than restore the people of Israel to me. I will make you a light to the Gentiles, and you will bring my salvation to the ends of the earth."

[7]The LORD, the Redeemer and Holy One of Israel, says to the one who is

---

I BELIEVE the Lord restrained his anger for the sake of his honor, even though the Israelites had rebelled and betrayed him. (48:9)

I BELIEVE the Lord is God alone, the First and Last. (48:12)

I LISTEN to the Lord's commands, follow him, and enjoy peace. (48:18)

I BELIEVE the Israelites would not have faced destruction and exile in Babylon if they had heeded the Lord's commands. (48:19)

I BELIEVE the Lord kept his promise to give his servant, Jesus, words of judgment like a sword (Revelation 1:16). (49:2)

I BELIEVE the Lord kept his promise to use his servant, Jesus, to bring the Gentiles to salvation (Luke 2:32; Acts 13:47). (49:6)

48:14 Or Chaldean. 48:20a Or the Chaldeans. 48:20b Hebrew his servant, Jacob.

despised and rejected by a nation, to the one who is the servant of rulers: "Kings will stand at attention when you pass by. Princes will bow low because the LORD has chosen you. He, the faithful LORD, the Holy One of Israel, chooses you."

Promises of Israel's Restoration
[8]This is what the LORD says: "At just the right time, I will respond to you. On the day of salvation, I will help you. I will give you as a token and pledge to Israel. This will prove that I will reestablish the land of Israel and reassign it to its own people again. [9]Through you I am saying to the prisoners of darkness, 'Come out! I am giving you your freedom!' They will be my sheep, grazing in green pastures and on hills that were previously bare. [10]They will neither hunger nor thirst. The searing sun and scorching desert winds will not reach them anymore. For the LORD in his mercy will lead them beside cool waters. [11]And I will make my mountains into level paths for them. The highways will be raised above the valleys. [12]See, my people will return from far away, from lands to the north and west, and from as far south as Egypt.*"

> I RESPOND to the Lord's invitation of salvation (2 Corinthians 6:2). (49:8)

[13]Sing for joy, O heavens! Rejoice, O earth! Burst into song, O mountains! For the LORD has comforted his people and will have compassion on them in their sorrow.

> I BELIEVE the Lord longs to comfort and show compassion to his people. (49:13)

[14]Yet Jerusalem* says, "The LORD has deserted us; the Lord has forgotten us."

[15]"Never! Can a mother forget her nursing child? Can she feel no love for a child she has borne? But even if that were possible, I would not forget you! [16]See, I have written your name on my hand. Ever before me is a picture of Jerusalem's walls in ruins. [17]Soon your descendants will come back, and all who are trying to destroy you will go away. [18]Look and see, for all your children will come back to you. As surely as I live," says the LORD, "they will be like jewels or bridal ornaments for you to display.

[19]"Even the most desolate parts of your abandoned land will soon be crowded with your people. Your enemies who enslaved you will be far away. [20]The generations born in exile will return and say, 'We need more room! It's crowded here!' [21]Then you will think to yourself, 'Who has given me all these descendants? For most of my children were killed, and the rest were carried away into exile. I was left here all alone. Who bore these children? Who raised them for me?' "

[22]This is what the Sovereign LORD says: "See, I will give a signal to the godless nations. They will carry your little sons back to you in their arms; they will bring your daughters on their shoulders. [23]Kings and queens will serve you. They will care for all your needs. They will bow to the earth before you and lick the dust from your feet. Then you will know that I am the LORD. Those who wait for me will never be put to shame."

> I BELIEVE the Lord kept his promise to bring back the Israelites with honor from the nations where they were scattered. (49:22)

[24]Who can snatch the plunder of war from the hands of a warrior? Who can demand that a tyrant* let his captives go? [25]But the LORD says, "The captives of warriors will be released, and the plunder of tyrants will be retrieved. For I will fight those who fight you, and I will save your children. [26]I will feed your enemies with their own flesh. They will be drunk with rivers of their own blood. All the world will know that I, the LORD, am your Savior and Redeemer, the Mighty One of Israel.*"

CHAPTER 50

The LORD asks, "Did I sell you as slaves to my creditors? Is that why you are not here? Is your mother gone because I divorced her and sent her away? No,

49:12 As in Dead Sea Scrolls, which read *from the region of Aswan*, which is in southern Egypt. Masoretic Text reads *from the region of Sinim.* 49:14 Hebrew *Zion.* 49:24 As in Dead Sea Scrolls, Syriac version, and Latin Vulgate (also see 49:25); Masoretic Text reads *a righteous person.* 49:26 Hebrew *of Jacob.*

I BELIEVE the Israelites suffered exile in Babylon because of their sins—certainly not because the Lord was too weak to save them. (50:1)

you went away as captives because of your sins. And your mother, too, was taken because of your sins. ²Was I too weak to save you? Is that why the house is silent and empty when I come home? Is it because I have no power to rescue? No, that is not the reason! For I can speak to the sea and make it dry! I can turn rivers into deserts covered with dying fish. ³I am the one who sends darkness out across the skies, bringing it to a state of mourning."

The LORD's Obedient Servant

I BELIEVE the Lord accurately foretold that his servant, Jesus, would endure beatings and mocking (Matthew 26:67; 27:26). (50:6)

⁴The Sovereign LORD has given me his words of wisdom, so that I know what to say to all these weary ones. Morning by morning he wakens me and opens my understanding to his will. ⁵The Sovereign LORD has spoken to me, and I have listened. I do not rebel or turn away. ⁶I give my back to those who beat me and my cheeks to those who pull out my beard. I do not hide from shame, for they mock me and spit in my face.

⁷Because the Sovereign LORD helps me, I will not be dismayed. Therefore, I have set my face like a stone, determined to do his will. And I know that I will triumph. ⁸He who gives me justice is near. Who will dare to oppose me now? Where are my enemies? Let them appear! ⁹See, the Sovereign LORD is on my side! Who will declare me guilty? All my enemies will be destroyed like old clothes that have been eaten by moths!

I TRUST AND RELY on the Lord, not on my own human understanding. (50:10)

¹⁰Who among you fears the LORD and obeys his servant? If you are walking in darkness, without a ray of light, trust in the LORD and rely on your God. ¹¹But watch out, you who live in your own light and warm yourselves by your own fires. This is the reward you will receive from me: You will soon lie down in great torment.

CHAPTER 51

A Call to Trust the LORD

"Listen to me, all who hope for deliverance—all who seek the LORD! Consider the quarry from which you were mined, the rock from which you were cut! ²Yes, think about your ancestors Abraham and Sarah, from whom you came. Abraham was alone when I called him. But when I blessed him, he became a great nation."

See the profiles for Abraham (page 19) and Sarah (page 25) at Genesis 15:6 and Genesis 21:1.

³The LORD will comfort Israel* again and make her deserts blossom. Her barren wilderness will become as beautiful as Eden—the garden of the LORD. Joy and gladness will be found there. Lovely songs of thanksgiving will fill the air.

⁴"Listen to me, my people. Hear me, Israel, for my law will be proclaimed, and my justice will become a light to the nations. ⁵My mercy and justice are coming soon. Your salvation is on the way. I will rule the nations. They will wait for me and long for my power. ⁶Look up to the skies above, and gaze down on the earth beneath. For the skies will disappear like smoke, and the earth will wear out like a piece of clothing. The people of the earth will die like flies, but my salvation lasts forever. My righteous rule will never end!

I BELIEVE the Lord's promise that he one day will establish his righteous rule on the earth. (51:6)

⁷"Listen to me, you who know right from wrong and cherish my law in your hearts. Do not be afraid of people's scorn or their slanderous talk. ⁸For the moth will destroy them as it destroys clothing. The worm will eat away at them as it eats wool. But my righteousness will last forever. My salvation will continue from generation to generation."

I BELIEVE the Lord's righteousness and salvation last forever. (51:8)

⁹Wake up, LORD! Robe yourself with strength! Rouse yourself as in the days of old when you slew Egypt, the dragon of the Nile.* ¹⁰Are you not the same today, the one who dried up the sea, making a path of escape when you saved your people? ¹¹Those who have been ransomed by the LORD will return to Jerusalem,* singing songs of everlasting joy. Sorrow and mourning will disappear, and they will be overcome with joy and gladness.

I BELIEVE the Lord kept his promise to bring back his ransomed people to Jerusalem with great joy and singing. (51:11)

51:3 Hebrew Zion; also in 51:16.   51:9 Hebrew slew Rahab the dragon. Rahab is the name of a mythical sea monster that represents chaos in ancient literature. The name is used here as a poetic name for Egypt.
51:11 Hebrew Zion.

¹²"I, even I, am the one who comforts you. So why are you afraid of mere humans, who wither like the grass and disappear? ¹³Yet you have forgotten the LORD, your Creator, the one who put the stars in the sky and established the earth. Will you remain in constant dread of human oppression? Will you continue to fear the anger of your enemies from morning till night? ¹⁴Soon all you captives will be released! Imprisonment, starvation, and death will not be your fate! ¹⁵For I am the LORD your God, who stirs up the sea, causing its waves to roar. My name is the LORD Almighty. ¹⁶And I have put my words in your mouth and hidden you safely within my hand. I set all the stars in space and established the earth. I am the one who says to Israel, 'You are mine!' "

¹⁷Wake up, wake up, O Jerusalem! You have drunk enough from the cup of the LORD's fury. You have drunk the cup of terror, tipping out its last drops. ¹⁸Not one of your children is left alive to help you or tell you what to do. ¹⁹These two things have been your lot: desolation and destruction, famine and war. And who is left to sympathize? Who is left to comfort you? ²⁰For your children have fainted and lie in the streets, helpless as antelopes caught in a net. The LORD has poured out his fury; God has rebuked them.

²¹But now listen to this, you afflicted ones, who sit in a drunken stupor, though not from drinking wine. ²²This is what the Sovereign LORD, your God and Defender, says: "See, I am taking the terrible cup from your hands. You will drink no more of my fury. It is gone at last! ²³But I will put that cup into the hands of those who tormented you. I will give it to those who trampled you into the dust and walked on your backs."

CHAPTER 52

Deliverance for Jerusalem

Wake up, wake up, O Zion! Clothe yourselves with strength. Put on your beautiful clothes, O holy city of Jerusalem, for unclean and godless people will no longer enter your gates. ²Rise from the dust, O Jerusalem. Remove the slave bands from your neck, O captive daughter of Zion. ³For this is what the LORD says: "When I sold you into exile, I received no payment. Now I can redeem you without paying for you."

⁴This is what the Sovereign LORD says: "Long ago my people went to live as resident foreigners in Egypt. Now they have been oppressed without cause by Assyria. ⁵And now, what is this?" asks the LORD. "Why are my people enslaved again? Those who rule them shout in exultation. My name is being blasphemed all day long. ⁶But I will reveal my name to my people, and they will come to know its power. Then at last they will recognize that it is I who speaks to them."

⁷How beautiful on the mountains are the feet of those who bring good news of peace and salvation, the news that the God of Israel* reigns! ⁸The watchmen shout and sing with joy, for before their very eyes they see the LORD bringing his people home to Jerusalem.* ⁹Let the ruins of Jerusalem break into joyful song, for the LORD has comforted his people. He has redeemed Jerusalem. ¹⁰The LORD will demonstrate his holy power before the eyes of all the nations. The ends of the earth will see the salvation of our God.

¹¹Go now, leave your bonds and slavery. Put Babylon behind you, with everything it represents, for it is unclean to you. You are the LORD's holy people. Purify yourselves, you who carry home the vessels of the LORD. ¹²You will not leave in a hurry, running for your lives. For the LORD will go ahead of you, and the God of Israel will protect you from behind.

The LORD's Suffering Servant

¹³See, my servant will prosper; he will be highly exalted. ¹⁴Many were amazed when they saw him*—beaten and bloodied, so disfigured one would

52:7 Hebrew of Zion.   52:8 Hebrew to Zion.   52:14 As in Syriac version; Hebrew reads you.

I DO NOT DREAD human oppression, because I remember the Lord, my Creator, will comfort me. (51:13)

I AM CONFIDENT, because the Lord Almighty, who set the stars and the earth in place, is the one who hides me in his hand. (51:16)

Ask God to cleanse your heart as you read his Word (Psalm 51:10).

I AM GLAD to proclaim the good news that God reigns! (52:7)

I LEAVE BEHIND my slavery to sin and live a pure life as one of the Lord's holy people (2 Corinthians 6:17; 2 Timothy 2:19). (52:11)

I BELIEVE the Lord exalted his servant, Jesus, after he was beaten and humiliated (Philippians 2:9-10). (52:13)

scarcely know he was a person. [15]And he will again startle* many nations. Kings will stand speechless in his presence. For they will see what they had not previously been told about; they will understand what they had not heard about.

CHAPTER 53

Who has believed our message? To whom will the LORD reveal his saving power? [2]My servant grew up in the LORD's presence like a tender green shoot, sprouting from a root in dry and sterile ground. There was nothing beautiful or majestic about his appearance, nothing to attract us to him. [3]He was despised and rejected—a man of sorrows, acquainted with bitterest grief. We turned our backs on him and looked the other way when he went by. He was despised, and we did not care.

[4]Yet it was our weaknesses he carried; it was our sorrows* that weighed him down. And we thought his troubles were a punishment from God for his own sins! [5]But he was wounded and crushed for our sins. He was beaten that we might have peace. He was whipped, and we were healed! [6]All of us have strayed away like sheep. We have left God's paths to follow our own. Yet the LORD laid on him the guilt and sins of us all.

[7]He was oppressed and treated harshly, yet he never said a word. He was led as a lamb to the slaughter. And as a sheep is silent before the shearers, he did not open his mouth. [8]From prison and trial they led him away to his death. But who among the people realized that he was dying for their sins—that he was suffering their punishment? [9]He had done no wrong, and he never deceived anyone. But he was buried like a criminal; he was put in a rich man's grave.

[10]But it was the LORD's good plan to crush him and fill him with grief. Yet when his life is made an offering for sin, he will have a multitude of children, many heirs. He will enjoy a long life, and the LORD's plan will prosper in his hands. [11]When he sees all that is accomplished by his anguish, he will be satisfied. And because of what he has experienced, my righteous servant will make it possible for many to be counted righteous, for he will bear all their sins. [12]I will give him the honors of one who is mighty and great, because he exposed himself to death. He was counted among those who were sinners. He bore the sins of many and interceded for sinners.

CHAPTER 54

Future Glory for Jerusalem

"Sing, O childless woman! Break forth into loud and joyful song, O Jerusalem, even though you never gave birth to a child. For the woman who could bear no children now has more than all the other women," says the LORD. [2]"Enlarge your house; build an addition; spread out your home! [3]For you will soon be bursting at the seams. Your descendants will take over other nations and live in their cities.

[4]"Fear not; you will no longer live in shame. The shame of your youth and the sorrows of widowhood will be remembered no more, [5]for your Creator will be your husband. The LORD Almighty is his name! He is your Redeemer, the Holy One of Israel, the God of all the earth. [6]For the LORD has called you back from your grief—as though you were a young wife abandoned by her husband," says your God. [7]"For a brief moment I abandoned you, but with great compassion I will take you back. [8]In a moment of anger I turned my face away for a little while. But with everlasting love I will have compassion on you," says the LORD, your Redeemer.

[9]"Just as I swore in the time of Noah that I would never again let a flood

I BELIEVE the Lord accurately foretold that Jesus would be wounded to heal his people from their sins (1 Peter 2:24). (53:5)

I BELIEVE Jesus did not protest before he died for the sins of the people (Matthew 27:12-14). (53:7)

I BELIEVE the Lord promised to be a husband to Israel and restore her to a loving relationship with him. (54:5)

See Noah's profile (page 13) at Genesis 6:9.

52:15 Or *cleanse.*   53:4 Or *Yet it was our sicknesses he carried; it was our diseases.*

cover the earth and destroy its life, so now I swear that I will never again pour out my anger on you. ¹⁰For the mountains may depart and the hills disappear, but even then I will remain loyal to you. My covenant of blessing will never be broken," says the LORD, who has mercy on you.

¹¹"O storm-battered city, troubled and desolate! I will rebuild you on a foundation of sapphires and make the walls of your houses from precious jewels. ¹²I will make your towers of sparkling rubies and your gates and walls of shining gems. ¹³I will teach all your citizens, and their prosperity will be great. ¹⁴You will live under a government that is just and fair. Your enemies will stay far away; you will live in peace. Terror will not come near. ¹⁵If any nation comes to fight you, it will not be because I sent them to punish you. Your enemies will always be defeated because I am on your side. ¹⁶I have created the blacksmith who fans the coals beneath the forge and makes the weapons of destruction. And I have created the armies that destroy. ¹⁷But in that coming day, no weapon turned against you will succeed. And everyone who tells lies in court will be brought to justice. These benefits are enjoyed by the servants of the LORD; their vindication will come from me. I, the LORD, have spoken!

CHAPTER 55

Invitation to the LORD's Salvation

"Is anyone thirsty? Come and drink—even if you have no money! Come, take your choice of wine or milk—it's all free! ²Why spend your money on food that does not give you strength? Why pay for food that does you no good? Listen, and I will tell you where to get food that is good for the soul!

³"Come to me with your ears wide open. Listen, for the life of your soul is at stake. I am ready to make an everlasting covenant with you. I will give you all the mercies and unfailing love that I promised to David. ⁴He displayed my power by being my witness and a leader among the nations. ⁵You also will command the nations, and they will come running to obey, because I, the LORD your God, the Holy One of Israel, have made you glorious."

⁶Seek the LORD while you can find him. Call on him now while he is near. ⁷Let the people turn from their wicked deeds. Let them banish from their minds the very thought of doing wrong! Let them turn to the LORD that he may have mercy on them. Yes, turn to our God, for he will abundantly pardon.

⁸"My thoughts are completely different from yours," says the LORD. "And my ways are far beyond anything you could imagine. ⁹For just as the heavens are higher than the earth, so are my ways higher than your ways and my thoughts higher than your thoughts.

¹⁰"The rain and snow come down from the heavens and stay on the ground to water the earth. They cause the grain to grow, producing seed for the farmer and bread for the hungry. ¹¹It is the same with my word. I send it out, and it always produces fruit. It will accomplish all I want it to, and it will prosper everywhere I send it. ¹²You will live in joy and peace. The mountains and hills will burst into song, and the trees of the field will clap their hands! ¹³Where once there were thorns, cypress trees will grow. Where briers grew, myrtles will sprout up. This miracle will bring great honor to the LORD's name; it will be an everlasting sign of his power and love.

CHAPTER 56

Blessings for All Nations

"Be just and fair to all," says the LORD. "Do what is right and good, for I am coming soon to rescue you. ²Blessed are those who are careful to do this. Blessed are those who honor my Sabbath days of rest by refusing to work. And blessed are those who keep themselves from doing wrong.

I BELIEVE the Lord will never break his covenant of blessing with Israel. (54:10)

I BELIEVE the Lord's promise to one day make Jerusalem a city full of justice and peace. (54:14)

I BELIEVE the Lord has promised one day to bring victory, justice, and peace to his servants in Jerusalem. (54:17)

See David's profile (page 629) at Psalm 3:1.

I TURN from my sin and find mercy and pardon from God. (55:7)

I KNOW God's thoughts and ways are far beyond my understanding. (55:8)

I BELIEVE the Lord's words always come true and fulfill his purposes. (55:11)

I BELIEVE God offers salvation to anyone— Jew or Gentile—who trusts him (Ephesians 2:11–22). (56:3)

I COMMIT my life to God and live to please him. (56:4)

³"And my blessings are for Gentiles, too, when they commit themselves to the LORD. Do not let them think that I consider them second-class citizens. And my blessings are also for the eunuchs. They are as much mine as anyone else. ⁴For I say this to the eunuchs who keep my Sabbath days holy, who choose to do what pleases me and commit their lives to me: ⁵I will give them—in my house, within my walls—a memorial and a name far greater than the honor they would have received by having sons and daughters. For the name I give them is an everlasting one. It will never disappear!

⁶"I will also bless the Gentiles who commit themselves to the LORD and serve him and love his name, who worship him and do not desecrate the Sabbath day of rest, and who have accepted his covenant. ⁷I will bring them also to my holy mountain of Jerusalem and will fill them with joy in my house of prayer. I will accept their burnt offerings and sacrifices, because my Temple will be called a house of prayer for all nations. ⁸For the Sovereign LORD, who brings back the outcasts of Israel, says: I will bring others, too, besides my people Israel."

Sinful Leaders Condemned

⁹Come, wild animals of the field! Come, wild animals of the forest! Come and devour my people! ¹⁰For the leaders of my people—the LORD's watchmen, his shepherds—are blind to every danger. They are like silent watchdogs that give no warning when danger comes. They love to lie around, sleeping and dreaming. ¹¹And they are as greedy as dogs, never satisfied. They are stupid shepherds, all following their own path, all of them intent on personal gain.

¹²"Come," they say. "We will get some wine and have a party. Let's all get drunk. Let this go on and on, and tomorrow will be even better."

CHAPTER 57

The righteous pass away; the godly often die before their time. And no one seems to care or wonder why. No one seems to understand that God is protecting them from the evil to come. ²For the godly who die will rest in peace.

Idolatrous Worship Condemned

I BELIEVE that God may allow his righteous people to die prematurely to protect them from even greater suffering. (57:1)

³"But you—come here, you witches' children, you offspring of adulterers and prostitutes! ⁴Whom do you mock, making faces and sticking out your tongues? You children of sinners and liars! ⁵You worship your idols with great passion beneath every green tree. You slaughter your children as human sacrifices down in the valleys, under overhanging rocks. ⁶Your gods are the smooth stones in the valleys. You worship them with drink offerings and grain offerings. They, not I, are your inheritance. Does all this make me happy? ⁷You have committed adultery on the mountaintops by worshiping idols there, and so you have been unfaithful to me. ⁸Behind closed doors, you have set up your idols and worship them instead of me. This is adultery, for you are loving these idols instead of loving me. You have climbed right into bed with these detestable gods. ⁹You have given olive oil and perfume to Molech* as your gift. You have traveled far, even into the world of the dead,* to find new gods to love. ¹⁰You grew weary in your search, but you never gave up. You strengthened yourself and went on. ¹¹Why were you more afraid of them than of me? How is it that you don't even remember me or think about me? Is it because I have not corrected you that you have no fear of me?

I DO NOT BREAK the Lord's heart by worshiping other gods. (57:7)

¹²"Now I will expose your so-called good deeds that you consider so righteous. None of them will benefit or save you. ¹³Let's see if your idols can do anything for you when you cry to them for help. They are so helpless that a breath of wind can knock them down! But whoever trusts in me will possess

57:9a Or *to the king.*   57:9b Hebrew *into Sheol.*

the land and inherit my holy mountain. ¹⁴I will say, 'Rebuild the road! Clear away the rocks and stones so my people can return from captivity.' "

God Forgives the Repentant

¹⁵The high and lofty one who inhabits eternity, the Holy One, says this: "I live in that high and holy place with those whose spirits are contrite and humble. I refresh the humble and give new courage to those with repentant hearts. ¹⁶For I will not fight against you forever; I will not always show my anger. If I did, all people would pass away—all the souls I have made. ¹⁷I was angry and punished these greedy people. I withdrew myself from them, but they went right on sinning. ¹⁸I have seen what they do, but I will heal them anyway! I will lead them and comfort those who mourn. ¹⁹Then words of praise will be on their lips. May they have peace, both near and far, for I will heal them all," says the LORD. ²⁰"But those who still reject me are like the restless sea. It is never still but continually churns up mire and dirt. ²¹There is no peace for the wicked," says my God.

I BELIEVE the Lord is high and holy, yet he gladly lives with and refreshes the humble and contrite. (57:15)

I BELIEVE God heals and restores all those who come to him. (57:19)

CHAPTER 58

True and False Worship

"Shout with the voice of a trumpet blast. Tell my people Israel* of their sins! ²Yet they act so pious! They come to the Temple every day and seem delighted to hear my laws. You would almost think this was a righteous nation that would never abandon its God. They love to make a show of coming to me and asking me to take action on their behalf. ³'We have fasted before you!' they say. 'Why aren't you impressed? We have done much penance, and you don't even notice it!'

"I will tell you why! It's because you are living for yourselves even while you are fasting. You keep right on oppressing your workers. ⁴What good is fasting when you keep on fighting and quarreling? This kind of fasting will never get you anywhere with me. ⁵You humble yourselves by going through the motions of penance, bowing your heads like a blade of grass in the wind. You dress in sackcloth and cover yourselves with ashes. Is this what you call fasting? Do you really think this will please the LORD?

⁶"No, the kind of fasting I want calls you to free those who are wrongly imprisoned and to stop oppressing those who work for you. Treat them fairly and give them what they earn. ⁷I want you to share your food with the hungry and to welcome poor wanderers into your homes. Give clothes to those who need them, and do not hide from relatives who need your help.

⁸"If you do these things, your salvation will come like the dawn. Yes, your healing will come quickly. Your godliness will lead you forward, and the glory of the LORD will protect you from behind. ⁹Then when you call, the LORD will answer. 'Yes, I am here,' he will quickly reply.

"Stop oppressing the helpless and stop making false accusations and spreading vicious rumors! ¹⁰Feed the hungry and help those in trouble. Then your light will shine out from the darkness, and the darkness around you will be as bright as day. ¹¹The LORD will guide you continually, watering your life when you are dry and keeping you healthy, too. You will be like a well-watered garden, like an ever-flowing spring. ¹²Your children will rebuild the deserted ruins of your cities. Then you will be known as the people who rebuild their walls and cities.

¹³"Keep the Sabbath day holy. Don't pursue your own interests on that day, but enjoy the Sabbath and speak of it with delight as the LORD's holy day. Honor the LORD in everything you do, and don't follow your own desires or talk idly. If you do this, ¹⁴the LORD will be your delight. I will give you

I DO NOT LIVE for myself while pretending to live for God. (58:3)

I PLEASE God by giving justice to the oppressed and food to the needy. (58:6)

I PLEASE the Lord when I help others and experience his guidance and blessing in my life. (58:11)

58:1 Hebrew *Jacob.*

See Jacob's profile (page 43) at Genesis 32:9.

great honor and give you your full share of the inheritance I promised to Jacob, your ancestor. I, the LORD, have spoken!"

CHAPTER 59

Warnings against Sin

Listen! The LORD is not too weak to save you, and he is not becoming deaf. He can hear you when you call. [2]But there is a problem—your sins have cut you off from God. Because of your sin, he has turned away and will not listen anymore. [3]Your hands are the hands of murderers, and your fingers are filthy with sin. Your mouth is full of lies, and your lips are tainted with corruption.

[4]No one cares about being fair and honest. Their lawsuits are based on lies. They spend their time plotting evil deeds and then doing them. [5]They spend their time and energy spinning evil plans that end up in deadly actions. [6]They cheat and shortchange everyone. Nothing they do is productive; all their activity is filled with sin. Violence is their trademark. [7]Their feet run to do evil, and they rush to commit murder. They think only about sinning. Wherever they go, misery and destruction follow them. [8]They do not know what true peace is or what it means to be just and good. They continually do wrong, and those who follow them cannot experience a moment's peace.

[9]It is because of all this evil that deliverance is far from us. That is why God doesn't punish those who injure us. No wonder we are in darkness when we expected light. No wonder we are walking in the gloom. [10]No wonder we grope like blind people and stumble along. Even at brightest noontime, we fall down as though it were dark. No wonder we are like corpses when compared to vigorous young men! [11]We growl like hungry bears; we moan like mournful doves. We look for justice, but it is nowhere to be found. We look to be rescued, but it is far away from us. [12]For our sins are piled up before God and testify against us. Yes, we know what sinners we are. [13]We know that we have rebelled against the LORD. We have turned our backs on God. We know how unfair and oppressive we have been, carefully planning our deceitful lies. [14]Our courts oppose people who are righteous, and justice is nowhere to be found. Truth falls dead in the streets, and fairness has been outlawed. [15]Yes, truth is gone, and anyone who tries to live a godly life is soon attacked.

The LORD looked and was displeased to find that there was no justice. [16]He was amazed to see that no one intervened to help the oppressed. So he himself stepped in to save them with his mighty power and justice. [17]He put on righteousness as his body armor and placed the helmet of salvation on his head. He clothed himself with the robes of vengeance and godly fury. [18]He will repay his enemies for their evil deeds. His fury will fall on his foes in distant lands. [19]Then at last they will respect and glorify the name of the LORD throughout the world. For he will come like a flood tide driven by the breath of the LORD.

[20]"The Redeemer will come to Jerusalem,* " says the LORD, "to buy back those in Israel* who have turned from their sins. [21]And this is my covenant with them," says the LORD. "My Spirit will not leave them, and neither will these words I have given you. They will be on your lips and on the lips of your children and your children's children forever. I, the LORD, have spoken!

CHAPTER 60

Future Glory for Jerusalem

"Arise, Jerusalem! Let your light shine for all the nations to see! For the glory of the LORD is shining upon you. [2]Darkness as black as night will cover all the nations of the earth, but the glory of the LORD will shine over you. [3]All nations will come to your light. Mighty kings will come to see your radiance.

59:20a Hebrew *to Zion.* 59:20b Hebrew *in Jacob.*

I KNOW the Lord may stop listening to me if I stubbornly continue to sin against him. (59:2)

I AM COMMITTED to being honest and fair. (59:4)

I BELIEVE the Lord kept his promise to send a Redeemer to buy back all who turn from their sins. (59:20)

I BELIEVE the Lord kept his promise to send his Spirit to be with his redeemed people always (Romans 8:9). (59:21)

I BELIEVE the Lord's promise to make his glory shine over and from Jerusalem (see also Revelation 21:24-25). (60:1)

[4]"Look and see, for everyone is coming home! Your sons are coming from distant lands; your little daughters will be carried home. [5]Your eyes will shine, and your hearts will thrill with joy, for merchants from around the world will come to you. They will bring you the wealth of many lands. [6]Vast caravans of camels will converge on you, the camels of Midian and Ephah. From Sheba they will bring gold and incense for the worship of the LORD. [7]The flocks of Kedar will be given to you, and the rams of Nebaioth will be brought for my altars. In that day I will make my Temple glorious.

[8]"And what do I see flying like clouds to Israel, like doves to their nests? [9]They are the ships of Tarshish, reserved to bring the people of Israel home. They will bring their wealth with them, and it will bring great honor to the LORD your God, the Holy One of Israel, for he will fill you with splendor.

[10]"Foreigners will come to rebuild your cities. Kings and rulers will send you aid. For though I have destroyed you in my anger, I will have mercy on you through my grace. [11]Your gates will stay open around the clock to receive the wealth of many lands. The kings of the world will be led as captives in a victory procession. [12]For the nations that refuse to be your allies will be destroyed. [13]The glory of Lebanon will be yours—the forests of cypress, fir, and pine—to beautify my sanctuary. My Temple will be glorious!

[14]"The children of your tormentors will come and bow before you. Those who despised you will kiss your feet. They will call you the City of the LORD, and Zion of the Holy One of Israel.

[15]"Though you were once despised and hated and rebuffed by all, you will be beautiful forever. You will be a joy to all generations, for I will make you so. [16]Powerful kings and mighty nations will bring the best of their goods to satisfy your every need. You will know at last that I, the LORD, am your Savior and Redeemer, the Mighty One of Israel.* [17]I will exchange your bronze for gold, your iron for silver, your wood for bronze, and your stones for iron. Peace and righteousness will be your leaders! [18]Violence will disappear from your land; the desolation and destruction of war will end. Salvation will surround you like city walls, and praise will be on the lips of all who enter there.

[19]"No longer will you need the sun or moon to give you light, for the LORD your God will be your everlasting light, and he will be your glory. [20]The sun will never set; the moon will not go down. For the LORD will be your everlasting light. Your days of mourning will come to an end. [21]All your people will be righteous. They will possess their land forever, for I will plant them there with my own hands in order to bring myself glory. [22]The smallest family will multiply into a large clan. The tiniest group will become a mighty nation. I, the LORD, will bring it all to pass at the right time."

CHAPTER 61

Good News for the Oppressed

The Spirit of the Sovereign LORD is upon me, because the LORD has appointed me to bring good news to the poor. He has sent me to comfort the brokenhearted and to announce that captives will be released and prisoners will be freed.* [2]He has sent me to tell those who mourn that the time of the LORD's favor has come,* and with it, the day of God's anger against their enemies. [3]To all who mourn in Israel,* he will give beauty for ashes, joy instead of mourning, praise instead of despair. For the LORD has planted them like strong and graceful oaks for his own glory.

[4]They will rebuild the ancient ruins, repairing cities long ago destroyed. They will revive them, though they have been empty for many generations. [5]Foreigners will be your servants. They will feed your flocks and plow your fields and tend your vineyards. [6]You will be called priests of the LORD, ministers

I BELIEVE the Lord kept his promise to bring his people back to Jerusalem. (60:4)

I BELIEVE the Lord kept his promise to rebuild Jerusalem with the wealth of the nations (Ezra 1:3-4; 5:8-10; see also Revelation 21:26). (60:10)

I BELIEVE the Lord's promise to make Jerusalem a place of joy and beauty forever (Revelation 21:18-22). (60:15)

I BELIEVE the Lord will one day be the light of his people (Revelation 21:23-24). (60:19)

I BELIEVE the Lord ultimately sent Jesus Christ to bring good news to the poor and the message of freedom to the captives of sin (Luke 4:18-19). (61:1)

60:16 Hebrew *of Jacob.*   61:1 Greek version reads *and the blind will see.*   61:2 Or *to proclaim the acceptable year of the LORD.*   61:3 Hebrew *in Zion.*

of our God. You will be fed with the treasures of the nations and will boast in their riches. ⁷Instead of shame and dishonor, you will inherit a double portion of prosperity and everlasting joy.

⁸"For I, the LORD, love justice. I hate robbery and wrongdoing. I will faithfully reward my people for their suffering and make an everlasting covenant with them. ⁹Their descendants will be known and honored among the nations. Everyone will realize that they are a people the LORD has blessed."

¹⁰I am overwhelmed with joy in the LORD my God! For he has dressed me with the clothing of salvation and draped me in a robe of righteousness. I am like a bridegroom in his wedding suit or a bride with her jewels. ¹¹The Sovereign LORD will show his justice to the nations of the world. Everyone will praise him! His righteousness will be like a garden in early spring, filled with young plants springing up everywhere.

CHAPTER 62

Isaiah's Prayer for Jerusalem

Because I love Zion, because my heart yearns for Jerusalem, I cannot remain silent. I will not stop praying for her until her righteousness shines like the dawn, and her salvation blazes like a burning torch.

²The nations will see your righteousness. Kings will be blinded by your glory. And the LORD will give you a new name. ³The LORD will hold you in his hands for all to see—a splendid crown in the hands of God. ⁴Never again will you be called the Godforsaken City* or the Desolate Land.* Your new name will be the City of God's Delight* and the Bride of God,* for the LORD delights in you and will claim you as his own. ⁵Your children will care for you with joy, O Jerusalem, just as a young man cares for his bride. Then God will rejoice over you as a bridegroom rejoices over his bride.

⁶O Jerusalem, I have posted watchmen on your walls; they will pray to the LORD day and night for the fulfillment of his promises. Take no rest, all you who pray. ⁷Give the LORD no rest until he makes Jerusalem the object of praise throughout the earth. ⁸The LORD has sworn to Jerusalem by his own strength: "I will never again hand you over to your enemies. Never again will foreign warriors come and take away your grain and wine. ⁹You raised it, and you will keep it, praising the LORD. Within the courtyards of the Temple, you yourselves will drink the wine that you have pressed."

¹⁰Go out! Prepare the highway for my people to return! Smooth out the road; pull out the boulders; raise a flag for all the nations to see. ¹¹The LORD has sent this message to every land: "Tell the people of Israel,* 'Look, your Savior is coming. See, he brings his reward with him as he comes.' " ¹²They will be called the Holy People and the People Redeemed by the LORD. And Jerusalem will be known as the Desirable Place and the City No Longer Forsaken.

CHAPTER 63

Judgment against the LORD's Enemies

Who is this who comes from Edom, from the city of Bozrah, with his clothing stained red? Who is this in royal robes, marching in the greatness of his strength?

"It is I, the LORD, announcing your salvation! It is I, the LORD, who is mighty to save!"

²Why are your clothes so red, as if you have been treading out grapes?

³"I have trodden the winepress alone; no one was there to help me. In my anger I have trampled my enemies as if they were grapes. In my fury I have

---

I PRAISE the Lord with joy because of the salvation and righteousness he gives. (61:10)

I BELIEVE the Lord delights in Jerusalem and one day will adorn her as a bride (Revelation 21:2). (62:4)

I LONG AND PRAY for the fulfillment of God's promises. (62:6)

I HELP proclaim the message of salvation to people everywhere. (62:11)

62:4a Hebrew *Azubah,* which means "forsaken." 62:4b Hebrew *Shemamah,* which means "desolate."
62:4c Hebrew *Hephzibah,* which means "my delight is in her." 62:4d Hebrew *Beulah,* which means "married."
62:11 Hebrew *Tell the daughter of Zion.*

trampled my foes. It is their blood that has stained my clothes. ⁴For the time has come for me to avenge my people, to ransom them from their oppressors. ⁵I looked, but no one came to help my people. I was amazed and appalled at what I saw. So I executed vengeance alone; unaided, I passed down judgment. ⁶I crushed the nations in my anger and made them stagger and fall to the ground."

Praise for Deliverance
⁷I will tell of the LORD's unfailing love. I will praise the LORD for all he has done. I will rejoice in his great goodness to Israel, which he has granted according to his mercy and love. ⁸He said, "They are my very own people. Surely they will not be false again." And he became their Savior. ⁹In all their suffering he also suffered, and he personally rescued them. In his love and mercy he redeemed them. He lifted them up and carried them through all the years.

¹⁰But they rebelled against him and grieved his Holy Spirit. That is why he became their enemy and fought against them. ¹¹Then they remembered those days of old when Moses led his people out of Egypt. They cried out, "Where is the one who brought Israel through the sea, with Moses as their shepherd? Where is the one who sent his Holy Spirit to be among his people? ¹²Where is the one whose power divided the sea before them, when Moses lifted up his hand, establishing his reputation forever? ¹³Where is the one who led them through the bottom of the sea? They were like fine stallions racing through the desert, never stumbling. ¹⁴As with cattle going down into a peaceful valley, the Spirit of the LORD gave them rest. You led your people, LORD, and gained a magnificent reputation."

Prayer for Mercy and Pardon
¹⁵LORD, look down from heaven and see us from your holy, glorious home. Where is the passion and the might you used to show on our behalf? Where are your mercy and compassion now? ¹⁶Surely you are still our Father! Even if Abraham and Jacob* would disown us, LORD, you would still be our Father. You are our Redeemer from ages past. ¹⁷LORD, why have you allowed us to turn from your path? Why have you given us stubborn hearts so we no longer fear you? Return and help us, for we are your servants and your special possession. ¹⁸How briefly your holy people possessed the holy place, and now our enemies have destroyed it. ¹⁹LORD, why do you treat us as though we never belonged to you? Why do you act as though we had never been known as your people?

CHAPTER 64

Oh, that you would burst from the heavens and come down! How the mountains would quake in your presence! ²As fire causes wood to burn and water to boil, your coming would make the nations tremble. Then your enemies would learn the reason for your fame! ³When you came down long ago, you did awesome things beyond our highest expectations. And oh, how the mountains quaked! ⁴For since the world began, no ear has heard, and no eye has seen a God like you, who works for those who wait for him! ⁵You welcome those who cheerfully do good, who follow godly ways.

But we are not godly. We are constant sinners, so your anger is heavy on us. How can people like us be saved? ⁶We are all infected and impure with sin. When we proudly display our righteous deeds, we find they are but filthy rags. Like autumn leaves, we wither and fall. And our sins, like the wind, sweep us away. ⁷Yet no one calls on your name or pleads with you for mercy. Therefore, you have turned away from us and turned us over to our sins.

63:16 Hebrew *Israel.*

I BELIEVE the Lord alone will bring justice for his people and vengeance against their enemies. (63:5)

I PRAISE the Lord and tell of his goodness, mercy, and love. (63:7)

I BELIEVE the Lord suffered along with his people and personally rescued and redeemed them. (63:9)

See Moses' profile (page 73) at Exodus 5:1.

See the profiles for Abraham (page 19) and Jacob (page 43) at Genesis 15:6 and Genesis 32:9.

I BELIEVE God works for those who wait for him! (64:4)

I ACKNOWLEDGE that all people are impure—even their righteous deeds are filthy and fleeting. (64:6)

I BELIEVE God is my Father, my Maker, my Redeemer. (64:8)

⁸And yet, LORD, you are our Father. We are the clay, and you are the potter. We are all formed by your hand. ⁹Oh, don't be so angry with us, LORD. Please don't remember our sins forever. Look at us, we pray, and see that we are all your people.

¹⁰Your holy cities are destroyed; even Jerusalem is a desolate wilderness. ¹¹The holy, beautiful Temple where our ancestors praised you has been burned down, and all the things of beauty are destroyed. ¹²After all this, LORD, must you still refuse to help us? Will you continue to be silent and punish us?

CHAPTER 65

Judgment and Final Salvation

I BELIEVE God kept his promise to reveal himself to those who had not been looking for him (Romans 10:20-21). (65:1)

The LORD says, "People who never before inquired about me are now asking about me. I am being found by people who were not looking for me. To them I have said, 'I am here!'

²"I opened my arms to my own people all day long, but they have rebelled. They follow their own evil paths and thoughts. ³All day long they insult me to my face by worshiping idols in their sacred gardens. They burn incense on the rooftops of their homes. ⁴At night they go out among the graves and secret places to worship evil spirits. They also eat pork and other forbidden foods. ⁵Yet they say to each other, 'Don't come too close or you will defile me! I am holier than you!' They are a stench in my nostrils, an acrid smell that never goes away.

I BELIEVE the Lord accurately foretold that he would punish those Israelites who rejected him and worshiped other gods. (65:6)

⁶"Look, my decree is written out in front of me: I will not stand silent; I will repay them in full! Yes, I will repay them—⁷both for their own sins and for those of their ancestors," says the LORD. "For they also burned incense on the mountains and insulted me on the hills. I will pay them back in full!

I BELIEVE the Lord kept his promise to preserve a remnant of his people Israel to serve him. (65:9)

⁸"But I will not destroy them all," says the LORD. "For just as good grapes are found among a cluster of bad ones (and someone will say, 'Don't throw them all away—there are some good grapes there!'), so I will not destroy all Israel. For I still have true servants there. ⁹I will preserve a remnant of the people of Israel* and of Judah to possess my land. Those I choose will inherit it and serve me there. ¹⁰For my people who have searched for me, the plain of Sharon will again be filled with flocks, and the valley of Achor will be a place to pasture herds.

I LISTEN to the Lord and do not deliberately choose to sin against him. (65:12)

¹¹"But because the rest of you have forsaken the LORD and his Temple and worship the gods of Fate and Destiny, ¹²I will 'destine' you to the sword. All of you will bow before the executioner, for when I called, you did not answer. When I spoke, you did not listen. You deliberately sinned—before my very eyes—and chose to do what you know I despise."

¹³Therefore, this is what the Sovereign LORD says: "You will starve, but my servants will eat. You will be thirsty, but they will drink. You will be sad and ashamed, but they will rejoice. ¹⁴You will cry in sorrow and despair, while my servants sing for joy. ¹⁵Your name will be a curse word among my people, for the Sovereign LORD will destroy you and call his true servants by another name. ¹⁶All who invoke a blessing or take an oath will do so by the God of truth. For I will put aside my anger and forget the evil of earlier days.

I BELIEVE and look forward to the Lord's promise to create new heavens and a new earth (2 Peter 3:13; Revelation 21:1). (65:17)

¹⁷"Look! I am creating new heavens and a new earth—so wonderful that no one will even think about the old ones anymore. ¹⁸Be glad; rejoice forever in my creation! And look! I will create Jerusalem as a place of happiness. Her people will be a source of joy. ¹⁹I will rejoice in Jerusalem and delight in my people. And the sound of weeping and crying will be heard no more.

²⁰"No longer will babies die when only a few days old. No longer will adults die before they have lived a full life. No longer will people be considered old

65:9 Hebrew *remnant of Jacob.*

at one hundred! Only sinners will die that young! ²¹In those days, people will live in the houses they build and eat the fruit of their own vineyards. ²²It will not be like the past, when invaders took the houses and confiscated the vineyards. For my people will live as long as trees and will have time to enjoy their hard-won gains. ²³They will not work in vain, and their children will not be doomed to misfortune. For they are people blessed by the LORD, and their children, too, will be blessed. ²⁴I will answer them before they even call to me. While they are still talking to me about their needs, I will go ahead and answer their prayers! ²⁵The wolf and lamb will feed together. The lion will eat straw like the ox. Poisonous snakes will strike no more. In those days, no one will be hurt or destroyed on my holy mountain. I, the LORD, have spoken!"

CHAPTER 66

This is what the LORD says: "Heaven is my throne, and the earth is my footstool. Could you ever build me a temple as good as that? Could you build a dwelling place for me? ²My hands have made both heaven and earth, and they are mine. I, the LORD, have spoken!

"I will bless those who have humble and contrite hearts, who tremble at my word. ³But those who choose their own ways, delighting in their sins, are cursed. Their offerings will not be accepted. When such people sacrifice an ox, it is no more acceptable than a human sacrifice. When they sacrifice a lamb or bring an offering of grain, it is as bad as putting a dog or the blood of a pig on the altar! When they burn incense, it is as if they had blessed an idol. ⁴I will send great troubles against them—all the things they feared. For when I called, they did not answer. When I spoke, they did not listen. They deliberately sinned—before my very eyes—and chose to do what they know I despise."

⁵Hear this message from the LORD, and tremble at his words: "Your close relatives hate you and throw you out for being loyal to my name. 'Let the LORD be honored!' they scoff. 'Be joyful in him!' But they will be put to shame. ⁶What is all the commotion in the city? What is that terrible noise from the Temple? It is the voice of the LORD taking vengeance against his enemies.

⁷"Before the birth pains even begin, Jerusalem gives birth to a son. ⁸Who has ever seen or heard of anything as strange as this? Has a nation ever been born in a single day? Has a country ever come forth in a mere moment? But by the time Jerusalem's* birth pains begin, the baby will be born; the nation will come forth. ⁹Would I ever bring this nation to the point of birth and then not deliver it?" asks the LORD. "No! I would never keep this nation from being born," says your God.

¹⁰"Rejoice with Jerusalem! Be glad with her, all you who love her and mourn for her. ¹¹Delight in Jerusalem! Drink deeply of her glory even as an infant drinks at its mother's generous breasts. ¹²Peace and prosperity will overflow Jerusalem like a river," says the LORD. "The wealth of the nations will flow to her. Her children will be nursed at her breasts, carried in her arms, and treated with love. ¹³I will comfort you there as a child is comforted by its mother."

¹⁴When you see these things, your heart will rejoice. Vigorous health will be yours! Everyone will see the good hand of the LORD on his people—and his anger against his enemies. ¹⁵See, the LORD is coming with fire, and his swift chariots of destruction roar like a whirlwind. He will bring punishment with the fury of his anger and the flaming fire of his hot rebuke. ¹⁶The LORD

I BELIEVE heaven is the Lord's throne and the earth is his footstool—no person or place can contain him. (66:1)

I TREMBLE at the Lord's Word with a contrite heart and receive his blessing. (66:2)

I BELIEVE the Lord will bring troubles and judgment to those who deliberately reject him. (66:4)

I BELIEVE the Lord kept his promise to bring the nation of Israel back into being suddenly and miraculously. (66:8)

66:8 Hebrew *Zion's.*

will punish the world by fire and by his sword, and many will be killed by the LORD.

¹⁷ "Those who 'purify' themselves in a sacred garden, feasting on pork and rats and other forbidden meats, will come to a terrible end," says the LORD. ¹⁸ "I can see what they are doing, and I know what they are thinking. So I will gather all nations and peoples together, and they will see my glory. ¹⁹ I will perform a sign among them. And I will send those who survive to be messengers to the nations—to Tarshish, to the Libyans* and Lydians* (who are famous as archers), to Tubal and Greece,* and to all the lands beyond the sea that have not heard of my fame or seen my glory. There they will declare my glory to the nations. ²⁰ They will bring the remnant of your people back from every nation. They will bring them to my holy mountain in Jerusalem as an offering to the LORD. They will ride on horses, in chariots and wagons, and on mules and camels," says the LORD. ²¹ "And I will appoint some of those who return to be my priests and Levites. I, the LORD, have spoken!

²² "As surely as my new heavens and earth will remain, so will you always be my people, with a name that will never disappear," says the LORD. ²³ "All humanity will come to worship me from week to week and from month to month. ²⁴ And as they go out, they will see the dead bodies of those who have rebelled against me. For the worms that devour them will never die, and the fire that burns them will never go out. All who pass by will view them with utter horror."

I BELIEVE the Lord one day will cause all humanity to worship him. (66:23)

66:19a As in some Greek manuscripts, which read *Put* [Libya]; Hebrew reads *Pul*.   66:19b Hebrew *Lud*. 66:19c Hebrew *Javan*.

JEREMIAH

THIS SECOND OF FOUR "major" Old Testament prophets urges readers then (and now) to come back to the Lord.

The theme of returning or coming back recurs nearly fifty times in Jeremiah. The prophet urges his fellow citizens in the kingdom of Judah to repent and turn back to the Lord—before it's too late.

The Lord calls Jeremiah to prophesy when he is still a very young man (chapter 1). More than a century has passed since Isaiah began prophesying. The kingdom of Israel had fallen three generations earlier.

Now, the Lord says, it's Judah's turn because of its pride, idolatry, and oppression of the poor. For more than forty years, Jeremiah warns of impending judgment against Judah (chapters 2–38), but virtually no one heeds his warnings to repent.

As predicted, the kingdom of Judah is finally crushed (chapter 39). The surviving remnant refuses to repent and continues to rebel against the Lord (chapters 40–44).

Toward the end of the book, Jeremiah includes a brief warning to his assistant, Baruch (chapter 45), and a series of prophecies against other nations (chapters 46–51).

A historical appendix (chapter 52) adds more details about the complete destruction of Judah's capital, Jerusalem.

Famous verses in Jeremiah abound, including

- ○ "[My people] have forsaken me—the fountain of living water" (2:13)
- ○ "Plow up the hard ground of your hearts!" (4:3)
- ○ Not one person is just and honest; all are corrupt (5:1; 6:28)
- ○ "They give assurances of peace when all is war" (6:14; 8:11)
- ○ The Temple is a den of thieves (7:11)
- ○ "Pray no more for these people, Jeremiah" (7:16; 11:14; see 14:11)
- ○ "The summer is gone . . . yet we are not saved!" (8:20)
- ○ "Let them boast in this alone: that they truly know me" (9:24)
- ○ "Cursed is anyone who does not obey the terms of my covenant!" (11:3)
- ○ "Can a leopard take away its spots? Neither can you start doing good" (13:23)
- ○ "Your words are what sustain me. They bring me great joy" (15:16)
- ○ "The human heart is most deceitful" (17:9)
- ○ "[The Lord's] word burns in my heart like a fire" (20:9; see 23:29)
- ○ "Take your choice of life or death!" (21:8)
- ○ "I will place a righteous Branch on King David's throne" (23:5; see 30:9; 33:14-26)
- ○ Seventy years of Babylonian captivity predicted (25:11-12; 29:10)
- ○ "For I know the plans I have for you" (29:11)
- ○ "I have loved you, my people, with an everlasting love" (31:3)
- ○ "I will make a new covenant" (31:31)

CHAPTER 1

These are the words of Jeremiah son of Hilkiah, one of the priests from Anathoth, a town in the land of Benjamin. ²The LORD first gave messages to Jeremiah during the thirteenth year of King Josiah's reign in Judah.* ³He continued to give messages throughout the reign of Josiah's son, King Jehoiakim, until the eleventh year of King Zedekiah's reign in Judah. In August of that year,* the people of Jerusalem were taken away as captives.

Jeremiah's Call and First Visions

⁴The LORD gave me a message. He said, ⁵"I knew you before I formed you in your mother's womb. Before you were born I set you apart and appointed you as my spokesman to the world."

⁶"O Sovereign LORD," I said, "I can't speak for you! I'm too young!"

⁷"Don't say that," the LORD replied, "for you must go wherever I send you and say whatever I tell you. ⁸And don't be afraid of the people, for I will be with you and take care of you. I, the LORD, have spoken!"

⁹Then the LORD touched my mouth and said, "See, I have put my words in your mouth! ¹⁰Today I appoint you to stand up against nations and kingdoms. You are to uproot some and tear them down, to destroy and overthrow them. You are to build others up and plant them."

¹¹Then the LORD said to me, "Look, Jeremiah! What do you see?"

And I replied, "I see a branch from an almond tree."

¹²And the LORD said, "That's right, and it means that I am watching,* and I will surely carry out my threats of punishment."

¹³Then the LORD spoke to me again and asked, "What do you see now?"

And I replied, "I see a pot of boiling water, tipping from the north."

¹⁴"Yes," the LORD said, "for terror from the north will boil out on the people of this land. ¹⁵Listen! I am calling the armies of the kingdoms of the north to come to Jerusalem. They will set their thrones at the gates of the city. They will attack its walls and all the other towns of Judah. ¹⁶I will pronounce judgment on my people for all their evil—for deserting me and worshiping other gods. Yes, they worship idols that they themselves have made!

¹⁷"Get up and get dressed. Go out, and tell them whatever I tell you to say. Do not be afraid of them, or I will make you look foolish in front of them. ¹⁸For see, today I have made you immune to their attacks. You are strong like a fortified city that cannot be captured, like an iron pillar or a bronze wall. None of the kings, officials, priests, or people of Judah will be able to stand against you. ¹⁹They will try, but they will fail. For I am with you, and I will take care of you. I, the LORD, have spoken!"

CHAPTER 2

The LORD's Case against His People

The LORD gave me another message. He said, ²"Go and shout in Jerusalem's streets: 'This is what the LORD says: I remember how eager you were to please me as a young bride long ago, how you loved me and followed me even through the barren wilderness. ³In those days Israel was holy to the LORD, the first of my children.* All who harmed my people were considered guilty, and disaster fell upon them. I, the LORD, have spoken!' "

⁴Listen to the word of the LORD, people of Jacob—all you families of Israel! ⁵This is what the LORD says: "What sin did your ancestors find in me that led them to stray so far? They worshiped foolish idols, only to become foolish themselves. ⁶They did not ask, 'Where is the LORD who brought us safely

Margin notes (left column):

See Josiah's profile (page 461) at 2 Kings 23:25.

I BELIEVE the Lord knew me long before I was ever conceived in my mother's womb. (1:5)

I AM CONFIDENT that the Lord is with me and will take care of me when I obey his commands. (1:7)

I BELIEVE the Lord will surely carry out his threats of punishment against those who rebel against him. (1:12)

I ABHOR idolatry and pledge never to desert the Lord. (1:16)

I NEVER WANT to lose my love for the Lord (Revelation 2:4–5). (2:2)

See Jacob's profile (page 43) at Genesis 32:9.

1:2 The thirteenth year of Josiah's reign was 627 B.C.   1:3 Hebrew *In the fifth month,* of the Hebrew calendar. A number of events in Jeremiah can be cross-checked with dates in surviving Babylonian records and related accurately to our modern calendar. This month in the eleventh year of Zedekiah's reign occurred in August and September 586 B.C. Also see 52:12 and the note there.   1:12 The Hebrew word for "watching" sounds like the word for "almond tree."   2:3 Hebrew *the firstfruits of his harvest.*

out of Egypt and led us through the barren wilderness—a land of deserts and pits, of drought and death, where no one lives or even travels?'

7"And when I brought you into a fruitful land to enjoy its bounty and goodness, you defiled my land and corrupted the inheritance I had promised you. 8The priests did not ask, 'Where is the LORD?' The judges ignored me, the rulers turned against me, and the prophets spoke in the name of Baal, wasting their time on nonsense. 9Therefore, I will bring my case against you and will keep on accusing you, even against your children's children in the years to come. I, the LORD, have spoken!

I NEVER WANT to take the Lord's blessings for granted. (2:7)

I DO NOT WASTE my time on nonsense, on myths that contradict God's Word. (2:8)

LIKE JEREMIAH

Jeremiah 1:19

I continue to do God's will, even if many oppose me.

Like thousands of army recruits, Jeremiah was drafted into a vocation where ongoing enemy assaults were all but guaranteed. But unlike army soldiers, Jeremiah had the Lord's assurance he would survive.

The Lord enlisted young Jeremiah for life. His only mission? To proclaim the Lord's message without fear.

Sure enough, those who did not want to hear God's truth attacked Jeremiah repeatedly and from every angle. Over the years, his fellow citizens fanned rumors into flame and hoped to watch him burn. Jeremiah's enemies imprisoned him, flogged him, put him in stocks, and made preparations for his execution. Later, they threw him into a muddy cistern and left him to die. Even former friends sought to take their revenge against this man from Anathoth.

Each time, the Lord rescued Jeremiah—but not always before he was scarred. His foes definitely couldn't kill him—but they could wound him. The Lord's promise of protection didn't exclude the possibility of having to endure great pain.

More than once, Jeremiah was tempted to hang up his prophet's hat and go home. He agonized over the prosperity of the wicked while he suffered miserably. He felt so terrible he wished he'd never been born. He wept over his nation's self-destructive rebellion against God and cried out to the Lord because of his own incurable wound.

Like Jeremiah, we are promised persecution (John 15:18-21; 2 Timothy 3:12). Like him, we also can cling to the promise of the Lord's protecting presence (Matthew 28:20; John 16:33). And we can rest assured that while pain and problems are inevitable, they cannot stop us from fulfilling God's will in this generation (Romans 8:35-39).

○ *Today's Scripture reading is Jeremiah 1, 18, and 32.*

10"Go west to the land of Cyprus*; go east to the land of Kedar. Think about what you see there. See if anyone has ever heard of anything as strange as this. 11Has any nation ever exchanged its gods for another god, even though its gods are nothing? Yet my people have exchanged their glorious God* for worthless idols! 12The heavens are shocked at such a thing and shrink back in horror and dismay, says the LORD. 13For my people have done two evil things: They have forsaken me—the fountain of living water. And they have dug for themselves cracked cisterns that can hold no water at all!

I DO NOT SUBSTITUTE any god or philosophy for the Lord (Romans 1:23). (2:11)

The Results of Israel's Sin

14"Why has Israel become a nation of slaves? Why has she been carried away as plunder? 15Lions have roared against her. The land has been destroyed, and the cities are now in ruins. No one lives in them anymore. 16Egyptians, marching from their cities of Memphis* and Tahpanhes, have utterly destroyed Israel's glory and power. 17And you have brought this on yourselves by rebelling against the LORD your God when he wanted to lead you and show you the way!

I DO NOT REBEL against the Lord's Word and ways. (2:17)

2:10 Hebrew *Kittim.*   2:11 Hebrew *their Glory.*   2:16 Hebrew *Noph.*

¹⁸"What have you gained by your alliances with Egypt and Assyria? What good to you are the waters of the Nile* and the Euphrates*? ¹⁹Your own wickedness will punish you. You will see what an evil, bitter thing it is to forsake the LORD your God, having no fear of him. I, the Lord, the LORD Almighty, have spoken! ²⁰Long ago I broke your yoke and tore away the chains of your slavery, but still you would not obey me. On every hill and under every green tree, you have prostituted yourselves by bowing down to idols.

²¹"How could this happen? When I planted you, I chose a vine of the purest stock—the very best. How did you grow into this corrupt wild vine? ²²No amount of soap or lye can make you clean. You are stained with guilt that cannot be washed away. I, the Sovereign LORD, have spoken!

Israel, an Unfaithful Wife

²³"You say, 'That's not true! We haven't worshiped the images of Baal!' But how can you say that? Go and look in any valley in the land! Face the awful sins you have done. You are like a restless female camel, desperate for a male! ²⁴You are like a wild donkey, sniffing the wind at mating time. Who can restrain your lust? Those who desire you do not even need to search, for you come running to them! ²⁵Why do you refuse to turn from all this running after other gods? But you say, 'Don't waste your breath. I have fallen in love with these foreign gods, and I can't stop loving them now!'

²⁶"Like a thief, Israel feels shame only when she gets caught. Kings, officials, priests, and prophets—all are alike in this. ²⁷To an image carved from a piece of wood they say, 'You are my father.' To an idol chiseled out of stone they say, 'You are my mother.' They turn their backs on me, but in times of trouble they cry out for me to save them! ²⁸Why don't you call on these gods you have made? When danger comes, let them save you if they can! For you have as many gods as there are cities and towns in Judah. ²⁹Why do you accuse me of doing wrong? You are the ones who have rebelled, says the LORD. ³⁰I have punished your children, but it did them no good. They still refuse to obey. You yourselves have killed your prophets as a lion kills its prey.

³¹"O my people, listen to the words of the LORD! Have I been like a desert to Israel? Have I been to them a land of darkness? Why then do my people say, 'At last we are free from God! We won't have anything to do with him anymore!' ³²Does a young woman forget her jewelry? Does a bride hide her wedding dress? No! Yet for years on end my people have forgotten me.

³³"How you plot and scheme to win your lovers. The most experienced prostitute could learn from you! ³⁴Your clothing is stained with the blood of the innocent and the poor. You killed them even though they didn't break into your houses! ³⁵And yet you say, 'I haven't done anything wrong. Surely he isn't angry with me!' Now I will punish you severely because you claim you have not sinned.

³⁶"First here, then there—you flit from one ally to another asking for help. But your new friends in Egypt will let you down, just as Assyria did before. ³⁷In despair, you will be led into exile with your hands on your heads, for the LORD has rejected the nations you trust. You will not succeed despite their help.

CHAPTER **3**

"If a man divorces a woman and she marries someone else, he is not to take her back again, for that would surely corrupt the land. But you have prostituted yourself with many lovers, says the LORD. Yet I am still calling you to come back to me.

²"Look all around you. Is there anywhere in the entire land where you have not been defiled by your adulteries? You sit like a prostitute beside the

---

I BELIEVE forgiveness and cleansing come only from the Lord (1 John 1:9). (2:22)

I DO NOT REFUSE to obey the Lord. (2:30)

I ACKNOWLEDGE when I have sinned against the Lord (1 John 1:8-10). (2:35)

2:18a Hebrew *of Shihor*, a branch of the Nile River.   2:18b Hebrew *the river*.

road waiting for a client. You sit alone like a nomad in the desert. You have polluted the land with your prostitution and wickedness. ³That is why even the spring rains have failed. For you are a prostitute and are completely unashamed. ⁴Yet you say to me, 'Father, you have been my guide since the days of my youth. ⁵Surely you won't be angry about such a little thing! Surely you can forget it!' So you talk, and keep right on doing all the evil you can."

Judah Follows Israel's Example

⁶During the reign of King Josiah, the LORD said to me, "Have you seen what fickle Israel does? Like a wife who commits adultery, Israel has worshiped other gods on every hill and under every green tree. ⁷I thought that after she had done all this she would return to me. But she did not come back. And though her faithless sister Judah saw this, ⁸she paid no attention. She saw that I had divorced faithless Israel and sent her away. But now Judah, too, has left me and given herself to prostitution. ⁹Israel treated it all so lightly—she thought nothing of committing adultery by worshiping idols made of wood and stone. So now the land has been greatly defiled. ¹⁰But in spite of all this, her faithless sister Judah has never sincerely returned to me. She has only pretended to be sorry," says the LORD.

Hope for Wayward Israel

¹¹Then the LORD said to me, "Even faithless Israel is less guilty than treacherous Judah! ¹²Therefore, go and say these words to Israel,* 'This is what the LORD says: O Israel, my faithless people, come home to me again, for I am merciful. I will not be angry with you forever. ¹³Only acknowledge your guilt. Admit that you rebelled against the LORD your God and committed adultery against him by worshiping idols under every green tree. Confess that you refused to follow me. I, the LORD, have spoken!' "

¹⁴"Return home, you wayward children," says the LORD, "for I am your husband. I will bring you again to the land of Israel*—one from here and two from there, from wherever you are scattered. ¹⁵And I will give you leaders after my own heart, who will guide you with knowledge and understanding.

¹⁶"And when your land is once more filled with people," says the LORD, "you will no longer wish for 'the good old days' when you possessed the Ark of the LORD's covenant. Those days will not be missed or even thought about, and there will be no need to rebuild the Ark. ¹⁷In that day Jerusalem will be known as The Throne of the LORD. All nations will come there to honor the LORD. They will no longer stubbornly follow their own evil desires. ¹⁸In those days the people of Judah and Israel will return together from exile in the north. They will return to the land I gave their ancestors as an inheritance forever.

¹⁹"I thought to myself, 'I would love to treat you as my own children!' I wanted nothing more than to give you this beautiful land—the finest inheritance in the world. I looked forward to your calling me 'Father,' and I thought you would never turn away from me again. ²⁰But you have betrayed me, you people of Israel! You have been like a faithless wife who leaves her husband," says the LORD.

²¹Voices are heard high on the windswept mountains, the weeping and pleading of Israel's people. For they have forgotten the LORD their God and wandered far from his ways.

²²"My wayward children," says the LORD, "come back to me, and I will heal your wayward hearts."

"Yes, we will come," the people reply, "for you are the LORD our God. ²³Our worship of idols and our religious orgies on the hills and mountains are completely false. Only in the LORD our God will Israel ever find salvation.

I DO NOT PRETEND that sin doesn't matter. (3:5)

See Josiah's profile (page 461) at 2 Kings 23:25.

I PAY ATTENTION to the consequences of sin. (3:8)

I REPENT honestly before the Lord and don't pretend to be sorry for my sins. (3:10)

Recommit yourself to loving the Lord with all your heart, soul, strength, and mind.

I BELIEVE the Lord is calling people from all nations to honor him. (3:17)

I NEVER WANT to forget the Lord my God and wander from his ways. (3:21)

3:12 Hebrew *toward the north.*   3:14 Hebrew *to Zion.*

²⁴From childhood we have watched as everything our ancestors worked for—their flocks and herds, their sons and daughters—was squandered on a delusion. ²⁵Let us now lie down in shame and dishonor, for we and our ancestors have always sinned against the LORD our God. We have never obeyed him."

CHAPTER 4

"O Israel, come back to me," says the LORD. "If you will throw away your detestable idols and go astray no more, ²and if you will swear by my name alone, and begin to live good, honest lives and uphold justice, then you will be a blessing to the nations of the world, and all people will come and praise my name."

Coming Judgment against Judah

³This is what the LORD says to the people of Judah and Jerusalem: "Plow up the hard ground of your hearts! Do not waste your good seed among thorns. ⁴Cleanse your minds and hearts before the LORD, or my anger will burn like an unquenchable fire because of all your sins.

⁵"Shout to Jerusalem and to all Judah! Tell them to sound the alarm throughout the land: 'Run for your lives! Flee to the fortified cities!' ⁶Send a signal toward Jerusalem*: 'Flee now! Do not delay!' For I am bringing terrible destruction upon you from the north."

⁷A lion stalks from its den, a destroyer of nations. And it is headed for your land! Your towns will lie in ruins, empty of people. ⁸So put on clothes of mourning and weep with broken hearts, for the fierce anger of the LORD is still upon us.

⁹"In that day," says the LORD, "the king and the officials will tremble in fear. The priests and the prophets will be struck with horror."

¹⁰Then I said, "O Sovereign LORD, the people have been deceived by what you said, for you promised peace for Jerusalem. Yet the sword is even now poised to strike them dead!"

¹¹The time is coming when the LORD will say to the people of Jerusalem, "A burning wind is blowing in from the desert. It is not a gentle breeze useful for winnowing grain. ¹²It is a roaring blast sent by me! Now I will pronounce your destruction!"

¹³Our enemy rushes down on us like a storm wind! His chariots are like whirlwinds; his horses are swifter than eagles. How terrible it will be! Our destruction is sure! ¹⁴O Jerusalem, cleanse your hearts that you may be saved. How long will you harbor your evil thoughts? ¹⁵From Dan and the hill country of Ephraim, your destruction has been announced.

¹⁶"Warn the surrounding nations and announce to Jerusalem: 'The enemy is coming from a distant land, raising a battle cry against the towns of Judah. ¹⁷They surround Jerusalem like watchmen surrounding a field, for my people have rebelled against me,' " says the LORD. ¹⁸"Your own actions have brought this upon you. This punishment is a bitter dose of your own medicine. It has pierced you to the heart!"

Jeremiah Weeps for His People

¹⁹My heart, my heart—I writhe in pain! My heart pounds within me! I cannot be still. For I have heard the blast of enemy trumpets and the roar of their battle cries. ²⁰Waves of destruction roll over the land, until it lies in complete desolation. Suddenly, every tent is destroyed; in a moment, every shelter is crushed. ²¹How long must this go on? How long must I be surrounded by war and death?

²²"My people are foolish and do not know me," says the LORD. "They are

I BELIEVE the Lord wanted the Israelites to be a blessing to the nations of the world (Genesis 12:3). (4:2)

I AM BROKENHEARTED and mourn when I realize I have been persistently sinning against the Lord (James 4:9-10). (4:8)

I DO NOT LISTEN to false prophets who pretend to speak for the Lord (Jeremiah 23:16-17). (4:10)

I ASK the Lord to cleanse my heart from evil thoughts. (4:14)

I WEEP when I think of the coming judgment against those who won't stop rebelling against the Lord. (4:19)

4:6 Hebrew Zion.

senseless children who have no understanding. They are clever enough at doing wrong, but they have no talent at all for doing right!"

Jeremiah's Vision of Coming Disaster

²³I looked at the earth, and it was empty and formless. I looked at the heavens, and there was no light. ²⁴I looked at the mountains and hills, and they trembled and shook. ²⁵I looked, and all the people were gone. All the birds of the sky had flown away. ²⁶I looked, and the fertile fields had become a wilderness. The cities lay in ruins, crushed by the LORD's fierce anger.

²⁷This is what the LORD says: "The whole land will be ruined, but I will not destroy it completely. ²⁸The earth will mourn, the heavens will be draped in black, because of my decree against my people. I have made up my mind and will not change it."

²⁹At the noise of marching armies, the people flee in terror from the cities. They hide in the bushes and run for the mountains. All the cities have been abandoned—not a person remains! ³⁰What are you doing, you who have been plundered? Why do you dress up in your most beautiful clothing and jewelry? Why do you brighten your eyes with mascara? It will do you no good! Your allies despise you and will kill you.

³¹I hear a great cry, like that of a woman giving birth to her first child. It is the cry of Jerusalem's people* gasping for breath, pleading for help, prostrate before their murderers.

CHAPTER 5

The Sins of Judah

"Run up and down every street in Jerusalem," says the LORD. "Look high and low; search throughout the city! If you can find even one person who is just and honest, I will not destroy the city. ²Even when they are under oath, saying, 'As surely as the LORD lives,' they all tell lies!"

³LORD, you are searching for honesty. You struck your people, but they paid no attention. You crushed them, but they refused to turn from sin. They are determined, with faces set like stone; they have refused to repent.

⁴Then I said, "But what can we expect from the poor and ignorant? They don't know the ways of the LORD. They don't understand what God expects of them. ⁵I will go and speak to their leaders. Surely they will know the LORD's ways and what God requires of them." But the leaders, too, had utterly rejected their God. ⁶So now a lion from the forest will attack them; a wolf from the desert will pounce on them. A leopard will lurk near their towns, tearing apart any who dare to venture out. For their rebellion is great, and their sins are many.

⁷"How can I pardon you? For even your children have turned from me. They have sworn by gods that are not gods at all! I fed my people until they were fully satisfied. But they thanked me by committing adultery and lining up at the city's brothels. ⁸They are well-fed, lusty stallions, each neighing for his neighbor's wife. ⁹Should I not punish them for this?" asks the LORD. "Should I not avenge myself against a nation such as this?

¹⁰"Go down the rows of the vineyards and destroy them, but leave a scattered few alive. Strip the branches from the vine, for they do not belong to the LORD. ¹¹The people of Israel and Judah are full of treachery against me," says the LORD. ¹²"They have lied about the LORD and have said, 'He won't bother us! No disasters will come upon us! There will be no war or famine! ¹³God's prophets are windbags full of words with no divine authority. Their predictions of disaster will fall on themselves!'"

¹⁴Therefore, this is what the LORD God Almighty says: "Because the people are talking like this, I will give you messages that will burn them up as if they

4:31 Hebrew *the daughter of Zion.*

I WANT to become talented at doing right and stay innocent of doing wrong (Romans 16:19). (4:22)

I BELIEVE all have sinned (Romans 3:23). (5:2)

I DO NOT LIE about the Lord and contradict his Word. (5:12)

I BELIEVE the Lord's prophets spoke with divine authority (2 Peter 1:20-21). (5:13)

were kindling wood. ¹⁵O Israel, I will bring a distant nation against you," says the LORD. "It is a mighty nation, an ancient nation, a people whose language you do not know, whose speech you cannot understand. ¹⁶Their weapons are deadly; their warriors are mighty. ¹⁷They will eat your harvests and your children's bread, your flocks of sheep and your herds of cattle. Yes, they will eat your grapes and figs. And they will destroy your fortified cities, which you think are so safe.

¹⁸"Yet even in those days I will not blot you out completely," says the LORD. ¹⁹"And when your people ask, 'Why is the LORD our God doing this to us?' you must reply, 'You rejected him and gave yourselves to foreign gods in your own land. Now you will serve foreigners in a land that is not your own.'

A Warning for God's People

²⁰"Make this announcement to Israel* and to Judah: ²¹Listen, you foolish and senseless people—who have eyes but do not see, who have ears but do not hear. ²²Do you have no respect for me? Why do you not tremble in my presence? I, the LORD, am the one who defines the ocean's sandy shoreline, an everlasting boundary that the waters cannot cross. The waves may toss and roar, but they can never pass the bounds I set.

²³"But my people have stubborn and rebellious hearts. They have turned against me and have chosen to practice idolatry. ²⁴They do not say from the heart, 'Let us live in awe of the LORD our God, for he gives us rain each spring and fall, assuring us of plentiful harvests.' ²⁵Your wickedness has deprived you of these wonderful blessings. Your sin has robbed you of all these good things.

²⁶"Among my people are wicked men who lie in wait for victims like a hunter hiding in a blind. They are continually setting traps for other people. ²⁷Like a cage filled with birds, their homes are filled with evil plots. And the result? Now they are great and rich. ²⁸They are well fed and well groomed, and there is no limit to their wicked deeds. They refuse justice to orphans and deny the rights of the poor. ²⁹Should I not punish them for this?" asks the LORD. "Should I not avenge myself against a nation such as this?

³⁰"A horrible and shocking thing has happened in this land—³¹the prophets give false prophecies, and the priests rule with an iron hand. And worse yet, my people like it that way! But what will you do when the end comes?

CHAPTER 6

Jerusalem's Last Warning

"Run for your lives, you people of Benjamin! Flee from Jerusalem! Sound the alarm in Tekoa! Send up a signal at Beth-hakkerem! Warn everyone that a powerful army is coming from the north to destroy this nation. ²O Jerusalem,* you are my beautiful and delicate daughter—but I will destroy you! ³Enemy shepherds will surround you. They will set up camp around the city and divide your pastures for their flocks. ⁴They shout, 'Prepare for battle and attack at noon! But now the day is fading, and the evening shadows are falling. ⁵So let us attack by night and destroy her palaces!' "

⁶This is what the LORD Almighty says: "Cut down the trees for battering rams. Build ramps against the walls of Jerusalem. This is the city to be punished, for she is wicked through and through. ⁷She spouts evil like a fountain! Her streets echo with the sounds of violence and destruction. Her sickness and sores are ever before me. ⁸This is your last warning, Jerusalem! If you do not listen, I will empty the land."

⁹This is what the LORD Almighty says: "Disaster will fall upon you. Even the few who remain in Israel will be gleaned again, as when a harvester checks each vine a second time to pick the grapes that were missed."

I LIVE in awe of the Lord my God. (5:24)

I UPHOLD the rights of the poor and needy. (5:28)

I GRIEVE when religious leaders abuse their authority. (5:31)

I BELIEVE that those who won't stop rebelling against the Lord face sure judgment. (6:6)

5:20 Hebrew *to the house of Jacob.*   6:2 Hebrew *Zion.*

Israel's Constant Rebellion

¹⁰To whom can I give warning? Who will listen when I speak? Their ears are closed, and they cannot hear. They scorn the word of the LORD. They don't want to listen at all. ¹¹So now I am filled with the LORD's fury. Yes, I am weary of holding it in!

"I will pour out my fury over Jerusalem, even on children playing in the streets, on gatherings of young men, and on husbands and wives and grandparents. ¹²Their homes will be turned over to their enemies, and so will their fields and their wives. For I will punish the people of this land," says the LORD.

¹³"From the least to the greatest, they trick others to get what does not belong to them. Yes, even my prophets and priests are like that! ¹⁴They offer superficial treatments for my people's mortal wound. They give assurances of peace when all is war. ¹⁵Are they ashamed when they do these disgusting things? No, not at all—they don't even blush! Therefore, they will lie among the slaughtered. They will be humbled beneath my punishing anger," says the LORD.

Israel Rejects the LORD's Way

¹⁶So now the LORD says, "Stop right where you are! Look for the old, godly way, and walk in it. Travel its path, and you will find rest for your souls. But you reply, 'No, that's not the road we want!' ¹⁷I set watchmen over you who said, 'Listen for the sound of the trumpet!' But you replied, 'No! We won't pay attention!'

¹⁸"Therefore, listen to this, all you nations. Take note of my people's condition. ¹⁹Listen, all the earth! I will bring disaster upon my people. It is the fruit of their own sin because they refuse to listen to me. They have rejected all my instructions. ²⁰There is no use now in offering me sweet incense from Sheba. Keep your expensive perfumes! I cannot accept your burnt offerings. Your sacrifices have no sweet fragrance for me."

²¹Therefore, this is what the LORD says: "I will put obstacles in my people's path. Fathers and sons will both fall over them. Neighbors and friends will collapse together."

An Invasion from the North

²²This is what the LORD says: "See a great army marching from the north! A great nation is rising against you from far-off lands. ²³They are fully armed for slaughter. They are cruel and show no mercy. As they ride forward, the noise of their army is like a roaring sea. They are marching in battle formation to destroy you, Jerusalem.*"

²⁴We have heard reports about the enemy, and we are weak with fright. Fear and pain have gripped us, like that of a woman about to give birth. ²⁵Don't go out to the fields! Don't travel the roads! The enemy is everywhere, and they are ready to kill. We are terrorized at every turn! ²⁶Now my people, dress yourselves in sackcloth, and sit among the ashes. Mourn and weep bitterly, as for the loss of an only son. For suddenly, the destroying armies will be upon you!

²⁷"Jeremiah, I have made you a tester of metals, that you may determine the quality of my people. ²⁸Are they not the worst of rebels, full of slander? They are as insolent as bronze, as hard and cruel as iron. All of them lead others into corruption. ²⁹The bellows blow fiercely. The refining fire grows hotter. But it will never purify and cleanse them because there is no purity in them to refine. ³⁰I will label them 'Rejected Silver' because I, the LORD, am discarding them."

6:23 Hebrew *daughter of Zion.*

I ALWAYS WANT to have eyes to see and ears to hear the Word of the Lord. (6:10)

I DO NOT USE deception to get what I want. (6:13)

I FIND rest for my soul by continually going back to God's Word and obeying what it says. (6:16)

I AM BROKENHEARTED and mourn when I realize I have been persistently sinning against the Lord (James 4:9-10). (6:26)

CHAPTER 7

Jeremiah Speaks at the Temple

The LORD gave another message to Jeremiah. He said, ²"Go to the entrance of the LORD's Temple, and give this message to the people: 'O Judah, listen to this message from the LORD! Listen to it, all of you who worship here! ³The LORD Almighty, the God of Israel, says: Even now, if you quit your evil ways, I will let you stay in your own land. ⁴But do not be fooled by those who repeatedly promise your safety because the Temple of the LORD is here. ⁵I will be merciful only if you stop your wicked thoughts and deeds and are fair to others; ⁶and if you stop exploiting foreigners, orphans, and widows; and if you stop your murdering; and if you stop worshiping idols as you now do to your own harm. ⁷Then I will let you stay in this land that I gave to your ancestors to keep forever.

⁸" 'Do you think that because the Temple is here you will never suffer? Don't fool yourselves! ⁹Do you really think you can steal, murder, commit adultery, lie, and worship Baal and all those other new gods of yours, ¹⁰and then come here and stand before me in my Temple and chant, "We are safe!"—only to go right back to all those evils again? ¹¹Do you think this Temple, which honors my name, is a den of thieves? I see all the evil going on there, says the LORD.

¹²" 'Go to the place at Shiloh where I once put the Tabernacle to honor my name. See what I did there because of all the wickedness of my people, the Israelites. ¹³While you were doing these wicked things, says the LORD, I spoke to you about it repeatedly, but you would not listen. I called out to you, but you refused to answer. ¹⁴So just as I destroyed Shiloh, I will now destroy this Temple that was built to honor my name, this Temple that you trust for help, this place that I gave to you and your ancestors. ¹⁵And I will send you into exile, just as I did your relatives, the people of Israel.*'

Judah's Persistent Idolatry

¹⁶"Pray no more for these people, Jeremiah. Do not weep or pray for them, and don't beg me to help them, for I will not listen to you. ¹⁷Do you not see what they are doing throughout the towns of Judah and in the streets of Jerusalem? ¹⁸No wonder I am so angry! Watch how the children gather wood and the fathers build sacrificial fires. See how the women knead dough and make cakes to offer to the Queen of Heaven. And they give drink offerings to their other idol gods! ¹⁹Am I the one they are hurting?" asks the LORD. "Most of all, they hurt themselves, to their own shame."

²⁰So the Sovereign LORD says: "I will pour out my terrible fury on this place. Its people, animals, trees, and crops will be consumed by the unquenchable fire of my anger."

²¹This is what the LORD Almighty, the God of Israel, says: "Away with your burnt offerings and sacrifices! Eat them yourselves! ²²When I led your ancestors out of Egypt, it was not burnt offerings and sacrifices I wanted from them. ²³This is what I told them: 'Obey me, and I will be your God, and you will be my people. Only do as I say, and all will be well!'

²⁴"But my people would not listen to me. They kept on doing whatever they wanted, following the stubborn desires of their evil hearts. They went backward instead of forward. ²⁵From the day your ancestors left Egypt until now, I have continued to send my prophets—day in and day out. ²⁶But my people have not listened to me or even tried to hear. They have been stubborn and sinful—even worse than their ancestors.

²⁷"Tell them all this, but do not expect them to listen. Shout out your warnings, but do not expect them to respond. ²⁸Say to them, 'This is the nation whose people will not obey the LORD their God and who refuse to be taught.

Side notes:
I FIX my thoughts on doing what is true and honorable and right (Philippians 4:8). (7:5)

I CARE for foreigners, orphans, and widows and refuse to let the world corrupt me (James 1:27). (7:6)

I LISTEN to the Lord's warnings and repent of my sins. (7:13)

I BELIEVE idolatry degrades those who practice it. (7:19)

I OBEY the Lord and love him with all of my heart (Mark 12:32-34). (7:23)

I OBEY the Lord and tell others what he has said. (7:28)

7:15 Hebrew *of Ephraim*, referring to the northern kingdom of Israel.

Truth has vanished from among them; it is no longer heard on their lips. ²⁹O Jerusalem, shave your head in mourning, and weep alone on the mountains. For the LORD has rejected and forsaken this generation that has provoked his fury.'

The Valley of Slaughter

³⁰"The people of Judah have sinned before my very eyes," says the LORD. "They have set up their abominable idols right in my own Temple, defiling it. ³¹They have built the pagan shrines of Topheth in the valley of the son of Hinnom, where they sacrifice their little sons and daughters in the fire. I have never commanded such a horrible deed; it never even crossed my mind to command such a thing! ³²So beware, for the time is coming," says the LORD, "when that place will no longer be called Topheth or the valley of the son of Hinnom, but the Valley of Slaughter. They will bury so many bodies in Topheth that there won't be room for all the graves. ³³The corpses of my people will be food for the vultures and wild animals, and no one will be left to scare them away. ³⁴I will put an end to the happy singing and laughter in the streets of Jerusalem. The joyful voices of bridegrooms and brides will no longer be heard in the towns of Judah. The land will lie in complete desolation.

I ABHOR child sacrifice. (7:31)

CHAPTER 8

"In that day," says the LORD, "the enemy will break open the graves of the kings and officials of Judah, and the graves of the priests, prophets, and common people. ²They will dig out their bones and spread them out on the ground before the sun, moon, and stars—the gods my people have loved, served, and worshiped. Their bones will not be gathered up again or buried but will be scattered on the ground like dung. ³And the people of this evil nation who survive will wish to die rather than live where I will send them. I, the LORD Almighty, have spoken!

Deception by False Prophets

⁴"Jeremiah, say to the people, 'This is what the LORD says: When people fall down, don't they get up again? When they start down the wrong road and discover their mistake, don't they turn back? ⁵Then why do these people keep going along their self-destructive path, refusing to turn back, even though I have warned them? ⁶I listen to their conversations, and what do I hear? Is anyone sorry for sin? Does anyone say, "What a terrible thing I have done"? No! All are running down the path of sin as swiftly as a horse rushing into battle! ⁷The stork knows the time of her migration, as do the turtledove, the swallow, and the crane.* They all return at the proper time each year. But not my people! They do not know what the LORD requires of them.

I REPENT when I realize I've sinned against the Lord. (8:5)

⁸" 'How can you say, "We are wise because we have the law of the LORD," when your teachers have twisted it so badly? ⁹These wise teachers will be shamed by exile for their sin, for they have rejected the word of the LORD. Are they so wise after all? ¹⁰I will give their wives and their farms to others. From the least to the greatest, they trick others to get what does not belong to them. Yes, even my prophets and priests are like that. ¹¹They offer superficial treatments for my people's mortal wound. They give assurances of peace when all is war. ¹²Are they ashamed when they do these disgusting things? No, not at all—they don't even blush! Therefore, they will lie among the slaughtered. They will be humbled when they are punished, says the LORD. ¹³I will take away their rich harvests of figs and grapes. Their fruit trees will all die. All the good things I prepared for them will soon be gone. I, the LORD, have spoken!'

I DO NOT TWIST God's Word or reject what he has said. (8:8)

¹⁴"Then the people will say, 'Why should we wait here to die? Come, let's

I BELIEVE that those who won't stop rebelling against the Lord face sure judgment. (8:13)

8:7 The identification of some of these birds is uncertain.

go to the fortified cities to die there. For the LORD our God has decreed our destruction and has given us a cup of poison to drink because we sinned against the LORD. [15]We hoped for peace, but no peace came. We hoped for a time of healing, but found only terror. [16]The snorting of the enemies' warhorses can be heard all the way from the land of Dan in the north! The whole land trembles at the approach of the terrible army, for it is coming to devour the land and everything in it—cities and people alike.'

[17]"I will send these enemy troops among you like poisonous snakes you cannot charm," says the LORD. "No matter what you do, they will bite you, and you will die."

Jeremiah Weeps for Sinful Judah

I WEEP when I think of the coming judgment against those who won't stop rebelling against the Lord. (8:18)

[18]My grief is beyond healing; my heart is broken. [19]Listen to the weeping of my people; it can be heard all across the land.

"Has the LORD abandoned Jerusalem*?" the people ask. "Is her King no longer there?"

"Oh, why have they angered me with their carved idols and worthless gods?" asks the LORD.

[20]"The harvest is finished, and the summer is gone," the people cry, "yet we are not saved!"

[21]I weep for the hurt of my people. I am stunned and silent, mute with grief. [22]Is there no medicine in Gilead? Is there no physician there? Why is there no healing for the wounds of my people?

CHAPTER 9

Oh, that my eyes were a fountain of tears; I would weep forever! I would sob day and night for all my people who have been slaughtered. [2]Oh, that I could go away and forget them and live in a shack in the desert, for they are all adulterous and treacherous.

Judgment for Disobedience

I STAND UP for what is right. (9:3)

[3]"My people bend their tongues like bows to shoot lies. They refuse to stand up for the truth. And they only go from bad to worse! They care nothing for me," says the LORD.

I CONSISTENTLY TELL the truth, not lies. (9:5)

[4]"Beware of your neighbor! Beware of your brother! They all take advantage of one another and spread their slanderous lies. [5]They all fool and defraud each other; no one tells the truth. With practiced tongues they tell lies; they wear themselves out with all their sinning. [6]They pile lie upon lie and utterly refuse to come to me," says the LORD.

[7]Therefore, the LORD Almighty says, "See, I will melt them in a crucible and test them like metal. What else can I do with them? [8]For their tongues aim lies like poisoned arrows. They promise peace to their neighbors while planning to kill them. [9]Should I not punish them for this?" asks the LORD. "Should I not avenge myself against a nation such as this?"

[10]I will weep for the mountains and wail for the desert pastures. For they are desolate and empty of life; the lowing of cattle is heard no more; the birds and wild animals all have fled.

[11]"I will make Jerusalem into a heap of ruins," says the LORD. "It will be a place haunted by jackals. The towns of Judah will be ghost towns, with no one living in them."

[12]Who is wise enough to understand all this? Who has been instructed by the LORD and can explain it to others? Why has the land been ruined so completely that no one even dares to travel through it?

I CHERISH God's Word and obey his commands. (9:13)

[13]The LORD replies, "This has happened because my people have abandoned the instructions I gave them; they have refused to obey my law.

8:19 Hebrew Zion.

[14]Instead, they have stubbornly followed their own desires and worshiped the images of Baal, as their ancestors taught them. [15]So now, listen to what the LORD Almighty, the God of Israel, says: Look! I will feed them with bitterness and give them poison to drink. [16]I will scatter them around the world, and they will be strangers in distant lands. Their enemies will chase them with the sword until I have destroyed them completely."

Weeping in Jerusalem

[17]This is what the LORD Almighty says: "Think about what is going on! Call for the mourners to come. [18]Quick! Begin your weeping! Let the tears flow from your eyes. [19]Hear the people of Jerusalem* crying in despair, 'We are ruined! Disaster has come upon us! We must leave our land, because our homes have been torn down.' "

> I WEEP when I think of the coming judgment against those who won't stop rebelling against the Lord. (9:17)

[20]Listen, you women, to the words of the LORD; open your ears to what he has to say. Teach your daughters to wail; teach one another how to lament. [21]For death has crept in through our windows and has entered our mansions. It has killed off the flower of our youth: Children no longer play in the streets, and young men no longer gather in the squares. [22]And the LORD says, "Bodies will be scattered across the fields like dung, or like bundles of grain after the harvest. No one will be left to bury them."

[23]This is what the LORD says: "Let not the wise man gloat in his wisdom, or the mighty man in his might, or the rich man in his riches. [24]Let them boast in this alone: that they truly know me and understand that I am the LORD who is just and righteous, whose love is unfailing, and that I delight in these things. I, the LORD, have spoken!

> I KNOW that the Lord is just and righteous and that his love never fails. (9:24)

[25]"A time is coming," says the LORD, "when I will punish all those who are circumcised in body but not in spirit—[26]the Egyptians, Edomites, Ammonites, Moabites, the people who live in distant places,* and yes, even the people of Judah. Like all these pagan nations, the people of Israel also have uncircumcised hearts."

CHAPTER 10

Idolatry Brings Destruction

Hear the word of the LORD, O Israel! [2]This is what the LORD says: "Do not act like other nations who try to read their future in the stars. Do not be afraid of their predictions, even though other nations are terrified by them. [3]Their ways are futile and foolish. They cut down a tree and carve an idol. [4]They decorate it with gold and silver and then fasten it securely with hammer and nails so it won't fall over. [5]There stands their god like a helpless scarecrow in a garden! It cannot speak, and it needs to be carried because it cannot walk. Do not be afraid of such gods, for they can neither harm you nor do you any good."

> I ABHOR astrology and fortune-telling. (10:2)

[6]LORD, there is no one like you! For you are great, and your name is full of power. [7]Who would not fear you, O King of nations? That title belongs to you alone! Among all the wise people of the earth and in all the kingdoms of the world, there is no one like you.

> I WORSHIP the Lord, who is the great and mighty King of kings. (10:6)

[8]The wisest of people who worship idols are stupid and foolish. The things they worship are made of wood! [9]They bring beaten sheets of silver from Tarshish and gold from Uphaz, and they give these materials to skillful craftsmen who make their idols. Then they dress these gods in royal purple robes made by expert tailors. [10]But the LORD is the only true God, the living God. He is the everlasting King! The whole earth trembles at his anger. The nations hide before his wrath.

> I WORSHIP the Lord, who is the only true God. (10:10)

[11]Say this to those who worship other gods: "Your so-called gods, who did not make the heavens and earth, will vanish from the earth."*

9:19 Hebrew *Zion.*   **9:26** Or *the people who clip the corners of their hair.*   **10:11** The original text of this verse is in Aramaic.

¹² But God made the earth by his power,
and he preserves it by his wisdom.
He has stretched out the heavens
by his understanding.
¹³ When he speaks, there is thunder in the heavens.
He causes the clouds to rise over the earth.
He sends the lightning with the rain
and releases the wind from his storehouses.
¹⁴ Compared to him, all people are foolish
and have no knowledge at all!
They make idols, but the idols will disgrace their makers,
for they are frauds.
They have no life or power in them.
¹⁵ Idols are worthless; they are lies!
The time is coming when they will all be destroyed.
¹⁶ But the God of Israel* is no idol!
He is the Creator of everything that exists,
including Israel, his own special possession.
The LORD Almighty is his name!

I WORSHIP the Lord, who is the Creator of the heavens and earth. (10:16)

The Coming Destruction

¹⁷ "Pack your bag and prepare to leave; the siege is about to begin," ¹⁸says the LORD. "For suddenly, I will fling you from this land and pour great troubles upon you. At last you will feel my anger."

¹⁹ My wound is desperate, and my grief is great. My sickness is incurable, but I must bear it. ²⁰My home is gone, and no one is left to help me rebuild it. My children have been taken away, and I will never see them again. ²¹The shepherds of my people have lost their senses. They no longer follow the LORD or ask what he wants of them. Therefore, they fail completely, and their flocks are scattered. ²²Listen! Hear the terrifying roar of great armies as they roll down from the north. The towns of Judah will be destroyed and will become a haunt for jackals.

I FOLLOW the Lord and ask what he wants of me. (10:21)

Jeremiah's Prayer

²³ I know, LORD, that a person's life is not his own. No one is able to plan his own course. ²⁴So correct me, LORD, but please be gentle. Do not correct me in anger, for I would die. ²⁵Pour out your wrath on the nations that refuse to recognize you—on nations that do not call upon your name. For they have utterly devoured your people Israel,* making the land a desolate wilderness.

CHAPTER 11

Judah's Broken Covenant

The LORD gave another message to Jeremiah. He said, ²"Remind the people of Judah and Jerusalem about the terms of their covenant with me. ³Say to them, 'This is what the LORD, the God of Israel, says: Cursed is anyone who does not obey the terms of my covenant! ⁴For I said to your ancestors when I brought them out of slavery in Egypt, "If you obey me and do whatever I command you, then you will be my people, and I will be your God." ⁵I said this so I could keep my promise to your ancestors to give you a land flowing with milk and honey—the land you live in today.' "

I OBEY the Lord and do whatever he commands. (11:4)

Then I replied, "So be it,* LORD!"

⁶ Then the LORD said, "Broadcast this message in the streets of Jerusalem. Go from town to town throughout the land and say, 'Remember the covenant your ancestors made, and do everything they promised. ⁷For I solemnly warned your ancestors when I brought them out of Egypt, repeating over and

10:16 Hebrew *the Portion of Jacob.*   10:25 Hebrew *Jacob.*   11:5 Hebrew *Amen.*

over again to this day: "Obey me!" [8]But your ancestors did not pay any attention; they would not even listen. Instead, they stubbornly followed their own evil desires. And because they refused to obey, I brought upon them all the curses described in our covenant.' "

[9]Again the LORD spoke to me and said, "I have discovered a conspiracy against me among the people of Judah and Jerusalem. [10]They have returned to the sins of their forefathers. They have refused to listen to me and are worshiping idols. Israel and Judah have both broken the covenant I made with their ancestors. [11]Therefore, says the LORD, I am going to bring calamity upon them, and they will not escape. Though they beg for mercy, I will not listen to their cries. [12]Then the people of Judah and Jerusalem will pray to their idols and offer incense before them. But the idols will not save them when disaster strikes! [13]Look now, people of Judah, you have as many gods as there are cities and towns. Your altars of shame—altars for burning incense to your god Baal—are along every street in Jerusalem.

[14]"Pray no more for these people, Jeremiah. Do not weep or pray for them, for I will not listen to them when they cry out to me in distress. [15]What right do my beloved people have to come to my Temple, where they have done so many immoral things? Can their sacrifices avert their destruction? They actually rejoice in doing evil!

[16]"I, the LORD, once called them a thriving olive tree, beautiful to see and full of good fruit. But now I have sent the fury of their enemies to burn them with fire, leaving them charred and broken. [17]I, the LORD Almighty, who planted this olive tree, have ordered it destroyed. For the people of Israel and Judah have done evil, provoking my anger by offering incense to Baal."

A Plot against Jeremiah

[18]Then the LORD told me about the plots my enemies were making against me. [19]I had been as unaware as a lamb on the way to its slaughter. I had no idea that they were planning to kill me! "Let's destroy this man and all his words," they said. "Let's kill him, so his name will be forgotten forever."

[20]O LORD Almighty, you are just, and you examine the deepest thoughts of hearts and minds. Let me see your vengeance against them, for I have committed my cause to you.

[21]The men of Anathoth wanted me dead. They said they would kill me if I did not stop speaking in the LORD's name. [22]So this is what the LORD Almighty says about them: "I will punish them! Their young men will die in battle, and their little boys and girls will starve. [23]Not one of these plotters from Anathoth will survive, for I will bring disaster upon them when their time of punishment comes."

CHAPTER 12

Jeremiah Questions the LORD's Justice

LORD, you always give me justice when I bring a case before you. Now let me bring you this complaint: Why are the wicked so prosperous? Why are evil people so happy? [2]You have planted them, and they have taken root and prospered. Your name is on their lips, but in their hearts they give you no credit at all. [3]But as for me, LORD, you know my heart. You see me and test my thoughts. Drag these people away like helpless sheep to be butchered! Set them aside to be slaughtered!

[4]How long must this land weep? Even the grass in the fields has withered. The wild animals and birds have disappeared because of the evil in the land. Yet the people say, "The LORD won't do anything!"

The LORD's Reply to Jeremiah

[5]Then the LORD replied to me, "If racing against mere men makes you tired, how will you race against horses? If you stumble and fall on open ground,

I CHOOSE God's will over my own evil desires. (11:8)

I REJOICE in doing what is right. (11:15)

I DO NOT TRY to avenge myself but leave that to God (Romans 12:19). (11:20)

I BRING my toughest questions to the Lord. (12:1)

I KNOW the Lord will not let the wicked prosper forever. (12:4)

what will you do in the thickets near the Jordan? [6]Even your own brothers, members of your own family, have turned on you. They have plotted, raising a cry against you. Do not trust them, no matter how pleasantly they speak.

[7]"I have abandoned my people, my special possession. I have surrendered my dearest ones to their enemies. [8]My chosen people have roared at me like a lion of the forest, so I have treated them as though I hated them. [9]My chosen people have become as disgusting to me as a vulture. And indeed, they are surrounded by vultures. Bring on the wild beasts to pick their corpses clean!

[10]"Many rulers have ravaged my vineyard, trampling down the vines and turning all its beauty into a barren wilderness. [11]They have made it an empty wasteland; I hear its mournful cry. The whole land is desolate, and no one even cares. [12]Destroying armies plunder the land. The sword of the LORD kills people from one end of the nation to the other. No one will escape! [13]My people have planted wheat but are harvesting thorns. They have worked hard, but it has done them no good. They will harvest a crop of shame, for the fierce anger of the LORD is upon them."

A Message for Israel's Neighbors

[14]Now this is what the LORD says: "As for all the evil nations reaching out for the inheritance I gave my people Israel, I will uproot them from their lands just as Judah will be uprooted from hers. [15]But afterward I will return and have compassion on all of them. I will bring them home to their own lands again, each nation to its own inheritance. [16]And if these nations quickly learn the ways of my people, and if they learn to swear by my name, saying, 'As surely as the LORD lives' (just as they taught my people to swear by the name of Baal), then they will be given a place among my people. [17]But any nation who refuses to obey me will be uprooted and destroyed. I, the LORD, have spoken!"

CHAPTER 13

Jeremiah's Linen Belt

This is what the LORD said to me: "Go and buy a linen belt and put it around your waist, but do not wash it." [2]So I bought the belt as the LORD directed me and put it around my waist. [3]Then the LORD gave me another message: [4]"Take the linen belt you are wearing, and go to the Euphrates River.* Hide it there in a hole in the rocks." [5]So I went and hid it at the Euphrates as the LORD had instructed me.

[6]A long time afterward, the LORD said to me, "Go back to the Euphrates and get the linen belt that I told you to hide there." [7]So I went to the Euphrates and dug it out of the hole where I had hidden it. But now it was mildewed and falling apart. The belt was useless.

[8]Then I received this message from the LORD: [9]"The LORD says: This illustrates how I will rot away the pride of Judah and Jerusalem. [10]These wicked people refuse to listen to me. They stubbornly follow their own desires and worship idols. Therefore, they will become like this linen belt—good for nothing! [11]As a belt clings to a person's waist, so I created Judah and Israel to cling to me," says the LORD. "They were to be my people, my pride, my glory—an honor to my name. But they would not listen to me.

[12]"So tell them, 'The LORD, the God of Israel, says: All your wineskins will be full of wine.' And they will reply, 'Of course, you don't need to tell us how prosperous we will be!' [13]Then tell them, 'No, this is what the LORD means: I will make everyone in this land so confused that they will seem drunk—from the king sitting on David's throne and from the priests and the prophets, right on down to the common people. [14]I will smash them one against the

13:4 Hebrew *Perath*; also in 13:5, 6, 7.

I ABHOR blatant opposition to the Lord. (12:8)

I BELIEVE the Lord wants people from every nation to worship him. (12:16)

I DO what the Lord says. (13:2)

I HUMBLE myself before the Lord and obey his commands. (13:9)

I LISTEN to the Lord and choose his will over my own evil desires. (13:10)

other, even parents against children, says the LORD. I will not let my pity or mercy or compassion keep me from destroying them.' "

A Warning against Pride

¹⁵Listen! Do not be proud, for the LORD has spoken. ¹⁶Give glory to the LORD your God before it is too late. Acknowledge him before he brings darkness upon you, causing you to stumble and fall on the dark mountains. For then, when you look for light, you will find only terrible darkness. ¹⁷And if you still refuse to listen, I will weep alone because of your pride. My eyes will overflow with tears because the LORD's flock will be led away into exile.

¹⁸Say to the king and his mother, "Come down from your thrones and sit in the dust, for your glorious crowns will soon be snatched from your heads." ¹⁹The towns of the Negev will close their gates, and no one will be able to open them. The people of Judah will be taken away as captives. They will all be carried into exile.

²⁰See the armies marching down from the north! Where is your flock— your beautiful flock—that he gave you to care for? ²¹How will you feel when the LORD sets your foreign allies over you as rulers? You will writhe in pain like a woman giving birth! ²²You may ask yourself, "Why is all this happening to me?" It is because of your many sins! That is why you have been raped and destroyed by invading armies. ²³Can an Ethiopian* change the color of his skin? Can a leopard take away its spots? Neither can you start doing good, for you always do evil.

²⁴"I will scatter you, just as chaff is scattered by the winds blowing in from the desert. ²⁵This is your allotment, that which is due you," says the LORD. "I have measured it out especially for you, because you have forgotten me and put your trust in false gods. ²⁶I myself will expose you to shame. ²⁷I am keenly aware of your adultery and lust, and your abominable idol worship out in the fields and on the hills. Your destruction is sure, Jerusalem! How long will it be before you are pure?"

CHAPTER 14

Judah's Terrible Drought

This message came to Jeremiah from the LORD, explaining why he was holding back the rain: ²"Judah wilts; her businesses have ground to a halt. All the people sit on the ground in mourning, and a great cry rises from Jerusalem. ³The nobles send servants to get water, but all the wells are dry. The servants return with empty pitchers, confused and desperate, covering their heads in grief. ⁴The ground is parched and cracked for lack of rain. The farmers are afraid; they, too, cover their heads. ⁵The deer abandons her newborn fawn because there is no grass. ⁶The wild donkeys stand on the bare hills panting like thirsty jackals. They strain their eyes looking for grass to eat, but there is none to be found."

⁷The people say, "LORD, our wickedness has caught up with us. We have sinned against you. So please, help us for the sake of your own reputation. ⁸O Hope of Israel, our Savior in times of trouble! Why are you like a stranger to us? Why are you like someone passing through the land, stopping only for the night? ⁹Are you also confused? Are you helpless to save us? You are right here among us, LORD. We are known as your people. Please don't abandon us now!"

¹⁰So the LORD replies to his people, "You love to wander far from me and do not follow in my paths. Now I will no longer accept you as my people. I will remember all your wickedness and will punish you for your sins."

13:23 Hebrew *a Cushite.*

I GIVE glory to the Lord my God. (13:16)

I FEAR the Lord and quickly repent of my sins. (13:22)

I BELIEVE the Lord governs everything— even the rain. (14:1)

I FOLLOW the Lord and do not wander from him. (14:10)

The LORD Forbids Jeremiah to Intercede

11 Then the LORD said to me, "Do not pray for these people anymore. 12 When they fast in my presence, I will pay no attention. When they present their burnt offerings and grain offerings to me, I will not accept them. In return, I will give them only war, famine, and disease."

13 Then I said, "O Sovereign LORD, their prophets are telling them, 'All is well—no war or famine will come. The LORD will surely send you peace.'"

14 Then the LORD said, "These prophets are telling lies in my name. I did not send them or tell them to speak. I did not give them any messages. They prophesy of visions and revelations they have never seen or heard. They speak foolishness made up in their own lying hearts. 15 Therefore, says the LORD, I will punish these lying prophets, for they have spoken in my name even though I never sent them. They say that no war or famine will come, but they themselves will die by war and famine! 16 As for the people to whom they prophesy—their bodies will be thrown out into the streets of Jerusalem, victims of famine and war. There will be no one left to bury them. Husbands, wives, sons, and daughters—all will be gone. For I will pour out their own wickedness on them.

17 "Now, Jeremiah, say this to them: 'Night and day my eyes overflow with tears. I cannot stop weeping, for my virgin daughter—my precious people—has been run through with a sword and lies mortally wounded on the ground. 18 If I go out into the fields, I see the bodies of people slaughtered by the enemy. If I walk the city streets, there I see people who have died of starvation. The prophets and priests continue with their work, but they do not know what they are doing.'"

A Prayer for Healing

19 LORD, have you completely rejected Judah? Do you really hate Jerusalem*? Why have you wounded us past all hope of healing? We hoped for peace, but no peace came. We hoped for a time of healing but found only terror.

20 LORD, we confess our wickedness and that of our ancestors, too. We all have sinned against you. 21 For the sake of your own name, LORD, do not abandon us. Do not disgrace yourself and the throne of your glory. Do not break your covenant with us. Please don't forget us!

22 Can any of the foreign gods send us rain? Does it fall from the sky by itself? No, it comes from you, the LORD our God! Only you can do such things. So we will wait for you to help us.

CHAPTER 15

Judah's Inevitable Doom

Then the LORD said to me, "Even if Moses and Samuel stood before me pleading for these people, I wouldn't help them. Away with them! Get them out of my sight! 2 And if they say to you, 'But where can we go?' tell them, 'This is what the LORD says: Those who are destined for death, to death; those who are destined for war, to war; those who are destined for famine, to famine; those who are destined for captivity, to captivity.'

3 "I will send four kinds of destroyers against them," says the LORD. "I will send the sword to kill, the dogs to drag away, the vultures to devour, and the wild animals to finish up what is left. 4 Because of the wicked things Manasseh son of Hezekiah, king of Judah, did in Jerusalem, I will make my people an object of horror to all the kingdoms of the earth.

5 "Who will feel sorry for you, Jerusalem? Who will weep for you? Who will even bother to ask how you are? 6 You have forsaken me and turned your back on me," says the LORD. "Therefore, I will raise my clenched fists to destroy you. I am tired of always giving you another chance. 7 I will winnow you like

I IGNORE the assurances of false prophets (Jeremiah 23:16-17). (14:13)

I WEEP when I think of the coming judgment against those who won't stop rebelling against the Lord. (14:17)

I WAIT for the Lord to help me. (14:22)

See the profiles for Moses (page 73) and Samuel (page 323) at Exodus 5:1 and 1 Samuel 3:1.

See the profiles for Manasseh (page 543) and Hezekiah (page 825) at 2 Chronicles 33:13 and Isaiah 37:1.

I DO NOT FORSAKE the Lord or turn my back on him. (15:6)

14:19 Hebrew *Zion.*

grain at the gates of your cities and take away everything you hold dear. I will destroy my own people, because they refuse to turn back to me from all their evil ways.

⁸"There will be more widows than the grains of sand along the seashore. At noontime I will bring a destroyer against the mothers of young men. I will cause anguish and terror to come upon them suddenly. ⁹The mother of seven grows faint and gasps for breath; her sun has gone down while it is yet day. She sits childless now, disgraced and humiliated. And those who are left, I will hand over to the enemy to be killed," says the LORD.

Jeremiah's Complaint

¹⁰Then I said, "What sadness is mine, my mother. Oh, that I had died at birth! I am hated everywhere I go. I am neither a lender who has threatened to foreclose nor a borrower who refuses to pay—yet they all curse me."

¹¹The LORD replied, "All will be well with you, Jeremiah. Your enemies will ask you to plead on their behalf in times of trouble and distress. ¹²Can a man break a bar of iron from the north, or a bar of bronze? ¹³Because of all my people's sins against me, I will hand over their wealth and treasures as plunder to the enemy. ¹⁴I will tell their enemies to take them as captives to a foreign land. For my anger blazes forth like fire, and it will consume them."

I TRUST in the Lord when others oppose me. (15:11)

¹⁵Then I said, "LORD, you know I am suffering for your sake. Punish my persecutors! Don't let them kill me! Be merciful to me and give them what they deserve! ¹⁶Your words are what sustain me. They bring me great joy and are my heart's delight, for I bear your name, O LORD God Almighty. ¹⁷I never joined the people in their merry feasts. I sat alone because your hand was on me. I burst with indignation at their sins. ¹⁸Why then does my suffering continue? Why is my wound so incurable? Your help seems as uncertain as a seasonal brook. It is like a spring that has gone dry."

I THANK the Lord, whose words bring me great joy and delight. (15:16)

I TRUST in the Lord in even the most uncertain of times. (15:18)

¹⁹The LORD replied, "If you return to me, I will restore you so you can continue to serve me. If you speak words that are worthy, you will be my spokesman. You are to influence them; do not let them influence you! ²⁰They will fight against you like an attacking army, but I will make you as secure as a fortified wall. They will not conquer you, for I will protect and deliver you. I, the LORD, have spoken! ²¹Yes, I will certainly keep you safe from these wicked men. I will rescue you from their cruel hands."

CHAPTER 16

Jeremiah Forbidden to Marry

The LORD gave me another message. He said, ²"Do not marry or have children in this place. ³For this is what the LORD says about the children born here in this city and about their mothers and fathers: ⁴They will die from terrible diseases. No one will mourn for them or bury them, and they will lie scattered on the ground like dung. They will die from war and famine, and their bodies will be food for the vultures and wild animals.

I BELIEVE God gives some the gift of singleness (1 Corinthians 7:7). (16:2)

Judah's Coming Punishment

⁵"Do not go to their funerals to mourn and show sympathy for them," says the LORD, "for I have removed my protection and peace from them. I have taken away my unfailing love and my mercy. ⁶Both the great and the lowly will die in this land. No one will bury them or mourn for them. Their friends will not cut themselves or shave their heads in sadness. ⁷No one will offer a meal to comfort those who mourn for the dead—not even for the death of a mother or a father. No one will send a cup of wine to console them.

⁸"And do not go to their feasts and parties. Do not eat and drink with them at all. ⁹For the LORD Almighty, the God of Israel, says: In your own lifetime, before your very eyes, I will put an end to the happy singing and laughter in

In response to these affirmations, tell the Lord what you obey—or find easy to disobey.

this land. The joyful voices of bridegrooms and brides will no longer be heard.

I DO NOT PRETEND to be ignorant of my sin against the Lord. (16:10)

[10] "When you tell the people all these things, they will ask, 'Why has the LORD decreed such terrible things against us? What have we done to deserve such treatment? What is our sin against the LORD our God?' [11] Tell them that this is the LORD's reply: It is because your ancestors were unfaithful to me. They worshiped other gods and served them. They abandoned me. They did not keep my law. [12] And you are even worse than your ancestors! You stubbornly follow your own evil desires and refuse to listen to me. [13] So I will throw you out of this land and send you into a foreign land where you and your ancestors have never been. There you can worship idols all you like—and I will grant you no favors!

I LISTEN to the Lord and choose his will over my own evil desires. (16:12)

Hope despite the Disaster

[14] "But the time is coming," says the LORD, "when people who are taking an oath will no longer say, 'As surely as the LORD lives, who rescued the people of Israel from the land of Egypt.' [15] Instead, they will say, 'As surely as the LORD lives, who brought the people of Israel back to their own land from the land of the north and from all the countries to which he had exiled them.' For I will bring them back to this land that I gave their ancestors.

[16] "But now I am sending for many fishermen who will catch them," says the LORD. "I am sending for hunters who will search for them in the forests and caves. [17] I am watching them closely, and I see every sin. They cannot hope to hide from me. [18] I will punish them doubly for all their sins, because they have defiled my land with lifeless images of their detestable gods and filled my inheritance with their evil deeds."

I BELIEVE the Lord sees every sin I commit. (16:17)

Jeremiah's Prayer of Confidence

[19] LORD, you are my strength and fortress, my refuge in the day of trouble! Nations from around the world will come to you and say, "Our ancestors were foolish, for they worshiped worthless idols. [20] Can people make their own god? The gods they make are not real gods at all!"

[21] "So now I will show them my power and might," says the LORD. "At last they will know that I am the LORD."

CHAPTER 17

Judah's Sin and Punishment

The LORD says, "My people act as though their evil ways are laws to be obeyed, inscribed with a diamond point on their stony hearts, or with an iron chisel on the corners of their altars. [2] Even their children go to worship at their sacred altars and Asherah poles, beneath every green tree and on every high hill. [3] So I will give all your wealth and treasures—together with your pagan shrines—as plunder to your enemies, for sin runs rampant in your land. [4] The wonderful inheritance I have reserved for you will slip out of your hands, and I will send you away as captives to a foreign land. For you have kindled my anger into a roaring fire that will burn forever."

I CONFESS my sins and ask the Lord to keep my heart soft toward him. (17:1)

Wisdom from the LORD

[5] This is what the LORD says: "Cursed are those who put their trust in mere humans and turn their hearts away from the LORD. [6] They are like stunted shrubs in the desert, with no hope for the future. They will live in the barren wilderness, on the salty flats where no one lives.

[7] "But blessed are those who trust in the LORD and have made the LORD their hope and confidence. [8] They are like trees planted along a riverbank, with roots that reach deep into the water. Such trees are not bothered by the heat or worried by long months of drought. Their leaves stay green, and they go right on producing delicious fruit.

I TRUST in the Lord and make him my hope and confidence. (17:7)

[9]"The human heart is most deceitful and desperately wicked. Who really knows how bad it is? [10]But I know! I, the LORD, search all hearts and examine secret motives. I give all people their due rewards, according to what their actions deserve."

Jeremiah's Trust in the LORD

[11]Like a bird that hatches eggs she has not laid, so are those who get their wealth by unjust means. Sooner or later they will lose their riches and, at the end of their lives, will become poor old fools.

[12]But we worship at your throne—eternal, high, and glorious! [13]O LORD, the hope of Israel, all who turn away from you will be disgraced and shamed. They will be buried in a dry and dusty grave, for they have forsaken the LORD, the fountain of living water.

[14]O LORD, you alone can heal me; you alone can save. My praises are for you alone! [15]People scoff at me and say, "What is this 'message from the LORD' you keep talking about? Why don't your predictions come true?"

[16]LORD, I have not abandoned my job as a shepherd for your people. I have not urged you to send disaster. It is your message I have given them, not my own. [17]LORD, do not desert me now! You alone are my hope in the day of disaster. [18]Bring shame and terror on all who persecute me, but give me peace. Yes, bring double destruction upon them!

Observing the Sabbath

[19]Then the LORD said to me, "Go and stand in the gates of Jerusalem, first at the gate where the king goes out, and then at each of the other gates. [20]Say to all the people, 'Listen to this message from the LORD, you kings of Judah and all you people of Judah and everyone living in Jerusalem. [21]This is what the LORD says: Listen to my warning and live! Stop carrying on your trade at Jerusalem's gates on the Sabbath day. [22]Do not do your work on the Sabbath, but make it a holy day. I gave this command to your ancestors, [23]but they did not listen or obey. They stubbornly refused to pay attention and would not respond to discipline.

[24]" 'But if you obey me, says the LORD, and do not carry on your trade or work on the Sabbath day, and if you keep it holy, [25]then this nation will continue forever. There will always be a descendant of David sitting on the throne here in Jerusalem. Kings and their officials will always ride among the people of Judah in chariots and on horses, and this city will remain forever. [26]And from all around Jerusalem, from the towns of Judah and Benjamin, from the western foothills* and the hill country and the Negev, the people will come with their burnt offerings and sacrifices. They will bring their grain offerings, incense, and thanksgiving offerings to the LORD's Temple.

[27]" 'But if you do not listen to me and refuse to keep the Sabbath holy, and if on the Sabbath day you bring loads of merchandise through the gates of Jerusalem just as on other days, then I will set fire to these gates. The fire will spread to the palaces, and no one will be able to put out the roaring flames.' "

CHAPTER 18

The Potter and the Clay

The LORD gave another message to Jeremiah. He said, [2]"Go down to the shop where clay pots and jars are made. I will speak to you while you are there." [3]So I did as he told me and found the potter working at his wheel. [4]But the jar he was making did not turn out as he had hoped, so the potter squashed the jar into a lump of clay and started again.

[5]Then the LORD gave me this message: [6]"O Israel, can I not do to you as this potter has done to his clay? As the clay is in the potter's hand, so are you in

17:26 Hebrew *the Shephelah.*

I BELIEVE the Lord searches my heart and examines my motives. (17:10)

I BELIEVE the Lord alone is the fountain of living water (John 4:10). (17:13)

I HOPE in the Lord alone in the day of disaster. (17:17)

I LISTEN to the Lord's warnings and obey his commands. (17:21)

See David's profile (page 629) at Psalm 3:1.

I BELIEVE the Lord is sovereign and can do whatever he wants. (18:6)

my hand. ⁷If I announce that a certain nation or kingdom is to be uprooted, torn down, and destroyed, ⁸but then that nation renounces its evil ways, I will not destroy it as I had planned. ⁹And if I announce that I will build up and plant a certain nation or kingdom, making it strong and great, ¹⁰but then that nation turns to evil and refuses to obey me, I will not bless that nation as I had said I would.

¹¹"Therefore, Jeremiah, go and warn all Judah and Jerusalem. Say to them, 'This is what the LORD says: I am planning disaster against you instead of good. So turn from your evil ways, each of you, and do what is right.' "

¹²But they replied, "Don't waste your breath. We will continue to live as we want to, following our own evil desires."

¹³Then the LORD said, "Has anyone ever heard of such a thing, even among the pagan nations? My virgin Israel has done something too terrible to understand! ¹⁴Does the snow ever melt high up in the mountains of Lebanon? Do the cold, flowing streams from the crags of Mount Hermon ever run dry? ¹⁵These can be counted on, but not my people! For they have deserted me and turned to worthless idols. They have stumbled off the ancient highways of good, and they walk the muddy paths of sin. ¹⁶Therefore, their land will become desolate, a monument to their stupidity. All who pass by will be astonished and shake their heads in amazement at its utter desolation. ¹⁷I will scatter my people before their enemies as the east wind scatters dust. And in all their trouble I will turn my back on them and refuse to notice their distress."

A Plot against Jeremiah

¹⁸Then the people said, "Come on, let's find a way to stop Jeremiah. We have our own priests and wise men and prophets. We don't need him to teach the law and give us advice and prophecies. Let's spread rumors about him and ignore what he says."

¹⁹LORD, help me! Listen to what they are planning to do to me! ²⁰Should they repay evil for good? They have set a trap to kill me, though I pleaded for them and tried to protect them from your anger. ²¹So let their children starve! Let the sword pour out their blood! Let their wives become widows without any children! Let their old men die in a plague, and let their young men be killed in battle! ²²Let screaming be heard from their homes as warriors come suddenly upon them. For they have dug a pit for me, and they have hidden traps along my path.

²³LORD, you know all about their murderous plots against me. Don't forgive their crimes and blot out their sins. Let them die before you. Deal with them in your anger.

CHAPTER 19

Jeremiah's Shattered Jar

The LORD said to me, "Go and buy a clay jar. Then ask some of the leaders of the people and of the priests to follow you. ²Go out into the valley of the son of Hinnom by the entrance to the Potsherd Gate, and repeat to them the words that I give you. ³Say to them, 'Listen to this message from the LORD, you kings of Judah and citizens of Jerusalem! This is what the LORD Almighty, the God of Israel, says: I will bring such a terrible disaster on this place that the ears of those who hear about it will ring!

⁴" 'For Israel has forsaken me and turned this valley into a place of wickedness. The people burn incense to foreign gods—idols never before worshiped by this generation, by their ancestors, or by the kings of Judah. And they have filled this place with the blood of innocent children. ⁵They have built pagan shrines to Baal, and there they burn their sons as sacrifices to Baal. I have never commanded such a horrible deed; it never even crossed my

---

I LISTEN to the Lord and choose his will over my own evil desires. (18:12)

I DO NOT WALK in the muddy paths of sin. (18:15)

I DO NOT TRY to avenge myself but leave that to God (Romans 12:19). (18:19)

I DO whatever the Lord commands. (19:1)

I ABHOR the murder of innocent children. (19:5)

mind to command such a thing! ⁶So beware, for the time is coming, says the LORD, when this place will no longer be called Topheth or the valley of the son of Hinnom, but the Valley of Slaughter. ⁷For I will upset the battle plans of Judah and Jerusalem and let invading armies slaughter them. The enemy will leave the dead bodies as food for the vultures and wild animals. ⁸I will wipe Jerusalem from the face of the earth, making it a monument to their stupidity. All who pass by will be appalled and will gasp at the destruction they see there. ⁹I will see to it that your enemies lay siege to the city until all the food is gone. Then those trapped inside will have to eat their own sons and daughters and friends. They will be driven to utter despair.'

¹⁰"As these men watch, Jeremiah, smash the jar you brought with you. ¹¹Then say to them, 'This is what the LORD Almighty says: As this jar lies shattered, so I will shatter the people of Judah and Jerusalem beyond all hope of repair. They will bury the bodies in Topheth until there is no more room. ¹²This is what I will do to this place and its people, says the LORD. I will cause this city to become defiled like Topheth. ¹³Yes, all the houses in Jerusalem, including the palace of Judah's kings, will become like Topheth—all the houses where you burned incense on the rooftops to your star gods, and where drink offerings were poured out to your idols.' "

¹⁴Then Jeremiah returned from Topheth where he had delivered this message, and he stopped in front of the Temple of the LORD. He said to the people there, ¹⁵"This is what the LORD Almighty, the God of Israel, says: I will bring disaster upon this city and its surrounding towns just as I promised, because you have stubbornly refused to listen to me."

CHAPTER 20

Jeremiah and Pashhur

Now Pashhur son of Immer, the priest in charge of the Temple of the LORD, heard what Jeremiah was saying. ²So he arrested Jeremiah the prophet and had him whipped and put in stocks at the Benjamin Gate of the LORD's Temple.

³The next day, when Pashhur finally released him, Jeremiah said, "Pashhur, the LORD has changed your name. From now on you are to be called 'The Man Who Lives in Terror.'* ⁴For this is what the LORD says: I will send terror upon you and all your friends, and you will watch as they are slaughtered by the swords of the enemy. I will hand the people of Judah over to the king of Babylon. He will take them captive to Babylon or run them through with the sword. ⁵And I will let your enemies plunder Jerusalem. All the famed treasures of the city—the precious jewels and gold and silver of your kings—will be carried off to Babylon. ⁶As for you, Pashhur, you and all your household will go as captives to Babylon. There you will die and be buried, you and all your friends to whom you promised that everything would be all right."

Jeremiah's Complaint

⁷O LORD, you persuaded me, and I allowed myself to be persuaded. You are stronger than I am, and you overpowered me. Now I am mocked by everyone in the city. ⁸Whenever I speak, the words come out in a violent outburst. "Violence and destruction!" I shout. So these messages from the LORD have made me a household joke. ⁹And I can't stop! If I say I'll never mention the LORD or speak in his name, his word burns in my heart like a fire. It's like a fire in my bones! I am weary of holding it in!

¹⁰I have heard the many rumors about me. They call me "The Man Who Lives in Terror." And they say, "If you say anything, we will report it." Even

I BELIEVE the wages of sin is death (Romans 6:23). (19:7)

I ABHOR astrology and idolatry. (19:13)

I DO NOT TRY to avenge myself but leave that to God (Romans 12:19). (20:3)

I RECOGNIZE that the Lord is sovereign and can do whatever he wants in my life. (20:7)

20:3 Hebrew *Magor-missabib*, which means "surrounded by terror"; also in 20:10.

my old friends are watching me, waiting for a fatal slip. "He will trap himself," they say, "and then we will get our revenge on him."

[11]But the LORD stands beside me like a great warrior. Before him they will stumble. They cannot defeat me. They will be shamed and thoroughly humiliated. Their dishonor will never be forgotten. [12]O LORD Almighty! You know those who are righteous, and you examine the deepest thoughts of hearts and minds. Let me see your vengeance against them, for I have committed my cause to you. [13]Now I will sing out my thanks to the LORD! Praise the LORD! For though I was poor and needy, he delivered me from my oppressors.

[14]Yet I curse the day I was born! May the day of my birth not be blessed. [15]I curse the messenger who told my father, "Good news—you have a son!" [16]Let him be destroyed like the cities of old that the LORD overthrew without mercy. Terrify him all day long with battle shouts, [17]for he did not kill me at birth. Oh, that I had died in my mother's womb, that her body had been my grave! [18]Why was I ever born? My entire life has been filled with trouble, sorrow, and shame.

CHAPTER 21

No Deliverance from Babylon

The LORD spoke through Jeremiah when King Zedekiah sent Pashhur son of Malkijah and Zephaniah son of Maaseiah, the priest, to speak with him. They begged Jeremiah, [2]"Please ask the LORD to help us. King Nebuchadnezzar* of Babylon has begun his attack on Judah. Perhaps the LORD will be gracious and do a mighty miracle as he has done in the past. Perhaps he will force Nebuchadnezzar to withdraw his armies."

[3]Jeremiah replied, "Go back to King Zedekiah and tell him, [4]'This is what the LORD, the God of Israel, says: I will make your weapons useless against the king of Babylon and the Babylonians* who are attacking you. Yes, I will bring your enemies right into the heart of this city. [5]I myself will fight against you with great power, for I am very angry. You have made me furious! [6]I will send a terrible plague upon this city, and both people and animals will die. [7]And then, says the LORD, even after King Zedekiah, his officials, and everyone else in the city have survived war, famine, and disease, I will hand them over to King Nebuchadnezzar of Babylon. He will slaughter them all without mercy, pity, or compassion.'

[8]"Tell all the people, 'This is what the LORD says: Take your choice of life or death! [9]Everyone who stays in Jerusalem will die from war, famine, or disease, but those who go out and surrender to the Babylonians will live. [10]For I have decided to bring disaster and not good upon this city, says the LORD. It will be captured by the king of Babylon, and he will reduce it to ashes.'

Judgment on Judah's Kings

[11]"Say to the royal family of Judah, 'Listen to this message from the LORD! [12]This is what the LORD says to the dynasty of David: Give justice to the people you judge! Help those who have been robbed; rescue them from their oppressors. Do what is right, or my anger will burn like an unquenchable fire because of all your sins. [13]I will fight against this city of Jerusalem that boasts, "We are safe on our mountain! No one can touch us here." [14]And I myself will punish you for your sinfulness, says the LORD. I will light a fire in your forests that will burn up everything around you.'"

CHAPTER 22

A Message for Judah's Kings

Then the LORD said to me, "Go over and speak directly to the king of Judah. Say to him, [2]'Listen to this message from the LORD, you king of Judah, sitting

---

See Nebuchadnezzar's profile (page 985) at Daniel 4:37.

I DO NOT BELIEVE the Lord is under any obligation to do a miracle for those who sin against him. (21:4)

I BELIEVE the wages of sin is death (Romans 6:23). (21:6)

I CHOOSE life and do whatever the Lord commands. (21:8)

I TRUST in the Lord when others oppose me. (20:11)

I BELIEVE the Lord knows my deepest thoughts and feelings. (20:12)

I DO what is right by showing justice to others and helping the oppressed. (21:12)

See David's profile (page 629) at Psalm 3:1.

21:2 Hebrew *Nebuchadrezzar*, a variant name for Nebuchadnezzar; also in 21:7.   21:4 Or *Chaldeans*; also in 21:9.

on David's throne. Let your officials and your people listen, too. ³This is what the LORD says: Be fair-minded and just. Do what is right! Help those who have been robbed; rescue them from their oppressors. Quit your evil deeds! Do not mistreat foreigners, orphans, and widows. Stop murdering the innocent! ⁴If you obey me, there will always be a descendant of David sitting on the throne here in Jerusalem. The king will ride through the palace gates in chariots and on horses, with his parade of officials and subjects. ⁵But if you refuse to pay attention to this warning, I swear by my own name, says the LORD, that this palace will become a pile of rubble.' "

A Message about the Palace

⁶Now this is what the LORD says concerning the royal palace: "You are as beloved to me as fruitful Gilead and the green forests of Lebanon. But I will destroy you and leave you deserted, with no one living within your walls. ⁷I will call for wreckers, who will bring out their tools to dismantle you. They will tear out all your fine cedar beams and throw them on the fire. ⁸People from many nations will pass by the ruins of this city and say to one another, 'Why did the LORD destroy such a great city?' ⁹And the answer will be, 'Because they violated their covenant with the LORD their God by worshiping other gods.' "

I DO NOT BETRAY God and worship false gods. (22:9)

A Message about Jehoahaz

¹⁰Do not weep for the dead king or mourn his loss. Instead, weep for the captive king being led away! For he will never return to see his native land again. ¹¹For this is what the LORD says about Jehoahaz,* who succeeded his father, King Josiah, and was taken away as a captive: "He will never return. ¹²He will die in a distant land and never again see his own country."

See Josiah's profile (page 461) at 2 Kings 23:25.

A Message about Jehoiakim

¹³And the LORD says, "Destruction is certain for Jehoiakim,* who builds his palace with forced labor.* By not paying wages, he builds injustice into its walls and oppression into its doorframes and ceilings. ¹⁴He says, 'I will build a magnificent palace with huge rooms and many windows, paneled throughout with fragrant cedar and painted a lovely red.'

I ABHOR slavery and oppressive labor practices. (22:13)

¹⁵"But a beautiful palace does not make a great king! Why did your father, Josiah, reign so long? Because he was just and right in all his dealings. That is why God blessed him. ¹⁶He made sure that justice and help were given to the poor and needy, and everything went well for him. Isn't that what it means to know me?" asks the LORD. ¹⁷"But you! You are full of selfish greed and dishonesty! You murder the innocent, oppress the poor, and reign ruthlessly."

I AM JUST AND RIGHT in all my dealings. (22:15)

I KNOW the Lord and long to see justice and help given to the poor and needy (James 1:27). (22:16)

¹⁸Therefore, this is the LORD's decree of punishment against King Jehoiakim, who succeeded his father, Josiah, on the throne: "His family will not weep for him when he dies. His subjects will not even care that he is dead. ¹⁹He will be buried like a dead donkey—dragged out of Jerusalem and dumped outside the gate! ²⁰Weep, for your allies are all gone. Search for them in Lebanon. Shout for them at Bashan. Search for them in the regions east of the river.* See, they are all destroyed. Not one is left to help you.

²¹"When you were prosperous, I warned you, but you replied, 'Don't bother me.' Since childhood you have been that way—you simply will not listen! ²²And now your allies have all disappeared with a puff of wind. All your friends have been taken away as captives. Surely at last you will see your wickedness and be ashamed. ²³It may be nice to live in a beautiful palace lined with lumber from the cedars of Lebanon, but soon you will cry and groan in anguish—anguish like that of a woman about to give birth.

I LISTEN to the Lord and heed his warnings. (22:21)

22:11 Hebrew *Shallum*, another name for Jehoahaz.   22:13a The brother and successor of the exiled Jehoahaz.
22:13b Hebrew *by unrighteousness*.   22:20 Hebrew *in Abarim*.

I BELIEVE that King
Jehoiachin fell into
Nebuchadnezzar's
hands and that none
of his descendants
ruled from David's
throne, just as the
Lord had said. (22:25)

See Nebuchadnezzar's
profile (page 985) at
Daniel 4:37.

See David's profile
(page 629) at Psalm 3:1.

A Message for Jehoiachin

24"And as surely as I live," says the LORD, "I will abandon you, Jehoiachin* son of Jehoiakim, king of Judah. Even if you were the signet ring on my right hand, I would pull you off. 25I will hand you over to those who seek to kill you, of whom you are so desperately afraid—to King Nebuchadnezzar* of Babylon and the mighty Babylonian* army. 26I will expel you and your mother from this land, and you will die in a foreign country. 27You will never again return to the land of your desire.

28"Why is this man Jehoiachin like a discarded, broken dish? Why are he and his children to be exiled to distant lands? 29O earth, earth, earth! Listen to this message from the LORD! 30This is what the LORD says: Let the record show that this man Jehoiachin was childless, for none of his children will ever sit on the throne of David to rule in Judah. His life will amount to nothing."

CHAPTER 23

The Righteous Branch

"I will send disaster upon the leaders of my people—the shepherds of my sheep—for they have destroyed and scattered the very ones they were expected to care for," says the LORD.

I BELIEVE the Lord will
hold ungodly leaders
accountable for their
actions. (23:2)

2This is what the LORD, the God of Israel, says to these shepherds: "Instead of leading my flock to safety, you have deserted them and driven them to destruction. Now I will pour out judgment on you for the evil you have done to them. 3But I will gather together the remnant of my flock from wherever I have driven them. I will bring them back into their own fold, and they will be fruitful and increase in number. 4Then I will appoint responsible shepherds to care for them, and they will never be afraid again. Not a single one of them will be lost or missing," says the LORD.

I BELIEVE the Lord
Jesus Christ is the
Branch who will rule
on King David's throne
with wisdom, justice,
and righteousness.
(23:5)

5"For the time is coming," says the LORD, "when I will place a righteous Branch on King David's throne. He will be a King who rules with wisdom. He will do what is just and right throughout the land. 6And this is his name: 'The LORD Is Our Righteousness.'* In that day Judah will be saved, and Israel will live in safety.

I BELIEVE that the Lord
kept his promise to
bring the people of
Israel back to their
own land after the
Babylonian captivity.
(23:8)

7"In that day," says the LORD, "when people are taking an oath, they will no longer say, 'As surely as the LORD lives, who rescued the people of Israel from the land of Egypt.' 8Instead, they will say, 'As surely as the LORD lives, who brought the people of Israel back to their own land from the land of the north and from all the countries to which he had exiled them.' Then they will live in their own land."

Judgment on False Prophets

9My heart is broken because of the false prophets, and I tremble uncontrollably. I stagger like a drunkard, like someone overcome by wine, because of the holy words the LORD has spoken against them. 10For the land is full of adultery, and it lies under a curse. The land itself is in mourning—its pastures are dried up. For the prophets do evil and abuse their power.

11"The priests are like the prophets, all ungodly, wicked men. I have seen their despicable acts right here in my own Temple," says the LORD. 12"Therefore, their paths will be dark and slippery. They will be chased down dark and treacherous trails, where they will fall. For I will bring disaster upon them when their time of punishment comes. I, the LORD, have spoken!

I LOVE what is pure,
true, and right
(Philippians 4:8).
(23:14)

13"I saw that the prophets of Samaria were terribly evil, for they prophesied by Baal and led my people of Israel into sin. 14But now I see that the prophets of Jerusalem are even worse! They commit adultery, and they love dishonesty. They encourage those who are doing evil instead of turning them away

22:24 Hebrew Coniah, a variant name for Jehoiachin; also in 22:28, 30. 22:25a Hebrew Nebuchadrezzar, a variant name for Nebuchadnezzar. 22:25b Or Chaldean. 23:6 Hebrew Yahweh Tsidqenu.

from their sins. These prophets are as wicked as the people of Sodom and Gomorrah once were."

¹⁵Therefore, this is what the LORD Almighty says concerning the prophets: "I will feed them with bitterness and give them poison to drink. For it is because of Jerusalem's prophets that wickedness fills this land. ¹⁶This is my warning to my people," says the LORD Almighty. "Do not listen to these prophets when they prophesy to you, filling you with futile hopes. They are making up everything they say. They do not speak for the LORD! ¹⁷They keep saying to these rebels who despise my word, 'Don't worry! The LORD says you will have peace!' And to those who stubbornly follow their own evil desires, they say, 'No harm will come your way!'

¹⁸"But can you name even one of these prophets who knows the LORD well enough to hear what he is saying? Has even one of them cared enough to listen? ¹⁹Look! The LORD's anger bursts out like a storm, a whirlwind that swirls down on the heads of the wicked. ²⁰The anger of the LORD will not diminish until it has finished all his plans. In the days to come, you will understand all this very clearly.

²¹"I have not sent these prophets, yet they claim to speak for me. I have given them no message, yet they prophesy. ²²If they had listened to me, they would have spoken my words and turned my people from their evil ways. ²³Am I a God who is only in one place?" asks the LORD. "Do they think I cannot see what they are doing? ²⁴Can anyone hide from me? Am I not everywhere in all the heavens and earth?" asks the LORD.

²⁵"I have heard these prophets say, 'Listen to the dream I had from God last night.' And then they proceed to tell lies in my name. ²⁶How long will this go on? If they are prophets, they are prophets of deceit, inventing everything they say. ²⁷By telling these false dreams, they are trying to get my people to forget me, just as their ancestors did by worshiping the idols of Baal. ²⁸Let these false prophets tell their dreams, but let my true messengers faithfully proclaim my every word. There is a difference between chaff and wheat! ²⁹Does not my word burn like fire?" asks the LORD. "Is it not like a mighty hammer that smashes rock to pieces?

³⁰"Therefore," says the LORD, "I stand against these prophets who get their messages from each other—³¹these smooth-tongued prophets who say, 'This prophecy is from the LORD!' ³²Their imaginary dreams are flagrant lies that lead my people into sin. I did not send or appoint them, and they have no message at all for my people," says the LORD.

False Prophecies and False Prophets

³³"Suppose one of the people or one of the prophets or priests asks you, 'What prophecy has the LORD burdened you with now?' You must reply, 'You are the burden!* The LORD says he will abandon you!' ³⁴If any prophet, priest, or anyone else says, 'I have a prophecy from the LORD,' I will punish that person along with his entire family. ³⁵You should keep asking each other, 'What is the LORD's answer?' or 'What is the LORD saying?' ³⁶But stop using this phrase, 'prophecy from the LORD.' For people are using it to give authority to their own ideas, turning upside down the words of our God, the living God, the LORD Almighty.

³⁷"This is what you should say to the prophets: 'What is the LORD's answer?' or 'What is the LORD saying?' ³⁸But suppose they respond, 'This is a prophecy from the LORD!' Then you should say, 'This is what the LORD says: Because you have used this phrase, "prophecy from the LORD," even though I warned you not to use it, ³⁹I will forget you completely. I will expel you from my presence, along with this city that I gave to you and your ancestors. ⁴⁰And

I DO NOT LISTEN to those who claim to speak for the Lord yet make up what they say. (23:16)

I LISTEN to the Lord's Word and choose his will over my own evil desires. (23:17)

I DO NOT TELL lies, especially not in the Lord's name. (23:25)

I FAITHFULLY PROCLAIM God's Word. (23:28)

I DO NOT CONTRADICT God's Word by giving equal or greater authority to my own ideas. (23:36)

23:33 As in Greek version and Latin Vulgate; Hebrew reads *What burden?*

I will make you an object of ridicule, and your name will be infamous throughout the ages.' "

CHAPTER 24

Good and Bad Figs

See Nebuchadnezzar's profile (page 985) at Daniel 4:37.

After King Nebuchadnezzar* of Babylon exiled Jehoiachin* son of Jehoiakim, king of Judah, to Babylon along with the princes of Judah and all the skilled craftsmen, the LORD gave me this vision. I saw two baskets of figs placed in front of the LORD's Temple in Jerusalem. ²One basket was filled with fresh, ripe figs, while the other was filled with figs that were spoiled and could not be eaten.

³Then the LORD said to me, "What do you see, Jeremiah?"

I replied, "Figs, some very good and some very bad."

⁴Then the LORD gave me this message: ⁵"This is what the LORD, the God of Israel, says: The good figs represent the exiles I sent from Judah to the land of the Babylonians.* ⁶I have sent them into captivity for their own good. I will see that they are well treated, and I will bring them back here again. I will build them up and not tear them down. I will plant them and not uproot them. ⁷I will give them hearts that will recognize me as the LORD. They will be my people, and I will be their God, for they will return to me wholeheartedly.

I RETURN to the Lord wholeheartedly after I sin. (24:7)

⁸"But the rotten figs," the LORD said, "represent King Zedekiah of Judah, his officials, all the people left in Jerusalem, and those who live in Egypt. I will treat them like spoiled figs, too rotten to eat. ⁹I will make them an object of horror and evil to every nation on earth. They will be disgraced and mocked, taunted and cursed, wherever I send them. ¹⁰I will send war, famine, and disease until they have vanished from the land of Israel, which I gave to them and their ancestors."

CHAPTER 25

Seventy Years of Captivity

See Nebuchadnezzar's profile (page 985) at Daniel 4:37.

This message for all the people of Judah came to Jeremiah from the LORD during the fourth year of Jehoiakim's reign* over Judah. This was the year when King Nebuchadnezzar* of Babylon began his reign.

I DO what the Lord commands year after year after year. (25:3)

²Jeremiah the prophet said to the people in Judah and Jerusalem, ³"For the past twenty-three years—from the thirteenth year of Josiah son of Amon,* king of Judah, until now—the LORD has been giving me his messages. I have faithfully passed them on to you, but you have not listened.

See Josiah's profile (page 461) at 2 Kings 23:25.

⁴"Again and again, the LORD has sent you his prophets, but you have not listened or even tried to hear. ⁵Each time the message was this: 'Turn from the evil road you are traveling and from the evil things you are doing. Only then will I let you live in this land that the LORD gave to you and your ancestors forever. ⁶Do not make me angry by worshiping the idols you have made. Then I will not harm you.'

I TURN BACK to the Lord when I've done evil things. (25:5)

⁷"But you would not listen to me," says the LORD. "You made me furious by worshiping your idols, bringing on yourselves all the disasters you now suffer. ⁸And now the LORD Almighty says: Because you have not listened to me, ⁹I will gather together all the armies of the north under King Nebuchadnezzar of Babylon, whom I have appointed as my deputy. I will bring them all against this land and its people and against the other nations near you. I will completely destroy* you and make you an object of horror and contempt and a ruin forever. ¹⁰I will take away your happy singing and laughter.

I BELIEVE the wages of sin is death (Romans 6:23). (25:9)

24:1a Hebrew *Nebuchadrezzar*, a variant name for Nebuchadnezzar.   24:1b Hebrew *Jeconiah*, a variant name for Jehoiachin.   24:5 Or *Chaldeans*.   25:1a The fourth year of Jehoiakim's reign and the accession year of Nebuchadnezzar's reign was 605 B.C.   25:1b Hebrew *Nebuchadrezzar*, a variant name for Nebuchadnezzar; also in 25:9.   25:3 The thirteenth year of Josiah's reign was 627 B.C.   25:9 The Hebrew term used here refers to the complete consecration of things or people to the LORD, either by destroying them or by giving them as an offering.

The joyful voices of bridegrooms and brides will no longer be heard. Your businesses will fail, and all your homes will stand silent and dark. ¹¹This entire land will become a desolate wasteland. Israel and her neighboring lands will serve the king of Babylon for seventy years.

¹²"Then, after the seventy years of captivity are over, I will punish the king of Babylon and his people for their sins, says the LORD. I will make the country of the Babylonians* an everlasting wasteland. ¹³I will bring upon them all the terrors I have promised in this book—all the penalties announced by Jeremiah against the nations. ¹⁴Many nations and great kings will enslave the Babylonians, just as they enslaved my people. I will punish them in proportion to the suffering they cause my people."

The Cup of the LORD's Anger

¹⁵Then the LORD, the God of Israel, said to me, "Take from my hand this cup filled to the brim with my anger, and make all the nations to whom I send you drink from it. ¹⁶When they drink from it, they will stagger, crazed by the warfare I will send against them."

¹⁷So I took the cup of anger from the LORD and made all the nations drink from it—every nation the LORD sent me to. ¹⁸I went to Jerusalem and the other towns of Judah, and their kings and officials drank from the cup. From that day until this, they have been a desolate ruin, an object of horror, contempt, and cursing. ¹⁹I went to Egypt and spoke to Pharaoh, his officials, his princes, and his people. They, too, drank from that terrible cup, ²⁰along with all the foreigners living in that land. So did all the kings of the land of Uz and the kings of the Philistine cities of Ashkelon, Gaza, Ekron, and what remains of Ashdod. ²¹Then I went to the nations of Edom, Moab, and Ammon, ²²and the kings of Tyre and Sidon, and the kings of the regions across the sea. ²³I went to Dedan, Tema, and Buz, and to the people who live in distant places.* ²⁴I went to the kings of Arabia, the kings of the nomadic tribes of the desert, ²⁵and to the kings of Zimri, Elam, and Media. ²⁶And I went to the kings of the northern countries, far and near, one after the other—all the kingdoms of the world. And finally, the king of Babylon* himself drank from the cup of the LORD's anger.

²⁷Then the LORD said to me, "Now tell them, 'The LORD Almighty, the God of Israel, says: Drink from this cup of my anger. Get drunk and vomit, and you will fall to rise no more, for I am sending terrible wars against you.' ²⁸And if they refuse to accept the cup, tell them, 'The LORD Almighty says: You must drink from it. You cannot escape! ²⁹I have begun to punish Jerusalem, the city where my own name is honored. Now should I let you go unpunished? No, you will not escape disaster. I will call for war against all the nations of the earth. I, the LORD Almighty, have spoken!'

³⁰"Now prophesy all these things, and say to them, 'The LORD will roar loudly against his own land from his holy dwelling in heaven. He will shout against everyone on the earth, like the harvesters do as they crush juice from the grapes. ³¹His cry of judgment will reach the ends of the earth, for the LORD will bring his case against all the nations. He will judge all the people of the earth, slaughtering the wicked with his sword. The LORD has spoken!' "

³²This is what the LORD Almighty says: "Look! Disaster will fall upon nation after nation! A great whirlwind of fury is rising from the most distant corners of the earth!"

³³In that day those the LORD has slaughtered will fill the earth from one end to the other. No one will mourn for them or gather up their bodies to bury them. They will be scattered like dung on the ground.

³⁴Weep and moan, you evil shepherds! Roll in the dust, you leaders of the

I BELIEVE the nation of Babylon was utterly defeated after keeping the people of Judah in captivity for seventy years, just as the Lord said. (25:12)

I BELIEVE the Lord judged all the nations—not just Judah. (25:17)

I BELIEVE the Lord Almighty is sovereign over all the nations. (25:27)

I BELIEVE a day is coming when the Lord Jesus Christ will judge all the nations (Revelation 19:11–16). (25:30)

I BELIEVE the Lord will severely judge ungodly leaders. (25:34)

25:12 Or Chaldeans.   25:23 Or who clip the corners of their hair.   25:26 Hebrew of Sheshach, a code name for Babylon.

flock! The time of your slaughter has arrived; you will fall and shatter like fragile pottery. ³⁵You will find no place to hide; there will be no way to escape.

³⁶Listen to the frantic cries of the shepherds, to the leaders of the flock shouting in despair, for the LORD is spoiling their pastures. ³⁷Peaceful meadows will be turned into a wasteland by the LORD's fierce anger. ³⁸He has left his den like a lion seeking its prey, and their land will be made desolate by the sword of the enemy and the LORD's fierce anger.

CHAPTER 26

Jeremiah's Escape from Death

This message came to Jeremiah from the LORD early in the reign of Jehoiakim son of Josiah,* king of Judah. ²The LORD said, "Stand out in front of the Temple of the LORD, and make an announcement to the people who have come there to worship from all over Judah. Give them my entire message; include every word. ³Perhaps they will listen and turn from their evil ways. Then I will be able to withhold the disaster I am ready to pour out on them because of their sins.

⁴"Say to them, 'This is what the LORD says: If you will not listen to me and obey the law I have given you, ⁵and if you will not listen to my servants, the prophets—for I sent them again and again to warn you, but you would not listen to them—⁶then I will destroy this Temple as I destroyed Shiloh, the place where the Tabernacle was located. And I will make Jerusalem an object of cursing in every nation on earth.'"

⁷The priests, the prophets, and all the people listened to Jeremiah as he spoke in front of the LORD's Temple. ⁸But when Jeremiah had finished his message, saying everything the LORD had told him to say, the priests and prophets and all the people at the Temple mobbed him. "Kill him!" they shouted. ⁹"What right do you have to prophesy in the LORD's name that this Temple will be destroyed like Shiloh? What do you mean, saying that Jerusalem will be destroyed?" And all the people threatened him as he stood in front of the Temple.

¹⁰When the officials of Judah heard what was happening, they rushed over from the palace and sat down at the New Gate of the Temple to hold court. ¹¹The priests and prophets presented their accusations to the officials and the people. "This man should die!" they said. "You have heard with your own ears what a traitor he is, for he has prophesied against this city."

¹²Then Jeremiah spoke in his own defense. "The LORD sent me to prophesy against this Temple and this city," he said. "The LORD gave me every word that I have spoken. ¹³But if you stop your sinning and begin to obey the LORD your God, he will cancel this disaster that he has announced against you. ¹⁴As for me, I am helpless and in your power—do with me as you think best. ¹⁵But if you kill me, rest assured that you will be killing an innocent man! The responsibility for such a deed will lie on you, on this city, and on every person living in it. For it is absolutely true that the LORD sent me to speak every word you have heard."

¹⁶Then the officials and the people said to the priests and prophets, "This man does not deserve the death sentence, for he has spoken to us in the name of the LORD our God."

¹⁷Then some of the wise old men stood and spoke to the people there. ¹⁸They said, "Think back to the days when Micah of Moresheth prophesied during the reign of King Hezekiah of Judah. He told the people of Judah, 'This is what the LORD Almighty says: Mount Zion will be plowed like an open field; Jerusalem will be reduced to rubble! A great forest will grow on the hilltop, where the Temple now stands.'* ¹⁹But did King Hezekiah and the

See Josiah's profile (page 461) at 2 Kings 23:25.

I BELIEVE the Lord does not want anyone to perish, so he gives an opportunity for everyone to repent (2 Peter 3:9). (26:3)

I KEEP DOING exactly what the Lord commands, even when my life is threatened. (26:8)

I HEED the biblical examples of men and women who obeyed the Lord and proclaimed his Word (Micah 1:1; 3:12). (26:18)

See Hezekiah's profile (page 825) at Isaiah 37:1.

26:1 The first year of Jehoiakim's reign was 608 B.C. 26:18 Mic 3:12.

people kill him for saying this? No, they turned from their sins and worshiped the LORD. They begged him to have mercy on them. Then the LORD held back the terrible disaster he had pronounced against them. If we kill Jeremiah, who knows what will happen to us?"

²⁰(At this time, Uriah son of Shemaiah from Kiriath-jearim was also prophesying for the LORD. And he predicted the same terrible disaster against the city and nation as Jeremiah did. ²¹When King Jehoiakim and the army officers and officials heard what he was saying, the king sent someone to kill him. But Uriah heard about the plot and escaped to Egypt. ²²Then King Jehoiakim sent Elnathan son of Acbor to Egypt along with several other men to capture Uriah. ²³They took him prisoner and brought him back to King Jehoiakim. The king then killed Uriah with a sword and had him buried in an unmarked grave.)

²⁴Ahikam son of Shaphan also stood with Jeremiah and persuaded the court not to turn him over to the mob to be killed.

CHAPTER 27

Jeremiah Wears an Ox Yoke

This message came to Jeremiah from the LORD early in the reign of Zedekiah* son of Josiah, king of Judah.

²The LORD said to me, "Make a yoke, and fasten it on your neck with leather thongs. ³Then send messages to the kings of Edom, Moab, Ammon, Tyre, and Sidon through their ambassadors to King Zedekiah in Jerusalem. ⁴Give them this message for their masters: 'This is what the LORD Almighty, the God of Israel, says: ⁵By my great power I have made the earth and all its people and every animal. I can give these things of mine to anyone I choose. ⁶Now I will give your countries to King Nebuchadnezzar of Babylon, who is my servant. I have put everything, even the wild animals, under his control. ⁷All the nations will serve him and his son and his grandson until his time is up. But then many nations and great kings will conquer and rule over Babylon. ⁸So you must submit to Babylon's king and serve him; put your neck under Babylon's yoke! I will punish any nation that refuses to be his slave, says the LORD. I will send war, famine, and disease upon that nation until Babylon has conquered it.

⁹" 'Do not listen to your false prophets, fortune-tellers, interpreters of dreams, mediums, and sorcerers who say, "The king of Babylon will not conquer you." ¹⁰They are all liars, and I will drive you from your land and send you far away to die. ¹¹But the people of any nation that submits to the king of Babylon will be allowed to stay in their own country to farm the land as usual. I, the LORD, have spoken!' "

¹²Then I repeated this same message to King Zedekiah of Judah. "If you want to live, submit to the king of Babylon and his people," I said. ¹³"Why do you insist on dying—you and your people? Why should you choose war, famine, and disease, which the LORD will bring against every nation that refuses to submit to Babylon's king? ¹⁴Do not listen to the false prophets who keep telling you, 'The king of Babylon will not conquer you.' They are liars. ¹⁵This is what the LORD says: I have not sent these prophets! They are telling you lies in my name, so I will drive you from this land. You will all die—you and all these prophets, too."

¹⁶Then I spoke to the priests and the people and said, "This is what the LORD says: Do not listen to your prophets who claim that soon the gold utensils taken from my Temple will be returned from Babylon. It is all a lie! ¹⁷Do not listen to them. Surrender to the king of Babylon, and you will live. Why should this whole city be destroyed? ¹⁸If they really are the LORD's prophets,

---

I RECOGNIZE that godly individuals are not exempt from persecution (2 Timothy 3:12). (26:21)

I STAND UP for those who are on trial for obeying God. (26:24)

See Josiah's profile (page 461) at 2 Kings 23:25.

I DO exactly what the Lord commands. (27:2)

I BELIEVE the Lord Almighty is sovereign over the nations. (27:6)

See Nebuchadnezzar's profile (page 985) at Daniel 4:37.

I DO NOT LISTEN to those who rebel against the Lord and are involved in the occult. (27:9)

In response to these affirmations, tell the Lord what you believe—or find hard to believe.

27:1 As in some Hebrew manuscripts and Syriac version (see also 27:3, 12); most Hebrew manuscripts read *Jehoiakim.*

let them pray to the LORD Almighty about the gold utensils that are still left in the LORD's Temple and in the king's palace and in the palaces of Jerusalem. Let them pray that these remaining articles will not be carried away with you to Babylon!

[19]"For this is what the LORD Almighty says about the bronze pillars in front of the Temple, the bronze Sea in the Temple courtyard, the bronze water carts, and all the other ceremonial articles. [20]King Nebuchadnezzar of Babylon left them here when he exiled Jehoiachin* son of Jehoiakim, king of Judah, to Babylon, along with all the other important people of Judah and Jerusalem. [21]Yes, this is what the LORD Almighty, the God of Israel, says about the precious things kept in the Temple and in the palace of Judah's king: [22]They will all be carried away to Babylon and will stay there until I send for them, says the LORD. But someday I will bring them back to Jerusalem again."

CHAPTER 28

Jeremiah Condemns Hananiah

One day in late summer* of that same year—the fourth year of the reign of Zedekiah, king of Judah—Hananiah son of Azzur, a prophet from Gibeon, addressed me publicly in the Temple while all the priests and people listened. He said, [2]"The LORD Almighty, the God of Israel, says: I will remove the yoke of the king of Babylon from your necks. [3]Within two years, I will bring back all the Temple treasures that King Nebuchadnezzar carried off to Babylon. [4]And I will bring back Jehoiachin* son of Jehoiakim, king of Judah, and all the other captives that were taken to Babylon. I will surely break the yoke that the king of Babylon has put on your necks. I, the LORD, have spoken!"

[5]Jeremiah responded to Hananiah as they stood in front of all the priests and people at the Temple. [6]He said, "Amen! May your prophecies come true! I hope the LORD does everything you say. I hope he does bring back from Babylon the treasures of this Temple and all our loved ones. [7]But listen now to the solemn words I speak to you in the presence of all these people. [8]The ancient prophets who preceded you and me spoke against many nations, always warning of war, famine, and disease. [9]So a prophet who predicts peace must carry the burden of proof. Only when his predictions come true can it be known that he is really from the LORD."

[10]Then Hananiah the prophet took the yoke off Jeremiah's neck and broke it. [11]And Hananiah said again to the crowd that had gathered, "The LORD has promised that within two years he will break the yoke of oppression from all the nations now subject to King Nebuchadnezzar of Babylon." At that, Jeremiah left the Temple area.

[12]Soon afterward the LORD gave this message to Jeremiah: [13]"Go and tell Hananiah, 'This is what the LORD says: You have broken a wooden yoke, but you have replaced it with a yoke of iron. [14]The LORD Almighty, the God of Israel, says: I have put a yoke of iron on the necks of all these nations, forcing them into slavery under King Nebuchadnezzar of Babylon. I have put everything, even the wild animals, under his control.' "

[15]Then Jeremiah the prophet said to Hananiah, "Listen, Hananiah! The LORD has not sent you, but the people believe your lies. [16]Therefore, the LORD says you must die. Your life will end this very year because you have rebelled against the LORD."

[17]Two months later,* Hananiah died.

See Nebuchadnezzar's profile (page 985) at Daniel 4:37.

I DO NOT PRETEND to speak for the Lord. (28:4)

I HEED the words of the Lord through his Old Testament prophets. (28:8)

I REJECT the words of prophets whose predictions don't come true (Deuteronomy 18:20-22). (28:9)

27:20 Hebrew *Jeconiah*, a variant name for Jehoiachin. 28:1 Hebrew *In the fifth month*, of the Hebrew calendar. This month in the fourth year of Zedekiah's reign occurred in August and September 593 B.C. Also see note on 1:3. 28:4 Hebrew *Jeconiah*, a variant name for Jehoiachin. 28:17 Hebrew *In the seventh month of that same year*. See 28:1 and the note there.

CHAPTER 29

A Letter to the Exiles

Jeremiah wrote a letter from Jerusalem to the elders, priests, prophets, and all the people who had been exiled to Babylon by King Nebuchadnezzar. ²This was after King Jehoiachin,* the queen mother, the court officials, the leaders of Judah, and all the craftsmen had been deported from Jerusalem. ³He sent the letter with Elasah son of Shaphan and Gemariah son of Hilkiah, when they went to Babylon as King Zedekiah's ambassadors to Nebuchadnezzar. This is what Jeremiah's letter said:

⁴The LORD Almighty, the God of Israel, sends this message to all the captives he has exiled to Babylon from Jerusalem: ⁵"Build homes, and plan to stay. Plant gardens, and eat the food you produce. ⁶Marry, and have children. Then find spouses for them, and have many grandchildren. Multiply! Do not dwindle away! ⁷And work for the peace and prosperity of Babylon. Pray to the LORD for that city where you are held captive, for if Babylon has peace, so will you."

⁸The LORD Almighty, the God of Israel, says, "Do not let the prophets and mediums who are there in Babylon trick you. Do not listen to their dreams ⁹because they prophesy lies in my name. I have not sent them," says the LORD. ¹⁰"The truth is that you will be in Babylon for seventy years. But then I will come and do for you all the good things I have promised, and I will bring you home again. ¹¹For I know the plans I have for you," says the LORD. "They are plans for good and not for disaster, to give you a future and a hope. ¹²In those days when you pray, I will listen. ¹³If you look for me in earnest, you will find me when you seek me. ¹⁴I will be found by you," says the LORD. "I will end your captivity and restore your fortunes. I will gather you out of the nations where I sent you and bring you home again to your own land."

¹⁵You may claim that the LORD has raised up prophets for you in Babylon. ¹⁶But this is what the LORD says about the king who sits on David's throne and all those still living here in Jerusalem—your relatives who were not exiled to Babylon. ¹⁷This is what the LORD Almighty says: "I will send war, famine, and disease upon them and make them like rotting figs—too bad to eat. ¹⁸Yes, I will pursue them with war, famine, and disease, and I will scatter them around the world. In every nation where I send them, I will make them an object of damnation, horror, contempt, and mockery. ¹⁹For they refuse to listen to me, though I have spoken to them repeatedly through my prophets. And you who are in exile have not listened either," says the LORD.

²⁰Therefore, listen to this message from the LORD, all you captives there in Babylon. ²¹This is what the LORD Almighty, the God of Israel, says about your prophets—Ahab son of Kolaiah and Zedekiah son of Maaseiah—who are telling you lies in my name: "I will turn them over to Nebuchadnezzar* for a public execution. ²²Their terrible fate will become proverbial, so that whenever the Judean exiles want to curse someone they will say, 'May the LORD make you like Zedekiah and Ahab, whom the king of Babylon burned alive!' ²³For these men have done terrible things among my people. They have committed adultery with their neighbors' wives and have lied in my name. I am a witness to this," says the LORD.

A Message for Shemaiah

²⁴ The LORD sent this message to Shemaiah the Nehelamite in Babylon: ²⁵"This is what the LORD Almighty, the God of Israel, says: You wrote a letter

---

See Nebuchadnezzar's profile (page 985) at Daniel 4:37.

I WORK for the peace and prosperity of my nation, so that God will be glorified. (29:7)

I BELIEVE my future is in the Lord's hands. (29:11)

I REMEMBER that the punishment for false prophets was death (Deuteronomy 13:5; 18:20–22). (29:21)

I DO NOT COMMIT adultery or misuse the Lord's name (Exodus 20:7, 14). (29:23)

I DO NOT CONTRADICT God's Word by giving equal or greater authority to my own ideas. (29:25)

29:2 Hebrew *Jeconiah*, a variant name for Jehoiachin. 29:21 Hebrew *Nebuchadrezzar*, a variant name for Nebuchadnezzar.

on your own authority to Zephaniah son of Maaseiah, the priest, and you sent copies to the other priests and people in Jerusalem. You said to Zephaniah, ²⁶"The LORD has appointed you to replace Jehoiada as the priest in charge of the house of the LORD. You are responsible to put anyone who claims to be a prophet in the stocks and neck irons. ²⁷So why have you done nothing to stop Jeremiah from Anathoth, who pretends to be a prophet among you? ²⁸Jeremiah sent a letter here to Babylon, predicting that our captivity will be a long one. He said we should build homes and plan to stay for many years. He said we should plant fruit trees, because we will be here to eat the fruit for many years to come.' "

²⁹But when Zephaniah the priest received Shemaiah's letter, he took it to Jeremiah and read it to him. ³⁰Then the LORD gave this message to Jeremiah: ³¹"Send an open letter to all the exiles in Babylon. Tell them, 'This is what the LORD says concerning Shemaiah the Nehelamite: Since he has prophesied to you when I did not send him and has tricked you into believing his lies, ³²I will punish him and his family. None of his descendants will see the good things I will do for my people, for he has taught you to rebel against me. I, the LORD, have spoken!' "

I URGE others not to rebel against the Lord's commands. (29:32)

CHAPTER 30
Promises of Deliverance

The LORD gave another message to Jeremiah. He said, ²"This is what the LORD, the God of Israel, says: Write down for the record everything I have said to you, Jeremiah. ³For the time is coming when I will restore the fortunes of my people of Israel and Judah. I will bring them home to this land that I gave to their ancestors, and they will possess it and live here again. I, the LORD, have spoken!"

I BELIEVE everything the Lord has spoken. (30:3)

⁴This is the message the LORD gave concerning Israel and Judah. ⁵"This is what the LORD says: I have heard the people crying; there is only fear and trembling. ⁶Now let me ask you a question: Do men give birth to babies? Then why do they stand there, ashen-faced, hands pressed against their sides like women about to give birth? ⁷In all history there has never been such a time of terror. It will be a time of trouble for my people Israel.* Yet in the end, they will be saved!

⁸"For in that day, says the LORD Almighty, I will break the yoke from their necks and snap their chains. Foreigners will no longer be their masters. ⁹For my people will serve the LORD their God and David their king, whom I will raise up for them.

I SERVE the Lord Jesus Christ as my God and King (Luke 1:32). (30:9)

See David's profile (page 629) at Psalm 3:1.

I BELIEVE the Lord disciplines those he loves (Hebrews 12:5-6). (30:11)

¹⁰"So do not be afraid, Jacob, my servant; do not be dismayed, Israel, says the LORD. For I will bring you home again from distant lands, and your children will return from their exile. Israel will return and will have peace and quiet in their own land, and no one will make them afraid. ¹¹For I am with you and will save you, says the LORD. I will completely destroy the nations where I have scattered you, but I will not destroy you. But I must discipline you; I cannot let you go unpunished.

¹²"This is what the LORD says: Yours is an incurable bruise, a terrible wound. ¹³There is no one to help you or bind up your injury. You are beyond the help of any medicine. ¹⁴All your allies have left you and do not care about you anymore. I have wounded you cruelly, as though I were your enemy. For your sins are many, and your guilt is great. ¹⁵Why do you protest your punishment—this wound that has no cure? I have had to punish you because your sins are many and your guilt is great.

¹⁶"But in that coming day, all who destroy you will be destroyed, and all your enemies will be sent into exile. Those who plunder you will be plundered,

30:7 Hebrew *Jacob;* also in 30:10b.

and those who attack you will be attacked. [17]I will give you back your health and heal your wounds, says the LORD.

"Now you are called an outcast—'Jerusalem* for whom nobody cares.' [18]But the LORD says this: When I bring you home again from your captivity and restore your fortunes, Jerusalem will be rebuilt on her ruins. The palace will be reconstructed as it was before. [19]There will be joy and songs of thanksgiving, and I will multiply my people and make of them a great and honored nation. [20]Their children will prosper as they did long ago. I will establish them as a nation before me, and I will punish anyone who hurts them. [21]They will have their own ruler again, and he will not be a foreigner. I will invite him to approach me, says the LORD, for who would dare to come unless invited? [22]You will be my people, and I will be your God."

[23]Look! The LORD's anger bursts out like a storm, a driving wind that swirls down on the heads of the wicked. [24]The fierce anger of the LORD will not diminish until it has finished all his plans. In the days to come, you will understand all this.

CHAPTER 31

Hope for Restoration

"In that day," says the LORD, "I will be the God of all the families of Israel, and they will be my people. [2]I will care for the survivors as they travel through the wilderness. I will again come to give rest to the people of Israel."

[3]Long ago the LORD said to Israel: "I have loved you, my people, with an everlasting love. With unfailing love I have drawn you to myself. [4]I will rebuild you, my virgin Israel. You will again be happy and dance merrily with tambourines. [5]Again you will plant your vineyards on the mountains of Samaria and eat from your own gardens there. [6]The day will come when watchmen will shout from the hill country of Ephraim, 'Come, let us go up to Jerusalem* to worship the LORD our God.' "

[7]Now this is what the LORD says: "Sing with joy for Israel*! Shout for the greatest of nations! Shout out with praise and joy: 'Save your people, O LORD, the remnant of Israel!' [8]For I will bring them from the north and from the distant corners of the earth. I will not forget the blind and lame, the expectant mothers and women about to give birth. A great company will return! [9]Tears of joy will stream down their faces, and I will lead them home with great care. They will walk beside quiet streams and not stumble. For I am Israel's father, and Ephraim is my oldest child.

[10]"Listen to this message from the LORD, you nations of the world; proclaim it in distant coastlands: The LORD, who scattered his people, will gather them together and watch over them as a shepherd does his flock. [11]For the LORD has redeemed Israel from those too strong for them. [12]They will come home and sing songs of joy on the heights of Jerusalem. They will be radiant because of the many gifts the LORD has given them—the good crops of wheat, wine, and oil, and the healthy flocks and herds. Their life will be like a watered garden, and all their sorrows will be gone. [13]The young women will dance for joy, and the men—old and young—will join in the celebration. I will turn their mourning into joy. I will comfort them and exchange their sorrow for rejoicing. [14]I will supply the priests with an abundance of offerings. I will satisfy my people with my bounty. I, the LORD, have spoken!"

Rachel's Sadness Turns to Joy

[15]This is what the LORD says: "A cry of anguish is heard in Ramah—mourning and weeping unrestrained. Rachel weeps for her children, refusing to be comforted—for her children are dead."

[16]But now the LORD says, "Do not weep any longer, for I will reward you.

I BELIEVE the Lord alone can heal those mortally wounded by sin. (30:17)

I BELONG to the Lord my God. (30:22)

I AM SO THANKFUL the Lord has drawn me to himself with everlasting love (Romans 8:38–39). (31:3)

I AM THANKFUL the Lord has turned my mourning into joy. (31:13)

30:17 Hebrew *Zion.*   31:6 Hebrew *Zion;* also in 31:12.   31:7 Hebrew *Jacob;* also in 31:11.

Your children will come back to you from the distant land of the enemy. [17] There is hope for your future," says the LORD. "Your children will come again to their own land. [18] I have heard Israel* saying, 'You disciplined me severely, but I deserved it. I was like a calf that needed to be trained for the yoke and plow. Turn me again to you and restore me, for you alone are the LORD my God. [19] I turned away from God, but then I was sorry. I kicked myself for my stupidity! I was thoroughly ashamed of all I did in my younger days.'

[20] "Is not Israel still my son, my darling child?" asks the LORD. "I had to punish him, but I still love him. I long for him and surely will have mercy on him.

[21] "Set up road signs; put up guideposts. Mark well the path by which you came. Come back again, my virgin Israel; return to your cities here. [22] How long will you wander, my wayward daughter? For the LORD will cause something new and different to happen—Israel will embrace her God.*"

[23] This is what the LORD Almighty, the God of Israel, says: "When I bring them back again, the people of Judah and its cities will again say, 'The LORD bless you—O righteous home, O holy mountain!' [24] And city dwellers and farmers and shepherds alike will live together in peace and happiness. [25] For I have given rest to the weary and joy to the sorrowing."

[26] At this, I woke up and looked around. My sleep had been very sweet.

[27] "The time will come," says the LORD, "when I will greatly increase the population and multiply the number of cattle here in Israel and Judah. [28] In the past I uprooted and tore down this nation. I overthrew it, destroyed it, and brought disaster upon it. But in the future I will plant it and build it up," says the LORD.

[29] "The people will no longer quote this proverb: 'The parents eat sour grapes, but their children's mouths pucker at the taste.' [30] All people will die for their own sins—those who eat the sour grapes will be the ones whose mouths will pucker.

[31] "The day will come," says the LORD, "when I will make a new covenant with the people of Israel and Judah. [32] This covenant will not be like the one I made with their ancestors when I took them by the hand and brought them out of the land of Egypt. They broke that covenant, though I loved them as a husband loves his wife," says the LORD.

[33] "But this is the new covenant I will make with the people of Israel on that day," says the LORD. "I will put my laws in their minds, and I will write them on their hearts. I will be their God, and they will be my people. [34] And they will not need to teach their neighbors, nor will they need to teach their family, saying, 'You should know the LORD.' For everyone, from the least to the greatest, will already know me," says the LORD. "And I will forgive their wickedness and will never again remember their sins."

[35] It is the LORD who provides the sun to light the day and the moon and stars to light the night. It is he who stirs the sea into roaring waves. His name is the LORD Almighty, and this is what he says: [36] "I am as likely to reject my people Israel as I am to do away with the laws of nature! [37] Just as the heavens cannot be measured and the foundation of the earth cannot be explored, so I will not consider casting them away forever for their sins. I, the LORD, have spoken!

[38] "The time is coming," says the LORD, "when all Jerusalem will be rebuilt for me, from the Tower of Hananel to the Corner Gate. [39] A measuring line will be stretched out over the hill of Gareb and across to Goah. [40] And the entire area—including the graveyard and ash dump in the valley, and all the fields out to the Kidron Valley on the east as far as the Horse Gate—will be holy to the LORD. The city will never again be captured or destroyed."

31:18 Hebrew *Ephraim*, referring to the northern kingdom of Israel; also in 31:20.   31:22 Hebrew *a woman will court a suitor.*

Sidebar annotations:

I HAVE TURNED BACK to the Lord and told him I'm sorry for the sins of my youth. (31:19)

I BELIEVE the Lord disciplines those he loves (Hebrews 12:5-6). (31:20)

I BELIEVE the Lord holds each person accountable for his or her own sin. (31:30)

I AM THANKFUL the Lord has forgiven my wickedness and will never again remember my sins (Hebrews 10:17). (31:34)

I BELIEVE the Lord will not reject his people Israel forever (Romans 11:1). (31:36)

I BELIEVE the new Jerusalem will never be destroyed (Revelation 21:2). (31:40)

CHAPTER 32

Jeremiah's Land Purchase

The following message came to Jeremiah from the LORD in the tenth year of the reign of Zedekiah,* king of Judah. This was also the eighteenth year of the reign of King Nebuchadnezzar.* ²Jerusalem was under siege from the Babylonian army, and Jeremiah was imprisoned in the courtyard of the guard in the royal palace. ³King Zedekiah had put him there because he continued to give this prophecy: "This is what the LORD says: I am about to hand this city over to the king of Babylon. ⁴King Zedekiah will be captured by the Babylonians* and taken to the king of Babylon to be judged and sentenced. ⁵I will take Zedekiah to Babylon and will deal with him there. If you fight against the Babylonians, you will never succeed."

⁶At that time the LORD sent me a message. He said, ⁷"Your cousin Hanamel son of Shallum will come and say to you, 'Buy my field at Anathoth. By law you have the right to buy it before it is offered to anyone else.' "

⁸Then, just as the LORD had said he would, Hanamel came and visited me in the prison. He said, "Buy my field at Anathoth in the land of Benjamin. By law you have the right to buy it before it is offered to anyone else, so buy it for yourself." Then I knew for sure that the message I had heard was from the LORD.

⁹So I bought the field at Anathoth, paying Hanamel seventeen pieces* of silver for it. ¹⁰I signed and sealed the deed of purchase before witnesses, weighed out the silver, and paid him. ¹¹Then I took the sealed deed and an unsealed copy of the deed, which contained the terms and conditions of the purchase, ¹²and I handed them to Baruch son of Neriah and grandson of Mahseiah. I did all this in the presence of my cousin Hanamel, the witnesses who had signed the deed, and all the men of Judah who were there.

¹³Then I said to Baruch as they all listened, ¹⁴"The LORD Almighty, the God of Israel, says: Take both this sealed deed and the unsealed copy, and put them into a pottery jar to preserve them for a long time. ¹⁵For the LORD Almighty, the God of Israel, says: Someday people will again own property here in this land and will buy and sell houses and vineyards and fields."

Jeremiah's Prayer

¹⁶Then after I had given the papers to Baruch, I prayed to the LORD: ¹⁷"O Sovereign LORD! You have made the heavens and earth by your great power. Nothing is too hard for you! ¹⁸You are loving and kind to thousands, though children suffer for their parents' sins. You are the great and powerful God, the LORD Almighty. ¹⁹You have all wisdom and do great and mighty miracles. You are very aware of the conduct of all people, and you reward them according to their deeds. ²⁰You performed miraculous signs and wonders in the land of Egypt—things still remembered to this day! And you have continued to do great miracles in Israel and all around the world. You have made your name very great, as it is today.

²¹"You brought Israel out of Egypt with mighty signs and wonders, with great power and overwhelming terror. ²²You gave the people of Israel this land that you had promised their ancestors long before—a land flowing with milk and honey. ²³Our ancestors came and conquered it and lived in it, but they refused to obey you or follow your law. They have hardly done one thing you told them to! That is why you have sent this terrible disaster upon them.

²⁴"See how the siege ramps have been built against the city walls! Because of war, famine, and disease, the city has been handed over to the Babylonians, who will conquer it. Everything has happened just as you said it

---

See Nebuchadnezzar's profile (page 985) at Daniel 4:37.

I RECOGNIZE that godly individuals are not exempt from persecution (2 Timothy 3:12). (32:2)

I DO whatever the Lord commands. (32:9)

I BELIEVE nothing is too hard for the Lord, who made the heavens and the earth by his great power. (32:17)

I BELIEVE the Lord is loving and kind to those who trust him and obey what he commands. (32:18)

I BELIEVE the Lord knows the conduct of all people and rewards each person according to his or her deeds (Romans 2:6). (32:19)

I BELIEVE the Lord himself delivered the Israelites from Egypt with a great display of power. (32:21)

32:1a The tenth year of Zedekiah's reign and the eighteenth year of Nebuchadnezzar's reign was 587 B.C.
32:1b Hebrew *Nebuchadrezzar*, a variant name for Nebuchadnezzar; also in 32:28.   32:4 Or *Chaldeans*; also in
32:5, 24, 25, 28, 29, 43.   32:9 Hebrew *17 shekels*, about 7 ounces or 194 grams in weight.

I DO whatever the Lord commands, even if it doesn't seem to make sense in my particular situation. (32:25)

I BELIEVE the Lord is the God of all the peoples of the world. (32:27)

I ABHOR idolatry and child sacrifice. (32:35)

I LONG for my family and descendants to worship the Lord forever. (32:39)

would. ²⁵And yet, O Sovereign LORD, you have told me to buy the field—paying good money for it before these witnesses—even though the city will soon belong to the Babylonians."

A Prediction of Jerusalem's Fall

²⁶Then this message came to Jeremiah from the LORD: ²⁷"I am the LORD, the God of all the peoples of the world. Is anything too hard for me? ²⁸I will hand this city over to the Babylonians and to Nebuchadnezzar, king of Babylon, and he will capture it. ²⁹The Babylonians outside the walls will come in and set fire to the city. They will burn down all these houses, where the people caused my fury to rise by offering incense to Baal on the rooftops and by pouring out drink offerings to other gods. ³⁰Israel and Judah have done nothing but wrong since their earliest days. They have infuriated me with all their evil deeds," says the LORD. ³¹"From the time this city was built until now, it has done nothing but anger me, so I am determined to get rid of it.

³²"The sins of Israel and Judah—the sins of the people of Jerusalem, the kings, the officials, the priests, and the prophets—stir up my anger. ³³My people have turned their backs on me and have refused to return. Day after day, year after year, I taught them right from wrong, but they would not listen or obey. ³⁴They have set up their abominable idols right in my own Temple, defiling it. ³⁵They have built pagan shrines to Baal in the valley of the son of Hinnom, and there they sacrifice their sons and daughters to Molech. I have never commanded such a horrible deed; it never even crossed my mind to command such a thing. What an incredible evil, causing Judah to sin so greatly!

A Promise of Restoration

³⁶"Now I want to say something more about this city. You have been saying, 'It will fall to the king of Babylon through war, famine, and disease.' But this is what the LORD, the God of Israel, says: ³⁷I will surely bring my people back again from all the countries where I will scatter them in my fury. I will bring them back to this very city and let them live in peace and safety. ³⁸They will be my people, and I will be their God. ³⁹And I will give them one heart and mind to worship me forever, for their own good and for the good of all their descendants.

⁴⁰"And I will make an everlasting covenant with them, promising not to stop doing good for them. I will put a desire in their hearts to worship me, and they will never leave me. ⁴¹I will rejoice in doing good to them and will faithfully and wholeheartedly replant them in this land. ⁴²Just as I have sent all these calamities upon them, so I will do all the good I have promised them. I, the LORD, have spoken!

⁴³"Fields will again be bought and sold in this land about which you now say, 'It has been ravaged by the Babylonians, a land where people and animals have all disappeared.' ⁴⁴Yes, fields will once again be bought and sold—deeds signed and sealed and witnessed—in the land of Benjamin and here in Jerusalem, in the towns of Judah and in the hill country, in the foothills of Judah* and in the Negev, too. For someday I will restore prosperity to them. I, the LORD, have spoken!"

CHAPTER 33

Promises of Peace and Prosperity

While Jeremiah was still confined in the courtyard of the guard, the LORD gave him this second message: ²"The LORD, the Maker of the heavens and earth—the LORD is his name—says this: ³Ask me and I will tell you some remarkable secrets about what is going to happen here. ⁴For this is what the

32:44 Hebrew *the Shephelah.*

LORD, the God of Israel, says: Though you have torn down the houses of this city and even the king's palace to get materials to strengthen the walls against the siege weapons of the enemy, [5]the Babylonians* will still enter. The men of this city are already as good as dead, for I have determined to destroy them in my terrible anger. I have abandoned them because of all their wickedness.

[6]"Nevertheless, the time will come when I will heal Jerusalem's damage and give her prosperity and peace. [7]I will restore the fortunes of Judah and Israel and rebuild their cities. [8]I will cleanse away their sins against me, and I will forgive all their sins of rebellion. [9]Then this city will bring me joy, glory, and honor before all the nations of the earth! The people of the world will see the good I do for my people and will tremble with awe!

[10]"This is what the LORD says: You say, 'This land has been ravaged, and the people and animals have all disappeared.' Yet in the empty streets of Jerusalem and Judah's other towns, there will be heard once more [11]the sounds of joy and laughter. The joyful voices of bridegrooms and brides will be heard again, along with the joyous songs of people bringing thanksgiving offerings to the LORD. They will sing,

'Give thanks to the LORD Almighty, for the LORD is good.
His faithful love endures forever!'

For I will restore the prosperity of this land to what it was in the past, says the LORD.

[12]"This is what the LORD Almighty says: This land—though it is now desolate and the people and animals have all disappeared—will once more see shepherds leading sheep and lambs. [13]Once again their flocks will prosper in the towns of the hill country, the foothills of Judah,* the Negev, the land of Benjamin, the vicinity of Jerusalem, and all the towns of Judah. I, the LORD, have spoken!

[14]"The day will come, says the LORD, when I will do for Israel and Judah all the good I have promised them. [15]At that time I will bring to the throne of David a righteous descendant,* and he will do what is just and right throughout the land. [16]In that day Judah will be saved, and Jerusalem will live in safety. And their motto will be 'The LORD is our righteousness!' [17]For this is what the LORD says: David will forever have a descendant sitting on the throne of Israel. [18]And there will always be Levitical priests to offer burnt offerings and grain offerings and sacrifices to me."

[19]Then this message came to Jeremiah from the LORD: [20]"If you can break my covenant with the day and the night so that they do not come on their usual schedule, [21]only then will my covenant with David, my servant, be broken. Only then will he no longer have a descendant to reign on his throne. The same is true for my covenant with the Levitical priests who minister before me. [22]And as the stars cannot be counted and the sand on the seashores cannot be measured, so I will multiply the descendants of David, my servant, and the Levites who minister before me."

[23]The LORD gave another message to Jeremiah. He said, [24]"Have you heard what people are saying?—'The LORD chose Judah and Israel and then abandoned them!' They are sneering and saying that Israel is not worthy to be counted as a nation. [25]But this is the LORD's reply: I would no more reject my people than I would change my laws of night and day, of earth and sky. [26]I will never abandon the descendants of Jacob or David, my servant, or change the plan that David's descendants will rule the descendants of Abraham, Isaac, and Jacob. Instead, I will restore them to their land and have mercy on them."

I BELIEVE that after many decades the Lord kept his promise to bring the people of Israel back to their own land. (33:6)

I THANK the Lord that he has washed away my sins and forgiven my rebellion. (33:8)

I WILL HONOR the Lord Jesus Christ as my righteous King forever (Luke 1:32-33). (33:15)

See David's profile (page 629) at Psalm 3:1.

I BELIEVE the Lord always will keep his covenant promises. (33:21)

I AM THANKFUL the Lord will never abandon me (Hebrews 13:5-6). (33:25)

See the profiles for Abraham (page 19), Isaac (page 31), and Jacob (page 43) at Genesis 15:6, Genesis 25:19, and Genesis 32:9.

33:5 Or *Chaldeans.*   33:13 Hebrew *the Shephelah.*   33:15 Hebrew *a righteous Branch.*

CHAPTER 34

A Warning for Zedekiah

See Nebuchadnezzar's profile (page 985) at Daniel 4:37.

I DO whatever the Lord commands. (34:2)

I BELIEVE the Lord's unconditional promises always come true. (34:4)

King Nebuchadnezzar of Babylon came with all the armies from the kingdoms he ruled, and he fought against Jerusalem and the towns of Judah. At that time this message came to Jeremiah from the LORD: ²"Go to King Zedekiah of Judah, and tell him, 'This is what the LORD, the God of Israel, says: I am about to hand this city over to the king of Babylon, and he will burn it. ³You will not escape his grasp but will be taken into captivity. You will stand before the king of Babylon to be judged and sentenced. Then you will be exiled to Babylon.'

⁴"But listen to this promise from the LORD, O Zedekiah, king of Judah. This is what the LORD says: 'You will not be killed in war ⁵but will die peacefully among your people. They will burn incense in your memory, just as they did for your ancestors. They will weep for you and say, "Alas, our king is dead!" This I have decreed, says the LORD.' "

⁶So Jeremiah the prophet delivered the message to King Zedekiah of Judah. ⁷At this time the Babylonian army was besieging Jerusalem, Lachish, and Azekah—the only cities of Judah with their walls still standing.

Freedom for Hebrew Slaves

⁸This message came to Jeremiah from the LORD after King Zedekiah made a covenant with the people, proclaiming freedom for the slaves. ⁹He had ordered all the people to free their Hebrew slaves—both men and women. No one was to keep a fellow Judean in bondage. ¹⁰The officials and all the people had obeyed the king's command, ¹¹but later they changed their minds. They took back the people they had freed, making them slaves again.

I DO NOT MAKE a vow to obey the Lord and then change my mind. (34:11)

I BELIEVE the Lord opposes slavery. (34:13)

¹²So the LORD gave them this message through Jeremiah: ¹³"This is what the LORD, the God of Israel, says: I made a covenant with your ancestors long ago when I rescued them from their slavery in Egypt. ¹⁴I told them that every Hebrew slave must be freed after serving six years. But this was never done. ¹⁵Recently you repented and did what was right, following my command. You freed your slaves and made a solemn covenant with me in my Temple. ¹⁶But now you have shrugged off your oath and defiled my name by taking back the men and women you had freed, making them slaves once again.

I OBEY the Lord's commands, no matter how costly they may be. (34:17)

¹⁷"Therefore, this is what the LORD says: Since you have not obeyed me by setting your countrymen free, I will set you free to be destroyed by war, famine, and disease. You will be considered a disgrace by all the nations of the earth. ¹⁸Because you have refused the terms of our covenant, I will cut you apart just as you cut apart the calf when you walked between its halves to solemnize your vows. ¹⁹Yes, I will cut you apart, whether you are officials of Judah or Jerusalem, court officials, priests, or common people—for you have broken your oath. ²⁰I will give you to your enemies, and they will kill you. Your bodies will be food for the vultures and wild animals. ²¹I will hand over King Zedekiah of Judah and his officials to the army of the king of Babylon. And though Babylon's king has left this city for a while, ²²I will call the Babylonian armies back again. They will fight against this city and will capture and burn it. I will see to it that all the towns of Judah are destroyed and left completely empty."

CHAPTER 35

The Faithful Recabites

See Josiah's profile (page 461) at 2 Kings 23:25.

I DO whatever the Lord commands. (35:2)

This is the message the LORD gave Jeremiah when Jehoiakim son of Josiah was king of Judah: ²"Go to the settlement where the families of the Recabites live, and invite them to the LORD's Temple. Take them into one of the inner rooms, and offer them some wine."

³So I went to see Jaazaniah son of Jeremiah and grandson of Habazziniah and all his brothers and sons—representing all the Recabite families. ⁴I took them to the Temple, and we went into the room assigned to the sons of

Hanan son of Igdaliah, a man of God. This room was located next to the one used by the palace officials, directly above the room of Maaseiah son of Shallum, the Temple gatekeeper. ⁵I set cups and jugs of wine before them and invited them to have a drink, ⁶but they refused. "No," they said. "We don't drink wine, because Jehonadab* son of Recab, our ancestor, gave us this command: 'You and your descendants must never drink wine. ⁷And do not build houses or plant crops or vineyards, but always live in tents. If you follow these commands, you will live long, good lives in the land.' ⁸So we have obeyed him in all these things. We have never had a drink of wine since then, nor have our wives, our sons, or our daughters. ⁹We haven't built houses or owned vineyards or farms or planted crops. ¹⁰We have lived in tents and have fully obeyed all the commands of Jehonadab, our ancestor. ¹¹But when King Nebuchadnezzar* of Babylon arrived in this country, we were afraid of the Babylonian* and Aramean armies. So we decided to move to Jerusalem. That is why we are here."

I REFUSE to compromise my family's integrity. (35:8)

See Nebuchadnezzar's profile (page 985) at Daniel 4:37.

¹²Then the LORD gave this message to Jeremiah: ¹³"The LORD Almighty, the God of Israel, says: Go and say to the people in Judah and Jerusalem, 'Come and learn a lesson about how to obey me. ¹⁴The Recabites do not drink wine because their ancestor Jehonadab told them not to. But I have spoken to you again and again, and you refuse to listen or obey. ¹⁵I have sent you prophet after prophet to tell you to turn from your wicked ways and to stop worshiping other gods, so that you might live in peace here in the land I gave to you and your ancestors. But you would not listen to me or obey. ¹⁶The families of Recab have obeyed their ancestor completely, but you have refused to listen to me.'

I OBEY the Lord completely in everything. (35:16)

¹⁷"Therefore, the LORD God Almighty, the God of Israel, says: Because you refuse to listen or answer when I call, I will send upon Judah and Jerusalem all the disasters I have threatened."

LIKE JEHONADAB   *I refuse to compromise my integrity.*
Jeremiah 35:19

Jehonadab son of Recab must have been either one incredibly great leader or one extremely domineering dad. At Jehonadab's directive, an entire family agreed to become a clan of teetotaling nomads.

Years later, Jeremiah invited the Recabites not to taste wine but to test their convictions. Without flinching, they remained true—and received a lasting reward from God. They also became examples of fidelity for believers down through the ages.

In the New Testament, we're told that drinking wine or eating meat is not a big deal. What matters to God is that we listen to him, trust him wholeheartedly, hold fast to what we know is true, and not violate our conscience (Romans 14:17-18, 23).

Like Jehonadab and his clan, may we never lose sight of what matters to God.

○ *Today's Scripture reading is Jeremiah 33–35.*

---

¹⁸Then Jeremiah turned to the Recabites and said, "This is what the LORD Almighty, the God of Israel, says: You have obeyed your ancestor Jehonadab in every respect, following all his instructions. ¹⁹Because of this, Jehonadab son of Recab will always have descendants who serve me. I, the LORD Almighty, the God of Israel, have spoken!"

I DESIRE to always have descendants who serve the Lord. (35:19)

CHAPTER 36

Baruch Reads the LORD's Messages
During the fourth year that Jehoiakim son of Josiah was king in Judah,* the LORD gave this message to Jeremiah: ²"Get a scroll, and write down all my

I BELIEVE the Holy Spirit moved Jeremiah to write down each of the Lord's messages against Israel and the other nations. (36:2)

35:6 Hebrew *Jonadab,* a variant name for Jehonadab; also in 35:10, 14, 18, 19. See 2 Kgs 10:15.   35:11a Hebrew *Nebuchadrezzar,* a variant name for Nebuchadnezzar.   35:11b Or *Chaldean.*   36:1 The fourth year of Jehoiakim's reign was 605 B.C.

See Josiah's profile (page 461) at 2 Kings 23:25.

messages against Israel, Judah, and the other nations. Begin with the first message back in the days of Josiah, and write down every message you have given, right up to the present time. ³Perhaps the people of Judah will repent if they see in writing all the terrible things I have planned for them. Then I will be able to forgive their sins and wrongdoings."

⁴So Jeremiah sent for Baruch son of Neriah, and as Jeremiah dictated, Baruch wrote down all the prophecies that the LORD had given him. ⁵Then Jeremiah said to Baruch, "I am a prisoner here and unable to go to the Temple. ⁶So you go to the Temple on the next day of fasting, and read the messages from the LORD that are on this scroll. On that day people will be there from all over Judah. ⁷Perhaps even yet they will turn from their evil ways and ask the LORD's forgiveness before it is too late. For the LORD's terrible anger has been pronounced against them."

⁸Baruch did as Jeremiah told him and read these messages from the LORD to the people at the Temple. ⁹This happened on the day of sacred fasting held in late autumn,* during the fifth year of the reign of Jehoiakim son of Josiah. People from all over Judah came to attend the services at the Temple on that day. ¹⁰Baruch read Jeremiah's words to all the people from the Temple room of Gemariah son of Shaphan. This room was just off the upper courtyard of the Temple, near the New Gate entrance.

I PROCLAIM God's Word to others. (36:10)

¹¹When Micaiah son of Gemariah and grandson of Shaphan heard the messages from the LORD, ¹²he went down to the secretary's room in the palace where the administrative officials were meeting. Elishama the secretary was there, along with Delaiah son of Shemaiah, Elnathan son of Acbor, Gemariah son of Shaphan, Zedekiah son of Hananiah, and all the others with official responsibilities. ¹³When Micaiah told them about the messages Baruch was reading to the people, ¹⁴the officials sent Jehudi son of Nethaniah, grandson of Shelemiah, and great-grandson of Cushi, to ask Baruch to come and read the messages to them, too. So Baruch took the scroll and went to them. ¹⁵"Sit down and read the scroll to us," the officials said, and Baruch did as they requested.

I TAKE God's Word very seriously. (36:16)

¹⁶By the time Baruch had finished reading, they were badly frightened. "We must tell the king what we have heard," they said. ¹⁷"But first, tell us how you got these messages. Did they come directly from Jeremiah?"

¹⁸So Baruch explained, "Jeremiah dictated them to me word by word, and I wrote down his words with ink on this scroll."

¹⁹"You and Jeremiah should both hide," the officials told Baruch. "Don't tell anyone where you are!" ²⁰Then the officials left the scroll for safekeeping in the room of Elishama the secretary and went to tell the king.

King Jehoiakim Burns the Scroll

I DO NOT DISREGARD, despise, or destroy God's written Word. (36:23)

²¹The king sent Jehudi to get the scroll. Jehudi brought it from Elishama's room and read it to the king as all his officials stood by. ²²It was late autumn, and the king was in a winterized part of the palace, sitting in front of a fire to keep warm. ²³Whenever Jehudi finished reading three or four columns, the king took his knife and cut off that section of the scroll. He then threw it into the fire, section by section, until the whole scroll was burned up. ²⁴Neither the king nor his officials showed any signs of fear or repentance at what they heard. ²⁵Even when Elnathan, Delaiah, and Gemariah begged the king not to burn the scroll, he wouldn't listen.

I TRY to protect God's written Word from destruction. (36:25)

I BELIEVE the Holy Spirit moved Jeremiah to once again write down (as dictated to Baruch) all the Lord's messages. (36:28)

²⁶Then the king commanded his son Jerahmeel, Seraiah son of Azriel, and Shelemiah son of Abdeel to arrest Baruch and Jeremiah. But the LORD had hidden them.

Jeremiah Rewrites the Scroll

²⁷After the king had burned Jeremiah's scroll, the LORD gave Jeremiah another message. He said, ²⁸"Get another scroll, and write everything again just as you

36:9 Hebrew *in the ninth month*, of the Hebrew calendar (also in 36:22). This month in the fifth year of Jehoiakim's reign occurred in November and December 604 B.C. Also see note on 1:3.

did on the scroll King Jehoiakim burned. [29]Then say to the king, 'This is what the LORD says: You burned the scroll because it said the king of Babylon would destroy this land and everything in it. [30]Now this is what the LORD says about King Jehoiakim of Judah: He will have no heirs to sit on the throne of David. His dead body will be thrown out to lie unburied—exposed to hot days and frosty nights. [31]I will punish him and his family and his officials because of their sins. I will pour out on them and on all the people of Judah and Jerusalem all the disasters I have promised, for they would not listen to my warnings.' "

[32]Then Jeremiah took another scroll and dictated again to his secretary Baruch. He wrote everything that had been on the scroll King Jehoiakim had burned in the fire. Only this time, he added much more!

CHAPTER 37

Zedekiah Calls for Jeremiah

Zedekiah son of Josiah succeeded Jehoiachin* son of Jehoiakim as the king of Judah. He was appointed by King Nebuchadnezzar* of Babylon. [2]But neither King Zedekiah nor his officials nor the people who were left in the land listened to what the LORD said through Jeremiah. [3]Nevertheless, King Zedekiah sent Jehucal son of Shelemiah and Zephaniah the priest, son of Maaseiah, to ask Jeremiah, "Please pray to the LORD our God for us." [4]Jeremiah had not yet been imprisoned, so he could come and go as he pleased.

[5]At this time the army of Pharaoh Hophra* of Egypt appeared at the southern border of Judah. When the Babylonian* army heard about it, they withdrew from their siege of Jerusalem. [6]Then the LORD gave this message to Jeremiah: [7]"This is what the LORD, the God of Israel, says: Tell the king of Judah, who sent you to ask me what is going to happen, that Pharaoh's army is about to return to Egypt, though he came here to help you. [8]Then the Babylonians* will come back and capture this city and burn it to the ground. [9]The LORD says: Do not fool yourselves that the Babylonians are gone for good. They aren't! [10]Even if you were to destroy the entire Babylonian army, leaving only a handful of wounded survivors, they would still stagger from their tents and burn this city to the ground!"

Jeremiah Is Imprisoned

[11]When the Babylonian army left Jerusalem because of Pharaoh's approaching army, [12]Jeremiah started to leave the city on his way to the land of Benjamin, to see the property he had bought. [13]But as he was walking through the Benjamin Gate, a sentry arrested him and said, "You are defecting to the Babylonians!" The sentry making the arrest was Irijah son of Shelemiah and grandson of Hananiah.

[14]"That's not true!" Jeremiah protested. "I had no intention of doing any such thing." But Irijah wouldn't listen, and he took Jeremiah before the officials. [15]They were furious with Jeremiah and had him flogged and imprisoned in the house of Jonathan the secretary. Jonathan's house had been converted into a prison. [16]Jeremiah was put into a dungeon cell, where he remained for many days.

[17]Later King Zedekiah secretly requested that Jeremiah come to the palace, where the king asked him, "Do you have any messages from the LORD?"

"Yes, I do!" said Jeremiah. "You will be defeated by the king of Babylon."

[18]Then Jeremiah asked the king, "What crime have I committed? What have I done against you, your officials, or the people that I should be imprisoned like this? [19]Where are your prophets now who told you the king of Babylon

See David's profile (page 629) at Psalm 3:1.

See the profiles for Josiah (page 461) and Nebuchadnezzar (page 985) at 2 Kings 23:25 and Daniel 4:37.

I DO NOT REBEL against the Lord and then ask someone who is godly to pray for me. (37:3)

I BELIEVE the Lord is sovereign over all the nations and that what he says will happen. (37:7)

I DO NOT JUDGE someone else's motives, let alone falsely accuse him or her of wrongdoing. (37:13)

I RECOGNIZE that godly individuals are not exempt from persecution (2 Timothy 3:12). (37:15)

I DO NOT TWIST God's Word for any reason. (37:17)

37:1a Hebrew *Coniah*, a variant name for Jehoiachin.　37:1b Hebrew *Nebuchadrezzar*, a variant name for Nebuchadnezzar.　37:5a Hebrew *army of Pharaoh*; see 44:30.　37:5b Or *Chaldean*; also in 37:10, 11.　37:8 Or *Chaldeans*; also in 37:9, 13.

would not attack you? [20]Listen, my lord the king, I beg you. Don't send me back to the dungeon in the house of Jonathan the secretary, for I will die there."

[21]So King Zedekiah commanded that Jeremiah not be returned to the dungeon. Instead, he was imprisoned in the courtyard of the guard in the royal palace. The king also commanded that Jeremiah be given a loaf of fresh bread every day as long as there was any left in the city. So Jeremiah was put in the palace prison.

CHAPTER 38

Jeremiah in a Cistern

Now Shephatiah son of Mattan, Gedaliah son of Pashhur, Jehucal* son of Shelemiah, and Pashhur son of Malkijah heard what Jeremiah had been telling the people. He was saying, [2]"This is what the LORD says: Everyone who stays in Jerusalem will die from war, famine, or disease, but those who surrender to the Babylonians* will live. [3]The LORD also says: The city of Jerusalem will surely be handed over to the army of the king of Babylon, who will capture it."

[4]So these officials went to the king and said, "Sir, this man must die! That kind of talk will undermine the morale of the few fighting men we have left, as well as that of all the people, too. This man is a traitor!"

[5]So King Zedekiah agreed. "All right," he said. "Do as you like. I will do nothing to stop you."

[6]So the officials took Jeremiah from his cell and lowered him by ropes into an empty cistern in the prison yard. It belonged to Malkijah, a member of the royal family. There was no water in the cistern, but there was a thick layer of mud at the bottom, and Jeremiah sank down into it.

[7]But Ebed-melech the Ethiopian,* an important palace official, heard that Jeremiah was in the cistern. At that time the king was holding court at the Benjamin Gate, [8]so Ebed-melech rushed from the palace to speak with him. [9]"My lord the king," he said, "these men have done a very evil thing in putting Jeremiah the prophet into the cistern. He will soon die of hunger, for almost all the bread in the city is gone."

[10]So the king told Ebed-melech, "Take along thirty of my men, and pull Jeremiah out of the cistern before he dies."

[11]So Ebed-melech took the men with him and went to a room in the palace beneath the treasury, where he found some old rags and discarded clothing. He carried these to the cistern and lowered them to Jeremiah on a rope. [12]Ebed-melech called down to Jeremiah, "Put these rags under your armpits to protect you from the ropes." Then when Jeremiah was ready, [13]they pulled him out. So Jeremiah was returned to the courtyard of the guard—the palace prison—where he remained.

Zedekiah Questions Jeremiah

[14]One day King Zedekiah sent for Jeremiah to meet him at the third entrance of the LORD's Temple. "I want to ask you something," the king said. "And don't try to hide the truth."

[15]Jeremiah said, "If I tell you the truth, you will kill me. And if I give you advice, you won't listen to me anyway."

[16]So King Zedekiah secretly promised him, "As surely as the LORD our Creator lives, I will not kill you or hand you over to the men who want you dead."

[17]Then Jeremiah said to Zedekiah, "The LORD God Almighty, the God of Israel, says: If you surrender to Babylon, you and your family will live, and the city will not be burned. [18]But if you refuse to surrender, you will not escape!

I WOULD NOT CONTRADICT God's Word even if my life were threatened. (38:3)

I RECOGNIZE that godly individuals are not exempt from persecution (2 Timothy 3:12). (38:6)

I DO whatever I can to help those who are being wrongly persecuted. (38:9)

I KNOW I cannot make someone else accept God's truth. (38:15)

38:1 Hebrew *Jucal*, a variant name for Jehucal; see 37:3. 38:2 Or *Chaldeans*; also in 38:18, 19, 23. 38:7 Hebrew *the Cushite*.

This city will be handed over to the Babylonians, and they will burn it to the ground."

¹⁹"But I am afraid to surrender," the king said, "for the Babylonians will hand me over to the Judeans who have defected to them. And who knows what they will do to me?"

²⁰Jeremiah replied, "You won't be handed over to them if you choose to obey the LORD. Your life will be spared, and all will go well for you. ²¹But if you refuse to surrender, this is what the LORD has revealed to me: ²²All the women left in your palace will be brought out and given to the officers of the Babylonian army. Then the women will taunt you, saying, 'What fine friends you have! They have betrayed and misled you. When your feet sank in the mud, they left you to your fate!' ²³All your wives and children will be led out to the Babylonians, and you will not escape. You will be seized by the king of Babylon, and this city will be burned."

²⁴Then Zedekiah said to Jeremiah, "Don't tell anyone you told me this, or you will die! ²⁵My officials may hear that I spoke to you. Then they may say to you, 'Tell us what you and the king were talking about. If you don't tell us, we will kill you.' ²⁶If this happens, just tell them you begged me not to send you back to Jonathan's dungeon, for fear you would die there."

²⁷Sure enough, it wasn't long before the king's officials came to Jeremiah and asked him why the king had called for him. But Jeremiah followed the king's instructions, and they left without finding out the truth. No one had overheard the conversation between Jeremiah and the king. ²⁸And Jeremiah remained a prisoner in the courtyard of the guard until the day Jerusalem was captured.

> I AM NOT OBLIGATED to tell the whole truth to evil, murderous men. (38:27)

CHAPTER 39

The Fall of Jerusalem

It was in January* during the ninth year of King Zedekiah's reign that King Nebuchadnezzar* and his army returned to besiege Jerusalem. ²Two and a half years later, on July 18,* the Babylonians broke through the wall, and the city fell. ³All the officers of the Babylonian army came in and sat in triumph at the Middle Gate: Nergal-sharezer of Samgar, and Nebo-sarsekim,* a chief officer, and Nergal-sharezer, the king's adviser, and many others.

> See Nebuchadnezzar's profile (page 985) at Daniel 4:37.

> I BELIEVE the people of Judah were utterly defeated by the Babylonians just as the Lord said. (39:2)

⁴King Zedekiah and his royal guard saw the Babylonians in the city gate, so they fled when the darkness of night arrived. They went out through a gate between the two walls behind the king's garden and headed toward the Jordan Valley.* ⁵But the Babylonians* chased the king and caught him on the plains of Jericho. They took him to King Nebuchadnezzar of Babylon, who was at Riblah in the land of Hamath. There the king of Babylon pronounced judgment upon Zedekiah. ⁶He made Zedekiah watch as they killed his sons and all the nobles of Judah. ⁷Then he gouged out Zedekiah's eyes, bound him in chains, and sent him away to exile in Babylon.

> I BELIEVE King Zedekiah died in exile yet never saw Babylon, just as the Lord said (Ezekiel 12:13). (39:7)

⁸Meanwhile, the Babylonians burned Jerusalem, including the palace, and tore down the walls of the city. ⁹Then Nebuzaradan, the captain of the guard, sent to Babylon the remnant of the population as well as those who had defected to him. ¹⁰But Nebuzaradan left a few of the poorest people in Judah, and he assigned them fields and vineyards to care for.

Jeremiah Remains in Judah

¹¹King Nebuchadnezzar had told Nebuzaradan to find Jeremiah. ¹²"See that he isn't hurt," he had said. "Look after him well, and give him anything he

39:1a Hebrew *in the tenth month*, of the Hebrew calendar. A number of events in Jeremiah can be cross-checked with dates in surviving Babylonian records and related accurately to our modern calendar. This event occurred on January 15, 588 B.C.; see 52:4 and the note there. 39:1b Hebrew *Nebuchadrezzar*, a variant name for Nebuchadnezzar; also in 39:11. 39:2 Hebrew *On the ninth day of the fourth month of the eleventh year of Zedekiah*. This event occurred on July 18, 586 B.C.; also see note on 39:1. 39:3 Or *Nergal-sharezer, Samgar-nebo, Sarsekim*. 39:4 Hebrew *the Arabah*. 39:5 Or *Chaldeans*; also in 39:8.

wants." ¹³So Nebuzaradan, the captain of the guard, and Nebushazban, a chief officer, and Nergal-sharezer, the king's adviser, and the other officers of Babylon's king ¹⁴sent messengers to bring Jeremiah out of the prison. They put him under the care of Gedaliah son of Ahikam and grandson of Shaphan, who was to take him back to his home. So Jeremiah stayed in Judah among his own people.

¹⁵The LORD had given the following message to Jeremiah while he was still in prison: ¹⁶"Say to Ebed-melech the Ethiopian,* 'The LORD Almighty, the God of Israel, says: I will do to this city everything I have threatened. I will send disaster, not prosperity. You will see its destruction, ¹⁷but I will rescue you from those you fear so much. ¹⁸Because you trusted me, I will preserve your life and keep you safe. I, the LORD, have spoken!' "

CHAPTER 40

The LORD gave a message to Jeremiah after Nebuzaradan, captain of the guard, had released him at Ramah. He had found Jeremiah bound in chains among the captives of Jerusalem and Judah who were being sent to exile in Babylon.

²The captain of the guard called for Jeremiah and said, "The LORD your God has brought this disaster on this land, ³just as he said he would. For these people have sinned against the LORD and disobeyed him. That is why it happened. ⁴Now I am going to take off your chains and let you go. If you want to come with me to Babylon, you are welcome. I will see that you are well cared for. But if you don't want to come, you may stay here. The whole land is before you—go wherever you like. ⁵If you decide to stay, then return to Gedaliah son of Ahikam and grandson of Shaphan. He has been appointed governor of Judah by the king of Babylon. Stay there with the people he rules. But it's up to you; go wherever you like."

Then Nebuzaradan gave Jeremiah some food and money and let him go. ⁶So Jeremiah returned to Gedaliah son of Ahikam at Mizpah and lived in Judah with the few who were still left in the land.

Gedaliah Governs in Judah

⁷The leaders of the Judean guerrilla bands in the countryside heard that the king of Babylon had appointed Gedaliah son of Ahikam as governor over the poor people who were left behind in Judah, and that he hadn't exiled everyone to Babylon. ⁸So they came to see Gedaliah at Mizpah. These are the names of the leaders who came: Ishmael son of Nethaniah, Johanan and Jonathan, sons of Kareah, Seraiah son of Tanhumeth, the sons of Ephai the Netophathite, Jaazaniah* son of the Maacathite, and all their men.

⁹Gedaliah assured them that it would be safe for them to surrender to the Babylonians.* "Stay here, and serve the king of Babylon," he said, "and all will go well for you. ¹⁰As for me, I will stay at Mizpah to represent you before the Babylonians who come to meet with us. Settle in any town you wish, and live off the land. Harvest the grapes and summer fruits and olives, and store them away."

¹¹When the Judeans in Moab, Ammon, Edom, and the other nearby countries heard that the king of Babylon had left a few people in Judah and that Gedaliah was the governor, ¹²they began to return to Judah from the places to which they had fled. They stopped at Mizpah to discuss their plans with Gedaliah and then went out into the Judean countryside to gather a great harvest of grapes and other crops.

A Plot against Gedaliah

¹³Soon after this, Johanan son of Kareah and the other guerrilla leaders came to Gedaliah at Mizpah. ¹⁴They said to him, "Did you know that Baalis, king of

---

I BELIEVE the Lord kept his promise to spare the lives of Jeremiah and Ebed-melech (Jeremiah 1:8; 38:7-13). (39:14)

I BELIEVE the people of Judah were utterly defeated by the Babylonians just as the Lord said. (40:2)

I LISTEN to the counsel of wise, discerning individuals. (40:6)

I BELIEVE those left in Judea could have prospered under Babylonian rule if they hadn't rebelled against the Lord. (40:10)

39:16 Hebrew *the Cushite.* **40:8** As in parallel text at 2 Kgs 25:23; Hebrew reads *Jezaniah,* a variant name for Jaazaniah. **40:9** Or *Chaldeans;* also in 40:10.

Ammon, has sent Ishmael son of Nethaniah to assassinate you?" But Gedaliah refused to believe them.

[15]Later Johanan had a private conference with Gedaliah and volunteered to kill Ishmael secretly. "Why should we let him come and murder you?" Johanan asked. "What will happen then to the Judeans who have returned? Why should the few of us who are still left be scattered and lost?"

[16]But Gedaliah said to Johanan, "I forbid you to do any such thing, for you are lying about Ishmael."

I DO NOT foolishly dismiss real threats against my life. (40:16)

CHAPTER 41
The Murder of Gedaliah

But in midautumn,* Ishmael son of Nethaniah and grandson of Elishama, who was a member of the royal family, arrived in Mizpah accompanied by ten men. Gedaliah invited them to dinner. While they were eating, [2]Ishmael and his ten men suddenly drew their swords and killed Gedaliah, whom the king of Babylon had appointed governor. [3]Then they went out and slaughtered all the Judean officials and Babylonian* soldiers who were with Gedaliah at Mizpah.

I DO NOT foolishly leave myself unprotected if I am in a position of political leadership. (41:1)

[4]The next day, before anyone had heard about Gedaliah's murder, [5]eighty men arrived from Shechem, Shiloh, and Samaria. They had come to worship at the Temple of the LORD. They had shaved off their beards, torn their clothes, and cut themselves, and had brought along grain offerings and incense. [6]Ishmael left Mizpah to meet them, weeping as he went. When he reached them, he said, "Oh, come and see what has happened to Gedaliah!"

[7]But as soon as they were all inside the town, Ishmael and his men killed all but ten of them and threw their bodies into a cistern. [8]The other ten had talked Ishmael into letting them go by promising to bring him their stores of wheat, barley, oil, and honey that they had hidden away. [9]The cistern where Ishmael dumped the bodies of the men that he murdered was the large one made by King Asa when he fortified Mizpah to protect himself against King Baasha of Israel. Ishmael son of Nethaniah filled it with corpses.

I ABHOR the slaughter of innocent people. (41:7)

See Asa's profile (page 521) at 2 Chronicles 16:9.

[10]Ishmael made captives of the king's daughters and the other people who had been left under Gedaliah's care in Mizpah by Nebuzaradan, captain of the guard. Taking them with him, he started back toward the land of Ammon.

[11]But when Johanan son of Kareah and the rest of the guerrilla leaders heard what Ishmael had done, [12]they took all their men and set out to stop him. They caught up with him at the pool near Gibeon. [13]The people Ishmael had captured shouted for joy when they saw Johanan and his men. [14]And all the captives from Mizpah escaped and began to help Johanan. [15]Meanwhile, Ishmael and eight of his men escaped from Johanan into the land of Ammon.

I DO NOT SEEK help from the enemy of God's people. (41:15)

[16]Then Johanan son of Kareah and his officers led away all the people they had rescued—warriors, women, children, and palace officials.* [17]They took them all to the village of Geruth-kimham near Bethlehem, where they prepared to leave for Egypt. [18]They were afraid of what the Babylonians* would do when they heard that Ishmael had killed Gedaliah, the governor appointed by the Babylonian king.

I DO NOT FEAR what people might do to me (Matthew 10:28). (41:18)

CHAPTER 42
Warning to Stay in Judah

Then all the army officers, including Johanan son of Kareah and Jezaniah* son of Hoshaiah, and all the people, from the least to the greatest, approached

41:1 Hebrew *in the seventh month,* of the Hebrew calendar. This month occurred in October and November 586 B.C. Also see note on 39:1. 41:3 Or *Chaldean.* 41:16 Or *eunuchs.* 41:18 Or *Chaldeans.* 42:1 Greek version reads *Azariah;* compare 43:2.

I DO NOT PLAN to rebel against the Lord and then ask someone who is godly to pray for me. (42:2)

[2]Jeremiah the prophet. They said, "Please pray to the LORD your God for us. As you know, we are only a tiny remnant compared to what we were before. [3]Beg the LORD your God to show us what to do and where to go."

[4]"All right," Jeremiah replied. "I will pray to the LORD your God, and I will tell you everything he says. I will hide nothing from you."

[5]Then they said to Jeremiah, "May the LORD your God be a faithful witness against us if we refuse to obey whatever he tells us to do! [6]Whether we like it or not, we will obey the LORD our God to whom we send you with our plea. For if we obey him, everything will turn out well for us."

I DO NOT BELIEVE the Lord Almighty is somehow obligated to answer my prayers instantaneously. (42:7)

[7]Ten days later, the LORD gave his reply to Jeremiah. [8]So he called for Johanan son of Kareah and the army officers, and for all the people, from the least to the greatest. [9]He said to them, "You sent me to the LORD, the God of Israel, with your request, and this is his reply: [10]'Stay here in this land. If you do, I will build you up and not tear you down; I will plant you and not uproot you. For I am sorry for all the punishment I have had to bring upon you. [11]Do not fear the king of Babylon anymore, says the LORD. For I am with you and will save you and rescue you from his power. [12]I will be merciful to you by making him kind, so he will let you stay here in your land.'

I DO NOT FEAR what people might do to me (Matthew 10:28). (42:11)

[13]"But if you refuse to obey the LORD your God and say, 'We will not stay here,' [14]and if you insist on going to live in Egypt where you think you will be free from war, famine, and alarms, [15]then this is what the LORD says to the remnant of Judah. The LORD Almighty, the God of Israel, says: 'If you insist on going to Egypt, [16]the war and famine you fear will follow close behind you, and you will die there. [17]That is the fate awaiting every one of you who insists on going to live in Egypt. Yes, you will die from war, famine, and disease. None of you will escape from the disaster I will bring upon you there.'

I BELIEVE the wages of sin is death (Romans 6:23). (42:17)

[18]"For the LORD Almighty, the God of Israel, says: 'Just as my anger and fury were poured out on the people of Jerusalem, so they will be poured out on you when you enter Egypt. You will become an object of damnation, horror, cursing, and mockery. And you will never see your homeland again.'

[19]"Listen, you remnant of Judah. The LORD has told you: 'Do not go to Egypt!' Don't forget this warning I have given you today. [20]For you were deceitful when you sent me to pray to the LORD your God for you, saying, 'Just tell us what the LORD our God says, and we will do it!' [21]And today I have told you exactly what he said, but you will not obey the LORD your God any better now than you have in the past. [22]So you can be sure that you will die from war, famine, and disease in Egypt, where you insist on going."

I DO NOT MAKE false vows to the Lord. (42:20)

CHAPTER 43

Jeremiah Taken to Egypt

When Jeremiah had finished giving this message from the LORD their God to all the people, [2]Azariah son of Hoshaiah and Johanan son of Kareah and all the other proud men said to Jeremiah, "You lie! The LORD our God hasn't forbidden us to go to Egypt! [3]Baruch son of Neriah has convinced you to say this, so we will stay here and be killed by the Babylonians* or be carried off into exile."

I DO NOT CONTRADICT God's Word. (43:2)

I DO NOT falsely accuse someone of wrongdoing. (43:3)

I DO NOT REFUSE to obey the Lord's commands. (43:4)

[4]So Johanan and all the army officers and all the people refused to obey the LORD's command to stay in Judah. [5]Johanan and his officers took with them all the people who had returned from the nearby countries to which they had fled. [6]In the crowd were men, women, and children, the king's daughters, and all those whom Nebuzaradan, the captain of the guard, had left with Gedaliah. Also included were the prophet Jeremiah and Baruch. [7]The people refused to obey the LORD and went to Egypt, going as far as the city of Tahpanhes.

43:3 Or *Chaldeans*.

⁸Then at Tahpanhes, the LORD gave another message to Jeremiah. He said, ⁹"While the people of Judah are watching, bury large rocks between the pavement stones at the entrance of Pharaoh's palace here in Tahpanhes. ¹⁰Then say to the people of Judah, 'The LORD Almighty, the God of Israel, says: I will surely bring my servant Nebuchadnezzar,* king of Babylon, here to Egypt. I will set his throne on these stones that I have hidden. He will spread his royal canopy over them. ¹¹And when he comes, he will destroy the land of Egypt. He will bring death to those destined for death; he will bring captivity to those destined for captivity; he will bring the sword against those destined for the sword. ¹²He will set fire to the temples of Egypt's gods, burning all their idols and carrying away the people as captives. He will pick clean the land of Egypt as a shepherd picks fleas from his cloak. And he himself will leave unharmed. ¹³He will break down the sacred pillars standing in the temple of the sun* in Egypt, and he will burn down the temples of Egypt's gods.' "

See Nebuchadnezzar's profile (page 985) at Daniel 4:37.

CHAPTER 44

Judgment for Idolatry

This is the message Jeremiah received concerning the Judeans living in northern Egypt in the cities of Migdol, Tahpanhes, and Memphis,* and throughout southern Egypt as well: ²"This is what the LORD Almighty, the God of Israel, says: You saw what I did to Jerusalem and to all the towns of Judah. They now lie in ruins, and no one lives in them. ³Because of all their wickedness, my anger rose high against them. They burned incense and worshiped other gods—gods that neither they nor you nor any of your ancestors have ever known.

⁴"Again and again I sent my servants, the prophets, to plead with them, 'Don't do these horrible things that I hate so much.' ⁵But my people would not listen or turn back from their wicked ways. They kept right on burning incense to these gods. ⁶And so my fury boiled over and fell like fire on the towns of Judah and into the streets of Jerusalem, and now they are a desolate ruin.

⁷"And now the LORD God Almighty, the God of Israel, asks you: Why are you destroying yourselves? For not one of you will survive—not a man, woman, or child among you who has come here from Judah, not even the babies in your arms. ⁸Why arouse my anger by burning incense to the idols you have made here in Egypt? You will only destroy yourselves and make yourselves an object of cursing and mockery for all the nations of the earth. ⁹Have you forgotten the sins of your ancestors, the sins of the kings and queens of Judah, and the sins you and your wives committed in Judah and Jerusalem? ¹⁰To this very hour you have shown no remorse or reverence. No one has chosen to follow my law and the decrees I gave to you and your ancestors before you.

¹¹"Therefore, the LORD Almighty, the God of Israel, says: I have made up my mind to destroy every one of you! ¹²I will take this remnant of Judah that insisted on coming here to Egypt, and I will consume them. They will fall here in Egypt, killed by war and famine. All will die, from the least to the greatest. They will be an object of damnation, horror, cursing, and mockery. ¹³I will punish them in Egypt just as I punished them in Jerusalem, by war, famine, and disease. ¹⁴Of those who fled to Egypt with dreams of returning home to Judah, only a handful will escape."

¹⁵Then all the women present and all the men who knew that their wives had burned incense to idols—a great crowd of all the Judeans living in Pathros, the southern region of Egypt—answered Jeremiah, ¹⁶"We will not listen to your messages from the LORD! ¹⁷We will do whatever we want. We will burn incense to the Queen of Heaven and sacrifice to her just as much as we like—just as we and our ancestors did before us, and as our kings and princes have always done in the towns of Judah and in the streets of

I LISTEN to the Lord and turn back from my wicked ways. (44:5)

I FEAR the Lord and obey his commands. (44:10)

I BELIEVE the Lord used the Babylonians to judge the rebellious people who fled from Judah to Egypt. (44:12)

I CHOOSE the Lord's will over my own evil desires. (44:17)

43:10 Hebrew *Nebuchadrezzar*, a variant name for Nebuchadnezzar.   43:13 Or *in Heliopolis*.   44:1 Hebrew *Noph*.

Jerusalem. For in those days we had plenty to eat, and we were well off and had no troubles! ¹⁸But ever since we quit burning incense to the Queen of Heaven and stopped worshiping her, we have been in great trouble and have suffered the effects of war and famine."

I ABHOR idolatry, even if loved ones engage in the worship of false gods. (44:19)

¹⁹"And," the women added, "do you suppose that we were worshiping the Queen of Heaven, pouring out drink offerings to her, and making cakes marked with her image, without our husbands knowing it and helping us? Of course not!"

²⁰Then Jeremiah said to all of them, men and women alike, who had given him that answer, ²¹"Do you think the LORD did not know that you and your ancestors, your kings and officials, and all the people were burning incense to idols in the towns of Judah and in the streets of Jerusalem? ²²It was because the LORD could no longer bear all the evil things you were doing that he made your land an object of cursing—a desolate ruin without a single inhabitant—as it is today. ²³The very reason all these terrible things have happened to you is because you have burned incense to idols and sinned against the LORD, refusing to obey him and follow his instructions, laws, and stipulations."

I DO NOT stubbornly and persistently refuse to obey the Lord. (44:23)

²⁴Then Jeremiah said to them all, including the women, "Listen to this message from the LORD, all you citizens of Judah who live in Egypt. ²⁵The LORD Almighty, the God of Israel, says: You and your wives have said that you will never give up your devotion and sacrifices to the Queen of Heaven, and you have proved it by your actions. Then go ahead and carry out your promises and vows to her!

Ask the Lord to speak to you. After all, this is his Word!

²⁶But listen to this message from the LORD, all you Judeans now living in Egypt: I have sworn by my great name, says the LORD, that my name will no longer be spoken by any of the Judeans in the land of Egypt. None of you may invoke my name or use this oath: 'As surely as the Sovereign LORD lives!' ²⁷For I will watch over you to bring you disaster and not good. You will suffer war and famine until all of you are dead.

²⁸Only a small number will escape death and return to Judah from Egypt. Then all those who came to Egypt will find out whose words are true, mine or theirs! ²⁹And this is the proof I give you, says the LORD, that all I have threatened will happen to you and that I will punish you here: ³⁰I will turn Pharaoh Hophra, king of Egypt, over to his enemies who want to kill him, just as I turned King Zedekiah of Judah over to King Nebuchadnezzar* of Babylon. I, the LORD, have spoken!"

See Nebuchadnezzar's profile (page 985) at Daniel 4:37.

CHAPTER 45

A Message for Baruch

The prophet Jeremiah gave a message to Baruch son of Neriah in the fourth year of the reign of Jehoiakim son of Josiah,* after Baruch had written down everything Jeremiah had dictated to him. He said, ²"This is what the LORD, the God of Israel, says to you, Baruch: ³You have said, 'I am overwhelmed with trouble! Haven't I had enough pain already? And now the LORD has added more! I am weary of my own sighing and can find no rest.'

I BELIEVE Baruch wrote down everything Jeremiah dictated to him. (45:1)

See Josiah's profile (page 461) at 2 Kings 23:25.

I DO NOT SEEK great things for myself. (45:5)

⁴"Baruch, this is what the LORD says: I will destroy this nation that I built. I will uproot what I planted. ⁵Are you seeking great things for yourself? Don't do it! But don't be discouraged. I will bring great disaster upon all these people, but I will protect you wherever you go. I, the LORD, have spoken!"

CHAPTER 46

Messages for the Nations

The following messages were given to Jeremiah the prophet from the LORD concerning foreign nations.

44:30 Hebrew *Nebuchadrezzar,* a variant name for Nebuchadnezzar. 45:1 The fourth year of Jehoiakim's reign was 605 B.C.

Messages about Egypt

²This message concerning Egypt was given in the fourth year of the reign of Jehoiakim son of Josiah,* the king of Judah, on the occasion of the battle of Carchemish when Pharaoh Neco, king of Egypt, and his army were defeated beside the Euphrates River by King Nebuchadnezzar* of Babylon.

³"Buckle on your armor and advance into battle! ⁴Harness the horses, and prepare to mount them. Put on your helmets, sharpen your spears, and prepare your armor. ⁵But look! The Egyptian army flees in terror. The bravest of its fighting men run without a backward glance. They are terrorized at every turn, says the LORD. ⁶The swiftest cannot flee; the mightiest warriors cannot escape. By the Euphrates River to the north they stumble and fall.

I BELIEVE the Lord used the Babylonians to defeat idolatrous Egypt (Jeremiah 46:25). (46:2)

See the profiles for Josiah (page 461) and Nebuchadnezzar (page 985) at 2 Kings 23:25 and Daniel 4:37.

LIKE BARUCH
Jeremiah 45:5

I am content to do God's will instead of longing for something that seems more rewarding.

What do people look for in a career?

Benefits and perks carry clout. A good salary or hefty 401k retirement plan is nice. Other factors like safe working conditions, upward mobility, flex schedules, and job satisfaction are even more important to many job seekers.

As Jeremiah's humble scribe, Baruch was guaranteed none of the above. "Just write down my words—every one of them," he was told. "And if the king burns the scroll when you're finished, start over and do it all again."

As Baruch leaned over Jeremiah's scroll day after day, he probably didn't know the words flowing from his pen would endure for thousands of years and be translated into hundreds of languages. He only knew for certain that Jeremiah's words often provoked taunts, threats, imprisonment, and attempts on the prophet's life. They even endangered Baruch's survival. No wonder he sometimes felt overwhelmed, weary, and restless!

God's direct message of comfort and challenge to Baruch foreshadowed his words to you and me:

- In Jeremiah's day, the Lord assured Baruch that his labor was not in vain. Every word would come true. Today, Scripture tells us that nothing we do for Jesus Christ is ever useless (1 Corinthians 15:58).
- The Lord exhorted Baruch to forget about promoting himself. Today, Jesus calls us not to worry about our physical needs but to make his kingdom our primary concern (Matthew 6:32-33).
- God guaranteed Baruch's physical protection, and today he grants us his constant presence and protection (Matthew 28:20; Hebrews 13:5-6).

The tasks in front of you and me may seem to produce greater pain than profit. The immediate rewards may seem few. But any troubles we face while doing God's will are nothing compared to the joy to come (2 Corinthians 4:18).

○ *Today's Scripture reading is Jeremiah 36, 43, and 45.*

---

⁷"Who is this, rising like the Nile River at floodtime, overflowing all the land? ⁸It is the Egyptian army, boasting that it will cover the earth like a flood, destroying every foe. ⁹Then come, you horses and chariots and mighty warriors of Egypt! Come, all you allies from Ethiopia, Libya, and Lydia* who are skilled with the shield and bow! ¹⁰For this is the day of the Lord, the LORD Almighty, a day of vengeance on his enemies. The sword will devour until it is satisfied, yes, drunk with your blood! The Lord, the LORD Almighty, will receive a sacrifice today in the north country beside the Euphrates River. ¹¹Go up to Gilead to get ointment, O virgin daughter of Egypt! But your many medicines will bring you no healing. ¹²The nations have heard of your shame. The earth is filled with your cries of despair. Your mightiest warriors will stumble across each other and fall together."

I DO NOT arrogantly boast about what I will do. (46:8)

I BELIEVE the day of the Lord will be a terrible day of judgment. (46:10)

46:2a The fourth year of Jehoiakim's reign was 605 B.C. 46:2b Hebrew *Nebuchadrezzar*, a variant name for Nebuchadnezzar; also in 46:13, 26. 46:9 Hebrew *Cush, Put, and Lud.*

¹³Then the LORD gave the prophet Jeremiah this message about King Nebuchadnezzar's plans to attack Egypt.

¹⁴"Shout it out in Egypt! Publish it in the cities of Migdol, Memphis,* and Tahpanhes! Mobilize for battle, for the sword of destruction will devour everyone around you. ¹⁵Why have your warriors fled in terror? They cannot stand because the LORD has driven them away. ¹⁶They stumble and fall over each other and say among themselves, 'Come, let's go back to our homeland where we were born. Let's get away from the sword of the enemy!' ¹⁷There they will say, 'Pharaoh, the king of Egypt, is a loudmouth who missed his opportunity!'

¹⁸"As surely as I live," says the King, whose name is the LORD Almighty, "one is coming against Egypt who is as tall as Mount Tabor or Mount Carmel by the sea! ¹⁹Pack up! Get ready to leave for exile, you citizens of Egypt! The city of Memphis will be destroyed, without a single person living there. ²⁰Egypt is as sleek as a young cow, but a gadfly from the north is on its way! ²¹Egypt's famed mercenaries have become like fattened calves. They turn and run, for it is a day of great disaster for Egypt, a time of great punishment. ²²Silent as a serpent gliding away, Egypt flees. The invading army marches in; they come against her with axes like woodsmen. ²³They will cut down her people like trees," says the LORD, "for they are more numerous than grasshoppers. ²⁴Egypt will be humiliated; she will be handed over to men from the north."

²⁵The LORD Almighty, the God of Israel, says: "I will punish Amon, the god of Thebes,* and all the other gods of Egypt. I will punish its rulers and Pharaoh, too, and all who trust in him. ²⁶I will hand them over to those who want them killed—to King Nebuchadnezzar of Babylon and his army. But afterward the land will recover from the ravages of war. I, the LORD, have spoken!

²⁷"But do not be afraid, Jacob, my servant; do not be dismayed, Israel. For I will bring you home again from distant lands, and your children will return from their exile. Israel* will return and will have peace and quiet, and nothing will make them afraid. ²⁸Fear not, Jacob, my servant," says the LORD, "for I am with you. I will destroy the nations to which I have exiled you, but I will not destroy you. But I must discipline you; I cannot let you go unpunished."

CHAPTER 47

A Message about Philistia

This is the LORD's message to the prophet Jeremiah concerning the Philistines of Gaza, before it was captured by the Egyptian army.

²This is what the LORD says: "A flood is coming from the north to overflow the land. It will destroy the land and everything in it—cities and people alike. People will scream in terror, and everyone in the land will weep. ³Hear the clatter of hooves and the rumble of wheels as the chariots rush by. Terrified fathers run madly, without a backward glance at their helpless children.

⁴"The time has come for the Philistines to be destroyed, along with their allies from Tyre and Sidon. Yes, the LORD is destroying the Philistines, those colonists from Crete.* ⁵The city of Gaza will be demolished; Ashkelon will lie in ruins. You remnant of the Mediterranean plain,* how long will you lament and mourn?

⁶"Now, O sword of the LORD, when will you be at rest again? Go back into your sheath; rest and be still! ⁷But how can it be still when the LORD has sent it on an errand? For the city of Ashkelon and the people living along the sea must be destroyed."

I HONOR the Lord Almighty as my King. (46:18)

I HATE idolatry and know the Lord does too. (46:25)

I BELIEVE the Lord disciplines those he loves (Hebrews 12:5-6). (46:28)

I BELIEVE the Lord used the Egyptians to demolish the idolatrous Philistines. (47:1)

46:14 Hebrew *Noph*; also in 46:19.　46:25 Hebrew *No.*　46:27 Hebrew *Jacob.*　47:4 Hebrew *from Caphtor.*
47:5 Hebrew *the plain.*

CHAPTER 48

A Message about Moab

This message was given concerning Moab.

This is what the LORD Almighty, the God of Israel, says: "Destruction is certain for the city of Nebo; it will soon lie in ruins. The city of Kiriathaim will be humiliated and captured; the fortress will be humiliated and broken down. [2]No one will ever brag about Moab again, for there is a plot against her life. In Heshbon plans have been completed to destroy her. 'Come,' they say, 'we will cut her off from being a nation.' The city of Madmen,* too, will be silenced; the sword will follow you there. [3]And then the roar of battle will surge against Horonaim, [4]for all Moab is being destroyed. Her little ones will cry out.* [5]Her refugees will climb the hills of Luhith, weeping bitterly, while cries of terror rise from Horonaim below. [6]Flee for your lives! Hide in the wilderness!* [7]Because you have trusted in your wealth and skill, you will be taken captive. Your god Chemosh, with his priests and princes, will be exiled to distant lands!

[8]"All the towns will be destroyed, both on the plateaus and in the valleys, for the LORD has spoken. [9]Oh, that Moab had wings so she could fly away, for her cities will be left empty, with no one living in them. [10]Cursed be those who refuse to do the work the LORD has given them, who hold back their swords from shedding blood!

[11]"From her earliest history, Moab has lived in peace. She is like wine that has been allowed to settle. She has not been poured from flask to flask, and she is now fragrant and smooth. [12]But the time is coming soon," says the LORD, "when I will send troublemakers to pour her from her jar. They will pour her out, then shatter the jar! [13]At last Moab will be ashamed of her idol Chemosh, as Israel was ashamed of her gold calf at Bethel.*

[14]"You used to boast, 'We are heroes, mighty men of war.' [15]But now Moab and her towns will be destroyed. Her most promising youth are doomed to slaughter," says the King, whose name is the LORD Almighty. [16]"Calamity is coming fast to Moab; it threatens ominously.

[17]"You friends of Moab, weep for her and cry! See how the strong scepter is broken, how the beautiful staff is shattered! [18]Come down from your glory and sit in the dust, you people of Dibon, for those who destroy Moab will shatter Dibon, too. They will tear down all your towers. [19]The people of Aroer stand anxiously beside the road to watch. They shout to those who flee from Moab, 'What has happened there?'

[20]"And the reply comes back, 'Moab lies in ruins; weep and wail! Tell it by the banks of the Arnon River: Moab has been destroyed!' [21]All the cities of the plateau lie in ruins, too. Judgment has been poured out on them all—on Holon and Jahaz* and Mephaath, [22]and on Dibon and Nebo and Bethdiblathaim, [23]and on Kiriathaim and Beth-gamul and Beth-meon, [24]and on Kerioth and Bozrah—all the cities of Moab, far and near.

[25]"The strength of Moab has ended. Her horns have been cut off, and her arms have been broken," says the LORD. [26]"Let her stagger and fall like a drunkard, for she has rebelled against the LORD. Moab will wallow in her own vomit, ridiculed by all. [27]Did you not make Israel the object of your ridicule? Was she caught in the company of thieves that you should despise her as you do?

[28]"You people of Moab, flee from your cities and towns! Live in the caves like doves that nest in the clefts of the rocks. [29]We have heard of the pride of Moab, for it is very great. We know of her loftiness, her arrogance, and her haughty heart. [30]I know about her insolence," says the LORD, "but her boasts

---

I BELIEVE the idolatrous Moabites were destroyed just as the Lord said (Jeremiah 48:7). (48:1)

I PUT no trust in my wealth or skills. (48:7)

I DO NOT BOAST about my strength. (48:14)

I HONOR the Lord Almighty as my King. (48:15)

I DO NOT REBEL against the Lord. (48:26)

I AM NOT FULL of pride and arrogance. (48:29)

48:2 *Madmen sounds like the Hebrew word for "silence"; it should not be confused with the English word* madmen. 48:4 Greek version reads *Her cries are heard as far away as Zoar.* 48:6 Or *Be like* [the town of] *Aroer in the wilderness.* 48:13 Hebrew *ashamed when they trusted in Bethel.* 48:21 Hebrew *Jahzah,* a variant name for Jahaz.

are false; they accomplish nothing. [31]Yes, I wail for Moab; my heart is broken for the men of Kir-hareseth.*

[32]"You people of Sibmah, rich in vineyards, I will weep for you even more than I did for Jazer. Your spreading vines once reached as far as the Dead Sea,* but the destroyer has stripped you bare! He has harvested your grapes and summer fruits. [33]Joy and gladness are gone from fruitful Moab. The presses yield no wine. No one treads the grapes with shouts of joy. There is shouting, yes, but not of joy. [34]Instead, their awful cries of terror can be heard from Heshbon clear across to Elealeh and Jahaz; from Zoar all the way to Horonaim and Eglath-shelishiyah. Even the waters of Nimrim are dried up now.

[35]"I will put an end to Moab," says the LORD, "for they offer sacrifices at the pagan shrines and burn incense to their false gods. [36]My heart moans like a flute for Moab and Kir-hareseth, for all their wealth has disappeared. [37]They shave their heads and beards in mourning. They slash their hands and put on clothes made of sackcloth. [38]Crying and sorrow will be in every Moabite home and on every street. For I have smashed Moab like an old, unwanted bottle. [39]How it is broken! Hear the wailing! See the shame of Moab! She has become an object of ridicule, an example of ruin to all her neighbors.

[40]"An eagle swoops down on the land of Moab," says the LORD. [41]"Her cities will fall; her strongholds will be seized. Even the mightiest warriors will be as frightened as a woman about to give birth. [42]Moab will no longer be a nation, for she has boasted against the LORD.

[43]"Terror and traps and snares will be your lot, O Moab," says the LORD. [44]"Those who flee in terror will fall into a trap, and those who escape the trap will step into a snare. I will see to it that you do not get away, for the time of your judgment has come," says the LORD. [45]"The people flee as far as Heshbon but are unable to go on. For a fire comes from Heshbon, King Sihon's ancestral home, to devour the entire land with all its rebellious people.

[46]"O Moab, your destruction is sure! The people of the god Chemosh are destroyed! Your sons and daughters have been taken away as captives. [47]But in the latter days I will restore the fortunes of Moab," says the LORD.

This is the end of Jeremiah's prophecy concerning Moab.

CHAPTER 49

A Message about Ammon

This message was given concerning the Ammonites.

This is what the LORD says: "What are you doing? Are there no descendants of Israel to inherit the land of Gad? Why are you, who worship Molech,* living in its towns? [2]I will punish you for this," says the LORD, "by destroying your city of Rabbah. It will become a desolate heap, and the neighboring towns will be burned. Then Israel will come and take back the land you took from her," says the LORD.

[3]"Cry out, O Heshbon, for the town of Ai is destroyed. Weep, O people of Rabbah! Put on your clothes of mourning. Weep and wail, hiding in the hedges, for your god Molech will be exiled along with his princes and priests. [4]You are proud of your fertile valleys, but they will soon be ruined. You rebellious daughter, you trusted in your wealth and thought no one could ever harm you. [5]But look! I will bring terror upon you," says the Lord, the LORD Almighty. "Your neighbors will chase you from your land, and no one will help your exiles as they flee. [6]But afterward I will restore the fortunes of the Ammonites," says the LORD.

I ABHOR idolatry. (48:35)

I BOAST only of what the Lord has done (1 Corinthians 1:31). (48:42)

I BELIEVE the idolatrous Ammonites were destroyed just as the Lord said. (49:1)

I DO NOT TRUST in my wealth or boast about my strength. (49:4)

48:31 Hebrew *Kir-heres*, a variant name for Kir-hareseth; also in 48:36. 48:32 Hebrew *the sea of Jazer*. 49:1 Hebrew *Milcom*, a variant name for Molech; also in 49:3.

Messages about Edom

[7] This message was given concerning Edom.

This is what the LORD Almighty says: "Where are all the wise men of Teman? Is there no one left to give wise counsel? [8] Turn and flee! Hide in deep caves, you people of Dedan! For when I bring disaster on Edom,* I will punish you, too! [9] Those who harvest grapes always leave a few for the poor. If thieves came at night, even they would not take everything. [10] But I will strip bare the land of Edom, and there will be no place left to hide. Its children, its brothers, and its neighbors—all will be destroyed—and Edom itself will be no more. [11] But I will preserve the orphans who remain among you. Your widows, too, will be able to depend on me for help."

[12] And this is what the LORD says: "If the innocent must suffer, how much more must you! You will not go unpunished! You must drink this cup of judgment! [13] For I have sworn by my own name," says the LORD, "that Bozrah will become an object of horror and a heap of rubble; it will be mocked and cursed. All its towns and villages will be desolate forever."

[14] I have heard a message from the LORD that an ambassador was sent to the nations to say, "Form a coalition against Edom, and prepare for battle!"

[15] This is what the LORD says: "I will cut you down to size among the nations, Edom. You will be despised by all. [16] You are proud that you inspire fear in others. And you are proud because you live in a rock fortress and hide high in the mountains. But don't fool yourselves! Though you live among the peaks with the eagles, I will bring you crashing down," says the LORD.

[17] "Edom will be an object of horror. All who pass by will be appalled and will gasp at the destruction they see there. [18] It will be like the destruction of Sodom and Gomorrah and their neighboring towns," says the LORD. "No one will live there anymore. [19] I will come like a lion from the thickets of the Jordan, leaping on the sheep in the pasture. I will chase Edom from its land, and I will appoint the leader of my choice. For who is like me, and who can challenge me? What ruler can oppose my will?"

[20] Listen to the LORD's plans for Edom and the people of Teman. Even the little children will be dragged off, and their homes will be empty. [21] The earth will shake with the noise of Edom's fall, and its cry of despair will be heard all the way to the Red Sea.* [22] The enemy will come as swiftly as an eagle, and he will spread his wings against Bozrah. Even the mightiest warriors will be as frightened as a woman about to give birth.

A Message about Damascus

[23] This message was given concerning Damascus.

This is what the LORD says: "The towns of Hamath and Arpad are struck with fear, for they have heard the news of their destruction. Their hearts are troubled like a wild sea in a raging storm. [24] Damascus has become feeble, and all her people turn to flee. Fear, anguish, and pain have gripped her as they do a woman giving birth. [25] That famous city, a city of joy, will be forsaken! [26] Her young men will fall in the streets and die. Her warriors will all be killed," says the LORD Almighty. [27] "And I will start a fire at the edge of Damascus that will burn up the palaces of Ben-hadad."

A Message about Kedar and Hazor

[28] This message was given concerning Kedar and the kingdoms of Hazor, which were attacked by King Nebuchadnezzar* of Babylon.

This is what the LORD says: "Advance against Kedar! Blot out the warriors from the East! [29] Their flocks and tents will be captured, and their household goods and camels will be taken away. Everywhere shouts of panic will be heard: 'We are terrorized at every turn!' [30] Flee for your lives," says the LORD.

I BELIEVE the wicked Edomites were destroyed just as the Lord said. (49:8)

I BELIEVE the Lord cares for widows and orphans (James 1:27). (49:11)

I AM NOT FULL of pride and arrogance. (49:16)

I BELIEVE the Lord Almighty is sovereign over all nations. (49:19)

I BELIEVE the wicked people of Damascus were destroyed just as the Lord said. (49:23)

See Nebuchadnezzar's profile (page 985) at Daniel 4:37.

49:8 Hebrew *Esau*; also in 49:10.   49:21 Hebrew *sea of reeds*.   49:28 Hebrew *Nebuchadrezzar*, a variant name for Nebuchadnezzar; also in 49:30.

"Hide yourselves in deep caves, you people of Hazor, for King Nebuchadnezzar of Babylon has plotted against you and is preparing to destroy you. ³¹"Go up and attack those self-sufficient nomadic tribes," says the LORD. "They live alone in the desert without walls or gates. ³²Their camels and cattle will all be yours. I will scatter to the winds these people who live in distant places.* I will bring calamity upon them from every direction," says the LORD. ³³"Hazor will be inhabited by jackals, and it will be desolate forever. No one will live there anymore."

A Message about Elam

³⁴This message concerning Elam came to the prophet Jeremiah from the LORD at the beginning of the reign of King Zedekiah of Judah.

³⁵This is what the LORD Almighty says: "I will destroy the archers of Elam—the best of their marksmen. ³⁶I will bring enemies from all directions, and I will scatter the people of Elam to the four winds. They will be exiled to countries around the world. ³⁷I myself will go with Elam's enemies to shatter it. My fierce anger will bring great disaster upon the people of Elam," says the LORD. "Their enemies will chase them with the sword until I have destroyed them completely. ³⁸I will set my throne in Elam," says the LORD, "and I will destroy its king and princes. ³⁹But in the latter days I will restore the fortunes of Elam," says the LORD.

CHAPTER 50

A Message about Babylon

The LORD gave Jeremiah the prophet this message concerning Babylon and the land of the Babylonians.*

²This is what the LORD says: "Tell the whole world, and keep nothing back! Raise a signal flag so everyone will know that Babylon will fall! Her images and idols will be shattered. Her gods Bel and Marduk will be utterly disgraced. ³For a nation will attack her from the north and bring such destruction that no one will live in her again. Everything will be gone; both people and animals will flee.

Hope for Israel and Judah

⁴"Then the people of Israel and Judah will join together," says the LORD, "weeping and seeking the LORD their God. ⁵They will ask the way to Jerusalem* and will start back home again. They will bind themselves to the LORD with an eternal covenant that will never again be broken.

⁶"My people have been lost sheep. Their shepherds have led them astray and turned them loose in the mountains. They have lost their way and cannot remember how to get back to the fold. ⁷All who found them devoured them. Their enemies said, 'We are allowed to attack them freely, for they have sinned against the LORD, their place of rest, the hope of their ancestors.'

⁸"But now, flee from Babylon! Leave the land of the Babylonians. Lead my people home again. ⁹For look, I am raising up an army of great nations from the north. I will bring them against Babylon to attack her, and she will be captured. The enemies' arrows will go straight to the mark; they will not miss! ¹⁰Babylonia* will be plundered until the attackers are glutted with plunder," says the LORD.

Babylon's Sure Fall

¹¹"You rejoice and are glad, you plunderers of my chosen people. You frisk about like a calf in a meadow and neigh like a stallion. ¹²But your homeland* will be overwhelmed with shame and disgrace. You will become the least of nations—a wilderness, a dry and desolate land. ¹³Because of the LORD's anger,

I BELIEVE the wicked Elamites were destroyed just as the Lord said. (49:35)

I BELIEVE the idolatrous Babylonians were destroyed just as the Lord said. (50:2)

I HAVE REPENTED of my sins and sought the Lord my God. (50:4)

I WAS like a lost sheep before the Lord saved me (Matthew 9:36). (50:6)

49:32 Or *who clip the corners of their hair.* 50:1 Or *Chaldeans;* also in 50:8, 25, 35, 45. 50:5 Hebrew *Zion;* also in 50:28. 50:10 Or *Chaldea.* 50:12 Hebrew *your mother.*

Babylon will become a deserted wasteland. All who pass by will be horrified and will gasp at the destruction they see there.

¹⁴"Yes, prepare to attack Babylon, all you nations round about. Let your archers shoot at her. Spare no arrows, for she has sinned against the LORD. ¹⁵Shout against her from every side. Look! She surrenders! Her walls have fallen. The LORD has taken vengeance, so do not spare her. Do to her as she has done to others! ¹⁶Lead from Babylon all those who plant crops; send all the harvesters away. Let the captives escape the sword of the enemy and rush back to their own lands.

Hope for God's People

¹⁷"The Israelites are like sheep that have been scattered by lions. First the king of Assyria ate them up. Then King Nebuchadnezzar* of Babylon cracked their bones." ¹⁸Therefore, the LORD Almighty, the God of Israel, says: "Now I will punish the king of Babylon and his land, just as I punished the king of Assyria. ¹⁹And I will bring Israel home again to her own land, to feed in the fields of Carmel and Bashan, and to be satisfied once more on the hill country of Ephraim and Gilead. ²⁰In those days," says the LORD, "no sin will be found in Israel or in Judah, for I will forgive the remnant I preserve.

The LORD's Judgment on Babylon

²¹"Go up, my warriors, against the land of Merathaim and against the people of Pekod. Yes, march against Babylon, the land of rebels, a land that I will judge! Pursue, kill, and completely destroy* them, as I have commanded you," says the LORD. ²²"Let the battle cry be heard in the land, a shout of great destruction. ²³Babylon, the mightiest hammer in all the earth, lies broken and shattered. Babylon is desolate among the nations! ²⁴Listen, Babylon, for I have set a trap for you. You are caught, for you have fought against the LORD.

²⁵"The LORD has opened his armory and brought out weapons to vent his fury against his enemies. The terror that falls upon the Babylonians will be the work of the Sovereign LORD Almighty. ²⁶Yes, come against her from distant lands. Break open her granaries. Crush her walls and houses into heaps of rubble. Destroy her completely, and leave nothing! ²⁷Even destroy her cattle—it will be terrible for them, too! Slaughter them all! For the time has come for Babylon to be devastated. ²⁸Listen to the people who have escaped from Babylon, as they declare in Jerusalem how the LORD our God has taken vengeance against those who destroyed his Temple.

²⁹"Send out a call for archers to come to Babylon. Surround the city so none can escape. Do to her as she has done to others, for she has defied the LORD, the Holy One of Israel. ³⁰Her young men will fall in the streets and die. Her warriors will all be killed," says the LORD.

³¹"See, I am your enemy, O proud people," says the Lord, the LORD Almighty. "Your day of reckoning has arrived. ³²O land of pride, you will stumble and fall, and no one will raise you up. For I will light a fire in the cities of Babylon that will burn everything around them."

³³And now the LORD Almighty says this: "The people of Israel and Judah have been wronged. Their captors hold them and refuse to let them go. ³⁴But the one who redeems them is strong. His name is the LORD Almighty. He will defend them and give them rest again in Israel. But the people of Babylon—there will be no rest for them!

³⁵"The sword of destruction will strike the Babylonians," says the LORD. "It will strike the people of Babylon—her princes and wise men, too. ³⁶And when it strikes her wise counselors, they will become fools! When it strikes her mightiest warriors, panic will seize them! ³⁷When it strikes her horses and

I DO NOT CONTINUE sinning against the Lord. (50:14)

See Nebuchadnezzar's profile (page 985) at Daniel 4:37.

I DO NOT FIGHT against the Lord. (50:24)

I DO NOT DEFY the Lord, who is holy. (50:29)

I PRAISE the Lord Almighty, my Redeemer. (50:34)

50:17 Hebrew *Nebuchadrezzar*, a variant name for Nebuchadnezzar.   50:21 The Hebrew term used here refers to the complete consecration of things or people to the LORD, either by destroying them or by giving them as an offering.

I AM NOT in love with false gods. (50:38)

chariots, her allies from other lands will become as weak as women. When it strikes her treasures, they all will be plundered. [38]It will even strike her water supply, causing it to dry up. And why? Because the whole land is filled with idols, and the people are madly in love with them.

[39]"Soon this city of Babylon will be inhabited by ostriches and jackals. It will be a home for the wild animals of the desert. Never again will people live there; it will lie desolate forever. [40]I will destroy it just as I* destroyed Sodom and Gomorrah and their neighboring towns," says the LORD. "No one will live there anymore.

[41]"Look! A great army is marching from the north! A great nation and many kings are rising against you from far-off lands. [42]They are fully armed for slaughter. They are cruel and show no mercy. As they ride forward, the noise of their army is like a roaring sea. They are marching in battle formation to destroy you, Babylon. [43]The king of Babylon has received reports about the enemy, and he is weak with fright. Fear and pain have gripped him, like that of a woman about to give birth.

I BELIEVE the Lord Almighty is sovereign over all nations. (50:44)

[44]"I will come like a lion from the thickets of the Jordan, leaping on the sheep in the pasture. I will chase Babylon from its land, and I will appoint the leader of my choice. For who is like me, and who can challenge me? What ruler can oppose my will?"

[45]Listen to the LORD's plans against Babylon and the land of the Babylonians. Even little children will be dragged off, and their homes will be empty. [46]The earth will shake with the noise of Babylon's fall, and her cry of despair will be heard around the world.

CHAPTER 51

This is what the LORD says: "I will stir up a destroyer against Babylon and the people of Babylonia.* [2]Foreigners will come and winnow her, blowing her away as chaff. They will come from every side to rise against her in her day of trouble. [3]Don't let the archers put on their armor or draw their bows. No one will be spared! Young and old alike will be completely destroyed.* [4]They will fall dead in the land of the Babylonians,* slashed to death in her streets. [5]For the LORD Almighty has not forsaken Israel and Judah. He is still their God, even though their land was filled with sin against the Holy One of Israel."

I BELIEVE the Lord will never forsake me (Hebrews 13:5). (51:5)

[6]Flee from Babylon! Save yourselves! Don't get trapped in her punishment! It is the LORD's time for vengeance; he will fully repay her. [7]Babylon has been like a golden cup in the LORD's hands, a cup from which he made the whole earth drink and go mad. [8]But now suddenly, Babylon, too, has fallen. Weep for her, and give her medicine. Perhaps she can yet be healed. [9]We would have helped her if we could, but nothing can save her now. Let her go; abandon her. Return now to your own land, for her judgment will be so great it cannot be measured. [10]The LORD has vindicated us. Come, let us announce in Jerusalem* everything the LORD our God has done.

I TELL others what the Lord my God has done. (51:10)

[11]Sharpen the arrows! Lift up the shields! For the LORD has stirred up the spirit of the kings of the Medes to march against Babylon and destroy her. This is his vengeance against those who desecrated his Temple. [12]Raise the battle flag against Babylon! Reinforce the guard and station the watchmen. Prepare an ambush, for the LORD will fulfill all his plans against Babylon.

I BELIEVE the Lord fulfilled all his plans against Babylon, just as he said. (51:12)

[13]You are a city rich with water, a great center of commerce, but your end has come. The thread of your life is cut. [14]The LORD Almighty has taken this vow and has sworn to it by his own name: "Your cities will be filled with enemies, like fields filled with locusts, and they will lift their shouts of triumph over you."

50:40 Hebrew *just as God.*   51:1 Hebrew *of Leb-kamai,* a code name for Babylonia.   51:3 The Hebrew term used here refers to the complete consecration of things or people to the LORD, either by destroying them or by giving them as an offering.   51:4 Or *Chaldeans;* also in 51:54.   51:10 Hebrew *Zion;* also in 51:24, 35a.

A Hymn of Praise to the LORD

¹⁵ He made the earth by his power,
   and he preserves it by his wisdom.
He has stretched out the heavens
   by his understanding.
¹⁶ When he speaks, there is thunder in the heavens.
   He causes the clouds to rise over the earth.
He sends the lightning with the rain
   and releases the wind from his storehouses.
¹⁷ Compared to him, all people are foolish
   and have no knowledge at all!
They make idols, but the idols will disgrace their makers,
   for they are frauds.
They have no life or power in them.
¹⁸ Idols are worthless; they are lies!
   The time is coming when they will all be destroyed.
¹⁹ But the God of Israel* is no idol!
   He is the Creator of everything that exists,
   including his people, his own special possession.
The LORD Almighty is his name!

Babylon's Great Punishment

²⁰"You* are my battle-ax and sword," says the LORD. "With you I will shatter nations and destroy many kingdoms. ²¹With you I will shatter armies, destroying the horse and rider, the chariot and charioteer. ²²With you I will shatter men and women, old people and children, young men and maidens. ²³With you I will shatter shepherds and flocks, farmers and oxen, captains and rulers.

²⁴"As you watch, I will repay Babylon and the people of Babylonia* for all the wrong they have done to my people in Jerusalem," says the LORD.

²⁵"Look, O mighty mountain, destroyer of the earth! I am your enemy," says the LORD. "I will raise my fist against you, to roll you down from the heights. When I am finished, you will be nothing but a heap of rubble. ²⁶You will be desolate forever. Even your stones will never again be used for building. You will be completely wiped out," says the LORD.

²⁷Signal many nations to mobilize for war against Babylon. Sound the battle cry! Bring out the armies of Ararat, Minni, and Ashkenaz. Appoint a leader, and bring a multitude of horses! ²⁸Bring against her the armies of the kings of the Medes and their generals, and the armies of all the countries they rule.

²⁹Babylon trembles and writhes in pain, for everything the LORD has planned against her stands unchanged. Babylon will be left desolate without a single inhabitant. ³⁰Her mightiest warriors no longer fight. They stay in their barracks. Their courage is gone. They have become as fearful as women. The invaders have burned the houses and broken down the city gates. ³¹Messengers from every side come running to the king to tell him all is lost! ³²All the escape routes are blocked. The fortifications are burning, and the army is in panic.

³³For the LORD Almighty, the God of Israel, says: "Babylon is like wheat on a threshing floor, about to be trampled. In just a little while her harvest will begin."

³⁴"King Nebuchadnezzar* of Babylon has eaten and crushed us and emptied out our strength. He has swallowed us like a great monster and filled his

---

I BELIEVE the Lord made the heavens and the earth. (51:15)

I BELIEVE the Lord is infinitely wise. (51:17)

I BELIEVE Babylon was destroyed forever just as the Lord said. (51:26)

I BELIEVE the Lord used the Medes to destroy the proud, cruel, and idolatrous Babylonians. (51:28)

51:19 Hebrew *the Portion of Jacob.*   **51:20** Possibly Cyrus, who was used of God to conquer Babylon. Compare Isa 44:28; 45:1.   **51:24** Or *Chaldea*; also in 51:35.   **51:34** Hebrew *Nebuchadrezzar*, a variant name for Nebuchadnezzar.

belly with our riches. He has thrown us out of our own country. [35]May Babylon be repaid for all the violence she did to us," say the people of Jerusalem. "May the people of Babylonia be paid in full for all the blood they spilled," says Jerusalem.

The LORD's Vengeance on Babylon

[36]The LORD says to Jerusalem, "I will be your lawyer to plead your case, and I will avenge you. I will dry up her river, her water supply, [37]and Babylon will become a heap of rubble, haunted by jackals. It will be an object of horror and contempt, without a single person living there.

[38]"In their drunken feasts, the people of Babylon roar like lions. [39]And while they lie inflamed with all their wine, I will prepare a different kind of feast for them. I will make them drink until they fall asleep, never again to waken," says the LORD. [40]"I will bring them like lambs to the slaughter, like rams and goats to be sacrificed.

[41]"How Babylon* is fallen—great Babylon, praised throughout the earth! The world can scarcely believe its eyes at her fall! [42]The sea has risen over Babylon; she is covered by its waves. [43]Her cities now lie in ruins; she is a dry wilderness where no one lives or even passes by. [44]And I will punish Bel, the god of Babylon, and pull from his mouth what he has taken. The nations will no longer come and worship him. The wall of Babylon has fallen.

A Message for the Exiles

[45]"Listen, my people, flee from Babylon. Save yourselves! Run from the LORD's fierce anger. [46]But do not panic when you hear the first rumor of approaching forces. For rumors will keep coming year by year. Then there will be a time of violence as the leaders fight against each other. [47]For the time is surely coming when I will punish this great city and all her idols. Her whole land will be disgraced, and her dead will lie in the streets. [48]The heavens and earth will rejoice, for out of the north will come destroying armies against Babylon," says the LORD. [49]"Just as Babylon killed the people of Israel and others throughout the world, so must her people be killed. [50]Go, you who escaped the sword! Do not stand and watch—flee while you can! Remember the LORD, even though you are in a far-off land, and think about your home in Jerusalem."

[51]"We are ashamed," the people say. "We are insulted and disgraced because the LORD's Temple has been defiled by foreigners."

[52]"Yes," says the LORD, "but the time is coming when Babylon's idols will be destroyed. The groans of her wounded people will be heard throughout the land. [53]Though Babylon reaches as high as the heavens, and though she increases her strength immeasurably, I will send enemies to plunder her," says the LORD.

Babylon's Complete Destruction

[54]Listen! Hear the cry of Babylon, the sound of great destruction from the land of the Babylonians. [55]For the LORD is destroying Babylon. He will silence her. Waves of enemies pound against her; the noise of battle rings through the city. [56]Destroying armies come against Babylon. Her mighty men are captured, and their weapons break in their hands. For the LORD is a God who gives just punishment, and he is giving Babylon all she deserves.

[57]"I will make drunk her officials, wise men, rulers, captains, and warriors," says the King, whose name is the LORD Almighty. "They will fall asleep and never wake up again!"

[58]This is what the LORD Almighty says: "The wide walls of Babylon will be leveled to the ground, and her high gates will be burned. The builders from many lands have worked in vain, for their work will be destroyed by fire!"

51:41 Hebrew *Sheshach*, a code name for Babylon.

I DO NOT TRY to avenge myself but leave that to God (Romans 12:19). (51:36)

I BELIEVE the wages of sin is death (Romans 6:23). (51:39)

I BELIEVE Babylon became a deserted wasteland just as the Lord said. (51:43)

I HATE idolatry and know the Lord does too. (51:44)

I REMEMBER the Lord and return to him after I have sinned. (51:50)

I BELIEVE the Lord is a God who gives just punishment. (51:56)

Jeremiah's Message Sent to Babylon

⁵⁹The prophet Jeremiah gave this message to Zedekiah's staff officer, Seraiah son of Neriah and grandson of Mahseiah, when he went to Babylon with King Zedekiah of Judah. This was during the fourth year of Zedekiah's reign.* ⁶⁰Jeremiah had recorded on a scroll all the terrible disasters that would soon come upon Babylon. ⁶¹He said to Seraiah, "When you get to Babylon, read aloud everything on this scroll. ⁶²Then say, 'LORD, you have said that you will destroy Babylon so that neither people nor animals will remain here. She will lie empty and abandoned forever.' ⁶³Then, when you have finished reading the scroll, tie it to a stone, and throw it into the Euphrates River. ⁶⁴Then say, 'In this same way Babylon and her people will sink, never again to rise, because of the disasters I will bring upon her.' "

This is the end of Jeremiah's messages.

CHAPTER 52

The Fall of Jerusalem

Zedekiah was twenty-one years old when he became king, and he reigned in Jerusalem eleven years. His mother's name was Hamutal, the daughter of Jeremiah from Libnah. ²But Zedekiah did what was evil in the LORD's sight, just as Jehoiakim had done. ³So the LORD, in his anger, finally banished the people of Jerusalem and Judah from his presence and sent them into exile.

Then Zedekiah rebelled against the king of Babylon. ⁴So on January 15,* during the ninth year of Zedekiah's reign, King Nebuchadnezzar* of Babylon led his entire army against Jerusalem. They surrounded the city and built siege ramps against its walls. ⁵Jerusalem was kept under siege until the eleventh year of King Zedekiah's reign.

⁶By July 18 of Zedekiah's eleventh year,* the famine in the city had become very severe, with the last of the food entirely gone. ⁷Then a section of the city wall was broken down, and all the soldiers made plans to escape from the city. But since the city was surrounded by the Babylonians,* they waited for nightfall and fled through the gate between the two walls behind the king's gardens. They made a dash across the fields, in the direction of the Jordan Valley.*

⁸But the Babylonians chased after them and caught King Zedekiah on the plains of Jericho, for by then his men had all abandoned him. ⁹They brought him to the king of Babylon at Riblah, in the land of Hamath, where sentence was passed against him. ¹⁰There at Riblah, the king of Babylon made Zedekiah watch as all his sons were killed; they also killed all the other leaders of Judah. ¹¹Then they gouged out Zedekiah's eyes, bound him in bronze chains, and led him away to Babylon. Zedekiah remained there in prison for the rest of his life.

The Temple Destroyed

¹²On August 17 of that year,* which was the nineteenth year of Nebuchadnezzar's reign, Nebuzaradan, captain of the guard, an official of the Babylonian king, arrived in Jerusalem. ¹³He burned down the Temple of the LORD, the royal palace, and all the houses of Jerusalem. He destroyed all the important buildings in the city. ¹⁴Then the captain of the guard supervised the entire Babylonian* army as they tore down the walls of Jerusalem. ¹⁵Nebuzaradan, captain of the guard, then took as exiles some of the poorest of

I DO what is good and right in the Lord's sight. (52:2)

See Nebuchadnezzar's profile (page 985) at Daniel 4:37.

I BELIEVE the people of Judah were utterly defeated by the Babylonians just as the Lord said. (52:7)

I BELIEVE King Zedekiah died in exile, yet never saw Babylon, just as the Lord said (Ezekiel 12:13). (52:11)

I BELIEVE the Babylonians destroyed the Temple just as the Lord said. (52:13)

51:59 The fourth year of Zedekiah's reign was 593 B.C. 52:4a Hebrew *on the tenth day of the tenth month,* of the Hebrew calendar. A number of events in Jeremiah can be cross-checked with dates in surviving Babylonian records and related accurately to our modern calendar. This event occurred on January 15, 588 B.C. 52:4b Hebrew *Nebuchadrezzar,* a variant name for Nebuchadnezzar; also in 52:12, 28, 29, 30. 52:6 Hebrew *By the ninth day of the fourth month* [of Zedekiah's eleventh year]. This event of the Hebrew lunar calendar occurred on July 18, 586 B.C.; also see note on 52:4a. 52:7a Or *Chaldeans;* also in 52:8, 17. 52:7b Hebrew *the Arabah.* 52:12 Hebrew *On the tenth day of the fifth month,* of the Hebrew calendar. This day was August 17, 586 B.C.; also see note on 52:4a. 52:14 Or *Chaldean.*

the people and those who remained in the city, along with the rest of the craftsmen and the troops who had declared their allegiance to the king of Babylon. ¹⁶But Nebuzaradan allowed some of the poorest people to stay behind in Judah to care for the vineyards and fields.

¹⁷The Babylonians broke up the bronze pillars, the bronze water carts, and the bronze Sea that were at the LORD's Temple, and they carried all the bronze away to Babylon. ¹⁸They also took all the pots, shovels, lamp snuffers, basins, dishes, and all the other bronze utensils used for making sacrifices at the Temple. ¹⁹Nebuzaradan, captain of the guard, also took the small bowls, firepans, basins, pots, lampstands, dishes, bowls used for drink offerings, and all the other utensils made of pure gold or silver.

²⁰The bronze from the two pillars, the water carts, and the Sea with the twelve bulls beneath it was too great to be measured. These things had been made for the LORD's Temple in the days of King Solomon. ²¹Each of the pillars was 27 feet tall and 18 feet in circumference.* They were hollow, with walls 3 inches thick.* ²²The bronze capital on top of each pillar was 7¹/₂ feet* high and was decorated with a network of bronze pomegranates all the way around. ²³There were ninety-six pomegranates on the sides, and a total of one hundred on the network around the top.

²⁴The captain of the guard took with him as prisoners Seraiah the chief priest, his assistant Zephaniah, and the three chief gatekeepers. ²⁵And of the people still hiding in the city, he took an officer of the Judean army, seven of the king's personal advisers, the army commander's chief secretary, who was in charge of recruitment, and sixty other citizens. ²⁶Nebuzaradan the commander took them all to the king of Babylon at Riblah. ²⁷And there at Riblah in the land of Hamath, the king of Babylon had them all put to death. So the people of Judah were sent into exile from their land.

²⁸The number of captives taken to Babylon in the seventh year of Nebuchadnezzar's reign* was 3,023. ²⁹Then in Nebuchadnezzar's eighteenth year* he took 832 more. ³⁰In his twenty-third year* he sent Nebuzaradan, his captain of the guard, who took 745 more—a total of 4,600 captives in all.

Hope for Israel's Royal Line

³¹In the thirty-seventh year of King Jehoiachin's exile in Babylon, Evil-merodach ascended to the Babylonian throne. He was kind to Jehoiachin and released him from prison on March 31 of that year.* ³²He spoke pleasantly to Jehoiachin and gave him preferential treatment over all the other exiled kings in Babylon. ³³He supplied Jehoiachin with new clothes to replace his prison garb and allowed him to dine at the king's table for the rest of his life. ³⁴The Babylonian king also gave him a regular allowance to cover his living expenses until the day of his death.

52:21a Hebrew *18 cubits* [8.1 meters] *tall and 12 cubits* [5.4 meters] *in circumference.* 52:21b Hebrew *4 fingers thick* [8 centimeters]. 52:22 Hebrew *5 cubits* [2.3 meters]. 52:28 This exile in the seventh year of Nebuchadnezzar's reign occurred in 597 B.C. 52:29 This exile in the eighteenth year of Nebuchadnezzar's reign occurred in 586 B.C. 52:30 This exile in the twenty-third year of Nebuchadnezzar's reign occurred in 581 B.C. 52:31 Hebrew *on the twenty-fifth day of the twelfth month,* of the Hebrew calendar. This day was March 31, 561 B.C.; also see note on 52:4a.

I BELIEVE the Babylonians carried away many valuable items from the Temple. (52:17)

See Solomon's profile (page 753) at Proverbs 2:9.

I BELIEVE the Babylonians took thousands of people from Judah into captivity. (52:28)

LAMENTATIONS

THIS SHORT BOOK records the lyrics of a series of sad, sorrowful songs that Jeremiah wrote after the destruction of Jerusalem.

In many ways, this is an appendix to the book of Jeremiah. In fact, in some ancient versions of the Old Testament, these five chapters appear at the end of Jeremiah—not as a separate book.

This isn't the first set of funeral songs or laments that Jeremiah composed (see 2 Chronicles 35:25), but over the centuries it has been the most remembered. Even today Jewish people read these songs aloud in mid-July, remembering how Jerusalem fell first to the Babylonian Empire and much later to the Roman Empire.

These laments clearly weren't written in a day. In the original Hebrew language, Lamentations is a superb example of carefully and beautifully crafted poetry.

In these poems, the weeping prophet expresses to the Lord the sorrows of the Jewish people. In the first funeral song (chapter 1), Jeremiah weeps over the ruined capital of Judah. In the second song (chapter 2), the prophet laments the destruction of the city. In the third song (chapter 3), he tries to come to grips with what he's experienced. In the fourth song (chapter 4), he describes the horror of the Babylonian siege. In the last song (chapter 5), Jeremiah cries out to the Lord for mercy.

Other laments in Scripture include 2 Samuel 1:17-27; 3:33-34; Psalms 88; 102; Ezekiel 19:1-14; 26:17-18; 27:32-36; 32:2-16; and Amos 5:1-2.

Famous verses in Lamentations include

- ○ "Look around and see if there is any suffering like mine" (1:12)
- ○ "The LORD has blotted out all memory of the holy festivals and Sabbath days" (2:6)
- ○ "I am the one who has seen the afflictions" (3:1)
- ○ "And though I cry and shout, he shuts out my prayers" (3:8)
- ○ "Yet I still dare to hope when I remember this" (3:21)
- ○ "The unfailing love of the LORD never ends!" (3:22)
- ○ "Great is his faithfulness; his mercies begin afresh" (3:23)
- ○ "The LORD is wonderfully good to those who wait for him" (3:25)
- ○ "Restore us, O LORD, and bring us back to you again!" (5:21)

CHAPTER 1

Sorrow in Jerusalem

Jerusalem's streets, once bustling with people, are now silent. Like a widow broken with grief, she sits alone in her mourning. Once the queen of nations, she is now a slave.

²She sobs through the night; tears stream down her cheeks. Among all her lovers, there is no one left to help her. All her friends have betrayed her; they are now her enemies.

1:1 Each of the first four chapters of this book is an acrostic, laid out in the order of the Hebrew alphabet. The first word of each verse begins with a successive Hebrew letter. Chapters 1, 2, and 4 have one verse for each of the 22 Hebrew letters. Chapter 3 contains 22 stanzas of three verses each. Though chapter 5 is not an acrostic, it also has 22 verses.

³Judah has been led away into captivity, afflicted and enslaved. She lives among foreign nations and has no place of rest. Her enemies have chased her down, and she has nowhere to turn.

⁴The roads to Jerusalem* are in mourning, no longer filled with crowds on their way to celebrate the Temple festivals. The city gates are silent, her priests groan, her young women are crying—how bitterly Jerusalem weeps!

I BELIEVE the Lord punished Jerusalem for her many sins. (1:5)

⁵Her oppressors have become her masters, and her enemies prosper, for the LORD has punished Jerusalem for her many sins. Her children have been captured and taken away to distant lands.

⁶All the beauty and majesty of Jerusalem* are gone. Her princes are like starving deer searching for pasture, too weak to run from the pursuing enemy.

⁷And now in the midst of her sadness and wandering, Jerusalem remembers her ancient splendor. But then she fell to her enemy, and there was no one to help her. Her enemy struck her down and laughed as she fell.

⁸Jerusalem has sinned greatly, so she has been tossed away like a filthy rag. All who once honored her now despise her, for they have seen her stripped naked and humiliated. All she can do is groan and hide her face.

I ABHOR sexual and spiritual immorality. (1:9)

⁹She defiled herself with immorality with no thought of the punishment that would follow. Now she lies in the gutter with no one to lift her out. "LORD, see my deep misery," she cries. "The enemy has triumphed."

¹⁰The enemy has plundered her completely, taking everything precious that she owns. She has seen foreigners violate her sacred Temple, the place the LORD had forbidden them to enter.

¹¹Her people groan as they search for bread. They have sold their treasures for food to stay alive. "O LORD, look," she mourns, "and see how I am despised.

¹²"Is it nothing to you, all you who pass by? Look around and see if there is any suffering like mine, which the LORD brought on me in the day of his fierce anger.

¹³"He has sent fire from heaven that burns in my bones. He has placed a trap in my path and turned me back. He has made me desolate, racked with sickness all day long.

¹⁴"He wove my sins into ropes to hitch me to a yoke of captivity. The Lord sapped my strength and gave me to my enemies; I am helpless in their hands.

¹⁵"The Lord has treated my mighty men with contempt. At his command a great army has come to crush my young warriors. The Lord has trampled his beloved city* as grapes are trampled in a winepress.

¹⁶"For all these things I weep; tears flow down my cheeks. No one is here to comfort me; any who might encourage me are far away. My children have no future, for the enemy has conquered us."

¹⁷Jerusalem pleads for help, but no one comforts her. Regarding his people,* the LORD has said, "Let their neighbors be their enemies! Let them be thrown away like a filthy rag!"

I BELIEVE the Lord was right to punish his rebellious people. (1:18)

¹⁸"And the LORD is right," she groans, "for I rebelled against him. Listen, people everywhere; look upon my anguish and despair, for my sons and daughters have been taken captive to distant lands.

¹⁹"I begged my allies for help, but they betrayed me. My priests and leaders starved to death in the city, even as they searched for food to save their lives.

I DO NOT REBEL against the Lord. (1:20)

²⁰"LORD, see my anguish! My heart is broken and my soul despairs, for I have rebelled against you. In the streets the sword kills, and at home there is only death.

²¹"Others heard my groans, but no one turned to comfort me. When my enemies heard of my troubles, they were happy to see what you had done. Oh, bring the day you promised, when you will destroy them as you have destroyed me.

²²"Look at all their evil deeds, LORD. Punish them, as you have punished me for all my sins. My groans are many, and my heart is faint."

1:4 Hebrew Zion; also in 1:17.   1:6 Hebrew the daughter of Zion.   1:15 Hebrew the virgin daughter of Judah.
1:17 Hebrew Jacob.

CHAPTER 2

God's Anger at Sin

The Lord in his anger has cast a dark shadow over Jerusalem.* The fairest of Israel's cities lies in the dust, thrown down from the heights of heaven. In his day of awesome fury, the Lord has shown no mercy even to his Temple.*

²Without mercy the Lord has destroyed every home in Israel.* In his anger he has broken down the fortress walls of Jerusalem.* He has brought to dust the kingdom and all its rulers.

³All the strength of Israel vanishes beneath his fury. The Lord has withdrawn his protection as the enemy attacks. He consumes the whole land of Israel like a raging fire.

⁴He bends his bow against his people as though he were their enemy. His strength is used against them to kill their finest youth. His fury is poured out like fire on beautiful Jerusalem.*

⁵Yes, the Lord has vanquished Israel like an enemy. He has destroyed her forts and palaces. He has brought unending sorrow and tears to Jerusalem.

⁶He has broken down his Temple as though it were merely a garden shelter. The LORD has blotted out all memory of the holy festivals and Sabbath days. Kings and priests fall together before his anger.

⁷The Lord has rejected his own altar; he despises his own sanctuary. He has given Jerusalem's palaces to her enemies. They shout in the LORD's Temple as though it were a day of celebration.

⁸The LORD was determined to destroy the walls of Jerusalem. He made careful plans for their destruction, then he went ahead and did it. Therefore, the ramparts and walls have fallen down before him.

⁹Jerusalem's gates have sunk into the ground. All their locks and bars are destroyed, for he has smashed them. Her kings and princes have been exiled to distant lands; the law is no more. Her prophets receive no more visions from the LORD.

¹⁰The leaders of Jerusalem sit on the ground in silence, clothed in sackcloth. They throw dust on their heads in sorrow and despair. The young women of Jerusalem hang their heads in shame.

¹¹I have cried until the tears no longer come. My heart is broken, my spirit poured out, as I see what has happened to my people. Little children and tiny babies are fainting and dying in the streets.

¹²"Mama, we want food," they cry, and then collapse in their mothers' arms. Their lives ebb away like the life of a warrior wounded in battle.

¹³In all the world has there ever been such sorrow? O daughter of Jerusalem, to what can I compare your anguish? O virgin daughter of Zion, how can I comfort you? For your wound is as deep as the sea. Who can heal you?

¹⁴Your "prophets" have said so many foolish things, false to the core. They did not try to hold you back from exile by pointing out your sins. Instead, they painted false pictures, filling you with false hope.

¹⁵All who pass by jeer at you. They scoff and insult Jerusalem,* saying, "Is this the city called 'Most Beautiful in All the World' and 'Joy of All the Earth'?"

¹⁶All your enemies deride you. They scoff and grind their teeth and say, "We have destroyed her at last! Long have we awaited this day, and it is finally here!"

¹⁷But it is the LORD who did it just as he warned. He has fulfilled the promises of disaster he made long ago. He has destroyed Jerusalem without mercy and caused her enemies to rejoice over her and boast of their power.

¹⁸Cry aloud* before the Lord, O walls of Jerusalem! Let your tears flow like a river. Give yourselves no rest from weeping day or night.

¹⁹Rise during the night and cry out. Pour out your hearts like water to the

I BELIEVE the Lord withdrew his protection when the Babylonians attacked Jerusalem. (2:3)

I WEEP when I remember the Lord's judgment against those who would not stop rebelling against him. (2:11)

I DISMISS the words of "prophets" who fill people with false hope and do not point out their sins. (2:14)

I BELIEVE the Lord did everything he planned against Jerusalem. (2:17)

2:1a Hebrew *the daughter of Zion;* also in 2:8, 10, 18.   2:1b Hebrew *footstool.*   2:2a Hebrew *Jacob;* also in 2:3.   2:2b Hebrew *the daughter of Judah;* also in 2:5.   2:4 Hebrew *on the tent of the daughter of Zion.* 2:15 Hebrew *the daughter of Jerusalem.*   2:18 Hebrew *Their heart cried.*

Lord. Lift up your hands to him in prayer. Plead for your children as they faint with hunger in the streets.

²⁰"O LORD, think about this!" Jerusalem cries. "You are doing this to your own people! Should mothers eat their little children, those they once bounced on their knees? Should priests and prophets die within the Lord's Temple?

²¹"See them lying in the streets—young and old, boys and girls, killed by the swords of the enemy. You have killed them in your anger, slaughtering them without mercy.

²²"You have invited terrors from all around as though you were calling them to a day of feasting. In the day of the LORD's anger, no one has escaped or survived. The enemy has killed all the children I bore and raised."

CHAPTER 3

Hope in the LORD's Faithfulness

I am the one who has seen the afflictions that come from the rod of the LORD's anger. ²He has brought me into deep darkness, shutting out all light. ³He has turned against me. Day and night his hand is heavy upon me.

⁴He has made my skin and flesh grow old. He has broken my bones. ⁵He has attacked me and surrounded me with anguish and distress. ⁶He has buried me in a dark place, like a person long dead.

⁷He has walled me in, and I cannot escape. He has bound me in heavy chains. ⁸And though I cry and shout, he shuts out my prayers. ⁹He has blocked my path with a high stone wall. He has twisted the road before me with many detours.

¹⁰He hid like a bear or a lion, waiting to attack me. ¹¹He dragged me off the path and tore me with his claws, leaving me helpless and desolate. ¹²He bent his bow and aimed it squarely at me.

¹³He shot his arrows deep into my heart. ¹⁴My own people laugh at me. All day long they sing their mocking songs. ¹⁵He has filled me with bitterness. He has given me a cup of deep sorrow to drink.

¹⁶He has made me grind my teeth on gravel. He has rolled me in the dust. ¹⁷Peace has been stripped away, and I have forgotten what prosperity is. ¹⁸I cry out, "My splendor is gone! Everything I had hoped for from the LORD is lost!"

¹⁹The thought of my suffering and homelessness is bitter beyond words.* ²⁰I will never forget this awful time, as I grieve over my loss. ²¹Yet I still dare to hope when I remember this:

²²The unfailing love of the LORD never ends! By his mercies we have been kept from complete destruction. ²³Great is his faithfulness; his mercies begin afresh each day. ²⁴I say to myself, "The LORD is my inheritance; therefore, I will hope in him!"

²⁵The LORD is wonderfully good to those who wait for him and seek him. ²⁶So it is good to wait quietly for salvation from the LORD. ²⁷And it is good for the young to submit to the yoke of his discipline.

²⁸Let them sit alone in silence beneath the LORD's demands. ²⁹Let them lie face down in the dust; then at last there is hope for them. ³⁰Let them turn the other cheek to those who strike them. Let them accept the insults of their enemies.

³¹For the Lord does not abandon anyone forever. ³²Though he brings grief, he also shows compassion according to the greatness of his unfailing love. ³³For he does not enjoy hurting people or causing them sorrow.

³⁴But the leaders of his people trampled prisoners underfoot. ³⁵They deprived people of their God-given rights in defiance of the Most High. ³⁶They perverted justice in the courts. Do they think the Lord didn't see it?

³⁷Can anything happen without the Lord's permission? ³⁸Is it not the Most High who helps one and harms another? ³⁹Then why should we, mere humans, complain when we are punished for our sins?

3:19 Hebrew *is wormwood and gall.*

I BELIEVE the wages of sin is death (Romans 6:23). (2:21)

I PUT my hope in the Lord, even as I grieve over deep pain and loss in my life. (3:21)

I KNOW the unfailing love of the Lord never ends (Romans 8:38-39). (3:22)

I REJOICE in the Lord's great faithfulness and mercy to me. (3:23)

I NEVER STOP placing my hope and trust in the Lord, no matter what happens. (3:24)

I WAIT for the Lord and seek him, for he is wonderfully good. (3:25)

I LOVE the Lord and submit to the yoke of his discipline when I have sinned (Hebrews 12:5-6). (3:27)

I TURN the other cheek to those who strike me (Matthew 5:39). (3:30)

I DO NOT DEPRIVE others of their God-given rights. (3:35)

I DO NOT COMPLAIN when I am punished for my sins. (3:39)

⁴⁰Instead, let us test and examine our ways. Let us turn again in repentance to the LORD. ⁴¹Let us lift our hearts and hands to God in heaven and say, ⁴²"We have sinned and rebelled, and you have not forgiven us.

⁴³"You have engulfed us with your anger, chased us down, and slaughtered us without mercy. ⁴⁴You have hidden yourself in a cloud so our prayers cannot reach you. ⁴⁵You have discarded us as refuse and garbage among the nations.

⁴⁶"All our enemies have spoken out against us. ⁴⁷We are filled with fear, for we are trapped, desolate, and ruined." ⁴⁸Streams of tears flow from my eyes because of the destruction of my people!

⁴⁹My tears flow down endlessly. They will not stop ⁵⁰until the LORD looks down from heaven and sees. ⁵¹My heart is breaking over the fate of all the women of Jerusalem.

⁵²My enemies, whom I have never harmed, chased me like a bird. ⁵³They threw me into a pit and dropped stones on me. ⁵⁴The water flowed above my head, and I cried out, "This is the end!"

⁵⁵But I called on your name, LORD, from deep within the well, ⁵⁶and you heard me! You listened to my pleading; you heard my weeping! ⁵⁷Yes, you came at my despairing cry and told me, "Do not fear."

⁵⁸Lord, you are my lawyer! Plead my case! For you have redeemed my life. ⁵⁹You have seen the wrong they have done to me, LORD. Be my judge, and prove me right. ⁶⁰You have seen the plots my enemies have laid against me.

⁶¹LORD, you have heard the vile names they call me. You know all about the plans they have made—⁶²the plots my enemies whisper and mutter against me all day long. ⁶³Look at them! In all their activities, they constantly mock me with their songs.

⁶⁴Pay them back, LORD, for all the evil they have done. ⁶⁵Give them hard and stubborn hearts, and then let your curse fall upon them! ⁶⁶Chase them down in your anger, destroying them from beneath the LORD's heavens.

CHAPTER 4

God's Anger Satisfied

How the gold has lost its luster! Even the finest gold has become dull. The sacred gemstones lie scattered in the streets!

²See how the precious children of Jerusalem,* worth their weight in gold, are now treated like pots of clay.

³Even the jackals feed their young, but not my people Israel. They ignore their children's cries, like the ostriches of the desert.

⁴The parched tongues of their little ones stick with thirst to the roofs of their mouths. The children cry for bread, but no one has any to give them.

⁵The people who once ate only the richest foods now beg in the streets for anything they can get. Those who once lived in palaces now search the garbage pits for food.

⁶The guilt* of my people is greater than that of Sodom, where utter disaster struck in a moment with no one to help them.

⁷Our princes were once glowing with health; they were as clean as snow and as elegant as jewels.

⁸But now their faces are blacker than soot. No one even recognizes them. Their skin sticks to their bones; it is as dry and hard as wood.

⁹Those killed by the sword are far better off than those who die of hunger, wasting away for want of food.

¹⁰Tenderhearted women have cooked their own children and eaten them in order to survive the siege.

¹¹But now the anger of the LORD is satisfied. His fiercest anger has now

I WEEP when I remember the Lord's judgment against those who wouldn't stop rebelling against him. (3:48)

I RECOGNIZE that godly individuals are not exempt from persecution (2 Timothy 3:12). (3:53)

I DO NOT TRY to avenge myself but leave that to God (Romans 12:19). (3:64)

I NEVER want to experience the disastrous consequences of unconfessed sin and unresolved guilt. (4:6)

4:2 Hebrew *sons of Zion.*   4:6 Or *punishment.*

been poured out. He started a fire in Jerusalem* that burned the city to its foundations.

¹²Not a king in all the earth—no one in all the world—would have believed an enemy could march through the gates of Jerusalem.

I ABHOR murder. (4:13)

¹³Yet it happened because of the sins of her prophets and priests, who defiled the city by shedding innocent blood.

¹⁴They wandered blindly through the streets, so defiled by blood that no one dared to touch them.

¹⁵"Get away!" the people shouted at them. "You are defiled! Don't touch us!" So they fled to distant lands and wandered there among foreign nations, but none would let them stay.

¹⁶The LORD himself has scattered them, and he no longer helps them. The priests and leaders are no longer honored and respected.

I LOOK to the Lord alone for salvation. (4:17)

¹⁷We looked in vain for our allies to come and save us, but we were looking to nations that could offer no help at all.

¹⁸We couldn't go into the streets without danger to our lives. Our end was near; our days were numbered. We were doomed!

¹⁹Our enemies were swifter than the eagles. If we fled to the mountains, they found us. If we hid in the wilderness, they were waiting for us there.

I DO NOT arrogantly boast about what I will do. (4:20)

²⁰Our king, the LORD's anointed, the very life of our nation, was caught in their snares. We had foolishly boasted that under his protection we could hold our own against any nation on earth!

²¹Are you rejoicing in the land of Uz, O people of Edom? But you, too, must drink from the cup of the LORD's anger. You, too, will be stripped naked in your drunkenness.

²²O Jerusalem,* your punishment will end; you will soon return from exile. But Edom, your punishment is just beginning; soon your many sins will be revealed.

CHAPTER 5

Prayer for Restoration

LORD, remember everything that has happened to us. See all the sorrows we bear! ²Our inheritance has been turned over to strangers, our homes to foreigners. ³We are orphaned and fatherless. Our mothers are widowed. ⁴We have to pay for water to drink, and even firewood is expensive. ⁵Those who pursue us are at our heels; we are exhausted but are given no rest. ⁶We submitted to Egypt and Assyria to get enough food to survive. ⁷It was our ancestors who sinned, but they died before the hand of judgment fell. We have suffered the punishment they deserved!

I BELIEVE the wages of sin is death (Romans 6:23). (5:7)

I ABHOR rape and other horrible acts of violence. (5:11)

I NEVER WANT to experience the disastrous consequences of unconfessed sin. (5:16)

I AM THANKFUL that the Lord remains the same forever! (5:19)

I ASK the Lord to renew my strength with his joy (Nehemiah 8:10). (5:21)

⁸Slaves have now become our masters; there is no one left to rescue us. ⁹We must hunt for food in the wilderness at the risk of our lives. ¹⁰Because of the famine, our skin has been blackened as though baked in an oven. ¹¹Our enemies rape the women and young girls in Jerusalem* and throughout the towns of Judah. ¹²Our princes are being hanged by their thumbs, and the old men are treated with contempt. ¹³The young men are led away to work at millstones, and the children stagger under heavy loads of wood. ¹⁴The old men no longer sit in the city gates; the young men no longer dance and sing.

¹⁵The joy of our hearts has ended; our dancing has turned to mourning. ¹⁶The garlands have* fallen from our heads. Disaster has fallen upon us because we have sinned. ¹⁷Our hearts are sick and weary, and our eyes grow dim with tears. ¹⁸For Jerusalem* is empty and desolate, a place haunted by jackals.

¹⁹But LORD, you remain the same forever! Your throne continues from generation to generation. ²⁰Why do you continue to forget us? Why have you forsaken us for so long? ²¹Restore us, O LORD, and bring us back to you again! Give us back the joys we once had! ²²Or have you utterly rejected us? Are you angry with us still?

4:11 Hebrew *in Zion.* 4:22 Hebrew *daughter of Zion.* 5:11 Hebrew *Zion.* 5:16 Or *The crown has.* 5:18 Hebrew *Mount Zion.*

EZEKIEL

THIS THIRD "MAJOR" Old Testament prophet urges readers to "know that I am the LORD."

The phrase, "know that I am the LORD," appears dozens of times throughout the book of Ezekiel. The phrase speaks of the Lord's great desire to love and be loved by his people. Sadly, most people in Ezekiel's day rebel against the Lord and become engrossed either in themselves or in materialism, immorality, and idolatry.

As an introduction to his prophecies, Ezekiel recounts seeing the Lord's glory (chapter 1) and receiving God's call at age thirty to be a prophet, not a priest (chapters 2–3). Ezekiel then warns the kingdom of Judah of coming judgment (chapters 4–7), sees visions of the Lord's glory departing from the Temple (chapters 8–11), continues to exhort the people of Judah to repent (chapters 12–24), and prophesies against other nations (chapters 25–32). After Jerusalem's fall, Ezekiel speaks of the nation's travails and future restoration (chapters 33–39).

More than a dozen years after Jerusalem's fall, Ezekiel prophesies again (chapters 40–48). His last major prophecy speaks of a new Temple to be built in Jerusalem—and filled with the Lord's glory—if the exiled Jewish people would truly repent (43:11).

In his public ministry and writings, Ezekiel uses signs, visions, direct prophecy, parables, poems, proverbs, and conditional promises to urge the people of Judah to repent and know the Lord.

Famous verses in Ezekiel include

- ○ Ezekiel sees God's glory (1:26-28; 3:23; 8:4; 9:3; 10:4, 18-19; 11:22-23; 43:2-5)
- ○ God commands Ezekiel to speak even if the people will not listen (2:7; 3:4-8, 11; 33:30-33)
- ○ God commands Ezekiel to be a watchman warning his people (3:16-21; 18:1-32; 33:1-33)
- ○ God says he will judge the people for their actions (7:3, 9, 27; 18:30; 24:14; 33:20; 36:19; 39:24)
- ○ God promises to restore his people if they repent (11:16-20; 18:31; 36:26-28; 43:11)
- ○ "The parents have eaten sour grapes, but their children's mouths . . ." (18:2)
- ○ "I don't want you to die. . . . Turn back and live!" (18:32; see 33:11)
- ○ "I gave them my laws so they could live by keeping them" (20:11; see 20:13, 21)
- ○ "And I gave them my Sabbath days of rest as a sign" (20:12; see 20:13, 21)
- ○ "I searched for someone to stand in the gap" (22:30)
- ○ "You were the perfection of wisdom and beauty. You were in Eden" (28:12-13)
- ○ "I myself will search and find my sheep. I will be like a shepherd" (34:11-12)

CHAPTER 1

A Vision of Living Beings

On July 31* of my thirtieth year,* while I was with the Judean exiles beside the Kebar River in Babylon, the heavens were opened to me, and I saw visions of God. ²This happened during the fifth year of King Jehoiachin's captivity. ³The LORD gave a message to me, Ezekiel son of Buzi, a priest, there beside the Kebar River in the land of the Babylonians,* and I felt the hand of the LORD take hold of me.

⁴As I looked, I saw a great storm coming toward me from the north, driving before it a huge cloud that flashed with lightning and shone with brilliant light. The fire inside the cloud glowed like gleaming amber. ⁵From the center of the cloud came four living beings that looked human, ⁶except that each had four faces and two pairs of wings. ⁷Their legs were straight like human legs, but their feet were split like calves' feet and shone like burnished bronze. ⁸Beneath each of their wings I could see human hands. ⁹The wings of each living being touched the wings of the two beings beside it. The living beings were able to fly in any direction without turning around. ¹⁰Each had a human face in the front, the face of a lion on the right side, the face of an ox on the left side, and the face of an eagle at the back. ¹¹Each had two pairs of outstretched wings—one pair stretched out to touch the wings of the living beings on either side of it, and the other pair covered its body. ¹²They went in whatever direction the spirit chose, and they moved straight forward in all directions without having to turn around.

¹³The living beings looked like bright coals of fire or brilliant torches, and it looked as though lightning was flashing back and forth among them. ¹⁴And the living beings darted to and fro like flashes of lightning.

¹⁵As I looked at these beings, I saw four wheels on the ground beneath them, one wheel belonging to each. ¹⁶The wheels sparkled as if made of chrysolite. All four wheels looked the same; each wheel had a second wheel turning crosswise within it. ¹⁷The beings could move forward in any of the four directions they faced, without turning as they moved. ¹⁸The rims of the four wheels were awesomely tall, and they were covered with eyes all around the edges. ¹⁹When the four living beings moved, the wheels moved with them. When they flew upward, the wheels went up, too. ²⁰The spirit of the four living beings was in the wheels. So wherever the spirit went, the wheels and the living beings went, too. ²¹When the living beings moved, the wheels moved. When the living beings stopped, the wheels stopped. When the living beings flew into the air, the wheels rose up. For the spirit of the living beings was in the wheels.

²²There was a surface spread out above them like the sky. It sparkled like crystal. ²³Beneath this surface the wings of each living being stretched out to touch the others' wings, and each had two wings covering its body. ²⁴As they flew their wings roared like waves crashing against the shore, or like the voice of the Almighty,* or like the shouting of a mighty army. When they stopped, they let down their wings. ²⁵As they stood with their wings lowered, a voice spoke from beyond the crystal surface above them.

²⁶Above the surface over their heads was what looked like a throne made of blue sapphire. And high above this throne was a figure whose appearance was like that of a man. ²⁷From his waist up, he looked like gleaming amber, flickering like a fire. And from his waist down, he looked like a burning flame, shining with splendor. ²⁸All around him was a glowing halo, like a rainbow shining through the clouds. This was the way the glory of the LORD appeared to me. When I saw it, I fell face down in the dust, and I heard someone's voice speaking to me.

*Sidebar notes:*

I BELIEVE Ezekiel saw visions of God while in Babylon with the exiles. (1:1)

I BELIEVE the Lord gave his message to Ezekiel. (1:3)

I BELIEVE Ezekiel saw four supernatural beings—the four living beings. (1:5)

Ask God to open your eyes as you read his Word (Psalm 119:18).

I BELIEVE Ezekiel saw the glory of the Lord on his throne, like the appearance of a man gleaming with brightness. (1:26)

I FALL DOWN in worship before the glory of the Lord. (1:28)

1:1a Hebrew *On the fifth day of the fourth month,* of the Hebrew calendar. A number of dates in Ezekiel can be cross-checked with dates in surviving Babylonian records and related accurately to our modern calendar. This event occurred on July 31, 593 B.C. 1:1b Or *in the thirtieth year.* 1:3 Or *Chaldeans.* 1:24 Hebrew *Shaddai.*

CHAPTER 2

Ezekiel's Call and Commission

"Stand up, son of man," said the voice. "I want to speak with you." ²The Spirit came into me as he spoke and set me on my feet. I listened carefully to his words. ³"Son of man," he said, "I am sending you to the nation of Israel, a nation that is rebelling against me. Their ancestors have rebelled against me from the beginning, and they are still in revolt to this very day. ⁴They are a hard-hearted and stubborn people. But I am sending you to say to them, 'This is what the Sovereign LORD says!' ⁵And whether they listen or not—for remember, they are rebels—at least they will know they have had a prophet among them.

⁶"Son of man, do not fear them. Don't be afraid even though their threats are sharp as thorns and barbed like briers, and they sting like scorpions. Do not be dismayed by their dark scowls. For remember, they are rebels! ⁷You must give them my messages whether they listen or not. But they won't listen, for they are completely rebellious! ⁸Son of man, listen to what I say to you. Do not join them in being a rebel. Open your mouth, and eat what I give you."

⁹Then I looked and saw a hand reaching out to me, and it held a scroll. ¹⁰He unrolled it, and I saw that both sides were covered with funeral songs, other words of sorrow, and pronouncements of doom.

I AM NOT AFRAID or dismayed by the threats of those who rebel against God's Word. (2:6)

I DO NOT JOIN others in rebelling against the Lord. (2:8)

LIKE EZEKIEL   *I long to experience God's glory and presence.*

Ezekiel 1:28

If only someone could have put a video camera in Ezekiel's hands before God transported him in a series of visions to see the Lord's glory and watch it slowly depart from the Temple. This was no Hollywood production—the producer, actor, soundman, and scriptwriter were all God himself.

Without a camera, Ezekiel tried to use words to describe the color and splendor of God's glorious throne. He found it difficult to portray the all-consuming experience—the sound and lights, the motion and emotion of being in the Lord's presence.

True, Ezekiel had been exiled to Babylon—hundreds of miles from the Temple. Nevertheless, he experienced what other priests only dreamed of. Ezekiel didn't just step into the Most Holy Place and stand in awe of the Lord's invisible presence above the gold cherubim on the Ark of the Covenant. Instead, Ezekiel was ushered into the very presence of God where real cherubim moved about and the voice of God thundered like many waters.

Having seen beyond the symbolic to the reality of the Lord's glory, Ezekiel spoke to the exiles with inflamed passion. He knew the glory the Israelites were rejecting when they turned to bow before grotesque and useless idols. So he constantly urged them to repent and turn back to the Lord.

Like Ezekiel, you and I can experience the glory and presence of God. How? Through his Son Jesus Christ (John 1:14) and through his Holy Spirit who makes our hearts God's new Temple (2 Corinthians 6:16).

While we have not seen God yet, we can display and portray his glory so others may choose life and dwell in his presence, as well (1 Peter 1:8; Matthew 5:16).

○ *Today's Scripture reading is Ezekiel 1–3.*

CHAPTER 3

The voice said to me, "Son of man, eat what I am giving you—eat this scroll! Then go and give its message to the people of Israel." ²So I opened my mouth, and he fed me the scroll. ³"Eat it all," he said. And when I ate it, it tasted as sweet as honey.

⁴Then he said, "Son of man, go to the people of Israel with my messages. ⁵I am not sending you to some foreign people whose language you cannot understand. ⁶No, I am not sending you to people with strange and difficult speech. If I did, they would listen! ⁷I am sending you to the people of Israel, but they

I DO whatever the Lord commands. (3:1)

I BELIEVE God accurately warned Ezekiel ahead of time that his people would not listen to the Lord's message. (3:7)

won't listen to you any more than they listen to me! For the whole lot of them are hard-hearted and stubborn. ⁸But look, I have made you as hard and stubborn as they are. ⁹I have made you as hard as rock! So don't be afraid of them or fear their angry looks, even though they are such rebels."

¹⁰Then he added, "Son of man, let all my words sink deep into your own heart first. Listen to them carefully for yourself. ¹¹Then go to your people in exile and say to them, 'This is what the Sovereign LORD says!' Do this whether they listen to you or not."

¹²Then the Spirit lifted me up, and I heard a loud rumbling sound behind me. (May the glory of the LORD be praised in his place!)* ¹³It was the sound of the wings of the living beings as they brushed against each other and the rumbling of their wheels beneath them.

¹⁴The Spirit lifted me up and took me away. I went in bitterness and turmoil, but the LORD's hold on me was strong. ¹⁵Then I came to the colony of Judean exiles in Tel-abib, beside the Kebar River. I sat there among them for seven days, overwhelmed.

A Watchman for Israel

¹⁶At the end of the seven days, the LORD gave me a message. He said, ¹⁷"Son of man, I have appointed you as a watchman for Israel. Whenever you receive a message from me, pass it on to the people immediately. ¹⁸If I warn the wicked, saying, 'You are under the penalty of death,' but you fail to deliver the warning, they will die in their sins. And I will hold you responsible, demanding your blood for theirs. ¹⁹If you warn them and they keep on sinning and refuse to repent, they will die in their sins. But you will have saved your life because you did what you were told to do. ²⁰If good people turn bad and don't listen to my warning, they will die. If you did not warn them of the consequences, then they will die in their sins. Their previous good deeds won't help them, and I will hold you responsible, demanding your blood for theirs. ²¹But if you warn them and they repent, they will live, and you will have saved your own life, too."

²²Then the LORD took hold of me, and he said to me, "Go out into the valley, and I will talk to you there." ²³So I got up and went, and there I saw the glory of the LORD, just as I had seen it in my first vision by the Kebar River. And I fell face down in the dust.

²⁴Then the Spirit came into me and set me on my feet. He talked to me and said, "Go, shut yourself up in your house. ²⁵There you will be bound with ropes so you cannot go out among the people. ²⁶And I will make your tongue stick to the roof of your mouth so you won't be able to pray for them, for they are rebellious. ²⁷But whenever I give you a message, I will loosen your tongue and let you speak. Then you will say to them, 'This is what the Sovereign LORD says!' Some of them will listen, but some will ignore you, for they are rebels.

CHAPTER 4

A Sign of the Coming Siege

"And now, son of man, take a large brick and set it down in front of you. Then draw a map of the city of Jerusalem on it. ²Build siege ramps against the city walls. Surround it with enemy camps and battering rams. ³Then take an iron griddle and place it between you and the city. Turn toward it and demonstrate how the enemy will attack Jerusalem. This will be a warning to the people of Israel.

⁴"Now lie on your left side and place the sins of Israel on yourself. You are to bear their sins for the number of days you lie there on your side. ⁵You will bear Israel's sins for 390 days—one day for each year of their sin. ⁶After that,

---

I TAKE God's words to heart before I present them to others. (3:10)

I SPEAK God's words whether people listen or not. (3:11)

I BELIEVE the Lord appointed Ezekiel as a watchman to the people of Israel in exile. (3:17)

I BELIEVE Ezekiel saw the glory of the Lord. (3:23)

I BELIEVE the Lord instructed Ezekiel to build a model of Jerusalem to picture how the enemy would attack. (4:3)

I BELIEVE the Lord instructed Ezekiel to lie on his side for 430 days to represent the years of Israel and Judah's sin. (4:4)

3:12 A likely reading for this verse is *Then the Spirit lifted me up, and as the glory of the LORD rose from its place, I heard behind me a loud rumbling sound.*

turn over and lie on your right side for 40 days—one day for each year of Judah's sin.

⁷"Meanwhile, continue your demonstration of the siege of Jerusalem. Lie there with your arm bared and prophesy her destruction. ⁸I will tie you up with ropes so you won't be able to turn from side to side until the days of your siege have been completed.

⁹"Now go and get some wheat, barley, beans, lentils, millet, and spelt, and mix them together in a storage jar. Use this food to make bread for yourself during the 390 days you will be lying on your side. ¹⁰Ration this out to yourself, eight ounces* of food for each day, and eat it at set times. ¹¹Then measure out a jar* of water for each day, and drink it at set times. ¹²Each day prepare your bread as you would barley cakes. While all the people are watching, bake it over a fire using dried human dung as fuel and then eat the bread. ¹³For this is what the LORD says: Israel will eat defiled bread in the Gentile lands, where I will banish them!"

¹⁴Then I said, "O Sovereign LORD, must I be defiled by using human dung? For I have never been defiled before. From the time I was a child until now I have never eaten any animal that died of sickness or that I found dead. And I have never eaten any of the animals that our laws forbid."

¹⁵"All right," the LORD said. "You may bake your bread with cow dung instead of human dung." ¹⁶Then he told me, "Son of man, I will cause food to be very scarce in Jerusalem. It will be weighed out with great care and eaten fearfully. The water will be portioned out drop by drop, and the people will drink it with dismay. ¹⁷Food and water will be so scarce that the people will look at one another in terror, and they will waste away under their punishment.

CHAPTER 5

A Sign of the Coming Judgment

"Son of man, take a sharp sword and use it as a razor to shave your head and beard. Use a scale to weigh the hair into three equal parts. ²Place a third of it at the center of your map of Jerusalem. After acting out the siege, burn it there. Scatter another third across your map and slash at it with a sword. Scatter the last third to the wind, for I will scatter my people with the sword. ³Keep just a bit of the hair and tie it up in your robe. ⁴Then take a few of these hairs out and throw them into the fire, burning them up. A fire will then spread from this remnant and destroy all of Israel.

⁵"This is what the Sovereign LORD says: This is an illustration of what will happen to Jerusalem. I placed her at the center of the nations, ⁶but she has rebelled against my regulations and has been even more wicked than the surrounding nations. She has refused to obey the laws I gave her to follow. ⁷So this is what the Sovereign LORD says: Since you have refused to obey my laws and regulations and have behaved even worse than your neighbors, ⁸I myself, the Sovereign LORD, am now your enemy. I will punish you publicly while all the nations watch. ⁹Because of your detestable idols, I will punish you more severely than I have punished anyone before or ever will again. ¹⁰Parents will eat their own children, and children will eat their parents. And I will punish you by scattering the few who survive to the far reaches of the earth.

¹¹"As surely as I live, says the Sovereign LORD, I will cut you off completely. I will show you no pity at all because you have defiled my Temple with idols and vile practices. ¹²A third of your people will die in the city from famine and disease. A third of them will be slaughtered by the enemy outside the city walls. And I will scatter a third to the winds and chase them with my sword. ¹³Then at last my anger will be spent, and I will be satisfied. And when my fury against them has subsided, all Israel will know that I, the LORD, have spoken to them in my jealous anger.

4:10 Hebrew *20 shekels* [228 grams].   4:11 Hebrew ⅙ *of a hin,* about 1.3 pints or 0.6 liters.

I BELIEVE the Lord instructed Ezekiel to make defiled bread to demonstrate how the Israelites would eat defiled bread while in exile. (4:9)

I BELIEVE the Lord instructed Ezekiel to shave his hair and use it to show how Jerusalem would be burned and the people scattered. (5:1)

I BELIEVE the Israelites were punished severely because of their detestable idolatry. (5:9)

I BELIEVE the Lord kept his promise that his anger against Israel would subside and that they would know that he is the Lord. (5:13)

I BELIEVE the Lord
would show the
nations what happens
when the Lord rebukes
a nation who deserts
him. (5:15)

¹⁴"So I will turn you into a ruin, a mockery in the eyes of the surrounding nations and to everyone who travels by. ¹⁵You will become an object of mockery and taunting and horror. You will be a warning to all the nations around you. They will see what happens when the LORD turns against a nation in furious rebuke. I, the LORD, have spoken!

¹⁶"I will shower you with the deadly arrows of famine to destroy you. The famine will become more and more severe until every crumb of food is gone. ¹⁷And along with the famine, wild animals will attack you, robbing you of your children. Disease and war will stalk your land, and I will bring the sword of the enemy against you. I, the LORD, have spoken!"

CHAPTER 6

Judgment against Israel's Mountains

Again a message came to me from the LORD: ²"Son of man, look over toward the mountains of Israel and prophesy against them. ³Give the mountains of Israel this message from the Sovereign LORD. This is what the Sovereign LORD says to the mountains and hills and to the ravines and valleys: I am about to bring war upon you, and I will destroy your pagan shrines. ⁴All your altars will be demolished, and your incense altars will be smashed. I will kill your people in front of your idols. ⁵I will lay your corpses in front of your idols and scatter your bones around your altars. ⁶Wherever you live there will be desolation. I will destroy your pagan shrines, your altars, your idols, your incense altars, and all the other religious objects you have made. ⁷Then when the place is littered with corpses, you will know that I am the LORD.

⁸"But I will let a few of my people escape destruction, and they will be scattered among the nations of the world. ⁹Then when they are exiled among the nations, they will remember me. They will recognize how grieved I am by their unfaithful hearts and lustful eyes that long for other gods. Then at last they will hate themselves for all their wickedness. ¹⁰They will know that I alone am the LORD and that I was serious when I predicted that all this would happen to them.

¹¹"This is what the Sovereign LORD says: Clap your hands in horror, and stamp your feet. Cry out, 'Alas!' because of all the evil that the people of Israel have done. Now they are going to die from war and famine and disease. ¹²Disease will strike down those who are far away in exile. War will destroy those who are nearby. And anyone who survives will be killed by famine. So at last I will spend my fury on them. ¹³When their dead lie scattered among their idols and altars, on every hill and mountain and under every green tree and great oak where they offered incense to their gods, then they will know that I alone am the LORD. ¹⁴I will crush them and make their cities desolate from the wilderness in the south to Riblah* in the north. Then they will know that I am the LORD."

CHAPTER 7

The Coming of the End

Then this message came to me from the LORD: ²"Son of man, this is what the Sovereign LORD says to Israel: The end is here! Wherever you look—east, west, north, or south—your land is finished. ³No hope remains, for I will unleash my anger against you. I will call you to account for all your disgusting behavior. ⁴I will turn my eyes away and show no pity, repaying you in full for all your evil. Then you will know that I am the LORD!

⁵"This is what the Sovereign LORD says: With one blow after another I will bring total disaster! ⁶The end has come! It has finally arrived! Your final doom is waiting! ⁷O people of Israel, the day of your destruction is dawning.

I BELIEVE the Lord
accurately foretold the
coming destruction of
the pagan shrines in
the mountains of
Israel. (6:3)

I BELIEVE the Israelites
learned God is the
Lord when he destroyed
their pagan idols. (6:7)

I RECOGNIZE the Lord
is grieved when his
people have unfaithful
hearts. (6:9)

I BELIEVE the Lord
called Israel to
account for all of
their disgusting, evil
behavior against him.
(7:3)

6:14 As in some Hebrew manuscripts; most Hebrew manuscripts read *Diblah.*

The time has come; the day of trouble is near. It will ring with shouts of anguish, not shouts of joy. ⁸Soon I will pour out my fury to complete your punishment for all your disgusting behavior. ⁹I will neither spare nor pity you. I will repay you for all your detestable practices. Then you will know that it is I, the LORD, who is striking the blow.

¹⁰"The day of judgment is here; your destruction awaits! The people's wickedness and pride have reached a climax. ¹¹Their violence will fall back on them as punishment for their wickedness. None of these proud and wicked people will survive. All their wealth will be swept away. ¹²Yes, the time has come; the day is here! There is no reason for buyers to rejoice over the bargains they find or for sellers to grieve over their losses, for all of them will fall under my terrible anger. ¹³And if any merchants should survive, they will never return to their business. For what God has said applies to everyone—it will not be changed! Not one person whose life is twisted by sin will recover.

The Desolation of Israel

¹⁴"The trumpets call Israel's army to mobilize, but no one listens, for my fury is against them all. ¹⁵Any who leave the city walls will be killed by enemy swords. Those who stay inside will die of famine and disease. ¹⁶The few who survive and escape to the mountains will moan like doves, weeping for their sins. ¹⁷Everyone's hands will be feeble; their knees will be as weak as water. ¹⁸They will dress themselves in sackcloth; horror and shame will cover them. They will shave their heads in sorrow and remorse.

¹⁹"They will throw away their money, tossing it out like worthless trash. It won't buy their deliverance in that day of the LORD's anger. It will neither satisfy nor feed them, for their love of money made them stumble into sin. ²⁰They were proud of their gold jewelry and used it to make vile and detestable idols. That is why I will make all their wealth disgusting to them. ²¹I will give it as plunder to foreigners from the most wicked of nations, and they will defile it. ²²I will hide my eyes as these robbers invade my treasured land and corrupt it.

²³"Prepare chains for my people, for the land is bloodied by terrible crimes. Jerusalem is filled with violence. ²⁴I will bring the most ruthless of nations to occupy their homes. I will break down their proud fortresses and defile their sanctuaries. ²⁵Terror and trembling will overcome my people. They will look for peace but will not find it. ²⁶Calamity will follow calamity; rumor will follow rumor. They will look in vain for a vision from the prophets. They will receive no teaching from the priests and no counsel from the leaders. ²⁷The king and the prince will stand helpless, weeping in despair, and the people's hands will tremble with fear. I will bring against them the evil they have done to others, and they will receive the punishment they so richly deserve. Then they will know that I am the LORD!"

CHAPTER 8

Idolatry in the Temple

Then on September 17,* during the sixth year of King Jehoiachin's captivity, while the leaders of Judah were in my home, the Sovereign LORD took hold of me. ²I saw a figure that appeared to be a man. From the waist down he looked like a burning flame. From the waist up he looked like gleaming amber. ³He put out what seemed to be a hand and took me by the hair. Then the Spirit lifted me up into the sky and transported me in a vision of God to Jerusalem. I was taken to the north gate of the inner courtyard of the Temple, where there is a large idol that has made the LORD very angry. ⁴Suddenly, the glory of the God of Israel was there, just as I had seen it before in the valley.

⁵Then the LORD said to me, "Son of man, look toward the north." So I

I BELIEVE the Lord's day of judgment came when the wickedness and pride of the people of Israel reached its climax. (7:10)

I DO NOT LOVE money or trust in it to buy my deliverance from God's judgment. (7:19)

I BELIEVE the Lord prepared chains for his people Israel because their land was filled with violence. (7:23)

I LISTEN intently and immediately to God's Word. (7:26)

I BELIEVE the Lord supernaturally transported Ezekiel in the midst of a vision to see the idolatry back in Jerusalem. (8:3)

8:1 Hebrew *on the fifth day of the sixth month*, of the Hebrew calendar. This event occurred on September 17, 592 B.C.; also see note on 1:1.

I KNOW the Lord is angered when his people worship idols instead of him. (8:5)

looked, and there to the north, beside the entrance to the gate of the altar, stood the idol that had made the LORD so angry.

⁶"Son of man," he said, "do you see what they are doing? Do you see the great sins the people of Israel are doing to drive me from my Temple? But come, and you will see even greater sins than these!" ⁷Then he brought me to the door of the Temple courtyard, where I could see an opening in the wall. ⁸He said to me, "Now, son of man, dig into the wall." So I dug into the wall and uncovered a door to a hidden room.

⁹"Go in," he said, "and see the unspeakable wickedness going on in there!" ¹⁰So I went in and saw the walls engraved with all kinds of snakes, lizards, and hideous creatures. I also saw the various idols worshiped by the people of Israel. ¹¹Seventy leaders of Israel were standing there with Jaazaniah son of Shaphan in the middle. Each of them held an incense burner, so there was a thick cloud of incense above their heads.

I DO NOT SIN in secret and think the Lord somehow does not see me. (8:12)

¹²Then the LORD said to me, "Son of man, have you seen what the leaders of Israel are doing with their idols in dark rooms? They are saying, 'The LORD doesn't see us; he has deserted our land!' " ¹³Then he added, "Come, and I will show you greater sins than these!"

¹⁴He brought me to the north gate of the LORD's Temple, and some women were sitting there, weeping for the god Tammuz. ¹⁵"Have you seen this?" he asked. "But I will show you even greater sins than these!"

¹⁶Then he brought me into the inner courtyard of the LORD's Temple. At the entrance, between the foyer and the bronze altar, about twenty-five men were standing with their backs to the LORD's Temple. They were facing eastward, worshiping the sun!

I ABHOR the terrible sins of Judah which provoked the Lord's anger. (8:17)

¹⁷"Have you seen this, son of man?" he asked. "Is it nothing to the people of Judah that they commit these terrible sins, leading the whole nation into violence, thumbing their noses at me, and rousing my fury against them? ¹⁸Therefore, I will deal with them in fury. I will neither pity nor spare them. And though they scream for mercy, I will not listen."

CHAPTER 9

The Slaughter of Idolaters

Then the LORD thundered, "Bring on the men appointed to punish the city! Tell them to bring their weapons with them!" ²Six men soon appeared from the upper gate that faces north, each carrying a battle club in his hand. One of them was dressed in linen and carried a writer's case strapped to his side. They all went into the Temple courtyard and stood beside the bronze altar.

I BELIEVE Ezekiel saw the Lord's glory begin to depart from the Temple. (9:3)

I BELIEVE God sees and sets apart those who grieve over the sin around them. (9:4)

³Then the glory of the God of Israel rose up from between the cherubim, where it had rested, and moved to the entrance of the Temple. And the LORD called to the man dressed in linen who was carrying the writer's case. ⁴He said to him, "Walk through the streets of Jerusalem and put a mark on the foreheads of all those who weep and sigh because of the sins they see around them."

⁵Then I heard the LORD say to the other men, "Follow him through the city and kill everyone whose forehead is not marked. Show no mercy; have no pity! ⁶Kill them all—old and young, girls and women and little children. But do not touch anyone with the mark. Begin your task right here at the Temple." So they began by killing the seventy leaders. ⁷"Defile the Temple!" the LORD commanded. "Fill its courtyards with the bodies of those you kill! Go!" So they went throughout the city and did as they were told.

⁸While they were carrying out their orders, I was all alone. I fell face down in the dust and cried out, "O Sovereign LORD! Will your fury against Jerusalem wipe out everyone left in Israel?"

I ABHOR murder and injustice. (9:9)

⁹Then he said to me, "The sins of the people of Israel and Judah are very great. The entire land is full of murder; the city is filled with injustice. They are saying, 'The LORD doesn't see it! The LORD has forsaken the land!' ¹⁰So I

will not spare them or have any pity on them. I will fully repay them for all they have done."

[11] Then the man in linen clothing, who carried the writer's case, reported back and said, "I have finished the work you gave me to do."

CHAPTER 10

The LORD's Glory Leaves the Temple

As I looked, I saw what appeared to be a throne of blue sapphire above the crystal surface over the heads of the cherubim. [2]Then the LORD spoke to the man in linen clothing and said, "Go in between the whirling wheels beneath the cherubim, and take a handful of glowing coals and scatter them over the city." He did this as I watched. [3]The cherubim were standing at the south end of the Temple when the man went in, and the cloud of glory filled the inner courtyard. [4]Then the glory of the LORD rose up from above the cherubim and went over to the door of the Temple. The Temple was filled with this cloud of glory, and the Temple courtyard glowed brightly with the glory of the LORD. [5]The moving wings of the cherubim sounded like the voice of God Almighty and could be heard clearly in the outer courtyard.

> I BELIEVE Ezekiel saw the Lord's glory move to the door of the Temple. (10:4)

[6]The LORD said to the man in linen clothing, "Go between the cherubim and take some burning coals from between the wheels." So the man went in and stood beside one of the wheels. [7]Then one of the cherubim reached out his hand and took some live coals from the fire burning among them. He put the coals into the hands of the man in linen clothing, and the man took them and went out. [8](All the cherubim had what looked like human hands hidden beneath their wings.)

[9]Each of the four cherubim had a wheel beside him, and the wheels sparkled like chrysolite. [10]All four wheels looked the same; each wheel had a second wheel turning crosswise within it. [11]The cherubim could move forward in any of the four directions they faced, without turning as they moved. They went straight in the direction in which their heads were turned, never turning aside. [12]Both the cherubim and the wheels were covered with eyes. The cherubim had eyes all over their bodies, including their hands, their backs, and their wings. [13]I heard someone refer to the wheels as "the whirling wheels." [14]Each of the four cherubim had four faces—the first was the face of an ox,* the second was a human face, the third was the face of a lion, and the fourth was the face of an eagle.

> I BELIEVE the cherubim are awesome angelic creatures. (10:9)

[15]Then the cherubim rose upward. These were the same living beings I had seen beside the Kebar River. [16]When the cherubim moved, the wheels moved with them. When they rose into the air, the wheels stayed beside them, going with them as they flew. [17]When the cherubim stood still, the wheels also stopped, for the spirit of the living beings was in the wheels.

[18]Then the glory of the LORD moved from the door of the Temple and hovered above the cherubim. [19]And as I watched, the cherubim flew with their wheels to the east gate of the LORD's Temple. And the glory of the God of Israel hovered above them.

> I BELIEVE Ezekiel saw the glory of the Lord leave the Temple and move to the east gate. (10:18)

[20]These were the same living beings I had seen beneath the God of Israel when I was by the Kebar River. I knew they were cherubim, [21]for each had four faces and four wings and what looked like human hands under their wings. [22]Their faces, too, were just like the faces of the beings I had seen at the Kebar, and they traveled straight ahead, just as the others had.

CHAPTER 11

Judgment on Israel's Leaders

Then the Spirit lifted me and brought me over to the east gateway of the LORD's Temple, where I saw twenty-five prominent men of the city. Among

10:14 Hebrew *the face of a cherub;* compare 1:10.

them were Jaazaniah son of Azzur and Pelatiah son of Benaiah, who were leaders among the people.

²Then the Spirit said to me, "Son of man, these are the men who are responsible for the wicked counsel being given in this city. ³They say to the people, 'Is it not a good time to build houses? Our city is like an iron pot. Inside it we will be like meat—safe from all harm.*' ⁴Therefore, son of man, prophesy against them loudly and clearly."

⁵Then the Spirit of the LORD came upon me, and he told me to say, "This is what the LORD says to the people of Israel: Is that what you are saying? Yes, I know it is, for I know every thought that comes into your minds. ⁶You have murdered endlessly and filled your streets with the dead.

⁷"Therefore, this is what the Sovereign LORD says: This city is an iron pot, but the victims of your injustice are the pieces of meat. And you are not safe, for I will soon drag you from the city. ⁸I will expose you to the war you so greatly fear, says the Sovereign LORD. ⁹I will drive you out of Jerusalem and hand you over to foreigners who will carry out my judgments against you. ¹⁰You will be slaughtered all the way to the borders of Israel, and then you will know that I am the LORD. ¹¹No, this city will not be an iron pot for you, and you will not be the meat, safe inside. I will judge you even to the borders of Israel, ¹²and you will know that I am the LORD. For you have refused to obey me; instead, you have copied the sins of the nations around you."

¹³While I was still speaking, Pelatiah son of Benaiah suddenly died. Then I fell face down in the dust and cried out, "O Sovereign LORD, are you going to kill everyone in Israel?"

Hope for Exiled Israel

¹⁴Then this message came to me from the LORD: ¹⁵"Son of man, the people still left in Jerusalem are talking about their relatives in exile, saying, 'They are far away from the LORD, so now he has given their land to us!' ¹⁶Therefore, give the exiles this message from the Sovereign LORD: Although I have scattered you in the countries of the world, I will be a sanctuary to you during your time in exile. ¹⁷I, the Sovereign LORD, will gather you back from the nations where you are scattered, and I will give you the land of Israel once again.

¹⁸"When the people return to their homeland, they will remove every trace of their detestable idol worship. ¹⁹And I will give them singleness of heart and put a new spirit within them. I will take away their hearts of stone and give them tender hearts* instead, ²⁰so they will obey my laws and regulations. Then they will truly be my people, and I will be their God. ²¹But as for those who long for idols, I will repay them fully for their sins, says the Sovereign LORD."

The LORD's Glory Leaves Jerusalem

²²Then the cherubim lifted their wings and rose into the air with their wheels beside them, and the glory of the God of Israel hovered above them. ²³Then the glory of the LORD went up from the city and stopped above the mountain to the east.

²⁴Afterward the Spirit of God carried me back again to Babylonia,* to the Judeans in exile there. And so ended the vision of my visit to Jerusalem. ²⁵And I told the exiles everything the LORD had shown me.

CHAPTER 12

Signs of the Coming Exile

Again a message came to me from the LORD: ²"Son of man, you live among rebels who could see the truth if they wanted to, but they don't want to. They

---

I DO NOT GIVE counsel that ignores the consequences and dangers of rebelling against God. (11:2)

I BELIEVE God knows and sees every thought of violence that comes to mind. (11:5)

I DO NOT REFUSE to obey the Lord and copy the sins of the pagan society around me. (11:12)

I BELIEVE the Lord kept his promise to give his people a new spirit and a new heart eager to obey him. (11:19)

I BELIEVE Ezekiel saw the glory of the Lord leave Jerusalem. (11:23)

I WANT to listen to and obey the Lord's truth. (12:2)

11:3 Hebrew *This city is the pot, and we are the meat.*   11:19 Hebrew *hearts of flesh.*   11:24 Or *Chaldea.*

could hear me if they would listen, but they won't listen because they are rebellious. ³So now put on a demonstration to show them what it will be like to go off into exile. Pack whatever you can carry on your back and leave your home to go on a journey. Make your preparations in broad daylight so the people can see you, for perhaps they will even yet consider what this means, even though they are such rebels. ⁴Bring your baggage outside during the day so they can watch you. Then as they are watching, leave your house in the evening, just as captives do when they begin a long march to distant lands. ⁵Dig a hole through the wall while they are watching and carry your possessions out through it. ⁶As they watch, lift your pack to your shoulders and walk away into the night. Cover your face and don't look around. All of these actions will be a sign for the people of Israel."

⁷So I did as I was told. In broad daylight I brought my pack outside, filled with the things I might carry into exile. Then in the evening while the people looked on, I dug through the wall with my hands and went out into the darkness with my pack on my shoulder.

⁸The next morning this message came to me from the LORD: ⁹"Son of man, these rebels, the people of Israel, have asked you what all this means. ¹⁰Say to them, 'This is what the Sovereign LORD says: These actions contain a message for Zedekiah in Jerusalem* and for all the people of Israel.' ¹¹Then explain that your actions are a demonstration of what will soon happen to them, for they will be driven from their homes and sent away into exile.

¹²"Even Zedekiah will leave Jerusalem at night through a hole in the wall, taking only what he can carry with him. He will cover his face, and his eyes will never see his homeland again. ¹³Then I will spread out my net and capture him in my snare. I will bring him to Babylon, the land of the Babylonians,* though he will never see it, and he will die there. ¹⁴I will scatter his servants and guards to the four winds and send the sword after them. ¹⁵And when I scatter them among the nations, they will know that I am the LORD. ¹⁶But I will spare a few of them from death by war, famine, or disease, so they can confess to their captors about how wicked they have been. Then they will know that I am the LORD!"

¹⁷Then this message came to me from the LORD: ¹⁸"Son of man, tremble as you eat your food. Drink your water with fear, as if it were your last. ¹⁹Give the people this message from the Sovereign LORD concerning those living in Israel and Jerusalem: They will eat their food with trembling and sip their tiny portions of water in utter despair, because their land will be stripped bare on account of their violence. ²⁰The cities will be destroyed and the farmland deserted. Then you will know that I am the LORD."

A New Proverb for Israel

²¹Again a message came to me from the LORD: ²²"Son of man, what is that proverb they quote in Israel: 'Time passes, making a liar of every prophet'? ²³Give the people this message from the Sovereign LORD: I will put an end to this proverb, and you will soon stop quoting it. Now give them this new proverb to replace the old one: 'The time has come for every prophecy to be fulfilled!'

²⁴"Then you will see what becomes of all the false visions and misleading predictions about peace in Israel. ²⁵For I am the LORD! What I threaten always happens. There will be no more delays, you rebels of Israel! I will fulfill my threat of destruction in your own lifetime, says the Sovereign LORD."

²⁶Then this message came to me from the LORD: ²⁷"Son of man, the people of Israel are saying, 'His visions won't come true for a long, long time.' ²⁸Therefore, give them this message from the Sovereign LORD: No more delay! I will now do everything I have threatened! I, the Sovereign LORD, have spoken!"

12:10 Hebrew *the prince in Jerusalem;* also in 12:12.   12:13 Or *Chaldeans.*

I BELIEVE the Lord instructed Ezekiel to pack his bags as a picture of the coming exile. (12:3)

I EXPLAIN God's Word to his people. (12:11)

I BELIEVE the Lord instructed Ezekiel to tremble while he ate and drank to demonstrate how those living in Jerusalem would tremble during the coming siege. (12:18)

I BELIEVE every prophecy of the Lord is fulfilled at the right time. (12:23)

I BELIEVE the Lord declared through Ezekiel that the time had come when he would do everything he threatened. (12:28)

CHAPTER 13

Judgment against False Prophets

Then this message came to me from the LORD: ²"Son of man, speak against the false prophets of Israel who are inventing their own prophecies. Tell them to listen to the word of the LORD. ³This is what the Sovereign LORD says: Destruction is certain for the false prophets who are following their own imaginations and have seen nothing at all!

⁴"O people of Israel, these prophets of yours are like jackals digging around in the ruins. ⁵They have done nothing to strengthen the breaks in the walls around the nation. They have not helped it to stand firm in battle on the day of the LORD. ⁶Instead, they have lied and said, 'My message is from the LORD,' even though the LORD never sent them. And yet they expect him to fulfill their prophecies! ⁷Can your visions be anything but false if you claim, 'This message is from the LORD,' when I have not even spoken to you?

⁸"Therefore, this is what the Sovereign LORD says: Because what you say is false and your visions are a lie, I will stand against you, says the Sovereign LORD. ⁹I will raise my fist against all the lying prophets, and they will be banished from the community of Israel. I will blot their names from Israel's record books, and they will never again see their own land. Then you will know that I am the Sovereign LORD!

¹⁰"These evil prophets deceive my people by saying, 'All is peaceful!' when there is no peace at all! It's as if the people have built a flimsy wall, and these prophets are trying to hold it together by covering it with whitewash! ¹¹Tell these whitewashers that their wall will soon fall down. A heavy rainstorm will undermine it; great hailstones and mighty winds will knock it down. ¹²And when the wall falls, the people will cry out, 'Where is the whitewash you applied?'

¹³"Therefore, this is what the Sovereign LORD says: I will sweep away your whitewashed wall with a storm of indignation, with a great flood of anger, and with hailstones of fury. ¹⁴I will break down your wall right to the foundation, and when it falls, it will crush you. Then you will know that I am the LORD! ¹⁵At last my anger against the wall and those who covered it with whitewash will be satisfied. Then I will say to you: 'The wall and those who whitewashed it are both gone. ¹⁶They were lying prophets who claimed peace would come to Jerusalem when there was no peace. I, the Sovereign LORD, have spoken!'

Judgment against False Women Prophets

¹⁷"Now, son of man, also speak out against the women who prophesy from their own imaginations. ¹⁸This is what the Sovereign LORD says: Destruction is certain for you women who are ensnaring the souls of my people, both young and old alike. You tie magic charms on their wrists and furnish them with magic veils. Do you think you can trap others without bringing destruction on yourselves? ¹⁹You turn my people away from me for a few handfuls of barley or a piece of bread. By lying to my people who love to listen to lies, you kill those who should not die, and you promise life to those who should not live.

²⁰"And so the Sovereign LORD says: I am against all your magic charms, which you use to ensnare my people like birds. I will tear them from your arms, setting my people free like birds set free from a cage. ²¹I will tear off the magic veils and save my people from your grasp. They will no longer be your victims. Then you will know that I am the LORD. ²²You have discouraged the righteous with your lies, when I didn't want them to suffer grief. And you have encouraged the wicked by promising them life, even though they continue in their sins. ²³But you will no longer talk of seeing visions that you

---

I DO NOT FALSELY CLAIM to have a message from the Lord. (13:6)

I BELIEVE the Lord stands against those who tell lies in his name. (13:8)

I DO NOT DECEIVE people into thinking they have peace with God when they do not. (13:10)

I BELIEVE the Lord kept his promise to destroy those women who deceived his people with magic charms and false prophecies. (13:18)

I ENCOURAGE the righteous and urge the wicked to stop sinning. (13:22)

never saw, nor will you practice your magic. For I will rescue my people from your grasp. Then you will know that I am the LORD."

CHAPTER 14

The Idolatry of Israel's Leaders

Then some of the leaders of Israel visited me, and while they were there, [2]this message came to me from the LORD: [3]"Son of man, these leaders have set up idols in their hearts. They have embraced things that lead them into sin. Why should I let them ask me anything? [4]Give them this message from the Sovereign LORD: I, the LORD, will punish the people of Israel who set up idols in their hearts so they fall into sin and then come to a prophet asking for help. [5]I will do this to capture the minds and hearts of all my people who have turned from me to worship their detestable idols.

[6]"Therefore, give the people of Israel this message from the Sovereign LORD: Repent and turn away from your idols, and stop all your loathsome practices. [7]I, the LORD, will punish all those, both Israelites and foreigners, who reject me and set up idols in their hearts so they fall into sin, and who then come to a prophet asking for my advice. [8]I will turn against such people and make a terrible example of them, destroying them. Then you will know that I am the LORD. [9]And if a prophet is deceived and gives a message anyway, it is because I, the LORD, have deceived that prophet. I will stand against such prophets and cut them off from the community of Israel. [10]False prophets and hypocrites—evil people who claim to want my advice—will all be punished for their sins. [11]In this way, the people of Israel will learn not to stray from me, polluting themselves with sin. They will be my people, and I will be their God, says the Sovereign LORD."

The Certainty of the LORD's Judgment

[12]Then this message came to me from the LORD: [13]"Son of man, suppose the people of a country were to sin against me, and I lifted my fist to crush them, cutting off their food supply and sending a famine to destroy both people and animals alike. [14]Even if Noah, Daniel, and Job were there, their righteousness would save no one but themselves, declares the Sovereign LORD.

[15]"Or suppose I were to send an invasion of dangerous wild animals to devastate the land and kill the people. [16]Even if these three men were there, the Sovereign LORD swears that it would do no good—it wouldn't save the people from destruction. Those three alone would be saved, but the land would be devastated.

[17]"Or suppose I were to bring war against the land, and I told enemy armies to come and destroy everything. [18]Even if these three men were in the land, the Sovereign LORD swears that they could not save the people. They alone would be saved.

[19]"Or suppose I were to pour out my fury by sending an epidemic of disease into the land, and the plague killed people and animals alike. [20]Even if Noah, Daniel, and Job were living there, the Sovereign LORD swears that they could not save the people. They alone would be saved by their righteousness.

[21]"Now this is what the Sovereign LORD says: How terrible it will be when all four of these fearsome punishments fall upon Jerusalem—war, famine, beasts, and plague—destroying all her people and animals. [22]Yet there will be survivors, and they will come here to join you as exiles in Babylon. You will see with your own eyes how wicked they are, and then you will feel better about what I have done to Jerusalem. [23]When you meet them and see their behavior, you will agree that these things are not being done to Israel without cause, says the Sovereign LORD."

I DO NOT SET UP idols in my heart or embrace things that lead me into sin. (14:3)

I BELIEVE the Lord kept his promise to punish those who rejected him, worshiped idols, and then sought his help. (14:7)

I BELIEVE the Lord longed for his people to learn not to stray from him. (14:11)

See the profiles for Noah (page 13), Daniel (page 979), and Job (page 599) at Genesis 6:9, Daniel 1:21, and Job 1:21.

I BELIEVE even the most righteous individuals cannot save their nation when it comes time for God's judgment. (14:18)

I BELIEVE the Lord does not judge or punish his people without cause. (14:23)

CHAPTER 15

Jerusalem—a Useless Vine

Then this message came to me from the LORD: ²"Son of man, how does a grapevine compare to a tree? Is a vine's wood as useful as the wood of a tree? ³Can its wood be used for making things, like pegs to hang up pots and pans? ⁴No, it can only be used for fuel, and even as fuel, it burns too quickly. ⁵Vine branches are useless both before and after being put into the fire!

⁶"And this is what the Sovereign LORD says: The people of Jerusalem are like grapevines growing among the trees of the forest. Since they are useless, I have set them aside to be burned! ⁷And I will see to it that if they escape from one fire, they will fall into another. When this happens, you will know that I am the LORD. ⁸And I will make the land desolate because my people have been unfaithful to me, says the Sovereign LORD."

CHAPTER 16

Jerusalem—an Unfaithful Wife

Then another message came to me from the LORD: ²"Son of man, confront Jerusalem with her loathsome sins. ³Give her this message from the Sovereign LORD: You are nothing but a Canaanite! Your father was an Amorite and your mother a Hittite! ⁴When you were born, no one cared about you. Your umbilical cord was left uncut, and you were never washed, rubbed with salt, and dressed in warm clothing. ⁵No one had the slightest interest in you; no one pitied you or cared for you. On the day you were born, you were dumped in a field and left to die, unwanted.

⁶"But I came by and saw you there, helplessly kicking about in your own blood. As you lay there, I said, 'Live!' ⁷And I helped you to thrive like a plant in the field. You grew up and became a beautiful jewel. Your breasts became full, and your hair grew, though you were still naked. ⁸And when I passed by and saw you again, you were old enough to be married. So I wrapped my cloak around you to cover your nakedness and declared my marriage vows. I made a covenant with you, says the Sovereign LORD, and you became mine.

⁹"Then I bathed you and washed off your blood, and I rubbed fragrant oils into your skin. ¹⁰I gave you expensive clothing of linen and silk, beautifully embroidered, and sandals made of fine leather. ¹¹I gave you lovely jewelry, bracelets, and beautiful necklaces, ¹²a ring for your nose and earrings for your ears, and a lovely crown for your head. ¹³And so you were made beautiful with gold and silver. Your clothes were made of fine linen and were beautifully embroidered. You ate the finest foods—fine flour, honey, and olive oil—and became more beautiful than ever. You looked like a queen, and so you were! ¹⁴Your fame soon spread throughout the world on account of your beauty, because the splendor I bestowed on you perfected your beauty, says the Sovereign LORD.

¹⁵"But you thought you could get along without me, so you trusted instead in your fame and beauty. You gave yourself as a prostitute to every man who came along. Your beauty was theirs for the asking! ¹⁶You used the lovely things I gave you to make shrines for idols, where you carried out your acts of prostitution. Unbelievable! How could such a thing ever happen? ¹⁷You took the very jewels and gold and silver ornaments I had given you and made statues of men and worshiped them, which is adultery against me. ¹⁸You used the beautifully embroidered clothes I gave you to cover your idols. Then you used my oil and incense to worship them. ¹⁹Imagine it! You set before them as a lovely sacrifice the fine flour and oil and honey I had given you, says the Sovereign LORD.

²⁰"Then you took your sons and daughters—the children you had borne to me—and sacrificed them to your gods. Was it not enough that you should be a prostitute? ²¹Must you also slaughter my children by sacrificing them to

I BELIEVE the Lord accurately predicted that Jerusalem would be burned because its people worshiped worthless idols and became worthless themselves. (15:6)

I BELIEVE the Lord gave Ezekiel another message to confront Jerusalem with her loathsome sins. (16:1)

I BELIEVE the Lord gave the nation Israel her very life and nurtured her. (16:6)

I BELIEVE the Lord made a special covenant with the nation of Israel. (16:8)

I BELIEVE the Lord bestowed splendor and beauty on his beloved nation of Israel. (16:14)

I BELIEVE the Lord was grieved that the nation of Israel took his good gifts and engaged in spiritual prostitution. (16:16)

I BELIEVE the Lord was appalled that the people of Israel sacrificed their own children to false gods. (16:20)

idols? ²²In all your years of adultery and loathsome sin, you have not once thought of the days long ago when you lay naked in a field, kicking about in your own blood.

²³"Your destruction is certain, says the Sovereign LORD. In addition to all your other wickedness, ²⁴you built a pagan shrine and put altars to idols in every town square. ²⁵On every street corner you defiled your beauty, offering your body to every passerby in an endless stream of prostitution. ²⁶Then you added lustful Egypt to your lovers, fanning the flames of my anger with your increasing promiscuity. ²⁷That is why I struck you with my fist and reduced your boundaries. I handed you over to your enemies, the Philistines, and even they were shocked by your lewd conduct! ²⁸You have prostituted yourselves with the Assyrians, too. It seems you can never find enough new lovers! And after your prostitution there, you still were not satisfied. ²⁹You added to your lovers by embracing that great merchant land of Babylonia*—but you still weren't satisfied!

³⁰"What a sick heart you have, says the Sovereign LORD, to do such things as these, acting like a shameless prostitute. ³¹You build your pagan shrines on every street corner and your altars to idols in every square. You have been worse than a prostitute, so eager for sin that you have not even demanded payment for your love! ³²Yes, you are an adulterous wife who takes in strangers instead of her own husband. ³³Prostitutes charge for their services—but not you! You give gifts to your lovers, bribing them to come to you. ³⁴So you are the opposite of other prostitutes. No one pays you; instead, you pay them!

Judgment on Jerusalem's Prostitution

³⁵"Therefore, you prostitute, listen to this message from the LORD! ³⁶This is what the Sovereign LORD says: Because you have exposed yourself in prostitution to all your lovers, and because you have worshiped detestable idols, and because you have slaughtered your children as sacrifices to your gods, ³⁷this is what I am going to do. I will gather together all your allies—these lovers of yours with whom you have sinned, both those you loved and those you hated—and I will strip you naked in front of them so they can stare at you. ³⁸I will punish you for your murder and adultery. I will cover you with blood in my jealous fury. ³⁹Then I will give you to your lovers—these many nations—and they will destroy you. They will knock down your pagan shrines and the altars to your idols. They will strip you and take your beautiful jewels, leaving you completely naked and ashamed. ⁴⁰They will band together in a mob to stone you and run you through with swords. ⁴¹They will burn your homes and punish you in front of many women. I will see to it that you stop your prostitution and end your payments to your many lovers.

⁴²"Then at last my fury against you will be spent, and my jealous anger will subside. I will be calm and will not be angry with you anymore. ⁴³But first, because you have not remembered your youth but have angered me by doing all these evil things, I will fully repay you for all of your sins, says the Sovereign LORD. For to all your disgusting sins, you have added these lewd acts. ⁴⁴Everyone who makes up proverbs will say of you, 'Like mother, like daughter.' ⁴⁵For your mother loathed her husband and her children, and so do you. And you are exactly like your sisters, for they despised their husbands and their children. Truly your mother must have been a Hittite and your father an Amorite.

⁴⁶"Your older sister was Samaria, who lived with her daughters in the north. Your younger sister was Sodom, who lived with her daughters in the south. ⁴⁷But you have not merely sinned as they did—no, that was nothing to

I BELIEVE the Lord repeatedly warned Israel of coming judgment. (16:23)

I BELIEVE Israel thoroughly rejected the Lord and became a lewd spiritual prostitute. (16:30)

I ABHOR adultery, idolatry, and murder. (16:38)

I BELIEVE the Lord kept his promise that his fury and anger would subside against Israel. (16:42)

16:29 Or Chaldea.

I BELIEVE the people of Judah became even more wicked than the wicked people of Sodom and Samaria. (16:48)

I BELIEVE the Lord vowed to give the people of Judah what they deserved for breaking their covenant with him. (16:59)

I AM SO THANKFUL the Lord has forgiven all my sins. (16:63)

I BELIEVE the Lord's next message for the people of Israel came to Ezekiel in the form of a riddle. (17:1)

I BELIEVE the Lord explained the riddle of the eagles. (17:12)

you. In a very short time you far surpassed them! ⁴⁸As surely as I live, says the Sovereign LORD, Sodom and her daughters were never as wicked as you and your daughters. ⁴⁹Sodom's sins were pride, laziness, and gluttony, while the poor and needy suffered outside her door. ⁵⁰She was proud and did loathsome things, so I wiped her out, as you have seen.

⁵¹"Even Samaria did not commit half your sins. You have done far more loathsome things than your sisters ever did. They seem righteous compared to you! ⁵²You should be deeply ashamed because your sins are so terrible. In comparison, you make your sisters seem innocent!

⁵³"But someday I will restore the fortunes of Sodom and Samaria, and I will restore you, too. ⁵⁴Then you will be truly ashamed of everything you have done, for your sins make them feel good in comparison. ⁵⁵Yes, your sisters, Sodom and Samaria, and all their people will be restored, and at that time you also will be restored. ⁵⁶In your proud days you held Sodom in contempt. ⁵⁷But now your greater wickedness has been exposed to all the world, and you are the one who is scorned—by Edom* and all her neighbors and by Philistia. ⁵⁸This is your punishment for all your disgusting sins, says the LORD.

⁵⁹"Now this is what the Sovereign LORD says: I will give you what you deserve, for you have taken your solemn vows lightly by breaking your covenant. ⁶⁰Yet I will keep the covenant I made with you when you were young, and I will establish an everlasting covenant with you. ⁶¹Then you will remember with shame all the evil you have done. I will make your sisters, Samaria and Sodom, to be your daughters, even though they are not part of our covenant. ⁶²And I will reaffirm my covenant with you, and you will know that I am the LORD. ⁶³You will remember your sins and cover your mouth in silence and shame when I forgive you of all that you have done, says the Sovereign LORD."

CHAPTER 17

A Story of Two Eagles

Then this message came to me from the LORD: ²"Son of man, tell this story to the people of Israel. ³Give them this message from the Sovereign LORD: A great eagle with broad wings full of many-colored feathers came to Lebanon. He took hold of the highest branch of a cedar tree ⁴and plucked off its topmost shoot. Then he carried it away to a city filled with merchants, where he planted it.

⁵"Then he planted one of its seedlings in fertile ground beside a broad river, where it would grow as quickly as a willow tree. ⁶It took root there and grew into a low, spreading vine. Its branches turned up toward the eagle, and its roots grew down beneath it. It soon produced strong branches and luxuriant leaves. ⁷But then another great eagle with broad wings and full plumage came along. So the vine sent its roots and branches out toward him for water. ⁸The vine did this even though it was already planted in good soil and had plenty of water so it could grow into a splendid vine and produce rich leaves and luscious fruit.

⁹"So now the Sovereign LORD asks: Should I let this vine grow and prosper? No! I will pull it out, roots and all! I will cut off its fruit and let its leaves wither and die. I will pull it out easily enough—it won't take a strong arm or a large army to do it. ¹⁰Then when the vine is transplanted, will it thrive? No, it will wither away completely when the east wind blows against it. It will die in the same good soil where it had grown so well."

The Riddle Explained

¹¹Then this message came to me from the LORD: ¹²"Say to these rebels of Israel: Don't you understand the meaning of this riddle of the eagles? I will

16:57 Many ancient manuscripts read *Aram.*

tell you, says the Sovereign LORD. The king of Babylon came to Jerusalem, took away her king and princes, and brought them to Babylon. [13]He made a treaty with a member of the royal family and made him take an oath of loyalty. He also exiled Israel's most influential leaders, [14]so Israel would not become strong again and revolt. Only by keeping her treaty with Babylon could Israel maintain her national identity.

[15]"Nevertheless, this man of Israel's royal family rebelled against Babylon, sending ambassadors to Egypt to request a great army and many horses. Can Israel break her sworn treaties like that and get away with it? [16]No! For as surely as I live, says the Sovereign LORD, the king of Israel will die in Babylon, the land of the king who put him in power and whose treaty he despised and broke. [17]Pharaoh and all his mighty army will fail to help Israel when the king of Babylon lays siege to Jerusalem again and destroys the lives of many. [18]For the king of Israel broke his treaty after swearing to obey; therefore, he will not escape.

[19]"So this is what the Sovereign LORD says: As surely as I live, I will punish him for breaking my covenant and despising the solemn oath he made in my name. [20]I will throw my net over him and capture him in my snare. I will bring him to Babylon and deal with him there for this treason against me. [21]And all the best warriors of Israel will be killed in battle, and those remaining in the city will be scattered to the four winds. Then you will know that I, the LORD, have spoken these words.

[22]"And the Sovereign LORD says: I will take a tender shoot from the top of a tall cedar, and I will plant it on the top of Israel's highest mountain. [23]It will become a noble cedar, sending forth its branches and producing seed. Birds of every sort will nest in it, finding shelter beneath its branches. [24]And all the trees will know that it is I, the LORD, who cuts down the tall tree and helps the short tree to grow tall. It is I who makes the green tree wither and gives new life to the dead tree. I, the LORD, have spoken! I will do what I have said."

CHAPTER 18

The Justice of a Righteous God

Then another message came to me from the LORD: [2]"Why do you quote this proverb in the land of Israel: 'The parents have eaten sour grapes, but their children's mouths pucker at the taste'? [3]As surely as I live, says the Sovereign LORD, you will not say this proverb anymore in Israel. [4]For all people are mine to judge—both parents and children alike. And this is my rule: The person who sins is the one who dies.

[5]"Suppose a certain man is just and does what is lawful and right, [6]and he has not feasted in the mountains before Israel's idols or worshiped them. And suppose he does not commit adultery or have intercourse with a woman during her menstrual period. [7]Suppose he is a merciful creditor, not keeping the items given in pledge by poor debtors, and does not rob the poor but instead gives food to the hungry and provides clothes for people in need. [8]And suppose he grants loans without interest, stays away from injustice, is honest and fair when judging others, [9]and faithfully obeys my laws and regulations. Anyone who does these things is just and will surely live, says the Sovereign LORD.

[10]"But suppose that man has a son who grows up to be a robber or murderer and refuses to do what is right. [11]And suppose that son does all the evil things his father would never do—worships idols on the mountains, commits adultery, [12]oppresses the poor and helpless, steals from debtors by refusing to let them redeem what they have given in pledge, worships idols and takes part in loathsome practices, [13]and lends money at interest. Should such a sinful person live? No! He must die and must take full blame.

[14]"But suppose that sinful son, in turn, has a son who sees his father's

I BELIEVE the Lord rebuked Israel for breaking their treaty with Babylon and seeking help from Pharaoh of Egypt. (17:15)

I DO NOT BREAK the Lord's covenant and despise the oaths I make in his name. (17:19)

I BELIEVE the Lord kept his promise to restore a remnant of Israel so other nations would know he is the Lord. (17:24)

I BELIEVE all people are the Lord's to judge and that each person is accountable to him. (18:4)

I BELIEVE the Lord sees the righteous and gives them life. (18:9)

I BELIEVE the Lord sees the wicked and holds them accountable for sin. (18:13)

wickedness but decides against that kind of life. [15]Suppose this son refuses to worship idols on the mountains, does not commit adultery, [16]and does not exploit the poor, but instead is fair to debtors and does not rob them. And suppose this son feeds the hungry, provides clothes for the needy, [17]helps the poor, does not lend money at interest, and obeys all my regulations and laws. Such a person will not die because of his father's sins; he will surely live. [18]But the father will die for the many sins he committed—for being cruel and robbing close relatives, doing what was clearly wrong among his people.

[19]" 'What?' you ask. 'Doesn't the child pay for the parent's sins?' No! For if the child does what is right and keeps my laws, that child will surely live. [20]The one who sins is the one who dies. The child will not be punished for the parent's sins, and the parent will not be punished for the child's sins. Righteous people will be rewarded for their own goodness, and wicked people will be punished for their own wickedness. [21]But if wicked people turn away from all their sins and begin to obey my laws and do what is just and right, they will surely live and not die. [22]All their past sins will be forgotten, and they will live because of the righteous things they have done.

[23]"Do you think, asks the Sovereign LORD, that I like to see wicked people die? Of course not! I only want them to turn from their wicked ways and live. [24]However, if righteous people turn to sinful ways and start acting like other sinners, should they be allowed to live? No, of course not! All their previous goodness will be forgotten, and they will die for their sins.

[25]"Yet you say, 'The Lord isn't being just!' Listen to me, O people of Israel. Am I the one who is unjust, or is it you? [26]When righteous people turn from being good and start doing sinful things, they will die for it. Yes, they will die because of their sinful deeds. [27]And if wicked people turn away from their wickedness, obey the law, and do what is just and right, they will save their lives. [28]They will live, because after thinking it over, they decided to turn from their sins. Such people will not die. [29]And yet the people of Israel keep saying, 'The Lord is unjust!' O people of Israel, it is you who are unjust, not I.

[30]"Therefore, I will judge each of you, O people of Israel, according to your actions, says the Sovereign LORD. Turn from your sins! Don't let them destroy you! [31]Put all your rebellion behind you, and get for yourselves a new heart and a new spirit. For why should you die, O people of Israel? [32]I don't want you to die, says the Sovereign LORD. Turn back and live!

CHAPTER 19

A Funeral Song for Israel's Kings

"Sing this funeral song for the princes of Israel:

[2] 'What is your mother?
    A lioness among lions!
She lay down among the young lions
    and reared her cubs.
[3] She raised one of her cubs
    to become a strong young lion.
He learned to catch and devour prey,
    and he became a man-eater.
[4] Then the nations heard about him,
    and he was trapped in their pit.
They led him away in chains
    to the land of Egypt.

[5] 'When the mother lion saw
    that all her hopes for him were gone,
she took another of her cubs
    and taught him to be a strong lion.

I BELIEVE the Lord will not hold children accountable for the sins of their parents. (18:19)

I BELIEVE the Lord does not want the wicked to die for their sins—he wants them to turn from their sin and live (2 Peter 3:9). (18:23)

I BELIEVE the Lord wants each person to turn back to him and live. (18:32)

I BELIEVE several kings of Judah were taken captive before the Babylonians destroyed Jerusalem. (19:4)

⁶He prowled among the other lions
  and became a leader among them.
He learned to catch and devour prey,
  and he, too, became a man-eater.
⁷He demolished fortresses in nearby nations*
  and destroyed their towns and cities.
Their farms were desolated,
  and their crops were destroyed.
Everyone in the land trembled in fear
  when they heard him roar.
⁸Then the armies of the nations attacked him,
  surrounding him from every direction.
They spread out their nets for him
  and captured him in their pit.
⁹With hooks, they dragged him into a cage
  and brought him before the king of Babylon.
They held him in captivity,
  so his voice could never again be heard
  on the mountains of Israel.

¹⁰'Your mother was like a vine
  planted by the water's edge.
It had lush, green foliage
  because of the abundant water.
¹¹Its branches became very strong,
  strong enough to be a ruler's scepter.
It soon became very tall,
  towering above all the others.
It stood out because of its height
  and because of its many lush branches.
¹²But the vine was uprooted in fury
  and thrown down to the ground.
The desert wind dried up its fruit
  and tore off its branches.
Its stem was destroyed by fire.
¹³Now the vine is growing in the wilderness,
  where the ground is hard and dry.
¹⁴A fire has come from its branches
  and devoured its fruit.
None of the remaining limbs
  is strong enough to be a ruler's scepter.'

This is a funeral song, and it is now time for the funeral."

CHAPTER 20

The Rebellion of Israel

On August 14,* during the seventh year of King Jehoiachin's captivity, some of the leaders of Israel came to request a message from the LORD. They sat down in front of me to wait for his reply. ²Then this message came to me from the LORD: ³"Son of man, give the leaders of Israel this message from the Sovereign LORD: How dare you come to ask for my help? As surely as I live, I will tell you nothing. This is the word of the Sovereign LORD!

⁴"Son of man, bring judgment against them and condemn them. Make them realize how loathsome the actions of their ancestors really were. ⁵Give them this message from the Sovereign LORD: When I chose Israel and revealed

Pray that the Holy Spirit will guide you into all truth (John 16:13).

I BELIEVE the Lord uprooted the kingdom of Judah in his anger. (19:12)

I BELIEVE the Lord knows the heart and motives of every person. (20:3)

I ABHOR idolatry, and the Lord finds it loathsome, too. (20:4)

19:7 As in Greek version; Hebrew reads *He consorted with widows.* 20:1 Hebrew *In the fifth month, on the tenth day,* of the Hebrew calendar. This event occurred on August 14, 591 B.C.; also see note on 1:1.

myself to her in Egypt, I swore that I, the LORD, would be her God. ⁶I promised that I would bring her and her descendants out of Egypt to a land I had discovered and explored for them—a good land, a land flowing with milk and honey, the best of all lands anywhere. ⁷Then I said to them, 'Each of you, get rid of your idols. Do not defile yourselves with the Egyptian gods, for I am the LORD your God.'

⁸"But they rebelled against me and would not listen. They did not get rid of their idols or forsake the gods of Egypt. Then I threatened to pour out my fury on them to satisfy my anger while they were still in Egypt. ⁹But I didn't do it, for I acted to protect the honor of my name. That way the surrounding nations wouldn't be able to laugh at Israel's God, who had promised to deliver his people. ¹⁰So I brought my people out of Egypt and led them into the wilderness. ¹¹There I gave them my laws so they could live by keeping them. Yes, all those who keep them will live! ¹²And I gave them my Sabbath days of rest as a sign between them and me. It was to remind them that I, the LORD, had set them apart to be holy, making them my special people.

> I BELIEVE the Lord gave the Sabbath to Israel as a sign of their covenant as God's special people. (20:12)

¹³"But the people of Israel rebelled against me, and they refused to obey my laws there in the wilderness. They wouldn't obey my instructions even though obedience would have given them life. And they also violated my Sabbath days. So I threatened to pour out my fury on them, and I made plans to utterly consume them in the desert. ¹⁴But again I held back in order to protect the honor of my name. That way the nations who saw me lead my people out of Egypt wouldn't be able to claim I destroyed them because I couldn't take care of them. ¹⁵But I swore to them in the wilderness that I would not bring them into the land I had given them, a land flowing with milk and honey, the most beautiful place on earth. ¹⁶I told them this because they had rejected my laws, ignored my will for them, and violated my Sabbath days. Their hearts were given to their idols. ¹⁷Nevertheless, I pitied them and held back from destroying them in the wilderness.

¹⁸"Then I warned their children and told them not to follow in their parents' footsteps, defiling themselves with their idols. ¹⁹'I am the LORD your God,' I told them. 'Follow my laws, pay attention to my instructions, ²⁰and keep my Sabbath days holy, for they are a sign to remind you that I am the LORD your God.'

> I FOLLOW the Lord and obey him because he is my God. (20:19)

²¹"But their children, too, rebelled against me. They refused to keep my laws and follow my instructions, even though obeying them would have given them life. And they also violated my Sabbath days. So again I threatened to pour out my fury on them in the wilderness. ²²Nevertheless, I withdrew my judgment against them to protect the honor of my name among the nations who had seen my power in bringing them out of Egypt. ²³But I took a solemn oath against them while they were in the wilderness. I vowed I would scatter them among all the nations ²⁴because they did not obey my laws. They scorned my instructions by violating my Sabbath days and longing for the idols of their ancestors. ²⁵I gave them over to worthless customs and laws that would not lead to life. ²⁶I let them pollute themselves with the very gifts I had given them, and I allowed them to give their firstborn children as offerings to their gods—so I might devastate them and show them that I alone am the LORD.

> I DO NOT CONTINUE to resist the Lord so long that he must devastate me. (20:26)

Judgment and Restoration

²⁷"Therefore, son of man, give the people of Israel this message from the Sovereign LORD: Your ancestors continued to blaspheme and betray me, ²⁸for when I brought them into the land I had promised them, they offered sacrifices and incense on every high hill and under every green tree they saw! They roused my fury as they offered up sacrifices to their gods. They brought their perfumes and incense and poured out their drink offerings to them! ²⁹I

said to them, 'What is this high place where you are going?' (This idol shrine has been called Bamah—'high place'—ever since.)

³⁰"Therefore, give the people of Israel this message from the Sovereign LORD: Do you plan to pollute yourselves just as your ancestors did? Do you intend to keep prostituting yourselves by worshiping detestable idols? ³¹For when you offer gifts to them and give your little children to be burned as sacrifices,* you continue to pollute yourselves to this day. Should I listen to you or help you, O people of Israel? As surely as I live, says the Sovereign LORD, I will not give you a message even though you have come to me requesting one.

³²"You say, 'We want to be like the nations all around us, who serve idols of wood and stone.' But what you have in mind will never happen. ³³As surely as I live, says the Sovereign LORD, I will rule you with an iron fist in great anger and with awesome power. ³⁴With might and fury I will bring you out from the lands where you are scattered. ³⁵I will bring you into the wilderness of the nations, and there I will judge you face to face. ³⁶I will judge you there just as I did your ancestors in the wilderness after bringing them out of Egypt, says the Sovereign LORD. ³⁷I will count you carefully and hold you to the terms of the covenant. ³⁸I will purge you of all those who rebel and sin against me. I will bring them out of the countries where they are in exile, but they will never enter the land of Israel. And when that happens, you will know that I am the LORD.

³⁹"As for you, O people of Israel, this is what the Sovereign LORD says: If you insist, go right ahead and worship your idols, but then don't turn around and bring gifts to me. Such desecration of my holy name must stop! ⁴⁰For on my holy mountain, says the Sovereign LORD, the people of Israel will someday worship me, and I will accept them. There I will require that you bring me all your offerings and choice gifts and sacrifices. ⁴¹When I bring you home from exile, you will be as pleasing to me as an offering of perfumed incense. And I will display my holiness in you as all the nations watch. ⁴²Then when I have brought you home to the land I promised your ancestors, you will know that I am the LORD. ⁴³You will look back at all your sins and hate yourselves because of the evil you have done. ⁴⁴You will know that I am the LORD, O people of Israel, when I have honored my name by treating you mercifully in spite of your wickedness, says the Sovereign LORD."

Judgment against the Negev

⁴⁵Then this message came to me from the LORD: ⁴⁶"Son of man, look toward the south* and speak out against it; prophesy against the fields of the Negev. ⁴⁷Give the southern wilderness this message from the Sovereign LORD: Hear the word of the LORD! I will set you on fire, O forest, and every tree will be burned—green and dry trees alike. The terrible flames will not be quenched; they will scorch everything from south to north. ⁴⁸And all the world will see that I, the LORD, have set this fire. It will not be put out."

⁴⁹Then I said, "O Sovereign LORD, they are saying of me, 'He only talks in riddles!' "

CHAPTER 21

The LORD's Sword of Judgment

Then this message came to me from the LORD: ²"Son of man, look toward Jerusalem and prophesy against Israel and her sanctuaries. ³Give her this message from the LORD: I am your enemy, O Israel, and I am about to unsheath my sword to destroy your people—the righteous and the wicked alike. ⁴Yes, I will not spare even the righteous! I will make a clean sweep throughout the land from south to north. ⁵All the world will know that I am the LORD. My

I HEED the Lord's warning to forsake the wickedness of previous generations. (20:30)

I DO NOT WANT to imitate the pagan society around me. (20:32)

I KNOW the Lord rejects the worship of those who also worship other gods. (20:39)

I BELIEVE the Israelites would know the Lord when he honored his name by showing mercy to them. (20:44)

I REALIZE that sometimes the righteous suffer when God judges the wicked. (21:4)

20:31 Or *and make your little children pass through the fire.*   20:46 Hebrew *Teman.*

sword is in my hand, and it will not return to its sheath until its work is finished.

⁶"Son of man, groan before the people! Groan before them with bitter anguish and a broken heart. ⁷When they ask you why, tell them, 'I groan because of the terrifying news I have heard. When it comes true, the boldest heart will melt with fear; all strength will disappear. Every spirit will faint; strong knees will tremble and become as weak as water. And the Sovereign LORD says: It is coming! It's on its way!' "

⁸Then the LORD said to me, ⁹"Son of man, give the people this message from the LORD: A sword is being sharpened and polished. ¹⁰It is being prepared for terrible slaughter; it will flash like lightning! Now will you laugh? Those far stronger than you have fallen beneath its power!* ¹¹Yes, the sword is now being sharpened and polished; it is being prepared for the executioner!

¹²"Son of man, cry out and wail; pound your thighs in anguish, for that sword will slaughter my people and their leaders—everyone will die! ¹³It will put them all to the test! So now the Sovereign LORD asks: What chance do they have?*

¹⁴"Son of man, prophesy to them and clap your hands vigorously. Then take the sword and brandish it twice, even three times, to symbolize the great massacre they will face! ¹⁵Let their hearts melt with terror, for the sword glitters at every gate. It flashes like lightning; it is polished for slaughter! ¹⁶O sword, slash to the right, and slash to the left, wherever you will, wherever you want. ¹⁷I, too, will clap my hands, and I will satisfy my fury. I, the LORD, have spoken!"

A Signpost for Babylon's King

¹⁸Then this message came to me from the LORD: ¹⁹"Son of man, make a map and trace two routes on it for the sword of Babylon's king to follow. Put a signpost on the road that comes out of Babylon where the road forks into two—²⁰one road going to Ammon and its capital, Rabbah, and the other to Judah and fortified Jerusalem. ²¹The king of Babylon now stands at the fork, uncertain whether to attack Jerusalem or Rabbah. He will call his magicians to use divination. They will cast lots by shaking arrows from the quiver. They will inspect the livers of their animal sacrifices. ²²Then they will decide to turn toward Jerusalem! With battering rams they will go against the gates, shouting for the kill. They will put up siege towers and build ramps against the walls to reach the top. ²³The people of Jerusalem will think it is a mistake, because of their treaty with the Babylonians. But the king of Babylon will remind the people of their rebellion. Then he will attack and capture them.

²⁴"Therefore, this is what the Sovereign LORD says: Again and again your guilt cries out against you, for you are not ashamed of your sin. You don't even try to hide it! Wherever you go, whatever you do, all your actions are filled with sin. So now the time of your punishment has come!

²⁵"O you corrupt and wicked prince of Israel, your final day of reckoning is here! ²⁶Take off your jeweled crown, says the Sovereign LORD. The old order changes—now the lowly are exalted, and the mighty are brought low. ²⁷Destruction! Destruction! I will surely destroy the kingdom. And it will not be restored until the one appears who has the right to judge it. Then I will hand it over to him.

A Message for the Ammonites

²⁸"And now, son of man, prophesy concerning the Ammonites and their mockery. Give them this message from the Sovereign LORD: My sword is drawn for your slaughter; it is sharpened to destroy, flashing like lightning!

I BELIEVE the Lord accurately warned his people that judgment was coming swiftly. (21:9)

I BELIEVE the Lord told Ezekiel to clap his hands and brandish a sword to picture the judgment by the sword that was coming to Israel. (21:14)

I BELIEVE the Lord instructed Ezekiel to make a map to demonstrate how the king of Babylon would choose to attack Jerusalem. (21:19)

I BELIEVE the Israelites were punished because they were not ashamed of their many sins. (21:24)

21:10 The meaning of the Hebrew is uncertain.   21:13 The meaning of the Hebrew is uncertain.

²⁹Your magicians and false prophets have given false visions and told lies about the sword. And now it will fall with even greater force on the wicked for whom the day of final reckoning has come. ³⁰Should I return my sword to its sheath before I deal with you? No, I will destroy you in your own country, the land of your birth. ³¹I will pour out my fury on you and blow on you with the fire of my anger. I will hand you over to cruel men who are skilled in destruction. ³²You are fuel for the fire, and your blood will be spilled in your own land. You will be utterly wiped out, your memory lost to history. I, the LORD, have spoken!"

CHAPTER 22

The Sins of Jerusalem

Now this message came to me from the LORD: ²"Son of man, are you ready to judge Jerusalem? Are you ready to judge this city of murderers? Denounce her terrible deeds in public, ³and give her this message from the Sovereign LORD: O city of murderers, doomed and damned—city of idols, filthy and foul— ⁴you are guilty of both murder and idolatry. Your day of destruction has come! You have reached the end of your years. I will make you an object of mockery throughout the world. ⁵O infamous city, filled with confusion, you will be mocked by people both far and near.

⁶"Every leader in Israel who lives within your walls is bent on murder. ⁷Fathers and mothers are contemptuously ignored. Resident foreigners are forced to pay for protection. Orphans and widows are wronged and oppressed. ⁸Inside your walls you despise my holy things and violate my Sabbath days of rest. ⁹People accuse others falsely and send them to their death. You are filled with idol worshipers and people who take part in lewd activities. ¹⁰Men sleep with their fathers' wives and have intercourse with women who are menstruating. ¹¹Within your walls live men who commit adultery with their neighbors' wives, who defile their daughters-in-law or who rape their own sisters. ¹²There are hired murderers, loan racketeers, and extortioners everywhere! They never even think of me and my commands, says the Sovereign LORD.

¹³"But now I clap my hands in indignation over your dishonest gain and bloodshed. ¹⁴How strong and courageous will you be in my day of reckoning? I, the LORD, have spoken! I will do what I have said. ¹⁵I will scatter you among the nations and purge you of your wickedness. ¹⁶And when you have been dishonored among the nations, you will know that I am the LORD."

The LORD's Refining Furnace

¹⁷Then this message came to me from the LORD: ¹⁸"Son of man, the people of Israel are the worthless slag that remains after silver is smelted. They are the dross that is left over—a useless mixture of copper, tin, iron, and lead. ¹⁹So give them this message from the Sovereign LORD: Because you are all worthless slag, I will bring you to my crucible in Jerusalem. ²⁰I will melt you down in the heat of my fury, just as copper, tin, iron, and lead are melted down in a furnace. ²¹I will gather you together and blow the fire of my anger upon you, ²²and you will melt like silver in fierce heat. Then you will know that I, the LORD, have poured out my fury on you."

The Sins of Israel's Leaders

²³Again a message came to me from the LORD: ²⁴"Son of man, give the people of Israel this message: In the day of my indignation, you will become like an uncleared wilderness or a desert without rain. ²⁵Your princes* plot conspiracies just as lions stalk their prey. They devour innocent people, seizing treasures and extorting wealth. They increase the number of widows

22:25 As in Greek version; Hebrew reads *prophets.*

I BELIEVE the Lord called on Ezekiel to denounce the city of Jerusalem for its terrible deeds. (22:2)

I AM NOT CONSUMED with hateful thoughts toward others (see 1 John 3:15). (22:6)

I ABHOR adultery, incest, and rape. (22:11)

I BELIEVE the Lord punished the Israelites to purge them and cause them to know that he is the Lord. (22:15)

I BELIEVE the Lord made the Promised Land like a desert in the day of his indignation. (22:24)

in the land. ²⁶Your priests have violated my laws and defiled my holy things. To them there is no difference between what is holy and what is not. And they do not teach my people the difference between what is ceremonially clean and unclean. They disregard my Sabbath days so that my holy name is greatly dishonored among them. ²⁷Your leaders are like wolves, who tear apart their victims. They actually destroy people's lives for profit! ²⁸And your prophets announce false visions and speak false messages. They say, 'My message is from the Sovereign LORD,' when the LORD hasn't spoken a single word to them. They repair cracked walls with whitewash! ²⁹Even common people oppress the poor, rob the needy, and deprive foreigners of justice.

³⁰"I looked for someone who might rebuild the wall of righteousness that guards the land. I searched for someone to stand in the gap in the wall so I wouldn't have to destroy the land, but I found no one. ³¹So now I will pour out my fury on them, consuming them in the fire of my anger. I will heap on them the full penalty for all their sins, says the Sovereign LORD."

CHAPTER 23

The Adultery of Two Sisters

This message came to me from the LORD: ²"Son of man, once there were two sisters who were daughters of the same mother. ³They became prostitutes in Egypt. Even as young girls, they allowed themselves to be fondled and caressed. ⁴The older girl was named Oholah, and her sister was Oholibah. I married them, and they bore me sons and daughters. I am speaking of Samaria and Jerusalem, for Oholah is Samaria and Oholibah is Jerusalem.

⁵"Then Oholah lusted after other lovers instead of me, and she gave her love to the Assyrians, her neighbors. ⁶They were all attractive young men, captains and commanders dressed in handsome blue, dashing about on their horses. ⁷And so she prostituted herself with the most desirable men of Assyria, worshiping their idols and defiling herself. ⁸For when she left Egypt, she did not leave her spirit of prostitution behind. She was still as lewd as in her youth, when the Egyptians satisfied their lusts with her and robbed her of her virginity. ⁹And so I handed her over to her Assyrian lovers, whom she desired so much. ¹⁰They stripped her and killed her and took away her children as their slaves. Her name was known to every woman in the land as a sinner who had received what she deserved.

¹¹"Yet even though Oholibah saw what had happened to Oholah, her sister, she followed right in her footsteps. And she was even more depraved, abandoning herself to her lust and prostitution. ¹²She fawned over her Assyrian neighbors, those handsome young men on fine horses, those captains and commanders in handsome uniforms—all of them desirable. ¹³I saw the way she was going, defiling herself just like her older sister.

¹⁴"Then she carried her prostitution even further. She fell in love with pictures that were painted on a wall—pictures of Babylonian* military officers, outfitted in striking red uniforms. ¹⁵Handsome belts encircled their waists, and flowing turbans crowned their heads. They were dressed like chariot officers from the land of Babylonia.* ¹⁶When she saw these paintings, she longed to give herself to them, so she sent messengers to Babylonia to invite them to come to her. ¹⁷So they came and committed adultery with her, defiling her in the bed of love. But later, she became disgusted with them and broke off their relationship.

¹⁸"So I became disgusted with Oholibah, just as I was with her sister, because she flaunted herself before them and gave herself to satisfy their lusts. ¹⁹But that didn't bother her. She turned to even greater prostitution, remembering her youth when she was a prostitute in Egypt. ²⁰She lusted after lovers

23:14 Or *Chaldean.*   23:15 Or *Chaldea;* also in 23:16.

I DO NOT OPPRESS, rob, and destroy others in a mad pursuit of wealth. (22:27)

I DO NOT GIVE my love, which belongs to the Lord, to any other god or power. (23:5)

I BELIEVE idolatry is spiritual lewdness in the eyes of the Lord. (23:7)

I DO NOT FOLLOW in the footsteps of those who prostitute themselves by loving other gods besides the Lord. (23:11)

I BELIEVE the Lord became disgusted with the spiritual lewdness of his people. (23:18)

whose attentions were gross and bestial. [21]And so, Oholibah, you celebrated your former days as a young girl in Egypt, when you first allowed yourself to be fondled and caressed.

The LORD's Judgment of Oholibah

[22]"Therefore, Oholibah, this is what the Sovereign LORD says: I will send your lovers against you—those very nations from which you turned away in disgust. [23]For the Babylonians will come with all the Chaldeans from Pekod and Shoa and Koa. And all the Assyrians will come with them—handsome young captains, commanders, chariot officers, and other high-ranking officers, riding their horses. [24]They will all come against you from the north with chariots, wagons, and a great army fully prepared for attack. They will take up positions on every side, surrounding you with men armed for battle. And I will hand you over to them so they can do with you as they please. [25]I will turn my jealous anger against you, and they will deal furiously with you. They will cut off your nose and ears, and any survivors will then be slaughtered by the sword. Your children will be taken away as captives, and everything that is left will be burned. [26]They will strip you of your beautiful clothes and jewels. [27]In this way, I will put a stop to the lewdness and prostitution you brought from Egypt. You will never again cast longing eyes on those things or fondly remember your time in Egypt.

[28]"For this is what the Sovereign LORD says: I will surely hand you over to your enemies, to those you loathe. [29]They will deal with you in hatred and rob you of all you own, leaving you naked and bare. The shame of your prostitution will be exposed to all the world. [30]You brought all this on yourself by prostituting yourself to other nations, defiling yourself with all their idols. [31]Because you have followed in your sister's footsteps, I will punish you with the same terrors that destroyed her.

[32]"Yes, this is what the Sovereign LORD says: You will drink from the same cup of terror as your sister—a cup that is large and deep. And all the world will mock and scorn you in your desolation. [33]You will reel like a drunkard beneath the awful blows of sorrow and distress, just as your sister Samaria did. [34]In deep anguish you will drain that cup of terror to the very bottom. Then you will smash it to pieces and beat your breast in anguish. For I, the Sovereign LORD, have spoken! [35]And because you have forgotten me and turned your back on me, says the Sovereign LORD, you must bear the consequences of all your lewdness and prostitution."

The LORD's Judgment on Both Sisters

[36]The LORD said to me, "Son of man, you must accuse Oholah and Oholibah of all their awful deeds. [37]They have committed both adultery and murder—adultery by worshiping idols and murder by burning their children as sacrifices on their altars. [38]Then after doing these terrible things, they defiled my Temple and violated my Sabbath day! [39]On the very day that they murdered their children in front of their idols, they boldly came into my Temple to worship! They came in and defiled my house!

[40]"You sisters sent messengers to distant lands to get men. Then when they arrived, you bathed yourselves, painted your eyelids, and put on your finest jewels for them. [41]You sat with them on a beautifully embroidered couch and put my incense and my oil on a table that was spread before you. [42]From your room came the sound of many men carousing. They were lustful men and drunkards from the wilderness, who put bracelets on your wrists and beautiful crowns on your heads. [43]Then I said, 'If they really want to sleep with worn-out, old prostitutes like these, let them!' [44]And that is what they did. They slept with Oholah and Oholibah, these shameless prostitutes, with all the zest of lustful young men. [45]But righteous people will judge these sister

---

I BELIEVE the Lord turned Jerusalem's lovers—foreign gods and nations—against her. (23:22)

I BELIEVE Israel brought on herself the terrors of warfare. (23:30)

I DO NOT FORGET the Lord and turn against him. (23:35)

cities for what they really are—adulteresses and murderers. They will sentence them to all the punishment they deserve. [46]"Now this is what the Sovereign LORD says: Bring an army against them and hand them over to be terrorized and plundered. [47]For their enemies will stone them and kill them with swords. They will butcher their sons and daughters and burn their homes. [48]In this way, I will put an end to lewdness and idolatry in the land, and my judgment will be a warning to others not to follow their wicked example. [49]You will be fully repaid for all your prostitution—your worship of idols. Yes, you will suffer the full penalty! Then you will know that I am the Sovereign LORD."

CHAPTER 24

The Sign of the Cooking Pot

On January 15,* during the ninth year of King Jehoiachin's captivity, this message came to me from the LORD: [2]"Son of man, write down today's date, because on this very day the king of Babylon is beginning his attack against Jerusalem. [3]Then show these rebels an illustration; give them a message from the Sovereign LORD. Put a pot of water on the fire to boil. [4]Fill it with choice meat—the rump and the shoulder and all the most tender cuts. [5]Use only the best sheep from the flock and heap fuel on the fire beneath the pot. Bring the pot to a boil, and cook the bones along with the meat.

[6]"Now this is what the Sovereign LORD says: Destruction is certain for Jerusalem, the city of murderers! She is a pot filled with corruption. So take the meat out chunk by chunk in whatever order it comes, [7]for her wickedness is evident to all. She murders boldly, leaving blood on the rocks for all to see. She doesn't even try to cover it! [8]So I will splash her blood on a rock as an open expression of my anger and vengeance against her.

[9]"This is what the Sovereign LORD says: Destruction is certain for Jerusalem, the city of murderers! I myself will pile up the fuel beneath her. [10]Yes, heap on the wood! Let the fire roar to make the pot boil. Cook the meat well with many spices. Then empty the pot and burn the bones. [11]Now set the empty pot on the coals to scorch away the filth and corruption. [12]But it's hopeless; the corruption remains. So throw it into the fire! [13]It is the filth and corruption of your lewdness and idolatry. And now, because I tried to cleanse you but you refused, you will remain filthy until my fury against you has been satisfied. [14]I, the LORD, have spoken! The time has come and I won't hold back; I will not change my mind. You will be judged on the basis of all your wicked actions, says the Sovereign LORD."

The Death of Ezekiel's Wife

[15]Then this message came to me from the LORD: [16]"Son of man, I am going to take away your dearest treasure. Suddenly she will die. Yet you must not show any sorrow. Do not weep; let there be no tears. [17]You may sigh but only quietly. Let there be no wailing at her grave. Do not uncover your head or take off your sandals. Do not perform the rituals of mourning or accept any food brought to you by consoling friends."

[18]So I proclaimed this to the people the next morning, and in the evening my wife died. The next morning I did everything I had been told to do. [19]Then the people asked, "What does all this mean? What are you trying to tell us?"

[20]So I said to them, "A message came to me from the LORD, [21]and I was told to give this message to the people of Israel. This is what the Sovereign LORD says: I will desecrate my Temple, the source of your security and pride. Your sons and daughters in Judea will be slaughtered by the sword. [22]Then you will do as Ezekiel has done. You will not mourn in public or console yourselves

I BELIEVE God is the Sovereign Lord. (23:49)

I BELIEVE the Lord told Ezekiel the very day the attack on Jerusalem began. (24:2)

I BELIEVE the Lord told Ezekiel to put a pot of meat on the fire to boil to picture the wickedness of Jerusalem and its coming judgment. (24:3)

I ABHOR cold-blooded murder. (24:7)

I DO NOT RESIST the Lord when he desires to cleanse me. (24:13)

I OBEY the Lord even in the most painful times of my life. (24:18)

24:1 Hebrew *On the tenth day of the tenth month,* of the Hebrew calendar. This event occurred on January 15, 588 B.C.; also see note on 1:1.

by eating the food brought to you by sympathetic friends. [23]Your heads must remain covered, and your sandals must not be taken off. You will not mourn or weep, but you will waste away because of your sins. You will mourn privately for all the evil you have done. [24]Ezekiel is an example for you to follow; you will do as he has done. And when that time comes, you will know that I am the LORD."

[25]Then the LORD said to me, "Son of man, on the day I take away their stronghold—their joy and glory, their heart's desire, their dearest treasure—I will also take away their sons and daughters. [26]And on that day a refugee from Jerusalem will come to you in Babylon and tell you what has happened. [27]And when he arrives, your voice will suddenly return so you can talk to him, and you will be a symbol for these people. Then they will know that I am the LORD."

> I BELIEVE the Lord called on Ezekiel to be a symbol to his people by taking away and then restoring his voice when the news of Jerusalem's fall came. (24:27)

CHAPTER 25

A Message for Ammon

Then this message came to me from the LORD: [2]"Son of man, look toward the land of Ammon and prophesy against its people. [3]Give the Ammonites this message from the Sovereign LORD: Hear the word of the Sovereign LORD! Because you scoffed when my Temple was desecrated, mocked Israel in her desolation, and laughed at Judah as she went away into exile, [4]I will allow nomads from the eastern deserts to overrun your country. They will set up their camps among you and pitch their tents on your land. They will harvest all your fruit and steal your livestock. [5]And I will turn the city of Rabbah into a pasture for camels, and all the land of the Ammonites into an enclosure for sheep. Then you will know that I am the LORD.

> I LISTEN to the word of the Sovereign Lord. (25:3)

[6]"And the Sovereign LORD says: Because you clapped and stamped and cheered with glee at the destruction of my people, [7]I will lift up my fist against you. I will give you as plunder to many nations. I will cut you off from being a nation and destroy you completely. Then you will know that I am the LORD.

> I DO NOT CHEER and mock when other people are punished for their sins. (25:6)

A Message for Moab

[8]"And the Sovereign LORD says: Because the people of Moab have said that Judah is just like all the other nations, [9]I will open up their eastern flank and wipe out their glorious frontier cities—Beth-jeshimoth, Baal-meon, and Kiriathaim. [10]And I will hand Moab over to nomads from the eastern deserts, just as I handed over Ammon. Yes, the Ammonites will no longer be counted among the nations. [11]And in the same way, I will bring my judgment down on the Moabites. Then they will know that I am the LORD.

> I BELIEVE God judged Israel's enemies so that they would know he is the Lord. (25:11)

A Message for Edom

[12]"And the Sovereign LORD says: The people of Edom have sinned greatly by avenging themselves against the people of Judah. [13]Therefore, says the Sovereign LORD, I will raise my fist of judgment against Edom. I will wipe out their people, cattle, and flocks with the sword. I will make a wasteland of everything from Teman to Dedan. [14]By the hand of my people of Israel, I will accomplish this. They will carry out my furious vengeance, and Edom will know it is from me. I, the Sovereign LORD, have spoken!

A Message for Philistia

[15]"And the Sovereign LORD says: The people of Philistia have acted against Judah out of revenge and long-standing contempt. [16]Therefore, says the Sovereign LORD, I will raise my fist of judgment against the land of the Philistines. I will wipe out the Kerethites and utterly destroy the people who live by the sea. [17]I will execute terrible vengeance against them to rebuke them for what they have done. And when I have inflicted my revenge, then they will know that I am the LORD."

CHAPTER 26

A Message for Tyre

On February 3, during the twelfth year of King Jehoiachin's captivity,* this message came to me from the LORD: ²"Son of man, Tyre has rejoiced over the fall of Jerusalem, saying, 'Ha! She who controlled the rich trade routes to the east has been broken, and I am the heir! Because she has been destroyed, I will become wealthy!'

³"Therefore, this is what the Sovereign LORD says: I am your enemy, O Tyre, and I will bring many nations against you, like the waves of the sea crashing against your shoreline. ⁴They will destroy the walls of Tyre and tear down its towers. I will scrape away its soil and make it a bare rock! ⁵The island of Tyre will become uninhabited. It will be a place for fishermen to spread their nets, for I have spoken, says the Sovereign LORD. Tyre will become the prey of many nations, ⁶and its mainland villages will be destroyed by the sword. Then they will know that I am the LORD.

⁷"For the Sovereign LORD says: I will bring King Nebuchadnezzar* of Babylon—the king of kings from the north—against Tyre with his cavalry, chariots, and great army. ⁸First he will destroy your mainland villages. Then he will attack you by building a siege wall, constructing a ramp, and raising a roof of shields against you. ⁹He will pound your walls with battering rams and demolish your towers with sledgehammers. ¹⁰The hooves of his cavalry will choke the city with dust, and your walls will shake as the horses gallop through your broken gates, pulling chariots behind them. ¹¹His horsemen will trample every street in the city. They will butcher your people, and your famous pillars will topple.

¹²"They will plunder all your riches and merchandise and break down your walls. They will destroy your lovely homes and dump your stones and timbers and even your dust into the sea. ¹³I will stop the music of your songs. No more will the sound of harps be heard among your people. ¹⁴I will make your island a bare rock, a place for fishermen to spread their nets. You will never be rebuilt, for I, the LORD, have spoken! This is the word of the Sovereign LORD.

The Effect of Tyre's Destruction

¹⁵"This is what the Sovereign LORD says to Tyre: The whole coastline will tremble at the sound of your fall, as the screams of the wounded echo in the continuing slaughter. ¹⁶All the seaport rulers will step down from their thrones and take off their royal robes and beautiful clothing. They will sit on the ground trembling with horror at what they have seen. ¹⁷Then they will wail for you, singing this funeral song:

'O famous island city,
   once ruler of the sea,
   how you have been destroyed!
Your people, with their naval power,
   once spread fear around the world.
¹⁸Now the coastlands tremble at your fall.
   The islands are dismayed as you pass away.'

¹⁹"For the Sovereign LORD says: I will make Tyre an uninhabited ruin. You will sink beneath the terrible waves of enemy attack. Great seas will swallow you. ²⁰I will send you to the pit to lie there with those who descended there long ago. Your city will lie in ruins, buried beneath the earth, like those in the pit who have entered the world of the dead. Never again will you be given a

---

I DO NOT GLOAT when God punishes other people. (26:2)

I BELIEVE the Lord accurately predicted the coming of King Nebuchadnezzar to attack and destroy Tyre. (26:7)

See Nebuchadnezzar's profile (page 985) at Daniel 4:37.

I BELIEVE the Lord will do everything he has promised and foretold. (26:14)

I BELIEVE the Lord accurately foretold that Tyre would become an uninhabited ruin. (26:19)

26:1 Hebrew *In the eleventh year, on the first day of the month,* of the Hebrew calendar year. Since an element is missing in the date formula here, scholars have reconstructed this probable reading: *In the eleventh [month of the twelfth] year, on the first day of the month.* This reading would put this message on February 3, 585 B.C.; also see note on 1:1.   26:7 Hebrew *Nebuchadrezzar,* a variant name for Nebuchadnezzar.

position of respect here in the land of the living. [21]I will bring you to a terrible end, and you will be no more. You will be looked for, but you will never be found. I, the Sovereign LORD, have spoken!"

CHAPTER 27

The End of Tyre's Glory

Then this message came to me from the LORD: [2]"Son of man, sing a funeral song for Tyre, [3]that mighty gateway to the sea, the trading center of the world. Give Tyre this message from the Sovereign LORD: You claimed, O Tyre, to be perfect in beauty. [4]You extended your boundaries into the sea. Your builders made you glorious! [5]You were like a great ship built of the finest cypress from Senir.* They took a cedar from Lebanon to make a mast for you. [6]They carved oars for you from the oaks of Bashan. They made your deck of pine wood, brought from the southern coasts of Cyprus.* Then they inlaid it with ivory. [7]Your sails were made of Egypt's finest linen, and they flew as a banner above you. You stood beneath blue and purple awnings made bright with dyes from the coasts of Elishah.

[8]"Your oarsmen came from Sidon and Arvad; your helmsmen were skilled men from Tyre itself. [9]Wise old craftsmen from Gebal did all the caulking. Ships came with goods from every land to barter for your trade. [10]Men from distant Persia, Lydia, and Libya* served in your great army. They hung their shields and helmets on your walls, giving you great honor. [11]Men from Arvad and from Helech stood on your walls as sentinels. Your towers were manned by men from Gammad. Their shields hung on your walls, perfecting your splendor.

[12]"Tarshish was your agent, trading your wares in exchange for silver, iron, tin, and lead. [13]Merchants from Greece,* Tubal, and Meshech brought slaves and bronze dishes. [14]From Togarmah came riding horses, chariot horses, and mules. All these were exchanged for your manufactured goods. [15]Merchants came to you from Dedan.* Numerous coastlands were your captive markets; they brought payment in ivory tusks and ebony wood.

[16]"Aram* sent merchants to buy your wares. They traded turquoise, purple dyes, embroidery, fine linen, and jewelry of coral and rubies. [17]Judah and Israel traded for your wares, offering wheat from Minnith, early figs,* honey, oil, and balm. [18]Damascus traded for your rich variety of goods, bringing wine from Helbon and white wool from Zahar. [19]Greeks from Uzal* came to trade for your merchandise. Wrought iron, cassia, and calamus were bartered for your wares. [20]Dedan traded their expensive saddle blankets with you.

[21]"The Arabians and the princes of Kedar brought lambs and rams and goats in trade for your goods. [22]The merchants of Sheba and Raamah came with all kinds of spices, jewels, and gold in exchange for your wares. [23]Haran, Canneh, Eden, Sheba, Asshur, and Kilmad came with their merchandise, too. [24]They brought choice fabrics to trade—blue cloth, embroidery, and many-colored carpets bound with cords and made secure. [25]The ships of Tarshish were your ocean caravans. Your island warehouse was filled to the brim!

The Destruction of Tyre

[26]"But look! Your oarsmen are rowing your ship of state into a hurricane! Your mighty vessel flounders in the heavy eastern gale. You are shipwrecked in the heart of the sea! [27]Everything is lost—your riches and wares, your sailors and helmsmen, your ship builders, merchants, and warriors. On that day of vast ruin, everyone on board sinks into the depths of the sea.

I DO NOT BOAST about my own self-sufficiency and claim I have no need of God. (27:3)

I ABHOR slavery. (27:13)

I BELIEVE the Lord accurately foretold that all of Tyre's riches would be ruined and lost. (27:27)

27:5 Or *Hermon.*   27:6 Hebrew *Kittim.*   27:10 Hebrew *Paras, Lud, and Put.*   27:13 Hebrew *Javan.*   27:15 Greek version reads *Rhodes.*   27:16 Some manuscripts read *Edom.*   27:17 The meaning of the Hebrew is uncertain.   27:19 Hebrew *Vedan and Javan from Uzal.* The meaning of the Hebrew is uncertain.

[28] "Your cities by the sea tremble as your helmsmen cry out in terror. [29] All the oarsmen abandon their ships; the sailors and helmsmen come to stand on the shore. [30] They weep bitterly as they throw dust on their heads and roll in ashes. [31] They shave their heads in grief because of you and dress themselves in sackcloth. They weep for you with bitter anguish and deep mourning. [32] As they wail and mourn, they sing this sad funeral song:

'Was there ever such a city as Tyre,
    now silent at the bottom of the sea?
[33] The merchandise you traded
    satisfied the needs of many nations.
Kings at the ends of the earth
    were enriched by your trade.
[34] Now you are a wrecked ship,
    broken at the bottom of the sea.
All your merchandise and your crew
    have passed away with you.
[35] All who live along the coastlands
    are appalled at your terrible fate.
Their kings are filled with horror
    and look on with twisted faces.
[36] The merchants of the nations
    shake their heads at the sight of you,*
for you have come to a horrible end
    and will be no more.' "

CHAPTER 28

A Message for Tyre's King

Then this message came to me from the LORD: [2] "Son of man, give the prince of Tyre this message from the Sovereign LORD: In your great pride you claim, 'I am a god! I sit on a divine throne in the heart of the sea.' But you are only a man and not a god, though you boast that you are like a god. [3] You regard yourself as wiser than Daniel and think no secret is hidden from you. [4] With your wisdom and understanding you have amassed great wealth—gold and silver for your treasuries. [5] Yes, your wisdom has made you very rich, and your riches have made you very proud.

[6] "Therefore, this is what the Sovereign LORD says: Because you think you are as wise as a god, [7] I will bring against you an enemy army, the terror of the nations. They will suddenly draw their swords against your marvelous wisdom and defile your splendor! [8] They will bring you down to the pit, and you will die there on your island home in the heart of the sea, pierced with many wounds. [9] Will you then boast, 'I am a god!' to those who kill you? To them you will be no god but merely a man! [10] You will die like an outcast at the hands of foreigners. I, the Sovereign LORD, have spoken!"

[11] Then this further message came to me from the LORD: [12] "Son of man, weep for the king of Tyre. Give him this message from the Sovereign LORD: You were the perfection of wisdom and beauty. [13] You were in Eden, the garden of God. Your clothing was adorned with every precious stone*—red carnelian, chrysolite, white moonstone, beryl, onyx, jasper, sapphire, turquoise, and emerald—all beautifully crafted for you and set in the finest gold. They were given to you on the day you were created. [14] I ordained and anointed you as the mighty angelic guardian.* You had access to the holy mountain of God and walked among the stones of fire.

[15] "You were blameless in all you did from the day you were created until

---

*Sidebar notes (left margin):*

I BELIEVE the Lord accurately foretold that many people would mourn the destruction of Tyre. (27:31)

See Daniel's profile (page 979) at Daniel 1:21.

I AM NOT PROUD of my wisdom or wealth. (28:5)

I BELIEVE the Lord humbles those who think they are as wise as he is. (28:6)

I RECOGNIZE that wisdom and beauty are fleeting if someone doesn't have a deep, abiding love for the Lord. (28:12)

27:36 Hebrew *hiss at you.* 28:13 The identification of some of these gemstones is uncertain. 28:14 Hebrew *guardian cherub;* also in 28:16.

the day evil was found in you. [16]Your great wealth filled you with violence, and you sinned. So I banished you from the mountain of God. I expelled you, O mighty guardian, from your place among the stones of fire. [17]Your heart was filled with pride because of all your beauty. You corrupted your wisdom for the sake of your splendor. So I threw you to the earth and exposed you to the curious gaze of kings. [18]You defiled your sanctuaries with your many sins and your dishonest trade. So I brought fire from within you, and it consumed you. I let it burn you to ashes on the ground in the sight of all who were watching. [19]All who knew you are appalled at your fate. You have come to a terrible end, and you are no more."

A Message for Sidon

[20]Then another message came to me from the LORD: [21]"Son of man, look toward the city of Sidon and prophesy against it. [22]Give the people of Sidon this message from the Sovereign LORD: I am your enemy, O Sidon, and I will reveal my glory by what happens to you. When I bring judgment against you and reveal my holiness among you, everyone watching will know that I am the LORD. [23]I will send a plague against you, and blood will be spilled in your streets. The attack will come from every direction, and your people will lie slaughtered within your walls. Then everyone will know that I am the LORD. [24]No longer will Israel's scornful neighbors prick and tear at her like thorns and briers. For then they will know that I am the Sovereign LORD.

Restoration for Israel

[25]"This is what the Sovereign LORD says: The people of Israel will again live in their own land, the land I gave my servant Jacob. For I will gather them from the distant lands where I have scattered them. I will reveal to the nations of the world my holiness among my people. [26]They will live safely in Israel and build their homes and plant their vineyards. And when I punish the neighboring nations that treated them with contempt, they will know that I am the LORD their God."

CHAPTER 29

A Message for Egypt

On January 7,* during the tenth year of King Jehoiachin's captivity, this message came to me from the LORD: [2]"Son of man, turn toward Egypt and prophesy against Pharaoh the king and all the people of Egypt. [3]Give them this message from the Sovereign LORD: I am your enemy, O Pharaoh, king of Egypt—you great monster, lurking in the streams of the Nile. For you have said, 'The Nile River is mine; I made it for myself!' [4]I will put hooks in your jaws and drag you out on the land with fish sticking to your scales. [5]I will leave you and all your fish stranded in the desert to die. You will lie unburied on the open ground, for I have given you as food to the wild animals and birds.

[6]"All the people of Egypt will discover that I am the LORD, for you collapsed like a reed when Israel looked to you for help. [7]Israel leaned on you, but like a cracked staff, you splintered and stabbed her in the armpit. When she put her weight on you, you gave way, and her back was thrown out of joint. [8]So now the Sovereign LORD says: I will bring an army against you, O Egypt, and destroy both people and animals. [9]The land of Egypt will become a desolate wasteland, and the Egyptians will know that I am the LORD.

"Because you said, 'The Nile River is mine; I made it,' [10]I am now the enemy of both you and your river. I will utterly destroy the land of Egypt, from Migdol to Aswan, as far south as the border of Ethiopia.* [11]For forty years not

I ABHOR violence and oppression. (28:16)

I BELIEVE the Lord revealed his glory and holiness when he judged Sidon. (28:22)

I BELIEVE the Lord kept his promise to return his people Israel to their land from all the nations where they were scattered. (28:25)

See Jacob's profile (page 43) at Genesis 32:9.

I DO NOT CLAIM to have created my own power, success, and wealth. (29:3)

I LEAN on the Lord for help, not on human powers, which will only fail me. (29:6)

29:1 Hebrew *On the twelfth day of the tenth month,* of the Hebrew calendar. A number of dates in Ezekiel can be cross-checked with dates in surviving Babylonian records and related accurately to our modern calendar. This event occurred on January 7, 587 B.C. **29:10** Hebrew *Cush.*

a soul will pass that way, neither people nor animals. It will be completely uninhabited. ¹²I will make Egypt desolate, and it will be surrounded by other desolate nations. Its cities will be empty and desolate for forty years, surrounded by other desolate cities. I will scatter the Egyptians to distant lands.

¹³"But the Sovereign LORD also says: At the end of the forty years I will bring the Egyptians home again from the nations to which they have been scattered. ¹⁴I will restore the prosperity of Egypt and bring its people back to the land of Pathros in southern Egypt from which they came. But Egypt will remain an unimportant, minor kingdom. ¹⁵It will be the lowliest of all the nations, never again great enough to rise above its neighbors.

¹⁶"Then Israel will no longer be tempted to trust in Egypt for help. Egypt's shattered condition will remind Israel of how sinful she was to trust Egypt in earlier days. Then Israel will know that I alone am the Sovereign LORD."

Nebuchadnezzar to Conquer Egypt

¹⁷On April 26,* during the twenty-seventh year of King Jehoiachin's captivity, this message came to me from the LORD: ¹⁸"Son of man, the army of King Nebuchadnezzar* of Babylon fought so hard against Tyre that the warriors' heads were rubbed bare and their shoulders were raw and blistered. Yet Nebuchadnezzar and his army won no plunder to compensate them for all their work. ¹⁹Therefore, this is what the Sovereign LORD says: I will give the land of Egypt to Nebuchadnezzar, king of Babylon. He will carry off their wealth, plundering everything they have to pay his army. ²⁰Yes, I have given him the land of Egypt as a reward for his work, says the Sovereign LORD, because he was working for me when he destroyed Tyre.

²¹"And the day will come when I will cause the ancient glory of Israel to revive, and then at last your words will be respected. Then they will know that I am the LORD."

CHAPTER 30

A Sad Day for Egypt

This is another message that came to me from the LORD: ²"Son of man, prophesy and give this message from the Sovereign LORD: Weep, ³for the terrible day is almost here—the day of the LORD! It is a day of clouds and gloom, a day of despair for the nations! ⁴A sword will come against Egypt, and those who are slaughtered will cover the ground. Their wealth will be carried away and their foundations destroyed. The land of Ethiopia* will be ravished. ⁵Ethiopia, Libya,* and Lydia,* and Arabia, with all their other allies, will be destroyed in that war.

⁶"For this is what the LORD says: All of Egypt's allies will fall, and the pride of their power will end. From Migdol to Aswan they will be slaughtered by the sword, says the Sovereign LORD. ⁷Egypt will be desolate, surrounded by desolate nations, and its cities will be in ruins, surrounded by other ruined cities. ⁸And the people of Egypt will know that I am the LORD when I have set Egypt on fire and destroyed all their allies. ⁹At that time I will send swift messengers in ships to terrify the complacent Ethiopians. Great panic will come upon them on that day of Egypt's certain destruction.

¹⁰"For this is what the Sovereign LORD says: Through King Nebuchadnezzar* of Babylon, I will destroy the hordes of Egypt. ¹¹He and his armies—ruthless among the nations—have been sent to demolish the land. They will make war against Egypt until slaughtered Egyptians cover the ground. ¹²I will dry up the Nile River and hand the land over to wicked men. I

I BELIEVE the Lord kept his promise to restore the Egyptians to their cities but never to their former power and glory. (29:14)

See Nebuchadnezzar's profile (page 985) at Daniel 4:37.

I BELIEVE the Lord accurately foretold that King Nebuchadnezzar would plunder Egypt after he destroyed Tyre. (29:19)

I BELIEVE the Lord uses human governments and powers to accomplish his purposes. (29:20)

I MOURN the despair that will come in the day of God's judgment against those who hate him. (30:3)

I BELIEVE the Lord punished Egypt and her allies so that people would know he is the Lord. (30:8)

See Nebuchadnezzar's profile (page 985) at Daniel 4:37.

I BELIEVE the Lord accurately foretold that the Babylonian armies would destroy Egypt. (30:12)

29:17 Hebrew *On the first day of the first month*, of the Hebrew calendar. This event occurred on April 26, 571 B.C.; also see note on 29:1.   29:18 Hebrew *Nebuchadrezzar*, a variant name for Nebuchadnezzar; also in 29:19.
30:4 Hebrew *Cush*; also in 30:5, 9.   30:5a Hebrew *Put . . . Kub*. Both *Put* and *Kub* are associated with Libya.
30:5b Hebrew *Lud*.   30:10 Hebrew *Nebuchadrezzar*, a variant name for Nebuchadnezzar.

will destroy the land of Egypt and everything in it, using foreigners to do it. I, the LORD, have spoken!

¹³"This is what the Sovereign LORD says: I will smash the idols of Egypt and the images at Memphis.* There will be no rulers left in Egypt; anarchy will prevail throughout the land! ¹⁴I will destroy Pathros, Zoan, and Thebes,* and they will lie in ruins, burned up by my anger. ¹⁵I will pour out my fury on Pelusium,* the strongest fortress of Egypt, and I will stamp out the people of Thebes. ¹⁶Yes, I will set fire to all Egypt! Pelusium will be racked with pain; Thebes will be torn apart; Memphis will live in constant terror. ¹⁷The young men of Heliopolis and Bubastis* will die in battle, and the women* will be taken away as slaves. ¹⁸When I come to break the proud strength of Egypt, it will be a dark day for Tahpanhes, too. A dark cloud will cover Tahpanhes, and its daughters will be led away as captives. ¹⁹And so I will greatly punish Egypt, and they will know that I am the LORD."

The Broken Arms of Pharaoh

²⁰On April 29,* during the eleventh year of King Jehoiachin's captivity, this message came to me from the LORD: ²¹"Son of man, I have broken the arm of Pharaoh, the king of Egypt. His arm has not been put in a cast so that it may heal. Neither has it been bound up with a splint to make it strong enough to hold a sword. ²²Therefore, this is what the Sovereign LORD says: I am the enemy of Pharaoh, the king of Egypt! I will break both of his arms—the good arm along with the broken one—and I will make his sword clatter to the ground. ²³I will scatter the Egyptians to many lands throughout the world. ²⁴I will strengthen the arms of Babylon's king and put my sword in his hand. But I will break the arms of Pharaoh, king of Egypt, and he will lie there mortally wounded, groaning in pain. ²⁵I will strengthen the arms of the king of Babylon, while the arms of Pharaoh fall useless to his sides. And when I put my sword in the hand of Babylon's king and he brings it against the land of Egypt, Egypt will know that I am the LORD. ²⁶I will scatter the Egyptians among the nations. Then they will know that I am the LORD."

CHAPTER 31

Egypt Compared to Fallen Assyria

On June 21,* during the eleventh year of King Jehoiachin's captivity, this message came to me from the LORD: ²"Son of man, give this message to Pharaoh, king of Egypt, and all his people: To whom would you compare your greatness? ³You are as Assyria was—a great and mighty nation. Assyria, too, was once like a cedar of Lebanon, full of thick branches that cast deep forest shade with its top high among the clouds. ⁴Deep springs watered it and helped it to grow tall and luxuriant. The water was so abundant that there was enough for all the trees nearby. ⁵This great tree towered above all the other trees around it. It prospered and grew long thick branches because of all the water at its roots. ⁶The birds nested in its branches, and in its shade all the wild animals gave birth to their young. All the great nations of the world lived in its shadow. ⁷It was strong and beautiful, for its roots went deep into abundant water. ⁸This tree became taller than any of the other cedars in the garden of God. No cypress had branches equal to it; no plane tree had boughs to compare. No tree in the garden of God came close to it in beauty. ⁹Because of the magnificence I gave this tree, it was the envy of all the other trees of Eden, the garden of God.

¹⁰"Therefore, this is what the Sovereign LORD says: Because it became proud and arrogant, and because it set itself so high above the others, reaching

I BELIEVE the Lord humbles the proud who live as if they don't need him. (30:18)

I BELIEVE the Lord sent many Egyptians into exile for their sins. (30:23)

I BELIEVE the Egyptians were just as proud—and vulnerable—as the Assyrians. (31:2)

I BELIEVE the Lord punished the Assyrians because of their arrogance and pride. (31:10)

30:13 Hebrew *Noph;* also in 30:16.   30:14 Hebrew *No;* also in 30:15, 16.   30:15 Hebrew *Sin;* also in 30:16.
30:17a Hebrew *of Awen and Pi-beseth.*   30:17b Or *her cities.*   30:20 Hebrew *On the seventh day of the first month,* of the Hebrew calendar. This event occurred on April 29, 587 B.C.; also see note on 29:1.   31:1 Hebrew *On the first day of the third month,* of the Hebrew calendar. This event occurred on June 21, 587 B.C.; also see note on 29:1.

to the clouds, ¹¹I handed it over to a mighty nation that destroyed it as its wickedness deserved. I myself discarded it. ¹²A foreign army—the terror of the nations—cut it down and left it fallen on the ground. Its branches were scattered across the mountains and valleys and ravines of the land. All those who lived beneath its shadow went away and left it lying there. ¹³The birds roosted on its fallen trunk, and the wild animals lay among its branches. ¹⁴Let no other nation proudly exult in its own prosperity, though it be higher than the clouds, for all are doomed. They will land in the pit along with all the proud people of the world.

¹⁵"This is what the Sovereign LORD says: When Assyria went down into the grave,* I made the deep places mourn, and I restrained the mighty waters. I clothed Lebanon in black and caused the trees of the field to wilt. ¹⁶I made the nations shake with fear at the sound of its fall, for I sent it down to the grave with all the others like it. And all the other proud trees of Eden, the most beautiful and the best of Lebanon, the ones whose roots went deep into the water, were relieved to find it there with them in the pit. ¹⁷Its allies, too, were all destroyed and had passed away. They had gone down to the grave—all those nations that had lived in its shade.

¹⁸"O Egypt, to which of the trees of Eden will you compare your strength and glory? You, too, will be brought down to the pit with all these other nations. You will lie there among the outcasts who have died by the sword. This will be the fate of Pharaoh and all his teeming hordes. I, the Sovereign LORD, have spoken!"

CHAPTER 32

A Warning for Pharaoh

On March 3,* during the twelfth year of King Jehoiachin's captivity, this message came to me from the LORD: ²"Son of man, mourn for Pharaoh, king of Egypt, and give him this message: You think of yourself as a strong young lion among the nations, but you are really just a sea monster, heaving around in your own rivers, stirring up mud with your feet.

³"Therefore, this is what the Sovereign LORD says: I will send many people to catch you in my net and haul you out of the water. ⁴I will leave you stranded on the land to die. All the birds of the heavens will land on you, and the wild animals of the whole earth will gorge themselves on you. ⁵I will cover the hills with your flesh and fill the valleys with your bones. ⁶I will drench the earth with your gushing blood all the way to the mountains, filling the ravines to the brim. ⁷When I blot you out, I will veil the heavens and darken the stars. I will cover the sun with a cloud, and the moon will not give you its light. ⁸Yes, I will bring darkness everywhere across your land. Even the brightest stars will become dark above you. I, the Sovereign LORD, have spoken!

⁹"And when I bring your shattered remains to distant nations that you have never seen, I will disturb many hearts. ¹⁰Yes, I will bring terror to many lands, and their kings will be terrified because of all I do to you. They will shudder in fear for their lives as I brandish my sword before them on the day of your fall.

¹¹"For this is what the Sovereign LORD says: The sword of the king of Babylon will come against you. ¹²I will destroy you with the swords of mighty warriors—the terror of the nations. They will shatter the pride of Egypt, and all its hordes will be destroyed. ¹³I will destroy all your flocks and herds that graze beside the streams. Never again will people or animals disturb those waters with their feet. ¹⁴Then I will let the waters of Egypt become calm again, and they will flow as smoothly as olive oil, says the Sovereign LORD. ¹⁵And

I DO NOT proudly exult in the prosperity of my nation—for it, too, will be judged. (31:14)

I BELIEVE the Lord accurately warned Egypt that it would be punished just as Assyria and other nations were. (31:18)

I MOURN for those who must face God's judgment because of their sin. (32:2)

I BELIEVE the Lord's coming punishment of Egypt was as sure as his Word. (32:8)

I BELIEVE the Lord's judgment of Egypt would cause other nations to shudder. (32:10)

I BELIEVE the Lord accurately foretold that the king of Babylon would destroy Egypt for its pride. (32:12)

31:15 Hebrew *to Sheol*; also in 31:16, 17. 32:1 Hebrew *On the first day of the twelfth month*, of the Hebrew calendar. This event occurred on March 3, 585 B.C.; also see note on 29:1.

when I destroy Egypt and wipe out everything you have and strike down all your people, then you will know that I am the LORD. ¹⁶Yes, this is the funeral song they will sing for Egypt. Let all the nations mourn for Egypt and its hordes. I, the Sovereign LORD, have spoken!"

Egypt Falls into the Pit

¹⁷On March 17,* during the twelfth year, another message came to me from the LORD: ¹⁸"Son of man, weep for the hordes of Egypt and for the other mighty nations. For I will send them down to the world below in company with those who descend to the pit. ¹⁹Say to them, 'O Egypt, are you lovelier than the other nations? No! So go down to the pit and lie there among the outcasts.' ²⁰The Egyptians will fall with the many who have died by the sword, for the sword is drawn against them. Egypt will be dragged away to its judgment. ²¹Down in the grave* mighty leaders will mockingly welcome Egypt and its allies, saying, 'They have come down; they lie among the outcasts, all victims of the sword.'

²²"Assyria lies there surrounded by the graves of all its people, those who were slaughtered by the sword. ²³Their graves are in the depths of the pit, and they are surrounded by their allies. These mighty men who once struck terror in the hearts of people everywhere are now dead at the hands of their enemies.

²⁴"Elam lies there buried with its hordes who descended as outcasts to the world below. They terrorized the nations while they lived, but now they lie in the pit and share the humiliation of those who have gone to the world of the dead. ²⁵They have a resting place among the slaughtered, surrounded by the graves of all their people. Yes, they terrorized the nations while they lived, but now they lie in shame in the pit, all of them outcasts, slaughtered by the sword.

²⁶"Meshech and Tubal are there, surrounded by the graves of all their hordes. They once struck terror into the hearts of all people. But now they are outcasts, all victims of the sword. ²⁷They are not buried in honor like the fallen heroes of the outcasts, who went down to the grave* with their weapons—their shields covering their bodies,* and their swords beneath their heads. They brought terror to everyone while they were still alive.

²⁸"You too, Egypt, will lie crushed and broken among the outcasts, all victims of the sword.

²⁹"Edom is there with its kings and princes. Mighty as they were, they also lie among those killed by the sword, with the outcasts who have gone down to the pit. ³⁰All the princes of the north and the Sidonians are there, all victims of the sword. Once a terror, they now lie there in shame. They lie there as outcasts with all the other dead who have descended to the pit.

³¹"When Pharaoh arrives, he will be relieved to find that he is not alone in having his entire army killed, says the Sovereign LORD. ³²For I have caused my terror to fall upon all the living. And Pharaoh and his hordes will lie there among the outcasts who have died by the sword. I, the Sovereign LORD, have spoken!"

CHAPTER 33

Ezekiel as Israel's Watchman

Once again a message came to me from the LORD: ²"Son of man, give your people this message: When I bring an army against a country, the people of that land choose a watchman. ³When the watchman sees the enemy coming,

---

I BELIEVE the Lord accurately foretold the destiny of the leaders and armies of Egypt. (32:18)

I BELIEVE all the proud and violent in this life share the same horrible fate after death. (32:24)

Recommit yourself to loving your neighbor as yourself.

32:17 Hebrew *On the fifteenth day of the month,* presumably in the twelfth month of the Hebrew calendar (see 32:1). This would put this message at the end of King Jehoiachin's twelfth year of captivity, on March 17, 585 B.C.; also see note on 29:1. Greek version reads *On the fifteenth day of the first month,* which would put this message on April 27, 586 B.C., at the beginning of Jehoiachin's twelfth year.   32:21 Hebrew *in Sheol.*
32:27a Hebrew *to Sheol.*   32:27b The meaning of the Hebrew phrase here is uncertain.

he blows the alarm to warn the people. ⁴Then if those who hear the alarm refuse to take action—well, it is their own fault if they die. ⁵They heard the warning but wouldn't listen, so the responsibility is theirs. If they had listened to the warning, they could have saved their lives. ⁶But if the watchman sees the enemy coming and doesn't sound the alarm to warn the people, he is responsible for their deaths. They will die in their sins, but I will hold the watchman accountable.

⁷"Now, son of man, I am making you a watchman for the people of Israel. Therefore, listen to what I say and warn them for me. ⁸If I announce that some wicked people are sure to die and you fail to warn them about changing their ways, then they will die in their sins, but I will hold you responsible for their deaths. ⁹But if you warn them to repent and they don't repent, they will die in their sins, but you will not be held responsible.

The Watchman's Message

¹⁰"Son of man, give the people of Israel this message: You are saying, 'Our sins are heavy upon us; we are wasting away! How can we survive?' ¹¹As surely as I live, says the Sovereign LORD, I take no pleasure in the death of wicked people. I only want them to turn from their wicked ways so they can live. Turn! Turn from your wickedness, O people of Israel! Why should you die?

¹²"Son of man, give your people this message: The good works of righteous people will not save them if they turn to sin, nor will the sins of evil people destroy them if they repent and turn from their sins. ¹³When I tell righteous people that they will live, but then they sin, expecting their past righteousness to save them, then none of their good deeds will be remembered. I will destroy them for their sins. ¹⁴And suppose I tell some wicked people that they will surely die, but then they turn from their sins and do what is just and right. ¹⁵For instance, they might give back a borrower's pledge, return what they have stolen, and obey my life-giving laws, no longer doing what is evil. If they do this, then they will surely live and not die. ¹⁶None of their past sins will be brought up again, for they have done what is just and right, and they will surely live.

¹⁷"Your people are saying, 'The Lord is not just,' but it is they who are not just. ¹⁸For again I say, when righteous people turn to evil, they will die. ¹⁹But if wicked people turn from their wickedness and do what is just and right, they will live. ²⁰O people of Israel, you are saying, 'The Lord is not just.' But I will judge each of you according to your deeds."

Explanation of Jerusalem's Fall

²¹On January 8,* during the twelfth year of our captivity, a man who had escaped from Jerusalem came to me and said, "The city has fallen!" ²²The previous evening the LORD had taken hold of me and opened my mouth, so I would be able to speak when this man arrived the next morning.

²³Then this message came to me from the LORD: ²⁴"Son of man, the scattered remnants of Judah living among the ruined cities keep saying, 'Abraham was only one man, and yet he gained possession of the entire land! We are many; surely the land should be given to us as a possession.' ²⁵Now give these people this message from the Sovereign LORD: You eat meat with blood in it, you worship idols, and you murder the innocent. Do you really think the land should be yours? ²⁶Murderers! Idolaters! Adulterers! Should the land belong to you?

²⁷"Give them this message from the Sovereign LORD: As surely as I live, those living in the ruins will die by the sword. Those living in the open fields will be eaten by wild animals. Those hiding in the forts and caves will die of disease. ²⁸I will destroy the land and demolish her pride. Her arrogant power

I URGE others to change their ways and turn from their sins. (33:8)

I KNOW that the Lord does not enjoy punishing the wicked—he longs for them to turn to him and live (2 Peter 3:9). (33:11)

I KNOW the Lord will not hold my past sins against me when I repent and turn to him. (33:16)

I BELIEVE God will judge each person according to his or her own deeds. (33:20)

I BELIEVE the Lord called on Ezekiel to be a symbol to his people by taking away and then restoring his voice when the news of Jerusalem's fall came (Ezekiel 24:26-27). (33:22)

I DO NOT EXPECT spiritual blessings when I persist in living in sin against God. (33:24)

See Abraham's profile (page 19) at Genesis 15:6.

33:21 Hebrew *On the fifth day of the tenth month,* of the Hebrew calendar. This event occurred on January 8, 585 B.C.; also see note on 29:1.

will come to an end. The mountains of Israel will be so ruined that no one will even travel through them. ²⁹When I have ruined the land because of their disgusting sins, then they will know that I am the LORD.

³⁰"Son of man, your people are whispering behind your back. They talk about you in their houses and whisper about you at the doors, saying, 'Come on, let's have some fun! Let's go hear the prophet tell us what the LORD is saying!' ³¹So they come pretending to be sincere and sit before you listening. But they have no intention of doing what I tell them. They express love with their mouths, but their hearts seek only after money. ³²You are very entertaining to them, like someone who sings love songs with a beautiful voice or plays fine music on an instrument. They hear what you say, but they don't do it! ³³But when all these terrible things happen to them—as they certainly will—then they will know a prophet has been among them."

CHAPTER 34

The Shepherds of Israel

Then this message came to me from the LORD: ²"Son of man, prophesy against the shepherds, the leaders of Israel. Give them this message from the Sovereign LORD: Destruction is certain for you shepherds who feed yourselves instead of your flocks. Shouldn't shepherds feed their sheep? ³You drink the milk, wear the wool, and butcher the best animals, but you let your flocks starve. ⁴You have not taken care of the weak. You have not tended the sick or bound up the broken bones. You have not gone looking for those who have wandered away and are lost. Instead, you have ruled them with force and cruelty. ⁵So my sheep have been scattered without a shepherd. They are easy prey for any wild animal. ⁶They have wandered through the mountains and hills, across the face of the earth, yet no one has gone to search for them.

⁷"Therefore, you shepherds, hear the word of the LORD: ⁸As surely as I live, says the Sovereign LORD, you abandoned my flock and left them to be attacked by every wild animal. Though you were my shepherds, you didn't search for my sheep when they were lost. You took care of yourselves and left the sheep to starve. ⁹Therefore, you shepherds, hear the word of the LORD. ¹⁰This is what the Sovereign LORD says: I now consider these shepherds my enemies, and I will hold them responsible for what has happened to my flock. I will take away their right to feed the flock, along with their right to feed themselves. I will rescue my flock from their mouths; the sheep will no longer be their prey.

The Good Shepherd

¹¹"For this is what the Sovereign LORD says: I myself will search and find my sheep. ¹²I will be like a shepherd looking for his scattered flock. I will find my sheep and rescue them from all the places to which they were scattered on that dark and cloudy day. ¹³I will bring them back home to their own land of Israel from among the peoples and nations. I will feed them on the mountains of Israel and by the rivers in all the places where people live. ¹⁴Yes, I will give them good pastureland on the high hills of Israel. There they will lie down in pleasant places and feed in lush mountain pastures. ¹⁵I myself will tend my sheep and cause them to lie down in peace, says the Sovereign LORD. ¹⁶I will search for my lost ones who strayed away, and I will bring them safely home again. I will bind up the injured and strengthen the weak. But I will destroy those who are fat and powerful. I will feed them, yes—feed them justice!

¹⁷"And as for you, my flock, my people, this is what the Sovereign LORD says: I will judge between one sheep and another, separating the sheep from the goats. ¹⁸Is it not enough for you to keep the best of the pastures for yourselves? Must you also trample down the rest? Is it not enough for you to take

I LISTEN to the Lord's Word with sincerity and obey him from a loving heart. (33:31)

I CARE for the Lord's people—putting their needs above my own. (34:2)

I BELIEVE the Lord held the Israelite leaders responsible for what happened to his people. (34:10)

I BELIEVE the Lord Jesus kept his promise to be the Good Shepherd, who searched for and found his own sheep (John 10:11-16). (34:11)

I BELIEVE the Lord will keep his promise to separate his people from imposters. (34:17)

the best water for yourselves? Must you also muddy the rest with your feet? [19]All that is left for my flock to eat is what you have trampled down. All they have to drink is water that you have fouled.

[20]"Therefore, this is what the Sovereign LORD says: I will surely judge between the fat sheep and the scrawny sheep. [21]For you fat sheep push and butt and crowd my sick and hungry flock until they are scattered to distant lands. [22]So I will rescue my flock, and they will no longer be abused and destroyed. And I will judge between one sheep and another. [23]And I will set one shepherd over them, even my servant David. He will feed them and be a shepherd to them. [24]And I, the LORD, will be their God, and my servant David will be a prince among my people. I, the LORD, have spoken!

The LORD's Covenant of Peace

[25]"I will make a covenant of peace with them and drive away the dangerous animals from the land. Then my people will be able to camp safely in the wildest places and sleep in the woods without fear. [26]I will cause my people and their homes around my holy hill to be a blessing. And I will send showers, showers of blessings, which will come just when they are needed. [27]The orchards and fields of my people will yield bumper crops, and everyone will live in safety. When I have broken their chains of slavery and rescued them from those who enslaved them, then they will know that I am the LORD. [28]They will no longer be prey for other nations, and wild animals will no longer attack them. They will live in safety, and no one will make them afraid.

[29]"And I will give them a land famous for its crops, so my people will never again go hungry or be shamed by the scorn of foreign nations. [30]In this way, they will know that I, the LORD their God, am with them. And they will know that they, the people of Israel, are my people, says the Sovereign LORD. [31]You are my flock, the sheep of my pasture. You are my people, and I am your God, says the Sovereign LORD."

CHAPTER 35

A Message for Edom

Again a message came to me from the LORD: [2]"Son of man, turn toward Mount Seir, and prophesy against its people. [3]Give them this message from the Sovereign LORD: I am your enemy, O Mount Seir, and I will raise my fist against you to destroy you completely. [4]I will demolish your cities and make you desolate, and then you will know that I am the LORD. [5]Your continual hatred for the people of Israel led you to butcher them when they were helpless, when I had already punished them for all their sins. [6]As surely as I live, says the Sovereign LORD, since you show no distaste for blood, I will give you a bloodbath of your own. Your turn has come! [7]I will make Mount Seir utterly desolate, killing off all who try to escape and any who return. [8]I will fill your mountains with the dead. Your hills, your valleys, and your streams will be filled with people slaughtered by the sword. [9]I will make you desolate forever. Your cities will never be rebuilt. Then you will know that I am the LORD.

[10]"For you said, 'The lands of Israel and Judah will be ours. We will take possession of them. What do we care that the LORD is there!' [11]Therefore, as surely as I live, says the Sovereign LORD, I will pay back your angry deeds with mine. I will punish you for all your acts of anger, envy, and hatred. And I will bring honor to my name by what I do to you. [12]Then you will know that I, the LORD, have heard every contemptuous word you spoke against the mountains of Israel. For you said, 'They have been destroyed; they have been given to us as food to eat!' [13]In saying that, you boasted proudly against me, and I have heard it all!

[14]"This is what the Sovereign LORD says: The whole world will rejoice when

---

I BELIEVE the Lord kept his promise to send one shepherd, Jesus Christ, to be over and care for all his people (John 10:11; Hebrews 13:20). (34:23)

See David's profile (page 629) at Psalm 3:1.

I BELIEVE the Lord promised to restore his people so they would know that he is their God and they are his people. (34:30)

I BELIEVE the Lord judged the Edomites because they hated and butchered the Israelites. (35:5)

I ABHOR violence and bloodshed. (35:6)

I BELIEVE the Lord hears every contemptuous word spoken against him and his people. (35:12)

I make you desolate. ¹⁵You rejoiced at the desolation of Israel's inheritance. Now I will rejoice at yours! You will be wiped out, you people of Mount Seir and all who live in Edom! Then you will know that I am the LORD!

CHAPTER 36

Restoration for Israel

"Son of man, prophesy to Israel's mountains. Give them this message: O mountains of Israel, hear the word of the LORD! ²This is what the Sovereign LORD says: Your enemies have taunted you, saying, 'Aha! Now the ancient heights belong to us!' ³Therefore, son of man, give the mountains of Israel this message from the Sovereign LORD: Your enemies have attacked you from all directions, and now you are possessed by many nations. You are the object of much mocking and slander. ⁴Therefore, O mountains of Israel, hear the word of the Sovereign LORD. He speaks to the hills and mountains, ravines and valleys, and to ruined wastes and long-deserted cities that have been destroyed and mocked by foreign nations everywhere. ⁵This is what the Sovereign LORD says: My jealous anger is on fire against these nations, especially Edom, because they have shown utter contempt for me by gleefully taking my land for themselves as plunder.

⁶"Therefore, prophesy to the hills and mountains, the ravines and valleys of Israel. Give them this message from the Sovereign LORD: I am full of fury because you have suffered shame before the surrounding nations. ⁷Therefore, says the Sovereign LORD, I have raised my hand and sworn an oath that those nations will soon have their turn at suffering shame. ⁸But the mountains of Israel will produce heavy crops of fruit to prepare for my people's return—and they will be coming home again soon! ⁹See, I am concerned for you, and I will come to help you. Your ground will be tilled and your crops planted. ¹⁰I will greatly increase the population of Israel, and the ruined cities will be rebuilt and filled with people. ¹¹Not only the people, but your flocks and herds will also greatly multiply. O mountains of Israel, I will bring people to live on you once again. I will make you even more prosperous than you were before. Then you will know that I am the LORD. ¹²I will cause my people to walk on you once again, and you will be their inheritance. You will never again devour their children.

¹³"This is what the Sovereign LORD says: Now the other nations taunt you, saying, 'Israel is a land that devours her own people!' ¹⁴But you will never again devour your people or bereave your nation, says the Sovereign LORD. ¹⁵I will not allow those foreign nations to sneer at you, and you will no longer be shamed by them or cause your nation to fall, says the Sovereign LORD."

¹⁶Then this further message came to me from the LORD: ¹⁷"Son of man, when the people of Israel were living in their own land, they defiled it by their evil deeds. To me their conduct was as filthy as a bloody rag. ¹⁸They polluted the land with murder and by worshiping idols, so I poured out my fury on them. ¹⁹I scattered them to many lands to punish them for the evil way they had lived. ²⁰But when they were scattered among the nations, they brought dishonor to my holy name. For the nations said, 'These are the people of the LORD, and he couldn't keep them safe in his own land!' ²¹Then I was concerned for my holy name, which had been dishonored by my people throughout the world.

²²"Therefore, give the people of Israel this message from the Sovereign LORD: I am bringing you back again but not because you deserve it. I am doing it to protect my holy name, which you dishonored while you were scattered among the nations. ²³I will show how holy my great name is—the name you dishonored among the nations. And when I reveal my holiness through you before their very eyes, says the Sovereign LORD, then the nations

I BELIEVE the Lord knows and cares when his people are mocked and attacked. (36:3)

I BELIEVE the Lord kept his promise to restore his blessings on the Israelites. (36:10)

I BELIEVE the Lord promised a time would come when Israel would no longer suffer shame or ruinous sin. (36:15)

I BELIEVE the Lord scattered the Israelites because they polluted his land with murder and idolatry. (36:19) will know that I am the LORD. ²⁴For I will gather you up from all the nations and bring you home again to your land.

²⁵"Then I will sprinkle clean water on you, and you will be clean. Your filth will be washed away, and you will no longer worship idols. ²⁶And I will give you a new heart with new and right desires, and I will put a new spirit in you. I will take out your stony heart of sin and give you a new, obedient heart.* ²⁷And I will put my Spirit in you so you will obey my laws and do whatever I command.

²⁸"And you will live in Israel, the land I gave your ancestors long ago. You will be my people, and I will be your God. ²⁹I will cleanse you of your filthy behavior. I will give you good crops, and I will abolish famine in the land. ³⁰I will give you great harvests from your fruit trees and fields, and never again will the surrounding nations be able to scoff at your land for its famines. ³¹Then you will remember your past sins and hate yourselves for all the evil things you did. ³²But remember, says the Sovereign LORD, I am not doing this because you deserve it. O my people of Israel, you should be utterly ashamed of all you have done!

³³"This is what the Sovereign LORD says: When I cleanse you from your sins, I will bring people to live in your cities, and the ruins will be rebuilt. ³⁴The fields that used to lie empty and desolate—a shock to all who passed by—will again be farmed. ³⁵And when I bring you back, people will say, 'This godforsaken land is now like Eden's garden! The ruined cities now have strong walls, and they are filled with people!' ³⁶Then the nations all around—all those still left—will know that I, the LORD, rebuilt the ruins and planted lush crops in the wilderness. For I, the LORD, have promised this, and I will do it.

³⁷"This is what the Sovereign LORD says: I am ready to hear Israel's prayers for these blessings, and I am ready to grant them their requests. ³⁸I will multiply them like the sacred flocks that fill Jerusalem's streets at the time of her festivals. The ruined cities will be crowded with people once more, and everyone will know that I am the LORD."

CHAPTER 37

A Valley of Dry Bones

The LORD took hold of me, and I was carried away by the Spirit of the LORD to a valley filled with bones. ²He led me around among the old, dry bones that covered the valley floor. They were scattered everywhere across the ground. ³Then he asked me, "Son of man, can these bones become living people again?"

"O Sovereign LORD," I replied, "you alone know the answer to that."

⁴Then he said to me, "Speak to these bones and say, 'Dry bones, listen to the word of the LORD! ⁵This is what the Sovereign LORD says: Look! I am going to breathe into you and make you live again! ⁶I will put flesh and muscles on you and cover you with skin. I will put breath into you, and you will come to life. Then you will know that I am the LORD.' "

⁷So I spoke these words, just as he told me. Suddenly as I spoke, there was a rattling noise all across the valley. The bones of each body came together and attached themselves as they had been before. ⁸Then as I watched, muscles and flesh formed over the bones. Then skin formed to cover their bodies, but they still had no breath in them.

⁹Then he said to me, "Speak to the winds and say: 'This is what the Sovereign LORD says: Come, O breath, from the four winds! Breathe into these dead bodies so that they may live again.' "

¹⁰So I spoke as he commanded me, and the wind entered the bodies, and

---

I HAVE ASKED the Lord to give me a new heart—ready to do whatever he commands. (36:26)

I BELIEVE the Lord promised to bring the Israelites back to the land to honor his name—not because they somehow deserved his favor. (36:32)

I BELIEVE the Lord is ready to hear and answer my prayers. (36:37)

I BELIEVE the Lord kept his promise to bring the nation of Israel back to life. (37:5)

36:26 Hebrew *a heart of flesh.*

they began to breathe. They all came to life and stood up on their feet—a great army of them.

[11]Then he said to me, "Son of man, these bones represent the people of Israel. They are saying, 'We have become old, dry bones—all hope is gone.' [12]Now give them this message from the Sovereign LORD: O my people, I will open your graves of exile and cause you to rise again. Then I will bring you back to the land of Israel. [13]When this happens, O my people, you will know that I am the LORD. [14]I will put my Spirit in you, and you will live and return home to your own land. Then you will know that I am the LORD. You will see that I have done everything just as I promised. I, the LORD, have spoken!"

Reunion of Israel and Judah

[15]Again a message came to me from the LORD: [16]"Son of man, take a stick and carve on it these words: 'This stick represents Judah and its allied tribes.' Then take another stick and carve these words on it: 'This stick represents the northern tribes of Israel.'* [17]Now hold them together in your hand as one stick. [18]When your people ask you what your actions mean, [19]say to them, 'This is what the Sovereign LORD says: I will take the northern tribes and join them to Judah. I will make them one stick in my hand.' [20]Then hold out the sticks you have inscribed, so the people can see them. [21]And give them this message from the Sovereign LORD: I will gather the people of Israel from among the nations. I will bring them home to their own land from the places where they have been scattered. [22]I will unify them into one nation in the land. One king will rule them all; no longer will they be divided into two nations. [23]They will stop polluting themselves with their detestable idols and other sins, for I will save them from their sinful backsliding. I will cleanse them. Then they will truly be my people, and I will be their God.

[24]"My servant David will be their king, and they will have only one shepherd. They will obey my regulations and keep my laws. [25]They will live in the land of Israel where their ancestors lived, the land I gave my servant Jacob. They and their children and their grandchildren after them will live there forever, generation after generation. And my servant David will be their prince forever. [26]And I will make a covenant of peace with them, an everlasting covenant. I will give them their land and multiply them, and I will put my Temple among them forever. [27]I will make my home among them. I will be their God, and they will be my people. [28]And since my Temple will remain among them forever, the nations will know that I, the LORD, have set Israel apart for myself to be holy."

CHAPTER 38

A Message for Gog

This is another message that came to me from the LORD: [2]"Son of man, prophesy against Gog of the land of Magog, the prince who rules over the nations of Meshech and Tubal. [3]Give him this message from the Sovereign LORD: Gog, I am your enemy! [4]I will turn you around and put hooks into your jaws to lead you out to your destruction. I will mobilize your troops and cavalry and make you a vast and mighty horde, all fully armed. [5]Persia, Ethiopia, and Libya* will join you, too, with all their weapons. [6]Gomer and all its hordes will also join you, along with the armies of Beth-togarmah from the distant north and many others.

[7]"Get ready; be prepared! Keep all the armies around you mobilized, and take command of them. [8]A long time from now you will be called into action. In the distant future you will swoop down on the land of Israel, which will be lying in peace after her recovery from war and after the return of her

I BELIEVE the Lord kept his promise to restore his people to the land of Israel. (37:12)

I BELIEVE the Lord kept his promise to put his Spirit in his people. (37:14)

I BELIEVE the Lord kept his promise to make his servant, the Lord Jesus, the great Shepherd of his people (Hebrews 13:20). (37:24)

See David's profile (page 629) at Psalm 3:1.

See Jacob's profile (page 43) at Genesis 32:9.

I BELIEVE the Lord kept his promise to make an everlasting covenant with his people (Hebrews 13:20). (37:26)

I BELIEVE the Lord has foretold the assembling and attack of the army of Gog in the distant future. (38:8)

37:16 Hebrew *Ephraim's stick, representing Joseph and all the house of Israel.*   38:5 Hebrew *Paras, Cush, and Put.*

people from many lands. ⁹You and all your allies—a vast and awesome horde—will roll down on them like a storm and cover the land like a cloud.

¹⁰"This is what the Sovereign LORD says: At that time evil thoughts will come to your mind, and you will devise a wicked scheme. ¹¹You will say, 'Israel is an unprotected land filled with unwalled villages! I will march against her and destroy these people who live in such confidence! ¹²I will go to those once-desolate cities that are again filled with people who have returned from exile in many nations. I will capture vast amounts of plunder and take many slaves, for the people are rich with cattle now, and they think the whole world revolves around them!' ¹³But Sheba and Dedan and the merchants of Tarshish will ask, 'Who are you to rob them of silver and gold? Who are you to drive away their cattle and seize their goods and make them poor?'

¹⁴"Therefore, son of man, prophesy against Gog. Give him this message from the Sovereign LORD: When my people are living in peace in their land, then you will rouse yourself.* ¹⁵You will come from your homeland in the distant north with your vast cavalry and your mighty army, ¹⁶and you will cover the land like a cloud. This will happen in the distant future. I will bring you against my land as everyone watches, and my holiness will be displayed by what happens to you. Then all the nations will know that I am the LORD.

¹⁷"This is what the Sovereign LORD says: You are the one I was talking about long ago, when I announced through Israel's prophets that in future days I would bring you against my people. ¹⁸But when Gog invades the land of Israel, says the Sovereign LORD, my fury will rise! ¹⁹For in my jealousy and blazing anger, I promise a mighty shaking in the land of Israel on that day. ²⁰All living things—all the fish, birds, animals, and people—will quake in terror at my presence. Mountains will be thrown down; cliffs will crumble; walls will fall to the earth. ²¹I will summon the sword against you throughout Israel, says the Sovereign LORD. Your men will turn against each other in mortal combat. ²²I will punish you and your hordes with disease and bloodshed; I will send torrential rain, hailstones, fire, and burning sulfur! ²³Thus will I show my greatness and holiness, and I will make myself known to all the nations of the world. Then they will know that I am the LORD!

CHAPTER 39

The Slaughter of Gog's Armies

"Son of man, prophesy against Gog. Give him this message from the Sovereign LORD: I am your enemy, O Gog, ruler of the nations of Meshech and Tubal. ²I will turn you and drive you toward the mountains of Israel, bringing you from the distant north. ³I will knock your weapons from your hands and leave you helpless. ⁴You and all your vast hordes will die on the mountains. I will give you as food to the vultures and wild animals. ⁵You will fall in the open fields, for I have spoken, says the Sovereign LORD. ⁶And I will rain down fire on Magog and on all your allies who live safely on the coasts. Then they will know that I am the LORD.

⁷"Thus, I will make known my holy name among my people of Israel. I will not let it be desecrated anymore. And the nations, too, will know that I am the LORD, the Holy One of Israel. ⁸That day of judgment will come, says the Sovereign LORD. Everything will happen just as I have declared it.

⁹"Then the people in the towns of Israel will go out and pick up your small and large shields, bows and arrows, javelins and spears, and they will use them for fuel. There will be enough to last them seven years! ¹⁰They will need nothing else for their fires. They won't need to cut wood from the fields or forests, for these weapons will give them all they need. They will take plunder from those who planned to plunder them, says the Sovereign LORD.

I BELIEVE the Lord promises to display his holiness when the army of Gog attacks the land of Israel. (38:16)

I BELIEVE the Lord will punish the army of Gog when they attack Israel. (38:21)

I BELIEVE the Lord will show his greatness and make himself known to the world when Gog is punished. (38:23)

I BELIEVE the Lord will make himself known as the Holy One of Israel. (39:7)

I BELIEVE the Lord's day of judgment will come just as he said. (39:8)

38:14 As in Greek version; Hebrew reads *then you will know.*

11"And I will make a vast graveyard for Gog and his hordes in the Valley of the Travelers, east of the Dead Sea.* The path of those who travel there will be blocked by this burial ground, and they will change the name of the place to the Valley of Gog's Hordes. 12It will take seven months for the people of Israel to cleanse the land by burying the bodies. 13Everyone in Israel will help, for it will be a glorious victory for Israel when I demonstrate my glory on that day, says the Sovereign LORD. 14At the end of the seven months, special crews will be appointed to search the land for any skeletons and to bury them, so the land will be made clean again. 15Whenever some bones are found, a marker will be set up beside them so the burial crews will see them and take them to be buried in the Valley of Gog's Hordes. 16(There will be a town there named Hamonah—which means 'horde.') And so the land will finally be cleansed.

17"And now, son of man, call all the birds and wild animals, says the Sovereign LORD. Say to them: Gather together for my great sacrificial feast. Come from far and near to the mountains of Israel, and there eat the flesh and drink the blood! 18Eat the flesh of mighty men and drink the blood of princes as though they were rams, lambs, goats, and fat young bulls of Bashan! 19Gorge yourselves with flesh until you are glutted; drink blood until you are drunk. This is the sacrificial feast I have prepared for you. 20Feast at my banquet table—feast on horses, riders, and valiant warriors, says the Sovereign LORD.

21"Thus, I will demonstrate my glory among the nations. Everyone will see the punishment I have inflicted on them and the power I have demonstrated. 22And from that time on the people of Israel will know that I am the LORD their God. 23The nations will then know why Israel was sent away to exile—it was punishment for sin, for they acted in treachery against their God. Therefore, I turned my back on them and let their enemies destroy them. 24I turned my face away and punished them in proportion to the vileness of their sins.

I BELIEVE the Lord will demonstrate his glory in his glorious victory over Gog. (39:13)

Restoration for God's People
25"So now the Sovereign LORD says: I will end the captivity of my people*; I will have mercy on Israel, for I am jealous for my holy reputation! 26They will accept responsibility for their past shame and treachery against me after they come home to live in peace and safety in their own land. And then no one will bother them or make them afraid. 27When I bring them home from the lands of their enemies, my holiness will be displayed to the nations. 28Then my people will know that I am the LORD their God—responsible for sending them away to exile and responsible for bringing them home. I will leave none of my people behind. 29And I will never again turn my back on them, for I will pour out my Spirit upon them, says the Sovereign LORD."

I BELIEVE the Lord will have mercy on Israel for the sake of his holy name. (39:25)

CHAPTER 40
The New Temple Area
On April 28,* during the twenty-fifth year of our captivity—fourteen years after the fall of Jerusalem—the LORD took hold of me. 2In a vision of God he took me to the land of Israel and set me down on a very high mountain. From there I could see what appeared to be a city across from me toward the south. 3As he brought me nearer, I saw a man whose face shone like bronze standing beside a gateway entrance. He was holding in his hand a measuring tape and a measuring rod.

4He said to me, "Son of man, watch and listen. Pay close attention to everything I show you. You have been brought here so I can show you many things. Then you will return to the people of Israel and tell them everything you have seen."

I BELIEVE the Lord transported Ezekiel in a vision to view a new glorious Temple—to be built if the people were ashamed of their wickedness and embraced absolute holiness (Ezekiel 43:11-12). (40:2)

39:11 Hebrew *the sea.* 39:25 Hebrew *of Jacob.* 40:1 Hebrew *At the beginning of the year, on the tenth day of the month,* of the Hebrew calendar. A number of dates in Ezekiel can be cross-checked with dates in surviving Babylonian records and related accurately to our modern calendar. This event occurred on April 28, 573 B.C.

The East Gateway

I BELIEVE Ezekiel carefully described the east gateway of the new Temple. (40:6)

⁵I could see a wall completely surrounding the Temple area. The man took a measuring rod that was 10¹/₂ feet* long and measured the wall, and the wall was 10¹/₂ feet thick and 10¹/₂ feet high.

⁶Then he went over to the gateway that goes through the eastern wall. He climbed the steps and measured the threshold of the gateway; it was 10¹/₂ feet deep.* ⁷There were guard alcoves on each side built into the gateway passage. Each of these alcoves was 10¹/₂ feet square, with a distance between them of 8³/₄ feet along the passage wall. The gateway's inner threshold, which led to the foyer at the inner end of the gateway passage, was 10¹/₂ feet deep. ⁸He also measured the foyer of the gateway* ⁹and found it to be 14 feet deep, with supporting columns 3¹/₂ feet thick. This foyer was at the inner end of the gateway structure, facing toward the Temple.

¹⁰There were three guard alcoves on each side of the gateway passage. Each had the same measurements, and the dividing walls separating them were also identical. ¹¹The man measured the gateway entrance, which was 17¹/₂ feet wide at the opening and 22³/₄ feet wide in the gateway passage. ¹²In front of each of the guard alcoves was a 21-inch curb. The alcoves themselves were 10¹/₂ feet square.

¹³Then he measured the entire width of the gateway, measuring the distance between the back walls of facing guard alcoves; this distance was 43³/₄ feet. ¹⁴He measured the dividing walls all along the inside of the gateway up to the gateway's foyer; this distance was 105 feet.* ¹⁵The full length of the gateway passage was 87¹/₂ feet from one end to the other. ¹⁶There were recessed windows that narrowed inward through the walls of the guard alcoves and their dividing walls. There were also windows in the foyer structure. The surfaces of the dividing walls were decorated with carved palm trees.

The Outer Courtyard

I BELIEVE Ezekiel carefully described the outer courtyard of the new Temple. (40:17)

¹⁷Then the man brought me through the gateway into the outer courtyard of the Temple. A stone pavement ran along the walls of the courtyard, and thirty rooms were built against the walls, opening onto the pavement. ¹⁸This pavement flanked the gates and extended out from the walls into the courtyard the same distance as the gateway entrance. This was the lower pavement. ¹⁹Then the man measured across the Temple's outer courtyard between the outer and inner gateways; the distance was 175 feet.

The North Gateway

I BELIEVE Ezekiel carefully described the north gateway of the new Temple. (40:20)

²⁰There was a gateway on the north just like the one on the east, and the man measured it. ²¹Here, too, there were three guard alcoves on each side, with dividing walls and a foyer. All the measurements matched those of the east gateway. The gateway passage was 87¹/₂ feet long and 43³/₄ feet wide between the back walls of facing guard alcoves. ²²The windows, the foyer, and the palm tree decorations were identical to those in the east gateway. There were seven steps leading up to the gateway entrance, and the foyer was at the inner end of the gateway passage. ²³Here on the north side, just as on the east, there was another gateway leading to the Temple's inner courtyard directly opposite this outer gateway. The distance between the two gateways was 175 feet.

The South Gateway

I BELIEVE Ezekiel carefully described the south gateway of the new Temple. (40:24)

²⁴Then the man took me around to the south gateway and measured its various parts, and he found they were exactly the same as in the others. ²⁵It

40:5 Hebrew 6 long cubits [3.2 meters], each being a cubit [18 inches or 45 centimeters] and a handbreadth [3 inches or 8 centimeters] in length. In this chapter, the distance measures are calculated using the Hebrew long cubit, which equals 21 inches or 53 centimeters.   40:6 Greek version; Hebrew reads one rod [10.5 feet or 3.2 meters] deep, and one threshold, one rod deep.   40:8 Many Hebrew manuscripts add which faced inward toward the Temple; it was one rod [10.5 feet or 3.2 meters] deep. ⁹Then he measured the foyer of the gateway, . . .   40:14 The meaning of the Hebrew in this verse is uncertain.

had windows along the walls as the others did, and there was a foyer where the gateway passage opened into the outer courtyard. And like the others, the gateway passage was 87½ feet long and 43¾ feet wide between the back walls of facing guard alcoves. ²⁶ This gateway also had a stairway of seven steps leading up to it, and there were palm tree decorations along the dividing walls. ²⁷And here again, directly opposite the outer gateway, was another gateway that led into the inner courtyard. The distance between the two gateways was 175 feet.

Gateways to the Inner Courtyard

²⁸ Then the man took me to the south gateway leading into the inner courtyard. He measured it and found that it had the same measurements as the other gateways. ²⁹Its guard alcoves, dividing walls, and foyer were the same size as those in the others. It also had windows along its walls and in the foyer structure. And like the others, the gateway passage was 87½ feet long and 43¾ feet wide. ³⁰(The foyers of the gateways leading into the inner courtyard were 8¾ feet deep and 43¾ feet wide.) ³¹ The foyer of the south gateway faced into the outer courtyard. It had palm tree decorations on its columns, and there were eight steps leading to its entrance.

³²Then he took me to the east gateway leading into the inner courtyard. He measured it and found that it had the same measurements as the other gateways. ³³Its guard alcoves, dividing walls, and foyer were the same size as those of the others, and there were windows along the walls and in the foyer structure. The gateway passage measured 87½ feet long and 43¾ feet wide. ³⁴Its foyer faced into the outer courtyard. It had palm tree decorations on its columns, and there were eight steps leading to its entrance.

³⁵Then he took me around to the north gateway leading to the inner courtyard. He measured it and found that it had the same measurements as the other gateways. ³⁶The guard alcoves, dividing walls, and foyer of this gateway had the same measurements as in the others and the same window arrangements. The gateway passage measured 87½ feet long and 43¾ feet wide. ³⁷Its foyer faced into the outer courtyard, and it had palm tree decorations on the columns. There were eight steps leading to its entrance.

Rooms for Preparing Sacrifices

³⁸A door led from the foyer of the inner gateway on the north side into a side room where the meat for sacrifices was washed before being taken to the altar. ³⁹On each side of this foyer were two tables, where the sacrificial animals were slaughtered for the burnt offerings, sin offerings, and guilt offerings. ⁴⁰Outside the foyer, on each side of the stairs going up to the north entrance, there were two more tables. ⁴¹So there were eight tables in all, four inside and four outside, where the sacrifices were cut up and prepared. ⁴² There were also four tables of hewn stone for preparation of the burnt offerings, each 31½ inches square and 21 inches high. On these tables were placed the butchering knives and other implements and the sacrificial animals. ⁴³There were hooks, each three inches* long, fastened to the foyer walls and set on the tables where the sacrificial meat was to be laid.

Rooms for the Priests

⁴⁴Inside the inner courtyard there were two one-room buildings for the singers, one beside the north gateway, facing south, and the other beside the south* gateway, facing north. ⁴⁵And the man said to me, "The building beside the north inner gate is for the priests who supervise the Temple maintenance. ⁴⁶The building beside the south inner gate is for the priests in charge of the altar—the descendants of Zadok—for they alone of all the Levites may approach the LORD to minister to him."

40:43 Hebrew *a handbreadth* [8 centimeters]. 40:44 As in Greek version; Hebrew reads *east*.

I BELIEVE Ezekiel carefully described the gateways to the inner courtyard of the new Temple. (40:28)

I BELIEVE Ezekiel carefully described the rooms for preparing sacrifices within the new Temple. (40:38)

I BELIEVE Ezekiel carefully described the rooms for the priests within the new Temple. (40:44)

The Inner Courtyard and Temple

Then the man measured the inner courtyard and found it to be 175 feet square. The altar stood there in the courtyard in front of the Temple. Then he brought me to the foyer of the Temple. He measured its supporting columns and found them to be 8³/₄ feet square. The entrance was 24¹/₂ feet wide with walls 5¹/₄ feet thick. The depth of the foyer was 35 feet and the width was 19¹/₄ feet. There were ten steps leading up to it, with a column on each side.

CHAPTER 41

After that, the man brought me into the Holy Place, the large main room of the Temple, and he measured the columns that framed its doorway. They were 10¹/₂ feet* square. ²The entrance was 17¹/₂ feet wide, and the walls on each side were 8³/₄ feet wide. The Holy Place itself was 70 feet long and 35 feet wide.

³Then he went into the inner room at the end of the Holy Place. He measured the columns at the entrance and found them to be 3¹/₂ feet thick. The entrance was 10¹/₂ feet wide, and the walls on each side of the entrance extended 12¹/₄ feet to the corners of the inner room. ⁴The inner room was 35 feet square. "This," he told me, "is the Most Holy Place."

⁵Then he measured the wall of the Temple and found that it was 10¹/₂ feet thick. There was a row of rooms along the outside wall; each room was 7 feet wide. ⁶These rooms were built in three levels, one above the other, with thirty rooms on each level. The supports for these rooms rested on ledges in the Temple wall, but the supports did not extend into the wall. ⁷Each level was wider than the one below it, corresponding to the narrowing of the Temple wall as it rose higher. A stairway led up from the bottom level through the middle level to the top level.

⁸I noticed that the Temple was built on a terrace, which provided a foundation for the side rooms. This terrace was 10¹/₂ feet high. ⁹The outer wall of the Temple's side rooms was 8³/₄ feet thick. This left an open area between these side rooms ¹⁰and the row of rooms along the outer wall of the inner courtyard. This open area measured 35 feet in width, and it went all the way around the Temple. ¹¹Two doors opened from the side rooms into the terrace yard, which was 8³/₄ feet wide. One door faced north and the other south.

¹²A large building stood on the west, facing the Temple courtyard. It was 122¹/₂ feet wide and 157¹/₂ feet long, and its walls were 8³/₄ feet thick. ¹³Then the man measured the Temple, and he found it to be 175 feet long. The courtyard around the building, including its walls, was an additional 175 feet in length. ¹⁴The inner courtyard to the east of the Temple was also 175 feet wide. ¹⁵The building to the west, including its two walls, was also 175 feet wide.

The Holy Place, the Most Holy Place, and the foyer of the Temple were all paneled with wood, ¹⁶as were the frames of the recessed windows. The inner walls of the Temple were paneled with wood above and below the windows. ¹⁷The space above the door leading into the Most Holy Place was also paneled. ¹⁸All the walls were decorated with carvings of cherubim, each with two faces, and there was a palm tree carving between each of the cherubim. ¹⁹One face—that of a man—looked toward the palm tree on one side. The other face—that of a young lion—looked toward the palm tree on the other side. The figures were carved all along the inside of the Temple, ²⁰from the floor to the top of the walls, including the outer wall of the Holy Place.

²¹There were square columns at the entrance to the Holy Place, and the ones at the entrance of the Most Holy Place were similar. ²²There was an altar made of wood, 3¹/₂ feet square and 5¹/₄ feet high. Its corners, base, and sides

I BELIEVE Ezekiel carefully described the inner courtyard of the new Temple. (40:47)

I BELIEVE Ezekiel carefully described the Holy Place of the new Temple. (41:1)

I BELIEVE Ezekiel carefully described the rooms along the walls of the new Temple. (41:5)

I BELIEVE Ezekiel carefully described the measurements of the walls of the new Temple. (41:8)

I BELIEVE Ezekiel carefully described the decorations and carvings on the walls of the new Temple. (41:18)

I BELIEVE Ezekiel carefully described the altar of the Lord's presence in the new Temple. (41:22)

41:1 Hebrew *6 cubits* [3.2 meters]. In this chapter, the distance measures are calculated using the Hebrew long cubit, which equals 21 inches or 53 centimeters.

were all made of wood. "This," the man told me, "is the table that stands in the LORD's presence."

²³Both the Holy Place and the Most Holy Place had double doorways, ²⁴each with two swinging doors. ²⁵The doors leading into the Holy Place were decorated with carved cherubim and palm trees just as on the walls. And there was a wooden canopy over the front of the Temple's foyer. ²⁶On both sides of the foyer there were recessed windows decorated with carved palm trees.

CHAPTER 42

Rooms for the Priests

Then the man led me out of the Temple courtyard by way of the north gateway. We entered the outer courtyard and came to a group of rooms against the north wall of the inner courtyard. ²This group of structures, whose entrance opened toward the north, was 175 feet long and 87½ feet wide.* ³One block of rooms overlooked the 35-foot width of the inner courtyard. Another block of rooms looked out onto the pavement of the outer courtyard. The two blocks were built three levels high and stood across from each other. ⁴Between the two blocks of rooms ran a walkway 17½ feet wide. It extended the entire 175 feet of the complex, and all the doors faced toward the north. ⁵Each of the two upper levels of rooms was narrower than the one beneath it because the upper levels had to allow space for walkways in front of them. ⁶Since there were three levels and they did not have supporting columns as in the courtyards, each of the upper levels was set back from the level beneath it. ⁷There was an outer wall that separated the rooms from the outer courtyard; it was 87½ feet long. ⁸This wall added length to the outer block of rooms, which extended for only 87½ feet, while the inner block—the rooms toward the Temple—extended for 175 feet. ⁹There was an entrance from the outer courtyard to these rooms from the east.

¹⁰On the south* side of the Temple there were two blocks of rooms just south of the inner courtyard between the Temple and the outer courtyard. These rooms were arranged just like the rooms on the north. ¹¹There was a walkway between the two blocks of rooms just like the complex on the north side of the Temple. This complex of rooms was the same length and width as the other one, and it had the same entrances and doors. The dimensions of each were identical. ¹²So there was an entrance in the wall facing the doors of the inner block of rooms, and another on the east at the end of the interior walkway.

¹³Then the man told me, "These rooms that overlook the Temple from the north and south are holy. It is there that the priests who offer sacrifices to the LORD will eat the most holy offerings. And they will use these rooms to store the grain offerings, sin offerings, and guilt offerings because these rooms are holy. ¹⁴When the priests leave the Holy Place, they must not go directly to the outer courtyard. They must first take off the clothes they wore while ministering because these clothes are holy. They must put on other clothes before entering the parts of the building complex open to the public."

¹⁵When the man had finished taking these measurements, he led me out through the east gateway to measure the entire Temple area. ¹⁶He measured the east side; it was 875 feet long. ¹⁷He also measured the north side and got the same measurement. ¹⁸The south side was the same length, ¹⁹and so was the west side. ²⁰So the area was 875 feet on each side with a wall all around it to separate the holy places from the common.

I BELIEVE Ezekiel carefully described the rooms for the priests within the new Temple. (42:1)

I BELIEVE Ezekiel heard and described the instructions for the use of the rooms for the priests within the new Temple. (42:13)

I BELIEVE Ezekiel carefully described the measurements of the entire area of the new Temple. (42:15)

42:2 Hebrew *100 cubits* [53 meters] *long and 50 cubits* [26.5 meters] *wide.* In this chapter, the distance measures are calculated using the Hebrew long cubit, which equals 21 inches or 53 centimeters.   42:10 As in Greek version; Hebrew reads *east.*

CHAPTER 43

The LORD's Glory Returns

After this, the man brought me back around to the east gateway. ²Suddenly, the glory of the God of Israel appeared from the east. The sound of his coming was like the roar of rushing waters, and the whole landscape shone with his glory. ³This vision was just like the others I had seen, first by the Kebar River and then when he came to destroy Jerusalem. And I fell down before him with my face in the dust. ⁴And the glory of the LORD came into the Temple through the east gateway.

⁵Then the Spirit took me up and brought me into the inner courtyard, and the glory of the LORD filled the Temple. ⁶And I heard someone speaking to me from within the Temple. (The man who had been measuring was still standing beside me.) ⁷And the LORD said to me, "Son of man, this is the place of my throne and the place where I will rest my feet. I will remain here forever, living among the people of Israel. They and their kings will not defile my holy name any longer by their adulterous worship of other gods or by raising monuments in honor of their dead kings.* ⁸They put their idol altars right next to mine with only a wall between them and me. They defiled my holy name by such wickedness, so I consumed them in my anger. ⁹Now let them put away their idols and the sacred pillars erected to honor their kings, and I will live among them forever.

¹⁰"Son of man, describe to the people of Israel the Temple I have shown you. Tell them its appearance and its plan so they will be ashamed of all their sins. ¹¹And if they are ashamed of what they have done, describe to them all the specifications of its construction—including its entrances and doors—and everything else about it. Write down all these specifications and directions as they watch so they will be sure to remember them. ¹²And this is the basic law of the Temple: absolute holiness! The entire top of the hill where the Temple is built is holy. Yes, this is the primary law of the Temple.

The Altar

¹³"These are the measurements of the altar*: There is a gutter all around the altar 21 inches wide and 21 inches deep, with a curb 9 inches* wide around its edge. And this is the height of the altar: ¹⁴From the gutter the altar rises 3½ feet to a ledge that surrounds the altar; this lower ledge is 21 inches wide. From the lower ledge the altar rises 7 feet to the upper ledge; this upper ledge is also 21 inches wide. ¹⁵The top of the altar, the hearth, rises still 7 feet higher, with a horn rising up from each of the four corners. ¹⁶The top of the altar is square, measuring 21 feet by 21 feet. ¹⁷The upper ledge also forms a square, measuring 24½ feet on each side, with a 21-inch gutter and a 10½-inch curb all around the edge. There are steps going up the east side of the altar."

¹⁸Then he said to me, "Son of man, this is what the Sovereign LORD says: These will be the regulations for the burning of offerings and the sprinkling of blood when the altar is built. ¹⁹At that time, the Levitical priests of the family of Zadok, who minister before me, are to be given a young bull for a sin offering, says the Sovereign LORD. ²⁰You will take some of its blood and smear it on the four horns of the altar, the four corners of the upper ledge, and the curb that runs around that ledge. This will cleanse and make atonement for the altar. ²¹Then take the young bull for the sin offering and burn it at the appointed place outside the Temple area.

²²"On the second day, sacrifice as a sin offering a young male goat that has no physical defects. Then cleanse and make atonement for the altar again,

---

43:7 Or *by raising pillars on their high places.* 43:13a Hebrew *measurements of the altar in long cubits, each being a cubit* [18 inches or 45 centimeters] *and a handbreadth* [3 inches or 8 centimeters] *in length.* In this chapter, the distance measures are calculated using the Hebrew long cubit, which equals 21 inches or 53 centimeters. 43:13b Hebrew *1 span* [23 centimeters].

I BOW in worship before the Lord's glory. (43:3)

I BELIEVE Ezekiel saw the glory of the Lord return to the new Temple. (43:5)

I BELIEVE the Lord called on his people to put away their idols so that he could live among them. (43:9)

I BELIEVE the Lord instructed Ezekiel to give the Israelites the specifications for constructing the new Temple if they were ashamed of their sins and embraced absolute holiness. (43:11)

I BELIEVE the Lord gave Ezekiel the measurements of the altar. (43:13)

I BELIEVE the Lord gave Ezekiel the regulations for the offerings. (43:18)

just as you did with the young bull. ²³When you have finished the cleansing ceremony, offer another young bull that has no defects and a perfect ram from the flock. ²⁴You are to present them to the LORD, and the priests are to sprinkle salt on them and offer them as a burnt offering to the LORD.

²⁵"Every day for seven days a male goat, a young bull, and a ram from the flock will be sacrificed as a sin offering. None of these animals may have physical defects of any kind. ²⁶Do this each day for seven days to cleanse and make atonement for the altar, thus setting it apart for holy use. ²⁷On the eighth day, and on each day afterward, the priests will sacrifice on the altar the burnt offerings and peace offerings of the people. Then I will accept you, says the Sovereign LORD."

CHAPTER 44

The Prince, Levites, and Priests

Then the man brought me back to the east gateway in the outer wall, but it was closed. ²And the LORD said to me, "This gate must remain closed; it will never again be opened. No man will ever pass through it, for the LORD, the God of Israel, entered here. Thus, it must always remain shut. ³Only the prince himself may sit inside this gateway to feast in the LORD's presence. But he may come and go only through the gateway's foyer."

⁴Then the man brought me through the north gateway to the front of the Temple. I looked and saw that the glory of the LORD filled the Temple of the LORD, and I fell to the ground with my face in the dust.

⁵And the LORD said to me, "Son of man, take careful notice; use your eyes and ears. Listen to everything I tell you about the regulations concerning the LORD's Temple. Take careful note of who may be admitted to the Temple and who is to be excluded from it. ⁶And give these rebels, the people of Israel, this message from the Sovereign LORD: O people of Israel, enough of your disgusting sins! ⁷You have brought uncircumcised foreigners into my sanctuary—people who have no heart for God. In this way, you profaned my Temple even as you offered me my food, the fat and blood of sacrifices. Thus, in addition to all your other disgusting sins, you have broken my covenant. ⁸You have not kept the laws I gave you concerning these sacred rituals, for you have hired foreigners to take charge of my sanctuary.

⁹"So this is what the Sovereign LORD says: No foreigners, including those who live among the people of Israel, will enter my sanctuary if they have not been circumcised and do not love the LORD. ¹⁰And the men of the tribe of Levi who abandoned me when Israel strayed away from me to worship idols must bear the consequences of their unfaithfulness. ¹¹They may still be Temple guards and gatemen, and they may still slaughter the animals brought for burnt offerings and be present to help the people. ¹²But they encouraged my people to worship other gods, causing Israel to fall into deep sin. So I have raised my hand and taken an oath that they must bear the consequences for their sins, says the Sovereign LORD. ¹³They may not approach me to minister as priests. They may not touch any of my holy things or the holy offerings, for they must bear the shame of all the sins they have committed. ¹⁴They are to serve as the Temple caretakers and are relegated to doing maintenance work and helping the people in a general way.

¹⁵"However, the Levitical priests of the family of Zadok continued to minister faithfully in the Temple when Israel abandoned me for idols. These men will serve as my ministers. They will stand in my presence and offer the fat and blood of the sacrifices, says the Sovereign LORD. ¹⁶They are the ones who will enter my sanctuary and approach my table to serve me. They are the ones who will fulfill all my requirements. ¹⁷When they enter the gateway to the inner courtyard, they must wear only linen clothing. They must wear no wool while on duty in the inner courtyard or in the Temple itself. ¹⁸They must wear

I BELIEVE the Lord gave Ezekiel the regulations concerning who might be admitted and excluded from the Lord's new Temple. (44:5)

I BELIEVE only those who love and commit themselves to the Lord may enter his presence. (44:9)

I BELIEVE the consequences of leading people away from the Lord are severe. (44:12)

I BELIEVE the Lord gave Ezekiel the personal and ministry regulations for the Levitical priests. (44:15)

linen turbans and linen undergarments. They must not wear anything that would cause them to perspire. ¹⁹When they return to the outer courtyard where the people are, they must take off the clothes they wear while ministering to me. They must leave them in the sacred rooms and put on other clothes so they do not harm the people by transmitting holiness to them through this clothing.

²⁰"They must neither let their hair grow too long nor shave it off completely. Instead, they must trim it regularly. ²¹The priests must never drink wine before entering the inner courtyard. ²²They may choose their wives only from among the virgins of Israel or the widows of the priests. They may not marry other widows or divorced women. ²³They will teach my people the difference between what is holy and what is common, what is ceremonially clean and unclean.

²⁴"They will serve as judges to resolve any disagreements among my people. Their decisions must be based on my regulations. And the priests themselves must obey my instructions and laws at all the sacred festivals, and they will see to it that the Sabbath is set apart as a holy day. ²⁵A priest must never defile himself by being in the presence of a dead person unless it is his father, mother, child, brother, or unmarried sister. In such cases it is permitted. ²⁶But such a priest can only return to his Temple duties after being ritually cleansed and then waiting for seven days. ²⁷The first day he returns to work and enters the inner courtyard and the sanctuary, he must offer a sin offering for himself, says the Sovereign LORD.

²⁸"As to property, the priests will not have any, for I alone am their inheritance. ²⁹Their food will come from the gifts and sacrifices brought to the Temple by the people—the grain offerings, the sin offerings, and the guilt offerings. Whatever anyone sets apart* for the LORD will belong to the priests. ³⁰The first of the ripe fruits and all the gifts brought to the LORD will go to the priests. The first samples of each grain harvest and the first of your flour must also be given to the priests so the LORD will bless your homes. ³¹The priests may never eat meat from any bird or animal that dies a natural death or that dies after being attacked by another animal.

CHAPTER 45

Division of the Land

"When you divide the land among the tribes of Israel, you must set aside a section of it for the LORD as his holy portion. This piece of land will be 8¹/₃ miles long and 6²/₃ miles wide.* The entire area will be holy ground. ²A section of this land, measuring 875 feet by 875 feet, will be set aside for the Temple. An additional strip of land 87¹/₂ feet wide is to be left empty all around it. ³Within the larger sacred area, measure out a portion of land 8¹/₃ miles long and 3¹/₃ miles wide. Within it the sanctuary of the Most Holy Place will be located. ⁴This area will be a holy land, set aside for the priests who minister to the LORD in the sanctuary. They will use it for their homes, and my Temple will be located within it. ⁵The strip of sacred land next to it, also 8¹/₃ miles long and 3¹/₃ miles wide, will be a living area for the Levites who work at the Temple. It will be their possession and a place for their towns.*

⁶"Adjacent to the larger sacred area will be a section of land 8¹/₃ miles long and 1²/₃ miles wide. This will be set aside to be a city where anyone in Israel can come and live.

⁷"Two special sections of land will be set apart for the prince. One section

I BELIEVE the Lord gave Ezekiel instructions for the roles and ritual cleansing of the priests of the new Temple. (44:24)

I BELIEVE the Lord gave Ezekiel instructions for providing for the Levitical priests of the new Temple. (44:29)

I BELIEVE the Lord gave Ezekiel instructions for dividing the land. (45:1)

44:29 The Hebrew term used here refers to the complete consecration of things or people to the LORD, either by destroying them or by giving them as an offering. 45:1 Reflecting the Greek reading 25,000 cubits [13.3 kilometers] long and 20,000 cubits [10.6 kilometers] wide; Hebrew reads 25,000 cubits long and 10,000 cubits wide. Compare 45:3, 5; 48:9. In this chapter, the distance measures are calculated using the Hebrew long cubit, which equals 21 inches or 53 centimeters. 45:5 As in Greek version; Hebrew reads They will have as their possession 20 rooms.

will share a border with the east side of the sacred lands and city, and the second section will share a border on the west side. Then the far eastern and western borders of the prince's lands will line up with the eastern and western boundaries of the tribal areas. [8]These sections of land will be the prince's allotment.

Rules for the Prince

"My princes will no longer oppress and rob my people; they will assign the rest of the land to the people, giving an allotment to each tribe. [9]For this is what the Sovereign LORD says: Enough, you princes of Israel! Stop all your violence and oppression and do what is just and right. Quit robbing and cheating my people out of their land! Stop expelling them from their homes! [10]You must use only honest weights and scales, honest dry volume measures, and honest liquid volume measures.* [11]The homer* will be your standard unit for measuring volume. The ephah and the bath* will each measure one-tenth of a homer. [12]The standard unit for weight will be the silver shekel.* One shekel consists of twenty gerahs, and sixty shekels are equal to one mina.*

I BELIEVE the Lord demands justice and honesty from the leaders of his people. (45:9)

Special Offerings and Celebrations

[13]"This is the tax you must give to the prince: one bushel of wheat or barley for every sixty* you harvest, [14]one percent of your olive oil,* [15]and one sheep for every two hundred in your flocks in Israel. These will be the grain offerings, burnt offerings, and peace offerings that will make atonement for the people who bring them, says the Sovereign LORD. [16]All the people of Israel must join the prince in bringing their offerings. [17]The prince will be required to provide offerings that are given at the religious festivals, the new moon celebrations, the Sabbath days, and all other similar occasions. He will provide the sin offerings, burnt offerings, grain offerings, drink offerings, and peace offerings to make reconciliation for the people of Israel.

I BELIEVE the Lord gave Ezekiel instructions for the taxes to be paid to support the offerings at the new Temple. (45:13)

[18]"This is what the Sovereign LORD says: In early spring, on the first day of each new year,* sacrifice a young bull with no physical defects to purify the Temple. [19]The priest will take some of the blood of this sin offering and put it on the doorposts of the Temple, the four corners of the upper ledge on the altar, and the gateposts at the entrance to the inner courtyard. [20]Do this also on the seventh day of the new year for anyone who has sinned through error or ignorance. In that way, you will make atonement for the Temple.

I BELIEVE the Lord gave Ezekiel instructions for the yearly offerings to purify the new Temple. (45:18)

[21]"On the fourteenth day of the new year, you must celebrate the Passover. This festival will last for seven days. Only bread without yeast may be eaten during that time. [22]On the day of Passover the prince will provide a young bull as a sin offering for himself and the people of Israel. [23]On each of the seven days of the feast he will prepare a burnt offering to the LORD. This daily offering will consist of seven young bulls and seven rams without any defects. A male goat will also be given each day for a sin offering. [24]The prince will provide a half bushel of flour as a grain offering and a gallon of olive oil* with each young bull and ram.

I BELIEVE the Lord gave Ezekiel instructions for the yearly celebration of the Passover. (45:21)

[25]"During the seven days of the Festival of Shelters, which occurs every year in early autumn,* the prince will provide these same sacrifices for the sin offering, the burnt offering, and the grain offering, along with the required olive oil.

45:10 Hebrew use honest scales, an honest ephah, and an honest bath.   45:11a The homer measures about 40 gallons or 182 liters.   45:11b The ephah is a dry measure; the bath is a liquid measure.   45:12a The shekel weighs about 0.4 ounces or 11 grams.   45:12b Elsewhere the mina is equated to 50 shekels.   45:13 Hebrew $^1/_6$ of an ephah from each homer of wheat . . . and of barley.   45:14 Hebrew the portion of oil, measured by the bath, is $^1/_{10}$ of a bath from each cor, which consists of 10 baths or 1 homer, for 10 baths are equivalent to a homer.
45:18 Hebrew On the first day of the first month, of the Hebrew calendar. This day of the Hebrew lunar calendar occurs in late March or early April.   45:24 Hebrew an ephah [18 liters] of flour . . . a hin [3.8 liters] of olive oil.
45:25 Hebrew the festival which begins on the fifteenth day of the seventh month (see Lev 23:33). This day of the Hebrew lunar calendar occurs in late September or October.

CHAPTER 46

I BELIEVE the Lord gave
Ezekiel instructions
for how the prince
and commoners were
to worship the Lord at
the east gateway.
(46:1)

I BELIEVE the Lord gave
Ezekiel instructions
for the prince's
Sabbath offerings.
(46:4)

I BELIEVE the Lord gave
Ezekiel instructions
for the morning burnt
sacrifice. (46:13)

I BELIEVE the Lord does
not want any of his
people unjustly
evicted by a greedy
ruler. (46:18)

¹"This is what the Sovereign LORD says: The east gateway of the inner wall will be closed during the six workdays each week, but it will be open on Sabbath days and the days of new moon celebrations. ²The prince will enter the foyer of the gateway from the outside. Then he will stand by the gatepost while the priest offers his burnt offering and peace offering. He will worship inside the gateway passage and then go back out the way he came. The gateway will not be closed until evening. ³The common people will worship the LORD in front of this gateway on Sabbath days and the days of new moon celebrations.

⁴"Each Sabbath day the prince will present to the LORD a burnt offering of six lambs and one ram, all with no physical defects. ⁵He will present a grain offering of a half bushel of flour to go with the ram and whatever amount of flour he chooses to go with each lamb. He is to offer one gallon of olive oil* for each half bushel of flour. ⁶At the new moon celebrations, he will bring one young bull, six lambs, and one ram, all with no physical defects. ⁷With the young bull he must bring a half bushel of flour for a grain offering. With the ram he must bring another half bushel of flour. And with each lamb he is to bring whatever amount of flour that he decides to give. With each half bushel of flour he must offer one gallon of olive oil.

⁸"The prince must enter the gateway through the foyer, and he must leave the same way he came. ⁹But when the people come in through the north gateway to worship the LORD during the religious festivals, they must leave by the south gateway. And those who entered through the south gateway must leave by the north gateway. They must never leave by the same gateway they came in; they must always use the opposite gateway. ¹⁰The prince will enter and leave with the people on these occasions.

¹¹"So at the special feasts and sacred festivals, the grain offering will be a half bushel of flour with each young bull, another half bushel of flour with each ram, and as much flour as the prince chooses to give with each lamb. One gallon of oil is to be given with each half bushel of flour. ¹²Whenever the prince offers a voluntary burnt offering or peace offering to the LORD, the east gateway to the inner courtyard will be opened for him to enter, and he will offer his sacrifices just as he does on Sabbath days. Then he will turn and leave the way he entered, and the gateway will be shut behind him.

¹³"Each morning a year-old lamb with no physical defects must be sacrificed as a burnt offering to the LORD. ¹⁴With the lamb, a grain offering must also be given to the LORD—about two and a half quarts of flour with a third of a gallon of olive oil* to moisten the flour. This will be a permanent law for you. ¹⁵The lamb, the grain offering, and the olive oil must be given as a daily sacrifice every morning without fail.

¹⁶"This is what the Sovereign LORD says: If the prince gives a gift of land to one of his sons, it will belong to him and his descendants forever. ¹⁷But if he gives a gift of land to one of his servants, the servant may keep it only until the Year of Jubilee, which comes every fiftieth year.* At that time the servant will be set free, and the land will return to the prince. Only the gifts given to the prince's sons will be permanent. ¹⁸And the prince may never take anyone's property by force. If he gives property to his sons, it must be from his own land, for I do not want any of my people unjustly evicted from their property."

The Temple Kitchens

¹⁹Then the man brought me through the entrance beside the gateway and led me to the sacred rooms assigned to the priests, which faced toward the north. He showed me a place at the extreme west end of these rooms. ²⁰He

46:5 Hebrew *an ephah* [18 liters] *of flour . . . a hin* [3.8 liters] *of olive oil;* also in 46:7, 11.   46:14 Hebrew ¹⁄₆ *of an ephah* [2.9 liters] *of flour with* ¹⁄₃ *of a hin* [1.3 liters] *of olive oil.*   46:17 Hebrew *until the Year of Release;* see Lev 25:8-17.

explained, "This is where the priests will cook the meat from the guilt offerings and sin offerings and bake the flour from the grain offerings into bread. They will do it here to avoid carrying the sacrifices through the outer courtyard and harming the people by transmitting holiness to them."

²¹Then he brought me back to the outer courtyard and led me to each of its four corners. In each corner I saw an enclosure. ²²Each of these enclosures was 70 feet long and 52¹/₂ feet wide,* surrounded by walls. ²³Along the inside of these walls was a ledge of stone with fireplaces under the ledge all the way around. ²⁴The man said to me, "These are the kitchens to be used by the Temple assistants to boil the sacrifices offered by the people."

CHAPTER 47

The River of Healing

Then the man brought me back to the entrance of the Temple. There I saw a stream flowing eastward from beneath the Temple threshold. This stream then passed to the right of the altar on its south side. ²The man brought me outside the wall through the north gateway and led me around to the eastern entrance. There I could see the stream flowing out through the south side of the east gateway. ³Measuring as he went, he led me along the stream for 1,750 feet* and told me to go across. At that point the water was up to my ankles. ⁴He measured off another 1,750 feet and told me to go across again. This time the water was up to my knees. After another 1,750 feet, it was up to my waist. ⁵Then he measured another 1,750 feet, and the river was too deep to cross without swimming.

⁶He told me to keep in mind what I had seen; then he led me back along the riverbank. ⁷Suddenly, to my surprise, many trees were now growing on both sides of the river! ⁸Then he said to me, "This river flows east through the desert into the Jordan Valley,* where it enters the Dead Sea.* The waters of this stream will heal the salty waters of the Dead Sea and make them fresh and pure. ⁹Everything that touches the water of this river will live. Fish will abound in the Dead Sea, for its waters will be healed. Wherever this water flows, everything will live. ¹⁰Fishermen will stand along the shores of the Dead Sea, fishing all the way from En-gedi to En-eglaim. The shores will be covered with nets drying in the sun. Fish of every kind will fill the Dead Sea, just as they fill the Mediterranean*! ¹¹But the marshes and swamps will not be purified; they will be sources of salt. ¹²All kinds of fruit trees will grow along both sides of the river. The leaves of these trees will never turn brown and fall, and there will always be fruit on their branches. There will be a new crop every month, without fail! For they are watered by the river flowing from the Temple. The fruit will be for food and the leaves for healing."

Boundaries for the Land

¹³This is what the Sovereign LORD says: "Follow these instructions for dividing the land for the twelve tribes of Israel: The tribe of Joseph will be given two shares of land.* ¹⁴Otherwise each tribe will receive an equal share. I swore that I would give this land to your ancestors, and it will now come to you as your inheritance.

¹⁵"The northern border will run from the Mediterranean toward Hethlon, then on through Lebo-hamath to Zedad; ¹⁶then it will run to Berothah and Sibraim, which are on the border between Damascus and Hamath, and finally to Hazer-hatticon, on the border of Hauran. ¹⁷So the

I BELIEVE the Lord gave Ezekiel instructions for the kitchens of the new Temple. (46:20)

I BELIEVE the Lord showed Ezekiel a stream flowing from the new Temple. (47:1)

I BELIEVE the river that flowed from the new Temple caused the trees to produce abundant fruit and leaves for healing (see Revelation 22:1–2). (47:12)

I BELIEVE the Lord gave Ezekiel instructions for dividing the land for the twelve tribes of Israel within its new borders. (47:13)

46:22 Hebrew *40 cubits* [21.2 meters] *long and 30 cubits* [15.9 meters] *wide.* The distances are calculated using the Hebrew long cubit, which equals 21 inches or 53 centimeters.　47:3 Hebrew *1,000 cubits* [530 meters]; also in 47:4, 5. The distances are calculated using the Hebrew long cubit, which equals 21 inches or 53 centimeters. 47:8a Hebrew *the Arabah.*　47:8b Hebrew *the sea;* also in 47:10.　47:10 Hebrew *the great sea;* also in 47:15, 17, 19, 20.　47:13 A share of land for each of Joseph's two oldest sons, Ephraim and Manasseh.

northern border will run from the Mediterranean to Hazar-enan, on the border between Hamath to the north and Damascus to the south. ¹⁸"The eastern border starts at a point between Hauran and Damascus and runs southward along the Jordan River between Israel and Gilead, past the Dead Sea* and as far south as Tamar.* This will be the eastern border. ¹⁹"The southern border will go west from Tamar to the waters of Meribah at Kadesh* and then follow the course of the brook of Egypt to the Mediterranean. This will be the southern border. ²⁰"On the west side the Mediterranean itself will be your border from the southern border to the point where the northern border begins, opposite Lebo-hamath.

²¹"Divide the land within these boundaries among the tribes of Israel. ²²Distribute the land as an inheritance for yourselves and for the foreigners who have joined you and are raising their families among you. They will be just like native-born Israelites to you, and they will receive an inheritance among the tribes. ²³All these immigrants are to be given land within the territory of the tribe with whom they now live. I, the Sovereign LORD, have spoken!

CHAPTER 48

Division of the Land

"Here is the list of the tribes of Israel and the territory each is to receive. The territory of Dan is in the extreme north. Its boundary line follows the Hethlon road to Lebo-hamath and then runs on to Hazar-enan on the border of Damascus, with Hamath to the north. Dan's territory extends all the way across the land of Israel from east to west. ²Asher's territory lies south of Dan's and also extends from east to west. ³Naphtali's land lies south of Asher's, also extending from east to west. ⁴Then comes Manasseh south of Naphtali, and its territory also extends from east to west. ⁵South of Manasseh is Ephraim, ⁶and then Reuben, ⁷and then Judah, all of whose boundaries extend from east to west.

⁸"South of Judah is the land set aside for a special purpose. It will be 8¹/₃ miles wide and will extend as far east and west as the tribal territories, with the Temple at the center.

⁹"The area set aside for the LORD's Temple will be 8¹/₃ miles long and 6²/₃ miles wide.* ¹⁰For the priests there will be a strip of land measuring 8¹/₃ miles long by 3¹/₃ miles wide, with the LORD's Temple at the center. ¹¹This area is set aside for the ordained priests, the descendants of Zadok who obeyed me and did not go astray when the people of Israel and the rest of the Levites did. ¹²It will be their special portion when the land is distributed, the most sacred land of all. Next to the priests' territory will lie the land where the other Levites will live. ¹³The land allotted to the Levites will be the same size and shape as that belonging to the priests—8¹/₃ miles long and 3¹/₃ miles wide. Together these portions of land will measure 8¹/₃ miles long by 6²/₃ miles wide.* ¹⁴None of this special land will ever be sold or traded or used by others, for it belongs to the LORD; it is set apart as holy.

¹⁵"An additional strip of land 8¹/₃ miles long by 1²/₃ miles wide, south of the sacred Temple area, will be allotted for public use—homes, pasturelands, and common lands, with a city at the center. ¹⁶The city will measure 1¹/₂ miles* on each side. ¹⁷Open lands will surround the city for 150 yards* in

I BELIEVE the Lord commanded that those who joined his people to worship him were to be treated as equal citizens. (47:22)

I BELIEVE the Lord gave Ezekiel instructions for the territories to be given to each tribe. (48:1)

I BELIEVE the Lord gave Ezekiel instructions for the area set aside for his new Temple. (48:9)

I BELIEVE the Lord required that the holy land for the Levites must never be sold. (48:14)

I BELIEVE the Lord gave Ezekiel instructions for allotting land around the new Temple for a city and farmlands for the people. (48:15)

47:18a Hebrew *the eastern sea.* 47:18b As in Greek version; Hebrew reads *you will measure.* 47:19 Hebrew *waters of Meribath-kadesh.* 48:9 Reflecting the Greek reading in 45:1: *25,000 cubits* [13.3 kilometers] *long and 20,000 cubits* [10.6 kilometers] *wide*; Hebrew reads *25,000 cubits long and 10,000 cubits wide.* Compare 45:1-5; 48:10-13. In this chapter, the distance measures are calculated using the Hebrew long cubit, which equals 21 inches or 53 centimeters. 48:13 See note on 48:9. 48:16 Hebrew *4,500 cubits* [2.4 kilometers]; also in 48:30, 32, 33, 34. 48:17 Hebrew *250 cubits* [133 meters].

every direction. [18]Outside the city there will be a farming area that stretches 3$\frac{1}{3}$ miles to the east and 3$\frac{1}{3}$ miles to the west along the border of the sacred area. This farmland will produce food for the people working in the city. [19]Those who come from the various tribes to work in the city may farm it. [20]This entire area—including the sacred lands and the city—is a square that measures 8$\frac{1}{3}$ miles on each side.

[21]"The areas that remain, to the east and to the west of the sacred lands and the city, will belong to the prince. Each of these areas will be 8$\frac{1}{3}$ miles wide, extending in opposite directions to the eastern and western borders of Israel. [22]So the prince's land will include everything between the territories allotted to Judah and Benjamin, except for the areas set aside for the sacred lands and the city.

I BELIEVE the Lord gave Ezekiel instructions for the land allotted to the prince. (48:21)

[23]"These are the territories allotted to the rest of the tribes. Benjamin's territory lies just south of the prince's lands, and it extends across the entire land of Israel from east to west. [24]South of Benjamin's territory lies that of Simeon, also extending across the land from east to west. [25]Next is the territory of Issachar with the same eastern and western boundaries. [26]Then comes the territory of Zebulun, which also extends across the land from east to west. [27]The territory of Gad is just south of Zebulun with the same borders to the east and west. [28]The southern border of Gad runs from Tamar to the waters of Meribah at Kadesh* and then follows the brook of Egypt to the Mediterranean.* [29]These are the allotments that will be set aside for each tribe's inheritance, says the Sovereign LORD.

I BELIEVE the Lord gave instructions for allotments for each of the tribes of Israel. (48:29)

The Gates of the City

[30]"These will be the exits to the city: On the north wall, which is 1$\frac{1}{2}$ miles long, [31]there will be three gates, each one named after a tribe of Israel. The first will be named for Reuben, the second for Judah, and the third for Levi. [32]On the east wall, also 1$\frac{1}{2}$ miles long, the gates will be named for Joseph, Benjamin, and Dan. [33]The south wall, also 1$\frac{1}{2}$ miles long, will have gates named for Simeon, Issachar, and Zebulun. [34]And on the west wall, also 1$\frac{1}{2}$ miles long, the gates will be named for Gad, Asher, and Naphtali.

[35]"The distance around the entire city will be six miles.* And from that day the name of the city will be 'The LORD Is There.'* "

I BELIEVE the Lord longs for a place to live among his people. (48:35)

48:28a Hebrew *waters of Meribath-kadesh.*   48:28b Hebrew *the great sea.*   48:35a Hebrew *18,000 cubits* [9.6 kilometers].   48:35b Hebrew *Yahweh Shammah.*

DANIEL

THIS FOURTH "MAJOR" Old Testament prophet urges readers to remember that God is directing all of history and in the end will judge each of us.

This book is major because of its substance, not its length. It presents some of the world's best-known and best-loved Bible stories, as well as the Old Testament's most detailed prophetic outlines of future events.

In the dramatic first half of the book, we read of Daniel's refusal to eat King Nebuchadnezzar's food (chapter 1) and of Nebuchadnezzar's plan to kill Daniel unless he can accurately tell what the king dreamed the previous night (chapter 2). We read about the time three of Daniel's friends are thrown into a fiery furnace (chapter 3) and Daniel's prediction that Nebuchadnezzar will go insane (chapter 4). We read of Daniel's ability to read the divine handwriting on King Belshazzar's wall (chapter 5) and the time Daniel is thrown into a lions' den by King Darius (chapter 6). These events take place over a period of nearly seventy years.

In the more prophetic second half of the book, we read of four visions that Daniel received predicting the fall of the Babylonian Empire; the rise and fall of the Persian, Grecian, and Roman Empires; and the last days before the Lord judges the living and the dead (chapters 7–12). A few of these predictions come true in Daniel's later years; most are fulfilled hundreds of years later; some have yet to happen.

Famous verses in Daniel include

- ○ "Daniel made up his mind not to defile himself" (1:8)
- ○ "There is a God in heaven who reveals secrets" (2:28)
- ○ "Truly, your God is the God of gods, the Lord over kings" (2:47)
- ○ "O Nebuchadnezzar, we do not need to defend ourselves before you" (3:16)
- ○ "The God whom we serve is able to save us. He will rescue us" (3:17)
- ○ "But even if he doesn't, . . . we will never serve your gods" (3:18)
- ○ "There is no other god who can rescue like this!" (3:29)
- ○ "O King Nebuchadnezzar, please listen to me. Stop sinning" (4:27)
- ○ "You will eat grass like a cow. . . . until you learn that the Most High rules" (4:32)
- ○ "This is the message that was written: MENE, MENE, TEKEL, PARSIN" (5:25)
- ○ "Was your God . . . able to rescue you from the lions?" (6:20)
- ○ "I watched as thrones were put in place and the Ancient One sat down to judge" (7:9)
- ○ "Then the court began its session, and the books were opened" (7:10)
- ○ "I saw someone who looked like a man coming with the clouds of heaven" (7:13)
- ○ "A period of seventy sets of seven has been decreed for your people" (9:24)
- ○ "But the people who know their God will be strong" (11:32)
- ○ "Many of those whose bodies lie dead and buried will rise up" (12:2)
- ○ "Those who are wise will shine as bright as the sky" (12:3)
- ○ "Many will rush here and there, and knowledge will increase" (12:4)
- ○ "At the end of the days, you will rise again to receive the inheritance set aside for you" (12:13)

CHAPTER 1

Daniel in Nebuchadnezzar's Court

During the third year of King Jehoiakim's reign in Judah,* King Nebuchadnezzar of Babylon came to Jerusalem and besieged it with his armies. ²The Lord gave him victory over King Jehoiakim of Judah. When Nebuchadnezzar returned to Babylon, he took with him some of the sacred objects from the Temple of God and placed them in the treasure-house of his god in the land of Babylonia.*

³Then the king ordered Ashpenaz, who was in charge of the palace officials, to bring to the palace some of the young men of Judah's royal family and other noble families, who had been brought to Babylon as captives. ⁴"Select only strong, healthy, and good-looking young men," he said. "Make sure they are well versed in every branch of learning, are gifted with knowledge and good sense, and have the poise needed to serve in the royal palace. Teach these young men the language and literature of the Babylonians.*" ⁵The king assigned them a daily ration of the best food and wine from his own kitchens. They were to be trained for a three-year period, and then some of them would be made his advisers in the royal court.

⁶Daniel, Hananiah, Mishael, and Azariah were four of the young men chosen, all from the tribe of Judah. ⁷The chief official renamed them with these Babylonian names:

Daniel was called Belteshazzar.
Hananiah was called Shadrach.
Mishael was called Meshach.
Azariah was called Abednego.

⁸But Daniel made up his mind not to defile himself by eating the food and wine given to them by the king. He asked the chief official for permission to eat other things instead. ⁹Now God had given the chief official great respect for Daniel. ¹⁰But he was alarmed by Daniel's suggestion. "My lord the king has ordered that you eat this food and wine," he said. "If you become pale and thin compared to the other youths your age, I am afraid the king will have me beheaded for neglecting my duties."

¹¹Daniel talked it over with the attendant who had been appointed by the chief official to look after Daniel, Hananiah, Mishael, and Azariah. ¹²"Test us for ten days on a diet of vegetables and water," Daniel said. ¹³"At the end of the ten days, see how we look compared to the other young men who are eating the king's rich food. Then you can decide whether or not to let us continue eating our diet." ¹⁴So the attendant agreed to Daniel's suggestion and tested them for ten days.

¹⁵At the end of the ten days, Daniel and his three friends looked healthier and better nourished than the young men who had been eating the food assigned by the king. ¹⁶So after that, the attendant fed them only vegetables instead of the rich foods and wines. ¹⁷God gave these four young men an unusual aptitude for learning the literature and science of the time. And God gave Daniel special ability in understanding the meanings of visions and dreams.

¹⁸When the three-year training period ordered by the king was completed, the chief official brought all the young men to King Nebuchadnezzar. ¹⁹The king talked with each of them, and none of them impressed him as much as Daniel, Hananiah, Mishael, and Azariah. So they were appointed to his regular staff of advisers. ²⁰In all matters requiring wisdom and balanced judgment, the king found the advice of these young men to be ten times better than that of all the magicians and enchanters in his entire kingdom.

²¹Daniel remained there until the first year of King Cyrus's reign.*

I BELIEVE the Babylonians crushed the kingdom of Judah just as the Lord said (Isaiah 39:5-7). (1:2)

I BELIEVE the Lord wanted the Israelites to be ceremonially clean, free from any kind of defilement (Leviticus 11:46-47). (1:8)

I CONTINUE to protect my purity before God in compromising situations. (1:11)

I BELIEVE God blesses the efforts of those who honor and obey him. (1:15)

I BELIEVE the Lord gave Daniel special ability in understanding the meaning of visions and dreams. (1:17)

1:1 The third year of Jehoiakim's reign, according to the Hebrew system of reckoning, was 605 B.C.   1:2 Hebrew *the land of Shinar.*   1:4 Or *of the Chaldeans.*   1:21 The first year of Cyrus's reign was 538 B.C.

CHAPTER 2
Nebuchadnezzar's Dream

One night during the second year of his reign,* Nebuchadnezzar had a dream that disturbed him so much that he couldn't sleep. ²He called in his magicians, enchanters, sorcerers, and astrologers,* and he demanded that they tell him what he had dreamed. As they stood before the king, ³he said, "I have had a dream that troubles me. Tell me what I dreamed, for I must know what it means."

⁴Then the astrologers answered the king in Aramaic,* "Long live the king! Tell us the dream, and we will tell you what it means."

⁵But the king said to the astrologers, "I am serious about this. If you don't tell me what my dream was and what it means, you will be torn limb from limb, and your houses will be demolished into heaps of rubble! ⁶But if you tell me what I dreamed and what the dream means, I will give you many wonderful gifts and honors. Just tell me the dream and what it means!"

⁷They said again, "Please, Your Majesty. Tell us the dream, and we will tell you what it means."

In response to the profiles, tell the Lord whose example you want to imitate—and whose failures you don't want to repeat.

LIKE DANIEL
Daniel 1:21

I remain true to God in the midst of compromising situations.

Can someone serve the Lord as a ranking member of China's Communist Party? As a trusted adviser to an immoral prime minister? As the secretary of state for a country on the brink of collapse?

Daniel shows us that—in any situation or station of life—we can remain true to the Lord our God.

Taken from his family and homeland as a youth and then thoroughly educated in the pagan beliefs of his day, Daniel had no props on which to lean his faith in the Lord. Yet Daniel never used excuses for halfhearted obedience to God. Others may have cited circumstances, lack of believing friends, political pressures, and even the threat of death as reasons for not serving God. But not Daniel.

Daniel served in one prominent position after another but always was willing to forsake politics rather than compromise his integrity. From his youth on, Daniel's first priority was to remain true to God—whether that meant using diplomacy to avoid ceremonial uncleanness, asking God for wisdom to answer the king's harsh demands, or calmly going to the lions' den instead of forsaking his faith.

Opportunities for wealth and power came and went (2:48; 5:17), but Daniel either spurned them or used them as an expression of his uncompromising service to the King of kings.

No matter what political or personal waves beat against him, like a rock, Daniel would not waver from his steadfast devotion to the Lord Almighty.

You and I may wonder about the difficult places God sometimes puts his servants. Yet Daniel's example reminds us it's never impossible to remain true to the Lord.

○ *Today's Scripture reading is Daniel 1–2 and 6.*

---

⁸The king replied, "I can see through your trick! You are trying to stall for time because you know I am serious about what I said. ⁹If you don't tell me the dream, you will be condemned. You have conspired to tell me lies in hopes that something will change. But tell me the dream, and then I will know that you can tell me what it means."

¹⁰The astrologers replied to the king, "There isn't a man alive who can tell Your Majesty his dream! And no king, however great and powerful, has ever asked such a thing of any magician, enchanter, or astrologer! ¹¹This is an impossible thing the king requires. No one except the gods can tell you your dream, and they do not live among people."

I BELIEVE that what is humanly impossible is possible with God (Matthew 19:26). (2:11)

2:1 The second year of Nebuchadnezzar's reign was 603 B.C.   2:2 Or *Chaldeans;* also in 2:4, 5, 10.   2:4 The original text from this point through chapter 7 is in Aramaic.

¹²The king was furious when he heard this, and he sent out orders to execute all the wise men of Babylon. ¹³And because of the king's decree, men were sent to find and kill Daniel and his friends. ¹⁴When Arioch, the commander of the king's guard, came to kill them, Daniel handled the situation with wisdom and discretion. ¹⁵He asked Arioch, "Why has the king issued such a harsh decree?" So Arioch told him all that had happened. ¹⁶Daniel went at once to see the king and requested more time so he could tell the king what the dream meant.

¹⁷Then Daniel went home and told his friends Hananiah, Mishael, and Azariah what had happened. ¹⁸He urged them to ask the God of heaven to show them his mercy by telling them the secret, so they would not be executed along with the other wise men of Babylon. ¹⁹That night the secret was revealed to Daniel in a vision. Then Daniel praised the God of heaven, ²⁰saying,

"Praise the name of God forever and ever,
  for he alone has all wisdom and power.
²¹He determines the course of world events;
  he removes kings and sets others on the throne.
He gives wisdom to the wise
  and knowledge to the scholars.
²²He reveals deep and mysterious things
  and knows what lies hidden in darkness,
  though he himself is surrounded by light.
²³I thank and praise you, God of my ancestors,
  for you have given me wisdom and strength.
You have told me what we asked of you
  and revealed to us what the king demanded."

Daniel Interprets the Dream

²⁴Then Daniel went in to see Arioch, who had been ordered to execute the wise men of Babylon. Daniel said to him, "Don't kill the wise men. Take me to the king, and I will tell him the meaning of his dream."

²⁵Then Arioch quickly took Daniel to the king and said, "I have found one of the captives from Judah who will tell Your Majesty the meaning of your dream!"

²⁶The king said to Daniel (also known as Belteshazzar), "Is this true? Can you tell me what my dream was and what it means?"

²⁷Daniel replied, "There are no wise men, enchanters, magicians, or fortunetellers who can tell the king such things. ²⁸But there is a God in heaven who reveals secrets, and he has shown King Nebuchadnezzar what will happen in the future. Now I will tell you your dream and the visions you saw as you lay on your bed.

²⁹"While Your Majesty was sleeping, you dreamed about coming events. The revealer of mysteries has shown you what is going to happen. ³⁰And it is not because I am wiser than any living person that I know the secret of your dream, but because God wanted you to understand what you were thinking about.

³¹"Your Majesty, in your vision you saw in front of you a huge and powerful statue of a man, shining brilliantly, frightening and awesome. ³²The head of the statue was made of fine gold, its chest and arms were of silver, its belly and thighs were of bronze, ³³its legs were of iron, and its feet were a combination of iron and clay. ³⁴But as you watched, a rock was cut from a mountain by supernatural means.* It struck the feet of iron and clay, smashing them to bits. ³⁵The whole statue collapsed into a heap of iron, clay, bronze, silver, and

2:34 Aramaic *not by human hands;* also in 2:45.

I BELIEVE Daniel handled the order of his execution with wisdom and discretion. (2:14)

I ASK the God of heaven to show others his mercy. (2:18)

I BELIEVE God revealed the king's dream to Daniel in a vision. (2:19)

I BELIEVE the Lord is sovereign over all the nations. (2:21)

I BELIEVE the Lord is infinitely wise. (2:22)

I BELIEVE God in heaven reveals secrets, including what will happen in the future. (2:28) gold. The pieces were crushed as small as chaff on a threshing floor, and the wind blew them all away without a trace. But the rock that knocked the statue down became a great mountain that covered the whole earth.

³⁶"That was the dream; now I will tell Your Majesty what it means. ³⁷Your Majesty, you are a king over many kings. The God of heaven has given you sovereignty, power, strength, and honor. ³⁸He has made you the ruler over all the inhabited world and has put even the animals and birds under your control. You are the head of gold.

I BELIEVE the statue represents four great empires that arose over the course of five centuries. (2:38)

LIKE SHADRACH, MESHACH, AND ABEDNEGO

I will trust and worship God whether I experience physical deliverance or not.

Daniel 3:18

On April 20, 1999, an armed gunman challenged an outgoing seventeen-year-old Columbine High School student named Cassie Bernall. "Do you believe in God?" he demanded. She paused, then answered her fellow student with a definite yes. For her confession of faith, she was shot dead.

When Shadrach, Meshach, and Abednego faced the fiery furnace, they had no idea how their story would turn out. Theirs would be the first miraculous deliverance recorded in the book of Daniel—but they didn't know that. Their confidence in God's ability to save them was not based on any prior guarantee of deliverance. But neither was their worship. This was not a test to determine if God would come through and therefore deserve the faith and service of these three young men. Even if the outcome was death, Shadrach, Meshach, and Abednego were committed to God alone.

As these three friends faced the king, their confident words couldn't have been more different from a panicked "foxhole" prayer. They did not beg, "Save me, God, and I'll serve you." Instead they declared, "We will worship you alone, O Lord, whether you save us or not."

Elisabeth Elliot, whose husband Jim died a young martyr's death, once said, "There are a lot worse things that could happen to you than dying. Like living in disobedience." Disobedience was not an option for Shadrach, Meshach, and Abednego.

Sure enough, there was no last-minute change of the king's heart and no apparent angelic rescuers. As their bodies were sent hurtling into the flames, Shadrach, Meshach, and Abednego must have been prepared to die. Instead—in the midst of that fiery trial—their ropes fell off, they stood up, and one like God's Son appeared to them.

You and I will not know ahead of time whether the Lord intends to deliver our bodies from death. All that matters is if for the Lord's sake we're always willing to say yes.

○ *Today's Scripture reading is Daniel 3.*

---

³⁹"But after your kingdom comes to an end, another great kingdom, inferior to yours, will rise to take your place. After that kingdom has fallen, yet a third great kingdom, represented by the bronze belly and thighs, will rise to rule the world. ⁴⁰Following that kingdom, there will be a fourth great kingdom, as strong as iron. That kingdom will smash and crush all previous empires, just as iron smashes and crushes everything it strikes. ⁴¹The feet and toes you saw that were a combination of iron and clay show that this kingdom will be divided. ⁴²Some parts of it will be as strong as iron, and others as weak as clay. ⁴³This mixture of iron and clay also shows that these kingdoms will try to strengthen themselves by forming alliances with each other through intermarriage. But this will not succeed, just as iron and clay do not mix.

⁴⁴"During the reigns of those kings, the God of heaven will set up a kingdom that will never be destroyed; no one will ever conquer it. It will shatter all these kingdoms into nothingness, but it will stand forever. ⁴⁵That is the meaning of the rock cut from the mountain by supernatural means, crushing to dust the statue of iron, bronze, clay, silver, and gold.

I BELIEVE Jesus Christ will be King over all the nations forever (Luke 1:32-33). (2:44)

"The great God has shown Your Majesty what will happen in the future. The dream is true, and its meaning is certain."

Nebuchadnezzar Rewards Daniel

⁴⁶Then King Nebuchadnezzar bowed to the ground before Daniel and worshiped him, and he commanded his people to offer sacrifices and burn sweet incense before him. ⁴⁷The king said to Daniel, "Truly, your God is the God of gods, the Lord over kings, a revealer of mysteries, for you have been able to reveal this secret."

⁴⁸Then the king appointed Daniel to a high position and gave him many valuable gifts. He made Daniel ruler over the whole province of Babylon, as well as chief over all his wise men. ⁴⁹At Daniel's request, the king appointed Shadrach, Meshach, and Abednego to be in charge of all the affairs of the province of Babylon, while Daniel remained in the king's court.

CHAPTER 3

Nebuchadnezzar's Gold Statue

King Nebuchadnezzar made a gold statue ninety feet tall and nine feet wide* and set it up on the plain of Dura in the province of Babylon. ²Then he sent messages to the princes, prefects, governors, advisers, counselors, judges, magistrates, and all the provincial officials to come to the dedication of the statue he had set up. ³When all these officials* had arrived and were standing before the image King Nebuchadnezzar had set up, ⁴a herald shouted out, "People of all races and nations and languages, listen to the king's command! ⁵When you hear the sound of the horn, flute, zither, lyre, harp, pipes, and other instruments,* bow to the ground to worship King Nebuchadnezzar's gold statue. ⁶Anyone who refuses to obey will immediately be thrown into a blazing furnace."

⁷So at the sound of the musical instruments,* all the people, whatever their race or nation or language, bowed to the ground and worshiped the statue that King Nebuchadnezzar had set up.

⁸But some of the astrologers* went to the king and informed on the Jews. ⁹They said to King Nebuchadnezzar, "Long live the king! ¹⁰You issued a decree requiring all the people to bow down and worship the gold statue when they hear the sound of the musical instruments.* ¹¹That decree also states that those who refuse to obey must be thrown into a blazing furnace. ¹²But there are some Jews—Shadrach, Meshach, and Abednego—whom you have put in charge of the province of Babylon. They have defied Your Majesty by refusing to serve your gods or to worship the gold statue you have set up."

¹³Then Nebuchadnezzar flew into a rage and ordered Shadrach, Meshach, and Abednego to be brought before him. When they were brought in, ¹⁴Nebuchadnezzar said to them, "Is it true, Shadrach, Meshach, and Abednego, that you refuse to serve my gods or to worship the gold statue I have set up? ¹⁵I will give you one more chance. If you bow down and worship the statue I have made when you hear the sound of the musical instruments, all will be well. But if you refuse, you will be thrown immediately into the blazing furnace. What god will be able to rescue you from my power then?"

¹⁶Shadrach, Meshach, and Abednego replied, "O Nebuchadnezzar, we do not need to defend ourselves before you. ¹⁷If we are thrown into the blazing furnace, the God whom we serve is able to save us. He will rescue us from your power, Your Majesty. ¹⁸But even if he doesn't, Your Majesty can be sure that we will never serve your gods or worship the gold statue you have set up."

I BELIEVE God is the God of gods and Lord of kings. (2:47)

I ABHOR the worship of idols. (3:5)

I WORSHIP the Lord alone and serve him wholeheartedly, no matter what the cost. (3:12)

I RECOGNIZE that godly individuals are not exempt from persecution (2 Timothy 3:12). (3:15)

I BELIEVE God is able to save me from the evil intentions of powerful individuals. (3:17)

3:1 Aramaic *60 cubits* [27 meters] *tall and 6 cubits* [2.7 meters] *wide.* 3:3 Aramaic *the princes, prefects, governors, advisers, counselors, judges, magistrates, and all the provincial officials.* 3:5 The identification of some of these musical instruments is uncertain. 3:7 Aramaic *the horn, flute, zither, lyre, harp, and other instruments of the musical ensemble.* 3:8 Aramaic *Chaldeans.* 3:10 Aramaic *the horn, flute, zither, lyre, harp, pipes, and other instruments of the musical ensemble; also in 3:15.*

The Blazing Furnace

[19]Nebuchadnezzar was so furious with Shadrach, Meshach, and Abednego that his face became distorted with rage. He commanded that the furnace be heated seven times hotter than usual. [20]Then he ordered some of the strongest men of his army to bind Shadrach, Meshach, and Abednego and throw them into the blazing furnace. [21]So they tied them up and threw them into the furnace, fully clothed. [22]And because the king, in his anger, had demanded such a hot fire in the furnace, the flames leaped out and killed the soldiers as they threw the three men in! [23]So Shadrach, Meshach, and Abednego, securely tied, fell down into the roaring flames.

[24]But suddenly, as he was watching, Nebuchadnezzar jumped up in amazement and exclaimed to his advisers, "Didn't we tie up three men and throw them into the furnace?"

"Yes," they said, "we did indeed, Your Majesty."

[25]"Look!" Nebuchadnezzar shouted. "I see four men, unbound, walking around in the fire. They aren't even hurt by the flames! And the fourth looks like a divine being*!"

[26]Then Nebuchadnezzar came as close as he could to the door of the flaming furnace and shouted: "Shadrach, Meshach, and Abednego, servants of the Most High God, come out! Come here!" So Shadrach, Meshach, and Abednego stepped out of the fire. [27]Then the princes, prefects, governors, and advisers crowded around them and saw that the fire had not touched them. Not a hair on their heads was singed, and their clothing was not scorched. They didn't even smell of smoke!

[28]Then Nebuchadnezzar said, "Praise to the God of Shadrach, Meshach, and Abednego! He sent his angel to rescue his servants who trusted in him. They defied the king's command and were willing to die rather than serve or worship any god except their own God. [29]Therefore, I make this decree: If any people, whatever their race or nation or language, speak a word against the God of Shadrach, Meshach, and Abednego, they will be torn limb from limb, and their houses will be crushed into heaps of rubble. There is no other god who can rescue like this!" [30]Then the king promoted Shadrach, Meshach, and Abednego to even higher positions in the province of Babylon.

CHAPTER 4

Nebuchadnezzar's Dream about a Tree

King Nebuchadnezzar sent this message to the people of every race and nation and language throughout the world:

"Peace and prosperity to you!

[2]"I want you all to know about the miraculous signs and wonders the Most High God has performed for me.

[3]How great are his signs,
   how powerful his wonders!
His kingdom will last forever,
   his rule through all generations.

[4]"I, Nebuchadnezzar, was living in my palace in comfort and prosperity. [5]But one night I had a dream that greatly frightened me; I saw visions that terrified me as I lay in my bed. [6]So I issued an order calling in all the wise men of Babylon, so they could tell me what my dream meant. [7]When all the magicians, enchanters, astrologers,* and fortunetellers came in, I told them the dream, but they could not tell me what it meant. [8]At last Daniel came in before me, and I told him the dream. (He

---

I BELIEVE the Lord delivered Shadrach, Meshach, and Abednego from almost instantaneous death in the fiery furnace. (3:25)

I WOULD RATHER DIE than serve or worship a false god. (3:28)

I BELIEVE Jesus Christ will be King over all the nations forever (Luke 1:32-33). (4:3)

3:25 Aramaic *like a son of the gods.* 4:7 Or *Chaldeans.*

I KNOW that the Spirit of the Lord lives in me, since I am a Christian (Romans 8:9). (4:8)

was named Belteshazzar after my god, and the spirit of the holy gods is in him.)

⁹"I said to him, 'O Belteshazzar, master magician, I know that the spirit of the holy gods is in you and that no mystery is too great for you to solve. Now tell me what my dream means.

¹⁰" 'While I was lying in my bed, this is what I dreamed. I saw a large tree in the middle of the earth. ¹¹The tree grew very tall and strong, reaching high into the heavens for all the world to see. ¹²It had fresh green leaves, and it was loaded with fruit for all to eat. Wild animals lived in its shade, and birds nested in its branches. All the world was fed from this tree.

¹³" 'Then as I lay there dreaming, I saw a messenger,* a holy one, coming down from heaven. ¹⁴The messenger shouted, "Cut down the tree; lop off its branches! Shake off its leaves, and scatter its fruit! Chase the animals from its shade and the birds from its branches. ¹⁵But leave the stump and the roots in the ground, bound with a band of iron and bronze and surrounded by tender grass. Now let him be drenched with the dew of heaven, and let him live like an animal among the plants of the fields. ¹⁶For seven periods of time, let him have the mind of an animal instead of a human. ¹⁷For this has been decreed by the messengers*; it is commanded by the holy ones. The purpose of this decree is that the whole world may understand that the Most High rules over the kingdoms of the world and gives them to anyone he chooses—even to the lowliest of humans."

I UNDERSTAND that the Lord is sovereign over all the nations. (4:17)

¹⁸" 'O Belteshazzar, that was the dream that I, King Nebuchadnezzar, had. Now tell me what it means, for no one else can help me. All the wisest men of my kingdom have failed me. But you can tell me because the spirit of the holy gods is in you.'

Daniel Explains the Dream

¹⁹"Upon hearing this, Daniel (also known as Belteshazzar) was overcome for a time, aghast at the meaning of the dream. Finally, the king said to him, 'Belteshazzar, don't be alarmed by the dream and what it means.'

"Belteshazzar replied, 'Oh, how I wish the events foreshadowed in this dream would happen to your enemies, my lord, and not to you! ²⁰You saw a tree growing very tall and strong, reaching high into the heavens for all the world to see. ²¹It had fresh green leaves, and it was loaded with fruit for all to eat. Wild animals lived in its shade, and birds nested in its branches. ²²That tree, Your Majesty, is you. For you have grown strong and great; your greatness reaches up to heaven, and your rule to the ends of the earth.

²³" 'Then you saw a messenger, a holy one, coming down from heaven and saying, "Cut down the tree and destroy it. But leave the stump and the roots in the ground, bound with a band of iron and bronze and surrounded by tender grass. Let him be drenched with the dew of heaven. Let him eat grass with the animals of the field for seven periods of time."

²⁴" 'This is what the dream means, Your Majesty, and what the Most High has declared will happen to you. ²⁵You will be driven from human society, and you will live in the fields with the wild animals. You will eat grass like a cow, and you will be drenched with the dew of heaven. Seven periods of time will pass while you live this way, until you learn that the Most High rules over the kingdoms of the world and gives them to anyone he chooses. ²⁶But the stump and the roots were left in the ground. This means that you will receive your kingdom back again when you have learned that heaven rules.

4:13 Aramaic *a watcher;* also in 4:23. 4:17 Aramaic *the watchers.*

²⁷" 'O King Nebuchadnezzar, please listen to me. Stop sinning and do what is right. Break from your wicked past by being merciful to the poor. Perhaps then you will continue to prosper.'

I DO what is right and show mercy to the poor. (4:27)

The Dream's Fulfillment

²⁸"But all these things did happen to King Nebuchadnezzar. ²⁹Twelve months later, he was taking a walk on the flat roof of the royal palace in Babylon. ³⁰As he looked out across the city, he said, 'Just look at this great city of Babylon! I, by my own mighty power, have built this beautiful city as my royal residence and as an expression of my royal splendor.'

³¹"While he was still speaking these words, a voice called down from heaven, 'O King Nebuchadnezzar, this message is for you! You are no longer ruler of this kingdom. ³²You will be driven from human society. You will live in the fields with the wild animals, and you will eat grass like a cow. Seven periods of time will pass while you live this way, until you learn that the Most High rules over the kingdoms of the world and gives them to anyone he chooses.'

UNLIKE NEBUCHADNEZZAR *I do not become arrogant, proud, and boastful.*

Daniel 4:37

On April 14, 1912, the massive *Titanic*, a masterpiece of human craftsmanship, plunged beneath the cold waters of the North Atlantic. The unsinkable sank—and only God knows how much arrogance played into the shocking tragedy.

Some twenty-five hundred years earlier, Nebuchadnezzar had built a vast masterpiece. Not a ship, but an entire empire with a capital city so splendid that its Hanging Gardens became known as one of the Seven Wonders of the Ancient World.

God gave Nebuchadnezzar enormous privileges—incredible power and wealth, and divinely appointed dreams detailing the future and warning him not to become too proud. But Nebuchadnezzar ignored the warnings and lost everything the day he surveyed his glorious city and said to himself, "I did this all, and I did it myself."

As predicted, Nebuchadnezzar almost instantly lost his sanity and was herded away into an animal-like existence.

When Nebuchadnezzar's sanity later returned, he exalted the Most High as the king of the universe, and God restored him to previous position. The Lord then used this pagan ruler to proclaim the power and majesty of the living God to the whole world.

Then as now, the biblical principle is true, "God sets himself against the proud, but he shows favor to the humble" (1 Peter 5:5).

Neither you nor I shall ever reign as king of the world. However, as we survey our businesses, our ministries, our possessions, or our families, whom do we credit (in our heart of hearts) for our successes?

Unlike Nebuchadnezzar, we don't have to suffer a devastating fall to learn how to walk humbly before our God.

○ *Today's Scripture reading is Daniel 4.*

³³"That very same hour the prophecy was fulfilled, and Nebuchadnezzar was driven from human society. He ate grass like a cow, and he was drenched with the dew of heaven. He lived this way until his hair was as long as eagles' feathers and his nails were like birds' claws.

Nebuchadnezzar Praises God

³⁴"After this time had passed, I, Nebuchadnezzar, looked up to heaven. My sanity returned, and I praised and worshiped the Most High and honored the one who lives forever.

I PRAISE AND WORSHIP the Most High. (4:34)

His rule is everlasting,
  and his kingdom is eternal.

I BELIEVE God has the power to do as he pleases in heaven and on earth. (4:35)

35 All the people of the earth
    are nothing compared to him.
He has the power to do as he pleases
    among the angels of heaven
    and with those who live on earth.
No one can stop him or challenge him,
    saying, 'What do you mean by doing these things?'

36 "When my sanity returned to me, so did my honor and glory and kingdom. My advisers and officers sought me out, and I was reestablished as head of my kingdom, with even greater honor than before.

I BELIEVE God is able to humble those who are proud. (4:37)

37 "Now I, Nebuchadnezzar, praise and glorify and honor the King of heaven. All his acts are just and true, and he is able to humble those who are proud."

CHAPTER 5

The Writing on the Wall

I DO NOT DESECRATE what is dedicated to God. (5:2)

I ABHOR the worship of idols. (5:4)

A number of years later, King Belshazzar gave a great feast for a thousand of his nobles and drank wine with them. 2While Belshazzar was drinking, he gave orders to bring in the gold and silver cups that his predecessor,* Nebuchadnezzar, had taken from the Temple in Jerusalem, so that he and his nobles, his wives, and his concubines might drink from them. 3So they brought these gold cups taken from the Temple of God in Jerusalem, and the king and his nobles, his wives, and his concubines drank from them. 4They drank toasts from them to honor their idols made of gold, silver, bronze, iron, wood, and stone.

5At that very moment they saw the fingers of a human hand writing on the plaster wall of the king's palace, near the lampstand. The king himself saw the hand as it wrote, 6and his face turned pale with fear. Such terror gripped him that his knees knocked together and his legs gave way beneath him.

7The king shouted for the enchanters, astrologers,* and fortune-tellers to be brought before him. He said to these wise men of Babylon, "Whoever can read this writing and tell me what it means will be dressed in purple robes of royal honor and will wear a gold chain around his neck. He will become the third highest ruler in the kingdom!" 8But when all the king's wise men came in, none of them could read the writing or tell him what it meant. 9So the king grew even more alarmed, and his face turned ashen white. His nobles, too, were shaken.

10But when the queen mother heard what was happening, she hurried to the banquet hall. She said to Belshazzar, "Long live the king! Don't be so pale and afraid about this. 11There is a man in your kingdom who has within him the spirit of the holy gods. During Nebuchadnezzar's reign, this man was found to have insight, understanding, and wisdom as though he himself were a god. Your predecessor, King Nebuchadnezzar, made him chief over all the magicians, enchanters, astrologers, and fortune-tellers of Babylon. 12This man Daniel, whom the king named Belteshazzar, has a sharp mind and is filled with divine knowledge and understanding. He can interpret dreams, explain riddles, and solve difficult problems. Call for Daniel, and he will tell you what the writing means."

Daniel Explains the Writing

13So Daniel was brought in before the king. The king asked him, "Are you Daniel, who was exiled from Judah by my predecessor, King Nebuchadnezzar? 14I have heard that you have the spirit of the gods within you and that you are filled with insight, understanding, and wisdom. 15My wise men and

5:2 Aramaic *father*; also in 5:11, 13, 18.   5:7 Or *Chaldeans*; also in 5:11.

enchanters have tried to read this writing on the wall, but they cannot. ¹⁶I am told that you can give interpretations and solve difficult problems. If you can read these words and tell me their meaning, you will be clothed in purple robes of royal honor, and you will wear a gold chain around your neck. You will become the third highest ruler in the kingdom."

¹⁷Daniel answered the king, "Keep your gifts or give them to someone else, but I will tell you what the writing means. ¹⁸Your Majesty, the Most High God gave sovereignty, majesty, glory, and honor to your predecessor, Nebuchadnezzar. ¹⁹He made him so great that people of all races and nations and languages trembled before him in fear. He killed those he wanted to kill and spared those he wanted to spare. He honored those he wanted to honor and disgraced those he wanted to disgrace. ²⁰But when his heart and mind were hardened with pride, he was brought down from his royal throne and stripped of his glory. ²¹He was driven from human society. He was given the mind of an animal, and he lived among the wild donkeys. He ate grass like a cow, and he was drenched with the dew of heaven, until he learned that the Most High God rules the kingdoms of the world and appoints anyone he desires to rule over them.

I UNDERSTAND that the Lord is sovereign over all the nations. (5:21)

UNLIKE BELSHAZZAR
Daniel 5:23

I abhor the thought of defying the God of heaven.

According to *The Dictionary of Cultural Literacy*, when you see the handwriting on the wall, "misfortune is impending." The phrase was coined after the Lord made a you-can't-ignore-this-no-matter-how-drunk-you-are announcement to the acting king of Babylon.

That evening, in a drunken act of defiance against the Lord, King Belshazzar had chosen to use holy cups for profane purposes. The cups meant for worshiping the God of heaven instead were used to honor horrific idols (5:4).

Instead of such gross blasphemy, Belshazzar should have been among the first to acknowledge that (1) God gives power to whomever he chooses, and (2) God alone deserves honor for ruling the world. Nebuchadnezzar had not kept these facts a secret. The royal records testified, and Belshazzar should have known that ignoring the God of heaven and exalting himself would bring his downfall.

When the handwriting appeared on the wall, though, it wasn't a warning. Instead, Belshazzar heard the verdict for his life of sin. That very night he was killed as the Medes and Persians overtook his city.

Except for this Scripture passage, Belshazzar's memory was quickly erased from history. In recent centuries some skeptics even denied his existence—just as Belshazzar had denied God's.

Sadly, the writing already is on the wall, so to speak, when individuals today defy the Lord and refuse to trust him. If they don't repent, their punishment will ultimately be death, just as it was for Belshazzar (John 3:18-20).

Even as believers, we can dishonor the Lord by using what belongs to him—our bodies and our very lives—to worship something or someone else (1 Corinthians 6:19-20).

Unlike Belshazzar, let's give ourselves completely to God, honoring and obeying him instead of serving sin (Romans 6:13-14; 12:1-2).

○ *Today's Scripture reading is Daniel 5.*

²²"You are his successor,* O Belshazzar, and you knew all this, yet you have not humbled yourself. ²³For you have defied the Lord of heaven and have had these cups from his Temple brought before you. You and your nobles and your wives and concubines have been drinking wine from them while praising gods of silver, gold, bronze, iron, wood, and stone—gods that neither see nor hear nor know anything at all. But you have not honored the God who gives you the breath of life and controls your destiny! ²⁴So God has sent this hand to write a message.

I HAVE humbled myself before the Lord. (5:22)

I BELIEVE God gives me the breath of life and controls my destiny. (5:23)

5:22 Aramaic *son.*

²⁵"This is the message that was written: MENE, MENE, TEKEL, PARSIN. ²⁶This is what these words mean:

Mene means 'numbered'—God has numbered the days of your reign and has brought it to an end.
²⁷ Tekel means 'weighed'—you have been weighed on the balances and have failed the test.
²⁸ Parsin* means 'divided'—your kingdom has been divided and given to the Medes and Persians."

²⁹Then at Belshazzar's command, Daniel was dressed in purple robes, a gold chain was hung around his neck, and he was proclaimed the third highest ruler in the kingdom.

³⁰That very night Belshazzar, the Babylonian* king, was killed.* ³¹And Darius the Mede took over the kingdom at the age of sixty-two.

CHAPTER 6
Daniel in the Lions' Den

Darius the Mede decided to divide the kingdom into 120 provinces, and he appointed a prince to rule over each province. ²The king also chose Daniel and two others as administrators to supervise the princes and to watch out for the king's interests. ³Daniel soon proved himself more capable than all the other administrators and princes. Because of his great ability, the king made plans to place him over the entire empire. ⁴Then the other administrators and princes began searching for some fault in the way Daniel was handling his affairs, but they couldn't find anything to criticize. He was faithful and honest and always responsible. ⁵So they concluded, "Our only chance of finding grounds for accusing Daniel will be in connection with the requirements of his religion."

⁶So the administrators and princes went to the king and said, "Long live King Darius! ⁷We administrators, prefects, princes, advisers, and other officials have unanimously agreed that Your Majesty should make a law that will be strictly enforced. Give orders that for the next thirty days anyone who prays to anyone, divine or human—except to Your Majesty—will be thrown to the lions. ⁸And let Your Majesty issue and sign this law so it cannot be changed, a law of the Medes and Persians, which cannot be revoked." ⁹So King Darius signed the law.

¹⁰But when Daniel learned that the law had been signed, he went home and knelt down as usual in his upstairs room, with its windows open toward Jerusalem. He prayed three times a day, just as he had always done, giving thanks to his God. ¹¹The officials went together to Daniel's house and found him praying and asking for God's help. ¹²So they went back to the king and reminded him about his law. "Did you not sign a law that for the next thirty days anyone who prays to anyone, divine or human—except to Your Majesty—will be thrown to the lions?"

"Yes," the king replied, "that decision stands; it is a law of the Medes and Persians, which cannot be revoked."

¹³Then they told the king, "That man Daniel, one of the captives from Judah, is paying no attention to you or your law. He still prays to his God three times a day."

¹⁴Hearing this, the king was very angry with himself for signing the law, and he tried to find a way to save Daniel. He spent the rest of the day looking for a way to get Daniel out of this predicament. ¹⁵In the evening the men went together to the king and said, "Your Majesty knows that according to the law of the Medes and the Persians, no law that the king signs can be changed."

I BELIEVE the Lord decreed that the Medo-Persian Empire would capture Babylon that very night. (5:28)

I DO NOT maliciously look for faults in others. (6:4)

I DO NOT lie to or flatter others, especially not out of blind ambition. (6:7)

I KEEP praying and giving thanks to God, no matter what happens (1 Thessalonians 5:17-18). (6:10)

5:28 Aramaic Peres, the singular of Parsin. 5:30a Or Chaldean. 5:30b The Persians and Medes conquered Babylon in October 539 B.C.

¹⁶So at last the king gave orders for Daniel to be arrested and thrown into the den of lions. The king said to him, "May your God, whom you worship continually, rescue you." ¹⁷A stone was brought and placed over the mouth of the den. The king sealed the stone with his own royal seal and the seals of his nobles, so that no one could rescue Daniel from the lions. ¹⁸Then the king returned to his palace and spent the night fasting. He refused his usual entertainment and couldn't sleep at all that night.

¹⁹Very early the next morning, the king hurried out to the lions' den. ²⁰When he got there, he called out in anguish, "Daniel, servant of the living God! Was your God, whom you worship continually, able to rescue you from the lions?"

²¹Daniel answered, "Long live the king! ²²My God sent his angel to shut the lions' mouths so that they would not hurt me, for I have been found innocent in his sight. And I have not wronged you, Your Majesty."

²³The king was overjoyed and ordered that Daniel be lifted from the den. Not a scratch was found on him because he had trusted in his God. ²⁴Then the king gave orders to arrest the men who had maliciously accused Daniel. He had them thrown into the lions' den, along with their wives and children. The lions leaped on them and tore them apart before they even hit the floor of the den.

²⁵Then King Darius sent this message to the people of every race and nation and language throughout the world:

"Peace and prosperity to you!

²⁶"I decree that everyone throughout my kingdom should tremble with fear before the God of Daniel.

For he is the living God,
and he will endure forever.
His kingdom will never be destroyed,
and his rule will never end.
²⁷ He rescues and saves his people;
he performs miraculous signs and wonders
in the heavens and on earth.
He has rescued Daniel
from the power of the lions."

²⁸So Daniel prospered during the reign of Darius and the reign of Cyrus the Persian.*

CHAPTER 7

Daniel's Vision of Four Beasts

Earlier, during the first year of King Belshazzar's reign in Babylon, Daniel had a dream and saw visions as he lay in his bed. He wrote the dream down, and this is what he saw.

²In my vision that night, I, Daniel, saw a great storm churning the surface of a great sea, with strong winds blowing from every direction. ³Then four huge beasts came up out of the water, each different from the others.

⁴The first beast was like a lion with eagles' wings. As I watched, its wings were pulled off, and it was left standing with its two hind feet on the ground, like a human being. And a human mind was given to it.

⁵Then I saw a second beast, and it looked like a bear. It was rearing up on one side, and it had three ribs in its mouth between its teeth. And I heard a voice saying to it, "Get up! Devour many people!"

⁶Then the third of these strange beasts appeared, and it looked like a leopard.

I WORSHIP God continually. (6:16)

I AM a servant of the living God. (6:20)

I FEAR the living God who reigns over all forever. (6:26)

I BELIEVE Daniel wrote down the dreams and visions he received from the Lord. (7:1)

6:28 Or *of Darius, that is, the reign of Cyrus the Persian.*

It had four wings like birds' wings on its back, and it had four heads. Great authority was given to this beast.

⁷Then in my vision that night, I saw a fourth beast, terrifying, dreadful, and very strong. It devoured and crushed its victims with huge iron teeth and trampled what was left beneath its feet. It was different from any of the other beasts, and it had ten horns. ⁸As I was looking at the horns, suddenly another small horn appeared among them. Three of the first horns were wrenched out, roots and all, to make room for it. This little horn had eyes like human eyes and a mouth that was boasting arrogantly.

⁹I watched as thrones were put in place and the Ancient One* sat down to judge. His clothing was as white as snow, his hair like whitest wool. He sat on a fiery throne with wheels of blazing fire, ¹⁰and a river of fire flowed from his presence. Millions of angels ministered to him, and a hundred million stood to attend him. Then the court began its session, and the books were opened.

¹¹I continued to watch because I could hear the little horn's boastful speech. I kept watching until the fourth beast was killed and its body was destroyed by fire. ¹²As for the other three beasts, their authority was taken from them, but they were allowed to live for a while longer.*

¹³As my vision continued that night, I saw someone who looked like a man* coming with the clouds of heaven. He approached the Ancient One and was led into his presence. ¹⁴He was given authority, honor, and royal power over all the nations of the world, so that people of every race and nation and language would obey him. His rule is eternal—it will never end. His kingdom will never be destroyed.

The Vision Is Explained

¹⁵I, Daniel, was troubled by all I had seen, and my visions terrified me. ¹⁶So I approached one of those standing beside the throne and asked him what it all meant. He explained it to me like this: ¹⁷"These four huge beasts represent four kingdoms that will arise from the earth. ¹⁸But in the end, the holy people of the Most High will be given the kingdom, and they will rule forever and ever."

¹⁹Then I wanted to know the true meaning of the fourth beast, the one so different from the others and so terrifying. It devoured and crushed its victims with iron teeth and bronze claws, and it trampled what was left beneath its feet. ²⁰I also asked about the ten horns on the fourth beast's head and the little horn that came up afterward and destroyed three of the other horns. This was the horn that seemed greater than the others and had human eyes and a mouth that was boasting arrogantly. ²¹As I watched, this horn was waging war against the holy people and was defeating them, ²²until the Ancient One came and judged in favor of the holy people of the Most High. Then the time arrived for the holy people to take over the kingdom.

²³Then he said to me, "This fourth beast is the fourth world power that will rule the earth. It will be different from all the others. It will devour the whole world, trampling everything in its path. ²⁴Its ten horns are ten kings that will rule that empire. Then another king will arise, different from the other ten, who will subdue three of them. ²⁵He will defy the Most High and wear down the holy people of the Most High. He will try to change their sacred festivals and laws, and they will be placed under his control for a time, times, and half a time.

²⁶"But then the court will pass judgment, and all his power will be taken away and completely destroyed. ²⁷Then the sovereignty, power, and greatness of all the kingdoms under heaven will be given to the holy people of the Most High. They will rule forever, and all rulers will serve and obey them."

I BELIEVE God is awesome in appearance. (7:9)

I OBEY Jesus Christ and believe he will be King over all the nations forever (Luke 1:32-33). (7:14)

I RECOGNIZE that godly individuals are not exempt from persecution (2 Timothy 3:12). (7:21)

I BELIEVE that God's people will reign with him forever (Revelation 20:4). (7:27)

7:9 Aramaic *an Ancient of Days;* also in 7:13, 22.   7:12 Aramaic *for a season and a time.*   7:13 Or *like a Son of Man;* Aramaic reads *like a son of man.*

[28] That was the end of the vision. I, Daniel, was terrified by my thoughts and my face was pale with fear, but I kept these things to myself.

CHAPTER 8

Daniel's Vision of a Ram and Goat

During the third year of King Belshazzar's reign, I, Daniel, saw another vision, following the one that had already appeared to me. [2] This time I was at the fortress of Susa, in the province of Elam, standing beside the Ulai River.*

[3] As I looked up, I saw in front of me a ram with two long horns standing beside the river.* One of the horns was longer than the other, even though it had begun to grow later than the shorter one. [4] The ram butted everything out of its way to the west, to the north, and to the south, and no one could stand against it or help its victims. It did as it pleased and became very great.

[5] While I was watching, suddenly a male goat appeared from the west, crossing the land so swiftly that it didn't even touch the ground. This goat, which had one very large horn between its eyes, [6] headed toward the two-horned ram that I had seen standing beside the river. [7] The goat charged furiously at the ram and struck it, breaking off both its horns. Now the ram was helpless, and the goat knocked it down and trampled it. There was no one who could rescue the ram from the goat's power.

[8] The goat became very powerful. But at the height of its power, its large horn was broken off. In the large horn's place grew four prominent horns pointing in the four directions of the earth. [9] From one of the prominent horns came a small horn whose power grew very great. It extended toward the south and the east and toward the glorious land of Israel. [10] His power reached to the heavens where it attacked the heavenly armies, throwing some of the heavenly beings and stars to the ground and trampling them. [11] He even challenged the Commander of heaven's armies by canceling the daily sacrifices offered to him and by destroying his Temple. [12] But the army of heaven was restrained from destroying him for this sin. As a result, sacrilege was committed against the Temple ceremonies, and truth was overthrown. The horn succeeded in everything it did.*

[13] Then I heard two of the holy ones talking to each other. One of them said, "How long will the events of this vision last? How long will the rebellion that causes desecration stop the daily sacrifices? How long will the Temple and heaven's armies be trampled on?"

[14] The other replied, "It will take twenty-three hundred evenings and mornings; then the Temple will be restored."

Gabriel Explains the Vision

[15] As I, Daniel, was trying to understand the meaning of this vision, someone who looked like a man suddenly stood in front of me. [16] And I heard a human voice calling out from the Ulai River, "Gabriel, tell this man the meaning of his vision."

[17] As Gabriel approached the place where I was standing, I became so terrified that I fell to the ground. "Son of man," he said, "you must understand that the events you have seen in your vision relate to the time of the end."

[18] While he was speaking, I fainted and lay there with my face to the ground. But Gabriel roused me with a touch and helped me to my feet. [19] Then he said, "I am here to tell you what will happen later in the time of wrath. What you have seen pertains to the very end of time. [20] The two-horned ram represents the kings of Media and Persia. [21] The shaggy male goat represents the king of Greece,* and the large horn between its eyes represents the first king of the Greek Empire. [22] The four prominent horns that replaced the

I BELIEVE the ram represents the Medo–Persian Empire that arose a few years after Daniel's vision (Daniel 8:20). (8:3)

I BELIEVE the goat represents the Greek Empire that quickly rose to power nearly two centuries after Daniel's vision (Daniel 8:21). (8:7)

I BELIEVE the small horn represents Antiochus IV Epiphanes, who defied God, oppressed God's people, and temporarily halted worship in the Temple nearly four centuries after Daniel's vision. (8:11)

I BELIEVE angels are awesome creatures sent from God to care for believers (Hebrews 1:14). (8:18)

8:2 Or *the Ulai Gate*; also in 8:16.   8:3 Or *the gate*; also in 8:6.   8:11-12 The meaning of the Hebrew for these verses is uncertain.   8:21 Hebrew *of Javan*.

I BELIEVE the four horns represent the division of the Greek Empire into four sections after the death of Alexander the Great. (8:22)

I BELIEVE the events foretold in this vision didn't happen for a long time. (8:26)

I BELIEVE Daniel studied the writings of the prophet Jeremiah and learned that the Babylonian exile would last for seventy years (Jeremiah 25:11-12; 29:10). (9:2)

See Jeremiah's profile (page 855) at Jeremiah 1:19.

I PRAISE the Lord because he is a great and awesome God! (9:4)

I DO NOT REFUSE to listen to the Lord's Word through the writings of his prophets. (9:5)

I BELIEVE the Lord is merciful and forgiving. (9:9)

See Moses' profile (page 73) at Exodus 5:1.

I BELIEVE the Lord is just in everything he does. (9:14)

one large horn show that the Greek Empire will break into four sections with four kings, none of them as great as the first.

23 "At the end of their rule, when their sin is at its height, a fierce king, a master of intrigue, will rise to power. 24 He will become very strong, but not by his own power. He will cause a shocking amount of destruction and succeed in everything he does. He will destroy powerful leaders and devastate the holy people. 25 He will be a master of deception, defeating many by catching them off guard. Without warning he will destroy them. He will even take on the Prince of princes in battle, but he will be broken, though not by human power.

26 "This vision about the twenty-three hundred evenings and mornings* is true. But none of these things will happen for a long time, so do not tell anyone about them yet."

27 Then I, Daniel, was overcome and lay sick for several days. Afterward I got up and performed my duties for the king, but I was greatly troubled by the vision and could not understand it.

CHAPTER 9

Daniel's Prayer for His People

It was the first year of the reign of Darius the Mede, the son of Ahasuerus, who became king of the Babylonians.* 2 During the first year of his reign, I, Daniel, was studying the writings of the prophets. I learned from the word of the LORD, as recorded by Jeremiah the prophet, that Jerusalem must lie desolate for seventy years.* 3 So I turned to the Lord God and pleaded with him in prayer and fasting. I wore rough sackcloth and sprinkled myself with ashes.

4 I prayed to the LORD my God and confessed: "O Lord, you are a great and awesome God! You always fulfill your promises of unfailing love to those who love you and keep your commands. 5 But we have sinned and done wrong. We have rebelled against you and scorned your commands and regulations. 6 We have refused to listen to your servants the prophets, who spoke your messages to our kings and princes and ancestors and to all the people of the land.

7 "Lord, you are in the right; but our faces are covered with shame, just as you see us now. This is true of us all, including the people of Judah and Jerusalem and all Israel, scattered near and far, wherever you have driven us because of our disloyalty to you. 8 O LORD, we and our kings, princes, and ancestors are covered with shame because we have sinned against you. 9 But the Lord our God is merciful and forgiving, even though we have rebelled against him. 10 We have not obeyed the LORD our God, for we have not followed the laws he gave us through his servants the prophets. 11 All Israel has disobeyed your law and turned away, refusing to listen to your voice.

"So now the solemn curses and judgments written in the law of Moses, the servant of God, have been poured out against us because of our sin. 12 You have done exactly what you warned you would do against us and our rulers. Never in all history has there been a disaster like the one that happened in Jerusalem. 13 Every curse written against us in the law of Moses has come true. All the troubles he predicted have taken place. But we have refused to seek mercy from the LORD our God by turning from our sins and recognizing his truth. 14 The LORD has brought against us the disaster he prepared, for we did not obey him, and the LORD our God is just in everything he does.

15 "O Lord our God, you brought lasting honor to your name by rescuing your people from Egypt in a great display of power. But we have sinned and are full of wickedness. 16 In view of all your faithful mercies, Lord, please turn your furious anger away from your city of Jerusalem, your holy mountain. All

8:26 Hebrew *about the evenings and mornings;* compare 8:14.   9:1 Or *the Chaldeans.*   9:2 See Jer 25:11-12; 29:10.

the neighboring nations mock Jerusalem and your people because of our sins and the sins of our ancestors.

¹⁷"O our God, hear your servant's prayer! Listen as I plead. For your own sake, Lord, smile again on your desolate sanctuary.

¹⁸"O my God, listen to me and hear my request. Open your eyes and see our wretchedness. See how your city lies in ruins—for everyone knows that it is yours. We do not ask because we deserve help, but because you are so merciful.

¹⁹"O Lord, hear. O Lord, forgive. O Lord, listen and act! For your own sake, O my God, do not delay, for your people and your city bear your name."

Gabriel's Message about the Exile
²⁰I went on praying and confessing my sin and the sins of my people, pleading with the LORD my God for Jerusalem, his holy mountain. ²¹As I was praying, Gabriel, whom I had seen in the earlier vision, came swiftly to me at the time of the evening sacrifice. ²²He explained to me, "Daniel, I have come here to give you insight and understanding. ²³ The moment you began praying, a command was given. I am here to tell you what it was, for God loves you very much. Now listen, so you can understand the meaning of your vision.

²⁴"A period of seventy sets of seven* has been decreed for your people and your holy city to put down rebellion, to bring an end to sin, to atone for guilt, to bring in everlasting righteousness, to confirm the prophetic vision, and to anoint the Most Holy Place.* ²⁵Now listen and understand! Seven sets of seven plus sixty-two sets of seven* will pass from the time the command is given to rebuild Jerusalem until the Anointed One* comes. Jerusalem will be rebuilt with streets and strong defenses,* despite the perilous times.

²⁶"After this period of sixty-two sets of seven,* the Anointed One will be killed, appearing to have accomplished nothing, and a ruler will arise whose armies will destroy the city and the Temple. The end will come with a flood, and war and its miseries are decreed from that time to the very end. ²⁷He will make a treaty with the people for a period of one set of seven,* but after half this time, he will put an end to the sacrifices and offerings. Then as a climax to all his terrible deeds,* he will set up a sacrilegious object that causes desecration,* until the end that has been decreed is poured out on this defiler."

CHAPTER 10

Daniel's Vision of a Messenger
In the third year of the reign of King Cyrus of Persia, Daniel (also known as Belteshazzar) had another vision. It concerned events certain to happen in the future—times of war and great hardship—and Daniel understood what the vision meant.

²When this vision came to me, I, Daniel, had been in mourning for three weeks. ³All that time I had eaten no rich food or meat, had drunk no wine, and had used no fragrant oils. ⁴On April 23,* as I was standing beside the great Tigris River, ⁵I looked up and saw a man dressed in linen clothing, with a belt of pure gold around his waist. ⁶His body looked like a dazzling gem. From his face came flashes like lightning, and his eyes were like flaming torches. His arms and feet shone like polished bronze, and his voice was like the roaring of a vast multitude of people.

⁷I, Daniel, am the only one who saw this vision. The men with me saw

I BELIEVE the Lord hears my prayers when I ask for something in line with his will (1 John 5:14). (9:17)

I CONFESS my sins and the sins of my people. (9:20)

I BELIEVE the Lord, through the angel Gabriel, gave Daniel visions and understanding about what would happen to his people in the future. (9:23)

I BELIEVE Daniel had another vision and understood what it meant. (10:1)

9:24a Hebrew *70 sevens.*   9:24b Or *the Most Holy One.*   9:25a Hebrew *Seven sevens plus 62 sevens.*   9:25b Or *an anointed one.*   9:25c Or *and a moat, or and trenches.*   9:26 Hebrew *After 62 sevens.*   9:27a Hebrew *for one seven.* 9:27b Hebrew *on the wing of abominations;* the meaning of the Hebrew is uncertain.   9:27c Hebrew *an abomination of desolation.*   10:4 Hebrew *On the twenty-fourth day of the first month.* This date in the book of Daniel can be cross-checked with dates in surviving Persian records and can be related accurately to our modern calendar. This day of the Hebrew lunar calendar occurred on April 23, 536 B.C.

nothing, but they were suddenly terrified and ran away to hide. ⁸So I was left there all alone to watch this amazing vision. My strength left me, my face grew deathly pale, and I felt very weak. ⁹When I heard him speak, I fainted and lay there with my face to the ground.

¹⁰Just then a hand touched me and lifted me, still trembling, to my hands and knees. ¹¹And the man said to me, "O Daniel, greatly loved of God, listen carefully to what I have to say to you. Stand up, for I have been sent to you." When he said this to me, I stood up, still trembling with fear.

¹²Then he said, "Don't be afraid, Daniel. Since the first day you began to pray for understanding and to humble yourself before your God, your request has been heard in heaven. I have come in answer to your prayer. ¹³But for twenty-one days the spirit prince* of the kingdom of Persia blocked my way. Then Michael, one of the archangels,* came to help me, and I left him there with the spirit prince of the kingdom of Persia.* ¹⁴Now I am here to explain what will happen to your people in the future, for this vision concerns a time yet to come."

¹⁵While he was speaking to me, I looked down at the ground, unable to say a word. ¹⁶Then the one who looked like a man* touched my lips, and I opened my mouth and began to speak. I said to the one standing in front of me, "I am terrified by the vision I have seen, my lord, and I am very weak. ¹⁷How can someone like me, your servant, talk to you, my lord? My strength is gone, and I can hardly breathe."

¹⁸Then the one who looked like a man touched me again, and I felt my strength returning. ¹⁹"Don't be afraid," he said, "for you are deeply loved by God. Be at peace; take heart and be strong!"

As he spoke these words, I suddenly felt stronger and said to him, "Now you may speak, my lord, for you have strengthened me."

²⁰He replied, "Do you know why I have come? Soon I must return to fight against the spirit prince of the kingdom of Persia, and then against the spirit prince of the kingdom of Greece.* ²¹But before I do that, I will tell you what is written in the Book of Truth. (There is no one to help me against these spirit princes except Michael, your spirit prince.* ¹I have been standing beside Michael* as his support and defense since the first year of the reign of Darius the Mede.)

CHAPTER 11

Kings of the South and North

²"Now then, I will reveal the truth to you. Three more Persian kings will reign, to be succeeded by a fourth, far richer than the others. Using his wealth for political advantage, he will stir up everyone to war against the kingdom of Greece.*

³"Then a mighty king will rise to power who will rule a vast kingdom and accomplish everything he sets out to do. ⁴But at the height of his power, his kingdom will be broken apart and divided into four parts. It will not be ruled by the king's descendants, nor will the kingdom hold the authority it once had. For his empire will be uprooted and given to others.

⁵"The king of the south will increase in power, but one of this king's own officials will become more powerful than he and will rule his kingdom with great strength.

⁶"Some years later, an alliance will be formed between the king of the north and the king of the south. The daughter of the king of the south will be given in marriage to the king of the north to secure the alliance, but she will

---

I AM GREATLY LOVED of God and listen to what he says. (10:11)

I DO NOT EXPECT the Lord to always answer my prayers instantaneously. (10:12)

I BELIEVE Michael is one of God's mightiest angels (Daniel 12:1; Jude 1:9; Revelation 12:7). (10:13)

I BELIEVE it would be terrifying to see an angel. (10:15)

I BELIEVE the Medo-Persian Empire failed to crush the rising Greek Empire two centuries after Daniel's vision. (11:2)

I BELIEVE the Greek Empire quickly broke into four sections two centuries after Daniel's vision. (11:4)

10:13a Hebrew *the prince;* also in 10:13c, 20.   10:13b Hebrew *the chief princes.*   10:13c As in one Greek version; Hebrew reads *and I was left there with the kings of Persia.* The meaning of the Hebrew is uncertain. 10:16 As in most manuscripts of the Masoretic Text; one manuscript of the Masoretic Text and one Greek version read *Then something that looked like a human hand.*   10:20 Hebrew *of Javan.*   10:21 Hebrew *against these except Michael, your prince.*   11:1 Hebrew *him.*   11:2 Hebrew *of Javan.*

lose her influence over him, and so will her father. She will be given up along with her supporters. [7]But when one of her relatives* becomes king of the south, he will raise an army and enter the fortress of the king of the north and defeat him. [8]When he returns again to Egypt, he will carry back their idols with him, along with priceless gold and silver dishes. For some years afterward he will leave the king of the north alone.

[9]"Later the king of the north will invade the realm of the king of the south but will soon return to his own land. [10]However, the sons of the king of the north will assemble a mighty army that will advance like a flood and carry the battle as far as the enemy's fortress. [11]Then the king of the south, in great anger, will rally against the vast forces assembled by the king of the north and will defeat them. [12]After the enemy army is swept away, the king of the south will be filled with pride and will have many thousands of his enemies killed. But his success will be short lived.

[13]"A few years later, the king of the north will return with a fully equipped army far greater than the one he lost. [14]At that time there will be a general uprising against the king of the south. Lawless ones among your own people will join them in order to fulfill the vision, but they will not succeed. [15]Then the king of the north will come and lay siege to a fortified city and capture it. The best troops of the south will not be able to stand in the face of the onslaught.

[16]"The king of the north will march onward unopposed; none will be able to stop him. He will pause in the glorious land of Israel, intent on destroying it. [17]He will make plans to come with the might of his entire kingdom and will form an alliance with the king of the south. He will give him a daughter in marriage in order to overthrow the kingdom from within, but his plan will fail.

[18]"After this, he will turn his attention to the coastal cities and conquer many. But a commander from another land will put an end to his insolence and will cause him to retreat in shame. [19]He will take refuge in his own fortresses but will stumble and fall, and he will be seen no more.

[20]"His successor will be remembered as the king who sent a tax collector to maintain the royal splendor, but after a very brief reign, he will die, though neither in battle nor open conflict.

[21]"The next to come to power will be a despicable man who is not directly in line for royal succession. But he will slip in when least expected and take over the kingdom by flattery and intrigue. [22]Before him great armies will be swept away, including a covenant prince. [23]By making deceitful promises, he will make various alliances. With a mere handful of followers, he will become strong. [24]Without warning he will enter the richest areas of the land and do something that none of his predecessors ever did—distribute among his followers the plunder and wealth of the rich. He will plot the overthrow of strongholds, but this will last for only a short while.

[25]"Then he will stir up his courage and raise a great army against the king of the south. The king of the south will go to battle with a mighty army, but to no avail, for plots against him will succeed. [26]Those of his own household will bring his downfall. His army will be swept away, and many will be killed. [27]Seeking nothing but each other's harm, these kings will plot against each other at the conference table, attempting to deceive each other. But it will make no difference, for an end will still come at the appointed time.

[28]"The king of the north will then return home with great riches. On the way he will set himself against the people of the holy covenant, doing much damage before continuing his journey.

[29]"Then at the appointed time he will once again invade the south, but this

I THINK idols are powerless objects. (11:8)

I BELIEVE the Egyptian and Syrian kings fought against each other more than three centuries after Daniel's vision. (11:11)

I BELIEVE the Lord is sovereign and can thwart the plans of great rulers. (11:17)

I BELIEVE Antiochus IV Epiphanes came to power nearly four centuries after Daniel's vision. (11:21)

11:7 Hebrew *a branch from her roots.*

time the result will be different. [30]For warships from western coastlands* will scare him off, and he will withdraw and return home. But he will vent his anger against the people of the holy covenant and reward those who forsake the covenant. [31]His army will take over the Temple fortress, polluting the sanctuary, putting a stop to the daily sacrifices, and setting up the sacrilegious object that causes desecration.* [32]He will flatter those who have violated the covenant and win them over to his side. But the people who know their God will be strong and will resist him.

[33]"Those who are wise will give instruction to many. But for a time many of these teachers will die by fire and sword, or they will be jailed and robbed. [34]While all these persecutions are going on, a little help will arrive, though many who join them will not be sincere. [35]And some who are wise will fall victim to persecution. In this way, they will be refined and cleansed and made pure until the time of the end, for the appointed time is still to come.

[36]"The king will do as he pleases, exalting himself and claiming to be greater than every god there is, even blaspheming the God of gods. He will succeed—until the time of wrath is completed. For what has been determined will surely take place. [37]He will have no regard for the gods of his ancestors, or for the god beloved of women, or for any other god, for he will boast that he is greater than them all. [38]Instead of these, he will worship the god of fortresses—a god his ancestors never knew—and lavish on him gold, silver, precious stones, and costly gifts. [39]Claiming this foreign god's help, he will attack the strongest fortresses. He will honor those who submit to him, appointing them to positions of authority and dividing the land among them as their reward.*

[40]"Then at the time of the end, the king of the south will attack him, and the king of the north will storm out against him with chariots, cavalry, and a vast navy. He will invade various lands and sweep through them like a flood. [41]He will enter the glorious land of Israel, and many nations will fall, but Moab, Edom, and the best part of Ammon will escape. [42]He will conquer many countries, and Egypt will not escape. [43]He will gain control over the gold, silver, and treasures of Egypt, and the Libyans and Ethiopians* will be his servants.

[44]"But then news from the east and the north will alarm him, and he will set out in great anger to destroy many as he goes. [45]He will halt between the glorious holy mountain and the sea and will pitch his royal tents there, but while he is there, his time will suddenly run out, and there will be no one to help him.

CHAPTER 12

The Time of the End

"At that time Michael, the archangel* who stands guard over your nation, will arise. Then there will be a time of anguish greater than any since nations first came into existence. But at that time every one of your people whose name is written in the book will be rescued. [2]Many of those whose bodies lie dead and buried will rise up, some to everlasting life and some to shame and everlasting contempt. [3]Those who are wise will shine as bright as the sky, and those who turn many to righteousness will shine like stars forever. [4]But you, Daniel, keep this prophecy a secret; seal up the book until the time of the end. Many will rush here and there, and knowledge will increase."

[5]Then I, Daniel, looked and saw two others standing on opposite banks of the river. [6]One of them asked the man dressed in linen, who was now standing above the river, "How long will it be until these shocking events happen?"

I BELIEVE Antiochus IV Epiphanes viciously attacked God's people, desecrated the Temple, and temporarily halted worship there. (11:31)

I BELIEVE someone worse than Antiochus IV Epiphanes will rise to power at the time of the end. (11:35)

I BELIEVE the Antichrist will be enormously proud and blasphemous. (11:36)

I BELIEVE the Antichrist will wage fierce wars during the Great Tribulation. (11:40)

I BELIEVE everyone will receive eternal rewards in heaven or punishment in hell (Matthew 25:46; Revelation 20:11–21:8). (12:2)

I LONG to be wise and turn many to righteousness. (12:3)

11:30 Hebrew *from Kittim.* 11:31 Hebrew *the abomination of desolation.* 11:39 Or *at a price.* 11:43 Hebrew *Cushites.* 12:1 Hebrew *the great prince.*

[7]The man dressed in linen, who was standing above the river, raised both his hands toward heaven and took this solemn oath by the one who lives forever: "It will go on for a time, times, and half a time. When the shattering of the holy people has finally come to an end, all these things will have happened."

[8]I heard what he said, but I did not understand what he meant. So I asked, "How will all this finally end, my lord?"

[9]But he said, "Go now, Daniel, for what I have said is for the time of the end. [10]Many will be purified, cleansed, and refined by these trials. But the wicked will continue in their wickedness, and none of them will understand. Only those who are wise will know what it means.

I DO NOT WANT to continue in wickedness. (12:10)

[11]"From the time the daily sacrifice is taken away and the sacrilegious object that causes desecration* is set up to be worshiped, there will be 1,290 days. [12]And blessed are those who wait and remain until the end of the 1,335 days!

[13]"As for you, go your way until the end. You will rest, and then at the end of the days, you will rise again to receive the inheritance set aside for you."

12:11 Hebrew *the abomination of desolation.*

HOSEA

THIS FIRST OF TWELVE "minor" prophetic books in the Old Testament urges readers to turn back to the Lord.

The theme of returning or coming back recurs nearly two dozen times in Hosea. The prophet urges the citizens of the northern kingdom of Israel to repent and turn back to the Lord—before it's too late. Nearly a century later, Jeremiah proclaims a very similar message to the southern kingdom of Judah.

Jeremiah and Hosea are similar in many respects. Both are called to the ministry as young men. Both watch their kingdoms rush headlong toward judgment. Both feel deep personal grief when their urgent warnings go unheeded.

Unlike Jeremiah, however, who is told not to marry, Hosea is commanded by God to marry a woman who turns out to be a prostitute.

The promiscuity of Hosea's wife, Gomer, paints a vivid picture of the faithlessness of the kingdom of Israel, and Hosea's efforts to redeem Gomer serve as an extraordinary illustration of the Lord's desire to win back the Israelites (chapters 1–14).

Famous verses in Hosea include

- "It will be said, 'You are children of the living God'" (1:10)
- "I will put an end to . . . her Sabbath days—all her appointed festivals" (2:11)
- "I will show love to those I called 'Not loved'" (2:23)
- "They will come trembling in awe to the LORD . . . in the last days" (3:5)
- "Don't point your finger at someone else and try to pass the blame!" (4:4)
- "They have exchanged the glory of God for the disgrace of idols" (4:7)
- "As soon as trouble comes, they will search for me" (5:15)
- "Come, let us return to the LORD!" (6:1)
- "Oh, that we might know the LORD! Let us press on to know him!" (6:3)
- "I don't want your sacrifices. I want you to know God" (6:6)
- "But like Adam, you broke my covenant and rebelled against me" (6:7)
- "Their sinful deeds are all around them; I see them all!" (7:2)
- "They look everywhere except to heaven, to the Most High" (7:16)
- "They have planted the wind and will harvest the whirlwind" (8:7)
- "Even though I gave them all my laws, they act as if those laws don't apply to them" (8:12)
- "Plow up the hard ground of your hearts, for now is the time to seek the LORD" (10:12)
- "But you have cultivated wickedness and raised a thriving crop of sins" (10:13)
- "My people . . . call me the Most High, but they don't truly honor me" (11:7)
- "O death, bring forth your terrors! O grave, bring forth your plagues!" (13:14)
- "Return to the LORD. Say to him, 'Forgive all our sins and graciously receive us'" (14:2)

CHAPTER 1

See the profiles for
Uzziah (page 533) and
Hezekiah (page 825) at
2 Chronicles 26:16 and
Isaiah 37:1.

The LORD gave these messages to Hosea son of Beeri during the years when Uzziah, Jotham, Ahaz, and Hezekiah were kings of Judah, and Jeroboam son of Jehoash* was king of Israel.

Hosea's Wife and Children

I BELIEVE the Lord called upon Hosea to marry an unfaithful woman to illustrate the unfaithfulness of Israel in worshiping other gods. (1:2)

²When the LORD first began speaking to Israel through Hosea, he said to him, "Go and marry a prostitute,* so some of her children will be born to you from other men. This will illustrate the way my people have been untrue to me, openly committing adultery against the LORD by worshiping other gods."

I OBEY the Lord, even when it will cause me deep and personal pain. (1:3)

³So Hosea married Gomer, the daughter of Diblaim, and she became pregnant and gave Hosea a son. ⁴And the LORD said, "Name the child Jezreel, for I am about to punish King Jehu's dynasty to avenge the murders he committed at Jezreel. ⁵In fact, I will put an end to Israel's independence by breaking its military power in the Jezreel Valley."

⁶Soon Gomer became pregnant again and gave birth to a daughter. And the LORD said to Hosea, "Name your daughter Lo-ruhamah—'Not loved'—for I will no longer show love to the people of Israel or forgive them. ⁷But I, the LORD their God, will show love to the people of Judah. I will personally free them from their enemies without any help from weapons or armies."

Make a commitment to read from God's Word daily.

⁸After Gomer had weaned Lo-ruhamah, she again became pregnant and gave birth to a second son. ⁹And the LORD said, "Name him Lo-ammi—'Not my people'—for Israel is not my people, and I am not their God. ¹⁰Yet the time will come when Israel will prosper and become a great nation. In that day its people will be like the sands of the seashore—too many to count! Then, at the place where they were told, 'You are not my people,' it will be said, 'You are children of the living God.' ¹¹Then the people of Judah and Israel will unite under one leader, and they will return from exile together. What a day that will be—the day of Jezreel*—when God will again plant his people in his land. ¹In that day you will call your brothers Ammi—'My people.' And you will call your sisters Ruhamah—'The ones I love.'

CHAPTER 2

Charges against an Unfaithful Wife

I DO NOT DESTROY and disdain my relationship with God by seeking other gods to love and worship. (2:2)

²"But now, call Israel* to account, for she is no longer my wife, and I am no longer her husband. Tell her to take off her garish makeup and suggestive clothing and to stop playing the prostitute. ³If she doesn't, I will strip her as naked as she was on the day she was born. I will leave her to die of thirst, as in a desert or a dry and barren wilderness. ⁴And I will not love her children as I would my own because they are not my children! They were conceived in adultery. ⁵For their mother is a shameless prostitute and became pregnant in a shameful way. She said, 'I'll run after other lovers and sell myself to them for food and drink, for clothing of wool and linen, and for olive oil.'

⁶"But I will fence her in with thornbushes. I will block the road to make her lose her way. ⁷When she runs after her lovers, she won't be able to catch up with them. She will search for them but not find them. Then she will think, 'I might as well return to my husband because I was better off with him than I am now.' ⁸She doesn't realize that it was I who gave her everything she has—the grain, the wine, the olive oil. Even the gold and silver she used in worshiping the god Baal were gifts from me!

I RECOGNIZE that it is the Lord who gives me every good thing—even when I am in rebellion to him. (2:8)

⁹"But now I will take back the wine and ripened grain I generously provided each harvest season. I will take away the linen and wool clothing I gave her to

---

1:1 Hebrew *Joash*, a variant name for Jehoash. 1:2 Or *a promiscuous woman.* 1:11 *Jezreel* means "God plants."
2:2 Hebrew *call your mother.*

cover her nakedness. ¹⁰I will strip her naked in public, while all her lovers look on. No one will be able to rescue her from my hands. ¹¹I will put an end to her annual festivals, her new moon celebrations, and her Sabbath days—all her appointed festivals. ¹²I will destroy her vineyards and orchards, things she claims her lovers gave her. I will let them grow into tangled thickets, where only wild animals will eat the fruit. ¹³I will punish her for all the times she deserted me, when she burned incense to her images of Baal, put on her earrings and jewels, and went out looking for her lovers," says the LORD.

The LORD's Love for Unfaithful Israel

¹⁴"But then I will win her back once again. I will lead her out into the desert and speak tenderly to her there. ¹⁵I will return her vineyards to her and transform the Valley of Trouble* into a gateway of hope. She will give herself to me there, as she did long ago when she was young, when I freed her from her captivity in Egypt.

¹⁶"In that coming day," says the LORD, "you will call me 'my husband' instead of 'my master.'* ¹⁷O Israel, I will cause you to forget your images of Baal; even their names will no longer be spoken. ¹⁸At that time I will make a covenant with all the wild animals and the birds and the animals that scurry along the ground so that they will not harm you. I will remove all weapons of war from the land, all swords and bows, so you can live unafraid in peace and safety. ¹⁹I will make you my wife forever, showing you righteousness and justice, unfailing love and compassion. ²⁰I will be faithful to you and make you mine, and you will finally know me as LORD.

²¹"In that day," says the LORD, "I will answer the pleading of the sky for clouds, which will pour down water on the earth in answer to its cries for rain. ²²Then the earth will answer the thirsty cries of the grain, the grapes, and the olive trees for moisture. And the whole grand chorus will sing together, 'Jezreel'—'God plants!'

²³"At that time I will plant a crop of Israelites and raise them for myself! I will show love to those I called 'Not loved.'* And to those I called 'Not my people,'* I will say, 'Now you are my people.' Then they will reply, 'You are our God!' "

CHAPTER 3

Hosea's Wife Is Redeemed

Then the LORD said to me, "Go and get your wife again. Bring her back to you and love her, even though she loves adultery. For the LORD still loves Israel even though the people have turned to other gods, offering them choice gifts.*"

²So I bought her back for fifteen pieces of silver* and about five bushels of barley and a measure of wine.* ³Then I said to her, "You must live in my house for many days and stop your prostitution. During this time, you will not have sexual intercourse with anyone, not even with me.*"

⁴This illustrates that Israel will be a long time without a king or prince, and without sacrifices, temple, priests, or even idols! ⁵But afterward the people will return to the LORD their God and to David's descendant, their king.* They will come trembling in awe to the LORD, and they will receive his good gifts in the last days.

CHAPTER 4

The LORD's Case against Israel

Hear the word of the LORD, O people of Israel! The LORD has filed a lawsuit against you, saying: "There is no faithfulness, no kindness, no knowledge of

I BELIEVE the Lord is both deeply hurt and rightly angry when his people seek other gods to love and worship. (2:13)

I BELIEVE the Lord's promise to forever restore and deepen his relationship of love with his people Israel. (2:19)

I BELIEVE the Lord offers the opportunity for the unloved and those who are not his people to become his own dearly loved people. (2:23)

I OFFER forgiving, faithful love to others, just as the Lord continues to love his people who turn from him. (3:1)

2:15 Hebrew *valley of Achor.*   2:16 Hebrew *'my baal.'*   2:23a Hebrew *Lo-ruhamah;* see 1:6.   2:23b Hebrew *Lo-ammi;* see 1:9.   3:1 Hebrew *raisin cakes.*   3:2a Hebrew *15 shekels of silver,* about 6 ounces or 171 grams in weight.   3:2b As in Greek version, which reads *a homer* [182 liters] *of barley and a measure of wine;* Hebrew reads *a homer of barley and a lethech* [2.5 bushels or 91 liters] *of barley.*   3:3 Or *and I will live with you.*   3:5 Hebrew *to David their king.*

God in your land. ²You curse and lie and kill and steal and commit adultery. There is violence everywhere, with one murder after another. ³That is why your land is not producing. It is filled with sadness, and all living things are becoming sick and dying. Even the animals, birds, and fish have begun to disappear.

I ACCEPT responsibility for my sins. (4:4)

⁴"Don't point your finger at someone else and try to pass the blame! Look, you priests, my complaint is with you!* ⁵As a sentence for your crimes, you will stumble in broad daylight, just as you might at night, and so will your false prophets. And I will destroy your mother, Israel. ⁶My people are being destroyed because they don't know me. It is all your fault, you priests, for you yourselves refuse to know me. Now I refuse to recognize you as my priests. Since you have forgotten the laws of your God, I will forget to bless your children. ⁷The more priests there are, the more they sin against me. They have exchanged* the glory of God for the disgrace of idols.

I DO NOT EXCHANGE the Lord's glory for the disgrace of false gods (Romans 1:23). (4:7)

⁸"The priests get fed when the people sin and bring their sin offerings to them. So the priests are glad when the people sin! ⁹'Like priests, like people'—since the priests are wicked, the people are wicked, too. So now I will punish both priests and people for all their wicked deeds. ¹⁰They will eat and still be hungry. Though they do a big business as prostitutes, they will have no children, for they have deserted the LORD to worship other gods.

I LOOK to the Lord—not inanimate objects or false gods—for guidance in my life. (4:12)

¹¹"Alcohol and prostitution have robbed my people of their brains. ¹²They are asking a piece of wood to tell them what to do! They think a stick can tell them the future! Longing after idols has made them foolish. They have played the prostitute, serving other gods and deserting their God. ¹³They offer sacrifices to idols on the tops of mountains. They go up into the hills to burn incense in the pleasant shade of oaks, poplars, and other trees.

"That is why your daughters turn to prostitution, and your daughters-in-law commit adultery. ¹⁴Why should I punish them? For you men are doing the same thing, sinning with whores and shrine prostitutes. O foolish people! You will be destroyed, for you refuse to understand.

I DO NOT USE a show of worship as a cover up for my sin. (4:15)

¹⁵"Though Israel is a prostitute, may Judah avoid such guilt. O Judah, do not join with those who worship me insincerely at Gilgal and at Beth-aven.* Their worship is mere pretense as they take oaths in the LORD's name. ¹⁶Israel is as stubborn as a heifer, so the LORD will put her out to pasture. She will stand alone and unprotected, like a helpless lamb in an open field. ¹⁷Leave her alone because she is married to idolatry. ¹⁸The men of Israel finish up their drinking bouts and off they go to find some prostitutes. Their love for shame is greater than their love for honor.* ¹⁹So a mighty wind will sweep them away. They will die in shame because they offer sacrifices to idols.

CHAPTER 5

The Failure of Israel's Leaders

"Hear this, you priests and all of Israel's leaders! Listen, all you men of the royal family! These words of judgment are for you: You are doomed! For you have led the people into a snare by worshiping the idols at Mizpah and Tabor. ²You have dug a deep pit to trap them at Acacia.* But never forget—I will settle with all of you for what you have done. ³I know what you are like, O Israel! You have left me as a prostitute leaves her husband; you are utterly

---

4:4 Hebrew *Your people are like those with a complaint against the priests.* 4:7 As in Syriac version and an ancient Hebrew tradition; Masoretic Text reads *I will exchange.* 4:15 *Beth-aven* means "house of wickedness"; it is being used as another name for Bethel, which means "house of God." 4:18 As in Greek version; the meaning of the Hebrew is uncertain. 5:2 Hebrew *at Shittim.* The meaning of the Hebrew for this sentence is uncertain.

defiled. [4]Your deeds won't let you return to your God. You are a prostitute through and through, and you cannot know the LORD.

[5]"The arrogance of Israel* testifies against her; she will stumble under her load of guilt. Judah, too, will fall with her. [6]Then at last, they will come with their flocks and herds to offer sacrifices to the LORD. But it will be too late! They will not find him, because he has withdrawn from them, and they are now alone. [7]For they have betrayed the honor of the LORD, bearing children that aren't his. Now their false religion will devour them, along with their wealth.

> I DO NOT WAIT until it is too late to seek and serve the Lord. (5:6)

LIKE HOSEA   *I show how much God loves those who reject him.*

Hosea 3:1

Who would want Hosea's assignment from the Lord? Want to marry someone who will break your heart? Or be a flesh-and-blood demonstration of how God's heart was broken by Israel's rejection?

Amazingly, there is no record that Hosea objected to the Lord's command. Instead, we read only of the outpouring of love reflected through the passionate words of God himself.

Hosea truly loved his wife—he didn't merely put up with her. He accepted Gomer's daughter and son as his own. Though they deserved to be called "Not loved" and "Not my people," their names became "The ones I love" and "My people" (1:6-2:1). Later Hosea paid to rescue his wife from the bondage of prostitution and the shame of her many sins (3:1-2).

Hosea and Gomer's actions were an object lesson to Israel and Judah: "This is how you have treated your Lord God. Your rejection of him for the love of idols is as detestable as a well-loved wife prostituting herself."

But this wasn't merely an allegory. Gomer was a real woman with a particular personality, distinct preferences, annoying habits, and varying moods. She was a human being who was the recipient of God's loyal, forgiving love through the forgiveness and affection of another human being—her husband Hosea.

You and I are not called to marry a rebellious, unfaithful lover. But like Hosea, we are called to make God's love tangible to others around us—especially to those who are running from him.

Hosea's sacrificial love for Gomer was a glimpse of the coming Lover of our souls—Jesus Christ. Jesus paid more than silver and barley. He paid his own life to buy us back (Romans 5:6-8).

If Hosea could obey God and love an unfaithful wife, because of Jesus we can love anyone God brings into our lives—good, rude, rebellious, or annoying. And we can demonstrate the Lord's compassion to a watching world (John 15:12-13).

○ *Today's Scripture reading is Hosea 1–3.*

---

[8]"Blow the ram's horn in Gibeah! Sound the alarm in Ramah! Raise the battle cry in Beth-aven*! Lead on into battle, O warriors of Benjamin! [9]One thing is certain, Israel*: When your day of punishment comes, you will become a heap of rubble.

[10]"The leaders of Judah have become as bad as thieves.* So I will pour my anger down on them like a waterfall. [11]The people of Israel will be crushed and broken by my judgment because they are determined to worship idols. [12]I will destroy Israel as a moth consumes wool. I will sap Judah's strength as dry rot weakens wood.

[13]"When Israel and Judah saw how sick they were, Israel turned to Assyria, to the great king there, but he could neither help nor cure them. [14]I will tear at Israel and Judah as a lion rips apart its prey. I will carry them off, and there will be no one left to rescue them. [15]Then I will return to my place until they admit

> I BELIEVE the people of Israel and Judah were judged severely because they loved and worshiped idols instead of the Lord. (5:11)

> I DO NOT LOOK to anyone besides the Lord to cure my moral and spiritual ills. (5:13)

5:5 Hebrew *Israel and Ephraim.*   5:8 *Beth-aven* means "house of wickedness"; it is being used as another name for Bethel, which means "house of God."   5:9 Hebrew *Ephraim,* referring to the northern kingdom of Israel; also in 5:11, 12, 13, 14.   5:10 Hebrew *have become as those who move a boundary marker.*

their guilt and look to me for help. For as soon as trouble comes, they will search for me."

CHAPTER 6
A Call to Repentance

"Come, let us return to the LORD! He has torn us in pieces; now he will heal us. He has injured us; now he will bandage our wounds. ²In just a short time, he will restore us so we can live in his presence. ³Oh, that we might know the LORD! Let us press on to know him! Then he will respond to us as surely as the arrival of dawn or the coming of rains in early spring."

⁴"O Israel* and Judah, what should I do with you?" asks the LORD. "For your love vanishes like the morning mist and disappears like dew in the sunlight. ⁵I sent my prophets to cut you to pieces. I have slaughtered you with my words, threatening you with death. My judgment will strike you as surely as day follows night. ⁶I want you to be merciful; I don't want your sacrifices. I want you to know God; that's more important than burnt offerings.

⁷"But like Adam, you broke my covenant and rebelled against me. ⁸Gilead is a city of sinners, tracked with footprints of blood. ⁹Its citizens are bands of robbers, lying in ambush for their victims. Gangs of priests murder travelers along the road to Shechem and practice every kind of sin. ¹⁰Yes, I have seen a horrible thing in Israel: My people have defiled themselves by chasing after other gods!

¹¹"O Judah, a harvest of punishment is also waiting for you, though I wanted so much to restore the fortunes of my people!

CHAPTER 7
Israel's Love for Wickedness

"I wanted to heal Israel, but its sins were far too great. Samaria is filled with liars, thieves, and bandits! ²Its people don't realize I am watching them. Their sinful deeds are all around them; I see them all! ³The people make the king glad with their wickedness. The princes laugh about the people's many lies. ⁴They are all adulterers, always aflame with lust. They are like an oven that is kept hot even while the baker is still kneading the dough.

⁵"On royal holidays, the princes get drunk. The king makes a fool of himself and drinks with those who are making fun of him. ⁶Their hearts blaze like a furnace with intrigue. Their plot smolders through the night, and in the morning it flames forth like a raging fire. ⁷They kill their kings one after another, and no one cries out to me for help.

⁸"My people of Israel* mingle with godless foreigners, picking up their evil ways. Now they have become as worthless as a half-baked cake! ⁹Worshiping foreign gods has sapped their strength, but they don't even know it. Israel is like an old man with graying hair, unaware of how weak and old he has become. ¹⁰His arrogance testifies against him, yet he doesn't return to the LORD his God or even try to find him.

¹¹"The people of Israel have become like silly, witless doves, first calling to Egypt, then flying to Assyria. ¹²But as they fly about, I will throw my net over them and bring them down like a bird from the sky. I will punish them for all their evil ways.*

¹³"How terrible it will be for my people who have deserted me! Let them die, for they have rebelled against me. I wanted to redeem them, but they have only spoken lies about me. ¹⁴They do not cry out to me with sincere hearts. Instead, they sit on their couches and wail. They cut themselves, begging foreign gods for crops and prosperity.

Margin notes (left column)

I SINCERELY RETURN to the Lord for healing after he has disciplined me. (6:1)

I PROVE my love for God by knowing him and showing mercy, not by participating in religious rituals. (6:6)

See Adam's profile (page 5) at Genesis 1:26.

I BELIEVE the Lord wanted desperately to bless his people rather than punish them. (6:11)

I REALIZE the Lord watches everyone and sees all of their sins. (7:2)

I CRY OUT to the Lord for help in the midst of social decay and destruction. (7:7)

I CRY OUT to the Lord with a sincere heart, trusting him alone for redemption and deliverance. (7:14)

6:4 Hebrew *Ephraim*, referring to the northern kingdom of Israel. 7:8 Hebrew *Ephraim*, referring to the northern kingdom of Israel; also in 7:11. 7:12 Hebrew *I will punish them because of what was reported against them in the assembly.*

[15] "I trained them and made them strong, yet now they plot evil against me. [16] They look everywhere except to heaven, to the Most High. They are like a crooked bow that always misses its target. Their leaders will be killed by their enemies because of their insolence toward me. Then the people of Egypt will laugh at them.

CHAPTER 8

Israel Harvests the Whirlwind

"Sound the alarm! The enemy descends like an eagle on the people of the LORD, for they have broken my covenant and revolted against my law. [2] Now Israel pleads with me, 'Help us, for you are our God!' [3] But it is too late! The people of Israel have rejected what is good, and now their enemies will chase after them. [4] The people have appointed kings and princes, but not with my consent. By making idols for themselves from their silver and gold, they have brought about their own destruction.

I DO NOT EXPECT God to rescue me when I continue to rebel against him. (8:3)

[5] "O Samaria, I reject this calf—this idol you have made. My fury burns against you. How long will you be incapable of innocence? [6] This calf you worship was crafted by your own hands! It is not God! Therefore, it must be smashed to bits.

I BELIEVE the Lord must destroy anything I set up as a substitute for him. (8:6)

[7] "They have planted the wind and will harvest the whirlwind. The stalks of wheat wither, producing no grain. And if there is any grain, foreigners will eat it. [8] The people of Israel have been swallowed up; they lie among the nations like an old pot that no one wants. [9] Like a wild donkey looking for a mate, they have gone up to Assyria. The people of Israel* have sold themselves to many lovers. [10] But though they have sold themselves to many lands, I will now gather them together. Then they will writhe under the burden of the great king!

[11] "Israel has built many altars to take away sin, but these very altars became places for sinning! [12] Even though I gave them all my laws, they act as if those laws don't apply to them. [13] The people of Israel love their rituals of sacrifice, but to me their sacrifices are all meaningless! I will call my people to account for their sins, and I will punish them. They will go back down to Egypt.

[14] "Israel has built great palaces, and Judah has fortified its cities. But they have both forgotten their Maker. Therefore, I will send down fire on their palaces and burn their fortresses."

I DO NOT FORGET the Lord, my Maker, in the midst of my prosperity and success. (8:14)

CHAPTER 9

Hosea Announces Israel's Punishment

O people of Israel, do not rejoice as others do. For you have been unfaithful to your God, hiring yourselves out like prostitutes, offering sacrifices to other gods on every threshing floor. [2] So now your harvests will be too small to feed you. The grapes you gather will not quench your thirst. [3] You may no longer stay here in this land of the LORD. You will be carried off to Egypt and Assyria, where you will live on food that is ceremonially unclean.

[4] There, far from home, you will not be allowed to pour out wine as a sacrifice to the LORD. None of the sacrifices you offer there will please him. Such sacrifices will be unclean, just as food touched by a person in mourning is unclean. All who present such sacrifices will be defiled. They may eat this food to feed themselves, but they may not offer it to the LORD.

[5] What then will you do on festival days? What will you do on days of feasting in the LORD's presence? [6] Even if you escape destruction from Assyria, you will be conquered by Egypt. Memphis* will bury you. Briers will take over your treasures of silver; brambles will fill your homes.

I BELIEVE the Lord accurately foretold that Israel would be taken to Assyria and Egypt because they followed other gods. (9:3)

8:9 Hebrew *Ephraim*, referring to the northern kingdom of Israel; also in 8:11. 9:6 Memphis was the capital of northern Egypt.

I DO NOT RESIST the Lord's Word or taunt those who warn me about the consequences for sin. (9:7)

I BELIEVE the Lord was filled with love and desire for the Israelites, but they deserted him. (9:10)

I BELIEVE the Lord declared that Israel would be driven away from their land—unloved and rejected—because of their wickedness and rebellion against him. (9:15)

I AM CAREFUL to keep the promises that I make. (10:4)

I ABHOR and do not repeat the disgusting sins of my ancestors (Judges 19–21). (10:9)

7 The time of Israel's punishment has come; the day of payment is almost here. Soon Israel will know this all too well. "The prophets are crazy!" the people shout. "The inspired men are mad!" So they taunt, for the nation is burdened with sin and shows only hatred for those who love God.

8 The prophet is a watchman for my God over Israel,* yet traps are laid in front of him wherever he goes. He faces hostility even in the house of God. 9 The things my people do are as depraved as what they did in Gibeah long ago. God will not forget. He will surely punish them for their sins.

10 The LORD says, "O Israel, when I first found you, it was like finding fresh grapes in the desert! When I saw your ancestors, it was like seeing the first ripe figs of the season! But then they deserted me for Baal-peor, giving themselves to that shameful idol. Soon they became as vile as the god they worshiped. 11 The glory of Israel will fly away like a bird, for your children will die at birth or perish in the womb or never even be conceived. 12 Even if your children do survive to grow up, I will take them from you. It will be a terrible day when I turn away and leave you alone. 13 I have watched Israel become as beautiful and pleasant as Tyre. But now Israel will bring out her children to be slaughtered."

14 O LORD, what should I request for your people? I will ask for wombs that don't give birth and breasts that give no milk.

15 The LORD says, "All their wickedness began at Gilgal; there I began to hate them. I will drive them from my land because of their evil actions. I will love them no more because all their leaders are rebels. 16 The people of Israel are stricken. Their roots are dried up; they will bear no more fruit. And if they give birth, I will slaughter their beloved children."

17 My God will reject the people of Israel because they will not listen or obey. They will be wanderers, homeless among the nations.

CHAPTER 10

The LORD's Judgment against Israel

How prosperous Israel is—a luxuriant vine loaded with fruit! But the more wealth the people got, the more they poured it on the altars of their foreign gods. The richer the harvests they brought in, the more beautiful the statues and idols they built. 2 The hearts of the people are fickle; they are guilty and must be punished. The LORD will break down their foreign altars and smash their many idols.

3 Then they will say, "We have no king because we didn't fear the LORD. But what's the difference? What could a king do for us anyway?" 4 They spout empty words and make promises they don't intend to keep. So perverted justice springs up among them like poisonous weeds in a farmer's field.

5 The people of Samaria tremble for their calf idol at Beth-aven.* The people mourn over it, and the priests wail for it, because its glory will be stripped away. 6 This idol they love so much will be carted away with them when they go as captives to Assyria, a gift to the great king there. Israel will be laughed at and shamed because its people have trusted in this idol. 7 Samaria will be cut off, and its king will disappear like a chip of wood on an ocean wave. 8 And the pagan shrines of Aven,* the place of Israel's sin, will crumble. Thorns and thistles will grow up around them. They will beg the mountains to bury them and the hills to fall on them.

9 The LORD says, "O Israel, ever since that awful night in Gibeah, there has been only sin and more sin! You have made no progress whatsoever. Was it not right that the wicked men of Gibeah were attacked? 10 Now I will attack you, too, for your rebellion and disobedience. I will call out the armies of the nations to punish you for your multiplied sins.

9:8 Hebrew *Ephraim*, referring to the northern kingdom of Israel; also in 9:11, 13, 16. 10:5 *Beth-aven* means "house of wickedness"; it is being used as another name for Bethel, which means "house of God." 10:8 *Aven* is a reference to Beth-aven; see 10:5 and the note there.

[11]"Israel* is like a trained heifer accustomed to treading out the grain—an easy job that she loves. Now I will put a heavy yoke on her tender neck. I will drive her in front of the plow. Israel* and Judah must now break up the hard ground; their days of ease are gone. [12]I said, 'Plant the good seeds of righteousness, and you will harvest a crop of my love. Plow up the hard ground of your hearts, for now is the time to seek the LORD, that he may come and shower righteousness upon you.'

[13]"But you have cultivated wickedness and raised a thriving crop of sins. You have eaten the fruit of lies—trusting in your military might, believing that great armies could make your nation safe! [14]Now the terrors of war will rise among your people. All your fortifications will fall, just as they did when Shalman destroyed Beth-arbel. Even mothers and children were dashed to death there. [15]You will share that fate, Bethel, because of your great wickedness. When the day of judgment dawns, the king of Israel will be completely destroyed.

> I SOFTEN my heart to the Lord and invest my life in righteousness in order to experience his love and blessing. (10:12)

CHAPTER 11

The LORD's Love for Israel

"When Israel was a child, I loved him as a son, and I called my son out of Egypt. [2]But the more I* called to him, the more he rebelled, offering sacrifices to the images of Baal and burning incense to idols. [3]It was I who taught Israel* how to walk, leading him along by the hand. But he doesn't know or even care that it was I who took care of him. [4]I led Israel along with my ropes of kindness and love. I lifted the yoke from his neck, and I myself stooped to feed him.

> I BELIEVE the Lord brought Israel out of Egypt—and brought his beloved son, Jesus, out of Egypt, too (Matthew 2:15). (11:1)

[5]"But since my people refuse to return to me, they will go back to Egypt and will be forced to serve Assyria. [6]War will swirl through their cities; their enemies will crash through their gates and destroy them, trapping them in their own evil plans. [7]For my people are determined to desert me. They call me the Most High, but they don't truly honor me.

[8]"Oh, how can I give you up, Israel? How can I let you go? How can I destroy you like Admah and Zeboiim? My heart is torn within me, and my compassion overflows. [9]No, I will not punish you as much as my burning anger tells me to. I will not completely destroy Israel, for I am God and not a mere mortal. I am the Holy One living among you, and I will not come to destroy.

> I DO NOT DESERT the Lord or falsely claim to honor him. (11:7)

[10]"For someday the people will follow the LORD. I will roar like a lion, and my people will return trembling from the west. [11]Like a flock of birds, they will come from Egypt. Flying like doves, they will return from Assyria. And I will bring them home again," says the LORD.

Charges against Israel and Judah

[12]Israel surrounds me with lies and deceit, but Judah still walks with God and is faithful to the Holy One.*

CHAPTER 12

The people of Israel* feed on the wind; they chase after the east wind all day long. They multiply lies and violence; they make alliances with Assyria and cut deals with the Egyptians.

[2]Now the LORD is bringing a lawsuit against Judah. He is about to punish Jacob* for all his deceitful ways. [3]Before Jacob was born, he struggled with his brother; when he became a man, he even fought with God. [4]Yes, he wrestled with the angel and won. He wept and pleaded for a blessing from him. There

> See the profiles for Jacob (page 43) and Esau (page 33) at Genesis 32:9 and Genesis 25:34.

10:11a Hebrew *Ephraim*, referring to the northern kingdom of Israel. 10:11b Hebrew *Jacob*. 11:2 As in Greek version; Hebrew reads *they*. 11:3 Hebrew *Ephraim*, referring to the northern kingdom of Israel; also in 11:8, 9, 12. 11:12 Or *and Judah is unruly against God, the faithful Holy One*. 12:1 Hebrew *Ephraim*, referring to the northern kingdom of Israel; also in 12:8, 14. 12:2 *Jacob* means "he grasps at the heel"; this can also figuratively mean "he deceives."

I LIVE in dependence on God, following the principles of love and justice. (12:6)

I DO NOT BOAST about my sins or independence from God. (12:8)

I BELIEVE the wages of sin is death (Romans 6:23). (12:14)

I DO NOT WANT to become proud and forget the Lord after enjoying the blessings of his salvation. (13:6)

I HAVE GLADLY ACCPETED the new birth the Lord offers (John 3:3-7). (13:13)

I TREMBLE at the terrible consequences of rebelling aainst God. (13:16)

at Bethel he met God face to face, and God spoke to him*—⁵the LORD God Almighty, the LORD is his name! ⁶So now, come back to your God! Act on the principles of love and justice, and always live in confident dependence on your God.

⁷But no, the people are like crafty merchants selling from dishonest scales— they love to cheat. ⁸Israel boasts, "I am rich, and I've gotten it all by myself! No one can say I got it by cheating! My record is spotless!"

⁹"I am the LORD your God, who rescued you from your slavery in Egypt. And I will make you live in tents again, as you do each year when you celebrate the Festival of Shelters.* ¹⁰I sent my prophets to warn you with many visions and parables."

¹¹But Gilead is filled with sinners who worship idols. And in Gilgal, too, they sacrifice bulls; their altars are lined up like the heaps of stone along the edges of a plowed field. ¹²Jacob fled to the land of Aram and earned a wife by tending sheep. ¹³Then the LORD led Jacob's descendants, the Israelites, out of Egypt by a prophet, who guided and protected them. ¹⁴But the people of Israel have bitterly provoked the LORD, so their Lord will now sentence them to death in payment for their sins.

CHAPTER 13

The LORD's Anger against Israel

In the past when the tribe of Ephraim spoke, the people shook with fear because the other Israelite tribes looked up to them. But the people of Ephraim sinned by worshiping Baal and thus sealed their destruction. ²Now they keep on sinning by making silver idols to worship—images shaped skillfully with human hands. "Sacrifice to these," they cry, "and kiss the calf idols!" ³Therefore, they will disappear like the morning mist, like dew in the morning sun, like chaff blown by the wind, like smoke from a chimney.

⁴"I am the LORD your God, who rescued you from your slavery in Egypt. You have no God but me, for there is no other savior. ⁵I took care of you in the wilderness, in that dry and thirsty land. ⁶But when you had eaten and were satisfied, then you became proud and forgot me. ⁷So now I will attack you like a lion, or like a leopard that lurks along the road. ⁸I will rip you to pieces like a bear whose cubs have been taken away. I will tear you apart and devour you like a hungry lion.

⁹"You are about to be destroyed, O Israel, though I am your helper. ¹⁰Where now is* your king? Why don't you call on him for help? Where are all the leaders of the land? You asked for them, now let them save you! ¹¹In my anger I gave you kings, and in my fury I took them away.

¹²"The sins of Ephraim have been collected and stored away for punishment. ¹³The people have been offered new birth, but they are like a child who resists being born. How stubborn they are! How foolish! ¹⁴Should I ransom them from the grave? Should I redeem them from death? O death, bring forth your terrors! O grave, bring forth your plagues! For I will not relent! ¹⁵Ephraim was the most fruitful of all his brothers, but the east wind—a blast from the LORD—will arise in the desert. It will blow hard against the people of Ephraim, drying up their land. All their flowing springs and wells will disappear. Every precious thing they have will be plundered and carried away. ¹⁶The people of Samaria must bear the consequences of their guilt because they rebelled against their God. They will be killed by an invading army, their little ones dashed to death against the ground, their pregnant women ripped open by swords."

12:4 As in Greek and Syriac versions; Hebrew reads *to us.* 12:9 Hebrew *as in the days of your appointed feast.* 13:10 As in Greek and Syriac versions and Latin Vulgate; Hebrew reads *I will be.*

CHAPTER 14

Healing for the Repentant

Return, O Israel, to the LORD your God, for your sins have brought you down. ²Bring your petitions, and return to the LORD. Say to him, "Forgive all our sins and graciously receive us, so that we may offer you the sacrifice of praise. ³Assyria cannot save us, nor can our strength in battle. Never again will we call the idols we have made 'our gods.' No, in you alone do the orphans find mercy."

⁴The LORD says, "Then I will heal you of your idolatry and faithlessness, and my love will know no bounds, for my anger will be gone forever! ⁵I will be to Israel like a refreshing dew from heaven. It will blossom like the lily; it will send roots deep into the soil like the cedars in Lebanon. ⁶Its branches will spread out like those of beautiful olive trees, as fragrant as the cedar forests of Lebanon. ⁷My people will return again to the safety of their land. They will flourish like grain and blossom like grapevines. They will be as fragrant as the wines of Lebanon.

⁸"O Israel,* stay away from idols! I am the one who looks after you and cares for you. I am like a tree that is always green, giving my fruit to you all through the year."

⁹Let those who are wise understand these things. Let those who are discerning listen carefully. The paths of the LORD are true and right, and righteous people live by walking in them. But sinners stumble and fall along the way.

14:8 Hebrew *Ephraim*, referring to the northern kingdom of Israel.

I AM THANKFUL the Lord lavishes his love on those who return to him. (14:4)

I WALK in the righteous paths of the Lord. (14:9)

JOEL

THIS SECOND OF TWELVE "minor" Old Testament prophets urges readers to repent for "the day of the LORD" is on its way.

The phrase "the day of the LORD" appears repeatedly in Joel (chapters 1–3). The phrase speaks of the Lord's terrifying judgments at various points in time.

During a terrible locust plague, Joel warns his people of even greater judgments ahead. He calls individuals from all walks of life to humble themselves, turn from their sins, and return to the Lord. He urges them to beg God to spare their lives and pour out his blessings again.

Joel's prophecies address events in his own day, other events during the founding of the early church, and still other events at the climax of history.

Famous verses in Joel include

- ○ "In all your history, has anything like this ever happened before?" (1:2)
- ○ "The day of the LORD is on the way, the day when destruction comes" (1:15)
- ○ "Let everyone tremble in fear because the day of the LORD is upon us" (2:1)
- ○ "It is a day of darkness and gloom, a day of thick clouds and deep blackness" (2:2)
- ○ "The sun and moon grow dark, and the stars no longer shine" (2:10; see 2:30-31; 3:15)
- ○ "Then . . . I will pour out my Spirit upon all people. Your sons and daughters will prophesy" (2:28)
- ○ "And anyone who calls on the name of the LORD will be saved" (2:32)
- ○ "Beat your plowshares into swords and your pruning hooks into spears" (3:10)
- ○ "Thousands upon thousands are waiting in the valley of decision" (3:14)

CHAPTER 1

The LORD gave this message to Joel son of Pethuel.

Mourning over the Locust Plague

²Hear this, you leaders of the people! Everyone listen! In all your history, has anything like this ever happened before? ³Tell your children about it in the years to come. Pass the awful story down from generation to generation. ⁴After the cutting locusts finished eating the crops, the swarming locusts took what was left! After them came the hopping locusts, and then the stripping locusts,* too!

⁵Wake up, you drunkards, and weep! All the grapes are ruined, and all your new wine is gone! ⁶A vast army of locusts* has invaded my land. It is a terrible army, too numerous to count! Its teeth are as sharp as the teeth of lions! ⁷They have destroyed my grapevines and fig trees, stripping their bark and leaving the branches white and bare.

⁸Weep with sorrow, as a virgin weeps when her fiancé has died. ⁹There is no grain or wine to offer at the Temple of the LORD. The priests are mourning because there are no offerings. Listen to the weeping of these ministers of the

I BELIEVE the Lord gave a message to the prophet Joel. (1:1)

I LISTEN to the Lord's Word and pay attention to the lessons from history. (1:2)

I MOURN when disaster strikes. (1:8)

1:4 The precise identification of the four kinds of locusts mentioned here is uncertain. 1:6 Hebrew *A nation.*

LORD! ¹⁰The fields are ruined and empty of crops. The grain, the wine, and the olive oil are gone.

¹¹Despair, all you farmers! Wail, all you vine growers! Weep, because the wheat and barley—yes, all the field crops—are ruined. ¹²The grapevines and the fig trees have all withered. The pomegranate trees, palm trees, and apple trees—yes, all the fruit trees—have dried up. All joy has dried up with them.

¹³Dress yourselves in sackcloth, you priests! Wail, you who serve before the altar! Come, spend the night in sackcloth, you ministers of my God! There is no grain or wine to offer at the Temple of your God. ¹⁴Announce a time of fasting; call the people together for a solemn meeting. Bring the leaders and all the people into the Temple of the LORD your God, and cry out to him there. ¹⁵The day of the LORD is on the way, the day when destruction comes from the Almighty. How terrible that day will be!

¹⁶We watch as our food disappears before our very eyes. There are no joyful celebrations in the house of our God. ¹⁷The seeds die in the parched ground, and the grain crops fail. The barns and granaries stand empty and abandoned. ¹⁸How the animals moan with hunger! The cattle wander about confused because there is no pasture for them. The sheep bleat in misery.

¹⁹LORD, help us! The fire has consumed the pastures and burned up all the trees. ²⁰Even the wild animals cry out to you because they have no water to drink. The streams have dried up, and fire has consumed the pastures.

CHAPTER 2

Locusts Invade like an Army

Blow the trumpet in Jerusalem*! Sound the alarm on my holy mountain! Let everyone tremble in fear because the day of the LORD is upon us. ²It is a day of darkness and gloom, a day of thick clouds and deep blackness. Suddenly, like dawn spreading across the mountains, a mighty army appears! How great and powerful they are! The likes of them have not been seen before and never will be seen again.

³Fire burns in front of them and follows them in every direction! Ahead of them the land lies as fair as the Garden of Eden in all its beauty. Behind them is nothing but desolation; not one thing escapes. ⁴They look like tiny horses, and they run as fast. ⁵Look at them as they leap along the mountaintops! Listen to the noise they make—like the rumbling of chariots, like the roar of a fire sweeping across a field, or like a mighty army moving into battle.

⁶Fear grips all the people; every face grows pale with fright. ⁷The attackers march like warriors and scale city walls like trained soldiers. Straight forward they march, never breaking rank. ⁸They never jostle each other; each moves in exactly the right place. They lunge through the gaps, and no weapon can stop them. ⁹They swarm over the city and run along its walls. They enter all the houses, climbing like thieves through the windows.

¹⁰The earth quakes as they advance, and the heavens tremble. The sun and moon grow dark, and the stars no longer shine. ¹¹The LORD leads them with a shout! This is his mighty army, and they follow his orders. The day of the LORD is an awesome, terrible thing. Who can endure it?

A Call to Repentance

¹²That is why the LORD says, "Turn to me now, while there is time! Give me your hearts. Come with fasting, weeping, and mourning. ¹³Don't tear your clothing in your grief; instead, tear your hearts." Return to the LORD your God, for he is gracious and merciful. He is not easily angered. He is filled with kindness and is eager not to punish you. ¹⁴Who knows? Perhaps even yet he will give you a reprieve, sending you a blessing instead of this terrible curse.

I JOIN with the Lord's people to pray when disaster strikes. (1:14)

I BELIEVE the day of the Lord's judgment will be a day of darkness and gloom. (2:2)

I TURN to the Lord wholeheartedly now while there is still time. (2:12)

2:1 Hebrew *Zion;* also in 2:15, 23.

Perhaps he will give you so much that you will be able to offer grain and wine to the LORD your God as before!

[15]Blow the trumpet in Jerusalem! Announce a time of fasting; call the people together for a solemn meeting. [16]Bring everyone—the elders, the children, and even the babies. Call the bridegroom from his quarters and the bride from her private room. [17]The priests, who minister in the LORD's presence, will stand between the people and the altar, weeping. Let them pray, "Spare your people, LORD! They belong to you, so don't let them become an object of mockery. Don't let their name become a proverb of unbelieving foreigners who say, 'Where is the God of Israel? He must be helpless!' "

The LORD's Promise of Restoration
[18]Then the LORD will pity his people and be indignant for the honor of his land! [19]He will reply, "Look! I am sending you grain and wine and olive oil, enough to satisfy your needs. You will no longer be an object of mockery among the surrounding nations. [20]I will remove these armies from the north and send them far away. I will drive them back into the parched wastelands, where they will die. Those in the rear will go into the Dead Sea; those at the front will go into the Mediterranean.* The stench of their rotting bodies will rise over the land."

Surely the LORD has done great things! [21]Don't be afraid, my people! Be glad now and rejoice because the LORD has done great things. [22]Don't be afraid, you animals of the field! The pastures will soon be green. The trees will again be filled with luscious fruit; fig trees and grapevines will flourish once more. [23]Rejoice, you people of Jerusalem! Rejoice in the LORD your God! For the rains he sends are an expression of his grace. Once more the autumn rains will come, as well as the rains of spring. [24]The threshing floors will again be piled high with grain, and the presses will overflow with wine and olive oil.

[25]The LORD says, "I will give you back what you lost to the stripping locusts, the cutting locusts, the swarming locusts, and the hopping locusts.* It was I who sent this great destroying army against you. [26]Once again you will have all the food you want, and you will praise the LORD your God, who does these miracles for you. Never again will my people be disgraced like this. [27]Then you will know that I am here among my people of Israel and that I alone am the LORD your God. My people will never again be disgraced like this.

The LORD's Promise of His Spirit
[28]"Then after I have poured out my rains again, I will pour out my Spirit upon all people. Your sons and daughters will prophesy. Your old men will dream dreams. Your young men will see visions. [29]In those days, I will pour out my Spirit even on servants, men and women alike.

[30]"I will cause wonders in the heavens and on the earth—blood and fire and pillars of smoke. [31]The sun will be turned into darkness, and the moon will turn bloodred before that great and terrible day of the LORD arrives. [32]And anyone who calls on the name of the LORD will be saved. There will be people on Mount Zion in Jerusalem who escape, just as the LORD has said. These will be among the survivors whom the LORD has called.

CHAPTER 3

Judgment against Enemy Nations
"At that time, when I restore the prosperity of Judah and Jerusalem," says the LORD, [2]"I will gather the armies of the world into the valley of Jehoshaphat.* There I will judge them for harming my people, for scattering my inheritance

I BELIEVE all people—regardless of age, class, or gender—need to pray for the Lord's mercy. (2:16)

I REJOICE because of the great things the Lord has done to rescue and restore his people. (2:21)

I BELIEVE the Lord kept his promise to pour out his Spirit on all people, regardless of age, class, or gender (Acts 2:16-21). (2:28)

I BELIEVE anyone who calls on the name of the Lord will be saved (Romans 10:13). (2:32)

I BELIEVE the Lord will judge the nations of the world after he restores Judah and Jerusalem. (3:2)

2:20 Hebrew *the eastern sea; . . . the western sea.* 2:25 The precise identification of the four kinds of locusts mentioned here is uncertain. 3:2 *Jehoshaphat* means "the LORD judges."

among the nations, and for dividing up my land. ³They cast lots to decide which of my people would be their slaves. They traded young boys for prostitutes and little girls for enough wine to get drunk.

⁴"What do you have against me, Tyre and Sidon and you cities of Philistia? Are you trying to take revenge on me? If you are, then watch out! I will strike swiftly and pay you back for everything you have done. ⁵You have taken my silver and gold and all my precious treasures, and you have carried them off to your pagan temples. ⁶You have sold the people of Judah and Jerusalem to the Greeks,* who took them far from their homeland. ⁷But I will bring them back again from all these places to which you sold them, and I will pay you back for all you have done. ⁸I will sell your sons and daughters to the people of Judah, and they will sell them to the peoples of Arabia,* a nation far away. I, the LORD, have spoken!"

⁹Say to the nations far and wide: "Get ready for war! Call out your best warriors! Let all your fighting men advance for the attack! ¹⁰Beat your plowshares into swords and your pruning hooks into spears. Train even your weaklings to be warriors. ¹¹Come quickly, all you nations everywhere! Gather together in the valley."

And now, O LORD, call out your warriors!

¹²"Let the nations be called to arms. Let them march to the valley of Jehoshaphat. There I, the LORD, will sit to pronounce judgment on them all. ¹³Now let the sickle do its work, for the harvest is ripe. Come, tread the winepress because it is full. The storage vats are overflowing with the wickedness of these people."

¹⁴Thousands upon thousands are waiting in the valley of decision. It is there that the day of the LORD will soon arrive. ¹⁵The sun and moon will grow dark, and the stars will no longer shine. ¹⁶The LORD's voice will roar from Zion and thunder from Jerusalem, and the earth and heavens will begin to shake. But to his people of Israel, the LORD will be a welcoming refuge and a strong fortress.

Blessings for God's People

¹⁷"Then you will know that I, the LORD your God, live in Zion, my holy mountain. Jerusalem will be holy forever, and foreign armies will never conquer her again. ¹⁸In that day the mountains will drip with sweet wine, and the hills will flow with milk. Water will fill the dry streambeds of Judah, and a fountain will burst forth from the LORD's Temple, watering the arid valley of acacias.* ¹⁹Egypt will become a wasteland and Edom a wilderness, because they attacked Judah and killed her innocent people.

²⁰"But Judah will remain forever, and Jerusalem will endure through all future generations. ²¹I will pardon my people's crimes, which I have not yet pardoned; and I, the LORD, will make my home in Jerusalem* with my people."

3:6 Hebrew *to the peoples of Javan.* 3:8 Hebrew *to the Sabeans.* 3:18 Hebrew *valley of Shittim.* 3:21 Hebrew *Zion.*

I BELIEVE the Lord will judge all the nations who try to fight against him. (3:12)

I BELIEVE the Lord's judgment will come because of the immense wickedness of humanity. (3:13)

I ASK the Lord to be my strength and fortress at all times. (3:16)

AMOS

THIS THIRD "MINOR" prophet urges readers to pursue righteousness and justice.

Many citizens of the northern kingdom of Israel probably applauded Amos when he warned of God's coming judgment against neighboring pagan nations (1:1-2:3) and the southern kingdom of Judah (2:4-5), where Amos was a shepherd and a farmer.

But the Israelites must have hissed when their country cousin prophesied against them (2:6-6:14) and proclaimed five visions confirming the Lord's decision to destroy them (7:1-9:10) within a generation.

The sins of these nations included the torture of prisoners of war, the inhumane treatment of fellow citizens, the enslavement of enemies, the slaughter of innocent individuals, the desecration of tombs, the rejection of God's revelation, and the corruption of what should be holy.

Amos's prophecies conclude with a brief glimmer of hope for the future (9:11-15) that has yet to be fully realized.

Famous verses in Amos include

- "The people . . . have sinned again and again" (1:3, 6, 9, 11, 13; 2:1, 4, 6)
- "Can two people walk together without agreeing on the direction?" (3:3)
- "The lion has roared—tremble in fear! The Sovereign LORD has spoken" (3:8)
- "Listen to me, you 'fat cows' of Samaria, you women who oppress" (4:1)
- "Prepare to meet your God as he comes in judgment" (4:12)
- "Come back to me and live!" (5:4)
- "Do what is good and run from evil—that you may live!" (5:14)
- "I want to see a mighty flood of justice, a river of righteous living" (5:24)
- "I will make the sun go down at noon and darken the earth while it is still day" (8:9)
- "I will send a famine . . . of hearing the words of the LORD" (8:11)
- "I will restore the fallen kingdom of David" (9:11)

CHAPTER 1

This message was given to Amos, a shepherd from the town of Tekoa in Judah. He received this message in visions two years before the earthquake, when Uzziah was king of Judah and Jeroboam II, the son of Jehoash,* was king of Israel.

²This is his report of what he saw and heard: "The LORD's voice roars from his Temple on Mount Zion; he thunders from Jerusalem! Suddenly, the lush pastures of the shepherds dry up. All the grass on Mount Carmel withers and dies."

God's Judgment on Israel's Neighbors

³This is what the LORD says: "The people of Damascus have sinned again and again, and I will not forget it. I will not let them go unpunished any longer!

1:1 Hebrew *Joash,* a variant name for Jehoash.

See Uzziah's profile (page 533) at 2 Chronicles 26:16.

I BELIEVE the Lord punishes cruelty and abuse. (1:3)

They beat down my people in Gilead as grain is threshed with threshing sledges of iron. ⁴So I will send down fire on King Hazael's palace, and the fortresses of King Ben-hadad will be destroyed. ⁵I will break down the gates of Damascus and slaughter its people all the way to the valley of Aven.* I will destroy the ruler in Beth-eden, and the people of Aram will return to Kir as slaves. I, the LORD, have spoken!"

⁶This is what the LORD says: "The people of Gaza have sinned again and again, and I will not forget it. I will not let them go unpunished any longer! They sent my people into exile, selling them as slaves in Edom. ⁷So I will send down fire on the walls of Gaza, and all its fortresses will be destroyed. ⁸I will slaughter the people of Ashdod and destroy the king of Ashkelon. Then I will turn to attack Ekron, and the few Philistines still left will be killed. I, the Sovereign LORD, have spoken!"

I BELIEVE the Lord punishes the breaking of treaties and selling of slaves. (1:9)

⁹This is what the LORD says: "The people of Tyre have sinned again and again, and I will not forget it. I will not let them go unpunished any longer! They broke their treaty of brotherhood with Israel, selling whole villages as slaves to Edom. ¹⁰So I will send down fire on the walls of Tyre, and all its fortresses will be destroyed."

I BELIEVE the Lord punishes unwarranted and ruthless attacks against others. (1:11)

¹¹This is what the LORD says: "The people of Edom have sinned again and again, and I will not forget it. I will not let them go unpunished any longer! They chased down their relatives, the Israelites, with swords. They showed them no mercy and were unrelenting in their anger. ¹²So I will send down fire on Teman, and the fortresses of Bozrah will be destroyed."

¹³This is what the LORD says: "The people of Ammon have sinned again and again, and I will not forget it. I will not let them go unpunished any longer! When they attacked Gilead to extend their borders, they committed cruel crimes, ripping open pregnant women with their swords. ¹⁴So I will send down fire on the walls of Rabbah, and all its fortresses will be destroyed. There will be wild shouts during the battle, swirling like a whirlwind in a mighty storm. ¹⁵And their king* and his princes will go into exile together. I, the LORD, have spoken!"

CHAPTER 2

I BELIEVE the Lord punishes the desecration of graves. (2:1)

This is what the LORD says: "The people of Moab have sinned again and again, and I will not forget it. I will not let them go unpunished any longer! They desecrated the tomb of Edom's king and burned his bones to ashes. ²So I will send down fire on the land of Moab, and all the fortresses in Kerioth will be destroyed. The people will fall in the noise of battle, as the warriors shout and the trumpets blare. ³And I will destroy their king and slaughter all their princes. I, the LORD, have spoken!"

God's Judgment on Judah and Israel

I BELIEVE the Lord punishes the rejection of his laws. (2:4)

⁴This is what the LORD says: "The people of Judah have sinned again and again, and I will not forget it. I will not let them go unpunished any longer! They have rejected the laws of the LORD, refusing to obey him. They have been led astray by the same lies that deceived their ancestors. ⁵So I will send down fire on Judah, and all the fortresses of Jerusalem will be destroyed."

⁶This is what the LORD says: "The people of Israel have sinned again and again, and I will not forget it. I will not let them go unpunished any longer! They have perverted justice by selling honest people for silver and poor people for a pair of sandals. ⁷They trample helpless people in the dust and deny justice to those who are oppressed. Both father and son sleep with the same woman, corrupting my holy name. ⁸At their religious festivals, they lounge around in clothing stolen from their debtors. In the house of their god, they present offerings of wine purchased with stolen money.

I HONOR God's holy name by bringing help and justice to the poor and by living in personal purity. (2:7)

1:5 Aven means "wickedness." 1:15 Hebrew malcam, possibly referring to their god Molech.

⁹"Yet think of all I did for my people! I destroyed the Amorites before my people arrived in the land. The Amorites were as tall as cedar trees and strong as oaks, but I destroyed their fruit and dug out their roots. ¹⁰It was I who rescued you from Egypt and led you through the desert for forty years so you could possess the land of the Amorites. ¹¹I chose some of your sons to be prophets and others to be Nazirites. Can you deny this, my people of Israel?" asks the LORD. ¹²"But you caused the Nazirites to sin by making them drink your wine, and you said to my prophets, 'Shut up!'

¹³"So I will make you groan as a wagon groans when it is loaded down with grain. ¹⁴Your fastest runners will not get away. The strongest among you will become weak. Even the mightiest warriors will be unable to save themselves. ¹⁵The archers will fail to stand their ground. The swiftest soldiers won't be fast enough to escape. Even warriors on horses won't be able to outrun the danger. ¹⁶On that day, the most courageous of your fighting men will drop their weapons and run for their lives. I, the LORD, have spoken!"

CHAPTER 3

Listen to this message that the LORD has spoken against you, O people of Israel and Judah—the entire family I rescued from Egypt: ²"From among all the families on the earth, I chose you alone. That is why I must punish you for all your sins."

Witnesses against Guilty Israel
³Can two people walk together without agreeing on the direction? ⁴Does a lion ever roar in a thicket without first finding a victim? Does a young lion growl in its den without first catching its prey? ⁵Does a bird ever get caught in a trap that has no bait? Does a trap ever spring shut when there's nothing there to catch? ⁶When the war trumpet blares, shouldn't the people be alarmed? When disaster comes to a city, isn't it because the LORD planned it?

⁷"But always, first of all, I warn you through my servants the prophets. I, the Sovereign LORD, have now done this."

⁸The lion has roared—tremble in fear! The Sovereign LORD has spoken—I dare not refuse to proclaim his message!

⁹Announce this to the leaders of Philistia* and Egypt: "Take your seats now on the hills around Samaria, and witness the scandalous spectacle of all Israel's crimes."

¹⁰"My people have forgotten what it means to do right," says the LORD. "Their fortresses are filled with wealth taken by theft and violence. ¹¹Therefore," says the Sovereign LORD, "an enemy is coming! He will surround them and shatter their defenses. Then he will plunder all their fortresses."

¹²This is what the LORD says: "A shepherd who tries to rescue a sheep from a lion's mouth will recover only two legs and a piece of ear. So it will be when the Israelites in Samaria are rescued with only a broken chair and a tattered pillow. ¹³Now listen to this, and announce it throughout all Israel,*" says the Lord, the LORD God Almighty. ¹⁴"On the very day I punish Israel for its sins, I will destroy the pagan altars at Bethel. The horns of the altar will be cut off and fall to the ground. ¹⁵And I will destroy the beautiful homes of the wealthy—their winter mansions and their summer houses, too—all their palaces filled with ivory. I, the LORD, have spoken!"

CHAPTER 4

Israel's Failure to Learn
Listen to me, you "fat cows" of Samaria, you women who oppress the poor and crush the needy and who are always asking your husbands for another drink! ²The Sovereign LORD has sworn this by his holiness: "The time will

3:9 Hebrew *Ashdod.*   3:13 Hebrew *the house of Jacob.*

I SUBMIT to God's discipline because I belong to him. (3:2)

Ask God to cleanse your heart as you read his Word (Psalm 51:10).

I LISTEN to the Lord's repeated warnings to forsake sin and follow him. (3:7)

I DO NOT SEEK to gain wealth in ways that hurt or take advantage of others. (3:10)

I DO NOT BEG for more and more luxuries at the expense of the poor and needy. (4:1) come when you will be led away with hooks in your noses. Every last one of you will be dragged away like a fish on a hook! ³You will leave by going straight through the breaks in the wall; you will be thrown from your fortresses.* I, the LORD, have spoken!

⁴"Go ahead and offer your sacrifices to the idols at Bethel and Gilgal. Keep on disobeying—your sins are mounting up! Offer sacrifices each morning and bring your tithes every three days! ⁵Present your bread made with yeast as an offering of thanksgiving. Then give your extra voluntary offerings so you can brag about it everywhere! This is the kind of thing you Israelites love to do," says the Sovereign LORD.

⁶"I brought hunger to every city and famine to every town. But still you wouldn't return to me," says the LORD.

⁷"I kept the rain from falling when you needed it the most, ruining all your crops. I sent rain on one town but withheld it from another. Rain fell on one field, while another field withered away. ⁸People staggered from one town to another for a drink of water, but there was never enough. But still you wouldn't return to me," says the LORD.

⁹"I struck your farms and vineyards with blight and mildew. Locusts devoured all your fig and olive trees. But still you wouldn't return to me," says the LORD.

¹⁰"I sent plagues against you like the plagues I sent against Egypt long ago. I killed your young men in war and slaughtered all your horses. The stench of death filled the air! But still you wouldn't return to me," says the LORD.

¹¹"I destroyed some of your cities, as I destroyed* Sodom and Gomorrah. Those of you who survived were like half-burned sticks snatched from a fire. But still you wouldn't return to me," says the LORD.

¹²"Therefore, I will bring upon you all these further disasters I have announced. Prepare to meet your God as he comes in judgment, you people of Israel!"

¹³For the LORD is the one who shaped the mountains, stirs up the winds, and reveals his every thought. He turns the light of dawn into darkness and treads the mountains under his feet. The LORD God Almighty is his name!

CHAPTER 5

A Call to Repentance

Listen, you people of Israel! Listen to this funeral song I am singing:

² "The virgin Israel has fallen,
   never to rise again!
She lies forsaken on the ground,
   with none to raise her up."

³The Sovereign LORD says: "When one of your cities sends a thousand men to battle, only a hundred will return. When a town sends a hundred, only ten will come back alive."

⁴Now this is what the LORD says to the family of Israel: "Come back to me and live! ⁵Don't go to worship the idols of Bethel, Gilgal, or Beersheba. For the people of Gilgal will be dragged off into exile, and the people of Bethel will come to nothing."

⁶Come back to the LORD and live! If you don't, he will roar through Israel* like a fire, devouring you completely. Your gods in Bethel certainly won't be able to quench the flames! ⁷You wicked people! You twist justice, making it a bitter pill for the poor and oppressed. Righteousness and fair play are meaningless fictions to you.

⁸It is the LORD who created the stars, the Pleiades and Orion. It is he who

I DO NOT PRETEND to worship the Lord while deliberately continuing to sin against him. (4:4)

I RETURN to the Lord when he disciplines me. (4:11)

I HEED the Lord's warnings about the judgment awaiting those who continue to sin against him. (5:1)

I BELIEVE the Lord, the Creator, has every right to judge me. (5:8)

4:3 Hebrew *thrown out toward Harmon,* possibly a reference to Mount Hermon.   4:11 Hebrew *as when God destroyed.*   5:6 Hebrew *the house of Joseph.*

turns darkness into morning and day into night. It is he who draws up water from the oceans and pours it down as rain on the land. The LORD is his name! [9]With blinding speed and power he destroys the strong, crushing all their defenses.

[10]How you hate honest judges! How you despise people who tell the truth! [11]You trample the poor and steal what little they have through taxes and unfair rent. Therefore, you will never live in the beautiful stone houses you are building. You will never drink wine from the lush vineyards you are planting. [12]For I know the vast number of your sins and rebellions. You oppress good people by taking bribes and deprive the poor of justice in the courts. [13]So those who are wise will keep quiet, for it is an evil time.

[14]Do what is good and run from evil—that you may live! Then the LORD God Almighty will truly be your helper, just as you have claimed he is. [15]Hate evil and love what is good; remodel your courts into true halls of justice. Perhaps even yet the LORD God Almighty will have mercy on his people who remain.*

> I HATE evil, love good, and pursue justice for all. (5:15)

[16]Therefore, this is what the Lord, the LORD God Almighty, says: "There will be crying in all the public squares and in every street. Call for the farmers to weep with you, and summon professional mourners to wail and lament. [17]There will be wailing in every vineyard, for I will pass through and destroy them all. I, the LORD, have spoken!"

Warning of Coming Judgment

[18]How terrible it will be for you who say, "If only the day of the LORD were here! For then the LORD would rescue us from all our enemies." But you have no idea what you are wishing for. That day will not bring light and prosperity, but darkness and disaster. [19]In that day you will be like a man who runs from a lion—only to meet a bear. After escaping the bear, he leans his hand against a wall in his house—and is bitten by a snake. [20]Yes, the day of the LORD will be a dark and hopeless day, without a ray of joy or hope.

[21]"I hate all your show and pretense—the hypocrisy of your religious festivals and solemn assemblies. [22]I will not accept your burnt offerings and grain offerings. I won't even notice all your choice peace offerings. [23]Away with your hymns of praise! They are only noise to my ears. I will not listen to your music, no matter how lovely it is. [24]Instead, I want to see a mighty flood of justice, a river of righteous living that will never run dry.

> I DO NOT MAKE a hypocritical show of worshiping the Lord. (5:21)
>
> I WORSHIP the Lord by living a life devoted to righteousness and justice. (5:24)

[25]"Was it to me you were bringing sacrifices and offerings during the forty years in the wilderness, Israel? [26]No, your real interest was in your pagan gods—Sakkuth your king god and Kaiwan your star god—the images you yourselves made.* [27]So I will send you into exile, to a land east of Damascus," says the LORD, whose name is God Almighty.

CHAPTER 6

How terrible it will be for you who lounge in luxury and think you are secure in Jerusalem* and Samaria! You are famous and popular in Israel, you to whom the people go for help. [2]Go over to Calneh and see what happened there. Then go to the great city of Hamath and on down to the Philistine city of Gath. You are no better than they were, and look at how they were destroyed. [3]You push away every thought of coming disaster, but your actions only bring the day of judgment closer.

[4]How terrible it will be for you who sprawl on ivory beds surrounded with luxury, eating the meat of tender lambs and choice calves. [5]You sing idle songs to the sound of the harp, and you fancy yourselves to be great musicians, as King David was. [6]You drink wine by the bowlful, and you perfume

> I DO NOT IGNORE the consequences that come from sinning against the Lord. (6:3)
>
> See David's profile (page 629) at Psalm 3:1.

5:15 Hebrew *on the remnant of Joseph.* 5:26 Greek version reads *You took up the shrine of Molech, and the star of your god Rephan, and the images you made for yourselves.* 6:1 Hebrew *Zion.*

yourselves with exotic fragrances, caring nothing at all that your nation* is going to ruin. ⁷Therefore, you will be the first to be led away as captives. Suddenly, all your revelry will end.

I AM NOT FILLED with arrogance and pride. (6:8)

⁸The Sovereign LORD has sworn by his own name, and this is what he, the LORD God Almighty, says: "I despise the pride and false glory of Israel,* and I hate their beautiful homes. I will give this city and everything in it to their enemies."

⁹If there are ten men left in one house, they will all die. ¹⁰And when a close relative—one who is responsible for burning the dead—goes into the house to carry away a dead body, he will ask the last survivor, "Is there anyone else with you?" And the person will answer, "No!" Then he will say, "Hush! Don't even whisper the name of the LORD. He might hear you!"

I ABHOR the poisoning of justice and righteousness. (6:12)

¹¹When the LORD gives the command, homes both great and small will be smashed to pieces. ¹²Can horses gallop over rocks? Can oxen be used to plow rocks? Stupid even to ask—but that's how stupid you are when you turn justice into poison and make bitter the sweet fruit of righteousness. ¹³And just as stupid is this bragging about your conquest of Lo-debar.* You boast, "Didn't we take Karnaim* by our own strength and power?"

¹⁴"O people of Israel, I am about to bring an enemy nation against you," says the LORD God Almighty. "It will oppress you bitterly throughout your land—from Lebo-hamath in the north to the Arabah Valley in the south."

CHAPTER 7

A Vision of Locusts

The Sovereign LORD showed me a vision. I saw him preparing to send a vast swarm of locusts over the land. This was after the king's share had been harvested from the fields and as the main crop was coming up. ²In my vision the locusts ate everything in sight that was green. Then I said, "O Sovereign LORD, please forgive your people! Unless you relent, Israel* will not survive, for we are only a small nation."

I PLEAD with the Lord to show mercy and forgive his people. (7:2)

³So the LORD relented and did not fulfill the vision. "I won't do it," he said.

A Vision of Fire

⁴Then the Sovereign LORD showed me another vision. I saw him preparing to punish his people with a great fire. The fire had burned up the depths of the sea and was devouring the entire land. ⁵Then I said, "O Sovereign LORD, please don't do it. Unless you relent, Israel will not survive, for we are only a small nation."

⁶Then the LORD turned from this plan, too. "I won't do that either," said the Sovereign LORD.

A Vision of a Plumb Line

⁷Then he showed me another vision. I saw the Lord standing beside a wall that had been built using a plumb line. He was checking it with a plumb line to see if it was straight. ⁸And the LORD said to me, "Amos, what do you see?"

I answered, "A plumb line."

I BELIEVE a time comes when the Lord must punish sin—when judgment cannot be postponed any longer. (7:8)

And the Lord replied, "I will test my people with this plumb line. I will no longer ignore all their sins. ⁹The pagan shrines of your ancestors* and the temples of Israel will be destroyed, and I will bring the dynasty of King Jeroboam to a sudden end."

Amos and Amaziah

¹⁰But when Amaziah, the priest of Bethel, heard what Amos was saying, he rushed a message to King Jeroboam: "Amos is hatching a plot against you right here on your very doorstep! What he is saying is intolerable. It will lead

---

6:6 Hebrew *Joseph.*   6:8 Hebrew *Jacob.*   6:13a *Lo-debar* means "nothing."   6:13b *Karnaim* means "horns," a term that symbolizes strength.   7:2 Hebrew *Jacob;* also in 7:5.   7:9 Hebrew *of Isaac.*

to rebellion all across the land. ¹¹He is saying, 'Jeroboam will soon be killed and the people of Israel will be sent away into exile.' "

¹²Then Amaziah sent orders to Amos: "Get out of here, you seer! Go on back to the land of Judah and do your preaching there! ¹³Don't bother us here in Bethel with your prophecies, especially not here where the royal sanctuary is!"

¹⁴But Amos replied, "I'm not one of your professional prophets. I certainly never trained to be one. I'm just a shepherd, and I take care of fig trees. ¹⁵But the LORD called me away from my flock and told me, 'Go and prophesy to my people in Israel.'

¹⁶"Now then, listen to this message from the LORD! You say, 'Don't prophesy against Israel. Stop preaching against my people.*' ¹⁷But this is what the LORD says: Because you have refused to listen, your wife will become a prostitute in this city, and your sons and daughters will be killed. Your land will be divided up, and you yourself will die in a foreign land. And the people of Israel will certainly become captives in exile, far from their homeland."

I DO whatever the Lord commands. (7:15)

CHAPTER 8

A Vision of Ripe Fruit

Then the Sovereign LORD showed me another vision. In it I saw a basket filled with ripe fruit. ²"What do you see, Amos?" he asked.

I replied, "A basket full of ripe fruit."

Then the LORD said, "This fruit represents my people of Israel—ripe for punishment! I will not delay their punishment again. ³In that day the riotous sounds of singing in the Temple will turn to wailing. Dead bodies will be scattered everywhere. They will be carried out of the city in silence. I, the Sovereign LORD, have spoken!"

⁴Listen to this, you who rob the poor and trample the needy! ⁵You can't wait for the Sabbath day to be over and the religious festivals to end so you can get back to cheating the helpless. You measure out your grain in false measures and weigh it out on dishonest scales. ⁶And you mix the wheat you sell with chaff swept from the floor! Then you enslave poor people for a debt of one piece of silver or a pair of sandals.

⁷Now the LORD has sworn this oath by his own name, the Pride of Israel*: "I will never forget the wicked things you have done! ⁸The earth will tremble for your deeds, and everyone will mourn. The land will rise up like the Nile River at floodtime, toss about, and sink again. ⁹At that time," says the Sovereign LORD, "I will make the sun go down at noon and darken the earth while it is still day. ¹⁰I will turn your celebrations into times of mourning, and your songs of joy will be turned to weeping. You will wear funeral clothes and shave your heads as signs of sorrow, as if your only son had died. How very bitter that day will be!

¹¹"The time is surely coming," says the Sovereign LORD, "when I will send a famine on the land—not a famine of bread or water but of hearing the words of the LORD. ¹²People will stagger everywhere from sea to sea, searching for the word of the LORD, running here and going there, but they will not find it. ¹³Beautiful girls and fine young men will grow faint and weary, thirsting for the LORD's word. ¹⁴And those who worship and swear by the idols of Samaria, Dan, and Beersheba will fall down, never to rise again."

I BELIEVE the Lord punished the Israelites at exactly the right time. (8:2)

I ALWAYS CONDUCT my business with utmost integrity. (8:5)

I OBEY God's Word now while I have the opportunity. (8:11)

CHAPTER 9

A Vision of God at the Altar

Then I saw a vision of the Lord standing beside the altar. He said, "Strike the tops of the Temple columns so hard that the foundation will shake. Smash

7:16 Hebrew *against the house of Isaac.* 8:7 Hebrew *the pride of Jacob.*

the columns so the roof will crash down on the people below. Then those who survive will be slaughtered in battle. No one will escape!

2"Even if they dig down to the place of the dead,* I will reach down and pull them up. Even if they climb up into the heavens, I will bring them down. 3Even if they hide at the very top of Mount Carmel, I will search them out and capture them. Even if they hide at the bottom of the ocean, I will send the great sea serpent after them to bite and destroy them. 4Even if they are driven into exile, I will command the sword to kill them there. I am determined to bring disaster upon them and not to help them."

5The Lord, the LORD Almighty, touches the land and it melts, and all its people mourn. The ground rises like the Nile River at floodtime, and then it sinks again. 6The upper stories of the LORD's home are in the heavens, while its foundation is on the earth. He draws up water from the oceans and pours it down as rain on the land. The LORD is his name!

7"Do you Israelites think you are more important to me than the Ethiopians*?" asks the LORD. "I brought you out of Egypt, but have I not done as much for other nations, too? I brought the Philistines from Crete* and led the Arameans out of Kir.

8"I, the Sovereign LORD, am watching this sinful nation of Israel, and I will uproot it and scatter its people across the earth. Yet I have promised that I will never completely destroy the family of Israel,*" says the LORD. 9"For I have commanded that Israel be persecuted by the other nations as grain is sifted in a sieve, yet not one true kernel will be lost. 10But all the sinners will die by the sword—all those who say, 'Nothing bad will happen to us.'

A Promise of Restoration

11"In that day I will restore the fallen kingdom of David. It is now like a house in ruins, but I will rebuild its walls and restore its former glory. 12And Israel will possess what is left of Edom and all the nations I have called to be mine. I, the LORD, have spoken, and I will do these things.

13"The time will come," says the LORD, "when the grain and grapes will grow faster than they can be harvested. Then the terraced vineyards on the hills of Israel will drip with sweet wine! 14I will bring my exiled people of Israel back from distant lands, and they will rebuild their ruined cities and live in them again. They will plant vineyards and gardens; they will eat their crops and drink their wine. 15I will firmly plant them there in the land I have given them," says the LORD your God. "Then they will never be uprooted again."

9:2 Hebrew to Sheol.   9:7a Hebrew the Cushites.   9:7b Hebrew Caphtor.   9:8 Hebrew the house of Jacob.

I KNOW no one can escape the just judgments of the Lord. (9:4)

I BELIEVE the Lord saves all who are true to him. (9:9)

I BELIEVE the Lord will keep his promise to restore the fallen kingdom of David. (9:11)

See David's profile (page 629) at Psalm 3:1.

OBADIAH

THIS FOURTH "MINOR" prophet warns of the Lord's coming judgment of the nation of Edom.

The Edomites were descendants of Esau, the twin brother of Jacob—the father of the twelve tribes of Israel. Despite the close family connection, the Edomites despised the Lord and rejected his chosen people.

Shortly after the fall of Jerusalem, Obadiah receives a brief but stirring message from the Lord that Edom is next in line for destruction (1:1-14, 18). In fact, the Lord plans to judge each of the godless nations (1:15-16). The sins of Edom include acting arrogantly, deserting the southern kingdom of Judah, plundering Judah's wealth, killing those who tried to escape, and handing over survivors to the dreaded Babylonians.

The Lord also promises to regather his exiled people so that they once again occupy the Promised Land (1:17, 19-21).

Other important Scriptures about Edom include Numbers 20:14-22; Psalm 137:7; Isaiah 21:11-12; 34:5-10; Jeremiah 49:7-22; Lamentations 4:21-22; Ezekiel 25:12-14; 35:1-15; Amos 1:6, 9, 11-12; and Malachi 1:2-4.

Famous verse in Obadiah include

- ○ "You are proud because you live in a rock fortress" (1:3)
- ○ "Your enemeies will wipe you out completely!" (1:5)
- ○ "The day is near when I, the LORD, will judge the godless nations!" (1:15)
- ○ "Yes, you nations will drink and stagger and disappear from history" (1:16)
- ○ "But Jerusalem will become a refuge for those who escape" (1:17)
- ○ "And the LORD himself will be king!" (1:21)

This is the vision that the Sovereign LORD revealed to Obadiah concerning the land of Edom.

Edom's Judgment Announced

We have heard a message from the LORD that an ambassador was sent to the nations to say, "Get ready, everyone! Let's assemble our armies and attack Edom!"

²The LORD says, "I will cut you down to size among the nations, Edom; you will be small and despised. ³You are proud because you live in a rock fortress and make your home high in the mountains. 'Who can ever reach us way up here?' you ask boastfully. Don't fool yourselves! ⁴Though you soar as high as eagles and build your nest among the stars, I will bring you crashing down. I, the LORD, have spoken!

⁵"If thieves came at night and robbed you, they would not take everything. Those who harvest grapes always leave a few for the poor. But your enemies will wipe you out completely! ⁶Every nook and cranny of Edom* will be searched and looted. Every treasure will be found and taken.

I DO NOT BOAST about my apparent self-sufficiency. (1:3)

6 Hebrew *Esau*; also in 8b, 9, 18, 19, 21.

I BELIEVE the Lord
accurately foretold
the destruction of
Edom. (1:7)

[7] "All your allies will turn against you. They will help to chase you from your land. They will promise you peace, while plotting your destruction. Your trusted friends will set traps for you, and you won't even know about it. [8] At that time not a single wise person will be left in the whole land of Edom!" says the LORD. "For on the mountains of Edom I will destroy everyone who has wisdom and understanding. [9] The mightiest warriors of Teman will be terrified, and everyone on the mountains of Edom will be cut down in the slaughter.

Reasons for Edom's Punishment

[10] "And why? Because of the violence you did to your close relatives in Israel.* Now you will be destroyed completely and filled with shame forever. [11] For you deserted your relatives in Israel during their time of greatest need. You stood aloof, refusing to lift a finger to help when foreign invaders carried off their wealth and cast lots to divide up Jerusalem. You acted as though you were one of Israel's enemies.

[12] "You shouldn't have done this! You shouldn't have gloated when they exiled your relatives to distant lands. You shouldn't have rejoiced because they were suffering such misfortune. You shouldn't have crowed over them as they suffered these disasters. [13] You shouldn't have plundered the land of Israel when they were suffering such calamity. You shouldn't have gloated over the destruction of your relatives, looting their homes and making your-

I ABHOR any kind of
violence against
refugees. (1:14)

selves rich at their expense. [14] You shouldn't have stood at the crossroads, killing those who tried to escape. You shouldn't have captured the survivors, handing them over to their enemies in that terrible time of trouble.

Edom Destroyed, Israel Restored

I BELIEVE the Lord will
judge the nations for
their evil deeds. (1:15)

[15] "The day is near when I, the LORD, will judge the godless nations! As you have done to Israel, so it will be done to you. All your evil deeds will fall back on your own heads. [16] Just as you swallowed up my people on my holy mountain, so you and the surrounding nations will swallow the punishment I pour out on you. Yes, you nations will drink and stagger and disappear from history, as though you had never even existed.

[17] "But Jerusalem* will become a refuge for those who escape; it will be a holy place. And the people of Israel* will come back to reclaim their inheritance. [18] At that time Israel will be a raging fire, and Edom, a field of dry stubble. The fire will roar across the field, devouring everything and leaving no survivors in Edom. I, the LORD, have spoken!

[19] "Then my people living in the Negev will occupy the mountains of Edom. Those living in the foothills of Judah* will possess the Philistine plains and take over the fields of Ephraim and Samaria. And the people of Benjamin will occupy the land of Gilead. [20] The exiles of Israel will return to their land and occupy the Phoenician coast as far north as Zarephath. The captives from Jerusalem exiled in the north* will return to their homeland

I LOOK FORWARD to
the day when the Lord
himself reigns as king!
(1:21)

and resettle the villages of the Negev. [21] Deliverers will go up to* Mount Zion in Jerusalem to rule over the mountains of Edom. And the LORD himself will be king!"

10 Hebrew *your brother Jacob.* 17a Hebrew *Mount Zion.* 17b Hebrew *house of Jacob;* also in 18. 19 Hebrew *the Shephelah.* 20 Hebrew *in Sepharad.* 21 Or *from.*

JONAH

THIS FIFTH "MINOR" prophet urges readers to remember that God loves all people and doesn't want any to perish.

Interestingly, Jonah is the last person who wants to hear this message. Even so, his book is one of the world's best-known and best-loved Bible stories.

When the Lord calls Jonah to go preach against the wicked Assyrian capital of Nineveh, Jonah fears they might repent and experience God's compassion. So what does Jonah do? Run from God, which proves disastrous (chapter 1).

After Jonah finds himself in the belly of a great fish, he cries out to the Lord for mercy (chapter 2) and then preaches a stirring message of God's pending judgment against Nineveh (3:1-4). Amazingly, the entire city humbles itself before the Lord and repents (3:5-9), and God chooses not to carry out the destruction he had threatened (3:10). So what does Jonah do? He gets angry with God. And Jonah wishes he could just die (chapter 4).

Interestingly, the Lord turns around and uses the Assyrians to bring judgment on the wicked northern kingdom of Israel a few decades later (2 Kings 15:19-17:23). Within several generations, however, the Assyrians become more pagan than ever, and God is compelled to pronounce final judgment on Nineveh (see the book of Nahum).

Famous verses in Jonah include

- "Get up and go to the great city of Ninevah!" (1:2; 3:2)
- "But Jonah got up and went in the opposite direction in order to get away from the LORD" (1:3)
- "Get up and pray to your god! Maybe he will have mercy on us" (1:6)
- "I am a Hebrew, and I worship the LORD, the God of heaven, who made the sea" (1:9)
- "Then they cried out to the LORD, Jonah's God. 'O LORD,' they pleaded, 'don't make us die'" (1:14)
- "The sailors were awestruck by the LORD's great power, and they offered him a sacrifice" (1:16)
- "Now the LORD had arranged for a great fish to swallow Jonah" (1:17)
- "Then Jonah prayed to the LORD his God from inside the fish" (2:1)
- "Then the LORD ordered the fish to spit up Jonah on the beach" (2:10)
- "This time Jonah obeyed the LORD's command and went to Nineveh" (3:3)
- "Forty days from now Nineveh will be destroyed!" (3:4)
- "Perhaps even yet God will have pity on us and hold back his fierce anger" (3:9)
- "When God saw . . . he had mercy on them" (3:10)
- "Didn't I say before I left home that you would do this, LORD? That is why I ran away" (4:2)
- "I knew that you were a gracious and compassionate God, slow to get angry" (4:2)
- Jonah asks to die (4:3, 8)
- "Shouldn't I feel sorry for such a great city?" (4:11)

CHAPTER 1

Jonah Runs from the LORD

The LORD gave this message to Jonah son of Amittai: ²"Get up and go to the great city of Nineveh! Announce my judgment against it because I have seen how wicked its people are."

³But Jonah got up and went in the opposite direction in order to get away from the LORD. He went down to the seacoast, to the port of Joppa, where he found a ship leaving for Tarshish. He bought a ticket and went on board, hoping that by going away to the west he could escape from the LORD.

⁴But as the ship was sailing along, suddenly the LORD flung a powerful wind over the sea, causing a violent storm that threatened to send them to the bottom. ⁵Fearing for their lives, the desperate sailors shouted to their gods for help and threw the cargo overboard to lighten the ship. And all this time Jonah was sound asleep down in the hold. ⁶So the captain went down after him. "How can you sleep at a time like this?" he shouted. "Get up and pray to your god! Maybe he will have mercy on us and spare our lives."

⁷Then the crew cast lots to see which of them had offended the gods and caused the terrible storm. When they did this, Jonah lost the toss. ⁸"What have you done to bring this awful storm down on us?" they demanded. "Who are you? What is your line of work? What country are you from? What is your nationality?"

⁹And Jonah answered, "I am a Hebrew, and I worship the LORD, the God of heaven, who made the sea and the land." ¹⁰Then he told them that he was running away from the LORD.

The sailors were terrified when they heard this. "Oh, why did you do it?" they groaned. ¹¹And since the storm was getting worse all the time, they asked him, "What should we do to you to stop this storm?"

¹²"Throw me into the sea," Jonah said, "and it will become calm again. For I know that this terrible storm is all my fault."

¹³Instead, the sailors tried even harder to row the boat ashore. But the stormy sea was too violent for them, and they couldn't make it. ¹⁴Then they cried out to the LORD, Jonah's God. "O LORD," they pleaded, "don't make us die for this man's sin. And don't hold us responsible for his death, because it isn't our fault. O LORD, you have sent this storm upon him for your own good reasons."

¹⁵Then the sailors picked Jonah up and threw him into the raging sea, and the storm stopped at once! ¹⁶The sailors were awestruck by the LORD's great power, and they offered him a sacrifice and vowed to serve him.

¹⁷Now the LORD had arranged for a great fish to swallow Jonah. And Jonah was inside the fish for three days and three nights.

CHAPTER 2

Jonah's Prayer

Then Jonah prayed to the LORD his God from inside the fish. ²He said, "I cried out to the LORD in my great trouble, and he answered me. I called to you from the world of the dead,* and LORD, you heard me! ³You threw me into the ocean depths, and I sank down to the heart of the sea. I was buried beneath your wild and stormy waves. ⁴Then I said, 'O LORD, you have driven me from your presence. How will I ever again see your holy Temple?'

⁵"I sank beneath the waves, and death was very near. The waters closed in around me, and seaweed wrapped itself around my head. ⁶I sank down to the very roots of the mountains. I was locked out of life and imprisoned in the

---

I DO NOT TRY to run away from the Lord or the responsibilities he has given me. (1:3)

Today what command(s) are you choosing to obey?

I KNOW I cannot run away from the Lord. (1:10)

I ACCEPT the responsibility for my sins so others aren't hurt worse than they already have been. (1:12)

I BELIEVE God hears me when I cry to him in the midst of terrible circumstances. (2:2)

2:2 Hebrew *from Sheol.*

land of the dead. But you, O LORD my God, have snatched me from the yawning jaws of death!

[7]"When I had lost all hope, I turned my thoughts once more to the LORD. And my earnest prayer went out to you in your holy Temple. [8]Those who worship false gods turn their backs on all God's mercies. [9]But I will offer sacrifices to you with songs of praise, and I will fulfill all my vows. For my salvation comes from the LORD alone."

[10]Then the LORD ordered the fish to spit up Jonah on the beach, and it did.

> I TURN my thoughts to the Lord when I've lost all earthly hope of deliverance. (2:7)
>
> I PRAISE the Lord because salvation comes from him alone. (2:9)

CHAPTER 3

Jonah Goes to Nineveh

Then the LORD spoke to Jonah a second time: [2]"Get up and go to the great city of Nineveh, and deliver the message of judgment I have given you."

[3]This time Jonah obeyed the LORD's command and went to Nineveh, a city so large that it took three days to see it all. [4]On the day Jonah entered the city, he shouted to the crowds: "Forty days from now Nineveh will be destroyed!" [5]The people of Nineveh believed God's message, and from the greatest to the least, they decided to go without food and wear sackcloth to show their sorrow.

> I OBEY the Lord when he gives me a second chance. (3:3)

UNLIKE JONAH

I am glad God extends his love to even the most rebellious of people.

Jonah 4:2

Like all the other prophets, Jonah knew God's heart. The only problem was that, as well as he *knew* the heart of the Lord—he didn't share it.

Jonah knew God's heart longed to embrace sinners instead of judging them (2 Peter 3:9). Jonah knew God's mercy firsthand and wanted that mercy kept "right where it belonged" (as he saw it)—blessing the Jewish nation.

After all, why should our enemies—who kill without mercy—receive mercy from the Almighty God? he thought.

Perhaps Jonah's frigid heart seems many degrees colder than our own. If so, we need to imagine forging into the territory of those who hate us—warning them of God's imminent judgment and watching God grant his grace instead. Or we need to remember people torn apart by war—Irish Catholics and Protestants, Arabs and Jews, Hutu and Tutsi, Albanians and Serbs—and realize Christians on both sides are risking their lives to reach others with God's message of salvation.

You and I cannot read the prophets and not know that God hates sin and will judge it with all severity. At the same time, like Jonah, you and I cannot read the same prophets and not know the Lord passionately desires to demonstrate his love and mercy.

Do our hearts reflect the Lord's? Will we, as the Lord commands through Micah (Micah 6:8), *do* justly and *love* mercy?

Unlike Jonah, may we never merely stand behind sandwich boards that proclaim "God Hates Sin." Instead, like the Lord, may we long for sinners to turn from their sins and rejoice when they escape eternal wrath.

○ *Today's Scripture reading is Jonah 1–4.*

---

[6]When the king of Nineveh heard what Jonah was saying, he stepped down from his throne and took off his royal robes. He dressed himself in sackcloth and sat on a heap of ashes. [7]Then the king and his nobles sent this decree throughout the city: "No one, not even the animals, may eat or drink anything at all. [8]Everyone is required to wear sackcloth and pray earnestly to God. Everyone must turn from their evil ways and stop all their violence. [9]Who can tell? Perhaps even yet God will have pity on us and hold back his fierce anger from destroying us."

I BELIEVE God delights to show mercy to those who repent (2 Peter 3:9). (3:10)

I DO NOT BECOME angry when God is merciful to violent, evil people who repent. (4:1)

[10]When God saw that they had put a stop to their evil ways, he had mercy on them and didn't carry out the destruction he had threatened.

CHAPTER 4

Jonah's Anger at the LORD's Mercy

This change of plans upset Jonah, and he became very angry. [2]So he complained to the LORD about it: "Didn't I say before I left home that you would do this, LORD? That is why I ran away to Tarshish! I knew that you were a gracious and compassionate God, slow to get angry and filled with unfailing love. I knew how easily you could cancel your plans for destroying these people. [3]Just kill me now, LORD! I'd rather be dead than alive because nothing I predicted is going to happen."

[4]The LORD replied, "Is it right for you to be angry about this?"

[5]Then Jonah went out to the east side of the city and made a shelter to sit under as he waited to see if anything would happen to the city. [6]And the LORD God arranged for a leafy plant to grow there, and soon it spread its broad leaves over Jonah's head, shading him from the sun. This eased some of his discomfort, and Jonah was very grateful for the plant.

[7]But God also prepared a worm! The next morning at dawn the worm ate through the stem of the plant, so that it soon died and withered away. [8]And as the sun grew hot, God sent a scorching east wind to blow on Jonah. The sun beat down on his head until he grew faint and wished to die. "Death is certainly better than this!" he exclaimed.

[9]Then God said to Jonah, "Is it right for you to be angry because the plant died?"

"Yes," Jonah retorted, "even angry enough to die!"

I BELIEVE the Lord feels sorry for the lost souls of a wicked city. (4:11)

[10]Then the LORD said, "You feel sorry about the plant, though you did nothing to put it there. And a plant is only, at best, short lived. [11]But Nineveh has more than 120,000 people living in spiritual darkness,* not to mention all the animals. Shouldn't I feel sorry for such a great city?"

4:11 Hebrew *people who don't know their right hands from their left.*

MICAH

THIS SIXTH "MINOR" prophet urges readers to pay "Attention!" to the Lord's warnings of impending judgment.

Like his contemporary Isaiah and several other prophets who would come later, Micah repeatedly urges God's people to listen. Why? Because their sins are many and their judgment sure.

Like Isaiah, Micah doesn't hesitate to denounce the godless rulers, corrupt priests, false prophets, and degenerate people who filled the kingdoms of Israel and Judah (chapters 1–3). Like Isaiah, Micah speaks of days far into the future (chapters 4–5). Like Isaiah, Micah pictures the Lord as putting his people on trial (chapter 6). And like Isaiah, Micah contrasts the godlessness of his day with the glorious future ahead (chapter 7).

Famous verses in Micah include

- ○ "Listen!" (1:2; 3:1, 9; 6:1, 2, 9)
- ○ "For my people's wound is far too deep to heal" (1:9)
- ○ "If you would do what is right, you would find my words to be good" (2:7)
- ○ "You are supposed to know right from wrong, but . . ." (3:1-2)
- ○ "I am filled with power and the Spirit of the LORD. I am filled with justice and might" (3:8)
- ○ "In the last days, the Temple of the LORD in Jerusalem will become the most important place on earth" (4:1)
- ○ "Many nations will come and say, 'Come, let us go up to the mountain of the LORD'" (4:2)
- ○ "The LORD will settle international disputes. All the nations will beat their swords into plowshares" (4:3)
- ○ "But you, O Bethlehem Ephrathah, are only a small village in Judah. Yet a ruler of Israel will come from you" (5:2)
- ○ "The LORD has already told you what is good, and this is what he requires" (6:8)
- ○ "Fear the LORD if you are wise!" (6:9)
- ○ "As for me, I look to the LORD for his help. I wait confidently for God to save me" (7:7)
- ○ "All the nations of the world will stand amazed at what the LORD will do for you" (7:16)
- ○ "Where is another God like you, who pardons the sins of the survivors . . . ?" (7:18)
- ○ "You will trample our sins under your feet and throw them into the depths of the ocean!" (7:19)
- ○ "You will show us your faithfulness and unfailing love as you promised" (7:20)

CHAPTER 1

The LORD gave these messages to Micah of Moresheth during the years when Jotham, Ahaz, and Hezekiah were kings of Judah. The messages concerned both Samaria and Jerusalem, and they came to Micah in the form of visions.

Grief over Samaria and Jerusalem

²Attention! Let all the people of the world listen! The Sovereign LORD has made accusations against you; the Lord speaks from his holy Temple.

³Look! The LORD is coming! He leaves his throne in heaven and comes to earth, walking on the high places. ⁴They melt beneath his feet and flow into the valleys like wax in a fire, like water pouring down a hill.

⁵And why is this happening? Because of the sins and rebellion of Israel and Judah.* Who is to blame for Israel's rebellion? Samaria, its capital city! Where is the center of idolatry in Judah? In Jerusalem, its capital!

⁶"So I, the LORD, will make the city of Samaria a heap of rubble. Her streets will be plowed up for planting vineyards. I will roll the stones of her walls down into the valley below, exposing all her foundations. ⁷All her carved images will be smashed to pieces. All her sacred treasures will be burned up. These things were bought with the money earned by her prostitution, and they will now be carried away to pay prostitutes elsewhere."

⁸Because of all this, I will mourn and lament. I will walk around naked and barefoot in sorrow and shame. I will howl like a jackal and wail like an ostrich. ⁹For my people's wound is far too deep to heal. It has reached into Judah, even to the gates of Jerusalem.

¹⁰Don't tell our enemies in the city of Gath*; don't weep at all.* You people in Beth-leaphrah,* roll in the dust to show your anguish and despair. ¹¹You people of Shaphir,* go as captives into exile—naked and ashamed. The people of Zaanan* dare not come outside their walls. The people of Beth-ezel* mourn because the very foundations of their city have been swept away. ¹²The people of Maroth* anxiously wait for relief, but only bitterness awaits them as the LORD's judgment reaches even to the gates of Jerusalem.

¹³Quick! Use your swiftest chariots and flee, you people of Lachish.* You were the first city in Judah to follow Israel in the sin of idol worship, and so you led Jerusalem* into sin. ¹⁴Send a farewell gift to Moresheth-gath; there is no hope of saving it. The town of Aczib* has deceived the kings of Israel, for it promised help it could not give. ¹⁵You people of Mareshah,* I will bring a conqueror to capture your town. And the leaders* of Israel will go to Adullam.

¹⁶Weep, you people of Judah! Shave your heads in sorrow, for the children you love will be snatched away, and you will never see them again. Make yourselves as bald as an eagle, for your little ones will be exiled to distant lands.

CHAPTER 2

Judgment against Wealthy Oppressors

How terrible it will be for you who lie awake at night, thinking up evil plans. You rise at dawn and hurry to carry out any of the wicked schemes you have power to accomplish. ²When you want a certain piece of land, you find a way to seize it. When you want someone's house, you take it by fraud and violence. No one's family or inheritance is safe with you around!

³But this is what the LORD says: "I will reward your evil with evil; you won't be able to escape! After I am through with you, none of you will ever again walk proudly in the streets."

1:5 Hebrew *and Jacob.* 1:10a *Gath* sounds like the Hebrew term for "tell." 1:10b Greek version reads *weep not in Acco.* 1:10c *Beth-leaphrah* means "house of dust." 1:11a *Shaphir* means "pleasant." 1:11b *Zaanan* sounds like the Hebrew term for "come out." 1:11c *Beth-ezel* means "adjoining house." 1:12 *Maroth* sounds like the Hebrew term for "bitter." 1:13a *Lachish* sounds like the Hebrew term for "team of horses." 1:13b Hebrew *the daughter of Zion.* 1:14 *Aczib* means "deception." 1:15a *Mareshah* sounds like the Hebrew term for "conqueror." 1:15b Hebrew *the glory.*

See Hezekiah's profile (page 825) at Isaiah 37:1.

I PAY ATTENTION to God's warnings about sinning against him. (1:2)

I MOURN deeply when God punishes those who refuse to follow him. (1:8)

Start each day reviewing the previous day's affirmations.

I WEEP over the devastating consequences of sin in my extended family. (1:16)

I ABHOR fraud and violence. (2:2)

[4]In that day your enemies will make fun of you by singing this song of despair about your experience:

"We are finished,
  completely ruined!
God has confiscated our land,
  taking it from us.
He has given our fields
  to those who betrayed us.*"

[5]Others will set your boundaries then, and the LORD's people will have no say in how the land is divided.

True and False Prophets

[6]"Don't say such things," the people say. "Don't prophesy like that. Such disasters will never come our way!"

[7]Should you talk that way, O family of Israel*? Will the LORD have patience with such behavior? If you would do what is right, you would find my words to be good. [8]Yet to this very hour my people rise against me! You steal the shirts right off the backs of those who trusted you, making them as ragged as men who have just come home from battle. [9]You have evicted women from their homes and stripped their children of all their God-given rights. [10]Up! Begone! This is no longer your land and home, for you have filled it with sin and ruined it completely.

[11]Suppose a prophet full of lies were to say to you, "I'll preach to you the joys of wine and drink!" That's just the kind of prophet you would like!

Hope for Restoration

[12]"Someday, O Israel, I will gather the few of you who are left. I will bring you together again like sheep in a fold, like a flock in its pasture. Yes, your land will again be filled with noisy crowds! [13]Your leader will break out and lead you out of exile. He will bring you through the gates of your cities of captivity, back to your own land. Your king will lead you; the LORD himself will guide you."

CHAPTER 3

Judgment against Israel's Leaders

Listen, you leaders of Israel! You are supposed to know right from wrong, [2]but you are the very ones who hate good and love evil. You skin my people alive and tear the flesh off their bones. [3]You eat my people's flesh, cut away their skin, and break their bones. You chop them up like meat for the cooking pot. [4]Then you beg the LORD for help in times of trouble! Do you really expect him to listen? After all the evil you have done, he won't even look at you!

[5]This is what the LORD says to you false prophets: "You are leading my people astray! You promise peace for those who give you food, but you declare war on anyone who refuses to pay you. [6]Now the night will close around you, cutting off all your visions. Darkness will cover you, making it impossible for you to predict the future. The sun will set for you prophets, and your day will come to an end. [7]Then you seers will cover your faces in shame, and you diviners will be disgraced. And you will admit that your messages were not from God."

[8]But as for me, I am filled with power and the Spirit of the LORD. I am filled with justice and might, fearlessly pointing out Israel's sin and rebellion. [9]Listen to me, you leaders of Israel! You hate justice and twist all that is right. [10]You are building Jerusalem on a foundation of murder and corruption. [11]You rulers govern for the bribes you can get; you priests teach God's laws only for a price; you prophets won't prophesy unless you are paid. Yet all of

I DO what is right and find God's words to be good. (2:7)

I ENSURE the rights of women and children to have adequate housing, protection, and care. (2:9)

I HATE evil and love what is good. (3:2)

I PROCLAIM God's Word fearlessly in the power of his Spirit. (3:8)

I ABHOR murder and corruption in government. (3:10)

2:4 Or to those who took us captive.　2:7 Hebrew house of Jacob.

you claim you are depending on the LORD. "No harm can come to us," you say, "for the LORD is here among us."

¹²So because of you, Mount Zion will be plowed like an open field; Jerusalem will be reduced to rubble! A great forest will grow on the hilltop, where the Temple now stands.

CHAPTER 4

The LORD's Future Reign

In the last days, the Temple of the LORD in Jerusalem will become the most important place on earth. People from all over the world will go there to worship. ²Many nations will come and say, "Come, let us go up to the mountain of the LORD, to the Temple of the God of Israel.* There he will teach us his ways, so that we may obey him." For in those days the LORD's teaching and his word will go out from Jerusalem.

³The LORD will settle international disputes. All the nations will beat their swords into plowshares and their spears into pruning hooks. All wars will stop, and military training will come to an end. ⁴Everyone will live quietly in their own homes in peace and prosperity, for there will be nothing to fear. The LORD Almighty has promised this! ⁵Even though the nations around us worship idols, we will follow the LORD our God forever and ever.

Israel's Return from Exile

⁶"In that coming day," says the LORD, "I will gather together my people who are lame, who have been exiles, filled with grief. ⁷They are weak and far from home, but I will make them strong again, a mighty nation. Then I, the LORD, will rule from Jerusalem* as their king forever."

⁸As for you, O Jerusalem, the citadel of God's people, your royal might and power will come back to you again. The kingship will be restored to my precious Jerusalem. ⁹But why are you now screaming in terror? Have you no king to lead you? He is dead! Have you no wise people to counsel you? All are gone! Pain has gripped you like it does a woman in labor. ¹⁰Writhe and groan in terrible pain, you people of Jerusalem,* for you must leave this city to live in the open fields. You will soon be sent into exile in distant Babylon. But the LORD will rescue you there; he will redeem you from the grip of your enemies.

¹¹True, many nations have gathered together against you, calling for your blood, eager to gloat over your destruction. ¹²But they do not know the LORD's thoughts or understand his plan. These nations don't know that he is gathering them together to be beaten and trampled like bundles of grain on a threshing floor.

¹³"Rise up and destroy the nations, O Jerusalem!"* says the LORD. "For I will give you iron horns and bronze hooves, so you can trample many nations to pieces. Then you will give all the wealth they acquired as offerings to me, the Lord of all the earth."

CHAPTER 5

A Ruler from Bethlehem

Mobilize! Marshal your troops! The enemy is laying siege to Jerusalem. With a rod they will strike the leader of Israel in the face.

²But you, O Bethlehem Ephrathah, are only a small village in Judah. Yet a ruler of Israel will come from you, one whose origins are from the distant past. ³The people of Israel will be abandoned to their enemies until the time when the woman in labor gives birth to her son. Then at last his fellow countrymen will return from exile to their own land. ⁴And he will stand to lead his flock with the LORD's strength, in the majesty of the name of the LORD his God.

I BELIEVE the Lord's promise that in the last days people from all over the world will come to worship and learn about the Lord in Jerusalem. (4:1)

I BELIEVE the Lord's promise to one day bring international and domestic peace to everyone. (4:4)

I BELIEVE the Lord accurately foretold that the Messiah, Jesus Christ, would be born in Bethlehem (Matthew 2:4-6). (5:2)

4:2 Hebrew *of Jacob.*   4:7 Hebrew *Mount Zion.*   4:10 Hebrew *O daughter of Zion.*   4:13 Hebrew *"Rise up and thresh, O daughter of Zion."*

Then his people will live there undisturbed, for he will be highly honored all around the world. ⁵And he will be the source of our peace.

When the Assyrians invade our land and break through our defenses, we will appoint seven rulers to watch over us, eight princes to lead us. ⁶They will rule Assyria with drawn swords and enter the gates of the land of Nimrod. They* will rescue us from the Assyrians when they pour over the borders to invade our land.

The Remnant Purified

⁷Then the few left in Israel* will go out among the nations. They will be like dew sent by the LORD or like rain falling on the grass, which no one can hold back. ⁸The remnant of Israel will go out among the nations and be as strong as a lion. And the other nations will be like helpless sheep, with no one to rescue them. ⁹The people of Israel will stand up to their foes, and all their enemies will be wiped out.

¹⁰"At that same time," says the LORD, "I will destroy all your weapons—your horses and chariots. ¹¹I will tear down your walls and demolish the defenses of your cities. ¹²I will put an end to all witchcraft; there will be no more fortune-tellers to consult. ¹³I will destroy all your idols and sacred pillars, so you will never again worship the work of your own hands. ¹⁴I will abolish your pagan shrines with their Asherah poles and destroy the cities where your idol temples stand. ¹⁵I will pour out my vengeance on all the nations that refuse to obey me."

CHAPTER 6

The LORD's Case against Israel

Listen to what the LORD is saying: "Stand up and state your case against me. Let the mountains and hills be called to witness your complaints.

²"And now, O mountains, listen to the LORD's complaint! He has a case against his people Israel! He will prosecute them to the full extent of the law. ³O my people, what have I done to make you turn from me? Tell me why your patience is exhausted! Answer me! ⁴For I brought you out of Egypt and redeemed you from your slavery. I sent Moses, Aaron, and Miriam to help you.

⁵"Don't you remember, my people, how King Balak of Moab tried to have you cursed and how Balaam son of Beor blessed you instead? And remember your journey from Acacia* to Gilgal, when I, the LORD, did everything I could to teach you about my faithfulness."

⁶What can we bring to the LORD to make up for what we've done? Should we bow before God with offerings of yearling calves? ⁷Should we offer him thousands of rams and tens of thousands of rivers of olive oil? Would that please the LORD? Should we sacrifice our firstborn children to pay for the sins of our souls? Would that make him glad?

⁸No, O people, the LORD has already told you what is good, and this is what he requires: to do what is right, to love mercy, and to walk humbly with your God.

Israel's Guilt and Punishment

⁹Listen! Fear the LORD if you are wise! His voice is calling out to everyone in Jerusalem: "The armies of destruction are coming; the LORD is sending them.* ¹⁰Will there be no end of your getting rich by cheating? The homes of the wicked are filled with treasures gained by dishonestly measuring out grain in short measures.* ¹¹And how can I tolerate all your merchants who use dishonest scales and weights? ¹²The rich among you have become wealthy through extortion and violence. Your citizens are so used to lying that their tongues can no longer tell the truth.

¹³"Therefore, I will wound you! I will bring you to ruin for all your sins. ¹⁴You will eat but never have enough. Your hunger pangs and emptiness will still remain. And though you try to save your money, it will come to nothing in the end. You will save a little, but I will give it to those who conquer you. ¹⁵You will plant crops but not harvest them. You will press your olives but not get

I BELIEVE the Lord's promise that Jesus will be highly honored all around the world (Philippians 2:9-11). (5:4)

I ABHOR all witchcraft and idolatry. (5:12)

See the profiles for Moses (page 73), Aaron (page 107), and Miriam (page 87) at Exodus 5:1, Exodus 32:2, and Exodus 15:20.

I BELIEVE the Lord did everything he could to try to teach his people about his faithfulness. (6:5)

I KNOW nothing I might sacrifice can pay for my sins. (6:6)

I LOVE mercy, do justly, and walk humbly with God because that is what he requires. (6:8)

I KNOW the consequences of ignoring God and hurting others are severe. (6:13)

5:6 Hebrew He.   5:7 Hebrew Jacob; also in 5:8.   6:5 Hebrew Shittim.   6:9 Hebrew "Listen to the rod. Who appointed it?"   6:10 Hebrew by using the short ephah; the ephah was a unit for measuring grain.

enough oil to anoint yourselves. You will trample the grapes but get no juice to make your wine.

See Ahab's profile (page 417) at 1 Kings 16:31.

[16] "The only laws you keep are those of evil King Omri; the only example you follow is that of wicked King Ahab! Therefore, I will make an example of you, bringing you to complete ruin. You will be treated with contempt, mocked by all who see you."

CHAPTER 7

Misery Turned to Hope

I LONG for the refreshing fellowship of godly people. (7:1)

I ABHOR bribery and perverted justice. (7:3)

What misery is mine! I feel like the fruit picker after the harvest who can find nothing to eat. Not a cluster of grapes or a single fig can be found to satisfy my hunger. [2]The godly people have all disappeared; not one fair-minded person is left on the earth. They are all murderers, even setting traps for their own brothers. [3]They go about their evil deeds with both hands. How skilled they are at using them! Officials and judges alike demand bribes. The people with money and influence pay them off, and together they scheme to twist justice. [4]Even the best of them is like a brier; the straightest is more crooked than a hedge of thorns. But your judgment day is coming swiftly now. Your time of punishment is here.

[5]Don't trust anyone—not your best friend or even your wife! [6]For the son despises his father. The daughter defies her mother. The daughter-in-law defies her mother-in-law. Your enemies will be right in your own household.

I AM CONFIDENT that the Lord will be with me, even if I fall. (7:8)

[7]As for me, I look to the LORD for his help. I wait confidently for God to save me, and my God will certainly hear me. [8]Do not gloat over me, my enemies! For though I fall, I will rise again. Though I sit in darkness, the LORD himself will be my light. [9]I will be patient as the LORD punishes me, for I have sinned against him. But after that, he will take up my case and punish my enemies for all the evil they have done to me. The LORD will bring me out of my darkness into the light, and I will see his righteousness. [10]Then my enemies will see that the LORD is on my side. They will be ashamed that they taunted me, saying, "Where is the LORD—that God of yours?" With my own eyes I will see them trampled down like mud in the streets.

[11]In that day, Israel, your cities will be rebuilt, and your borders will be extended. [12]People from many lands will come and honor you—from Assyria all the way to the towns of Egypt, and from Egypt all the way to the Euphrates River,* and from many distant seas and mountains. [13]But the land* will become empty and desolate because of the wickedness of those who live there.

The LORD's Compassion on Israel

[14]O LORD, come and rule your people; lead your flock in green pastures. Help them to live in peace and prosperity. Let them enjoy the fertile pastures of Bashan and Gilead as they did long ago.

[15]"Yes," says the LORD, "I will do mighty miracles for you, like those I did when I rescued you from slavery in Egypt."

[16]All the nations of the world will stand amazed at what the LORD will do for you. They will be embarrassed that their power is so insignificant. They will stand in silent awe, deaf to everything around them. [17]They will come to realize what lowly creatures they really are. Like snakes crawling from their holes, they will come out to meet the LORD our God. They will fear him greatly, trembling in terror at his presence.

I AM THANKFUL for the Lord's compassion and forgiveness. (7:19)

See the profiles for Abraham (page 19) and Jacob (page 43) at Genesis 15:6 and Genesis 32:9.

[18]Where is another God like you, who pardons the sins of the survivors among his people? You cannot stay angry with your people forever, because you delight in showing mercy. [19]Once again you will have compassion on us. You will trample our sins under your feet and throw them into the depths of the ocean! [20]You will show us your faithfulness and unfailing love as you promised with an oath to our ancestors Abraham and Jacob long ago.

7:12 Hebrew *the river.* · 7:13 Or *earth.*

NAHUM

THIS SEVENTH "MINOR" prophet warns of the Lord's coming judgment of the city of Nineveh, the capital of Assyria.

Even though the entire population of Nineveh had repented of their sins and worshiped the Lord a century earlier (see the book of Jonah), subsequent generations reject what they know to be true and grow increasingly rebellious, murderous, and vile. As a result, God calls the prophet Nahum to pronounce final judgment on the city.

The sins of Nineveh include acting arrogantly because of its vast power and wealth, plotting against the Lord God, brutally slaying people without cause, crushing the northern kingdom of Israel, plotting against the southern kingdom of Judah, and actively promoting the worship of horrid idols.

In this book, Nahum describes the greatness of the Lord (1:1-7), the fierceness of his anger against the sworn enemy of his people (1:8-15), and the impending total destruction of Nineveh (2:1–3:19). The Babylonians so obliterated the city that its location was hidden for twenty-four centuries.

Famous verses in Nahum include

- ○ "The LORD is slow to get angry, but his power is great, . . ." (1:3)
- ○ "The LORD is good. . . . He is a strong refuge. And he knows everyone who trusts in him" (1:7)
- ○ "Why are you scheming against the LORD? He will destroy you with one blow" (1:9)
- ○ "Look! A messenger is coming . . . with good news! He is bringing a message of peace" (1:15)
- ○ "Nineveh's exile has been decreed" (2:7)
- ○ "Where now is that great Nineveh, lion of the nations . . . ?" (2:11)
- ○ "How terrible it will be for Nineveh, the city of murder and lies!" (3:1)
- ○ "Yet no one anywhere will regret your destruction" (3:7)

CHAPTER 1

This message concerning Nineveh came as a vision to Nahum, who lived in Elkosh.

The LORD's Anger against Nineveh

²The LORD is a jealous God, filled with vengeance and wrath. He takes revenge on all who oppose him and furiously destroys his enemies! ³The LORD is slow to get angry, but his power is great, and he never lets the guilty go unpunished. He displays his power in the whirlwind and the storm. The billowing clouds are the dust beneath his feet. ⁴At his command the oceans and rivers dry up, the lush pastures of Bashan and Carmel fade, and the green forests of Lebanon wilt. ⁵In his presence the mountains quake, and the hills melt away; the earth trembles, and its people are destroyed. ⁶Who can stand before his fierce anger? Who can survive his burning fury? His rage blazes forth like fire, and the mountains crumble to dust in his presence.

I BELIEVE the Lord is slow to get angry but at the right time will punish the guilty with great power (2 Peter 3:9-10). (1:3)

I BELIEVE the Lord is good—a refuge to all those who trust in him. (1:7)

I BELIEVE the Lord accurately foretold the destruction of Nineveh. (1:14)

I BELIEVE the Lord's promise to restore Israel. (2:2)

I REALIZE the Lord's judgment against the wicked must be fearful and awesome. (2:10)

I ABHOR murder and falsehood. (3:1)

[7] The LORD is good. When trouble comes, he is a strong refuge. And he knows everyone who trusts in him. [8] But he sweeps away his enemies in an overwhelming flood. He pursues his foes into the darkness of night.

[9] Why are you scheming against the LORD? He will destroy you with one blow; he won't need to strike twice! [10] His enemies, tangled up like thorns, staggering like drunks, will be burned like dry straw in a field. [11] Who is this king of yours who dares to plot evil against the LORD?

[12] This is what the LORD says: "Even though the Assyrians have many allies, they will be destroyed and disappear. O my people, I have already punished you once, and I will not do it again. [13] Now I will break your chains and release you from Assyrian oppression."

[14] And this is what the LORD says concerning the Assyrians in Nineveh: "You will have no more children to carry on your name. I will destroy all the idols in the temples of your gods. I am preparing a grave for you because you are despicable and don't deserve to live!"

[15] Look! A messenger is coming over the mountains with good news! He is bringing a message of peace. Celebrate your festivals, O people of Judah, and fulfill all your vows, for your enemies from Nineveh will never invade your land again. They have been completely destroyed!

CHAPTER 2

The Fall of Nineveh

Nineveh, you are already surrounded by enemy armies! Sound the alarm! Man the ramparts! Muster your defenses, and keep a sharp watch for the enemy attack to begin! [2] For the land of Israel lies empty and broken after your attacks, but the LORD will restore its honor and power again.

[3] Shields flash red in the sunlight! The attack begins! See their scarlet uniforms! Watch as their glittering chariots move into position, with a forest of spears waving above them. [4] The chariots race recklessly along the streets and through the squares, swift as lightning, flickering like torches. [5] The king shouts to his officers; they stumble in their haste, rushing to the walls to set up their defenses. [6] But too late! The river gates are open! The enemy has entered! The palace is about to collapse!

[7] Nineveh's exile has been decreed, and all the servant girls mourn its capture. Listen to them moan like doves; watch them beat their breasts in sorrow. [8] Nineveh is like a leaking water reservoir! The people are slipping away. "Stop, stop!" someone shouts, but the people just keep on running.

[9] Loot the silver! Plunder the gold! There seems no end to Nineveh's many treasures—its vast, uncounted wealth. [10] Soon the city is an empty shambles, stripped of its wealth. Hearts melt in horror, and knees shake. The people stand aghast, their faces pale and trembling.

[11] Where now is that great Nineveh, lion of the nations, full of fight and boldness, where the old and feeble and the young and tender lived with nothing to fear? [12] O Nineveh, you were once a mighty lion! You crushed your enemies to feed your cubs and your mate. You filled your city and your homes with captives and plunder.

[13] "I am your enemy!" says the LORD Almighty. "Your chariots will soon go up in smoke. The finest of your youth will be killed in battle. Never again will you bring back plunder from conquered nations. Never again will the voices of your proud messengers be heard."

CHAPTER 3

The LORD's Judgment against Nineveh

How terrible it will be for Nineveh, the city of murder and lies! She is crammed with wealth to be plundered. [2] Listen! Hear the crack of the whips as the chariots rush forward against her. Wheels rumble, horses' hooves pound, and chariots clatter as they bump wildly through the streets. ³See the flashing swords and glittering spears in the upraised arms of the cavalry! The dead are lying in the streets—dead bodies, heaps of bodies, everywhere. People stumble over them, scramble to their feet, and fall again. ⁴All this because Nineveh, the beautiful and faithless city, mistress of deadly charms, enticed the nations with her beauty. She taught them all to worship her false gods, enchanting people everywhere.

⁵"No wonder I am your enemy!" declares the LORD Almighty. "And now I will lift your skirts so all the earth will see your nakedness and shame. ⁶I will cover you with filth and show the world how vile you really are. ⁷All who see you will shrink back in horror and say, 'Nineveh lies in utter ruin.' Yet no one anywhere will regret your destruction."

⁸Are you any better than Thebes,* surrounded by rivers, protected by water on all sides? ⁹Ethiopia* and the land of Egypt were the source of her strength, which seemed without limit. The nations of Put and Libya also helped and supported her. ¹⁰Yet Thebes fell, and her people were led away as captives. Her babies were dashed to death against the stones of the streets. Soldiers cast lots to see who would get the Egyptian officers as servants. All their leaders were bound in chains.

¹¹And you, Nineveh, will also stagger like a drunkard. You will hide for fear of the attacking enemy. ¹²All your fortresses will fall. They will be devoured like the ripe figs that fall into the mouths of those who shake the trees. ¹³Your troops will be as weak and helpless as women. The gates of your land will be opened wide to the enemy and set on fire and burned.

¹⁴Get ready for the siege! Store up water! Strengthen the defenses! Make bricks to repair the walls! Go into the pits to trample clay, and pack it into molds! ¹⁵But in the middle of your preparations, the fire will devour you; the sword will cut you down. The enemy will consume you like locusts, devouring everything they see. There will be no escape, even if you multiply like grasshoppers. ¹⁶Merchants, as numerous as the stars, have filled your city with vast wealth. But like a swarm of locusts, they strip the land and then fly away. ¹⁷Your princes and officials are also like locusts, crowding together in the hedges to survive the cold. But like locusts that fly away when the sun comes up to warm the earth, all of them will fly away and disappear.

¹⁸O Assyrian king, your princes lie dead in the dust. Your people are scattered across the mountains. There is no longer a shepherd to gather them together. ¹⁹There is no healing for your wound; your injury is fatal. All who hear of your destruction will clap their hands for joy. Where can anyone be found who has not suffered from your cruelty?

3:8 Hebrew *No-amon;* also in 3:10.   3:9 Hebrew *Cush.*

I AM HORRIFIED by the destructive power of the Lord's judgments but do not doubt his justice. (3:7)

I BELIEVE the Lord's judgment on Nineveh was a final and just reward for their wickedness and cruelty. (3:19)

HABAKKUK

THIS EIGHTH "MINOR" prophet urges readers to continue trusting the Lord when evil overruns the world.

This book features a unique dialogue between the Lord and the best-known "doubting Thomas" of the Old Testament.

"O Lord," Habakkuk asks, how long will you allow the southern kingdom of Judah to perpetrate wickedness before you judge it? (1:1-4).

"Look," the Lord replies, I'm already raising up the Babylonians to carry off the people of Judah into exile (1:5-11).

This answer astonishes the prophet.

"O Lord," Habakkuk asks, how could you plan to use such a vile and pagan nation to judge Judah? (1:12-2:1).

"Look," the Lord replies, I'll take care of judging the Babylonians later. Don't stop placing your faith in me (2:2-20).

As an expression of faith, Habakkuk concludes his book with a beautiful song of praise to the Lord (3:1-19).

The most famous phrase in Habakkuk—"The righteous will live by their faith"—is quoted three times by New Testament writers in Romans 1:17, Galatians 3:11, and Hebrews 10:38.

Other famous verses in Habakkuk include

- ○ "How long, O LORD, must I call for help? . . . I cry, but you do not come to save" (1:2)
- ○ "The LORD replied, 'Look at the nations and be amazed! Watch and be astounded'" (1:5)
- ○ "O LORD my God, my Holy One, you who are eternal—is your plan in all of this to wipe us out?" (1:12)
- ○ "I will climb up into my watchtower now and wait to see what the LORD will say to me" (2:1)
- ○ "Then the LORD said to me, 'Write my answer in large, clear letters'" (2:2)
- ○ "Look at the proud! They trust in themselves" (2:4)
- ○ "For the time will come when all the earth will be filled . . . with an awareness of the glory of the LORD" (2:14; see 3:3)
- ○ "But the LORD is in his holy Temple. Let all the earth be silent before him" (2:20)
- ○ "In your anger, remember your mercy" (3:2)
- ○ "Even though the fig trees have no blossoms, . . . yet I will rejoice in the LORD!" (3:17-18)
- ○ "The Sovereign LORD is my strength! He will make me as surefooted as a deer" (3:19)

CHAPTER 1

This is the message that the prophet Habakkuk received from the LORD in a vision.

Habakkuk's Complaint

²How long, O LORD, must I call for help? But you do not listen! "Violence!" I cry, but you do not come to save. ³Must I forever see this sin and misery all around me? Wherever I look, I see destruction and violence. I am surrounded by people who love to argue and fight. ⁴The law has become paralyzed and useless, and there is no justice given in the courts. The wicked far outnumber the righteous, and justice is perverted with bribes and trickery.

The LORD's Reply

⁵ The LORD replied, "Look at the nations and be amazed! Watch and be astounded at what I will do! For I am doing something in your own day, something you wouldn't believe even if someone told you about it. ⁶I am raising up the Babylonians* to be a new power on the world scene. They are a cruel and violent nation who will march across the world and conquer it. ⁷They are notorious for their cruelty. They do as they like, and no one can stop them. ⁸Their horses are swifter than leopards. They are a fierce people, more fierce than wolves at dusk. Their horsemen race forward from distant places. Like eagles they swoop down to pounce on their prey.

⁹"On they come, all of them bent on violence. Their hordes advance like a wind from the desert, sweeping captives ahead of them like sand. ¹⁰They scoff at kings and princes and scorn all their defenses. They simply pile ramps of earth against their walls and capture them! ¹¹They sweep past like the wind and are gone. But they are deeply guilty, for their own strength is their god."

Habakkuk's Second Complaint

¹²O LORD my God, my Holy One, you who are eternal—is your plan in all of this to wipe us out? Surely not! O LORD our Rock, you have decreed the rise of these Babylonians to punish and correct us for our terrible sins. ¹³You are perfectly just in this. But will you, who cannot allow sin in any form, stand idly by while they swallow us up? Should you be silent while the wicked destroy people who are more righteous than they?

¹⁴Are we but fish to be caught and killed? Are we but creeping things that have no leader to defend them from their enemies? ¹⁵Must we be strung up on their hooks and dragged out in their nets while they rejoice? ¹⁶Then they will worship their nets and burn incense in front of them. "These nets are the gods who have made us rich!" they will claim.

¹⁷Will you let them get away with this forever? Will they succeed forever in their heartless conquests?

CHAPTER 2

I will climb up into my watchtower now and wait to see what the LORD will say to me and how he will answer my complaint.

The LORD's Second Reply

²Then the LORD said to me, "Write my answer in large, clear letters on a tablet, so that a runner can read it and tell everyone else. ³But these things I plan won't happen right away. Slowly, steadily, surely, the time approaches when the vision will be fulfilled. If it seems slow, wait patiently, for it will surely take place. It will not be delayed.

⁴"Look at the proud! They trust in themselves, and their lives are crooked;* but the righteous will live by their faith.* ⁵Wealth* is treacherous, and the arrogant are never at rest. They range far and wide, with their mouths opened as

---

I CRY OUT to the Lord for answers when I feel overwhelmed by the violence and injustice I see around me. (1:3)

I BELIEVE the Lord is working in the affairs of the nations. (1:5)

I BELIEVE the Lord accurately predicted the coming of the Babylonians to punish the kingdom of Judah. (1:6)

I BELIEVE the Lord has every right to punish sin. (1:12)

Keep a prayer journal. This is where life changes often begin!

I WAIT patiently for the Lord's promises and purposes to be fulfilled. (2:3)

I LIVE by faith while I wait for the Lord. (2:4)

1:6 Or *Chaldeans.*   2:4a Greek version reads *I will have no pleasure in anyone who turns away.*   2:4b Or *the just will live by their faithfulness.*   2:5a As in Dead Sea Scroll 1QpHab; other Hebrew manuscripts read *Wine.*

wide as death,* but they are never satisfied. In their greed they have gathered up many nations and peoples. ⁶But the time is coming when all their captives will taunt them, saying, 'You thieves! At last justice has caught up with you! Now you will get what you deserve for your oppression and extortion!' ⁷Suddenly, your debtors will rise up in anger. They will turn on you and take all you have, while you stand trembling and helpless. ⁸You have plundered many nations; now they will plunder you. You murderers! You have filled the countryside with violence and all the cities, too.

⁹"How terrible it will be for you who get rich by unjust means! You believe your wealth will buy security, putting your families beyond the reach of danger. ¹⁰But by the murders you committed, you have shamed your name and forfeited your lives. ¹¹The very stones in the walls of your houses cry out against you, and the beams in the ceilings echo the complaint.

¹²"How terrible it will be for you who build cities with money gained by murder and corruption! ¹³Has not the LORD Almighty promised that the wealth of nations will turn to ashes? They work so hard, but all in vain! ¹⁴For the time will come when all the earth will be filled, as the waters fill the sea, with an awareness of the glory of the LORD.

I BELIEVE the wealth of the nations will one day turn to ashes. (2:13)

I LOOK forward to the day when the whole earth will be aware of the Lord's glory. (2:14)

LIKE HABAKKUK   *I live by faith, not by sight.*
Habakkuk 2:4

The morning news blares out another daily dose of reality—students killing classmates, government officials committing crimes, celebrities divorcing, wars erupting over race and religion. How should we respond?

Habakkuk heard the news on the streets of Jerusalem and asked a classic question: "How much longer, Lord?"

Surprisingly, Habakkuk was even more troubled by God's answer: Soon the violence and corruption of Judah would be punished by the fierce Babylonians.

Habakkuk was shocked: "Not them, Lord! How could you? They deserve worse judgment than we do!"

God's next reply came like the sun breaking over the horizon. The light of God's truth cleared Habakkuk's troubled vision. Past his current darkness Habakkuk saw the glorious Lord of life and light. He remembered God's power to save his people in the past. He believed God would again show mercy. As a result, the peace of faith replaced the panic of fear.

Habakkuk teaches us that the righteous live by faith in the one who alone can answer our toughest questions, no matter how difficult or unclear our circumstances may seem.

You and I may weep in frustration when life is hard and unfair—the business fails, the tumor is malignant, the child doesn't come home, the wrong side wins. Living by faith means seeing, through our tears, beyond the bleak picture on the screen to the certainty that God's promises will come true.

Like Habakkuk, we can know the vivid reality that the Sovereign Lord of glory will surely triumph. That is the real news—worth celebrating!

○ *Today's Scripture reading is Habakkuk 1–3.*

¹⁵"How terrible it will be for you who make your neighbors drunk! You force your cup on them so that you can gloat over their nakedness and shame. ¹⁶But soon it will be your turn! Come, drink and be exposed! Drink from the cup of the LORD's judgment, and all your glory will be turned to shame. ¹⁷You cut down the forests of Lebanon. Now you will be cut down! You terrified the wild animals you caught in your traps. Now terror will strike you because of your murder and violence in cities everywhere!

¹⁸"What have you gained by worshiping all your man-made idols? How foolish to trust in something made by your own hands! What fools you are to believe such lies! ¹⁹How terrible it will be for you who beg lifeless wooden

2:5b Hebrew *as Sheol.*

idols to save you. You ask speechless stone images to tell you what to do. Can an idol speak for God? They may be overlaid with gold and silver, but they are lifeless inside. ²⁰But the LORD is in his holy Temple. Let all the earth be silent before him. "

CHAPTER 3

Habakkuk's Prayer
This prayer was sung by the prophet Habakkuk:*

²I have heard all about you, LORD, and I am filled with awe by the amazing things you have done. In this time of our deep need, begin again to help us, as you did in years gone by. Show us your power to save us. And in your anger, remember your mercy.

³I see God, the Holy One, moving across the deserts from Edom* and Mount Paran.* His brilliant splendor fills the heavens, and the earth is filled with his praise! What a wonderful God he is! ⁴Rays of brilliant light flash from his hands. He rejoices in his awesome power.* ⁵Pestilence marches before him; plague follows close behind. ⁶When he stops, the earth shakes. When he looks, the nations tremble. He shatters the everlasting mountains and levels the eternal hills. But his power is not diminished in the least! ⁷I see the peoples of Cushan and Midian trembling in terror.

⁸Was it in anger, LORD, that you struck the rivers and parted the sea? Were you displeased with them? No, you were sending your chariots of salvation! ⁹You were commanding your weapons of power! You split open the earth with flowing rivers! ¹⁰The mountains watched and trembled. Onward swept the raging waters. The mighty deep cried out, lifting its hands to the LORD. ¹¹The lofty sun and moon began to fade, obscured by brilliance from your arrows and the flashing of your glittering spear.

¹²You marched across the land in awesome anger and trampled the nations in your fury. ¹³You went out to rescue your chosen people, to save your anointed ones. You crushed the heads of the wicked and laid bare their bones from head to toe. ¹⁴With their own weapons, you destroyed those who rushed out like a whirlwind, thinking Israel would be easy prey. ¹⁵You trampled the sea with your horses, and the mighty waters piled high.

¹⁶I trembled inside when I heard all this; my lips quivered with fear. My legs gave way beneath me,* and I shook in terror. I will wait quietly for the coming day when disaster will strike the people who invade us. ¹⁷Even though the fig trees have no blossoms, and there are no grapes on the vine; even though the olive crop fails, and the fields lie empty and barren; even though the flocks die in the fields, and the cattle barns are empty, ¹⁸yet I will rejoice in the LORD! I will be joyful in the God of my salvation! ¹⁹The Sovereign LORD is my strength! He will make me as surefooted as a deer* and bring me safely over the mountains.

(For the choir director: This prayer is to be accompanied by stringed instruments.)

I AM FILLED with awe because of all the amazing things the Lord has done. (3:2)

I BELIEVE the Lord's power is never diminished in the least. (3:6)

I TREMBLE over the awful consequences that come from sinning against the Lord. (3:16)

I RECEIVE my strength from the Sovereign Lord. (3:19)

3:1 Hebrew adds *according to shigionoth,* probably indicating the musical setting for the prayer. 3:3a Hebrew *Teman.* 3:3b Hebrew adds *selah;* also in 3:9, 13. The meaning of this Hebrew term is uncertain; it is probably a musical or literary term. 3:4 Or *He veils his awesome power.* 3:16 Hebrew *Decay entered my bones.* 3:19 Or *will give me the speed of a deer.*

ZEPHANIAH

THIS NINTH "MINOR" prophet urges readers to repent for "the day of the LORD" is on its way.

As in the book of Joel, "the day of the LORD" appears repeatedly in Zephaniah. The phrase speaks of the Lord's terrifying judgments at various points in time.

During King Josiah's reign, Zephaniah warns of God's coming judgment against the southern kingdom of Judah (1:1-18; 3:1-7), urges the people to repent (2:1-3), and speaks of God's future blessings on the kingdom (3:10-20).

The sins of Judah include prolific wickedness, rampant idolatry, astrology, child sacrifice, anarchy, shamelessness, pride, and complete indifference to the things of the Lord. Zephaniah also predicts God's coming judgment against other nations (2:4-15; 3:8) and speaks of God's future blessings on those nations (3:9).

The sins of Philistia, Moab, Ammon, Ethiopia, and Assyria include mocking the things of God, attacking the people of God, rampant idolatry, and pride.

Zephaniah's prophecies address events near at hand and far into the future.

Famous verses in Zephaniah include

- "Stand in silence . . . for the awesome day of the LORD's judgment has come" (1:7)
- "I will search . . . and punish those who sit contented in their sins, indifferent to the LORD" (1:12)
- "That terrible day of the LORD is near. Swiftly it comes" (1:14)
- "Gather together and pray, you shameless nation. Gather while there is still time" (2:1-2)
- "Beg the LORD to save you. . . . Walk humbly and do what is right" (2:3)
- "For the LORD their God will visit his people in kindness and restore their prosperity again" (2:7)
- Moab and Ammon "will receive the wages of their pride" (2:10)
- "Then people from nations around the world will worship the LORD" (2:11)
- "But the LORD is still there in the city, and he does no wrong. Day by day his justice is more evident" (3:5)
- "On that day I will purify the lips of all people, so that everyone will be able to worship the LORD together" (3:9)
- "The lowly and the humble . . . trust in the name of the LORD" (3:12)
- Everyone will sing for joy when the Lord restores the fortunes of his people (3:14-20)

CHAPTER 1

The LORD gave these messages to Zephaniah when Josiah son of Amon was king of Judah. Zephaniah was the son of Cushi, son of Gedaliah, son of Amariah, son of Hezekiah.

Coming Judgment against Judah

²"I will sweep away everything in all your land," says the LORD. ³"I will sweep away both people and animals alike. Even the birds of the air and the fish in

See the profiles for Hezekiah (page 825) and Josiah (page 461) at Isaiah 37:1 and 2 Kings 23:25.

I BELIEVE the Lord has predicted the great day of his judgment on the earth. (1:3)

the sea will die. I will reduce the wicked to heaps of rubble,* along with the rest of humanity," says the LORD. [4]"I will crush Judah and Jerusalem with my fist and destroy every last trace of their Baal worship. I will put an end to all the idolatrous priests, so that even the memory of them will disappear. [5]For they go up to their roofs and bow to the sun, moon, and stars. They claim to follow the LORD, but then they worship Molech,* too. So now I will destroy them! [6]And I will destroy those who used to worship me but now no longer do. They no longer ask for the LORD's guidance or seek my blessings."

[7]Stand in silence in the presence of the Sovereign LORD, for the awesome day of the LORD's judgment has come. The LORD has prepared his people for a great slaughter and has chosen their executioners.* [8]"On that day of judgment," says the LORD, "I will punish the leaders and princes of Judah and all those following pagan customs. [9]Yes, I will punish those who participate in pagan worship ceremonies, and those who steal and kill to fill their masters' homes with loot.

[10]"On that day," says the LORD, "a cry of alarm will come from the Fish Gate and echo throughout the newer Mishneh section* of the city. And a great crashing sound will come from the surrounding hills. [11]Wail in sorrow, all you who live in the market area, for all who buy and sell there will die.

[12]"I will search with lanterns in Jerusalem's darkest corners to find and punish those who sit contented in their sins, indifferent to the LORD, thinking he will do nothing at all to them. [13]They are the very ones whose property will be plundered by the enemy, whose homes will be ransacked. They will never have a chance to live in the new homes they have built. They will never drink wine from the vineyards they have planted.

[14]"That terrible day of the LORD is near. Swiftly it comes—a day when strong men will cry bitterly. [15]It is a day when the LORD's anger will be poured out. It is a day of terrible distress and anguish, a day of ruin and desolation, a day of darkness and gloom, of clouds, blackness, [16]trumpet calls, and battle cries. Down go the walled cities and strongest battlements!

[17]"Because you have sinned against the LORD, I will make you as helpless as a blind man searching for a path. Your blood will be poured out into the dust, and your bodies will lie there rotting on the ground."

[18]Your silver and gold will be of no use to you on that day of the LORD's anger. For the whole land will be devoured by the fire of his jealousy. He will make a terrifying end of all the people on earth.*

CHAPTER 2

A Call to Repentance

Gather together and pray, you shameless nation. [2]Gather while there is still time, before judgment begins and your opportunity is blown away like chaff. Act now, before the fierce fury of the LORD falls and the terrible day of the LORD's anger begins. [3]Beg the LORD to save you—all you who are humble, all you who uphold justice. Walk humbly and do what is right. Perhaps even yet the LORD will protect you from his anger on that day of destruction.

Judgment against Philistia

[4]Gaza, Ashkelon, Ashdod, Ekron—these Philistine cities, too, will be rooted out and left in desolation. [5]And how terrible it will be for you Philistines* who live along the coast and in the land of Canaan, for this judgment is against you, too! The LORD will destroy you until not one of you is left. [6]The coastal area will become a pasture, a place of shepherd camps and enclosures for sheep.

I BELIEVE the Lord accurately foretold the destruction of the kingdom of Judah. (1:4)

I DO NOT foolishly assume the Lord will not punish me if I continue sinning. (1:12)

I DO NOT TRUST wealth to protect me from the Lord's anger and final judgment. (1:18)

I REPENT now—while I have the opportunity—before the day of God's anger and judgment comes. (2:2)

I BELIEVE the Lord accurately foretold the judgment of Judah's pagan neighbors. (2:5)

1:3 The meaning of the Hebrew is uncertain. 1:5 Hebrew *Malcam*, another name for Molech; or it could possibly mean *their king*. 1:7 Hebrew *has prepared a sacrifice and sanctified his guests*. 1:10 Or *the Second Quarter*, a newer section of Jerusalem. 1:18 Or *the people living in the land*. 2:5 Hebrew *Kerethites*.

[7] The few survivors of the tribe of Judah will pasture there. They will lie down to rest in the abandoned houses in Ashkelon. For the LORD their God will visit his people in kindness and restore their prosperity again.

Judgment against Moab and Ammon

[8] "I have heard the taunts of the people of Moab and Ammon, mocking my people and invading their borders. [9] Now, as surely as I live," says the LORD Almighty, the God of Israel, "Moab and Ammon will be destroyed as completely as Sodom and Gomorrah. Their land will become a place of stinging nettles, salt pits, and eternal desolation. Those of my people who are left will plunder them and take their land."

[10] They will receive the wages of their pride, for they have scoffed at the people of the LORD Almighty. [11] The LORD will terrify them as he destroys all the gods in the land. Then people from nations around the world will worship the LORD, each in their own land.

Judgment against Ethiopia and Assyria

[12] "You Ethiopians* will also be slaughtered by my sword," says the LORD.

[13] And the LORD will strike the lands of the north with his fist. He will destroy Assyria and make its great capital, Nineveh, a desolate wasteland, parched like a desert. [14] The city that once was so proud will become a pasture for sheep and cattle. All sorts of wild animals will settle there. Owls of many kinds will live among the ruins of its palaces, hooting from the gaping windows. Rubble will block all the doorways, and the cedar paneling will lie open to the wind and weather.

[15] This is the fate of that boisterous city, once so secure. "In all the world there is no city as great as I," it boasted. But now, look how it has become an utter ruin, a place where animals live! Everyone passing that way will laugh in derision or shake a defiant fist.

CHAPTER 3

Jerusalem's Rebellion and Redemption

How terrible it will be for rebellious, polluted Jerusalem, the city of violence and crime. [2] It proudly refuses to listen even to the voice of the LORD. No one can tell it anything; it refuses all correction. It does not trust in the LORD or draw near to its God.

[3] Its leaders are like roaring lions hunting for their victims—out for everything they can get. Its judges are like ravenous wolves at evening time, who by dawn have left no trace of their prey. [4] Its prophets are arrogant liars seeking their own gain. Its priests defile the Temple by disobeying God's laws. [5] But the LORD is still there in the city, and he does no wrong. Day by day his justice is more evident, but no one takes notice—the wicked know no shame.

[6] "I have wiped out many nations, devastating their fortress walls and towers. Their cities are now deserted; their streets are in silent ruin. There are no survivors to even tell what happened. [7] I thought, 'Surely they will have reverence for me now! Surely they will listen to my warnings, so I won't need to strike again.' But no; however much I punish them, they continue their evil practices from dawn till dusk and dusk till dawn." [8] So now the LORD says: "Be patient; the time is coming soon when I will stand up and accuse these evil nations. For it is my decision to gather together the kingdoms of the earth and pour out my fiercest anger and fury on them. All the earth will be devoured by the fire of my jealousy.

[9] "On that day I will purify the lips of all people, so that everyone will be able to worship the LORD together. [10] My scattered people who live beyond the rivers of Ethiopia* will come to present their offerings. [11] And then you

I BELIEVE the Lord judged the nations for their pride and arrogance against him. (2:10)

I ABHOR injustice and greed. (3:3)

I BELIEVE the Lord will purify the lips of all people so they may worship him. (3:9)

2:12 Hebrew *Cushites*.   3:10 Hebrew *Cush*.

will no longer need to be ashamed of yourselves, for you will no longer be rebels against me. I will remove all the proud and arrogant people from among you. There will be no pride on my holy mountain. [12]Those who are left will be the lowly and the humble, for it is they who trust in the name of the LORD. [13]The people of Israel who survive will do no wrong to each other, never telling lies or deceiving one another. They will live peaceful lives, lying down to sleep in safety; there will be no one to make them afraid."

[14]Sing, O daughter of Zion; shout aloud, O Israel! Be glad and rejoice with all your heart, O daughter of Jerusalem! [15]For the LORD will remove his hand of judgment and will disperse the armies of your enemy. And the LORD himself, the King of Israel, will live among you! At last your troubles will be over, and you will fear disaster no more.

[16]On that day the announcement to Jerusalem will be, "Cheer up, Zion! Don't be afraid! [17]For the LORD your God has arrived to live among you. He is a mighty savior. He will rejoice over you with great gladness. With his love, he will calm all your fears. He will exult over you by singing a happy song."

[18]"I will gather you who mourn for the appointed festivals; you will be disgraced no more.* [19]And I will deal severely with all who have oppressed you. I will save the weak and helpless ones; I will bring together those who were chased away. I will give glory and renown to my former exiles, who have been mocked and shamed. [20]On that day I will gather you together and bring you home again. I will give you a good name, a name of distinction among all the nations of the earth. They will praise you as I restore your fortunes before their very eyes. I, the LORD, have spoken!"

3:18 The meaning of the Hebrew for this verse is uncertain.

I HUMBLY TRUST in the name of the Lord. (3:12)

I REJOICE that one day the Lord will reign as King among his people. (3:15)

HAGGAI

THIS TENTH "MINOR" prophet urges readers to repent of their misplaced priorities.

Haggai is the first of three prophets to rebuke God's people after the Babylonian Captivity.

Although more than fifty thousand forsake their idolatrous ways, return to the land of Judah, and start to rebuild the Temple, they have not wholeheartedly committed themselves to serving the Lord.

Eventually, the preparatory work to lay the Temple foundation stops. Years go by. Nothing happens. Then the Lord gives Haggai a series of five messages for the leaders of his people. The Lord exhorts the governor and high priest and the people to consider their miserable plight and start building the Temple (1:1-11). The Lord commends them for obeying him (1:12-15). The Lord urges them to take courage even though the task before them seems impossible (2:1-9). The Lord promises to bless his people from that day forward (2:10-19). And the Lord promises to bless the governor in the future (2:20-23).

The people are quick to obey the Lord and claim his promises. True, they experience fierce opposition from their pagan neighbors. But the Persian king Darius comes to their aid and generously supports the rebuilding of the Temple. The Jewish people complete the work in less than five years, dedicate the Temple, and celebrate the Passover with great rejoicing (see Ezra 5-6).

Famous verses in Haggai include

- "Why are you living in luxurious houses while my house lies in ruins?" (1:4; see 1:9)
- "Consider how things are going for you!" (1:5, 7; see 2:15, 18)
- "You have planted much but harvested little" (1:6)
- "The whole remnant of God's people obeyed the message from the LORD their God" (1:12)
- "The people worshiped the LORD in earnest" (1:12)
- "I am with you, says the LORD!" (1:13)
- "Take courage and work, for I am with you, says the LORD Almighty" (2:4)
- "In just a little while I will again shake the heavens and the earth" (2:6; see 2:21)
- "I will fill this place with glory, says the LORD Almighty" (2:7)
- "The silver is mine, and the gold is mine, says the LORD Almighty" (2:8)
- "The future glory of this Temple will be greater than its past glory" (2:9)
- "From this day onward I will bless you" (2:19)
- "I will treat you like a signet ring on my finger" (2:23)

CHAPTER 1

A Call to Rebuild the Temple

On August 29* of the second year of King Darius's reign, the LORD gave a message through the prophet Haggai to Zerubbabel son of Shealtiel, governor of Judah, and to Jeshua* son of Jehozadak, the high priest. ²"This is what the LORD Almighty says: The people are saying, 'The time has not yet come to rebuild the LORD's house—the Temple.' "

³So the LORD sent this message through the prophet Haggai: ⁴"Why are you living in luxurious houses while my house lies in ruins? ⁵This is what the LORD Almighty says: Consider how things are going for you! ⁶You have planted much but harvested little. You have food to eat, but not enough to fill you up. You have wine to drink, but not enough to satisfy your thirst. You have clothing to wear, but not enough to keep you warm. Your wages disappear as though you were putting them in pockets filled with holes!

⁷"This is what the LORD Almighty says: Consider how things are going for you! ⁸Now go up into the hills, bring down timber, and rebuild my house. Then I will take pleasure in it and be honored, says the LORD. ⁹You hoped for rich harvests, but they were poor. And when you brought your harvest home, I blew it away. Why? Because my house lies in ruins, says the LORD Almighty, while you are all busy building your own fine houses. ¹⁰That is why the heavens have withheld the dew and the earth has withheld its crops. ¹¹I have called for a drought on your fields and hills—a drought to wither the grain and grapes and olives and all your other crops, a drought to starve both you and your cattle and to ruin everything you have worked so hard to get."

Obedience to God's Call

¹²Then Zerubbabel son of Shealtiel, Jeshua son of Jehozadak, the high priest, and the whole remnant of God's people obeyed the message from the LORD their God. It had been delivered by the prophet Haggai, whom the LORD their God had sent, and the people worshiped the LORD in earnest. ¹³Then Haggai, the LORD's messenger, gave the people this message from the LORD: "I am with you, says the LORD!" ¹⁴So the LORD sparked the enthusiasm of Zerubbabel son of Shealtiel, governor of Judah, Jeshua son of Jehozadak, the high priest, and the whole remnant of God's people. They came and began their work on the house of the LORD Almighty, their God. ¹⁵This was on September 21* of the second year of King Darius's reign.

CHAPTER 2

The New Temple's Splendor

Then on October 17* of that same year, the LORD sent another message through the prophet Haggai. ²"Say this to Zerubbabel son of Shealtiel, governor of Judah, and to Jeshua* son of Jehozadak, the high priest, and to the remnant of God's people there in the land: ³Is there anyone who can remember this house—the Temple—as it was before? In comparison, how does it look to you now? It must seem like nothing at all! ⁴But now take courage, Zerubbabel, says the LORD. Take courage, Jeshua son of Jehozadak, the high priest. Take courage, all you people still left in the land, says the LORD. Take courage and work, for I am with you, says the LORD Almighty. ⁵My Spirit remains among you, just as I promised when you came out of Egypt. So do not be afraid.

⁶"For this is what the LORD Almighty says: In just a little while I will again

I DO NOT NEGLECT my relationship with the Lord to fulfill my own wants and needs. (1:4)

I KNOW difficult circumstances can be a result of my disobedience to the Lord. (1:9)

I ASK the Lord to stir my heart to obey him enthusiastically. (1:14)

I TAKE COURAGE in the Lord's presence whenever my efforts to obey him seem to produce puny results. (2:4)

1:1a Hebrew *On the first day of the sixth month,* of the Hebrew calendar. A number of dates in Haggai can be cross-checked with dates in surviving Persian records and related accurately to our modern calendar. This event occurred on August 29, 520 B.C. **1:1b** Hebrew *Joshua,* a variant name for Jeshua; also in 1:12, 14. **1:15** Hebrew *on the twenty-fourth day of the sixth month,* of the Hebrew calendar. This event occurred on September 21, 520 B.C.; also see note on 1:1a. **2:1** Hebrew *on the twenty-first day of the seventh month,* of the Hebrew calendar. This event occurred on October 17, 520 B.C.; also see note on 1:1a. **2:2** Hebrew *Joshua,* a variant name for Jeshua; also in 2:4.

shake the heavens and the earth. I will shake the oceans and the dry land, too. ⁷I will shake all the nations, and the treasures of all the nations will come to this Temple. I will fill this place with glory, says the LORD Almighty. ⁸The silver is mine, and the gold is mine, says the LORD Almighty. ⁹The future glory of this Temple will be greater than its past glory, says the LORD Almighty. And in this place I will bring peace. I, the LORD Almighty, have spoken!"

Blessings Promised for Obedience
¹⁰On December 18* of the second year of King Darius's reign, the LORD sent this message to the prophet Haggai: ¹¹"This is what the LORD Almighty says! Ask the priests this question about the law: ¹²If one of you is carrying a holy sacrifice in his robes and happens to brush against some bread or stew, wine or oil, or any other kind of food, will it also become holy?"

The priests replied, "No."

¹³Then Haggai asked, "But if someone becomes ceremonially unclean by touching a dead person and then brushes against any of the things mentioned, will it be defiled?"

And the priests answered, "Yes."

¹⁴Then Haggai said, "That is how it is with this people and this nation, says the LORD. Everything they do and everything they offer is defiled. ¹⁵So think about this from now on—consider how things were going for you before you began to lay the foundation of the LORD's Temple. ¹⁶When you hoped for a twenty-bushel crop, you harvested only ten. When you expected to draw fifty gallons from the winepress, you found only twenty. ¹⁷I sent blight and mildew and hail to destroy all the produce of your labor. Yet, even so, you refused to return to me, says the LORD.

¹⁸"On this eighteenth day of December—the day when the foundation of the LORD's Temple was laid—carefully consider this: ¹⁹I am giving you a promise now while the seed is still in the barn, before you have harvested your grain and before the grapevine, the fig tree, the pomegranate, and the olive tree have produced their crops. From this day onward I will bless you."

Promises for Zerubbabel
²⁰The LORD sent this second message to Haggai on December 18*: ²¹"Tell Zerubbabel, the governor of Judah, that I am about to shake the heavens and the earth. ²²I will overthrow royal thrones, destroying the power of foreign kingdoms. I will overturn their chariots and charioteers. The horses will fall, and their riders will kill each other. ²³But when this happens, says the LORD Almighty, I will honor you, Zerubbabel son of Shealtiel, my servant. I will treat you like a signet ring on my finger, says the LORD, for I have specially chosen you. I, the LORD Almighty, have spoken!"

2:10 Hebrew *On the twenty-fourth day of the ninth month,* of the Hebrew calendar (also in 2:18). This event occurred on December 18, 520 B.C.; also see note on 1:1a. 2:20 Hebrew *on the twenty-fourth day of the month;* see note on 2:10.

I BELIEVE the Lord one day will shake the heavens and the earth and fill his Temple with treasures and glory (Hebrews 12:26-27). (2:6)

I DO NOT REFUSE to return to the Lord when he disciplines me. (2:17)

I BELIEVE the Lord will bless me and meet my needs as I step out in obedience to him. (2:19)

ZECHARIAH

THIS ELEVENTH "MINOR" prophet urges the people to repent, finish building the Temple, and look forward to the coming Messiah.

In the midst of the five messages that Haggai received from the Lord, Zechariah receives a series of prophetic visions (chapters 1–6). The dramatic visions reveal that (1) the Lord has not forgotten Jerusalem and Judah; (2) the Lord will destroy the world powers who have oppressed God's people; (3) the godly will return to the Lord; (4) Jerusalem will be rebuilt and filled with the Lord's glory again; (5) God's people must be cleansed before the Lord's glory returns; (6) all this will occur by the Lord's Spirit; and (7) the Lord has much more in store in the distant future.

Two years later, in response to a question from the town of Bethel, Zechariah receives another prophetic word from the Lord (chpaters 7–8), again urging God's people to repent and pursue true godliness.

Later, Zechariah receives several more messages (chapters 9–14) addressing events near at hand, other events during the Messiah's first coming (more details than any other prophet except Isaiah), and still other events at the climax of history.

Famous verses in Zechariah abound, including

- ○ "Return to me, and I will return to you, says the LORD Almighty" (1:3)
- ○ "Be silent before the LORD, all humanity" (2:13)
- ○ "I, the LORD, reject your accusations, Satan" (3:2)
- ○ "Listen to me, O Jeshua." You are a symbol of my servant, the Branch (3:8; see 6:12)
- ○ "It is not by force nor by strength, but by my Spirit, says the LORD Almighty" (4:6)
- ○ "Do not despise these small beginnings, for the LORD rejoices to see the work begin" (4:10)
- ○ "All this will happen if you carefully obey the commands of the LORD your God" (6:15)
- ○ "Was it really for me that you were fasting?" (7:5)
- ○ "This is what the LORD Almighty says: Judge fairly and honestly, and show mercy . . ." (7:9-10; see 8:16-17)
- ○ "Look, your king is coming to you. He is . . . riding on a donkey—even on a donkey's colt" (9:9)
- ○ "They counted out for my wages thirty pieces of silver" (11:12)
- ○ "And the LORD said to me, 'Throw it to the potters'—this magnificent sum at which they valued me!" (11:13)
- ○ "They will look on me whom they have pierced and mourn for him as for an only son" (12:10)
- ○ "On that day a fountain will be opened for the dynasty of David . . . a fountain to cleanse them" (13:1)
- ○ "Strike down the shepherd, and the sheep will be scattered" (13:7)
- ○ "On that day the sources of light will no longer shine, yet there will be continuous day!" (14:6-7)
- ○ "And the LORD will be king over all the earth" (14:9)

CHAPTER 1

A Call to Return to the LORD

In midautumn* of the second year of King Darius's reign, the LORD gave this message to the prophet Zechariah son of Berekiah and grandson of Iddo.

²"I, the LORD, was very angry with your ancestors. ³Therefore, say to the people, 'This is what the LORD Almighty says: Return to me, and I will return to you, says the LORD Almighty.' ⁴Do not be like your ancestors who would not listen when the earlier prophets said to them, 'This is what the LORD Almighty says: Turn from your evil ways and stop all your evil practices.'

⁵"Your ancestors and their prophets are now long dead. ⁶But all the things I said through my servants the prophets happened to your ancestors, just as I said they would. As a result, they repented and said, 'We have received what we deserved from the LORD Almighty. He has done what he said he would do.'"

A Man among the Myrtle Trees

⁷Then on February 15* of the second year of King Darius's reign, the LORD sent another message to the prophet Zechariah son of Berekiah and grandson of Iddo. Zechariah said:

⁸In a vision during the night, I saw a man sitting on a red horse that was standing among some myrtle trees in a small valley. Behind him were red, brown, and white horses, each with its own rider. ⁹I asked the angel who was talking with me, "My lord, what are all those horses for?"

"I will show you," the angel replied.

¹⁰So the man standing among the myrtle trees explained, "They are the ones the LORD has sent out to patrol the earth."

¹¹Then the other riders reported to the angel of the LORD, who was standing among the myrtle trees, "We have patrolled the earth, and the whole earth is at peace."

¹²Upon hearing this, the angel of the LORD prayed this prayer: "O LORD Almighty, for seventy years now you have been angry with Jerusalem and the towns of Judah. How long will it be until you again show mercy to them?" ¹³And the LORD spoke kind and comforting words to the angel who talked with me.

¹⁴Then the angel said to me, "Shout this message for all to hear: 'This is what the LORD Almighty says: My love for Jerusalem and Mount Zion is passionate and strong. ¹⁵But I am very angry with the other nations that enjoy peace and security. I was only a little angry with my people, but the nations punished them far beyond my intentions.

¹⁶"'Therefore, this is what the LORD says: I have returned to show mercy to Jerusalem. My Temple will be rebuilt, says the LORD Almighty, and plans will be made for the reconstruction of Jerusalem.*' ¹⁷Say this also: 'This is what the LORD Almighty says: The towns of Israel will again overflow with prosperity, and the LORD will again comfort Zion and choose Jerusalem as his own.'"

Four Horns and Four Blacksmiths

¹⁸Then I looked up and saw four animal horns. ¹⁹"What are these?" I asked the angel who was talking with me.

He replied, "These horns represent the world powers that scattered Judah, Israel, and Jerusalem."

²⁰Then the LORD showed me four blacksmiths. ²¹"What are these men coming to do?" I asked.

I LEARN from the disobedience and repentance of those who have come before me. (1:6)

I BELIEVE the Lord sees and controls the whole earth. (1:10)

I BELIEVE the Lord kept his promise to show mercy to Jerusalem and rebuild his Temple. (1:16)

I BELIEVE the Lord kept his promise to judge the nations that exiled Israel and Judah. (1:20)

1:1 Hebrew *In the eighth month.* A number of dates in Zechariah can be cross-checked with dates in surviving Persian records and related accurately to our modern calendar. This month of the Hebrew lunar calendar occurred in October and November 520 B.C.   1:7 Hebrew *on the twenty-fourth day of the eleventh month, the month of Shebat,* of the Hebrew calendar. This event occurred on February 15, 519 B.C.; also see note on 1:1. 1:16 Hebrew *and the measuring line will be stretched out over Jerusalem.*

The angel replied, "The blacksmiths have come to terrify the four horns that scattered and humbled Judah. They will throw them down and destroy them."

CHAPTER 2
Future Prosperity of Jerusalem
When I looked around me again, I saw a man with a measuring line in his hand. ²"Where are you going?" I asked.

He replied, "I am going to measure Jerusalem, to see how wide and how long it is."

³Then the angel who was with me went to meet a second angel who was coming toward him. ⁴The other angel said, "Hurry, and say to that young man, 'Jerusalem will someday be so full of people that it won't have room enough for everyone! Many will live outside the city walls, with all their livestock—and yet they will be safe. ⁵For I, myself, will be a wall of fire around Jerusalem, says the LORD. And I will be the glory inside the city!' "

The Exiles Are Called Home
⁶The LORD says, "Come away! Flee from the north, for I have scattered you to the four winds. ⁷Come away! Escape to Jerusalem,* you who are exiled in Babylon!"

⁸"After a period of glory, the LORD Almighty sent me against the nations who oppressed you. For he said, 'Anyone who harms you harms my most precious possession.* ⁹I will raise my fist to crush them, and their own slaves will plunder them.' Then you will know that the LORD Almighty has sent me."

¹⁰The LORD says, "Shout and rejoice, O Jerusalem,* for I am coming to live among you. ¹¹Many nations will join themselves to the LORD on that day, and they, too, will be my people. I will live among you, and you will know that the LORD Almighty sent me to you. ¹²The land of Judah will be the LORD's inheritance in the holy land, and he will once again choose Jerusalem to be his own city. ¹³Be silent before the LORD, all humanity, for he is springing into action from his holy dwelling."

CHAPTER 3
Cleansing for the High Priest
Then the angel showed me Jeshua* the high priest standing before the angel of the LORD. Satan* was there at the angel's right hand, accusing Jeshua of many things. ²And the LORD said to Satan, "I, the LORD, reject your accusations, Satan. Yes, the LORD, who has chosen Jerusalem, rebukes you. This man is like a burning stick that has been snatched from a fire."

³Jeshua's clothing was filthy as he stood there before the angel. ⁴So the angel said to the others standing there, "Take off his filthy clothes." And turning to Jeshua he said, "See, I have taken away your sins, and now I am giving you these fine new clothes."

⁵Then I said, "Please, could he also have a clean turban on his head?" So they put a clean priestly turban on his head and dressed him in new clothes while the angel of the LORD stood by.

⁶Then the angel of the LORD spoke very solemnly to Jeshua and said, ⁷"This is what the LORD Almighty says: If you follow my ways and obey my requirements, then you will be given authority over my Temple and its courtyards. I will let you walk in and out of my presence along with these others standing here. ⁸Listen to me, O Jeshua the high priest, and all you other priests. You are

Ask the Lord to make you "totally committed to doing what is right" (Titus 2:14).

I BELIEVE the Lord himself one day will be the protection around Jerusalem and the glory within the city (Revelation 21:23). (2:5)

I AM AGAINST the oppression of the Jewish people— the Lord's precious possession (Romans 11:28-29). (2:8)

I AM SILENT before the Lord as I wait for him to act. (2:13)

I AM CONFIDENT the Lord will reject Satan's accusations against his chosen ones (1 John 2:1; Revelation 12:10-11). (3:2)

I ASK the Lord to cleanse me and make me fit to serve him. (3:4)

2:7 Hebrew to Zion. 2:8 Hebrew harms the apple of my eye. 2:10 Hebrew O daughter of Zion. 3:1a Hebrew Joshua, a variant name for Jeshua; also in 3:3, 4, 6, 8, 9. 3:1b Or The Accuser; Hebrew reads The Adversary; also in 3:2.

symbols of the good things to come. Soon I am going to bring my servant, the Branch. [9]Now look at the jewel I have set before Jeshua, a single stone with seven facets.* I will engrave an inscription on it, says the LORD Almighty, and I will remove the sins of this land in a single day. [10]And on that day, says the LORD Almighty, each of you will invite your neighbor into your home to share your peace and prosperity."

CHAPTER 4

A Lampstand and Two Olive Trees

Then the angel who had been talking with me returned and woke me, as though I had been asleep. [2]"What do you see now?" he asked.

I answered, "I see a solid gold lampstand with a bowl of oil on top of it. Around the bowl are seven lamps, each one having seven spouts with wicks. [3]And I see two olive trees, one on each side of the bowl."

[4]Then I asked the angel, "What are these, my lord? What do they mean?"

[5]"Don't you know?" the angel asked.

"No, my lord," I replied.

[6]Then he said to me, "This is what the LORD says to Zerubbabel: It is not by force nor by strength, but by my Spirit, says the LORD Almighty. [7]Nothing, not even a mighty mountain, will stand in Zerubbabel's way; it will flatten out before him! Then Zerubbabel will set the final stone of the Temple in place, and the people will shout: 'May God bless it! May God bless it!' "

[8]Then another message came to me from the LORD: [9]"Zerubbabel is the one who laid the foundation of this Temple, and he will complete it. Then you will know that the LORD Almighty has sent me. [10]Do not despise these small beginnings, for the LORD rejoices to see the work begin, to see the plumb line in Zerubbabel's hand. For these seven lamps represent the eyes of the LORD that search all around the world."

[11]Then I asked the angel, "What are these two olive trees on each side of the lampstand, [12]and what are the two olive branches that pour out golden oil through two gold tubes?"

[13]"Don't you know?" he asked.

"No, my lord," I replied.

[14]Then he said to me, "They represent the two anointed ones who assist the Lord of all the earth."

CHAPTER 5

A Flying Scroll

I looked up again and saw a scroll flying through the air.

[2]"What do you see?" the angel asked.

"I see a flying scroll," I replied. "It appears to be about thirty feet long and fifteen feet wide.*"

[3]Then he said to me, "This scroll contains the curse that is going out over the entire land. One side says that those who steal will be banished from the land; the other side says that those who swear falsely will be banished from the land. [4]And this is what the LORD Almighty says: I am sending this curse into the house of every thief and into the house of everyone who swears falsely by my name. And my curse will remain in that house until it is completely destroyed—even its timbers and stones."

A Woman in a Basket

[5]Then the angel who was talking with me came forward and said, "Look up! Something is appearing in the sky."

[6]"What is it?" I asked.

I BELIEVE the Spirit of the Lord Almighty is far more powerful than human force or strength. (4:6)

I REJOICE, as the Lord does, when his people begin to obey him and accomplish his purposes. (4:10)

I BELIEVE the Lord's promise one day to cleanse sinners from his land (Revelation 21:8, 27). (5:3)

3:9 Hebrew *7 eyes.*   5:2 Hebrew *20 cubits* [9 meters] *long and 10 cubits* [4.5 meters] *wide.*

He replied, "It is a basket for measuring grain,* and it is filled with the sins* of everyone throughout the land."

⁷When the heavy lead cover was lifted off the basket, there was a woman sitting inside it. ⁸The angel said, "The woman's name is Wickedness," and he pushed her back into the basket and closed the heavy lid again.

⁹Then I looked up and saw two women flying toward us, with wings gliding on the wind. Their wings were like those of a stork, and they picked up the basket and flew with it into the sky.

¹⁰"Where are they taking the basket?" I asked the angel.

¹¹He replied, "To the land of Babylonia,* where they will build a temple for the basket. And when the temple is ready, they will set the basket there on its pedestal."

I ABHOR wickedness. (5:8)

CHAPTER 6

Four Chariots

Then I looked up again and saw four chariots coming from between two bronze mountains. ²The first chariot was pulled by red horses, the second by black horses, ³the third by white horses, and the fourth by dappled-gray horses. ⁴"And what are these, my lord?" I asked the angel who was talking with me.

⁵He replied, "These are the four spirits* of heaven who stand before the Lord of all the earth. They are going out to do his work. ⁶The chariot with black horses is going north, the chariot with white horses is going west,* and the chariot with dappled-gray horses is going south."

⁷The powerful horses were eager to be off, to patrol back and forth across the earth. And the LORD said, "Go and patrol the earth!" So they left at once on their patrol.

⁸Then the LORD summoned me and said, "Those who went north have vented the anger of my Spirit* there."

I BELIEVE the Lord accomplishes his work in all the earth. (6:5)

The Crowning of Jeshua

⁹Then I received another message from the LORD: ¹⁰"Heldai, Tobijah, and Jedaiah will bring gifts of silver and gold from the Jews exiled in Babylon. As soon as they arrive, meet them at the home of Josiah son of Zephaniah. ¹¹Accept their gifts and make a crown* from the silver and gold. Then put the crown on the head of Jeshua* son of Jehozadak, the high priest. ¹²Tell him that the LORD Almighty says: Here is the man called the Branch. He will branch out where he is and build the Temple of the LORD. ¹³He will build the LORD's Temple, and he will receive royal honor and will rule as king from his throne. He will also serve as priest from his throne,* and there will be perfect harmony between the two.

¹⁴"The crown will be a memorial in the Temple of the LORD to honor those who gave it—Heldai,* Tobijah, Jedaiah, and Josiah* son of Zephaniah."

¹⁵Many will come from distant lands to rebuild the Temple of the LORD. And when this happens, you will know my messages have been from the LORD Almighty. All this will happen if you carefully obey the commands of the LORD your God.

I BELIEVE the Lord accurately foretold that his Branch—Jesus the Messiah—would be both priest and king. (6:13)

I OBEY the Lord's commands and see his promises fulfilled. (6:15)

CHAPTER 7

A Call to Justice and Mercy

On December 7* of the fourth year of King Darius's reign, another message came to Zechariah from the LORD. ²The people of Bethel had sent Sharezer

5:6a Hebrew *an ephah*, about half a bushel or 18 liters; also in 5:7, 8, 9, 10, 11.   5:6b As in Greek version; Hebrew reads *the appearance*.   5:11 Hebrew *the land of Shinar*.   6:5 Or *the four winds*.   6:6 Hebrew *is going after them*.   6:8 Hebrew *have given my Spirit rest*.   6:11a As in Greek and Syriac versions; Hebrew reads *crowns*.   6:11b Hebrew *Joshua*, a variant name for Jeshua.   6:13 Or *There will be a priest by his throne*.   6:14a As in Syriac version (compare 6:10); Hebrew reads *Helem*.   6:14b As in Syriac version (compare 6:10); Hebrew reads *Hen*.   7:1 Hebrew *On the fourth day of the ninth month, the month of Kislev*, of the Hebrew calendar. This event occurred on December 7, 518 B.C.; also see note on 1:1.

and Regemmelech,* along with their men, to seek the LORD's favor. ³They were to ask this question of the prophets and of the priests at the Temple of the LORD Almighty: "Should we continue to mourn and fast each summer on the anniversary of the Temple's destruction,* as we have done for so many years?"

⁴The LORD Almighty sent me this message: ⁵"Say to all your people and your priests, 'During those seventy years of exile, when you fasted and mourned in the summer and at the festival in early autumn,* was it really for me that you were fasting? ⁶And even now in your holy festivals, you don't think about me but only of pleasing yourselves. ⁷Isn't this the same message the LORD proclaimed through the prophets years ago when Jerusalem and the towns of Judah were bustling with people, and the Negev and the foothills of Judah* were populated areas?' "

⁸Then this message came to Zechariah from the LORD: ⁹"This is what the LORD Almighty says: Judge fairly and honestly, and show mercy and kindness to one another. ¹⁰Do not oppress widows, orphans, foreigners, and poor people. And do not make evil plans to harm each other.

¹¹"Your ancestors would not listen to this message. They turned stubbornly away and put their fingers in their ears to keep from hearing. ¹²They made their hearts as hard as stone, so they could not hear the law or the messages that the LORD Almighty had sent them by his Spirit through the earlier prophets. That is why the LORD Almighty was so angry with them.

¹³"Since they refused to listen when I called to them, I would not listen when they called to me, says the LORD Almighty. ¹⁴I scattered them as with a whirlwind among the distant nations, where they lived as strangers. Their land became so desolate that no one even traveled through it. The land that had been so pleasant became a desert."

CHAPTER 8

Promised Blessings for Jerusalem

Then another message came to me from the LORD Almighty: ²"This is what the LORD Almighty says: My love for Mount Zion is passionate and strong; I am consumed with passion for Jerusalem! ³And now the LORD says: I am returning to Mount Zion, and I will live in Jerusalem. Then Jerusalem will be called the Faithful City; the mountain of the LORD Almighty will be called the Holy Mountain. ⁴This is what the LORD Almighty says: Once again old men and women will walk Jerusalem's streets with a cane and sit together in the city squares. ⁵And the streets of the city will be filled with boys and girls at play.

⁶"This is what the LORD Almighty says: All this may seem impossible to you now, a small and discouraged remnant of God's people. But do you think this is impossible for me, the LORD Almighty? ⁷This is what the LORD Almighty says: You can be sure that I will rescue my people from the east and from the west. ⁸I will bring them home again to live safely in Jerusalem. They will be my people, and I will be faithful and just toward them as their God.

⁹"This is what the LORD Almighty says: Take heart and finish the task! You have heard what the prophets have been saying about building the Temple of the LORD Almighty ever since the foundation was laid. ¹⁰Before the work on the Temple began, there were no jobs and no wages for either people or animals. No traveler was safe from the enemy, for there were enemies on all sides. I had turned everyone against each other. ¹¹But now I will not treat the remnant of my people as I treated them before, says the LORD Almighty. ¹²For I am planting seeds of peace and prosperity among you. The grapevines will

---

I FAST to please the Lord, not to feel sorry for myself. (7:5)

I PLEASE the Lord by living honestly and showing mercy and kindness. (7:9)

I KEEP my heart sensitive to God's Word. (7:12)

I BELIEVE the Lord's promise to one day return and live among his people in Jerusalem (Revelation 21:1-3). (8:3)

I BELIEVE the Lord is able to accomplish anything, even what seems humanly impossible. (8:6)

7:2 Or *Bethel-sharezer had sent Regemmelech.*   7:3 Hebrew *mourn and fast in the fifth month.* This month of the Hebrew lunar calendar usually occurs in July and August.   7:5 Hebrew *fasted and mourned in the fifth and seventh months.* The fifth month of the Hebrew lunar calendar usually occurs in July and August. The seventh month usually occurs in September and October; both the Day of Atonement and the Festival of Shelters were celebrated in the seventh month.   7:7 Hebrew *the Shephelah.*

be heavy with fruit. The earth will produce its crops, and the sky will release the dew. Once more I will make the remnant in Judah and Israel the heirs of these blessings. ¹³Among the nations, Judah and Israel had become symbols of what it means to be cursed. But no longer! Now I will rescue you and make you both a symbol and a source of blessing! So don't be afraid or discouraged, but instead get on with rebuilding the Temple!

¹⁴"For this is what the LORD Almighty says: I did not change my mind when your ancestors angered me and I promised to punish them, says the LORD Almighty. ¹⁵Neither will I change my decision to bless Jerusalem and the people of Judah. So don't be afraid. ¹⁶But this is what you must do: Tell the truth to each other. Render verdicts in your courts that are just and that lead to peace. ¹⁷Do not make evil plots to harm each other. And stop this habit of swearing to things that are false. I hate all these things, says the LORD."

¹⁸Here is another message that came to me from the LORD Almighty. ¹⁹"This is what the LORD Almighty says: The traditional fasts and times of mourning you have kept in early summer, midsummer, autumn, and winter* are now ended. They will become festivals of joy and celebration for the people of Judah. So love truth and peace.

²⁰"This is what the LORD Almighty says: People from nations and cities around the world will travel to Jerusalem. ²¹The people of one city will say to the people in another, 'Let us go to Jerusalem to ask the LORD to bless us and to seek the LORD Almighty. We are planning to go ourselves.' ²²People from many nations, even powerful nations, will come to Jerusalem to seek the LORD Almighty and to ask the LORD to bless them.

²³"This is what the LORD Almighty says: In those days ten people from nations and languages around the world will clutch at the hem of one Jew's robe. And they will say, 'Please let us walk with you, for we have heard that God is with you.'"

CHAPTER 9

Judgment against Israel's Enemies

This is the message* from the LORD against the land of Aram* and the city of Damascus, for the eyes of all humanity, including the people of Israel, are on the LORD. ²Doom is certain for Hamath, near Damascus, and for the cities of Tyre and Sidon, too, though they are so clever. ³Tyre has built a strong fortress and has piled up so much silver and gold that it is as common as dust in the streets! ⁴But now the Lord will strip away Tyre's possessions and hurl its fortifications into the Mediterranean Sea.* Tyre will be set on fire and burned to the ground.

⁵The city of Ashkelon will see Tyre fall and will be filled with fear. Gaza will shake with terror, and so will Ekron, for their hopes will be dashed. Gaza will be conquered and its king killed, and Ashkelon will be completely deserted. ⁶Foreigners will occupy the city of Ashdod. Thus, I will destroy the pride of the Philistines. ⁷They will no longer eat meat with blood in it or feed on other forbidden foods. All the surviving Philistines will worship our God and be adopted as a new clan in Judah.* And the Philistines of Ekron will join my people, just as the Jebusites once did. ⁸I will guard my Temple and protect it from invading armies. I am closely watching their movements. No foreign oppressor will ever again overrun my people's land.

Zion's Coming King

⁹Rejoice greatly, O people* of Zion! Shout in triumph, O people of Jerusalem! Look, your king is coming to you. He is righteous and victorious, yet he is humble,

---

I LIVE a truthful life—in public and in private. (8:16)

I LOVE truth and peace. (8:19)

I BELIEVE the Lord's promise that Jerusalem one day will be a place where all peoples come to seek the Lord. (8:22)

I BELIEVE the Lord accurately foretold the destruction of Tyre. (9:4)

I BELIEVE the Lord promised to make the surviving Philistines part of his people. (9:7)

I BELIEVE the Lord accurately foretold that the coming King, Jesus, would be righteous and victorious, yet humble—riding on a donkey (Matthew 21:5). (9:9)

8:19 Hebrew *in the fourth, fifth, seventh, and tenth months.* The fourth month of the Hebrew lunar calendar usually occurs in June and July. The fifth month usually occurs in July and August. The seventh month usually occurs in September and October. The tenth month usually occurs in December and January.   9:1a Hebrew *An Oracle: The message.*   9:1b Hebrew *land of Hadrach.*   9:4 Hebrew *the sea.*   9:7 Hebrew *and will become a leader in Judah.* 9:9 Hebrew *daughter.*

I BELIEVE Jesus one day will bring peace to all nations and rule the earth. (9:10)

riding on a donkey—even on a donkey's colt. [10]I will remove the battle chariots from Israel* and the warhorses from Jerusalem, and I will destroy all the weapons used in battle. Your king will bring peace to the nations. His realm will stretch from sea to sea and from the Euphrates River* to the ends of the earth.*

[11]Because of the covenant I made with you, sealed with blood, I will free your prisoners from death in a waterless dungeon. [12]Come back to the place of safety, all you prisoners, for there is yet hope! I promise this very day that I will repay you two mercies for each of your woes! [13]Judah is my bow, and Israel is my arrow! Jerusalem* is my sword, and like a warrior, I will brandish it against the Greeks.*

[14]The LORD will appear above his people; his arrows will fly like lightning! The Sovereign LORD will sound the trumpet; he will go out against his enemies like a whirlwind from the southern desert. [15]The LORD Almighty will protect his people, and they will subdue their enemies with sling stones. They will shout in battle as though drunk with wine, shedding the blood of their enemies. They will be filled with blood like a bowl, drenched with blood like the corners of the altar.

[16]When that day arrives, the LORD their God will rescue his people, just as a shepherd rescues his sheep. They will sparkle in his land like jewels in a crown. [17]How wonderful and beautiful they will be! The young men and women will thrive on the abundance of grain and new wine.

CHAPTER 10

The LORD Will Restore His People

Ask the LORD for rain in the spring, and he will give it. It is the LORD who makes storm clouds that drop showers of rain so that every field becomes a lush pasture.

[2]Household gods give false advice, fortune-tellers predict only lies, and interpreters of dreams pronounce comfortless falsehoods. So my people are wandering like lost sheep, without a shepherd to protect and guide them.

I ASK the Lord—not false religions or fallen people—to supply all my needs (Philippians 4:19). (10:1)

I BELIEVE the Lord himself will be the shepherd of his people. (10:3)

[3]"My anger burns against your shepherds, and I will punish these leaders.* For the LORD Almighty has arrived to look after his flock of Judah; he will make them strong and glorious, like a proud warhorse in battle. [4]From Judah will come the cornerstone, the tent peg, the battle bow, and all the rulers. [5]They will be like mighty warriors in battle, trampling their enemies in the mud under their feet. Since the LORD is with them as they fight, they will overthrow even the horsemen of the enemy.

[6]"I will strengthen Judah and save Israel*; I will reestablish them because I love them. It will be as though I had never rejected them, for I am the LORD their God, who will hear their cries. [7]The people of Israel* will become like mighty warriors, and their hearts will be happy as if by wine. Their children, too, will see it all and be glad; their hearts will rejoice in the LORD. [8]When I whistle to them, they will come running, for I have redeemed them. From the few that are left, their population will grow again to its former size. [9]Though I have scattered them like seeds among the nations, still they will remember me in distant lands. With their children, they will survive and come home again to Israel. [10]I will bring them back from Egypt and Assyria and resettle them in Gilead and Lebanon. There won't be enough room for them all! [11]They will pass safely through the sea of distress,* for the waves of the sea will be held back. And the waters of the Nile will become dry. The pride of Assyria will be crushed, and the rule of Egypt will end. [12]I will make my people strong in my power, and they will go wherever they wish by my authority. I, the LORD, have spoken!"

I BELIEVE the Lord's promise one day to fill his people with his authority and power. (10:12)

9:10a Hebrew *from Ephraim*; also in 9:13. 9:10b Hebrew *the river*. 9:10c Or *the end of the land*. 9:13a Hebrew *Zion*. 9:13b Hebrew *the sons of Javan*. 10:3 Or *these male goats*. 10:6 Hebrew *save the house of Joseph*. 10:7 Hebrew *of Ephraim*. 10:11 Or *the sea of Egypt*, referring to the Red Sea.

CHAPTER 11

Open your doors, Lebanon, so that fire may sweep through your cedar forests. ²Weep, you cypress trees, for all the ruined cedars; the tallest and most beautiful of them are fallen. Weep, you oaks of Bashan, as you watch the thickest forests being felled. ³Listen to the wailing of the shepherds, for their wealth is gone. Hear the young lions roaring, for their thickets in the Jordan Valley have been destroyed.

The Good and Evil Shepherds

⁴This is what the LORD my God says: "Go and care for a flock that is intended for slaughter. ⁵The buyers will slaughter their sheep without remorse. The sellers will say, 'Praise the LORD, I am now rich!' Even the shepherds have no compassion for them. ⁶And likewise, I will no longer have pity on the inhabitants of the land," says the LORD. "I will let them fall into each other's clutches, as well as into the clutches of their king. They will turn the land into a wilderness, and I will not protect them."

⁷So I cared for the flock intended for slaughter—the flock that was oppressed. Then I took two shepherd's staffs and named one Favor and the other Union. ⁸I got rid of their three evil shepherds in a single month. But I became impatient with these sheep—this nation—and they hated me, too. ⁹So I told them, "I won't be your shepherd any longer. If you die, you die. If you are killed, you are killed. And those who remain will devour each other!"

¹⁰Then I took my staff called Favor and snapped it in two, showing that I had revoked the covenant I had made with all the nations. ¹¹That was the end of my covenant with them. Those who bought and sold sheep were watching me, and they knew that the LORD was speaking to them through my actions. ¹²And I said to them, "If you like, give me my wages, whatever I am worth; but only if you want to." So they counted out for my wages thirty pieces* of silver.

¹³And the LORD said to me, "Throw it to the potters*"—this magnificent sum at which they valued me! So I took the thirty coins and threw them to the potters in the Temple of the LORD. ¹⁴Then I broke my other staff, Union, to show that the bond of unity between Judah and Israel was broken.

¹⁵Then the LORD said to me, "Go again and play the part of a worthless shepherd. ¹⁶This will illustrate how I will give this nation a shepherd who will not care for the sheep that are threatened by death, nor look after the young, nor heal the injured, nor feed the healthy. Instead, this shepherd will eat the meat of the fattest sheep and tear off their hooves. ¹⁷Doom is certain for this worthless shepherd who abandons the flock! The sword will cut his arm and pierce his right eye! His arm will become useless, and his right eye completely blind!"

CHAPTER 12

Future Deliverance for Jerusalem

This* message concerning the fate of Israel came from the LORD: "This message is from the LORD, who stretched out the heavens, laid the foundations of the earth, and formed the spirit within humans. ²I will make Jerusalem and Judah like an intoxicating drink to all the nearby nations that send their armies to besiege Jerusalem. ³On that day I will make Jerusalem a heavy stone, a burden for the world. None of the nations who try to lift it will escape unscathed.

⁴"On that day, says the LORD, I will cause every horse to panic and every rider to lose his nerve. I will watch over the people of Judah, but I will blind

I BELIEVE the Lord accurately foretold the destruction of Lebanon. (11:1)

I BELIEVE the Lord told Zechariah to act out the role of the coming shepherd, the Messiah, who would be rejected. (11:4)

I BELIEVE the Lord used Zechariah as a picture of how the Messiah would be rejected and valued at a mere thirty pieces of silver (Matthew 27:9-10; see Acts 1:18-19). (11:12)

I BELIEVE the Lord made the heavens and the earth and all humanity. (12:1)

11:12 Hebrew *30 shekels*, about 12 ounces or 342 grams in weight.   11:13 Syriac version reads *into the treasury*; also in 11:13b.   12:1 Hebrew *An Oracle: This.*

the horses of her enemies. ⁵And the clans of Judah will say to themselves, 'The people of Jerusalem have found strength in the LORD Almighty, their God.'

⁶"On that day I will make the clans of Judah like a brazier that sets a woodpile ablaze or like a burning torch among sheaves of grain. They will burn up all the neighboring nations right and left, while the people living in Jerusalem remain secure. ⁷The LORD will give victory to the rest of Judah first, before Jerusalem, so that the people of Jerusalem and the royal line of David will not have greater honor than the rest of Judah. ⁸On that day the LORD will defend the people of Jerusalem; the weakest among them will be as mighty as King David! And the royal descendants will be like God, like the angel of the LORD who goes before them! ⁹For my plan is to destroy all the nations that come against Jerusalem.

¹⁰"Then I will pour out a spirit of grace and prayer on the family of David and on all the people of Jerusalem. They will look on me whom they have pierced and mourn for him as for an only son. They will grieve bitterly for him as for a firstborn son who has died. ¹¹The sorrow and mourning in Jerusalem on that day will be like the grievous mourning of Hadad-rimmon in the valley of Megiddo.

¹²"All Israel will weep in profound sorrow, each family by itself, with the husbands and wives in separate groups. The family of David will mourn, along with the family of Nathan, ¹³the family of Levi, and the family of Shimei. ¹⁴Each of the surviving families from Judah will mourn separately, husbands and wives apart.

CHAPTER 13

A Fountain of Cleansing

"On that day a fountain will be opened for the dynasty of David and for the people of Jerusalem, a fountain to cleanse them from all their sins and defilement.

²"And on that day, says the LORD Almighty, I will get rid of every trace of idol worship throughout the land, so that even the names of the idols will be forgotten. I will remove from the land all false prophets and the unclean spirits that inspire them. ³If anyone begins prophesying again, his own father and mother will tell him, 'You must die, for you have prophesied lies in the name of the LORD.' Then his own father and mother will stab him.

⁴"No one will be boasting then of a prophetic gift! No one will wear prophet's clothes to try to fool the people. ⁵'No,' he will say. 'I'm not a prophet; I'm a farmer. The soil has been my means of livelihood from my earliest youth.' ⁶And if someone asks, 'Then what are those scars on your chest*?' he will say, 'I was wounded at the home of friends!'

The Scattering of the Sheep

⁷"Awake, O sword, against my shepherd, the man who is my partner, says the LORD Almighty. Strike down the shepherd, and the sheep will be scattered, and I will turn against the lambs. ⁸Two-thirds of the people in the land will be cut off and die, says the LORD. But a third will be left in the land. ⁹I will bring that group through the fire and make them pure, just as gold and silver are refined and purified by fire. They will call on my name, and I will answer them. I will say, 'These are my people,' and they will say, 'The LORD is our God.' "

CHAPTER 14

The LORD Will Rule the Earth

Watch, for the day of the LORD is coming when your possessions will be plundered right in front of you! ²On that day I will gather all the nations to fight against Jerusalem. The city will be taken, the houses plundered, and the

13:6 Or *scars between your hands.*

See David's profile (page 629) at Psalm 3:1.

I BELIEVE the Lord's promise one day to defend and honor the people of Judah and Jerusalem. (12:8)

I BELIEVE the Lord one day will pour out grace on his people Israel, who will mourn that they rejected and killed the Savior, Jesus (John 19:34-37). (12:10)

I BELIEVE the people of Israel one day will repent and be cleansed from all their sins. (13:1)

See David's profile (page 629) at Psalm 3:1.

I BELIEVE the Lord accurately foretold that Jesus would be struck down and his disciples scattered (Matthew 26:31; Mark 14:27). (13:7)

I BELIEVE the Lord's promise to a people who call on the Lord as their own. (13:9)

I BELIEVE the Lord accurately foretold the coming destruction of Jerusalem. (14:1)

women raped. Half the population will be taken away into captivity, and half will be left among the ruins of the city.

³Then the LORD will go out to fight against those nations, as he has fought in times past. ⁴On that day his feet will stand on the Mount of Olives, which faces Jerusalem on the east. And the Mount of Olives will split apart, making a wide valley running from east to west, for half the mountain will move toward the north and half toward the south. ⁵You will flee through this valley, for it will reach across to Azal.* Yes, you will flee as you did from the earthquake in the days of King Uzziah of Judah. Then the LORD my God will come, and all his holy ones with him.*

See Uzziah's profile (page 533) at 2 Chronicles 26:16.

⁶On that day the sources of light will no longer shine,* ⁷yet there will be continuous day! Only the LORD knows how this could happen! There will be no normal day and night, for at evening time it will still be light. ⁸On that day life-giving waters will flow out from Jerusalem, half toward the Dead Sea and half toward the Mediterranean,* flowing continuously both in summer and in winter.

⁹And the LORD will be king over all the earth. On that day there will be one LORD—his name alone will be worshiped. ¹⁰All the land from Geba, north of Judah, to Rimmon, south of Jerusalem, will become one vast plain. But Jerusalem will be raised up in its original place and will be inhabited all the way from the Benjamin Gate over to the site of the old gate, then to the Corner Gate, and from the Tower of Hananel to the king's winepresses. ¹¹And Jerusalem will be filled, safe at last, never again to be cursed and destroyed.

I LOOK FORWARD to when the Lord is worshiped as king over all the earth. (14:9)

¹²And the LORD will send a plague on all the nations that fought against Jerusalem. Their people will become like walking corpses, their flesh rotting away. Their eyes will shrivel in their sockets, and their tongues will decay in their mouths. ¹³On that day they will be terrified, stricken by the LORD with great panic. They will fight against each other in hand-to-hand combat; ¹⁴Judah, too, will be fighting at Jerusalem. The wealth of all the neighboring nations will be captured—great quantities of gold and silver and fine clothing. ¹⁵This same plague will strike the horses, mules, camels, donkeys, and all the other animals in the enemy camps.

¹⁶In the end, the enemies of Jerusalem who survive the plague will go up to Jerusalem each year to worship the King, the LORD Almighty, and to celebrate the Festival of Shelters. ¹⁷And any nation anywhere in the world that refuses to come to Jerusalem to worship the King, the LORD Almighty, will have no rain. ¹⁸And if the people of Egypt refuse to attend the festival, the LORD will punish them with the same plague that he sends on the other nations who refuse to go. ¹⁹Egypt and the other nations will all be punished if they don't go to celebrate the festival.

I BELIEVE the Lord's promise that all survivors will worship him. (14:16)

²⁰On that day even the harness bells of the horses will be inscribed with these words: SET APART AS HOLY TO THE LORD. And the cooking pots in the Temple of the LORD will be as sacred as the basins used beside the altar. ²¹In fact, every cooking pot in Jerusalem and Judah will be set apart as holy to the LORD Almighty. All who come to worship will be free to use any of these pots to boil their sacrifices. And on that day there will no longer be traders* in the Temple of the LORD Almighty.

I BELIEVE the Lord's holiness one day will pervade and prevail. (14:20)

14:5a The meaning of the Hebrew is uncertain.   14:5b As in Greek version; Hebrew reads *with you.*
14:6 Hebrew *there will be no light, no cold or frost.* The meaning of the Hebrew is uncertain.   14:8 Hebrew *half toward the eastern sea and half toward the western sea.*   14:21 Hebrew *Canaanites.*

MALACHI

THIS LAST "MINOR" prophet urges readers to quit playing games with God.

During the days of Ezra and Nehemiah, the Israelites finished rebuilding Jerusalem yet quickly turned away from the Lord. Oh, they had a form of religion. But their worship was a sham.

The prophet Malachi challenges the insincerity and corruption of his people with hard-hitting exhortations. Many of these exhortations take the form of a dialogue between the Lord and the Jewish people. In those dialogues, the Lord makes a statement, only to be countered by his people: "Really? How?"

Like the book of James, the book of Malachi is a rapid-fire series of mini-sermons on practicing true religion, honoring the Lord's name, obeying God's Word, teaching what is right, doing what is just, living in light of the Lord's coming judgment, not oppressing the downtrodden, forsaking pride, fearing the Lord, and loving him with all one's heart, soul, strength, and mind.

Malachi concludes the writings of the Old Testament with prophetic words about Jesus Christ's first and second comings.

Famous verses in Malachi include

- ○ "'I have loved you deeply,' says the LORD. But you retort, 'Really? How . . . ?'" (1:2)
- ○ "Try giving gifts like that to your governor, and see how pleased he is!" (1:8)
- ○ "I wish that someone among you would shut the Temple doors" (1:10)
- ○ "The purpose of my covenant with the Levites was to bring life and peace" (2:5)
- ○ "Remain loyal to the wife of your youth. 'For I hate divorce!' says the LORD" (2:15-16)
- ○ "Look! I am sending my messenger, and he will prepare the way before me" (3:1; see 4:5)
- ○ "Then the Lord you are seeking will suddenly come to his Temple" (3:1)
- ○ "I am the LORD, and I do not change. That is why you . . . are not already completely destroyed" (3:6)
- ○ "Bring all the tithes into the storehouse. . . . If you do, . . . I will open the windows of heaven" (3:10)
- ○ "Then those who feared the LORD spoke with each other, and the LORD listened" (3:16)
- ○ "But for you who fear my name, the Sun of Righteousness will rise with healing" (4:2)
- ○ "Remember to obey the instructions of my servant Moses" (4:4)
- ○ "Look, I am sending you the prophet Elijah before the great and dreadful day" (4:5)
- ○ "His preaching will turn the hearts of parents to their children" (4:6)
- ○ "Otherwise I will come and strike the land with a curse" (4:6)

CHAPTER 1

This is the message* that the LORD gave to Israel through the prophet Malachi.*

The LORD's Love for Israel

²"I have loved you deeply," says the LORD.

But you retort, "Really? How have you loved us?"

And the LORD replies, "I showed my love for you by loving your ancestor Jacob. Yet Esau was Jacob's brother, ³and I rejected Esau and devastated his hill country. I turned Esau's inheritance into a desert for jackals."

⁴And Esau's descendants in Edom may say, "We have been shattered, but we will rebuild the ruins."

But this is what the LORD Almighty says: "They may try to rebuild, but I will demolish them again! Their country will be known as 'The Land of Wickedness,' and their people will be called 'The People with Whom the LORD Is Forever Angry.' ⁵When you see the destruction for yourselves, you will say, 'Truly, the LORD's great power reaches far beyond our borders!'"

Unworthy Sacrifices

⁶ The LORD Almighty says to the priests: "A son honors his father, and a servant respects his master. I am your father and master, but where are the honor and respect I deserve? You have despised my name!

"But you ask, 'How have we ever despised your name?'

⁷"You have despised my name by offering defiled sacrifices on my altar.

"Then you ask, 'How have we defiled the sacrifices*?'

"You defile them by saying the altar of the LORD deserves no respect. ⁸When you give blind animals as sacrifices, isn't that wrong? And isn't it wrong to offer animals that are crippled and diseased? Try giving gifts like that to your governor, and see how pleased he is!" says the LORD Almighty.

⁹"Go ahead, beg God to be merciful to you! But when you bring that kind of offering, why should he show you any favor at all?" asks the LORD Almighty.

¹⁰"I wish that someone among you would shut the Temple doors so that these worthless sacrifices could not be offered! I am not at all pleased with you," says the LORD Almighty, "and I will not accept your offerings. ¹¹But my name is honored by people of other nations from morning till night. All around the world they offer sweet incense and pure offerings in honor of my name. For my name is great among the nations," says the LORD Almighty. ¹²"But you dishonor my name with your actions. By bringing contemptible food, you are saying it's all right to defile the Lord's table. ¹³You say, 'It's too hard to serve the LORD,' and you turn up your noses at his commands," says the LORD Almighty. "Think of it! Animals that are stolen and mutilated, crippled and sick—presented as offerings! Should I accept from you such offerings as these?" asks the LORD. ¹⁴"Cursed is the cheat who promises to give a fine ram from his flock but then sacrifices a defective one to the Lord. For I am a great king," says the LORD Almighty, "and my name is feared among the nations!

CHAPTER 2

A Warning for the Priests

"Listen, you priests; this command is for you! ²Listen to me and take it to heart. Honor my name," says the LORD Almighty, "or I will bring a terrible curse against you. I will curse even the blessings you receive. Indeed, I have already cursed them, because you have not taken my warning seriously. ³I will rebuke your descendants and splatter your faces with the dung of your

---

I DO NOT QUESTION the Lord's deep love for me. (1:2)

See the profiles for Jacob (page 43) and Esau (page 33) at Genesis 32:9 and Genesis 25:34.

I RECOGNIZE the Lord's great power and ability to destroy all who reject him. (1:5)

I HONOR AND RESPECT the Lord and give him my best. (1:6)

If something in this Bible helps you experience a closer walk with God, why not share it with others?

I TAKE the Lord's warnings to heart. (2:2)

1:1a Hebrew *An Oracle: The message.* **1:1b** *Malachi* means "my messenger." **1:7** As in Greek version; Hebrew reads *defiled you.*

festival sacrifices, and I will add you to the dung heap. [4]Then at last you will know it was I who sent you this warning so that my covenant with the Levites may continue," says the LORD Almighty.

[5]"The purpose of my covenant with the Levites was to bring life and peace, and this is what I gave them. This called for reverence from them, and they greatly revered me and stood in awe of my name. [6]They passed on to the people all the truth they received from me. They did not lie or cheat; they walked with me, living good and righteous lives, and they turned many from lives of sin. [7]The priests' lips should guard knowledge, and people should go to them for instruction, for the priests are the messengers of the LORD Almighty. [8]But not you! You have left God's paths. Your 'guidance' has caused many to stumble into sin. You have corrupted the covenant I made with the Levites," says the LORD Almighty. [9]"So I have made you despised and humiliated in the eyes of all the people. For you have not obeyed me but have shown partiality in your interpretation of the law."

A Call to Faithfulness

[10]Are we not all children of the same Father? Are we not all created by the same God? Then why are we faithless to each other, violating the covenant of our ancestors? [11]In Judah, in Israel, and in Jerusalem there is treachery, for the men of Judah have defiled the LORD's beloved sanctuary by marrying women who worship idols. [12]May the LORD cut off from the nation of Israel* every last man who has done this and yet brings an offering to the LORD Almighty.

[13]Here is another thing you do. You cover the LORD's altar with tears, weeping and groaning because he pays no attention to your offerings, and he doesn't accept them with pleasure. [14]You cry out, "Why has the LORD abandoned us?" I'll tell you why! Because the LORD witnessed the vows you and your wife made to each other on your wedding day when you were young. But you have been disloyal to her, though she remained your faithful companion, the wife of your marriage vows. [15]Didn't the LORD make you one with your wife? In body and spirit you are his.* And what does he want? Godly children from your union. So guard yourself; remain loyal to the wife of your youth. [16]"For I hate divorce!" says the LORD, the God of Israel. "It is as cruel as putting on a victim's bloodstained coat," says the LORD Almighty. "So guard yourself; always remain loyal to your wife."

[17]You have wearied the LORD with your words.

"Wearied him?" you ask. "How have we wearied him?"

You have wearied him by suggesting that the LORD favors evildoers since he does not punish them. You have wearied him by asking, "Where is the God of justice?"

CHAPTER 3

The Coming Day of Judgment

"Look! I am sending my messenger, and he will prepare the way before me. Then the Lord you are seeking will suddenly come to his Temple. The messenger of the covenant, whom you look for so eagerly, is surely coming," says the LORD Almighty. [2]"But who will be able to endure it when he comes? Who will be able to stand and face him when he appears? For he will be like a blazing fire that refines metal or like a strong soap that whitens clothes. [3]He will sit and judge like a refiner of silver, watching closely as the dross is burned away. He will purify the Levites, refining them like gold or silver, so that they may once again offer acceptable sacrifices to the LORD. [4]Then once more the LORD will accept the offerings brought to him by the people of Judah and Jerusalem, as he did in former times. [5]At that time I will put you on trial. I will

I REVERE the Lord and stand in awe of his name. (2:5)

I DO NOT SHOW partiality in how I interpret God's Word. (2:9)

I REMAIN loyal and committed to my spouse. (2:15)

I DO NOT WEARY the Lord by accusing him of injustice. (2:17)

I BELIEVE the Lord kept his promise to send a messenger before his coming (Mark 1:2; Luke 7:27). (3:1)

2:12 Hebrew *from the tents of Jacob.* 2:15 Or *Did not one God make us and preserve our life and breath?* or *Did not one God make her, both flesh and spirit?* The meaning of the Hebrew is uncertain.

be a ready witness against all sorcerers and adulterers and liars. I will speak against those who cheat employees of their wages, who oppress widows and orphans, or who deprive the foreigners living among you of justice, for these people do not fear me," says the LORD Almighty.

A Call to Repentance

⁶"I am the LORD, and I do not change. That is why you descendants of Jacob are not already completely destroyed. ⁷Ever since the days of your ancestors, you have scorned my laws and failed to obey them. Now return to me, and I will return to you," says the LORD Almighty.

"But you ask, 'How can we return when we have never gone away?'

⁸"Should people cheat God? Yet you have cheated me!

"But you ask, 'What do you mean? When did we ever cheat you?'

"You have cheated me of the tithes and offerings due to me. ⁹You are under a curse, for your whole nation has been cheating me. ¹⁰Bring all the tithes into the storehouse so there will be enough food in my Temple. If you do," says the LORD Almighty, "I will open the windows of heaven for you. I will pour out a blessing so great you won't have enough room to take it in! Try it! Let me prove it to you! ¹¹Your crops will be abundant, for I will guard them from insects and disease.* Your grapes will not shrivel before they are ripe," says the LORD Almighty. ¹²"Then all nations will call you blessed, for your land will be such a delight," says the LORD Almighty.

¹³"You have said terrible things about me," says the LORD.

"But you say, 'What do you mean? How have we spoken against you?'

¹⁴"You have said, 'What's the use of serving God? What have we gained by obeying his commands or by trying to show the LORD Almighty that we are sorry for our sins? ¹⁵From now on we will say, "Blessed are the arrogant." For those who do evil get rich, and those who dare God to punish them go free of harm.'"

The LORD's Promise of Mercy

¹⁶Then those who feared the LORD spoke with each other, and the LORD listened to what they said. In his presence, a scroll of remembrance was written to record the names of those who feared him and loved to think about him. ¹⁷"They will be my people," says the LORD Almighty. "On the day when I act, they will be my own special treasure. I will spare them as a father spares an obedient and dutiful child. ¹⁸Then you will again see the difference between the righteous and the wicked, between those who serve God and those who do not."

CHAPTER 4

The Coming Day of Judgment

The LORD Almighty says, "The day of judgment is coming, burning like a furnace. The arrogant and the wicked will be burned up like straw on that day. They will be consumed like a tree—roots and all.

²"But for you who fear my name, the Sun of Righteousness will rise with healing in his wings.* And you will go free, leaping with joy like calves let out to pasture. ³On the day when I act, you will tread upon the wicked as if they were dust under your feet," says the LORD Almighty.

⁴"Remember to obey the instructions of my servant Moses, all the laws and regulations that I gave him on Mount Sinai* for all Israel.

⁵"Look, I am sending you the prophet Elijah before the great and dreadful day of the LORD arrives. ⁶His preaching will turn the hearts of parents* to their children, and the hearts of children to their parents. Otherwise I will come and strike the land with a curse."

I TRUST in the Lord's unchanging love and faithfulness. (3:6)

See Jacob's profile (page 43) at Genesis 32:9.

I PROVE the Lord's faithfulness by giving generously to him. (3:10)

I DO NOT INSULT God by saying it is worthless to repent and obey him. (3:14)

I FEAR the Lord and obey him. (3:17)

I BELIEVE the day of the Lord's judgment is coming. (4:1)

I FEAR the Lord's name and find healing in Jesus, the Sun of Righteousness. (4:2)

See Moses' profile (page 73) at Exodus 5:1.

I BELIEVE the Lord kept his promise to send Elijah before the day of his judgment (Mark 9:11-13). (4:5)

See the profiles for Elijah (page 421) and John the Baptist (page 1117) at 1 Kings 19:18 and Mark 1:4.

3:11 Hebrew *from the devourer.* 4:2 Or *the sun of righteousness will rise with healing in its wings.* 4:4 Hebrew *Horeb,* another name for Sinai. 4:6 Hebrew *fathers;* also in 4:6b.

NEW
testament

MATTHEW

THIS FIRST BOOK in the New Testament challenges us to trust Jesus Christ as Savior and obey him as Lord.

As one of Jesus' original twelve disciples, Matthew writes as an eyewitness of Jesus' itinerant ministry, death, and resurrection. Tradition says the apostle traveled far and wide proclaiming the Good News of Jesus for more than thirty years—until he was martyred for his faith.

Many of Matthew's original readers may have wondered if Jesus truly was the long awaited King of the Jews. In this Gospel, Matthew frequently refers back to the Old Testament writings to prove that Jesus is indeed the Messiah.

In this book, Matthew speaks about his calling and first evangelistic dinner party (9:9-13), his appointment as an apostle (10:1-4), and much more.

Favorite passages in this Gospel include
- ○ The Christmas story (2:1-12)
- ○ The Beatitudes (5:3-10)
- ○ The Lord's Prayer (6:9-13)
- ○ Jesus' prayer promise (7:7-8)
- ○ Jesus' invitation to rest (11:28-30)
- ○ Peter's confession of faith (16:13-20)
- ○ Jesus' discourse on the end of the age (24:1-44)
- ○ Jesus' resurrection (28:1-10)
- ○ The Great Commission (28:18-20)

CHAPTER 1

The Record of Jesus' Ancestors

This is a record of the ancestors of Jesus the Messiah, a descendant of King David and of Abraham:

² Abraham was the father of Isaac.
Isaac was the father of Jacob.
Jacob was the father of Judah and his brothers.
³ Judah was the father of Perez and Zerah (their mother was Tamar).
Perez was the father of Hezron.
Hezron was the father of Ram.*
⁴ Ram was the father of Amminadab.
Amminadab was the father of Nahshon.
Nahshon was the father of Salmon.
⁵ Salmon was the father of Boaz (his mother was Rahab).
Boaz was the father of Obed (his mother was Ruth).
Obed was the father of Jesse.

See the profiles for David (page 629) and Abraham (page 19) at Psalm 3:1 and Genesis 15:6.

See the profiles for Isaac (page 31) and Jacob (page 43) at Genesis 25:19 and Genesis 32:9.

See the profiles for Rahab (page 251) and Ruth (page 311) at Joshua 2:11 and Ruth 1:16.

1:3 Greek *Aram;* also in 1:4. See 1 Chr 2:9-10.

See Solomon's profile (page 753) at Proverbs 2:9.

See the profiles for Rehoboam (page 409) and Asa (page 521) at 1 Kings 12:8 and 2 Chronicles 16:9.

See the profiles for Jehoshaphat (page 527) and Uzziah (page 533) at 2 Chronicles 20:21 and 2 Chronicles 26:16.

See Hezekiah's profile (page 825) at Isaiah 37:1.

See the profiles for Manasseh (page 543) and Josiah (page 461) at 2 Chronicles 33:13 and 2 Kings 23:25.

See Mary's profile (page 1149) at Luke 1:38.

I BELIEVE in Jesus Christ, born of the virgin Mary. (1:18)

I TREAT others with consideration instead of humiliation, even when it appears they are in the wrong. (1:19)

I BELIEVE AND ACCEPT God's workings, even when they are out of the realm of my previous experience. (1:20)

I BELIEVE Jesus is Immanuel—God with us. (1:23)

I TAKE God's messages seriously and obey them in every detail. (1:24)

⁶ Jesse was the father of King David.
David was the father of Solomon (his mother was Bathsheba, the widow of Uriah).
⁷ Solomon was the father of Rehoboam.
Rehoboam was the father of Abijah.
Abijah was the father of Asaph.*
⁸ Asaph was the father of Jehoshaphat.
Jehoshaphat was the father of Jehoram.*
Jehoram was the father* of Uzziah.
⁹ Uzziah was the father of Jotham.
Jotham was the father of Ahaz.
Ahaz was the father of Hezekiah.
¹⁰ Hezekiah was the father of Manasseh.
Manasseh was the father of Amos.*
Amos was the father of Josiah.
¹¹ Josiah was the father of Jehoiachin* and his brothers (born at the time of the exile to Babylon).
¹² After the Babylonian exile:
Jehoiachin was the father of Shealtiel.
Shealtiel was the father of Zerubbabel.
¹³ Zerubbabel was the father of Abiud.
Abiud was the father of Eliakim.
Eliakim was the father of Azor.
¹⁴ Azor was the father of Zadok.
Zadok was the father of Akim.
Akim was the father of Eliud.
¹⁵ Eliud was the father of Eleazar.
Eleazar was the father of Matthan.
Matthan was the father of Jacob.
¹⁶ Jacob was the father of Joseph, the husband of Mary.
Mary was the mother of Jesus, who is called the Messiah.

¹⁷All those listed above include fourteen generations from Abraham to King David, and fourteen from David's time to the Babylonian exile, and fourteen from the Babylonian exile to the Messiah.

The Birth of Jesus the Messiah

¹⁸Now this is how Jesus the Messiah was born. His mother, Mary, was engaged to be married to Joseph. But while she was still a virgin, she became pregnant by the Holy Spirit. ¹⁹Joseph, her fiancé, being a just man, decided to break the engagement quietly, so as not to disgrace her publicly.

²⁰As he considered this, he fell asleep, and an angel of the Lord appeared to him in a dream. "Joseph, son of David," the angel said, "do not be afraid to go ahead with your marriage to Mary. For the child within her has been conceived by the Holy Spirit. ²¹And she will have a son, and you are to name him Jesus,* for he will save his people from their sins." ²²All of this happened to fulfill the Lord's message through his prophet:

²³ "Look! The virgin will conceive a child!
She will give birth to a son,
and he will be called Immanuel*
(meaning, God is with us)."

²⁴When Joseph woke up, he did what the angel of the Lord commanded. He

1:7 Asaph is the same person as Asa; also in 1:8. See 1 Chr 3:10. 1:8a Greek Joram. See 1 Kgs 22:50 and note at 1 Chr 3:11. 1:8b Or ancestor; also in 1:11. 1:10 Amos is the same person as Amon. See 1 Chr 3:14. 1:11 Greek Jeconiah; also in 1:12. See 2 Kgs 24:6 and note at 1 Chr 3:16. 1:21 Jesus means "The LORD saves." 1:23 Isa 7:14; 8:8, 10.

brought Mary home to be his wife, ²⁵but she remained a virgin until her son was born. And Joseph named him Jesus.

Today what truth(s) are you choosing to believe?

CHAPTER 2

The Visit of the Wise Men

Jesus was born in the town of Bethlehem in Judea, during the reign of King Herod. About that time some wise men* from eastern lands arrived in Jerusalem, asking, ²"Where is the newborn king of the Jews? We have seen his star as it arose,* and we have come to worship him."

³Herod was deeply disturbed by their question, as was all of Jerusalem. ⁴He called a meeting of the leading priests and teachers of religious law. "Where did the prophets say the Messiah would be born?" he asked them.

I FOCUS intently on seeking Jesus to worship him as King. (2:2)

LIKE JOSEPH   *I know God's ways are right and true.*

Matthew 1:24

Have you ever been credited—or blamed—for something you didn't do? Have you ever wished you could change your reputation?

Only after Jesus Christ's death and resurrection did people come to think of Jesus Christ as "the son of the virgin Mary." For more than thirty years Jesus was commonly referred to as "Jesus, the son of Joseph" (Luke 3:23; John 1:45). The assumption was obvious and the social stigma great.

In all probability, for many years only Mary's elderly relatives Elizabeth and Zechariah, and Mary and Joseph themselves, knew (beyond question) that Joseph wasn't Jesus' real father. After all, no one else had received a divine revelation announcing this spectacular miracle. Not surprisingly, many chose to believe the rumors whispered about Joseph, Mary, and Jesus (see John 8:41).

To his credit, Joseph believed what the Lord revealed to him in a series of dreams—no matter how incredible those revelations were. Each time, Joseph quickly translated his belief into action—at great personal cost.

Consider what Joseph lost by following God's instructions:
- His reputation as a godly individual
- His extended family relationships
- His home and country
- His security

Not once, however, does Scripture record that Joseph hesitated to instantly follow God's leading. He took to heart the reality that "just as the heavens are higher than the earth, so are my [the Lord's] ways higher than your ways and my thoughts higher than your thoughts" (Isaiah 55:9).

Like Joseph, you and I have a choice to make. Each day, will we choose God's will and ways no matter what the cost? Or today will we decide to go our own way?

○ *Today's Scripture reading is Matthew 1:18-25 and 2:13-23.*

---

⁵"In Bethlehem," they said, "for this is what the prophet wrote:

⁶'O Bethlehem of Judah,
you are not just a lowly village in Judah,
for a ruler will come from you
who will be the shepherd for my people Israel.'* "

I KNOW the Scriptures so I can direct others intent on seeking Jesus Christ (Micah 5:2). (2:6)

⁷Then Herod sent a private message to the wise men, asking them to come see him. At this meeting he learned the exact time when they first saw the star. ⁸Then he told them, "Go to Bethlehem and search carefully for the child. And when you find him, come back and tell me so that I can go and worship him, too!"

⁹After this interview the wise men went their way. Once again the star appeared to them, guiding them to Bethlehem. It went ahead of them and

2:1 Or *royal astrologers*; Greek reads *magi*; also in 2:7, 16.   2:2 Or *in the east.*   2:6 Mic 5:2; 2 Sam 5:2.

I WORSHIP Jesus with joy, humility, and offerings. (2:10)

See Mary's profile (page 1149) at Luke 1:38.

See Jeremiah's profile (page 855) at Jeremiah 1:19.

I OBEY what the Lord says—promptly and willingly. (2:21)

See John the Baptist's profile (page 1117) at Mark 1:4.

See Isaiah's profile (page 801) at Isaiah 6:13.

I HAVE BEEN BAPTIZED as a public testimony that I have repented and believe in Jesus Christ for salvation. (3:6)

See the profiles for the Pharisees (page 1087) and the Sadducees (page 1103) at Matthew 12:14 and Matthew 22:23.

See Abraham's profile (page 19) at Genesis 15:6.

stopped over the place where the child was. [10]When they saw the star, they were filled with joy! [11] They entered the house where the child and his mother, Mary, were, and they fell down before him and worshiped him. Then they opened their treasure chests and gave him gifts of gold, frankincense, and myrrh. [12]But when it was time to leave, they went home another way, because God had warned them in a dream not to return to Herod.

The Escape to Egypt

[13]After the wise men were gone, an angel of the Lord appeared to Joseph in a dream. "Get up and flee to Egypt with the child and his mother," the angel said. "Stay there until I tell you to return, because Herod is going to try to kill the child." [14]That night Joseph left for Egypt with the child and Mary, his mother, [15]and they stayed there until Herod's death. This fulfilled what the Lord had spoken through the prophet: "I called my Son out of Egypt."*

[16]Herod was furious when he learned that the wise men had outwitted him. He sent soldiers to kill all the boys in and around Bethlehem who were two years old and under, because the wise men had told him the star first appeared to them about two years earlier.* [17]Herod's brutal action fulfilled the prophecy of Jeremiah:

[18] "A cry of anguish is heard in Ramah—
weeping and mourning unrestrained.
Rachel weeps for her children,
refusing to be comforted—for they are dead."*

The Return to Nazareth

[19]When Herod died, an angel of the Lord appeared in a dream to Joseph in Egypt and told him, [20]"Get up and take the child and his mother back to the land of Israel, because those who were trying to kill the child are dead." [21]So Joseph returned immediately to Israel with Jesus and his mother. [22]But when he learned that the new ruler was Herod's son Archelaus, he was afraid. Then, in another dream, he was warned to go to Galilee. [23]So they went and lived in a town called Nazareth. This fulfilled what was spoken by the prophets concerning the Messiah: "He will be called a Nazarene."

CHAPTER 3

John the Baptist Prepares the Way

In those days John the Baptist began preaching in the Judean wilderness. His message was, [2]"Turn from your sins and turn to God, because the Kingdom of Heaven is near.*" [3]Isaiah had spoken of John when he said,

"He is a voice shouting in the wilderness:
'Prepare a pathway for the Lord's coming!
Make a straight road for him!' "*

[4]John's clothes were woven from camel hair, and he wore a leather belt; his food was locusts and wild honey. [5]People from Jerusalem and from every section of Judea and from all over the Jordan Valley went out to the wilderness to hear him preach. [6]And when they confessed their sins, he baptized them in the Jordan River.

[7]But when he saw many Pharisees and Sadducees coming to be baptized, he denounced them. "You brood of snakes!" he exclaimed. "Who warned you to flee God's coming judgment? [8]Prove by the way you live that you have really turned from your sins and turned to God. [9]Don't just say, 'We're safe—we're the descendants of Abraham.' That proves nothing. God can change these stones here into children of Abraham. [10]Even now the ax of

2:15 Hos 11:1.   2:16 Or according to the time he calculated from the wise men.   2:18 Jer 31:15.   3:2 Or has come or is coming soon.   3:3 Isa 40:3.

God's judgment is poised, ready to sever your roots. Yes, every tree that does not produce good fruit will be chopped down and thrown into the fire.

[11]"I baptize with* water those who turn from their sins and turn to God. But someone is coming soon who is far greater than I am—so much greater that I am not even worthy to be his slave.* He will baptize you with the Holy Spirit and with fire.* [12]He is ready to separate the chaff from the grain with his winnowing fork. Then he will clean up the threshing area, storing the grain in his barn but burning the chaff with never-ending fire."

I HUMBLY ACKNOWLEDGE that I am a servant of the Lord God Almighty. (3:11)

LIKE THE MAGI *I seek the Lord with all my heart.*
Matthew 2:1

If you're not married, how long have you sought a spouse? If you are married, how long did you seek your spouse's "I do"?

The Magi risked everything, seeking the Christ child for many months. They traveled perhaps a thousand miles or more in a small camel caravan to find "the newborn king of the Jews" (2:2).

These wise men may have come from a prestigious city of the ancient Medes, Persians, or Chaldeans—they were almost certainly not Jews. Why then their intense dedication to find Jesus Christ?

Somehow, these men knew that God in heaven had sent his Son to earth. Nothing more spectacular had ever happened in human history. They felt compelled to welcome this awesome child and to present him with exquisite gifts of great wealth.

Braving extreme heat, sandstorms, and the constant threat of thieves, these Magi traveled through many foreign lands to the far west—to within a day of the great Mediterranean Sea.

God rewarded the dedication of these wise men and protected them as they returned home with the great news that God's Son indeed was visiting earth.

Like the Magi, you and I have a choice to make. With other believers, let's seek the Lord with all our hearts.

○ *Today's Scripture reading is Matthew 2.*

The Baptism of Jesus

[13]Then Jesus went from Galilee to the Jordan River to be baptized by John. [14]But John didn't want to baptize him. "I am the one who needs to be baptized by you," he said, "so why are you coming to me?"

[15]But Jesus said, "It must be done, because we must do everything that is right.*" So then John baptized him.

[16]After his baptism, as Jesus came up out of the water, the heavens were opened and he saw the Spirit of God descending like a dove and settling on him. [17]And a voice from heaven said, "This is my beloved Son, and I am fully pleased with him."

I DO whatever Jesus says, even if I don't understand everything he commands. (3:15)

I BELIEVE in Jesus, the Son of God, who is greatly loved by the Father and well pleasing to him. (3:17)

CHAPTER 4
The Temptation of Jesus

Then Jesus was led out into the wilderness by the Holy Spirit to be tempted there by the Devil. [2]For forty days and forty nights he ate nothing and became very hungry. [3]Then the Devil* came and said to him, "If you are the Son of God, change these stones into loaves of bread."

[4]But Jesus told him, "No! The Scriptures say,

'People need more than bread for their life;
    they must feed on every word of God.'* "

[5]Then the Devil took him to Jerusalem, to the highest point of the Temple, [6]and said, "If you are the Son of God, jump off! For the Scriptures say,

I FOLLOW Jesus' example, responding to temptation with truth from God's Word. (4:4)

I DO NOT TWIST and misuse Scripture to fit my own ideas and desires (Psalm 91:11-12). (4:6)

3:11a Or in. 3:11b Greek *to carry his sandals.* 3:11c Or *in the Holy Spirit and in fire.* 3:15 Or *we must fulfill all righteousness.* 4:3 Greek *the tempter.* 4:4 Deut 8:3.

'He orders his angels to protect you.
And they will hold you with their hands
   to keep you from striking your foot on a stone.'* "

I DO NOT TEST God
with flagrant
requests. (4:7)

[7]Jesus responded, "The Scriptures also say, 'Do not test the Lord your God.'* "

[8]Next the Devil took him to the peak of a very high mountain and showed him the nations of the world and all their glory. [9]"I will give it all to you," he said, "if you will only kneel down and worship me."

[10]"Get out of here, Satan," Jesus told him. "For the Scriptures say,

I WORSHIP AND SERVE
the Lord alone,
rejecting Satan's
enticements. (4:10)

'You must worship the Lord your God;
   serve only him.'* "

[11]Then the Devil went away, and angels came and cared for Jesus.

The Ministry of Jesus Begins

See John the Baptist's
profile (page 1117) at
Mark 1:4.

[12]When Jesus heard that John had been arrested, he left Judea and returned to Galilee. [13]But instead of going to Nazareth, he went to Capernaum, beside the Sea of Galilee, in the region of Zebulun and Naphtali. [14]This fulfilled Isaiah's prophecy:

[15] "In the land of Zebulun and of Naphtali,
   beside the sea, beyond the Jordan River—
   in Galilee where so many Gentiles live—
[16] the people who sat in darkness
   have seen a great light.
And for those who lived in the land where death casts its shadow,
   a light has shined."*

[17]From then on, Jesus began to preach, "Turn from your sins and turn to God, because the Kingdom of Heaven is near.* "

The First Disciples

See the profiles for
Peter (page 1111) and
Andrew (page 1199) at
Matthew 26:75 and
John 1:42.

[18]One day as Jesus was walking along the shore beside the Sea of Galilee, he saw two brothers—Simon, also called Peter, and Andrew—fishing with a net, for they were commercial fishermen. [19]Jesus called out to them, "Come, be my disciples, and I will show you how to fish for people!" [20]And they left their nets at once and went with him.

[21]A little farther up the shore he saw two other brothers, James and John, sitting in a boat with their father, Zebedee, mending their nets. And he called them to come, too. [22]They immediately followed him, leaving the boat and their father behind.

I LEAVE BEHIND
anything that keeps
me from following
Jesus. (4:20)

See John's profile
(page 1435) at
Revelation 1:9.

The Ministry of Jesus in Galilee

[23]Jesus traveled throughout Galilee teaching in the synagogues, preaching everywhere the Good News about the Kingdom. And he healed people who had every kind of sickness and disease. [24]News about him spread far beyond the borders of Galilee so that the sick were soon coming to be healed from as far away as Syria. And whatever their illness and pain, or if they were possessed by demons, or were epileptics, or were paralyzed—he healed them all. [25]Large crowds followed him wherever he went—people from Galilee, the Ten Towns,* Jerusalem, from all over Judea, and from east of the Jordan River.

CHAPTER 5

The Sermon on the Mount

One day as the crowds were gathering, Jesus went up the mountainside with his disciples and sat down to teach them.

4:6 Ps 91:11-12.   4:7 Deut 6:16.   4:10 Deut 6:13.   4:15-16 Isa 9:1-2.   4:17 Or has come or is coming soon.
4:25 Greek Decapolis.

The Beatitudes

²This is what he taught them:

³ "God blesses those who realize their need for him,*
for the Kingdom of Heaven is given to them.

⁴ God blesses those who mourn,
for they will be comforted.

⁵ God blesses those who are gentle and lowly,
for the whole earth will belong to them.

⁶ God blesses those who are hungry and thirsty for justice,
for they will receive it in full.

⁷ God blesses those who are merciful,
for they will be shown mercy.

⁸ God blesses those whose hearts are pure,
for they will see God.

⁹ God blesses those who work for peace,
for they will be called the children of God.

¹⁰ God blesses those who are persecuted because they live for God,
for the Kingdom of Heaven is theirs.

¹¹ "God blesses you when you are mocked and persecuted and lied about because you are my followers. ¹²Be happy about it! Be very glad! For a great reward awaits you in heaven. And remember, the ancient prophets were persecuted, too.

Teaching about Salt and Light

¹³ "You are the salt of the earth. But what good is salt if it has lost its flavor? Can you make it useful again? It will be thrown out and trampled underfoot as worthless. ¹⁴You are the light of the world—like a city on a mountain, glowing in the night for all to see. ¹⁵Don't hide your light under a basket! Instead, put it on a stand and let it shine for all. ¹⁶In the same way, let your good deeds shine out for all to see, so that everyone will praise your heavenly Father.

Teaching about the Law

¹⁷ "Don't misunderstand why I have come. I did not come to abolish the law of Moses or the writings of the prophets. No, I came to fulfill them. ¹⁸I assure you, until heaven and earth disappear, even the smallest detail of God's law will remain until its purpose is achieved. ¹⁹So if you break the smallest commandment and teach others to do the same, you will be the least in the Kingdom of Heaven. But anyone who obeys God's laws and teaches them will be great in the Kingdom of Heaven.

²⁰ "But I warn you—unless you obey God better than the teachers of religious law and the Pharisees do, you can't enter the Kingdom of Heaven at all!

Teaching about Anger

²¹ "You have heard that the law of Moses says, 'Do not murder. If you commit murder, you are subject to judgment.'* ²²But I say, if you are angry with someone,* you are subject to judgment! If you call someone an idiot,* you are in danger of being brought before the high council. And if you curse someone,* you are in danger of the fires of hell.

²³ "So if you are standing before the altar in the Temple, offering a sacrifice to God, and you suddenly remember that someone has something against you, ²⁴leave your sacrifice there beside the altar. Go and be reconciled to that person. Then come and offer your sacrifice to God. ²⁵Come to terms quickly

---

I LIVE humbly before God and other people, knowing God will reward me. (5:5)

I SHOW mercy toward others and receive mercy from God. (5:7)

I KEEP my heart pure in order to know God more intimately. (5:8)

I SEEK peace in my relationships, as befits a child of God. (5:9)

Today what command(s) are you choosing to obey?

See Moses' profile (page 73) at Exodus 5:1.

I OBEY God's commands from the heart and encourage others to do the same. (5:19)

See the profile for the Pharisees (page 1087) at Matthew 12:14.

I TAKE the initiative to be reconciled to others. (5:23)

5:3 Greek *the poor in spirit.*   5:21 Exod 20:13; Deut 5:17.   5:22a Greek *your brother;* also in 5:23. Some manuscripts add *without cause.*   5:22b Greek uses an Aramaic term of contempt: *If you say to your brother, 'Raca.'*   5:22c Greek *if you say, 'You fool.'*

with your enemy before it is too late and you are dragged into court, handed over to an officer, and thrown in jail. ²⁶I assure you that you won't be free again until you have paid the last penny.

Teaching about Adultery

²⁷"You have heard that the law of Moses says, 'Do not commit adultery.'* ²⁸But I say, anyone who even looks at a woman with lust in his eye has already committed adultery with her in his heart. ²⁹So if your eye—even if it is your good eye*—causes you to lust, gouge it out and throw it away. It is better for you to lose one part of your body than for your whole body to be thrown into hell. ³⁰And if your hand—even if it is your stronger hand*— causes you to sin, cut it off and throw it away. It is better for you to lose one part of your body than for your whole body to be thrown into hell.

Teaching about Divorce

³¹"You have heard that the law of Moses says, 'A man can divorce his wife by merely giving her a letter of divorce.'* ³²But I say that a man who divorces his wife, unless she has been unfaithful, causes her to commit adultery. And anyone who marries a divorced woman commits adultery.

Teaching about Vows

³³"Again, you have heard that the law of Moses says, 'Do not break your vows; you must carry out the vows you have made to the Lord.'* ³⁴But I say, don't make any vows! If you say, 'By heaven!' it is a sacred vow because heaven is God's throne. ³⁵And if you say, 'By the earth!' it is a sacred vow because the earth is his footstool. And don't swear, 'By Jerusalem!' for Jerusalem is the city of the great King. ³⁶Don't even swear, 'By my head!' for you can't turn one hair white or black. ³⁷Just say a simple, 'Yes, I will,' or 'No, I won't.' Your word is enough. To strengthen your promise with a vow shows that something is wrong.*

Teaching about Revenge

³⁸"You have heard that the law of Moses says, 'If an eye is injured, injure the eye of the person who did it. If a tooth gets knocked out, knock out the tooth of the person who did it.'* ³⁹But I say, don't resist an evil person! If you are slapped on the right cheek, turn the other, too. ⁴⁰If you are ordered to court and your shirt is taken from you, give your coat, too. ⁴¹If a soldier demands that you carry his gear for a mile,* carry it two miles. ⁴²Give to those who ask, and don't turn away from those who want to borrow.

Teaching about Love for Enemies

⁴³"You have heard that the law of Moses says, 'Love your neighbor'* and hate your enemy. ⁴⁴But I say, love your enemies!* Pray for those who persecute you! ⁴⁵In that way, you will be acting as true children of your Father in heaven. For he gives his sunlight to both the evil and the good, and he sends rain on the just and on the unjust, too. ⁴⁶If you love only those who love you, what good is that? Even corrupt tax collectors do that much. ⁴⁷If you are kind only to your friends,* how are you different from anyone else? Even pagans do that. ⁴⁸But you are to be perfect, even as your Father in heaven is perfect.

CHAPTER 6

Teaching about Giving to the Needy

"Take care! Don't do your good deeds publicly, to be admired, because then you will lose the reward from your Father in heaven. ²When you give a gift to someone in need, don't shout about it as the hypocrites do—blowing

---

5:27 Exod 20:14; Deut 5:18.   **5:29** Greek *your right eye.*   **5:30** Greek *your right hand.*   **5:31** Deut 24:1.
5:33 Num 30:2.   **5:37** Or *Anything beyond this is from the evil one.*   **5:38** Greek *'An eye for an eye and a tooth for a tooth.'* Exod 21:24; Lev 24:20; Deut 19:21.   **5:41** Greek *milion* [4,854 feet or 1,478 meters].   **5:43** Lev 19:18.
5:44 Some manuscripts add *Bless those who curse you, do good to those who hate you.*   **5:47** Greek *your brothers.*

I REJECT impure, lustful thoughts and desires. (5:27)

I AM TRUSTWORTHY in everything I promise. (5:33)

I BLESS those who hate me and make compassion, not personal vengeance, my higher priority. (5:39)

I LOVE those who hate me and pray for them. (5:43)

I EXERCISE the spiritual disciplines of giving, praying, and fasting for God—not for the praise of others. (6:1)

trumpets in the synagogues and streets to call attention to their acts of charity! I assure you, they have received all the reward they will ever get. ³But when you give to someone, don't tell your left hand what your right hand is doing. ⁴Give your gifts in secret, and your Father, who knows all secrets, will reward you.

Teaching about Prayer and Fasting

⁵"And now about prayer. When you pray, don't be like the hypocrites who love to pray publicly on street corners and in the synagogues where everyone can see them. I assure you, that is all the reward they will ever get. ⁶But when you pray, go away by yourself, shut the door behind you, and pray to your Father secretly. Then your Father, who knows all secrets, will reward you.

⁷"When you pray, don't babble on and on as people of other religions do. They think their prayers are answered only by repeating their words again and again. ⁸Don't be like them, because your Father knows exactly what you need even before you ask him! ⁹Pray like this:

> Our Father in heaven,
> may your name be honored.
> ¹⁰ May your Kingdom come soon.
> May your will be done here on earth,
> just as it is in heaven.
> ¹¹ Give us our food for today,*
> ¹² and forgive us our sins,
> just as we have forgiven those who have sinned against us.
> ¹³ And don't let us yield to temptation,
> but deliver us from the evil one.*

¹⁴"If you forgive those who sin against you, your heavenly Father will forgive you. ¹⁵But if you refuse to forgive others, your Father will not forgive your sins.

¹⁶"And when you fast, don't make it obvious, as the hypocrites do, who try to look pale and disheveled so people will admire them for their fasting. I assure you, that is the only reward they will ever get. ¹⁷But when you fast, comb your hair and wash your face. ¹⁸Then no one will suspect you are fasting, except your Father, who knows what you do in secret. And your Father, who knows all secrets, will reward you.

Teaching about Money and Possessions

¹⁹"Don't store up treasures here on earth, where they can be eaten by moths and get rusty, and where thieves break in and steal. ²⁰Store your treasures in heaven, where they will never become moth-eaten or rusty and where they will be safe from thieves. ²¹Wherever your treasure is, there your heart and thoughts will also be.

²²"Your eye is a lamp for your body. A pure eye lets sunshine into your soul. ²³But an evil eye shuts out the light and plunges you into darkness. If the light you think you have is really darkness, how deep that darkness will be!

²⁴"No one can serve two masters. For you will hate one and love the other, or be devoted to one and despise the other. You cannot serve both God and money.

²⁵"So I tell you, don't worry about everyday life—whether you have enough food, drink, and clothes. Doesn't life consist of more than food and clothing? ²⁶Look at the birds. They don't need to plant or harvest or put food in barns because your heavenly Father feeds them. And you are far more valuable to him than they are. ²⁷Can all your worries add a single moment to your life? Of course not.

I SPEAK intimately with my Father instead of just babbling rote prayers. (6:7)

I FORGIVE those who hurt me so that I may fully experience God's forgiveness of me. (6:14)

I MAKE eternal riches, not monetary wealth, the primary focus of my life and investments. (6:19)

I DO NOT PUT all my energy into worrying about my daily needs. (6:25)

6:11 Or *for tomorrow*. 6:13 Or *from evil*. Some manuscripts add *For yours is the kingdom and the power and the glory forever. Amen.*

See Solomon's profile
(page 753) at Proverbs
2:9.

I TRUST my heavenly
Father who knows,
cares about, and
supplies my needs.
(6:30)

I FOCUS my life and
energy on serving God
and his Kingdom each
day that he gives me.
(6:33)

I SCRUTINIZE my own
life before I judge
others. (7:1)

I SEEK good things
from God, knowing he
will answer. (7:7)

I WISELY DISCERN a
person's teaching and
actions to see if they
are true or false.
(7:15)

²⁸"And why worry about your clothes? Look at the lilies and how they grow. They don't work or make their clothing, ²⁹yet Solomon in all his glory was not dressed as beautifully as they are. ³⁰And if God cares so wonderfully for flowers that are here today and gone tomorrow, won't he more surely care for you? You have so little faith!

³¹"So don't worry about having enough food or drink or clothing. ³²Why be like the pagans who are so deeply concerned about these things? Your heavenly Father already knows all your needs, ³³and he will give you all you need from day to day if you live for him and make the Kingdom of God your primary concern.

³⁴"So don't worry about tomorrow, for tomorrow will bring its own worries. Today's trouble is enough for today.

CHAPTER 7

Don't Condemn Others

"Stop judging others, and you will not be judged. ²For others will treat you as you treat them.* Whatever measure you use in judging others, it will be used to measure how you are judged. ³And why worry about a speck in your friend's eye* when you have a log in your own? ⁴How can you think of saying, 'Let me help you get rid of that speck in your eye,' when you can't see past the log in your own eye? ⁵Hypocrite! First get rid of the log from your own eye; then perhaps you will see well enough to deal with the speck in your friend's eye.

⁶"Don't give what is holy to unholy people.* Don't give pearls to swine! They will trample the pearls, then turn and attack you.

Effective Prayer

⁷"Keep on asking, and you will be given what you ask for. Keep on looking, and you will find. Keep on knocking, and the door will be opened. ⁸For everyone who asks, receives. Everyone who seeks, finds. And the door is opened to everyone who knocks. ⁹You parents—if your children ask for a loaf of bread, do you give them a stone instead? ¹⁰Or if they ask for a fish, do you give them a snake? Of course not! ¹¹If you sinful people know how to give good gifts to your children, how much more will your heavenly Father give good gifts to those who ask him.

The Golden Rule

¹²"Do for others what you would like them to do for you. This is a summary of all that is taught in the law and the prophets.

The Narrow Gate

¹³"You can enter God's Kingdom only through the narrow gate. The highway to hell* is broad, and its gate is wide for the many who choose the easy way. ¹⁴But the gateway to life is small, and the road is narrow, and only a few ever find it.

The Tree and Its Fruit

¹⁵"Beware of false prophets who come disguised as harmless sheep, but are really wolves that will tear you apart. ¹⁶You can detect them by the way they act, just as you can identify a tree by its fruit. You don't pick grapes from thornbushes, or figs from thistles. ¹⁷A healthy tree produces good fruit, and an unhealthy tree produces bad fruit. ¹⁸A good tree can't produce bad fruit, and a bad tree can't produce good fruit. ¹⁹So every tree that does not produce good fruit is chopped down and thrown into the fire. ²⁰Yes, the way to identify a tree or a person is by the kind of fruit that is produced.

7:2 Or For God will treat you as you treat others; Greek reads For with the judgment you judge you will be judged.
7:3 Greek your brother's eye; also in 7:5.   7:6 Greek Don't give the sacred to dogs.   7:13 Greek The way that leads to destruction.

True Disciples

²¹"Not all people who sound religious are really godly. They may refer to me as 'Lord,' but they still won't enter the Kingdom of Heaven. The decisive issue is whether they obey my Father in heaven. ²²On judgment day many will tell me, 'Lord, Lord, we prophesied in your name and cast out demons in your name and performed many miracles in your name.' ²³But I will reply, 'I never knew you. Go away; the things you did were unauthorized.*'

Building on a Solid Foundation

²⁴"Anyone who listens to my teaching and obeys me is wise, like a person who builds a house on solid rock. ²⁵Though the rain comes in torrents and the floodwaters rise and the winds beat against that house, it won't collapse, because it is built on rock. ²⁶But anyone who hears my teaching and ignores it is foolish, like a person who builds a house on sand. ²⁷When the rains and floods come and the winds beat against that house, it will fall with a mighty crash."

²⁸After Jesus finished speaking, the crowds were amazed at his teaching, ²⁹for he taught as one who had real authority—quite unlike the teachers of religious law.

CHAPTER 8

Jesus Heals a Man with Leprosy

Large crowds followed Jesus as he came down the mountainside. ²Suddenly, a man with leprosy approached Jesus. He knelt before him, worshiping. "Lord," the man said, "if you want to, you can make me well again."

³Jesus touched him. "I want to," he said. "Be healed!" And instantly the leprosy disappeared. ⁴Then Jesus said to him, "Go right over to the priest and let him examine you. Don't talk to anyone along the way. Take along the offering required in the law of Moses for those who have been healed of leprosy, so everyone will have proof of your healing."

Faith of the Roman Officer

⁵When Jesus arrived in Capernaum, a Roman officer came and pleaded with him, ⁶"Lord, my young servant lies in bed, paralyzed and racked with pain."

⁷Jesus said, "I will come and heal him."

⁸Then the officer said, "Lord, I am not worthy to have you come into my home. Just say the word from where you are, and my servant will be healed! ⁹I know, because I am under the authority of my superior officers and I have authority over my soldiers. I only need to say, 'Go,' and they go, or 'Come,' and they come. And if I say to my slaves, 'Do this or that,' they do it."

¹⁰When Jesus heard this, he was amazed. Turning to the crowd, he said, "I tell you the truth, I haven't seen faith like this in all the land of Israel! ¹¹And I tell you this, that many Gentiles will come from all over the world and sit down with Abraham, Isaac, and Jacob at the feast in the Kingdom of Heaven. ¹²But many Israelites—those for whom the Kingdom was prepared—will be cast into outer darkness, where there will be weeping and gnashing of teeth."

¹³Then Jesus said to the Roman officer, "Go on home. What you have believed has happened." And the young servant was healed that same hour.

Jesus Heals Many People

¹⁴When Jesus arrived at Peter's house, Peter's mother-in-law was in bed with a high fever. ¹⁵But when Jesus touched her hand, the fever left her. Then she got up and prepared a meal for him.

¹⁶That evening many demon-possessed people were brought to Jesus. All the spirits fled when he commanded them to leave; and he healed all the sick. ¹⁷This fulfilled the word of the Lord through Isaiah, who said, "He took our sicknesses and removed our diseases."*

7:23 Or *unlawful.* 8:17 Isa 53:4.

I PAY ATTENTION to Jesus Christ's words and practice them. (7:24)

I BELIEVE Jesus taught with true authority. (7:29)

I BELIEVE Jesus is willing to make me clean. (8:3)

See Moses' profile (page 73) at Exodus 5:1.

I BELIEVE Jesus has the authority to heal. (8:8)

I BELIEVE people from all over the world will come into God's Kingdom. (8:11)

See the profiles for Abraham (page 19), Isaac (page 31), and Jacob (page 43) at Genesis 15:6, Genesis 25:19, and Genesis 32:9.

See Peter's profile (page 1111) at Matthew 26:75.

I BRING all my diseases and infirmities of body, mind, and spirit to Jesus. (8:16)

See Isaiah's profile (page 801) at Isaiah 6:13.

The Cost of Following Jesus

¹⁸When Jesus noticed how large the crowd was growing, he instructed his disciples to cross to the other side of the lake.

¹⁹Then one of the teachers of religious law said to him, "Teacher, I will follow you no matter where you go!"

²⁰But Jesus said, "Foxes have dens to live in, and birds have nests, but I, the Son of Man, have no home of my own, not even a place to lay my head."

²¹Another of his disciples said, "Lord, first let me return home and bury my father."

²²But Jesus told him, "Follow me now! Let those who are spiritually dead care for their own dead."*

Jesus Calms the Storm

²³Then Jesus got into the boat and started across the lake with his disciples. ²⁴Suddenly, a terrible storm came up, with waves breaking into the boat. But Jesus was sleeping. ²⁵The disciples went to him and woke him up, shouting, "Lord, save us! We're going to drown!"

²⁶And Jesus answered, "Why are you afraid? You have so little faith!" Then he stood up and rebuked the wind and waves, and suddenly all was calm. ²⁷The disciples just sat there in awe. "Who is this?" they asked themselves. "Even the wind and waves obey him!"

Jesus Heals Two Demon-Possessed Men

²⁸When Jesus arrived on the other side of the lake in the land of the Gadarenes,* two men who were possessed by demons met him. They lived in a cemetery and were so dangerous that no one could go through that area. ²⁹They began screaming at him, "Why are you bothering us, Son of God? You have no right to torture us before God's appointed time!" ³⁰A large herd of pigs was feeding in the distance, ³¹so the demons begged, "If you cast us out, send us into that herd of pigs."

³²"All right, go!" Jesus commanded them. So the demons came out of the men and entered the pigs, and the whole herd plunged down the steep hillside into the lake and drowned in the water. ³³The herdsmen fled to the nearby city, telling everyone what happened to the demon-possessed men. ³⁴The entire town came out to meet Jesus, but they begged him to go away and leave them alone.

CHAPTER 9

Jesus Heals a Paralyzed Man

Jesus climbed into a boat and went back across the lake to his own town. ²Some people brought to him a paralyzed man on a mat. Seeing their faith, Jesus said to the paralyzed man, "Take heart, son! Your sins are forgiven."

³"Blasphemy! This man talks like he is God!" some of the teachers of religious law said among themselves.

⁴Jesus knew what they were thinking, so he asked them, "Why are you thinking such evil thoughts? ⁵Is it easier to say, 'Your sins are forgiven' or 'Get up and walk'? ⁶I will prove that I, the Son of Man, have the authority on earth to forgive sins." Then Jesus turned to the paralyzed man and said, "Stand up, take your mat, and go on home, because you are healed!"

⁷And the man jumped up and went home! ⁸Fear swept through the crowd as they saw this happen right before their eyes. They praised God for sending a man with such great authority.

Jesus Calls Matthew

⁹As Jesus was going down the road, he saw Matthew sitting at his tax-collection

---

I AM WILLING to leave behind the securities of home and family to follow Jesus. (8:20)

I TRUST that Jesus is with me and am not afraid. (8:26)

I DO NOT RESIST but rejoice in Jesus' miracles in my life and in the lives of others. (8:34)

I BELIEVE Jesus when he says that my sins are forgiven. (9:2)

8:22 Greek *Let the dead bury their own dead.*   **8:28** Some manuscripts read *Gerasenes;* other manuscripts read *Gergesenes.* See Mark 5:1; Luke 8:26.

booth. "Come, be my disciple," Jesus said to him. So Matthew got up and followed him.

[10] That night Matthew invited Jesus and his disciples to be his dinner guests, along with his fellow tax collectors and many other notorious sinners. [11] The Pharisees were indignant. "Why does your teacher eat with such scum*?" they asked his disciples.

[12] When he heard this, Jesus replied, "Healthy people don't need a doctor—sick people do." [13] Then he added, "Now go and learn the meaning of this Scripture: 'I want you to be merciful; I don't want your sacrifices.'* For I have come to call sinners, not those who think they are already good enough."

I COME to Jesus as a sinner in need of forgiveness, not as a self-righteous performer looking for approval. (9:10)

See the profile for the Pharisees (page 1087) at Matthew 12:14.

LIKE MATTHEW   *I invite my friends to meet the Lord.*
Matthew 9:9

Do you like going to banquets? Jesus did! He enjoyed the opportunity to meet new people and whet their appetites for the Kingdom of God.

The Gospel accounts make it clear that Jesus loved to have others—friends, disciples, new converts, even religious leaders who opposed his ministry—throw parties for him.

In his preaching and teaching, Jesus spoke of the "feast in the Kingdom of Heaven" and how great it will be for those who accept his invitation. He also warned of how terrible it will be for those who are excluded because of their unbelief.

In the first three Gospels, we learn that after Matthew (aka Levi) got to know Jesus and heard his preaching, he was invited to become one of Jesus' twelve disciples. Matthew must have been shocked: After all, Jewish teachers normally weren't even willing to associate with tax collectors and other notorious "sinners."

After overcoming his initial shock, Matthew immediately gave up his lucrative tax-collecting business and held a huge banquet that evening. The banquet wasn't in Matthew's honor—a "retirement" party of sorts. Instead, Matthew somehow knew Jesus wanted to meet his friends. So he invited them all over to his home.

Sure enough, the word about Matthew's party got out to that city's religious elite, who condemned Jesus. Jesus used their harsh criticisms, however, as an opportunity to demonstrate his love and compassion for the "scum" of the earth.

Like Matthew, you and I have work associates, friends, neighbors, and relatives who don't know the Lord yet. Some may be rather shady characters. But the Lord loves them and wants us to invite them over and find a way to introduce them to the Savior.

To read parallel accounts to this story, see Mark 2:14-17 and Luke 5:27-32.

○ *Today's Scripture reading is Matthew 8:10-9:13.*

A Discussion about Fasting

[14] One day the disciples of John the Baptist came to Jesus and asked him, "Why do we and the Pharisees fast, but your disciples don't fast?"

[15] Jesus responded, "Should the wedding guests mourn while celebrating with the groom? Someday he will be taken from them, and then they will fast. [16] And who would patch an old garment with unshrunk cloth? For the patch shrinks and pulls away from the old cloth, leaving an even bigger hole than before. [17] And no one puts new wine into old wineskins. The old skins would burst from the pressure, spilling the wine and ruining the skins. New wine must be stored in new wineskins. That way both the wine and the wineskins are preserved."

See John the Baptist's profile (page 1117) at Mark 1:4.

I DO NOT TRY to force God's way of grace and salvation into a box of legalistic codes. (9:17)

Jesus Heals in Response to Faith

[18] As Jesus was saying this, the leader of a synagogue came and knelt down

9:11 Greek *with tax collectors and sinners.*   9:13 Hos 6:6.

before him. "My daughter has just died," he said, "but you can bring her back to life again if you just come and lay your hand upon her."

[19] As Jesus and the disciples were going to the official's home, [20] a woman who had had a hemorrhage for twelve years came up behind him. She touched the fringe of his robe, [21] for she thought, "If I can just touch his robe, I will be healed."

[22] Jesus turned around and said to her, "Daughter, be encouraged! Your faith has made you well." And the woman was healed at that moment.

[23] When Jesus arrived at the official's home, he noticed the noisy crowds and heard the funeral music. [24] He said, "Go away, for the girl isn't dead; she's only asleep." But the crowd laughed at him. [25] When the crowd was finally outside, Jesus went in and took the girl by the hand, and she stood up! [26] The report of this miracle swept through the entire countryside.

Jesus Heals the Blind and Mute

[27] After Jesus left the girl's home, two blind men followed along behind him, shouting, "Son of David, have mercy on us!"

[28] They went right into the house where he was staying, and Jesus asked them, "Do you believe I can make you see?"

"Yes, Lord," they told him, "we do."

[29] Then he touched their eyes and said, "Because of your faith, it will happen." [30] And suddenly they could see! Jesus sternly warned them, "Don't tell anyone about this." [31] But instead, they spread his fame all over the region.

[32] When they left, some people brought to him a man who couldn't speak because he was possessed by a demon. [33] So Jesus cast out the demon, and instantly the man could talk. The crowds marveled. "Nothing like this has ever happened in Israel!" they exclaimed.

[34] But the Pharisees said, "He can cast out demons because he is empowered by the prince of demons."

The Need for Workers

[35] Jesus traveled through all the cities and villages of that area, teaching in the synagogues and announcing the Good News about the Kingdom. And wherever he went, he healed people of every sort of disease and illness. [36] He felt great pity for the crowds that came, because their problems were so great and they didn't know where to go for help. They were like sheep without a shepherd. [37] He said to his disciples, "The harvest is so great, but the workers are so few. [38] So pray to the Lord who is in charge of the harvest; ask him to send out more workers for his fields."

CHAPTER 10

Jesus Sends Out the Twelve Apostles

Jesus called his twelve disciples to him and gave them authority to cast out evil spirits and to heal every kind of disease and illness. [2] Here are the names of the twelve apostles:

first Simon (also called Peter),
then Andrew (Peter's brother),
James (son of Zebedee),
John (James's brother),
[3] Philip,
Bartholomew,
Thomas,
Matthew (the tax collector),
James (son of Alphaeus),
Thaddaeus,
[4] Simon (the Zealot*),
Judas Iscariot (who later betrayed him).

10:4 Greek *the Cananean.*

I AM ENCOURAGED because I trusted in Jesus and he healed me. (9:22)

I DO NOT LAUGH at the promises of Jesus. (9:24)

I ASK Jesus for mercy because I believe in him. (9:27)

See David's profile (page 629) at Psalm 3:1.

I HAVE COMPASSION on people who are lost and wandering. (9:36)

I ASK the Lord of the harvest to send out more workers. (9:37)

See the profiles for Peter (page 1111), Andrew (page 1199), and John (page 1435) at Matthew 26:75, John 1:42, and Revelation 1:9.

See Thomas's profile (page 1231) at John 20:28.

See Judas's profile (page 1121) at Mark 3:19.

5Jesus sent the twelve disciples out with these instructions: "Don't go to the Gentiles or the Samaritans, 6but only to the people of Israel—God's lost sheep. 7Go and announce to them that the Kingdom of Heaven is near.* 8Heal the sick, raise the dead, cure those with leprosy, and cast out demons. Give as freely as you have received!

9"Don't take any money with you. 10Don't carry a traveler's bag with an extra coat and sandals or even a walking stick. Don't hesitate to accept hospitality, because those who work deserve to be fed.* 11Whenever you enter a city or village, search for a worthy man and stay in his home until you leave for the next town. 12When you are invited into someone's home, give it your blessing. 13If it turns out to be a worthy home, let your blessing stand; if it is not, take back the blessing. 14If a village doesn't welcome you or listen to you, shake off the dust of that place from your feet as you leave. 15I assure you, the wicked cities of Sodom and Gomorrah will be better off on the judgment day than that place will be.

16"Look, I am sending you out as sheep among wolves. Be as wary as snakes and harmless as doves. 17But beware! For you will be handed over to the courts and beaten in the synagogues. 18And you must stand trial before governors and kings because you are my followers. This will be your opportunity to tell them about me—yes, to witness to the world. 19When you are arrested, don't worry about what to say in your defense, because you will be given the right words at the right time. 20For it won't be you doing the talking—it will be the Spirit of your Father speaking through you.

21"Brother will betray brother to death, fathers will betray their own children, and children will rise against their parents and cause them to be killed. 22And everyone will hate you because of your allegiance to me. But those who endure to the end will be saved. 23When you are persecuted in one town, flee to the next. I assure you that I, the Son of Man, will return before you have reached all the towns of Israel.

24"A student is not greater than the teacher. A servant is not greater than the master. 25The student shares the teacher's fate. The servant shares the master's fate. And since I, the master of the household, have been called the prince of demons,* how much more will it happen to you, the members of the household! 26But don't be afraid of those who threaten you. For the time is coming when everything will be revealed; all that is secret will be made public. 27What I tell you now in the darkness, shout abroad when daybreak comes. What I whisper in your ears, shout from the housetops for all to hear!

28"Don't be afraid of those who want to kill you. They can only kill your body; they cannot touch your soul. Fear only God, who can destroy both soul and body in hell. 29Not even a sparrow, worth only half a penny, can fall to the ground without your Father knowing it. 30And the very hairs on your head are all numbered. 31So don't be afraid; you are more valuable to him than a whole flock of sparrows.

32"If anyone acknowledges me publicly here on earth, I will openly acknowledge that person before my Father in heaven. 33But if anyone denies me here on earth, I will deny that person before my Father in heaven.

34"Don't imagine that I came to bring peace to the earth! No, I came to bring a sword. 35I have come to set a man against his father, and a daughter against her mother, and a daughter-in-law against her mother-in-law. 36Your enemies will be right in your own household! 37If you love your father or mother more than you love me, you are not worthy of being mine; or if you love your son or daughter more than me, you are not worthy of being mine. 38If you refuse to take up your cross and follow me, you are not worthy of

I GIVE to others from the abundance of mercy and gifts God has given to me. (10:8)

Make a commitment to read from God's Word daily.

I AM DISCERNING in dealing with people, yet never deceitful. (10:16)

I TRUST the Holy Spirit to help me answer when I am attacked for my faith. (10:19)

I WILL NOT BE AFRAID to suffer for Jesus Christ, who suffered for me. (10:25)

I BOLDLY ACKNOWLEDGE my allegiance to Jesus Christ. (10:32)

I LOVE AND OBEY Jesus Christ above all other persons, no matter how dear they are to me. (10:37)

10:7 Or *has come* or *is coming soon.*   10:10 Or *the worker is worthy of support.*   10:25 Greek *Beelzeboul.*

I GIVE myself up wholly to Jesus, knowing that is the only way I will ever find myself. (10:39)

I CARE for children and those who belong to Jesus as if they were Jesus himself. (10:40)

I SEEK reassurance from Jesus when I cannot understand why life's circumstances are not working out as I expected. (11:2)

See John the Baptist's profile (page 1117) at Mark 1:4.

I AM NOT OFFENDED when the Lord Jesus chooses to work out his plan differently than I expected. (11:6)

I BELIEVE John the Baptist was the messenger that Scripture predicted would prepare the way for Jesus Christ (Malachi 3:1). (11:10)

I BELIEVE all the Hebrew Scriptures pointed to the coming of Jesus Christ. (11:13)

See Elijah's profile (page 421) at 1 Kings 19:18.

I REPENT when I hear the gospel and see God's work. (11:20)

---

being mine. ³⁹If you cling to your life, you will lose it; but if you give it up for me, you will find it.

⁴⁰"Anyone who welcomes you is welcoming me, and anyone who welcomes me is welcoming the Father who sent me. ⁴¹If you welcome a prophet as one who speaks for God,* you will receive the same reward a prophet gets. And if you welcome good and godly people because of their godliness, you will be given a reward like theirs. ⁴²And if you give even a cup of cold water to one of the least of my followers, you will surely be rewarded."

CHAPTER 11

Jesus and John the Baptist

When Jesus had finished giving these instructions to his twelve disciples, he went off teaching and preaching in towns throughout the country.

²John the Baptist, who was now in prison, heard about all the things the Messiah was doing. So he sent his disciples to ask Jesus, ³"Are you really the Messiah we've been waiting for, or should we keep looking for someone else?"

⁴Jesus told them, "Go back to John and tell him about what you have heard and seen—⁵the blind see, the lame walk, the lepers are cured, the deaf hear, the dead are raised to life, and the Good News is being preached to the poor. ⁶And tell him: 'God blesses those who are not offended by me.*'"

⁷When John's disciples had gone, Jesus began talking about him to the crowds. "Who is this man in the wilderness that you went out to see? Did you find him weak as a reed, moved by every breath of wind? ⁸Or were you expecting to see a man dressed in expensive clothes? Those who dress like that live in palaces, not out in the wilderness. ⁹Were you looking for a prophet? Yes, and he is more than a prophet. ¹⁰John is the man to whom the Scriptures refer when they say,

'Look, I am sending my messenger before you,
    and he will prepare your way before you.'*

¹¹"I assure you, of all who have ever lived, none is greater than John the Baptist. Yet even the most insignificant person in the Kingdom of Heaven is greater than he is! ¹²And from the time John the Baptist began preaching and baptizing until now, the Kingdom of Heaven has been forcefully advancing, and violent people attack it.* ¹³For before John came, all the teachings of the Scriptures looked forward to this present time. ¹⁴And if you are willing to accept what I say, he is Elijah, the one the prophets said would come.* ¹⁵Anyone who is willing to hear should listen and understand!

¹⁶"How shall I describe this generation? These people are like a group of children playing a game in the public square. They complain to their friends, ¹⁷'We played wedding songs, and you weren't happy, so we played funeral songs, but you weren't sad.' ¹⁸For John the Baptist didn't drink wine and he often fasted, and you say, 'He's demon possessed.' ¹⁹And I, the Son of Man, feast and drink, and you say, 'He's a glutton and a drunkard, and a friend of the worst sort of sinners!' But wisdom is shown to be right by what results from it."

Judgment for the Unbelievers

²⁰Then Jesus began to denounce the cities where he had done most of his miracles, because they hadn't turned from their sins and turned to God. ²¹"What horrors await you, Korazin and Bethsaida! For if the miracles I did in you had been done in wicked Tyre and Sidon, their people would have sat in deep repentance long ago, clothed in sackcloth and throwing ashes on their

---

10:41 Greek *welcome a prophet in the name of a prophet.* 11:6 Or *who don't fall away because of me.* 11:10 Mal 3:1. 11:12 Or *until now, eager multitudes have been pressing into the Kingdom of Heaven.* 11:14 See Mal 4:5.

heads to show their remorse. [22]I assure you, Tyre and Sidon will be better off on the judgment day than you! [23]And you people of Capernaum, will you be exalted to heaven? No, you will be brought down to the place of the dead.* For if the miracles I did for you had been done in Sodom, it would still be here today. [24]I assure you, Sodom will be better off on the judgment day than you."

Jesus' Prayer of Thanksgiving

[25]Then Jesus prayed this prayer: "O Father, Lord of heaven and earth, thank you for hiding the truth from those who think themselves so wise and clever, and for revealing it to the childlike. [26]Yes, Father, it pleased you to do it this way!

[27]"My Father has given me authority over everything. No one really knows the Son except the Father, and no one really knows the Father except the Son and those to whom the Son chooses to reveal him."

[28]Then Jesus said, "Come to me, all of you who are weary and carry heavy burdens, and I will give you rest. [29]Take my yoke upon you. Let me teach you, because I am humble and gentle, and you will find rest for your souls. [30]For my yoke fits perfectly, and the burden I give you is light."

CHAPTER 12

Controversy about the Sabbath

At about that time Jesus was walking through some grainfields on the Sabbath. His disciples were hungry, so they began breaking off heads of wheat and eating the grain. [2]Some Pharisees saw them do it and protested, "Your disciples shouldn't be doing that! It's against the law to work by harvesting grain on the Sabbath."

[3]But Jesus said to them, "Haven't you ever read in the Scriptures what King David did when he and his companions were hungry? [4]He went into the house of God, and they ate the special bread reserved for the priests alone. That was breaking the law, too. [5]And haven't you ever read in the law of Moses that the priests on duty in the Temple may work on the Sabbath? [6]I tell you, there is one here who is even greater than the Temple! [7]But you would not have condemned those who aren't guilty if you knew the meaning of this Scripture: 'I want you to be merciful; I don't want your sacrifices.'* [8]For I, the Son of Man, am master even of the Sabbath."

[9]Then he went over to the synagogue, [10]where he noticed a man with a deformed hand. The Pharisees asked Jesus, "Is it legal to work by healing on the Sabbath day?" (They were, of course, hoping he would say yes, so they could bring charges against him.)

[11]And he answered, "If you had one sheep, and it fell into a well on the Sabbath, wouldn't you get to work and pull it out? Of course you would. [12]And how much more valuable is a person than a sheep! Yes, it is right to do good on the Sabbath." [13]Then he said to the man, "Reach out your hand." The man reached out his hand, and it became normal, just like the other one. [14]Then the Pharisees called a meeting and discussed plans for killing Jesus.

Jesus, God's Chosen Servant

[15]But Jesus knew what they were planning. He left that area, and many people followed him. He healed all the sick among them, [16]but he warned them not to say who he was. [17]This fulfilled the prophecy of Isaiah concerning him:

[18]"Look at my Servant,
  whom I have chosen.
He is my Beloved,
  and I am very pleased with him.

I PRAISE the Father for choosing to reveal his truth to me. (11:25)

I COME to Jesus with my burdens and receive rest. (11:28)

I ACCEPT the demands that Jesus places on those who follow him. (11:29)

See David's profile (page 629) at Psalm 3:1.

See Moses' profile (page 73) at Exodus 5:1.

I DO NOT PUT man's interpretations and rules above God's Word. (12:6)

I ACKNOWLEDGE Jesus Christ as Lord of every day and every act of obedience. (12:8)

I CARE more about helping individuals in need than about looking righteous. (12:12)

See Isaiah's profile (page 801) at Isaiah 6:13.

I BELIEVE Jesus fulfilled the prophecy about God's Servant. (12:18)

11:23 Greek *to Hades.*   12:7 Hos 6:6.

I will put my Spirit upon him,
  and he will proclaim justice to the nations.
[19] He will not fight or shout;
  he will not raise his voice in public.
[20] He will not crush those who are weak,
  or quench the smallest hope,
  until he brings full justice with his final victory.
[21] And his name will be the hope
  of all the world."*

Jesus and the Prince of Demons

[22]Then a demon-possessed man, who was both blind and unable to talk, was brought to Jesus. He healed the man so that he could both speak and see. [23] The crowd was amazed. "Could it be that Jesus is the Son of David, the Messiah?" they wondered out loud.

[24]But when the Pharisees heard about the miracle, they said, "No wonder he can cast out demons. He gets his power from Satan,* the prince of demons."

[25]Jesus knew their thoughts and replied, "Any kingdom at war with itself is doomed. A city or home divided against itself is doomed. [26]And if Satan is casting out Satan, he is fighting against himself. His own kingdom will not survive. [27]And if I am empowered by the prince of demons,* what about your own followers? They cast out demons, too, so they will judge you for what you have said. [28]But if I am casting out demons by the Spirit of God, then the Kingdom of God has arrived among you. [29]Let me illustrate this. You can't enter a strong man's house and rob him without first tying him up. Only then can his house be robbed!* [30]Anyone who isn't helping me opposes me, and anyone who isn't working with me is actually working against me.

[31]"Every sin or blasphemy can be forgiven—except blasphemy against the Holy Spirit, which can never be forgiven. [32]Anyone who blasphemes against me, the Son of Man, can be forgiven, but blasphemy against the Holy Spirit will never be forgiven, either in this world or in the world to come.

[33]"A tree is identified by its fruit. Make a tree good, and its fruit will be good. Make a tree bad, and its fruit will be bad. [34]You brood of snakes! How could evil men like you speak what is good and right? For whatever is in your heart determines what you say. [35]A good person produces good words from a good heart, and an evil person produces evil words from an evil heart. [36]And I tell you this, that you must give an account on judgment day of every idle word you speak. [37]The words you say now reflect your fate then; either you will be justified by them or you will be condemned."

The Sign of Jonah

[38]One day some teachers of religious law and Pharisees came to Jesus and said, "Teacher, we want you to show us a miraculous sign to prove that you are from God."

[39]But Jesus replied, "Only an evil, faithless generation would ask for a miraculous sign; but the only sign I will give them is the sign of the prophet Jonah. [40]For as Jonah was in the belly of the great fish for three days and three nights, so I, the Son of Man, will be in the heart of the earth for three days and three nights. [41]The people of Nineveh will rise up against this generation on judgment day and condemn it, because they repented at the preaching of Jonah. And now someone greater than Jonah is here—and you refuse to repent. [42] The queen of Sheba* will also rise up against this generation on judgment day and condemn it, because she came from a distant land to hear

I BELIEVE that Jesus is the Son of David, the Messiah. (12:23)

I BELIEVE Jesus cast out demons by the Spirit of God. (12:28)

I GUARD my heart and words, knowing that out of the first flows the second. (12:34)

I GUARD my words carefully, knowing I will have to give account for every one. (12:36)

I KNOW that Jesus is from God the Father because of the sign of his resurrection. (12:39)

See Jonah's profile (page 1027) at Jonah 4:2.

12:18-21 Isa 42:1-4.   12:24 Greek *Beelzeboul*.   12:27 Greek *by Beelzeboul*.   12:29 Or *One cannot rob Satan's kingdom without first tying him up. Only then can his demons be cast out*.   12:42 Greek *The queen of the south*.

the wisdom of Solomon. And now someone greater than Solomon is here—and you refuse to listen to him.

See Solomon's profile (page 753) at Proverbs 2:9.

⁴³"When an evil spirit leaves a person, it goes into the desert, seeking rest but finding none. ⁴⁴Then it says, 'I will return to the person I came from.' So it returns and finds its former home empty, swept, and clean. ⁴⁵Then the spirit finds seven other spirits more evil than itself, and they all enter the person and live there. And so that person is worse off than before. That will be the experience of this evil generation."

The True Family of Jesus

⁴⁶As Jesus was speaking to the crowd, his mother and brothers were outside, wanting to talk with him. ⁴⁷Someone told Jesus, "Your mother and your brothers are outside, and they want to speak to you."

⁴⁸Jesus asked, "Who is my mother? Who are my brothers?" ⁴⁹ Then he pointed to his disciples and said, "These are my mother and brothers. ⁵⁰Anyone who does the will of my Father in heaven is my brother and sister and mother!"

I DO the will of my Father in heaven. (12:50)

UNLIKE THE PHARISEES *I am not a self-centered legalist.*
Matthew 12:14

Talk about a bunch of hypocrites.

The Pharisees said they believed in God, angels, miracles, the Ten Commandments, and the prophecies of old. They went so far as to reinterpret the Scriptures and follow strict rules governing all manner of external behavior in order to look ultrareligious. Yet Jesus warned, "Unless you obey God better than the teachers of religious law and the Pharisees do, you can't enter the Kingdom of Heaven at all!" (5:20). Why such a harsh rebuke?

It turns out that the Pharisees in Jesus' day had placed their own rules above God's Word and looked down on everyone else. They were far more interested in their own power and prestige than in God's glory and honor.

When Jesus started going out of his way to break the minute "laws" invented and revered by these people, the Pharisees saw red. They couldn't stand it when he emphasized obeying the spirit of Scripture from the heart. Why, here was a commoner asserting his authority over their centuries of hallowed tradition!

The more convincingly Jesus demonstrated his deity, the more bloodthirsty the Pharisees became. Finally, they decided to work out a plan to assassinate this subversive folk hero from Galilee. So much for heeding God's Word and his promised Messiah.

Sadly, many religious hypocrites seek to wield power in our own day. If we're not careful, you and I also can end up focusing merely on the external aspects of Christianity instead of on an ongoing, daily, heartfelt relationship with the Lord himself.

Unlike the Pharisees, let's take God at his Word and daily choose to love him with all our heart, soul, strength, and mind (22:34-40).

To discover more about what Jesus thought of the Pharisees, see Matthew 15:1-20; 16:5-12; 21:33–22:22; and 23:1-36.

○ *Today's Scripture reading is Matthew 12:1-45.*

CHAPTER 13

Story of the Farmer Scattering Seed

Later that same day, Jesus left the house and went down to the shore, ²where an immense crowd soon gathered. He got into a boat, where he sat and taught as the people listened on the shore. ³He told many stories such as this one:

I LISTEN to Jesus' words whenever I have the opportunity. (13:2)

"A farmer went out to plant some seed. ⁴As he scattered it across his field, some seeds fell on a footpath, and the birds came and ate them. ⁵Other seeds fell on shallow soil with underlying rock. The plants sprang up quickly, ⁶but they soon wilted beneath the hot sun and died because the roots had no nourishment in the shallow soil. [7]Other seeds fell among thorns that shot up and choked out the tender blades. [8]But some seeds fell on fertile soil and produced a crop that was thirty, sixty, and even a hundred times as much as had been planted. [9]Anyone who is willing to hear should listen and understand!"

[10]His disciples came and asked him, "Why do you always tell stories when you talk to the people?"

[11]Then he explained to them, "You have been permitted to understand the secrets of the Kingdom of Heaven, but others have not. [12]To those who are open to my teaching, more understanding will be given, and they will have an abundance of knowledge. But to those who are not listening, even what they have will be taken away from them. [13]That is why I tell these stories, because people see what I do, but they don't really see. They hear what I say, but they don't really hear, and they don't understand. [14]This fulfills the prophecy of Isaiah, which says:

'You will hear my words,
    but you will not understand;
you will see what I do,
    but you will not perceive its meaning.
[15]For the hearts of these people are hardened,
    and their ears cannot hear,
    and they have closed their eyes—
so their eyes cannot see,
    and their ears cannot hear,
    and their hearts cannot understand,
and they cannot turn to me
    and let me heal them.'*

[16]"But blessed are your eyes, because they see; and your ears, because they hear. [17]I assure you, many prophets and godly people have longed to see and hear what you have seen and heard, but they could not.

[18]"Now here is the explanation of the story I told about the farmer sowing grain: [19]The seed that fell on the hard path represents those who hear the Good News about the Kingdom and don't understand it. Then the evil one comes and snatches the seed away from their hearts. [20]The rocky soil represents those who hear the message and receive it with joy. [21]But like young plants in such soil, their roots don't go very deep. At first they get along fine, but they wilt as soon as they have problems or are persecuted because they believe the word. [22]The thorny ground represents those who hear and accept the Good News, but all too quickly the message is crowded out by the cares of this life and the lure of wealth, so no crop is produced. [23]The good soil represents the hearts of those who truly accept God's message and produce a huge harvest—thirty, sixty, or even a hundred times as much as had been planted."

Story of the Wheat and Weeds

[24]Here is another story Jesus told: "The Kingdom of Heaven is like a farmer who planted good seed in his field. [25]But that night as everyone slept, his enemy came and planted weeds among the wheat. [26]When the crop began to grow and produce grain, the weeds also grew. [27]The farmer's servants came and told him, 'Sir, the field where you planted that good seed is full of weeds!'

[28]"'An enemy has done it!' the farmer exclaimed.

"'Shall we pull out the weeds?' they asked.

[29]"He replied, 'No, you'll hurt the wheat if you do. [30]Let both grow together

I SEEK to build upon the understanding of God and his Word that I already have. (13:12)

See Isaiah's profile (page 801) at Isaiah 6:13.

I DO NOT HARDEN my heart or ignore the truth God has already revealed to me. (13:15)

I THANK God for giving me understanding of his truth. (13:16)

I GROW in my understanding of the Good News so that I won't give up in times of trouble. (13:21)

I FOCUS on understanding the Good News so financial worries don't crowd out its importance. (13:22)

I UNDERSTAND AND BELIEVE the Good News wholeheartedly to be saved and live a productive life. (13:23)

13:14-15 Isa 6:9-10.

until the harvest. Then I will tell the harvesters to sort out the weeds and burn them and to put the wheat in the barn.' "

Illustration of the Mustard Seed

³¹Here is another illustration Jesus used: "The Kingdom of Heaven is like a mustard seed planted in a field. ³²It is the smallest of all seeds, but it becomes the largest of garden plants and grows into a tree where birds can come and find shelter in its branches."

I BELIEVE the Kingdom of Heaven is growing. (13:32)

Illustration of the Yeast

³³Jesus also used this illustration: "The Kingdom of Heaven is like yeast used by a woman making bread. Even though she used a large amount* of flour, the yeast permeated every part of the dough."

³⁴Jesus always used stories and illustrations like these when speaking to the crowds. In fact, he never spoke to them without using such parables. ³⁵This fulfilled the prophecy that said,

"I will speak to you in parables.
I will explain mysteries hidden since the creation of the world."*

The Wheat and Weeds Explained

³⁶Then, leaving the crowds outside, Jesus went into the house. His disciples said, "Please explain the story of the weeds in the field."

³⁷"All right," he said. "I, the Son of Man, am the farmer who plants the good seed. ³⁸The field is the world, and the good seed represents the people of the Kingdom. The weeds are the people who belong to the evil one. ³⁹The enemy who planted the weeds among the wheat is the Devil. The harvest is the end of the world, and the harvesters are the angels.

I BELONG to God and am a member of the Kingdom of Heaven. (13:38)

⁴⁰"Just as the weeds are separated out and burned, so it will be at the end of the world. ⁴¹I, the Son of Man, will send my angels, and they will remove from my Kingdom everything that causes sin and all who do evil, ⁴²and they will throw them into the furnace and burn them. There will be weeping and gnashing of teeth. ⁴³Then the godly will shine like the sun in their Father's Kingdom. Anyone who is willing to hear should listen and understand!

I WAIT for God's time to determine who has lived his or her life in hypocrisy or in true belief. (13:41)

Illustration of the Hidden Treasure

⁴⁴"The Kingdom of Heaven is like a treasure that a man discovered hidden in a field. In his excitement, he hid it again and sold everything he owned to get enough money to buy the field—and to get the treasure, too!

I GIVE anything to be part of God's Kingdom. (13:44)

Illustration of the Pearl Merchant

⁴⁵"Again, the Kingdom of Heaven is like a pearl merchant on the lookout for choice pearls. ⁴⁶When he discovered a pearl of great value, he sold everything he owned and bought it!

Illustration of the Fishing Net

⁴⁷"Again, the Kingdom of Heaven is like a fishing net that is thrown into the water and gathers fish of every kind. ⁴⁸When the net is full, they drag it up onto the shore, sit down, sort the good fish into crates, and throw the bad ones away. ⁴⁹That is the way it will be at the end of the world. The angels will come and separate the wicked people from the godly, ⁵⁰throwing the wicked into the fire. There will be weeping and gnashing of teeth. ⁵¹Do you understand?"

"Yes," they said, "we do."

I BELIEVE God will judge the wicked at the end of the world. (13:50)

⁵²Then he added, "Every teacher of religious law who has become a disciple in the Kingdom of Heaven is like a person who brings out of the storehouse the new teachings as well as the old."

13:33 Greek 3 measures.   13:35 Ps 78:2.

Jesus Rejected at Nazareth

[53]When Jesus had finished telling these stories, he left that part of the country. [54]He returned to Nazareth, his hometown. When he taught there in the synagogue, everyone was astonished and said, "Where does he get his wisdom and his miracles? [55]He's just a carpenter's son, and we know Mary, his mother, and his brothers—James, Joseph, Simon, and Judas. [56]All his sisters live right here among us. What makes him so great?" [57]And they were deeply offended and refused to believe in him.

Then Jesus told them, "A prophet is honored everywhere except in his own hometown and among his own family." [58]And so he did only a few miracles there because of their unbelief.

CHAPTER 14

The Death of John the Baptist

When Herod Antipas* heard about Jesus, [2]he said to his advisers, "This must be John the Baptist come back to life again! That is why he can do such miracles." [3]For Herod had arrested and imprisoned John as a favor to his wife Herodias (the former wife of Herod's brother Philip). [4]John kept telling Herod, "It is illegal for you to marry her." [5]Herod would have executed John, but he was afraid of a riot, because all the people believed John was a prophet.

[6]But at a birthday party for Herod, Herodias's daughter performed a dance that greatly pleased him, [7]so he promised with an oath to give her anything she wanted. [8]At her mother's urging, the girl asked, "I want the head of John the Baptist on a tray!" [9]The king was sorry, but because of his oath and because he didn't want to back down in front of his guests, he issued the necessary orders. [10]So John was beheaded in the prison, [11]and his head was brought on a tray and given to the girl, who took it to her mother. [12]John's disciples came for his body and buried it. Then they told Jesus what had happened.

Jesus Feeds Five Thousand

[13]As soon as Jesus heard the news, he went off by himself in a boat to a remote area to be alone. But the crowds heard where he was headed and followed by land from many villages. [14]A vast crowd was there as he stepped from the boat, and he had compassion on them and healed their sick.

[15] That evening the disciples came to him and said, "This is a desolate place, and it is getting late. Send the crowds away so they can go to the villages and buy food for themselves."

[16]But Jesus replied, "That isn't necessary—you feed them."

[17]"Impossible!" they exclaimed. "We have only five loaves of bread and two fish!"

[18]"Bring them here," he said. [19]Then he told the people to sit down on the grass. And he took the five loaves and two fish, looked up toward heaven, and asked God's blessing on the food. Breaking the loaves into pieces, he gave some of the bread and fish to each disciple, and the disciples gave them to the people. [20]They all ate as much as they wanted, and they picked up twelve baskets of leftovers. [21]About five thousand men had eaten from those five loaves, in addition to all the women and children!

Jesus Walks on Water

[22]Immediately after this, Jesus made his disciples get back into the boat and cross to the other side of the lake while he sent the people home. [23]Afterward he went up into the hills by himself to pray. Night fell while he was there

---

I AM NOT OFFENDED by anything Jesus said. (13:55)

See Mary's profile (page 1149) at Luke 1:38.

See John the Baptist's profile (page 1117) at Mark 1:4.

I LISTEN AND HEED when others warn me about sin in my life. (14:4)

I DO NOT LET peer pressure and my own public image keep me from doing what is right. (14:9)

I TAKE TIME to grieve. (14:13)

I AM SENSITIVE to the spiritual and physical needs of others, even when I am in need myself. (14:14)

I ALLOW Jesus to use whatever I have to meet the needs of others. (14:19)

14:1 Greek *Herod the tetrarch.* He was a son of King Herod and was ruler over one of the four districts in Palestine.

alone. [24]Meanwhile, the disciples were in trouble far away from land, for a strong wind had risen, and they were fighting heavy waves.

[25]About three o'clock in the morning* Jesus came to them, walking on the water. [26]When the disciples saw him, they screamed in terror, thinking he was a ghost. [27]But Jesus spoke to them at once. "It's all right," he said. "I am here! Don't be afraid."

[28]Then Peter called to him, "Lord, if it's really you, tell me to come to you by walking on water."

[29]"All right, come," Jesus said.

So Peter went over the side of the boat and walked on the water toward Jesus. [30]But when he looked around at the high waves, he was terrified and began to sink. "Save me, Lord!" he shouted.

[31]Instantly Jesus reached out his hand and grabbed him. "You don't have much faith," Jesus said. "Why did you doubt me?" [32]And when they climbed back into the boat, the wind stopped.

[33]Then the disciples worshiped him. "You really are the Son of God!" they exclaimed.

[34]After they had crossed the lake, they landed at Gennesaret. [35]The news of their arrival spread quickly throughout the whole surrounding area, and soon people were bringing all their sick to be healed. [36]The sick begged him to let them touch even the fringe of his robe, and all who touched it were healed.

CHAPTER 15

Jesus Teaches about Inner Purity

Some Pharisees and teachers of religious law now arrived from Jerusalem to interview Jesus. [2]"Why do your disciples disobey our age-old traditions?" they demanded. "They ignore our tradition of ceremonial hand washing before they eat."

[3]Jesus replied, "And why do you, by your traditions, violate the direct commandments of God? [4]For instance, God says, 'Honor your father and mother,' and 'Anyone who speaks evil of father or mother must be put to death.'* [5]But you say, 'You don't need to honor your parents by caring for their needs if you give the money to God instead.' [6]And so, by your own tradition, you nullify the direct commandment of God. [7]You hypocrites! Isaiah was prophesying about you when he said,

[8]'These people honor me with their lips,
   but their hearts are far away.
[9]Their worship is a farce,
   for they replace God's commands with their own man-made
      teachings.'* "

[10]Then Jesus called to the crowds and said, "Listen to what I say and try to understand. [11]You are not defiled by what you eat; you are defiled by what you say and do.*"

[12]Then the disciples came to him and asked, "Do you realize you offended the Pharisees by what you just said?"

[13]Jesus replied, "Every plant not planted by my heavenly Father will be rooted up, [14]so ignore them. They are blind guides leading the blind, and if one blind person guides another, they will both fall into a ditch."

[15]Then Peter asked Jesus, "Explain what you meant when you said people aren't defiled by what they eat."

[16]"Don't you understand?" Jesus asked him. [17]"Anything you eat passes through the stomach and then goes out of the body. [18]But evil words come from an evil heart and defile the person who says them. [19]For from the heart

---

I HAVE faith and courage in a threatening situation because Jesus is with me. (14:24)

See Peter's profile (page 1111) at Matthew 26:75.

I KEEP my focus on Jesus in every threatening situation of life. (14:30)

I DO NOT LOOK for loopholes to get around obeying God's commands. (15:6)

See Isaiah's profile (page 801) at Isaiah 6:13.

I WILL SPEAK the truth, even if it offends those who disobey God. (15:12)

See Peter's profile (page 1111) at Matthew 26:75.

I EXAMINE my heart so that what comes out of my mouth is pure. (15:18)

14:25 Greek *In the fourth watch of the night.*   15:4 Exod 20:12; 21:17; Lev 20:9; Deut 5:16.   15:8-9 Isa 29:13.
15:11 Or *what comes out of the mouth defiles a person.*

come evil thoughts, murder, adultery, all other sexual immorality, theft, lying, and slander. ²⁰These are what defile you. Eating with unwashed hands could never defile you and make you unacceptable to God!"

The Faith of a Gentile Woman

²¹Jesus then left Galilee and went north to the region of Tyre and Sidon. ²²A Gentile* woman who lived there came to him, pleading, "Have mercy on me, O Lord, Son of David! For my daughter has a demon in her, and it is severely tormenting her."

²³But Jesus gave her no reply—not even a word. Then his disciples urged him to send her away. "Tell her to leave," they said. "She is bothering us with all her begging."

²⁴Then he said to the woman, "I was sent only to help the people of Israel—God's lost sheep—not the Gentiles."

²⁵But she came and worshiped him and pleaded again, "Lord, help me!"

²⁶"It isn't right to take food from the children and throw it to the dogs," he said.

²⁷"Yes, Lord," she replied, "but even dogs are permitted to eat crumbs that fall beneath their master's table."

²⁸"Woman," Jesus said to her, "your faith is great. Your request is granted." And her daughter was instantly healed.

Jesus Heals Many People

²⁹Jesus returned to the Sea of Galilee and climbed a hill and sat down. ³⁰A vast crowd brought him the lame, blind, crippled, mute, and many others with physical difficulties, and they laid them before Jesus. And he healed them all. ³¹The crowd was amazed! Those who hadn't been able to speak were talking, the crippled were made well, the lame were walking around, and those who had been blind could see again! And they praised the God of Israel.

Jesus Feeds Four Thousand

³²Then Jesus called his disciples to him and said, "I feel sorry for these people. They have been here with me for three days, and they have nothing left to eat. I don't want to send them away hungry, or they will faint along the road."

³³The disciples replied, "And where would we get enough food out here in the wilderness for all of them to eat?"

³⁴Jesus asked, "How many loaves of bread do you have?"

They replied, "Seven, and a few small fish." ³⁵So Jesus told all the people to sit down on the ground. ³⁶Then he took the seven loaves and the fish, thanked God for them, broke them into pieces, and gave them to the disciples, who distributed the food to the crowd.

³⁷They all ate until they were full, and when the scraps were picked up, there were seven large baskets of food left over! ³⁸There were four thousand men who were fed that day, in addition to all the women and children. ³⁹Then Jesus sent the people home, and he got into a boat and crossed over to the region of Magadan.

CHAPTER 16

Leaders Demand a Miraculous Sign

One day the Pharisees and Sadducees came to test Jesus' claims by asking him to show them a miraculous sign from heaven.

²He replied, "You know the saying, 'Red sky at night means fair weather tomorrow, ³red sky in the morning means foul weather all day.' You are good at reading the weather signs in the sky, but you can't read the obvious signs of the times!* ⁴Only an evil, faithless generation would ask for a miraculous sign, but the only sign I will give them is the sign of the prophet Jonah." Then Jesus left them and went away.

I BELIEVE Jesus seeks anyone anywhere who needs and wants him. (15:21)

I SEEK mercy from Jesus by expressing my need to him both publicly and privately. (15:22)

See the profiles for the Gentile Woman (page 1129) and David (page 629) at Mark 7:30 and Psalm 3:1.

I PERSIST in prayer, completely dependent on the Lord. (15:25)

I HAVE COMPASSION for the physical and spiritual needs of others. (15:32)

I LEARN to trust Jesus to meet the needs of others through me—especially because I have seen him do it before. (15:33)

See the profile for the Sadducees (page 1103) at Matthew 22:23.

I DO NOT DEMAND extra proof as an excuse for unbelief. (16:4)

See Jonah's profile (page 1027) at Jonah 4:2.

15:22 Greek Canaanite.   16:2-3 Several manuscripts do not include any of the words in 16:2-3 after He replied.

Yeast of the Pharisees and Sadducees

[5]Later, after they crossed to the other side of the lake, the disciples discovered they had forgotten to bring any food. [6]"Watch out!" Jesus warned them. "Beware of the yeast of the Pharisees and Sadducees."

[7]They decided he was saying this because they hadn't brought any bread. [8]Jesus knew what they were thinking, so he said, "You have so little faith! Why are you worried about having no food? [9]Won't you ever understand? Don't you remember the five thousand I fed with five loaves, and the baskets of food that were left over? [10]Don't you remember the four thousand I fed with seven loaves, with baskets of food left over? [11]How could you even think I was talking about food? So again I say, 'Beware of the yeast of the Pharisees and Sadducees.'"

[12]Then at last they understood that he wasn't speaking about yeast or bread but about the false teaching of the Pharisees and Sadducees.

Peter's Declaration about Jesus

[13]When Jesus came to the region of Caesarea Philippi, he asked his disciples, "Who do people say that the Son of Man is?"

[14]"Well," they replied, "some say John the Baptist, some say Elijah, and others say Jeremiah or one of the other prophets."

[15]Then he asked them, "Who do you say I am?"

[16]Simon Peter answered, "You are the Messiah, the Son of the living God."

[17]Jesus replied, "You are blessed, Simon son of John,* because my Father in heaven has revealed this to you. You did not learn this from any human being. [18]Now I say to you that you are Peter,* and upon this rock I will build my church, and all the powers of hell* will not conquer it. [19]And I will give you the keys of the Kingdom of Heaven. Whatever you lock on earth will be locked in heaven, and whatever you open on earth will be opened in heaven." [20]Then he sternly warned them not to tell anyone that he was the Messiah.

Jesus Predicts His Death

[21]From then on Jesus began to tell his disciples plainly that he had to go to Jerusalem, and he told them what would happen to him there. He would suffer at the hands of the leaders and the leading priests and the teachers of religious law. He would be killed, and he would be raised on the third day.

[22]But Peter took him aside and corrected him. "Heaven forbid, Lord," he said. "This will never happen to you!"

[23]Jesus turned to Peter and said, "Get away from me, Satan! You are a dangerous trap to me. You are seeing things merely from a human point of view, and not from God's."

[24]Then Jesus said to the disciples, "If any of you wants to be my follower, you must put aside your selfish ambition, shoulder your cross, and follow me. [25]If you try to keep your life for yourself, you will lose it. But if you give up your life for me, you will find true life. [26]And how do you benefit if you gain the whole world but lose your own soul* in the process? Is anything worth more than your soul? [27]For I, the Son of Man, will come in the glory of my Father with his angels and will judge all people according to their deeds. [28]And I assure you that some of you standing here right now will not die before you see me, the Son of Man, coming in my Kingdom."

CHAPTER 17

The Transfiguration

Six days later Jesus took Peter and the two brothers, James and John, and led them up a high mountain. [2]As the men watched, Jesus' appearance changed so that his face shone like the sun, and his clothing became dazzling white.

I REMEMBER God's provision in the past and trust him for future provision. (16:8)

See the profiles for John the Baptist (page 1117), Elijah (page 421), and Jeremiah (page 855) at Mark 1:4, 1 Kings 19:18, and Jeremiah 1:19.

I BELIEVE Jesus is the Christ, the Son of God. (16:16)

See Peter's profile (page 1111) at Matthew 26:75.

I DO NOT TELL God how to run the universe. (16:22)

I GAIN meaning and fulfillment in life by giving myself freely to Jesus. (16:25)

I AM WILLING to "lose out" in this world to gain the salvation and reward of God. (16:26)

See the profiles for Peter (page 1111) and John (page 1435) at Matthew 26:75 and Revelation 1:9.

I WORSHIP the glorified Lord Jesus Christ (1 Corinthians 15:35-55). (17:1)

16:17 Greek *Simon son of Jonah;* see John 1:42; 21:15-17. 16:18a *Peter* means "stone" or "rock." 16:18b Greek *and the gates of Hades.* 16:26 Or *your life;* also in 16:26b.

See the profiles for Moses (page 73) and Elijah (page 421) at Exodus 5:1 and 1 Kings 19:18.

I LISTEN to what God commands instead of rushing around pursuing my own little agenda. (17:4)

I FOCUS on Jesus alone, who is preeminent above all human spiritual leaders. (17:8)

I ASK the Lord for mercy on those I love. (17:15)

I AM WILLING to go beyond my duty so that I do not purposely offend unbelievers. (17:27)

³Suddenly, Moses and Elijah appeared and began talking with Jesus. ⁴Peter blurted out, "Lord, this is wonderful! If you want me to, I'll make three shrines,* one for you, one for Moses, and one for Elijah."

⁵But even as he said it, a bright cloud came over them, and a voice from the cloud said, "This is my beloved Son, and I am fully pleased with him. Listen to him." ⁶The disciples were terrified and fell face down on the ground.

⁷Jesus came over and touched them. "Get up," he said, "don't be afraid." ⁸And when they looked, they saw only Jesus with them. ⁹As they descended the mountain, Jesus commanded them, "Don't tell anyone what you have seen until I, the Son of Man, have been raised from the dead."

¹⁰His disciples asked, "Why do the teachers of religious law insist that Elijah must return before the Messiah comes*?"

¹¹Jesus replied, "Elijah is indeed coming first to set everything in order. ¹²But I tell you, he has already come, but he wasn't recognized, and he was badly mistreated. And soon the Son of Man will also suffer at their hands." ¹³Then the disciples realized he had been speaking of John the Baptist.

Jesus Heals a Demon-Possessed Boy

¹⁴When they arrived at the foot of the mountain, a huge crowd was waiting for them. A man came and knelt before Jesus and said, ¹⁵"Lord, have mercy on my son, because he has seizures and suffers terribly. He often falls into the fire or into the water. ¹⁶So I brought him to your disciples, but they couldn't heal him."

¹⁷Jesus replied, "You stubborn, faithless people! How long must I be with you until you believe? How long must I put up with you? Bring the boy to me." ¹⁸Then Jesus rebuked the demon in the boy, and it left him. From that moment the boy was well.

¹⁹Afterward the disciples asked Jesus privately, "Why couldn't we cast out that demon?"

²⁰"You didn't have enough faith," Jesus told them. "I assure you, even if you had faith as small as a mustard seed you could say to this mountain, 'Move from here to there,' and it would move. Nothing would be impossible."*

Jesus Again Predicts His Death

²²One day after they had returned to Galilee, Jesus told them, "The Son of Man is going to be betrayed. ²³He will be killed, but three days later he will be raised from the dead." And the disciples' hearts were filled with grief.

Payment of the Temple Tax

²⁴On their arrival in Capernaum, the tax collectors for the Temple tax came to Peter and asked him, "Doesn't your teacher pay the Temple tax?"

²⁵"Of course he does," Peter replied. Then he went into the house to talk to Jesus about it.

But before he had a chance to speak, Jesus asked him, "What do you think, Peter*? Do kings tax their own people or the foreigners they have conquered?"

²⁶"They tax the foreigners," Peter replied.

"Well, then," Jesus said, "the citizens are free! ²⁷However, we don't want to offend them, so go down to the lake and throw in a line. Open the mouth of the first fish you catch, and you will find a coin. Take the coin and pay the tax for both of us."

CHAPTER 18

The Greatest in the Kingdom

About that time the disciples came to Jesus and asked, "Which of us is greatest in the Kingdom of Heaven?"

²Jesus called a small child over to him and put the child among them.

17:4 Or *shelters*; Greek reads *tabernacles.* **17:10** Greek *that Elijah must come first.* **17:20** Some manuscripts add verse 21, *But this kind of demon won't leave unless you have prayed and fasted.* **17:25** Greek *Simon.*

³Then he said, "I assure you, unless you turn from your sins and become as little children, you will never get into the Kingdom of Heaven. ⁴Therefore, anyone who becomes as humble as this little child is the greatest in the Kingdom of Heaven. ⁵And anyone who welcomes a little child like this on my behalf is welcoming me. ⁶But if anyone causes one of these little ones who trusts in me to lose faith, it would be better for that person to be thrown into the sea with a large millstone tied around the neck.

⁷"How terrible it will be for anyone who causes others to sin. Temptation to do wrong is inevitable, but how terrible it will be for the person who does the tempting. ⁸So if your hand or foot causes you to sin, cut it off and throw it away. It is better to enter heaven* crippled or lame than to be thrown into the unquenchable fire with both of your hands and feet. ⁹And if your eye causes you to sin, gouge it out and throw it away. It is better to enter heaven half blind than to have two eyes and be thrown into hell.

¹⁰"Beware that you don't despise a single one of these little ones. For I tell you that in heaven their angels are always in the presence of my heavenly Father.*

Story of the Lost Sheep

¹²"If a shepherd has one hundred sheep, and one wanders away and is lost, what will he do? Won't he leave the ninety-nine others and go out into the hills to search for the lost one? ¹³And if he finds it, he will surely rejoice over it more than over the ninety-nine that didn't wander away! ¹⁴In the same way, it is not my heavenly Father's will that even one of these little ones should perish.

Correcting a Fellow Believer

¹⁵"If another believer* sins against you, go privately and point out the fault. If the other person listens and confesses it, you have won that person back. ¹⁶But if you are unsuccessful, take one or two others with you and go back again, so that everything you say may be confirmed by two or three witnesses. ¹⁷If that person still refuses to listen, take your case to the church. If the church decides you are right, but the other person won't accept it, treat that person as a pagan or a corrupt tax collector. ¹⁸I tell you this: Whatever you prohibit on earth is prohibited in heaven, and whatever you allow on earth is allowed in heaven.

¹⁹"I also tell you this: If two of you agree down here on earth concerning anything you ask, my Father in heaven will do it for you. ²⁰For where two or three gather together because they are mine,* I am there among them."

Story of the Unforgiving Debtor

²¹Then Peter came to him and asked, "Lord, how often should I forgive someone* who sins against me? Seven times?"

²²"No!" Jesus replied, "seventy times seven!*

²³"For this reason, the Kingdom of Heaven can be compared to a king who decided to bring his accounts up to date with servants who had borrowed money from him. ²⁴In the process, one of his debtors was brought in who owed him millions of dollars.* ²⁵He couldn't pay, so the king ordered that he, his wife, his children, and everything he had be sold to pay the debt. ²⁶But the man fell down before the king and begged him, 'Oh, sir, be patient with me, and I will pay it all.' ²⁷Then the king was filled with pity for him, and he released him and forgave his debt.

²⁸"But when the man left the king, he went to a fellow servant who owed him a few thousand dollars.* He grabbed him by the throat and demanded instant payment. ²⁹His fellow servant fell down before him and begged for a little

I BECOME great through childlike humility. (18:4)

I WELCOME AND CARE for children, protecting them from sin. (18:6)

I RID my life of anything that makes it easy to sin against God. (18:8)

I RESPECT children, knowing their angels are in God's own presence. (18:10)

I DEAL with offenses against me first in private. (18:15)

I CALL ON others as helpers and witnesses to seek reconciliation with one who has wronged me. (18:16)

See Peter's profile (page 1111) at Matthew 26:75.

I EMULATE God in forgiving others because he has forgiven me so much. (18:23)

18:8 Greek *enter life;* also in 18:9.   18:10 Some manuscripts add verse 11, *And I, the Son of Man, have come to save the lost.*   18:15 Greek *your brother.*   18:20 Greek *gather together in my name.*   18:21 Greek *my brother.* 18:22 Or *77 times.*   18:24 Greek *10,000 talents.*   18:28 Greek *100 denarii.* A denarius was the equivalent of a full day's wage.

more time. 'Be patient and I will pay it,' he pleaded. [30]But his creditor wouldn't wait. He had the man arrested and jailed until the debt could be paid in full.

[31]"When some of the other servants saw this, they were very upset. They went to the king and told him what had happened. [32]Then the king called in the man he had forgiven and said, 'You evil servant! I forgave you that tremendous debt because you pleaded with me. [33]Shouldn't you have mercy on your fellow servant, just as I had mercy on you?' [34]Then the angry king sent the man to prison until he had paid every penny.

[35]"That's what my heavenly Father will do to you if you refuse to forgive your brothers and sisters* in your heart."

CHAPTER 19

Discussion about Divorce and Marriage

After Jesus had finished saying these things, he left Galilee and went southward to the region of Judea and into the area east of the Jordan River. [2]Vast crowds followed him there, and he healed their sick.

[3]Some Pharisees came and tried to trap him with this question: "Should a man be allowed to divorce his wife for any reason?"

[4]"Haven't you read the Scriptures?" Jesus replied. "They record that from the beginning 'God made them male and female.'* [5]And he said, 'This explains why a man leaves his father and mother and is joined to his wife, and the two are united into one.'* [6]Since they are no longer two but one, let no one separate them, for God has joined them together."

[7]"Then why did Moses say a man could merely write an official letter of divorce and send her away?"* they asked.

[8]Jesus replied, "Moses permitted divorce as a concession to your hard-hearted wickedness, but it was not what God had originally intended. [9]And I tell you this, a man who divorces his wife and marries another commits adultery—unless his wife has been unfaithful.*"

[10]Jesus' disciples then said to him, "Then it is better not to marry!"

[11]"Not everyone can accept this statement," Jesus said. "Only those whom God helps. [12]Some are born as eunuchs, some have been made that way by others, and some choose not to marry for the sake of the Kingdom of Heaven. Let anyone who can, accept this statement."

Jesus Blesses the Children

[13]Some children were brought to Jesus so he could lay his hands on them and pray for them. The disciples told them not to bother him. [14]But Jesus said, "Let the children come to me. Don't stop them! For the Kingdom of Heaven belongs to such as these." [15]And he put his hands on their heads and blessed them before he left.

The Rich Young Man

[16]Someone came to Jesus with this question: "Teacher,* what good things must I do to have eternal life?"

[17]"Why ask me about what is good?" Jesus replied. "Only God is good. But to answer your question, you can receive eternal life if you keep the commandments."

[18]"Which ones?" the man asked.

And Jesus replied: " 'Do not murder. Do not commit adultery. Do not steal. Do not testify falsely. [19]Honor your father and mother. Love your neighbor as yourself.'* "

[20]"I've obeyed all these commandments," the young man replied. "What else must I do?"

I HONOR marriage as God created it from the beginning—one man and one woman for life (Genesis 1:27; 2:24). (19:4)

See Moses' profile (page 73) at Exodus 5:1.

I KEEP my heart soft toward God and my spouse. (19:8)

I ACCEPT God's call to singleness if that is clearly his will for me. (19:11)

I DO NOT HINDER children from coming to Jesus. (19:13)

Ask the Lord to speak to you. After all, this is his Word!

18:35 Greek *your brother.* 19:4 Gen 1:27; 5:2. 19:5 Gen 2:24. 19:7 Deut 24:1. 19:9 Some manuscripts add *And the man who marries a divorced woman commits adultery.* 19:16 Some manuscripts read *Good Teacher.* 19:18-19 Exod 20:12-16; Lev 19:18; Deut 5:16-20.

²¹Jesus told him, "If you want to be perfect, go and sell all you have and give the money to the poor, and you will have treasure in heaven. Then come, follow me." ²²But when the young man heard this, he went sadly away because he had many possessions.

²³Then Jesus said to his disciples, "I tell you the truth, it is very hard for a rich person to get into the Kingdom of Heaven. ²⁴I say it again—it is easier for a camel to go through the eye of a needle than for a rich person to enter the Kingdom of God!"

²⁵The disciples were astounded. "Then who in the world can be saved?" they asked.

²⁶Jesus looked at them intently and said, "Humanly speaking, it is impossible. But with God everything is possible."

²⁷Then Peter said to him, "We've given up everything to follow you. What will we get out of it?"

²⁸And Jesus replied, "I assure you that when I, the Son of Man, sit upon my glorious throne in the Kingdom,* you who have been my followers will also sit on twelve thrones, judging the twelve tribes of Israel. ²⁹And everyone who has given up houses or brothers or sisters or father or mother or children or property, for my sake, will receive a hundred times as much in return and will have eternal life. ³⁰But many who seem to be important now will be the least important then, and those who are considered least here will be the greatest then.*

CHAPTER 20

Story of the Vineyard Workers

"For the Kingdom of Heaven is like the owner of an estate who went out early one morning to hire workers for his vineyard. ²He agreed to pay the normal daily wage* and sent them out to work.

³"At nine o'clock in the morning he was passing through the marketplace and saw some people standing around doing nothing. ⁴So he hired them, telling them he would pay them whatever was right at the end of the day. ⁵At noon and again around three o'clock he did the same thing. ⁶At five o'clock that evening he was in town again and saw some more people standing around. He asked them, 'Why haven't you been working today?'

⁷"They replied, 'Because no one hired us.'

"The owner of the estate told them, 'Then go on out and join the others in my vineyard.'

⁸"That evening he told the foreman to call the workers in and pay them, beginning with the last workers first. ⁹When those hired at five o'clock were paid, each received a full day's wage. ¹⁰When those hired earlier came to get their pay, they assumed they would receive more. But they, too, were paid a day's wage. ¹¹When they received their pay, they protested, ¹²'Those people worked only one hour, and yet you've paid them just as much as you paid us who worked all day in the scorching heat.'

¹³"He answered one of them, 'Friend, I haven't been unfair! Didn't you agree to work all day for the usual wage? ¹⁴Take it and go. I wanted to pay this last worker the same as you. ¹⁵Is it against the law for me to do what I want with my money? Should you be angry because I am kind?'

¹⁶"And so it is, that many who are first now will be last then; and those who are last now will be first then."

Jesus Again Predicts His Death

¹⁷As Jesus was on the way to Jerusalem, he took the twelve disciples aside privately and told them what was going to happen to him. ¹⁸"When we get to Jerusalem," he said, "the Son of Man will be betrayed to the leading priests

I PUT ASIDE all that would keep me from following Jesus Christ. (19:21)

See the Rich Young Man's profile (page 1133) at Mark 10:22.

I CAN GIVE UP temporary possessions and pleasures, knowing Jesus Christ will amply provide for me and reward me, both in this life and the next. (19:27)

See Peter's profile (page 1111) at Matthew 26:75.

I SERVE God with my whole life, not comparing my service and rewards with others. (20:1)

I DO NOT ENVY others when God is generous to them. (20:15)

19:28 Greek *in the regeneration.* 19:30 Greek *But many who are first will be last; and the last, first.* 20:2 Greek *a denarius,* the payment for a full day's labor; also in 20:9, 10, 13.

and the teachers of religious law. They will sentence him to die. [19]Then they will hand him over to the Romans to be mocked, whipped, and crucified. But on the third day he will be raised from the dead."

Jesus Teaches about Serving Others

[20]Then the mother of James and John, the sons of Zebedee, came to Jesus with her sons. She knelt respectfully to ask a favor. [21]"What is your request?" he asked.

She replied, "In your Kingdom, will you let my two sons sit in places of honor next to you, one at your right and the other at your left?"

[22]But Jesus told them, "You don't know what you are asking! Are you able to drink from the bitter cup of sorrow I am about to drink?"

"Oh yes," they replied, "we are able!"

[23]"You will indeed drink from it," he told them. "But I have no right to say who will sit on the thrones next to mine. My Father has prepared those places for the ones he has chosen."

[24]When the ten other disciples heard what James and John had asked, they were indignant. [25]But Jesus called them together and said, "You know that in this world kings are tyrants, and officials lord it over the people beneath them. [26]But among you it should be quite different. Whoever wants to be a leader among you must be your servant, [27]and whoever wants to be first must become your slave. [28]For even I, the Son of Man, came here not to be served but to serve others, and to give my life as a ransom for many."

Jesus Heals Two Blind Men

[29]As Jesus and the disciples left the city of Jericho, a huge crowd followed behind. [30]Two blind men were sitting beside the road. When they heard that Jesus was coming that way, they began shouting, "Lord, Son of David, have mercy on us!" [31]The crowd told them to be quiet, but they only shouted louder, "Lord, Son of David, have mercy on us!"

[32]Jesus stopped in the road and called, "What do you want me to do for you?" [33]"Lord," they said, "we want to see!" [34]Jesus felt sorry for them and touched their eyes. Instantly they could see! Then they followed him.

CHAPTER 21

The Triumphal Entry

As Jesus and the disciples approached Jerusalem, they came to the town of Bethphage on the Mount of Olives. Jesus sent two of them on ahead. [2]"Go into the village over there," he said, "and you will see a donkey tied there, with its colt beside it. Untie them and bring them here. [3]If anyone asks what you are doing, just say, 'The Lord needs them,' and he will immediately send them." [4]This was done to fulfill the prophecy,

[5] "Tell the people of Israel,*
  'Look, your King is coming to you.
  He is humble, riding on a donkey—
    even on a donkey's colt.' "*

[6]The two disciples did as Jesus said. [7]They brought the animals to him and threw their garments over the colt, and he sat on it.*

[8]Most of the crowd spread their coats on the road ahead of Jesus, and others cut branches from the trees and spread them on the road. [9]He was in the center of the procession, and the crowds all around him were shouting,

"Praise God* for the Son of David!
Bless the one who comes in the name of the Lord!
Praise God in highest heaven!"*

21:5a Greek *Tell the daughter of Zion.* Isa 62:11.   21:5b Zech 9:9.   21:7 Greek *over them, and he sat on them.*   21:9a Greek *Hosanna,* an exclamation of praise that literally means "save now"; also in 21:9b, 15.   21:9b Pss 118:25-26; 148:1.

Margin notes:

See John's profile (page 1435) at Revelation 1:9.

I AM WILLING to lay down my life for Jesus Christ. (20:22)

I LEAVE the details of my eternal reward and position of honor to the Father. (20:23)

I SERVE those over whom I have authority. (20:25)

I FOLLOW Jesus' example of serving others and laying down my life for them. (20:28)

I PLEAD for the Lord's mercy. (20:30)

See the profiles for Blind Bartimaeus (page 1135) and David (page 629) at Mark 10:52 and Psalm 3:1.

I OBEY Jesus' commands, even if others question me. (21:6)

I WORSHIP Jesus, the King who comes in gentleness. (21:9)

See David's profile (page 629) at Psalm 3:1.

[10]The entire city of Jerusalem was stirred as he entered. "Who is this?" they asked.

[11]And the crowds replied, "It's Jesus, the prophet from Nazareth in Galilee."

Jesus Clears the Temple

[12]Jesus entered the Temple and began to drive out the merchants and their customers. He knocked over the tables of the money changers and the stalls of those selling doves. [13]He said, "The Scriptures declare, 'My Temple will be called a place of prayer,' but you have turned it into a den of thieves!"*

[14]The blind and the lame came to him, and he healed them there in the Temple. [15]The leading priests and the teachers of religious law saw these wonderful miracles and heard even the little children in the Temple shouting, "Praise God for the Son of David." But they were indignant [16]and asked Jesus, "Do you hear what these children are saying?"

"Yes," Jesus replied. "Haven't you ever read the Scriptures? For they say, 'You have taught children and infants to give you praise.'* " [17]Then he returned to Bethany, where he stayed overnight.

Jesus Curses the Fig Tree

[18]In the morning, as Jesus was returning to Jerusalem, he was hungry, [19]and he noticed a fig tree beside the road. He went over to see if there were any figs on it, but there were only leaves. Then he said to it, "May you never bear fruit again!" And immediately the fig tree withered up.

[20]The disciples were amazed when they saw this and asked, "How did the fig tree wither so quickly?"

[21]Then Jesus told them, "I assure you, if you have faith and don't doubt, you can do things like this and much more. You can even say to this mountain, 'May God lift you up and throw you into the sea,' and it will happen. [22]If you believe, you will receive whatever you ask for in prayer."

The Authority of Jesus Challenged

[23]When Jesus returned to the Temple and began teaching, the leading priests and other leaders came up to him. They demanded, "By whose authority did you drive out the merchants from the Temple?* Who gave you such authority?"

[24]"I'll tell you who gave me the authority to do these things if you answer one question," Jesus replied. [25]"Did John's baptism come from heaven or was it merely human?"

They talked it over among themselves. "If we say it was from heaven, he will ask why we didn't believe him. [26]But if we say it was merely human, we'll be mobbed, because the people think he was a prophet." [27]So they finally replied, "We don't know."

And Jesus responded, "Then I won't answer your question either.

Story of the Two Sons

[28]"But what do you think about this? A man with two sons told the older boy, 'Son, go out and work in the vineyard today.' [29]The son answered, 'No, I won't go,' but later he changed his mind and went anyway. [30]Then the father told the other son, 'You go,' and he said, 'Yes, sir, I will.' But he didn't go. [31]Which of the two was obeying his father?"

They replied, "The first, of course."

Then Jesus explained his meaning: "I assure you, corrupt tax collectors and prostitutes will get into the Kingdom of God before you do. [32]For John the Baptist came and showed you the way to life, and you didn't believe him,

I DO NOT HINDER others from coming to God in prayer. (21:13)

I DO NOT RESENT it when others praise God from the heart. (21:15)

I BELIEVE I will receive what I ask for from the Lord in prayer. (21:22)

I SAY yes to the Lord. (21:29)

I OBEY the Lord in my actions, not just my words. (21:30)

I REPENT of my sin and believe in Jesus Christ. (21:32)

See John the Baptist's profile (page 1117) at Mark 1:4.

21:13 Isa 56:7; Jer 7:11.   21:16 Ps 8:2.   21:23 Or *By whose authority do you do these things?*

while tax collectors and prostitutes did. And even when you saw this happening, you refused to turn from your sins and believe him.

Story of the Evil Farmers

³³"Now listen to this story. A certain landowner planted a vineyard, built a wall around it, dug a pit for pressing out the grape juice, and built a lookout tower. Then he leased the vineyard to tenant farmers and moved to another country. ³⁴At the time of the grape harvest he sent his servants to collect his share of the crop. ³⁵But the farmers grabbed his servants, beat one, killed one, and stoned another. ³⁶So the landowner sent a larger group of his servants to collect for him, but the results were the same.

³⁷"Finally, the owner sent his son, thinking, 'Surely they will respect my son.'

³⁸"But when the farmers saw his son coming, they said to one another, 'Here comes the heir to this estate. Come on, let's kill him and get the estate for ourselves!' ³⁹So they grabbed him, took him out of the vineyard, and murdered him.

⁴⁰"When the owner of the vineyard returns," Jesus asked, "what do you think he will do to those farmers?"

⁴¹The religious leaders replied, "He will put the wicked men to a horrible death and lease the vineyard to others who will give him his share of the crop after each harvest."

⁴²Then Jesus asked them, "Didn't you ever read this in the Scriptures?

'The stone rejected by the builders
has now become the cornerstone.
This is the Lord's doing,
and it is marvelous to see.'*

⁴³What I mean is that the Kingdom of God will be taken away from you and given to a nation that will produce the proper fruit. ⁴⁴Anyone who stumbles over that stone will be broken to pieces, and it will crush anyone on whom it falls.*"

⁴⁵When the leading priests and Pharisees heard Jesus, they realized he was pointing at them—that they were the farmers in his story. ⁴⁶They wanted to arrest him, but they were afraid to try because the crowds considered Jesus to be a prophet.

CHAPTER 22

Story of the Great Feast

Jesus told them several other stories to illustrate the Kingdom. He said, ²"The Kingdom of Heaven can be illustrated by the story of a king who prepared a great wedding feast for his son. ³Many guests were invited, and when the banquet was ready, he sent his servants to notify everyone that it was time to come. But they all refused! ⁴So he sent other servants to tell them, 'The feast has been prepared, and choice meats have been cooked. Everything is ready. Hurry!' ⁵But the guests he had invited ignored them and went about their business, one to his farm, another to his store. ⁶Others seized his messengers and treated them shamefully, even killing some of them.

⁷"Then the king became furious. He sent out his army to destroy the murderers and burn their city. ⁸And he said to his servants, 'The wedding feast is ready, and the guests I invited aren't worthy of the honor. ⁹Now go out to the street corners and invite everyone you see.'

¹⁰"So the servants brought in everyone they could find, good and bad alike, and the banquet hall was filled with guests. ¹¹But when the king came in to meet the guests, he noticed a man who wasn't wearing the proper clothes for a

I TRUST AND OBEY the Son of God. (21:37)

I ACCEPT God's invitation to join his Kingdom. (22:3)

21:42 Ps 118:22-23.   21:44 This verse is omitted in some early manuscripts.

wedding. ¹²'Friend,' he asked, 'how is it that you are here without wedding clothes?' And the man had no reply. ¹³Then the king said to his aides, 'Bind him hand and foot and throw him out into the outer darkness, where there is weeping and gnashing of teeth.' ¹⁴For many are called, but few are chosen."

Taxes for Caesar

¹⁵Then the Pharisees met together to think of a way to trap Jesus into saying something for which they could accuse him. ¹⁶They decided to send some of their disciples, along with the supporters of Herod, to ask him this question: "Teacher, we know how honest you are. You teach about the way of God regardless of the consequences. You are impartial and don't play favorites. ¹⁷Now tell us what you think about this: Is it right to pay taxes to the Roman government or not?"

¹⁸But Jesus knew their evil motives. "You hypocrites!" he said. "Whom are you trying to fool with your trick questions? ¹⁹Here, show me the Roman coin used for the tax." When they handed him the coin,* ²⁰he asked, "Whose picture and title are stamped on it?"

²¹"Caesar's," they replied.

"Well, then," he said, "give to Caesar what belongs to him. But everything that belongs to God must be given to God." ²²His reply amazed them, and they went away.

Discussion about Resurrection

²³That same day some Sadducees stepped forward—a group of Jews who say there is no resurrection after death. They posed this question: ²⁴"Teacher, Moses said, 'If a man dies without children, his brother should marry the widow and have a child who will be the brother's heir.'* ²⁵Well, there were seven brothers. The oldest married and then died without children, so the second brother married the widow. ²⁶This brother also died without children, and the wife was married to the next brother, and so on until she had been the wife of each of them. ²⁷And then she also died. ²⁸So tell us, whose wife will she be in the resurrection? For she was the wife of all seven of them!"

²⁹Jesus replied, "Your problem is that you don't know the Scriptures, and you don't know the power of God. ³⁰For when the dead rise, they won't be married. They will be like the angels in heaven. ³¹But now, as to whether there will be a resurrection of the dead—haven't you ever read about this in the Scriptures? Long after Abraham, Isaac, and Jacob had died, God said,* ³²'I am the God of Abraham, the God of Isaac, and the God of Jacob.'* So he is the God of the living, not the dead."

³³When the crowds heard him, they were impressed with his teaching.

The Most Important Commandment

³⁴But when the Pharisees heard that he had silenced the Sadducees with his reply, they thought up a fresh question of their own to ask him. ³⁵One of them, an expert in religious law, tried to trap him with this question: ³⁶"Teacher, which is the most important commandment in the law of Moses?"

³⁷Jesus replied, " 'You must love the Lord your God with all your heart, all your soul, and all your mind.'* ³⁸This is the first and greatest commandment. ³⁹A second is equally important: 'Love your neighbor as yourself.'* ⁴⁰All the other commandments and all the demands of the prophets are based on these two commandments."

Whose Son Is the Messiah?

⁴¹Then, surrounded by the Pharisees, Jesus asked them a question: ⁴²"What do you think about the Messiah? Whose son is he?"

They replied, "He is the son of David."

I DO NOT TRY to enter God's Kingdom on my own terms. (22:12)

I DO NOT QUESTION God in a futile attempt to justify myself. (22:15)

I FULFILL my human and social responsibilities, but my life and allegiance ultimately belong to God. (22:21)

See Moses' profile (page 73) at Exodus 5:1.

I LEARN the Scriptures and believe the power of God. (22:29)

I BELIEVE in eternal life and the future resurrection of all who are righteous in God's eyes. (22:31)

See the profiles for Abraham (page 19), Isaac (page 31), and Jacob (page 43) at Genesis 15:6, Genesis 25:19, and Genesis 32:9.

I LOVE the Lord my God with my entire being—intellect, emotion, and spirit. (22:37)

I LOVE others as myself as an expression of my love for God. (22:39)

See David's profile (page 629) at Psalm 3:1.

22:19 Greek *a denarius.*   22:24 Deut 25:5-6.   22:31 Greek *in the Scriptures? God said.*   22:32 Exod 3:6.
22:37 Deut 6:5.   22:39 Lev 19:18.

[43]Jesus responded, "Then why does David, speaking under the inspiration of the Holy Spirit, call him Lord? For David said,

[44] 'The LORD said to my Lord,
   Sit in honor at my right hand
      until I humble your enemies beneath your feet.'*

[45]Since David called him Lord, how can he be his son at the same time?"

[46]No one could answer him. And after that, no one dared to ask him any more questions.

CHAPTER 23

Jesus Warns the Religious Leaders

Then Jesus said to the crowds and to his disciples, [2]"The teachers of religious law and the Pharisees are the official interpreters of the Scriptures. [3]So practice and obey whatever they say to you, but don't follow their example. For they don't practice what they teach. [4]They crush you with impossible religious demands and never lift a finger to help ease the burden.

[5]"Everything they do is for show. On their arms they wear extra wide prayer boxes with Scripture verses inside,* and they wear extra long tassels on their robes. [6]And how they love to sit at the head table at banquets and in the most prominent seats in the synagogue! [7]They enjoy the attention they get on the streets, and they enjoy being called 'Rabbi.'* [8]Don't ever let anyone call you 'Rabbi,' for you have only one teacher, and all of you are on the same level as brothers and sisters.* [9]And don't address anyone here on earth as 'Father,' for only God in heaven is your spiritual Father. [10]And don't let anyone call you 'Master,' for there is only one master, the Messiah. [11]The greatest among you must be a servant. [12]But those who exalt themselves will be humbled, and those who humble themselves will be exalted.

[13]"How terrible it will be for you teachers of religious law and you Pharisees. Hypocrites! For you won't let others enter the Kingdom of Heaven, and you won't go in yourselves.* [15]Yes, how terrible it will be for you teachers of religious law and you Pharisees. For you cross land and sea to make one convert, and then you turn him into twice the son of hell as you yourselves are.

[16]"Blind guides! How terrible it will be for you! For you say that it means nothing to swear 'by God's Temple'—you can break that oath. But then you say that it is binding to swear 'by the gold in the Temple.' [17]Blind fools! Which is greater, the gold, or the Temple that makes the gold sacred? [18]And you say that to take an oath 'by the altar' can be broken, but to swear 'by the gifts on the altar' is binding! [19]How blind! For which is greater, the gift on the altar, or the altar that makes the gift sacred? [20]When you swear 'by the altar,' you are swearing by it and by everything on it. [21]And when you swear 'by the Temple,' you are swearing by it and by God, who lives in it. [22]And when you swear 'by heaven,' you are swearing by the throne of God and by God, who sits on the throne.

[23]"How terrible it will be for you teachers of religious law and you Pharisees. Hypocrites! For you are careful to tithe even the tiniest part of your income,* but you ignore the important things of the law—justice, mercy, and faith. You should tithe, yes, but you should not leave undone the more important things. [24]Blind guides! You strain your water so you won't accidentally swallow a gnat; then you swallow a camel!

[25]"How terrible it will be for you teachers of religious law and you Pharisees. Hypocrites! You are so careful to clean the outside of the cup and the

---

I BELIEVE Jesus Christ is the Messiah, the Son of David and Lord of all (Psalm 110:1). (22:44)

I PRACTICE what I preach. (23:3)

I DO NOT SEEK to be exalted by others by assuming impressive titles and authority. (23:8)

I DO NOT CREATE religious barriers that keep people from God's Kingdom. (23:13)

I AM true to my word. (23:16)

I OBEY the small details of God's Word without neglecting to obey the foundational principles of justice, mercy, and faith. (23:23)

22:44 Ps 110:1. 23:5 Greek *They enlarge their phylacteries.* 23:7 *Rabbi,* from Aramaic, means "master" or "teacher." 23:8 Greek *brothers.* 23:13 Some manuscripts add verse 14, *How terrible it will be for you teachers of religious law and you Pharisees. Hypocrites! You shamelessly cheat widows out of their property, and then, to cover up the kind of people you really are, you make long prayers in public. Because of this, your punishment will be the greater.* 23:23 Greek *to tithe the mint, the dill, and the cumin.*

dish, but inside you are filthy—full of greed and self-indulgence! ²⁶Blind Pharisees! First wash the inside of the cup, and then the outside will become clean, too.

²⁷"How terrible it will be for you teachers of religious law and you Pharisees. Hypocrites! You are like whitewashed tombs—beautiful on the outside but filled on the inside with dead people's bones and all sorts of impurity. ²⁸You try to look like upright people outwardly, but inside your hearts are filled with hypocrisy and lawlessness.

²⁹"How terrible it will be for you teachers of religious law and you Pharisees. Hypocrites! For you build tombs for the prophets your ancestors killed and decorate the graves of the godly people your ancestors destroyed. ³⁰Then you say, 'We never would have joined them in killing the prophets.'

I DEVELOP a pure character within instead of hiding impurity behind a good outward show. (23:28)

UNLIKE THE SADDUCEES *I am not a total skeptic.*

Matthew 22:23

Talk about a bunch of rich fools.

Around the time Matthew wrote his Gospel, the high priest and his fellow Sadducees acted like Jewish aristocrats. They ruled the Temple and ran the Lord right out the door. They denied some of the most basic teachings of Scripture—life after death, heaven, hell, angels, demons, miracles (see Acts 23:8)—to the point of casting doubt on God himself. No wonder Jesus harshly rebuked them and said, "Your problem is that you don't know the Scriptures, and you don't know the power of God" (Matthew 22:29).

After Pentecost (Acts 2:1-42), the Sadducees "were very disturbed that Peter and John were claiming, on the authority of Jesus, that there is a resurrection of the dead." They arrested the two leading apostles (Acts 4:1-3) and later threw the whole lot—including Matthew—into jail (Acts 5:17-18). The apostles must have seen the irony when God sent an angel to perform a spectacular miracle that threw the Sadducees into a fit.

Like the Sadducees, you and I can be tempted to doubt the supernatural details of God's Word. Yet if God is God, nothing is impossible!

Unlike the Sadducees, let's stand in awe of the Lord God, gladly acknowledge his mighty power, and heed his every word.

○ *Today's Scripture reading is Matthew 22:23-46.*

³¹"In saying that, you are accusing yourselves of being the descendants of those who murdered the prophets. ³²Go ahead. Finish what they started. ³³Snakes! Sons of vipers! How will you escape the judgment of hell? ³⁴I will send you prophets and wise men and teachers of religious law. You will kill some by crucifixion and whip others in your synagogues, chasing them from city to city. ³⁵As a result, you will become guilty of murdering all the godly people from righteous Abel to Zechariah son of Barachiah, whom you murdered in the Temple between the altar and the sanctuary. ³⁶I assure you, all the accumulated judgment of the centuries will break upon the heads of this very generation.

See Abel's profile (page 9) at Genesis 4:4.

Jesus Grieves over Jerusalem

³⁷"O Jerusalem, Jerusalem, the city that kills the prophets and stones God's messengers! How often I have wanted to gather your children together as a hen protects her chicks beneath her wings, but you wouldn't let me. ³⁸And now look, your house is left to you, empty and desolate. ³⁹For I tell you this, you will never see me again until you say, 'Bless the one who comes in the name of the Lord!'* "

I GRIEVE over those who will not let the Lord Jesus lovingly gather them in. (23:37)

23:39 Ps 118:26.

CHAPTER 24

Jesus Foretells the Future

As Jesus was leaving the Temple grounds, his disciples pointed out to him the various Temple buildings. [2]But he told them, "Do you see all these buildings? I assure you, they will be so completely demolished that not one stone will be left on top of another!"

[3]Later, Jesus sat on the slopes of the Mount of Olives. His disciples came to him privately and asked, "When will all this take place? And will there be any sign ahead of time to signal your return and the end of the world*?"

[4]Jesus told them, "Don't let anyone mislead you. [5]For many will come in my name, saying, 'I am the Messiah.' They will lead many astray. [6]And wars will break out near and far, but don't panic. Yes, these things must come, but the end won't follow immediately. [7]The nations and kingdoms will proclaim war against each other, and there will be famines and earthquakes in many parts of the world. [8]But all this will be only the beginning of the horrors to come.

[9]"Then you will be arrested, persecuted, and killed. You will be hated all over the world because of your allegiance to me. [10]And many will turn away from me and betray and hate each other. [11]And many false prophets will appear and will lead many people astray. [12]Sin will be rampant everywhere, and the love of many will grow cold. [13]But those who endure to the end will be saved. [14]And the Good News about the Kingdom will be preached throughout the whole world, so that all nations will hear it; and then, finally, the end will come.

[15]"The time will come when you will see what Daniel the prophet spoke about: the sacrilegious object that causes desecration* standing in the Holy Place"—reader, pay attention! [16]"Then those in Judea must flee to the hills. [17]A person outside the house* must not go inside to pack. [18]A person in the field must not return even to get a coat. [19]How terrible it will be for pregnant women and for mothers nursing their babies in those days. [20]And pray that your flight will not be in winter or on the Sabbath. [21]For that will be a time of greater horror than anything the world has ever seen or will ever see again. [22]In fact, unless that time of calamity is shortened, the entire human race will be destroyed. But it will be shortened for the sake of God's chosen ones.

[23]"Then if anyone tells you, 'Look, here is the Messiah,' or 'There he is,' don't pay any attention. [24]For false messiahs and false prophets will rise up and perform great miraculous signs and wonders so as to deceive, if possible, even God's chosen ones. [25]See, I have warned you.

[26]"So if someone tells you, 'Look, the Messiah is out in the desert,' don't bother to go and look. Or, 'Look, he is hiding here,' don't believe it! [27]For as the lightning lights up the entire sky, so it will be when the Son of Man comes. [28]Just as the gathering of vultures shows there is a carcass nearby, so these signs indicate that the end is near.*

[29]"Immediately after those horrible days end,

the sun will be darkened,
the moon will not give light,
the stars will fall from the sky,
and the powers of heaven will be shaken.*

[30]And then at last, the sign of the coming of the Son of Man will appear in the heavens, and there will be deep mourning among all the nations of the earth. And they will see the Son of Man arrive on the clouds of heaven with power and great glory.* [31]And he will send forth his angels with the sound of a

---

I AM NOT DECEIVED by those who call themselves the Messiah. (24:4)

I NOTE world events as they lead up to Jesus Christ's return, but I am not alarmed. (24:6)

I EXPECT persecution as a believer in Jesus Christ. (24:9)

I AM NOT CAUGHT OFF GUARD by the rise of wickedness in society. (24:10)

I ADVANCE the preaching of the Good News to all the nations of the world. (24:14)

See Daniel's profile (page 979) at Daniel 1:21.

I AM PREPARED for Jesus Christ's return. (24:25)

I BELIEVE Jesus Christ will return with power and great glory to judge the earth. (24:30)

24:3 Or *the age.*   24:15 Greek *the abomination of desolation.* See Dan 9:27; 11:31; 12:11.   24:17 Greek *on the roof.*   24:28 Greek *Wherever the carcass is, the vultures gather.*   24:29 See Isa 13:10; 34:4; Joel 2:10.   24:30 See Dan 7:13.

mighty trumpet blast, and they will gather together his chosen ones from the farthest ends of the earth and heaven.

[32]"Now learn a lesson from the fig tree. When its buds become tender and its leaves begin to sprout, you know without being told that summer is near. [33]Just so, when you see the events I've described beginning to happen, you can know his return is very near, right at the door. [34]I assure you, this generation* will not pass from the scene before all these things take place. [35]Heaven and earth will disappear, but my words will remain forever.

[36]"However, no one knows the day or the hour when these things will happen, not even the angels in heaven or the Son himself.* Only the Father knows.

[37]"When the Son of Man returns, it will be like it was in Noah's day. [38]In those days before the Flood, the people were enjoying banquets and parties and weddings right up to the time Noah entered his boat. [39]People didn't realize what was going to happen until the Flood came and swept them all away. That is the way it will be when the Son of Man comes.

[40]"Two men will be working together in the field; one will be taken, the other left. [41]Two women will be grinding flour at the mill; one will be taken, the other left. [42]So be prepared, because you don't know what day your Lord is coming.

[43]"Know this: A homeowner who knew exactly when a burglar was coming would stay alert and not permit the house to be broken into. [44]You also must be ready all the time. For the Son of Man will come when least expected.

[45]"Who is a faithful, sensible servant, to whom the master can give the responsibility of managing his household and feeding his family? [46]If the master returns and finds that the servant has done a good job, there will be a reward. [47]I assure you, the master will put that servant in charge of all he owns. [48]But if the servant is evil and thinks, 'My master won't be back for a while,' [49]and begins oppressing the other servants, partying, and getting drunk—[50]well, the master will return unannounced and unexpected. [51]He will tear the servant apart and banish him with the hypocrites. In that place there will be weeping and gnashing of teeth.

CHAPTER 25

Story of the Ten Bridesmaids

"The Kingdom of Heaven can be illustrated by the story of ten bridesmaids* who took their lamps and went to meet the bridegroom. [2]Five of them were foolish, and five were wise. [3]The five who were foolish took no oil for their lamps, [4]but the other five were wise enough to take along extra oil. [5]When the bridegroom was delayed, they all lay down and slept. [6]At midnight they were roused by the shout, 'Look, the bridegroom is coming! Come out and welcome him!'

[7]"All the bridesmaids got up and prepared their lamps. [8]Then the five foolish ones asked the others, 'Please give us some of your oil because our lamps are going out.' [9]But the others replied, 'We don't have enough for all of us. Go to a shop and buy some for yourselves.'

[10]"But while they were gone to buy oil, the bridegroom came, and those who were ready went in with him to the marriage feast, and the door was locked. [11]Later, when the other five bridesmaids returned, they stood outside, calling, 'Sir, open the door for us!' [12]But he called back, 'I don't know you!'

[13]"So stay awake and be prepared, because you do not know the day or hour of my return.

Story of the Three Servants

[14]"Again, the Kingdom of Heaven can be illustrated by the story of a man going on a trip. He called together his servants and gave them money to

I LIVE my life with the expectancy of Jesus Christ's soon return. (24:33)

I KNOW that no one can know the exact day and hour of Christ's return. (24:36)

See Noah's profile (page 13) at Genesis 6:9.

I SERVE my master, Jesus Christ, faithfully until the moment he returns. (24:46)

I AM PREPARED to serve the Lord for my whole lifetime. (25:4)

I AM PREPARED for the Lord's return at any moment. (25:13)

24:34 Or *this age*, or *this nation.*   **24:36** Some manuscripts omit the phrase *or the Son himself.*   **25:1** Or *virgins;* also in 25:7, 11.

I BELIEVE the Lord does not give the same gifts or responsibilities to each person. (25:15)

I BELIEVE the Lord will ask for an account of everything he has given to his servants. (25:19)

I EMPLOY all the abilities and resources God has given me, no matter how small, to the best use for his Kingdom. (25:21)

I DO NOT MISJUDGE the Lord's character. (25:24)

invest for him while he was gone. ¹⁵He gave five bags of gold* to one, two bags of gold to another, and one bag of gold to the last—dividing it in proportion to their abilities—and then left on his trip. ¹⁶The servant who received the five bags of gold began immediately to invest the money and soon doubled it. ¹⁷The servant with two bags of gold also went right to work and doubled the money. ¹⁸But the servant who received the one bag of gold dug a hole in the ground and hid the master's money for safekeeping.

¹⁹"After a long time their master returned from his trip and called them to give an account of how they had used his money. ²⁰The servant to whom he had entrusted the five bags of gold said, 'Sir, you gave me five bags of gold to invest, and I have doubled the amount.' ²¹The master was full of praise. 'Well done, my good and faithful servant. You have been faithful in handling this small amount, so now I will give you many more responsibilities. Let's celebrate together!'

²²"Next came the servant who had received the two bags of gold, with the report, 'Sir, you gave me two bags of gold to invest, and I have doubled the amount.' ²³The master said, 'Well done, my good and faithful servant. You have been faithful in handling this small amount, so now I will give you many more responsibilities. Let's celebrate together!'

²⁴"Then the servant with the one bag of gold came and said, 'Sir, I know you are a hard man, harvesting crops you didn't plant and gathering crops you didn't cultivate. ²⁵I was afraid I would lose your money, so I hid it in the earth and here it is.'

²⁶"But the master replied, 'You wicked and lazy servant! You think I'm a hard man, do you, harvesting crops I didn't plant and gathering crops I didn't cultivate? ²⁷Well, you should at least have put my money into the bank so I could have some interest. ²⁸Take the money from this servant and give it to the one with the ten bags of gold. ²⁹To those who use well what they are given, even more will be given, and they will have an abundance. But from those who are unfaithful,* even what little they have will be taken away. ³⁰Now throw this useless servant into outer darkness, where there will be weeping and gnashing of teeth.'

The Final Judgment

I BELIEVE that the Lord Jesus Christ will judge all people when he comes again to rule the earth. (25:32)

³¹"But when the Son of Man comes in his glory, and all the angels with him, then he will sit upon his glorious throne. ³²All the nations will be gathered in his presence, and he will separate them as a shepherd separates the sheep from the goats. ³³He will place the sheep at his right hand and the goats at his left. ³⁴Then the King will say to those on the right, 'Come, you who are blessed by my Father, inherit the Kingdom prepared for you from the foundation of the world. ³⁵For I was hungry, and you fed me. I was thirsty, and you gave me a drink. I was a stranger, and you invited me into your home. ³⁶I was naked, and you gave me clothing. I was sick, and you cared for me. I was in prison, and you visited me.'

³⁷"Then these righteous ones will reply, 'Lord, when did we ever see you hungry and feed you? Or thirsty and give you something to drink? ³⁸Or a stranger and show you hospitality? Or naked and give you clothing? ³⁹When did we ever see you sick or in prison, and visit you?' ⁴⁰And the King will tell them, 'I assure you, when you did it to one of the least of these my brothers and sisters,* you were doing it to me!'

I MINISTER to those in need as though they themselves were Jesus Christ. (25:40)

⁴¹"Then the King will turn to those on the left and say, 'Away with you, you cursed ones, into the eternal fire prepared for the Devil and his demons! ⁴²For I was hungry, and you didn't feed me. I was thirsty, and you didn't give me anything to drink. ⁴³I was a stranger, and you didn't invite me into your

25:15 Greek *talents;* also throughout the story. A talent is equal to 75 pounds or 34 kilograms.   25:29 Or *who have nothing.*   25:40 Greek *my brothers.*

home. I was naked, and you gave me no clothing. I was sick and in prison, and you didn't visit me.'

⁴⁴"Then they will reply, 'Lord, when did we ever see you hungry or thirsty or a stranger or naked or sick or in prison, and not help you?' ⁴⁵And he will answer, 'I assure you, when you refused to help the least of these my brothers and sisters, you were refusing to help me.' ⁴⁶And they will go away into eternal punishment, but the righteous will go into eternal life."

CHAPTER 26

The Plot to Kill Jesus

When Jesus had finished saying these things, he said to his disciples, ²"As you know, the Passover celebration begins in two days, and I, the Son of Man, will be betrayed and crucified."

³At that same time the leading priests and other leaders were meeting at the residence of Caiaphas, the high priest, ⁴to discuss how to capture Jesus secretly and put him to death. ⁵"But not during the Passover," they agreed, "or there will be a riot."

Jesus Anointed at Bethany

⁶Meanwhile, Jesus was in Bethany at the home of Simon, a man who had leprosy. ⁷During supper, a woman came in with a beautiful jar* of expensive perfume and poured it over his head. ⁸The disciples were indignant when they saw this. "What a waste of money," they said. ⁹"She could have sold it for a fortune and given the money to the poor."

¹⁰But Jesus replied, "Why berate her for doing such a good thing to me? ¹¹You will always have the poor among you, but I will not be here with you much longer. ¹²She has poured this perfume on me to prepare my body for burial. ¹³I assure you, wherever the Good News is preached throughout the world, this woman's deed will be talked about in her memory."

Judas Agrees to Betray Jesus

¹⁴Then Judas Iscariot, one of the twelve disciples, went to the leading priests ¹⁵and asked, "How much will you pay me to betray Jesus to you?" And they gave him thirty pieces of silver. ¹⁶From that time on, Judas began looking for the right time and place to betray Jesus.

The Last Supper

¹⁷On the first day of the Festival of Unleavened Bread, the disciples came to Jesus and asked, "Where do you want us to prepare the Passover supper?"

¹⁸"As you go into the city," he told them, "you will see a certain man. Tell him, 'The Teacher says, My time has come, and I will eat the Passover meal with my disciples at your house.' " ¹⁹So the disciples did as Jesus told them and prepared the Passover supper there.

²⁰When it was evening, Jesus sat down at the table with the twelve disciples. ²¹While they were eating, he said, "The truth is, one of you will betray me."

²²Greatly distressed, one by one they began to ask him, "I'm not the one, am I, Lord?"

²³He replied, "One of you who is eating with me now* will betray me. ²⁴For I, the Son of Man, must die, as the Scriptures declared long ago. But how terrible it will be for my betrayer. Far better for him if he had never been born!"

²⁵Judas, the one who would betray him, also asked, "Teacher, I'm not the one, am I?"

And Jesus told him, "You have said it yourself."

²⁶As they were eating, Jesus took a loaf of bread and asked God's blessing

I RECOGNIZE that those who reject God's people are rejecting Jesus Christ as well. (25:45)

I AM LAVISH in my expressions of love to Jesus. (26:7)

I EVALUATE a person's service by what it means to the Lord, not by financial measures. (26:8)

I WOULD NEVER ALLOW money to lure me into harming Jesus Christ and his people in any way. (26:14)

See Judas's profile (page 1121) at Mark 3:19.

I WELCOME Jesus and his followers into my home. (26:18)

I DO NOT EVER WANT to betray the Lord Jesus. (26:22)

I TAKE the bread of the Lord's Supper as a reminder of Christ's body given for me. (26:26)

26:7 Greek an alabaster jar.   26:23 Or The one who has dipped his hand in the bowl with me.

on it. Then he broke it in pieces and gave it to the disciples, saying, "Take it and eat it, for this is my body." ²⁷And he took a cup of wine and gave thanks to God for it. He gave it to them and said, "Each of you drink from it, ²⁸for this is my blood, which seals the covenant* between God and his people. It is poured out to forgive the sins of many. ²⁹Mark my words—I will not drink wine again until the day I drink it new with you in my Father's Kingdom." ³⁰Then they sang a hymn and went out to the Mount of Olives.

Jesus Predicts Peter's Denial

³¹"Tonight all of you will desert me," Jesus told them. "For the Scriptures say,

'God* will strike the Shepherd,
and the sheep of the flock will be scattered.'*

³²But after I have been raised from the dead, I will go ahead of you to Galilee and meet you there."

³³Peter declared, "Even if everyone else deserts you, I never will."

³⁴"Peter," Jesus replied, "the truth is, this very night, before the rooster crows, you will deny me three times."

³⁵"No!" Peter insisted. "Not even if I have to die with you! I will never deny you!" And all the other disciples vowed the same.

Jesus Prays in Gethsemane

³⁶Then Jesus brought them to an olive grove called Gethsemane, and he said, "Sit here while I go on ahead to pray." ³⁷He took Peter and Zebedee's two sons, James and John, and he began to be filled with anguish and deep distress. ³⁸He told them, "My soul is crushed with grief to the point of death. Stay here and watch with me."

³⁹He went on a little farther and fell face down on the ground, praying, "My Father! If it is possible, let this cup of suffering be taken away from me. Yet I want your will, not mine." ⁴⁰Then he returned to the disciples and found them asleep. He said to Peter, "Couldn't you stay awake and watch with me even one hour? ⁴¹Keep alert and pray. Otherwise temptation will overpower you. For though the spirit is willing enough, the body is weak!"

⁴²Again he left them and prayed, "My Father! If this cup cannot be taken away until I drink it, your will be done." ⁴³He returned to them again and found them sleeping, for they just couldn't keep their eyes open.

⁴⁴So he went back to pray a third time, saying the same things again. ⁴⁵Then he came to the disciples and said, "Still sleeping? Still resting?* Look, the time has come. I, the Son of Man, am betrayed into the hands of sinners. ⁴⁶Up, let's be going. See, my betrayer is here!"

Jesus Is Arrested

⁴⁷And even as he said this, Judas, one of the twelve disciples, arrived with a mob that was armed with swords and clubs. They had been sent out by the leading priests and other leaders of the people. ⁴⁸Judas had given them a prearranged signal: "You will know which one to arrest when I go over and give him the kiss of greeting." ⁴⁹So Judas came straight to Jesus. "Greetings, Teacher!" he exclaimed and gave him the kiss.

⁵⁰Jesus said, "My friend, go ahead and do what you have come for." Then the others grabbed Jesus and arrested him. ⁵¹One of the men with Jesus pulled out a sword and slashed off an ear of the high priest's servant.

⁵²"Put away your sword," Jesus told him. "Those who use the sword will be killed by the sword. ⁵³Don't you realize that I could ask my Father for thousands* of angels to protect us, and he would send them instantly? ⁵⁴But if I did, how would the Scriptures be fulfilled that describe what must happen now?"

I TAKE the cup of the Lord's Supper as a reminder of Christ's blood shed to seal God's new covenant with his people. (26:28)

I AM HONEST about my weaknesses and recognize that I am prone to sin. (26:33)

See John's profile (page 1435) at Revelation 1:9.

I OFFER to stay with those in spiritual anguish. (26:38)

I ASK God for deliverance from difficulties as I surrender myself fully to his will. (26:39)

I PERSEVERE in prayer, always alert to temptation. (26:41)

I BELIEVE all the writings of the biblical prophets will be fulfilled. (26:54)

26:28 Some manuscripts read *the new covenant.*   26:31a Greek *I.*   26:31b Zech 13:7.   26:45 Or *Sleep on, take your rest.*   26:53 Greek *12 legions.*

[55] Then Jesus said to the crowd, "Am I some dangerous criminal, that you have come armed with swords and clubs to arrest me? Why didn't you arrest me in the Temple? I was there teaching every day. [56] But this is all happening to fulfill the words of the prophets as recorded in the Scriptures." At that point, all the disciples deserted him and fled.

Jesus before the Council

[57] Then the people who had arrested Jesus led him to the home of Caiaphas, the high priest, where the teachers of religious law and other leaders had gathered. [58] Meanwhile, Peter was following far behind and eventually came to the courtyard of the high priest's house. He went in, sat with the guards, and waited to see what was going to happen to Jesus.

[59] Inside, the leading priests and the entire high council* were trying to find witnesses who would lie about Jesus, so they could put him to death. [60] But even though they found many who agreed to give false witness, there was no testimony they could use. Finally, two men were found [61] who declared, "This man said, 'I am able to destroy the Temple of God and rebuild it in three days.' "

[62] Then the high priest stood up and said to Jesus, "Well, aren't you going to answer these charges? What do you have to say for yourself?" [63] But Jesus remained silent. Then the high priest said to him, "I demand in the name of the living God that you tell us whether you are the Messiah, the Son of God."

[64] Jesus replied, "Yes, it is as you say. And in the future you will see me, the Son of Man, sitting at God's right hand in the place of power and coming back on the clouds of heaven."*

[65] Then the high priest tore his clothing to show his horror, shouting, "Blasphemy! Why do we need other witnesses? You have all heard his blasphemy. [66] What is your verdict?"

"Guilty!" they shouted. "He must die!"

[67] Then they spit in Jesus' face and hit him with their fists. And some slapped him, [68] saying, "Prophesy to us, you Messiah! Who hit you that time?"

Peter Denies Jesus

[69] Meanwhile, as Peter was sitting outside in the courtyard, a servant girl came over and said to him, "You were one of those with Jesus the Galilean."

[70] But Peter denied it in front of everyone. "I don't know what you are talking about," he said.

[71] Later, out by the gate, another servant girl noticed him and said to those standing around, "This man was with Jesus of Nazareth."

[72] Again Peter denied it, this time with an oath. "I don't even know the man," he said.

[73] A little later some other bystanders came over to him and said, "You must be one of them; we can tell by your Galilean accent."

[74] Peter said, "I swear by God, I don't know the man." And immediately the rooster crowed. [75] Suddenly, Jesus' words flashed through Peter's mind: "Before the rooster crows, you will deny me three times." And he went away, crying bitterly.

CHAPTER 27

Judas Hangs Himself

Very early in the morning, the leading priests and other leaders met again to discuss how to persuade the Roman government to sentence Jesus to death. [2] Then they bound him and took him to Pilate, the Roman governor.

[3] When Judas, who had betrayed him, realized that Jesus had been condemned to die, he was filled with remorse. So he took the thirty pieces of

I BELIEVE Jesus is the Christ, the Son of God. (26:63)

I BELIEVE that Jesus is sitting at the right hand of God Almighty and that one day he will come back on the clouds of heaven. (26:64)

I DO NOT DENY that I belong to Jesus Christ. (26:74)

See Peter's profile (page 1111) at Matthew 26:75.

See Pilate's profile (page 1229) at John 19:16.

I REALIZE it's not enough merely to feel remorse, so I confess my sins to God and ask for his forgiveness. (27:3)

See Judas's profile (page 1121) at Mark 3:19.

26:59 Greek *the Sanhedrin.*   26:64 See Ps 110:1; Dan 7:13.

silver back to the leading priests and other leaders. [4]"I have sinned," he declared, "for I have betrayed an innocent man."

"What do we care?" they retorted. "That's your problem." [5]Then Judas threw the money onto the floor of the Temple and went out and hanged himself. [6]The leading priests picked up the money. "We can't put it in the Temple treasury," they said, "since it's against the law to accept money paid for murder." [7]After some discussion they finally decided to buy the potter's field, and they made it into a cemetery for foreigners. [8]That is why the field is still called the Field of Blood. [9]This fulfilled the prophecy of Jeremiah that says,

"They took* the thirty pieces of silver—
  the price at which he was valued by the people of Israel—
[10]and purchased the potter's field,
  as the Lord directed.*"

Jesus' Trial before Pilate

[11]Now Jesus was standing before Pilate, the Roman governor. "Are you the King of the Jews?" the governor asked him.

Jesus replied, "Yes, it is as you say."

[12]But when the leading priests and other leaders made their accusations against him, Jesus remained silent. [13]"Don't you hear their many charges against you?" Pilate demanded. [14]But Jesus said nothing, much to the governor's great surprise.

[15]Now it was the governor's custom to release one prisoner to the crowd each year during the Passover celebration—anyone they wanted. [16]This year there was a notorious criminal in prison, a man named Barabbas.* [17]As the crowds gathered before Pilate's house that morning, he asked them, "Which one do you want me to release to you—Barabbas, or Jesus who is called the Messiah?" [18](He knew very well that the Jewish leaders had arrested Jesus out of envy.)

[19]Just then, as Pilate was sitting on the judgment seat, his wife sent him this message: "Leave that innocent man alone, because I had a terrible nightmare about him last night."

[20]Meanwhile, the leading priests and other leaders persuaded the crowds to ask for Barabbas to be released and for Jesus to be put to death. [21]So when the governor asked again, "Which of these two do you want me to release to you?" the crowd shouted back their reply: "Barabbas!"

[22]"But if I release Barabbas," Pilate asked them, "what should I do with Jesus who is called the Messiah?"

And they all shouted, "Crucify him!"

[23]"Why?" Pilate demanded. "What crime has he committed?"

But the crowd only roared the louder, "Crucify him!"

[24]Pilate saw that he wasn't getting anywhere and that a riot was developing. So he sent for a bowl of water and washed his hands before the crowd, saying, "I am innocent of the blood of this man. The responsibility is yours!"

[25]And all the people yelled back, "We will take responsibility for his death—we and our children!"*

[26]So Pilate released Barabbas to them. He ordered Jesus flogged with a lead-tipped whip, then turned him over to the Roman soldiers to crucify him.

The Soldiers Mock Jesus

[27]Some of the governor's soldiers took Jesus into their headquarters and called out the entire battalion. [28]They stripped him and put a scarlet robe on him. [29]They made a crown of long, sharp thorns and put it on his head, and they placed a stick in his right hand as a scepter. Then they knelt before him in mockery, yelling, "Hail! King of the Jews!" [30]And they spit on him and

---

I BELIEVE the priests bought a field with betrayal money, just as the prophet Jeremiah had foretold. (27:9)

See Jeremiah's profile (page 855) at Jeremiah 1:19.

I BELIEVE Jesus is the King of the Jews. (27:11)

I LISTEN to loved ones who urge me to show mercy. (27:19)

I DO NOT MAKE excuses for avoiding my responsibility to do what is just and right. (27:24)

I GRIEVE over the mockery and beatings that Jesus endured. (27:29)

27:9 Or *I took.*   27:9-10 Greek *as the Lord directed me.* Zech 11:12-13; Jer 32:6-9.   27:16 Some manuscripts read *Jesus Barabbas;* also in 27:17.   27:25 Greek *"His blood be on us and on our children."*

grabbed the stick and beat him on the head with it. [31]When they were finally tired of mocking him, they took off the robe and put his own clothes on him again. Then they led him away to be crucified.

The Crucifixion

[32]As they were on the way, they came across a man named Simon, who was from Cyrene,* and they forced him to carry Jesus' cross. [33]Then they went out to a place called Golgotha (which means Skull Hill). [34]The soldiers gave him wine mixed with bitter gall, but when he had tasted it, he refused to drink it.

[35]After they had nailed him to the cross, the soldiers gambled for his clothes by throwing dice.* [36]Then they sat around and kept guard as he hung there. [37]A signboard was fastened to the cross above Jesus' head, announcing the charge against him. It read: "This is Jesus, the King of the Jews."

I BELIEVE Jesus refused to accept anything to diminish his pain. (27:34)

LIKE PETER

Matthew 26:75

I know that no matter how often I let God down, he won't give up on me.

From the time we were kids, we've been told: Three strikes and you're out.

In life, we get only so many opportunities to blow it. In many competitive situations, no wonder our first reaction is to tense up. It seems as if everyone struggles with the fear of failure, at least occasionally. Every time we hear about another friend or colleague losing his job, we automatically wonder, "Will I be next?"

Thankfully, God's Kingdom operates on an entirely different basis. We can never let God down one too many times. If we love him and own up to our sins, confessing them and asking for his forgiveness, God keeps right on forgiving us and putting us back in the game.

If anyone has ever understood the marvel of God's goodness to keep giving us second chances, it was the apostle Peter (aka Simon). In the course of a single evening, Peter denied Jesus Christ three times: first to a maid, then in front of a couple of her friends, and finally before an entire group of bystanders. Yet after his resurrection, Jesus made a point of repeatedly reassuring Peter that he still had great things in store for this very human, less-than-perfect disciple.

Later in life, Peter looked back on this experience and reminded his fellow Christians that Jesus "personally carried away our sins in his own body on the cross so we can be dead to sin and live for what is right. You have been healed by his wounds! Once you were wandering like lost sheep. But now you have turned to your Shepherd, the Guardian of your souls" (1 Peter 2:24-25).

As Peter discovered, it's not too late for you and me to return to Jesus Christ today, confess our sins, ask for his forgiveness, and receive a second chance. The Lord hasn't given up on anyone yet.

To read the other Gospel accounts about Peter's three denials, see Mark 14:66-72; Luke 22:54-62; and John 18:15-18, 25-27.

○ Today's Scripture reading is Matthew 26:20-75.

---

[38]Two criminals were crucified with him, their crosses on either side of his. [39]And the people passing by shouted abuse, shaking their heads in mockery. [40]"So! You can destroy the Temple and build it again in three days, can you? Well then, if you are the Son of God, save yourself and come down from the cross!"

[41]The leading priests, the teachers of religious law, and the other leaders also mocked Jesus. [42]"He saved others," they scoffed, "but he can't save himself! So he is the king of Israel, is he? Let him come down from the cross, and we will believe in him! [43]He trusted God—let God show his approval by delivering him! For he said, 'I am the Son of God.' " [44]And the criminals who were crucified with him also shouted the same insults at him.

See the Dying Thief's profile (page 1191) at Luke 23:42.

I DO NOT REFUSE to believe in Jesus Christ as the King of Israel and the Son of God. (27:42)

The Death of Jesus

[45]At noon, darkness fell across the whole land until three o'clock. [46]At about

27:32 Cyrene was a city in northern Africa. 27:35 Greek by casting lots. A few late manuscripts add This fulfilled the word of the prophet: "They divided my clothes among themselves and cast lots for my robe." See Ps 22:18.

three o'clock, Jesus called out with a loud voice, *"Eli, Eli, lema sabachthani?"* which means, "My God, my God, why have you forsaken me?" *

⁴⁷Some of the bystanders misunderstood and thought he was calling for the prophet Elijah. ⁴⁸One of them ran and filled a sponge with sour wine, holding it up to him on a stick so he could drink. ⁴⁹But the rest said, "Leave him alone. Let's see whether Elijah will come and save him." *

See Elijah's profile (page 421) at 1 Kings 19:18.

I BELIEVE Jesus gave up his spirit willingly—no one took it from him. (27:50)

⁵⁰Then Jesus shouted out again, and he gave up his spirit. ⁵¹At that moment the curtain in the Temple was torn in two, from top to bottom. The earth shook, rocks split apart, ⁵²and tombs opened. The bodies of many godly men and women who had died were raised from the dead ⁵³after Jesus' resurrection. They left the cemetery, went into the holy city of Jerusalem, and appeared to many people. *

⁵⁴The Roman officer and the other soldiers at the crucifixion were terrified by the earthquake and all that had happened. They said, "Truly, this was the Son of God!"

I WILLINGLY IDENTIFY with Jesus in his suffering. (27:55)

See the profiles for Mary Magdalene (page 1163) and John (page 1435) at Luke 8:2 and Revelation 1:9.

⁵⁵And many women who had come from Galilee with Jesus to care for him were watching from a distance. ⁵⁶Among them were Mary Magdalene, Mary (the mother of James and Joseph), and Zebedee's wife, the mother of James and John.

The Burial of Jesus

⁵⁷As evening approached, Joseph, a rich man from Arimathea who was one of Jesus' followers, ⁵⁸went to Pilate and asked for Jesus' body. And Pilate issued an order to release it to him. ⁵⁹Joseph took the body and wrapped it in a long linen cloth. ⁶⁰He placed it in his own new tomb, which had been carved out of the rock. Then he rolled a great stone across the entrance as he left. ⁶¹Both Mary Magdalene and the other Mary were sitting nearby watching.

I BELIEVE that Jesus died and that his body was buried in a tomb. (27:60)

The Guard at the Tomb

⁶²The next day—on the first day of the Passover ceremonies*—the leading priests and Pharisees went to see Pilate. ⁶³They told him, "Sir, we remember what that deceiver once said while he was still alive: 'After three days I will be raised from the dead.' ⁶⁴So we request that you seal the tomb until the third day. This will prevent his disciples from coming and stealing his body and then telling everyone he came back to life! If that happens, we'll be worse off than we were at first."

I BELIEVE Jesus' tomb was sealed so that no one could have stolen his body. (27:66)

⁶⁵Pilate replied, "Take guards and secure it the best you can." ⁶⁶So they sealed the tomb and posted guards to protect it.

CHAPTER 28

The Resurrection

Early on Sunday morning,* as the new day was dawning, Mary Magdalene and the other Mary went out to see the tomb. ²Suddenly there was a great earthquake, because an angel of the Lord came down from heaven and rolled aside the stone and sat on it. ³His face shone like lightning, and his clothing was as white as snow. ⁴The guards shook with fear when they saw him, and they fell into a dead faint.

⁵Then the angel spoke to the women. "Don't be afraid!" he said. "I know you are looking for Jesus, who was crucified. ⁶He isn't here! He has been raised from the dead, just as he said would happen. Come, see where his body was lying. ⁷And now, go quickly and tell his disciples he has been raised from the dead, and he is going ahead of you to Galilee. You will see him there. Remember, I have told you."

27:46 Ps 22:1.   27:49 Some manuscripts add *And another took a spear and pierced his side, and out came water and blood.*   27:51-53 Or *The earth shook, rocks split apart, tombs opened, and the bodies of many godly men and women who had died were raised from the dead. After Jesus' resurrection, they left the cemetery, went into the holy city of Jerusalem, and appeared to many people.*   27:62 Or *On the next day, which is after the Preparation.*   28:1 Greek *After the Sabbath, on the first day of the week.*

[8]The women ran quickly from the tomb. They were very frightened but also filled with great joy, and they rushed to find the disciples to give them the angel's message. [9]And as they went, Jesus met them. "Greetings!" he said. And they ran to him, held his feet, and worshiped him. [10]Then Jesus said to them, "Don't be afraid! Go tell my brothers to leave for Galilee, and they will see me there."

I BELIEVE Jesus rose from the dead—and I rejoice. (28:8)

I WORSHIP the resurrected Lord Jesus. (28:9)

LIKE JOSEPH OF ARIMATHEA   *I don't hide my faith in the Lord Jesus.*
Matthew 27:57

Each of the Gospel writers had a unique purpose, audience, and vantage point from which he communicated the Good News of Jesus Christ.

As a result, the cast of characters always changes from one Gospel to the next—except for John the Baptist, Mary, the apostles, the Pharisees, Pilate . . . and somebody named Joseph of Arimathea, who appears on the stage for a brief moment, then exits, never to be heard from again.

Scripture tells us that Joseph was from a village in the hill country north and west of Jerusalem. It tells us he was rich, "an honored member of the high council . . . who was waiting for the Kingdom of God to come" (Mark 15:43), "a good and righteous man" who "had not agreed with the decision and actions of the other religious leaders" (Luke 23:50-51) and "who had been a secret disciple of Jesus (because he feared the Jewish leaders)" (John 19:38).

All four Gospel writers note that it was Joseph of Arimathea—not one of the apostles—who had the courage to ask Pilate for permission to take Jesus' body down from the cross and give it a proper burial in his own tomb.

As far as we can tell, Joseph had no idea he was fulfilling the prophecy that the Messiah's body would be "buried . . . in a rich man's grave" (Isaiah 53:9; see also 1 Corinthians 15:4).

Today we remember Joseph as the one who gathered his courage and risked his life to obey the Holy Spirit's prompting to ensure that the Messiah's body had a dignified burial. Let's not forget: If Joseph hadn't stepped out and declared his allegiance to the Lord, Jesus' body would have been tossed in a heap with dozens of other crucified Jews—and three days later there wouldn't have been an empty tomb.

To one degree or another, most Christians find it hard to be outspoken about our faith in Jesus Christ. You and I certainly are not alone when we feel nervous, hesitant, or afraid. But like Joseph, let's gather our courage and obey the Holy Spirit. The results of even one conversation could prove to be far greater than anyone right now could possibly imagine.

○ *Today's Scripture reading is Matthew 27:32-61.*

The Report of the Guard

[11]As the women were on their way into the city, some of the men who had been guarding the tomb went to the leading priests and told them what had happened. [12]A meeting of all the religious leaders was called, and they decided to bribe the soldiers. [13]They told the soldiers, "You must say, 'Jesus' disciples came during the night while we were sleeping, and they stole his body.' [14]If the governor hears about it, we'll stand up for you and everything will be all right." [15]So the guards accepted the bribe and said what they were told to say. Their story spread widely among the Jews, and they still tell it today.

I DO NOT LOSE faith even though others seek to undermine the truth about Jesus Christ. (28:15)

The Great Commission

[16]Then the eleven disciples left for Galilee, going to the mountain where Jesus had told them to go. [17]When they saw him, they worshiped him—but some of them still doubted!

[18]Jesus came and told his disciples, "I have been given complete authority in heaven and on earth. [19]Therefore, go and make disciples of all the nations, baptizing them in the name of the Father and the Son and the Holy Spirit. [20]Teach these new disciples to obey all the commands I have given you. And be sure of this: I am with you always, even to the end of the age."

I BELIEVE God the Father has given Jesus all authority in heaven and on earth. (28:18)

I OBEY Jesus Christ's command to make disciples of all nations. (28:19)

I OBEY everything Jesus has commanded and rejoice in his abiding presence. (28:20)

MARK

THIS SECOND New Testament book challenges us to consider Jesus' life and then choose for or against him.

As a close associate of the apostles, John Mark (aka Mark) retells many of Peter's stories about Jesus' public ministry and the final days surrounding Jesus' crucifixion, burial, resurrection, and ascension. Mark writes his Gospel with an emphasis on Jesus' actions and other people's reactions.

Many of Mark's original readers were Roman citizens who had heard about the miracle worker from Galilee. Mark knows they're more interested in what Jesus did than where he came from or what he said. So while Luke takes 183 verses to introduce Jesus' public ministry, Mark takes only 13. And while Matthew uses eleven long chapters to recount several of Jesus' most important sermons, Mark uses just one.

Famous passages in this Gospel include
- ◯ Huge crowds surround Jesus during the early days of his ministry (1:33, 45; 2:2, 13; 3:7; 4:1)
- ◯ Jesus tells the story about the rich young man (10:17-31)
- ◯ "For even I, the Son of Man, came here not to be served but to serve others, and to give my life as a ransom for many" (10:45)
- ◯ Jesus tells the story about blind Bartimaeus (10:46-52)
- ◯ Jesus predicts that Peter will deny him three times "before the rooster crows twice" (14:30; see 14:68, 72)
- ◯ A young man—possibly Mark—is with Jesus and the apostles at Gethsemane (14:51-52)
- ◯ Shorter ending of Mark (16:8)
- ◯ Longer ending of Mark (16:9-20)

CHAPTER 1

John the Baptist Prepares the Way

Here begins the Good News about Jesus the Messiah, the Son of God.* ²In the book of the prophet Isaiah, God said,

"Look, I am sending my messenger before you,
and he will prepare your way.*
³ He is a voice shouting in the wilderness:
'Prepare a pathway for the Lord's coming!
Make a straight road for him!'* "

⁴ This messenger was John the Baptist. He lived in the wilderness and was preaching that people should be baptized to show that they had turned from their sins and turned to God to be forgiven.* ⁵ People from Jerusalem and from

See John Mark's profile (page 1255) at Acts 13:13.

See Isaiah's profile (page 801) at Isaiah 6:13.

1:1 Some manuscripts do not include *the Son of God.*   1:2 Mal 3:1.   1:3 Isa 40:3.   1:4 Greek *preaching a baptism of repentance for the forgiveness of sins.*

I BELIEVE John the
Baptist baptized
people who turned
from their sins to God.
(1:5)

all over Judea traveled out into the wilderness to see and hear John. And when they confessed their sins, he baptized them in the Jordan River. ⁶His clothes were woven from camel hair, and he wore a leather belt; his food was locusts and wild honey. ⁷He announced: "Someone is coming soon who is far greater than I am—so much greater that I am not even worthy to be his slave.* ⁸I baptize you with* water, but he will baptize you with the Holy Spirit!"

The Baptism of Jesus

⁹One day Jesus came from Nazareth in Galilee, and he was baptized by John in the Jordan River. ¹⁰And when Jesus came up out of the water, he saw the heavens split open and the Holy Spirit descending like a dove on him. ¹¹And a voice came from heaven saying, "You are my beloved Son, and I am fully pleased with you."

I BELIEVE the Holy
Spirit descended on
Jesus when he was
baptized. (1:10)

I BELIEVE God the
Father's voice from
heaven declared that
Jesus was his beloved
Son who fully pleased
him. (1:11)

The Temptation of Jesus

¹²Immediately the Holy Spirit compelled Jesus to go into the wilderness. ¹³He was there for forty days, being tempted by Satan. He was out among the wild animals, and angels took care of him.

The First Disciples

I BELIEVE Jesus
preached the Good
News that the
Kingdom of God was
near. (1:14)

See the profiles for
Peter (page 1111) and
Andrew (page 1199) at
Matthew 26:75 and
John 1:42.

I FOLLOW the Lord
Jesus when he calls
me. (1:18)

See John's profile (page
1435) at Revelation 1:9.

I BELIEVE Jesus taught
with real authority.
(1:22)

¹⁴Later on, after John was arrested by Herod Antipas, Jesus went to Galilee to preach God's Good News. ¹⁵"At last the time has come!" he announced. "The Kingdom of God is near! Turn from your sins and believe this Good News!"

¹⁶One day as Jesus was walking along the shores of the Sea of Galilee, he saw Simon* and his brother, Andrew, fishing with a net, for they were commercial fishermen. ¹⁷Jesus called out to them, "Come, be my disciples, and I will show you how to fish for people!" ¹⁸And they left their nets at once and went with him.

¹⁹A little farther up the shore Jesus saw Zebedee's sons, James and John, in a boat mending their nets. ²⁰He called them, too, and immediately they left their father, Zebedee, in the boat with the hired men and went with him.

Jesus Casts Out an Evil Spirit

²¹Jesus and his companions went to the town of Capernaum, and every Sabbath day he went into the synagogue and taught the people. ²²They were amazed at his teaching, for he taught as one who had real authority—quite unlike the teachers of religious law.

²³A man possessed by an evil spirit was in the synagogue, ²⁴and he began shouting, "Why are you bothering us, Jesus of Nazareth? Have you come to destroy us? I know who you are—the Holy One sent from God!"

²⁵Jesus cut him short. "Be silent! Come out of the man." ²⁶At that, the evil spirit screamed and threw the man into a convulsion, but then he left him.

²⁷Amazement gripped the audience, and they began to discuss what had happened. "What sort of new teaching is this?" they asked excitedly. "It has such authority! Even evil spirits obey his orders!" ²⁸The news of what he had done spread quickly through that entire area of Galilee.

Jesus Heals Many People

I BELIEVE Jesus healed
many people from
many different
diseases and from
demon possession.
(1:34)

²⁹After Jesus and his disciples left the synagogue, they went over to Simon and Andrew's home, and James and John were with them. ³⁰Simon's mother-in-law was sick in bed with a high fever. They told Jesus about her right away. ³¹He went to her bedside, and as he took her by the hand and helped her to sit up, the fever suddenly left, and she got up and prepared a meal for them.

³²That evening at sunset, many sick and demon-possessed people were brought to Jesus. ³³And a huge crowd of people from all over Capernaum gathered outside the door to watch. ³⁴So Jesus healed great numbers of sick

1:7 Greek *to stoop down and untie his sandals.* **1:8** Or *in;* also in 1:8b. **1:16** *Simon* is called *Peter* in 3:16 and thereafter.

people who had many different kinds of diseases, and he ordered many demons to come out of their victims. But because they knew who he was, he refused to allow the demons to speak.

Jesus Preaches in Galilee

³⁵The next morning Jesus awoke long before daybreak and went out alone into the wilderness to pray. ³⁶Later Simon and the others went out to find him. ³⁷They said, "Everyone is asking for you."

³⁸But he replied, "We must go on to other towns as well, and I will preach to them, too, because that is why I came." ³⁹So he traveled throughout the region of Galilee, preaching in the synagogues and expelling demons from many people.

I FOLLOW Jesus' example and spend time alone in prayer. (1:35)

LIKE JOHN THE BAPTIST *I recognize and exalt the preeminence of the Lord Jesus.*

Mark 1:4

Poor John the Baptist. Talk about a guy who needed to see a media specialist to improve his public image and a psychological guru to boost his self-esteem. Right?

Actually, John didn't really care what others thought of him—of his wild appearance, eccentric diet, prophetic speech, and all. John knew he was just a messenger—it was the Messiah's image and esteem John was interested in exalting.

John the Baptist had no lack of confidence as he bucked society's fashions and conventions to proclaim a radical message from his wilderness platform. He wasn't afraid to insult the establishment and challenge the religious leaders who shackled the people with their tradition but lived in covert rebellion against God. Yet this prophet wasn't interested in gaining a following for himself.

Instead, this fiery man thundered out the call for people to repent and turn to the Lord. Then in the waters of the Jordan River he baptized those who meant business.

John's intensity and bold actions weren't a by-product of climbing his own ladder to fame and success. And his obvious humility did not spring from self-hate or low self-esteem, either. He simply recognized that this life wasn't all about John—it was all about Jesus.

Even before his birth, John's life purpose was extraordinarily clear (Luke 1:11-17, 67-80). John knew exactly who he was in God's plan—and pursued that purpose wholeheartedly for God's glory, not his own. Even when his disciples left him (John 1:19-41). Even when he ended up caged before his own prophecies could come true (Luke 7:18-35). Even when his message of repentance cost him his head (Matthew 14:1-12).

Granted, the short-term benefits of exalting Jesus Christ above self seemed bleak at best. But John the Baptist reaped rich, eternal rewards. Jesus himself honored John, declaring that no prophet—not even Moses—was greater.

You and I may not have a mission revealed by ancient prophecies (Malachi 4:5-6), but our purpose can be the same as John's. Like him, we are to be Jesus Christ's ambassadors to the world (2 Corinthians 5:18-20).

○ *Today's Scripture reading is Mark 1:1-11; 2:18-22; and 6:14-29.*

Jesus Heals a Man with Leprosy

⁴⁰A man with leprosy came and knelt in front of Jesus, begging to be healed. "If you want to, you can make me well again," he said.

⁴¹Moved with pity,* Jesus touched him. "I want to," he said. "Be healed!" ⁴²Instantly the leprosy disappeared—the man was healed. ⁴³Then Jesus sent him on his way and told him sternly, ⁴⁴"Go right over to the priest and let him examine you. Don't talk to anyone along the way. Take along the offering required in the law of Moses for those who have been healed of leprosy, so everyone will have proof of your healing."

⁴⁵But as the man went on his way, he spread the news, telling everyone

I BELIEVE Jesus can make me well. (1:40)

See Moses' profile (page 73) at Exodus 5:1.

1:41 Some manuscripts read *Moved with anger.*

what had happened to him. As a result, such crowds soon surrounded Jesus that he couldn't enter a town anywhere publicly. He had to stay out in the secluded places, and people from everywhere came to him there.

CHAPTER 2

Jesus Heals a Paralyzed Man

Several days later Jesus returned to Capernaum, and the news of his arrival spread quickly through the town. ²Soon the house where he was staying was so packed with visitors that there wasn't room for one more person, not even outside the door. And he preached the word to them. ³Four men arrived carrying a paralyzed man on a mat. ⁴They couldn't get to Jesus through the crowd, so they dug through the clay roof above his head. Then they lowered the sick man on his mat, right down in front of Jesus. ⁵Seeing their faith, Jesus said to the paralyzed man, "My son, your sins are forgiven."

⁶But some of the teachers of religious law who were sitting there said to themselves, ⁷"What? This is blasphemy! Who but God can forgive sins!"

⁸Jesus knew what they were discussing among themselves, so he said to them, "Why do you think this is blasphemy? ⁹Is it easier to say to the paralyzed man, 'Your sins are forgiven' or 'Get up, pick up your mat, and walk'? ¹⁰I will prove that I, the Son of Man, have the authority on earth to forgive sins." Then Jesus turned to the paralyzed man and said, ¹¹"Stand up, take your mat, and go on home, because you are healed!"

¹²The man jumped up, took the mat, and pushed his way through the stunned onlookers. Then they all praised God. "We've never seen anything like this before!" they exclaimed.

Jesus Calls Levi (Matthew)

¹³Then Jesus went out to the lakeshore again and taught the crowds that gathered around him. ¹⁴As he walked along, he saw Levi son of Alphaeus sitting at his tax-collection booth. "Come, be my disciple," Jesus said to him. So Levi got up and followed him.

¹⁵That night Levi invited Jesus and his disciples to be his dinner guests, along with his fellow tax collectors and many other notorious sinners. (There were many people of this kind among the crowds that followed Jesus.) ¹⁶But when some of the teachers of religious law who were Pharisees* saw him eating with people like that, they said to his disciples, "Why does he eat with such scum*?"

¹⁷When Jesus heard this, he told them, "Healthy people don't need a doctor—sick people do. I have come to call sinners, not those who think they are already good enough."

A Discussion about Fasting

¹⁸John's disciples and the Pharisees sometimes fasted. One day some people came to Jesus and asked, "Why do John's disciples and the Pharisees fast, but your disciples don't fast?"

¹⁹Jesus replied, "Do wedding guests fast while celebrating with the groom? Of course not. They can't fast while they are with the groom. ²⁰But someday he will be taken away from them, and then they will fast. ²¹And who would patch an old garment with unshrunk cloth? For the new patch shrinks and pulls away from the old cloth, leaving an even bigger hole than before. ²²And no one puts new wine into old wineskins. The wine would burst the wineskins, spilling the wine and ruining the skins. New wine needs new wineskins."

A Discussion about the Sabbath

²³One Sabbath day as Jesus was walking through some grainfields, his disciples began breaking off heads of wheat. ²⁴But the Pharisees said to Jesus,

Today what example(s) are you choosing to heed?

I OVERCOME obstacles to bring my friends to Jesus. (2:4)

I BELIEVE Jesus has the authority to forgive sins. (2:10)

See Matthew's profile (page 1081) at Matthew 9:9.

I INVITE my friends to my home and introduce them to Jesus. (2:15)

See the profile for the Pharisees (page 1087) at Matthew 12:14.

I BELIEVE Jesus spent time with sinners and called them to follow him. (2:17)

2:16a Greek *the scribes of the Pharisees.*   2:16b Greek *with tax collectors and sinners.*

"They shouldn't be doing that! It's against the law to work by harvesting grain on the Sabbath."

²⁵But Jesus replied, "Haven't you ever read in the Scriptures what King David did when he and his companions were hungry? ²⁶He went into the house of God (during the days when Abiathar was high priest), ate the special bread reserved for the priests alone, and then gave some to his companions. That was breaking the law, too." ²⁷Then he said to them, "The Sabbath was made to benefit people, and not people to benefit the Sabbath. ²⁸And I, the Son of Man, am master even of the Sabbath!"

CHAPTER 3

Jesus Heals on the Sabbath

Jesus went into the synagogue again and noticed a man with a deformed hand. ²Since it was the Sabbath, Jesus' enemies watched him closely. Would he heal the man's hand on the Sabbath? If he did, they planned to condemn him. ³Jesus said to the man, "Come and stand in front of everyone." ⁴Then he turned to his critics and asked, "Is it legal to do good deeds on the Sabbath, or is it a day for doing harm? Is this a day to save life or to destroy it?" But they wouldn't answer him. ⁵He looked around at them angrily, because he was deeply disturbed by their hard hearts. Then he said to the man, "Reach out your hand." The man reached out his hand, and it became normal again! ⁶At once the Pharisees went away and met with the supporters of Herod to discuss plans for killing Jesus.

Crowds Follow Jesus

⁷Jesus and his disciples went out to the lake, followed by a huge crowd from all over Galilee, Judea, ⁸Jerusalem, Idumea, from east of the Jordan River, and even from as far away as Tyre and Sidon. The news about his miracles had spread far and wide, and vast numbers of people came to see him for themselves.

⁹Jesus instructed his disciples to bring around a boat and to have it ready in case he was crowded off the beach. ¹⁰There had been many healings that day. As a result, many sick people were crowding around him, trying to touch him. ¹¹And whenever those possessed by evil spirits caught sight of him, they would fall down in front of him shrieking, "You are the Son of God!" ¹²But Jesus strictly warned them not to say who he was.

Jesus Chooses the Twelve Apostles

¹³Afterward Jesus went up on a mountain and called the ones he wanted to go with him. And they came to him. ¹⁴Then he selected twelve of them to be his regular companions, calling them apostles.* He sent them out to preach, ¹⁵and he gave them authority to cast out demons. ¹⁶These are the names of the twelve he chose:

Simon (he renamed him Peter),
¹⁷ James and John (the sons of Zebedee, but Jesus nicknamed them "Sons of Thunder"*),
¹⁸ Andrew,
Philip,
Bartholomew,
Matthew,
Thomas,
James (son of Alphaeus),
Thaddaeus,
Simon (the Zealot*),
¹⁹ Judas Iscariot (who later betrayed him).

3:14 Some manuscripts do not include *calling them apostles.* 3:17 Greek *whom he named Boanerges, which means Sons of Thunder.* 3:18 Greek *the Cananean.*

I READ all the Scriptures. (2:25)

See David's profile (page 629) at Psalm 3:1.

I BELIEVE the Sabbath was made to benefit people and was not intended to be a rigid rule for all people all the time. (2:27)

I DO NOT CONDEMN others for serving the Lord. (3:2)

I BELIEVE Jesus felt genuinely angry because of the hard hearts of his enemies. (3:5)

See the profile for the Pharisees (page 1087) at Matthew 12:14.

I BELIEVE Jesus chose twelve apostles and gave them authority to preach and cast out demons. (3:14)

See Peter's profile (page 1111) at Matthew 26:75.

See John's profile (page 1435) at Revelation 1:9.

See the profiles for Andrew (page 1199), Matthew (page 1081), and Thomas (page 1231) at John 1:42, Matthew 9:9, and John 20:28.

Jesus and the Prince of Demons

²⁰When Jesus returned to the house where he was staying, the crowds began to gather again, and soon he and his disciples couldn't even find time to eat. ²¹When his family heard what was happening, they tried to take him home with them. "He's out of his mind," they said.

²²But the teachers of religious law who had arrived from Jerusalem said, "He's possessed by Satan,* the prince of demons. That's where he gets the power to cast out demons."

²³Jesus called them over and said to them by way of illustration, "How can Satan cast out Satan? ²⁴A kingdom at war with itself will collapse. ²⁵A home divided against itself is doomed. ²⁶And if Satan is fighting against himself, how can he stand? He would never survive. ²⁷Let me illustrate this. You can't enter a strong man's house and rob him without first tying him up. Only then can his house be robbed!*

²⁸"I assure you that any sin can be forgiven, including blasphemy; ²⁹but anyone who blasphemes against the Holy Spirit will never be forgiven. It is an eternal sin." ³⁰He told them this because they were saying he had an evil spirit.

The True Family of Jesus

³¹Jesus' mother and brothers arrived at the house where he was teaching. They stood outside and sent word for him to come out and talk with them. ³²There was a crowd around Jesus, and someone said, "Your mother and your brothers and sisters* are outside, asking for you."

³³Jesus replied, "Who is my mother? Who are my brothers?" ³⁴Then he looked at those around him and said, "These are my mother and brothers. ³⁵Anyone who does God's will is my brother and sister and mother."

CHAPTER 4

Story of the Farmer Scattering Seed

Once again Jesus began teaching by the lakeshore. There was such a large crowd along the shore that he got into a boat and sat down and spoke from there. ²He began to teach the people by telling many stories such as this one:

³"Listen! A farmer went out to plant some seed. ⁴As he scattered it across his field, some seed fell on a footpath, and the birds came and ate it. ⁵Other seed fell on shallow soil with underlying rock. The plant sprang up quickly, ⁶but it soon wilted beneath the hot sun and died because the roots had no nourishment in the shallow soil. ⁷Other seed fell among thorns that shot up and choked out the tender blades so that it produced no grain. ⁸Still other seed fell on fertile soil and produced a crop that was thirty, sixty, and even a hundred times as much as had been planted." Then he said, ⁹"Anyone who is willing to hear should listen and understand!"

¹⁰Later, when Jesus was alone with the twelve disciples and with the others who were gathered around, they asked him, "What do your stories mean?"

¹¹He replied, "You are permitted to understand the secret about the Kingdom of God. But I am using these stories to conceal everything about it from outsiders, ¹²so that the Scriptures might be fulfilled:

'They see what I do,
    but they don't perceive its meaning.
They hear my words,
    but they don't understand.
So they will not turn from their sins
    and be forgiven.'*

I DO NOT CALL people crazy when I don't understand what they are doing for the Lord. (3:21)

I BELIEVE God can forgive any sin. (3:28)

I BELIEVE someone who refuses to stop blaspheming against the Holy Spirit by attributing the works of Jesus to demons will never experience God's forgiveness. (3:30)

I BELIEVE those who do God's will are part of Jesus' spiritual family. (3:34)

I AM WILLING AND EAGER to hear and to understand Jesus' teachings. (4:9)

I BELIEVE Jesus spoke in parables to conceal new spiritual truths from those who continually refused to turn from their sins. (4:12)

3:22 Greek *Beelzeboul.* 3:27 Or *One cannot rob Satan's kingdom without first tying him up. Only then can his demons be cast out.* 3:32 Some manuscripts do not include *and sisters.* 4:12 Isa 6:9-10.

¹³"But if you can't understand this story, how will you understand all the others I am going to tell? ¹⁴The farmer I talked about is the one who brings God's message to others. ¹⁵The seed that fell on the hard path represents those who hear the message, but then Satan comes at once and takes it away from them. ¹⁶The rocky soil represents those who hear the message and receive it with joy. ¹⁷But like young plants in such soil, their roots don't go very deep. At first they get along fine, but they wilt as soon as they have problems or are persecuted because they believe the word. ¹⁸The thorny ground represents those who hear and accept the Good News, ¹⁹but all too quickly the message is crowded out by the cares of this life, the lure of wealth, and the desire for nice things, so no crop is produced. ²⁰But the good soil represents those who hear and accept God's message and produce a huge harvest—thirty, sixty, or even a hundred times as much as had been planted."

I BELIEVE some individuals receive God's message with joy for a time until they have problems. (4:17)

I BELIEVE some individuals accept God's message and produce many visible results. (4:20)

UNLIKE JUDAS   *I do not follow Jesus Christ out of selfish, ulterior motives.*
Mark 3:19

The history of the nineteenth and twentieth centuries contains numerous stories of men and women who formed their own religious cults to make a fortune from gullible souls. Judas apparently had dreams of fame and riches as grand as those of any charlatan. And he saw Jesus as his sure ticket to achieving them.

From the first time he "borrowed" a little money from the apostles' fund to the moment he pocketed thirty pieces of silver (Matthew 26:14-16), Judas was looking out for his own best interests. When he objected to a woman's lavish outpouring of perfume on Jesus, for instance, it wasn't because Judas really cared about the poor. What Jesus saw as an act of worship, Judas calculated as a loss of funds to pilfer (John 12:1-6).

As Jesus approached Jerusalem and began predicting his sufferings, Judas counted the cost—and decided to cash in while he could. Whether he wanted to destroy Jesus or merely force Jesus to seize power, Judas's focus was solely on his own agenda, not on the will of God. With ease, Satan entered Judas's heart and propelled him to cut a deal with the leading priests and plot a way to betray Jesus (Luke 22:1-6).

Even when Judas was later filled with remorse, he never turned back to God in repentance. He simply regretted the tragic turn of events and took what appeared to be the easiest way out (Matthew 27:5).

Scripture warns us not to even consider the possibility of following the Lord as a means to financial gain and personal profit (1 Peter 1:13-19; 2 Peter 2:1-16). Unlike Judas, let's value Jesus far above silver—for who he is, not for what we can get from him.

○ *Today's Scripture reading is Mark 3:19 and 14:3-11, 43-49.*

Illustration of the Lamp
²¹Then Jesus asked them, "Would anyone light a lamp and then put it under a basket or under a bed to shut out the light? Of course not! A lamp is placed on a stand, where its light will shine.

²²"Everything that is now hidden or secret will eventually be brought to light. ²³Anyone who is willing to hear should listen and understand! ²⁴And be sure to pay attention to what you hear. The more you do this, the more you will understand—and even more, besides. ²⁵To those who are open to my teaching, more understanding will be given. But to those who are not listening, even what they have will be taken away from them."

I PAY ATTENTION to what I hear from God's Word so I can understand more and more. (4:24)

Illustration of the Growing Seed
²⁶Jesus also said, "Here is another illustration of what the Kingdom of God is like: A farmer planted seeds in a field, ²⁷and then he went on with his other activities. As the days went by, the seeds sprouted and grew without the farmer's help, ²⁸because the earth produces crops on its own. First a leaf blade

pushes through, then the heads of wheat are formed, and finally the grain ripens. ²⁹And as soon as the grain is ready, the farmer comes and harvests it with a sickle."

Illustration of the Mustard Seed

³⁰Jesus asked, "How can I describe the Kingdom of God? What story should I use to illustrate it? ³¹It is like a tiny mustard seed. Though this is one of the smallest of seeds, ³²it grows to become one of the largest of plants, with long branches where birds can come and find shelter."

³³He used many such stories and illustrations to teach the people as much as they were able to understand. ³⁴In fact, in his public teaching he taught only with parables, but afterward when he was alone with his disciples, he explained the meaning to them.

Jesus Calms the Storm

³⁵As evening came, Jesus said to his disciples, "Let's cross to the other side of the lake." ³⁶He was already in the boat, so they started out, leaving the crowds behind (although other boats followed). ³⁷But soon a fierce storm arose. High waves began to break into the boat until it was nearly full of water.

³⁸Jesus was sleeping at the back of the boat with his head on a cushion. Frantically they woke him up, shouting, "Teacher, don't you even care that we are going to drown?"

³⁹When he woke up, he rebuked the wind and said to the water, "Quiet down!" Suddenly the wind stopped, and there was a great calm. ⁴⁰And he asked them, "Why are you so afraid? Do you still not have faith in me?"

⁴¹And they were filled with awe and said among themselves, "Who is this man, that even the wind and waves obey him?"

CHAPTER 5

Jesus Heals a Demon-Possessed Man

So they arrived at the other side of the lake, in the land of the Gerasenes.* ²Just as Jesus was climbing from the boat, a man possessed by an evil spirit ran out from a cemetery to meet him. ³This man lived among the tombs and could not be restrained, even with a chain. ⁴Whenever he was put into chains and shackles—as he often was—he snapped the chains from his wrists and smashed the shackles. No one was strong enough to control him. ⁵All day long and throughout the night, he would wander among the tombs and in the hills, screaming and hitting himself with stones.

⁶When Jesus was still some distance away, the man saw him. He ran to meet Jesus and fell down before him. ⁷He gave a terrible scream, shrieking, "Why are you bothering me, Jesus, Son of the Most High God? For God's sake, don't torture me!" ⁸For Jesus had already said to the spirit, "Come out of the man, you evil spirit."

⁹Then Jesus asked, "What is your name?"

And the spirit replied, "Legion, because there are many of us here inside this man." ¹⁰Then the spirits begged him again and again not to send them to some distant place. ¹¹There happened to be a large herd of pigs feeding on the hillside nearby. ¹²"Send us into those pigs," the evil spirits begged. ¹³Jesus gave them permission. So the evil spirits came out of the man and entered the pigs, and the entire herd of two thousand pigs plunged down the steep hillside into the lake, where they drowned.

¹⁴The herdsmen fled to the nearby city and the surrounding countryside, spreading the news as they ran. Everyone rushed out to see for themselves. ¹⁵A crowd soon gathered around Jesus, but they were frightened when they saw the man who had been demon possessed, for he was sitting there fully

I BELIEVE God will finish and fulfill his purposes for his Kingdom at just the right time. (4:29)

I BELIEVE the Kingdom of God has grown tremendously from its small start. (4:32)

I BELIEVE the waves and winds calmed when Jesus rebuked them. (4:39)

I BELIEVE Jesus truly is the Son of the Most High God. (5:7)

I BELIEVE Jesus brought sanity to a man after he freed him from many evil spirits. (5:15)

5:1 Some manuscripts read *Gadarenes*; others read *Gergesenes*. See Matt 8:28; Luke 8:26.

clothed and perfectly sane. ¹⁶Those who had seen what happened to the man and to the pigs told everyone about it, ¹⁷and the crowd began pleading with Jesus to go away and leave them alone.

¹⁸When Jesus got back into the boat, the man who had been demon possessed begged to go, too. ¹⁹But Jesus said, "No, go home to your friends, and tell them what wonderful things the Lord has done for you and how merciful he has been." ²⁰So the man started off to visit the Ten Towns* of that region and began to tell everyone about the great things Jesus had done for him; and everyone was amazed at what he told them.

> I TELL my friends about the wonderful things the Lord has done for me. (5:20)

Jesus Heals in Response to Faith

²¹When Jesus went back across to the other side of the lake, a large crowd gathered around him on the shore. ²²A leader of the local synagogue, whose name was Jairus, came and fell down before him, ²³pleading with him to heal his little daughter. "She is about to die," he said in desperation. "Please come and place your hands on her; heal her so she can live."

> I PLEAD with Jesus to heal my child if he or she is sick. (5:23)

LIKE JAIRUS *I believe God can do miracles.*
Mark 5:23

Imagine what emotions Jairus must have experienced the day he almost lost his daughter. After reading Mark's account, you can almost see Jairus holding his daughter's trembling hand as his wife cooled the girl's forehead. "Jairus," his wife whispered, "what are we going to do? She hasn't eaten in days. Her fever grows only worse. She hasn't said a word or woken even once today. I'm . . . I'm so afraid." Jairus was a synagogue leader—a man of faith. Yet he and his wife both knew the horrible truth. They had cried out to the Lord until they couldn't pray anymore. Yet it seemed they were about to lose their precious daughter.

Just then, Jairus heard a commotion and stepped outside. A large crowd was gathering along the shore in front of the village. It was Jesus! In desperation, Jairus threw aside all decorum and pushed his way forcefully through the crowd. Falling at Jesus' feet, Jairus pleaded with the Lord to heal his daughter.

Jesus agreed and started toward Jairus's home—but then stopped for what seemed like an eternity. While Jesus talked at length with an elderly woman, Jairus languished. *Oh, Jesus,* he thought, *Please! Let's come back and talk with her later. My daughter! Oh, please save my daughter!*

Then came the worst news a father could ever hear. Jairus fell to his knees in grief, only to feel Jesus' hand upon his shoulder. "Get up, Jairus," Jesus said. "Don't be afraid. Just trust me." Slowly, Jairus stood up and started walking back, half in a daze, to his house. Then the sounds of wailing started to fill the air. "Don't stop, Jairus," Jesus said. "Just believe."

Later that night, after kissing their daughter good night, Jairus and his wife fell into each other's arms and wept great tears of joy. Jesus now calls you and me to believe.

○ *Today's Scripture reading is Mark 5:21-43.*

---

²⁴Jesus went with him, and the crowd thronged behind. ²⁵And there was a woman in the crowd who had had a hemorrhage for twelve years. ²⁶She had suffered a great deal from many doctors through the years and had spent everything she had to pay them, but she had gotten no better. In fact, she was worse. ²⁷She had heard about Jesus, so she came up behind him through the crowd and touched the fringe of his robe. ²⁸For she thought to herself, "If I can just touch his clothing, I will be healed." ²⁹Immediately the bleeding stopped, and she could feel that she had been healed!

³⁰Jesus realized at once that healing power had gone out from him, so he turned around in the crowd and asked, "Who touched my clothes?"

> I REACH OUT to Jesus for healing. (5:27)
>
> I BELIEVE the woman was healed of her hemorrhaging when she touched Jesus. (5:29)

5:20 Greek *Decapolis.*

I BELIEVE Jesus wanted to interview a woman who had just been healed and confirm for her that her faith in him had made her well. (5:32)

I IGNORE those who discourage me from trusting Jesus and seeking his help. (5:36)

See the profiles for Peter (page 1111) and John (page 1435) at Matthew 26:75 and Revelation 1:9.

I BELIEVE Jesus brought a little girl back to life. (5:42)

I DO NOT REFUSE to believe Jesus' teaching. (6:3)

See the profiles for Mary (page 1149) and James (page 1407) at Luke 1:38 and James 2:18.

I BELIEVE Jesus gave his disciples authority to cast out evil spirits. (6:7)

[31]His disciples said to him, "All this crowd is pressing around you. How can you ask, 'Who touched me?' "

[32]But he kept on looking around to see who had done it. [33]Then the frightened woman, trembling at the realization of what had happened to her, came and fell at his feet and told him what she had done. [34]And he said to her, "Daughter, your faith has made you well. Go in peace. You have been healed."

[35]While he was still speaking to her, messengers arrived from Jairus's home with the message, "Your daughter is dead. There's no use troubling the Teacher now."

[36]But Jesus ignored their comments and said to Jairus, "Don't be afraid. Just trust me." [37]Then Jesus stopped the crowd and wouldn't let anyone go with him except Peter and James and John. [38]When they came to the home of the synagogue leader, Jesus saw the commotion and the weeping and wailing. [39]He went inside and spoke to the people. "Why all this weeping and commotion?" he asked. "The child isn't dead; she is only asleep."

[40]The crowd laughed at him, but he told them all to go outside. Then he took the girl's father and mother and his three disciples into the room where the girl was lying. [41]Holding her hand, he said to her, "Get up, little girl!"* [42]And the girl, who was twelve years old, immediately stood up and walked around! Her parents were absolutely overwhelmed. [43]Jesus commanded them not to tell anyone what had happened, and he told them to give her something to eat.

CHAPTER 6

Jesus Rejected at Nazareth

Jesus left that part of the country and returned with his disciples to Nazareth, his hometown. [2]The next Sabbath he began teaching in the synagogue, and many who heard him were astonished. They asked, "Where did he get all his wisdom and the power to perform such miracles? [3]He's just the carpenter, the son of Mary and brother of James, Joseph,* Judas, and Simon. And his sisters live right here among us." They were deeply offended and refused to believe in him.

[4]Then Jesus told them, "A prophet is honored everywhere except in his own hometown and among his relatives and his own family." [5]And because of their unbelief, he couldn't do any mighty miracles among them except to place his hands on a few sick people and heal them. [6]And he was amazed at their unbelief.

Jesus Sends Out the Twelve Apostles

Then Jesus went out from village to village, teaching. [7]And he called his twelve disciples together and sent them out two by two, with authority to cast out evil spirits. [8]He told them to take nothing with them except a walking stick—no food, no traveler's bag, no money. [9]He told them to wear sandals but not to take even an extra coat. [10]"When you enter each village, be a guest in only one home," he said. [11]"And if a village won't welcome you or listen to you, shake off its dust from your feet as you leave. It is a sign that you have abandoned that village to its fate."

[12]So the disciples went out, telling all they met to turn from their sins. [13]And they cast out many demons and healed many sick people, anointing them with olive oil.

The Death of John the Baptist

[14]Herod Antipas, the king, soon heard about Jesus, because people everywhere were talking about him. Some were saying,* "This must be John

---

5:41 Greek text uses Aramaic *"Talitha cumi"* and then translates it as "Get up, little girl." 6:3 Greek *Joses*; see Matt 13:55. 6:14 Some manuscripts read *He was saying.*

the Baptist come back to life again. That is why he can do such miracles." [15]Others thought Jesus was the ancient prophet Elijah. Still others thought he was a prophet like the other great prophets of the past. [16]When Herod heard about Jesus, he said, "John, the man I beheaded, has come back from the dead." [17]For Herod had sent soldiers to arrest and imprison John as a favor to Herodias. She had been his brother Philip's wife, but Herod had married her. [18]John kept telling Herod, "It is illegal for you to marry your brother's wife." [19]Herodias was enraged and wanted John killed in revenge, but without Herod's approval she was powerless. [20]And Herod respected John, knowing that he was a good and holy man, so he kept him under his protection. Herod was disturbed whenever he talked with John, but even so, he liked to listen to him.

[21]Herodias's chance finally came. It was Herod's birthday, and he gave a party for his palace aides, army officers, and the leading citizens of Galilee. [22]Then his daughter, also named Herodias,* came in and performed a dance that greatly pleased them all. "Ask me for anything you like," the king said to the girl, "and I will give it to you." [23]Then he promised, "I will give you whatever you ask, up to half of my kingdom!"

[24]She went out and asked her mother, "What should I ask for?"

Her mother told her, "Ask for John the Baptist's head!"

[25]So the girl hurried back to the king and told him, "I want the head of John the Baptist, right now, on a tray!"

[26]Then the king was very sorry, but he was embarrassed to break his oath in front of his guests. [27]So he sent an executioner to the prison to cut off John's head and bring it to him. The soldier beheaded John in the prison, [28]brought his head on a tray, and gave it to the girl, who took it to her mother. [29]When John's disciples heard what had happened, they came for his body and buried it in a tomb.

Jesus Feeds Five Thousand

[30]The apostles returned to Jesus from their ministry tour and told him all they had done and what they had taught. [31]Then Jesus said, "Let's get away from the crowds for a while and rest." There were so many people coming and going that Jesus and his apostles didn't even have time to eat. [32]They left by boat for a quieter spot. [33]But many people saw them leaving, and people from many towns ran ahead along the shore and met them as they landed. [34]A vast crowd was there as he stepped from the boat, and he had compassion on them because they were like sheep without a shepherd. So he taught them many things.

[35]Late in the afternoon his disciples came to him and said, "This is a desolate place, and it is getting late. [36]Send the crowds away so they can go to the nearby farms and villages and buy themselves some food."

[37]But Jesus said, "You feed them."

"With what?" they asked. "It would take a small fortune* to buy food for all this crowd!"

[38]"How much food do you have?" he asked. "Go and find out."

They came back and reported, "We have five loaves of bread and two fish." [39]Then Jesus told the crowd to sit down in groups on the green grass. [40]So they sat in groups of fifty or a hundred.

[41]Jesus took the five loaves and two fish, looked up toward heaven, and asked God's blessing on the food. Breaking the loaves into pieces, he kept giving the bread and fish to the disciples to give to the people. [42]They all ate as much as they wanted, [43]and they picked up twelve baskets of leftover bread and fish. [44]Five thousand men had eaten from those five loaves!

I RECOGNIZE many people thought Jesus was Elijah or another prophet or John the Baptist raised from the dead. (6:15)

See Elijah's profile (page 421) at 1 Kings 19:18.

I DO NOT TRY to destroy those who confront me with my own sins. (6:19)

I DO NOT ALLOW myself to be influenced by individuals who arouse my lust. (6:22)

I DO NOT FOLLOW through on a terrible, destructive promise simply to avoid embarrassment. (6:26)

I BELIEVE Jesus cared about his disciples' need for rest after an intense period of ministry. (6:31)

I BELIEVE Jesus had compassion on people because they needed a shepherd. (6:34)

I BELIEVE Jesus challenged his disciples to meet the needs of the crowds. (6:37)

I BELIEVE Jesus fed thousands of people with five loaves and two fish. (6:44)

6:22 Some manuscripts read *the daughter of Herodias herself.*   6:37 Greek *200 denarii.* A denarius was the equivalent of a full day's wage.

Jesus Walks on Water

⁴⁵Immediately after this, Jesus made his disciples get back into the boat and head out across the lake to Bethsaida, while he sent the people home. ⁴⁶Afterward he went up into the hills by himself to pray.

⁴⁷During the night, the disciples were in their boat out in the middle of the lake, and Jesus was alone on land. ⁴⁸He saw that they were in serious trouble, rowing hard and struggling against the wind and waves. About three o'clock in the morning* he came to them, walking on the water. He started to go past them, ⁴⁹but when they saw him walking on the water, they screamed in terror, thinking he was a ghost. ⁵⁰They were all terrified when they saw him. But Jesus spoke to them at once. "It's all right," he said. "I am here! Don't be afraid." ⁵¹Then he climbed into the boat, and the wind stopped. They were astonished at what they saw. ⁵²They still didn't understand the significance of the miracle of the multiplied loaves, for their hearts were hard and they did not believe.

⁵³When they arrived at Gennesaret on the other side of the lake, they anchored the boat ⁵⁴and climbed out. The people standing there recognized him at once, ⁵⁵and they ran throughout the whole area and began carrying sick people to him on mats. ⁵⁶Wherever he went—in villages and cities and out on the farms—they laid the sick in the market plazas and streets. The sick begged him to let them at least touch the fringe of his robe, and all who touched it were healed.

CHAPTER 7

Jesus Teaches about Inner Purity

One day some Pharisees and teachers of religious law arrived from Jerusalem to confront Jesus. ²They noticed that some of Jesus' disciples failed to follow the usual Jewish ritual of hand washing before eating. ³(The Jews, especially the Pharisees, do not eat until they have poured water over their cupped hands,* as required by their ancient traditions. ⁴Similarly, they eat nothing bought from the market unless they have immersed their hands in water. This is but one of many traditions they have clung to—such as their ceremony of washing cups, pitchers, and kettles.*) ⁵So the Pharisees and teachers of religious law asked him, "Why don't your disciples follow our age-old customs? For they eat without first performing the hand-washing ceremony."

⁶Jesus replied, "You hypocrites! Isaiah was prophesying about you when he said,

⁷'These people honor me with their lips,
     but their hearts are far away.
  Their worship is a farce,
     for they replace God's commands with their own man-made
        teachings.'*

⁸For you ignore God's specific laws and substitute your own traditions."

⁹Then he said, "You reject God's laws in order to hold on to your own traditions. ¹⁰For instance, Moses gave you this law from God: 'Honor your father and mother,' and 'Anyone who speaks evil of father or mother must be put to death.'* ¹¹But you say it is all right for people to say to their parents, 'Sorry, I can't help you. For I have vowed to give to God what I could have given to you.'* ¹²You let them disregard their needy parents. ¹³As such, you break the law of God in order to protect your own tradition. And this is only one example. There are many, many others."

¹⁴Then Jesus called to the crowd to come and hear. "All of you listen," he

I GO AWAY by myself to pray to God. (6:46)

I BELIEVE Jesus walked on the water of a large lake. (6:48)

I BELIEVE Jesus reassured his disciples with his presence. (6:50)

I DO NOT HARDEN my heart to the meaning of Jesus' miracles. (6:52)

I BELIEVE Jesus healed the sick wherever he went. (6:56)

See the profile for the Pharisees (page 1087) at Matthew 12:14.

See Isaiah's profile (page 801) at Isaiah 6:13.

I DO NOT REPLACE God's commands with man-made teachings. (7:7)

See Moses' profile (page 73) at Exodus 5:1.

I DO NOT GIVE people excuses for ignoring God's laws. (7:11)

I DO NOT DISREGARD my parents' needs. (7:12)

I DO NOT BREAK God's law to protect my own traditions. (7:13)

6:48 Greek *About the fourth watch of the night.*   **7:3** Greek *washed with the fist.*   **7:4** Some Greek manuscripts add *and dining couches.*   **7:7** Isa 29:13.   **7:10** Exod 20:12; 21:17; Lev 20:9; Deut 5:16.   **7:11** Greek *'What I could have given to you is Corban' (that is, a gift).*

said, "and try to understand. ¹⁵You are not defiled by what you eat; you are defiled by what you say and do!*"

¹⁷Then Jesus went into a house to get away from the crowds, and his disciples asked him what he meant by the statement he had made. ¹⁸"Don't you understand either?" he asked. "Can't you see that what you eat won't defile you? ¹⁹Food doesn't come in contact with your heart, but only passes through the stomach and then comes out again." (By saying this, he showed that every kind of food is acceptable.)

²⁰And then he added, "It is the thought-life that defiles you. ²¹For from within, out of a person's heart, come evil thoughts, sexual immorality, theft, murder, ²²adultery, greed, wickedness, deceit, eagerness for lustful pleasure, envy, slander, pride, and foolishness. ²³All these vile things come from within; they are what defile you and make you unacceptable to God."

The Faith of a Gentile Woman

²⁴Then Jesus left Galilee and went north to the region of Tyre.* He tried to keep it secret that he was there, but he couldn't. As usual, the news of his arrival spread fast. ²⁵Right away a woman came to him whose little girl was possessed by an evil spirit. She had heard about Jesus, and now she came and fell at his feet. ²⁶She begged him to release her child from the demon's control.

Since she was a Gentile, born in Syrian Phoenicia, ²⁷Jesus told her, "First I should help my own family, the Jews.* It isn't right to take food from the children and throw it to the dogs."

²⁸She replied, "That's true, Lord, but even the dogs under the table are given some crumbs from the children's plates."

²⁹"Good answer!" he said. "And because you have answered so well, I have healed your daughter." ³⁰And when she arrived home, her little girl was lying quietly in bed, and the demon was gone.

Jesus Heals a Deaf and Mute Man

³¹Jesus left Tyre and went to Sidon, then back to the Sea of Galilee and the region of the Ten Towns.* ³²A deaf man with a speech impediment was brought to him, and the people begged Jesus to lay his hands on the man to heal him. ³³Jesus led him to a private place away from the crowd. He put his fingers into the man's ears. Then, spitting onto his own fingers, he touched the man's tongue with the spittle. ³⁴And looking up to heaven, he sighed and commanded, "Be opened!"* ³⁵Instantly the man could hear perfectly and speak plainly!

³⁶Jesus told the crowd not to tell anyone, but the more he told them not to, the more they spread the news, ³⁷for they were completely amazed. Again and again they said, "Everything he does is wonderful. He even heals those who are deaf and mute."

CHAPTER 8

Jesus Feeds Four Thousand

About this time another great crowd had gathered, and the people ran out of food again. Jesus called his disciples and told them, ²"I feel sorry for these people. They have been here with me for three days, and they have nothing left to eat. ³And if I send them home without feeding them, they will faint along the road. For some of them have come a long distance."

⁴"How are we supposed to find enough food for them here in the wilderness?" his disciples asked.

⁵"How many loaves of bread do you have?" he asked.

7:15 Some manuscripts add verse 16, *Anyone who is willing to hear should listen and understand.* 7:24 Some Greek manuscripts add *and Sidon.* 7:27 Greek *Let the children eat first.* 7:31 Greek *Decapolis.* 7:34 Greek text uses Aramaic *"Ephphatha"* and then translates it as *"Be opened."*

I KNOW I become defiled by my wrong words and actions, not by my diet. (7:15)

I BELIEVE Jesus declared that all food was acceptable to eat. (7:19)

I BELIEVE that defilement comes from the heart first. (7:21)

I COME to Jesus for help when my children are in danger. (7:25)

I BELIEVE Jesus has mercy and power enough for everyone. (7:28)

I BELIEVE Jesus healed a woman's daughter from demon possession. (7:30)

I BRING my friends to Jesus. (7:32)

I BELIEVE Jesus healed a deaf man so he could hear and speak. (7:35)

I OBEY Jesus' instructions even if I do not understand them. (7:36)

I THANK God for all the food he provides, and I give to others in need. (8:6)

"Seven," they replied. ⁶So Jesus told all the people to sit down on the ground. Then he took the seven loaves, thanked God for them, broke them into pieces, and gave them to his disciples, who distributed the bread to the crowd. ⁷A few small fish were found, too, so Jesus also blessed these and told the disciples to pass them out.

⁸They ate until they were full, and when the scraps were picked up, there were seven large baskets of food left over! ⁹There were about four thousand people in the crowd that day, and he sent them home after they had eaten. ¹⁰Immediately after this, he got into a boat with his disciples and crossed over to the region of Dalmanutha.

Pharisees Demand a Miraculous Sign

¹¹When the Pharisees heard that Jesus had arrived, they came to argue with him. Testing him to see if he was from God, they demanded, "Give us a miraculous sign from heaven to prove yourself."

I DO NOT DEMAND signs from God. (8:11)

See the profile for the Pharisees (page 1087) at Matthew 12:14.

¹²When he heard this, he sighed deeply and said, "Why do you people keep demanding a miraculous sign? I assure you, I will not give this generation any such sign." ¹³So he got back into the boat and left them, and he crossed to the other side of the lake.

Yeast of the Pharisees and Herod

¹⁴But the disciples discovered they had forgotten to bring any food, so there was only one loaf of bread with them in the boat. ¹⁵As they were crossing the lake, Jesus warned them, "Beware of the yeast of the Pharisees and of Herod."

I WATCH OUT for hypocrisy and unbelief. (8:15)

¹⁶They decided he was saying this because they hadn't brought any bread. ¹⁷Jesus knew what they were thinking, so he said, "Why are you so worried about having no food? Won't you ever learn or understand? Are your hearts too hard to take it in? ¹⁸'You have eyes—can't you see? You have ears—can't you hear?'* Don't you remember anything at all? ¹⁹What about the five thousand men I fed with five loaves of bread? How many baskets of leftovers did you pick up afterward?"

"Twelve," they said.

²⁰"And when I fed the four thousand with seven loaves, how many large baskets of leftovers did you pick up?"

"Seven," they said.

²¹"Don't you understand even yet?" he asked them.

Jesus Heals a Blind Man

²²When they arrived at Bethsaida, some people brought a blind man to Jesus, and they begged him to touch and heal the man. ²³Jesus took the blind man by the hand and led him out of the village. Then, spitting on the man's eyes, he laid his hands on him and asked, "Can you see anything now?"

²⁴The man looked around. "Yes," he said, "I see people, but I can't see them very clearly. They look like trees walking around."

²⁵Then Jesus placed his hands over the man's eyes again. As the man stared intently, his sight was completely restored, and he could see everything clearly. ²⁶Jesus sent him home, saying, "Don't go back into the village on your way home."

Peter's Declaration about Jesus

²⁷Jesus and his disciples left Galilee and went up to the villages of Caesarea Philippi. As they were walking along, he asked them, "Who do people say I am?"

See Elijah's profile (page 421) at 1 Kings 19:18.

²⁸"Well," they replied, "some say John the Baptist, some say Elijah, and others say you are one of the other prophets."

8:18 Jer 5:21.

²⁹Then Jesus asked, "Who do you say I am?"

Peter replied, "You are the Messiah." ³⁰But Jesus warned them not to tell anyone about him.

Jesus Predicts His Death

³¹Then Jesus began to tell them that he, the Son of Man, would suffer many terrible things and be rejected by the leaders, the leading priests, and the teachers of religious law. He would be killed, and three days later he would rise again. ³²As he talked about this openly with his disciples, Peter took him aside and told him he shouldn't say things like that.*

> I BELIEVE Jesus is the Messiah, not simply a great man. (8:29)
>
> *See Peter's profile (page 1111) at Matthew 26:75.*
>
> I BELIEVE Jesus accurately predicted his suffering, death, and resurrection. (8:31)

LIKE THE GENTILE WOMAN *I persist in seeking God with my need, believing in his power and willingness to help me.*

Mark 7:30

Living in Tyre, surrounded by the pagan Gentile culture of her birth, this woman from Syrian Phoenicia seemed far removed from the promises and blessings of God. Yet she was a woman in desperate need. That desperation produced great faith in her. Jesus came to her town specifically to highlight and reward her faith.

This woman's heart tore daily for months as she watched how a demon tormented her dear little daughter. She experienced the despair of being powerless to rescue her. Then one day this woman heard of the great Jewish rabbi, Jesus, who healed the sick and freed others from their bondage of demons.

Moved by God's Holy Spirit, this woman believed in him, without seeing his miracles for herself. What incredible joy when she realized he was coming to her village! This belief, coupled with love for her daughter, drove her to seek Jesus out and beg for her daughter's deliverance.

The woman knew very well before she ever approached Jesus that she was an outsider to God's promises, undeserving of his riches. Jesus seemed to put her off—not because he begrudged sharing his power, but to allow her to express the depth of her faith in the mercy of the God of Israel. She knew that God had something even for the "dogs"—those outside of Israel—and knew he longed to bless any who believed, Jew or Gentile.

Jesus gladly rewarded this remarkable woman's faith—and taught his disciples an important lesson at the same time. This Gentile went home to find her daughter healed—and completely free from demonic oppression.

How often we wonder why we have to express our needs in prayer when God already knows our circumstances. We wonder why we need to ask others to petition God as well. God rewards those who, like this Gentile woman, express their need—and faith—to him.

To read more about this remarkable woman of faith, see Matthew 15:21-28.

○ *Today's Scripture reading is Mark 7:24-30.*

---

³³Jesus turned and looked at his disciples and then said to Peter very sternly, "Get away from me, Satan! You are seeing things merely from a human point of view, not from God's."

³⁴Then he called his disciples and the crowds to come over and listen. "If any of you wants to be my follower," he told them, "you must put aside your selfish ambition, shoulder your cross, and follow me. ³⁵If you try to keep your life for yourself, you will lose it. But if you give up your life for my sake and for the sake of the Good News, you will find true life. ³⁶And how do you benefit if you gain the whole world but lose your own soul* in the process? ³⁷Is anything worth more than your soul? ³⁸If a person is ashamed of me and my message in these adulterous and sinful days, I, the Son of Man, will be ashamed of that person when I return in the glory of my Father with the holy angels."

> I PUT ASIDE my selfish ambition, give up my life, and follow the Lord Jesus. (8:34)
>
> I BELIEVE nothing in life is worth more than my soul. (8:37)

8:32 Or *and began to correct him.* 8:36 Or *your life;* also in 8:37.

CHAPTER 9

Jesus went on to say, "I assure you that some of you standing here right now will not die before you see the Kingdom of God arrive in great power!"

The Transfiguration

[2]Six days later Jesus took Peter, James, and John to the top of a mountain. No one else was there. As the men watched, Jesus' appearance changed, [3]and his clothing became dazzling white, far whiter than any earthly process could ever make it. [4]Then Elijah and Moses appeared and began talking with Jesus.

[5]"Teacher, this is wonderful!" Peter exclaimed. "We will make three shrines*—one for you, one for Moses, and one for Elijah." [6]He didn't really know what to say, for they were all terribly afraid.

[7]Then a cloud came over them, and a voice from the cloud said, "This is my beloved Son. Listen to him." [8]Suddenly they looked around, and Moses and Elijah were gone, and only Jesus was with them. [9]As they descended the mountainside, he told them not to tell anyone what they had seen until he, the Son of Man, had risen from the dead. [10]So they kept it to themselves, but they often asked each other what he meant by "rising from the dead."

[11]Now they began asking him, "Why do the teachers of religious law insist that Elijah must return before the Messiah comes?"

[12]Jesus responded, "Elijah is indeed coming first to set everything in order. Why then is it written in the Scriptures that the Son of Man must suffer and be treated with utter contempt? [13]But I tell you, Elijah has already come, and he was badly mistreated, just as the Scriptures predicted."

Jesus Heals a Boy Possessed by an Evil Spirit

[14]At the foot of the mountain they found a great crowd surrounding the other disciples, as some teachers of religious law were arguing with them. [15]The crowd watched Jesus in awe as he came toward them, and then they ran to greet him. [16]"What is all this arguing about?" he asked.

[17]One of the men in the crowd spoke up and said, "Teacher, I brought my son for you to heal him. He can't speak because he is possessed by an evil spirit that won't let him talk. [18]And whenever this evil spirit seizes him, it throws him violently to the ground and makes him foam at the mouth and grind his teeth and become rigid.* So I asked your disciples to cast out the evil spirit, but they couldn't do it."

[19]Jesus said to them, "You faithless people! How long must I be with you until you believe? How long must I put up with you? Bring the boy to me." [20]So they brought the boy. But when the evil spirit saw Jesus, it threw the child into a violent convulsion, and he fell to the ground, writhing and foaming at the mouth. [21]"How long has this been happening?" Jesus asked the boy's father.

He replied, "Since he was very small. [22]The evil spirit often makes him fall into the fire or into water, trying to kill him. Have mercy on us and help us. Do something if you can."

[23]"What do you mean, 'If I can'?" Jesus asked. "Anything is possible if a person believes."

[24]The father instantly replied, "I do believe, but help me not to doubt!"

[25]When Jesus saw that the crowd of onlookers was growing, he rebuked the evil spirit. "Spirit of deafness and muteness," he said, "I command you to come out of this child and never enter him again!" [26]Then the spirit screamed and threw the boy into another violent convulsion and left him. The boy lay there motionless, and he appeared to be dead. A murmur ran through the crowd, "He's dead." [27]But Jesus took him by the hand and helped him to his feet, and he stood up.

9:5 Or shelters; Greek reads tabernacles.   9:18 Or become weak.

I BELIEVE Jesus accurately predicted that some of his disciples would see his glory revealed. (9:1)

See the profiles for Peter (page 1111) and John (page 1435) at Matthew 26:75 and Revelation 1:9.

See the profiles for Moses (page 73) and Elijah (page 421) at Exodus 5:1 and 1 Kings 19:18.

I FOCUS my attention on Jesus, not on spiritual experiences. (9:5)

I BELIEVE God spoke from heaven, commanding Peter, James, and John to listen to his beloved Son. (9:7)

I BELIEVE Jesus Christ taught his disciples clearly that the Scriptures said he must suffer. (9:12)

I DO NOT DOUBT Jesus can help me, even in the most difficult of circumstances. (9:23)

[28]Afterward, when Jesus was alone in the house with his disciples, they asked him, "Why couldn't we cast out that evil spirit?"

[29]Jesus replied, "This kind can be cast out only by prayer.*"

Jesus Again Predicts His Death

[30]Leaving that region, they traveled through Galilee. Jesus tried to avoid all publicity [31]in order to spend more time with his disciples and teach them. He said to them, "The Son of Man is going to be betrayed. He will be killed, but three days later he will rise from the dead." [32]But they didn't understand what he was saying, and they were afraid to ask him what he meant.

The Greatest in the Kingdom

[33]After they arrived at Capernaum, Jesus and his disciples settled in the house where they would be staying. Jesus asked them, "What were you discussing out on the road?" [34]But they didn't answer, because they had been arguing about which of them was the greatest. [35]He sat down and called the twelve disciples over to him. Then he said, "Anyone who wants to be the first must take last place and be the servant of everyone else."

I AM WILLING to take last place and become the servant of everyone else. (9:35)

[36]Then he put a little child among them. Taking the child in his arms, he said to them, [37]"Anyone who welcomes a little child like this on my behalf welcomes me, and anyone who welcomes me welcomes my Father who sent me."

Using the Name of Jesus

[38]John said to Jesus, "Teacher, we saw a man using your name to cast out demons, but we told him to stop because he isn't one of our group."

I DO NOT HINDER the ministry of others simply because they don't belong to my group. (9:38)

[39]"Don't stop him!" Jesus said. "No one who performs miracles in my name will soon be able to speak evil of me. [40]Anyone who is not against us is for us. [41]If anyone gives you even a cup of water because you belong to the Messiah, I assure you, that person will be rewarded.

I BELIEVE the Lord will reward anyone who does something good to those who belong to him. (9:41)

[42]"But if anyone causes one of these little ones who trusts in me to lose faith, it would be better for that person to be thrown into the sea with a large millstone tied around the neck. [43]If your hand causes you to sin, cut it off. It is better to enter heaven* with only one hand than to go into the unquenchable fires of hell with two hands.* [45]If your foot causes you to sin, cut it off. It is better to enter heaven with only one foot than to be thrown into hell with two feet.* [47]And if your eye causes you to sin, gouge it out. It is better to enter the Kingdom of God half blind than to have two eyes and be thrown into hell, [48]where the worm never dies and the fire never goes out.'*

I CONTINUE to purify my life and live at peace with other believers. (9:50)

[49]"For everyone will be purified with fire.* [50]Salt is good for seasoning. But if it loses its flavor, how do you make it salty again? You must have the qualities of salt among yourselves and live in peace with each other."

CHAPTER 10

Discussion about Divorce and Marriage

Then Jesus left Capernaum and went southward to the region of Judea and into the area east of the Jordan River. As always there were the crowds, and as usual he taught them.

[2]Some Pharisees came and tried to trap him with this question: "Should a man be allowed to divorce his wife?"

See the profile for the Pharisees (page 1087) at Matthew 12:14.

[3]"What did Moses say about divorce?" Jesus asked them.

I POINT people to the Scriptures when they have questions. (10:3)

[4]"Well, he permitted it," they replied. "He said a man merely has to write his wife an official letter of divorce and send her away."*

See Moses' profile (page 73) at Exodus 5:1.

[5]But Jesus responded, "He wrote those instructions only as a concession to

9:29 Some manuscripts add *and fasting.* 9:43a Greek *enter life;* also in 9:45. 9:43b Some manuscripts add verse 44 (which is identical with 9:48). 9:45 Some manuscripts add verse 46 (which is identical with 9:48). 9:48 Isa 66:24. 9:49 Greek *salted with fire.* Some manuscripts add *and every sacrifice will be salted with salt.* 10:4 Deut 24:1.

your hard-hearted wickedness. [6]But God's plan was seen from the beginning of creation, for 'He made them male and female.'* [7]This explains why a man leaves his father and mother and is joined to his wife,* [8]and the two are united into one.'* Since they are no longer two but one, [9]let no one separate them, for God has joined them together."

[10]Later, when he was alone with his disciples in the house, they brought up the subject again. [11]He told them, "Whoever divorces his wife and marries someone else commits adultery against her. [12]And if a woman divorces her husband and remarries, she commits adultery."

Jesus Blesses the Children

[13]One day some parents brought their children to Jesus so he could touch them and bless them, but the disciples told them not to bother him. [14]But when Jesus saw what was happening, he was very displeased with his disciples. He said to them, "Let the children come to me. Don't stop them! For the Kingdom of God belongs to such as these. [15]I assure you, anyone who doesn't have their kind of faith will never get into the Kingdom of God." [16]Then he took the children into his arms and placed his hands on their heads and blessed them.

The Rich Man

[17]As he was starting out on a trip, a man came running up to Jesus, knelt down, and asked, "Good Teacher, what should I do to get eternal life?"

[18]"Why do you call me good?" Jesus asked. "Only God is truly good. [19]But as for your question, you know the commandments: 'Do not murder. Do not commit adultery. Do not steal. Do not testify falsely. Do not cheat. Honor your father and mother.'* "

[20]"Teacher," the man replied, "I've obeyed all these commandments since I was a child."

[21]Jesus felt genuine love for this man as he looked at him. "You lack only one thing," he told him. "Go and sell all you have and give the money to the poor, and you will have treasure in heaven. Then come, follow me." [22]At this, the man's face fell, and he went sadly away because he had many possessions.

[23]Jesus looked around and said to his disciples, "How hard it is for rich people to get into the Kingdom of God!" [24]This amazed them. But Jesus said again, "Dear children, it is very hard* to get into the Kingdom of God. [25]It is easier for a camel to go through the eye of a needle than for a rich person to enter the Kingdom of God!"

[26]The disciples were astounded. "Then who in the world can be saved?" they asked.

[27]Jesus looked at them intently and said, "Humanly speaking, it is impossible. But not with God. Everything is possible with God."

[28]Then Peter began to mention all that he and the other disciples had left behind. "We've given up everything to follow you," he said.

[29]And Jesus replied, "I assure you that everyone who has given up house or brothers or sisters or mother or father or children or property, for my sake and for the Good News, [30]will receive now in return, a hundred times over, houses, brothers, sisters, mothers, children, and property—with persecutions. And in the world to come they will have eternal life. [31]But many who seem to be important now will be the least important then, and those who are considered least here will be the greatest then.* "

I BELIEVE God's plan for marriage is evident from the creation (Genesis 1:27; 2:24). (10:6)

I BRING my children to Jesus and ask for his blessing. (10:13)

I RECOGNIZE that Jesus is the Son of God, not simply a good teacher. (10:18)

I AM WILLING to give up whatever Jesus asks in order to follow him. (10:21)

I BELIEVE everything—no matter how difficult—is possible with God. (10:27)

See Peter's profile (page 1111) at Matthew 26:75.

I BELIEVE that God will abundantly reward those who give up things for his sake. (10:29)

10:6 Gen 1:27; 5:2.　10:7 Some manuscripts do not include *and is joined to his wife.*　10:7-8 Gen 2:24.
10:19 Exod 20:12-16; Deut 5:16-20.　10:24 Some manuscripts add *for those who trust in riches.*　10:31 Greek
But many who are first will be last; and the last, first.

Jesus Again Predicts His Death

³²They were now on the way to Jerusalem, and Jesus was walking ahead of them. The disciples were filled with dread and the people following behind were overwhelmed with fear. Taking the twelve disciples aside, Jesus once more began to describe everything that was about to happen to him in Jerusalem. ³³"When we get to Jerusalem," he told them, "the Son of Man will be betrayed to the leading priests and the teachers of religious law. They will sentence him to die and hand him over to the Romans. ³⁴They will mock him, spit on him, beat him with their whips, and kill him, but after three days he will rise again."

I BELIEVE Jesus accurately predicted that he would be beaten and killed and that he would rise again. (10:33)

UNLIKE THE RICH YOUNG MAN
Mark 10:22

I let nothing stand in the way of coming to Jesus Christ.

Every eleven-year-old wants his weekly allowance as soon as possible—until his mother points out all the chores that still need to be finished.

When the rich young man came to Jesus, he sincerely thought he wanted eternal life, and he asked Jesus most earnestly what he could do to get it. Jesus felt genuine love for the man—so much so that he pinpointed the one obstacle that had to be removed first. In doing so, Jesus revealed that the man's wealth consumed him. As much as he loved the thought of eternal life, the young man loved his current lifestyle and prestige even more.

This particular man, like many other rich men, wanted to *do* something to gain eternal life. Money makes you feel like you can do anything, doesn't it? He had his financial portfolio and professional résumé all in order. Alongside his impeccable character qualifications, his résumé even listed all his favorite charities. That always looks good when closing a deal. But Jesus wasn't interested in dealing—he wanted the man's heart.

Once again, Jesus saw clearly into the man's life and spoke words that went directly to the point. The man had indeed obeyed the everyday commands Jesus listed—but not the greatest command of all. He *didn't* love the Lord his God with all his heart and soul and strength. He *did* have other gods before the true God. He wanted eternal life, for sure, but not if that meant forsaking his gods of money, possessions, and influence.

Nothing in this life is more important than loving and following the Lord Jesus Christ. Not family relationships or financial security, not fulfilled dreams or temporal fame. Unlike the rich young man, you and I can make the right choice to let go of anything that keeps us from enjoying the Lord's very best.

You can read more about the rich young man in Matthew 19:16-30 and Luke 18:18-30.

○ *Today's Scripture reading is Mark 10:17-31.*

Jesus Teaches about Serving Others

³⁵Then James and John, the sons of Zebedee, came over and spoke to him. "Teacher," they said, "we want you to do us a favor."

³⁶"What is it?" he asked.

³⁷"In your glorious Kingdom, we want to sit in places of honor next to you," they said, "one at your right and the other at your left."

³⁸But Jesus answered, "You don't know what you are asking! Are you able to drink from the bitter cup of sorrow I am about to drink? Are you able to be baptized with the baptism of suffering I must be baptized with?"

³⁹"Oh yes," they said, "we are able!"

And Jesus said, "You will indeed drink from my cup and be baptized with my baptism, ⁴⁰but I have no right to say who will sit on the thrones next to mine. God has prepared those places for the ones he has chosen."

⁴¹When the ten other disciples discovered what James and John had asked, they were indignant. ⁴²So Jesus called them together and said, "You know that in this world kings are tyrants, and officials lord it over the people beneath them. ⁴³But among you it should be quite different. Whoever wants to

See John's profile (page 1435) at Revelation 1:9.

be a leader among you must be your servant, ⁴⁴and whoever wants to be first must be the slave of all. ⁴⁵For even I, the Son of Man, came here not to be served but to serve others, and to give my life as a ransom for many."

Jesus Heals Blind Bartimaeus

⁴⁶And so they reached Jericho. Later, as Jesus and his disciples left town, a great crowd was following. A blind beggar named Bartimaeus (son of Timaeus) was sitting beside the road as Jesus was going by. ⁴⁷When Bartimaeus heard that Jesus from Nazareth was nearby, he began to shout out, "Jesus, Son of David, have mercy on me!"

⁴⁸"Be quiet!" some of the people yelled at him.

But he only shouted louder, "Son of David, have mercy on me!"

⁴⁹When Jesus heard him, he stopped and said, "Tell him to come here."

So they called the blind man. "Cheer up," they said. "Come on, he's calling you!" ⁵⁰Bartimaeus threw aside his coat, jumped up, and came to Jesus.

⁵¹"What do you want me to do for you?" Jesus asked.

"Teacher," the blind man said, "I want to see!"

⁵²And Jesus said to him, "Go your way. Your faith has healed you." And instantly the blind man could see! Then he followed Jesus down the road.*

CHAPTER 11

The Triumphal Entry

As Jesus and his disciples approached Jerusalem, they came to the towns of Bethphage and Bethany, on the Mount of Olives. Jesus sent two of them on ahead. ²"Go into that village over there," he told them, "and as soon as you enter it, you will see a colt tied there that has never been ridden. Untie it and bring it here. ³If anyone asks what you are doing, just say, 'The Lord needs it and will return it soon.' "

⁴The two disciples left and found the colt standing in the street, tied outside a house. ⁵As they were untying it, some bystanders demanded, "What are you doing, untying that colt?" ⁶They said what Jesus had told them to say, and they were permitted to take it. ⁷Then they brought the colt to Jesus and threw their garments over it, and he sat on it.

⁸Many in the crowd spread their coats on the road ahead of Jesus, and others cut leafy branches in the fields and spread them along the way. ⁹He was in the center of the procession, and the crowds all around him were shouting,

"Praise God!*
  Bless the one who comes in the name of the Lord!
¹⁰Bless the coming kingdom of our ancestor David!
  Praise God in highest heaven!"*

¹¹So Jesus came to Jerusalem and went into the Temple. He looked around carefully at everything, and then he left because it was late in the afternoon. Then he went out to Bethany with the twelve disciples.

Jesus Curses the Fig Tree

¹²The next morning as they were leaving Bethany, Jesus felt hungry. ¹³He noticed a fig tree a little way off that was in full leaf, so he went over to see if he could find any figs on it. But there were only leaves because it was too early in the season for fruit. ¹⁴Then Jesus said to the tree, "May no one ever eat your fruit again!" And the disciples heard him say it.

Jesus Clears the Temple

¹⁵When they arrived back in Jerusalem, Jesus entered the Temple and began to drive out the merchants and their customers. He knocked over the tables

I BELIEVE Jesus did not come to be served but to serve and give his life as a ransom for many. (10:45)

See David's profile (page 629) at Psalm 3:1.

I DO NOT LET others dissuade me from seeking Jesus. (10:48)

I OBEY Jesus' instructions. (11:4)

See David's profile (page 629) at Psalm 3:1.

I BELIEVE Jesus experienced physical hunger. (11:12)

10:52 Or *on the way.*   11:9 Greek *Hosanna,* an exclamation of praise that literally means "save now"; also in 11:10.   11:9-10 Pss 118:25-26; 148:1.

of the money changers and the stalls of those selling doves, ¹⁶and he stopped everyone from bringing in merchandise. ¹⁷He taught them, "The Scriptures declare, 'My Temple will be called a place of prayer for all nations,' but you have turned it into a den of thieves."*

¹⁸When the leading priests and teachers of religious law heard what Jesus had done, they began planning how to kill him. But they were afraid of him because the people were so enthusiastic about Jesus' teaching. ¹⁹That evening Jesus and the disciples* left the city.

²⁰The next morning as they passed by the fig tree he had cursed, the disciples noticed it was withered from the roots. ²¹Peter remembered what Jesus had said to the tree on the previous day and exclaimed, "Look, Teacher! The fig tree you cursed has withered!"

> I DO NOT ALLOW money to keep people from coming to God in prayer and worship. (11:17)

> See Peter's profile (page 1111) at Matthew 26:75.

LIKE BLIND BARTIMAEUS
Mark 10:52

I am confident that God delights in hearing and answering my prayers.

The next time you see a blind beggar sitting on the sidewalk, clutching his belongings with one hand and holding out a cup in the other, stop for a minute. Say hello, introduce yourself, ask his name, give him a couple dollars, and tell him the story of blind Bartimaeus. Then ask the man what he'd like Jesus to do, and say a prayer. You'll never be the same.

Scripture doesn't tell us why Bartimaeus was blind—perhaps he lost his sight after a tragic accident. It doesn't even tell us his first name—we just know he was the son of Timaeus and was sitting alongside the road with another blind man (Matthew 20:30) when he heard Jesus was coming!

Bartimaeus was desperate for a miracle and started shouting at the top of his lungs, "Jesus, Son of David, have mercy on me!" The crowds yelled back, telling Bartimaeus to be quiet, but the beggar only shouted louder, "Son of David, have mercy on me!"

Interestingly, Jesus didn't answer Bartimaeus. Instead, he commanded the crowd: "Tell him to come here." In response to Jesus' command, Bartimaeus threw aside his coat—something a blind man would never do—and rushed toward the sound of Jesus' voice. He knew exactly what he wanted Jesus to do for him and believed—without a shadow of doubt—that his prayer of a lifetime was about to be answered!

Like Bartimaeus, you and I may find ourselves praying week after week, month after month, year after year, for God to answer one of our most heartfelt prayers. Let's never stop asking (Matthew 7:7). Instead, with great confidence, let's step out in faith and depend on the Lord's answer.

○ Today's Scripture reading is Mark 10:46-52.

---

²²Then Jesus said to the disciples, "Have faith in God. ²³I assure you that you can say to this mountain, 'May God lift you up and throw you into the sea,' and your command will be obeyed. All that's required is that you really believe and do not doubt in your heart. ²⁴Listen to me! You can pray for anything, and if you believe, you will have it. ²⁵But when you are praying, first forgive anyone you are holding a grudge against, so that your Father in heaven will forgive your sins, too.*"

> I BELIEVE in God and don't harbor doubts in my heart when I pray. (11:23)

> I DO NOT HOLD grudges but forgive others before I pray. (11:25)

The Authority of Jesus Challenged

²⁷By this time they had arrived in Jerusalem again. As Jesus was walking through the Temple area, the leading priests, the teachers of religious law, and the other leaders came up to him. They demanded, ²⁸"By whose authority did you drive out the merchants from the Temple?* Who gave you such authority?"

²⁹"I'll tell who gave me authority to do these things if you answer one

11:17 Isa 56:7; Jer 7:11.   11:19 Greek *they*; some manuscripts read *he*.   11:25 Some manuscripts add verse 26, *But if you do not forgive, neither will your Father who is in heaven forgive your sins.*   11:28 Or *By whose authority do you do these things?*

question," Jesus replied. ³⁰"Did John's baptism come from heaven or was it merely human? Answer me!"

³¹They talked it over among themselves. "If we say it was from heaven, he will ask why we didn't believe him. ³²But do we dare say it was merely human?" For they were afraid that the people would start a riot, since everyone thought that John was a prophet. ³³So they finally replied, "We don't know."

And Jesus responded, "Then I won't answer your question either."

CHAPTER 12

Story of the Evil Farmers

Then Jesus began telling them stories: "A man planted a vineyard, built a wall around it, dug a pit for pressing out the grape juice, and built a lookout tower. Then he leased the vineyard to tenant farmers and moved to another country. ²At grape-picking time he sent one of his servants to collect his share of the crop. ³But the farmers grabbed the servant, beat him up, and sent him back empty-handed.

⁴"The owner then sent another servant, but they beat him over the head and treated him shamefully. ⁵The next servant he sent was killed. Others who were sent were either beaten or killed, ⁶until there was only one left—his son whom he loved dearly. The owner finally sent him, thinking, 'Surely they will respect my son.'

⁷"But the farmers said to one another, 'Here comes the heir to this estate. Let's kill him and get the estate for ourselves!' ⁸So they grabbed him and murdered him and threw his body out of the vineyard.

⁹"What do you suppose the owner of the vineyard will do?" Jesus asked. "I'll tell you—he will come and kill them all and lease the vineyard to others. ¹⁰Didn't you ever read this in the Scriptures?

'The stone rejected by the builders
    has now become the cornerstone.
¹¹This is the Lord's doing,
    and it is marvelous to see.'* "

¹²The Jewish leaders wanted to arrest him for using this illustration because they realized he was pointing at them—they were the wicked farmers in his story. But they were afraid to touch him because of the crowds. So they left him and went away.

Taxes for Caesar

¹³The leaders sent some Pharisees and supporters of Herod to try to trap Jesus into saying something for which he could be arrested. ¹⁴"Teacher," these men said, "we know how honest you are. You are impartial and don't play favorites. You sincerely teach the ways of God. Now tell us—is it right to pay taxes to the Roman government or not? ¹⁵Should we pay them, or should we not?"

Jesus saw through their hypocrisy and said, "Whom are you trying to fool with your trick questions? Show me a Roman coin,* and I'll tell you." ¹⁶When they handed it to him, he asked, "Whose picture and title are stamped on it?"

"Caesar's," they replied.

¹⁷"Well, then," Jesus said, "give to Caesar what belongs to him. But everything that belongs to God must be given to God." This reply completely amazed them.

Discussion about Resurrection

¹⁸Then the Sadducees stepped forward—a group of Jews who say there is no resurrection after death. They posed this question: ¹⁹"Teacher, Moses gave us

---

I DO NOT NEED to give a direct answer to those who question me insincerely. (11:33)

I BELIEVE Jesus was rejected, just as the Scriptures predicted. (12:10)

See the profile for the Pharisees (page 1087) at Matthew 12:14.

I PAY whatever I owe my government and give my life wholly to God. (12:17)

I BELIEVE in the resurrection of the dead. (12:18)

See the profile for the Sadducees (page 1103) at Matthew 22:23.

See Moses' profile (page 73) at Exodus 5:1.

12:10-11 Ps 118:22-23.   12:15 Greek *a denarius*.

a law that if a man dies, leaving a wife without children, his brother should marry the widow and have a child who will be the brother's heir.* ²⁰Well, there were seven brothers. The oldest of them married and then died without children. ²¹So the second brother married the widow, but soon he too died and left no children. Then the next brother married her and died without children. ²²This continued until all the brothers had married her and died, and still there were no children. Last of all, the woman died, too. ²³So tell us, whose wife will she be in the resurrection? For all seven were married to her."

²⁴Jesus replied, "Your problem is that you don't know the Scriptures, and you don't know the power of God. ²⁵For when the dead rise, they won't be married. They will be like the angels in heaven. ²⁶But now, as to whether the dead will be raised—haven't you ever read about this in the writings of Moses, in the story of the burning bush? Long after Abraham, Isaac, and Jacob had died, God said to Moses,* 'I am the God of Abraham, the God of Isaac, and the God of Jacob.'* ²⁷So he is the God of the living, not the dead. You have made a serious error."

The Most Important Commandment

²⁸One of the teachers of religious law was standing there listening to the discussion. He realized that Jesus had answered well, so he asked, "Of all the commandments, which is the most important?"

²⁹Jesus replied, "The most important commandment is this: 'Hear, O Israel! The Lord our God is the one and only Lord. ³⁰And you must love the Lord your God with all your heart, all your soul, all your mind, and all your strength.'* ³¹The second is equally important: 'Love your neighbor as yourself.'* No other commandment is greater than these."

³²The teacher of religious law replied, "Well said, Teacher. You have spoken the truth by saying that there is only one God and no other. ³³And I know it is important to love him with all my heart and all my understanding and all my strength, and to love my neighbors as myself. This is more important than to offer all of the burnt offerings and sacrifices required in the law."

³⁴Realizing this man's understanding, Jesus said to him, "You are not far from the Kingdom of God." And after that, no one dared to ask him any more questions.

Whose Son Is the Messiah?

³⁵Later, as Jesus was teaching the people in the Temple, he asked, "Why do the teachers of religious law claim that the Messiah will be the son of David? ³⁶For David himself, speaking under the inspiration of the Holy Spirit, said,

'The LORD said to my Lord,
Sit in honor at my right hand
until I humble your enemies beneath your feet.'*

³⁷Since David himself called him Lord, how can he be his son at the same time?" And the crowd listened to him with great interest.

³⁸Here are some of the other things he taught them at this time: "Beware of these teachers of religious law! For they love to parade in flowing robes and to have everyone bow to them as they walk in the marketplaces. ³⁹And how they love the seats of honor in the synagogues and at banquets. ⁴⁰But they shamelessly cheat widows out of their property, and then, to cover up the kind of people they really are, they make long prayers in public. Because of this, their punishment will be the greater."

The Widow's Offering

⁴¹Jesus went over to the collection box in the Temple and sat and watched as the crowds dropped in their money. Many rich people put in large amounts.

I DO NOT INVENT hypothetical stories to try to disprove God's Word. (12:20)

See the profiles for Abraham (page 19), Isaac (page 31), and Jacob (page 43) at Genesis 15:6, Genesis 25:19, and Genesis 32:9.

I BELIEVE God is the God of the living—that is, every believer who has died is alive with him. (12:27)

I LOVE the Lord my God with all my heart, soul, mind, and strength. (12:30)

I LOVE my neighbor as myself. (12:31)

See David's profile (page 629) at Psalm 3:1.

I BELIEVE Jesus is the Messiah, the Son of David, yet also his Lord, as the Scripture predicted. (12:36)

I WATCH OUT for individuals who try to cover up their sins by acting religious. (12:40)

12:19 Deut 25:5-6.   12:26a Greek *in the story of the bush? God said to him.*   12:26b Exod 3:6.   12:29-30 Deut 6:4-5.   12:31 Lev 19:18.   12:36 Ps 110:1.

I GIVE even out of my
need, not simply out
of my abundance.
(12:44)

⁴²Then a poor widow came and dropped in two pennies.* ⁴³He called his disciples to him and said, "I assure you, this poor widow has given more than all the others have given. ⁴⁴For they gave a tiny part of their surplus, but she, poor as she is, has given everything she has."

CHAPTER 13

Jesus Foretells the Future

As Jesus was leaving the Temple that day, one of his disciples said, "Teacher, look at these tremendous buildings! Look at the massive stones in the walls!"

I BELIEVE Jesus
accurately predicted
the destruction of the
Temple in Jerusalem.
(13:2)

*See the profiles for
Peter (page 1111),
John (page 1435), and
Andrew (page 1199)
at Matthew 26:75,
Revelation 1:9, and
John 1:42.*

²Jesus replied, "These magnificent buildings will be so completely demolished that not one stone will be left on top of another."

³Later, Jesus sat on the slopes of the Mount of Olives across the valley from the Temple. Peter, James, John, and Andrew came to him privately and asked him, ⁴"When will all this take place? And will there be any sign ahead of time to show us when all this will be fulfilled?"

⁵Jesus replied, "Don't let anyone mislead you, ⁶because many will come in my name, claiming to be the Messiah.* They will lead many astray. ⁷And wars will break out near and far, but don't panic. Yes, these things must come, but the end won't follow immediately. ⁸Nations and kingdoms will proclaim war against each other, and there will be earthquakes in many parts of the world, and famines. But all this will be only the beginning of the horrors to come. ⁹But when these things begin to happen, watch out! You will be handed over to the courts and beaten in the synagogues. You will be accused before governors and kings of being my followers. This will be your opportunity to tell them about me.* ¹⁰And the Good News must first be preached to every nation. ¹¹But when you are arrested and stand trial, don't worry about what to say in your defense. Just say what God tells you to. Then it is not you who will be speaking, but the Holy Spirit.

I AM NOT MISLED by
those who claim to be
the Messiah. (13:5)

I WATCH FOR the signs
of the Lord's return.
(13:9)

I HELP preach the
Good News to every
nation. (13:10)

I ENDURE to the end,
even though others
will hate me because
of my allegiance to
Christ. (13:13)

¹²"Brother will betray brother to death, fathers will betray their own children, and children will rise against their parents and cause them to be killed. ¹³And everyone will hate you because of your allegiance to me. But those who endure to the end will be saved.

¹⁴"The time will come when you will see the sacrilegious object that causes desecration* standing where it should not be"—reader, pay attention! "Then those in Judea must flee to the hills. ¹⁵A person outside the house* must not go back into the house to pack. ¹⁶A person in the field must not return even to get a coat. ¹⁷How terrible it will be for pregnant women and for mothers nursing their babies in those days. ¹⁸And pray that your flight will not be in winter. ¹⁹For those will be days of greater horror than at any time since God created the world. And it will never happen again. ²⁰In fact, unless the Lord shortens that time of calamity, the entire human race will be destroyed. But for the sake of his chosen ones he has shortened those days.

I BELIEVE a time of
calamity is coming
that will be shortened
only for the sake of
God's chosen ones.
(13:20)

²¹"And then if anyone tells you, 'Look, here is the Messiah,' or, 'There he is,' don't pay any attention. ²²For false messiahs and false prophets will rise up and perform miraculous signs and wonders so as to deceive, if possible, even God's chosen ones. ²³Watch out! I have warned you!

²⁴"At that time, after those horrible days end,

the sun will be darkened,
    the moon will not give light,
²⁵the stars will fall from the sky,
    and the powers of heaven will be shaken.*

I BELIEVE everyone will
see Jesus when he
returns in great power
and glory. (13:26)

²⁶Then everyone will see the Son of Man arrive on the clouds with great power and glory.* ²⁷And he will send forth his angels to gather together his

12:42 Greek *2 lepta, which is a kodrantes.*   13:6 Greek *name, saying, 'I am.'*   13:9 Or *This will be your testimony against them.*   13:14 Greek *the abomination of desolation.* See Dan 9:27; 11:31; 12:11.   13:15 Greek *on the roof.* 13:24-25 See Isa 13:10; 34:4; Joel 2:10.   13:26 See Dan 7:13.

chosen ones from all over the world—from the farthest ends of the earth and heaven. [28] "Now, learn a lesson from the fig tree. When its buds become tender and its leaves begin to sprout, you know without being told that summer is near. [29] Just so, when you see the events I've described beginning to happen, you can be sure that his return is very near, right at the door. [30] I assure you, this generation* will not pass from the scene until all these events have taken place. [31] Heaven and earth will disappear, but my words will remain forever.

[32] "However, no one knows the day or hour when these things will happen, not even the angels in heaven or the Son himself. Only the Father knows. [33] And since you don't know when they will happen, stay alert and keep watch.*

I BELIEVE only God the Father knows the exact moment when Jesus will return. (13:32)

LIKE THE POOR WIDOW
Mark 12:42

I know that God will multiply my gifts a hundredfold.

Anyone else watching the collection box earlier that day wouldn't have even noticed the poor widow's two pennies tossed in among the silver and gold coins that had poured in. But it wasn't just anyone standing nearby—it was Jesus.

The widow's pennies caught Jesus' eye as they quietly plinked into the offering box. Suddenly, the widow had his full attention. Oh, Jesus had seen the other gifts all right—and he did not condemn them. But with his words he honored this poor widow for millennia to come. He set the worth of her gift far above any other given that day.

God doesn't judge and use our offerings based on any human standards of measurement. What could those two pennies possibly buy for the Temple service? Were they well spent or squandered by the youngest son of some corrupt religious leader? No matter. God viewed them as far more valuable than the donations of the wealthiest king—because they were given out of the heart of a woman who loved and trusted him enough to give everything she had. Her gift was a blessing to him—and to others. For with the poor widow's example, the Lord has opened the hearts and pockets of believers down through the centuries. From her two pennies have flowed other offerings too great to ever be counted.

Like the poor widow, you and I delight the Lord when we trust him and give out of our need, instead of only out of our surplus (2 Corinthians 8:2-3; 9:6-14).

The poor widow's story is also told in Luke 21:1-4.

○ Today's Scripture reading is Mark 12:41-44.

---

[34] "The coming of the Son of Man can be compared with that of a man who left home to go on a trip. He gave each of his employees instructions about the work they were to do, and he told the gatekeeper to watch for his return. [35] So keep a sharp lookout! For you do not know when the homeowner will return—at evening, midnight, early dawn, or late daybreak. [36] Don't let him find you sleeping when he arrives without warning. [37] What I say to you I say to everyone: Watch for his return!"

CHAPTER 14

Jesus Anointed at Bethany

It was now two days before the Passover celebration and the Festival of Unleavened Bread. The leading priests and the teachers of religious law were still looking for an opportunity to capture Jesus secretly and put him to death. [2] "But not during the Passover," they agreed, "or there will be a riot."

[3] Meanwhile, Jesus was in Bethany at the home of Simon, a man who had leprosy. During supper, a woman came in with a beautiful jar of expensive perfume.* She broke the seal and poured the perfume over his head. [4] Some

13:30 Or *this age,* or *this nation.*   13:33 Some manuscripts add *and pray.*   14:3 Greek *an alabaster jar of expensive ointment, pure nard.*

of those at the table were indignant. "Why was this expensive perfume wasted?" they asked. ⁵"She could have sold it for a small fortune* and given the money to the poor!" And they scolded her harshly.

⁶But Jesus replied, "Leave her alone. Why berate her for doing such a good thing to me? ⁷You will always have the poor among you, and you can help them whenever you want to. But I will not be here with you much longer. ⁸She has done what she could and has anointed my body for burial ahead of time. ⁹I assure you, wherever the Good News is preached throughout the world, this woman's deed will be talked about in her memory."

Judas Agrees to Betray Jesus

¹⁰Then Judas Iscariot, one of the twelve disciples, went to the leading priests to arrange to betray Jesus to them. ¹¹The leading priests were delighted when they heard why he had come, and they promised him a reward. So he began looking for the right time and place to betray Jesus.

The Last Supper

¹²On the first day of the Festival of Unleavened Bread (the day the Passover lambs were sacrificed), Jesus' disciples asked him, "Where do you want us to go to prepare the Passover supper?"

¹³So Jesus sent two of them into Jerusalem to make the arrangements. "As you go into the city," he told them, "a man carrying a pitcher of water will meet you. Follow him. ¹⁴At the house he enters, say to the owner, 'The Teacher asks, Where is the guest room where I can eat the Passover meal with my disciples?' ¹⁵He will take you upstairs to a large room that is already set up. That is the place; go ahead and prepare our supper there." ¹⁶So the two disciples went on ahead into the city and found everything just as Jesus had said, and they prepared the Passover supper there.

¹⁷In the evening Jesus arrived with the twelve disciples. ¹⁸As they were sitting around the table eating, Jesus said, "The truth is, one of you will betray me, one of you who is here eating with me."

¹⁹Greatly distressed, one by one they began to ask him, "I'm not the one, am I?"

²⁰He replied, "It is one of you twelve, one who is eating with me now.* ²¹For I, the Son of Man, must die, as the Scriptures declared long ago. But how terrible it will be for my betrayer. Far better for him if he had never been born!"

²²As they were eating, Jesus took a loaf of bread and asked God's blessing on it. Then he broke it in pieces and gave it to the disciples, saying, "Take it, for this is my body."

²³And he took a cup of wine and gave thanks to God for it. He gave it to them, and they all drank from it. ²⁴And he said to them, "This is my blood, poured out for many, sealing the covenant* between God and his people. ²⁵I solemnly declare that I will not drink wine again until that day when I drink it new in the Kingdom of God." ²⁶Then they sang a hymn and went out to the Mount of Olives.

Jesus Predicts Peter's Denial

²⁷"All of you will desert me," Jesus told them. "For the Scriptures say,

'God* will strike the Shepherd,
    and the sheep will be scattered.'*

²⁸But after I am raised from the dead, I will go ahead of you to Galilee and meet you there."

²⁹Peter said to him, "Even if everyone else deserts you, I never will."

I DO NOT BERATE others who give sacrificially to the Lord. (14:6)

I BELIEVE Jesus knew exactly who would betray him. (14:18)

I BELIEVE Jesus gave the bread to his disciples as a symbol of his body, which would be broken for them. (14:22)

I BELIEVE Jesus gave the cup of wine to his disciples as a symbol of his blood, which would seal the new covenant between God and his people. (14:23)

I BELIEVE Jesus accurately predicted that his disciples would leave him, just as the Scriptures said. (14:27)

See Peter's profile (page 1111) at Matthew 26:75.

14:5 Greek *300 denarii*. A denarius was the equivalent of a full day's wage.   **14:20** Or *one who is dipping bread into the bowl with me*.   **14:24** Some manuscripts read *the new covenant*.   **14:27a** Greek *I*.   **14:27b** Zech 13:7.

³⁰"Peter," Jesus replied, "the truth is, this very night, before the rooster crows twice, you will deny me three times."

³¹"No!" Peter insisted. "Not even if I have to die with you! I will never deny you!" And all the others vowed the same.

Jesus Prays in Gethsemane

³²And they came to an olive grove called Gethsemane, and Jesus said, "Sit here while I go and pray." ³³He took Peter, James, and John with him, and he began to be filled with horror and deep distress. ³⁴He told them, "My soul is crushed with grief to the point of death. Stay here and watch with me."

³⁵He went on a little farther and fell face down on the ground. He prayed that, if it were possible, the awful hour awaiting him might pass him by. ³⁶"Abba,* Father," he said, "everything is possible for you. Please take this cup of suffering away from me. Yet I want your will, not mine."

³⁷Then he returned and found the disciples asleep. "Simon!" he said to Peter. "Are you asleep? Couldn't you stay awake and watch with me even one hour? ³⁸Keep alert and pray. Otherwise temptation will overpower you. For though the spirit is willing enough, the body is weak."

³⁹Then Jesus left them again and prayed, repeating his pleadings. ⁴⁰Again he returned to them and found them sleeping, for they just couldn't keep their eyes open. And they didn't know what to say.

⁴¹When he returned to them the third time, he said, "Still sleeping? Still resting?* Enough! The time has come. I, the Son of Man, am betrayed into the hands of sinners. ⁴²Up, let's be going. See, my betrayer is here!"

Jesus Is Betrayed and Arrested

⁴³And immediately, as he said this, Judas, one of the twelve disciples, arrived with a mob that was armed with swords and clubs. They had been sent out by the leading priests, the teachers of religious law, and the other leaders. ⁴⁴Judas had given them a prearranged signal: "You will know which one to arrest when I go over and give him the kiss of greeting. Then you can take him away under guard."

⁴⁵As soon as they arrived, Judas walked up to Jesus. "Teacher!" he exclaimed, and gave him the kiss. ⁴⁶Then the others grabbed Jesus and arrested him. ⁴⁷But someone pulled out a sword and slashed off an ear of the high priest's servant.

⁴⁸Jesus asked them, "Am I some dangerous criminal, that you come armed with swords and clubs to arrest me? ⁴⁹Why didn't you arrest me in the Temple? I was there teaching every day. But these things are happening to fulfill what the Scriptures say about me."

⁵⁰Meanwhile, all his disciples deserted him and ran away. ⁵¹There was a young man following along behind, clothed only in a linen nightshirt. When the mob tried to grab him, ⁵²they tore off his clothes, but he escaped and ran away naked.

Jesus before the Council

⁵³Jesus was led to the high priest's home where the leading priests, other leaders, and teachers of religious law had gathered. ⁵⁴Meanwhile, Peter followed far behind and then slipped inside the gates of the high priest's courtyard. For a while he sat with the guards, warming himself by the fire.

⁵⁵Inside, the leading priests and the entire high council* were trying to find witnesses who would testify against Jesus, so they could put him to death. But their efforts were in vain. ⁵⁶Many false witnesses spoke against him, but they contradicted each other. ⁵⁷Finally, some men stood up to testify against him with this lie: ⁵⁸"We heard him say, 'I will destroy this Temple made with

I BELIEVE Jesus accurately predicted that Peter would deny him three times. (14:30)

I DO NOT DENY that I can sin and fail the Lord. (14:31)

See John's profile (page 1435) at Revelation 1:9.

I BELIEVE Jesus sincerely prayed that the cup of suffering might pass from him, if it were possible. (14:36)

I STAY ALERT in prayer so that temptation will not overpower me. (14:38)

I BELIEVE Jesus was arrested to begin to fulfill what the Scriptures said would happen to him (Isaiah 53:7-9). (14:49)

I BELIEVE the disciples all deserted Jesus after his arrest, just as he said they would (Mark 14:27). (14:50)

14:36 *Abba* is an Aramaic term for "father." 14:41 Or *Sleep on, take your rest.* 14:55 Greek *the Sanhedrin.*

human hands, and in three days I will build another, made without human hands.' " [59]But even then they didn't get their stories straight!

[60]Then the high priest stood up before the others and asked Jesus, "Well, aren't you going to answer these charges? What do you have to say for yourself?" [61]Jesus made no reply. Then the high priest asked him, "Are you the Messiah, the Son of the blessed God?"

[62]Jesus said, "I am, and you will see me, the Son of Man, sitting at God's right hand in the place of power and coming back on the clouds of heaven."*

[63]Then the high priest tore his clothing to show his horror and said, "Why do we need other witnesses? [64]You have all heard his blasphemy. What is your verdict?" And they all condemned him to death.

[65]Then some of them began to spit at him, and they blindfolded him and hit his face with their fists. "Who hit you that time, you prophet?" they jeered. And even the guards were hitting him as they led him away.

Peter Denies Jesus

[66]Meanwhile, Peter was below in the courtyard. One of the servant girls who worked for the high priest [67]noticed Peter warming himself at the fire. She looked at him closely and then said, "You were one of those with Jesus, the Nazarene."

[68]Peter denied it. "I don't know what you're talking about," he said, and he went out into the entryway. Just then, a rooster crowed.*

[69]The servant girl saw him standing there and began telling the others, "That man is definitely one of them!" [70]Peter denied it again.

A little later some other bystanders began saying to Peter, "You must be one of them because you are from Galilee."

[71]Peter said, "I swear by God, I don't know this man you're talking about." [72]And immediately the rooster crowed the second time. Suddenly, Jesus' words flashed through Peter's mind: "Before the rooster crows twice, you will deny me three times." And he broke down and cried.

CHAPTER 15

Jesus' Trial before Pilate

Very early in the morning the leading priests, other leaders, and teachers of religious law—the entire high council*—met to discuss their next step. They bound Jesus and took him to Pilate, the Roman governor.

[2]Pilate asked Jesus, "Are you the King of the Jews?"

Jesus replied, "Yes, it is as you say."

[3]Then the leading priests accused him of many crimes, [4]and Pilate asked him, "Aren't you going to say something? What about all these charges against you?" [5]But Jesus said nothing, much to Pilate's surprise.

[6]Now it was the governor's custom to release one prisoner each year at Passover time—anyone the people requested. [7]One of the prisoners at that time was Barabbas, convicted along with others for murder during an insurrection. [8]The mob began to crowd in toward Pilate, asking him to release a prisoner as usual. [9]"Should I give you the King of the Jews?" Pilate asked. [10](For he realized by now that the leading priests had arrested Jesus out of envy.) [11]But at this point the leading priests stirred up the mob to demand the release of Barabbas instead of Jesus. [12]"But if I release Barabbas," Pilate asked them, "what should I do with this man you call the King of the Jews?"

[13]They shouted back, "Crucify him!"

[14]"Why?" Pilate demanded. "What crime has he committed?"

But the crowd only roared the louder, "Crucify him!"

[15]So Pilate, anxious to please the crowd, released Barabbas to them. He

---

I BELIEVE Jesus is the Messiah, the Son of God, who will return in power and glory. (14:62)

I WILL NOT DENY my relationship with Jesus Christ. (14:68)

I BELIEVE Peter denied Jesus three times, just as Jesus said he would (Mark 14:30). (14:71)

I WEEP in repentance when I sin and fail the Lord. (14:72)

See Pilate's profile (page 1229) at John 19:16.

I BELIEVE Jesus is the King of the Jews. (15:2)

I BELIEVE some leading priests stirred up a mob to ask for Barabbas to be released instead of Jesus. (15:11)

I DO NOT PUNISH the innocent and let the guilty go unpunished for selfish, political ends. (15:15)

14:62 See Ps 110:1; Dan 7:13. 14:68 Some manuscripts do not include *Just then, a rooster crowed.* 15:1 Greek *the Sanhedrin;* also in 15:43.

ordered Jesus flogged with a lead-tipped whip, then turned him over to the Roman soldiers to crucify him.

The Soldiers Mock Jesus

[16] The soldiers took him into their headquarters* and called out the entire battalion. [17] They dressed him in a purple robe and made a crown of long, sharp thorns and put it on his head. [18] Then they saluted, yelling, "Hail! King of the Jews!" [19] And they beat him on the head with a stick, spit on him, and dropped to their knees in mock worship. [20] When they were finally tired of mocking him, they took off the purple robe and put his own clothes on him again. Then they led him away to be crucified.

> I MOURN the mockery and beatings Jesus endured at the hands of the soldiers. (15:17)

The Crucifixion

[21] A man named Simon, who was from Cyrene,* was coming in from the country just then, and they forced him to carry Jesus' cross. (Simon is the father of Alexander and Rufus.) [22] And they brought Jesus to a place called Golgotha (which means Skull Hill). [23] They offered him wine drugged with myrrh, but he refused it. [24] Then they nailed him to the cross. They gambled for his clothes, throwing dice* to decide who would get them.

> I BELIEVE Jesus fully endured the pain of dying on a Roman cross. (15:23)

[25] It was nine o'clock in the morning when the crucifixion took place. [26] A signboard was fastened to the cross above Jesus' head, announcing the charge against him. It read: "The King of the Jews." [27] Two criminals were crucified with him, their crosses on either side of his.* [29] And the people passing by shouted abuse, shaking their heads in mockery. "Ha! Look at you now!" they yelled at him. "You can destroy the Temple and rebuild it in three days, can you? [30] Well then, save yourself and come down from the cross!"

[31] The leading priests and teachers of religious law also mocked Jesus. "He saved others," they scoffed, "but he can't save himself! [32] Let this Messiah, this king of Israel, come down from the cross so we can see it and believe him!" Even the two criminals who were being crucified with Jesus ridiculed him.

> See the Dying Thief's profile (page 1191) at Luke 23:42.

> I MOURN the mockery and abuse Jesus endured as he hung on the cross. (15:29)

> I BELIEVE Jesus truly is the Messiah. (15:32)

The Death of Jesus

[33] At noon, darkness fell across the whole land until three o'clock. [34] Then, at that time Jesus called out with a loud voice, "*Eloi, Eloi, lema sabachthani?*" which means, "My God, my God, why have you forsaken me?"*

[35] Some of the bystanders misunderstood and thought he was calling for the prophet Elijah. [36] One of them ran and filled a sponge with sour wine, holding it up to him on a stick so he could drink. "Leave him alone. Let's see whether Elijah will come and take him down!" he said.

[37] Then Jesus uttered another loud cry and breathed his last. [38] And the curtain in the Temple was torn in two, from top to bottom. [39] When the Roman officer who stood facing him saw how he had died, he exclaimed, "Truly, this was the Son of God!"

[40] Some women were there, watching from a distance, including Mary Magdalene, Mary (the mother of James the younger and of Joseph*), and Salome. [41] They had been followers of Jesus and had cared for him while he was in Galilee. Then they and many other women had come with him to Jerusalem.

> See Elijah's profile (page 421) at 1 Kings 19:18.

> I BELIEVE Jesus truly is the Son of God. (15:39)

> See Mary Magdalene's profile (page 1163) at Luke 8:2.

The Burial of Jesus

[42] This all happened on Friday, the day of preparation,* the day before the Sabbath. As evening approached, [43] an honored member of the high council, Joseph from Arimathea (who was waiting for the Kingdom of God to come), gathered his courage and went to Pilate to ask for Jesus' body. [44] Pilate couldn't believe that Jesus was already dead, so he called for the Roman

> I GATHER COURAGE to make bold requests for the Lord's sake. (15:43)

> See Joseph of Arimathea's profile (page 1113) at Matthew 27:57.

15:16 Greek *the courtyard, which is the praetorium.* 15:21 Cyrene was a city in northern Africa. 15:24 Greek *casting lots.* See Ps 22:18. 15:27 Some manuscripts add verse 28, *And the Scripture was fulfilled that said, "He was counted among those who were rebels."* See Isa 53:12. 15:34 Ps 22:1. 15:40 Greek *Joses;* also in 15:47. See Matt 27:56. 15:42 Greek *on the day of preparation.*

military officer in charge and asked him. ⁴⁵The officer confirmed the fact, and Pilate told Joseph he could have the body. ⁴⁶Joseph bought a long sheet of linen cloth, and taking Jesus' body down from the cross, he wrapped it in the cloth and laid it in a tomb that had been carved out of the rock. Then he rolled a stone in front of the entrance. ⁴⁷Mary Magdalene and Mary the mother of Joseph saw where Jesus' body was laid.

CHAPTER 16

The Resurrection

The next evening, when the Sabbath ended, Mary Magdalene and Salome and Mary the mother of James went out and purchased burial spices to put on Jesus' body. ²Very early on Sunday morning,* just at sunrise, they came to the tomb. ³On the way they were discussing who would roll the stone away from the entrance to the tomb. ⁴But when they arrived, they looked up and saw that the stone—a very large one—had already been rolled aside. ⁵So they entered the tomb, and there on the right sat a young man clothed in a white robe. The women were startled, ⁶but the angel said, "Do not be so surprised. You are looking for Jesus, the Nazarene, who was crucified. He isn't here! He has been raised from the dead! Look, this is where they laid his body. ⁷Now go and give this message to his disciples, including Peter: Jesus is going ahead of you to Galilee. You will see him there, just as he told you before he died!" ⁸The women fled from the tomb, trembling and bewildered, saying nothing to anyone because they were too frightened to talk.*

[Shorter Ending of Mark]

Then they reported all these instructions briefly to Peter and his companions. Afterward Jesus himself sent them out from east to west with the sacred and unfailing message of salvation that gives eternal life. Amen.

[Longer Ending of Mark]

⁹It was early on Sunday morning when Jesus rose from the dead, and the first person who saw him was Mary Magdalene, the woman from whom he had cast out seven demons. ¹⁰She went and found the disciples, who were grieving and weeping. ¹¹But when she told them that Jesus was alive and she had seen him, they didn't believe her.

¹²Afterward he appeared to two who were walking from Jerusalem into the country, but they didn't recognize him at first because he had changed his appearance. ¹³When they realized who he was, they rushed back to tell the others, but no one believed them.

¹⁴Still later he appeared to the eleven disciples as they were eating together. He rebuked them for their unbelief—their stubborn refusal to believe those who had seen him after he had risen.

¹⁵And then he told them, "Go into all the world and preach the Good News to everyone, everywhere. ¹⁶Anyone who believes and is baptized will be saved. But anyone who refuses to believe will be condemned. ¹⁷These signs will accompany those who believe: They will cast out demons in my name, and they will speak new languages.* ¹⁸They will be able to handle snakes with safety, and if they drink anything poisonous, it won't hurt them. They will be able to place their hands on the sick and heal them."

¹⁹When the Lord Jesus had finished talking with them, he was taken up into heaven and sat down in the place of honor at God's right hand. ²⁰And the disciples went everywhere and preached, and the Lord worked with them, confirming what they said by many miraculous signs.

I BELIEVE Jesus rose from the dead! (16:6)

See Peter's profile (page 1111) at Matthew 26:75.

I BELIEVE the Good News of Jesus' resurrection. (16:11)

I BELIEVE the witnesses of Jesus' resurrection. (16:14)

I HELP proclaim the Good News of Jesus to everyone, everywhere. (16:15)

I BELIEVE Jesus was taken up to heaven to the place of honor at God the Father's right hand. (16:19)

16:2 Greek *on the first day of the week;* also in 16:9. 16:8 The most reliable early manuscripts conclude the Gospel of Mark at verse 8. Other manuscripts include various endings to the Gospel. Two of the more noteworthy endings are printed here. 16:17 Or *new tongues.* Some manuscripts omit *new.*

LUKE

THIS THIRD GOSPEL challenges us to take the time to carefully consider Jesus' life, ministry, teachings, death, burial, resurrection, and ascension.

As an associate of the apostle Paul, Luke had the opportunity to travel widely and interview many of those most closely associated with Jesus. He even won the confidence of Jesus' mother, Mary, and reports far more about Jesus' birth and childhood than all the other Gospel writers combined.

Many of Luke's original readers, like Luke himself, were Gentiles. With that audience in mind, Luke gives special emphasis to poetry, prayers, poverty and wealth, repentance, and women of faith.

Famous passages in this Gospel include
- The Christmas story (1:26-56; 2:1-39)
- Jesus' childhood (2:40-52)
- Violent reaction to Jesus' first sermon in Nazareth (4:14-30)
- Peter's response to Jesus' sermon on the Sea of Galilee (5:1-11)
- The Beatitudes and sorrows (6:20-26)
- Jesus' raising of a widow's son from the dead (7:11-17)
- The inclusion of women in Jesus' ministry team (8:2-3)
- Jesus' transfiguration (9:28-36)
- James and John want to order down fire from heaven (9:51-56)
- Jesus' sending out of the seventy-two disciples (10:1-20)
- The story of the shrewd manager (16:1-13)
- The story of the ten lepers (17:11-19)
- The Last Supper (22:7-30)
- Jesus' appearance to two disciples from Emmaus (24:13-35)

CHAPTER 1

Introduction

Most honorable Theophilus:

Many people have written accounts about the events that took place* among us. ²They used as their source material the reports circulating among us from the early disciples and other eyewitnesses of what God has done in fulfillment of his promises. ³Having carefully investigated all of these accounts from the beginning, I have decided to write a careful summary for you, ⁴to reassure you of the truth of all you were taught.

See Luke's profile (page 1379) at 2 Timothy 4:11.

The Birth of John the Baptist Foretold

⁵It all begins with a Jewish priest, Zechariah, who lived when Herod was king of Judea. Zechariah was a member of the priestly order of Abijah. His wife,

1:1 Or *have been fulfilled.*

See Aaron's profile (page 107) at Exodus 32:2.

I AM RIGHTEOUS in the sight of God, observing all the Lord's commandments and regulations. (1:6)

I OBEY the Lord's commands and believe my prayers have been heard by the Lord. (1:13)

See John the Baptist's profile (page 1117) at Mark 1:4.

I DESIRE to turn the hearts of the fathers to their children and of the disobedient to the wisdom of the righteous. (1:17)

See Elijah's profile (page 421) at 1 Kings 19:18.

I RECOGNIZE what the Lord has done for me, how he has shown his favor to me. (1:25)

See the profiles for Joseph (page 1071) and David (page 629) at Matthew 1:24 and Psalm 3:1.

I AM HIGHLY FAVORED whenever I experience the Lord's presence in my life. (1:28)

I BELIEVE Jesus is great, the Son of the Most High, to whom the Lord God has given the throne of his ancestor David. (1:32)

I AM the Lord's servant; may his Word be accomplished in my life. (1:38)

Elizabeth, was also from the priestly line of Aaron. ⁶Zechariah and Elizabeth were righteous in God's eyes, careful to obey all of the Lord's commandments and regulations. ⁷They had no children because Elizabeth was barren, and now they were both very old.

⁸One day Zechariah was serving God in the Temple, for his order was on duty that week. ⁹As was the custom of the priests, he was chosen by lot to enter the sanctuary and burn incense in the Lord's presence. ¹⁰While the incense was being burned, a great crowd stood outside, praying.

¹¹Zechariah was in the sanctuary when an angel of the Lord appeared, standing to the right of the incense altar. ¹²Zechariah was overwhelmed with fear. ¹³But the angel said, "Don't be afraid, Zechariah! For God has heard your prayer, and your wife, Elizabeth, will bear you a son! And you are to name him John. ¹⁴You will have great joy and gladness, and many will rejoice with you at his birth, ¹⁵for he will be great in the eyes of the Lord. He must never touch wine or hard liquor, and he will be filled with the Holy Spirit, even before his birth.* ¹⁶And he will persuade many Israelites to turn to the Lord their God. ¹⁷He will be a man with the spirit and power of Elijah, the prophet of old. He will precede the coming of the Lord, preparing the people for his arrival. He will turn the hearts of the fathers to their children, and he will change disobedient minds to accept godly wisdom."*

¹⁸Zechariah said to the angel, "How can I know this will happen? I'm an old man now, and my wife is also well along in years."

¹⁹Then the angel said, "I am Gabriel! I stand in the very presence of God. It was he who sent me to bring you this good news! ²⁰And now, since you didn't believe what I said, you won't be able to speak until the child is born. For my words will certainly come true at the proper time."

²¹Meanwhile, the people were waiting for Zechariah to come out, wondering why he was taking so long. ²²When he finally did come out, he couldn't speak to them. Then they realized from his gestures that he must have seen a vision in the Temple sanctuary.

²³He stayed at the Temple until his term of service was over, and then he returned home. ²⁴Soon afterward his wife, Elizabeth, became pregnant and went into seclusion for five months. ²⁵"How kind the Lord is!" she exclaimed. "He has taken away my disgrace of having no children!"

The Birth of Jesus Foretold

²⁶In the sixth month of Elizabeth's pregnancy, God sent the angel Gabriel to Nazareth, a village in Galilee, ²⁷to a virgin named Mary. She was engaged to be married to a man named Joseph, a descendant of King David. ²⁸Gabriel appeared to her and said, "Greetings, favored woman! The Lord is with you!*"

²⁹Confused and disturbed, Mary tried to think what the angel could mean. ³⁰"Don't be frightened, Mary," the angel told her, "for God has decided to bless you! ³¹You will become pregnant and have a son, and you are to name him Jesus. ³²He will be very great and will be called the Son of the Most High. And the Lord God will give him the throne of his ancestor David. ³³And he will reign over Israel* forever; his Kingdom will never end!"

³⁴Mary asked the angel, "But how can I have a baby? I am a virgin."

³⁵The angel replied, "The Holy Spirit will come upon you, and the power of the Most High will overshadow you. So the baby born to you will be holy, and he will be called the Son of God. ³⁶What's more, your relative Elizabeth has become pregnant in her old age! People used to say she was barren, but she's already in her sixth month. ³⁷For nothing is impossible with God."

³⁸Mary responded, "I am the Lord's servant, and I am willing to accept whatever he wants. May everything you have said come true." And then the angel left.

1:15 Or *even from birth.* 1:17 See Mal 4:5-6. 1:28 Some manuscripts add *Blessed are you among women.* 1:33 Greek *over the house of Jacob.*

Mary Visits Elizabeth

³⁹A few days later Mary hurried to the hill country of Judea, to the town ⁴⁰where Zechariah lived. She entered the house and greeted Elizabeth. ⁴¹At the sound of Mary's greeting, Elizabeth's child leaped within her, and Elizabeth was filled with the Holy Spirit.

I AM FILLED with the Holy Spirit. (1:41)

⁴²Elizabeth gave a glad cry and exclaimed to Mary, "You are blessed by God above all other women, and your child is blessed. ⁴³What an honor this is, that the mother of my Lord should visit me! ⁴⁴When you came in and greeted me, my baby jumped for joy the instant I heard your voice! ⁴⁵You are blessed, because you believed that the Lord would do what he said."

I AM BLESSED because I have believed that what the Lord has said will be accomplished. (1:45)

UNLIKE ZECHARIAH   *I do not doubt God's ability to answer my prayers.*

Luke 1:18

Who's more anxious to see our most heartfelt prayers answered? You and I? Or God?

In the very last paragraph of the Old Testament, the Lord declared: "Look, I am sending you the prophet Elijah before the great and dreadful day of the Lord arrives. His preaching will turn the hearts of parents to their children, and the hearts of children to their parents. Otherwise I will come and strike the land with a curse" (Malachi 4:5-6).

Four hundred years later, it was time for that prophecy to be fulfilled. By lot, a priest named Zechariah was chosen to enter the sanctuary and burn incense to the Lord. He had probably waited his entire adult life for the privilege to approach God's presence and pray. What was foremost on his mind? The deep yearning he and his wife, Elizabeth, had for her to bear a son.

Of course, Zechariah wasn't expecting God to answer him audibly. But he did answer him by sending the angel Gabriel—the same angel who had explained part of the Lord's timetable to the prophet Daniel six hundred years earlier. Gabriel announced to Zechariah that his wife indeed would have a son who "will be a man with the spirit and power of Elijah, the prophet of old" (Luke 1:17).

Even though he was a righteous and godly priest, Zechariah's first response was one of unbelief!

Like Zechariah, you and I may find it hard to believe that God will ever answer some of our most important prayer requests. But why do we doubt?

Unlike Zechariah, let's never question God's greatness and goodness (Hebrews 11:1-2, 6 and James 1:6-8, 17).

○ *Today's Scripture reading is Luke 1:1-25, 57-80.*

The Magnificat: Mary's Song of Praise

⁴⁶Mary responded,

"Oh, how I praise the Lord.
⁴⁷ How I rejoice in God my Savior!

I GLORIFY the Lord and rejoice in God my Savior. (1:46)

⁴⁸ For he took notice of his lowly servant girl,
      and now generation after generation
         will call me blessed.

I BELIEVE God has been mindful of me, his servant, no matter what my circumstances. (1:48)

⁴⁹ For he, the Mighty One, is holy,
      and he has done great things for me.
⁵⁰ His mercy goes on from generation to generation,
      to all who fear him.

I BELIEVE the Lord's mercy extends to those who fear him (Psalm 103:17). (1:50)

⁵¹ His mighty arm does tremendous things!
      How he scatters the proud and haughty ones!
⁵² He has taken princes from their thrones
      and exalted the lowly.

I BELIEVE the Lord lifts up the humble. (1:52)

⁵³ He has satisfied the hungry with good things
      and sent the rich away with empty hands.
⁵⁴ And how he has helped his servant Israel!
      He has not forgotten his promise to be merciful.

See Abraham's profile (page 19) at Genesis 15:6.

[55] For he promised our ancestors—Abraham and his children—
to be merciful to them forever."

[56] Mary stayed with Elizabeth about three months and then went back to her own home.

The Birth of John the Baptist

I SHARE the joy of others when the Lord shows them great mercy. (1:58)

[57] Now it was time for Elizabeth's baby to be born, and it was a boy. [58] The word spread quickly to her neighbors and relatives that the Lord had been very kind to her, and everyone rejoiced with her.

[59] When the baby was eight days old, all the relatives and friends came for the circumcision ceremony. They wanted to name him Zechariah, after his father. [60] But Elizabeth said, "No! His name is John!"

[61] "What?" they exclaimed. "There is no one in all your family by that name."
[62] So they asked the baby's father, communicating to him by making gestures.
[63] He motioned for a writing tablet, and to everyone's surprise he wrote, "His

I SPEAK God's praises. (1:64)

name is John!" [64] Instantly Zechariah could speak again, and he began praising God.

[65] Wonder fell upon the whole neighborhood, and the news of what had happened spread throughout the Judean hills. [66] Everyone who heard about it reflected on these events and asked, "I wonder what this child will turn out to be? For the hand of the Lord is surely upon him in a special way."

Zechariah's Prophecy

[67] Then his father, Zechariah, was filled with the Holy Spirit and gave this prophecy:

I PRAISE the Lord, because he has come and has redeemed his people. (1:68)

[68] "Praise the Lord, the God of Israel,
because he has visited his people and redeemed them.
[69] He has sent us a mighty Savior
from the royal line of his servant David,
[70] just as he promised
through his holy prophets long ago.
[71] Now we will be saved from our enemies
and from all who hate us.

Keep a prayer journal. This is where life changes often begin!

[72] He has been merciful to our ancestors
by remembering his sacred covenant with them,
[73] the covenant he gave to our ancestor Abraham.
[74] We have been rescued from our enemies,
so we can serve God without fear,
[75] in holiness and righteousness forever.

[76] "And you, my little son,
will be called the prophet of the Most High,
because you will prepare the way for the Lord.

I TELL people how to find salvation through the forgiveness of their sins. (1:77)

[77] You will tell his people how to find salvation
through forgiveness of their sins.
[78] Because of God's tender mercy,
the light from heaven is about to break upon us,
[79] to give light to those who sit in darkness and in the shadow of death,
and to guide us to the path of peace."

[80] John grew up and became strong in spirit. Then he lived out in the wilderness until he began his public ministry to Israel.

CHAPTER 2

The Birth of Jesus

At that time the Roman emperor, Augustus, decreed that a census should be taken throughout the Roman Empire. [2] (This was the first census taken when

Quirinius was governor of Syria.) ³All returned to their own towns to register for this census. ⁴And because Joseph was a descendant of King David, he had to go to Bethlehem in Judea, David's ancient home. He traveled there from the village of Nazareth in Galilee. ⁵He took with him Mary, his fiancée, who was obviously pregnant by this time.

⁶And while they were there, the time came for her baby to be born. ⁷She gave birth to her first child, a son. She wrapped him snugly in strips of cloth and laid him in a manger, because there was no room for them in the village inn.

See the profiles for Joseph (page 1071) and David (page 629) at Matthew 1:24 and Psalm 3:1.

I BELIEVE Jesus was born of the virgin Mary. (2:7)

The Shepherds and Angels
⁸That night some shepherds were in the fields outside the village, guarding their flocks of sheep. ⁹Suddenly, an angel of the Lord appeared among them, and the radiance of the Lord's glory surrounded them. They were terribly frightened, ¹⁰but the angel reassured them. "Don't be afraid!" he said. "I bring you good news of great joy for everyone! ¹¹The Savior—yes, the Messiah, the Lord—has been born tonight in Bethlehem, the city of David! ¹²And this is how you will recognize him: You will find a baby lying in a manger, wrapped snugly in strips of cloth!"

I BELIEVE Jesus truly is the Savior, the Messiah, and the Lord. (2:11)

LIKE MARY
Luke 1:38

I am the Lord's servant, willing to affirm whatever he says.

How many times has a young woman trembled with trepidation or delight when her doctor announces, "You're pregnant"?

It's almost too hard to believe that a child is growing inside when everything still looks the same. Even the most ordinary, well-planned pregnancy seems like a dream at first. No wonder the angel's announcement left Mary astounded.

How could Mary really fathom becoming pregnant when she knew beyond question she still was a virgin? Of course, she couldn't figure it out—but she could believe the Holy Spirit would fulfill the angel's words. And she could eagerly anticipate mothering the baby who would fulfill the prophets' promises from long ago.

While her elderly relative Zechariah couldn't fathom the angel's announcement that his wife was going to bear a baby, Mary readily believed God could do something new and unheard of. Mary willingly accepted the miracle of this unique pregnancy and all the consequences that followed.

In all likelihood, the Lord could have asked Mary to do *anything*. As a humble servant of the Lord God, she was dedicated to doing whatever she could for him.

Whether it's a high calling or difficult chore that the Lord gives us, are you and I ready to respond like Mary?

○ *Today's Scripture reading is Luke 1:26-56 and 2:1-7.*

---

¹³Suddenly, the angel was joined by a vast host of others—the armies of heaven—praising God:

¹⁴ "Glory to God in the highest heaven,
   and peace on earth to all whom God favors.*"

I BELIEVE vast numbers of angels praised God after Jesus' birth. (2:14)

¹⁵When the angels had returned to heaven, the shepherds said to each other, "Come on, let's go to Bethlehem! Let's see this wonderful thing that has happened, which the Lord has told us about."

¹⁶They ran to the village and found Mary and Joseph. And there was the baby, lying in the manger. ¹⁷Then the shepherds told everyone what had happened and what the angel had said to them about this child. ¹⁸All who heard the shepherds' story were astonished, ¹⁹but Mary quietly treasured these

I TELL others about Jesus. (2:17)

2:14 Or *and peace on earth for all those pleasing God.* Some manuscripts read *and peace on earth, goodwill among people.*

I GLORIFY AND PRAISE God for what he has done. (2:20)

things in her heart and thought about them often. ²⁰The shepherds went back to their fields and flocks, glorifying and praising God for what the angels had told them, and because they had seen the child, just as the angel had said.

Jesus Is Presented in the Temple

²¹Eight days later, when the baby was circumcised, he was named Jesus, the name given him by the angel even before he was conceived.

See Moses' profile (page 73) at Exodus 5:1.

I DEDICATE each of my children to the Lord. (2:23)

²²Then it was time for the purification offering, as required by the law of Moses after the birth of a child; so his parents took him to Jerusalem to present him to the Lord. ²³The law of the Lord says, "If a woman's first child is a boy, he must be dedicated to the Lord."* ²⁴So they offered a sacrifice according to what was required in the law of the Lord—"either a pair of turtledoves or two young pigeons."*

The Prophecy of Simeon

²⁵Now there was a man named Simeon who lived in Jerusalem. He was a righteous man and very devout. He was filled with the Holy Spirit, and he eagerly expected the Messiah to come and rescue Israel. ²⁶The Holy Spirit had revealed to him that he would not die until he had seen the Lord's Messiah. ²⁷That day the Spirit led him to the Temple. So when Mary and Joseph came to present the baby Jesus to the Lord as the law required, ²⁸Simeon was there. He took the child in his arms and praised God, saying,

I AM THANKFUL the Messiah has come. (2:28)

²⁹ "Lord, now I can die in peace!
    As you promised me,
³⁰ I have seen the Savior
³¹   you have given to all people.
³² He is a light to reveal God to the nations,
       and he is the glory of your people Israel!"

I BELIEVE Jesus came to be the Savior of people from all nations. (2:32)

³³Joseph and Mary were amazed at what was being said about Jesus. ³⁴Then Simeon blessed them, and he said to Mary, "This child will be rejected by many in Israel, and it will be their undoing. But he will be the greatest joy to many others. ³⁵Thus, the deepest thoughts of many hearts will be revealed. And a sword will pierce your very soul."

The Prophecy of Anna

³⁶Anna, a prophet, was also there in the Temple. She was the daughter of Phanuel, of the tribe of Asher, and was very old. She was a widow, for her husband had died when they had been married only seven years. ³⁷She was now eighty-four years old. She never left the Temple but stayed there day and night, worshiping God with fasting and prayer. ³⁸She came along just as Simeon was talking with Mary and Joseph, and she began praising God. She talked about Jesus to everyone who had been waiting for the promised King to come and deliver Jerusalem.

I OBEY all of the Lord's commands. (2:39)

³⁹When Jesus' parents had fulfilled all the requirements of the law of the Lord, they returned home to Nazareth in Galilee. ⁴⁰There the child grew up healthy and strong. He was filled with wisdom beyond his years, and God placed his special favor upon him.

Jesus Speaks with the Teachers

⁴¹Every year Jesus' parents went to Jerusalem for the Passover festival. ⁴²When Jesus was twelve years old, they attended the festival as usual. ⁴³After the celebration was over, they started home to Nazareth, but Jesus stayed behind in Jerusalem. His parents didn't miss him at first, ⁴⁴because they assumed he was with friends among the other travelers. But when he didn't show up that evening, they started to look for him among their relatives and friends.

2:23 Exod 13:2.   2:24 Lev 12:8.

⁴⁵When they couldn't find him, they went back to Jerusalem to search for him there. ⁴⁶Three days later they finally discovered him. He was in the Temple, sitting among the religious teachers, discussing deep questions with them. ⁴⁷And all who heard him were amazed at his understanding and his answers.

⁴⁸His parents didn't know what to think. "Son!" his mother said to him. "Why have you done this to us? Your father and I have been frantic, searching for you everywhere."

⁴⁹"But why did you need to search?" he asked. "You should have known that I would be in my Father's house."* ⁵⁰But they didn't understand what he meant.

I BELIEVE Jesus was God the Father's Son. (2:49)

⁵¹Then he returned to Nazareth with them and was obedient to them; and his mother stored all these things in her heart. ⁵²So Jesus grew both in height and in wisdom, and he was loved by God and by all who knew him.

LIKE THE SHEPHERDS   *I joyfully share the Good News with others.*

Luke 2:17

God had visited the fields of Bethlehem with singing before. A thousand years earlier, his Spirit inspired a shepherd boy to sing dozens of great melodies of praise. Every Israelite knew of that shepherd boy who left the fields to become Israel's greatest king.

But no one had such hopes for these particular shepherds. Much more highly esteemed persons—King David's direct descendants—filled the rooms of Bethlehem's inns as they came back to be counted in their ancestral home.

Yet it was not to any of the VIPs that God sent his angel and the armies of heaven to announce the birth of the Savior, the Son of David. Instead, God displayed his extraordinary concert and light show to these shepherds—and invited them to come and see the Messiah everyone else had been waiting for.

Although initially stunned by the glory of God and the message of the angel, these shepherds immediately ran to see this miracle. There lay the baby, wrapped in strips of cloth and snuggled in the hay—just as the angel had said. This baby fulfilled every Israelite's deepest hope and answered every Gentile's greatest longings. His birth was "good news for everyone"!

The shepherds couldn't stick around all day, of course. But as they headed back to the hills and their sleeping sheep, Scripture tells us that they told the miraculous news to everyone they met. After being silent for so many centuries, God had just announced the Messiah's birth with multitudes of angels. They had seen the Christ child with their own eyes, just as the angel had said! Who could keep quiet?

You and I don't need angels to spur us on to share the Good News. After all, we have already met the Savior. With joy, let's help proclaim the Good News!

○ *Today's Scripture reading is Luke 2:8-20.*

CHAPTER 3

John the Baptist Prepares the Way

It was now the fifteenth year of the reign of Tiberius, the Roman emperor. Pilate was governor over Judea; Herod Antipas was ruler* over Galilee; his brother Philip was ruler* over Iturea and Traconitis; Lysanias was ruler over Abilene. ²Annas and Caiaphas were the high priests. At this time a message from God came to John son of Zechariah, who was living out in the wilderness. ³Then John went from place to place on both sides of the Jordan River, preaching that people should be baptized to show that they had turned from their sins and turned to God to be forgiven.* ⁴Isaiah had spoken of John when he said,

See Pilate's profile (page 1229) at John 19:16.

See John the Baptist's profile (page 1117) at Mark 1:4.

I HAVE REPENTED, received God's forgiveness for my sins, and been baptized. (3:3)

2:49 Or *"Didn't you realize that I should be involved with my Father's affairs?"*   3:1a Greek *Herod was tetrarch.* Herod Antipas was a son of King Herod.   3:1b Greek *tetrarch;* also in 3:1c, 19.   3:3 Greek *preaching a baptism of repentance for the forgiveness of sins.*

See Isaiah's profile
(page 801) at Isaiah
6:13.

"He is a voice shouting in the wilderness:
'Prepare a pathway for the Lord's coming!
   Make a straight road for him!
⁵Fill in the valleys,
   and level the mountains and hills!
Straighten the curves,
   and smooth out the rough places!
⁶And then all people will see
   the salvation sent from God.' "*

⁷Here is a sample of John's preaching to the crowds that came for baptism: "You brood of snakes! Who warned you to flee God's coming judgment? ⁸Prove by the way you live that you have really turned from your sins and turned to God. Don't just say, 'We're safe—we're the descendants of Abraham.' That proves nothing. God can change these stones here into children of Abraham. ⁹Even now the ax of God's judgment is poised, ready to sever your roots. Yes, every tree that does not produce good fruit will be chopped down and thrown into the fire."

I DEMONSTRATE my
repentance by living
in a way that pleases
God. (3:8)

See Abraham's profile
(page 19) at Genesis
15:6.

¹⁰The crowd asked, "What should we do?"

¹¹John replied, "If you have two coats, give one to the poor. If you have food, share it with those who are hungry."

¹²Even corrupt tax collectors came to be baptized and asked, "Teacher, what should we do?"

¹³"Show your honesty," he replied. "Make sure you collect no more taxes than the Roman government requires you to."

¹⁴"What should we do?" asked some soldiers.

John replied, "Don't extort money, and don't accuse people of things you know they didn't do. And be content with your pay."

I AM CONTENT with my
pay and do not extort
money or accuse
people falsely. (3:14)

I BELIEVE Jesus is the
Christ, the Messiah,
and have been
baptized by the Holy
Spirit. (3:16)

¹⁵Everyone was expecting the Messiah to come soon, and they were eager to know whether John might be the Messiah. ¹⁶John answered their questions by saying, "I baptize with* water; but someone is coming soon who is greater than I am—so much greater that I am not even worthy to be his slave.* He will baptize you with the Holy Spirit and with fire.* ¹⁷He is ready to separate the chaff from the grain with his winnowing fork. Then he will clean up the threshing area, storing the grain in his barn but burning the chaff with never-ending fire." ¹⁸John used many such warnings as he announced the Good News to the people.

¹⁹John also publicly criticized Herod Antipas, ruler of Galilee, for marrying Herodias, his brother's wife, and for many other wrongs he had done. ²⁰So Herod put John in prison, adding this sin to his many others.

The Baptism of Jesus

I BELIEVE in the
Trinity—God the
Father, God the Son,
and God the Holy
Spirit. (3:22)

I BELIEVE Jesus is
God's only Son—a
descendant of Joseph
and David and
Abraham and Adam.
(3:23)

See Joseph's profile
(page 1071) at
Matthew 1:24.

²¹One day when the crowds were being baptized, Jesus himself was baptized. As he was praying, the heavens opened, ²²and the Holy Spirit descended on him in the form of a dove. And a voice from heaven said, "You are my beloved Son, and I am fully pleased with you.*"

The Record of Jesus' Ancestors

²³Jesus was about thirty years old when he began his public ministry.

Jesus was known as the son of Joseph.
Joseph was the son of Heli.
²⁴ Heli was the son of Matthat.
Matthat was the son of Levi.
Levi was the son of Melki.
Melki was the son of Jannai.

3:4-6 Isa 40:3-5. 3:16a Or in. 3:16b Greek to untie his sandals. 3:16c Or in the Holy Spirit and in fire.
3:22 Some manuscripts read and today I have become your Father.

Jannai was the son of Joseph.
25 Joseph was the son of Mattathias.
Mattathias was the son of Amos.
Amos was the son of Nahum.
Nahum was the son of Esli.
Esli was the son of Naggai.
26 Naggai was the son of Maath.
Maath was the son of Mattathias.
Mattathias was the son of Semein.
Semein was the son of Josech.
Josech was the son of Joda.
27 Joda was the son of Joanan.
Joanan was the son of Rhesa.
Rhesa was the son of Zerubbabel.
Zerubbabel was the son of Shealtiel.
Shealtiel was the son of Neri.

LIKE SIMEON AND ANNA *I believe I will experience tremendous answers to prayer in my lifetime.*

Luke 2:38

Simeon and Anna were quite elderly, but they certainly weren't waiting around to die. Instead, every day they woke up with the expectation that today could be the day they had dreamed about for decades.

Simeon had the Lord's promise that he would not die until he saw the Lord's Messiah. Anna had no such guarantee, but, like many others, she knew the time of the Messiah's coming was near (Daniel 9:20-25). While they waited, they lived righteous and devout lives, walking with God in obedience and worshiping him with all their hearts.

As Mary and Joseph entered the Temple one morning with baby Jesus cradled in their arms, they looked like any other devout couple fulfilling their duty to God. But to an old man led by the Holy Spirit, they stood out like a beacon. The small child and his parents were welcomed to God's house as no family before had ever been greeted.

Like Simeon and Anna, you and I can wake up each day looking forward to the promise of Jesus' coming—again (Titus 2:11-14; 1 Peter 1:3-13). True, we may not see Jesus Christ's return in our lifetime. But as we anticipate that day, our eyes will be opened to see how many promises God fulfills along the way.

○ Today's Scripture reading is Luke 2:21-38.

28 Neri was the son of Melki.
Melki was the son of Addi.
Addi was the son of Cosam.
Cosam was the son of Elmadam.
Elmadam was the son of Er.
29 Er was the son of Joshua.
Joshua was the son of Eliezer.
Eliezer was the son of Jorim.
Jorim was the son of Matthat.
Matthat was the son of Levi.
30 Levi was the son of Simeon.
Simeon was the son of Judah.
Judah was the son of Joseph.
Joseph was the son of Jonam.
Jonam was the son of Eliakim.
31 Eliakim was the son of Melea.
Melea was the son of Menna.

Menna was the son of Mattatha.
Mattatha was the son of Nathan.
Nathan was the son of David.
³² David was the son of Jesse.
Jesse was the son of Obed.
Obed was the son of Boaz.
Boaz was the son of Salmon.*
Salmon was the son of Nahshon.
³³ Nahshon was the son of Amminadab.
Amminadab was the son of Admin.
Admin was the son of Arni.*
Arni was the son of Hezron.
Hezron was the son of Perez.
Perez was the son of Judah.
³⁴ Judah was the son of Jacob.
Jacob was the son of Isaac.
Isaac was the son of Abraham.
Abraham was the son of Terah.
Terah was the son of Nahor.
³⁵ Nahor was the son of Serug.
Serug was the son of Reu.
Reu was the son of Peleg.
Peleg was the son of Eber.
Eber was the son of Shelah.
³⁶ Shelah was the son of Cainan.
Cainan was the son of Arphaxad.
Arphaxad was the son of Shem.
Shem was the son of Noah.
Noah was the son of Lamech.
³⁷ Lamech was the son of Methuselah.
Methuselah was the son of Enoch.
Enoch was the son of Jared.
Jared was the son of Mahalalel.
Mahalalel was the son of Kenan.
³⁸ Kenan was the son of Enosh.*
Enosh was the son of Seth.
Seth was the son of Adam.
Adam was the son of God.

CHAPTER 4

The Temptation of Jesus

Then Jesus, full of the Holy Spirit, left the Jordan River. He was led by the Spirit to go out into the wilderness, ²where the Devil tempted him for forty days. He ate nothing all that time and was very hungry.

³Then the Devil said to him, "If you are the Son of God, change this stone into a loaf of bread."

⁴But Jesus told him, "No! The Scriptures say, 'People need more than bread for their life.'* "

⁵Then the Devil took him up and revealed to him all the kingdoms of the world in a moment of time. ⁶The Devil told him, "I will give you the glory of these kingdoms and authority over them—because they are mine to give to anyone I please. ⁷I will give it all to you if you will bow down and worship me."

⁸Jesus replied, "The Scriptures say,

Marginal notes:
See David's profile (page 629) at Psalm 3:1.

See the profiles for Jacob (page 43), Isaac (page 31), and Abraham (page 19) at Genesis 32:9, Genesis 25:19, and Genesis 15:6.

See Noah's profile (page 13) at Genesis 6:9.

See Enoch's profile (page 11) at Genesis 5:24.

See Adam's profile (page 5) at Genesis 1:26.

I DO NOT LIVE on bread alone but on every word that comes from the mouth of the Lord. (4:4)

I WORSHIP the Lord my God and serve him only. (4:8)

3:32 Greek Sala; see Ruth 4:22. 3:33 Arni is the same person as Ram; see 1 Chr 2:9-10. 3:38 Greek Enos; see Gen 5:6. 4:4 Deut 8:3.

'You must worship the Lord your God;
serve only him.'* "

⁹Then the Devil took him to Jerusalem, to the highest point of the Temple, and said, "If you are the Son of God, jump off! ¹⁰For the Scriptures say,

'He orders his angels to protect and guard you.
¹¹ And they will hold you with their hands
to keep you from striking your foot on a stone.'* "

¹²Jesus responded, "The Scriptures also say, 'Do not test the Lord your God.'* "

¹³When the Devil had finished tempting Jesus, he left him until the next opportunity came.

I DO NOT PUT the Lord my God to the test. (4:12)

Jesus Rejected at Nazareth

¹⁴Then Jesus returned to Galilee, filled with the Holy Spirit's power. Soon he became well known throughout the surrounding country. ¹⁵He taught in their synagogues and was praised by everyone.

¹⁶When he came to the village of Nazareth, his boyhood home, he went as usual to the synagogue on the Sabbath and stood up to read the Scriptures. ¹⁷The scroll containing the messages of Isaiah the prophet was handed to him, and he unrolled the scroll to the place where it says:

I MAKE it my usual habit to attend worship services. (4:16)

See Isaiah's profile (page 801) at Isaiah 6:13.

¹⁸ "The Spirit of the Lord is upon me,
for he has appointed me to preach Good News to the poor.
He has sent me to proclaim
that captives will be released,
that the blind will see,
that the downtrodden will be freed from their oppressors,
¹⁹ and that the time of the Lord's favor has come.* "

²⁰He rolled up the scroll, handed it back to the attendant, and sat down. Everyone in the synagogue stared at him intently. ²¹Then he said, "This Scripture has come true today before your very eyes!"

²²All who were there spoke well of him and were amazed by the gracious words that fell from his lips. "How can this be?" they asked. "Isn't this Joseph's son?"

I BELIEVE Jesus fulfilled the Old Testament prophecies about the Messiah. (4:21)

²³Then he said, "Probably you will quote me that proverb, 'Physician, heal yourself'—meaning, 'Why don't you do miracles here in your hometown like those you did in Capernaum?' ²⁴But the truth is, no prophet is accepted in his own hometown.

²⁵"Certainly there were many widows in Israel who needed help in Elijah's time, when there was no rain for three and a half years and hunger stalked the land. ²⁶Yet Elijah was not sent to any of them. He was sent instead to a widow of Zarephath—a foreigner in the land of Sidon. ²⁷Or think of the prophet Elisha, who healed Naaman, a Syrian, rather than the many lepers in Israel who needed help."

See Elijah's profile (page 421) at 1 Kings 19:18.

See Elisha's profile (page 431) at 2 Kings 2:14.

²⁸When they heard this, the people in the synagogue were furious. ²⁹Jumping up, they mobbed him and took him to the edge of the hill on which the city was built. They intended to push him over the cliff, ³⁰but he slipped away through the crowd and left them.

Jesus Casts Out a Demon

³¹Then Jesus went to Capernaum, a town in Galilee, and taught there in the synagogue every Sabbath day. ³²There, too, the people were amazed at the things he said, because he spoke with authority.

I AM AMAZED at Jesus' teaching, for his message has authority and power. (4:32)

4:8 Deut 6:13.   4:10-11 Ps 91:11-12.   4:12 Deut 6:16.   4:18-19 Or *and to proclaim the acceptable year of the Lord.* Isa 61:1-2.

[33]Once when he was in the synagogue, a man possessed by a demon began shouting at Jesus, [34]"Go away! Why are you bothering us, Jesus of Nazareth? Have you come to destroy us? I know who you are—the Holy One sent from God."

[35]Jesus cut him short. "Be silent!" he told the demon. "Come out of the man!" The demon threw the man to the floor as the crowd watched; then it left him without hurting him further.

[36]Amazed, the people exclaimed, "What authority and power this man's words possess! Even evil spirits obey him and flee at his command!" [37]The story of what he had done spread like wildfire throughout the whole region.

Jesus Heals Many People

[38]After leaving the synagogue that day, Jesus went to Simon's home, where he found Simon's mother-in-law very sick with a high fever. "Please heal her," everyone begged. [39]Standing at her bedside, he spoke to the fever, rebuking it, and immediately her temperature returned to normal. She got up at once and prepared a meal for them.

[40]As the sun went down that evening, people throughout the village brought sick family members to Jesus. No matter what their diseases were, the touch of his hand healed every one. [41]Some were possessed by demons; and the demons came out at his command, shouting, "You are the Son of God." But because they knew he was the Messiah, he stopped them and told them to be silent.

Jesus Continues to Preach

[42]Early the next morning Jesus went out into the wilderness. The crowds searched everywhere for him, and when they finally found him, they begged him not to leave them. [43]But he replied, "I must preach the Good News of the Kingdom of God in other places, too, because that is why I was sent." [44]So he continued to travel around, preaching in synagogues throughout Judea.*

CHAPTER 5

The First Disciples

One day as Jesus was preaching on the shore of the Sea of Galilee,* great crowds pressed in on him to listen to the word of God. [2]He noticed two empty boats at the water's edge, for the fishermen had left them and were washing their nets. [3]Stepping into one of the boats, Jesus asked Simon,* its owner, to push it out into the water. So he sat in the boat and taught the crowds from there.

[4]When he had finished speaking, he said to Simon, "Now go out where it is deeper and let down your nets, and you will catch many fish."

[5]"Master," Simon replied, "we worked hard all last night and didn't catch a thing. But if you say so, we'll try again." [6]And this time their nets were so full they began to tear! [7]A shout for help brought their partners in the other boat, and soon both boats were filled with fish and on the verge of sinking.

[8]When Simon Peter realized what had happened, he fell to his knees before Jesus and said, "Oh, Lord, please leave me—I'm too much of a sinner to be around you." [9]For he was awestruck by the size of their catch, as were the others with him. [10]His partners, James and John, the sons of Zebedee, were also amazed.

Jesus replied to Simon, "Don't be afraid! From now on you'll be fishing for people!" [11]And as soon as they landed, they left everything and followed Jesus.

I ASK Jesus to heal those who are sick, believing he can heal anyone. (4:38)

I SERVE others as an expression of thanks to the Lord for healing me. (4:39)

I TAKE TIME to meet with the Lord early in the morning. (4:42)

I LISTEN to the Word of God. (5:1)

See Peter's profile (page 1111) at Matthew 26:75.

I DO whatever Jesus asks, even if it doesn't seem to make sense from a human viewpoint. (5:5)

I AM NOT AFRAID to leave everything and follow Jesus. (5:10)

See John's profile (page 1435) at Revelation 1:9.

4:44 Some manuscripts read *Galilee.*   5:1 Greek *Lake Gennesaret,* another name for the Sea of Galilee.   5:3 *Simon* is called *Peter* in 6:14 and thereafter.

Jesus Heals a Man with Leprosy

[12]In one of the villages, Jesus met a man with an advanced case of leprosy. When the man saw Jesus, he fell to the ground, face down in the dust, begging to be healed. "Lord," he said, "if you want to, you can make me well again."

[13]Jesus reached out and touched the man. "I want to," he said. "Be healed!" And instantly the leprosy disappeared. [14]Then Jesus instructed him not to tell anyone what had happened. He said, "Go right to the priest and let him examine you. Take along the offering required in the law of Moses for those who have been healed of leprosy, so everyone will have proof of your healing." [15]Yet despite Jesus' instructions, the report of his power spread even faster, and vast crowds came to hear him preach and to be healed of their diseases. [16]But Jesus often withdrew to the wilderness for prayer.

I GIVE testimony to Jesus' cleansing and healing power in my life. (5:14)

See Moses' profile (page 73) at Exodus 5:1.

I OFTEN WITHDRAW to private places and pray. (5:16)

Jesus Heals a Paralyzed Man

[17]One day while Jesus was teaching, some Pharisees and teachers of religious law were sitting nearby. (It seemed that these men showed up from every village in all Galilee and Judea, as well as from Jerusalem.) And the Lord's healing power was strongly with Jesus. [18]Some men came carrying a paralyzed man on a sleeping mat. They tried to push through the crowd to Jesus, [19]but they couldn't reach him. So they went up to the roof, took off some tiles, and lowered the sick man down into the crowd, still on his mat, right in front of Jesus. [20]Seeing their faith, Jesus said to the man, "Son, your sins are forgiven."

See the profile for the Pharisees (page 1087) at Matthew 12:14.

I DO whatever it takes to bring my friends to Jesus. (5:18)

[21]"Who does this man think he is?" the Pharisees and teachers of religious law said to each other. "This is blasphemy! Who but God can forgive sins?"

[22]Jesus knew what they were thinking, so he asked them, "Why do you think this is blasphemy? [23]Is it easier to say, 'Your sins are forgiven' or 'Get up and walk'? [24]I will prove that I, the Son of Man, have the authority on earth to forgive sins." Then Jesus turned to the paralyzed man and said, "Stand up, take your mat, and go on home, because you are healed!"

[25]And immediately, as everyone watched, the man jumped to his feet, picked up his mat, and went home praising God. [26]Everyone was gripped with great wonder and awe. And they praised God, saying over and over again, "We have seen amazing things today."

I BELIEVE the greatest miracle is spiritual healing—especially the forgiveness of sins. (5:24)

Jesus Calls Levi (Matthew)

[27]Later, as Jesus left the town, he saw a tax collector named Levi sitting at his tax-collection booth. "Come, be my disciple!" Jesus said to him. [28]So Levi got up, left everything, and followed him.

[29]Soon Levi held a banquet in his home with Jesus as the guest of honor. Many of Levi's fellow tax collectors and other guests were there. [30]But the Pharisees and their teachers of religious law complained bitterly to Jesus' disciples, "Why do you eat and drink with such scum*?"

[31]Jesus answered them, "Healthy people don't need a doctor—sick people do. [32]I have come to call sinners to turn from their sins, not to spend my time with those who think they are already good enough."

See Matthew's profile (page 1081) at Matthew 9:9.

I SPEND time with sinful people who need to know about Jesus. (5:30)

A Discussion about Fasting

[33]The religious leaders complained that Jesus' disciples were feasting instead of fasting. "John the Baptist's disciples always fast and pray," they declared, "and so do the disciples of the Pharisees. Why are yours always feasting?"

[34]Jesus asked, "Do wedding guests fast while celebrating with the groom? [35]Someday he will be taken away from them, and then they will fast."

[36]Then Jesus gave them this illustration: "No one tears a piece of cloth from a new garment and uses it to patch an old garment. For then the new

See John the Baptist's profile (page 1117) at Mark 1:4.

5:30 Greek *with tax collectors and sinners.*

garment would be torn, and the patch wouldn't even match the old garment. [37]And no one puts new wine into old wineskins. The new wine would burst the old skins, spilling the wine and ruining the skins. [38]New wine must be put into new wineskins. [39]But no one who drinks the old wine seems to want the fresh and the new. 'The old is better,' they say."

CHAPTER 6

A Discussion about the Sabbath

One Sabbath day as Jesus was walking through some grainfields, his disciples broke off heads of wheat, rubbed off the husks in their hands, and ate the grains. [2]But some Pharisees said, "You shouldn't be doing that! It's against the law to work by harvesting grain on the Sabbath."

[3]Jesus replied, "Haven't you ever read in the Scriptures what King David did when he and his companions were hungry? [4]He went into the house of God, ate the special bread reserved for the priests alone, and then gave some to his friends. That was breaking the law, too." [5]And Jesus added, "I, the Son of Man, am master even of the Sabbath."

Jesus Heals on the Sabbath

[6]On another Sabbath day, a man with a deformed right hand was in the synagogue while Jesus was teaching. [7] The teachers of religious law and the Pharisees watched closely to see whether Jesus would heal the man on the Sabbath, because they were eager to find some legal charge to bring against him. [8]But Jesus knew their thoughts. He said to the man with the deformed hand, "Come and stand here where everyone can see." So the man came forward. [9]Then Jesus said to his critics, "I have a question for you. Is it legal to do good deeds on the Sabbath, or is it a day for doing harm? Is this a day to save life or to destroy it?" [10]He looked around at them one by one and then said to the man, "Reach out your hand." The man reached out his hand, and it became normal again! [11]At this, the enemies of Jesus were wild with rage and began to discuss what to do with him.

Jesus Chooses the Twelve Apostles

[12]One day soon afterward Jesus went to a mountain to pray, and he prayed to God all night. [13]At daybreak he called together all of his disciples and chose twelve of them to be apostles. Here are their names:

[14] Simon (he also called him Peter),
 Andrew (Peter's brother),
 James,
 John,
 Philip,
 Bartholomew,
[15] Matthew,
 Thomas,
 James (son of Alphaeus),
 Simon (the Zealot),
[16] Judas (son of James),
 Judas Iscariot (who later betrayed him).

Crowds Follow Jesus

[17]When they came down the slopes of the mountain, the disciples stood with Jesus on a large, level area, surrounded by many of his followers and by the crowds. There were people from all over Judea and from Jerusalem and from as far north as the seacoasts of Tyre and Sidon. [18]They had come to hear him and to be healed, and Jesus cast out many evil spirits. [19]Everyone was trying to touch him, because healing power went out from him, and they were all cured.

See the profile for the Pharisees (page 1087) at Matthew 12:14.

See David's profile (page 629) at Psalm 3:1.

I BELIEVE Jesus, the Son of Man, is Lord of all—including the Sabbath. (6:5)

I SPEND time at night praying to God. (6:12)

See the profiles for Peter (page 1111), Andrew (page 1199), and John (page 1435) at Matthew 26:75, John 1:42, and Revelation 1:9.

See the profiles for Matthew (page 1081) and Thomas (page 1231) at Matthew 9:9 and John 20:28.

See Judas's profile (page 1121) at Mark 3:19.

The Beatitudes

[20]Then Jesus turned to his disciples and said,

"God blesses you who are poor,
for the Kingdom of God is given to you.
[21] God blesses you who are hungry now,
for you will be satisfied.
God blesses you who weep now,
for the time will come when you will laugh with joy.
[22] God blesses you who are hated and excluded and mocked and cursed
because you are identified with me, the Son of Man.

[23]"When that happens, rejoice! Yes, leap for joy! For a great reward awaits you in heaven. And remember, the ancient prophets were also treated that way by your ancestors.

Sorrows Foretold

[24] "What sorrows await you who are rich,
for you have your only happiness now.
[25] What sorrows await you who are satisfied and prosperous now,
for a time of awful hunger is before you.
What sorrows await you who laugh carelessly,
for your laughing will turn to mourning and sorrow.
[26] What sorrows await you who are praised by the crowds,
for their ancestors also praised false prophets.

Love for Enemies

[27]"But if you are willing to listen, I say, love your enemies. Do good to those who hate you. [28]Pray for the happiness of those who curse you. Pray for those who hurt you. [29]If someone slaps you on one cheek, turn the other cheek. If someone demands your coat, offer your shirt also. [30]Give what you have to anyone who asks you for it; and when things are taken away from you, don't try to get them back. [31]Do for others as you would like them to do for you.

[32]"Do you think you deserve credit merely for loving those who love you? Even the sinners do that! [33]And if you do good only to those who do good to you, is that so wonderful? Even sinners do that much! [34]And if you lend money only to those who can repay you, what good is that? Even sinners will lend to their own kind for a full return.

[35]"Love your enemies! Do good to them! Lend to them! And don't be concerned that they might not repay. Then your reward from heaven will be very great, and you will truly be acting as children of the Most High, for he is kind to the unthankful and to those who are wicked. [36]You must be compassionate, just as your Father is compassionate.

Don't Condemn Others

[37]"Stop judging others, and you will not be judged. Stop criticizing others, or it will all come back on you. If you forgive others, you will be forgiven. [38]If you give, you will receive. Your gift will return to you in full measure, pressed down, shaken together to make room for more, and running over. Whatever measure you use in giving—large or small—it will be used to measure what is given back to you."

[39]Then Jesus gave the following illustration: "What good is it for one blind person to lead another? The first one will fall into a ditch and pull the other down also. [40]A student is not greater than the teacher. But the student who works hard will become like the teacher.

[41]"And why worry about a speck in your friend's eye* when you have a log in your own? [42]How can you think of saying, 'Friend,* let me help you get rid

---

I AM CONTENT with my lot in life, knowing the ultimate reality is spiritual—God's eternal Kingdom (1 Corinthians 7:17-24). (6:20)

I AM CONTENT in times of need and sorrow, knowing God will meet my every need. (6:21)

I AM CONTENT—even exuberant—in times of ridicule and persecution, knowing my reward in heaven is great. (6:23)

I AM CAUTIOUS in times of prosperity, remembering the ultimate reality is spiritual—God's eternal Kingdom—not the temporal stuff of this life. (6:24)

I LOVE my enemies and do good to those who mistreat me. (6:27)

I DO to others as I would have them to do me. (6:31)

I AM COMPASSIONATE, just as my Father in heaven is compassionate. (6:36)

I EXAMINE myself and repent of any known sin. (6:42)

6:41 Greek *your brother's eye*; also in 6:42.   6:42 Greek *Brother.*

of that speck in your eye,' when you can't see past the log in your own eye? Hypocrite! First get rid of the log from your own eye; then perhaps you will see well enough to deal with the speck in your friend's eye.

The Tree and Its Fruit

[43] "A good tree can't produce bad fruit, and a bad tree can't produce good fruit. [44] A tree is identified by the kind of fruit it produces. Figs never grow on thornbushes or grapes on bramble bushes. [45] A good person produces good deeds from a good heart, and an evil person produces evil deeds from an evil heart. Whatever is in your heart determines what you say.

Building on a Solid Foundation

[46] "So why do you call me 'Lord,' when you won't obey me? [47] I will show you what it's like when someone comes to me, listens to my teaching, and then obeys me. [48] It is like a person who builds a house on a strong foundation laid upon the underlying rock. When the floodwaters rise and break against the house, it stands firm because it is well built. [49] But anyone who listens and doesn't obey is like a person who builds a house without a foundation. When the floods sweep down against that house, it will crumble into a heap of ruins."

CHAPTER 7

Faith of the Roman Officer

When Jesus had finished saying all this, he went back to Capernaum. [2] Now the highly valued slave of a Roman officer was sick and near death. [3] When the officer heard about Jesus, he sent some respected Jewish leaders to ask him to come and heal his slave. [4] So they earnestly begged Jesus to come with them and help the man. "If anyone deserves your help, it is he," they said, [5] "for he loves the Jews and even built a synagogue for us."

[6] So Jesus went with them. But just before they arrived at the house, the officer sent some friends to say, "Lord, don't trouble yourself by coming to my home, for I am not worthy of such an honor. [7] I am not even worthy to come and meet you. Just say the word from where you are, and my servant will be healed. [8] I know because I am under the authority of my superior officers, and I have authority over my soldiers. I only need to say, 'Go,' and they go, or 'Come,' and they come. And if I say to my slaves, 'Do this or that,' they do it."

[9] When Jesus heard this, he was amazed. Turning to the crowd, he said, "I tell you, I haven't seen faith like this in all the land of Israel!" [10] And when the officer's friends returned to his house, they found the slave completely healed.

Jesus Raises a Widow's Son

[11] Soon afterward Jesus went with his disciples to the village of Nain, with a great crowd following him. [12] A funeral procession was coming out as he approached the village gate. The boy who had died was the only son of a widow, and many mourners from the village were with her. [13] When the Lord saw her, his heart overflowed with compassion. "Don't cry!" he said. [14] Then he walked over to the coffin and touched it, and the bearers stopped. "Young man," he said, "get up." [15] Then the dead boy sat up and began to talk to those around him! And Jesus gave him back to his mother.

[16] Great fear swept the crowd, and they praised God, saying, "A mighty prophet has risen among us," and "We have seen the hand of God at work today." [17] The report of what Jesus had done that day spread all over Judea and even out across its borders.

Jesus and John the Baptist

[18] The disciples of John the Baptist told John about everything Jesus was doing. So John called for two of his disciples, [19] and he sent them to the Lord

I CALL Jesus "Lord" and do what he says. (6:46)

I LISTEN to Jesus' words and put them into practice, for his Word is the foundation upon which I build my life. (6:47)

I PLEAD earnestly with Jesus to help those I care about and to heal those I love. (7:4)

I PRAY to the Lord on behalf of my friends and loved ones. (7:6)

I BELIEVE Jesus can merely say the word and anything will happen. (7:7)

I PRAISE God when I see his hand at work in miraculous ways. (7:16)

See John the Baptist's profile (page 1117) at Mark 1:4.

to ask him, "Are you the Messiah we've been expecting, or should we keep looking for someone else?"

²⁰John's two disciples found Jesus and said to him, "John the Baptist sent us to ask, 'Are you the Messiah we've been expecting, or should we keep looking for someone else?' "

²¹At that very time, he cured many people of their various diseases, and he cast out evil spirits and restored sight to the blind. ²²Then he told John's disciples, "Go back to John and tell him what you have seen and heard—the blind see, the lame walk, the lepers are cured, the deaf hear, the dead are raised to life, and the Good News is being preached to the poor. ²³And tell him, 'God blesses those who are not offended by me.*' "

²⁴After they left, Jesus talked to the crowd about John. "Who is this man in the wilderness that you went out to see? Did you find him weak as a reed, moved by every breath of wind? ²⁵Or were you expecting to see a man dressed in expensive clothes? No, people who wear beautiful clothes and live in luxury are found in palaces, not in the wilderness. ²⁶Were you looking for a prophet? Yes, and he is more than a prophet. ²⁷John is the man to whom the Scriptures refer when they say,

'Look, I am sending my messenger before you,
    and he will prepare your way before you.'*

²⁸I tell you, of all who have ever lived, none is greater than John. Yet even the most insignificant person in the Kingdom of God is greater than he is!"

²⁹When they heard this, all the people, including the unjust tax collectors, agreed that God's plan was right,* for they had been baptized by John. ³⁰But the Pharisees and experts in religious law had rejected God's plan for them, for they had refused John's baptism.

³¹"How shall I describe this generation?" Jesus asked. "With what will I compare them? ³²They are like a group of children playing a game in the public square. They complain to their friends, 'We played wedding songs, and you weren't happy, so we played funeral songs, but you weren't sad.' ³³For John the Baptist didn't drink wine and he often fasted, and you say, 'He's demon possessed.' ³⁴And I, the Son of Man, feast and drink, and you say, 'He's a glutton and a drunkard, and a friend of the worst sort of sinners!' ³⁵But wisdom is shown to be right by the lives of those who follow it.*"

Jesus Anointed by a Sinful Woman

³⁶One of the Pharisees asked Jesus to come to his home for a meal, so Jesus accepted the invitation and sat down to eat. ³⁷A certain immoral woman heard he was there and brought a beautiful jar* filled with expensive perfume. ³⁸Then she knelt behind him at his feet, weeping. Her tears fell on his feet, and she wiped them off with her hair. Then she kept kissing his feet and putting perfume on them.

³⁹When the Pharisee who was the host saw what was happening and who the woman was, he said to himself, "This proves that Jesus is no prophet. If God had really sent him, he would know what kind of woman is touching him. She's a sinner!"

⁴⁰Then Jesus spoke up and answered his thoughts. "Simon," he said to the Pharisee, "I have something to say to you."

"All right, Teacher," Simon replied, "go ahead."

⁴¹Then Jesus told him this story: "A man loaned money to two people— five hundred pieces of silver* to one and fifty pieces to the other. ⁴²But neither of them could repay him, so he kindly forgave them both, canceling their debts. Who do you suppose loved him more after that?"

I BELIEVE that Jesus is the promised Messiah. (7:19)

I BELIEVE John the Baptist was more than a prophet—he was God's messenger to prepare the way for Jesus' public ministry. (7:27)

See the profile for the Pharisees (page 1087) at Matthew 12:14.

I BELIEVE Jesus knows each and every person through and through. (7:39)

7:23 Or *who don't fall away because of me.*   7:27 Mal 3:1.   7:29 Or *praised God.*   7:35 Or *But wisdom is justified by all her children.*   7:37 Greek *an alabaster jar.*   7:41 Greek *500 denarii.* A denarius was the equivalent of a full day's wage.

⁴³Simon answered, "I suppose the one for whom he canceled the larger debt."

"That's right," Jesus said. ⁴⁴Then he turned to the woman and said to Simon, "Look at this woman kneeling here. When I entered your home, you didn't offer me water to wash the dust from my feet, but she has washed them with her tears and wiped them with her hair. ⁴⁵You didn't give me a kiss of greeting, but she has kissed my feet again and again from the time I first came in. ⁴⁶You neglected the courtesy of olive oil to anoint my head, but she has anointed my feet with rare perfume. ⁴⁷I tell you, her sins—and they are many—have been forgiven, so she has shown me much love. But a person who is forgiven little shows only little love." ⁴⁸Then Jesus said to the woman, "Your sins are forgiven."

⁴⁹The men at the table said among themselves, "Who does this man think he is, going around forgiving sins?"

⁵⁰And Jesus said to the woman, "Your faith has saved you; go in peace."

CHAPTER 8

Women Who Followed Jesus

Not long afterward Jesus began a tour of the nearby cities and villages to announce the Good News concerning the Kingdom of God. He took his twelve disciples with him, ²along with some women he had healed and from whom he had cast out evil spirits. Among them were Mary Magdalene, from whom he had cast out seven demons; ³Joanna, the wife of Chuza, Herod's business manager; Susanna; and many others who were contributing from their own resources to support Jesus and his disciples.

Story of the Farmer Scattering Seed

⁴One day Jesus told this story to a large crowd that had gathered from many towns to hear him: ⁵"A farmer went out to plant some seed. As he scattered it across his field, some seed fell on a footpath, where it was stepped on, and the birds came and ate it. ⁶Other seed fell on shallow soil with underlying rock. This seed began to grow, but soon it withered and died for lack of moisture. ⁷Other seed fell among thorns that shot up and choked out the tender blades. ⁸Still other seed fell on fertile soil. This seed grew and produced a crop one hundred times as much as had been planted." When he had said this, he called out, "Anyone who is willing to hear should listen and understand!"

⁹His disciples asked him what the story meant. ¹⁰He replied, "You have been permitted to understand the secrets of the Kingdom of God. But I am using these stories to conceal everything about it from outsiders, so that the Scriptures might be fulfilled:

'They see what I do,
  but they don't really see;
they hear what I say,
  but they don't understand.'*

¹¹"This is the meaning of the story: The seed is God's message. ¹²The seed that fell on the hard path represents those who hear the message, but then the Devil comes and steals it away and prevents them from believing and being saved. ¹³The rocky soil represents those who hear the message with joy. But like young plants in such soil, their roots don't go very deep. They believe for a while, but they wilt when the hot winds of testing blow. ¹⁴The thorny ground represents those who hear and accept the message, but all too quickly the message is crowded out by the cares and riches and pleasures of this life. And so they never grow into maturity. ¹⁵But the good soil represents honest,

8:10 Isa 6:9.

I LOVE the Lord all the more for all he has forgiven me. (7:47)

I BELIEVE Jesus indeed forgives sins. (7:49)

I TRUST Jesus for salvation, the forgiveness of sins, and daily peace. (7:50)

I HELP to support the Lord's workers out of my own means. (8:3)

I DO NOT GO my own way and become choked by life's worries and pleasures after I have believed. (8:14)

good-hearted people who hear God's message, cling to it, and steadily produce a huge harvest.

Illustration of the Lamp

[16] "No one would light a lamp and then cover it up or put it under a bed. No, lamps are mounted in the open, where they can be seen by those entering the house. [17] For everything that is hidden or secret will eventually be brought to light and made plain to all. [18] So be sure to pay attention to what you hear. To those who are open to my teaching, more understanding will be given. But to those who are not listening, even what they think they have will be taken away from them."

The True Family of Jesus

[19] Once when Jesus' mother and brothers came to see him, they couldn't get to him because of the crowds. [20] Someone told Jesus, "Your mother and your brothers are outside, and they want to see you."

[21] Jesus replied, "My mother and my brothers are all those who hear the message of God and obey it."

> I HEAR the Word of God, embrace it, and continue to produce a good crop. (8:15)

> I HEAR God's Word and put it into practice. (8:21)

LIKE MARY MAGDALENE *I believe God can deliver me from any nightmare.*

Luke 8:2

Mary experienced a never-ending nightmare at the hands of demons. Not overwhelming life circumstances, but seven wicked spiritual beings who invaded her body and tormented her spirit. Mary found no way of escape—until the day she met Jesus.

When Mary came face-to-face with Jesus, he immediately cast out the demons, and she awoke to the glories of his salvation. She never went back to her old life. Instead, Mary became one of a handful of female disciples who stayed close to Jesus. She traveled with him, supported him financially, stood by and wept at his crucifixion, and saw him first after his resurrection.

How many demons bind lost people in horrible nightmares in our day? Millions suffer from true demonic possession or from the "demons" of sexual abuse, alcoholism, drugs, suicidal depression, and extreme insecurity about the future.

Mary came to Jesus, not for a quick fix to her nightmares, but for complete freedom and lifelong dependence and relationship.

Jesus still delivers people from nightmares today. No nightmare is too awful. He can cast them all away. Like Mary, you and I can come to him for complete salvation today.

To read more about Mary Magdalene, see Luke 24:1-12 and John 20:1-18.

○ *Today's Scripture reading is Luke 7:36–8:3.*

Jesus Calms the Storm

[22] One day Jesus said to his disciples, "Let's cross over to the other side of the lake." So they got into a boat and started out. [23] On the way across, Jesus lay down for a nap, and while he was sleeping the wind began to rise. A fierce storm developed that threatened to swamp them, and they were in real danger.

[24] The disciples woke him up, shouting, "Master, Master, we're going to drown!"

So Jesus rebuked the wind and the raging waves. The storm stopped and all was calm! [25] Then he asked them, "Where is your faith?"

And they were filled with awe and amazement. They said to one another, "Who is this man, that even the winds and waves obey him?"

> I PLACE my faith in the Lord, the Creator and governor of the entire universe. (8:25)

Jesus Heals a Demon-Possessed Man

[26] So they arrived in the land of the Gerasenes,* across the lake from Galilee. [27] As Jesus was climbing out of the boat, a man who was possessed by demons

8:26 Some manuscripts read *Gadarenes*; other manuscripts read *Gergesenes.* See Matt 8:28; Mark 5:1.

came out to meet him. Homeless and naked, he had lived in a cemetery for a long time. [28]As soon as he saw Jesus, he shrieked and fell to the ground before him, screaming, "Why are you bothering me, Jesus, Son of the Most High God? Please, I beg you, don't torture me!" [29]For Jesus had already commanded the evil spirit to come out of him. This spirit had often taken control of the man. Even when he was shackled with chains, he simply broke them and rushed out into the wilderness, completely under the demon's power.

[30]"What is your name?" Jesus asked.

"Legion," he replied—for the man was filled with many demons. [31]The demons kept begging Jesus not to send them into the Bottomless Pit. [32]A large herd of pigs was feeding on the hillside nearby, and the demons pleaded with him to let them enter into the pigs. Jesus gave them permission. [33]So the demons came out of the man and entered the pigs, and the whole herd plunged down the steep hillside into the lake, where they drowned.

[34]When the herdsmen saw it, they fled to the nearby city and the surrounding countryside, spreading the news as they ran. [35]A crowd soon gathered around Jesus, for they wanted to see for themselves what had happened. And they saw the man who had been possessed by demons sitting quietly at Jesus' feet, clothed and sane. And the whole crowd was afraid. [36]Then those who had seen what happened told the others how the demon-possessed man had been healed. [37]And all the people in that region begged Jesus to go away and leave them alone, for a great wave of fear swept over them.

So Jesus returned to the boat and left, crossing back to the other side of the lake. [38]The man who had been demon possessed begged to go, too, but Jesus said, [39]"No, go back to your family and tell them all the wonderful things God has done for you." So he went all through the city telling about the great thing Jesus had done for him.

Jesus Heals in Response to Faith

[40]On the other side of the lake the crowds received Jesus with open arms because they had been waiting for him. [41]And now a man named Jairus, a leader of the local synagogue, came and fell down at Jesus' feet, begging him to come home with him. [42]His only child was dying, a little girl twelve years old.

As Jesus went with him, he was surrounded by the crowds. [43]And there was a woman in the crowd who had had a hemorrhage for twelve years. She had spent everything she had on doctors* and still could find no cure. [44]She came up behind Jesus and touched the fringe of his robe. Immediately, the bleeding stopped.

[45]"Who touched me?" Jesus asked.

Everyone denied it, and Peter said, "Master, this whole crowd is pressing up against you."

[46]But Jesus told him, "No, someone deliberately touched me, for I felt healing power go out from me." [47]When the woman realized that Jesus knew, she began to tremble and fell to her knees before him. The whole crowd heard her explain why she had touched him and that she had been immediately healed. [48]"Daughter," he said to her, "your faith has made you well. Go in peace."

[49]While he was still speaking to her, a messenger arrived from Jairus's home with the message, "Your little girl is dead. There's no use troubling the Teacher now."

[50]But when Jesus heard what had happened, he said to Jairus, "Don't be afraid. Just trust me, and she will be all right."

[51]When they arrived at the house, Jesus wouldn't let anyone go in with him except Peter, James, John, and the little girl's father and mother. [52]The house

---

I AM a different person because of what the Lord Jesus has done in my life. (8:35)

I TELL others how much the Lord has done for me. (8:39)

I PLEAD with Jesus to heal my loved one who is dying. (8:41)

See Jairus's profile (page 1123) at Mark 5:23.

I BELIEVE Jesus can bring about instantaneous healing. (8:44)

See Peter's profile (page 1111) at Matthew 26:75.

I ENJOY a profound peace because Jesus has healed me. (8:48)

I CHOOSE to believe Jesus in the midst of fear. (8:50)

See John's profile (page 1435) at Revelation 1:9.

8:43 Some manuscripts omit *She had spent everything she had on doctors.*

was filled with people weeping and wailing, but he said, "Stop the weeping! She isn't dead; she is only asleep."

[53]But the crowd laughed at him because they all knew she had died. [54]Then Jesus took her by the hand and said in a loud voice, "Get up, my child!" [55]And at that moment her life returned, and she immediately stood up! Then Jesus told them to give her something to eat. [56]Her parents were overwhelmed, but Jesus insisted that they not tell anyone what had happened.

I DO NOT LAUGH AT or mock the Word of the Lord. (8:53)

CHAPTER 9

Jesus Sends Out the Twelve Apostles

One day Jesus called together his twelve apostles and gave them power and authority to cast out demons and to heal all diseases. [2]Then he sent them out to tell everyone about the coming of the Kingdom of God and to heal the sick. [3]"Don't even take along a walking stick," he instructed them, "nor a traveler's bag, nor food, nor money. Not even an extra coat. [4]When you enter each village, be a guest in only one home. [5]If the people of the village won't receive your message when you enter it, shake off its dust from your feet as you leave. It is a sign that you have abandoned that village to its fate."

[6]So they began their circuit of the villages, preaching the Good News and healing the sick.

I TRUST God to provide my needs when I minister in his name. (9:3)

Herod's Confusion

[7]When reports of Jesus' miracles reached Herod Antipas,* he was worried and puzzled because some were saying, "This is John the Baptist come back to life again." [8]Others were saying, "It is Elijah or some other ancient prophet risen from the dead."

[9]"I beheaded John," Herod said, "so who is this man about whom I hear such strange stories?" And he tried to see him.

See John the Baptist's profile (page 1117) at Mark 1:4.

See Elijah's profile (page 421) at 1 Kings 19:18.

Jesus Feeds Five Thousand

[10]When the apostles returned, they told Jesus everything they had done. Then he slipped quietly away with them toward the town of Bethsaida. [11]But the crowds found out where he was going, and they followed him. And he welcomed them, teaching them about the Kingdom of God and curing those who were ill. [12]Late in the afternoon the twelve disciples came to him and said, "Send the crowds away to the nearby villages and farms, so they can find food and lodging for the night. There is nothing to eat here in this deserted place."

[13]But Jesus said, "You feed them."

"Impossible!" they protested. "We have only five loaves of bread and two fish. Or are you expecting us to go and buy enough food for this whole crowd?" [14]For there were about five thousand men there.

"Just tell them to sit down on the ground in groups of about fifty each," Jesus replied. [15]So the people all sat down. [16]Jesus took the five loaves and two fish, looked up toward heaven, and asked God's blessing on the food. Breaking the loaves into pieces, he kept giving the bread and fish to the disciples to give to the people. [17]They all ate as much as they wanted, and they picked up twelve baskets of leftovers!

I WELCOME people who come to me and speak about the Kingdom of God. (9:11)

I DO NOT TELL Jesus what to do. (9:12)

I GIVE THANKS before I eat. (9:16)

Peter's Declaration about Jesus

[18]One day as Jesus was alone, praying, he came over to his disciples and asked them, "Who do people say I am?"

[19]"Well," they replied, "some say John the Baptist, some say Elijah, and others say you are one of the other ancient prophets risen from the dead."

[20]Then he asked them, "Who do you say I am?"

Peter replied, "You are the Messiah sent from God!"

See Peter's profile (page 1111) at Matthew 26:75.

I BELIEVE Jesus is the Messiah sent from God. (9:20)

9:7 Greek *Herod the tetrarch.* He was a son of King Herod and was ruler over one of the four districts in Palestine.

Jesus Predicts His Death

²¹Jesus warned them not to tell anyone about this. ²²"For I, the Son of Man, must suffer many terrible things," he said. "I will be rejected by the leaders, the leading priests, and the teachers of religious law. I will be killed, but three days later I will be raised from the dead."

²³Then he said to the crowd, "If any of you wants to be my follower, you must put aside your selfish ambition, shoulder your cross daily, and follow me. ²⁴If you try to keep your life for yourself, you will lose it. But if you give up your life for me, you will find true life. ²⁵And how do you benefit if you gain the whole world but lose or forfeit your own soul in the process? ²⁶If a person is ashamed of me and my message, I, the Son of Man, will be ashamed of that person when I return in my glory and in the glory of the Father and the holy angels. ²⁷And I assure you that some of you standing here right now will not die before you see the Kingdom of God."

The Transfiguration

²⁸About eight days later Jesus took Peter, James, and John to a mountain to pray. ²⁹And as he was praying, the appearance of his face changed, and his clothing became dazzling white. ³⁰Then two men, Moses and Elijah, appeared and began talking with Jesus. ³¹They were glorious to see. And they were speaking of how he was about to fulfill God's plan by dying in Jerusalem.

³²Peter and the others were very drowsy and had fallen asleep. Now they woke up and saw Jesus' glory and the two men standing with him. ³³As Moses and Elijah were starting to leave, Peter, not even knowing what he was saying, blurted out, "Master, this is wonderful! We will make three shrines*—one for you, one for Moses, and one for Elijah." ³⁴But even as he was saying this, a cloud came over them; and terror gripped them as it covered them.

³⁵Then a voice from the cloud said, "This is my Son, my Chosen One.* Listen to him." ³⁶When the voice died away, Jesus was there alone. They didn't tell anyone what they had seen until long after this happened.

Jesus Heals a Demon-Possessed Boy

³⁷The next day, after they had come down the mountain, a huge crowd met Jesus. ³⁸A man in the crowd called out to him, "Teacher, look at my boy, who is my only son. ³⁹An evil spirit keeps seizing him, making him scream. It throws him into convulsions so that he foams at the mouth. It is always hitting and injuring him. It hardly ever leaves him alone. ⁴⁰I begged your disciples to cast the spirit out, but they couldn't do it."

⁴¹"You stubborn, faithless people," Jesus said, "how long must I be with you and put up with you? Bring him here." ⁴²As the boy came forward, the demon knocked him to the ground and threw him into a violent convulsion. But Jesus rebuked the evil spirit and healed the boy. Then he gave him back to his father. ⁴³Awe gripped the people as they saw this display of God's power.

Jesus Again Predicts His Death

While everyone was marveling over all the wonderful things he was doing, Jesus said to his disciples, ⁴⁴"Listen to me and remember what I say. The Son of Man is going to be betrayed." ⁴⁵But they didn't know what he meant. Its significance was hidden from them, so they could not understand it, and they were afraid to ask him about it.

The Greatest in the Kingdom

⁴⁶Then there was an argument among them as to which of them would be the greatest. ⁴⁷But Jesus knew their thoughts, so he brought a little child to his side. ⁴⁸Then he said to them, "Anyone who welcomes a little child like this on

I LIVE my life for Jesus, not for my own selfish ambition. (9:24)

See John's profile (page 1435) at Revelation 1:9.

See the profiles for Moses (page 73) and Elijah (page 421) at Exodus 5:1 and 1 Kings 19:18.

I LISTEN to Jesus, God's Son, who is far superior to even Moses or Elijah. (9:35)

I BRING my loved ones to Jesus. (9:41)

I AM AMAZED at the greatness of God and marvel at all that Jesus has done. (9:43)

I AM NOT AFRAID to ask the Lord questions when I do not understand. (9:45)

I WELCOME little children in Jesus' name. (9:48)

9:33 Or *shelters*; Greek reads *tabernacles*.   9:35 Some manuscripts read *This is my beloved Son.*

my behalf welcomes me, and anyone who welcomes me welcomes my Father who sent me. Whoever is the least among you is the greatest."

Using the Name of Jesus

49John said to Jesus, "Master, we saw someone using your name to cast out demons. We tried to stop him because he isn't in our group."

50But Jesus said, "Don't stop him! Anyone who is not against you is for you."

Opposition from Samaritans

51As the time drew near for his return to heaven, Jesus resolutely set out for Jerusalem. 52He sent messengers ahead to a Samaritan village to prepare for his arrival. 53But they were turned away. The people of the village refused to have anything to do with Jesus because he had resolved to go to Jerusalem. 54When James and John heard about it, they said to Jesus, "Lord, should we order down fire from heaven to burn them up*?" 55But Jesus turned and rebuked them.* 56So they went on to another village.

The Cost of Following Jesus

57As they were walking along someone said to Jesus, "I will follow you no matter where you go."

58But Jesus replied, "Foxes have dens to live in, and birds have nests, but I, the Son of Man, have no home of my own, not even a place to lay my head."

59He said to another person, "Come, be my disciple."

The man agreed, but he said, "Lord, first let me return home and bury my father."

60Jesus replied, "Let those who are spiritually dead care for their own dead.* Your duty is to go and preach the coming of the Kingdom of God."

61Another said, "Yes, Lord, I will follow you, but first let me say good-bye to my family."

62But Jesus told him, "Anyone who puts a hand to the plow and then looks back is not fit for the Kingdom of God."

I FOLLOW Jesus wholeheartedly without regrets. (9:62)

CHAPTER 10

Jesus Sends Out His Disciples

The Lord now chose seventy-two* other disciples and sent them on ahead in pairs to all the towns and villages he planned to visit. 2These were his instructions to them: "The harvest is so great, but the workers are so few. Pray to the Lord who is in charge of the harvest, and ask him to send out more workers for his fields. 3Go now, and remember that I am sending you out as lambs among wolves. 4Don't take along any money, or a traveler's bag, or even an extra pair of sandals. And don't stop to greet anyone on the road.

5"Whenever you enter a home, give it your blessing. 6If those who live there are worthy, the blessing will stand; if they are not, the blessing will return to you. 7When you enter a town, don't move around from home to home. Stay in one place, eating and drinking what they provide you. Don't hesitate to accept hospitality, because those who work deserve their pay.

8"If a town welcomes you, eat whatever is set before you 9and heal the sick. As you heal them, say, 'The Kingdom of God is near you now.' 10But if a town refuses to welcome you, go out into its streets and say, 11'We wipe the dust of your town from our feet as a public announcement of your doom. And don't forget the Kingdom of God is near!' 12The truth is, even wicked Sodom will be better off than such a town on the judgment day.

13"What horrors await you, Korazin and Bethsaida! For if the miracles I did

I ASK the Lord of the harvest to send out workers into his harvest field. (10:2)

I WILLINGLY GO where the Lord sends me, despite potential dangers or risks. (10:3)

9:54 Some manuscripts add *as Elijah did.*   9:55 Some manuscripts add *And he said, "You don't realize what your hearts are like.* 56*For the Son of Man has not come to destroy men's lives, but to save them."*   9:60 Greek *Let the dead bury their own dead.*   10:1 Some manuscripts read *70;* also in 10:17.

in you had been done in wicked Tyre and Sidon, their people would have sat in deep repentance long ago, clothed in sackcloth and throwing ashes on their heads to show their remorse. ¹⁴Yes, Tyre and Sidon will be better off on the judgment day than you. ¹⁵And you people of Capernaum, will you be exalted to heaven? No, you will be brought down to the place of the dead.*"

¹⁶Then he said to the disciples, "Anyone who accepts your message is also accepting me. And anyone who rejects you is rejecting me. And anyone who rejects me is rejecting God who sent me."

¹⁷When the seventy-two disciples returned, they joyfully reported to him, "Lord, even the demons obey us when we use your name!"

¹⁸"Yes," he told them, "I saw Satan falling from heaven as a flash of lightning! ¹⁹And I have given you authority over all the power of the enemy, and you can walk among snakes and scorpions and crush them. Nothing will injure you. ²⁰But don't rejoice just because evil spirits obey you; rejoice because your names are registered as citizens of heaven."

Jesus' Prayer of Thanksgiving

²¹Then Jesus was filled with the joy of the Holy Spirit and said, "O Father, Lord of heaven and earth, thank you for hiding the truth from those who think themselves so wise and clever, and for revealing it to the childlike. Yes, Father, it pleased you to do it this way.

²²"My Father has given me authority over everything. No one really knows the Son except the Father, and no one really knows the Father except the Son and those to whom the Son chooses to reveal him."

²³Then when they were alone, he turned to the disciples and said, "How privileged you are to see what you have seen. ²⁴I tell you, many prophets and kings have longed to see and hear what you have seen and heard, but they could not."

The Most Important Commandment

²⁵One day an expert in religious law stood up to test Jesus by asking him this question: "Teacher, what must I do to receive eternal life?"

²⁶Jesus replied, "What does the law of Moses say? How do you read it?"

²⁷The man answered, " 'You must love the Lord your God with all your heart, all your soul, all your strength, and all your mind.' And, 'Love your neighbor as yourself.' "*

²⁸"Right!" Jesus told him. "Do this and you will live!"

²⁹The man wanted to justify his actions, so he asked Jesus, "And who is my neighbor?"

Story of the Good Samaritan

³⁰Jesus replied with an illustration: "A Jewish man was traveling on a trip from Jerusalem to Jericho, and he was attacked by bandits. They stripped him of his clothes and money, beat him up, and left him half dead beside the road.

³¹"By chance a Jewish priest came along; but when he saw the man lying there, he crossed to the other side of the road and passed him by. ³²A Temple assistant* walked over and looked at him lying there, but he also passed by on the other side.

³³"Then a despised Samaritan came along, and when he saw the man, he felt deep pity. ³⁴Kneeling beside him, the Samaritan soothed his wounds with medicine and bandaged them. Then he put the man on his own donkey and took him to an inn, where he took care of him. ³⁵The next day he handed the innkeeper two pieces of silver* and told him to take care of the man. 'If his

---

I LISTEN intently to God's Word and have high regard for those who teach it faithfully. (10:16)

I REJOICE that my name is written in heaven. (10:20)

I AM THANKFUL that Jesus chose to reveal his Father to me. (10:22)

See Moses' profile (page 73) at Exodus 5:1.

I LOVE the Lord with all my heart, soul, strength, and mind and love my neighbor as myself. (10:27)

I BELIEVE everyone I meet is my neighbor. (10:29)

I GET PERSONALLY INVOLVED in meeting the pressing needs of others. (10:34)

10:15 Greek *to Hades.*   10:27 Deut 6:5; Lev 19:18.   10:32 Greek *A Levite.*   10:35 Greek *2 denarii.* A denarius was the equivalent of a full day's wage.

bill runs higher than that,' he said, 'I'll pay the difference the next time I am here.'

³⁶"Now which of these three would you say was a neighbor to the man who was attacked by bandits?" Jesus asked.

³⁷The man replied, "The one who showed him mercy."

Then Jesus said, "Yes, now go and do the same."

Jesus Visits Martha and Mary

³⁸As Jesus and the disciples continued on their way to Jerusalem, they came to a village where a woman named Martha welcomed them into her home. ³⁹Her sister, Mary, sat at the Lord's feet, listening to what he taught. ⁴⁰But Martha was worrying over the big dinner she was preparing. She came to Jesus and said, "Lord, doesn't it seem unfair to you that my sister just sits here while I do all the work? Tell her to come and help me."

⁴¹But the Lord said to her, "My dear Martha, you are so upset over all these details! ⁴²There is really only one thing worth being concerned about. Mary has discovered it—and I won't take it away from her."

I AVOID distractions that keep me from spending time with the Lord and learning from him. (10:40)

LIKE THE GOOD SAMARITAN *I do good to others from all walks of life.*

Luke 10:35

The Jewish people despised few groups more than the Samaritans, whom they considered renegade, cheating, blasphemous half-breeds.

The Samaritans were a hybrid nationality that rose after the kingdom of Israel was exiled by the Assyrians seven and a half centuries before Jesus Christ's crucifixion. Originally polytheistic (2 Kings 17:24-41), the Samaritans eventually embraced the writings of Moses, though they changed several key teachings (see John 4:20, for instance). Their faith had become monotheistic, but it was still fatally corrupted in the eyes of virtually all Jews.

As the Savior of the world, however, Jesus reached out to the Samaritan people (John 4:1-42) and used the story of the Good Samaritan to paint a vivid, dramatic example of what it means to "love your neighbor as yourself" (Leviticus 19:18).

Later, one of the first New Testament deacons, Philip, demonstrated his newfound love for all humanity by preaching the good news about Jesus to the "despised" Samaritans (Acts 8:4-13), and the apostles Peter and John did the same (Acts 8:25).

Jesus calls all Christians—including you and me—to be good Samaritans, doing good deeds to others in need and then sharing with them the greatest story ever told.

○ *Today's Scripture reading is Luke 10:25-37.*

CHAPTER 11

Teaching about Prayer

Once when Jesus had been out praying, one of his disciples came to him as he finished and said, "Lord, teach us to pray, just as John taught his disciples."

²He said, "This is how you should pray:

"Father, may your name be honored.
    May your Kingdom come soon.
³Give us our food day by day.
⁴And forgive us our sins—
    just as we forgive those who have sinned against us.
    And don't let us yield to temptation.*"

⁵Then, teaching them more about prayer, he used this illustration: "Suppose you went to a friend's house at midnight, wanting to borrow three

See John the Baptist's profile (page 1117) at Mark 1:4.

I PRAY as the Lord Jesus taught his disciples to pray. (11:2)

I DEPEND each day on God's provision of my basic needs. (11:3)

I FORGIVE everyone who sins against me and ask God to forgive me as well. (11:4)

11:2-4 Some manuscripts add additional portions of the Lord's Prayer as it reads in Matt 6:9-13.

loaves of bread. You would say to him, ⁶'A friend of mine has just arrived for a visit, and I have nothing for him to eat.' ⁷He would call out from his bedroom, 'Don't bother me. The door is locked for the night, and we are all in bed. I can't help you this time.' ⁸But I tell you this—though he won't do it as a friend, if you keep knocking long enough, he will get up and give you what you want so his reputation won't be damaged.*

⁹"And so I tell you, keep on asking, and you will be given what you ask for. Keep on looking, and you will find. Keep on knocking, and the door will be opened. ¹⁰For everyone who asks, receives. Everyone who seeks, finds. And the door is opened to everyone who knocks.

¹¹"You fathers—if your children ask* for a fish, do you give them a snake instead? ¹²Or if they ask for an egg, do you give them a scorpion? Of course not! ¹³If you sinful people know how to give good gifts to your children, how much more will your heavenly Father give the Holy Spirit to those who ask him."

Jesus and the Prince of Demons

¹⁴One day Jesus cast a demon out of a man who couldn't speak, and the man's voice returned to him. The crowd was amazed, ¹⁵but some said, "No wonder he can cast out demons. He gets his power from Satan,* the prince of demons!" ¹⁶ Trying to test Jesus, others asked for a miraculous sign from heaven to see if he was from God.

¹⁷He knew their thoughts, so he said, "Any kingdom at war with itself is doomed. A divided home is also doomed. ¹⁸You say I am empowered by the prince of demons.* But if Satan is fighting against himself by empowering me to cast out his demons, how can his kingdom survive? ¹⁹And if I am empowered by the prince of demons, what about your own followers? They cast out demons, too, so they will judge you for what you have said. ²⁰But if I am casting out demons by the power of God, then the Kingdom of God has arrived among you. ²¹For when Satan,* who is completely armed, guards his palace, it is safe—²²until someone who is stronger attacks and overpowers him, strips him of his weapons, and carries off his belongings.

²³"Anyone who isn't helping me opposes me, and anyone who isn't working with me is actually working against me.

²⁴"When an evil spirit leaves a person, it goes into the desert, searching for rest. But when it finds none, it says, 'I will return to the person I came from.' ²⁵So it returns and finds that its former home is all swept and clean. ²⁶Then the spirit finds seven other spirits more evil than itself, and they all enter the person and live there. And so that person is worse off than before."

²⁷As he was speaking, a woman in the crowd called out, "God bless your mother—the womb from which you came, and the breasts that nursed you!"

²⁸He replied, "But even more blessed are all who hear the word of God and put it into practice."

The Sign of Jonah

²⁹As the crowd pressed in on Jesus, he said, "These are evil times, and this evil generation keeps asking me to show them a miraculous sign. But the only sign I will give them is the sign of the prophet Jonah. ³⁰What happened to him was a sign to the people of Nineveh that God had sent him. What happens to me will be a sign that God has sent me, the Son of Man, to these people.

³¹"The queen of Sheba* will rise up against this generation on judgment day and condemn it, because she came from a distant land to hear the wisdom of Solomon. And now someone greater than Solomon is here—and

I PETITION God for my every need, knowing he—and he alone—can meet each need. (11:9)

I BELIEVE God the Father gives the Holy Spirit to those who ask him. (11:13)

I BELIEVE that the Kingdom of God came when Jesus was here on earth. (11:20)

I AM GENUINELY BLESSED because I hear the Word of God and do what it says. (11:28)

See Jonah's profile (page 1027) at Jonah 4:2.

See Solomon's profile (page 753) at Proverbs 2:9.

11:8 Greek *in order to avoid shame,* or *because of [your] persistence.* 11:11 Some manuscripts add *for bread, do you give them a stone? Or if they ask.* 11:15 Greek *Beelzeboul.* 11:18 Greek *by Beelzeboul;* also in 11:19. 11:21 Greek *the strong one.* 11:31 Greek *the queen of the south.*

you refuse to listen to him. ³²The people of Nineveh, too, will rise up against this generation on judgment day and condemn it, because they repented at the preaching of Jonah. And now someone greater than Jonah is here—and you refuse to repent.

Receiving the Light

³³"No one lights a lamp and then hides it or puts it under a basket. Instead, it is put on a lampstand to give light to all who enter the room. ³⁴Your eye is a lamp for your body. A pure eye lets sunshine into your soul. But an evil eye shuts out the light and plunges you into darkness. ³⁵Make sure that the light you think you have is not really darkness. ³⁶If you are filled with light, with no dark corners, then your whole life will be radiant, as though a floodlight is shining on you."

I LIVE in the light of God's presence (1 John 1:5–2:10). (11:36)

Jesus Criticizes the Religious Leaders

³⁷As Jesus was speaking, one of the Pharisees invited him home for a meal. So he went in and took his place at the table. ³⁸His host was amazed to see that he sat down to eat without first performing the ceremonial washing required by Jewish custom. ³⁹Then the Lord said to him, "You Pharisees are so careful to clean the outside of the cup and the dish, but inside you are still filthy—full of greed and wickedness! ⁴⁰Fools! Didn't God make the inside as well as the outside? ⁴¹So give to the needy what you greedily possess, and you will be clean all over.

See the profile for the Pharisees (page 1087) at Matthew 12:14.

LIKE MARY AND MARTHA

Luke 10:42

I have discovered my relationship with Jesus is more important than any job I could do for him.

No matter what the centuries have done to the reputation of Mary and Martha, there's no doubt that Jesus loved them both—Scripture plainly says so (John 11:5).

What both women needed to discover was that—more than anything else—Jesus wanted their love in return.

For some reason, Mary learned this lesson more easily. In childlike trust she began to sit at Jesus' feet, opening her ears and heart and waiting eagerly for him to fill them. Not even the most sacrificial good works mattered as much as spending time with the Lord (John 12:1-8).

For Martha, learning this lesson came harder. She, too, believed Jesus was the Messiah, the Son of God (John 11:27). But Martha apparently felt she had to do something big to impress the Lord—and complained when Mary wouldn't help. But Jesus refused to replace Mary's fellowship with a list of worries and concerns.

How often, even in our quiet times, are you and I "upset over all these details"? We may think we're sitting at Jesus' feet, but our minds are rushing through the day checking details, making lists, and then rattling off worries and complaints to the Lord. Our Bible may be open, but are we really listening to Jesus?

Like Mary and Martha, we aren't called by God to wear ourselves out. Instead, we're invited to find rest for our souls (Matthew 11:28-30).

○ Today's Scripture reading is Luke 10:38-42.

---

⁴²"But how terrible it will be for you Pharisees! For you are careful to tithe even the tiniest part of your income,* but you completely forget about justice and the love of God. You should tithe, yes, but you should not leave undone the more important things.

⁴³"How terrible it will be for you Pharisees! For how you love the seats of honor in the synagogues and the respectful greetings from everyone as you walk through the markets! ⁴⁴Yes, how terrible it will be for you. For you are

I GIVE God a tithe of all I have without neglecting justice and the love of God. (11:42)

I MAKE SURE my life is pure inside, not just impressive outside. (11:44)

11:42 Greek *to tithe the mint and the rue and every herb.*

like hidden graves in a field. People walk over them without knowing the corruption they are stepping on."

⁴⁵"Teacher," said an expert in religious law, "you have insulted us, too, in what you just said."

⁴⁶"Yes," said Jesus, "how terrible it will be for you experts in religious law! For you crush people beneath impossible religious demands, and you never lift a finger to help ease the burden. ⁴⁷How terrible it will be for you! For you build tombs for the very prophets your ancestors killed long ago. ⁴⁸Murderers! You agree with your ancestors that what they did was right. You would have done the same yourselves. ⁴⁹This is what God in his wisdom said about you:* 'I will send prophets and apostles to them, and they will kill some and persecute the others.'

⁵⁰"And you of this generation will be held responsible for the murder of all God's prophets from the creation of the world—⁵¹from the murder of Abel to the murder of Zechariah, who was killed between the altar and the sanctuary. Yes, it will surely be charged against you.

⁵²"How terrible it will be for you experts in religious law! For you hide the key to knowledge from the people. You don't enter the Kingdom yourselves, and you prevent others from entering."

⁵³As Jesus finished speaking, the Pharisees and teachers of religious law were furious. From that time on they grilled him with many hostile questions, ⁵⁴trying to trap him into saying something they could use against him.

CHAPTER 12

A Warning against Hypocrisy

Meanwhile, the crowds grew until thousands were milling about and crushing each other. Jesus turned first to his disciples and warned them, "Beware of the yeast of the Pharisees—beware of their hypocrisy. ²The time is coming when everything will be revealed; all that is secret will be made public. ³Whatever you have said in the dark will be heard in the light, and what you have whispered behind closed doors will be shouted from the housetops for all to hear!

⁴"Dear friends, don't be afraid of those who want to kill you. They can only kill the body; they cannot do any more to you. ⁵But I'll tell you whom to fear. Fear God, who has the power to kill people and then throw them into hell.

⁶"What is the price of five sparrows? A couple of pennies? Yet God does not forget a single one of them. ⁷And the very hairs on your head are all numbered. So don't be afraid; you are more valuable to him than a whole flock of sparrows.

⁸"And I assure you of this: If anyone acknowledges me publicly here on earth, I, the Son of Man, will openly acknowledge that person in the presence of God's angels. ⁹But if anyone denies me here on earth, I will deny that person before God's angels. ¹⁰Yet those who speak against the Son of Man may be forgiven, but anyone who speaks blasphemies against the Holy Spirit will never be forgiven.

¹¹"And when you are brought to trial in the synagogues and before rulers and authorities, don't worry about what to say in your defense, ¹²for the Holy Spirit will teach you what needs to be said even as you are standing there."

Story of the Rich Fool

¹³Then someone called from the crowd, "Teacher, please tell my brother to divide our father's estate with me."

¹⁴Jesus replied, "Friend, who made me a judge over you to decide such things as that?" ¹⁵Then he said, "Beware! Don't be greedy for what you don't have. Real life is not measured by how much we own."

11:49 Greek Therefore, the wisdom of God said.

See Abel's profile (page 9) at Genesis 4:4.

I KEEP on guard against hypocrisy in my life. (12:1)

See the profile for the Pharisees (page 1087) at Matthew 12:14.

I DO NOT FEAR what mere humans can do to me. (12:4)

I TRUST that the Lord himself will teach me what to say when I must defend myself as a believer. (12:11)

I KEEP ON GUARD against all kinds of greed. (12:15)

[16]And he gave an illustration: "A rich man had a fertile farm that produced fine crops. [17]In fact, his barns were full to overflowing. [18]So he said, 'I know! I'll tear down my barns and build bigger ones. Then I'll have room enough to store everything. [19]And I'll sit back and say to myself, My friend, you have enough stored away for years to come. Now take it easy! Eat, drink, and be merry!'

[20]"But God said to him, 'You fool! You will die this very night. Then who will get it all?'

[21]"Yes, a person is a fool to store up earthly wealth but not have a rich relationship with God."

I ACTIVELY SEEK to be rich toward God. (12:21)

UNLIKE THE RICH FOOL
Luke 12:20

I do not trust in wealth alone to make me happy.

What's the Rich Fool's name?

If you asked the judge Ehud, he would have told you King Eglon of Moab, an extremely wealthy and obese tyrant who oppressed God's people for eighteen long years before his gruesome demise (Judges 3:12-30).

If you asked the prophet Samuel, he would have told you Eli, a well-to-do priest who scorned the things of God and suffered the same fate the Lord had predicted would befall Eli's two utterly wicked sons (1 Samuel 2:27-4:18).

If you asked King David, he would have told you Nabal, a mean and dishonest man who had grown rich, threw a big party in his own honor and then was struck dead by the Lord (1 Samuel 25:2-38).

Scripture makes it clear that wealth can be a blessing of God. But it also can be a snare of the Devil, turning our heart from the eternal to the temporal—from wisely choosing God's will to blindly pursuing our own pleasures (Deuteronomy 8:1-20; 1 Timothy 6:6-10).

Unlike the Rich Fool, let's remember that everything we have is God's and do all we can to store up treasure in heaven.

○ *Today's Scripture reading is Luke 12:13-34.*

Teaching about Money and Possessions

[22]Then turning to his disciples, Jesus said, "So I tell you, don't worry about everyday life—whether you have enough food to eat or clothes to wear. [23]For life consists of far more than food and clothing. [24]Look at the ravens. They don't need to plant or harvest or put food in barns because God feeds them. And you are far more valuable to him than any birds! [25]Can all your worries add a single moment to your life? Of course not! [26]And if worry can't do little things like that, what's the use of worrying over bigger things?

[27]"Look at the lilies and how they grow. They don't work or make their clothing, yet Solomon in all his glory was not dressed as beautifully as they are. [28]And if God cares so wonderfully for flowers that are here today and gone tomorrow, won't he more surely care for you? You have so little faith! [29]And don't worry about food—what to eat and drink. Don't worry whether God will provide it for you. [30]These things dominate the thoughts of most people, but your Father already knows your needs. [31]He will give you all you need from day to day if you make the Kingdom of God your primary concern.

[32]"So don't be afraid, little flock. For it gives your Father great happiness to give you the Kingdom.

[33]"Sell what you have and give to those in need. This will store up treasure for you in heaven! And the purses of heaven have no holes in them. Your treasure will be safe—no thief can steal it and no moth can destroy it. [34]Wherever your treasure is, there your heart and thoughts will also be.

See Solomon's profile (page 753) at Proverbs 2:9.

I BELIEVE God the Father knows exactly what I need. (12:30)

I AM STORING UP treasure in heaven when I willingly sell my possessions and give to the poor—to those in greater need than me. (12:33)

Be Ready for the Lord's Coming

I DO NOT PUT OFF doing what the Lord asks; I'm ready and willing to do whatever he asks, whenever he asks—day or night. (12:35)

35"Be dressed for service and well prepared, 36as though you were waiting for your master to return from the wedding feast. Then you will be ready to open the door and let him in the moment he arrives and knocks. 37There will be special favor for those who are ready and waiting for his return. I tell you, he himself will seat them, put on an apron, and serve them as they sit and eat! 38He may come in the middle of the night or just before dawn.* But whenever he comes, there will be special favor for his servants who are ready!

39"Know this: A homeowner who knew exactly when a burglar was coming would not permit the house to be broken into. 40You must be ready all the time, for the Son of Man will come when least expected."

See Peter's profile (page 1111) at Matthew 26:75.

41Peter asked, "Lord, is this illustration just for us or for everyone?"

I BELIEVE the Lord will richly reward those who long for his coming (2 Timothy 4:6-8). (12:44)

42And the Lord replied, "I'm talking to any faithful, sensible servant to whom the master gives the responsibility of managing his household and feeding his family. 43If the master returns and finds that the servant has done a good job, there will be a reward. 44I assure you, the master will put that servant in charge of all he owns. 45But if the servant thinks, 'My master won't be back for a while,' and begins oppressing the other servants, partying, and getting drunk—46well, the master will return unannounced and unexpected. He will tear the servant apart and banish him with the unfaithful. 47The servant will be severely punished, for though he knew his duty, he refused to do it.

I BELIEVE the Lord will judge individuals according to both their knowledge and their actions. (12:48)

48"But people who are not aware that they are doing wrong will be punished only lightly. Much is required from those to whom much is given, and much more is required from those to whom much more is given.

Jesus Causes Division

I RECOGNIZE that heartfelt belief for or against the Lord Jesus Christ sometimes divides families. (12:51)

I RECOGNIZE the signs of the times. (12:54)

49"I have come to bring fire to the earth, and I wish that my task were already completed! 50There is a terrible baptism ahead of me, and I am under a heavy burden until it is accomplished. 51Do you think I have come to bring peace to the earth? No, I have come to bring strife and division! 52From now on families will be split apart, three in favor of me, and two against—or the other way around. 53There will be a division between father and son, mother and daughter, mother-in-law and daughter-in-law."

54Then Jesus turned to the crowd and said, "When you see clouds beginning to form in the west, you say, 'Here comes a shower.' And you are right. 55When the south wind blows, you say, 'Today will be a scorcher.' And it is. 56You hypocrites! You know how to interpret the appearance of the earth and the sky, but you can't interpret these present times.

57"Why can't you decide for yourselves what is right? 58If you are on the way to court and you meet your accuser, try to settle the matter before it reaches the judge, or you may be sentenced and handed over to an officer and thrown in jail. 59And if that happens, you won't be free again until you have paid the last penny."

CHAPTER 13

A Call to Repentance

See Pilate's profile (page 1229) at John 19:16.

I BELIEVE that those who do not repent face God's judgment. (13:3)

I HAVE TURNED from my evil ways and turned to God. (13:5)

About this time Jesus was informed that Pilate had murdered some people from Galilee as they were sacrificing at the Temple in Jerusalem. 2"Do you think those Galileans were worse sinners than other people from Galilee?" he asked. "Is that why they suffered? 3Not at all! And you will also perish unless you turn from your evil ways and turn to God. 4And what about the eighteen men who died when the Tower of Siloam fell on them? Were they the worst sinners in Jerusalem? 5No, and I tell you again that unless you repent, you will also perish."

12:38 Greek *in the second or third watch.*

Illustration of the Barren Fig Tree

⁶Then Jesus used this illustration: "A man planted a fig tree in his garden and came again and again to see if there was any fruit on it, but he was always disappointed. ⁷Finally, he said to his gardener, 'I've waited three years, and there hasn't been a single fig! Cut it down. It's taking up space we can use for something else.'

⁸"The gardener answered, 'Give it one more chance. Leave it another year, and I'll give it special attention and plenty of fertilizer. ⁹If we get figs next year, fine. If not, you can cut it down.' "

Jesus Heals on the Sabbath

¹⁰One Sabbath day as Jesus was teaching in a synagogue, ¹¹he saw a woman who had been crippled by an evil spirit. She had been bent double for eighteen years and was unable to stand up straight. ¹²When Jesus saw her, he called her over and said, "Woman, you are healed of your sickness!" ¹³Then he touched her, and instantly she could stand straight. How she praised and thanked God!

¹⁴But the leader in charge of the synagogue was indignant that Jesus had healed her on the Sabbath day. "There are six days of the week for working," he said to the crowd. "Come on those days to be healed, not on the Sabbath."

¹⁵But the Lord replied, "You hypocrite! You work on the Sabbath day! Don't you untie your ox or your donkey from their stalls on the Sabbath and lead them out for water? ¹⁶Wasn't it necessary for me, even on the Sabbath day, to free this dear woman* from the bondage in which Satan has held her for eighteen years?" ¹⁷This shamed his enemies. And all the people rejoiced at the wonderful things he did.

Illustration of the Mustard Seed

¹⁸Then Jesus said, "What is the Kingdom of God like? How can I illustrate it? ¹⁹It is like a tiny mustard seed planted in a garden; it grows and becomes a tree, and the birds come and find shelter among its branches."

Illustration of the Yeast

²⁰He also asked, "What else is the Kingdom of God like? ²¹It is like yeast used by a woman making bread. Even though she used a large amount* of flour, the yeast permeated every part of the dough."

The Narrow Door

²²Jesus went through the towns and villages, teaching as he went, always pressing on toward Jerusalem. ²³Someone asked him, "Lord, will only a few be saved?"

He replied, ²⁴"The door to heaven is narrow. Work hard to get in, because many will try to enter, ²⁵but when the head of the house has locked the door, it will be too late. Then you will stand outside knocking and pleading, 'Lord, open the door for us!' But he will reply, 'I do not know you.' ²⁶You will say, 'But we ate and drank with you, and you taught in our streets.' ²⁷And he will reply, 'I tell you, I don't know you. Go away, all you who do evil.'

²⁸"And there will be great weeping and gnashing of teeth, for you will see Abraham, Isaac, Jacob, and all the prophets within the Kingdom of God, but you will be thrown out. ²⁹Then people will come from all over the world to take their places in the Kingdom of God. ³⁰And note this: Some who are despised now will be greatly honored then; and some who are greatly honored now will be despised then.*"

I BELIEVE Jesus longs to heal those who have been kept in bondage by Satan. (13:16)

I REJOICE at the wonderful things Jesus does. (13:17)

I BELIEVE that those who continue to refuse to turn from their evil ways and turn to God will one day find it's too late to repent and be saved. (13:27)

See the profiles for Abraham (page 19), Isaac (page 31), and Jacob (page 43) at Genesis 15:6, Genesis 25:19, and Genesis 32:9.

I BELIEVE God's Kingdom includes individuals from all over the world. (13:29)

I BELIEVE that some who are despised here on earth will be greatly honored in God's Kingdom some day. (13:30)

13:16 Greek *this woman, a daughter of Abraham.*   13:21 Greek *3 measures.*   13:30 Greek *Some are last who will be first, and some are first who will be last.*

Jesus Grieves over Jerusalem

[31]A few minutes later some Pharisees said to him, "Get out of here if you want to live, because Herod Antipas wants to kill you!"

[32]Jesus replied, "Go tell that fox that I will keep on casting out demons and doing miracles of healing today and tomorrow; and the third day I will accomplish my purpose. [33]Yes, today, tomorrow, and the next day I must proceed on my way. For it wouldn't do for a prophet of God to be killed except in Jerusalem!

[34]"O Jerusalem, Jerusalem, the city that kills the prophets and stones God's messengers! How often I have wanted to gather your children together as a hen protects her chicks beneath her wings, but you wouldn't let me. [35]And now look, your house is left to you empty. And you will never see me again until you say, 'Bless the one who comes in the name of the Lord!'* "

CHAPTER 14

Jesus Heals on the Sabbath

See the profile for the Pharisees (page 1087) at Matthew 12:14.

One Sabbath day Jesus was in the home of a leader of the Pharisees. The people were watching him closely, [2]because there was a man there whose arms and legs were swollen.* [3]Jesus asked the Pharisees and experts in religious law, "Well, is it permitted in the law to heal people on the Sabbath day, or not?" [4]When they refused to answer, Jesus touched the sick man and healed him and sent him away. [5]Then he turned to them and asked, "Which of you doesn't work on the Sabbath? If your son* or your cow falls into a pit, don't you proceed at once to get him out?" [6]Again they had no answer.

I TOUCH the sick. (14:4)

Jesus Teaches about Humility

[7]When Jesus noticed that all who had come to the dinner were trying to sit near the head of the table, he gave them this advice: [8]"If you are invited to a wedding feast, don't always head for the best seat. What if someone more respected than you has also been invited? [9]The host will say, 'Let this person sit here instead.' Then you will be embarrassed and will have to take whatever seat is left at the foot of the table!

I DO NOT TRY to take the seat of honor at special events. (14:8)

[10]"Do this instead—sit at the foot of the table. Then when your host sees you, he will come and say, 'Friend, we have a better place than this for you!' Then you will be honored in front of all the other guests. [11]For the proud will be humbled, but the humble will be honored."

I BELIEVE God will honor the humble. (14:11)

[12]Then he turned to his host. "When you put on a luncheon or a dinner," he said, "don't invite your friends, brothers, relatives, and rich neighbors. For they will repay you by inviting you back. [13]Instead, invite the poor, the crippled, the lame, and the blind. [14]Then at the resurrection of the godly, God will reward you for inviting those who could not repay you."

I EXTEND hospitality to those who cannot repay me. (14:13)

Story of the Great Feast

[15]Hearing this, a man sitting at the table with Jesus exclaimed, "What a privilege it would be to have a share in the Kingdom of God!"

[16]Jesus replied with this illustration: "A man prepared a great feast and sent out many invitations. [17]When all was ready, he sent his servant around to notify the guests that it was time for them to come. [18]But they all began making excuses. One said he had just bought a field and wanted to inspect it, so he asked to be excused. [19]Another said he had just bought five pair of oxen and wanted to try them out. [20]Another had just been married, so he said he couldn't come.

I RESPOND to the Lord's invitation and come into his Kingdom. (14:18)

[21]"The servant returned and told his master what they had said. His master was angry and said, 'Go quickly into the streets and alleys of the city and invite the poor, the crippled, the lame, and the blind.' [22]After the servant had

13:35 Ps 118:26. 14:2 Traditionally translated *who had dropsy.* 14:5 Some manuscripts read *donkey.*

done this, he reported, 'There is still room for more.' ²³So his master said, 'Go out into the country lanes and behind the hedges and urge anyone you find to come, so that the house will be full. ²⁴For none of those I invited first will get even the smallest taste of what I had prepared for them.' "

The Cost of Being a Disciple

²⁵Great crowds were following Jesus. He turned around and said to them, ²⁶"If you want to be my follower you must love me more than* your own father and mother, wife and children, brothers and sisters—yes, more than your own life. Otherwise, you cannot be my disciple. ²⁷And you cannot be my disciple if you do not carry your own cross and follow me.

²⁸"But don't begin until you count the cost. For who would begin construction of a building without first getting estimates and then checking to see if there is enough money to pay the bills? ²⁹Otherwise, you might complete only the foundation before running out of funds. And then how everyone would laugh at you! ³⁰They would say, 'There's the person who started that building and ran out of money before it was finished!'

³¹"Or what king would ever dream of going to war without first sitting down with his counselors and discussing whether his army of ten thousand is strong enough to defeat the twenty thousand soldiers who are marching against him? ³²If he is not able, then while the enemy is still far away, he will send a delegation to discuss terms of peace. ³³So no one can become my disciple without giving up everything for me.

³⁴"Salt is good for seasoning. But if it loses its flavor, how do you make it salty again? ³⁵Flavorless salt is good neither for the soil nor for fertilizer. It is thrown away. Anyone who is willing to hear should listen and understand!"

CHAPTER 15

Story of the Lost Sheep

Tax collectors and other notorious sinners often came to listen to Jesus teach. ²This made the Pharisees and teachers of religious law complain that he was associating with such despicable people—even eating with them!

³So Jesus used this illustration: ⁴"If you had one hundred sheep, and one of them strayed away and was lost in the wilderness, wouldn't you leave the ninety-nine others to go and search for the lost one until you found it? ⁵And then you would joyfully carry it home on your shoulders. ⁶When you arrived, you would call together your friends and neighbors to rejoice with you because your lost sheep was found. ⁷In the same way, heaven will be happier over one lost sinner who returns to God than over ninety-nine others who are righteous and haven't strayed away!

Story of the Lost Coin

⁸"Or suppose a woman has ten valuable silver coins* and loses one. Won't she light a lamp and look in every corner of the house and sweep every nook and cranny until she finds it? ⁹And when she finds it, she will call in her friends and neighbors to rejoice with her because she has found her lost coin. ¹⁰In the same way, there is joy in the presence of God's angels when even one sinner repents."

Story of the Lost Son

¹¹To illustrate the point further, Jesus told them this story: "A man had two sons. ¹²The younger son told his father, 'I want my share of your estate now, instead of waiting until you die.' So his father agreed to divide his wealth between his sons.

¹³"A few days later this younger son packed all his belongings and took a trip to a distant land, and there he wasted all his money on wild living.

I LOVE Jesus more than anyone—including myself. (14:26)

I HAVE COUNTED the cost of following Jesus. (14:28)

I HAVE LET GO of everything to be Jesus' disciple. (14:33)

I LISTEN to what Jesus says and take heed. (14:35)

I BEFRIEND AND SOCIALIZE with people who need the Lord. (15:2)

See the profile for the Pharisees (page 1087) at Matthew 12:14.

I REJOICE with others when even one person returns to God. (15:7)

I REJOICE greatly when even one person returns to God. (15:10)

I DO NOT WASTE my money on wild living. (15:13)

14:26 Greek *you must hate.*   15:8 Greek *10 drachmas.* A drachma was the equivalent of a full day's wage.

[14]About the time his money ran out, a great famine swept over the land, and he began to starve. [15]He persuaded a local farmer to hire him to feed his pigs. [16]The boy became so hungry that even the pods he was feeding the pigs looked good to him. But no one gave him anything.

[17]"When he finally came to his senses, he said to himself, 'At home even the hired men have food enough to spare, and here I am, dying of hunger! [18]I will go home to my father and say, "Father, I have sinned against both heaven and you, [19]and I am no longer worthy of being called your son. Please take me on as a hired man."'

[20]"So he returned home to his father. And while he was still a long distance away, his father saw him coming. Filled with love and compassion, he ran to his son, embraced him, and kissed him. [21]His son said to him, 'Father, I have sinned against both heaven and you, and I am no longer worthy of being called your son.*'

I HUMBLY REPENT when I realize I have sinned against God and hurt others. (15:21)

[22]"But his father said to the servants, 'Quick! Bring the finest robe in the house and put it on him. Get a ring for his finger, and sandals for his feet. [23]And kill the calf we have been fattening in the pen. We must celebrate with a feast, [24]for this son of mine was dead and has now returned to life. He was lost, but now he is found.' So the party began.

I CELEBRATE when a loved one or friend returns to God. (15:23)

[25]"Meanwhile, the older son was in the fields working. When he returned home, he heard music and dancing in the house, [26]and he asked one of the servants what was going on. [27]'Your brother is back,' he was told, 'and your father has killed the calf we were fattening and has prepared a great feast. We are celebrating because of his safe return.'

[28]"The older brother was angry and wouldn't go in. His father came out and begged him, [29]but he replied, 'All these years I've worked hard for you and never once refused to do a single thing you told me to. And in all that time you never gave me even one young goat for a feast with my friends. [30]Yet when this son of yours comes back after squandering your money on prostitutes, you celebrate by killing the finest calf we have.'

I DO NOT BECOME ANGRY when a repentant sinner is welcomed back with rejoicing. (15:28)

[31]"His father said to him, 'Look, dear son, you and I are very close, and everything I have is yours. [32]We had to celebrate this happy day. For your brother was dead and has come back to life! He was lost, but now he is found!'"

CHAPTER 16

Story of the Shrewd Manager

Jesus told this story to his disciples: "A rich man hired a manager to handle his affairs, but soon a rumor went around that the manager was thoroughly dishonest. [2]So his employer called him in and said, 'What's this I hear about your stealing from me? Get your report in order, because you are going to be dismissed.'

[3]"The manager thought to himself, 'Now what? I'm through here, and I don't have the strength to go out and dig ditches, and I'm too proud to beg. [4]I know just the thing! And then I'll have plenty of friends to take care of me when I leave!'

[5]"So he invited each person who owed money to his employer to come and discuss the situation. He asked the first one, 'How much do you owe him?' [6]The man replied, 'I owe him eight hundred gallons of olive oil.' So the manager told him, 'Tear up that bill and write another one for four hundred gallons.*'

[7]"'And how much do you owe my employer?' he asked the next man. 'A thousand bushels of wheat,' was the reply. 'Here,' the manager said, 'take your bill and replace it with one for only eight hundred bushels.*'

15:21 Some manuscripts add *Please take me on as a hired man.* 16:6 Greek *100 baths . . . 50 [baths].* 16:7 Greek *100 korous . . . 80 [korous].*

[8]"The rich man had to admire the dishonest rascal for being so shrewd. And it is true that the citizens of this world are more shrewd than the godly are. [9]I tell you, use your worldly resources to benefit others and make friends. In this way, your generosity stores up a reward for you in heaven.*

[10]"Unless you are faithful in small matters, you won't be faithful in large ones. If you cheat even a little, you won't be honest with greater responsibilities. [11]And if you are untrustworthy about worldly wealth, who will trust you with the true riches of heaven? [12]And if you are not faithful with other people's money, why should you be trusted with money of your own?

[13]"No one can serve two masters. For you will hate one and love the other, or be devoted to one and despise the other. You cannot serve both God and money."

[14]The Pharisees, who dearly loved their money, naturally scoffed at all this. [15]Then he said to them, "You like to look good in public, but God knows your evil hearts. What this world honors is an abomination in the sight of God.

I USE money to help others and befriend them for God's Kingdom. (16:9)

I AM TRUSTWORTHY with other people's money. (16:12)

I DEARLY LOVE God, not money. (16:14)

See the profile for the Pharisees (page 1087) at Matthew 12:14.

LIKE THE LOST SON
Luke 15:21

I experience God's warm embrace and complete forgiveness.

The Bible is full of the stories of parents and their wayward children.

Consider, for instance, the stories of Adam and Eve and their son Cain (Genesis 4:1-16), of Lot and his two daughters (Genesis 19:30-38), of Gideon and his son Abimelech (Judges 8:22-9:57), of Eli and his sons (1 Samuel 2:12-4:22), of Samuel and his sons (1 Samuel 8:1-5), and of David and two of his sons (2 Samuel 13-18). In each of these particular stories, Scripture gives us no indication that the prodigals ever repented.

Here Jesus tells of another prodigal who, in essence, slapped his father in the face and said, "I wish you were dead! Give me my share of the inheritance now!" Jesus' listeners probably were aghast that the father complied with his younger son's request. They were probably even more aghast when, apparently many months later, that same father pulled out all the stops to welcome back his utterly wretched son.

God's love is like that—no matter how badly we've failed him, if we come to our senses and truly repent of our sins, he warmly embraces us and completely forgives our sins. Here is a message of hope for everyone—even the worst of sinners (see 1 Timothy 1:12-17).

○ *Today's Scripture reading is Luke 15.*

---

[16]"Until John the Baptist began to preach, the laws of Moses and the messages of the prophets were your guides. But now the Good News of the Kingdom of God is preached, and eager multitudes are forcing their way in. [17]But that doesn't mean that the law has lost its force in even the smallest point. It is stronger and more permanent than heaven and earth.

[18]"Anyone who divorces his wife and marries someone else commits adultery, and anyone who marries a divorced woman commits adultery."

The Rich Man and Lazarus

[19]Jesus said, "There was a certain rich man who was splendidly clothed and who lived each day in luxury. [20]At his door lay a diseased beggar named Lazarus. [21]As Lazarus lay there longing for scraps from the rich man's table, the dogs would come and lick his open sores. [22]Finally, the beggar died and was carried by the angels to be with Abraham.* The rich man also died and was buried, [23]and his soul went to the place of the dead.* There, in torment, he saw Lazarus in the far distance with Abraham.

[24]"The rich man shouted, 'Father Abraham, have some pity! Send Lazarus

See the profiles for John the Baptist (page 1117) and Moses (page 73) at Mark 1:4 and Exodus 5:1.

I HONOR AND VALUE both the Old and New Testaments—God's eternal Word. (16:17)

I REFUSE to entertain the idea of divorcing my spouse to marry someone else. (16:18)

See Abraham's profile (page 19) at Genesis 15:6.

I BELIEVE in the awful reality of hell, and I shudder. (16:23)

16:9 Or *Then when you run out at the end of this life, your friends will welcome you into eternal homes.*   16:22 Greek *into Abraham's bosom.*   16:23 Greek *to Hades.*

over here to dip the tip of his finger in water and cool my tongue, because I am in anguish in these flames.'

²⁵"But Abraham said to him, 'Son, remember that during your lifetime you had everything you wanted, and Lazarus had nothing. So now he is here being comforted, and you are in anguish. ²⁶And besides, there is a great chasm separating us. Anyone who wanted to cross over to you from here is stopped at its edge, and no one there can cross over to us.'

²⁷"Then the rich man said, 'Please, Father Abraham, send him to my father's home. ²⁸For I have five brothers, and I want him to warn them about this place of torment so they won't have to come here when they die.'

²⁹"But Abraham said, 'Moses and the prophets have warned them. Your brothers can read their writings anytime they want to.'

³⁰"The rich man replied, 'No, Father Abraham! But if someone is sent to them from the dead, then they will turn from their sins.'

³¹"But Abraham said, 'If they won't listen to Moses and the prophets, they won't listen even if someone rises from the dead.' "

CHAPTER 17

Teachings about Forgiveness and Faith

One day Jesus said to his disciples, "There will always be temptations to sin, but how terrible it will be for the person who does the tempting. ²It would be better to be thrown into the sea with a large millstone tied around the neck than to face the punishment in store for harming one of these little ones. ³I am warning you! If another believer* sins, rebuke him; then if he repents, forgive him. ⁴Even if he wrongs you seven times a day and each time turns again and asks forgiveness, forgive him."

⁵One day the apostles said to the Lord, "We need more faith; tell us how to get it."

⁶"Even if you had faith as small as a mustard seed," the Lord answered, "you could say to this mulberry tree, 'May God uproot you and throw you into the sea,' and it would obey you!

⁷"When a servant comes in from plowing or taking care of sheep, he doesn't just sit down and eat. ⁸He must first prepare his master's meal and serve him his supper before eating his own. ⁹And the servant is not even thanked, because he is merely doing what he is supposed to do. ¹⁰In the same way, when you obey me you should say, 'We are not worthy of praise. We are servants who have simply done our duty.' "

Ten Healed of Leprosy

¹¹As Jesus continued on toward Jerusalem, he reached the border between Galilee and Samaria. ¹²As he entered a village there, ten lepers stood at a distance, ¹³crying out, "Jesus, Master, have mercy on us!"

¹⁴He looked at them and said, "Go show yourselves to the priests." And as they went, their leprosy disappeared.

¹⁵One of them, when he saw that he was healed, came back to Jesus, shouting, "Praise God, I'm healed!" ¹⁶He fell face down on the ground at Jesus' feet, thanking him for what he had done. This man was a Samaritan.

¹⁷Jesus asked, "Didn't I heal ten men? Where are the other nine? ¹⁸Does only this foreigner return to give glory to God?" ¹⁹And Jesus said to the man, "Stand up and go. Your faith has made you well."

The Coming of the Kingdom

²⁰One day the Pharisees asked Jesus, "When will the Kingdom of God come?"

Jesus replied, "The Kingdom of God isn't ushered in with visible signs.*

17:3 Greek *your brother.* 17:20 Or *by your speculations.*

I BELIEVE God's Word clearly warns the unrepentant of the error of their ways. (16:29)

I DO NOT TEMPT others to sin. (17:1)

I WOULD DO nothing to harm a little child. (17:2)

I AM ALWAYS READY to forgive someone who wrongs me and then repents. (17:4)

I PRAY believing God can do anything. (17:6)

I AM QUICK to thank and praise God when he heals me. (17:15)

See the profile for the Pharisees (page 1087) at Matthew 12:14.

²¹You won't be able to say, 'Here it is!' or 'It's over there!' For the Kingdom of God is among you.*"

²²Later he talked again about this with his disciples. "The time is coming when you will long to share in the days of the Son of Man, but you won't be able to," he said. ²³"Reports will reach you that the Son of Man has returned and that he is in this place or that. Don't believe such reports or go out to look for him. ²⁴For when the Son of Man returns, you will know it beyond all doubt. It will be as evident as the lightning that flashes across the sky. ²⁵But first the Son of Man must suffer terribly* and be rejected by this generation.

²⁶"When the Son of Man returns, the world will be like the people were in Noah's day. ²⁷In those days before the flood, the people enjoyed banquets and parties and weddings right up to the time Noah entered his boat and the flood came to destroy them all.

²⁸"And the world will be as it was in the days of Lot. People went about their daily business—eating and drinking, buying and selling, farming and building—²⁹until the morning Lot left Sodom. Then fire and burning sulfur rained down from heaven and destroyed them all. ³⁰Yes, it will be 'business as usual' right up to the hour when the Son of Man returns.* ³¹On that day a person outside the house* must not go into the house to pack. A person in the field must not return to town. ³²Remember what happened to Lot's wife! ³³Whoever clings to this life will lose it, and whoever loses this life will save it. ³⁴That night two people will be asleep in one bed; one will be taken away, and the other will be left. ³⁵Two women will be grinding flour together at the mill; one will be taken, the other left.*"

³⁷"Lord, where will this happen?" the disciples asked.

Jesus replied, "Just as the gathering of vultures shows there is a carcass nearby, so these signs indicate that the end is near."*

CHAPTER 18

Story of the Persistent Widow

One day Jesus told his disciples a story to illustrate their need for constant prayer and to show them that they must never give up. ²"There was a judge in a certain city," he said, "who was a godless man with great contempt for everyone. ³A widow of that city came to him repeatedly, appealing for justice against someone who had harmed her. ⁴The judge ignored her for a while, but eventually she wore him out. 'I fear neither God nor man,' he said to himself, ⁵'but this woman is driving me crazy. I'm going to see that she gets justice, because she is wearing me out with her constant requests!' "

⁶Then the Lord said, "Learn a lesson from this evil judge. ⁷Even he rendered a just decision in the end, so don't you think God will surely give justice to his chosen people who plead with him day and night? Will he keep putting them off? ⁸I tell you, he will grant justice to them quickly! But when I, the Son of Man, return, how many will I find who have faith?"

Story of the Pharisee and Tax Collector

⁹Then Jesus told this story to some who had great self-confidence and scorned everyone else: ¹⁰"Two men went to the Temple to pray. One was a Pharisee, and the other was a dishonest tax collector. ¹¹The proud Pharisee stood by himself and prayed this prayer: 'I thank you, God, that I am not a sinner like everyone else, especially like that tax collector over there! For I never cheat, I don't sin, I don't commit adultery, ¹²I fast twice a week, and I give you a tenth of my income.'

¹³"But the tax collector stood at a distance and dared not even lift his eyes

I REFUSE to believe any report that says Jesus has returned to earth and is in this or that place, waiting to be revealed. (17:23)

See Noah's profile (page 13) at Genesis 6:9.

I REFUSE to cling to this life and will follow Jesus even to death. (17:33)

I BELIEVE many will be taken away in judgment when Jesus returns. (17:35)

I NEED TO PRAY constantly and never give up. (18:1)

I KNOW God will not put off his children who plead with him. (18:7)

See the profile for the Pharisees (page 1087) at Matthew 12:14.

17:21 Or *within you.* 17:25 Or *suffer many things.* 17:30 Or *on the day the Son of Man is revealed.* 17:31 Greek *on the roof.* 17:35 Some manuscripts add verse 36, *Two men will be working in the field; one will be taken, the other left.* 17:37 Greek *Wherever the carcass is, the vultures gather.*

I HAVE ASKED God to be merciful to me, a sinner, and now am justified before him. (18:13)

to heaven as he prayed. Instead, he beat his chest in sorrow, saying, 'O God, be merciful to me, for I am a sinner.' [14]I tell you, this sinner, not the Pharisee, returned home justified before God. For the proud will be humbled, but the humble will be honored."

Jesus Blesses the Children

I ACTIVELY ENCOURAGE children to come to Jesus. (18:16)

[15]One day some parents brought their little children to Jesus so he could touch them and bless them, but the disciples told them not to bother him. [16]Then Jesus called for the children and said to the disciples, "Let the children come to me. Don't stop them! For the Kingdom of God belongs to such as these. [17]I assure you, anyone who doesn't have their kind of faith will never get into the Kingdom of God."

The Rich Man

[18]Once a religious leader asked Jesus this question: "Good teacher, what should I do to get eternal life?"

[19]"Why do you call me good?" Jesus asked him. "Only God is truly good. [20]But as for your question, you know the commandments: 'Do not commit adultery. Do not murder. Do not steal. Do not testify falsely. Honor your father and mother.'* "

[21]The man replied, "I've obeyed all these commandments since I was a child."

I LET nothing keep me from gaining eternal life. (18:22)

See the Rich Young Man's profile (page 1133) at Mark 10:22.

[22]"There is still one thing you lack," Jesus said. "Sell all you have and give the money to the poor, and you will have treasure in heaven. Then come, follow me." [23]But when the man heard this, he became sad because he was very rich.

[24]Jesus watched him go and then said to his disciples, "How hard it is for rich people to get into the Kingdom of God! [25]It is easier for a camel to go through the eye of a needle than for a rich person to enter the Kingdom of God!"

[26]Those who heard this said, "Then who in the world can be saved?"

I BELIEVE God can save anyone, no matter what his or her past deeds or current circumstances. (18:27)

See Peter's profile (page 1111) at Matthew 26:75.

[27]He replied, "What is impossible from a human perspective is possible with God."

[28]Peter said, "We have left our homes and followed you."

I BELIEVE the Lord rewards me both now and eternally for sacrificing for his sake here on earth. (18:29)

[29]"Yes," Jesus replied, "and I assure you, everyone who has given up house or wife or brothers or parents or children, for the sake of the Kingdom of God, [30]will be repaid many times over in this life, as well as receiving eternal life in the world to come."

Jesus Again Predicts His Death

I BELIEVE all the predictions of the Old Testament prophets concerning Jesus' first coming came true. (18:31)

[31]Gathering the twelve disciples around him, Jesus told them, "As you know, we are going to Jerusalem. And when we get there, all the predictions of the ancient prophets concerning the Son of Man will come true. [32]He will be handed over to the Romans to be mocked, treated shamefully, and spit upon. [33]They will whip him and kill him, but on the third day he will rise again."

[34]But they didn't understand a thing he said. Its significance was hidden from them, and they failed to grasp what he was talking about.

Jesus Heals a Blind Beggar

See Blind Bartimaeus's profile (page 1135) at Mark 10:52.

See David's profile (page 629) at Psalm 3:1.

[35]As they approached Jericho, a blind beggar was sitting beside the road. [36]When he heard the noise of a crowd going past, he asked what was happening. [37]They told him that Jesus of Nazareth was going by. [38]So he began shouting, "Jesus, Son of David, have mercy on me!" [39]The crowds ahead of Jesus tried to hush the man, but he only shouted louder, "Son of David, have mercy on me!"

18:20 Exod 20:12-16; Deut 5:16-20.

⁴⁰When Jesus heard him, he stopped and ordered that the man be brought to him. ⁴¹Then Jesus asked the man, "What do you want me to do for you?"

"Lord," he pleaded, "I want to see!"

⁴²And Jesus said, "All right, you can see! Your faith has healed you." ⁴³Instantly the man could see, and he followed Jesus, praising God. And all who saw it praised God, too.

I PRAISE God each time he heals someone. (18:43)

CHAPTER 19

Jesus and Zacchaeus

Jesus entered Jericho and made his way through the town. ²There was a man there named Zacchaeus. He was one of the most influential Jews in the Roman tax-collecting business, and he had become very rich. ³He tried to get a look at Jesus, but he was too short to see over the crowds. ⁴So he ran ahead and climbed a sycamore tree beside the road, so he could watch from there.

⁵When Jesus came by, he looked up at Zacchaeus and called him by name. "Zacchaeus!" he said. "Quick, come down! For I must be a guest in your home today."

I AM THANKFUL that Jesus knows me by name. (19:5)

⁶Zacchaeus quickly climbed down and took Jesus to his house in great excitement and joy. ⁷But the crowds were displeased. "He has gone to be the guest of a notorious sinner," they grumbled.

⁸Meanwhile, Zacchaeus stood there and said to the Lord, "I will give half my wealth to the poor, Lord, and if I have overcharged people on their taxes, I will give them back four times as much!"

I PAY restitution to those from whom I have stolen. (19:8)

⁹Jesus responded, "Salvation has come to this home today, for this man has shown himself to be a son of Abraham. ¹⁰And I, the Son of Man, have come to seek and save those like him who are lost."

I BELIEVE the Lord rejoices when he sees the fruits of repentance in our lives. (19:9)

See Abraham's profile (page 19) at Genesis 15:6.

Story of the Ten Servants

¹¹ The crowd was listening to everything Jesus said. And because he was nearing Jerusalem, he told a story to correct the impression that the Kingdom of God would begin right away. ¹²He said, "A nobleman was called away to a distant empire to be crowned king and then return. ¹³Before he left, he called together ten servants and gave them ten pounds of silver* to invest for him while he was gone. ¹⁴But his people hated him and sent a delegation after him to say they did not want him to be their king.

I VERY MUCH WANT Jesus to be my King. (19:14)

¹⁵"When he returned, the king called in the servants to whom he had given the money. He wanted to find out what they had done with the money and what their profits were. ¹⁶The first servant reported a tremendous gain—ten times as much as the original amount! ¹⁷'Well done!' the king exclaimed. 'You are a trustworthy servant. You have been faithful with the little I entrusted to you, so you will be governor of ten cities as your reward.'

I STRIVE to be trustworthy and faithful with whatever the Lord entrusts to me. (19:17)

¹⁸"The next servant also reported a good gain—five times the original amount. ¹⁹'Well done!' the king said. 'You can be governor over five cities.'

²⁰"But the third servant brought back only the original amount of money and said, 'I hid it and kept it safe. ²¹I was afraid because you are a hard man to deal with, taking what isn't yours and harvesting crops you didn't plant.'

²²"'You wicked servant!' the king roared. 'Hard, am I? If you knew so much about me and how tough I am, ²³why didn't you deposit the money in the bank so I could at least get some interest on it?' ²⁴Then turning to the others standing nearby, the king ordered, 'Take the money from this servant, and give it to the one who earned the most.'

I BELIEVE those who use well what the Lord gives them will be given even more. (19:26)

²⁵"'But, master,' they said, 'that servant has enough already!'

²⁶"'Yes,' the king replied, 'but to those who use well what they are given, even more will be given. But from those who are unfaithful,* even what little they have will be taken away. ²⁷And now about these enemies of mine who

I BELIEVE those who hate the Lord face certain judgment if they do not repent. (19:27)

19:13 Greek 10 minas; 1 mina was was worth about 3 months' wages.   19:26 Or who have nothing.

didn't want me to be their king—bring them in and execute them right here in my presence.' "

The Triumphal Entry

²⁸After telling this story, Jesus went on toward Jerusalem, walking ahead of his disciples. ²⁹As they came to the towns of Bethphage and Bethany, on the Mount of Olives, he sent two disciples ahead. ³⁰"Go into that village over there," he told them, "and as you enter it, you will see a colt tied there that has never been ridden. Untie it and bring it here. ³¹If anyone asks what you are doing, just say, 'The Lord needs it.' "

³²So they went and found the colt, just as Jesus had said. ³³And sure enough, as they were untying it, the owners asked them, "Why are you untying our colt?"

³⁴And the disciples simply replied, "The Lord needs it." ³⁵So they brought the colt to Jesus and threw their garments over it for him to ride on.

³⁶Then the crowds spread out their coats on the road ahead of Jesus. ³⁷As they reached the place where the road started down from the Mount of Olives, all of his followers began to shout and sing as they walked along, praising God for all the wonderful miracles they had seen.

³⁸"Bless the King who comes in the name of the Lord!
　Peace in heaven
　　and glory in highest heaven!"*

³⁹But some of the Pharisees among the crowd said, "Teacher, rebuke your followers for saying things like that!"

⁴⁰He replied, "If they kept quiet, the stones along the road would burst into cheers!"

Jesus Weeps over Jerusalem

⁴¹But as they came closer to Jerusalem and Jesus saw the city ahead, he began to cry. ⁴²"I wish that even today you would find the way of peace. But now it is too late, and peace is hidden from you. ⁴³Before long your enemies will build ramparts against your walls and encircle you and close in on you. ⁴⁴They will crush you to the ground, and your children with you. Your enemies will not leave a single stone in place, because you have rejected the opportunity God offered you."

Jesus Clears the Temple

⁴⁵Then Jesus entered the Temple and began to drive out the merchants from their stalls. ⁴⁶He told them, "The Scriptures declare, 'My Temple will be a place of prayer,' but you have turned it into a den of thieves."*

⁴⁷After that, he taught daily in the Temple, but the leading priests, the teachers of religious law, and the other leaders of the people began planning how to kill him. ⁴⁸But they could think of nothing, because all the people hung on every word he said.

CHAPTER 20

The Authority of Jesus Challenged

One day as Jesus was teaching and preaching the Good News in the Temple, the leading priests and teachers of religious law and other leaders came up to him. ²They demanded, "By whose authority did you drive out the merchants from the Temple?* Who gave you such authority?"

³"Let me ask you a question first," he replied. ⁴"Did John's baptism come from heaven, or was it merely human?"

⁵They talked it over among themselves. "If we say it was from heaven, he will ask why we didn't believe him. ⁶But if we say it was merely human, the

---

I AM WILLING to give to the Lord whatever he asks. (19:34)

See the profile for the Pharisees (page 1087) at Matthew 12:14.

I WEEP over the tragedy awaiting those who continue to reject Jesus. (19:41)

I HANG on every word Jesus has said. (19:48)

I RESPECT Jesus' authority as God's Son. (20:2)

See John the Baptist's profile (page 1117) at Mark 1:4.

19:38 Pss 118:26; 148:1.　19:46 Isa 56:7; Jer 7:11.　20:2 Or *By whose authority do you do these things?*

people will stone us, because they are convinced he was a prophet." ⁷Finally they replied, "We don't know."

⁸And Jesus responded, "Then I won't answer your question either."

Story of the Evil Farmers

⁹Now Jesus turned to the people again and told them this story: "A man planted a vineyard, leased it out to tenant farmers, and moved to another country to live for several years. ¹⁰At grape-picking time, he sent one of his servants to collect his share of the crop. But the farmers attacked the servant, beat him up, and sent him back empty-handed. ¹¹So the owner sent another servant, but the same thing happened; he was beaten up and treated shamefully, and he went away empty-handed. ¹²A third man was sent and the same thing happened. He, too, was wounded and chased away.

¹³" 'What will I do?' the owner asked himself. 'I know! I'll send my cherished son. Surely they will respect him.'

¹⁴"But when the farmers saw his son, they said to each other, 'Here comes the heir to this estate. Let's kill him and get the estate for ourselves!' ¹⁵So they dragged him out of the vineyard and murdered him.

LIKE ZACCHAEUS   *I demonstrate my faith by making restitution*
Luke 19:10   *and asking others for forgiveness.*

Ever climb a tree? If so, why?

Zacchaeus may have convinced himself he only wanted to get a better look at Jesus when he climbed—very ungentlemanly—up the sycamore tree. But his heart must have been wanting more. One upward look from the Lord and the words "I must be your guest today," and Zacchaeus was scrambling back down in excitement. He didn't need the crowds to tell him he was a notorious sinner, but now he saw the way out. The love and attention of the Messiah were enough to flood Zacchaeus's heart with the desire to shed his old sinful life and start anew with God—and with everyone else, too.

With the enthusiasm of a true businessman, Zacchaeus began making plans for his new life. It would take a lot of research, paperwork, and humility, but he planned to repay everyone he had overcharged—four times what he owed them. And what good he could do by designating half of his wealth to improve the lives of the poor.

True faith produces in us a desire to live a just life!

Jesus recognized this sign of salvation and Zacchaeus' true identity. This man had been lost but now was saved. This man, like Abraham of old, had believed and received righteousness. And like Abraham, he demonstrated his obedience by obeying God's commands. As a result, Zacchaeus gained new, eternal life with God. From that day on, he was a different person—and it was obvious for everyone to see!

Like Zacchaeus, our faith cannot remain an ethereal experience between us and God. We cannot simply bask in the blessings of being loved by the Lord. Whether it means repaying what we've stolen (Ephesians 4:28) or correcting falsehoods (Ephesians 4:25), you and I are compelled by God to make things right with others.

○ *Today's Scripture reading is Luke 19:1-10.*

"What do you suppose the owner of the vineyard will do to those farmers?" Jesus asked. ¹⁶"I'll tell you—he will come and kill them all and lease the vineyard to others."

"But God forbid that such a thing should ever happen," his listeners protested.

¹⁷Jesus looked at them and said, "Then what do the Scriptures mean?

I GLADLY ACCEPT Jesus.
(20:17)

'The stone rejected by the builders
has now become the cornerstone.'*

20:17 Ps 118:22.

¹⁸All who stumble over that stone will be broken to pieces, and it will crush anyone on whom it falls."

¹⁹When the teachers of religious law and the leading priests heard this story, they wanted to arrest Jesus immediately because they realized he was pointing at them—that they were the farmers in the story. But they were afraid there would be a riot if they arrested him.

Taxes for Caesar

²⁰Watching for their opportunity, the leaders sent secret agents pretending to be honest men. They tried to get Jesus to say something that could be reported to the Roman governor so he would arrest Jesus. ²¹They said, "Teacher, we know that you speak and teach what is right and are not influenced by what others think. You sincerely teach the ways of God. ²²Now tell us—is it right to pay taxes to the Roman government or not?"

²³He saw through their trickery and said, ²⁴"Show me a Roman coin.* Whose picture and title are stamped on it?"

"Caesar's," they replied.

²⁵"Well then," he said, "give to Caesar what belongs to him. But everything that belongs to God must be given to God." ²⁶So they failed to trap him in the presence of the people. Instead, they were amazed by his answer, and they were silenced.

Discussion about Resurrection

²⁷Then some Sadducees stepped forward—a group of Jews who say there is no resurrection after death. ²⁸They posed this question: "Teacher, Moses gave us a law that if a man dies, leaving a wife but no children, his brother should marry the widow and have a child who will be the brother's heir.* ²⁹Well, there were seven brothers. The oldest married and then died without children. ³⁰His brother married the widow, but he also died. Still no children. ³¹And so it went, one after the other, until each of the seven had married her and died, leaving no children. ³²Finally, the woman died, too. ³³So tell us, whose wife will she be in the resurrection? For all seven were married to her!"

³⁴Jesus replied, "Marriage is for people here on earth. ³⁵But that is not the way it will be in the age to come. For those worthy of being raised from the dead won't be married then. ³⁶And they will never die again. In these respects they are like angels. They are children of God raised up to new life. ³⁷But now, as to whether the dead will be raised—even Moses proved this when he wrote about the burning bush. Long after Abraham, Isaac, and Jacob had died, he referred to the Lord* as 'the God of Abraham, the God of Isaac, and the God of Jacob.'* ³⁸So he is the God of the living, not the dead. They are all alive to him."

³⁹"Well said, Teacher!" remarked some of the teachers of religious law who were standing there. ⁴⁰And that ended their questions; no one dared to ask any more.

Whose Son Is the Messiah?

⁴¹Then Jesus presented them with a question. "Why is it," he asked, "that the Messiah is said to be the son of David? ⁴²For David himself wrote in the book of Psalms:

'The Lord said to my Lord,
Sit in honor at my right hand
⁴³   until I humble your enemies,
    making them a footstool under your feet.'*

⁴⁴Since David called him Lord, how can he be his son at the same time?"

⁴⁵Then, with the crowds listening, he turned to his disciples and said,

---

I DO NOT PRETEND to have more faith in Jesus than I really have. (20:21)

I ACKNOWLEDGE that everything I have is given to me by God. (20:25)

See the profile for the Sadducees (page 1103) at Matthew 22:23.

See Moses' profile (page 73) at Exodus 5:1.

I BELIEVE marriage is for people here on earth, not for those in heaven. (20:34)

I AM WORTHY of being raised from the dead because God has made me his child and given me new, eternal life. (20:35)

I HAVE no question that the dead will be raised. (20:37)

See Abraham's profile (page 19) at Genesis 15:6.

I BELIEVE God is the God of the living— that is every believer who has died is alive with him. (20:38)

See David's profile (page 629) at Psalm 3:1.

I BELIEVE Jesus is the Messiah, the son of David, the Lord of lords, who sits at God the Father's right hand. (20:42)

20:24 Greek *a denarius.*   20:28 Deut 25:5-6.   20:37a Greek *when he wrote about the bush. He referred to the Lord.*
20:37b Exod 3:6.   20:42-43 Ps 110:1.

[46]"Beware of these teachers of religious law! For they love to parade in flowing robes and to have everyone bow to them as they walk in the marketplaces. And how they love the seats of honor in the synagogues and at banquets. [47]But they shamelessly cheat widows out of their property, and then, to cover up the kind of people they really are, they make long prayers in public. Because of this, their punishment will be the greater."

CHAPTER 21

The Widow's Offering

While Jesus was in the Temple, he watched the rich people putting their gifts into the collection box. [2]Then a poor widow came by and dropped in two pennies.* [3]"I assure you," he said, "this poor widow has given more than all the rest of them. [4]For they have given a tiny part of their surplus, but she, poor as she is, has given everything she has."

Jesus Foretells the Future

[5]Some of his disciples began talking about the beautiful stonework of the Temple and the memorial decorations on the walls. But Jesus said, [6]"The time is coming when all these things will be so completely demolished that not one stone will be left on top of another."

[7]"Teacher," they asked, "when will all this take place? And will there be any sign ahead of time?"

[8]He replied, "Don't let anyone mislead you. For many will come in my name, claiming to be the Messiah* and saying, 'The time has come!' But don't believe them. [9]And when you hear of wars and insurrections, don't panic. Yes, these things must come, but the end won't follow immediately." [10]Then he added, "Nations and kingdoms will proclaim war against each other. [11]There will be great earthquakes, and there will be famines and epidemics in many lands, and there will be terrifying things and great miraculous signs in the heavens.

[12]"But before all this occurs, there will be a time of great persecution. You will be dragged into synagogues and prisons, and you will be accused before kings and governors of being my followers. [13]This will be your opportunity to tell them about me. [14]So don't worry about how to answer the charges against you, [15]for I will give you the right words and such wisdom that none of your opponents will be able to reply! [16]Even those closest to you—your parents, brothers, relatives, and friends—will betray you. And some of you will be killed. [17]And everyone will hate you because of your allegiance to me. [18]But not a hair of your head will perish! [19]By standing firm, you will win your souls.

[20]"And when you see Jerusalem surrounded by armies, then you will know that the time of its destruction has arrived. [21]Then those in Judea must flee to the hills. Let those in Jerusalem escape, and those outside the city should not enter it for shelter. [22]For those will be days of God's vengeance, and the prophetic words of the Scriptures will be fulfilled. [23]How terrible it will be for pregnant women and for mothers nursing their babies. For there will be great distress in the land and wrath upon this people. [24]They will be brutally killed by the sword or sent away as captives to all the nations of the world. And Jerusalem will be conquered and trampled down by the Gentiles until the age of the Gentiles comes to an end.

[25]"And there will be strange events in the skies—signs in the sun, moon, and stars. And down here on earth the nations will be in turmoil, perplexed by the roaring seas and strange tides. [26]The courage of many people will falter because of the fearful fate they see coming upon the earth, because the stability of the very heavens will be broken up. [27]Then everyone will see the Son of

I AM ON MY GUARD against spiritual leaders who do not live out God's principles in their private lives. (20:46)

See the Poor Widow's profile (page 1139) at Mark 12:42.

I GIVE sacrificially to the Lord, not just a tiny part of my surplus, trusting in his provision for all my needs. (21:4)

I BELIEVE the Temple and city of Jerusalem were completely destroyed in A.D. 70 as Lord Jesus foretold. (21:6)

I DO NOT PANIC when I hear of wars and natural disasters, because they are the beginning signs of Jesus' return. (21:9)

I USE harsh accusations as opportunities to tell my persecutors about Jesus. (21:13)

I KNOW many Christians will face and have faced intense hatred, betrayal, and even martyrdom for Jesus' sake, only to gain eternal life. (21:16)

I BELIEVE great signs will accompany Jesus' second coming. (21:25)

21:2 Greek 2 lepta.   21:8 Greek name, saying, 'I am.'

I BELIEVE everyone will see Jesus arrive on the clouds with power and great glory. (21:27)

Man arrive on the clouds with power and great glory.* [28] So when all these things begin to happen, stand straight and look up, for your salvation is near!"

[29] Then he gave them this illustration: "Notice the fig tree, or any other tree. [30] When the leaves come out, you know without being told that summer is near. [31] Just so, when you see the events I've described taking place, you can be sure that the Kingdom of God is near. [32] I assure you, this generation* will not pass from the scene until all these events have taken place. [33] Heaven and earth will disappear, but my words will remain forever.

I LIVE my life in constant preparation for Jesus' return, not wasting my time with temporal worries and careless living. (21:34)

[34] "Watch out! Don't let me find you living in careless ease and drunkenness, and filled with the worries of this life. Don't let that day catch you unaware, [35] as in a trap. For that day will come upon everyone living on the earth. [36] Keep a constant watch. And pray that, if possible, you may escape these horrors and stand before the Son of Man."

[37] Every day Jesus went to the Temple to teach, and each evening he returned to spend the night on the Mount of Olives. [38] The crowds gathered early each morning to hear him.

CHAPTER 22

Judas Agrees to Betray Jesus

The Festival of Unleavened Bread, which begins with the Passover celebration, was drawing near. [2] The leading priests and teachers of religious law were actively plotting Jesus' murder. But they wanted to kill him without starting a riot, a possibility they greatly feared.

See Judas's profile (page 1121) at Mark 3:19.

I DO NOT DELIGHT in evil plans. (22:5)

[3] Then Satan entered into Judas Iscariot, who was one of the twelve disciples, [4] and he went over to the leading priests and captains of the Temple guard to discuss the best way to betray Jesus to them. [5] They were delighted that he was ready to help them, and they promised him a reward. [6] So he began looking for an opportunity to betray Jesus so they could arrest him quietly when the crowds weren't around.

The Last Supper

See the profiles for Peter (page 1111) and John (page 1435) at Matthew 26:75 and Revelation 1:9.

I ASK, "Where?" when Jesus says, "Go." (22:9)

[7] Now the Festival of Unleavened Bread arrived, when the Passover lambs were sacrificed. [8] Jesus sent Peter and John ahead and said, "Go and prepare the Passover meal, so we can eat it together."

[9] "Where do you want us to go?" they asked him.

[10] He replied, "As soon as you enter Jerusalem, a man carrying a pitcher of water will meet you. Follow him. At the house he enters, [11] say to the owner, 'The Teacher asks, Where is the guest room where I can eat the Passover meal with my disciples?' [12] He will take you upstairs to a large room that is already set up. That is the place. Go ahead and prepare our supper there." [13] They went off to the city and found everything just as Jesus had said, and they prepared the Passover supper there.

I BELIEVE the Passover meal pictures God's new covenant of salvation through Jesus' death, burial, and resurrection. (22:15)

I BELIEVE the bread represents Jesus' body, broken on the cross for my salvation. (22:19)

[14] Then at the proper time Jesus and the twelve apostles sat down together at the table. [15] Jesus said, "I have looked forward to this hour with deep longing, anxious to eat this Passover meal with you before my suffering begins. [16] For I tell you now that I won't eat it again until it comes to fulfillment in the Kingdom of God."

[17] Then he took a cup of wine, and when he had given thanks for it, he said, "Take this and share it among yourselves. [18] For I will not drink wine again until the Kingdom of God has come."

[19] Then he took a loaf of bread; and when he had thanked God for it, he broke it in pieces and gave it to the disciples, saying, "This is my body, given for you. Do this in remembrance of me." [20] After supper he took another cup

21:27 See Dan 7:13. 21:32 Or this age, or this nation.

of wine and said, "This wine is the token of God's new covenant to save you—an agreement sealed with the blood I will pour out for you.*

²¹"But here at this table, sitting among us as a friend, is the man who will betray me. ²²For I, the Son of Man, must die since it is part of God's plan. But how terrible it will be for my betrayer!" ²³Then the disciples began to ask each other which of them would ever do such a thing.

²⁴And they began to argue among themselves as to who would be the greatest in the coming Kingdom. ²⁵Jesus told them, "In this world the kings and great men order their people around, and yet they are called 'friends of the people.' ²⁶But among you, those who are the greatest should take the lowest rank, and the leader should be like a servant. ²⁷Normally the master sits at the table and is served by his servants. But not here! For I am your servant. ²⁸You have remained true to me in my time of trial. ²⁹And just as my Father has granted me a Kingdom, I now grant you the right ³⁰to eat and drink at my table in that Kingdom. And you will sit on thrones, judging the twelve tribes of Israel.

Jesus Predicts Peter's Denial

³¹"Simon, Simon, Satan has asked to have all of you, to sift you like wheat. ³²But I have pleaded in prayer for you, Simon, that your faith should not fail. So when you have repented and turned to me again, strengthen and build up your brothers."

³³Peter said, "Lord, I am ready to go to prison with you, and even to die with you."

³⁴But Jesus said, "Peter, let me tell you something. The rooster will not crow tomorrow morning until you have denied three times that you even know me."

³⁵Then Jesus asked them, "When I sent you out to preach the Good News and you did not have money, a traveler's bag, or extra clothing, did you lack anything?"

"No," they replied.

³⁶"But now," he said, "take your money and a traveler's bag. And if you don't have a sword, sell your clothes and buy one! ³⁷For the time has come for this prophecy about me to be fulfilled: 'He was counted among those who were rebels.'* Yes, everything written about me by the prophets will come true."

³⁸"Lord," they replied, "we have two swords among us."

"That's enough," he said.

Jesus Prays on the Mount of Olives

³⁹Then, accompanied by the disciples, Jesus left the upstairs room and went as usual to the Mount of Olives. ⁴⁰There he told them, "Pray that you will not be overcome by temptation."

⁴¹He walked away, about a stone's throw, and knelt down and prayed, ⁴²"Father, if you are willing, please take this cup of suffering away from me. Yet I want your will, not mine." ⁴³Then an angel from heaven appeared and strengthened him. ⁴⁴He prayed more fervently, and he was in such agony of spirit that his sweat fell to the ground like great drops of blood.* ⁴⁵At last he stood up again and returned to the disciples, only to find them asleep, exhausted from grief. ⁴⁶"Why are you sleeping?" he asked. "Get up and pray. Otherwise temptation will overpower you."

Jesus Is Betrayed and Arrested

⁴⁷But even as he said this, a mob approached, led by Judas, one of his twelve disciples. Judas walked over to Jesus and greeted him with a kiss. ⁴⁸But Jesus said, "Judas, how can you betray me, the Son of Man, with a kiss?"

I BELIEVE the wine represents Jesus' blood, poured out for my salvation. (22:20)

I AM HUMBLED to think that Jesus made himself a servant of all—even to the point of death on the cross. (22:27)

I KNOW that Satan would like to ruin me. (22:31)

I UNDERSTAND that God's Good News never changes, but his methods for proclaiming it can vary. (22:36)

I PRAY that I will not be overcome by temptation. (22:40)

I KNEEL DOWN AND PRAY for God's will, not my own, to be done. (22:41)

22:19-20 Some manuscripts omit 22:19b-20, *given for you . . . I will pour out for you.* 22:37 Isa 53:12.
22:43-44 These verses are not included in many ancient manuscripts.

⁴⁹When the other disciples saw what was about to happen, they exclaimed, "Lord, should we fight? We brought the swords!" ⁵⁰And one of them slashed at the high priest's servant and cut off his right ear.

⁵¹But Jesus said, "Don't resist anymore." And he touched the place where the man's ear had been and healed him. ⁵²Then Jesus spoke to the leading priests and captains of the Temple guard and the other leaders who headed the mob. "Am I some dangerous criminal," he asked, "that you have come armed with swords and clubs to arrest me? ⁵³Why didn't you arrest me in the Temple? I was there every day. But this is your moment, the time when the power of darkness reigns."

Peter Denies Jesus

⁵⁴So they arrested him and led him to the high priest's residence, and Peter was following far behind. ⁵⁵The guards lit a fire in the courtyard and sat around it, and Peter joined them there. ⁵⁶A servant girl noticed him in the firelight and began staring at him. Finally she said, "This man was one of Jesus' followers!"

⁵⁷Peter denied it. "Woman," he said, "I don't even know the man!"

⁵⁸After a while someone else looked at him and said, "You must be one of them!"

"No, man, I'm not!" Peter replied.

⁵⁹About an hour later someone else insisted, "This must be one of Jesus' disciples because he is a Galilean, too."

⁶⁰But Peter said, "Man, I don't know what you are talking about." And as soon as he said these words, the rooster crowed. ⁶¹At that moment the Lord turned and looked at Peter. Then Peter remembered that the Lord had said, "Before the rooster crows tomorrow morning, you will deny me three times." ⁶²And Peter left the courtyard, crying bitterly.

⁶³Now the guards in charge of Jesus began mocking and beating him. ⁶⁴They blindfolded him; then they hit him and asked, "Who hit you that time, you prophet?" ⁶⁵And they threw all sorts of terrible insults at him.

Jesus before the Council

⁶⁶At daybreak all the leaders of the people assembled, including the leading priests and the teachers of religious law. Jesus was led before this high council,* ⁶⁷and they said, "Tell us if you are the Messiah."

But he replied, "If I tell you, you won't believe me. ⁶⁸And if I ask you a question, you won't answer. ⁶⁹But the time is soon coming when I, the Son of Man, will be sitting at God's right hand in the place of power."*

⁷⁰They all shouted, "Then you claim you are the Son of God?"

And he replied, "You are right in saying that I am."

⁷¹"What need do we have for other witnesses?" they shouted. "We ourselves heard him say it."

CHAPTER 23

Jesus' Trial before Pilate

Then the entire council took Jesus over to Pilate, the Roman governor. ²They began at once to state their case: "This man has been leading our people to ruin by telling them not to pay their taxes to the Roman government and by claiming he is the Messiah, a king."

³So Pilate asked him, "Are you the King of the Jews?"

Jesus replied, "Yes, it is as you say."

⁴Pilate turned to the leading priests and to the crowd and said, "I find nothing wrong with this man!"

22:66 Greek *before their Sanhedrin.*   22:69 See Ps 110:1.

I DO NOT BELIEVE Jesus wants me to take up armed resistance against those who oppose his name. (22:51)

I KNOW Jesus turns to look at me when I fail him; he doesn't turn away and forsake me. (22:61)

I BELIEVE Jesus is the Messiah, the Son of God who sits in the place of power. (22:67)

See Pilate's profile (page 1229) at John 19:16.

I BELIEVE Jesus truly is the Messiah, the King of the Jews, the Lord of all. (23:2)

⁵Then they became desperate. "But he is causing riots everywhere he goes, all over Judea, from Galilee to Jerusalem!"

⁶"Oh, is he a Galilean?" Pilate asked. ⁷When they answered that he was, Pilate sent him to Herod Antipas, because Galilee was under Herod's jurisdiction, and Herod happened to be in Jerusalem at the time.

⁸Herod was delighted at the opportunity to see Jesus, because he had heard about him and had been hoping for a long time to see him perform a miracle. ⁹He asked Jesus question after question, but Jesus refused to answer. ¹⁰Meanwhile, the leading priests and the teachers of religious law stood there shouting their accusations. ¹¹Now Herod and his soldiers began mocking and ridiculing Jesus. Then they put a royal robe on him and sent him back to Pilate. ¹²Herod and Pilate, who had been enemies before, became friends that day.

I WOULD NEVER DREAM of mocking Jesus. (23:11)

¹³Then Pilate called together the leading priests and other religious leaders, along with the people, ¹⁴and he announced his verdict. "You brought this man to me, accusing him of leading a revolt. I have examined him thoroughly on this point in your presence and find him innocent. ¹⁵Herod came to the same conclusion and sent him back to us. Nothing this man has done calls for the death penalty. ¹⁶So I will have him flogged, but then I will release him."*

I BELIEVE Jesus had done nothing deserving of punishment, let alone the death penalty. (23:15)

LIKE THE DYING THIEF
Luke 23:42

I trust God today and receive forgiveness of sins and eternal life with God forever.

The young man leaned over the bed, his strong hands surrounding the old man's frail ones. "Do you believe Jesus died for you, Grandpa? Do you want to trust him to save you?" The old man nodded his head and gave up his lifelong antagonism toward his Creator. He whispered, "Yes, I do want Jesus to be my Savior." His head fell back on the pillow, and a few hours later he slipped into the presence of God. Once again, God's mercy pursued a sinner right to death's door. With simple faith, that sinner was instantly snatched from judgment and shortly thereafter entered into glory.

The thief hung contorted and writhing for breath on a Roman cross. Anger and hatred raged in his bursting heart—until he realized who the man was hanging beside him. Was it something Jesus said or the sheer presence of God that convinced him? The thief quieted down, had a complete change of heart, and offered an amazing prayer to the one dying beside him.

Jesus granted the thief his simple request—and more! "Today you will be with me in paradise." There was no time for probation or restitution for this man, but salvation came immediately. Right then, Jesus was paying for his sins. That day Jesus would walk with him in paradise!

Scripture makes it clear that Jesus welcomes you and me into his family the moment we believe. The transfer is swift and sure—whether we live on earth another fifty years or enter heaven within a few heartbeats.

Augustine once observed, "There is one case of deathbed repentance recorded, that of the penitent thief, that none should despair; and only one that none should presume."

Why put off trusting Jesus for a day longer? Now is the day of salvation! (2 Corinthians 6:1-2).

○ *Today's Scripture reading is Luke 23:26-43.*

---

¹⁸Then a mighty roar rose from the crowd, and with one voice they shouted, "Kill him, and release Barabbas to us!" ¹⁹(Barabbas was in prison for murder and for taking part in an insurrection in Jerusalem against the government.) ²⁰Pilate argued with them, because he wanted to release Jesus. ²¹But they shouted, "Crucify him! Crucify him!"

²²For the third time he demanded, "Why? What crime has he committed? I have found no reason to sentence him to death. I will therefore flog him and let him go."

23:16 Some manuscripts add verse 17, *For it was necessary for him to release one [prisoner] for them during the feast.*

I DO NOT GIVE IN to the sinful demands of the crowd, no matter how long and hard they insist. (23:24)

I BELIEVE Jesus willingly died for the sins of the whole world, even those of his executioners. (23:34)

I BELIEVE Jesus truly is God's Chosen One, the Messiah, the King of the Jews, the Lord of all. (23:35)

I BELIEVE Jesus willingly died to save us, even though he could have saved himself. (23:37)

I BELIEVE Jesus gladly welcomed the repentant thief into paradise. (23:42)

I BELIEVE God the Father created many spectacular signs to prove it was his Son, Jesus, dying on the cross. (23:44)

I BELIEVE Jesus willingly gave his life on the cross—no one took it from him. (23:46)

I AM FILLED with sorrow to think of all Jesus suffered on the cross to pay the penalty for my sins. (23:48)

See *Joseph of Arimathea's profile (page 1113) at Matthew 27:57.*

---

²³But the crowd shouted louder and louder for Jesus' death, and their voices prevailed. ²⁴So Pilate sentenced Jesus to die as they demanded. ²⁵As they had requested, he released Barabbas, the man in prison for insurrection and murder. But he delivered Jesus over to them to do as they wished.

The Crucifixion

²⁶As they led Jesus away, Simon of Cyrene,* who was coming in from the country just then, was forced to follow Jesus and carry his cross. ²⁷Great crowds trailed along behind, including many grief-stricken women. ²⁸But Jesus turned and said to them, "Daughters of Jerusalem, don't weep for me, but weep for yourselves and for your children. ²⁹For the days are coming when they will say, 'Fortunate indeed are the women who are childless, the wombs that have not borne a child and the breasts that have never nursed.' ³⁰People will beg the mountains to fall on them and the hills to bury them. ³¹For if these things are done when the tree is green, what will happen when it is dry?*"

³² Two others, both criminals, were led out to be executed with him. ³³Finally, they came to a place called The Skull.* All three were crucified there—Jesus on the center cross, and the two criminals on either side. ³⁴Jesus said, "Father, forgive these people, because they don't know what they are doing."* And the soldiers gambled for his clothes by throwing dice.* ³⁵The crowd watched, and the leaders laughed and scoffed. "He saved others," they said, "let him save himself if he is really God's Chosen One, the Messiah." ³⁶The soldiers mocked him, too, by offering him a drink of sour wine. ³⁷They called out to him, "If you are the King of the Jews, save yourself!" ³⁸A signboard was nailed to the cross above him with these words: "This is the King of the Jews."

³⁹One of the criminals hanging beside him scoffed, "So you're the Messiah, are you? Prove it by saving yourself—and us, too, while you're at it!" ⁴⁰But the other criminal protested, "Don't you fear God even when you are dying? ⁴¹We deserve to die for our evil deeds, but this man hasn't done anything wrong." ⁴² Then he said, "Jesus, remember me when you come into your Kingdom."

⁴³And Jesus replied, "I assure you, today you will be with me in paradise."

The Death of Jesus

⁴⁴By this time it was noon, and darkness fell across the whole land until three o'clock. ⁴⁵ The light from the sun was gone. And suddenly, the thick veil hanging in the Temple was torn apart. ⁴⁶Then Jesus shouted, "Father, I entrust my spirit into your hands!"* And with those words he breathed his last.

⁴⁷When the captain of the Roman soldiers handling the executions saw what had happened, he praised God and said, "Surely this man was innocent.*" ⁴⁸And when the crowd that came to see the crucifixion saw all that had happened, they went home in deep sorrow.* ⁴⁹But Jesus' friends, including the women who had followed him from Galilee, stood at a distance watching.

The Burial of Jesus

⁵⁰Now there was a good and righteous man named Joseph. He was a member of the Jewish high council, ⁵¹but he had not agreed with the decision and actions of the other religious leaders. He was from the town of Arimathea in Judea, and he had been waiting for the Kingdom of God to come. ⁵²He went to Pilate and asked for Jesus' body. ⁵³Then he took the body down from the cross and wrapped it in a long linen cloth and laid it in a new tomb that had

---

23:26 *Cyrene* was a city in northern Africa. **23:31** Or *If these things are done to me, the living tree, what will happen to you, the dry tree?* **23:33** Sometimes rendered *Calvary*, which comes from the Latin word for "skull." **23:34a** This sentence is not included in many ancient manuscripts. **23:34b** Greek *by casting lots.* See Ps 22:18. **23:46** Ps 31:5. **23:47** Or *righteous.* **23:48** Greek *beating their breasts.*

been carved out of rock. ⁵⁴This was done late on Friday afternoon, the day of preparation* for the Sabbath.

⁵⁵As his body was taken away, the women from Galilee followed and saw the tomb where they placed his body. ⁵⁶Then they went home and prepared spices and ointments to embalm him. But by the time they were finished it was the Sabbath, so they rested all that day as required by the law.

I BELIEVE Jesus' body was buried publicly in the presence of several known witnesses soon after he died on the cross. (23:55)

CHAPTER 24

The Resurrection

But very early on Sunday morning* the women came to the tomb, taking the spices they had prepared. ²They found that the stone covering the entrance had been rolled aside. ³So they went in, but they couldn't find the body of the Lord Jesus. ⁴They were puzzled, trying to think what could have happened to it. Suddenly, two men appeared to them, clothed in dazzling robes. ⁵The women were terrified and bowed low before them. Then the men asked, "Why are you looking in a tomb for someone who is alive? ⁶He isn't here! He has risen from the dead! Don't you remember what he told you back in Galilee, ⁷that the Son of Man must be betrayed into the hands of sinful men and be crucified, and that he would rise again the third day?"

I BELIEVE the Good News that Jesus died for my sins, was buried, and rose again on the third day! (24:7)

LIKE CLEOPAS   *I look to God every time I break bread.*

Luke 24:31

Doesn't it seem a bit unusual that Jesus spent so much time eating and drinking with his disciples? What does stopping to have a meal have to do with anything? It's something we do all the time—which is exactly why Jesus seized upon it.

Repeatedly throughout his earthly ministry, Jesus talked about the wonderful feast in the Kingdom of Heaven, when the Lord would celebrate with believers from all ages in glory. It's a banquet no one wants to miss!

Jesus also used meals as opportunities to pray to God the Father (9:16) and to tell his disciples, "sinners," Pharisees, and the crowds something about the Kingdom of Heaven (14:7-24; 19:1-10).

Right before his death, Jesus transformed the bread and wine of the Passover feast into powerful symbols of what the Christian faith is all about (22:7-30).

After his resurrection, Jesus kept right on eating with his disciples. His first meal was with an otherwise unknown disciple named Cleopas, who rushed back to Jerusalem to tell the apostles that he had seen the resurrected Lord Jesus. Imagine his surprise when the Lord suddenly appeared among them and asked for something else to eat!

Cleopas never looked at another meal the same. Every piece of fresh-baked bread, every piece of broiled fish, every cup of wine became an instant reminder to seize the opportunity to look to the resurrected Lord Jesus with thanksgiving, to fellowship with other believers, and to share his faith with others who hadn't trusted God yet.

The apostle Paul makes it clear the same experience can be ours today (1 Corinthians 10:16-31; 11:17-34).

○ *Today's Scripture reading is Luke 24.*

⁸Then they remembered that he had said this. ⁹So they rushed back to tell his eleven disciples—and everyone else—what had happened. ¹⁰The women who went to the tomb were Mary Magdalene, Joanna, Mary the mother of James, and several others. They told the apostles what had happened, ¹¹but the story sounded like nonsense, so they didn't believe it. ¹²However, Peter ran to the tomb to look. Stooping, he peered in and saw the empty linen wrappings; then he went home again, wondering what had happened.*

I AM ANXIOUS to tell others the Good News about Jesus. (24:9)

See Peter's profile (page 1111) at Matthew 26:75.

23:54 Greek *on the day of preparation.*   24:1 Greek *But on the first day of the week, very early in the morning.*
24:12 Some manuscripts do not include this verse.

The Walk to Emmaus

[13]That same day two of Jesus' followers were walking to the village of Emmaus, seven miles* out of Jerusalem. [14]As they walked along they were talking about everything that had happened. [15]Suddenly, Jesus himself came along and joined them and began walking beside them. [16]But they didn't know who he was, because God kept them from recognizing him.

[17]"You seem to be in a deep discussion about something," he said. "What are you so concerned about?"

They stopped short, sadness written across their faces. [18]Then one of them, Cleopas, replied, "You must be the only person in Jerusalem who hasn't heard about all the things that have happened there the last few days."

[19]"What things?" Jesus asked.

"The things that happened to Jesus, the man from Nazareth," they said. "He was a prophet who did wonderful miracles. He was a mighty teacher, highly regarded by both God and all the people. [20]But our leading priests and other religious leaders arrested him and handed him over to be condemned to death, and they crucified him. [21]We had thought he was the Messiah who had come to rescue Israel. That all happened three days ago. [22]Then some women from our group of his followers were at his tomb early this morning, and they came back with an amazing report. [23]They said his body was missing, and they had seen angels who told them Jesus is alive! [24]Some of our men ran out to see, and sure enough, Jesus' body was gone, just as the women had said."

[25]Then Jesus said to them, "You are such foolish people! You find it so hard to believe all that the prophets wrote in the Scriptures. [26]Wasn't it clearly predicted by the prophets that the Messiah would have to suffer all these things before entering his time of glory?" [27]Then Jesus quoted passages from the writings of Moses and all the prophets, explaining what all the Scriptures said about himself.

[28]By this time they were nearing Emmaus and the end of their journey. Jesus would have gone on, [29]but they begged him to stay the night with them, since it was getting late. So he went home with them. [30]As they sat down to eat, he took a small loaf of bread, asked God's blessing on it, broke it, then gave it to them. [31]Suddenly, their eyes were opened, and they recognized him. And at that moment he disappeared!

[32]They said to each other, "Didn't our hearts feel strangely warm as he talked with us on the road and explained the Scriptures to us?" [33]And within the hour they were on their way back to Jerusalem, where the eleven disciples and the other followers of Jesus were gathered. When they arrived, they were greeted with the report, [34]"The Lord has really risen! He appeared to Peter*!"

Jesus Appears to the Disciples

[35]Then the two from Emmaus told their story of how Jesus had appeared to them as they were walking along the road and how they had recognized him as he was breaking the bread. [36]And just as they were telling about it, Jesus himself was suddenly standing there among them. He said, "Peace be with you."* [37]But the whole group was terribly frightened, thinking they were seeing a ghost! [38]"Why are you frightened?" he asked. "Why do you doubt who I am? [39]Look at my hands. Look at my feet. You can see that it's really me. Touch me and make sure that I am not a ghost, because ghosts don't have bodies, as you see that I do!" [40]As he spoke, he held out his hands for them to see, and he showed them his feet.*

[41]Still they stood there doubting, filled with joy and wonder. Then he asked them, "Do you have anything here to eat?" [42]They gave him a piece of broiled fish, [43]and he ate it as they watched.

I BELIEVE all that the Old Testament prophets wrote about the Messiah's sufferings and time of glory. (24:25)

See Moses' profile (page 73) at Exodus 5:1.

I BELIEVE Jesus could appear and disappear at will after his resurrection. (24:31)

I BELIEVE Jesus appeared to Peter and the other disciples shortly after his resurrection. (24:34)

I BELIEVE Jesus had a tangible, physical body after his resurrection. (24:39)

I BELIEVE Jesus' hands and feet still bear the marks of his brutal execution. (24:40)

24:13 Greek *60 stadia* [11.1 kilometers].　24:34 Greek *Simon.*　24:36 Some manuscripts do not include *He said, "Peace be with you."*　24:40 Some manuscripts do not include this verse.

44 Then he said, "When I was with you before, I told you that everything written about me by Moses and the prophets and in the Psalms must all come true." 45 Then he opened their minds to understand these many Scriptures. 46 And he said, "Yes, it was written long ago that the Messiah must suffer and die and rise again from the dead on the third day. 47 With my authority, take this message of repentance to all the nations, beginning in Jerusalem: 'There is forgiveness of sins for all who turn to me.' 48 You are witnesses of all these things.

49 "And now I will send the Holy Spirit, just as my Father promised. But stay here in the city until the Holy Spirit comes and fills you with power from heaven."

The Ascension

50 Then Jesus led them to Bethany, and lifting his hands to heaven, he blessed them. 51 While he was blessing them, he left them and was taken up to heaven.* 52 They worshiped him and* then returned to Jerusalem filled with great joy. 53 And they spent all of their time in the Temple, praising God.

24:51 Some manuscripts do not include *and was taken up to heaven.*   24:52 Some manuscripts do not include *worshiped him and.*

I BELIEVE everything written in the Old Testament about Jesus is true. (24:44)

I CLAIM Jesus' authority to proclaim to everyone: "There is forgiveness of sins for all who turn to [Jesus]." (24:47)

I BELIEVE Jesus ascended to heaven a few weeks after his resurrection. (24:51)

I WORSHIP Jesus and am filled with great joy. (24:52)

JOHN

THIS FOURTH New Testament book calls us to "believe that Jesus is the Messiah, the Son of God" (John 20:31).

Most of what John writes here is unique to his Gospel. John's focus is on the deity of Jesus Christ and thus on his miraculous signs, Jesus' behind-the-scenes discussions with various individuals (3:1–4:42), the violent reactions to Jesus' claims (6:15–12:50), and Jesus' lengthy teachings and prayer for his disciples on the night before his crucifixion (13:1–17:26).

Unlike the other Gospel writers, John deliberately sets out to write to everyone, everywhere, down through the ages.

Favorite passages in this Gospel include

- ○ John gives a prologue about Jesus Christ's deity (1:1-18)
- ○ Jesus turns water into wine (2:1-12)
- ○ "Unless you are born again, you can never see the Kingdom of God" (3:3)
- ○ "For God so loved the world that he gave his only Son . . ." (3:16)
- ○ "He [Jesus] must become greater . . . and I [John] must become less . . ." (3:30)
- ○ Jesus heals a man who has been lame for thirty-eight years (5:1-15)
- ○ Jesus claims to be the Son of God (5:16-47)
- ○ Jesus feeds over five thousand people (6:1-15)
- ○ "If you are thirsty, come to me! If you believe in me . . ." (7:37-39)
- ○ "My purpose is to give life in all its fullness" (10:10)
- ○ "I am the good shepherd . . ." (10:11-18)
- ○ "Despite all the miraculous signs he had done, most of the people did not believe in him" (12:37)
- ○ "I am going to prepare a place for you" (14:2)
- ○ "I am the way, the truth, and the life. No one can come to the Father except through me" (14:6)
- ○ Jesus appears to some of his disciples after his resurrection (21:1-25)

CHAPTER 1

Christ, the Eternal Word

In the beginning the Word already existed. He was with God, and he was God. ²He was in the beginning with God. ³He created everything there is. Nothing exists that he didn't make. ⁴Life itself was in him, and this life gives light to everyone. ⁵The light shines through the darkness, and the darkness can never extinguish it.

⁶God sent John the Baptist ⁷to tell everyone about the light so that everyone might believe because of his testimony. ⁸John himself was not the light; he was only a witness to the light. ⁹The one who is the true light, who gives light to everyone, was going to come into the world.

¹⁰But although the world was made through him, the world didn't recognize

I BELIEVE Jesus Christ—the eternal Word—existed with God and was God. (1:1)

I BELIEVE Jesus created everything there is. (1:3)

See John the Baptist's profile (page 1117) at Mark 1:4.

I HAVE BEEN GIVEN the right to become a child of God because I have believed Jesus and accepted him as my Lord and Savior. (1:12)

I BELIEVE Jesus, as God the Father's only Son, became human to reveal God's glory to humanity. (1:14)

I HAVE BENEFITED from the rich and gracious blessings brought by Jesus Christ. (1:16)

See Moses' profile (page 73) at Exodus 5:1.

See Elijah's profile (page 421) at 1 Kings 19:18.

I BELIEVE John was the messenger sent to prepare the way for the Messiah. (1:23)

See Isaiah's profile (page 801) at Isaiah 6:13.

See the profile for the Pharisees (page 1087) at Matthew 12:14.

I BELIEVE Jesus is the Lamb of God who takes away the sin of the world. (1:29)

I BELIEVE God the Father confirmed that Jesus is the Savior of the world when the Holy Spirit descended and rested upon him after his baptism (Luke 3:21–22). (1:33)

him when he came. [11]Even in his own land and among his own people, he was not accepted. [12]But to all who believed him and accepted him, he gave the right to become children of God. [13]They are reborn! This is not a physical birth resulting from human passion or plan—this rebirth comes from God.

[14]So the Word became human and lived here on earth among us. He was full of unfailing love and faithfulness.* And we have seen his glory, the glory of the only Son of the Father.

[15]John pointed him out to the people. He shouted to the crowds, "This is the one I was talking about when I said, 'Someone is coming who is far greater than I am, for he existed long before I did.' "

[16]We have all benefited from the rich blessings he brought to us—one gracious blessing after another.* [17]For the law was given through Moses; God's unfailing love and faithfulness came through Jesus Christ. [18]No one has ever seen God. But his only Son, who is himself God,* is near to the Father's heart; he has told us about him.

The Testimony of John the Baptist

[19]This was the testimony of John when the Jewish leaders sent priests and Temple assistants* from Jerusalem to ask John whether he claimed to be the Messiah. [20]He flatly denied it. "I am not the Messiah," he said.

[21]"Well then, who are you?" they asked. "Are you Elijah?"

"No," he replied.

"Are you the Prophet?"*

"No."

[22]"Then who are you? Tell us, so we can give an answer to those who sent us. What do you have to say about yourself?"

[23]John replied in the words of Isaiah:

"I am a voice shouting in the wilderness,
 'Prepare a straight pathway for the Lord's coming!' "*

[24]Then those who were sent by the Pharisees [25]asked him, "If you aren't the Messiah or Elijah or the Prophet, what right do you have to baptize?"

[26]John told them, "I baptize with* water, but right here in the crowd is someone you do not know, [27]who will soon begin his ministry. I am not even worthy to be his slave.*" [28]This incident took place at Bethany, a village east of the Jordan River, where John was baptizing.

Jesus, the Lamb of God

[29]The next day John saw Jesus coming toward him and said, "Look! There is the Lamb of God who takes away the sin of the world! [30]He is the one I was talking about when I said, 'Soon a man is coming who is far greater than I am, for he existed long before I did.' [31]I didn't know he was the one, but I have been baptizing with water in order to point him out to Israel."

[32]Then John said, "I saw the Holy Spirit descending like a dove from heaven and resting upon him. [33]I didn't know he was the one, but when God sent me to baptize with water, he told me, 'When you see the Holy Spirit descending and resting upon someone, he is the one you are looking for. He is the one who baptizes with the Holy Spirit.' [34]I saw this happen to Jesus, so I testify that he is the Son of God.*"

The First Disciples

[35]The following day, John was again standing with two of his disciples. [36]As Jesus walked by, John looked at him and then declared, "Look! There is the Lamb of God!" [37]Then John's two disciples turned and followed Jesus.

1:14 Greek *grace and truth*; also in 1:17.   1:16 Greek *grace upon grace*.   1:18 Some manuscripts read *his one and only Son*.   1:19 Greek *and Levites*.   1:21 See Deut 18:15, 18; Mal 4:5-6.   1:23 Isa 40:3.   1:26 Or *in*; also in 1:31, 33.   1:27 Greek *to untie his sandals*.   1:34 Some manuscripts read *the chosen One of God*.

³⁸Jesus looked around and saw them following. "What do you want?" he asked them.

They replied, "Rabbi" (which means Teacher), "where are you staying?"

³⁹"Come and see," he said. It was about four o'clock in the afternoon when they went with him to the place, and they stayed there the rest of the day.

⁴⁰Andrew, Simon Peter's brother, was one of these men who had heard what John said and then followed Jesus. ⁴¹The first thing Andrew did was to find his brother, Simon, and tell him, "We have found the Messiah" (which means the Christ).

⁴²Then Andrew brought Simon to meet Jesus. Looking intently at Simon, Jesus said, "You are Simon, the son of John—but you will be called Cephas" (which means Peter*).

See Peter's profile (page 1111) at Matthew 26:75.

LIKE ANDREW   *I tell others about the Lord Jesus.*
John 1:42

What's your greatest passion in life?
To be rich? To be famous? To be number one?
Andrew's greatest joy in life was telling others about the Lord Jesus.

Andrew had been a disciple of John the Baptist, who was actively preparing the way for the Messiah. As soon as John the Baptist saw Jesus and said, "There he is," Andrew went up to Jesus, introduced himself, and invited himself over to Jesus' place for the rest of the day.

Afterward, Andrew was so excited he immediately went to find his brother, Peter, and bring him back to meet Jesus, too. Andrew also made sure Jesus met their fishing partners—two other brothers named James and John. It was no small matter that these four men later became Jesus' first disciples (Matthew 4:18-22; Mark 1:16-20; Luke 5:1-11). Imagine if Andrew hadn't been passionate about telling others about Jesus!

Scripture tells us Andrew never lost his zeal for introducing others to his Savior. Right before the feeding of the five thousand, for instance, it was Andrew that said, in effect, "Excuse me, Jesus. I'd like to introduce you to a little boy here who's offered to give you his sack lunch" (see John 6:1-13). On yet another occasion, it was Andrew who helped introduce Jesus to some friends of Philip visiting from Greece (12:20-36).

Andrew served as one of the key leaders of the early church (Acts 1:13) and tradition says he was eventually martyred—after still telling others about the Lord Jesus. Like Andrew, let's look for opportunities to share the Good News with those we know and love who don't know the Lord yet.

○ *Today's Scripture reading is John 1:35-42; 6:1-13; 12:20-36.*

---

⁴³The next day Jesus decided to go to Galilee. He found Philip and said to him, "Come, be my disciple." ⁴⁴Philip was from Bethsaida, Andrew and Peter's hometown.

⁴⁵Philip went off to look for Nathanael and told him, "We have found the very person Moses and the prophets wrote about! His name is Jesus, the son of Joseph from Nazareth."

⁴⁶"Nazareth!" exclaimed Nathanael. "Can anything good come from there?"

"Just come and see for yourself," Philip said.

⁴⁷As they approached, Jesus said, "Here comes an honest man—a true son of Israel."

⁴⁸"How do you know about me?" Nathanael asked.

And Jesus replied, "I could see you under the fig tree before Philip found you."

⁴⁹Nathanael replied, "Teacher, you are the Son of God—the King of Israel!"

I RECOGNIZE Jesus as the fulfillment of all the Old Testament prophets wrote about the Messiah. (1:45)

See Joseph's profile (page 1071) at Matthew 1:24.

1:42 The names *Cephas* and *Peter* both mean "rock."

⁵⁰Jesus asked him, "Do you believe all this just because I told you I had seen you under the fig tree? You will see greater things than this." ⁵¹Then he said, "The truth is, you will all see heaven open and the angels of God going up and down upon the Son of Man."*

CHAPTER 2

The Wedding at Cana

The next day* Jesus' mother was a guest at a wedding celebration in the village of Cana in Galilee. ²Jesus and his disciples were also invited to the celebration. ³The wine supply ran out during the festivities, so Jesus' mother spoke to him about the problem. "They have no more wine," she told him.

⁴"How does that concern you and me?" Jesus asked. "My time has not yet come."

⁵But his mother told the servants, "Do whatever he tells you."

⁶Six stone waterpots were standing there; they were used for Jewish ceremonial purposes and held twenty to thirty gallons* each. ⁷Jesus told the servants, "Fill the jars with water." When the jars had been filled to the brim, ⁸he said, "Dip some out and take it to the master of ceremonies." So they followed his instructions.

⁹When the master of ceremonies tasted the water that was now wine, not knowing where it had come from (though, of course, the servants knew), he called the bridegroom over. ¹⁰"Usually a host serves the best wine first," he said. "Then, when everyone is full and doesn't care, he brings out the less expensive wines. But you have kept the best until now!"

¹¹This miraculous sign at Cana in Galilee was Jesus' first display of his glory. And his disciples believed in him.

¹²After the wedding he went to Capernaum for a few days with his mother, his brothers, and his disciples.

Jesus Clears the Temple

¹³It was time for the annual Passover celebration, and Jesus went to Jerusalem. ¹⁴In the Temple area he saw merchants selling cattle, sheep, and doves for sacrifices; and he saw money changers behind their counters. ¹⁵Jesus made a whip from some ropes and chased them all out of the Temple. He drove out the sheep and oxen, scattered the money changers' coins over the floor, and turned over their tables. ¹⁶Then, going over to the people who sold doves, he told them, "Get these things out of here. Don't turn my Father's house into a marketplace!"

¹⁷Then his disciples remembered this prophecy from the Scriptures: "Passion for God's house burns within me."*

¹⁸"What right do you have to do these things?" the Jewish leaders demanded. "If you have this authority from God, show us a miraculous sign to prove it."

¹⁹"All right," Jesus replied. "Destroy this temple, and in three days I will raise it up."

²⁰"What!" they exclaimed. "It took forty-six years to build this Temple, and you can do it in three days?" ²¹But by "this temple," Jesus meant his body. ²²After he was raised from the dead, the disciples remembered that he had said this. And they believed both Jesus and the Scriptures.

²³Because of the miraculous signs he did in Jerusalem at the Passover celebration, many people were convinced that he was indeed the Messiah. ²⁴But Jesus didn't trust them, because he knew what people were really like. ²⁵No one needed to tell him about human nature.

Margin notes

I BELIEVE Jesus is the way to heaven (John 14:6). (1:51)

I DO whatever Jesus tells me to do. (2:8)

I BELIEVE Jesus turned water into wine to display his glory to his disciples. (2:11)

I DO NOT TURN the Lord's house into a marketplace. (2:16)

I BELIEVE Jesus accurately predicted that he would rise from the dead, just as the Scriptures said (Psalm 16:10; Acts 2:24-32; 13:35-37). (2:22)

I BELIEVE Jesus knows the truth about each person's heart. (2:24)

1:51 See Gen 28:10-17, the account of Jacob's ladder.   2:1 Greek *On the third day;* see 1:35, 43.   2:6 Greek *2 or 3 measures* [75 to 113 liters].   2:17 Or *"Concern for God's house will be my undoing."* Ps 69:9.

CHAPTER 3

Jesus and Nicodemus

After dark one evening, a Jewish religious leader named Nicodemus, a Pharisee, ²came to speak with Jesus. "Teacher," he said, "we all know that God has
sent you to teach us. Your miraculous signs are proof enough that God is with
you."

³Jesus replied, "I assure you, unless you are born again,* you can never see
the Kingdom of God."

⁴"What do you mean?" exclaimed Nicodemus. "How can an old man go
back into his mother's womb and be born again?"

⁵Jesus replied, "The truth is, no one can enter the Kingdom of God without
being born of water and the Spirit.* ⁶Humans can reproduce only human
life, but the Holy Spirit gives new life from heaven. ⁷So don't be surprised at
my statement that you* must be born again. ⁸Just as you can hear the wind
but can't tell where it comes from or where it is going, so you can't explain
how people are born of the Spirit."

See the profile for the Pharisees (page 1087) at Matthew 12:14.

I BELIEVE a person must be born again in order to see the Kingdom of God. (3:3)

I BELIEVE the Holy Spirit gives new life from heaven. (3:6)

LIKE NATHANAEL   *I am known by the Lord and loved.*

John 1:49

Who's Nathanael?

Near the beginning and end of his Gospel, John describes Nathanael as one of Jesus' first
disciples. Yet he's not listed by Matthew, Mark, and Luke as one of the twelve apostles. Some biblical
scholars believe that's because Nathanael also went by the name of Bartholomew—much as Matthew
also went by Levi, and Peter also went by Simon.

Like the apostles Matthew, James, John, Andrew, Peter, and Philip, Nathanael had an intriguing
first encounter with the Lord Jesus.

John tells us that Nathanael was under a fig tree when Philip interrupted him and said, "We have
found the very person Moses and the prophets wrote about!" What was Nathanael doing under that
fig tree? Presumably, he was resting. It's very possible he was praying. Perhaps he was asking the
Lord to make him an honest man—a true son of Israel. Perhaps he was meditating on a prophetic
passage from Isaiah's scroll read at the synagogue that previous Sabbath. Or perhaps he was
dreaming about the day when the Messiah would come and and every fruit tree would bear "a new
crop every month, without fail!" (Ezekiel 47:12). In any case, God was preparing Nathanael's heart.

When Philip and Nathanael walked toward Jesus, the Lord said straight out what kind of man
Nathanael was and where he had just been. Nathanael was amazed and immediately declared his
faith in the Lord Jesus.

Like Nathanael, we can rest assured that the Lord loves us so much that he always knows where
we are and what's on our heart (Psalm 139:1-18; Isaiah 40:9-27).

○ *Today's Scripture reading is John 1:43–2:11 and 21:1-13.*

---

⁹"What do you mean?" Nicodemus asked.

¹⁰Jesus replied, "You are a respected Jewish teacher, and yet you don't understand these things? ¹¹I assure you, I am telling you what we know and have
seen, and yet you won't believe us. ¹²But if you don't even believe me when I
tell you about things that happen here on earth, how can you possibly believe if I tell you what is going on in heaven? ¹³For only I, the Son of Man,*
have come to earth and will return to heaven again. ¹⁴And as Moses lifted up
the bronze snake on a pole in the wilderness, so I, the Son of Man, must be
lifted up on a pole,* ¹⁵so that everyone who believes in me will have eternal
life.

I BELIEVE Jesus had to be lifted up to die so everyone who believes in him would have eternal life (Numbers 21:9). (3:14)

See Moses' profile (page 73) at Exodus 5:1.

3:3 Or *born from above*; also in 3:7.   3:5 Or *spirit*. The Greek word for *Spirit* can also be translated *wind*; see 3:8.
3:7 The Greek word for *you* is plural; also in 3:12.   3:13 Some manuscripts add *who lives in heaven*.   3:14 Greek
must be lifted up.

I BELIEVE God loves me and gave his Son to die so that I will not perish but have eternal life (Romans 5:8). (3:16)

I KNOW there is no judgment waiting for me because I trust in Jesus (Romans 5:9-10). (3:18)

See John the Baptist's profile (page 1117) at Mark 1:4.

I AM FILLED with joy when Jesus is glorified and honored. (3:29)

I BELIEVE Jesus has been given authority over everything. (3:35)

See the profiles for the Pharisees (page 1087) and John the Baptist (page 1117) at Matthew 12:14 and Mark 1:4.

See the profiles for Jacob (page 43) and Joseph (page 51) at Genesis 32:9 and Genesis 39:2.

I AM NOT SURPRISED that Jesus reaches out to everyone, no matter what their nationality, race, or gender. (4:9)

[16]"For God so loved the world that he gave his only Son, so that everyone who believes in him will not perish but have eternal life. [17]God did not send his Son into the world to condemn it, but to save it.

[18]"There is no judgment awaiting those who trust him. But those who do not trust him have already been judged for not believing in the only Son of God. [19]Their judgment is based on this fact: The light from heaven came into the world, but they loved the darkness more than the light, for their actions were evil. [20]They hate the light because they want to sin in the darkness. They stay away from the light for fear their sins will be exposed and they will be punished. [21]But those who do what is right come to the light gladly, so everyone can see that they are doing what God wants."

John the Baptist Exalts Jesus

[22]Afterward Jesus and his disciples left Jerusalem, but they stayed in Judea for a while and baptized there.

[23]At this time John the Baptist was baptizing at Aenon, near Salim, because there was plenty of water there and people kept coming to him for baptism. [24]This was before John was put into prison. [25]At that time a certain Jew began an argument with John's disciples over ceremonial cleansing. [26]John's disciples came to him and said, "Teacher, the man you met on the other side of the Jordan River, the one you said was the Messiah, is also baptizing people. And everybody is going over there instead of coming here to us."

[27]John replied, "God in heaven appoints each person's work. [28]You yourselves know how plainly I told you that I am not the Messiah. I am here to prepare the way for him—that is all. [29]The bride will go where the bridegroom is. A bridegroom's friend rejoices with him. I am the bridegroom's friend, and I am filled with joy at his success. [30]He must become greater and greater, and I must become less and less.

[31]"He has come from above and is greater than anyone else. I am of the earth, and my understanding is limited to the things of earth, but he has come from heaven.* [32]He tells what he has seen and heard, but how few believe what he tells them! [33]Those who believe him discover that God is true. [34]For he is sent by God. He speaks God's words, for God's Spirit is upon him without measure or limit. [35]The Father loves his Son, and he has given him authority over everything. [36]And all who believe in God's Son have eternal life. Those who don't obey the Son will never experience eternal life, but the wrath of God remains upon them."

CHAPTER 4

Jesus and the Samaritan Woman

Jesus* learned that the Pharisees had heard, "Jesus is baptizing and making more disciples than John" [2](though Jesus himself didn't baptize them—his disciples did). [3]So he left Judea to return to Galilee.

[4]He had to go through Samaria on the way. [5]Eventually he came to the Samaritan village of Sychar, near the parcel of ground that Jacob gave to his son Joseph. [6]Jacob's well was there; and Jesus, tired from the long walk, sat wearily beside the well about noontime. [7]Soon a Samaritan woman came to draw water, and Jesus said to her, "Please give me a drink." [8]He was alone at the time because his disciples had gone into the village to buy some food.

[9]The woman was surprised, for Jews refuse to have anything to do with Samaritans. She said to Jesus, "You are a Jew, and I am a Samaritan woman. Why are you asking me for a drink?"

[10]Jesus replied, "If you only knew the gift God has for you and who I am, you would ask me, and I would give you living water."

[11]"But sir, you don't have a rope or a bucket," she said, "and this is a very

3:31 Some manuscripts omit *but he has come from heaven.* 4:1 Some manuscripts read *The Lord.*

deep well. Where would you get this living water? ¹²And besides, are you greater than our ancestor Jacob who gave us this well? How can you offer better water than he and his sons and his cattle enjoyed?"

¹³Jesus replied, "People soon become thirsty again after drinking this water. ¹⁴But the water I give them takes away thirst altogether. It becomes a perpetual spring within them, giving them eternal life."

¹⁵"Please, sir," the woman said, "give me some of that water! Then I'll never be thirsty again, and I won't have to come here to haul water."

¹⁶"Go and get your husband," Jesus told her.

¹⁷"I don't have a husband," the woman replied.

I BELIEVE Jesus gives supernatural water that takes away one's thirst and gives eternal life (John 7:37-39). (4:14)

I BELIEVE Jesus knows everything about me. (4:17)

LIKE NICODEMUS   *I must be born again by believing in Jesus Christ.*
John 3:3

Driving down an unfamiliar route, the sign ahead warns: "Wrong Way. Do Not Enter." Wise drivers heed the warning, turn around, and search for signs that redirect them to their desired destination.

When Nicodemus came to Jesus, he was a man heading the wrong way down a one-way street. He desperately wanted to get to heaven and wanted to know if Jesus could tell him how. Unlike the other Pharisees, Nicodemus didn't visit Jesus to trap him with a question or denounce him as a devil. Jesus knew Nicodemus's driving desire really was to enter God's Kingdom.

To a hungry, searching heart, Jesus spoke plainly, "You must be born again" (see 3:3).

Like other Pharisees, Nicodemus had been trying to get into God's Kingdom by dependence on his Jewish lineage and by slavery to human traditions—and he was frustrated. "You'll never get there that way," Jesus told him. "Time to change direction. You can only get where you want to go by being born again."

Jesus' directions perplexed Nicodemus's earthbound mind. So Jesus explained what he meant. To live in heaven requires a new birth from above. Nicodemus had no idea what Jesus was talking about. But this wasn't such a radical idea. Nicodemus should have remembered that God had said the Israelites would need new hearts (Ezekiel 11:19).

As if writing down the directions to make sure Nicodemus wouldn't miss a single turn, Jesus patiently explained the way in even more detail. Jesus said, in effect: "In a mysterious way, the Holy Spirit brings about new birth. It happens when you believe in me, for I will be lifted up so you can be healed and forgiven from all sin. When you trust in me, I'll give you eternal life. The only way you can get to heaven from here is if I take you. Believe me, I've been there before and I'm going back" (see John 3:5-15).

Jesus was waving a warning sign right in front of Nicodemus: "You can't make your own way into heaven." You and I can't get there on our own either. We must follow Jesus, believe in him, and be born again.

○ *Today's Scripture reading is John 3:1-21.*

Jesus said, "You're right! You don't have a husband—¹⁸for you have had five husbands, and you aren't even married to the man you're living with now."

¹⁹"Sir," the woman said, "you must be a prophet. ²⁰So tell me, why is it that you Jews insist that Jerusalem is the only place of worship, while we Samaritans claim it is here at Mount Gerizim,* where our ancestors worshiped?"

²¹Jesus replied, "Believe me, the time is coming when it will no longer matter whether you worship the Father here or in Jerusalem. ²²You Samaritans know so little about the one you worship, while we Jews know all about him, for salvation comes through the Jews. ²³But the time is coming and is already here when true worshipers will worship the Father in spirit and in truth. The Father is looking for anyone who will worship him that way. ²⁴For God is Spirit, so those who worship him must worship in spirit and in truth."

I WORSHIP the Father in spirit and truth. (4:24)

4:20 Greek *on this mountain.*

²⁵The woman said, "I know the Messiah will come—the one who is called Christ. When he comes, he will explain everything to us."

²⁶Then Jesus told her, "I am the Messiah!"*

²⁷Just then his disciples arrived. They were astonished to find him talking to a woman, but none of them asked him why he was doing it or what they had been discussing. ²⁸The woman left her water jar beside the well and went back to the village and told everyone, ²⁹"Come and meet a man who told me everything I ever did! Can this be the Messiah?" ³⁰So the people came streaming from the village to see him.

³¹Meanwhile, the disciples were urging Jesus to eat. ³²"No," he said, "I have food you don't know about."

³³"Who brought it to him?" the disciples asked each other.

³⁴Then Jesus explained: "My nourishment comes from doing the will of God, who sent me, and from finishing his work. ³⁵Do you think the work of harvesting will not begin until the summer ends four months from now? Look around you! Vast fields are ripening all around us and are ready now for the harvest. ³⁶The harvesters are paid good wages, and the fruit they harvest is people brought to eternal life. What joy awaits both the planter and the harvester alike! ³⁷You know the saying, 'One person plants and someone else harvests.' And it's true. ³⁸I sent you to harvest where you didn't plant; others had already done the work, and you will gather the harvest."

Many Samaritans Believe

³⁹Many Samaritans from the village believed in Jesus because the woman had said, "He told me everything I ever did!" ⁴⁰When they came out to see him, they begged him to stay at their village. So he stayed for two days, ⁴¹long enough for many of them to hear his message and believe. ⁴²Then they said to the woman, "Now we believe because we have heard him ourselves, not just because of what you told us. He is indeed the Savior of the world."

Jesus Heals an Official's Son

⁴³At the end of the two days' stay, Jesus went on into Galilee. ⁴⁴He had previously said, "A prophet is honored everywhere except in his own country." ⁴⁵The Galileans welcomed him, for they had been in Jerusalem at the Passover celebration and had seen all his miraculous signs.

⁴⁶In the course of his journey through Galilee, he arrived at the town of Cana, where he had turned the water into wine. There was a government official in the city of Capernaum whose son was very sick. ⁴⁷When he heard that Jesus had come from Judea and was traveling in Galilee, he went over to Cana. He found Jesus and begged him to come to Capernaum with him to heal his son, who was about to die.

⁴⁸Jesus asked, "Must I do miraculous signs and wonders before you people will believe in me?"

⁴⁹The official pleaded, "Lord, please come now before my little boy dies."

⁵⁰Then Jesus told him, "Go back home. Your son will live!" And the man believed Jesus' word and started home.

⁵¹While he was on his way, some of his servants met him with the news that his son was alive and well. ⁵²He asked them when the boy had begun to feel better, and they replied, "Yesterday afternoon at one o'clock his fever suddenly disappeared!" ⁵³Then the father realized it was the same time that Jesus had told him, "Your son will live." And the officer and his entire household believed in Jesus. ⁵⁴This was Jesus' second miraculous sign in Galilee after coming from Judea.

4:26 Greek "I am, the one speaking to you."

I GAIN greatest satisfaction in doing God's will. (4:34)

I LOOK AROUND AND SEE opportunities to bring people to eternal life. (4:35)

I TAKE TIME to tell others about the Good News of salvation. (4:40)

I BELIEVE in Jesus because of his Word, not just because of the testimony of others. (4:42)

I BEG Jesus for healing if my child is seriously ill. (4:47)

I CARE more about my child's well-being than about proving God's power through a miracle. (4:49)

I BELIEVE Jesus healed the boy at the moment he spoke the words, "Your son will live." (4:53)

CHAPTER 5

Jesus Heals a Lame Man

Afterward Jesus returned to Jerusalem for one of the Jewish holy days. ²Inside the city, near the Sheep Gate, was the pool of Bethesda,* with five covered porches. ³Crowds of sick people—blind, lame, or paralyzed—lay on the porches.* ⁵One of the men lying there had been sick for thirty-eight years. ⁶When Jesus saw him and knew how long he had been ill, he asked him, "Would you like to get well?"

⁷"I can't, sir," the sick man said, "for I have no one to help me into the pool when the water is stirred up. While I am trying to get there, someone else always gets in ahead of me."

LIKE THE SAMARITAN WOMAN
I am satisfied because God knows, loves, and fills me.
John 4:14

What does it take to satisfy your deepest thirst for *life?*

Plenty of fashionable clothes? A successful career? The perfect job? Status and power? A beautiful home? Security? All of the above and committed, loving relationships, too?

When the Samaritan woman came to the well, she craved the satisfaction of her physical thirst. When she got there, she met a man who promised not only to quench her thirst but also to fill her life with living water that would never run dry.

Even though this woman didn't fully understand her own thirst, Jesus knew her parched heart. She was looking for the Messiah, who would explain all things. To the searching sinner, Jesus did not speak in parables. He told her something he hadn't told anyone else straight out: "I am the Messiah."

But why should she believe him? After all, Jesus had asked her for water and then claimed he had something better. He then declared her national religion inadequate and revealed the pain and shame of her life. Yet in exposing all her insufficiencies, Jesus also shared a beautiful secret: The Father is looking for men and women who will worship him in spirit and in truth.

Instead of running back to the safety of her sin and old way of life, this hurting woman grabbed hold of Jesus' invitation to come into a loving relationship with the Father. In her excitement, she forgot all about her empty water jug and ran back to town and told others about her newfound Savior. What clear evidence that the water of eternal life was beginning to well up within her!

Only God can satisfy the human heart and all its longings. Like the Samaritan woman, you and I can find true satisfaction nowhere else.

○ *Today's Scripture reading is John 4:1-42.*

---

⁸Jesus told him, "Stand up, pick up your sleeping mat, and walk!"

⁹Instantly, the man was healed! He rolled up the mat and began walking! But this miracle happened on the Sabbath day. ¹⁰So the Jewish leaders objected. They said to the man who was cured, "You can't work on the Sabbath! It's illegal to carry that sleeping mat!"

¹¹He replied, "The man who healed me said to me, 'Pick up your sleeping mat and walk.' "

¹²"Who said such a thing as that?" they demanded.

¹³The man didn't know, for Jesus had disappeared into the crowd. ¹⁴But afterward Jesus found him in the Temple and told him, "Now you are well; so stop sinning, or something even worse may happen to you." ¹⁵Then the man went to find the Jewish leaders and told them it was Jesus who had healed him.

Jesus Claims to Be the Son of God

¹⁶So the Jewish leaders began harassing Jesus for breaking the Sabbath rules. ¹⁷But Jesus replied, "My Father never stops working, so why should I?" ¹⁸So

I BELIEVE Jesus could speak the word and heal anyone, no matter how long that person had been sick or crippled. (5:9)

I OBEY Jesus. (5:11)

I DO NOT CONTINUE sinning. (5:14)

5:2 Some manuscripts read *Beth-zatha;* other manuscripts read *Bethsaida.* 5:3 Some manuscripts add *waiting for a certain movement of the water,* ⁴*for an angel of the Lord came from time to time and stirred up the water. And the first person to step down into it afterward was healed.*

I BELIEVE Jesus made himself equal with God when he spoke of God as his Father. (5:18)

the Jewish leaders tried all the more to kill him. In addition to disobeying the Sabbath rules, he had spoken of God as his Father, thereby making himself equal with God.

[19]Jesus replied, "I assure you, the Son can do nothing by himself. He does only what he sees the Father doing. Whatever the Father does, the Son also does. [20]For the Father loves the Son and tells him everything he is doing, and the Son will do far greater things than healing this man. You will be astonished at what he does. [21]He will even raise from the dead anyone he wants to, just as the Father does. [22]And the Father leaves all judgment to his Son, [23]so that everyone will honor the Son, just as they honor the Father. But if you refuse to honor the Son, then you are certainly not honoring the Father who sent him.

I BELIEVE Jesus deserves the same honor as his Father. (5:23)

[24]"I assure you, those who listen to my message and believe in God who sent me have eternal life. They will never be condemned for their sins, but they have already passed from death into life.

[25]"And I assure you that the time is coming, in fact it is here, when the dead will hear my voice—the voice of the Son of God. And those who listen will live. [26]The Father has life in himself, and he has granted his Son to have life in himself. [27]And he has given him authority to judge all mankind because he is the Son of Man. [28]Don't be so surprised! Indeed, the time is coming when all the dead in their graves will hear the voice of God's Son, [29]and they will rise again. Those who have done good will rise to eternal life, and those who have continued in evil will rise to judgment. [30]But I do nothing without consulting the Father. I judge as I am told. And my judgment is absolutely just, because it is according to the will of God who sent me; it is not merely my own.

I BELIEVE Jesus always works in complete harmony with the Father's will. (5:30)

Witnesses to Jesus

[31]"If I were to testify on my own behalf, my testimony would not be valid. [32]But someone else is also testifying about me, and I can assure you that everything he says about me is true. [33]In fact, you sent messengers to listen to John the Baptist, and he preached the truth. [34]But the best testimony about me is not from a man, though I have reminded you about John's testimony so you might be saved. [35]John shone brightly for a while, and you benefited and rejoiced. [36]But I have a greater witness than John—my teachings and my miracles. They have been assigned to me by the Father, and they testify that the Father has sent me. [37]And the Father himself has also testified about me. You have never heard his voice or seen him face to face, [38]and you do not have his message in your hearts, because you do not believe me—the one he sent to you.

See John the Baptist's profile (page 1117) at Mark 1:4.

[39]"You search the Scriptures because you believe they give you eternal life. But the Scriptures point to me! [40]Yet you refuse to come to me so that I can give you this eternal life.

I BELIEVE the Old Testament Scriptures point to Jesus Christ. (5:39)

[41]"Your approval or disapproval means nothing to me, [42]because I know you don't have God's love within you. [43]For I have come to you representing my Father, and you refuse to welcome me, even though you readily accept others who represent only themselves. [44]No wonder you can't believe! For you gladly honor each other, but you don't care about the honor that comes from God alone.

[45]"Yet it is not I who will accuse you of this before the Father. Moses will accuse you! Yes, Moses, on whom you set your hopes. [46]But if you had believed Moses, you would have believed me because he wrote about me. [47]And since you don't believe what he wrote, how will you believe what I say?"

See Moses' profile (page 73) at Exodus 5:1.

I BELIEVE that Moses wrote about Jesus Christ. (5:46)

CHAPTER 6

Jesus Feeds Five Thousand

After this, Jesus crossed over the Sea of Galilee, also known as the Sea of Tiberias. [2]And a huge crowd kept following him wherever he went, because they saw his miracles as he healed the sick. ³Then Jesus went up into the hills and sat down with his disciples around him. ⁴(It was nearly time for the annual Passover celebration.) ⁵Jesus soon saw a great crowd of people climbing the hill, looking for him. Turning to Philip, he asked, "Philip, where can we buy bread to feed all these people?" ⁶He was testing Philip, for he already knew what he was going to do.

⁷Philip replied, "It would take a small fortune* to feed them!"

⁸Then Andrew, Simon Peter's brother, spoke up. ⁹"There's a young boy here with five barley loaves and two fish. But what good is that with this huge crowd?"

¹⁰"Tell everyone to sit down," Jesus ordered. So all of them—the men alone numbered five thousand—sat down on the grassy slopes. ¹¹Then Jesus took the loaves, gave thanks to God, and passed them out to the people. Afterward he did the same with the fish. And they all ate until they were full. ¹²"Now gather the leftovers," Jesus told his disciples, "so that nothing is wasted." ¹³There were only five barley loaves to start with, but twelve baskets were filled with the pieces of bread the people did not eat!

¹⁴When the people saw this miraculous sign, they exclaimed, "Surely, he is the Prophet* we have been expecting!" ¹⁵Jesus saw that they were ready to take him by force and make him king, so he went higher into the hills alone.

Jesus Walks on Water

¹⁶That evening his disciples went down to the shore to wait for him. ¹⁷But as darkness fell and Jesus still hadn't come back, they got into the boat and headed out across the lake toward Capernaum. ¹⁸Soon a gale swept down upon them as they rowed, and the sea grew very rough. ¹⁹They were three or four miles* out when suddenly they saw Jesus walking on the water toward the boat. They were terrified, ²⁰but he called out to them, "I am here! Don't be afraid." ²¹Then they were eager to let him in, and immediately the boat arrived at their destination!

Jesus, the Bread of Life

²²The next morning, back across the lake, crowds began gathering on the shore, waiting to see Jesus. For they knew that he and his disciples had come over together and that the disciples had gone off in their boat, leaving him behind. ²³Several boats from Tiberias landed near the place where the Lord had blessed the bread and the people had eaten. ²⁴When the crowd saw that Jesus wasn't there, nor his disciples, they got into the boats and went across to Capernaum to look for him. ²⁵When they arrived and found him, they asked, "Teacher, how did you get here?"

²⁶Jesus replied, "The truth is, you want to be with me because I fed you, not because you saw the miraculous sign. ²⁷But you shouldn't be so concerned about perishable things like food. Spend your energy seeking the eternal life that I, the Son of Man, can give you. For God the Father has sent me for that very purpose."

²⁸They replied, "What does God want us to do?"

²⁹Jesus told them, "This is what God wants you to do: Believe in the one he has sent."

³⁰They replied, "You must show us a miraculous sign if you want us to believe in you. What will you do for us? ³¹After all, our ancestors ate manna while they journeyed through the wilderness! As the Scriptures say, 'Moses gave them bread from heaven to eat.'* "

³²Jesus said, "I assure you, Moses didn't give them bread from heaven. My Father did. And now he offers you the true bread from heaven. ³³The true

I BELIEVE Jesus always knows what he is going to do. (6:6)

I KNOW Jesus can provide, no matter how great the need. (6:7)

See Peter's profile (page 1111) at Matthew 26:75.

I DO NOT UNDERESTIMATE what God can do with the smallest of contributions. (6:9)

I THANK God for my food. (6:11)

I DO NOT WASTE what God has provided. (6:12)

I AM NOT AFRAID when I know Jesus is with me. (6:20)

I BELIEVE it is vastly more important to gain eternal life through Jesus than to have all my physical needs met. (6:27)

I DO NOT DEMAND a miraculous sign before I believe in Jesus Christ, God's Son. (6:30)

See Moses' profile (page 73) at Exodus 5:1.

6:7 Greek 200 denarii. A denarius was the equivalent of a full day's wage.   6:14 See Deut 18:15, 18.
6:19 Greek 25 or 30 stadia [4.6 or 5.5 kilometers].   6:31 Exod 16:4; Ps 78:24.

bread of God is the one who comes down from heaven and gives life to the world."

³⁴"Sir," they said, "give us that bread every day of our lives."

³⁵Jesus replied, "I am the bread of life. No one who comes to me will ever be hungry again. Those who believe in me will never thirst. ³⁶But you haven't believed in me even though you have seen me. ³⁷However, those the Father has given me will come to me, and I will never reject them. ³⁸For I have come down from heaven to do the will of God who sent me, not to do what I want. ³⁹And this is the will of God, that I should not lose even one of all those he has given me, but that I should raise them to eternal life at the last day. ⁴⁰For it is my Father's will that all who see his Son and believe in him should have eternal life—that I should raise them at the last day."

⁴¹ Then the people* began to murmur in disagreement because he had said, "I am the bread from heaven." ⁴²They said, "This is Jesus, the son of Joseph. We know his father and mother. How can he say, 'I came down from heaven'?"

⁴³But Jesus replied, "Don't complain about what I said. ⁴⁴For people can't come to me unless the Father who sent me draws them to me, and at the last day I will raise them from the dead. ⁴⁵As it is written in the Scriptures, 'They will all be taught by God.'* Everyone who hears and learns from the Father comes to me. ⁴⁶(Not that anyone has ever seen the Father; only I, who was sent from God, have seen him.)

⁴⁷"I assure you, anyone who believes in me already has eternal life. ⁴⁸Yes, I am the bread of life! ⁴⁹Your ancestors ate manna in the wilderness, but they all died. ⁵⁰However, the bread from heaven gives eternal life to everyone who eats it. ⁵¹I am the living bread that came down out of heaven. Anyone who eats this bread will live forever; this bread is my flesh, offered so the world may live."

⁵² Then the people began arguing with each other about what he meant. "How can this man give us his flesh to eat?" they asked.

⁵³So Jesus said again, "I assure you, unless you eat the flesh of the Son of Man and drink his blood, you cannot have eternal life within you. ⁵⁴But those who eat my flesh and drink my blood have eternal life, and I will raise them at the last day. ⁵⁵For my flesh is the true food, and my blood is the true drink. ⁵⁶All who eat my flesh and drink my blood remain in me, and I in them. ⁵⁷I live by the power of the living Father who sent me; in the same way, those who partake of me will live because of me. ⁵⁸I am the true bread from heaven. Anyone who eats this bread will live forever and not die as your ancestors did, even though they ate the manna."

⁵⁹He said these things while he was teaching in the synagogue in Capernaum.

Many Disciples Desert Jesus

⁶⁰Even his disciples said, "This is very hard to understand. How can anyone accept it?"

⁶¹Jesus knew within himself that his disciples were complaining, so he said to them, "Does this offend you? ⁶²Then what will you think if you see me, the Son of Man, return to heaven again? ⁶³It is the Spirit who gives eternal life. Human effort accomplishes nothing. And the very words I have spoken to you are spirit and life. ⁶⁴But some of you don't believe me." (For Jesus knew from the beginning who didn't believe, and he knew who would betray him.) ⁶⁵ Then he said, "That is what I meant when I said that people can't come to me unless the Father brings them to me."

⁶⁶At this point many of his disciples turned away and deserted him. ⁶⁷Then Jesus turned to the Twelve and asked, "Are you going to leave, too?"

I BELIEVE Jesus will raise to eternal life every person who believes in him. (6:40)

See Joseph's profile (page 1071) at Matthew 1:24.

I BELIEVE in Jesus, the bread of life, and have eternal life. (6:47)

In response to these affirmations, tell the Lord what you believe— or find hard to believe.

I BELIEVE Jesus knows the thoughts of every person. (6:61)

I BELIEVE no amount of human effort can give someone eternal life. (6:63)

6:41 Greek *Jewish people*; also in 6:52.   6:45 Isa 54:13.

[68]Simon Peter replied, "Lord, to whom would we go? You alone have the words that give eternal life. [69]We believe them, and we know you are the Holy One of God."

[70]Then Jesus said, "I chose the twelve of you, but one is a devil." [71]He was speaking of Judas, son of Simon Iscariot, one of the Twelve, who would betray him.

CHAPTER 7

Jesus and His Brothers

After this, Jesus stayed in Galilee, going from village to village. He wanted to stay out of Judea where the Jewish leaders were plotting his death. [2]But soon it was time for the Festival of Shelters, [3]and Jesus' brothers urged him to go to Judea for the celebration. "Go where your followers can see your miracles!" they scoffed. [4]"You can't become a public figure if you hide like this! If you can do such wonderful things, prove it to the world!" [5]For even his brothers didn't believe in him.

[6]Jesus replied, "Now is not the right time for me to go. But you can go anytime, and it will make no difference. [7]The world can't hate you, but it does hate me because I accuse it of sin and evil. [8]You go on. I am not yet* ready to go to this festival, because my time has not yet come." [9]So Jesus remained in Galilee.

Jesus Teaches Openly at the Temple

[10]But after his brothers had left for the festival, Jesus also went, though secretly, staying out of public view. [11]The Jewish leaders tried to find him at the festival and kept asking if anyone had seen him. [12]There was a lot of discussion about him among the crowds. Some said, "He's a wonderful man," while others said, "He's nothing but a fraud, deceiving the people." [13]But no one had the courage to speak favorably about him in public, for they were afraid of getting in trouble with the Jewish leaders.

[14]Then, midway through the festival, Jesus went up to the Temple and began to teach. [15]The Jewish leaders were surprised when they heard him. "How does he know so much when he hasn't studied everything we've studied?" they asked.

[16]So Jesus told them, "I'm not teaching my own ideas, but those of God who sent me. [17]Anyone who wants to do the will of God will know whether my teaching is from God or is merely my own. [18]Those who present their own ideas are looking for praise for themselves, but those who seek to honor the one who sent them are good and genuine. [19]None of you obeys the law of Moses! In fact, you are trying to kill me."

[20]The crowd replied, "You're demon possessed! Who's trying to kill you?"

[21]Jesus replied, "I worked on the Sabbath by healing a man, and you were offended. [22]But you work on the Sabbath, too, when you obey Moses' law of circumcision. (Actually, this tradition of circumcision is older than the law of Moses; it goes back to Abraham.) [23]For if the correct time for circumcising your son falls on the Sabbath, you go ahead and do it, so as not to break the law of Moses. So why should I be condemned for making a man completely well on the Sabbath? [24]Think this through and you will see that I am right."

Is Jesus the Messiah?

[25]Some of the people who lived there in Jerusalem said among themselves, "Isn't this the man they are trying to kill? [26]But here he is, speaking in public, and they say nothing to him. Can it be that our leaders know that he really is the Messiah? [27]But how could he be? For we know where this man comes

7:8 Some manuscripts omit yet.

I BELIEVE Jesus alone has the words that give eternal life. (6:68)

See Peter's profile (page 1111) at Matthew 26:75.

See Judas's profile (page 1121) at Mark 3:19.

I BELIEVE Jesus knew the right time for everything he did. (7:8)

I HAVE the courage to speak favorably of Jesus always, even if it means getting in trouble. (7:13)

I BELIEVE Jesus taught the truths of God. (7:16)

See Moses' profile (page 73) at Exodus 5:1.

I AM NOT OFFENDED by anything Jesus does. (7:21)

See Abraham's profile (page 19) at Genesis 15:6.

from. When the Messiah comes, he will simply appear; no one will know where he comes from."

[28]While Jesus was teaching in the Temple, he called out, "Yes, you know me, and you know where I come from. But I represent one you don't know, and he is true. [29]I know him because I have come from him, and he sent me to you." [30]Then the leaders tried to arrest him; but no one laid a hand on him, because his time had not yet come.

[31]Many among the crowds at the Temple believed in him. "After all," they said, "would you expect the Messiah to do more miraculous signs than this man has done?"

[32]When the Pharisees heard that the crowds were murmuring such things, they and the leading priests sent Temple guards to arrest Jesus. [33]But Jesus told them, "I will be here a little longer. Then I will return to the one who sent me. [34]You will search for me but not find me. And you won't be able to come where I am."

[35]The Jewish leaders were puzzled by this statement. "Where is he planning to go?" they asked. "Maybe he is thinking of leaving the country and going to the Jews in other lands, or maybe even to the Gentiles! [36]What does he mean when he says, 'You will search for me but not find me,' and 'You won't be able to come where I am'?"

Jesus Promises Living Water

[37]On the last day, the climax of the festival, Jesus stood and shouted to the crowds, "If you are thirsty, come to me! [38]If you believe in me, come and drink! For the Scriptures declare that rivers of living water will flow out from within."* [39](When he said "living water," he was speaking of the Spirit, who would be given to everyone believing in him. But the Spirit had not yet been given, because Jesus had not yet entered into his glory.)

Division and Unbelief

[40]When the crowds heard him say this, some of them declared, "This man surely is the Prophet."* [41]Others said, "He is the Messiah." Still others said, "But he can't be! Will the Messiah come from Galilee? [42]For the Scriptures clearly state that the Messiah will be born of the royal line of David, in Bethlehem, the village where King David was born."* [43]So the crowd was divided in their opinion about him. [44]And some wanted him arrested, but no one touched him.

[45]The Temple guards who had been sent to arrest him returned to the leading priests and Pharisees. "Why didn't you bring him in?" they demanded.

[46]"We have never heard anyone talk like this!" the guards responded.

[47]"Have you been led astray, too?" the Pharisees mocked. [48]"Is there a single one of us rulers or Pharisees who believes in him? [49]These ignorant crowds do, but what do they know about it? A curse on them anyway!"

[50]Nicodemus, the leader who had met with Jesus earlier, then spoke up. [51]"Is it legal to convict a man before he is given a hearing?" he asked.

[52]They replied, "Are you from Galilee, too? Search the Scriptures and see for yourself—no prophet ever comes from Galilee!"

[*The most ancient Greek manuscripts do not include John 7:53–8:11.*]

[53]Then the meeting broke up and everybody went home.

CHAPTER 8

A Woman Caught in Adultery

Jesus returned to the Mount of Olives, [2]but early the next morning he was back again at the Temple. A crowd soon gathered, and he sat down and taught them. [3]As he was speaking, the teachers of religious law and Pharisees

---

I BELIEVE the religious leaders could not arrest Jesus or kill him before the time appointed by God. (7:30)

See the profile for the Pharisees (page 1087) at Matthew 12:14.

I BELIEVE Jesus accurately predicted that he would return to the Father in heaven. (7:33)

I BELIEVE every Christian has received the Holy Spirit (Romans 8:9). (7:38)

I DO NOT LET my lack of knowledge keep me from believing in Jesus and his Word. (7:41)

See David's profile (page 629) at Psalm 3:1.

I DO NOT UNDERESTIMATE how many people believe in Jesus at all levels of society. (7:48)

I SPEAK UP for Jesus always, even in hostile situations. (7:50)

I SEARCH the Scriptures and see that Jesus fulfills every Old Testament prediction about the Messiah. (7:52)

See the profile for the Pharisees (page 1087) at Matthew 12:14.

7:37-38 Or *"Let anyone who is thirsty come to me and drink.* [38]*For the Scriptures declare that rivers of living water will flow from the heart of those who believe in me."* 7:40 See Deut 18:15, 18. 7:42 See Mic 5:2.

brought a woman they had caught in the act of adultery. They put her in front of the crowd.

[4]"Teacher," they said to Jesus, "this woman was caught in the very act of adultery. [5]The law of Moses says to stone her. What do you say?"

[6]They were trying to trap him into saying something they could use against him, but Jesus stooped down and wrote in the dust with his finger. [7]They kept demanding an answer, so he stood up again and said, "All right, stone her. But let those who have never sinned throw the first stones!" [8]Then he stooped down again and wrote in the dust.

[9]When the accusers heard this, they slipped away one by one, beginning with the oldest, until only Jesus was left in the middle of the crowd with the woman. [10]Then Jesus stood up again and said to her, "Where are your accusers? Didn't even one of them condemn you?"

[11]"No, Lord," she said.

And Jesus said, "Neither do I. Go and sin no more."

I BELIEVE Jesus has the authority to judge sin. (8:5)

See Moses' profile (page 73) at Exodus 5:1.

I FORSAKE my sin, thankful that Jesus has forgiven me instead of condemning me. (8:11)

LIKE THE ADULTEROUS WOMAN *I forsake my sin because God has forgiven all my past.*

John 8:11

"Guilty as charged"—no doubt about it.

The woman tossed to the ground in front of Jesus had nothing to say. Dragged weeping from her bedroom to the somber Temple floor, she had no advocate—because she had no excuse. God's law clearly commanded, "Do not commit adultery" (Exodus 20:14). She couldn't deny the sordid facts.

Of course, the religious leaders gathered around her cared little for the woman's fate. They cared even less for Moses' law, which required punishing both the woman *and* the man caught in adultery (Leviticus 20:10). They only wanted to trap Jesus after demanding that he pass judgment on her behavior. But Jesus ignored their twisted game, stooped down, and apparently wrote out his verdict against the hypocrites who stood ready to condemn him. After realizing that *their* sins had been exposed, they quickly slipped from the crowd.

Jesus kept writing on the ground. The adulterous woman sat there quietly as the Lord spoke to her heart. She suddenly realized that Jesus cared as much about not breaking God's law as about not breaking God's heart. Quietly, she repented. When he stood up, Jesus asked where her accusers were and then declared her forgiven, cleansed, and new! (See 2 Corinthians 5:17.)

Like the adulterous woman, you and I no longer face condemnation if we belong to Jesus Christ (Romans 8:1), no matter what we've done.

○ *Today's Scripture reading is John 8:1-11.*

Jesus, the Light of the World

[12]Jesus said to the people, "I am the light of the world. If you follow me, you won't be stumbling through the darkness, because you will have the light that leads to life."

[13]The Pharisees replied, "You are making false claims about yourself!"

[14]Jesus told them, "These claims are valid even though I make them about myself. For I know where I came from and where I am going, but you don't know this about me. [15]You judge me with all your human limitations,* but I am not judging anyone. [16]And if I did, my judgment would be correct in every respect because I am not alone—I have with me the Father who sent me. [17]Your own law says that if two people agree about something, their witness is accepted as fact.* [18]I am one witness, and my Father who sent me is the other."

[19]"Where is your father?" they asked.

Jesus answered, "Since you don't know who I am, you don't know who my Father is. If you knew me, then you would know my Father, too." [20]Jesus

I BELIEVE Jesus knew exactly who he was, where he had come from, and where he was going. (8:14)

I KNOW my limitations and would never try to judge God. (8:15)

8:15 Or *judge me by human standards.*   8:17 See Deut 19:15.

made these statements while he was teaching in the section of the Temple known as the Treasury. But he was not arrested, because his time had not yet come.

The Unbelieving People Warned

²¹Later Jesus said to them again, "I am going away. You will search for me and die in your sin. You cannot come where I am going."

²²The Jewish leaders asked, "Is he planning to commit suicide? What does he mean, 'You cannot come where I am going'?"

²³Then he said to them, "You are from below; I am from above. You are of this world; I am not. ²⁴That is why I said that you will die in your sins; for unless you believe that I am who I say I am, you will die in your sins."

²⁵"Tell us who you are," they demanded.

Jesus replied, "I am the one I have always claimed to be.* ²⁶I have much to say about you and much to condemn, but I won't. For I say only what I have heard from the one who sent me, and he is true." ²⁷But they still didn't understand that he was talking to them about his Father.

²⁸So Jesus said, "When you have lifted up the Son of Man on the cross, then you will realize that I am he and that I do nothing on my own, but I speak what the Father taught me. ²⁹And the one who sent me is with me—he has not deserted me. For I always do those things that are pleasing to him." ³⁰Then many who heard him say these things believed in him.

Jesus and Abraham

³¹Jesus said to the people* who believed in him, "You are truly my disciples if you keep obeying my teachings. ³²And you will know the truth, and the truth will set you free."

³³"But we are descendants of Abraham," they said. "We have never been slaves to anyone on earth. What do you mean, 'set free'?"

³⁴Jesus replied, "I assure you that everyone who sins is a slave of sin. ³⁵A slave is not a permanent member of the family, but a son is part of the family forever. ³⁶So if the Son sets you free, you will indeed be free. ³⁷Yes, I realize that you are descendants of Abraham. And yet some of you are trying to kill me because my message does not find a place in your hearts. ³⁸I am telling you what I saw when I was with my Father. But you are following the advice of your father."

³⁹"Our father is Abraham," they declared.

"No," Jesus replied, "for if you were children of Abraham, you would follow his good example.* ⁴⁰I told you the truth I heard from God, but you are trying to kill me. Abraham wouldn't do a thing like that. ⁴¹No, you are obeying your real father when you act that way."

They replied, "We were not born out of wedlock! Our true Father is God himself."

⁴²Jesus told them, "If God were your Father, you would love me, because I have come to you from God. I am not here on my own, but he sent me. ⁴³Why can't you understand what I am saying? It is because you are unable to do so! ⁴⁴For you are the children of your father the Devil, and you love to do the evil things he does. He was a murderer from the beginning and has always hated the truth. There is no truth in him. When he lies, it is consistent with his character; for he is a liar and the father of lies. ⁴⁵So when I tell the truth, you just naturally don't believe me! ⁴⁶Which of you can truthfully accuse me of sin? And since I am telling you the truth, why don't you believe me? ⁴⁷Anyone whose Father is God listens gladly to the words of God. Since you don't, it proves you aren't God's children."

I WILL NOT DIE in my sins, because I believe Jesus is who he says he is—the one sent from God. (8:24)

I KEEP OBEYING Jesus' commands and teachings because I am his disciple (Matthew 28:20). (8:31)

I BELIEVE God's truth sets me free from sin. (8:32)

See Abraham's profile (page 19) at Genesis 15:6.

I KNOW God is my true Father because I love his Son, Jesus Christ. (8:42)

I BELIEVE the devil was a murderer and liar from the beginning (Genesis 3:4; 1 John 3:8). (8:44)

I GLADLY LISTEN to the words of God because I am a child of God. (8:47)

8:25 Or "Why do I speak to you at all?" 8:31 Greek *Jewish people;* also in 8:48, 52, 57. 8:39 Some manuscripts read *if you are children of Abraham, follow his example.*

⁴⁸The people retorted, "You Samaritan devil! Didn't we say all along that you were possessed by a demon?"

⁴⁹"No," Jesus said, "I have no demon in me. For I honor my Father—and you dishonor me. ⁵⁰And though I have no wish to glorify myself, God wants to glorify me. Let him be the judge. ⁵¹I assure you, anyone who obeys my teaching will never die!"

⁵²The people said, "Now we know you are possessed by a demon. Even Abraham and the prophets died, but you say that those who obey your teaching will never die! ⁵³Are you greater than our father Abraham, who died? Are you greater than the prophets, who died? Who do you think you are?"

⁵⁴Jesus answered, "If I am merely boasting about myself, it doesn't count. But it is my Father who says these glorious things about me. You say, 'He is our God,' ⁵⁵but you do not even know him. I know him. If I said otherwise, I would be as great a liar as you! But it is true—I know him and obey him. ⁵⁶Your ancestor Abraham rejoiced as he looked forward to my coming. He saw it and was glad."

⁵⁷The people said, "You aren't even fifty years old. How can you say you have seen Abraham?*"

⁵⁸Jesus answered, "The truth is, I existed before Abraham was even born!"* ⁵⁹At that point they picked up stones to kill him. But Jesus hid himself from them and left the Temple.

CHAPTER 9

Jesus Heals a Man Born Blind

As Jesus was walking along, he saw a man who had been blind from birth. ²"Teacher," his disciples asked him, "why was this man born blind? Was it a result of his own sins or those of his parents?"

³"It was not because of his sins or his parents' sins," Jesus answered. "He was born blind so the power of God could be seen in him. ⁴All of us must quickly carry out the tasks assigned us by the one who sent me, because there is little time left before the night falls and all work comes to an end. ⁵But while I am still here in the world, I am the light of the world."

⁶Then he spit on the ground, made mud with the saliva, and smoothed the mud over the blind man's eyes. ⁷He told him, "Go and wash in the pool of Siloam" (Siloam means Sent). So the man went and washed, and came back seeing!

⁸His neighbors and others who knew him as a blind beggar asked each other, "Is this the same man—that beggar?" ⁹Some said he was, and others said, "No, but he surely looks like him!"

And the beggar kept saying, "I am the same man!"

¹⁰They asked, "Who healed you? What happened?"

¹¹He told them, "The man they call Jesus made mud and smoothed it over my eyes and told me, 'Go to the pool of Siloam and wash off the mud.' I went and washed, and now I can see!"

¹²"Where is he now?" they asked.

"I don't know," he replied.

¹³Then they took the man to the Pharisees. ¹⁴Now as it happened, Jesus had healed the man on a Sabbath. ¹⁵The Pharisees asked the man all about it. So he told them, "He smoothed the mud over my eyes, and when it was washed away, I could see!"

¹⁶Some of the Pharisees said, "This man Jesus is not from God, for he is working on the Sabbath." Others said, "But how could an ordinary sinner do such miraculous signs?" So there was a deep division of opinion among them.

I BELIEVE Jesus is far greater than Abraham or any of the prophets. (8:53)

I BELIEVE Jesus existed with the Father from all eternity. (8:58)

I BELIEVE God can use disabilities and disease to show his power. (9:3)

I TELL others how Jesus has changed my life. (9:11)

See the profile for the Pharisees (page 1087) at Matthew 12:14.

I KNOW my limitations and would never try to judge God. (9:16)

8:57 Some manuscripts read *How can you say Abraham has seen you?* 8:58 Or *"Truly, truly, before Abraham was, I am."*

[17] Then the Pharisees once again questioned the man who had been blind and demanded, "This man who opened your eyes—who do you say he is?"

The man replied, "I think he must be a prophet."

[18] The Jewish leaders wouldn't believe he had been blind, so they called in his parents. [19] They asked them, "Is this your son? Was he born blind? If so, how can he see?"

[20] His parents replied, "We know this is our son and that he was born blind, [21] but we don't know how he can see or who healed him. He is old enough to speak for himself. Ask him." [22] They said this because they were afraid of the Jewish leaders, who had announced that anyone saying Jesus was the Messiah would be expelled from the synagogue. [23] That's why they said, "He is old enough to speak for himself. Ask him."

[24] So for the second time they called in the man who had been blind and told him, "Give glory to God by telling the truth,* because we know Jesus is a sinner."

[25] "I don't know whether he is a sinner," the man replied. "But I know this: I was blind, and now I can see!"

[26] "But what did he do?" they asked. "How did he heal you?"

[27] "Look!" the man exclaimed. "I told you once. Didn't you listen? Why do you want to hear it again? Do you want to become his disciples, too?"

[28] Then they cursed him and said, "You are his disciple, but we are disciples of Moses. [29] We know God spoke to Moses, but as for this man, we don't know anything about him."

[30] "Why, that's very strange!" the man replied. "He healed my eyes, and yet you don't know anything about him! [31] Well, God doesn't listen to sinners, but he is ready to hear those who worship him and do his will. [32] Never since the world began has anyone been able to open the eyes of someone born blind. [33] If this man were not from God, he couldn't do it."

[34] "You were born in sin!" they answered. "Are you trying to teach us?" And they threw him out of the synagogue.

Spiritual Blindness

[35] When Jesus heard what had happened, he found the man and said, "Do you believe in the Son of Man*?"

[36] The man answered, "Who is he, sir, because I would like to."

[37] "You have seen him," Jesus said, "and he is speaking to you!"

[38] "Yes, Lord," the man said, "I believe!" And he worshiped Jesus.

[39] Then Jesus told him, "I have come to judge the world. I have come to give sight to the blind and to show those who think they see that they are blind."

[40] The Pharisees who were standing there heard him and asked, "Are you saying we are blind?"

[41] "If you were blind, you wouldn't be guilty," Jesus replied. "But you remain guilty because you claim you can see."

CHAPTER 10

The Good Shepherd and His Sheep

"I assure you, anyone who sneaks over the wall of a sheepfold, rather than going through the gate, must surely be a thief and a robber! [2] For a shepherd enters through the gate. [3] The gatekeeper opens the gate for him, and the sheep hear his voice and come to him. He calls his own sheep by name and leads them out. [4] After he has gathered his own flock, he walks ahead of them, and they follow him because they recognize his voice. [5] They won't follow a stranger; they will run from him because they don't recognize his voice."

[6] Those who heard Jesus use this illustration didn't understand what he meant, [7] so he explained it to them. "I assure you, I am the gate for the sheep,"

**Sidebar notes (left margin):**

I AM NOT AFRAID of religious leaders. (9:22)

I WANT to be a disciple of Jesus for the rest of my life. (9:27)

See Moses' profile (page 73) at Exodus 5:1.

I BELIEVE God is ready to hear those who worship and obey him. (9:31)

I BELIEVE in Jesus and worship him. (9:38)

I FOLLOW Jesus and recognize him as my good shepherd (Psalm 23:1). (10:4)

9:24 Or *Give glory to God, not to Jesus;* Greek reads *Give glory to God.*   9:35 Some manuscripts read *the Son of God.*

he said. [8]"All others who came before me were thieves and robbers. But the true sheep did not listen to them. [9]Yes, I am the gate. Those who come in through me will be saved. Wherever they go, they will find green pastures. [10]The thief's purpose is to steal and kill and destroy. My purpose is to give life in all its fullness.

[11]"I am the good shepherd. The good shepherd lays down his life for the sheep. [12]A hired hand will run when he sees a wolf coming. He will leave the sheep because they aren't his and he isn't their shepherd. And so the wolf attacks them and scatters the flock. [13]The hired hand runs away because he is merely hired and has no real concern for the sheep.

[14]"I am the good shepherd; I know my own sheep, and they know me, [15]just as my Father knows me and I know the Father. And I lay down my life for the sheep. [16]I have other sheep, too, that are not in this sheepfold. I must bring them also, and they will listen to my voice; and there will be one flock with one shepherd.

[17]"The Father loves me because I lay down my life that I may have it back again. [18]No one can take my life from me. I lay down my life voluntarily. For I have the right to lay it down when I want to and also the power to take it again. For my Father has given me this command."

[19]When he said these things, the people* were again divided in their opinions about him. [20]Some of them said, "He has a demon, or he's crazy. Why listen to a man like that?" [21]Others said, "This doesn't sound like a man possessed by a demon! Can a demon open the eyes of the blind?"

Jesus Claims to Be the Son of God

[22]It was now winter, and Jesus was in Jerusalem at the time of Hanukkah.* [23]He was at the Temple, walking through the section known as Solomon's Colonnade. [24]The Jewish leaders surrounded him and asked, "How long are you going to keep us in suspense? If you are the Messiah, tell us plainly."

[25]Jesus replied, "I have already told you, and you don't believe me. The proof is what I do in the name of my Father. [26]But you don't believe me because you are not part of my flock. [27]My sheep recognize my voice; I know them, and they follow me. [28]I give them eternal life, and they will never perish. No one will snatch them away from me, [29]for my Father has given them to me, and he is more powerful than anyone else. So no one can take them from me. [30]The Father and I are one."

[31]Once again the Jewish leaders picked up stones to kill him. [32]Jesus said, "At my Father's direction I have done many things to help the people. For which one of these good deeds are you killing me?"

[33]They replied, "Not for any good work, but for blasphemy, because you, a mere man, have made yourself God."

[34]Jesus replied, "It is written in your own law that God said to certain leaders of the people, 'I say, you are gods!'* [35]And you know that the Scriptures cannot be altered. So if those people, who received God's message, were called 'gods,' [36]why do you call it blasphemy when the Holy One who was sent into the world by the Father says, 'I am the Son of God'? [37]Don't believe me unless I carry out my Father's work. [38]But if I do his work, believe in what I have done, even if you don't believe me. Then you will realize that the Father is in me, and I am in the Father."

[39]Once again they tried to arrest him, but he got away and left them. [40]He went beyond the Jordan River to stay near the place where John was first baptizing. [41]And many followed him. "John didn't do miracles," they remarked to one another, "but all his predictions about this man have come true." [42]And many believed in him there.

10:19 Greek *Jewish people.*   10:22 Or *the Festival of Dedication.*   10:34 Ps 82:6.

I BELIEVE Jesus is the gate to eternal life for those who believe in him. (10:9)

I BELIEVE Jesus gives life in all its fullness. (10:10)

I BELIEVE Jesus accurately predicted that many peoples would believe in him. (10:16)

I BELIEVE Jesus laid down his life and took it up again voluntarily—no one took it from him. (10:18)

See Solomon's profile (page 753) at Proverbs 2:9.

I KNOW that I have eternal life and that no one can snatch me away from Jesus. (10:28)

I BELIEVE Jesus and the Father are one. (10:38)

See John the Baptist's profile (page 1117) at Mark 1:4.

CHAPTER 11

The Death of Lazarus

A man named Lazarus was sick. He lived in Bethany with his sisters, Mary and Martha. ²This is the Mary who poured the expensive perfume on the Lord's feet and wiped them with her hair.* Her brother, Lazarus, was sick. ³So the two sisters sent a message to Jesus telling him, "Lord, the one you love is very sick."

⁴But when Jesus heard about it he said, "Lazarus's sickness will not end in death. No, it is for the glory of God. I, the Son of God, will receive glory from this." ⁵Although Jesus loved Martha, Mary, and Lazarus, ⁶he stayed where he was for the next two days and did not go to them. ⁷Finally after two days, he said to his disciples, "Let's go to Judea again."

⁸But his disciples objected. "Teacher," they said, "only a few days ago the Jewish leaders in Judea were trying to kill you. Are you going there again?"

⁹Jesus replied, "There are twelve hours of daylight every day. As long as it is light, people can walk safely. They can see because they have the light of this world. ¹⁰Only at night is there danger of stumbling because there is no light." ¹¹Then he said, "Our friend Lazarus has fallen asleep, but now I will go and wake him up."

¹²The disciples said, "Lord, if he is sleeping, that means he is getting better!" ¹³They thought Jesus meant Lazarus was having a good night's rest, but Jesus meant Lazarus had died.

¹⁴Then he told them plainly, "Lazarus is dead. ¹⁵And for your sake, I am glad I wasn't there, because this will give you another opportunity to believe in me. Come, let's go see him."

¹⁶Thomas, nicknamed the Twin,* said to his fellow disciples, "Let's go, too—and die with Jesus."

¹⁷When Jesus arrived at Bethany, he was told that Lazarus had already been in his grave for four days. ¹⁸Bethany was only a few miles* down the road from Jerusalem, ¹⁹and many of the people* had come to pay their respects and console Martha and Mary on their loss. ²⁰When Martha got word that Jesus was coming, she went to meet him. But Mary stayed at home. ²¹Martha said to Jesus, "Lord, if you had been here, my brother would not have died. ²²But even now I know that God will give you whatever you ask."

²³Jesus told her, "Your brother will rise again."

²⁴"Yes," Martha said, "when everyone else rises, on resurrection day."

²⁵Jesus told her, "I am the resurrection and the life.* Those who believe in me, even though they die like everyone else, will live again. ²⁶They are given eternal life for believing in me and will never perish. Do you believe this, Martha?"

²⁷"Yes, Lord," she told him. "I have always believed you are the Messiah, the Son of God, the one who has come into the world from God." ²⁸Then she left him and returned to Mary. She called Mary aside from the mourners and told her, "The Teacher is here and wants to see you." ²⁹So Mary immediately went to him.

³⁰Now Jesus had stayed outside the village, at the place where Martha met him. ³¹When the people who were at the house trying to console Mary saw her leave so hastily, they assumed she was going to Lazarus's grave to weep. So they followed her there. ³²When Mary arrived and saw Jesus, she fell down at his feet and said, "Lord, if you had been here, my brother would not have died."

³³When Jesus saw her weeping and saw the other people wailing with her, he was moved with indignation and was deeply troubled. ³⁴"Where have you put him?" he asked them.

See the profiles for Lazarus (page 1219) and Mary and Martha (page 1171) at John 12:11 and Luke 10:42.

I TELL Jesus when my loved ones are sick. (11:3)

I BELIEVE Jesus can and did use sickness and even death to bring glory to God the Father. (11:4)

I AM NOT AFRAID of those who threaten me when I am walking in the light with Jesus. (11:9)

I AM WILLING to go into dangerous situations with the Lord. (11:16)

See Thomas's profile (page 1231) at John 20:28.

I BELIEVE Jesus is the resurrection and the life, the one who gives eternal life to those who believe in him. (11:25)

I BELIEVE Jesus is the Messiah, the Son of God. (11:27)

I OFFER true comfort to those who are grieving. (11:31)

11:2 This incident is recorded in chapter 12. **11:16** Greek *the one who was called Didymus*. **11:18** Greek *was about 15 stadia* [about 2.8 kilometers]. **11:19** Greek *Jewish people;* also 11:31, 33, 36, 45, 54. **11:25** Some manuscripts do not include *and the life*.

They told him, "Lord, come and see." [35] Then Jesus wept. [36] The people who were standing nearby said, "See how much he loved him." [37] But some said, "This man healed a blind man. Why couldn't he keep Lazarus from dying?"

Jesus Raises Lazarus from the Dead

[38] And again Jesus was deeply troubled. Then they came to the grave. It was a cave with a stone rolled across its entrance. [39] "Roll the stone aside," Jesus told them.

But Martha, the dead man's sister, said, "Lord, by now the smell will be terrible because he has been dead for four days."

[40] Jesus responded, "Didn't I tell you that you will see God's glory if you believe?" [41] So they rolled the stone aside. Then Jesus looked up to heaven and said, "Father, thank you for hearing me. [42] You always hear me, but I said it out loud for the sake of all these people standing here, so they will believe you sent me." [43] Then Jesus shouted, "Lazarus, come out!" [44] And Lazarus came out, bound in graveclothes, his face wrapped in a headcloth. Jesus told them, "Unwrap him and let him go!"

The Plot to Kill Jesus

[45] Many of the people who were with Mary believed in Jesus when they saw this happen. [46] But some went to the Pharisees and told them what Jesus had done. [47] Then the leading priests and Pharisees called the high council* together to discuss the situation. "What are we going to do?" they asked each other. "This man certainly performs many miraculous signs. [48] If we leave him alone, the whole nation will follow him, and then the Roman army will come and destroy both our Temple and our nation."

[49] And one of them, Caiaphas, who was high priest that year, said, "How can you be so stupid? [50] Why should the whole nation be destroyed? Let this one man die for the people."

[51] This prophecy that Jesus should die for the entire nation came from Caiaphas in his position as high priest. He didn't think of it himself; he was inspired to say it. [52] It was a prediction that Jesus' death would be not for Israel only, but for the gathering together of all the children of God scattered around the world.

[53] So from that time on the Jewish leaders began to plot Jesus' death. [54] As a result, Jesus stopped his public ministry among the people and left Jerusalem. He went to a place near the wilderness, to the village of Ephraim, and stayed there with his disciples.

[55] It was now almost time for the celebration of Passover, and many people from the country arrived in Jerusalem several days early so they could go through the cleansing ceremony before the Passover began. [56] They wanted to see Jesus, and as they talked in the Temple, they asked each other, "What do you think? Will he come for the Passover?" [57] Meanwhile, the leading priests and Pharisees had publicly announced that anyone seeing Jesus must report him immediately so they could arrest him.

CHAPTER 12

Jesus Anointed at Bethany

Six days before the Passover ceremonies began, Jesus arrived in Bethany, the home of Lazarus—the man he had raised from the dead. [2] A dinner was prepared in Jesus' honor. Martha served, and Lazarus sat at the table with him. [3] Then Mary took a twelve-ounce jar* of expensive perfume made from essence of nard, and she anointed Jesus' feet with it and wiped his feet with her hair. And the house was filled with fragrance.

[4] But Judas Iscariot, one of his disciples—the one who would betray him—

I BELIEVE Jesus brought glory to God when he raised Lazarus from the dead. (11:40)

I BELIEVE Jesus spoke the word and raised Lazarus from the dead. (11:44)

See the profile for the Pharisees (page 1087) at Matthew 12:14.

I CARE more about God's truth and salvation than about my political security. (11:48)

See Mary and Martha's profile (page 1171) at Luke 10:42.

See Judas's profile (page 1121) at Mark 3:19.

11:47 Greek *the Sanhedrin.* 12:3 Greek *took 1 litra* [327 grams].

said, [5]"That perfume was worth a small fortune.* It should have been sold and the money given to the poor." [6]Not that he cared for the poor—he was a thief who was in charge of the disciples' funds, and he often took some for his own use.

[7]Jesus replied, "Leave her alone. She did it in preparation for my burial. [8]You will always have the poor among you, but I will not be here with you much longer."

[9]When all the people* heard of Jesus' arrival, they flocked to see him and also to see Lazarus, the man Jesus had raised from the dead. [10]Then the leading priests decided to kill Lazarus, too, [11]for it was because of him that many of the people had deserted them and believed in Jesus.

The Triumphal Entry

[12] The next day, the news that Jesus was on the way to Jerusalem swept through the city. A huge crowd of Passover visitors [13]took palm branches and went down the road to meet him. They shouted,

"Praise God!*
Bless the one who comes in the name of the Lord!
Hail to the King of Israel!"*

[14]Jesus found a young donkey and sat on it, fulfilling the prophecy that said:

[15] "Don't be afraid, people of Israel.*
Look, your King is coming,
    sitting on a donkey's colt."*

[16]His disciples didn't realize at the time that this was a fulfillment of prophecy. But after Jesus entered into his glory, they remembered that these Scriptures had come true before their eyes.

[17]Those in the crowd who had seen Jesus call Lazarus back to life were telling others all about it. [18]That was the main reason so many went out to meet him—because they had heard about this mighty miracle. [19]Then the Pharisees said to each other, "We've lost. Look, the whole world has gone after him!"

Jesus Predicts His Death

[20]Some Greeks who had come to Jerusalem to attend the Passover [21]paid a visit to Philip, who was from Bethsaida in Galilee. They said, "Sir, we want to meet Jesus." [22]Philip told Andrew about it, and they went together to ask Jesus.

[23]Jesus replied, "The time has come for the Son of Man to enter into his glory. [24]The truth is, a kernel of wheat must be planted in the soil. Unless it dies it will be alone—a single seed. But its death will produce many new kernels—a plentiful harvest of new lives. [25] Those who love their life in this world will lose it. Those who despise their life in this world will keep it for eternal life. [26]All those who want to be my disciples must come and follow me, because my servants must be where I am. And if they follow me, the Father will honor them. [27]Now my soul is deeply troubled. Should I pray, 'Father, save me from what lies ahead'? But that is the very reason why I came! [28]Father, bring glory to your name."

Then a voice spoke from heaven, saying, "I have already brought it glory, and I will do it again." [29]When the crowd heard the voice, some thought it was thunder, while others declared an angel had spoken to him.

[30]Then Jesus told them, "The voice was for your benefit, not mine. [31]The time of judgment for the world has come, when the prince of this world* will

---

I DO NOT STEAL money from offerings given to God's work. (12:6)

I BELIEVE Jesus truly did raise Lazarus from the dead. (12:11)

I BELIEVE Jesus fulfilled the prophecy that the Messiah would enter Jerusalem riding a donkey. (12:15)

I TELL others about the miraculous things Jesus has done. (12:17)

See the profile for the Pharisees (page 1087) at Matthew 12:14.

I BELIEVE God brought glory to his name through Jesus' life and death. (12:28)

12:5 Greek *300 denarii.* A denarius was equivalent to a full day's wage.   12:9 Greek *Jewish people;* also in 12:11.
12:13a Greek *Hosanna,* an exclamation of praise that literally means "save now."   12:13b Ps 118:25-26; Zeph 3:15.   12:15a Greek *daughter of Zion.*   12:15b Zech 9:9.   12:31 *The prince of this world* is a name for Satan.

be cast out. [32]And when I am lifted up on the cross,* I will draw everyone to myself." [33]He said this to indicate how he was going to die.

[34]"Die?" asked the crowd. "We understood from Scripture that the Messiah would live forever. Why are you saying the Son of Man will die? Who is this Son of Man you are talking about?"

[35]Jesus replied, "My light will shine out for you just a little while longer. Walk in it while you can, so you will not stumble when the darkness falls. If you walk in the darkness, you cannot see where you are going. [36]Believe in the light while there is still time; then you will become children of the light." After saying these things, Jesus went away and was hidden from them.

I MAKE the most of every opportunity to understand and believe God's truth. (12:35)

LIKE LAZARUS   *I believe God one day will raise me from the dead.*
John 12:11

What would you want more than anything after your death?

Throughout the Scriptures, the Lord offers the promise of resurrection and eternal life to those who believe in him. That hope takes the sting out of death, but not the grief.

Before his martyrdom, the apostle Paul admitted: "I'm torn between two desires: Sometimes I want to live, and sometimes I long to go and be with Christ. That would be far better for me, but it is better for you that I live" (Philippians 1:23-24).

When they think of going to be with the Lord, many hesitate and wonder, "What about all the loved ones I'll leave behind?"

Lazarus had the unique privilege of being raised from the dead to be reunited with his loved ones *and* still be with the Lord.

Like his sisters, Lazarus had a deep love for and faith in the Lord Jesus. They looked forward to the resurrection. Still, Lazarus must have hoped and prayed that Jesus would arrive in time to heal him before he died.

Like people in Jesus' day, you and I may not understand why the Lord heals some and allows others to die. We ourselves may face the prospect of an early death. Even Lazarus eventually had to face death again. But the second time, he died confident that he would receive a heavenly body that will never die.

Like Lazarus, let us never lose the hope and joy of knowing that after this life "we will be at home with the Lord" (2 Corinthians 5:8).

○ *Today's Scripture reading is John 11:1–12:36.*

The Unbelief of the People
[37]But despite all the miraculous signs he had done, most of the people did not believe in him. [38]This is exactly what Isaiah the prophet had predicted:

I BELIEVE Isaiah accurately predicted the nation of Israel's unbelief. (12:38)

See Isaiah's profile (page 801) at Isaiah 6:13.

"Lord, who has believed our message?
   To whom will the Lord reveal his saving power?"*

[39]But the people couldn't believe, for as Isaiah also said,

[40]"The Lord has blinded their eyes
   and hardened their hearts—
so their eyes cannot see,
   and their hearts cannot understand,
and they cannot turn to me
   and let me heal them."*

[41]Isaiah was referring to Jesus when he made this prediction, because he was given a vision of the Messiah's glory. [42]Many people, including some of the Jewish leaders, believed in him. But they wouldn't admit it to anyone because

12:32 Greek *lifted up from the earth.*   12:38 Isa 53:1.   12:40 Isa 6:10.

I LOVE God's praise more than human praise. (12:43)

I AM no longer in darkness, because I trust in Jesus, the light of the world. (12:46)

of their fear that the Pharisees would expel them from the synagogue. [43]For they loved human praise more than the praise of God.

[44]Jesus shouted to the crowds, "If you trust me, you are really trusting God who sent me. [45]For when you see me, you are seeing the one who sent me. [46]I have come as a light to shine in this dark world, so that all who put their trust in me will no longer remain in the darkness. [47]If anyone hears me and doesn't obey me, I am not his judge—for I have come to save the world and not to judge it. [48]But all who reject me and my message will be judged at the day of judgment by the truth I have spoken. [49]I don't speak on my own authority. The Father who sent me gave me his own instructions as to what I should say. [50]And I know his instructions lead to eternal life; so I say whatever the Father tells me to say!"

CHAPTER 13

Jesus Washes His Disciples' Feet

I BELIEVE Jesus showed the full extent of his love when he washed his disciples' feet. (13:1)

See Judas's profile (page 1121) at Mark 3:19.

I BELIEVE Jesus knew exactly who he was, where he had come from, and where he was going. (13:3)

See Peter's profile (page 1111) at Matthew 26:75.

Before the Passover celebration, Jesus knew that his hour had come to leave this world and return to his Father. He now showed the disciples the full extent of his love.* [2]It was time for supper, and the Devil had already enticed Judas, son of Simon Iscariot, to carry out his plan to betray Jesus. [3]Jesus knew that the Father had given him authority over everything and that he had come from God and would return to God. [4]So he got up from the table, took off his robe, wrapped a towel around his waist, [5]and poured water into a basin. Then he began to wash the disciples' feet and to wipe them with the towel he had around him.

[6]When he came to Simon Peter, Peter said to him, "Lord, why are you going to wash my feet?"

[7]Jesus replied, "You don't understand now why I am doing it; someday you will."

[8]"No," Peter protested, "you will never wash my feet!"

Jesus replied, "But if I don't wash you, you won't belong to me."

[9]Simon Peter exclaimed, "Then wash my hands and head as well, Lord, not just my feet!"

I HAVE BEEN MADE clean by Jesus. (13:10)

[10]Jesus replied, "A person who has bathed all over does not need to wash, except for the feet,* to be entirely clean. And you are clean, but that isn't true of everyone here." [11]For Jesus knew who would betray him. That is what he meant when he said, "Not all of you are clean."

[12]After washing their feet, he put on his robe again and sat down and asked, "Do you understand what I was doing? [13]You call me 'Teacher' and 'Lord,' and you are right, because it is true. [14]And since I, the Lord and Teacher, have washed your feet, you ought to wash each other's feet. [15]I have given you an example to follow. Do as I have done to you. [16]How true it is that a servant is not greater than the master. Nor are messengers more important than the one who sends them. [17]You know these things—now do them! That is the path of blessing.

I FOLLOW Jesus' example and humble myself to serve others. (13:14)

Jesus Predicts His Betrayal

I BELIEVE Jesus knew all about his disciples, including which one would betray him. (13:18)

[18]"I am not saying these things to all of you; I know so well each one of you I chose. The Scriptures declare, 'The one who shares my food has turned against me,'* and this will soon come true. [19]I tell you this now, so that when it happens you will believe I am the Messiah. [20]Truly, anyone who welcomes my messenger is welcoming me, and anyone who welcomes me is welcoming the Father who sent me."

[21]Now Jesus was in great anguish of spirit, and he exclaimed, "The truth is, one of you will betray me!"

See John's profile (page 1435) at Revelation 1:9.

[22]The disciples looked at each other, wondering whom he could mean. [23]One

13:1 Or *He loved his disciples to the very end.* 13:10 Some manuscripts do not include *except for the feet.*
13:18 Ps 41:9.

of Jesus' disciples, the one Jesus loved, was sitting next to Jesus at the table.* ²⁴Simon Peter motioned to him to ask who would do this terrible thing. ²⁵Leaning toward Jesus, he asked, "Lord, who is it?"

²⁶Jesus said, "It is the one to whom I give the bread dipped in the sauce." And when he had dipped it, he gave it to Judas, son of Simon Iscariot. ²⁷As soon as Judas had eaten the bread, Satan entered into him. Then Jesus told him, "Hurry. Do it now." ²⁸None of the others at the table knew what Jesus meant. ²⁹Since Judas was their treasurer, some thought Jesus was telling him to go and pay for the food or to give some money to the poor. ³⁰So Judas left at once, going out into the night.

Jesus Predicts Peter's Denial

³¹As soon as Judas left the room, Jesus said, "The time has come for me, the Son of Man, to enter into my glory, and God will receive glory because of all that happens to me. ³²And God will bring* me into my glory very soon. ³³Dear children, how brief are these moments before I must go away and leave you! Then, though you search for me, you cannot come to me—just as I told the Jewish leaders. ³⁴So now I am giving you a new commandment: Love each other. Just as I have loved you, you should love each other. ³⁵Your love for one another will prove to the world that you are my disciples."

I PROVE that I am Jesus' disciple when I love others. (13:35)

³⁶Simon Peter said, "Lord, where are you going?"

And Jesus replied, "You can't go with me now, but you will follow me later."

³⁷"But why can't I come now, Lord?" he asked. "I am ready to die for you."

³⁸Jesus answered, "Die for me? No, before the rooster crows tomorrow morning, you will deny three times that you even know me.

I BELIEVE Jesus accurately predicted that Peter would deny him. (13:38)

CHAPTER 14

Jesus, the Way to the Father

"Don't be troubled. You trust God, now trust in me. ²There are many rooms in my Father's home, and I am going to prepare a place for you. If this were not so, I would tell you plainly. ³When everything is ready, I will come and get you, so that you will always be with me where I am. ⁴And you know where I am going and how to get there."

I BELIEVE Jesus is preparing a place for me in heaven and will come again to take me there. (14:3)

⁵"No, we don't know, Lord," Thomas said. "We haven't any idea where you are going, so how can we know the way?"

⁶Jesus told him, "I am the way, the truth, and the life. No one can come to the Father except through me. ⁷If you had known who I am, then you would have known who my Father is.* From now on you know him and have seen him!"

See Thomas's profile (page 1231) at John 20:28.

⁸Philip said, "Lord, show us the Father and we will be satisfied."

⁹Jesus replied, "Philip, don't you even yet know who I am, even after all the time I have been with you? Anyone who has seen me has seen the Father! So why are you asking to see him? ¹⁰Don't you believe that I am in the Father and the Father is in me? The words I say are not my own, but my Father who lives in me does his work through me. ¹¹Just believe that I am in the Father and the Father is in me. Or at least believe because of what you have seen me do.

I BELIEVE Jesus is the way, the truth, and the life, and that I can come to the Father only through him. (14:6)

¹²"The truth is, anyone who believes in me will do the same works I have done, and even greater works, because I am going to be with the Father. ¹³You can ask for anything in my name, and I will do it, because the work of the Son brings glory to the Father. ¹⁴Yes, ask anything in my name, and I will do it!

I BELIEVE Jesus is the exact representation of the Father (Colossians 1:15; Hebrews 1:3). (14:9)

Jesus Promises the Holy Spirit

¹⁵"If you love me, obey my commandments. ¹⁶And I will ask the Father, and he will give you another Counselor,* who will never leave you. ¹⁷He is the

I LOVE Jesus and keep his commands. (14:15)

13:23 Greek *was reclining on Jesus' bosom.* The "disciple whom Jesus loved" was probably John.   **13:32** Some manuscripts read *And if God is glorified in him [the Son of Man], God will bring.*   **14:7** Some manuscripts read *If you really have known me, you will know who my Father is.*   **14:16** Or *Comforter,* or *Encourager,* or *Advocate.* Greek *Paraclete;* also in 14:26.

Holy Spirit, who leads into all truth. The world at large cannot receive him, because it isn't looking for him and doesn't recognize him. But you do, because he lives with you now and later will be in you. [18]No, I will not abandon you as orphans—I will come to you. [19]In just a little while the world will not see me again, but you will. For I will live again, and you will, too. [20]When I am raised to life again, you will know that I am in my Father, and you are in me, and I am in you. [21]Those who obey my commandments are the ones who love me. And because they love me, my Father will love them, and I will love them. And I will reveal myself to each one of them."

[22]Judas (not Judas Iscariot, but the other disciple with that name) said to him, "Lord, why are you going to reveal yourself only to us and not to the world at large?"

[23]Jesus replied, "All those who love me will do what I say. My Father will love them, and we will come to them and live with them. [24]Anyone who doesn't love me will not do what I say. And remember, my words are not my own. This message is from the Father who sent me. [25]I am telling you these things now while I am still with you. [26]But when the Father sends the Counselor as my representative—and by the Counselor I mean the Holy Spirit—he will teach you everything and will remind you of everything I myself have told you.

[27]"I am leaving you with a gift—peace of mind and heart. And the peace I give isn't like the peace the world gives. So don't be troubled or afraid. [28]Remember what I told you: I am going away, but I will come back to you again. If you really love me, you will be very happy for me, because now I can go to the Father, who is greater than I am. [29]I have told you these things before they happen so that you will believe when they do happen.

[30]"I don't have much more time to talk to you, because the prince of this world approaches. He has no power over me, [31]but I will do what the Father requires of me, so that the world will know that I love the Father. Come, let's be going.

CHAPTER 15

Jesus, the True Vine

"I am the true vine, and my Father is the gardener. [2]He cuts off every branch that doesn't produce fruit, and he prunes the branches that do bear fruit so they will produce even more. [3]You have already been pruned for greater fruitfulness by the message I have given you. [4]Remain in me, and I will remain in you. For a branch cannot produce fruit if it is severed from the vine, and you cannot be fruitful apart from me.

[5]"Yes, I am the vine; you are the branches. Those who remain in me, and I in them, will produce much fruit. For apart from me you can do nothing. [6]Anyone who parts from me is thrown away like a useless branch and withers. Such branches are gathered into a pile to be burned. [7]But if you stay joined to me and my words remain in you, you may ask any request you like, and it will be granted! [8]My true disciples produce much fruit. This brings great glory to my Father.

[9]"I have loved you even as the Father has loved me. Remain in my love. [10]When you obey me, you remain in my love, just as I obey my Father and remain in his love. [11]I have told you this so that you will be filled with my joy. Yes, your joy will overflow! [12]I command you to love each other in the same way that I love you. [13]And here is how to measure it—the greatest love is shown when people lay down their lives for their friends. [14]You are my friends if you obey me. [15]I no longer call you servants, because a master doesn't confide in his servants. Now you are my friends, since I have told you everything the Father told me. [16]You didn't choose me. I chose you. I appointed

---

See Judas's profile (page 1121) at Mark 3:19.

I BELIEVE the Father loves me and comes to live with those who love and obey his Son, Jesus. (14:23)

I BELIEVE Jesus is coming again. (14:28)

I BELIEVE I can do nothing fruitful unless I remain connected to Jesus. (15:4)

I REMAIN in Jesus' love by obeying him. (15:10)

you to go and produce fruit that will last, so that the Father will give you whatever you ask for, using my name. ¹⁷I command you to love each other.

The World's Hatred

¹⁸"When the world hates you, remember it hated me before it hated you. ¹⁹The world would love you if you belonged to it, but you don't. I chose you to come out of the world, and so it hates you. ²⁰Do you remember what I told you? 'A servant is not greater than the master.' Since they persecuted me, naturally they will persecute you. And if they had listened to me, they would listen to you! ²¹The people of the world will hate you because you belong to me, for they don't know God who sent me. ²²They would not be guilty if I had not come and spoken to them. But now they have no excuse for their sin. ²³Anyone who hates me hates my Father, too. ²⁴If I hadn't done such miraculous signs among them that no one else could do, they would not be counted guilty. But as it is, they saw all that I did and yet hated both of us—me and my Father. ²⁵This has fulfilled what the Scriptures said: 'They hated me without cause.'*

²⁶"But I will send you the Counselor*—the Spirit of truth. He will come to you from the Father and will tell you all about me. ²⁷And you must also tell others about me because you have been with me from the beginning.

I REMEMBER the world hated Jesus and am not surprised if it hates his followers. (15:18)

I TELL others about Jesus. (15:27)

CHAPTER 16

"I have told you these things so that you won't fall away. ²For you will be expelled from the synagogues, and the time is coming when those who kill you will think they are doing God a service. ³This is because they have never known the Father or me. ⁴Yes, I'm telling you these things now, so that when they happen, you will remember I warned you. I didn't tell you earlier because I was going to be with you for a while longer.

I REMEMBER Jesus' warning when I am ridiculed, threatened, and persecuted. (16:4)

The Work of the Holy Spirit

⁵"But now I am going away to the one who sent me, and none of you has asked me where I am going. ⁶Instead, you are very sad. ⁷But it is actually best for you that I go away, because if I don't, the Counselor* won't come. If I do go away, he will come because I will send him to you. ⁸And when he comes, he will convince the world of its sin, and of God's righteousness, and of the coming judgment. ⁹The world's sin is unbelief in me. ¹⁰Righteousness is available because I go to the Father, and you will see me no more. ¹¹Judgment will come because the prince of this world has already been judged.

I BELIEVE the Holy Spirit convinces the world of sin, of God's righteousness, and of coming judgment. (16:8)

¹²"Oh, there is so much more I want to tell you, but you can't bear it now. ¹³When the Spirit of truth comes, he will guide you into all truth. He will not be presenting his own ideas; he will be telling you what he has heard. He will tell you about the future. ¹⁴He will bring me glory by revealing to you whatever he receives from me. ¹⁵All that the Father has is mine; this is what I mean when I say that the Spirit will reveal to you whatever he receives from me.

I BELIEVE the Holy Spirit brings glory to the Lord Jesus. (16:14)

Sadness Will Be Turned to Joy

¹⁶"In just a little while I will be gone, and you won't see me anymore. Then, just a little while after that, you will see me again."

¹⁷The disciples asked each other, "What does he mean when he says, 'You won't see me, and then you will see me'? And what does he mean when he says, 'I am going to the Father'? ¹⁸And what does he mean by 'a little while'? We don't understand."

¹⁹Jesus realized they wanted to ask him, so he said, "Are you asking yourselves what I meant? I said in just a little while I will be gone, and you won't see me anymore. Then, just a little while after that, you will see me again.

15:25 Pss 35:19; 69:4.   15:26 Or *Comforter,* or *Encourager,* or *Advocate.* Greek *Paraclete.*   16:7 Or *Comforter,* or *Encourager,* or *Advocate.* Greek *Paraclete.*

I BELIEVE Jesus accurately predicted that the disciples would mourn when he went away and rejoice when he came back to life. (16:20)

I BELIEVE the Father loves me because I love Jesus and believe in him. (16:27)

I TAKE HEART in the midst of my trials and sorrows because Jesus has overcome the world. (16:33)

I BELIEVE Jesus brought the Father glory by his complete obedience. (17:4)

I BELIEVE Jesus prayed earnestly for his disciples. (17:9)

I DO NOT BELONG to the world. (17:14)

[20] Truly, you will weep and mourn over what is going to happen to me, but the world will rejoice. You will grieve, but your grief will suddenly turn to wonderful joy when you see me again. [21] It will be like a woman experiencing the pains of labor. When her child is born, her anguish gives place to joy because she has brought a new person into the world. [22] You have sorrow now, but I will see you again; then you will rejoice, and no one can rob you of that joy. [23] At that time you won't need to ask me for anything. The truth is, you can go directly to the Father and ask him, and he will grant your request because you use my name. [24] You haven't done this before. Ask, using my name, and you will receive, and you will have abundant joy.

[25] "I have spoken of these matters in parables, but the time will come when this will not be necessary, and I will tell you plainly all about the Father. [26] Then you will ask in my name. I'm not saying I will ask the Father on your behalf, [27] for the Father himself loves you dearly because you love me and believe that I came from God. [28] Yes, I came from the Father into the world, and I will leave the world and return to the Father."

[29] Then his disciples said, "At last you are speaking plainly and not in parables. [30] Now we understand that you know everything and don't need anyone to tell you anything.* From this we believe that you came from God."

[31] Jesus asked, "Do you finally believe? [32] But the time is coming—in fact, it is already here—when you will be scattered, each one going his own way, leaving me alone. Yet I am not alone because the Father is with me. [33] I have told you all this so that you may have peace in me. Here on earth you will have many trials and sorrows. But take heart, because I have overcome the world."

CHAPTER 17

The Prayer of Jesus

When Jesus had finished saying all these things, he looked up to heaven and said, "Father, the time has come. Glorify your Son so he can give glory back to you. [2] For you have given him authority over everyone in all the earth. He gives eternal life to each one you have given him. [3] And this is the way to have eternal life—to know you, the only true God, and Jesus Christ, the one you sent to earth. [4] I brought glory to you here on earth by doing everything you told me to do. [5] And now, Father, bring me into the glory we shared before the world began.

[6] "I have told these men about you. They were in the world, but then you gave them to me. Actually, they were always yours, and you gave them to me; and they have kept your word. [7] Now they know that everything I have is a gift from you, [8] for I have passed on to them the words you gave me; and they accepted them and know that I came from you, and they believe you sent me.

[9] "My prayer is not for the world, but for those you have given me, because they belong to you. [10] And all of them, since they are mine, belong to you; and you have given them back to me, so they are my glory! [11] Now I am departing the world; I am leaving them behind and coming to you. Holy Father, keep them and care for them—all those you have given me—so that they will be united just as we are. [12] During my time here, I have kept them safe.* I guarded them so that not one was lost, except the one headed for destruction, as the Scriptures foretold.

[13] "And now I am coming to you. I have told them many things while I was with them so they would be filled with my joy. [14] I have given them your word. And the world hates them because they do not belong to the world, just as I do not. [15] I'm not asking you to take them out of the world, but to keep them safe from the evil one. [16] They are not part of this world any more

16:30 Or *don't need that anyone should ask you anything.* 17:12 Greek *I have kept in your name those whom you have given me.*

than I am. [17]Make them pure and holy by teaching them your words of truth. [18]As you sent me into the world, I am sending them into the world. [19]And I give myself entirely to you so they also might be entirely yours.

[20]"I am praying not only for these disciples but also for all who will ever believe in me because of their testimony. [21]My prayer for all of them is that they will be one, just as you and I are one, Father—that just as you are in me and I am in you, so they will be in us, and the world will believe you sent me.

[22]"I have given them the glory you gave me, so that they may be one, as we are—[23]I in them and you in me, all being perfected into one. Then the world will know that you sent me and will understand that you love them as much as you love me. [24]Father, I want these whom you've given me to be with me, so they can see my glory. You gave me the glory because you loved me even before the world began!

[25]"O righteous Father, the world doesn't know you, but I do; and these disciples know you sent me. [26]And I have revealed you to them and will keep on revealing you. I will do this so that your love for me may be in them and I in them."

CHAPTER 18

Jesus Is Betrayed and Arrested

After saying these things, Jesus crossed the Kidron Valley with his disciples and entered a grove of olive trees. [2]Judas, the betrayer, knew this place, because Jesus had gone there many times with his disciples. [3]The leading priests and Pharisees had given Judas a battalion of Roman soldiers and Temple guards to accompany him. Now with blazing torches, lanterns, and weapons, they arrived at the olive grove.

[4]Jesus fully realized all that was going to happen to him. Stepping forward to meet them, he asked, "Whom are you looking for?"

[5]"Jesus of Nazareth," they replied.

"I am he,"* Jesus said. Judas was standing there with them when Jesus identified himself. [6]And as he said, "I am he," they all fell backward to the ground! [7]Once more he asked them, "Whom are you searching for?"

And again they replied, "Jesus of Nazareth."

[8]"I told you that I am he," Jesus said. "And since I am the one you want, let these others go." [9]He did this to fulfill his own statement: "I have not lost a single one of those you gave me."*

[10]Then Simon Peter drew a sword and slashed off the right ear of Malchus, the high priest's servant. [11]But Jesus said to Peter, "Put your sword back into its sheath. Shall I not drink from the cup the Father has given me?"

Annas Questions Jesus

[12]So the soldiers, their commanding officer, and the Temple guards arrested Jesus and tied him up. [13]First they took him to Annas, the father-in-law of Caiaphas, the high priest that year. [14]Caiaphas was the one who had told the other Jewish leaders, "Better that one should die for all."

Peter's First Denial

[15]Simon Peter followed along behind, as did another of the disciples. That other disciple was acquainted with the high priest, so he was allowed to enter the courtyard with Jesus. [16]Peter stood outside the gate. Then the other disciple spoke to the woman watching at the gate, and she let Peter in. [17]The woman asked Peter, "Aren't you one of Jesus' disciples?"

"No," he said, "I am not."

[18]The guards and the household servants were standing around a charcoal

---

I BELIEVE Jesus has prayed for everyone who has believed in him—including me (Romans 8:34). (17:20)

I LOOK FORWARD to seeing Jesus' glory, which he wants to show to all his disciples. (17:24)

See Judas's profile (page 1121) at Mark 3:19.

See the profile for the Pharisees (page 1087) at Matthew 12:14.

I BELIEVE Jesus knew exactly what was going to happen when Judas and the soldiers came after him in the olive grove. (18:4)

I BELIEVE Judas and the soldiers all fell back onto the ground when Jesus said who he was. (18:6)

See Peter's profile (page 1111) at Matthew 26:75.

I BELIEVE Jesus willingly took the cup of suffering the Father had given him. (18:11)

I DO NOT DENY that I am one of Jesus' disciples, no matter what the danger or threat. (18:17)

18:5 Greek *I am;* also in 18:6, 8.   18:9 See John 6:39 and 17:12.

fire they had made because it was cold. And Peter stood there with them, warming himself.

The High Priest Questions Jesus

[19]Inside, the high priest began asking Jesus about his followers and what he had been teaching them. [20]Jesus replied, "What I teach is widely known, because I have preached regularly in the synagogues and the Temple. I have been heard by people* everywhere, and I teach nothing in private that I have not said in public. [21]Why are you asking me this question? Ask those who heard me. They know what I said."

[22]One of the Temple guards standing there struck Jesus on the face. "Is that the way to answer the high priest?" he demanded.

[23]Jesus replied, "If I said anything wrong, you must give evidence for it. Should you hit a man for telling the truth?"

[24]Then Annas bound Jesus and sent him to Caiaphas, the high priest.

Peter's Second and Third Denials

[25]Meanwhile, as Simon Peter was standing by the fire, they asked him again, "Aren't you one of his disciples?"

"I am not," he said.

[26]But one of the household servants of the high priest, a relative of the man whose ear Peter had cut off, asked, "Didn't I see you out there in the olive grove with Jesus?" [27]Again Peter denied it. And immediately a rooster crowed.

Jesus' Trial before Pilate

[28]Jesus' trial before Caiaphas ended in the early hours of the morning. Then he was taken to the headquarters of the Roman governor. His accusers didn't go in themselves because it would defile them, and they wouldn't be allowed to celebrate the Passover feast. [29]So Pilate, the governor, went out to them and asked, "What is your charge against this man?"

[30]"We wouldn't have handed him over to you if he weren't a criminal!" they retorted.

[31]"Then take him away and judge him by your own laws," Pilate told them.

"Only the Romans are permitted to execute someone," the Jewish leaders replied. [32]This fulfilled Jesus' prediction about the way he would die.*

[33]Then Pilate went back inside and called for Jesus to be brought to him. "Are you the King of the Jews?" he asked him.

[34]Jesus replied, "Is this your own question, or did others tell you about me?"

[35]"Am I a Jew?" Pilate asked. "Your own people and their leading priests brought you here. Why? What have you done?"

[36]Then Jesus answered, "I am not an earthly king. If I were, my followers would have fought when I was arrested by the Jewish leaders. But my Kingdom is not of this world."

[37]Pilate replied, "You are a king then?"

"You say that I am a king, and you are right," Jesus said. "I was born for that purpose. And I came to bring truth to the world. All who love the truth recognize that what I say is true."

[38]"What is truth?" Pilate asked. Then he went out again to the people and told them, "He is not guilty of any crime. [39]But you have a custom of asking me to release someone from prison each year at Passover. So if you want me to, I'll release the King of the Jews."

[40]But they shouted back, "No! Not this man, but Barabbas!" (Barabbas was a criminal.)

I BELIEVE Jesus told the truth without hesitation while under arrest. (18:23)

I ABHOR the hypocrisy of attempting to maintain ceremonial purity while rebelling against the Lord. (18:28)

See Pilate's profile (page 1229) at John 19:16.

I BELIEVE Jesus accurately predicted the way he would die. (18:32)

I BELIEVE Jesus truly is the King of kings and Lord of lords (Revelation 19:16). (18:36)

18:20 Greek *Jewish people*; also in 18:38. **18:32** See John 12:32-33.

CHAPTER 19

Jesus Sentenced to Death

Then Pilate had Jesus flogged with a lead-tipped whip. ²The soldiers made a crown of long, sharp thorns and put it on his head, and they put a royal purple robe on him. ³"Hail! King of the Jews!" they mocked, and they hit him with their fists.

⁴Pilate went outside again and said to the people, "I am going to bring him out to you now, but understand clearly that I find him not guilty." ⁵Then Jesus came out wearing the crown of thorns and the purple robe. And Pilate said, "Here is the man!"

⁶When they saw him, the leading priests and Temple guards began shouting, "Crucify! Crucify!"

"You crucify him," Pilate said. "I find him not guilty."

⁷The Jewish leaders replied, "By our laws he ought to die because he called himself the Son of God."

⁸When Pilate heard this, he was more frightened than ever. ⁹He took Jesus back into the headquarters again and asked him, "Where are you from?" But Jesus gave no answer. ¹⁰"You won't talk to me?" Pilate demanded. "Don't you realize that I have the power to release you or to crucify you?"

¹¹Then Jesus said, "You would have no power over me at all unless it were given to you from above. So the one who brought me to you has the greater sin."

¹²Then Pilate tried to release him, but the Jewish leaders told him, "If you release this man, you are not a friend of Caesar. Anyone who declares himself a king is a rebel against Caesar."

¹³When they said this, Pilate brought Jesus out to them again. Then Pilate sat down on the judgment seat on the platform that is called the Stone Pavement (in Hebrew, *Gabbatha*). ¹⁴It was now about noon of the day of preparation for the Passover. And Pilate said to the people,* "Here is your king!"

¹⁵"Away with him," they yelled. "Away with him—crucify him!"

"What? Crucify your king?" Pilate asked.

"We have no king but Caesar," the leading priests shouted back.

¹⁶Then Pilate gave Jesus to them to be crucified.

The Crucifixion

So they took Jesus and led him away. ¹⁷Carrying the cross by himself, Jesus went to the place called Skull Hill (in Hebrew, *Golgotha*). ¹⁸There they crucified him. There were two others crucified with him, one on either side, with Jesus between them. ¹⁹And Pilate posted a sign over him that read, "Jesus of Nazareth, the King of the Jews." ²⁰The place where Jesus was crucified was near the city; and the sign was written in Hebrew, Latin, and Greek, so that many people could read it.

²¹Then the leading priests said to Pilate, "Change it from 'The King of the Jews' to 'He said, I am King of the Jews.' "

²²Pilate replied, "What I have written, I have written. It stays exactly as it is."

²³When the soldiers had crucified Jesus, they divided his clothes among the four of them. They also took his robe, but it was seamless, woven in one piece from the top. ²⁴So they said, "Let's not tear it but throw dice* to see who gets it." This fulfilled the Scripture that says, "They divided my clothes among them and threw dice for my robe."* So that is what they did.

²⁵Standing near the cross were Jesus' mother, and his mother's sister, Mary (the wife of Clopas), and Mary Magdalene. ²⁶When Jesus saw his mother standing there beside the disciple he loved, he said to her, "Woman, he is your son." ²⁷And he said to this disciple, "She is your mother." And from then on this disciple took her into his home.

19:14 Greek *Jewish people;* also in 19:20.   19:24a Greek *cast lots.*   19:24b Ps 22:18.

I BELIEVE Jesus was flogged and beaten, just as the Scriptures predicted (Isaiah 53:5). (19:1)

I BELIEVE Jesus was innocent of any sin or wrongdoing. (19:4)

I BELIEVE Jesus truly was and is the Son of God. (19:7)

I ABHOR the hypocrisy of attempting to maintain political peace while rebelling against the Lord. (19:12)

See the Dying Thief's profile (page 1191) at Luke 23:42.

I BELIEVE Jesus is the King of all humanity, Jews and Gentiles alike. (19:19)

See the profiles for Mary (page 1149) and Mary Magdalene (page 1163) at Luke 1:38 and Luke 8:2.

See John's profile (page 1435) at Revelation 1:9.

I BELIEVE Jesus continued to demonstrate great love and compassion even while dying on the cross. (19:27)

The Death of Jesus

[28]Jesus knew that everything was now finished, and to fulfill the Scriptures he said, "I am thirsty."* [29]A jar of sour wine was sitting there, so they soaked a sponge in it, put it on a hyssop branch, and held it up to his lips. [30]When Jesus had tasted it, he said, "It is finished!" Then he bowed his head and gave up his spirit.

[31]The Jewish leaders didn't want the victims hanging there the next day, which was the Sabbath (and a very special Sabbath at that, because it was the Passover), so they asked Pilate to hasten their deaths by ordering that their legs be broken. Then their bodies could be taken down. [32]So the soldiers came and broke the legs of the two men crucified with Jesus. [33]But when they came to Jesus, they saw that he was dead already, so they didn't break his legs. [34]One of the soldiers, however, pierced his side with a spear, and blood and water flowed out. [35]This report is from an eyewitness giving an accurate account; it is presented so that you also can believe. [36]These things happened in fulfillment of the Scriptures that say, "Not one of his bones will be broken,"* [37]and "They will look on him whom they pierced."*

The Burial of Jesus

[38]Afterward Joseph of Arimathea, who had been a secret disciple of Jesus (because he feared the Jewish leaders), asked Pilate for permission to take Jesus' body down. When Pilate gave him permission, he came and took the body away. [39]Nicodemus, the man who had come to Jesus at night, also came, bringing about seventy-five pounds* of embalming ointment made from myrrh and aloes. [40]Together they wrapped Jesus' body in a long linen cloth with the spices, as is the Jewish custom of burial. [41]The place of crucifixion was near a garden, where there was a new tomb, never used before. [42]And so, because it was the day of preparation before the Passover and since the tomb was close at hand, they laid Jesus there.

CHAPTER 20

The Resurrection

Early Sunday morning,* while it was still dark, Mary Magdalene came to the tomb and found that the stone had been rolled away from the entrance. [2]She ran and found Simon Peter and the other disciple, the one whom Jesus loved. She said, "They have taken the Lord's body out of the tomb, and I don't know where they have put him!"

[3]Peter and the other disciple ran to the tomb to see. [4]The other disciple outran Peter and got there first. [5]He stooped and looked in and saw the linen cloth lying there, but he didn't go in. [6]Then Simon Peter arrived and went inside. He also noticed the linen wrappings lying there, [7]while the cloth that had covered Jesus' head was folded up and lying to the side. [8]Then the other disciple also went in, and he saw and believed—[9]for until then they hadn't realized that the Scriptures said he would rise from the dead. [10]Then they went home.

Jesus Appears to Mary Magdalene

[11]Mary was standing outside the tomb crying, and as she wept, she stooped and looked in. [12]She saw two white-robed angels sitting at the head and foot of the place where the body of Jesus had been lying. [13]"Why are you crying?" the angels asked her.

"Because they have taken away my Lord," she replied, "and I don't know where they have put him."

[14]She glanced over her shoulder and saw someone standing behind her. It was

---

I BELIEVE Jesus gave up his spirit—no one took it from him. (19:30)

I BELIEVE the Scriptures accurately predicted what would happen right after Jesus died. (19:37)

See Joseph of Arimathea's profile (page 1113) at Matthew 27:57.

See Nicodemus's profile (page 1203) at John 3:3.

See Mary Magdalene's profile (page 1163) at Luke 8:2.

See the profiles for Peter (page 1111) and John (page 1435) at Matthew 26:75 and Revelation 1:9.

I BELIEVE the Scriptures accurately predicted that Jesus would rise from the dead. (20:9)

19:28 See Pss 22:15; 69:21.   19:36 Exod 12:46; Num 9:12; Ps 34:20.   19:37 Zech 12:10.   19:39 Greek *100 litras* [32.7 kilograms].   20:1 Greek *On the first day of the week.*

Jesus, but she didn't recognize him. [15]"Why are you crying?" Jesus asked her. "Who are you looking for?"

She thought he was the gardener. "Sir," she said, "if you have taken him away, tell me where you have put him, and I will go and get him."

[16]"Mary!" Jesus said.

She turned toward him and exclaimed, "Teacher!"*

[17]"Don't cling to me," Jesus said, "for I haven't yet ascended to the Father. But go find my brothers and tell them that I am ascending to my Father and your Father, my God and your God."

[18]Mary Magdalene found the disciples and told them, "I have seen the Lord!" Then she gave them his message.

I BELIEVE Jesus knows me by name. (20:16)

UNLIKE PILATE   *I embrace God's truth wholeheartedly.*

John 19:16

What's your greatest claim to fame?

Besides Jesus, few people are spoken of more often in churches around the world every Sunday than Pontius Pilate. Of all people he's even mentioned by name in the Apostles' Creed.

Why all the attention?

History portrays Pilate as a rash, capricious, and ultimately ineffective Roman provincial governor. At his greatest hour of testing, Pilate failed miserably by condemning the world's only innocent man—God's Son, Jesus Christ—to death by crucifixion.

Each Gospel writer records this trial at length. Ironically, they make it sound almost as if Pilate were on trial, not Jesus. And for good reason. If Pilate committed one more blunder, he knew Caesar might forcefully throw him out of office, disgraced. Yet when the pressure was on, Pilate listened to everyone—except the one person telling him the truth!

Despite his better judgment and the urgent warning of his wife (Matthew 27:19), Pilate rejected the lordship of Jesus and bowed to the political will of the chief priests. In a futile attempt to save his own neck, Pilate washed his hands of the truth and secured his infamous place in history.

To discover more about Pilate's fatal error, see Matthew 27:11-26; Mark 15:1-15; and Luke 23:1-25.

○ *Today's Scripture reading is John 18:28–19:16.*

Jesus Appears to His Disciples

[19] That evening, on the first day of the week, the disciples were meeting behind locked doors because they were afraid of the Jewish leaders. Suddenly, Jesus was standing there among them! "Peace be with you," he said. [20]As he spoke, he held out his hands for them to see, and he showed them his side. They were filled with joy when they saw their Lord! [21]He spoke to them again and said, "Peace be with you. As the Father has sent me, so I send you." [22]Then he breathed on them and said to them, "Receive the Holy Spirit. [23]If you forgive anyone's sins, they are forgiven. If you refuse to forgive them, they are unforgiven."

I BELIEVE the disciples were filled with joy when they saw the risen Lord Jesus! (20:20)

I BELIEVE every Christian has received the Holy Spirit (Romans 8:9). (20:22)

Jesus Appears to Thomas

[24]One of the disciples, Thomas (nicknamed the Twin*), was not with the others when Jesus came. [25]They told him, "We have seen the Lord!" But he replied, "I won't believe it unless I see the nail wounds in his hands, put my fingers into them, and place my hand into the wound in his side."

[26]Eight days later the disciples were together again, and this time Thomas was with them. The doors were locked; but suddenly, as before, Jesus was standing among them. He said, "Peace be with you." [27]Then he said to Thomas,

20:16 Greek *and said in Hebrew, "Rabboni," which means "Teacher."*   20:24 Greek *the one who was called Didymus.*

"Put your finger here and see my hands. Put your hand into the wound in my side. Don't be faithless any longer. Believe!"

28"My Lord and my God!" Thomas exclaimed.

29Then Jesus told him, "You believe because you have seen me. Blessed are those who haven't seen me and believe anyway."

Purpose of the Book

30Jesus' disciples saw him do many other miraculous signs besides the ones recorded in this book. 31But these are written so that you may believe* that Jesus is the Messiah, the Son of God, and that by believing in him you will have life.

CHAPTER 21

Jesus Appears to Seven Disciples

Later Jesus appeared again to the disciples beside the Sea of Galilee.* This is how it happened. 2Several of the disciples were there—Simon Peter, Thomas (nicknamed the Twin*), Nathanael from Cana in Galilee, the sons of Zebedee, and two other disciples.

3Simon Peter said, "I'm going fishing."

"We'll come, too," they all said. So they went out in the boat, but they caught nothing all night.

4At dawn the disciples saw Jesus standing on the beach, but they couldn't see who he was. 5He called out, "Friends, have you caught any fish?"

"No," they replied.

6Then he said, "Throw out your net on the right-hand side of the boat, and you'll get plenty of fish!" So they did, and they couldn't draw in the net because there were so many fish in it.

7Then the disciple whom Jesus loved said to Peter, "It is the Lord!" When Simon Peter heard that it was the Lord, he put on his tunic (for he had stripped for work), jumped into the water, and swam ashore. 8The others stayed with the boat and pulled the loaded net to the shore, for they were only out about three hundred feet.* 9When they got there, they saw that a charcoal fire was burning and fish were frying over it, and there was bread.

10"Bring some of the fish you've just caught," Jesus said. 11So Simon Peter went aboard and dragged the net to the shore. There were 153 large fish, and yet the net hadn't torn.

12"Now come and have some breakfast!" Jesus said. And no one dared ask him if he really was the Lord because they were sure of it. 13Then Jesus served them the bread and the fish. 14This was the third time Jesus had appeared to his disciples since he had been raised from the dead.

Jesus Challenges Peter

15After breakfast Jesus said to Simon Peter, "Simon son of John, do you love me more than these?"

"Yes, Lord," Peter replied, "you know I love you."

"Then feed my lambs," Jesus told him.

16Jesus repeated the question: "Simon son of John, do you love me?"

"Yes, Lord," Peter said, "you know I love you."

"Then take care of my sheep," Jesus said.

17Once more he asked him, "Simon son of John, do you love me?"

Peter was grieved that Jesus asked the question a third time. He said, "Lord, you know everything. You know I love you."

Jesus said, "Then feed my sheep. 18The truth is, when you were young, you were able to do as you liked and go wherever you wanted to. But when you are old, you will stretch out your hands, and others will direct you and take

Margin notes:

I ACKNOWLEDGE Jesus as my Lord and my God. (20:28)

I BELIEVE Jesus is the Messiah, the Son of God. (20:31)

See the profiles for Peter (page 1111), Nathanael (page 1201), and John (page 1435) at Matthew 26:75, John 1:49, and Revelation 1:9.

I ACKNOWLEDGE Jesus as my Lord. (21:7)

I BELIEVE the Lord Jesus revealed himself repeatedly to his disciples after his resurrection. (21:14)

I LOVE the Lord Jesus more than anything or anyone else. (21:15)

I DEMONSTRATE active caring and concern for other believers. (21:16)

20:31 Some manuscripts read *may continue to believe.*   **21:1** Greek *Sea of Tiberias,* another name for the Sea of Galilee.   **21:2** Greek *the one who was called Didymus.*   **21:8** Greek *200 cubits* [90 meters].

you where you don't want to go." ¹⁹Jesus said this to let him know what kind of death he would die to glorify God. Then Jesus told him, "Follow me."

²⁰Peter turned around and saw the disciple Jesus loved following them—the one who had leaned over to Jesus during supper and asked, "Lord, who among us will betray you?" ²¹Peter asked Jesus, "What about him, Lord?"

I BELIEVE Jesus accurately predicted Peter's death (2 Peter 1:14). (21:19)

LIKE THOMAS *I claim Jesus as my Lord and my God.*

John 20:28

Meet the original doubting Thomas.

The Twin, as he was called by his friends, wasn't afraid to speak his mind. And he was no wimp, either.

Just a short time after some of the Jewish leaders threatened to arrest Jesus and picked up stones to kill him, Jesus urged his disciples to go back to Jerusalem with him. The apostles all were shaking in their boots except Thomas, who said to them, "Let's go, too—and die with Jesus" (11:16).

A few days later, while Jesus was presenting some difficult new truths to his disciples, it was Thomas again who spoke up and said, "We haven't any idea where you are going, so how can we know the way?" (14:5).

So it doesn't come as a complete surprise when, after Jesus' resurrection, it was Thomas who found it so hard to believe—until he saw Jesus with his own eyes. Suddenly, Thomas's doubts crumbled and he said, "My Lord and my God!" Scripture and tradition indicate Thomas never again wavered in his faith and trust. With Peter and the other apostles, the Twin proclaimed Jesus as his Lord and his God until his dying day.

While you and I haven't seen the Lord Jesus with our own eyes, it doesn't matter. God's blessings are still ours to enjoy if we've heard the Good News and placed our trust in Jesus (1 Peter 1:8-9).

○ *Today's Scripture reading is John 20:1-29.*

---

²²Jesus replied, "If I want him to remain alive until I return, what is that to you? You follow me." ²³So the rumor spread among the community of believers* that that disciple wouldn't die. But that isn't what Jesus said at all. He only said, "If I want him to remain alive until I return, what is that to you?"

Conclusion

²⁴This is that disciple who saw these events and recorded them here. And we all know that his account of these things is accurate.

²⁵And I suppose that if all the other things Jesus did were written down, the whole world could not contain the books.

21:23 Greek *the brothers.*

I BELIEVE John accurately recorded what he had witnessed of Jesus' life, ministry, death, and resurrection. (21:24)

ACTS

THIS FIFTH New Testament book records how the church started and spread throughout the Roman empire.

In many ways, this book provides a natural bridge between the four Gospels and the letters by Paul (and others) that follow.

Luke's account of the early church begins in Jerusalem, where Jesus' followers wait, just as he instructed them before his ascension (chapter 1). About ten days after Jesus' departure, the Holy Spirit fills the believers (2:1-13), who proclaim the Good News to the city (2:14-7:60).

When persecution breaks out, most Christians scatter throughout Judea and neighboring regions, where they lead other Jews and even Samaritans to faith in Jesus Christ (8:1-9:43). Then Peter receives a vision from the Lord and proclaims the Good News to Gentiles as well (10:1-11:18).

The evangelization of Gentiles continues in neighboring countries, including the establishment of a vibrant church in the city of Antioch (11:19-12:25). From Antioch, Paul and others go out on several Christian missionary journeys to other parts of the Roman empire (13:1-21:16).

While in Jerusalem, near the end of his third missionary journey, Paul is arrested and eventually taken to Rome. Along the way, he takes the opportunity to proclaim the Good News to many top Roman government officials. Luke's account ends with Paul still under house arrest, awaiting trial (21:17-28:31).

Famous passages in Acts include

- "Tell people about me everywhere—in Jerusalem, throughout Judea, in Samaria, and to the ends of the earth" (1:8)
- "They . . . devoted themselves to the apostles' teaching and fellowship, sharing in the Lord's Supper and in prayer" (2:42)
- "And each day the Lord added to their group those who were being saved" (2:47)
- "There is salvation in no one else [besides Jesus]! There is no other name in all of heaven for people to call on to save them" (4:12)
- "Do you think God wants us to obey you rather than him?" (4:19; see 5:29)
- Saul becomes a follower of Christ (9:1-19; see 22:1-16 and 26:9-19)
- Peter miraculously escapes from prison (12:3-19)
- The first church council meets in Jerusalem (15:1-21)
- Paul and Silas are imprisoned (16:16-40)
- Paul preaches in Athens (17:16-34)
- Paul escapes a riot in Ephesus (19:23-20:1)
- Paul is arrested during a riot in Jerusalem (21:26-36)

CHAPTER 1

The Promise of the Holy Spirit

Dear Theophilus:

In my first book* I told you about everything Jesus began to do and teach ²until the day he ascended to heaven after giving his chosen apostles further instructions from the Holy Spirit. ³During the forty days after his crucifixion, he appeared to the apostles from time to time and proved to them in many ways that he was actually alive. On these occasions he talked to them about the Kingdom of God.

⁴In one of these meetings as he was eating a meal with them, he told them, "Do not leave Jerusalem until the Father sends you what he promised. Remember, I have told you about this before. ⁵John baptized with* water, but in just a few days you will be baptized with the Holy Spirit."

The Ascension of Jesus

⁶When the apostles were with Jesus, they kept asking him, "Lord, are you going to free Israel now and restore our kingdom?"

⁷"The Father sets those dates," he replied, "and they are not for you to know. ⁸But when the Holy Spirit has come upon you, you will receive power and will tell people about me everywhere—in Jerusalem, throughout Judea, in Samaria, and to the ends of the earth."

⁹It was not long after he said this that he was taken up into the sky while they were watching, and he disappeared into a cloud. ¹⁰As they were straining their eyes to see him, two white-robed men suddenly stood there among them. ¹¹They said, "Men of Galilee, why are you standing here staring at the sky? Jesus has been taken away from you into heaven. And someday, just as you saw him go, he will return!"

Matthias Replaces Judas

¹²The apostles were at the Mount of Olives when this happened, so they walked the half mile* back to Jerusalem. ¹³Then they went to the upstairs room of the house where they were staying. Here is the list of those who were present:

> Peter,
> John,
> James,
> Andrew,
> Philip,
> Thomas,
> Bartholomew,
> Matthew,
> James (son of Alphaeus),
> Simon (the Zealot),
> and Judas (son of James).

¹⁴They all met together continually for prayer, along with Mary the mother of Jesus, several other women, and the brothers of Jesus.

¹⁵During this time, on a day when about 120 believers* were present, Peter stood up and addressed them as follows:

¹⁶"Brothers, it was necessary for the Scriptures to be fulfilled concerning Judas, who guided the Temple police to arrest Jesus. This was predicted long ago by the Holy Spirit, speaking through King David. ¹⁷Judas was one of us, chosen to share in the ministry with us."

¹⁸(Judas bought a field with the money he received for his treachery, and falling there, he burst open, spilling out his intestines. ¹⁹The news of his

---

See Luke's profile (page 1379) at 2 Timothy 4:11.

I BELIEVE Jesus Christ appeared to his disciples after his resurrection and proved he was alive! (1:3)

See John the Baptist's profile (page 1117) at Mark 1:4.

I HELP obey Jesus Christ's command to tell people about him everywhere—to the ends of the earth (Matthew 28:18-20). (1:8)

I BELIEVE Jesus Christ will one day return! (1:11)

See the profiles for Peter (page 1111), John (page 1435), Andrew (page 1199), Thomas (page 1231), and Matthew (page 1081) at Matthew 26:75, Revelation 1:9, John 1:42, John 20:28, and Matthew 9:9.

I MEET with other believers for prayer. (1:14)

See Mary's profile (page 1149) at Luke 1:38.

See the profiles for Judas (page 1121) and David (page 629) at Mark 3:19 and Psalm 3:1.

1:1 The reference is to the book of Luke.   1:5 Or *in;* also in 1:5b.   1:12 Greek *a Sabbath day's journey.*
1:15 Greek *brothers.*

death spread rapidly among all the people of Jerusalem, and they gave the place the Aramaic name *Akeldama*, which means "Field of Blood.")

[20]Peter continued, "This was predicted in the book of Psalms, where it says, 'Let his home become desolate, with no one living in it.' And again, 'Let his position be given to someone else.'*

[21]"So now we must choose another man to take Judas's place. It must be someone who has been with us all the time that we were with the Lord Jesus— [22]from the time he was baptized by John until the day he was taken from us into heaven. Whoever is chosen will join us as a witness of Jesus' resurrection."

[23]So they nominated two men: Joseph called Barsabbas (also known as Justus) and Matthias. [24]Then they all prayed for the right man to be chosen. "O Lord," they said, "you know every heart. Show us which of these men you have chosen [25]as an apostle to replace Judas the traitor in this ministry, for he has deserted us and gone where he belongs." [26]Then they cast lots, and in this way Matthias was chosen and became an apostle with the other eleven.

CHAPTER 2

The Holy Spirit Comes

On the day of Pentecost, seven weeks after Jesus' resurrection,* the believers were meeting together in one place. [2]Suddenly, there was a sound from heaven like the roaring of a mighty windstorm in the skies above them, and it filled the house where they were meeting. [3]Then, what looked like flames or tongues of fire appeared and settled on each of them. [4]And everyone present was filled with the Holy Spirit and began speaking in other languages,* as the Holy Spirit gave them this ability.

[5]Godly Jews from many nations were living in Jerusalem at that time. [6]When they heard this sound, they came running to see what it was all about, and they were bewildered to hear their own languages being spoken by the believers.

[7]They were beside themselves with wonder. "How can this be?" they exclaimed. "These people are all from Galilee, [8]and yet we hear them speaking the languages of the lands where we were born! [9]Here we are—Parthians, Medes, Elamites, people from Mesopotamia, Judea, Cappadocia, Pontus, the province of Asia, [10]Phrygia, Pamphylia, Egypt, and the areas of Libya toward Cyrene, visitors from Rome (both Jews and converts to Judaism), [11]Cretans, and Arabians. And we all hear these people speaking in our own languages about the wonderful things God has done!" [12]They stood there amazed and perplexed. "What can this mean?" they asked each other. [13]But others in the crowd were mocking. "They're drunk, that's all!" they said.

Peter Preaches to a Crowd

[14]Then Peter stepped forward with the eleven other apostles and shouted to the crowd, "Listen carefully, all of you, fellow Jews and residents of Jerusalem! Make no mistake about this. [15]Some of you are saying these people are drunk. It isn't true! It's much too early for that. People don't get drunk by nine o'clock in the morning. [16]No, what you see this morning was predicted centuries ago by the prophet Joel:

[17]'In the last days, God said,
  I will pour out my Spirit upon all people.
 Your sons and daughters will prophesy,
   your young men will see visions,
   and your old men will dream dreams.
[18]In those days I will pour out my Spirit

I PRAY for the right church leaders to be chosen, no matter what method of selection is used. (1:24)

I BELIEVE the Holy Spirit filled the first Christians on the day of Pentecost and gave them the ability to speak in other languages. (2:4)

I BELIEVE God allowed the first Christians to proclaim the Good News of Jesus Christ to Jews from every part of the world in their own language. (2:11)

See Peter's profile (page 1111) at Matthew 26:75.

I BELIEVE the events on the day of Pentecost were a fulfillment of prophecy. (2:16)

1:20 Pss 69:25; 109:8.   2:1 Greek *When the day of Pentecost arrived.* This annual celebration came 50 days after the Passover ceremonies. See Lev 23:16.   2:4 Or *in other tongues.*

upon all my servants, men and women alike,
and they will prophesy.
[19] And I will cause wonders in the heavens above
and signs on the earth below—
blood and fire and clouds of smoke.
[20] The sun will be turned into darkness,
and the moon will turn bloodred,
before that great and glorious day of the Lord arrives.
[21] And anyone who calls on the name of the Lord
will be saved.'*

[22] "People of Israel, listen! God publicly endorsed Jesus of Nazareth by doing wonderful miracles, wonders, and signs through him, as you well know. [23] But you followed God's prearranged plan. With the help of lawless Gentiles, you nailed him to the cross and murdered him. [24] However, God released him from the horrors of death and raised him back to life again, for death could not keep him in its grip. [25] King David said this about him:

'I know the Lord is always with me.
I will not be shaken, for he is right beside me.
[26] No wonder my heart is filled with joy,
and my mouth shouts his praises!
My body rests in hope.
[27] For you will not leave my soul among the dead*
or allow your Holy One to rot in the grave.
[28] You have shown me the way of life,
and you will give me wonderful joy in your presence.'*

[29] "Dear brothers, think about this! David wasn't referring to himself when he spoke these words I have quoted, for he died and was buried, and his tomb is still here among us. [30] But he was a prophet, and he knew God had promised with an oath that one of David's own descendants would sit on David's throne as the Messiah. [31] David was looking into the future and predicting the Messiah's resurrection. He was saying that the Messiah would not be left among the dead and that his body would not rot in the grave.

[32] "This prophecy was speaking of Jesus, whom God raised from the dead, and we all are witnesses of this. [33] Now he sits on the throne of highest honor in heaven, at God's right hand. And the Father, as he had promised, gave him the Holy Spirit to pour out upon us, just as you see and hear today. [34] For David himself never ascended into heaven, yet he said,

'The LORD said to my Lord,
Sit in honor at my right hand
[35] until I humble your enemies,
making them a footstool under your feet.'*

[36] So let it be clearly known by everyone in Israel that God has made this Jesus whom you crucified to be both Lord and Messiah!"

[37] Peter's words convicted them deeply, and they said to him and to the other apostles, "Brothers, what should we do?"

[38] Peter replied, "Each of you must turn from your sins and turn to God, and be baptized in the name of Jesus Christ for the forgiveness of your sins. Then you will receive the gift of the Holy Spirit. [39] This promise is to you and to your children, and even to the Gentiles*—all who have been called by the Lord our God." [40] Then Peter continued preaching for a long time, strongly

---

I HAVE CALLED UPON the name of the Lord and am saved. (2:21)

I BELIEVE God released Jesus Christ from the horrors of death. (2:24)

See David's profile (page 629) at Psalm 3:1.

I BELIEVE Jesus Christ rose from the dead, just as David predicted (Psalm 16:8-11). (2:31)

I BELIEVE Jesus Christ sits on the throne in heaven beside the Father (Psalm 110:1). (2:34)

I BELIEVE the promise of salvation is to all peoples down through the ages. (2:39)

2:17-21 Joel 2:28-32. 2:27 Greek in Hades; also in 2:31. 2:25-28 Ps 16:8-11. 2:34-35 Ps 110:1. 2:39 Greek to those far away.

urging all his listeners, "Save yourselves from this generation that has gone astray!"

[41] Those who believed what Peter said were baptized and added to the church—about three thousand in all. [42] They joined with the other believers and devoted themselves to the apostles' teaching and fellowship, sharing in the Lord's Supper and in prayer.

The Believers Meet Together

[43] A deep sense of awe came over them all, and the apostles performed many miraculous signs and wonders. [44] And all the believers met together constantly and shared everything they had. [45] They sold their possessions and shared the proceeds with those in need. [46] They worshiped together at the Temple each day, met in homes for the Lord's Supper, and shared their meals with great joy and generosity—[47] all the while praising God and enjoying the goodwill of all the people. And each day the Lord added to their group those who were being saved.

CHAPTER 3

Peter Heals a Crippled Beggar

Peter and John went to the Temple one afternoon to take part in the three o'clock prayer service. [2] As they approached the Temple, a man lame from birth was being carried in. Each day he was put beside the Temple gate, the one called the Beautiful Gate, so he could beg from the people going into the Temple. [3] When he saw Peter and John about to enter, he asked them for some money.

[4] Peter and John looked at him intently, and Peter said, "Look at us!" [5] The lame man looked at them eagerly, expecting a gift. [6] But Peter said, "I don't have any money for you. But I'll give you what I have. In the name of Jesus Christ of Nazareth, get up and walk!"

[7] Then Peter took the lame man by the right hand and helped him up. And as he did, the man's feet and anklebones were healed and strengthened. [8] He jumped up, stood on his feet, and began to walk! Then, walking, leaping, and praising God, he went into the Temple with them.

[9] All the people saw him walking and heard him praising God. [10] When they realized he was the lame beggar they had seen so often at the Beautiful Gate, they were absolutely astounded! [11] They all rushed out to Solomon's Colonnade, where he was holding tightly to Peter and John. Everyone stood there in awe of the wonderful thing that had happened.

Peter Preaches in the Temple

[12] Peter saw his opportunity and addressed the crowd. "People of Israel," he said, "what is so astounding about this? And why look at us as though we had made this man walk by our own power and godliness? [13] For it is the God of Abraham, the God of Isaac, the God of Jacob, the God of all our ancestors who has brought glory to his servant Jesus by doing this. This is the same Jesus whom you handed over and rejected before Pilate, despite Pilate's decision to release him. [14] You rejected this holy, righteous one and instead demanded the release of a murderer. [15] You killed the author of life, but God raised him to life. And we are witnesses of this fact!

[16] "The name of Jesus has healed this man—and you know how lame he was before. Faith in Jesus' name has caused this healing before your very eyes.

[17] "Friends,* I realize that what you did to Jesus was done in ignorance; and the same can be said of your leaders. [18] But God was fulfilling what all the prophets had declared about the Messiah beforehand—that he must suffer all these things. [19] Now turn from your sins and turn to God, so you can be

3:17 Greek Brothers.

I JOIN with other believers and devote myself to the apostles' teaching (now found in the Bible), to fellowship, to taking communion, and to prayer. (2:42)

I AM WILLING to share anything I own to provide for my Christian brothers and sisters in need. (2:44)

See the profiles for Peter (page 1111) and John (page 1435) at Matthew 26:75 and Revelation 1:9.

I SHARE the Good News of Jesus Christ with others in need whether or not I can help them financially. (3:6)

See Solomon's profile (page 753) at Proverbs 2:9.

I TAKE ADVANTAGE of opportunities to share the Good News of Jesus Christ with others. (3:12)

See the profiles for Abraham (page 19), Isaac (page 31), Jacob (page 43), and Pilate (page 1229) at Genesis 15:6, Genesis 25:19, Genesis 32:9, and John 19:16.

I TURN AWAY from my sins to God and experience his cleansing and refreshment. (3:19)

cleansed of your sins. [20]Then wonderful times of refreshment will come from the presence of the Lord, and he will send Jesus your Messiah to you again. [21]For he must remain in heaven until the time for the final restoration of all things, as God promised long ago through his prophets. [22]Moses said, 'The Lord your God will raise up a Prophet like me from among your own people. Listen carefully to everything he tells you.'* [23]Then Moses said, 'Anyone who will not listen to that Prophet will be cut off from God's people and utterly destroyed.'*

[24]"Starting with Samuel, every prophet spoke about what is happening today. [25]You are the children of those prophets, and you are included in the covenant God promised to your ancestors. For God said to Abraham, 'Through your descendants all the families on earth will be blessed.'* [26]When God raised up his servant, he sent him first to you people of Israel, to bless you by turning each of you back from your sinful ways."

CHAPTER 4

Peter and John before the Council

While Peter and John were speaking to the people, the leading priests, the captain of the Temple guard, and some of the Sadducees came over to them. [2]They were very disturbed that Peter and John were claiming, on the authority of Jesus, that there is a resurrection of the dead. [3]They arrested them and, since it was already evening, jailed them until morning. [4]But many of the people who heard their message believed it, so that the number of believers totaled about five thousand men, not counting women and children.*

[5]The next day the council of all the rulers and elders and teachers of religious law met in Jerusalem. [6]Annas the high priest was there, along with Caiaphas, John, Alexander, and other relatives of the high priest. [7]They brought in the two disciples and demanded, "By what power, or in whose name, have you done this?"

[8]Then Peter, filled with the Holy Spirit, said to them, "Leaders and elders of our nation, [9]are we being questioned because we've done a good deed for a crippled man? Do you want to know how he was healed? [10]Let me clearly state to you and to all the people of Israel that he was healed in the name and power of Jesus Christ from Nazareth, the man you crucified, but whom God raised from the dead. [11]For Jesus is the one referred to in the Scriptures, where it says,

'The stone that you builders rejected
    has now become the cornerstone.'*

[12]There is salvation in no one else! There is no other name in all of heaven for people to call on to save them."

[13]The members of the council were amazed when they saw the boldness of Peter and John, for they could see that they were ordinary men who had had no special training. They also recognized them as men who had been with Jesus. [14]But since the man who had been healed was standing right there among them, the council had nothing to say. [15]So they sent Peter and John out of the council chamber* and conferred among themselves.

[16]"What should we do with these men?" they asked each other. "We can't deny they have done a miraculous sign, and everybody in Jerusalem knows about it. [17]But perhaps we can stop them from spreading their propaganda. We'll warn them not to speak to anyone in Jesus' name again." [18]So they called the apostles back in and told them never again to speak or teach about Jesus.

[19]But Peter and John replied, "Do you think God wants us to obey you

---

I BELIEVE Jesus Christ will remain in heaven until the final restoration of all things. (3:21)

I BELIEVE God fulfilled his promise to bless all peoples through Abraham's descendants (Genesis 22:18) when he sent his servant, Jesus Christ. (3:25)

I BELIEVE in and proclaim the resurrection based on the authority of Jesus Christ, my risen Lord and Savior. (4:2)

I TAKE NOTE each time another large number of people in my city believe the Good News of Jesus Christ. (4:4)

See the profiles for Peter (page 1111), John (page 1435), and the Sadducees (page 1103) at Matthew 26:75, Revelation 1:9, and Matthew 22:23.

I BELIEVE Jesus Christ alone is the Savior—there is no one else! (4:12)

I DO NOT OBEY people when it means disobeying God. (4:19)

3:22 Deut 18:15.   3:23 Deut 18:19; Lev 23:29.   3:25 Gen 22:18.   4:4 Greek *5,000 adult males.*   4:11 Ps 118:22.
4:15 Greek *the Sanhedrin.*

rather than him? [20]We cannot stop telling about the wonderful things we have seen and heard."

[21]The council then threatened them further, but they finally let them go because they didn't know how to punish them without starting a riot. For everyone was praising God [22]for this miraculous sign—the healing of a man who had been lame for more than forty years.

The Believers Pray for Courage

[23]As soon as they were freed, Peter and John found the other believers and told them what the leading priests and elders had said. [24]Then all the believers were united as they lifted their voices in prayer: "O Sovereign Lord, Creator of heaven and earth, the sea, and everything in them—[25]you spoke long ago by the Holy Spirit through our ancestor King David, your servant, saying,

'Why did the nations rage?
Why did the people waste their time with futile plans?
[26]The kings of the earth prepared for battle;
the rulers gathered together
against the Lord
and against his Messiah.'*

[27]"That is what has happened here in this city! For Herod Antipas, Pontius Pilate the governor, the Gentiles, and the people of Israel were all united against Jesus, your holy servant, whom you anointed. [28]In fact, everything they did occurred according to your eternal will and plan. [29]And now, O Lord, hear their threats, and give your servants great boldness in their preaching. [30]Send your healing power; may miraculous signs and wonders be done through the name of your holy servant Jesus."

[31]After this prayer, the building where they were meeting shook, and they were all filled with the Holy Spirit. And they preached God's message with boldness.

The Believers Share Their Possessions

[32]All the believers were of one heart and mind, and they felt that what they owned was not their own; they shared everything they had. [33]And the apostles gave powerful witness to the resurrection of the Lord Jesus, and God's great favor was upon them all. [34]There was no poverty among them, because people who owned land or houses sold them [35]and brought the money to the apostles to give to others in need.

[36]For instance, there was Joseph, the one the apostles nicknamed Barnabas (which means "Son of Encouragement"). He was from the tribe of Levi and came from the island of Cyprus. [37]He sold a field he owned and brought the money to the apostles for those in need.

CHAPTER 5

Ananias and Sapphira

There was also a man named Ananias who, with his wife, Sapphira, sold some property. [2]He brought part of the money to the apostles, but he claimed it was the full amount. His wife had agreed to this deception.

[3]Then Peter said, "Ananias, why has Satan filled your heart? You lied to the Holy Spirit, and you kept some of the money for yourself. [4]The property was yours to sell or not sell, as you wished. And after selling it, the money was yours to give away. How could you do a thing like this? You weren't lying to us but to God."

[5]As soon as Ananias heard these words, he fell to the floor and died. Everyone

I UNITE with other believers in prayer and praise to the Sovereign Lord. (4:24)
See David's profile (page 629) at Psalm 3:1.

See Pilate's profile (page 1229) at John 19:16.

I BELIEVE everything that happened to Jesus Christ occurred according to God's eternal plan. (4:28)

I UNITE with other Christians and care for fellow believers who are in need. (4:32)
See Barnabas's profile (page 1253) at Acts 11:23.

I AM WILLING to sell some of my property to help provide for Christians in need. (4:37)

See Peter's profile (page 1111) at Matthew 26:75.

I DO NOT LIE to God or others about the amount of money I give to God's work. (5:4)

4:25-26 Ps 2:1-2.

who heard about it was terrified. [6]Then some young men wrapped him in a sheet and took him out and buried him.

[7]About three hours later his wife came in, not knowing what had happened. [8]Peter asked her, "Was this the price you and your husband received for your land?"

"Yes," she replied, "that was the price."

[9]And Peter said, "How could the two of you even think of doing a thing like this—conspiring together to test the Spirit of the Lord? Just outside that door are the young men who buried your husband, and they will carry you out, too."

[10]Instantly, she fell to the floor and died. When the young men came in and saw that she was dead, they carried her out and buried her beside her husband. [11]Great fear gripped the entire church and all others who heard what had happened.

The Apostles Heal Many

[12]Meanwhile, the apostles were performing many miraculous signs and wonders among the people. And the believers were meeting regularly at the Temple in the area known as Solomon's Colonnade. [13]No one else dared to join them, though everyone had high regard for them. [14]And more and more people believed and were brought to the Lord—crowds of both men and women. [15]As a result of the apostles' work, sick people were brought out into the streets on beds and mats so that Peter's shadow might fall across some of them as he went by. [16]Crowds came in from the villages around Jerusalem, bringing their sick and those possessed by evil spirits, and they were all healed.

The Apostles Meet Opposition

[17]The high priest and his friends, who were Sadducees, reacted with violent jealousy. [18]They arrested the apostles and put them in the jail. [19]But an angel of the Lord came at night, opened the gates of the jail, and brought them out. Then he told them, [20]"Go to the Temple and give the people this message of life!" [21]So the apostles entered the Temple about daybreak and immediately began teaching.

When the high priest and his officials arrived, they convened the high council,* along with all the elders of Israel. Then they sent for the apostles to be brought for trial. [22]But when the Temple guards went to the jail, the men were gone. So they returned to the council and reported, [23]"The jail was locked, with the guards standing outside, but when we opened the gates, no one was there!"

[24]When the captain of the Temple guard and the leading priests heard this, they were perplexed, wondering where it would all end. [25]Then someone arrived with the news that the men they had jailed were out in the Temple, teaching the people.

[26]The captain went with his Temple guards and arrested them, but without violence, for they were afraid the people would kill them if they treated the apostles roughly. [27]Then they brought the apostles in before the council. [28]"Didn't we tell you never again to teach in this man's name?" the high priest demanded. "Instead, you have filled all Jerusalem with your teaching about Jesus, and you intend to blame us for his death!"

[29]But Peter and the apostles replied, "We must obey God rather than human authority. [30]The God of our ancestors raised Jesus from the dead after you killed him by crucifying him. [31]Then God put him in the place of honor at his right hand as Prince and Savior. He did this to give the people of Israel an opportunity to turn from their sins and turn to God so their sins would be forgiven. [32]We are witnesses of these things and so is the Holy Spirit, who is given by God to those who obey him."

5:21 Greek *Sanhedrin;* also in 5:27, 41.

I DO NOT TEST the Holy Spirit by trying to get away with sin. (5:9)

I MEET together regularly with other believers. (5:12)

See Solomon's profile (page 753) at Proverbs 2:9.

See the profile for the Sadducees (page 1103) at Matthew 22:23.

I BELIEVE an angel of the Lord released the apostles from prison. (5:19)

I DO NOT LET anything stop me from giving out the message of life. (5:21)

I DO NOT HESITATE to speak God's truth— even if I must disobey or offend those in authority. (5:29)

I BELIEVE God honored Jesus Christ as Prince and Savior to give individuals the opportunity to turn from their sins and be forgiven. (5:31)

³³At this, the high council was furious and decided to kill them. ³⁴But one member had a different perspective. He was a Pharisee named Gamaliel, who was an expert on religious law and was very popular with the people. He stood up and ordered that the apostles be sent outside the council chamber for a while. ³⁵Then he addressed his colleagues as follows: "Men of Israel, take care what you are planning to do to these men! ³⁶Some time ago there was that fellow Theudas, who pretended to be someone great. About four hundred others joined him, but he was killed, and his followers went their various ways. The whole movement came to nothing. ³⁷After him, at the time of the census, there was Judas of Galilee. He got some people to follow him, but he was killed, too, and all his followers were scattered.

See the profile for the Pharisees (page 1087) at Matthew 12:14.

UNLIKE ANANIAS AND SAPPHIRA — I do not try to fool God and others.

Acts 5:4

The exuberant crowd applauded as the president of a medium-sized Christian college climbed the podium for the last speech of the day. At the culmination of the groundbreaking ceremony for the college's new library, he opened an envelope handed to him by a businessman who was smiling and waving to the media. Instead of holding a promised million-dollar gift, however, the envelope contained an IOU. Not a dollar of that IOU was ever paid. Who was jilted worse? The struggling college—or God?

Ananias and Sapphira's ploy was much more subtle—subtle enough that they thought they could get away with it. Yet God always knows the true value of one's giving. More importantly, he knows the exact condition of every heart.

Of course, Ananias and Sapphira were under no obligation to give anything to the church. Though the early believers shared freely, no one was pressured to give up ownership of personal property or to tithe a certain amount of each sale. Still, because of greed or vanity, Ananias and Sapphira chose to falsify the size of their gift. That premeditated sin brought severe judgment upon their heads.

Ananias and Sapphira were not judged for their lack of generosity. Instead, they were judged for trying to deceive God. They presented themselves as something very different than they actually were.

You and I may be inclined to overlook a lie, judging its severity by the perceived damage that's been done. But every lie is in reality a bold statement of unbelief against the omniscient Lord God.

Someone very well may try to fool other believers, but who in his or her right mind would try to deceive the all-seeing and all-knowing Lord?

Unlike Ananias and Sapphira, let's make a point of telling the truth to God and others.

○ Today's Scripture reading is Acts 4:32–5:11.

³⁸"So my advice is, leave these men alone. If they are teaching and doing these things merely on their own, it will soon be overthrown. ³⁹But if it is of God, you will not be able to stop them. You may even find yourselves fighting against God."

⁴⁰The council accepted his advice. They called in the apostles and had them flogged. Then they ordered them never again to speak in the name of Jesus, and they let them go. ⁴¹The apostles left the high council rejoicing that God had counted them worthy to suffer dishonor for the name of Jesus. ⁴²And every day, in the Temple and in their homes,* they continued to teach and preach this message: "The Messiah you are looking for is Jesus."

I BELIEVE God's enemies cannot stop the Christian faith from spreading. (5:39)

I REJOICE when I have the privilege of suffering for Jesus Christ. (5:41)

CHAPTER 6

Seven Men Chosen to Serve

But as the believers* rapidly multiplied, there were rumblings of discontent. Those who spoke Greek complained against those who spoke Hebrew, saying

5:42 Greek *from house to house.* 6:1 Greek *disciples;* also in 6:2, 7.

that their widows were being discriminated against in the daily distribution of food. ²So the Twelve called a meeting of all the believers.

"We apostles should spend our time preaching and teaching the word of God, not administering a food program," they said. ³"Now look around among yourselves, brothers, and select seven men who are well respected and are full of the Holy Spirit and wisdom. We will put them in charge of this business. ⁴Then we can spend our time in prayer and preaching and teaching the word."

⁵This idea pleased the whole group, and they chose the following: Stephen (a man full of faith and the Holy Spirit), Philip, Procorus, Nicanor, Timon, Parmenas, and Nicolas of Antioch (a Gentile convert to the Jewish faith, who had now become a Christian). ⁶These seven were presented to the apostles, who prayed for them as they laid their hands on them.

⁷God's message was preached in ever-widening circles. The number of believers greatly increased in Jerusalem, and many of the Jewish priests were converted, too.

Stephen Is Arrested

⁸Stephen, a man full of God's grace and power, performed amazing miracles and signs among the people. ⁹But one day some men from the Synagogue of Freed Slaves, as it was called, started to debate with him. They were Jews from Cyrene, Alexandria, Cilicia, and the province of Asia. ¹⁰None of them was able to stand against the wisdom and Spirit by which Stephen spoke.

¹¹So they persuaded some men to lie about Stephen, saying, "We heard him blaspheme Moses, and even God." ¹²Naturally, this roused the crowds, the elders, and the teachers of religious law. So they arrested Stephen and brought him before the high council.* ¹³The lying witnesses said, "This man is always speaking against the Temple and against the law of Moses. ¹⁴We have heard him say that this Jesus of Nazareth will destroy the Temple and change the customs Moses handed down to us." ¹⁵At this point everyone in the council stared at Stephen because his face became as bright as an angel's.

CHAPTER 7

Stephen Addresses the Council

Then the high priest asked Stephen, "Are these accusations true?"

²This was Stephen's reply: "Brothers and honorable fathers, listen to me. Our glorious God appeared to our ancestor Abraham in Mesopotamia before he moved to Haran.* ³God told him, 'Leave your native land and your relatives, and come to the land that I will show you.'* ⁴So Abraham left the land of the Chaldeans and lived in Haran until his father died. Then God brought him here to the land where you now live. ⁵But God gave him no inheritance here, not even one square foot of land. God did promise, however, that eventually the whole country would belong to Abraham and his descendants—though he had no children yet. ⁶But God also told him that his descendants would live in a foreign country where they would be mistreated as slaves for four hundred years. ⁷'But I will punish the nation that enslaves them,' God told him, 'and in the end they will come out and worship me in this place.'* ⁸God also gave Abraham the covenant of circumcision at that time. And so Isaac, Abraham's son, was circumcised when he was eight days old. Isaac became the father of Jacob, and Jacob was the father of the twelve patriarchs of the Jewish nation.

⁹"These sons of Jacob were very jealous of their brother Joseph, and they sold him to be a slave in Egypt. But God was with him ¹⁰and delivered him from his anguish. And God gave him favor before Pharaoh, king of Egypt.

I DO NOT TRY to do more work than God has called me to do. (6:2)

I BELIEVE church leaders should be selected on the basis of their faith and dependence on the Holy Spirit. (6:3)

See the profiles for Stephen (page 1245) and Philip (page 1269) at Acts 7:60 and Acts 21:8.

I DO NOT LIE (Exodus 20:16). (6:11)

See Moses' profile (page 73) at Exodus 5:1.

I RESPECTFULLY ADDRESS those who oppose me. (7:2)

See Abraham's profile (page 19) at Genesis 15:6.

I BELIEVE God spoke to Abraham, who obeyed God's commands. (7:4)

See the profiles for Isaac (page 31) and Jacob (page 43) at Genesis 25:19 and Genesis 32:9.

See Joseph's profile (page 51) at Genesis 39:2.

6:12 Greek *Sanhedrin;* also in 6:15. 7:2 *Mesopotamia* was the region now called Iraq. *Haran* was a city in what is now called Syria. 7:3 Gen 12:1. 7:5-7 Gen 12:7; 15:13-14; Exod 3:12.

God also gave Joseph unusual wisdom, so that Pharaoh appointed him governor over all of Egypt and put him in charge of all the affairs of the palace.

[11]"But a famine came upon Egypt and Canaan. There was great misery for our ancestors, as they ran out of food. [12]Jacob heard that there was still grain in Egypt, so he sent his sons* to buy some. [13]The second time they went, Joseph revealed his identity to his brothers, and they were introduced to Pharaoh. [14]Then Joseph sent for his father, Jacob, and all his relatives to come to Egypt, seventy-five persons in all. [15]So Jacob went to Egypt. He died there, as did all his sons. [16]All of them were taken to Shechem and buried in the tomb Abraham had bought from the sons of Hamor in Shechem.

[17]"As the time drew near when God would fulfill his promise to Abraham, the number of our people in Egypt greatly increased. [18]But then a new king came to the throne of Egypt who knew nothing about Joseph. [19]This king plotted against our people and forced parents to abandon their newborn babies so they would die.

[20]"At that time Moses was born—a beautiful child in God's eyes. His parents cared for him at home for three months. [21]When at last they had to abandon him, Pharaoh's daughter found him and raised him as her own son. [22]Moses was taught all the wisdom of the Egyptians, and he became mighty in both speech and action.

[23]"One day when he was forty years old, he decided to visit his relatives, the people of Israel. [24]During this visit, he saw an Egyptian mistreating a man of Israel. So Moses came to his defense and avenged him, killing the Egyptian. [25]Moses assumed his brothers would realize that God had sent him to rescue them, but they didn't.

[26]"The next day he visited them again and saw two men of Israel fighting. He tried to be a peacemaker. 'Men,' he said, 'you are brothers. Why are you hurting each other?'

[27]"But the man in the wrong pushed Moses aside and told him to mind his own business. 'Who made you a ruler and judge over us?' he asked. [28]'Are you going to kill me as you killed that Egyptian yesterday?' [29]When Moses heard that, he fled the country and lived as a foreigner in the land of Midian, where his two sons were born.

[30]"Forty years later, in the desert near Mount Sinai, an angel appeared to Moses in the flame of a burning bush. [31]Moses saw it and wondered what it was. As he went to see, the voice of the Lord called out to him, [32]'I am the God of your ancestors—the God of Abraham, Isaac, and Jacob.' Moses shook with terror and dared not look.

[33]"And the Lord said to him, 'Take off your sandals, for you are standing on holy ground. [34]You can be sure that I have seen the misery of my people in Egypt. I have heard their cries. So I have come to rescue them. Now go, for I will send you to Egypt.'* [35]And so God sent back the same man his people had previously rejected by demanding, 'Who made you a ruler and judge over us?' Through the angel who appeared to him in the burning bush, Moses was sent to be their ruler and savior. [36]And by means of many miraculous signs and wonders, he led them out of Egypt, through the Red Sea, and back and forth through the wilderness for forty years.

[37]"Moses himself told the people of Israel, 'God will raise up a Prophet like me from among your own people.'* [38]Moses was with the assembly of God's people in the wilderness. He was the mediator between the people of Israel and the angel who gave him life-giving words on Mount Sinai to pass on to us.

[39]"But our ancestors rejected Moses and wanted to return to Egypt. [40]They told Aaron, 'Make us some gods who can lead us, for we don't know what has become of this Moses, who brought us out of Egypt.' [41]So they made an idol

7:12 Greek *our fathers;* also in 7:15.   7:31-34 Exod 3:5-10.   7:37 Deut 18:15.

I BELIEVE God was with Joseph and gave him unusual wisdom and favor before Pharaoh. (7:10)

I BELIEVE God fulfilled his promise to Abraham's descendants at just the right time. (7:17)

See the profiles for Moses (page 73) and Moses' Parents (page 69) at Exodus 5:1 and Exodus 2:3.

I BELIEVE God had a special purpose for Moses' birth and upbringing in Pharaoh's family. (7:21)

I BELIEVE Moses failed in his first attempt to rescue the Israelites. (7:27)

I BELIEVE the Lord spoke to Moses from the burning bush. (7:31)

I BELIEVE the Lord sent Moses back as savior for the Israelites— forty years after they had rejected him. (7:35)

I BELIEVE the Lord raised up Jesus Christ, another prophet like Moses, just as he said he would do (Deuteronomy 18:15). (7:37)

See Aaron's profile (page 107) at Exodus 32:2.

I BELIEVE the Lord
finally gave up the
Israelites to follow the
idols they had been
worshiping all along.
(7:42)

See the profiles for
Joshua (page 275) and
David (page 629) at
Joshua 23:14 and
Psalm 3:1.
See Solomon's profile
(page 753) at Proverbs
2:9.

I BELIEVE the Lord
doesn't live in the
Tabernacle, the
Temple, or any
building made by
human hands. (7:48)

I DO NOT RESIST the
Holy Spirit. (7:51)

See Paul's profile (page
1333) at Galatians 2:5.

shaped like a calf, and they sacrificed to it and rejoiced in this thing they had made. ⁴²Then God turned away from them and gave them up to serve the sun, moon, and stars as their gods! In the book of the prophets it is written,

'Was it to me you were bringing sacrifices
    during those forty years in the wilderness, Israel?
⁴³No, your real interest was in your pagan gods—
    the shrine of Molech,
    the star god Rephan,
    and the images you made to worship them.
So I will send you into captivity
    far away in Babylon.'*

⁴⁴"Our ancestors carried the Tabernacle* with them through the wilderness. It was constructed in exact accordance with the plan shown to Moses by God. ⁴⁵Years later, when Joshua led the battles against the Gentile nations that God drove out of this land, the Tabernacle was taken with them into their new territory. And it was used there until the time of King David.

⁴⁶"David found favor with God and asked for the privilege of building a permanent Temple for the God of Jacob.* ⁴⁷But it was Solomon who actually built it. ⁴⁸However, the Most High doesn't live in temples made by human hands. As the prophet says,

⁴⁹'Heaven is my throne,
    and the earth is my footstool.
Could you ever build me a temple as good as that?'
    asks the Lord.
'Could you build a dwelling place for me?
⁵⁰ Didn't I make everything in heaven and earth?'*

⁵¹"You stubborn people! You are heathen at heart and deaf to the truth. Must you forever resist the Holy Spirit? But your ancestors did, and so do you! ⁵²Name one prophet your ancestors didn't persecute! They even killed the ones who predicted the coming of the Righteous One—the Messiah whom you betrayed and murdered. ⁵³You deliberately disobeyed God's law, though you received it from the hands of angels.*"

⁵⁴The Jewish leaders were infuriated by Stephen's accusation, and they shook their fists in rage.* ⁵⁵But Stephen, full of the Holy Spirit, gazed steadily upward into heaven and saw the glory of God, and he saw Jesus standing in the place of honor at God's right hand. ⁵⁶And he told them, "Look, I see the heavens opened and the Son of Man standing in the place of honor at God's right hand!"

⁵⁷Then they put their hands over their ears, and drowning out his voice with their shouts, they rushed at him. ⁵⁸They dragged him out of the city and began to stone him. The official witnesses took off their coats and laid them at the feet of a young man named Saul.*

⁵⁹And as they stoned him, Stephen prayed, "Lord Jesus, receive my spirit." ⁶⁰And he fell to his knees, shouting, "Lord, don't charge them with this sin!" And with that, he died.

CHAPTER 8

Saul was one of the official witnesses at the killing of Stephen.

Persecution Scatters the Believers

A great wave of persecution began that day, sweeping over the church in Jerusalem, and all the believers except the apostles fled into Judea and Samaria.

7:42-43 Amos 5:25-27. 7:44 Greek *the tent of witness.* 7:46 Some manuscripts read *the house of Jacob.* 7:49-50 Isa 66:1-2. 7:53 Greek *received the Law as it was ordained by angels.* 7:54 Greek *they were grinding their teeth against him.* 7:58 *Saul* is later called Paul; see 13:9.

[2](Some godly men came and buried Stephen with loud weeping.) [3]Saul was going everywhere to devastate the church. He went from house to house, dragging out both men and women to throw them into jail.

LIKE STEPHEN   *I stand up for the Lord no matter what.*

Acts 7:60

When you think of the word *martyr,* who comes to mind?

During the past century, millions of men, women, and young people have died because of their faith in Jesus Christ.

One of the twentieth century's most famous martyrs, Jim Elliot, once said: "He is no fool who gives what he cannot keep to gain what he cannot lose."

Like Jim Elliot, Stephen was an outstanding individual who was wholeheartedly committed to the Lord. Scripture tells us he was "well respected," "full of the Holy Spirit and wisdom," "full of faith," and "full of God's grace and power" (6:3, 5, 8).

In life and in death, Stephen imitated his Lord and Savior. Like Jesus and the twelve apostles, Stephen "performed amazing miracles and signs among the people" (6:8) and was arrested for preaching about Jesus. Like Jesus and the apostles, Stephen was tried by the Jewish high council in Jerusalem. Like Moses and Jesus, Stephen's face "became as bright as an angel's" (6:15).

Stephen was filled with the Holy Spirit and in obedience to Jesus (Luke 12:11-12) boldly answered the false charges leveled against him. Far from boring his listeners, Stephen infuriated the Jewish leaders by using a summary of Israel's history to accuse them of stubbornly fighting against the Lord—just as their ancestors had.

While his accusers shook their fists in rage, Stephen saw a glorious vision of Jesus. Then, like Jesus, Stephen was dragged outside the city of Jerusalem to be killed. Before collapsing, Stephen echoed two of the most famous prayers the Lord had cried out from the cross (Luke 23:34, 46).

Today Stephen is remembered as the first Christian *martyr.* But first and foremost, he was a true *Christian.* He consciously determined to trust the Lord Jesus and obey him—no matter what.

The Lord now calls you and me to follow in his footsteps.

○ *Today's Scripture reading is Acts 6–7.*

Philip Preaches in Samaria

[4]But the believers who had fled Jerusalem went everywhere preaching the Good News about Jesus. [5]Philip, for example, went to the city of Samaria and told the people there about the Messiah. [6]Crowds listened intently to what he had to say because of the miracles he did. [7]Many evil spirits were cast out, screaming as they left their victims. And many who had been paralyzed or lame were healed. [8]So there was great joy in that city.

[9]A man named Simon had been a sorcerer there for many years, claiming to be someone great. [10]The Samaritan people, from the least to the greatest, often spoke of him as "the Great One—the Power of God." [11]He was very influential because of the magic he performed. [12]But now the people believed Philip's message of Good News concerning the Kingdom of God and the name of Jesus Christ. As a result, many men and women were baptized. [13]Then Simon himself believed and was baptized. He began following Philip wherever he went, and he was amazed by the great miracles and signs Philip performed.

[14]When the apostles back in Jerusalem heard that the people of Samaria had accepted God's message, they sent Peter and John there. [15]As soon as they arrived, they prayed for these new Christians to receive the Holy Spirit. [16]The Holy Spirit had not yet come upon any of them, for they had only been baptized in the name of the Lord Jesus. [17]Then Peter and John laid their hands upon these believers, and they received the Holy Spirit.

[18]When Simon saw that the Holy Spirit was given when the apostles placed

I CONTINUE sharing the Good News about Jesus Christ no matter what. (8:4)

See Philip's profile (page 1269) at Acts 21:8.

I AM THANKFUL that the Lord used someone to persuade me to believe in Jesus Christ. (8:6)

I COME to the support of new believers. (8:14)

See the profiles for Peter (page 1111) and John (page 1435) at Matthew 26:75 and Revelation 1:9.

I BELIEVE the Samaritan believers received the Holy Spirit—confirming that they too were true believers. (8:17)

their hands upon people's heads, he offered money to buy this power. [19]"Let me have this power, too," he exclaimed, "so that when I lay my hands on people, they will receive the Holy Spirit!"

[20]But Peter replied, "May your money perish with you for thinking God's gift can be bought! [21]You can have no part in this, for your heart is not right before God. [22]Turn from your wickedness and pray to the Lord. Perhaps he will forgive your evil thoughts, [23]for I can see that you are full of bitterness and held captive by sin."

[24]"Pray to the Lord for me," Simon exclaimed, "that these terrible things won't happen to me!"

[25]After testifying and preaching the word of the Lord in Samaria, Peter and John returned to Jerusalem. And they stopped in many Samaritan villages along the way to preach the Good News to them, too.

Philip and the Ethiopian Eunuch

[26]As for Philip, an angel of the Lord said to him, "Go south* down the desert road that runs from Jerusalem to Gaza." [27]So he did, and he met the treasurer of Ethiopia, a eunuch of great authority under the queen of Ethiopia.* The eunuch had gone to Jerusalem to worship, [28]and he was now returning. Seated in his carriage, he was reading aloud from the book of the prophet Isaiah.

[29]The Holy Spirit said to Philip, "Go over and walk along beside the carriage."

[30]Philip ran over and heard the man reading from the prophet Isaiah; so he asked, "Do you understand what you are reading?"

[31]The man replied, "How can I, when there is no one to instruct me?" And he begged Philip to come up into the carriage and sit with him. [32]The passage of Scripture he had been reading was this:

"He was led as a sheep to the slaughter.
And as a lamb is silent before the shearers,
    he did not open his mouth.
[33]He was humiliated and received no justice.
    Who can speak of his descendants?
    For his life was taken from the earth."*

[34]The eunuch asked Philip, "Was Isaiah talking about himself or someone else?" [35]So Philip began with this same Scripture and then used many others to tell him the Good News about Jesus.

[36]As they rode along, they came to some water, and the eunuch said, "Look! There's some water! Why can't I be baptized?"* [38]He ordered the carriage to stop, and they went down into the water, and Philip baptized him.

[39]When they came up out of the water, the Spirit of the Lord caught Philip away. The eunuch never saw him again but went on his way rejoicing. [40]Meanwhile, Philip found himself farther north at the city of Azotus! He preached the Good News there and in every city along the way until he came to Caesarea.

CHAPTER 9

Saul's Conversion

Meanwhile, Saul was uttering threats with every breath. He was eager to destroy the Lord's followers,* so he went to the high priest. [2]He requested letters addressed to the synagogues in Damascus, asking their cooperation in the arrest of any followers of the Way he found there. He wanted to bring them—both men and women—back to Jerusalem in chains.

I KNOW the gift of the Holy Spirit cannot be bought with money. (8:20)

See Isaiah's profile (page 801) at Isaiah 6:13.

I TALK with those who seem interested in understanding God's Word. (8:30)

I USE the Scriptures to explain the Good News about Jesus Christ. (8:35)

I SHARE the Good News of Jesus Christ everywhere I go. (8:40)

See Paul's profile (page 1333) at Galatians 2:5.

8:26 Or Go at noon.   8:27 Greek under the Candace, the queen of Ethiopia.   8:32-33 Isa 53:7-8.   8:36 Some manuscripts add verse 37, "You can," Philip answered, "if you believe with all your heart." And the eunuch replied, "I believe that Jesus Christ is the Son of God."   9:1 Greek disciples.

[3]As he was nearing Damascus on this mission, a brilliant light from heaven suddenly beamed down upon him! [4]He fell to the ground and heard a voice saying to him, "Saul! Saul! Why are you persecuting me?"

[5]"Who are you, sir?" Saul asked.

And the voice replied, "I am Jesus, the one you are persecuting! [6]Now get up and go into the city, and you will be told what you are to do."

[7]The men with Saul stood speechless with surprise, for they heard the sound of someone's voice, but they saw no one! [8]As Saul picked himself up off the ground, he found that he was blind. [9]So his companions led him by the hand to Damascus. He remained there blind for three days. And all that time he went without food and water.

[10]Now there was a believer* in Damascus named Ananias. The Lord spoke to him in a vision, calling, "Ananias!"

"Yes, Lord!" he replied.

I BELIEVE Jesus Christ blinded Saul physically and then spoke to him. (9:5)

UNLIKE SIMON THE SORCERER   *I do not view the Holy Spirit as a magical power to manipulate for my own purposes.*

Acts 8:24

Do you know the difference between a miracle and a magic trick? Can you discern between the Holy Spirit's activity and the special effects of those who use his name while conjuring up remarkable displays of power?

Simon knew all about power. In Samaria, he was billed as "the Great One—the Power of God" (8:10)—until Philip came preaching the Good News about Jesus Christ. Through Philip's prayers, the sick were healed, the demon possessed were released from bondage, and hearts were transformed. Simon was so impressed that he made a profession of faith and followed Philip and the apostles around. Yet was Simon a sincere believer? Or was he jealously looking for a way to steal back the show from the visiting Jews?

The truth came out when Simon watched the Holy Spirit given to the Samaritan believers. He was amazed and thought to himself, *I must get that power!* So he offered cash to Peter, who sternly rebuked Simon for his evil thoughts and bitter heart.

Why does the Holy Spirit come to live in everyone who becomes a Christian (Romans 8:9)? His power works in you and me to further God's glory, honor, and praise—not to make us rich or famous.

Unlike Simon, let's honor the Holy Spirit for who he is—and not try to manipulate him for our own glory.

○ *Today's Scripture reading is Acts 8:9-25.*

---

[11]The Lord said, "Go over to Straight Street, to the house of Judas. When you arrive, ask for Saul of Tarsus. He is praying to me right now. [12]I have shown him a vision of a man named Ananias coming in and laying his hands on him so that he can see again."

[13]"But Lord," exclaimed Ananias, "I've heard about the terrible things this man has done to the believers in Jerusalem! [14]And we hear that he is authorized by the leading priests to arrest every believer in Damascus."

[15]But the Lord said, "Go and do what I say. For Saul is my chosen instrument to take my message to the Gentiles and to kings, as well as to the people of Israel. [16]And I will show him how much he must suffer for me."

[17]So Ananias went and found Saul. He laid his hands on him and said, "Brother Saul, the Lord Jesus, who appeared to you on the road, has sent me so that you may get your sight back and be filled with the Holy Spirit." [18]Instantly something like scales fell from Saul's eyes, and he regained his sight. Then he got up and was baptized. [19]Afterward he ate some food and was strengthened.

I DO NOT HESITATE to obey God's commands. (9:13)

I BELIEVE the Lord chose to use Saul to take the message of salvation to many people, even kings. (9:15)

I AM WILLING to pray with anyone who has committed his or her life to Jesus Christ. (9:17)

9:10 Greek *disciple*; also in 9:36.

Saul in Damascus and Jerusalem

Saul stayed with the believers* in Damascus for a few days. [20]And immediately he began preaching about Jesus in the synagogues, saying, "He is indeed the Son of God!"

[21]All who heard him were amazed. "Isn't this the same man who persecuted Jesus' followers with such devastation in Jerusalem?" they asked. "And we understand that he came here to arrest them and take them in chains to the leading priests."

[22]Saul's preaching became more and more powerful, and the Jews in Damascus couldn't refute his proofs that Jesus was indeed the Messiah. [23]After a while the Jewish leaders decided to kill him. [24]But Saul was told about their plot, and that they were watching for him day and night at the city gate so they could murder him. [25]So during the night, some of the other believers* let him down in a large basket through an opening in the city wall.

[26]When Saul arrived in Jerusalem, he tried to meet with the believers, but they were all afraid of him. They thought he was only pretending to be a believer! [27]Then Barnabas brought him to the apostles and told them how Saul had seen the Lord on the way to Damascus. Barnabas also told them what the Lord had said to Saul and how he boldly preached in the name of Jesus in Damascus. [28]Then the apostles accepted Saul, and after that he was constantly with them in Jerusalem, preaching boldly in the name of the Lord. [29]He debated with some Greek-speaking Jews, but they plotted to murder him. [30]When the believers* heard about it, however, they took him to Caesarea and sent him on to his hometown of Tarsus.

[31]The church then had peace throughout Judea, Galilee, and Samaria, and it grew in strength and numbers. The believers were walking in the fear of the Lord and in the comfort of the Holy Spirit.

Peter Heals Aeneas and Raises Dorcas

[32]Peter traveled from place to place to visit the believers, and in his travels he came to the Lord's people in the town of Lydda. [33]There he met a man named Aeneas, who had been paralyzed and bedridden for eight years. [34]Peter said to him, "Aeneas, Jesus Christ heals you! Get up and make your bed!" And he was healed instantly. [35]Then the whole population of Lydda and Sharon turned to the Lord when they saw Aeneas walking around.

[36]There was a believer in Joppa named Tabitha (which in Greek is Dorcas*). She was always doing kind things for others and helping the poor. [37]About this time she became ill and died. Her friends prepared her for burial and laid her in an upstairs room. [38]But they had heard that Peter was nearby at Lydda, so they sent two men to beg him, "Please come as soon as possible!"

[39]So Peter returned with them; and as soon as he arrived, they took him to the upstairs room. The room was filled with widows who were weeping and showing him the coats and other garments Dorcas had made for them. [40]But Peter asked them all to leave the room; then he knelt and prayed. Turning to the body he said, "Get up, Tabitha." And she opened her eyes! When she saw Peter, she sat up! [41]He gave her his hand and helped her up. Then he called in the widows and all the believers, and he showed them that she was alive.

[42]The news raced through the whole town, and many believed in the Lord. [43]And Peter stayed a long time in Joppa, living with Simon, a leatherworker.

CHAPTER 10

Cornelius Calls for Peter

In Caesarea there lived a Roman army officer named Cornelius, who was a captain of the Italian Regiment. [2]He was a devout man who feared the God of

Margin notes

I HELP those who are in danger. (9:25)

I WELCOME new believers to the family of God and introduce them to older Christians. (9:27)
See Barnabas's profile (page 1253) at Acts 11:23.

I WALK in the fear of the Lord and in the comfort of the Holy Spirit. (9:31)

See Peter's profile (page 1111) at Matthew 26:75.

I CONTINUALLY FIND ways to do kind things for others and help the poor. (9:36)

I MOURN deeply when a godly Christian friend dies. (9:39)

I AM a devout person who fears God. (10:2)

9:19 Greek *disciples;* also in 9:26.   9:25 Greek *his disciples.*   9:30 Greek *brothers.*   9:36 The names *Tabitha* in Aramaic and *Dorcas* in Greek both mean "gazelle."

Israel, as did his entire household. He gave generously to charity and was a man who regularly prayed to God. ³One afternoon about three o'clock, he had a vision in which he saw an angel of God coming toward him. "Cornelius!" the angel said.

⁴Cornelius stared at him in terror. "What is it, sir?" he asked the angel.

And the angel replied, "Your prayers and gifts to the poor have not gone unnoticed by God! ⁵Now send some men down to Joppa to find a man named Simon Peter. ⁶He is staying with Simon, a leatherworker who lives near the shore. Ask him to come and visit you."

⁷As soon as the angel was gone, Cornelius called two of his household servants and a devout soldier, one of his personal attendants. ⁸He told them what had happened and sent them off to Joppa.

> I BELIEVE my prayers and gifts to the poor do not go unnoticed by God. (10:4)
>
> I BELIEVE the Lord sometimes uses extraordinary means to tell others about himself. (10:5)
>
> See Peter's profile (page 1111) at Matthew 26:75.

LIKE ANANIAS
Acts 9:17

I believe God can change the heart of even the hardest person.

What's your first reaction when you hear about a notorious sinner who claims to have been converted?

Ananias wasn't sure he had heard the Lord right. Go and visit Saul the Persecutor? Didn't the Lord know about this man? Hadn't Saul viciously attacked the Christians in Jerusalem and come to destroy the believers in Damascus?

Ananias's questions were normal. But the Lord told Ananias to do what he had said. Why? Because the Lord had already dealt with Saul and chosen him to proclaim God's message throughout the world—and to endure much suffering as a result.

Ananias proved he believed the Lord by going to Straight Street. When he found Saul, Ananias placed his hands on him and called Saul his "brother." As a result of his obedience, Ananias witnessed the power of God filling Saul with his Holy Spirit and freeing him from his blindness.

Immediately afterward, other Christians feared that Saul was an imposter waiting to trap them. They hadn't received a vision from Jesus confirming Saul's conversion. But soon they saw his changed life and heard his bold testimony that Jesus "is indeed the Son of God!" (9:20). Joy swept through the church.

When you and I hear about those who oppose the Christian faith and hate us as Christians, let's pray for their salvation. After all, God wants everyone to repent (2 Peter 3:9)—even those who seem the farthest from his grace.

○ Today's Scripture reading is Acts 9:1-18.

Peter Visits Cornelius

⁹The next day as Cornelius's messengers were nearing the city, Peter went up to the flat roof to pray. It was about noon, ¹⁰and he was hungry. But while lunch was being prepared, he fell into a trance. ¹¹He saw the sky open, and something like a large sheet was let down by its four corners. ¹²In the sheet were all sorts of animals, reptiles, and birds. ¹³Then a voice said to him, "Get up, Peter; kill and eat them."

¹⁴"Never, Lord," Peter declared. "I have never in all my life eaten anything forbidden by our Jewish laws.*"

¹⁵The voice spoke again, "If God says something is acceptable, don't say it isn't."* ¹⁶The same vision was repeated three times. Then the sheet was pulled up again to heaven.

¹⁷Peter was very perplexed. What could the vision mean? Just then the men sent by Cornelius found the house and stood outside at the gate. ¹⁸They asked if this was the place where Simon Peter was staying. ¹⁹Meanwhile, as Peter was puzzling over the vision, the Holy Spirit said to him, "Three men have

> I BELIEVE God used a dramatic vision to teach an important truth to the apostle Peter. (10:11)
>
> I DO NOT REFUSE to accept what God commands me to accept. (10:14)

10:14 Greek *anything common and unclean.*   10:15 Greek *"What God calls clean you must not call unclean."*

I OBEY the Lord
without hesitation.
(10:20)

come looking for you. ²⁰Go down and go with them without hesitation. All is well, for I have sent them."

²¹So Peter went down and said, "I'm the man you are looking for. Why have you come?"

²²They said, "We were sent by Cornelius, a Roman officer. He is a devout man who fears the God of Israel and is well respected by all the Jews. A holy angel instructed him to send for you so you can go to his house and give him a message." ²³So Peter invited the men to be his guests for the night. The next day he went with them, accompanied by some other believers* from Joppa.

I CALL my friends and
relatives together to
hear the Good News
of Jesus Christ. (10:24)

²⁴They arrived in Caesarea the following day. Cornelius was waiting for him and had called together his relatives and close friends to meet Peter. ²⁵As Peter entered his home, Cornelius fell to the floor before him in worship. ²⁶But Peter pulled him up and said, "Stand up! I'm a human being like you!" ²⁷So Cornelius got up, and they talked together and went inside where the others were assembled.

²⁸Peter told them, "You know it is against the Jewish laws for me to come into a Gentile home like this. But God has shown me that I should never think of anyone as impure. ²⁹So I came as soon as I was sent for. Now tell me why you sent for me."

³⁰Cornelius replied, "Four days ago I was praying in my house at three o'clock in the afternoon. Suddenly, a man in dazzling clothes was standing in front of me. ³¹He told me, 'Cornelius, your prayers have been heard, and your gifts to the poor have been noticed by God! ³²Now send some men to Joppa and summon Simon Peter. He is staying in the home of Simon, a leatherworker who lives near the shore.' ³³So I sent for you at once, and it was good of you to come. Now here we are, waiting before God to hear the message the Lord has given you."

The Gentiles Hear the Good News

I BELIEVE God accepts
anyone who fears and
obeys him. (10:35)

*See John the Baptist's
profile (page 1117) at
Mark 1:4.*

³⁴Then Peter replied, "I see very clearly that God doesn't show partiality. ³⁵In every nation he accepts those who fear him and do what is right. ³⁶I'm sure you have heard about the Good News for the people of Israel—that there is peace with God through Jesus Christ, who is Lord of all. ³⁷You know what happened all through Judea, beginning in Galilee after John the Baptist began preaching. ³⁸And no doubt you know that God anointed Jesus of Nazareth with the Holy Spirit and with power. Then Jesus went around doing good and healing all who were oppressed by the Devil, for God was with him.

³⁹"And we apostles are witnesses of all he did throughout Israel and in Jerusalem. They put him to death by crucifying him, ⁴⁰but God raised him to life three days later. Then God allowed him to appear, ⁴¹not to the general public,* but to us whom God had chosen beforehand to be his witnesses. We were those who ate and drank with him after he rose from the dead. ⁴²And he ordered us to preach everywhere and to testify that Jesus is ordained of God

I BELIEVE Jesus Christ
will forgive the sins of
anyone who believes
in him. (10:43)

to be the judge of all—the living and the dead. ⁴³He is the one all the prophets testified about, saying that everyone who believes in him will have their sins forgiven through his name."

The Gentiles Receive the Holy Spirit

⁴⁴Even as Peter was saying these things, the Holy Spirit fell upon all who had heard the message. ⁴⁵The Jewish believers who came with Peter were amazed that the gift of the Holy Spirit had been poured out upon the Gentiles, too. ⁴⁶And there could be no doubt about it, for they heard them speaking in tongues and praising God.

Then Peter asked, ⁴⁷"Can anyone object to their being baptized, now that

10:23 Greek *brothers.*   10:41 Greek *the people.*

they have received the Holy Spirit just as we did?" ⁴⁸So he gave orders for them to be baptized in the name of Jesus Christ. Afterward Cornelius asked him to stay with them for several days.

CHAPTER 11

Peter Explains His Actions

Soon the news reached the apostles and other believers* in Judea that the Gentiles had received the word of God. ²But when Peter arrived back in Jerusalem, some of the Jewish believers* criticized him. ³"You entered the home of Gentiles* and even ate with them!" they said.

⁴Then Peter told them exactly what had happened. ⁵"One day in Joppa," he said, "while I was praying, I went into a trance and saw a vision. Something like a large sheet was let down by its four corners from the sky. And it came right down to me. ⁶When I looked inside the sheet, I saw all sorts of small animals, wild animals, reptiles, and birds that we are not allowed to eat. ⁷And I heard a voice say, 'Get up, Peter; kill and eat them.'

I ACTIVELY SUPPORT those who share the Good News of Jesus Christ to people of other nationalities. (11:2)

See Peter's profile (page 1111) at Matthew 26:75.

LIKE CORNELIUS

Acts 10:33

I am so glad God's salvation is freely offered to all people.

If "God so loved the world" (John 3:16), what about the Gentile heathen down through the ages?

The Scriptures clearly demonstrate that God never meant for his message of salvation to be hidden within the nation of Israel. Through the edicts of the mighty pagan emperors Nebuchadnezzar, Darius, and Xerxes, the Lord demonstrated his glory to the far reaches of the known world. God even went out of his way—as he had for Abraham—to call out Rahab and Ruth and Naaman and other individuals from paganism to know and serve him.

Like those earlier Gentiles who believed in God, Cornelius sought to enter God's kingdom through the Jewish faith.

Cornelius followed the tenets of Israel's religion—whatever it would take for him, as an outsider, to get to God. He lived to please the Lord, praying earnestly and giving generously to the poor. He also proved himself to be a man who responded to every bit of truth God revealed along the way.

When the angel appeared to him one afternoon, Cornelius discovered God wanted to answer his prayers in a bigger way than the Roman officer had ever hoped or dreamed. Cornelius immediately obeyed the angel and sent for the apostle Peter. He then gathered his family and friends in eager anticipation of God's special message.

Who was more amazed, Peter or Cornelius, when the Holy Spirit came upon the Romans who listened to Peter's message? Cornelius and his relatives and friends suddenly found themselves equal members of God's family through faith in Jesus Christ, Abraham's promised descendant (Galatians 3:15-22).

Through Jesus Christ, you and I are welcomed into God's family regardless of our race, language, or place of birth. Like Cornelius, let's praise God that nothing can stop him from drawing us into his family.

○ *Today's Scripture reading is Acts 10:1–11:18.*

---

⁸"'Never, Lord,' I replied. 'I have never eaten anything forbidden by our Jewish laws.*'

⁹"But the voice from heaven came again, 'If God says something is acceptable, don't say it isn't.'*

¹⁰"This happened three times before the sheet and all it contained was pulled back up to heaven. ¹¹Just then three men who had been sent from Caesarea arrived at the house where I was staying. ¹²The Holy Spirit told me to go with them and not to worry about their being Gentiles. These six

I DO NOT REFUSE to accept what God commands me to accept. (11:9)

11:1 Greek *brothers*. 11:2 Greek *those of the circumcision*. 11:3 Greek *of uncircumcised men*. 11:8 Greek *anything common or unclean*. 11:9 Greek *'What God calls clean you must not call unclean.'*

brothers here accompanied me, and we soon arrived at the home of the man who had sent for us. [13]He told us how an angel had appeared to him in his home and had told him, 'Send messengers to Joppa to find Simon Peter. [14]He will tell you how you and all your household will be saved!'

[15]"Well, I began telling them the Good News, but just as I was getting started, the Holy Spirit fell on them, just as he fell on us at the beginning. [16]Then I thought of the Lord's words when he said, 'John baptized with* water, but you will be baptized with the Holy Spirit.' [17]And since God gave these Gentiles the same gift he gave us when we believed in the Lord Jesus Christ, who was I to argue?"

[18]When the others heard this, all their objections were answered and they began praising God. They said, "God has also given the Gentiles the privilege of turning from sin and receiving eternal life."

The Church in Antioch of Syria

[19]Meanwhile, the believers who had fled from Jerusalem during the persecution after Stephen's death traveled as far as Phoenicia, Cyprus, and Antioch of Syria. They preached the Good News, but only to Jews. [20]However, some of the believers who went to Antioch from Cyprus and Cyrene began preaching to Gentiles* about the Lord Jesus. [21]The power of the Lord was upon them, and large numbers of these Gentiles believed and turned to the Lord.

[22]When the church at Jerusalem heard what had happened, they sent Barnabas to Antioch. [23]When he arrived and saw this proof of God's favor, he was filled with joy, and he encouraged the believers to stay true to the Lord. [24]Barnabas was a good man, full of the Holy Spirit and strong in faith. And large numbers of people were brought to the Lord.

[25]Then Barnabas went on to Tarsus to find Saul. [26]When he found him, he brought him back to Antioch. Both of them stayed there with the church for a full year, teaching great numbers of people. (It was there at Antioch that the believers* were first called Christians.)

[27]During this time, some prophets traveled from Jerusalem to Antioch. [28]One of them named Agabus stood up in one of the meetings to predict by the Spirit that a great famine was coming upon the entire Roman world. (This was fulfilled during the reign of Claudius.) [29]So the believers in Antioch decided to send relief to the brothers and sisters* in Judea, everyone giving as much as they could. [30]This they did, entrusting their gifts to Barnabas and Saul to take to the elders of the church in Jerusalem.

CHAPTER 12

James Is Killed and Peter Is Imprisoned

About that time King Herod Agrippa* began to persecute some believers in the church. [2]He had the apostle James (John's brother) killed with a sword. [3]When Herod saw how much this pleased the Jewish leaders, he arrested Peter during the Passover celebration* [4]and imprisoned him, placing him under the guard of four squads of four soldiers each. Herod's intention was to bring Peter out for public trial after the Passover. [5]But while Peter was in prison, the church prayed very earnestly for him.

Peter's Miraculous Escape from Prison

[6]The night before Peter was to be placed on trial, he was asleep, chained between two soldiers, with others standing guard at the prison gate. [7]Suddenly, there was a bright light in the cell, and an angel of the Lord stood before Peter. The angel tapped him on the side to awaken him and said, "Quick! Get up!" And the chains fell off his wrists. [8]Then the angel told him,

See *John the Baptist's profile (page 1117) at Mark 1:4.*

I BELIEVE God gave the same gift of the Holy Spirit to Jewish and Gentile believers alike. (11:17)

I PRAISE God for offering eternal life to people from all nations. (11:18)

I REJOICE when I meet new believers and encourage them to stay true to the faith. (11:23)

See *Paul's profile (page 1333) at Galatians 2:5.*

I GIVE as much as I can to help other believers in need—even if I know I could face difficult times, too. (11:29)

See *John's profile (page 1435) at Revelation 1:9.*

See *Peter's profile (page 1111) at Matthew 26:75.*

I JOIN with others to pray for believers suffering persecution for their faith. (12:5)

I SLEEP soundly because I know the Lord is with me even in the midst of difficult circumstances. (12:6)

11:16 Or *in*; also in 11:16b. 11:20 Greek *the Greeks*; other manuscripts read *the Hellenists*. 11:26 Greek *disciples*; also in 11:29. 11:29 Greek *the brothers*. 12:1 Greek *Herod the king*. He was the nephew of Herod Antipas and a grandson of Herod the Great. 12:3 Greek *the days of unleavened bread*.

"Get dressed and put on your sandals." And he did. "Now put on your coat and follow me," the angel ordered.

⁹So Peter left the cell, following the angel. But all the time he thought it was a vision. He didn't realize it was really happening. ¹⁰They passed the first and second guard posts and came to the iron gate to the street, and this opened to them all by itself. So they passed through and started walking down the street, and then the angel suddenly left him.

LIKE BARNABAS *I encourage other brothers and sisters in Christ.*
Acts 11:23

Some people are best known by their nicknames.

Mention "Joseph—the Levite from Cyprus" to your Christian friends, and few will know whom you're talking about. After he's first introduced in Acts 4:36-37, Joseph is always called by his nickname: Barnabas (that is, "Son of Encouragement").

And what an encourager he was! Scripture tells us that Barnabas "was filled with joy," "was a good man, full of the Holy Spirit and strong in faith," and was a powerful evangelist (11:23-24). It also says he "encouraged the believers to stay true to the Lord" (11:23). Humanly speaking, the church wouldn't have grown as fast and half the New Testament wouldn't have been written without Barnabas's encouragement. Consider:

- After quitting the first missionary team ever sent by the church to evangelize unreached territories, John Mark could have disappeared from history. But his cousin Barnabas came alongside Mark, encouraged him, and enlisted him back into the Lord's service. Later, tradition holds that Mark had the courage to write the Gospel that bears his name.
- Several years after his dramatic conversion, Saul (aka Paul) wanted to meet with the believers in Jerusalem. Of course, the last time Saul was in town he had been trying to destroy them, so they were afraid for their lives. Barnabas intervened, convincing the apostles to embrace this new brother in Christ. Later, Barnabas enlisted Saul to help him establish a vibrant church in the city of Antioch—and from there teamed up to evangelize various cities throughout Asia Minor. Afterward, Paul wrote more than a dozen letters accepted by the apostles as part of God's inspired Word.

True, at one point Barnabas and Paul had a sharp disagreement—ironically, over John Mark. Yet God clearly brought good out of their decision to form separate missionary teams (15:36-41), and the men held each other in high esteem for many years (1 Corinthians 9:6; Galatians 2:1-13; Colossians 4:10; 2 Timothy 4:11; Philemon 1:24).

Few Christians have contributed more to the advancement of the church than Barnabas. Like him, let's go out of our way to encourage others, too.

○ *Today's Scripture reading is Acts 11:19-30 and 13:1–14:28.*

---

¹¹Peter finally realized what had happened. "It's really true!" he said to himself. "The Lord has sent his angel and saved me from Herod and from what the Jews were hoping to do to me!"

¹²After a little thought, he went to the home of Mary, the mother of John Mark, where many were gathered for prayer. ¹³He knocked at the door in the gate, and a servant girl named Rhoda came to open it. ¹⁴When she recognized Peter's voice, she was so overjoyed that, instead of opening the door, she ran back inside and told everyone, "Peter is standing at the door!"

¹⁵"You're out of your mind," they said. When she insisted, they decided, "It must be his angel."

¹⁶Meanwhile, Peter continued knocking. When they finally went out and opened the door, they were amazed. ¹⁷He motioned for them to quiet down and told them what had happened and how the Lord had led him out of jail. "Tell James and the other brothers what happened," he said. And then he went to another place.

I BELIEVE the Lord sent an angel to rescue Peter from prison. (12:11)

See John Mark's profile (page 1255) at Acts 13:13.

I AM NOT SURPRISED when God answers my prayers. (12:15)

[18]At dawn, there was a great commotion among the soldiers about what had happened to Peter. [19]Herod Agrippa ordered a thorough search for him. When he couldn't be found, Herod interrogated the guards and sentenced them to death. Afterward Herod left Judea to stay in Caesarea for a while.

The Death of Herod Agrippa

[20]Now Herod was very angry with the people of Tyre and Sidon. So they sent a delegation to make peace with him because their cities were dependent upon Herod's country for their food. They made friends with Blastus, Herod's personal assistant, [21]and an appointment with Herod was granted. When the day arrived, Herod put on his royal robes, sat on his throne, and made a speech to them. [22]The people gave him a great ovation, shouting, "It is the voice of a god, not of a man!"

[23]Instantly, an angel of the Lord struck Herod with a sickness, because he accepted the people's worship instead of giving the glory to God. So he was consumed with worms and died.

[24]But God's Good News was spreading rapidly, and there were many new believers.

[25]When Barnabas and Saul had finished their mission in Jerusalem, they returned to Antioch, taking John Mark with them.

CHAPTER 13

Barnabas and Saul Are Sent Out

Among the prophets and teachers of the church at Antioch of Syria were Barnabas, Simeon (called "the black man"*), Lucius (from Cyrene), Manaen (the childhood companion of King Herod Antipas*), and Saul. [2]One day as these men were worshiping the Lord and fasting, the Holy Spirit said, "Dedicate Barnabas and Saul for the special work I have for them." [3]So after more fasting and prayer, the men laid their hands on them and sent them on their way.

Paul's First Missionary Journey

[4]Sent out by the Holy Spirit, Saul and Barnabas went down to the seaport of Seleucia and then sailed for the island of Cyprus. [5]There, in the town of Salamis, they went to the Jewish synagogues and preached the word of God. (John Mark went with them as their assistant.)

[6]Afterward they preached from town to town across the entire island until finally they reached Paphos, where they met a Jewish sorcerer, a false prophet named Bar-Jesus. [7]He had attached himself to the governor, Sergius Paulus, a man of considerable insight and understanding. The governor invited Barnabas and Saul to visit him, for he wanted to hear the word of God. [8]But Elymas, the sorcerer (as his name means in Greek), interfered and urged the governor to pay no attention to what Saul and Barnabas said. He was trying to turn the governor away from the Christian faith.

[9]Then Saul, also known as Paul, filled with the Holy Spirit, looked the sorcerer in the eye and said, [10]"You son of the Devil, full of every sort of trickery and villainy, enemy of all that is good, will you never stop perverting the true ways of the Lord? [11]And now the Lord has laid his hand of punishment upon you, and you will be stricken awhile with blindness." Instantly mist and darkness fell upon him, and he began wandering around begging for someone to take his hand and lead him. [12]When the governor saw what had happened, he believed and was astonished at what he learned about the Lord.

Paul Preaches in Antioch of Pisidia

[13]Now Paul and those with him left Paphos by ship for Pamphylia,* landing at the port town of Perga. There John Mark left them and returned to Jerusalem. [14]But Barnabas and Paul traveled inland to Antioch of Pisidia.*

13:1a Greek who was called Niger.   13:1b Greek Herod the tetrarch.   13:13-14 Pamphylia and Pisidia were districts in the land now called Turkey.

I ALWAYS GIVE glory to God. (12:23)

See Paul's profile (page 1333) at Galatians 2:5.

I FAST sometimes when I am worshiping the Lord. (13:2)

I LOOK for opportunities to present the Good News to those in authority. (13:8)

I DO NOT LET DOWN my ministry team by suddenly quitting and leaving. (13:13)

On the Sabbath they went to the synagogue for the services. [15]After the usual readings from the books of Moses and from the Prophets, those in charge of the service sent them this message: "Brothers, if you have any word of encouragement for us, come and give it!"

[16]So Paul stood, lifted his hand to quiet them, and started speaking. "People of Israel," he said, "and you devout Gentiles who fear the God of Israel, listen to me.

[17]"The God of this nation of Israel chose our ancestors and made them prosper in Egypt. Then he powerfully led them out of their slavery. [18]He put up with them* through forty years of wandering around in the wilderness. [19]Then he destroyed seven nations in Canaan and gave their land to Israel as an inheritance. [20]All this took about 450 years. After that, judges ruled until the time of Samuel the prophet. [21]Then the people begged for a king, and God gave them Saul son of Kish, a man of the tribe of Benjamin, who reigned for forty years. [22]But God removed him from the kingship and replaced him with David, a man about whom God said, 'David son of Jesse is a man after my own heart, for he will do everything I want him to.'*

See Moses' profile (page 73) at Exodus 5:1.

I TAKE ADVANTAGE of opportunities to present God's message of Good News. (13:16)

See Samuel's profile (page 323) at 1 Samuel 3:1.

See Saul's profile (page 339) at 1 Samuel 18:9.

See David's profile (page 629) at Psalm 3:1.

LIKE JOHN MARK
Acts 13:13

I do not let past failures keep me from serving God today.

John Mark was no marine. When the going got tough, he got going—home.

Traveling as an assistant to the greatest missionary of all time on the first official missions trip in all of church history, John Mark bailed out before the missions-team members faced their first flogging. Scripture makes no mention of disease or a death in the family that compelled Mark to return to Jerusalem. Only that he deserted. No wonder Paul refused to take him on his second trip (15:38).

No one denied that Mark blew it. Perhaps it wasn't even the first time he bolted. Some biblical scholars identify him as the young man who fled the scene when Jesus was arrested (Mark 14:51-52).

But even with a blemished résumé, Mark had a place in God's service. God saw Mark's potential and his cousin Barnabas saw it, too. Yet Mark could have refused, wallowing in his own failure and inadequacy.

Instead, Mark grasped the grace of God and returned with Barnabas to bless the saints in Cyprus. Then later, when God's Spirit called him to pick up his pen and write, Mark willingly recorded the account of the Good News of Jesus Christ that bears his name. Rather than letting his failure stunt him, Mark grew spiritually and became dear to Peter (1 Peter 5:13) and useful to Paul, too (2 Timothy 4:11).

You and I might be able to produce a long list of mistakes and immature actions from days gone by. But like Mark, let's grasp God's grace and refuse to let past failures keep us from serving God today.

○ Today's Scripture reading is Acts 13:1-13.

[23]"And it is one of King David's descendants, Jesus, who is God's promised Savior of Israel! [24]But before he came, John the Baptist preached the need for everyone in Israel to turn from sin and turn to God and be baptized. [25]As John was finishing his ministry he asked, 'Do you think I am the Messiah? No! But he is coming soon—and I am not even worthy to be his slave.*'

[26]"Brothers—you sons of Abraham, and also all of you devout Gentiles who fear the God of Israel—this salvation is for us! [27]The people in Jerusalem and their leaders fulfilled prophecy by condemning Jesus to death. They didn't recognize him or realize that he is the one the prophets had written about,

I BELIEVE Jesus Christ is God's promised Savior! (13:23)

See John the Baptist's profile (page 1117) at Mark 1:4.

See Abraham's profile (page 19) at Genesis 15:6.

13:18 Other manuscripts read *He cared for them;* compare Deut 1:31. 13:22 1 Sam 13:14. 13:25 Greek *to untie his sandals.*

See Pilate's profile (page 1229) at John 19:16.

though they hear the prophets' words read every Sabbath. [28] They found no just cause to execute him, but they asked Pilate to have him killed anyway.

[29] "When they had fulfilled all the prophecies concerning his death, they took him down from the cross and placed him in a tomb. [30] But God raised him from the dead! [31] And he appeared over a period of many days to those who had gone with him from Galilee to Jerusalem—these are his witnesses to the people of Israel.

I BELIEVE God's ancient promises came true when he raised Jesus Christ from the dead. (13:32)

[32] "And now Barnabas and I are here to bring you this Good News. God's promise to our ancestors has come true in our own time, [33] in that God raised Jesus. This is what the second psalm is talking about when it says concerning Jesus,

'You are my Son.
    Today I have become your Father.*'

[34] For God had promised to raise him from the dead, never again to die. This is stated in the Scripture that says, 'I will give you the sacred blessings I promised to David.'* [35] Another psalm explains more fully, saying, 'You will not allow your Holy One to rot in the grave.'* [36] Now this is not a reference to David, for after David had served his generation according to the will of God, he died and was buried, and his body decayed. [37] No, it was a reference to someone else—someone whom God raised and whose body did not decay.

I BELIEVE in Jesus Christ and am freed from all guilt and declared right with God. (13:39)

[38] "Brothers, listen! In this man Jesus there is forgiveness for your sins. [39] Everyone who believes in him is freed from all guilt and declared right with God—something the Jewish law could never do. [40] Be careful! Don't let the prophets' words apply to you. For they said,

[41] 'Look, you mockers,
    be amazed and die!
For I am doing something in your own day,
    something you wouldn't believe
    even if someone told you about it.'* "

I URGE new believers to remain faithful to God by his grace. (13:43)

[42] As Paul and Barnabas left the synagogue that day, the people asked them to return again and speak about these things the next week. [43] Many Jews and godly converts to Judaism who worshiped at the synagogue followed Paul and Barnabas, and the two men urged them, "By God's grace, remain faithful."

Paul Turns to the Gentiles

[44] The following week almost the entire city turned out to hear them preach the word of the Lord. [45] But when the Jewish leaders saw the crowds, they were jealous; so they slandered Paul and argued against whatever he said.

[46] Then Paul and Barnabas spoke out boldly and declared, "It was necessary that this Good News from God be given first to you Jews. But since you have rejected it and judged yourselves unworthy of eternal life—well, we will offer it to Gentiles. [47] For this is as the Lord commanded us when he said,

'I have made you a light to the Gentiles,
    to bring salvation to the farthest corners of the earth.'* "

I BELIEVE all who are appointed to eternal life become believers. (13:48)

[48] When the Gentiles heard this, they were very glad and thanked the Lord for his message; and all who were appointed to eternal life became believers. [49] So the Lord's message spread throughout that region. [50] Then the Jewish leaders stirred up both the influential religious women and the leaders of the city, and they incited a mob against Paul and Barnabas and ran them out of town. [51] But they shook off the dust of their feet against them and went to the city of Iconium. [52] And the believers* were filled with joy and with the Holy Spirit.

13:33 Or *Today I reveal you as my Son.* Ps 2:7.   13:34 Isa 55:3.   13:35 Ps 16:10.   13:41 Hab 1:5.   13:47 Isa 49:6.   13:52 Greek *the disciples.*

CHAPTER 14

Paul and Barnabas in Iconium

In Iconium,* Paul and Barnabas went together to the synagogue and preached with such power that a great number of both Jews and Gentiles believed. ²But the Jews who spurned God's message stirred up distrust among the Gentiles against Paul and Barnabas, saying all sorts of evil things about them. ³The apostles stayed there a long time, preaching boldly about the grace of the Lord. The Lord proved their message was true by giving them power to do miraculous signs and wonders. ⁴But the people of the city were divided in their opinion about them. Some sided with the Jews, and some with the apostles.

⁵A mob of Gentiles and Jews, along with their leaders, decided to attack and stone them. ⁶When the apostles learned of it, they fled for their lives. They went to the region of Lycaonia, to the cities of Lystra and Derbe and the surrounding area, ⁷and they preached the Good News there.

Paul and Barnabas in Lystra and Derbe

⁸While they were at Lystra, Paul and Barnabas came upon a man with crippled feet. He had been that way from birth, so he had never walked. ⁹He was listening as Paul preached, and Paul noticed him and realized he had faith to be healed. ¹⁰So Paul called to him in a loud voice, "Stand up!" And the man jumped to his feet and started walking.

¹¹When the listening crowd saw what Paul had done, they shouted in their local dialect, "These men are gods in human bodies!" ¹²They decided that Barnabas was the Greek god Zeus and that Paul, because he was the chief speaker, was Hermes. ¹³The temple of Zeus was located on the outskirts of the city. The priest of the temple and the crowd brought oxen and wreaths of flowers, and they prepared to sacrifice to the apostles at the city gates.

¹⁴But when Barnabas and Paul heard what was happening, they tore their clothing in dismay and ran out among the people, shouting, ¹⁵"Friends,* why are you doing this? We are merely human beings like yourselves! We have come to bring you the Good News that you should turn from these worthless things to the living God, who made heaven and earth, the sea, and everything in them. ¹⁶In earlier days he permitted all the nations to go their own ways, ¹⁷but he never left himself without a witness. There were always his reminders, such as sending you rain and good crops and giving you food and joyful hearts." ¹⁸But even so, Paul and Barnabas could scarcely restrain the people from sacrificing to them.

¹⁹Now some Jews arrived from Antioch and Iconium and turned the crowds into a murderous mob. They stoned Paul and dragged him out of the city, apparently dead. ²⁰But as the believers* stood around him, he got up and went back into the city. The next day he left with Barnabas for Derbe.

Paul and Barnabas Return to Antioch of Syria

²¹After preaching the Good News in Derbe and making many disciples, Paul and Barnabas returned again to Lystra, Iconium, and Antioch of Pisidia, ²²where they strengthened the believers. They encouraged them to continue in the faith, reminding them that they must enter into the Kingdom of God through many tribulations. ²³Paul and Barnabas also appointed elders in every church and prayed for them with fasting, turning them over to the care of the Lord, in whom they had come to trust. ²⁴Then they traveled back through Pisidia to Pamphylia. ²⁵They preached again in Perga, then went on to Attalia.

²⁶Finally, they returned by ship to Antioch of Syria, where their journey had begun and where they had been committed to the grace of God for the

See Paul's profile (page 1333) at Galatians 2:5.

I PRESENT the grace of God with boldness in the midst of opposition. (14:3)

I GIVE glory to God for making heaven and earth, the sea, and everything in them. (14:15)

I BELIEVE God has revealed truths about himself in creation for all humanity to see and understand (Romans 1:19-20). (14:17)

I BELIEVE evangelism and discipleship go hand in hand. (14:21)

14:1 *Iconium,* as well as *Lystra* and *Derbe* (14:6), were cities in the land now called Turkey. 14:15 Greek *Men.* 14:20 Greek *disciples;* also in 14:22, 28.

I REJOICE in all the great things God has done to further his kingdom. (14:27)

See the profiles for Paul (page 1333) and Moses (page 73) at Galatians 2:5 and Exodus 5:1.

I BRING questions of important doctrine to the spiritual elders of my church. (15:2)

See the profile for the Pharisees (page 1087) at Matthew 12:14.

See Peter's profile (page 1111) at Matthew 26:75.

I BELIEVE God accepts all people who believe in Jesus Christ by giving them the Holy Spirit, whether they're Jews or Gentiles. (15:8)

I BELIEVE that all are saved the same way— by the favor of Jesus Christ. (15:11)

See James's profile (page 1407) at James 2:18.

I BELIEVE the conversion of the Gentiles was clearly predicted by the Old Testament prophets. (15:15)

See David's profile (page 629) at Psalm 3:1.

I REFRAIN from practices that would needlessly offend people who haven't yet heard the Good News and trusted Jesus Christ. (15:21)

work they had now completed. [27]Upon arriving in Antioch, they called the church together and reported about their trip, telling all that God had done and how he had opened the door of faith to the Gentiles, too. [28]And they stayed there with the believers in Antioch for a long time.

CHAPTER 15

The Council at Jerusalem

While Paul and Barnabas were at Antioch of Syria, some men from Judea arrived and began to teach the Christians*: "Unless you keep the ancient Jewish custom of circumcision taught by Moses, you cannot be saved." [2]Paul and Barnabas, disagreeing with them, argued forcefully and at length. Finally, Paul and Barnabas were sent to Jerusalem, accompanied by some local believers, to talk to the apostles and elders about this question. [3]The church sent the delegates to Jerusalem, and they stopped along the way in Phoenicia and Samaria to visit the believers.* They told them—much to everyone's joy—that the Gentiles, too, were being converted.

[4]When they arrived in Jerusalem, Paul and Barnabas were welcomed by the whole church, including the apostles and elders. They reported on what God had been doing through their ministry. [5]But then some of the men who had been Pharisees before their conversion stood up and declared that all Gentile converts must be circumcised and be required to follow the law of Moses.

[6]So the apostles and church elders got together to decide this question. [7]At the meeting, after a long discussion, Peter stood and addressed them as follows: "Brothers, you all know that God chose me from among you some time ago to preach to the Gentiles so that they could hear the Good News and believe. [8]God, who knows people's hearts, confirmed that he accepts Gentiles by giving them the Holy Spirit, just as he gave him to us. [9]He made no distinction between us and them, for he also cleansed their hearts through faith. [10]Why are you now questioning God's way by burdening the Gentile believers* with a yoke that neither we nor our ancestors were able to bear? [11]We believe that we are all saved the same way, by the special favor of the Lord Jesus."

[12]There was no further discussion, and everyone listened as Barnabas and Paul told about the miraculous signs and wonders God had done through them among the Gentiles.

[13]When they had finished, James stood and said, "Brothers, listen to me. [14]Peter* has told you about the time God first visited the Gentiles to take from them a people for himself. [15]And this conversion of Gentiles agrees with what the prophets predicted. For instance, it is written:

[16]'Afterward I will return,
  and I will restore the fallen kingdom of David.
From the ruins I will rebuild it,
  and I will restore it,
[17]so that the rest of humanity might find the Lord,
  including the Gentiles—
  all those I have called to be mine.
This is what the Lord says,
[18] he who made these things known long ago.'*

[19]And so my judgment is that we should stop troubling the Gentiles who turn to God, [20]except that we should write to them and tell them to abstain from eating meat sacrificed to idols, from sexual immorality, and from consuming blood or eating the meat of strangled animals. [21]For these laws of Moses have been preached in Jewish synagogues in every city on every Sabbath for many generations."

15:1 Greek brothers; also in 15:32, 33.   15:3 Greek brothers; also in 15:23, 36, 40.   15:10 Greek disciples.
15:14 Greek Simon.   15:16-18 Amos 9:11-12; Isa 45:21.

The Letter for Gentile Believers

²² Then the apostles and elders and the whole church in Jerusalem chose delegates, and they sent them to Antioch of Syria with Paul and Barnabas to report on this decision. The men chosen were two of the church leaders*— Judas (also called Barsabbas) and Silas. ²³ This is the letter they took along with them:

"This letter is from the apostles and elders, your brothers in Jerusalem. It is written to the Gentile believers in Antioch, Syria, and Cilicia. Greetings!

²⁴ "We understand that some men from here have troubled you and upset you with their teaching, but they had no such instructions from us. ²⁵ So it seemed good to us, having unanimously agreed on our decision, to send you these official representatives, along with our beloved Barnabas and Paul, ²⁶ who have risked their lives for the sake of our Lord Jesus Christ. ²⁷ So we are sending Judas and Silas to tell you what we have decided concerning your question.

²⁸ "For it seemed good to the Holy Spirit and to us to lay no greater burden on you than these requirements: ²⁹ You must abstain from eating food offered to idols, from consuming blood or eating the meat of strangled animals, and from sexual immorality. If you do this, you will do well. Farewell."

³⁰ The four messengers went at once to Antioch, where they called a general meeting of the Christians and delivered the letter. ³¹ And there was great joy throughout the church that day as they read this encouraging message.

³² Then Judas and Silas, both being prophets, spoke extensively to the Christians, encouraging and strengthening their faith. ³³ They stayed for a while, and then Judas and Silas were sent back to Jerusalem, with the blessings of the Christians, to those who had sent them.* ³⁵ Paul and Barnabas stayed in Antioch to assist many others who were teaching and preaching the word of the Lord there.

> I SEEK to encourage and strengthen the faith of other Christians. (15:32)

Paul and Barnabas Separate

³⁶ After some time Paul said to Barnabas, "Let's return to each city where we previously preached the word of the Lord, to see how the new believers are getting along." ³⁷ Barnabas agreed and wanted to take along John Mark. ³⁸ But Paul disagreed strongly, since John Mark had deserted them in Pamphylia and had not shared in their work. ³⁹ Their disagreement over this was so sharp that they separated. Barnabas took John Mark with him and sailed for Cyprus. ⁴⁰ Paul chose Silas, and the believers sent them off, entrusting them to the Lord's grace. ⁴¹ So they traveled throughout Syria and Cilicia to strengthen the churches there.

> I VISIT AND ENCOURAGE new believers I have led to the Lord. (15:36)

> I ENTRUST fellow Christians to the grace of God when they are ready to leave and serve him in another land. (15:40)

CHAPTER 16

Paul's Second Missionary Journey

Paul and Silas went first to Derbe and then on to Lystra. There they met Timothy, a young disciple whose mother was a Jewish believer, but whose father was a Greek. ² Timothy was well thought of by the believers* in Lystra and Iconium, ³ so Paul wanted him to join them on their journey. In deference to the Jews of the area, he arranged for Timothy to be circumcised before they left, for everyone knew that his father was a Greek. ⁴ Then they went from town to town, explaining the decision regarding the commandments that were to be obeyed, as decided by the apostles and elders in Jerusalem. ⁵ So the churches were strengthened in their faith and grew daily in numbers.

> *See the profiles for Paul (page 1333) and Timothy (page 1373) at Galatians 2:5 and 1 Timothy 4:12.*

15:22 Greek *were leaders among the brothers.* 15:33 Some manuscripts add verse 34, *But Silas decided to stay there.* 16:2 Greek *brothers;* also in 16:40.

A Call from Macedonia

[6]Next Paul and Silas traveled through the area of Phrygia and Galatia, because the Holy Spirit had told them not to go into the province of Asia at that time. [7]Then coming to the borders of Mysia, they headed for the province of Bithynia,* but again the Spirit of Jesus did not let them go. [8]So instead, they went on through Mysia to the city of Troas.

[9]That night Paul had a vision. He saw a man from Macedonia in northern Greece, pleading with him, "Come over here and help us." [10]So we* decided to leave for Macedonia at once, for we could only conclude that God was calling us to preach the Good News there.

Lydia of Philippi Believes in Jesus

[11]We boarded a boat at Troas and sailed straight across to the island of Samothrace, and the next day we landed at Neapolis. [12]From there we reached Philippi, a major city of the district of Macedonia and a Roman colony; we stayed there several days.

[13]On the Sabbath we went a little way outside the city to a riverbank, where we supposed that some people met for prayer, and we sat down to speak with some women who had come together. [14]One of them was Lydia from Thyatira, a merchant of expensive purple cloth. She was a worshiper of God. As she listened to us, the Lord opened her heart, and she accepted what Paul was saying. [15]She was baptized along with other members of her household, and she asked us to be her guests. "If you agree that I am faithful to the Lord," she said, "come and stay at my home." And she urged us until we did.

Paul and Silas in Prison

[16]One day as we were going down to the place of prayer, we met a demon-possessed slave girl. She was a fortune-teller who earned a lot of money for her masters. [17]She followed along behind us shouting, "These men are servants of the Most High God, and they have come to tell you how to be saved."

[18]This went on day after day until Paul got so exasperated that he turned and spoke to the demon within her. "I command you in the name of Jesus Christ to come out of her," he said. And instantly it left her.

[19]Her masters' hopes of wealth were now shattered, so they grabbed Paul and Silas and dragged them before the authorities at the marketplace. [20]"The whole city is in an uproar because of these Jews!" they shouted. [21]"They are teaching the people to do things that are against Roman customs."

[22]A mob quickly formed against Paul and Silas, and the city officials ordered them stripped and beaten with wooden rods. [23]They were severely beaten, and then they were thrown into prison. The jailer was ordered to make sure they didn't escape. [24]So he took no chances but put them into the inner dungeon and clamped their feet in the stocks.

[25]Around midnight, Paul and Silas were praying and singing hymns to God, and the other prisoners were listening. [26]Suddenly, there was a great earthquake, and the prison was shaken to its foundations. All the doors flew open, and the chains of every prisoner fell off! [27]The jailer woke up to see the prison doors wide open. He assumed the prisoners had escaped, so he drew his sword to kill himself. [28]But Paul shouted to him, "Don't do it! We are all here!"

[29]Trembling with fear, the jailer called for lights and ran to the dungeon and fell down before Paul and Silas. [30]He brought them out and asked, "Sirs, what must I do to be saved?"

[31]They replied, "Believe on the Lord Jesus and you will be saved, along with your entire household." [32]Then they shared the word of the Lord with

---

I AM SENSITIVE to the leading of the Holy Spirit. (16:6)

I BELIEVE God used a vision to call Paul to preach the Good News in Macedonia. (16:9)

I ACTIVELY LOOK for individuals who appear to be searching for God. (16:13)

I OFFER hospitality to Christian workers who are ministering in my area. (16:15)

I BELIEVE demons recognize the servants and message of the Most High God. (16:17)

I SING praises to God even in the midst of suffering. (16:25)

I SHARE the Good News of salvation with individuals and their families whenever possible. (16:32)

16:6-7 *Phrygia, Galatia, Asia, Mysia,* and *Bithynia* were all districts in the land now called Turkey.   16:10 Luke, the writer of this book, here joined Paul and accompanied him on his journey.

him and all who lived in his household. [33] That same hour the jailer washed their wounds, and he and everyone in his household were immediately baptized. [34] Then he brought them into his house and set a meal before them. He and his entire household rejoiced because they all believed in God.

[35] The next morning the city officials sent the police to tell the jailer, "Let those men go!" [36] So the jailer told Paul, "You and Silas are free to leave. Go in peace."

[37] But Paul replied, "They have publicly beaten us without trial and jailed us—and we are Roman citizens. So now they want us to leave secretly? Certainly not! Let them come themselves to release us!"

> I USE the privileges of my citizenship to further the work of the Lord. (16:37)

[38] When the police made their report, the city officials were alarmed to learn that Paul and Silas were Roman citizens. [39] They came to the jail and apologized to them. Then they brought them out and begged them to leave the city. [40] Paul and Silas then returned to the home of Lydia, where they met with the believers and encouraged them once more before leaving town.

CHAPTER 17

Paul Preaches in Thessalonica

Now Paul and Silas traveled through the towns of Amphipolis and Apollonia and came to Thessalonica, where there was a Jewish synagogue. [2] As was Paul's custom, he went to the synagogue service, and for three Sabbaths in a row he interpreted the Scriptures to the people. [3] He was explaining and proving the prophecies about the sufferings of the Messiah and his rising from the dead. He said, "This Jesus I'm telling you about is the Messiah." [4] Some who listened were persuaded and became converts, including a large number of godly Greek men and also many important women of the city.*

> See Paul's profile (page 1333) at Galatians 2:5.

> I USE the Scriptures—not my logic or eloquence—to explain and prove that Jesus is the Messiah, the Savior of the world. (17:3)

[5] But the Jewish leaders were jealous, so they gathered some worthless fellows from the streets to form a mob and start a riot. They attacked the home of Jason, searching for Paul and Silas so they could drag them out to the crowd.* [6] Not finding them there, they dragged out Jason and some of the other believers* instead and took them before the city council. "Paul and Silas have turned the rest of the world upside down, and now they are here disturbing our city," they shouted. [7] "And Jason has let them into his home. They are all guilty of treason against Caesar, for they profess allegiance to another king, Jesus."

[8] The people of the city, as well as the city officials, were thrown into turmoil by these reports. [9] But the officials released Jason and the other believers after they had posted bail.

Paul and Silas in Berea

[10] That very night the believers sent Paul and Silas to Berea. When they arrived there, they went to the synagogue. [11] And the people of Berea were more open-minded than those in Thessalonica, and they listened eagerly to Paul's message. They searched the Scriptures day after day to check up on Paul and Silas, to see if they were really teaching the truth. [12] As a result, many Jews believed, as did some of the prominent Greek women and many men.

> I ENCOURAGE non-Christians to search the Scriptures for themselves—not to put their faith in me. (17:11)

[13] But when some Jews in Thessalonica learned that Paul was preaching the word of God in Berea, they went there and stirred up trouble. [14] The believers acted at once, sending Paul on to the coast, while Silas and Timothy remained behind. [15] Those escorting Paul went with him to Athens; then they returned to Berea with a message for Silas and Timothy to hurry and join him.

> See Timothy's profile (page 1373) at 1 Timothy 4:12.

Paul Preaches in Athens

[16] While Paul was waiting for them in Athens, he was deeply troubled by all the idols he saw everywhere in the city. [17] He went to the synagogue to debate

> I AM DEEPLY TROUBLED by the idolatry I see around me. (17:16)

17:4 Some manuscripts read *many of the wives of the leading men.*   17:5 Or *the city council.*   17:6 Greek *brothers;* also in 17:10, 14.

with the Jews and the God-fearing Gentiles, and he spoke daily in the public square to all who happened to be there.

[18]He also had a debate with some of the Epicurean and Stoic philosophers. When he told them about Jesus and his resurrection, they said, "This babbler has picked up some strange ideas." Others said, "He's pushing some foreign religion."

[19]Then they took him to the Council of Philosophers.* "Come and tell us more about this new religion," they said. [20]"You are saying some rather startling things, and we want to know what it's all about." [21](It should be explained that all the Athenians as well as the foreigners in Athens seemed to spend all their time discussing the latest ideas.)

[22]So Paul, standing before the Council,* addressed them as follows: "Men of Athens, I notice that you are very religious, [23]for as I was walking along I saw your many altars. And one of them had this inscription on it—'To an Unknown God.' You have been worshiping him without knowing who he is, and now I wish to tell you about him.

[24]"He is the God who made the world and everything in it. Since he is Lord of heaven and earth, he doesn't live in man-made temples, [25]and human hands can't serve his needs—for he has no needs. He himself gives life and breath to everything, and he satisfies every need there is. [26]From one man he created all the nations throughout the whole earth. He decided beforehand which should rise and fall, and he determined their boundaries.

[27]"His purpose in all of this was that the nations should seek after God and perhaps feel their way toward him and find him—though he is not far from any one of us. [28]For in him we live and move and exist. As one of your own poets says, 'We are his offspring.' [29]And since this is true, we shouldn't think of God as an idol designed by craftsmen from gold or silver or stone. [30]God overlooked people's former ignorance about these things, but now he commands everyone everywhere to turn away from idols and turn to him.* [31]For he has set a day for judging the world with justice by the man he has appointed, and he proved to everyone who this is by raising him from the dead."

[32]When they heard Paul speak of the resurrection of a person who had been dead, some laughed, but others said, "We want to hear more about this later." [33]That ended Paul's discussion with them, [34]but some joined him and became believers. Among them were Dionysius, a member of the Council,* a woman named Damaris, and others.

CHAPTER 18

Paul Meets Priscilla and Aquila in Corinth

Then Paul left Athens and went to Corinth.* [2]There he became acquainted with a Jew named Aquila, born in Pontus, who had recently arrived from Italy with his wife, Priscilla. They had been expelled from Italy as a result of Claudius Caesar's order to deport all Jews from Rome. [3]Paul lived and worked with them, for they were tentmakers* just as he was.

[4]Each Sabbath found Paul at the synagogue, trying to convince the Jews and Greeks alike. [5]And after Silas and Timothy came down from Macedonia, Paul spent his full time preaching and testifying to the Jews, telling them, "The Messiah you are looking for is Jesus." [6]But when the Jews opposed him and insulted him, Paul shook the dust from his robe and said, "Your blood be upon your own heads—I am innocent. From now on I will go to the Gentiles."

[7]After that he stayed with Titius Justus, a Gentile who worshiped God and

---

I TAKE ADVANTAGE of opportunities to proclaim the Good News of Jesus Christ in secular forums. (17:19)

I BELIEVE God has revealed truths about himself in creation for all humanity to see and understand (Romans 1:19-20). (17:24)

I BELIEVE from one man God created all the nations throughout the whole earth. (17:26)

See Adam's profile (page 5) at Genesis 1:26.

I BELIEVE God wants all nations to seek after him and find him. (17:27)

I BOLDLY PROCLAIM the resurrection of Jesus Christ and his coming judgment of the world. (17:31)

See Paul's profile (page 1333) at Galatians 2:5.

I CONSISTENTLY SEEK to convince others about the Good News of Jesus Christ. (18:4)

See Timothy's profile (page 1373) at 1 Timothy 4:12.

17:19 Greek *the Areopagus.* 17:22 Or *in the middle of Mars Hill;* Greek reads *in the middle of the Areopagus.* 17:30 Greek *everywhere to repent.* 17:34 Greek *an Areopagite.* 18:1 *Athens* and *Corinth* were major cities in Achaia, the region on the southern end of the Greek peninsula. 18:3 Or *leatherworkers.*

lived next door to the synagogue. ⁸Crispus, the leader of the synagogue, and all his household believed in the Lord. Many others in Corinth also became believers and were baptized.

⁹One night the Lord spoke to Paul in a vision and told him, "Don't be afraid! Speak out! Don't be silent! ¹⁰For I am with you, and no one will harm you because many people here in this city belong to me." ¹¹So Paul stayed there for the next year and a half, teaching the word of God.

¹²But when Gallio became governor of Achaia, some Jews rose in concerted action against Paul and brought him before the governor for judgment. ¹³They accused Paul of "persuading people to worship God in ways that are contrary to the law." ¹⁴But just as Paul started to make his defense, Gallio turned to Paul's accusers and said, "Listen, you Jews, if this were a case involving some wrongdoing or a serious crime, I would be obliged to listen to you. ¹⁵But since it is merely a question of words and names and your Jewish laws, you take care of it. I refuse to judge such matters." ¹⁶And he drove them out of the courtroom. ¹⁷The mob had grabbed Sosthenes, the leader of the synagogue, and had beaten him right there in the courtroom. But Gallio paid no attention.

Paul Returns to Antioch of Syria
¹⁸Paul stayed in Corinth for some time after that and then said good-bye to the brothers and sisters* and sailed for the coast of Syria, taking Priscilla and Aquila with him. (Earlier, at Cenchrea, Paul had shaved his head according to Jewish custom, for he had taken a vow.) ¹⁹When they arrived at the port of Ephesus, Paul left the others behind. But while he was there, he went to the synagogue to debate with the Jews. ²⁰They asked him to stay longer, but he declined. ²¹So he left, saying, "I will come back later,* God willing." Then he set sail from Ephesus. ²²The next stop was at the port of Caesarea. From there he went up and visited the church at Jerusalem* and then went back to Antioch.

²³After spending some time in Antioch, Paul went back to Galatia and Phrygia, visiting all the believers,* encouraging them and helping them to grow in the Lord.

Apollos Instructed at Ephesus
²⁴Meanwhile, a Jew named Apollos, an eloquent speaker who knew the Scriptures well, had just arrived in Ephesus from Alexandria in Egypt. ²⁵He had been taught the way of the Lord and talked to others with great enthusiasm and accuracy about Jesus. However, he knew only about John's baptism. ²⁶When Priscilla and Aquila heard him preaching boldly in the synagogue, they took him aside and explained the way of God more accurately.

²⁷Apollos had been thinking about going to Achaia, and the brothers and sisters in Ephesus encouraged him in this. They wrote to the believers in Achaia, asking them to welcome him. When he arrived there, he proved to be of great benefit to those who, by God's grace, had believed. ²⁸He refuted all the Jews with powerful arguments in public debate. Using the Scriptures, he explained to them, "The Messiah you are looking for is Jesus."

CHAPTER 19
Paul's Third Missionary Journey
While Apollos was in Corinth, Paul traveled through the interior provinces. Finally, he came to Ephesus, where he found several believers.* ²"Did you receive the Holy Spirit when you believed?" he asked them.

I BELIEVE God used a vision to urge Paul to continue to preach the Word of God boldly in Corinth. (18:9)

I BELIEVE God kept his promise to rescue Paul from harm during his time in Corinth. (18:14)

I VISIT AND ENCOURAGE the believers I have led to the Lord. (18:23)

See John the Baptist's profile (page 1117) at Mark 1:4.

I INSTRUCT, personally and privately, new believers who need to know the way of God more accurately. (18:26)

I USE the Scriptures to prove that Jesus is the Messiah, the Savior of the world. (18:28)

See Paul's profile (page 1333) at Galatians 2:5.

18:18 Greek brothers; also in 18:27.   18:21 Some manuscripts read "I must by all means be at Jerusalem for the upcoming festival, but I will come back later."   18:22 Greek the church.   18:23 Greek disciples; also in 18:27. 19:1 Greek disciples; also in 19:9, 30.

"No," they replied, "we don't know what you mean. We haven't even heard that there is a Holy Spirit."

3"Then what baptism did you experience?" he asked.

And they replied, "The baptism of John."

4Paul said, "John's baptism was to demonstrate a desire to turn from sin and turn to God. John himself told the people to believe in Jesus, the one John said would come later."

5As soon as they heard this, they were baptized in the name of the Lord Jesus. 6Then when Paul laid his hands on them, the Holy Spirit came on them, and they spoke in other tongues and prophesied. 7There were about twelve men in all.

Paul Ministers in Ephesus

8Then Paul went to the synagogue and preached boldly for the next three months, arguing persuasively about the Kingdom of God. 9But some rejected his message and publicly spoke against the Way, so Paul left the synagogue and took the believers with him. Then he began preaching daily at the lecture hall of Tyrannus. 10This went on for the next two years, so that people throughout the province of Asia—both Jews and Greeks—heard the Lord's message.

11God gave Paul the power to do unusual miracles, 12so that even when handkerchiefs or cloths that had touched his skin were placed on sick people, they were healed of their diseases, and any evil spirits within them came out.

13A team of Jews who were traveling from town to town casting out evil spirits tried to use the name of the Lord Jesus. The incantation they used was this: "I command you by Jesus, whom Paul preaches, to come out!" 14Seven sons of Sceva, a leading priest, were doing this. 15But when they tried it on a man possessed by an evil spirit, the spirit replied, "I know Jesus, and I know Paul. But who are you?" 16And he leaped on them and attacked them with such violence that they fled from the house, naked and badly injured.

17The story of what happened spread quickly all through Ephesus, to Jews and Greeks alike. A solemn fear descended on the city, and the name of the Lord Jesus was greatly honored. 18Many who became believers confessed their sinful practices. 19A number of them who had been practicing magic brought their incantation books and burned them at a public bonfire. The value of the books was several million dollars.* 20So the message about the Lord spread widely and had a powerful effect.

The Riot in Ephesus

21Afterward Paul felt impelled by the Holy Spirit* to go over to Macedonia and Achaia before returning to Jerusalem. "And after that," he said, "I must go on to Rome!" 22He sent his two assistants, Timothy and Erastus, on ahead to Macedonia while he stayed awhile longer in the province of Asia.

23But about that time, serious trouble developed in Ephesus concerning the Way. 24It began with Demetrius, a silversmith who had a large business manufacturing silver shrines of the Greek goddess Artemis.* He kept many craftsmen busy. 25He called the craftsmen together, along with others employed in related trades, and addressed them as follows:

"Gentlemen, you know that our wealth comes from this business. 26As you have seen and heard, this man Paul has persuaded many people that handmade gods aren't gods at all. And this is happening not only here in Ephesus but throughout the entire province! 27Of course, I'm not just talking about the loss of public respect for our business. I'm also concerned that the temple of the great goddess Artemis will lose its influence and that Artemis—this magnificent goddess worshiped throughout the province of Asia and all around the world—will be robbed of her prestige!"

See John the Baptist's profile (page 1117) at Mark 1:4.

I BELIEVE John's baptism prepared people to believe in Jesus Christ. (19:4)

I ACTIVELY TRY to persuade others to accept the Good News of Jesus Christ. (19:8)

I BELIEVE God gave Paul the power to do unusual miracles. (19:11)

I BELIEVE evil spirits can tell if a person belongs to Jesus Christ or not. (19:15)

I DESTROY the tools of my former evil practices, no matter what the cost. (19:19)

See Timothy's profile (page 1373) at 1 Timothy 4:12.

I RECOGNIZE that opposition is inevitable when many people turn to Jesus Christ. (19:26)

19:19 Greek *50,000 pieces of silver,* each of which was the equivalent of a day's wage. 19:21 Or *purposed in his spirit.* 19:24 *Artemis* is otherwise known as Diana.

[28]At this their anger boiled, and they began shouting, "Great is Artemis of the Ephesians!" [29]A crowd began to gather, and soon the city was filled with confusion. Everyone rushed to the amphitheater, dragging along Gaius and Aristarchus, who were Paul's traveling companions from Macedonia. [30]Paul wanted to go in, but the believers wouldn't let him. [31]Some of the officials of the province, friends of Paul, also sent a message to him, begging him not to risk his life by entering the amphitheater.

I LOOK OUT for the safety of fellow believers. (19:30)

LIKE PRISCILLA AND AQUILA   *I help others understand God's truth better.*

Acts 18:26

The hardworking, blue-collar couple from Italy approached the young, eloquent scholar from Egypt. Would he care to come over for supper? Along with the pasta or the pita bread, they served up more of what the preacher wanted most—further truth about God and his wonderful Son, Jesus Christ.

As brilliant as he was, Apollos had not yet heard the whole message of Jesus Christ. Like someone who has read the first two books of a trilogy, he needed to be filled in on the exciting conclusion. Priscilla and Aquila gave him the wonderful news—there was more to believing in Jesus as Messiah than simply following John's baptism to show one's desire to be right with God. Now that desire could be fulfilled! How? Because Jesus had died on the cross to pay for our sins and had risen from the grave completely victorious over death.

It's important to note that when Priscilla and Aquila heard Apollos's impassioned but inadequate preaching in the synagogue, they approached him as a brother instead of as an enemy. They graciously instructed him in private instead of blasting him in public.

Interestingly, differences in age, occupation, and nationality didn't matter. Why? Because Priscilla and Aquila knew the Scriptures, they had studied under Paul, they cared about Apollos, and they wanted to see God's message of salvation continue to go forth in full truth. Apollos could see that and welcomed their instruction. Scripture tells us that when he departed, Apollos was an even more powerful tool in the hand of God.

You and I are surrounded by individuals who believe in Jesus—yet who need to know more. Like Priscilla and Aquila, let's help others learn more about God's way and then rejoice when God's kingdom grows as a result.

○ *Today's Scripture reading is Acts 18.*

[32]Inside, the people were all shouting, some one thing and some another. Everything was in confusion. In fact, most of them didn't even know why they were there. [33]Alexander was thrust forward by some of the Jews, who encouraged him to explain the situation. He motioned for silence and tried to speak in defense. [34]But when the crowd realized he was a Jew, they started shouting again and kept it up for two hours: "Great is Artemis of the Ephesians! Great is Artemis of the Ephesians!"

[35]At last the mayor was able to quiet them down enough to speak. "Citizens of Ephesus," he said. "Everyone knows that Ephesus is the official guardian of the temple of the great Artemis, whose image fell down to us from heaven. [36]Since this is an indisputable fact, you shouldn't be disturbed, no matter what is said. Don't do anything rash. [37]You have brought these men here, but they have stolen nothing from the temple and have not spoken against our goddess. [38]If Demetrius and the craftsmen have a case against them, the courts are in session and the judges can take the case at once. Let them go through legal channels. [39]And if there are complaints about other matters, they can be settled in a legal assembly. [40]I am afraid we are in danger of being charged with rioting by the Roman government, since there is no cause for all this commotion. And if Rome demands an explanation, we won't know what to say." [41]Then he dismissed them, and they dispersed.

I USE legal channels— not public riots—to solve disputes. (19:38)

CHAPTER 20

Paul Goes to Macedonia and Greece

See Paul's profile (page 1333) at Galatians 2:5.

When it was all over, Paul sent for the believers* and encouraged them. Then he said good-bye and left for Macedonia. ²Along the way, he encouraged the believers in all the towns he passed through. Then he traveled down to Greece, ³where he stayed for three months. He was preparing to sail back to Syria when he discovered a plot by some Jews against his life, so he decided to return through Macedonia.

I ENCOURAGE believers I meet when traveling. (20:2)

I TAKE necessary precautions to thwart plots against my life. (20:3)

See Timothy's profile (page 1373) at 1 Timothy 4:12.

⁴Several men were traveling with him. They were Sopater of Berea, the son of Pyrrhus; Aristarchus and Secundus, from Thessalonica; Gaius, from Derbe; Timothy; and Tychicus and Trophimus, who were from the province of Asia. ⁵They went ahead and waited for us at Troas. ⁶As soon as the Passover season* ended, we boarded a ship at Philippi in Macedonia and five days later arrived in Troas, where we stayed a week.

Paul's Final Visit to Troas

I GATHER with other Christians to observe the Lord's Supper. (20:7)

⁷On the first day of the week, we gathered to observe the Lord's Supper.* Paul was preaching; and since he was leaving the next day, he talked until midnight. ⁸The upstairs room where we met was lighted with many flickering lamps. ⁹As Paul spoke on and on, a young man named Eutychus, sitting on the windowsill, became very drowsy. Finally, he sank into a deep sleep and fell three stories to his death below. ¹⁰Paul went down, bent over him, and took him into his arms. "Don't worry," he said, "he's alive!" ¹¹Then they all went back upstairs and ate the Lord's Supper together.* And Paul continued talking to them until dawn; then he left. ¹²Meanwhile, the young man was taken home unhurt, and everyone was greatly relieved.

Paul Meets the Ephesian Elders

¹³Paul went by land to Assos, where he had arranged for us to join him, and we went on ahead by ship. ¹⁴He joined us there and we sailed together to Mitylene. ¹⁵The next day we passed the island of Kios. The following day, we crossed to the island of Samos. And a day later we arrived at Miletus.

¹⁶Paul had decided against stopping at Ephesus this time because he didn't want to spend further time in the province of Asia. He was hurrying to get to Jerusalem, if possible, for the Festival of Pentecost. ¹⁷But when we landed at Miletus, he sent a message to the elders of the church at Ephesus, asking them to come down to meet him.

I DO NOT SHRINK from telling the truth from God's Word. (20:20)

I SHARE the same message of salvation with everyone—the necessity of turning from sin and turning to God, and of faith in the Lord Jesus Christ. (20:21)

¹⁸When they arrived he declared, "You know that from the day I set foot in the province of Asia until now ¹⁹I have done the Lord's work humbly—yes, and with tears. I have endured the trials that came to me from the plots of the Jews. ²⁰Yet I never shrank from telling you the truth, either publicly or in your homes. ²¹I have had one message for Jews and Gentiles alike—the necessity of turning from sin and turning to God, and of faith in our Lord Jesus.

I BELIEVE my life's work ultimately is to do what God commands me to do. (20:24)

²²"And now I am going to Jerusalem, drawn there irresistibly by the Holy Spirit,* not knowing what awaits me, ²³except that the Holy Spirit has told me in city after city that jail and suffering lie ahead. ²⁴But my life is worth nothing unless I use it for doing the work assigned me by the Lord Jesus—the work of telling others the Good News about God's wonderful kindness and love.

I BELIEVE God holds church leaders responsible for the pastoral care of his people. (20:28)

²⁵"And now I know that none of you to whom I have preached the Kingdom will ever see me again. ²⁶Let me say plainly that I have been faithful. No one's damnation can be blamed on me,* ²⁷for I didn't shrink from declaring all that God wants for you. ²⁸"And now beware! Be sure that you feed and shepherd God's flock—his church, purchased with his blood—over whom the Holy Spirit has appointed

20:1 Greek *disciples.*   20:6 Greek *the days of unleavened bread.*   20:7 Greek *to break bread.*   20:11 Greek *broke the bread.*   20:22 Or *by my spirit,* or *by an inner compulsion.* Greek reads *by the spirit.*   20:26 Greek *I am innocent of the blood of all.*

you as elders.* ²⁹I know full well that false teachers, like vicious wolves, will come in among you after I leave, not sparing the flock. ³⁰Even some of you will distort the truth in order to draw a following. ³¹Watch out! Remember the three years I was with you—my constant watch and care over you night and day, and my many tears for you.

³²"And now I entrust you to God and the word of his grace—his message that is able to build you up and give you an inheritance with all those he has set apart for himself.

³³"I have never coveted anyone's money or fine clothing. ³⁴You know that these hands of mine have worked to pay my own way, and I have even supplied the needs of those who were with me. ³⁵And I have been a constant example of how you can help the poor by working hard. You should remember the words of the Lord Jesus: 'It is more blessed to give than to receive.' "

³⁶When he had finished speaking, he knelt and prayed with them. ³⁷They wept aloud as they embraced him in farewell, ³⁸sad most of all because he had said that they would never see him again. Then they accompanied him down to the ship.

I DO NOT COVET other people's money but work hard to provide for myself and help those in need. (20:33)

CHAPTER 21

Paul's Journey to Jerusalem

After saying farewell to the Ephesian elders, we sailed straight to the island of Cos. The next day we reached Rhodes and then went to Patara. ²There we boarded a ship sailing for the Syrian province of Phoenicia. ³We sighted the island of Cyprus, passed it on our left, and landed at the harbor of Tyre, in Syria, where the ship was to unload. ⁴We went ashore, found the local believers,* and stayed with them a week. These disciples prophesied through the Holy Spirit that Paul should not go on to Jerusalem. ⁵When we returned to the ship at the end of the week, the entire congregation, including wives and children, came down to the shore with us. There we knelt, prayed, ⁶and said our farewells. Then we went aboard, and they returned home.

⁷The next stop after leaving Tyre was Ptolemais, where we greeted the brothers and sisters* but stayed only one day. ⁸Then we went on to Caesarea and stayed at the home of Philip the Evangelist, one of the seven men who had been chosen to distribute food. ⁹He had four unmarried daughters who had the gift of prophecy.

¹⁰During our stay of several days, a man named Agabus, who also had the gift of prophecy, arrived from Judea. ¹¹When he visited us, he took Paul's belt and bound his own feet and hands with it. Then he said, "The Holy Spirit declares, 'So shall the owner of this belt be bound by the Jewish leaders in Jerusalem and turned over to the Romans.' " ¹²When we heard this, we who were traveling with him, as well as the local believers, begged Paul not to go on to Jerusalem.

¹³But he said, "Why all this weeping? You are breaking my heart! For I am ready not only to be jailed at Jerusalem but also to die for the sake of the Lord Jesus." ¹⁴When it was clear that we couldn't persuade him, we gave up and said, "The will of the Lord be done."

Paul Arrives at Jerusalem

¹⁵Shortly afterward we packed our things and left for Jerusalem. ¹⁶Some believers from Caesarea accompanied us, and they took us to the home of Mnason, a man originally from Cyprus and one of the early disciples. ¹⁷All the brothers and sisters in Jerusalem welcomed us cordially.

¹⁸The next day Paul went in with us to meet with James, and all the elders of the Jerusalem church were present. ¹⁹After greetings were exchanged, Paul

See Paul's profile (page 1333) at Galatians 2:5.

I PRAY when I say good-bye to fellow believers who are leaving to serve the Lord elsewhere. (21:5)

I AM WILLING to suffer for the Lord Jesus Christ. (21:13)

I COMMIT another person's decision to the Lord's will when my counsel is not taken. (21:14)

I CORDIALLY WELCOME those who are servants of the Lord. (21:17)

See James's profile (page 1407) at James 2:18.

20:28 Greek *overseers.* 21:4 Greek *disciples;* also in 21:16. 21:7 Greek *brothers;* also in 21:17.

gave a detailed account of the things God had accomplished among the Gentiles through his ministry.

I REJOICE in all the great things God has done to further his kingdom. (21:20)

See Moses' profile (page 73) at Exodus 5:1.

[20]After hearing this, they praised God. But then they said, "You know, dear brother, how many thousands of Jews have also believed, and they all take the law of Moses very seriously. [21]Our Jewish Christians here at Jerusalem have been told that you are teaching all the Jews living in the Gentile world to turn their backs on the laws of Moses. They say that you teach people not to circumcise their children or follow other Jewish customs. [22]Now what can be done? For they will certainly hear that you have come.

[23]"Here's our suggestion. We have four men here who have taken a vow and are preparing to shave their heads. [24]Go with them to the Temple and join them in the purification ceremony, and pay for them to have their heads shaved. Then everyone will know that the rumors are all false and that you yourself observe the Jewish laws.

I DO my best to prevent misunder-standings and thwart false rumors. (21:24)

[25]"As for the Gentile Christians, all we ask of them is what we already told them in a letter: They should not eat food offered to idols, nor consume blood, nor eat meat from strangled animals, and they should stay away from all sexual immorality."

Paul Is Arrested

[26]So Paul agreed to their request, and the next day he went through the purification ritual with the men and went to the Temple. Then he publicly announced the date when their vows would end and sacrifices would be offered for each of them.

[27]The seven days were almost ended when some Jews from the province of Asia saw Paul in the Temple and roused a mob against him. They grabbed him, [28]yelling, "Men of Israel! Help! This is the man who teaches against our people and tells everybody to disobey the Jewish laws. He speaks against the Temple—and he even defiles it by bringing Gentiles in!" [29](For earlier that day they had seen him in the city with Trophimus, a Gentile from Ephesus,* and they assumed Paul had taken him into the Temple.)

I REALIZE my best intentions and efforts may not thwart false rumors and accusations. (21:30)

[30]The whole population of the city was rocked by these accusations, and a great riot followed. Paul was dragged out of the Temple, and immediately the gates were closed behind him. [31]As they were trying to kill him, word reached the commander of the Roman regiment that all Jerusalem was in an uproar. [32]He immediately called out his soldiers and officers and ran down among the crowd. When the mob saw the commander and the troops coming, they stopped beating Paul. [33]The commander arrested him and ordered him bound with two chains. Then he asked the crowd who he was and what he had done. [34]Some shouted one thing and some another. He couldn't find out the truth in all the uproar and confusion, so he ordered Paul to be taken to the fortress. [35]As they reached the stairs, the mob grew so violent the soldiers had to lift Paul to their shoulders to protect him. [36]And the crowd followed behind shouting, "Kill him, kill him!"

Paul Speaks to the Crowd

[37]As Paul was about to be taken inside, he said to the commander, "May I have a word with you?"

"Do you know Greek?" the commander asked, surprised. [38]"Aren't you the Egyptian who led a rebellion some time ago and took four thousand members of the Assassins out into the desert?"

I CALMLY REQUEST the opportunity to defend myself when I am falsely accused. (21:39)

[39]"No," Paul replied, "I am a Jew from Tarsus in Cilicia, which is an important city. Please, let me talk to these people." [40]The commander agreed, so Paul stood on the stairs and motioned to the people to be quiet. Soon a deep silence enveloped the crowd, and he addressed them in their own language, Aramaic.*

21:29 Greek *Trophimus, the Ephesian.*   21:40 Or *Hebrew.*

CHAPTER 22

"Brothers and esteemed fathers," Paul said, "listen to me as I offer my defense." ²When they heard him speaking in their own language,* the silence was even greater. ³"I am a Jew, born in Tarsus, a city in Cilicia, and I was brought up and educated here in Jerusalem under Gamaliel. At his feet I learned to follow our Jewish laws and customs very carefully. I became very zealous to honor God in everything I did, just as all of you are today. ⁴And I persecuted the followers of the Way, hounding some to death, binding and delivering both men and women to prison. ⁵The high priest and the whole council of leaders can testify that this is so. For I received letters from them to our Jewish brothers in Damascus, authorizing me to bring the Christians from there to Jerusalem, in chains, to be punished.

See Paul's profile (page 1333) at Galatians 2:5.

I COMMEND others who have demonstrated religious zeal when I begin to tell them about the Good News of Jesus Christ. (22:3)

LIKE PHILIP   *I can tell anyone about the Lord.*

Acts 21:8

The apostle Philip and the Philip whose stories are told in Acts knew each other and were both evangelists. The apostle Philip loved introducing people to Jesus Christ while he walked the land of Judea. And the other Philip loved telling people about his Lord and Savior who died and rose again.

The latter Philip eventually became the more famous of the two men. Acts 6:3 tells us that he was "well respected" and "full of the Holy Spirit and wisdom." For a time, he actively served within the church in Jerusalem at the request of the apostles. When Stephen was martyred, however, Philip was forced to flee Judea.

Instead of running straight back home to Caesarea, Philip fulfilled the Lord's Great Commission to "tell people about me everywhere . . . and to the ends of the earth" (1:8). Philip started by preaching the Good News to crowds of Samaritans, many of whom believed his message and were baptized (8:4-12). From Samaria, Philip traveled south for a divine appointment with an Ethiopian eunuch and then journeyed north, telling others about the Lord "in every city along the way until he came to Caesarea" (8:40).

From that point on, he was known as "Philip the Evangelist" (21:8). His home became a powerful lighthouse for the Good News for several decades.

The Great Commission applies to all Christians down through the ages—including you and me. Like Philip, let's shine the light of Jesus where we are to all we meet.

❍ *Today's Scripture reading is Acts 8:4-12 and 8:26-40.*

---

⁶"As I was on the road, nearing Damascus, about noon a very bright light from heaven suddenly shone around me. ⁷I fell to the ground and heard a voice saying to me, 'Saul, Saul, why are you persecuting me?'

⁸"'Who are you, sir?' I asked. And he replied, 'I am Jesus of Nazareth, the one you are persecuting.' ⁹The people with me saw the light but didn't hear the voice.

¹⁰"I said, 'What shall I do, Lord?' And the Lord told me, 'Get up and go into Damascus, and there you will be told all that you are to do.'

¹¹"I was blinded by the intense light and had to be led into Damascus by my companions. ¹²A man named Ananias lived there. He was a godly man in his devotion to the law, and he was well thought of by all the Jews of Damascus. ¹³He came to me and stood beside me and said, 'Brother Saul, receive your sight.' And that very hour I could see him!

¹⁴"Then he told me, 'The God of our ancestors has chosen you to know his will and to see the Righteous One and hear him speak. ¹⁵You are to take his message everywhere, telling the whole world what you have seen and heard. ¹⁶And now, why delay? Get up and be baptized, and have your sins washed away, calling on the name of the Lord.'

I TELL others how I became a Christian. (22:6)

See Ananias's profile (page 1249) at Acts 9:17.

I BELIEVE the Lord Jesus Christ chose Paul as one of his ambassadors. (22:15)

22:2 Greek in Aramaic.

[17]"One day after I returned to Jerusalem, I was praying in the Temple, and I fell into a trance. [18]I saw a vision of Jesus saying to me, 'Hurry! Leave Jerusalem, for the people here won't believe you when you give them your testimony about me.'

[19]"'But Lord,' I argued, 'they certainly know that I imprisoned and beat those in every synagogue who believed on you. [20]And when your witness Stephen was killed, I was standing there agreeing. I kept the coats they laid aside as they stoned him.'

[21]"But the Lord said to me, 'Leave Jerusalem, for I will send you far away to the Gentiles!'"

[22]The crowd listened until Paul came to that word; then with one voice they shouted, "Away with such a fellow! Kill him! He isn't fit to live!" [23]They yelled, threw off their coats, and tossed handfuls of dust into the air.

Paul Reveals His Roman Citizenship

[24]The commander brought Paul inside and ordered him lashed with whips to make him confess his crime. He wanted to find out why the crowd had become so furious. [25]As they tied Paul down to lash him, Paul said to the officer standing there, "Is it legal for you to whip a Roman citizen who hasn't even been tried?"

[26]The officer went to the commander and asked, "What are you doing? This man is a Roman citizen!"

[27]So the commander went over and asked Paul, "Tell me, are you a Roman citizen?"

"Yes, I certainly am," Paul replied.

[28]"I am, too," the commander muttered, "and it cost me plenty!"

"But I am a citizen by birth!"

[29]The soldiers who were about to interrogate Paul quickly withdrew when they heard he was a Roman citizen, and the commander was frightened because he had ordered him bound and whipped.

Paul before the High Council

[30]The next day the commander freed Paul from his chains and ordered the leading priests into session with the Jewish high council.* He had Paul brought in before them to try to find out what the trouble was all about.

CHAPTER 23

Gazing intently at the high council,* Paul began: "Brothers, I have always lived before God in all good conscience!"

[2]Instantly Ananias the high priest commanded those close to Paul to slap him on the mouth. [3]But Paul said to him, "God will slap you, you whitewashed wall! What kind of judge are you to break the law yourself by ordering me struck like that?"

[4]Those standing near Paul said to him, "Is that the way to talk to God's high priest?"

[5]"I'm sorry, brothers. I didn't realize he was the high priest," Paul replied, "for the Scriptures say, 'Do not speak evil of anyone who rules over you.'*"

[6]Paul realized that some members of the high council were Sadducees and some were Pharisees, so he shouted, "Brothers, I am a Pharisee, as were all my ancestors! And I am on trial because my hope is in the resurrection of the dead!"

[7]This divided the council—the Pharisees against the Sadducees—[8]for the Sadducees say there is no resurrection or angels or spirits, but the Pharisees believe in all of these. [9]So a great clamor arose. Some of the teachers of religious law who were Pharisees jumped up to argue that Paul was all right. "We

Margin notes

See Stephen's profile (page 1245) at Acts 7:60.

I BELIEVE the Lord Jesus Christ sent Paul as one of his ambassadors to the Gentile world. (22:21)

I USE my privileges as a citizen to obtain justice. (22:25)

I LIVE in good conscience before God. (23:1)

See Paul's profile (page 1333) at Galatians 2:5.

I DO NOT PURPOSELY SPEAK evil of my leaders. (23:5)

I POINT OUT the contradictory beliefs of my listeners when I proclaim God's message. (23:6)

I BELIEVE what the Bible says about the resurrection, angels, and spirits. (23:8)

22:30 Greek *Sanhedrin.*   23:1 Greek *Sanhedrin;* also in 23:6, 15, 20, 28.   23:5 Exod 22:28.

see nothing wrong with him," they shouted. "Perhaps a spirit or an angel spoke to him." [10] The shouting grew louder and louder, and the men were tugging at Paul from both sides, pulling him this way and that. Finally, the commander, fearing they would tear him apart, ordered his soldiers to take him away from them and bring him back to the fortress.

[11] That night the Lord appeared to Paul and said, "Be encouraged, Paul. Just as you have told the people about me here in Jerusalem, you must preach the Good News in Rome."

The Plan to Kill Paul

[12] The next morning a group of Jews got together and bound themselves with an oath to neither eat nor drink until they had killed Paul. [13] There were more than forty of them. [14] They went to the leading priests and other leaders and told them what they had done. "We have bound ourselves under oath to neither eat nor drink until we have killed Paul. [15] You and the high council should tell the commander to bring Paul back to the council again," they requested. "Pretend you want to examine his case more fully. We will kill him on the way."

[16] But Paul's nephew heard of their plan and went to the fortress and told Paul. [17] Paul called one of the officers and said, "Take this young man to the commander. He has something important to tell him."

[18] So the officer did, explaining, "Paul, the prisoner, called me over and asked me to bring this young man to you because he has something to tell you."

[19] The commander took him by the arm, led him aside, and asked, "What is it you want to tell me?"

[20] Paul's nephew told him, "Some Jews are going to ask you to bring Paul before the Jewish high council tomorrow, pretending they want to get some more information. [21] But don't do it! There are more than forty men hiding along the way ready to jump him and kill him. They have vowed not to eat or drink until they kill him. They are ready, expecting you to agree to their request."

[22] "Don't let a soul know you told me this," the commander warned the young man as he sent him away.

Paul Is Sent to Caesarea

[23] Then the commander called two of his officers and ordered, "Get two hundred soldiers ready to leave for Caesarea at nine o'clock tonight. Also take two hundred spearmen and seventy horsemen. [24] Provide horses for Paul to ride, and get him safely to Governor Felix." [25] Then he wrote this letter to the governor:

[26] "From Claudius Lysias, to his Excellency, Governor Felix. Greetings! [27] This man was seized by some Jews, and they were about to kill him when I arrived with the troops. When I learned that he was a Roman citizen, I removed him to safety. [28] Then I took him to their high council to try to find out what he had done. [29] I soon discovered it was something regarding their religious law—certainly nothing worthy of imprisonment or death. [30] But when I was informed of a plot to kill him, I immediately sent him on to you. I have told his accusers to bring their charges before you."

[31] So that night, as ordered, the soldiers took Paul as far as Antipatris. [32] They returned to the fortress the next morning, while the horsemen took him on to Caesarea. [33] When they arrived in Caesarea, they presented Paul and the letter to Governor Felix. [34] He read it and then asked Paul what province he was from. "Cilicia," Paul answered.

[35] "I will hear your case myself when your accusers arrive," the governor told him. Then the governor ordered him kept in the prison at Herod's headquarters.

I BELIEVE the Lord Jesus Christ commissioned Paul to preach his Good News in Rome. (23:11)

I DO what I can to protect Christian workers who are in danger. (23:16)

In response to the profiles, tell the Lord whose example you want to imitate— and whose failures you don't want to repeat.

CHAPTER 24

Paul Appears before Felix

See Paul's profile (page 1333) at Galatians 2:5.

Five days later Ananias, the high priest, arrived with some of the Jewish leaders and the lawyer* Tertullus, to press charges against Paul. ²When Paul was called in, Tertullus laid charges against Paul in the following address to the governor:

"Your Excellency, you have given peace to us Jews and have enacted reforms for us. ³And for all of this we are very grateful to you. ⁴But lest I bore you, kindly give me your attention for only a moment as I briefly outline our case against this man. ⁵For we have found him to be a troublemaker, a man who is constantly inciting the Jews throughout the world to riots and rebellions against the Roman government. He is a ringleader of the sect known as the Nazarenes. ⁶Moreover he was trying to defile the Temple when we arrested him.* ⁸You can find out the truth of our accusations by examining him yourself." ⁹Then the other Jews chimed in, declaring that everything Tertullus said was true.

I DO NOT BRING false accusations against God's servants. (24:5)

¹⁰Now it was Paul's turn. The governor motioned for him to rise and speak. Paul said, "I know, sir, that you have been a judge of Jewish affairs for many years, and this gives me confidence as I make my defense. ¹¹You can quickly discover that it was no more than twelve days ago that I arrived in Jerusalem to worship at the Temple. ¹²I didn't argue with anyone in the Temple, nor did I incite a riot in any synagogue or on the streets of the city. ¹³These men certainly cannot prove the things they accuse me of doing.

I TAKE the opportunity to defend myself in court. (24:10)

¹⁴"But I admit that I follow the Way, which they call a sect. I worship the God of our ancestors, and I firmly believe the Jewish law and everything written in the books of prophecy. ¹⁵I have hope in God, just as these men do, that he will raise both the righteous and the ungodly. ¹⁶Because of this, I always try to maintain a clear conscience before God and everyone else.

I BELIEVE God will raise both the righteous and the ungodly from the dead. (24:15)

I CAREFULLY STATE the facts to correct false accusations against me. (24:18)

¹⁷"After several years away, I returned to Jerusalem with money to aid my people and to offer sacrifices to God. ¹⁸My accusers saw me in the Temple as I was completing a purification ritual. There was no crowd around me and no rioting. ¹⁹But some Jews from the province of Asia were there—and they ought to be here to bring charges if they have anything against me! ²⁰Ask these men here what wrongdoing the Jewish high council* found in me, ²¹except for one thing I said when I shouted out, 'I am on trial before you today because I believe in the resurrection of the dead!'"

²²Felix, who was quite familiar with the Way, adjourned the hearing and said, "Wait until Lysias, the garrison commander, arrives. Then I will decide the case." ²³He ordered an officer to keep Paul in custody but to give him some freedom and allow his friends to visit him and take care of his needs.

I MINISTER to imprisoned Christians when given the opportunity to do so. (24:23)

²⁴A few days later Felix came with his wife, Drusilla, who was Jewish. Sending for Paul, they listened as he told them about faith in Christ Jesus. ²⁵As he reasoned with them about righteousness and self-control and the judgment to come, Felix was terrified. "Go away for now," he replied. "When it is more convenient, I'll call for you again." ²⁶He also hoped that Paul would bribe him, so he sent for him quite often and talked with him.

²⁷Two years went by in this way; then Felix was succeeded by Porcius Festus. And because Felix wanted to gain favor with the Jewish leaders, he left Paul in prison.

CHAPTER 25

Paul Appears before Festus

See Paul's profile (page 1333) at Galatians 2:5.

Three days after Festus arrived in Caesarea to take over his new responsibilities, he left for Jerusalem, ²where the leading priests and other Jewish leaders

24:1 Greek *some elders and an orator.* 24:6 Some manuscripts add *We would have judged him by our law,* ⁷*but Lysias, the commander of the garrison, came and took him violently away from us,* ⁸*commanding his accusers to come before you.* 24:20 Greek *Sanhedrin.*

met with him and made their accusations against Paul. ³They asked Festus as a favor to transfer Paul to Jerusalem. (Their plan was to waylay and kill him.) ⁴But Festus replied that Paul was at Caesarea and he himself would be returning there soon. ⁵So he said, "Those of you in authority can return with me. If Paul has done anything wrong, you can make your accusations."

⁶Eight or ten days later he returned to Caesarea, and on the following day Paul's trial began. ⁷On Paul's arrival in court, the Jewish leaders from Jerusalem gathered around and made many serious accusations they couldn't prove. ⁸Paul denied the charges. "I am not guilty," he said. "I have committed no crime against the Jewish laws or the Temple or the Roman government."

⁹Then Festus, wanting to please the Jews, asked him, "Are you willing to go to Jerusalem and stand trial before me there?"

¹⁰But Paul replied, "No! This is the official Roman court, so I ought to be tried right here. You know very well I am not guilty. ¹¹If I have done something worthy of death, I don't refuse to die. But if I am innocent, neither you nor anyone else has a right to turn me over to these men to kill me. I appeal to Caesar!"

¹²Festus conferred with his advisers and then replied, "Very well! You have appealed to Caesar, and to Caesar you shall go!"

¹³A few days later King Agrippa arrived with his sister, Bernice,* to pay their respects to Festus. ¹⁴During their stay of several days, Festus discussed Paul's case with the king. "There is a prisoner here," he told him, "whose case was left for me by Felix. ¹⁵When I was in Jerusalem, the leading priests and other Jewish leaders pressed charges against him and asked me to sentence him. ¹⁶Of course, I quickly pointed out to them that Roman law does not convict people without a trial. They are given an opportunity to defend themselves face to face with their accusers.

¹⁷"When they came here for the trial, I called the case the very next day and ordered Paul brought in. ¹⁸But the accusations made against him weren't at all what I expected. ¹⁹It was something about their religion and about someone called Jesus who died, but whom Paul insists is alive. ²⁰I was perplexed as to how to conduct an investigation of this kind, and I asked him whether he would be willing to stand trial on these charges in Jerusalem. ²¹But Paul appealed to the emperor. So I ordered him back to jail until I could arrange to send him to Caesar."

²²"I'd like to hear the man myself," Agrippa said.

And Festus replied, "You shall—tomorrow!"

Paul Speaks to Agrippa

²³So the next day Agrippa and Bernice arrived at the auditorium with great pomp, accompanied by military officers and prominent men of the city. Festus ordered that Paul be brought in. ²⁴Then Festus said, "King Agrippa and all present, this is the man whose death is demanded both by the local Jews and by those in Jerusalem. ²⁵But in my opinion he has done nothing worthy of death. However, he appealed his case to the emperor, and I decided to send him. ²⁶But what shall I write the emperor? For there is no real charge against him. So I have brought him before all of you, and especially you, King Agrippa, so that after we examine him, I might have something to write. ²⁷For it doesn't seem reasonable to send a prisoner to the emperor without specifying the charges against him!"

CHAPTER 26

Then Agrippa said to Paul, "You may speak in your defense."

So Paul, with a gesture of his hand, started his defense: ²"I am fortunate, King Agrippa, that you are the one hearing my defense against all these

I DENY false charges against me. (25:8)

I REFUSE to put myself in harm's way. (25:10)

I USE my rights as a citizen to prevent being unjustly punished. (25:11)

See Agrippa's profile (page 1275) at Acts 26:28.

I BELIEVE Jesus Christ is alive. (25:19)

See Paul's profile (page 1333) at Galatians 2:5.

25:13 Greek *Agrippa the king and Bernice arrived.*

I APPEAL to the knowledge a person already has when explaining the Good News of Jesus Christ. (26:3)

See the profile (page 1087) for the Pharisees at Matthew 12:14.

accusations made by the Jewish leaders, [3]for I know you are an expert on Jewish customs and controversies. Now please listen to me patiently!

[4]"As the Jewish leaders are well aware, I was given a thorough Jewish training from my earliest childhood among my own people and in Jerusalem. [5]If they would admit it, they know that I have been a member of the Pharisees, the strictest sect of our religion. [6]Now I am on trial because I am looking forward to the fulfillment of God's promise made to our ancestors. [7]In fact, that is why the twelve tribes of Israel worship God night and day, and they share the same hope I have. Yet, O king, they say it is wrong for me to have this hope! [8]Why does it seem incredible to any of you that God can raise the dead?

[9]"I used to believe that I ought to do everything I could to oppose the followers of Jesus of Nazareth.* [10]Authorized by the leading priests, I caused many of the believers in Jerusalem to be sent to prison. And I cast my vote against them when they were condemned to death. [11]Many times I had them whipped in the synagogues to try to get them to curse Christ. I was so violently opposed to them that I even hounded them in distant cities of foreign lands.

I TELL others how I became a Christian. (26:13)

[12]"One day I was on such a mission to Damascus, armed with the authority and commission of the leading priests. [13]About noon, Your Majesty, a light from heaven brighter than the sun shone down on me and my companions. [14]We all fell down, and I heard a voice saying to me in Aramaic,* 'Saul, Saul, why are you persecuting me? It is hard for you to fight against my will.*'

[15]" 'Who are you, sir?' I asked.

"And the Lord replied, 'I am Jesus, the one you are persecuting. [16]Now stand up! For I have appeared to you to appoint you as my servant and my witness. You are to tell the world about this experience and about other times I will appear to you. [17]And I will protect you from both your own people and the Gentiles. Yes, I am going to send you to the Gentiles, [18]to open their eyes so they may turn from darkness to light, and from the power of Satan to God. Then they will receive forgiveness for their sins and be given a place among God's people, who are set apart by faith in me.'

I BELIEVE the Lord Jesus Christ offers forgiveness and a place among God's people of faith to everyone, whatever their race or nationality. (26:18)

See Moses' profile (page 73) at Exodus 5:1.

I BELIEVE Jesus Christ died and rose again in fulfillment of the Old Testament prophecies about the Messiah. (26:23)

[19]"And so, O King Agrippa, I was not disobedient to that vision from heaven. [20]I preached first to those in Damascus, then in Jerusalem and throughout all Judea, and also to the Gentiles, that all must turn from their sins and turn to God—and prove they have changed by the good things they do. [21]Some Jews arrested me in the Temple for preaching this, and they tried to kill me. [22]But God protected me so that I am still alive today to tell these facts to everyone, from the least to the greatest. I teach nothing except what the prophets and Moses said would happen—[23]that the Messiah would suffer and be the first to rise from the dead as a light to Jews and Gentiles alike."

[24]Suddenly, Festus shouted, "Paul, you are insane. Too much study has made you crazy!"

[25]But Paul replied, "I am not insane, Most Excellent Festus. I am speaking the sober truth. [26]And King Agrippa knows about these things. I speak frankly, for I am sure these events are all familiar to him, for they were not done in a corner! [27]King Agrippa, do you believe the prophets? I know you do—"

[28]Agrippa interrupted him. "Do you think you can make me a Christian so quickly?"*

[29]Paul replied, "Whether quickly or not, I pray to God that both you and everyone here in this audience might become the same as I am, except for these chains."

I PRAY that each person who hears the Good News will become a Christian. (26:29)

[30]Then the king, the governor, Bernice, and all the others stood and left. [31]As they talked it over they agreed, "This man hasn't done anything worthy of death or imprisonment." [32]And Agrippa said to Festus, "He could be set free if he hadn't appealed to Caesar!"

26:9 Greek *oppose the name of Jesus the Nazarene.*   26:14a Or *Hebrew.*   26:14b Greek *It is hard for you to kick against the oxgoads.*   26:28 Or *"A little more, and your arguments would make me a Christian."*

CHAPTER 27

Paul Sails for Rome

When the time came, we set sail for Italy. Paul and several other prisoners were placed in the custody of an army officer named Julius, a captain of the Imperial Regiment. ²And Aristarchus, a Macedonian from Thessalonica, was also with us. We left on a boat whose home port was Adramyttium; it was scheduled to make several stops at ports along the coast of the province of Asia.

³The next day when we docked at Sidon, Julius was very kind to Paul and let him go ashore to visit with friends so they could provide for his needs. ⁴Putting out to sea from there, we encountered headwinds that made it difficult to keep the ship on course, so we sailed north of Cyprus between the island and the mainland. ⁵We passed along the coast of the provinces of Cilicia and Pamphylia, landing at Myra, in the province of Lycia. ⁶There the officer found an Egyptian ship from Alexandria that was bound for Italy, and he put us on board.

See Paul's profile (page 1333) at Galatians 2:5.

I ACKNOWLEDGE acts of kindness shown by those in authority over me. (27:3)

UNLIKE AGRIPPA *I do not want merely intellectual knowledge of the Lord.*

Acts 26:28

King Agrippa should have known better.

In the middle of a stirring presentation of the Good News of Jesus Christ, Agrippa interrupted the great apostle Paul, then stood up and left the auditorium.

It wasn't that Agrippa couldn't grasp what Paul was saying. Paul could say, apparently without flattery, that Agrippa was "an expert on Jewish customs and controversies" and that "these events [related to Paul] are all familiar to him" (26:3, 26).

And it wasn't that Agrippa couldn't choose to believe what Paul was declaring. Paul confidently urged Agrippa to affirm the belief that God can raise the dead, that Paul's testimony was true, and that Jesus Christ fulfilled the Old Testament prophecies about the Messiah (26:8, 22-23).

Agrippa didn't deny his knowledge of the facts. In fact, the king knew more than enough to explain the Good News to others. But that Good News stayed in his head—he refused to embrace it in his heart.

A short time after Paul's death, Agrippa turned against Jerusalem, helped destroy the Jewish nation, and then moved to Rome, where he retired from politics and lived for another thirty years. History gives no indication, though, that Agrippa ever repented and became a Christian.

Sadly, many Agrippas fill the pews of this nation's churches any given Sunday. Granted, they may not walk out halfway through the sermon. But they persistently refuse to open the door of their heart (Revelation 3:20).

The Lord urges you and me to let him come in. Why not say "Yes"?

○ *Today's Scripture reading is Acts 25–26.*

---

⁷We had several days of rough sailing, and after great difficulty we finally neared Cnidus. But the wind was against us, so we sailed down to the leeward side of Crete, past the cape of Salmone. ⁸We struggled along the coast with great difficulty and finally arrived at Fair Havens, near the city of Lasea. ⁹We had lost a lot of time. The weather was becoming dangerous for long voyages by then because it was so late in the fall,* and Paul spoke to the ship's officers about it.

¹⁰"Sirs," he said, "I believe there is trouble ahead if we go on—shipwreck, loss of cargo, injuries, and danger to our lives." ¹¹But the officer in charge of the prisoners listened more to the ship's captain and the owner than to Paul. ¹²And since Fair Havens was an exposed harbor—a poor place to spend the winter—most of the crew wanted to go to Phoenix, farther up the coast of

I AM NOT AFRAID to warn others of impending danger. (27:9)

27:9 Greek *because the fast was now already gone by.* This fast happened on the Day of Atonement *(Yom Kippur),* which occurred in late September or early October.

Crete, and spend the winter there. Phoenix was a good harbor with only a southwest and northwest exposure.

The Storm at Sea

[13] When a light wind began blowing from the south, the sailors thought they could make it. So they pulled up anchor and sailed along close to shore. [14] But the weather changed abruptly, and a wind of typhoon strength (a "northeaster," they called it) caught the ship and blew it out to sea. [15] They couldn't turn the ship into the wind, so they gave up and let it run before the gale.

[16] We sailed behind a small island named Cauda,* where with great difficulty we hoisted aboard the lifeboat that was being towed behind us. [17] Then we banded the ship with ropes to strengthen the hull. The sailors were afraid of being driven across to the sandbars of Syrtis off the African coast, so they lowered the sea anchor and were thus driven before the wind.

[18] The next day, as gale-force winds continued to batter the ship, the crew began throwing the cargo overboard. [19] The following day they even threw out the ship's equipment and anything else they could lay their hands on. [20] The terrible storm raged unabated for many days, blotting out the sun and the stars, until at last all hope was gone.

[21] No one had eaten for a long time. Finally, Paul called the crew together and said, "Men, you should have listened to me in the first place and not left Fair Havens. You would have avoided all this injury and loss. [22] But take courage! None of you will lose your lives, even though the ship will go down. [23] For last night an angel of the God to whom I belong and whom I serve stood beside me, [24] and he said, 'Don't be afraid, Paul, for you will surely stand trial before Caesar! What's more, God in his goodness has granted safety to everyone sailing with you.' [25] So take courage! For I believe God. It will be just as he said. [26] But we will be shipwrecked on an island."

The Shipwreck

[27] About midnight on the fourteenth night of the storm, as we were being driven across the Sea of Adria,* the sailors sensed land was near. [28] They took soundings and found the water was only 120 feet deep. A little later they sounded again and found only 90 feet.* [29] At this rate they were afraid we would soon be driven against the rocks along the shore, so they threw out four anchors from the stern and prayed for daylight. [30] Then the sailors tried to abandon the ship; they lowered the lifeboat as though they were going to put out anchors from the prow. [31] But Paul said to the commanding officer and the soldiers, "You will all die unless the sailors stay aboard." [32] So the soldiers cut the ropes and let the boat fall off.

[33] As the darkness gave way to the early morning light, Paul begged everyone to eat. "You haven't touched food for two weeks," he said. [34] "Please eat something now for your own good. For not a hair of your heads will perish." [35] Then he took some bread, gave thanks to God before them all, and broke off a piece and ate it. [36] Then everyone was encouraged, [37] and all 276 of us began eating—for that is the number we had aboard. [38] After eating, the crew lightened the ship further by throwing the cargo of wheat overboard.

[39] When morning dawned, they didn't recognize the coastline, but they saw a bay with a beach and wondered if they could get between the rocks and get the ship safely to shore. [40] So they cut off the anchors and left them in the sea. Then they lowered the rudders, raised the foresail, and headed toward shore. [41] But the ship hit a shoal and ran aground. The bow of the ship stuck fast, while the stern was repeatedly smashed by the force of the waves and began to break apart.

[42] The soldiers wanted to kill the prisoners to make sure they didn't swim

I ALWAYS TRY to encourage others, even when they are suffering the consequences of rejecting wise counsel. (27:22)

I BELIEVE an angel revealed to Paul that he would reach Rome and that everyone sailing with him would be safe. (27:24)

I WARN others to follow God's will or suffer the consequences. (27:31)

I ENCOURAGE people to take care of themselves when they are under severe stress. (27:33)

I THANK God for my food even in the most difficult circumstances. (27:35)

27:16 Some manuscripts read *Clauda.* 27:27 The *Sea of Adria* is in the central Mediterranean; it is not to be confused with the Adriatic Sea. 27:28 Greek *20 fathoms . . . 15 fathoms* [37 meters . . . 27 meters].

ashore and escape. ⁴³But the commanding officer wanted to spare Paul, so he didn't let them carry out their plan. Then he ordered all who could swim to jump overboard first and make for land, ⁴⁴and he told the others to try for it on planks and debris from the broken ship. So everyone escaped safely ashore!

CHAPTER **28**

Paul on the Island of Malta

Once we were safe on shore, we learned that we were on the island of Malta. ²The people of the island were very kind to us. It was cold and rainy, so they built a fire on the shore to welcome us and warm us.

³As Paul gathered an armful of sticks and was laying them on the fire, a poisonous snake, driven out by the heat, fastened itself onto his hand. ⁴The people of the island saw it hanging there and said to each other, "A murderer, no doubt! Though he escaped the sea, justice will not permit him to live." ⁵But Paul shook off the snake into the fire and was unharmed. ⁶The people waited for him to swell up or suddenly drop dead. But when they had waited a long time and saw no harm come to him, they changed their minds and decided he was a god.

⁷Near the shore where we landed was an estate belonging to Publius, the chief official of the island. He welcomed us courteously and fed us for three days. ⁸As it happened, Publius's father was ill with fever and dysentery. Paul went in and prayed for him, and laying his hands on him, he healed him. ⁹Then all the other sick people on the island came and were cured. ¹⁰As a result we were showered with honors, and when the time came to sail, people put on board all sorts of things we would need for the trip.

Paul Arrives at Rome

¹¹It was three months after the shipwreck that we set sail on another ship that had wintered at the island—an Alexandrian ship with the twin gods* as its figurehead. ¹²Our first stop was Syracuse,* where we stayed three days. ¹³From there we sailed across to Rhegium.* A day later a south wind began blowing, so the following day we sailed up the coast to Puteoli. ¹⁴There we found some believers,* who invited us to stay with them seven days. And so we came to Rome.

¹⁵The brothers and sisters* in Rome had heard we were coming, and they came to meet us at the Forum* on the Appian Way. Others joined us at The Three Taverns.* When Paul saw them, he thanked God and took courage.

¹⁶When we arrived in Rome, Paul was permitted to have his own private lodging, though he was guarded by a soldier.

Paul Preaches at Rome under Guard

¹⁷Three days after Paul's arrival, he called together the local Jewish leaders. He said to them, "Brothers, I was arrested in Jerusalem and handed over to the Roman government, even though I had done nothing against our people or the customs of our ancestors. ¹⁸The Romans tried me and wanted to release me, for they found no cause for the death sentence. ¹⁹But when the Jewish leaders protested the decision, I felt it necessary to appeal to Caesar, even though I had no desire to press charges against my own people. ²⁰I asked you to come here today so we could get acquainted and so I could tell you that I am bound with this chain because I believe that the hope of Israel—the Messiah—has already come."

²¹They replied, "We have heard nothing against you. We have had no letters

I PROTECT those under my care. (27:43)

I EXTEND hospitality to individuals who survive a disaster. (28:2)

See Paul's profile (page 1333) at Galatians 2:5.

I PRAY for the sick relatives of those who show kindness and hospitality to me. (28:8)

I WELCOME missionaries and other traveling Christian workers into my home. (28:14)

I INVITE others to my home so I may share the Good News of salvation with them. (28:20)

28:11 The *twin gods* were the Roman gods Castor and Pollux. 28:12 *Syracuse* was on the island of Sicily.
28:13 *Rhegium* was on the southern tip of Italy. 28:14 Greek *brothers*. 28:15a Greek *brothers*. 28:15b *The Forum* was about 43 miles (70 kilometers) from Rome. 28:15c *The Three Taverns* was about 35 miles (57 kilometers) from Rome.

from Judea or reports from anyone who has arrived here. [22]But we want to hear what you believe, for the only thing we know about these Christians* is that they are denounced everywhere."

[23]So a time was set, and on that day a large number of people came to Paul's house. He told them about the Kingdom of God and taught them about Jesus from the Scriptures—from the five books of Moses and the books of the prophets. He began lecturing in the morning and went on into the evening. [24]Some believed and some didn't. [25]But after they had argued back and forth among themselves, they left with this final word from Paul: "The Holy Spirit was right when he said to our ancestors through Isaiah the prophet,

[26]'Go and say to my people,
You will hear my words,
but you will not understand;
you will see what I do,
but you will not perceive its meaning.
[27]For the hearts of these people are hardened,
and their ears cannot hear,
and they have closed their eyes—
so their eyes cannot see,
and their ears cannot hear,
and their hearts cannot understand,
and they cannot turn to me
and let me heal them.'*

[28]So I want you to realize that this salvation from God is also available to the Gentiles, and they will accept it."*

[30]For the next two years, Paul lived in his own rented house.* He welcomed all who visited him, [31]proclaiming the Kingdom of God with all boldness and teaching about the Lord Jesus Christ. And no one tried to stop him.

28:22 Greek *this sect.* 28:26-27 Isa 6:9-10. 28:28 Some manuscripts add verse 29, *And when he had said these words, the Jews departed, greatly disagreeing with each other.* 28:30 Or *at his own expense.*

I USE the Scriptures to present the Good News to others. (28:23)

See Moses' profile (page 73) at Exodus 5:1.

See Isaiah's profile (page 801) at Isaiah 6:13.

I BELIEVE God makes his message of salvation available to all who will accept it. (28:28)

I BOLDLY TELL others about the Lord Jesus Christ. (28:31)

ROMANS

THIS FIRST OF TWENTY-ONE New Testament letters answers many basic questions about Christian faith and practice.

In chapters 1–8, the apostle Paul presents basic teachings about humanity's bent toward sin, God's judgment of sin, and God's free offer of salvation through Jesus Christ. Paul also explains the difference between faith and works, between Adam and Christ, between slavery to sin and freedom to obey God, and between our present sufferings and the glorious future awaiting us with God in heaven.

In chapters 9–11, Paul elaborates on God's plans for the Jewish nation in the past, at that point in history, and in the future. He cites many Old Testament verses that show that God planned all along to make salvation available to everyone—Jews and Gentiles alike.

In chapters 12–16, Paul describes how Christians should live out their faith through service to other believers, respect for governmental authorities, holy living before a watching world, and consideration of other believers. He also reminds them of his plans to visit them, greets a number of the believers in Rome, and closes with some final words of instruction.

Famous verses in Romans include
- ○ "I am not ashamed of this Good News about Christ" (1:16)
- ○ "No one is good—not even one" (3:10)
- ○ "For all have sinned; all fall short of God's glorious standard" (3:23)
- ○ "When we were utterly helpless, Christ came at just the right time and died for us sinners" (5:6)
- ○ "Adam's sin brought death, so death spread to everyone, for everyone sinned" (5:12)
- ○ "Do not let sin control the way you live; do not give in to its lustful desires" (6:12)
- ○ "For the wages of sin is death, but the free gift of God is eternal life through Christ Jesus our Lord" (6:23)
- ○ "God causes everything to work together for the good of those who love God and are called according to his purpose for them" (8:28)
- ○ "If you confess with your mouth that Jesus is Lord and believe in your heart that God raised him from the dead, you will be saved" (10:9)
- ○ "Give your bodies to God. Let them be a living and holy sacrifice—the kind he will accept" (12:1)
- ○ "Pay all your debts, except the debt of love for others. You can never finish paying that!" (13:8)

CHAPTER **1**

Greetings from Paul

This letter is from Paul, Jesus Christ's slave, chosen by God to be an apostle and sent out to preach his Good News. [2]This Good News was promised long ago by God through his prophets in the holy Scriptures. [3]It is the Good News about his Son, Jesus, who came as a man, born into King David's royal family line. [4]And Jesus Christ our Lord was shown to be the Son of God when God powerfully raised him from the dead by means of the Holy Spirit.* [5]Through Christ, God has given us the privilege and authority to tell Gentiles everywhere what God has done for them, so that they will believe and obey him, bringing glory to his name.

[6]You are among those who have been called to belong to Jesus Christ, [7]dear friends in Rome. God loves you dearly, and he has called you to be his very own people.

May grace and peace be yours from God our Father and the Lord Jesus Christ.

God's Good News

[8]Let me say first of all that your faith in God is becoming known throughout the world. How I thank God through Jesus Christ for each one of you. [9]God knows how often I pray for you. Day and night I bring you and your needs in prayer to God, whom I serve with all my heart* by telling others the Good News about his Son.

[10]One of the things I always pray for is the opportunity, God willing, to come at last to see you. [11]For I long to visit you so I can share a spiritual blessing with you that will help you grow strong in the Lord. [12]I'm eager to encourage you in your faith, but I also want to be encouraged by yours. In this way, each of us will be a blessing to the other.

[13]I want you to know, dear brothers and sisters,* that I planned many times to visit you, but I was prevented until now. I want to work among you and see good results, just as I have done among other Gentiles. [14]For I have a great sense of obligation to people in our culture and to people in other cultures,* to the educated and uneducated alike. [15]So I am eager to come to you in Rome, too, to preach God's Good News.

[16]For I am not ashamed of this Good News about Christ. It is the power of God at work, saving everyone who believes—Jews first and also Gentiles. [17]This Good News tells us how God makes us right in his sight. This is accomplished from start to finish by faith. As the Scriptures say, "It is through faith that a righteous person has life."*

God's Anger at Sin

[18]But God shows his anger from heaven against all sinful, wicked people who push the truth away from themselves.* [19]For the truth about God is known to them instinctively.* God has put this knowledge in their hearts. [20]From the time the world was created, people have seen the earth and sky and all that God made. They can clearly see his invisible qualities—his eternal power and divine nature. So they have no excuse whatsoever for not knowing God.

[21]Yes, they knew God, but they wouldn't worship him as God or even give him thanks. And they began to think up foolish ideas of what God was like. The result was that their minds became dark and confused. [22]Claiming to be wise, they became utter fools instead. [23]And instead of worshiping the glorious, ever-living God, they worshiped idols made to look like mere people, or birds and animals and snakes.

[24]So God let them go ahead and do whatever shameful things their hearts desired. As a result, they did vile and degrading things with each other's

---

See Paul's profile (page 1333) at Galatians 2:5.

I BELIEVE the Good News about Jesus Christ. (1:2)

See David's profile (page 629) at Psalm 3:1.

I BELIEVE Jesus Christ was shown to be the Son of God when God the Father raised him from the dead. (1:4)

I BELIEVE God loves me dearly and has called me to be one of his very own people. (1:7)

I PRAY daily for other believers and speak to unbelievers about God's Son. (1:9)

I AM NOT ASHAMED of the Good News of Jesus Christ. (1:16)

I BELIEVE God has revealed himself to all people as the Creator of the heavens and the earth. (1:20)

1:4 Or *the Spirit of holiness.*   1:9 Or *in my spirit.*   1:13 Greek *brothers.*   1:14 Greek *to Greeks and to barbarians.*
1:17 Hab 2:4.   1:18 Or *who prevent the truth from being known.*   1:19 Greek *is manifest in them.*

bodies. ²⁵Instead of believing what they knew was the truth about God, they deliberately chose to believe lies. So they worshiped the things God made but not the Creator himself, who is to be praised forever. Amen.

²⁶That is why God abandoned them to their shameful desires. Even the women turned against the natural way to have sex and instead indulged in sex with each other. ²⁷And the men, instead of having normal sexual relationships with women, burned with lust for each other. Men did shameful things with other men and, as a result, suffered within themselves the penalty they so richly deserved.

²⁸When they refused to acknowledge God, he abandoned them to their evil minds and let them do things that should never be done. ²⁹Their lives became full of every kind of wickedness, sin, greed, hate, envy, murder, fighting, deception, malicious behavior, and gossip. ³⁰They are backstabbers, haters of God, insolent, proud, and boastful. They are forever inventing new ways of sinning and are disobedient to their parents. ³¹They refuse to understand, break their promises, and are heartless and unforgiving. ³²They are fully aware of God's death penalty for those who do these things, yet they go right ahead and do them anyway. And, worse yet, they encourage others to do them, too.

CHAPTER 2

God's Judgment of Sin

You may be saying, "What terrible people you have been talking about!" But you are just as bad, and you have no excuse! When you say they are wicked and should be punished, you are condemning yourself, for you do these very same things. ²And we know that God, in his justice, will punish anyone who does such things. ³Do you think that God will judge and condemn others for doing them and not judge you when you do them, too? ⁴Don't you realize how kind, tolerant, and patient God is with you? Or don't you care? Can't you see how kind he has been in giving you time to turn from your sin?

⁵But no, you won't listen. So you are storing up terrible punishment for yourself because of your stubbornness in refusing to turn from your sin. For there is going to come a day of judgment when God, the just judge of all the world, ⁶will judge all people according to what they have done. ⁷He will give eternal life to those who persist in doing what is good, seeking after the glory and honor and immortality that God offers. ⁸But he will pour out his anger and wrath on those who live for themselves, who refuse to obey the truth and practice evil deeds. ⁹There will be trouble and calamity for everyone who keeps on sinning—for the Jew first and also for the Gentile. ¹⁰But there will be glory and honor and peace from God for all who do good—for the Jew first and also for the Gentile. ¹¹For God does not show favoritism.

¹²God will punish the Gentiles when they sin, even though they never had God's written law. And he will punish the Jews when they sin, for they do have the law. ¹³For it is not merely knowing the law that brings God's approval. Those who obey the law will be declared right in God's sight. ¹⁴Even when Gentiles, who do not have God's written law, instinctively follow what the law says, they show that in their hearts they know right from wrong. ¹⁵They demonstrate that God's law is written within them, for their own consciences either accuse them or tell them they are doing what is right. ¹⁶The day will surely come when God, by Jesus Christ, will judge everyone's secret life. This is my message.

The Jews and the Law

¹⁷If you are a Jew, you are relying on God's law for your special relationship with him. You boast that all is well between yourself and God. ¹⁸Yes, you know what he wants; you know right from wrong because you have been

---

I WORSHIP the Creator—not the creation. (1:25)

Start each day by reviewing the previous day's faith affirmations.

I AM THANKFUL that God has been kind, tolerant, and patient with me. (2:4)

I BELIEVE God will one day judge all people for what they have done. (2:6)

I BELIEVE obedience—not knowledge—is what makes a person right before God. (2:13)

I DO NOT RELY on my heritage or knowledge to make me right with God. (2:17)

taught his law. [19]You are convinced that you are a guide for the blind and a beacon light for people who are lost in darkness without God. [20]You think you can instruct the ignorant and teach children the ways of God. For you are certain that in God's law you have complete knowledge and truth.

[21]Well then, if you teach others, why don't you teach yourself? You tell others not to steal, but do you steal? [22]You say it is wrong to commit adultery, but do you do it? You condemn idolatry, but do you steal from pagan temples? [23]You are so proud of knowing the law, but you dishonor God by breaking it. [24]No wonder the Scriptures say, "The world blasphemes the name of God because of you."*

I DO NOT DISHONOR God's law by breaking it. (2:23)

[25]The Jewish ceremony of circumcision is worth something only if you obey God's law. But if you don't obey God's law, you are no better off than an uncircumcised Gentile. [26]And if the Gentiles obey God's law, won't God give them all the rights and honors of being his own people? [27]In fact, uncircumcised Gentiles who keep God's law will be much better off than you Jews who are circumcised and know so much about God's law but don't obey it.

I BECOME RIGHT with God through a change of heart produced by the Holy Spirit. (2:29)

[28]For you are not a true Jew just because you were born of Jewish parents or because you have gone through the Jewish ceremony of circumcision. [29]No, a true Jew is one whose heart is right with God. And true circumcision is not a cutting of the body but a change of heart produced by God's Spirit. Whoever has that kind of change seeks praise from God, not from people.

CHAPTER 3

God Remains Faithful

Then what's the advantage of being a Jew? Is there any value in the Jewish ceremony of circumcision? [2]Yes, being a Jew has many advantages. First of all, the Jews were entrusted with the whole revelation of God.*

I BELIEVE the Jews were entrusted with God's revelation in Old Testament times. (3:2)

[3]True, some of them were unfaithful; but just because they broke their promises, does that mean God will break his promises? [4]Of course not! Though everyone else in the world is a liar, God is true. As the Scriptures say, "He will be proved right in what he says, and he will win his case in court."*

[5]"But," some say, "our sins serve a good purpose, for people will see God's goodness when he declares us sinners to be innocent. Isn't it unfair, then, for God to punish us?" (That is actually the way some people talk.) [6]Of course not! If God is not just, how is he qualified to judge the world? [7]"But," some might still argue, "how can God judge and condemn me as a sinner if my dishonesty highlights his truthfulness and brings him more glory?" [8]If you follow that kind of thinking, however, you might as well say that the more we sin the better it is! Those who say such things deserve to be condemned, yet some slander me by saying this is what I preach!

I BELIEVE God is completely just and qualified to judge the world. (3:6)

All People Are Sinners

[9]Well then, are we Jews better than others?* No, not at all, for we have already shown that all people, whether Jews or Gentiles, are under the power of sin. [10]As the Scriptures say,

I BELIEVE all people are under the power of sin. (3:9)

"No one is good—
    not even one.
[11]No one has real understanding;
    no one is seeking God.
[12]All have turned away from God;
    all have gone wrong.
No one does good,
    not even one."*

2:24 Isa 52:5.   3:2 Greek *the oracles of God.*   3:4 Ps 51:4.   3:9 Greek *Are we better?*   3:10-12 Pss 14:1-3; 53:1-3.

13 "Their talk is foul, like the stench from an open grave.
　Their speech is filled with lies."
　"The poison of a deadly snake drips from their lips."*
14 　"Their mouths are full of cursing and bitterness."*
15 "They are quick to commit murder.
16 　Wherever they go, destruction and misery follow them.
17 They do not know what true peace is."*
18 　"They have no fear of God to restrain them."*

19Obviously, the law applies to those to whom it was given, for its purpose is to keep people from having excuses and to bring the entire world into judgment before God. 20For no one can ever be made right in God's sight by doing what his law commands. For the more we know God's law, the clearer it becomes that we aren't obeying it.

Christ Took Our Punishment
21But now God has shown us a different way of being right in his sight—not by obeying the law but by the way promised in the Scriptures long ago. 22We are made right in God's sight when we trust in Jesus Christ to take away our sins. And we all can be saved in this same way, no matter who we are or what we have done.

23For all have sinned; all fall short of God's glorious standard. 24Yet now God in his gracious kindness declares us not guilty. He has done this through Christ Jesus, who has freed us by taking away our sins. 25For God sent Jesus to take the punishment for our sins and to satisfy God's anger against us. We are made right with God when we believe that Jesus shed his blood, sacrificing his life for us. God was being entirely fair and just when he did not punish those who sinned in former times. 26And he is entirely fair and just in this present time when he declares sinners to be right in his sight because they believe in Jesus.

27Can we boast, then, that we have done anything to be accepted by God? No, because our acquittal is not based on our good deeds. It is based on our faith. 28So we are made right with God through faith and not by obeying the law.

29After all, God is not the God of the Jews only, is he? Isn't he also the God of the Gentiles? Of course he is. 30There is only one God, and there is only one way of being accepted by him. He makes people right with himself only by faith, whether they are Jews or Gentiles. 31Well then, if we emphasize faith, does this mean that we can forget about the law? Of course not! In fact, only when we have faith do we truly fulfill the law.

CHAPTER 4
The Faith of Abraham
Abraham was, humanly speaking, the founder of our Jewish nation. What were his experiences concerning this question of being saved by faith? 2Was it because of his good deeds that God accepted him? If so, he would have had something to boast about. But from God's point of view Abraham had no basis at all for pride. 3For the Scriptures tell us, "Abraham believed God, so God declared him to be righteous."*

4When people work, their wages are not a gift. Workers earn what they receive. 5But people are declared righteous because of their faith, not because of their work.

6King David spoke of this, describing the happiness of an undeserving sinner who is declared to be righteous:

7 "Oh, what joy for those whose disobedience is forgiven,
　whose sins are put out of sight.

I KNOW the purpose of the law is to show God's righteousness and my sinfulness. (3:19)

I AM MADE RIGHT in God's sight when I trust Jesus Christ to take away my sins. (3:22)

I BELIEVE Jesus Christ took the punishment for my sins and satisfied God's anger against me. (3:25)

See Abraham's profile (page 19) at Genesis 15:6.

I BELIEVE God declared Abraham to be righteous because he believed God. (4:3)

See David's profile (page 629) at Psalm 3:1.

3:13 Pss 5:9; 140:3.　3:14 Ps 10:7.　3:15-17 Isa 59:7-8.　3:18 Ps 36:1.　4:3 Gen 15:6.

⁸Yes, what joy for those
whose sin is no longer counted against them by the Lord."*

⁹Now then, is this blessing only for the Jews, or is it for Gentiles, too? Well, what about Abraham? We have been saying he was declared righteous by God because of his faith. ¹⁰But how did his faith help him? Was he declared righteous only after he had been circumcised, or was it before he was circumcised? The answer is that God accepted him first, and then he was circumcised later!

¹¹The circumcision ceremony was a sign that Abraham already had faith and that God had already accepted him and declared him to be righteous—even before he was circumcised. So Abraham is the spiritual father of those who have faith but have not been circumcised. They are made right with God by faith. ¹²And Abraham is also the spiritual father of those who have been circumcised, but only if they have the same kind of faith Abraham had before he was circumcised.

¹³It is clear, then, that God's promise to give the whole earth to Abraham and his descendants was not based on obedience to God's law, but on the new relationship with God that comes by faith. ¹⁴So if you claim that God's promise is for those who obey God's law and think they are "good enough" in God's sight, then you are saying that faith is useless. And in that case, the promise is also meaningless. ¹⁵But the law brings punishment on those who try to obey it. (The only way to avoid breaking the law is to have no law to break!)

¹⁶So that's why faith is the key! God's promise is given to us as a free gift. And we are certain to receive it, whether or not we follow Jewish customs, if we have faith like Abraham's. For Abraham is the father of all who believe. ¹⁷That is what the Scriptures mean when God told him, "I have made you the father of many nations."* This happened because Abraham believed in the God who brings the dead back to life and who brings into existence what didn't exist before.

¹⁸When God promised Abraham that he would become the father of many nations, Abraham believed him. God had also said, "Your descendants will be as numerous as the stars,"* even though such a promise seemed utterly impossible! ¹⁹And Abraham's faith did not weaken, even though he knew that he was too old to be a father at the age of one hundred and that Sarah, his wife, had never been able to have children.

²⁰Abraham never wavered in believing God's promise. In fact, his faith grew stronger, and in this he brought glory to God. ²¹He was absolutely convinced that God was able to do anything he promised. ²²And because of Abraham's faith, God declared him to be righteous.

²³Now this wonderful truth—that God declared him to be righteous—wasn't just for Abraham's benefit. ²⁴It was for us, too, assuring us that God will also declare us to be righteous if we believe in God, who brought Jesus our Lord back from the dead. ²⁵He was handed over to die because of our sins, and he was raised from the dead to make us right with God.

CHAPTER 5

Faith Brings Joy

Therefore, since we have been made right in God's sight by faith, we have peace with God because of what Jesus Christ our Lord has done for us. ²Because of our faith, Christ has brought us into this place of highest privilege where we now stand, and we confidently and joyfully look forward to sharing God's glory.

³We can rejoice, too, when we run into problems and trials, for we know

---

I BELIEVE circumcision was a sign that Abraham already believed God. (4:11)

I RECEIVE God's promise—like Abraham—by faith as a free gift. (4:16)

See Sarah's profile (page 25) at Genesis 21:1.

I BRING glory to God as my faith grows stronger. (4:20)

I AM ABSOLUTELY CONVINCED that God is able to do anything he has promised. (4:21)

I CHOOSE to rejoice when I run into problems, because they help me learn to endure. (5:3)

4:7-8 Ps 32:1-2.   4:17 Gen 17:5.   4:18 Gen 15:5.

that they are good for us—they help us learn to endure. [4]And endurance develops strength of character in us, and character strengthens our confident expectation of salvation. [5]And this expectation will not disappoint us. For we know how dearly God loves us, because he has given us the Holy Spirit to fill our hearts with his love.

[6]When we were utterly helpless, Christ came at just the right time and died for us sinners. [7]Now, no one is likely to die for a good person, though someone might be willing to die for a person who is especially good. [8]But God showed his great love for us by sending Christ to die for us while we were still sinners. [9]And since we have been made right in God's sight by the blood of Christ, he will certainly save us from God's judgment. [10]For since we were restored to friendship with God by the death of his Son while we were still his enemies, we will certainly be delivered from eternal punishment by his life. [11]So now we can rejoice in our wonderful new relationship with God—all because of what our Lord Jesus Christ has done for us in making us friends of God.

Adam and Christ Contrasted

[12]When Adam sinned, sin entered the entire human race. Adam's sin brought death, so death spread to everyone, for everyone sinned. [13]Yes, people sinned even before the law was given. And though there was no law to break, since it had not yet been given, [14]they all died anyway—even though they did not disobey an explicit commandment of God, as Adam did. What a contrast between Adam and Christ, who was yet to come! [15]And what a difference between our sin and God's generous gift of forgiveness. For this one man, Adam, brought death to many through his sin. But this other man, Jesus Christ, brought forgiveness to many through God's bountiful gift. [16]And the result of God's gracious gift is very different from the result of that one man's sin. For Adam's sin led to condemnation, but we have the free gift of being accepted by God, even though we are guilty of many sins. [17]The sin of this one man, Adam, caused death to rule over us, but all who receive God's wonderful, gracious gift of righteousness will live in triumph over sin and death through this one man, Jesus Christ.

[18]Yes, Adam's one sin brought condemnation upon everyone, but Christ's one act of righteousness makes all people right in God's sight and gives them life. [19]Because one person disobeyed God, many people became sinners. But because one other person obeyed God, many people will be made right in God's sight.

[20]God's law was given so that all people could see how sinful they were. But as people sinned more and more, God's wonderful kindness became more abundant. [21]So just as sin ruled over all people and brought them to death, now God's wonderful kindness rules instead, giving us right standing with God and resulting in eternal life through Jesus Christ our Lord.

CHAPTER 6

Sin's Power Is Broken

Well then, should we keep on sinning so that God can show us more and more kindness and forgiveness? [2]Of course not! Since we have died to sin, how can we continue to live in it? [3]Or have you forgotten that when we became Christians and were baptized to become one with Christ Jesus, we died with him? [4]For we died and were buried with Christ by baptism. And just as Christ was raised from the dead by the glorious power of the Father, now we also may live new lives.

[5]Since we have been united with him in his death, we will also be raised as he was. [6]Our old sinful selves were crucified with Christ so that sin might lose its power in our lives. We are no longer slaves to sin. [7]For when we died with Christ we were set free from the power of sin. [8]And since we died with Christ,

I KNOW I am dearly loved by God because he has given me his Holy Spirit to fill my heart with his love. (5:5)

I BELIEVE God showed his great love by sending his Son to die for us while we were still sinners. (5:8)

I BELIEVE sin entered the human race when Adam sinned. (5:12)

See Adam's profile (page 5) at Genesis 1:26.

I BELIEVE Adam's sin brought condemnation to everyone, but Jesus Christ's righteousness makes us right in God's sight and gives us life. (5:18)

I WAS SET FREE from the power of sin when I became a Christian. (6:7)

we know we will also share his new life. ⁹We are sure of this because Christ rose from the dead, and he will never die again. Death no longer has any power over him. ¹⁰He died once to defeat sin, and now he lives for the glory of God. ¹¹So you should consider yourselves dead to sin and able to live for the glory of God through Christ Jesus.

¹²Do not let sin control the way you live;* do not give in to its lustful desires. ¹³Do not let any part of your body become a tool of wickedness, to be used for sinning. Instead, give yourselves completely to God since you have been given new life. And use your whole body as a tool to do what is right for the glory of God. ¹⁴Sin is no longer your master, for you are no longer subject to the law, which enslaves you to sin. Instead, you are free by God's grace.

Freedom to Obey God

¹⁵So since God's grace has set us free from the law, does this mean we can go on sinning? Of course not! ¹⁶Don't you realize that whatever you choose to obey becomes your master? You can choose sin, which leads to death, or you can choose to obey God and receive his approval. ¹⁷Thank God! Once you were slaves of sin, but now you have obeyed with all your heart the new teaching God has given you. ¹⁸Now you are free from sin, your old master, and you have become slaves to your new master, righteousness.

¹⁹I speak this way, using the illustration of slaves and masters, because it is easy to understand. Before, you let yourselves be slaves of impurity and lawlessness. Now you must choose to be slaves of righteousness so that you will become holy.

²⁰In those days, when you were slaves of sin, you weren't concerned with doing what was right. ²¹And what was the result? It was not good, since now you are ashamed of the things you used to do, things that end in eternal doom. ²²But now you are free from the power of sin and have become slaves of God. Now you do those things that lead to holiness and result in eternal life. ²³For the wages of sin is death, but the free gift of God is eternal life through Christ Jesus our Lord.

CHAPTER 7

No Longer Bound to the Law

Now, dear brothers and sisters*—you who are familiar with the law—don't you know that the law applies only to a person who is still living? ²Let me illustrate. When a woman marries, the law binds her to her husband as long as he is alive. But if he dies, the laws of marriage no longer apply to her. ³So while her husband is alive, she would be committing adultery if she married another man. But if her husband dies, she is free from that law and does not commit adultery when she remarries.

⁴So this is the point: The law no longer holds you in its power, because you died to its power when you died with Christ on the cross. And now you are united with the one who was raised from the dead. As a result, you can produce good fruit, that is, good deeds for God. ⁵When we were controlled by our old nature, sinful desires were at work within us, and the law aroused these evil desires that produced sinful deeds, resulting in death. ⁶But now we have been released from the law, for we died with Christ, and we are no longer captive to its power. Now we can really serve God, not in the old way by obeying the letter of the law, but in the new way, by the Spirit.

God's Law Reveals Our Sin

⁷Well then, am I suggesting that the law of God is evil? Of course not! The law is not sinful, but it was the law that showed me my sin. I would never have known that coveting is wrong if the law had not said, "Do not covet."* ⁸But

I CONSIDER myself dead to sin and able to live for the glory of God through Jesus Christ. (6:11)

I GIVE myself completely to God instead of letting sin control the way I live. (6:13)

I AM A SLAVE of righteousness, not of sin. (6:18)

I AM GOD'S SLAVE and do those things that lead to holiness and result in eternal life. (6:22)

I CAN SERVE God now by the power of the Holy Spirit, who lives in me. (7:6)

6:12 Or *Do not let sin reign in your body, which is subject to death.* 7:1 Greek *brothers.* 7:7 Exod 20:17; Deut 5:21.

sin took advantage of this law and aroused all kinds of forbidden desires within me! If there were no law, sin would not have that power.

⁹I felt fine when I did not understand what the law demanded. But when I learned the truth, I realized I had broken the law and was a sinner, doomed to die. ¹⁰So the good law, which was supposed to show me the way of life, instead gave me the death penalty. ¹¹Sin took advantage of the law and fooled me; it took the good law and used it to make me guilty of death. ¹²But still, the law itself is holy and right and good.

¹³But how can that be? Did the law, which is good, cause my doom? Of course not! Sin used what was good to bring about my condemnation. So we can see how terrible sin really is. It uses God's good commandment for its own evil purposes.

Struggling with Sin

¹⁴The law is good, then. The trouble is not with the law but with me, because I am sold into slavery, with sin as my master. ¹⁵I don't understand myself at all, for I really want to do what is right, but I don't do it. Instead, I do the very thing I hate. ¹⁶I know perfectly well that what I am doing is wrong, and my bad conscience shows that I agree that the law is good. ¹⁷But I can't help myself, because it is sin inside me that makes me do these evil things.

¹⁸I know I am rotten through and through so far as my old sinful nature is concerned. No matter which way I turn, I can't make myself do right. I want to, but I can't. ¹⁹When I want to do good, I don't. And when I try not to do wrong, I do it anyway. ²⁰But if I am doing what I don't want to do, I am not really the one doing it; the sin within me is doing it.

²¹It seems to be a fact of life that when I want to do what is right, I inevitably do what is wrong. ²²I love God's law with all my heart. ²³But there is another law at work within me that is at war with my mind. This law wins the fight and makes me a slave to the sin that is still within me. ²⁴Oh, what a miserable person I am! Who will free me from this life that is dominated by sin?* ²⁵Thank God! The answer is in Jesus Christ our Lord. So you see how it is: In my mind I really want to obey God's law, but because of my sinful nature I am a slave to sin.

CHAPTER 8

Life in the Spirit

So now there is no condemnation for those who belong to Christ Jesus. ²For the power* of the life-giving Spirit has freed you* through Christ Jesus from the power of sin that leads to death. ³The law of Moses could not save us, because of our sinful nature. But God put into effect a different plan to save us. He sent his own Son in a human body like ours, except that ours are sinful. God destroyed sin's control over us by giving his Son as a sacrifice for our sins. ⁴He did this so that the requirement of the law would be fully accomplished for us* who no longer follow our sinful nature but instead follow the Spirit.

⁵Those who are dominated by the sinful nature think about sinful things, but those who are controlled by the Holy Spirit think about things that please the Spirit. ⁶If your sinful nature controls your mind, there is death. But if the Holy Spirit controls your mind, there is life and peace. ⁷For the sinful nature is always hostile to God. It never did obey God's laws, and it never will. ⁸That's why those who are still under the control of their sinful nature can never please God.

⁹But you are not controlled by your sinful nature. You are controlled by the Spirit if you have the Spirit of God living in you. (And remember that those

I BELIEVE God's Old Testament law is holy and right and good. (7:12)

I BELIEVE the problem is never with God's law but with me—if sin is my master. (7:14)

I KNOW I cannot make myself do right if I am under the power of my sinful nature. (7:18)

I THANK God for freeing me from a life that is dominated by sin. (7:25)

I BELIEVE God destroyed sin's control over me by giving his Son as a sacrifice for my sins. (8:3)

See Moses' profile (page 73) at Exodus 5:1.

I BELIEVE the Holy Spirit lives in every Christian. (8:9)

7:24 Greek *from this body of death?* 8:2a Greek *the law;* also in 8:2b. 8:2b Some manuscripts read *me.* 8:4 Or *accomplished by us.*

who do not have the Spirit of Christ living in them are not Christians at all.) [10]Since Christ lives within you, even though your body will die because of sin, your spirit is alive* because you have been made right with God. [11]The Spirit of God, who raised Jesus from the dead, lives in you. And just as he raised Christ from the dead, he will give life to your mortal body by this same Spirit living within you.

[12]So, dear brothers and sisters,* you have no obligation whatsoever to do what your sinful nature urges you to do. [13]For if you keep on following it, you will perish. But if through the power of the Holy Spirit you turn from it* and its evil deeds, you will live. [14]For all who are led by the Spirit of God are children* of God.

[15]So you should not be like cowering, fearful slaves. You should behave instead like God's very own children, adopted into his family*—calling him "Father, dear Father."* [16]For his Holy Spirit speaks to us deep in our hearts and tells us that we are God's children. [17]And since we are his children, we will share his treasures—for everything God gives to his Son, Christ, is ours, too. But if we are to share his glory, we must also share his suffering.

The Future Glory

[18]Yet what we suffer now is nothing compared to the glory he will give us later. [19]For all creation is waiting eagerly for that future day when God will reveal who his children really are. [20]Against its will, everything on earth was subjected to God's curse. [21]All creation anticipates the day when it will join God's children in glorious freedom from death and decay. [22]For we know that all creation has been groaning as in the pains of childbirth right up to the present time. [23]And even we Christians, although we have the Holy Spirit within us as a foretaste of future glory, also groan to be released from pain and suffering. We, too, wait anxiously for that day when God will give us our full rights as his children,* including the new bodies he has promised us. [24]Now that we are saved, we eagerly look forward to this freedom. For if you already have something, you don't need to hope for it. [25]But if we look forward to something we don't have yet, we must wait patiently and confidently.

[26]And the Holy Spirit helps us in our distress. For we don't even know what we should pray for, nor how we should pray. But the Holy Spirit prays for us with groanings that cannot be expressed in words. [27]And the Father who knows all hearts knows what the Spirit is saying, for the Spirit pleads for us believers in harmony with God's own will. [28]And we know that God causes everything to work together* for the good of those who love God and are called according to his purpose for them. [29]For God knew his people in advance, and he chose them to become like his Son, so that his Son would be the firstborn, with many brothers and sisters. [30]And having chosen them, he called them to come to him. And he gave them right standing with himself, and he promised them his glory.

Nothing Can Separate Us from God's Love

[31]What can we say about such wonderful things as these? If God is for us, who can ever be against us? [32]Since God did not spare even his own Son but gave him up for us all, won't God, who gave us Christ, also give us everything else?

[33]Who dares accuse us whom God has chosen for his own? Will God? No! He is the one who has given us right standing with himself. [34]Who then will condemn us? Will Christ Jesus? No, for he is the one who died for us and was

---

I HAVE no obligation to do what the sinful nature urges me to do. (8:12)

I KNOW what I suffer now is nothing compared to the glory God will give me later. (8:18)

I AWAIT anxiously the day when God will release me from suffering and give me the new body he has promised. (8:23)

I KNOW that God causes all things to work together for the good of those who love him and are called according to his purpose for them. (8:28)

I BELIEVE Jesus Christ will never condemn me, because he is the one who died for me. (8:34)

8:10 Or *the Spirit will bring you eternal life.*   8:12 Greek *brothers;* also in 8:29.   8:13 Greek *put it to death.*
8:14 Greek *sons;* also in 8:19.   8:15a Greek *You received a spirit of sonship.*   8:15b Greek *"Abba, Father."* Abba is an Aramaic term for "father."   8:23 Greek *wait anxiously for sonship.*   8:28 Some manuscripts read *And we know that everything works together.*

raised to life for us and is sitting at the place of highest honor next to God, pleading for us.

[35]Can anything ever separate us from Christ's love? Does it mean he no longer loves us if we have trouble or calamity, or are persecuted, or are hungry or cold or in danger or threatened with death? [36](Even the Scriptures say, "For your sake we are killed every day; we are being slaughtered like sheep."*) [37]No, despite all these things, overwhelming victory is ours through Christ, who loved us.

[38]And I am convinced that nothing can ever separate us from his love. Death can't, and life can't. The angels can't, and the demons can't. Our fears for today, our worries about tomorrow, and even the powers of hell can't keep God's love away. [39]Whether we are high above the sky or in the deepest ocean, nothing in all creation will ever be able to separate us from the love of God that is revealed in Christ Jesus our Lord.

CHAPTER 9

God's Selection of Israel

In the presence of Christ, I speak with utter truthfulness—I do not lie—and my conscience and the Holy Spirit confirm that what I am saying is true. [2]My heart is filled with bitter sorrow and unending grief [3]for my people, my Jewish brothers and sisters.* I would be willing to be forever cursed—cut off from Christ!—if that would save them. [4]They are the people of Israel, chosen to be God's special children.* God revealed his glory to them. He made covenants with them and gave his law to them. They have the privilege of worshiping him and receiving his wonderful promises. [5]Their ancestors were great people of God, and Christ himself was a Jew as far as his human nature is concerned. And he is God, who rules over everything and is worthy of eternal praise! Amen.*

[6]Well then, has God failed to fulfill his promise to the Jews? No, for not everyone born into a Jewish family is truly a Jew! [7]Just the fact that they are descendants of Abraham doesn't make them truly Abraham's children. For the Scriptures say, "Isaac is the son through whom your descendants will be counted,"* though Abraham had other children, too. [8]This means that Abraham's physical descendants are not necessarily children of God. It is the children of the promise who are considered to be Abraham's children. [9]For God had promised, "Next year I will return, and Sarah will have a son."*

[10]This son was our ancestor Isaac. When he grew up, he married Rebekah, who gave birth to twins. [11]But before they were born, before they had done anything good or bad, she received a message from God. (This message proves that God chooses according to his own plan, [12]not according to our good or bad works.) She was told, "The descendants of your older son will serve the descendants of your younger son."* [13]In the words of the Scriptures, "I loved Jacob, but I rejected Esau."*

[14]What can we say? Was God being unfair? Of course not! [15]For God said to Moses,

"I will show mercy to anyone I choose,
    and I will show compassion to anyone I choose."*

[16]So receiving God's promise is not up to us. We can't get it by choosing it or working hard for it. God will show mercy to anyone he chooses.

[17]For the Scriptures say that God told Pharaoh, "I have appointed you for the very purpose of displaying my power in you, and so that my fame

I AM CONVINCED nothing can ever separate me from God's love. (8:38)

I BELIEVE being born Jewish does not make a person a true son of Abraham. (9:6)

See the profiles for Abraham (page 19) and Isaac (page 31) at Genesis 15:6 and Genesis 25:19.

I BELIEVE those who trust God's promises through Jesus Christ are Abraham's true descendants. (9:8)

See Sarah's profile (page 25) at Genesis 21:1.

See the profiles for Rebekah (page 35), Jacob (page 43), and Esau (page 44) at Genesis 27:10, Genesis 32:9, and Genesis 25:34.

See Moses' profile (page 73) at Exodus 5:1.

I DO NOT RECEIVE God's promise by working hard for it but because God chose to show mercy to me. (9:16)

8:36 Ps 44:22.   9:3 Greek *my brothers.*   9:4 Greek *chosen for sonship.*   9:5 Or *May God, who rules over everything, be praised forever. Amen.*   9:7 Gen 21:12.   9:9 Gen 18:10, 14.   9:12 Gen 25:23.   9:13 Mal 1:2-3.   9:15 Exod 33:19.

might spread throughout the earth."* ¹⁸So you see, God shows mercy to some just because he wants to, and he chooses to make some people refuse to listen.

¹⁹Well then, you might say, "Why does God blame people for not listening? Haven't they simply done what he made them do?"

²⁰No, don't say that. Who are you, a mere human being, to criticize God? Should the thing that was created say to the one who made it, "Why have you made me like this?" ²¹When a potter makes jars out of clay, doesn't he have a right to use the same lump of clay to make one jar for decoration and another to throw garbage into? ²²God has every right to exercise his judgment and his power, but he also has the right to be very patient with those who are the objects of his judgment and are fit only for destruction. ²³He also has the right to pour out the riches of his glory upon those he prepared to be the objects of his mercy—²⁴even upon us, whom he selected, both from the Jews and from the Gentiles.

²⁵Concerning the Gentiles, God says in the prophecy of Hosea,

"Those who were not my people,
  I will now call my people.
And I will love those
  whom I did not love before."*

²⁶And,

"Once they were told,
  'You are not my people.'
But now he will say,
  'You are children of the living God.'* "

²⁷Concerning Israel, Isaiah the prophet cried out,

"Though the people of Israel are as numerous as the sand on the
    seashore,
  only a small number will be saved.
²⁸ For the Lord will carry out his sentence upon the earth
  quickly and with finality."*

²⁹And Isaiah said in another place,

"If the Lord Almighty
  had not spared a few of us,
we would have been wiped out
  as completely as Sodom and Gomorrah."*

Israel's Unbelief

³⁰Well then, what shall we say about these things? Just this: The Gentiles have been made right with God by faith, even though they were not seeking him. ³¹But the Jews, who tried so hard to get right with God by keeping the law, never succeeded. ³²Why not? Because they were trying to get right with God by keeping the law and being good instead of by depending on faith. They stumbled over the great rock in their path. ³³God warned them of this in the Scriptures when he said,

"I am placing a stone in Jerusalem* that causes people to stumble,
  and a rock that makes them fall.*
But anyone who believes in him
  will not be disappointed.*"

I DO NOT CRITICIZE God. (9:20)

I BELIEVE God has every right to show judgment and mercy as he desires. (9:22)

See Hosea's profile (page 1003) at Hosea 3:1.

See Isaiah's profile (page 801) at Isaiah 6:13.

I BELIEVE God predicted through prophecy that only a portion of his people Israel would be saved. (9:29)

I BELIEVE God told the Jews throughout Old Testament times that they must come to him by faith. (9:33)

9:17 Exod 9:16. 9:25 Hos 2:23. 9:26 Greek *You are sons of the living God.* Hos 1:10. 9:27-28 Isa 10:22-23.
9:29 Isa 1:9. 9:33a Greek *in Zion.* 9:33b Isa 8:14. 9:33c Or *will not be put to shame.* Isa 28:16.

CHAPTER 10

Dear brothers and sisters,* the longing of my heart and my prayer to God is that the Jewish people might be saved. ²I know what enthusiasm they have for God, but it is misdirected zeal. ³For they don't understand God's way of making people right with himself. Instead, they are clinging to their own way of getting right with God by trying to keep the law. They won't go along with God's way. ⁴For Christ has accomplished the whole purpose* of the law. All who believe in him are made right with God.

Salvation Is for Everyone

⁵For Moses wrote that the law's way of making a person right with God requires obedience to all of its commands.* ⁶But the way of getting right with God through faith says, "You don't need to go to heaven" (to find Christ and bring him down to help you). ⁷And it says, "You don't need to go to the place of the dead" (to bring Christ back to life again). ⁸Salvation that comes from trusting Christ—which is the message we preach—is already within easy reach. In fact, the Scriptures say, "The message is close at hand; it is on your lips and in your heart."*

⁹For if you confess with your mouth that Jesus is Lord and believe in your heart that God raised him from the dead, you will be saved. ¹⁰For it is by believing in your heart that you are made right with God, and it is by confessing with your mouth that you are saved. ¹¹As the Scriptures tell us, "Anyone who believes in him will not be disappointed."* ¹²Jew and Gentile are the same in this respect. They all have the same Lord, who generously gives his riches to all who ask for them. ¹³For "Anyone who calls on the name of the Lord will be saved."*

¹⁴But how can they call on him to save them unless they believe in him? And how can they believe in him if they have never heard about him? And how can they hear about him unless someone tells them? ¹⁵And how will anyone go and tell them without being sent? That is what the Scriptures mean when they say, "How beautiful are the feet of those who bring good news!"*

¹⁶But not everyone welcomes the Good News, for Isaiah the prophet said, "Lord, who has believed our message?"* ¹⁷Yet faith comes from listening to this message of good news—the Good News about Christ.

¹⁸But what about the Jews? Have they actually heard the message? Yes, they have:

"The message of God's creation has gone out to everyone,
and its words to all the world."*

¹⁹But did the people of Israel really understand? Yes, they did, for even in the time of Moses, God had said,

"I will rouse your jealousy by blessing other nations.
I will make you angry by blessing the foolish Gentiles."*

²⁰And later Isaiah spoke boldly for God:

"I was found by people
who were not looking for me.
I showed myself to those
who were not asking for me."*

²¹But regarding Israel, God said,

"All day long I opened my arms to them,
but they kept disobeying me and arguing with me."*

I BELIEVE I am made right with God by believing in Christ, because Jesus Christ accomplished the whole purpose of the law. (10:4)

See Moses' profile (page 73) at Exodus 5:1.

I CONFESS with my mouth that Jesus Christ is Lord and believe in my heart that God raised him from the dead. (10:9)

I BELIEVE Jews and Gentiles are saved in the same way: by believing in the Lord Jesus Christ. (10:12)

See Isaiah's profile (page 801) at Isaiah 6:13.

I BELIEVE faith comes by listening to the message of God's Good News about Christ. (10:17)

I BELIEVE God continually reached out to save the ancient nation of Israel, which repeatedly rejected him. (10:21)

10:1 Greek Brothers. 10:4 Or the end. 10:5 Lev 18:5. 10:6-8 Deut 30:12-14. 10:11 Or will not be put to shame. Isa 28:16. 10:13 Joel 2:32. 10:15 Isa 52:7. 10:16 Isa 53:1. 10:18 Ps 19:4. 10:19 Deut 32:21. 10:20 Isa 65:1. 10:21 Isa 65:2.

CHAPTER 11

God's Mercy on Israel

I BELIEVE God has not rejected his people, the Jews. (11:1)

See Abraham's profile (page 19) at Genesis 15:6.

See Elijah's profile (page 421) at 1 Kings 19:18.

I ask, then, has God rejected his people, the Jews? Of course not! Remember that I myself am a Jew, a descendant of Abraham and a member of the tribe of Benjamin.

²No, God has not rejected his own people, whom he chose from the very beginning. Do you remember what the Scriptures say about this? Elijah the prophet complained to God about the people of Israel and said, ³"Lord, they have killed your prophets and torn down your altars. I alone am left, and now they are trying to kill me, too."*

⁴And do you remember God's reply? He said, "You are not the only one left. I have seven thousand others who have never bowed down to Baal!"*

⁵It is the same today, for not all the Jews have turned away from God. A few* are being saved as a result of God's kindness in choosing them. ⁶And if they are saved by God's kindness, then it is not by their good works. For in that case, God's wonderful kindness would not be what it really is—free and undeserved.

I BELIEVE God has chosen and saved some of the Jews, while the others have been unresponsive. (11:7)

⁷So this is the situation: Most of the Jews have not found the favor of God they are looking for so earnestly. A few have—the ones God has chosen—but the rest were made unresponsive. ⁸As the Scriptures say,

"God has put them into a deep sleep.
To this very day he has shut their eyes so they do not see,
and closed their ears so they do not hear."*

See David's profile (page 629) at Psalm 3:1.

⁹David spoke of this same thing when he said,

"Let their bountiful table become a snare,
a trap that makes them think all is well.
Let their blessings cause them to stumble.
¹⁰Let their eyes go blind so they cannot see,
and let their backs grow weaker and weaker."*

I BELIEVE God's purpose was to make his salvation available to the Gentiles so the Jews would want to be saved, too. (11:11)

¹¹Did God's people stumble and fall beyond recovery? Of course not! His purpose was to make his salvation available to the Gentiles, and then the Jews would be jealous and want it for themselves. ¹²Now if the Gentiles were enriched because the Jews turned down God's offer of salvation, think how much greater a blessing the world will share when the Jews finally accept it.

¹³I am saying all of this especially for you Gentiles. God has appointed me as the apostle to the Gentiles. I lay great stress on this, ¹⁴for I want to find a way to make the Jews want what you Gentiles have, and in that way I might save some of them. ¹⁵For since the Jews' rejection meant that God offered salvation to the rest of the world, how much more wonderful their acceptance will be. It will be life for those who were dead! ¹⁶And since Abraham and the other patriarchs were holy, their children will also be holy.* For if the roots of the tree are holy, the branches will be, too.

See the profiles for Isaac (page 31) and Jacob (page 43) at Genesis 25:19 and Genesis 32:9.

I SHARE in the blessings of Abraham. (11:17)

¹⁷But some of these branches from Abraham's tree, some of the Jews, have been broken off. And you Gentiles, who were branches from a wild olive tree, were grafted in. So now you also receive the blessing God has promised Abraham and his children, sharing in God's rich nourishment of his special olive tree. ¹⁸But you must be careful not to brag about being grafted in to replace the branches that were broken off. Remember, you are just a branch, not the root.

¹⁹"Well," you may say, "those branches were broken off to make room for me." ²⁰Yes, but remember—those branches, the Jews, were broken off because they didn't believe God, and you are there because you do believe.

11:3 1 Kgs 19:10, 14.   11:4 1 Kgs 19:18.   11:5 Greek *A remnant.*   11:8 Deut 29:4; Isa 29:10.   11:9-10 Ps 69:22-23.   11:16 Greek *If the dough offered as firstfruits is holy, so is the whole lump.*

Don't think highly of yourself, but fear what could happen. [21]For if God did not spare the branches he put there in the first place, he won't spare you either.

[22]Notice how God is both kind and severe. He is severe to those who disobeyed, but kind to you as you continue to trust in his kindness. But if you stop trusting, you also will be cut off. [23]And if the Jews turn from their unbelief, God will graft them back into the tree again. He has the power to do it.

[24]For if God was willing to take you who were, by nature, branches from a wild olive tree and graft you into his own good tree—a very unusual thing to do—he will be far more eager to graft the Jews back into the tree where they belong.

God's Mercy Is for Everyone

[25]I want you to understand this mystery, dear brothers and sisters,* so that you will not feel proud and start bragging. Some of the Jews have hard hearts, but this will last only until the complete number of Gentiles comes to Christ. [26]And so all Israel will be saved. Do you remember what the prophets said about this?

"A Deliverer will come from Jerusalem,*
    and he will turn Israel* from all ungodliness.
[27]And then I will keep my covenant with them
    and take away their sins."*

[28]Many of the Jews are now enemies of the Good News. But this has been to your benefit, for God has given his gifts to you Gentiles. Yet the Jews are still his chosen people because of his promises to Abraham, Isaac, and Jacob. [29]For God's gifts and his call can never be withdrawn. [30]Once, you Gentiles were rebels against God, but when the Jews refused his mercy, God was merciful to you instead. [31]And now, in the same way, the Jews are the rebels, and God's mercy has come to you. But someday they,* too, will share in God's mercy. [32]For God has imprisoned all people in their own disobedience so he could have mercy on everyone.

[33]Oh, what a wonderful God we have! How great are his riches and wisdom and knowledge! How impossible it is for us to understand his decisions and his methods! [34]For who can know what the Lord is thinking? Who knows enough to be his counselor?* [35]And who could ever give him so much that he would have to pay it back? [36]For everything comes from him; everything exists by his power and is intended for his glory. To him be glory evermore. Amen.

CHAPTER 12

A Living Sacrifice to God

And so, dear brothers and sisters,* I plead with you to give your bodies to God. Let them be a living and holy sacrifice—the kind he will accept. When you think of what he has done for you, is this too much to ask? [2]Don't copy the behavior and customs of this world, but let God transform you into a new person by changing the way you think. Then you will know what God wants you to do, and you will know how good and pleasing and perfect his will really is.

[3]As God's messenger, I give each of you this warning: Be honest in your estimate of yourselves, measuring your value by how much faith God has given you. [4]Just as our bodies have many parts and each part has a special function, [5]so it is with Christ's body. We are all parts of his one body, and each of us has

---

I BELIEVE God is kind to those who trust him and severe to those who won't. (11:22)

I BELIEVE the Jews are still God's chosen people because God is still keeping his promises to Abraham, Isaac, and Jacob. (11:28)

I EXALT in God's wonderful wisdom and understanding! (11:33)

I GIVE my body to God as a living and holy sacrifice. (12:1)

11:25 Greek *brothers*.   11:26a Greek *from Zion*.   11:26b Greek *Jacob*.   11:26-27 Isa 59:20-21.   11:31 Some manuscripts read *But now they*; other manuscripts read *But they*.   11:34 See Isa 40:13.   12:1 Greek *brothers*.

different work to do. And since we are all one body in Christ, we belong to each other, and each of us needs all the others.

⁶God has given each of us the ability to do certain things well. So if God has given you the ability to prophesy, speak out when you have faith that God is speaking through you. ⁷If your gift is that of serving others, serve them well. If you are a teacher, do a good job of teaching. ⁸If your gift is to encourage others, do it! If you have money, share it generously. If God has given you leadership ability, take the responsibility seriously. And if you have a gift for showing kindness to others, do it gladly.

I DO my best to use my God-given abilities to serve other Christians. (12:6)

⁹Don't just pretend that you love others. Really love them. Hate what is wrong. Stand on the side of the good. ¹⁰Love each other with genuine affection,* and take delight in honoring each other. ¹¹Never be lazy in your work, but serve the Lord enthusiastically.

I LOVE other people sincerely, not just for show. (12:9)

¹²Be glad for all God is planning for you. Be patient in trouble, and always be prayerful. ¹³When God's children are in need, be the one to help them out. And get into the habit of inviting guests home for dinner or, if they need lodging, for the night.

I OPEN my wallet and my home willingly and regularly to other Christians. (12:13)

¹⁴If people persecute you because you are a Christian, don't curse them; pray that God will bless them. ¹⁵When others are happy, be happy with them. If they are sad, share their sorrow. ¹⁶Live in harmony with each other. Don't try to act important, but enjoy the company of ordinary people. And don't think you know it all!

¹⁷Never pay back evil for evil to anyone. Do things in such a way that everyone can see you are honorable. ¹⁸Do your part to live in peace with everyone, as much as possible.

I DO my part to live in peace with others. (12:18)

¹⁹Dear friends, never avenge yourselves. Leave that to God. For it is written,

"I will take vengeance;
I will repay those who deserve it,"*
says the Lord.

²⁰Instead, do what the Scriptures say:

"If your enemies are hungry, feed them.
If they are thirsty, give them something to drink,
  and they will be ashamed of what they have done to you."*

²¹Don't let evil get the best of you, but conquer evil by doing good.

CHAPTER 13

Respect for Authority

Obey the government, for God is the one who put it there. All governments have been placed in power by God. ²So those who refuse to obey the laws of the land are refusing to obey God, and punishment will follow. ³For the authorities do not frighten people who are doing right, but they frighten those who do wrong. So do what they say, and you will get along well. ⁴The authorities are sent by God to help you. But if you are doing something wrong, of course you should be afraid, for you will be punished. The authorities are established by God for that very purpose, to punish those who do wrong. ⁵So you must obey the government for two reasons: to keep from being punished and to keep a clear conscience.

⁶Pay your taxes, too, for these same reasons. For government workers need to be paid so they can keep on doing the work God intended them to do. ⁷Give to everyone what you owe them: Pay your taxes and import duties, and give respect and honor to all to whom it is due.

I PAY taxes and respect those in authority to show my reverence for God's authority. (13:7)

12:10 Greek *with brotherly love.*   12:19 Deut 32:35.   12:20 Greek *and you will heap burning coals on their heads.* Prov 25:21-22.

Love Fulfills God's Requirements

[8]Pay all your debts, except the debt of love for others. You can never finish paying that! If you love your neighbor, you will fulfill all the requirements of God's law. [9]For the commandments against adultery and murder and stealing and coveting—and any other commandment—are all summed up in this one commandment: "Love your neighbor as yourself."* [10]Love does no wrong to anyone, so love satisfies all of God's requirements.

[11]Another reason for right living is that you know how late it is; time is running out. Wake up, for the coming of our salvation is nearer now than when we first believed. [12]The night is almost gone; the day of salvation will soon be here. So don't live in darkness. Get rid of your evil deeds. Shed them like dirty clothes. Clothe yourselves with the armor of right living, as those who live in the light. [13]We should be decent and true in everything we do, so that everyone can approve of our behavior. Don't participate in wild parties and getting drunk, or in adultery and immoral living, or in fighting and jealousy. [14]But let the Lord Jesus Christ take control of you, and don't think of ways to indulge your evil desires.

CHAPTER 14

The Danger of Criticism

Accept Christians who are weak in faith, and don't argue with them about what they think is right or wrong. [2]For instance, one person believes it is all right to eat anything. But another believer who has a sensitive conscience will eat only vegetables. [3]Those who think it is all right to eat anything must not look down on those who won't. And those who won't eat certain foods must not condemn those who do, for God has accepted them. [4]Who are you to condemn God's servants? They are responsible to the Lord, so let him tell them whether they are right or wrong. The Lord's power will help them do as they should.

[5]In the same way, some think one day is more holy than another day, while others think every day is alike. Each person should have a personal conviction about this matter. [6]Those who have a special day for worshiping the Lord are trying to honor him. Those who eat all kinds of food do so to honor the Lord, since they give thanks to God before eating. And those who won't eat everything also want to please the Lord and give thanks to God. [7]For we are not our own masters when we live or when we die. [8]While we live, we live to please the Lord. And when we die, we go to be with the Lord. So in life and in death, we belong to the Lord. [9]Christ died and rose again for this very purpose, so that he might be Lord of those who are alive and of those who have died.

[10]So why do you condemn another Christian*? Why do you look down on another Christian? Remember, each of us will stand personally before the judgment seat of God. [11]For the Scriptures say,

" 'As surely as I live,' says the Lord,
'every knee will bow to me
and every tongue will confess allegiance to God.' "*

[12]Yes, each of us will have to give a personal account to God. [13]So don't condemn each other anymore. Decide instead to live in such a way that you will not put an obstacle in another Christian's path.

[14]I know and am perfectly sure on the authority of the Lord Jesus that no food, in and of itself, is wrong to eat. But if someone believes it is wrong, then for that person it is wrong. [15]And if another Christian is distressed by what you eat, you are not acting in love if you eat it. Don't let your eating ruin

I PAY all my debts—except the debt of love for others. (13:8)

I LIVE a pure life because Jesus Christ's return is closer every day. (13:11)

I ACCEPT Christians with differing convictions without condemning them. (14:1)

I DO NOT CONDEMN other Christians with differing convictions, because I remember that each Christian is responsible to the Lord. (14:4)

I DO NOT CONDEMN other Christians but live in keeping with my convictions so that I will not confuse other believers. (14:14)

13:9 Lev 19:18. 14:10 Greek *your brother;* also in 14:10b, 13, 15, 21. 14:11 Isa 45:23.

someone for whom Christ died. [16]Then you will not be condemned for doing something you know is all right.

[17]For the Kingdom of God is not a matter of what we eat or drink, but of living a life of goodness and peace and joy in the Holy Spirit. [18]If you serve Christ with this attitude, you will please God. And other people will approve of you, too. [19]So then, let us aim for harmony in the church and try to build each other up.

[20]Don't tear apart the work of God over what you eat. Remember, there is nothing wrong with these things in themselves. But it is wrong to eat anything if it makes another person stumble. [21]Don't eat meat or drink wine or do anything else if it might cause another Christian to stumble. [22]You may have the faith to believe that there is nothing wrong with what you are doing, but keep it between yourself and God. Blessed are those who do not condemn themselves by doing something they know is all right. [23]But if people have doubts about whether they should eat something, they shouldn't eat it. They would be condemned for not acting in faith before God. If you do anything you believe is not right, you are sinning.

CHAPTER 15

Living to Please Others

We may know that these things make no difference, but we cannot just go ahead and do them to please ourselves. We must be considerate of the doubts and fears of those who think these things are wrong. [2]We should please others. If we do what helps them, we will build them up in the Lord. [3]For even Christ didn't please himself. As the Scriptures say, "Those who insult you are also insulting me."* [4]Such things were written in the Scriptures long ago to teach us. They give us hope and encouragement as we wait patiently for God's promises.

[5]May God, who gives this patience and encouragement, help you live in complete harmony with each other—each with the attitude of Christ Jesus toward the other. [6]Then all of you can join together with one voice, giving praise and glory to God, the Father of our Lord Jesus Christ.

[7]So accept each other just as Christ has accepted you; then God will be glorified. [8]Remember that Christ came as a servant to the Jews to show that God is true to the promises he made to their ancestors. [9]And he came so the Gentiles might also give glory to God for his mercies to them. That is what the psalmist meant when he wrote:

"I will praise you among the Gentiles;
    I will sing praises to your name."*

[10]And in another place it is written,

"Rejoice, O you Gentiles,
    along with his people, the Jews."*

[11]And yet again,

"Praise the Lord, all you Gentiles;
    praise him, all you people of the earth."*

[12]And the prophet Isaiah said,

"The heir to David's throne* will come,
    and he will rule over the Gentiles.
    They will place their hopes on him."*

[13]So I pray that God, who gives you hope, will keep you happy and full of peace as you believe in him. May you overflow with hope through the power of the Holy Spirit.

I FOCUS on living by the Holy Spirit, not on living by secondary concerns or rules. (14:17)

I DO NOT SIN by going against my personal convictions. (14:23)

I LIVE to build up others in the Lord. (15:2)

I GLORIFY God by accepting others just as Jesus Christ has accepted me. (15:7)

See David's profile (page 629) at Psalm 3:1.

See Isaiah's profile (page 801) at Isaiah 6:13.

I ENJOY happiness, peace, hope, and power through the Holy Spirit. (15:13)

15:3 Ps 69:9.   15:9 Ps 18:49.   15:10 Deut 32:43.   15:11 Ps 117:1.   15:12a Greek *The root of Jesse.* 15:12b Isa 11:10.

Paul's Reason for Writing

[14]I am fully convinced, dear brothers and sisters,* that you are full of goodness. You know these things so well that you are able to teach others all about them. [15]Even so, I have been bold enough to emphasize some of these points, knowing that all you need is this reminder from me. For I am, by God's grace, [16]a special messenger from Christ Jesus to you Gentiles. I bring you the Good News and offer you up as a fragrant sacrifice to God so that you might be pure and pleasing to him by the Holy Spirit. [17]So it is right for me to be enthusiastic about all Christ Jesus has done through me in my service to God. [18]I dare not boast of anything else. I have brought the Gentiles to God by my message and by the way I lived before them. [19]I have won them over by the miracles done through me as signs from God—all by the power of God's Spirit. In this way, I have fully presented the Good News of Christ all the way from Jerusalem clear over into Illyricum.*

[20]My ambition has always been to preach the Good News where the name of Christ has never been heard, rather than where a church has already been started by someone else. [21]I have been following the plan spoken of in the Scriptures, where it says,

"Those who have never been told about him will see,
  and those who have never heard of him will understand."*

[22]In fact, my visit to you has been delayed so long because I have been preaching in these places.

I AM ENTHUSIASTIC about all God has done through me by the power of his Holy Spirit. (15:17)

Paul's Travel Plans

[23]But now I have finished my work in these regions, and after all these long years of waiting, I am eager to visit you. [24]I am planning to go to Spain, and when I do, I will stop off in Rome. And after I have enjoyed your fellowship for a little while, you can send me on my way again.

[25]But before I come, I must go down to Jerusalem to take a gift to the Christians there. [26]For you see, the believers in Greece* have eagerly taken up an offering for the Christians in Jerusalem, who are going through such hard times. [27]They were very glad to do this because they feel they owe a real debt to them. Since the Gentiles received the wonderful spiritual blessings of the Good News from the Jewish Christians, they feel the least they can do in return is help them financially. [28]As soon as I have delivered this money and completed this good deed of theirs, I will come to see you on my way to Spain. [29]And I am sure that when I come, Christ will give me a great blessing for you.

I AM GENEROUS to other Christians in need. (15:25)

[30]Dear brothers and sisters, I urge you in the name of our Lord Jesus Christ to join me in my struggle by praying to God for me. Do this because of your love for me, given to you by the Holy Spirit. [31]Pray that I will be rescued from those in Judea who refuse to obey God. Pray also that the Christians there will be willing to accept the donation I am bringing them. [32]Then, by the will of God, I will be able to come to you with a happy heart, and we will be an encouragement to each other.

[33]And now may God, who gives us his peace, be with you all. Amen.

I PRAY for Christians who are actively serving the Lord. (15:30)

CHAPTER 16

Paul Greets His Friends

Our sister Phoebe, a deacon in the church in Cenchrea, will be coming to see you soon. [2]Receive her in the Lord, as one who is worthy of high honor. Help her in every way you can, for she has helped many in their needs, including me.

[3]Greet Priscilla and Aquila. They have been co-workers in my ministry for

See the profile for Priscilla and Aquila (page 1265) at Acts 18:26.

15:14 Greek brothers; also in 15:30.   15:19 Illyricum was a region northeast of Italy.   15:21 Isa 52:15.
15:26 Greek Macedonia and Achaia, the northern and southern regions of Greece.

Christ Jesus. [4]In fact, they risked their lives for me. I am not the only one who is thankful to them; so are all the Gentile churches. [5]Please give my greetings to the church that meets in their home.

Greet my dear friend Epenetus. He was the very first person to become a Christian in the province of Asia. [6]Give my greetings to Mary, who has worked so hard for your benefit. [7]Then there are Andronicus and Junia,* my relatives,* who were in prison with me. They are respected among the apostles and became Christians before I did. Please give them my greetings. [8]Say hello to Ampliatus, whom I love as one of the Lord's own children, [9]and Urbanus, our co-worker in Christ, and beloved Stachys.

[10]Give my greetings to Apelles, a good man whom Christ approves. And give my best regards to the members of the household of Aristobulus. [11]Greet Herodion, my relative.* Greet the Christians in the household of Narcissus. [12]Say hello to Tryphena and Tryphosa, the Lord's workers, and to dear Persis, who has worked so hard for the Lord. [13]Greet Rufus, whom the Lord picked out to be his very own; and also his dear mother, who has been a mother to me.

[14]And please give my greetings to Asyncritus, Phlegon, Hermes, Patrobas, Hermas, and the brothers and sisters* who are with them. [15]Give my greetings to Philologus, Julia, Nereus and his sister, and to Olympas and all the other believers who are with them. [16]Greet each other in Christian love.* All the churches of Christ send you their greetings.

Paul's Final Instructions

[17]And now I make one more appeal, my dear brothers and sisters. Watch out for people who cause divisions and upset people's faith by teaching things that are contrary to what you have been taught. Stay away from them. [18]Such people are not serving Christ our Lord; they are serving their own personal interests. By smooth talk and glowing words they deceive innocent people. [19]But everyone knows that you are obedient to the Lord. This makes me very happy. I want you to see clearly what is right and to stay innocent of any wrong. [20]The God of peace will soon crush Satan under your feet. May the grace of our Lord Jesus Christ be with you.

[21]Timothy, my fellow worker, and Lucius, Jason, and Sosipater, my relatives, send you their good wishes.

[22]I, Tertius, the one who is writing this letter for Paul, send my greetings, too, as a Christian brother.

[23]Gaius says hello to you. I am his guest, and the church meets here in his home. Erastus, the city treasurer, sends you his greetings, and so does Quartus, a Christian brother.*

[25]God is able to make you strong, just as the Good News says. It is the message about Jesus Christ and his plan for you Gentiles, a plan kept secret from the beginning of time. [26]But now as the prophets* foretold and as the eternal God has commanded, this message is made known to all Gentiles everywhere, so that they might believe and obey Christ. [27]To God, who alone is wise, be the glory forever through Jesus Christ. Amen.

16:7a Or *Junias;* some manuscripts read *Julia.* 16:7b Or *compatriots;* also in 16:21. 16:11 Or *compatriot.* 16:14 Greek *brothers;* also in 16:17. 16:16 Greek *with a sacred kiss.* 16:23 Some manuscripts add verse 24, *May the grace of our Lord Jesus Christ be with you all. Amen.* 16:26 Greek *the prophetic writings.*

I WORK hard for the benefit of other Christians. (16:6)

I HONOR Christians who work hard for the Lord. (16:12)

I WATCH OUT for and stay away from individuals who cause problems by teaching falsehoods within the church. (16:17)

See Timothy's profile (page 1373) at 1 Timothy 4:12.

I BELIEVE God's Good News is the message about Jesus Christ's offer of salvation to all who believe. (16:25)

1 CORINTHIANS

THIS SECOND New Testament letter answers many tough questions about living out the Christian faith as a church.

The apostle Paul wrote this letter to the church he had established in the city of Corinth during one of his missionary journeys (Acts 18:1-18).

In chapters 1-4, Paul explains the difference between Christian unity and divisions, between the wisdom of God and the world's wisdom, and between spiritual maturity and immaturity.

In chapters 5-15, Paul addresses specific concerns within the Corinthian church regarding spiritual pride, immorality, and lawsuits among Christians. He also answers their questions about marriage, meat sacrificed to idols, Paul's apostolic authority, public worship, spiritual gifts, and the resurrection.

In chapter 16, Paul reminds them of his plans to visit them again and closes with some final words of instruction.

Famous passages in 1 Corinthians include

- ○ "No eye has seen, no ear has heard, and no mind has imagined what God has prepared for those who love him" (2:9)
- ○ "Don't you realize that all of you together are the temple of God . . . ?" (3:16)
- ○ "You are not to associate with anyone who claims to be a Christian yet indulges in sexual sin, or is greedy" (5:11)
- ○ "But now your sins have been washed away, and you have been set apart for God. You have been made right with God" (6:11)
- ○ "Or don't you know that your body is the temple of the Holy Spirit, who lives in you . . . ?" (6:19)
- ○ "It is love that really builds up the church" (8:1)
- ○ "I try to find common ground with everyone so that I might bring them to Christ" (9:22)
- ○ "Run in such a way that you will win" (9:24)
- ○ "God is faithful. He will keep the temptation from becoming so strong that you can't stand up against it" (10:13)
- ○ "Whatever you do, you must do all for the glory of God" (10:31)
- ○ Instructions about the Lord's Supper (11:23-32)
- ○ "A spiritual gift is given to each of us as a means of helping the entire church" (12:7)
- ○ Love is the greatest virtue (12:31-13:13)
- ○ A synopsis of the message of Good News (15:1-8)
- ○ "Flesh and blood cannot inherit the Kingdom of God" (15:50)
- ○ Our bodies will be transformed (15:51-54)
- ○ "Be strong and steady, always enthusiastic about the Lord's work" (15:58)

CHAPTER 1

Greetings from Paul

This letter is from Paul, chosen by the will of God to be an apostle of Christ Jesus, and from our brother Sosthenes.

²We are writing to the church of God in Corinth, you who have been called by God to be his own holy people. He made you holy by means of Christ Jesus, just as he did all Christians everywhere—whoever calls upon the name of Jesus Christ, our Lord and theirs.

³May God our Father and the Lord Jesus Christ give you his grace and peace.

Paul Gives Thanks to God

⁴I can never stop thanking God for all the generous gifts he has given you, now that you belong to Christ Jesus. ⁵He has enriched your church with the gifts of eloquence and every kind of knowledge. ⁶This shows that what I told you about Christ is true. ⁷Now you have every spiritual gift you need as you eagerly wait for the return of our Lord Jesus Christ. ⁸He will keep you strong right up to the end, and he will keep you free from all blame on the great day when our Lord Jesus Christ returns. ⁹God will surely do this for you, for he always does just what he says, and he is the one who invited you into this wonderful friendship with his Son, Jesus Christ our Lord.

Divisions in the Church

¹⁰Now, dear brothers and sisters,* I appeal to you by the authority of the Lord Jesus Christ to stop arguing among yourselves. Let there be real harmony so there won't be divisions in the church. I plead with you to be of one mind, united in thought and purpose. ¹¹For some members of Chloe's household have told me about your arguments, dear brothers and sisters. ¹²Some of you are saying, "I am a follower of Paul." Others are saying, "I follow Apollos," or "I follow Peter,*" or "I follow only Christ." ¹³Can Christ be divided into pieces?

Was I, Paul, crucified for you? Were any of you baptized in the name of Paul? ¹⁴I thank God that I did not baptize any of you except Crispus and Gaius, ¹⁵for now no one can say they were baptized in my name. ¹⁶(Oh yes, I also baptized the household of Stephanas. I don't remember baptizing anyone else.) ¹⁷For Christ didn't send me to baptize, but to preach the Good News—and not with clever speeches and high-sounding ideas, for fear that the cross of Christ would lose its power.

The Wisdom of God

¹⁸I know very well how foolish the message of the cross sounds to those who are on the road to destruction. But we who are being saved recognize this message as the very power of God. ¹⁹As the Scriptures say,

"I will destroy human wisdom
 and discard their most brilliant ideas."*

²⁰So where does this leave the philosophers, the scholars, and the world's brilliant debaters? God has made them all look foolish and has shown their wisdom to be useless nonsense. ²¹Since God in his wisdom saw to it that the world would never find him through human wisdom, he has used our foolish preaching to save all who believe. ²²God's way seems foolish to the Jews because they want a sign from heaven to prove it is true. And it is foolish to the Greeks because they believe only what agrees with their own wisdom. ²³So when we preach that Christ was crucified, the Jews are offended, and the Gentiles say it's all nonsense. ²⁴But to those called by God to salvation, both Jews and Gentiles,* Christ is the mighty power of God and the wonderful wisdom of God. ²⁵This "foolish" plan of God is far wiser than the wisest of

---

See Paul's profile (page 1333) at Galatians 2:5.

I AM a Christian—someone who has called upon the name of Jesus Christ and been made one of God's holy people. (1:2)

I AM THANKFUL God invited me into a wonderful friendship with his Son, Jesus Christ my Lord. (1:9)

I DO NOT continually argue with other believers. (1:10)

See Peter's profile (page 1111) at Matthew 26:75.

I BELIEVE the message of the cross is the very power of God (Romans 1:16). (1:18)

I BELIEVE the smallest part of God's wisdom and power far exceeds the greatest human potential. (1:25)

1:10 Greek *brothers*; also in 1:11, 26.　1:12 Greek *Cephas*.　1:19 Isa 29:14.　1:24 Greek *Greeks*.

human plans, and God's weakness is far stronger than the greatest of human strength. [26]Remember, dear brothers and sisters, that few of you were wise in the world's eyes, or powerful, or wealthy when God called you. [27]Instead, God deliberately chose things the world considers foolish in order to shame those who think they are wise. And he chose those who are powerless to shame those who are powerful. [28]God chose things despised by the world, things counted as nothing at all, and used them to bring to nothing what the world considers important, [29]so that no one can ever boast in the presence of God. [30]God alone made it possible for you to be in Christ Jesus. For our benefit God made Christ to be wisdom itself. He is the one who made us acceptable to God. He made us pure and holy, and he gave himself to purchase our freedom. [31]As the Scriptures say,

"The person who wishes to boast
should boast only of what the Lord has done."*

Pray that the Holy Spirit will guide you into all truth (John 16:13).

I BELIEVE Jesus Christ made us pure, holy, and acceptable to God. (1:30)

CHAPTER 2

Paul Preaches Wisdom

Dear brothers and sisters,* when I first came to you I didn't use lofty words and brilliant ideas to tell you God's message.* [2]For I decided to concentrate only on Jesus Christ and his death on the cross. [3]I came to you in weakness—timid and trembling. [4]And my message and my preaching were very plain. I did not use wise and persuasive speeches, but the Holy Spirit was powerful among you. [5]I did this so that you might trust the power of God rather than human wisdom.

[6]Yet when I am among mature Christians, I do speak with words of wisdom, but not the kind of wisdom that belongs to this world, and not the kind that appeals to the rulers of this world, who are being brought to nothing. [7]No, the wisdom we speak of is the secret wisdom of God,* which was hidden in former times, though he made it for our benefit before the world began. [8]But the rulers of this world have not understood it; if they had, they would never have crucified our glorious Lord. [9]That is what the Scriptures mean when they say,

"No eye has seen, no ear has heard,
and no mind has imagined
what God has prepared
for those who love him."*

I TRUST the power of God rather than human wisdom. (2:5)

I KNOW I can't begin to imagine what God has prepared for me. (2:9)

[10]But we know these things because God has revealed them to us by his Spirit, and his Spirit searches out everything and shows us even God's deep secrets. [11]No one can know what anyone else is really thinking except that person alone, and no one can know God's thoughts except God's own Spirit. [12]And God has actually given us his Spirit (not the world's spirit) so we can know the wonderful things God has freely given us. [13]When we tell you this, we do not use words of human wisdom. We speak words given to us by the Spirit, using the Spirit's words to explain spiritual truths.* [14]But people who aren't Christians can't understand these truths from God's Spirit. It all sounds foolish to them because only those who have the Spirit can understand what the Spirit means. [15]We who have the Spirit understand these things, but others can't understand us at all. [16]How could they? For,

I BELIEVE individuals who aren't Christians can't understand the truths from God's Spirit. (2:14)

"Who can know what the Lord is thinking?
Who can give him counsel?"*

But we can understand these things, for we have the mind of Christ.

1:31 Jer 9:24.   2:1a Greek *Brothers*.   2:1b Greek *mystery*; other manuscripts read *testimony*.   2:7 Greek *we speak God's wisdom in a mystery*.   2:9 Isa 64:4.   2:13 Or *explaining spiritual truths in spiritual language*, or *explaining spiritual truths to spiritual people*.   2:16 Isa 40:13.

CHAPTER 3

Paul and Apollos, Servants of Christ

Dear brothers and sisters,* when I was with you I couldn't talk to you as I would to mature Christians. I had to talk as though you belonged to this world or as though you were infants in the Christian life.* ²I had to feed you with milk and not with solid food, because you couldn't handle anything stronger. And you still aren't ready, ³for you are still controlled by your own sinful desires. You are jealous of one another and quarrel with each other. Doesn't that prove you are controlled by your own desires? You are acting like people who don't belong to the Lord. ⁴When one of you says, "I am a follower of Paul," and another says, "I prefer Apollos," aren't you acting like those who are not Christians?*

⁵Who is Apollos, and who is Paul, that we should be the cause of such quarrels? Why, we're only servants. Through us God caused you to believe. Each of us did the work the Lord gave us. ⁶My job was to plant the seed in your hearts, and Apollos watered it, but it was God, not we, who made it grow. ⁷The ones who do the planting or watering aren't important, but God is important because he is the one who makes the seed grow. ⁸The one who plants and the one who waters work as a team with the same purpose. Yet they will be rewarded individually, according to their own hard work. ⁹We work together as partners who belong to God. You are God's field, God's building—not ours.

¹⁰Because of God's special favor to me, I have laid the foundation like an expert builder. Now others are building on it. But whoever is building on this foundation must be very careful. ¹¹For no one can lay any other foundation than the one we already have—Jesus Christ. ¹²Now anyone who builds on that foundation may use gold, silver, jewels, wood, hay, or straw. ¹³But there is going to come a time of testing at the judgment day to see what kind of work each builder has done. Everyone's work will be put through the fire to see whether or not it keeps its value. ¹⁴If the work survives the fire, that builder will receive a reward. ¹⁵But if the work is burned up, the builder will suffer great loss. The builders themselves will be saved, but like someone escaping through a wall of flames.

¹⁶Don't you realize that all of you together are the temple of God and that the Spirit of God lives in* you? ¹⁷God will bring ruin upon anyone who ruins this temple. For God's temple is holy, and you Christians are that temple.

¹⁸Stop fooling yourselves. If you think you are wise by this world's standards, you will have to become a fool so you can become wise by God's standards. ¹⁹For the wisdom of this world is foolishness to God. As the Scriptures say,

"God catches those who think they are wise
in their own cleverness."*

²⁰And again,

"The Lord knows the thoughts of the wise,
that they are worthless."*

²¹So don't take pride in following a particular leader. Everything belongs to you: ²²Paul and Apollos and Peter*; the whole world and life and death; the present and the future. Everything belongs to you, ²³and you belong to Christ, and Christ belongs to God.

CHAPTER 4

Paul and the Corinthians

So look at Apollos and me as mere servants of Christ who have been put in charge of explaining God's secrets. ²Now, a person who is put in charge as a

I AM NOT JEALOUS and do not quarrel with others. (3:3)

See Paul's profile (page 1333) at Galatians 2:5.

I WORK as a team with other Christians for the same purpose—glorifying God. (3:8)

I SEEK to do work that God will judge as having lasting value. (3:13)

I RECOGNIZE that human wisdom by itself amounts to nothing in God's sight. (3:19)

I DO NOT TAKE PRIDE in following a particular leader. (3:21)

See Peter's profile (page 1111) at Matthew 26:75.

I AM FAITHFUL as a servant of Christ. (4:2)

3:1a Greek *Brothers.* 3:1b Greek *in Christ.* 3:4 Greek *aren't you merely human?* 3:16 Or *among.* 3:19 Job 5:13. 3:20 Ps 94:11. 3:22 Greek *Cephas.*

manager must be faithful. [3]What about me? Have I been faithful? Well, it matters very little what you or anyone else thinks. I don't even trust my own judgment on this point. [4]My conscience is clear, but that isn't what matters. It is the Lord himself who will examine me and decide.

[5]So be careful not to jump to conclusions before the Lord returns as to whether or not someone is faithful. When the Lord comes, he will bring our deepest secrets to light and will reveal our private motives. And then God will give to everyone whatever praise is due.

[6]Dear brothers and sisters,* I have used Apollos and myself to illustrate what I've been saying. If you pay attention to the Scriptures,* you won't brag about one of your leaders at the expense of another. [7]What makes you better than anyone else? What do you have that God hasn't given you? And if all you have is from God, why boast as though you have accomplished something on your own?

[8]You think you already have everything you need! You are already rich! Without us you have become kings! I wish you really were on your thrones already, for then we would be reigning with you! [9]But sometimes I think God has put us apostles on display, like prisoners of war at the end of a victor's parade, condemned to die. We have become a spectacle to the entire world—to people and angels alike.

[10]Our dedication to Christ makes us look like fools, but you are so wise! We are weak, but you are so powerful! You are well thought of, but we are laughed at. [11]To this very hour we go hungry and thirsty, without enough clothes to keep us warm. We have endured many beatings, and we have no homes of our own. [12]We have worked wearily with our own hands to earn our living. We bless those who curse us. We are patient with those who abuse us. [13]We respond gently when evil things are said about us. Yet we are treated like the world's garbage, like everybody's trash—right up to the present moment.

[14]I am not writing these things to shame you, but to warn you as my beloved children. [15]For even if you had ten thousand others to teach you about Christ, you have only one spiritual father. For I became your father in Christ Jesus when I preached the Good News to you. [16]So I ask you to follow my example and do as I do.

[17]That is the very reason I am sending Timothy—to help you do this. For he is my beloved and trustworthy child in the Lord. He will remind you of what I teach about Christ Jesus in all the churches wherever I go.

[18]I know that some of you have become arrogant, thinking I will never visit you again. [19]But I will come—and soon—if the Lord will let me, and then I'll find out whether these arrogant people are just big talkers or whether they really have God's power. [20]For the Kingdom of God is not just fancy talk; it is living by God's power. [21]Which do you choose? Should I come with punishment and scolding, or should I come with quiet love and gentleness?

CHAPTER 5

Paul Condemns Spiritual Pride

I can hardly believe the report about the sexual immorality going on among you, something so evil that even the pagans don't do it. I am told that you have a man in your church who is living in sin with his father's wife. [2]And you are so proud of yourselves! Why aren't you mourning in sorrow and shame? And why haven't you removed this man from your fellowship?

[3]Even though I am not there with you in person, I am with you in the Spirit.* Concerning the one who has done this, I have already passed judgment [4]in the name of the Lord Jesus. You are to call a meeting of the church,*

I BELIEVE when the Lord comes, he will bring my deepest secrets to light and will reveal my private motives. (4:5)

I RESPOND gently when evil things are said about me. (4:13)

See Timothy's profile (page 1373) at 1 Timothy 4:12.

I LIVE by God's power and do not merely speak with empty words. (4:20)

I BELIEVE the open sexual immorality of a church member is cause for deep mourning, not for pride! (5:2)

4:6a Greek *Brothers.* 4:6b Or *You must learn not to go beyond "what is written,"* so that. 5:3 Or *in spirit.*
5:4 Or *In the name of the Lord Jesus, you are to call a meeting of the church.*

and I will be there in spirit, and the power of the Lord Jesus will be with you as you meet. ⁵Then you must cast this man out of the church and into Satan's hands, so that his sinful nature will be destroyed* and he himself* will be saved when the Lord returns.

⁶How terrible that you should boast about your spirituality, and yet you let this sort of thing go on. Don't you realize that if even one person is allowed to go on sinning, soon all will be affected? ⁷Remove this wicked person from among you so that you can stay pure.* Christ, our Passover Lamb, has been sacrificed for us. ⁸So let us celebrate the festival, not by eating the old bread* of wickedness and evil, but by eating the new bread* of purity and truth.

⁹When I wrote to you before, I told you not to associate with people who indulge in sexual sin. ¹⁰But I wasn't talking about unbelievers who indulge in sexual sin, or who are greedy or are swindlers or idol worshipers. You would have to leave this world to avoid people like that. ¹¹What I meant was that you are not to associate with anyone who claims to be a Christian* yet indulges in sexual sin, or is greedy, or worships idols, or is abusive, or a drunkard, or a swindler. Don't even eat with such people.

¹²It isn't my responsibility to judge outsiders, but it certainly is your job to judge those inside the church who are sinning in these ways. ¹³God will judge those on the outside; but as the Scriptures say, "You must remove the evil person from among you."*

CHAPTER 6

Avoiding Lawsuits with Christians

When you have something against another Christian, why do you file a lawsuit and ask a secular court to decide the matter, instead of taking it to other Christians to decide who is right? ²Don't you know that someday we Christians are going to judge the world? And since you are going to judge the world, can't you decide these little things among yourselves? ³Don't you realize that we Christians will judge angels? So you should surely be able to resolve ordinary disagreements here on earth. ⁴If you have legal disputes about such matters, why do you go to outside judges who are not respected by the church? ⁵I am saying this to shame you. Isn't there anyone in all the church who is wise enough to decide these arguments? ⁶But instead, one Christian* sues another—right in front of unbelievers!

⁷To have such lawsuits at all is a real defeat for you. Why not just accept the injustice and leave it at that? Why not let yourselves be cheated? ⁸But instead, you yourselves are the ones who do wrong and cheat even your own Christian brothers and sisters.*

Avoiding Sexual Sin

⁹Don't you know that those who do wrong will have no share in the Kingdom of God? Don't fool yourselves. Those who indulge in sexual sin, who are idol worshipers, adulterers, male prostitutes, homosexuals, ¹⁰thieves, greedy people, drunkards, abusers, and swindlers—none of these will have a share in the Kingdom of God. ¹¹There was a time when some of you were just like that, but now your sins have been washed away,* and you have been set apart for God. You have been made right with God because of what the Lord Jesus Christ and the Spirit of our God have done for you.

¹²You may say, "I am allowed to do anything." But I reply, "Not everything is good for you." And even though "I am allowed to do anything," I must not become a slave to anything. ¹³You say, "Food is for the stomach, and the

I DO NOT ASSOCIATE with anyone who claims to be a Christian and yet indulges in a blatantly sinful lifestyle. (5:11)

I BELIEVE it is not yet my responsibility to judge those outside the church. (5:12)

I BELIEVE someday Christians will judge the world. (6:2)

I WOULD RATHER ACCEPT an injustice than sue another Christian in a human court of law. (6:7)

I HAVE BEEN WASHED, set apart, and made right with God because of what the Lord Jesus Christ and the Holy Spirit have done for me. (6:11)

5:5a Or *so that he will die*; Greek reads *for the destruction of the flesh.*   5:5b Greek *and the spirit.*   5:6-7 Greek *Don't you realize that even a little leaven spreads quickly through the whole batch of dough? ⁷Purge out the old leaven so that you can be a new batch of dough, just as you are already unleavened.*   5:8a Greek *not with old leaven.*
5:8b Greek *but with unleavened [bread].*   5:11 Greek *a brother.*   5:13 Deut 17:7.   6:6 Greek *one brother.*
6:8 Greek *brothers.*   6:11 Or *you have been cleansed.*

stomach is for food." This is true, though someday God will do away with both of them. But our bodies were not made for sexual immorality. They were made for the Lord, and the Lord cares about our bodies. ¹⁴And God will raise our bodies from the dead by his marvelous power, just as he raised our Lord from the dead. ¹⁵Don't you realize that your bodies are actually parts of Christ? Should a man take his body, which belongs to Christ, and join it to a prostitute? Never! ¹⁶And don't you know that if a man joins himself to a prostitute, he becomes one body with her? For the Scriptures say, "The two are united into one."* ¹⁷But the person who is joined to the Lord becomes one spirit with him.

¹⁸Run away from sexual sin! No other sin so clearly affects the body as this one does. For sexual immorality is a sin against your own body. ¹⁹Or don't you know that your body is the temple of the Holy Spirit, who lives in you and was given to you by God? You do not belong to yourself, ²⁰for God bought you with a high price. So you must honor God with your body.

CHAPTER 7

Instruction on Marriage

Now about the questions you asked in your letter. Yes, it is good to live a celibate life. ²But because there is so much sexual immorality, each man should have his own wife, and each woman should have her own husband.

³The husband should not deprive his wife of sexual intimacy, which is her right as a married woman, nor should the wife deprive her husband. ⁴The wife gives authority over her body to her husband, and the husband also gives authority over his body to his wife. ⁵So do not deprive each other of sexual relations. The only exception to this rule would be the agreement of both husband and wife to refrain from sexual intimacy for a limited time, so they can give themselves more completely to prayer. Afterward they should come together again so that Satan won't be able to tempt them because of their lack of self-control. ⁶This is only my suggestion. It's not meant to be an absolute rule. ⁷I wish everyone could get along without marrying, just as I do. But we are not all the same. God gives some the gift of marriage, and to others he gives the gift of singleness.

⁸Now I say to those who aren't married and to widows—it's better to stay unmarried, just as I am. ⁹But if they can't control themselves, they should go ahead and marry. It's better to marry than to burn with lust.

¹⁰Now, for those who are married I have a command that comes not from me, but from the Lord.* A wife must not leave her husband. ¹¹But if she does leave him, let her remain single or else go back to him. And the husband must not leave his wife.

¹²Now, I will speak to the rest of you, though I do not have a direct command from the Lord. If a Christian man* has a wife who is an unbeliever and she is willing to continue living with him, he must not leave her. ¹³And if a Christian woman has a husband who is an unbeliever, and he is willing to continue living with her, she must not leave him. ¹⁴For the Christian wife brings holiness to her marriage, and the Christian husband brings holiness to his marriage. Otherwise, your children would not have a godly influence, but now they are set apart for him. ¹⁵(But if the husband or wife who isn't a Christian insists on leaving, let them go. In such cases the Christian husband or wife is not required to stay with them, for God wants his children to live in peace.) ¹⁶You wives must remember that your husbands might be converted because of you. And you husbands must remember that your wives might be converted because of you.

¹⁷You must accept whatever situation the Lord has put you in, and continue

I BELIEVE God will raise my body from the dead by his marvelous power, just as he raised the Lord Jesus Christ from the dead. (6:14)

I HONOR God with my body, which is a temple of the Holy Spirit, who lives in me. (6:19)

I BELIEVE God gives some the gift of marriage, and to others he gives the gift of singleness. (7:7)

I BELIEVE a married person who leaves his or her spouse should remain single or else go back to his or her spouse. (7:11)

I ACCEPT whatever situation the Lord has put me in. (7:17)

6:16 Gen 2:24.   7:10 See Matt 5:32; 19:9; Mark 10:11-12; Luke 16:18.   7:12 Greek *a brother*.

on as you were when God first called you. This is my rule for all the churches. [18]For instance, a man who was circumcised before he became a believer should not try to reverse it. And the man who was uncircumcised when he became a believer should not be circumcised now. [19]For it makes no difference whether or not a man has been circumcised. The important thing is to keep God's commandments.

[20]You should continue on as you were when God called you. [21]Are you a slave? Don't let that worry you—but if you get a chance to be free, take it. [22]And remember, if you were a slave when the Lord called you, the Lord has now set you free from the awful power of sin. And if you were free when the Lord called you, you are now a slave of Christ. [23]God purchased you at a high price. Don't be enslaved by the world.* [24]So, dear brothers and sisters,* whatever situation you were in when you became a believer, stay there in your new relationship with God.

[25]Now, about the young women who are not yet married. I do not have a command from the Lord for them. But the Lord in his kindness has given me wisdom that can be trusted, and I will share it with you. [26]Because of the present crisis,* I think it is best to remain just as you are. [27]If you have a wife, do not end the marriage. If you do not have a wife, do not get married. [28]But if you do get married, it is not a sin. And if a young woman gets married, it is not a sin. However, I am trying to spare you the extra problems that come with marriage.

[29]Now let me say this, dear brothers and sisters: The time that remains is very short, so husbands should not let marriage be their major concern. [30]Happiness or sadness or wealth should not keep anyone from doing God's work. [31]Those in frequent contact with the things of the world should make good use of them without becoming attached to them, for this world and all it contains will pass away. [32]In everything you do, I want you to be free from the concerns of this life. An unmarried man can spend his time doing the Lord's work and thinking how to please him. [33]But a married man can't do that so well. He has to think about his earthly responsibilities and how to please his wife. [34]His interests are divided. In the same way, a woman who is no longer married or has never been married can be more devoted to the Lord in body and in spirit, while the married woman must be concerned about her earthly responsibilities and how to please her husband.

[35]I am saying this for your benefit, not to place restrictions on you. I want you to do whatever will help you serve the Lord best, with as few distractions as possible. [36]But if a man thinks he ought to marry his fiancée because he has trouble controlling his passions and time is passing, it is all right; it is not a sin. Let them marry. [37]But if he has decided firmly not to marry and there is no urgency and he can control his passion, he does well not to marry. [38]So the person who marries does well, and the person who doesn't marry does even better.

[39]A wife is married to her husband as long as he lives. If her husband dies, she is free to marry whomever she wishes, but this must be a marriage acceptable to the Lord.* [40]But in my opinion it will be better for her if she doesn't marry again, and I think I am giving you counsel from God's Spirit when I say this.

CHAPTER 8

Food Sacrificed to Idols

Now let's talk about food that has been sacrificed to idols. You think that everyone should agree with your perfect knowledge. While knowledge may make us feel important, it is love that really builds up the church. [2]Anyone

---

I OBEY God's commands. (7:19)

I AM a slave of Jesus Christ. (7:22)

I DO NOT LET happiness or sadness or wealth or marital status keep me from obeying God and serving him. (7:30)

I DO whatever will help me serve the Lord best, with as few distractions as possible. (7:35)

I BELIEVE a Christian should marry someone who is acceptable to the Lord—another growing, committed believer. (7:39)

I BELIEVE love is what really builds up the church. (8:1)

7:23 Greek *don't become slaves of people.*   7:24 Greek *brothers;* also in 7:29.   7:26 Or *pressures of life.*
7:39 Or *but only to a Christian;* Greek reads *but only in the Lord.*

who claims to know all the answers doesn't really know very much. [3]But the person who loves God is the one God knows and cares for.

[4]So now, what about it? Should we eat meat that has been sacrificed to idols? Well, we all know that an idol is not really a god and that there is only one God and no other. [5]According to some people, there are many so-called gods and many lords, both in heaven and on earth. [6]But we know that there is only one God, the Father, who created everything, and we exist for him. And there is only one Lord, Jesus Christ, through whom God made everything and through whom we have been given life.

[7]However, not all Christians realize this. Some are accustomed to thinking of idols as being real, so when they eat food that has been offered to idols, they think of it as the worship of real gods, and their weak consciences are violated. [8]It's true that we can't win God's approval by what we eat. We don't miss out on anything if we don't eat it, and we don't gain anything if we do. [9]But you must be careful with this freedom of yours. Do not cause a brother or sister with a weaker conscience to stumble.

[10]You see, this is what can happen: Weak Christians who think it is wrong to eat this food will see you eating in the temple of an idol. You know there's nothing wrong with it, but they will be encouraged to violate their conscience by eating food that has been dedicated to the idol. [11]So because of your superior knowledge, a weak Christian,* for whom Christ died, will be destroyed. [12]And you are sinning against Christ when you sin against other Christians* by encouraging them to do something they believe is wrong. [13]If what I eat is going to make another Christian sin, I will never eat meat again as long as I live—for I don't want to make another Christian stumble.

CHAPTER 9

Paul Gives Up His Rights

Do I not have as much freedom as anyone else?* Am I not an apostle? Haven't I seen Jesus our Lord with my own eyes? Isn't it because of my hard work that you are in the Lord? [2]Even if others think I am not an apostle, I certainly am to you, for you are living proof that I am the Lord's apostle.

[3]This is my answer to those who question my authority as an apostle.* [4]Don't we have the right to live in your homes and share your meals? [5]Don't we have the right to bring a Christian wife* along with us as the other disciples and the Lord's brothers and Peter* do? [6]Or is it only Barnabas and I who have to work to support ourselves? [7]What soldier has to pay his own expenses? And have you ever heard of a farmer who harvests his crop and doesn't have the right to eat some of it? What shepherd takes care of a flock of sheep and isn't allowed to drink some of the milk? [8]And this isn't merely human opinion. Doesn't God's law say the same thing? [9]For the law of Moses says, "Do not keep an ox from eating as it treads out the grain."* Do you suppose God was thinking only about oxen when he said this? [10]Wasn't he also speaking to us? Of course he was. Just as farm workers who plow fields and thresh the grain expect a share of the harvest, Christian workers should be paid by those they serve.

[11]We have planted good spiritual seed among you. Is it too much to ask, in return, for mere food and clothing? [12]If you support others who preach to you, shouldn't we have an even greater right to be supported? Yet we have never used this right. We would rather put up with anything than put an obstacle in the way of the Good News about Christ.

[13]Don't you know that those who work in the Temple get their meals from the food brought to the Temple as offerings? And those who serve at the altar get a share of the sacrificial offerings. [14]In the same way, the Lord gave orders

I BELIEVE there is only one God and that idols are not really gods. (8:4)

I BELIEVE I cannot win God's approval by what I eat. (8:8)

I DO NOT ENCOURAGE another Christian to do something he or she believes is wrong. (8:12)

See Peter's profile (page 1111) at Matthew 26:75.

See Barnabas's profile (page 1253) at Acts 11:23.

See Moses' profile (page 73) at Exodus 5:1.

I BELIEVE Christian workers are entitled to be paid by those they serve. (9:10)

I WOULD RATHER PUT UP with anything than put an obstacle in the way of the Good News about Jesus Christ. (9:12)

8:11 Greek *brother;* also in 8:13.   8:12 Greek *brothers.*   9:1 Greek *Am I not free?*   9:3 Greek *those who examine me.*   9:5a Greek *a sister, a wife.*   9:5b Greek *Cephas.*   9:9 Deut 25:4.

that those who preach the Good News should be supported by those who benefit from it. [15]Yet I have never used any of these rights. And I am not writing this to suggest that I would like to start now. In fact, I would rather die than lose my distinction of preaching without charge. [16]For preaching the Good News is not something I can boast about. I am compelled by God to do it. How terrible for me if I didn't do it!

[17]If I were doing this of my own free will, then I would deserve payment. But God has chosen me and given me this sacred trust, and I have no choice. [18]What then is my pay? It is the satisfaction I get from preaching the Good News without expense to anyone, never demanding my rights as a preacher.

[19]This means I am not bound to obey people just because they pay me, yet I have become a servant of everyone so that I can bring them to Christ. [20]When I am with the Jews, I become one of them so that I can bring them to Christ. When I am with those who follow the Jewish laws, I do the same, even though I am not subject to the law, so that I can bring them to Christ. [21]When I am with the Gentiles who do not have the Jewish law,* I fit in with them as much as I can. In this way, I gain their confidence and bring them to Christ. But I do not discard the law of God; I obey the law of Christ.

[22]When I am with those who are oppressed, I share their oppression so that I might bring them to Christ. Yes, I try to find common ground with everyone so that I might bring them to Christ. [23]I do all this to spread the Good News, and in doing so I enjoy its blessings.

[24]Remember that in a race everyone runs, but only one person gets the prize. You also must run in such a way that you will win. [25]All athletes practice strict self-control. They do it to win a prize that will fade away, but we do it for an eternal prize. [26]So I run straight to the goal with purpose in every step. I am not like a boxer who misses his punches.* [27]I discipline my body like an athlete, training it to do what it should. Otherwise, I fear that after preaching to others I myself might be disqualified.

CHAPTER 10

Warnings against Idolatry

I don't want you to forget, dear brothers and sisters,* what happened to our ancestors in the wilderness long ago. God guided all of them by sending a cloud that moved along ahead of them, and he brought them all safely through the waters of the sea on dry ground. [2]As followers of Moses, they were all baptized in the cloud and the sea. [3]And all of them ate the same miraculous* food, [4]and all of them drank the same miraculous water. For they all drank from the miraculous rock that traveled with them, and that rock was Christ. [5]Yet after all this, God was not pleased with most of them, and he destroyed them in the wilderness.

[6]These events happened as a warning to us, so that we would not crave evil things as they did [7]or worship idols as some of them did. For the Scriptures say, "The people celebrated with feasting and drinking, and they indulged themselves in pagan revelry."* [8]And we must not engage in sexual immorality as some of them did, causing 23,000 of them to die in one day. [9]Nor should we put Christ* to the test, as some of them did and then died from snakebites. [10]And don't grumble as some of them did, for that is why God sent his angel of death to destroy them. [11]All these events happened to them as examples for us. They were written down to warn us, who live at the time when this age is drawing to a close.

[12]If you think you are standing strong, be careful, for you, too, may fall into the same sin. [13]But remember that the temptations that come into your life are no different from what others experience. And God is faithful. He will

---

I BECOME a servant of others so that I can bring them to Christ. (9:19)

I OBEY the law of Christ and do not discard the law of God. (9:21)

I TRY to find common ground with everyone so that I might bring them to Christ. (9:22)

I PRACTICE strict self-control, living with purpose in every step, in order to gain an eternal prize. (9:25)

See Moses' profile (page 73) at Exodus 5:1.

I DO NOT CRAVE evil things as the Israelites did on the way to the Promised Land. (10:6)

I HEED the examples recorded in the Old Testament. (10:11)

9:21 Greek *those without the law.*   9:26 Or *I am not just shadowboxing.*   10:1 Greek *brothers.*   10:3 Greek *spiritual;* also in 10:4.   10:7 Exod 32:6.   10:9 Some manuscripts read *the Lord.*

keep the temptation from becoming so strong that you can't stand up against it. When you are tempted, he will show you a way out so that you will not give in to it.

[14]So, my dear friends, flee from the worship of idols. [15]You are reasonable people. Decide for yourselves if what I am about to say is true. [16]When we bless the cup at the Lord's Table, aren't we sharing in the benefits of the blood of Christ? And when we break the loaf of bread, aren't we sharing in the benefits of the body of Christ? [17]And we all eat from one loaf, showing that we are one body. [18]And think about the nation of Israel; all who eat the sacrifices are united by that act.

[19]What am I trying to say? Am I saying that the idols to whom the pagans bring sacrifices are real gods and that these sacrifices are of some value? [20]No, not at all. What I am saying is that these sacrifices are offered to demons, not to God. And I don't want any of you to be partners with demons. [21]You cannot drink from the cup of the Lord and from the cup of demons, too. You cannot eat at the Lord's Table and at the table of demons, too. [22]What? Do you dare to rouse the Lord's jealousy as Israel did? Do you think we are stronger than he is?

[23]You say, "I am allowed to do anything"—but not everything is helpful. You say, "I am allowed to do anything"—but not everything is beneficial. [24]Don't think only of your own good. Think of other Christians and what is best for them.

[25]Here's what you should do. You may eat any meat that is sold in the marketplace. Don't ask whether or not it was offered to idols, and then your conscience won't be bothered. [26]For "the earth is the Lord's, and everything in it."*

[27]If someone who isn't a Christian asks you home for dinner, go ahead; accept the invitation if you want to. Eat whatever is offered to you and don't ask any questions about it. Your conscience should not be bothered by this. [28]But suppose someone warns you that this meat has been offered to an idol. Don't eat it, out of consideration for the conscience of the one who told you. [29]It might not be a matter of conscience for you, but it is for the other person.

Now, why should my freedom be limited by what someone else thinks? [30]If I can thank God for the food and enjoy it, why should I be condemned for eating it? [31]Whatever you eat or drink or whatever you do, you must do all for the glory of God. [32]Don't give offense to Jews or Gentiles or the church of God. [33]That is the plan I follow, too. I try to please everyone in everything I do. I don't just do what I like or what is best for me, but what is best for them so they may be saved.

CHAPTER 11

And you should follow my example, just as I follow Christ's.

Instructions for Public Worship

[2]I am so glad, dear friends, that you always keep me in your thoughts and you are following the Christian teaching I passed on to you. [3]But there is one thing I want you to know: A man is responsible to Christ, a woman is responsible to her husband, and Christ is responsible to God. [4]A man dishonors Christ* if he covers his head while praying or prophesying. [5]But a woman dishonors her husband* if she prays or prophesies without a covering on her head, for this is the same as shaving her head. [6]Yes, if she refuses to wear a head covering, she should cut off all her hair. And since it is shameful for a woman to have her hair cut or her head shaved, then she should wear a covering.* [7]A man should not wear anything on his head when worshiping, for man is God's glory, made in God's own image, but woman is the glory of man. [8]For the first man didn't come from woman, but the first

I BELIEVE God will always provide a way for me to escape from temptation and keep it from becoming so strong that I can't stand up against it. (10:13)

I BELIEVE that partaking of the bread and the cup with other believers demonstrates our unity in Jesus Christ. (10:17)

I WOULD NOT DARE to arouse the Lord's jealousy by practicing rituals that demonstrate loyalty to pagan beliefs. (10:22)

I THINK of other Christians and what is best for them regarding the way I live. (10:24)

I BELIEVE the earth is the Lord's and everything in it (Psalm 24:1). (10:26)

I EAT AND DRINK and do everything else for God's glory. (10:31)

I AM CAREFUL not to dishonor Jesus Christ, the church, or my spouse. (11:4)

See the profiles for Adam (page 5) and Eve (page 7) at Genesis 1:26 and Genesis 3:21.

10:26 Ps 24:1.   11:4 Greek his head.   11:5 Greek her head.   11:6 Or then she should have long hair.

woman came from man. [9]And man was not made for woman's benefit, but woman was made for man. [10]So a woman should wear a covering on her head as a sign of authority because the angels are watching.

[11]But in relationships among the Lord's people, women are not independent of men, and men are not independent of women. [12]For although the first woman came from man, all men have been born from women ever since, and everything comes from God.

[13]What do you think about this? Is it right for a woman to pray to God in public without covering her head? [14]Isn't it obvious that it's disgraceful for a man to have long hair? [15]And isn't it obvious that long hair is a woman's pride and joy? For it has been given to her as a covering. [16]But if anyone wants to argue about this, all I can say is that we have no other custom than this, and all the churches of God feel the same way about it.

Order at the Lord's Supper

[17]But now when I mention this next issue, I cannot praise you. For it sounds as if more harm than good is done when you meet together. [18]First of all, I hear that there are divisions among you when you meet as a church, and to some extent I believe it. [19]But, of course, there must be divisions among you so that those of you who are right will be recognized!

[20]It's not the Lord's Supper you are concerned about when you come together. [21]For I am told that some of you hurry to eat your own meal without sharing with others. As a result, some go hungry while others get drunk. [22]What? Is this really true? Don't you have your own homes for eating and drinking? Or do you really want to disgrace the church of God and shame the poor? What am I supposed to say about these things? Do you want me to praise you? Well, I certainly do not!

[23]For this is what the Lord himself said, and I pass it on to you just as I received it. On the night when he was betrayed, the Lord Jesus took a loaf of bread, [24]and when he had given thanks, he broke it and said, "This is my body, which is given* for you. Do this in remembrance of me." [25]In the same way, he took the cup of wine after supper, saying, "This cup is the new covenant between God and you, sealed by the shedding of my blood. Do this in remembrance of me as often as you drink it." [26]For every time you eat this bread and drink this cup, you are announcing the Lord's death until he comes again.

[27]So if anyone eats this bread or drinks this cup of the Lord unworthily, that person is guilty of sinning against the body and the blood of the Lord. [28]That is why you should examine yourself before eating the bread and drinking from the cup. [29]For if you eat the bread or drink the cup unworthily, not honoring the body of Christ,* you are eating and drinking God's judgment upon yourself. [30]That is why many of you are weak and sick and some have even died.

[31]But if we examine ourselves, we will not be examined by God and judged in this way. [32]But when we are judged and disciplined by the Lord, we will not be condemned with the world. [33]So, dear brothers and sisters,* when you gather for the Lord's Supper, wait for each other. [34]If you are really hungry, eat at home so you won't bring judgment upon yourselves when you meet together.

I'll give you instructions about the other matters after I arrive.

CHAPTER 12

Spiritual Gifts

And now, dear brothers and sisters,* I will write about the special abilities the Holy Spirit gives to each of us, for I must correct your misunderstandings about

---

I BELIEVE Christian husbands and wives need each other. (11:11)

I GRIEVE when divisions exist within a church. (11:18)

I AM CAREFUL not to disgrace the church or shame the poor. (11:22)

I TAKE the bread and the cup as the Lord Jesus Christ instructed. (11:23)

I EXAMINE my heart for unconfessed sins before taking the bread and the cup. (11:28)

11:24 Some manuscripts read *broken*. 11:29 Greek *the body*; some manuscripts read *the Lord's body*. 11:33 Greek *brothers*. 12:1 Greek *brothers*.

them. [2]You know that when you were still pagans you were led astray and swept along in worshiping speechless idols. [3]So I want you to know how to discern what is truly from God: No one speaking by the Spirit of God can curse Jesus, and no one is able to say, "Jesus is Lord," except by the Holy Spirit.

[4]Now there are different kinds of spiritual gifts, but it is the same Holy Spirit who is the source of them all. [5]There are different kinds of service in the church, but it is the same Lord we are serving. [6]There are different ways God works in our lives, but it is the same God who does the work through all of us. [7]A spiritual gift is given to each of us as a means of helping the entire church.

[8]To one person the Spirit gives the ability to give wise advice; to another he gives the gift of special knowledge. [9]The Spirit gives special faith to another, and to someone else he gives the power to heal the sick. [10]He gives one person the power to perform miracles, and to another the ability to prophesy. He gives someone else the ability to know whether it is really the Spirit of God or another spirit that is speaking. Still another person is given the ability to speak in unknown languages,* and another is given the ability to interpret what is being said. [11]It is the one and only Holy Spirit who distributes these gifts. He alone decides which gift each person should have.

One Body with Many Parts

[12]The human body has many parts, but the many parts make up only one body. So it is with the body of Christ. [13]Some of us are Jews, some are Gentiles, some are slaves, and some are free. But we have all been baptized into Christ's body by one Spirit, and we have all received the same Spirit.*

[14]Yes, the body has many different parts, not just one part. [15]If the foot says, "I am not a part of the body because I am not a hand," that does not make it any less a part of the body. [16]And if the ear says, "I am not part of the body because I am only an ear and not an eye," would that make it any less a part of the body? [17]Suppose the whole body were an eye—then how would you hear? Or if your whole body were just one big ear, how could you smell anything?

[18]But God made our bodies with many parts, and he has put each part just where he wants it. [19]What a strange thing a body would be if it had only one part! [20]Yes, there are many parts, but only one body. [21]The eye can never say to the hand, "I don't need you." The head can't say to the feet, "I don't need you."

[22]In fact, some of the parts that seem weakest and least important are really the most necessary. [23]And the parts we regard as less honorable are those we clothe with the greatest care. So we carefully protect from the eyes of others those parts that should not be seen, [24]while other parts do not require this special care. So God has put the body together in such a way that extra honor and care are given to those parts that have less dignity. [25]This makes for harmony among the members, so that all the members care for each other equally. [26]If one part suffers, all the parts suffer with it, and if one part is honored, all the parts are glad.

[27]Now all of you together are Christ's body, and each one of you is a separate and necessary part of it. [28]Here is a list of some of the members that God has placed in the body of Christ:

first are apostles,
second are prophets,
third are teachers,
then those who do miracles,
those who have the gift of healing,
those who can help others,
those who can get others to work together,
those who speak in unknown languages.

12:10 Or *in tongues;* also in 12:28, 30.   12:13 Greek *we were all given one Spirit to drink.*

I BELIEVE no one is truly able to say, "Jesus is Lord," except by the Holy Spirit. (12:3)

I BELIEVE the Holy Spirit gives spiritual gifts to individual Christians as a means of helping the entire church. (12:7)

I BELIEVE the Holy Spirit alone decides which gift each Christian should have. (12:11)

I BELIEVE all Christians have received the same Spirit (Romans 8:9). (12:13)

I NEED other Christians. (12:21)

I BELIEVE if one part of the church suffers, all the parts suffer with it. (12:26)

I BELIEVE no one spiritual gift has been given to every Christian. (12:29)

²⁹Is everyone an apostle? Of course not. Is everyone a prophet? No. Are all teachers? Does everyone have the power to do miracles? ³⁰Does everyone have the gift of healing? Of course not. Does God give all of us the ability to speak in unknown languages? Can everyone interpret unknown languages? No! ³¹And in any event, you should desire the most helpful gifts.

Love Is the Greatest
First, however, let me tell you about something else that is better than any of them!

CHAPTER 13

If I could speak in any language in heaven or on earth* but didn't love others, I would only be making meaningless noise like a loud gong or a clanging cymbal. ²If I had the gift of prophecy, and if I knew all the mysteries of the future and knew everything about everything, but didn't love others, what good would I be? And if I had the gift of faith so that I could speak to a mountain and make it move, without love I would be no good to anybody. ³If I gave everything I have to the poor and even sacrificed my body, I could boast about it;* but if I didn't love others, I would be of no value whatsoever.

I BELIEVE nothing in my life is of any value if I don't love others. (13:3)

I AM patient and kind, not jealous or boastful or proud. (13:4)

I DO NOT DEMAND my own way or keep records of when I've been wronged. (13:5)

⁴Love is patient and kind. Love is not jealous or boastful or proud ⁵or rude. Love does not demand its own way. Love is not irritable, and it keeps no record of when it has been wronged. ⁶It is never glad about injustice but rejoices whenever the truth wins out. ⁷Love never gives up, never loses faith, is always hopeful, and endures through every circumstance.

⁸Love will last forever, but prophecy and speaking in unknown languages* and special knowledge will all disappear. ⁹Now we know only a little, and even the gift of prophecy reveals little! ¹⁰But when the end comes, these special gifts will all disappear.

¹¹It's like this: When I was a child, I spoke and thought and reasoned as a child does. But when I grew up, I put away childish things. ¹²Now we see things imperfectly as in a poor mirror, but then we will see everything with perfect clarity.* All that I know now is partial and incomplete, but then I will know everything completely, just as God knows me now.

¹³There are three things that will endure—faith, hope, and love—and the greatest of these is love.

CHAPTER 14

The Gifts of Tongues and Prophecy
Let love be your highest goal, but also desire the special abilities the Spirit gives, especially the gift of prophecy. ²For if your gift is the ability to speak in tongues,* you will be talking to God but not to people, since they won't be able to understand you. You will be speaking by the power of the Spirit, but it will all be mysterious. ³But one who prophesies is helping others grow in the Lord, encouraging and comforting them. ⁴A person who speaks in tongues is strengthened personally in the Lord, but one who speaks a word of prophecy strengthens the entire church.

I HAVE MADE love my highest goal in life (Mark 12:28-31). (14:1)

⁵I wish you all had the gift of speaking in tongues, but even more I wish you were all able to prophesy. For prophecy is a greater and more useful gift than speaking in tongues, unless someone interprets what you are saying so that the whole church can get some good out of it.

⁶Dear brothers and sisters,* if I should come to you talking in an unknown language,* how would that help you? But if I bring you some revelation or some special knowledge or some prophecy or some teaching—that is what

13:1 Greek *in tongues of people and angels.* 13:3 Some manuscripts read *and even gave my body to be burned.* 13:8 Or *in tongues.* 13:12 Greek *see face to face.* 14:2 Or *in unknown languages;* also in 14:4, 5, 13, 14, 18, 22, 28, 39. 14:6a Greek *brothers;* also in 14:20, 26, 39. 14:6b Or *in tongues;* also in 14:19, 23, 26, 27.

will help you. [7]Even musical instruments like the flute or the harp, though they are lifeless, are examples of the need for speaking in plain language. For no one will recognize the melody unless the notes are played clearly. [8]And if the bugler doesn't sound a clear call, how will the soldiers know they are being called to battle? [9]And it's the same for you. If you talk to people in a language they don't understand, how will they know what you mean? You might as well be talking to an empty room.

[10]There are so many different languages in the world, and all are excellent for those who understand them, [11]but to me they mean nothing. I will not understand people who speak those languages, and they will not understand me. [12]Since you are so eager to have spiritual gifts, ask God for those that will be of real help to the whole church.

[13]So anyone who has the gift of speaking in tongues should pray also for the gift of interpretation in order to tell people plainly what has been said. [14]For if I pray in tongues, my spirit is praying, but I don't understand what I am saying.

[15]Well then, what shall I do? I will do both. I will pray in the spirit,* and I will pray in words I understand. I will sing in the spirit, and I will sing in words I understand. [16]For if you praise God only in the spirit, how can those who don't understand you praise God along with you? How can they join you in giving thanks when they don't understand what you are saying? [17]You will be giving thanks very nicely, no doubt, but it doesn't help the other people present.

[18]I thank God that I speak in tongues more than all of you. [19]But in a church meeting I would much rather speak five understandable words that will help others than ten thousand words in an unknown language.

[20]Dear brothers and sisters, don't be childish in your understanding of these things. Be innocent as babies when it comes to evil, but be mature and wise in understanding matters of this kind. [21]It is written in the Scriptures,*

> "I will speak to my own people
>   through unknown languages
>   and through the lips of foreigners.
> But even then, they will not listen to me,"*
>   says the Lord.

[22]So you see that speaking in tongues is a sign, not for believers, but for unbelievers; prophecy, however, is for the benefit of believers, not unbelievers. [23]Even so, if unbelievers or people who don't understand these things come into your meeting and hear everyone talking in an unknown language, they will think you are crazy. [24]But if all of you are prophesying, and unbelievers or people who don't understand these things come into your meeting, they will be convicted of sin, and they will be condemned by what you say. [25]As they listen, their secret thoughts will be laid bare, and they will fall down on their knees and worship God, declaring, "God is really here among you."

A Call to Orderly Worship

[26]Well, my brothers and sisters, let's summarize what I am saying. When you meet, one will sing, another will teach, another will tell some special revelation God has given, one will speak in an unknown language, while another will interpret what is said. But everything that is done must be useful to all and build them up in the Lord. [27]No more than two or three should speak in an unknown language. They must speak one at a time, and someone must be ready to interpret what they are saying. [28]But if no one is present who can interpret, they must be silent in your church meeting and speak in tongues to God privately.

I ASK God for spiritual gifts that will help other believers. (14:12)

I AM INNOCENT concerning evil but mature in understanding spiritual matters. (14:20)

I LONG for people to declare that "God is really here" in my church. (14:25)

I BELIEVE everything during a church service must be useful to all and build them up in the Lord. (14:26)

14:15 Or *in the Spirit;* also in 14:15b, 16.   14:21a Greek *in the law.*   14:21b Isa 28:11-12.

²⁹Let two or three prophesy, and let the others evaluate what is said. ³⁰But if someone is prophesying and another person receives a revelation from the Lord, the one who is speaking must stop. ³¹In this way, all who prophesy will have a turn to speak, one after the other, so that everyone will learn and be encouraged. ³²Remember that people who prophesy are in control of their spirit and can wait their turn. ³³For God is not a God of disorder but of peace, as in all the other churches.*

³⁴Women should be silent during the church meetings. It is not proper for them to speak. They should be submissive, just as the law says. ³⁵If they have any questions to ask, let them ask their husbands at home, for it is improper for women to speak in church meetings.*

³⁶Do you think that the knowledge of God's word begins and ends with you Corinthians? Well, you are mistaken! ³⁷If you claim to be a prophet or think you are very spiritual, you should recognize that what I am saying is a command from the Lord himself. ³⁸But if you do not recognize this, you will not be recognized.*

³⁹So, dear brothers and sisters, be eager to prophesy, and don't forbid speaking in tongues. ⁴⁰But be sure that everything is done properly and in order.

CHAPTER 15

The Resurrection of Christ

Now let me remind you, dear brothers and sisters,* of the Good News I preached to you before. You welcomed it then and still do now, for your faith is built on this wonderful message. ²And it is this Good News that saves you if you firmly believe it—unless, of course, you believed something that was never true in the first place.

³I passed on to you what was most important and what had also been passed on to me—that Christ died for our sins, just as the Scriptures said. ⁴He was buried, and he was raised from the dead on the third day, as the Scriptures said. ⁵He was seen by Peter* and then by the twelve apostles. ⁶After that, he was seen by more than five hundred of his followers* at one time, most of whom are still alive, though some have died by now. ⁷Then he was seen by James and later by all the apostles. ⁸Last of all, I saw him, too, long after the others, as though I had been born at the wrong time. ⁹For I am the least of all the apostles, and I am not worthy to be called an apostle after the way I persecuted the church of God.

¹⁰But whatever I am now, it is all because God poured out his special favor on me—and not without results. For I have worked harder than all the other apostles, yet it was not I but God who was working through me by his grace. ¹¹So it makes no difference whether I preach or they preach. The important thing is that you believed what we preached to you.

The Resurrection of the Dead

¹²But tell me this—since we preach that Christ rose from the dead, why are some of you saying there will be no resurrection of the dead? ¹³For if there is no resurrection of the dead, then Christ has not been raised either. ¹⁴And if Christ was not raised, then all our preaching is useless, and your trust in God is useless. ¹⁵And we apostles would all be lying about God, for we have said that God raised Christ from the grave, but that can't be true if there is no resurrection of the dead. ¹⁶If there is no resurrection of the dead, then Christ has not been raised. ¹⁷And if Christ has not been raised, then your faith is useless, and you are still under condemnation for your sins. ¹⁸In that case, all

---

I BELIEVE God is a God of peace, not of disorder. (14:33)

I RECOGNIZE that others have an understanding of God's Word that I can learn from. (14:37)

I HAVE BUILT my faith on the wonderful message of salvation—the Good News of Jesus Christ. (15:1)

I BELIEVE Jesus Christ died for my sins, was buried, and was raised from the dead on the third day, just as the Old Testament predicted. (15:4)

See Peter's profile (page 1111) at Matthew 26:75.

See James's profile (page 1407) at James 2:18.

I BELIEVE God raised Christ from the grave. (15:15)

14:33 The phrase *as in all the other churches* could be joined to the beginning of 14:34.   14:35 Some manuscripts place verses 34-35 after 14:40.   14:38 Some manuscripts read *If you are ignorant of this, stay in your ignorance.*
15:1 Greek *brothers;* also in 15:31, 50, 58.   15:5 Greek *Cephas.*   15:6 Greek *the brothers.*

who have died believing in Christ have perished! ¹⁹And if we have hope in Christ only for this life, we are the most miserable people in the world.

²⁰But the fact is that Christ has been raised from the dead. He has become the first of a great harvest of those who will be raised to life again.

²¹So you see, just as death came into the world through a man, Adam, now the resurrection from the dead has begun through another man, Christ. ²²Everyone dies because all of us are related to Adam, the first man. But all who are related to Christ, the other man, will be given new life. ²³But there is an order to this resurrection: Christ was raised first; then when Christ comes back, all his people will be raised.

²⁴After that the end will come, when he will turn the Kingdom over to God the Father, having put down all enemies of every kind.* ²⁵For Christ must reign until he humbles all his enemies beneath his feet. ²⁶And the last enemy to be destroyed is death. ²⁷For the Scriptures say, "God has given him authority over all things."* (Of course, when it says "authority over all things," it does not include God himself, who gave Christ his authority.) ²⁸Then, when he has conquered all things, the Son will present himself to God, so that God, who gave his Son authority over all things, will be utterly supreme over everything everywhere.

²⁹If the dead will not be raised, then what point is there in people being baptized for those who are dead? Why do it unless the dead will someday rise again?

³⁰And why should we ourselves be continually risking our lives, facing death hour by hour? ³¹For I swear, dear brothers and sisters, I face death daily. This is as certain as my pride in what the Lord Jesus Christ has done in you. ³²And what value was there in fighting wild beasts—those men of Ephesus*—if there will be no resurrection from the dead? If there is no resurrection,

> "Let's feast and get drunk,
>   for tomorrow we die!"*

³³Don't be fooled by those who say such things, for "bad company corrupts good character." ³⁴Come to your senses and stop sinning. For to your shame I say that some of you don't even know God.

The Resurrection Body

³⁵But someone may ask, "How will the dead be raised? What kind of bodies will they have?" ³⁶What a foolish question! When you put a seed into the ground, it doesn't grow into a plant unless it dies first. ³⁷And what you put in the ground is not the plant that will grow, but only a dry little seed of wheat or whatever it is you are planting. ³⁸Then God gives it a new body—just the kind he wants it to have. A different kind of plant grows from each kind of seed. ³⁹And just as there are different kinds of seeds and plants, so also there are different kinds of flesh—whether of humans, animals, birds, or fish.

⁴⁰There are bodies in the heavens, and there are bodies on earth. The glory of the heavenly bodies is different from the beauty of the earthly bodies. ⁴¹The sun has one kind of glory, while the moon and stars each have another kind. And even the stars differ from each other in their beauty and brightness.

⁴²It is the same way for the resurrection of the dead. Our earthly bodies, which die and decay, will be different when they are resurrected, for they will never die. ⁴³Our bodies now disappoint us, but when they are raised, they will be full of glory. They are weak now, but when they are raised, they will be full of power. ⁴⁴ They are natural human bodies now, but when they are

I BELIEVE Jesus Christ became the first of a great harvest of those who will be raised from the dead. (15:20)

See Adam's profile (page 5) at Genesis 1:26.

I BELIEVE everyone dies because all of us are related to Adam, the first man. (15:22)

I BELIEVE when Christ comes back, all his people will be raised from the dead. (15:23)

I BELIEVE that even death will be conquered when Christ comes back (Revelation 20:14; 21:4). (15:26)

I DO NOT LIVE foolishly, as if there were no resurrection. (15:32)

I DO NOT KEEP close company with those whose behavior corrupts good morals. (15:33)

I BELIEVE my resurrected body will be full of power and glory and will never die. (15:43)

15:24 Greek *every ruler and every authority and power.*   15:27 Ps 8:6.   15:32a Greek *fighting wild beasts in Ephesus.*
15:32b Isa 22:13.

raised, they will be spiritual bodies. For just as there are natural bodies, so also there are spiritual bodies.

⁴⁵The Scriptures tell us, "The first man, Adam, became a living person."* But the last Adam—that is, Christ—is a life-giving Spirit. ⁴⁶What came first was the natural body, then the spiritual body comes later. ⁴⁷Adam, the first man, was made from the dust of the earth, while Christ, the second man, came from heaven. ⁴⁸Every human being has an earthly body just like Adam's, but our heavenly bodies will be just like Christ's. ⁴⁹Just as we are now like Adam, the man of the earth, so we will someday be like Christ, the man from heaven.

⁵⁰What I am saying, dear brothers and sisters, is that flesh and blood cannot inherit the Kingdom of God. These perishable bodies of ours are not able to live forever.

⁵¹But let me tell you a wonderful secret God has revealed to us. Not all of us will die, but we will all be transformed. ⁵²It will happen in a moment, in the blinking of an eye, when the last trumpet is blown. For when the trumpet sounds, the Christians who have died* will be raised with transformed bodies. And then we who are living will be transformed so that we will never die. ⁵³For our perishable earthly bodies must be transformed into heavenly bodies that will never die.

⁵⁴When this happens—when our perishable earthly bodies have been transformed into heavenly bodies that will never die—then at last the Scriptures will come true:

"Death is swallowed up in victory.*
⁵⁵ O death, where is your victory?
O death, where is your sting?"*

⁵⁶For sin is the sting that results in death, and the law gives sin its power. ⁵⁷How we thank God, who gives us victory over sin and death through Jesus Christ our Lord!

⁵⁸So, my dear brothers and sisters, be strong and steady, always enthusiastic about the Lord's work, for you know that nothing you do for the Lord is ever useless.

CHAPTER 16

The Collection for Jerusalem

Now about the money being collected for the Christians in Jerusalem: You should follow the same procedures I gave to the churches in Galatia. ²On every Lord's Day,* each of you should put aside some amount of money in relation to what you have earned and save it for this offering. Don't wait until I get there and then try to collect it all at once. ³When I come I will write letters of recommendation for the messengers you choose to deliver your gift to Jerusalem. ⁴And if it seems appropriate for me also to go along, then we can travel together.

Paul's Final Instructions

⁵I am coming to visit you after I have been to Macedonia, for I am planning to travel through Macedonia. ⁶It could be that I will stay awhile with you, perhaps all winter, and then you can send me on my way to the next destination. ⁷This time I don't want to make just a short visit and then go right on. I want to come and stay awhile, if the Lord will let me. ⁸In the meantime, I will be staying here at Ephesus until the Festival of Pentecost, ⁹for there is a wide-open door for a great work here, and many people are responding. But there are many who oppose me.

15:45 Gen 2:7. 15:52 Greek *the dead*. 15:54 Isa 25:8. 15:55 Hos 13:14. 16:2 Greek *every first day of the week*.

Margin notes:

I BELIEVE someday I will have a heavenly body like Jesus Christ's resurrected body. (15:49)

I BELIEVE someday the body of every Christian will be transformed into a heavenly body. (15:54)

I AM strong and steady and always enthusiastic about the Lord's work, for I know that nothing I do for the Lord is ever useless. (15:58)

I PLAN for consistent giving to help other Christians. (16:2)

[10]When Timothy comes, treat him with respect. He is doing the Lord's work, just as I am. [11]Don't let anyone despise him. Send him on his way with your blessings when he returns to me. I am looking forward to seeing him soon, along with the other brothers.

[12]Now about our brother Apollos—I urged him to join the other brothers when they visit you, but he was not willing to come right now. He will be seeing you later, when the time is right.

[13]Be on guard. Stand true to what you believe. Be courageous. Be strong. [14]And everything you do must be done with love.

[15]You know that Stephanas and his household were the first to become Christians in Greece,* and they are spending their lives in service to other Christians. I urge you, dear brothers and sisters,* [16]to respect them fully and others like them who serve with such real devotion. [17]I am so glad that Stephanas, Fortunatus, and Achaicus have come here. They have been making up for the help you weren't here to give me. [18]They have been a wonderful encouragement to me, as they have been to you, too. You must give proper honor to all who serve so well.

Paul's Final Greetings

[19]The churches here in the province of Asia* greet you heartily in the Lord, along with Aquila and Priscilla and all the others who gather in their home for church meetings. [20]All the brothers and sisters here have asked me to greet you for them. Greet each other in Christian love.*

[21]Here is my greeting, which I write with my own hand—PAUL.

[22]If anyone does not love the Lord, that person is cursed. Our Lord, come!*

[23]May the grace of the Lord Jesus be with you.

[24]My love to all of you in Christ Jesus.*

16:15a Greek *were the firstfruits in Achaia*, the southern region of the Greek peninsula.　16:15b Greek *brothers*; also in 16:20.　16:19 *Asia* was a Roman province in what is now western Turkey.　16:20 Greek *with a sacred kiss*.　16:22 From Aramaic, *Marana tha*.　16:24 Some manuscripts add *Amen*.

I SHOW respect to anyone who is doing the Lord's work, no matter what his or her age or social standing. (16:10)

See Timothy's profile (page 1373) at 1 Timothy 4:12.

I STAND TRUE to what I believe with courage and strength. (16:13)

I DO everything with love. (16:14)

I AM SPENDING my life in service to other Christians. (16:15)

I GIVE proper honor to other Christians who serve well. (16:18)

See the profile of Priscilla and Aquila (page 1265) at Acts 18:26.

See Paul's profile (page 1333) at Galatians 2:5.

2 CORINTHIANS

THIS THIRD New Testament letter contrasts the authority of Paul and false teachers who had set up themselves as "super apostles."

In chapters 1–7, Paul talks about how he almost died, how his plans had changed, how much he cared about the church in Corinth, and how carefully he proclaimed the message of Good News—which is so much better than the old covenant. He then elaborates on his severe trials, on the sure hope of heaven, on our obligations as God's ambassadors, and on the need for repentance from sin.

In chapters 8–9, Paul urges the believers in Corinth to fulfill their promise to take up a generous offering for the persecuted believers in Jerusalem.

In chapters 10–13, Paul contrasts his authority with the claims of false teachers who had infiltrated the church, describes his credentials as an apostle, reminds them of his plans to visit them again, and closes with a final challenge.

Famous verses in 2 Corinthians include

- ❍ "He [God] comforts us in all our troubles so that we can comfort others" (1:4)
- ❍ "Our only power and success come from God" (3:5)
- ❍ "Though our bodies are dying, our spirits are being renewed every day" (4:16)
- ❍ "For we must all stand before Christ to be judged. We will each receive whatever we deserve" (5:10)
- ❍ "Those who become Christians become new persons. They are not the same anymore, for the old life is gone. A new life has begun!" (5:17)
- ❍ "We are Christ's ambassadors" (5:20)
- ❍ "Today is the day of salvation" (6:2)
- ❍ "Don't team up with those who are unbelievers" (6:14)
- ❍ "God loves the person who gives cheerfully" (9:7)
- ❍ "And God will generously provide all you need" (9:8)
- ❍ "We use God's mighty weapons, not mere worldly weapons, to knock down the Devil's strongholds" (10:4)
- ❍ "Each time he [the Lord] said, 'My gracious favor is all you need. My power works best in your weakness'" (12:9)
- ❍ "Examine yourselves to see if your faith is really genuine" (13:5)

CHAPTER 1

Greetings from Paul

This letter is from Paul, appointed by God to be an apostle of Christ Jesus, and from our dear brother Timothy.

We are writing to God's church in Corinth and to all the Christians throughout Greece.*

See the profiles for Paul (page 1333) and Timothy (page 1373) at Galatians 2:5 and 1 Timothy 4:12.

1:1 Greek *Achaia,* the southern region of the Greek peninsula.

²May God our Father and the Lord Jesus Christ give you his grace and peace.

God Offers Comfort to All

³All praise to the God and Father of our Lord Jesus Christ. He is the source* of every mercy and the God who comforts us. ⁴He comforts us in all our troubles so that we can comfort others. When others are troubled, we will be able to give them the same comfort God has given us. ⁵You can be sure that the more we suffer for Christ, the more God will shower us with his comfort through Christ. ⁶So when we are weighed down with troubles, it is for your benefit and salvation! For when God comforts us, it is so that we, in turn, can be an encouragement to you. Then you can patiently endure the same things we suffer. ⁷We are confident that as you share in suffering, you will also share God's comfort.

⁸I think you ought to know, dear brothers and sisters,* about the trouble we went through in the province of Asia. We were crushed and completely overwhelmed, and we thought we would never live through it. ⁹In fact, we expected to die. But as a result, we learned not to rely on ourselves, but on God who can raise the dead. ¹⁰And he did deliver us from mortal danger. And we are confident that he will continue to deliver us. ¹¹He will rescue us because you are helping by praying for us. As a result, many will give thanks to God because so many people's prayers for our safety have been answered.

Paul's Change of Plans

¹²We can say with confidence and a clear conscience that we have been honest* and sincere in all our dealings. We have depended on God's grace, not on our own earthly wisdom. That is how we have acted toward everyone, and especially toward you. ¹³My letters have been straightforward, and there is nothing written between the lines and nothing you can't understand. I hope someday you will fully understand us, ¹⁴even if you don't fully understand us now. Then on the day when our Lord Jesus comes back again, you will be proud of us in the same way we are proud of you.

¹⁵Since I was so sure of your understanding and trust, I wanted to give you a double blessing. ¹⁶I wanted to stop and see you on my way to Macedonia and again on my return trip. Then you could send me on my way to Judea.

¹⁷You may be asking why I changed my plan. Hadn't I made up my mind yet? Or am I like people of the world who say yes when they really mean no? ¹⁸As surely as God is true, I am not that sort of person. My yes means yes ¹⁹because Jesus Christ, the Son of God, never wavers between yes and no. He is the one whom Timothy, Silas,* and I preached to you, and he is the divine Yes—God's affirmation. ²⁰For all of God's promises have been fulfilled in him. That is why we say "Amen" when we give glory to God through Christ. ²¹It is God who gives us, along with you, the ability to stand firm for Christ.* He has commissioned us, ²²and he has identified us as his own by placing the Holy Spirit in our hearts as the first installment of everything he will give us.

²³Now I call upon God as my witness that I am telling the truth. The reason I didn't return to Corinth was to spare you from a severe rebuke. ²⁴But that does not mean we want to tell you exactly how to put your faith into practice.* We want to work together with you so you will be full of joy as you stand firm in your faith.

CHAPTER 2

So I said to myself, "No, I won't do it. I won't make them unhappy with another painful visit." ²For if I cause you pain and make you sad, who is going to make me glad? ³That is why I wrote as I did in my last letter, so that when I

I COMFORT others with the same comfort God gives me in all my troubles. (1:4)

I RELY on God when I am crushed and completely overwhelmed. (1:9)

I AM honest and sincere in all my dealings. (1:12)

I MEAN what I say and say what I mean, because that is what Jesus Christ does. (1:18)

I AM IDENTIFIED as God's own because God has placed his Holy Spirit in my heart. (1:22)

1:3 Greek *the Father.*   1:8 Greek *brothers.*   1:12 Some manuscripts read *holy.*   1:19 Greek *Silvanus.*
1:21 Or *who has identified us and you as genuine Christians.*   1:24 Greek *want to lord it over your faith.*

do come, I will not be made sad by the very ones who ought to give me the greatest joy. Surely you know that my happiness depends on your happiness. [4]How painful it was to write that letter! Heartbroken, I cried over it. I didn't want to hurt you, but I wanted you to know how very much I love you.

Forgiveness for the Sinner

[5]I am not overstating it when I say that the man who caused all the trouble hurt your entire church more than he hurt me. [6]He was punished enough when most of you were united in your judgment against him. [7]Now it is time to forgive him and comfort him. Otherwise he may become so discouraged that he won't be able to recover. [8]Now show him that you still love him.

[9]I wrote to you as I did to find out how far you would go in obeying me. [10]When you forgive this man, I forgive him, too. And when I forgive him (for whatever is to be forgiven), I do so with Christ's authority for your benefit, [11]so that Satan will not outsmart us. For we are very familiar with his evil schemes.

Ministers of the New Covenant

[12]Well, when I came to the city of Troas to preach the Good News of Christ, the Lord gave me tremendous opportunities. [13]But I couldn't rest because my dear brother Titus hadn't yet arrived with a report from you. So I said good-bye and went on to Macedonia to find him.

[14]But thanks be to God, who made us his captives and leads us along in Christ's triumphal procession. Now wherever we go he uses us to tell others about the Lord and to spread the Good News like a sweet perfume. [15]Our lives are a fragrance presented by Christ to God. But this fragrance is perceived differently by those being saved and by those perishing. [16]To those who are perishing we are a fearful smell of death and doom. But to those who are being saved we are a life-giving perfume. And who is adequate for such a task as this? [17]You see, we are not like those hucksters—and there are many of them—who preach just to make money. We preach God's message with sincerity and with Christ's authority. And we know that the God who sent us is watching us.

CHAPTER 3

Are we beginning again to tell you how good we are? Some people need to bring letters of recommendation with them or ask you to write letters of recommendation for them. [2]But the only letter of recommendation we need is you yourselves! Your lives are a letter written in our* hearts, and everyone can read it and recognize our good work among you. [3]Clearly, you are a letter from Christ prepared by us. It is written not with pen and ink, but with the Spirit of the living God. It is carved not on stone, but on human hearts.

[4]We are confident of all this because of our great trust in God through Christ. [5]It is not that we think we can do anything of lasting value by ourselves. Our only power and success come from God. [6]He is the one who has enabled us to represent his new covenant. This is a covenant, not of written laws, but of the Spirit. The old way ends in death; in the new way, the Holy Spirit gives life.

The Glory of the New Covenant

[7]That old system of law etched in stone led to death, yet it began with such glory that the people of Israel could not bear to look at Moses' face. For his face shone with the glory of God, even though the brightness was already fading away. [8]Shouldn't we expect far greater glory when the Holy Spirit is giving life? [9]If the old covenant, which brings condemnation, was glorious, how much more glorious is the new covenant, which makes us right with

3:2 Some manuscripts read *your*.

I AM HEARTBROKEN when I must confront other Christians with their sin and their need to change. (2:4)

I FORGIVE Christian brothers and sisters who sin against my church and then repent. (2:7)

See Titus's profile (page 1385) at Titus 1:5.

I THANK God, who made me a part of his kingdom and uses me to spread his Good News. (2:14)

I CAN DO something of lasting value only through the power and success that comes from God. (3:5)

See Moses' profile (page 73) at Exodus 5:1.

I BELIEVE the new covenant, which makes us right with God, is much more glorious than the old covenant under Moses. (3:9)

I AM BOLD for Jesus Christ because the glory of the new covenant will not fade away or be replaced. (3:12)

I BELIEVE only Jesus Christ can remove the veil that keeps people from understanding the truth. (3:14)

I BECOME more like the Lord and reflect more of his glory as he works within me. (3:18)

God! [10]In fact, that first glory was not glorious at all compared with the overwhelming glory of the new covenant. [11]So if the old covenant, which has been set aside, was full of glory, then the new covenant, which remains forever, has far greater glory.

[12]Since this new covenant gives us such confidence, we can be very bold. [13]We are not like Moses, who put a veil over his face so the people of Israel would not see the glory fading away. [14]But the people's minds were hardened, and even to this day whenever the old covenant is being read, a veil covers their minds so they cannot understand the truth. And this veil can be removed only by believing in Christ. [15]Yes, even today when they read Moses' writings, their hearts are covered with that veil, and they do not understand.

[16]But whenever anyone turns to the Lord, then the veil is taken away. [17]Now, the Lord is the Spirit, and wherever the Spirit of the Lord is, he gives freedom. [18]And all of us have had that veil removed so that we can be mirrors that brightly reflect* the glory of the Lord. And as the Spirit of the Lord works within us, we become more and more like him and reflect his glory even more.

CHAPTER 4

Treasure in Perishable Containers

And so, since God in his mercy has given us this wonderful ministry, we never give up. [2]We reject all shameful and underhanded methods. We do not try to trick anyone, and we do not distort the word of God. We tell the truth before God, and all who are honest know that.

[3]If the Good News we preach is veiled from anyone, it is a sign that they are perishing. [4]Satan, the god of this evil world, has blinded the minds of those who don't believe, so they are unable to see the glorious light of the Good News that is shining upon them. They don't understand the message we preach about the glory of Christ, who is the exact likeness of God.

I BELIEVE Satan has blinded the minds of unbelievers. (4:4)

In response to these affirmations, tell the Lord what you obey—or find easy to disobey.

I BELIEVE God put his glorious power in our weak bodies so everyone can see it is his, not ours. (4:7)

[5]We don't go around preaching about ourselves; we preach Christ Jesus, the Lord. All we say about ourselves is that we are your servants because of what Jesus has done for us. [6]For God, who said, "Let there be light in the darkness," has made us understand that this light is the brightness of the glory of God that is seen in the face of Jesus Christ.

[7]But this precious treasure—this light and power that now shine within us—is held in perishable containers, that is, in our weak bodies.* So everyone can see that our glorious power is from God and is not our own.

[8]We are pressed on every side by troubles, but we are not crushed and broken. We are perplexed, but we don't give up and quit. [9]We are hunted down, but God never abandons us. We get knocked down, but we get up again and keep going. [10]Through suffering, these bodies of ours constantly share in the death of Jesus so that the life of Jesus may also be seen in our bodies.

[11]Yes, we live under constant danger of death because we serve Jesus, so that the life of Jesus will be obvious in our dying bodies. [12]So we live in the face of death, but it has resulted in eternal life for you.

[13]But we continue to preach because we have the same kind of faith the psalmist had when he said, "I believed in God, and so I speak."* [14]We know that the same God who raised our Lord Jesus will also raise us with Jesus and present us to himself along with you. [15]All of these things are for your benefit. And as God's grace brings more and more people to Christ, there will be great thanksgiving, and God will receive more and more glory.

I BELIEVE God receives more and more glory as his grace brings more and more people to Christ. (4:15)

I BELIEVE my present troubles for Christ's sake will result in eternal glory. (4:17)

[16]That is why we never give up. Though our bodies are dying, our spirits are* being renewed every day. [17]For our present troubles are quite small and won't last very long. Yet they produce for us an immeasurably great glory that will last forever! [18]So we don't look at the troubles we can see right now;

3:18 Or *so that we can see in a mirror.* 4:7 Greek *But we have this treasure in earthen vessels.* 4:13 Ps 116:10.
4:16 Greek *our inner being is.*

rather, we look forward to what we have not yet seen. For the troubles we see will soon be over, but the joys to come will last forever.

CHAPTER 5

New Bodies

For we know that when this earthly tent we live in is taken down—when we die and leave these bodies—we will have a home in heaven, an eternal body made for us by God himself and not by human hands. ²We grow weary in our present bodies, and we long for the day when we will put on our heavenly bodies like new clothing. ³For we will not be spirits without bodies, but we will put on new heavenly bodies. ⁴Our dying bodies make us groan and sigh, but it's not that we want to die and have no bodies at all. We want to slip into our new bodies so that these dying bodies will be swallowed up by everlasting life. ⁵God himself has prepared us for this, and as a guarantee he has given us his Holy Spirit.

⁶So we are always confident, even though we know that as long as we live in these bodies we are not at home with the Lord. ⁷That is why we live by believing and not by seeing. ⁸Yes, we are fully confident, and we would rather be away from these bodies, for then we will be at home with the Lord. ⁹So our aim is to please him always, whether we are here in this body or away from this body. ¹⁰For we must all stand before Christ to be judged. We will each receive whatever we deserve for the good or evil we have done in our bodies.

We Are God's Ambassadors

¹¹It is because we know this solemn fear of the Lord that we work so hard to persuade others. God knows we are sincere, and I hope you know this, too. ¹²Are we trying to pat ourselves on the back again? No, we are giving you a reason to be proud of us, so you can answer those who brag about having a spectacular ministry rather than having a sincere heart before God. ¹³If it seems that we are crazy, it is to bring glory to God. And if we are in our right minds, it is for your benefit. ¹⁴Whatever we do, it is because Christ's love controls us.* Since we believe that Christ died for everyone, we also believe that we have all died to the old life we used to live.* ¹⁵He died for everyone so that those who receive his new life will no longer live to please themselves. Instead, they will live to please Christ, who died and was raised for them.

¹⁶So we have stopped evaluating others by what the world thinks about them. Once I mistakenly thought of Christ that way, as though he were merely a human being. How differently I think about him now! ¹⁷What this means is that those who become Christians become new persons. They are not the same anymore, for the old life is gone. A new life has begun!

¹⁸All this newness of life is from God, who brought us back to himself through what Christ did. And God has given us the task of reconciling people to him. ¹⁹For God was in Christ, reconciling the world to himself, no longer counting people's sins against them. This is the wonderful message he has given us to tell others. ²⁰We are Christ's ambassadors, and God is using us to speak to you. We urge you, as though Christ himself were here pleading with you, "Be reconciled to God!" ²¹For God made Christ, who never sinned, to be the offering for our sin, so that we could be made right with God through Christ.

CHAPTER 6

As God's partners,* we beg you not to reject this marvelous message of God's great kindness. ²For God says,

"At just the right time, I heard you.
On the day of salvation, I helped you."*

Indeed, God is ready to help you right now. Today is the day of salvation.

I BELIEVE the Holy Spirit guarantees God's promise to give us everlasting life. (5:5)

I AIM to please the Lord always. (5:9)

I KNOW I will receive whatever I deserve for the good or evil I have done. (5:10)

I LIVE to please Jesus Christ. (5:15)

I HAVE BEEN MADE right with God through Jesus Christ. (5:21)

5:14a Or *urges us on.*   5:14b Greek *Since one died on behalf of all, then all died.*   6:1 Or *As we work together.*   6:2 Isa 49:8.

Paul's Hardships

³We try to live in such a way that no one will be hindered from finding the Lord by the way we act, and so no one can find fault with our ministry. ⁴In everything we do we try to show that we are true ministers of God. We patiently endure troubles and hardships and calamities of every kind. ⁵We have been beaten, been put in jail, faced angry mobs, worked to exhaustion, endured sleepless nights, and gone without food. ⁶We have proved ourselves by our purity, our understanding, our patience, our kindness, our sincere love, and the power of the Holy Spirit.* ⁷We have faithfully preached the truth. God's power has been working in us. We have righteousness as our weapon, both to attack and to defend ourselves. ⁸We serve God whether people honor us or despise us, whether they slander us or praise us. We are honest, but they call us impostors. ⁹We are well known, but we are treated as unknown. We live close to death, but here we are, still alive. We have been beaten within an inch of our lives. ¹⁰Our hearts ache, but we always have joy. We are poor, but we give spiritual riches to others. We own nothing, and yet we have everything.

¹¹Oh, dear Corinthian friends! We have spoken honestly with you. Our hearts are open to you. ¹²If there is a problem between us, it is not because of a lack of love on our part, but because you have withheld your love from us. ¹³I am talking now as I would to my own children. Open your hearts to us!

The Temple of the Living God

¹⁴Don't team up with those who are unbelievers. How can goodness be a partner with wickedness? How can light live with darkness? ¹⁵What harmony can there be between Christ and the Devil*? How can a believer be a partner with an unbeliever? ¹⁶And what union can there be between God's temple and idols? For we are the temple of the living God. As God said:

"I will live in them
    and walk among them.
I will be their God,
    and they will be my people.*
¹⁷Therefore, come out from them
    and separate yourselves from them, says the Lord.
Don't touch their filthy things,
    and I will welcome you.*
¹⁸And I will be your Father,
    and you will be my sons and daughters,
    says the Lord Almighty.*"

CHAPTER 7

Because we have these promises, dear friends, let us cleanse ourselves from everything that can defile our body or spirit. And let us work toward complete purity because we fear God.

Paul's Joy at the Church's Repentance

²Please open your hearts to us. We have not done wrong to anyone. We have not led anyone astray. We have not taken advantage of anyone. ³I'm not saying this to condemn you, for I said before that you are in our hearts forever. We live or die together with you. ⁴I have the highest confidence in you, and my pride in you is great. You have greatly encouraged me; you have made me happy despite all our troubles.

⁵When we arrived in Macedonia there was no rest for us. Outside there was conflict from every direction, and inside there was fear. ⁶But God, who encourages

---

I SHOW I am God's servant by enduring hardship and living a pure life. (6:4)

I SERVE God whether I am despised or honored, slandered or praised. (6:8)

I BELIEVE a Christian should not marry an unbeliever. (6:14)

I FEAR God and continually cleanse my life from anything impure. (7:1)

I BELIEVE God encourages those who are discouraged. (7:6)

6:6 Or the holiness of spirit.   6:15 Greek and Beliar.   6:16 Lev 26:12; Ezek 37:27.   6:17 Isa 52:11; Ezek 20:34.
6:18 2 Sam 7:14.

those who are discouraged, encouraged us by the arrival of Titus. ⁷His presence was a joy, but so was the news he brought of the encouragement he received from you. When he told me how much you were looking forward to my visit, and how sorry you were about what had happened, and how loyal your love is for me, I was filled with joy!

⁸I am no longer sorry that I sent that letter to you, though I was sorry for a time, for I know that it was painful to you for a little while. ⁹Now I am glad I sent it, not because it hurt you, but because the pain caused you to have remorse and change your ways. It was the kind of sorrow God wants his people to have, so you were not harmed by us in any way. ¹⁰For God can use sorrow in our lives to help us turn away from sin and seek salvation. We will never regret that kind of sorrow. But sorrow without repentance is the kind that results in death.

¹¹Just see what this godly sorrow produced in you! Such earnestness, such concern to clear yourselves, such indignation, such alarm, such longing to see me, such zeal, and such a readiness to punish the wrongdoer. You showed that you have done everything you could to make things right. ¹²My purpose was not to write about who did the wrong or who was wronged. I wrote to you so that in the sight of God you could show how much you really do care for us. ¹³We have been encouraged by this.

In addition to our own encouragement, we were especially delighted to see how happy Titus was at the way you welcomed him and set his mind at ease. ¹⁴I had told him how proud I was of you—and you didn't disappoint me. I have always told you the truth, and now my boasting to Titus has also proved true! ¹⁵Now he cares for you more than ever when he remembers the way you listened to him and welcomed him with such respect and deep concern. ¹⁶I am very happy now because I have complete confidence in you.

CHAPTER 8

A Call to Generous Giving

Now I want to tell you, dear brothers and sisters,* what God in his kindness has done for the churches in Macedonia. ²Though they have been going through much trouble and hard times, their wonderful joy and deep poverty have overflowed in rich generosity. ³For I can testify that they gave not only what they could afford but far more. And they did it of their own free will. ⁴They begged us again and again for the gracious privilege of sharing in the gift for the Christians in Jerusalem. ⁵Best of all, they went beyond our highest hopes, for their first action was to dedicate themselves to the Lord and to us for whatever directions God might give them.

⁶So we have urged Titus, who encouraged your giving in the first place, to return to you and encourage you to complete your share in this ministry of giving. ⁷Since you excel in so many ways—you have so much faith, such gifted speakers, such knowledge, such enthusiasm, and such love for us*—now I want you to excel also in this gracious ministry of giving. ⁸I am not saying you must do it, even though the other churches are eager to do it. This is one way to prove your love is real.

⁹You know how full of love and kindness our Lord Jesus Christ was. Though he was very rich, yet for your sakes he became poor, so that by his poverty he could make you rich.

¹⁰I suggest that you finish what you started a year ago, for you were the first to propose this idea, and you were the first to begin doing something about it. ¹¹Now you should carry this project through to completion just as enthusiastically as you began it. Give whatever you can according to what you have. ¹²If you are really eager to give, it isn't important how much you are able to

8:1 Greek *brothers.* 8:7 Some manuscripts read *love from us to you.*

See Titus's profile (page 1385) at Titus 1:5.

I BELIEVE God often uses sorrow to cause me to repent and turn away from sin. (7:10)

I HAVE DEDICATED myself wholeheartedly to the Lord. (8:5)

See Titus's profile (page 1385) at Titus 1:5.

I KNOW the Lord Jesus Christ showed the depth of his great love when he became physically poor in order to make me spiritually rich. (8:9)

I GIVE to other
Christians when they
are in need and I have
plenty. (8:14)

give. God wants you to give what you have, not what you don't have. ¹³Of course, I don't mean you should give so much that you suffer from having too little. I only mean that there should be some equality. ¹⁴Right now you have plenty and can help them. Then at some other time they can share with you when you need it. In this way, everyone's needs will be met. ¹⁵Do you remember what the Scriptures say about this? "Those who gathered a lot had nothing left over, and those who gathered only a little had enough."*

Titus and His Companions
¹⁶I am thankful to God that he has given Titus the same enthusiasm for you that I have. ¹⁷He welcomed our request that he visit you again. In fact, he himself was eager to go and see you. ¹⁸We are also sending another brother with Titus. He is highly praised in all the churches as a preacher of the Good News. ¹⁹He was appointed by the churches to accompany us as we take the offering to Jerusalem*—a service that glorifies the Lord and shows our eagerness to help. ²⁰By traveling together we will guard against any suspicion, for we are anxious that no one should find fault with the way we are handling this generous gift. ²¹We are careful to be honorable before the Lord, but we also want everyone else to know we are honorable.

I SEEK to live honorably
before God and others.
(8:21)

²²And we are also sending with them another brother who has been thoroughly tested and has shown how earnest he is on many occasions. He is now even more enthusiastic because of his increased confidence in you. ²³If anyone asks about Titus, say that he is my partner who works with me to help you. And these brothers are representatives* of the churches. They are splendid examples of those who bring glory to Christ. ²⁴So show them your love, and prove to all the churches that our boasting about you is justified.

CHAPTER 9

The Collection for Christians in Jerusalem
I really don't need to write to you about this gift for the Christians in Jerusalem.* ²For I know how eager you are to help, and I have been boasting to our friends in Macedonia that you Christians in Greece* were ready to send an offering a year ago. In fact, it was your enthusiasm that stirred up many of them to begin helping. ³But I am sending these brothers just to be sure that you really are ready, as I told them you would be, with your money all collected. I don't want it to turn out that I was wrong in my boasting about you. ⁴I would be humiliated—and so would you—if some Macedonian Christians came with me, only to find that you still weren't ready after all I had told them! ⁵So I thought I should send these brothers ahead of me to make sure the gift you promised is ready. But I want it to be a willing gift, not one given under pressure.

I HELP others to
succeed in fulfilling
their Christian
commitments. (9:5)

I GIVE money to God
cheerfully, willingly,
and purposefully. (9:7)

⁶Remember this—a farmer who plants only a few seeds will get a small crop. But the one who plants generously will get a generous crop. ⁷You must each make up your own mind as to how much you should give. Don't give reluctantly or in response to pressure. For God loves the person who gives cheerfully. ⁸And God will generously provide all you need. Then you will always have everything you need and plenty left over to share with others. ⁹As the Scriptures say,

"Godly people give generously to the poor.
Their good deeds will never be forgotten."*

¹⁰For God is the one who gives seed to the farmer and then bread to eat. In the same way, he will give you many opportunities to do good, and he will produce a great harvest of generosity* in you.

8:15 Exod 16:18. 8:19 See 1 Cor 16:3-4. 8:23 Greek *apostles.* 9:1 Greek *about the offering for the saints.*
9:2 Greek *Achaia,* the southern region of the Greek peninsula. 9:9 Ps 112:9. 9:10 Greek *righteousness.*

[11]Yes, you will be enriched so that you can give even more generously. And when we take your gifts to those who need them, they will break out in thanksgiving to God. [12]So two good things will happen—the needs of the Christians in Jerusalem will be met, and they will joyfully express their thanksgiving to God. [13]You will be glorifying God through your generous gifts. For your generosity to them will prove that you are obedient to the Good News of Christ. [14]And they will pray for you with deep affection because of the wonderful grace of God shown through you.

[15]Thank God for his Son—a gift too wonderful for words!*

CHAPTER 10

Paul Defends His Authority

Now I, Paul, plead with you. I plead with the gentleness and kindness that Christ himself would use, even though some of you say I am bold in my letters but timid in person. [2]I hope it won't be necessary, but when I come I may have to be very bold with those who think we act from purely human motives. [3]We are human, but we don't wage war with human plans and methods. [4]We use God's mighty weapons, not mere worldly weapons, to knock down the Devil's strongholds. [5]With these weapons we break down every proud argument that keeps people from knowing God. With these weapons we conquer their rebellious ideas, and we teach them to obey Christ. [6]And we will punish those who remained disobedient after the rest of you became loyal and obedient.

[7]The trouble with you is that you make your decisions on the basis of appearance.* You must recognize that we belong to Christ just as much as those who proudly declare that they belong to Christ. [8]I may seem to be boasting too much about the authority given to us by the Lord. But this authority is to build you up, not to tear you down. And I will not be put to shame by having my work among you destroyed.

[9]Now this is not just an attempt to frighten you by my letters. [10]For some say, "Don't worry about Paul. His letters are demanding and forceful, but in person he is weak, and his speeches are really bad!" [11]The ones who say this must realize that we will be just as demanding and forceful in person as we are in our letters.

[12]Oh, don't worry; I wouldn't dare say that I am as wonderful as these other men who tell you how important they are! But they are only comparing themselves with each other, and measuring themselves by themselves. What foolishness!

[13]But we will not boast of authority we do not have. Our goal is to stay within the boundaries of God's plan for us, and this plan includes our working there with you. [14]We are not going too far when we claim authority over you, for we were the first to travel all the way to you with the Good News of Christ. [15]Nor do we claim credit for the work someone else has done. Instead, we hope that your faith will grow and that our work among you will be greatly enlarged. [16]Then we will be able to go and preach the Good News in other places that are far beyond you, where no one else is working. Then there will be no question about being in someone else's territory. [17]As the Scriptures say,

"The person who wishes to boast
should boast only of what the Lord has done."*

[18]When people boast about themselves, it doesn't count for much. But when the Lord commends someone, that's different!

I GLORIFY God and draw closer to other Christians by giving generously. (9:12)

I THANK God for generously giving his wonderful Son! (9:15)

See Paul's profile (page 1333) at Galatians 2:5.

I DO NOT ACT from purely human motives. (10:2)

I JOIN with other believers to use God's weapons to break down proud, rebellious arguments that keep people from obeying Jesus Christ. (10:5)

I DO NOT MEASURE or compare myself with others. (10:12)

I BOAST only about what the Lord has done. (10:17)

9:15 Greek *Thank God for his indescribable gift.*   10:7 Or *Look at the obvious facts.*   10:17 Jer 9:24.

CHAPTER 11

Paul and the False Apostles

I hope you will be patient with me as I keep on talking like a fool. Please bear with me. ²I am jealous for you with the jealousy of God himself. For I promised you as a pure bride* to one husband, Christ. ³But I fear that somehow you will be led away from your pure and simple devotion to Christ, just as Eve was deceived by the serpent. ⁴You seem to believe whatever anyone tells you, even if they preach about a different Jesus than the one we preach, or a different Spirit than the one you received, or a different kind of gospel than the one you believed. ⁵But I don't think I am inferior to these "super apostles." ⁶I may not be a trained speaker, but I know what I am talking about. I think you realize this by now, for we have proved it again and again.

⁷Did I do wrong when I humbled myself and honored you by preaching God's Good News to you without expecting anything in return? ⁸I "robbed" other churches by accepting their contributions so I could serve you at no cost. ⁹And when I was with you and didn't have enough to live on, I did not ask you to help me. For the brothers who came from Macedonia brought me another gift. I have never yet asked you for any support, and I never will. ¹⁰As surely as the truth of Christ is in me, I will never stop boasting about this all over Greece.* ¹¹Why? Because I don't love you? God knows I do.

¹²But I will continue doing this to cut the ground out from under the feet of those who boast that their work is just like ours. ¹³These people are false apostles. They have fooled you by disguising themselves as apostles of Christ. ¹⁴But I am not surprised! Even Satan can disguise himself as an angel of light. ¹⁵So it is no wonder his servants can also do it by pretending to be godly ministers. In the end they will get every bit of punishment their wicked deeds deserve.

Paul's Many Trials

¹⁶Once again, don't think that I have lost my wits to talk like this. But even if you do, listen to me, as you would to a foolish person, while I also boast a little. ¹⁷Such bragging is not something the Lord wants, but I am acting like a fool. ¹⁸And since others boast about their human achievements, I will, too. ¹⁹After all, you, who think you are so wise, enjoy listening to fools! ²⁰You put up with it when they make you their slaves, take everything you have, take advantage of you, put on airs, and slap you in the face. ²¹I'm ashamed to say that we were not strong enough to do that!

But whatever they dare to boast about—I'm talking like a fool again—I can boast about it, too. ²²They say they are Hebrews, do they? So am I. And they say they are Israelites? So am I. And they are descendants of Abraham? So am I. ²³They say they serve Christ? I know I sound like a madman, but I have served him far more! I have worked harder, been put in jail more often, been whipped times without number, and faced death again and again. ²⁴Five different times the Jews gave me thirty-nine lashes. ²⁵Three times I was beaten with rods. Once I was stoned. Three times I was shipwrecked. Once I spent a whole night and a day adrift at sea. ²⁶I have traveled many weary miles. I have faced danger from flooded rivers and from robbers. I have faced danger from my own people, the Jews, as well as from the Gentiles. I have faced danger in the cities, in the deserts, and on the stormy seas. And I have faced danger from men who claim to be Christians but are not.* ²⁷I have lived with weariness and pain and sleepless nights. Often I have been hungry and thirsty and have gone without food. Often I have shivered with cold, without enough clothing to keep me warm.

²⁸Then, besides all this, I have the daily burden of how the churches are getting along. ²⁹Who is weak without my feeling that weakness? Who is led astray, and I do not burn with anger?

11:2 Greek *a virgin.* 11:10 Greek *Achaia.* 11:26 Greek *from false brothers.*

See Eve's profile (page 7) at Genesis 3:21.

I DO NOT BELIEVE anyone who teaches something different from what God's Word says about Jesus Christ, the Holy Spirit, and the Good News of salvation. (11:4)

I BELIEVE Satan's servants can convincingly disguise themselves as godly ministers. (11:15)

I BOAST about my human achievements only when necessary to gain the attention of those who are listening to false teachers. (11:18)

I DO NOT LISTEN to fools. (11:19)

[30]If I must boast, I would rather boast about the things that show how weak I am. [31]God, the Father of our Lord Jesus, who is to be praised forever, knows I tell the truth. [32]When I was in Damascus, the governor under King Aretas kept guards at the city gates to catch me. [33]But I was lowered in a basket through a window in the city wall, and that's how I got away!

I PREFER to boast about how God uses me in spite of my weaknesses. (11:30)

CHAPTER 12

Paul's Vision and His Thorn in the Flesh

This boasting is all so foolish, but let me go on. Let me tell about the visions and revelations I received from the Lord. [2]I* was caught up into the third heaven fourteen years ago. [3]Whether my body was there or just my spirit, I don't know; only God knows. [4]But I do know that I* was caught up into paradise and heard things so astounding that they cannot be told. [5]That experience is something worth boasting about, but I am not going to do it. I am going to boast only about my weaknesses. [6]I have plenty to boast about and would be no fool in doing it, because I would be telling the truth. But I won't do it. I don't want anyone to think more highly of me than what they can actually see in my life and my message, [7]even though I have received wonderful revelations from God. But to keep me from getting puffed up, I was given a thorn in my flesh, a messenger from Satan to torment me and keep me from getting proud.

I BELIEVE Paul experienced a heavenly vision. (12:4)

[8]Three different times I begged the Lord to take it away. [9]Each time he said, "My gracious favor is all you need. My power works best in your weakness." So now I am glad to boast about my weaknesses, so that the power of Christ may work through me. [10]Since I know it is all for Christ's good, I am quite content with my weaknesses and with insults, hardships, persecutions, and calamities. For when I am weak, then I am strong.

I BELIEVE God's gracious favor and power are all I need if I have physical weaknesses. (12:9)

Paul's Concern for the Corinthians

[11]You have made me act like a fool—boasting like this. You ought to be writing commendations for me, for I am not at all inferior to these "super apostles," even though I am nothing at all. [12]When I was with you, I certainly gave you every proof that I am truly an apostle, sent to you by God himself. For I patiently did many signs and wonders and miracles among you. [13]The only thing I didn't do, which I do in the other churches, was to become a burden to you. Please forgive me for this wrong!

[14]Now I am coming to you for the third time, and I will not be a burden to you. I don't want what you have; I want you. And anyway, little children don't pay for their parents' food. It's the other way around; parents supply food for their children. [15]I will gladly spend myself and all I have for your spiritual good, even though it seems that the more I love you, the less you love me.

[16]Some of you admit I was not a burden to you. But they still think I was sneaky and took advantage of you by trickery. [17]But how? Did any of the men I sent to you take advantage of you? [18]When I urged Titus to visit you and sent our other brother with him, did Titus take advantage of you? No, of course not! For we both have the same Spirit and walk in each other's steps, doing things the same way.

I DO NOT TAKE advantage of or become a burden to the people I serve. (12:16)

See Titus's profile (page 1385) at Titus 1:5.

[19]Perhaps you think we are saying all this just to defend ourselves. That isn't it at all. We tell you this as Christ's servants, and we know that God is listening. Everything we do, dear friends, is for your benefit. [20]For I am afraid that when I come to visit you I won't like what I find, and then you won't like my response. I am afraid that I will find quarreling, jealousy, outbursts of anger, selfishness, backstabbing, gossip, conceit, and disorderly behavior. [21]Yes, I am afraid that when I come, God will humble me again because of you. And I will have to grieve because many of you who sinned earlier have not repented of your impurity, sexual immorality, and eagerness for lustful pleasure.

I GRIEVE whenever a Christian friend sins and refuses to repent. (12:21)

12:2 Greek *I know a man in Christ who.*   12:4 Greek *he.*

CHAPTER 13

Paul's Final Advice

This is the third time I am coming to visit you. As the Scriptures say, "The facts of every case must be established by the testimony of two or three witnesses."* ²I have already warned those who had been sinning when I was there on my second visit. Now I again warn them and all others, just as I did before, that this next time I will not spare them.

³I will give you all the proof you want that Christ speaks through me. Christ is not weak in his dealings with you; he is a mighty power among you. ⁴Although he died on the cross in weakness, he now lives by the mighty power of God. We, too, are weak, but we live in him and have God's power—the power we use in dealing with you.

⁵Examine yourselves to see if your faith is really genuine. Test yourselves. If you cannot tell that Jesus Christ is among you,* it means you have failed the test. ⁶I hope you recognize that we have passed the test and are approved by God.

⁷We pray to God that you will not do anything wrong. We pray this, not to show that our ministry to you has been successful, but because we want you to do right even if we ourselves seem to have failed. ⁸Our responsibility is never to oppose the truth, but to stand for the truth at all times. ⁹We are glad to be weak, if you are really strong. What we pray for is your restoration to maturity.

¹⁰I am writing this to you before I come, hoping that I won't need to deal harshly with you when I do come. For I want to use the authority the Lord has given me to build you up, not to tear you down.

Paul's Final Greetings

¹¹Dear brothers and sisters,* I close my letter with these last words: Rejoice. Change your ways. Encourage each other. Live in harmony and peace. Then the God of love and peace will be with you.

¹²Greet each other in Christian love.* All the Christians here send you their greetings.

¹³May the grace of our Lord Jesus Christ, the love of God, and the fellowship of the Holy Spirit be with you all.*

13:1 Deut 19:15. 13:5 Or *in you.* 13:11 Greek *Brothers.* 13:12 Greek *with a sacred kiss.* 13:12-13 Some English versions divide verse 12 into verses 12 and 13, and then verse 13 becomes verse 14.

I LIVE in Jesus Christ, who lives by the mighty power of God. (13:4)

I HAVE EXAMINED myself to see if my faith is genuine. (13:5)

I STAND for the truth at all times. (13:8)

I LIVE in harmony and peace with other Christians in my church. (13:11)

GALATIANS

THIS FOURTH New Testament letter contrasts the message of Paul with that of false teachers who had completely distorted the Good News.

Paul wrote this letter to a group of churches he had helped establish in the province of Galatia during one of his missionary journeys.

In chapters 1–5, Paul expresses his shock that the Galatian believers were so confused about the Good News. He reminds them that Jesus Christ revealed the message, the apostles confirmed it, and the Old Testament Scriptures looked forward to it. He then exposes the motives of the false teachers and urges the Galatian believers to live in freedom by the Holy Spirit.

In chapter 6, Paul closes with some final words of instruction and challenge.

Famous verses in Galatians include

- ○ "I myself no longer live, but Christ lives in me" (2:20)
- ○ "Christ has rescued us from the curse pronounced by the law" (3:13)
- ○ "There is no longer Jew or Gentile, slave or free, male or female. For you are all Christians—you are one in Christ Jesus" (3:28)
- ○ "When the right time came, God sent his Son" (4:4)
- ○ "God has sent the Spirit of his Son into your hearts, and now you can call God your dear Father" (4:6)
- ○ "Christ has really set us free. Now make sure that you stay free" (5:1)
- ○ "Live according to your new life in the Holy Spirit" (5:16)
- ○ "When the Holy Spirit controls our lives, he will produce this kind of fruit in us: love, joy, peace, patience, kindness, goodness, faithfulness, gentleness, and self-control" (5:22-23)
- ○ "If another Christian is overcome by some sin, you who are godly should gently and humbly help that person back onto the right path" (6:1)
- ○ "You will always reap what you sow!" (6:7)
- ○ "Don't get discouraged and give up, for we will reap a harvest of blessing at the appropriate time" (6:9)
- ○ "Whenever we have the opportunity, we should do good to everyone, especially to our Christian brothers and sisters" (6:10)

CHAPTER 1

Greetings from Paul

This letter is from Paul, an apostle. I was not appointed by any group or by human authority. My call is from Jesus Christ himself and from God the Father, who raised Jesus from the dead.

²All the brothers and sisters* here join me in sending greetings to the churches of Galatia.

1:2 Greek *brothers;* also in 1:11.

I BELIEVE Jesus Christ died for my sins in order to rescue me from this evil world. (1:4)

I GIVE God the glory for rescuing me from this evil world. (1:5)

I CAREFULLY STUDY the New Testament so that I can discern the truth about Jesus Christ. (1:7)

I AM Jesus Christ's servant and try to please God rather than people. (1:10)

I BELIEVE the Good News of salvation is based on God's revelation, not human reasoning or logic. (1:12)

See Peter's profile (page 1111) at Matthew 26:75.

See James's profile (page 1407) at James 2:18.

See the profiles for Barnabas (page 1253) and Titus (page 1385) at Acts 11:23 and Titus 1:5.

³May grace and peace be yours from God our Father and from the Lord Jesus Christ. ⁴He died for our sins, just as God our Father planned, in order to rescue us from this evil world in which we live. ⁵That is why all glory belongs to God through all the ages of eternity. Amen.

There Is Only One Good News

⁶I am shocked that you are turning away so soon from God, who in his love and mercy called you to share the eternal life he gives through Christ. You are already following a different way ⁷that pretends to be the Good News but is not the Good News at all. You are being fooled by those who twist and change the truth concerning Christ.

⁸Let God's curse fall on anyone, including myself, who preaches any other message than the one we told you about. Even if an angel comes from heaven and preaches any other message, let him be forever cursed. ⁹I will say it again: If anyone preaches any other gospel than the one you welcomed, let God's curse fall upon that person.

¹⁰Obviously, I'm not trying to be a people pleaser! No, I am trying to please God. If I were still trying to please people, I would not be Christ's servant.

Paul's Message Comes from Christ

¹¹Dear brothers and sisters, I solemnly assure you that the Good News of salvation which I preach is not based on mere human reasoning or logic. ¹²For my message came by a direct revelation from Jesus Christ himself. No one else taught me.

¹³You know what I was like when I followed the Jewish religion—how I violently persecuted the Christians.* I did my best to get rid of them. ¹⁴I was one of the most religious Jews of my own age, and I tried as hard as possible to follow all the old traditions of my religion.

¹⁵But then something happened! For it pleased God in his kindness to choose me and call me, even before I was born! What undeserved mercy! ¹⁶Then he revealed his Son to me* so that I could proclaim the Good News about Jesus to the Gentiles. When all this happened to me, I did not rush out to consult with anyone else; ¹⁷nor did I go up to Jerusalem to consult with those who were apostles before I was. No, I went away into Arabia and later returned to the city of Damascus. ¹⁸It was not until three years later that I finally went to Jerusalem for a visit with Peter* and stayed there with him for fifteen days. ¹⁹And the only other apostle I met at that time was James, our Lord's brother. ²⁰You must believe what I am saying, for I declare before God that I am not lying. ²¹Then after this visit, I went north into the provinces of Syria and Cilicia. ²²And still the Christians in the churches in Judea didn't know me personally. ²³All they knew was that people were saying, "The one who used to persecute us now preaches the very faith he tried to destroy!" ²⁴And they gave glory to God because of me.

CHAPTER 2

The Apostles Accept Paul

Then fourteen years later I went back to Jerusalem again, this time with Barnabas; and Titus came along, too. ²I went there because God revealed to me that I should go. While I was there I talked privately with the leaders of the church. I wanted them to understand what I had been preaching to the Gentiles. I wanted to make sure they did not disagree, or my ministry would have been useless. ³And they did agree. They did not even demand that my companion Titus be circumcised, though he was a Gentile.*

⁴Even that question wouldn't have come up except for some so-called Christians there—false ones, really*—who came to spy on us and see our

1:13 Greek *the church of God.*   1:16 Or *in me.*   1:18 Greek *Cephas.*   2:3 Greek *a Greek.*   2:4 Greek *some false brothers.*

freedom in Christ Jesus. They wanted to force us, like slaves, to follow their Jewish regulations. ⁵But we refused to listen to them for a single moment. We wanted to preserve the truth of the Good News for you.

> I REFUSE to listen to those who try to add rules as a requirement for salvation. (2:5)

LIKE PAUL
Galatians 2:5

I earnestly strive to preserve the purity of the Good News of Jesus Christ.

In remote stands of old-growth forests on the West Coast of the United States, zealous environmentalists sometimes chain themselves to ancient trees to temporarily stop a logging company from moving into that area. These environmentalists are fiercely focused and willing to do anything to preserve the purity of the virgin forests.

The apostle Paul (aka Saul) knew what that kind of zeal was all about. But he dedicated his life to protect not a natural wonder but a supernatural truth.

Before he met Jesus Christ, Paul poured all his energy into preserving the Jewish religion and wiping out those who taught the way of Christ (1:13-14). After his dramatic encounter with the risen Lord on the Damascus road, however, Paul saw the pure truth of the Good News of salvation with brilliant clarity. His physical eyes were blinded temporarily, but his spiritual eyes were finally opened to God's truth. Never again would anything be more important in Paul's life than (a) proclaiming the Good News of God's simple and free offer of salvation through Jesus Christ and (b) protecting it from destruction or dilution.

If anyone had good reason to add something to the gospel, it would have been Paul. His whole life had been steeped in Jewish learning and tradition, preparing him to be a leader among the Pharisees, one of the strictest and most respected Jewish sects (Acts 22:1-5; 26:4-5). He could have fallen back on his training and rich heritage to cloak or embellish the Good News.

Instead, Paul saw clearly the danger of adding regulations or requirements to the simple command to believe on the Lord Jesus Christ to be saved. So with the intensity of a jealous husband, Paul took aim at anything that would lead the believers away from their trust in and devotion to Christ (2 Corinthians 11:2-3).

As a result, Paul alternately endured the wrath of unbelievers and confronted apostles, boasted of his background, and called himself the worst of sinners (2 Corinthians 11:16-30; Galatians 2:11-16; 1 Timothy 1:15). To protect the purity of the Good News, Paul also railed against false teachers in blistering language and pleaded with believers in tears (Galatians 1:8-9; 5:11-12).

You and I have not been given the position of apostles. Yet, like Paul, we can preserve the purity of the Good News through our faith and life:

- When we live by the power of the Spirit, depending upon him for our righteousness.
- When we confront false teaching that adds human requirements to God's gift of salvation.
- When we lead believers to depend on Christ and Christ alone.

Even if it means putting our lives in harm's way, let's never abandon the essential truths of the Christian faith.

○ *Today's Scripture reading is Galatians 1–2.*

⁶And the leaders of the church who were there had nothing to add to what I was preaching. (By the way, their reputation as great leaders made no difference to me, for God has no favorites.) ⁷They saw that God had given me the responsibility of preaching the Good News to the Gentiles, just as he had given Peter the responsibility of preaching to the Jews. ⁸For the same God who worked through Peter for the benefit of the Jews worked through me for the benefit of the Gentiles. ⁹In fact, James, Peter,* and John, who were known as pillars of the church, recognized the gift God had given me, and they accepted Barnabas and me as their co-workers. They encouraged us to keep preaching to the Gentiles, while they continued their work with the Jews. ¹⁰The only thing they suggested was that we remember to help the poor, and I have certainly been eager to do that.

See Peter's profile (page 1111) at Matthew 26:75.

See the profiles for James (page 1407) and John (page 1435) at James 2:18 and Revelation 1:9.

2:9 Greek *Cephas;* also in 2:11, 14.

Paul Confronts Peter

[11]But when Peter came to Antioch, I had to oppose him publicly, speaking strongly against what he was doing, for it was very wrong. [12]When he first arrived, he ate with the Gentile Christians, who don't bother with circumcision. But afterward, when some Jewish friends of James came, Peter wouldn't eat with the Gentiles anymore because he was afraid of what these legalists would say. [13]Then the other Jewish Christians followed Peter's hypocrisy, and even Barnabas was influenced to join them in their hypocrisy.

[14]When I saw that they were not following the truth of the Good News, I said to Peter in front of all the others, "Since you, a Jew by birth, have discarded the Jewish laws and are living like a Gentile, why are you trying to make these Gentiles obey the Jewish laws you abandoned? [15]You and I are Jews by birth, not 'sinners' like the Gentiles. [16]And yet we Jewish Christians know that we become right with God, not by doing what the law commands, but by faith in Jesus Christ. So we have believed in Christ Jesus, that we might be accepted by God because of our faith in Christ—and not because we have obeyed the law. For no one will ever be saved by obeying the law."*

[17]But what if we seek to be made right with God through faith in Christ and then find out that we are still sinners? Has Christ led us into sin? Of course not! [18]Rather, I make myself guilty if I rebuild the old system I already tore down. [19]For when I tried to keep the law, I realized I could never earn God's approval. So I died to the law so that I might live for God. I have been crucified with Christ. [20]I myself no longer live, but Christ lives in me. So I live my life in this earthly body by trusting in the Son of God, who loved me and gave himself for me. [21]I am not one of those who treats the grace of God as meaningless. For if we could be saved by keeping the law, then there was no need for Christ to die.

CHAPTER 3

The Law and Faith in Christ

Oh, foolish Galatians! What magician has cast an evil spell on you? For you used to see the meaning of Jesus Christ's death as clearly as though I had shown you a signboard with a picture of Christ dying on the cross. [2]Let me ask you this one question: Did you receive the Holy Spirit by keeping the law? Of course not, for the Holy Spirit came upon you only after you believed the message you heard about Christ. [3]Have you lost your senses? After starting your Christian lives in the Spirit, why are you now trying to become perfect by your own human effort? [4]You have suffered so much for the Good News. Surely it was not in vain, was it? Are you now going to just throw it all away?

[5]I ask you again, does God give you the Holy Spirit and work miracles among you because you obey the law of Moses? Of course not! It is because you believe the message you heard about Christ.

[6]In the same way, "Abraham believed God, so God declared him righteous because of his faith."* [7]The real children of Abraham, then, are all those who put their faith in God.

[8]What's more, the Scriptures looked forward to this time when God would accept the Gentiles, too, on the basis of their faith. God promised this good news to Abraham long ago when he said, "All nations will be blessed through you."* [9]And so it is: All who put their faith in Christ share the same blessing Abraham received because of his faith.

[10]But those who depend on the law to make them right with God are under his curse, for the Scriptures say, "Cursed is everyone who does not observe and obey all these commands that are written in God's Book of the Law."* [11]Consequently, it is clear that no one can ever be right with God by trying to keep the law. For the Scriptures say, "It is through faith that a righteous

I BELIEVE leaders who lead others astray by their hypocrisy need to be corrected. (2:14)

I AM ACCEPTED by God because of my faith in Jesus Christ, not because I have obeyed the Old Testament laws. (2:16)

I LIVE by trusting in Jesus Christ, who loves me and gave himself for me. (2:20)

I BELIEVE the Holy Spirit lives in me because I have trusted Jesus Christ. (3:2)

See Moses' profile (page 73) at Exodus 5:1.

See Abraham's profile (page 19) at Genesis 15:6.

I AM a real child of Abraham because I have put my faith in God. (3:7)

I RECEIVE the same blessing as Abraham because I have put my faith in Jesus Christ. (3:9)

2:16 Some translators hold that the quotation extends through verse 14; others through verse 16; and still others through verse 21. 3:6 Gen 15:6. 3:8 Gen 12:3; 18:18; 22:18. 3:10 Deut 27:26.

person has life."* ¹²How different from this way of faith is the way of law, which says, "If you wish to find life by obeying the law, you must obey all of its commands."* ¹³But Christ has rescued us from the curse pronounced by the law. When he was hung on the cross, he took upon himself the curse for our wrongdoing. For it is written in the Scriptures, "Cursed is everyone who is hung on a tree."* ¹⁴Through the work of Christ Jesus, God has blessed the Gentiles with the same blessing he promised to Abraham, and we Christians receive the promised Holy Spirit through faith.

The Law and God's Promises
¹⁵Dear brothers and sisters,* here's an example from everyday life. Just as no one can set aside or amend an irrevocable agreement, so it is in this case. ¹⁶God gave the promise to Abraham and his child.* And notice that it doesn't say the promise was to his children,* as if it meant many descendants. But the promise was to his child—and that, of course, means Christ. ¹⁷This is what I am trying to say: The agreement God made with Abraham could not be canceled 430 years later when God gave the law to Moses. God would be breaking his promise. ¹⁸For if the inheritance could be received only by keeping the law, then it would not be the result of accepting God's promise. But God gave it to Abraham as a promise.

¹⁹Well then, why was the law given? It was given to show people how guilty they are. But this system of law was to last only until the coming of the child to whom God's promise was made. And there is this further difference. God gave his laws to angels to give to Moses, who was the mediator between God and the people. ²⁰Now a mediator is needed if two people enter into an agreement, but God acted on his own when he made his promise to Abraham.

²¹Well then, is there a conflict between God's law and God's promises? Absolutely not! If the law could have given us new life, we could have been made right with God by obeying it. ²²But the Scriptures have declared that we are all prisoners of sin, so the only way to receive God's promise is to believe in Jesus Christ.

²³Until faith in Christ was shown to us as the way of becoming right with God, we were guarded by the law. We were kept in protective custody, so to speak, until we could put our faith in the coming Savior.

God's Children through Faith
²⁴Let me put it another way. The law was our guardian and teacher to lead us until Christ came. So now, through faith in Christ, we are made right with God. ²⁵But now that faith in Christ has come, we no longer need the law as our guardian. ²⁶So you are all children* of God through faith in Christ Jesus. ²⁷And all who have been united with Christ in baptism have been made like him. ²⁸There is no longer Jew or Gentile,* slave or free, male or female. For you are all Christians—you are one in Christ Jesus. ²⁹And now that you belong to Christ, you are the true children of Abraham. You are his heirs, and now all the promises God gave to him belong to you.

CHAPTER 4

Think of it this way. If a father dies and leaves great wealth for his young children, those children are not much better off than slaves until they grow up, even though they actually own everything their father had. ²They have to obey their guardians until they reach whatever age their father set.

³And that's the way it was with us before Christ came. We were slaves to the spiritual powers of this world. ⁴But when the right time came, God sent his Son, born of a woman, subject to the law. ⁵God sent him to buy freedom for us who were slaves to the law, so that he could adopt us as his very own

I AM RESCUED from the curse of the law because Jesus Christ took the curse upon himself when he hung on the cross. (3:13)

I BELIEVE the law was given to show people their guilt before God. (3:19)

I BELIEVE all Christians—regardless of race, gender, or social status—are one in Jesus Christ. (3:28)

See Mary's profile (page 1149) at Luke 1:38.

I BELIEVE God the Father sent Jesus Christ in order to buy my freedom and adopt me as his child. (4:5)

3:11 Hab 2:4. 3:12 Lev 18:5. 3:13 Deut 21:23. 3:15 Greek *Brothers.* 3:16a Greek *seed;* also in 3:16c, 19. See Gen 12:7. 3:16b Greek *seeds.* 3:26 Greek *sons.* 3:28 Greek *Jew or Greek.*

I CALL God my Father because he has sent the Spirit of his Son into my heart. (4:6)

I NEVER WANT to be enslaved again to the spiritual powers of this world. (4:9)

I AM CONCERNED about the spiritual growth of those whom I have helped lead to the Lord. (4:19)

See the profiles for Abraham (page 19), Isaac (page 31), and Sarah (page 25) at Genesis 15:6, Genesis 25:19, and Genesis 21:1.

See Isaiah's profile (page 801) at Isaiah 6:13.

I BELIEVE that those who trust in Jesus Christ are children of the promise God made to Abraham. (4:28)

children.* 6And because you Gentiles have become his children, God has sent the Spirit of his Son into your hearts, and now you can call God your dear Father.* 7Now you are no longer a slave but God's own child.* And since you are his child, everything he has belongs to you.

Paul's Concern for the Galatians

8Before you Gentiles knew God, you were slaves to so-called gods that do not even exist. 9And now that you have found God (or should I say, now that God has found you), why do you want to go back again and become slaves once more to the weak and useless spiritual powers of this world? 10You are trying to find favor with God by what you do or don't do on certain days or months or seasons or years. 11I fear for you. I am afraid that all my hard work for you was worth nothing. 12Dear brothers and sisters,* I plead with you to live as I do in freedom from these things, for I have become like you Gentiles were—free from the law.

You did not mistreat me when I first preached to you. 13Surely you remember that I was sick when I first brought you the Good News of Christ. 14But even though my sickness was revolting to you, you did not reject me and turn me away. No, you took me in and cared for me as though I were an angel from God or even Christ Jesus himself. 15Where is that joyful spirit we felt together then? In those days, I know you would gladly have taken out your own eyes and given them to me if it had been possible. 16Have I now become your enemy because I am telling you the truth?

17Those false teachers who are so anxious to win your favor are not doing it for your good. They are trying to shut you off from me so that you will pay more attention to them. 18Now it's wonderful if you are eager to do good, and especially when I am not with you. 19But oh, my dear children! I feel as if I am going through labor pains for you again, and they will continue until Christ is fully developed in your lives. 20How I wish I were there with you right now, so that I could be more gentle with you. But at this distance I frankly don't know what else to do.

Abraham's Two Children

21Listen to me, you who want to live under the law. Do you know what the law really says? 22The Scriptures say that Abraham had two sons, one from his slave-wife and one from his freeborn wife.* 23The son of the slave-wife was born in a human attempt to bring about the fulfillment of God's promise. But the son of the freeborn wife was born as God's own fulfillment of his promise.

24Now these two women serve as an illustration of God's two covenants. Hagar, the slave-wife, represents Mount Sinai where people first became enslaved to the law. 25And now Jerusalem is just like Mount Sinai in Arabia, because she and her children live in slavery. 26But Sarah, the free woman, represents the heavenly Jerusalem. And she is our mother. 27That is what Isaiah meant when he prophesied,

"Rejoice, O childless woman!
Break forth into loud and joyful song,
    even though you never gave birth to a child.
For the woman who could bear no children
    now has more than all the other women!"*

28And you, dear brothers and sisters, are children of the promise, just like Isaac. 29And we who are born of the Holy Spirit are persecuted by those who

4:5 Greek sons; also in 4:6.   4:6 Greek into your hearts, crying, "Abba, Father." Abba is an Aramaic term for "father."   4:7 Greek son; also in 4:7b.   4:12 Greek brothers; also in 4:28, 31.   4:22 See Gen 16:15; 21:2-3.   4:27 Isa 54:1.

want us to keep the law, just as Isaac, the child of promise, was persecuted by Ishmael, the son of the slave-wife.

³⁰But what do the Scriptures say about that? "Get rid of the slave and her son, for the son of the slave woman will not share the family inheritance with the free woman's son."* ³¹So, dear brothers and sisters, we are not children of the slave woman, obligated to the law. We are children of the free woman, acceptable to God because of our faith.

I AM ACCEPTABLE to God because of my faith. (4:31)

CHAPTER 5
Freedom in Christ

So Christ has really set us free. Now make sure that you stay free, and don't get tied up again in slavery to the law.

²Listen! I, Paul, tell you this: If you are counting on circumcision to make you right with God, then Christ cannot help you. ³I'll say it again. If you are trying to find favor with God by being circumcised, you must obey all of the regulations in the whole law of Moses. ⁴For if you are trying to make yourselves right with God by keeping the law, you have been cut off from Christ! You have fallen away from God's grace.

⁵But we who live by the Spirit eagerly wait to receive everything promised to us who are right with God through faith. ⁶For when we place our faith in Christ Jesus, it makes no difference to God whether we are circumcised or not circumcised. What is important is faith expressing itself in love.

⁷You were getting along so well. Who has interfered with you to hold you back from following the truth? ⁸It certainly isn't God, for he is the one who called you to freedom. ⁹But it takes only one wrong person among you to infect all the others—a little yeast spreads quickly through the whole batch of dough! ¹⁰I am trusting the Lord to bring you back to believing as I do about these things. God will judge that person, whoever it is, who has been troubling and confusing you.

¹¹Dear brothers and sisters,* if I were still preaching that you must be circumcised—as some say I do—why would the Jews persecute me? The fact that I am still being persecuted proves that I am still preaching salvation through the cross of Christ alone. ¹²I only wish that those troublemakers who want to mutilate you by circumcision would mutilate themselves.*

¹³For you have been called to live in freedom—not freedom to satisfy your sinful nature, but freedom to serve one another in love. ¹⁴For the whole law can be summed up in this one command: "Love your neighbor as yourself."* ¹⁵But if instead of showing love among yourselves you are always biting and devouring one another, watch out! Beware of destroying one another.

See Moses' profile (page 73) at Exodus 5:1.

I FIND favor with God by depending on Jesus Christ, not on my own efforts. (5:4)

I KNOW it is important to express my faith in love. (5:6)

I DO NOT ALLOW anyone to hold me back from following the truth. (5:7)

Living by the Spirit's Power

¹⁶So I advise you to live according to your new life in the Holy Spirit. Then you won't be doing what your sinful nature craves. ¹⁷The old sinful nature loves to do evil, which is just opposite from what the Holy Spirit wants. And the Spirit gives us desires that are opposite from what the sinful nature desires. These two forces are constantly fighting each other, and your choices are never free from this conflict. ¹⁸But when you are directed by the Holy Spirit, you are no longer subject to the law.

¹⁹When you follow the desires of your sinful nature, your lives will produce these evil results: sexual immorality, impure thoughts, eagerness for lustful pleasure, ²⁰idolatry, participation in demonic activities, hostility, quarreling, jealousy, outbursts of anger, selfish ambition, divisions, the feeling that everyone is wrong except those in your own little group, ²¹envy, drunkenness, wild parties, and other kinds of sin. Let me tell you again, as I

I LIVE in freedom by serving others in love. (5:13)

I DO NOT FOLLOW the desires of my sinful nature. (5:19)

4:30 Gen 21:10.   5:11 Greek *Brothers.*   5:12 Or *castrate themselves;* Greek reads *cut themselves off.*
5:14 Lev 19:18.

have before, that anyone living that sort of life will not inherit the Kingdom of God. ²²But when the Holy Spirit controls our lives, he will produce this kind of fruit in us: love, joy, peace, patience, kindness, goodness, faithfulness, ²³gentleness, and self-control. Here there is no conflict with the law.

²⁴Those who belong to Christ Jesus have nailed the passions and desires of their sinful nature to his cross and crucified them there. ²⁵If we are living now by the Holy Spirit, let us follow the Holy Spirit's leading in every part of our lives. ²⁶Let us not become conceited, or irritate one another, or be jealous of one another.

CHAPTER 6

We Reap What We Sow

Dear brothers and sisters, if another Christian* is overcome by some sin, you who are godly should gently and humbly help that person back onto the right path. And be careful not to fall into the same temptation yourself. ²Share each other's troubles and problems, and in this way obey the law of Christ. ³If you think you are too important to help someone in need, you are only fooling yourself. You are really a nobody.

⁴Be sure to do what you should, for then you will enjoy the personal satisfaction of having done your work well, and you won't need to compare yourself to anyone else. ⁵For we are each responsible for our own conduct.

⁶Those who are taught the word of God should help their teachers by paying them.

⁷Don't be misled. Remember that you can't ignore God and get away with it. You will always reap what you sow! ⁸Those who live only to satisfy their own sinful desires will harvest the consequences of decay and death. But those who live to please the Spirit will harvest everlasting life from the Spirit. ⁹So don't get tired of doing what is good. Don't get discouraged and give up, for we will reap a harvest of blessing at the appropriate time. ¹⁰Whenever we have the opportunity, we should do good to everyone, especially to our Christian brothers and sisters.

Paul's Final Advice

¹¹Notice what large letters I use as I write these closing words in my own handwriting. ¹²Those who are trying to force you to be circumcised are doing it for just one reason. They don't want to be persecuted for teaching that the cross of Christ alone can save. ¹³And even those who advocate circumcision don't really keep the whole law. They only want you to be circumcised so they can brag about it and claim you as their disciples.

¹⁴As for me, God forbid that I should boast about anything except the cross of our Lord Jesus Christ. Because of that cross,* my interest in this world died long ago, and the world's interest in me is also long dead. ¹⁵It doesn't make any difference now whether we have been circumcised or not. What counts is whether we really have been changed into new and different people. ¹⁶May God's mercy and peace be upon all those who live by this principle. They are the new people of God.*

¹⁷From now on, don't let anyone trouble me with these things. For I bear on my body the scars that show I belong to Jesus.

¹⁸My dear brothers and sisters,* may the grace of our Lord Jesus Christ be with you all. Amen.

6:1 Greek *Brothers, if a man.*   6:14 Or *Because of him.*   6:16 Greek *the Israel of God.*   6:18 Greek *Brothers.*

I ALLOW the Holy Spirit to control my life and produce his fruit in me. (5:22)

I GENTLY AND HUMBLY HELP other Christians return to a life of godliness after they have sinned. (6:1)

I OBEY Jesus Christ's law of love by sharing the troubles and problems of other Christians. (6:2)

I DO NOT GIVE UP doing good for others, especially other Christians. (6:10)

I DO NOT BOAST about anything except what Jesus Christ did for me on the cross. (6:14)

EPHESIANS

THIS FIFTH New Testament letter answers many basic questions about Christian faith and practice.

Paul apparently wrote this letter not only to the church in Ephesus, but also to the churches in other cities where he had ministered during his missionary journeys. In any case, it's an important letter that was widely circulated after Paul wrote it.

In chapters 1–3, Paul marvels over the amazing spiritual realities of the Christian faith. He praises God and prays that his readers will gain a much greater understanding of those spiritual realities.

In chapters 4–6, Paul urges his readers to live in unity and purity by the Spirit's power. He then gives specific instructions about Spirit-guided relationships and concludes with a challenge to stand firm against the Devil's strategies.

Famous verses in Ephesians include

- ○ "God . . . has blessed us with every spiritual blessing in the heavenly realms" (1:3)
- ○ "The Spirit is God's guarantee that he will give us everything he promised" (1:14)
- ○ "God saved you by his special favor when you believed. And you can't take credit for this; it is a gift from God" (2:8)
- ○ "We are God's masterpiece" (2:10)
- ○ "He [God] is able to accomplish infinitely more than we would ever dare to ask or hope" (3:20)
- ○ "There is only one Lord, one faith, one baptism" (4:5)
- ○ "Don't let the sun go down while you are still angry" (4:26)
- ○ "Make the most of every opportunity for doing good in these evil days" (5:16)
- ○ "Let the Holy Spirit fill and control you" (5:18)
- ○ "Submit to one another out of reverence for Christ" (5:21)
- ○ "Remember that the Lord will reward each one of us for the good we do" (6:8)
- ○ "Put on all of God's armor so that you will be able to stand firm against all strategies and tricks of the Devil" (6:11)

CHAPTER 1

Greetings from Paul

This letter is from Paul, chosen by God to be an apostle of Christ Jesus.

It is written to God's holy people in Ephesus,* who are faithful followers of Christ Jesus.

²May grace and peace be yours, sent to you from God our Father and Jesus Christ our Lord.

Spiritual Blessings

³How we praise God, the Father of our Lord Jesus Christ, who has blessed us with every spiritual blessing in the heavenly realms because we belong to

See Paul's profile (page 1333) at Galatians 2:5.

I PRAISE God for blessing me with every spiritual blessing in the heavenly realms. (1:3)

1:1 Some manuscripts do not include in Ephesus.

Christ. [4]Long ago, even before he made the world, God loved us and chose us in Christ to be holy and without fault in his eyes. [5]His unchanging plan has always been to adopt us into his own family by bringing us to himself through Jesus Christ. And this gave him great pleasure.

[6]So we praise God for the wonderful kindness he has poured out on us because we belong to his dearly loved Son. [7]He is so rich in kindness that he purchased our freedom through the blood of his Son, and our sins are forgiven. [8]He has showered his kindness on us, along with all wisdom and understanding.

[9]God's secret plan has now been revealed to us; it is a plan centered on Christ, designed long ago according to his good pleasure. [10]And this is his plan: At the right time he will bring everything together under the authority of Christ—everything in heaven and on earth. [11]Furthermore, because of Christ, we have received an inheritance from God,* for he chose us from the beginning, and all things happen just as he decided long ago. [12]God's purpose was that we who were the first to trust in Christ should praise our glorious God. [13]And now you also have heard the truth, the Good News that God saves you. And when you believed in Christ, he identified you as his own by giving you the Holy Spirit, whom he promised long ago. [14]The Spirit is God's guarantee that he will give us everything he promised and that he has purchased us to be his own people. This is just one more reason for us to praise our glorious God.

Paul's Prayer for Spiritual Wisdom

[15]Ever since I first heard of your strong faith in the Lord Jesus and your love for Christians everywhere, [16]I have never stopped thanking God for you. I pray for you constantly, [17]asking God, the glorious Father of our Lord Jesus Christ, to give you spiritual wisdom and understanding, so that you might grow in your knowledge of God. [18]I pray that your hearts will be flooded with light so that you can understand the wonderful future he has promised to those he called. I want you to realize what a rich and glorious inheritance he has given to his people.*

[19]I pray that you will begin to understand the incredible greatness of his power for us who believe him. This is the same mighty power [20]that raised Christ from the dead and seated him in the place of honor at God's right hand in the heavenly realms. [21]Now he is far above any ruler or authority or power or leader or anything else in this world or in the world to come. [22]And God has put all things under the authority of Christ, and he gave him this authority for the benefit of the church. [23]And the church is his body; it is filled by Christ, who fills everything everywhere with his presence.

CHAPTER 2

Made Alive with Christ

Once you were dead, doomed forever because of your many sins. [2]You used to live just like the rest of the world, full of sin, obeying Satan, the mighty prince of the power of the air. He is the spirit at work in the hearts of those who refuse to obey God. [3]All of us used to live that way, following the passions and desires of our evil nature. We were born with an evil nature, and we were under God's anger just like everyone else.

[4]But God is so rich in mercy, and he loved us so very much, [5]that even while we were dead because of our sins, he gave us life when he raised Christ from the dead. (It is only by God's special favor that you have been saved!) [6]For he raised us from the dead along with Christ, and we are seated with him in the heavenly realms—all because we are one with Christ Jesus. [7]And so God can always point to us as examples of the incredible wealth of

---

I BELIEVE God's plan has always been to bring people into his own family through Jesus Christ. (1:5)

I PRAISE God for the wonderful kindness he has poured out to me. (1:6)

I BELIEVE God the Father identified me as his own by giving me the Holy Spirit when I believed in Christ. (1:13)

I PRAY that I will begin to understand the incredible greatness of God's power for those who believe him. (1:19)

I BELIEVE I was born with an evil nature and under God's anger—until he saved me. (2:3)

I BELIEVE God is rich in mercy and loved me deeply even though I was a sinner just like everyone else. (2:4)

1:11 Or *we have become God's inheritance.*   1:18 Or *realize how much God has been honored by acquiring his people.*

his favor and kindness toward us, as shown in all he has done for us through Christ Jesus.

[8]God saved you by his special favor when you believed. And you can't take credit for this; it is a gift from God. [9]Salvation is not a reward for the good things we have done, so none of us can boast about it. [10]For we are God's masterpiece. He has created us anew in Christ Jesus, so that we can do the good things he planned for us long ago.

Oneness and Peace in Christ

[11]Don't forget that you Gentiles used to be outsiders by birth. You were called "the uncircumcised ones" by the Jews, who were proud of their circumcision, even though it affected only their bodies and not their hearts. [12]In those days you were living apart from Christ. You were excluded from God's people, Israel, and you did not know the promises God had made to them. You lived in this world without God and without hope. [13]But now you belong to Christ Jesus. Though you once were far away from God, now you have been brought near to him because of the blood of Christ.

[14]For Christ himself has made peace between us Jews and you Gentiles by making us all one people. He has broken down the wall of hostility that used to separate us. [15]By his death he ended the whole system of Jewish law that excluded the Gentiles. His purpose was to make peace between Jews and Gentiles by creating in himself one new person from the two groups. [16]Together as one body, Christ reconciled both groups to God by means of his death, and our hostility toward each other was put to death. [17]He has brought this Good News of peace to you Gentiles who were far away from him, and to us Jews who were near. [18]Now all of us, both Jews and Gentiles, may come to the Father through the same Holy Spirit because of what Christ has done for us.

A Temple for the Lord

[19]So now you Gentiles are no longer strangers and foreigners. You are citizens along with all of God's holy people. You are members of God's family. [20]We are his house, built on the foundation of the apostles and the prophets. And the cornerstone is Christ Jesus himself. [21]We who believe are carefully joined together, becoming a holy temple for the Lord. [22]Through him you Gentiles are also joined together as part of this dwelling where God lives by his Spirit.

CHAPTER 3

God's Secret Plan Revealed

I, Paul, am a prisoner of Christ Jesus because of my preaching to you Gentiles. [2]As you already know, God has given me this special ministry of announcing his favor to you Gentiles. [3]As I briefly mentioned earlier in this letter, God himself revealed his secret plan to me. [4]As you read what I have written, you will understand what I know about this plan regarding Christ. [5]God did not reveal it to previous generations, but now he has revealed it by the Holy Spirit to his holy apostles and prophets.

[6]And this is the secret plan: The Gentiles have an equal share with the Jews in all the riches inherited by God's children. Both groups have believed the Good News, and both are part of the same body and enjoy together the promise of blessings through Christ Jesus. [7]By God's special favor and mighty power, I have been given the wonderful privilege of serving him by spreading this Good News.

[8]Just think! Though I did nothing to deserve it, and though I am the least deserving Christian there is, I was chosen for this special joy of telling the Gentiles about the endless treasures available to them in Christ. [9]I was chosen to explain to everyone this plan that God, the Creator of all things, had kept secret from the beginning.

I DO NOT TAKE CREDIT for saving myself—my salvation is a gift from God. (2:8)

I DO good things for others for God's glory. (2:10)

Ask God to open your eyes as you read his Word (Psalm 119:18).

I COME to God the Father through the Holy Spirit because of what Jesus Christ has done for me. (2:18)

See Paul's profile (page 1333) at Galatians 2:5.

I HAVE BELIEVED the Good News and enjoy the promise of blessings through Jesus Christ. (3:6)

I BELIEVE God showed his rich wisdom by bringing both Jews and Gentiles into his church. (3:10)

I COME fearlessly into God's presence because of Jesus Christ and my faith in him. (3:12)

I PRAY that I will experience the love of Christ and be filled with the fullness of life and power that comes from God. (3:19)

I PRAISE God that he is able to accomplish infinitely more than I could ever dare to ask or hope. (3:20)

I DEMONSTRATE my love for other Christians by showing grace when they sin. (4:2)

I BELIEVE God has given each Christian a special spiritual gift. (4:7)

I STRIVE to become mature in the Lord so that I will not constantly change my mind about what I believe every time I hear something new. (4:14)

[10]God's purpose was to show his wisdom in all its rich variety to all the rulers and authorities in the heavenly realms. They will see this when Jews and Gentiles are joined together in his church. [11]This was his plan from all eternity, and it has now been carried out through Christ Jesus our Lord.

[12]Because of Christ and our faith in him, we can now come fearlessly into God's presence, assured of his glad welcome. [13]So please don't despair because of what they are doing to me here. It is for you that I am suffering, so you should feel honored and encouraged.

Paul's Prayer for Spiritual Empowering

[14]When I think of the wisdom and scope of God's plan, I fall to my knees and pray to the Father,* [15]the Creator of everything in heaven and on earth. [16]I pray that from his glorious, unlimited resources he will give you mighty inner strength through his Holy Spirit. [17]And I pray that Christ will be more and more at home in your hearts as you trust in him. May your roots go down deep into the soil of God's marvelous love. [18]And may you have the power to understand, as all God's people should, how wide, how long, how high, and how deep his love really is. [19]May you experience the love of Christ, though it is so great you will never fully understand it. Then you will be filled with the fullness of life and power that comes from God.

[20]Now glory be to God! By his mighty power at work within us, he is able to accomplish infinitely more than we would ever dare to ask or hope. [21]May he be given glory in the church and in Christ Jesus forever and ever through endless ages. Amen.

CHAPTER 4

Unity in the Body

Therefore I, a prisoner for serving the Lord, beg you to lead a life worthy of your calling, for you have been called by God. [2]Be humble and gentle. Be patient with each other, making allowance for each other's faults because of your love. [3]Always keep yourselves united in the Holy Spirit, and bind yourselves together with peace.

[4]We are all one body, we have the same Spirit, and we have all been called to the same glorious future. [5]There is only one Lord, one faith, one baptism, [6]and there is only one God and Father, who is over us all and in us all and living through us all. [7]However, he has given each one of us a special gift according to the generosity of Christ. [8]That is why the Scriptures say,

"When he ascended to the heights,
  he led a crowd of captives
  and gave gifts to his people."*

[9]Notice that it says "he ascended." This means that Christ first came down to the lowly world in which we live.* [10]The same one who came down is the one who ascended higher than all the heavens, so that his rule might fill the entire universe.

[11]He is the one who gave these gifts to the church: the apostles, the prophets, the evangelists, and the pastors and teachers. [12]Their responsibility is to equip God's people to do his work and build up the church, the body of Christ, [13]until we come to such unity in our faith and knowledge of God's Son that we will be mature and full grown in the Lord, measuring up to the full stature of Christ.

[14]Then we will no longer be like children, forever changing our minds about what we believe because someone has told us something different or because someone has cleverly lied to us and made the lie sound like the truth. [15]Instead, we will hold to the truth in love, becoming more and more

3:14 Some manuscripts read *the Father of our Lord Jesus Christ.*   4:8 Ps 68:18.   4:9 Or *to the lowest parts of the earth.*

in every way like Christ, who is the head of his body, the church. [16]Under his direction, the whole body is fitted together perfectly. As each part does its own special work, it helps the other parts grow, so that the whole body is healthy and growing and full of love.

Living as Children of Light

[17]With the Lord's authority let me say this: Live no longer as the ungodly* do, for they are hopelessly confused. [18]Their closed minds are full of darkness; they are far away from the life of God because they have shut their minds and hardened their hearts against him. [19]They don't care anymore about right and wrong, and they have given themselves over to immoral ways. Their lives are filled with all kinds of impurity and greed.

[20]But that isn't what you were taught when you learned about Christ. [21]Since you have heard all about him and have learned the truth that is in Jesus, [22]throw off your old evil nature and your former way of life, which is rotten through and through, full of lust and deception. [23]Instead, there must be a spiritual renewal of your thoughts and attitudes. [24]You must display a new nature because you are a new person, created in God's likeness—righteous, holy, and true.

[25]So put away all falsehood and "tell your neighbor the truth"* because we belong to each other. [26]And "don't sin by letting anger gain control over you."* Don't let the sun go down while you are still angry, [27]for anger gives a mighty foothold to the Devil.

[28]If you are a thief, stop stealing. Begin using your hands for honest work, and then give generously to others in need. [29]Don't use foul or abusive language. Let everything you say be good and helpful, so that your words will be an encouragement to those who hear them.

[30]And do not bring sorrow to God's Holy Spirit by the way you live. Remember, he is the one who has identified you as his own, guaranteeing that you will be saved on the day of redemption.

[31]Get rid of all bitterness, rage, anger, harsh words, and slander, as well as all types of malicious behavior. [32]Instead, be kind to each other, tenderhearted, forgiving one another, just as God through Christ has forgiven you.

CHAPTER 5

Living in the Light

Follow God's example in everything you do, because you are his dear children. [2]Live a life filled with love for others, following the example of Christ, who loved you and gave himself as a sacrifice to take away your sins. And God was pleased, because that sacrifice was like sweet perfume to him.

[3]Let there be no sexual immorality, impurity, or greed among you. Such sins have no place among God's people. [4]Obscene stories, foolish talk, and coarse jokes—these are not for you. Instead, let there be thankfulness to God. [5]You can be sure that no immoral, impure, or greedy person will inherit the Kingdom of Christ and of God. For a greedy person is really an idolater who worships the things of this world. [6]Don't be fooled by those who try to excuse these sins, for the terrible anger of God comes upon all those who disobey him. [7]Don't participate in the things these people do. [8]For though your hearts were once full of darkness, now you are full of light from the Lord, and your behavior should show it! [9]For this light within you produces only what is good and right and true.

[10]Try to find out what is pleasing to the Lord. [11]Take no part in the worthless deeds of evil and darkness; instead, rebuke and expose them. [12]It is shameful even to talk about the things that ungodly people do in secret. [13]But when the light shines on them, it becomes clear how evil these things are.

I NO LONGER LIVE like the ungodly do. (4:17)

I DO NOT SIN by letting anger control me. (4:26)

I SPEAK what is good and helpful, not foul and abusive. (4:29)

I FORGIVE others just as God through Christ has forgiven me. (4:32)

I FOLLOW Jesus Christ's example by living a life filled with love for others. (5:2)

I USE my mouth to give thanks to God, not to repeat coarse jokes or obscenities. (5:4)

I DO what is pleasing to the Lord. (5:10)

4:17 Greek *Gentiles.*   4:25 Zech 8:16.   4:26 Ps 4:4.

[14]And where your light shines, it will expose their evil deeds. This is why it is said,

"Awake, O sleeper,
rise up from the dead,
and Christ will give you light."

Living by the Spirit's Power

[15]So be careful how you live, not as fools but as those who are wise. [16]Make the most of every opportunity for doing good in these evil days. [17]Don't act thoughtlessly, but try to understand what the Lord wants you to do. [18]Don't be drunk with wine, because that will ruin your life. Instead, let the Holy Spirit fill and control you. [19] Then you will sing psalms and hymns and spiritual songs among yourselves, making music to the Lord in your hearts. [20]And you will always give thanks for everything to God the Father in the name of our Lord Jesus Christ.

Spirit-Guided Relationships: Wives and Husbands

[21]And further, you will submit to one another out of reverence for Christ. [22]You wives will submit to your husbands as you do to the Lord. [23]For a husband is the head of his wife as Christ is the head of his body, the church; he gave his life to be her Savior. [24]As the church submits to Christ, so you wives must submit to your husbands in everything.

[25]And you husbands must love your wives with the same love Christ showed the church. He gave up his life for her [26]to make her holy and clean, washed by baptism and God's word.* [27]He did this to present her to himself as a glorious church without a spot or wrinkle or any other blemish. Instead, she will be holy and without fault. [28]In the same way, husbands ought to love their wives as they love their own bodies. For a man is actually loving himself when he loves his wife. [29]No one hates his own body but lovingly cares for it, just as Christ cares for his body, which is the church. [30]And we are his body.

[31]As the Scriptures say, "A man leaves his father and mother and is joined to his wife, and the two are united into one."* [32]This is a great mystery, but it is an illustration of the way Christ and the church are one. [33]So again I say, each man must love his wife as he loves himself, and the wife must respect her husband.

CHAPTER 6

Children and Parents

Children, obey your parents because you belong to the Lord, for this is the right thing to do. [2]"Honor your father and mother." This is the first of the Ten Commandments that ends with a promise. [3]And this is the promise: If you honor your father and mother, "you will live a long life, full of blessing."*

[4]And now a word to you fathers. Don't make your children angry by the way you treat them. Rather, bring them up with the discipline and instruction approved by the Lord.

Slaves and Masters

[5]Slaves, obey your earthly masters with deep respect and fear. Serve them sincerely as you would serve Christ. [6]Work hard, but not just to please your masters when they are watching. As slaves of Christ, do the will of God with all your heart. [7]Work with enthusiasm, as though you were working for the Lord rather than for people. [8]Remember that the Lord will reward each one of us for the good we do, whether we are slaves or free.

[9]And in the same way, you masters must treat your slaves right. Don't

---

I LET the Holy Spirit fill and control my life. (5:18)

I SUBMIT to other Christians out of love and reverence for the Lord Jesus Christ. (5:21)

I BELIEVE Christ loves and cares for his body, the church. (5:29)

I BELIEVE marriage illustrates the way Christ and his church are one. (5:32)

I OBEY my parents when I am a child and honor them even when I am grown. (6:2)

I DO my best at work because I am working to please the Lord. (6:7)

5:26 Greek *having cleansed her by the washing of water with the word.*   5:31 Gen 2:24.   6:2-3 Exod 20:12; Deut 5:16.

threaten them; remember, you both have the same Master in heaven, and he has no favorites.

The Whole Armor of God

[10]A final word: Be strong with the Lord's mighty power. [11]Put on all of God's armor so that you will be able to stand firm against all strategies and tricks of the Devil. [12]For we are not fighting against people made of flesh and blood, but against the evil rulers and authorities of the unseen world, against those mighty powers of darkness who rule this world, and against wicked spirits in the heavenly realms.

[13]Use every piece of God's armor to resist the enemy in the time of evil, so that after the battle you will still be standing firm. [14]Stand your ground, putting on the sturdy belt of truth and the body armor of God's righteousness. [15]For shoes, put on the peace that comes from the Good News, so that you will be fully prepared.* [16]In every battle you will need faith as your shield to stop the fiery arrows aimed at you by Satan.* [17]Put on salvation as your helmet, and take the sword of the Spirit, which is the word of God. [18]Pray at all times and on every occasion in the power of the Holy Spirit. Stay alert and be persistent in your prayers for all Christians everywhere.

[19]And pray for me, too. Ask God to give me the right words as I boldly explain God's secret plan that the Good News is for the Gentiles, too.* [20]I am in chains now for preaching this message as God's ambassador. But pray that I will keep on speaking boldly for him, as I should.

Final Greetings

[21]Tychicus, a much loved brother and faithful helper in the Lord's work, will tell you all about how I am getting along. [22]I am sending him to you for just this purpose. He will let you know how we are, and he will encourage you.

[23]May God give you peace, dear brothers and sisters,* and love with faith, from God the Father and the Lord Jesus Christ. [24]May God's grace be upon all who love our Lord Jesus Christ with an undying love.

6:15 Or *For shoes, put on the readiness to preach the Good News of peace with God.*   6:16 Greek *by the evil one.*
6:19 Greek *explain the mystery of the gospel.*   6:23 Greek *brothers.*

I STAND firm against all the Devil's tricks by putting on all of God's armor. (6:11)

I PRAY earnestly for Christians who are experiencing persecution and other kinds of spiritual attack. (6:18)

I LOVE the Lord Jesus Christ with an undying love. (6:24)

PHILIPPIANS

THIS SIXTH New Testament letter answers many basic questions about Christian faith and practice.

Paul wrote this letter to a church he had established during one of his missionary journeys (Acts 16:12-40).

In this letter, Paul describes his joy because
- he knows the Philippian believers have placed their faith in Jesus Christ
- he has heard that many are preaching the Good News of Jesus Christ
- he has a sure hope of heaven when he dies
- he has the privilege of knowing Christ

Paul also urges the Philippian believers to be steadfast in the face of opposition, to be Christ-like in their service toward other believers, to be shining witnesses in a dark world, to watch out for false teachers, to follow his example, and to be Christ centered in their outlook on life. In addition, he commends Timothy and Epaphroditus for their outstanding work for the Lord's sake and commends the Philippian believers for their generous support of Paul's ministry.

Famous verses in Philippians include
- "I am sure that God, who began the good work within you, will continue his work until it is finally finished" (1:6)
- "For to me, living is for Christ, and dying is even better" (1:21)
- "Your attitude should be the same that Christ Jesus had" (2:5)
- "Live clean, innocent lives as children of God in a dark world" (2:15)
- "Everything else is worthless when compared with the priceless gain of knowing Christ Jesus my Lord" (3:8)
- "I strain to . . . receive the prize for which God, through Christ Jesus, is calling us up to heaven" (3:14)
- "Don't worry about anything; instead, pray about everything" (4:6)
- "Fix your thoughts on what is true and honorable and right" (4:8)
- "I can do everything with the help of Christ who gives me the strength I need" (4:13)

CHAPTER 1

Greetings from Paul

This letter is from Paul and Timothy, slaves of Christ Jesus.

It is written to all of God's people in Philippi, who believe in Christ Jesus, and to the elders* and deacons.

²May God our Father and the Lord Jesus Christ give you grace and peace.

Paul's Thanksgiving and Prayer

³Every time I think of you, I give thanks to my God. ⁴I always pray for you, and I make my requests with a heart full of joy ⁵because you have been my

See the profiles for Paul (page 1333) and Timothy (page 1373) at Galatians 2:5 and 1 Timothy 4:12.

I PRAY continually and joyfully for other Christians who serve the Lord with me. (1:4)

1:1 Greek *overseers.*

partners in spreading the Good News about Christ from the time you first heard it until now. ⁶And I am sure that God, who began the good work within you, will continue his work until it is finally finished on that day when Christ Jesus comes back again.

⁷It is right that I should feel as I do about all of you, for you have a very special place in my heart. We have shared together the blessings of God, both when I was in prison and when I was out, defending the truth and telling others the Good News. ⁸God knows how much I love you and long for you with the tender compassion of Christ Jesus. ⁹I pray that your love for each other will overflow more and more, and that you will keep on growing in your knowledge and understanding. ¹⁰For I want you to understand what really matters, so that you may live pure and blameless lives until Christ returns. ¹¹May you always be filled with the fruit of your salvation*—those good things that are produced in your life by Jesus Christ—for this will bring much glory and praise to God.

I BELIEVE God has begun a good work among his people and will continue it until it is finished. (1:6)

I PRAY that I will bring glory to God by living a life that honors Jesus Christ. (1:11)

Paul's Joy That Christ Is Preached

¹²And I want you to know, dear brothers and sisters,* that everything that has happened to me here has helped to spread the Good News. ¹³For everyone here, including all the soldiers in the palace guard, knows that I am in chains because of Christ. ¹⁴And because of my imprisonment, many of the Christians* here have gained confidence and become more bold in telling others about Christ.

¹⁵Some are preaching out of jealousy and rivalry. But others preach about Christ with pure motives. ¹⁶They preach because they love me, for they know the Lord brought me here to defend the Good News. ¹⁷Those others do not have pure motives as they preach about Christ. They preach with selfish ambition, not sincerely, intending to make my chains more painful to me. ¹⁸But whether or not their motives are pure, the fact remains that the message about Christ is being preached, so I rejoice. And I will continue to rejoice. ¹⁹For I know that as you pray for me and as the Spirit of Jesus Christ helps me, this will all turn out for my deliverance.

I REJOICE whenever the life-changing message of Jesus Christ is proclaimed. (1:18)

Paul's Life for Christ

²⁰For I live in eager expectation and hope that I will never do anything that causes me shame, but that I will always be bold for Christ, as I have been in the past, and that my life will always honor Christ, whether I live or I die. ²¹For to me, living is for Christ, and dying is even better. ²²Yet if I live, that means fruitful service for Christ. I really don't know which is better. ²³I'm torn between two desires: Sometimes I want to live, and sometimes I long to go and be with Christ. That would be far better for me, ²⁴but it is better for you that I live.

I AM DETERMINED to honor Jesus Christ with my life, no matter what. (1:20)

²⁵I am convinced of this, so I will continue with you so that you will grow and experience the joy of your faith. ²⁶Then when I return to you, you will have even more reason to boast about what Christ Jesus has done for me.

Live as Citizens of Heaven

²⁷But whatever happens to me, you must live in a manner worthy of the Good News about Christ, as citizens of heaven. Then, whether I come and see you again or only hear about you, I will know that you are standing side by side, fighting together for the Good News. ²⁸Don't be intimidated by your enemies. This will be a sign to them that they are going to be destroyed, but that you are going to be saved, even by God himself. ²⁹For you have been given not only the privilege of trusting in Christ but also the privilege of suffering for him. ³⁰We are in this fight together. You have seen me suffer for him in the past, and you know that I am still in the midst of this great struggle.

I BELIEVE it is a privilege to trust in Jesus Christ and to suffer for him. (1:29)

1:11 Greek *the fruit of righteousness.*   1:12 Greek *brothers.*   1:14 Greek *brothers in the Lord.*

CHAPTER 2

Unity through Humility

Is there any encouragement from belonging to Christ? Any comfort from his love? Any fellowship together in the Spirit? Are your hearts tender and sympathetic? ²Then make me truly happy by agreeing wholeheartedly with each other, loving one another, and working together with one heart and purpose.

³Don't be selfish; don't live to make a good impression on others. Be humble, thinking of others as better than yourself. ⁴Don't think only about your own affairs, but be interested in others, too, and what they are doing.

Christ's Humility and Exaltation

⁵Your attitude should be the same that Christ Jesus had. ⁶Though he was God, he did not demand and cling to his rights as God. ⁷He made himself nothing;* he took the humble position of a slave and appeared in human form.* ⁸And in human form he obediently humbled himself even further by dying a criminal's death on a cross. ⁹Because of this, God raised him up to the heights of heaven and gave him a name that is above every other name, ¹⁰so that at the name of Jesus every knee will bow, in heaven and on earth and under the earth, ¹¹and every tongue will confess that Jesus Christ is Lord, to the glory of God the Father.

Shine Brightly for Christ

¹²Dearest friends, you were always so careful to follow my instructions when I was with you. And now that I am away you must be even more careful to put into action God's saving work in your lives, obeying God with deep reverence and fear. ¹³For God is working in you, giving you the desire to obey him and the power to do what pleases him.

¹⁴In everything you do, stay away from complaining and arguing, ¹⁵so that no one can speak a word of blame against you. You are to live clean, innocent lives as children of God in a dark world full of crooked and perverse people. Let your lives shine brightly before them. ¹⁶Hold tightly to the word of life, so that when Christ returns, I will be proud that I did not lose the race and that my work was not useless. ¹⁷But even if my life is to be poured out like a drink offering to complete the sacrifice of your faithful service (that is, if I am to die for you), I will rejoice, and I want to share my joy with all of you. ¹⁸And you should be happy about this and rejoice with me.

Paul Commends Timothy

¹⁹If the Lord Jesus is willing, I hope to send Timothy to you soon. Then when he comes back, he can cheer me up by telling me how you are getting along. ²⁰I have no one else like Timothy, who genuinely cares about your welfare. ²¹All the others care only for themselves and not for what matters to Jesus Christ. ²²But you know how Timothy has proved himself. Like a son with his father, he has helped me in preaching the Good News. ²³I hope to send him to you just as soon as I find out what is going to happen to me here. ²⁴And I have confidence from the Lord that I myself will come to see you soon.

Paul Commends Epaphroditus

²⁵Meanwhile, I thought I should send Epaphroditus back to you. He is a true brother, a faithful worker, and a courageous soldier. And he was your messenger to help me in my need. ²⁶Now I am sending him home again, for he has been longing to see you, and he was very distressed that you heard he was ill. ²⁷And he surely was ill; in fact, he almost died. But God had mercy on him—and also on me, so that I would not have such unbearable sorrow. ²⁸So I am all the more anxious to send him back to you, for I know you will be glad to see him, and that will lighten all my cares. ²⁹Welcome him with

I ENCOURAGE my spiritual leaders by loving and working together with other believers. (2:2)

I SHARE the attitude of Jesus Christ when I live to serve others instead of insisting on my own rights. (2:5)

I BELIEVE God raised Jesus Christ to the highest place of honor, authority, and worship. (2:9)

I LIVE a pure life—free from complaining and arguing—to show God's light to this dark world. (2:15)

See Timothy's profile (page 1373) at 1 Timothy 4:12.

I CARE about what matters to Jesus Christ, not just about my own interests. (2:21)

2:7a Or *He laid aside his mighty power and glory.* 2:7b Greek *and was born in the likeness of men and was found in appearance as a man.*

Christian love* and with great joy, and be sure to honor people like him. ³⁰For he risked his life for the work of Christ, and he was at the point of death while trying to do for me the things you couldn't do because you were far away.

CHAPTER 3

The Priceless Gain of Knowing Christ

Whatever happens, dear brothers and sisters,* may the Lord give you joy. I never get tired of telling you this. I am doing this for your own good.

²Watch out for those dogs, those wicked men and their evil deeds, those mutilators who say you must be circumcised to be saved. ³For we who worship God in the Spirit* are the only ones who are truly circumcised. We put no confidence in human effort. Instead, we boast about what Christ Jesus has done for us.

⁴Yet I could have confidence in myself if anyone could. If others have reason for confidence in their own efforts, I have even more! ⁵For I was circumcised when I was eight days old, having been born into a pure-blooded Jewish family that is a branch of the tribe of Benjamin. So I am a real Jew if there ever was one! What's more, I was a member of the Pharisees, who demand the strictest obedience to the Jewish law. ⁶And zealous? Yes, in fact, I harshly persecuted the church. And I obeyed the Jewish law so carefully that I was never accused of any fault.

⁷I once thought all these things were so very important, but now I consider them worthless because of what Christ has done. ⁸Yes, everything else is worthless when compared with the priceless gain of knowing Christ Jesus my Lord. I have discarded everything else, counting it all as garbage, so that I may have Christ ⁹and become one with him. I no longer count on my own goodness or my ability to obey God's law, but I trust Christ to save me. For God's way of making us right with himself depends on faith. ¹⁰As a result, I can really know Christ and experience the mighty power that raised him from the dead. I can learn what it means to suffer with him, sharing in his death, ¹¹so that, somehow, I can experience the resurrection from the dead!

Pressing toward the Goal

¹²I don't mean to say that I have already achieved these things or that I have already reached perfection! But I keep working toward that day when I will finally be all that Christ Jesus saved me for and wants me to be. ¹³No, dear brothers and sisters, I am still not all I should be,* but I am focusing all my energies on this one thing: Forgetting the past and looking forward to what lies ahead, ¹⁴I strain to reach the end of the race and receive the prize for which God, through Christ Jesus, is calling us up to heaven.*

¹⁵I hope all of you who are mature Christians will agree on these things. If you disagree on some point, I believe God will make it plain to you. ¹⁶But we must be sure to obey the truth we have learned already.

¹⁷Dear brothers and sisters, pattern your lives after mine, and learn from those who follow our example. ¹⁸For I have told you often before, and I say it again with tears in my eyes, that there are many whose conduct shows they are really enemies of the cross of Christ. ¹⁹Their future is eternal destruction. Their god is their appetite, they brag about shameful things, and all they think about is this life here on earth. ²⁰But we are citizens of heaven, where the Lord Jesus Christ lives. And we are eagerly waiting for him to return as our Savior. ²¹He will take these weak mortal bodies of ours and change them into glorious bodies like his own, using the same mighty power that he will use to conquer everything, everywhere.

2:29 Greek *in the Lord.* 3:1 Greek *brothers;* also in 3:13, 17. 3:3 Or *in spirit;* some manuscripts read *worship by the Spirit of God.* 3:13 Some manuscripts read *I am not all I should be.* 3:14 Or *from heaven.*

I HONOR those Christians who work hard and sacrifice to serve the Lord. (2:29)

I WORSHIP God in the Spirit and put no spiritual confidence in my own human effort. (3:3)

I TRUST in Jesus Christ alone—not my own goodness or right living—to save me. (3:8)

I FOCUS on pushing forward to grow in Jesus Christ and please him. (3:13)

I LIVE as a citizen of heaven as I eagerly wait for Jesus Christ to take me there. (3:20)

I BELIEVE Jesus Christ will change my body into one like his own by his resurrection power. (3:21)

CHAPTER 4

Dear brothers and sisters,* I love you and long to see you, for you are my joy and the reward for my work. So please stay true to the Lord, my dear friends.

Paul's Final Thoughts

²And now I want to plead with those two women, Euodia and Syntyche. Please, because you belong to the Lord, settle your disagreement. ³And I ask you, my true teammate,* to help these women, for they worked hard with me in telling others the Good News. And they worked with Clement and the rest of my co-workers, whose names are written in the Book of Life.

LIKE EPAPHRODITUS *I am willing to risk my life for the work of Jesus Christ.*

Philippians 2:30

Around the world every day thousands of Christian ambassadors say good-bye to loved ones and journey along wilderness paths and crude roads marred by huge potholes and threats of attack.

These missionaries willingly make their homes in the midst of urban paganism and tropical diseases, aware that deteriorating health or escalating violence could force them to flee at a moment's notice. They don't fly in small airplanes or ford rivers for the thrill of adventure but as a necessary task in order to bring the Good News of Jesus Christ to those who still need to hear it.

Like these men and women, Epaphroditus took great risks for the sake of Christ, yet he wasn't even a missionary. He was an ordinary guy sent by his church to bring practical help and assistance to their beloved Paul. For the Lord's sake, Epaphroditus undertook the long trip, spent time with the great apostle inside a Roman prison, and then contracted a nearly fatal illness.

Like the Lord Jesus Christ, Epaphroditus obeyed God—even to the point of death. God may not call you and me to make an arduous journey to some faraway land. Then again, he may. Are you and I willing to leave the comfort and safety of home?

Like Epaphroditus, are we willing to serve the Lord at any cost?

○ *Today's Scripture reading is Philippians 1–2.*

---

⁴Always be full of joy in the Lord. I say it again—rejoice! ⁵Let everyone see that you are considerate in all you do. Remember, the Lord is coming soon.

⁶Don't worry about anything; instead, pray about everything. Tell God what you need, and thank him for all he has done. ⁷If you do this, you will experience God's peace, which is far more wonderful than the human mind can understand. His peace will guard your hearts and minds as you live in Christ Jesus.

⁸And now, dear brothers and sisters, let me say one more thing as I close this letter. Fix your thoughts on what is true and honorable and right. Think about things that are pure and lovely and admirable. Think about things that are excellent and worthy of praise. ⁹Keep putting into practice all you learned from me and heard from me and saw me doing, and the God of peace will be with you.

Paul's Thanks for Their Gifts

¹⁰How grateful I am, and how I praise the Lord that you are concerned about me again. I know you have always been concerned for me, but for a while you didn't have the chance to help me. ¹¹Not that I was ever in need, for I have learned how to get along happily whether I have much or little. ¹²I know how to live on almost nothing or with everything. I have learned the secret of living in every situation, whether it is with a full stomach or empty, with plenty or little. ¹³For I can do everything with the help of Christ who gives me the strength I need. ¹⁴But even so, you have done well to share with me in my present difficulty.

I ALWAYS AM FULL of joy in the Lord. (4:4)

I PRAY about everything instead of worrying about anything. (4:6)

I HEED godly examples so I can enjoy God's peace in my life. (4:9)

I CAN DO everything with the help of Jesus Christ, who gives me the strength I need. (4:13)

4:1 Greek *brothers*; also in 4:8.   4:3 Greek *true yokefellow*, or *loyal Syzygus*.

[15]As you know, you Philippians were the only ones who gave me financial help when I brought you the Good News and then traveled on from Macedonia. No other church did this. [16]Even when I was in Thessalonica you sent help more than once. [17]I don't say this because I want a gift from you. What I want is for you to receive a well-earned reward because of your kindness.

[18]At the moment I have all I need—more than I need! I am generously supplied with the gifts you sent me with Epaphroditus. They are a sweet-smelling sacrifice that is acceptable to God and pleases him. [19]And this same God who takes care of me will supply all your needs from his glorious riches, which have been given to us in Christ Jesus. [20]Now glory be to God our Father forever and ever. Amen.

I AM CONFIDENT God will meet all my needs from his glorious riches in Christ Jesus. (4:19)

Paul's Final Greetings

[21]Give my greetings to all the Christians there. The brothers who are with me here send you their greetings. [22]And all the other Christians send their greetings, too, especially those who work in Caesar's palace.

[23]May the grace of the Lord Jesus Christ be with your spirit.

COLOSSIANS

THIS SEVENTH New Testament letter contrasts Christian faith and practice with false teachings. Paul had not visited Colosse yet when he wrote this important letter to the church in that city.

In chapters 1–2, Paul contrasts the supremacy of Jesus Christ with every other authority in heaven and earth. He urges the believers in Colosse to stay true to Christ and not be led astray by false teachers.

In chapters 3–4, Paul urges his readers to be Christ-centered in their outlook on life, gives them specific instructions about Christ-honoring relationships, and asks them to pray for his ministry. He concludes with some final words of instruction and greetings.

Famous verses in Colossians include

○ "Christ is the visible image of the invisible God" (1:15)
○ "Christ is the one through whom God created everything" (1:16)
○ "For God in all his fullness was pleased to live in Christ" (1:19)
○ "In him [Christ] lie hidden all the treasures of wisdom and knowledge" (2:3)
○ "Don't let anyone lead you astray with empty philosophy and high-sounding nonsense" (2:8)
○ "Since you have been raised to new life with Christ, set your sights on the realities of heaven" (3:1)
○ "Remember, the Lord forgave you, so you must forgive others" (3:13)
○ "Let the peace that comes from Christ rule in your hearts" (3:15)
○ "Let the words of Christ, in all their richness, live in your hearts and make you wise" (3:16)
○ "And whatever you do or say, let it be as a representative of the Lord Jesus" (3:17)
○ "Work hard and cheerfully at whatever you do, as though you were working for the Lord" (3:23)
○ "Devote yourselves to prayer with an alert mind and a thankful heart" (4:2)
○ "Live wisely among those who are not Christians, and make the most of every opportunity" (4:5)

CHAPTER 1

Greetings from Paul

This letter is from Paul, chosen by God to be an apostle of Christ Jesus, and from our brother Timothy.

²It is written to God's holy people in the city of Colosse, who are faithful brothers and sisters* in Christ.

May God our Father give you grace and peace.

See the profiles for Paul (page 1333) and Timothy (page 1373) at Galatians 2:5 and 1 Timothy 4:12.

Paul's Thanksgiving and Prayer

³We always pray for you, and we give thanks to God the Father of our Lord Jesus Christ, ⁴for we have heard that you trust in Christ Jesus and that you

I TRUST in Jesus Christ and love God's people. (1:4)

1:2 Greek *faithful brothers.*

love all of God's people. [5]You do this because you are looking forward to the joys of heaven—as you have been ever since you first heard the truth of the Good News. [6]This same Good News that came to you is going out all over the world. It is changing lives everywhere, just as it changed yours that very first day you heard and understood the truth about God's great kindness to sinners.

[7]Epaphras, our much loved co-worker, was the one who brought you the Good News. He is Christ's faithful servant, and he is helping us in your place.* [8]He is the one who told us about the great love for others that the Holy Spirit has given you.

[9]So we have continued praying for you ever since we first heard about you. We ask God to give you a complete understanding of what he wants to do in your lives, and we ask him to make you wise with spiritual wisdom. [10]Then the way you live will always honor and please the Lord, and you will continually do good, kind things for others. All the while, you will learn to know God better and better.

[11]We also pray that you will be strengthened with his glorious power so that you will have all the patience and endurance you need. May you be filled with joy, [12]always thanking the Father, who has enabled you to share the inheritance that belongs to God's holy people, who live in the light. [13]For he has rescued us from the one who rules in the kingdom of darkness, and he has brought us into the Kingdom of his dear Son. [14]God has purchased our freedom with his blood* and has forgiven all our sins.

Christ Is Supreme

[15]Christ is the visible image of the invisible God. He existed before God made anything at all and is supreme over all creation.* [16]Christ is the one through whom God created everything in heaven and earth. He made the things we can see and the things we can't see—kings, kingdoms, rulers, and authorities. Everything has been created through him and for him. [17]He existed before everything else began, and he holds all creation together.

[18]Christ is the head of the church, which is his body. He is the first of all who will rise from the dead,* so he is first in everything. [19]For God in all his fullness was pleased to live in Christ, [20]and by him God reconciled everything to himself. He made peace with everything in heaven and on earth by means of his blood on the cross. [21]This includes you who were once so far away from God. You were his enemies, separated from him by your evil thoughts and actions, [22]yet now he has brought you back as his friends. He has done this through his death on the cross in his own human body. As a result, he has brought you into the very presence of God, and you are holy and blameless as you stand before him without a single fault. [23]But you must continue to believe this truth and stand in it firmly. Don't drift away from the assurance you received when you heard the Good News. The Good News has been preached all over the world, and I, Paul, have been appointed by God to proclaim it.

Paul's Work for the Church

[24]I am glad when I suffer for you in my body, for I am completing what remains of Christ's sufferings for his body, the church. [25]God has given me the responsibility of serving his church by proclaiming his message in all its fullness to you Gentiles. [26]This message was kept secret for centuries and generations past, but now it has been revealed to his own holy people. [27]For it has pleased God to tell his people that the riches and glory of Christ are for you Gentiles, too. For this is the secret: Christ lives in you, and this is your assurance that you will share in his glory.

I ASK God for the spiritual wisdom to understand what he wants me to do. (1:9)

I BELIEVE Jesus Christ is the visible image of the invisible God. (1:15)

I BELIEVE God brought me back as his friend through Jesus Christ's death on the cross. (1:22)

I HOLD FIRMLY to the truth and the assurance of the Good News without drifting away. (1:23)

I AM ASSURED that I will share in Jesus Christ's glory because he lives in me. (1:27)

1:7 Greek *he is ministering on your behalf*; other manuscripts read *he is ministering on our behalf*. 1:14 Some manuscripts do not include *with his blood*. 1:15 Greek *He is the firstborn of all creation*. 1:18 Greek *He is the beginning, the firstborn from the dead*.

[28]So everywhere we go, we tell everyone about Christ. We warn them and teach them with all the wisdom God has given us, for we want to present them to God, perfect* in their relationship to Christ. [29]I work very hard at this, as I depend on Christ's mighty power that works within me.

Recommit yourself to following the Lord with all your heart, soul, strength, and mind.

CHAPTER 2

I want you to know how much I have agonized for you and for the church at Laodicea, and for many other friends who have never known me personally. [2]My goal is that they will be encouraged and knit together by strong ties of love. I want them to have full confidence because they have complete understanding of God's secret plan, which is Christ himself. [3]In him lie hidden all the treasures of wisdom and knowledge.

[4]I am telling you this so that no one will be able to deceive you with persuasive arguments. [5]For though I am far away from you, my heart is with you. And I am very happy because you are living as you should and because of your strong faith in Christ.

Freedom from Rules and New Life in Christ

[6]And now, just as you accepted Christ Jesus as your Lord, you must continue to live in obedience to him. [7]Let your roots grow down into him and draw up nourishment from him, so you will grow in faith, strong and vigorous in the truth you were taught. Let your lives overflow with thanksgiving for all he has done.

I DRAW NOURISHMENT from Jesus Christ and am growing in my faith in him. (2:7)

[8]Don't let anyone lead you astray with empty philosophy and high-sounding nonsense that come from human thinking and from the evil powers of this world,* and not from Christ. [9]For in Christ the fullness of God lives in a human body,* [10]and you are complete through your union with Christ. He is the Lord over every ruler and authority in the universe.

I AM NOT LED ASTRAY by human thinking and worldly philosophies. (2:8)

[11]When you came to Christ, you were "circumcised," but not by a physical procedure. It was a spiritual procedure—the cutting away of your sinful nature. [12]For you were buried with Christ when you were baptized. And with him you were raised to a new life because you trusted the mighty power of God, who raised Christ from the dead.

[13]You were dead because of your sins and because your sinful nature was not yet cut away. Then God made you alive with Christ. He forgave all our sins. [14]He canceled the record that contained the charges against us. He took it and destroyed it by nailing it to Christ's cross. [15]In this way, God disarmed the evil rulers and authorities. He shamed them publicly by his victory over them on the cross of Christ.

I BELIEVE God canceled the record of wrongs I've done when he nailed it to Christ's cross. (2:14)

[16]So don't let anyone condemn you for what you eat or drink, or for not celebrating certain holy days or new-moon ceremonies or Sabbaths. [17]For these rules were only shadows of the real thing, Christ himself. [18]Don't let anyone condemn you by insisting on self-denial. And don't let anyone say you must worship angels, even though they say they have had visions about this. These people claim to be so humble, but their sinful minds have made them proud. [19]But they are not connected to Christ, the head of the body. For we are joined together in his body by his strong sinews, and we grow only as we get our nourishment and strength from God.

[20]You have died with Christ, and he has set you free from the evil powers of this world. So why do you keep on following rules of the world, such as, [21]"Don't handle, don't eat, don't touch." [22]Such rules are mere human teaching about things that are gone as soon as we use them. [23]These rules may seem wise because they require strong devotion, humility, and severe bodily discipline. But they have no effect when it comes to conquering a person's evil thoughts and desires.

I BELIEVE Jesus Christ has set me free from the evil powers of the world. (2:20)

I BELIEVE human rules are powerless to change a person's thoughts and desires. (2:23)

1:28 Or *mature.*   2:8 Or *from the basic principles of this world;* also in 2:20.   2:9 Greek *in him dwells all the fullness of the Godhead bodily.*

CHAPTER 3

Living the New Life

Since you have been raised to new life with Christ, set your sights on the realities of heaven, where Christ sits at God's right hand in the place of honor and power. [2]Let heaven fill your thoughts. Do not think only about things down here on earth. [3]For you died when Christ died, and your real life is hidden with Christ in God. [4]And when Christ, who is your* real life, is revealed to the whole world, you will share in all his glory.

[5]So put to death the sinful, earthly things lurking within you. Have nothing to do with sexual sin, impurity, lust, and shameful desires. Don't be greedy for the good things of this life, for that is idolatry. [6]God's terrible anger will come upon those who do such things. [7]You used to do them when your life was still part of this world. [8]But now is the time to get rid of anger, rage, malicious behavior, slander, and dirty language. [9]Don't lie to each other, for you have stripped off your old evil nature and all its wicked deeds. [10]In its place you have clothed yourselves with a brand-new nature that is continually being renewed as you learn more and more about Christ, who created this new nature within you. [11]In this new life, it doesn't matter if you are a Jew or a Gentile,* circumcised or uncircumcised, barbaric, uncivilized,* slave, or free. Christ is all that matters, and he lives in all of us.

[12]Since God chose you to be the holy people whom he loves, you must clothe yourselves with tenderhearted mercy, kindness, humility, gentleness, and patience. [13]You must make allowance for each other's faults and forgive the person who offends you. Remember, the Lord forgave you, so you must forgive others. [14]And the most important piece of clothing you must wear is love. Love is what binds us all together in perfect harmony. [15]And let the peace that comes from Christ rule in your hearts. For as members of one body you are all called to live in peace. And always be thankful.

[16]Let the words of Christ, in all their richness, live in your hearts and make you wise. Use his words to teach and counsel each other. Sing psalms and hymns and spiritual songs to God with thankful hearts. [17]And whatever you do or say, let it be as a representative of the Lord Jesus, all the while giving thanks through him to God the Father.

Instructions for Christian Households

[18]You wives must submit to your husbands, as is fitting for those who belong to the Lord. [19]And you husbands must love your wives and never treat them harshly.

[20]You children must always obey your parents, for this is what pleases the Lord. [21]Fathers, don't aggravate your children. If you do, they will become discouraged and quit trying.

[22]You slaves must obey your earthly masters in everything you do. Try to please them all the time, not just when they are watching you. Obey them willingly because of your reverent fear of the Lord. [23]Work hard and cheerfully at whatever you do, as though you were working for the Lord rather than for people. [24]Remember that the Lord will give you an inheritance as your reward, and the Master you are serving is Christ. [25]But if you do what is wrong, you will be paid back for the wrong you have done. For God has no favorites who can get away with evil.

CHAPTER 4

You slave owners must be just and fair to your slaves. Remember that you also have a Master—in heaven.

An Encouragement for Prayer

[2]Devote yourselves to prayer with an alert mind and a thankful heart. [3]Don't

---

I AM NOT GREEDY for the good things of this life. (3:5)

I REPLACE my sinful habits and desires with the new nature Jesus Christ creates and renews within me. (3:10)

I FORGIVE others and make allowances for their faults. (3:13)

I ALLOW Jesus Christ's words to be absorbed into my heart and life—and I use those words to bless others. (3:16)

I WORK HARD on the job as though I were working for the Lord, not merely for my boss. (3:23)

I DEVOTE myself to prayer with an alert mind and a thankful heart. (4:2)

3:4 Some manuscripts read *our.*   3:11a Greek *Greek.*   3:11b Greek *Barbarian, Scythian.*

forget to pray for us, too, that God will give us many opportunities to preach about his secret plan—that Christ is also for you Gentiles. That is why I am here in chains. ⁴Pray that I will proclaim this message as clearly as I should.

⁵Live wisely among those who are not Christians, and make the most of every opportunity. ⁶Let your conversation be gracious and effective so that you will have the right answer for everyone.

Paul's Final Instructions and Greetings

⁷Tychicus, a much loved brother, will tell you how I am getting along. He is a faithful helper who serves the Lord with me. ⁸I have sent him on this special trip to let you know how we are doing and to encourage you. ⁹I am also sending Onesimus, a faithful and much loved brother, one of your own people. He and Tychicus will give you all the latest news.

¹⁰Aristarchus, who is in prison with me, sends you his greetings, and so does Mark, Barnabas's cousin. And as you were instructed before, make Mark welcome if he comes your way. ¹¹Jesus (the one we call Justus) also sends his greetings. These are the only Jewish Christians among my co-workers; they are working with me here for the Kingdom of God. And what a comfort they have been!

¹²Epaphras, from your city, a servant of Christ Jesus, sends you his greetings. He always prays earnestly for you, asking God to make you strong and perfect, fully confident of the whole will of God. ¹³I can assure you that he has agonized for you and also for the Christians in Laodicea and Hierapolis.

¹⁴Dear Doctor Luke sends his greetings, and so does Demas. ¹⁵Please give my greetings to our Christian brothers and sisters* at Laodicea, and to Nympha and those who meet in her house.

¹⁶After you have read this letter, pass it on to the church at Laodicea so they can read it, too. And you should read the letter I wrote to them. ¹⁷And say to Archippus, "Be sure to carry out the work the Lord gave you."

¹⁸Here is my greeting in my own handwriting—PAUL.

Remember my chains.

May the grace of God be with you.

4:15 Greek *brothers.*

I LOOK for opportunities to tell others the Good News of Jesus Christ. (4:5)

See the profiles for John Mark (page 1255) and Barnabas (page 1253) at Acts 13:13 and Acts 11:23.

I SEEK to obey all of God's commands. (4:12)

See Luke's profile (page 1379) at 2 Timothy 4:11.

I ENCOURAGE other believers to continue in the work the Lord has given them. (4:17)

See Paul's profile (page 1333) at Galatians 2:5.

1 THESSALONIANS

THIS EIGHTH New Testament letter urges new believers to live for the Lord in the face of adversity.

Paul wrote this letter to a church he had established a short time earlier during one of his missionary journeys (Acts 17:1-10).

In chapters 1-3, Paul praises God for the faith of the Thessalonian believers, describes his ministry among them, expresses his concern for them ever since persecution had broken out, explains why he felt compelled to send Timothy back to visit them, and thanks God that their faith is still strong.

In chapters 4-5, Paul urges the Thessalonian believers to live in a way that pleases God, to encourage each other with the hope of heaven, and to remember that Jesus Christ is coming back again. He concludes with some final words of instruction and challenge.

Famous verses in 1 Thessalonians include

- ○ "We always thank God for all of you and pray for you constantly" (1:2)
- ○ "And now the word of the Lord is ringing out from you to people everywhere" (1:8)
- ○ "You turned away from idols to serve the true and living God" (1:9)
- ○ "We were as gentle among you as a mother feeding and caring for her own children" (2:7)
- ○ "We treated each of you as a father treats his own children" (2:11)
- ○ "God wants you to be holy" (4:3)
- ○ "Live a quiet life, minding your own business and working with your hands" (4:11)
- ○ "I want you to know what will happen to the Christians who have died" (4:13)
- ○ "The day of the Lord will come unexpectedly, like a thief in the night" (5:2)
- ○ "He [Christ] died for us so that we can live with him forever" (5:10)
- ○ "Honor those who are your leaders in the Lord's work" (5:12)
- ○ "Always be joyful. Keep on praying. No matter what happens, always be thankful" (5:16-18)
- ○ "Do not stifle the Holy Spirit" (5:19)
- ○ "Keep away from every kind of evil" (5:22)
- ○ "May your whole spirit and soul and body be kept blameless until that day when our Lord Jesus Christ comes again" (5:23)

CHAPTER 1

Greetings from Paul

This letter is from Paul, Silas,* and Timothy.

It is written to the church in Thessalonica, you who belong to God the Father and the Lord Jesus Christ.

May his grace and peace be yours.

The Faith of the Thessalonian Believers

²We always thank God for all of you and pray for you constantly. ³As we talk to our God and Father about you, we think of your faithful work, your

See the profiles for Paul (page 1333) and Timothy (page 1373) at Galatians 2:5 and 1 Timothy 4:12.

1:1 Greek *Silvanus.*

loving deeds, and your continual anticipation of the return of our Lord Jesus Christ.

⁴We know that God loves you, dear brothers and sisters,* and that he chose you to be his own people. ⁵For when we brought you the Good News, it was not only with words but also with power, for the Holy Spirit gave you full assurance that what we said was true. And you know that the way we lived among you was further proof of the truth of our message. ⁶So you received the message with joy from the Holy Spirit in spite of the severe suffering it brought you. In this way, you imitated both us and the Lord. ⁷As a result, you yourselves became an example to all the Christians in Greece.* ⁸And now the word of the Lord is ringing out from you to people everywhere, even beyond Greece, for wherever we go we find people telling us about your faith in God. We don't need to tell them about it, ⁹for they themselves keep talking about the wonderful welcome you gave us and how you turned away from idols to serve the true and living God. ¹⁰And they speak of how you are looking forward to the coming of God's Son from heaven—Jesus, whom God raised from the dead. He is the one who has rescued us from the terrors of the coming judgment.

CHAPTER 2

Paul Remembers His Visit

You yourselves know, dear brothers and sisters,* that our visit to you was not a failure. ²You know how badly we had been treated at Philippi just before we came to you and how much we suffered there. Yet our God gave us the courage to declare his Good News to you boldly, even though we were surrounded by many who opposed us. ³So you can see that we were not preaching with any deceit or impure purposes or trickery.

⁴For we speak as messengers who have been approved by God to be entrusted with the Good News. Our purpose is to please God, not people. He is the one who examines the motives of our hearts. ⁵Never once did we try to win you with flattery, as you very well know. And God is our witness that we were not just pretending to be your friends so you would give us money! ⁶As for praise, we have never asked for it from you or anyone else. ⁷As apostles of Christ we certainly had a right to make some demands of you, but we were as gentle among you as a mother* feeding and caring for her own children. ⁸We loved you so much that we gave you not only God's Good News but our own lives, too.

⁹Don't you remember, dear brothers and sisters, how hard we worked among you? Night and day we toiled to earn a living so that our expenses would not be a burden to anyone there as we preached God's Good News among you. ¹⁰You yourselves are our witnesses—and so is God—that we were pure and honest and faultless toward all of you believers. ¹¹And you know that we treated each of you as a father treats his own children. ¹²We pleaded with you, encouraged you, and urged you to live your lives in a way that God would consider worthy. For he called you into his Kingdom to share his glory.

¹³And we will never stop thanking God that when we preached his message to you, you didn't think of the words we spoke as being just our own. You accepted what we said as the very word of God—which, of course, it was. And this word continues to work in you who believe.

¹⁴And then, dear brothers and sisters, you suffered persecution from your own countrymen. In this way, you imitated the believers in God's churches in Judea who, because of their belief in Christ Jesus, suffered from their own people, the Jews.

I BELIEVE God loves me and chose me to be part of his family. (1:4)

I LOOK FORWARD to Jesus Christ's return from heaven. (1:10)

I DO NOT USE flattery or deceit when I share the Good News of Jesus Christ. (2:5)

I GIVE myself to others and present the Good News to them in love. (2:8)

I TREAT new Christians as a loving parent would treat a child. (2:11)

I CONTINUALLY THANK God for the individuals who trust the Lord through me. (2:13)

1:4 Greek *brothers.* 1:7 Greek *Macedonia and Achaia,* the northern and southern regions of Greece; also in 1:8. 2:1 Greek *brothers;* also in 2:9, 14, 17. 2:7 Some manuscripts read *we were as infants among you; we were as a mother.*

¹⁵For some of the Jews had killed their own prophets, and some even killed the Lord Jesus. Now they have persecuted us and driven us out. They displease God and oppose everyone ¹⁶by trying to keep us from preaching the Good News to the Gentiles, for fear some might be saved. By doing this, they continue to pile up their sins. But the anger of God has caught up with them at last.

Timothy's Good Report about the Church

¹⁷Dear brothers and sisters, after we were separated from you for a little while (though our hearts never left you), we tried very hard to come back because of our intense longing to see you again. ¹⁸We wanted very much to come, and I, Paul, tried again and again, but Satan prevented us. ¹⁹After all, what gives us hope and joy, and what is our proud reward and crown? It is you! Yes, you will bring us much joy as we stand together before our Lord Jesus when he comes back again. ²⁰For you are our pride and joy.

See Paul's profile (page 1333) at Galatians 2:5.

CHAPTER 3

Finally, when we could stand it no longer, we decided that I should stay alone in Athens, ²and we sent Timothy to visit you. He is our co-worker for God and our brother in proclaiming the Good News of Christ. We sent him to strengthen you, to encourage you in your faith, ³and to keep you from becoming disturbed by the troubles you were going through. But, of course, you know that such troubles are going to happen to us Christians. ⁴Even while we were with you, we warned you that troubles would soon come— and they did, as you well know.

⁵That is why, when I could bear it no longer, I sent Timothy to find out whether your faith was still strong. I was afraid that the Tempter had gotten the best of you and that all our work had been useless. ⁶Now Timothy has just returned, bringing the good news that your faith and love are as strong as ever. He reports that you remember our visit with joy and that you want to see us just as much as we want to see you. ⁷So we have been greatly comforted, dear brothers and sisters,* in all of our own crushing troubles and suffering, because you have remained strong in your faith. ⁸It gives us new life, knowing you remain strong in the Lord.

⁹How we thank God for you! Because of you we have great joy in the presence of God. ¹⁰Night and day we pray earnestly for you, asking God to let us see you again to fill up anything that may still be missing in your faith.

¹¹May God himself, our Father, and our Lord Jesus make it possible for us to come to you very soon. ¹²And may the Lord make your love grow and overflow to each other and to everyone else, just as our love overflows toward you. ¹³As a result, Christ will make your hearts strong, blameless, and holy when you stand before God our Father on that day when our Lord Jesus comes with all those who belong to him.

See Timothy's profile (page 1373) at 1 Timothy 4:12.

I WARN new believers that suffering is part of the Christian life. (3:4)

I TAKE COURAGE when my fellow Christians stand strong in their faith. (3:7)

I ASK God to give me more opportunities to be with new Christians and help them grow in their faith. (3:10)

I BELIEVE Jesus Christ is the one who makes me stand holy and blameless before God. (3:13)

CHAPTER 4

Live to Please God

Finally, dear brothers and sisters,* we urge you in the name of the Lord Jesus to live in a way that pleases God, as we have taught you. You are doing this already, and we encourage you to do so more and more. ²For you remember what we taught you in the name of the Lord Jesus. ³God wants you to be holy, so you should keep clear of all sexual sin. ⁴Then each of you will control your body* and live in holiness and honor—⁵not in lustful passion as the pagans do, in their ignorance of God and his ways.

⁶Never cheat a Christian brother in this matter by taking his wife, for the

I LIVE in holiness and honor. (4:4)

3:7 Greek brothers. 4:1 Greek brothers; also in 4:10, 13. 4:4 Or will know how to take a wife for himself; Greek reads will know how to possess his own vessel.

Lord avenges all such sins, as we have solemnly warned you before. [7]God has called us to be holy, not to live impure lives. [8]Anyone who refuses to live by these rules is not disobeying human rules but is rejecting God, who gives his Holy Spirit to you.

[9]But I don't need to write to you about the Christian love* that should be shown among God's people. For God himself has taught you to love one another. [10]Indeed, your love is already strong toward all the Christians* in all of Macedonia. Even so, dear brothers and sisters, we beg you to love them more and more. [11]This should be your ambition: to live a quiet life, minding your own business and working with your hands, just as we commanded you before. [12]As a result, people who are not Christians will respect the way you live, and you will not need to depend on others to meet your financial needs.

The Hope of the Resurrection

[13]And now, brothers and sisters, I want you to know what will happen to the Christians who have died so you will not be full of sorrow like people who have no hope. [14]For since we believe that Jesus died and was raised to life again, we also believe that when Jesus comes, God will bring back with Jesus all the Christians who have died.

[15]I can tell you this directly from the Lord: We who are still living when the Lord returns will not rise to meet him ahead of those who are in their graves. [16]For the Lord himself will come down from heaven with a commanding shout, with the call of the archangel, and with the trumpet call of God. First, all the Christians who have died will rise from their graves. [17]Then, together with them, we who are still alive and remain on the earth will be caught up in the clouds to meet the Lord in the air and remain with him forever. [18]So comfort and encourage each other with these words.

CHAPTER 5

I really don't need to write to you about how and when all this will happen, dear brothers and sisters.* [2]For you know quite well that the day of the Lord will come unexpectedly, like a thief in the night. [3]When people are saying, "All is well; everything is peaceful and secure," then disaster will fall upon them as suddenly as a woman's birth pains begin when her child is about to be born. And there will be no escape.

[4]But you aren't in the dark about these things, dear brothers and sisters, and you won't be surprised when the day of the Lord comes like a thief. [5]For you are all children of the light and of the day; we don't belong to darkness and night. [6]So be on your guard, not asleep like the others. Stay alert and be sober. [7]Night is the time for sleep and the time when people get drunk. [8]But let us who live in the light think clearly, protected by the body armor of faith and love, and wearing as our helmet the confidence of our salvation. [9]For God decided to save us through our Lord Jesus Christ, not to pour out his anger on us. [10]He died for us so that we can live with him forever, whether we are dead or alive at the time of his return. [11]So encourage each other and build each other up, just as you are already doing.

Paul's Final Advice

[12]Dear brothers and sisters, honor those who are your leaders in the Lord's work. They work hard among you and warn you against all that is wrong. [13]Think highly of them and give them your wholehearted love because of their work. And remember to live peaceably with each other.

[14]Brothers and sisters, we urge you to warn those who are lazy. Encourage those who are timid. Take tender care of those who are weak. Be patient with everyone.

4:9 Greek *brotherly love.* 4:10 Greek *the brothers.* 5:1 Greek *brothers*; also in 5:4, 12, 14, 25, 26, 27.

I DO NOT REJECT God by living in sexual impurity. (4:8)

I BELIEVE all the Christians who have died will rise first when the Lord comes from heaven. (4:16)

I ENCOURAGE other Christians with the hope that all believers—living or dead—will meet the Lord Jesus Christ in the air when he returns. (4:18)

I KNOW the day of the Lord's judgment will come unexpectedly. (5:2)

I STAY alert and watch for the Lord's coming. (5:6)

I AM GLAD God decided to save me, not pour out his anger on me. (5:9)

I HONOR AND LOVE those in my church who work hard for the Lord and for his people. (5:13)

¹⁵See that no one pays back evil for evil, but always try to do good to each other and to everyone else.

¹⁶Always be joyful. ¹⁷Keep on praying. ¹⁸No matter what happens, always be thankful, for this is God's will for you who belong to Christ Jesus.

¹⁹Do not stifle the Holy Spirit. ²⁰Do not scoff at prophecies, ²¹but test everything that is said. Hold on to what is good. ²²Keep away from every kind of evil.

I BELIEVE God wants me to be thankful, no matter what happens. (5:18)

Paul's Final Greetings

²³Now may the God of peace make you holy in every way, and may your whole spirit and soul and body be kept blameless until that day when our Lord Jesus Christ comes again. ²⁴God, who calls you, is faithful; he will do this.

²⁵Dear brothers and sisters, pray for us.

²⁶Greet all the brothers and sisters in Christian love.*

²⁷I command you in the name of the Lord to read this letter to all the brothers and sisters.

²⁸And may the grace of our Lord Jesus Christ be with all of you.

I BELIEVE God is faithful to make me holy and keep me blameless until Jesus Christ comes. (5:24)

5:26 Greek *with a holy kiss.*

2 THESSALONIANS

THIS NINTH New Testament letter urges confused believers to stand firm for the Lord despite persecution and false teachings.

In chapters 1–2, Paul praises God for the faith of the Thessalonian believers, promises that God will bless them and judge those who are persecuting them, instructs them about the Lord's second coming, and urges them to stand firm.

In chapter 3, Paul asks the Thessalonian believers to pray for his ministry and exhorts them to get back to work, even though the Lord is coming back.

Famous verses in 2 Thessalonians include

- ○ What will happen when the Lord Jesus comes back (1:7-10)
- ○ "We pray that God, by his power, will fulfill all your good intentions" (1:11)
- ○ What will happen before the Lord Jesus comes back (2:1-12)
- ○ "May our Lord . . . comfort your hearts and give you strength in every good thing you do and say" (2:16-17)
- ○ "Pray first that the Lord's message will spread rapidly and be honored wherever it goes" (3:1)
- ○ "May the Lord of peace himself always give you his peace no matter what happens" (3:16)

CHAPTER 1

Greetings from Paul

This letter is from Paul, Silas,* and Timothy.

It is written to the church in Thessalonica, you who belong to God our Father and the Lord Jesus Christ.

²May God our Father and the Lord Jesus Christ give you grace and peace.

See the profiles for Paul (page 1333) and Timothy (page 1373) at Galatians 2:5 and 1 Timothy 4:12.

Encouragement during Persecution

³Dear brothers and sisters,* we always thank God for you, as is right, for we are thankful that your faith is flourishing and you are all growing in love for each other. ⁴We proudly tell God's other churches about your endurance and faithfulness in all the persecutions and hardships you are suffering. ⁵But God will use this persecution to show his justice. For he will make you worthy of his Kingdom, for which you are suffering, ⁶and in his justice he will punish those who persecute you. ⁷And God will provide rest for you who are being persecuted and also for us when the Lord Jesus appears from heaven. He will come with his mighty angels, ⁸in flaming fire, bringing judgment on those who don't know God and on those who refuse to obey the Good News of our Lord Jesus. ⁹They will be punished with everlasting destruction, forever separated from the Lord and from his glorious power ¹⁰when he comes to receive glory and praise from his holy people. And you will be among those praising him on that day, for you believed what we testified about him.

¹¹And so we keep on praying for you, that our God will make you worthy of the life to which he called you. And we pray that God, by his power, will

I BELIEVE God uses the persecution of Christians to show his justice. (1:5)

I BELIEVE God will provide rest for Christians and punishment for those who have persecuted them when the Lord Jesus Christ comes again. (1:7)

I PRAY that God will make me worthy of the life to which he called me. (1:11)

1:1 Greek *Silvanus*.   1:3 Greek *Brothers*.

fulfill all your good intentions and faithful deeds. [12] Then everyone will give honor to the name of our Lord Jesus because of you, and you will be honored along with him. This is all made possible because of the undeserved favor of our God and Lord, Jesus Christ.*

CHAPTER 2

Events prior to the Lord's Second Coming

And now, brothers and sisters,* let us tell you about the coming again of our Lord Jesus Christ and how we will be gathered together to meet him. [2] Please don't be so easily shaken and troubled by those who say that the day of the Lord has already begun. Even if they claim to have had a vision, a revelation, or a letter supposedly from us, don't believe them. [3] Don't be fooled by what they say.

For that day will not come until there is a great rebellion against God and the man of lawlessness is revealed—the one who brings destruction.* [4] He will exalt himself and defy every god there is and tear down every object of adoration and worship. He will position himself in the temple of God, claiming that he himself is God. [5] Don't you remember that I told you this when I was with you? [6] And you know what is holding him back, for he can be revealed only when his time comes.

[7] For this lawlessness is already at work secretly, and it will remain secret until the one who is holding it back steps out of the way. [8] Then the man of lawlessness will be revealed, whom the Lord Jesus will consume with the breath of his mouth and destroy by the splendor of his coming. [9] This evil man will come to do the work of Satan with counterfeit power and signs and miracles. [10] He will use every kind of wicked deception to fool those who are on their way to destruction because they refuse to believe the truth that would save them. [11] So God will send great deception upon them, and they will believe all these lies. [12] Then they will be condemned for not believing the truth and for enjoying the evil they do.

Believers Should Stand Firm

[13] As for us, we always thank God for you, dear brothers and sisters loved by the Lord. We are thankful that God chose you to be among the first* to experience salvation, a salvation that came through the Spirit who makes you holy and by your belief in the truth. [14] He called you to salvation when we told you the Good News; now you can share in the glory of our Lord Jesus Christ.

[15] With all these things in mind, dear brothers and sisters, stand firm and keep a strong grip on everything we taught you both in person and by letter.

[16] May our Lord Jesus Christ and God our Father, who loved us and in his special favor gave us everlasting comfort and good hope, [17] comfort your hearts and give you strength in every good thing you do and say.

CHAPTER 3

Paul's Request for Prayer

Finally, dear brothers and sisters,* I ask you to pray for us. Pray first that the Lord's message will spread rapidly and be honored wherever it goes, just as when it came to you. [2] Pray, too, that we will be saved from wicked and evil people, for not everyone believes in the Lord. [3] But the Lord is faithful; he will make you strong and guard you from the evil one.* [4] And we are confident in the Lord that you are practicing the things we commanded you, and that you always will. [5] May the Lord bring you into an ever deeper understanding of the love of God and the endurance that comes from Christ.

I ABHOR blasphemy.
(2:4)

I WHOLEHEARTEDLY AFFIRM the truth of God that saves me.
(2:10)

I KEEP a firm grip on all the biblical truth I have been taught.
(2:15)

I PRAY that God's message will spread quickly and be honored wherever it goes. (3:1)

I PRAY that God will give me a deeper understanding of his love. (3:5)

1:12 Or *of our God and the Lord Jesus Christ.* 2:1 Greek *brothers;* also in 2:13, 15. 2:3 Greek *the son of destruction.* 2:13 Some manuscripts read *God chose you from the very beginning.* 3:1 Greek *brothers;* also in 3:6, 13. 3:3 Or *from evil.*

An Exhortation to Proper Living

⁶And now, dear brothers and sisters, we give you this command with the authority of our Lord Jesus Christ: Stay away from any Christian* who lives in idleness and doesn't follow the tradition of hard work we gave you. ⁷For you know that you ought to follow our example. We were never lazy when we were with you. ⁸We never accepted food from anyone without paying for it. We worked hard day and night so that we would not be a burden to any of you. ⁹It wasn't that we didn't have the right to ask you to feed us, but we wanted to give you an example to follow. ¹⁰Even while we were with you, we gave you this rule: "Whoever does not work should not eat."

¹¹Yet we hear that some of you are living idle lives, refusing to work and wasting time meddling in other people's business. ¹²In the name of the Lord Jesus Christ, we appeal to such people—no, we command them: Settle down and get to work. Earn your own living. ¹³And I say to the rest of you, dear brothers and sisters, never get tired of doing good.

> I NEVER GET TIRED of doing good. (3:13)

¹⁴Take note of those who refuse to obey what we say in this letter. Stay away from them so they will be ashamed. ¹⁵Don't think of them as enemies, but speak to them as you would to a Christian who needs to be warned.

> I WARN Christian friends who refuse to obey God's truth. (3:15)

Paul's Final Greetings

¹⁶May the Lord of peace himself always give you his peace no matter what happens. The Lord be with you all.

¹⁷Now here is my greeting, which I write with my own hand—PAUL. I do this at the end of all my letters to prove that they really are from me.

¹⁸May the grace of our Lord Jesus Christ be with you all.

> See Paul's profile (page 1333) at Galatians 2:5.

3:6 Greek *brother;* also in 3:15.

1 TIMOTHY

IN THIS FIRST OF THREE pastoral letters, Paul answers many of Timothy's basic questions about living out the Christian faith as a church leader.

Paul wrote this letter to a young man he had mentored and then commissioned to build up the church in the city of Ephesus.

In chapter 1, Paul reminds Timothy to continue to oppose false teachers, reminds him of God's calling, and urges him to cling tightly to his faith in Jesus Christ.

In chapters 2–3, Paul gives Timothy instructions about leading public worship and about appointing elders and deacons for the church at Ephesus. He also gives Timothy a concise affirmation of the key truths of the Christian faith.

In chapters 4–6, Paul urges Timothy to wholeheartedly fulfill his duties as a Christian leader, gives him specific instructions about Christ-honoring relationships, and instructs him about false teachings and true riches.

Famous verses in 1 Timothy include

- ○ "Christ Jesus came into the world to save sinners—and I was the worst of them all" (1:15)
- ○ Don't let your faith be shipwrecked (1:19)
- ○ "I urge you, first of all, to pray for all people" (2:1)
- ○ "God our Savior . . . wants everyone to be saved and to understand the truth" (2:3-4)
- ○ "For there is only one God and one Mediator who can reconcile God and people. He is the man Christ Jesus" (2:5)
- ○ "It is a true saying that if someone wants to be an elder, he desires an honorable responsibility. For an elder must be a man whose life cannot be spoken against" (3:1-2)
- ○ "In the same way, deacons must be people who are respected" (3:8)
- ○ "Without question, this is the great mystery of our faith . . ." (3:16)
- ○ "Now the Holy Spirit tells us clearly that in the last times . . ." (4:1)
- ○ "Physical exercise has some value, but spiritual exercise is much more important" (4:8)
- ○ "Don't let anyone think less of you because you are young. Be an example to all believers" (4:12)
- ○ "True religion with contentment is great wealth" (6:6)
- ○ "We didn't bring anything with us when we came into the world, and we certainly cannot carry anything with us when we die" (6:7)
- ○ "The love of money is at the root of all kinds of evil" (6:10)
- ○ "Fight the good fight" (6:12)

CHAPTER 1

Greetings from Paul

This letter is from Paul, an apostle of Christ Jesus, appointed by the command of God our Savior and by Christ Jesus our hope.

[2]It is written to Timothy, my true child in the faith.

May God our Father and Christ Jesus our Lord give you grace, mercy, and peace.

Warnings against False Teachings

[3]When I left for Macedonia, I urged you to stay there in Ephesus and stop those who are teaching wrong doctrine. [4]Don't let people waste time in endless speculation over myths and spiritual pedigrees.* For these things only cause arguments; they don't help people live a life of faith in God.* [5]The purpose of my instruction is that all the Christians there would be filled with love that comes from a pure heart, a clear conscience, and sincere faith.

[6]But some teachers have missed this whole point. They have turned away from these things and spend their time arguing and talking foolishness. [7]They want to be known as teachers of the law of Moses, but they don't know what they are talking about, even though they seem so confident. [8]We know these laws are good when they are used as God intended. [9]But they were not made for people who do what is right. They are for people who are disobedient and rebellious, who are ungodly and sinful, who consider nothing sacred and defile what is holy, who murder their father or mother or other people. [10]These laws are for people who are sexually immoral, for homosexuals and slave traders, for liars and oath breakers, and for those who do anything else that contradicts the right teaching [11]that comes from the glorious Good News entrusted to me by our blessed God.

Paul's Gratitude for God's Mercy

[12]How thankful I am to Christ Jesus our Lord for considering me trustworthy and appointing me to serve him, [13]even though I used to scoff at the name of Christ. I hunted down his people, harming them in every way I could. But God had mercy on me because I did it in ignorance and unbelief. [14]Oh, how kind and gracious the Lord was! He filled me completely with faith and the love of Christ Jesus.

[15]This is a true saying, and everyone should believe it: Christ Jesus came into the world to save sinners—and I was the worst of them all. [16]But that is why God had mercy on me, so that Christ Jesus could use me as a prime example of his great patience with even the worst sinners. Then others will realize that they, too, can believe in him and receive eternal life. [17]Glory and honor to God forever and ever. He is the eternal King, the unseen one who never dies; he alone is God. Amen.

Timothy's Responsibility

[18]Timothy, my son, here are my instructions for you, based on the prophetic words spoken about you earlier. May they give you the confidence to fight well in the Lord's battles. [19]Cling tightly to your faith in Christ, and always keep your conscience clear. For some people have deliberately violated their consciences; as a result, their faith has been shipwrecked. [20]Hymenaeus and Alexander are two examples of this. I turned them over to Satan so they would learn not to blaspheme God.

CHAPTER 2

Instructions about Worship

I urge you, first of all, to pray for all people. As you make your requests, plead for God's mercy upon them, and give thanks. [2]Pray this way for kings and all

---

See Paul's profile (page 1333) at Galatians 2:5.

See Timothy's profile (page 1373) at 1 Timothy 4:12.

I SPEND my time developing a life of faith, not pursuing foolish theological arguments. (1:6)

See Moses' profile (page 73) at Exodus 5:1.

I BELIEVE the law of Moses was designed to convict sinners, not save believers. (1:9)

I THANK the Lord for showing mercy and saving me. (1:13)

I BELIEVE Jesus Christ came into the world to save even the worst of sinners. (1:15)

I PRAY for those in authority so I can live in peace and quietness, in godliness and dignity. (2:2)

1:4a Greek *in myths and endless genealogies, which cause speculation.* 1:4b Greek *a stewardship of God in faith.*

others who are in authority, so that we can live in peace and quietness, in godliness and dignity. ³This is good and pleases God our Savior, ⁴for he wants everyone to be saved and to understand the truth. ⁵For there is only one God and one Mediator who can reconcile God and people. He is the man Christ Jesus. ⁶He gave his life to purchase freedom for everyone. This is the message that God gave to the world at the proper time. ⁷And I have been chosen—this is the absolute truth—as a preacher and apostle to teach the Gentiles about faith and truth.

⁸So wherever you assemble, I want men to pray with holy hands lifted up to God, free from anger and controversy. ⁹And I want women to be modest in their appearance. They should wear decent and appropriate clothing and not draw attention to themselves by the way they fix their hair or by wearing gold or pearls or expensive clothes. ¹⁰For women who claim to be devoted to God should make themselves attractive by the good things they do.

¹¹Women should listen and learn quietly and submissively. ¹²I do not let women teach men or have authority over them. Let them listen quietly. ¹³For God made Adam first, and afterward he made Eve. ¹⁴And it was the woman, not Adam, who was deceived by Satan, and sin was the result. ¹⁵But women will be saved through childbearing* and by continuing to live in faith, love, holiness, and modesty.

CHAPTER 3

Leaders in the Church

It is a true saying that if someone wants to be an elder,* he desires an honorable responsibility. ²For an elder must be a man whose life cannot be spoken against. He must be faithful to his wife.* He must exhibit self-control, live wisely, and have a good reputation. He must enjoy having guests in his home and must be able to teach. ³He must not be a heavy drinker or be violent. He must be gentle, peace loving, and not one who loves money. ⁴He must manage his own family well, with children who respect and obey him. ⁵For if a man cannot manage his own household, how can he take care of God's church?

⁶An elder must not be a new Christian, because he might be proud of being chosen so soon, and the Devil will use that pride to make him fall.* ⁷Also, people outside the church must speak well of him so that he will not fall into the Devil's trap and be disgraced.

⁸In the same way, deacons must be people who are respected and have integrity. They must not be heavy drinkers and must not be greedy for money. ⁹They must be committed to the revealed truths of the Christian faith and must live with a clear conscience. ¹⁰Before they are appointed as deacons, they should be given other responsibilities in the church as a test of their character and ability. If they do well, then they may serve as deacons.

¹¹In the same way, their wives* must be respected and must not speak evil of others. They must exercise self-control and be faithful in everything they do. ¹²A deacon must be faithful to his wife, and he must manage his children and household well. ¹³Those who do well as deacons will be rewarded with respect from others and will have increased confidence in their faith in Christ Jesus.

The Truths of Our Faith

¹⁴I am writing these things to you now, even though I hope to be with you soon, ¹⁵so that if I can't come for a while, you will know how people must conduct themselves in the household of God. This is the church of the living God, which is the pillar and support of the truth.

I BELIEVE Jesus Christ is the only one who can reconcile people to God because he gave his life to purchase our freedom. (2:6)

I WORSHIP together with other Christians in a spirit of holiness, not strife. (2:8)

See the profiles for Adam (page 5) and Eve (page 7) at Genesis 1:26 and 3:21.

I BELIEVE an elder must be faithful to his wife, exhibit self-control, live wisely, and have a good reputation. (3:2)

I BELIEVE Christians should be given opportunities to serve in the church before they are put in positions of authority. (3:10)

2:15 Or *will be saved by accepting their role as mothers,* or *will be saved by the birth of the Child.* 3:1 Greek *overseer;* also in 3:2. 3:2 Greek *be the husband of one wife;* also in 3:12. 3:6 Or *he might fall into the same judgment as the Devil.* 3:11 Or *the women deacons.* The Greek word can be translated *women* or *wives.*

¹⁶Without question, this is the great mystery of our faith:

Christ* appeared in the flesh
  and was shown to be righteous by the Spirit.*
He was seen by angels
  and was announced to the nations.
He was believed on in the world
  and was taken up into heaven.*

CHAPTER 4

Warnings against False Teachers

Now the Holy Spirit tells us clearly that in the last times some will turn away from what we believe; they will follow lying spirits and teachings that come from demons. ²These teachers are hypocrites and liars. They pretend to be religious, but their consciences are dead.*

³They will say it is wrong to be married and wrong to eat certain foods. But God created those foods to be eaten with thanksgiving by people who know and believe the truth. ⁴Since everything God created is good, we should not reject any of it. We may receive it gladly, with thankful hearts. ⁵For we know it is made holy by the word of God and prayer.

A Good Servant of Christ Jesus

⁶If you explain this to the brothers and sisters,* you will be doing your duty as a worthy servant of Christ Jesus, one who is fed by the message of faith and the true teaching you have followed. ⁷Do not waste time arguing over godless ideas and old wives' tales. Spend your time and energy in training yourself for spiritual fitness. ⁸Physical exercise has some value, but spiritual exercise is much more important, for it promises a reward in both this life and the next. ⁹This is true, and everyone should accept it. ¹⁰We work hard and suffer much* in order that people will believe the truth, for our hope is in the living God, who is the Savior of all people, and particularly of those who believe.

¹¹Teach these things and insist that everyone learn them. ¹²Don't let anyone think less of you because you are young. Be an example to all believers in what you teach, in the way you live, in your love, your faith, and your purity. ¹³Until I get there, focus on reading the Scriptures to the church, encouraging the believers, and teaching them.

¹⁴Do not neglect the spiritual gift you received through the prophecies spoken to you when the elders of the church laid their hands on you. ¹⁵Give your complete attention to these matters. Throw yourself into your tasks so that everyone will see your progress. ¹⁶Keep a close watch on yourself and on your teaching. Stay true to what is right, and God will save you and those who hear you.

CHAPTER 5

Never speak harshly to an older man,* but appeal to him respectfully as though he were your own father. Talk to the younger men as you would to your own brothers. ²Treat the older women as you would your mother, and treat the younger women with all purity as your own sisters.

Advice about Widows, Elders, and Slaves

³The church should care for any widow who has no one else to care for her. ⁴But if she has children or grandchildren, their first responsibility is to show godliness at home and repay their parents by taking care of them. This is something that pleases God very much.

⁵But a woman who is a true widow, one who is truly alone in this world,

---

**Sidebar notes (left margin):**

I BELIEVE Jesus Christ came in the flesh, was shown to be righteous by the Spirit, was believed on in the world, and was taken up into heaven. (3:16)

I THANK God for all foods instead of rejecting some as less spiritual than others. (4:4)

I EXERCISE spiritually by ministering to other believers and reaching out to others who aren't Christians yet. (4:8)

I AM COMMITTED to staying true to what is right. (4:16)

I TREAT individuals in my church with respect, love, and purity. (5:1)

I CARE for my mother or father if she or he is elderly, ill, or widowed. (5:4)

3:16a Greek *Who*; some manuscripts read *God*.   3:16b Or *in his spirit*.   3:16c Greek *in glory*.   4:2 Greek *are seared*.   4:6 Greek *brothers*.   4:10 Some manuscripts read *and strive*.   5:1 Or *an elder*.

has placed her hope in God. Night and day she asks God for help and spends much time in prayer. ⁶But the widow who lives only for pleasure is spiritually dead. ⁷Give these instructions to the church so that the widows you support* will not be criticized.

⁸But those who won't care for their own relatives, especially those living in the same household, have denied what we believe. Such people are worse than unbelievers.

⁹A widow who is put on the list for support must be a woman who is at least sixty years old and was faithful to her husband.* ¹⁰She must be well respected by everyone because of the good she has done. Has she brought up her children well? Has she been kind to strangers? Has she served other Christians humbly?* Has she helped those who are in trouble? Has she always been ready to do good?

Ask the Lord to make you "totally committed to doing what is right" (Titus 2:14).

LIKE TIMOTHY
I am an example of godly living, even in my youth.

1 Timothy 4:12

"Young people these days!" Older folks have been shaking their heads and complaining about every generation from Roman times until now. Paul exhorted Timothy not to let that negative attitude get to him and definitely not to let it hinder him from diligently and deliberately setting an example for the believers in Ephesus.

No one knows Timothy's exact age when Paul wrote him this letter from one servant of God to another. He was clearly young enough to have his ministry questioned, yet mature enough in his faith to be entrusted with the spiritual leadership and training of the church in a rather large city.

Timothy's spiritual maturity was carefully nurtured over the course of many years. Although Timothy's father apparently was not a Christian, his Jewish mother and grandmother had saturated his young heart and mind with the Holy Scriptures (2 Timothy 1:5; 3:15).

By the time he met Paul, Timothy was ready to convert his well-rounded biblical knowledge into active service for the Lord (Acts 16:1-4). When Timothy was commissioned, Paul and the elders at his church laid their hands on him and publicly prophesied that the Lord had uniquely equipped him to minister to others (1 Timothy 4:14; 2 Timothy 1:6).

After that, Timothy traveled with the apostle and his evangelistic team for at least a year and a half (Acts 16:5–18:19). During that time, Timothy learned by experience how to preach the Good News, care for new believers, and build up thriving new churches.

Even with all those spiritual advantages, Timothy still had to make a daily choice to follow the Lord wholeheartedly. So Paul urged Timothy to work hard, to pursue godliness, to hold tightly to the truth day after day (1 Timothy 4:7; 6:11-12; 2 Timothy 2:3, 15). Why? Because young Timothy was a spiritual leader—and other believers were watching.

You and I may or may not enjoy a rich spiritual heritage. But like Timothy, you and I can choose today to live as examples of godliness, no matter what our age.

○ *Today's Scripture reading is 1 Timothy 3–4.*

¹¹The younger widows should not be on the list, because their physical desires will overpower their devotion to Christ and they will want to remarry. ¹²Then they would be guilty of breaking their previous pledge. ¹³Besides, they are likely to become lazy and spend their time gossiping from house to house, getting into other people's business and saying things they shouldn't. ¹⁴So I advise these younger widows to marry again, have children, and take care of their own homes. Then the enemy will not be able to say anything against them. ¹⁵For I am afraid that some of them have already gone astray and now follow Satan.

¹⁶If a Christian woman has relatives who are widows, she must take care of them and not put the responsibility on the church. Then the church can care for widows who are truly alone.

5:7 Or *so the church*; Greek reads *so they.* 5:9 Greek *was the wife of one man.* 5:10 Greek *Has she washed the feet of saints?*

I BELIEVE elders who work hard at preaching and teaching should be paid well. (5:17)

I DO NOT LISTEN to unsubstantiated complaints against my church leaders. (5:19)

I BELIEVE the true nature of every life—good or sinful—will eventually be revealed. (5:25)

I DO NOT BRING shame on the name of God by acting disrespectfully toward my boss or employer. (6:1)

I AM CONTENT with what I have. (6:8)

I PURSUE what is right, good, and godly. (6:11)

See Pilate's profile (page 1229) at John 19:16.

[17]Elders who do their work well should be paid well,* especially those who work hard at both preaching and teaching. [18]For the Scripture says, "Do not keep an ox from eating as it treads out the grain." And in another place, "Those who work deserve their pay!"*

[19]Do not listen to complaints against an elder unless there are two or three witnesses to accuse him. [20]Anyone who sins should be rebuked in front of the whole church so that others will have a proper fear of God.

[21]I solemnly command you in the presence of God and Christ Jesus and the holy angels to obey these instructions without taking sides or showing special favor to anyone. [22]Never be in a hurry about appointing an elder. Do not participate in the sins of others. Keep yourself pure.

[23]Don't drink only water. You ought to drink a little wine for the sake of your stomach because you are sick so often.

[24]Remember that some people lead sinful lives, and everyone knows they will be judged. But there are others whose sin will not be revealed until later. [25]In the same way, everyone knows how much good some people do, but there are others whose good deeds won't be known until later.

CHAPTER 6

Christians who are slaves should give their masters full respect so that the name of God and his teaching will not be shamed. [2]If your master is a Christian, that is no excuse for being disrespectful. You should work all the harder because you are helping another believer* by your efforts.

False Teaching and True Riches

Teach these truths, Timothy, and encourage everyone to obey them. [3]Some false teachers may deny these things, but these are the sound, wholesome teachings of the Lord Jesus Christ, and they are the foundation for a godly life. [4]Anyone who teaches anything different is both conceited and ignorant. Such a person has an unhealthy desire to quibble over the meaning of words. This stirs up arguments ending in jealousy, fighting, slander, and evil suspicions. [5]These people always cause trouble. Their minds are corrupt, and they don't tell the truth. To them religion is just a way to get rich.

[6]Yet true religion with contentment is great wealth. [7]After all, we didn't bring anything with us when we came into the world, and we certainly cannot carry anything with us when we die. [8]So if we have enough food and clothing, let us be content. [9]But people who long to be rich fall into temptation and are trapped by many foolish and harmful desires that plunge them into ruin and destruction. [10]For the love of money is at the root of all kinds of evil. And some people, craving money, have wandered from the faith and pierced themselves with many sorrows.

Paul's Final Instructions

[11]But you, Timothy, belong to God; so run from all these evil things, and follow what is right and good. Pursue a godly life, along with faith, love, perseverance, and gentleness. [12]Fight the good fight for what we believe. Hold tightly to the eternal life that God has given you, which you have confessed so well before many witnesses. [13]And I command you before God, who gives life to all, and before Christ Jesus, who gave a good testimony before Pontius Pilate, [14]that you obey his commands with all purity. Then no one can find fault with you from now until our Lord Jesus Christ returns. [15]For at the right time Christ will be revealed from heaven by the blessed and only almighty God, the King of kings and Lord of lords. [16]He alone can never die, and he lives in light so brilliant that no human can approach him. No

5:17 Greek *should be worthy of double honor.*   5:18 Deut 25:4; Luke 10:7.   6:2 Greek *a brother.*

one has ever seen him, nor ever will. To him be honor and power forever. Amen.

[17]Tell those who are rich in this world not to be proud and not to trust in their money, which will soon be gone. But their trust should be in the living God, who richly gives us all we need for our enjoyment. [18]Tell them to use their money to do good. They should be rich in good works and should give generously to those in need, always being ready to share with others whatever God has given them. [19]By doing this they will be storing up their treasure as a good foundation for the future so that they may take hold of real life.

[20]Timothy, guard what God has entrusted to you. Avoid godless, foolish discussions with those who oppose you with their so-called knowledge. [21]Some people have wandered from the faith by following such foolishness.

May God's grace be with you all.

I MAKE eternal investments by using the money God gives me to do good and share with others. (6:19)

2 TIMOTHY

IN THIS SECOND pastoral letter, Paul urges Timothy to stand firm for the Lord despite persecution.

In chapters 1-3, Paul exhorts Timothy to hold fast to his Christian faith and maintain his ministry at all costs, despite the perilous times, remembering the faith of those most dear to him.

In chapter 4, Paul reiterates his key themes and records his final words of instruction and challenge.

Famous verses in 2 Timothy include

- "God has not given us a spirit of fear and timidity, but of power, love, and self-discipline" (1:7)
- "I know the one in whom I trust, and I am sure that he is able to guard what I have entrusted to him until the day of his return" (1:12)
- "Teach these great truths to trustworthy people who are able to pass them on to others" (2:2)
- "This is a true saying . . ." (2:11)
- "Work hard so God can approve you. Be a good worker, one who does not need to be ashamed and who correctly explains the word of truth" (2:15)
- "Run away from anything that stimulates youthful lust" (2:22)
- "In the last days there will be very difficult times" (3:1)
- "Everyone who wants to live a godly life in Christ Jesus will suffer persecution" (3:12)
- "All Scripture is inspired by God and is useful . . ." (3:16-17)
- "Preach the word of God. Be persistent, whether the time is favorable or not" (4:2)
- "I have fought a good fight, I have finished the race, and I have remained faithful. And now the prize awaits me" (4:7-8)

CHAPTER 1

Greetings from Paul

This letter is from Paul, an apostle of Christ Jesus by God's will, sent out to tell others about the life he has promised through faith in Christ Jesus. ²It is written to Timothy, my dear son.

May God our Father and Christ Jesus our Lord give you grace, mercy, and peace.

Encouragement to Be Faithful

³Timothy, I thank God for you. He is the God I serve with a clear conscience, just as my ancestors did. Night and day I constantly remember you in my prayers. ⁴I long to see you again, for I remember your tears as we parted. And I will be filled with joy when we are together again.

⁵I know that you sincerely trust the Lord, for you have the faith of your mother, Eunice, and your grandmother, Lois. ⁶This is why I remind you to

See Paul's profile (page 1333) at Galatians 2:5.

See Timothy's profile (page 1373) at 1 Timothy 4:12.

I THANK God for my Christian brothers and sisters, and I pray for them constantly. (1:3)

fan into flames the spiritual gift God gave you when I laid my hands on you. [7]For God has not given us a spirit of fear and timidity, but of power, love, and self-discipline. [8]So you must never be ashamed to tell others about our Lord. And don't be ashamed of me, either, even though I'm in prison for Christ. With the strength God gives you, be ready to suffer with me for the proclamation of the Good News.

[9]It is God who saved us and chose us to live a holy life. He did this not because we deserved it, but because that was his plan long before the world began—to show his love and kindness to us through Christ Jesus. [10]And now he has made all of this plain to us by the coming of Christ Jesus, our Savior, who broke the power of death and showed us the way to everlasting life through the Good News. [11]And God chose me to be a preacher, an apostle, and a teacher of this Good News.

[12]And that is why I am suffering here in prison. But I am not ashamed of it, for I know the one in whom I trust, and I am sure that he is able to guard what I have entrusted to him* until the day of his return.

[13]Hold on to the pattern of right teaching you learned from me. And remember to live in the faith and love that you have in Christ Jesus. [14]With the help of the Holy Spirit who lives within us, carefully guard what has been entrusted to you.

[15]As you know, all the Christians who came here from the province of Asia have deserted me; even Phygelus and Hermogenes are gone. [16]May the Lord show special kindness to Onesiphorus and all his family because he often visited and encouraged me. He was never ashamed of me because I was in prison. [17]When he came to Rome, he searched everywhere until he found me. [18]May the Lord show him special kindness on the day of Christ's return. And you know how much he helped me at Ephesus.

CHAPTER 2

A Good Soldier of Christ Jesus

Timothy, my dear son, be strong with the special favor God gives you in Christ Jesus. [2]You have heard me teach many things that have been confirmed by many reliable witnesses. Teach these great truths to trustworthy people who are able to pass them on to others.

[3]Endure suffering along with me, as a good soldier of Christ Jesus. [4]And as Christ's soldier, do not let yourself become tied up in the affairs of this life, for then you cannot satisfy the one who has enlisted you in his army. [5]Follow the Lord's rules for doing his work, just as an athlete either follows the rules or is disqualified and wins no prize. [6]Hardworking farmers are the first to enjoy the fruit of their labor. [7]Think about what I am saying. The Lord will give you understanding in all these things.

[8]Never forget that Jesus Christ was a man born into King David's family and that he was raised from the dead. This is the Good News I preach. [9]And because I preach this Good News, I am suffering and have been chained like a criminal. But the word of God cannot be chained. [10]I am willing to endure anything if it will bring salvation and eternal glory in Christ Jesus to those God has chosen.

[11]This is a true saying:

If we die with him,
  we will also live with him.
[12]If we endure hardship,
  we will reign with him.
If we deny him,
  he will deny us.

Margin notes

I AM NOT ASHAMED of the Lord or of his servants. (1:8)

I TRUST God to guard everything I have entrusted to him until the day of his return. (1:12)

See Timothy's profile (page 1373) at 1 Timothy 4:12.

I TEACH God's great truths to trustworthy people who can teach them to others. (2:2)

I STAY FOCUSED on serving the Lord and do not become tied up in worldly distractions. (2:4)

See David's profile (page 629) at Psalm 3:1.

I WILLINGLY SUFFER anything to bring glory to God. (2:10)

1:12 Or *what has been entrusted to me.*

¹³ If we are unfaithful,
    he remains faithful,
    for he cannot deny himself.

An Approved Worker

¹⁴Remind everyone of these things, and command them in God's name to stop fighting over words. Such arguments are useless, and they can ruin those who hear them. ¹⁵Work hard so God can approve you. Be a good worker, one who does not need to be ashamed and who correctly explains the word of truth. ¹⁶Avoid godless, foolish discussions that lead to more and more ungodliness. ¹⁷This kind of talk spreads like cancer. Hymenaeus and Philetus are examples of this. ¹⁸They have left the path of truth, preaching the lie that the resurrection of the dead has already occurred; and they have undermined the faith of some.

LIKE LUKE

2 Timothy 4:11

I make sure those who work hard for the Lord can depend on me for help and support.

When Luke joined Paul's evangelistic team, they gained a sea-loving companion who meticulously documented all their travels. And they gained a physician who provided compassionate attention when they suffered physical ailments. When their journey led to prison, though, Luke proved his greatest asset to Paul by remaining a loyal brother and friend.

Luke stood by Paul during his imprisonment and a harrowing voyage to Rome. Together, they survived political persecution, a terrible storm, and shipwreck (Acts 27:1–28:16). Then, during Paul's house arrest in Rome, Luke apparently worked very hard for many months to help the apostle prepare to appear in Caesar's court. Some scholars believe that during this time Luke wrote the carefully researched and divinely inspired accounts of Jesus Christ's life (which we know as the Gospel of Luke) and of the Holy Spirit's work among the first believers and missionaries (that we know as Acts).

Even though he penned far more pages of the New Testament than the apostle Paul did, during his lifetime Luke was not known as an exemplary ambassador of Jesus Christ. That was Paul's role—and Luke willingly fortified him in it. No wonder Paul greatly valued Luke as a coworker in Christ.

Like Luke, you and I can strengthen individuals we know who serve the Lord by coming alongside them and helping them get the job done. That may mean traveling overseas for several months to assist a missionary friend or perhaps developing a committed, uncritical relationship with a staff member at church.

Whatever we do, let's not desert God's servants in their time of need.

○ *Today's Scripture reading is 2 Timothy 3:10–4:22.*

---

¹⁹But God's truth stands firm like a foundation stone with this inscription: "The Lord knows those who are his,"* and "Those who claim they belong to the Lord must turn away from all wickedness."*

²⁰In a wealthy home some utensils are made of gold and silver, and some are made of wood and clay. The expensive utensils are used for special occasions, and the cheap ones are for everyday use. ²¹If you keep yourself pure, you will be a utensil God can use for his purpose. Your life will be clean, and you will be ready for the Master to use you for every good work.

I KEEP my life pure and ready to be used by God for his special purposes. (2:21)

²²Run from anything that stimulates youthful lust. Follow anything that makes you want to do right. Pursue faith and love and peace, and enjoy the companionship of those who call on the Lord with pure hearts.

²³Again I say, don't get involved in foolish, ignorant arguments that only start fights. ²⁴The Lord's servants must not quarrel but must be kind to everyone. They must be able to teach effectively and be patient with difficult

I AM KIND and do not quarrel, even with difficult people. (2:24)

2:19a Num 16:5.   **2:19b** See Isa 52:11.

people. ²⁵They should gently teach those who oppose the truth. Perhaps God will change those people's hearts, and they will believe the truth. ²⁶Then they will come to their senses and escape from the Devil's trap. For they have been held captive by him to do whatever he wants.

CHAPTER 3

The Dangers of the Last Days

You should also know this, Timothy, that in the last days there will be very difficult times. ²For people will love only themselves and their money. They will be boastful and proud, scoffing at God, disobedient to their parents, and ungrateful. They will consider nothing sacred. ³They will be unloving and unforgiving; they will slander others and have no self-control; they will be cruel and have no interest in what is good. ⁴They will betray their friends, be reckless, be puffed up with pride, and love pleasure rather than God. ⁵They will act as if they are religious, but they will reject the power that could make them godly. You must stay away from people like that.

⁶They are the kind who work their way into people's homes and win the confidence of* vulnerable women who are burdened with the guilt of sin and controlled by many desires. ⁷Such women are forever following new teachings, but they never understand the truth. ⁸And these teachers fight the truth just as Jannes and Jambres fought against Moses. Their minds are depraved, and their faith is counterfeit. ⁹But they won't get away with this for long. Someday everyone will recognize what fools they are, just as happened with Jannes and Jambres.

Paul's Charge to Timothy

¹⁰But you know what I teach, Timothy, and how I live, and what my purpose in life is. You know my faith and how long I have suffered. You know my love and my patient endurance. ¹¹You know how much persecution and suffering I have endured. You know all about how I was persecuted in Antioch, Iconium, and Lystra—but the Lord delivered me from all of it. ¹²Yes, and everyone who wants to live a godly life in Christ Jesus will suffer persecution. ¹³But evil people and impostors will flourish. They will go on deceiving others, and they themselves will be deceived.

¹⁴But you must remain faithful to the things you have been taught. You know they are true, for you know you can trust those who taught you. ¹⁵You have been taught the holy Scriptures from childhood, and they have given you the wisdom to receive the salvation that comes by trusting in Christ Jesus. ¹⁶All Scripture is inspired by God and is useful to teach us what is true and to make us realize what is wrong in our lives. It straightens us out and teaches us to do what is right. ¹⁷It is God's way of preparing us in every way, fully equipped for every good thing God wants us to do.

CHAPTER 4

And so I solemnly urge you before God and before Christ Jesus—who will someday judge the living and the dead when he appears to set up his Kingdom: ²Preach the word of God. Be persistent, whether the time is favorable or not. Patiently correct, rebuke, and encourage your people with good teaching.

³For a time is coming when people will no longer listen to right teaching. They will follow their own desires and will look for teachers who will tell them whatever they want to hear. ⁴They will reject the truth and follow strange myths.

⁵But you should keep a clear mind in every situation. Don't be afraid of

---

See Timothy's profile (page 1373) at 1 Timothy 4:12.

I AVOID people who claim to be religious but reject God's power that could make them godly. (3:5)

See Moses' profile (page 73) at Exodus 5:1.

I RECOGNIZE that everyone who wants to live a godly life will suffer persecution. (3:12)

I BELIEVE all Scripture is inspired by God and teaches me what is true and what I should do. (3:16)

I BELIEVE Jesus Christ will one day judge the living and the dead. (4:1)

3:6 Greek *and take captive.*

suffering for the Lord. Work at bringing others to Christ. Complete the ministry God has given you.

Paul's Final Words

⁶As for me, my life has already been poured out as an offering to God. The time of my death is near. ⁷I have fought a good fight, I have finished the race, and I have remained faithful. ⁸And now the prize awaits me—the crown of righteousness that the Lord, the righteous Judge, will give me on that great day of his return. And the prize is not just for me but for all who eagerly look forward to his glorious return.

⁹Please come as soon as you can. ¹⁰Demas has deserted me because he loves the things of this life and has gone to Thessalonica. Crescens has gone to Galatia, and Titus has gone to Dalmatia. ¹¹Only Luke is with me. Bring Mark with you when you come, for he will be helpful to me. ¹²I sent Tychicus to Ephesus. ¹³When you come, be sure to bring the coat I left with Carpus at Troas. Also bring my books, and especially my papers.*

¹⁴Alexander the coppersmith has done me much harm, but the Lord will judge him for what he has done. ¹⁵Be careful of him, for he fought against everything we said.

¹⁶The first time I was brought before the judge, no one was with me. Everyone had abandoned me. I hope it will not be counted against them. ¹⁷But the Lord stood with me and gave me strength, that I might preach the Good News in all its fullness for all the Gentiles to hear. And he saved me from certain death.* ¹⁸Yes, and the Lord will deliver me from every evil attack and will bring me safely to his heavenly Kingdom. To God be the glory forever and ever. Amen.

Paul's Final Greetings

¹⁹Give my greetings to Priscilla and Aquila and those living at the household of Onesiphorus. ²⁰Erastus stayed at Corinth, and I left Trophimus sick at Miletus.

²¹Hurry so you can get here before winter. Eubulus sends you greetings, and so do Pudens, Linus, Claudia, and all the brothers and sisters.*

²²May the Lord be with your spirit. Grace be with you all.

4:13 Greek *especially the parchments.*   4:17 Greek *from the mouth of a lion.*   4:21 Greek *brothers.*

I WORK at bringing others to Jesus Christ. (4:5)

I LOOK FORWARD to the glorious return of Jesus Christ and the prize he will give to those who eagerly await him. (4:8)

See John Mark's profile (page 1255) at Acts 13:13.

I BELIEVE the Lord will bring me safely into his heavenly Kingdom. (4:18)

See the profile for Priscilla and Aquila (page 1265) at Acts 18:26.

TITUS

IN THIS THIRD pastoral letter, Paul answers many of Titus's basic questions about living out the Christian faith as a church leader.

Paul wrote this letter to a young man he had mentored and then commissioned to build up the church on the island of Crete.

In chapter 1, Paul reminds Titus to appoint elders and oppose the false teachers who are fighting against the teachings of the church.

In chapters 2–3, Paul gives Titus specific instructions about Christ-honoring relationships and right living in order to please God our Savior. He concludes with another warning and some final instructions.

Famous verses in Titus include

- ○ "An elder must be well thought of for his good life. He must be faithful . . ." (1:6)
- ○ "Everything is pure to those whose hearts are pure" (1:15)
- ○ "Make the teaching about God our Savior attractive in every way" (2:10)
- ○ "He [Christ] gave his life to free us from every kind of sin, to cleanse us, and to make us his very own people, totally committed to doing what is right" (2:14)
- ○ "God our Savior showed us his kindness and love. He saved us, not because of the good things we did, but because of his mercy" (3:4-5)

CHAPTER 1

Greetings from Paul

This letter is from Paul, a slave of God and an apostle of Jesus Christ. I have been sent to bring faith to those God has chosen and to teach them to know the truth that shows them how to live godly lives. ²This truth gives them the confidence of eternal life, which God promised them before the world began—and he cannot lie. ³And now at the right time he has revealed this Good News, and we announce it to everyone. It is by the command of God our Savior that I have been trusted to do this work for him.

⁴This letter is written to Titus, my true child in the faith that we share.

May God the Father and Christ Jesus our Savior give you grace and peace.

See Paul's profile (page 1333) at Galatians 2:5.

I BELIEVE God does not lie. (1:2)

Titus's Work in Crete

⁵I left you on the island of Crete so you could complete our work there and appoint elders in each town as I instructed you. ⁶An elder must be well thought of for his good life. He must be faithful to his wife,* and his children must be believers who are not wild or rebellious. ⁷An elder* must live a blameless life because he is God's minister. He must not be arrogant or quick-tempered; he must not be a heavy drinker, violent, or greedy for money. ⁸He must enjoy having guests in his home and must love all that is good. He must live wisely and be fair. He must live a devout and disciplined life. ⁹He must have a strong and steadfast belief in the trustworthy message he

I BELIEVE an elder should live a blameless life as one of God's ministers. (1:7)

1:6 Or *have only one wife*, or *be married only once*; Greek reads *be the husband of one wife.* 1:7 Greek *overseer.*

was taught; then he will be able to encourage others with right teaching and show those who oppose it where they are wrong.

¹⁰For there are many who rebel against right teaching; they engage in useless talk and deceive people. This is especially true of those who insist on circumcision for salvation. ¹¹They must be silenced. By their wrong teaching, they have already turned whole families away from the truth. Such teachers only want your money. ¹²One of their own men, a prophet from Crete, has said about them, "The people of Crete are all liars; they are cruel animals and lazy gluttons." ¹³This is true. So rebuke them as sternly as necessary to make them strong in the faith. ¹⁴They must stop listening to Jewish myths and the commands of people who have turned their backs on the truth.

¹⁵Everything is pure to those whose hearts are pure. But nothing is pure to those who are corrupt and unbelieving, because their minds and consciences are defiled. ¹⁶Such people claim they know God, but they deny him by the way they live. They are despicable and disobedient, worthless for doing anything good.

CHAPTER 2

Promote Right Teaching

But as for you, promote the kind of living that reflects right teaching. ²Teach the older men to exercise self-control, to be worthy of respect, and to live wisely. They must have strong faith and be filled with love and patience.

³Similarly, teach the older women to live in a way that is appropriate for someone serving the Lord. They must not go around speaking evil of others and must not be heavy drinkers. Instead, they should teach others what is good. ⁴These older women must train the younger women to love their husbands and their children, ⁵to live wisely and be pure, to take care of their homes, to do good, and to be submissive to their husbands. Then they will not bring shame on the word of God.

⁶In the same way, encourage the young men to live wisely in all they do. ⁷And you yourself must be an example to them by doing good deeds of every kind. Let everything you do reflect the integrity and seriousness of your teaching. ⁸Let your teaching be so correct that it can't be criticized. Then those who want to argue will be ashamed because they won't have anything bad to say about us.

⁹Slaves must obey their masters and do their best to please them. They must not talk back ¹⁰or steal, but they must show themselves to be entirely trustworthy and good. Then they will make the teaching about God our Savior attractive in every way.

¹¹For the grace of God has been revealed, bringing salvation to all people. ¹²And we are instructed to turn from godless living and sinful pleasures. We should live in this evil world with self-control, right conduct, and devotion to God, ¹³while we look forward to that wonderful event when the glory of our great God and Savior, Jesus Christ, will be revealed. ¹⁴He gave his life to free us from every kind of sin, to cleanse us, and to make us his very own people, totally committed to doing what is right. ¹⁵You must teach these things and encourage your people to do them, correcting them when necessary. You have the authority to do this, so don't let anyone ignore you or disregard what you say.

CHAPTER 3

Do What Is Good

Remind your people to submit to the government and its officers. They should be obedient, always ready to do what is good. ²They must not speak evil of anyone, and they must avoid quarreling. Instead, they should be gentle and show true humility to everyone.

I KEEP my heart pure. (1:15)

I AM AN EXAMPLE to others by my good deeds. (2:7)

I MAKE the teaching about God attractive to others by the way I live. (2:10)

I BELIEVE Jesus Christ gave his life to free us from sin and make us his own people. (2:14)

³Once we, too, were foolish and disobedient. We were misled by others and became slaves to many wicked desires and evil pleasures. Our lives were full of evil and envy. We hated others, and they hated us.

⁴But then God our Savior showed us his kindness and love. ⁵He saved us, not because of the good things we did, but because of his mercy. He washed away our sins and gave us a new life through the Holy Spirit.* ⁶He generously poured out the Spirit upon us because of what Jesus Christ our Savior did. ⁷He declared us not guilty because of his great kindness. And now we know that we will inherit eternal life. ⁸These things I have told you are all true. I want you to insist on them so that everyone who trusts in God will be careful to do good deeds all the time. These things are good and beneficial for everyone.

I BELIEVE God showed his kindness and love to me even while I was foolish, disobedient, and hateful. (3:4)

I AM CONFIDENT I will inherit eternal life because God has graciously declared me not guilty. (3:7)

LIKE TITUS   *I seek God's blessings for his church.*

Titus 1:5

As one of the apostle Paul's coworkers, Titus must have accumulated quite a few Empire Express mileage points. Each time we read about Titus, Paul was sending him on another missions trip across the Mediterranean.

In the city of Corinth, Titus arrived as the not-so-lucky bearer of bad news—a written rebuke from Paul. Instead of sidestepping this painful path to blessing, Titus faithfully delivered the message that was meant to spur repentance and spiritual healing. He actively ministered among the Corinthian believers and then carried back a positive report to Paul (2 Corinthians 7:6-13). Afterward, Titus gladly accepted the assignment to turn right back around and visit them again (2 Corinthians 8:16-18).

Later, Paul asked Titus to minister on the island of Crete. This time Titus blessed the believers by—among other things—selecting and training a group of older men who could lead the church when no apostles or other itinerant Christian workers were around (Titus 1:5). A short time later, Paul instructed Titus to head to Nicopolis to meet him (3:12) and receive his next assignment.

Unlike Titus, you and I don't have to travel a lot to bless the church. We can seek God's best for the believers with whom we fellowship each week. How? Like Titus, by affirming God's truth, obeying his commands, and consciously and consistently setting an example others can follow.

○ *Today's Scripture reading is Titus 1–3.*

Paul's Final Remarks and Greetings

⁹Do not get involved in foolish discussions about spiritual pedigrees* or in quarrels and fights about obedience to Jewish laws. These kinds of things are useless and a waste of time. ¹⁰If anyone is causing divisions among you, give a first and second warning. After that, have nothing more to do with that person. ¹¹For people like that have turned away from the truth. They are sinning, and they condemn themselves.

¹²I am planning to send either Artemas or Tychicus to you. As soon as one of them arrives, do your best to meet me at Nicopolis as quickly as you can, for I have decided to stay there for the winter. ¹³Do everything you can to help Zenas the lawyer and Apollos with their trip. See that they are given everything they need. ¹⁴For our people should not have unproductive lives. They must learn to do good by helping others who have urgent needs.

I LEARN to do good by helping others. (3:14)

¹⁵Everybody here sends greetings. Please give my greetings to all of the believers who love us.

May God's grace be with you all.

3:5 Greek *He saved us through the washing of regeneration and renewing of the Holy Spirit.*   3:9 Greek *discussions and genealogies.*

PHILEMON

THIS IS ONE OF FOUR New Testament "postcard epistles"—brief letters consisting of only one chapter.

Paul wrote this postcard epistle to a good friend named Philemon. The letter is short yet very moving. In it, the apostle strongly urges Philemon to forgive his former slave and accept him back as a brother in Christ. As such, it is a masterful example of persuasive writing.

Paul may have written this letter in conjunction with his letter to the church at Colosse, which met (at least in part) in Philemon's house.

Famous verses in Philemon include

- ○ "Take this as a request from your friend Paul, an old man, now in prison for the sake of Christ Jesus" (1:9)
- ○ "My plea is that you show kindness to Onesimus. I think of him as my own son" (1:10)
- ○ "Onesimus ran away for a little while so you could have him back forever" (1:15)
- ○ "So if you consider me your partner, give him the same welcome you would give me if I were coming" (1:17)
- ○ "If he has . . . stolen anything from you, charge me for it . . . " (1:18-19)

Greetings from Paul

This letter is from Paul, in prison for preaching the Good News about Christ Jesus, and from our brother Timothy.

It is written to Philemon, our much loved co-worker, ²and to our sister Apphia and to Archippus, a fellow soldier of the cross. I am also writing to the church that meets in your house.

³May God our Father and the Lord Jesus Christ give you grace and peace.

See the profiles for Paul (page 1333) and Timothy (page 1373) at Galatians 2:5 and 1 Timothy 4:12.

Paul's Thanksgiving and Prayer

⁴I always thank God when I pray for you, Philemon, ⁵because I keep hearing of your trust in the Lord Jesus and your love for all of God's people. ⁶You are generous because of your faith. And I am praying that you will really put your generosity to work, for in so doing you will come to an understanding of all the good things we can do for Christ. ⁷I myself have gained much joy and comfort from your love, my brother, because your kindness has so often refreshed the hearts of God's people.

I TRUST the Lord and love God's people. (1:5)

I REFRESH the hearts of God's people by my kindness. (1:7)

Paul's Appeal for Onesimus

⁸That is why I am boldly asking a favor of you. I could demand it in the name of Christ because it is the right thing for you to do, ⁹but because of our love, I prefer just to ask you. So take this as a request from your friend Paul, an old man, now in prison for the sake of Christ Jesus.

¹⁰My plea is that you show kindness to Onesimus. I think of him as my own son because he became a believer as a result of my ministry here in prison. ¹¹Onesimus* hasn't been of much use to you in the past, but now he

11 *Onesimus* means "useful."

I BELIEVE our mutual relationship with the Lord changes my relationships with other Christians and makes us brothers and sisters. (1:16)

I AM WILLING to pay the debts of a repentant person if it will help mend a broken relationship with a Christian brother or sister. (1:18)

is very useful to both of us. [12]I am sending him back to you, and with him comes my own heart.

[13]I really wanted to keep him here with me while I am in these chains for preaching the Good News, and he would have helped me on your behalf. [14]But I didn't want to do anything without your consent. And I didn't want you to help because you were forced to do it but because you wanted to. [15]Perhaps you could think of it this way: Onesimus ran away for a little while so you could have him back forever. [16]He is no longer just a slave; he is a beloved brother, especially to me. Now he will mean much more to you, both as a slave and as a brother in the Lord.

[17]So if you consider me your partner, give him the same welcome you would give me if I were coming. [18]If he has harmed you in any way or stolen anything from you, charge me for it. [19]I, Paul, write this in my own handwriting: "I will repay it." And I won't mention that you owe me your very soul!

LIKE PHILEMON
Philemon 1:10

I forgive past offenses in order to welcome someone into God's family.

George Washington was definitely ahead of his time when he freed his slaves the day he died. Like Washington, Philemon legally owned slaves. Given his kind and generous character, he presumably treated them better than most masters.

Still, when one of his slaves ran away, Philemon's generosity was put to the test. For, in God's good plan, the slave ran all the way from Colosse to Rome—and straight into the life of Philemon's dear friend, the apostle Paul.

This slave, Onesimus, heard Paul's message of salvation, trusted Jesus Christ, and became a dear son in the faith. Becoming a Christian did not change Onesimus's legal obligations, however, or his precarious circumstances as Philemon's runaway slave. So, as much as he wanted Onesimus's fellowship, Paul wrote an urgent letter and sent him back to Philemon.

Paul knew all about Philemon's kindness to God's people and how he and his wife, Apphia, had opened their home to the church in the city of Colosse. So in his letter, the aged apostle asked for a room when he came—and begged Philemon to extend the same hospitality and welcome to Onesimus, his newest brother in Jesus Christ.

When a person becomes a Christian, he or she instantly becomes a member of the family of God, but that doesn't erase the past. If he or she has hurt us, or others we love, you and I have a tough choice to make. Will we accept this new believer anyway—for the Lord's sake?

To read about Paul's own difficulties in being accepted by other Christians after his dramatic conversion, see Acts 9:19-28.

○ *Today's Scripture reading is Philemon 1.*

I AM ALWAYS READY to welcome God's servants into my home. (1:22)

See the profiles for John Mark (page 1255) and Luke (page 1379) at Acts 13:13 and 2 Timothy 4:11.

[20]Yes, dear brother, please do me this favor for the Lord's sake. Give me this encouragement in Christ. [21]I am confident as I write this letter that you will do what I ask and even more!

[22]Please keep a guest room ready for me, for I am hoping that God will answer your prayers and let me return to you soon.

Paul's Final Greetings

[23]Epaphras, my fellow prisoner in Christ Jesus, sends you his greetings. [24]So do Mark, Aristarchus, Demas, and Luke, my co-workers.

[25]The grace of the Lord Jesus Christ be with your spirit.

HEBREWS

THIS IS THE FIRST in a series of general letters. The original audience for this letter included a large number of Jews who had embraced the Christian faith but now were tempted to turn back.

The author of this letter is unknown. It may have been Paul or perhaps Apollos, Barnabas, or even Priscilla—all of whom were well respected for their ability to teach God's Word in depth.

In chapters 1–12, the author presents Jesus Christ as God's Son, the promised Messiah, our eternal High Priest, the perfect fulfillment of the Old Testament law and sacrificial system, and far superior to the greatest of Old Testament heroes. The author urges his readers to persevere in their faith because God's Word is sure, because all the great heroes of the faith persevered, and because great rewards await the faithful in heaven and terrible judgment awaits those who reject Christ.

In chapter 13, the author closes with some final words of instruction and challenge.

Famous verses in Hebrews include

- "Long ago God spoke . . . to our ancestors through the prophets. But now in these final days, he has spoken to us through his Son" (1:1-2)
- "The Son reflects God's own glory, and everything about him represents God exactly" (1:3)
- "Since he himself [Jesus] has gone through suffering and temptation, he is able to help us when we are being tempted" (2:18)
- "The word of God is full of living power. It is sharper than the sharpest knife" (4:12)
- "So let us come boldly to the throne of our gracious God" (4:16)
- "It is impossible to restore to repentance those who were once enlightened . . . and who then turn away from God" (6:4-6)
- "This confidence is like a strong and trustworthy anchor for our souls" (6:19)
- "He [Jesus] is able, once and forever, to save everyone who comes to God through him" (7:25)
- "It is destined that each person dies only once and after that comes judgment" (9:27)
- "Let us not neglect our meeting together, as some people do, but encourage and warn each other" (10:25)
- "What is faith? It is the confident assurance that . . ." (11:1-2)
- "It is impossible to please God without faith" (11:6)
- "Let us run with endurance the race that God has set before us" (12:1)
- "Watch out that no bitter root of unbelief rises up among you" (12:15)
- "Our God is a consuming fire" (12:29)
- "Jesus Christ is the same yesterday, today, and forever" (13:8)
- "Let us continually offer our sacrifice of praise to God" (13:15)

CHAPTER 1

Jesus Christ Is God's Son

Long ago God spoke many times and in many ways to our ancestors through the prophets. ²But now in these final days, he has spoken to us through his Son. God promised everything to the Son as an inheritance, and through the Son he made the universe and everything in it. ³The Son reflects God's own glory, and everything about him represents God exactly. He sustains the universe by the mighty power of his command. After he died to cleanse us from the stain of sin, he sat down in the place of honor at the right hand of the majestic God of heaven.

Christ Is Greater Than the Angels

⁴This shows that God's Son is far greater than the angels, just as the name God gave him is far greater than their names. ⁵For God never said to any angel what he said to Jesus:

"You are my Son.
Today I have become your Father.*"

And again God said,

"I will be his Father,
and he will be my Son."*

⁶And then, when he presented his honored* Son to the world, God said, "Let all the angels of God worship him."* ⁷God calls his angels

"messengers swift as the wind,
and servants made of flaming fire."*

⁸But to his Son he says,

"Your throne, O God, endures forever and ever.
Your royal power is expressed in righteousness.
⁹You love what is right and hate what is wrong.
Therefore God, your God, has anointed you,
pouring out the oil of joy on you more than on anyone else."*

¹⁰And,

"Lord, in the beginning you laid the foundation of the earth,
and the heavens are the work of your hands.
¹¹Even they will perish, but you remain forever.
They will wear out like old clothing.
¹²You will roll them up like an old coat.
They will fade away like old clothing.
But you are always the same;
you will never grow old."*

¹³And God never said to an angel, as he did to his Son,

"Sit in honor at my right hand
until I humble your enemies,
making them a footstool under your feet."*

¹⁴But angels are only servants. They are spirits sent from God to care for those who will receive salvation.

CHAPTER 2

A Warning against Drifting Away

So we must listen very carefully to the truth we have heard, or we may drift away from it. ²The message God delivered through angels has always proved

---

I BELIEVE Jesus Christ is the Creator and Sustainer of the universe. (1:2)

I BELIEVE Jesus Christ is God the Son. (1:8)

I BELIEVE God sends angels as servants to care for his people. (1:14)

1:5a Or *Today I reveal you as my Son.* Ps 2:7. **1:5b** 2 Sam 7:14. **1:6a** Greek *firstborn.* **1:6b** Deut 32:43. **1:7** Ps 104:4. **1:8-9** Ps 45:6-7. **1:10-12** Ps 102:25-27. **1:13** Ps 110:1.

true, and the people were punished for every violation of the law and every act of disobedience. ³What makes us think that we can escape if we are indifferent to this great salvation that was announced by the Lord Jesus himself? It was passed on* to us by those who heard him speak, ⁴and God verified the message by signs and wonders and various miracles and by giving gifts of the Holy Spirit whenever he chose to do so.

Jesus, the Man

⁵And furthermore, the future world we are talking about will not be controlled by angels. ⁶For somewhere in the Scriptures it says,

"What is man that you should think of him,
 and the son of man* that you should care for him?
⁷For a little while you made him lower than the angels,
 and you crowned him with glory and honor.*
⁸You gave him authority over all things."*

I BELIEVE the future world will not be controlled by angels but by the Lord Jesus Christ. (2:5)

Now when it says "all things," it means nothing is left out. But we have not yet seen all of this happen. ⁹What we do see is Jesus, who "for a little while was made lower than the angels" and now is "crowned with glory and honor" because he suffered death for us. Yes, by God's grace, Jesus tasted death for everyone in all the world. ¹⁰And it was only right that God—who made everything and for whom everything was made—should bring his many children into glory. Through the suffering of Jesus, God made him a perfect leader, one fit to bring them into their salvation.

I BELIEVE Jesus Christ tasted death for everyone. (2:9)

¹¹So now Jesus and the ones he makes holy have the same Father. That is why Jesus is not ashamed to call them his brothers and sisters.* ¹²For he said to God,

"I will declare the wonder of your name to my brothers and sisters.*
 I will praise you among all your people."

¹³He also said, "I will put my trust in him." And in the same context he said, "Here I am—together with the children God has given me."* ¹⁴Because God's children are human beings—made of flesh and blood— Jesus also became flesh and blood by being born in human form. For only as a human being could he die, and only by dying could he break the power of the Devil, who had the power of death. ¹⁵Only in this way could he deliver those who have lived all their lives as slaves to the fear of dying.

I BELIEVE Jesus Christ came in human form so that, by dying, he could break the power of death and the Devil. (2:14)

See Abraham's profile (page 19) at Genesis 15:6.

¹⁶We all know that Jesus came to help the descendants of Abraham, not to help the angels. ¹⁷Therefore, it was necessary for Jesus to be in every respect like us, his brothers and sisters, so that he could be our merciful and faithful High Priest before God. He then could offer a sacrifice that would take away the sins of the people. ¹⁸Since he himself has gone through suffering and temptation, he is able to help us when we are being tempted.

I BELIEVE Jesus Christ is able to help me when I am tempted. (2:18)

CHAPTER 3

Jesus Is Greater Than Moses

And so, dear brothers and sisters who belong to God* and are bound for heaven, think about this Jesus whom we declare to be God's Messenger and High Priest. ²For he was faithful to God, who appointed him, just as Moses served faithfully and was entrusted with God's entire house. ³But Jesus deserves far more glory than Moses, just as a person who builds a fine house deserves more praise than the house itself. ⁴For every house has a builder, but God is the one who made everything.

I BELIEVE Jesus Christ deserves glory as God's Messenger and High Priest. (3:1)

See Moses' profile (page 73) at Exodus 5:1.

2:3 Or *and confirmed.* 2:6 Or *Son of Man.* 2:7 Some manuscripts add *You put him in charge of everything you made.* 2:6-8 Ps 8:4-6. 2:11 Greek *his brothers;* also in 2:17. 2:12 Greek *my brothers.* Ps 22:22. 2:13 Isa 8:17-18. 3:1 Greek *And so, holy brothers.*

I BELIEVE Moses' work was an illustration of the truths God would reveal later about his Son. (3:5)

[5]Moses was certainly faithful in God's house, but only as a servant. His work was an illustration of the truths God would reveal later. [6]But Christ, the faithful Son, was in charge of the entire household. And we are God's household, if we keep up our courage and remain confident in our hope in Christ. [7]That is why the Holy Spirit says,

"Today you must listen to his voice.
[8]Don't harden your hearts against him
    as Israel did when they rebelled,
    when they tested God's patience in the wilderness.
[9]There your ancestors tried my patience,
    even though they saw my miracles for forty years.
[10]So I was angry with them, and I said,
'Their hearts always turn away from me.
    They refuse to do what I tell them.'
[11]So in my anger I made a vow:
'They will never enter my place of rest.' "*

[12]Be careful then, dear brothers and sisters.* Make sure that your own hearts are not evil and unbelieving, turning you away from the living God. [13]You must warn each other every day, as long as it is called "today," so that none of you will be deceived by sin and hardened against God. [14]For if we are faithful to the end, trusting God just as firmly as when we first believed, we will share in all that belongs to Christ. [15]But never forget the warning:

I AM COMMITTED to trusting God to my dying day. (3:14)

"Today you must listen to his voice.
    Don't harden your hearts against him
    as Israel did when they rebelled."*

[16]And who were those people who rebelled against God, even though they heard his voice? Weren't they the ones Moses led out of Egypt? [17]And who made God angry for forty years? Wasn't it the people who sinned, whose bodies fell in the wilderness? [18]And to whom was God speaking when he vowed that they would never enter his place of rest? He was speaking to those who disobeyed him. [19]So we see that they were not allowed to enter his rest because of their unbelief.

I BELIEVE unbelief keeps a person from entering God's rest or experiencing his blessing. (3:19)

CHAPTER 4

Promised Rest for God's People

God's promise of entering his place of rest still stands, so we ought to tremble with fear that some of you might fail to get there. [2]For this Good News—that God has prepared a place of rest—has been announced to us just as it was to them. But it did them no good because they didn't believe what God told them.* [3]For only we who believe can enter his place of rest. As for those who didn't believe, God said,

"In my anger I made a vow:
'They will never enter my place of rest,' "*

even though his place of rest has been ready since he made the world. [4]We know it is ready because the Scriptures mention the seventh day, saying, "On the seventh day God rested from all his work."* [5]But in the other passage God said, "They will never enter my place of rest."* [6]So God's rest is there for people to enter. But those who formerly heard the Good News failed to enter because they disobeyed God. [7]So God set another time for entering his place of rest, and that time is today. God announced this through David a long time later in the words already quoted:

I LISTEN to God's Word and obey it. (4:6)

See David's profile (page 629) at Psalm 3:1.

3:7-11 Ps 95:7-11.   3:12 Greek *brothers*.   3:15 Ps 95:7-8.   4:2 Some manuscripts read *they didn't share the faith of those who listened [to God]*.   4:3 Ps 95:11.   4:4 Gen 2:2.   4:5 Ps 95:11.

"Today you must listen to his voice.
   Don't harden your hearts against him."*

[8]This new place of rest was not the land of Canaan, where Joshua led them. If it had been, God would not have spoken later about another day of rest. [9]So there is a special rest* still waiting for the people of God. [10]For all who enter into God's rest will find rest from their labors, just as God rested after creating the world. [11]Let us do our best to enter that place of rest. For anyone who disobeys God, as the people of Israel did, will fall.

   [12]For the word of God is full of living power. It is sharper than the sharpest knife, cutting deep into our innermost thoughts and desires. It exposes us for what we really are. [13]Nothing in all creation can hide from him. Everything is naked and exposed before his eyes. This is the God to whom we must explain all that we have done.

Christ Is Our High Priest

[14]That is why we have a great High Priest who has gone to heaven, Jesus the Son of God. Let us cling to him and never stop trusting him. [15]This High Priest of ours understands our weaknesses, for he faced all of the same temptations we do, yet he did not sin. [16]So let us come boldly to the throne of our gracious God. There we will receive his mercy, and we will find grace to help us when we need it.

CHAPTER 5

Now a high priest is a man chosen to represent other human beings in their dealings with God. He presents their gifts to God and offers their sacrifices for sins. [2]And because he is human, he is able to deal gently with the people, though they are ignorant and wayward. For he is subject to the same weaknesses they have. [3]That is why he has to offer sacrifices, both for their sins and for his own sins. [4]And no one can become a high priest simply because he wants such an honor. He has to be called by God for this work, just as Aaron was.

   [5]That is why Christ did not exalt himself to become High Priest. No, he was chosen by God, who said to him,

"You are my Son.
   Today I have become your Father.*"

[6]And in another passage God said to him,

"You are a priest forever
   in the line of Melchizedek."*

   [7]While Jesus was here on earth, he offered prayers and pleadings, with a loud cry and tears, to the one who could deliver him out of death. And God heard his prayers because of his reverence for God. [8]So even though Jesus was God's Son, he learned obedience from the things he suffered. [9]In this way, God qualified him as a perfect High Priest, and he became the source of eternal salvation for all those who obey him. [10]And God designated him to be a High Priest in the line of Melchizedek.

A Call to Spiritual Growth

[11]There is so much more we would like to say about this. But you don't seem to listen, so it's hard to make you understand. [12]You have been Christians a long time now, and you ought to be teaching others. Instead, you need someone to teach you again the basic things a beginner must learn about the Scriptures.* You are like babies who drink only milk and cannot eat solid

See Joshua's profile (page 275) at Joshua 23:14.

I BELIEVE God's Word is full of living power. (4:12)

I COME boldly to God's throne and find grace and mercy because Jesus Christ is my High Priest. (4:16)

See Aaron's profile (page 107) at Exodus 32:2.

I BELIEVE Jesus Christ, God's Son, experientially learned obedience through the things he suffered. (5:8)

I BELIEVE God the Father qualified Jesus Christ, through his perfect obedience in the midst of great suffering, to be the source of salvation for all who obey him. (5:9)

4:7 Ps 95:7-8.   4:9 Or *Sabbath rest.*   5:5 Or *Today I reveal you as my Son.* Ps 2:7.   5:6 Ps 110:4.   5:12 Or *about the oracles of God.*

I TRAIN myself to
recognize the difference
between right and
wrong and then to do
the right thing. (5:14)

food. [13]And a person who is living on milk isn't very far along in the Christian life and doesn't know much about doing what is right. [14]Solid food is for those who are mature, who have trained themselves to recognize the difference between right and wrong and then do what is right.

CHAPTER 6

So let us stop going over the basics of Christianity* again and again. Let us go on instead and become mature in our understanding. Surely we don't need to start all over again with the importance of turning away from evil deeds and placing our faith in God. [2]You don't need further instruction about baptisms, the laying on of hands, the resurrection of the dead, and eternal judgment. [3]And so, God willing, we will move forward to further understanding.

I HAVE REPENTED—I
have turned away
from evil deeds and
placed my faith in
God. (6:1)

[4]For it is impossible to restore to repentance those who were once enlightened—those who have experienced the good things of heaven and shared in the Holy Spirit, [5]who have tasted the goodness of the word of God and the power of the age to come—[6]and who then turn away from God. It is impossible to bring such people to repentance again because they are nailing the Son of God to the cross again by rejecting him, holding him up to public shame.

I ABHOR turning away
from God and
rejecting Jesus Christ.
(6:6)

[7]When the ground soaks up the rain that falls on it and bears a good crop for the farmer, it has the blessing of God. [8]But if a field bears thistles and thorns, it is useless. The farmer will condemn that field and burn it.

[9]Dear friends, even though we are talking like this, we really don't believe that it applies to you. We are confident that you are meant for better things, things that come with salvation. [10]For God is not unfair. He will not forget how hard you have worked for him and how you have shown your love to him by caring for other Christians, as you still do. [11]Our great desire is that you will keep right on loving others as long as life lasts, in order to make certain that what you hope for will come true. [12]Then you will not become spiritually dull and indifferent. Instead, you will follow the example of those who are going to inherit God's promises because of their faith and patience.

I FOLLOW the example
of other faithful
Christians so I won't
become spiritually
indifferent. (6:12)

God's Promises Bring Hope

[13]For example, there was God's promise to Abraham. Since there was no one greater to swear by, God took an oath in his own name, saying:

See Abraham's profile
(page 19) at Genesis
15:6.

[14] "I will certainly bless you richly,
    and I will multiply your descendants into countless millions."*

[15]Then Abraham waited patiently, and he received what God had promised.

[16]When people take an oath, they call on someone greater than themselves to hold them to it. And without any question that oath is binding. [17]God also bound himself with an oath, so that those who received the promise could be perfectly sure that he would never change his mind. [18]So God has given us both his promise and his oath. These two things are unchangeable because it is impossible for God to lie. Therefore, we who have fled to him for refuge can take new courage, for we can hold on to his promise with confidence.

I HOLD ON TO God's
promise with
confidence because he
does not lie. (6:18)

[19]This confidence is like a strong and trustworthy anchor for our souls. It leads us through the curtain of heaven into God's inner sanctuary. [20]Jesus has already gone in there for us. He has become our eternal High Priest in the line of Melchizedek.

CHAPTER 7

Melchizedek Is Compared to Abraham

This Melchizedek was king of the city of Salem and also a priest of God Most High. When Abraham was returning home after winning a great battle against many kings, Melchizedek met him and blessed him. [2]Then Abraham took a

See Abraham's profile
(page 19) at Genesis
15:6.

6:1 Or *the basics about Christ.*   6:14 Gen 22:17.

tenth of all he had won in the battle and gave it to Melchizedek. His name means "king of justice." He is also "king of peace" because *Salem* means "peace." ³There is no record of his father or mother or any of his ancestors—no beginning or end to his life. He remains a priest forever, resembling the Son of God.

⁴Consider then how great this Melchizedek was. Even Abraham, the great patriarch of Israel, recognized how great Melchizedek was by giving him a tenth of what he had taken in battle. ⁵Now the priests, who are descendants of Levi, are commanded in the law of Moses to collect a tithe from all the people, even though they are their own relatives.* ⁶But Melchizedek, who was not even related to Levi, collected a tenth from Abraham. And Melchizedek placed a blessing upon Abraham, the one who had already received the promises of God. ⁷And without question, the person who has the power to bless is always greater than the person who is blessed.

⁸In the case of Jewish priests, tithes are paid to men who will die. But Melchizedek is greater than they are, because we are told that he lives on. ⁹In addition, we might even say that Levi's descendants, the ones who collect the tithe, paid a tithe to Melchizedek through their ancestor Abraham. ¹⁰For although Levi wasn't born yet, the seed from which he came was in Abraham's loins when Melchizedek collected the tithe from him.

¹¹And finally, if the priesthood of Levi could have achieved God's purposes—and it was that priesthood on which the law was based—why did God need to send a different priest from the line of Melchizedek, instead of from the line of Levi and Aaron?*

¹²And when the priesthood is changed, the law must also be changed to permit it. ¹³For the one we are talking about belongs to a different tribe, whose members do not serve at the altar. ¹⁴What I mean is, our Lord came from the tribe of Judah, and Moses never mentioned Judah in connection with the priesthood.

Christ Is like Melchizedek

¹⁵The change in God's law is even more evident from the fact that a different priest, who is like Melchizedek, has now come. ¹⁶He became a priest, not by meeting the old requirement of belonging to the tribe of Levi, but by the power of a life that cannot be destroyed. ¹⁷And the psalmist pointed this out when he said of Christ,

"You are a priest forever
  in the line of Melchizedek."*

¹⁸Yes, the old requirement about the priesthood was set aside because it was weak and useless. ¹⁹For the law made nothing perfect, and now a better hope has taken its place. And that is how we draw near to God.

²⁰God took an oath that Christ would always be a priest, but he never did this for any other priest. ²¹Only to Jesus did he say,

"The Lord has taken an oath
  and will not break his vow:
  'You are a priest forever.' "*

²²Because of God's oath, it is Jesus who guarantees the effectiveness of this better covenant.

²³Another difference is that there were many priests under the old system. When one priest died, another had to take his place. ²⁴But Jesus remains a priest forever; his priesthood will never end. ²⁵Therefore he is able, once and forever, to save* everyone who comes to God through him. He lives forever to plead with God on their behalf.

See Moses' profile (page 73) at Exodus 5:1.

See Aaron's profile (page 107) at Exodus 32:2.

I BELIEVE Jesus Christ became a priest because his life will never end. (7:16)

I BELIEVE a better hope has taken the place of the Old Testament law. (7:19)

I BELIEVE Jesus Christ lives forever to save and plead for all who come to God through him. (7:25)

7:5 Greek *their brothers, who are descendants of Abraham.*   7:11 Greek *according to the order of Aaron.*
7:17 Ps 110:4.   7:21 Ps 110:4.   7:25 Or *able to save completely.*

I BELIEVE Jesus Christ
offered himself as a
sacrifice for sins once
for all people. (7:27)

I BELIEVE God appointed
Jesus Christ as the
perfect priest forever.
(7:28)

²⁶He is the kind of high priest we need because he is holy and blameless, unstained by sin. He has now been set apart from sinners, and he has been given the highest place of honor in heaven. ²⁷He does not need to offer sacrifices every day like the other high priests. They did this for their own sins first and then for the sins of the people. But Jesus did this once for all when he sacrificed himself on the cross. ²⁸Those who were high priests under the law of Moses were limited by human weakness. But after the law was given, God appointed his Son with an oath, and his Son has been made perfect forever.

CHAPTER 8

Christ Is Our High Priest

Here is the main point: Our High Priest sat down in the place of highest honor in heaven, at God's right hand. ²There he ministers in the sacred tent, the true place of worship that was built by the Lord and not by human hands.

³And since every high priest is required to offer gifts and sacrifices, our High Priest must make an offering, too. ⁴If he were here on earth, he would not even be a priest, since there already are priests who offer the gifts required by the law of Moses. ⁵They serve in a place of worship that is only a copy, a shadow of the real one in heaven. For when Moses was getting ready to build the Tabernacle, God gave him this warning: "Be sure that you make everything according to the design I have shown you here on the mountain."* ⁶But our High Priest has been given a ministry that is far superior to the ministry of those who serve under the old laws, for he is the one who guarantees for us a better covenant with God, based on better promises.

⁷If the first covenant had been faultless, there would have been no need for a second covenant to replace it. ⁸But God himself found fault with the old one when he said:

"The day will come, says the Lord,
    when I will make a new covenant
    with the people of Israel and Judah.
⁹This covenant will not be like the one
    I made with their ancestors
when I took them by the hand
    and led them out of the land of Egypt.
They did not remain faithful to my covenant,
    so I turned my back on them, says the Lord.
¹⁰But this is the new covenant I will make
    with the people of Israel on that day, says the Lord:
I will put my laws in their minds
    so they will understand them,
and I will write them on their hearts
    so they will obey them.
I will be their God,
    and they will be my people.
¹¹And they will not need to teach their neighbors,
    nor will they need to teach their family,
    saying, 'You should know the Lord.'
For everyone, from the least to the greatest,
    will already know me.
¹²And I will forgive their wrongdoings,
    and I will never again remember their sins."*

¹³When God speaks of a new covenant, it means he has made the first one obsolete. It is now out of date and ready to be put aside.

*See Moses' profile
(page 73) at Exodus 5:1.*

I BELIEVE Jesus Christ
has a better ministry
and guarantees a
better covenant than
the Old Testament
priests. (8:6)

I BELIEVE God keeps
his promise to put his
laws into the hearts
and minds of his
people. (8:10)

I BELIEVE God promises
to forgive and never
again remember the
sins of his people.
(8:12)

8:5 Exod 25:40; 26:30.   8:8-12 Jer 31:31-34.

CHAPTER 9

Old Rules about Worship

Now in that first covenant between God and Israel, there were regulations for worship and a sacred tent here on earth. ²There were two rooms in this tent. In the first room were a lampstand, a table, and loaves of holy bread on the table. This was called the Holy Place. ³Then there was a curtain, and behind the curtain was the second room called the Most Holy Place. ⁴In that room were a gold incense altar and a wooden chest called the Ark of the Covenant, which was covered with gold on all sides. Inside the Ark were a gold jar containing some manna, Aaron's staff that sprouted leaves, and the stone tablets of the covenant with the Ten Commandments written on them. ⁵The glorious cherubim were above the Ark. Their wings were stretched out over the Ark's cover, the place of atonement. But we cannot explain all of these things now.

⁶When these things were all in place, the priests went in and out of the first room* regularly as they performed their religious duties. ⁷But only the high priest goes into the Most Holy Place, and only once a year, and always with blood, which he offers to God to cover his own sins and the sins the people have committed in ignorance. ⁸By these regulations the Holy Spirit revealed that the Most Holy Place was not open to the people as long as the first room and the entire system it represents were still in use.

⁹This is an illustration pointing to the present time. For the gifts and sacrifices that the priests offer are not able to cleanse the consciences of the people who bring them. ¹⁰For that old system deals only with food and drink and ritual washing—external regulations that are in effect only until their limitations can be corrected.

Christ Is the Perfect Sacrifice

¹¹So Christ has now become the High Priest over all the good things that have come. He has entered that great, perfect sanctuary in heaven, not made by human hands and not part of this created world. ¹²Once for all time he took blood into that Most Holy Place, but not the blood of goats and calves. He took his own blood, and with it he secured our salvation forever.

¹³Under the old system, the blood of goats and bulls and the ashes of a young cow could cleanse people's bodies from ritual defilement. ¹⁴Just think how much more the blood of Christ will purify our hearts from deeds that lead to death so that we can worship the living God. For by the power of the eternal Spirit, Christ offered himself to God as a perfect sacrifice for our sins. ¹⁵That is why he is the one who mediates the new covenant between God and people, so that all who are invited can receive the eternal inheritance God has promised them. For Christ died to set them free from the penalty of the sins they had committed under that first covenant.

¹⁶Now when someone dies and leaves a will, no one gets anything until it is proved that the person who wrote the will* is dead.* ¹⁷The will goes into effect only after the death of the person who wrote it. While the person is still alive, no one can use the will to get any of the things promised to them.

¹⁸That is why blood was required under the first covenant as a proof of death. ¹⁹For after Moses had given the people all of God's laws, he took the blood of calves and goats, along with water, and sprinkled both the book of God's laws and all the people, using branches of hyssop bushes and scarlet wool. ²⁰Then he said, "This blood confirms the covenant God has made with you."* ²¹And in the same way, he sprinkled blood on the sacred tent and on everything used for worship. ²²In fact, we can say that according to the law of

See Aaron's profile *(page 107) at Exodus 32:2.*

I BELIEVE the gifts and sacrifices of the priests were not able to cleanse anyone's conscience. (9:9)

I BELIEVE Jesus Christ secured my salvation forever when he offered his own blood for my sins. (9:12)

I BELIEVE the blood of Jesus Christ purifies my heart to worship the living God. (9:14)

See Moses' profile *(page 73) at Exodus 5:1.*

9:6 Greek *first tent;* also in 9:8.　9:16a Or *covenant.*　9:16b Or *Now when someone makes a covenant, it is necessary to ratify it with the death of a sacrifice.*　9:20 Exod 24:8.

I BELIEVE there is no forgiveness of sins without the shedding of blood. (9:22)

Moses, nearly everything was purified by sprinkling with blood. Without the shedding of blood, there is no forgiveness of sins.

²³That is why the earthly tent and everything in it—which were copies of things in heaven—had to be purified by the blood of animals. But the real things in heaven had to be purified with far better sacrifices than the blood of animals.

²⁴For Christ has entered into heaven itself to appear now before God as our Advocate.* He did not go into the earthly place of worship, for that was merely a copy of the real Temple in heaven. ²⁵Nor did he enter heaven to offer himself again and again, like the earthly high priest who enters the Most Holy Place year after year to offer the blood of an animal. ²⁶If that had been necessary, he would have had to die again and again, ever since the world began. But no! He came once for all time, at the end of the age, to remove the power of sin forever by his sacrificial death for us.

I BELIEVE each person dies once and after that comes judgment. (9:27)

²⁷And just as it is destined that each person dies only once and after that comes judgment, ²⁸so also Christ died only once as a sacrifice to take away the sins of many people. He will come again but not to deal with our sins again. This time he will bring salvation to all those who are eagerly waiting for him.

CHAPTER 10

Christ's Sacrifice Once for All

I BELIEVE the law of Moses was only a shadow of the reality of the good things Jesus Christ has done for me. (10:1)

See Moses' profile (page 73) at Exodus 5:1.

The old system in the law of Moses was only a shadow of the things to come, not the reality of the good things Christ has done for us. The sacrifices under the old system were repeated again and again, year after year, but they were never able to provide perfect cleansing for those who came to worship. ²If they could have provided perfect cleansing, the sacrifices would have stopped, for the worshipers would have been purified once for all time, and their feelings of guilt would have disappeared.

I BELIEVE the sacrifices in Old Testament times reminded the Israelite people of their sins. (10:3)

³But just the opposite happened. Those yearly sacrifices reminded them of their sins year after year. ⁴For it is not possible for the blood of bulls and goats to take away sins. ⁵That is why Christ, when he came into the world, said,

"You did not want animal sacrifices and grain offerings.
　But you have given me a body so that I may obey you.
⁶No, you were not pleased with animals burned on the altar
　or with other offerings for sin.
⁷Then I said, 'Look, I have come to do your will, O God—
　just as it is written about me in the Scriptures.' "*

I BELIEVE Jesus Christ canceled the old sacrificial system when he established the new covenant. (10:9)

⁸Christ said, "You did not want animal sacrifices or grain offerings or animals burned on the altar or other offerings for sin, nor were you pleased with them" (though they are required by the law of Moses). ⁹Then he added, "Look, I have come to do your will." He cancels the first covenant in order to establish the second. ¹⁰And what God wants is for us to be made holy by the sacrifice of the body of Jesus Christ once for all time.

¹¹Under the old covenant, the priest stands before the altar day after day, offering sacrifices that can never take away sins. ¹²But our High Priest offered himself to God as one sacrifice for sins, good for all time. Then he sat down at the place of highest honor at God's right hand. ¹³There he waits until his enemies are humbled as a footstool under his feet. ¹⁴For by that one offering he perfected forever all those whom he is making holy.

I BELIEVE Jesus Christ perfected forever all whom he is making holy by sacrificing himself for their sins once for all time. (10:14)

¹⁵And the Holy Spirit also testifies that this is so. First he says,

¹⁶ "This is the new covenant I will make
　with my people on that day, says the Lord:

9:24 Greek *on our behalf.*　10:5-7 Ps 40:6-8.

I will put my laws in their hearts
so they will understand them,
and I will write them on their minds
so they will obey them."

[17]Then he adds,

"I will never again remember
their sins and lawless deeds."*

[18]Now when sins have been forgiven, there is no need to offer any more sacrifices.

A Call to Persevere

[19]And so, dear brothers and sisters,* we can boldly enter heaven's Most Holy Place because of the blood of Jesus. [20]This is the new, life-giving way that Christ has opened up for us through the sacred curtain, by means of his death for us.*

[21]And since we have a great High Priest who rules over God's people, [22]let us go right into the presence of God, with true hearts fully trusting him. For our evil consciences have been sprinkled with Christ's blood to make us clean, and our bodies have been washed with pure water.

[23]Without wavering, let us hold tightly to the hope we say we have, for God can be trusted to keep his promise. [24]Think of ways to encourage one another to outbursts of love and good deeds. [25]And let us not neglect our meeting together, as some people do, but encourage and warn each other, especially now that the day of his coming back again is drawing near.

[26]Dear friends, if we deliberately continue sinning after we have received a full knowledge of the truth, there is no other sacrifice that will cover these sins. [27]There will be nothing to look forward to but the terrible expectation of God's judgment and the raging fire that will consume his enemies. [28]Anyone who refused to obey the law of Moses was put to death without mercy on the testimony of two or three witnesses. [29]Think how much more terrible the punishment will be for those who have trampled on the Son of God and have treated the blood of the covenant as if it were common and unholy. Such people have insulted and enraged the Holy Spirit who brings God's mercy to his people.

[30]For we know the one who said,

"I will take vengeance.
I will repay those who deserve it."

He also said,

"The Lord will judge his own people."*

[31]It is a terrible thing to fall into the hands of the living God.

[32]Don't ever forget those early days when you first learned about Christ. Remember how you remained faithful even though it meant terrible suffering. [33]Sometimes you were exposed to public ridicule and were beaten, and sometimes you helped others who were suffering the same things. [34]You suffered along with those who were thrown into jail. When all you owned was taken from you, you accepted it with joy. You knew you had better things waiting for you in eternity.

[35]Do not throw away this confident trust in the Lord, no matter what happens. Remember the great reward it brings you! [36]Patient endurance is what you need now, so you will continue to do God's will. Then you will receive all that he has promised.

I CAN GO into God's presence with my conscience made clean with Jesus Christ's blood. (10:22)

I DO NOT NEGLECT meeting together regularly with other Christians. (10:25)

I REMEMBER the great reward that awaits me in heaven whenever I face persecution here on earth. (10:35)

10:16-17 Jer 31:33-34.   10:19 Greek *brothers*.   10:20 Greek *his flesh*.   10:30 Deut 32:35-36.

³⁷ "For in just a little while,
the Coming One will come and not delay.
³⁸ And a righteous person will live by faith.
But I will have no pleasure in anyone who turns away." *

I LIVE by faith and will not turn away from the Lord, no matter what happens. (10:38)

³⁹But we are not like those who turn their backs on God and seal their fate. We have faith that assures our salvation.

CHAPTER 11

Great Examples of Faith

I REGARD faith as evidence for things I cannot yet see. (11:1)

What is faith? It is the confident assurance that what we hope for is going to happen. It is the evidence of things we cannot yet see. ²God gave his approval to people in days of old because of their faith.

I BELIEVE the whole universe was formed at God's command. (11:3)

³By faith we understand that the entire universe was formed at God's command, that what we now see did not come from anything that can be seen.

See Abel's profile (page 9) at Genesis 4:4.

⁴It was by faith that Abel brought a more acceptable offering to God than Cain did. God accepted Abel's offering to show that he was a righteous man. And although Abel is long dead, he still speaks to us because of his faith.

See Enoch's profile (page 11) at Genesis 5:24.

⁵It was by faith that Enoch was taken up to heaven without dying—"suddenly he disappeared because God took him." * But before he was taken up, he was approved as pleasing to God. ⁶So, you see, it is impossible to please God without faith. Anyone who wants to come to him must believe that there is a God and that he rewards those who sincerely seek him.

I COME to God believing that he exists and that he rewards me when I seek him. (11:6)

⁷It was by faith that Noah built an ark to save his family from the flood. He obeyed God, who warned him about something that had never happened before. By his faith he condemned the rest of the world and was made right in God's sight.

See Noah's profile (page 13) at Genesis 6:9.

⁸It was by faith that Abraham obeyed when God called him to leave home and go to another land that God would give him as his inheritance. He went without knowing where he was going. ⁹And even when he reached the land God promised him, he lived there by faith—for he was like a foreigner, living in a tent. And so did Isaac and Jacob, to whom God gave the same promise. ¹⁰Abraham did this because he was confidently looking forward to a city with eternal foundations, a city designed and built by God.

See Abraham's profile (page 19) at Genesis 15:6.

See the profiles for Isaac (page 31) and Jacob (page 43) at Genesis 25:19 and Genesis 32:9.

¹¹It was by faith that Sarah together with Abraham was able to have a child, even though they were too old and Sarah was barren. Abraham believed that God would keep his promise.* ¹²And so a whole nation came from this one man, Abraham, who was too old to have any children—a nation with so many people that, like the stars of the sky and the sand on the seashore, there is no way to count them.

I LIVE as a foreigner here on earth and look forward to a city with eternal foundations. (11:10)

¹³All these faithful ones died without receiving what God had promised them, but they saw it all from a distance and welcomed the promises of God. They agreed that they were no more than foreigners and nomads here on earth. ¹⁴And obviously people who talk like that are looking forward to a country they can call their own. ¹⁵If they had meant the country they came from, they would have found a way to go back. ¹⁶But they were looking for a better place, a heavenly homeland. That is why God is not ashamed to be called their God, for he has prepared a heavenly city for them.

See Sarah's profile (page 25) at Genesis 21:1.

I BELIEVE the promises of God, even if I do not experience their fulfillment during my lifetime. (11:13)

¹⁷It was by faith that Abraham offered Isaac as a sacrifice when God was testing him. Abraham, who had received God's promises, was ready to sacrifice his only son, Isaac, ¹⁸though God had promised him, "Isaac is the son through whom your descendants will be counted." * ¹⁹Abraham assumed

I BELIEVE God is able to bring the dead back to life again. (11:19)

10:37-38 Hab 2:3-4.   11:5 Gen 5:24.   11:11 Some manuscripts read *It was by faith that Sarah was able to have a child, even though she was too old and barren. Sarah believed that God would keep his promise.*   11:18 Gen 21:12.

that if Isaac died, God was able to bring him back to life again. And in a sense, Abraham did receive his son back from the dead.

²⁰It was by faith that Isaac blessed his two sons, Jacob and Esau. He had confidence in what God was going to do in the future.

²¹It was by faith that Jacob, when he was old and dying, blessed each of Joseph's sons and bowed in worship as he leaned on his staff.

²²And it was by faith that Joseph, when he was about to die, confidently spoke of God's bringing the people of Israel out of Egypt. He was so sure of it that he commanded them to carry his bones with them when they left!

²³It was by faith that Moses' parents hid him for three months. They saw that God had given them an unusual child, and they were not afraid of what the king might do.

²⁴It was by faith that Moses, when he grew up, refused to be treated as the son of Pharaoh's daughter. ²⁵He chose to share the oppression of God's people instead of enjoying the fleeting pleasures of sin. ²⁶He thought it was better to suffer for the sake of the Messiah than to own the treasures of Egypt, for he was looking ahead to the great reward that God would give him. ²⁷It was by faith that Moses left the land of Egypt. He was not afraid of the king. Moses kept right on going because he kept his eyes on the one who is invisible. ²⁸It was by faith that Moses commanded the people of Israel to keep the Passover and to sprinkle blood on the doorposts so that the angel of death would not kill their firstborn sons.

²⁹It was by faith that the people of Israel went right through the Red Sea as though they were on dry ground. But when the Egyptians followed, they were all drowned.

³⁰It was by faith that the people of Israel marched around Jericho seven days, and the walls came crashing down.

³¹It was by faith that Rahab the prostitute did not die with all the others in her city who refused to obey God. For she had given a friendly welcome to the spies.

³²Well, how much more do I need to say? It would take too long to recount the stories of the faith of Gideon, Barak, Samson, Jephthah, David, Samuel, and all the prophets. ³³By faith these people overthrew kingdoms, ruled with justice, and received what God had promised them. They shut the mouths of lions, ³⁴quenched the flames of fire, and escaped death by the edge of the sword. Their weakness was turned to strength. They became strong in battle and put whole armies to flight. ³⁵Women received their loved ones back again from death.

But others trusted God and were tortured, preferring to die rather than turn from God and be free. They placed their hope in the resurrection to a better life. ³⁶Some were mocked, and their backs were cut open with whips. Others were chained in dungeons. ³⁷Some died by stoning, and some were sawed in half; others were killed with the sword. Some went about in skins of sheep and goats, hungry and oppressed and mistreated. ³⁸They were too good for this world. They wandered over deserts and mountains, hiding in caves and holes in the ground.

³⁹All of these people we have mentioned received God's approval because of their faith, yet none of them received all that God had promised. ⁴⁰For God had far better things in mind for us that would also benefit them, for they can't receive the prize at the end of the race until we finish the race.*

CHAPTER 12

God's Discipline Proves His Love

Therefore, since we are surrounded by such a huge crowd of witnesses to the life of faith, let us strip off every weight that slows us down, especially the sin

11:40 Greek *for us, for they apart from us can't finish.*

I HAVE CONFIDENCE in what God is going to do in the future. (11:20)

See Esau's profile (page 33) at Genesis 25:34.

See Joseph's profile (page 51) at Genesis 39:2.

See the profile (page 69) for Moses' Parents at Exodus 2:3.

See Moses' profile (page 73) at Exodus 5:1.

I VALUE my future reward in heaven more than any temporal pleasures. (11:25)

See Rahab's profile (page 251) at Joshua 2:11.

See the profiles for Gideon (page 289), Samson (page 301), Jephthah (page 295), David (page 629), and Samuel (page 323) at Judges 7:15, Judges 16:1, Judges 11:31, Psalm 3:1, and 1 Samuel 3:1.

I RUN God's race with endurance, getting rid of anything that hinders me. (12:1)

that so easily hinders our progress. And let us run with endurance the race that God has set before us. ²We do this by keeping our eyes on Jesus, on whom our faith depends from start to finish.* He was willing to die a shameful death on the cross because of the joy he knew would be his afterward. Now he is seated in the place of highest honor beside God's throne in heaven. ³Think about all he endured when sinful people did such terrible things to him, so that you don't become weary and give up. ⁴After all, you have not yet given your lives in your struggle against sin.

⁵And have you entirely forgotten the encouraging words God spoke to you, his children? He said,

"My child, don't ignore it when the Lord disciplines you,
 and don't be discouraged when he corrects you.
⁶For the Lord disciplines those he loves,
 and he punishes those he accepts as his children."*

⁷As you endure this divine discipline, remember that God is treating you as his own children. Whoever heard of a child who was never disciplined? ⁸If God doesn't discipline you as he does all of his children, it means that you are illegitimate and are not really his children after all. ⁹Since we respect our earthly fathers who disciplined us, should we not all the more cheerfully submit to the discipline of our heavenly Father and live forever*?

¹⁰For our earthly fathers disciplined us for a few years, doing the best they knew how. But God's discipline is always right and good for us because it means we will share in his holiness. ¹¹No discipline is enjoyable while it is happening—it is painful! But afterward there will be a quiet harvest of right living for those who are trained in this way.

¹²So take a new grip with your tired hands and stand firm on your shaky legs. ¹³Mark out a straight path for your feet. Then those who follow you, though they are weak and lame, will not stumble and fall but will become strong.

A Call to Listen to God

¹⁴Try to live in peace with everyone, and seek to live a clean and holy life, for those who are not holy will not see the Lord. ¹⁵Look after each other so that none of you will miss out on the special favor of God. Watch out that no bitter root of unbelief rises up among you, for whenever it springs up, many are corrupted by its poison. ¹⁶Make sure that no one is immoral or godless like Esau. He traded his birthright as the oldest son for a single meal. ¹⁷And afterward, when he wanted his father's blessing, he was rejected. It was too late for repentance, even though he wept bitter tears.

¹⁸You have not come to a physical mountain, to a place of flaming fire, darkness, gloom, and whirlwind, as the Israelites did at Mount Sinai when God gave them his laws. ¹⁹For they heard an awesome trumpet blast and a voice with a message so terrible that they begged God to stop speaking. ²⁰They staggered back under God's command: "If even an animal touches the mountain, it must be stoned to death."* ²¹Moses himself was so frightened at the sight that he said, "I am terrified and trembling."*

²²No, you have come to Mount Zion, to the city of the living God, the heavenly Jerusalem, and to thousands of angels in joyful assembly. ²³You have come to the assembly of God's firstborn children, whose names are written in heaven. You have come to God himself, who is the judge of all people. And you have come to the spirits of the redeemed in heaven who have now been made perfect. ²⁴You have come to Jesus, the one who mediates the new covenant between God and people, and to the sprinkled

I DO NOT GET TIRED of struggling against sin, because I remember all that Jesus Christ endured. (12:3)

I BELIEVE God is my loving heavenly Father and accept and learn from his discipline. (12:9)

I ABHOR bitterness and unbelief. (12:15)

See Esau's profile (page 33) at Genesis 25:34.

See Isaac's profile (page 31) at Genesis 25:19.

See Moses' profile (page 73) at Exodus 5:1.

12:2 Or *Jesus, the Originator and Perfecter of our faith.*   **12:5-6** Prov 3:11-12.   **12:9** Or *really live.*   **12:20** Exod 19:13.   **12:21** Deut 9:19.

blood, which graciously forgives instead of crying out for vengeance as the blood of Abel did.

See Abel's profile (page 9) at Genesis 4:4.

²⁵See to it that you obey God, the one who is speaking to you. For if the people of Israel did not escape when they refused to listen to Moses, the earthly messenger, how terrible our danger if we reject the One who speaks to us from heaven! ²⁶When God spoke from Mount Sinai his voice shook the earth, but now he makes another promise: "Once again I will shake not only the earth but the heavens also."* ²⁷This means that the things on earth will be shaken, so that only eternal things will be left.

²⁸Since we are receiving a Kingdom that cannot be destroyed, let us be thankful and please God by worshiping him with holy fear and awe. ²⁹For our God is a consuming fire.

I PLEASE God by worshiping him with holy fear and awe. (12:28)

CHAPTER 13
Concluding Words

Continue to love each other with true Christian love.* ²Don't forget to show hospitality to strangers, for some who have done this have entertained angels without realizing it! ³Don't forget about those in prison. Suffer with them as though you were there yourself. Share the sorrow of those being mistreated, as though you feel their pain in your own bodies.

I SHOW hospitality to other Christians—even those I haven't met before. (13:2)

⁴Give honor to marriage, and remain faithful to one another in marriage. God will surely judge people who are immoral and those who commit adultery.

⁵Stay away from the love of money; be satisfied with what you have. For God has said,

I BELIEVE God will never forsake me. (13:5)

"I will never fail you.
I will never forsake you."*

⁶That is why we can say with confidence,

"The Lord is my helper,
so I will not be afraid.
What can mere mortals do to me?"*

⁷Remember your leaders who first taught you the word of God. Think of all the good that has come from their lives, and trust the Lord as they do.

⁸Jesus Christ is the same yesterday, today, and forever. ⁹So do not be attracted by strange, new ideas. Your spiritual strength comes from God's special favor, not from ceremonial rules about food, which don't help those who follow them.

I AM NOT DISTRACTED by new, strange spiritual ideas. (13:9)

¹⁰We have an altar from which the priests in the Temple on earth have no right to eat. ¹¹Under the system of Jewish laws, the high priest brought the blood of animals into the Holy Place as a sacrifice for sin, but the bodies of the animals were burned outside the camp. ¹²So also Jesus suffered and died outside the city gates in order to make his people holy by shedding his own blood. ¹³So let us go out to him outside the camp and bear the disgrace he bore. ¹⁴For this world is not our home; we are looking forward to our city in heaven, which is yet to come.

I AM LOOKING FORWARD to my real home in heaven. (13:14)

¹⁵With Jesus' help, let us continually offer our sacrifice of praise to God by proclaiming the glory of his name. ¹⁶Don't forget to do good and to share what you have with those in need, for such sacrifices are very pleasing to God.

I PLEASE God by offering him the sacrifices of praise and right living. (13:15)

¹⁷Obey your spiritual leaders and do what they say. Their work is to watch over your souls, and they know they are accountable to God. Give them reason to do this joyfully and not with sorrow. That would certainly not be for your benefit.

12:26 Hag 2:6.   13:1 Greek *with brotherly love.*   13:5 Deut 31:6, 8.   13:6 Ps 118:6.

[18]Pray for us, for our conscience is clear and we want to live honorably in everything we do. [19]I especially need your prayers right now so that I can come back to you soon.

[20-21]And now, may the God of peace, who brought again from the dead our Lord Jesus, equip you with all you need for doing his will. May he produce in you, through the power of Jesus Christ, all that is pleasing to him. Jesus is the great Shepherd of the sheep by an everlasting covenant, signed with his blood. To him be glory forever and ever. Amen.

[22]I urge you, dear brothers and sisters,* please listen carefully to what I have said in this brief letter.

See Timothy's profile (page 1373) at 1 Timothy 4:12.

[23]I want you to know that our brother Timothy is now out of jail. If he comes here soon, I will bring him with me to see you.

[24]Give my greetings to all your leaders and to the other believers there. The Christians from Italy send you their greetings.

[25]May God's grace be with you all.

13:22 Greek *brothers*.

JAMES

THIS IS THE SECOND general letter distributed to the church at large.

The original audience for this letter was Jewish Christians scattered throughout the Roman empire.

The author, James, presents a number of minisermons on important issues of Christian faith and practice. In many passages, he echoes important themes that Jesus addressed during his earthly ministry.

In chapters 1–2, James challenges his readers about faith and endurance, faith and obedience, faith and love, and faith and good deeds.

In chapters 3–4, James warns his readers about untamed speech, earthly wisdom, ungodly desires, harsh criticism, and prideful boasting.

In chapter 5, James urges his readers to be patient in suffering and to persevere in prayer. Famous verses in James include

- ○ "If you want to know what God wants you to do—ask him, and he will gladly tell you" (1:5)
- ○ "God blesses the people who patiently endure testing" (1:12)
- ○ "Whatever is good and perfect comes to us from God above" (1:17)
- ○ "Be quick to listen, slow to speak, and slow to get angry" (1:19)
- ○ "Pure and lasting religion in the sight of God our Father means that we must care for orphans and widows" (1:27)
- ○ "Hasn't God chosen the poor in this world to be rich in faith?" (2:5)
- ○ "The person who keeps all the laws except one is as guilty as the person who has broken all of God's laws" (2:10)
- ○ "Faith that doesn't show itself by good deeds is no faith at all—it is dead and useless" (2:17)
- ○ "The wisdom that comes from heaven is first of all pure" (3:17)
- ○ "Don't you realize that friendship with this world makes you an enemy of God?" (4:4)
- ○ "So humble yourselves before God. Resist the Devil" (4:7)
- ○ "What you ought to say is, 'If the Lord wants us to, we will live and do this or that'" (4:15)
- ○ "Confess your sins to each other and pray for each other" (5:16)

CHAPTER 1

Greetings from James

This letter is from James, a slave of God and of the Lord Jesus Christ.

It is written to Jewish Christians scattered among the nations.* Greetings!

See James's profile (page 1407) at James 2:18.

Faith and Endurance

²Dear brothers and sisters,* whenever trouble comes your way, let it be an opportunity for joy. ³For when your faith is tested, your endurance has a chance to grow. ⁴So let it grow, for when your endurance is fully developed, you will be strong in character and ready for anything.

1:1 Greek *To the twelve tribes in the dispersion.*   1:2 Greek *brothers;* also in 1:16, 19.

I ASK God for wisdom to know what he wants me to do. (1:5)

⁵If you need wisdom—if you want to know what God wants you to do—ask him, and he will gladly tell you. He will not resent your asking. ⁶But when you ask him, be sure that you really expect him to answer, for a doubtful mind is as unsettled as a wave of the sea that is driven and tossed by the wind. ⁷People like that should not expect to receive anything from the Lord. ⁸They can't make up their minds. They waver back and forth in everything they do.

⁹Christians who are* poor should be glad, for God has honored them. ¹⁰And those who are rich should be glad, for God has humbled them. They will fade away like a flower in the field. ¹¹The hot sun rises and dries up the grass; the flower withers, and its beauty fades away. So also, wealthy people will fade away with all of their achievements.

I KNOW God does not tempt anyone to sin. (1:13)

¹²God blesses the people who patiently endure testing. Afterward they will receive the crown of life that God has promised to those who love him. ¹³And remember, no one who wants to do wrong should ever say, "God is tempting me." God is never tempted to do wrong, and he never tempts anyone else either. ¹⁴Temptation comes from the lure of our own evil desires. ¹⁵These evil desires lead to evil actions, and evil actions lead to death. ¹⁶So don't be misled, my dear brothers and sisters.

I BELIEVE every good gift is from God. (1:17)

¹⁷Whatever is good and perfect comes to us from God above, who created all heaven's lights.* Unlike them, he never changes or casts shifting shadows. ¹⁸In his goodness he chose to make us his own children by giving us his true word. And we, out of all creation, became his choice possession.

Listening and Doing

I AM QUICK to listen, slow to speak, and slow to get angry. (1:19)

¹⁹My dear brothers and sisters, be quick to listen, slow to speak, and slow to get angry. ²⁰Your anger can never make things right in God's sight.

²¹So get rid of all the filth and evil in your lives, and humbly accept the message God has planted in your hearts, for it is strong enough to save your souls.

²²And remember, it is a message to obey, not just to listen to. If you don't obey, you are only fooling yourself. ²³For if you just listen and don't obey, it is like looking at your face in a mirror but doing nothing to improve your appearance. ²⁴You see yourself, walk away, and forget what you look like. ²⁵But if you keep looking steadily into God's perfect law—the law that sets you free—and if you do what it says and don't forget what you heard, then God will bless you for doing it.

I CARE for widows and orphans. (1:27)

²⁶If you claim to be religious but don't control your tongue, you are just fooling yourself, and your religion is worthless. ²⁷Pure and lasting religion in the sight of God our Father means that we must care for orphans and widows in their troubles, and refuse to let the world corrupt us.

CHAPTER 2

A Warning against Prejudice

My dear brothers and sisters,* how can you claim that you have faith in our glorious Lord Jesus Christ if you favor some people more than others?

²For instance, suppose someone comes into your meeting* dressed in fancy clothes and expensive jewelry, and another comes in who is poor and dressed in shabby clothes. ³If you give special attention and a good seat to the rich person, but you say to the poor one, "You can stand over there, or else sit on the floor"—well, ⁴doesn't this discrimination show that you are guided by wrong motives?

I DO NOT DISCRIMINATE against a person because he or she is poor. (2:3)

⁵Listen to me, dear brothers and sisters. Hasn't God chosen the poor in this world to be rich in faith? Aren't they the ones who will inherit the Kingdom

1:9 Greek *The brother who is.* 1:17 Greek *from above, from the Father of lights.* 2:1 Greek *brothers;* also in 2:5, 14. 2:2 Greek *synagogue.*

he promised to those who love him? ⁶And yet, you insult the poor man! Isn't it the rich who oppress you and drag you into court? ⁷Aren't they the ones who slander Jesus Christ, whose noble name you bear?

⁸Yes indeed, it is good when you truly obey our Lord's royal command found in the Scriptures: "Love your neighbor as yourself."* ⁹But if you pay special attention to the rich, you are committing a sin, for you are guilty of breaking that law.

¹⁰And the person who keeps all of the laws except one is as guilty as the person who has broken all of God's laws. ¹¹For the same God who said, "Do not commit adultery," also said, "Do not murder."* So if you murder someone, you have broken the entire law, even if you do not commit adultery.

> I BELIEVE that breaking even one commandment makes someone guilty of breaking God's law. (2:10)

¹²So whenever you speak, or whatever you do, remember that you will be judged by the law of love, the law that set you free. ¹³For there will be no mercy for you if you have not been merciful to others. But if you have been merciful, then God's mercy toward you will win out over his judgment against you.

LIKE JAMES
James 2:18

I demonstrate my faith in God by living a good life for him.

Once you know the real thing, a counterfeit doesn't have a chance. Whether it's a hundred-dollar bill or a famous work of art, imitations don't measure up.

James knew what genuine holiness looked like. After all, he grew up with the sinless Son of God for an older brother. Of course, for several decades James didn't recognize Jesus' divinity (John 7:1-10). But once James believed, he was quick to tell the difference between true godliness and insincere religious talk.

As an elder and leader of the church in Jerusalem, James's own faith was plain for all to see. When Paul and Barnabas presented their case for not burdening the Gentiles with circumcision, James was the one who spoke up. He made the motion to accept the conversion of these Gentiles as a fulfillment of God's ancient prophetic promises. He affirmed *faith* as the way to salvation for Jews and Gentiles alike. At the same time, he asked that these brand-new Gentile believers be instructed to *practice* their faith before a watching world in accordance with basic, well-known biblical principles (Acts 15:13-21).

Like James, let's encourage one another to demonstrate the reality of our faith through our godly speech, helpful actions, respectful gestures, and generous gifts to others in need.

○ Today's Scripture reading is James 1–2.

Faith without Good Deeds Is Dead

¹⁴Dear brothers and sisters, what's the use of saying you have faith if you don't prove it by your actions? That kind of faith can't save anyone. ¹⁵Suppose you see a brother or sister who needs food or clothing, ¹⁶and you say, "Well, good-bye and God bless you; stay warm and eat well"—but then you don't give that person any food or clothing. What good does that do?

> I PROVE my faith by my actions. (2:14)

¹⁷So you see, it isn't enough just to have faith. Faith that doesn't show itself by good deeds is no faith at all—it is dead and useless.

> Recommit yourself to loving your neighbor as yourself.

¹⁸Now someone may argue, "Some people have faith; others have good deeds." I say, "I can't see your faith if you don't have good deeds, but I will show you my faith through my good deeds."

¹⁹Do you still think it's enough just to believe that there is one God? Well, even the demons believe this, and they tremble in terror! ²⁰Fool! When will you ever learn that faith that does not result in good deeds is useless? ²¹Don't you remember that our ancestor Abraham was declared right with God because of what he did when he offered his son Isaac on the altar?

> See the profiles for Abraham (page 19) and Isaac (page 31) at Genesis 15:6 and Genesis 25:19.

2:8 Lev 19:18.   2:11 Exod 20:13-14; Deut 5:17-18.

I TRUST God enough to do whatever he tells me to do. (2:22)

See Rahab's profile (page 251) at Joshua 2:11.

I KNOW faith without good deeds is dead faith. (2:26)

I CONTROL my tongue so I can control myself in all other ways. (3:2)

I DO NOT CURSE others, because I know they, too, are made in God's image. (3:10)

I DO NOT BRAG about the good that I do. (3:13)

I PLANT seeds of peace to reap a harvest of goodness. (3:18)

²²You see, he was trusting God so much that he was willing to do whatever God told him to do. His faith was made complete by what he did—by his actions. ²³And so it happened just as the Scriptures say: "Abraham believed God, so God declared him to be righteous."* He was even called "the friend of God."* ²⁴So you see, we are made right with God by what we do, not by faith alone.

²⁵Rahab the prostitute is another example of this. She was made right with God by her actions—when she hid those messengers and sent them safely away by a different road. ²⁶Just as the body is dead without a spirit, so also faith is dead without good deeds.

CHAPTER 3

Controlling the Tongue

Dear brothers and sisters,* not many of you should become teachers in the church, for we who teach will be judged by God with greater strictness.

²We all make many mistakes, but those who control their tongues can also control themselves in every other way. ³We can make a large horse turn around and go wherever we want by means of a small bit in its mouth. ⁴And a tiny rudder makes a huge ship turn wherever the pilot wants it to go, even though the winds are strong. ⁵So also, the tongue is a small thing, but what enormous damage it can do. A tiny spark can set a great forest on fire. ⁶And the tongue is a flame of fire. It is full of wickedness that can ruin your whole life. It can turn the entire course of your life into a blazing flame of destruction, for it is set on fire by hell itself.

⁷People can tame all kinds of animals and birds and reptiles and fish, ⁸but no one can tame the tongue. It is an uncontrollable evil, full of deadly poison. ⁹Sometimes it praises our Lord and Father, and sometimes it breaks out into curses against those who have been made in the image of God. ¹⁰And so blessing and cursing come pouring out of the same mouth. Surely, my brothers and sisters, this is not right! ¹¹Does a spring of water bubble out with both fresh water and bitter water? ¹²Can you pick olives from a fig tree or figs from a grapevine? No, and you can't draw fresh water from a salty pool.

True Wisdom Comes from God

¹³If you are wise and understand God's ways, live a life of steady goodness so that only good deeds will pour forth. And if you don't brag about the good you do, then you will be truly wise! ¹⁴But if you are bitterly jealous and there is selfish ambition in your hearts, don't brag about being wise. That is the worst kind of lie. ¹⁵For jealousy and selfishness are not God's kind of wisdom. Such things are earthly, unspiritual, and motivated by the Devil. ¹⁶For wherever there is jealousy and selfish ambition, there you will find disorder and every kind of evil.

¹⁷But the wisdom that comes from heaven is first of all pure. It is also peace loving, gentle at all times, and willing to yield to others. It is full of mercy and good deeds. It shows no partiality and is always sincere. ¹⁸And those who are peacemakers will plant seeds of peace and reap a harvest of goodness.

CHAPTER 4

Drawing Close to God

What is causing the quarrels and fights among you? Isn't it the whole army of evil desires at war within you? ²You want what you don't have, so you scheme and kill to get it. You are jealous for what others have, and you can't possess it, so you fight and quarrel to take it away from them. And yet the reason you don't have what you want is that you don't ask God for it. ³And even when

2:23a Gen 15:6.   2:23b See Isa 41:8.   3:1 Greek *brothers;* also in 3:10.

you do ask, you don't get it because your whole motive is wrong—you want only what will give you pleasure.

⁴You adulterers! Don't you realize that friendship with this world makes you an enemy of God? I say it again, that if your aim is to enjoy this world, you can't be a friend of God. ⁵What do you think the Scriptures mean when they say that the Holy Spirit, whom God has placed within us, jealously longs for us to be faithful*? ⁶He gives us more and more strength to stand against such evil desires. As the Scriptures say,

> "God sets himself against the proud,
>   but he shows favor to the humble."*

⁷So humble yourselves before God. Resist the Devil, and he will flee from you. ⁸Draw close to God, and God will draw close to you. Wash your hands, you sinners; purify your hearts, you hypocrites. ⁹Let there be tears for the wrong things you have done. Let there be sorrow and deep grief. Let there be sadness instead of laughter, and gloom instead of joy. ¹⁰When you bow down before the Lord and admit your dependence on him, he will lift you up and give you honor.

Warning against Judging Others

¹¹Don't speak evil against each other, my dear brothers and sisters.* If you criticize each other and condemn each other, then you are criticizing and condemning God's law. But you are not a judge who can decide whether the law is right or wrong. Your job is to obey it. ¹²God alone, who made the law, can rightly judge among us. He alone has the power to save or to destroy. So what right do you have to condemn your neighbor?

Warning about Self-Confidence

¹³Look here, you people who say, "Today or tomorrow we are going to a certain town and will stay there a year. We will do business there and make a profit." ¹⁴How do you know what will happen tomorrow? For your life is like the morning fog—it's here a little while, then it's gone. ¹⁵What you ought to say is, "If the Lord wants us to, we will live and do this or that." ¹⁶Otherwise you will be boasting about your own plans, and all such boasting is evil.

¹⁷Remember, it is sin to know what you ought to do and then not do it.

CHAPTER 5

Warning to the Rich

Look here, you rich people, weep and groan with anguish because of all the terrible troubles ahead of you. ²Your wealth is rotting away, and your fine clothes are moth-eaten rags. ³Your gold and silver have become worthless. The very wealth you were counting on will eat away your flesh in hell.* This treasure you have accumulated will stand as evidence against you on the day of judgment. ⁴For listen! Hear the cries of the field workers whom you have cheated of their pay. The wages you held back cry out against you. The cries of the reapers have reached the ears of the Lord Almighty.

⁵You have spent your years on earth in luxury, satisfying your every whim. Now your hearts are nice and fat, ready for the slaughter. ⁶You have condemned and killed good people who had no power to defend themselves against you.

Patience in Suffering

⁷Dear brothers and sisters,* you must be patient as you wait for the Lord's return. Consider the farmers who eagerly look for the rains in the fall and in

I AM a friend of God, not of the world. (4:4)

I HUMBLE myself before God, so that I will receive strength to stand against evil desires. (4:6)

I RECOGNIZE my dependence on God, knowing that he will lift me up. (4:10)

I DO NOT CRITICIZE AND CONDEMN other believers, since God alone has the right to judge his people. (4:12)

I KNOW worldly wealth will one day be worthless. (5:3)

4:5 Or *the spirit that God placed within us tends to envy*, or *the Holy Spirit, whom God has placed within us, opposes our envy.*   4:6 Prov 3:34.   4:11 Greek *brothers.*   5:3 Or *will eat your flesh like fire.*   5:7 Greek *brothers*; also in 5:9, 10, 12, 19.

I TAKE COURAGE because the Lord's coming is near. (5:8)

See Job's profile (page 599) at Job 1:21.

I BELIEVE God can heal me when I am sick. (5:15)

I PRAY earnestly. (5:16)

See Elijah's profile (page 421) at 1 Kings 19:18.

the spring. They patiently wait for the precious harvest to ripen. [8]You, too, must be patient. And take courage, for the coming of the Lord is near.

[9]Don't grumble about each other, my brothers and sisters, or God will judge you. For look! The great Judge is coming. He is standing at the door!

[10]For examples of patience in suffering, dear brothers and sisters, look at the prophets who spoke in the name of the Lord. [11]We give great honor to those who endure under suffering. Job is an example of a man who endured patiently. From his experience we see how the Lord's plan finally ended in good, for he is full of tenderness and mercy.

[12]But most of all, my brothers and sisters, never take an oath, by heaven or earth or anything else. Just say a simple yes or no, so that you will not sin and be condemned for it.

The Power of Prayer

[13]Are any among you suffering? They should keep on praying about it. And those who have reason to be thankful should continually sing praises to the Lord.

[14]Are any among you sick? They should call for the elders of the church and have them pray over them, anointing them with oil in the name of the Lord. [15]And their prayer offered in faith will heal the sick, and the Lord will make them well. And anyone who has committed sins will be forgiven.

[16]Confess your sins to each other and pray for each other so that you may be healed. The earnest prayer of a righteous person has great power and wonderful results. [17]Elijah was as human as we are, and yet when he prayed earnestly that no rain would fall, none fell for the next three and a half years! [18]Then he prayed for rain, and down it poured. The grass turned green, and the crops began to grow again.

Restore Wandering Believers

[19]My dear brothers and sisters, if anyone among you wanders away from the truth and is brought back again, [20]you can be sure that the one who brings that person back will save that sinner from death and bring about the forgiveness of many sins.

1 PETER

THIS IS THE THIRD general letter distributed to the church at large.

In this letter, the apostle Peter urges Christians to live for the Lord in the face of adversity.

In chapter 1, Peter urges his readers to thank God for their precious salvation, to see beyond their current trials, to look forward to how God will richly bless them in heaven, to sincerely love their Christian brothers and sisters, and to keep from slipping back into their old ways of doing evil.

In chapters 2–4, Peter reminds his readers of their new identity as Christians and then gives them specific instructions about Christ-honoring relationships. He also challenges them to live for God, no matter how much they must suffer for their faith.

In chapter 5, Peter exhorts Christian men—those in and under leadership—and then closes with some final instructions.

Famous verses in 1 Peter include

○ "God has given us the privilege of being born again" (1:3; see 1:23)

○ "Your faith is far more precious to God than mere gold" (1:7; see 1:18-19)

○ "You must be holy in everything you do" (1:15)

○ "Crave pure spiritual milk so that you can grow into the fullness of your salvation" (2:2)

○ "You are a chosen people. You are a kingdom of priests, God's holy nation, his very own possession" (2:9)

○ "Keep away from evil desires because they fight against your very souls" (2:11)

○ "Christ, who suffered for you, is your example. Follow in his steps" (2:21)

○ "He [Christ] personally carried away our sins in his own body on the cross" (2:24)

○ "Don't repay evil for evil" (3:9)

○ "Worship Christ as Lord of your life. And if you are asked about your Christian hope, always be ready to explain it" (3:15)

○ "Love covers a multitude of sins" (4:8)

○ "Humble yourselves under the mighty power of God, and in his good time he will honor you" (5:6)

○ "Give all your worries and cares to God, for he cares about what happens to you" (5:7)

○ "Watch out for attacks from the Devil. . . . He prowls around like a roaring lion" (5:8)

CHAPTER 1

Greetings from Peter

This letter is from Peter, an apostle of Jesus Christ.

I am writing to God's chosen people who are living as foreigners in the lands of Pontus, Galatia, Cappadocia, the province of Asia, and Bithynia. ²God the Father chose you long ago, and the Spirit has made you holy. As a result, you have obeyed Jesus Christ and are cleansed by his blood.

May you have more and more of God's special favor and wonderful peace.

See Peter's profile (page 1111) at Matthew 26:75.

I BELIEVE God the Father chose me and the Holy Spirit made me holy. (1:2)

The Hope of Eternal Life

³All honor to the God and Father of our Lord Jesus Christ, for it is by his boundless mercy that God has given us the privilege of being born again. Now we live with a wonderful expectation because Jesus Christ rose again from the dead. ⁴For God has reserved a priceless inheritance for his children. It is kept in heaven for you, pure and undefiled, beyond the reach of change and decay. ⁵And God, in his mighty power, will protect you until you receive this salvation, because you are trusting him. It will be revealed on the last day for all to see. ⁶So be truly glad!* There is wonderful joy ahead, even though it is necessary for you to endure many trials for a while.

⁷These trials are only to test your faith, to show that it is strong and pure. It is being tested as fire tests and purifies gold—and your faith is far more precious to God than mere gold. So if your faith remains strong after being tried by fiery trials, it will bring you much praise and glory and honor on the day when Jesus Christ is revealed to the whole world.

⁸You love him even though you have never seen him. Though you do not see him, you trust him; and even now you are happy with a glorious, inexpressible joy. ⁹Your reward for trusting him will be the salvation of your souls.

¹⁰This salvation was something the prophets wanted to know more about. They prophesied about this gracious salvation prepared for you, even though they had many questions as to what it all could mean. ¹¹They wondered what the Spirit of Christ within them was talking about when he told them in advance about Christ's suffering and his great glory afterward. They wondered when and to whom all this would happen.

¹²They were told that these things would not happen during their lifetime, but many years later, during yours. And now this Good News has been announced by those who preached to you in the power of the Holy Spirit sent from heaven. It is all so wonderful that even the angels are eagerly watching these things happen.

A Call to Holy Living

¹³So think clearly and exercise self-control. Look forward to the special blessings that will come to you at the return of Jesus Christ. ¹⁴Obey God because you are his children. Don't slip back into your old ways of doing evil; you didn't know any better then. ¹⁵But now you must be holy in everything you do, just as God—who chose you to be his children—is holy. ¹⁶For he himself has said, "You must be holy because I am holy."*

¹⁷And remember that the heavenly Father to whom you pray has no favorites when he judges. He will judge or reward you according to what you do. So you must live in reverent fear of him during your time as foreigners here on earth. ¹⁸For you know that God paid a ransom to save you from the empty life you inherited from your ancestors. And the ransom he paid was not mere gold or silver. ¹⁹He paid for you with the precious lifeblood of Christ, the sinless, spotless Lamb of God. ²⁰God chose him for this purpose long before the world began, but now in these final days, he was sent to the earth for all to see. And he did this for you.

²¹Through Christ you have come to trust in God. And because God raised Christ from the dead and gave him great glory, your faith and hope can be placed confidently in God. ²²Now you can have sincere love for each other as brothers and sisters* because you were cleansed from your sins when you accepted the truth of the Good News. So see to it that you really do love each other intensely with all your hearts.*

²³For you have been born again. Your new life did not come from your

I LOVE Jesus Christ and trust him, even though I have never seen him. (1:8)

I BELIEVE the Spirit of Jesus Christ told the Old Testament prophets in advance about his suffering and glory. (1:11)

I LIVE in reverent fear of God. (1:17)

I SINCERELY LOVE my brothers and sisters in Christ. (1:22)

1:6 Or *So you are truly glad.* 1:16 Lev 11:44-45; 19:2; 20:7. 1:22a Greek *can have brotherly love.* 1:22b Some manuscripts read *with a pure heart.*

earthly parents because the life they gave you will end in death. But this new life will last forever because it comes from the eternal, living word of God. ²⁴As the prophet says,

"People are like grass that dies away;
  their beauty fades as quickly as the beauty of wildflowers.
The grass withers,
  and the flowers fall away.
²⁵But the word of the Lord will last forever."*

And that word is the Good News that was preached to you.

CHAPTER 2

So get rid of all malicious behavior and deceit. Don't just pretend to be good! Be done with hypocrisy and jealousy and backstabbing. ²You must crave pure spiritual milk so that you can grow into the fullness of your salvation. Cry out for this nourishment as a baby cries for milk, ³now that you have had a taste of the Lord's kindness.

Living Stones for God's House
⁴Come to Christ, who is the living cornerstone of God's temple. He was rejected by the people, but he is precious to God who chose him.

⁵And now God is building you, as living stones, into his spiritual temple. What's more, you are God's holy priests, who offer the spiritual sacrifices that please him because of Jesus Christ. ⁶As the Scriptures express it,

"I am placing a stone in Jerusalem,*
  a chosen cornerstone,
and anyone who believes in him
  will never be disappointed.*"

⁷Yes, he is very precious to you who believe. But for those who reject him,

"The stone that was rejected by the builders
  has now become the cornerstone."*

⁸And the Scriptures also say,

"He is the stone that makes people stumble,
  the rock that will make them fall."*

They stumble because they do not listen to God's word or obey it, and so they meet the fate that has been planned for them.

⁹But you are not like that, for you are a chosen people. You are a kingdom of priests, God's holy nation, his very own possession. This is so you can show others the goodness of God, for he called you out of the darkness into his wonderful light.

¹⁰ "Once you were not a people;
  now you are the people of God.
Once you received none of God's mercy;
  now you have received his mercy."*

¹¹Dear brothers and sisters, you are foreigners and aliens here. So I warn you to keep away from evil desires because they fight against your very souls. ¹²Be careful how you live among your unbelieving neighbors. Even if they accuse you of doing wrong, they will see your honorable behavior, and they will believe and give honor to God when he comes to judge the world.*

I DO NOT JUST PRETEND to be good—I get rid of all wrong behaviors and destructive attitudes. (2:1)

I BELIEVE God made me his own so I can show his goodness to others. (2:9)

1:24-25 Isa 40:6-8. 2:6a Greek *in Zion.* 2:6b Or *will never be put to shame.* Isa 28:16. 2:7 Ps 118:22.
2:8 Isa 8:14. 2:10 Hos 1:6, 9; 2:23. 2:12 Or *on the day of visitation.*

Respecting People in Authority

¹³For the Lord's sake, accept all authority—the king as head of state, ¹⁴and the officials he has appointed. For the king has sent them to punish all who do wrong and to honor those who do right.

¹⁵It is God's will that your good lives should silence those who make foolish accusations against you. ¹⁶You are not slaves; you are free. But your freedom is not an excuse to do evil. You are free to live as God's slaves. ¹⁷Show respect for everyone. Love your Christian brothers and sisters.* Fear God. Show respect for the king.

Slaves

¹⁸You who are slaves must accept the authority of your masters. Do whatever they tell you—not only if they are kind and reasonable, but even if they are harsh. ¹⁹For God is pleased with you when, for the sake of your conscience, you patiently endure unfair treatment. ²⁰Of course, you get no credit for being patient if you are beaten for doing wrong. But if you suffer for doing right and are patient beneath the blows, God is pleased with you.

²¹This suffering is all part of what God has called you to. Christ, who suffered for you, is your example. Follow in his steps. ²²He never sinned, and he never deceived anyone. ²³He did not retaliate when he was insulted. When he suffered, he did not threaten to get even. He left his case in the hands of God, who always judges fairly. ²⁴He personally carried away our sins in his own body on the cross so we can be dead to sin and live for what is right. You have been healed by his wounds! ²⁵Once you were wandering like lost sheep. But now you have turned to your Shepherd, the Guardian of your souls.

CHAPTER 3

Wives

In the same way, you wives must accept the authority of your husbands, even those who refuse to accept the Good News. Your godly lives will speak to them better than any words. They will be won over ²by watching your pure, godly behavior.

³Don't be concerned about the outward beauty that depends on fancy hairstyles, expensive jewelry, or beautiful clothes. ⁴You should be known for the beauty that comes from within, the unfading beauty of a gentle and quiet spirit, which is so precious to God. ⁵That is the way the holy women of old made themselves beautiful. They trusted God and accepted the authority of their husbands. ⁶For instance, Sarah obeyed her husband, Abraham, when she called him her master. You are her daughters when you do what is right without fear of what your husbands might do.

Husbands

⁷In the same way, you husbands must give honor to your wives. Treat her with understanding as you live together. She may be weaker than you are, but she is your equal partner in God's gift of new life. If you don't treat her as you should, your prayers will not be heard.

All Christians

⁸Finally, all of you should be of one mind, full of sympathy toward each other, loving one another with tender hearts and humble minds. ⁹Don't repay evil for evil. Don't retaliate when people say unkind things about you. Instead, pay them back with a blessing. That is what God wants you to do, and he will bless you for it. ¹⁰For the Scriptures say,

"If you want a happy life and good days,
    keep your tongue from speaking evil,

2:17 Greek *Love the brotherhood.*

I ACCEPT human authority for the Lord's sake. (2:13)

I SHOW RESPECT to everyone, including those in government. (2:17)

I BELIEVE Jesus Christ carried away my sins in his own body on the cross. (2:24)

I AM MORE CONCERNED about inner beauty than physical attractiveness. (3:4)

See the profiles for Abraham (page 19) and Sarah (page 25) at Genesis 15:6 and Genesis 21:1.

I BELIEVE a Christian husband and wife are equal partners in God's gift of new life. (3:7)

and keep your lips from telling lies.
¹¹Turn away from evil and do good.
    Work hard at living in peace with others.
¹²The eyes of the Lord watch over those who do right,
    and his ears are open to their prayers.
But the Lord turns his face
    against those who do evil."*

Suffering for Doing Good

¹³Now, who will want to harm you if you are eager to do good? ¹⁴But even if you suffer for doing what is right, God will reward you for it. So don't be afraid and don't worry. ¹⁵Instead, you must worship Christ as Lord of your life. And if you are asked about your Christian hope, always be ready to explain it. ¹⁶But you must do this in a gentle and respectful way. Keep your conscience clear. Then if people speak evil against you, they will be ashamed when they see what a good life you live because you belong to Christ. ¹⁷Remember, it is better to suffer for doing good, if that is what God wants, than to suffer for doing wrong!

¹⁸Christ also suffered when he died for our sins once for all time. He never sinned, but he died for sinners that he might bring us safely home to God. He suffered physical death, but he was raised to life in the Spirit.*

¹⁹So he went and preached to the spirits in prison—²⁰those who disobeyed God long ago when God waited patiently while Noah was building his boat. Only eight people were saved from drowning in that terrible flood.* ²¹And this is a picture of baptism, which now saves you by the power of Jesus Christ's resurrection. Baptism is not a removal of dirt from your body; it is an appeal to God from* a clean conscience.

²²Now Christ has gone to heaven. He is seated in the place of honor next to God, and all the angels and authorities and powers are bowing before him.

CHAPTER 4

Living for God

So then, since Christ suffered physical pain, you must arm yourselves with the same attitude he had, and be ready to suffer, too. For if you are willing to suffer for Christ, you have decided to stop sinning. ²And you won't spend the rest of your life chasing after evil desires, but you will be anxious to do the will of God. ³You have had enough in the past of the evil things that godless people enjoy—their immorality and lust, their feasting and drunkenness and wild parties, and their terrible worship of idols.

⁴Of course, your former friends are very surprised when you no longer join them in the wicked things they do, and they say evil things about you. ⁵But just remember that they will have to face God, who will judge everyone, both the living and the dead. ⁶That is why the Good News was preached even to those who have died—so that although their bodies were punished with death, they could still live in the spirit as God does.

⁷The end of the world is coming soon. Therefore, be earnest and disciplined in your prayers. ⁸Most important of all, continue to show deep love for each other, for love covers a multitude of sins. ⁹Cheerfully share your home with those who need a meal or a place to stay.

¹⁰God has given gifts to each of you from his great variety of spiritual gifts. Manage them well so that God's generosity can flow through you. ¹¹Are you called to be a speaker? Then speak as though God himself were speaking through you. Are you called to help others? Do it with all the strength and energy that God supplies. Then God will be given glory in everything through Jesus Christ. All glory and power belong to him forever and ever. Amen.

I AM NOT AFRAID when I suffer for doing right, because I know God will reward me for it. (3:14)

I AM always ready to explain my hope in Jesus Christ in a gentle and respectful way. (3:15)

See Noah's profile (page 13) at Genesis 6:9.

I BELIEVE Jesus Christ is in heaven and all the angels are bowing before him. (3:22)

I AM ANXIOUS to do God's will. (4:2)

I PRAY earnestly, both for other believers and for those who haven't trusted Jesus Christ yet, because the end of the world is coming soon. (4:7)

I MAKE good use of my spiritual gifts so God will be given great glory. (4:10)

3:10-12 Ps 34:12-16.   3:18 Or *spirit*.   3:20 Greek *saved through water*.   3:21 Or *for*.

Suffering for Being a Christian

[12]Dear friends, don't be surprised at the fiery trials you are going through, as if something strange were happening to you. [13]Instead, be very glad—because these trials will make you partners with Christ in his suffering, and afterward you will have the wonderful joy of sharing his glory when it is displayed to all the world.

[14]Be happy if you are insulted for being a Christian, for then the glorious Spirit of God will come upon you. [15]If you suffer, however, it must not be for murder, stealing, making trouble, or prying into other people's affairs. [16]But it is no shame to suffer for being a Christian. Praise God for the privilege of being called by his wonderful name! [17]For the time has come for judgment, and it must begin first among God's own children. And if even we Christians must be judged, what terrible fate awaits those who have never believed God's Good News? [18]And

> "If the righteous are barely saved,
>   what chance will the godless and sinners have?"*

[19]So if you are suffering according to God's will, keep on doing what is right, and trust yourself to the God who made you, for he will never fail you.

CHAPTER 5

Advice for Elders and Young Men

And now, a word to you who are elders in the churches. I, too, am an elder and a witness to the sufferings of Christ. And I, too, will share his glory and his honor when he returns. As a fellow elder, this is my appeal to you: [2]Care for the flock of God entrusted to you. Watch over it willingly, not grudgingly—not for what you will get out of it, but because you are eager to serve God. [3]Don't lord it over the people assigned to your care, but lead them by your good example. [4]And when the head Shepherd comes, your reward will be a never-ending share in his glory and honor.

[5]You younger men, accept the authority of the elders. And all of you, serve each other in humility, for

> "God sets himself against the proud,
>   but he shows favor to the humble."*

[6]So humble yourselves under the mighty power of God, and in his good time he will honor you. [7]Give all your worries and cares to God, for he cares about what happens to you.

[8]Be careful! Watch out for attacks from the Devil, your great enemy. He prowls around like a roaring lion, looking for some victim to devour. [9]Take a firm stand against him, and be strong in your faith. Remember that your Christian brothers and sisters* all over the world are going through the same kind of suffering you are.

[10]In his kindness God called you to his eternal glory by means of Jesus Christ. After you have suffered a little while, he will restore, support, and strengthen you, and he will place you on a firm foundation. [11]All power is his forever and ever. Amen.

Peter's Final Greetings

[12]I have written this short letter to you with the help of Silas,* whom I consider a faithful brother. My purpose in writing is to encourage you and assure you that the grace of God is with you no matter what happens.

[13]Your sister church here in Rome* sends you greetings, and so does my son Mark. [14]Greet each other in Christian love.*

Peace be to all of you who are in Christ.

I KEEP DOING what is right and trust God even when I must suffer as a result. (4:19)

I WILLINGLY SERVE other Christians in humility. (5:5)

I GIVE all my worries and cares to God because he cares for me. (5:7)

I BELIEVE God's grace is with me, no matter what happens. (5:12)

See John Mark's profile (page 1255) at Acts 13:13.

4:18 Prov 11:31.   5:5 Prov 3:34.   5:9 Greek *your brothers.*   5:12 Greek *Silvanus.*   5:13 Greek *The elect one in Babylon.* Babylon was probably a code name for Rome.   5:14 Greek *with a kiss of love.*

2 PETER

THIS IS THE FOURTH general letter distributed to the church at large.

In this letter, Peter urges confused believers to stand firm for the Lord despite false teachers.

In chapter 1, Peter challenges his readers to grow in their knowledge of God so they won't stumble or fall away. He also challenges them to pay attention to the Scriptures and the teachings of the apostles.

In chapter 2, Peter exposes the ungodliness and impure motives of the false teachers who sought to undermine the faith of Peter's readers. He makes it clear that God's judgment awaits them.

In chapter 3, Peter reminds his readers that the Lord Jesus is definitely coming back and urges them to live godly, pure, and holy lives. He concludes with a final warning about false teachers.

Famous verses in 2 Peter include

- ○ "His [Jesus'] divine power gives us everything we need for living a godly life" (1:3)
- ○ "So make every effort to apply the benefits of these promises to your life" (1:5)
- ○ "Doing this, you will never stumble or fall away" (1:10)
- ○ "We were not making up clever stories when we told you about the power of our Lord Jesus Christ and his coming again" (1:16)
- ○ "No prophecy in Scripture ever came from the prophets themselves. . . . It was the Holy Spirit who moved the prophets to speak from God" (1:20-21)
- ○ "The Lord knows how to rescue godly people from their trials" (2:9)
- ○ "They promise freedom, but they themselves are slaves to sin and corruption" (2:19)
- ○ "God has also commanded that the heavens and the earth will be consumed by fire" (3:7)
- ○ "A day is like a thousand years to the Lord, and a thousand years is like a day" (3:8)
- ○ "He [the Lord] does not want anyone to perish, so he is giving more time for everyone to repent" (3:9; see 3:15)

CHAPTER 1

Greetings from Peter

This letter is from Simon* Peter, a slave and apostle of Jesus Christ.

I am writing to all of you who share the same precious faith we have, faith given to us by Jesus Christ, our God and Savior, who makes us right with God.

²May God bless you with his special favor and wonderful peace as you come to know Jesus, our God and Lord,* better and better.

See Peter's profile (page 1111) at Matthew 26:75.

Growing in the Knowledge of God

³As we know Jesus better, his divine power gives us everything we need for living a godly life. He has called us to receive his own glory and goodness! ⁴And by that same mighty power, he has given us all of his rich and wonderful

I BELIEVE Jesus Christ's divine power gives me everything I need to live a godly life. (1:3)

1:1 Greek *Simeon.*   1:2 Or *come to know God and Jesus our Lord.*

promises. He has promised that you will escape the decadence all around you caused by evil desires and that you will share in his divine nature.

⁵So make every effort to apply the benefits of these promises to your life. Then your faith will produce a life of moral excellence. A life of moral excellence leads to knowing God better. ⁶Knowing God leads to self-control. Self-control leads to patient endurance, and patient endurance leads to godliness. ⁷Godliness leads to love for other Christians,* and finally you will grow to have genuine love for everyone. ⁸The more you grow like this, the more you will become productive and useful in your knowledge of our Lord Jesus Christ. ⁹But those who fail to develop these virtues are blind or, at least, very shortsighted. They have already forgotten that God has cleansed them from their old life of sin.

> I CONTINUALLY develop the virtues of moral excellence, knowing God better, self-control, patient endurance, godliness, and love. (1:9)

¹⁰So, dear brothers and sisters,* work hard to prove that you really are among those God has called and chosen. Doing this, you will never stumble or fall away. ¹¹And God will open wide the gates of heaven for you to enter into the eternal Kingdom of our Lord and Savior Jesus Christ.

Paying Attention to Scripture

¹²I plan to keep on reminding you of these things—even though you already know them and are standing firm in the truth. ¹³Yes, I believe I should keep on reminding you of these things as long as I live. ¹⁴But the Lord Jesus Christ has shown me that my days here on earth are numbered and I am soon to die.* ¹⁵So I will work hard to make these things clear to you. I want you to remember them long after I am gone.

> I BELIEVE the apostle Peter saw the Lord Jesus Christ's power and glory. (1:16)

¹⁶For we were not making up clever stories when we told you about the power of our Lord Jesus Christ and his coming again. We have seen his majestic splendor with our own eyes. ¹⁷And he received honor and glory from God the Father when God's glorious, majestic voice called down from heaven, "This is my beloved Son; I am fully pleased with him." ¹⁸We ourselves heard the voice when we were there with him on the holy mountain.

> I UNDERSTAND that the Old Testament prophets spoke because the Holy Spirit moved them. (1:21)

¹⁹Because of that, we have even greater confidence in the message proclaimed by the prophets. Pay close attention to what they wrote, for their words are like a light shining in a dark place—until the day Christ appears and his brilliant light shines in your hearts.* ²⁰Above all, you must understand that no prophecy in Scripture ever came from the prophets themselves* ²¹or because they wanted to prophesy. It was the Holy Spirit who moved the prophets to speak from God.

CHAPTER 2

The Danger of False Teachers

But there were also false prophets in Israel, just as there will be false teachers among you. They will cleverly teach their destructive heresies about God and even turn against their Master who bought them. Theirs will be a swift and terrible end. ²Many will follow their evil teaching and shameful immorality. And because of them, Christ and his true way will be slandered. ³In their greed they will make up clever lies to get hold of your money. But God condemned them long ago, and their destruction is on the way.

> I KNOW that God will condemn and punish false teachers who cheat and deceive his people. (2:3)

⁴For God did not spare even the angels when they sinned; he threw them into hell,* in gloomy caves* and darkness until the judgment day. ⁵And God did not spare the ancient world—except for Noah and his family of seven. Noah warned the world of God's righteous judgment. Then God destroyed the whole world of ungodly people with a vast flood. ⁶Later, he turned the cities of Sodom and Gomorrah into heaps of ashes and swept them off the face

> See Noah's profile (page 13) at Genesis 6:9.

1:7 Greek *brotherly love.*   1:10 Greek *brothers.*   1:14 Greek *I must soon put off this earthly tent.*   1:19 Or *until the day dawns and the morning star rises in your hearts.*   1:20 Or *is a matter of one's own interpretation.*   2:4a Greek *Tartaros.*   2:4b Some manuscripts read *chains of gloom.*

of the earth. He made them an example of what will happen to ungodly people. [7]But at the same time, God rescued Lot out of Sodom because he was a good man who was sick of all the immorality and wickedness around him. [8]Yes, he was a righteous man who was distressed by the wickedness he saw and heard day after day.

[9]So you see, the Lord knows how to rescue godly people from their trials, even while punishing the wicked right up until the day of judgment. [10]He is especially hard on those who follow their own evil, lustful desires and who despise authority. These people are proud and arrogant, daring even to scoff at the glorious ones* without so much as trembling. [11]But the angels, even though they are far greater in power and strength than these false teachers, never speak out disrespectfully against* the glorious ones.

[12]These false teachers are like unthinking animals, creatures of instinct, who are born to be caught and killed. They laugh at the terrifying powers they know so little about, and they will be destroyed along with them. [13]Their destruction is their reward for the harm they have done. They love to indulge in evil pleasures in broad daylight. They are a disgrace and a stain among you. They revel in deceitfulness while they feast with you. [14]They commit adultery with their eyes, and their lust is never satisfied. They make a game of luring unstable people into sin. They train themselves to be greedy; they are doomed and cursed. [15]They have wandered off the right road and followed the way of Balaam son of Beor,* who loved to earn money by doing wrong. [16]But Balaam was stopped from his mad course when his donkey rebuked him with a human voice.

[17]These people are as useless as dried-up springs of water or as clouds blown away by the wind—promising much and delivering nothing. They are doomed to blackest darkness. [18]They brag about themselves with empty, foolish boasting. With lustful desire as their bait, they lure back into sin those who have just escaped from such wicked living. [19]They promise freedom, but they themselves are slaves to sin and corruption. For you are a slave to whatever controls you. [20]And when people escape from the wicked ways of the world by learning about our Lord and Savior Jesus Christ and then get tangled up with sin and become its slave again, they are worse off than before. [21]It would be better if they had never known the right way to live than to know it and then reject the holy commandments that were given to them. [22]They make these proverbs come true: "A dog returns to its vomit,"* and "A washed pig returns to the mud."

CHAPTER 3

The Day of the Lord Is Coming

This is my second letter to you, dear friends, and in both of them I have tried to stimulate your wholesome thinking and refresh your memory. [2]I want you to remember and understand what the holy prophets said long ago and what our Lord and Savior commanded through your apostles.

[3]First, I want to remind you that in the last days there will be scoffers who will laugh at the truth and do every evil thing they desire. [4]This will be their argument: "Jesus promised to come back, did he? Then where is he? Why, as far back as anyone can remember, everything has remained exactly the same since the world was first created."

[5]They deliberately forget that God made the heavens by the word of his command, and he brought the earth up from the water and surrounded it with water. [6]Then he used the water to destroy the world with a mighty flood. [7]And God has also commanded that the heavens and the earth will be consumed by fire on the day of judgment, when ungodly people will perish.

I BELIEVE God knows how to rescue godly people from their trials. (2:9)

I BELIEVE God will punish false teachers who mock spiritual authorities and powers. (2:10)

I ABHOR adultery and greed. (2:14)

I REMEMBER the words of the Old Testament prophets and the commands of the Lord Jesus Christ. (3:2)

I RECOGNIZE that scoffers will doubt God's Word and Jesus Christ's promise to return. (3:3)

2:10 *The glorious ones* are probably evil angels; also in 2:11.   2:11 Greek *never bring blasphemous judgment from the Lord against.*   2:15 Other manuscripts read *Bosor.*   2:22 Prov 26:11.

I BELIEVE the Lord has not returned yet because he does not want anyone to perish and is giving people time to repent. (3:9)

I LOOK FORWARD to the new heavens and new earth, where everyone is right with God. (3:13)

See Paul's profile (page 1333) at Galatians 2:5.

[8]But you must not forget, dear friends, that a day is like a thousand years to the Lord, and a thousand years is like a day. [9]The Lord isn't really being slow about his promise to return, as some people think. No, he is being patient for your sake. He does not want anyone to perish, so he is giving more time for everyone to repent. [10]But the day of the Lord will come as unexpectedly as a thief. Then the heavens will pass away with a terrible noise, and everything in them will disappear in fire, and the earth and everything on it will be exposed to judgment.*

[11]Since everything around us is going to melt away, what holy, godly lives you should be living! [12]You should look forward to that day and hurry it along—the day when God will set the heavens on fire and the elements will melt away in the flames. [13]But we are looking forward to the new heavens and new earth he has promised, a world where everyone is right with God.

[14]And so, dear friends, while you are waiting for these things to happen, make every effort to live a pure and blameless life. And be at peace with God.

[15]And remember, the Lord is waiting so that people have time to be saved. This is just as our beloved brother Paul wrote to you with the wisdom God gave him—[16]speaking of these things in all of his letters. Some of his comments are hard to understand, and those who are ignorant and unstable have twisted his letters around to mean something quite different from what he meant, just as they do the other parts of Scripture—and the result is disaster for them.

Peter's Final Words

[17]I am warning you ahead of time, dear friends, so that you can watch out and not be carried away by the errors of these wicked people. I don't want you to lose your own secure footing. [18]But grow in the special favor and knowledge of our Lord and Savior Jesus Christ.

To him be all glory and honor, both now and forevermore. Amen.

3:10 Some manuscripts read *will be burned up.*

1 JOHN

THIS IS THE FIFTH general letter distributed to the church at large.

In this letter, the apostle John urges Christians to be pure in their faith and loving in their practice, despite intense pressures from false teachers.

In chapters 1–2, John contrasts
- walking in God's light vs. stumbling in spiritual darkness
- confessing any known sins vs. practicing spiritual dishonesty
- obeying God's commands vs. participating in spiritual deception
- growing in Christian maturity vs. continuing in spiritual lostness
- doing God's will vs. giving in to temporal lusts
- continuing to live for Christ vs. heeding antichrists

In chapters 3–5, John contrasts
- living as children of God vs. living as children of the Devil
- growing in Christian love vs. fostering hatred
- obeying God's commands vs. participating in spiritual deception
- believing in Jesus Christ vs. facing spiritual death

Famous verses in 1 John include
- "If we are living in the light of God's presence, just as Christ is, then we have fellowship with each other" (1:7)
- "If we confess our sins to him [God], he is faithful and just to forgive us and to cleanse us from every wrong" (1:9)
- "He [Jesus Christ] is the sacrifice for our sins" (2:2)
- "Stop loving this evil world and all that it offers you" (2:15)
- "The Spirit teaches you all things" (2:27)
- "See how very much our heavenly Father loves us, for he allows us to be called his children, and we really are!" (3:1)
- "When he [Christ] comes we will be like him, for we will see him as he really is" (3:2)
- "If anyone has enough money to live well and sees a brother or sister in need and refuses to help—how can God's love be in that person?" (3:17)
- "Let us stop just saying we love each other . . . " (3:18)
- "The Spirit who lives in you is greater than the spirit who lives in the world" (4:4)
- "He [God] loved us and sent his Son as a sacrifice to take away our sins" (4:10)
- "Perfect love expels all fear" (4:18)
- "Whoever has God's Son has life; whoever does not have his Son does not have life" (5:12)
- "I write this to you who believe in the Son of God, so that you may know you have eternal life" (5:13)
- "We can be confident that he will listen to us whenever we ask him for anything in line with his will" (5:14)
- "Keep away from anything that might take God's place in your hearts" (5:21)

CHAPTER 1

Introduction

I BELIEVE Jesus Christ
gives life to all who
believe his message of
Good News. (1:1)

*See John's profile (page
1435) at Revelation 1:9.*

The one who existed from the beginning* is the one we have heard and seen. We saw him with our own eyes and touched him with our own hands. He is Jesus Christ, the Word of life. ²This one who is life from God was shown to us, and we have seen him. And now we testify and announce to you that he is the one who is eternal life. He was with the Father, and then he was shown to us. ³We are telling you about what we ourselves have actually seen and heard, so that you may have fellowship with us. And our fellowship is with the Father and with his Son, Jesus Christ.

*Ask God to cleanse your
heart as you read his
Word (Psalm 51:10).*

⁴We are writing these things so that our* joy will be complete.

Living in the Light

I LIVE in the light of
God's presence and,
as a result, enjoy
forgiveness from God
and fellowship with
other believers. (1:7)

I CONFESS my sin and
receive God's just
forgiveness. (1:9)

⁵This is the message he has given us to announce to you: God is light and there is no darkness in him at all. ⁶So we are lying if we say we have fellowship with God but go on living in spiritual darkness. We are not living in the truth. ⁷But if we are living in the light of God's presence, just as Christ is, then we have fellowship with each other, and the blood of Jesus, his Son, cleanses us from every sin.

⁸If we say we have no sin, we are only fooling ourselves and refusing to accept the truth. ⁹But if we confess our sins to him, he is faithful and just to forgive us and to cleanse us from every wrong. ¹⁰If we claim we have not sinned, we are calling God a liar and showing that his word has no place in our hearts.

CHAPTER 2

I BELIEVE Jesus Christ
pleads before God for
me when I sin. (2:1)

My dear children, I am writing this to you so that you will not sin. But if you do sin, there is someone to plead for you before the Father. He is Jesus Christ, the one who pleases God completely.* ²He is the sacrifice for our sins. He takes away not only our sins but the sins of all the world.

I KNOW I belong to
God because I obey
him. (2:3)

³And how can we be sure that we belong to him? By obeying his commandments. ⁴If someone says, "I belong to God," but doesn't obey God's commandments, that person is a liar and does not live in the truth. ⁵But those who obey God's word really do love him. That is the way to know whether or not we live in him. ⁶Those who say they live in God should live their lives as Christ did.

A New Commandment

I LOVE other believers.
(2:7)

⁷Dear friends, I am not writing a new commandment, for it is an old one you have always had, right from the beginning. This commandment—to love one another—is the same message you heard before. ⁸Yet it is also new. This commandment is true in Christ and is true among you, because the darkness is disappearing and the true light is already shining.

⁹If anyone says, "I am living in the light," but hates a Christian brother or sister,* that person is still living in darkness. ¹⁰Anyone who loves other Christians* is living in the light and does not cause anyone to stumble. ¹¹Anyone who hates a Christian brother or sister is living and walking in darkness. Such a person is lost, having been blinded by the darkness.

¹²I am writing to you, my dear children, because your sins have been forgiven because of Jesus.

¹³I am writing to you who are mature because you know Christ, the one who is from the beginning.

1:1 Greek *What was from the beginning.*   1:4 Some manuscripts read *your.*   2:1 Greek *Jesus Christ, the righteous.*
2:9 Greek *his brother;* also in 2:11.   2:10 Greek *his brother.*

I am writing to you who are young because you have won your battle with Satan.

[14]I have written to you, children, because you have known the Father.

I have written to you who are mature because you know Christ, the one who is from the beginning.

I have written to you who are young because you are strong with God's word living in your hearts, and you have won your battle with Satan.

[15]Stop loving this evil world and all that it offers you, for when you love the world, you show that you do not have the love of the Father in you. [16]For the world offers only the lust for physical pleasure, the lust for everything we see, and pride in our possessions. These are not from the Father. They are from this evil world. [17]And this world is fading away, along with everything it craves. But if you do the will of God, you will live forever.

[18]Dear children, the last hour is here. You have heard that the Antichrist is coming, and already many such antichrists have appeared. From this we know that the end of the world has come. [19]These people left our churches because they never really belonged with us; otherwise they would have stayed with us. When they left us, it proved that they do not belong with us. [20]But you are not like that, for the Holy Spirit has come upon you,* and all of you know the truth. [21]So I am writing to you not because you don't know the truth but because you know the difference between truth and falsehood. [22]And who is the great liar? The one who says that Jesus is not the Christ. Such people are antichrists, for they have denied the Father and the Son. [23]Anyone who denies the Son doesn't have the Father either. But anyone who confesses the Son has the Father also.

[24]So you must remain faithful to what you have been taught from the beginning. If you do, you will continue to live in fellowship with the Son and with the Father. [25]And in this fellowship we enjoy the eternal life he promised us.

[26]I have written these things to you because you need to be aware of those who want to lead you astray. [27]But you have received the Holy Spirit,* and he lives within you, so you don't need anyone to teach you what is true. For the Spirit teaches you all things, and what he teaches is true—it is not a lie. So continue in what he has taught you, and continue to live in Christ.

[28]And now, dear children, continue to live in fellowship with Christ so that when he returns, you will be full of courage and not shrink back from him in shame. [29]Since we know that God is always right, we also know that all who do what is right are his children.

I LOVE the Father, not the world and all it offers. (2:15)

I KNOW the last hour is here because many deny Jesus Christ. (2:18)

I CONTINUE to live in close fellowship with Jesus Christ, looking forward to his return without fear or shame. (2:28)

CHAPTER 3

Living as Children of God

See how very much our heavenly Father loves us, for he allows us to be called his children, and we really are! But the people who belong to this world don't know God, so they don't understand that we are his children. [2]Yes, dear friends, we are already God's children, and we can't even imagine what we will be like when Christ returns. But we do know that when he comes we will be like him, for we will see him as he really is. [3]And all who believe this will keep themselves pure, just as Christ is pure.

[4]Those who sin are opposed to the law of God, for all sin opposes the law of God. [5]And you know that Jesus came to take away our sins, for there is no sin in him. [6]So if we continue to live in him, we won't sin either. But those who keep on sinning have never known him or understood who he is.

[7]Dear children, don't let anyone deceive you about this: When people do

2:20 Greek *But you have an anointing from the Holy One.*   **2:27** Greek *the anointing.*

what is right, it is because they are righteous, even as Christ is righteous. ⁸But when people keep on sinning, it shows they belong to the Devil, who has been sinning since the beginning. But the Son of God came to destroy these works of the Devil. ⁹Those who have been born into God's family do not sin, because God's life is in them. So they can't keep on sinning, because they have been born of God. ¹⁰So now we can tell who are children of God and who are children of the Devil. Anyone who does not obey God's commands and does not love other Christians* does not belong to God.

Love One Another

¹¹This is the message we have heard from the beginning: We should love one another. ¹²We must not be like Cain, who belonged to the evil one and killed his brother. And why did he kill him? Because Cain had been doing what was evil, and his brother had been doing what was right. ¹³So don't be surprised, dear brothers and sisters,* if the world hates you.

¹⁴If we love our Christian brothers and sisters, it proves that we have passed from death to eternal life. But a person who has no love is still dead. ¹⁵Anyone who hates another Christian* is really a murderer at heart. And you know that murderers don't have eternal life within them. ¹⁶We know what real love is because Christ gave up his life for us. And so we also ought to give up our lives for our Christian brothers and sisters. ¹⁷But if anyone has enough money to live well and sees a brother or sister in need and refuses to help—how can God's love be in that person?

¹⁸Dear children, let us stop just saying we love each other; let us really show it by our actions. ¹⁹It is by our actions that we know we are living in the truth, so we will be confident when we stand before the Lord, ²⁰even if our hearts condemn us. For God is greater than our hearts, and he knows everything.

²¹Dear friends, if our conscience is clear, we can come to God with bold confidence. ²²And we will receive whatever we request because we obey him and do the things that please him. ²³And this is his commandment: We must believe in the name of his Son, Jesus Christ, and love one another, just as he commanded us. ²⁴Those who obey God's commandments live in fellowship with him, and he with them. And we know he lives in us because the Holy Spirit lives in us.

CHAPTER 4

Discerning False Prophets

Dear friends, do not believe everyone who claims to speak by the Spirit. You must test them to see if the spirit they have comes from God. For there are many false prophets in the world. ²This is the way to find out if they have the Spirit of God: If a prophet acknowledges that Jesus Christ became a human being, that person has the Spirit of God. ³If a prophet does not acknowledge Jesus, that person is not from God. Such a person has the spirit of the Antichrist. You have heard that he is going to come into the world, and he is already here.

⁴But you belong to God, my dear children. You have already won your fight with these false prophets, because the Spirit who lives in you is greater than the spirit who lives in the world. ⁵These people belong to this world, so they speak from the world's viewpoint, and the world listens to them. ⁶But we belong to God; that is why those who know God listen to us. If they do not belong to God, they do not listen to us. That is how we know if someone has the Spirit of truth or the spirit of deception.

Loving One Another

⁷Dear friends, let us continue to love one another, for love comes from God.

I DO NOT KEEP on sinning, because I have been born of God. (3:9)

See Abel's profile (page 9) at Genesis 4:4.

I AM NOT SURPRISED when the world hates me, because it is evil and I do what is right. (3:13)

I AM WILLING to show true love for other believers by giving up my life for them, just as Jesus Christ gave up his life for me. (3:16)

I DO NOT JUST SAY I love other Christians but show it by my actions. (3:18)

I RECEIVE what I request from God because I believe in his Son and love other believers. (3:22)

I TEST spiritual teachers and ideas according to belief in Jesus Christ, the Son of God, who came as a human being. (4:2)

I BELIEVE the Spirit who lives in me is greater than the spirit of the world. (4:4)

3:10 Greek *his brother.* 3:13 Greek *brothers;* also in 3:14, 16. 3:15 Greek *his brother.*

Anyone who loves is born of God and knows God. [8]But anyone who does not love does not know God—for God is love.

[9]God showed how much he loved us by sending his only Son into the world so that we might have eternal life through him. [10]This is real love. It is not that we loved God, but that he loved us and sent his Son as a sacrifice to take away our sins.

[11]Dear friends, since God loved us that much, we surely ought to love each other. [12]No one has ever seen God. But if we love each other, God lives in us, and his love has been brought to full expression through us.

[13]And God has given us his Spirit as proof that we live in him and he in us. [14]Furthermore, we have seen with our own eyes and now testify that the Father sent his Son to be the Savior of the world. [15]All who proclaim that Jesus is the Son of God have God living in them, and they live in God. [16]We know how much God loves us, and we have put our trust in him.

God is love, and all who live in love live in God, and God lives in them. [17]And as we live in God, our love grows more perfect. So we will not be afraid on the day of judgment, but we can face him with confidence because we are like Christ here in this world.

[18]Such love has no fear because perfect love expels all fear. If we are afraid, it is for fear of judgment, and this shows that his love has not been perfected in us. [19]We love each other* as a result of his loving us first.

[20]If someone says, "I love God," but hates a Christian brother or sister,* that person is a liar; for if we don't love people we can see, how can we love God, whom we have not seen? [21]And God himself has commanded that we must love not only him but our Christian brothers and sisters, too.

CHAPTER 5

Faith in the Son of God

Everyone who believes that Jesus is the Christ is a child of God. And everyone who loves the Father loves his children, too. [2]We know we love God's children if we love God and obey his commandments. [3]Loving God means keeping his commandments, and really, that isn't difficult. [4]For every child of God defeats this evil world by trusting Christ to give the victory. [5]And the ones who win this battle against the world are the ones who believe that Jesus is the Son of God.

[6]And Jesus Christ was revealed as God's Son by his baptism in water and by shedding his blood on the cross*—not by water only, but by water and blood. And the Spirit also gives us the testimony that this is true. [7]So we have these three witnesses*—[8]the Spirit, the water, and the blood—and all three agree. [9]Since we believe human testimony, surely we can believe the testimony that comes from God. And God has testified about his Son. [10]All who believe in the Son of God know that this is true. Those who don't believe this are actually calling God a liar because they don't believe what God has testified about his Son.

[11]And this is what God has testified: He has given us eternal life, and this life is in his Son. [12]So whoever has God's Son has life; whoever does not have his Son does not have life.

Conclusion

[13]I write this to you who believe in the Son of God, so that you may know you have eternal life. [14]And we can be confident that he will listen to us whenever we ask him for anything in line with his will. [15]And if we know he is listening when we make our requests, we can be sure that he will give us what we ask for.

I LOVE other Christians because God has shown his great love for me by sending his Son to take away my sin. (4:11)

I KNOW how much God loves me, and I put my trust in him. (4:16)

I GROW in love and am not afraid to face the day of judgment. (4:17)

I DEFEAT this evil world by trusting Jesus Christ, the Son of God. (5:4)

I HAVE life because I have Jesus Christ. (5:12)

4:19 Or *We love him;* Greek reads *We love.*   4:20 Greek *brother;* also in 4:21.   5:6 Greek *This is he who came by water and blood.*   5:7 Some very late manuscripts add *in heaven—the Father, the Word, and the Holy Spirit, and these three are one. And we have three witnesses on earth.*

I PRAY for other Christians who are sinning. (5:16)

[16]If you see a Christian brother or sister* sinning in a way that does not lead to death, you should pray, and God will give that person life. But there is a sin that leads to death, and I am not saying you should pray for those who commit it. [17]Every wrong is sin, but not all sin leads to death.

[18]We know that those who have become part of God's family do not make a practice of sinning, for God's Son holds them securely, and the evil one cannot get his hands on them. [19]We know that we are children of God and that the world around us is under the power and control of the evil one. [20]And we know that the Son of God has come, and he has given us understanding so that we can know the true God. And now we are in God because we are in his Son, Jesus Christ. He is the only true God, and he is eternal life.

I KEEP AWAY from anything that takes God's place in my heart. (5:21)

[21]Dear children, keep away from anything that might take God's place in your hearts.*

5:16 Greek *your brother.* 5:21 Greek *keep yourselves from idols.*

2 JOHN

THIS IS THE SECOND of four New Testament "postcard epistles"—brief letters consisting of only one chapter.

John wrote this postcard epistle to a group of Christians—either an extended family or a local church. The letter is short yet urgent. In it, the apostle warns his readers to watch out for false teachers and to have nothing to do with them.

Famous verses in 2 John include

- ○ "Love means doing what God has commanded us, and he has commanded us to love one another" (1:6)
- ○ "Many deceivers have gone out into the world" (1:7)
- ○ "Watch out, so that you do not lose the prize for which we have been working so hard" (1:8)
- ○ "Anyone who encourages him [a spiritual deceiver] becomes a partner in his evil work" (1:11)

Greetings

This letter is from John the Elder.*

It is written to the chosen lady and to her children,* whom I love in the truth, as does everyone else who knows God's truth—²the truth that lives in us and will be in our hearts forever.

³May grace, mercy, and peace, which come from God our Father and from Jesus Christ his Son, be with us who live in truth and love.

See John's profile (page 1435) at Revelation 1:9.

Live in the Truth

⁴How happy I was to meet some of your children and find them living in the truth, just as we have been commanded by the Father.

⁵And now I want to urge you, dear lady, that we should love one another. This is not a new commandment, but one we had from the beginning. ⁶Love means doing what God has commanded us, and he has commanded us to love one another, just as you heard from the beginning.

I LOVE other believers, just as God has commanded. (1:6)

⁷Many deceivers have gone out into the world. They do not believe that Jesus Christ came to earth in a real body. Such a person is a deceiver and an antichrist. ⁸Watch out, so that you do not lose the prize for which we* have been working so hard. Be diligent so that you will receive your full reward. ⁹For if you wander beyond the teaching of Christ, you will not have fellowship with God. But if you continue in the teaching of Christ, you will have fellowship with both the Father and the Son.

I CONTINUE to follow Jesus Christ's teaching and live in fellowship with God. (1:9)

¹⁰If someone comes to your meeting and does not teach the truth about Christ, don't invite him into your house or encourage him in any way. ¹¹Anyone who encourages him becomes a partner in his evil work.

I DO NOT ENCOURAGE false teachers in any way. (1:10)

1a Greek From the elder. 1b Or the church God has chosen and her members, or the chosen Kyria and her children.
8 Some manuscripts read you.

Conclusion

[12]Well, I have much more to say to you, but I don't want to say it in a letter. For I hope to visit you soon and to talk with you face to face. Then our joy will be complete.

[13]Greetings from the children of your sister,* chosen by God.

13 Or *from the members of your sister church.*

3 JOHN

THIS IS THE THIRD New Testament "postcard epistle."
John wrote this brief letter to a good friend named Gaius. The letter is short yet urgent.
In it, the apostle praises Gaius for showing hospitality to Christian teachers and urges him to
continue to do so despite opposition from a corrupt church leader named Diotrephes.

Famous verses in 3 John include

- ○ "I am praying that all is well with you and that your body is as healthy as I know
  your soul is" (1:2)
- ○ "I could have no greater joy than to hear that my children live in the truth" (1:4)
- ○ "Those who do good prove that they are God's children" (1:11)

Greetings

This letter is from John the Elder.*

It is written to Gaius, my dear friend, whom I love in the truth.

²Dear friend, I am praying that all is well with you and that your body is as healthy as I know your soul is. ³Some of the brothers recently returned and made me very happy by telling me about your faithfulness and that you are living in the truth. ⁴I could have no greater joy than to hear that my children live in the truth.

Caring for the Lord's Workers

⁵Dear friend, you are doing a good work for God when you take care of the traveling teachers* who are passing through, even though they are strangers to you. ⁶They have told the church here of your friendship and your loving deeds. You do well to send them on their way in a manner that pleases God. ⁷For they are traveling for the Lord* and accept nothing from those who are not Christians.* ⁸So we ourselves should support them so that we may become partners with them for the truth.

⁹I sent a brief letter to the church about this, but Diotrephes, who loves to be the leader, does not acknowledge our authority. ¹⁰When I come, I will report some of the things he is doing and the wicked things he is saying about us. He not only refuses to welcome the traveling teachers, he also tells others not to help them. And when they do help, he puts them out of the church.

¹¹Dear friend, don't let this bad example influence you. Follow only what is good. Remember that those who do good prove that they are God's children, and those who do evil prove that they do not know God. ¹²But everyone speaks highly of Demetrius, even truth itself. We ourselves can say the same for him, and you know we speak the truth.

Conclusion

¹³I have much to tell you, but I don't want to do it in a letter. ¹⁴For I hope to see you soon, and then we will talk face to face.

¹⁵May God's peace be with you.

Your friends here send you their greetings. Please give my personal greetings to each of our friends there.

See John's profile (page 1435) at Revelation 1:9.

I PRAY for the physical and spiritual well-being of my friends. (1:2)

I AM HAPPIEST when those I lead to Jesus Christ continue to live in his truth. (1:4)

I HELP care for and support those who travel and work for the Lord. (1:8)

1 Greek *From the elder.*   5 Greek *the brothers;* also in verse 10.   7a Greek *the Name.*   7b Greek *from Gentiles.*

JUDE

THIS IS THE FOURTH New Testament "postcard epistle."

Jude wrote this brief letter to the church at large. The letter is short yet urgent. In it, Jude urges confused believers to stand firm for the Lord despite false teachers. His letter echoes several themes discussed in Peter's longer letters.

Key verses in Jude include

- ○ "Some godless people have wormed their way in among you, saying that God's forgiveness allows us to live immoral lives" (1:4)
- ○ "When these people join you in fellowship meals celebrating the love of the Lord, they are like dangerous reefs that can shipwreck you" (1:12)
- ○ "They are wandering stars, heading for everlasting gloom and darkness" (1:13)
- ○ "Remember what the apostles of our Lord Jesus Christ told you" (1:17)
- ○ "Continue to build your lives on the foundation of your holy faith" (1:20)
- ○ "Show mercy to those whose faith is wavering" (1:22)
- ○ "All glory to God, who is able to keep you from stumbling, and who will bring you into his glorious presence innocent of sin and with great joy" (1:24)

Greetings from Jude

This letter is from Jude, a slave of Jesus Christ and a brother of James.

I am writing to all who are called to live in the love of God the Father and the care of Jesus Christ.

²May you receive more and more of God's mercy, peace, and love.

See James's profile (page 1407) at James 2:18.

The Danger of False Teachers

³Dearly loved friends, I had been eagerly planning to write to you about the salvation we all share. But now I find that I must write about something else, urging you to defend the truth of the Good News.* God gave this unchanging truth once for all time to his holy people. ⁴I say this because some godless people have wormed their way in among you, saying that God's forgiveness allows us to live immoral lives. The fate of such people was determined long ago, for they have turned against our only Master and Lord, Jesus Christ.

I REJECT the false idea that God's forgiveness allows us to live immoral lives. (1:4)

⁵I must remind you—and you know it well—that even though the Lord* rescued the whole nation of Israel from Egypt, he later destroyed every one of those who did not remain faithful. ⁶And I remind you of the angels who did not stay within the limits of authority God gave them but left the place where they belonged. God has kept them chained in prisons of darkness, waiting for the day of judgment. ⁷And don't forget the cities of Sodom and Gomorrah and their neighboring towns, which were filled with sexual immorality and every kind of sexual perversion. Those cities were destroyed by fire and are a warning of the eternal fire that will punish all who are evil.

I WATCH OUT for false teachers who live immoral lives, mocking and despising spiritual powers and authorities. (1:8)

⁸Yet these false teachers, who claim authority from their dreams, live immoral lives, defy authority, and scoff at the power of the glorious ones.* ⁹But

See Moses' profile (page 73) at Exodus 5:1.

3 Greek *to contend for the faith.* 5 Some manuscripts read *Jesus.* 8 *The glorious ones* are probably evil angels.

even Michael, one of the mightiest of the angels, did not dare accuse Satan of blasphemy, but simply said, "The Lord rebuke you." (This took place when Michael was arguing with Satan about Moses' body.) [10]But these people mock and curse the things they do not understand. Like animals, they do whatever their instincts tell them, and they bring about their own destruction. [11]How terrible it will be for them! For they follow the evil example of Cain, who killed his brother. Like Balaam, they will do anything for money. And like Korah, they will perish because of their rebellion.

[12]When these people join you in fellowship meals celebrating the love of the Lord, they are like dangerous reefs that can shipwreck you.* They are shameless in the way they care only about themselves. They are like clouds blowing over dry land without giving rain, promising much but producing nothing. They are like trees without fruit at harvesttime. They are not only dead but doubly dead, for they have been pulled out by the roots. [13]They are like wild waves of the sea, churning up the dirty foam of their shameful deeds. They are wandering stars, heading for everlasting gloom and darkness.

[14]Now Enoch, who lived seven generations after Adam, prophesied about these people. He said,

"Look, the Lord is coming
    with thousands of his holy ones.
[15] He will bring the people of the world
    to judgment.
He will convict the ungodly of all the evil things
    they have done in rebellion
and of all the insults that godless sinners
    have spoken against him."*

[16]These people are grumblers and complainers, doing whatever evil they feel like. They are loudmouthed braggarts, and they flatter others to get favors in return.

A Call to Remain Faithful

[17]But you, my dear friends, must remember what the apostles of our Lord Jesus Christ told you, [18]that in the last times there would be scoffers whose purpose in life is to enjoy themselves in every evil way imaginable. [19]Now they are here, and they are the ones who are creating divisions among you. They live by natural instinct because they do not have God's Spirit living in them.

[20]But you, dear friends, must continue to build your lives on the foundation of your holy faith. And continue to pray as you are directed by the Holy Spirit.* [21]Live in such a way that God's love can bless you as you wait for the eternal life that our Lord Jesus Christ in his mercy is going to give you. [22]Show mercy to those whose faith is wavering. [23]Rescue others by snatching them from the flames of judgment. There are still others to whom you need to show mercy, but be careful that you aren't contaminated by their sins.*

A Prayer of Praise

[24]And now, all glory to God, who is able to keep you from stumbling, and who will bring you into his glorious presence innocent of sin and with great joy. [25]All glory to him, who alone is God our Savior, through Jesus Christ our Lord. Yes, glory, majesty, power, and authority belong to him, in the beginning, now, and forevermore. Amen.

See Abel's profile (page 9) at Genesis 4:4.

See the profiles for Enoch (page 11) and Adam (page 5) at Genesis 5:24 and Genesis 1:26.

I TAKE HEED of the apostles' warning that evil scoffers will come and promote sin and divisions among God's people. (1:17)

I DO whatever it takes to help other Christians stay strong in their faith and holy living. (1:22)

I GIVE all glory to God my Savior. (1:25)

12 Or they are contaminants among you, or they are stains.   14-15 The quotation comes from the Apocrypha: Enoch 1:9.   20 Greek Pray in the Holy Spirit.   23 Greek mercy, hating even the clothing stained by the flesh.

REVELATION

THIS LAST BOOK of the Bible is concerned with the *future.*

Surprisingly, however, the overriding question in this book isn't how the world is going to end. Instead, the big question is: How are *you* going to finish up your life? Are you going to be strong in your Christian faith, no matter what happens?

In chapters 1–3, the aged apostle John sees an awe-inspiring vision of the resurrected and exalted Lord Jesus Christ, who dictates brief letters to the seven churches in the Roman province of Asia Minor. He urges these first-century Christians to be faithful in the face of temptations, false teachings, persecution, and even martyrdom.

In chapters 4–20, John sees awe-inspiring visions of heaven and describes how terrible judgments will destroy all those who refuse to stop rebelling against the Lord God Almighty.

In chapters 21–22, John sees awe-inspiring visions of the new heaven and earth, where God will dwell with his people forever.

Famous verses in Revelation include

- ○ "God blesses . . . all who listen to it [this prophecy] and obey what it says" (1:3; see 22:7)
- ○ "Write down what you have seen—both the things that are now happening and the things that will happen later" (1:19)
- ○ "Look how far you have fallen from your first love!" (2:5)
- ○ "Remain faithful even when facing death, and I will give you the crown of life" (2:10)
- ○ "Look! Here I stand at the door and knock" (3:20)
- ○ "Holy, holy, holy is the Lord God Almighty—the one who always was, who is, and who is still to come" (4:8)
- ○ "You are worthy" (4:11; 5:9)
- ○ "Your blood has ransomed people for God from every tribe and language and people and nation" (5:9)
- ○ "Terror will come on the earth and the sea. For the Devil has come down to you in great anger, and he knows that he has little time" (12:12)
- ○ "Take note: I will come as unexpectedly as a thief!" (16:15; see 3:3)
- ○ "He [Jesus Christ] is Lord over all lords and King over all kings" (17:14; see 19:16)
- ○ "I saw the dead . . . standing before God's throne. And the books were opened, including the Book of Life" (20:12)
- ○ "Then I saw a new heaven and a new earth" (21:1)
- ○ "Look, the home of God is now among his people!" (21:3)
- ○ "I am coming soon!" (22:7, 12, 20)
- ○ A final warning (22:18-19)

CHAPTER 1

Prologue

This is a revelation from* Jesus Christ, which God gave him concerning the events that will happen soon. An angel was sent to God's servant John so that John could share the revelation with God's other servants. ²John faithfully reported the word of God and the testimony of Jesus Christ—everything he saw.

³God blesses the one who reads this prophecy to the church, and he blesses all who listen to it and obey what it says. For the time is near when these things will happen.

John's Greeting to the Seven Churches

⁴This letter is from John to the seven churches in the province of Asia. Grace and peace from the one who is, who always was, and who is still to come; from the sevenfold Spirit* before his throne; ⁵and from Jesus Christ, who is the faithful witness to these things, the first to rise from the dead, and the commander of all the rulers of the world.

All praise to him who loves us and has freed us from our sins by shedding his blood for us. ⁶He has made us his Kingdom and his priests who serve before God his Father. Give to him everlasting glory! He rules forever and ever! Amen!

⁷Look! He comes with the clouds of heaven. And everyone will see him— even those who pierced him. And all the nations of the earth will weep because of him. Yes! Amen!

⁸"I am the Alpha and the Omega—the beginning and the end," says the Lord God. "I am the one who is, who always was, and who is still to come, the Almighty One."

Vision of the Son of Man

⁹I am John, your brother. In Jesus we are partners in suffering and in the Kingdom and in patient endurance. I was exiled to the island of Patmos for preaching the word of God and speaking about Jesus. ¹⁰It was the Lord's Day, and I was worshiping in the Spirit.* Suddenly, I heard a loud voice behind me, a voice that sounded like a trumpet blast. ¹¹It said, "Write down what you see, and send it to the seven churches: Ephesus, Smyrna, Pergamum, Thyatira, Sardis, Philadelphia, and Laodicea."

¹²When I turned to see who was speaking to me, I saw seven gold lampstands. ¹³And standing in the middle of the lampstands was the Son of Man.* He was wearing a long robe with a gold sash across his chest. ¹⁴His head and his hair were white like wool, as white as snow. And his eyes were bright like flames of fire. ¹⁵His feet were as bright as bronze refined in a furnace, and his voice thundered like mighty ocean waves. ¹⁶He held seven stars in his right hand, and a sharp two-edged sword came from his mouth. And his face was as bright as the sun in all its brilliance.

¹⁷When I saw him, I fell at his feet as dead. But he laid his right hand on me and said, "Don't be afraid! I am the First and the Last. ¹⁸I am the living one who died. Look, I am alive forever and ever! And I hold the keys of death and the grave.* ¹⁹Write down what you have seen—both the things that are now happening and the things that will happen later. ²⁰This is the meaning of the seven stars you saw in my right hand and the seven gold lampstands: The seven stars are the angels of* the seven churches, and the seven lampstands are the seven churches.

CHAPTER 2

The Message to the Church in Ephesus

"Write this letter to the angel of* the church in Ephesus. This is the message from the one who holds the seven stars in his right hand, the one who walks among the seven gold lampstands:

Margin notes

I GIVE praise and everlasting glory to Jesus Christ, who loves me and freed me from my sins by shedding his blood for me. (1:5)

I BELIEVE the Lord God is the one who is, who always was, and who is still to come. (1:8)

I BELIEVE Jesus Christ's appearance is awe inspiring. (1:13)

I BELIEVE Jesus Christ is the one who died, rose again three days later, and is alive forever! (1:18)

1:1 Or *of.* 1:4 Greek *the seven spirits.* 1:10 Or *in spirit.* 1:13 Or *one who looked like a man;* Greek reads *one like a son of man.* See Dan 7:13. 1:18 Greek *and Hades.* 1:20 Or *the messengers for.* 2:1 Or *the messenger for;* also in 2:8, 12, 18.

²"I know all the things you do. I have seen your hard work and your patient endurance. I know you don't tolerate evil people. You have examined the claims of those who say they are apostles but are not. You have discovered they are liars. ³You have patiently suffered for me without quitting. ⁴But I have this complaint against you. You don't love me or each other as you did at first! ⁵Look how far you have fallen from your first love! Turn back to me again and work as you did at first. If you don't, I will come and remove your lampstand from its place among the churches. ⁶But there is this about you that is good: You hate the deeds of the immoral Nicolaitans, just as I do.

I AM WILLING to suffer patiently for Jesus Christ without quitting. (2:3)

I LOVE my Lord and Savior above all else. (2:5)

LIKE JOHN   *I wait expectantly for Jesus Christ to come again!*

Revelation 1:9

How many a young woman has waited weeks and months, even years, for a sweetheart's return from duty overseas? She pores over every letter that arrives and clings to the pictures and memories of every moment she and her loved one spent together before his departure.

More than any fiancée, John longed for Jesus Christ's return. He wasn't looking forward to witnessing a spectacular event or to escaping life's troubles. Instead, he daily desired more than anything to see the Lord he knew and adored.

From the first day the Savior called him to leave his nets, John longed for a deeper friendship with the Lord. He walked hundreds of miles of dusty roads with Jesus and shared thousands of meals with him. He heard Jesus teach the multitudes and in amazement read the Scriptures that spoke of this promised Messiah. John's hands frequently touched Jesus when they worked and when they embraced after a child's miraculous healing.

To John's delight, Jesus invited him into his closest circle of friends and shared with him his moments of brightest glory and deepest grief (Matthew 17:1-9; 26:36-46). John saw Jesus transfigured into his glorious, shining appearance on the mountain. He also watched as Jesus' frail human body went limp on the cross (John 19:25-27). Three days later, John entered the empty tomb and realized Jesus had risen from the dead! Afterward for nearly six weeks, he fellowshiped with the Lord and then watched him rise into the clouds while two angels promised that "someday, just as you saw him go, he will return!" (Acts 1:11).

Contrary to rumors popular at the time, John knew he might die before that great coming (John 21:22-23). But each day of his long life he held on to the *promise* that Jesus would come, and the *possibility* that it could be that very day.

Some mornings, John must have scanned the skies, searching for a glimpse of that glorious brightness he had seen once before. One morning, he did see the Lord's glory again—though he was not transported by the Lord's return but by the Lord's Spirit (Revelation 1:9-19). What unfolded before John's aged and amazed eyes became his desire and ours as his heart burst out, "Amen! Come, Lord Jesus!" (see 22:20).

You and I have good reason to eagerly await Jesus' return. Unlike John, we haven't seen Jesus Christ shining in all his brilliant glory (Mark 9:2-10; Revelation 1:13-16; 21:23). But we can love him just the same (1 Peter 1:8).

Like John, let's live in close fellowship with the Lord until we see him as he really is (1 John 2:28; 3:2). After all, today may be the day!

○ *Today's Scripture reading is Revelation 1–3.*

---

⁷"Anyone who is willing to hear should listen to the Spirit and understand what the Spirit is saying to the churches. Everyone who is victorious will eat from the tree of life in the paradise of God.

The Message to the Church in Smyrna
⁸"Write this letter to the angel of the church in Smyrna. This is the message from the one who is the First and the Last, who died and is alive:

⁹"I know about your suffering and your poverty—but you are rich! I know the slander of those opposing you. They say they are Jews, but

I AM COMMITTED to remaining faithful to Jesus Christ, no matter what persecution I must face. (2:10)

they really aren't because theirs is a synagogue of Satan. [10]Don't be afraid of what you are about to suffer. The Devil will throw some of you into prison and put you to the test. You will be persecuted for 'ten days.' Remain faithful even when facing death, and I will give you the crown of life.

[11]"Anyone who is willing to hear should listen to the Spirit and understand what the Spirit is saying to the churches. Whoever is victorious will not be hurt by the second death.

The Message to the Church in Pergamum

[12]"Write this letter to the angel of the church in Pergamum. This is the message from the one who has a sharp two-edged sword:

[13]"I know that you live in the city where that great throne of Satan is located, and yet you have remained loyal to me. And you refused to deny me even when Antipas, my faithful witness, was martyred among you by Satan's followers. [14]And yet I have a few complaints against you. You tolerate some among you who are like Balaam, who showed Balak how to trip up the people of Israel. He taught them to worship idols by eating food offered to idols and by committing sexual sin. [15]In the same way, you have some Nicolaitans among you—people who follow the same teaching and commit the same sins. [16]Repent, or I will come to you suddenly and fight against them with the sword of my mouth.

I DO NOT FELLOWSHIP with individuals who claim to be Christians but who continue to indulge in sexual sins, idolatry, and other abhorrent practices (1 Corinthians 5:11). (2:14)

[17]"Anyone who is willing to hear should listen to the Spirit and understand what the Spirit is saying to the churches. Everyone who is victorious will eat of the manna that has been hidden away in heaven. And I will give to each one a white stone, and on the stone will be engraved a new name that no one knows except the one who receives it.

The Message to the Church in Thyatira

[18]"Write this letter to the angel of the church in Thyatira. This is the message from the Son of God, whose eyes are bright like flames of fire, whose feet are like polished bronze:

[19]"I know all the things you do—your love, your faith, your service, and your patient endurance. And I can see your constant improvement in all these things. [20]But I have this complaint against you. You are permitting that woman—that Jezebel who calls herself a prophet—to lead my servants astray. She is encouraging them to worship idols, eat food offered to idols, and commit sexual sin. [21]I gave her time to repent, but she would not turn away from her immorality. [22]Therefore, I will throw her upon a sickbed, and she will suffer greatly with all who commit adultery with her, unless they turn away from all their evil deeds. [23]I will strike her children dead. And all the churches will know that I am the one who searches out the thoughts and intentions of every person. And I will give to each of you whatever you deserve. [24]But I also have a message for the rest of you in Thyatira who have not followed this false teaching ('deeper truths,' as they call them—depths of Satan, really). I will ask nothing more of you [25]except that you hold tightly to what you have until I come.

I BELIEVE Jesus Christ searches out the thoughts and intentions of every person. (2:23)

I BELIEVE Satan is the source of false teachings. (2:24)

I AM COMMITTED to obeying Jesus Christ to the very end. (2:26)

[26]"To all who are victorious, who obey me to the very end, I will give authority over all the nations. [27]They will rule the nations with an iron rod and smash them like clay pots. [28]They will have the same authority I received from my Father, and I will also give them the morning star! [29]Anyone who is willing to hear should listen to the Spirit and understand what the Spirit is saying to the churches.

CHAPTER 3

The Message to the Church in Sardis

"Write this letter to the angel of* the church in Sardis. This is the message from the one who has the sevenfold Spirit* of God and the seven stars:

"I know all the things you do, and that you have a reputation for being alive—but you are dead. ²Now wake up! Strengthen what little remains, for even what is left is at the point of death. Your deeds are far from right in the sight of God. ³Go back to what you heard and believed at first; hold to it firmly and turn to me again. Unless you do, I will come upon you suddenly, as unexpected as a thief.

⁴"Yet even in Sardis there are some who have not soiled their garments with evil deeds. They will walk with me in white, for they are worthy. ⁵All who are victorious will be clothed in white. I will never erase their names from the Book of Life, but I will announce before my Father and his angels that they are mine. ⁶Anyone who is willing to hear should listen to the Spirit and understand what the Spirit is saying to the churches.

I WALK in obedience to the Lord Jesus Christ. (3:4)

The Message to the Church in Philadelphia

⁷"Write this letter to the angel of the church in Philadelphia. This is the message from the one who is holy and true. He is the one who has the key of David. He opens doors, and no one can shut them; he shuts doors, and no one can open them.

See David's profile (page 629) at Psalm 3:1.

⁸"I know all the things you do, and I have opened a door for you that no one can shut. You have little strength, yet you obeyed my word and did not deny me. ⁹Look! I will force those who belong to Satan—those liars who say they are Jews but are not—to come and bow down at your feet. They will acknowledge that you are the ones I love.

¹⁰"Because you have obeyed my command to persevere, I will protect you from the great time of testing that will come upon the whole world to test those who belong to this world. ¹¹Look, I am coming quickly. Hold on to what you have, so that no one will take away your crown. ¹²All who are victorious will become pillars in the Temple of my God, and they will never have to leave it. And I will write my God's name on them, and they will be citizens in the city of my God—the new Jerusalem that comes down from heaven from my God. And they will have my new name inscribed upon them. ¹³Anyone who is willing to hear should listen to the Spirit and understand what the Spirit is saying to the churches.

I PERSEVERE in obeying Jesus Christ, who loves me as his own. (3:10)

The Message to the Church in Laodicea

¹⁴"Write this letter to the angel of the church in Laodicea. This is the message from the one who is the Amen—the faithful and true witness, the ruler* of God's creation:

I BELIEVE Jesus Christ is the ruler of God's creation. (3:14)

¹⁵"I know all the things you do, that you are neither hot nor cold. I wish you were one or the other! ¹⁶But since you are like lukewarm water, I will spit you out of my mouth! ¹⁷You say, 'I am rich. I have everything I want. I don't need a thing!' And you don't realize that you are wretched and miserable and poor and blind and naked. ¹⁸I advise you to buy gold from me—gold that has been purified by fire. Then you will be rich. And also buy white garments so you will not be shamed by your nakedness. And buy ointment for your eyes so you will be able to see. ¹⁹I am the one who corrects and disciplines everyone I love. Be diligent and turn from your indifference.

I ACKNOWLEDGE who I am in God's sight— that I have nothing without him. (3:17)

I ACCEPT Jesus Christ's discipline and am not indifferent to him. (3:19)

3:1a Or *the messenger for*; also in 3:7, 14.   3:1b Greek *the seven spirits*.   3:14 Or *the source*.

²⁰"Look! Here I stand at the door and knock. If you hear me calling and open the door, I will come in, and we will share a meal as friends. ²¹I will invite everyone who is victorious to sit with me on my throne, just as I was victorious and sat with my Father on his throne. ²²Anyone who is willing to hear should listen to the Spirit and understand what the Spirit is saying to the churches."

CHAPTER 4

Worship in Heaven

Then as I looked, I saw a door standing open in heaven, and the same voice I had heard before spoke to me with the sound of a mighty trumpet blast. The voice said, "Come up here, and I will show you what must happen after these things." ²And instantly I was in the Spirit,* and I saw a throne in heaven and someone sitting on it! ³ The one sitting on the throne was as brilliant as gemstones—jasper and carnelian. And the glow of an emerald circled his throne like a rainbow. ⁴Twenty-four thrones surrounded him, and twenty-four elders sat on them. They were all clothed in white and had gold crowns on their heads. ⁵And from the throne came flashes of lightning and the rumble of thunder. And in front of the throne were seven lampstands with burning flames. They are the seven spirits* of God. ⁶In front of the throne was a shiny sea of glass, sparkling like crystal.

In the center and around the throne were four living beings, each covered with eyes, front and back. ⁷The first of these living beings had the form of a lion; the second looked like an ox; the third had a human face; and the fourth had the form of an eagle with wings spread out as though in flight. ⁸Each of these living beings had six wings, and their wings were covered with eyes, inside and out. Day after day and night after night they keep on saying,

"Holy, holy, holy is the Lord God Almighty—
    the one who always was, who is, and who is still to come."

⁹Whenever the living beings give glory and honor and thanks to the one sitting on the throne, the one who lives forever and ever, ¹⁰the twenty-four elders fall down and worship the one who lives forever and ever. And they lay their crowns before the throne and say,

¹¹ "You are worthy, O Lord our God,
    to receive glory and honor and power.
For you created everything,
    and it is for your pleasure that they exist and were created."

CHAPTER 5

The Lamb Opens the Scroll

And I saw a scroll in the right hand of the one who was sitting on the throne. There was writing on the inside and the outside of the scroll, and it was sealed with seven seals. ²And I saw a strong angel, who shouted with a loud voice: "Who is worthy to break the seals on this scroll and unroll it?" ³But no one in heaven or on earth or under the earth was able to open the scroll and read it.

⁴Then I wept because no one could be found who was worthy to open the scroll and read it. ⁵But one of the twenty-four elders said to me, "Stop weeping! Look, the Lion of the tribe of Judah, the heir to David's throne,* has conquered. He is worthy to open the scroll and break its seven seals."

⁶I looked and I saw a Lamb that had been killed but was now standing between the throne and the four living beings and among the twenty-four elders. He had seven horns and seven eyes, which are the seven spirits* of

I BELIEVE the appearance of God on his throne is awe inspiring. (4:3)

I BELIEVE the Lord God Almighty is exceedingly holy. (4:8)

I BELIEVE the Lord God created everything for his pleasure. (4:11)

I BELIEVE Jesus Christ is the great Lion of the tribe of Judah, the heir to David's throne (Genesis 49:9-10; Isaiah 11:1, 10). (5:5)

See David's profile (page 629) at Psalm 3:1.

4:2 Or *in spirit.*   4:5 See 1:4 and 3:1, where the same expression is translated *the sevenfold Spirit.*   5:5 Greek *the root of David.*   5:6 See note on 4:5.

God that are sent out into every part of the earth. [7]He stepped forward and took the scroll from the right hand of the one sitting on the throne. [8]And as he took the scroll, the four living beings and the twenty-four elders fell down before the Lamb. Each one had a harp, and they held gold bowls filled with incense—the prayers of God's people!

[9]And they sang a new song with these words:

"You are worthy to take the scroll
  and break its seals and open it.
For you were killed, and your blood has ransomed people for God
  from every tribe and language and people and nation.
[10]And you have caused them to become God's Kingdom and his priests.
  And they will reign* on the earth."

[11]Then I looked again, and I heard the singing of thousands and millions of angels around the throne and the living beings and the elders. [12]And they sang in a mighty chorus:

"The Lamb is worthy—the Lamb who was killed.
  He is worthy to receive power and riches
  and wisdom and strength
  and honor and glory and blessing."

[13]And then I heard every creature in heaven and on earth and under the earth and in the sea. They also sang:

"Blessing and honor and glory and power
  belong to the one sitting on the throne
  and to the Lamb forever and ever."

[14]And the four living beings said, "Amen!" And the twenty-four elders fell down and worshiped God and the Lamb.

CHAPTER 6

The Lamb Breaks the First Six Seals

As I watched, the Lamb broke the first of the seven seals on the scroll. Then one of the four living beings called out with a voice that sounded like thunder, "Come!" [2]I looked up and saw a white horse. Its rider carried a bow, and a crown was placed on his head. He rode out to win many battles and gain the victory.

[3]When the Lamb broke the second seal, I heard the second living being say, "Come!" [4]And another horse appeared, a red one. Its rider was given a mighty sword and the authority to remove peace from the earth. And there was war and slaughter everywhere.

[5]When the Lamb broke the third seal, I heard the third living being say, "Come!" And I looked up and saw a black horse, and its rider was holding a pair of scales in his hand. [6]And a voice from among the four living beings said, "A loaf of wheat bread or three loaves of barley for a day's pay.* And don't waste* the olive oil and wine."

[7]And when the Lamb broke the fourth seal, I heard the fourth living being say, "Come!" [8]And I looked up and saw a horse whose color was pale green like a corpse. And Death was the name of its rider, who was followed around by the Grave.* They were given authority over one-fourth of the earth, to kill with the sword and famine and disease* and wild animals.

[9]And when the Lamb broke the fifth seal, I saw under the altar the souls of all who had been martyred for the word of God and for being faithful in their witness. [10]They called loudly to the Lord and said, "O Sovereign Lord, holy

I BELIEVE Jesus Christ ransomed people for God from every nation by his death on the cross. (5:9)

I BELIEVE Jesus Christ is worthy to receive power, riches, wisdom, strength, honor, glory, and blessing. (5:12)

I BELIEVE the Lord is sovereign, holy, true, patient, faithful, and just. (6:10)

5:10 Some manuscripts read *they are reigning.*   6:6a Greek *A choinix of wheat for a denarius, and 3 choinix of barley for a denarius.*   6:6b Or *hurt.*   6:8a Greek *by Hades.*   6:8b Greek *death.*

and true, how long will it be before you judge the people who belong to this world for what they have done to us? When will you avenge our blood against these people?" [11] Then a white robe was given to each of them. And they were told to rest a little longer until the full number of their brothers and sisters*—their fellow servants of Jesus—had been martyred.

[12] I watched as the Lamb broke the sixth seal, and there was a great earthquake. The sun became as dark as black cloth, and the moon became as red as blood. [13] Then the stars of the sky fell to the earth like green figs falling from trees shaken by mighty winds. [14] And the sky was rolled up like a scroll and taken away. And all of the mountains and all of the islands disappeared. [15] Then the kings of the earth, the rulers, the generals, the wealthy people, the people with great power, and every slave and every free person—all hid themselves in the caves and among the rocks of the mountains. [16] And they cried to the mountains and the rocks, "Fall on us and hide us from the face of the one who sits on the throne and from the wrath of the Lamb. [17] For the great day of their wrath has come, and who will be able to survive?"

CHAPTER 7

God's People Will Be Preserved

Then I saw four angels standing at the four corners of the earth, holding back the four winds from blowing upon the earth. Not a leaf rustled in the trees, and the sea became as smooth as glass. [2] And I saw another angel coming from the east, carrying the seal of the living God. And he shouted out to those four angels who had been given power to injure land and sea, [3] "Wait! Don't hurt the land or the sea or the trees until we have placed the seal of God on the foreheads of his servants."

[4] And I heard how many were marked with the seal of God. There were 144,000 who were sealed from all the tribes of Israel:

[5]	from Judah	12,000
	from Reuben	12,000
	from Gad	12,000
[6]	from Asher	12,000
	from Naphtali	12,000
	from Manasseh	12,000
[7]	from Simeon	12,000
	from Levi	12,000
	from Issachar	12,000
[8]	from Zebulun	12,000
	from Joseph	12,000
	from Benjamin	12,000

Praise from the Great Multitude

[9] After this I saw a vast crowd, too great to count, from every nation and tribe and people and language, standing in front of the throne and before the Lamb. They were clothed in white and held palm branches in their hands. [10] And they were shouting with a mighty shout, "Salvation comes from our God on the throne and from the Lamb!"

[11] And all the angels were standing around the throne and around the elders and the four living beings. And they fell face down before the throne and worshiped God. [12] They said,

"Amen! Blessing and glory and wisdom
and thanksgiving and honor and power and strength
belong to our God forever and forever. Amen!"

6:11 Greek *their brothers.*

I AM a servant of Jesus Christ—even to death. (6:11)

I BELIEVE even the most powerful individuals in the world will tremble in fear at the prospect of the Lord's wrath. (6:15)

I BELIEVE people from every nation, tribe, people, and language will be in heaven. (7:9)

I BELIEVE blessing, glory, wisdom, thanksgiving, honor, power, and strength belong to God forever. (7:12)

¹³ Then one of the twenty-four elders asked me, "Who are these who are clothed in white? Where do they come from?"

¹⁴ And I said to him, "Sir, you are the one who knows."

Then he said to me, "These are the ones coming out of the great tribulation. They washed their robes in the blood of the Lamb and made them white. ¹⁵ That is why they are standing in front of the throne of God, serving him day and night in his Temple. And he who sits on the throne will live among them and shelter them. ¹⁶ They will never again be hungry or thirsty, and they will be fully protected from the scorching noontime heat. ¹⁷ For the Lamb who stands in front of the throne will be their Shepherd. He will lead them to the springs of life-giving water. And God will wipe away all their tears."

> I BELIEVE God will one day wipe away all tears. (7:17)

CHAPTER 8

The Lamb Breaks the Seventh Seal

When the Lamb broke the seventh seal, there was silence throughout heaven for about half an hour. ² And I saw the seven angels who stand before God, and they were given seven trumpets.

³ Then another angel with a gold incense burner came and stood at the altar. And a great quantity of incense was given to him to mix with the prayers of God's people, to be offered on the gold altar before the throne. ⁴ The smoke of the incense, mixed with the prayers of the saints, ascended up to God from the altar where the angel had poured them out. ⁵ Then the angel filled the incense burner with fire from the altar and threw it down upon the earth; and thunder crashed, lightning flashed, and there was a terrible earthquake.

> I BELIEVE the prayers of God's people are like sweet-smelling incense to him. (8:3)

The First Four Trumpets

⁶ Then the seven angels with the seven trumpets prepared to blow their mighty blasts.

⁷ The first angel blew his trumpet, and hail and fire mixed with blood were thrown down upon the earth, and one-third of the earth was set on fire. One-third of the trees were burned, and all the grass was burned.

> I BELIEVE God's judgments on the earth will be terrible. (8:7)

⁸ Then the second angel blew his trumpet, and a great mountain of fire was thrown into the sea. And one-third of the water in the sea became blood. ⁹ And one-third of all things living in the sea died. And one-third of all the ships on the sea were destroyed.

¹⁰ Then the third angel blew his trumpet, and a great flaming star fell out of the sky, burning like a torch. It fell upon one-third of the rivers and on the springs of water. ¹¹ The name of the star was Bitterness.* It made one-third of the water bitter, and many people died because the water was so bitter.

¹² Then the fourth angel blew his trumpet, and one-third of the sun was struck, and one-third of the moon, and one-third of the stars, and they became dark. And one-third of the day was dark and one-third of the night also.

¹³ Then I looked up. And I heard a single eagle crying loudly as it flew through the air, "Terror, terror, terror to all who belong to this world because of what will happen when the last three angels blow their trumpets."

CHAPTER 9

The Fifth Trumpet Brings the First Terror

Then the fifth angel blew his trumpet, and I saw a star that had fallen to earth from the sky, and he was given the key to the shaft of the bottomless pit. ² When he opened it, smoke poured out as though from a huge furnace, and the sunlight and air were darkened by the smoke.

³ Then locusts came from the smoke and descended on the earth, and they

> I BELIEVE the world will one day experience great terrors of God's judgment. (9:3)

8:11 Greek *Wormwood.*

were given power to sting like scorpions. ⁴They were told not to hurt the grass or plants or trees but to attack all the people who did not have the seal of God on their foreheads. ⁵They were told not to kill them but to torture them for five months with agony like the pain of scorpion stings. ⁶In those days people will seek death but will not find it. They will long to die, but death will flee away!

⁷The locusts looked like horses armed for battle. They had gold crowns on their heads, and they had human faces. ⁸Their hair was long like the hair of a woman, and their teeth were like the teeth of a lion. ⁹They wore armor made of iron, and their wings roared like an army of chariots rushing into battle. ¹⁰They had tails that stung like scorpions, with power to torture people. This power was given to them for five months. ¹¹Their king is the angel from the bottomless pit; his name in Hebrew is *Abaddon,* and in Greek, *Apollyon*—the Destroyer.

¹²The first terror is past, but look, two more terrors are coming!

The Sixth Trumpet Brings the Second Terror

¹³Then the sixth angel blew his trumpet, and I heard a voice speaking from the four horns of the gold altar that stands in the presence of God. ¹⁴And the voice spoke to the sixth angel who held the trumpet: "Release the four angels who are bound at the great Euphrates River." ¹⁵And the four angels who had been prepared for this hour and day and month and year were turned loose to kill one-third of all the people on earth. ¹⁶They led an army of 200 million mounted troops—I heard an announcement of how many there were.

¹⁷And in my vision, I saw the horses and the riders sitting on them. The riders wore armor that was fiery red and sky blue and yellow. The horses' heads were like the heads of lions, and fire and smoke and burning sulfur billowed from their mouths. ¹⁸One-third of all the people on earth were killed by these three plagues—by the fire and the smoke and burning sulfur that came from the mouths of the horses. ¹⁹Their power was in their mouths, but also in their tails. For their tails had heads like snakes, with the power to injure people.

²⁰But the people who did not die in these plagues still refused to turn from their evil deeds. They continued to worship demons and idols made of gold, silver, bronze, stone, and wood—idols that neither see nor hear nor walk! ²¹And they did not repent of their murders or their witchcraft or their immorality or their thefts.

CHAPTER 10

The Angel and the Small Scroll

Then I saw another mighty angel coming down from heaven, surrounded by a cloud, with a rainbow over his head. His face shone like the sun, and his feet were like pillars of fire. ²And in his hand was a small scroll, which he had unrolled. He stood with his right foot on the sea and his left foot on the land. ³And he gave a great shout, like the roar of a lion. And when he shouted, the seven thunders answered.

⁴When the seven thunders spoke, I was about to write. But a voice from heaven called to me: "Keep secret what the seven thunders said. Do not write it down."

⁵Then the mighty angel standing on the sea and on the land lifted his right hand to heaven. ⁶And he swore an oath in the name of the one who lives forever and ever, who created heaven and everything in it, the earth and everything in it, and the sea and everything in it. He said, "God will wait no longer. ⁷But when the seventh angel blows his trumpet, God's mysterious plan will be fulfilled. It will happen just as he announced it to his servants the prophets."

I BELIEVE Satan's hordes will one day afflict the world with great suffering. (9:10)

I BELIEVE Satan is the Destroyer from the bottomless pit of hell. (9:11)

I ABHOR idolatry, the worship of demons, murder, and witch-craft. (9:20)

I BELIEVE God chooses to keep some things secret (Deuteronomy 29:29). (10:4)

I BELIEVE God created everything. (10:6)

I BELIEVE God's mysterious plan will one day be fulfilled, just as he predicted through his prophets. (10:7)

⁸Then the voice from heaven called to me again: "Go and take the unrolled scroll from the angel who is standing on the sea and on the land."

⁹So I approached him and asked him to give me the little scroll. "Yes, take it and eat it," he said. "At first it will taste like honey, but when you swallow it, it will make your stomach sour!" ¹⁰So I took the little scroll from the hands of the angel, and I ate it! It was sweet in my mouth, but it made my stomach sour. ¹¹Then he said to me, "You must prophesy again about many peoples, nations, languages, and kings."

CHAPTER 11

The Two Witnesses

Then I was given a measuring stick, and I was told, "Go and measure the Temple of God and the altar, and count the number of worshipers. ²But do not measure the outer courtyard, for it has been turned over to the nations. They will trample the holy city for 42 months. ³And I will give power to my two witnesses, and they will be clothed in sackcloth and will prophesy during those 1,260 days."

I BELIEVE God will one day give special power to his two prophets. (11:3)

⁴These two prophets are the two olive trees and the two lampstands that stand before the Lord of all the earth. ⁵If anyone tries to harm them, fire flashes from the mouths of the prophets and consumes their enemies. This is how anyone who tries to harm them must die. ⁶They have power to shut the skies so that no rain will fall for as long as they prophesy. And they have the power to turn the rivers and oceans into blood, and to send every kind of plague upon the earth as often as they wish.

⁷When they complete their testimony, the beast that comes up out of the bottomless pit will declare war against them. He will conquer them and kill them. ⁸And their bodies will lie in the main street of Jerusalem,* the city which is called "Sodom" and "Egypt," the city where their Lord was crucified. ⁹And for three and a half days, all peoples, tribes, languages, and nations will come to stare at their bodies. No one will be allowed to bury them. ¹⁰All the people who belong to this world will give presents to each other to celebrate the death of the two prophets who had tormented them.

¹¹But after three and a half days, the spirit of life from God entered them, and they stood up! And terror struck all who were staring at them. ¹²Then a loud voice shouted from heaven, "Come up here!" And they rose to heaven in a cloud as their enemies watched.

I BELIEVE God will raise the two prophets from the dead. (11:11)

¹³And in the same hour there was a terrible earthquake that destroyed a tenth of the city. Seven thousand people died in that earthquake. And everyone who did not die was terrified and gave glory to the God of heaven.

I GIVE glory to God in both the best and the worst of times. (11:13)

¹⁴ The second terror is past, but look, now the third terror is coming quickly.

The Seventh Trumpet Brings the Third Terror

¹⁵ Then the seventh angel blew his trumpet, and there were loud voices shouting in heaven: "The whole world has now become the Kingdom of our Lord and of his Christ, and he will reign forever and ever."

¹⁶And the twenty-four elders sitting on their thrones before God fell on their faces and worshiped him. ¹⁷And they said,

"We give thanks to you, Lord God Almighty,
   the one who is and who always was,
for now you have assumed your great power
   and have begun to reign.
¹⁸The nations were angry with you,
   but now the time of your wrath has come.

11:8 Greek *the great city.*

I BELIEVE the Lord will one day judge the dead and reward all those who serve him and fear his name. (11:18)

It is time to judge the dead and reward your servants.
You will reward your prophets and your holy people,
all who fear your name, from the least to the greatest.
And you will destroy all who have caused destruction on the earth."

[19] Then, in heaven, the Temple of God was opened and the Ark of his covenant could be seen inside the Temple. Lightning flashed, thunder crashed and roared; there was a great hailstorm, and the world was shaken by a mighty earthquake.

CHAPTER 12

The Woman and the Dragon

Then I witnessed in heaven an event of great significance. I saw a woman clothed with the sun, with the moon beneath her feet, and a crown of twelve stars on her head. [2]She was pregnant, and she cried out in the pain of labor as she awaited her delivery.

[3]Suddenly, I witnessed in heaven another significant event. I saw a large red dragon with seven heads and ten horns, with seven crowns on his heads. [4]His tail dragged down one-third of the stars, which he threw to the earth. He stood before the woman as she was about to give birth to her child, ready to devour the baby as soon as it was born.

[5]She gave birth to a boy who was to rule all nations with an iron rod. And the child was snatched away from the dragon and was caught up to God and to his throne. [6]And the woman fled into the wilderness, where God had prepared a place to give her care for 1,260 days.

I BELIEVE God's angels oppose the Devil and his demons. (12:7)

[7]Then there was war in heaven. Michael and the angels under his command fought the dragon and his angels. [8]And the dragon lost the battle and was forced out of heaven. [9]This great dragon—the ancient serpent called the Devil, or Satan, the one deceiving the whole world—was thrown down to the earth with all his angels.

I BELIEVE the Devil—Satan—futilely accuses Christians before God. (12:10)

[10]Then I heard a loud voice shouting across the heavens,

"It has happened at last—the salvation and power and kingdom of our God, and the authority of his Christ! For the Accuser has been thrown down to earth—the one who accused our brothers and sisters* before our God day and night. [11]And they have defeated him because of the blood of the Lamb and because of their testimony. And they were not afraid to die. [12]Rejoice, O heavens! And you who live in the heavens, rejoice! But terror will come on the earth and the sea. For the Devil has come down to you in great anger, and he knows that he has little time."

[13]And when the dragon realized that he had been thrown down to the earth, he pursued the woman who had given birth to the child. [14]But she was given two wings like those of a great eagle. This allowed her to fly to a place prepared for her in the wilderness, where she would be cared for and protected from the dragon* for a time, times, and half a time.

[15]Then the dragon tried to drown the woman with a flood of water that flowed from its mouth. [16]But the earth helped her by opening its mouth and swallowing the river that gushed out from the mouth of the dragon. [17]Then the dragon became angry at the woman, and he declared war against the rest of her children—all who keep God's commandments and confess that they belong to Jesus.

I KEEP God's commands and belong to Jesus Christ. (12:17)

The Beast out of the Sea

[18]Then he stood* waiting on the shore of the sea.

12:10 Greek *brothers.*   12:14 Greek *the serpent;* also in 12:15. See 12:9.   12:18 Some manuscripts read *Then I stood,* and some translations put this entire sentence into 13:1.

CHAPTER 13

And now in my vision I saw a beast rising up out of the sea. It had seven heads and ten horns, with ten crowns on its horns. And written on each head were names that blasphemed God. ²This beast looked like a leopard, but it had bear's feet and a lion's mouth! And the dragon gave him his own power and throne and great authority.

³I saw that one of the heads of the beast seemed wounded beyond recovery—but the fatal wound was healed! All the world marveled at this miracle and followed the beast in awe. ⁴They worshiped the dragon for giving the beast such power, and they worshiped the beast. "Is there anyone as great as the beast?" they exclaimed. "Who is able to fight against him?"

⁵Then the beast was allowed to speak great blasphemies against God. And he was given authority to do what he wanted for forty-two months. ⁶And he spoke terrible words of blasphemy against God, slandering his name and all who live in heaven, who are his temple. ⁷And the beast was allowed to wage war against God's holy people and to overcome them. And he was given authority to rule over every tribe and people and language and nation. ⁸And all the people who belong to this world worshiped the beast. They are the ones whose names were not written in the Book of Life, which belongs to the Lamb who was killed before the world was made.

⁹Anyone who is willing to hear should listen and understand. ¹⁰The people who are destined for prison will be arrested and taken away. Those who are destined for death will be killed. But do not be dismayed, for here is your opportunity to have endurance and faith.

The Beast out of the Earth

¹¹Then I saw another beast come up out of the earth. He had two horns like those of a lamb, and he spoke with the voice of a dragon. ¹²He exercised all the authority of the first beast. And he required all the earth and those who belong to this world to worship the first beast, whose death-wound had been healed. ¹³He did astounding miracles, such as making fire flash down to earth from heaven while everyone was watching. ¹⁴And with all the miracles he was allowed to perform on behalf of the first beast, he deceived all the people who belong to this world. He ordered the people of the world to make a great statue of the first beast, who was fatally wounded and then came back to life. ¹⁵He was permitted to give life to this statue so that it could speak. Then the statue commanded that anyone refusing to worship it must die.

¹⁶He required everyone—great and small, rich and poor, slave and free—to be given a mark on the right hand or on the forehead. ¹⁷And no one could buy or sell anything without that mark, which was either the name of the beast or the number representing his name. ¹⁸Wisdom is needed to understand this. Let the one who has understanding solve the number of the beast, for it is the number of a man.* His number is 666.*

CHAPTER 14

The Lamb and the 144,000

Then I saw the Lamb standing on Mount Zion, and with him were 144,000 who had his name and his Father's name written on their foreheads. ²And I heard a sound from heaven like the roaring of a great waterfall or the rolling of mighty thunder. It was like the sound of many harpists playing together.

³This great choir sang a wonderful new song in front of the throne of God and before the four living beings and the twenty-four elders. And no one could learn this song except those 144,000 who had been redeemed from the earth. ⁴For they are spiritually undefiled, pure as virgins,* following the Lamb

I ABHOR blasphemy. (13:1)

I BELONG to Jesus Christ, and, because of this, I know that my name is written in the Book of Life. (13:8)

I AM COMMITTED to enduring in my faith in Jesus Christ, no matter what persecution I must face. (13:10)

I ABHOR idolatry. (13:12)

13:18a Or *of humanity.* 13:18b Some manuscripts read *616.* 14:4a Greek *they are virgins who have not defiled themselves with women.*

wherever he goes. They have been purchased from among the people on the earth as a special offering* to God and to the Lamb. ⁵No falsehood can be charged against them; they are blameless.

The Three Angels
⁶And I saw another angel flying through the heavens, carrying the everlasting Good News to preach to the people who belong to this world—to every nation, tribe, language, and people. ⁷"Fear God," he shouted. "Give glory to him. For the time has come when he will sit as judge. Worship him who made heaven and earth, the sea, and all the springs of water."

⁸Then another angel followed him through the skies, shouting, "Babylon is fallen—that great city is fallen—because she seduced the nations of the world and made them drink the wine of her passionate immorality."

⁹Then a third angel followed them, shouting, "Anyone who worships the beast and his statue or who accepts his mark on the forehead or the hand ¹⁰must drink the wine of God's wrath. It is poured out undiluted into God's cup of wrath. And they will be tormented with fire and burning sulfur in the presence of the holy angels and the Lamb. ¹¹The smoke of their torment rises forever and ever, and they will have no relief day or night, for they have worshiped the beast and his statue and have accepted the mark of his name. ¹²Let this encourage God's holy people to endure persecution patiently and remain firm to the end, obeying his commands and trusting in Jesus."

¹³And I heard a voice from heaven saying, "Write this down: Blessed are those who die in the Lord from now on. Yes, says the Spirit, they are blessed indeed, for they will rest from all their toils and trials; for their good deeds follow them!"

The Harvest of the Earth
¹⁴Then I saw the Son of Man* sitting on a white cloud. He had a gold crown on his head and a sharp sickle in his hand.

¹⁵Then an angel came from the Temple and called out in a loud voice to the one sitting on the cloud, "Use the sickle, for the time has come for you to harvest; the crop is ripe on the earth." ¹⁶So the one sitting on the cloud swung his sickle over the earth, and the whole earth was harvested.

¹⁷After that, another angel came from the Temple in heaven, and he also had a sharp sickle. ¹⁸Then another angel, who has power to destroy the world with fire, shouted to the angel with the sickle, "Use your sickle now to gather the clusters of grapes from the vines of the earth, for they are fully ripe for judgment." ¹⁹So the angel swung his sickle on the earth and loaded the grapes into the great winepress of God's wrath. ²⁰And the grapes were trodden in the winepress outside the city, and blood flowed from the winepress in a stream about 180 miles* long and as high as a horse's bridle.

CHAPTER 15

The Song of Moses and of the Lamb
Then I saw in heaven another significant event, and it was great and marvelous. Seven angels were holding the seven last plagues, which would bring God's wrath to completion. ²I saw before me what seemed to be a crystal sea mixed with fire. And on it stood all the people who had been victorious over the beast and his statue and the number representing his name. They were all holding harps that God had given them. ³And they were singing the song of Moses, the servant of God, and the song of the Lamb:

"Great and marvelous are your actions,
Lord God Almighty.

I FEAR God, give glory to him, and worship him. (14:7)

I ABHOR idolatry. (14:9)

I AM COMMITTED to trusting Jesus Christ and obeying his commands, no matter what persecution I must face. (14:12)

I BELIEVE the good deeds of those who die for Jesus Christ will be rewarded in heaven. (14:13)

I BELIEVE God's judgments will one day bring his wrath to completion. (15:1)

See Moses' profile (page 73) at Exodus 5:1.

14:4b Greek as firstfruits. 14:14 Or one who looked like a man; Greek reads one like a son of man. 14:20 Greek 1,600 stadia [296 kilometers].

Just and true are your ways,
  O King of the nations.*
⁴Who will not fear, O Lord, and glorify your name?
  For you alone are holy.
All nations will come and worship before you,
  for your righteous deeds have been revealed."

I FEAR the Lord and glorify his holy name. (15:4)

The Seven Bowls of the Seven Plagues

⁵Then I looked and saw that the Temple in heaven, God's Tabernacle, was thrown wide open! ⁶The seven angels who were holding the bowls of the seven plagues came from the Temple, clothed in spotless white linen* with gold belts across their chests. ⁷And one of the four living beings handed each of the seven angels a gold bowl filled with the terrible wrath of God, who lives forever and forever. ⁸The Temple was filled with smoke from God's glory and power. No one could enter the Temple until the seven angels had completed pouring out the seven plagues.

CHAPTER 16

Then I heard a mighty voice shouting from the Temple to the seven angels, "Now go your ways and empty out the seven bowls of God's wrath on the earth."

²So the first angel left the Temple and poured out his bowl over the earth, and horrible, malignant sores broke out on everyone who had the mark of the beast and who worshiped his statue.

³Then the second angel poured out his bowl on the sea, and it became like the blood of a corpse. And everything in the sea died.

⁴Then the third angel poured out his bowl on the rivers and springs, and they became blood. ⁵And I heard the angel who had authority over all water saying, "You are just in sending this judgment, O Holy One, who is and who always was. ⁶For your holy people and your prophets have been killed, and their blood was poured out on the earth. So you have given their murderers blood to drink. It is their just reward." ⁷And I heard a voice from the altar saying, "Yes, Lord God Almighty, your punishments are true and just."

⁸Then the fourth angel poured out his bowl on the sun, causing it to scorch everyone with its fire. ⁹Everyone was burned by this blast of heat, and they cursed the name of God, who sent all of these plagues. They did not repent and give him glory.

¹⁰Then the fifth angel poured out his bowl on the throne of the beast, and his kingdom was plunged into darkness. And his subjects ground their teeth in anguish, ¹¹and they cursed the God of heaven for their pains and sores. But they refused to repent of all their evil deeds.

¹²Then the sixth angel poured out his bowl on the great Euphrates River, and it dried up so that the kings from the east could march their armies westward without hindrance. ¹³And I saw three evil spirits that looked like frogs leap from the mouth of the dragon, the beast, and the false prophet. ¹⁴These miracle-working demons caused all the rulers of the world to gather for battle against the Lord on that great judgment day of God Almighty.

¹⁵"Take note: I will come as unexpectedly as a thief! Blessed are all who are watching for me, who keep their robes ready so they will not need to walk naked and ashamed."

¹⁶And they gathered all the rulers and their armies to a place called *Armageddon* in Hebrew.

¹⁷Then the seventh angel poured out his bowl into the air. And a mighty

I BELIEVE God will be perfectly just in sending judgment on the whole earth. (16:5)

I BELIEVE God's punishments are true and just. (16:7)

I ABHOR blasphemy. (16:9)

I BELIEVE Jesus Christ's coming will catch the world by surprise. (16:15)

15:3 Some manuscripts read *King of the ages;* other manuscripts read *King of the saints.* 15:6 Some manuscripts read *in bright and sparkling stone.*

shout came from the throne of the Temple in heaven, saying, "It is finished!" [18]Then the thunder crashed and rolled, and lightning flashed. And there was an earthquake greater than ever before in human history. [19]The great city of Babylon split into three pieces, and cities around the world fell into heaps of rubble. And so God remembered all of Babylon's sins, and he made her drink the cup that was filled with the wine of his fierce wrath. [20]And every island disappeared, and all the mountains were leveled. [21]There was a terrible hailstorm, and hailstones weighing seventy-five pounds* fell from the sky onto the people below. They cursed God because of the hailstorm, which was a very terrible plague.

CHAPTER 17

The Great Prostitute

One of the seven angels who had poured out the seven bowls came over and spoke to me. "Come with me," he said, "and I will show you the judgment that is going to come on the great prostitute, who sits on many waters. [2]The rulers of the world have had immoral relations with her, and the people who belong to this world have been made drunk by the wine of her immorality."

I ABHOR blasphemy. (17:3)

[3]So the angel took me in spirit* into the wilderness. There I saw a woman sitting on a scarlet beast that had seven heads and ten horns, written all over with blasphemies against God. [4]The woman wore purple and scarlet clothing and beautiful jewelry made of gold and precious gems and pearls. She held in her hand a gold goblet full of obscenities and the impurities of her immorality. [5]A mysterious name was written on her forehead: "Babylon the Great, Mother of All Prostitutes and Obscenities in the World." [6]I could see that she was drunk—drunk with the blood of God's holy people who were witnesses for Jesus. I stared at her completely amazed.

I BELONG to Jesus Christ, and my name is written in the Book of Life. (17:8)

[7]"Why are you so amazed?" the angel asked. "I will tell you the mystery of this woman and of the beast with seven heads and ten horns. [8]The beast you saw was alive but isn't now. And yet he will soon come up out of the bottomless pit and go to eternal destruction. And the people who belong to this world, whose names were not written in the Book of Life from before the world began, will be amazed at the reappearance of this beast who had died.

[9]"And now understand this: The seven heads of the beast represent the seven hills of the city where this woman rules. They also represent seven kings. [10]Five kings have already fallen, the sixth now reigns, and the seventh is yet to come, but his reign will be brief. [11]The scarlet beast that was alive and then died is the eighth king. He is like the other seven, and he, too, will go to his doom. [12]His ten horns are ten kings who have not yet risen to power; they will be appointed to their kingdoms for one brief moment to reign with the beast. [13]They will all agree to give their power and authority to him. [14]To-

I BELIEVE Jesus Christ is the King of kings and Lord of lords. (17:14)

gether they will wage war against the Lamb, but the Lamb will defeat them because he is Lord over all lords and King over all kings, and his people are the called and chosen and faithful ones."

[15]And the angel said to me, "The waters where the prostitute is sitting represent masses of people of every nation and language. [16]The scarlet beast and his ten horns—which represent ten kings who will reign with him—all hate the prostitute. They will strip her naked, eat her flesh, and burn her remains with fire. [17]For God has put a plan into their minds, a plan that will carry out his purposes. They will mutually agree to give their authority to the scarlet beast, and so the words of God will be fulfilled. [18]And this woman you saw in your vision represents the great city that rules over the kings of the earth."

I BELIEVE the words of God will one day be fulfilled just as he predicted through his prophets. (17:17)

16:21 Greek *1 talent* [34 kilograms]. 17:3 Or *in the Spirit.*

CHAPTER 18

The Fall of Babylon

After all this I saw another angel come down from heaven with great authority, and the earth grew bright with his splendor. ²He gave a mighty shout, "Babylon is fallen—that great city is fallen! She has become the hideout of demons and evil spirits, a nest for filthy buzzards, and a den for dreadful beasts. ³For all the nations have drunk the wine of her passionate immorality. The rulers of the world have committed adultery with her, and merchants throughout the world have grown rich as a result of her luxurious living."

⁴Then I heard another voice calling from heaven, "Come away from her, my people. Do not take part in her sins, or you will be punished with her. ⁵For her sins are piled as high as heaven, and God is ready to judge her for her evil deeds. ⁶Do to her as she has done to your people. Give her a double penalty for all her evil deeds. She brewed a cup of terror for others, so give her twice as much as she gave out. ⁷She has lived in luxury and pleasure, so match it now with torments and sorrows. She boasts, 'I am queen on my throne. I am no helpless widow. I will not experience sorrow.' ⁸Therefore, the sorrows of death and mourning and famine will overtake her in a single day. She will be utterly consumed by fire, for the Lord God who judges her is mighty."

⁹And the rulers of the world who took part in her immoral acts and enjoyed her great luxury will mourn for her as they see the smoke rising from her charred remains. ¹⁰They will stand at a distance, terrified by her great torment. They will cry out, "How terrible, how terrible for Babylon, that great city! In one single moment God's judgment came on her."

¹¹The merchants of the world will weep and mourn for her, for there is no one left to buy their goods. ¹²She bought great quantities of gold, silver, jewels, pearls, fine linen, purple dye, silk, scarlet cloth, every kind of perfumed wood, ivory goods, objects made of expensive wood, bronze, iron, and marble. ¹³She also bought cinnamon, spice, incense, myrrh, frankincense, wine, olive oil, fine flour, wheat, cattle, sheep, horses, chariots, and slaves—yes, she even traded in human lives.

¹⁴"All the fancy things you loved so much are gone," they cry. "The luxuries and splendor that you prized so much will never be yours again. They are gone forever."

¹⁵The merchants who became wealthy by selling her these things will stand at a distance, terrified by her great torment. They will weep and cry. ¹⁶"How terrible, how terrible for that great city! She was so beautiful—like a woman clothed in finest purple and scarlet linens, decked out with gold and precious stones and pearls! ¹⁷And in one single moment all the wealth of the city is gone!"

And all the shipowners and captains of the merchant ships and their crews will stand at a distance. ¹⁸They will weep as they watch the smoke ascend, and they will say, "Where in all the world is there another city like this?" ¹⁹And they will throw dust on their heads to show their great sorrow. And they will say, "How terrible, how terrible for the great city! She made us all rich from her great wealth. And now in a single hour it is all gone."

²⁰But you, O heaven, rejoice over her fate. And you also rejoice, O holy people of God and apostles and prophets! For at last God has judged her on your behalf.

²¹Then a mighty angel picked up a boulder as large as a great millstone. He threw it into the ocean and shouted, "Babylon, the great city, will be thrown down as violently as I have thrown away this stone, and she will disappear forever. ²²Never again will the sound of music be heard there—no more harps, songs, flutes, or trumpets. There will be no industry of any kind, and no more milling of grain. ²³Her nights will be dark, without a single lamp.

I DO NOT TAKE PART in the abhorrent sins of this world. (18:4)

I BELIEVE the Lord God is the mighty judge of all that exists. (18:8)

I DO NOT PRIZE temporal luxuries. (18:14)

I LOOK FORWARD to the day when God judges the world for persecuting his people. (18:20)

There will be no happy voices of brides and grooms. This will happen because her merchants, who were the greatest in the world, deceived the nations with her sorceries. ²⁴In her streets the blood of the prophets was spilled. She was the one who slaughtered God's people all over the world."

I ABHOR the murder of God's people. (18:24)

CHAPTER 19

Songs of Victory in Heaven

After this, I heard the sound of a vast crowd in heaven shouting, "Hallelujah! Salvation is from our God. Glory and power belong to him alone. ²His judgments are just and true. He has punished the great prostitute who corrupted the earth with her immorality, and he has avenged the murder of his servants." ³Again and again their voices rang, "Hallelujah! The smoke from that city ascends forever and forever!"

⁴Then the twenty-four elders and the four living beings fell down and worshiped God, who was sitting on the throne. They cried out, "Amen! Hallelujah!"

⁵And from the throne came a voice that said, "Praise our God, all his servants, from the least to the greatest, all who fear him."

I BELIEVE the Lord God Almighty reigns forever. (19:6)

⁶Then I heard again what sounded like the shout of a huge crowd, or the roar of mighty ocean waves, or the crash of loud thunder: "Hallelujah! For the Lord our God, the Almighty, reigns. ⁷Let us be glad and rejoice and honor him. For the time has come for the wedding feast of the Lamb, and his bride has prepared herself. ⁸She is permitted to wear the finest white linen." (Fine linen represents the good deeds done by the people of God.)

I BELIEVE the good deeds of God's people will be rewarded in heaven. (19:8)

⁹And the angel said, "Write this: Blessed are those who are invited to the wedding feast of the Lamb." And he added, "These are true words that come from God."

I SERVE God and worship him alone. (19:10)

¹⁰Then I fell down at his feet to worship him, but he said, "No, don't worship me. For I am a servant of God, just like you and other brothers and sisters* who testify of their faith in Jesus. Worship God. For the essence of prophecy is to give a clear witness for Jesus.*"

The Rider on the White Horse

¹¹Then I saw heaven opened, and a white horse was standing there. And the one sitting on the horse was named Faithful and True. For he judges fairly and then goes to war. ¹²His eyes were bright like flames of fire, and on his head were many crowns. A name was written on him, and only he knew what it meant. ¹³He was clothed with a robe dipped in blood, and his title was the Word of God. ¹⁴The armies of heaven, dressed in pure white linen, followed him on white horses. ¹⁵From his mouth came a sharp sword, and with it he struck down the nations. He ruled them with an iron rod, and he trod the winepress of the fierce wrath of almighty God. ¹⁶On his robe and thigh was written this title: King of kings and Lord of lords.

I BELIEVE Jesus Christ is the King of kings and Lord of lords. (19:16)

¹⁷Then I saw an angel standing in the sun, shouting to the vultures flying high in the sky: "Come! Gather together for the great banquet God has prepared. ¹⁸Come and eat the flesh of kings, captains, and strong warriors; of horses and their riders; and of all humanity, both free and slave, small and great."

¹⁹Then I saw the beast gathering the kings of the earth and their armies in order to fight against the one sitting on the horse and his army. ²⁰And the beast was captured, and with him the false prophet who did mighty miracles on behalf of the beast—miracles that deceived all who had accepted the mark of the beast and who worshiped his statue. Both the beast and his false prophet were thrown alive into the lake of fire that burns with sulfur. ²¹Their entire army was killed by the sharp sword that came out of the mouth of the one riding the white horse. And all the vultures of the sky gorged themselves on the dead bodies.

19:10a Greek *brothers.*   19:10b Or *is the message confirmed by Jesus.*

CHAPTER 20

The Thousand Years

Then I saw an angel come down from heaven with the key to the bottomless pit and a heavy chain in his hand. ²He seized the dragon—that old serpent, the Devil, Satan—and bound him in chains for a thousand years. ³The angel threw him into the bottomless pit, which he then shut and locked so Satan could not deceive the nations anymore until the thousand years were finished. Afterward he would be released again for a little while.

⁴Then I saw thrones, and the people sitting on them had been given the authority to judge. And I saw the souls of those who had been beheaded for their testimony about Jesus, for proclaiming the word of God. And I saw the souls of those who had not worshiped the beast or his statue, nor accepted his mark on their forehead or their hands. They came to life again, and they reigned with Christ for a thousand years. ⁵This is the first resurrection. (The rest of the dead did not come back to life until the thousand years had ended.) ⁶Blessed and holy are those who share in the first resurrection. For them the second death holds no power, but they will be priests of God and of Christ and will reign with him a thousand years.

The Defeat of Satan

⁷When the thousand years end, Satan will be let out of his prison. ⁸He will go out to deceive the nations from every corner of the earth, which are called Gog and Magog. He will gather them together for battle—a mighty host, as numberless as sand along the shore. ⁹And I saw them as they went up on the broad plain of the earth and surrounded God's people and the beloved city. But fire from heaven came down on the attacking armies and consumed them.

¹⁰Then the Devil, who betrayed them, was thrown into the lake of fire that burns with sulfur, joining the beast and the false prophet. There they will be tormented day and night forever and ever.

The Final Judgment

¹¹And I saw a great white throne, and I saw the one who was sitting on it. The earth and sky fled from his presence, but they found no place to hide. ¹²I saw the dead, both great and small, standing before God's throne. And the books were opened, including the Book of Life. And the dead were judged according to the things written in the books, according to what they had done. ¹³The sea gave up the dead in it, and death and the grave* gave up the dead in them. They were all judged according to their deeds. ¹⁴And death and the grave were thrown into the lake of fire. This is the second death—the lake of fire. ¹⁵And anyone whose name was not found recorded in the Book of Life was thrown into the lake of fire.

CHAPTER 21

The New Jerusalem

Then I saw a new heaven and a new earth, for the old heaven and the old earth had disappeared. And the sea was also gone. ²And I saw the holy city, the new Jerusalem, coming down from God out of heaven like a beautiful bride prepared for her husband.

³I heard a loud shout from the throne, saying, "Look, the home of God is now among his people! He will live with them, and they will be his people. God himself will be with them.* ⁴He will remove all of their sorrows, and there will be no more death or sorrow or crying or pain. For the old world and its evils are gone forever."

⁵And the one sitting on the throne said, "Look, I am making all things

I BELIEVE Satan will one day be bound for a thousand years while Christ reigns on the earth. (20:2)

I BELIEVE the Devil will one day be thrown into the lake of fire to be tormented forever. (20:10)

I BELIEVE all people will one day be judged according to the things they have done. (20:12)

I BELIEVE death, the grave, and those whose names are not in the Book of Life will one day be thrown into the lake of fire. (20:14)

I BELIEVE God will one day make a new heaven and a new earth. (21:1)

I BELIEVE God himself will one day live with his people. (21:3)

I BELIEVE God will one day eliminate all death, sorrow, crying, and pain. (21:4)

20:13 Greek *and Hades; also in 20:14.*   21:3 Some manuscripts read *God himself will be with them, their God.*

new!" And then he said to me, "Write this down, for what I tell you is trustworthy and true." ⁶And he also said, "It is finished! I am the Alpha and the Omega—the Beginning and the End. To all who are thirsty I will give the springs of the water of life without charge! ⁷All who are victorious will inherit all these blessings, and I will be their God, and they will be my children. ⁸But cowards who turn away from me, and unbelievers, and the corrupt, and murderers, and the immoral, and those who practice witchcraft, and idol worshipers, and all liars—their doom is in the lake that burns with fire and sulfur. This is the second death."

⁹Then one of the seven angels who held the seven bowls containing the seven last plagues came and said to me, "Come with me! I will show you the bride, the wife of the Lamb."

¹⁰So he took me in spirit* to a great, high mountain, and he showed me the holy city, Jerusalem, descending out of heaven from God. ¹¹It was filled with the glory of God and sparkled like a precious gem, crystal clear like jasper. ¹²Its walls were broad and high, with twelve gates guarded by twelve angels. And the names of the twelve tribes of Israel were written on the gates. ¹³There were three gates on each side—east, north, south, and west. ¹⁴The wall of the city had twelve foundation stones, and on them were written the names of the twelve apostles of the Lamb.

¹⁵The angel who talked to me held in his hand a gold measuring stick to measure the city, its gates, and its wall. ¹⁶When he measured it, he found it was a square, as wide as it was long. In fact, it was in the form of a cube, for its length and width and height were each 1,400 miles.* ¹⁷Then he measured the walls and found them to be 216 feet thick* (the angel used a standard human measure).

¹⁸The wall was made of jasper, and the city was pure gold, as clear as glass. ¹⁹The wall of the city was built on foundation stones inlaid with twelve gems: the first was jasper, the second sapphire, the third agate, the fourth emerald, ²⁰the fifth onyx, the sixth carnelian, the seventh chrysolite, the eighth beryl, the ninth topaz, the tenth chrysoprase, the eleventh jacinth, the twelfth amethyst.

²¹The twelve gates were made of pearls—each gate from a single pearl! And the main street was pure gold, as clear as glass.

²²No temple could be seen in the city, for the Lord God Almighty and the Lamb are its temple. ²³And the city has no need of sun or moon, for the glory of God illuminates the city, and the Lamb is its light. ²⁴The nations of the earth will walk in its light, and the rulers of the world will come and bring their glory to it. ²⁵Its gates never close at the end of day because there is no night. ²⁶And all the nations will bring their glory and honor into the city. ²⁷Nothing evil will be allowed to enter—no one who practices shameful idolatry and dishonesty—but only those whose names are written in the Lamb's Book of Life.

CHAPTER 22

And the angel showed me a pure river with the water of life, clear as crystal, flowing from the throne of God and of the Lamb, ²coursing down the center of the main street. On each side of the river grew a tree of life, bearing twelve crops of fruit,* with a fresh crop each month. The leaves were used for medicine to heal the nations.

³No longer will anything be cursed. For the throne of God and of the Lamb will be there, and his servants will worship him. ⁴And they will see his face, and his name will be written on their foreheads. ⁵And there will be no night

I ABHOR unbelief, murder, immorality, witchcraft, and idolatry. (21:8)

I BELIEVE the appearance of the new Jerusalem will be awe inspiring. (21:18)

I BELIEVE no evil will be allowed within the new Jerusalem. (21:27)

If something in this Bible helps you experience a closer walk with God, why not share it with others?

21:10 Or *in the Spirit.*   21:16 Greek *12,000 stadia* [2,220 kilometers].   21:17 Greek *144 cubits* [65 meters].
22:2 Or *12 kinds of fruit.*

there—no need for lamps or sun—for the Lord God will shine on them. And they will reign forever and ever.

⁶Then the angel said to me, "These words are trustworthy and true: ' The Lord God, who tells his prophets what the future holds, has sent his angel to tell you what will happen soon.' "

Jesus Is Coming

⁷"Look, I am coming soon! Blessed are those who obey the prophecy written in this scroll."

⁸I, John, am the one who saw and heard all these things. And when I saw and heard these things, I fell down to worship the angel who showed them to me. ⁹But again he said, "No, don't worship me. I am a servant of God, just like you and your brothers the prophets, as well as all who obey what is written in this scroll. Worship God!"

¹⁰Then he instructed me, "Do not seal up the prophetic words you have written, for the time is near. ¹¹Let the one who is doing wrong continue to do wrong; the one who is vile, continue to be vile; the one who is good, continue to do good; and the one who is holy, continue in holiness."

¹²"See, I am coming soon, and my reward is with me, to repay all according to their deeds. ¹³I am the Alpha and the Omega, the First and the Last, the Beginning and the End."

¹⁴Blessed are those who wash their robes so they can enter through the gates of the city and eat the fruit from the tree of life. ¹⁵Outside the city are the dogs—the sorcerers, the sexually immoral, the murderers, the idol worshipers, and all who love to live a lie.

¹⁶"I, Jesus, have sent my angel to give you this message for the churches. I am both the source of David and the heir to his throne.* I am the bright morning star."

¹⁷The Spirit and the bride say, "Come." Let each one who hears them say, "Come." Let the thirsty ones come—anyone who wants to. Let them come and drink the water of life without charge. ¹⁸And I solemnly declare to everyone who hears the prophetic words of this book: If anyone adds anything to what is written here, God will add to that person the plagues described in this book. ¹⁹And if anyone removes any of the words of this prophetic book, God will remove that person's share in the tree of life and in the holy city that are described in this book.

²⁰He who is the faithful witness to all these things says, "Yes, I am coming soon!"

Amen! Come, Lord Jesus!

²¹The grace of the Lord Jesus be with you all.

22:16 Greek *I am the root and offspring of David.*

I BELIEVE the words of Revelation are trustworthy and true. (22:6)

I BELIEVE God blesses each person who reads Revelation, listens to it, and obeys what it says. (22:7)

I CONTINUE TO BE holy and do good just as God commands. (22:11)

I BELIEVE Jesus Christ is the source of David and heir to his throne (Isaiah 11:1, 10). (22:16)

See David's profile (page 629) at Psalm 3:1.

I LONG for the Lord Jesus Christ's return! (22:20)

Famous Bible Passages

Adam and Eve's fall **Genesis 3:6-7**

Abraham is declared righteous because of his faith **Genesis 15:6**

Moses and the burning bush **Exodus 3:2-10**

The Israelites flee from Egypt **Exodus 12:37-38**

God splits the Red Sea **Exodus 14:15-22**

Ten Commandments **Exodus 20:1-17**

"Be holy because I am holy" **Leviticus 11:44-45; 19:2; 20:7, 26; 21:8**

"Love your neighbor as yourself" **Leviticus 19:18, 34**

Bitter complaining by the Israelites **Numbers 11:1-6**

The Ten Commandments repeated **Deuteronomy 5:6-21**

The command to love the Lord wholeheartedly **Deuteronomy 6:4-9; 10:12-13**

The walls of Jericho come tumbling down **Joshua 6:20**

"As for me and my family, we will serve the Lord" **Joshua 24:15**

Samson's exploits **Judges 15:1-20**

Ruth pledges her unfailing loyalty **Ruth 1:16-17**

"The LORD has sought out a man after his own heart" **1 Samuel 13:14**

David defeats the giant Goliath **1 Samuel 17:1-51**

David's adulterous affair with Bathsheba **2 Samuel 11:1-27**

Solomon's judgment regarding two prostitutes and a baby **1 Kings 3:16-28**

Elijah calls down fire from heaven **2 Kings 1:9-12**

Jabez's remarkable prayer and God's answer **1 Chronicles 4:9-10**

The Israelites' celebration of the Ark's arrival in Jerusalem **1 Chronicles 15:25-16:43**

The glory of the Lord filling the Temple **2 Chronicles 5:13-6:2; 7:1-3**

"If my people who are called by my name will humble themselves . . ." **2 Chronicles 7:14**

"The eyes of the LORD search the whole earth" **2 Chronicles 16:9**

"Ezra had determined to study and obey the law of the LORD" **Ezra 7:10**

Nehemiah's prayer of repentance to the Lord **Nehemiah 1:4-11**

"If I must die, I am willing to die" **Esther 4:16**

"The LORD gave me everything I had, and the LORD has taken it away" **Job 1:21**

The benefits of meditating on God's Word **Psalms 1, 19, and 119**

The psalmist's humble confession of sin **Psalms 32 and 51**

The psalmist's intense desire for the Lord **Psalms 42:1-4; 63:1-8**

The importance of fearing the Lord **Proverbs 1:7; 3:7; 9:10; 15:33; 16:6; 22:4**

"Teach your children to choose the right path" **Proverbs 22:6**

"There is a time for everything . . ." **Ecclesiastes 3:1-8**

God "has planted eternity in the human heart" **Ecclesiastes 3:11**

"For love is as strong as death" **Song of Songs 8:6**

"Look! The virgin will conceive a child!" **Isaiah 7:14**

"For a child is born to us, a son is given to us" **Isaiah 9:6**

"You will keep in perfect peace all who trust in you" **Isaiah 26:3**

"But those who wait on the LORD will find new strength" **Isaiah 40:31**

"All of us have strayed away like sheep" **Isaiah 53:6**

"So are my ways higher than your ways" **Isaiah 55:9**

"Our righteous deeds . . . are but filthy rags" **Isaiah 64:6**

"[My people] have forsaken me—the fountain of living water" **Jeremiah 2:13**

"The human heart is most deceitful" **Jeremiah 17:9**

"For I know the plans I have for you" **Jeremiah 29:11**

"I have loved you, my people, with an everlasting love" **Jeremiah 31:3**

"Great is his faithfulness; his mercies begin afresh" **Lamentations 3:23**

"I searched for someone to stand in the gap" **Ezekiel 22:30**

"Daniel made up his mind not to defile himself" **Daniel 1:8**

"Was your God . . . able to rescue you from the lions?" **Daniel 6:20**

"Oh, that we might know the LORD! Let us press on to know him!" **Hosea 6:3**

"Then . . . I will pour out my Spirit upon all people. Your sons and daughters will prophesy" **Joel 2:28**

"Prepare to meet your God as he comes in judgment" **Amos 4:12**

"The day is near when I, the LORD, will judge the godless nations!" **Obadiah 1:15**

"Now the LORD had arrange for a great fish to swallow Jonah" **Jonah 1:17**

"But you, O Bethlehem Ephrathah, are only a small village in Judah. Yet a ruler will come for you" **Micah 5:2**

"The LORD has already told you what is good, and this is what he requires" **Micah 6:8**

"Look! A messenger is coming . . . with good news! He is bringing a message of peace" **Nahum 1:15**

"I will climb up into my watchtower now and wait to see what the Lord will say to me" **Habakkuk 2:1**

"Even though the fig trees have no blossoms, . . . yet I will rejoice in the LORD!" **Habakkuk 3:17-18**

"Stand in silence . . . for the awesome day of the LORD's judgment has come" **Zephaniah 1:7**

"In just a little while I will again shake the heavens and the earth" **Haggai 2:6; see 2:21**

"It is not by force nor by strength, but by my Spirit, says the LORD Almighty" **Zechariah 4:6**

"Look! I am sending my messenger, and he will prepare the way before me" **Malachi 3:1; see 4:5**

The Christmas story **Matthew 2:1-12; Luke 1:26-56; Luke 2:1-39**

The Beatitudes and sorrows **Matthew 5:3-10; Luke 6:20-26**

Peter's confession of faith **Matthew 16:13-20**

Jesus' discourse on the end of the age **Matthew 24:1-44**

The Great Commission **Matthew 28:18-20; Mark 16:15; Luke 24:47-48; Acts 1:8**

"For even I, the Son of Man, came here not to be served but to serve others, and to give my life as a ransom for many" **Mark 10:45**

Jesus' appearance to two disciples from Emmaus **Luke 24:13-35**

John gives a prologue about Jesus Christ's deity **John 1:1-18**

"Unless you are born again, you can never see the Kingdom of God" **John 3:3**

"For God so loved the world that he gave his only Son . . . " **John 3:16**

"My purpose is to give life in all its fullness" **John 10:10**

"I am going to prepare a place for you" **John 14:2**

"I am the way, the truth, and the life. No one can come to the Father except through me" **John 14:6**

"They . . . devoted themselves to the apostles' teaching and fellowship, sharing in the Lord's Supper and in prayer" **Acts 2:42**

"There is salvation in no one else [besides Jesus]! There is no other name in all of heaven for people to call on to save them" **Acts 4:12**

"I am not ashamed of this Good News about Christ" **Romans 1:16**

"For all have sinned; all fall short of God's glorious standard" **Romans 3:23**

"For the wages of sin is death, but the free gift of God is eternal life through Christ Jesus our Lord" **Romans 6:23**

"God causes everything to work together for the good of those who love God and are called according to his purpose for them" **Romans 8:28**

"If you confess with your mouth that Jesus is Lord and believe in your heart that God raised him from the dead, you will be saved" **Romans 10:9**

"Give your bodies to God. Let them be a living and holy sacrifice—the kind he will accept" **Romans 12:1**

"No eye has seen, no ear has heard, and no mind has imagined what God has prepared for those who love him" **1 Corinthians 2:9**

"God is faithful. He will keep the temptation from becoming so strong that you can't stand up against it" **1 Corinthians 10:13**

Love is the greatest virtue **1 Corinthians 12:31–13:13**

"Those who become Christians become new persons. They are not the same anymore, for the old life is gone. A new life has begun!" **2 Corinthians 5:17**

"Each time he [the Lord] said, 'My gracious favor is all you need. My power works best in your weakness'" **2 Corinthians 12:9**

"I myself no longer live, but Christ lives in me" **Galatians 2:20**

"When the Holy Spirit controls our lives, he will produce this kind of fruit in us: love, joy, peace, patience, kindness, goodness, faithfulness, gentleness, and self-control" **Galatians 5:22–23**

"God saved you by his special favor when you believed. And you can't take credit for this; it is a gift from God" **Ephesians 2:8**

"He [God] is able to accomplish infinitely more than we would ever dare to ask or hope" **Ephesians 3:20**

"Put on all of God's armor so that you will be able to stand firm against all the strategies and tricks of the Devil" **Ephesians 6:11**

"I am sure that God, who began the good work within you, will continue his work until it is finally finished" **Philippians 1:6**

"For to me, living is for Christ, and dying is even better" **Philippians 1:21**

"Your attitude should be the same that Christ Jesus had" **Philippians 2:5**

"Don't worry about anything; instead, pray about everything" **Philippians 4:6**

"Since you have been raised to new life with Christ, set your sights on the realities of heaven" **Colossians 3:1**

"Live wisely among those who are not Christians, and make the most of every opportunity" **Colossians 4:5**

"I want you to know what will happen to the Christians who have died" **1 Thessalonians 4:13**

"We pray that God, by his power, will fulfill all your good intentions" **2 Thessalonians 2:11**

"God our Savior . . . wants everyone to be saved and to understand the truth" **1 Timothy 2:3-4**

"Don't let anyone think less of you because you are young. Be an example to all believers . . . "
1 Timothy 4:12

"The love of money is at the root of all kinds of evil" **1 Timothy 6:10**

"God has not given us a spirit of fear and timidity, but of power, love, and self-discipline" **2 Timothy 1:7**

"All Scripture is inspired by God and is useful . . . " **2 Timothy 3:16–17**

"He [Christ] gave his life to free us from every kind of sin, to cleanse us, and to make us his very own people, totally committed to doing what is right" **Titus 2:14**

"God our Savior showed us his kindness and love. He saved us, not because of the good things we did, but because of his mercy" **Titus 3:4–5**

"Take this as a request from your friend Paul, an old man, now in prison for the sake of Christ Jesus" **Philemon 1:9**

"The word of God is full of living power. It is sharper than the sharpest knife . . . " **Hebrews 4:12**

"It is destined that each person dies only once and after that comes judgment" **Hebrews 9:27**

"Let us run with endurance the race that God has set before us" **Hebrews 12:1**

"Faith that doesn't show itself by good deeds is no faith at all—it is dead and useless" **James 2:17**

"What you ought to say is, 'If the Lord wants us to, we will live and do this or that'" **James 4:15**

"God has given us the privilege of being born again" **1 Peter 1:3; see 1:23**

"Keep away from evil desires because they fight against your very souls" **1 Peter 2:11**

"Worship Christ as Lord of your life. And if you are asked about your Christian hope, always be ready to explain it" **1 Peter 3:15**

"Give all your worries and cares to God, for he cares about what happens to you" **1 Peter 5:7**

"No prophecy in Scripture ever came from the prophets themselves. . . . It was the Holy Spirit who moved the prophets to speak from God" **2 Peter 1:20–21**

"A day is like a thousand years to the Lord, and a thousand years is like a day" **2 Peter 3:8**

"If we confess our sins to him [God], he is faithful and just to forgive us and to cleanse us from every wrong" **1 John 1:9**

"See how very much our heavenly Father loves us, for he allows us to be called his children, and we really are!" **1 John 3:1**

"Love means doing what God has commanded us, and he has commanded us to love one another" **2 John 1:6**

"I am praying that all is well with you and that your body is as healthy as I know your soul is" **3 John 1:2**

"All glory to God, who is able to keep you from stumbling, and who will bring you into his glorious presence innocent of sin and with great joy" **Jude 1:24**

"Look! Here I stand at the door and knock" **Revelation 3:20**

"Take note: I will come as unexpectedly as a thief!" **Revelation 16:15; see 3:3**

"I saw the dead . . . standing before God's throne. And the books were opened, including the Book of Life" **Revelation 20:12**

"Look, the home of God is now among his people!" **Revelation 21:3**

Examples to Heed

LIKE ADAM I am created by God and endowed with eternal dignity and value. **Genesis 1:26** *page 5*

LIKE EVE I know for certain that God forgives even the worst of sins. **Genesis 3:21** *page 7*

LIKE ABEL I am righteous in God's eyes by faith alone. **Genesis 4:4** *page 9*

LIKE ENOCH I can walk in close fellowship with God my entire life. **Genesis 5:24** *page 11*

LIKE NOAH I live a blameless life, even if I am the only one who does so. **Genesis 6:9** *page 13*

LIKE ABRAHAM I am the recipient of incredible blessings when I believe God. **Genesis 15:6** *page 19*

LIKE SARAH I know God will always keep his promises. **Genesis 21:1** *page 25*

LIKE ISAAC I am blessing my family for generations to come by passing on a spiritual heritage to my children. **Genesis 25:19** *page 31*

UNLIKE ESAU I value my relationship with God and the spiritual blessings he offers me. **Genesis 25:34** *page 33*

UNLIKE REBEKAH I do not attempt to obtain God's blessings through my own schemes. **Genesis 27:10** *page 35*

LIKE JACOB I always recognize God's hand on my life as I pursue his blessings. **Genesis 32:9** *page 43*

LIKE JOSEPH I trust the Lord to use difficulties in my life to bring about good. **Genesis 39:2** *page 51*

LIKE MOSES' PARENTS I do what is right for my family in obedience to God. **Exodus 2:3** *page 69*

LIKE MOSES I value my relationship to God more than any earthly possessions or fame. **Exodus 5:1** *page 73*

LIKE MIRIAM I lead others in praise to God for his goodness. **Exodus 15:20** *page 87*

UNLIKE AARON I do not give in to the pressure of others to redefine God. **Exodus 32:2** *page 107*

LIKE RAHAB I believe the Lord gladly saves all who turn to him, regardless of their nationality or background. **Joshua 2:11** *page 251*

LIKE CALEB I never stop taking on challenges to trust and obey God. **Joshua 14:12** *page 265*

LIKE JOSHUA I am filled with courage because of God's exceedingly great promises to me. **Joshua 23:14** *page 275*

LIKE DEBORAH I bring glory to God by leading others to face difficult battles. **Judges 4:9** *page 283*

LIKE GIDEON I increase my faith by obeying God. **Judges 7:15** *page 289*

UNLIKE JEPHTHAH I do not make a foolish vow to God. **Judges 11:31** *page 295*

UNLIKE SAMSON I will not let myself be ruled by passions and lusts. **Judges 16:1** *page 301*

LIKE RUTH I faithfully care for my loved ones. **Ruth 1:16** *page 311*

LIKE HANNAH I am confident that God brings joy out of sorrow. **1 Samuel 2:8** *page 319*

UNLIKE ELI I do not devalue God in my heart and affections. **1 Samuel 2:30** *page 321*

LIKE SAMUEL I allow God to use me for his glory no matter what my age. **1 Samuel 3:1** *page 323*

LIKE JONATHAN I can overcome any odds by God's power. **1 Samuel 14:6** *page 331*

UNLIKE SAUL I am not jealous when God chooses to honor and use someone else more than me. **1 Samuel 18:9** *page 339*

LIKE ABIGAIL I appeal to other believers to resist sinful choices and continue in godliness. **1 Samuel 25:31** *page 349*

UNLIKE AMNON I do not allow lust to rule my life. **2 Samuel 13:15** *page 369*

UNLIKE ABSALOM I do not grab for power. **2 Samuel 15:6** *page 373*

UNLIKE REHOBOAM I do not listen to foolish counsel. **1 Kings 12:8** *page 409*

UNLIKE JEROBOAM I do not turn my back on God, the Giver, to grasp his gifts. **1 Kings 13:4** *page 411*

UNLIKE AHAB I do not marry someone who opposes God or follow my spouse in worshiping other gods. **1 Kings 16:31** *page 417*

LIKE ELIJAH I know God will meet my needs even in the most desperate of circumstances. **1 Kings 19:18** *page 421*

LIKE ELISHA I experience the power of God in my own life. **2 Kings 2:14** *page 431*

UNLIKE GEHAZI I do not grasp wealth that rightly belongs to God or others. **2 Kings 5:22** *page 435*

LIKE JOSIAH I lead others by word and example to hear and obey God's Word. **2 Kings 23:25** *page 461*

LIKE JABEZ I know God wants to prosper me no matter how humble my birth. **1 Chronicles 4:10** *page 471*

UNLIKE ASA I want to be true to God to the very end. **2 Chronicles 16:9** *page 521*

LIKE JEHOSHAPHAT I face trials and danger with songs of praise for God's faithful love. **2 Chronicles 20:21** *page 527*

UNLIKE UZZIAH I humbly keep the Lord as king of my heart and life. **2 Chronicles 26:16** *page 533*

LIKE MANASSEH I know it's never too late to turn to God for forgiveness, no matter how horrible my sins. **2 Chronicles 33:13** *page 543*

LIKE HILKIAH I can experience the power of God's Word today. **2 Chronicles 34:14** *page 549*

LIKE EZRA I pray to God for safety and protection. **Ezra 8:21** *page 559*

LIKE NEHEMIAH I seek God's very best despite the obstacles in my way. **Nehemiah 1:11** *page 567*

LIKE ESTHER I act courageously even when I am afraid because I know that God is in control. **Esther 4:16** *page 591*

LIKE MORDECAI I use every opportunity to work for the good of others. **Esther 10:3** *page 593*

LIKE JOB I cling to God in the midst of my deepest pain. **Job 1:21** *page 599*

UNLIKE ELIPHAZ, BILDAD, AND ZOPHAR I do not assume God must be punishing those who suffer. **Job 4:7** *page 601*

UNLIKE ELIHU I do not presume I know God's reasons. **Job 32:10** *page 619*

LIKE DAVID I share my heart with God in any and every circumstance. **Psalm 3:1** *page 629*

LIKE ASAPH I turn to God when my faith is shaken. **Psalm 73:28** *page 687*

LIKE PHINEHAS I am willing to stand up for what's right. **Psalm 106:30** *page 717*

UNLIKE SOLOMON I apply the wisdom of God's Word to my everyday life. **Proverbs 2:9** *page 753*

LIKE ISAIAH I proclaim the Lord's salvation, knowing that I, too, need the Savior. **Isaiah 6:13** *page 801*

LIKE HEZEKIAH I go to God in prayer when I am attacked and the Lord is blasphemed. **Isaiah 37:1** *page 825*

LIKE JEREMIAH I continue to do God's will, even if many oppose me. **Jeremiah 1:19** *page 855*

LIKE JEHONADAB I refuse to compromise my integrity. **Jeremiah 35:19** *page 893*

LIKE BARUCH I am content to do God's will instead of longing for something more rewarding. **Jeremiah 45:5** *page 903*

LIKE EZEKIEL I long to experience God's glory and presence. **Ezekiel 1:28** *page 923*

LIKE DANIEL I remain true to God in the midst of compromising situations. **Daniel 1:21** *page 979*

LIKE SHADRACH, MESHACH, AND ABEDNEGO I will trust and worship God whether I experience physical deliverance or not. **Daniel 3:18** *page 981*

UNLIKE NEBUCHADNEZZAR I do not become arrogant, proud, and boastful. **Daniel 4:37** *page 985*

UNLIKE BELSHAZZAR I abhor the thought of defying the God of heaven. **Daniel 5:23** *page 987*

LIKE HOSEA I show how much God loves those who reject him. **Hosea 3:1** *page 1003*

UNLIKE JONAH I am glad God extends his love to even the most rebellious of people. **Jonah 4:2** *page 1027*

LIKE HABAKKUK I live by faith, not by sight. **Habakkuk 2:4** *page 1041*

LIKE JOSEPH I know God's ways are right and true. **Matthew 1:24** *page 1071*

LIKE THE MAGI I seek the Lord with all my heart. **Matthew 2:1** *page 1073*

LIKE MATTHEW I invite my friends to meet the Lord. **Matthew 9:9** *page 1081*

UNLIKE THE PHARISEES I am not a self-centered legalist. **Matthew 12:14** *page 1087*

UNLIKE THE SADDUCEES I am not a total skeptic. **Matthew 22:23** *page 1103*

LIKE PETER I know that no matter how often I let God down, he won't give up on me. **Matthew 26:75** *page 1111*

LIKE JOSEPH OF ARIMATHEA I don't hide my faith in the Lord Jesus. **Matthew 27:57** *page 1113*

LIKE JOHN THE BAPTIST I recognize and exalt the preeminence of the Lord Jesus. **Mark 1:4** *page 1117*

UNLIKE JUDAS I do not follow Jesus Christ out of selfish, ulterior motives. **Mark 3:19** *page 1121*

LIKE JAIRUS I believe God can do miracles. **Mark 5:23** *page 1123*

LIKE THE GENTILE WOMAN I persist in seeking God with my need, believing in his power and willingness to help me. **Mark 7:30** *page 1129*

UNLIKE THE RICH YOUNG MAN I let nothing stand in the way of coming to Jesus Christ. **Mark 10:22** *page 1133*

LIKE BLIND BARTIMAEUS I am confident that God delights in hearing and answering my prayers. **Mark 10:52** *page 1135*

LIKE THE POOR WIDOW I know that God will multiply my gifts a hundredfold. **Mark 12:42** *page 1139*

UNLIKE ZECHARIAH I do not doubt God's ability to answer my prayers. **Luke 1:18** *page 1147*

LIKE MARY I am the Lord's servant, willing to affirm whatever he says. **Luke 1:38** *page 1149*

LIKE THE SHEPHERDS I joyfully share the Good News with others. **Luke 2:17** *page 1151*

LIKE SIMEON AND ANNA I believe I will experience tremendous answers to prayer in my lifetime. **Luke 2:38** *page 1153*

LIKE MARY MAGDALENE I believe God can deliver me from any nightmare. **Luke 8:2** *page 1163*

LIKE THE GOOD SAMARITAN I do good to people from all walks of life. **Luke 10:35** *page 1169*

LIKE MARY AND MARTHA I have discovered my relationship with Jesus is more important than any job I could do for him. **Luke 10:42** *page 1171*

UNLIKE THE RICH FOOL I do not trust in wealth alone to make me happy. **Luke 12:20** *page 1173*

LIKE THE LOST SON I experience God's warm embrace and complete forgiveness. **Luke 15:21** *page 1179*

LIKE ZACCHAEUS I demonstrate my faith by making restitution and asking others for forgiveness. **Luke 19:10** *page 1185*

LIKE THE DYING THIEF I trust God today and receive forgiveness of sins and eternal life with God forever. **Luke 23:42** *page 1191*

LIKE CLEOPAS I look to God every time I break bread. **Luke 24:31** *page 1193*

LIKE ANDREW I tell others about the Lord Jesus. **John 1:42** *page 1199*

LIKE NATHANAEL I am known by the Lord and loved. **John 1:49** *page 1201*

LIKE NICODEMUS I must be born again by believing in Jesus Christ. **John 3:3** *page 1203*

LIKE THE SAMARITAN WOMAN I am satisfied because God knows, loves, and fills me. **John 4:14** *page 1205*

LIKE THE ADULTEROUS WOMAN I forsake my sin, because God has forgiven all my past. **John 8:11** *page 1211*

LIKE LAZARUS I believe God one day will raise me from the dead. **John 12:11** *page 1219*

UNLIKE PILATE I embrace God's truth wholeheartedly. **John 19:16** *page 1229*

LIKE THOMAS I claim Jesus as my Lord and my God. **John 20:28** *page 1231*

UNLIKE ANANIAS AND SAPPHIRA I do not try to fool God and others. **Acts 5:4** *page 1241*

LIKE STEPHEN I stand up for the Lord no matter what. **Acts 7:60** *page 1245*

UNLIKE SIMON THE SORCERER I do not view the Holy Spirit as a magical power to manipulate for my own purposes. **Acts 8:24** *page 1247*

LIKE ANANIAS I believe God can change the heart of even the hardest person. **Acts 9:17** *page 1249*

LIKE CORNELIUS I am so glad God's salvation is freely offered to all people. **Acts 10:33** *page 1251*

LIKE BARNABAS I encourage other brothers and sisters in Christ. **Acts 11:23** *page 1253*

LIKE JOHN MARK I do not let past failures keep me from serving God today. **Acts 13:13** *page 1255*

LIKE PRISCILLA AND AQUILA I help others understand God's truth better. **Acts 18:26** *page 1265*

LIKE PHILIP I can tell anyone about the Lord. **Acts 21:8** *page 1269*

UNLIKE AGRIPPA I do not want merely intellectual knowledge of the Lord. **Acts 26:28** *page 1275*

LIKE PAUL I earnestly strive to preserve the purity of the Good News of Jesus Christ. **Galatians 2:5** *page 1333*

LIKE EPAPHRODITUS I am willing to risk my life for the work of Jesus Christ. **Philippians 2:30** *page 1351*

LIKE TIMOTHY I am an example of godly living, even in my youth. **1 Timothy 4:12** *page 1373*

LIKE LUKE I make sure those who work hard for the Lord can depend on me for help and support. **2 Timothy 4:11** *page 1379*

LIKE TITUS I seek God's blessings for his church. **Titus 1:5** *page 1385*

LIKE PHILEMON I forgive past offenses in order to welcome someone into God's family. **Philemon 1:10** *page 1388*

LIKE JAMES I demonstrate my faith in God by living a good life for him. **James 2:18** *page 1407*

LIKE JOHN I wait expectantly for Jesus Christ to come again! **Revelation 1:9** *page 1435*

Truths to Believe

ABUNDANCE

I believe God blessed some Old Testament believers with great wealth and an abundance of other blessings.

Genesis 13:2 *page 16*

Genesis 24:1 *page 27*

Genesis 26:12-14 *page 32*

Genesis 32:9-10 *page 41*

1 Kings 3:13 *page 394*

1 Chronicles 29:1-4 *page 502*

Job 1:1-3 *page 598*

I believe God promised to give great abundance to all of his people if they obeyed his commands.

Deuteronomy 8:9 *page 215*

Deuteronomy 28:11, 47 *pages 234, 235*

Deuteronomy 30:9 *page 238*

Deuteronomy 33:15 *page 244*

Nehemiah 9:25 *page 576*

Psalm 36:8 *page 655*

Psalm 66:12 *page 678*

Proverbs 10:22 *page 759*

Malachi 3:11 *page 1066*

I believe the Lord desires to abundantly bless me spiritually.

John 10:10 *page 1215*

John 16:24 *page 1224*

Romans 5:20 *page 1284*

Ephesians 1:3-18 *pages 1339-1340*

APPEARING

I believe the Lord appeared to some Old Testament believers.

Genesis 3:8 *page 6*

Genesis 18:1 *page 20*

Genesis 26:23 *page 32*

Genesis 28:13 *page 36*

Exodus 3:2 *page 70*

Exodus 33:11, 21-23 *page 108*

Numbers 11:16 *page 170*

Joshua 5:13-14 *page 252*

Judges 6:12 *page 285*

1 Kings 3:5 *page 394*

1 Kings 19:5-9 *pages 419-420*

Isaiah 6:1 *page 800*

Ezekiel 1:1 *page 922*

Acts 7:2, 30 *pages 1242, 1243*

I believe the Lord appeared to his people during the exodus from Egypt.

Exodus 19:11 *page 90*

Exodus 20:20 *page 92*

Leviticus 9:23 *page 128*

Numbers 9:15 *page 168*

Numbers 14:10, 14 *page 173*

Numbers 16:19, 42 *pages 177, 178*

Numbers 20:6 *page 181*

Deuteronomy 31:15 *page 239*

I believe Jesus, God's Son, came in human appearance and lived here on earth for more than thirty years.

Luke 3:23 *page 1152*

John 1:1-18 *pages 1197-1198*

Philippians 2:7 *page 1349*

1 Timothy 3:16 *page 1372*

Hebrews 1:1-3 *page 1390*

I believe Jesus repeatedly appeared to his disciples after his resurrection from the dead.

Matthew 28:16 *page 1113*

Luke 24:36 *page 1194*

John 20:19, 26 *page 1129*

John 21:1 *page 1230*

Acts 10:40 *page 1250*

1 Corinthians 15:3-8 *page 1314*

I believe Jesus will appear once more.
Matthew 24:30 *page 1104*
2 Thessalonians 1:7 *page 1365*
2 Timothy 4:1 *page 1380*

2 Peter 1:19 *page 1418*
Revelation 19:11 *page 1450*

ASSURANCE

I believe Jesus assured his disciples of many important truths.
Matthew 5:18, 26 *pages 1075, 1076*
Matthew 11:11 *page 1084*
Matthew 13:17 *page 1088*
Matthew 24:2 *page 1104*
Mark 10:15 *page 1132*
Mark 12:43 *page 1138*

Luke 12:8 *page 1172*
Luke 18:29-30 *page 1182*
John 3:3 *page 1201*
John 6:32 *page 1207*
John 8:34 *page 1212*
John 10:7 *page 1214*

AWESOME

I believe God's presence is awesome.
Genesis 31:53 *page 41*
Exodus 15:11 *page 85*
Exodus 16:10 *page 86*
2 Chronicles 2:5 *page 507*

Psalm 68:35 *page 681*
Psalm 89:7 *page 701*
Isaiah 6:1-5 *page 800*

I believe God's deeds are awesome.
Deuteronomy 4:34 *page 211*
2 Samuel 7:23 *page 363*
1 Chronicles 17:21 *page 490*

Psalm 65:5 *page 677*
Psalm 66:3 *page 678*
Psalm 77:14 *page 690*

I believe God's judgments are awesome.
Deuteronomy 5:25 *page 212*
Psalm 90:11 *page 703*
Lamentations 2:1 *page 916*

Joel 2:11 *page 1012*
Zephaniah 1:7 *page 1044*

BAPTISM

I believe Jesus was revealed as God's Son by his baptism.
Matthew 3:13-17 *page 1073*
Mark 1:9-11 *page 1116*
Luke 3:21-22 *page 1152*

John 1:29-34 *page 1198*
1 John 5:6 *page 1425*

I believe water baptism is an important step of discipleship—and an act of obedience to Jesus Christ.
Matthew 28:19 *page 1113*
Acts 2:38 *page 1236*

Acts 22:16 *page 1269*

I believe the early church baptized new believers in water.
Acts 2:41 *page 1237*
Acts 8:12, 38 *pages 1245, 1246*
Acts 9:18 *page 1247*
Acts 10:48 *page 1251*

Acts 16:15, 33 *page 1260*
Acts 18:8 *page 1263*
Acts 19:5 *page 1264*

I believe the Holy Spirit baptizes all believers.
Matthew 3:11 *page 1073*
Mark 1:8 *page 1116*
Luke 3:16 *page 1152*

John 1:33 *page 1198*
Acts 11:16 *page 1252*
Romans 6:4 *page 1285*

BLESSING
I believe God longs to bless his people if they believe him, obey his commands, and do what he says.

Matthew 5:3-11 *page 1075*
Matthew 11:6 *page 1084*
Luke 6:20-23 *page 1159*
Luke 7:23 *page 1161*
John 13:17 *page 1220*
John 20:29 *page 1230*

Galatians 6:9 *page 1338*
Ephesians 1:3 *page 1339*
James 1:12 *page 1406*
Revelation 1:3 *page 1434*
Revelation 22:7 *page 1453*

BLOOD
I believe the blood Jesus shed on the cross cleanses me from all sin.

Matthew 26:28 *page 1108*
Mark 14:24 *page 1140*
Luke 22:20 *page 1188*
John 19:34 *page 1228*
Acts 20:28 *page 1266*
Romans 3:25 *page 1283*
Romans 5:9 *page 1285*
1 Corinthians 11:25 *page 1310*
Ephesians 1:7 *page 1340*
Ephesians 2:13 *page 1341*

Colossians 1:14, 20 *page 1354*
Hebrews 9:14, 22 *page 1397*
Hebrews 10:4, 19-22 *pages 1398, 1399*
Hebrews 13:12, 20-21 *pages 1403, 1404*
1 Peter 1:2 *page 1411*
1 John 1:7 *page 1422*
1 John 5:6-8 *page 1425*
Revelation 1:5 *page 1434*
Revelation 5:9 *page 1439*

BODY
I believe Jesus had a physical human body.

Matthew 1:18-25 *pages 1070–1071*
Matthew 8:24 *page 1080*
Luke 2:52 *page 1151*
Luke 22:8 *page 1188*
John 1:14 *page 1198*

John 4:6-7 *page 1202*
Romans 8:3 *page 1287*
Hebrews 10:5 *page 1398*
1 John 1:1 *page 1422*
2 John 1:7 *page 1427*

I believe Jesus gave his body as a sacrifice for my sins.

Matthew 20:28 *page 1098*
Romans 8:3 *page 1287*
Ephesians 5:2 *page 1343*

Hebrews 10:10 *page 1398*
1 Peter 2:24 *page 1414*
1 John 2:2 *page 1422*

I believe that Jesus' body was buried for three days and then he rose from the dead.

Matthew 12:40 *page 1086*
Matthew 16:21 *page 1903*
Mark 15:42–16:6 *pages 1143–1144*
Luke 23:50–24:6 *pages 1192–1193*

John 19:38–20:16 *pages 1228–1229*
Acts 13:37 *page 1256*
Romans 10:9 *page 1291*
1 Corinthians 15:4 *page 1314*

I understand that all believers belong to the body of Christ.

Romans 12:5 *page 1293*
1 Corinthians 12:13 *page 1311*

Ephesians 1:23 *page 1340*
Colossians 1:18 *page 1354*

I believe I will receive a new body when Christ comes again.

1 Corinthians 15:35-58 *pages 1315–1316*
2 Corinthians 5:1 *page 1323*

1 Thessalonians 4:13-18 *page 1362*

BORN AGAIN
I believe someone must be born again to become part of God's family forever.

John 1:12-13 *page 1198*
John 3:3-7 *page 1201*
1 Peter 1:3, 23 *page 1412*

1 John 3:9 *page 1424*
1 John 4:7 *page 1425*

BURIAL

I believe Jesus died, was buried, and rose again from the dead three days later.

Isaiah 53:9 *page 842*

Matthew 27:60 *page 1112*

Mark 15:46-47 *page 1144*

Mark 16:6 *page 1144*

Luke 23:53 *page 1192*

John 19:42 *page 1228*

1 Corinthians 15:4 *page 1314*

CALLING

I believe I can count on the Lord to respond when I call on him.

Deuteronomy 4:7 *page 210*

2 Samuel 22:7 *page 382*

Job 12:4 *page 606*

Psalm 4:3 *page 630*

Psalm 31:17 *page 650*

Psalm 34:17 *page 652*

Psalm 55:16 *page 671*

Psalm 86:7 *page 699*

Psalm 91:15 *page 704*

Psalm 102:2 *page 709*

Psalm 116:4 *page 724*

Psalm 130:1 *page 736*

Isaiah 58:9 *page 845*

Isaiah 59:1 *page 846*

Isaiah 65:24 *page 851*

Lamentations 3:55 *page 918*

Habakkuk 1:2 *page 1040*

Zechariah 13:9 *page 1060*

Acts 4:12 *page 1238*

Romans 10:14 *page 1291*

CHOOSING

I choose to love the Lord, live for him, and enjoy his rich blessings.

Deuteronomy 30:19-20 *page 238*

Joshua 24:15 *page 275*

Psalm 25:12 *page 645*

Psalm 65:4 *page 677*

Proverbs 22:6 *page 770*

Isaiah 56:4 *page 844*

Romans 6:16-19 *page 1286*

CHURCH

I believe the early church suffered intense persecution.

Acts 8:1 *page 1244*

Acts 12:1 *page 1252*

1 Corinthians 15:9 *page 1314*

Philippians 3:10 *page 1350*

Colossians 1:24 *page 1354*

I believe the Lord is blessing and building his church for his glory.

Matthew 16:18 *page 1093*

1 Corinthians 12:5-7 *page 1311*

1 Corinthians 14:4-19 *pages 1312–1313*

Ephesians 1:22-23 *page 1340*

Ephesians 4:11-15 *page 1342*

Colossians 1:18-25 *page 1354*

COMPASSION

I believe God is compassionate.

Deuteronomy 13:17 *page 221*

Psalm 25:6 *page 645*

Psalm 51:1 *page 667*

Psalm 103:13 *page 711*

Psalm 145:9 *page 746*

Isaiah 30:18 *page 820*

Isaiah 49:13 *page 839*

Isaiah 54:8 *page 842*

Jonah 4:2 *page 1028*

Luke 15:20 *page 1178*

CONDEMNATION

I believe God will judge the wicked who refuse to repent.

Genesis 19:24-25 *page 23*

Deuteronomy 28:15-19 *page 234*

Joshua 24:20 *page 275*

Psalm 26:9 *page 646*

Isaiah 1:20 *page 796*

Jeremiah 15:6 *page 870*

Romans 2:5-6 *page 1281*

COVENANT

I believe God made covenants with some of the great Old Testament believers.

Genesis 9:9-17 *page 12*
Genesis 15:18 *page 18*
Genesis 26:23-25 *page 32*
Genesis 28:13-15 *page 36*
Exodus 2:4 *page 68*
Exodus 19:5 *page 90*

Leviticus 2:13 *page 120*
Numbers 1:53 *page 156*
Deuteronomy 4:13 *page 210*
Joshua 7:11 *page 254*
Judges 2:1 *page 279*
2 Samuel 23:5 *page 384*

I believe the Lord has kept his promise to make a new covenant with his people—with those who trust in him.

Isaiah 55:3 *page 843*
Isaiah 59:21 *page 846*
Isaiah 61:8 *page 848*
Jeremiah 31:31 *page 888*
Ezekiel 16:60 *page 936*
Matthew 26:28 *page 1108*

Mark 14:24 *page 1140*
Luke 22:20 *page 1188*
1 Corinthians 11:3 *page 1309*
2 Corinthians 3:6 *page 1321*
Hebrews 8:6 *page 1396*
Hebrews 12:24 *page 1402*

CREATION

I believe creation still suffers the effects of humanity's fall into sin.

Genesis 3:17-19 *page 6*
Isaiah 24:5-6 *page 814*
Jeremiah 12:4 *page 867*

Hosea 4:3 *page 1002*
Romans 8:19 *page 1288*

I believe God one day will make new heavens and a new earth!

Isaiah 65:17 *page 850*
Isaiah 66:22 *page 852*
Haggai 2:6 *page 1048*
Hebrews 12:26-27 *page 1403*

2 Peter 3:13 *page 1420*
Revelation 20:11 *page 1451*
Revelation 21:1 *page 1451*

DARKNESS

I believe those who refuse to repent are in darkness and face God's terrible judgment.

Psalm 35:6 *page 653*
Proverbs 2:13 *page 753*
Isaiah 8:22 *page 802*
Hebrews 12:18 *page 1402*

2 Peter 2:4, 17 *pages 1418, 1419*
Jude 1:6, 13 *pages 1431, 1432*
Revelation 16:10 *page 1447*

DEATH

I believe the wages of sin is death.

Genesis 2:17 *page 5*
Genesis 3:3-4 *page 6*
Genesis 5:5 *page 8*
Numbers 16:38 *page 177*
Deuteronomy 30:15-20 *page 238*
Joshua 1:18 *page 248*
Proverbs 10:16 *page 759*
Proverbs 11:18-19 *page 760*
Isaiah 22:14 *page 813*

Ezekiel 18:4, 9, 13, 17 *pages 937, 938*
Romans 1:32 *page 1281*
Romans 5:12 *page 1285*
Romans 6:16, 21-23 *page 1286*
Romans 7:5 *page 1286*
Romans 8:2, 6, 13 *pages 1287, 1288*
Galatians 6:8 *page 1338*
2 Peter 2:12-13 *page 1419*

I believe the Lord Jesus was raised from the dead three days after his crucifixion.

Matthew 12:40 *page 1086*
Matthew 16:21 *page 1093*
Matthew 28:6 *page 1112*
Mark 15:42-16:6 *pages 1143-1144*
Luke 23:50-24:6 *pages 1192-1193*

John 19:38-20:16 *pages 1228-1229*
Acts 13:37 *page 1256*
Romans 10:9 *page 1291*
1 Corinthians 15:4 *page 1314*

I believe God doesn't want any to perish but all to repent and choose life.

Exodus 34:6 *page 108*

Deuteronomy 30:15, 19 *page 238*

Isaiah 30:18 *page 820*

Romans 2:4 *page 1281*

1 Timothy 1:16 *page 1370*

1 Timothy 2:4 *page 1371*

2 Peter 3:9 *page 1420*

I believe God one day will destroy death.

Isaiah 25:8 *page 815*

Hosea 13:14 *page 1008*

Luke 20:36 *page 1186*

1 Corinthians 15:26, 54-56 *pages 1315, 1316*

Revelation 1:18 *page 1434*

Revelation 20:14 *page 1451*

DEEDS

I believe God will judge each person's deeds—good or bad.

Psalm 62:12 *page 676*

Proverbs 24:12 *page 772*

Ecclesiastes 12:14 *page 788*

Isaiah 3:10-11 *page 798*

Isaiah 59:18 *page 846*

Jeremiah 17:10 *page 873*

Jeremiah 21:14 *page 876*

Jeremiah 32:19 *page 889*

Ezekiel 7:3, 9, 27 *pages 926, 927*

Ezekiel 18:30 *page 938*

Ezekiel 24:14 *page 946*

Ezekiel 33:20 *page 956*

Ezekiel 36:19 *page 959*

Ezekiel 39:24 *page 963*

Matthew 12:36 *page 1086*

Matthew 16:27 *page 1903*

Romans 14:12 *page 1295*

1 Corinthians 3:8, 13-15 *page 1302*

1 Corinthians 4:5 *page 1303*

2 Corinthians 5:10 *page 1323*

Ephesians 6:8 *page 1344*

Colossians 3:24-25 *page 1356*

1 Peter 4:5 *page 1415*

Revelation 2:23 *page 1436*

Revelation 20:12-13 *page 1451*

Revelation 22:12 *page 1453*

ETERNALITY

I believe God is eternal, without beginning or end.

Genesis 21:33 *page 25*

Psalm 90:2 *page 703*

Psalm 93:2 *page 705*

Psalm 102:24-27 *page 710*

Isaiah 40:28 *page 830*

Isaiah 44:6 *page 834*

Micah 5:2 *page 1032*

1 Timothy 1:17 *page 1370*

Revelation 1:8 *page 1434*

I believe God's Word is eternal—it will never disappear.

Psalm 119:89, 152, 160 *pages 730, 731*

Isaiah 40:7 *pages 829, 830*

Matthew 5:18 *page 1075*

Matthew 24:35 *page 1105*

1 Peter 1:25 *page 1413*

I believe God's kingdom is eternal.

Psalm 10:16 *page 634*

Psalm 145:13 *page 746*

Isaiah 9:7 *page 804*

Jeremiah 10:10 *page 865*

Daniel 2:44 *page 981*

Daniel 4:34 *page 985*

Daniel 7:14 *page 990*

Micah 4:7 *page 1032*

Luke 1:33 *page 1146*

Revelation 11:15 *page 1443*

I believe nothing is more pressing or urgent than for someone to make sure he or she receives eternal life.

Isaiah 55:2 *page 843*

Habakkuk 2:13-14 *page 1041*

Matthew 19:16 *page 1096*

Luke 10:40-42 *page 1169*

John 6:27 *page 1207*

Acts 16:30-31 *page 1260*

1 Corinthians 7:30 *page 1306*

2 Corinthians 4:18 *page 1322*

Hebrews 12:16 *page 1402*

1 Peter 1:24-25 *page 1413*

I believe those who refuse to repent will face eternal destruction.
Isaiah 8:22 *page 803*
Matthew 25:41 *page 1106*
Philippians 3:19 *page 1350*
2 Thessalonians 1:9 *page 1365*

Hebrews 10:29 *page 1399*
2 Peter 2:4, 17 *pages 1418, 1419*
Jude 1:6, 13 *pages 1431, 1432*
Revelation 16:10 *page 1447*

EVIL

I believe God cannot tolerate evil in his presence.
Leviticus 22:3 *page 144*
Psalm 68:2 *page 679*
1 Corinthians 6:9-10 *page 1304*
Galatians 5:19-21 *page 1337*

2 Thessalonians 1:7-9 *page 1365*
Hebrews 10:22 *page 1399*
Revelation 21:27 *page 1452*

I believe Satan is the evil one—the author of all evil.
Matthew 6:13 *page 1077*
John 8:44 *page 1212*
Acts 13:10 *page 1254*

1 John 3:8, 12 *page 1424*
1 John 5:19 *page 1426*

I believe Satan has many evil spirits under his command.
Matthew 25:41 *page 1106*
Luke 9:1 *page 1165*

Jude 1:6 *page 1431*
Revelation 12:7-9 *page 1444*

I believe the world is filled with evil.
Ecclesiastes 3:16 *page 782*
Ecclesiastes 4:3 *page 782*
Jeremiah 17:9 *page 873*
John 16:8-9 *page 1223*

Ephesians 6:12 *page 1345*
1 John 2:15-16 *page 1423*
Revelation 21:4 *page 1451*

I believe people are naturally bent toward doing evil.
Psalm 14:2-3 *page 636*
Ecclesiastes 7:20, 29 *pages 784, 785*
Isaiah 53:6 *page 842*
Isaiah 59:4-8 *page 846*
Isaiah 64:6 *page 849*
Jeremiah 17:9 *page 873*
Romans 3:10-12 *page 1282*

Romans 8:7 *page 1287*
Matthew 15:19 *page 1091*
Galatians 5:19-21 *page 1337*
Ephesians 2:1-2 *page 1340*
Colossians 3:5-7 *page 1356*
Titus 3:3 *page 1385*
1 John 1:8 *page 1422*

I believe God urges sinners to turn from their wicked ways.
Exodus 34:6 *page 108*
Deuteronomy 30:15, 19 *page 238*
Isaiah 30:18 *page 820*
Romans 2:4 *page 1281*

1 Timothy 1:16 *page 1370*
1 Timothy 2:4 *page 1371*
2 Peter 3:9 *page 1420*

FAITH

I believe Abraham is the father of all who place their faith in God.
Genesis 15:6 *page 18*
Luke 19:9 *page 1183*
Romans 4:3, 9, 20-22 *pages 1283, 1284*

Galatians 3:6-7 *page 1334*
Hebrews 11:8-11, 17 *page 1400*
James 2:23 *page 1408*

I believe not everyone has the same amount of faith—some have little faith, and some have great faith.
Matthew 6:30 *page 1078*
Matthew 8:10 *page 1079*
Matthew 17:20 *page 1094*
Acts 6:5 *page 1242*

Acts 11:22-24 *page 1252*
1 Corinthians 12:9 *page 1311*
2 Corinthians 10:15 *page 1327*
James 2:5 *page 1406*

FORGIVENESS

I believe the Lord Jesus has the authority to forgive sins.

Matthew 9:6 *page 1080*
Luke 7:48 *page 1162*
Acts 5:31 *page 1240*

Acts 13:38 *page 1256*
Hebrews 12:24 *page 1402*

FULFILLMENT

I believe God fulfills all of his promises.

Deuteronomy 7:9 *page 214*
Deuteronomy 8:18 *page 215*
Deuteronomy 9:5 *page 216*
Joshua 14:10 *page 263*
1 Kings 8:15, 24 *page 401*
Nehemiah 1:5 *page 566*

Nehemiah 9:32 *page 577*
Psalm 146:6 *page 747*
Lamentations 2:17 *page 917*
Daniel 9:4 *page 992*
2 Corinthians 1:20 *page 1320*

I believe God fulfills all his prophecies.

Exodus 8:24 *page 77*
Deuteronomy 34:5 *page 245*
1 Samuel 28:17 *page 351*
2 Kings 23:26-27 *page 461*
2 Chronicles 36:21 *page 548*
Jeremiah 32:8 *page 889*
Jeremiah 40:2-3 *page 898*

Zechariah 1:6 *page 1052*
Matthew 26:24 *page 1107*
Matthew 26:56 *page 1109*
Mark 9:13 *page 1130*
Luke 24:25-27 *page 1194*
John 17:12 *page 1224*

GIFTS

I believe every Christian should exercise his or her spiritual gift.

Romans 12:7-8 *page 1294*
1 Corinthians 1:7 *page 1300*
1 Corinthians 12:7 *page 1311*

Ephesians 4:7 *page 1342*
1 Timothy 4:14 *page 1372*
1 Peter 4:10 *page 1415*

GLORY

I believe the glory of the Lord appeared often in Old Testament times.

Exodus 16:7, 10 *page 86*
Exodus 24:17 *page 97*
Exodus 40:35 *page 117*

Ezekiel 1:28 *page 922*
Ezekiel 3:23 *page 924*

I believe the earth is filled with the Lord's glory.

Numbers 14:21 *page 174*
Psalm 8:1 *page 632*

Isaiah 6:3 *page 800*

I believe the Lord Jesus is seated on a glorious throne at God the Father's right hand.

Matthew 19:28 *page 1097*
Matthew 25:31 *page 1106*
Acts 2:33 *page 1236*
Ephesians 1:20 *page 1340*

Hebrews 1:3 *page 1390*
Hebrews 8:1 *page 1396*
Hebrews 10:12 *page 1398*

I believe the Lord Jesus one day will return with majesty and glory.

Matthew 16:27 *page 1093*
Matthew 24:30, 64 *page 1104*
Acts 1:11 *page 1234*

Philippians 2:10-11 *page 1348*
2 Thessalonians 1:7-8 *page 1365*
Revelation 22:12 *page 1453*

I believe all glory belongs to the Lord forever and ever.

1 Chronicles 16:29 *page 488*
1 Chronicles 29:11 *page 503*
Psalm 8:1 *page 632*
Psalm 29:1 *page 648*
Psalm 86:12 *page 699*
Psalm 96:8 *page 707*

Psalm 113:4 *page 723*
Psalm 115:1 *page 723*
Psalm 148:13 *page 748*
Isaiah 42:8 *page 832*
Jude 1:25 *page 1432*
Revelation 4:11 *page 1438*

GOODNESS

I believe God is good.

1 Chronicles 16:34 *page 488*
Psalm 25:8 *page 645*
Psalm 31:19 *page 650*
Psalm 34:8 *page 652*
Psalm 35:28 *page 654*
Psalm 86:5 *page 699*
Psalm 92:15 *page 705*

Psalm 129:4 *page 736*
Psalm 135:3 *page 738*
Nahum 1:7 *page 1036*
Matthew 19:17 *page 1096*
1 Peter 2:9 *page 1413*
2 Peter 1:3 *page 1417*

I believe no one is good—unless God makes them good, righteous, and pure.

1 Kings 8:46 *page 402*
2 Chronicles 6:36 *page 511*
Psalm 14:1-3 *page 636*
Psalm 53:1-4 *page 669*
Psalm 143:2 *page 744*
Proverbs 20:9 *page 768*
Ecclesiastes 7:20 *page 784*

Jeremiah 2:29 *page 856*
Jeremiah 5:1-9 *page 859*
Jeremiah 6:28 *page 861*
Micah 7:2 *page 1034*
Romans 3:10-12 *page 1282*
James 3:2 *page 1408*
1 John 1:8, 10 *page 1422*

I believe in the Lord and do what is good as a demonstration of my faith.

Psalm 34:14 *page 652*
Psalm 37:3 *page 655*
Isaiah 1:17 *page 796*
Amos 5:14 *page 1019*
Matthew 5:16 *page 1075*
Luke 6:27 *page 1159*
Romans 6:4 *page 1285*
Romans 13:12 *page 1295*
Galatians 5:6 *page 1337*
Galatians 6:10 *page 1338*

Ephesians 2:10 *page 1341*
Ephesians 4:24 *page 1343*
1 Thessalonians 5:15 *page 1363*
Titus 2:14 *page 1384*
Titus 3:8 *page 1385*
Hebrews 13:16 *page 1403*
James 1:22 *page 1406*
1 Peter 3:11 *page 1415*
1 John 2:5 *page 1422*
3 John 11 *page 1429*

GRACE

I am saved by God's grace.

John 3:36 *page 1202*
Romans 6:23 *page 1286*
2 Corinthians 4:15 *page 1322*

Ephesians 2:5, 8 *pages 1340, 1341*
1 Peter 1:3 *page 1412*

HEAVEN

I believe God one day will make new heavens and a new earth!

Isaiah 65:17 *page 850*
Isaiah 66:22 *page 852*
Haggai 2:6 *page 1048*
Hebrews 12:26-27 *page 1403*

2 Peter 3:13 *page 1420*
Revelation 20:11 *page 1451*
Revelation 21:1 *page 1451*

I believe I will receive a new body and spend eternity with God in the new heavens and new earth.

John 14:2-3 *page 1221*
1 Corinthians 15:35-58 *pages 1315–1316*
2 Corinthians 5:1 *page 1323*

1 Thessalonians 4:13-18 *page 1362*
2 Peter 3:13 *page 1420*
Revelation 21:1 *page 1451*

HELL

I believe in the reality of hell.

Job 31:12 *page 617*
Proverbs 2:18 *page 753*
Matthew 5:22, 29-30 *pages 1075, 1076*
Matthew 7:13 *page 1078*
Matthew 10:28 *page 1083*

Matthew 16:18 *page 1093*
Matthew 18:9 *page 1095*
Matthew 23:15, 33 *pages 1102, 1103*
Mark 9:43-47 *page 1131*
Luke 12:5 *page 1172*

Romans 8:38 *page 1289*
James 3:6 *page 1408*

James 5:3 *page 1409*
2 Peter 2:4 *page 1418*

HOLINESS
I believe God is absolutely holy.
Exodus 3:2-5 *page 70*
Exodus 15:11 *page 85*
Exodus 19:16-24 *page 91*
Leviticus 11:44 *page 131*
1 Samuel 6:20 *page 323*

Psalm 99:5 *page 708*
Isaiah 6:3 *page 800*
Isaiah 57:15 *page 845*
Revelation 4:8 *page 1438*
Revelation 15:4 *page 1447*

I believe only those who are holy will live in God's presence forever.
Psalm 15:1-5 *page 636*
Matthew 5:8 *page 1075*
1 Corinthians 1:30 *page 1301*
Ephesians 1:4-5 *page 1340*
Ephesians 5:25-27 *page 1344*

Colossians 1:19-22 *page 1354*
1 Thessalonians 3:13 *page 1361*
Hebrews 10:10-14, 22 *pages 1398, 1399*
Hebrews 13:12 *page 1403*

HOLY SPIRIT
I believe the Holy Spirit inspired the Scriptures.
2 Samuel 23:2 *page 384*
Nehemiah 9:20, 30 *pages 576, 577*
Ezekiel 2:2 *page 923*
Ezekiel 11:2 *page 930*
Micah 3:8 *page 1031*
Zechariah 7:12 *page 1056*
Matthew 22:43 *page 1102*

Mark 12:36 *page 1137*
Acts 1:16 *page 1234*
Acts 4:25 *page 1239*
Ephesians 6:17 *page 1345*
2 Timothy 3:16 *page 1380*
Hebrews 1:1 *page 1390*
2 Peter 1:21 *page 1418*

I believe the Holy Spirit filled some believers temporarily before Jesus Christ's ascension to heaven.
Exodus 31:3 *page 104*
Exodus 35:31 *page 111*
Numbers 11:17 *page 170*
Judges 3:10 *page 280*
Judges 6:34 *page 286*
Judges 11:29 *page 294*
Judges 13:25 *page 297*
Judges 14:6, 19 *pages 297, 298*

Judges 15:14 *page 298*
1 Samuel 10:6 *page 327*
1 Samuel 16:13 *page 335*
2 Chronicles 20:14 *page 525*
Ezekiel 11:5 *page 930*
Micah 3:8 *page 1031*
Matthew 1:18 *page 1070*
John 20:22 *page 1229*

I believe the Holy Spirit lives within every believer today.
John 7:39 *page 1210*
Acts 2:4, 17 *page 1235*
Acts 10:45 *page 1250*
Romans 8:9 *page 1287*
1 Corinthians 2:12 *page 1301*
1 Corinthians 3:16-17 *page 1302*

2 Corinthians 1:22 *page 1320*
Galatians 3:2 *page 1334*
Ephesians 1:13 *page 1340*
Titus 3:5-6 *page 1385*
1 John 3:24 *page 1424*
1 John 4:13 *page 1425*

HONOR
I believe Jesus is seated in honor at God the Father's right hand.
Psalm 110:1 *page 721*
Matthew 19:28 *page 1097*
Matthew 22:44 *page 1102*
Matthew 25:31 *page 1106*
Mark 12:36 *page 1137*
Mark 16:19 *page 1144*
Luke 20:42 *page 1186*
Acts 2:33-34 *page 1236*

Acts 5:31 *page 1240*
Acts 7:55-56 *page 1244*
Romans 8:34 *page 1288*
Ephesians 1:20 *page 1340*
Hebrews 1:3 *page 1390*
Hebrews 8:1 *page 1396*
Hebrews 10:12 *page 1398*

I believe Jesus is deserving of all honor, glory, and praise.

John 5:23 *page 1206*

2 Thessalonians 1:12 *page 1366*

1 Timothy 6:15-16 *page 1374*

Hebrews 1:6 *page 1390*

2 Peter 1:17 *page 1418*

2 Peter 3:18 *page 1420*

Revelation 5:12-13 *page 1439*

HUMILITY

I believe God blesses those who are humble.

Psalm 18:27 *page 639*

Psalm 138:6 *page 741*

Psalm 147:6 *page 747*

Psalm 149:4 *page 749*

Proverbs 3:34 *page 754*

Isaiah 29:19 *page 819*

Isaiah 57:15 *page 845*

Isaiah 66:2 *page 851*

Matthew 23:12 *page 1102*

James 4:6 *page 1409*

1 Peter 5:5 *page 1416*

JEALOUSY

I believe God is jealous for my wholehearted commitment and love.

Exodus 20:5 *page 91*

Deuteronomy 4:24 *page 210*

Deuteronomy 5:9 *page 212*

Deuteronomy 6:15 *page 213*

Joshua 24:19 *page 275*

Psalm 78:58 *page 693*

Ezekiel 5:13 *page 925*

1 Corinthians 10:22 *page 1309*

2 Corinthians 11:2 *page 1328*

James 4:5 *page 1409*

JESUS CHRIST

I believe Jesus created all that is.

John 1:3 *page 1197*

1 Corinthians 8:5-6 *page 1307*

Colossians 1:15-16 *page 1354*

Hebrews 1:2 *page 1390*

I believe Jesus came to earth and lived here for more than thirty years.

Matthew 1:18 *page 1070*

Luke 2:7 *page 1149*

Luke 3:23 *page 1152*

John 1:14 *page 1198*

Hebrews 2:14 *page 1391*

I believe Jesus is eternally and fully God and that more than two thousand years ago he became fully human, too.

John 1:1, 14, 18 *pages 1197, 1198*

John 14:9 *page 1221*

2 Corinthians 4:4 *page 1322*

Philippians 2:6-8 *page 1349*

Colossians 1:15-16 *page 1354*

Hebrews 1:2 *page 1390*

1 John 1:1 *page 1422*

I believe Jesus performed many great miracles while here on earth.

Matthew 8:3 *page 1079*

Mark 3:8 *page 1119*

Luke 19:37 *page 1184*

John 2:23 *page 1200*

John 12:37 *page 1219*

I believe Jesus proclaimed Good News to humanity.

Matthew 4:17, 23 *page 1074*

Matthew 9:35 *page 1082*

Matthew 11:5 *page 1084*

Mark 1:14 *page 1116*

Luke 4:18, 43 *pages 1155, 1156*

Luke 20:1 *page 1184*

I believe Jesus was crucified on the cross in my place for my sins.

Isaiah 53:8, 12 *page 842*

Mark 10:45 *page 1134*

Romans 4:23-25 *page 1284*

1 Corinthians 15:3-5 *page 1314*

1 Peter 2:24 *page 1414*

I believe Jesus offers eternal life to any who trust him.

John 3:16, 36 *page 1202*

John 5:24 *page 1206*

John 6:40 *page 1208*

John 11:25-26 *page 1216*

John 20:31 *page 1230*   1 John 5:13 *page 1425*
1 Timothy 1:16 *page 1370*

I believe Jesus forgives the sins of all who trust him.
Mark 2:3-12 *page 1118*   Acts 10:43 *page 1250*
John 5:24 *page 1206*   Romans 3:22-26 *page 1283*

I believe Jesus gives the right to become children of God to all who trust him.
John 1:12 *page 1198*   Ephesians 1:5 *page 1340*
Romans 8:14 *page 1288*   Ephesians 5:1 *page 1343*
2 Corinthians 6:18 *page 1324*   Hebrews 2:10 *page 1391*
Galatians 3:26 *page 1335*   1 John 3:1 *page 1423*

I believe Jesus is coming back to earth one day.
Matthew 16:27 *page 1093*
Matthew 24:30 *page 1104*   1 Thessalonians 4:14 *page 1362*
Matthew 25:31 *page 1106*   2 Thessalonians 1:7-8 *page 1365*
Mark 8:38 *page 1129*   Titus 2:13 *page 1384*
John 14:1-3 *page 1221*   Hebrews 9:28 *page 1398*
Acts 1:11 *page 1234*   2 Peter 3:10 *page 1420*

JUDGMENT

I believe the Lord is and will be the judge of all, living and dead.
Genesis 18:25 *page 21*   John 9:39 *page 1214*
Deuteronomy 32:36 *page 242*   Acts 10:42 *page 1250*
Psalm 7:8, 11 *page 632*   Romans 2:16 *page 1281*
Psalm 9:7-8 *page 633*   1 Corinthians 5:13 *page 1304*
Psalm 50:6 *page 667*   2 Corinthians 5:10 *page 1323*
Psalm 62:12 *page 676*   2 Timothy 4:1, 8 *pages 1380, 1381*
Psalm 75:7 *page 689*   Hebrews 12:23 *page 1402*
Psalm 96:13 *page 707*   James 5:9 *page 1410*
Proverbs 24:12 *page 772*   1 Peter 2:12 *page 1413*
Isaiah 33:22 *page 823*   2 Peter 3:10 *page 1420*
Matthew 19:28 *page 1097*   Revelation14:7 *page 1446*

I believe individuals need to exercise great care when they are put in a position to judge others who are accused of breaking the law.
Leviticus 19:15 *page 141*   Proverbs 18:5 *page 766*
Deuteronomy 16:18 *page 224*   Proverbs 24:23-25 *page 772*
1 Samuel 16:7 *page 335*   1 Corinthians 5:12-13 *page 1304*

I believe Christians need to exercise great care in judging fellow believers.
Matthew 7:1-2 *page 1078*   1 Corinthians 6:2 *page 1304*
Luke 6:37 *page 1159*   2 Corinthians 2:6 *page 1321*
1 Corinthians 5:12 *page 1304*   Galatians 6:1 *page 1338*

I believe Christians will help the Lord judge the world and angelic beings.
Luke 22:30 *page 1189*   Revelation 20:4 *page 1451*
1 Corinthians 6:2-3 *page 1304*

JUSTICE

I believe God is just in all he does.
Deuteronomy 32:4 *page 240*   Psalm 101:1 *page 709*
Ezra 9:15 *page 561*   Psalm 103:6 *page 711*
Psalm 7:17 *page 632*   Isaiah 1:27 *page 797*
Psalm 9:16 *page 633*   Isaiah 5:16 *page 800*
Psalm 11:7 *page 635*   Isaiah 61:8 *page 848*
Psalm 45:6 *page 663*   Jeremiah 9:24 *page 865*

Jeremiah 11:20 *page 867*
Romans 2:5 *page 1281*

Romans 3:25 *page 1283*
1 John 1:9 *page 1422*

I believe God calls us to do what is right and just.

Genesis 18:19 *page 21*
Exodus 23:6 *page 95*
Deuteronomy 16:19-20 *page 224*
Deuteronomy 24:17 *page 231*
Proverbs 31:8-9 *page 778*

Isaiah 1:17 *page 796*
Hosea 12:6 *page 1008*
Amos 5:24 *page 1019*
Micah 6:8 *page 1033*

I believe God will judge those who pervert justice.

Exodus 23:6 *page 95*
2 Chronicles 19:7 *page 524*
Isaiah 5:23-24 *page 800*

Amos 2:6 *page 1016*
Matthew 23:23 *page 1102*

KINGDOM

I believe the Lord God is King over all.

1 Chronicles 16:31 *page 488*
Psalm 2:4 *page 628*
Psalm 9:7 *page 633*
Psalm 10:16 *page 634*
Psalm 11:4 *page 635*
Psalm 22:28 *page 643*
Psalm 29:10 *page 648*
Psalm 47:8 *page 664*
Psalm 93:1 *page 705*

Psalm 97:1 *page 707*
Psalm 99:1 *page 708*
Psalm 103:19 *page 711*
Psalm 146:10 *page 747*
Isaiah 52:7 *page 841*
Daniel 5:21 *page 987*
Romans 9:5 *page 1289*
Revelation 1:6 *page 1434*
Revelation 19:6 *page 1450*

KNOWLEDGE

I believe God knows everything, even what is in the human heart.

Genesis 20:6 *page 23*
1 Kings 8:39 *page 402*
1 Chronicles 29:17 *page 503*
Psalm 44:21 *page 662*
Psalm 94:11 *page 705*

Proverbs 24:12 *page 772*
Matthew 6:4 *page 1077*
Luke 16:15 *page 1179*
Acts 15:8 *page 1258*

I believe God is far wiser than anyone can imagine.

Deuteronomy 29:29 *page 237*
Psalm 147:5 *page 747*
Jeremiah 32:19 *page 889*
Daniel 2:20 *page 980*

Romans 11:33 *page 1293*
Romans 16:27 *page 1298*
1 Corinthians 1:20-25 *page 1300*

I believe nothing is more important than knowing God.

Matthew 4:18-20 *page 1074*
Matthew 6:24, 31-33 *pages 1077, 1078*
Matthew 10:37 *page 1083*

Matthew 16:19-22 *page 1093*
Mark 2:14 *page 1118*

I believe all who refuse to know God will face judgment.

Matthew 7:22-23 *page 1079*
John 3:18-19 *page 1202*

John 16:8-9 *page 1223*

I believe God is the source of all true knowledge and wisdom.

1 Kings 4:29 *page 396*
Proverbs 2:6 *page 752*
Daniel 2:21 *page 980*

Romans 11:33 *page 1293*
Colossians 2:3 *page 1355*
James 1:5 *page 1406*

I believe that human wisdom is futile apart from God.

Isaiah 29:14 *page 819*
Daniel 2:10-11 *page 979*

1 Corinthians 1:19 *page 1300*
1 Corinthians 13:1-2 *page 1312*

I believe God gives some individuals special knowledge, wisdom, and insight.

Numbers 23:5 *page 186*

1 Kings 4:29-34 *page 396*

1 Kings 6:11 *page 398*

Jeremiah 2:1 *page 854*

Ezekiel 1:3 *page 922*

Joel 1:1 *page 1011*

Jonah 1:1 *page 1026*

Haggai 1:1 *page 1048*

Zechariah 1:1 *page 1052*

Malachi 1:1 *page 1064*

Luke 2:40 *page 1150*

1 Corinthians 12:8 *page 1311*

LIFE

I believe God created all living creatures.

Genesis 1:11-12, 20-27 *page 4*

Genesis 2:8-9, 19, 22 *pages 5, 6*

Numbers 16:22 *page 177*

Nehemiah 9:6 *page 576*

Isaiah 45:12 *page 835*

Jeremiah 51:19 *page 911*

Acts 17:24 *page 1262*

1 Corinthians 8:6 *page 1307*

Ephesians 3:9 *page 1341*

Revelation 10:6 *page 1442*

I believe God wants me to live for him all of my life.

Genesis 5:24 *page 9*

Genesis 17:1 *page 19*

Deuteronomy 6:2 *page 213*

Joshua 24:15 *page 275*

Galatians 5:25 *page 1338*

Ephesians 2:10 *page 1341*

1 John 2:3-6 *page 1422*

I believe sin produces countless struggles and sorrows in this life.

Genesis 3:17-19 *page 6*

Exodus 34:7 *page 108*

Leviticus 26:18 *page 151*

Numbers 14:18 *page 174*

Deuteronomy 5:9 *page 212*

Joshua 22:20 *page 273*

Ezra 9:13 *page 561*

Nehemiah 9:33 *page 577*

Psalm 32:10 *page 651*

Psalm 34:21 *page 653*

Isaiah 13:11 *page 807*

Ezekiel 18:20 *page 938*

Amos 3:2 *page 1017*

Romans 2:5 *page 1281*

Galatians 6:7 *page 1338*

I believe life on this earth is only temporal.

2 Kings 19:26 *page 455*

Job 14:1 *page 607*

Psalm 39:4-5 *page 658*

Psalm 89:47-48 *page 702*

Psalm 90:5 *page 703*

Isaiah 40:6 *page 829*

Matthew 6:27 *page 1077*

James 1:10 *page 1406*

James 4:14 *page 1409*

1 Peter 1:24 *page 1413*

I believe God offers eternal life to all who trust him.

John 3:16, 36 *page 1202*

John 5:24 *page 1206*

John 6:40 *page 1208*

John 11:25-26 *page 1216*

John 20:31 *page 1230*

1 Timothy 1:16 *page 1370*

1 John 5:13 *page 1425*

I believe God alone is the source of eternal life.

John 3:16, 36 *page 1202*

John 5:24 *page 1206*

John 6:40 *page 1208*

John 11:25-26 *page 1216*

John 20:31 *page 1230*

1 Timothy 1:16 *page 1370*

1 John 5:13 *page 1425*

I believe God wants me to trust him, obey him, and enjoy many of his blessings in this life.

Genesis 48:15-16 *page 62*

Exodus 20:12 *page 91*

Leviticus 18:5 *page 140*

Deuteronomy 30:19-20 *page 238*

Joshua 24:15 *page 275*

Psalm 25:12 *page 645*

Psalm 65:4 *page 677*

Proverbs 22:6 *page 770*

Isaiah 56:4 *page 844*

Romans 6:16-19 *page 1286*

Galatians 2:20 *page 1334*

I believe God wants to demonstrate his new life at work in me.

Romans 8:1 *page 1287*
Romans 14:17 *page 1296*
2 Corinthians 5:15 *page 1323*
Galatians 2:20 *page 1334*

Galatians 5:16 *page 1337*
Galatians 6:8 *page 1338*
Ephesians 3:19 *page 1343*

LIGHT

I believe God created light and the sun, moon, and stars.

Genesis 1:3-5 *page 3*
Genesis 1:15-18 *page 4*
Nehemiah 9:6 *page 576*
Job 9:9 *page 604*
Psalm 33:6 *page 651*
Psalm 74:16 *page 688*

Psalm 104:19 *page 712*
Isaiah 40:26 *page 830*
Isaiah 45:12 *page 835*
Amos 5:8 *page 1018*
2 Corinthians 4:6 *page 1322*

I believe God is my light—my source of hope, protection, truth, and joy.

2 Samuel 22:29 *page 383*
Psalm 18:28 *page 639*
Psalm 27:1 *page 646*
Psalm 84:11 *page 698*

Luke 2:32 *page 1150*
1 John 1:5 *page 1422*
Revelation 21:23 *page 1452*

I believe Christians are to be lights in this world—beacons of hope, protection, truth, and joy.

Isaiah 49:6 *page 838*
Isaiah 58:10 *page 845*
Matthew 5:14-15 *page 1075*
Luke 11:36 *page 1171*
John 3:21 *page 1202*

Acts 13:47 *page 1256*
Romans 13:12 *page 1295*
2 Corinthians 4:6-7 *page 1322*
1 Thessalonians 5:5 *page 1362*

I believe the sun, moon, and stars are temporal and that God himself will illumine the new heavens and earth.

Psalm 102:25-26 *page 710*
Isaiah 51:6 *page 840*
Isaiah 60:19-20 *page 847*
Matthew 24:35 *page 1105*

Hebrews 1:11-12 *page 1390*
2 Peter 3:10 *page 1420*
Revelation 21:1, 22-23 *pages 1451, 1452*

LOSTNESS

I believe everyone is lost until God finds, rescues, and saves them.

Psalm 119:176 *page 733*
Isaiah 53:6 *page 842*
Jeremiah 50:6 *page 908*

Ezekiel 34:16 *page 957*
Romans 3:12 *page 1282*
1 Peter 2:25 *page 1414*

LOVE

I believe God is rich in unfailing love to all who love him, trust him, confess their sins, experience his forgiveness, and obey him wholeheartedly.

Exodus 34:6-7 *page 108*
Deuteronomy 7:12 *page 214*
1 Kings 8:23 *page 401*

Nehemiah 1:5 *page 566*
Psalm 25:10 *page 645*
Psalm 32:10 *page 651*

MERCY

I believe I am saved by God's mercy.

Genesis 19:16 *page 22*
Luke 18:13 *page 1181*
Romans 6:14 *page 1286*

Ephesians 2:8-9 *page 1341*
Titus 3:5 *page 1385*
1 Peter 1:3 *page 1412*

OBEDIENCE
I believe God blesses and rewards those who love him and obey his commands.

Genesis 48:15-16 *page 62*
Exodus 19:5 *page 90*
Exodus 20:6, 12 *page 91*
Exodus 23:13 *page 95*
Leviticus 18:5 *page 140*
Deuteronomy 30:19-20 *page 238*
Joshua 24:15 *page 275*

Psalm 25:12 *page 645*
Psalm 65:4 *page 677*
Proverbs 22:6 *page 770*
Isaiah 56:4 *page 844*
Romans 6:16-19 *page 1286*
Galatians 2:20 *page 1334*

I believe people face grave consequences when they persistently disobey God's commands.

Genesis 3:17-19 *page 6*
Exodus 16:28 *page 88*
Exodus 34:7 *page 108*
Leviticus 26:14, 18 *page 151*
Numbers 14:18 *page 174*
Deuteronomy 5:9 *page 212*
Joshua 22:20 *page 273*
Ezra 9:13 *page 561*

Nehemiah 9:33 *page 577*
Psalm 32:10 *page 651*
Psalm 34:21 *page 653*
Isaiah 13:11 *page 807*
Ezekiel 18:20 *page 938*
Amos 3:2 *page 1017*
Romans 2:5 *page 1281*
Galatians 6:7 *page 1338*

OPPRESSION
I believe God cares for the oppressed and commands people not to oppose them.

Exodus 9:2 *page 77*
Exodus 22:21 *page 94*
Psalm 9:9 *page 633*
Psalm 10:18 *page 634*
Psalm 12:7 *page 635*
Psalm 37:14-15 *page 656*
Psalm 72:12-14 *page 685*

Psalm 82:3-4 *page 696*
Isaiah 1:17 *page 796*
Ezekiel 22:7 *page 943*
Amos 5:7 *page 1019*
Matthew 25:31-46 *pages 1106-1107*
James 1:27 *page 1406*

PATIENCE
I believe people face grave consequences when they test God's great patience.

Numbers 14:22-23 *page 174*
Psalm 78:41, 56-59 *pages 692, 693*

1 Corinthians 10:9 *page 1308*

PEACE
I believe God offers peace to those who love him and obey what he commands.

Psalm 119:165 *page 732*
Luke 2:14 *page 1149*

2 John 1:3 *page 1427*

PERISHING
I believe God doesn't want anyone to perish.

Luke 21:18 *page 1187*
John 3:16 *page 1202*
John 10:28 *page 1215*

John 11:26 *page 1216*
Acts 27:34 *page 1276*
2 Peter 3:9 *page 1420*

I believe the wicked will perish if they refuse to turn to God for salvation.

Leviticus 26:14, 18 *page 151*
1 Samuel 2:9 *page 317*
Psalm 32:10 *page 651*
Psalm 34:21 *page 653*

Isaiah 13:11 *page 807*
Ezekiel 18:20 *page 938*
Romans 2:5 *page 1281*
Galatians 6:7 *page 1338*

PERSECUTION
I know God's people have suffered persecution through the ages.

Psalm 109:16 *page 720*
Psalm 129:1-2 *page 736*
Matthew 5:12 *page 1075*
Matthew 13:21 *page 1088*
Luke 11:49 *page 1172*
John 15:20 *page 1223*
Acts 7:52 *page 1244*

Acts 12:1 *page 1252*
Galatians 1:23 *page 1332*
Galatians 5:11 *page 1337*
1 Thessalonians 2:14 *page 1360*
2 Timothy 3:12 *page 1380*
Hebrews 10:34 *page 1399*
Revelation 2:3 *page 1435*

I believe God will judge those who persecute his people.

Deuteronomy 32:35 *page 242*
Psalm 76:9 *page 689*
Psalm 119:84 *page 729*

Jeremiah 17:18 *page 873*
Romans 12:19 *page 1294*
2 Thessalonians 1:6 *page 1365*

PRAYER
I believe God hears the prayers of sinners who call out to him.

Psalm 51:17 *page 668*
Psalm 145:18 *page 746*

Luke 15:10 *page 1177*
Luke 24:47 *page 1195*

I believe God answers prayer.

Genesis 20:17 *page 24*
Deuteronomy 9:20 *page 216*
Psalm 34:17 *page 652*
Psalm 55:17 *page 671*

Psalm 69:33 *page 683*
Psalm 116:1 *page 724*
Psalm 145:18 *page 746*
Proverbs 15:29 *page 764*

PRIDE
I recognize that the godless are often very proud.

Job 20:6 *page 611*
Psalm 10:4 *page 634*
Ezekiel 7:10 *page 927*

Malachi 4:1 *page 1066*
Mark 7:21-22 *page 1127*
2 Timothy 3:2 *page 1380*

I believe God hates self-centered pride and arrogance.

2 Samuel 22:28 *page 383*
Psalm 5:5 *page 630*
Psalm 138:6 *page 741*
Proverbs 6:16-17 *page 756*

Proverbs 8:13 *page 757*
Luke 1:15 *page 1146*
James 4:6 *page 1409*
1 Peter 5:5 *page 1416*

PROMISES
I believe God always tells the truth and keeps every promise he makes.

Joshua 21:45 *page 272*
Joshua 23:14 *page 274*
2 Samuel 22:31 *page 383*
1 Kings 8:56 *page 403*

Psalm 119:41 *page 728*
Proverbs 30:5 *page 777*
Titus 1:2 *page 1383*

I believe God kept all his promises to various Old Testament believers.

Genesis 9:11-13 *page 12*
Genesis 26:24 *page 32*
Exodus 2:24 *page 70*
Joshua 21:45 *page 272*
Jeremiah 33:20-21 *page 891*

Acts 7:5, 17 *pages 1242, 1243*
Acts 13:32 *page 1256*
Acts 26:6 *page 1274*
Romans 4:13 *page 1284*

I wholeheartedly believe God's promises for believers today.

Acts 2:38-39 *page 1236*
Ephesians 3:6 *page 1341*
Hebrews 4:1 *page 1392*
Hebrews 6:17-18 *page 1394*

Hebrews 10:23 *page 1399*
Hebrews 12:26 *page 1403*
2 Peter 3:9 *page 1420*

PROPHECY

I believe God always fulfills what he predicts through his prophets.

1 Kings 12:15 *page 408*

1 Kings 13:26 *page 411*

2 Chronicles 10:15 *page 515*

2 Chronicles 36:21-22 *page 548*

Daniel 4:33 *page 985*

Matthew 1:22 *page 1070*

Luke 21:22 *page 1187*

Acts 3:18 *page 1237*

2 Peter 1:20-21 *page 1418*

Revelation 10:7 *page 1442*

I believe God judges false prophets who make big claims but don't speak for him.

Deuteronomy 13:1-5 *page 220*

Deuteronomy 18:20-22 *page 225*

Ezekiel 13:3 *page 932*

Ezekiel 14:10 *page 933*

2 Peter 2:1 *page 1418*

Revelation 20:10 *page 1451*

PURITY

I believe God wants every person to be pure and clean in his sight.

2 Samuel 22:27 *page 383*

Isaiah 1:16-18 *page 796*

Ezekiel 36:25 *page 960*

John 13:4-10 *page 1220*

1 Corinthians 5:8 *page 1304*

2 Corinthians 7:1 *page 1324*

Ephesians 5:25-27 *page 1344*

Philippians 2:15 *page 1349*

1 Timothy 4:12 *page 1372*

I believe no one in all the earth can be pure unless God washes and cleanses that person from his or her sins.

Job 25:4 *page 614*

1 Corinthians 1:30 *page 1301*

Hebrews 10:22 *page 1399*

SALVATION

I believe nothing is more important than receiving God's salvation from sin, death, and eternal punishment.

Isaiah 55:2 *page 843*

Habakkuk 2:13-14 *page 1041*

Matthew 19:16 *page 1096*

Luke 10:40-42 *page 1169*

John 6:27 *page 1207*

Acts 16:30-31 *page 1260*

1 Corinthians 7:30 *page 1306*

2 Corinthians 4:18 *page 1322*

Hebrews 12:16 *page 1402*

1 Peter 1:24-25 *page 1413*

I believe God doesn't want anyone to perish but all to come to repentance and experience his eternal salvation.

Luke 21:18 *page 1187*

John 3:16 *page 1202*

John 10:28 *page 1215*

John 11:26 *page 1216*

Acts 27:34 *page 1276*

2 Peter 3:9 *page 1420*

I believe salvation is found in Jesus Christ alone.

Mark 16:8 *page 1144*

John 10:7 *page 1214*

John 14:6 *page 1221*

Acts 4:12 *page 1238*

Romans 10:8-10, 13 *page 1291*

1 John 2:23 *page 1423*

SATAN

I believe Satan is evil.

John 8:44 *page 1212*

2 Corinthians 2:11 *page 1321*

1 Peter 5:8 *page 1416*

I believe Satan is crafty and deceitful.

Genesis 3:1 *page 6*

John 8:44 *page 1212*

2 Corinthians 11:14 *page 1328*

I believe Satan attacks the godly.

1 Chronicles 21:1 *page 492*
Job 1:6 *page 598*
Zechariah 3:1 *page 1053*
Matthew 4:1 *page 1073*
Luke 22:31 *page 1189*
1 Corinthians 7:5 *page 1305*
2 Corinthians 2:11 *page 1320*
2 Corinthians 12:7 *page 1329*

Ephesians 4:27 *page 1343*
Ephesians 6:10, 16 *page 1345*
1 Thessalonians 2:18 *page 1361*
1 Timothy 3:6 *page 1371*
James 4:7 *page 1409*
1 Peter 5:8 *page 1416*
Revelation 2:10 *page 1436*

I believe Satan is limited in what he can do, what he knows, and where he goes.

Zechariah 3:2 *page 1053*
Luke 22:31 *page 1189*

Ephesians 6:10, 16 *page 1345*
James 4:7 *page 1409*

I believe Satan cannot stay in God's presence.

Job 1:12 *page 598*
Job 2:7 *page 599*
Matthew 4:10 *page 1073*

Matthew 16:23 *page 1093*
Mark 8:33 *page 1129*
Luke 10:18 *page 1168*

I believe the Lord will crush Satan and punish him forever.

Genesis 3:15 *page 6*
Romans 16:20 *page 1298*

Revelation 20:10 *page 1451*

SCRIPTURES

I believe the Scriptures are inspired by God.

2 Samuel 23:2 *page 384*
Nehemiah 9:20, 30 *pages 576, 577*
Ezekiel 2:2 *page 923*
Ezekiel 11:2 *page 930*
Micah 3:8 *page 1031*
Zechariah 7:12 *page 1056*
Matthew 22:43 *page 1102*

Mark 12:36 *page 1137*
Acts 1:16 *page 1234*
Acts 4:25 *page 1239*
Ephesians 6:17 *page 1345*
2 Timothy 3:16 *page 1380*
Hebrews 1:1 *page 1390*
2 Peter 1:21 *page 1418*

I believe the Scriptures are completely true and trustworthy.

Psalm 19:7 *page 641*
Psalm 33:4 *page 651*
Psalm 119:142 *page 731*

Proverbs 30:5 *page 777*
1 Peter 1:23-25 *pages 1412–1413*
Revelation 22:6 *page 1453*

I believe the Scriptures are eternal.

Psalm 119:89 *page 730*
Isaiah 40:8 *page 830*

Matthew 5:18 *page 1075*
1 Peter 1:23-25 *pages 1412–1413*

I believe the Scriptures reveal the truth about God, creation, humanity, sin, salvation, eternity, and everything else we need to know in this life.

Deuteronomy 29:29 *page 237*
2 Timothy 3:16 *page 1380*

Hebrews 4:12 *page 1392*
1 Peter 1:23-25 *pages 1412–1413*

SOUL

I believe God cares about the salvation, purity, and protection of my soul.

Psalm 16:10 *page 637*
Psalm 19:7 *page 641*
Psalm 31:7 *page 649*
Matthew 10:28 *page 1083*
Matthew 11:29 *page 1085*

Matthew 16:26 *page 1093*
1 Thessalonians 5:23 *page 1363*
Hebrews 6:19 *page 1394*
1 Peter 1:9 *page 1412*
1 Peter 2:25 *page 1414*

SPIRIT

I believe God cares about the salvation, purity, and protection of my spirit.

Romans 8:10 *page 1288*

Romans 15:27 *page 1297*

1 Corinthians 1:7 *page 1300*

1 Corinthians 6:17 *page 1305*

1 Corinthians 7:34 *page 1306*

1 Corinthians 14:15-16 *page 1313*

2 Corinthians 7:1 *page 1324*

Galatians 4:15 *page 1336*

Ephesians 1:3, 17 *pages 1339, 1340*

Ephesians 4:23 *page 1343*

Philippians 4:23 *page 1352*

Colossians 1:9 *page 1354*

1 Thessalonians 5:23 *page 1363*

1 Timothy 4:7-8 *page 1372*

2 Timothy 1:7 *page 1378*

2 Timothy 4:22 *page 1381*

Philemon 1:25 *page 1388*

Hebrews 13:9 *page 1403*

1 Peter 2:2, 5 *page 1413*

1 Peter 3:4 *page 1414*

SUFFERING

I believe God allows both the godly and the godless to experience trials, suffering, and pain in this life.

Ruth 1:13 *page 310*

Job 1:1, 13-19 *page 598*

Psalm 9:13 *page 633*

Psalm 38:6 *page 657*

Ecclesiastes 2:22-23 *page 781*

Jeremiah 7:8 *page 862*

Matthew 17:12 *page 1094*

Matthew 26:39 *page 1108*

Luke 4:25-27 *page 1155*

John 9:1-3 *page 1213*

John 16:33 *page 1224*

Acts 8:1 *page 1244*

Acts 20:19 *page 1266*

Romans 1:27 *page 1281*

Romans 8:17-23 *page 1288*

Philippians 1:29 *page 1348*

1 Thessalonians 2:14 *page 1360*

2 Thessalonians 1:4-5 *page 1365*

Hebrews 10:32-34 *page 1399*

1 Peter 1:6-7 *page 1412*

1 Peter 2:21-23 *page 1414*

Revelation 16:10-11 *page 1447*

I believe Satan sometimes causes believers to experience terrible suffering.

Job 2:6 *page 599*

2 Corinthians 12:7 *page 1329*

Revelation 2:10 *page 1436*

I believe the wicked can cause believers much suffering and anguish.

Psalm 9:13 *page 633*

Psalm 120:5 *page 733*

Matthew 17:12 *page 1094*

Acts 8:1 *page 1244*

Acts 20:19 *page 1266*

Philippians 1:29 *page 1348*

1 Thessalonians 2:14 *page 1360*

2 Thessalonians 1:4-5 *page 1365*

I believe the sins and foolishness of family members and friends can cause needless suffering and pain in someone's life.

Genesis 3:16-17 *page 6*

Exodus 20:5 *page 91*

Joshua 7:24-26 *page 255*

Romans 5:12 *page 1285*

I believe my own sins can cause needless suffering and pain.

Genesis 3:16-17 *page 6*

Exodus 20:5 *page 91*

Psalm 38:5-6 *page 657*

I believe this world won't be free of suffering until the Lord makes the new heavens and new earth.

Isaiah 25:6-8 *page 815*

Romans 8:20-21 *page 1288*

Revelation 21:4 *page 1451*

TEACHING

I believe what God teaches through his Word.

Micah 4:2 *page 1031*

Matthew 11:13-15 *page 1084*

John 17:17 *page 1225*

Colossians 3:16 *page 1356*

2 Timothy 3:16 *page 1380*

TRUTH

I believe God's Word is always true and trustworthy.

Joshua 21:45 *page 272*

Joshua 23:14 *page 274*

1 Samuel 2:34 *page 318*

2 Samuel 22:31 *page 383*

2 Kings 15:12 *page 449*

Nehemiah 9:8, 13 *page 576*

Psalm 18:30 *page 639*

Psalm 33:4 *page 651*

Psalm 119:160 *page 732*

Proverbs 30:5 *page 777*

Revelation 22:6 *page 1453*

I wholeheartedly believe what is true and live accordingly.

2 Corinthians 3:14 *page 1321*

Ephesians 1:13 *page 1340*

Ephesians 4:14 *page 1342*

Colossians 1:23 *page 1354*

1 Timothy 1:15 *page 1370*

1 Timothy 4:10 *page 1372*

2 Timothy 2:25 *page 1380*

1 John 5:10 *page 1425*

I believe Jesus is the Truth.

John 1:9 *page 1197*

John 3:33 *page 1202*

John 14:6 *page 1221*

John 17:3 *page 1224*

John 18:37 *page 1226*

WORLD

I believe God created the world.

Genesis 1:1 *page 3*

Genesis 14:19, 22 *pages 17, 18*

Exodus 20:11 *page 91*

2 Kings 19:15 *page 454*

1 Chronicles 16:26 *page 488*

Nehemiah 9:6 *page 576*

Psalm 33:6-9 *page 651*

Psalm 104:24 *page 712*

Psalm 121:1-2 *page 733*

Psalm 146:5-7 *pages 746–747*

Isaiah 42:5 *page 832*

Isaiah 45:12 *page 835*

Jeremiah 27:4-5 *page 883*

Jeremiah 32:17 *page 889*

Jonah 1:9 *page 1026*

Acts 14:15 *page 1257*

Colossians 1:15-16 *page 1354*

Revelation 14:7 *page 1446*

I believe sin has wreaked havoc in this world.

Genesis 3:16-17 *page 6*

Genesis 6:5-7 *pages 9–10*

Romans 5:12 *page 1285*

Galatians 5:19-21 *page 1337*

I believe Satan is the prince of this world.

Matthew 4:8 *page 1074*

2 Corinthians 4:4 *page 1322*

Ephesians 2:2 *page 1340*

1 John 5:19 *page 1426*

Revelation 12:9 *page 1444*

I believe the people of this world are bound in sin and lost without Jesus Christ.

John 1:29 *page 1198*

John 8:34-36 *page 1212*

Romans 5:15-17 *page 1285*

Romans 6:6-7 *page 1285*

Romans 6:23 *page 1286*

Romans 7:24-25 *page 1287*

Galatians 3:22 *page 1335*

I believe God one day will make new heavens and a new earth.

Isaiah 65:17 *page 850*

Romans 8:20-21 *page 1288*

2 Peter 3:13 *page 1420*

Revelation 21:4 *page 1451*

Commands to Obey

ABSTAINING
I abstain from that which God forbids.

Exodus 20:1-17 *pages 91–92*
Leviticus 18:3 *page 140*
Acts 15:20 *page 1258*
2 Corinthians 6:17 *page 1324*

Galatians 5:19-21 *page 1337*
1 Timothy 6:11 *page 1374*
2 Timothy 2:22 *page 1379*
1 John 5:21 *page 1426*

ADOPTION
I am so thankful the Lord has adopted me into his family.

Romans 8:15 *page 1288*
Galatians 4:5 *page 1335*
Ephesians 1:5 *page 1340*

Hebrews 2:11-13 *page 1391*
1 John 3:1 *page 1423*

ADULTERY
I abhor adultery.

Exodus 20:14 *page 91*
Matthew 5:27-28, 32 *page 1076*

Matthew 19:9 *page 1096*
1 Corinthians 6:18-20 *page 1305*

BITTERNESS
I do not harbor bitterness in my heart.

Philippians 1:12-14 *page 1348*
Hebrews 12:15 *page 1402*

James 2:5 *page 1406*
1 John 3:15 *page 1424*

BLAMELESSNESS
I live a blameless life in God's sight.

Genesis 17:1 *page 19*
Leviticus 19:2 *page 141*
Deuteronomy 18:13 *page 225*
Matthew 5:48 *page 1076*

1 Timothy 3:2 *page 1371*
Titus 1:7 *page 1383*
1 Peter 1:15-16 *page 1412*

I do not envy those who are wicked.

Psalm 37:1-2 *page 655*
Psalm 73:3-18 *pages 685–686*

Proverbs 24:19 *page 771*

BLASPHEMY
I do not blaspheme the Lord's name.

Exodus 20:7 *page 91*
Exodus 22:28 *page 95*
Leviticus 24:10-16 *page 148*

Numbers 15:30-31 *page 176*
Deuteronomy 5:11 *page 212*
1 Timothy 1:20 *page 1370*

BLESSING
I bless the Lord, who is great and deserves my praise.

1 Chronicles 16:36 *page 488*
Nehemiah 9:5 *page 576*

Job 1:21 *page 598*
Psalm 18:46 *page 640*

Psalm 89:52 *page 702*
Psalm 113:2 *page 723*
Psalm 119:12 *page 727*
Daniel 2:19-23 *page 980*
Matthew 21:9 *page 1098*
Luke 1:68 *page 1148*

Luke 24:53 *page 1195*
2 Corinthians 1:3 *page 1320*
Ephesians 1:3 *page 1339*
1 Peter 1:3 *page 1412*
Revelation 5:12-13 *page 1439*

I bless others.
Genesis 24:60 *page 29*
Numbers 6:24 *page 163*

Romans 1:10-12 *page 1280*

BODY

I willingly give my body to God as a living and holy sacrifice.
Numbers 8:5 *page 167*
Jeremiah 1:4-10, 17-19 *page 854*
Daniel 3:28 *page 983*
Malachi 2:15 *page 1065*
Romans 6:13, 16, 19 *page 1286*
Romans 12:1 *page 1293*
1 Corinthians 9:27 *page 1308*
Galatians 2:20 *page 1334*

Galatians 6:17 *page 1338*
Philippians 1:20-24 *page 1348*
Colossians 1:24 *page 1354*
1 Thessalonians 4:4 *page 1361*
1 Thessalonians 5:23 *page 1363*
2 Timothy 4:6 *page 1381*
Hebrews 12:1-4 *pages 1401–1402*
2 Peter 1:14 *page 1418*

CALLING

I am thankful the Lord called me to turn from my sins, trust him, become part of his family forever, and live for him.
1 Kings 8:33 *page 402*
2 Chronicles 6:24 *page 511*
Isaiah 55:6 *page 843*
Isaiah 64:7 *page 849*
Isaiah 66:4 *page 851*
Jeremiah 3:1, 19 *pages 856, 857*
Jeremiah 35:17 *page 893*
Hosea 2:23 *page 1001*
Hosea 11:2 *page 1007*
Joel 2:32 *page 1013*
Zechariah 7:13 *page 1056*
Matthew 9:13 *page 1081*
Matthew 22:14 *page 1101*
Mark 2:17 *page 1118*
Luke 5:32 *page 1157*
John 10:3 *page 1214*
Acts 2:21, 39 *page 1236*
Acts 22:16 *page 1269*
Romans 1:6-7 *page 1280*
Romans 8:28-30 *page 1288*
Romans 10:13 *page 1291*

1 Corinthians 1:2, 24, 26 *pages 1300, 1301*
1 Corinthians 7:17, 20, 22 *pages 1305, 1306*
Galatians 1:6, 15 *page 1332*
Galatians 5:8, 13 *page 1337*
Ephesians 1:18 *page 1340*
Ephesians 4:1, 4 *page 1342*
Colossians 3:15 *page 1356*
1 Thessalonians 2:12 *page 1360*
1 Thessalonians 4:7 *page 1362*
1 Thessalonians 5:24 *page 1363*
2 Thessalonians 1:11 *page 1365*
2 Thessalonians 2:14 *page 1366*
Hebrews 11:8 *page 1400*
1 Peter 2:9 *page 1413*
1 Peter 4:16 *page 1416*
1 Peter 5:10 *page 1416*
2 Peter 1:3, 10 *pages 1417, 1418*
1 John 3:1 *page 1423*
Jude 1:1 *page 1431*
Revelation 3:20 *page 1438*

CHOOSING

I choose to love the Lord, live for him, and enjoy his rich blessings.
Deuteronomy 30:19-20 *page 238*
Joshua 24:15 *page 275*
Psalm 25:12 *page 645*
Psalm 65:4 *page 677*

Proverbs 22:6 *page 770*
Isaiah 56:4 *page 844*
Romans 6:16, 19 *page 1286*

CHURCH
I long for harmony and holiness within the church.

Matthew 18:17 *page 1095*
Acts 5:11 *page 1240*
Romans 14:19 *page 1296*
1 Corinthians 1:10 *page 1300*
1 Corinthians 5:1, 4-5, 12 *pages 1303, 1304*
1 Corinthians 6:4, 6 *page 1304*
1 Corinthians 8:1 *page 1306*
1 Corinthians 11:18, 22 *page 1310*

2 Corinthians 2:5 *page 1321*
Ephesians 3:10 *page 1342*
Ephesians 5:23-25, 27, 29, 32 *page 1344*
Titus 3:5, 7, 10, 15 *page 1385*
James 3:1 *page 1408*
3 John 1:9 *page 1429*
Revelation 2:1, 8, 12, 18 *pages 1434-1436*
Revelation 3:1, 7, 14 *page 1437*

COMFORT
I look to the Lord, who comforts me.

Psalm 10:17 *page 634*
Psalm 23:4 *page 644*
Psalm 71:20-21 *page 684*
Psalm 119:50 *page 728*
Isaiah 52:9 *page 841*

Matthew 5:4 *page 1075*
Acts 9:31 *page 1248*
2 Corinthians 1:3-7 *page 1320*
Philippians 2:1 *page 1349*
2 Thessalonians 2:16-17 *page 1366*

COMMANDS
I obey all the Lord's commands.

Exodus 24:7 *page 96*
Leviticus 22:31 *page 145*
Deuteronomy 11:22 *page 218*
Joshua 22:5 *page 272*
1 Kings 8:58 *page 403*
2 Kings 17:37 *page 452*

Psalm 119:168 *page 732*
Ecclesiastes 12:13 *page 788*
John 14:15 *page 1221*
1 Timothy 6:13-14 *page 1374*
1 John 3:24 *page 1424*
Revelation 14:12 *page 1446*

I urge other believers to keep obeying the Lord's commands.

Deuteronomy 6:4-9 *page 213*
Joshua 8:34-35 *page 256*
Psalm 119:46 *page 728*

Matthew 5:19 *page 1075*
Matthew 28:19-20 *page 1113*

CONDEMNATION
I am thankful that God doesn't condemn those who have trusted in Jesus Christ.

John 3:16 *page 1202*
John 5:24 *page 1206*

Romans 8:34 *page 1288*

CONFESSION
I confess my sins to the Lord and ask for his cleansing and forgiveness.

Deuteronomy 10:16 *page 217*
Deuteronomy 30:6 *page 238*
Psalm 19:12 *page 641*
Psalm 51:2, 7, 10 *page 668*
Proverbs 20:9 *page 768*
Isaiah 1:18 *page 796*
Jeremiah 4:4 *page 858*
Daniel 11:35 *page 996*
Daniel 12:10 *page 997*

Acts 3:19 *page 1237*
Acts 15:9 *page 1258*
2 Corinthians 7:1 *page 1324*
Ephesians 5:26 *page 1344*
Titus 2:14 *page 1384*
Hebrews 1:3 *page 1390*
Hebrews 10:2 *page 1398*
1 Peter 1:2, 22 *pages 1411, 1412*
1 John 1:7-9 *page 1422*

I seek to live a clean, holy life in God's sight.

Leviticus 20:7-8 *page 142*
Psalm 119:10-11 *page 727*
Isaiah 1:16 *page 796*
Philippians 2:15 *page 1349*

2 Timothy 2:21 *page 1379*
Hebrews 12:14 *page 1402*
1 Peter 3:21 *page 1415*

CONTENTMENT
I find my contentment in the Lord.
Exodus 20:17 *page 92*
Psalm 16:5 *page 637*
Matthew 6:25-33 *pages 1077–1078*

Philippians 4:10-13 *page 1351*
1 Timothy 6:6-8 *page 1374*

COURAGE
I take courage in the Lord.
Joshua 1:9 *page 248*
1 Chronicles 28:20 *page 502*
Psalm 27:14 *page 647*

Haggai 2:4 *page 1048*
John 16:33 *page 1224*
1 John 5:5 *page 1425*

I urge other believers to continue trusting the Lord.
Numbers 14:6-9 *page 173*
Deuteronomy 31:6 *page 238*
Joshua 1:9 *page 248*

1 Corinthians 16:13 *page 1317*
1 Timothy 6:11-12 *page 1374*

COVETING
I do not covet.
Exodus 20:17 *page 92*
Deuteronomy 5:21 *page 212*
Acts 20:33 *page 1267*

Romans 7:7 *page 1286*
Romans 13:9 *page 1295*

CREATION
I praise God, who created the heavens and earth—the whole universe.
Genesis 1:1 *page 3*
Exodus 20:11 *page 91*
2 Kings 19:15 *page 454*
1 Chronicles 16:26 *page 488*
Nehemiah 9:6 *page 576*
Psalm 33:6-9 *page 651*
Psalm 104:24 *page 712*
Psalm 121:1-2 *page 733*
Psalm 146:5-7 *page 746*

Isaiah 42:5 *page 832*
Isaiah 45:12 *page 835*
Jeremiah 27:4-5 *page 883*
Jeremiah 32:17 *page 889*
Jonah 1:9 *page 1026*
Acts 14:15 *page 1257*
Colossians 1:15-16 *page 1354*
Revelation 14:7 *page 1446*

I praise God for making me a new person.
2 Corinthians 5:17 *page 1323*
Ephesians 2:10 *page 1341*

Ephesians 4:24 *page 1343*
Colossians 3:10 *page 1356*

CROSS
I thank the Lord Jesus for being willing to die on a cross in my place for my sins.
Isaiah 53:8, 12 *page 842*
Matthew 27:35 *page 1111*
Mark 10:45 *page 1134*

Romans 4:23-25 *page 1284*
1 Corinthians 15:3-5 *page 1314*
1 Peter 2:24 *page 1414*

DARKNESS
I thank God for delivering me from darkness and for blessing me with his light.
Isaiah 9:1-2 *page 803*
Isaiah 58:10 *page 845*
Matthew 4:16 *page 1074*
Luke 1:79 *page 1148*
John 1:5 *page 1197*

John 12:46 *page 1220*
Acts 26:18 *page 1274*
Romans 2:19 *page 1282*
2 Corinthians 4:6 *page 1322*
1 Peter 2:9 *page 1413*

I walk in the light, not in darkness.

Romans 13:12 *page 1295*

2 Corinthians 6:14 *page 1324*

Ephesians 5:11 *page 1343*

1 Thessalonians 5:5 *page 1362*

1 John 1:5-6 *page 1422*

1 John 2:8-9, 11 *page 1422*

DEATH

I thank the Lord Jesus for dying in my place for my sins.

Isaiah 53:8, 12 *page 842*

Matthew 27:35 *page 1111*

Mark 10:45 *page 1134*

Romans 4:23-25 *page 1284*

1 Corinthians 15:3-5 *page 1314*

1 Peter 2:24 *page 1414*

I have died to sin, and I live for Jesus Christ.

Romans 6:11 *page 1286*

Galatians 2:20 *page 1334*

Colossians 2:20 *page 1355*

DISCIPLINE

I gladly and humbly accept God's discipline in my life.

Deuteronomy 8:5 *page 215*

Psalm 94:12 *page 705*

Proverbs 1:3 *page 752*

1 Corinthians 11:32 *page 1310*

Hebrews 12:5-11 *page 1402*

Revelation 3:19 *page 1437*

ENDURANCE

I carefully guard against walking away from God or forsaking my faith.

Psalm 125:1 *page 735*

Matthew 10:22 *page 1083*

Matthew 24:13 *page 1104*

Mark 13:13 *page 1138*

Romans 5:3-4 *pages 1284–1285*

2 Corinthians 1:6 *page 1320*

2 Corinthians 6:4 *page 1324*

Colossians 1:11 *page 1354*

2 Thessalonians 1:4 *page 1365*

2 Thessalonians 3:5 *page 1366*

1 Timothy 6:11 *page 1374*

2 Timothy 2:3, 10, 12 *page 1378*

2 Timothy 3:10 *page 1380*

Hebrews 10:36 *page 1399*

Hebrews 12:1, 7 *pages 1401, 1402*

James 1:3-4, 12 *pages 1405, 1406*

James 5:11 *page 1410*

1 Peter 1:6 *page 1412*

1 Peter 2:19 *page 1414*

2 Peter 1:6 *page 1418*

Revelation 1:9 *page 1434*

Revelation 2:2, 19 *pages 1435, 1436*

Revelation 3:10 *page 1437*

Revelation 13:10 *page 1445*

Revelation 14:12 *page 1446*

ENVY

I do not envy others, especially not those who are wicked.

Exodus 20:17 *page 92*

Psalm 37:1-4 *page 655*

Psalm 73:3, 16-18 *pages 685, 686*

Proverbs 3:31 *page 754*

Proverbs 24:19 *page 772*

1 Corinthians 13:4 *page 1312*

Galatians 5:26 *page 1338*

James 3:13-16 *page 1408*

ETERNALITY

I have trusted Jesus Christ and thank him for giving me eternal life.

Matthew 7:13-14 *page 1078*

Mathew 19:29 *page 1097*

John 3:16 *page 1202*

John 5:24 *page 1206*

John 11:25-26 *page 1216*

John 17:3 *page 1224*

Acts 11:18 *page 1252*

Romans 6:23 *page 1286*

1 Timothy 1:16 *page 1370*

2 Timothy 1:10 *page 1378*

1 John 4:9 *page 1425*

1 John 5:11-13 *page 1425*

EVIL

I do not follow the example of the wicked.

Psalm 1:1 *page 627*
Psalm 18:21 *page 639*
Proverbs 4:14 *page 755*

2 Peter 2:1-3 *page 1418*
Jude 1:8-11 *pages 1431–1432*

I fear God and do not partner with evildoers.

Exodus 23:2 *page 95*
Psalm 1:1 *page 627*
Psalm 26:5 *page 646*

Proverbs 24:21 *page 772*
2 Corinthians 6:14-15 *page 1324*
1 Peter 4:4 *page 1415*

EXALTATION

I exalt the Lord!

Exodus 15:2 *page 84*
2 Samuel 22:47 *page 384*
Psalm 34:3 *page 652*
Psalm 57:5 *page 672*

Psalm 99:5-9 *pages 708–709*
Psalm 107:31-32 *pages 718–719*
Psalm 118:28 *page 726*
Isaiah 52:13 *page 841*

FAITH

I place my faith and trust in God alone—who saves me, makes me righteous, answers my prayers, and gives me the sure hope of eternal life.

Genesis 15:6 *page 18*
Psalm 116:6 *page 724*
Habakkuk 2:4 *page 1040*
Matthew 7:13-14 *page 1078*
Matthew 9:22 *page 1082*
Mathew 19:29 *page 1097*
John 3:16 *page 1202*
John 5:24 *page 1206*
John 11:25-26 *page 1216*

John 17:3 *page 1224*
Acts 11:18 *page 1252*
Acts 15:8-9 *page 1258*
Romans 6:23 *page 1286*
1 Timothy 1:16 *page 1370*
2 Timothy 1:10 *page 1378*
1 Peter 1:21 *page 1412*
1 John 4:9 *page 1425*
1 John 5:11-13 *page 1425*

I place my faith in God without wavering or doubting.

1 Kings 18:21 *page 418*
Psalm 17:5 *page 637*
Psalm 26:1 *page 646*
Matthew 21:21 *page 1099*

Mark 9:24 *page 1130*
Romans 4:20-22 *page 1284*
Hebrews 10:23 *page 1399*
Jude 1:21 *page 1432*

I demonstrate and strengthen my faith by obeying God and doing what is good and right.

Genesis 22:1 *page 25*
Psalm 106:31 *page 716*
2 Corinthians 1:24 *page 1320*
Galatians 5:6 *page 1337*

Philippians 1:25 *page 1348*
Colossians 2:7 *page 1355*
2 Thessalonians 1:3 *page 1365*
James 2:14 *page 1407*

I guard against losing my faith.

1 Corinthians 13:7 *page 1312*
1 Timothy 6:10 *page 1374*

1 Peter 5:8-11 *page 1416*

I keep my faith even in the midst of trials.

Romans 5:3 *page 1284*
2 Corinthians 6:4 *page 1324*
2 Thessalonians 1:4-5 *page 1365*
2 Timothy 2:3 *page 1378*
Hebrews 10:35-36 *page 1399*

James 1:3 *page 1405*
James 5:11 *page 1410*
1 Peter 1:5-7 *page 1412*
1 Peter 5:8-11 *page 1416*
Revelation 2:10 *page 1436*

FEAR

I fear the Lord, which is the beginning of true wisdom.

Job 28:28 *page 616*

Psalm 111:10 *page 722*

Proverbs 1:7 *page 752*

Proverbs 9:10 *page 758*

Proverbs 15:33 *page 764*

Ecclesiastes 12:13 *page 788*

I fear the Lord and do what he says.

Genesis 22:12 *page 26*

Deuteronomy 5:29 *page 213*

Deuteronomy 10:12, 20 *pages 217, 218*

Psalm 112:1 *page 722*

Ecclesiastes 12:13 *page 788*

Philippians 2:12 *page 1349*

I trust God and do not fear what others might do to me.

Joshua 5:1 *page 251*

2 Chronicles 20:15 *page 525*

Nehemiah 4:14 *page 570*

Psalm 118:6 *page 725*

Isaiah 8:13 *page 803*

Isaiah 40:9-11 *page 830*

Isaiah 41:10 *page 831*

Matthew 10:28 *page 1083*

FORGIVENESS

I pray to God and ask him to forgive my sins.

1 Kings 8:30 *page 402*

Psalm 25:7 *page 645*

Psalm 51:7 *page 668*

Psalm 79:8-9 *page 694*

Daniel 9:19 *page 993*

Matthew 6:12 *page 1077*

Luke 8:13-14 *page 1162*

I forgive those who sin against me.

Matthew 6:12, 14-15 *page 1077*

Matthew 18:21-35 *pages 1095–1096*

Ephesians 4:32 *page 1343*

Colossians 3:13 *page 1356*

FREE

I rejoice in God's free gift of salvation.

Psalm 42:5 *page 660*

Isaiah 12:1-6 *page 806*

Luke 10:20 *page 1168*

Romans 4:16 *page 1284*

Romans 5:16 *page 1285*

Ephesians 2:8-9 *page 1340*

I am thankful God has set me free from sin and slavery to serve him.

Isaiah 44:22 *page 835*

Luke 4:18-19 *page 1155*

John 8:32 *page 1212*

Romans 3:23 *page 1283*

Romans 6:6-22 *pages 1285–1286*

1 Corinthians 1:30 *page 1301*

1 Corinthians 7:22-23 *page 1306*

Galatians 4:5 *page 1335*

Ephesians 1:7 *page 1340*

Colossians 1:14 *page 1354*

1 Timothy 2:6 *page 1371*

Titus 2:14 *page 1384*

1 Peter 2:16 *page 1414*

2 Peter 2:19-20 *page 1419*

Revelation 1:5 *page 1434*

FULFILLMENT

I fulfill all my promises to God.

Deuteronomy 23:21 *page 230*

Psalm 22:25 *page 643*

Psalm 76:11 *page 689*

Ecclesiastes 5:4-5 *page 783*

GIFTS

I give gifts to the Lord.

1 Chronicles 16:29 *page 488*

Psalm 96:8 *page 707*

Matthew 22:21 *page 1101*

Romans 6:13 *page 1286*

Romans 12:1 *page 1293*

Hebrews 13:15-16 *page 1403*

I thank the Lord for the free gift of salvation.

Psalm 42:5 *page 660*
Isaiah 12:1-6 *page 806*
Luke 10:20 *page 1168*
Romans 4:16 *page 1284*

Romans 5:16 *page 1285*
2 Corinthians 9:15 *page 1327*
Ephesians 2:8-9 *page 1341*

I give gifts to others in need.

Deuteronomy 15:7 *page 222*
Matthew 6:2 *page 1076*
2 Corinthians 8:1-15 *pages 1325–1326*
1 Timothy 6:17-18 *page 1375*

Hebrews 13:16 *page 1403*
James 2:16 *page 1407*
1 John 3:17 *page 1424*

GLORY

I praise the Lord, who is glorious.

Exodus 15:11 *page 85*
1 Chronicles 29:13 *page 503*
Nehemiah 9:5-6 *pages 575–576*
Psalm 44:8 *page 662*
Psalm 138:5 *page 741*

Psalm 148:13 *page 748*
Isaiah 6:3 *page 800*
Ephesians 1:12-14 *page 1340*
Hebrews 13:15 *page 1403*

I do everything for the glory of the Lord.

Romans 6:11 *page 1286*
1 Corinthians 10:31 *page 1309*
Colossians 3:17 *page 1356*

1 Peter 4:11 *page 1415*
Revelation 4:11 *page 1438*

I tell others about the Lord's glory.

Deuteronomy 32:3 *page 240*
1 Chronicles 16:24 *page 488*
1 Chronicles 22:5 *page 494*
Psalm 21:13 *page 642*
Psalm 46:8 *page 664*

Psalm 78:4 *page 690*
Psalm 148:11 *page 748*
Hebrews 13:15 *page 1403*
Revelation 19:1 *page 1450*

I look forward to my glorious future with the Lord forever.

Daniel 12:3 *page 966*
1 Corinthians 15:42-57 *pages 1315–1316*
Ephesians 1:17-19 *page 1340*
Colossians 3:4 *page 1356*

1 Thessalonians 4:17-18 *page 1362*
Hebrews 11:16 *page 1400*
1 Peter 1:3-9 *page 1412*
Revelation 21:1-7 *pages 1451–1452*

GOOD

I hate evil and love what is good.

Psalm 34:14 *page 652*
Proverbs 11:27 *page 759*
Amos 5:14-15 *page 1019*

1 Timothy 6:11 *page 1374*
1 Peter 3:11 *page 1415*
3 John 1:11 *page 1429*

I proclaim the Good News of salvation to others.

2 Kings 7:9 *page 437*
1 Chronicles 16:23 *page 488*
Isaiah 40:9 *page 830*
Matthew 4:23 *page 1074*
Luke 1:77 *page 1148*
Luke 4:18 *page 1155*

Acts 8:35 *page 1246*
Acts 20:24 *page 1266*
Romans 10:15 *page 1291*
2 Corinthians 2:14 *page 1321*
2 Timothy 1:8 *page 1378*

GRACE

I experience more and more of God's grace in my life.

Psalm 67:1 *page 679*
Psalm 84:11 *page 698*
Acts 6:8 *page 1242*

Romans 1:7 *page 1280*
1 Corinthians 1:3 *page 1300*
Ephesians 6:24 *page 1343*

2 Timothy 2:1 *page 1378*
Hebrews 13:9 *page 1403*
1 Peter 5:12 *page 1416*

2 Peter 3:18 *page 1420*
Revelation 22:21 *page 1453*

I ask God to give more of his grace to others.
Acts 14:26 *page 1257*
Acts 15:40 *page 1259*
Acts 20:32 *page 1267*
Romans 1:7 *page 1280*

Romans 16:20 *page 1298*
1 Corinthians 1:3 *page 1300*
Ephesians 6:24 *page 1343*
Revelation 22:21 *page 1453*

HATE
I hate what is wrong and love what is good and right.
Psalm 5:5 *page 630*
Psalm 45:7 *page 663*
Psalm 97:10 *page 707*
Proverbs 11:27 *page 760*

Amos 5:14-15 *page 1019*
1 Timothy 6:11 *page 1374*
1 Peter 3:11 *page 1415*
3 John 1:11 *page 1429*

HEAVEN
I worship God, who is the creator of the heavens and earth.
Genesis 1:1 *page 3*
Genesis 14:19, 22 *pages 17, 18*
Exodus 20:11 *page 91*
2 Kings 19:15 *page 454*
1 Chronicles 16:26 *page 488*
Nehemiah 9:6 *page 576*
Psalm 33:6-9 *page 651*
Psalm 104:24 *page 712*
Psalm 121:1-2 *page 733*

Psalm 146:5-7 *pages 746–747*
Isaiah 42:5 *page 832*
Isaiah 45:12 *page 835*
Jeremiah 27:4-5 *page 883*
Jeremiah 32:17 *page 889*
Jonah 1:9 *page 1026*
Acts 14:15 *page 1257*
Colossians 1:15-16 *page 1354*
Revelation 14:7 *page 1446*

I pray to God in heaven, who hears my prayers and answers me.
1 Kings 8:22 *page 401*
2 Kings 19:15-16 *page 454*
2 Chronicles 6:21 *page 511*

2 Chronicles 7:14 *page 512*
Daniel 10:12 *page 994*
Matthew 7:11 *page 1078*

I am storing up treasures in heaven.
Matthew 5:12 *page 1075*
Matthew 6:20 *page 1077*
Matthew 19:21 *page 1097*
Luke 16:9 *page 1179*

1 Timothy 6:19 *page 1375*
2 Timothy 4:8 *page 1381*
James 1:12 *page 1406*
Revelation 2:10 *page 1436*

HOLINESS
I am holy because God has made me holy and I obey his commands.
Leviticus 11:44-45 *page 131*
Numbers 15:40 *page 176*
Deuteronomy 7:6-11 *page 214*
Deuteronomy 26:18-19 *page 233*
Romans 12:1-2 *page 1293*
1 Corinthians 1:2 *page 1300*
Ephesians 1:4 *page 1340*
Ephesians 5:27 *page 1344*
Philippians 1:10 *page 1348*
Colossians 1:11-12 *page 1354*
Colossians 3:12 *page 1356*
1 Thessalonians 4:3-8 *pages 1361–1362*

1 Thessalonians 5:23-24 *page 1363*
2 Thessalonians 2:13 *page 1366*
1 Timothy 4:12 *page 1372*
2 Timothy 1:9 *page 1378*
2 Timothy 2:21 *page 1379*
Hebrews 9:14 *page 1397*
Hebrews 10:10 *page 1398*
Hebrews 12:14 *page 1402*
1 Peter 1:15-16 *page 1412*
1 Peter 2:5 *page 1413*
2 Peter 3:11, 14 *page 1420*

HOLY SPIRIT
I repent whenever I grieve the Holy Spirit.

Isaiah 63:10 *page 849*

Acts 5:3, 9 *pages 1239, 1240*

Acts 7:51 *page 1244*

Ephesians 4:30 *page 1343*

1 Thessalonians 5:19 *page 1363*

HONOR
I honor my father and mother.

Exodus 20:12 *page 91*

Deuteronomy 5:16 *page 212*

Matthew 15:4 *page 1091*

Matthew 19:19 *page 1096*

Mark 7:10 *page 1126*

Mark 10:19 *page 1132*

Luke 18:20 *page 1182*

Ephesians 6:2-3 *page 1344*

I honor the Lord wholeheartedly and serve him gladly.

Joshua 24:14 *page 275*

Psalm 29:2 *page 648*

Psalm 31:19 *page 650*

Psalm 34:9 *page 652*

Psalm 63:4 *page 676*

Psalm 85:9 *page 698*

Psalm 86:11 *page 699*

Psalm 147:11 *page 747*

Proverbs 3:9 *page 754*

Proverbs 14:31 *page 763*

Ecclesiastes 12:1 *page 787*

Isaiah 25:1 *page 815*

Isaiah 29:13 *page 819*

Isaiah 58:13 *page 845*

1 Corinthians 6:20 *page 1305*

I marvel that God desires to honor those who obey him.

Deuteronomy 26:19 *page 233*

Psalm 8:5 *page 632*

Psalm 15:4 *page 636*

Psalm 62:7 *page 676*

Proverbs 21:21 *page 769*

Proverbs 22:4 *page 770*

John 12:26 *page 1218*

Romans 2:10 *page 1281*

HOPE
I put my hope and trust in God.

Psalm 25:5, 21 *pages 645, 646*

Psalm 31:14 *page 650*

Psalm 34:8 *page 652*

Psalm 56:4 *page 671*

Psalm 62:8 *page 676*

Psalm 130:7 *page 737*

Psalm 146:5 *page 746*

Proverbs 3:5 *page 754*

Proverbs 22:19 *page 770*

Isaiah 26:4 *page 816*

Isaiah 50:10 *page 840*

Lamentations 3:24 *page 918*

John 3:18 *page 1202*

John 12:44 *page 1220*

John 14:1 *page 1221*

Galatians 2:20 *page 1334*

1 Timothy 4:10 *page 1372*

1 Timothy 6:17 *page 1375*

Hebrews 4:14 *page 1393*

Hebrews 10:23 *page 1399*

I put my hope and trust in God's Word.

Psalm 19:7 *page 641*

Psalm 33:4 *page 651*

Psalm 119:43, 74, 81, 114, 147
pages 728-730, 732

Psalm 130:5 *page 736*

HUMILITY
I humble myself before God.

2 Chronicles 7:14 *page 512*

Ezra 8:21 *page 559*

Psalm 138:6 *page 741*

Micah 6:8 *page 1033*

Luke 18:9-14 *pages 1181-1182*

James 1:21 *page 1406*

James 4:7 *page 1409*

1 Peter 5:6 *page 1416*

I wait for the Lord to lift me up.

1 Samuel 2:7 *page 317*

Psalm 3:3 *page 629*

Psalm 145:14 *page 746*

James 4:7-8 *page 1409*

1 Peter 5:6 *page 1416*

IMMORALITY

I abstain from sexual immorality.

Proverbs 2:16 *page 753*

Proverbs 5:3 *page 755*

Matthew 15:19-20 *pages 1091–1092*

Acts 15:20 *page 1258*

1 Corinthians 6:13-20 *pages 1304–1305*

1 Corinthians 10:8 *page 1308*

Galatians 5:19 *page 1337*

Ephesians 5:3 *page 1343*

Revelation 22:15 *page 1453*

INHERITANCE

I am thankful for the inheritance God is giving to all believers.

Daniel 12:13 *page 997*

Matthew 25:34 *page 1106*

Acts 20:32 *page 1267*

1 Corinthians 15:50 *page 1316*

Ephesians 1:11, 18 *page 1340*

Colossians 1:12 *page 1354*

Colossians 3:24 *page 1356*

Titus 3:7 *page 1385*

Hebrews 6:12 *page 1394*

Hebrews 9:15 *page 1397*

James 2:5 *page 1406*

1 Peter 1:4 *page 1412*

Revelation 21:7 *page 1452*

INTEGRITY

I seek to please God by acting with integrity.

1 Kings 9:4 *page 403*

1 Chronicles 29:17 *page 503*

Job 1:1 *page 598*

Psalm 18:25 *page 639*

Psalm 26:1 *page 646*

Psalm 101:2 *page 709*

Psalm 119:1 *page 726*

Proverbs 2:7, 21 *page 752*

Proverbs 20:7 *page 768*

1 Timothy 3:8 *page 1371*

Titus 2:7 *page 1384*

JEALOUSY

I do not display jealousy or hostility toward others.

Romans 13:13 *page 1295*

1 Corinthians 3:3 *page 1302*

1 Corinthians 13:4 *page 1312*

2 Corinthians 12:20 *page 1329*

Galatians 5:20, 26 *pages 1337, 1338*

Philippians 1:15 *page 1348*

1 Timothy 6:4 *page 1374*

James 3:14-16 *page 1408*

James 4:2 *page 1408*

1 Peter 2:1 *page 1413*

JOY

I find my joy in the Lord.

Deuteronomy 12:7 *page 219*

1 Samuel 2:1 *page 317*

Nehemiah 8:10 *page 575*

Psalm 32:11 *page 651*

Psalm 64:10 *page 677*

Isaiah 41:16 *page 831*

Isaiah 61:10 *page 848*

Joel 2:23 *page 1013*

Habakkuk 3:17-19 *page 1042*

Philippians 4:4 *page 1351*

KINGDOM

I rejoice that God has called me into his kingdom.

Matthew 8:11 *page 1079*

Matthew 19:28 *page 1097*

Luke 13:29 *page 1175*

John 3:3 *page 1201*

1 Corinthians 15:50-53 *page 1316*

Colossians 1:13 *page 1354*

1 Thessalonians 2:12 *page 1360*

2 Timothy 4:18 *page 1381*

KNOWLEDGE

LOVE

I love my neighbors as myself.
Leviticus 19:18, 34 *pages 141, 142*
Matthew 22:39 *page 1101*
Romans 13:8 *page 1295*
Galatians 5:14 *page 1337*
James 2:8 *page 1407*

I love those in need—widows, orphans, the poor, immigrants, refugees, and others who are downtrodden and oppressed.
Leviticus 19:33-34 *page 142*
Deuteronomy 10:19 *page 218*
Proverbs 29:7 *page 776*
1 Corinthians 13:3 *page 1312*
1 Timothy 5:3 *page 1372*
1 Timothy 5:16 *page 1373*
James 1:27 *page 1406*
James 2:5 *page 1406*
1 John 3:17 *page 1424*

I do not love the things of this world, which are temporal at best.
Psalm 119:36 *page 728*
Ecclesiastes 5:10-11 *page 783*
Matthew 6:24 *page 1077*
Mark 10:21-22 *page 1132*
John 12:25 *page 1218*
1 Timothy 6:10 *page 1374*
Hebrews 13:5 *page 1403*
James 2:5 *page 1406*
1 John 2:15 *page 1423*

MERCY

I thank God for showing mercy to me.
Psalm 89:1 *page 700*
Psalm 103:4 *page 711*
Lamentations 3:22-23 *page 918*
Daniel 9:9 *page 992*
Micah 7:18 *page 1034*
Luke 17:11-19 *page 1180*
Romans 15:9 *page 1296*
2 Corinthians 1:3 *page 1320*
Ephesians 2:4-5 *page 1340*
1 Peter 1:3 *page 1412*
1 Peter 2:10 *page 1413*

I call out to God for mercy in times of distress.
Exodus 22:27 *page 94*
Psalm 40:11 *page 659*
Psalm 52:9 *page 669*
Psalm 79:8 *page 694*
Isaiah 33:2 *page 822*
Daniel 9:16 *page 992*
Matthew 15:22 *page 1092*
Matthew 20:30-31 *page 1098*
Luke 18:13 *page 1181*

I show mercy to others.
Daniel 4:27 *page 985*
Hosea 6:6 *page 1004*
Matthew 5:7 *page 1075*
Matthew 9:13 *page 1081*
Matthew 12:7 *page 1085*
Luke 6:36 *page 1159*
James 2:13 *page 1407*
Jude 1:22-23 *page 1432*

I pray for God to show his mercy to others.
Genesis 43:14 *page 55*
Matthew 17:15 *page 1094*
Galatians 6:16 *page 1338*
1 Timothy 1:2 *page 1370*
1 Timothy 2:1 *page 1370*
2 John 1:3 *page 1427*
Jude 1:2 *page 1431*

MURDER

I abhor murder.
Genesis 9:5 *page 12*
Exodus 20:3 *page 91*
Exodus 21:12 *page 92*
Leviticus 24:17 *page 148*
Matthew 5:21 *page 1075*
1 John 3:15 *page 1424*

OPPRESSION
I obey God's commands to help the poor and oppressed.

Leviticus 19:10 *page 141*
Leviticus 23:22 *page 146*
Deuteronomy 15:7, 11 *page 222*
Deuteronomy 24:12, 14-15 *page 231*
Esther 9:22 *page 594*
Proverbs 29:7 *page 776*

Isaiah 1:17 *page 796*
1 Corinthians 9:22 *page 1308*
1 Timothy 5:3 *page 1372*
James 1:27 *page 1406*
1 John 3:17 *page 1424*

PATIENCE
I am patient, even in the midst of difficult circumstances.

Psalm 27:14 *page 647*
Proverbs 25:15 *page 773*
Ecclesiastes 7:8 *page 784*
Romans 8:25 *page 1288*
Romans 12:12 *page 1294*
2 Corinthians 6:6 *page 1324*
Galatians 5:22 *page 1338*

Colossians 1:11 *page 1354*
Colossians 3:12 *page 1356*
Titus 2:2 *page 1384*
Hebrews 10:36 *page 1399*
James 1:12 *page 1406*
James 5:10-11 *page 1410*
1 Peter 2:19-20 *page 1414*

PEACE
I experience and live in God's peace.

Judges 6:24 *page 286*
Psalm 4:8 *page 630*
Acts 10:36 *page 1250*
Romans 5:1 *page 1284*
Romans 14:17 *page 1296*
2 Corinthians 13:11 *page 1330*
Galatians 6:16 *page 1338*

Philippians 4:6-7 *page 1351*
Hebrews 12:14 *page 1402*
1 Peter 1:2 *page 1411*
2 Peter 1:2 *page 1417*
2 Peter 3:14 *page 1420*
2 John 1:3 *page 1427*

I pray for others to experience temporal and lasting peace.

Numbers 6:26 *page 163*
1 Samuel 20:42 *page 342*
1 Samuel 25:6, 35 *pages 346, 348*
Psalm 122:7-8 *page 734*
Psalm 128:6 *page 736*
Jeremiah 29:7 *page 885*
Romans 1:7 *page 1280*
Romans 1:17 *page 1280*

Romans 15:13 *page 1296*
1 Corinthians 1:3 *page 1300*
2 Corinthians 1:2 *page 1320*
Galatians 1:3 *page 1332*
Ephesians 6:23 *page 1345*
Philippians 1:2 *page 1347*
Jude 1:2 *page 1431*

PERSECUTION
I stand true for God when I suffer persecution.

Psalm 119:157 *page 732*
Daniel 3:16-18 *page 982*
Matthew 5:10-11, 44 *pages 1075, 1076*
Matthew 10:22-39 *pages 1083–1084*
Matthew 24:9, 13 *page 1104*

Romans 12:14 *page 1294*
2 Thessalonians 1:4-5 *page 1365*
2 Timothy 1:8 *page 1378*
1 Peter 3:14-17 *page 1415*
Revelation 2:10 *page 1436*

PRAISE
I praise the Lord for his greatness and glory.

1 Chronicles 16:25 *page 488*
Nehemiah 9:5 *page 575*
Psalm 21:13 *page 642*
Psalm 48:1 *page 665*
Psalm 104:1 *page 712*

Matthew 6:9-10 *page 1077*
Luke 11:2 *page 1169*
Hebrews 13:15 *page 1403*
Revelation 7:12 *page 1440*
Revelation 11:17 *page 1443*

I praise the Lord for his righteousness and goodness.
Genesis 24:27 *page 28*
1 Chronicles 16:34 *page 488*
2 Chronicles 5:13 *page 510*
Ezra 3:11 *page 553*
Psalm 71:16 *page 684*
Psalm 106:1 *page 715*

Isaiah 5:16 *page 800*
Isaiah 24:15-16 *page 815*
Isaiah 61:11 *page 848*
Isaiah 63:7 *page 849*
Revelation 15:4 *page 1447*

I praise the Lord for saving me.
Exodus 15:2 *page 84*
2 Samuel 22:4 *page 382*
2 Kings 17:39 *page 452*
Psalm 9:14 *page 633*
Psalm 18:3 *page 638*
Psalm 30:1 *page 648*
Psalm 35:10 *page 653*

Psalm 42:5 *page 660*
Psalm 116:13 *page 725*
Jeremiah 17:14 *page 873*
Zephaniah 3:17 *page 1046*
Luke 1:68 *page 1148*
Jude 1:24-25 *page 1432*

I praise the Lord with music and song.
Exodus 15:1-2 *page 84*
1 Chronicles 16:42 *page 489*
1 Chronicles 23:5, 30 *pages 494, 495*
1 Chronicles 25:3 *page 497*
2 Chronicles 5:13 *page 510*
2 Chronicles 20:21 *page 525*
2 Chronicles 29:27-28 *pages 536–537*
Psalm 7:17 *page 632*
Psalm 21:13 *page 642*
Psalm 30:4-5 *page 648*
Psalm 47:6 *page 664*
Psalm 68:4 *page 679*

Psalm 81:1-3 *page 695*
Psalm 100:2-3 *page 709*
Psalm 135:3 *page 738*
Psalm 150:6 *page 749*
Isaiah 12:1 *page 806*
Isaiah 12:5 *page 806*
Isaiah 42:10-12 *page 832*
Jeremiah 20:13 *page 876*
Jeremiah 33:11 *page 891*
Jonah 2:9 *page 1027*
Colossians 3:16 *page 1356*
James 5:13 *page 1410*

I urge others to praise the Lord.
1 Chronicles 16:7-8 *page 487*
1 Chronicles 29:20 *page 503*
Nehemiah 9:5 *page 575*
Psalm 33:1 *page 651*

Psalm 103:22 *page 711*
Psalm 107:8 *page 718*
Matthew 5:16 *page 1075*

PRAYER

I confess my sins when I pray to God.
Ezra 9:6 *page 560*
Ezra 10:1 *page 561*
Nehemiah 1:6 *page 566*
Nehemiah 9:1-3 *page 576*

Isaiah 59:12-13 *page 846*
Daniel 9:4-5, 20 *pages 992, 993*
Matthew 6:12 *page 1077*
Luke 11:4 *page 1169*

I pray to God alone.
Exodus 23:13 *page 95*
Isaiah 17:7-8 *page 810*
Isaiah 44:9-20 *pages 834–835*
Jeremiah 7:18 *page 862*

Jeremiah 10:14 *page 866*
Jeremiah 14:22 *page 870*
Revelation 21:27 *page 1452*

I participate in public prayer on special occasions.
1 Kings 8:30 *page 402*
Ezra 10:1 *page 561*

Acts 3:1 *page 1237*

I pray in times of crisis.
Exodus 2:23 *page 70*
Judges 4:3 *page 281*
2 Kings 19:1 *page 454*

2 Kings 19:4 *page 454*
Ezra 9:5-15 *pages 560–561*
Nehemiah 9:1-38 *pages 575–576*

Psalm 5:2 *page 630*
Psalm 30:10 *page 649*
Psalm 55:1 *page 670*
Psalm 71:2 *page 683*

Psalm 109:21-31 *page 721*
Psalm 141:1 *page 743*
Daniel 9:1-19 *pages 992–993*
Matthew 26:42 *page 1108*

I pray privately.
Matthew 6:5-6 *page 1077*
Matthew 14:23 *page 1090*

Luke 9:18 *page 1165*

I pray concisely and thoughtfully.
Ecclesiastes 5:1-5 *page 783*
Matthew 6:7-9 *page 1077*

Luke 11:2 *page 1169*

I do not make rash promises to God.
Judges 11:30-35 *page 294*
1 Samuel 14:24-45 *pages 332–333*

Ecclesiastes 5:2-6 *page 783*

I pray regularly.
Daniel 6:10 *page 988*
Romans 1:9 *page 1280*
Ephesians 1:16 *page 1340*
Philippians 1:4 *page 1347*

Colossians 1:3 *page 1353*
1 Thessalonians 1:2 *page 1359*
1 Thessalonians 3:10 *page 1361*

I pray for others.
Genesis 20:7 *page 23*
Exodus 8:9 *page 76*
Numbers 21:7 *page 183*
1 Samuel 12:19, 23 *page 329*
2 Kings 4:32-35 *page 433*
2 Chronicles 30:18 *page 538*
Job 42:8 *page 625*
Acts 6:5-6 *page 1242*
Acts 12:4-5 *page 1252*
Acts 14:23 *page 1257*
Acts 28:8 *page 1277*
Romans 1:9 *page 1280*

Ephesians 1:16-19 *page 1340*
Ephesians 6:18 *page 1345*
Philippians 1:3 *page 1347*
Colossians 1:3 *page 1353*
Colossians 4:3-4, 12 *pages 1356, 1357*
2 Thessalonians 3:1-2 *page 1366*
1 Timothy 2:1-2 *pages 1370–1371*
2 Timothy 1:2 *page 1377*
Philemon 1:4 *page 1387*
Hebrews 13:18-19 *page 1404*
James 5:14-16 *page 1410*

I pray about my own needs.
Matthew 6:11, 13 *page 1077*
Luke 11:3-4 *page 1169*

Philippians 4:6 *page 1351*
James 5:13 *page 1410*

PRIDE
I rejoice in what God has done in my life and in the lives of other believers, but I don't act arrogant or proud.
Psalm 16:3 *page 637*
Romans 15:17-18 *page 1297*
1 Corinthians 1:31 *page 1301*
1 Corinthians 9:16 *page 1308*
2 Corinthians 7:4 *page 1324*
Galatians 6:14 *page 1338*

Ephesians 2:9-10 *page 1341*
Philippians 3:3 *page 1350*
1 Thessalonians 2:20 *page 1361*
James 4:16 *page 1409*
1 John 2:16 *page 1423*

PURITY
I rejoice that God has made me pure in his sight.
Ezekiel 36:25 *page 960*
Zechariah 13:1 *page 1060*
Acts 15:8-9 *page 1258*
Romans 15:15-16 *page 1297*
1 Corinthians 1:30 *page 1301*

1 Corinthians 6:11 *page 1304*
Ephesians 5:25-26 *page 1344*
Titus 2:14 *page 1384*
Titus 3:5 *page 1385*
Hebrews 1:3 *page 1390*

Hebrews 9:14 *page 1397*
Hebrews 10:22 *page 1399*
1 Peter 1:2, 22 *pages 1411, 1412*

1 John 1:7-9 *page 1422*
Revelation 22:14 *page 1453*

I thank God for my salvation and seek to live a pure life.
2 Corinthians 7:1 *page 1324*
Philippians 1:10 *page 1348*
1 Timothy 4:11 *page 1372*

2 Timothy 2:21 *page 1379*
Titus 2:4-5 *page 1384*
2 Peter 3:14 *page 1420*

I confess my sins when I fail God.
Ezra 9:6 *page 560*
Ezra 10:1 *page 561*
Nehemiah 1:6 *page 566*
Nehemiah 9:1-3 *page 575*
Isaiah 59:12-13 *page 846*

Daniel 9:4-5, 20 *pages 992, 993*
Matthew 6:12 *page 1077*
Luke 11:4 *page 1169*
James 5:16 *page 1410*
1 John 1:9 *page 1422*

I look forward to the absolute purity I'll enjoy in God's presence forever.
1 Peter 1:4 *page 1412*
Revelation 14:4-5 *pages 1445–1446*

Revelation 22:14 *page 1453*

SALVATION
I cry out to God for deliverance in the midst of desperate circumstances.
Exodus 2:23 *page 70*
Judges 4:3 *page 281*
2 Kings 19:1 *page 454*
2 Kings 19:4 *page 454*
Ezra 9:5-15 *pages 560–561*
Nehemiah 9:1-38 *pages 575–577*
Psalm 5:2 *page 630*

Psalm 30:10 *page 649*
Psalm 55:1 *page 670*
Psalm 71:2 *page 683*
Psalm 109:21-31 *page 721*
Psalm 141:1 *page 743*
Daniel 9:1-19 *pages 992–993*
Matthew 26:42 *page 1108*

I thank God for saving me.
Exodus 15:2 *page 94*
2 Samuel 22:4 *page 382*
2 Kings 17:39 *page 452*
Psalm 9:14 *page 633*
Psalm 18:3 *page 638*
Psalm 30:1 *page 648*
Psalm 35:10 *page 653*

Psalm 42:5 *page 660*
Psalm 51:12 *page 668*
Psalm 116:13 *page 725*
Jeremiah 17:14 *page 873*
Zephaniah 3:17 *page 1046*
Luke 1:68 *page 1148*
Jude 1:24-25 *page 1432*

I tell others the Good News about salvation in Jesus Christ.
Matthew 4:23 *page 1074*
Acts 4:8-12 *page 1238*
Acts 8:4 *page 1245*
Acts 10:36 *page 1250*
Romans 1:16 *page 1280*

Romans 10:16-17 *page 1291*
Philippians 1:4-5 *page 1347*
2 Timothy 1:8 *page 1378*
Revelation 14:6 *page 1446*

I long to see the Good News of salvation proclaimed around the world.
Psalm 96:2-3 *pages 706–707*
Matthew 28:19 *page 1113*
Mark 16:15 *page 1144*

Acts 1:8 *page 1234*
Romans 10:14-15 *page 1291*
Revelation 14:6 *page 1446*

SATAN
I ask God to protect me from Satan's attacks.
Matthew 6:13 *page 1077*
John 17:15 *page 1224*
Ephesians 6:16-17 *page 1345*
2 Thessalonians 3:13 *page 1367*

James 4:7-8 *page 1409*
1 Peter 5:8 *page 1416*
1 John 2:13 *page 1422*
Revelation 2:10 *page 1436*

STEALING
I do not steal.
Exodus 20:15 *page 92*
Leviticus 19:11 *page 141*
Proverbs 22:28 *page 770*
Proverbs 29:24 *page 776*

Romans 13:9 *page 1295*
Ephesians 4:28 *page 1343*
1 Peter 4:15 *page 1416*

I pay my debts to others.
Leviticus 24:18 *page 148*
Romans 13:8 *page 1295*

Philemon 1:18-19 *page 1388*

I do not ask others to co-sign loans and end up forcing them to pay my debts.
Proverbs 6:1 *page 756*
Proverbs 20:16 *page 768*

Proverbs 27:13 *page 774*

TEACHING
I teach others from God's Word.
Deuteronomy 6:4-9 *page 213*
Ezra 7:8-10 *page 557*
Psalm 78:5-6 *page 691*
Acts 17:11 *page 1261*

1 Timothy 4:13 *page 1372*
2 Timothy 3:16 *page 1380*
2 Timothy 4:2 *page 1380*
Hebrews 5:12 *page 1393*

TRUST
I always put my trust in the Lord and in his Word.
Genesis 49:18 *page 63*
Deuteronomy 1:32 *page 206*
Psalm 19:7 *page 641*
Psalm 25:5, 21 *pages 645, 646*
Psalm 31:14 *page 650*
Psalm 33:4 *page 651*
Psalm 34:8 *page 652*
Psalm 56:4 *page 671*
Psalm 62:8 *page 676*
Psalm 119:43, 74, 81, 114, 147
pages 728–730, 732
Psalm 130:5-7 *pages 736–737*
Psalm 146:5 *page 746*

Proverbs 3:5 *page 754*
Proverbs 22:19 *page 770*
Isaiah 26:4 *page 816*
Isaiah 50:10 *page 840*
Lamentations 3:24 *page 918*
John 3:18 *page 1202*
John 12:44 *page 1220*
John 14:1 *page 1221*
Galatians 2:20 *page 1334*
1 Timothy 4:10 *page 1372*
1 Timothy 6:17 *page 1375*
Hebrews 4:14 *page 1393*
Hebrews 10:23 *page 1399*

TRUTH
I tell the truth to God and others.
Exodus 20:16 *page 92*
Leviticus 19:11 *page 141*
Joshua 7:11, 19 *page 254*
Psalm 5:6 *page 630*
Psalm 7:14 *page 632*
Psalm 12:1-2 *page 635*
Psalm 15:2 *page 636*
Psalm 34:12-13 *page 652*

Proverbs 6:16-17 *page 756*
Proverbs 24:28 *page 772*
Proverbs 25:18 *page 773*
Zechariah 8:16 *page 1057*
Acts 5:3 *page 1239*
Acts 20:20 *page 1266*
Ephesians 4:25 *page 1343*
Colossians 3:9 *page 1356*

WILL
I choose God's will over my own will.
Genesis 6:9 *page 10*
Numbers 15:39 *page 176*
1 Kings 8:58 *page 403*
Matthew 12:50 *page 1087*

John 4:34 *page 1204*
John 5:30 *page 1206*
Ephesians 6:6 *page 1344*
1 Thessalonians 5:18 *page 1363*

WORSHIP

I worship the Lord alone.

I abhor the worship of false gods.